THE
OXFORD COMPANION TO
POLITICS OF THE WORLD

THE OXFORD
COMPANION TO
POLITICS OF THE WORLD

SECOND EDITION

Editor in Chief
Joel Krieger

Editors
Margaret E. Crahan   Lawrence R. Jacobs   William A. Joseph
Georges Nzongola-Ntalaja   James A. Paul

OXFORD
UNIVERSITY PRESS
2001

OXFORD
UNIVERSITY PRESS

Oxford   New York
Athens   Auckland   Bangkok   Bogotá   Buenos Aires   Calcutta
Cape Town   Chennai   Dar es Salaam   Delhi   Florence   Hong Kong   Istanbul
Karachi   Kuala Lumpur   Madrid   Melbourne   Mexico City   Mumbai
Nairobi   Paris   São Paulo   Shanghai   Singapore   Taipei   Tokyo   Toronto   Warsaw

and associated companies in
Berlin   Ibadan

Copyright © 2001 by Oxford University Press, Inc.
Second Edition

Published by Oxford University Press, Inc.
198 Madison Avenue, New York, NY 10016
www.oup.com

Oxford is a registered trademark of Oxford University Press

Library of Congress Cataloging-in-Publication Data
The Oxford companion to politics of the world / editor in chief, Joel Krieger; editors,
Margaret E. Crahan . . . [et al.].—2nd ed.
Includes bibliographical references and index.
ISBN 0-19-511739-5 (alk. paper)
1. Political science—Encyclopedias.   2. World politics—Encyclopedias.   I. Krieger, Joel.
JA61 .O95 2001
320'.03—dc21   00-051023

1 3 5 7 9 8 6 4 2

Printed in the United States of America
on acid-free paper

CONTENTS

CRITICAL ISSUES

Critical Issues articles appear alphabetically in the text, easily identifiable by the black title bar starting at the *top* of the page.

INTERPRETIVE ESSAYS

Interpretive Essays appear alphabetically in the text, easily identifiable by the black title bar starting at the *bottom* of the page.

PREFACE

The world of politics seems more unsettled today and the challenges more daunting than many anticipated when we began work more than a decade ago on the first edition of the *Oxford Companion to Politics of the World*. Published in 1993, the first edition of the *Companion* took shape as 1989 ushered in democratic transitions throughout Eastern and Central Europe, as Nelson Mandela's release from prison promised a new era in South Africa, and as democratic ideals swept away authoritarian regimes throughout much of the world.

Of course, despite high expectations, signs of uncertainty abounded even then. One could foresee how difficult it might be to stabilize both the economies and the political institutions in transitional democracies, to unify peoples torn by ethnic and nationalist strife and divided by socioeconomic disparities, and to narrow the gap between the developing and the developed world. In addition, it was clear that the nation-state faced a host of challenges from above and below, by regional and global forces outside, and by ethnic-nationalist, separatist, and religious forces within. Indeed the very definitions of the nation-state, nationalism, and citizenship were changing under pressures such as the emergence of global cities as major international actors and the escalation of worldwide immigration. Nonetheless it was still possible to interpret the epoch-making events of the post-1989 world as the herald of a more cooperative, integrated, prosperous world order.

As the new century unfolds, conflict and squalor—expressed in brutal brushfire wars, horrifying epidemics, and chronic underdevelopment—vie with equally dramatic accounts of the widening circle of opportunities associated with a liberal political order and the global, albeit unequal, diffusion of trade, investment, production, and communications. More than a decade has passed since the grim predictability of East-West rivalries and static geopolitical alliances shattered into a kaleidoscopic pattern of overlapping and contested sovereignties driven as much by global economic competition as by national affinities or shared security interests.

In writing the second edition of the *Companion*, we therefore have much more evidence to marshal in analyzing the processes of change that have reshaped every dimension of political life in this uncertain post-cold war order. For better or worse, however, the issues and challenges seem far clearer than the ultimate assessments. Will the processes of globalization deliver on the promises of a worldwide diffusion of wealth and opportunity as well as greater international harmony—or will they reinforce the comparative advantages of the more prosperous regions and peoples, undermine local cultures, foment conflict, and intensify environmental degradation? How effectively will politics— within and among nations—meld the dynamism of capitalist markets with historic concerns for equality, social justice, and humane sustainable development? Can we create a system of institutions for international governance that fosters cooperation, provides for national as well as personal security, and enjoys widespread support from both "haves" and "have-nots"? Designed to explain the world of politics through article-by-article discussion of questions such as these, the *Companion* hopes to lend perspective and depth to contemporary political developments.

APPROACH

In a single volume, *The Oxford Companion to Politics of the World*, Second Edition, provides a comprehensive guide to international relations and national domestic politics throughout the world. It does so through 672 articles that represent the contributions of over 500 contributors from 40 countries, including 87 completely new entries commissioined for this edition. Contributors have been drawn from a host of disciplines in the social sciences and humanities, including political science, economics, women's studies, sociology, anthropology, philosophy, law, history, international studies, and business. All are specialists chosen for the originality and importance of their contributions to the study of world politics. The contributors also include many practitioners: advisors, policy analysts and activists, journalists, political leaders from national governments and international organizations, and diplomats. The diversity of the contributors' experiences and perspectives ensures the vital interaction of wide-ranging national, regional, and international perspectives from a host of political and intellectual traditions.

In the *Companion*, we strive to provide accurate, definitive treatments of important subjects consistent with the highest standards of scholarship while conveying a sense of the excitement of world politics. In this way, we hope to contribute to understandings that challenge parochialism and transcend narrow disciplinary divisions as well as to offer the reader many and varied examples of vibrant, cutting-edge interpretation and analysis.

ORGANIZATION AND USE

The editors have worked to devise a conceptual scheme for the book that allows an enormous amount of information about politics throughout the world to be conveyed in a single volume. All told, the 672 articles are distributed among eleven substantive categories and vary in length from short factual pieces of several hundred words to major essays of 4,000 words or more. Written with a diverse array of readers in mind, the articles are intended to appeal to general readers fascinated by politics, students from high school through graduate study, and scholars throughout the social sciences disciplines, philosophy, religion, women's studies, law, and business. In addition, the *Companion* is intended to meet the professional needs of journalists, diplomats, people working in foundations, government offices, and international organizations, as well as those engaged in international business or law.

Inevitably, in a project of this scope, principles of selectivity are crucial. Rather than dispersing information through a multitude of short, dry articles on narrowly defined topics, the editors devised a system of coverage in which recurring patterns of information are located within particular types of articles. For example, the *Companion* contains articles on nearly every country in the world. These articles convey extensive information about national institutions and organizations, political leaders, parties, political economy, the social bases of politics and political divisions (class, race, ethnicity, ideology, religion, gender, traditional forces), patterns of conflict and prospects for change, and foreign affairs.

Also included in the *Companion* are biographies of leaders and intellectual figures who have shaped the world as we know it. These articles include biographical information and assessments of the national and international significance of figures as diverse as Mohandas Gandhi, Eva Perón, Mao Zedong, Julius Nyerere, David Ben-Gurion, Margaret Thatcher, Aleksandr Solzhenitsyn, Charles de Gaulle, Hannah Arendt, Michel Foucault, Martin Luther King, Jr., Jawaharial Nehru and some eighty other persons who have played exceptionally significant roles in shaping contemporary political life.

In addition, the *Companion* features twenty-three *interpretive essays*. These are major analytic treatments of particularly significant and far-reaching themes. Addressing such topics as ethnicity, nationalism, gender and politics, development and underdevelopment, war, democracy, class and politics, political parties and party competition, globalization, race and racism, humanitarian intervention, and environmentalism, the interpretive essays provide a thematic scaffold for the work as a whole. We also include four interpretive essays that identify debates, analyze directions, and assess the contributions of the academic fields that frame the *Companion*: political science, comparative politics, international relations, and international law. Black title bars at the bottom corner of the page identify this type of essay.

For the second edition, we have added a new article format called *critical issues*, six pairs of essays by contributors with different perspectives and interpretations of the same theme. Providing informed and often passionate debates on affirmative action, the United Nations, the future of entitlements, sustainable development, censorship, and the limits of liberal democracy, critical issues are distinguished by their intellectual and policy significance. Each contributor to the critical issues section is a political or intellectual figure who has helped shape public discussion of these enduring political themes. Black title bars at the top corner of the page identify critical issues essays.

Along with the country articles, biographies, interpretive essays, and critical issues, the *Companion* includes seven other categories for communicating critical information about world affairs and conveying the range and depth of contemporary interpretation:

- *concepts* (e.g. sovereignty, political violence, citizenship, communitarianism, decolonization, rational choice, multiculturalism)
- *conventions, treaties, and developments in international law* (e.g. Balfour Declaration, law of the sea, Maastricht Treaty, Lomé Convention/Cotonou Agreement, NAFTA)
- *forms of government and institutions* (e.g., apartheid, military rule, U.S. Congress, totalitarianism, post-communism, Supreme Court of the United States)
- *historical events* (e.g. World War II, Chernobyl nuclear accident, Cuban middle crisis, Holocaust, Kosovo War, Tiananmen Square, Rwandan Genocide)

- *international issues* (e.g. AIDS, antisemitism, liberation theology, information technology, refugees, security, terrorism)
- *international organizations* (e.g., Roman Catholic Church, European Union, Amnesty International, World Trade Organization, Organization of American States, Security Council)
- *domestic political, economic, and social issues* (e.g., elections and voting behavior, reproductive rights, psychology and politics, civil rights movement, democratic transitions, Medicare and Medicaid)

The Companion relies on several cross-referencing schemes to guide readers from their initial point of entry to related articles throughout the volume. Entry titles with no article following refer the reader to a substantive entry under which the topic is discussed. Within the body of an article, cross-references may also be indicated by the insertion of an asterisk. Topics marked in this way will be found elsewhere in the volume as separate entries. Finally, when the use of an asterisk would be misleading or unclear, or when the entry term of a related article does not appear within the body of the text, cross-references are listed within parentheses at the end of the article.

More generally, the cross-referencing scheme will help users gain an in-depth understanding of comprehensive themes. For example, cross-references will direct readers interested in women's studies to an ensemble of articles on topics including feminism, feminist theory, gender and politics, patriarchy, women and development, the Equal Rights Amendment, gender gap, and reproductive rights. Similarly, readers interested in business and economics will be led from articles on international finance, political economy, and international debt to related articles discussing balance of payments, the International Monetary Fund, World Bank, and protection, and in turn to articles on North-South relations, newly industrializing economies, World Trade Organization, and many others.

In addition, the index will help readers following a line of reasoning, to locate particular information, or seek references to political figures not covered by independent articles. The bibliographies at the end of articles suggest sources that may prove helpful for those wanting to pursue more intensive research into an area of interest or professional concern. The Directory of Contributors (page xiii) identifies all of the articles by author. Finally, despite the boundary disputes that beset contemporary world politics and the uncertain future of quite a few countries, six regional maps are included in the *Companion*. The maps reflect the balance of international consensus and common usage in the summer of 2000, and are presented with the knowledge that country names and borders are subject to change.

With considerations of space and focus in mind, coverage has been limited, with a few significant exceptions, to the issues and personalities of the twentieth century; a vast majority of the articles treats the period since World War II.

The *Companion* is the work of many people. With the assistance of an international advisory board, the project was conceived and directed by an editorial board consisting of Margaret E. Crahan, Lawrence R. Jacobs, William A. Joseph, Georges Nzongola-Ntalaja, and James A. Paul. The editors worked tirelessly through every phase of the project with enormous intelligence, skill, and boundless reservoirs of good humor for which I am immensely grateful. They tapped their endless networks to unearth contributors for the volume and provided the intellectual compass for the work. The editorial board for the second edition benefited greatly from the contributions that Miles Kahler, Barbara B. Stallings, and Margaret Weir made to the first edition.

A number of friends and colleagues were especially generous in the advice and assistance they provided the editorial board: Ivo Banac, Walter Clemens, Selwyn Cudjoe, Alex N. Dragnich, Greg Gause, Anne Gillespie, David Held, Martin Sánchez Jankowski, Stuart J. Kaufman, Mark Kesselman, Craig Murphy, George Ross, and Gordon Silverstein. Several editors at Oxford University Press have helped in various phases of the project, including Katherine Adzima, Karen Fein, Linda Halvorson, Ellen Satrom, and Nancy Toff. Special thanks are due to the project editor, Fritz McDonald. We would also like to thank David Gombac, who copyedited the manuscript with exceptional skill and sensitivity. Finally I would like to thank my wife, Carol, for her enthusiasm and forbearance, and my children, Nathan and Megan, for the welcome distractions they provided.

Of course, the ultimate value of the *Companion* depends on the commitment and talent of the contributors, some of whom worked on their articles under extraordinarily difficult conditions and all of whom graciously invested their wisdom and scholarship in the project. The fast-paced developments and ever-shifting terrain of contemporary politics present special challenges as well as satisfactions to the editors and authors alike. We hope readers will share our sense of excitement and that the Companion will help capture for them the complexity, vitality, and endless fascination of contemporary world affairs.

Joel Krieger
Jamaica Plain, Massachusetts
August 2000

EDITORS AND ADVISERS

DIRECTORY OF CONTRIBUTORS

Philip Abbott, *Professor of Political Science, Wayne State University*
Roosevelt, Franklin Delano

Levon Abrahamian, *Senior Researcher, Institute of Archaeology and Ethnography, National Academy of Sciences of Armenia, Yerevan*
Armenia

Joan R. Acker, *Professor of Sociology, University of Oregon*
Comparable Worth

Sean Aday, *Professor, The Annenberg School of Communications*
Media and Politics

John A. Agnew, *Professor and Chair, Department of Geography, University of California, Los Angeles*
Geopolitics

Feroz Ahmad, *Professor of History and University Research Professor, University of Massachusetts, Boston*
Atatürk, Kemal; Kemalism; Turkey

Claude Ake, *Director, Centre for Advanced Social Science, Port Harcourt, Nigeria*
Development and Underdevelopment

Mateo Alaluf, *Professor in Labor and Social Thought, University of Brussels*
Luxembourg

Herbert E. Alexander, *Professor Emeritus of Political Science, and Director Emeritus of Citizens' Research Foundation, University of Southern California*
Political Action Committee

Hayward R. Alker, *Professor, School of International Relations, University of Southern California*
International Systems; Thucydides

Erik Allardt, *Professor, Department of Sociology, University of Helsinki*
Finland

Christopher S. Allen, *Associate Professor of Political Science, University of Georgia*
Codetermination; Kohl, Helmut; Proportional Representation; Schröder, Gerhard; Social Market Economy

Stephen E. Ambrose, *Thomas Byrd Professor of History and Director, The Eisenhower Center*
Eisenhower, Dwight D.

Benedict R. O'Gorman Anderson, *Aaron L. Binenkorb Professor of International Studies, Cornell University and Director; Cornell Modern Indonesia Project*
Nationalism

Lamis Andoni, *Journalist*
Jordan

Peggy Antrobus, *Tutor/Co-ordinator, Women and Development Unit (WAND), Barbados*
Women and Development

Cynthia Arnson, *Assistant Director, Latin American Program, Woodrow Wilson International Center for Scholars*
U.S.–Latin American Relations

Robert J. Art, *Christian A. Herter Professor of International Relations, Brandeis University*
Bureaucratic Politics; Security

S. K. B. Asante, *Professor and former Senior Regional Advisor, Cabinet Office, United Nations Economic Commission for Africa, Addis Ababa, Ethiopia*
Economic Community of West African States

Adrienne Asch, *Henry R. Luce Professor, Wellesley College*
Disability Politics

G. Pope Atkins, *Professor of Political Science, United States Naval Academy*
Inter-American Development Bank; Latin American and Caribbean Regional Organizations; Monroe Doctrine; Organization of American States; Rio Treaty

Lloyd Axworthy, *Minister of Foreign Affairs, Canada*
The United Nations

Mario J. Azevedo, *Chair and Frank Porter Graham Professor, Department of African-American and African Studies, The University of North Carolina at Charlotte*
Equatorial Guinea; Guinea-Bissau; Lusophone Africa; Mozambique

Don Babai, *Associate for the Center for International Affairs, Harvard University*
International Monetary Fund; World Bank; World Trade Organization

Les Back, *Department of Sociology, Goldsmith's College, University of London*
Race and Racism

John H. Badgley, *Adjunct Professor, Department of Asian Studies, Cornell University*
Aung San Suu Kyi; Myanmar [Burma]

Ben H. Bagdikian, *Former Dean of the Graduate School of Journalism, The University of California at Berkeley*
Information Technology

Raymond William Baker, *Dean of Faculty, Trinity College, Connecticut*
Sadat, Anwar

Ivo Banac, *Bradford Durfee Professor of History and Chair, Council on European Studies, Yale University*
Croatia; Serbia and Montenegro; Tito; Yugoslavia

Lok Raj Baral, *Professor of Political Science, Tribhuvan University, Kathmandu, Nepal*
Nepal

William J. Barber, *Andrews Professor of Economics, Emeritus, Wesleyan University*
Keynesianism

Zygmunt Bauman, *Emeritus Professor of Sociology, University of Leeds*
Holocaust; Modernity

Kenneth Baynes, *Associate Professor of Philosophy, State University of New York at Stony Brook*
Legitimacy

David Beetham, *Professor of Politics, University of Leeds, United Kingdom*
Weber, Max

Joel Beinin, *Professor of Middle East History, Department of History, Stanford University*
Nasser, Gamal Abdel; Nasserism

Mark R. Beissinger, *Associate Professor of Policial Science, University of Wisconsin-Madison*
Commonwealth of Independent States; Russia

Benjamin Beit Hallahmi, *Professor of Psychology, Department of Psychology, University of Haifa*
Fundamentalism

Getinet Belay, *Assistant Professor of Communications Studies, Rutgers University*
Information Society

Daniel Bell, *Scholar in Residence, American Academy of Arts and Sciences, Cambridge, Mass.*
Postindustrial Society

Thomas J. Bellows, *Professor, Department of Political Science, The University of Texas at San Antonio*
Singapore

Shlomo Ben-Ami, *Acting Foreign Minister, Israel*
Franco, Francisco; Spanish Civil War

Phyllis Bennis, *Fellow of the Institute for Policy Studies and Director of the New Internationalism Project, Institute for Policy Studies*
Annan, Kofi

Larry Berman, *Director, University of California Washington Center and Professor of Political Science, UC Davis*
Reagan, Ronald Wilson

Marshall Berman, *Professor of Political Science, City College/CUNY*
Postmodernism

Serge Berstein, *Professeur des Universités à l'Institut d'Etudes Politiques de Paris and Directeur du Cycle Superieur d'Histoire du XX Siècle, Institut d'Etudes Politiques de Paris*
Gaullism

Lucien Bianco, *Director of Studies, Centre de Recherches et de Documentation sur la Chine Contemporaine, Paris*
Chinese Revolution

Henry S. Bienen, *Dean, Woodrow Wilson School of Public and International Affairs, Princeton University*
Military Rule

Harry W. Blair, *Professor of Political Science, Bucknell University*
Bangladesh; Grameen Bank

Lee Bollinger, *President, The University of Michigan*
Censorship

John R. Bolton, *Senior Vice President, American Enterprise Institute for Public Policy Research, Washington, D.C.*
The United Nations

Heraclio Bonilla, *Coordinator, History Section, Latin American Faculty for Social Sciences (FLACSO), Equador*
Bolívar, Simón; Mariátegui, José Carlos; Martí, José

John A. Booth, *Regents Professor of Political Science, University of North Texas*
Nicaragua

Sylvia Borren, *Novib*
Gay and Lesbian Politics

Steven J. Brams, *Professor of Politics, New York University*
Game Theory

Gerard Braunthal, *Professor Emeritus of Political Science, University of Massachusetts/Amherst*
Germany, Federal Republic of

Jacqueline Anne Braveboy-Wagner, *Professor of Political Science and Director, M.A. in International Relations, The Graduate School and University Center of the City University of New York*
   English-Speaking Caribbean; Grenada; Trinidad and Tobago

Judith Brett, *Reader School of Sociology, Politics and Anthropology, La Trobe University, Melbourne Australia*
   Australia

Alan Brinkley, *Allan Nevins Professor of History, Columbia University*
   New Deal

Festus Brotherson, *Senior Research Associate, North-South Center, University of Miami, Florid.*
   Guyana

Archie Brown, *Professor of Politics, University of Oxford, and Director of Russian and East European Centre, St. Antony's College, Oxford*
   Gorbachev, Mikhail

Robert Buijtenhuijs, *Director of Research, Department of Political and Historical Studies, African Studies Centre, The Netherlands*
   Chad

Charlotte Bunch, *Professor, School of Planning and Executive Director, Center for Women's Global Leadership, Rutgers University*
   Feminism

Stephen G. Bunker, *Professor of Sociology, University of Wisconsin, Madison*
   Amazon Development

David Calleo, *Dean Acheson Professor and Director of European Studies, Nitze School of Advanced International Studies, Johns Hopkins University*
   German Unification

Charles Cameron, *Associate Professor of Political Science, Columbia University, New York, NY*
   Veto

Maxwell Cameron, *Associate Professor, Department of Political Science, University of British Columbia*
   NAFTA

Horace Campbell, *Professor of African Politics, Syracuse University*
   Cabral, Amílcar; Cuito Cuanavale; Nyerere, Julius; Pan-Africanism

Christopher Candland, *Assistant Professor, Department of Political Science, Wellesley College*
   Civil Society; Social Capital

Clayborne Carson, *Professor of History and Editor of the Papers of Martin Luther King, Jr., Stanford University*
   African Americans

Pablo Gonzales Casanova, *Research Professor, Instituto de Investigaciones Sociales, Universidad Nacional Autonoma de Mexico*
   Imperialism

Antonio Cassese, *Professor of International Law, European University Institute*
   International Law

David Chalmers, *Distinguished Service Professor of History, University of Florida*
   Ku Klux Klan

Ming K. Chan, *Research Fellow and Executive Coordinator, Hong Kong Documentary Archive, Hoover Institution, Stanford University*
   Hong Kong

David P. Chandler, *Emeritus Professor of History, Monash University*
   Cambodia; Pol Pot

Eugenio Chang-Rodríguez, *New York, NY*
   Haya de la Torre, Víctor Raúl

Margaret Chatterjee, *Professor of Philosophy, University of Delhi*
   Gandhi, Mohandas

Fantu Cheru, *Associate Professor of African and Development Studies, The American University*
   Kenya

Daniel Chirot, *Professor of Sociology and International Studies, University of Washington*
   Romania

Nazli Choucri, *Professor, Department of Political Science, Massachusetts Institute of Technology*
   Environmentalism

Andrew Clapham, *Associate Professor of Public International Law, Graduate Institute of International Studies, Geneva, Switzerland*
   Human Rights; International Law

Christopher Clapham, *Professor of Politics & International Relations, Lancaster University, United Kingdom*
   One-Party System; Patron-Client Politics

Cal Clark, *Alumni Professor of Political Science, Department of Political Science, Auburn University*
   Taiwan

James W. Clarke, *Professor of Political Science, University of Arizona*
   Assassination

Walter Clemens, *Professor of Political Science, Boston University; Associate, Davis Center for Russian Studies, Harvard University*
  Baltic States

Gregory Cleva, *Arlington, Va.*
  Kissinger, Henry

Helena Cobban, *Contributing Writer, The Christian Science Monitor*
  Arafat, Yasir

David Collier, *Professor of Political Science, University of California, Berkeley*
  Bureaucratic Authoritarianism

Michael L. Conniff, *Professor of History, Auburn University*
  Vargas, Getúlio

Allan D. Cooper, *Professor of Political Science, Department of History and Political Science, Otterbein College*
  Namibia

Michael Coppedge, *Professor, The Helen Kellogg Institute for International Studies, The University of Notre Dame*
  Venezuela

Stephen Cornell, *Professor of Sociology and Director of the Udall Center for Studies in Public Policy at The University of Arizona*
  Native Americans

Margaret E. Crahan, *Dorothy Epstein Professor in Latin American History, Hunter College*
  Arias, Oscar

Russell Crandall, *Latin American Studies Program, Johns Hopkins University*
  Brazil

Barbara B. Crane, *Senior Policy Adviser, Centre for Development and Population Activities and Executive Vice President for Policy, Research and Evaluation, Ipas*
  Population Policy

Markus Crepaz, *Associate Professor, Department of Political Science, The University of Georgia*
  Austria

Robert Cribb, *Reader in Modern Southeast Asian History, University of Queensland*
  Timor

Donald K. Crone, *Dean of Faculty and Professor of International Relations, Scripps College*
  Association of Southeast Asian Nations

William E. Crowther, *Professor, Department of Political Science, University of North Carolina*
  Moldova

Selwyn R. Cudjoe, *Professor of Africana Studies, Wellesley College*
  James, C. L. R.

Roy Culpeper, *President of the North-South Institute*
  Regional Development Banks

Bruce Cumings, *Norman and Edna Freehling Professor, Department of History, University of Chicago*
  Korea, Democratic People's Republic of; Korean War

Michael Curtis, *Professor, Department of Political Science Rutgers University*
  Anti-semitism

Robert A. Dahl, *Sterling Professor Emeritus of Political Science, Yale University*
  Pluralism

Richard Dale, *Associate Professor Emeritus of Political Science, Southern Illinois University at Carbondale*
  Botswana

Dana G. Dalrymple, *Research Advisor, Office of Agriculture and Food Security, Global Bureau, U.S. Agency for International Development*
  Green Revolution

Russell J. Dalton, *Professor of Political Science, University of California, Irvine*
  New Social Movements

Robert V. Daniels, *Professor Emeritus of History, University of Vermont*
  Stalin, Joseph

Kishore C. Dash, *Professor of International Studies, Department of International Studies, Thunderbird, The American Graduate School of International Management*
  South Asian Association for Regional Cooperation

Roger H. Davidson, *Professor of Government and Politics, University of Maryland*
  Congress, U.S.

Professor Thomas M. Davies, Jr., *Department of History, San Diego State University*
  Guevara, Ernesto

Richard B. Day, *Professor, University of Toronto*
  Trotsky, Lev

Samuel Decalo, *Professor of African Politics, University of Natal*
  Central African Republic; Togo

Mark W. Delancey, *Professor, Department of Government and International Studies, University of South Carolina*
  Cameroon

Lual Deng, *Managing Director and Founder, African Development Center (ADC) Nairobi, Kenya*
  African Development Bank; Sudan

James Der Derian, *Professor of Political Science, University of Massachusetts, Amherst and Professor of International Relations, Watson Institute for International Studies, Brown University*
Diplomacy

Allison Des Forges, *Human Rights Watch*
Rwandan Genocide

Meghnad Desai, *Professor of Economics and Director, The Centre for the Study of Global Governance, London School of Economics and Political Science*
Capitalism

Edward M. Dew, *Professor, Department of Politics, Fairfield University*
Suriname

Yoram Dinstein, *Yanowicz Professor of Human Rights and Pro-President, Tel Aviv University; Member, Institute of International Law*
Nuremberg Trials; War Crimes; War Crimes Tribunals; War, Rules of

Lowell Dittmer, *Professor, Department of Political Science, University of California, Berkeley*
Deng Xiaoping

George W. Downs, *Class of 1942 Professor of Peace and War, Department of Politics and Woodrow Wilson School, Princeton University*
Arms Race

Margaret Doxey, *Professor Emeritus & Senior Research Associate, Department of Political Studies, Trent University*
Sanctions

Paul W. Drake, *Institute of America Professor of Inter-American Affairs, University of California, San Diego*
Allende, Salvador; Chile; Pinochet, Augusto

Alasdair Drysdale, *Chairman, Department of Geography, University of New Hampshire*
Syria

Peter D. Drysdale, *Professor in the Asia Pacific School of Economics and Management, and the Economics Division, Research School of Pacific and Asian Studies, Australian National University (ANU), and Executive Director of the Australia-Japan Research Centre (AJRC)*
Asia Pacific Economic Cooperation (APEC); Pacific Region

William J. Duiker, *Liberal Arts Professor Emeritus of East Asian Studies, The Pennsylvania State University*
Ho Chi Minh

Alex Dupuy, *Professor of Sociology, Wesleyan University*
Haiti

Ronald S. Edari, *Associate Professor of Sociology and Urban Studies, University of Wisconsin, Milwaukee*
Urbanization

S. N. Eisenstadt, *Rose Isaacs Professor Emeritus of Sociology, The Hebrew University of Jerusalem*
Modernization

Zillah Eisenstein, *Professor of Politics, Ithaca College*
Feminist Theory

Samuel J. Eldersveld, *Professor Emeritus of Political Science, University of Michigan*
Elites

Charlotte Elton, *San Lorenzo Project Coordinator, Panamanian Center for Research and Social Action, CEASPA, Panama*
Panama

Anne Emig, *The Japan Program, Inter-American Development Bank*
Asian Development Bank

Donald K. Emmerson, *Senior Fellow, Asia/Pacific Research Center, Stanford University*
Indonesia

Robert D. English, *Assistant Professor, School of International Relations, University of Southern California*
Kosovo War

Cynthia H. Enloe, *Professor of Government, Clark University*
Gender and Politics

Kenneth Paul Erickson, *Professor, Department of Political Science, Hunter College*
Drugs

Amitai Etzioni, *University Professor, George Washington University*
Communitarianism

Peter B. Evans, *Professor of Sociology, University of California, Berkeley*
Dependency

Richard Falk, *Albert G. Milbank Professor of International Law and Practice, Princeton University*
Hiroshima; International Court of Justice; Rights; Sovereignty

M. Patricia Fernández Kelly, *Research Scientist, Department of Sociology and Office of Population Research, Princeton University*
Maquiladoras

José María Figueres Olsen, *Chairman, Costa Rica Foundation for Sustainable Development*
U.S.–Central American Relations

Kenneth Finegold, *Associate Professor of Government, Eastern Washington University*
Progressive Movement, U.S.

Milton Fisk, *Professor Emeritus, Department of Philosophy, Indiana University at Bloomington*
The Limits of Liberal Democracy

E. V. K. FitzGerald, *Director of Financial Studies, International Development Centre, University of Oxford*
Economic Commission for Latin America and the Carribbean

John Fitzmaurice, *Lecturer, Institut d'Etudes Européennes at the Université Libre de Bruxelles*
Belgium

Michael Fleet, *Professor of Political Science, Marquette University*
Christian Democracy

David P. Forsythe, *Professor of Political Science, University of Nebraska-Lincoln*
Helsinki Accords

Jeffry A. Frieden, *Professor of Government, Harvard University*
International Debt

Haruhiro Fukui, *Professor Emeritus, Department of Political Science, University of California, Santa Barbara*
Hirohito; Japan

Francis Fukuyama, *Omer L. and Nancy Hirst Professor of Public Policy, School of Public Policy, George Mason University*
The Limits of Liberal Democracy

Johan Galtung, *Professor of Peace Studies, University of Hawaii, and Director of TRANSCEND, a Peace and Development Network*
Peace

Eduardo A. Gamarra, *Professor of Political Science and Director, Latin American and Caribbean Center, Florida International University*
Bolivia

F. Chris Garcia, *Professor of Political Science, Department of Political Science, University of New Mexico*
Hispanic Americans

David E. Gardinier, *Professor of History, Marquette University*
Gabon

Raymond L. Garthoff, *Foreign Policy Studies Program, The Brookings Institution*
Warsaw Treaty Organization

John Garver; *Professor, Sam Nunn School of International Affairs, Georgia Institute of Technology*
Sino-American Relations

Joyce Gelb, *Professor of Political Science, City College and Graduate Center, City University of New York*
Gender Gap

Julie George, *Graduate Student*
Georgia

Stephen George, *Jean Monnet Professor of Politics, University of Sheffield*
Rome, Treaty of

David N. Gibbs, *Associate Professor of Political Science, University of Arizona*
Mauritania

Hashim T. Gibrill, *Professor, Department of Political Science, Clark Atlanta University*
South-South Cooperation

Martin Gilbert, *Honorary Fellow, Merton College, Oxford*
Churchill, Winston

Stephen Gill, *Professor of Political Science, York University*
Group of 7; Hegemony

Michael Gilsenan, *David B. Kleiser Chair of the Humanities, Department of Middle Eastern Studies, New York University*
Islam; Jihad

Benjamin Ginsberg, *David Bernstein Professor of Political Science, Director, Center for Governmental Studies, The Johns Hopkins University*
Elections and Voting Behavior

Todd Gitlin, *Professor of Culture, Journalism and Sociology, New York University*
New Left

Betty Glad, *Olin P. Johnston Professor of Political Science, University of South Carolina, Columbia*
Carter, Jimmy

Abbott Gleason, *Keeney Professor of History, Department of History, Brown University*
Totalitarianism

Michael J. Glennon, *Professor of Law, School of Law, University of California at Davis*
War Powers Resolution

Jack A. Goldstone, *Professor of Sociology and International Relations, University of California-Davis*
Revolution

Richard Gordon, *Associate Professor of Politics, University of California, Santa Cruz, deceased*
Fordism

Lewis L. Gould, *Eugene C. Barker Centennial Professor Emeritus in American History, University of Texas at Austin*
Johnson, Lyndon Baines

Peter A. Gourevitch, *Professor, Graduate School of International Relations and Pacific Studies, University of California, San Diego*
Political Economy

Doris A. Graber, *Professor of Political Science, University of Illinois at Chicago*
Psychology and Politics

Mark Graber, *Associate Professor, Department of Government and Politics, University of Maryland, College Park*
Roe v. Wade

Norman A. Graebuer, *Randolph P. Compton Professor of History and Public Affairs Emeritus, University of Virginia*
Isolationism

Sarah Graham-Brown, *Writer and Researcher on the Middle East and on development issues*
Palestine

Donald Green, *Professor of Political Science, Department of Political Science, and Director of the Institution for Social and Policy Studies, Yale University*
Rational Choice

Beverly Grier, *Associate Professor of Government and International Relations, Clark University*
Niger

Merilee S. Grindle, *Edward S. Mason Professor of International Development, John F. Kennedy School of Government, Harvard University*
Rural Development

Bertram Gross, *Distinguished Professor Emeritus, City University of New York and Visiting Professor, World Classics, Saint Mary's College of California*
Planning

Jan T. Gross, *Professor of Politics, New York University*
Central Europe

A. Tom Grunfeld, *Associate Professor of History, Empire State College, SUNY*
Tibet

Lani Guinier, *Professor of Law, Harvard Law School*
Affirmative Action

Richard Gunther, *Professor of Political Science, Ohio State University*
Spain

Ted Robert Gurr, *Distinguished University Professor, Department of Government and Politics, and Director, Minorities at Risk Project, Center for International Development and Conflict Management, University of Maryland*
Political Violence

Stephan Haggard, *Professor, Graduate School of International Relations and Pacific Studies, University of California, San Diego*
Export-Led Growth; Import-Substitution Industrialization; Newly Industrializing Economies

Mehrdad Haghayeghi, *Associate Professor of Political Science, Department of Political Science, Southwest Missouri State University*
Central Asia

John A. Hall, *Professor of Sociology, McGill University*
Liberalism; State

Kermit L. Hall, *Provost and Vice Chancellor for Academic Affairs, North Carolina State University, Raleigh, North Carolina*
Supreme Court of the United States

Linda Hall, *Albuquerque, NM*
Mexico

Peter A. Hall, *Frank G. Thomson Professor of Government at Harvard University*
Monetarism

Fred Halliday, *Professor of International Relations, London School of Economics and Political Science*
Cold War; Iranian Revolution; Terrorism; Yemen

Nora Hamilton, *Associate Professor of Political Science, University of Southern California*
Cárdenas, Lázaro

Phillip Hansen, *Professor of Political Science, Department of Political Science, University of Regina*
Arendt, Hannah

B. E. Harrell-Bond, *Distinguished Adjunct Professor, Forced Migration and Refugee Studies, American University in Cairo*
Refugees

Tom Harrison, *History Teacher, The Brearley School, New York*
Nineteen Eighty-Nine

Jonathan Hartlyn, *Professor of Political Science and Director, Institute of Latin American Studies, University of North Carolina at Chapel Hill*
Colombia; Dominican Republic

Ronald L. Hatchett, *Cullen/Sarofim Professor of International Studies and Director, Center for International Studies, The University of St. Thomas, Houston, Texas*
Bosnia and Herzegovina

Fred M. Hayward, *Senior Associate, International Initiatives, American Council on Education, Washington, DC*
  Sierra Leone

Michael Hechter, *Professor of Sociology, The University of Washington*
  Internal Colonialism

J. Bryan Hehir, *Professor of the Practice in Religion and Society, Weatherhead Center for International Affairs, Harvard University*
  Roman Catholic Church

David Held, *Graham Wallas Chair in Political Science, London School of Economics and Political Science*
  Democracy; Globalization

Suzette Hemberger, *Independent scholar, Washington, DC*
  Constitution

Phillip G. Henderson, *Associate Professor of Political Science, The Catholic University of America*
  Bush, George Herbert Walker

Charles F. Hermann, *Associate Dean for International Programs at the George Bush School of Government and Professor of Political Science, Texas A&M University*
  Crisis

Carolina G. Hernandez, *President, Institute for Strategic and Development Studies, Philippines and Professor of Political Science, University of the Philippines, Diliman, Quezon City*
  Aquino, Corazon; Marcos, Ferdinand; Philippines

Christopher Hill, *Montague Burton Professor of International Relations, London School of Economics and Political Science*
  Foreign Policy

Enid Hill, *Professor, American University in Cairo*
  Ibn Khaldun

Ronald J. Hill, *Professor of Comparative Government, Trinity College, Dublin, Ireland*
  Soviet Union

Stanley Hoffmann, *Paul and Catherine Buttenwieser University Professor, Harvard University*
  Gaulle, Charles de

Kalevi J. Holsti, *University Killam Professor, Department of Political Science, University of British Columbia*
  League of Nations

Roger G. Hood, *Professor of Criminology, Director of the Centre for Criminological Research, University of Oxford and Fellow of All Souls College*
  Capital Punishment

Eric Hooglund, *Editor, Middle East Journal*
  Iran; Khomeini, Ruhollah

Michael Hout, *Department of Sociology, University of California, Berkeley*
  Social Mobility

Evelyne Huber, *Morehead Alumni Distinguished Professor in Latin American Politics, University of North Carolina, Chapel Hill*
  Jamaica

Shirley Hune, *Professor of Urban Planning, School of Public Policy and Social Research, and Associate Dean, Graduate Division, University of California, Los Angeles*
  Nonaligned Movement

Richard M. Hunt, *Senior Lecturer on Social Studies and University Marshal, Harvard University*
  Hitler, Adolf

Ronald Inglehart, *Professor of Political Science and Program Director, Center for Political Studies, Institute for Social Research, University of Michigan*
  Postmaterialism

Maurice Isserman, *William R. Kenan, Jr. Professor of History, Hamilton College*
  Left

Ruth Iyob, *Professor, Department of Political Science, University of Missouri, Saint Louis*
  Intergovernmental Authority for Development (IGAD)

Keith Jackson, *Emeritus Professor of Political Science, Department of Political Science, University of Canterbury, New Zealand*
  ANZUS Treaty; New Zealand

Lawrence R. Jacobs, *Associate Professor, Department of Political Science, University of Minnesota*
  Medicare and Medicaid

Ayesha Jalal, *Professor of History, Tufts University*
  Pakistan

Kathleen Hall Jamieson, *Professor of Communication and Dean, The Annenberg School for Communication, University of Pennsylvania*
  Media and Politics

Martín Sánchez Jankowski, *Professor, Department of Sociology, University of California, Berkeley*
  Gangs

Jane Jenson, *Professor, Department of Political Science, Universite De Montreal*
  Canada; Trudeau, Pierre

Bruce W. Jentleson, *Director, Terry Sanford Institute of Public Policy, Duke University*
  Domino Theory

Dong Youl Jeong, *Assistant Professor of Library and Information Science, Ewha University*
Information Society

Bob Jessop, *Professor of Sociology, Department of Sociology, Lancaster University, England*
Thatcherism

L. Adele Jinadu, *Professor, Department of Social Sciences, Logos State University*
Fanon, Frantz

George Joffé, *Centre for International Studies in the London School of Economics, and Political Science, London University, and Visiting Fellow at the Centre for International Studies, Cambridge University*
Libya; Qaddafi, Muammar

Michael Johnston, *Professor of Political Science, Department of Political Science, Colgate University*
Corruption

Susanne Jonas, *Professor of Latin American & Latino Studies, University of California, Santa Cruz*
Guatemala

William A. Joseph, *M. Margaret Ball Professor of International Relations, Department of Political Science, Wellesley College*
China; Cultural Revolution

Christopher C. Joyner, *Professor, Department of Government, Georgetown University*
Treaty

Samba Ka, *ACBF, Zimbabwe*
Senegal

Lawrence C. Katzenstein, *Lecturer, Department of Political Science, University of Minnesota, Twin Cities*
Multinational Corporations

Dennis Kavanagh, *Professor, School of Politics and Communication Studies, University of Liverpool*
Thatcher, Margaret

John T. S. Keeler, *Professor of Political Science and Director of the European Union Center, University of Washington*
Reform

Rich Keiser, *Associate Professor of Political Science, Department of Political Science, Carleton College*
Political Machine

Robert O. Keohane, *Professor, James B. Duke Professor of Political Science, Duke University*
Reciprocity; Regime

Mark Kesselman, *Professor of Political Science, Department of Political Science, Columbia University*
Mitterrand, François

Moncef M. Khaddar, *Professor, Department of Political Science, American University in Cairo*
Tunisia

Rashid I. Khalidi, *Professor of Middle East History and Director, Center for International Studies, University of Chicago*
Intifada; Resolution 242

Baruch Kimmerling, *Professor of Sociology in Politics, The Hebrew University*
Israel

Desmond King, *Official Fellow in Politics, St. John's College, University of Oxford*
New Right; Right

Eric R. Kingson, *Professor of Social Work and Public Administration, School of Social Work, Syracuse University*
Baby Boomer; Social Security

Richard S. Kirkendall, *Bullitt Professor of American History Emeritus, University of Washington*
Truman, Harry S.

Michael T. Klare, *Five College Professor of Peace and World Security Studies, Hampshire College*
Militarism

Franklin Knight, *Leonard and Helen R. Stulman Professor of History, Johns Hopkins University*
Cuba

Jack Knight, *Assistant Professor of Political Science, Washington University in St. Louis*
Public Good

Atul Kohli, *Wilson School of Public and International Affairs, Robertson Hall, Princeton University*
Nehru, Jawaharlal

Walter S. G. Kohn, *Emeritus Professor of Political Science, Illinois State University, deceased*
Switzerland

George Kolankiewicz, *Professor of Sociology, Department of Social Sciences, The School of Slavonic and East European Studies, University College London*
Poland; Wałęsa, Lech

Bennett Kovrig, *Professor Emeritus of Political Science, University of Toronto*
Hungary

Stephen D. Krasner, *Graham H. Stuart Professor of International Relations, Stanford University*
International Political Economy

Joel Krieger, *Norma Wilentz Hess Professor of Political Science, Wellesley College*
Britain

Jacek Kugler, *Elizabeth Helm Rosecrans Professor of World Politics, School for Politics and Economics, Claremont Graduate University*
    War

Charles Kupchan, *Associate Professor of International Affairs, Georgetown University, and Senior Fellow, Council on Foreign Relations*
    Strategy

James Kurth, *Claude Smith Professor of Political Science, Department of Political Science, Swarthmore College*
    Military-Industrial Complex

Walter LaFeber, *Noll Professor of American History, Cornell University*
    Truman Doctrine

Anthony Lake, *Distinguished Professor, Edmund A. Walsh School of Foreign Service, Georgetown University, Washington, D.C.*
    Vietnam War

David A. Lake, *Professor and Chair, Department of Political Science, University of California, San Diego*
    Balance of Power; Realism

Carol Lancaster, *Associate Professor and Director of the Masters of Science in Foreign Service, School of Foreign Service, Georgetown University*
    Paris Club

Fred H. Lawson, *Professor of Government, Mills College*
    Arab League; Gulf States; Kuwait

Kay Lawson, *Professor of Political Science and International Relations, San Francisco State University*
    Political Parties and Party Competition

Margaret C. Lee, *Professor, African Studies Program, School of Foreign Service, Georgetown University*
    Southern Africa; Southern African Development Community; Truth and Reconciliation Commission; Zimbabwe

Carol Skalnik Leff, *Associate Professor of Political Science, University of Illinois at Urbana-Champaign*
    Slovakia

Christiane Lemke, *Lecturer in Political Science, Freie Universitat Berlin*
    German Democratic Republic

Stephanie Lenway, *Professor, Carlson School of Management, University of Minnesota*
    Multinational Corporations

Ann M. Lesch, *Professor of Political Science and Associate Director, Center for Arab and Islamic Studies, Villanova University*
    Palestine Liberation Organization

David Levering Lewis, *Martin Luther King, Jr., Professor of History, Rutgers University*
    Du Bois, W. E. B.

Lars T. Lih, *Freelance writer, Montreal, Quebec*
    Stalinism; Yeltsin, Boris

Arend Lijphart, *Profesor of Political Science, University of California, San Diego*
    Consociational Democracy

Héctor Lindo-Fuentes, *Professor of History, Department of History, Fordham University*
    El Salvador

Juan J. Linz, *Emeritus Sterling Professor of Political and Social Science, Yale University*
    Authoritarianism

Seymour Martin Lipset, *Virginia E. Hazel and John T. Hazel, Jr. Professor of Public Policy, George Mason University and Senior Fellow, Hoover Institution, Stanford University*
    United States

Charles Lipson, *Associate Professor of Political Science; Chair, Committee on International Relations; Director, the Programs on International Politics, Economics, and Security (PIPES), University of Chicago*
    Finance, International; Nationalization

Robert S. Litwak, *Director, Division of International Studies, Woodrow Wilson International Center for Scholars*
    Containment; Détente

Zachary Lockman, *Professor of Middle Eastern Studies and History, New York University*
    Balfour Declaration; Ben-Gurion, David; Zionism

Tom Lodge, *Professor of Political Studies, University of the Witwatersrand*
    Mandela, Nelson

John Logsdon, Director, *Space Policy Institute, Elliott School of International Affairs, George Washington University*
    Space

John Logue, *Professor of Political Science, Kent State*
    Denmark

Glenn C. Loury, *University Professor, Professor of Economics, and Director of the Institute on Race and Social Division, Boston University*
    Affirmative Action

Joseph L. Love, *Professor of History, University of Illinois at Urbana-Champaign*
    Prebisch, Raúl

Brian Loveman, *Professor of Political Science, San Diego State University*
    Guerrilla Warfare; Guevara, Ernesto

Steven Lukes, *Professor, Department of Sociology, New York University*
  Power

Igor Luksic, *Professor, Faculty of Social Sciences, University of Ljubljana*
  Slovenia

S. Neil MacFarlane, *Professor, St. Anne's College, Oxford*
  National Liberation Movements

Henri Madelin, *Associate Professor of Political Science, Institut d'Etudes Politiques de Paris*
  John Paul II; Vatican City State; Vatican II

Archie Mafeje, *Professor, Department of Sociology, American University in Cairo*
  Tribalism

Victor V. Magagna, *Associate Professor of Political Science, University of California, San Diego*
  Peasants

Bernard Magubane, *Retired Professor Emeritus, Department of Anthropology, University of Connecticut*
  Apartheid; South Africa

N. J. Ku-Ntima Makidi, *Professor of Political Science, Director of International Studies, Paine College Augusta, Georgia, and Research Fellow, African Studies Center, University of Florida, Gainesville*
  Congo, Republic of

Assis V. Malaquias, *Assistant Professor, Department of Government, St. Lawrence University, Canton, NY*
  Humanitarian Intervention

William Maley, *Associate Professor of Politics, University College, University of New South Wales, Australia*
  Afghanistan

Chibli Mallat, *Lecturer in Islamic Law, School of Oriental and African Studies, University of London*
  Shari'a

Patrick Manning, *Director of the World History Center and Professor of History and African-American Studies, Northeastern University*
  Francophone Africa

Jane J. Mansbridge, *Professor, Kennedy School of Government, Harvard University*
  Equal Rights Amendment

John Markakis, *Professor of African Studies, University of Crete*
  Ethiopia

Andrei S. Markovits, *Professor of Politics, Department of Germanic Languages and Literatures, The University of Michigan, Ann Arbor*
  Ostpolitik

Theodore R. Marmor, *Professor of Public Policy and Management and the Yale School of Management, and Professor Political Science, Yale University*
  The Future of Entitlements

David Marples, *Professor, Department of History and Classics, University of Alberta*
  Belarus

Peter Marshall, *Chairman of the Joint Commonwealth Societies' Council, London*
  Commonwealth

Jens Martens, *Member of the Executive Board, World Economy, Ecology, and Development (WEED)*
  Sustainable Development

Guy Martin, *Visiting Associate Professor of Government and Foreign Affairs, University of Virginia*
  Benin; Burkina Faso; Lomé Convention/Cotonou Agreement; Mali

J. Paul Martin, *Executive Director, Center for the Study of Human Rights, Columbia University*
  Amnesty International

Lisa L. Martin, *Professor of Government, Harvard University*
  International Cooperation

Jerry L. Mashaw, *Sterling Professor of Law at the Yale School of Law, and Professor, Institute for Social and Policy Studies, Yale University*
  The Future of Entitlements

James Mayall, *Sir Patrick Sheehy Professor of International Relations and Director, Centre of International Studies, University of Cambridge*
  Mercantilism

David Mayers, *Professor of History and Political Science, Boston University*
  Kennan, George

Anthony McGrew, *Professor of International Relations, Southampton University*
  Globalization

Robert J. McIntyre, *United Nations Development Programme*
  Bulgaria

Timothy J. McKeown, *Associate Professor of Political Science, Department of Political Science, University of North Carolina, Chapel Hill*
  Protection

David McLellan, *Professor of Political Theory, University of Kent*
  Acheson, Dean; Communism; Marx, Karl

Kenneth McRoberts, *Professor of Political Science and Director, Robbarts Centre for Canadian Studies*
Quebec

Andy McSmith, *Chief Political Correspondent, The Observer, London, England*
Blair, Tony

Zhores A. Medvedev, *Retired, Formerly with National Institute for Medical Research, United Kingdom*
Chernobyl Nuclear Accident

Pratap Mehta, *Assistant Professor of Government, Harvard University*
Gandhi, Indira; India; Nehru, Jawaharlal

Maurice Meisner, *Harvey Goldberg Professor of History, University of Wisconsin, Madison*
Mao Zedong

Ruben P. Mendez, *Historian, UNDP and Adjunct Professor and Fellow, New York and Yale Universities*
International Public Finance

Berhanu Mengistu, *Professor of Urban Studies and Public Administration, College of Business and Public Administration, Old Dominion University*
Parastatals; Privatization

Anthony M. Messina, *Associate Professor, Department of Government and International Studies, University of Notre Dame*
Foreign Workers

Steven Metz, *Research Professor of National Security Affairs, U.S. Army War College Strategic Studies Institute, Carlisle Barracks, Pennsylvania*
Counterinsurgency

Alfred G. Meyer, *Professor Emeritus of Political Science, University of Michigan, deceased*
Leninism

Michael L. Mezey, *Professor of Political Science and Dean of the College of Liberal Arts and Sciences, DePaul University, Chicago*
Legislature

William Minter, *Senior Research Fellow, Africa Policy Information Center*
Angola

Bruce Miroff, *Professor and Chair of Political Science, Department of Political Science, State University of New York, Albany*
Kennedy, John Fitzgerald

Timothy Mitchell, *Associate Professor of Politics, New York University*
Egypt

William C. Mitchell, *Professor of Political Science Emeritus, University of Oregon*
Public Choice Theory

James H. Mittelman, *Professor of International Relations, School of International Service, American University, Washington, DC*
Third World

Lars Mjøset, *Research Director, Comparative Studies, Institute for Social Research, Oslo*
Iceland; Norway; Scandinavia

Tariq Modood, *Professor of Sociology, Politics and Public Policy and Director, Centre for the Study of Ethnicity and Citizenship, Department of Sociology, University of Bristol*
Multiculturalism

Bruce Moon, *Professor of International Relations, Department of International Relations, Lehigh University*
Structural Adjustment Program

Patrick Morgan, *Thomas and Elizabeth Tierney Professor of Peace Research, University of California, Irvine*
Arms Control; Disarmament

Aldon Morris, *Professor of Sociology, Department of Sociology, Northwestern University*
Civil Rights Movement

Lorenzo Morris, *Professor of Political Science, Department of Political Science, Howard University*
Public Policy

Robert A. Mortimer, *Professor of Political Science, Haverford College*
Algeria; Algerian War of Independence; Maghreb

Chantal Mouffe, *Professor of Political Theory, Centre for the Study of Democracy, University of Westminster, London*
Citizenship

Gary Mucciaroni, *Associate Professor, Department of Political Science, Temple University*
Political Business Cycle; Watergate

Craig N. Murphy, *Professor of Political Science, Wellesley College*
Gramsci, Antonio; International Labor Organization; Organization for Economic Co-operation and Development

Walusako A. Mwalilino, *Library Technician, The Library of Congress*
Malawi

Musifiky Mwanasali, *Professor, Department of Political Science, Sarah Lawrence College*
Burundi; Lumumba, Patrice

Richard P. Nathan, *Director, Rockefeller Institute of Government, SUNY, Albany*
Federalism

Marysa Navarro-Aranguren, *Department of History, Dartmouth College*
Perón, Eva Duarte de

Mohamed Saidou N'Daou, *Chicago, IL*
Guinea

Clark D. Neher, *Professor of Political Science, Northern Illinois University*
Thailand

Joan M. Nelson, *Senior Associate, Overseas Development Council*
Political Participation

Michael Nelson, *Professor of Political Science, Rhodes College*
Presidency, U.S.

Catharine Newbury, *Associate Professor of Political Science and African Studies, The University of North Carolina at Chapel Hill*
Rwanda

Jan Nijman, *Professor of Geography and Regional Studies, School of International Studies, University of Miami*
Foreign Aid

August H. Nimtz, Jr., *Professor of Political Science, University of Minnesota*
Marxism

Okwudiba Nnoli, *Coordinator-General, Pan African Centre for Research on Peace anbd Conflict Resolution*
Ethnicity

Emile Noël, *Principal, European University Institute, deceased*
Monnet, Jean

Philip Norton, *Professor The Lord Norton of Louth, Professor of Government, University of Hull, Director of Center for Legislative Studies.*
Cabinet Government; Constitutional Monarchy; Parliamentary Democracy; Parliamentary Sovereignty

Sulayman S. Nyang, *Chairman and Professor, Department of African Studies, Howard University*
Gambia

Georges Nzongola-Ntalaja, *Professor Emeritus, African Studies, Howard University and Senior Technical Adviser for Governance, United Nations Development Programme*
Congo, Democratic Republic of; Great Lakes Region

Michael O'Neill, *Professor, Department of Politics, Nottingham Trent University*
Green Parties

Rowena Olegario, *Assistant Professor, University of Michigan Business School*
Malcolm X

Bamidele Olowu, *Public Policy and Administration, Institute of Social Studies, The Hague, Netherlands*
Economic Commission for Africa

Adebayo O. Olukoshi, *Research Professor and Research Programme Coordinator, The Nordic Africa Institute, Uppsala, Sweden*
Nigeria

Amii Omara-Otunnu, *Associate Professor of History and Director, Center for Contemporary African Studies, University of Connecticut*
Uganda

Akwasi P. Osei, *Associate Professor of History and Political Science, Dept of History, Political Science, and Philosophy, Delaware State University*
Ghana; Nkrumah, Kwame

David Ost, *Professor of Political Science, Hobart and William Smith Colleges, and Visiting Professor, Central European University, Warsaw*
Solidarity

Roger Owen, *Lecturer in the Recent Economic History of the Middle East and Director, St. Antony's College, University of Oxford*
Suez Crisis

Robert Paarlberg, *Professor of Political Science, Wellesley College*
Famine; Food Politics

David Scott Palmer, *Professor of International Relations and Political Science and Chairman of the Department of Political Science at Boston University*
Peru

Nicholas C. Pano, *Professor of History and Associate Dean, College of Arts and Science, Western Illinois University*
Albania; Balkans

Peter Paret, *Professor, School of Historical Studies, Institute for Advanced Study, Princeton*
Clausewitz, Carl von

Jane L. Parpart, *Professor of History, Women's Studies, and International Development, Dalousie University, Halifax, Canada and Visiting Professor of Political Science at the University of Stellenbosch, South Africa*
Zambia

Gianfranco Pasquino, *Professor of Political Science, University of Bologna, Italy and Adjunct Professor of Politics, Bologna Center of the Johns Hopkins University*
Italy; Secularization

Robert A. Pastor, *Goodrich C. White Professor of International Relations, Department of Political Science, Emory University*
Panama Canal Treaty

James A. Paul, *Executive Director, Global Policy Forum*
Gulf War; Lebanon; Middle East; Morocco; Non-Governmental Organizations; Small States and Territories; Tunisia

J. Roland Pennock, *Richter Professor Emeritus of Political Science, Swarthmore College, deceased*
Equality and Inequality

Don Peretz, *Professor Emeritus of Political Science, State University of New York at Binghamton*
Arab-Israeli Conflict

Marifeli Perez-Stable, *Visiting Professor, Department of Sociology and Anthropology, Florida International University*
Castro, Fidel

Rosalind Pollack Petchesky, *Professor of Political Science, Hunter College of the City University of New York*
Reproductive Politics

M. J. Peterson, *Professor of Political Science, University of Massachusetts, Amherst*
Antarctica; Law of the Sea

Peter G. Peterson, *Chairman, The Blackstone Group, New York, NY, Chairman, The Federal Reserve Bank, New York, Chairman, The Council on Foreign Relations*
The Future of Entitlements

Karen Pfeifer, *Associate Professor of Economics, Smith College*
Infitah

Gail Pheterson, *Associate Professor of Psychology, University of Picardie, Amiens, France*
Prostitution

Richard M. Pious, *Adolph and Effie Ochs Professor and Chair of Department of Political Science, Barnard College*
Separation of Powers

Adamantia Pollis, *Professor, Graduate Faculty of Political and Social Science, New School University*
Cyprus; Greece

Jonas Pontusson, *Associate Professor of Government, Cornell University*
Sweden

Mark Poster, *Professor of History, University of California,*
Foucault, Michel

Hugh Poulton, *Consultant for the Minority Rights Group, London, and ARTICLE 19, the Global Campaign for Free Expression*
Macedonia, the Former Yugoslav Republic of

Alex Pravda, *Professor, St. Antony's College, Oxford*
Prague Spring

Victor Prescott, *Professor, Department of Geography, University of Melbourne*
Boundary Disputes

Roy L. Prosterman, *Professor of Law, University of Washington, President, Rural Development Institute*
Land Reform

Adam Przeworski, *Martin A. Ryerson Distinguished Social Science Professor, University of Chicago*
Socialism and Social Democracy

Louis Putterman, *Professor of Economics, Brown University*
Collectivization

Lucian W. Pye, *Ford Professor of Political Science, Emeritus, Massachusetts Institute of Technology*
Political Culture; Political Science

George H. Quester, *Professor of Government and Politics, University of Maryland*
U.S. Foreign Policy

Paul J. Quirk, *Associate Professor, Department of Political Science and Institute of Government and Public Affairs, University of Illinois, Urbana*
Deregulation

Jeremy A. Rabkin, *Professor, Department of Government, Cornell University*
Censorship; Conservatism

John Ranelagh, *Author of* The Agency: The Rise and Decline of the CIA
Central Intelligence Agency

Mark Robert Rank, *Professor of Social Work, George Warren Brown School of Social Work, Washington University*
Welfare

Arati Rao, *Adjunct Assistant Professor, School of International and Public Affairs, Columbia University*
Patriarchy

Thomas C. Reeves, *Professor of History, University of Wisconsin, Parkside*
McCarthyism

Robert B. Reich, *University Professor and the Maurice B. Hexter Professor of Social and Economic Policy, Brandeis University and Heller Graduate School*
Deindustrialization

Mitchell Reiss, *Guest Scholar, Woodrow Wilson International Center for Scholars, Washington, D.C.*
Nonproliferation, Nuclear

Robert B. Marks Ridinger, Chair, *Electronic Information Resources Management and Professor, University Libraries, Northern Illinois University*
  Peace Corps

Mitchell S. Ritchie, *College of Law, University of Florida*
  Supreme Court of the United States

Adam Roberts, *Montague Burton Professor of International Relations at Oxford University; Fellow of Balliol College; Fellow of the British Academy*
  Grotius, Hugo; United Nations

Richard A. H. Robinson, *Reader in Iberian History, School of Historical Studies, The University of Birmingham*
  Portugal

William I. Robinson, *Professor, Department of Sociology and Anthropology, New Mexico State University*
  Intervention

Thomas R. Rochon, *Associate Professor of Politics, Center for Politics and Policy, Claremont Graduate School*
  Peace Movement

Luis G. Rodríguez, *Professor of Political and Social Sciences, Cayey University College, Puerto Rico*
  Puerto Rico

Riordan Roett, *The Sarita and Don Johnston Professor and Director Western Hemisphere Program, Paul H. Nitze School of Advanced International Studies, Johns Hopkins University*
  Brazil

John D. Rogers, *Lecturer, Department of History, Tufts University*
  Sri Lanka

Leo E. Rose, *Professor Emeritus of Political Science and Editor Emeritus of Asian Survey, University of California, Berkeley*
  Bhutan

Richard Rosecrance, *Professor, Department of Political Science, University of California, Los Angeles*
  Interdependence

James N. Rosenau, *University Professor of International Affairs, The George Washington University*
  International Relations

Mark B. Rosenberg, *Professor of Political Science and Director, Latin American and Caribbean Center, Florida International University*
  Honduras

George Ross, *Professor, Center for European Studies, Harvard University; Morris Hillquit Professor of Labor and Social Thought, Brandeis University*
  Economic and Monetary Union; European Union; France; Labor Movement; Maastricht Treaty; May 1968

Donald Rothchild, *Professor of Political Science, University of California, Davis*
  Secessionist Movements

Robert L. Rothstein, *Harvey Picker Distinguished Professor of International Relations, Colgate University*
  North-South Relations; United Nations Conference on Trade and Development

Stephen R. Routh, *Doctoral Candidate in Political Science, UC Davis*
  Reagan, Ronald Wilson

Joshua Rubenstein, *Northeast Regional Director, Amnesty International USA, and Associate, Davis Center for Russian Studies, Harvard University*
  Solzhenitsyn, Aleksandr; Soviet Dissent

Bruce Russett, *Dean Acheson Professor of International Relations and Political Science, Yale University*
  Deterrence; Security Dilemma

Peter Rutland, *Tenured Professor of Political Science, Wesleyan University*
  Command Economy

Tony Saich, *Daewoo Professor of International Affairs, Kennedy School of Government, Harvard University*
  Chinese Communist Party; Tiananmen Square

Ghassan Salame, *Director of Studies, Centre National de la Recherche Scientifique, Université de Paris I (Panthéon-Sorbonne)*
  Arab Nationalism; Saudi Arabia

Ahmed I. Samatar, *James Wallace Professor and Dean of International Studies and Programming at Macalester College in St. Paul, Minnesota*
  Somalia

Joel Samoff, *Consulting Professor, Center for African Studies, Stanford University*
  Tanzania

Alan J. K. Sanders, *Lecturer in Mongolian Studies, School of Oriental and African Studies, University of London*
  Mongolia

Ellis Sandoz, *Director, Hermann Moyse, Jr., Distinguished Professor of Political Science, Eric Voegelin Institute for American Renaissance Studies, Louisiana State University*
  Bill of Rights

Danesh D. Sarooshi, *Senior Lecturer in Public International Law, University College London, University of London*
  Security Council

Jorge Reina Schement, *Co-Director, Institute for Information Policy Professor of Communications and Information Policy, Penn State University*
  Information Society

Klaus Schilder, *Project Manager, World Economy, Ecology, and Development Association (WEED)*
Sustainable Development

Jennifer Schirmer, *Director of Program on Conflict Resolution & Peacebuilding, International Peace Research Institute of Oslo*
Torture

Kay Lehman Schlozman, *Professor of Political Science, Boston College*
Interest Groups

Philippe C. Schmitter, *Professor of Political and Social Sciences European University Institute*
Comparative Politics; Corporatism

Brooke Grundfest Schoepf, *Lecturer, Department of Social Medicine, Harvard Medical School*
AIDS

Lars Schoultz, *Kenan Professor, Political Science Department, University of North Carolina, Chapel Hill*
U.S.–Latin American Relations

Joseph M. Schwartz, *Associate Professor of Political Science, Temple University*
Left

Thomas Alan Schwartz, *Associate Professor of History, Vanderbilt University*
Marshall Plan; Potsdam Conference; Yalta Conference

Richard Scotch, *Professor, School of Social Sciences, University of Texas at Dallas*
Disability Politics

Katherine O'Sullivan See, *Professor of Sociology, James Madison College, Michigan State University*
Northern Ireland

Monique Segarra, *New York, NY*
Ecuador

Claudio G. Segrè, *Professor of History, University of Texas at Austin*
Fascism; Mussolini, Benito

Bereket Habte Selassie, *William E. Leuchtenburg Professor of African Studies in the University of North Carolina at Chapel Hill*
Eritrea; Eritrean War of Independence; Haile Selassie I; Horn of Africa; Organization of African Unity; Self-Determination

Mitchell A. Seligson, *Daniel H. Wallace Professor of Political Science, Department of Political Science, University of Pittsburgh*
Costa Rica

Rebecca Sevilla, *Novib*
Gay and Lesbian Politics

Ian Shapiro, *Professor of Political Science, Yale University*
Rational Choice

Robert Y. Shapiro, *Professor of Political Science and Department Chair, 2000–2003, Department of Political Science, Columbia University*
Public Opinion

Gene Sharp, *Senior Scholar, The Albert Einstein Institution*
Civil Disobedience; Nonviolent Action

Jeremy F. Shearmur, *Political Science, Faculties, Australian National University*
Libertarianism

Andrew Shennan, *Class of 1966 Associate Professor of History, Wellesley College*
World War II

Paul E. Sigmund, *Professor of Politics, Princeton University*
Liberation Theology

Joel H. Silbey, *President White Professor of History, Cornell University*
Political Realignment

Harvey G. Simmons, *Professor, Department of Political Science, York University, Toronto*
Le Pen, Jean Marie

John Simons, *Doctoral Candidate in Political Science, Hebrew University and Visiting Scholar, Department of Government, Harvard University*
Israel

D. S. Ranjit Singh, *Professor, Department of History, Faculty of Arts and Social Sciences, University of Malaya, Kuala Lumpur*
Brunei

Richard Sinnott, *Director, Centre for European Economic and Public Affairs, University College, Dublin*
Ireland

Carmen Sirianni, *Associate Professor of Sociology, Brandeis University*
Industrial Democracy; Workers' Control

Ian Skeet, *Editor, Oxford Energy Forum and Consultant, Oxford Institute for Energy Studies*
Organization of Petroleum Exporting Countries

Marion Farouk Sluglett, *Lecturer, Politics, University College of Wales, Swansea, and Visiting Associate Professor of Political Science, University of Utah, Salt Lake City, deceased*
Hussein, Saddam; Iraq

Peter Sluglett, *Professor of History, University of Utah, Salt Lake City*
Hussein, Saddam; Iraq

Ninian Smart, *J. F. Rowny Professor of Comparative Religions and Chair of the Religious Studies Department, University of California, Santa Barbara*
Religion and Politics

Michael Joseph Smith, *Professor of Political Science, School of International Studies, University of Miami*
Anarchy; Idealism

Steven S. Smith, *Distinguished McKnight University Professor of Political Science and Law, University of Minnesota*
Filibuster

Tony Smith, *Cornelia Jackson Professor of Political Science, Tufts University*
Decolonization; Political Development

William C. Smith, *Associate Professor of Political Science, University of Miami*
Argentina

Richard Smoke, *Professor of Political Science and Research Director, Center for Foreign Policy Development, Watson Institute, Brown University, deceased*
Nuclear Weapons

Luis Guillermo Solís, *Vice Dean, School of Social Sciences, University of Costa Rica*
U.S.–Central American Relations

John Solomos, *Professor, Faculty of Humanities and Social Sciences, South Bank University*
Race and Racism

James M. SoRelle, *Professor, Department of History, Baylor University*
King, Martin Luther, Jr.

Donald L. Sparks, *Professor of International Economics, The Citadel*
Indian Ocean Region; Madagascar

Barbara B. Stallings, *Director, Economic Development Division, U.N. Economic Commission for Latin America and the Caribbean*
Balance of Payments

Sven Steinmo, *Associate Professor of Political Science, University of Colorado, Boulder*
Taxes and Taxation

John D. Stephens, *Gerhard E. Lenski, Jr. Distinguished Professor of Political Science and Sociology, University of North Carolina, Chapel Hill*
Jamaica

Björn Stigson, *President, World Business Council for Sustainable Development*
Sustainable Development

Joe Stork, *Advocacy Director, Middle East and North Africa Division, Human Rights Watch*
Eisenhower Doctrine; Iran-Iraq War

Susan Strange, *Professor of International Relations and Director, European Policy Unit, European University Institute, Florence*
Gold Standard

Paul Streeten, *Professor Emeritus, Boston University*
Basic Needs; Brain Drain; Human Development Index; Purchasing Power Parity

Martin Stuart-Fox, *Professor and Head of the Department of History, University of Queensland*
Laos

Jomo Kwame Sundaram, *Professor, Faculty of Economics and Administration, University of Malaya*
Malaysia

Ronald Grigor Suny, *Professor of Political Science, The University of Chicago*
Russian Revolution

Abram de Swaan, *Chairman, Amsterdam School for Social Science Research, University of Amsterdam*
Welfare State

Donald K. Swearer, *Professor of Asian Religions, Swarthmore College*
Buddhism

Tadeusz Swietochowski, *Executive Committee Member, The Columbia Caspian Project, School of International and Public Affairs*
Azerbaijan

Roman Szporluk, *M. S. Hrushevsky Professor of Ukrainian History, Harvard University; Director, Ukrainian Research Institute, Harvard University*
Ukraine

Hung-chao Tai, *Professor of Political Science, University of Detroit*
Confucianism

Carlyle A. Thayer, *Professor of Southeast Asia Security Studies, Asia-Pacific Center for Security Studies, Honolulu, Hawaii*
Vietnam

John B. Thompson, *Reader in Sociology and Fellow of Jesus College, University of Cambridge*
Ideology

Hugh Tinker, *Emeritus Professor of Politics, University of Lancaster*
Colonial Empires

Jeanne Maddox Toungara, *Associate Professor of History* *Howard University*
   Côte d'Ivoire

Gregory F. Treverton, *Vice President and Director of Studies, Pacific Council on International Policy*
   Intelligence

Srdja Trifkovic, *Foreign Affairs Editor,* Chronicles: A Magazine of American Culture *and Director, International Studies Program, The Rockford Institute*
   Bosnian War

Yoshi Tsurumi, *Professor of International Business, Zicklin Graduate School of Business, Baruch College, the City University of New York*
   Japan-U.S. Relations

Danilo Türk, *Professor of International Law, Faculty of Law, University of Ljubljana, and Permanent Representative of Slovenia to the United Nations*
   Genocide

Blair P. Turner, *Professor of History and Political Science, Virginia Military Institute*
   Malvinas/Falklands War

Frederick C. Turner, *Professor of Political Science, Universidad de San Andres*
   Perón, Juan Domingo

Thomas Turner, *Professor of Political Science, National University of Rwanda*
   Mercenaries; Warlordism

Meredeth Turshen, *Associate Professor of Urban Studies and Community Health, Rutgers, The State University of New Jersey*
   World Health Organization

Brian Urquhart, *Former Under-Secretary General of the United Nations*
   Hammarskjöld, Dag

Aldo C. Vacs, *Associate Professor of Government, Skidmore College*
   Argentina

Martin van Bruinessen, *ISIM Chair for the Study of Contemporary Muslim Societies, Department of Oriental Studies, Utrecht University*
   Kurdistan

Peter van der Veer, *Professor of Comparative Religion, University of Amsterdam*
   Hinduism

Guglielmo Verdirame, *Fellow, Merton College, University of Oxford*
   Refugees

John R. Vile, *Professor and Chair, Department of Political Science, Middle Tennessee State University*
   Judicial Review

Paul R. Viotti, *Professor, Graduate School of International Studies, University of Denver*
   Force, Use of; North Atlantic Treaty Organization

Stephen M. Walt, *Kirkpatrick Professor of International Affairs, John F. Kennedy School of Government, Harvard University*
   Alliance

Ronald Walters, *Distinguished Leadership Scholar, Director of the African American Leadership Institute in the Burns Academy of Leadership, and Professor of Government and Politics at the University of Maryland College Park*
   U.S.-Africa Relations

M. Stephen Weatherford, *Professor of Political Science, University of California, Santa Barbara*
   Policy Coordination, Economic

Steven Weatherill, *Jacques Delors Professor of European Community Law, Faculty of Law, Somerville College, Oxford University*
   European Court of Justice

Brian Weinstein, *Professor, Department of Political Science, Howard University*
   Language Policy

Martin Weinstein, *Professor of Political Science, William Paterson University of New Jersey*
   Paraguay; Uruguay

Margaret Weir, *Professor of Sociology and Political Science, University of California, Berkeley*
   Entitlements; Great Society; Underclass

Claude E. Welch, *SUNY Distinguished Service Professor, Department of Political Science, State University of New York at Buffalo*
   Coup d'État

David A. Welch, *Assistant Professor of Political Science, University of Toronto*
   Bay of Pigs Invasion; Cuban Missile Crisis

Joseph White, *Professor of Politics, Department of Politics and Institute of Central and East European Studies, University of Glasgow*
   Budget

Stephen White, *Professor of Politics, University of Glasgow*
   Communist Party States; Perestroika; Post-Communism

Laurence Whitehead, *Official Fellow in Politics, Senior Fellow, Nuffield College, Oxford*
   Democratic Transitions

Ife Williams, *Professor, International Education Center, Savannah State University*
  Liberia

Robert C. Williams, *Dean, Davidson College*
  Lenin, Vladimir Ilich

Samuel R. Williamson, *Vice-Chancellor and President Emeritus, Professor of History, The University of the South*
  World War I

Garry Wills, *Adjunct Professor of History, Northwestern University*
  Nixon, Richard Milhous

Graham K. Wilson, *Professor of Political Science, University of Wisconsin, Madison*
  American Federation of Labor and Congress of Industrial Organizations; Bureaucracy; Clinton, Bill

Ann Withorn, *Professor of Social Policy, College of Public and Community Service, University of Massachusetts, Boston*
  Feminization of Poverty

Sharon L. Wolchik, *Professor of Political Science and International Affairs, The George Washington University*
  Charter 77; Czech Republic; Czechoslovakia; Havel, Václav

Robert Paul Wolff, *Professor of Afro-American Studies and Graduate Program Director, University of Massachusetts, Amherst*
  Anarchism

Steven B. Wolinetz, *Professor of Political Science, Memorial University of Newfoundland*
  Netherlands

Meredith Woo-Cumings, *Professor of Political Science, Northwestern University*
  Korea, Republic of

Peter Worsley, *Professor Emeritus of the University of Manchester, U.K.*
  Populism

Erik Olin Wright, *Vilas Distinguished Research Professor and C. Wright Mills Professor of Sociology, Director, Havens Center for the Study of Social Structure and Social Change, University of Wisconsin, Madison*
  Class and Politics

Mark W. Zacher, *Professor of Political Science, University of British Columbia*
  International Organizations

Aristide R. Zolberg, *University-in-Exile Professor, Graduate Faculty, New School for Social Research & Director, International Center for Migration, Ethnicity and Citizenship*
  International Migration

Yahia H. Zoubir, *Associate Professor of International Studies at Thunderbird, The American Graduate School of International Management in Glendale, Arizona and Director of Thunderbird Europe, French-Geneva Center, in Archamps, France*
  Western Sahara

THE
OXFORD COMPANION TO
POLITICS OF THE WORLD

A

ABDEL NASSER, Gamal. See Nasser, Gamal Abdel.

ABORTION. See Reproductive Politics.

ACHESON, Dean. Born in 1893 in Middletown, Connecticut, Dean Acheson trained as a lawyer and developed formidable administrative talents. He first entered the State Department in the mid-1930s, as a protégé of Felix Frankfurter, and became under secretary of state in Franklin D. *Roosevelt's last administration. But it was while occupying the same position under Harry S. *Truman, with whom he enjoyed a close affinity, and later, as secretary of state in Truman's second administration, that Acheson reached the height of his influence.

As under secretary he represented the United States in establishing a number of international economic organizations immediately after World War II. With the Secretaries of State James F. Byrnes and his successor George C. Marshall abroad much of the time, Acheson was probably the main influence on the conduct of U.S. foreign policy in the crucial years of 1946 and 1947. During that period, and as secretary of state during Truman's second administration (1949–1953), Acheson probably exercised more influence on U.S. foreign policy than any of his predecessors in that office. In addition to the formulation of the *Truman Doctrine, he was particularly closely connected with U.S. proposals in March 1946 for international control of trade in fusionable materials, with the policy of the *containment of the Soviet Union through the *North Atlantic Treaty Organization (NATO), and with the apparent exclusion of Korea from the list of countries on the Asian periphery that the United States was prepared to defend. He was convinced that the active wielding of American political, economic, and military power was necessary for the preservation of world peace and that the United States should assume the duties of empire that had previously devolved upon Britain. In such areas as Greece, Indochina, and the Middle East, Acheson was prominent in advising Truman to assert boldly the newfound power and influence of the United States in the postwar world. Indeed, he was one of the main architects of the Truman Doctrine, which, in its more radical formulations, committed the United States to supporting anticommunist regimes everywhere in the world in a dangerously open-ended manner.

With the landslide victory of Eisenhower in 1953, Acheson returned to his law practice but continued to frame the foreign policy plank of the Democratic platform until the Kennedy era. He published his political memoirs, entitled *Present at the Creation*, in 1969, and died in 1971.

(See also American Foreign Policy; Cold War.)

Dean Acheson, *Present at the Creation: My Years in the State Department* (New York, 1969). Gaddis Smith, *Dean Acheson* (New York, 1972).
David McLellan

AFFIRMATIVE ACTION. See overleaf.

AFGHANISTAN. Modern-day Afghanistan, a landlocked state in Southwest Asia, emerged in the nineteenth century as a buffer between British India and the expanding Russian Empire. Given the diversity of ethnic groups within its borders (Pashtuns, Tajiks, Uzbeks, Hazaras, and many others), it has never been a "nation-state," and while the overwhelming majority of Afghanistan's estimated 20 million citizens are Muslims, they are more prone to bond with those who share common ethnic or linguistic backgrounds, tribal identifications, or sectarian commitments. After nearly five decades of relative stability, Afghanistan was thrown into turmoil by a communist coup in April 1978, followed by the Soviet invasion of Afghanistan in December 1979. Intense popular resistance within Afghanistan was a major factor prompting the withdrawal of Soviet forces, a process completed in February 1989; and in April 1992, the communist regime collapsed. However, it rapidly became clear that the Afghan state had collapsed as well, and ever since, the country has been wracked by a largely low-level but increasingly ethnicized struggle for control of the remaining symbols of nationwide power, notably the capital, Kabul, which suffered severe damage from rocket and artillery attacks by the Ḥizbi Islāmī ("Party of Islam"). Since 1994, this struggle has pitted the Pakistan-backed, ethnically Pashtun Ṭālibān "student" militia against the military forces, active in the northeast of the country, of the "government" of President Burhanuddin Rabbani and his principal military commander, Aḥmad Shāh Masʿūd.

Until 1973, Afghanistan had a monarchical system of government; the last king, Muḥammad Zāhir Shāh, occupied the throne from November 1933 until July 1973, when his cousin Muḥammad Dāʾūd overthrew him and established a short-lived republican regime. The monarchy presided over a ubiquitous but relatively weak array of state instruments, and during Zāhir Shāh's rule took care not to challenge the key interests expressed by tribal collective leaderships (*jirgas*). Nevertheless, the attempt from the mid-1950s to use foreign aid and asset-sales revenue to fund a centrally driven *modernization process had the perverse effect of creating a new stratum of politicized Afghans whose political and social aspirations the state was unable to satisfy. It was this stratum that provided cadres for the Afghan communist movement,

(cont. on p. 12)

3

AFFIRMATIVE ACTION. I have been known over the years as a critic of affirmative action policies. However, in the wake of a successful ballot initiative banning affirmative action in the state of California, I now find it necessary to reiterate the old, and in my view still valid, arguments on behalf of explicit public efforts to reduce racial inequality. In doing so, I want to stress that I am not defending racial quotas, or race-based allocations of public contracts, or racial double standards in the workplace, or huge disparities in the test scores of blacks and whites admitted to elite universities. These practices are deservedly under attack. But I do defend the U.S. Army's programs to commission more black officers, the public funding of efforts to bring blacks into science and engineering, the attempts by urban law enforcement agencies to recruit black personnel, and the goal of top universities—public and private—to retain some racial diversity in their student bodies. The mere fact that these efforts take race into account, I will argue here, should not be disqualifying.

My basic position is that the current campaign against "preferences" goes too far by turning what prior to Proposition 209 had been a reform movement to which I was happy to belong into an abolitionist crusade that I feel forced to oppose. Some say that all government policies should be "color blind." And, given our troubled racial history, the simplicity and clarity of this colorblind formulation can, indeed, seem compelling. But, the problem is more complicated than this "simple" position can accommodate. I maintain that procedural color blindness is neither a necessary nor a sufficient condition for the attainment of substantive racial justice.

Thus, we arrive at the fundamental question: Why should we care about racial inequality per se? What is wrong with a situation in which blacks are roughly 12 percent of the U.S. population, but some 40 percent of welfare recipients, 50 percent of incarcerated felons, and 3 percent of newly graduating engineers? Why should we care about the racial composition of the police forces in large cities, of presidential appointees to the federal bench, or of the freshman class at a state university? Why should a large corporation actively seek a qualified black candidate for a position in its upper management? After all, thinking in the abstract, a growing *welfare population or an increasing number of incarcerated felons is a problem for society no matter what the color of those citizens. What matters is that we reduce the total numbers, right?

Actually, I will argue that this is not right, or at least not for America, not today. A president who appoints hundreds of local federal judges among whom there are no blacks invites a wholly unnecessary political firestorm. He would rightly find himself in trouble. A corporation that neglects to bring along some blacks into upper management exposes itself needlessly to potential difficulties with its customers or

its lower-level employees. A racially diverse big city fielding a nearly all white police force is asking for big trouble the next time a drunken black motorist has to be forcibly subdued. A freshman class devoid of blacks teaches its students some lessons about our society that are not listed in the course catalog. And to accept with equanimity the blackening of our prisons or welfare rolls is to be indifferent, I suggest, to an important aspect of social justice.

Reasons to Care. One reason to care about racial inequality is that race forms an important part of the personal identity of many citizens. Ideally, these racial identities should be irrelevant to our dealings with one another. Yet clearly they are not. As a result, all kinds of circumstances, having nothing to do with "racial preferences," require a government to depart from the strictly "color blind" treatment of its citizens in order to discharge its legitimate function. To offer just one example, in the summer of 1996, the conservative federal judge Richard Posner upheld the preferential hiring of a black prison guard in an Illinois boot camp for young offenders. He argued that, with an inmate population that was three-quarters black, and given that "aversive training" methods familiar to marine enlistees were to be employed at the boot camp, the state might have a compelling and thus constitutionally justifiable interest in providing for some racial diversity in the camp's officer corps.

Faced with such an example, supporters of the "color blind" position invariably reply that race here simply serves as a proxy for some nonracial trait—like the ability to win the trust of black inmates. But this response is insufficient, for the crux of the matter is not the state's use of race as a proxy for some desirable characteristic in an employee, but rather some citizens' tendency to view the world through a racially tinted lens. In the boot camp, a young inmate is bullied mercilessly by guards who either have his best interests at heart or do not. When black youths refuse to believe that this bullying is for some useful purpose when none of the guards are black, then the success of the training technique requires racial diversity on the staff. And this is true no matter how sophisticated the prison personnel office may be at discovering, without using race, whether an applicant "truly cares" about his prospective charges.

Another reason to care about racial inequality is that race is an important source of information in many situations. Race is an easily observable trait that is correlated with some hard to observe traits about which employers, lenders, police officers and others are concerned. Direct evidence from employer interviews indicates that both black and white employers are reluctant to hire black, urban young males who exhibit lower-class behavioral styles. Racial identity is also used as information in a variety of ways by police. Some evidence indicates that it shapes their law enforcement decisions. Indeed, the dramatic disparity between the races in the rates of arrest and incarceration for criminal offenses must be taken into account when discussing racial differences in the labor market experiences of males, thought the direction of causality is difficult to untangle. The key to all of these examples is their self-reinforcing nature: they begin with racial beliefs that then bring about their own statistical confirmation.

Yet another reason to care about racial inequality is that race influences the social networks that are open to individuals, and these networks in turn have a major effect upon individuals' opportunities. Here are two observations that illustrate the key to my argument: First, all societies exhibit significant social segmentation. People make choices about whom to befriend, whom to marry, where to live, to which schools to send their children and so on. Factors like race, *ethnicity, social class, and religious affiliation influence these choices of association. Second, the processes through which individuals develop their productive capacities are shaped by custom, convention, and social norms, and are not fully responsive to market forces, or reflective of the innate abilities of persons. Networks of social affiliation are not usually the result of calculated economic decisions. They nevertheless help determine how resources important to the development of the productive capacities of human beings are made available to individuals.

It is a great impediment for a talented youngster to be embedded in a social network of peers whose values do not affirm the activities the youngster must undertake to develop his talent. Children do not freely choose their peers. To a significant degree they inherit these associations as a consequence of where they live, what their parents believe, what social group they belong to, and so on. In American society, given our history, racial identity is one important component of that complex of social characteristics that define the networks in which we live. Opportunity travels along the synapses of these networks. We learn about what we can do with our talents from the conversation taking place over dinner, from the family friend who says "Why doesn't your kid do this or that?" from the business owner who offers a summer job. These kinds of opportunity-enhancing associations are not just out there in the marketplace to be purchased by the highest bidder. Nor are they allocated randomly so as to create some kind of level playing field.

Racial Justice. Now as someone who values liberty it is my view that we cannot and should not seek to equalize for all persons access to such networks of social affiliation. They are to a large degree the inheritance of history, and we must take them as they come. But we do not have to accept the inegalitarian consequences of these structures without reflection, nor must we impute naturalness or an inevitability to those unequal consequences.

We do not, in other words, have to take one seventeen-year-old who has grown up in a suburban, affluent, two-parent family with wholesome neighbors and peers, attending schools that work, and compare him with another seventeen-year-old who has grown up under less felicitous circumstances, and then stamp on the forehead of the former the big M for merit and say of the latter, "He has not earned the right to further develop his talents." When it comes time to allocate state-funded opportunities for the intellectual development of the two youngsters, we need not pretend that the playing field has been level all the time and that, by favoring the first kid, we are merely giving scarce opportunities to the most deserving recipient.

I am arguing that inalienable non-marketed social and cultural resources play a critical role in the production and reproduction of economic inequality. In this context, it is crucial to realize that even the values, attitudes, and beliefs held by an individual—of central import for the attainment of success in life—are shaped by the cultural milieu in which that person develops. *Whom* one knows affects *what* one comes to believe, and in that way influences what one can do with one's God-given talents. Do we collectively, as a society, have any responsibility for the debilitating, even pathological cultural milieus that exist in our midst?

My claim here is that the "social pathology" to be observed in some quarters for our society did not come out of thin air, but to some extent is a consequence of historical practices, including, in the case of blacks, the practice of racial oppression. Moreover, the ongoing racial segmentation of our society—most clearly visible in the social isolation of today's urban black poor—is an important social inequity that helps to perpetuate the consequences of our troubled racial history. I believe this analysis has an important ethical implication: Because the creation of a skilled workforce is a social process, the meritocratic ideal—that in a free society individuals should be allowed to rise to the level of their competence—should be tempered with an understanding that no one travels that road alone. We should not embrace the notion that individuals have "merit" that must be rewarded without some awareness of the processes by which that merit is produced. Theses are social processes, with a racial dimension. It should be evident that, notwithstanding the establishment of a legal regime or equal opportunity, historically engendered economic differences between racial groups could well persist into the indefinite future, and not as some have argued, perniciously, because of the genetic inferiority of blacks. This is what I mean by the problem of racial injustice.

To the extent that past disparities reflect overt racial exclusion, the propriety of the contemporary order is called into question. I stress that this is not a reparations argument. I am not saying that some individuals are due something because of what was done to their ancestors. Neither is this a group *entitlement argument, in which racial collectivities are seen as having *rights that take precedence over those of individuals. Indeed, my argument here is entirely consistent with individualism as a core philosophical premise. I am simply acknowledging the additional fact that in society, people are not atoms. They are, rather situated within systems of mutual affiliation. And in our society, these systems are defined, in part, by race.

Taking note of this situatedness and understanding its historical roots leads me to some recognition of race as a legitimate factor in consideration of social justice. When the developmental prospects of individuals depend on the circumstances of those with whom they are socially affiliated, and when social affiliation reflects a tendency toward racial segregation, even a minimal commitment to equality of opportunity for individuals can require, I am arguing, a willingness to take racial identity into account. In our divided society, given our tragic past, this implies that public efforts to counter the effects of historical disadvantage among blacks are not only consistent with, but indeed are required by widely embraced, individualistic, democratic ideals.

Color-Blind Extremists. This argument leads naturally to the question of whether affirmative-action policies are necessary and justified. To emphasize that racial group disparities can be transmitted across generations through subtle and complex social processes is not necessarily to endorse employment or educational preferences based on race.

Yet, coming up with cases that challenge the absolutist claim is not difficult. How can a college educator convey to students the lesson that "not all blacks think alike," with too few blacks on campus for this truth to be evident? Can the police consider race when making undercover assignments? Can a black public employee use health insurance benefits to choose a black therapist with whom to discuss race-related anxieties? Can units in a public housing project be let with an eye to sustaining a racially integrated environment? What about a National Science Foundation that encourages gifted blacks to pursue careers in the fields where few now study? Clearly, there is no general rule that can resolve all of these case reasonably.

Costs of Racial Preferences. I want to be clear. This criticism of color blind absolutism is not an unqualified defense of the affirmative action status quo. There are many reasons to suspect that in particular contexts the costs of using racial preferences will outweigh the benefits. One such reason for questioning the wisdom of affirmative action in certain contexts is that the widespread use of preference can logically be expected to erode the perception of black competence.

Let some employer use a threshold of assessed productivity that is lower for hiring blacks than for hiring whites. The preferential hiring policy defines three categories of individuals within each of the two racial groups, which I will call "marginals," "successes," and "failures." Marginals are those whose hiring status is altered by the policy—either whites not hired who otherwise would have been, or blacks hired who otherwise would not have been. Successes are those who would be hired with or without the policy, and failures are those who would be passed over with or without the preferential policy. Let us consider how an outsider who can observe the hiring decision, but not the employer's productivity assessment, would estimate the productivity of those subject to this hiring process.

Notice that a lower hiring threshold for blacks causes the outside market to reduce its estimate of the productivity of black successes, since, on average, less is required to achieve that status. In addition, black failures, seen to have been passed over despite a lower hiring threshold, are thereby revealed as especially unproductive. On the other hand, a hiring process favoring blacks must enhance the reputations of white failures, as seen by outsiders, since they may have been artificially held back. And white successes, who are hired despite being disfavored in selection, have thereby been shown to be especially productive.

We have thus reached the result that, among blacks, only marginals gain from the establishment of a preferential hiring program—they do so because the outside observer lumps them together with black successes. They thus gain a job and a better reputation than they objectively deserve. Moreover, among whites, only marginals are harmed by the program, for only they lose the chance of securing a job and only they see their reputations harmed by virtue of being placed in the same category as white failures. In practical terms, since marginals are typically a minority of all workers, the outside reputations of most blacks will be lowered, and that of most whites enhanced, by preferential hiring. The inferential logic that leads to this arresting conclusion is particularly insidious, in that it can serve to legitimate otherwise indefensible negative stereotypes about blacks.

Another reason for being skeptical about the practice of affirmative action is that it can undercut the incentives for blacks to develop their competitive abilities. For instance, preferential treatment can lead to the patronization of black workers and students. By "patronization," I mean the setting of lower standards of expected accomplishment for blacks than for whites because of the belief that blacks are not as capable of meeting a higher, common standard. In the 1993 article I wrote with Steven Coate ("Anti-Discrimination Enforcement and the Problem of Patronization" *American Economic Review*, September, pp. 792–810), we show how behavior of this kind can be based on a self-fulfilling prophesy. That is, observed performance among blacks may be lower precisely because blacks are being patronized, a policy that is undertaken because of the need for an employer or admissions officer to meet affirmative action guidelines.

Consider a workplace in which a supervisor operating under some affirmative action guidelines must recommend subordinate workers for promotion. Suppose further that he is keen to promote blacks where possible, and that he monitors his subordinates' performance and bases his recommendations on these observations. Pressure to promote blacks might lead him to deemphasize deficiencies in the performance of black subordinates, recommending them for promotion when he would not have done so for whites. But his behavior could undermine the ability of black workers to identify and correct their deficiencies. They are denied honest feedback from their supervisor on their performance and are encouraged to think that one can get ahead without attaining the same degree of proficiency as whites.

Alternatively, consider a population of students applying to professional schools for admissions. The schools, due to affirmative action concerns, are eager to admit a certain percentage of blacks. They believe that to do so they must accept black applicants with test scores and grades below those of some whites whom they reject. If most schools follow this policy, the message sent out to black students is that the level of performance needed to gain admission is lower than that which white students know they must attain. If black and white students are, at least to some extent, responsive to these differing expectations, they might, as a result, achieve grades and test scores reflective of the expectation gap. In this way, the schools' belief that different admissions standards are necessary becomes a self-fulfilling prophecy.

Developmental Affirmative Action. The common theme in these two examples is that the desire to see greater black representation is pursued by using different criteria for the promotion or admission of black and white candidates. But the use of different criteria reduces the incentives that blacks have for developing needed skills. This argument does not presume that blacks are less capable than whites; it is based on the fact that an individual's need to make use of his abilities is undermined when that individual is patronized by the employer or the admissions committee.

This problem could be avoided if, instead of using different criteria of selection, the employers and schools in question sought to meet their desired level of black participation through a concerted effort to enhance performance, while maintaining common standards of evaluation. Call it "developmental," as opposed to "preferential," affirmative action. Such a targeted effort as performance enhancement among black employees or students is definitely not color blind behavior. It presumes a direct concern about racial inequality and involves allocating benefits on the basis of race. What distinguishes it from preferential hiring or admissions, though, is that it takes seriously the fact of differential performance and seeks to reverse it directly, rather than trying to hide from that fact by setting a different threshold of expectations for the performance of blacks.

For example, given that black students are far scarcer than white and Asian students in the fields of math and science, encouraging their entry into these areas without lowering standards—through summer workshops, support for curriculum development at historically black colleges, or the financing of research assistantships for promising graduate students—would be consistent with my distinction between "preferential" and "developmental" affirmative action. Also consistent would be the provision of management assistance to new black-owned businesses, which would then be expected to bid competitively for government contracts, or the provisional admission of black students to the state university, conditional on their raising their academic scores to competitive levels after a year or two of study at a local community college. The key is that the racially targeted assistance be short-lived and preparatory to the entry of its recipients into an arena of competition where they would be assessed in the same way as everyone else.

In conclusion, I am arguing that if our interest is achieving a just society, then there is nothing in the sorry history of affirmative action abuses that requires us to tie our hands with a color-blind formalism. The color blind principle, while consistent as a self-contained legal rule, is in my opinion neither morally nor politically coherent. It requires that we not care about racial inequality, per se, when, as I have argued above, there are many compelling reasons to reject that position.

(See also AFRICAN AMERICANS; CLASS AND POLITICS; EQUALITY AND INEQUALITY; RACE AND RACISM; RELIGION AND POLITICS.)

Glenn C. Loury, "How to Mend Affirmative Action" *The Public Interest* 127 (Spring 1997): 33–43. Charles Moskos and John Sibley Butler, *All That We Can Be: Black Leadership and Racial Integration the Army Way* (New York, 1997). Stephen Thernstrom and Abigail M. Thernstrom, *America in Black and White* (New York, 1997). William G. Bowen and Derek Bok, *The Shape of the River* (Princeton, N.J., 1998).

GLENN C. LOURY

AFFIRMATIVE ACTION. At the dawn of a new millennium, America's quest to overcome the lasting impact of centuries of racial inequality is on a collision course with its even more pervasive preoccupation with quantifiable measurements of that all American social good, "success." According to Nicholas Lemann in *The Big Test: the Secret History of the American Meritocracy* (New York, 1999), his masterful account of this impending collision course in higher education, "two conflicting sets of numbers" are being generated that spell mutually inconsistent solutions for distributing high-stakes educational opportunity. The first is "everyone's scores on standardized tests." The second is "the share of good jobs and educational billets" held by *African Americans or women. Those who believe in education by the first set of numbers allocate places in colleges or universities based on scores on mental aptitude tests. Deciding who "deserves" to benefit from admission to selective colleges and universities occurs within a *testocracy* which sorts, evaluates, and ranks measurable mental aptitude. Test scores are presumed to tell us all that what we can and need to know about each applicant's potential and future capacity, defined by "merit." Those committed to the second set of numbers believe just as fervently in discovering and promoting untapped, and perhaps immeasurable, human potential when it lives in dark-skinned or female bodies. Commitments to the second set of numbers are defended in the name of fairness. In recent years, claims of merit have trumped African American's claims of fairness.

The testocrats, those who believe in the first set of numbers, are certain that those who are capable of knowing the most will rise to become part of a competent and legitimate intellectual *elite or mental theocracy. Thus, they satisfy concerns about fairness and equal opportunity when access to higher education—or other opportunities such as jobs or public offices—is awarded in an open competition to those with the most merit, i.e., those with the highest test scores. While the old boys network of yore was an elite based on inherited privilege, this new elite claims to earn their places based on their inherited aptitude, legitimated by claims of democratic opportunity. Equal opportunity in this understanding means the opportunity to achieve one's just deserts based on one's measurable merit. Once a meritocracy is firmly in place, the equal opportunity society expects nothing further of its successes. Equality of results is anathema. Monitoring what anyone does with opportunity is tyrannical. Society will certainly benefit, since those who are most deserving will be justly rewarded, and thus presumably have incentive to keep climbing upward.

In contrast, those who emphasize the second set of numbers—defenders of affirmative action—seek to measure how far we have come from slavery and state-sanctioned segregation. They seek to redistribute opportunity to succeed based on principles of fairness to ensure that those who have traditionally been denied such opportunity are compensated or at least no longer held back. They argue that the traditional "test-centered" approaches to merit—based on fixed, one-size-fits-all tests of mental aptitude—simply fail to detect the actual potential of those who, because of the legacy of human bondage and Jim Crow, are ill prepared to excel on aptitude tests but can nevertheless succeed. This approach implicitly questions whether indicators of aptitude measured by standard tests are a true test of merits, but this critique is more often than not left unstated. Whether the "winners" deserve to succeed, i.e., whether they have "merit," is not the issue. The question is whether the particular losers of color deserve to lose.

The need to assure diversity among those admitted to elite universities, as with other educational opportunities, is one way this concern with fairness and compensatory justice has recently been articulated. Proponents of affirmative action, for example, often acknowledged that the criteria to assure a diverse class were often at odds with or at least supplemental to the criteria applied by the meritocrats. Advocates of diversity, as well as supporters of affirmative action, accepted the meritocrats' claim that standardized admission indices (relying on both grades and aptitude tests) generally predict one's capacity both to learn and to do. But principles of fairness and diversity made it necessary to compensate for underperformance among minority candidates on these conventional measures of "worth." Thus, under the rubric of "affirmative action," efforts were undertaken to recruit and admit minority candidates with less impressive test scores. These candidates were often selected, therefore, based on supplemental criteria such as leadership ability, community service, motivation (as evidenced in their ability to overcome obstacles), and unusual evidence of accomplishment that suggested the ability to follow through on goals.

In pursuit of racial diversity, proponents of the second set of numbers have failed to generalize beyond the experience of people of color or to question whether opportunity to succeed should be handed out in rank order of "desert" claims. What they argue instead is that opportunity should be given to those people of color who can take advantage of that opportunity, despite weaker test performance. In other words, they challenge us to open up to people of color the category of just who is "deserving" of opportunity. But they do not challenge the notion of creating such a category in the first place.

If we are to move beyond the present polarized debate, the issue of how to measure and what to call merit in a multiracial *democracy needs to be explored carefully. The same is true of what we call fairness. Such an inquiry would look at the question of merit as a functional rather than generic concept. It would keep more firmly in mind the democratic purposes of higher education as well as the specific mission of most institutions of higher education.

In this essay I shall argue that we need to take the lessons of this inquiry about merit to reconfirm the democratic role of higher education in a multiracial society and act to reconnect admissions processes to that democratic mission. By keeping the institutional mission at the forefront, we can begin to reconsider the relationship between individual merit and operational fairness, between claims of individual desert and societal needs. I tentatively call this a process of conformative action, because it takes lessons from both the meritocratic as well as affirmative action ideals to confirm a set of experimental and pragmatic actions that link all (ad)mission practices to the broad purposes and public character of higher education in a multiracial democracy.

The Democratic Mission of Higher Education. Despite the apparent clash in the meaning of equality and merit, both the affirmative action idea and the new meritocracy of mental test aptitude share two common principles: the fair and democratic distribution of opportunities and the public character and mission of educational institutions. These commitments also inform the stated mission of most public (and a good many private) institutions of higher education. Both the meritocracy and affirmative action ideals seek legitimacy in a more democratic distribution of opportunity to those who are competent to use that opportunity wisely or well, although they differ, of course, in their analysis.

While meritocrats find that standardized testing is a sufficient mechanism to ensure opportunity, it turns out, however, that the testocracy rewards those who are already privileged. Access to higher education and good jobs are simply passed from one generation to another. Those with social and economic privileges are able to learn the rules of the test either through explicit coaching, private school, or upper class, resource-rich suburban education and then successfully play the testing game to their own advantage.

Early in the new meritocracy, the experience of people of color, and in particular African Americans, as well as many white women became a lightening rod for identifying unfairness. A test-centered approach to allocating high-stakes opportunity left them out. But under the umbrella of affirmative action, their claims were made solely on their own behalf: They did not challenge the fundamental assumptions of conventional meritocracy. Thus, affirmative action was developed to compensate for the deficiencies in the new meritocracy and, unwittingly, it served not to delegitimize but to camouflage the serious flaws in the meritocracy's claims of democratic opportunity.

Another area of ostensible agreement masks significant policy distinctions. Those who appeal to meritocratic ideals as well as those who support affirmative action precepts recognize the public character and mission of educational institutions. For Glenn Loury, as well as many others who have been critics of affirmative action as well as for supporters of the principle, education has a sacred role to play in a democracy because it is so deeply intertwined with the tasks of preparing young people for the responsibilities of citizenship (including employment), the challenges of public participation, and the chance for leadership. Public schools in other words are public not just because they are supported by public monies but because they educate every student for the responsibilities and benefits of participating in public life. State-funded opportunities for intellectual development are scarce and play a critical role in the reproduction of social inequalities and the ongoing racial segmentation of society.

Training citizens means educating people to be able to participate in public life, to have opinions, to find out how to express opinions in ways that are persuasive. To train leaders, institutions educate people who will occupy positions of responsibility and power, people who will participate in their chosen discipline in ways that have lasting impact, people who contribute to civic life and people who are committed to public service. Therefore, the challenge of allocating high stakes opportunity is intimately connected to the challenge of training students to become public citizens, and even public-minded community, business, educational, and elected leaders.

The new meritocrats introduced aptitude testing as a way to broaden opportunity away from the old boys network of inherited and narrowly defined privilege; the proponents of affirmative action advocate broadening opportunity even further to include those people of color and women whom aptitude testing still leaves out. Starting from different places, they reach similar commitments to a system of admissions consistent with the equal opportunity ideals of American democracy. Unfortunately, what also unifies the two competing approaches is their failure to locate the conversation about selection explicitly within this larger democratic framework. And for the new meritocrats in particular, they have lost sight of the original connection between merit as competence and the expectation will be deployed to serve the society that made the opportunity to succeed available in the first place. The issue of leadership and public service or public spiritedness seems to have dropped out of the merit formula. Instead, the question of what we are looking for has simply collapsed into performance on an aptitude test.

Evaluating the Democratic Potential of Each Approach. There are three democratic values that are fundamentally at risk in the institutional practices put into place by the new meritocracy, even as they have been modified by a commitment to affirmative action: inclusiveness (no one is arbitrarily shut out or excluded), transparency (the processes employed are visibly apparent and are functionally linked to the public character or public mission of the institution), and accountability (the choice of beneficiaries is directly linked to a *public good). Here, I shall emphasize the first value—inclusiveness—and substantiate my claims by relying on a study of the University of Michigan Law School, a state-funded school that that deliberately practiced affirmative action and, as a consequence, finds itself in the midst of a lawsuit challenging its affirmative action policies.

A study of the careers of three generations of students of color admitted to the University of Michigan Law School (Richard Lempert, David Chambers, and Terry Adams, "Michigan's Minority Graduates in Practice: The River Runs Through Law School" *Law and Social Inquiry, Journal of the American Bar Foundation* 25, no. 2 [Spring 2000]: 395–505) concludes that traditional, "hard," test-score based, admissions processes are no better predictors of success after law school—whether success is measured by earned income, career satisfaction, or service contributions—than are "soft," more whole-person selection criteria. Those who graduate from the University of Michigan Law School tend to succeed, whether as applicants they were admitted, on the one hand, pursuant to criteria that emphasize "mental aptitude" for the study of law or on the other hand, by virtue of expectations about their capacity to contribute to the community of legal education, the legal profession, or citizens generally.

In other words, the "soft" processes predict alumni career success at least as well as the "hard" test-based criterion. The study also found that the "soft" processes gave birth to several previously undetected rewards: (1) a more diverse student body which the white and nonwhite graduates of the school now conclude was an educational good in itself; (2) a student body that will go on to serve historically underrepresented populations; and (3) a student body that will be more involved in giving back to—as well as providing leadership for—the larger community.

The study found that the minority graduates also succeeded—after graduation—in ways that eluded many of their white counterparts: (1) minority alumni provide, on average, considerably more service to minority clients than do white alumni; (2) among those Michigan graduates who enter the private practice of law, "minority alumni tend to do more pro bono work, sit on the boards of more community organizations and do more mentoring of younger attorneys than white alumni." The study found, in other words, that minority graduates use the opportunity provided by their legal education to accomplish, at higher rates than their white counterparts, two of the law school's goals. They provide legal service to an underrepresented segment of the population and they provide community service and leadership to the community as a whole. Indeed, the meritocrats' reliance on testing for admission proved a great failure in predicting leadership after graduation from law school. The higher one's LSAT score, the less likely one was to do public service or contribute to one's community as a lawyer.

The study shows that conventional test-based admission policies apparently both mask and support deep flaws in the way we allocate opportunity and privilege. They reward many people who then fail to give back to society. They also fail to identify those who in fact have much to give and do give in service of the profession and its larger goals.

The study, thus, helps us analyze the core democratic value of inclusiveness, which some might describe as the new meritocracy's commitment to "equal opportunity." Testing people for mental aptitude assumes that the concomitant sorting and ranking will be democratic in that all individuals, regardless of their social ranking or geographic location and regardless of whether they "win" or "lose," will nevertheless be treated equally because they enjoy the same initial opportunity to prove their worth—their merit—on objective tests. Even if this assumption is true—and the Michigan study as well as much of the literature suggests that it may not be—it is still only partially democratic because it leaves out so many. While the meritocracy is certainly more inclusive in the net it casts than the old boys network, some people, indeed many quite capable people, are excluded because they had lower test scores, even though in fact they could do the job once they graduated.

Moreover, to an important degree, it leaves those people out permanently. Exclusion from elite institutions is not just exclusion from a particular credential like the ability to take a bar examination. It is a continued exclusion from the paths to positions of leadership and influence within the society. Exclusion from access to such *social capital is hard to justify on democratic grounds when it merely reflects the unexamined preference for a specific form of intergenerational wealth transfer. The negative consequences for society at large are even greater if those excluded were more likely than those included to contribute to desirable social goals.

The new meritocracy may have started as an effort to re-place a system of inherited privilege, but as it ended the last century, it reproduced much of what it was designed to replace. Thus it seems that the testocracy can be criticized for doing two things that are inconsistent with an equal opportunity mandate: (1) it is credentializing those who are already quite privileged and (2) it is normalizing racial inequality or misleading us into seeing educational inequality in K-12 and beyond as "normal." It confuses inherited privilege with inherited aptitude, but in either case it makes an inherited resource a precondition for opportunity. The new meritocracy thus finds itself defending only a partially democratic version of opportunity that leaves out many people of color based on the unfair accumulation of resources that some bring to the test.

While any system of sorting and ranking will develop "losers," a truly democratic system needs to give those losers a sense of hope in the future. The development of a class of permanent losers and permanent winners violates the fundamental claim of democracy that "the people" shall rule. Instead, it purports to rest on the peculiarly prodemocratic idea that only some of the people will rule all of the time and it makes that prodemocratic judgment quite early in a person's life.

The Limits of Meritocratic "Testocracy." This analysis suggests that an argument against the meritocratic approach can be made on the first ground on which meritocracy claims to stand: it has failed to institutionalize the critical democratic value of inclusiveness. The Michigan study also shows that meritocracy, reduced as it has been by claims of efficiency at some public institutions to a mere "testocracy," does not even serve the need to elevate the most competent. The study challenges that widely shared, almost naturalized assumption, that tests of aptitude assure competence or even quality among those who perform well on the tests. It turns out the whole person, particularized selection criteria used to admit minority candidates actually correlate better with the career paths and service attributes of minority graduates. Yet despite the tenor of the present debate about affirmative action, the study finds a noticeable absence of such relationships between conventional predictors and what it is we expect lawyers to do. Test scores and comparable measures of either "legal aptitude" or general intelligence may correlate modestly with first year law school grades. But they do not predict or correlate with anything else that we claim to value. They fail to predict career success. They also fail to identify in advance those who will fulfill the mission of the public law school.

An empirical study like that of the Michigan Law School forces us to become more explicit about what, in fact, a school is attempting to measure or predict when it looks at an applicant. Usually we think a school is trying to measure a potentially "successful" applicant. And if we take "success" to mean anything other than high grades, including such things as contributing to the diversity of the educational experience for all students or providing leadership to the entire community, then the affirmative action processes of Michigan are the most empirically accountable tool for achieving this objective. The study also finds that on three important measures of success—financial satisfaction, career satisfaction and public service—conventional admissions practices are limited, short-sighted measures that are in many important ways *inferior* to the criterion used to select beneficiaries of affirmative action.

Although the lessons of a single study should not be overgeneralized, the Michigan case invites some provocative observations about admissions practices, more generally. Whether in schools, colleges and universities, or graduate and professional training, the study suggests that admissions practices may better serve both specific educational and training functions and the broader public mission when they focus on concrete measures of what applicants have accomplished rather than generic predictors of what candidates are considered capable of doing. The study shows that using an alternative measure for admission does not reduce the number of places available to qualified applicants. It simply alters, in an important way, how we view qualifications.

Confirmative Action. The Michigan study reveals the critical importance of linking institutional processes to institutional goals. Indeed, the study suggests that affirmative action is an experiment that should inform the way we admit everyone. If taxpayers are subsidizing opportunities for students to attend college or law school, what is it that the taxpayers legitimately can expect those students to "do" once they attain their degree?

One approach might be to use a mix of criteria, with a certain number of students admitted based on their test scores in relation, for example, to the predictive validity of such scores, that is no more than 20 percent of the entering class. The rest of the class would then be admitted based on a whole person evaluation that seeks to identify "the distance traveled" by the applicant in overcoming obstacles, the leadership and community service record, and the evidence of the applicant's long-term commitment to making a contribution to the community that is ultimately subsidizing his or her tuition. Or, perhaps more as a heuristic than a practical tool, public universities might consider using the tests as a floor, below which no one in recent memory has succeeded in graduating from the institution. Above that test-determined floor, applicants could be chosen by several alternatives, including a lottery, portfolio-based assessment, or a more structured and participatory decision making process. In addition, the challenge of embedding admissions into the institution's mission should prompt us to reconsider issues of curriculum, learning theory, and the ways to motivate members of a diverse population to each reach his or her full potential.

The recent experience of the University of Texas with its innovative 10% Plan is a worthwhile point of departure for such a conversation. If efficiency and equal opportunity are the driving values, then the Texas 10% Plan has much to recommend it. None of these alternatives to the testocracy, however, is easy to implement or operationalize without error. Yet, what the Lempert study makes clear is the need to pursue alternatives that are both experimental and affirmatively democratic. Merit becomes a function of societal needs and values rather than a fixed, quantifiable entity that, like one's blood pressure or body temperature, can be measured with the proper instruments. Merit, in other words, becomes dynamic. Dynamic merit involves a commitment to the distribution of opportunity not only at birth but also through one's life. It is contextual and resistant to standardized measurement. It requires modesty in our beliefs about what we can measure in human beings, even as it demands that we be clear about our institutional objectives.

Clearly, the goal is to make good on our educational institutions' commitment to democratic values in a multiracial society. The practice, what I am tentatively calling 'confirmative action,' is to adopt admissions' criteria that confirm that goal. This is not a plea for a specific magic bullet replacement for the testocracy. Nor is it an unqualified endorsement of affirmative action as the only tool to achieve coherence between what we say we want and what we are doing. Rather it is a claim that affirmative action is a valuable experiment from which we might learn. It is an experiment that teaches us to engage in a range of selection practices, each of which should be assessed in terms of its ability to realize the mission of the institution within the larger framework of a multiracial democracy.

Confirmative action, however, goes beyond affirming the experience of affirmative action for its specific beneficiaries. It decouples merit from testable mental aptitude for all applicants, thus freeing us to envision many more ways of experimenting with systems for allocating scarce resources.

Toward this end confirmative action builds on the values of affirmative action but does not limit the practice to an historically disadvantaged group. Confirmative action offers opportunity more broadly but without a one-size-fits-all metric. It joins the idea of opportunity for all that undergirds the new meritocracy to the idea that no one-size-fits-all gauge can fairly allocate such opportunity. It thus borrows from both the meritocratic and affirmative action approaches but situates the practices of admission or selection within a clearer understanding of institutional mission.

Confirmative action is a practice of social justice that is both experimental and contextual. It challenges the idea that those who are already privileged can be trusted to administer or justify a system for allocating opportunity. But it challenges that idea on behalf of all of those who have been left out, not just those who were deliberately excluded because of race, color or previous condition of servitude. Most of all, confirmative action reconnects issues of selection or admission to the democratic values of higher education.

Confirmative action, in other words, provides another and potentially more constructive way of framing the question of allocating high stakes opportunity by connecting it to a larger conversation about democracy.

(See also Equality and Inequality; Multiculturalism; Race and Racism; Social Mobility.)

Susan Sturm and Lani Guinier, *The Future of Affirmative Action: Reclaiming the Innovative Ideal*, 84 Cal. L. Rev. 953, 968 (1996). Christopher Jencks and Meredith Phillips, *The Black-White Test Score Gap* (Washington, D.C., 1998). Lani Guinier, "Commentary, Law School Affirmative Action: An Empirical Study" *Law and Social Inquiry, Journal of the American Bar Foundation* 25, no. 2 (Spring 2000): 565–583. Lani Guinier and Gerald Torres, *The Miners' Canary: Rethinking Race and Power* (Harvard University Press, 2001).

Lani Guinier

which was heavily involved both in the removal of the monarchy and in the 1978 coup; but it also provided the core of the Afghan Islamist movement, which in turn formed a part of the Mujāhidīn resistance to Marxist rule.

The communist regime, formally built around the bitterly factorized "People's Democratic Party of Afghanistan," suffered problems of legitimacy from its inception, and came to rely on nonlegitimate means of domination—notably coercion and the use of resources to "purchase" support—in order to survive. Following the Soviet invasion, a well-funded secret police force, KhAD (Khedamāt-i Eṭlāʿā-i Dawlatī, or "State Information Service"), was established under the tutelage of the Soviet KGB to identify and repress opponents of the regime, especially in urban areas. Rural areas were exposed to ferocious attacks by Soviet air and ground forces, resulting in the deaths of approximately 1 million Afghans, and the departure as refugees to Pakistan and Iran of a further 5–6 million. With the disintegration of the communist regime, over 4 million returned, but war damage, economic disruption, and fear of either persecution or antipersonnel mines blocked the return of the remainder.

As a result of this sequence of events, Afghanistan has no "national" political system. Rather, different groups claim "control" over different areas within the country. Despite the Ṭalibān movement's occupation of Kabul in September 1996, the Credentials Committee of the United Nations General Assembly declined to grant it Afghanistan's UN seat, which remained in the hands of the Rabbani government. This was partly in response to the Ṭalibān's antediluvian views on gender issues, but also because their ideological position—mixing Islamic precepts derived from the Deobandī school with a radical and antimodernist commitment to establishing a "pure" Islamic order with no direct precedent in Afghan history—put them at odds with a number of the key principles embodied in the UN Charter. In rural areas that the Ṭalibān purport to control, their actual presence is very light, and traditional structures of governance, notably the *jirga*, coexist with other local power-holders, especially wealthy traders. In urban areas, the control of the Ṭalibān is more direct, and is exercised not through cohesive bureaucratic structures, but rather the religious police, known as the department responsible for "the Promotion of Virtue and the Suppression of Vice." The Ṭalibān movement, which comprises not simply religious students, but also other Pashtuns (including former communists) who have joined it for reasons of either ethnic solidarity or prudence, is factionalized to a considerable degree: the authority of its leader, Muaḥammad ʿUmar, boosted by his claimed title of Amīr al-Muʾminīn ("Commander of the Faithful"), is therefore a vital unifying factor, although it is not remotely sufficient to ensure coherent policy-making.

Disorder in the political sphere has permitted the flourishing on Afghan soil of a number of "nontraditional," translational security threats. The first is opium cultivation. While Afghanistan's 1998 output of cereal crops, estimated by the UN Food and Agriculture Organization (FAO) to be 3.85 million tons, far exceeded that year's dry opium output of 3,269 tons, it was the latter statistic that received the most attention, since it established Afghanistan as one of the largest sources of opium in the world. The Ṭalibān were known to benefit from taxes on narcotics. The second "nontraditional" security threat arose from the entrenchment in Ṭalibān areas of a range of radical and militant Islamic groups, most notoriously that of the Saudi dissident Usama Bin Laden, but including Kashmiri terrorist groups such as the Ḥarakāt al-Mujāhidīn which won world coverage through the hijacking of an Indian Airlines aircraft to the Ṭalibān stronghold of Kandahar in December 1999.

These threats in turn engaged the attention of the United States, especially following the bombing in August 1998 of U.S. embassies in Tanzania and Kenya, for which Bin Laden was blamed. Within a month, the Clinton administration launched "Tomahawk" cruise missile strikes against suspected Bin Laden bases in eastern Afghanistan, which failed to kill Bin Laden, but resulted in the deaths of a number of Kashmiri militants whom his network had been training; these strikes were followed by a U.S. Executive Order in July 1999 blocking property and prohibiting transactions with the Ṭalibān (who continued to shelter Bin Laden), and ultimately, in November 1999, by the imposition of sanctions against the Ṭalibān by the UN Security Council in Resolution 1267.

Afghanistan's continuing problems are scarcely homegrown. Since 1994, an estimated 80,000–100,000 Pakistanis have reportedly trained and fought for the Ṭalibān in Afghanistan: this "creeping invasion" of Afghanistan has been a major factor in the expansion of Ṭalibān influence, and prompted other regional states to lend support to the anti-Ṭalibān opposition lest the movement become entrenched adjacent to their borders or spheres of influence. It is also a reminder of the extent to which two decades of strife not only opened the borders of Afghanistan to the predations of meddlesome neighbors, but turned Afghanistan into a theater of confrontation between antagonistic states in a region undergoing significant reconfiguration as a result of the 1979 Iranian revolution, the disintegration of the Soviet Union in 1991, and Pakistan's ongoing search for strategic depth in the context of its confrontation with India, especially over Kashmir. The war in Afghanistan is neither purely international nor purely civil, and this has made the crafting of a workable solution to Afghanistan's problems of political order prove almost insuperable.

While Afghanistan remains extremely isolated, it is linked to the wider world through a number of channels. The United Nations sought through various avenues—a Special Mission established by the General Assembly, and the appointment in 1997 of a distinguished diplomat, Ambassador Lakhdar Brahimi, as the UN secretary-general's special envoy to Afghanistan—to broker understandings between the various Afghan combatants, but met with little success, largely because the conflict had not ripened for settlement, and supplies of arms and fuel continued to flow freely to the Ṭalibān and their opponents. The UN's other main involvement in Afghanistan arose from its broader humanitarian mandate. Some humanitarian activities have been strikingly successful, such as the work of the Mine Action Programme, which, using Afghan organizations under a UN umbrella, succeeded in clearing mines and unexploded ordnance from many parts of the country. Other UN agencies have been hampered by the tensions between their operating principles and procedures, on the one hand, and the ideology and vision of the Ṭalibān, on the other. The International Committee of the Red Cross remains heavily involved in the provision of medical services, in the production of prosthetic and orthotic devices for disabled Afghans, and in the promotion of the principles of international humanitarian law through scripts of the BBC World Service "reconstruction serial" *New Home, New Life*, which secured a wide listening audience in Afghanistan.

Despite all the traumas through which Afghanistan has passed, its population—one of the poorest and most deprived in the world—is sustained by a remarkable degree of initiative (reflected in the activities of the private sector), by very strong norms of reciprocity, and by assistance from international agencies and a range of local and international nongovernmental organizations (NGOs) which seek to provide both emergency and development assistance. However, two decades of war have de-skilled a generation of Afghans, and this loss of human capital, together with the effects of suppressed trauma, poses a major threat to social order. Should this threat go unaddressed, the consequences both for Afghanistan and for its region could well be devastating.

(See also DRUGS; ISLAM; SOVIET UNION; TERRORISM.)

Barnett R. Rubin, *The Fragmentation of Afghanistan: State Formation and Collapse in the International System* (New Haven, Conn., 1995). William Maley, ed., *Fundamentalism Reborn? Afghanistan and the Taliban* (New York, 1998). Henry S. Bradsher, *Afghan Communism and Soviet Intervention* (Karachi, 1999).

WILLIAM MALEY

AFL-CIO. See AMERICAN FEDERATION OF LABOR AND CONGRESS OF INDUSTRIAL ORGANIZATIONS.

AFRICAN AMERICANS. More than 10 million people brought as slaves to the Americas during the period from the sixteenth to the nineteenth centuries confronted a situation that was historically unprecedented. Never before had such a large group of people been driven from their homelands and forced to labor for the remainder of their lives in distant societies dominated by culturally and racially different people. Deprived of their freedom and torn from their cultural roots, slaves and their descendants responded to their enslavement in varied and innovative ways.

Slaves born into African societies initially relied upon their cultural traditions as they struggled against chattel slavery, but life in Africa had not prepared them to challenge European technological superiority. Some slaves saw their situation as hopeless and committed suicide rather than endure the passage to the Americas or the harsh process of slave breaking once they arrived. Others fought their enslavers, rebelling aboard slave ships or in the Americas. Few rebellions succeeded, however, because slaves were closely supervised, unfamiliar with their new surroundings, often divided by linguistic and religious differences, and subjected to brutal punishments when disobedient. In addition, disease and malnutrition killed many slaves and weakened the ability of others to rebel. Most Africans who came to the Americas, particularly those brought to the sugar plantations of Brazil or the Caribbean islands, died without bearing children.

Those who survived found it necessary to undergo a cultural transformation. Africans from diverse cultural backgrounds became African Americans, a group stigmatized by the color of their skin and bound together by the common experience of being subordinate to Europeans. The most basic aspect of this cultural transformation involved the adoption of European languages, which not only enabled slaves to

communicate with their masters but also, in some cases, with each other. The transformation also involved the adoption of other European cultural, social, and political practices, but this did not constitute a complete abandonment of African cultural values, some of which persisted in the Americas. Nor did African slaves simply become Europeanized because they simultaneously transformed European culture as they infused it with their own insights. African Americans not only endured under oppression; over time they also established families, churches, schools, self-help groups, fraternal orders, and other institutions as they sought to improve their lives collectively and individually. These institutions conformed somewhat to European-American models, but they also reflected the distinctive common experiences and aspirations of slaves and their descendants.

The tendency of African Americans to utilize European cultural forms increased during the eighteenth and nineteenth centuries as a result of the religious "awakenings" and democratic revolutions that occurred in many European-dominated societies. Emerging forms of African-American Christianity combined residual elements of African religions and those aspects of Christianity that appealed to slaves and freed blacks. From the beginning of the slave era, conversion to Christianity sometimes offered a means for slaves to improve their lives or simply to find a degree of psychological solace. Although conversion rarely led directly to emancipation for slaves—indeed, most slave masters saw Christianity as compatible with or mandating slavery—in British North America democratic ideas accompanied the spread of evangelical Christianity during the eighteenth and nineteenth centuries. Methodist and Baptist religious practices in particular appealed to African Americans because they fostered democratic ideals and encouraged individuals to assert control over their spiritual lives as well as over congregational decision making. Prayer and prophecy became means for expressing African-American aspirations. As transformed by blacks struggling to free themselves, Christianity became a theology promoting freedom and social justice that was at least partially outside the control of whites.

The formation in 1793 of Philadelphia's Bethel African Methodist Episcopal (AME) church was an important step in the institutionalization of African-American culture and society. Bethel's minister, Richard Allen (1760–1831), initially remained within the Episcopal church hierarchy, but in 1816, when the AME church achieved full autonomy, he became the denomination's first bishop. Other blacks would join the AME Zion denomination or one of the hundreds of Baptist and Methodist churches that gained many members as a result of the religious revivals of the decades before the Civil War. Such religious institutions provided training grounds for the development of black leadership. Moreover, Christianity was a source of insight for African Americans seeking understanding of their history and plight. They could identify their enslavement with that of the Jews or see the Ethiopians mentioned in the Bible as their ancient ancestors.

While African Americans adapted Christianity to serve new purposes, they also transformed modern concepts of *nationalism into a set of political ideas that gave them a collective identity and informed their movements for advancement. Both the American and the French *revolutions of the late eighteenth century encouraged African Americans to hope that they might enjoy the *rights that were won by white people. The gradual movement in Europe and the Americas toward the ideal of universal rights influenced and was in turn influenced by African-American struggles for advancement. After the British colonies of North America gained their independence, blacks in the United States petitioned white leaders to end slavery and racial discrimination by pointing to the egalitarian sentiments expressed in revolutionary documents such as the Declaration of Independence. The French revolution of 1789 also strengthened antislavery sentiment in the Americas and prompted a successful slave rebellion, led by Toussaint L'Ouverture (1743–1803), in the colony that became Haiti. Taken together, the American and the French revolutions provided democratic ideals for many subsequent African-American political movements. The democratic idealism expressed in the American Declaration of Independence encouraged some blacks to believe the principles of equality were universal rather than limited to white men. The U.S. Constitution of 1787 reflected the postrevolutionary decline of democratic idealism, however, by reinforcing the legal rights of slaveholders and providing African Americans with few mechanisms for effective political action against the proslavery state governments.

Whether slaves could or should seek full citizenship in white-dominated societies became central questions for nineteenth- and twentieth-century African-American political movements. European Americans generally rejected the idea that African Americans should be granted equal rights. Such white resistance to racial equality led some African Americans to insist that their rights would be protected only in a black-controlled nation. In the United States, the strengthening of the slave economy after the invention of the cotton gin in 1793 lessened the possibility that slavery would be abolished peacefully. Although some emancipated blacks became politically active during the early nineteenth century, most states imposed special restrictions on their political freedom. After the exposure of major slave conspiracies in Virginia in 1800 and South Carolina in 1822, and the crushing of the Nat Turner (1800–1831) slave rebellion in Virginia in 1831, southern whites severely restricted the ability of slaves and free blacks to assemble. In addition, the desire of African Americans to emigrate back to Africa or at least out of the United States grew during the antebellum years. In 1815 Paul Cuffe (1759–1817), a wealthy African-American merchant mariner, brought a small group of settlers to Sierra Leone on the west coast of Africa. Most emancipated blacks found emigration to Africa impractical and undesirable, however, for they had been born in the United States and had little knowledge of life elsewhere. In 1817 a national meeting of black leaders rejected the efforts of white leaders of the American Colonization Society to encourage freed blacks to go to Africa.

The formation of the American Anti-Slavery Society in 1833 further encouraged African-American antislavery agitation. Although the society's leader, William Lloyd Garrison, was a white abolitionist who believed in "moral suasion" as the best means of ending slavery, by the 1840s many black abolitionists had begun to attack slavery politically by supporting antislavery parties and candidates for political office. The most well-known black abolitionist, Frederick Douglass (1817–1895), initially allied himself with Garrison, but by the end of the 1840s had become a proponent of political strategies. Other black leaders such as Henry Highland Garnet and Martin Delany urged not only political action but also slave rebellions as the best means of abolishing slavery. Garnet and Delany also became advocates of black nationalism, believing that there was little hope for black advancement in the United States. Delany's *Condition, Elevation, Emigration and Destiny of the Colored People of the United States, Politically Considered* (1852) argued that African Americans were "a nation within a nation" and recommended emigration to Central America or Africa. Pessimism increased among African Americans about their prospects in the United States after the Supreme Court's Dred Scott decision of 1857, which concluded that blacks were not citizens but were "a subordinate and inferior class of beings."

The Civil War marked a major turning point in African-American politics. Although President Abraham Lincoln initially did not see the war as a struggle against slavery, the increasing reliance of the Union army on black soldiers altered war objectives. In 1863, Lincoln's Emancipation Proclamation promised freedom to slaves in areas still held by the Confederacy. After the defeat of the Confederacy, Republican leaders recognized that citizenship rights for freed slaves were necessary for the party's success in the South during the Reconstruction period. They drafted and obtained ratification by the states of constitutional amendments designed to free all slaves (13th Amendment) and to eliminate racial discrimination of laws (14th) and voting (15th). During the Reconstruction period, African Americans participated in the southern political system, but black-supported Republican state governments in the region faced strong opposition from recalcitrant white segregationists, and none survived after the last federal troops were removed in 1877.

The end of Reconstruction led to a rapid decline in black political activity, and by the early twentieth century most southern states had enacted racially discriminatory laws that segregated blacks and prevented them from voting. Black political leaders responded to the imposition of this "Jim Crow" system in a variety of ways. Some leaders, including AME bishop Henry McNeal Turner (1834–1915), advocated black separatism and even emigration to Africa. Others, notably Booker T. Washington (1856–1915), founder of Tuskegee Institute in Alabama, urged blacks to forgo agitation for civil rights and instead develop skills that would be useful for white employers. Washington garnered the financial backing of white philanthropists, particularly after his conciliatory address at the Atlanta Exposition of 1895, and he dominated African-American politics at the national level at the beginning of the twentieth century.

The most innovative political thinker of the period was William E. B. *Du Bois (1868–1963), who combined elements of earlier nationalist thought, particularly an appreciation of the African roots of African-American culture, with a strong commitment to ending racial discrimination. In 1900, Du Bois, influenced by the earlier efforts of Alexander Crummell (1819–1898) and Edwart Wilmot Blyden (1932–1912), participated in the first Pan-African Conference in London, which advocated unity among all people of African ancestry. In 1905, Du Bois became a founding member of the Niagara movement, formed to promote protest activity on behalf of black civil rights, and, four years later, he joined with white reformers to establish the National Association for the Advancement of Colored People (NAACP).

Twentieth-century African-American politics were greatly affected by the migration of millions of blacks from the rural South to urban areas. A massive influx of blacks to northern cities during World War I strengthened existing African-American urban religious and fraternal institutions, and led to increasing political militancy in the growing black communities. Marcus Garvey (1887–1940) organized the most substantial manifestation of the new militancy, the Universal Negro Improvement Association (UNIA), which, according to some estimates, attracted several million followers. Garvey's ultimate goal was to create a strong, independent African nation that would advance the interests of black people throughout the world. Garvey's caustic criticisms of civil rights leaders such as Du Bois made him a controversial figure among blacks and a target of government persecution. He was convicted of mail fraud in connection with his fundraising for the Black Star steamship line, and his movement declined rapidly after his deportation in 1927 to Jamaica.

Despite the persecution of Garvey, African-American cultural distinctiveness continued to flourish through the movement known as the Harlem Renaissance. Poets, essayists, dramatists, novelists, and artists of the 1920s became increasingly concerned with depicting the lives of African Americans. Langston Hughes (1902–1967), the most popular and prolific of the poets of the period, summarized the sentiments of other writers when he announced in a 1926 article: "We younger Negro artists who create now intend to express our individual dark-skinned selves without fear or shame." ("The Negro Artist and the Racial Mountain," *The Nation*, June 23, 1926, pp. 692–694.) Other major intellectual figures of the movement included Alain Locke (1886–1954), Claude McKay (1890–1948), and Zora Neale Hurston (1901–1960). Innovative forms of African-American music also appeared during the 1920s as blues and jazz became increasingly popular in urban centers.

The worldwide economic depression of the 1930s strengthened the tendency of African Americans to seek advancement through interracial political movements and civil rights reform. A small minority of blacks, including a number of prominent artists and intellectuals, was drawn to the Communist Party, which identified itself with the ideal of universal rights and which fostered the notion that blacks could play a major role in radically transforming American society. Du Bois and Paul Robeson (1898–1976), a famed singer and actor, were prominent among blacks who remained close to the Communist Party during the 1940s and 1950s, even as other blacks, such as Hughes and novelist Richard Wright (1908–1960), became disillusioned with the party. The dominant direction of African-American political activity outside the South involved electoral participation and efforts to combat racial discrimination through litigation, lobbying efforts, and, to an increasing extent, protest activity. After 1932, black voters generally supported the Democratic Party in national elections, and most black leaders at the national level participated in interracial coalitions favoring civil rights reforms. The 1941 March on Washington movement, initiated by black union

leader A. Philip Randolph, demonstrated the potential for mass protest activity as a means of bringing about civil rights reform by prodding President Franklin D. *Roosevelt to establish a Fair Employment Practices Committee. Despite Randolph's success in using the threat of protest to achieve concessions, however, the strategy of nonviolent direct action had few practitioners outside of the Congress of Racial Equality (CORE), a small, interracial group formed in 1944.

The participation of black soldiers in the United States military during *World War II prompted intensified demands for racial equality, but, during the decade following the war, conventional electoral politics and civil rights lobbying rather than mass activism characterized African-American life. Both socialist and black nationalist radicalism had little impact on black politics, particularly at the national level. Instead, encouraged by the Supreme Court's *Brown v. Board of Education* (1954) decision, civil rights organizations and their leaders sought to strengthen federal and state antidiscrimination policies. The NAACP largely shaped the national civil rights agenda, but, after the Montgomery bus boycott movement of 1955–56, this organization faced competition from more militant local groups inspired by African independence movements, linked to black colleges and churches, as well as skilled in the use of nonviolent protest tactics. The Southern Christian Leadership Conference (SCLC), formed in 1957 and led by Montgomery protest leader Martin Luther *King, Jr. (1929–1968), was particularly effective in organizing massive protest campaigns in southern communities such as Birmingham in 1963 and Selma in 1965. CORE initiated a Freedom Ride campaign in 1961, pressuring the federal government to act against racial discrimination in interstate travel. The Student Nonviolent Coordinating Committee (SNCC), formed by student leaders of the sit-in movement of 1960, spearheaded the effort to achieve voting rights for blacks in Mississippi, Alabama, and southwest Georgia. The southern protest movement prodded the federal government to enact both the Civil Rights Act of 1964, which outlawed segregation in most public facilities, and the Voting Rights Act of 1965.

Even as the southern protest movement achieved its civil rights goals, it also revived feelings of racial consciousness among African Americans. Black nationalist sentiments were evident among urban blacks during the early 1960s, but the most effective proponent of these ideas, *Malcolm X (1925–1965), had little impact on national African-American politics until 1964 when he broke with the religious separatist group the Nation of Islam. In the months before his *assassination in 1965, Malcolm began to establish ties with militants who had been active in the civil rights movement. By 1966, both SNCC, under the leadership of Stokely Carmichael (1944–1998), and CORE became identified with the "Black Power" slogan, which symbolized the increasingly militant racial consciousness of African Americans. During the decade from 1965 to 1975, many new black-controlled cultural, social, political, educational, and economic institutions came into existence. The Black Panther Party, based in Oakland, California, reflected the widespread discontent of young northern blacks through the brash willingness of armed Panthers to confront police. For the most part, however, the majority of African-American institutions of the Black Power era did not pose direct political challenges to the state but instead emphasized African-American cultural distinctiveness. During the late 1960s and early 1970s internal ideological conflicts and external repression led to the decline of militant political groups. The National Black Political Assembly, founded at a 1972 convention in Gary, Indiana, could not reverse the disintegration of black nationalist political activity. Instead, black political activity increasingly focused on efforts to elect black politicians in predominantly black districts. In addition to the increasing number of African Americans holding elected or appointed offices, the most enduring outgrowths of the militancy of the 1960s were the black studies academic programs, businesses selling products designed for blacks, and associations formed to protect the interests of black professionals.

As popular support for governmental social reforms programs declined during the 1970s and 1980s, mass protest and militancy among African Americans was increasingly supplanted by efforts to utilize conventional tactics to achieve greater control over communities and institutions that were predominantly black. Many studies of American racial relations during this period noted the disjunction between the economic advances of middle-class blacks and the economic stagnation of large numbers of poor or working-class blacks. *Affirmative action programs came under attack not only from white conservatives but also from some blacks who noted the adverse psychological impact of such programs on some blacks. National black leaders largely focused their efforts on the consolidation of the civil rights gains of the 1960s, but many incorporated aspects of black nationalism and Pan-Africanism into their political perspectives. Jesse Jackson's (b. 1941) campaigns for the presidency in 1984 and 1988 demonstrated the potential strength of the black electorate. In addition, during the period after 1970, black women have increasingly won election to public office and assumed prominent roles in racial policy discussions.

The overriding concern of black political and intellectual life during the final decades of the twentieth century was the extent to which African Americans had become divided by class and gender identities. African-American leaders were unable to formulate successful strategies to deal with the serious economic problems of blacks who did not benefit economically from civil rights legislation and affirmative action programs. The combustible elements of political stagnation, endemic poverty, and police repression contributed to major racial riots in Miami in 1980 and Los Angeles in 1991. The increasing prevalence of households headed by single, jobless mothers; the high rates of mortality, unemployment, and incarceration among black males; and the reluctance of white Americans to support major new governmental social programs to deal with these problems led to a revival of strategies for African-American self-help and cultural uplift. The most notable expression of this revival was the ascendancy of Louis Farrakhan, leader of the Nation of Islam, to national prominence as a spokesperson for discontented blacks. Farrakhan played a major role in organizing the Million Man March in Washington, D.C., in October 1995, an event that was less a protest than a collective act of atonement by black males.

The Million Man March, with its emphasis on the distinctive problems of black males within the context of broader racial solidarity, served as a counterpoint to the emergence, during the previous two decades, of a vibrant black feminist (or womanist) movement. To some degree this movement was itself a reaction against the misogyny of some black male leaders as well as the lack of attention to black female concerns in the white feminist movement. Although black women had produced important and distinctive contributions to African-American history throughout the nineteenth and twentieth centuries, a concerted effort to promote a collective consciousness among African-American women was evident in numerous literary works that reached a wide readership after the mid-1970s. Seminal works in this literary and social movement were Alice Walker's *The Color Purple* (1982) and Toni Morrison's *Beloved* (1987).

Thus, at the end of the twentieth century, African Americans had succeeded in overcoming historic forms of racial discrimination, but some racial barriers remained. The economic success of some members of the group had brought about increasing diversity among African Americans, which in turn encouraged increasing variety in collective and individual advancement strategies. Increasingly likely to be involved in the mainstream of American life, African Americans continued to be concerned with distinctive and unresolved questions of group identity and destiny.

(See also CIVIL RIGHTS MOVEMENT; EQUALITY AND INEQUALITY; FEMINISM; NONVIOLENT ACTION; RACE AND RACISM; RELIGION AND POLITICS; SUPREME COURT OF THE UNITED STATES.)

Herbert Aptheker, ed., A *Documentary History of the Negro People in the United States* (New York: 1974). John Hope Franklin, with Alfred A. Moss, Jr., *From Slavery to Freedom: A History of Negro Americans* (New York, 1988). Darlene Clark Hine and Kathleen Thompson, *A Shining Thread of Hope: The History of Black Women in America* (New York, 1988). Jack Salzman, David Lionel Smith, and Cornel West, eds., *Encyclopedia of African American Culture and History* (New York, 1996). William Julius Wilson, *The Bridge over the Racial Divide* (Berkeley, Calif., 1999). David O. Sear, Jim Sidanius, and Lawrence Bobo, eds., *Racialized Politics: The Debate about Racism in America* (Chicago, 2000).

CLAYBORNE CARSON

AFRICAN DEVELOPMENT BANK. The African Development Bank (ADB) was established in 1964 by thirty-two independent African states. Article 1 of the agreement establishing it states that "the purpose of the Bank shall be to contribute to the economic development and social progress of its regional members—individually and jointly." Ten years later, its membership was extended to twenty-six non-African states through the creation of the African Development Fund (ADF). Resources of ADF are lent to poorer African countries at zero interest rates, with principal repayments spread over fifty years including a ten-year grace period. Moreover, a Nigerian Trust Fund (NTF) was established in 1976 to assist African states severely hit by the first oil shock.

The Bank Group—ADB, ADF, and NTF—currently has seventy-nine member states, of which fifty-three are African. Eritrea and South Africa are the new members. This expansion in membership has led to a substantial increase in the authorized capital of the bank from US$1.6 billion in 1979 to US$21.8 billion in 1988. It has also led to a significant increase in the volume of concessional lending, with two-thirds of the total number of loans now being funded through ADF.

Bank resources are managed by an executive president, assisted by three vice-presidents and 500 professional staff.

Moreover, there is an eighteen-person Board of Executive Directors representing its shareholders. Since 1986 the bank has enjoyed a triple-A rating in the international capital markets, which is a significant recognition.

The founders of the bank envisaged it as having a dual role of financing "investment projects and programmes relating to the economic and social development of its regional members" and of providing technical know-how in their design, implementation, and management. In this regard, the Bank Group has collaborated with a majority of multilateral and bilateral donors in cofinancing projects and programs in Africa.

The bank financed only investment projects during the first nineteen years (1967–1985) of its operations. With the African economic crisis at its peak in the mid-1980s, the Bank Group has added a new and quick disbursing instrument to the investment project financing device. Hence, as of 1986 it has allocated twenty-five percent of its annual lending to finance, with the *World Bank, policy-based operations in the framework of structural adjustment programs. This has resulted in a significant increase in the annual volume of loans as well as disbursements. For instance, loans worth about US$6.0 billion were approved during the period 1986–1988, compared to approximately US$7.0 billion during 1967–1985. By sectoral allocation, agriculture is the leading sector with about thirty-one percent of cumulative lending, followed by public utilities, transport, and industry with twenty-three percent, nineteen percent, and fourteen percent respectively. The share of education and health is only 8.2 percent.

In recognition of the challenges facing African economies, the bank in 1996 reorganized its internal organizational structures to better serve Africa. In this regard, it has reoriented its lending operations in support of strategies that focus on economic growth, poverty reduction, and protection of the environment, as well as private sector development.

(See also ASIAN DEVELOPMENT BANK; ECONOMIC COMMISSION FOR AFRICA; INTER-AMERICAN DEVELOPMENT BANK.)

African Development Bank, *Agreement Establishing the African Development Bank*, 2d ed. (Abidjan, 1988).

LUAL ACUEK DENG

AFRICAN NATIONAL CONGRESS. See MANDELA, NELSON; SOUTH AFRICA.

AGGRESSION. See FORCE, USE OF.

AGRARIAN REFORM. See LAND REFORM.

AIDS. AIDS is a fatal disease syndrome that emerged during the late 1970s in Africa and the United States. The slow-acting Human Immunodeficiency Virus (HIV) spread silently across the globe, causing the AIDS pandemic. Nineteen million people have died; more than 35 million now live with the virus. In some areas of the world the epidemic is just beginning. Ninety percent of the more than 54 million people who have contracted HIV/AIDS to date live in less developed countries, where health and social infrastructures weakened by economic crisis are unable to cope with severe new burdens of disease. More than 70 percent of the total are in Africa, where

some 25 million people live with HIV/AIDS. In the sixteen hardest-hit countries, life expectancy has declined sharply.

The HIV, which causes immune system damage leading to diseases of AIDS syndrome, is transmitted through sexual intercourse, blood, and from mother to infant. The virus uses the body's own immune system to reproduce itself and eventually damages its defenses against other diseases. These include virulent forms of tuberculosis, pneumonia, wasting diarrheas, cancers, and neurological disorders. Untreated classic sexually transmitted diseases (STDs) increase the likelihood of sexual transmission of HIV. The period between infection and the onset of disease symptoms is lengthy and varies between individuals, apparently according to their genetic makeup and that of the virus. In Africa and other developing areas, HIV testing is expensive and not widely available; most people who harbor the virus do not know that they are infected until several years later, when they fall sick. During this period, unless they use condom protection, they will have transmitted infection to their sex partners.

Although AIDS was first identified in 1981 in the United States among homosexual men, different transmission patterns predominate in different arts of the world and in different population subgroups within countries; these patterns have changed over time. Worldwide, about 70 percent of infections are believed to have been acquired during sexual intercourse; 45 percent of those infected are women, most of whom have acquired HIV from men who had sex with multiple partners and failed to use condom protection. The viral strain predominant in high prevalence areas of East and Southern Africa is HIV-1 type E, readily transmissible in heterosexual intercourse, which accounts for an estimated 80 or 90 percent of infections. There (as in the poverty-stricken ghettos of U.S. cities), AIDS is the leading cause of death in young adults. The highest prevalence is among young women, who account for over half of those infected. Adolescent girls are especially biologically and socially vulnerable to infection by older men; from two to six times more girls are infected than boys of their age. Many children—about 10 percent of the total number of AIDS sufferers—are infected in utero, during birth, or breast-feeding. In sixteen African countries 10 percent of people aged fifteen to forty-nine years are infected; the highest rate, 36 percent, is in Botswana. Ninety percent of deaths occur in adults aged twenty to forty-nine, the prime working years.

The prolonged disease process is extremely painful in its later stages and the sick require extensive care. Most of the care burden falls upon women who may be sick themselves, and without financial and other resources. With many people falling sick and others overworked and demoralized by so much death around them, the impact on all economic activities, and on family and social life in the affected areas is severe. Deaths of productive adults leave orphaned children and elders who depended upon them. Globally, an estimated 11 million children under fifteen have lost their mothers or both their parents to AIDS. Some 8 million of these are in Africa, where poverty makes them vulnerable to HIV infection in their turn. Gains made by child survival programs have been overtaken in high-prevalence areas, where AIDS has increased mortality in children by two or three times. More African children now die from AIDS than from either malaria or measles, which formerly were major killers. Money needed by families for food and other necessities is spent on medicines. Trained labor, previously scarce, has been lost to AIDS. Health systems face personnel crises; millions of school-age children have lost their teachers; factories and farms have lost workers and managers. In the villages, labor time lost by women caring for the sick creates substantial agricultural losses.

In the United States, before new disease-delaying anti-retroviral drugs became available in 1985, about half of those infected with HIV developed AIDS symptoms within ten years. Expensive new drug-combinations suppress viral replication and delay disease onset, but the rapidly mutating virus develops drug-resistance and many people experience harmful side-effects, so treatments must be carefully monitored. To date, no HIV-infected person has fully recovered; most are expected to progress to AIDS eventually. In Africa, public health systems have collapsed under the combined onslaughts of AIDS, economic crisis, and Structural Adjustment Programs (SAPs) that sacrificed social programs to debt reimbursement. Access to physicians, let alone to sophisticated drugs and laboratory monitoring are not widely available; death generally occurs within two years following the onset of AIDS diseases. Neither cure nor vaccine is likely to emerge in the near future, and when these do become available access will be limited by inability to pay, especially in the Third World. Even with substantial drug price reductions mooted by pharmaceutical companies, anti-retroviral therapies will not be affordable by the poor or middle classes.

An epidemic is an essentially social process, shaped by political economy and culture. AIDS has struck with particular severity in communities struggling under the burdens of economic crisis, the roots of which reside in a combination of internal and international processes. These include stagnation in the global economy, distorted internal production structures inherited from colonialism, unfavorable terms of trade, rapid class formation, landlessness, unemployment, the subordination of women, and widening disparities in wealth fueled by channeling public funds into private pockets. Many epidemiologists underestimated the potential magnitude of HIV/AIDS in Africa, believing that the heterosexual epidemic could be contained by focusing prevention efforts on "core transmitters," people such as sex workers and long-haul transporters known to have multiple sex partners. AIDS was constructed as an urban disease, from which "traditional" rural areas would be spared. Social scientists and physicians familiar with conditions in Africa, however, envisaged the impeding catastrophe. They pointed to poverty and gender inequality, especially to harsh socioeconomic conditions that have divided families, increased disparities in wealth and power, and altered behavioral norms in rural as well as urban areas. From the mid-1970s, increasing millions of Africans have lived in abject poverty, their survival precarious, deprived of hope for the future. Survival strategies include labor migration, long-distance trade, smuggling, and exchange of sex for the means of subsistence. Mines, plantations, trading towns, fishing camps, and ports attract job-seekers in large numbers. Most are men who come without their families. Their camps are visited by girls and women who arrive on paydays, often traveling long distances. Poor women have few income-earning opportunities as remunerative as sex; often they must support dependents as well

as provide for themselves. Deepening economic crisis and SAPs fell hardest on the poor; wars and military occupation brought civilian deaths, rape, and mass population displacement across the continent. These conditions set the stage for sex with multiple partners, and led to widespread dissemination of the new virus. Poverty and pervasive gender inequality make it especially difficult for women and girls to avoid unsafe sex. Their risk is further increased by sexual violence. Those with secondary-level education are more likely to protect themselves and sexual partners from HIV infection; thus, Africa's education crisis is another factor driving the AIDS pandemic.

AIDS prevention is exceedingly complex; response to AIDS is political, in Africa as elsewhere. Public health action takes place on a terrain of contested meanings and unequal power, where different knowledges struggle for control. AIDS is not just another disease; the HIV virus is not just one among many new microorganisms affecting humans. The biological disease processes are difficult for laypeople, including political leaders, to comprehend. Linked to reproduction and death, AIDS is emotionally and symbolically freighted. Some diseases of the AIDS syndrome are often culturally stigmatized. Furthermore, because it is sexually transmitted and incurable, AIDS may be attributed to moral transgressions and supernatural sanctions; response may include accusations of blame. Blaming others leads to denial of risk and failure to take realistic steps to protect oneself and others. Where AIDS is believed to be caused by women, by minorities, or by supernatural agency, scapegoating, witch-hunting, and social unrest compound socioeconomic disruption. AIDS often provokes fear and hostility toward the afflicted. Wives may be cast off by spouses. Families unable to dissemble the nature of the illness may find themselves isolated. AIDS orphans may be shunned and left to roam the streets, where they are particularly vulnerable to HIV infection.

In many countries around the world, powerful interest groups have treated AIDS, like classic STDs, as a moral, rather than a health issue. This makes it difficult for some governments to conduct rational prevention campaigns. Many hold (erroneously) that sex education and condoms will increase sexual activity ("immorality") among youth, or among women. Where national, community, and NGO leaders share these perspectives, the moralist stance inhibits effective prevention campaigns. In Uganda, Tanzania, and Senegal, resistance from many religious leaders and community elders was strong in the early 1990s. Alarmed governments nevertheless instituted strong safer sex education campaigns, and made STD treatment and condoms widely available and acceptable, especially among young people. The incidence of new infections began to decline these countries in 1996. Elsewhere, the virus continues to spread, not only in cities where the epidemic is well established, but also to rural areas and to countries apparently HIV-free in the 1980s.

Limiting sexual transmission requires empowering substantial numbers of people to alter highly valued behaviors, including sexual relations widely considered to be "natural" and essential to health. Condoms are not popular among men, many of whom enjoy a double standard with numerous, often younger, sex partners, while wives' sexuality is generally strictly controlled. Children are highly valued, and a means for women to hold a steady partner and gain respect.

Few women, married or single, can refuse to serve a steady partner, even if they suspect that he may be infected. nor can most propose condom protection. But knowledge that children can become infected through their mothers can act as an incentive to men to protect steady partners. Problem-posing empowerment methods that incorporate deep understanding of local cultures can be used by community groups to address broad issues of gender and social relations and discover powerful cultural symbols as a practical, if partial, means of prevention. Using social group dynamics, communities can model more egalitarian behaviors, placing changes in sexual behavior within the context of support for democracy, political accountability, and development. It may be this potential to bring about social change that makes many governments reluctant to use these methods against AIDS.

Africa is not the only continent to have experienced the effects of prolonged, multiplex crisis: a second major focus on HIV infection lies in South and Southeast Asia, home to one-half the world's population. Despite its rapid industrial development, Asia's economic crisis in the late 1990s increased poverty, and with it, increased the velocity of the AIDS pandemic, already rampant in the sex "industry," among the military, and among intravenous drug users. While vigorous condom promotion has slowed Thailand's epidemic, elsewhere the constraints described for Africa apply. The understandings on which this perspective is based, and the conclusions with respect to the need for global redistribution of wealth which follow, have not been readily accepted by policymakers. Instead, there is a tendency to seek panaceas, limited interventions that appear to offer hope of interrupting the epidemic without threatening vested interests. Unless the underlying struggles of millions to survive in the midst of poverty, powerlessness, and hopelessness are addressed, however, HIV infection will continue to spread among the world's poor. Since social structures circumscribe the choices people make, stopping AIDS requires eliminating the barriers that deny women control over sexual decisions, and poor men, women, and youth of control over their lives.

(See also GAY AND LESBIAN POLITICS; REPRODUCTIVE POLITICS; WOMEN AND DEVELOPMENT.)

African Urban Quarterly 5, no. 1–2, 1991. Special Issue on AIDS, STDs, and urbanization in Africa. B. G. Schoepf, "Ethical, Methodological and Political Issues of Aids Research in Central Africa," *Social Science and Medicine* 33, no. 7 (1991): 749–763. P. E. Farmer, *AIDS and Accusation: Haiti and the Geography of Blame* (Berkeley, Cal., 1992). B. G. Schoepf, "Women and AIDS: A Gender and Development Approach," in R. Gallin, A. Ferguson, and J. Harper, eds., *Women and International Development Annual* 3, (Boulder, Colo. 1992): 55–85. B. G. Schoepf, "Action Research on AIDS with Women in Kinshasa: Community-Based Risk Education Support," *Social Science and Medicine* 37, no. 11 (1993): 1401–1413. M. de Bruyn, et al., "Facing the Challenges of HIV/AIDS/STDs: A Gender-Based Response." World Health Organization, Global Program on AIDS (Geneva, 1995). P. E. Farmer, M Connors, and J. Simmons, eds., *Women, Poverty and AIDS: Sex Drugs and Structural Violence* (Monroe, Me., 1996). J. Mann, D. Tarantola, and T. Netter, eds. *AIDS in the World* (Cambridge, Mass., 1996). G. C. Bond, et al., eds., *AIDS in Africa and the Caribbean* (Boulder, Colo., 1997). J. P. M. Ntozi, J. K. Anarfi, J.C. Caldwell, and S. Jain, eds., "Vulnerability to HIV Infection and Effects of AIDS in Africa and Asia/India," *Health Transition Review* 7, supplement 1 (1997). P. W. Setel, W. C. Chinwa, and E. Preston-Whyte, eds., "Sexual Networking, Knowledge and Sexual Risk: Contextual Social Research for Confronting AIDS in Eastern and Southern ," *Health Transition Review* 7, supplement 3 (1997). C. Bawa Yamba, "Cosmologies in Turmoil: Withfinding and AIDS in Chiawa, Zambia," *Africa* 67, no. 2 (1997): 200–203. B. G. Schoepf, "Inscribing the Body Politic: Women and AIDS in Africa," in M. Lock and P. A. Kaufert, eds. *Pragmatic Women and Body Politics* (Cambridge, U.K. 1998): 98–126. P. E. Farmer, *Infections and Inequalities: The Modern Plagues* (Berkeley, Cal., 1999). B. G. Schoepf, C. Schoepf, and J. V. Millen, "Theoretical Therapies, Remote Remedies: SAPs and the Political Ecology of Poverty and Health in Africa," in J. Y. Kim, J. V. Millen, A. Irwin, and J. Gershman, eds., *Dying for Growth: Global Inequality and the Health of the Poor* (Monroe, Me., 2000): 91–126. UNAIDS, *Report on the Global HIV/AIDS Epidemic* (Geneva, June 2000).

BROOKE GRUNDFEST SCHOEPF

ALBANIA. The Republic of Albania is located in the southwestern quadrant of the Balkan Peninsula. With an area of 28,750 square kilometers (11,000 sq. mi.) and a population in 1999 of approximately 3.4 million, Albania is the smallest of the Balkan states in size and population. It is also one of the most ethnically homogeneous countries in Europe with Albanians in 1999 comprising 95 percent of the population. Prior to World War II, about 70 percent of the Albanians were Muslims, 20 percent Eastern Orthodox, and 10 percent Roman Catholic. Albania is thus the only predominantly Muslim country in Europe. With an estimated per capita GDP of US $1,490 in 1999, Albania is Europe's least-developed nation.

Albania was part of the Ottoman Empire for nearly 450 years prior to winning its independence in November 1912. After a period of political instability between 1912 and 1924, Ahmet Zogu (1895–1961) became president in 1925. In 1928 he transformed Albania into a monarchy and ruled as King Zog until 1939, when he fled the country following its invasion and occupation by Italy. After a power struggle between communist and noncommunist resistance groups during World War II, the Albanian Communist Party under the leadership of Enver Hoxha emerge1d victorious in 1945.

Hoxha ruled Albania from 1945 until his death in 1985. He was a staunch disciple of Soviet dictator Joseph Stalin and continued to pursue hard-line Stalinist policies even after the Soviet Union and its Eastern European allies had repudiated them.

Hoxha's successor Ramiz Alia was, however, compelled by growing popular pressure to institute a series of economic, legal, and social reforms. These culminated in December 1990 in the legalization of opposition parties. Albania's first contested election in March 1991 resulted in a victory for the Communist Party, which soon found it necessary to form a coalition government to address the severe problems confronting the country. Unable to cope with the situation it had inherited, the government called for new elections in March 1992. The opposition Democratic Party soundly defeated the Socialists (former Communist Party), and the Democratic Party leader, Sali Berisha, was elected president.

In 1997, Albania experienced a large-scale popular uprising following the collapse of speculative financial pyramid schemes into which thousands of Albanians had invested their savings. Following the restoration of order by a European peacekeeping force, new elections were held in June 1997. The Socialists won by a large margin, and Rexhep Mejdani replaced Berisha as president. In November 1998 Albania finally adopted a permanent post-communist constitution. During the Kosovo conflict of March–June 1999, Albania served as a refuge for compatriots who fled Yugoslavia and as a base for NATO forces and humanitarian organizations dispatched to the region. The country, however, continues to experience political instability, social unrest, and economic stagnation as its leaders strive to establish a market economy within a democratic multiparty system.

(See also KOSOVO WAR, POST-COMMUNISM.)

Nicholas C. Pano, "The Process of Democratization in Albania," in Karen Dawisha and Bruce Parrott, eds., *Politics, Power, and the Struggle for Democracy in South-East Europe* (Cambridge, U.K., 1997), pp. 285–352. Elez Biberaj. *Albania in Transition* (Boulder, Colo., 1998).

NICHOLAS C. PANO

ALGERIA. For a quarter-century after independence in 1962, Algeria's political system was strongly marked by the ideological and institutional heritage of the *Algerian War of Independence (1954–1962). The wartime conception of a "party-nation" was transformed into a hegemonic party-state overseen by a strong military establishment. Under Colonel Houari Boumédienne, who held power from 1965 to 1978, the regime pursued the socialist and anti-imperialist ideology of the wartime Front de Libération Nationale (FLN). As the postwar elite faltered in the face of burgeoning social problems and sinking oil revenues, a populist Islamic movement emerged in the 1980s to challenge the political and military regime.

The army was the first arbiter in postwar Algerian politics, installing Ahmed Ben Bella, one of the nine founders of the FLN, as head of government in a power struggle among wartime leaders during the summer of 1962. A charismatic politician, Ben Bella gained the support of the Armée de Libération Nationale led by Boumédienne. The early alliance of party leader and military officer laid the foundation for the postcolonial state, codified as a *one-party system with a strong head of state in the 1963 constitution. The principle of a single party guiding the action of the state remained in force until the 1989 constitutional revision.

Seizing power in 1965, Boumédienne strengthened the state. A handful of powerful ministers commanded the levers of the economy (finance, energy, heavy industry, planning) and society (information, justice, culture, youth, religious affairs). Associational life was largely controlled by official party-sponsored organizations. Within this institutional structure, the legislature played a distinctly secondary role. Elections were conducted under a system of multiple candidacies inside the single party. Suspended in 1965 and reinstituted in 1977, the National Assembly only played an important political role when multiparty parliamentary elections were held for the first time in 1991.

Although Chadli Benjedid, another military officer elected to the presidency in 1979 as the sole candidate named by the FLN, continued to operate within the same institutional environment, he incrementally chipped away at the ideological foundations of Algerian socialism. He broke up many of the state firms into smaller enterprises and encouraged a gradual shift toward private-sector initiatives. As Benjedid diluted the ideological militance of the regime without narrowing the FLN's prerogatives, disadvantaged social groups turned increasingly toward Islamist ideas for an alternative regime model. Accumulated disaffections forced the rulers to revise the constitution in 1989, terminating the FLN's monopoly status. In local elections in June 1990, the Front Islamique du Salut (FIS) ran well ahead of the FLN and captured control of numerous cities, towns, and regional assemblies. A sharp cleavage between secular and religious models of society emerged. Tensions between the rising Islamist movement and entrenched secular elite plagued the emergent multiparty system throughout 1991. With the FIS on the verge of gaining control of the National Assembly in December 1991, the army reasserted its power in January 1992 by canceling the election results, obliging Benjedid to resign, instituting a five-member High State Committee, and subsequently banning the FIS.

This military intervention plunged the country into a devastating civil war which claimed from 80,000 to 100,000 lives from 1992 through 1998. Islamists took up arms under such banners as the Armée Islamique du Salut (Army of Islamic Salvation) and the Groupe Islamique Armée (Armed Islamic Groups), the latter a terrorist band that carried out exceptionally brutal massacres. The army engineered the appointment of retired general Liamine Zeroual as head of state in 1994, and he was officially elected president in November 1995. Although the Zeroual government conducted parliamentary and local elections in 1997, it did not succeed in crushing the armed Islamist rebellion. The insurgency was waning, however, when Abdelaziz Pouteflika was elected president in 1999.

Algeria's original development strategy emphasized national self-sufficiency and state ownership of the principal means of production. During the war for independence, Algerian intellectuals formulated a critique of the colonialist and capitalist economic structures erected during 130 years of French rule and settlement. Ben Bella's government created the first state company, SONATRACH (Société Nationale de Transport et Commercialisation des Hydrocarbures), which grew into a huge enterprise managing Algeria's substantial oil and natural gas resources. By 1971, the state nationalized all foreign energy holdings and embarked on massive investments in other industrial sectors. Eighteen large national firms (*sociétés nationales*) in such domains as iron and steel, mechanical engineering, industrial vehicles, mining and metallurgy, and construction materials were established. A succession of three-year, four-year, and five-year plans directed state investment policy in both heavy and light industries.

The state-managed economy nevertheless failed to keep pace with the consumption and employment needs of a rapidly growing population (which increased from 10 to 23 million between 1962 and 1987). The rural sector received inadequate public investment, and food imports rose accordingly. During the 1980s, Benjedid began to shift toward free-market policies in an attempt to stimulate production, but shortages and social inequalities sparked massive riots in October 1988 that led to the constitutional reforms of 1989 and the electoral repudiation of the FLN in 1990–1991.

Algeria's model of self-reliant national development was grounded in a strategy of collective *Third World action. From 1962 through 1983, Algeria played an unusually active role in efforts to organize African states, oil-producing states, raw materials producers, and the Third World as a whole. The country organized a series of major conferences of developing countries including the first conference of the Group of 77 in 1967, the fourth summit meeting of nonaligned states in 1973, and the first *Organization of Petroleum Exporting Countries summit in 1975, all convened in Algiers. It also figured prominently in such major North-South negotiations as the Conference on International Economic Cooperation and the Sixth and Eleventh Special Sessions of the UN. This pronounced engagement in the international debate on global economic structures was one of the distinguishing characteristics of Algerian diplomacy.

Following independence, Algeria trained Africans from countries such as Angola, Mozambique, and South Africa in techniques of *guerrilla warfare. Closer to home, it supported the right of self-determination in *Western Sahara, producing strained relations with Morocco. However ambitious its goal of organizing a large Third World coalition, Algeria's power was objectively limited. As oil prices fell and material constraints grew, the voluntarism of the first two decades of Algerian foreign policy gave way to a narrower conception of national interest, namely, regional stability and economic integration in the *Maghreb.

For more that two decades after independence, power holders drew their political legitimacy from their service in the revolution against *France or from their role as managers of Algeria's development model. These two modes of legitimization gradually lost their force with the passage of time, the rise of a postwar generation, and economic setbacks. The Islamist challenge has left Algeria's military and secular regime in search of a new formula to restore political stability.

(See also DECOLONIZATION; ISLAM; NATIONAL LIBERATION MOVEMENTS; NONALIGNED MOVEMENT; RELIGION AND POLITICS; SOCIALISM AND SOCIAL DEMOCRACY.)

David and Marina Ottaway, *Algeria: The Politics of a Socialist Revolution* (Berkeley, Calif., 1970). Jean Leca and Jean-Claude Vatin, *L'Algérie politique: Institutions et régime* (Paris, 1975). Lahouari Addi, *L'Algérie et la démocratie* (Paris, 1994). William Quandt, *Between Ballots and Bullets* (Washington, D.C., 1998).

ROBERT A. MORTIMER

ALGERIAN WAR OF INDEPENDENCE. The Algerian war (November 1954–March 1962) was a major event in the history of *decolonization in Africa. The war mobilized the Algerian nation and deeply divided the French people. It impelled *France's president, Charles de *Gaulle, himself carried to power by a revolt of the European population of *Algeria in May 1958, to grant independence to the colonies of black Africa. Unable to stem the tide of indigenous Algerian support for the nationalist movement, de Gaulle eventually negotiated the terms of Algerian independence, bringing to power in July 1962 a militant anti-imperialist government that became a major actor in Arab, African, and *Nonaligned Movement affairs.

Nine "historic chiefs," young men who had been active in legal and clandestine political activity and who in several cases had served in the French army during World War II, formed the Comité Revolutionnaire de l'Unité et de l'Action (CRUA) early in 1954. This committee organized a network of resistants into the Front de Libération Nationale (FLN) and Arme, de Libération Nationale, which launched the insurrection with some seventy attacks across the country on 1 November 1954. France progressively committed hundreds of thousands of troops to the "pacification" of Algeria, a colony that some 1 million European settlers considered their home.

The FLN recruited a corps of rural and urban guerrilla fighters who tied down this large French military contingent. Terrible instances of *torture and *terrorism marked the conduct of the war. Although France largely succeeded in containing the insurgency on a strictly military plane, it could not extinguish the political force of the *revolution. The FLN moreover capitalized upon the accession of Morocco and Tunisia to independence in 1956 (itself attributable in part to the insecurity in Algeria) to assemble a sizable military force on Algeria's borders. The two countries provided bases of operations and gave ample logistic and diplomatic support to the FLN.

The institutions of the Algerian revolution evolved steadily as the rebellion gained force. In August 1956, the top internal guerrilla leadership met in the Soummam Valley. This congress constituted the first meeting of the Conseil National de la Révolution Algérienne (CNRA), an organ that met periodically to fix broad policy; after the cease-fire in 1962, the CNRA adopted the Tripoli Program, the first comprehensive statement of the FLN's intention to carry out a "democratic popular revolution" after independence. The CNRA created an executive committee, transformed in September 1958 into the Gouvernement Provisoire de la République Algérienne (GPRA), which henceforth assumed the functions of a government in exile, representing the nationalist movement in its relations with France and other governments. Meanwhile, as he explored avenues of a negotiated settlement, de Gaulle had to contend with an army-settler rebellion in January 1960 and an attempted military coup in April 1961.

Ferhat Abbas and Ben Youssef Ben Khedda served successively as prime ministers of the GPRA while the future leader of independent Algeria, Ahmed Ben Bella—a founder of the CRUA captured by France along with several other leaders in 1956—was an honorary minister of state in the GPRA. The provisional government was recognized by many Arab and other *Third World governments, and it maintained an effective lobbying presence at the UN, where French policy was strongly criticized. Ultimately the war was won not so much on the battlefield as in the arena of politics and *diplomacy where the FLN/GPRA captured the support of the great majority of Algerians and of international opinion. During the final phase of the war, as negotiations took place in Europe, the Organisation de l'Arme, Secrète, created by extremist proponents of French Algeria, conducted a savage rearguard scorched earth campaign.

As the first sustained armed uprising against colonial rule in Africa, the Algerian war had a major effect on movements of national liberation throughout the continent and beyond. The Algerian struggle prompted assertions of the right of independence elsewhere in Africa, and the cost of the war discouraged France and other colonial powers from seriously resisting the anti-imperialist tide. Algeria gave military training to the fledgling *national liberation movements of Angola, Mozambique, and South Africa, and Algiers became a haven for political exiles. Even before acquiring national sovereignty, the GPRA participated in numerous anticolonial conferences including the founding meeting of the Nonaligned Movement in which independent Algeria became a driving force. The militant ideology of national self-sustaining development forged by the Algerian intelligentsia during the war made Algiers a notable pole of attraction in Third World politics through the 1960s and 1970s. The war stirred deep passions on both shores of the Mediterranean and shaped the new era of post-colonial politics.

(See also GUERRILLA WARFARE; POLITICAL VIOLENCE.)

Alistair Horne, *A Savage War of Peace: Algeria, 1954–1962* (Harmondsworth, U.K., 1977). Slimane Chikh, *L'Algérie en armes ou le temps des certitudes* (Paris, 1981).

ROBERT A. MORTIMER

ALLENDE, Salvador. Salvador Allende Gossens became an international symbol of the attempt to create *socialism through nonviolent, democratic means. As a politician, Allende always exhibited a Marxist orientation, but he excelled as a practitioner rather than an ideologist or intellectual. He achieved fame in 1970 as the first Marxist ever freely elected president of Chile. Then a violent military *coup d'état on 11 September 1973 cut short his six-year term. The resultant death of Allende and *Chile's socialist experiment have stirred controversy ever since.

Born 26 July 1908 in the port city of Valparaíso, Allende entered medical studies in 1926. He became a student leader against a military dictatorship, and then received his medical degree in 1932. The following year he helped found the Partido Socialista of Chile. After working for the public health service, Allende won election to the national Chamber of Deputies in 1937. His career prospered in 1939 when he became minister of health in the Frente Popular government (1938–1942), based on a coalition among the Partido Socialista, the Partido Comunista, and the Partido Radical.

After serving as secretary general of the Socialist Party in 1943, Allende devoted his energies to the national Senate. He won election to that body in 1945, 1949, 1953, 1961, 1965, and 1969. A consummate congressional politician, he also served as the Senate's vice president in the 1940s and president in the 1960s.

In those same decades, Allende ran for president of Chile four times as the candidate of an alliance of the Socialist and Communist parties, usually known as the Frente de Acción Popular (FRAP). Those campaigns, mainly backed by organized labor, featured increasingly bold programs against the local upper class and the United States. Allende captured six percent of the total national votes in 1952, twenty-nine percent in 1958, thirty-nine percent in 1964, and thirty-six percent in 1970. Elected a minority president in a multiparty contest, Allende nonetheless tried to carry out his long-standing commitment to a democratic transition toward socialism. He headed a coalition government known as the Unidad Popular (UP), which encompassed Radicals, social democrats, and defectors from the left wing of the Christian Democrats, along with the dominant Socialists and Communists.

As president, Allende socialized the major means of production. Although the opposition complained about illegal measures, he enacted most of his reforms within the constitutional framework. The main targets for expropriation and redistribution were U.S. copper mines and other foreign-owned industries, banks, large corporations, and great estates. The government also recognized extensive private and mixed public-private sectors of the economy but failed to clearly demarcate those domains.

State intervention mainly benefited workers and peasants, whose share of national income rose. After Allende's first year

in office, however, investment and production fell while inflation soared, exacerbated by cutoffs of U.S. aid and credits. Amid economic shortages, *class conflict escalated. The middle class increasingly reacted against the degree to which Allende's project favored the proletariat at their expense.

Politics polarized between Allende's leftist coalition and his centrist and rightist opponents, backed by the United States. The president was unable to discipline his own supporters, who quarreled over offices, ideologies, and strategies. Some demanded and initiated on their own more rapid changes than Allende desired, especially in property transfers. Allende vacillated between compromise and confrontation with the increasingly disloyal opposition. His adversaries mobilized strikes and lockouts, mainly by truckers, shopkeepers, and professionals. They also launched media campaigns accusing the government of illegitimacy and totalitarian intentions.

Allende tried to restore order by appointing military commanders to top cabinet posts, but they did not want to take responsibility for his besieged government. In the showdown midterm congressional elections of March 1973, the opposition unified nearly all the centrist and rightist parties. They hoped that deteriorating economic conditions would allow them to win two-thirds of the congressional seats and thus impeach Allende. However, the UP increased its electoral share to forty-four percent.

Although civil liberties were still intact, representative *democracy was strained by the deadlock between the executive and legislature. Allende's decisions to resolve that stalemate through a plebiscite in September 1973 was blocked by the takeover by a junta led by Army General Augusto *Pinochet Ugarte. According to most accounts, Allende committed suicide during the attack on the presidential palace, but others maintain he was murdered. In any case, the military interred Allende's remains in an unmarked grave. The security forces also imprisoned, tortured, and assassinated or exiled thousands of Allende sympathizers. The subsequent dictatorship of the armed forces pledged to extirpate democracy as well as *Marxism.

Controversy has continued to swirl around the Allende government as to why if failed to construct socialism and why it failed to preserve democracy. On the first question of socialism, most analysts agree that the goal was too ambitious for the means. Whether Allende should have moderated his objectives or radicalized his methods remains in dispute. Equally debatable is the issue of whether the Chilean tragedy proved that there cannot be a peaceful path to socialism or merely showed that it was impossible under a minority government in the specific conditions in Chile in the early 1970s.

On the second question of democracy, scholars still argue as to whether the right, center, or left were primarily to blame for the inability to negotiate differences and avoid a breakdown. At the same time, most experts continue to criticize the United States for destabilizing the UP government through economic pressures and support for the subversive opposition. Virtually no one, however, assigns primary responsibility to the United States for the overthrow of Allende. Some early analysts contended that the clash within Chile of irreconcilable social and ideological forces made Allende's downfall inevitable. By contrast, subsequent research has suggested that greater political skill and flexibility on the part of the UP and its opponents might have averted Armageddon.

After harsh rule by the armed forces finally ended in a restoration of electoral democracy in 1990, most Chileans hoped to avoid any repetition of the conflicts of the Allende years. Polls showed that a majority looked back on his presidency as a disastrous period of economic crisis, social strife, and political extremism. A minority, however, still viewed Allende as a noble figure; they honored him as a leader who never forsook his dedication to both socialism and representative democracy—however incompatible—and who gave his life fighting for the working class.

(See also U.S.–LATIN AMERICAN RELATIONS.)

Paul W. Drake, *Socialism and Populism in Chile, 1932–52* (Urbana, Ill., 1978). Edy Kaufman, *Crisis in Allende's Chile* (New York, 1988).

PAUL W. DRAKE

ALLIANCE. An alliance is a cooperative security relationship between two or more states, usually taking the form of a written military commitment. In practice, however, the presence of a formal treaty says relatively little about the level of commitment or the extent of cooperation. Less formal arrangements—variously known as alignments, ententes, or coalitions—can perform similar functions and exert equally significant effects.

Efforts to explain why alliances form fall into two basic families. Within the realist tradition, alliances are seen as a way for *states to increase their security in response to an external threat. The greater the threat—a function of relative power, geographic proximity, and aggressive intentions—the greater the tendency for states to ally against it.

The tendency for states to balance threats is the main barrier to *hegemony in the *international system. As Louis XIV, Napoleon, and Adolf Hitler discovered, states that seek to dominate the system eventually provoke a powerful countervailing alliance. Similarly, the creation of the North Atlantic Treaty Organization (NATO) in 1949 was a response to the military power of the Soviet Union, its geographic proximity to Western Europe, and Western concerns about Soviet intentions.

By contrast, liberal or idealist approaches argue that alliances reflect the shared characteristics of the member states. They also suggest that these affinities are reinforced when intra-alliance decision making is governed by strong institutions, which can facilitate adaptation to new conditions. From this perspective, NATO's durability reflects both shared democratic ideals and the dense array of NATO-related institutions that have grown up over the past forty years. On the whole, however, shared beliefs and institutional bonds are less important than external threats in generating and preserving an alliance. States facing a common enemy usually overlook ideological differences (as the United States and Soviet Union did during World War II), while states proclaiming similar ideologies may be bitter rivals (as in the Sino-Soviet conflict or the various quarrels within the pan-Arab movement).

Alliances are often seen as a cause of war, but repeated efforts to verify this hypothesis have been unsuccessful. If anything, war is more likely when alliance formation does not proceed efficiently. If balancing coalitions form slowly or if alliance members try to "free-ride" on their partners' efforts, aggressors are likely to underestimate the opposition they will face and thus be more inclined to use force.

The end of the *Cold War has had powerful effects on existing alliances. The disintegration of the Soviet Union removed NATO's primary raison d'être, but the alliance has adopted the new mission of managing regional conflicts and in 1999 incorporated three former Warsaw Treaty Organization (Warsaw Pact) states, Poland, Hungary, and the Czech Republic. NATO's evolution suggests that alliances can persist even after the external threat is gone, but the growing signs of strain suggest that keeping NATO together will be increasingly difficult over time. Elsewhere, the end of the Soviet-American rivalry is forcing regional powers to rely on their own resources rather than on a friendly *superpower, which helps explain why India and Pakistan have recently intensified their nuclear weapons programs. Although few states seem inclined to oppose U.S. leadership at present, alliances designed to counter U.S. predominance will become more likely in the future, especially if the United States wields its power in a bellicose or domineering fashion.

(See also BALANCE OF POWER; IDEALISM; IDEOLOGY; LIBERALISM; REALISM.)

Stephen M. Walt, *The Origins of Alliances* (Ithaca, N.Y., 1987). Glenn Snyder, *Alliance Politics* (Ithaca, N.Y., 1997).

STEPHEN M. WALT

AMAZON DEVELOPMENT. Natural resource extraction has dominated regional economies of the Brazilian Amazon. During the rubber boom from the 1860s to 1910 and other, briefer episodes of prosperity, regional business elites and politicians proposed diversification as a shelter against the violent market fluctuations, high infrastructural costs of expansion, and heavy debt load occasioned by their dependence on natural resource exports. Sporadic attempts to promote manufacturing and agriculture in the region have succumbed to scanty budgets, topographic and climatological obstacles, and the allure of new extractive export booms.

A new effort began in the 1960s, with the Superintendência do Desenvolvimento da Amazonia (SUDAM) and the Banco da Amazonia (BASA) administering a program of fiscal incentives based on tax exemptions and tax holidays for investors in the region. Originally designed to promote industry, the fiscal incentives were soon expanded to include cattle ranching, an activity that vastly accelerated deforestation, speculation, and land conflicts, but engendered little permanent economic growth or employment. Only in the controversial free trade zone in Manaus did manufacturing dominate development budgets.

In 1970, agricultural development returned briefly to the fore. The Programa de Integraçao Nacional (PIN) stressed road building and colonization, with a strong emphasis on small farms, agricultural extension, and integrated rural development. By 1973 business criticism of PIN's social welfare provisions and of the agencies assigned to implement them, a growing government deficit combined with expanding foreign debt, and the administrative difficulties of the colonization programs led to substantial reductions in PIN budgets.

POLAMAZONIA, established the following year, was committed to large-scale extraction around sites chosen as "growth poles." POLAMAZONIA aimed to promote, in priority order: (1) mining, (2) lumbering, (3) ranching, (4) fishing, (5) agriculture, and (6) hydroelectric energy. Whereas PIN proposed to develop by distributing access to resources and infrastructure around domestic markets, POLAMAZONIA aimed to concentrate capital investments and resources in order to accelerate Amazonian exports, both to the rest of Brazil and to external markets.

The greatest numbers of subsidies were focused around three large mineral enterprises established by CVRD, a public/private company with the area around CVRD's huge Carajas iron mine receiving the greatest share. The Tocantins River, which flowed nearby, was dammed at Tucurui to provide electricity to a joint venture in aluminum smelting between a Japanese consortium and CVRD. Local business interests, politicians, and intellectuals protested against the environmental, demographic, and political consequences of granting huge tracts of land and extensive rights-of-way to mining companies and of damming a river whose navigability had been crucial to older local economies. These critical voices had little impact on the federal government whose centralizing policies since 1968 had been particularly debilitating for the poor, sparsely populated states in the Amazon. In 1980, it mounted a massive new fiscal incentives project, the Projeto Grande Carajas (PGC), to attract investment to the 900,000-square-kilometer (350,000 sq. mi.) area around the mine, the dam, and the railroad that took iron ore to the coast. PGC granted corporate tax exemptions on profits earned within its jurisdiction, so its main beneficiaries were the mining companies and the large construction companies that were engaged in infrastructural development.

Meanwhile, migrants had been flowing into the area around Carajas, encouraged by the prospects of jobs and by the certainty that the necessary roads and railroads would open up new lands for settlement. This migration intensified land conflicts. Indigenous groups in the area were clearly at risk of invasion owing to the mineral projects. The impoverished local state could not deal with the increased demands on its social welfare and security budgets. Its failure was used to justify further usurpations by the federal government and by the CVRD, even though the mining project itself had not yet achieved the international financing it had been seeking since 1977.

By 1982, it was clear that the Brazilian government was committed to a highly unfavorable deal when it assumed the entire cost of building the Tucurui dam and other infrastructure with no firm commitment from the Japanese on the scale of the aluminum smelter. Environmentalists in the European Parliament threatened to oppose European Community (EC) credits to the Carajas project. When the *World Bank coordinated the eventual Carajas loan agreement, it incorporated protections for both environment and indigenous groups, but as the loan was made to the mining company rather than to the state, these did not extend to the entire PGC region.

International concern, however, focused more on another World Bank–supported project, POLONOROESTE, in the south central Amazon, and on the plight of the indigenous groups in the northern Amazon whose lands are being invaded by gold miners. In negotiating a POLONOROESTE loan to asphalt a highway into Rondonia and to support small-scale colonization there, the World Bank demanded fewer environmental and indigenous rights guarantees than in Carajas. It conceded that making international groups beholden to the bank rather than to the nation would violate national sovereignty.

Deforestation, massive social upheavals, and the violence that attended the building of the BR-364 road from Cuiaba to Porto Velho and the flood of migrants and lumber mills, together with the clear failure of the Brazilian government to implement the controls the World Bank had demanded, greatly strengthened the international critics of large, highly capitalized projects in the Amazon. Though protesting that international criticism challenged its sovereignty, the central government began to respond to pressure from environmentalists and advocates of indigenous rights. Brazils chronic fiscal crisis, however, and its continued susceptibility to intromission by business and political groups have limited governmental response to highly publicized proclamations and occasional dramatic sanctions. A new constitution returns some powers over resource extraction and the environment to the local states, but they have neither the organization, the revenues, nor the political will to exercise their new powers. Some individual firms are doing well with the mineral boom and with the incentives that accompany it, but the local governments have received little additional revenue to offset the social and ecological problems that mineral extraction under external control has brought them. Furthermore, the privatization of CVRD in 1998 was followed by reductions in the company's environmental and social welfare programs. The same year, the national government exempted all exporters from paying taxes due to local states. This further diminished revenues in the Amazon states that face increasing environmental problems.

(See also ENVIRONMENTALISM.)

Stephen G. Bunker, *Underdeveloping the Amazon: Extraction, Unequal Exchange, and the Failure of the Modern State* (Urbana, Ill., 1985). Susanna B. Hecht, "Environment, Development, and Politics: Capital Accumulation and the Livestock Sector in Eastern Amazonia" *World Development* 13 (June 1985). Dennis Mahar, *Government Policies and Deforestation in Brazil's Amazon Region* (Washington, D.C., 1989). *Margaret E. Keck*, "Brazil's Planafloro: The Limits for Accountability," in Jonathan Fox and L. David Brown, *The Struggle for Accountability: The World Bank, NGOs, and Grassroots Movements* (Cambridge, Mass., 1998).
STEPHEN G. BUNKER

AMERICAN FEDERATION OF LABOR AND CONGRESS OF INDUSTRIAL ORGANIZATIONS. The American Federation of Labor and Congress of Industrial Organizations (AFL-CIO) is the peak association representing labor in the United States. At present, nearly all major unions are members; at times in the recent past, however, some of the very largest unions have not belonged for a variety of reasons ranging from the positions taken by the AFL-CIO on issues such as the Vietnam War, which caused the United Auto Workers to secede, to the suspension of unions for corruption, as in the case of the Teamsters in the 1960s and 1970s.

As the unwieldy title perhaps suggests, the merger of the AFL with the CIO in 1955 papered over important divisions in the ranks of American labor rather than fully resolving them. The AFL unions were predominantly though not exclusively craft unions representing workers organized on the basis of a skill, such as plumbers, bricklayers, and carpenters. The CIO unions were strongly committed to organizing workers on the basis of their employment in an industry such as steel or automobile production. Added to this difference in recruitment was a major difference in attitudes of AFL and CIO unions to politics.

In general, AFL unions came from the tradition associated with the founder of the AFL, Samuel Gompers, who advocated "unionism pure and simple." Gompers believed that the only way to overcome the opposition to unions in the pro-business, free market–oriented United States was to keep unions free from the taint of radicalism or socialism and to avoid antagonizing potential members by affiliating to one of the major political parties in an era in which their support was based on regional or ethnic loyalties, not class. While Gompers was successful in creating the first permanent organization of unions in the United States, his approach was seen as far too narrow by many union organizers after the First World War.

The CIO unions which emerged in the 1930s were aware from the first of the importance of politics. CIO unions had been able to organize in large part because of the protective legislation passed by pro-labor legislators known as the Wagner Act or, more correctly, the National Labor Relations Act, the beneficent attitude of some leading politicians including President Roosevelt, and the support of the new government agency, the National Labor Relations Board (NLRB), set up to enforce new federal labor laws. The Wagner Act overcame strong, even violent, opposition by industrialists such as Henry Ford to unions by requiring that employees be able vote in a secret ballot conducted by the NLRB on whether or not to have a union and that employers bargain in good faith with a union if it won such a ballot. Without this protection CIO unions would not have come into existence; not surprisingly, they were more actively involved in politics than AFL unions. Moreover, CIO unions tended to see themselves not merely as labor unions but as part of a social movement, the *labor movement, that sought both the amelioration of the condition of workers in the broadest sense and a more just society. In this, many of the unions were closer to the social democratic traditions of Europe than the AFL unions.

The AFL and CIO were prompted to merge in spite of these differences by political setbacks in the 1940s. A resurgent Republican Party passed revisions to the NLRA over the veto of President Truman. These revisions, known as the Taft-Hartley Act, substantially weakened the legal position of unions and may indeed have set in place forces that would undermine the unions in the long term. While the full dangers of Taft-Hartley may not have been apparent at the time, unions were shocked that they were not able to prevent its adoption. Yet the period around the merger of the AFL and CIO was in general the high water mark of unionism in the United States; some thirty-five percent of the workforce belonged to labor unions. The AFL-CIO, though not formally affiliated to the Democratic Party, played a crucial role within it, influencing the selection of presidential candidates and providing crucial support for liberal Democratic candidates through its Committee on Political Education (COPE), admired and feared as one of the best fund-raising and election organizations in the country. AFL-CIO lobbyists, also respected as among the most competent in Washington, were a central element in campaigns for progressive causes such as civil rights legislation as well as labor legislation. Yet though the AFL-CIO was respected and feared in Washington, it was unable to change the provisions of Taft-Hartley that impeded recruiting new members for unions. The AFL-CIO's relationship with the Democratic Party was always unbalanced; the AFL-CIO supported liberal Democrats and their causes far more loyally than liberal Democrats supported the AFL-CIO on issues, such as repealing Taft-Hartley, that were important to unions. Organized labor was a constituency that many liberal Democrats felt they could take for granted while they courted new support among the white collar, suburban, and non-union population. As employment drifted to regions of the United States in which unions were weak and industries traditionally difficult to organize expanded while industries in which unions were strong (such as automobiles and steel) declined, the percentage of the workforce unionized slowly but steadily sank. An aging union leadership epitomized by the president of the AFL-CIO from 1955 to 1978, George Meany, proved unwilling or unable to maintain the liberal coalition of which labor had been part. The AFL-CIO took positions on many of the "new politics" issues that emerged in the 1960s and 1970s that antagonized liberal Democrats with whom it had once been allied; Meany's determined support for U.S. involvement in the *Vietnam War and refusal to endorse the liberal, antiwar Democratic candidate in the 1972 presidential election crystallized an ill-founded but widely held belief among many liberals that unions were now part of the establishment, conservative, often corrupt, and resistant to fresh ideas.

The AFL-CIO found itself without much support outside the ranks of labor when the gentle decline in labor's strength in the thirty years after the Second World War turned into a collapse in the 1980s. The reasons for the collapse of union strength in the last two decades of the century were partly economic; industries in which unions were strong declined more rapidly in part because of foreign competition. However, unions also declined in part because of political reasons. The Reagan administration signaled its tough attitude to unions by breaking the air Traffic Controllers' union when it called an illegal strike. Reagan also appointed people to the NLRB who took a consistently anti-union position, facilitating determined efforts by corporations to weaken unions as a prerequisite for cutting costs and remaining competitive in globalized markets in which American wages and costs were high. Meany's successor, the quiet and studious Lane Kirkland, proved incapable of crafting a strategy for recovery. However, in the 1980s and 1990s some signs of recovery emerged. First, public sector unions showed great potential for growth; the National Education Association (NEA), for example, emerged as a force not only in bargaining but within the Democratic Party. Second, nearly all major unions were within the AFL-CIO as the United Auto Workers, the United Mine Workers, and the reformed Teamsters returned to the fold. Third, new leadership developed more imaginative plans to halt the decline in membership. A new president of the AFL-CIO, John Sweeney, came from a background in the Service Employees International Union in which he had succeeded in organizing people in the service sector. Fourth, relations between unions and liberals in politics were much improved. Both unions and liberals realized that their divisions had advantaged conservatives, resulting in policies during the Reagan and Bush years to the disadvantage of them both. Unions showed greater sympathy to issues, such as women's rights, dear to liberals; unions and groups such as environmentalists combined to oppose further trade liberalization, most notably during a conference of the *World Trade Organization in Seattle in 1999. Whereas environmental issues had divided labor from environmentalists in the 1960s and 1970s, in the 1990s both groups came to believe that they should make common cause in taking on the challenge *globalization posed for workers in the United States and abroad. The AFL-CIO was heartened at century's end by figures showing that the percentage of the unionized workforce had stopped declining, remaining at just under 14 percent of the workforce. The AFL-CIO could scarcely feel euphoric as only 9.4 percent of the private sector workforce was unionized. However, the AFL-CIO could hope that its decline had ended.

At the end of the twentieth century, organized labor in the United States was much weaker than in most advanced industrialized democracies. This would not be surprising to those who associate the United States with a strong commitment to individualism and free markets. It is important to remember, however, that at midcentury, deep-seated factors such as U.S. political culture, the size and diversity of the country, and its ethnic and racial heterogeneity did not prevent American unions from being as strong in terms of the proportion of the workforce unionized as British unions were in that era, or stronger than German unions are today. Reversing union decline in the United States may be merely an extremely difficult challenge for the AFL-CIO, not an actual impossibility.

(See also CLASS AND CLASS POLITICS; ENVIRONMENTALISM.)
GRAHAM K. WILSON

AMERICAN FOREIGN POLICY. See U.S. FOREIGN POLICY.

AMERICAN INDIANS. See NATIVE AMERICANS.

AMNESTY INTERNATIONAL. Founded in 1961 by the British lawyer Peter Benenson, Amnesty International is a *nongovernmental organization (NGO) which works primarily for the release of prisoners of conscience, fair and prompt trials for political prisoners (defined as persons in prison for their beliefs who have not practiced or advocated violence), and the abolition of the death penalty, extrajudicial killings, and all forms of torture. The organization took root quickly in Europe and the United States, but it was not until the mid-1970s that its numerical and geographical growth became remarkable. It is the largest human rights NGO in the world and sets the standards for human rights monitoring, reporting, and campaigns. It was awarded the Nobel Peace Prize in 1977.

In 1998, Amnesty claimed a membership of over 1 million active or dues-paying members in over 100 countries. Most are grouped in 54 national or country sections, of which 33 are now outside Europe and North America. The U.S. section is headquartered in New York, as is the Secretariat's UN office. More than 4,200 local groups and numerous other, unregistered school, university, and professional groups carry out Amnesty's projects around the world. They are served by the London Secretariat whose staff numbers over 300, assisted

by an additional 95 volunteers. In 1998 the annual budget of the Secretariat was over $24 million. National sections have their own administrative structures and budgets, and they also support the budget of the Secretariat. Amnesty has strict fund-raising rules. It does not accept government funds and limits the percentage of budgets at all levels that can come from a single source.

Amid the recent rapid growth in the number of human rights organizations, Amnesty International has remained unique in a number of important ways. It is a membership organization in the sense that it is supported financially and its work is carried out primarily by its worldwide membership. Policies are set every two years at International Council Meetings where decisions are all made by representatives of the worldwide membership. Amnesty is also unique among human rights NGOs in terms of the geographic spread of its membership, emphasized by a recent decision to open outreach offices overseas, notably in Uganda in Africa.

Amnesty seeks to remain independent of external influences, particularly of governments and ideologies. At the heart of Amnesty's commitment to independence are the standards it sets for its data collection, monitoring, and reporting. Accuracy and timeliness are major concerns of the professional staff in London who monitor countries around the world and prepare the reports for action campaigns, big and small. In addition to the rules about fund-raising, collaboration with other NGOs is limited by specific guidelines. To assure distance from national politics, Amnesty members—with one or two exceptions such as work on the death penalty or prisons—are not allowed to work on issues within their own country. Lobbying national legislatures is similarly limited. Amnesty, however, actively lobbies international organizations, notably the UN in New York and Geneva, UNESCO, the Council of Europe and the European Community, the Inter-American Commission on Human Rights, and the Organization of African Unity.

Amnesty's advocacy methods have evolved from Benenson's original idea that exposure to public view, especially through the media, would embarrass governments into improving their practices. To achieve this goal Amnesty has traditionally used many means: in addition to letter-writing and petitions to government officials, it sends out missions composed of experts to collect data and provide support for local human rights NGOs; it publishes reports and uses its members to bring them to the attention of officials around the world; it organizes campaigns to focus on a country or a form of violation and carries them out through national sections and members; it runs an urgent action network which makes use of the latest technologies to alert members on how to take immediate action on individual death penalty or prisoner of conscience cases. Increasingly Amnesty has devoted more of its budget to human rights education and training. Promotional activities have also included consciousness-raising concert tours, scholarships for student media projects, prisoner relief, and compensation programs for the victims of human rights abuse.

Under the influence of International Council meetings, Amnesty's mandate has expanded, reflecting the breadth and interests of its members. Today the mandate includes a concern for abuses faced by refugees, women, and children. Persons in prison for homosexuality can be classified as political prisoners. The International Council meeting in Cape Town, South Africa, in December 1997 was dominated by debates on the mandate. The participants, who came from Amnesty sections all over the world, agreed that Amnesty ought to act now, for example, to prevent abuses by non-state actors as well as by states, to work for the eradication of female genital mutilation, and to campaign against land mines and the use of children in armed conflict. The 1997 Council also agreed to launch a new four-year overall review of the mandate.

The significance of Amnesty International has been less in its individual achievements than in its success in mobilizing popular support for human rights. In this regard it has contributed more than any other single organization to the present world climate. Amnesty makes extensive use of its Web sites: that of its U.S. office is at www.amnesty-usa.org, and that of its Secretariat is at www.amnesty-usa.org, These are the easiest way to obtain recent and more detailed information on its work.

(See also HUMAN RIGHTS)

J. PAUL MARTIN

ANTIGUA AND BARBUDA. See ENGLISH-SPEAKING CARIBBEAN.

ANARCHISM. Anarchism is the political philosophy which holds that the putative authority of the *state is illegitimate, and therefore either *may* be, or *ought* to be, ignored, resisted, or undermined. The doctrine has antecedents in the teachings of the Skeptic philosophers of the classical period but finds its modern origins in the reaction to the theory of state authority advanced by sixteenth-, seventeenth-, and eighteenth-century social contract theorists and theorists of the absolute state.

There are two traditions of anarchist thought—libertarian, or extreme individualist, and communitarian—and each appears in three distinctively different variations, which may be labeled philosophical anarchism, ideal anarchism, and revolutionary anarchism. Philosophical anarchism is the thesis that there is not, and cannot be, a legitimate state—a state that has the moral right to demand the obedience of its subjects or citizens—because that demand by the state violates the moral autonomy of the individual. Ideal anarchism holds that, in addition to being illegitimate, the state is suboptimal—it performs less well the tasks of maintaining social order and providing essential services than would an association of free men and women without coercive state *power to compel their behavior. Revolutionary anarchism goes a step further and argues that the state is so immediately destructive of human well-being that it must be destroyed by force, so that a more humane and constructive social order can take its place. It is revolutionary anarchism that is associated in the popular mind with the term *anarchism.* In the United States, anarchists are popularly imagined to speak with Eastern European accents, to wear beards, and to favor the use of bombs.

Libertarian, or individualistic, anarchism is grounded in the laissez-faire theory of the capitalist economy. It holds that states are illegitimate interferences with the individual's *rights of contract; that the police power of the state is a violation of natural rights; and that all of the functions now performed by states, such as maintenance of public order,

provision of public services, even defense against foreign invasion, can be performed more efficiently and more legitimately by voluntary associations of free individuals. This line of attack on the *legitimacy of state authority can be found in such popular authors as the nineteenth-century U.S. lawyer Lysander Spooner and the twentieth-century Hungarian-American novelist Ayn Rand, as well as in the philosophical writings of the nineteenth-century German Max Stirner and the twentieth-century U.S. philosopher Robert Nozick and others.

Communitarian anarchism holds that in the absence of a coercive state, social life is most efficiently and humanely organized by means of cooperative communities in which the collective good, rather than one's own individual interest, is the primary motivating concern. (See Jean-Jacques Rousseau for a classic development of the distinction between the General, or Common, Good and Individual Interest.) Communitarian anarchists reject the libertarian anarchists' emphasis on mutually self-interested contractual agreements, and emphasize instead discussion, collective deliberation, and mutual understanding as a basis for social order. In the writings of some communitarian anarchists, such as the nineteenth-century Englishman William Godwin, the great Russian novelist Leo Tolstoy, and the Indian pacifist leader Mohandas *Gandhi, this doctrine is combined with the teaching of the natural goodness and sympathy of human beings. According to Godwin and other communitarians, it is modern civilization, *capitalism, and the state that corrupt human beings and turn them against one another.

The nineteenth and twentieth centuries have seen a number of important communitarian anarchist experimental communities in which a substantial effort was made to live out the ideals of the doctrine. These include New Lanark in England and New Harmony in Indiana, both organized by nineteenth-century Welsh industrialist Robert Owen; Brook Farm, a communitarian anarchist experimental community started by George Ripley outside Boston and inhabited, at one time or another, by such nineteenth-century literary figures as Ralph Waldo Emerson and Henry David Thoreau; and the kibbutzim, or collective agricultural experimental communities, started in Israel by early twentieth-century European émigrés.

The central theme of all strains of anarchist doctrine is the illegitimacy of the state. The central theme of all nonanarchist political philosophy is the legitimacy of the state—the right of the state to rule. Anarchism thus stands as the permanent. Other in the discourse of political philosophy. As such, it is reviled, condemned, ignored, but always present as a challenge to established political authority.

(See also CITIZENSHIP.)

ROBERT PAUL WOLFF

ANARCHY. As applied to *international relations, anarchy refers to the absence of authoritative institutions or norms above independent sovereign *states. Both the empirical and normative consequences of this international anarchy are subjects of debate. To adherents of *realism, anarchy is the defining feature of relations among states. Following *Thucydides and Hobbes, authors like Hans Morgenthau and Kenneth Waltz emphasize the permanent insecurity that follows from the absence of any institution to protect states from one another. No state can be secure in its borders from the ambitions of other states; trust among states is impossible because promises can be enforced only by self-help. The result is a permanent "*security-*power dilemma." Each state seeks greater security by adding to its military power; but in so doing it creates fear among other states that this power will be used against them, so they too seek to add to their power. A vicious circle of power and insecurity is thus established because there exists no authority above states to enforce order. Every state must permanently prepare for *war—or face extinction.

According to this view of international anarchy, states can mitigate, but never escape, the effects of their permanent rivalry. They may enter into *alliances with other states to prevent any one actor from becoming dominant; they may seek the protection of a single, powerful state at some cost to their external autonomy; they may seek to avoid permanent alliances altogether so as to maintain some degree of flexibility. All these strategies may help a state to survive, but they cannot negate the permanent structural feature of the *international system, i.e., anarchy. Depending on the skill, prudence, and ambitions of states making up the international system at a given historical moment, the competition among states may or may not result in general war; but general war is a permanent possibility. "Structural realists" therefore emphasize continuity in international relations and regard most schemes for institutionalized *international cooperation to be futile and utopian. States guard their independence; they will not willingly cede their sovereign authority to some higher institution, however "rational" such a scheme may be.

A consequence of this view of international anarchy is a tendency to treat individual states as unitary, rational actors competing in a fixed universe of power. Domestic determinants of *foreign policy are deprecated or largely ignored; the theoretical demands of the international structure are regarded in themselves as providing a parsimonious explanation of a given state's foreign policy. Anarchy in this sense becomes more than a description of the international milieu; it is a fundamental reality upon which to base a theory of international relations. Perhaps the best-known recent theory taking this approach is that of Kenneth Waltz in *Theory of International Politics*.

Other authors treat international anarchy less literally and as less important. In *The Anarchical Society* Hedley Bull argues that international relations resembles a society at least as much as it resembles Hobbesian anarchy—hence his oxymoronic title. Bull points out that international anarchy has not prevented the growth of trade and industry, and that it has not made life for individuals "solitary, poor, nasty, brutish, and short." Hobbes himself did not apply his description of the state of nature to the international milieu; he thought individual sovereign states would learn to control their disposition to go to war with one another. For thinkers like Bull, the absence of authoritative supranational organization or law does not necessarily rule out all forms of international society. International anarchy, in short, not only can be distinguished from domestic anarchy, but its consequences are not as deleterious.

On the normative level, thinkers who regard international anarchy as a primary and determining feature of international political life are usually pessimistic about the possibilities of taming the competition among states by means other than deterrent strategies based on military power. (Authors who share this diagnosis but are more sanguine about the possibilities of creating viable international organizations are normally classed as "idealists.") The best hope for moderation in the international system is a prudent calculation of the power interests of the state; theorists disagree about whether a bipolar or a multipolar system is more conducive to stability. Those who regard anarchy as less all-encompassing point to the increased possibilities of existing international institutions and believe that states can learn to guarantee their security by means other than war and the preparation for war. They are also more likely to regard differences in domestic regime to be key for an understanding of policy.

(See also Deterrence; Idealism; Security Dilemma; Sovereignty.)

Hedley Bull, *The Anarchical Society* (New York, 1977). Kenneth W. Waltz, *Theory of International Politics* (Reading, Mass., 1979). Stanley Hoffman, *Janus and Minerva* (Boulder, Colo., 1987).

Michael Joseph Smith

ANGOLA. The contours of Angola as a country, almost 1,300 kilometers from north to south and over 1,200 kilometers from west to east, were determined by Portuguese conquest at the end of the nineteenth century. Linked both to the central African and southern African regions, at the intersection of global, regional, and internal cleavages, this nation of 11 million has been at war almost without interruption since 1961. Since United Nations–monitored elections in 1992, a formal multiparty structure presided over by the Popular Movement for the Liberation of Angola (MPLA) has coexisted with a highly centralized national political economy based on oil, pervasive insecurity for civilians, and a patchwork of divided control over most of the national territory. Angola is potentially one of the richest of African countries and a continuing magnet for investment in offshore oil extraction. But the failure to achieve political stability after independence in 1975 has made it one of the continent's most recalcitrant cases of humanitarian crisis.

Angola's precolonial and colonial history set the stage for particularly deep internal cleavages after independence. The slave trade was the dominant feature of the political economy from the seventeenth through the early nineteenth centuries, and its impact was among the most sustained and pervasive anywhere on the continent. Portuguese colonization during this period planted deep roots in Luanda, Benguela, and an adjacent coastal strip. The gap with interior areas which were conquered later, combined with the centralizing tendencies of twentieth-century Portuguese colonial rule, lived on in splits within Angolan nationalism. At the same time, the economic and political backwardness of Portuguese colonialism left the country with weak national institutions and high illiteracy rates.

In their war for independence, which began in 1961, Angolans were divided. The National Front for the Liberation of Angola (FNLA) was based among Kikongo-speaking people in the north. Jonas Savimbi's National Union for the Total Independence of Angola (Unita) claimed leadership of Umbundu-speaking Angolans, from the central plateau. The MPLA had a national appeal, but its strongest base was among Kimbundu-speaking people in the Luanda area. The divisions were less ethnic than regional and political in character, but grew more rather than less intense with succeeding stages of conflict. Portuguese control began to crumble in 1974, and rivalry led to war the next year. U.S., Congo-Kinshasa, and South African military intervention in favor of the FNLA and Unita was countered by Cuban forces and Soviet supplies aiding the MPLA. After Angola's independence in November 1975, the victorious MPLA soon gained international recognition, except from the United States and South Africa. The U.S. Congress barred further U.S. military involvement in Angola. The South African troops then also withdrew.

Over 90 percent of the approximately 335,000 Portuguese settlers fled the country. Since they had monopolized almost all skilled jobs, the economy was devastated. State companies took over from the Portuguese, but lacked management skills. Only the oil sector, where the government worked with foreign companies, prospered. From 1976 through 1991, Angola suffered guerrilla warfare plus direct South African attacks. In retaliation for Angolan support for the freedom of South African–occupied Namibia, South Africa backed Unita on a massive scale until Namibia's independence in 1990. Conflict over Unita-occupied southeastern Angola led to large-scale battles involving South African and Cuban troops as well as Angolan government and Unita forces, ending in a military setback for South Africa in 1987–88.

Agreements in 1988 on Namibian independence and withdrawal of Cuban troops from Angola ended major South African military involvement. But the war continued. In May 1991, after two years of talks, the Angolan government and Unita signed a treaty providing for a cease-fire, troop demobilization, and multiparty elections. In the September 1992 elections, judged free and fair by UN observers, the MPLA won 54 percent and Unita 34 percent in the legislative race. President José Eduardo dos Santos, of the MPLA, fell just short of 50 percent in the presidential contest, while Unita leader Savimbi had 40 percent.

After Savimbi refused to accept the results, Angola returned to war. Unita, aided by supplies from Congo-Kinshasa and South Africa (then still under the apartheid regime), launched offensives around the country. The government responded, expelling Unita from Luanda while armed civilians took reprisals against Unita supporters. In 1993–94, Unita controlled much of the countryside and some inland cities. Bitter fighting raged in most areas, causing casualties of an estimated 1,000 people a day and physical damage to both towns and countryside far above that of the previous two decades of war.

Critics charged that inaction by the United States and the United Nations, which failed to protest Unita's failure to disarm before the election or to react quickly when the war resumed, was in part responsible for the catastrophe. In May 1993, the United States finally recognized the elected Angolan government. In September 1993 the UN imposed an arms and fuel embargo on Unita. New peace talks began in Lusaka, Zambia, in November 1993. A year later came a new peace treaty, including troop demobilization in exchange for a share of ministries and provincial governorships for Unita.

The Lusaka peace process was monitored by a new UN mission, including, 7,000 peacekeeping troops at its high point in 1995–96. An international "troika" of the United States, Russia, and Portugal served as guarantors of the peace process. Despite an elaborate demobilization exercise, in which many of Unita's troops were integrated into a new national army, Savimbi's hard-line faction of Unita succeeded in maintaining a well-trained army of at least 15,000 to 25,000 loyal troops. Unita joined in a government of national unity in April 1997, but refused to give up control of territory under its control. As Savimbi's intention to return to war became clearer, many of Unita's civilian leaders abandoned him. Both Unita and Angolan government troops became entangled in the conflict in neighboring Congo-Kinshasa in 1997 and 1998. After more than $1 billion over four years spent on UN peacekeeping, Angola faced the prospect of renewed war.

Any explanation of the persistent divisions in Angola must take into account multiple factors which reinforced each other over time. Precolonial and colonial-era divisions between groups linked more closely to the "central society" of the capital and those in the hinterland crystallized into political divisions within the nationalist movement. Those divisions were hardened by the polarizing tendencies of the global Cold War and the regional battle over white-minority rule. Jonas Savimbi's fanatic ambition and tight control over his militarized party proved the decisive stumbling block to post–Cold War, post-apartheid peace settlements, despite continuous erosion of his political base in the 1990s.

In the 1990s, with ideological divisions no longer relevant, Angola's links to the external world as well as its internal conflict were shaped even more clearly by the political economies of diamonds and oil. Unita's capacity to continue the war was based on sale of diamonds from areas under its control, estimated at $3.7 billion between 1992 and 1998. Oil production, meanwhile, ensured that Angola's exports grew at an annual rate of 7.4 percent from 1987 to 1997, with a 15.1 percent growth rate predicted for 1998–2002. The value of oil production rose from $1.2 billion in 1986 to $4.5 billion in 1997.

Continued war, population displacement, and the lack of government capacity to implement economic and social programs, however, left Angola with a life expectancy of only 47. In 1998 the country ranked 156th of 174 countries in the UN's Human Development Index, a full 28 steps below its ranking in GDP per capita. At least 1.2 million people were internally displaced, and more than 80 percent were living in poverty. With an external debt of $10.5 billion, export earnings subject to fluctuating oil prices, and fiscal management undermined by corruption as well as lack of technical capacity, the Angolan government also repeatedly failed to win the seal of economic approval from the World Bank and the International Monetary Fund.

Between independence in 1975 and the mid-1990s, Angola's ruling elite, in the government, military, and ruling MPLA party, consistently built good relations with major oil companies from the United States, France, and other countries. In the 1990s it also shed its socialist ideological coloration. Both by virtue of its national presence and by deliberate measures to co-opt political opponents, its top ranks became increasingly mixed in both ethnic and political origin. At the same time, however, its failure to deliver peace, to advance economic welfare, or to deliver government services left it more and more isolated from urban as well as rural citizens.

Disillusionment with both the government and Unita was

already pervasive at the time of the 1992 election, and continued to grow in the subsequent period. At the end of the 1990s, despite stirrings among non-governmental organizations, independent media, and workers in the education sector, there was little sign of emergence of significant new political forces. The perpetual emergency promoted a political climate in which popular energies were directed above all to day-to-day survival. Although commercial and communications links from Angola to South Africa and the world at large continued to grow rapidly, their impact on the internal political scene was still difficult to discern.

(See also GREAT LAKES REGION: LUSOPHONE AFRICA; SOUTHERN AFRICAN DEVELOPMENT COMMUNITY.)

F. W. Heimer, *The Decolonization Conflict in Angola, 1974–76* (Geneva, 1979). Tony Hodges, *Angola to 2000: Prospects for Recovery* (London, 1993). Karl Maier, *Angola: Promises and Lies* (London, 1996). William Minter, *Apartheid's Contras: An Inquiry into the Roots of War in Angola and Mozambique* (London, 1994). Inge Tvedten, *Angola: Struggle for Peace and Reconstruction* (Boulder, Colo., 1997).

WILLIAM MINTER

ANNAN, Kofi. On 1 January 1997, Kofi Annan became the seventh secretary general of the *United Nations. His election followed a bitterly-contested U.S. veto of a second term for his predecessor, Boutros Boutros-Ghali of Egypt. The *Security Council recognized it was still Africa's "turn" in the UN's highest office, and eventually selected the U.S.- and French-backed Annan, a soft-spoken Ghanaian then heading the UN's Peacekeeping Department.

Annan proved an innovative and surprisingly independent secretary general—far less in thrall to the United States than many had anticipated. Though his choices are severely limited by the UN's financial crisis and by unrelenting pressure from the United States and other major powers, Annan has won widespread support and learned to maximize his options. He moved quickly to reassert UN centrality in emergencies across the globe.

UN staffers have been largely delighted with their new chief, and morale within the organization has soared. Annan, the first black African secretary general and the first to rise to the top position from within the ranks of the UN staff, is appreciated not only for his political acumen, but for his respect for and willingness to work collaboratively with his colleagues.

Born in Ghana in 1938, Annan studied economics in Kumasi and earned a bachelor's degree at Macalester College in Minnesota in 1961. He did graduate work in Geneva and later earned a master's degree in management from the Massachusetts Institute of Technology in 1972.

Annan joined the United Nations system in 1962, working in financial and management posts with the *World Health Organization, the High Commissioner for Human Rights in Geneva, the UN Economic Commission for Africa, and at UN headquarters in New York. He headed the UN's Peacekeeping Department from 1993 to 1995, and again in 1996, during a period of unprecedented growth in the size and scope of United Nations peacekeeping operations. At its peak in 1995, the UN was fielding almost 70,000 military and civilian "Blue Helmets" from seventy-seven countries.

During Annan's tenure as head of UN peacekeeping, many problems and tragedies arose, as international crises in Bosnia and Rwanda overwhelmed the UN's capacity and demonstrated the insufficiency of support from major member states. While Annan shared some responsibility, and characteristically apologized for his judgment errors, the main crises resulted not from Secretariat or secretary-general failures, but from the refusal of the major Security Council members to adequately respond and back the UN efforts.

When Annan came into office in 1997, he faced formidable challenges. The organization was near bankruptcy and it faced serious criticism and hostility in Washington. In his first weeks in office, Annan traveled to Washington to build support in the conservative Congress. He promised to shrink the UN's operating budget, asking in return that the United States pay its $1.6 billion in back dues.

Annan continued his predecessor's cuts in UN staff and budget. At the same time he introduced many management reforms—a new post of deputy secretary general, a new office of financial oversight to keep watch for waste and *corruption, and a more efficient cabinet-style management. Still, the United States refused to pay its debts, prolonging the financial crisis and keeping Annan's UN very short of resources.

Faced with insufficient funds, Annan sought closer relations between the United Nations and the private sector. Amid some controversy, he joined the annual gatherings of corporate chief executives in Davos, Switzerland, and called for a strategic partnership between the UN and business. In 1999 he proposed "The Global Compact," nine principles on *human rights, labor standards, and the environment that corporations should adopt. At the same time, the UN muted its criticism of *globalization and gave stronger support to corporate-friendly open markets. He thus also set the stage for broader alliances between the UN and its agencies and multinational corporations. Many critics have noted the tarnished environmental, labor, and human rights records of some of these partner corporations. Critics are likewise skeptical about the threat to UN decision-making inherent in UN reliance on funds from private foundations, corporations, or individuals like Ted Turner of CNN. But Annan and his team have been strongly committed to this course.

Annan has not hesitated to tackle other controversial issues. Opening the 1999 General Assembly, he spoke in favor of "*humanitarian intervention," stating explicitly that national *sovereignty could no longer shield governments that massively violate human rights of their citizens. Many developing countries, fearing that only weaker states would face such response, reacted negatively, but Annan has persisted in raising this issue, acknowledging the UN Charter's contradictions between sovereignty and human rights. In another controversial field, Annan increasingly spoke out about how economic sanctions against Iraq were causing the UN to be blamed for the humanitarian crisis facing the Iraqi population.

Under Annan, the UN has greatly increased its use of modern communications and he has pushed the organization to be more open and accountable. In 1999 the UN released major reports on disasters in Rwanda and Srebrenica, assessments that were painfully self-critical and set a new standard for UN evaluation and transparency. Annan is credited with promotion of women to higher posts in the organization. And he will likely be remembered for his effective management and personal diplomacy, and his warmth and charm in even the most difficult international crises.

(See also BOSNIAN WAR; RWANDAN GENOCIDE.)

PHYLLIS BENNIS

ANTARCTICA. The international regime for Antarctica and the Southern Ocean is defined by the Antarctic Treaty System. Its main elements are expressed in the 1959 Antarctic Treaty, the 1972 Convention on the Conservation of Antarctic Seals, the 1980 Convention on the Conservation of Antarctic Marine Living Resources, and the 1991 Protocol on Environmental Protection (Madrid Protocol) plus annexes; finer details are elaborated in consultative parties' measures and recommendations.

The Antarctic Treaty was negotiated among the twelve states—seven territorial claimants (Argentina, Australia, Chile, France, New Zealand, Norway, United Kingdom), two superpowers (Soviet Union, United States), and three others (Belgium, Japan, South Africa) operating Antarctic research stations during the 1957–1958 International Geophysical Year (IGY). It established the four shared principles and one compromise basic to the regime. The shared principles are 1) existence of an "Antarctic community" using and managing the area jointly, 2) scientific cooperation, 3) nonmilitarization, and 4) environmental protection. The compromise sets aside disputes about sovereignty by putting territorial claims into abeyance for the treaty's duration.

Though "regional" in its focus on a particular geographical area, the Antarctic regime includes participating states from around the world self-selected according to the functional criterion of supporting scientific research. Like other regional regimes, it was created and operates outside the UN. More unusually, it comprises two classes of member states. The twelve original members plus any other state sponsoring "substantial scientific research" in Antarctica hold voting rights as "consultative parties"; in 1999 twenty-six states had that status. The other seventeen (the "nonconsultative parties") have sent observers to meetings since 1983 but have no vote. Increasing the number of consultative parties after 1977, particularly by including major Third World states like Brazil, China, and India, buttressed the regime's political strength but also increased the difficulties of intragroup functioning because most decisions must be made unanimously.

The low intensity and almost exclusively scientific focus of Antarctic activity in the 1960s and early 1970s allowed participating states to manage Antarctic affairs through biennial consultative meetings. The Scientific Committee on Antarctic Research—a transnational committee of the International Congress of Scientific Unions initially created to coordinate IGY programs—provided expert advice as needed. The increased prominence of resource and environmental issues in the 1980s plus higher levels of activity in the area led to creation of additional standing bodies: the Commission on Antarctic Marine Living Resources (1980), the Council of Managers of National Antarctic Programs (1988), and the Committee on Environmental Protection (1991). Resource issues also inspired two sets of outside challenges proposing replacement of the Antarctic Treaty System with alternate arrangements. The first, a group of nonmember states led by Malaysia, proposed creating a UN-based regime based on the common heritage of mankind principle; the second, a coali-

tion of environmentalist organizations, sought to have Antarctica declared a world park. Both challenges faded after the consultative parties abandoned a 1988 draft agreement on regulating mineral and fuel resource exploitation in favor of the fifty-year moratorium contained in the Madrid Protocol. The remnants of the Malaysia group dropped their challenge; the environmentalist organizations now focus on pressuring member states to adopt and enforce strong environmental commitments.

The major challenges facing the Antarctic regime today stem from the need to perfect and implement the Madrid Protocol and its annexes, the increased intensity of human activity on Antarctica and in the Southern Ocean, and new problems posed by privately organized tourist excursions. The consultative parties shifted to annual meetings beginning in 1995, have refined their decision-making procedures, and are seriously considering creation of a small full-time Antarctic secretariat. After a difficult start, the Commission on Antarctic Marine Living Resources is functioning as a reasonably effective fisheries regulator, but faces challenges as some states (notably Australia, Chile, and the United Kingdom) assert claims to maritime jurisdiction around non-Antarctic territories that extend into the Commission area and others seek to ensure access for their distant water fleets. The Committee on Environmental Protection has barely begun work; some of the annexes are still under negotiation, and incorporation of the Madrid Protocol into national legal systems and bureaucratic routines has just begun.

(See also ENVIRONMENTALISM.)

Sir Arthur Watts, *International Law and the Antarctic Treaty System* (Cambridge, U.K., 1992). Francisco Francioni and Tullio Scovazzi, eds., *International Law for Antarctic*, 2d ed. (The Hague, 1997). Olav Schram Stokke and Davor Vidas, eds., *Governing the Antarctic: The Effectiveness and Legitimacy of the Antarctic Treaty System* (Cambridge, U.K., 1997).

M. J. PETERSON

ANTI-SEMITISM. Discrimination, prejudice, bigotry, racism, and xenophobia have existed in all historical eras and in all countries, yet there is something distinctive in the extraordinary persistence of anti-Semitism, or hatred of Jews, historically and spatially. A wholly disproportionate amount of the attention given to the existence of Jews has been critical in character, irrespective of any specific behavior. Or it has focused for varied and often contradictory reasons on the alleged negative qualities of Jews. No other group of people has suffered from a regime like that of Nazi Germany, whose leaders had the total extermination of a whole people as a defining ideological motivation. Throughout history Jews have suffered from massacres, burning, expropriation of property, expulsions, wearing of special badges, imposition of quotas, legal and social discrimination, and denial of and limits on freedom.

Anti-Semitism has emanated from all political persuasions, from holders of all religious beliefs, from those critical of Christianity or Judaism, and from all social groups. Hatred of Jews has been manifested when they lived in segregated ghettoes and when they shared emancipated environments with non-Jews. It has persisted in an age of universal suffrage and change in the nature of economic systems.

What distinguishes anti-Semitism from the ever-present prejudice or hostility directed against other (non-Jewish) people and groups is not so much the strength and passion of this hatred as its many-faceted character and the range of arguments and doctrines that see Jews at best as peripheral in society and at worst as destructive monsters and forces of evil. Some arguments—whether of a political, economic, social, religious, or psychological nature—make a claim to rationality. The claim is that the Jews, because of their religious customs, insistence on monotheism, dietary habits, or tribal exclusiveness, are alien to the traditions and ways of life of the societies in which they live, try to subvert those societies, or are able to control both these societies and other diabolical forces in the world.

The uniqueness of anti-Semitism is that no other group of people in the world has been charged simultaneously with alienation from society and with cosmopolitanism; with being capitalist exploiters and agents of international finance and also revolutionary agitators; with having a materialist mentality and with being people of the Book; with acting as militant aggressors and with being cowardly; with adherence to a superstitious religion and with being agents of modernism; with upholding a rigid law and also being morally decadent; with being a chosen people and also having an inferior human nature; with both arrogance and timidity; with both individualism and communal adherence; with being guilty of the crucifixion of Christ and at the same time held to account for the invention of Christianity. Even in ancient Greece and Rome, the refusal of Jews to recognize pagan gods and their different rituals, their practice of circumcision, their observance of the Sabbath, their dietary laws, and intermarriage among Jews set them apart. Christian hostility was based on the responsibility of Jews, who rejected Christianity and the Messiah, for the crucifixion of Jesus, which justified their "perpetual servitude." From early modern European history on, Jews were castigated for their ethnic separation, culture, and autonomous community.

Logically, it might have been expected that the criticism of Jewish particularity would cease in the era of European emancipation and the gradual removal of many traditional restrictions and forms of discrimination. Emancipation would, it was believed, bring with it assimilation, if not religious conversion, and the elimination of supposedly Jewish behavioral characteristics.

The religious element of anti-Semitism, resting on Jewish rejection of the true faith, may indeed have been reduced, if not eliminated. But in its place greater prominence was given to Jewish characteristics, which were partly genetic in nature and partly the result of alien cultural and ethnic traditions. Purported characteristics such as moral insensitivity, superstitious habits, lack of social graces, and cultural inferiority now rendered Jews incapable of true citizenship.

Unexpectedly, the Enlightenment helped produce a new rationale for anti-Semitism. Some of its major figures, especially Voltaire, were instrumental in providing a secular anti-Jewish rhetoric in the name of European culture rather than religion.

Not surprisingly, the visibility of the Jewish community, especially in central Europe, buttressed the argument that Jews were cultural aliens who were disproportionately prominent in elite positions. Envy of economic success by Jews, resentment of their position in certain businesses and professions, criticism of their central role in the sphere of distribution and of their crucial situation as intermediaries, and jealousy of their conspicuous role in cultural and intellectual life led to the charge that Jews were subverting the economic basis of society and were responsible for its problems, economic crises, dislocation of individuals, and any reduction in the standard of living.

Reinforcing this charge of the alien nature of Jews has been a second, more recent one of racial inferiority. The very coining of the term "anti-Semitism" by Wilhelm Marr in 1879 suggested that opposition was being registered to racial characteristics rather than religious beliefs. Secular racial anti-Semitism has never really been anything other than antagonism to Jews. The myth of Jewish biological inferiority justified the continuing attacks in a more secular age because evils in society supposedly were traceable to the presence of the Jewish race. The argument of biological differences marks the emergence of the genocidal strain in modern anti-Semitism. The world, it was concluded, must be saved from Judaization.

In other words, Jews were considered a threat to culture itself, as the materialist spirit of their race presumably eroded true values. Much of the original support for Nazism rested on its claim that it was defending the true European values against the threat to Aryan virility—a claim that stemmed from the inculcation of the nineteenth-century and twentieth-century German ideology of the *Volk* in both racial and nonracial forms. The *Volk* must overcome and reject the materialism and capitalism symbolized by the urban and rationalistic Jew.

Paradoxically, the charge that Jews were a separate ethnic group, thus justifying denial of their individual rights, did not lead to a recognition that they were also members of a collective entity with its own self-consciousness and interest in collective self-determination as a nation-state. The price of civil and political equality in this view was renunciation of any collective identification by Jews. For two centuries this argument has been made, but in the present it has another dimension. The question of Jewish nationhood or collective identity is now linked with the state of Israel.

In world politics, the principle of Jewish self-determination as a people with the right to form its own state has often been regarded less sympathetically than in the case of other peoples. Not only has the creation of Israel been opposed by Arab and Muslim countries, but its claim to legitimacy as a sovereign state also troubles left-wing Western intellectuals who have no similar difficulty with the claims of other groups.

The establishment of the state led in part to the transformation of the traditionally perceived image of Jews. That image—of the sinister economic force, usurer, moneylender, landlord, parasite—still survives, if in much-reduced fashion, but it has now been superseded by that of the Israelis, or Zionists, who are criticized as arrogant, colonialist, imperialist, and racist.

In addition to the criticism of Jewish particularity, the concept of Jews as the "chosen people" has provided both a historical and a contemporary source of antagonism. The concept was meaningful for the early leaders of the church and of Islam. For anti-Semites the chosen people embody fanaticism, evil, or an attitude of superiority to other peoples. They perceive the Old Testament as the source of Jewish fanaticism, tribal nationalism, and communal exclusivism, and now as the basis for the aggressive attitude of the state of Israel.

To explain the pathological obsession with Jews some have resorted to psychological factors, as did Jean-Paul Sartre in his famous definition of the anti-Semite as a person who is afraid. Troubled people project their own anxieties, drives, impulses of which they are ashamed, and negative self-images onto Jews, who are then seen as aggressive, competitive, and secretive; are resented as a "chosen people"; and are made a scapegoat for both personal failures and the failures of society. In the United States, the militia movement with an estimated 15,000 participants, allied with white supremacist groups, hate groups, identity churches, skinheads, the Ku Klux Klan, and neo-Nazi groups, has stressed anti-Jewish themes, though it has mainly focused on hostility to the federal government and bureaucracy. A new phenomenon is the use of the Internet by anti-Semites and racists to promote their cause by hate mail.

Fear of a worldwide Jewish plot or conspiracy has been manifested in a variety of ways, whether Christian, Enlightenment, socialist, Marxist, Third World, or Nazi in form. The Nazi version was that Jews were destroyers of culture and constituted the basis of a worldwide conspiracy. The conclusion was that the Jewish race was a microbe or bacillus that had to be eliminated so that purification could be obtained. Thus the Nazis justified the policy of total extermination or *Holocaust of an entire people. The most recent significant argument about alleged Jewish conspiracy is that the Holocaust never happened and that the record of genocide of Jews is a hoax to discredit the Nazi regime for the benefit of world Jewry and the state of Israel. Holocaust denial, begun in the United States in 1979 as an organized propaganda movement, is now publicized in many countries.

Today, the virus of anti-Semitism continues to infect the rhetoric and actions of heterogeneous groups: religious fundamentalists, elements of the Right, blacks, Arab and Islamic countries, the Third World, the former Soviet Union, the political Left, and those who are critical of liberal democratic systems. Christian hostility toward Jews has declined considerably. But the 2,000-year-old Christian prejudice, with its negative moral and spiritual conception of Jews, has still not ended. In Western societies, now that Jews, the former pariahs, have moved into the center of society and compete on equal terms for its key positions, prejudice has become alloyed with resentment.

Yet hostility toward Jews has also come from the political Left. With the Socialist movement in the nineteenth century came sharp criticism of the role of Jews in capitalist systems. In this criticism Karl Marx (among others) was an influential figure in arguing that Judaism constituted the essence of capitalism. The contemporary hostility to Israel of the Left, which has associated it with imperialism, pronounced it a racist state, and regarded *Zionism as the only national liberation movement that is "reactionary" rather than progressive, suggests deeper emotions.

Anti-Semitic attitudes in the United States are higher in the African-American community than among whites. Black leaders (other than members of Congress) and the more politically conscious African Americans are more frequently negative than the majority of blacks. Although analytically quite distinct, this more negative attitude toward Jews overlaps in general with a less sympathetic attitude to Israel than that held by whites.

To the Islamic world, Jews no longer conform to the stereotype of a tolerated but subordinated minority. Muslim treatment of Jews has historically been less harsh than that in Western countries or that accorded Christians in Muslim countries, partly because Jews did not challenge the political supremacy of Muslims. But now Jews rule over Muslims. To this has been added the growing anti-Semitism first introduced by diplomatic and Christian missions to Arab countries and by anti-Semitic European works such as the *Protocols of the Elders of Zion*. Anti-Semitism in the Islamic world has dramatically increased since the formation of the state of Israel in 1948. Public figures and the state-controlled media in the Arab world, and the Palestinian Hamas Islamic organization, have frequently engaged in anti-Jewish rhetoric including statements from the Quran, Holocaust denial, characterizations of Jews in negative ways, and allegations of Zionist plots to control the world, in the effort to deny the legitimacy of Israel and to limit normalization of relations between Israel and the Arab countries.

In the Soviet Union anti-Semitism flourished for a variety of reasons: resentment of Jewish overrepresentation in certain occupations, annoyance at Jews who were critical of the system or who struggled for human rights, inherited prejudice from tsarist times, rancor at the desire of Jews to emigrate, and the use of anti-Semitism as an instrument for the regime to gain popularity among the population and to deflect attention from the country's pressing problems. Soviet anti-Semitism directly infected current thought in the rest of the world through its criticism of Jewish traits and behavior: moreover, until they abated during the Gorbachev era, Soviet attacks on the actions of Israel affected the international community, especially the UN, which reached its lowest point with the 1975 "Zionism is racism" resolution. After the collapse of communism in 1989–1990, Jewish life in central and eastern Europe has generally improved. Yet previously suppressed or controlled anti-Semitism has arisen among the population in those countries. Jews have been attacked as accomplices of the former communist elite, especially security officials, as responsible for miseries suffered under communism, as plutocratic economic exploiters, and as a foreign destabilizing element interfering with the new form of nationalism in eastern Europe. Zionism has been condemned as an expression of Jewish feelings of superiority and belief in being the chosen people.

In the postwar period there has been in democratic countries a significant decline in discriminatory attitudes and in the numbers of those who are strongly prejudiced against Jews. Anti-Semitism is now not politically or intellectually respectable. No important political organization in the United States or in other democratic countries openly advocates anti-Semitic views, nor are Jews denied civil or political rights in those countries. But the phenomenon of anti-Semitism has still not disappeared either in attitudes and beliefs or in patterns of behavior.

(See also RACE AND RACISM; ZIONISM.)

(Jacob Katz, *From Prejudice to Destruction* (Cambridge, Mass., 1980). Norman Cohn, *Warrant for Genocide* (Decatur, Ga., 1981). Michael Curtis, ed., *Antisemitism in the Contemporary World* (Boulder, Colo., 1985). Bernard Lewis, *Semites and Anti-Semites* (New York, 1987). Leon Poliakov, *The History of Antisemitism* (New York, 1987). Leonard Dinnerstein, Antisemitism in America (New York, 1993).

MICHAEL CURTIS

ANZUS TREATY. The ANZUS Treaty between Australia, New Zealand, and the United States was signed in San Francisco in September 1951. Although designed originally to afford United States *security backing for Australia and New Zealand against any future threat posed by a resurgent Japan, it is a very generalized document containing loose guarantees of support with no specific threat enumerated. The key article, Article IV, stipulates that "each Party recognises that an armed attack in the Pacific area on any of the Parties would be dangerous to its own peace and safety and declares that it would act to meet the common danger in accordance with its constitutional processes." The treaty was designed to remain in force indefinitely although any party could "cease to be a member of the Council" following one year's notice (Art. X). There is no provision for expulsion.

For more than a decade after it was signed ANZUS did not provide the primary basis for Australian and New Zealand defense. It was only with the advent of the *Vietnam War and the British policy of withdrawal east of Suez that ANZUS came to the forefront. Technically, Vietnam fell more under the Southeast Asia Treaty Organization arrangements than under ANZUS, but the ANZUS link was used to bring influence to bear upon New Zealand in particular.

In practice, the United States tended to regard Australia and New Zealand as one, and any important differences in approach between the two needed to be settled in advance in Canberra, or they tended to be ignored. Yet in reality Australia and New Zealand had divergent regional interests. The Australian focus was on neighboring Indonesia, on its security concerns in the divided island of New Guinea, and on the potentially troubled area of the Indian Ocean. New Zealand meanwhile tended to concentrate on the world of micro- or ministates in the Southwest Pacific. Also, New Zealand was not keyed into the U.S. global deterrence network through such facilities as the important communications and relay facilities at North West Cape, Pine Gap, or Nurrungar in Australia.

Strains in the alliance emerged in the late 1960s and early 1970s. Opposition to nuclear power in New Zealand came into conflict with a resumption of visits by nuclear-powered U.S. warships, which had been suspended pending acceptance of insurance liability for nuclear accident. By 1984, three of the four leading New Zealand political parties contesting the general election of that year advocated a ban on nuclear-ship visits. The ban covered both ships carrying—or likely to be carrying—*nuclear weapons and those that were nuclear-propelled. The remaining party, the National Party, adopted a similar policy before being returned to power in 1990, by which time the ban had been enshrined in legislation.

Subsequently, with the U.S. decision to remove nuclear weapons from its warships, a major obstacle was removed, but the legislation ensured that problems have continued to exist over the prohibition of nuclear propulsion. The ban was not intended as a rejection of ANZUS for, in effect, New Zealanders wanted both the ban and retention of the alliance. The United States claimed that the ban amounted to a nonfulfillment of New Zealand's obligations under the treaty and declared its security guarantee for New Zealand nonoperative.

In formal terms, the ANZUS Treaty continues, with one partner nonoperative. In practice, Australia and the United States have always been the dominant partners. New Zealand's relations with the United States have been downgraded from ally to friendly country while Australia continues to maintain close defense cooperation with both countries, only separately rather than as part of a tripartite *alliance.

(See also INDIAN OCEAN REGION; PACIFIC REGION.)

Jacob Bercovitch, ed., *ANZUS in Crisis: Alliance Management in International Affairs* (London, 1988). Michael C. Pugh, *The ANZUS Crisis, Nuclear Visiting and Deterrence* (Cambridge, U.K., 1989).

KEITH JACKSON

APARTHEID. In 1948 the Nationalist Party (NP) swept to power in South Africa, promising to bring a stop to the muddled situation created by the policies of segregation, which had guided "native policy" since the formation of the Union of *South Africa in 1910. The new policy was summed up in the word "apartheid" or "apartness." Segregation, by conceding the token franchise to the Africans and Coloureds (the African franchise was eliminated in 1936, the Coloured in 1953), had by 1948 become nothing more than a pragmatic plugging of leaks in the structure of segregation as they occurred. For NP race purists, segregation was judged to be undermining white supremacy. The ultimate aim was to make South Africa a "white man's country" built on black helots.

Apartheid represented a qualitatively new stage to entrench and guarantee white rule and black exploitation and oppression. In 1913 the principle of territorial segregation had been introduced and Africans could claim permanent residence in the reserves, which constituted 13 percent of South Africa. The Group Areas Act of 1952 extended this principle to segregate Coloured and Indian areas as well. It empowered the executive to declare areas reserved for particular races for residential purposes. The Suppression of Communism Act empowered the prime minister to draw up a list of persons declared to be Communists and to forbid any such person to be a member of Parliament, a provincial council, or any public organization. The governor-general could also prohibit any publication suspected as Communist. Any organization declared to be Communist could be banned and there would be no right to appeal against a proclamation declaring such an organization unlawful. Mixed marriages and carnal intercourse between white and black were made illegal.

Apartheid was racism unbridled and unrestrained. It was blatant and terroristic at home and abroad. It made racism and anticommunism the main principles of state policy. The NP gave the policy of white domination and black subordination and exploitability a sense of finality. At the heart of black exploitation and oppression were the pass laws, dating back to the early nineteenth century, designed to control and direct African labor to wherever it was needed.

The NP, which claimed to represent Afrikaner patrimony in South Africa, built an edifice of racist laws not only to guarantee white supremacy, but also to ensure that Afrikaners were on a par with their English counterparts in all spheres of South African life. The essential difference between apartheid and segregation was that, for the advocates of apartheid, white domination and black subservience were not a matter of negotiation. Africans had to accept ultimate submission or prepare for revolution. In 1960, rather than negotiate African grievances, the regime banned the African National Congress (ANC), which had been formed in 1912, and the Pan-African Congress, which had split from the ANC in 1958. The first political organization to be proscribed had been the Communist Party of South Africa in 1950. In 1977 the Black Consciousness Movement was banned. From September 1984 onwards, the confrontation between the regime and extraparliamentary forces intensified with the beginning of unrest in the Vaal Triangle, and in March 1985 innocent demonstrators, commemorating the Sharpeville slaughter twenty-five years earlier, were killed in Uitenhage. In July the regime imposed a state of emergency which tightened restrictions on the activities of the United Democratic Front and other organizations.

The whites-only franchise guaranteed that differences in the white community were contained within acceptable bounds. But the very success of building the white economy on disenfranchised black labor had undermined the basis of territorial apartheid. The influx control laws could not stem the tide of African urbanization. Thus, across the urban landscape of South Africa huge concentrations of African townships and slums whose residents defied ethnic fragmentation emerged, epitomized by Soweto. It was in these townships that the most radical challenge to the status quo would be launched in the 1970s.

The epic struggle was between Africans and white settlers. The subtext of that struggle was between Afrikaner *nationalism and British *imperialism. This latter struggle culminated in 1961, when South Africa withdrew from the multiracial *Commonwealth and became a republic. This was a crowning moment for Afrikaner nationalists. They had revenged the humiliations they suffered, first in the South African War of 1899–1902 when the Afrikaner republics of the Orange Free State and the Transvaal became British colonies, and then in 1910 when the Union was established and the British monarch became South Africa's head of state.

Even as the Afrikaners celebrated their victory over British imperialism, the real struggle for the future of South Africa had just begun. On 21 March 1960 the struggle had been joined when at Sharpeville, an African township in the industrial area near Vereeniging (where the Boer Republics surrendered their autonomy and became British colonies), the police opened fire and killed 69 innocent demonstrators and wounded 180 bystanders. The result was pandemonium in South Africa and throughout the world. A state of emergency was declared, giving the executive wide powers to crush the African revolt and to maintain law and order. The events at Sharpeville and after did irreparable harm to South Africa. An immediate consequence of the massacre was the outflow of £12.5 million and gold reserve. Shares in the Johannesburg stock fell by £500 million.

The brutality with which apartheid was maintained led the United Nations to declare it a crime against humanity. In 1963 the Organization of African Unity was formed, and one of its goals was to help African nationalists wage war against white colonial enclaves in Africa and apartheid in South Africa. From Sharpeville on, South Africa's international position deteriorated such that the Western powers, against their will, were forced by world public opinion to introduce various sanctions against their once-favored offspring. In 1976 the Soweto student uprising underlined further the brutality of apartheid. The collapse of Portuguese colonial rule in 1975

and the independence of Zimbabwe in 1980 left the apartheid regime without an overall strategy to control the regional political agenda. The theological foundations of apartheid also collapsed in the 1980s as the Dutch Reformed Church split into factions.

The assault from outside by the guerrilla forces of the ANC, the sanctions imposed by the international community, and the internal revolts rendered the political arrangements considered natural up to the end of World War II obsolete. They were now considered offensive abroad and an insult at home.

The tumultuous events unleashed by the student revolt in 1976 in Soweto and accelerated by the introduction of a new constitutional dispensation to the Coloureds and Indians in the early 1980s saw the NP split into various factions. This was the state of affairs in the mid-1980s when businessmen and other interested parties began talks with the ANC that led to the release of Nelson *Mandela in February 1990 and the unbanning of the ANC and other organizations. From 1990, even as the carnage escalated in the townships and in Natal, South Africans negotiated a new constitution, and in 1994 the first truly democratic elections were held, leading to the triumph of the ANC alliance. In a gesture of magnanimity the ANC agreed to a Government of National Unity of all parties that won twenty seats in the election. South Africa had avoided a bloodbath that everybody expected. What remains now is the ugly legacy of white supremacy with its deep-rooted structural inequalities. South Africa's structural integration remains an uncertain and contradictory process as long as disparities coincide with racial and class divisions.

(See also RACE AND RACISM.)

A. Hepple, *Verwoerd* (London, 1967). D. W. Krüger, *The Making of a Nation* (London, 1969). Dunbar Moodie, *The Rise of Afrikaner Power* (Berkeley, Calif., 1975). Dan O'Meare, *Volkskapitalisme, Class, Capital and Ideology in the Development of Afrikaner Nationalism, 1934–1948* (Johannesburg, 1983). Bernard Magubane, *The Political Economy of Race and Class in South Africa* (New York, 1989). Bernard Magubane, *The Making of a Racist State: British Imperialism and the Union of South Africa, 1875–1910* (Trenton, N.J., 1996).

BERNARD MAGUBANE

AQUINO, Corazon. On 25 February 1986 Corazon ("Cory") Cojuangco Aquino became become the first woman president of the *Philippines through a popular revolt following a failed coup attempt against Ferdinand *Marcos, her predecessor in office. Widow of former Senator Benigno ("Ninoy") Aquino, Marcos's principal political rival, she participated in the snap elections in February 1986 after more than one million Filipinos signed their names endorsing her candidacy.

She was born on 25 January 1933 of wealthy and politically prominent families in Luzon. Her father was a Filipino Chinese businessman and politician from Tarlac, her mother a member of a political clan in Rizal. Cory was educated in Catholic schools in Manila and the United States, receiving a bachelor's degree from the College of Mount St. Vincent in New York City.

Her marriage to Ninoy Aquino in 1954 brought two politically prominent Tarlac families together. He was an impressive journalist-politician—young, articulate, witty, dynamic—who went on to become his town's youngest mayor, his province's youngest vice-governor and governor, and, by 1967, the youngest Philippine senator.

When martial law was declared on 21 September 1972, Marcos ordered the arrest and prolonged imprisonment of his opponents, led by Ninoy Aquino. Aquino's seven-year detention was followed by exile in the United States on humanitarian grounds. His *assassination on his return to Manila on 21 August 1983 triggered middle-class protests against Marcos, culminating in the "People Power Revolt" that led to Marcos's fall and Cory Aquino's rise to power.

Her presidency began with overwhelming popularity. It was marked, however, by constant threat from military factions loyal to Marcos and closely identified with Juan Ponce Enrile, his former defense minister. Enrile, General Fidel V. Ramos, the vice chief of staff, and an organization called the Reform the Armed Forces of the Philippines Movement (RAM) had led a mutiny amid mass protest against the fraudulent February 1986 elections. Enlisting popular support, they claimed electoral victory for Cory Aquino. In 1986–1989, however, Enrile and RAM plotted against the government through a series of unsuccessful coups that undermined economic recovery.

Cory Aquino interpreted her role as a transition president whose tasks were to restore democracy and to revive the country's devastated economy. She was constrained, however, by the tenacity of inherited socioeconomic and politicomilitary problems. Her abhorrence of patronage and party politics caused her shaky coalition to fragment, thereby costing her a vehicle for effective governance. Reluctant to wield power, she sacrificed the opportunity to institute socioeconomic measures as lasting foundations for meaningful economic progress and political stability.

Aware of her country's vulnerabilities and cognizant of the imperative of national independence, she sought in 1990 to restructure her country's relations with the United States by serving notice to terminate the agreement on military basing rights. In mid-1992 her preferred successor, Fidel V. Ramos, won the presidency in a hotly contested multiparty election. Cory Aquino has since devoted her time to the institutionalization of democracy through the Benigno S. Aquino, Jr. Foundation, which undertakes programs to empower peoples, especially rural women. She continues to speak for democracy in national, regional, and global forums and to command respect and popular support against perceived threats to the constitutional order in her country. Her legacy of uniting Filipinos against authoritarian rule and defending the transition to democracy against its enemies became an inspiration for subsequent pro-democracy movements elsewhere in the world. She will be remembered as the frail, bespectacled widow in yellow courageously leading her people in nonviolent resistance against dictatorship.

(See also DEMOCRATIC TRANSITIONS.)

Claude A. Buss, *Cory Aquino and the People of the Philippines* (Stanford, Calif., 1987). *University of the Philippines Public Lectures on the Aquino Administration and the Post-EDSA Government 1986–1992)*, 2 vols. (Quezon City, 1992–1993. Robert H. Reid and Eileen Guerrero, *Corazon Aquino and the Brushfire Revolution* (Baton Rouge, La., 1995).

CAROLINA G. HERNANDEZ

ARAB LEAGUE. On 25 September 1944, representatives from Egypt, Iraq, Syria, Lebanon, and Transjordan met in Alexandria to draw up plans to enhance cooperation among Arab states through the creation of a General Arab Congress. The Alexandria Protocol, issued on 7 October, proposed the formation of a League of Arab States whose primary institutions would be a council, in which all Arab states would participate on an equal basis, and a number of specialized subcommittees charged with facilitating joint policies on such issues as economic *development, nationality and immigration, and Palestinian rights. The treaty formally establishing the League was signed on 22 March 1945 by the governments of Egypt, Iraq, Syria, Lebanon, Transjordan, Saudi Arabia, and (North) Yemen. It provided for a council in which each member-state would have a single vote; special standing committees to promote cooperation in economic and financial affairs, communications, cultural affairs, legal matters, social affairs, and public health; and a secretariat, consisting of a secretary general appointed by the council and confirmed by a two-thirds majority of the member-states along with supporting staff. Palestine was granted representation on the council, while Cairo was designated "the permanent seat of the League of Arab States." Membership in the organization was open to "any independent Arab State" upon application to the secretariat. Algeria, Bahrain, Kuwait, Libya, Morocco, Oman, Qatar, Tunisia, the United Arab Emirates, and the People's Democratic Republic of Yemen joined the League immediately after becoming independent; Djibouti, Mauritania, Somalia, and the Sudan made up the remainder of the League's twenty-two members.

League efforts to settle disputes among member-states have for the most part proven unsuccessful. Conflict between Egypt and Iraq over the latter's participation in the Baghdad Pact paralyzed the organization throughout the 1950s; attempts to mediate the fighting between Egypt and Saudi Arabia that attended the Yemeni civil war of 1962 foundered; calls for arbitration between the Jordanian government and the Palestinian national movement in the months leading up to the civil war of September 1970 went unheeded; successive plans to end the fighting in Lebanon after 1975 could not be implemented. In March 1979, following Cairo's signing a peace treaty with Israel, the council suspended Egypt's membership in the League and moved the secretariat to Tunis. Egypt was readmitted to full membership ten years later, but joined Saudi Arabia in sponsoring a resolution that condemned the Iraqi occupation of Kuwait in August 1990 and authorized Arab League forces to collaborate with U.S. and British troops in the Gulf. Tensions resulting from this decision led to the resignations of Secretary General Chadhli Klibi and the League's long-standing ambassador to the United Nations, Clovis Maksoud; ten member-states, led by Iraq, then boycotted an extraordinary council meeting in September 1990 that approved the transfer of the secretariat back to Cairo. The overall inactivity of the new Egyptian secretary general, Esmat 'Abd al-Majid, underlined the organization's growing dormancy. By the mid-1990s, conflicts among Arab states tended to be addressed through state-to-state mediation rather than deliberations by the League.

(See also ARAB NATIONALISM.)

Ahmad M. Gomaa, *The Foundation of the League of Arab States* (London, 1977).

FRED H. LAWSON

ARAB NATIONALISM. The concept of Arab nationalism has been invoked by Arab monarchs as well as revolutionists;

pro-Westerners and anti-Westerners; advocates of secularism and exponents of religion; capitalists and socialists; democrats and dictators. In fact, it has been put to so many contradictory uses that its meaning is far from clear. One thing is clear, however: *nationalism is a potent factor in Arab *political culture. *Public opinion surveys show that most Arabs feel an "Arab identity," though the meaning of such identity can range from a diffuse feeling of cultural belonging to a commitment to creating a unified Arab state.

Like other kinds of nationalism throughout the globe, Arab nationalism is quite recent, going back only to the late nineteenth century. Its earliest advocates worked to create a new "national" language by modernizing and purifying literary Arabic. That language is now standard throughout the Arab world in the mass media and most literature. But separate and quite distinct dialects are still used for ordinary discourse in the various Arab countries—a reminder that a unified Arab state was never created.

Early nationalists also created the myth of "Arabism," an ethnic and cultural unity that supposedly binds all people in the Arabic-speaking world. Arabism plays down the differences (and conflicts) between various Arab communities: Shi'i and Sunni, Copt and Muslim, for example. And it does not adequately account for the place of many non-Arabs like Kurds, Berbers, and Armenians who live in various Arab states.

Arab nationalism created myths about its ancient roots and past glories. Just as the French believe that modern France is the lineal descendant of Charlemagne's empire (a dubious proposition), so Arabs came to believe that the Arab Nation is the inheritor of the great Islamic empires of the past. The important role of Islam in this construct has created difficulty for secular Arab nationalists, including Christian Arabs who have often been active in the secular nationalist movements.

Arab nationalism was the invention of schoolteachers, journalists, and other intellectuals of the late Ottoman Empire. To this project they eventually won over the wealthy classes of merchants and landowners as well as large sections of the urban populace and even many rural dwellers. Socialist and religious movements also bid for mass support during this very turbulent time, but nationalism won out over its rivals.

Arab nationalism never successfully solved the problem as to what territory would constitute the Arab state. Early nationalists had only local ambitions, but there soon emerged pan-Arabists who called for unity of all the Arabic-speaking peoples—"from Baghdad to Tetouan," as a famous song went. A popular early poem by the Lebanese-born Ibrahim al-Yazigi caught the yearning of these early nationalists intellectuals and their sense that national identity was the safest psychic harbor in a stormy world: "Awaken, O Arabs and leave slumber aside/As danger's flood washes your knees in its tide!"

In the late nineteenth century, most Arabic-speaking lands were ruled by the Ottoman Empire, whose sultans and central bureaucracy were Turkish. Emerging Arab nationalism called for new relations of equality within the empire. Nationalists founded societies for literary revival and administrative autonomy and some younger radicals set up clandestine groups that began to work for independence. In 1908, reforms of the Young Turks in Istanbul further Turkified the empire (nationalism was emerging in Turkey, too). Arab nationalists responded with sharpened demands and they convened their first general congress in Paris in June 1913.

The British enlisted the aid of Arab nationalism during World War I. In return for Arab military aid against the Ottomans, they promised to support Arab independence after victory in the war. Simultaneously, however, the British gave assurances for a "Jewish National Home" in *Palestine, and they secretly planned to divide most of the area into British and French colonies. After the war, Arab nationalists tried to create a unified Arab Kingdom based in Damascus. It effectively governed only a small area, and after less than two years was snuffed out by the French military.

Arab nationalism then encountered a new and more powerful antagonist: European colonialism. The Arab world had been divided up, rather arbitrarily, into a number of colonial states. Nationalist anticolonial movements sprang up in nearly every one. Alongside pan-Arab national identity was born an identity based on the colonial units: Syrian, Lebanese, Iraqi, and Palestinian nationalism.

Throughout the colonial period, the nationalist movements grew in strength, though sometimes they faced cruel repression. European rulers made every effort to split up and isolate the nationalists, appealing especially to minority groups like Kurds, Berbers, Armenians, Jews, Druze, Alawis, and the like. These efforts at divide and rule, though ultimately unsuccessful, created animosities between communities that left a legacy of mutual suspicion and intolerance for the independence period.

After World War II, most Arab countries successfully gained their independence and assumed their separate places in the UN and the international state system. Though nationalism had won, many Arab nationalists were discontented. They were unhappy that the Arab world remained divided into some twenty states, that the new state of Israel had taken Arab land in 1948, and that most of the independent states were still dominated economically and politically by the former colonial powers. A new brand of postcolonial nationalism sought to battle against all three of these problems, while within each country, governments promoted a new nationalist identity—*citizenship in the new states.

In the 1950s and 1960s, a number of movements came into being to promote Arab nationalism throughout the region. The best-known and perhaps the most influential was *Nasserism, inspired by the Egyptian leader Gamal Abdel *Nasser. The Movement of Arab Nationalists was especially influential in Lebanon and among the Palestinians, while the Bath Party came to play an important role in Syria and Iraq. In the early 1960s, all of these groups gave greater emphasis to secularism and especially to socialism.

As the individual Arab states built up their structures of *power and *ideology, reinforced in many cases by oil wealth, the potential and support for larger Arab unity began to fade. Egypt and Syria merged but then split again (1958–1961), creating further skepticism about the project of unity. Other abortive unity efforts, especially those proclaimed by Libyan leader Muammar *Qaddafi in the 1970s and 1980s, began to seem almost comical.

But the earlier spirit of militant nationalism remained alive, kindled most often by the *Arab-Israeli conflict and the wars which it regularly produced. Some regimes, like those in Syria, Iraq, and Libya, used pan-Arabism in their official ideology. More common symbols, like a map of a pan-Arab state, appeared regularly throughout the region, even in such moderate venues as Egypt's semiofficial newspaper, al-Ahram. But for all the symbolic and rhetorical flourish, Arab nationalism failed to prevail over its Israeli antagonist, and no amount of talk about national unity could obscure the record of *authoritarianism and economic difficulties of the nationalist regimes. Feuds between Arab governments further weakened the pan-Arabist impulse, and even the *Arab League, the strongest inter-Arab organization, nearly disintegrated in 1990 under the pressure of the Iraqi invasion of Kuwait.

A different view of Arab nationalism gained ground in the 1980s, one based on regional economic integration and the free movement of people and capital. Local groupings of states took shape in this period, notably the Gulf Cooperation Council (1981) and the Arab Maghreb Union (1988). Such projects had none of the ideological fire of the earlier movements, but their gradualism appealed to many Arab intellectuals, business executives, and politicians, especially in light of the successes of European integration. This trend was slow to bear fruit, however, and inter-Arab trade, investment, and cooperation still remain quite limited.

The most formidable challenge to Arab nationalism in the late 1970s and after came from Islamic revivalism. Islamic groups bitterly opposed Arab nationalism because of its secularist approach to politics. During this period, secular governments cracked down harshly on their Islamic rivals in a number of countries, most notably in Syria during the Hama uprising of 1982. Later, however, as limited democratic openings led to elections in Jordan, Tunisia, and Algeria, the challenge of the Islamists reemerged in electoral successes. The ballot box seemed to show that sentiments of religious solidarity had at least partly replaced sentiments of nationalist identity. But Islamism and nationalism alike now confront international secular culture conveyed powerfully by satellite television, the Internet, and steadily-increasing ties of all kinds with Europe.

As Arab nationalism reconstructs once again, the 1990s synthesis with Islamic revivalism may now be waning, in favor of newer forms of identity. The regional integrationist project as a future direction of Arab nationalism remains the most appealing way forward, a path which would permit greater autonomy and self-expression for important minorities like the Kurds. As long as deep social crises afflict the region, however, dogmatic ideologies like authoritarian nationalism and Islamic fundamentalism will remain strong contenders for power.

(See also COLONIAL EMPIRES; DECOLONIZATION; GULF WAR; ISLAM; RELIGION AND POLITICS; SECULARIZATION.)

Albert Hourani, Arabic Thought in the Liberal Age, 1798–1939 (Cambridge, U.K., 1983). Giacomo Lucian and Ghassan Salame, eds., The Politics of Arab Integration (London, 1988). Rashid Khalidi et al., The Origins of Arab Nationalism (New York 1991). James P. Janowski and Israel Gershoni, Rethinking Nationalism in the Arab Middle East (New York, 1997).

GHASSAN SALAME

ARAB-ISRAELI CONFLICT. Since 1948, when Jewish inhabitants of the former British mandate of *Palestine established the state of *Israel, the Arab-Israeli conflict has appeared on the agenda of every session of the UN General Assembly.

The conflict has roots which go back to the 1890s when Jewish settlers first came from Europe and the Zionist movement began to lay the foundations for a future Jewish homeland in Palestine with its overwhelmingly Arab population. The clash of this Jewish state-building project with the emerging nationalist sentiment of the Palestinian Arabs aroused bitter intercommunal struggles during the mandate and led to the conflict that lay ahead. Though only a small territory was at stake—with few natural resources—the conflict was eventually magnified in international significance by the fact that the land in question is sacred to three of the world's great religions, by its intersection with politics in the world's most important oil-producing region, and by the connection of the conflict to the Cold War between the Soviet Union and the United States.

In November 1947, to the dismay of the Arabs, the UN partitioned Palestine into a Jewish and an Arab state (as well as an international enclave for Jerusalem), giving fifty-five percent of the territory to the Jewish state. As British forces withdrew, a civil war erupted between Jews and Arabs. When Israel declared independence in May 1948, several *Arab League members sent units of their regular armies to join guerrilla forces fighting in Palestine. Israel eventually won this war, aided by weapons received from the Soviet bloc. The poorly armed Arab armies and Palestinian irregulars, badly led and unable to coordinate their operations, were no match for the Jewish forces.

After the fighting stopped in 1949, Israel gained about 5,200 square kilometers (2,000 sq. mi.) beyond the area allocated in the UN partition plan, now occupying over seventy-five percent of Palestine. The UN-sponsored armistice agreements, signed between Israel and the Arab belligerents (*Egypt, *Jordan, *Lebanon, and *Syria), gave Egypt control of the Gaza Strip and Jordan some 5,200 square kilometers (2,000 sq. mi.) of eastern Palestine on the west bank of the Jordan River, including the Old City of Jerusalem. In spite of efforts by the UN Conciliation Commission for Palestine (CCP), which met separately with Arab and Israeli delegations in Lausanne, the parties made no lasting *peace agreement.

Over 700,000 Palestinian Arabs fled or were driven from their homes to surrounding Arab countries, mostly to Jordan, the Gaza Strip, Lebanon, and Syria. Both the host countries and the *refugees themselves insisted that those who left Palestine be permitted to return before direct negotiations with Israel. In its Resolution 194(III) of 11 December 1948 establishing the CCP, the UN General Assembly resolved "that the refugees wishing to return to their homes and live at peace with their neighbors should be permitted to do so at the earliest practicable date, and that compensation should be paid for the property of those choosing not to return . . ." During the interim period the refugees were to be assisted by the UN Relief and Works Agency for Palestine Refugees in the Near East (UNRWA).

International efforts to resolve the conflict attempted to find a compromise between the position of Israel, which insisted on direct negotiations, and Arab demands for refugee repatriation and/or compensation and Israeli withdrawal from land beyond the UN partition borders. Absent a settlement, the Arab states refused to recognize Israel or to have any relations with it.

The United States offered several proposals, including

plans for regional economic development that would have integrated refugees into the countries to which they had fled. All such proposals failed, however, because of political obstacles.

Political change in the Arab world sharpened the conflict between Israel and its neighbors during the 1950s. New military regimes came to power—in Syria in 1949 and in Egypt in 1952—geeking to throw off Western tutelage and to affirm Arab national identity. Gamal Abdel *Nasser of Egypt in particular symbolized the new radical nationalist leadership and the growing military, economic, and political strength of the Arab world.

Israeli leaders saw Nasser as a threat. In 1954, in an effort to undermine relations between Egypt and the West, Israeli agents set off a series of bombs at U.S. and Egyptian properties in Cairo and Alexandria. In February 1955, Israel carried out a large-scale attack on Gaza, in retaliation for infiltrators and guerrillas coming across the border.

For its part, Egypt contributed to heightened tensions by continuing to refuse Israeli passage through the Suez Canal. Nasser's bellicose public rhetoric also sharpened Israeli insecurity.

In 1954, Israel began to purchase extensive military equipment from France while Nasser tried unsuccessfully to obtain arms from Western sources, Egypt finally made a deal in 1955 to buy arms from the Soviet bloc. Soviet support had shifted away from Israel and began to favor Syria and Egypt.

In July 1956, Nasser nationalized the Suez Canal, after the United States and the West rejected his requests for assistance in constructing the Aswan High Dam. Both Britain and France saw the move as blow to their interests. Soon after, at secret meetings in Europe, Israeli, French, and British leaders agreed to launch a joint military action against Egypt to regain control of the canal and overthrow the Egyptian leader. Israel began the attack in October. After its forces seized the Gaza Strip and the Sinai Peninsula, and reached the Suez Canal, British and French forces occupied the northern Canal Zone.

With uncharacteristic unity, both the United States and the Soviet Union denounced the tripartite attack and joined in a call through the UN for immediate withdrawal of the invaders. The Soviets threatened military action against Britain and France and the United States withheld vital oil supplies from both countries. These moves soon forced the invaders to withdraw.

In November the General Assembly established the UN Emergency Force (UNEF) to supervise the withdrawal and to patrol the frontiers between Egypt and Israel. Israel left Gaza in March 1957 after receiving assurances that UNEF would remain along its border with Egypt and guarantee free passage from the Gulf of Akaba through the Straits of Tiran to the Red Sea.

Following the Suez War, UNEF assured relatively stable conditions on the frontier between Egypt and Israel, although the two countries remained officially at war. More serious were Israeli border clashes with Syria and Jordan, some over the Jordan River and its sources. The Arab states opposed Israeli plans to divert Jordan River waters to the arid Negev in southern Israel, plans that would diminish their scarce water supplies. In 1960 the Arab League charged that Israel's water scheme was "an act of aggression," and in 1963 the League adopted its own diversion blueprint. Israel nevertheless went ahead with its plan.

Israel's strategic doctrine required that it develop and maintain overwhelming military superiority over all potential Arab enemies. Close relations with France enabled Israel to purchase very advanced weapons; French experts also helped Israel set up a nuclear reactor and a *nuclear weapons program. Israel also developed a sophisticated weapons manufacturing capability of its own.

By 1967 tensions caused by the water dispute and by border incidents led to a number of military clashes. During May Syria protested that Israel was massing troops on its border. Nasser threatened to prevent Israel's passage through the Straits of Tiran, demanded that UNEF forces leave Egyptian territory, and moved troops towards the Sinai border with Israel.

In early June the situation led to a political crisis in Israel where the first national unity government was formed. On 5 June, Israeli leaders decided to make a "preemptive" strike against Egypt, Syria, and Iraq. After firing on Israeli-controlled Jerusalem, Jordanian forces were also involved. The fate of the Arab armies was determined in the first few hours of war when Israeli planes destroyed most of the opposing air fleets while they were still on the ground. Within six days, Israel conquered the Sinai Peninsula from Egypt, the West Bank and East Jerusalem from Jordan, and the Golan Heights from Syria.

As a result of the war, Israel emerged as the dominant regional power, the Arab states were thrown into disarray, and tensions deepened between the United States and the Soviet Union. After the war, the Soviet Union greatly increased support for Egypt, Syria, and Iraq, while the United States began to provide Israel with major arms and economic aid. A regional arms race began in earnest. With Israeli forces on the east bank of the Suez Canal, Egypt shut the waterway, badly damaging its own economy. Some 300,000 more Palestinians had been driven into exile as refugees as well as nearly 100,000 Syrians who lost homes in the Golan Heights.

Differences between the Soviet Union and the United States blocked efforts to end the twenty years of conflict through the UN. Moscow supported UN resolutions condemning Israel and calling on it to return territory gained in the war, while Washington supported Israel's insistence that territory could be returned only through a final peace settlement guaranteeing Israel's security.

The stalemate was broken in November 1967 when the United States and the Soviet Union agreed to a British-sponsored compromise, Security Council *Resolution 242. Its principal components included "the inadmissability of the acquisition of territory by war and the need to work for a just and lasting peace . . . Withdrawal of Israeli armed forces from territories of recent conflict; Termination of all claims or states of belligerency and respect for and acknowledgement of the sovereignty, territorial integrity and political independence of every State in the area . . . [and] a just settlement of the refugee problem . . ."

Parts of the resolution were ambiguous, but it remained the basis of future negotiations. Although the United States, the Soviet Union, Israel, and most Arab states accepted the resolution, they disagreed over the phrase, "withdrawal of Israeli armed forces from territories" occupied during the war.

The Arab states, supported by the Soviet Union and many other UN members, insisted that withdrawal had to be complete, whereas Israel and the United States argued that partial withdrawal could satisfy the resolution.

After the war most Arab states scaled down their terms for a settlement. Few demanded that Israel retreat to the 1947 partition borders or repatriate all the refugees. They now based their demands on Resolution 242: withdrawal to the 1949 armistice frontiers and a solution of the refugee problem that could include alternatives to repatriation.

An important consequence of the 1967 war was revival of Palestinian *Arab nationalism. Palestinians now became disenchanted with leaders of the defeated Arab states and supported recently founded Palestinian groups that proposed to liberate the country by *guerrilla warfare. The largest organization was Fatah; one of its leaders, Yasir *Arafat, soon became leader of the new umbrella group representing Palestinian nationalism—the *Palestine Liberation Organization (PLO).

The focus now shifted from conflict between Israel and Arab governments to conflict between Israel and Palestinian nationalists. The diverse Palestinian factions devised their own strategies to defeat Israel and establish an independent state. Until the 1970s, most Palestinian groups sought total victory though they insisted that Jews in Palestine before Israel was established would be welcome in the "secular, democratic state" they sought to found. Palestinian groups tried to infiltrate guerrillas into Israel; they sometimes struck at targets outside of Israel; some even hijacked civilian aircraft to advance their cause. Palestinian groups and Israeli security services also waged an underground war in Europe.

The Palestinian movement won formal support and even financial backing from most Arab states, although many Arab leaders viewed the Palestinians as dangerous antagonists. By striking at states that harbored Palestinian guerrillas, Israel sought to sharpen this conflict. In 1970, Jordan was the principal Palestinian base and their armed groups became a state within a state, threatening the royal government. In September, Jordan's Army attacked the Palestinians, reimposing control over the border. Because neither Syria nor Egypt permitted autonomous Palestinian presence and guerrilla bases, most Palestinian organizations withdrew to Lebanon; all but Israel's northern border was now relatively secure from guerrilla raids.

After several years Egyptian and Syrian leaders concluded they could not regain territory seized by Israel in 1967 through diplomacy alone. In 1972, Egyptian President Anwar *Sadat discharged his Soviet military advisers, hoping that closer ties with the West would lead to an agreement for Israeli withdrawal. Finally disappointed, he decided to force the issue by war. After secret negotiations, Egypt and Syria opened a two-front surprise attack in October 1973. Initially they drove back the Israelis, recapturing sectors of Sinai and the Golan. Eventually, the tide of battle turned and Israel regained most territories it had occupied before.

The war, known as the October, Yom Kippur, or Ramadan War, shattered the myth of an invincible Israeli army. It nearly became a confrontation between the United States and the Soviet Union when Moscow threatened to send troops to assist Egypt; the United States then declared a high-level military alert. Both superpowers sent airborne resupplies to their allies during the heat of battle. But as the fighting ended, tensions were diffused and the two countries agreed on another Security Council Resolution—338, reaffirming Resolution 242.

An international peace conference convened in Geneva under UN auspices during December of 1973, but broke up after two days. The United States then began a "step-by-step" approach mediated by Secretary of State Henry *Kissinger, who arranged a series of disengagement agreements, two with Egypt and one with Syria, providing for gradual Israeli withdrawal from parts of Sinai and the Golan.

President Sadat of Egypt turned again to diplomacy with a surprise announcement on 9 November 1977 declaring his desire to visit Jerusalem for peace talks with Israel. The Jerusalem visit opened a new phase in Arab-Israeli relations: the first time an Arab head of state traveled to Israel for direct negotiations. When the subsequent talks faltered, U.S. President Jimmy *Carter convened the Israeli and Egyptian leaders at Camp David in September 1978. After thirteen days of acrimonious debate, Carter convinced Sadat and Israeli Prime Minister Menachem Begin to sign accords on a framework for peace.

Following further negotiations, Israel and Egypt signed a peace treaty in Washington, D.C., on 26 March 1979 providing for phased withdrawal of Israeli forces from Sinai and establishing normal ties between the two countries. Because Syrian and Palestinian territories remained occupied, Arab opinion was incensed at the Egyptian step and the country stood isolated in the region for several years.

Relations between Egypt and Israel remained strained, worsened by disputes over implementation of the Camp David Accords and by Israel's hostile relations with other Arab states, especially its attack on Lebanon in 1982. Egypt interpreted the pact to mean full Palestinian self-government; the Israeli government insisted that it was responsible only to offer "autonomy."

Between 1967 and 1987, Palestinians increasingly resisted Israeli rule in the occupied West Bank and Gaza. Israel's leaders believed that Palestinian acts of rebellion were instigated by the PLO and struck at the organization's base in Lebanon. Israel supported anti-Palestinian Maronite forces in the Lebanese civil war which began in 1975. It also mounted air attacks against southern Lebanese towns and villages, culminating in the 1978 invasion taking Israeli forces up to the Litani River. When its forces later withdrew, Israel maintained control over a ten-mile-deep territory north of its border assisted by anti-government Lebanese militias.

In June 1982, Israel struck at Lebanon with a full-scale invasion by 40,000 Israeli troops, supported by massive armor and air raids. Neither the small Lebanese army, nor the Syrians (who occupied part of Lebanon), nor the Palestinian fighters were any match for this force. Israel's siege of Beirut led to international condemnation. Eventually, the United States persuaded Israel to withdraw provided Palestinian and Syrian troops also left the city. The evacuation culminated in the Sabra and Chatilla incident in which right-wing Lebanese Christian militia forces allied with Israel massacred hundreds of Palestinian civilians in the two refugee camps.

The Sabra and Chatilla incident sharpened opposition in Israel to the invasion of Lebanon, becoming a major issue in the 1982 election. After the election, Israel began a phased withdrawal, but left a fifteen-mile-wide strip in south Lebanon under its control and continued to carry out air strikes against Lebanese and Palestinian targets.

Unrest in the West Bank and Gaza erupted again in December 1987 with widespread strikes and demonstrations aimed at Israeli occupation forces. Unlike previous disturbances the demonstrations escalated into a unified uprising called the *intifada, refocusing international attention on the Palestine question. The central issue was the Palestinian demand for an independent state in the West Bank and Gaza alongside Israel.

As a result of the intifada and the confidence it inspired, the PLO recognized UN Resolutions 242 and 338 as the basis for peace discussions. It also renounced the use of *terrorism and agreed to mutual recognition between the Palestinians and Israel. This led to a public dialogue between the United States and the PLO which soon broke down. The Arabs continued to call for a return of all territories occupied in 1967, including East Jerusalem and the Golan Heights, for recognition of the PLO and creation of an independent Palestinian state. Israel refused to talk to the PLO and insisted that it would not give up any occupied territories—building Jewish settlements in the territories instead. Migrations of hundreds of thousands of Soviet Jews to Israel, beginning in 1989, further sharpened controversy.

After the *Gulf War of 1990–1991, the United States undertook yet another major effort to broker a peace agreement. A conference convened in Madrid during October 1991 to initiate bilateral negotiations between Israel and Syria, Lebanon, and Jordan. Israel agreed to Palestinian participation as part of the Jordanian delegation, provided no individuals affiliated with the PLO were represented. After a formal opening session, the conference reconvened into a series of meetings dealing with the disputed issues. A parallel phase convened parties interested in regional water, environment, development, refugee, and disarmament and regional security issues. The Israeli election for the thirteenth Knesset in June 1992 led to replacement of the hard-line Likud bloc by a new government headed by Labor Party leader Yitzhak Rabin.

Because the Madrid negotiations between Israel, Syria, Lebanon, Jordan, and the Palestinians became stalemated, the Rabin government participated in a series of secret talks with the Palestinians in Oslo, Norway, leading to mutual recognition of Israel and the PLO. The outline for a peace agreement between them was signed in Washington in September 1993 under the auspices of U.S. President Bill *Clinton. The agreement was followed by several years of intense negotiations over the details for a peace treaty to be signed by 1999. However, defeat of the Rabin government by Benjamin Netanyahu of the nationalist Likud bloc in 1996 slowed the negotiations. The Likud government accepted the peace treaty signed between Israel and Jordan in October 1994, although relations between Israel and the Arab states greatly deteriorated as a result of Netanyahu's policies. His government was defeated in 1999 by One Israel, a Labor-led coalition headed by former army Chief-of-Staff Ehud Barak, who promised to end the conflict with Syria and the Palestinians and to withdraw Israeli forces from the "security zone" they occupied in south Lebanon. The forces did leave in mid-2000 but negotiations with Syria failed despite U.S. intervention. Barak renewed discussions with PLO leader Arafat, leading to a summit

meeting in Washington in July 2000 sponsored by Clinton. Although progress was made toward agreement over borders between a Palestinian state and Israel, the summit broke down over differences on the future of Palestine refugees and Arab East Jerusalem, captured by Israel from Jordan in 1967.

(See also NATIONALISM; SUEZ CRISIS; UNITED NATIONS; ZIONISM.)

Martin Gilbert, *The Arab-Israeli Conflict, Its History in Maps,* 2d ed. (London, 1976). Walter Laqueur and Barry Rubin, eds., *The Israel-Arab Reader: A Documentary History* (New York, 1984). Don Peretz, *Intifada: The Palestinian Uprising* (Boulder, Colo., and London, 1990). Don Peretz, *Palestinians, Refugees, and the Middle East Peace Process* (Washington, D.C., 1993). Don Peretz, *The Arab-Israel Dispute—Library in a Book* (New York, 1996).

DON PERETZ

ARAFAT, Yasir. Born in Cairo in August 1929, Yasir Arafat was the sixth child of a Palestinian wholesale merchant. His mother died when he was 4 years old, and he was sent to Jerusalem to live with an uncle. As a seven-year-old, he observed at close hand the Arab Revolt of 1936. Returning to Cairo in 1937, he pursued his education and became involved in the Palestinian national movement at an early age.

Like other members of his generation, Arafat was deeply influenced by events of 1948, when 700,000 Palestinians lost their homes and Israel was created. While studying in Cairo, he became increasingly involved in the politics of the Egyptian capital, forming close ties to the Muslim Brotherhood and coming under the influence of radical *Arab nationalism. He soon joined with Salah Khalaf and others to form the Palestinian Student Union and was elected its first president.

After receiving his engineering degree from Cairo University in 1956, Arafat and some friends found work in the booming oil city of Kuwait. There, he took a post with the Kuwaiti Public Works Department, but politics continued to be his real vocation. During meetings held in Kuwait in 1958 and 1959, he joined with Salah Khalaf, Khalil al-Wazir, and others to found the Palestinian Liberation Movement—known as Fatah. For the next five years he devoted himself increasingly to organizing this movement, traveling throughout the *Middle East to contact potential supporters and adherents.

In December 1964, Arafat persuaded his comrades that the time had come to launch an armed struggle against Israel, as Algerians had done against French colonial power ten years before. He quit his job to work full-time for Fatah, and in January 1965, with scant resources, he organized the first guerrilla attacks on Israel from across the Jordanian border.

During this time, he lived on the move between Beirut, Damascus, and Palestinian camps in Jordan, traveling incognito, wearing disguises, and narrowly escaping danger. The guerrilla raids he organized did not affect Israel much—many were intercepted by Israeli security forces—but they won great approval and support among Palestinians and throughout the Arab world. Some Arab governments offered financial aid, although they were very wary of the new movement. In 1966, Arafat was arrested twice in Damascus on orders of Syrian Defense Minister Hafiz al-Asad.

After the Arab-Israeli war of 1967, in which the remainder of Palestine fell under Israeli rule, Arafat infiltrated across the border into the occupied West Bank and tried to build networks and train cadres to foment an uprising. But the population did not respond, and soon Arafat escaped back to Jordan.

In March 1968, hearing of an impending Israeli army attack on a Palestinian camp at Karameh in Jordan, Arafat and some of his Fatah comrades decided to disregard classic guerrilla strategy and engage the Israeli forces. With help from units of the Jordanian army, the Palestinian fighters inflicted heavy casualties on the Israelis. This broadly advertised victory brought Fatah a flood of support; thousands joined the guerrillas, and contributions of money and arms flowed in. Arafat then emerged from the anonymity of Fatah's collective leadership and soon was named the movement's official spokesman.

On 3 February 1969, the Palestine National Council elected Arafat chairman of the Executive Committee of the newly reorganized *Palestine Liberation Organization (PLO). Arafat then presided over the rapid development of the PLO, including the buildup of several thousand armed guerrillas in camps in Jordan. In 1970, Arafat was pushed by the most radical factions into an ill-judged confrontation with the monarchy there; the PLO armed presence in the country was then destroyed by King Hussein's army.

The PLO regrouped in Lebanon, and Arafat sought to build his forces anew. He presided over the organization as it created a state within a state, with military forces as well as many economic and social service organizations. He also gave some support to international terror operations designed to bring pressure on Israel and call attention to the Palestinian cause.

After Israel's victory in the October War of 1973, Arafat won unanimous support for the PLO from Arab heads of state, and in November 1974 he addressed the UN General Assembly. That same year, the PLO took steps toward accepting the existence of Israel and shifted its goals toward creating an independent Palestinian state in the territories occupied by Israel since 1967.

As civil war engulfed Lebanon in 1975, Arafat built the PLO fighters into a standing army outfitted with heavy weapons and even a few old tanks. When the Israeli army moved massively into Lebanon in 1982, PLO military installations in the south were quickly defeated, but Arafat nonetheless led his forces in an epic defense of Beirut. Eventually, he agreed to lead an evacuation of PLO forces from the city.

Shifting headquarters to Tunis, far from Israel's borders, Arafat led the PLO in an increasingly diplomatic strategy for Palestinian rights, first seeking a joint strategy with his old enemy King Hussein. For several years he faced fierce opposition to his leadership from a Syrian-sponsored breakaway group led by Abu Musa, but continuing efforts to evict him from the PLO leadership proved unavailing.

In 1983 he repaired relations with Cairo and began to develop more ties to European governments and improved relations with the United States. The *intifada, or Palestinian uprising in the Occupied Territories, gave new force to the Palestinian cause beginning in late 1987.

In November 1988, Arafat led the Palestine National Congress to support more conciliatory policies, and in December he announced recognition of Israel after addressing the UN General Assembly in Geneva. He was not able to establish a lasting dialogue with the United States at that point, however. After Arafat seemed to side with Iraq in the Gulf War of 1990–1991, the PLO was at first excluded from taking part in the Palestinian-Israeli peace talks that began in Madrid in November 1991.

In spring 1993, the Labor government in Israel established a secret dialogue with the PLO, through meetings held in Norway. In September, the two sides granted unprecedented public recognition to each other, and concluded a "Declaration of Principles" (DOP), which Arafat, Israeli Premier Yitzhak Rabin, and Foreign Minister Shimon Peres signed in a White House ceremony. Under the DOP, Israel allowed Arafat and many lieutenants to return to Gaza and Jericho to set up a self-governing authority; by January 1996, its jurisdiction included all other major Palestinian urban areas of the West Bank, except East Jerusalem. Residents of the West Bank and Gaza then elected a Palestinian legislature, which tried with little success to establish checks to Arafat's power.

The territorial basis for the Palestinian Authority remained problematic. The Rabin government had promised further interim withdrawals prior to implementation of a final status agreement, originally scheduled for May 1999, but after Benjamin Netanyahu won Israel's 1996 election, his government stonewalled on most further withdrawals. The Palestinians were left with varying levels of control over scores of unconnected parcels of land, amidst areas which remained under total Israeli control. Frequent blockades imposed by Israel on the Palestinians made the hoped-for economic boom impossible. The Palestinian economy deteriorated, the residents' disappointment in Arafat and the DOP rose, and Islamic organizations became more popular.

After half a century of effort, Arafat's achievements were partial. In the 1970s and 1980s, he was an important symbol of the rebirth of secular Palestinian nationalism. By the 1990s, he was also seen by many Palestinians as a tragic symbol of national impotence. In addition, his frequent use of "divide and rule" among subordinates—especially after the deaths of key colleagues in 1988 and 1991—left much of Palestinian political life unhealthily divided.

(See also ARAB-ISRAELI CONFLICT; GUERRILLA WARFARE, PALESTINE.)

Helena Cobban, *The Palestinian Liberation Movement* (New York, 1984). John Wallach and Janet Wallach, *Arafat: In the Eyes of the Beholder* (New York, 1990). Andrew Gowers and Tony Walker, *Yasser Arafat and the Palestinian Revolution* (London, 1991). Jane Corbin, *The Norway Channel* (New York, 1994).

HELENA COBBAN

ARENDT, Hannah. Born in Hanover, Germany, in 1906, Hannah Arendt was educated at the universities of Marburg and Heidelberg. At Marburg she studied with Martin Heidegger and Edmund Husserl. At Heidelberg she worked with Karl Jaspers, completing a doctorate on the concept of love in the work of Saint Augustine in 1929. Following Hitler's rise to power in Germany in 1933, she moved to Paris, where she was active in Jewish refugee organizations. In 1941, she escaped Nazi-occupied France and emigrated to the United States, eventually becoming a U.S. citizen. In the United States she taught and lectured at a number of institutions, notably the University of Chicago and the New School for

Social Research in New York City, and produced her best-known work in political thought. She died in New York in 1975.

Arendt was influenced by her teachers as well as by the central figures in German philosophy and culture, notably Immanuel Kant. However, she was no disciple of any of them, instead using their ideas to develop her own distinctive political and philosophical analysis. This has made it difficult to slot her in the ranks of political theorists and has contributed to widely divergent interpretations of her work.

The most powerful image raised by Arendt's work is her own: thinking without a banister. The banister is the Western tradition of political thought as it shaped Western experience from Greek antiquity until the late nineteenth century. Thinking without a banister means starting with the traditional framework and thinking through its limits. That is, one deals with radically new phenomena, especially *totalitarianism and *revolution, in new ways, while respecting the humanist concerns of traditional thought. This involves recovering the original meaning and significance of concepts and issues that the tradition itself has covered up.

Arendt's approach is evident in her account in *The Human Condition* (Chicago, 1950) of "public" and "private" realms. She provocatively argues that what we call the "public" and "private" are in reality neither, but that there has emerged in the modern era a new sphere, the "social." In this realm, private economic matters have become public political ones, to the detriment of both. People are reduced to the status of means to the satisfaction of material ends. Fueled by the requirements of labor, once the most despised but now the most honored of human activities, individuals increasingly relate to each other as interchangeable and dispensable parts of a complex division of labor rather than as citizens consciously sharing a common situation. Both totalitarianism and revolution express these developments (*On Revolution*, New York, 1965; *The Origins of Totalitarianism*, 3d ed., New York, 1973). Arendt finds widespread in the twentieth century a "normal" kind of thoughtlessness that could lead to political evil. The relation between thoughtlessness and the politically unconscionable is given its sharpest statement in Arendt's most controversial work, *Eichmann in Jerusalem* (New York, 1965). In it, she makes a distinctive contribution to political thought by confronting the question of what it means to think politically and the consequences of our failure to do so.

Thinking politically requires above all a strong sense of personal responsibility. *Citizenship involves a concern for a world that was here before we were born and will remain after we have died, a network of common involvements that do not simply serve the reproduction of life. Judging, for Arendt the most political of our mental faculties, allows us to rule on those things that should or should not inhabit this world. The capacity to judge has been seriously eroded in modern society and with it the ability to make distinctions important for both political theory and political practice. Because she wrote with a broad sweep about large-scale historical and philosophical developments, and because she criticized an obsessive focus on the self in modern life, Arendt's concern for the personal in a plural world of many persons can easily be missed. Arendt's "person" is no mere isolated individual. A person exists necessarily in, through, and for others, and they for him or her. Thus to assess or judge a persona is to assess or judge the policy of which this person is a member—and vice versa. The speculative treatment of Adolf Eichmann's motivations or the essays on specific individuals that are collected in *Men in Dark Times* (New York, 1968) are not simply biographical fragments but concrete political analyses whose very specificity brings the larger picture into a new, clearer light.

Hannah Arendt's political thought asks us to think about fundamental political distinctions without the assurance of a generally accepted tradition of cultural norms. It asks us to exercise our reason without assuming the possibility of transparent truths about social and political life. In defending a critical reason and personal responsibility, while at the same time stressing the limits of this reason, Arendt speaks powerfully to an age in which many of the utopian hopes of *modernity and the Enlightenment have been called into question, but which remains inescapably modern.

George Kateb, *Hannah Arendt: Politics, Conscience, Evil* (Totowa, N.J., 1983). Leah Bradshaw, *Acting and Thinking: The Political Thought of Hannah Arendt* (Toronto, 1989). Phillip Hansen, *Hannah Arendt: History, Politics and Citizenship* (Cambridge, U.K., 1991).

PHILIP HANSEN

ARGENTINA. At the beginning of the twentieth century, Argentina ranked among the privileged nations of the world, enjoying European levels of per capita income, urbanization, and literacy. Its sophisticated entrepreneurial class, large and prosperous middle class, relatively well paid urban working class, and the absence of an oppressed peasantry distinguished Argentina from most other Latin American societies. The contrast between its impressive socioeconomic potential and its political instability and economic stagnation since the 1930s has led to the frequent characterization of Argentina as a "riddle" or "paradox."

Historical Background. Independence from Spain in 1816 led to a succession of civil wars during the nineteenth century. On one side were the Buenos Aires-based "Unitarians" who controlled the vast fertile pampa grasslands and the main port, favoring free trade with Europe and a powerful centralized national state. Opposed were the regional elites, known as the "Federalists," who defended provincial autonomy and economic protectionism.

Following the overthrow of the federalist caudillo Juan Manuel de Rosas in 1852, the adroit use of military force, electoral fraud, political concessions, and economic might established the hegemony of the agro-export elite and allied commercial interests of Buenos Aires. These groups created conditions that favored rapid economic *modernization between 1862 and 1916. By World War I, Argentina had consolidated its status as a prosperous semiperipheral society and major exporter of temperate agricultural goods. The population had increased fivefold thanks to massive immigration from Europe.

This economic boom, however, contained the seeds of the destruction of the oligarchical order. The growth of the urban middle class and the resentment of those regional elites excluded from the economic bonanza led in 1891 to the creation of the Unión Cívica Radical (UCR), Argentina's first mass political party. The extraordinary increase in the number of immigrants and urban workers spurred the emergence of anarchist and socialist movements. The rise of militant labor and political organizations, the growing pressure from the moderate opposition, and the realization by the ruling conservative elites that the largely middle-class UCR had no revolutionary intentions facilitated liberalization of the oligarchical system and paved the way for the Radical leader Hipólito Yrigoyen to win the presidency in 1916.

During the period of democratic political stability from 1916 to 1930, conservative groups were partially displaced from political power, but only minor changes were introduced in the socioeconomic domain. The world economic crash of 1929 quickly led to a political crisis that culminated in 1930 in a *coup d'état against the Radical government. This coup orchestrated by the landed and commercial elites, implemented by the army, and supported by middle-class groups, marked a watershed in the country's modern history, inaugurating five decades of political upheaval.

Rise and Decline of Populist Political Economy. The use of coercion and fraud following the coup of 1930 ushered in the long "infamous decade" (1930–1943) of conservative rule. However, the attempt to re-create the traditional export economy and the oligarchic republic was a chimera in the changed domestic and international circumstances engendered by the Great Depression. The emergence of an entrepreneurial class based on *import-substitution industrialization, combined with massive rural-urban migration, sparked fundamental transformations in Argentina's social structure. The onset of World War II gave an additional impetus to industrialization and encouraged a coup against the conservative administration in 1943. Colonel Juan Domingo *Perón emerged as the most skillful of the new generation of politically inclined military officers. Perón moved rapidly to consolidate his popular support and to defeat his conservative and leftist opponents, winning the presidency in 1946.

The support Perón received from the new urban working class, inhabitants of poorer provinces, and substantial sectors of the lower middle class foreshadowed a remarkable transformation of the Argentine political scene. Perón successfully organized a state-controlled corporatist alliance whose bases were organized labor, industrialists producing for the domestic market, and nationalistic military officers. Peronist economic policy consisted of strong state intervention to promote light industrialization; income redistribution; and *nationalization of public utilities, railroads, and foreign trade. While the Peronist regime maintained democratic forms, it did not hesitate to utilize a broad array of authoritarian practices to harass its political adversaries and restrict opposition political parties.

By the 1950s, the regime began to crumble in the face of severe balance-of-payments problems, a swollen public sector deficit, and mounting inflationary pressures. Renewed struggles over income shares among members of the Peronist coalition, plus growing resistance to Perón by the military, rural producers and urban entrepreneurial interests, and the Catholic Church led to a military coup in September 1955 that toppled the regime.

Stalemate, Cyclical Crises, and Modern Authoritarianism. During the decade following Perón's overthrow, successive semidemocratic and dictatorial governments found it virtually impossible to implement the coherent macroeconomic policies necessary to modernize Argentina's semiclosed economy. In June 1966 a military coup overthrew the elected Radical government of Arturo Illia and imposed an authoritarian regime presided over by General Juan Carlos Onganía. The self-proclaimed "Argentine Revolution" sought to implement a new strategy of state-led development designed to deepen import-substitution industrialization. Following the 1969 Cordobazo, an unprecedented mass uprising, a confluence of factors—including military factionalism, the evaporation of entrepreneurial support, mounting mass mobilization, and increasingly radical opposition from revolutionary guerrilla groups—led to a spiral of *political violence and popular protests and the rebirth of the civilian opposition spearheaded by Peronists and Radicals. The armed forces' reluctant acceptance of a transition to civilian rule facilitated Juan Perón's return to Argentina in 1972 and paved the way for his electoral victory in 1973.

Hopes for a return to democracy and economic growth were dashed by Perón's death in 1974, the escalation of revolutionary and counterrevolutionary violence, and the vacillating performance of the government headed by his widow, María Estela Martínez de Perón. The discredited Peronist government was overthrown in March 1976.

The military conducted a "dirty war" of state terrorism against a wide array of regime opponents. The official number of reported deaths was nearly 10,000, while the unofficial tally of killed and "disappeared" was estimated at 25,000–30,000. Headed by General Jorge Rafael Videla, the military and their business and technocratic allies attempted to restructure the state, society, and economy following the tenets of "free-market" *monetarism. These economic policies provoked rampant financial speculation and triple-digit inflation, while much of the country's industrial base was dismantled and tens of thousands of blue- and white-collar jobs were eliminated in the manufacturing sector. Economic disaster was fueled by a massive foreign debt, which soared from US$7 billion to over US$43 billion in 1981. However, the subsequent collapse of the military dictatorship was less the result of the economic crisis than the consequence of the disastrous April 1982 decision to invade the Malvinas/Falkland Islands. Humiliating defeat at the hands of *Britain left the military regime with a bankrupt economy. Deep divisions within the armed forces, coupled with the resurgence of civilian opposition, forced the military to accede to elections.

Travails of Democratic Consolidation. Raúl Alfonsín and his Radical Party came to power in late 1983. The difficulties of reconciling growth, monetary stability, and service on the huge external debt with popular expectations for strong control over the military, income redistribution, and social justice proved insurmountable. The failure of the Radical "heterodox shock" economic policies led to hyperinflation and contributed to the victory of the Peronist Carlos Saúl Menem in the May 1989 presidential election.

Menem's government repudiated most of Peronism's populist and statist legacy and carried out a far-ranging project of neoliberal free-market economic reforms featuring privatization of state enterprises, financial deregulation, liberalization of international trade, and promotion of foreign investment, as well as labor market reforms that undercut the bargaining power of the Peronist-controlled trade unions. The cornerstone of the new economic program was the "Convertibility Plan" of 1991, which rapidly brought inflation under control, with prices rising at an annual rate of less than 1 percent by the end of the decade. The economy expanded by more than 30 percent between 1991 and 1994, before entering a new period of stagnation followed by a slow recovery and a new recession in 1999. This irregular pattern of growth took place in the context of the rapid economic integration within the MERCOSUR (Southern Cone Common Market), a regional trade bloc comprising Argentina, Brazil, Uruguay, and Paraguay. Menem also succeeded in significantly reducing the defense budget and restoring civilian control over the armed forces.

Market-oriented policies exacerbated social inequality and concentrated income and wealth in the hands of a minority. Unemployment rose to more than 18 percent in 1995, before declining to a still very high 13 percent in 2000. Consequently, although Argentina's per capita income of approximately US$9,000 ranks as the highest in Latin America, in the 1990s social inequality increased significantly and a third of the country's population remained below the official poverty line. Further underscoring the fragility of the new economic model, the foreign debt reached US140 billion in 1999 and the persistent trade deficit made Argentina increasingly vulnerable to the vagaries of highly volatile international capital flows.

Notwithstanding these problems, the newfound economic stability won Menem considerable support among all sectors of society and enabled him to garner the Radical Party's endorsement for constitutional reforms in 1994, including the incumbent president's right to stand for immediate reelection. A preference for continuity carried Menem to an impressive victory, with nearly 50 percent of the vote in the 1995 presidential election.

During Menem's second administration, high unemployment, widespread allegations of corruption and police brutality, growing insecurity, and distrust of the judiciary sharply eroded the government's popularity. Thus the two main opposition parties, the Radicals and a center-left coalition called FREPASO (Frente del País Solidario), established an electoral front calling for the maintenance of macroeconomic stability but with greater respect for democratic institutions and more emphasis on social programs to promote greater equity. Following its victory in the 1997 congressional elections, the new opposition "Alliance for Work, Justice, and Education" confronted Peronism for control over the national government. In the 1999 presidential elections, Fernando de la Rúa, the Alliance candidate and mayor of the city of Buenos Aires, received 48.5 percent of the popular vote, soundly defeating Eduardo Duhalde, the Peronist's standard-bearer.

Democratic governability in post-Menem Argentina faced multiple challenges. On the economic front, the De la Rúa government confronted persistent problems with the fiscal deficit, high unemployment, and difficulties in improving Argentina's competitiveness in global markets. On the political front, De la Rúa had to strengthen the cohesiveness of his center-left coalition and establish a *modus vivendi* with the Peronist opposition, which retained influence over the Supreme Court and control over the Federal Senate and a majority of provincial governorships.

Argentina is well advanced in the consolidation of a liberal and competitive democracy. This is a considerable achievement for a country that, from 1930 until 1983, had 26 successful military coups and 16 army generals among its 24 presidents. The groups that in the past had supported authoritarianism—the armed forces, the dominant classes, sectors of organized labor, and right-wing groups within the Peronist movement—all appear to have accepted the democratic rules of the game. With its democracy consolidated, Argentina's challenge for the future will be to improve the quality of its political institutions by assuring the accountability of the executive branch, respecting the independence of the Congress and the judicial system, and strengthening the democratic values and actors of civil society. Finally, to enhance democratic governability and legitimacy, Argentina will need to achieve stable long-term economic growth, significantly reducing poverty and social inequalities.

(See also AUTHORITARIANISM; DEMOCRATIC TRANSITIONS; MALVINAS/FALKLANDS WAR; MILITARY RULE; PERÓN, MARÍA EVA DUARTE DE; POPULISM.)

David Rock, *Argentina, 1516–1987: From Spanish Colonization to Alfonsín*, 2d ed. (Berkeley, Calif., 1987). Guillermo O'Donnell, *Bureaucratic Authoritarianism: Argentina, 1966–1973, in Comparative Perspective* (Berkeley, Calif., 1988). William C. Smith, *Authoritarianism and the Crisis of the Argentine Political Economy* (Stanford, Calif., 1991). Edward Gibson, *Class and Conservative Parties: Argentina in Comparative Perspective* (Baltimore, 1996). James W. McGuire, *Peronism Without Perón: Unions, Ties, and Democracy in Argentina* (Stanford, Calif., 1997). David Pion-Berlin, *Through the Corridors of Power: Institutions and Civil-Military Relations in Argentina* (University Park, Pa., 1997).

WILLIAM C. SMITH
ALDO C. VACS

ARIAS, Oscar. President of *Costa Rica from 1986 to 1990, Oscar Arias Sánchez received the Nobel Peace Prize in 1987 for his efforts to develop a peace plan to end the warfare that plagued *Nicaragua, *El Salvador, and *Guatemala in the 1980s. His proposal, commonly known as Esquipulas II, was originally sketched out on a napkin in the cafeteria of Washington's Mayflower Hotel in September 1985, eight months prior to Arias's election as president. Aimed at building on the efforts of the Contadora countries (Colombia, Mexico, Panama, and Venezuela), which had initiated a peace process in 1984, it called for internal dialogue within each country between the government and the opposition, a cease-fire and amnesty for guerrillas and political prisoners, freedom of speech, and free elections. It also called on foreign governments to stop aiding the guerrillas.

As president of the most democratic country in the region, which had eliminated its army in 1948, Arias used his moral authority, bolstered by the Nobel Peace Prize, to pressure the Central American presidents to abide by the plan. Ultimately it contributed to the end of warfare in Nicaragua in 1989, El Salvador in 1992, and Guatemala in 1996. The plan also emphasized greater regional political and economic cooperation and was regarded as a Central American declaration of independence from the superpowers.

Born into a wealthy coffee-growing family that had a long history of public service, Arias received degrees in law and economics from the University of Costa Rica in 1967 and in political science from the University of Essex in England in 1974. Arias entered government service in 1970 as a member of the economic council of President José Figueres (1970–1974) and as vice president of the Board of Directors of the Central Bank. From 1972 to 1975 he served as minister of national *planning and economic policy. In this post he followed a pragmatic course admitting the limits of state planning, particularly in small open economies such as Costa Rica's.

In February 1978 Arias was elected to the National Assembly where he promoted constitutional and electoral reform. In July 1979 he was chosen general secretary of the Partido de Liberación Nacional and was reelected in 1983. That post provided a base for his eventual campaign for his party's nomination for the presidency. During the campaign Arias portrayed himself as the candidate who was most likely to promote peace in the region.

As president Arias renegotiated Costa Rica's foreign debt—which in 1986 was estimated to be the highest per capita debt in the world (US$1,800)—providing some short-term relief. Efforts to deemphasize Costa Rica's dependence on coffee for export earnings by encouraging an expansion of nontraditional exports such as flowers and textiles had limited success. The government also encouraged a substantial expansion of tourist facilities to generate foreign exchange. Attempts to deal with deficit spending via cutbacks in government social welfare programs and reduction of consumer price subsidies brought dissension within Arias's cabinet as well as public opposition. Arias's administration was, however, successful in implementing a program to finance low-and middle-income housing and spent more than twenty times as much on education and health care as on security.

Arias nevertheless continues to be best known for his assidousness in convincing the Central American presidents to sign the Esquipulas II agreement on 7 August 1987 and then pressuring them, as well as the United States, Cuba, and the Soviet Union, to support the peace process. While President Reagan initially categorized the agreement as fatally flawed, it garnered considerable support in the U.S. Congress and ultimately undercut funding for the counterrevolutionary forces attempting to overthrow the Sandinista government in Nicaragua. The State Department and some members of Congress attempted to pressure Arias by intimating that U.S. economic aid might be cut. Once Arias received the Nobel Peace Prize, however, such pressures diminished.

Arias used the money from the Peace Prize to establish the Arias Foundation for Peace and Human Progress, which focuses on promoting nonviolent conflict resolution, demilitarization, ecological preservation, and the reduction of socioeconomic injustice. To those who have accused Arias of rampant idealism, he has replied: "Politicians have an obligation to be dreamers, to be idealists, to be Quixotes. It is our obligation to want to change things. Nobody in Central America can be satisfied with the status quo. There is too much poverty, violence, hunger, and misery."

(See also U.S.–LATIN AMERICAN RELATIONS.)

Oscar Arias Sánchez, *Nuevos rumbos para el desarrollo costarricense.* 2d ed. (San José, Costa Rica, 1984). Oscar Arias Sánchez, *Quién gobierna en Costa Rica?* (San José, Costa Rica, 1984). Guido Fernádez, *El primer domingo de febrero: Crónica interior de la elección de Oscar Arias* (San José, Costa Rica, 1986). Lowell Gudmundson, "Costa Rica's Arias at Midterm" *Current History* (December 1987): 417–420, 431–432. Edward J. Heubal, "Costa Rican Interpretations of Costa Rican Politics" *Latin American Research Review*, 25, no. 2 (1990): 217–225.

MARGARET E. CRAHAN

ARMENIA. Premodern Armenian society existed on the Anatolian plateau as early as the second millennium B.C.E. It gave rise to several important kingdoms and eventually produced a distinct language and alphabet and a distinct religious institution known as the Armenian Apostolic Church. Armenian territory passed under the rule of a number of foreign conquerors and was fought over between rival empires: Persians, Byzantines, Ottomans, and Russians. Thanks to their geographic position, Armenians played an important role in trade between Europe and Asia.

Modern Armenian *nationalism arose in the late nineteenth century, when the territory was under Ottoman and Russian rule. Armenian nationalists formed parties and secret societies to press for Ottoman reforms. Three major parties were formed during this period: the Armenakan, the social democratic party Hnchakian, and the Armenian Revolutionary Federation (Dashnaktsutiun). All such reform efforts were forcibly repressed, with large-scale massacres of Armenians taking place in Ottoman Armenia in 1895–1896.

During World War I, the Istanbul government regarded its Armenian population as unreliable and potentially subversive, despite Armenian declarations of loyalty. Consequently, in 1915 the government decided to deport the entire Armenian population—nearly 2 million people—to Syria and Mesopotamia. Deportations continued until 1918; it has been estimated that as many as 1.5 million Armenians died or were killed en route, in what became known as the Armenian *genocide. As a result of continuing persecution, Armenians emigrated throughout the world and today form significant communities in Russia (~200,000), the United States (~1,000,000), France (~400,000), Georgia (~350,000), Iran (~200,000), Lebanon (~190,000), Latin America (~180,000), and elsewhere.

In May 1918 Armenians established an independent republic, with the capital at Yerevan, in lands of the former Russian Empire. In late 1920 the Armenian government surrendered authority to the communists as Turkey pressed Armenia at its western border. By 1990 the population of Soviet Armenia had grown to about 3 million, and the republic had become relatively prosperous, with an industrialized economy and many cultural institutions.

The tumultuous changes occurring throughout the Soviet Union beginning in the late 1980s inevitably had repercussions in Armenia. A movement to unite the republic with the Armenian enclave in the Nagorno-Karabagh autonomous region inside neighboring Soviet Azerbaijan resulted in outbreaks of interethnic violence that drove some 300,000 Armenians from Azerbaijan between 1988 and 1990. In 1992 the independent Nagorno-Karabagh Republic was unilaterally declared. War between the breakaway republic and Azerbaijan ended with a cease-fire in 1994.

In 1990, in the first democratic election held in Armenia during the Soviet era, noncommunist parties, notably the Armenian Pan-National Movement, won a majority of seats in the legislature. In March 1991 the government announced Armenia's intention to withdraw from the Soviet Union, a process which was accomplished in September 1991. In October 1991 Levon Ter-Petrossian was elected the first president of Armenia. He was reelected in 1996 but resigned in February 1998. In March 1998 Robert Kocharian, the former president of the Nagorno-Karabagh Republic, was elected president.

Richard G. Hovannisian, *Armenia on the Road to Independence, 1918* (Berkeley, Calif., 1967). Richard G. Hovannisian, *The Republic of Armenia*, 4 vols. (Berkeley, Calif., 1971–1996). Claire Mouradian, *De Staline à Gorbatchev, histoire d'une république soviétique: L'Arménie* (Paris, 1990).
LEVON ABRAHAMAN

ARMS CONTROL. The precise origin of the term "arms control" is unclear, although arms control endeavors can be found throughout recorded history. The term came into wide use by the early 1960s to distinguish limitations on arms and forces from *disarmament. The most influential definition is the functional one offered by Thomas Schelling and Morton Halperin in *Strategy and Arms Control:* "all the forms of military cooperation between potential enemies in the interest of reducing the likelihood of war, its scope and violence if it occurs, and the political and economic costs of being prepared for it." This falls short of encompassing all arms control activities because some are not cooperative in nature and a few are not military-related (such as the Hot Line). It is also worth emphasizing that arms control is intended to enhance *security, and is often said to fulfill other functions such as strengthening political relationships among states or helping governments control their military establishments.

Although arms control can include selective reductions in, or elimination of, some weapons and forces, it differs from disarmament in its assumption that states continue to see military forces as useful or vital in international politics so they will continue to exist and be used. Disarmament is pursued in the belief that military forces are pernicious and should be eliminated so they cannot be used. Thus the two overlap in some actions but not in basic conception. From an arms control perspective, conditions sometimes make it wise to increase weapons or forces and undesirable to reduce them. Advocates have often seen arms control as a more realistic route to security than disarmament.

Historically, the urge to get *war and the burdens of preparing for it under more control can be traced to two broad impulses. One is a military distaste for weapons that discount martial values such as courage and honor. For instance, some military figures opposed the crossbow, the use of gunpowder, and the submarine on these grounds, and modern soldiers have condemned *nuclear weapons partly because they cancel the meaning of traditional military values in combat and call into question the use of military forces as instruments of *foreign policy. The other impulse is civilian repugnance at steadily more destructive weapons and wars. In this century the latter has dominated—arms control theory was largely developed by civilian analysts, and arms control proposals have generally had less support in military than civilian circles.

These impulses compete with offsetting ones. There is the compelling desire to survive and be victorious should war occur—arms control restraints risk defeat and death, and arms limitations are particularly difficult to sustain in a war. There is also suspicion about other governments' intentions, including the fear that they will evade or cheat on any arms control arrangements. Arms control thus becomes a variant of the problem of cooperation under *anarchy—a dilemma in which potentially beneficial cooperative limitations can allow someone to gain an advantage by evading them, breeding suspicion that others will cheat and the temptation to cheat oneself so that reaching and sustaining acceptable agreements is difficult.

Modern arms control theory was primarily developed in a brief period (roughly 1958–1962) in conjunction with *deterrence theory. It suggested that overcoming the cooperation-under-anarchy dilemma was both necessary and feasible in the context of nuclear deterrence. States had immense mutual interests in limiting the *arms race, in preventing nuclear deterrence from breaking down (keeping it "stable"), and in limiting any war that occurred. Thus even hostile states could and should cooperate for this common interest, while stable nuclear deterrence would curb the incentive to defect from the cooperation. Although this cooperation pertained to nuclear forces in particular, it was but a short step to suggest cooperation below the nuclear level as well, because conventional arms buildups and deployments, also costly, could readily lead to instability, confrontations, and fighting that might escalate to the nuclear level. The point of the theory was to assist governments in seeing the virtue and necessity of arms control and to help identify the steps that should (and should not) be taken. Given the overwhelming concern with nuclear weapons, the theory did not rest on a thorough analysis of parallel ideas and previous experience with arms control in the prenuclear era, and to this day no comprehensive history of arms control has been written.

Arms control measures can be unilateral (i.e., steps to prevent accidental or unauthorized firing of one's nuclear weapons), bilateral, or multilateral. Arms control can develop informal agreements or negotiated treaties. It can take effect at any stage in the life cycle of weapons and forces: development, deployment, decision to use, and use. It is often categorized by the nature of the weapons and forces involved or the functional purpose of the measures. The following typology offers examples and summarizes many current arms control initiatives venues:

• Control of strategic nuclear weapons: The Strategic Arms Limitation Talks (SALT) I ABM Treaty (1972) banned Soviet and American development and deployment of dense nationwide antiballistic missile defenses, to stabilize deterrence and reduce chances of war. The SALT I Interim Offensive Arms Agreement (1972) limited the number of Soviet and American intercontinental ballistic missiles and submarine-based missiles. The SALT II agreement (1979), never ratified but generally observed, set limits on the numbers of each type of Soviet and American strategic bombers and missiles and on the number of nuclear weapons each delivery vehicle could carry. The Strategic Arms Reduction Talks (START) I Treaty (1991) ordered cuts in U.S. and Soviet strategic nuclear weapons from roughly 12,000 to approximately 9,000 each, and the START II treaty (1993 but not ratified until 2000) lowered this limit to a maximum of 3,500 to be reached, under a 1998 amendment, by the year 2007. These agreements also order the deactivation of land-based missiles that carry more than one warhead each by 2003 and their destruction by 2007. The two parties have agreed to negotiate a follow-on agreement that will lower the maximum number to 2,000–2,500 by 2007.

• Control of intermediate-range or tactical nuclear weapons: the Intermediate Nuclear Forces (INF) Treaty (1987) banned development and deployment of nuclear-armed ballistic and cruise (land-based) missiles with ranges of 300 to 3,400 miles and ordered all existing ones in the Soviet, U.S., and West German arsenals destroyed.

- Control of nuclear proliferation: The Nuclear Nonproliferation Treaty (1968) seeks to prevent development/deployment of nuclear weapons by states that do not already possess them. It was indefinitely extended in 1995, with over 180 states now parties to it.
- Control of nuclear testing: the Limited Test Ban Treaty (1963) banned testing in the atmosphere or at sea to protect people from radioactive fallout. The subsequent Comprehensive Test Ban Treaty (1996) banned all nuclear tests, including ones below ground, and is aimed at preventing further development of nuclear weapons.
- Nuclear-free zones: the Antarctic Treaty (1959), the Treaty for Prohibition of Nuclear Weapons in Latin America (1967), the Outer Space Treaty (1967), and the Seabed Treaty (1971) barred nuclear weapons from their respective areas. Additional nuclear-free zones were established in Africa and Southeast Asia in 1996.
- Control of conventional forces: the Paris Treaty on Conventional Armed Forces in Europe (CFE) of 1990, with later amendments, limits forces in Europe so as to enhance deterrence by curbing the threat of large military attacks by surprise. The Land Mines Convention (1997) outlaws possession and use of anti-personnel mines, primarily to protect civilians.
- Control of chemical and biological weapons: the Geneva Protocol (1925) banned the use of chemical weapons; the Chemical Weapons Convention (1993) forbids development and deployment of all such weapons and ordered destruction of existing stocks. The Biological Weapons Convention (1972) did the same for those weapons, and efforts to add major verification requirements will be made when the convention is reviewed in 2000.
- Preventing accidental or unauthorized use: "Permissive Action Links" on American nuclear weapons make them inoperable when tampered with and unusable without inserting a code sent from the National Command Center. Other states have similar arrangements.
- Avoidance or management of dangerous situations: the U.S.-Soviet agreement on Measures to Reduce the Risk of Outbreak of Nuclear War (1971) called for immediate notification by the parties of any serious accident or unauthorized incident involving nuclear weapons. Hot Line agreements, which continue to multiply, have created continuous communications links among states for use in emergencies.
- Limiting wars: nonuse of the most destructive weapons is one way wars are limited. Another example is the Geneva Convention (latest version 1949) on humane treatment of prisoners of war.

Four concerns have been preeminent in shaping arms control since World War II. One is a desire to limit or outlaw particularly horrendous weapons. A second is to stabilize deterrence by restricting "provocative" weapons and forces, ones which could increase the incentives to initiate a war, particularly in a crisis. This includes nuclear weapons ideal for a war-winning initial attack, defensive systems that could undermine an opponent's deterrence threats, highly offensive-oriented conventional forces, forces unusually vulnerable to an attack, and command and control systems very vulnerable to attack. The third concern is to prevent accidental or unauthorized use of weapons by terrorists or unbalanced individuals or due to mechanical malfunctions. The final concern is to limit proliferation of nuclear weapons and related delivery systems.

Since arms control is an issue between states involved in a competitive, sometimes very hostile, relationship, progress is heavily dependent on a set of political factors. To begin with, arms control is normally affected by the tenor of the political relationships of the parties, and its status is often taken as a barometer of those relationships. There is debate about the necessity and wisdom of this linkage. One view holds that mutual interests in arms control should and can override a highly adversarial relationship—especially with respect to nuclear weapons. The opposite view, now fairly widely accepted, is that when political relationships are poor (especially if they are deteriorating) serious cooperation to limit arms is unlikely. Thus some analysts have charged that arms control is possible mainly when it is unnecessary, and unreachable when most needed.

Next, arms control is normally pursued within a strong concern for verification, and agreements are often confined to what states believe they can verify and will permit others to verify. This adds greatly to the complexities in negotiations, ratification, and implementation. Another factor is that arms control rarely restricts weapons and forces to which the parties attach great importance and strongly wish to refine or expand. States have also often designed around agreements, thereby circumventing their provisions. This incites complaints that arms control is peripheral, used at the margins and too often pursued to create an illusion of restraint that is politically appealing at home and abroad.

Finally, arms control is politically popular in principle but actual agreements and practices are often controversial. This makes it difficult for several parties to gain and sustain a sufficient domestic consensus simultaneously. Negotiations at home, on bargaining positions or for ratification of agreements, can be as difficult as those with other states. Hence, crafting acceptable agreements is often very complex and time consuming, with a good possibility of failure or of agreements being outmoded by political developments or technological change before they are finally signed. To avoid such problems, some analysts and officials favor taking informal unilateral (but parallel) steps to limit arms when conditions will permit and on those lines the United States and Russia at times have begun implementing agreements they cannot get ratified.

The theory of arms control can explain what it is, why and how it can be useful, and why it is possible. The theory is weaker concerning when and why it is attained or fails, with disagreement continuing about the factors involved (international system structure, technological change, bureaucratic interests, domestic politics, etc.) and their relative impact. As a result, there is little agreement about the status of arms control. Is it success independent of broader developments in international politics or determined by them?

International politics now operates within an elaborate web of arms control practices and agreements, and, in tandem with nuclear deterrence, arms control has been the foremost route to security adopted by major states in the past half-century. The CFE Agreement among virtually all governments in Europe and North America arranged for destruction or removal of over 100,000 pieces of military equipment and elaborate restraints on deployments of forces. The United States and Russia are destroying their huge chemical weapons stocks. The INF Treaty led to the elimination of 2,767 missiles. The START Agreements will slash strategic nuclear weapons to roughly one-sixth of Cold War levels; the United States and Russia have also undertaken unilateral elimination or storage of thousands of short-range nuclear weapons, and Britain and France have significantly reduced their nuclear arsenals. The number of nuclear weapons states has risen only slightly since 1990, and the number actively seeking nuclear weapons has not increased. The first UN effort to uproot a mass-destruction-weapons program was undertaken in Iraq. The capabilities of the International Atomic Energy Agency to detect clandestine nuclear programs have been greatly expanded. Nonproliferation agreements are bolstered by cooperation among suppliers of sensitive military systems—the Nuclear Suppliers Group, the Wassenaar Arrangement (on conventional weapons), the Missile Technology Control Regime, the Zangger Committee (on nuclear nonproliferation), and the Australia Group for chemical weapons control. These developments occurred following a period, 1975–1985, when optimism regarding and support for arms control were quite low, suggesting that it is a durable and significant phenomenon.

However, the arms control web is sometime fragile, incomplete, and not a fine mesh. Ballistic missiles and other nuclear delivery systems continue to proliferate widely, and fear of the resumption of outright proliferation was heightened by the 1998 nuclear tests by India and Pakistan. The Comprehensive Test Ban is not officially in force until the U.S., India, Pakistan, and Israel sign and ratify it, which they have yet to do—and this may force other states to use alternative arrangements to put it into operation. Several states have demonstrated that a substantial clandestine weapons program can still escape international detection. Japan has established a "virtual" nuclear arsenal by stockpiling plutonium and developing components for future delivery vehicles, and other states may follow suit. The five original nuclear powers have suspended production of fissionable material for weapons but a treaty on this has been blocked by India and Pakistan. The United States and Russia have sophisticated programs in place to refine their nuclear arsenals without nuclear testing and still possess over 10,000 nuclear weapons apiece. Conventional arms continue to spread, as does their manufacture, with almost no restraints. Technological change has produced numerous new weapons which could be destabilizing to deterrence and make verification more complicated. Arms control advocates fear that the ABM Treaty will soon be undermined by U.S. determination to build national and theater missile defenses. Chemical weapons were used in the Iran-Iraq war on a scale not seen since World War I. Thus, critics of arms control's utility have plenty of ammunition.

As the century begins, the main focus is on securing universal adherence to the Comprehensive Test Ban and the Land Mines Convention, generating further deep cuts in American and Russian nuclear arsenals, and drawing the other nuclear powers into nuclear reduction agreements. Campaigns will continue for adoption of no-first-use policies on nuclear weapons and their eventual elimination. The destruction of chemical weapons stocks must be completed. Concern about the poor controls on conventional weapons will continue, but serious progress here is much in doubt.

(See also ARMS RACE; BALANCE OF POWER; INTERNATIONAL COOPERATION; INTERNATIONAL LAW; STRATEGY; WAR CRIMES; WAR, RULES OF.)

Albert Carnesdale and Richard N. Haass, *Superpower Arms Control: Setting the Record Straight* (Cambridge, Mass., 1987). Patrick M. Morgan, "On Strategic Arms Control and International Security," in Edward A. Kolodziej and Patrick M. Morgan, eds., *Security and Arms Control: A Guide to International Policymaking, Volume Two* (New York, 1989): 299–318. Jeffrey A. Larsen and Gregory J. Rattray, eds., *Arms Control: Toward the Twenty-first Century* (Boulder, Colo., 1996). Jonathan Dean and Jeffrey Laurenti, *Options and Opportunities: Arms Control and Disarmament for the Twenty-first Century* (New York, 1997).

PATRICK M. MORGAN

ARMS RACE. The precise origin of the term *arms race* is obscure, but it seems to have first appeared in England during the late 1850s when journalists and politicians began to use it to describe the competitive, interstate accumulation of naval combat vessels by Britain and France. The timing of the term's appearance can probably be explained by the fact that it was around this time that technologically advanced and expensive weapons began to assume greater importance. A large number of infantry could be mobilized and sent into the field in a matter of months. The same thing could not be said about ironclad frigates. This meant that the nation with the largest number of such vessels at the outset of a *war possessed an important and potentially critical advantage. Not surprisingly, nations soon found themselves in a race to have the most modern as well as the largest navies. No less predictably, they turned to the technologies created by the emerging industrial revolution to help them accomplish their ends.

Both the scholarly and popular literatures have continued the tradition of applying the term *arms race* to describe a competition involving major weapons systems and technological innovations. A simpler troop buildup has rarely been viewed as an arms race. The Anglo-French arms race of 1859–1860 was precipitated by the French construction of the ironclad *La Gloire* and its plan to build sixteen others. The arms race between the United States and the Soviet Union focused on the development of *nuclear weapons and missile systems. The close historical relationship between arms races and technology explains why the arms race literature has had what might appear to be a myopic and discriminatory preoccupation with the arms races between European nations and those involving major world powers such as Japan and the United States. This situation has been changed somewhat in recent years with the growing technological character of the arms buildups in the Middle East and South Asia.

What Is an Arms Race? The 1850s common language definition of an arms race as an "intense competition over the rapid accumulation of weaponry that requires a significant amount of time and/or money to produce" is as relevant today as it was a century and a half ago, but scholars have disagreed about the degree of competition that must be present to justify the use of the term *arms race*. For example, the United States and Iran both initiated major new arms programs in the 1980s. However, no one would argue that they were in an arms race because it is obvious that neither program was inspired by the other. The buildups were not competitive. The same thing can be said of parts of the apparent arms race between the United States and the Soviet Union during a substantial portion of the *Cold War. For example, a close examination of the historical record during the years of the Reagan administration reveals that much of the increase in the defense budget of United States was inspired more by the domestic imperatives of the campaign strategy that Ronald *Reagan used against Jimmy *Carter than by the rate of Soviet arms procurement or the desire to establish strategic superiority. One important implication of the multitude of rationales that underlie arms races is that the dream of game theorists to characterize all arms races by reference to a single game such as the Prisoner's Dilemma will probably not be realized.

The pattern of arms growth that must be present is also problematic. Lewis Richardson, the best-known arms race theorist, argued that the rate of arms accumulation in an arms race either converges to a stable growth rate or continues to accelerate. This model provides an adequate description of the arms race preceding *World War I, the inspiration for much of Richardson's work, but it is now clear that most arms races do not fit this neat pattern. The arms race between the United States and Soviet Union provides one of the clearest exceptions. Over its forty-year history there were periods when both nations were accelerating their rates of arms acquisitions, periods when they both were reducing the rate of acquisitions, and periods when the growth in arms stocks of one nation was accelerating while that of the other was declining. This complexity characterizes any group of arms races as well. If one examines ten different arms races, it becomes clear that the pattern of growth rate varies across the races. While the arms race that culminated in World War I was characterized both by large increases in the number of weapons (an absolute measure of arms race intensity) and a proportionate increase in the number of weapons available in each nation's stockpile (a relative measure), this is not always the case. Many naval arms races of the nineteenth century involved only modest increases in absolute number of weapons, and some of those in the late twentieth century involve only modest relative increases in available forces.

Do Arms Races Cause Wars? After decades of systematic study, the relationship between arms races and wars remains a contentious issue. There is a general recognition that many wars have not been preceded by arms races (e.g., Boer War, *Vietnam War) and many arms races have not led to war (e.g., Anglo-French naval race of 1859, postwar arms race between the United States and Soviet Union). However, there is little agreement on whether the existence of an arms race increases or decreases the chances that an antagonism between two states will erupt into war. One tradition of scholarship believes that arms races increase the probability of war by mutually exacerbating the perception of hostility. This occurs because each nation sees the other as more aggressive because of its arms policy. Another tradition believes that arms races often reduce the probability by mutually increasing the cost of aggression.

Since 1970, a growing number of social scientists have begun to believe that there is no simple answer to the question of whether or not arms races cause wars. They argue that the empirical record reveals that there are times when arms races have increased the likelihood of conflict and other times when they have reduced it. Whether or not a particular arms race will increase the risk of war depends on a host of factors. These include national goals, strategic choices, the current technology of war, and the level of misperception and uncertainty that exist. Because these factors vary from case to case, the likelihood that an arms race will lead to war varies as well. If correct, this helps to account for why previous scholars from each competing tradition have been able to find evidence in support of their positions. To complicate matters still further, this third school believes that any estimate of the "average" likelihood that an arms race will lead to war can be expected to vary from decade to decade as technologies and the distribution of other key factors such as goals and resources change.

Despite the evolution of this more contingent vision of the relationship between arms races and war, policymakers faced with the choice of whether or not to develop a new weapons system can still find themselves in a quandary. The question is not whether the development of the system will increase the price that a rival perceives that it must pay for initiating conflict or whether it will increase the rival's perception of the offensive threat that can be mounted against it—except in rare cases it will do both. What matters is the precise trade-off between the *security induced by increasing the cost of aggression and the insecurity induced by increasing the perception of hostile intent. In some contexts this trade-off is fairly obvious. A nation in a situation of highly redundant mutually assured destruction (MAD) is unlikely to have its security threatened by a modest increase in the capabilities of its rival. On the other hand, a non-nuclear power with a significant arms advantage might be tempted to initiate a preventive war in order to stave off the impact of an arms race that it feels it will lose. Unfortunately, most intent/cost trade-offs are not so clear.

For now, two prescriptions are believed to hold across the widest variety of contexts. Decision makers should: 1) respond to an arms increase on the part of an adversary with a slightly smaller increase; and 2) concentrate on defense. It is recognized that few weapons will be viewed as being entirely defensive, but it is also true that some weapons will be viewed by a rival as much more defensive than others. These two prescriptions both possess the twin virtues of minimizing the chances that the action will be interpreted as indicating aggressive intent without signaling weakness or the willingness to be exploited.

(See also ARMS CONTROL; GAME THEORY; STRATEGIC ARMS LIMITATION TREATIES.)

Lewis F. Richardson, *Arms and Insecurity* (Pittsburgh, Pa., 1960): Evangelista, *Innovation and the Arms Race*. George W. Downs and David M. Rocke, *Tacit Bargaining, Arms Races, and Arms Control* (Ann Arbor, Mich., 1990).

GEORGE W. DOWNS

ATOMIC BOMB. See NUCLEAR WEAPONS.

ASIA PACIFIC ECONOMIC COOPERATION. The rise of the East Asian economies, led by Japan's reconstruction after the Second World War, saw growing economic *interdependence in the Pacific encourage moves toward arrangements for closer economic cooperation among Asia Pacific economies. This was given expression at the political level with the formation of the Asia Pacific Economic Cooperation (APEC) group at a meeting of regional foreign and trade ministers in Canberra in November 1989.

As the countries of East Asia became more important in the world economy and in world trade, they increasingly had to shape their approach to international economic policy in an environment in which their activities had an increasing influence on global outcomes. Shared experience of economic development based on internationally oriented industrialization provided a foundation for building a common approach through regional cooperation to issues of trade and economic diplomacy.

Japan in particular was under pressure in the 1990s to accept more responsibility in trade, finance, technology, and development cooperation policy. A regional arrangement encompassing North America enabled Japan and other East Asian economies to secure a new role in regional and international affairs without jeopardizing important links with the United States. This framework was especially important to Australia—with whom Japan cooperated closely in its conceptualization—given its increasingly strong trade, economic, and political links in East Asia and its established investment and security links with the United States.

Compared with the elaborate mechanisms for consultation on economic policy matters that have evolved within Europe, or that are incorporated in the Organization for Economic Cooperation and Development (OECD), those in the Pacific are in an early stage of development. Nonetheless, they have been built upon common interests in regional economic cooperation and incorporate unique features suited to managing the problems of policy coordination among Asia Pacific economies.

The process of establishing an infrastructure for closer economic cooperation was begun in September 1980, with what became the first Pacific Economic Cooperation Council (PECC) meeting in Canberra. PECC's forums and task forces, which dealt with regional cooperation in trade, fisheries, minerals and energy, and other issues, served both policy and commercial strategic purposes. PECC has a tripartite structure, including government officials, industry people, and academic researchers, and a small coordinating secretariat in Singapore. Discussions among economists, within the Pacific Trade and Development (PAFTAD) Conference series since 1968, and business people, within the Pacific Basin Economic Council (PBEC) since 1969, preceded its establishment.

At the end of the 1980s, Pacific economic cooperation activities underwent a significant change. On 6–7 November 1989, a ministerial level meeting on APEC was convened. This was the most powerful and representative group of ministers responsible for foreign economic policy ever to assemble in Asia and the Pacific (from Japan, Korea, the ASEAN countries, Canada, the United States, Australia, and New Zealand). In 1991 membership was expanded to include the three Chinese economies (China, Hong Kong, and Taiwan [Chinese Taipei]). In November 1993, President Clinton invited leaders to join the first annual APEC summit in Seattle. The APEC agenda is coordinated by Senior Officials Meetings (SOM) and developed within numerous APEC Working Groups. An APEC Business Advisory Council (ABAC) also has an input into ministerial and leaders' meetings. Membership has expanded to include Mexico, Papua New Guinea, Chile, Peru, Vietnam, and Russia.

The liberalization of trade and investment was from the beginning the core of APEC's economic policy agenda, but trade and investment facilitation and economic and technical cooperation (ecotech) are its other two pillars.

East Asia's economic and political ambitions are ordered critically around the goal of modernization. Trade liberalization and reform are the leading instruments of East Asia's industrial transformation through the deeper access they provide to international markets and capital. As "catching up" economies, East Asian countries have a profound interest in a trade regime that eschews discrimination in trade treatment as they expand market share. This is why the organizing idea for APEC was open regionalism and why APEC has sought to promote trade liberalization on a nondiscriminatory, multilateral basis.

Yet APEC is not simply a trading arrangement, although defense of an open trading system is the most important shared interest of Asia Pacific economies. The Asia Pacific is a vast zone of economic development, and economic and technical cooperation focused on capacity building and market strengthening in the course of economic transformation are essential complements to APEC's trade policy agenda.

While APEC was founded to address economic issues, an accompanying political objective was to accommodate East Asia's growing power without disturbing the balancing role played by North America in regional economic and political affairs. There was a happy coincidence of political and economic interests, encouraging regionalism based on a distinctly global agenda, at the end of the Cold War.

In little over a decade, APEC has had an impressive record of achievement. Through APEC, East Asian and Pacific countries have worked to define a strategy for trade and economic diplomacy—liberalization and reform organized around the principles of open regionalism—particularly suited to the development objectives and diversity of the Asia Pacific region. APEC has provided a framework for the accommodation of the three Chinese economies into mutually productive economic relationships, despite the diplomatic tensions across the Taiwan Straits. It progressed from official and ministerial level institutions to regular meetings of Asia Pacific leaders in a forum in which tensions can be diffused and calmed and political energies mobilized to deal with priority issues in each of its member states. It influenced the outcome of the Uruguay Round of trade negotiations and revealed its potential as a major coalition within the *World Trade Organization. At the same time, APEC has established a new mode in international trade liberalization through its commitment to free trade and investment by 2010 and 2020 and has provided a vehicle for carrying reform forward independently of formal international negotiations.

Despite the economic crisis in East Asia in 1997 and 1998, there was no sign of retreat on APEC's core agenda for trade and economic reform. Indeed, it has been extended to encompass financial and other market strengthening programs.

Developments at the end of the 1990s raised some questions about the way ahead for APEC because of the awakening interest in subregional cooperation in East Asia in response to the economic crisis and longer-term structural change. But the hosting of the APEC meetings by China in Shanghai in 2001 marks an important turning point in Asia Pacific diplomacy as China seeks to signal through APEC its global role and intentions.

(See also PACIFIC REGION.)

Yoichi Funabashi, *Asia Pacific Fusion: Japan's Role in APEC*, Institute for International Economies (Washington, D.C., 1995). Ross Garnaut, *Open Regionalism and Trade Liberalization: An Asia Pacific Contribution to the World Trade System*, Institute of Southeast Asian Studies (Singapore, 1996). APEC website, http:///www.apecsec.org.sg.

PETER D. DRYSDALE

ASIAN DEVELOPMENT BANK. The Asian Development Bank (ADB) is a multilateral *regional development bank that promotes poverty reduction and economic growth in Asia and the Pacific. Established in 1966 and headquartered in Manila, ADB is owned by its fifty-eight member countries, including forty-two regional and sixteen nonregional members.

ADB makes loans, provides technical assistance and equity investments, and offers advice to developing member countries. Since establishment, the bank has made $82 billion in loans. In 1999, loans reached nearly $5 billion, while technical assistance totaled $173 million and equity investment $154 million. The People's Republic of *China is the bank's number one borrower, followed by *Indonesia, *India, and *Pakistan.

Bank operations cover a wide range of sectors. Agriculture dominated early lending, but infrastructure projects, particularly energy, transportation, and communications, have historically accounted for the largest share of loans. In the 1990s, ADB expanded lending for social development and poverty has taken on new prominence since the 1997 Asian currency crisis.

Despite the region's record of high growth, Asia is also home to 900 million poor. In 1999, ADB adopted a new Poverty Reduction Strategy, making poverty reduction its paramount goal. Other objectives, as stated by the bank, are promoting growth, protecting the environment, supporting human development, and improving the status of women.

Bank operations are financed by ordinary capital resources, special funds, and other funds. Ordinary capital, including paid-in capital, reserves, borrowing, and accumulated retained income, supports nearly three-quarters of loans. The bank has $47.6 billion in subscribed capital, of which $3.3 billion is paid-in and $44.3 billion is callable. ADB, which has a triple-A credit rating, typically raises $4 billion–$5 billion per year from bond issues. The largest of the special funds, the Asian Development Fund (ADF), was established in 1974 to facilitate concessional lending to poorer developing member countries. Roughly one-quarter of ADB loans are made on concessional terms through ADF.

Like other multilateral development finance institutions, the bank is governed by its shareholders. The United States and Japan are the largest shareholders, each with 15.9 percent in 2000. Debate, and at times tension, between Japan and the United States over substance, priorities, and style are a persistent characteristic of ADB operations.

The board of governors, composed of one representative from each member, meets annually. Governors elect a twelve-member board of directors with authority to approve policy initiatives and financing operations. ADB is headed by a pres-

ident who is elected by the board of governors for a five-year term.

ADB is unique among multilateral development finance institutions for the large role the government of Japan plays in institutional management as well as funding. Japan is a founding member of ADB and the largest source of funds when ordinary capital and special funds are combined. The president of ADB is traditionally Japanese, and the bank is known for its pragmatic approach and relatively consensual decision-making style.

ADB is also the only international development finance institution in which both the People's Republic of China and *Taiwan—under the name Taipei, China—are members.

(See also AFRICAN DEVELOPMENT BANK; DEVELOPMENT AND UNDERDEVELOPMENT; INTER-AMERICAN DEVELOPMENT BANK; WORLD BANK.)

Nihal Kappagoda, *The Multilateral Development Banks: The Asian Development Bank* (Boulder, Colo., 1995). Barun Roy, *A Continent in Change: Thirty Years of the Asian Development Bank* (Manila, Philippines 1997). ADB homepage, http://www.adb.org.

ANNE EMIG

ASSASSINATION. The premeditated murder of a political figure for reasons associated with the victim's prominence, political perspective, or some combination of both is known as assassination. As a formal means of political action, assassination is usually traced historically to a secret Islamic order known as Nizaris that emerged (ca. 1090) in the region south of the Caspian Sea that is now encompassed by Syria and Iran. The members of this radical sect were distinguished by a fanatical devotion to their cause and a willingness to kill selectively on command to eliminate political opposition. The term "assassin" is derived from an Arabic word meaning user of hashish, the substance members of the sect used to prepare themselves psychologically for a politically inspired murder. In modern times, assassination occurs throughout the world and is not restricted to any particular religious sect, ethnic group, nationality, or culture. The distinction between assassination and lethal acts of *terrorism is based on the political prominence of the actual, or intended, victim(s). For example, the Irish Republican Army's (IRA) clandestine killings of British troops and Protestant civilians were often described as acts of terrorism, whereas the death of Lord Louis Mountbatten, killed by an IRA bomb in 1979, was considered an assassination.

Transnational research suggests that social and economic factors are not associated with assassinations in any interpretable way. Contrary to popular belief, assassination is less likely to occur in non-Western developing nations than it is in Western developed nations. Assassination is a much more frequent event in Italy, France, and the United States, for example, than it is in any African nation. Several other tentative conclusions are possible. Assassinations are more likely during times of political instability and domestic strife. Such acts are less frequent in the most permissive, democratic societies (e.g., the Scandinavian nations) as well as the most restrictive, authoritarian societies (e.g., China and the pre-perestroika East European bloc). Heads of state and high government officials remain the most frequent targets, but in recent years the attention of political extremist groups has shifted sharply to multinational business executives and members of the diplomatic corps (who are also more likely than heads of state to be killed when an attempt is made). Heads of state remain the preferred targets of lone assassins. Before 1970, most assassination attempts were carried out by lone assassins. The pattern has changed since then with political extremist groups accounting for the majority of assassination attempts, except in the United States where the earlier lone assassin pattern continues.

When a political figure does fall victim to a single assassin, attention necessarily shifts to the assailant's mental state. A psychological study of assassins and would-be assassins (James W. Clarke, *American Assassins: The Darker Side of Politics*, rev. ed., Princeton, N.J., 1990) identifies certain themes that define the motives of lone assassins in the United States that may have more universal applicability. Most assassins in the United States acted alone and were motivated primarily by personal problems (e.g., failed relationships and careers, or completely delusionary grievances) having little to do with political ideology or, for that matter, the public figures they attacked. This persistent, and possibly peculiar, American motivational strain, combined with the dramatic increase in successful and attempted assassinations from 1963 to 1998 (nine, which was the same as the number of presidential elections during the same period), the world prominence of the victims, and the corresponding sharp increase in the normally high levels of ordinary homicide, set the United States apart from other nations.

(See also NORTHERN IRELAND; POLITICAL VIOLENCE.)

Thomas H. Snitch, "Terrorism and Political Assassinations: A Transnational Assessment, 1968–80," *Annals of the American Academy of Political and Social Sciences* 463 (September 1982): 54–66. Franklin L. Ford, *Political Murder: From Tyrannicide to Terrorism* (Cambridge, Mass., 1985). Sonia L. Alianak, "Religion, Politics, and Assassination in the Middle East," World Affairs 160 (Winter 1998): 163–175.

JAMES W. CLARKE

ASSOCIATION OF SOUTHEAST ASIAN NATIONS. A change of government in Indonesia in 1965 that ended hostilities with Malaysia and a sense of external security threats to the region from China and the *Vietnam War combined to allow the creation of the Association of Southeast Asian Nations (ASEAN) in August 1967 through the Bangkok Declaration. The original members—Indonesia, Malaysia, the Philippines, Singapore, and Thailand—were joined by Brunei on its independence in 1984, by Vietnam in 1995, and by Laos and Burma (Myanmar) in 1997; Cambodia is slated to join as soon as its domestic political stability allows. ASEAN's work is conducted through intergovernmental committees, assisted since 1976 by a secretariat established in Jakarta (Indonesia). All decisions must be approved by foreign ministers or heads of state, representing national governments.

Formally a mechanism for regional coordination, ASEAN serves as one channel among its members and between them and a wide range of other states and international organizations, without replacing the members' own representations in those organizations. The range of issues considered by ASEAN has slowly grown to encompass almost all areas of policy, from the environment and the drug trade to financial stability and transportation. A wide network of *nongovernmental organizations among business, government, and professional groups provides another level of regional cooperation that leads some to speak of an ASEAN Community. Official and unofficial exchange of information about economic policies and problems has become extensive and is of great value to states primarily concerned with accelerating their economic development. But Southeast Asian nations' economic ties are so much more extensive outside the region than within that integration like that advanced by the *European Union is unlikely. This is considered by some to be ASEAN's signal failure.

The Treaty of Amity and Co-operation in Southeast Asia and the Declaration of ASEAN Concord, both signed in 1976, effectively established peaceful relations and dispute avoidance mechanisms among the members. These treaties, later signed by all Southeast Asian states and opened to others in the wider Asian region, are an important basis for a peace zone in Asia and the South Pacific. A concern to prevent intervention by outside powers resulted in the Declaration of a Zone of Peace, Freedom and Neutrality in Southeast Asia in 1971, and a Nuclear Weapons Free Zone has been approved to buttress this effort.

The winding down of the Cold War and the establishment of the Asia-Pacific Economic Cooperation forum (APEC) in 1989 combined to shift the emphasis of ASEAN. The end of the Cold War allowed the inclusion of political and security issues in ASEAN's agenda, resulting in the formation of the ASEAN Regional Forum (ARF) as an Asia-wide security conference in 1994. APEC is an alternative forum for economic discussions among the participants in ASEAN's annual Post-Ministerial Conference, shifting ASEAN's own programmatic development toward regional economic integration. Emphasis is placed on regional security and greater economic integration among the expanded members in ASEAN's Vision 2020, adopted in 1997. Key roles in regional security and economic affairs, combined with expansion to encompass all of Southeast Asia (with a combined population in 1997 of about 500 million), is thought by their leaders to provide the ASEAN members with a balance to the influence of China and Japan in Asia. ASEAN is considered the most successful regional organization among *Third World states.

Ron Edwards, ed., *ASEAN Business, Trade, and Development* (Singapore, 1996). Michael Leifer, *The ASEAN Regional Forum* (London, 1996).

DONALD K. CRONE

ATATÜRK, Kemal. Turkish nationalist leader and founder of modern *Turkey, Kemal Atatürk (originally Mustafa Kemal) was born in 1881 in what is now the Greek city of Salonika. He went to military school, one of the few options open to a lower-middle-class Muslim youth seeking a modern education and a career. Graduating as staff captain in 1905, he joined the Young Turk movement whose goal was to reform the Ottoman Empire. When the Young Turk revolution took place in July 1908, he pursued a military rather than a political career, serving in Albania (1910), Libya (1911–1912), and in the Balkans (1912–1913). He was military attaché to Sofia in October 1913 but returned to active command at Gallipoli where he made his reputation. Promoted to the rank of pasha (general) in April 1916, he was virtually exiled by his Young Turk rivals to the eastern front. Subsequently he recaptured the towns of Bitlis and Mus from the Russians and fought a defensive campaign in Palestine and Syria.

In October 1918 the Turks were forced to sign an armistice and await their fate. In May 1919 the sultan sent Kemal to disband Ottoman armies in Anatolia; instead Kemal decided to unify a fragmented resistance movement and reorganize the army. The Greek landing at Izmir on 15 May aroused passions throughout Anatolia and facilitated Kemal's task. He summoned nationalist congresses in Erzurum (July 1919) and Sivas (September 1919) where he was elected the chair. The sultan (and the Allies occupying Istanbul) responded with massive repression, and a court-martial in Istanbul sentenced Kemal to death in absentia. But the sultan's acceptance of the Treaty of Sèvres (August 1920) left the nationalists as sole guardians of national rights. After signing agreements with the Soviets and thus ending his isolation, Kemal concentrated on defeating the Greek invasion, finally succeeding in September 1922. The discredited sultan's attempt to participate in peace negotiations enabled Kemal to abolish the sultanate in November, and the Treaty of Lausanne (July 1923) gave European recognition of an independent sovereign Turkey.

Kemal now dealt with conservatives in his own ranks, most of whom were generals popular with the army. Because of their higher social status, they preferred an Islamist regime under the caliph. Kemal outflanked them by having the Assembly declare a republic on 29 October with himself as president. The caliphate was abolished in 1924 and the Kurdish rebellion of 1925 provided Kemal with the opportunity to crush all opposition. He then carried out a program of radical reform which transformed the entire institutional structure of the new state. Kemal had become the unrivaled master of the new state, ruling through the Republican People's Party and mediating between various factions. He strove to create a Turkey with a modern social structure and economy. He experimented briefly with an opposition in 1930 but abandoned the project when he found that conservative forces were aroused. That made him even more radical, for he assumed that the people needed to be educated in the values of the new Turkey. His radical ideas were formulated in an ideology known as *Kemalism. He was reelected president in 1927, 1931, and 1935, and the Assembly bestowed upon him the name Atatürk ("Father Turk") in 1934; soon after his death on 10 November 1938 he was proclaimed "eternal leader."

Lord Kinross, Ataturk: The Rebirth of a Nation (London, 1964). Bernard Lewis, The Emergence of Modern Turkey, 2d ed. (London, 1968). Turkish National Commission for UNESCO, Atatürk (Ankara, 1981). Vamik Volkan and Norman Itzkowitz, The Immortal Atatürk: A Psychobiography (Chicago, 1984).

FEROZ AHMAD

AUNG SAN SUU KYI. "The quest for democracy in Myanmar (Burma) is the struggle of a people to live whole, meaningful lives. . . . It is part of the unceasing human endeavour to prove that the spirit of man can transcend the flaws of his nature." Her words spoken by her son at the Nobel Peace Prize ceremony reveal Aung San Suu Kyi's character and commitment. Confined to house arrest in Burma, she was later released but stayed in the country to fight for democracy. Not only Burma's most prominent opposition leader, she has world stature as a spokesperson for social justice and non-violence. Her fluent command of English and Burmese; her wit and poise, her writing skill, and her resolve to face down the generals rank her among the commanding women of the twentieth century.

Born 19 June 1945, she is General Aung San's daughter. He founded Burma's independence army, negotiated independence, and established a bond with Burma's complex of minority leaders—all before his assassination at age thirty-two. Her father's sacrifice helps explain her legitimacy as a national leader; however Aung San Suu Kyi overcame political handicaps before gaining acceptance among Burmese. She was educated abroad, married a foreigner, Michael Aris (who died in 1999), and had two children. They never lived in Burma as a family. When she returned in 1988 to care for her dying mother she was swept into politics as a speaker at a democracy demonstration. Her oratorical skills were unrivaled.

The measure of her popularity came with the 1991 elections. Her National League of Democracy won eighty percent of the seats, so the junta commenced arresting and jailing NLD's members, some of whom died from torture. This confrontation continues, yet "Mrs. Aris," as the junta calls her, still speaks out for justice, democracy, and human rights.

(See also MYANMAR.)

JOHN H. BADGLEY

AUSTRALIA. With its legal, cultural, and political institutions modeled on those of the mother country, Australia developed as a British outpost in the South Pacific, with an economy based on the export of primary commodities, primarily wool and gold. A British penal colony was established at Sydney Cove in 1788, followed by the establishment of five more colonies during the first half of the nineteenth century, peopled predominantly with settlers from the British Isles. From the middle of the nineteenth century immigration restrictions were imposed, particularly with respect to Asians, to maintain a white Australia.

The effect of British settlement on the Australian Aborigines was devastating. The land was annexed under the doctrine of terra nullius—that Australia was an empty land belonging to no one. European infectious diseases, destruction of food sources, and armed conflict decimated the population, and those who survived were subject to restrictive and discriminatory legislation until the middle of this century. In 1992 a High Court judgment found that Australian law recognized a form of native title, thus overturning terra nullius and strengthening pressure for an act of reconciliation between indigenous and settled Australians.

In 1901 the six colonies federated to form the Commonwealth of Australia. The resulting political institutions combined the conventions of the Westminster system of responsible cabinet government with a federal system in which the colonies became states, retaining their own parliaments and bureaucracies and a considerable degree of sovereignty. The federal Parliament is a two-chamber legislature, elected on a universal franchise. The lower house (House of Representatives) employs a preferential voting system, the upper house (the Senate) a proportional system. Although designed as a state's house, with equal representation from each state, the Senate's operations have followed party lines for most of its history. Voting in elections at both federal and state levels is compulsory.

The constitution formally divided powers between the two levels of government and established the High Court of Australia to adjudicate disputes. The initial powers given to the new federal government seemed limited—mainly to do with external affairs such as defense and immigration and with matters such as currency and marriage laws on which uniformity seemed desirable. During the twentieth century, however, the scope of the federal government's powers has increased enormously, both because of judicial interpretation and because of the financial dominance held by the federal government since World War II. Friction between the two levels of government is a continuing feature of Australian political life, and the division of power has hindered reform efforts. Although the Australian federal system is unsupported by marked regional or ethnic differences, it is deeply embedded in the organizational life of Australian society and is unlikely to be seriously challenged in the foreseeable future.

The Commonwealth of Australia also includes the Northern Territory, which now has limited self-government and is pressing for full statehood, and the Australian Capital Territory, which is the location of Canberra, the federal capital. Apart from some islands in the Indian and Pacific Oceans and the Australian Antarctic Territory, Australia has no external territories. Papua New Guinea, which had been administered by Australia since World War II as a United Nations Trust Territory, became an independent nation in 1975.

Since 1910 the Australian party system has been dominated by three parties: the Australian Labor Party, formed in the 1890s as the political wing of the trade union movement; a nonlabor party committed to private enterprise and liberalism which has undergone several changes of identity and which was re-formed by Robert Menzies (1894–1978) in 1944 as the Liberal Party of Australia; and a rural-based party (originally the Country Party, now the National Party) which has regularly participated in coalition governments with the major non-Labor party. Until the early 1970s Australian patterns of party identification were relatively stable, but since then the electorate has become more volatile, with increasing numbers of independent and minor party candidates winning seats. The rural-based National Party has continued to exert considerable influence, despite a decline in the farm-based population. A new center-left party, the Australia Democrats, has achieved some success in Senate elections, and it is now unlikely that the governing party will also control the Senate.

Historically the two major parties have differed most markedly in the class orientation of their social outlook and in their attitude to government intervention in the economy, although both supported the postwar expansion of the government's role in the regulation of the economy and provision of social welfare, and both have retreated from this since the mid-1970s out of a concern to reduce the size and scope of government. Both have embraced economic liberalism but can be distinguished somewhat in terms of their social agenda.

Australia only slowly sought legal independence from Britain. Authority was increasingly delegated to governors and parliaments in Australia throughout the nineteenth century, although the British monarch and parliament possessed the theoretical legal power to rule Australia until 1986 when the U.K. Australia Act was proclaimed. Australia did not begin to assume independence in foreign affairs until 1917 and did not adopt the 1931 U.K. Statute of Westminster until 1942. Elizabeth II, the queen of England, is also queen of Australia and is represented in Australia by six state governors and by the governor general of the Commonwealth. Although on paper these governors have enormous power, they have rarely exercised it.

During the 1990s support for Australia becoming a republic gathered momentum. However, although there is strong support for replacing the monarch as head of state, there is considerable disagreement over the method of selection and the powers of office. A referendum on the issue in 1999 was defeated.

Until World War II, Australia looked to Britain for defense, for markets for its primary produce, for capital, for immigrants, and for its cultural standards. While Australia has remained a member of the *Commonwealth, the wartime alliance with the United States in the Pacific War, together with the latter's dominance of the postwar Western world, drew Australia closer to the United States, as a source of capital and cultural standards and as a major ally. In 1951 the *ANZUS Treaty was signed by Australia, New Zealand, and the United States. Australia aided the United States in the *Vietnam War and has allowed the United States to establish military bases on its soil. Since the end of the Cold War Australia has pursued closer engagement with the Asia-Pacific region. It was active in the establishment of the Asia-Pacific Economic Cooperation Forum and of the Association of Southeast Asian Nations Regional Forum. The region is now the focus of Australian economic policy and an increasingly important source of immigrants.

After World War II Australia embarked on a massive immigration program that has radically altered its demographic composition. More than half of the population increase since the war, from 7.5 million in 1947 to approximately 19 million in 1999, has been due to immigration and to children born to immigrant parents. While migrants continued to come from Britain and Ireland, they were also drawn from most parts of Europe, particularly Greece and Italy, and from the Middle East. Since the end of the 1960s with the dismantling of the white Australia policy there has been increasing immigration from Asia, which has met with some opposition. The Australian population has moved in less than fifty years from being one of the most homogeneous to one of the most diverse in the world, and an official policy of assimilation has been replaced, with some tension, by one of multiculturalism, which recognizes people's rights to maintain their separate cultural identities within a shared political and legal framework.

Australia has a mixed economy in which the government historically has played a large role in the development of infrastructure. Encouraged by the strength of the labor movement, Australia, like New Zealand, developed a system of industrial tribunals to settle disputes between employers and unions and to fix conditions of labor. Australia continues to have a highly unionized workforce by Western standards, although levels are declining. Throughout the twentieth century the Australian economy has relied heavily on the export of primary commodities, particularly wool and minerals. The manufacturing sector has been weak, developed for the domestic market rather than for export. Recently, Australia has experienced deteriorating terms of trade, chronic current account deficits, and escalating foreign debt. Government response has been to pursue the liberalization of world agricultural trade and to attempt to strengthen the export of manufactured goods through an economic liberal agenda of integrating Australia more fully into the world economy. Financial institutions have been deregulated, tariffs have been massively reduced, state-owned enterprises have been privatized, and there has been some deregulation of the labor market. Much of this has been done without widespread popular support and currently has led to some disenchantment with established political processes and institutions.

(See also COLONIAL EMPIRES; FEDERALISM; INTERNATIONAL MIGRATION; PACIFIC REGION.)

Geoffrey Sawer, *Australian Government Today*, 13th ed. (Melbourne, 1987). Geoffrey Bolton, *The Oxford History of Australia*, 2d ed., vol. 5 (Melbourne, 1996). Paul Kelly, *The End of Certainty: Power, Politics, and Business in Australia* (Sydney, 1994).

JUDITH BRETT

AUSTRIA. Today's Republic of Austria is a small (83,850 square kilometers, slightly smaller than the state of Maine), overwhelmingly German-speaking country, with a population of around 8 million. Seventy-eight percent of Austrians are Roman Catholic; 5 percent are Protestant; the remainder are made up of members of other religions. Austria is ranked as the ninth wealthiest country in the world, measured in GDP per capita purchasing power parities (1999). The country is located in the heart of Europe, at the crossroads between east and west, north and south. The centrality of its location is responsible for Austria's varied historical experiences and changing identities.

With the end of World War I (1918), Austria made the transition from the constitutional monarchy of Austria-Hungary to a republic. This new form of government, proclaimed on 12 November 1918, was declared the "German-Austrian Republic." The republic was drastically reduced in size and power compared to its former grandeur, which led to a widespread belief among the now almost exclusively German-speaking Austrian population that this republic was too small to survive economically as well as militarily.

Austrian society in the 1920s and 1930s was deeply divided into three distinct, mutually hostile *Lager* (camps or pillars): the reform-minded, progressive, anticlerical Social Democrats based in "red Vienna" and representing the emerging urban proletariat; the Christian Socialists, believers in Catholicism and strong government, supported by the rural peasantry and the petite bourgeoisie; and the German Nationalists, who openly favored *Anschluss* (annexation) with Germany. This group drew its support from white-collar employees and bureaucrats. These subcultures had their own paramilitary forces that regularly engaged each other in bloody confrontations, culminating in the Austrian civil war of February 1934, which cost the lives of 118 persons.

In 1938, when Chancellor Kurt von Schuschnigg attempted to stop continued Nazi infiltration by meeting with Adolf *Hitler in Berchtesgaden, he faced threats of military intervention in support of the Austrian Nazis. Schuschnigg determined to let the Austrian people decide for themselves whether they wanted to join Germany and announced a plebiscite for 13 March 1938. Furious about this plan, Hitler

openly threatened to invade Austria if the plebiscite were to take place, demanding in addition that Schuschnigg abdicate as chancellor in favor of a loyal follower of Hitler, Arthur Seiss-Inquart. Eventually, Austria gave in to the threats of violence and invasion by German troops. Nevertheless, on 12 March, Hitler marched into Vienna to the cheers of his Austrian sympathizers and Austria ceased to exist as an independent state and became the *Ostmark*, a part of the German Third Reich.

After ten years of occupation by France, Great Britain, the United States, and the Soviet Union, Austria signed the State Treaty on 15 May 1955 which fully restored Austria's sovereignty as a federal republic. In the same year, the lower chamber of the Austrian Parliament enacted the Federal Constitutional Law on Permanent Neutrality.

The catastrophic experiences of Austrian elites during World War II had a cathartic effect: Austria recovered very quickly thanks to a remarkable willingness among the leaders of the various *Lager* to cooperate with each other, the exact opposite of what had occurred during the interwar years. Cooperation took place at two levels: first, at the level of "grand coalitions" for significant periods (1945–1966, 1986–2000) of the Socialist Party of Austria (SPÖ) and the Austrian People's Party (ÖVP). Second, the representatives of the unions and employers' organizations fostered a unique form of social and economic cooperation which was responsible for the remarkable economic miracle that took place during the 1960s, characterized by quickly rising incomes, high economic growth low unemployment and inflation, and development towards a generous welfare state. The *Sozialpartnerschaft* (social partnership or neocorporatism) proved very successful again in 1974–75 when the quadrupling of oil prices led to stagflation in every European country except Austria. However, it appears that Austrian neocorporatism is not as influential as it used to be three decades ago.

With the demise of the Soviet Union and the end of the Cold War, Austria was permitted to apply for European Union membership. In June 1994, an overwhelming majority of Austrian people (67 percent) voted in favor of EU membership. Austria joined the EU on 1 January 1995.

Austria is a representative democracy. Article 1 of the federal constitution states: "Austria is a democratic republic. Its law emanates from the people." However, the constitution does contain some elements of direct democracy, such as provisions for referenda or popular initiatives and for the direct election of the head of state, the federal president, decided by all Austrian citizens eligible to vote.

Austria has a parliamentary form of government. The cabinet is politically responsible to the *Nationalrat* (lower chamber, House of Representatives), which is based on a proportional representation-list system, and which can by a simple majority depose the government by a vote of no confidence. A second chamber, called the *Bundesrat* (Senate) or upper chamber, which represents the various *Länder* (states). This system is considered a "weak" bicameral legislative system as the *Nationalrat* is clearly the more powerful of the two.

In 1986, the Green Party gained representation in Parliament for the first time. In the same year, Jörg Haider took over the reins of the Freedom Party of Austria (FPÖ), which at that time teetered on the brink of extinction. He drastically reorganized the party and stamped a strongly nationalist, anti-immigrant, far-right, and xenophobic character on it. His populist leadership style gained him many followers, and in the 1999 general election the FPÖ became the second largest party in Austria, polling almost 27 percent of the popular vote. In February 2000 the party formed a governing coalition with the ÖVP, which prompted a number of EU member states to impose unprecedented bilateral sanctions on Austria. While many observers agree that these EU member states may have overreacted, it will provide Austrians with an opportunity to critically examine their country's weak attempts to purge National Socialism after World War II and thereby make Austria a stronger member of the democratic family of nations.

(See also CORPORATISM.)

Anton Pelinka, *Austria: Out of the Shadow of the Past* (Boulder, Colo., 1998).

MARKUS CREPAZ

AUTHORITARIANISM. While authority refers to legitimate power, authoritarianism is associated with "arbitrary," illegitimate authority. Nondemocratic regimes share the following characteristics: those governing are self-appointed and, even if elected, cannot be displaced by citizens' free choice among competitors; and there is no freedom to create a broad range of groups, organizations, and political parties to compete for power or question the decisions of the rulers.

This essay deals with authoritarian regimes, which may be contrasted with competitive democracies (which enjoy almost *unlimited* rather than very confined *pluralism) and with totalitarian systems (where pluralism is entirely absent and mobilizational ideologies sustain the regime). We have previously defined authoritarian regimes as "political systems with limited, not responsible, political pluralism, without elaborate and guiding ideology, but with distinctive mentalities, without extensive nor intensive political mobilization, except at some points in their development, and in which a leader or occasionally a small group exercises power within formally ill-defined limits but actually quite predictable ones."

Operating with neither the resources of *legitimacy associated with competitive democracies nor the mobilizational capacities of totalitarian systems, the authoritarian regimes on the periphery of ideological centers feel the pressure to imitate, incorporate, and manipulate dominant ideological styles. Generic values like patriotism, *nationalism, economic development, social justice, order, and the pragmatic incorporation of ideological elements derived from the dominant political centers allow rulers without mobilized mass support to neutralize opponents, co-opt a variety of supporters, and decide policies pragmatically.

The lack of ideology limits the capacity to mobilize people and to create the psychological and emotional identification of the masses. Indeed, limited political mobilization is a characteristic of authoritarian regimes. In some, the depoliticization of the masses corresponds to the intent of the rulers; in others, the rulers initially intended to mobilize their supporters and the population. The struggle for national independence from a colonial power, the desire to incorporate into the political process sectors of the society untapped by any previous political leadership, or the defeat of a highly mobilized opponent in societies in which democracy had allowed and encouraged such mobilization do contribute to the emergence of mobilizational authoritarian regimes of a nationalist, populist, or fascist variety. The maintenance of equilibrium between limited pluralisms limits the effectiveness of the mobilization and can lead to apathy.

If our definition is useful, it should allow us to develop subtypes. Authoritarian regimes include 1) bureaucratic-military regimes; 2) organic statist regimes; 3) mobilizational regimes, including postdemocratic and postcolonial; 4) personal rulership; and 5) post-totalitarian regimes.

Bureaucratic-Military Regimes. The most frequent subtype are regimes in which a coalition predominantly, but not exclusively, controlled by army officers, bureaucrats, and technocrats establishes control of government and excludes or includes other groups without commitment to a specific ideology, acts pragmatically within the limits of their bureaucratic mentality, and neither creates nor allows a mass single party to play a dominant role. They may operate without parties, but frequently they have created an official government-sponsored single party. In a few cases they allow a multiparty system, but make sure that the elections do not offer an opportunity for free competition for popular support.

Organic Statism. Quite different from the bureaucratic-military-technocratic type, organic statism presupposes a corporatist mode of interest representation and participation or mobilization. Theorists of the organic statist authoritarian model contrast the natural (or organic) development of business and professional organizations, trade unions, universities, churches, workplace associations, neighborhood groups, etc., to the artificial formation of political parties and other institutions for interest representation and the organization of political life in competitive democracies.

A set of false assumptions pervades the model, beginning with the expectation that natural primary associations will not be troubled by internal conflicts of ideology or interests. Moreover, in historical terms, no political system has employed an exclusively organic or corporatist institutional format. Nevertheless, ideologies derived from organic statism and *corporatism have significantly influenced twentieth-century authoritarian regimes, including *Mussolini's.

Mobilizational Regimes: Postdemocratic and Postcolonial Societies. With the rise of *Leninism and *fascism in Europe after World War I, new antidemocratic and illiberal mobilizational regimes appeared, based on elite representation of the majority and driven by overarching historical goals, whether to liberate the proletariat or affirm a vision of national grandeur. Mobilizational authoritarian states emerged also with considerable frequency among postcolonial states where the struggle for independence would often become associated with an individual leader. In a context of arbitrary and often externally imposed national boundaries, fierce ethnic rivalries, religious and linguistic diversity, and the weak institutionalization of political representation and administration, the dilemmas of underdevelopment and state-building were met with authoritarian responses. *One-party systems and personalized charismatic leadership emerged as alternative authoritarian systems characterized by mass mobilization.

Personal Rulership. Personal rule is a system of relations linking rulers not with the "public" or even the ruled (at least not directly), but with patrons, associates, clients, supporters, and rivals, who constitute the "system." The system is structured not by institutions but by the politicians themselves, and this dependence on persons accounts for its essential vulnerability. It is severely restrictive with regard to political liberties while being generally tolerant of nonpolitical rights (except in the tyrannical regimes). Rulers exercise nearly unlimited legal competence. They use: 1) co-optation and consultation, 2) patronage, 3) agreement and accord, and 4) intimidation and coercion in different mixes. The fate of the ruler affects that of the political class that supports him and often the welfare of the political order. If we add the restraints and uncertainties posed by foreign political and economic factors, poor countries dependent on a few primary exports, and with crop fluctuations due to the weather, we can understand the instability of personal rule. Foreign economic and military assistance, including that given by neighboring countries to the ruler or to the exiles and rebels, is another factor. Personal rule therefore presents the paradox of relatively autonomous, even arbitrary power marked by coercion and the inability to implement policies owing to the lack of resources and trained officials. Personal rulership is more unpredictable, more paternalistic or arbitrary, tyrannical and corrupting, but ultimately weaker and more unstable than more "formed" authoritarian regimes.

There is a type of nondemocratic rule that is distinct, in its dynamic and consequences for the society, from *totalitarianism and authoritarian regimes; it has been called (using a term borrowed from Max Weber's description of extreme forms of patrimonialism) sultanistic. A rule not based on tradition, nor on ideology, nor on charismatic appeal, nor on the purpose of defending a particular social order (class structure, religious traditions), sultanistic rule benefits the ruler, his family, friends, cronies, and praetorian guards. It blurs the boundaries between the public treasury and the ruler's wealth and undermines the bureaucratic and military organizations. In this system business cannot base its decisions on the market or the legal system depending as it does on arbitrary and corrupt power. The result is a deinstitutionalization of society.

Post-Totalitarian Regimes. The changes in the USSR and Communist Eastern Europe provoked in an intense debate about the emerging regimes that could not anymore be conceptualized as totalitarian. The facts that those regimes came after the transformation of society by totalitarianism, that the institutions and organization that sustained it—particularly the single party—had not been dismantled (except for the extensive terror machine and the gulags), the use of the wooden language of "frozen ideology," and the memory of the recent past made them different from authoritarian systems. *Totalitarianism can be said to have failed in its most positive ambitions to change people, to provide a sense of purpose and meaning. But it succeeded in changing societies and largely destroying the bases of the social-cultural pluralism of civil society, the autonomy and self-assertiveness of their corporate groups, and (in socialist societies) the independence of economic actors. The result was that the social pluralism that could give rise to a latent and perhaps politically relevant pluralism did not exist. In addition, the relative closure of those societies and the control of the mass media made it impossible for the broader population to think about alternative political models (as in most authoritarian re-

gimes). There was room for *privatization and dissidence on a scale intolerable under totalitarianism, but not for the wide range of nonlegal and illegal oppositions as under most authoritarian regimes, partly because the civil society that might protect or encourage them did not exist.

The following developments' favored a move toward posttotalitarianism: the ossification of an ideology mechanically repeated, the growing acceptance of programmatic or rational criteria in policy making not derived from or even compatible with the ideological tenets, the ritualization of indoctrination, the growing lack of support by intellectuals, and the tolerance for esthetic expressions not subject to ideological dictates. Only the articulation and diffusion of dangerous ideas was still limited. Ideology, accepted in a diffuse and unarticulated way, could serve as a "mentality" to the apparatchiks, but did not occupy the central place it once did. The single party and its top leadership continued to be the central decision-making structure, but changes in the activities of the party organizations, in recruitment and promotion through nomenclature, and the composition of the top leadership could not be ignored. Bureaucratization and gerontocratic tendencies characterized the party. These changes resulted from the reconsideration by the elite of the cost, including to themselves, of the totalitarian model, particularly the insecurity (such as purges and the *Cultural Revolution) and considerations of efficacy in the competitive world system of economies, technology, and military capability. Without question, de-Stalinization, the liquidation of massive and indiscriminate terror, and the introduction of socialist legality (even when, for dissidents, a repressive legality) have contributed to the transformation of totalitarian systems.

Crises, Breakdown of Authoritarian Regimes, and Transition to Democracy. Since the 1970s a "third wave" of democratization has led to transitions to democracy in many authoritarian regimes, first in Southern Europe, then in Latin America and the Republic of Korea (South Korea), and most recently in the post-totalitarian communist countries of Eastern Europe and parts of the former Soviet Union. These developments have led to a growing literature that analyzes the crisis or breakdown of authoritarian regimes and the different paths to democratization. Those changes range from negotiated transitions imposed from above, reforma pactada—ruptura pactada, to overthrow by coup, abdication, or disintegration of the regime.

Although each transition has its own distinctive characteristics, the type of nondemocratic rule can make a difference in the path followed in the transition to and the legacy of the new *democracy. In a number of authoritarian military regimes, the military decided to end authoritarian rule, allowing free elections that transferred power to democratic presidents, but sometimes retaining certain privileges and the implicit threat to contest decisions affecting the armed forces. The limited changes in the society often led to the restoration of the old constitution and reemergence of the old party system and patterns of politics. More institutionalized authoritarian regimes did not lead to the restoration of the predictatorship democratic regimes, but to a new democratic regime owing to the social change that had taken place. In the case of civilian or civilianized regimes, the transition often was negotiated between reformist incumbents and the opposition.

The regimes we have characterized as sultanistic have not

led to such peaceful, orderly, and negotiated transitions, but to a broad and heterogeneous coalition that gains power violently and establishes a provisional government. Such a government in a number of cases has led to the establishment of a new authoritarian (sometimes revolutionary) rule rather than democracy, or to continued instability.

Despite the wave of democratization, totalitarian, or at least post-totalitarian and authoritarian, regimes still exist. The crisis of the ideologies that have supported these regimes (*Marxism-Leninism, communism, fascism, authoritarian corporatism, and derivatives like *African socialism or the national security state), together with growing recognition of the value of liberal democracy as something more than "formal" or "bourgeois" democracy, and the failure of centrally planned socialist economies make the establishment of nondemocratic regimes less attractive. Nonetheless, the failure of new democracies to satisfy popular expectations, social and economic conflict, ethnic violence, and aggressive nationalism can lead to authoritarian rule.

(See also COMMAND ECONOMY; COMMUNIST PARTY STATES; CORPORATISM; CORRUPTION; CULTURAL REVOLUTION; DECOLONIZATION; DEMOCRATIC TRANSITIONS; FASCISM; LEGITIMACY; LENINISM; MILITARY RULE; MUSSOLINI; NATIONALISM; NINETEEN EIGHTY-NINE; ONE-PARTY SYSTEM; PATRON-CLIENT POLITICS; PLURALISM; POPULISM; PRIVATIZATION; TOTALITARIANISM.)

Samuel P. Huntington and Clement H. Moore, eds., *Authoritarian Politics in Modern Society* (New York, 1970). Guillermo O'Donnell, *Modernization and Bureaucratic Authoritarianism* (Berkeley, Calif., 1973). Philippe Schmitter, "Still the Century of Corporatism?" *Review of Politics* 36 (1974): 85–131. Juan Linz and Alfred Stepan, eds., *The Breakdown of Democratic Regimes* (Baltimore, 1978). Alfred Stepan, *The State and Society* (Princeton, N.J., 1978). David Collier, ed., *The New Authoritarianism in Latin America* (Princeton, N.J., 1979) Adam Przeworski, *Democracy and the Market: Political and Economic Reforms in Eastern Europe and Latin America* (Cambridge, U.K., 1991). Juan Linz and Alfred Stepan, *Problems of Democratic Transition and Consolidation: Southern Europe, South America and Post-Communist Europe* (Baltimore, 1996). H. E. Chehabi and Juan J. Linz, eds., *Sultanistic Regimes* (Baltimore, 1998). Juan Linz, *Totalitarian and Authoritarian Regimes* (Boulder, Colo., 2000).

JUAN J. LINZ

AUTHORITY. See LEGITIMACY; SOVEREIGNTY.

AZERBAIJAN, an independent republic that emerged in 1991 from the dissolution of the Soviet Union, is the largest (33,500 sq. mil.) and the most populous (7.5 million inhabitants) part of the geographical region of Caucasia, south of the Caucasus Mountain range. The territory of Azerbaijan includes two administrative units of autonomous status, Nakhichevan, separated from the republic by a belt of Armenia, and the Nagorno-Karabagh district, in which the majority of the population is Armenian.

This chessboard pattern of ethnic distribution in the south-

western part of the country was the backdrop for the most violent and longest-lasting territorial dispute that followed the disintegration of the USSR, the Nagorno-Karabagh conflict. The war, which has been the chief national concern of Azerbaijan, resulted in the loss of a fifth of the country's territory and about 750,000 refugees or displaced persons. In the peace talks that came in the wake of the 1994 cease-fire, the gist of Armenian claims has been the "common state" based on a horizontal rather than a vertical relationship, in effect a form of confederation unacceptable to Azerbaijan.

According to the pattern of other post-Soviet republics, the 1995 constitution established the predominance of executive power in the hands of the president, with the legislative branch considerably weaker. The judiciary came to be seen as subject to executive influence. There are a number of political parties, some of them in opposition to the ruling New Azerbaijan Party, headed by the president of the republic, Haidar Aliyev. The main dimensions of the cleavage are not so much programs or even the personalities of leaders but rather the rivalry between the former Soviet power elite, still in control of many key positions, and the intelligentsia with its traditions of opposing the Soviet regime in its last years. Political transformations of the future are likely to come with generational change, coupled with the politics of succession.

Azerbaijan, a country endowed with a wealth of oil deposits, borders on incomparably more powerful neighbors—not only Russia, but also Iran, and Turkey. For all the differences between the ruling group and the opposition, there is a consensus as to the main direction of foreign relations, which aims at rapprochement with the West without antagonizing Russia. Because the 1999 war in Chechnya has been seen as an attempt by Russia to reassert its influence in Caucasia, elements inclined to be pro-Russian in Azerbaijani politics are gaining some strength.

The foreign policy orientation toward the West goes hand in hand with the growth of economic links to world oil markets and the influx of investments and technology in the Azerbaijani oil industry. The crucial problem remains the safe and economically viable transportation of the oil via pipelines which must pass through territories of neighboring countries, Georgia and Turkey (an option favored by the United States) or, alternatively, through Iran or Russia. The dilemma creates additional complexity for Azerbaijani foreign policy. Another attempt at integrating Azerbaijani within the global economy is the Europe-Caucasus-Asia Transport Corridor (TRACECA), also called the New Silk Road, linking Europe with the Far East, which is promoted by the European Union.

(See also POST-COMMUNISM.)

Tadeusz Swietochowski, *Russia and Azerbaijan: A Borderland in Transition* (New York, 1995). Thomas Goltz, *Azerbaijan Diary: A Rogue Reporter's Adventures in an Oil-Rich, War-Torn, Post-Soviet Republic* (Armonk, N.Y., 1998).

TADEUSZ SWIETOCHOWSKI

B

BABY BOOMER. Nineteen forty-six marks the beginning of a nineteen-year period of high birth rates. By 1964, some 17 million more people were born than would have been born had the fertility patterns of the early 1940s prevailed . . . 76 million new Americans! Today, counting immigration to the United States, baby boomers number 83 million persons.

No one explanation of the cause of the "baby boom" phenomenon is sufficient. In one sense, the explanation is simple—more women married, had children earlier, and had slightly larger families. Certainly, in the United States, as was true for most industrialized nations, the initial increase in fertility can be explained by the end of World War II. But this does not explain why the boom continued into the 1960s (Light, 1988). Landon Jones (1980) suggests cultural changes, including a return to normalcy, a growing economy, and a new "procreation ethic," help explain the trend. Demographer Richard Easterlin (1987) suggests that members of small cohorts, such as those born in the 1930s, usually experience favorable economic circumstances, including less competition for job advancement, and are therefore more likely to marry earlier and have more children.

The much-used "pig going through the python" metaphor provides a visual image of the effect of this change in the nation's age structure. As baby boomers moved from the nurseries to the schools, and then into the employment and housing markets, the very size of this cohort (really, cohorts) created strains. But, for the most part, these systems adjusted. For example, the primary, secondary, and then higher educational systems expanded and even prospered, providing baby boomers with more educational opportunities than previous cohorts.

Stereotypes abound about baby boomers and have structured much of the political discussion surrounding this phenomenon. Baby boomers have variously been described as a "lucky" and as an "unlucky" generation; as countercultural political activists and as materialistically driven "yuppies." But this huge grouping of people defies easy classification. Some among the oldest among them, including Bill *Clinton, have set their sights on "retirement." The youngest, those turning thirty-six in 2000, are on the cusp of middle age, more likely to be thinking about first mortgages and their young children than their retirement years. Indeed, the baby boom cohorts are diverse, with, as political scientist Paul Light notes, splits cutting across their numbers by income position, race, age, amount of education, gender, marital status, employment status, involvement with the Vietnam War, and geographic region. Add differences by ethnicity, immigration status, health, pension coverage, religion, and sexual orientation, and they are clearly far from homogeneous. Belonging to a nineteen-year cohort does not provide a central explanation of their behavior and decision-making. For example, class, race, gender, and geography have far more to do with their *political participation, party affiliation, or voting than timing of birth.

In recent years, attention has focused on the political and economic consequences of their aging. On the one hand, there are those who argue that their aging will precipitate a crisis in the ability of the public and private sectors to respond to growing pension, health, and long-term care costs, thereby undermining the economy and the well-being of today's young. Those seeking to advance an agenda of shrinking the public sector by privatizing *Social Security and Medicare often draw on these arguments.

However, just as educational institutions and family budgets adjusted to the passage of the baby boom cohorts through their doors, it seems likely the nation can adjust without catastrophe to the sixty-year transition of the baby boom into and through their older working years, old age, and, eventually, very old age. Modest economic growth seems likely to ease this adjustment. The improving health status of the old creates new possibilities of continued community and economic contributions during old age, including employment, full- or part-time. In spite of the privatization rhetoric, when future congresses come to terms with addressing projected shortfalls in Social Security and Medicare, they are likely to find incremental reforms—probably some combination of tax increases and benefit reductions—to be safer and more politically and administratively feasible than radical change.

As policy reforms are considered, it will be important to recognize diversity of the baby boom cohorts and to carefully consider the distributional implications of various alternatives, especially in terms of the effects on those at greatest economic and social risk. For example, partial privatization of Social Security is likely to improve the well-being of some groups (e.g., high-income males) and place others at greater risk (e.g., most women and low-income groups). Whatever the policy, careful political consideration needs to be given to balancing the costs and benefits of change across working persons and various groups of baby boomers.

(See also MEDICARE AND MEDICAID; ENTITLEMENTS, THE FUTURE OF.)

Landon Y. Jones, *Great Expectations: America and the Baby Boom Generation* (New York, 1980). Richard A. Easterlin, *Birth and Fortune: The Impact of Numbers on Personal Welfare* (Chicago, 1987). Paul C. Light, *Baby Boomers* (New York, 1988). Congressional Budget Office, *Baby Boomers in Retirement: An Early Perspective* (Washington, D.C., 1993). John M. Cornman and Eric R. Kingson, "Trends, Issues, Perspectives, and Values for the Aging of the Baby Boom Cohorts," *Gerontologist 36*, no. 1 (1996): 15–26.

ERIC R. KINGSON

BAHAMAS. See ENGLISH-SPEAKING CARIBBEAN.

BAHRAIN. See GULF STATES.

BALANCE OF PAYMENTS. The balance of payments is an accounting device for recording a country's economic transactions over a given period with the rest of the world. Although there are no universally accepted categories for constructing the balance of payments, the International Monetary Fund (IMF) has tried to establish a uniform set of criteria. In addition, the IMF's annual publication, *Balance of Payments Statistics*, is the main international source of data on the balance of payments.

The balance of payments is usually divided into three sets of categories. The first is the "current account": exports and imports of goods (the "trade balance"), exports and imports of services, investment income, and unrequited transfers. The current account mirrors a country's domestic accounts, i.e., a current account deficit reflects more domestic spending than saving and vice versa. The second set of categories is the "capital account": inward and outward flows of direct investment, portfolio investment, long-term loans, and short-term capital. The third set involves the items constituting a country's reserves: monetary gold, special drawing rights (SDRs), IMF credit, and foreign exchange assets. In principle, changes in a country's reserves must offset any difference between the current and capital account balances. In practice, since not all transactions are recorded, there is a residual item called "net errors and omissions."

Far from being only an accounting device, the balance of payments has crucial economic and even political consequences. Since the difference between the current and capital accounts must be offset by a country's reserves, the balance of payments represents a limit on a country's ability to obtain resources from the rest of the world. When that limit is reached, domestic economic policy must be changed in order to adjust. For example, a devaluation could be decreed in order to increase exports and lower imports, or domestic spending could be cut in order to achieve the same goals. A country could also try to increase capital inflows through higher interest rates or move favorable treatment of foreign capital. (While the need for adjustment theoretically applies to both surplus and deficit countries, there is no economic mechanism to force the former to change policy.)

The political consequences of the balance of payments arise in part because there are always winners and losers from the economic policy changes to deal with a balance-of-payments deficit. For example, a devaluation will favor exporters, while increasing costs for consumers and for producers who use imported inputs. Likewise, a rise in interests rates to attract foreign capital will mean that domestic savers will also increase their return while borrowers will have to pay more. The IMF itself frequently becomes involved in political conflicts over the balance of payments, since it has strong views on appropriate types of adjustment and considerable influence over lenders.

An overall pattern is supposed to characterize the balance of payments. A "mature economy" is expected to have a current account surplus offset by capital exports, meaning that it produces more than it uses domestically. A "developing economy" is supposed to have the opposite: it consumes more than it can produce, thus running a current account deficit financed through capital imports. This pattern has frequently been violated in recent years as the United States has run the world's largest current account deficit and absorbed a substantial share of the world's capital. The trade and investment dynamics underlying this situation have been another source of political friction, in this case among industrial countries, especially the United States and Japan.

International Monetary Fund, *Balance of Payments Statistics* (Washington, D.C., various years). Rudiger Dornbusch, *Open Economy Macroeconomics* (New York, 1980).

BARBARA B. STALLINGS

BALANCE OF POWER. The balance of power is one of the oldest concepts in *international relations. Apparently practiced since organized human societies first began to interact, and with certainty since the time of ancient Greece, it is said by some to be a universal law of history. Yet the term is used in a variety of different and occasionally incompatible ways. Descriptively, it can refer to any distribution of *power, an equality of power, a preponderance of power, a policy of equilibrium, or a policy of preponderance. Analytically, it can denote either a specific theory of *state behavior or *realism and other general theories that utilize power as a central organizing concept. Prescriptively, it is usually—but not always—invoked in support of national goals or policies associated with expanded military capabilities.

Although considerable ambiguity remains, the balance of power has come to mean, at least among scholars of international relations, an international process that, when operative, tends to create roughly equal distributions of power between opposing states or coalitions of states or a situation characterized by such a distribution. Preponderances of power, once confusingly referred to as "balances," are now commonly, but not universally, referred to as situations or structures of *hegemony.

By checking power with power—often through the formation of flexible, temporary *alliances—the balance of power purportedly works to limit expansionism, preserve the independence of states, and maintain the status quo. If scholars now generally agree on this more delimited conception of the balance of power, they disagree over whether it works automatically, as an inherent feature of *international systems, or only through conscious efforts to manage international politics. In other words, while they share a general consensus on the nature of the process, they subscribe to different theories of the balance of power.

In *System and Process in International Politics* (New York, 1957), Morton A. Kaplan develops the classic theory of conscious state action and balancing behavior. Assuming that actors have limited aims and seek to maintain the system itself, he identifies six "essential rules" that, when followed by at least five "essential actors" (or states), characterize a balance of power system:

1. Act to increase capabilities but negotiate rather than fight.

2. Fight rather than pass up an opportunity to increase capabilities.

3. Stop fighting rather than eliminate an essential national actor.

4. Act to oppose any coalition or single actor which tends to assume a position of predominance with respect to the rest of the system.

5. Act to constrain actors who subscribe to supranational organizing principles.

6. Permit defeated or constrained essential national actors to re-enter the system as acceptable role partners or act to bring some previously inessential actor within the essential actor classification. Treat all essential actors as acceptable role partners.

By following these rules, Kaplan argues, states guard against the ambitions of others. By rehabilitating the losers as potential allies, states also preserve the necessary conditions for the balance of power system to operate. Any failure by an essential national actor to follow one or more of these rules, for whatever reason, may destabilize the system and transform it into one of five other possible systems. It is this ability of states to choose whether to follow these rules, and especially the implied self-restraint required in rules three and six, that necessitates conscious management and creates a need for states to be socialized into the system. A balance of power system as described by these rules, Kaplan argues, existed in Europe during the eighteenth, nineteenth, and early twentieth centuries.

Other scholars see the balance of power as driven by the unconscious motivations and interests of states—with the exception of a "balancer" that throws its weight into one scale, and then the other, opposing whichever side appears to possess the greatest ambitions. This semiautomatic theory assumes that whereas every other state strives to enhance its power and resources, the balancer is curiously immune from this otherwise universal law. Motivated not by national egoism but by international altruism, the balancer forgoes potential national gains to preserve the stability of the system. Built largely on the experience of Britain in the eighteenth and nineteenth centuries, this perspective also draws some support from the balancing behavior of the United States in the first and second world wars.

In terms reminiscent of the operation and description of physical laws and purely competitive economic markets, the balance of power is understood by still others as an automatic process. According to Kenneth Waltz (*Theory of International Politics*, Reading Mass., 1979), the balance of power tends to produce roughly equal distributions of capabilities without any state deliberately willing this result. In this view, all states strive for predominance and, by doing so, naturally tend to check the aspirations and counter the successes of others. If one state threatens to rise above the rest, its competitors will redouble their own internal efforts, form countervailing alliances, or initiate preemptive *war. Although this equilibrating mechanism may be thwarted by the fortunes of economic growth or ineptitude of political leaders, the competition between states nonetheless tends to prevent any single state or coalition of states from dominating others.

While balance of power theory is often accepted as true, both because of its logical consistency and wide acceptance among policy makers, there is some debate as to whether roughly equal distributions of power do in fact tend to form within the international system—whether automatically or as the result of conscious efforts. In part, this debate is rooted in the different theories discussed above: proponents of theories based on conscious state action who assume that the balance of power requires at least three actors to function would exclude the period since 1945 as a potential case, but it is central, say, to Waltz's automatic balance of power theory. It also stems from inadequate definitions and measures of power; nineteenth-century Britain, for instance, is classified by some as a balancer and others as a hegemon.

Although exceptions do not disprove the rule, important empirical anomalies do exist. During the first and second world wars, for instance, the Allies possessed overwhelming power—whether measured by GNP, industrial production, or military expenditures, all standard indicators. "Bandwagoning" rather than balancing appears to have characterized the foreign policies of European states at these times. Working within the context of the theory but seeking to address such anomalies, Stephen M. Walt (*The Origins of Alliances*, Ithaca, N.Y., 1987) has hypothesized that states balance threats, not power—but this merely substitutes one ambiguous term for another without increasing our ability to test or falsify the theory.

While the balance of power is widely seen as a process that regulates international conflict and thereby preserves national independence and the status quo, analysts disagree over whether the balance of power promotes *peace or war. For some, war is often necessary to counter drives for hegemony, and power—in the end—is measured only on the battlefield; war, in this view, is an inherent part of the balancing process. For others, balances of power deter war, as risk-adverse states are normally reluctant to initiate hostilities in situations of approximate equality.

The gap between these positions is not as large as it seems. Both hold that the balance of power creates and preserves relatively equal distributions of power within the international system. For the former group, war is, on occasion, a necessary means toward this end. For the latter, balances typically inhibit aggressive action. It is not inconsistent to suggest that war may be required to establish a balance of power that subsequently will prevent war. This offers relatively little hope, however, for controlling or reducing the frequency of war; given the dynamic nature of the international system, propelled forward by varying rates of economic growth and military expenditures, states may be constantly moving toward but only occasionally reaching balances of power.

The current balance of power within the international system is highly ambiguous. For some, the United States has been the sole "superpower" since the end of the *Cold War. In this view, according to balance of power theory, other countries should now align against the United States. There is, at present, little evidence of this tendency, suggesting either that the United States is not dominant or that it is exerting, somewhat contrary to expectations, a benign and non-threatening influence in contemporary world affairs.

Others perceive the system to be more multipolar in structure. In this view, Russia remains a military power on the basis of its nuclear stockpile, despite its economic and political collapse; Japan possesses the world's second largest economy; Germany by itself, or perhaps within a more robust European Union, is increasingly a power on the world stage; and China is an emerging giant on the Eurasian continent. Balance of power theory predicts a competitive international environment of fluid alliances and, perhaps, greater conflict between countries in the future. To date, there is also little evidence to support this more grim prognosis.

One of the key questions for the future of international relations is whether the balance of power will eventually reassert itself. Will countries fall once again into suspicion and struggle, or has the community of democratic and economically interdependent states grown sufficiently large to transcend the supposedly iron law of the balance of power?

(See also FORCE, USE OF; FOREIGN POLICY; INTERDEPENDENCE; SECURITY.)

Ernst B. Haas, "The Balance of Power: Prescription, Concept, or Propaganda?," *World Politics* 5, no. 4 (July 1953): 442–477. Edward Vose Gulik, *Europe's Classical Balance of Power* (Ithaca, N.Y., 1955). Michael Mastanduno, "Preserving the Unipolar Moment: Realist Theories and U.S. Grand Strategy after the Cold War," *International Security* 21, no. 4 (Spring 1997): 49–88.

DAVID A. LAKE

BALFOUR DECLARATION. On 2 November 1917, Arthur Balfour, the British secretary of state for foreign affairs, announced that "His Majesty's Government view with favour the establishment in Palestine of a national home for the Jewish people, and will use their best endeavours to facilitate the achievement of this object." This declaration, which came as British forces were conquering *Palestine, hitherto part of the Ottoman Empire, marked the first time that major European power had extended official support to the Zionist movement's goal of making Palestine (ninety percent of whose population was at that time Arab) into a Jewish homeland.

In later years there would be considerable dispute about the extent of the commitment to *Zionism which the Balfour Declaration entailed, and about how to reconcile its promise to foster the development of the Jewish "national home" with its promise that "nothing shall be done which may prejudice the civil and religious rights of the existing non-Jewish communities in Palestine." Nonetheless, for two decades the Balfour Declaration stood as official policy, underlying British support for Jewish immigration, settlement, and statebuilding in Palestine. It was thus a tremendous achievement for Zionism, giving it the powerful patron without whose protection and support it could not have overcome the opposition of the indigenous Arab majority and laid the demographic, economic, political, and military foundations of the future State of *Israel.

Several considerations contributed to the British decision to endorse Zionism in 1917. Many imperial policymakers believed that a Jewish Palestine under British tutelage would strengthen British power in the postwar Middle East, protect the Suez Canal, and help secure control of the eastern Mediterranean. Foreign Office officials were convinced that the declaration would induce Jews in the United States and in Russia to support the Allied cause in World War I. Zionist leaders in Britain tirelessly and effectively lobbied the British government to adopt this new policy, with the support of a number of prominent Christian Zionists, including Prime Minister Lloyd George.

The Balfour Declaration was one of several mutually irreconcilable commitments which Britain made regarding the postwar disposition of the Arab provinces of the Ottoman Empire. In 1915–1916 Britain negotiated an agreement with Hussein, the sharif of Mecca, who with his Hashemite family wanted to break free of Ottoman rule (the so-called Hussein-McMahon Correspondence). Assured of British arms and money, and what they took to be a British commitment to support the postwar establishment of an independent Arab state in virtually all the former Ottoman Arab provinces, Hussein and his Arab nationalist allies launched a revolt against Ottoman rule. At the same time, however, Britain was secretly negotiating a treaty with France (the Sykes-Picot Agreement of May 1916) which divided the region between them.

After the war the British reneged on their promise to the Arabs: although two of Hussein's sons were ultimately installed on the thrones of the newly created British client-states of Iraq and Transjordan, France assumed control of Syria and Lebanon while Palestine came under British rule. Despite strong Palestinian Arab nationalist opposition, the Balfour Declaration's commitment to Zionism was incorporated into the mandate which Britain received from the *League of Nations. In 1939, however, anxious to win Arab support as war approached, Britain declared that it had fulfilled its commitments under the Balfour Declaration and imposed restrictions on Jewish immigration and land purchases. The resulting rupture of the British-Zionist alliance turned into open conflict after the war, leading ultimately to British withdrawal from Palestine and the establishment of the State of Israel in 1948.

(See also ARAB NATIONALISM; COLONIAL EMPIRES.)

Leonard Stein, *The Balfour Declaration* (New York, 1961). Christopher Sykes, *Crossroads to Israel, 1917–1948* (Bloomington, Ind., 1965).

ZACHARY LOCKMAN

BALKANS. The Balkans refers to both the Balkan Peninsula located in southeastern Europe and the nine countries of Albania, Bosnia-Herzegovina, Bulgaria, Croatia, Greece, Macedonia, Romania, Slovenia, and *Yugoslavia (Serbia and Montenegro) situated in this region. The term "Balkan" is derived from the Turkish word for "forested mountains." Beginning in the nineteenth century, the expression "Balkans" was used to describe the area in Europe dominated by the Ottoman Empire, and it is currently applied to the nine states of the region. In light of the diplomatic conflict, international rivalries, and ethnic conflicts along with the political fragmentation ("balkanization") that have characterized the history of the region, the more neutral term Southeast Europe is also used to designate the area.

The Balkan states have a combined area of 765,000 square kilometers (295,350 sq. mi.), slightly larger than the state of Texas. In 1999, the population of the region was approximately 70 million. There are three major religions practiced in the area: Eastern Orthodoxy, Roman Catholicism, and Islam, with the Eastern Orthodox divided into self-governing national churches. Reflecting the ethnic diversity of the Balkans, eight major languages (Albanian, Bulgarian, Croatian, Greek, Macedonian, Romanian, Serbian, and Slovene) are used by the peoples of the region. Until the 1960s, when they began to develop and diversify, the economies of the Balkan states were predominantly based on agriculture.

The strategic location of the Balkan Peninsula at the juncture of Europe and Asia has made it a "cockpit" for competing empires, peoples, and cultures. During the fourteenth and fifteenth centuries, most of the Balkans fell under the control of the Ottoman Empire.

With the decline of the Ottoman Empire and the growth of national consciousness on the part of the Balkan peoples during the nineteenth century, the region became a major focal point in European international relations between 1815 and 1914. During this period, the Eastern Question, the problem of determining the disposition of the European territories of the empire, occupied much of the attention of the major European powers of the era. The conflicting interests of the European powers in the Balkans coupled with the territorial disputes among the emerging Balkan states combined to transform the region into the so-called "powder keg" of Europe, and they were contributing factors to the outbreak of *World War I in 1914.

Prior to World War I, Serbia, Greece, Romania, Bulgaria, and Albania had in turn succeeded in winning their independence from the Ottoman Empire. Following the war, a Yugoslav state was created through the union of Serbia, Montenegro, Croatia, and Slovenia.

After World War II, communist governments were established in all the countries but Greece. Between 1989 and 1991 the Balkan communist regimes were overthrown, and these states have subsequently registered varying degrees of progress in effecting their transitions to political democracy and a market economy. These processes, however, have been hindered by the outbreak of two major armed conflicts in the region—Bosnia-Herzegovina, April 1992–November 1995; and Kosovo, March–June 1999.

The unity of Yugoslavia was destroyed when the Republics of Croatia and Slovenia declared their independence in 1991 following a civil war. Given the subsequent recognition of the independence of Bosnia-Herzegovina and Macedonia, the expressed desire for independence of the Albanians of Kosovo, and separatist sentiments in Montenegro, the end of the fragmentation of the former Yugoslavia may not have yet occurred. The political instability of the new Balkan regimes and the revival of ethnic conflicts in the region suggest that the Balkans may again become a "powder keg" in Europe.

(See also BOSNIAN WAR; NINETEEN EIGHTY-NINE; KOSOVO WAR; POST-COMMUNISM.)

Barbara Jelavich, *History of the Balkans*, 2 vols. (Cambridge, U.K., 1983). F. W. Carter and H. T. Norris, *The Changing Shape of the Balkans* (Boulder, Colo., 1996). Karen Dawisha and Bruce Parrott, eds., *Politics, Power, and the Struggle for Democracy in South-East Europe* (Cambridge, U.K., 1997).

NICHOLAS C. PANO

BALTIC STATES. The three Baltic states regained their independence in 1991 as the USSR disintegrated. Estonia, Latvia, and Lithuania had been independent states from 1920 until 1940, when they became "union-republics" of the Soviet Union. For most of the second millennium, however, Estonians and Latvians had been ruled by the descendants of German knights who conquered and Christianized much of the eastern Baltic shores, starting in the twelfth century. Indeed, these German-speaking "Baltic barons" ruled the Baltic lands much longer than Russians. With them came Christianity, then literacy, and, later still, *nationalism. Even when the Baltic lands became outlying provinces of Sweden and later of Tsarist Russia, Germanic merchants and seigneurs continued to dominate Baltic towns and commerce and the manors where Estonians and Latvians were enserfed.

Unlike Estonians and Latvians, Lithuanian tribes united and repulsed the German crusaders. Their Duchy of Lithuania stretched from the Baltic to the Black Sea. The last pagans in Europe, Lithuanians eventually accepted Catholicism as part of a strategic alliance with Poland in the fourteenth century. In the late eighteenth century, however, the Lithuanian lands as well as parts of Poland also became provinces of Tsarist Russia.

Balts fought and repulsed the Red Army in 1919–1920 but, after Hitler and Stalin partitioned Eastern Europe in 1939, did not resist when the Red Army and Soviet commissars took over Estonia, Latvia, and Lithuania. Baltic parliaments elected from one-party slates in 1940 asked for and received admission into the USSR. The Red Army was driven out by Hitler's troops in 1941 but reoccupied the Baltic lands again in 1944, harassed for a decade by "forest brethren" guerrillas.

The ethnic composition of Estonia and Latvia changed significantly after annexation by the USSR, owing to mass deportations of native Balts, World War II deaths, and "biological" losses—babies not born because prospective parents died young. Reduced numbers of Balts were more than offset by an influx of Russian-speaking soldiers, administrators, and workers from other parts of the Soviet Union. The share of Estonians in Estonia's population decreased from 88 percent in the late 1930s to 61 percent in 1989; the percentage of Latvians in Latvia's population decreased from 77 percent before World War II to 52 percent in 1989.

Lithuania, again, had a different fate. Slavs and other minorities made up only one-fifth of Lithuania's population in 1991, because Soviet leaders did not target Lithuania for industrialization as they did Estonia and Latvia, and dispatched fewer workers there. Many Slavs in Lithuania were Poles—many descended from persons who had lived there for generations or even centuries.

Hopes for restoration of the Baltic countries' independence were sustained by U.S. refusal, followed by most Western countries, to recognize their annexation by the USSR. Baltic activists seized on the 1975 *Helsinki Accords to demand respect for national and individual rights in the Baltic region. They shifted gears in the late 1980s and organized Popular Fronts to promote Mikhail *Gorbachev's campaigns for *perestroika (economic reconstruction) and glasnost' (openness). Soon the Popular Fronts went far beyond Gorbachev and demanded first "sovereignty" and then, when Moscow balked, "independence." Baltic willingness to face down Kremlin threats and "black beret" special forces inspired other Soviet republics—even the Russian Republic—to defy the Kremlin and go for independence. Following the abortive coup by hard-line Communists against Gorbachev, the world and the Kremlin recognized the reborn Baltic republics in August–September 1991.

Estonia and Lithuania adopted new constitutions by referenda in 1992 while Latvia adapted its 1922 constitution. Estonia and Latvia became the only ex-Soviet republics to adopt a parliamentary system, with the prime minister as head of government and an executive president as head of state. Lithuania opted for a semi-presidential system. The Lithuanian constitution, drafted by anti-Communists, established a strong presidency because they expected independence leader Vytautas Landsbergis to be elected president, but he lost to the former Communist Party leader, Algirdas Brazauskas. The Estonian constitution was also written by anti-Communists. They created a figurehead presidency because they feared that Soviet-era leader Arnold Rüütel would win the presidency, but the cultural historian and diplomat Lennart Meri prevailed and later won a second term.

Each Baltic parliament consisted of just one house in the 1990s. The Estonian *Riigikogu* had 101 members; the Latvian *Saeima*, 100; the Lithuanian *Seimas*, 141. All citizens aged eighteen and older could vote. The Riigikogu and Saeima were elected by proportional representation; in Lithuania seventy-one deputies to the Seimas were elected directly and seventy deputies on a proportional basis through party lists.

To limit the number of parties in parliament, each republic required that a party (or coalition of parties) pass a threshold—four percent of the total vote in Latvia, five percent in Estonia and Lithuania—to win a seat (though Lithuania waived this requirement for ethnic minority parties). The threshold made election results hard to predict. Many voters "wasted" their votes on small parties with little prospect of winning a seat in parliament.

Each Baltic republic in the 1990s was a unified state divided into counties. Administration was divided into central government and local authorities, with no intermediate level of government. Each republic had a national police force under the Ministry of the Interior.

Lithuania granted citizenship to all residents, while Estonia and Latvia (like most Western countries) made citizenship conditional on a term of residence and some knowledge of the titular language and constitution. Each republic pledged to uphold the *human* rights of all its residents, citizens or not.

Each republic had an independent judiciary with a supreme court, lower courts, and a constitutional court. In the 1990s Baltic judicial systems were inefficient, with long delays in court hearings and enforcement of decisions. Prisons were crowded; prosecutors and police were often rough.

The zigs and zags of Baltic politics in the 1990s followed a dialectical logic. Thesis: Communists fell and nationalists rose to power in the late 1980s–early 1990s. Antithesis: The nationalists were better at breaking from Soviet domination than at governing. Winning independence was different from managing a modern state and economy. Euphoria gave way to post-independence disenchantment. In the mid-1990s voters in each Baltic republic turned against the very leaders who had led the liberation struggle. Most voters were disappointed that living standards fell for most people except the newly rich business classes; many were also angry that some politicians profited from privatization of national resources; and some worried that nationalists might provoke Russia into an armed intervention. Synthesis: The tides turned again. Elections held from 1996 to 1999 put center-right coalitions at the helm in each Baltic republic. Some of the same nationalist leaders who appeared too naive or radical early in the decade now seemed more pragmatic and skillful.

Many factors drove the dialectic—ideology, ethnicity, trust in charismatic politicians, and economic interests. Voter moods oscillated between hope and anger. The transition to self-rule in the Baltics was not easy. Voters proved fickle or apathetic; many politicians proved venal or inept; many individuals and factions proved corrupt. Private enrichment often crowded out the common good. Still, laws proved more powerful than any personalities, political patronage, or partisanship. When voters chose to replace one set of politicians with another, change took place peacefully. Former Communists and anti-Communists with deep grudges against one another bowed to democratic procedure.

Baltic politics in the 1990s resembled more the fledgling democracies of the Czech Republic, Poland, and Hungary than Russia or other former Soviet union-republics. No strong man (or woman) dominated any Baltic country after the Soviet breakup; no congeries of bankers or entrepreneurs achieved decisive political influence; no armed battles took place between president and parliament. The gravity of the worst corruption scandals in the Baltic did not approach those that dominated Russian politics or that flared in Belgium and Japan.

Whether democracy could be consolidated would depend heavily on social and economic factors. The political culture of democracy was weak after fifty years of repression and dependency. Materialistic values were far stronger among young people than civic virtues. Few non-governmental organizations represented anything but parochial interests.

By 2000 real incomes per capita were slightly higher in each Baltic state than in 1989, but wealth and opportunity were skewed. There was a Generation of Winners—people in their thirties or early forties who took advantage of marketization; a Generation of Losers—those too old, sick, or unskilled to do so, and left with a weak social insurance safety net; and a New Youth Generation wanting to succeed economically but often closed out by those who were already winning.

The Baltic lands have been a strategic and commercial crossroads between Europe and Russia for ages. Their location and ports helped Hanseatic merchants become rich for many centuries; they could help the Baltic countries to prosper like Rotterdam or Singapore or Hong Kong. But these same factors tempt would-be conquerors as well as merchants.

The Baltic lands and populations are small relative to their mighty neighbors. Estonia occupies 17,666 square miles, an area the size of New Hampshire and Vermont. It borders on Latvia and Russia; its sea coasts look toward Finland and Sweden. Its population of 1,408,523 in 2000 gave it a population density of 77 persons per square mile.

Latvia covers 25,400 square miles—about the size of West Virginia. With 2,353,874 people, there were 93 per square mile. It borders Lithuania, Estonia, Belarus, and Russia.

Lithuania is slightly smaller than Latvia—25,212 square miles. But it had a much larger population: 3,584,966—a density of 142 per square mile. It borders Belarus, Latvia, Poland, and Russia at Kaliningrad.

The "clash of civilizations" echoed in the region as Balts strove to pull away from the East and join the West. Nearly every Baltic government after 1991 looked west and north for trade and security. Each Baltic country sought to break its dependence on Russia for food and other exports and its reliance on Russian oil.

The Baltic *drang nach Westen* might have been contained had Russian President Boris *Yeltsin continued the friendly support he gave to Baltic independence in 1990–1991. Instead, Yeltsin kept troops in the Baltic countries for three years and tried to boycott Baltic ports. The Kremlin and Russian legislators denounced Estonians and Latvians for "abusing the human rights" of their Russian-speaking residents, that is, instituting naturalization procedures. Instead of utilizing Baltic oil refineries and terminals for their exports to the West, Russian exporters became undependable suppliers quite ready to close the spigot for political reasons.

In the 1990s all Baltic governments pursued admission into NATO, the European Union, and other West European and Nordic associations. They spurned the Commonwealth of Independent States as a possible vehicle for Russian imperialism. The minuscule Baltic armies got training from European and U.S. instructors and some equipment from the United States. They took part in Partnership for Peace training and in peacekeeping missions from Lebanon to Bosnia. When NATO took in Poland, Hungary, and the Czech Republic in 1999, many Balts felt they were left in a no-man's land, and intensified their struggle for acceptance in a second wave of NATO expansion. Balts tried to meet the NATO standard of spending two percent of GDP on defense but fell short, as their economic growth stalled in the late 1990s. Some Balts hoped that, if and when they joined the EU, it would be a surrogate for a formal military alliance.

Despite many problems, the Baltic transformation was remarkable. Balts moved to self-rule and a market economy within a few years. Despite large populations of noncitizens, most of whom did not know the local language, there was almost no violence between Balts and Russian-speakers.

Gradually the non-native elements in the Baltic were being co-opted rather than repressed or driven out. Time, social change, and government policies gradually tipped the balance of incentives in the 1990s toward integration and assimilation in the Baltic lands.

The nonviolent transformation begun in the late 1980s looked set to continue along liberal and nonviolent lines in the early twenty-first century.

(See also DEMOCRATIC TRANSITIONS; POST-COMMUNISM.)

Anatol Lieven, *The Baltic Revolution: Estonia, Latvia, and Lithuania and the Path to Independence* (New Haven, Conn., 1993). David D. Laitin, *Identity in Formation: The Russian-Speaking Populations in the Near Abroad* (Ithaca, N.Y., 1998). Walter C. Clemens, Jr., *The Baltic Transformed: Complexity Theory and European Security* (forthcoming). *The Journal of Baltic Studies* (quarterly journal of the American Association for Baltic Studies). *The Baltic Times* (weekly newspaper, Riga).

WALTER C. CLEMENS, JR.

BANGLADESH. One of the world's poorest nations, Bangladesh is also one of the most populous and most densely populated. In the mid-1990s, its per capita income of less than US$250 placed it among the bottom fifteen nations ranked by the World Bank, while its 120 million people occupied an area roughly equal to that of the American state of Iowa (which has only 3 million inhabitants). And although it is rapidly urbanizing, the country is still overwhelmingly rural, with less than twenty percent of its population in urban areas. Correspondingly, about two-thirds of the labor force is in agriculture, producing around one-third of GDP. With its monsoon climate, Bangladesh has a larger proportion of its people at risk of flood and famine than virtually any other country.

Ethnically, Bangladesh is remarkably homogeneous, with more than 97 percent Bengalis (defined as those who speak the Bengali language) and a scattering of tribal groups mostly in the mountainous southeast. The country is also principally of one religion, being some 85–90 percent Muslim, with Hindus making up most of the remainder.

Bangladesh has in a sense achieved independence twice, first in 1947 when it emerged from British rule as the "eastern wing" of *Pakistan, separated from its western counterpart by 1,500 kilometers (900 mi.) of *India, and then again in 1971 when, with Indian help, it broke away from Pakistan to become a separate country in its own right after a brief but bloody civil war.

The country's politics were primarily authoritarian during its first two decades, with the Parliament serving largely as a creature of the executive. Changes of regime came through assassination and military coup. Major leaders during this period include Bangladesh's founding father, Sheikh Mujibur Rahman, usually referred to as "Mujib" (1972–75), Ziaur Rahman or "Zia" (1976–81), and Hussein Muhammad Ershad (1982–90). Each of the three founded a political party. First came Sheikh Mujib's Awami League (now led by his daughter Sheikh Hasina Wajed), then Zia's Bangladesh National Party or BNP (presently under the leadership of his widow, Begum Khaleda Zia), and finally Ershad's Jatiya Party.

All three groupings survived to become the principal parties of the 1990s. There is some ideological differentiation among the parties, with the Awami League professing a moderately left, secular, pro-India stance, while the BNP has been somewhat more capitalist, less secular, and anti-India. As the newest of the three, the Jatiya Party sought to establish its identity through a mildly pro-Islamic posture. There are a large number of smaller parties, but only one, the fundamentalist Jama'at-I-Islami, has had much following, and it has trailed far behind the other three.

Through most of the Ershad period in the 1980s, opposition parties engaged in a pattern of mobilization-demonstration-agitation-strike, to which the regime responded alternately with guile and harsh intimidation. In 1990 yet another cycle began, but to the surprise of most observers, this time the political dynamic emulated the overthrow of Ferdinand *Marcos in the Philippines in 1986 rather than the customary course of military repression. The army, called upon to impose martial law, instead instructed President Ershad to resign immediately, which he then did. Critical to the army's thinking, apparently, was the cumulative movement of civil society elements into the opposition camp. University campuses, professional groups, trade unions, government servants, and even the major foreign-funded development *nongovernmental organizations (NGOs) all deserted the regime—a pattern which surely proved instrumental in providing for a peaceful change from the Ershad dictatorship, but which also provided an unhappy precedent for the future.

On Ershad's resignation, an acting president was installed and elections, widely regarded as honest, were held in February 1991, returning the BNP to power with a hairline popular plurality but a large advantage in seats over the second-place Awami League. The new Parliament quickly scrapped the presidential system for a Westminster-style model, and Prime Minister Khaleda Zia embarked on an unsteady path that soon descended into political confusion and disruption, continuing the pattern of the Ershad period's latter days and setting the tone for the decade of the 1990s.

The abiding problem of Bangladesh politics has been the inability of the principal parties to agree to a set of working rules of the political game that provide for behavioral civility. In large part because of the eventual success of the anti-Ershad agitation, but also because that success was the only peaceful regime change that Bangladesh had seen up to that point, opposition parties have come to see the agitational approach as the only way to oppose the regime in power. Thus the Awami League spent most of its efforts after the 1991 election in mobilizing drives against the BNP government, mobilizing successive confrontations, parliamentary boycotts, and *hartals* (general shutdowns of all activity).

Despite its increasingly inept responses and declining popular favor, the BNP ministry did finish its five-year term and then held an election in February 1996, which it won. By this time, however, the Awami League had found a galvanizing issue with its demand for a caretaker government to supervise the elections, after the model of the 1991 poll. But the BNP refused to accede, opposition parties boycotted the February election, and the BNP found itself almost totally isolated. In the ensuing months the pattern of 1990 repeated itself, with the same civil society elements demanding a new election. The BNP government gave in, a caretaker regime was set up, and an election in June 1996, generally thought to be free and fair, returned an Awami League plurality, giving the prime ministership to Sheikh Hasina Wajed.

Khaleda Zia and the BNP then moved into the role earlier held by Sheikh Hasina and the Awami League, occasionally behaving as a loyal opposition within a parliamentary system but devoting most of their efforts to bringing down the government through the same pattern of mobilization-agitation-*hartal*. The result has been continual disruption of political and economic life, and a consequent dampening effect on badly needed foreign investment.

The political economy at all levels has centered around a patron-client structure in which the beneficiaries of government spending provide the regime with their support. In the urban areas finished garments have joined construction, contracting, and trading as the major sources of income for the regime's supporters, while in the countryside development project monies form the basis of linkage. The patron-client process has been fueled to a significant extent by ample foreign aid revenues averaging between US$1.5 and 2 billion yearly in the 1980s and 1990s, which have greatly facilitated an increasingly institutionalized *corruption.

Despite its authoritarian past, Bangladesh has over the years been remarkably receptive to experiments in rural development, and several NGOs have gained world-class reputations for their innovative strategies. In particular, the Grameen Bank has pioneered very small loans to landless people without collateral—mostly women—expanding to more than two million borrowers with almost no defaulters by the late 1980s, a most impressive record. Another notable NGO is the Bangladesh Rural Advancement Committee, which has evolved a "conscientization" approach to rural development in which village-level groups are encouraged to construct their own strategies for promoting increased income and control over their own lives.

Foreign relations for Bangladesh have focused primarily in three directions. India, with roughly eight times the population of Bangladesh and more than twelve times its GDP, is inevitably the major concern. Disputes over sharing water from the Ganges River have persistently been the main conflict here, followed by long-festering insurrectionary movements among tribal groups on both sides of Bangladesh's southeastern border with India. Both these problems have abated recently, with the new Awami League government agreeing to a thirty-year water-sharing treaty in 1997 and to some tribal refugee repatriation. In the longer term, successive Bangladesh governments have hoped that the *South Asian Association for Regional Cooperation (SAARC), formed in 1983, will establish some equilibrium between India and the other much smaller countries in the region.

A second major foreign policy concern has been dealing with international aid donors, led by the World Bank and the United States, which have pressed for policy reforms like *privatization, reducing subsidies, and encouraging export industries. The third major focus in foreign policy has been the Middle Eastern countries, chiefly Saudi Arabia, which has given significant aid while also encouraging Islamic fundamentalism in Bangladesh.

(See also Islam; Military Rule; Patron-Client Politics.)

Craig Baxter, *Bangladesh: From a Nation to a State* (Boulder, Colo., 1997). For an annual update, see *Asian Survey*'s yearly assessment, appearing every February, e.g., Elora Shehabuddin, "Bangladesh in 1999: Desperately Seeking a Responsible Opposition," *Asian Survey* 40, 1 (January–February 2000), 181–188. For current coverage, consult web sites at <http://bangladesh-web.com/news/> and <http://www.dailystarnews.com>.

Harry W. Blair

BARBADOS. See English-Speaking Caribbean.

BASIC NEEDS. The basic needs approach grew out of disappointment with policies for economic growth in the *Third World, which had left poverty and unemployment largely untouched. Basic needs emphasizes the need for concern for the poor by defining development as *"of the people, for the people, and by the people."* The simplest definition of the basic needs approach is "incomes plus social services plus participation." *Incomes* covers the creation of productive and remunerative jobs. *Social services* covers the provision of public goods such as health and education, as well as food subsidies. These raise the earning power of the poor. Transfer payments out of public revenue, charitable donations or gifts by the family, and payments in kind to temporarily or chronically unemployed (the latter include the handicapped, disabled, infirm, old, and chronically sick) are necessary to meet the needs of the unemployable.

Participation in its widest sense covers the nonmaterial aspects of basic needs: self-reliance, freedom, recognition of one's work, cultural identity, participation in the life of the community. Although this component is much more difficult to include in an economic analysis, it is nonetheless important—material basic needs may well be provided for in, for example, a well-run prison, yet we would not say that basic human needs are met there. Participation is both an end in itself and a means for the delivery of basic needs in an affordable way.

The basic needs sectors are normally regarded to be food

and nutrition, education, health, water and sanitation, and shelter. To these one may wish to add, in some circumstances, fuel and transport. There is controversy over who should determine what are basic needs: experts or the consumers themselves. When is there a case for intervening with free consumers' choices? What is the correct policy if people prefer circuses to bread?

An important lesson of work on the subject has been to show the absence of a rigid link between income per head and basic needs fulfillment. Countries such as Sri Lanka, Cuba, Chile, China, Costa Rica, and the state of Kerala in India have registered basic needs indicators, such as life expectancy, infant mortality, and literacy rates, that are similar to those of much more economically advanced countries, whereas countries such as South Africa, Saudi Arabia, and Brazil show poor basic needs performance despite much higher average incomes. This is, of course, partly a function of unequal income distribution, but other factors are also important. Among these are political organization (although many types of political regimes have shown good basic needs performance), whether the poor participate in the process of decision making, proportion of government budget spent on health and education, and whether this expenditure is directed to the poor.

Although there are technical and economic problems to be faced in the basic needs approach, the principal obstacles are administrative and political. The international community can help by supporting regimes that are intent on giving high priority to basic needs. The governments of some low-income countries are not always willing to devote resources to this purpose and have therefore objected to basic needs being introduced into the international development dialogue. They have charged donors with being intrusive and diversionary. On the other hand, donor countries have occasionally used basic needs as a way of reducing commitments by claiming that the ability to meet basic needs is largely a matter of local resources and action.

(See also DEVELOPMENT AND UNDERDEVELOPMENT; EQUALITY AND INEQUALITY; FOOD POLITICS.)

Paul Streeten et al., *First Things First: Meeting Basic Human Needs in Developing Countries* (New York, 1981).

PAUL STREETEN

BAY OF PIGS INVASION. The Bay of Pigs Invasion, launched on 17–19 April 1961, was the most serious attempt by the U.S. *Central Intelligence Agency to overthrow Fidel *Castro. Castro's rise to power in *Cuba upset a long-standing hemispheric status quo built upon a U.S. claim to an exclusive sphere of influence in Latin America and a prohibition against the spread of *communism into the region. U.S. opinion, both in the government and in the country at large, gradually turned to the conclusion that Castro had to be removed.

The scheme was hatched during the *Eisenhower administration, and called for training and equipping a force of Cuban exiles in Guatemala that would land, with U.S. air support, on the southern coast of the island near the Escambray mountains, move into the hills, and rally the Cuban people against the new dictator. The essence of the plan was to repeat the success of a similar operation against Guatemalan President Jacobo Arbenz Guzmán in July 1954. But the CIA grossly underestimated Castro's popularity, and the size, equipment, and training of the invasion force proved wholly inadequate to the task at hand. Moreover, the plan underwent a series of changes, right up until the day of the invasion itself, virtually guaranteeing its failure. The landing site was moved westward from Trinidad to Playa Girón, a flat, swampy area far away from the Escambray, affording no cover and no escape; the number of bombing runs on Cuban airfields authorized for the small exile air force was scaled back to the point where it failed to knock out Castro's air power; and at the last minute, President John F. *Kennedy decided to withhold the American air support needed to cover the landing. The invasion was quickly defeated by superior Cuban forces.

Kennedy had, in fact, inherited an almost impossible predicament from Eisenhower; Kennedy was reluctant to use U.S. military might directly against Castro because of the ill will it would generate in Latin America. He had high hopes that the Alliance for Progress would lead to an improvement in U.S. relations with its Latin American neighbors, and overt intervention against Cuba would frustrate that aim. At the same time, as CIA director Allen Dulles vehemently argued, once preparations for an exile invasion were under way in Guatemala, it would be difficult to turn back. If the invaders were brought back to the United States or dispersed, they would blow the cover on the operation and alienate the Right (who would conclude that the president lacked nerve), the Left (who would object to the very idea of intervention), and the Latin Americans (who would question the president's commitment to nonintervention). Perhaps most importantly, the Soviet Union would conclude that Kennedy was soft on communism, and Dulles worried that canceling the operation might trigger Communist takeovers throughout the hemisphere. It was also possible, Dulles noted, that the exile force would resist being disarmed.

Kennedy was well aware of the faults of the plan, and it met strong and vocal opposition from many of the administration's Latin American specialists and top military advisers. But Kennedy allowed himself to be persuaded that the landing should go ahead, with the United States distancing itself from it as far as possible. He would later take full public responsibility for the disaster.

The invasion generated considerable ill will in Latin America and exposed President Kennedy to severe criticism from both Right and Left. But the most important short-run effect of the invasion was to convince Castro of the United States' unrelenting hostility and drive Cuba further into the Soviet camp. It was partly to forestall a more decisive military assault that the Soviet Union attempted to deploy nuclear missiles to Cuba in 1962, although, ironically, the experience convinced Kennedy that a military solution to the Cuban problem was imprudent.

(See also COLD WAR; CUBAN MISSILE CRISIS; U.S.-LATIN AMERICAN RELATIONS.)

Peter Wyden, *Bay of Pigs: The Untold Story* (New York, 1979). Trumbull Higgins, *The Perfect Failure: Kennedy, Eisenhower, and the CIA at the Bay of Pigs* (New York, 1987).

DAVID A. WELCH

BELARUS proclaimed itself a sovereign state in the late Soviet period and became formally independent on 25 August

1991. Stanislau Shushevich, a physicist, became the Speaker of the assembly and de facto leader of the country until he was ousted in January 1994. However, parliament remained dominated by former Communists and leftist politicians, led by Prime Minister Vyachaslau Kebich. In 1994 a new Constitution was issued that introduced a mixed system with a president sharing power with the parliament. In July, a former KGB border guard and state farm chair, Alyaksander Lukashenka, was elected president, defeating Kebich on the second ballot.

Under Lukashenka, Belarus abandoned efforts at economic reform, and the new president began to alter radically the political structure of the country. Asserting control over the media, he initiated a referendum that supported the removal of national symbols and gave the presidency powers to dissolve parliament in times of crisis. In November 1996, a second referendum consolidated fully the power of the president by making fundamental changes to the 1994 Constitution. The parliament (thirteenth session) was dissolved and replaced with a bicameral structure: an upper house called the Council of the Republic and a lower House of Representatives composed of 110 members of the former parliament (excluding the opposition members). Concomitantly, the president also established control over the Constitutional Court.

Since 1996, Belarus has made several moves in line with the president's affirmed desire to "reunite" with *Russia. This began on 12 April 1994 with a treaty on a monetary union—eventually abandoned by the Russian side as unworkable. On 21 February 1995, Belarus signed a Treaty of Friendship and Cooperation with its larger eastern neighbor. On 2 April 1996, Russian President Boris *Yeltsin and Lukashenka formed a Community of Sovereign Republics. A year later a formal treaty turned the Community into a Union, though no loss of sovereignty by either country was specified. In December 1998, the two presidents announced that the union was to become deeper, but in practice, the Russian side remained wary of making financial commitments to Belarus.

Russia is quite willing to develop military cooperation with Belarus, however. Belarus is a training ground for Russian troops, of which about 80,000 are operating in the republic, in addition to Russian military facilities. Both the military and security forces of the two countries conduct joint maneuvers, and Lukashenka announced his goal of a joint force of 300,000 troops "to protect" the western border from *NATO.

Belarus is marked by internal repression, illegal detentions, and even the disappearance of several leading oppositionists. A mission of the Organization for Security and Cooperation in Europe has tried for two years, with little success, to facilitate a dialogue between the president and the opposition. On the positive side, Belarus ratified the START-1 Treaty (1993), joined NATO's Partnership for Peace program (1995), and had transported all Soviet *nuclear weapons to Russia by early 1995. Conversely, economic reform and *privatization are at a standstill, and Belarus is isolated from European institutions such as the EU and Council of Europe. Indeed, it appears to have reverted back to the former Soviet model.

(See also POST-COMMUNISM.)

Jan Zaprudnik, *Belarus: At a Crossroads in History* (Boulder, Colo., 1995). David R. Marples, *Belarus: A Denationalized Nation* (Amsterdam, 1999).
                                                    DAVID MARPLES

BELGIUM is a small, densely populated state located in northwest Europe, on the North Sea, sandwiched between France, Germany, and the Netherlands. Its population is just over 10 million, of which 59 percent (in the north) are Dutch speaking and 41 percent (in Brussels and the south) are French speaking. In addition, there are close to one million immigrants living in Belgium. The first country on the continent to industrialize, Belgium's heavy industries are now in terminal decline. The dynamic part of the economy involves lighter, high-tech industry, mainly in Flanders. The main towns are Brussels (the capital), Antwerp, and Liège.

Belgium came into existence as an independent state only in 1831, after the revolution against the Netherlands, with whom Belgium had been joined at the Congress of Vienna (1815). Before then, the areas that today make up Belgium were part of various principalities, mostly part of the Holy Roman Empire and part of the Spanish and later Austrian Netherlands. After 1831, Belgium's independence and were neutrality were guaranteed by all the great powers.

The new Belgian state was mostly governed by French speakers. From the second half of the nineteenth century, linguistic and cultural conflict between Flemish and French speakers came to dominate political life. The Flemish movement obtained first bilingualism, then the creation of separate language regions, and finally federalization after 1970.

Before the First World War, Belgian political life was dominated by rivalry between Catholics and the nonconfessional and at times anticlerical Liberals. After 1918, with the rise of the Socialists as the second largest party, there have been three national political families, taking part in alternating coalitions, either of the center-left (Catholics and Socialists) or center-right (Catholics and Liberals).

By 1920, the Belgian party system had settled into the pattern that was to prevail until the 1970s. The main characteristic of this system was consensus-seeking consociationalism, based on the three national political families, each surrounded by a dense network of "its" trade unions, social insurance funds, and youth, women's, and cultural organizations, catering to people's needs from cradle to grave. Other smaller parties such as the extreme right in the 1930s and the Communists briefly after 1945 achieved parliamentary representation, but remained marginal.

The system came under increasing pressure from the regional parties that achieved a peak of support at just over 20 percent in 1971. Distinctive Flemish and Walloon parties, fighting for language rights and more autonomy, if not outright independence, mobilized support. Under these pressures the hitherto unitary Christian, Socialist, and Liberal political families split into three pairs of parties. Growing antagonism between the sister parties across the language frontier made governing ever more complex.

The postmodern trend toward *secularization and greater freedom of choice and individualism spelled the end of the old political certainties and stabilities. The traditional political families saw their share of the vote and their dominance in society decline, as not only community parties emerged, but also other new political forces. Strong Green parties have emerged in both Wallonia and Flanders. Pressures of immigration, the breakdown of family life in the cities, and related problems of inner city poverty have created a growing protest and alienation from conventional politics. This has, on the one hand, fed single issue movements and, on the other, the extreme right, especially in Flanders and Brussels. Against this backdrop, the Christian Democrats are strongest in Flanders, the Socialists in Wallonia, and the Liberals in Brussels. The Greens do better in Wallonia.

Belgium is a constitutional monarchy and has been a federal state since 1993, with a complex and unique structure of asymmetrical communities, responsible for language, culture, education, and personal social services, and regions with socioeconomic powers. Each region and community has its own government and parliament, with wide-ranging devolved powers, including the right to conduct foreign relations within its own areas of competence. The federal government is responsible for defense, foreign affairs, internal security, and monetary policy, and retains important socioeconomic powers.

Executive power at the federal level is in the hands of a prime minister and cabinet that is responsible to the House of Representatives. Parliament is bicameral. The 150-member House is elected for a maximum term of four years by proportional representation. It alone can censure the government and has the last word on legislation and budgetary matters. The seventy-one-member Senate is mainly representative of the regions and communities. It only has delaying powers over ordinary legislation, but must approve constitutional legislation. The 1993 constitution included several devices to ensure the stability of the executive, including the constructive no-confidence motion, borrowed from Germany.

Electoral volatility has been increasing and coalition politics has become more open and complex, offering a wider range of options, as the 1999 coalition of Liberals, Socialists, and Greens illustrates. Federalism is entering the political culture, as different coalitions in the various regions become a real possibility. Despite the plethora of crises, intercommunity conflict and talk of the imminent implosion of Belgium have diminished; political energy instead has been redirected toward reducing popular alienation and distrust of government, brought on by a series of dramatic financial, judicial, and agricultural scandals.

Belgium was a colonial power in Africa until 1960 (Congo, Burundi, and Rwanda), and the experience of decolonization and continued involvement in its former colonies has played a critical role in Belgian foreign policy.

As a vulnerable small state, occupied in both world wars and with a very open economy strongly dependent on trade, Belgium was an early and enthusiastic supporter of both European integration and Western collective security, becoming a founder member of both the European Community and NATO. The Belgian franc is to be replaced by the euro in 2002, which should hasten the country's further integration into Europe.

(See also CONGO, DEMOCRATIC REPUBLIC OF; CONSOCIATIONAL DEMOCRACY.)

John Fitzmaurice, *The Politics of Belgium: A Unique Federalism* (London, 1996).

JOHN FITZMAURICE

BELIZE. See ENGLISH-SPEAKING CARIBBEAN.

BEN-GURION, David. For more than four decades David Ben-Gurion was one of the preeminent leaders of the Zionist labor movement in *Palestine, of that country's Jewish community (the *Yishuv*), of the international Zionist movement, and then of *Israel, whose political life he dominated for a decade and a half. He can safely be ranked foremost among the founders of the State of Israel.

David Ben-Gurion was born David Gruen in 1886 in the small town of Plonsk in Russian Poland. His father, an uncertified lawyer, was a secular Jew and fervent adherent of the proto-Zionist "Love of Zion" movement. While still an adolescent, young Gruen became an activist of the socialist-Zionist "Workers of Zion" party. Emigrating to Palestine in 1906, he adopted the Hebrew name Ben-Gurion and for a brief period worked in agriculture, after which he devoted himself to party work and several years of legal studies.

Deported by the Ottoman authorities when World War I broke out, Ben-Gurion spent most of the war years in the United States, where he married. In 1918 he made his way back to Palestine as a volunteer with the Jewish Legion, a unit of the British army created after the *Balfour Declaration of November 1917. Although away on a mission for his party when the *Histadrut* ("General Organization of Jewish Workers in the Land of Israel") was established in 1920, he became its secretary and leading figure soon after his return at the end of 1921.

The *Histadrut* was the vehicle through which Ben-Gurion built up not only his own personal power but also the power of the labor-Zionist movement (dominated by his party) within the broader *Yishuv* and the Zionist Organization. Ben-Gurion and his party struggled to have the Jewish working class in Palestine, organized in the highly centralized *Histadrut*, assume the role of state-building vanguard in the Zionist project by taking charge of immigration and settlement and creating its own network of economic enterprises in agriculture, industry, construction, and distribution, and its own social, educational, and cultural institutions. As part of the same strategy, Ben-Gurion and the *Histadrut* fought to compel Jewish employers to hire only Jewish workers, to the exclusion of cheaper Arab labor. In the 1920s, while advocating cooperation between Arab and Jewish workers, Ben-Gurion strongly rejected the authenticity of Palestinian *Arab nationalism and insisted on the Jews' superior claim to Palestine.

By the early 1930s Ben-Gurion's party, by then known as MAPAI (Workers' Party of the Land of Israel), had become the leading force within the *Yishuv* and the Zionist movement, a development signaled by Ben-Gurion's elevation in 1935 from the leadership of the *Histadrut* to the positions of chair of the Zionist Executive and of the Jewish Agency, the de facto political leadership of the *Yishuv*. From then until 1948 Ben-Gurion would be at the center of Zionist politics and diplomacy. While publicly calling for peace and reconciliation with Palestine's Arab majority, and favoring acceptance of a 1937 British proposal to establish a Jewish state in only a small part of Palestine, he insisted in private that ultimately all of Palestine must be Jewish, a position whose formal endorsement by the Zionist movement he secured in 1942. After World War II Ben-Gurion directed the Zionist political and military struggle, first to compel the British to open Palestine to Jewish immigration and then to secure the establishment of a Jewish state.

Ben-Gurion presided over the establishment of the State of Israel in May 1948 and became its first prime minister and defense minister, suppressing challenges to the authority of the new government and supervising military operations during the war that ensued. A skillful politician, Ben-Gurion held together fractious coalition governments severely tested by the new state's economic difficulties, the massive influx of Jewish immigrants, conflicts between secular and religious Jews, and the acceptance of reparations payments from the Federal Republic of Germany (FRG).

As the *Cold War got under way, Ben-Gurion aligned Israel with the Western camp. In the 1950s, with the United States declining to assume the role of Israel's big-power patron, he established close ties with France, based on a common interest in suppressing Arab nationalism. Convinced that Arabs understood only the language of power, Ben-Gurion opposed Israeli concessions and advocated an "activist" policy of large-scale military retaliation in response to border incidents.

In December 1953 Ben-Gurion abruptly resigned and, proposing to set an example to Israeli youth, "retired" to a desert kibbutz. Rising border tensions aggravated by Israeli raids paved the way for his return to power in 1955, whereupon he began (in collusion with Britain and France) to plan an attack on Egypt aimed at bringing down the nationalist regime of President *Nasser. A military success for Israel, the Suez War of October-November 1956 brought few lasting gains: under U.S. pressure Israel was soon forced to withdraw from the territories it had conquered.

Ben-Gurion remained prime minister until 1963 when, exhausted by party infighting, he again abruptly "retired" to his kibbutz. He soon returned to political life, however, and when his old party MAPAI refused to accommodate his demands, he and his younger protégés broke away to form a new party, RAFI (Israel Workers' List). Ben-Gurion now advocated "statism," which rejected MAPAI's social democratic ethos in favor of a nonclass ideology, proposed that the state assume many *Histadrut* functions, and demanded electoral reform. RAFI did poorly in the 1965 elections, however, and a few years later it merged with MAPAI into the new Israeli Labor Party. Old, in declining health, and no longer a serious candidate for national leadership, Ben-Gurion finally left political life for good in 1970. He died in December 1973 at the age of 87.

Ben-Gurion combined an unquestioning devotion to the achievement of his ultimate goal, the establishment and strengthening of the Jewish state, with considerable tactical flexibility. He possessed tremendous willpower, first-rate organizational ability, and a talent for political maneuvering. Ben-Gurion's critics on both left and right not inaccurately saw him as overbearing, self-righteous, and stubborn, while his supporters insisted that he was precisely the kind of tough and realistic leader *Zionism and later Israel needed. Certainly Ben-Gurion left a deep and enduring imprint on Israeli politics and policy.

(See also ARAB-ISRAELI CONFLICT; INTERNATIONAL MIGRATION; SUEZ CRISIS.)

Shabtai Teveth, *Ben-Gurion and the Palestinian Arabs* (Oxford, 1985). Shabtai Teveth, *Ben-Gurion: The Burning Ground, 1886–1948* (Boston, 1987).

ZACHARY LOCKMAN

BENIN. Until 1985 Benin (formerly Dahomey) held the unenviable record of the most coups since independence. Six times in ten years (1963–72) the army, or factions of it, successfully seized power, with the country also intermittently rocked by military mutinies, attempted *coups d'état, and internal army strife. Since independence, thirteen civilian or military presidents have governed the country. Benin's political institutions have been manipulated, subverted, and abused by civilians and military alike.

When Dahomey achieved internal self-government in 1958, clientelism, regionalism, and ethnicity, which were already well-entrenched, became institutionalized. Each of the parties—Hubert Maga's *Mouvement Démocratique du Dahomey* (MDD), Sourou Migan Apithy's *Parti Républicain du Dahomey* (PRD), Justin Ahomadegbe's *Union Démocratique Dahoméenne* (UDD), and Émile-Derlin Zinsou's *Union Progressiste Dahoméenne* (UPD) ?functioned strictly as a regional party. The regional exclusiveness of each of the three main political parties—MDD, PRD, and UDD, representing the north, Yoruba, and Fon, respectively—meant that no one of them could form an administration of its own, and that coalitions were essential. In October 1963, following a general strike, the army commander, Colonel Christophe Soglo, suspended the constitution and ended the Maga government. In November 1963, Sourou Migan Apithy and Justin Ahomadegbe created a new united party, which alone contested the 1964 elections. In this new government, Apithy became president, sharing power with Ahomadegbe, who became vice-president and head of government. As competition between the two increased, Ahomadegbe tried to evict Apithy from the presidential palace. Colonel Soglo then dismissed Apithy and Ahomadegbe and installed the president of the National Assembly, Tahirou Congacou, in their place. The refusal of the three civilian leaders to cooperate in attempts to create a new constitution and new regime, together with popular pressures, induced the military (at first reluctant) to take power just before Christmas 1965.

Soglo's regime (1965–1967) continued to practice regional spoils politics. The junior officers called for the establishment of a *Comité Militaire de Vigilance* (CMV) as a way of curbing the regime's excesses. In December 1967, Major Maurice Kouandété seized power. There followed a prolonged power struggle between Kouandété and Lt.-Colonel Alphonse Alley, Soglo's chief of staff. Alley acted briefly as head of state (December 1967–July 1968). In July 1968, the army appointed a politician from the old guard, Émile-Derlin Zinsou, as president. Like Soglo, Zinsou tried to reduce public spending, thus antagonizing both the unions and the southern elite and merchants. Undermined by internal conflict within the army and having lost Kouandété's support, Zinsou was overthrown by the former in December 1969. Following the coup, a military directorate of three—Lt.-Colonels de Souza, Sinzogan, and Kouandété—was appointed. This triumvirate called an election, held over three weeks and contested by region. Zinsou, who lacked a mass base, received only 3 percent of the vote, while the others (Ahomadegbe, Apithy, and Maga) easily carried their regions. With the regional conflict by then reaching a level of intensity bordering on civil war, a resolution formalizing spoils politics was eventually reached. The three rivals made up a presidential council; each in turn was to be head of state for two years, starting with Maga (May 1970). In spite of political violence, several mutinies, and a coup attempt, Ahomadegbe succeeded Maga as chairman of the presidential council in May 1972, only to be faced by a Maga-Apithy alliance which rendered his regime impotent. In October 1972 this regime was overthrown by junior army officers, led by Colonel Mathieu Kérékou, who removed their seniors from command positions and established their own regime.

The excesses of both civilian and military governments and their failure to deal with economic and social problems led to the alienation of the unions, students, intellectuals, and peasants from the political system. These groups pressed for reforms, which helped bring about Dahomey's radicalization and a break with the old system, symbolized in its adoption of *socialism in November 1974, and its change of name to Benin in November 1975. By that time, Kérékou had established himself as the dominant military figure, routed the former politicians, and neutralized his civilian left. A fifteen-member *Comité Militaire Révolutionnaire* (CMR), and an advisory *Conseil National de la Révolution* (CNR) of sixty-seven members were established. The most determined opposition came from the regime's civilian supporters—organized labor, radical students, and the left—who wanted a civilian, popularly-based regime. These groups were organized in the leftist *Union Générale des Étudiants et des Élèves Dahoméens* (UGEED), and the student-dominated *Front Unique Démocratique* (FUD), which called for the democratization and "civilianization" of the regime. In November 1972, Kérékou announced a program of "national independence." In the political sphere, attempts were made to create representative institutions, especially at the local level. Thus, some 1,500 rural revolutionary committees (*groupements villageois*) and two urban participatory institutions—Committees for the Defense of the Revolution/CDRs and *comités de gestion*/CGs—were set up in 1974 at all places of work or residence In November 1974, Kérékou announced that Dahomey was to adopt *Marxism-*Leninism as its *ideology and to create a socialist state and society. Key sectors of the economy were nationalized, leading to the creation of over 120 new state enterprises. Plagued by military factionalism, having alienated trade unionists, civil servants, students, and teachers, and constantly threatened by coups d'état, the Kérékou regime became increasingly repressive and authoritarian. Kérékou was able to survive only because his rivals were either dead, detained, or marginalized, and because he had built up a substantial popular following of his own. The left had little mass support, and its leaders (students included) were easily coopted by the regime.

In May 1976, the new party (*Parti Révolutionnaire du Peuple Béninois*/PRPB), created in 1975, elected a twenty-seven-person Central Committee (later increased to forty-five members) with a clear civilian majority. A process of institution-building designed to strengthen Kérékou's position and to centralize power and authority in the presidency was initiated. A new constitution was adopted in November 1977. The elections due under this constitution were postponed until November 1979 and resulted in the appointment of a more civilian cabinet, with only seven of twenty-two portfolios in military hands. The 1980s were marked in Benin by a sense of political and economic decline and failure. By 1979 it had become clear to the Kérékou regime that its external economic relations could be only with the West, particularly with France. Kérékou, still very much in control of the political

system, retired from the army in January 1987 in order to tackle the economic crisis. However, the combination of a huge salary bill, the oil price collapse in Nigeria (Benin's main trading partner), the collapse of the banking system, and the stalled economic reform process due to the regime's corrupt, nepotic, and predatory practices ushered in a major economic crisis which eventually led to the downfall of the Kérékou regime, following a wave of strikes and mass demonstrations in Cotonou in December 1989.

From 19–28 February 1990, a National Sovereign Conference (NSC)—which was to constitute a model for democratic transition throughout *Francophone Africa—brought together representatives of many socioeconomic and professional groups and more than fifty political parties. The 488 delegates elected Nicéphore Soglo (a former World Bank executive) as prime minister for the fourteen-month transition period, while Kérékou remained president with reduced powers. The army promised to return to the barracks. Kérékou's admission that his regime had been a failure, as well as his acceptance of the NSC's decisions as binding and of his 1991 electoral defeat constituted the basis for his national popular rehabilitation as a heroic figure who paved the way for African democracy. The *Haut Conseil de la République* (HCR), the quasi-legislative arm of the transition state under the leadership of Archbishop Isidore de Souza, approved the draft constitution and supervised the 1991 legislative and presidential elections. Nicéphore Soglo, the transition prime minister, was elected president and took office in February 1991. During the period 1991–1994, three parliamentary groups (pro-Soglo, opposition, independent) were evenly divided, and no real majority emerged until May 1992, when Soglo was able to build a fragile working majority, which collapsed in September 1993. Until the 1995 elections, Soglo could command only nineteen of the sixty-four votes in the National Assembly, a number that declined even further during the 1994 budget crisis. A decisive factor in Soglo's demise was the failure of his free-market reforms to revive the economy. Modest initial growth was seriously undermined in 1994 by the 50 percent devaluation of the CFA franc, while privatization led to the retrenchment of 10,000 public workers. Soglo's increased reliance on the authoritarian methods of the past eventually led to his defeat in the March 1996 presidential elections, which saw the surprising return to power of Mathieu Kérékou, now a born-again Christian and newly converted democrat, who garnered over 52 percent of the votes. The resignation of prime minister Adrien Houngbédji on 8 May 1998 dealt a fatal blow to the motley alliance of some twenty political parties who initially supported Kérékou. This political crisis occurred in a context of social unrest, protest, and strikes. Legislative elections designed to renew the National Assembly took place on 30 March 1999. Regrouped around three alliances, the opposition won forty-two seats while the governmental coalition obtained only forty seats (out of eighty-three contested seats). With twenty-seven deputies, the *Renaissance du Bénin* of former president Nicéphore Soglo was the main beneficiary of these elections, thus ideally positioning him for the March 2001 presidential elections. In early 2000, an alliance of ten opposition parties, led by Soglo and Adrien Houngbédji, now Speaker of the National Assembly, was formed. As a result, Kérékou was forced to resort once again to a coalition government based on a fragile partisan alliance. As the country celebrated the fortieth anniversary of its independence on 1 August 2000, Kérékou's *fin de règne* occurred in a gloomy political atmosphere rife with persistent rumors of corruption, financial scandals, and yet another military coup d'état.

(See also FRANCOPHONE AFRICA; SOCIALISM AND SOCIAL DEMOCRACY.)

Chris Allen, "Benin," in Bogdan Szajkowski, ed., *Benin, the Congo, Burkina Faso* (London and New York, 1989), pp. 1–144. Samuel Decalo, "Benin: First of the New Democracies," in John F. Clark and David E. Gardinier, eds., *Political Reform in Francophone Africa* (Boulder, Colo., 1997), pp. 43–61. Bruce A. Magnusson, "Testing Democracy in Benin: Experiments in Institutional Reform," in Richard Joseph, ed., *State, Conflict and Democracy in Africa* (Boulder, Colo., 1999), pp. 217–237.

GUY MARTIN

BHUTAN. The Kingdom of Bhutan, located on the southeast slope of the Himalayas, is bordered on the north by Tibet and on the south, east, and west by India. The population as of the mid-1990s was about 600,000. Historically, Bhutan had a theocratic system of government similar to that in Tibet, dominated by the Druk (dragon) Buddhist sect of Mahayana *Buddhism. But by the late nineteenth century the system had fallen apart, and was replaced by a hereditary monarchy in 1907. The first two rulers of the Wangchuk dynasty gradually extended their control over the disparate collection of monastic and local landed elites. The third ruler, Jigme Dorji Wangchuk (1952–1972), introduced basic political and economic reforms: a Tshogdu (elected national assembly) and a Lhengyel Tsok (council of ministers), but with the king serving as head of state. The present ruler, Jigme Singye Wangchuk, came to the throne in 1972 and continued his father's modernization programs. The central administrative system was greatly expanded and given a broad range of powers and responsibilities. An autonomous judiciary was established, with a high court in the capital, Thimphu, and courts in each district. A new legal code, based upon both modern principles of jurisprudence and Bhutan's customary Buddhist laws, was introduced.

By the mid-1980s, King Jigme Singye was concerned with the excessive concentration of power in the center and sought to introduce an ambitious decentralization program. But this was superseded in the late 1980s by a broad range of new policies—termed the *Drigham Namza*, or national culture principle, program—that had as its objective the preservation of Bhutan's national identity and traditional Buddhist culture. Dzongka, the official court language, became the national language by decree, replacing the various Tibetan dialects in eastern Bhutan and the Nepali spoken in southern Bhutan. These programs elicited a negative response from the large Hindu Nepali minority in the south and the various other ethnic and linguistic minorities in the eastern hills.

Under the *Drigham Namza* policy, the large number of "illegal" immigrants that had entered Bhutan since the 1970s were ordered to leave the country. Most of these were Nepalese who had settled in southern Bhutan. Also resident in this area was a Nepalese community of long standing, having been there since the early twentieth century. The order to leave did not extend to these legal Bhutanese citizens. But the confusion caused by the eviction program led to opposition to *Drigham Namza*, and many legal Nepali Bhutanese fled the

country. Approximately 120,000 Nepalese from Bhutan ended up in refugee camps in India and Nepal by 1995. This led to a bitter ongoing dispute between the Nepal and Bhutan governments that had not been resolved by 2000. Southern Bhutan thus was still an arena of Bhutanese/Nepalese conflict, though by 1998 at a reduced scale. In 1996–1997, a Buddhist community in eastern Bhutan, the Sherdopens, also emerged as a dissident force in Bhutan's polity that could pose a serious threat to the integrity of the monarchical system.

Michael Aris, and Michael Hutt, eds., *Bhutan: Aspects of Culture and Development*, Kiscadale Asian Research Series no. 6 (Gartmore, Scotland, 1994).

LEO E. ROSE

BILL OF RIGHTS. The Bill of Rights of the *United States *Constitution consists of the first ten amendments taken together, especially the first eight which identify specific individual rights. These were proposed in 1789 by Representative James Madison, who was solidly backed by President George Washington during the First Congress. Ten of the twelve congressionally approved amendments were ratified by ten states so as to take effect on 15 December 1791. Their general tenor is to protect individual personal, political, and religious liberties against infringement by government, principally by the national government in the original conception and down to 1925 when a process of "nationalization" gradually began that has brought protection against invasion by the states of most of the *rights listed and of a number only implied by (or "penumbral" to) the rights specified. The philosophical foundation of the Bill of Rights is set forth in the Declaration of Independence's first sentences, especially the announcement of "certain unalienable rights" grounded in the "laws of nature and nature's God." The effectiveness of the provisions of the Bill of Rights in protecting fundamental personal liberties through American law is uniquely dependent upon the power of *judicial review as exercised by the federal judiciary, with a last resort in the *Supreme Court of the United States. The judiciary determines with finality, on a case by case adversary basis, the meaning and force of laws under the Constitution considered as the Supreme Law of the Land (Art. VI).

The origins of the liberties protected and general theory of rights undergirding that protection are of great antiquity and grounded in immemorial usage (or *prescription*) and natural right, although meaning and importance were sharpened by the debate leading to American independence and Revolution and gained impetus from the eighteenth-century Enlightenment with its emphasis upon reason and the individual. It remains generally true, however, that the rights protected substantively were part and parcel of an inherited tradition of common law liberty and rule of law that originally emerged in medieval England and whose great monument is the Magna Carta (1215). Decisive for the continuity of this vision of liberty through law and limited government was the education of subsequent generations of lawyers, including the American revolutionary generation and beyond, by Sir Edward Coke's *Institutes* and *Reports*. After the Glorious Revolution, the English Bill of Rights was enacted as part of the constitutional settlement (1689). Following this precedent, the bill of rights concept today may be thought of as primarily

American. But the liberties protected, and institutional modes devised for their protection, are deeply moored in Anglo-American political and constitutional history, especially in the seventeenth-century resistance against absolute kingship—thereby avoided in England, unlike in most of the rest of Western Europe—with fateful consequences for free government into the present. Indeed, the securing of personal liberty and free government through rule of law is a legacy quite self-consciously reaching beyond the Magna Carta itself, back to Aristotle and Cicero in distant antiquity.

Well before 1789 when, under heavy political pressure from the Anti-Federalists and public sentiment fearful that personal liberties might be imperiled by the new Constitution, James Madison proposed his amendments, virtually *all* of the rights to be included in the federal Bill of Rights already had been set out in bills of rights ratified by eleven of the original thirteen states plus Vermont. North Carolina, for example, refused even to consider ratification until religious liberty was secured, and ratification elsewhere was conditioned on the promise of amendments to protect personal liberty and the states' integrity. *Critical rights* already adopted by one or another of the new American states included no establishment of religion, free exercise of religion, free speech, free press, assembly, petition, right to bear arms, searches and seizures protection, requirement of grand jury indictment and petit jury trial, protection against double jeopardy and self-incrimination, and guarantee of due process of law. The Massachusetts Declaration of Rights (1780), drafted by John Adams, even included a reserved powers clause (Art. IV) analogous to the Tenth Amendment's provision. The Massachusetts document also had the merit of partly replacing the admonitory language of *ought* used by George Mason in drafting the 1776 Virginia Declaration of Rights (the model for eight other states' bills of rights), with the imperative *shall* of legal command found (along with *shall not*) in Madison's Bill of Rights.

The Bill of Rights was originally applicable only to the federal government. The truly *critical rights*, especially those stated in the First Amendment, were considered to be the heart of "the laws of Nature and nature's God" invoked by the Declaration of Independence. These, it was thought, must at all costs be put beyond the reach of majorities because they were antecedent to the social compact and were the essential preconditions of free government itself. They were called "rights of conscience" and thought to be emblematic of the free human being (the Magna Carta's *liber homo*). Thomas Jefferson invoked them in the powerful opening sentence of the Virginia Statute of Religious Freedom (1786): "God Almighty hath created the mind free." There was virtually no case law and judicial elaboration of the meaning of the provisions of the Bill of Rights until well after adoption of the Civil War amendments, numbers thirteen, fourteen, and fifteen. A voluminous litigatory process of "absorption," "selective incorporation," and identification of liberties occupying a "preferred position" (First Amendment rights), or as being "fundamental rights," began in 1925 and 1931 Supreme Court decisions in the Gitlow and Near cases and accelerated in 1947 with the Adamson case. This has resulted in broad application of the Bill of Rights to state governments and even to private actions, no less than to actions of the federal government. Today the *liberty* protected against invasion by the states under the Due Process Clause of the Fourteenth Amendment embraces all provisions of the First Amendment and nearly all provisions of the Fourth, Fifth, Sixth, Seventh, and Eighth Amendments. The principal exceptions are the Fifth Amendment's right to a grand jury indictment in criminal cases and the Seventh Amendment's guarantee of a jury trial in civil cases. In addition, there is a substantial expanse of additional personal liberty, especially race-related "civil rights," protected by the Equal Protection Clause. This expansion includes strictly extraconstitutional rights (such as privacy and the right to travel) that an activist judiciary has discovered to be long-unsuspected implications of the express rights, or has construed as being included in the Retained Rights Clause of the Ninth Amendment and, perhaps, even hidden among the "Blessings of Liberty" spoken of in the Preamble to the Constitution.

(See also HUMAN RIGHTS.)

Bernard Schwartz, *The Great Rights of Mankind: A History of the American Bill of Rights* (New York, 1977). Ellis Sandoz, *A Government of Laws: Political Theory, Religion and the American Founding* (Baton Rouge, 1990). Helen Veit et al., *Creating the Bill of Rights: The Documentary Record of the First Federal Congress* (Baltimore, 1991). Gordon Lloyd and Margie Lloyd, eds., *The Essential Bill of Rights: Original Arguments and Fundamental Documents* (Lanham, Md., 1998).

ELLIS SANDOZ

BLAIR, Tony. The last and youngest U.K. prime minister of the twentieth century governs by consensus. Unlike the Victorian founders of the British Labour Party, Tony Blair is not trying to reform the capitalist system out of existence nor level out the disparities in wealth it generates. Averting social conflict is the central purpose of his domestic program. To achieve this, paradoxically, he needed to be a divisive leader of his own party, the Labour Party.

Born 6 May 1953, the son of a Conservative, Blair entered politics relatively late. As a young barrister based in London, he encountered other ambitious lawyers who were active in the Labour Party, including his future wife Cherie Booth, and their employer Alexander Irvine, who became lord chancellor in the Blair cabinet. However, once started, he made rapid progress. In May 1983, he became the youngest Labour MP, representing Sedgefield, in the north of England. By July 1994, after the sudden death of incumbent John Smith, he was the youngest-ever leader of the Labour Party.

He owed his position to a change in party rules introduced by Smith. He was elected by a plebiscite in which nearly a million supporters cast votes, which replaced the maneuvering and alliance building of previous leadership contests. He was thus freed from the normal political debts to fellow MPs, or to powerful trade unions which fund the Labour Party. His first display of this independence was to rewrite the party's seventy-six-year-old constitution, deleting its famous reference to "common ownership of the means of production." He submitted this proposal to a ballot of party members, who were persuaded to endorse what amounted to the burial of Labour's socialist past.

Blair's 1997 general election campaign was consciously modeled on Bill *Clinton's success. His continual references to New Labour, his promise to be "tough on crime, tough on the causes of crime," his promise to make "education, education, education" his first priority, campaigning techniques like "rapid rebuttal," and much else were borrowed from the Democrats. Blair was more cautious than Clinton about public spending, which he undertook to freeze for two years. He also promised no increase in income tax. Having thus reassured middle-class voters, on 1 May 1997 he became prime minister in Labour's biggest election victory for more than half a century.

During conflicts abroad, Blair consciously aped Margaret *Thatcher, by pushing earlier and harder for military intervention in the Gulf and in Kosovo. In both cases, his actions were popular in the country. The Kosovo conflict, unusually, carried left-wing approval. However, this eagerness to be tough in times of crisis disguises Blair's general wish to move with majority opinion and hold the middle ground. In *Northern Ireland, he overruled his own party's republican sympathies to ensure uninterrupted continuation of the painstaking diplomacy of his predecessor, John Major. In his anxiety to retain the confidence of Ulster's prickly Unionist leaders, he removed the Northern Ireland secretary, Mo Mowlam—whose two years in this role had made her the only cabinet minister more popular than Blair himself—and sent in his favorite, Peter Mandelson, whom the Unionists trusted.

Blair's other constitutional changes—including devolved assemblies in Scotland and Wales, the ending of the anachronistic right of hereditary peers to vote in the House of Lords, and the introduction of directly elected mayors to English cities like London—are all conciliatory moves despite their radical appearance. The Scottish Assembly, for example, is seen as a bulwark against Scottish separatism, while the House of Lords faced the risk of being abolished outright.

In other respects, Blair has risked disappointing his own supporters. There were high expectations that the U.K.'s National Health Service would improve under Labour, but Blair and his chancellor Gordon Brown made a greater priority out of holding down public spending. Labour MPs rebelled in large numbers when the government announced cuts in benefits for single mothers and for the disabled. Blair's home secretary, Jack Straw, courted unpopularity on the left with harsh measures to cut crime and illegal immigration—despite which, violent crime continued rising.

Blair has also disappointed his allies, the Liberal Democrats, by making no move to introduce *proportional representation to the House of Commons. His long-term ambition is a solid new alliance in the center of British politics, with the Liberals and possibly the left wing of the Conservative Party aligned with New Labour, leaving the Tory right and Labour's own left permanently excluded. Ironically, the size of his parliamentary majority—which far exceeded his own expectations—may have stymied this project. Most of his 418 MPs oppose changes in the Commons voting system or deals with other parties.

Blair also took care to avoid committing himself during his first term in office to a decision on whether sterling should join the European single currency. Both he and his chancellor are instinctively pro-Europe, unlike Thatcher and the majority of Tory MPs. Giving the Bank of England control over interest rates was seen as an opening move toward sterling's integration with the euro. But if Labour were to abolish sterling, they would risk antagonizing public opinion, as well as a rift with the feared media mogul, Rupert Murdoch.

None of these problems prevented Blair from enjoying more than two years as one of the most popular prime ministers the U.K. has ever had. Labour inherited a buoyant economy and took such meticulous care of it that by 2000, Britain had seen more than seven years of uninterrupted growth. Blair has also cut unemployment, restored some trade union bargaining rights, introduced a national minimum wage, and has begun to tackle poverty and decay in inner cities. During the twentieth century, the Labour Party was never able to win outright in two successive general elections, or hold onto office for more than six successive years. There is no reason to doubt that they will achieve that under Tony Blair.

(See also BRITAIN; ECONOMIC AND MONETARY UNION; SOCIALISM AND SOCIAL DEMOCRACY.)

Peter Mandelson and Roger Liddle, *The Blair Revolution: Can New Labour Deliver?* (London, 1996). Andy McSmith, *Faces of Labour: The Inside Story* (London, 1997). Philip Gould, *The Unfinished Revolution: How the Modernisers Saved the Labour Party* (London, 1998).

ANDY McSMITH

BLS STATES. See SOUTHERN AFRICA; SMALL STATES AND TERRITORIES.

BOLÍVAR, Simón. Best known of the heroes of the Latin American independence movement, Simón Bolívar was a brilliant military strategist and was responsible for the liberation of the five Andean countries from Spanish control. Equally important, Bolívar is remembered for his prophetic views about Latin American political problems and his aborted attempts to form a continent-wide federation rather than a proliferation of small nations.

Born in Caracas, *Venezuela, on 24 July 1783, Bolívar's wealthy background enabled him to combine military expertise with a broad general culture, frequently expressed through bitter statements regarding the present and future of Latin America. At a young age, he went to Spain and elsewhere in Europe. Back in Caracas in 1807, he began to militate for the independence of Latin America. He first participated in agitation and propaganda organizations such as the Sociedad Patriótica. Later he organized a liberation army that won the decisive battles leading to the independence of Venezuela, Colombia, Ecuador, Peru, and Bolivia.

After the military period was over, Bolívar became active as a political leader in several of the countries he had liberated. Unlike José de San Martín, leader of the independence movement in the southern part of the continent, Bolívar was a staunch republican. From the beginning, however, he argued that only a strong and centralized government could control the factional forces in the new republics and prevent national disintegration. For example, he was one of the first to suggest that the failure of the first republic in Venezuela did not result from the superiority of the monarchic forces but the establishment of a weak government in 1811. In his famous speech at the Congress of Angostura in February 1819, Bolívar voiced his preference for a central and unitary government as well as a hereditary senate; this anticipated his idea of a life-term president, which he elaborated for Bolivia's constitution. Latin America was not yet ready, he thought, for representative government.

In international terms, Bolívar also supported centralism.

He tried to persuade his contemporaries to form a large, unified nation rather than many small ones. This would provide a defensive mechanism against external aggression, he argued. Although his vision was adopted at the Congress of Panama in 1826, it was never implemented. Latin America fragmented, while its neighbor to the north followed the Bolivarian prescription. Partly as a consequence, the United States came to dominate Latin America, just as Bolívar had feared.

After twenty years of involvement in political and military struggles, and of controlling the public affairs of several countries, Bolívar admitted that "America is ungovernable for us." These words, written a month before his death in December 1830, summarized his profound pessimism. The next 150 years of history can be seen as confirmation of Bolívar's prophecies about domestic and international problems in the Western Hemisphere.

Simón Bolívar, *Cartas de Bolívar* (Albuquerque, N.Mex., 1948).

HERACLIO BONILLA

BOLIVIA. Bolivia's turbulent political history is rooted in its racial, geographic, and ethnic diversity. Approximately 60 percent of the country's 6.5 million inhabitants are Indians; another 30 percent are racially mixed. Bolivia's political life, however, has always been dominated by whites, who constitute less than 10 percent of the population. Moreover, Bolivia's geographic diversity has contributed to a profound sense of regional rivalry. Political conflict in Bolivia has been characterized by regional disputes, pitting the residents of the eastern lowlands against those of the Andean highlands. This pattern of regional and racial conflict has been largely responsible for undermining the effectiveness of national governments.

Owing primarily these factors, for the first fifty years after Bolivian independence in 1825, the country was dominated by strongmen (*caudillos*). The War of the Pacific in 1879 ended the *caudillo* period as the combined forces of Peru and Bolivia were defeated by Chile; as a result, Bolivia became a landlocked nation. The end of the war also coincided with Bolivia's integration into the world economy through the export of tin. For most of the next fifty years, Bolivia was ruled by a formally democratic system controlled by powerful tin barons. The Chaco War (1932–1935) pitted Bolivia against Paraguay in a bloody struggle that ended civilian rule and generated a turbulent that culminated in revolutionary upheaval in 1952.

Led by the Movimiento Nacionalista Revolucionario (MNR), Bolivian workers, middle sectors, and peasants overthrew the old order on 9 April 1952. For the next twelve years, the MNR carried out one of the most far-reaching social revolutions of the twentieth century, nationalizing the nation's tin industry, introducing a broad agrarian reform, and declaring universal suffrage. In the process, thirty years of state-led economic development began.

In November 1964, the Bolivian military overthrew the MNR, and over the next two decades military governments held power, ranging from the populist experiments of General Juan José Torres (1970) to the repressive right-wing government of General Hugo Banzer Suárez (1971–1978), and the corrupt administration of "Narco General" Luis García Meza (1980–1981). Following a dramatic institutional breakdown, the military transferred power to civilians in October 1982.

Since then Bolivia has held four national elections. The results have been determined by the Congress, which serves an electoral college when the winning candidate fails to obtain a majority of the vote. Coalitions between governing and opposition parties are the basis of contemporary Bolivian politics. In 1985, President Víctor Paz Estenssoro's MNR joined forces with General Hugo Banzer's Acción Democrática Nacionalista (ADN) party. Between 1989 and 1993 Jaime Paz Zamora of the Movimiento de Izquierda Revolucionaria (MIR) governed Bolivia with support from Banzer. The MNR returned to power in 1993 under the leadership of Gonzalo Sánchez de Lozada, a mining entrepreneur turned politician.

The main political actors in recent Bolivian history have been the political parties, labor, and the military. The largest party is the MNR, founded by Paz Estenssoro in 1941. Responsible for carrying out the 1952 revolution, the party switched positions when it returned to power in 1985. It imposed an economic program that ended hyperinflation and stabilized Bolivia's economy. It also ended state capitalism by decentralizing and privatizing state firms and opening up the economy through its neoliberal "new economic policy."

General Hugo Banzer's ADN was founded after Banzer was overthrown in 1978 and has been a key element of Bolivia's democratization. In 1985, the ADN won the presidential election but failed to reach the required fifty percent and was outmaneuvered in the Congress by Paz Estenssoro and the MNR. After co-governing between 1989 and 1993, Banzer finally won the elections in 1997 and assumed the presidency as a civilian democrat. The third party is the MIR, founded in 1971 to combat the Banzer dictatorship. In August 1989, the MIR's leader Jaime Paz Zamora was elected president by the Congress. In one of the most ironic twists in Bolivian politics, Paz Zamora was elected through a pact with Banzer's ADN. The MIR-ADN pact remained operative throughout the 1990s.

Historically, labor has been among Bolivia's most powerful institutions. Under the direction of the Central Obrera Boliviana (COB), labor was able to challenge the imposition of austerity measures while simultaneously obtaining concessions for the working classes. But years of struggle culminated pitifully in 1985 when the government launched its new economic policy. Mass firings of mine workers, who constituted the backbone of organized labor in Bolivia, proved to be the COB's downfall. After nearly fifteen years of rebuilding, the COB has failed to regain its once prominent position.

At the time of the transition to civilian government in 1982, the Bolivian armed forces were discredited by corruption, factionalism, and widespread human rights abuses committed while in power. Subsequent democratic governments attempted to rebuild the institution without challenging it. With U.S. aid, Bolivian governments have satisfied demands from officers for better equipment and training.

With the assistance of the armed forces the Bolivian government has also carried out a an effective "Dignity Plan" with the objective of stamping out the production of the coca leaf in Bolivia by the year 2002. By 2000 the campaign had successfully eradicated nearly fifty percent of all coca production. If such progress continues, Bolivia could become the first country in the region to extricate itself from the illicit *drugs industry. At the same time Bolivia would have to develop viable alternatives to ensure the livelihood of over 200,000 people who were engaged in the cultivation of coca.

(See also DEMOCRATIC TRANSITIONS.)

James Dunkerley, *Rebellion in the Veins: Political Struggle in Bolivia, 1952–1982* (London, 1984). James M. Malloy and Eduardo Gamarra, *Revolution and Reaction: Bolivia, 1964–1985* (New Brunswick, N.J., 1988). Kenneth D. Lehman, *Bolivia and the United States: A Limited Partnership* (Athens, Ga., 1999).

EDUARDO A. GAMARRA

BOLSHEVIK REVOLUTION. See RUSSIAN REVOLUTION.

BOSNIA AND HERZEGOVINA. The European Community and the United States recognized the modern state of Bosnia-Herzegovina on 6 and 7 April 1992, respectively, and the new state was admitted to the United Nations on 22 May 1992. But not all citizens of Bosnia-Herzegovina were supportive of its sovereignty or, indeed, its right to exist.

For centuries, a succession of *colonial empires created a complex interweaving of peoples in Bosnia-Herzegovina, each with their own religion, culture, and perception of history. When these peoples lived together in peace it was primarily because an occupying great power imposed its will over the aspirations of all three factions: from 1463 until 1878 it was the Turks; from 1878 to 1919, the Austrians; from 1919 to 1945, the king of Serbia and the Serbian aristocracy; and from 1945 to 1991, the communists.

In 1992 there were approximately 4.5 million people living in Bosnia-Herzegovina, divided into three major ethnic groups: Muslim Slavs (Bosniaks), who had converted to Islam during the Turkish occupation (40 percent of the population); Serbs, Slavs who were influenced by Byzantium and were Orthodox Christians (33 percent of the population); and Croats, Slavs who early on were influenced by the West, especially the Hungarians and Austrians, and had taken on the Roman Catholic Christian religion (17 percent of the population).

Encouraged by the willingness of the Europeans to recognize unilateral declarations of independence by *Croatia and *Slovenia, the Muslim-dominated Bosnian Assembly held a referendum on declaring independence on 29 February 1992. Sixty-three percent of the electorate turned out and over 90 percent voted for independence. But the voters were almost exclusively Muslims and Croats; the Serbs had boycotted the vote as illegal. Even the Muslim/Croat majority did not share objectives, however. The Muslims wanted a unitary state in which they would be the major power; the Croats wanted to take their lands out of Bosnia-Herzegovina and join the new Republic of Croatia.

The European Community (now the European Union or EU) recognized that maintaining a single multicultural state could only be done by force and tried to head off conflict by bringing the leaders of the three major ethnic factions to Lisbon in March 1992 for intensive negotiations. Under EC auspices, the leaders of the three main ethnic groups in Bosnia-Herzegovina signed an agreement in Sarajevo, providing for the division of the republic into three autonomous units along ethnic lines. But on 25 March, following a trip to Sarajevo by U.S. Ambassador to *Yugoslavia Warren Zimmerman in which Zimmerman implied that the United States would support a multicultural state headed by the Muslim plurality, President Alija Izetbegovic (a Muslim) rejected the division of the republic based on ethnicity and urged all Bosnians to accept the concept of a unitary state. Two days later, the Serbs in Bosnia proclaimed an independent Serbian Republic of Bosnia-Herzegovina. Almost immediately a war began with each of the three ethnic factions fighting the other two. Brutal combat continued for 44 months, despite the presence of a so-called "UN Protection Force."

To quell the conflict, UN and EC representatives put forward other plans to divide Bosnia-Herzegovina along ethnic lines in January 1993 and July 1993. The United States and the government of Alija Izetbegovic rejected partition and insisted that Bosnia-Herzegovina be a multicultural, unitary state. In October 1994, Bosnian Serb President Radovan Karadzic, in a private message to U.S. President Bill Clinton, said that the Bosnian Serbs would drop their insistence on an independent Serbian state if the Serbs were allowed to have a "Bosnian Serb Republic" with a high degree of autonomy within a Bosnia-Herzegovina with a weak central government whose role was limited to international matters. The idea was initially rejected by the United States and the Izetbegovic government, but by the fall of 1995, after more than 200,000 people had lost their lives and another two million had been driven from their homes, the factions agreed on 21 November 1995 in Dayton, Ohio, to a plan that essentially took Karadzic up on his offer.

The Republic of Bosnia-Herzegovina that emerged from Dayton and the subsequent peace treaty of 14 December 1995 is a federal state. It consists of two subunits: a Muslim/Croat Federation and a Bosnian Serb Republic (Republika Srbska). Each subunit has its own constitution, parliament, and Presidency. These regional governments control most day-to-day matters such as education, police force, taxation, and public services.

The national government of the Republic of Bosnia-Herzegovina consists of a bicameral legislature. The House of Representatives has 42 members who serve for two years: 28 from the Muslim Croat Federation (14 Muslim, 14 Croat) and 14 from the Bosnian Serb Republic. The representatives from the Muslim/Croat Federation are directly elected by Federation voters. The Serbian representatives are elected by the Bosnian Serb National Assembly. A House of People consists of 15 members elected for two-year terms: five Muslims, five Croats, and five Serbs. Croat and Muslim members are selected by the Federation House of People; the Serbian members are selected by the Bosnian Serb Republic National Assembly.

The executive branch of the Republic of Bosnia-Herzegovina consists of a Presidency and a Council of Ministers. The Presidency has three members elected for four-year terms: a Muslim, a Croat, and a Serb. The Muslim and Croat members are elected by the voters of the Federation; the Serb, by voters of the Bosnian Serb Republic. The Bosnia-Herzegovina Council of Ministers consists of two co-chairs (usually one from the Federation, one from the Bosnian Serb Republic), one deputy, and three ministers. All members of the Council of Ministers are appointed by the Bosnia-Herzegovina Presidency with the approval of the Bosnia-Herzegovina House of Representatives.

The national government of Bosnia-Herzegovina handles defense, diplomatic, and international economic matters for the country.

In practice the national government is very weak. Any proposal of the Presidency can be blocked if just one of the three members objects. In this event the issue is sent to the parliamentary members from the ethnic group of the member making the objection. If they agree with the Presidency member's position, the proposal is rejected. Similarly, decisions in the parliament can be blocked if one-third of the members of either house object. Each ethnic group, therefore, has a de facto veto over legislation.

Because of the weakness of the central government the real power in Bosnia-Herzegovina remains in the hands of a United Nations High Commissioner for Bosnia-Herzegovina, backed by 37,000 troops of a NATO-dominated international military force under UN auspices. The High Commissioner has the power to remove any elected official from office if, in his opinion, the official is not acting in the spirit of the Dayton accords and the constitution of Bosnia-Herzegovina. For example, the president of the Bosnian Serb Republic was removed from office in 1999 by the High Commissioner despite his having been elected by the voters of that republic. When the national government of Bosnia-Herzegovina has been unable to act, the High Commissioner has taken action in their stead. For example, the flag of the new country, its money, and license plates for automobiles were all designed by the UN High Commissioner.

As of March 2000, The Republic of Bosnia-Herzegovina is not yet a truly functioning sovereign state. Deep suspicions and fears continue to divide the people into ethnic enclaves. Few refugees have been allowed to return to their homes in areas dominated by other ethnic groups. The national government is little more than a debating society and the real focus of most citizens' loyalties remains upon the leaders of their respective ethnic groups and upon local political structures.

(See also BOSNIAN WAR; KOSOVO WAR; MACEDONIA; SERBIA AND MONTENEGRO; WAR.)

David Owen, *Balkan Odyssey* (New York, 1995). James A. Baker III, *The Politics of Diplomacy* (New York, 1995).

RONALD L. HATCHETT

BOSNIAN WAR. The war in Bosnia-Herzegovina (1992–1995) was the most destructive segment of the War of Yugoslav Dissolution that began when the Yugoslav republics of *Slovenia and *Croatia seceded in the summer of 1991. Because there was no ethnic majority within its boundaries and no "Bosnian" nation, of all six republics of the old Yugoslav federation the Republic of Bosnia-Herzegovina (hereafter "Bosnia") had most to fear from violent secession. A majority of its citizens would have preferred the then-existing Yugoslav framework to political experiments that could risk *war. But once reunited Germany was committed to the recognition of Croatia and Slovenia, the Muslim leadership in Sarajevo knew both that the old *Yugoslavia was impossible and that historic opportunities beckoned.

Of the three constituent peoples of Bosnia-Herzegovina, as defined by earlier Yugoslav constitutions, the Muslims were the most numerous (43 percent). Most of them were prepared

to accept a compromise that would fall short of full independence—especially if full independence risked war—but they nevertheless nervously followed their leaders in the Party of Democratic Action (Stranka Demokratske Akcije, SDA) who demanded a leap in the dark.

The Croats (17 percent) were the least numerous, but—especially in their stronghold of western Herzegovina—they were the most determined to get Bosnia out of Yugoslavia, and then to break away from Bosnia with the support of Croatia. Their party (Hrvatska Demokratska Zajednica, HDZ BH) was prepared to enter a tactical alliance with the Muslims to get the independence vote, but most Bosnian Croats were not prepared to see their long-term future in a sovereign Bosnia. Their leader, Mate Boban, did not believe in any permanent alliances, but clearly saw the interests of his people and their statelet ("Herceg-Bosna") in an extended Croatia.

The Serbs of Bosnia, overwhelmingly, refused to be ejected from Yugoslavia, especially as the Bosnian referendum on "sovereignty" (February 1992) was held in violation of the constitutional right of each of Bosnia's three peoples to veto any decision unacceptable to its vital interests. That they would have liked a "Greater Serbia" is certain. That they would have gone to war to get it is unlikely. Indeed, the Serbian Democratic Party (Srpska Demokratska Stranka, SDS) was willing to settle—before the war began—for a regional autonomy far less substantial than what the Serbs were subsequently offered in Geneva in 1993 and at Dayton in 1995.

In the aftermath of the first post-communist election in Bosnia (fall 1992) those three main ethnic political parties were included in a coalition government of anti-communist nationalists. The breakup of that coalition clearly reflected external pressure as Serbia tried to frighten Alija Izetbegovic, the Muslim leader, into passivity and Croatia, with German support, tried to win him for secession. There was never any prospect that Bosnia could be taken out of Yugoslavia, that is, detached from Serbia, without a war.

President Slobodan Milosevic of Serbia, however, played the Bosnian crisis primarily as a means of consolidating his power in Serbia proper and extending his influence without committing himself to any clearly defined strategic objective, such as the "Greater Serbian" project. A cynical apparatchik devoid of convictions rather than a "Serbian nationalist," he withdrew the Yugoslav National Army (JNA) from Bosnia (April 1992) and sent in his paramilitaries, who triggered ethnic cleansing. Ever the short-term manipulator, he imposed his control on the Bosnian Serbs, whom he managed to divide between a civilian faction in Pale (Radovan Karadzic, Momcilo Krajisnik) and the military HQ at Han Pijesak (General Ratko Mladic).

Milosevic in Serbia and President Franjo Tudjman in Croatia were both busy establishing a quasi-dictatorial post-communist regime, and they needed vulgar nationalism—for a time—to outbid the most vulgar nationalists. Tudjman, however, did not shed Marxist crocodile tears at the passing of the old Titoist certainties. Their respective struggles to impose themselves on their own republics may explain more about the war in Bosnia than the confused and variable goals of any of the Bosnian leaders.

When the Bosnian Serbs took control of the Serb-majority areas, they were well equipped and officered. But the numerical advantage lay with the Muslims, who hoped to win in the end with international help. The crucial military issue was whether the Serbs could bottle up superior Muslim forces by keeping an armed ring around Sarajevo. Consequently, cease-fires tended to favor the Serbs and to be broken by the Muslims. The Serb ring around Sarajevo held from first to last.

In addition the Serbs severely damaged the patience of western states by their mistreatment of prisoners in 1992 and by their expulsion ethnic cleansing of non-Serb civilians. Similar atrocities by Croats and Muslims were less conspicuous. The Western media chose their sympathies at the start and kept up an agitation in favor of military intervention against the Serbs.

Of several peace plans offered or mediated by the EC/EU from 1991 to 1993 the Serbs rejected the Vance-Owen Plan (May 1993) that would have divided Bosnia into ten "cantons," and Muslims rejected the Owen-Stoltenberg Plan that provided for a confederal model of three sovereign national entities (December 1993). A territorial plan that did not include a constitutional blueprint, presented by the "Contact Group" in 1994, was refused by the Serbs because it was nonnegotiable. It was quietly discarded in 1995.

The media call for intervention made the war the subject of international debate to an extent unknown since Vietnam. Many Europeans were inclined to support a compromise peace and a federalized Bosnia, supported no side, and wanted a real arms embargo; whereas the United States disliked European peace plans, broke the arms embargo from at least 1994, and overtly supported the Muslims.

In 1992–1993 the Serbs sat on their advantages and hoped that the world would recognize their apparent victory. But the war changed when the U.S. sponsored a Croat-Muslim alliance and the Europeans realized that there would be no settlement unless the EU surrendered political leadership to Washington. This was followed by a crisis in 1994 when a mortar shell fell on the crowded Markale market in Sarajevo. The Serbs were blamed, and evidence that the shell could not have been fired from Serbian lines became available too late to affect the crisis caused by the massacre.

The *North Atlantic Treaty Organization (NATO), in loose combination with the UN, demanded that Serbian artillery be removed from the vicinity of Sarajevo. A NATO attack on the Bosnian Serb Army (VRS) was obviated when the Russians agreed to send troops to help monitor the cease-fire. From this point the war became a matter of Muslim attempts to exploit the safe areas—in Sarajevo, Gorazde, Tuzla, Bihac, and finally Srebrenica—which had been declared by the UN but never demilitarized by UNPROFOR (United Nations Protecting Force). In short the Muslims were allowed to attack out of these areas but the Serbs were not allowed to pursue them back in.

This inequitable stance was disliked by the UNPROFOR commander, General Michael Rose, but it seemed just what the U.S. NATO commander, Admiral Leighton Smith, needed to get his aircraft into action. The first NATO bombs ever dropped in action fell on the VRS near Gorazde in April 1994. General Rose managed to contain the crisis, however, as he did during the even more alarming confrontation between the Serbs and NATO near Bihac in November.

The pursuit of peace by international threats, intermittent military intervention, sanctions, and sanctions-busting was extremely complicated and accompanied by a diplomatic and ideological debate of unusual emotional intensity. It transformed NATO from a purely defensive alliance into an "out-of-area" enforcement agency. The apparent success of the prointervention lobby in the media must be seen in the context of strong support for their agitation from parts of the U.S. administration.

Post-communist Russia was consistently reluctant to exert itself in the Balkan area. Russian policy began with an almost ideological commitment to accepting Western good faith, and there was severe disillusion in Russia when it became clear that much of the West wanted a peace settlement based on the defeat of the Serbs. By 1995 even informed Russian opinion was getting alarmed at the direction events were taking, but it was too late, and too difficult, for the Yeltsin presidency to devise a new policy.

In 1995 London and Paris reluctantly agreed to allow NATO to bomb the Serbs, while the United States accepted the sort of settlement the Europeans had recommended in 1993. But the bombing of the VRS in August 1995, which appeared to end the war, was probably less important than the entry of the Croatian army in Bosnia, now trained and extensively re-equipped at the initiative of the U.S. Even this Croatian intervention was only possible because the Yugoslav army refused to intervene to save its clients west of the Drina. The war ended because Milosevic of Serbia wanted it to end.

The chief outcome of the war was a transformed NATO, and the renewal of American leadership in Europe to an extent not seen since before the *Vietnam War. It established that America wanted to lead, and to be indispensable, in the process of European reorganization after *1989. Bosnia itself was not much affected by international intervention. The war took longer than it would have done, and the Serbian position is more uncertain, but the settlement that followed Dayton is not unlike a plausible compromise in April 1992.

In the last two centuries, *Balkan states have been employed to slow and control the collapse of the Ottoman Empire. Balkan nations were created, enlarged, and shrunk as the need arose. During the two world wars of the twentieth century, Balkan territories were bargaining chips for alliance construction and Balkan nationality and ethnicity were never taken too seriously. The war of 1992–1995 confirmed this trend.

Richard Holbrooke, the chief U.S. negotiator in 1995, boasted a year later: "We are re-engaged in the world, and Bosnia was the test." This "we" meant the United States, not "the West" or "the international community." Indeed, no nation-state started and finished the Bosnian story as a political actor with an unchanged diplomatic personality. All the major actors were uncertain and divided about their policies. Debate took place within and between agencies, departments, armies, and diplomatic chancelleries. Each great power became a forum for the global debate for and against intervention, the debate for and against a certain kind NATO and an associated, media-led international political process.

If the old Yugoslavia was untenable and eventually collapsed under the weight of the supposedly insurmountable differences among its constituent nations, it is unclear how Bosnia—the Yugoslav microcosm *par excellence*—can develop and sustain the dynamics of a viable polity. The answer will become known only when the outside powers lose their present interest in upholding the constitutional edifice made in Dayton.

(See also BOSNIA AND HERZEGOVINA; POST-COMMUNISM; SERBIA AND MONTENEGRO.)

Robert D. Kaplan, *Balkan Ghosts: A Journey through History* (New York, 1994). Susan L. Woodward, *Balkan Tragedy* (Washington, D.C., 1995). General Sir Michael Rose, *Fighting for Peace* (London, 1998). Robert M. Hayden, *Blueprints for a House Divided: The Constitutional Logic of the Yugoslav Conflicts* (Ann Arbor, Mich., 1999).

SRDA TRIFKOVIC

BOTSWANA, encircled by South Africa, Zimbabwe, Zambia, and Namibia in Southern Africa, achieved its independence from the United Kingdom on 30 September 1966. Although large in size (581,732 sq. km., or 224,607 sq. mi.—slightly less than twice the size of Arizona), it is sparsely populated (by 1.456 million people, known as Batswana, in 1995), and, like neighboring Namibia, suffers from droughts and supports livestock ranching, rather than extensive agriculture. Proclaimed a British protectorate (known as the Bechuanaland Protectorate) in 1885, it was of greater strategic than economic value to the British. Its role was to be a bridge to Southern Rhodesia (later Zimbabwe), forming part of the Cape-to-Cairo territorial ambition of Cecil Rhodes in South Africa. Once the Union of South Africa was created after the end of the 1899–1902 Anglo-Boer War, the British and the South Africans anticipated that Bechuanaland would be transferred to the Union. Time and again the South Africans requested the transfer, but the British declined, in large measure because both the British government and the Africans in Bechuanaland found South African racial policies to be increasingly unpalatable. As these policies hardened after the electoral victory of the South African National Party in 1948, the Batswana became more politically conscious, and political parties emerged in the early 1960s. The protectorate capital was moved from Mafikeng in South Africa to Gaborone in 1965, in time for the granting of self-government, which lasted less than two years.

The general elections of 1965, under the British first-past-the-post or plurality system, gave the newly formed Botswana Democratic Party (BDP) a decisive (80.4 percent of the votes cast) position within the newly-created nonracial legislature, and no further legislative elections were held in the preindependence period. General elections were held at five-year intervals (1969, 1974, 1979, 1984, 1989, 1994, and 1999), and in each the BDP emerged the winner. In the general elections of 16 October 1999, BDP secured thirty-three of the forty National Assembly seats, representing 57 percent of the votes cast, and the Botswana National Front, which first participated in the 1969 general election, became the premier opposition party (with six seats). The legislature has a dominant forty-four-member lower house, the National Assembly, and a nominal fifteen-member upper house, the House of Chiefs, that has a restricted legislative role, dealing with traditional law, privileges, rights, and leadership of the eight recognized ethnic groups in Botswana. This upper house accommodated the chiefs to the new political dispensation at independence, which reduced the powers of the chiefs, who usually benefited from the British system of indirect rule in the protectorate. The president, who is elected by the members of the lower house, enjoys veto powers concerning legislation as

well as a wide range of appointive powers. Although not without its critics, Botswana enjoys an enviable reputation for maintaining a stable, efficient, and honest democratic system. There has been considerable continuity in presidential leadership, starting with President Sir Seretse Khama and continuing through President J. Quett K. Masire, and then (on 1 April 1998) to President Festus Mogae. In addition, Sir Seretse's son, Ian Khama (who is a retired senior military officer), has served as vice president since 1997, and probably will be a future president.

Thanks to the discovery of profitable diamond pipes and copper-nickel deposits, Botswana has been able to advance economically from an exceptionally low preindependence level to one of the best in the continent. This, in turn, has facilitated the development of a sorely-needed economic infrastructure and the amelioration of the worst effects of periodic drought, which has a devastating impact on the beef industry. Nevertheless there is a strongly asymmetrical distribution of wealth in the country, which critics decry, and the government has had a sterling reputation for public probity, which impressed foreign aid donors. (Lately, there have been several well-publicized lapses in that probity.) Botswana has attempted to increase its economic independence relative to South Africa by creating its own banking system, currency, and stock market, although it continues to be a member of the Southern African Customs Union, which generates roughly a sixth of its annual revenue. Mining accounts for about half of the annual revenue, and the diamond mining industry is closely linked to De Beers, the giant South African multinational firm.

For much of its independent existence, Botswana attempted to balance its commitment to the achievement of African majority rule in Southern Africa with the stark reality of cross-border raids and the influx of political refugees. In 1977, it created the Botswana Defense Force (BDF), which now, critics claim, consumes too much of the national expenditures (at 7.3 percent), and whose growth has disturbed the Namibian government. Botswana and Namibia submitted their northern border dispute over Kasikili/Sedudu island in the Chobe River to the International Court of Justice, which decided in favor of Botswana's claims on 13 December 1999. The BDF has participated in the United Nations peacekeeping mission in Somalia, and Gaborone is the site of the administrative headquarters of the *Southern African Development Community.

(See also SOUTHERN AFRICA.)

Stephen J. Stedman, ed., *Botswana: The Political Economy of Development* (Boulder, Colo., 1993). Richard Dale, *Botswana's Search for Autonomy in Southern Africa* (Westport, Conn., 1995). Kenneth Good, *Realizing Democracy in Botswana, Namibia, and South Africa* (Pretoria, 1997).

RICHARD DALE

BOUNDARY DISPUTES. Except in the eastern half of the Arabian Peninsula, where the territory of Saudi Arabia joins the lands of Yemen, Oman, the United Arab Emirates, and Qatar, the nineteenth and early twentieth centuries witnessed the replacement of frontiers by boundaries. Everywhere else frontiers, which are zones of varying widths, were replaced by boundaries, which are lines. Unfortunately this improvement in the precise definition of national territory has not ended disputes associated with international boundaries, as the war following the Iraqi invasion of Kuwait in August 1990 readily attests. They exist in every continent except Australia, where there are instead boundary disputes between some of the states making up the federation.

The study of international boundary disputes provides an interdisciplinary focus for geographers, lawyers, and political scientists. Although there will be different approaches within and between disciplines, there is general agreement that there are four types of boundary disputes. Territorial disputes arise when one country claims adjoining land across the boundary because of some special quality that that area possesses. The qualities might relate, for example, to the history of the region, the population that occupies it, or its strategic character. The persistent dispute between Chile and Bolivia stems from the desire of the latter, landlocked country to regain access to the Pacific Ocean that was lost in 1879.

Positional disputes relate to some defect in the definition of the boundary. The Sino-Russian dispute over the island at the confluence of the Amur and Ussuri rivers in eastern Asia is based in the ambiguous description of their common boundary in the treaty of 1860. Other positional disputes occur when a river in which the international boundary is located changes its course suddenly, perhaps by cutting through the neck of a meander in its course. Such events bedeviled U.S.-Mexican relations along the Rio Grande until 1964, when a comprehensive treaty ended the uncertainty about the proper location of the boundary. In both territorial and positional disputes at least one side is arguing that the boundary should be moved either so that it can acquire territory to which it has a solid claim or so that the boundary will occupy the correct position fixed by an earlier treaty.

The other two kinds of boundary disputes can be solved without moving the line. Resource disputes occur when the boundary intersects some unitary resource, such as a lake or oil field, and the two neighbors disagree on how the resource should be exploited. In 1975 Bangladesh and India were involved in a resource development dispute when India built a barrage across the Ganges River, which reaches the sea on the coast of Bangladesh, in order to divert waters into the Hooghly River so that sediments silting the port of Calcutta could be flushed into the Bay of Bengal. Bangladesh was convinced that the scale of diversion proposed would adversely affect its coastal environments and its agricultural and fishing industries. The issue was resolved when India agreed to let a larger proportion of the Ganges' flow continue unimpeded to Bangladesh.

Functional boundary disputes occur when one country perceives that it is being adversely affected by rules and regulations being applied by its neighbor along the boundary and especially at crossing points. The detriment might be suffered by the people who live in the borderland or by the country's import and export industries. In the period between 1964 and 1977 there were twenty-four occasions when one African country closed its boundary, prompting strenuous objections, especially when the country affected was landlocked. Functional disputes can be solved by the designation of new regulations or the provision of exemptions from their operation in critical cases.

When scholars working on boundary disputes have decided into which category a particular dispute falls, the comprehensive analysis of the topic involves the following ele-

ments. First, it is necessary to identify the trigger action that persuaded the claimant country to initiate the dispute at that particular time. Some disputes, especially territorial disputes, last for long periods and pass through periods of intense activity and quiescence. The Iranian claim to three islands in the Persian Gulf was executed, at the expense of Sharjah, when British forces were withdrawn from the Gulf in November 1971.

Second, it is important to establish the aims of the government initiating the dispute. In most cases the desire will be for additional territory or relief from some administrative irritation connected with the boundary. However, apparently hopeless claims have been launched, to generate national cohesion when governments are facing serious domestic problems, for example, or for other reasons, as in the case of the Philippines' claim to North Sabah in 1960 to delay the inclusion of Sabah and Sarawak into Malaysia.

Third, the arguments deployed to justify the dispute and the policies designed to secure success must be identified and assessed. Finally the results of the dispute need to be cataloged. Do they relate directly to some aspect of the boundary or to some facet of bilateral relations or domestic politics?

Although it is rarely possible to predict when any particular boundary dispute will develop, there have been historical periods during the last two centuries when boundary disputes were more common than at other times. The acquisition of colonies by European powers in North America, Africa, and Asia prompted a rash of disputes as efforts were made to secure the best possible areas, sometimes with only imperfect knowledge of the human and physical geography of the regions involved. These unknown areas were often divided by straight lines or the course of a river or a watershed. The rectification of these lines once the area had been thoroughly explored created serious friction in the bilateral relations of Britain, France, and Germany. At the end of colonial periods boundary disputes will often erupt. In the 1820s, as Spanish rule was replaced by independent states in South America, disputes arose over the correct location of Spanish administrative boundaries, which were the lines of cleavage along which independence movements separated. In Africa in the 1960s, several African states found that colonial administrators had failed to correct evident positional problems on their boundaries.

In Europe the conclusions of wars have been marked by outbreaks of territorial claims by the victorious states against those defeated. The Congress of Vienna in 1815, the Congress of Berlin in 1878, the London Conference in 1913, and the Paris peace conferences in 1919 and 1945 were the events when territorial disputes were tackled and solved in large numbers.

Since 1945, when the United States laid claim to its continental margin, coastal states have made claims to a suite of maritime zones in addition to the long-standing territorial waters. The new areas consist of the continental margin and an exclusive economic zone. Because the latter zone is 200 nautical miles wide, adjacent coastal states and states separated by less than 400 nautical miles of sea have been faced with the need to fix common maritime limits. Whereas boundary disputes on land involve a boundary that already exists, maritime boundary disputes arise through overlapping claims to areas of the sea and seabed. Once the boundary is drawn, the dispute is settled; to date, the resulting boundary has never been challenged by either party. There seem to be three main reasons for this. First, both states ensure that they have complete and detailed knowledge about the physical, resource, and strategic qualities of the seas and seabed to be divided. Second, the selected line is often a compromise between the two extreme claims. Third, provisions in the boundary treaty deal with questions of developing resources intersected by the line and settling any future disagreements that might arise over interpretation.

(See also DECOLONIZATION; GULF WAR; LAW OF THE SEA.)

A. J. Day, ed., *Borders and Territorial Disputes* (Detroit, 1982). J. R. V. Prescott, *The Maritime Political Boundaries of the World* (New York, 1986). J. R. V. Prescott, *Political Frontiers and Boundaries* (London, 1987).

VICTOR PRESCOTT

BRAIN DRAIN. The debate about the benefits and damage of the brain drain, or the outflow of professional people trained in low-income countries to higher-income countries, has distinguished among three groups: the migrants, those they join, and those they leave behind. It is usually agreed that the first two groups gain, but controversy arises over the third.

On one side are those who point to benefits of the free movement of human beings. Above all, the migrating individuals and their families gain. In addition, migrants' contribution to knowledge is often greater abroad, where better facilities for work are available. This greater contribution to knowledge is often available to the whole world.

Occasionally migrant professionals return, after a period of self-improvement, to their own country; while away, they may send remittances to their family at home. And although they deprive their country of taxable capacity, the migrants relieve it of burdens such as educating their children. The home country may enjoy political benefits from having ex-nationals (if they have not been driven out), in positions of power and influence abroad. Worldwide living standards are improved by permitting talent to go to its highest-yielding activity, and equality is promoted by the weakening of monopoly positions.

Although this cosmopolitan line of reasoning has appeal, some qualifications are necessary. First, the home country has borne (some of) the costs of educating the migrants but loses the tax revenue from their incomes.

Second, there are intellectual as well as technical economies of scale, external economies, and complementarities. The emigration of leading professionals (e.g., teachers) can deprive those left behind of guidance and stimulus. There is also the loss of employment opportunities for less highly trained people, such as assistants.

Third, the problem is aggravated by the fact that the mobility is partial. Trained and skilled people move, while the unskilled and semiskilled, on the whole, do not. Although it may be best to permit both skilled and unskilled people to move freely, it does not follow that any step toward greater freedom of movement is good. If the skilled can move and the unskilled cannot, it may be better also to restrict the movement of the skilled.

Fourth, possibly the most important impact of the brain drain, or rather of attempts to plug it, is the impact on internal income distribution. In order to prevent skilled people from leaving, salary differentials have to be raised, reinforcing an initial inegalitarian income distribution. This adds obstacles to national integration, and retarded development adds to the temptations of the brain drain. This creates additional incentives to perpetuate inequalities, and so on in a vicious circle.

Fifth, the external brain drain is matched by an internal drain: the reference group for the professionals who remain is the group of their peers in the rich countries. For example, doctors go to the cities to practice expensive, private, curative medicine instead of to rural areas to provide preventive health services.

(See also DEVELOPMENT AND UNDERDEVELOPMENT; INTERNATIONAL MIGRATION.)

Walter Adams, ed., *The Brain Drain* (New York, 1968).

PAUL STREETEN

BRAZIL. The largest and most populous country in South America, with 165 million inhabitants and enormous natural resources, by the late 1990s Brazil had become the world's tenth largest economy. Its automobile, computer, and other manufacturing industries are among the most advanced in the developing world. This impressive industrialization, though, masks a very uneven distribution of wealth and income that contributes to political divisiveness.

Brazil's political system, rooted in a strong and sometimes paternalistic state structure, has acted both as a creative force in the country's development as a nation and as an obstacle to change. In various incarnations from colonial administration to monarchy, from early presidentialism to military *authoritarianism, the state apparatus has guided political decision making as much or more than any individual political actor or group of actors. Indeed, the state has rarely, if ever, ceded power to the majority.

Historical Background. Unlike any other Latin American country, Brazil was colonized by Portugal. In 1530, the Portuguese crown sent an expedition to establish fifteen captaincies to be administered by local rulers of Portuguese blood. These landowners enjoyed considerable autonomy from the Portuguese government in Lisbon until King João VI and his court were forced to flee to Brazil in 1808, fugitives from Napoleon's armies. Consolidation and centralization of economic life in the colony resulted. In 1821 the king returned to Portugal, and the following year his son Pedro, the regent whom he had left behind, declared himself emperor of an independent Brazil.

Confrontations between Emperor Pedro I and local Brazilian aristocracy over the degree of centralization became common occurrences. Indeed, it was one such clash—over the issue of slavery—which provoked Pedro's eventual downfall. The slave trade, which had begun in the mid-sixteenth century, was outlawed in 1850 and legal ownership of slaves was abolished in 1888. Growing discontent among the landed elites over this issue, as well as the emperor's administrative abilities and the prospect of his daughter Isabel taking the throne, provoked the creation of a political alternative: military leaders ousted the emperor in a bloodless coup in 1889 and ushered in Brazil's first attempt at republican government.

The political era that emerged after the monarchy, known as the "Old Republic," was characterized by a system in which two states, Minas Gerais and São Paulo, was first among equals. The elites of those areas—by custom, economic prowess, and geography—had grown close to the power center in the national capital at Rio de Janeiro. With the end of the monarchy and the beginning of the *política dos governadores* (polity of governors), they were allowed to assume preeminent responsibility in designing the economic policies of the nation. In exchange, the leaders of these two dominant states agreed not to interfere in the internal politics of the other states. Political participation in the Old Republic remained in the hands of regional oligarchies. Although the immigration of non-Portuguese Europeans to Brazil had quickened following the abolition of slavery—with colonies of Swiss, Germans, and Italians settling principally in the country's south—the new people enjoyed few civil rights or privileges. Expanded participation in politics was given force only when an iconoclast from the country's deep south emerged to challenge the rules of the game.

When political bosses in Minas Gerais and São Paulo failed to agree on the presidential succession in 1930, the time was right for a renegade candidate to seize power amid the confusion. With the tacit support of the armed forces and the church, the Old Republic was dissolved and *Getúlio Vargas became provisional president.

A political populist as well as opportunist, Vargas succeeded in perpetuating his rule by skillfully using political institutions so long as they contributed to his designs and abandoning them when they did not. In 1934, delegates approved a new constitution and elected Vargas as their first president. Three years later, Vargas ignored the constitution's one-term limit on the presidency, canceled the 1938 elections, and began eight years of dictatorship known as the *Estado Novo* (New State).

During the *Estado Novo*, Vargas consolidated the patrimonial state. Labor, which had been occasionally organized since colonial times but never united by class consciousness, was successfully drawn under direct state control; political parties—few of which had survived by 1937—were not allowed to operate. Whatever remnant of the *política dos governadores* that might have existed was swallowed up in the central powers accorded to the presidency.

By 1943 there was considerable pressure among the elites and military for a return to democratic government. Vargas acceded to the pressure and called elections for 1945, but when it looked like he would again subvert the electoral process, the military removed him from office.

Vargas would eventually return to the presidency for a final five-year term, although his legacy in political terms was largely concluded by the end of the *Estado Novo*. The central powers of the presidency, the weak and constantly shifting landscape of political parties, the cooptation and suppression of labor and other class-based movements, the consolidation of the patrimonial state in a national corporatist bureaucracy: these phenomena continue to channel, if not dictate, the progress of the Brazilian state today.

Postwar Politics. The end of the *Estado Novo* ushered in an era of ever-increasing military participation in national politics. Military candidates ran in every presidential election between 1945 and 1960, although only the first contender, Eurico Gaspar Dutra, ever won. The losers in the subsequent contests remained nominally on the sidelines, but a military coup in 1954 and attempted coups in 1955 and 1961 presaged the eventual 1964 coup that installed a military regime that endured for more than two decades.

In the years before the takeover, however, the country experienced a series of populist presidents: Vargas won election in 1950, followed by Juscelino Kubitschek in 1955 and Janio Quadros in 1960. With no strong ideological movements and a weak party tradition, the presidents of this period (called the 1946 Republic) tended to be little more than clientelist leaders, using the presidency to dole out favors to political supporters. Although social mobilization increased as the country's urban centers grew, political participation remained firmly in the hands of elites, which used the state apparatus to their own political and economic advantage.

It was a challenge to the perquisites of those political and economic elites that spurred the military to break decisively with constitutional democratic rule in 1964. João Goulart, who had assumed the presidency following the resignation of Quadros, was perceived by the traditional power centers as a reformer with a leftist bent. But before any major reform project even got under way, the military toppled his civilian regime. Commanders installed General Humberto Castello Branco as first of the five military presidents.

Although the ideological predilections of the armed forces were hardly homogeneous, the administrations between 1964 and 1985 were united in their determination to advance Brazilian economic development and to reorder (and at times brutally suppress) civil society to the extent necessary to sustain the economic project.

Following an era of increased repression under Castello Branco's two immediate successors, the armed forces began a program of *abertura*, or political opening, believing that a gradual liberalization of the political system would be in the best interest of both the military and Brazil in general. The government reestablished habeas corpus, initiated a political amnesty, granted increased press freedoms, and laid the groundwork for popular elections of regional and local officials as well as a civilian president.

This democratic opening culminated in the election of civilian candidate Tancredo Neves in 1985. Neves, however, died on the eve of his scheduled inauguration and never took office, leaving vice president José Sarney to become president. Since Sarney had been a military supporter until shortly before the election, he was unable to gain much legitimacy for his presidency. Moreover, the Sarney period saw public support for the traditional parties and politicians erode substantially. Thus, in the November 1989 presidential election, the two run-off candidates were political neophytes. Fernando Collor de Mello, wealthy former governor of a small northeastern state, advocated the neoliberal policies that were becoming increasingly popular in Latin America. Luis Ignacio "Lula" da Silva, a well-known labor leader and candidate of the Workers Party (PT), ran on a populist platform. Collor won a narrow victory, but governing proved difficult because he had no party to back him in Congress and had to improvise coalitions for each issue.

Collor's political fortunes came crashing down when Congress forced him from office following allegations of widespread corruption operated principally by his former campaign manager. Collor was replaced by his vice president Itamar Franco, who proved to be an uninspired leader not known for his political acumen. The presidential elections of 1994 pitted Fernando Henrique Cardoso, a world-renowned academic and Franco's finance minister, against Lula, who attempted to win the presidency for a second time. Cardoso, basking in the light of a highly successful economic reform plan that he implemented while working under Franco, won in a landslide. Cardoso's first term was judged to be sufficiently successful by the Brazilian people—they elected him for a second term in late 1998. Lula was again his principal rival. Soon after his inauguration in January 1999, Brazil was forced to devalue its currency. While the economy recovered relatively quickly, Cardoso's popularity dropped sharply and had not recovered by mid-term. Municipal elections in October 2000 signaled the beginning of the presidential campaign of 2002.

Political Economy. With its vast size, wealth of natural resources, and combination of tropical and temperate climates, during its entire history as an independent nation Brazil has had pretensions of becoming a world economic power.

From colonial times well into the twentieth century, the country's economy was driven by a steady flow of exports: sugar production, concentrated in the humid northeast, began as early as 1520 and thrived well into the seventeenth century; gold production took off with the discovery of major deposits in 1695 and dominated the export sector until the end of the eighteenth century; coffee production in the country's center-south emerged in the early nineteenth century. As late as the 1920s coffee still constituted 75 percent of Brazil's exports.

With the Great Depression of the 1930s, Brazil experienced difficulty in purchasing manufactured goods abroad and so began its first experiment with import-substitution industrialization (ISI). ISI was an economic strategy which relied upon high tariffs, an overvalued exchange rate, and other policies which attempted to promote domestic production and lessen dependence on industrialized nations such as the United States. The program was expanded after World War II as a new generation of economic planners sought to overcome the lagging expansion of primary product export markets with a major state-sponsored industrialization push. President Juscelino Kubitschek (1956–1961) captured the ethos of Brazilian economic pretensions in his promise to complete "fifty years of progress in five."

Between 1945 and 1962, Brazilian industrial production grew an average of 8 percent annually, although not without economic dislocations and major social costs. The economic policies implemented to protect industrial producers (especially the overvalued exchange rate) effectively penalized the primary product sector, leaving agricultural producers and workers demoralized and vulnerable in the face of a depressed world economy. The attempts of the Quadros and Goulart regimes to reconcile these competing economic interests were further complicated by the frustration of a growing urban working class, and the determination of landowners to forestall any major income redistribution. The resulting fissures in political society led to the military takeover in 1964.

Fiscal and monetary discipline imposed during the military years, together with high rates of investment, paid off with impressive rates of growth. GDP rose at an annual average of 10.9 percent from 1968 through 1974, the industrial sector flourished (but at the expense of agriculture), and the country's foreign exchange reserves expanded from US$656 million to US$6.417 billion in 1973. It is no wonder that, despite inflation averaging 17 percent during the same period, observers refer to those years as the "economic miracle."

In the latter half of the 1970s, however, growth began to wane and inflation raged. This inflation, coupled with an overvalued currency, fueled a unsustainable trade deficit. And rather than curtail imports, economic planners decided to borrow abroad to finance this trade deficit.

When it came time to repay, Brazil was ill equipped to do so. The oil shocks of 1973 and 1979 had led to a worldwide economic slump, and demand for Brazilian exports had fallen. In addition, international banks became reluctant to make loans to Third World countries following Mexico's announcement in August 1982 that it could no longer service its foreign debt. The better part of the 1980s was spent seeking new ways out of the debt crisis in which Brazil found itself.

The external debt problems were combined with internal mismanagement as the Sarney government proposed various economic "packages" to deal with runaway inflation. Some innovative economic plans were implemented but they all failed, mainly due to the inability to rein in the burgeoning fiscal deficit. This economic turmoil thus paved the way for the Collor victory in 1989, but his attempts to tame the economy were basically similar to Sarney's and the plans ended up making inflation even worse.

Economic mismanagement continued in the late 1980s and early 1990s and Brazil quickly found itself ravaged by hyperinflation with annual rates well above 1,000 percent. Relief finally came in 1994, when then Finance Minister Cardoso implemented the *Real Plan*, an economic package based upon a new, stronger currency, which immediately cut inflation down to barely 2 percent. Since that time inflation has been moderate by Brazilian standards and the *Real Plan* remains extremely popular among rich and poor Brazilians alike.

While by no means out of the woods, the Brazilian economy performed reasonably well during Cardoso's first term at office. The aforementioned *Real Plan* cut inflation considerably and Cardoso has been able to pass some economic reform legislature through the always obstinate Congress. This new economic responsibility was manifested in October 1997 when the Asian financial crisis sparked a run on the Brazilian currency. Instead of devaluing the currency (which would have provoked rampant inflation), the Cardoso administration responded by taking the politically more difficult route of raising interest rates and implementing an emergency fiscal spending package which quickly restored investor confidence in the Brazilian economy. Moreover, the creation of the Mercosur trade agreement that ties Brazil, Argentina, Paraguay, and Uruguay (Chile and Bolivia are associate members) is one signal that Brazil has begun to put behind its protectionist past and embrace international trade as a means to create larger markets for its products.

The good management of the economy had one weak spot—fiscal deficits. International markets became increasingly uneasy in late 1998 about the unwillingness of the Brazilian Congress to pass critical legislation to cut public spending and the ongoing deficits of the central and state governments. In spite of an emergency aid package from the international financial institutions, Brazil was forced to devalue its currency in January 1999. The impact was negative but not devastating. The Congress responded slowly in approving some legislation that will have a positive impact on the deficit problem. The economic team received high marks for its prudent management and restoration of confidence in 1999–2000. But many of the fundamental problems remain to be solved and they may need to await a new president and Congress in 2002.

Social Bases of Politics and Catalysts for Change. Amid the economic turmoil of the 1980s, political relations among various sectors of Brazilian society began transform themselves. While the state retained preeminence as the broker of civil discourse, the reshaping of major civil institutions outside the patrimonial state—organized labor, the Catholic Church, and the military, among others—is worth nothing. Although no one group has sufficient power to reshape the civil society of Brazil on its own, each contends for public attention and national power, and each stands to influence the shape of contemporary Brazil.

Organized labor is one group in particular whose achievements have greatly impacted Brazilian civil society, and in turn have transformed civil society's relationship with the state. Beginning in 1979 when the military was still in power, with major strikes in the industrial heartland of São Paulo state, Brazilian labor began to win an increasing level of autonomy from the state. Hamstrung since the Vargas years by corporatist labor laws that made the government the final arbiter of labor relations, by the early 1980s independent union leaders such as Lula were able to bargain directly with employees. It did not take long before Lula came to symbolize a "New Unionism," in which independent labor syndicates could hold legitimacy and contend vociferously for economic power. Furthermore, the political gains in the quest for such power were subsequently consolidated in the PT, an organization remarkable for its relative cohesion amid a system of weak political parties.

Brazil Today. While it is true that the economy has grown impressively—albeit usually with high inflation—over the past several decades, Brazil still is a country of tremendous inequality and injustice, with 41 percent of the population classified as living in poverty. The endless *favelas* (slums) in the major cities are a daily reminder to Brazilians of the tremendous social ills that plague their country. Indeed, when compared with countries such as Argentina, Mexico, and Chile, the Brazilian socioeconomic indicators—education, health, etc.—lag way behind. Thus, President Cardoso has his work cut out for him: Brazil needs to continue growing but this growth needs to be distributed much more equitably; primary health and education need to be greatly expanded; government subsidies and transfer payments that benefit the non-poor need to be reduced and this revenue needs to be redirected toward the poor sectors of society.

Moving into the twenty-first century, Brazil seems caught between its powerful state, which has traditionally dominated both economic and political life, and a set of new international trends which put more emphasis on the private sector and autonomous political groups. These opposing tendencies must be resolved in some way if the country is to move toward the world power status that its people have always sought.

Thomas E. Skidmore, *Politics in Brazil 1930–1964* (New York, 1967). Thomas E. Skidmore, *The Politics of Military Rule in Brazil, 1964–1985* (New York, 1988). Werner Baer, *The Brazilian Economy: Growth and Development* (New York; 1989). Alfred Stepan, ed., *Democratizing Brazil: Problems of Transition and Consolidation* (New York, 1989). Riordan Roett, *Brazil: Politics in a Patrimonial Society* (New York, 1992). Sebastian Edwards, *Crisis and Reform in Latin America* (New York, 1995).
RUSSELL C. CRANDALL
RIORDAN ROETT

BRETTON WOODS SYSTEM. See FINANCE, INTERNATIONAL; INTERNATIONAL MONETARY FUND; WORLD BANK.

BRITAIN. By contrast to Germany, the states of Eastern and Central Europe, or the post-Soviet republics, Britain at the start of the twenty-first century continues to enjoy a reputation for stability and continuity. Nevertheless, British politics and society have experienced some critical transitions in the period since World War II and in both domestic and international terms significant challenges lie ahead.

From Thatcherism to New Labour. In domestic terms, the premiership of Margaret *Thatcher from 1979 to 1990 marked a dramatic departure in the consensus politics that Britain's two leading parties (Labour and Conservative) had shared throughout the postwar period. Until she was abruptly replaced by John Major as Conservative Party leader and prime minister in November 1990, Thatcher challenged fundamental principles of British postwar politics including the egalitarian ethos of the *welfare state, commitment to a full-employment economy, an accepted role for trade unions in the formation of economic and social policy, a significant public sector economy based on nationalized industries, and state economic management to secure growth, stable prices, and desirable exchange rates and balance of payments through Keynesian demand management. *Thatcherism advanced neoliberalism and an "enterprise culture" that challenged the principles (but continued most of the policies) of the welfare state, preferred *monetarism to *Keynesianism, shifted the balance of resources from the public sector to the private sector, and helped forge a *political culture that prized individualism, selectivity, and competition.

In many ways, the period of Thatcher's leadership as prime minister (1979–1990) marks a critical dividing line in postwar British politics. She set the tone and redefined the goals of British politics like few before her. In November 1990, a leadership challenge within Thatcher's own Conservative Party—largely over her anti–European Community stance and high-handed leadership style—caused her sudden resignation and replacement by John Major. Major served as prime minister from 1990 to 1997, leading the Conservative Party to a victory in the 1992 general election before succumbing to Tony Blair's New Labour in May 1997.

Some twenty electoral records were broken in the 1997 election, as the Labour Party won 419 of the 658 seats in Parliament, the largest majority it has ever held. Blair became prime minister as the beneficiary of a 10 percent swing from Conservative to Labour, a postwar record. More women (119) and members of ethnic minorities (9) were elected than ever before. At the same time, the Conservative Party, one of Europe's most successful parties in the twentieth century, was badly humbled. More cabinet ministers lost their seats than ever before and the Conservatives were completely shut out in Scotland and Wales.

From the start, New Labour's signature claim to represent a "Third Way"—a model of government not simply between, but beyond neoliberalism and traditional European social democracy—generated enormous interest and mobilized important new recruits, most notable among them Germany's Chancellor Gerhard *Schröder. New Labour has placed very basic issues on the agenda, defining its governing project by reference to a set of modernizing challenges—to develop top-quality public services especially in education and health; reform welfare policy through "workfare" programs with job-training components; and reconfigure Britain's relationship with Europe. Most radical and far-reaching, the government has pressed an agenda of constitutional reforms, from the removal of the right of hereditary peers to speak and vote in the House of Lords to the formation of a Scottish Parliament and a Welsh Senedd (or Assembly), and the implementation of a peace agreement for Northern Ireland that would involve a set of new political institutions and power-sharing arrangements, some involving the Republic of Ireland.

In international terms, Britain has endured far greater changes and a longer-term and perhaps more enduring transition than it has experienced on the domestic political front. From hegemonic power in the nineteenth century, Britain has become a middle-level European power. Moreover, Britain's reluctance to participate fully in the *European Union's agenda of economic and political integration, underscored by its refusal to join the initial group of eleven at the launch of the European Unions single currency, the euro, in January 1999, heightens perceptions that geography has shaped destiny, with the U.K. loathe to surrender its position as a European outsider, yet keen to enhance its political influence in the EU.

Thatcher set out to redraw the domestic political map as the geopolitical map of Europe was being transformed. For his part, Blair is determined to use his decisive victory—and the advantages afforded by a very competitive and smooth running economy in 2000—to establish a legacy for New Labour of irreversible changes in policy orientations, constitutional arrangements, and relations with European partners. The equally bold and distinctive visions of Thatcherism and New Labour have contributed an unexpected air of volatility to U.K. politics and raised its international profile. Thatcher helped advance a global neoliberalism. Blair, in turn, has helped inspire far-reaching efforts to invent a Third Way model of government determined to pose pragmatic solutions to economic and social problems, reduce ideological divisions, and meld concerns for social justice with a commitment to innovative, market-based economies.

Dilemmas of State Formation. Britain is the largest of the British Isles, a group of islands off the northwest coast of Europe, and encompasses England, Scotland, and Wales. The second largest island comprises Northern Ireland and the Republic of *Ireland. *Britain* is shorthand for the United Kingdom of Great Britain and Northern Ireland (UK). The term *Great Britain* includes England, Wales, and Scotland, but not Northern Ireland. Covering an area of approximately 244,000 square kilometers (94,000 sq. mi.), Britain is roughly two-thirds the size of Japan or approximately half the size of France. In 1995 the population of the United Kingdom was 58.6 million people; the population is projected to peak at 61.2 million people in 2023.

Britain's location as an offshore island adjacent to Europe is significant. Historically, Britain's island destiny made it less subject to invasion and conquest than its continental counterparts, affording the country a sense of security. The geographic separation from mainland Europe has also created for many Britons a feeling that they are both apart from and a part of Europe, a factor that has complicated relations with Britain's European Union partners to this day.

Despite the longevity of Britain's constitutional order, dating from the Constitutional Settlement of 1688, complications remain concerning the identity of the nation-state and institutional and constitutional arrangements for its governance. In the 1970s declining economic fortunes deepened the pattern of uneven development in regional and national terms within the UK, in which England prospered, relatively when compared with Scotland and Wales. The discovery of oil reserves off Scotland's northern coast increased demands for greater autonomy, and at the same time culturally based nationalism flared in Wales. Support for devolution, the transferal of specified powers from the UK Parliament in Westminster to national bodies, gained considerable momentum in the 1970s, then reemerged in the 1990s as a key part of the New Labour government's reform agenda.

The relationship between Northern Ireland and Britain remains far more complicated. Soon after the failed Easter Rebellion in 1916, Britain partitioned Ireland (in 1920): the six northern counties that make up Northern Ireland today were split from the remaining twenty-six counties that became the Irish Free State and later the Republic of Ireland. The majority Protestant population of Northern Ireland is descended from English and Scottish settlers, dominates political and economic affairs, and endorses continued union with Britain (hence they are called "unionists"). The minority population of Northern Ireland are Catholic descendants from the original Irish inhabitants (like the vast majority in the Irish Republic), many of whom are nationalists who, in one form or another, want to sever or reduce ties with Britain and increase ties with the Republic of Ireland (hence they are called "republicans"). The British government rushed troops to Northern Ireland in 1969, after Catholic demands for economic and political equality provoked Protestant riots. Despite a series of efforts at negotiated agreements between the Northern Irish communities, the UK, and Ireland—including a series of much-anticipated, on-again, off-again talks beginning in the spring of 1991—the political deadlock endured for a quarter century. In the fall of 1994, cease-fire declarations made by the Irish Republican Army (IRA) and the Protestant paramilitary organizations renewed hope for a peace settlement. Then in a dramatic new development in early spring 1995, British Prime Minister John Major and Irish Prime Minister John Bruton jointly issued a Framework Agreement, inspiring mounting optimism about a political settlement.

Blair's decisive electoral victory created an opening for new initiatives. Under deadline pressure imposed by Blair and the new Irish prime minister, Bertie Ahern, an agreement was reached on Good Friday 1998. It specified elections for a

Northern Ireland assembly in which Protestants and Catholics would share power, and the creation of a North-South Council to facilitate "all-Ireland" cooperation on matters such as economic development, agriculture, transportation, and the environment. Much was left unclear, for example the details of how and when the IRA would give up its weapons, how to create a nonpartisan police force, and the release of prisoners affiliated with the paramilitary groups. Nevertheless, despite doubts about the fine print, in May 1998, both parts of Ireland voted yes in a referendum to approve the peace agreement. It appeared that a new era was dawning in Northern Ireland, but since early 1999, disputes over IRA disarmament and Sinn Fein ministerial representation in a new Northern Ireland government have raised fears of a new deadlock. Northern Ireland underscores the fact that the UK has yet to resolve some fundamental concerns linked to its formation as a nation-state.

Politics, Institutions, and Constitutional Reform. Even in Britain, issues about political institutions and democratic governance remain unresolved. Owing to its exceptional regime continuity, Britain must apply constitutional traditions and institutional arrangements that were developed in a very different age. In addition, the British constitution remains a patchwork of common law, convention, statutory law, and works of authority rather than a single document of preeminent authority. Fundamental constitutional principles are few, and even they are subject to change. Importantly, core principles of government and political institutions can be reformed through normal legislation without recourse to extraordinary procedures for amending constitutions (although governments have come to rely on referendums for added political cover).

Historically, the UK operates by a fusion of legislature and executive expressed in the cabinet, with the prime minister much more than the first among cabinet equals but less autonomously powerful than the chief executive in a presidential system. The prime minister is the head of government and leader of the party with a working majority in the House of Commons. Powerful programatically oriented parties still dominate the landscape of British politics, play a critical constitutional role in the formation of governments, and determine parliamentary behavior of MPs to a degree unimaginable in the United States. Party competition in Britain is framed by competition between Labour and Conservative parties, with a center party, the Liberal Democrats, looking for a strategic opening to assume a role in the UK akin to that played by the Free Democratic Party in Germany throughout most of the postwar period. Devolution seems likely to enhance the electoral as well as the agenda-setting significance of national parties: the Scottish National Party (SNP), founded in 1934, and in Wales the Plaid Cymru, which dates from 1925.

In the mid-1990s, publicity surrounding the marital problems of Princess Diana and Prince Charles subjected the monarchy to intense criticism and contributed to the growing debate about the undemocratic underpinning of the British state. In 1997 the initially cool and standoffish reaction of the royal family to Princess Diana's death inspired criticism of the Crown and helped place on the agenda broader issues about citizen control over government and constitutional reform. Added to these concerns are the role of the unelected House of Lords and the absence of an "entrenched" Bill of Rights (one that Parliament cannot override). Against this backdrop, the Blair government has begun to implement far-reaching reforms of Parliament including the removal of the right of hereditary Peers to speak and vote in the House of Lords and the redesign of the historic upper chamber. In addition, the European Convention on Human Rights has been incorporated into UK law. Moreover, new systems of proportional representation have been introduced for Welsh and Scottish elections as well as for the European Parliament, and the possible use of proportional representation in UK general elections has been placed on the reform agenda. New Labour's inability to control the outcome of London's historic mayoral contest in May 2000 illustrates the difficulties that may accompany far-reaching measures to devolve and decentralize power.

Finally, the initiatives in Northern Ireland and power-sharing arrangements between Westminster and national assemblies in Scotland and Wales raise the prospect of further basic modifications of UK constitutional principles. Devolution implies both an element of *federalism and some compromise in the historic "parliamentary sovereignty" at the heart of the Westminster model, with uncertain and potentially unsettling consequences. Constitutional reform may become New Labour's most enduring legacy, but for many the redefinition of Britain's post-hegemonic role—its relationship to Europe and the EU—remain the country's greatest challenge.

Britain and the European Union. From 1989 to 1997, seemingly endless backbiting over the Social Charter and Maastricht in the Conservative Party sidetracked Thatcher and Major and cost them dearly in political terms. Britain's traumatic withdrawal from the Exchange Rate Mechanism (ERM) in 1992 stands as a warning that deeper European integration can be economically disruptive and politically dangerous. In 2000, as the most important EU member not to be in the initial Euro-11 group, Britain faced mounting pressure to participate in the single currency. The government has resisted demands for a timetable and insisted that no final decision will be made until after the general election anticipated in 2001, or before the question has been subjected to a referendum. The euro's dramatic decline against the dollar since its launch in January 1999 made early entry increasingly unlikely.

In the end, the UK will be forced to resolve its ambivalence about the euro and its role in Europe. Only full participation in the agenda for *Economic and Monetary Union will permit the UK to redefine its relationship with the EU and assume a new leadership role on the continent. Inevitably, New Labour will have to face these issues, and the political divisions that will almost certainly follow. The euro will cast a long shadow over New Labour's economic strategies, and perceptions about Blair's handling of the UK position on this critical matter are likely to have tremendous political repercussions for years to come.

(See also MAASTRICHT TREATY.)

Samuel H. Beer, *Britain against Itself: The Political Contradictions of Collectivism* (New York, 1982). David Marquand, *The Progressive Dilemma* (London, 1991). Anthony Giddens, *The Third Way: The Renewal of Social Democracy* (Cambridge U.K., 1998). Geoffrey Evans and Pippa Norris, eds., *Critical Elections: British Parties and Voters in Long-Term Perspective*

(London, 1999). Joel Krieger, *British Politics in the Global Age. Can Social Democracy Survive?* (New York: 1999).

JOEL KRIEGER

BRUNEI, or Brunei Darussalam (Abode of Peace), became an independent nation on 1 January 1984. Once a sprawling empire but threatened with extinction in the nineteenth century, this tiny state of 2,226 square miles (5,788 sq. km.) on the northwestern portion of the island of Borneo survived under British protection from 1888 until independence. After World War II, the rapid increase in wealth from the petroleum industry, the British desire to withdraw, and the unpleasant experiences resulting from the abortive revolt of 1962 by the Parti Rakyat Brunei (People's Party of Brunei), caused Sultan Omar Ali Saifuddin III (r. 1950–1967) to opt for absolute monarchism.

In 1967 Omar abdicated in favor of his son, Hassanal Bolkiah. On independence day Brunei emerged as an absolute monarchy with a ministerial form of government in which members of the royal family and the Malay nobility (pengiran) were given key portfolios. Very little has changed since then. (The Brunei National Democratic Party, permitted since 1985, was dissolved in 1988 when it became too vocal in demanding reforms.) The sultan maintains his power through an alliance with the nobility by appeasing the Malays, who form 65 percent of a population of 320,000, and by invoking the concept of *Melayu Islam Beraja* (Malay Islamic Monarchy), which calls for unquestioned loyalty to the ruler.

The immense wealth derived from the hydrocarbon industry has enabled the population to enjoy an annual per capita income of US$25,000, and the government to install a welfare state. Income from its reserves of over US$45 billion, mostly invested abroad, will be able to sustain the welfare state even if the hydrocarbon deposits are depleted. The Chinese, who make up 20 percent of the population and are noncitizens, do not enjoy these benefits.

Given past trends, the policy of keeping the Malays economically happy but politically starved may not last forever. The monarchy is apprehensive about a recurrence of political unrest. An additional stimulus to discontent is the extravagance of the royal family and the fact that there is no distinction between the private purse of the sultan and state revenues. The sultan has surrounded himself with extensive security forces including the Royal Brunei Armed Forces (about 4,400 strong), the Royal Brunei Police (2,300), the Gurkha Reserve Unit (2,300), and the British Army Gurkha Battalion (1,000). Evolutionary change might be encouraged by the educated elite and the technocrats who are becoming increasingly powerful in the civil service.

Brunei's main fear externally is encroachment by its larger neighbors, especially Malaysia and Indonesia. To some extent it has immunized itself against external threat by becoming a member in 1984 of the Association of Southeast Asian Nations (ASEAN), the Organization of the Islamic Conference (OIC), and the UN. More important, since 1987 it has sought to play a more dynamic role in ASEAN economics, a move which has brought about cordial relations with its neighbors.

D. S. Ranjit Singh and Jatswan S. Sidhu, *Historical Dictionary of Brunei* (Lanham, Md., 1997). B. A. Hussaininiya, *Sultan Omar Ali Saifuddien III and Britain, The Making of Modern Brunei,* (Kuala Lumpur, 1995).

D. S. RANJIT SINGH

BUDDHISM. The term "Buddhism" is derived from the title of the founder of the tradition, the Buddha, meaning "the Enlightened One." From its beginnings in north India in the fifth century B.C.E. as a mendicant/monastic-based religion, Buddhism spread throughout the rest of Asia during the early centuries of the present era, becoming a major cultural, social, economic, and political force. In many cases Buddhism broadened local, animistically defined conceptions of political leadership. In particular, it formulated classical conceptions of kingship in the Indianized states of Sri Lanka, Myanmar (Burma), Thailand, Laos, and Cambodia. The Buddhist worldview legitimated the king as maintainer of the political, economic, social, and moral orders. The historical model for the mythic Buddhist world ruler was the great Indian monarch Asoka (third century B.C.E.), who established hegemony over virtually the entire Indian subcontinent. The quality of later Buddhist rulers—Sinhalese, Burmese, Thai, Lao—was measured by the idealized rule of this strong, righteous, benevolent monarch who, according to Asoka's own edicts and the Buddhist chronicles, created a welfare state dedicated to the pursuit of religious and humanitarian goals. This ideal has also been operative in the development of the modern nation-state, and still functions as a moral norm for political leadership.

In China, Korea, and Japan Buddhism competed with *Confucianism for influence in defining policy as well as court politics. By the end of the ninth century in China the political and economic power of Buddhist monasteries led to an attempt to disestablish the tradition; in eighth-century Japan the disruptive political and military power of the Buddhist monasteries in the hills surrounding the ancient city of Nara prompted the emperor to move the capital to Kyoto; and by the thirteenth century Tibet had become a Buddhist theocratic state. In short, Buddhism was a major factor in the historical development of the classical states in virtually all mainland South, Southeast, Central, and East Asian countries. Its worldview and its institutions have both legitimated and challenged traditional political structures and statuses. While various Buddhist religious ideals, e.g., nirvana, do not fit comfortably with power politics, throughout the centuries Buddhism has generally supported the state and been supported by it. In the twentieth century this traditional symbiotic relationship has been evolving and, in some cases, undergoing dramatic changes.

The fortunes of Buddhism in various Asian countries have been determined by three major factors: the policies of political regimes, economic and social change, and educational and cultural transformation. Buddhism played a major role in the nationalist resistance to Western colonialism in Sri Lanka and Burma in the late nineteenth and early twentieth centuries. In both cases Buddhism fueled pride in national identity. In Sri Lanka, S.W.R.D. Bandaranaike won election as prime minister in 1957 on a Buddhist ticket. His victory was arguably a key factor in the development of the chauvinistic Buddhist fundamentalism which has been such a potent political force in Sri Lanka's racial strife since the mid-1980s. In Burma (Myanmar), U Nu's attempt to create a Buddhist state in the decade after the end of World War II led to his ouster in 1962 by his colleague, General Ne Win. Ne Win's road to Burmese socialism has been an economic disaster. The government's recent attempts to bolster Buddhism seem to be a ploy to win support for an unpopular regime. In 1989 Buddhist monks joined demonstrations in support of Aung San Suu Kyi election. In Vietnam Buddhist protest against the Diem regime as a "Catholic police state" contributed to Diem's downfall in 1963. The creation of a Unified Buddhist church in 1964 and the Buddhist effort to forge a middle path between policies of China, the Soviet Union, and the United States proved to be politically naive and ineffective. Thich Nhat Hanh, the chief spokesperson for the Buddhist peace movement in Vietnam, has become the leader of the Engaged Buddhist movement in the West. In Thailand support of Buddhism has been a major element in the Thai government's efforts to fashion various nation-building programs ranging from hill tribe resettlement to rural development. A counterpoint to Japan's secular political and economic climate is the Komeito Party's affiliation with the Nichiren Shoshu sect of Japanese Buddhism.

Politically repressive states have undermined Buddhist institutions as in the case of *Mao's China and Pol Pot's Cambodia, although they have also supported them as in the case of Ne Win's Myanmar. Mao and Pol Pot saw Buddhism in traditional Marxist terms as a justification of class exploitation and, therefore, as something to be attacked or, in the extreme case of Cambodia, to be destroyed. Buddhist leaders in Tibet have been in exile in India since the Chinese occupation of that country in 1959. The Dalai Lama has appealed to Western democracies to exert pressure on China to stop what he considers to be the cultural genocide of his country. Politically he supports Tibetan autonomy within the Chinese political sphere rather than an independent Tibet. In 1980 Ne Win created a national organizational structure for Burmese Buddhism which provided more state support for Buddhism. At the same time, the government has exercised greater control over Buddhist institutions. Recalcitrant Buddhist monks, especially in the Mandalay area, resisted the Burmese military regime in 1989 and 1990. They were arrested and imprisoned.

Classical Asian Buddhism defined itself institutionally in relationship to the monarchical state, on the one hand, and a village, agricultural economy on the other. Buddhism has had some difficulty in redefining itself in a modern nation-state, urban, increasingly industrialized, world-market economic environment. Buddhist leaders have sought to create a viable social ethic which speaks to such a modern environment. Western-educated laypersons have played an important role in redefining Buddhist thought for the modern world. As a consequence, in the monastic-oriented Buddhist countries of Southeast Asia, the central place of the monk is being challenged. Furthermore, as increasing attention is being devoted to such issues as Buddhism and race relations, Buddhism and peace, Buddhism and nuclear development, Buddhism and the destruction of the environment and so on, critics argue that the specifically religious orientation of Buddhism is at risk. Yet a new international Buddhist leadership is emerging—both lay and monastic—which is fashioning a relevant Buddhist spirituality rooted in personal disciplines like meditation coupled with a Buddhist social ethic focused on particular economic, social, and political issues. Generally speaking, this international "Engaged Buddhism" has been critical of the exploitation of the *Third World by Western nations. Its proponents have argued for balanced, humane, and less exploitative forms of development that are more respectful of the cultural, religious, and natural environments of Asian countries. Currently, this critical role appears to be Buddhism's most important contribution to the political and economic climates not only of Asia but also of the West.

(See also RELIGION AND POLITICS; SECULARIZATION).

Heinz Bechert and Richard Gombrich, eds., *The World of Buddhism* (New York, 1984). Joseph H. Kitagawa and Mark D. Cummings, eds., *Buddhism and Asian History* (New York, 1989). Ian Harris, ed. *Buddhism and Politics in Twentieth Century Asia*. (London, 1999).

DONALD K. SWEARER

BUDGET. Any budget, public or private, is a statement about how money will be spent and raised over a period of time. To budget is, at least formally, to make those decisions. Budgeting is necessary to ensure resources are used for higher priorities, rather than being spent on a lesser purpose and then being unavailable when needed for a more important one. Identifying constraints in advance can allow measures to ameliorate their effects, or prevent making promises that cannot be kept.

Because recognizing and responding to constraints is never pleasant, government budgeting is usually contentious. It is made more difficult by multiple, often conflicting goals.

Governments are widely expected to "balance" their budgets—defined as revenue equaling or exceeding spending. Deficits are viewed as misgovernment. Similarly, the national debt, the total accrued borrowing, is especially suspect in the United States. Thus many systems require that budgets be balanced as part of the *constitution or other fundamental law. In practice, however, these requirements often include exclusions such as a separate budget for capital expenses that allows borrowing.

Popular or elite beliefs may be contradicted or rationalized by economic arguments. From a more right-wing perspective total spending is what matters, because government spending is inherently less efficient than decisions made in the market. More standard economic analysis emphasizes the deficit or surplus, and attends to total debt mainly because interest payments can become a large and disabling expense.

In the classic Keynesian analysis, deficits at any level of spending increase aggregate demand, so encourage inflation and employment; surpluses decrease demand, so encourage price stability (or in the extreme deflation) and unemployment. This analysis makes national budgets central subjects of class conflict, as "looser" fiscal policy (e.g., deficits) relatively favors labor, and the reverse favors capital. Although they still accept this analysis on the margins, Western macroeconomists now tend to argue that short-term economic management should rely on monetary policy, while the budget is managed to increase national savings. If the government saves or borrows less, and this is not offset by private behavior, national total savings will rise. More savings could increase investment and, thus, economic growth. In practice there are many offsetting effects. Moreover, the savings campaign assumes the main purpose of budgeting should be to impose pain (make citizens pay more relative to what government provides), so will not reduce conflict.

Conflict may also center on allocations of spending by broad categories, such as defense vs. education or health. Sometimes, however, these priorities follow more consensual trends determined by events. Thus U.S. defense spending grew quickly after the Soviet Union invaded Afghanistan and U.S. diplomats were taken hostage in Iran, and fell after the collapse of communism in 1989.

More detailed allocations can represent a "general financial and work plan" for government's agencies. Then both the documents and the review of those documents may help make bureaucrats accountable to political overseers and the public. Politicians and voters pay special attention to the distribution of projects across legislative districts ("pork-barrel" spending). Executives normally argue they should control such decisions so as to limit wasteful spending. But executives can also manipulate legislators through dispensing such patronage. In the U.S. federal government, the legislature largely controls such decisions. Advocates of a "line-item veto" assert that the president could prevent more projects if he did not have to accept or reject entire packages passed by the legislature. Whether potential savings would justify the shift in power is quite questionable.

Some critics argue that budgets should measure all ways that government affects society, such as regulation and loan guarantees. That would contradict the role of the budget in managing the government itself, and combine widely incomparable activities. Problems stemming from different forms of spending are challenging enough.

Most government programs create a bureau and promise the bureau will do something (fight crime, shoot people into space, shoot enemies, collect taxes, or whatever). Then the budget decision concerns how much to fund the bureau; debate will focus on how much the bureau "needs" to perform its (perhaps controversial) functions; and political authorities can argue that, with better management, more could be done with less. Much of that process focuses on inputs rather than outputs.

But many programs, spending most of the money in some governments, are *entitlements. An entitlement promises precise benefits, such as exact pensions or reimbursement for health services, to specific individuals. Then spending depends on explicit payment or eligibility rules, e.g., the pension rate or qualification. Inputs are outputs.

Spending for entitlements is the sum of the details created by its rules; spending for a bureau is what the bureau does with its total. Politicians can control a total and displace some of the blame for results to the managers of a bureau. They must change visible rules to control spending for an entitlement. Specificity, visibility, and the fact that groups that can win entitlement status are usually more powerful mean that entitlement spending is often viewed as "uncontrollable." The term really means that annual budget processes designed to set spending levels for bureaus are ill suited to change basic entitlement law, so are rarely used to do so. But a government can change entitlement law if it wishes. The United States, for example, abolished the Aid to Families with Dependent Children entitlement in 1996, and has frequently changed the conditions of payment for Medicare services.

These different functions of budgeting and forms of commitment create unavoidable tensions:

1. For administrative purposes, budgets should be routine and made in a timely manner (usually annually). Yet conflict inhibits keeping to a tight schedule.

2. Policy choice often fits poorly with the budget process calendar. Emergencies arise after the budget is settled. Many policies, especially entitlements, require commitments for much longer periods than a year. Contributory pensions cannot have their benefits revised each year, because voters would not contribute thirty years in advance on such terms. Businesses expect some predictability in their tax obligations.

3. Most political systems decentralize a lot of policy making, e.g., to committees in a legislature or agencies within an executive. But, because details must add to some total, budget processes require some central coordination. Since policy is often meaningless without money, central coordinators (the British Treasury or U.S. Senate Appropriations Committee, for example) inevitably are in continual conflict with the non-budgetary decision-makers in agencies and legislative committees.

4. The economy affects budget totals as much as the budget shapes the economy, so the government can chase its tail while pursuing "economic management."

The overall priorities and totals that emerge from each political system's process, the level of detail in allocations and the processes of decision vary. Most advanced industrial countries spend far larger shares of national product on government activities than does the United States; in most, the legislature is less influential. In all, however, the budget is a treaty among competing interests: an agreement as to who will contribute, and receive, how much. Like any treaty, its terms will depend on power relationships and who participates in the negotiations. Unlike others, it is renegotiated continually. Thus budgeting is one of the major decision processes in modern politics.

(See also KEYNESIANISM; WELFARE.)

Aaron Wildavsky, "A Budget for All Seasons? Why the Traditional Budget Lasts." *Public Administration Review* 38: 6 (Nov/Dec 1978): 501–509. Joseph White and Aaron Wildavsky, *The Deficit and the Public Interest: The Search for Responsible Budgeting in the 1980s* (Berkeley, Calif., and New York, 1991). Herbert Stein, "The Fiscal Revolution in America, Part II: 1964–1994," in W. Elliot Brownlee, ed., *Funding the Modern American State, 1941–1995: The Rise and Fall of the Era of Easy Finance* (Cambridge, U.K., 1996). Irene S. Rubin, *The Politics of Public Budgeting: Getting and Spending, Borrowing and Balancing*, 3d ed. (Chatham, 1997).
JOSEPH WHITE

BULGARIA. A Slavic country of approximately 8 million people in southeastern Europe, located between Romania and Turkey, Bulgaria achieved independence in 1908 after 500 years of Ottoman rule. Like many countries in the region, Bulgaria experienced considerable tumult and profound regime changes in the twentieth century. Bulgaria's participation in World War I on the side of the Central Powers had catastrophic results, including the imposed annexation of its of territory to Greece, Romania, and the Kingdom of Serbia, Croatia, and Slovenia as well as the loss of its outlet to the Aegean Sea. Bulgaria supported the losing side again in World War II, and the arrival of the Red Army in August 1944 inaugurated a period of Communist Party rule.

During the postwar period, the Bulgarian Communist Party (BCP), in alliance with the surviving radical splinter of the Agrarian Party, set about establishing a comprehensive set of Soviet-type political, economic, and social institutions. Starting from a low material level as well as unfavorable resource and energy endowments, Bulgaria achieved relatively dynamic and successful growth within Soviet forms. Comprehensive state ownership and central *planning characterized the rapidly expanding urban, industrial core. The rural economy was forcibly collectivized in a manner that led to rapid mechanization and improved high rural incomes, albeit in the presence of widespread corruption and the destruction of traditional family structures in the countryside.

As a result of these changes, Bulgaria experienced structural transformation of the economy, a rapid growth in incomes, and improvements in the quality and quantity of consumer goods availability during the 1945–1975 period. The country enjoyed less satisfactory economic results, however, in the following decade and severe problems from 1983 to 1985 were accompanied by rising political discontent. Bulgaria was deeply committed to the Council for Mutual Economic Assistance (CMEA) bilateral trade patterns, especially the Soviet Union as its major market for manufactured and agricultural output and principal source of raw materials. The decay of trade relationships beginning in the Andropov period sharply depressed Bulgarian economic performance. Soviet trade retrenchment after 1986 compounded the Bulgarian problem and it began to borrow heavily abroad. A crisis atmosphere developed in which mass expulsion of the Turkish minority took place.

The political effects of *perestroika and glasnost were late in arriving in Bulgaria, but struck with particular force since the collapse of the coordinating function of the BCP parallel hierarchy occurred in the context of already existing economic difficulties. The political crisis in the fall of *1989 produced the abrupt resignation of Todor Zhivkov after thirty-five years in power but left Bulgaria with a leadership vacuum when no alternative structures of coordination and control emerged. From a position of relative prosperity and seemingly successful development, Bulgarians suddenly faced the prospects of real deprivation at the same time that the creation of entirely new forms of economic organization was required.

The strong showing of the renamed Bulgarian Socialist Party (BSP) in the June 1990 parliamentary elections and the lack of a coherent program by the sixteen-party Union of Democratic Forces (UDF) initially suggested little support for a complete recasting of the system regardless of what happens elsewhere in Eastern Europe. After a six month political impasse, a coalition government dominated by the BSP and the Agrarians (eight and four ministers, respectively) was formed in December 1990 with an unaffiliated prime minister, Dimitar Popov, joined by three UDF and four independent members. New elections in November 1991 saw the BSP share of the vote fall to 34 percent, slightly less than the coalition total for the UDF. UDF Prime Minister Filip Dimitrov governed in tenuous coalition with the Turkish minority party, which drew barely 7 percent of the vote but is the only other participant in Parliament. The narrow 54 to 46 margin for the UDF candidate Zhelyu Zhelev over the BSP candidate in the January 1992 presidential election showed that the socialist party retained considerable appeal. Yet, the UDF alliance of pro-Democratic parties gained strength through the mid-1990s, however, with the UDF's Ivan Kostov serving as prime minister since 1997.

Following triple-digit inflation and declines in GDP in 1996 and 1997, the new UDF government has attempted to stabilize the economy through the implementation of an IMF package of credits and structural reforms, including privatization, efforts to fight *corruption and crime, and the liberalization (marketization) of agricultural policies. These policies, as well as a set of open-government reforms and changes in regional administration (program "Bulgaria 2001") lend the Kostov government a modernizing persona. Externally, Bulgaria, like all countries in Southeast Europe, faces the potential spillover consequences of instability from the recurring conflicts in the territories of the former Yugoslavia and the absence of a firm political settlement in Kosovo.

(See also COLLECTIVIZATION; COMMUNIST PARTY STATES; KOSOVO WAR; POST-COMMUNISM.)

R. J. McIntyre, *Bulgaria: Politics, Economics and Society* (London, 1988). R. J. Crampton, *A Short History of Modern Bulgaria* (Cambridge, U.K., 1989).

ROBERT J. MCINTYRE

BUREAUCRACY. In common with all advanced, industrialized nations, the United States needs a large bureaucracy to develop and implement a wide range of government programs. By the late 1990s, there were just under three million civilian federal government employees working on tasks that ranged from paying retirement pensions (*Social Security) to space exploration (the National Aeronautics and Space Administration). The federal civil service had been larger, reaching a peacetime peak of 3.5 million in 1990, and there were many more officials working for state governments than for the federal (approximately 4.5 million). In the last twenty years, federal government has adopted the practice of contracting out an increasing amount of work to private sector consultants, a practice that may well be more expensive than having the work done by civil servants but which allows politicians to boast of reducing the number of federal employees. Nonetheless, the federal bureaucracy was far larger than the framers of the Constitution (which does not mention the bureaucracy) could have imagined.

The United States has had a distinct experience of bureaucracy that contrasts with most if not all of the European democracies as well as Asian countries such as Japan. After a brief period from the adoption to the Constitution until the election of President Jackson, the bureaucracy was seen not as a prestigious career into which the best graduates of the best colleges or universities could be attracted (as in France, Japan, and Britain) but as a source of patronage for politicians to dispense to their supporters. The well-known phrase "to the victors the spoils" described accurately how government jobs, such as in the New York Customs House, which was the primary source of federal revenue in the nineteenth century, were used. As Stephen Skowronek has described, Progressive reformers in the late nineteenth century engaged in a long struggle to establish a system through which government employees were recruited on merit free from political patronage into a civil service system with job security. It might be argued that this development was not so much later in the United States than in Britain where the Northcote Trevelyan reforms established a career civil service recruited on merit at midcentury. Yet in contrast to Britain, the United States never imposed the merit system across the entire civil service. The proportion of U.S. federal civil servants under the merit system peaked at 88 percent in 1929 and today is only 54 percent. A newly elected president retains the right to make thousands (no one is even sure how many) of appointments, a degree of patronage that is unparalleled in other democracies.

Part of the reason for the incomplete triumph of the merit system in the United States is that politicians still value the power to make appointments as a political weapon. Appointments may no longer be made for running party *political machines, which have disappeared, but they are used to consolidate support among key constituencies. The determination of President *Clinton to form through his power of appointment an administration "that looks like America" meant that he was determined to reward African Americans, Latinos, and feminists for their support in the preceding election and to signal to those groups that he was sympathetic to their goals. The power of appointment can also be used, as it was by President *Reagan, to impose policies on a bureaucracy that might be unsympathetic to them. Reagan, for example, used his power to appoint numerous officials to regulatory agencies such as the Environmental Protection Agency (EPA) and Occupational Safety and Health Administration (OSHA) to ensure that they adopted a more conciliatory approach to business corporations. Presidents have also come to expect the right to appoint hundreds of people to work on their own staffs in the White House. On numerous issues ranging from economic policy to foreign policy, presidents expect to be able to have their own advisers in the White House who are political appointees, not civil servants. Presidents believe that these political appointees, who can be fired at will, reflect their views and interests better than career civil servants.

The career civil service in consequence at even its highest levels is quite different in character from those of most democracies. As Aberbach and Rockman have noted, even the higher civil service in the United States is composed primarily of people with a more technical training in contrast to the highest-level civil servants in Japan, Britain, or continental Europe. Civil servants are expected to give expert advice and not to participate as much as elsewhere in the formulation of policy alongside elected politicians. As noted earlier, only just over half of civilian federal government employees today hold jobs fully protected by civil service rules. This is in part because of the introduction of the Senior Executive Service during the Carter presidency, a body in which very senior officials hold supposedly better-paid jobs in return for less job security. Yet the constant increase in the number of political appointees in government departments, what Paul Light has termed the "thickening of government," has been more important in separating the career civil servant from policy making in Washington to a degree that is unequaled in Berlin, Tokyo, Paris, or London.

Stephen Skowronek, *Building a New American State: The Expansion of National Administrative Capacities, 1877–1920* (Cambridge, U.K. 1982). Paul Charles Light, *Thickening Government: Federal Hierarchy and the Diffusion of Responsibility* (Washington, D.C., 1995). Paul Charles Light, *The True Size of Government* (Washington, D.C., 1999). Joel D. Aberbach and Bert A. Rockman, *In the Web of Politics* (Washington, D.C., 2000).

GRAHAM K. WILSON

BUREAUCRATIC AUTHORITARIANISM. The concept of bureaucratic authoritarianism arose from the study of major episodes of authoritarian rule in South America between the 1960s and the 1980s: Brazil from 1964 to 1985, Argentina from 1966 to 1973 and later from 1976 to 1983, Chile from 1973 to 1990, and Uruguay from 1973 to 1985. This body of analysis is closely identified with the writings of Guillermo O'Donnell.

Bureaucratic authoritarianism is a type of *military rule often interpreted as novel in relation to the earlier history of Latin America. It was generally led by the military as an institution, in contrast to the personalistic rule of individual officers. Rotation in the presidency among military leaders was a common, though not universal, trait. This form of rule has been interpreted as distinctively bureaucratic because national leadership was dominated by individuals who had risen to prominence not through political careers but through bureaucratic careers in large public and private organizations, including international agencies and transnational corporations. Decision-making styles among these leaders were commonly technocratic.

This bureaucratic, technocratic orientation was generally accompanied by intense repression, which in most of the cases reached levels unprecedented in the region. Repression was unleashed against the *labor movement, political parties associated with labor, and other social sectors whose prior mobilization had seemed to threaten the existing political and economic system.

The phenomenon of bureaucratic authoritarianism commanded wide analytic interest, in part because its emergence seemed to contradict the hypothesis that socioeconomic *modernization might be supportive of *democracy. In terms of per capita indicators, Argentina, Chile, and Uruguay were among the most modernized countries in Latin America. Brazil was less modernized on a per capita basis, yet in absolute terms it had a large modern sector and its economic difficulties prior to the 1964 coup were in important respects those of an industrial economy. The appearance in these countries of an authoritarianism of unprecedented harshness thus challenged this earlier hypothesis.

Analysts explained this outcome by suggesting that the process of modernization had two consequences which collided: it intensified certain types of economic problems, and it augmented the capacity of the popular classes to resist an important spectrum of proposed solutions to these problems. It was argued that this collision increased pressures to inaugurate bureaucratic authoritarianism, as a means both of pursuing these proposed solutions and controlling resistance to them.

The rise of authoritarianism must be seen against the backdrop of abiding dilemmas in Latin American development: serious inequalities, which governments periodically sought to remedy through redistributive policies; inefficient industrial structures, sheltered from international competition by a high level of state protection which was strongly supported by a larger framework of economic *nationalism; and the contradictory role of labor movements that favored redistribution and protection. Latin America was able to confront governments when they abandoned such policies, and yet were often unable to enter coalitions that provided a stable basis for pursuing these policies.

The cases of bureaucratic authoritarianism shared a common approach to addressing these dilemmas. This approach included: (1) postponing redistribution, or even reversing it, in order to foster economic growth; (2) seeking to create a more efficient, internationally competitive economy and cultivating international economic actors as partners in the development model; and (3) attempting to control or destroy the labor movement, which in the past had often undermined these other policies. This policy mix had long been an option on the Latin American development agenda, and the initial success experienced by some of these new governments in implementing these policies commanded great attention, evoking both condemnation and praise.

The Concept. Bureaucratic authoritarianism has thus been understood as a form of bureaucratic and technocratic military rule that seeks to curtail popular mobilization and is built on a political coalition and a policy orientation that entails strong ties to international economic actors. It contrasts with *fascism, which is mobilizational and nationalistic. It lacks the comprehensive domination of *totalitarianism, notwithstanding the scope of repression in Chile and Uruguay, as well as Argentina in the 1970s. As a subtype of authoritarian rule, it may be distinguished from other subtypes: populist authoritarianism, which promotes popular mobilization rather than demobilization; and traditional authoritarianism, which is found prior to any extensive popular mobilization.

Bureaucratic authoritarianism is often referred to as a type of regime. Yet standard definitions of the term focus not just on what are conventionally thought of as regime characteristics—military rule, repression, demobilization, and bureaucratic orientation—but also on the composition of the dominant coalition and orientation of public policy. Hence, many scholars have labeled bureaucratic authoritarianism more broadly as a form of state or political system, not just a regime type. The broader definition has the merit of focusing attention on the links among these different elements; on the other hand, it may lump together so many attributes as to be analytically unwieldy.

As occurs with many concepts, scholars debated both the fit with the initial cases and the extension to other cases. In response to the evolving interpretations of the original four countries, analysts refined their definitions, and the question arose whether the concept really corresponded to these cases. A useful way to view this debate is to understand bureaucratic authoritarianism as an analytic construct referring to a syndrome of attributes, all of which may not be present in every case.

In the debate over extension to other cases, one candidate was Peru, which experienced institutional military rule around the same time—between 1968 and 1980. Yet many analysts interpret Peru, especially up to 1975, as a case of populist authoritarianism, owing to the scope of popular mobilization. The inclusion of Mexico was suggested in light of its conjunction of authoritarianism and technocratic policymaking. However, many scholars hesitated to include Mexico because organized labor was not excluded from the country's governing coalition and because the Mexican system during this period was not the outgrowth of an immediate prior polarization and was not a military regime.

With reference to non–Latin American cases, the concept has been applied to authoritarian Spain; to Poland, Hungary, and Austria during the interwar period; to Greece in the late 1960s and early 1970s; and to authoritarian experiences in East and Southeast Asia and in the Middle East. In these cases, many traits that Latin American specialists associate

with the original four countries may not be present, and hence the concept has served more generically to refer to modern (rather than traditional) authoritarianism that has a major bureaucratic dimension.

Explaining the Rise of Bureaucratic Authoritarianism. Economic issues were a contributing condition in the original four cases, though not a sufficient explanation. An initial hypothesis suggested that military and economic elites established bureaucratic authoritarianism with the specific goal of promoting long-term economic and political stability, which in turn would promote the vertical integration ("deepening") of the economy, i.e., increase the domestic production of industrial inputs. Although this specific hypothesis was not well supported, the broader set of economic priorities discussed above—within which vertical integration was sometimes an element—did represent both a source of pressure, and (for some actors) a political opportunity, for inaugurating bureaucratic authoritarianism. A global process of economic internationalization reinforced these economic priorities, and hence also the incentives for this new form of rule.

Three other contributing conditions merit note. One is the demonstration effect of the opposition movements, social protests, and new alternatives on the left that arose in Western Europe, the Communist world, and the Americas in the 1960s and early 1970s. In Latin America, this demonstration effect was intensified by the emergence of socialist Cuba. The survival of a socialist state in the region dramatically extended the political horizon of the Latin American left, and combined with the larger international context of political mobilization and protest, it played a role in escalating opposition and protest in the original four countries. This escalation also fueled conservative fears of popular mobilization, thereby intensifying polarization and subsequent repression.

Second, the structure of domestic politics had an impact. Its role can be seen in the contrast between the four cases discussed above and the experience of Venezuela and Mexico. Venezuela had a high level of modernization in per capita terms, and Mexico had one of the largest modern sectors in Latin America. In light of the modernization arguments noted above, these two countries might have experienced bureaucratic authoritarianism—yet they did not. This occurred partly because during an earlier period in Mexico and Venezuela, a cohesive political center had been constituted that commanded an electoral majority and incorporated organized labor. In the subsequent period of crisis and polarization, this broad center provided a basis for stable rule and mitigated some of the difficulties experienced in Argentina, Brazil, Chile, and Uruguay—none of which had formed an equivalent centrist bloc. Third, in Venezuela, and in Mexico late in the period under discussion, this political resource was supplemented by an important economic resource: massive oil revenues, which gave the state greater capacity to address distributional issues and hence may have reduced pressure for the measures entailed in bureaucratic authoritarianism.

Demise and Impact. As of the early 1990s, bureaucratic authoritarianism had disappeared in South America. Various factors contributed to this outcome. First, many Latin American countries have had difficulty establishing stable, legitimate political rule and have experienced long-term cycles of alternation between competitive and authoritarian regimes. Hence, this disappearance is part of a recurring pattern, the causes of which remain a matter of scholarly debate. Second, damaging tensions emerged within bureaucratic-authoritarian rule, for instance, between the internationalization promoted by the economic model and the nationalism of the military and of other sectors capable of mounting serious opposition. Third, severe economic problems, experienced throughout the region as part of the *international debt crisis, helped discredit authoritarianism. Finally, domestic and international protest against *human rights abuses, and somewhat later, the demonstration effect of a worldwide process of democratization, further debilitated authoritarian rule.

What was the impact of this authoritarian experience? The economic record is diverse. Notwithstanding ongoing economic difficulties, Brazil unquestionably saw a dramatic advance toward a modern industrial economy. In Chile a far more open economy was created, a transformation which a subsequent democratically elected government sought to build upon, not reverse. Argentina, by contrast, produced dramatic failures. The post-1966 government achieved initial economic success and then collapsed in an explosion of social protest. The post-1976 government imposed far more draconian economic measures and repression, yet it was unable to overcome a myriad of economic difficulties and left a deeply troubled economy. Uruguay experienced a revival of economic growth in the 1970s, reversing two decades of stagnation. These gains eroded in the early 1980s, however, owing to the combined effects of internal policy failure and the larger debt crisis.

Although the political record is likewise diverse, in two important respects the political legacies are convergent. Among substantial sectors of the population, the experience of preauthoritarian polarization and crisis, followed by the trauma of authoritarian rule, led to a greater appreciation of electoral democracy. In addition, the experience of this cycle of authoritarianism—along with the debt crisis, other economic difficulties, and later collapse of socialism in Eastern Europe and the Soviet Union—lowered developmental expectations and eroded the credibility of socialist and progressive political alternatives in these four countries. Consequently, in the aftermath of bureaucratic authoritarianism, there was evidence of greater support for democracy and a reduced likelihood of any immediate renewal of polarization.

(See also AUTHORITARIANISM; DEVELOPMENT AND UNDERDEVELOPMENT.)

Guillermo O'Donnell, *Modernization and Bureaucratic-Authoritarianism: Studies in South American Politics*, Politics of Modernization Series No. 9, Institute of International Studies, University of California, Berkeley (Berkeley, Calif., 1973; the 1998 edition includes a new preface). David Collier, ed., *The New Authoritarianism in Latin America* (Princeton, N.J., 1979). Karen L. Remmer and Gilbert W. Merkx, "Bureaucratic-Authoritarianism Revisited," with a reply by O'Donnell, *Latin America Research Review* 17, no. 2 (1982): 3–50. Guillermo O'Donnell, *Bureaucratic Authoritarianism: Argentina 1966–1973, in Comparative Perspective* (Berkeley, Calif., and Los Angeles, 1988). Ruth Berins Collier and David Collier, *Shaping the Political Arena: Critical Junctures, the Labor Movement, and Regime Dynamics in Latin America* (Princeton, N.J., 1991). Guillermo O'Donnell, *Counterpoints: Selected Essays on Authoritarianism and Democratization* (Notre Dame, Ind., 1999).

DAVID COLLIER

BUREAUCRATIC POLITICS. A term that came into vogue in the late 1960s in American political science, *bureaucratic politics* has become an accepted concept for the analysis of *foreign policy decision-making. The "bureaucratic politics model" purports to explain how bureaucracies affect both the formulation and implementation of a state's foreign policy. Proponents of the model claim that bargaining among foreign policy bureaucracies is the key to understanding a state's foreign policy output. Critics of the model claim that a focus solely on bureaucratic conflict is insufficient to explain a state's foreign policy, although such behavior must be taken into account.

At the outset, it would be absurd to deny either that bureaucracies exist or that they have influence. The modern *state is, above all else, the bureaucratic state. That is, bureaucracies are essential to both domestic and foreign policies. The earliest student of bureaucratic behavior, Max *Weber, applauded the bureaucratic mode of political organization as the most advanced and the form best suited to the administration of complex societies. Selection for a position within a bureaucracy would come through testing and merit, not favoritism or connections. Decisions would be made on the basis of expertise, not personal whim. Behavior would be predictable and regularized and occur within well-proscribed channels and procedures. In short, for Weber the bureaucratic mode was a clear advance on its predecessors.

What Weber saw as virtues, however, became vices in the eyes of later observers. What Weber found predictable and regularized others found deadening and stifling. Rules to provide regularized channels had become ends in themselves, not means to other goals. Advancement on the basics of merit had too easily become a lifelong sinecure for unimaginative bureaucrats. Injecting fresh approaches became difficult because elected leaders could not break the stranglehold that bureaucrats had on policy. The marshaling of expertise to solve difficult problems became a cover for bureaucrats to serve the interests of their own organizations at the expense of the public interest and other bureaucracies with which they competed for resources and influence. What for Weber had been the pinnacle of modern political organization had become the logjam in the machinery of government to successor observers.

In the late 1960s, students of foreign policy analysis in the United States built upon the basic insight these earliest critics had advanced about the pernicious effects of the bureaucratic mode and developed three propositions about how bureaucracies affected foreign policy. Their first proposition held that organizational position determined policy stance, that "where you stand (your policy stance on a given issue) depends on where you sit (your institutional position and responsibilities)." The best predictor of what position a bureaucrat would take on an issue was the interests of the organization that he or she represented. Their second proposition was that the foreign policy decisions and actions of a government do not represent the intent of any one figure, but rather are the unintended result of bargaining, pulling, hauling, and tugging by bureaucratic competitors in their ceaseless quest for more funds, resources, and influence. The policy a government might adopt is unpredictable because it is the result of a fierce bureaucratic struggle for power. The third proposition of the bureaucratic politics model asserted that there was a difference between formulating and implementing a policy. Even if top political decision makers prevailed over the bureaucrats in the formulation stage, they would lose out to them in the implementation stage because the bureaucrats implement the policy. There would be considerable slippage between governmental intent (the policy as formulated) and governmental action (what actually was done). Bureaucrats, in short, appeared to be both powerful and pernicious.

Accepted uncritically, the bureaucratic paradigm would lead one to look at bureaucrats, not elected political leaders, for the major initiatives in foreign policy; to focus on the internecine struggles among bureaucrats, not on the views and images that are held in common by them; and to look within a government to predict its actions, rather than observing the policies of other governments and how those actions affect the balance of competition among competing bureaucracies.

Critics of the bureaucratic politics model reacted to its exclusive focus on bureaucratic politics and its neglect of both domestic and international politics. Their criticisms did not imply that bureaucracies were irrelevant in explaining foreign policy outcomes, only that their role was circumscribed. The critics held that heads of government and top political leaders set the terms within which bureaucrats work, and that it was important to look at how top political decision makers constrained the bureaucrats below them, not simply at how the bureaucrats fought with one another. In this view bureaucrats derived their power, not from their bureaucratic position per se, but from the larger interests within society that they represented and especially from their close alliances with members of Congress. Shared images often characterized the top-level decision makers; where differences of opinion occurred, they were as often as not due to differences in intellectual outlook and past experiences rather than to bureaucratic position. Events in the international realm also constrained bureaucratic behavior by altering the balance of political power among the bureaucracies. In sum, critics of the bureaucratic politics school argued that more often than not bureaucratic factors took second place to both domestic and international politics as determinants of foreign policy. Bureaucratic politics was a necessary supplement to those two, but could never make much sense without them.

Ironically, the bureaucratic politics approach experienced its greatest popularity in the United States, a country where executive branch bureaucrats are subject to powerful presidential and congressional pressures. In a presidential system such as that of the United States, where power is shared between the executive and the Congress, bureaucratic power is severely constrained. In parliamentary systems, where parliaments are weak in relation to executives, bureaucrats have considerable power vis-à-vis the legislature; but even in these cases they are subject to prime ministers and cabinets whom they must serve, whatever the party or policy. Bureaucrats may thus retain more power in parliamentary than in presidential systems, but in both they are subject to popularly elected executives. Bureaucratic politics is important in modern government, but only within the parameters set by both domestic and international politics.

Graham T. Allison, *Essence of Decision* (Boston, 1971). I. M. Destler, *President, Bureaucrats, and Foreign Policy* (Princeton, N.J., 1972). Morton H. Halperin, *Bureaucracy and Foreign Policy* (Washington, D.C., 1974). Robert J. Art, "Bureaucratic Politics and American Foreign Policy—A Critique," reprinted in G. John Ikenberry, ed., *American Foreign Policy—Theoretical Essays* (New York, 1989): 433–457. Stephen C. Krasner, "Are Bureaucracies Important? (or Allison Wonderland)," reprinted in G. John Ikenberry, ed., *American Foreign Policy—Theoretical Essays* (New York, 1989): 419–433.

ROBERT J. ART

BURKINA FASO. A Sahelian, land-locked former French colony in West Africa, Burkina Faso (formerly Upper Volta) has a land area of 274,200 square kilometers (105,870 sq. mi.) and a population estimated at 11.5 million in 1999. In 1998, the GNP stood at US$2.6 billion, while GNP per capita was $240. The capital city is Ouagadougou, and *Islam and indigenous beliefs are the main religions.

In March 1959, the main nationalist party, the *Rassemblement Démocratique Africain* (RDA) won an overwhelming victory in the legislative elections which brought Maurice Yaméogo, a moderate, pro-French leader, to power first as prime minister, then as president after the country became independent from France on 5 August 1960. Politics then took the form of power struggles among rival factions and leaders within the RDA, with the trade unions acting as powerbrokers. Indeed, labor strikes contributed to the downfall of the corrupt Yaméogo regime, which was toppled on 3 January 1966 by a military *coup d'état led by General Sangoulé Lamizana. The RDA continued to dominate the country's political life under the military regime and was back in power by 1971. However, in February 1974, Lamizana and the military suspended the constitution and resumed power. The constitutional referendum of November 1977 and the legislative and presidential elections of April–May 1978 marked a return to traditional party politics characterized by increased factionalism and personal rivalries within the RDA.

The military coup of 25 November 1980, which overthrew Lamizana and brought Colonel Sayé Zerbo to power, marked the end of the RDA dominance. The loose coalition of nationalist and reform-minded army officers led by Sayé Zerbo ruled through the *Comité Militaire de Redressement pour le Progrès National* (CMRPN). The CMRPN embarked on a program of economic and financial austerity, coupled with restrictions on civil liberties, which put it on a collision course with the trade unions. This conflict resulted in yet another military coup on 7 November 1982, now led by a group of younger, more radical army officers. The new governing body, the *Conseil de Salut du Peuple* (CSP), headed by Major Jean-Baptiste Ouédraogo, promised to reinstate political freedom and to promote social justice. A major ideological cleavage soon emerged within the CSP and resulted in a third coup which, on 4 August 1983, brought to power the left-wing faction, led by a popular and charismatic young captain, Thomas Sankara.

Aimed at empowering the disenfranchised rural masses, the Burkinabè revolution institutionalized new agencies of popular power (the *Conseil National de la Révolution*, or CNR, and the *Comités de Défense de la Révolution*, or CDRs). A *basic needs-oriented economic and social development strategy was initiated, and a nonaligned foreign policy launched. The various Marxist-Leninist political parties, which had contributed to the seizure of power by the Sankara faction of the army, were absorbed into the new revolutionary structure. As a result of intense intra-left factional struggles, Sankara created an umbrella structure for all the extreme-left political factions as the nucleus of a future single party, the *Union des*

Communistes Burkinabè (UCB). As the CNR progressively cut itself off from the traditional social basis of previous regimes (the urban petty bourgeoisie) without gaining enough support among the peasantry, it became increasingly isolated. The Sankara faction became marginalized within both the CNR and the army. Growing disagreement on ideology, strategy, and security issues culminated in a bloody coup on 15 October 1987 engineered by Sankara's *alter ego*, Blaise Compaoré, which led to the violent death of Sankara, thirteen of his associates, and up to 100 other persons, and to the subsequent seizure of power by Compaoré and his faction.

Soon after assuming power, the Compaoré regime initiated a national rectification process designed to redress the perceived excesses of the previous government. The *Front Populaire* (FP), the organ that now replaced the CNR as the regime's main ruling body, embarked on a witchhunt designed to neutralize the extreme-leftist factions. In March 1988, the *Comités Révolutionnaires* (CRs) replaced the CDRs, with a somewhat reduced political role. On 19 September 1989, former Sankara associates Jean-Baptiste Lingani and Henri Zongo were arrested and executed on account of their "antirevolutionary" activities. On 2 June 1991 a new constitution was adopted by referendum.

Meanwhile, growing opposition to Compaoré and his party, the *Organisation Démocratique et Populaire-Mouvement du Travail* (ODP-MT), led to the creation in September 1991 of a broad coalition of democratic forces, the *Coordination des Forces Démocratiques* (CFD). In October 1991, Compaoré resisted the CFD's call for a popular and sovereign national conference and created another support group, the *Alliance pour le Respect et la Défense de la Constitution* (ARDC). Following the presidential elections of 1 December 1991, boycotted by the opposition candidates, Compaoré was voted back in office with 84.4 percent of the vote (but with only 25 percent of the electorate voting). In a repeat performance, Compaoré won 87.5 percent of the vote (with only 44 percent of the electorate voting) in the presidential elections of 15 November 1998, once again boycotted by the opposition. Beyond its core of support (sections of organized labor, civil servants, and the military), the ODP-MT government has generally been met with hostility or indifference.

While appearing to play by the rules of multiparty democracy, and thus endearing itself to the international financial institutions, the Compaoré regime in fact has persistently ignored the opposition's demands to progressively reinforce the hegemony of its party, the ODP-MT, which was later broadened and renamed the *Congrès pour la Démocratie et le Progrès* (CDP). The constitutional amendment of 27 January 1997 enabled the president to be reelected indefinitely. The legislative elections of 11 May 1997 saw the CDP win 101 out of 111 seats in the National Assembly. The creation of various watchdog agencies such as the national electoral commission (*Commission électorale nationale indépendante* [CENI]), the higher committee for information (*Comité supérieur de l'information* [CSI]), and the independent commission of inquiry (*Commission d'enquête indépendant* [CEI]), all tightly controlled by the government, appear as mere democratic window-dressing. The murder on 13 December 1998 of investigative journalist Norbert Zongo and three of his associates, which remains unsolved to this day despite strong evidence pointing to the presidential security force, further ex-

acerbated political tensions and became a political *cause célèbre* around which a broad-based opposition to the regime by mass democratic movements, including student organizations and the powerful trade union (the *Confédération Générale du Travail-Burkina*), has rallied. Ultimately, the obstinate refusal of the CDP regime to abide by the rules of multiparty democracy, its involvement with rebel forces in Sierra Leone and Angola, its frequent resort to political repression, incarceration, and assassination, its obstruction of justice, its constant abuses of *human rights, and its inexorable descent into authoritarian, one-party rule will undoubtedly lead to further social unrest and political violence.

(See also FRANCOPHONE AFRICA; SOCIALISM AND SOCIAL DEMOCRACY.)

Guy Martin, "Revolutionary Democracy, Social-Political Conflict and Militarization in Burkina Faso, 1983–1988," in Peter Meyns and Dan W. Nabudere, eds., *Democracy and the One-Party State in Africa* (Hamburg, 1989), pp. 57–77. Joan Baxter and Keith Somerville, "Burkina Faso," in Bogdan Szajkowski, ed., *Benin, the Congo, Burkina Faso* (London, 1989), pp. 237–286. Pierre Englebert, *Burkina Faso: Unsteady Statehood in West Africa* (Boulder, Colo., 1996). R. von Meijenfeld, C. Santiso, and R. Otayek, eds., *La Democratie au Burkina Faso* (Stockholm, 1998).

GUY MARTIN

BURMA. See MYANMAR.

BURUNDI. The Republic of Burundi is a landlocked country located in the Great Lakes region in Africa. Surrounded by the Democratic Republic of the Congo to the west, Rwanda to the north, and Tanzania to the south and the east, Burundi covers 27,834 square kilometers (10,747 miles) of luxuriant landscape. With 170 persons per square kilometer, it is ranked among the most densely populated countries in the world. Located on the shores of Lake Tanganyika, Bujumbura is the main city and the political and economic hub.

With the exception of tin and some gold, Burundi is poor in mineral resources. Its economy is enclaved and dependent for its growth on the goodwill of its equally poor neighbors and the vagaries of the world commodity market. Most Barundi are farmers or pastoralists. Coffee is the major export commodity, whereas cattle serve as symbol of both material wealth and social status. Burundi imports all necessary industrial goods, including oil.

Mwami (King) Ntare I is credited as the founder of this polity whose history would later be marked by many tribulations. In the early nineteenth century, his successors further unified and expanded the territory roughly to its present boundaries. By 1850, Uburundi, as the country was then known, was a powerful nation in East and Central Africa, with a homogenous, though socially variegated, population that spoke the same language (Kirundi) and was bound by the same culture.

German officers were the first Europeans to control Burundi by imposing a treaty in 1903 that made it part of German East Africa. After World War I, Belgium took over and, in 1924, began to implement a series of changes that still affect Burundi and its citizens. Among the most important colonial decisions were the dismantling of precolonial social arrangements and the replacement of century-old institutions by a new power structure.

At independence on 1 July 1962, Mwami Mwambutsa IV

briefly returned to power and set up a multiparty system. Soon, however, social turmoil swept the country, weakening the monarch's effectiveness as an arbiter of political disputes, and exacerbating communal violence among Hutu, Tutsi, and Twa, the three major ethnic communities. Colonel Micombero staged a coup and established the first republic in 1966. He was overthrown a few years later by another officer who, in turn, was toppled in 1989.

Since independence, Barundi and their leaders have vainly grappled with the formidable task of institutionalizing political openness, the participation of all citizens in the governing process, and the peaceful coexistence among the three major communities. In a move designed to bring lasting peace to his country, the third military ruler, Major Pierre Buyoya, courageously initiated political reform that led to the revision of the constitution, its adoption by referendum, and the organization of general elections. This process resulted in the return to a short-lived civilian rule under the presidential leadership of Melchior Ndadaye, the winner of the 1993 elections.

President Ndadaye's assassination three months after his election plunged Burundi into a renewed cycle of communal violence, armed provocation, and bloody retaliations. Although the army, which had been in power since 1968, succeeded in preventing mass atrocities committed in neighboring Rwanda from spilling over into Burundi, it failed to quell internal rebellion and repeated military incursions by Burundian opposition fighters who operated from neighboring Congo.

It was under these circumstances that a faction of the Tutsi-led army returned Major Buyoya to the presidency in 1996. Upon his return to power, President Buyoya set out to stop the nation's steady decline into anarchy. Once again, he pronounced himself in favor of political dialogue and reconciliation with willing members of the political opposition. With great difficulty, negotiations between the government and its foes began in neighboring Tanzania, amidst a highly polarized national climate and an international regime of economic sanctions against Burundi. Despite the existence of positive signs indicating that the government and part of the political opposition are moving towards a political settlement, the presence of a radical, anti-dialogue core within the army and the political elite suggests that the future of Burundi is still in the making.

(See also GREAT LAKES REGION; RWANDA.)

René Lemarchand, *Burundi: Ethnic Conflict and Genocide* (Washington, D.C., and New York, 1995). Jean-Pierre Chrétien, *Le Défi de l'ethnisme: Rwanda et Burundi, 1990–1996* (Paris, 1997).

MUSIFIKY MWANASALI

BUSH, George Herbert Walker. Forty-first president of the *United States, George Herbert Walker Bush was born on 12 June 1924 into a prosperous and politically active family. (His father, a partner in a Wall Street investment firm, served as a U.S. senator from Connecticut from 1952 until 1963.) Upon graduation from Phillips Academy, Andover, Bush entered the U.S. Navy, where he won the Distinguished Flying Cross and three air medals during World War II. At the end of the war, Bush attended Yale University, graduating Phi Beta Kappa in 1948.

In 1963, having made his own fortune in the Texas oil in-dustry, Bush entered Texas politics by winning election as a moderate candidate running against a conservative faction for the Republican Party chair of Harris County, Texas. In 1966, he was elected to represent the Seventh District of Houston, Texas, in the U.S. Congress. In Congress, Bush was a moderate Republican, supporting such measures as a 1968 national open housing bill despite the strong opposition of his constituents.

Bush made unsuccessful bids for a U.S. Senate seat in Texas in 1964 and in 1970. In 1971, President Richard *Nixon appointed Bush the U.S. ambassador to the UN. In 1974 he was appointed chief of the U.S. Liaison Office in China. Upon returning to the United States, Bush became chair of the Republican National Committee, a position which he held at the peak of the Watergate crisis. With the unpleasant task of presiding over Nixon's resignation behind him, Bush was asked by President Gerald Ford to assume the director's post at the *Central Intelligence Agency in 1976.

In 1980, with James Baker as his manager, Bush campaigned against Ronald *Reagan for the Republican presidential nomination. Bush positioned himself as the moderate challenger to Reagan but withdrew from the race late in the primaries after Reagan appeared to have the nomination locked up. Bush accepted Reagan's invitation to become the vice-presidential running mate on the 1980 ticket. As vice president, Bush chaired several task forces, including those on *drugs and *terrorism, traveled to seventy-four nations as the representative of the United States, and was designated by the president to chair the crisis management team in the White House.

After defeating Senator Robert Dole of Kansas in early contests for the Republican presidential nomination in 1988, Bush began to put some distance between himself and the Reagan administration with regard to his policy views on the environment, civil rights, and ethics in government. Bush, however, reiterated the Reagan philosophy of maintaining a strong national defense and pledged "no new taxes" during the 1988 election campaign on his way to defeating Democratic nominee Michael Dukakis in forty of fifty states.

Bush's early reputation as a moderate, pragmatic politician resurfaced in 1990 when he broke his tax pledge and supported non-income tax increases in order to curb the growing deficit. Bush's sponsorship of a comprehensive clean air program enacted by Congress also served to indicate a different policy perspective from that of his predecessor.

On the whole, however, foreign affairs dominated Bush's policy interests during the first two years of his presidency. He met with Soviet leader Mikhail *Gorbachev three times to discuss a wide array of issues including potential agreements on the reduction of strategic and chemical weapons and the issuance of a joint communiqué condemning Iraq for the invasion of neighboring Kuwait on 2 August 1990.

The joint communiqué on Iraq reinforced earlier U.S.-Soviet cooperation in forging a UN Security Council resolution authorizing the use of military force by U.S.-led coalition powers if economic sanctions and diplomacy failed to bring about a withdrawal of Iraqi forces from Kuwait by 15 January 1991. President Bush ordered a U.S.-led attack on military targets in Iraq and Kuwait when the government of Saddam Hussein showed no intention of abiding by the UN decree, and on 17 January a forty-three-day war erupted.

The war with Iraq marked the second occasion in which the Bush administration had resorted to the use of military force after diplomacy had failed to bring about its desired resolution to an international problem. On 20 December 1989, Bush ordered 10,000 American troops into Panama to restore order after General Manuel Noriega annulled the May 1989 elections, which had been won by U.S.-backed opposition candidate Guillermo Endara.

Bush's leadership was characterized by most observers as collegial, broadly consultative, and flexible. Friendship and loyalty were hallmarks of Bush's personal style and were central to his conduct of *foreign policy, upon which his success as president will likely be judged to a considerable degree.

Two of Bush's sons, George W. and Jeb, have followed their father into politics. Jeb was elected governor of Florida and George W. was elected governor of Texas and was nominated as the Republican presidential candidate in 2000.

(See also GULF WAR; PRESIDENCY, U.S.; TAXES AND TAXATION.)

Fitzhugh Green, *George Bush: An Intimate Portrait* (New York, 1989).

PHILLIP G. HENDERSON

C

CABINET GOVERNMENT. In its origins, cabinet government is an English concept, denoting government by a small collective decision-making body, answerable for its actions to—and, often, formally removable from office by—the legislature. The term "cabinet" derives from English practice in the seventeenth century, when the king found his principal body of advisers, the privy council, to be too large to assist effectively in the governing of the country and turned instead to a small group of council members. This group became known by different names, including the cabinet council, and in the following century the king's principal body of ministers became recognized as "the cabinet."

The nineteenth century witnessed the emergence of a mass franchise and the recognition of the need for the cabinet to maintain the support of the elected chamber. The century saw the confirmation of the concept of collective responsibility as a convention of the constitution, ministers remaining legally answerable to the monarch but politically answerable to Parliament. The convention entailed 1) that decisions must be collectively arrived at, with ministers then accepting decisions once made (or else resigning their seals of office) and 2) that the government must resign or request a dissolution of Parliament if defeated on a vote of confidence in the House of Commons. The body for collective decision-making was the cabinet, though all ministers (those outside as well as within the cabinet) were—and remain—bound by the convention of collective responsibility.

The functions of the British cabinet in the twentieth century were delineated by the Machinery of Government Committee in 1918 as: 1) the final determination of the policy to be submitted to Parliament; 2) the supreme control of the national executive in accordance with the policy prescribed by Parliament; and 3) the continuous coordination and delimitation of the activities of the several departments of state. Although the growth of political parties largely ensured parliamentary approval for measures presented by cabinet, the nexus between cabinet and the legislature is central to the concept of cabinet government. A political system may have a cabinet, but there is no cabinet government if the cabinet itself is not the decision-making body and is not collectively answerable to the legislature for its measures and conduct of government.

The concept of cabinet government was imparted to other countries that fell under the British flag and was adopted by various European states. Two types of cabinet government can be identified. The *Westminster model*, common to countries in the *Commonwealth, emulates the British system, with an emphasis on collective decision-making, limiting the independence of the individual minister. The *continental model*, prevalent in countries with multiparty systems and cabinets composed of members drawn from partners to a coalition, places less emphasis on the centrality of collective decision-making and gives greater scope for independent action by individual ministers. *France has a hybrid system in which executive power is shared by an elected president and a cabinet drawn from a separately elected national assembly. Hybrid systems have, in many cases, become a feature of the new democracies of central and eastern Europe.

The two models of cabinet government are distinguishable from presidential models, in which there is a cabinet but no collective responsibility to the legislature. Presidential systems are to be found especially in the Americas and in some of the new democracies of eastern Europe. Here, cabinets are appointed by the president, who has an electoral constituency distinct from that of the legislature, and the composition of the cabinet is not determined by the outcome of legislative elections. Though members of the cabinet may be confirmed by the legislature, they are essentially the creatures of the president. In the United States, Congress exercises power over the structure and funding of executive departments but its links are with individual departments and department heads. The cabinet is not collectively responsible to Congress. Instead, the body serves as an advisory body to the president and the president remains free to make as much or as little use of it as he pleases. The president is vested with the "executive power" which, in a system of cabinet government, is exercised collectively by the cabinet.

(See also BRITAIN.)

John P. Mackintosh, *The British Cabinet,* 3d ed. (London, 1977). M. S. Shugart and J. M. Carey, *Presidents and Assemblies: Constitutional Design and Electoral Dynamics* (Cambridge, U.K., 1992).

PHILIP NORTON

CABRAL, Amílcar. The preeminent theorist and guerrilla fighter in the period of the *decolonization of Africa, Amílcar Cabral was born on 12 September 1924 at Bafata in *Guinea-Bissau. Brought up in the period of the Second World War, he saw firsthand the impact of colonialism, especially at the hands of the poorest country in Europe. Amílcar Cabral went to Portugal to be educated in 1944 and later graduated as an agricultural engineer. In 1952 he returned to Guinea-Bissau to work as a colonial agronomy engineer. Having been trained at the agronomy center in *Portugal, Cabral was instructed to plan and execute the agricultural census of Guinea-Bissau in 1953. This study gave Cabral insight into the conditions of the majority of the population in Guinea-Bissau. This provided the raw material which was to be the basis of the theoretical contributions of Cabral on the social structure of

Guinea-Bissau. This study also gave him the opportunity to travel throughout the rural areas and gave him historical, racial, and cultural data on the ethnic makeup of Guinea-Bissau.

A job transfer to *Angola in 1955 brought him into direct contact with those elements in that society who were in the embryonic stages of forming the Movimento Popular de Libertação de Angola (MPLA). It was this sojourn in Angola along with his experience in Guinea-Bissau and *São Tomé which made Cabral a pivotal person in drawing up a plan for a coordinated struggle against Portuguese colonialism in Angola, Guinea-Bissau, *Mozambique, and São Tomé.

Cabral was one of the founding members of the Partido Áfricano da Indêpendencia da Guiné-Bissau e Cabo Verde (PAIGC). As the secretary-general of the organization, he molded a small guerrilla army into a fighting force that tied down the Portuguese army in Guinea-Bissau.

As a theoretician, diplomat, writer, and spokesperson for the forces of liberation, Amílcar Cabral distinguished himself inside and outside Africa. At the Tri-Continental Conference in Havana in 1966 Cabral delivered a major statement on the peculiarities of the historical process in Africa and made a unique contribution to the understanding of historical materialism in Africa. Cabral's position as a theorist of the African condition was reinforced by his analysis of the role of cultural resistance in the struggle for African liberation. His affirmation of African culture's important place in the universal culture of humanity was based in a conception of liberation not only for political sovereignty but also as true cultural liberation. In this context, he affirmed that national liberation was an act of culture.

Amílcar Cabral was assassinated in Conakry, *Guinea, on the night of 20 January 1973. Prior to his assassination, he had proclaimed that Guinea-Bissau would declare its independence from Portugal in that year. It was the protracted struggles of the Africans in Guinea-Bissau, Angola, and Mozambique which precipitated the coup in Portugal in April 1974. This change sped the process of decolonization in Africa in a very fundamental way. Cabral's writings and speeches have provided the basis for a new direction in the study of Africa.

(See also CAPE VERDE; GUERRILLA WARFARE; NATIONAL LIBERATION MOVEMENTS.)

Amílcar Cabral, *Unity and Struggle: Speeches and Writings* (New York, 1979).

HORACE CAMPBELL

CAMBODIA is a Southeast Asian constitutional monarchy (68,000 square miles in area, population c. 11 million) bordered by Thailand, Vietnam, Laos, and the Gulf of Thailand.

Between the ninth and fifteenth centuries A.D. a powerful kingdom in northwestern Cambodia, known today as Angkor (from the Sanskrit word for "city"), dominated much of Southeast Asia. An image of its famous temple, Angkor Wat, has appeared on five successive Cambodian flags since 1954.

Angkorean kings were in theory absolute but in practice constrained by the demands of relatives and subordinates and by pressures from outside powers. Later Cambodian rulers shared these absolutist notions, and in most cases operated under similar constraints.

After Angkor's decline in the 1400s, Cambodia became sub-

ordinate to the Thai kingdom of Ayudhya. In the seventeenth century, Vietnamese migration weakened Cambodian authority in the Mekong Delta, and for several hundred years Cambodia was hemmed in by its ambitious neighbors. In the 1830s and 1840s, racked by invasions, the kingdom almost disappeared. When French officials offered the Cambodian monarch protection in 1863, he readily accepted. France probably saved Cambodia from being absorbed by Thailand and Vietnam.

In the colonial era, which lasted ninety years, Cambodia suffered from benign neglect, although its population quadrupled, a basic infrastructure was installed, and the kingdom became an exporter of rubber and rice. A single high school catered to the elite. French scholars restored the temples at Angkor, and deciphered over a thousand Angkorean inscriptions. They bequeathed to Cambodians a glorious history which had been largely forgotten.

Cambodia was a component of French Indo-China, but in contrast to *Vietnam, anti-French feelings and nationalist fervor were slow to develop.

During World War II, French administrators allowed the Japanese to station troops in Indo-China, and retained administrative control. In 1945, the Japanese imprisoned all French civil servants and asked Cambodia's young king, Norodom Sihanouk, to declare the kingdom's independence. When the French returned in force they allowed Cambodia to form political parties and write a constitution. Cambodia was a backwater in the First Indo-China War (1946–1954). In 1952 King Sihanouk launched a personal Crusade for Independence, which embarrassed the French into granting Cambodia its freedom, ahead of Vietnam, in 1953. Two years later, Sihanouk abdicated and founded a political movement, which swept a national parliamentary election.

For the next fifteen years, Norodom Sihanouk tried to run Cambodia single-handedly. He was popular among the predominantly Buddhist population, tolerant of corrupt subordinates, and brutal with the fragmented opposition. In 1960, a clandestine Communist Party was formed, spearheaded by several Cambodians who had studied in France, including a schoolteacher named Saloth Sar, alias *Pol Pot. The party was small and ineffective. It received guidance from Vietnam.

As the second Indo-China War (1955–1975) intensified, the economy faltered, and Sihanouk's popularity declined. His policy of anti-American neutralism, which aimed to keep Cambodia out of the war, led him to permit the Vietnamese Communists to station troops on Cambodian soil. Local Communists, labeled the Khmer Rouge, gradually grew stronger.

In 1970, Sihanouk was overthrown in a bloodless coup while traveling abroad. An inept, pro-American government took his place, and waged war against the far more powerful Vietnamese Communists, who inflicted a series of defeats on them and also helped to train and equip the Khmer Rouge army.

In 1975 Khmer Rouge forces were victorious. Under Pol Pot, the Communist Party, calling itself "the organization," brutally restructured Cambodian society, following radical Maoist models. Money, private property, schools, and religion were banned; cities were emptied; everyone became an agricultural worker. Thousands of adherents of the former regime were killed, and later, tens of thousands of alleged "traitors" were also put to death. Over a million others, or one in seven

Cambodians, died of overwork and malnutrition. Because nearly all the victims were ethnic Cambodians, the process has been called "auto-genocide."

For over two years, the Communist Party remained concealed, emerging only at Chinese insistence in 1977. Khmer Rouge ideology stressed independence, especially from Vietnam. Vietnam, for its part, treated Cambodia as its subordinate. By the end of 1977, the two countries were at war. Vietnamese forces invaded Cambodia in late 1978, and occupied it as a satellite for ten years.

The Cambodian government installed by Vietnam struggled to revive normality, but over half a million Cambodians fled the country, the new regime retained a Marxist-Leninist focus, and Khmer Rouge forces, supported by Thailand and China, harassed the regime from their bases on the Thai border. The Khmer Rouge were recognized as Cambodia's legitimate government by the UN. By punishing Vietnam for invading Cambodia, larger powers cut Cambodia off from international assistance in the wake of the damage inflicted by the Khmer Rouge.

During the 1980s, Cambodia's foreign minister Hun Sen (b. 1952), a former Khmer Rouge military commander, became prime minister and displayed formidable political skills, while eschewing the fervent nationalism of the Khmer Rouge. When Vietnam withdrew its forces in 1989, the (ex-Communist) Cambodian People's Party (CPP) dominated Cambodian political life and Hun Sen consolidated his position.

An international peace conference in 1991 placed Cambodia under UN protection and removed foreign patronage from its warring factions. Under a UN protectorate in 1992–1993, a new constitution restored Sihanouk to the throne. A UN-brokered national election led to a fragile coalition between the royalist party that won the election and the incumbent CPP, which controlled the army and the police. The coalition came apart in 1997, when Hun Sen staged a coup against his partners. The coup shocked many foreign donors, and delayed Cambodia's entry into the *Association of Southeast Asia Nations (ASEAN).

Internationally monitored elections in 1998 resulted in another royalist-CCP coalition, with Hun Sen continuing as the country's strong man. No plausible successors and few checks and balances were in sight, aside from foreign aid donors, eager to obtain results from their infusions of assistance.

The Khmer Rouge, meanwhile, deprived of foreign patronage, had withered on the vine. For the first time since the 1960s, Cambodia was at peace. Hun Sen took personal credit for the achievement. His power base lay in the CPP, among entrepreneurs, and in the kingdom's 100,000-man army, which had no enemies to fight.

In 1999 Cambodia was admitted to ASEAN and faced the challenges of globalization. Its economy was weak; there were few exploitable raw materials, aside from timber, which had been heavily logged in the 1980s and 1990s, with severe ecological effects. Industrialization was in its infancy. Cambodia's work force was untrained, its birth rate high, and its education system understaffed and poorly funded. Some short-term foreign investments, particularly in tourism, showed promise, and local *human rights organizations displayed great courage in monitoring abuses throughout the country. Among those in power, there has never been much respect for the rule of law or human rights, and a culture of impunity encouraged the often rapacious conduct of the army and the police. Per capita incomes were among the lowest in Asia. Health care was rudimentary, and HIV/AIDS had reached epidemic proportions. Prospects for the early twenty-first century are bleak, as far as people's welfare and political freedoms are concerned, because most politicians concentrate on amassing personal wealth and because the concepts of loyal opposition, accountability, and civil society still find so little resonance among those in power.

(See also BUDDHISM; DECOLONIZATION.)

David Chandler, *The Tragedy of Cambodia History: Politics, War and Revolution Since 1945* (New Haven, Conn., 1991). Ian Mabbett and David Chandler, *The Khmers* (Oxford, U.K., 1995). Elizabeth Becker, *When the War Was Over: Cambodia and the Khmer Rouge Revolution*, 2d ed. (New York, 1998). David Chandler, *A History of Cambodia*, 3d ed. (Boulder, Colo., 2000).

DAVID CHANDLER

CAMEROON, on the Atlantic coast between Nigeria and the equator, suffered German colonial rule (1884–1916) and mandate/trust status under the British (in the west) and the French (in the east). The larger part became independent on 1 January 1960 and a portion of the British territory joined on 1 October 1960 to form the Federal Republic of Cameroon (after 1972 the United Republic of Cameroon and after 1984 the Republic of Cameroon).

The first president, Ahmadou Ahidjo (1924–1989), under French influence, accepted a constitution similar to that of de Gaulle's France. He quickly modified it, creating an authoritarian, centralized regime with the secret police as the ultimate arbiter of conflict. Paul Biya replaced Ahidjo in a constitutional transfer of power in 1982.

The 1996 constitution limits the president to two seven-year terms in office and there is a bicameral legislature. The president retains substantial powers and Biya, as president and head of the dominant party, the Cameroon People's Democratic Movement (CPDM), has vast powers of appointment and dismissal. He is a superpatron with government resources to maintain a clientele linking leaders from ethnic, regional, and other groups. However, Biya is less adept at manipulating this clientele than was Ahidjo; in recent years he has relied heavily on his ethnic group, the Beti, for support. The judiciary, the legislature, and the CPDM remain subservient. The military (which saved Biya in a violent coup attempt on 6 April 1982) and to a lesser extent the bureaucracy have been able to exert pressure on the president, but in recent years the domestic democracy movement and external actors pressuring for democratic and economic liberalization have become influential.

The most obvious source of cleavage is the more than 200 ethnic groups, but the more powerful division results from the dual colonial inheritance: between Anglophones, about twenty percent of the population, and Francophones, eighty percent. This split has been manipulated by Ahidjo and Biya to prevent the emergence of the potentially more dangerous north-south conflict, a mixture of religious (*Islam in the north, Christianity in the south), cultural (pastoral versus agricultural), and historical divisions. The Anglophone-Francophone issue allows a skillful politician room to maneuver. Ahidjo played this well, but Biya has lost the support of the Muslim northerners, although gaining strength in the substantial Christian community there, and in the 1990s an alliance across the language divide was forming in the south. This seems now to have weakened.

Class conflict is successfully smothered by other cleavages, although a substantial gap in income and lifestyle exists between the majority and a small elite. This gap, intensified by economic troubles in the late 1980s and 1990s, has found little political meaning.

The world *democracy movement has influenced Cameroon; courageous leaders and large numbers of citizens have faced the power of the regime to push for democracy. The oldest opposition movement, the Union des Populations du Cameroun (UPC), founded in the 1950s as a nationalist independence party, fought a violent civil war against French and Ahidjoist forces in the late 1950s and 1960s. Recently, the UPC returned from exile to participate in the electoral process, but it has lost its revolutionary fervor. In the 1990s the Social Democratic Front (SDF), led by John Fru Ndi, is the more nationalistic and grassroots party. Ndi was one of several persons who demanded the right to form political parties in 1990. At first, his support was among Anglophones. SDF rallies brought violent government repression and Ndi's popularity spread even into the southern French-speaking areas, especially among the Bamileke ethnic group. In 1991 parties were legalized, and many appeared. In the north the Union Nationale pour la Démocratie et la Progrès (UNDP), led by Bello Bouba Maigari, garnered most of the Ahidjo followers, while the SDF gained strength in the south. Strikes in 1992 in most southern cities, the *Ville Morte* or Ghost City campaign, brought significant economic pressure on Biya in an effort to win a new constitution. Biya stalled, played divide and rule, and gave little positive response to the massive demonstrations. Rigged parliamentary and presidential elections saw the CPDM and Biya remain in power. By the end of the decade, these tactics succeeded in wearing down the opposition. A new constitution did come into force in 1996, but it was imposed by Biya; it did not arise from a national conference of the representatives of the people. The democracy movement had restricted the powers of authoritarian rule, but such rule was still in effect.

Ahidjo and Biya followed similar foreign policies. At independence the French suppressed the UPC, the real nationalist party, and gave power to their protégé, Ahidjo, a conservative northerner. Several secret treaties gave France great influence over Cameroon policies. *Foreign policy has had a pro-West, pro-French, pro-capitalist orientation. The latter aspect has been accentuated in recent years under pressure from the *International Monetary Fund, France, and the United States. Privatization, free trade, and open access to foreign investors have been instituted. Trade and investment have become more diversified, although France remains the major economic and political relationship.

The major regional foreign policy issue is the relationship with the giant to the west, *Nigeria, seen by Cameroon as a threatening imperial power. Trade issues, smuggling, and the treatment of foreign nationals have been important, but the major issue has been the demarcation of the border, especially near the coast where significant petroleum reserves are located. Low intensity fighting has broken out on several occasions. Major attention is paid to regional affairs in the

Union Douanière et Economique de l'Afrique Centrale. Of the members, Cameroon has the most to gain from an enlarged market and as the hub of transportation and investment.

*Development policy is based on less central planning and more room for free enterprise than in the past. Agricultural expansion has shown some success and the country remains food self-sufficient. Some food is exported to neighboring countries. However, import-substitution and large-scale industrial development have not succeeded. The country suffered economic decline in the 1980s and 1990s and what was once considered an economic success story in Africa has become one of the more troubled of economies. Declines in prices for its petroleum, coffee, cocoa, and other exports (upon which the economy is dependent), rapidly declining petroleum reserves, corruption and politically based policy decisions, and a rapidly increasing debt situation are at the base of the problem. This decline in prosperity has had serious domestic political ramifications.

(See also FRANCOPHONE AFRICA.)

Mark W. DeLancey, *Cameroon: Dependence and Independence*. Profiles/ Nations of Contemporary Africa Series (Boulder, Colo., 1989). Joseph Takougang and Milton H. Krieger, *African State and Society in the 1990s: Cameroon's Political Crossroads* (Boulder, Colo., 1998).

MARK W. DeLANCEY

CANADA. Its immense landmass makes Canada the second-largest country in the world, but its population of 26 million as of 1990 leaves it only sparsely populated. Moreover, 90 percent of that population lives in a narrow 200-mile (320-kilometer) band along the border with the United States, with 62 percent concentrated in the two central provinces of Ontario and *Quebec. Such proximity to its southern neighbor and close cultural ties have made the Canada-U.S. relationship one of the most important factors in post-1945 economics and politics. Of equal importance, however, are the legacies of its colonial ties to France and Britain.

Much of the area that now is Canada was first explored and settled by the French in the sixteenth century. France controlled most of that territory until 1759 when British forces attacked Quebec City. Although the elite and colonial administrators returned to France after the conquest, the ordinary population of farmers and traders remained in place. Canada's first steps toward nationhood in the nineteenth century followed more than 100 years of political conflict between French and English colonists.

Canada's existence as an independent nation-state began with the British North America (BNA) Act, passed by the Parliament of the United Kingdom in 1867. That act set out the terms of unification of four British colonies in North America—Nova Scotia, New Brunswick, Lower Canada (Quebec), and Upper Canada (Ontario). Subsequent acts expanded the national territory by incorporating western lands belonging to the Hudson's Bay Company (much of Saskatchewan and Alberta), the Red River Colony (Manitoba), and the colony of British Columbia on the Pacific coast. A federal system of government with nine provinces was in place by 1905. The tenth province, Newfoundland and Labrador, joined the confederation in 1949.

Political institutions were modeled on those of the United Kingdom, albeit within a federal system of central and provincial governments. The central government (termed the federal government in Canadian political discourse) and all provinces have popularly elected assemblies whose business is organized by a system of competitive parties. The Parliament of Canada consists of the House of Commons and an appointed upper chamber, the Senate. The executive, comprising the prime minister and cabinet, is responsible to the House in accordance with the procedures of a responsible party system. The Senate was designed to provide provincial representation at the federal level. Its seats are apportioned unequally among the provinces, and it is appointed by the governor-general, on the recommendation of the prime minister. This procedure, as well as the unequal distribution of seats, has been a matter of great controversy for several decades. The head of state remains the British monarch, represented in Canada by a governor-general and ten lieutenant-governors.

Full independence from the British Parliament was achieved slowly and in recent years only with a great deal of domestic controversy. Created as a dominion in 1867, autonomy in international affairs came with Canada's participation in World War I and its separate signature of the Treaty of Versailles. The Statute of Westminster of 1931 confirmed this independence. The fundamental constitutional document—the BNA Act—set out, *inter alia,* the division of powers between the federal government and the provinces. The final court of appeal for disputes over this division of powers remained the Judicial Committee of the Privy Council of the British Parliament until 1949. That body quite systematically favored the powers of the provinces over those of the central government. Since 1949 the Canadian Supreme Court has been the final court of appeal. The final act severing the vestiges of colonial ties came only in 1982, with the patriation of the constitution. The British Parliament, at the request of Canadian government, passed the Constitution Act, which established new constitutional arrangements, including a Charter of Rights and Freedoms and a procedure for amending Canadian constitutional documents domestically.

Dispute over constitutional arrangements has been deeply divisive since the 1960s, and the 1982 arrangements did not settle the matter. Indeed they exacerbated the issue, because the new arrangements were put into place over the objections of the province of Quebec. Quebec did not accept the constitutional compromise worked out in the negotiations leading to the Constitution Act, but the prime minister and nine provincial premiers made the request to the British Parliament nonetheless.

Two fundamental social cleavages of Canadian society are language and culture. These issues have had profound effects on political conflict and the evolution of the federal institutions. The place in the Canadian community of the one-third of the citizens whose language is French has dominated political debate since the nineteenth century. At the heart of the dispute are differing visions or models of Canadian society. For many Francophones the model is that of two founding peoples—French and English—whose status is one of equality. Moreover, they consider the province of Quebec to be their homeland where they have constituted a distinct society and whose protection depends upon a powerful provincial government. Beginning in the 1960s a Québécois nationalist movement pressed for the recognition of this vision of society. An important test of the model occurred in a 1980 referendum organized by the nationalist government of the province of Quebec on the issue of changing Quebec's status within Canada to one of sovereignty-association. This referendum was defeated, but in subsequent years popular support within the province for such a change grew.

An alternative model of society, actively promoted from the late 1960s under the leadership of Prime Minister Pierre *Trudeau (1968–1979; 1980–1982), describes Canada as a bilingual and bicultural society, organized as ten equal provinces. Language rights are to be protected by the constitution and through the political process. By implication, the federal government has responsibility for guaranteeing that all Canadians, whether Francophone or Anglophone, may live and receive services anywhere in the country.

A third and competing alternative emerged out of the politics of the 1960s, in part as a result of the high rates of postwar immigration from Europe and the Third World and official encouragement to ethnic groups to retain their cultural distinctiveness. In this view Canada is a multicultural society in which no group merits being singled out for distinction. Canada is one of the three main immigrant-receiving countries of the world and has a continually high ratio of immigrants to population (16 percent in 1981). A new immigration policy instituted in the 1970s dropped a long-standing concern with whether newcomers could be "assimilated" to Canadian society and instituted an official policy of nondiscrimination, favoring entrepreneurs and family members, and recognizing the special needs of refugees. Sources of immigration have changed as a result. In the 1980s, the proportion of Europeans dropped below 30 percent, with more than two-fifths of immigrants coming from Asia and another fifth from the Americas, including the Caribbean. These patterns have strengthened the multicultural policy thrust and have led to new demands for state responses to discrimination and disadvantages suffered by "visible minorities."

The first two models of society had clear implications for constitutional politics and the relations between the central government and the provinces. Quebec, after 1960, demanded greater control over spending and policy-making in jurisdictions shared with the federal government. The response of the federal government was a compromise, which throughout the 1970s and 1980s gave greater powers to all provinces. In particular, the central government weakened its control over the major levers of social and economic policy, devolving them to the provinces or to intergovernmental institutions.

Conflict between the models came to a head in the constitutional negotiations of 1981. The federal government's document constitutionally entrenched the Trudeauian model by establishing language rights of French and English throughout the country and by establishing for the first time a Charter of Rights in fundamental law. There was no recognition of a distinct status for Quebec.

Premier René Lévesque of Quebec refused to approve the document and after 1982 that province rejected Canada's constitutional arrangements. New negotiations completed in 1987 produced a constitutional amendment—the Meech Lake Accord—which would have set out a definition of Quebec as a "distinct society" in the preamble to the 1982 document. Two provincial legislatures refused to ratify this accord, however, by the 1990 deadline, because of opposition to the notion of special status for Quebec. The leaders of all parties in the province of Quebec then began to prepare the way for a unilateral restructuring of the constitutional arrangements, in the direction of greater autonomy.

The longstanding ethnic and linguistic divisions within Canadian society have provided a constant source of political division. The other constant pole, also derivative of a powerful external force, is the relationship with the United States. With World War II and postwar reconstruction, the Canadian economy moved increasingly into the orbit of the U.S. economy. The development strategy of the federal government, supported by both the Liberals and Progressive Conservatives—the two major political parties—was moderately Keynesian in fiscal policy, modestly committed to social spending, and centered around the encouragement of both primary and secondary production via investment by foreign as well as Canadian firms. The economy grew, albeit unevenly, in the first postwar decades. One central aspect of the unevenness reflected profound regional differences in the distribution of resources and population. The province of Ontario was the only one that consistently benefited from the modern economy, while all others suffered from the lack of modern manufacturing or natural resources or both. Programs for regional development and redistribution of income from the richer provinces to the poorer began in the late 1950s. In the 1960s, in addition, new social programs (universal health care, state-funded old-age pensions, workforce training programs, etc.) were instituted jointly by the federal and provincial governments. Nevertheless, state spending for social programs still ranks behind levels observed in many European countries with a comparable political history.

Throughout the postwar decades the Canadian and U.S. economies became increasingly integrated. By 1987, 75 percent of Canadian exports went to the United States. Only 44 percent of Canadian exports were fully manufactured goods (the bulk of these were products fell under an agreement made in the 1960s for free trade in automobiles and parts); the rest were unprocessed or semiprocessed primary goods. Fully two-thirds of imports were manufactured goods, 68 percent of which came from the United States.

North American economic integration provoked opposition because of its perceived threat to Canadian political, economic and cultural sovereignty. Fears of job loss, weakening of research and development, and *deindustrialization provided a major focus for political conflict from the late 1960s. A nationalist movement in English Canada played a role in organizing such politics as well as helping to foster the institutional supports in communication and other arenas to sustain a distinct Canadian identity. Social democrats from the New Democratic Party consistently opposed the state's development strategy, as did a wing of the Liberal Party. Opposition also grew among intellectuals and trade unionists.

Nevertheless, despite widespread opposition in Anglophone Canada, in 1987–1988 the Canadian government, led by the Progressive Conservatives, negotiated the U.S.-Canada Free Trade Agreement, a precursor to *NAFTA. All tariffs fell and there was a substantial weakening of nontariff barriers. The establishment of free trade in the service sector was of particular importance both for economic restructuring in North America and as a model for international economic negotiations.

With this important step toward the constitution of a regional bloc, Canada clearly dedicated its economic future to North America. It remains, however, involved in the international economic and political community through its membership in North Atlantic Treaty Organization (NATO), the Commonwealth, *la Francophonie*, the UN, and the Group of 7. The country came out of World War II with a clear and active commitment to multilateral economic and political institutions. It played an important role in the founding of the UN and the General Agreement on Tariffs and Trade (GATT) and in the institutionalization of the Commonwealth and *la Francophonie* for a postcolonial world. Being a rich middle power with longstanding ties to the United States, two different European nations, and the Third World, Canada has preferred multilateral negotiations and peacekeeping activities. Recent political changes have brought a substantial reduction in Canada's role in providing development aid to the Third World. Military expenditures in recent decades have been restrained, concentrating on forces for peacekeeping and for defense of the sovereignty of the Canadian Arctic, including against incursions by the United States.

(See also FEDERALISM; INTERNATIONAL MIGRATION; NATIONALISM.)

Michael S. Cross and Gregory S. Kealey, eds., *Modern Canada: 1930–1980's*, Readings in Canadian Social History, vol. 5 (Toronto, 1984). Robert Bothwell, Ian Drummond, and John English, *Canada: 1900–1945* (Toronto, 1987). Janine Brodie and Jane Jenson, *Crisis, Challenge and Change: Party and Class in Canada Revisited* (Ottawa, 1988). Wallace Clement and Glen Williams, eds., *The New Canadian Political Economy* (Montreal, 1989). Michael Whittington and Glen Williams, eds., *Canadian Politics in the 1990s* (Toronto, 1990).

JANE JENSON

CAPITAL PUNISHMENT. The modern movement to abolish the death penalty has its roots in the liberal utilitarian and humanistic ideas spawned by the Enlightenment in Europe at the end of the eighteenth century. Cesare Beccaria's famous treatise *On Crimes and Punishments*, published in 1764, advocated the replacement of the old regime of maximum terror, randomly inflicted, by a graded system of penalties proportionate to the crime committed. Capital punishment was viewed as both inhumane and ineffective. In the 1780s the enlightened rulers of Tuscany and Austria abolished executions for a time and Imperial Russia came close to doing so. Pressure to restrict the death penalty to only the gravest crimes began to mount in Britain, the United States, and several European states.

Pennsylvania (in 1786) was the first U.S. state to abolish capital punishment for all crimes except first-degree murder. But another sixty years passed before any state abolished capital punishment for all murders—Michigan in 1846, followed by Rhode Island in 1852 (except for murder of a guard by a life-sentenced prisoner), and Wisconsin a year later. By the early years of the twentieth century eleven European countries—Portugal (the first in 1864), Italy, Holland, Romania, Sweden, Finland, Norway, Denmark, Austria, Prussia, and Switzerland—had all got rid of it, except in time of war, as had several South American states after gaining independence.

However, capital punishment was reinstated and expanded by various authoritarian regimes during the twentieth century. The demise of these regimes was often followed by an immediate abolition of the death penalty. Germany and Italy did so after the Second World War, and Romania after the fall of Ceaucescu in 1989. Especially notable was the declaration after the end of apartheid that the death penalty was unconstitutional in South Africa.

The last twenty-five years of the twentieth century saw a remarkable increase in the pace of abolition. By 1965, twenty-three countries had abandoned capital punishment for ordinary crimes (twelve of them having abolished it totally for all offenses in peacetime or war). By the beginning of the twenty-first century the number of abolitionist states had increased to eighty-five, the vast majority being totally abolitionist. A further thirty-eight have not executed anybody for at least ten years and therefore can be regarded as abolitionist de facto. No Western European country now has the death penalty. Most countries of Eastern Europe have abolished capital punishment. Albania and Armenia are committed to abolition and Turkey and Yugoslavia are abolitionist de facto. Belarus was the only country in the region to execute offenders as of 2000.

Nevertheless, at the end of 1999, seventy-one countries still retained it, thirty-four of them for trading in illegal drugs, compared with a total of twenty-two such countries identified in a UN survey in 1985. Another twenty-five states, at the minimum, maintain the death penalty for sexual crimes such as adultery, rape, aggravated rape, and sodomy. At least seventeen countries maintain it for property-related offenses such as robbery, aggravated theft, smuggling, speculation, and fraud. Capital punishment is embedded in the religion-based legal culture of the Islamic states of the Middle East, North Africa, and Asia; it is widely supported on the grounds of its supposed deterrent effects throughout Southeast Asia and the Caribbean. It is imposed, in some years very extensively, in campaigns to "crack down" on a wide range of crimes in China. Thirty-eight states of the United States cling tenaciously to capital punishment, although ten of them have yet to execute any person since the constitutionality of the death penalty was affirmed in 1976. Nearly two-thirds of executions have taken place in five states: Texas, Virginia, Florida, Missouri, and Louisiana. Some 3,600 inmates were housed on "death row" on 1 January 2000.

In 1999, thirty-one countries were known to have carried out judicial executions, but only four of them executed over a hundred people, while ninety-eight were executed in the United States. The total number judicially executed has fluctuated considerably year by year largely reflecting whether or not China pursued an anticrime campaign. Thus, during the "strike hard" crackdown of 1996 over 4,000 people were known to have been executed, accounting for over 80 percent of all global executions that year. The sharp fall in subsequent years reflected the implementation of China's Revised Criminal Law, which restricted somewhat the scope of capital crimes. But raw numbers can, of course, be misleading when countries vary so greatly in the size of their populations. Thus for the period 1994 to 1998 China, with a yearly average rate of 2.01, executed far fewer people per million population than did Singapore (13.73) and several other countries. The state of Virginia had the highest execution rate in the United States (1.09) in the years 1994 to 1998.

These figures for officially known executions fall short of the actual number judicially executed and of course do not include several thousand summary executions and "disappearances" throughout the world.

As more and more countries became abolitionist they acted to secure the adoption of international resolutions, agreements, and instruments to protect offenders in retentionist countries from excessive use of capital punishment. Thus, in 1977 the General Assembly of the United Nations called for "the progressive restriction of the number of offences for which the death penalty may be imposed with a view to the desirability of abolishing the punishment." In recognition that abolition itself was not always a feasible goal, the Economic and Social Council of the UN promulgated a list of Safeguards Guaranteeing the Protection of the Rights of Those Facing the Death Penalty in 1986, a list that was further extended in 1989.

Protocol Number 6 to the European Convention of Human Rights (ECHR), adopted in 1982, and the Second Optional Protocol to the International Covenant on Civil and Political Rights (ICCPR), adopted in 1989, have both provided opportunities for states to confirm abolition of the death penalty in peacetime. At the end of 1999, thirty-five countries were parties to Protocol Number 6 and seven others had signed but not yet ratified it. However, among the forty-four countries that had ratified or signed the Second Optional Protocol, only thirteen were from outside Europe or Australasia. Eight were South or Central American countries; three were from the African region—Djibouti, Mozambique, and Namibia—and two were from Asia and the Pacific region: Nepal and the Seychelles. Important as they are, these treaties have yet to gain the assent of Asian and Middle Eastern countries, some of which have stigmatized international pressure to abolish the death penalty as a form of cultural imperialism.

However, the United States has not seen ratification of the ICCPR as incompatible with its opposition to the Second Optional Protocol on the death penalty. The United States also entered reservations to the Convention both with respect to article 6(5), which prohibits the imposition of the death penalty on persons who committed the crime when under the age of eighteen, and to article 7, which proscribes cruel and unusual treatment or punishment. The United States declared that it would only be bound by the latter article to the extent that "cruel, inhuman or degrading treatment or punishment" means that as is defined by the Supreme Court's interpretation of the 5th, 8th, or 14th Amendments to the Constitution of the United States. Furthermore, Jamaica in 1997 followed by Trinidad and Tobago in 1998 withdrew from the Optional Protocol to the ICCPR. Trinidad and Tobago immediately reacceded but with a reservation that removed the right of prisoners under sentence of death in Trinidad and Tobago to file complaints to the UN Human Rights Committee, the body that monitors compliance with the provisions of the ICCPR.

Nevertheless, in 1997 the UN Commission on Human Rights was able to pass a resolution calling on all countries that retained capital punishment to consider suspending executions with a view to abolishing the death penalty completely. Resolutions to this effect were also successfully brought before the Commission in 1998, 1999, and 2000.

Abolition of the death penalty has now become a condition for membership of the Council of Europe and the European Union and both bodies promote abolition in nonmember states. When Russia and Ukraine failed to honor their agreement on becoming members of the Council of Europe to impose an immediate moratorium on executions, they were threatened with expulsion. Cessation of executions in both these countries in 1997 has signaled a remarkable change. Before its dissolution the Soviet Union had executed seven times as many offenders per capita than the United States.

International pressure against the death penalty triumphed when the maximum penalty that might be imposed by the International Criminal Court, established to try persons accused of genocide, other crimes against humanity, and war crimes, was fixed at life imprisonment. While this does not affect the legality of capital punishment in individual states, an international agreement that the death penalty is not appropriate even for the most heinous of crimes can be expected to have more than a symbolic political significance in the years ahead.

(See also HUMAN RIGHTS; SUPREME COURT OF THE UNITED STATES.)

Roger G. Hood, *The Death Penalty: A World-Wide Perspective* (Oxford, 1996). William Schabas, *The Abolition of the Death Penalty in International Law*, 2d ed. (Cambridge, U.K., 1997).

ROGER HOOD

CAPITALISM. Despite the suffix *-ism*, capitalism refers neither to an *ideology nor a movement. It refers, if anything, to a set of economic and legal institutions which together make the production of things for private profit the normal course of economic organization. In short, it is a mode of production, a way of organizing economic activity.

The word itself is of recent vintage, having been coined by William Makepeace Thackeray in the mid-nineteenth century. Capitalism may be said to have originated in Western Europe sometime in the 200 years or so following the Black Death of 1349. Like much else about the subject, this is a controversial assertion, for exactly what constitutes capitalism—certain features of which existed in earlier periods of history and on other continents—is open to debate. Capitalism as we now know it, however, arose in Western Europe between four and six centuries ago.

Capitalism is a system marked by 1) private property in the means of production, whether land, tools, machines, or ideas; 2) a legal framework entitling the owner of those means to the profits they generate subject only to nonarbitrary taxation; 3) a framework of contracts within which sales and purchases relevant to the production activity can be carried out, especially the right to hire and fire workers; and 4) the legal right of the owner to dispose of the profits as well as the property generating those profits in any way he or she chooses, subject to well-specified and justiciable limits.

The use of money and the existence of markets becomes ubiquitous as capitalism spreads, limited only by what individuals may hold property rights in. For its sustained growth capitalism requires investment on a continuing basis, either out of profits previously earned or from credit provided by financial intermediaries. But money, markets, and investment are necessary only inasmuch as they are instrumental to generating profits. The necessary conditions are profits in a system of private property with contractual rights.

Although money and markets have existed at least since

the early Phoenicians and sophisticated credit markets have existed in India and China for centuries, the identification of the rise of modern capitalism with Western Europe is beyond dispute. Why capitalism should have originated there rather than in the more prosperous and economically sophisticated (as of 1350) regions of Arabia or Asia, on the other hand, is a much-debated topic. The debate has been particularly strong among Marxists given that the transition from feudalism to capitalism forms a major part of *Marx's theory of history as well as a rehearsal for the presumed future transition from capitalism to *socialism.

The lines of debate are drawn according to whether forces internal to Western European societies or those external are said to form the crucial element. Thus advocates of the internal explanation stress the loosening of feudal bonds on serfs via the spread of monetization and the rise of absolutist monarchies dominating the feudal baronage, along with the development of urban settlements peopled by traders and artisans. The external explanation emphasizes the shock of the encounter with Islamic civilizations during the Crusades, the search for alternate trade routes in response to the capture of overland routes by the Arabs, and the innovation of the maneuverable cannon which fitted on to sailing ships and extended the capacity of European navies to sail farther away from their home base.

Each of these explanations is conditional upon the other, and a synthesis is needed. Any explanation must place Western Europe in a global context and must account for the force of ideas (especially religious) and technological innovations (especially in the military sphere). As yet, no theory has satisfactorily explained not only why the advent of capitalism was in Western Europe but also why other regions which may have stood a better chance in terms of prior conditions failed to develop anything similar. Explanations of the origins of capitalism have thus far taken its advent in Western Europe as a given rather than a contingent fact to be explained.

Until the eighteenth century capitalism existed side by side with feudal structures. Especially in the realm of the technology of production, changes, if any, had been gradual over the centuries, and in some areas even ancient Roman standards had not been reattained. Money, markets, contracts, and property rights were all more or less in place by the beginning of the eighteenth century, although much more development was yet to come here as well. It was the development of the steam engine during the eighteenth century that irreversibly set capitalism on its path of growth. Industrialism came to be synonymous with capitalism. The first Industrial Revolution of the 1770s in England was followed by several others over the next 200 years, each setting off a half-century wave of expansion and contraction only to be renewed by the next revolution. The key to capitalism seemed to lie in its releasing the potential of labor for infinite rises in productivity.

Population growth expanded in parallel with the Industrial Revolution and has been a major complementary feature wherever capitalism has developed. Factory production with large concentrations of workers in one place, the growth of rapid transport and of communications on a global scale, the growth of cities and the desertion of villages, and the breakdown of the household as a major center of production of consumables all gave capitalism a dynamism and a facility for "creative destruction" of all that was old or merely recent. Complaints of attendant social breakdown, of anomie and alienation, of the dissolution of marriage and households, of the decline of religion, were commonly—and perhaps too glibly—voiced.

It was in this combination of alienation from the rural, precontractual life and the concentration of large numbers in factories and towns that the first articulate opposition to capitalism arose in the form of socialism. Different schools of socialism combined the nostalgic and the futuristic elements in various ways, but as an ideology and as a movement socialism became a powerful force of resistance and reform in capitalism. Alongside these developments arose trade unions, a form of association hitherto unknown. While trade unions were not always socialist, their interest was in regulating the growth of capitalism in ways that would enhance the workers' share in the total surplus. The collectivism of trade unions was eminently adaptable to mass politics, which increasingly became the norm in advanced capitalist countries, and these led to major qualifications to laissez-faire in capitalist countries—pensions, social security, and other social provisions associated with the *welfare state. It was from these roots that in the course of the first half of the twentieth century the *state came to play a major role in the spheres of the economy involved with the welfare of the labor force.

In the period between World War I and World War II, capitalism faced its most severe challenge. Hyperinflation following upon war, the triumph of Bolshevism in Russia, the long depression of the 1930s, and the rise of *fascism in Germany and Italy were seen as demonstrating the weakness of individualist capitalism and the success of collectivist alternatives. The rise of welfare capitalism in the United States during the *New Deal and in Britain during World War II was a successful social innovation that revived the prospects of capitalism in the postwar period. The rise of mass consumerism with full employment was seen as a permanent solution to the problems of capitalism.

As full employment became the norm, however, the strength of the trade unions as well as the permanence of the welfare state threatened the sustainability of profits. By the 1970s everywhere in advanced capitalism the crisis of profitability led to stagflation. Reacting to these pressures, capitalism emerged in the late twentieth century renewed by new innovations in electronics and telecommunications and with a reduced commitment to the collectivist institutions of previous years. *Multinational corporations which had arisen in the early twentieth century became the major shaping force of the newly emerging global capitalism. Capitalism seems to proceed through alternating cycles of inward-looking and outward-looking developments, and the 1980s and 1990s suggest a return to the nineteenth century when an earlier phase of capitalism became entwined with *imperialism.

In its preindustrial phase Western European capitalism had already spread its trade network to all parts of the globe, and *colonial empires had been established in America, Africa, and Asia. At the outset these empires were sources for plunder of gold and silver and slaves. The influx of gold from South America into the Iberian empires may even have been the cause of the first century of sustained inflation in Western Europe. But after the Industrial Revolution the network of

formal and informal empires established through trade and credit offered ready markets for the industrial products of Western European capitalism. In return these peripheral regions became suppliers of nonslave but still relatively unfree labor and raw materials.

As informal trade links gave way to territorial conquest across Africa and Southeast and South Asia during the late nineteenth century, capitalism began to be widely identified with imperialism. Especially in South America, informal networks were just as influential as were formal networks. As growth spread, many former peripheral regions—North America, southern Europe, and finally during the late twentieth century East Asia—became fully capitalist and part of the advanced core.

Throughout its 200-year history industrial capitalism has continued to be productive at ever-increasing levels, despite prolonged periods of depression. The capacity of the system for sustained growth is often underestimated and does not seem to have diminished. What is more difficult is to establish the reasons for this sustained growth. Some attribute it to the innovating entrepreneur, ever seeking fabulous profits and willing to take enormous risks. Others attribute it to the combination of competition in the private sphere and the self-denying practice of laissez-faire on the part of the state. Others assign the state a more prominent role, especially in the earlier phases of industrial growth. Military expansionism, the Protestant ethic, gold discoveries, universalization of education and training, discoveries of science and technology—all these have been given their due prominence. The possibility of achieving large and sustained profits and the guarantee that these profits can be kept, augmented, and/or enjoyed would seem to be the one constant characteristic of capitalism. A variety of institutional arrangements have existed at different times within capitalism—competition and monopoly, inflation and stable prices, laissez-faire and interventionism, *authoritarianism and *democracy. In the end, as long as profit can be made and spent as the profit maker wishes within a nonarbitrary legal framework, capitalism—no matter how unclear its workings—will flourish.

(See also DEVELOPMENT AND UNDERDEVELOPMENT; LABOR MOVEMENT; MARXISM.)

MEGHNAD DESAI

CÁRDENAS, Lázaro. President of *Mexico between 1934 and 1940, Lázaro Cárdenas is widely recognized as the most progressive president of Mexico's postrevolutionary period. Born in 1895, of Damaso Cárdenas and Felicitas del Río in Jiquilpán, Michoacán, Cárdenas joined the Constitutionalist army at age 18, during the Mexican Revolution, and eventually rose to the rank of division general. In 1928 he was elected governor of Michoacán, where he promoted the organization of workers and peasants and carried out an extensive agrarian reform. In 1930 he became president of the executive committee of the governing Partido Nacional Revolucionario, and in 1931, secretary of government in the Ortiz Rubio administration.

The election of Cárdenas as president of Mexico in 1934 led to a decisive shift in government policy in the areas of labor relations, agrarian reform, and national control over natural resources. Throughout his campaign, Cárdenas had urged workers to organize and unite, and while he was president he supported workers in their strikes and other conflicts with both foreign and national capital. He also encouraged the formation of the Mexican Labor Confederation, which continued to be the major labor federation in Mexico for several decades.

Under Cárdenas, an extensive agrarian reform was implemented that distributed 44.5 million acres (18 million hectares), twice as much as all previous governments combined, to 810,000 peasants, generally in the form of *ejidos*—community-owned plots that could be farmed individually or collectively. The agrarian reform was innovative in that it was applied not only to traditional and often inefficient holdings but also to highly productive commercial estates, and collective *ejidos* were established as a means to maintain high levels of productivity (by maintaining economies of scale) while achieving the social goals of giving land to *peasants and rural workers.

In 1938, following a lengthy dispute between the newly organized confederation of petroleum workers and the U.S.- and British-owned petroleum companies, Cárdenas expropriated the companies, turning their administration over to a state-owned company, Petroleos Mexicanos (PEMEX), which became the largest company in Mexico's extensive *parastatal sector. The expropriation and *nationalization of the oil industry marked a significant step in eliminating foreign control of the export sector, affirmed the right of the Mexican *state to exercise control over critical resources, and positioned the state for more effective intervention in the economy.

Although the Cárdenas administration was a period of intense confrontation between the state and the private sector over such issues as agrarian reform and the rights of labor, groups within the private sector also benefited from government efforts to promote manufacturing and from loans by state development banks, as well as the expansion of the market resulting from wage increases and reforms in the rural areas. Nevertheless, polarization grew between an increasingly militant and organized urban and rural labor force, on the one hand, and business groups and landowners, often supported by state governors, military officers, and party officials, on the other. The growing polarization and fear of a split within the government were factors in what many have seen as a shift in the last years of the Cárdenas administration toward a moderation of reform efforts and attempts to control the militancy of labor and peasant groups.

In 1938 the government restructured the governing party on a corporate basis, changing its name to the Partido de la Revolución Mexicana. The party was composed of four sectors: labor, peasants, the military (later dropped), and the "popular sector" (consisting of organizations of state workers, teachers, small landowners, students, professionals, and women's groups). Ostensibly organized to institutionalize the influence of these sectors on the party and government, the party structure in fact reinforced hierarchical structures within the constituent organizations and eventually became a mechanism for the co-option and control of these sectors.

The election of General Manuel Avila Camacho as president in 1940 brought a formal end to the most progressive phase of Mexico's postrevolutionary history, and several of the reforms of the Cárdenas administration were subsequently reversed. Nevertheless, the Cárdenas government had an enduring effect on Mexican social, economic, and political life.

The agrarian reform effectively eliminated traditional forms of labor exploitation in the countryside, curtailed the political power of the landowning class, and provided land to a significant sector of the peasantry. The nationalization of the petroleum industry eliminated foreign control and confirmed that of the Mexican state over a critical resource, setting the stage for the growth of Mexico's public sector. The new corporate party structure institutionalized the relationship between the state and popular sector. At the same time, the reforms of the Cárdenas government reinforced the legitimacy of the state as heir of the Mexican Revolution, an important factor in Mexico's political stability over the next several decades.

Cárdenas continued to have a role in Mexican politics, holding several positions in government, including that of minister of defense in the Avila Camacho administration, and informally representing the left wing within the government party until his death in 1970. Recognition of his record in government and his continued support for reform, especially in issues affecting the peasantry, is evident in the general use of the term *cardenismo* to refer to progressive currents within the Mexican political system.

(See also LAND REFORM.)

Arnaldo Córdova, *La política de masas del cardenismo* (Mexico City, 1974). Fernando Benítez, *Lázaro Cárdenas y la Revolución Mexicana* (Mexico City, 1977). Nora Hamilton, *The Limits of the State Autonomy: Post-Revolutionary Mexico* (Princeton, N.J., 1982).

NORA HAMILTON

CARIBBEAN REGION. See ENGLISH-SPEAKING CARIBBEAN.

CARTER, Jimmy, the thirty-ninth president of the United States, was born in the small town of Plains, Georgia, on 21 October 1924. He was the eldest of the four children born to James Earl Carter, Sr., and Lillian Gordy Carter. After graduating from Plains High School (1941), he attended Georgia Southwestern College (1941–1942), the Georgia Institute of Technology (1942–1943), and the U.S. Naval Academy at Annapolis (1943–1946). In 1946 he married Rosalynn Smith and graduated from the Naval Academy (standing sixtieth academically in his class of 820). Between 1946 and 1953, he served, primarily, in the submarine service of the U.S. Navy (including a stint in the nuclear submarine service headed by Admiral Hyman Rickover). He obtained the rank of lieutenant, senior grade.

Upon the death of his father in 1953, Jimmy Carter returned to Plains to manage the family farm and peanut processing business. In 1962, he won a seat in the Georgia legislature. In 1966 he undertook an unsuccessful gubernatorial campaign. Four years later he defeated the popular and moderate former governor Carl Sanders in the Democratic primaries and won the governorship. Despite a stylistically "populist" campaign that contained some covert appeals to white racist sentiment, in office Carter proved to be a racial moderate and progressive. He reorganized the Georgia state government, reformed the state's mental health and environmental programs, hung Martin Luther King, Jr.'s portrait in the state capitol, and increased the number of black state employees.

A short-lived attempt to secure the Democratic vice presidential nomination in 1972 was followed by a four-year campaign for the Democratic presidential nomination. Not only did Carter outflank and outmaneuver his more prominent opponents, he used symbols to great advantage. His emphasis on his religious commitments (Baptist), regional base (the South, small town), and good relations with Georgia blacks appealed to voters wearied of *Watergate, big government, and racial divisions. His appeals, however, were so broad that his Republican opponent in the 1976 general election, incumbent President Gerald Ford, was able to cut into his strength with claims that he waffled on the issues. From a following of approximately 70 percent in the late summer of 1976, Carter was able to eke out only a narrow 50 to 48 percent victory over Ford.

As president Carter showed energy and intelligence in tackling several problems of his day. In his *foreign policy he attempted to deal with new world order problems. Thus he secured Senate approval of the treaty returning the Panama Canal to Panama, played a key role in securing the Camp David Accords between Egypt and Israel, and curbed the export of nuclear weapons technology to countries that did not possess them. He also put *human rights near the top of his foreign policy agenda and tried to adapt to revolutionary movements in the Third World (e.g., to the Sandinistas in Nicaragua).

Domestically, his presidency marked the turn of the Democratic Party toward a neoliberal program emphasizing *deregulation and the conservation of energy and the environment. His programmatic successes included the deregulation of the airline industry and interstate trucking; the creation of the Departments of Energy and Education; the passage of several conservation measures, including the Strip Mining Control and Reclamation Act of 1977; and the Alaska Land Act of 1980. After a long struggle, he also secured portions of his energy program. He also resisted AFL-CIO calls to raise the minimum wage to $3.00 per hour and deferred action for several months on the full employment provisions of the proposed Humphrey-Hawkins bill.

Several of his major policy goals, however, never were accomplished. Due to his inexperience in diplomacy, the Strategic Arms Limitation agreement was not concluded with the USSR until June 1979. Whatever chances it had for passage in the Senate were ended when the Soviets invaded Afghanistan in December 1979. He also failed in his attempts at welfare reform, as well as his endeavors to create a national no-fault insurance program and establish a federal consumer protection agency.

Despite Carter's intelligence and his energy, his popular support as president was shallow. A precipitous decline in his popularity toward the end of 1979 led Senator Ted Kennedy of the Democratic Party's liberal wing to compete with him for the party's nomination in 1980. Having fended off that challenge, Carter lost the general election of 1980 to the Republican candidate, Ronald *Reagan, by a vote of 41 to 51 percent. Independent candidate John B. Anderson carried 7 percent of the popular vote. It was the first time since Herbert Hoover that an elected president had run for and failed to win a second term.

The reasons for Carter's shallow support in the country and in the Democratic Party have been widely debated. Some scholars argue that his problems were due to one or more of the following forces: the growing factionalism in Congress, the lack of programmatic cohesion in the

Democratic Party, the difficulties the traditional Democrats have had in adapting to a more conservative political climate, and the intractable nature of the problems facing the country.

Others scholars see Carter as bearing more responsibility for his political problems. They note that he lacked the kinds of political skills requisite to successful governance. He had difficulties in determining his programmatic priorities and dealing with political tradeoffs; his congressional liaison operation was amateurish at the beginning; and he often failed to consult influentials in the relevant policy networks as a part of the coalition building process.

Certainly factors over which Carter had no clear control contributed to his failure to win reelection. The administration's inability to secure the release of the American hostages held in Iran caused some voters to shift toward Reagan. But most important was the double digit inflation of the economy. Many voters, as most of the exit polls showed, saw Carter as an ineffective president, and a plurality of the voters, for the first time since the New Deal, saw the Republican Party as the most likely to manage the economy in constructive ways.

As an ex-president Carter has shaped an unusually constructive role for himself. Working from the Carter Center in Atlanta, he has led a campaign to eradicate the Guinea worm disease and river blindness, monitored elections in Third World nations, and mediated international crises. His efforts were critical to the successful resolution of U.S. conflicts with the Democratic People's Republic of Korea or North Korea (1994) and Haiti (1994).

(See also PANAMA CANAL TREATY; PRESIDENCY, U.S.; U.S. FOREIGN POLICY.)

Betty Glad, *Jimmy Carter: In Search of the Great White House* (New York, 1980). Erwin C. Hargrove, *Jimmy Carter as President: Leadership and the Practice of the Public Good* (Baton Rouge, La., 1988). Jimmy Carter, *Keeping Faith: Memoirs of a President* (New York, 1982).

BETTY GLAD

CASTRO, Fidel. "He has good timber and the actor in him will not be lacking," observed the 1945 yearbook of Havana's prestigious Jesuit high school, *Belén*, about graduating senior Fidel Castro. Fourteen years later, Castro would bask in the glory bestowed upon him and the Rebel Army by the Cuban people. "This time the revolution is for real!" proclaimed by the young *Comandante* on 1 January 1959. Having launched an armed struggle only in December 1956, the rebels defeated Fulgencio Batista's dictatorship with lightning speed. "This is a decisive moment in our history. Our happiness is immense, but we have much yet to do," continued Fidel. By 2002, when the Cuban Republic commemorates its centennial, Castro will have been at the helm for more than four decades.

Fidel Castro was born in 1926, the year *Cuba was hit by one of the worst hurricanes ever recorded. His father Angel, a Spaniard, fought against Cuban independence in the 1895–1898 war, left after Spain was defeated, and returned as a poor immigrant shortly thereafter. During the early twentieth century, Cuba was a land of opportunity, and Angel Castro reaped the bounty of a booming sugar economy. He became a prosperous landowner in Oriente, Cuba's easternmost province. Lina, Castro's mother and Angel's second wife, was initially a maid in the first marriage's household; Angel and Lina did not marry until the young Fidel was five.

After spending the previous eleven years in Catholic boarding schools in Santiago (Oriente's capital) and Havana, Fidel entered the University of Havana in 1945, just as Ramón Grau was starting his presidency. In 1933, Cuba was shaken by a revolution against Gerardo Machado's dictatorship and against Washington's interference in Cuban affairs, sanctioned since the republic's founding by the U.S.-imposed Platt Amendment. A 100-day nationalist regime headed by Grau was deposed through U.S. pressure and the help of then-Sergeant Batista, who led a revolt against the army leadership amidst the anti-Machado maelstrom. During the 1930s, Batista restored an iron-fisted order while enacting socioeconomic reforms, and the Roosevelt administration abrogated the Platt Amendment. The progressive Constitution of 1940 embodied the compromise that defused the revolution of 1933. Batista won the first presidential election under the new charter; in 1944, he passed the sash to the opposition *Auténtico* party. Grau's return marked a moment of national euphoria as the citizenry expected fulfillment of his earlier tenure's ideals. The young Castro partook of these expectations, which were soon disappointed by continued political corruption and demagoguery.

During the late 1940s and early 1950s, Fidel inhabited the world of student politics in Havana. He failed to win a position in university government, but remained active in that complex world which often spilled over unto the larger political arena. In 1947, Castro joined the later aborted Cuban expedition to topple Dominican dictator Rafael Trujillo. The year 1948 found him in Bogotá for a Latin American student meeting when Colombian Liberal party leader Jorge Gaitán was assassinated and a bloody uprising ensued. Action groups emerged as extrainstitutional players in Havana politics, and Castro took part in their activities. In 1947, Eduardo Chibás broke with the *Auténticos*, founded the *Ortodoxo* party, and raised the banner of honesty in government and the ideals of 1933 with sound and fury. Castro joined the new party and was an *Ortodoxo* congressional candidate in the elections scheduled for June 1952. On 10 March, however, General Batista directed a coup d'état. Twenty-five years old, Castro reacted with indignation and filed a quickly dismissed court challenge to Batista's usurpation of constitutional rule. Tall and handsome, he had by then acquired a studiously patrician manner; love of food, passion for baseball, and insatiable energy were already trademarks as was his lack of interest in music.

Though the coup succeeded almost effortlessly, the general did not find it easy to consolidate his regime. From the start, calls were issued to restore the constitution and hold new elections. Random violence also marked the early *Batistato*; Castro's 26 July 1953 attack on Santiago's Moncada Barracks culminated the spiraling discontent. He comfortably fit into the reigning political ambience: a proclivity for violence, an intransigent impatience, an exasperating self-righteousness regarding what was best for *la patria* (the homeland). His grandiose rhetoric at the Moncada trial, "Condemn me, it does not matter. History will absolve me!" had a natural appeal to his contemporaries. A civic opposition also mobilized public opinion, which clamored for the reestablishment of the Constitution of 1940. When dialogue faltered, the advocates of violence gained ground; Castro's July 26th Movement

quickly seized the anti-Batista momentum. Once successfully ensconced in the Sierra Maestra, the Rebel Army trapped the regime: Fidel emanated an earnest, patriotic purpose that sparked the national imagination; the army's inability to inflict a defeat upon his guerrillas lent him an expanding aura of inevitability. On New Year's Eve, 1958, Fulgencio Batista fled Cuba.

The young revolution, indeed, had much to do. The leonine Fidel elicited an unbounded popular trust and challenged Cubans to accept the gauntlet history had thrown down: to make Cuba a just and sovereign nation. At dizzying speed, the new government enacted reforms aimed at improving the lot of the poor and defending the interests of the nation; none embodied the new Cuba better than the agrarian reform of May 1959. Wealthy Cubans and the United States reacted with alarm. By 1960's end, both had been dispossessed: upper- and many middle-class Cubans fleeing to Miami, and Washington preparing what turned out to be the Bay of Pigs fiasco, while popular fervor remained undiminished. Reading the list of confiscated U.S.-owned properties in August, the *Comandante* lost his voice and finished the inventory in searing whispers into the microphone as a human sea elatedly clamored, ¡Cuba Si! ¡Yanquis No! Shortly thereafter, large-scale Cuban businesses suffered the same fate. In April 1961, when the *Fidelistas* routed the U.S.-sponsored invasion, the Platt Amendment met its de facto end. Castro reaped a political windfall from the David-Goliath confrontation.

Fidel Castro was and is a nationalist. Cuban history has always marked his imagination and propelled his radicalism. That he thrust Cuba into the throes of the *Cold War was more a consequence of opportunity than of principle. Fidel, the revolutionary, defied the United States and needed allies; Castro, the dictator, conveniently assimilated *Marxism-*Leninism's formula for unchallenged power. Socialism also dovetailed into Cuba's radical nationalism: Cubans attained more equitable, if austere, living standards, and the nation deflected U.S. reversionary efforts. The alliance with the Soviet Union brought a basket of benefits that sustained the Cuban economy, supported universal access to health care, education, and social security, yielded Cuba a disproportionate presence in global affairs, and granted Castro a stage beyond the island upon which to seek recognition. Thus, when the Cold War finally ended, the sense of security that had set in during the 1970s and 1980s was badly jarred.

Castro and his regime survived the 1990s. A tightened U.S. embargo and the disappearance of Soviet subsidies did not provoke a popular uprising. Instead, Cubans took to the seas seeking a better life in the United States or retreated to their private lives, concerned only with putting food on the table. If the people's will, energy, and passion bolstered the young revolution, their fear, apathy, and sense of impotence now played an important part in Castro's resilience and ability to remain in power. Cuba's economy tottered on a seesaw of timid reforms and stubborn resistance; foreign investment, tourism, and the diaspora's remittances patched together a precarious lattice that impeded economic collapse without supporting future growth. Cuba's politics remained time warped in the rituals of mass mobilizations that gave the appearance of steely unity behind Castro, while remaining dismissive of elections that would have truly gauged the popular will. His words in January 1998 echoed an intractable defiance: "Cuba is not changing. Cuba is reaffirming its position, its ideals, its objectives. The world is the one changing." Until his passing, the formal trappings of contemporary Cuba seemed set, even if ordinary Cubans paid little heed to the ideals that once moved them to accept history's gauntlet.

Castro has avoided the world's harsh repudiation. Unabated U.S. hostility and the illusions once conjured by the revolution have perpetuated David's aura. The Cold War's aftermath also created an unexpected confluence of interests that extended Castro's international limelight. In a unipolar world, engaging Cuba has allowed Europe, Canada, and Latin America to assert their independence from the United States; Pope John Paul II now denounces the social ills of unfettered capitalism with almost the same zeal he mustered against communism. During the 1990s, Castro traveled the world and welcomed the visits of distinguished dignitaries such as the pope and Spain's King Juan Carlos. The costs of his rule have yet to be fully apprehended. There once were at least 30,000 political prisoners in Cuban jails, some 5,000 opponents fell before firing squads, untold thousands perished in the Florida Straits, about 15 percent of Cuba's population is exiled, and millions on the island are muzzled. After Castro's passing, a capitalist and democratic Cuba may yet be his sternest judge. History's sentence will likely value the accomplishments of Fidel, the great revolutionary, but Castro's record as one of the twentieth-century's longest running dictators will unlikely be absolved.

(See also U.S. FOREIGN POLICY; U.S.–LATIN AMERICAN RELATIONS.)

Tad Szulc, *Fidel: A Critical Portrait* (New York, 1986). Thomas G. Patterson, *Contesting Castro: The United States and the Triumph of the Cuban Revolution* (New York, 1994). Marifeli Pérez-Stable, *The Cuban Revolution: Origins, Course, and Legacy*, 2d ed. (New York, 1999).

MARIFELI PÉREZ-STABLE

CENSORSHIP. See overleaf.

CENTRAL AFRICAN REPUBLIC. The Central African Republic (CAR) is one of Africa's less-developed and least-known countries. A 1,967- to 2,953-foot-high (600- to 900-meter-high) landlocked plateau, the CAR is ecologically a transitional zone, its 241,314 square miles (625,000 sq. km.) stretching from savannah lands in the north to dense rain forests in the extreme south. The country possesses rich timber (hardwoods) and mineral resources (including diamonds, uranium, iron, and copper) and grows cash crops (cotton, coffee); however, poor roads and distance to the coast (all goods must travel via the shallow Ubangi River through the Congo River to Brazzaville) keep the economy depressed, resources underexploited, and imports costly.

The country's estimated population of 3 million is a complex mosaic of some eighty ethnic groups, the largest being the Gbaya, Banda, Zande, and Sara. Few are indigenous to the CAR, most arriving during the last 200 years. Prior to independence known as Oubangui-Chari (after two of its rivers) and part of French Equatorial Africa, at the outset the colony was carved into concessions and harshly exploited by private companies. Outcries in Paris (spearheaded by author André Gide) in due course alleviated some of the worst abuses. Still, to pay for its upkeep a poll tax forced farmers to grow cash crops, especially cotton, resulting in new abuses and unrest. Stagnating during the colonial era, the CAR emerged independent on 13 August 1960 under David Dacko. Barthélemy Boganda, the country's charismatic founding father, had died in an air crash in 1959. Social and budgetary stresses, Dacko's weak leadership, and inter-elite frictions set the stage for the coup of 31 December 1965, led by Chief of Staff Colonel Jean-Bedel Bokassa, a relative of both Boganda and Dacko.

Bokassa's bizarre fourteen-year rule was a vain tyranny with all domestic and foreign policy dictated by whim, culminating in his grandiose Napoleon-style coronation as emperor in 1977. National resources were looted; the CAR's minimal infrastructure fell into disrepair; the economy ground to a halt. Having directly sustained the regime owing to the CAR's mineral wealth and strategic location, France finally flew in troops to the capital, Bangui, to oust Bokassa on 20 September 1979 after he crushed student riots with great bloodshed and (personal) cruelty. (In 1986 Bokassa stunningly returned from exile to stand trial.) Dacko, reelevated to power by France, and "confirmed" in office in rigged presidential elections, again proved inept in governing the by-now-seething country. On 1 September 1981 he was himself ousted by General André Kolingba in a coup countenanced by France.

Though Kolingba civilianized his regime along the party-state lines already institutionalized by Mobutu in the Congo, Eyadema in Togo, and others, political stability and legitimacy eluded him. Ethnicity continued to polarize an increasingly urban and radical populace with pressing societal needs in an economy in shambles, rampant with corruption, and providing few employment prospects. The changed global context of the 1990s saw a dramatic shift in France's African policy and a decline in the commitment to sustain Kolingba. Although Kolingba sought to prolong his tenure in office by refusing to hold a sovereign national conference and attempting to derail the return to multipartyism, presidential elections were eventually held in 1993, and he lost them to Ange-Félix Patassé.

Despite its popular mandate, the new regime could not meet popular expectations for social change and development. A series of army mutinies based on economic and social grievances in 1996 led to a crisis situation that required intervention by African and UN peacekeeping forces to stabilize. Relative calm was reestablished between 1997 and 1999, but long-term stability will require sustained progress in the democratization process as well as in economic and social development.

(See also FRANCOPHONE AFRICA.)

Yarisse Zactizoum, *Histoire de la Centrafrique,* 2 vols. (Paris, 1983). Thomas O'Toole, *The Central African Republic* (Boulder, Colo., 1986). Samuel Decalo, "Jean-Bedel Bokassa," in *Psychoses of Power: African Personal Dictatorships* (Boulder, Colo., 1989). Elikia M'Bokolo, "Comparisons and Contrasts in Equatorial Africa: Gabon, Congo and the Central African Republic," in David Birmingham and Phyllis M. Martin, eds., *History of Central Africa: The Contemporary Years since 1960* (London, 1998).

SAMUEL DECALO

CENSORSHIP. There can be no doubt that censorship has a bad name in modern democratic societies. By "censorship" we generally mean any attempt to prohibit or punish those who exercise their "right" of freedom of speech or press. This is, indeed, a constitutional imperative in the United States, enshrined in the First Amendment: "Congress shall make no law . . . abridging the freedom of speech or of the press." Virtually all democratic societies throughout the world embrace some version of this legal principle. But the idea that censorship is an evil extends far beyond the legal realm and to a significant degree defines our understandings about social intercourse as well. Thus, we commonly hear how it is wrong to penalize anyone merely for what he or she says or thinks. Indeed, the great nineteenth century philosopher John Stuart Mill made the point rather emphatically that "private censorship" posed the greater threat for liberty of expression. The fear of censorship, therefore, cuts a wide swath through social life, and it behooves us to understand its intellectual roots and its general desirability as a legal and social norm.

We should begin with a very brief review of the development of the First Amendment, since our primary understandings of censorship have been formed in the crucible of that constitutional history.

Although the First Amendment was part of the original *Bill of Rights of the U.S. Constitution, it was not until 1919 that the *Supreme Court of the United States rendered its very first decision on its meaning. The Court was actually presented with a trilogy of cases arising out of antiwar activities during the First World War. One case (*Debs* v. *United States*, 1895) involved the presidential candidate for the Socialist Party, who had been arrested and convicted for giving a speech in which he praised individuals who had refused to be drafted. The famous justice Oliver Wendell Holmes, Jr., wrote for a unanimous Court in Debs and each of the other cases, holding that "When a nation is at war, many things that might be said in time of peace are such a hindrance to its effort that their utterance will not be endured so long as men fight and that no Court could regard them as protected by any constitutional *right." The overriding standard was "whether the words used are used in such circumstances and are of such a nature as to create a clear and present danger that they will bring about the substantive evils that Congress has a right to prevent." To Holmes this "was a question of proximity and degree." Certainly, he added, the "most stringent protection of free speech would not protect a man in falsely shouting fire in a theatre and causing a panic." The upshot was that all of these defendant went to jail—including Eugene Debs, who received, while in prison, over a million votes for president in the election of 1920.

These three cases inaugurated what can only be described as a century of debate over the scope and meaning of the right to be free of censorship in "speech" and the "press." For his part, Justice Holmes promptly departed from his initial perspective on the scope of free speech. In doing so, and in joining forces with the liberal justice Louis Brandeis, he became the celebrated architect of the modern idea that free speech means no censorship for the speech we hate, even appropriately hate. One year after the now infamous opening trilogy, in another World War I case involving protestors who distributed leaflets calling for a general strike (*Abrams* v. *United States*, 1919). Holmes and Brandeis magnificently articulated an anticensorship position and located the rationale of freedom of speech in the societal interest in achieving truth. Holmes wrote of how he had no sympathy with "these poor and puny anonymities" who advocated a "creed of ignorance and immaturity," and then added in immortal words:

"But when men have realized that time as upset many fighting faiths, they may come to believe even more than they believe the very foundations of their own conduct that the ultimate good desired is better reached by free trade in ideas—that the best test of truth is the power of the thought to get itself accepted in the competition of the market, and that truth is the only ground upon which their wishes safely can be carried out. That at any rate is the theory of our Constitution."

Over the succeeding decades, these sentiments and others in a similar vein set the tone for a rich and at times highly contentious debate over the limits of censorship. By the 1930s, it seemed as if Holmes and Brandeis had won the day, as case after case in the Supreme Court enunciated a strong free speech framework. The 1950s brought a setback, however, when *Communism seemed on the ascendancy around the globe and communist conspiracies were seen in every corner of social life. The tactics of stimulating group hatreds that had seemed to underlie the rise of *fascism and Nazism in Europe added to a more widespread anxiety about a nearly unbounded right of free speech. In *Dennis* v. *United States* (1951), the Supreme Court upheld the convictions of the top leadership of the Communist Party in the United States for advocating the overthrow of the government. To a majority of the Court it seemed senseless and rash to apply the same First Amendment principles to the street corner orator as to highly organized and disciplined groups bent on achieving a putsch at the propitious moment.

But the 1960s brought a return to the Holmes-Brandeis perspective and, in a series of notable and seminal cases, the Court laid the groundwork for the understanding of freedom of speech and the press that lives to this day. The most important was *Brandenburg* v. *Ohio* (1969), in which the Court upheld the right of groups such as the *Ku Klux Klan to march and speak. The "principle," according to the Court, is that the state may not censor speech "except where such advocacy [of the use of force or of law violation] is directed to inciting or producing imminent lawless action and is likely to incite or produce such action." This extraordinary protection against censorship has become part of the way of life in the United States. With only a few exceptions (e.g., obscenity, libel, fighting words), the First Amendment extends the bar on censorship far beyond what most people would consider "reasonable."

Now, the most important part of this process has been not the development of a "test" for the protection of speech (of which there have been many) but rather the articulation of the reasons why protection should extend this far. As one might expect, this has been a major occupation of judges and scholars. It is, therefore, a very complex body of literature on the subject. But, for our purposes, the following summary will have to suffice. It has been said, and fairly widely accepted, that our interest in finding the truth and in arriving at the best possible policies in a self-governing society requires us to be open to all ideas, even those we abhor or believe to be dangerous errors. Since we are not infallible, we ought to be prepared to listen to those who wish to say that what we believe is false. And, even if our beliefs really are true, we nevertheless benefit from confronting those who believe falsely. Beliefs, like muscles, quickly become flabby without meeting resistance. All in all, as Holmes famously said: "But when men have realized that time has upset many fighting faiths, they may come to believe even more than they believe the very foundations of their own conduct that the ultimate good desired is better reached by free trade in ideas—that the best test of truth is the power of the thought to get itself accepted in the competition of the market, and that truth is the only ground upon which their wishes safely can be carried out."

In addition to these theories about the benefits to truth and *democracy, another idea frequently deployed to justify extending the outer boundary of constitutional protection so far is that we need a barrier, or a fortress, to protect against the natural human impulse to censor. Censorship, in the First Amendment literature, is assumed to be a bad tendency we more or less all share. Holmes spoke memorably about this, as well: "Persecution for the expression of opinions seems to me perfectly logical. If you have no doubt of your premises or your power and want a certain result with all your heart you naturally express your wishes in law and sweep away all opposition. To allow opposition by speech seems to indicate that you think the speech impotent, as when a man says that he has squared the circle, or that you do not care wholeheartedly for the result, or that you doubt either your power or your premises." Censorship is natural, or "logical," but it's also dangerous and wrong. It deprives us of the truth, is a display of our own lack of courage to confront opposing beliefs and ideas, and strips the democracy of the opportunity to learn what all citizens think. Indeed, Justice Brandeis once compared it to the motivation for burning witches: "Men feared witches and burned women. It is the function of speech to free men from the bondage of irrational fears."

We see, then, that in this relatively brief time span of less than 100 years, even with the ebbing and flowing of constitutional protection for speech, the creation of a fundamental idea that censorship is a human impulse that threatens our realization of truth and democratic government. In this vision, speech is good and must be protected from the perils of the desire to suppress. I shall return to this conception, but first we need to explore an important variation on this central theme of the First Amendment.

It is not a very long leap to begin to see the world in a slightly different way. For if censorship is such a natural tendency, then we ought to see it manifest not only through government action but through private action as well. I mentioned at the outset that John Stuart Mill argued that private censorship was, indeed, the most dangerous of all for liberty of speech, primarily because it is so pervasive and so ineradicable compared to legislation, which may be judicially overturned. Social ostracism may be as powerful a deterrent as a fine, or even as a prison term. And, when the press is controlled by major corporations, whose self-interests may be furthered by denying access to those with troublesome viewpoints, this private censorship may be as pernicious to the search for truth and democratic decision making as any of the government variety.

It is precisely this realization that has led to significant debate within the First Amendment as to its proper reach. The question is, should it stand as a bar to any government regulation of expression, or should it draw a distinction between government regulation intended to prohibit speech deemed offensive or dangerous (which would not generally be allowed) and government regulation intended to minimize the adverse effects of private censorship and to expand and even equalize the opportunities for speech among the citizenry? On just a few occasions, the Court has actually gone further than this and held that private censorship itself can be prohibited under the First Amendment. A shopping center, for example, was once said to be the modern equivalent of the city for First Amendment purposes and, therefore, required to meet the same constitutional expectations. But that idea was later jettisoned by a subsequent Court and has not since been revived. The Court, however, has required government in this country to open up certain public property (notably streets and parks) to speech activities, on a first-come-first-served basis, as a means of equalizing citizen access to the marketplace of ideas. But the most significant issues for the First Amendment have arisen in the context of government regulations designed to enhance the opportunities of those marginalized by private control of the primary means of communication. And the context in which such regulations have been tried and allowed has been the new electronic media of broadcasting and cable.

In the United States, for these purposes, we have had a dual system of freedom of the press. The electronic media have been subject to a system of government licensing, under which licenses are allocated according to the determination of a federal agency (the Federal Communications Commission) as to which applicant would best serve the "public interest." All licensees, moreover, must comply with a set of regulations designed to enhance access for different points of view. The "equal time" provision requires broadcasters who let candidates for public office to "use" their stations to provide comparable access to all other candidates for those offices. The "fairness doctrine" required (until it was abandoned in the late 1980s) broadcasters to be "fair" in the coverage of all controversial issues of public importance.

No such regulations, however, have been constitutionally sanctioned for the print media. The official rationale for this differential treatment of electronic and print media has been that broadcasting must make use of a "scarce" resource, namely the electromagnetic spectrum. Since there are more people who would like to communicate over the airwaves than there are frequencies available, allocation was necessary and government allocation was permissible. Those "lucky enough" to receive these coveted permits to broadcast were then reasonably required to share and to meet the demands of the "public interest." There are, however, many problems with this theoretical distinction. The most significant is that it was not necessary for the government to be the method of allocation—the market would have worked, too, by selling property rights in the spectrum which could then be resold as any other property might. Of course, it still might be that there would be too few broadcasters controlling the medium, but that's a different argument and one difficult to sustain in the face of the near universal phenomenon of monopoly status for daily newspapers in cities across the country. In any event, the Court never confronted the issue. Rather in cases from each medium the Court simply stressed the evils of government censorship (with regard to print) or the evils of private censorship and the concomitant need for government intervention to protect the marketplace of ideas (electronic media).

This dual system, which still exists although in a somewhat less dichotomous state than in earlier decades, has been less about differences between the various media and more about the a deep ambivalence inside our concerns about censorship: Should we limit our efforts to controlling improper state interventions into the marketplace or should we take a broader perspective and attend to the myriad ways in which private power, especially that derived from money, can distort and "censor" speech? Each approach is not without its costs and limitations, and the twentieth-century solution of having a differential system of freedom of the press is in many ways a natural embodiment of our ambivalence and an experiment in ambiguity.

Up to now I have focused on the creation of the concept of censorship in First Amendment jurisprudence, where the classic understanding is of an evil (whether government or private) that must be curbed in order to protect something of great value (i.e., speech). This, however, needs substantial modification. Censorship is, as Holmes said, "perfectly logical." But there are several things more to be said about it. At the very least, it is important to recognize a vital distinction. "Censorship" is a pejorative term we have devised for attempts to prohibit speech. But that does not necessarily mean that prohibiting speech is intrinsically a bad thing. In fact, it would be unthinkable for us to accept a principle that there should be no coercion against speech or ideas. In ordinary life we regularly and appropriately penalize people for saying things that are wrongful and hurtful. It is, moreover, widely regarded as entirely acceptable to penalize those who have acted in bad ways in order to deter others, who may be "persuaded" by the bad conduct, to act similarly. Speech can hurt and it can hurt in ways that we should take cognizance of through our negative responses.

It is also important to realize that what we label "censorship" can be both "logical" and, indeed, desirable and further that it is really just a part of a much broader human tendency or impulse—which we might more or less call the desire to have your way and to want to stop those who either violate what you want or pose a threat to what you want. One might, in other words, take Holmes' definition of persecution, or censorship, and expand its effects. To "sweep away all opposition" may mean to prohibit and punish speech but it may also mean to refuse to compromise in the political process or to punish excessively those who violate your rules—or even to use speech as an instrument of oppression and intolerance. We are, then, talking about a human character flaw with adverse consequences that extend far beyond the realm of freedom of speech.

There is, however, another side to all this. We also want people to have the courage of their convictions and to stand up for them and insist that they be adhered to. This is certainly the case with our moral principles and with the fundamental values of our society, not least of which is freedom of speech itself. While intolerance is certainly a problem in human society, so is weakness of will and fecklessness.

What we can say, I believe, is that the greater risk is in the direction of excessive intolerance, that there is a bias in human affairs in that direction. We can also say, too, that it is hard, and perhaps nearly or even impossible, to say precisely, or with any helpful rule, when and how much it is appropriate to insist on having your way and to ignore or penalize those who would have it otherwise. And, yet, it is this reality of life that gives power and meaning to the very concept of freedom of speech and its correlative concept of censorship. In a profound sense, freedom of speech is as anticensorship as it is pro-speech. With a general human bias in the conduct of human affairs, and one not subject to rules of guidance, we benefit by taking a segment of human conduct—which we call "speech"—and fundamentally remove it from our normal methods of exerting our control. In this sense, we are not signifying the specialness of speech but the general concern we have with the underlying mentality inherent in the act of suppression. This we call "censorship."

There are many reasons why understanding this development of the concept of "censorship," so powerfully rendered through the First Amendment jurisprudence of the twentieth century, is important. But one is the need to recognize that what is "reasonable" under the First Amendment is not necessarily reasonable in the other realms of life. In building the First Amendment, perhaps we have had to overstate the virtues of speech and the evils of regulation and punishment of speech. In time, a more balanced picture of what we call "censorship" is needed, which should also better secure public confidence in the reasonableness of the First Amendment itself.

(See also MEDIA AND POLITICS; INFORMATION SOCIETY.)

LEE BOLLINGER

CENSORSHIP. In the most literal sense, censorship is the activity of a censor—an official with the responsibility to approve or deny distribution of particular texts to the general public. In early modern Europe, almost all printing was subject to some form of government licensing or censorship. But this practice was ended in England in 1694 and never took root in British colonies. It had ended in virtually all Western countries by the nineteenth century.

In modern liberal democracies, the term "censorship" is generally used in a more extended sense, often indeed in a rather metaphorical sense, to describe any obstruction to free communication. In this sense, there is still a good deal of censorship in Western countries. The term is almost always used reproachfully, but not everything called "censorship" will soon go the way of old licensing systems for printing houses.

There is one area where even modern liberal democracies often impose "prior restraint" on publication of information. Yet this one area of true censorship is, in fact, among the least controversial. Most governments try to restrict the dissemination of military secrets. They may impose limited forms of censorship on reporting from war zones or demand the right to screen publications by officials (or former officials) with knowledge of official secrets. Despite grumbling about overly restrictive controls in particular cases, such practices are not widely condemned. There is general acceptance that even democratic states need to protect secrets from external enemies, actual or potential. And prosecution after the fact cannot undo the damage when secrets are revealed. So, for example, the *Supreme Court of the United States has held that government would be justified in suppressing (in advance) publication of details about the movements of troopships in time of war.

What most people in democratic countries strongly oppose is control on information that simply shields the government from criticism. In the nineteenth century, most governments, even those with elements of *parliamentary democracy, did claim the authority to suppress subversive or seditious speech. Even though such restraints could operate by formal prosecution after publication—thereby escaping the odium of full censorship—they were largely abandoned in almost all Western countries in the course of the twentieth century. It is now generally thought that in a free country, government should not suppress any form of communication merely because it may have a bad influence on the political opinions of citizens.

Thoroughgoing censorship of this kind was prevalent in totalitarian states, which exercised tight controls on anything circulated to ordinary citizens. Such censorship remains a feature of the few remaining communist dictatorships such as China and Cuba. Not only do such governments try to suppress reporting of happenings in civil life—such as strikes, protests, or industrial accidents—but they also try to suppress unauthorized reports on what other citizens say or think about such embarrassments. In effect, extreme dictatorships view their own citizens as potential enemies and try to withhold information from their own citizens as they would from a foreign enemy. The degree to which independent news reporting is allowed to circulate in a society remains a very strong indication of its government's respect for democracy and human rights. Censorship, in this sense, is rightly a main focus of scrutiny for international *human rights advocates.

Yet censorship remains an issue in established liberal democracies and is likely to remain a matter of continuing controversy—at least in the extended sense in which the word censorship is now commonly used. Most Western governments, for example, enacted criminal penalties in the nineteenth century to restrain the distribution of obscene texts or images, as new technology created the potential for mass distribution of pornography. Most such controls were greatly relaxed in the second half of the twentieth century. Yet most governments still threaten criminal penalties against hardcore pornography, at least when it is particularly violent or degrading or involves sexualized depictions of children. Is this "censorship"?

Certainly, suppression of pornography is not designed to suppress the circulation of actual information, as all the acts or practices depicted in hard-core pornography can be adequately described without resort to extremely graphic imagery. Many commentators defend such controls on the ground that they are not designed to shield government from criticism but to protect society from affront or from an erosion of confidence in moral standards. But many publishers and artists vehemently dissent from particular acts of suppression. And certainly it is not easy to draw clear or firm lines between improper "political" controls and permissible "social" or "moral" forms of control.

It was common, particularly in the 1950s and 1960s, to associate opposition to all forms of "censorship" with "progressive opinion." As with obscenity controls, much remaining censorship seemed designed to uphold moral standards of an earlier time. As one country after another relaxed its restrictions on nudity and erotic imagery, in films and magazines and stage shows, it seemed that, at least in the Western world, all countries were moving toward greater permissiveness and remaining national differences would soon give way before the general trend.

But this has not happened. The new feminist movement that arose in the 1970s protested against pornographic imagery as degrading to women and inciting to sexual violence. Advocates for racial and ethnic minorities protested against all forms of expression they regarded as degrading to their own groups or tending to promote bigotry or incite violence against them. In the United States, some efforts to respond to feminist protests in the 1980s were judged by federal courts to violate constitutional rights to free speech. Similarly, some speech codes on university campuses, designed to restrict speech offensive to particular minorities, were struck down by courts. But these restrictions on speech had been applauded by many activists and scholars of the left. Somewhat similar measures, applying to publications in general circulation, were, in fact, sustained against constitutional challenge in neighboring Canada.

Most countries have established different standards for different communications media. There are more restrictive standards for what can be broadcast on television, for example, than for what can be shown in movie theaters; photographic imagery is often more restricted than the printed word. But there are notable differences between countries, as well. Compared to most European countries, the United States enforces tighter restrictions on nudity and offensive language in broadcasting, but it imposes less restrictive controls on the graphic depiction of violence.

Precisely because such measures are not about restricting

actual information, there is no reason to think most countries will arrive at the same ultimate standards. Information may leak across borders quite easily, undermining the authority of dictatorships that try to suppress knowledge of awkward facts. But restrictions on pornographic or extremely violent imagery are about censoring attitudes more than censoring information. Postwar Germany punishes political displays of the swastika as well as public denials of the historical fact of the *Holocaust. In the United States, the Supreme Court has severely limited regulation of anything that seems remotely connected to political expression but has accommodated much control over nudity and sexual imagery, particularly in broadcasting. Different countries, with different historic experiences and national cultures, are bound to respond somewhat differently to contemporary provocations.

Nor does the advent of global communication networks necessarily portend a trend toward greater permissiveness everywhere in the world. Just as movies and television productions can be dubbed into foreign languages, they can be edited to conform to differing national standards. Modern means of communication may spread cultural trends, but they also allow protest movements to mobilize more quickly, and protest movements—such as *feminism—often favor tighter local controls on certain forms of communication. It is too early to tell whether governments will succeed in efforts to impose differing local controls on the flow of imagery and invective on the Internet. But it is not clear that wider availability of Internet sources (e.g., for child pornography or Nazi paraphernalia) will, in any case, lead to demands for tighter controls. The availability of Internet access may reduce protest against existing controls on public distribution of embargoed materials, as taboo seekers turn to the utterly private channels of the Internet.

International standards are not likely to ensure standard responses, either. The International Covenant on Civil and Political Rights, for example, balances its broad affirmation of "freedom of expression" with the acknowledgment that this freedom "may be subject to certain restrictions . . . for the protection of national security or of public order or of public health or morals" (Art. 19). At the same time, it commits governments to prohibit "propaganda for war" and "advocacy of national, racial or religious hatred that constitutes incitement to discrimination, hostility or violence . . ." (Art. 20). The United States specifically disavowed any obligation to implement such restrictions when it ratified the Covenant in 1992 and it will be a long time, if ever, before a UN organ has the legal or moral authority to override strongly held national objections to differing policies on such matters. The European Convention on Human Rights has developed more authority among signatories, but here too general guarantees of free expression are balanced by recognition that controls may sometimes be appropriate. The European Court of Human Rights has so far been cautious in overriding differing national approaches to the exceptions.

Finally, the issue of "censorship" will remain alive in liberal democracies because the term has come to be used in such extended ways that policy disputes are almost inescapable. Many people protest when public museums decline to display certain works or public authorities refuse to fund certain displays. Others are outraged when public agencies lend support to displays accused of fostering degrading imagery or mockery toward religion or one-sided historical portrayals. In a number of cases, most prominently in the United States, museums have altered or revised displays that aroused great controversy and the National Endowment for the Arts has agreed to limit funding for obscene or sexually offensive art. Critics were quick to condemn this as censorship (though the Supreme Court gave wary approval to the NEA policy).

In the 1980s, American liberals charged the government with imposing "gag orders" on family planning services, when federal funding was made conditional on exclusion of counseling on abortion. Conservatives in the 1990s protested when government grants to religious colleges and religiously affiliated social service agencies were conditioned on exclusion of religious messages from the recipient programs. If such practices constitute censorship, then such censorship is not likely to disappear, because there is no agreed formula on how to distribute limited public funds and public pressure is bound to influence the funding policies of democratic governments.

The issues are still more complicated when protests against censorship are leveled against private firms or private institutions. Both the movie industry and the recording industry in the United States have responded to public protests by adopting labeling codes and promising to exercise self-restraint regarding extreme depictions of violence. Newspapers and professional journals reserve the right to refuse publication to articles they deem unsuitable. Those whose work gets rejected often charge that they have been censored. Others protest when copyright is enforced against those who want to republish extended excerpts of protected works.

Particular cases may raise legitimate questions about overly restrictive policies. But we are not likely to arrive at any enduring, universal consensus on neutral or proper standards in such matters. Protecting free expression is not the only governmental concern, even in liberal democracies. And even free expression sometimes requires restrictions to protect the rights of others or the ground rules for civil exchange of ideas. The right to speak freely must include the right to decide when and how to speak. When that right is exercised by private entities, some people are bound to find fault with the choices they make.

The term "censorship" carries emotive force because it calls to mind images of heavy-handed government repression. Such images are still true to the reality in some countries. But in Western-style democracies, where free expression is generally well protected, charges of "censorship" are often no more than vehement rhetoric, deployed to stigmatize particular decisions about the allocation of public subsidies or private resources, by those who feel disadvantaged by these decisions. In such circumstances, cries of censorship are really protests against perceived inequalities. And arguments about inequality are not likely to disappear from democratic politics.

(See also INFORMATION SOCIETY; INFORMATION TECHNOLOGY.)

Alexander Meicklejohn, "Free Speech and Its Relation to Self-Government," in *Political Freedom* (New York, 1965). Rodney Smolla, *Free Speech in an Open Society* (New York, 1992). Owen Fiss, *Liberalism Divided: Freedom of Speech and the Many Uses of State Power* (Boulder, Colo., 1996). Jeffrey A. Smith, *War and Press Freedom* (New York, 1999). James Weinstein, *Hate Speech, Pornography and the Radical Attack on Free Speech Doctrine* (Boulder, Colo., 1999). Jeremy Harris Lipschultz, *Free Expression in the Age of the Internet* (Boulder, Colo., 2000).

JEREMY A. RABKIN

CENTRAL ASIA. Surrounded by Russia to the north, China to the east, Iran and Afghanistan to the south, and the Caspian Sea to the west, Central Asia (Turkistan) is located at the crossroads of Europe and Asia. The emergence of modern Central Asia can be traced back to the aftermath of the Russian Revolution of 1917, which brought to power the Bolsheviks and established a communist party state in Russia. It took Lenin and his local cadre nearly seven years to consolidate their reign over Turkistan, inhabited by tribal Turkmen, Kazak, and Kyrgyz, as well as sedentary Tajiks and Uzbeks. Prior to 1924, however, the Bolsheviks only nominally altered the political structure of Central Asia, which had been under the czarist jurisdiction of the "governor general of Turkistan" and the "governor general of the Steppe." In 1918, the territory that covered much of the present Uzbekistan, Tajikistan, and Turkmenistan was renamed Turkistan Autonomous Soviet Socialist Republic, and the Steppe region—the current territory of Kazakstan and Kyrgyzstan—renamed Kyrgyz Autonomous Soviet Socialist Republic. In addition to these territories, two Uzbek principalities of Bukhara and Khiva were assigned new names—the Soviet People's Republic of Bukhara and the Soviet People's Republic of Khorezm—in 1920. Both, however, were considered outside the Soviet Union, yet tied to it by treaties of alliance.

In 1924 Stalin redrew the map of the region by eliminating the republics of Turkistan, Bukhara, and Khorezm. In their place he created the Soviet Socialist republics of Uzbekistan and Turkmenistan, the Autonomous Region of Kara Kyrgyz, and the Autonomous Republic of Tajikistan—formally within the boundaries of the Republic of Uzbekistan. The Steppe region was renamed the Kazak Autonomous Republic and the Autonomous Region of Kara Kyrgyz was subsequently renamed three times: Kyrgyz Autonomous Region in 1925, Kyrgyz Autonomous Republic in 1926, and Kyrgyz Soviet Socialist Republic in 1936. The Autonomous Republic of Tajikistan was transformed into the Soviet Socialist Republic of Tajikistan in 1929 and was formally severed from Uzbekistan territory. The last of the five republics of Central Asia, the Kazak Soviet Socialist Republic, was formally created in 1936.

The Central Asian republics declared their independence from the former *Soviet Union in 1991, putting an end to nearly sixty years of Soviet-style political governance, which in principle had placed the Supreme Soviet (people's assembly) at the center of the decision-making process. In reality, however, the decision-making power had been in the hands of the first secretary of the Republican Communist Party, whose activities were closely monitored by the Politburo in Moscow.

Although in some republics independence brought about major structural changes that aimed at altering the institutional and constitutional frameworks of politics, with the exception of Kyrgyzstan, power remained in the hands of the former Communist leaders who so far have hindered the process of post-communist democratization. And despite the theoretical separation of powers, the post-independence presidents have virtual control over all three branches of the government and dictate national policy priorities. The parliaments have been effectively sidelined, and organized opposition has been banned or kept under close scrutiny. This growing authoritarian tendency has been most visible in Uzbekistan and Turkmenistan, less apparent in Kyrgyzstan and Kazakstan. The civil war in Tajikistan (1992–1997), on the other hand, halted that republic's post-independence political and economic transition. However, the July 1997 peace agreement made possible the formation of a coalition government and hence offered better prospects for a gradual move toward democratization of politics in the future.

While political reform has been slow, economic reform has been enthusiastically embraced by some leaders, particularly President Nursultan Nazarbayev of Kazakstan and President Askar Akayev of Kyrgyzstan. But the region has been hard hit by the shocks of transition to a market economy, despite its vast energy and mineral resources. Three factors explain the economic difficulties facing the region. First, Central Asia is landlocked, and as such its economic fate hinges upon how quickly and successfully it can gain access to the world markets through neighboring countries. The precarious situation in *Afghanistan, U.S. opposition to Iran as a transit alternative, and the logistical problems involving the eastern route to China have left the region hopelessly dependent on Russia, whose ultimate goal is to maintain its economic hold on the region by perpetuating continued dependency. Second, despite marked variations, the overall attitude toward economic reform has been decidedly conservative in Turkmenistan and Uzbekistan and until recently in Tajikistan, where the state still owns and controls much of the economy. Although a respectable degree of privatization, trade liberalization, and currency reform have been carried out in these republics, economic transition has been very slow and limited in scope. Third, with the notable exception of Kyrgyzstan and perhaps Kazakstan, the attitude of leadership toward foreign investment has been less than enthusiastic. The main problems revolve around the uncertainties surrounding the legal framework for investment, which has created an undesirable environment for Western companies. In the absence of adequate foreign investment, the Central Asian economies have been unable to follow through with post-privatization restructuring, which is critical to a successful economic transition.

Consequently, economic stagnation has taken a toll on government finances, leading to chronic current account and budget deficits, as well as constant inflationary pressure that has ranged from moderate to severe over the past several years. To combat the budget deficit and inflation, the governments have relied upon tight monetary policies that include postponement in payments of wages in Kazakstan and Kyrgyzstan, thus raising the prospects for mass demonstrations and political instability. Elsewhere, frequent wage increases have only been implemented to keep pace with the rising inflation that has kept real wages from appreciating since 1992.

The Central Asian republics face a wide range of problems and challenges that have the potential to weaken severely the legitimacy of the current regimes and bring about chronic political instability. In most instances economic conditions have worsened for the average citizen since independence. Part of the problem may be attributed to widespread corruption that has enriched those closest to the centers of political power. No serious attempt has yet been made to combat corruption or improve the transparency of government financial activities in any of the republics.

Each republic faces unique challenges that have the potential to alter its political chemistry in the future. Kazakstan has been confronted with an ethnic dilemma since independence thanks to its Slavic population, which is estimated to be nearly 35 percent of the inhabitants. Secessionist expressions by some Slavic organizations are a serious concern of the Kazak government. Uzbekistan faces a growing Islamic threat that has been gathering strength because of the repressive policies of the government and the failure of economic reform. Kyrgyzstan also faces an Islamic threat, which has been exacerbated by pronounced economic inequality. Tajikistan's fragile stability has been constantly threatened by regionalism and drug lords who have continued to export large quantities of drugs through Central Asia to Europe. Finally, the Turkmen president has had serious health problems in the past, the recurrence of which could promote uncertainty regarding the transition of power.

None of the Central Asian republics has an adequate military force to defend the largely porous borders against potential security threats. Most have signed bilateral treaties with Russia for the purpose of territorial defense. In addition, several multilateral treaties under the jurisdiction of the *Commonwealth of Independent States (CIS) have been in effect since 1992, which in principle are designed to offer protection in case of an external military threat. Tajikistan has relied on Russia's heavy military presence to defend its border with Afghanistan both during and after that country's civil war. An estimated 19,000 Russian soldiers have been stationed in the republic.

Given its landlocked status and its strong ties to Russia, Central Asia will remain a minor player in the international politics of the early twenty-first century, one whose presence will be overshadowed by the Russian Federation and its desire to remain the dominant force in the region. Central Asia, however, is blessed with sizable hydrocarbon resources located predominantly in Kazakhstan and Turkmenistan, as well as mineral resources, including gold, titanium, uranium, and other nonferrous metals. But the development of hydrocarbon resources depends on the construction of new pipelines, which have proved to be costly and difficult to achieve politically. Russia has acted to prevent or to delay the construction of alternative pipeline routes that could bypass its territories. Disputes over the legal status of the Caspian Sea, where most of the oil deposits are located, have also been a critical factor in delaying offshore development of energy resources. Once completed, these pipelines could bring an estimated seven million barrels of oil per day to the world markets within two decades: it is only then that the region may play a pivotal role in global energy markets. China has also increased its involvement in the energy sector of Central Asia as it moves to secure its growing energy needs into the next century. In 1997, China signed a $9.5 billion oil contract with Kazakstan to build a pipeline to the east and to develop the Uzen oil field in the southwestern part of the republic.

The gradual incorporation of central Asia into the global economy so far has produced mixed results. On the positive side, independence has offered these republics the opportunity to diversify export destinations and demand world market prices for their raw materials. This has allowed the Central Asian republics to somewhat increase their revenues. On the negative side, fluctuations in world market prices have begun to create financial instability in some republics. Kazakstan, for instance, was hard hit in 1998 as oil prices began to plummet, thus causing a significant revenue shortfall, as budget estimates were calculated on the basis of higher export receipts. Central Asia has also been affected by the financial crisis in Asia, as many Southeast Asian countries have entered into commercial intercourse with the region. Consequently, the much-needed foreign investment projects and commercial activities have been put on hold to the detriment of the region.

Although the composition of the region's trading partners has changed since 1992, with many European and Asian countries involved in commerce, Russia is still the main trading partner. In the absence of adequate hard currency, the Central Asian republics have been engaged in barter trade with Russia and the other CIS countries to satisfy domestic needs. Central Asia will not be a significant factor affecting global economic processes in the near future; given its vast energy resources, however, it is certain that the region will assume a higher profile as it carries on its quest for true economic and political independence.

(See also ISLAM; POST-COMMUNISM.)

Alexander Bennigsen and S. Enders Wimbush, *Muslims of the Soviet Empire: A Guide* (Bloomington, Ind., 1986). Ali Banuazizi and Marvin Weiner, *The New Geopolitics of Central Asia and Its Borderlands* (Bloomington, Ind., 1994). Mehrdad Haghayeghi, *Islam and Politics in Central Asia* (New York, 1996).

MEHRDAD HAGHAYEGHI

CENTRAL EUROPE cannot be sharply delimited on a map. Although it is situated on the east-west axis of the continent—the adjective "central" here signifies an in-between (as in Central America) rather than being at a hub—Central Europe is less a geographical entity than an intellectual construct. Occasionally an alternative name—East-Central Europe—has been applied to it. And indeed, while the countries comprising it—with Poland, Hungary, and Czechoslovakia at the core—were part of the Soviet bloc, it used to be called Eastern Europe.

In its original German form, the term first gained wide currency beginning in 1915 with the publication of Friedrich Naumann's book *Mitteleuropa*. In *Mitteleuropa*—100,000 copies of which were sold within six months—Naumann evoked the idea of the common destiny of smaller European nations whose variety and distinct identities could be preserved in a supranational, federative organism. The Austro-Hungarian monarchy might have played this role if it had not disintegrated. A body of writings refers to the Danube as a geographical linchpin and cultural metaphor of identity *cum* variety embedded in the idea of Central Europe.

After World War I the map of Central Europe was redrawn to include a number of new or restored state entities: the so-called successor states. Following the lofty principles introduced at the Versailles peace conference (1919) by the U.S. President Woodrow Wilson, the inhabitants of reconstructed Europe were to live under self-government in their own nation-states. Neither ideal could be successfully implemented, however, because of the patchwork of ethnic settlements throughout Central Europe.

With the advent of *fascism in Italy and in Germany, aggressive *nationalism and authoritarian rule came to dominate politics in Central Europe. This brought the gradual erosion of democratic institutions in all countries of the region with the exception of Czechoslovakia. In the words of a contemporary historian, it was an epoch characterized by the rule of "little dictators." Appeasement of Hitler's territorial claims against Czechoslovakia by the Western powers at the Munich Conference (1938) revealed how defenseless small European countries were against more powerful and aggressive neighbors. After the conclusion of the Nazi-Soviet pact in August 1939 and the outbreak of World War II in September, some were directly occupied, some joined the Axis, and some were created anew (notably Slovakia and Croatia) under Nazi sponsorship eager to exploit ethnic resentments.

Central Europe suffered staggering material and human losses during World War II, the most devastating being the *Holocaust of European Jewry. But other national groups—notably Poles, Serbs, and Croats—lost several million people as well. Moreover, the war brought population transfers and boundary shifts to the region. Thus the Central Europe that emerged from the conflict was virtually uninhabited by Jews or Germans, two groups which until then had been a ubiquitous and essential component of its urban landscape. At the conference tables of Tehran (1943) and Yalta (1945), arrangements for the postwar world order made by Winston Churchill, Franklin D. Roosevelt, and Joseph Stalin recognized Central Europe as the Soviet Union's buffer zone. In the political vocabulary the term "Yalta" soon replaced "Munich" as a symbol of unprincipled and shortsighted Western realpolitik.

By 1948 in all countries of the region political pluralism was eradicated, Socialist parties were absorbed by local Communist parties, and an effective one-party system was installed under the close supervision of networks of Soviet advisers and a ubiquitous security police. The Iron Curtain fell over what was now known as Eastern Europe while local regimes, "people's democracies," proceeded to emulate the Soviet model. The state took ownership of material resources and control over production. Economic planning and collectivization of agriculture were implemented. *Secularization and indoctrination in Marxist ideology proceeded apace. In slavish replication of the Soviet paradigm, indigenous Communist Party leaders were idolized as "little Stalins," while many eminent Communists were purged in a series of show trials.

Thus, the European satellites of the Soviet Union—with the exception of Yugoslavia, whose Communist leader, Josip Broz *Tito, was branded a renegade by Stalin—became a part of "the Soviet bloc." Their economic integration was safeguarded through the Council for Mutual Economic Assistance (1949–1991), and military integration through membership in the *Warsaw Treaty Organization, or Warsaw Pact (1955–1991).

The mid-1950s, the years following Stalin's death, brought significant political change to Central Europe. Stalin's "personality cult" was denounced in the Soviet Union and a "thaw," a liberalization, followed in the Soviet bloc. In Hungary this led to the proclamation of neutrality by Imre Nagy, a Communist leader turned patriot, and a bloody military intervention by the Red Army to suppress the national uprising. In Czechoslovakia the process of de-Stalinization lasted longer and culminated only in 1968, when Alexander Dubcek committed the Communist Party to a reform policy dubbed "Socialism with a Human Face." Yet another military intervention by the Soviet Union (this time assisted by the other Warsaw Pact armies) cut the process short in August 1968.

In the 1970s there was détente with the West and mounting social tensions in the Soviet-bloc countries. In accordance with the "third basket" provisions of the *Helsinki Accords (1976) *human rights began to be invoked in political discourse. Human rights activists in Central Europe openly challenged the ruling Communist regimes. Opposition milieus evolved a new strategy of social action practicing freedom of speech, openly addressing their fellow citizens, and promoting *civil society. In the summer of 1980 *Solidarity was born in the Gdansk shipyards under the charismatic leadership of Lech Wałęsa.

Even though suffering organizational setbacks and imprisonment of their leaders in the 1980s, Solidarity in Poland and *Charter 77 in Czechoslovakia eventually prevailed and transformed East European politics. Ideas of empowered citizenship, emancipated society, political and cultural *pluralism, elaborated in the writings of numerous talented writers and essayists (Václav *Havel among them), brought forth the strength of spiritual links with European politics and tradition. The concept of Central Europe made its comeback.

In the climate induced by pursuit of glasnost and perestroika in the Soviet Union the *1989 "refolution" (akin simultaneously to reform and revolution) took place in Central Europe. With the exception of Romania, and until civil war broke out in Yugoslavia in 1991, it was a nonviolent, negotiated process of regime change. Popular protests led to round-table negotiations and then to free elections, and instead of "people's democracies" there were by the end of 1990 multiparty parliamentary republics in Central Europe. To be sure, institutionalization of political democracy was only slowly taking root there, but, surprisingly, it proved easier to accomplish than transformation of the economic system.

There was broad agreement that market institutions and private property ought to replace central planning and state ownership in economy. But the sheer scale of changes required to implement this transition was unprecedented. All of the Soviet-bloc countries suffered widespread environmental devastation. Banking systems, financial markets, unemployment services—infrastructure that was indispensable to the transition—were nonexistent. Resources necessary to sustain a market economy—institutions, procedures, managerial skills, adequately trained work force, capital—were sorely lacking.

In the decade following the 1989 revolutions, Poland, Hungary, and the Czech Republic have been accepted into *NATO (1999); their economies grow robustly in multiyear series; and their post-communist parties became loyal participants in the electoral process, occasionally winning (and then relinquishing) parliamentary majorities. As Central European states prepare to join the European Union in the first decade of the twenty-first century, liberty and the market economy appear to be solidly rooted in the region.

(See also NINETEEN EIGHTY-NINE; PRAGUE SPRING; POST-COMMUNISM.)

Anthony Polonsky, *The Little Dictators: The History of Eastern Europe Since 1918* (London, 1975). Timothy Garton Ash, *The Uses of Adversity:*

Essays on the Fate of Central Europe (New York, 1989). Joseph Rothschild, *Return to Diversity: A Political History of East Central Europe Since World War II* (New York, 1989). George Schopflin, ed., *In Search of Central Europe* (Totowa, N.J., 1989). Vladimir Tismaneanu, ed., *The Revolutions of 1989* (London, 1999).

JAN T. GROSS

CENTRAL INTELLIGENCE AGENCY. The shock of Pearl Harbor and the realization of the *Cold War prompted the 1947 National Security Act, which created the Central Intelligence Agency (CIA) as the United States' first peacetime foreign *intelligence organization, covering espionage, counterespionage, and intelligence analysis. The agency was prohibited from operating inside the United States and was placed under the direction of the president through the National Security Council (NSC). It coordinates intelligence from all sources and from all departments of U.S. government. The 1949 Central Intelligence Agency Act empowered the director of central intelligence (DCI) to spend agency money "without regard to the provisions of law and regulation": this provides the legal authority for covert actions (e.g., support for foreign political parties and trade unions) and operations (e.g., organizing the overthrow of a foreign government). In 1976 President Gerald Ford issued an executive order prohibiting the agency from conducting *assassinations. In 1981 President Ronald Reagan authorized the agency to operate within the United States to collect "significant" foreign intelligence as long as spying on the domestic operations of U.S. citizens and corporations is not involved. In 1982 the Boland amendment forbade the CIA to engage in or fund activities aimed at the overthrow of the Sandinista government in Nicaragua. In 1990 a congressional inspector general was appointed.

Extraordinary technical achievements characterized the CIA's first decades. Richard Bissell (deputy director responsible for operations, 1958–1962), a genius at intelligence management, developed the U-2 and SR-71 spy planes and the first spy satellites. The U-2 moved from the drawing board in 1954 to first flight in less than a year. It was at the experimental edge of aviation technology, flying higher and longer than any other airplane. U-2 photographs caused the U.S. Air Force to retarget and remap the USSR before Francis Gary Powers was shot down in a U-2 over the Soviet Union on 1 May 1960. The SR-71, operational from 1965, officially broke the world's speed and altitude records in 1990. Spy satellites became the principal means of intelligence collection from the early 1960s and remain so in the present day.

Until the mid-1970s, individual congressional leaders, rather than committees, exercised oversight of the CIA. With the *Vietnam War and *Watergate, attitudes changed, and the place—if any—for secrecy in the democracy became a political issue. President Ford's Rockefeller Commission (1975) and the Pike and Church congressional committees (1975–1976) revealed assassination plots against foreign leaders, notably Patrice *Lumumba in the Congo (1960) and Fidel *Castro (1961–1964); domestic surveillance of a number of U.S. citizens and journalists; mail opening; and possession of lethal toxins and devices. The investigations found that the agency had not been a "rogue elephant," but concluded that stricter authority and control were required. A new understanding developed between Congress, the presidency, and the agency, and a place for secrets was acknowledged by im-

plication. The CIA began to report not only to the president and the NSC but also to many congressional committees, in particular the Intelligence Oversight and the Appropriations committees, which in turn raised questions about CIA secrecy and security. Agency officers naturally grew reluctant to take decisions that might involve contentious sessions in Congress. In order to overcome this problem, Reagan's NSC staff itself organized support for anti-Sandinista forces, thus circumventing the Boland amendment but also setting the stage for the Iran-Contra scandal.

By 1994, as a consequence of the end of the Cold War and the Gulf War, the agency's focus had changed from analysis to providing support for the war-makers. In turn, this resulted in greater emphasis on technical development and collections systems, and less emphasis on political/analytical information. The ending of SR-71 spy plane operations in 1990 helped to compound the change. A perceived result was the acknowledged agency failure to predict nuclear weapons testing by India in May 1998. The DCI, while being the head of the agency, is also nominally the head of all U.S. intelligence and the president's chief intelligence officer. The relationship between the DCI and the president has been the key element determining the influence of the agency. Allen Dulles (DCI 1953–1961) was close to President Dwight Eisenhower, and oversaw many of the agency's most famous exploits, including the overthrow of Jacobo Arbenz in Guatemala (1954), the Berlin Tunnel tapping into Soviet land lines (1955), and the public failure to overthrow Castro via the Bay of Pigs Invasion (1961). Richard Helms (DCI 1966–1973) used his influence with Lyndon Johnson to warn about the growing dangers of U.S. involvement in Vietnam, and despite pressure from Richard Nixon, kept the agency out of the Watergate scandal. William Colby (DCI 1973–1976) consciously created the modern agency by revealing controversial secrets, forcing Congress, the presidency, and the population at large to accept the reality of an intelligence agency. William Casey (DCI 1981–1987) was the only DCI to achieve cabinet rank.

(See also CONGRESS, U.S.; PRESIDENCY, U.S.; SECURITY.)

John Ranelagh, *The Agency* (New York, 1987). Rhodri Jeffreys-Jones, *The CIA and American Democracy* (New Haven, Conn., 1989). Christopher Andrew, *For the President's Eyes Only* (New York, 1995).

JOHN RANELAGH

CENTRALLY PLANNED ECONOMY. See COMMAND ECONOMY.

CHAD. The recent history of Chad has been quite exceptional compared with that of other African polities south of the Sahara. When the country became independent in August 1960, after slightly more than half a century of French colonization, internal tensions were already building. Chad's first president, François (later N'Garta) Tombalbaye, came to power in the late 1950s as head of the then-dominant Parti Progressiste Tchadien, a party whose membership was drawn chiefly from the more developed south (about one-quarter of the national territory, comprising slightly less than 50 percent of the population, 6.2 million in 1993). The inhabitants of the north, almost entirely Muslim, were politically divided among themselves, but soon became antagonized by the increasingly authoritarian rule of President Tombalbaye. The antagonism was deepened by the presence in the northern provinces of a large number of civil servants from the south. Some of this stratum of officials were corrupt, and many, being Christians or believers in traditional African religions, did not understand local cultures and customs.

This uneasy situation led, in 1965–1968, to a series of grassroots peasant revolts in several of the northern provinces and to the creation of a nominally radical and anti-imperialist exile political movement, the Front de Libération Nationale du Tchad (FROLINAT), that endeavored to unite the various local peasant movements. At first the FROLINAT rebellion did not constitute a real menace to the Chadian state, although the Tombalbaye regime lost control over part of the north and had to turn to France for military assistance during 1969–1972. In 1977, however, branches of FROLINAT began to receive extensive support from *Libya, which claimed Chad's northern Aozou Strip as Libyan territory and, more generally, wanted to exercise greater influence over the Saharan and Sahelian regions of Chad. FROLINAT now represented a truly formidable rebel force. In the meantime, the Chadian army, headed by General Félix Malloum, had taken power in April 1975; Tombalbaye was killed in the coup.

A series of bloody battles and several rounds of diplomatic negotiations led to the formation in late 1979 of a national coalition government headed by Goukouni Weddeye, a FROLINAT leader. Soon afterward, in April 1980, new tensions developed when FROLINAT leaders quarreled among themselves about the proper extent of Libyan aid and influence in Chadian affairs. Hissein Habré, then minister of defense and a staunch anti-Qaddafi politician, left the government; another civil war erupted, ending in victory for Habré and his Forces Armées du Nord in June 1982 (marking, incidentally, the first time a guerrilla movement had ever come to power in independent Africa).

The protracted civil war had several important consequences. First, with the Libyan intervention, the conflict became fully internationalized. Habré received support from the Sudan, Egypt, Saudi Arabia, and the United States in his anti-Qaddafi crusade, while France came to his rescue in 1983 by sending troops in response to a thinly disguised Libyan invasion.

Second, during the turmoils of the civil war, Chad nearly ceased to exist as a political entity. From February 1979 until the summer of 1982, Chad's southern provinces functioned as an independent state in all but name, while various FROLINAT "warlords" exercised autonomous control over northern provinces. Only with Habré's military victory was central authority reestablished.

Third, the civil war virtually destroyed the economy of a country that, already at independence, had been counted among the poorest in the world, with virtually no resources except agriculture and animal husbandry. (Cotton is the main export crop; oil has been discovered in the south, but uncertainties remain about the exploitation. The stabilization of Habré's regime led to lavish economic aid, principally from France and the United States, but Chad nevertheless remains a poor and undeveloped country.

At the end of 1989, Habré's regime seemed rather stable. However, a split within the regime brought renewed warfare. In April 1989, several military commanders, led by Colonel Idriss Déby, had fled to the Sudan denouncing Habré's dic-

tatorial rule. They represented two ethnic groups from the center-east, the Zaghawa and the Hadjeraï, that had backed Habré when he came to power in 1982 but that now withdrew their allegiance.

In exile, Déby founded a new political movement, the Mouvement Patriotique du Salut (MPS), and started to build up his armed forces with limited help from Libya and the Sudan. Although he seemed at first no real menace to Habré, a surprise offensive in late 1990 led to the unexpected breakdown of the incumbent regime. On 1 December 1990 Habré went into exile in Senegal and Idriss Déby became Chad's new ruler.

The new regime's political record is rather contradictory. Freedom of the press was restored in late 1990, and political parties were permitted beginning in 1992. (As of 1998 there were more than sixty.) After a Sovereign National Conference in 1993 followed by a protracted transitional period, a new democratic constitution was adopted by referendum in March 1996. It provided for a presidential regime some parliamentary control. Idriss Déby won a landslide victory in the presidential elections of June–July 1996 and was confirmed as head of state, while his party, the MPS, obtained a narrow majority in the National Assembly in the 1997 parliamentary elections. The results of both elections, however, have been contested by Déby's principal opponents; in fact, they were not entirely "fair and free." Moreover, the regime does not really control the armed forces, which has led to acute security problems throughout the country and protests from *human rights organizations. Armed opposition groups are still active in some parts of the country, especially in the southern regions where oil has been discovered. The outcome of Chad's democratization process thus remains uncertain.

(See also GUERRILLA WARFARE.)

R. Buijtenhuijs, *La Conférence Nationale Souveraine du Tchad: Un essai d'histoire immédiate* (Paris, 1993). S. C. Nolutshungu, *Limits of Anarchy: Intervention and State Formation in Chad* (Charlottesville, Va., 1996).

ROBERT BUIJTENHUIJS

CHARTER 77. The most important dissident organization in *Czechoslovakia, Charter 77 was founded in January 1977. It was established by dissident writers, philosophers, and other intellectuals, including Václav *Havel, to protest against the systematic violation of *human rights in Czechoslovakia. The influence of the charter proved to be far greater than its 1,300 signatories. Charter activities helped to keep alive free thought during the communist period. Charter activists also founded the Civic Forum, the umbrella group that emerged in November 1989 to lead the Velvet Revolution that ousted the communist system.

Outraged by the harsh sentences meted out to a group of Czech rock musicians, the Plastic People of the Universe, and inspired by the *Helsinki Accords, the charter originally functioned as a human rights group. Its spokespersons called on Czech and Slovak leaders to observe the international agreements they had signed, as well as Czech and Slovak law. Despite harassment the charter continued its activities throughout the rest of the communist period in Czechoslovakia.

In the early 1980s, the emphasis of the charter's activities shifted. Charter spokespersons continued to defend human rights, but they also began issuing position papers that provided alternative perspectives on economic, political, and social problems. They also discussed issues that the communist authorities ignored. The charter thus came to serve as a focus of a second, independent intellectual community. Charter documents also came to be known to large circles of people still in the official world.

The charter's impact on policy making was extremely limited during the communist period due to its small numbers and the harsh response of the regime. At the same time, the continued existence of the charter was important not only to later developments in Czechoslovakia but throughout Central and Eastern Europe. Dissidents in Poland, Hungary, and elsewhere drew inspiration from the charter. As the Czechoslovak Communist Party leadership hesitatingly implemented certain aspects of Gorbachev's policies in Czechoslovakia, the ground that the charter's activities had helped to prepare bore fruit in the increased willingness of the population, including young people, to challenge the regime by engaging in open protests and founding illegal groups. In the early days after the brutal police attack on peaceful student demonstrators in November 1989, charter activists took the lead in organizing the Civic Forum and negotiating with the communist leadership to end communist rule.

The charter continued to exist after the end of communism in Czechoslovakia. Many charter activists held crucial positions after 1989. At a summer 1990 conference, charter activists decided to continue to serve as a watchdog to see that the new, democratic regime in Czechoslovakia respected human rights. However, in 1992, the charter was disbanded.

(See also CENTRAL EUROPE; COMMUNIST PARTY STATES; NINETEEN EIGHTY-NINE; PRAGUE SPRING.)

H. Gordon Skilling, *Samizdat and an Independent Society in Central and Eastern Europe* (Columbus, 1989).

SHARON L. WOLCHIK

CHERNOBYL NUCLEAR ACCIDENT. The nuclear accident that occurred on 26 April 1986 at Chernobyl, a town in Ukraine situated approximately 60 miles (100 km.) north of Kiev, is an event that seems to become increasingly important with time. The reason is that its impact on human health and on agriculture, the environment, the economy, and future energy strategies continues to mount each year. Moreover, its effects have extended beyond the former *Soviet Union to all states that use nuclear energy. For this reason, and because of public sensitivity about nuclear issues, neither the Soviet government nor other governments were eager to publish information about the accident and its consequences. As a result, new facts are still emerging, and assessments of the accident keep changing.

Most of the studies that have been made of the medical and environmental impact of the accident remain classified. The continued lack of openness about Chernobyl reflects the fact that the Soviet authorities did not have a consistent, rational policy and were unable to respond to the challenges that the accident produced. On the positive side, however, after Chernobyl there was more frankness about other accidents, both before and after, and the disaster can be seen as one of the triggers that stimulated *glasnost in the USSR.

There is no doubt that the Chernobyl accident dealt a

crushing blow to the prestige of Soviet science and technology. It also ruined the nuclear energy program in the Soviet Union and Eastern and Central Europe. It turned the embryonic Soviet environmental movement into a strong political force that formed links with local nationalist movements in key Soviet republics. Internationally it served as a stark warning that pollution cannot be contained within one country and that greater international cooperation is required to deal with it and other global problems. Furthermore, it demonstrated the need for stricter international supervision of nuclear facilities. As a result, the International Atomic Energy Agency (IAEA) gained prominence and became more effective.

Economic Cost and Impact on World Nuclear Industry. In purely financial terms the cost of the accident, initially estimated in July 1986 at 2 billion rubles (US$3 billion), increased to 8 billion rubles in 1987. By 1990, when the Soviet government allocated special funds to the most affected regions, the cost had escalated to 50 billion rubles. If one adds the costs of the tasks that remain to be done, together with those of canceled or frozen nuclear energy projects, the cost will rise to nearly 200 billion rubles by the year 2000, and it will continue to rise well into the next century.

The world nuclear energy industry was severely affected by the accident. Before 1986 it was assumed that in the unlikely event that a maximum nuclear reactor accident occurred, it would involve the meltdown of the reactor core owing to the accumulation of fission radionuclides. If this occurred at the end of the reactor cycle, the fission radionuclides would generate about 4 percent of the total thermal power of a working reactor. Most safety devices, therefore, were designed to protect the environment from such an accident.

What happened at Chernobyl was far worse. The total power of the reactor surged to about 100 and then to 440 times its normal full power within four seconds, provoking a "prompt criticality" explosion. The fuel channels ruptured, the reactor core was destroyed, and the 2,000-ton, three-meter-thick upper plate was displaced, shearing off more than 1,000 steel pipes attached to the primary circuit. The bottom 1,000-ton concrete plate was pressed down, smashing the metal structures beneath it. The local release of thermal energy in the reactor core was about 10,000 times higher than in the Three Mile Island nuclear accident in Pennsylvania in March 1979. Neither the safety regulations nor risk factor calculations had envisaged the possibility of this type of accident.

Although Western authorities insisted that the design flaws that made the accident possible were unique to that type of graphite-moderated, high-power, boiling channel type and were not to be found in Western or Japanese reactors, nuclear power everywhere was affected. The new safety regulations recommended by the IAEA made nuclear energy far more expensive. In 1986, 430 reactors in twenty-six countries generated nearly 16 percent of the world's electricity. A further 149 reactors were planned or under construction. Within two years this number had fallen to ninety-six. The Soviet energy program suffered most, but many projects in Eastern and Western Europe and in the developing countries were also canceled. All older Magnox-type, graphite-moderated reactors in Britain were shut down.

Impact on Soviet and East European Energy Programs. Because Soviet oil production had declined, nuclear power was given priority in the economic development plan proposed by Mikhail *Gorbachev for the period 1985–2000. Nuclear-generated electricity was expected to reach 40 percent of the total energy requirement toward the end of the century. Nearly half of the new capacity was planned to come from graphite-moderated, high-power, boiling channel reactors of the Chernobyl type. Studies of the causes of the accident, however, identified several fundamental design flaws in the reactor model. As a result, it was eliminated from the nuclear energy program and extensive modifications had to be made to the thirteen existing reactors of this type.

Several pressurized water reactors and five military plutonium-producing reactors were shut down for good. Others already under construction were canceled or temporarily halted for safety reasons. Levels of production of nuclear-generated electricity remained stagnant, causing an acute energy crisis that set back Soviet industrial development in 1986–1990. Energy shortages, compounded by a shortage of investment capital (owing both to the cost of Chernobyl and to reduced oil revenues) gradually caused the total failure of the "administrative command" economy, contributing significantly to the decision to adopt market-oriented economic principles as part of a new *perestroika package.

The use of crude oil and oil fuel to generate electricity and for heating increased. Soviet per capita oil consumption, already high (twelve barrels a year), rose even further. The result was a reduction in the amount of oil available for export. Eastern and Central European countries, heavily dependent on Soviet oil, were severely affected (they were further hit by the decision to charge them world prices in hard currency from the beginning of 1991) both by oil shortages and by the problems in the Soviet nuclear energy program: 49 percent of Hungarian, 36 percent of Bulgarian, 26 percent of Czechoslovakian, and 37 percent of Finnish electricity was produced by nuclear power stations built by the Soviet Union, as of 1989. Furthermore, in the future they will have to dispose of their own spent nuclear fuel and nuclear waste.

In the German Democratic Republic (GDR) there were four Soviet pressurized water reactors of the old type in 1990, producing 10 percent of the country's electricity. Five new units were under construction at the time of reunification. None of them met the safety standards of the Federal Republic of Germany (FRG). Because no alternative energy sources exist (except highly polluting lignite coal), it has been decided to close down the old reactors and to put the new models into operation after reequipping them.

Health Impact. After the accident 116,000 people were evacuated from the so-called exclusion zone, i.e., areas lying within a radius of 18.6 miles (30 km.) of the power station. Later, new areas of radioactive contamination were discovered to the west, north, and south of the exclusion zone, some with levels of radioactive cesium 137 well above 40 curies per square kilometer (above 1,500,000 Bq/m²). These were designated "special areas of strict radiological control," and about 600,000 inhabitants were registered to undergo periodic medical examinations for the rest of their lives. Their offspring would also be subject to lifelong medical checkups.

The permissible whole-life radiation exposure for these people was raised to 35 rem, higher than the permissible whole-life exposure for those working in the nuclear industry. But by 1990 some groups were already approaching the maximum level, and nearly 100,000 people from Byelorussia, the Ukraine, and the Bryansk region of the Russian Republic had to be resettled.

Nearly 500,000 people who had taken part in the initial stages of cleaning up, decontaminating the accident site and villages in the area, conducting dosimetry for radiation maps, patrolling the area, constructing protective dams and the cover for the damaged reactor, and so forth, had been exposed to high levels of radiation. They have established the Chernobyl Society to lobby for better medical care and financial compensation for health damage.

According to unofficial reports, radiation-linked health problems are affecting three groups in particular: evacuees from the exclusion zone, inhabitants of the special areas of strict radiological control, and people who were involved in dealing with the consequences of the accident. They are said to suffer both from specific conditions (increased incidence of thyroid deficiency and leukemia) and from nonspecific problems (especially nervous and respiratory disorders). However, there have been no official scientific or statistical reports of these problems.

The main delayed effect of radiation exposure—the increased incidence of cancer—will emerge twenty to forty years after the accident and will carry the problems of Chernobyl victims well into the twenty-first century. No information has been released about the incidence of genetic defects among newborn children or about the genetic effects on plants and animals in the exclusion zone and on farm animals near it.

Environmental and Antinuclear Movements. Before the Chernobyl disaster the Soviet environmental movement was weak and divided and there was no independent Soviet antinuclear movement. Officially sponsored groups campaigned against *nuclear weapons and nuclear war, not against nuclear power. After the accident antinuclear environmental groups began to emerge, and in some republics they combined nationalist grievances with their environmental concerns. The strongest opposition to nuclear power developed in the Ukraine and Byelorussia, the two republics that had suffered most from the accident.

There were more working and planned nuclear power stations in the Ukraine than in any other republic. The plan of the central government was to use nuclear-generated heat directly in some metallurgical technologies and to sell electricity from these power stations to Bulgaria, Hungary, and Romania. The planning, design, and implementation of all nuclear projects was done in Moscow, and there was little consultation with local communities about their need for power or the location of stations. When freely contested elections were held in 1989 and 1990, environmental movements used the opportunity to organize political campaigns and to elect representatives to the central and republican parliaments. In 1990 the Ukrainian Supreme Soviet declared the republic an "ecological disaster area" and demanded that the three remaining working reactors at Chernobyl be closed. The first *green party was officially registered in the Ukraine in 1990. In Lithuania antinuclear groups campaigned successfully against the construction of the third and fourth units at the Ignalina plant.

In 1988 the antinuclear movement also began to campaign against underground nuclear tests in the Semipalatinsk region of Kazakhstan, the main nuclear test site since the first Soviet atomic bomb was exploded in 1949. Despite strong resistance from the ministry of defense, the Semipalatinsk test site was closed in 1990.

Future Tasks. Recent calculations show that nearly 70 million curies of radioactivity were released by the Chernobyl accident. Half of them were deposited within the then Soviet Union. By 1990 only the long-lived radionuclides (cesium 137, strontium 90, and plutonium) were creating problems. The first maps published in 1990 showed the uneven, almost random distribution of these radionuclides. About half of the cesium and strontium and most of the plutonium remain inside the exclusion zone, which has now been converted into an ecological study area for research into plants and animals. A significant proportion (probably about 1 million curies) is located in hundreds of temporary waste disposal facilities where the topsoil that was scraped from a million hectares (2.5 million acres) of land in and around the Chernobyl station, asphalt and concrete from the roads, vehicles, and trees that were killed by the initial fallout have been stored.

There are about 1,540 lbs. (700 kg.) of plutonium, 95 lbs (43 kg.) of strontium 90, 179 lbs. (81 kg.) of cesium 137, and nearly 187 tons (170 metric tons) of uranium, totaling about 7 million curies of radioactivity, in the hastily constructed sarcophagus that covers the damaged reactor. But the metal structures inside the cover are rusting and becoming brittle, and volatile dust composed of "hot particles" from the melted fuel materials is building up. There is therefore a danger that some structures within the sarcophagus will collapse, allowing radioactivity to be released through holes in the cement. The present plan is to build a huge, solid cover that will seal the existing sarcophagus hermetically and serve as a safe tomb for at least 300 years.

Because of the very slow natural process of decontamination of soil tainted by strontium 90, cesium 137, and plutonium, the agricultural consequences will persist for forty to fifty years. About 2.5 million acres (1 million hectares) have been taken out of agricultural use and will be reforested. Field, meat, and dairy products from a further 5 million acres (2 million hectares) must checked for contamination and subjected to special processing methods to reduce radioactivity before consumption.

The Chernobyl accident was a turning point in Soviet history and in public perceptions of nuclear power. It reversed the trend toward wider reliance on nuclear power and discredited the belief that this was the ultimate answer to the world's energy needs.

(See also ENVIRONMENTALISM; NUCLEAR FREEZE.)

Report of the U.S. Department of Energy's Team Analyses of the Chernobyl-4 Atomic Energy Station Accident Sequence, U.S. Department of Energy (Washington, D.C., 1986). *Summary Report on the Post-Accident Review Meeting on the Chernobyl Accident,* INSAG-I Report, International Atomic Energy Agency, Safety Series (Vienna, 1986). Viktor Haynes and Marko Bojcun, *The Chernobyl Disaster* (London, 1988). Zhores A. Medvedev, *The Legacy of Chernobyl* (New York, 1990).

ZHORES A. MEDVEDEV

CHILE lies along the west coast of South America, stretching 2,600 miles (4,150 km.) from Peru to the Antarctic. Numbering approximately 14 million, its Spanish-speaking population is almost 90 percent Roman Catholic. Chile is distinctive in Latin America because it had one of the most stable, progressive constitutional democracies prior to 1973 and experienced one of the most durable, conservative military dictatorships from 1973 until the return of democracy in 1990. In the closing years of the twentieth century, its ability to consolidate civilian rule was a litmus test of the democratic trend that engulfed Latin America.

After independence from Spain in 1818, Chile suffered the civil strife typical of former colonies. Unlike its neighbors, however, it quickly established a stable republic under the constitution of 1833, which lasted until 1925. That oligarchic system concentrated power in the hands of the president, the landowning families, the merchants, and the Roman Catholic Church. It nevertheless sustained civilian rule and gradually incorporated new social groups and parties through peaceful elections. The only disruption of regular presidential turnover occurred during a brief civil war in 1891. That conflict between the legislative and executive branches resulted in a semiparliamentary republic in which congressional authority outweighed that of the presidency.

The constitution of 1925, which lasted until 1973, restored a strong presidential system, separated church and state, and codified rights for labor. After its enactment, a military dictatorship ruled from 1927 to 1931, undercut by the Great Depression of 1929. From 1932 until 1973, Chile maintained an unusually open, sturdy representative democracy. It was noteworthy for its multiparty system reminiscent of West European polities. It included three poles clearly defined by ideology and class: a conservative right based among the economic elites, a reformist center rooted in the middle strata, and a Marxist left anchored in the proletariat. From the 1930s through the 1960s, centrist coalition governments dedicated to *import-substitution industrialization and to welfare for the urban middle and working classes prevailed.

An erratic but persistent leftward trend in voting and policies culminated in the first free election anywhere of a Marxist president, Salvador *Allende Gossens in 1970. Mainly backed by the Socialist and Communist parties, he won with 36 percent of the popular vote in a three-way race. He greatly accelerated the reforms—especially *nationalization of U.S. copper mines and redistribution of agricultural lands—begun under his Christian Democrat predecessor, Eduardo Frei Montalva. In order to move the country from state capitalism toward state socialism, Allende expropriated the major means of production and promoted massive redistribution to urban and rural workers.

Backed by the United States, centrist forces (the Partido Demócrata Cristiano) joined rightists (the Partido Nacional) in an alliance against Allende's socialist project. Class conflict and political polarization escalated. On 11 September 1973, President Allende died defending his government, democracy, and socialism against a coup d'état led by Army General Augusto *Pinochet Ugarte.

For nearly a decade, Pinochet reigned without significant challenge. After exterminating, exiling, or imprisoning thousands of leaders of the left and labor, Pinochet relied on a coalition of military officers, technocrats, and capitalists. He constructed an extremely repressive system of one-man rule, giving the president iron control over both the government and the armed forces.

Pinochet ended not only democratic politics but also statist economic policies designed to subsidize manufacturing and social welfare. Guided by economists enamored of the neoliberal model associated with the University of Chicago, the government shrank the role of the state in favor of the market. It liberalized trade, promoted nontraditional exports, slashed fiscal outlays, privatized public enterprises, pruned social services, and crippled labor unions. An economic boom from 1977 to 1981, called the Chilean "miracle," was achieved at the cost of regressive income distribution and high unemployment.

At the pinnacle of his authoritarian politics and free-market economics, Pinochet convoked a noncompetitive plebiscite in 1980. It approved a constitution to continue him in office through 1988, when a subsequent plebiscite would be held to ratify his mandate for another eight years.

In the decade of the 1980s, Chile evolved from *authoritarianism to democracy as a result of five profound transformations. First, the international recession and debt crisis of 1981–1982 provoked modifications in the neoliberal economic model. After recovery began in 1985, the essential elements of the free enterprise approach were retained. Second, although most military and business leaders remained loyal to Pinochet, dissent grew in the previously solid ranks of regime supporters. Third, economic dislocations sparked massive social protests from 1983 to 1986. That mobilization of civil society spread from organized labor through the middle classes to end up concentrated in the urban shantytowns. Fourth, the previously shackled and dormant political parties recaptured center stage and took charge of the campaign to defeat Pinochet in the 1988 plebiscite. And fifth, the spread of democratization in the Western Hemisphere left the Pinochet regime isolated and defensive, particularly vis-à-vis pressures for liberalization from the United States.

An uneasy coalition of centrist and leftist parties known as the Concertation defeated Pinochet in the 1988 plebiscite, 55 percent to 43 percent. As a result, the government convened competitive presidential and congressional contests in 1989, won by the opposition by an identical margin. The opposition standard-bearer, Christian Democrat Patricio Aylwin, took office in March 1990. Thus ended peacefully seventeen years of harsh military rule within the legal framework erected by the dictatorship.

The Aylwin administration (1990–1994) was succeeded by that of another president from the Concertation, fellow Christian Democrat Eduardo Frei Ruiz Tagle (1994–2000). Both civilian governments in the 1990s pursued four main tasks. First, they maintained the market-oriented model, macroeconomic stability, and high rates of growth while reducing poverty. However, income distribution became more unequal, and many poorer Chileans complained about the continuing neglect of pent-up demands for social justice. Others lamented the deterioration of the environment that accompanied economic expansion.

Second, the Aylwin and Frei governments sought to consolidate and deepen democracy, mainly by whittling down the authoritarian impediments bequeathed by the Pinochet regime. They asserted civilian control over the armed forces, even though the military retained many prerogatives. In 1998, Pinochet stepped down as commander-in-chief of the army and became a senator for life. However, most attempts to reform the constitution and other key political institutions to eradicate the vestiges of authoritarianism, such as an electoral system biased toward the right and a judiciary relatively unresponsive to popular demands, were defeated by right-wing forces in Congress. At the same time, some social movements that had opposed the dictatorship lost momentum, and groups such as women and indigenous peoples protested insufficient government action on their behalf. While policy making became increasingly technocratic and pragmatic, political participation declined. Although polls revealed widespread support for the restored democracy, many citizens expressed little commitment to the system, and electoral turnout tapered off as the decade wore on.

Third, the Concertation labored to hold together its winning coalition, based mainly on the Christian Democrats and Socialists, bitter enemies under Allende who coalesced against Pinochet. Their continued electoral majorities maintained the alliance despite Socialist discontent over the Christian Democrats' monopoly of the presidency. Although unable to win the presidency in a popular vote against the Concertation, the rightist opposition controlled the Senate because the 1980 constitution reserved enough nonelected senatorial seats for conservatives. Torn between more democratic and more authoritarian elements, the right-wing groups were captained by two offshoots of the old National Party and the Pinochet camp: the Renovación Nacional and the Unión Democrática Independiente. The most ardent backers of the opposition were the business magnates and the armed forces.

Fourth, the first two democratic governments tried to deliver truth and justice to those who had suffered human rights abuses under Pinochet, without enraging the armed forces. A detailed report of the atrocities was issued by the government-appointed Truth and Reconciliation Commission and some compensation was paid to the victims. However, obstructionism from the military, the right, and the courts prevented a full accounting or retribution against the perpetrators. Forgetting and reconciling were limited, partly because new evidence of crimes kept surfacing, for example through discoveries of new burial grounds or revelations by foreign tribunals.

Despite shortcomings, Chile's redemocratization received high marks from most observers. In contrast with many Latin American countries, its transition took place under favorable economic circumstances and was regarded by some as a model for the rest of the hemisphere. Equally important, Chile's democratization entailed a return to deeply rooted values and institutions, now buttressed by a broad consensus against any return to the conflicts of the Allende and Pinochet years.

(See also DEMOCRATIC TRANSITIONS; MILITARY RULE; SOCIALISM AND SOCIAL DEMOCRACY; U.S.–LATIN AMERICAN RELATIONS.)

J. Samuel Valenzuela and Arturo Valenzuela, *Military Rule in Chile: Dictatorship and Oppositions* (Baltimore, 1986). Brian Loveman, *Chile: The Legacy of Hispanic Capitalism* (New York, 1988). Pamela Constable and Arturo Valenzuela, *A Nation of Enemies: Chile Under Pinochet* (New York, 1991). Timothy R. Scully, *Rethinking the Center: Party Politics in Nineteenth- and Twentieth-Century Chile* (Stanford, Calif., 1992). Leslie Bethell, ed., *Chile Since Independence* (Cambridge, U.K., 1993). Lois Hecht Oppenheim, *Politics in Chile: Democracy, Authoritarianism, and the Search for Development* (Boulder, Colo., 1993). Paul W. Drake and Iván

Jaksic, eds., *The Struggle for Democracy in Chile*, rev. ed. (Lincoln, Neb., 1995).

PAUL W. DRAKE

CHINA. The People's Republic of China (PRC) is one of the world's few remaining *communist party states. China, like Cuba, Vietnam, Laos, and North (the Democratic People's Republic of) Korea, is ruled by a political party that proclaims ideological allegiance to *Marxism-*Leninism, asserts the right to exercise leadership in nearly all spheres of society, and proscribes any opposition it judges to be a threat to its power. Why communist power survived in China after it collapsed in Russia and most other countries, and whether it will continue to survive, are two of the most intriguing and important questions in contemporary world politics.

Geography, Demography, and Administration. China occupies nearly 3.7 million square miles (9.5 million sq. km.) of the Asian continent with borders that stretch from India in the west to the Pacific Ocean in the east and from Russia in the north to Vietnam, Laos, and Burma in the south. In terms of area, it is the third largest country in the world, after Russia and Canada. It is the most populous country, with more than 1.2 billion people as of 2000. Owing to an aggressive—and sometimes coercive—family planning program, the population growth rate has been brought down to around 1.1 percent per year, very low for a country at China's level of economic development. China has not yet escaped its age-old dilemma of the race between the number of people and the availability of food: the country currently has about 20 percent of the world's population, but only 7 percent of its arable land.

Despite enormous economic progress since 1980, China is still among the poorer nations in the world. The GNP per capita, according to World Bank calculations, was US$750 (or US$3,220 at purchasing power parity) in 1998. Other indicators, however, suggest that the physical quality of life for the average citizen is better in China than it is most other developing countries. For example, life expectancy in China is seventy years (compared with sixty-three in India) and infant mortality is 31 per 1,000 live births (70 in India). Such figures reflect the relative priority that the Chinese government has given to basic health care and other welfare measures over the last several decades.

The PRC is made up of twenty-two provinces, five autonomous regions, and four centrally administered municipalities (including Beijing, the capital of the country, and Shanghai, its largest city). The autonomous regions are areas with high concentrations of non-Chinese ethnic minorities who altogether constitute approximately 8 percent of the total population. These regions (for example, *Tibet) are, according to the constitution, entitled to some measure of self-government in order to meet their special needs and to preserve their cultural identities; in reality, such autonomy, especially when it comes to political matters, is extremely limited.

The PRC is a unitary state in which the subnational levels are subordinate in all important matters to the center. Growing regional economic differentiation, ethnic assertiveness, and the complexity of modern administration in a continental-sized nation may increase centrifugal pressures on the PRC in the years ahead. Movement toward *federalism with more power sharing between the center and its constit-

uent units might ease some of these tensions. But such a trend would run against the grain of both deeply entrenched patterns formed when China was a highly centralized empire and the basic structure of the contemporary Chinese communist party state.

From Empire to People's Republic. China's birth as a modern nation-state was a painful one. The 2,000-year-old imperial system was destroyed by a combination of internal decline and external pressures that culminated in the Revolution of 1911 and the establishment of the Republic of China, whose first president was Sun Yat-sen. But the collapse of the empire was only the beginning of the *Chinese Revolution. The new republic quickly disintegrated into regional warlordism and ultimately civil war between two major claimants to national power, the Nationalist (or Kuomintang) Party led Chiang Kai-shek and the *Chinese Communist *Party (CCP). The CCP, under the leadership of Chairman *Mao Zedong, prevailed in this struggle and, in October 1949, proclaimed the establishment of the People's Republic of China. The Nationalists were forced to flee to the island of *Taiwan, ninety miles from the mainland, where, with American support and protection, they established a government in exile that retained the rubric of the Republic of China.

The first years of communist rule in China were dominated by the tasks of political consolidation, economic reconstruction, and social transformation. The early 1950s was a period of significant achievement for the new regime: a strong, effective central government was in place for the first time in nearly a century; industrial and agricultural production quickly reached and then surpassed prewar levels; and popular support was secured via successful campaigns to redistribute land to poor *peasants and eradicate long-standing social ills such as prostitution and opium addiction. Internationally, China asserted its reclaimed sovereignty by fighting the United States and its allies to a stalemate in the *Korean War; although this engagement was costly in economic and military terms, it bolstered the nation's pride and international prestige.

At the same time, there were clear signs that political repression and ideological dogmatism would be hallmarks of communist power. The party quickly backtracked from its initial pledges to go slow in the transition to socialism and to preside over a mixed economy and an inclusive polity. The socialization of the means of production in both industry and agriculture was set in motion and essentially completed by the mid-1950s, while substantial violence was unleashed against those judged to be enemies or doubters of the new order. The new state—with Mao Zedong in firm control of the party and Zhou Enlai overseeing the government bureaucracy as premier (or prime minister)—was structured in such a way as to ensure communist domination of the economy, politics, and cultural life.

In 1953, the PRC adopted its First Five-Year Plan. Based largely on the Soviet model, this plan put the greatest emphasis on the rapid expansion of heavy industry and the *collectivization of agriculture. The results of the plan in the industrial sector were quite impressive with overall output exceeding the target and rising more than 130 percent by 1957, the last year of the plan. In agriculture, the figures were less striking, although production did achieve a critical measure of success in outstripping population growth. However, the Chinese countryside was transformed during this period by the coercive establishment of large-scale cooperative farms (averaging 250 families) that expanded the scope of collective agriculture far beyond the more modest efforts that had been carried out in the wake of the earlier *land reform.

The central political event of this period—and one of the major turning points in the history of the PRC—was the "Hundred Flowers" movement of 1956, an ill-fated attempt initiated by Chairman Mao to liberalize China's political life and shake up the bureaucracy. Responding to what he perceived as the first manifestations of ideological retrogression in the Soviet Union and a flagging of revolutionary élan within the CCP, Mao let it be known that he welcomed public criticism of his regime's shortcomings ("Let a hundred flowers bloom"). But when the criticism became more intense than he expected and challenged the very nature of communist authority, he joined with the bureaucracy in sanctioning a vicious repression of all dissent. The subsequent "Anti-Rightist Campaign" of 1957 had the immediate result that hundreds of thousands of intellectuals were labeled as traitors; many of these were dismissed from their jobs or demoted, sent to jail, or banished to remote labor reform camps. More broadly, the campaign had the effect of casting a pall over China's intellectual life that would not be lifted until after Mao's death two decades later.

Radicalism Ascendant. The Hundred Flowers movement had occurred in the context of a debate within the CCP leadership about the path of China's future economic development. Some of the more conservative party leaders held to the view that the pattern established by the First Five-Year Plan was essentially correct and that, with moderate modifications stressing greater material incentives and technical assistance for the peasantry, agricultural production could be effectively stimulated to reach satisfactory levels. However, in the highly charged political milieu that followed the Anti-Rightist Campaign, Mao was able to prevail upon his colleagues to endorse his radical vision for a thorough break with the Soviet model of cautious planning and technocratic management. The result was the "Great Leap Forward" of 1958–1960.

This utopian campaign, with its stress on mass mobilization and moral-ideological incentives, was intended to be a great leap into both prosperity and *communism. In just a few years, it was hoped, China would jump into the forefront of industrial nations while at the same time completing the building of socialism to enter the more egalitarian communist stage of social development. The countryside was once more subjected to a precipitous reorganization when the agricultural cooperatives were merged into gigantic and unmanageable communes that encompassed as many as 20,000 families each. Fantastically high production targets were set for all sectors of the economy. More than a million backyard steel furnaces sprang up across the land in the effort to meet the goal of quickly overtaking Britain in steel production. Steel output did surge, but most of what was produced in these small-scale enterprises was useless. As the Leap unfolded, critics were silenced, either afraid to speak out or censured when they did.

The Great Leap turned into a great tragedy. Agricultural production plummeted as resources were wasted, the land was exhausted, and the labor force pushed beyond endurance. One result was the largest famine in human history, which directly or indirectly claimed between 20 and 30 million Chinese lives. Industrial production also collapsed, plunging the country into a deep depression. Poor weather and the withdrawal of Soviet advisers and technical assistance (a result of increasing ideological and strategic tensions in Sino-Soviet relations) played a role in exacerbating China's economic misfortunes during this time. But the major blame for the catastrophe must lie with the flawed vision and the political intolerance of China's top leaders—principally Mao Zedong.

The early 1960s was a time of recovery for the PRC. The Leap was abandoned and replaced by a more incremental development strategy that partook of elements of the First Five-Year Plan but allowed more leeway for market forces that had been squelched by both the Soviet model and the Maoist alternative. The communes were sharply reduced in size and function; bureaucratization supplanted mobilization; and meritocracy rather than equality was promoted as the guiding principle of China's *modernization. Although Mao retained significant power as chairman of the party during this period, his prestige was considerably diminished and day-to-day administration rested with other leaders, including Liu Shaoqi (president of the PRC), Zhou Enlai, and *Deng Xiaoping (secretary-general of the CCP).

By 1965, Chairman Mao had concluded that both he and China had been betrayed by some of the highest-ranking members of the CCP (especially Liu and Deng), and, indeed, that the whole party and country were in need of a reinfusion of revolutionary spirit. His solution was the "Great Proletarian Cultural Revolution," an engineered mass movement to isolate and remove those leaders who were seen to be leading China down the same "capitalist road" that the Soviet Union had already traversed. At the outset of the *Cultural Revolution, Mao forged an alliance of radical party ideologues, loyal military commanders, and tens of millions of student Red Guards to carry out his crusade against revisionism. From 1966 to 1969 (when the army, with Mao's blessing, stepped in to restore order), China was plunged into near anarchy: the economy was disrupted, the polity paralyzed, and society torn by a violent and vindictive witch-hunt for class enemies. Many of China's leaders were toppled from power and, along with numerous intellectuals, were publicly humiliated, physically abused, and imprisoned or sent into internal exile, where some (including President Liu Shaoqi) died of maltreatment.

During the next few years, the People's Liberation Army, under the command of a sycophantic Maoist, Lin Biao, dominated the Chinese political scene. A new wave of extreme leftist policies were implemented across a wide range of areas of life, including education, the arts, factory management, income distribution, and health care. Radicalism appeared triumphant.

But the 1970s turned out to be another decade of intense political and ideological struggle within China's communist party elite. In 1971, Lin Biao—Mao's closest ally during the Cultural Revolution and his chosen heir—allegedly attempted to have the chairman assassinated after the two parted ways on a number of issues including the new trend toward *détente in *Sino-American relations and the political role of the military. The mid-1970s witnessed a cataclysmic confrontation between the radical defenders of the legacies of the Cultural Revolution and more moderate leaders (including Zhou Enlai and the rehabilitated Deng Xiaoping) who urged that the nation's priorities be shifted from class struggle politics to economic modernization.

Reform and Repression in Post-Mao China. The death of Mao Zedong in September 1976 set the stage for the denouement of radical power in the PRC. A month later, Hua Guofeng, who had been lifted from relative obscurity by Mao as a compromise choice for premier following Zhou's death in January 1976, ordered the arrest of his radical rivals in the top leadership (the so-called Gang of Four, which included Mao's widow, Jiang Qing). Shortly thereafter, Hua was named to succeed Mao as chairman of the CCP.

But Hua himself was pushed aside in a few years. He was outmaneuvered by Deng Xiaoping, who had come back to the center of power from a second spell in political purgatory that had begun in mid-1976 after again incurring Mao's wrath because of his "heretical" views on economic policy. By the late 1970s, Deng Xiaoping was firmly installed as China's paramount leader, though he never took any of the highest formal positions in either the party or state hierarchy.

Under the rubric of building "socialism with Chinese characteristics," Deng used his position to launch China on an ambitious modernization drive. Eschewing many of the radical policies of the Maoist era, Deng oversaw the introduction of reforms in the 1980s that touched nearly every aspect of life in the PRC. Agriculture was decollectivized and authority for managing farm work devolved to the individual peasant household. Small-scale industrialization spread to such an extent in the countryside that an increasingly large proportion of the rural labor force began earning much of its income through nonfarm employment. Market mechanisms were allowed to supplement a greatly relaxed centrally planned *command economy. Enterprise management was decentralized and workers were induced to increase productivity by a host of material incentive schemes. Science, education, and cultural life in general were depoliticized in order to encourage China's intellectuals to devote their energies and talents to the country's modernization. A policy of "opening to the outside world" was introduced to encourage expanded trade, foreign investment, and cultural exchange. The overall effect of these reforms on the economy was tremendous, with GNP growth rates averaging about 10 percent per year for most of the 1980s and 1990s.

Political change was also on Deng's agenda. Curbs were placed on the arbitrary exercise of power and steps were taken to give some measure of regularity to the legal system. But Deng made it clear from the start of his reform effort that the political supremacy of the Communist Party was not to be challenged. He proved his inflexibility on this point by the ruthless suppression of a series of popular movements for greater democracy in 1979, 1986, and, most dramatically, in the crisis of June 1989, when hundreds of demonstrators were killed by army troops in the area around Beijing's *Tiananmen Square.

The brutal crushing of the Tiananmen protests ushered in a period of uneasy quiet in Chinese politics. Leaders considered too soft on the question of political reform, including party chief and one-time Deng protégé Zhao Ziyang, were purged or demoted. Power was in the hands of a coalition of octogenarians, headed by Deng Xiaoping, many of whom had made a pretense of retiring from active involvement in politics. The formal positions of state and party authority were held by their underlings, among them Jiang Zemin, a former mayor of Shanghai, who became CCP general secretary (the party's top office in the post-Mao era) in mid-1989.

Political repression and economic retrenchment characterized party-state policy in post-Tiananmen China, while anger, cynicism, and apathy best described the public mood in the very early 1990s. But in 1992, Deng, chastened by the collapse of communist regimes in the Soviet Union and East Central Europe, reignited economic reform, leading to more extensive marketization and *globalization of the Chinese economy. In the few years before his death in early 1997, Deng also gradually turned over greater power to Jiang Zemin, who, in addition to serving as head of the CCP, became president of the People's Republic in 1993. At century's end, Jiang was indisputably China's top leader and had proven to be a capable and faithful disciple of Deng Xiaoping's view that the prosperity and security of the PRC could best be gained by a combination of economic growth and communist rule.

China's Political System. The People's Republic of China is defined in the country's constitution as "a socialist state under the people's democratic dictatorship led by the working class and based on an alliance of workers and peasants." This formula effectively gives the CCP a monopoly on formal power and ostensibly legitimizes the proscription of meaningful opposition. There are a few noncommunist parties, but they are politically impotent and are allowed to function only so as long as they abide by strict guidelines set down by the CCP. There is considerably more latitude for the pursuit of independent nonpolitical interests than there was during the Maoist era. But most social organizations and professional or occupational associations serve as transmission belts for party policy or can operate openly only with official permission. The intensity of the crackdown that began in 1999 on the mystical Buddhist Falun Gong sect was motivated as much by the party's fear of the movement's popularity and autonomy as it was by the desire to suppress its religious views.

The constitutional structure of the PRC vests formal state authority in a hierarchically arranged system of people's congresses. These begin at the local level of the urban district and the rural township and culminate in the "highest organ of state power," the National People's Congress (NPC), which meets once a year for about two weeks. The NPC chooses the highest officials of the state, including the premier, who presides over the government's functional ministries and commissions, and the president, a largely ceremonial position that has always been held and used as an additional base of personal power by an influential individual party leader.

Elections to the people's congresses at the grass-roots level have become more democratic in recent years, as have elections for government positions in many of the one million rural villages where the majority of Chinese still live. However, CCP oversight of elections ensures that all candidates will be ideologically acceptable to the party.

Although CCP membership of around 60 million comprises less than 6 percent of the total population, the party is organized so that it penetrates society at every level, including places of work and residence through its weblike network of branches, committees, and congresses. There have been efforts to reduce the amount of political interference in economic, academic, and administrative matters, but little of importance is decided by factory managers, mayors, university presidents, or other responsible authorities without the concurrence of the ubiquitous party secretary. However, the capacity of the regime to control and monitor the lives of its citizens has diminished considerably, reflecting the fact that China's political system has moved a long way from the *totalitarianism of the Maoist period and has evolved toward a less intrusive, though still repressive, *bureaucratic authoritarianism under Deng and his successors.

The National Party Congress and the Central Committee are, in theory, the CCP's "highest leading bodies." But because of their large size and infrequent meetings, these organizations are relatively insignificant in terms of important decision-making. Much greater power resides in the much smaller Politburo and its even more exclusive Standing Committee headed by the general secretary.

One important innovation in Chinese politics—and one unprecedented for a communist system—is the imposition of term limits and mandatory retirement ages for party and state officials. The country has already gone through a routinized turnover in the position of premier (Li Peng was replaced by Zhu Rongji in 1998 after serving two terms) and Jiang Zemin has announced his intention to retire as both president and party general secretary at the end of his current term in 2003.

China's state and party constitutions depict a complex arrangement for the institutions and processes of government. But the realities of power in the PRC are often influenced in decisive ways by the workings of informal patterns of influence and decision-making. *Guanxi* (or "connections") are often more important for getting things done than is reliance on specified bureaucratic procedure. Patron-client relations and nepotism still dominate both elite and local politics, as does factionalism based as much on personal links as on ideological or political affinities.

Challenges of the New Century. China's rapid economic development was surely one of the great stories of the late twentieth century. Much of the country's population has seen a dramatic improvement in living standards (average income more than quadrupled between 1980 and 2000) and the PRC has been propelled into the ranks of the world's largest and most dynamic economies. But growth and modernization have also brought serious problems that will test the political and economic management skills of China's leadership. There are enormous and growing gaps between those people and regions that have benefited from the market reforms and those left behind—a particular quandary for a ruling communist party that is still theoretically committed to promoting equality. *Corruption is rampant, and environmental degradation has, in some parts of China, reached crisis proportions. China's vast peasantry (about 70 percent of the population is still classified as rural) may, as it has in the past, be a major factor in shaping the country's destiny. In some ways, economic reform has made rural dwellers into a force for conservatism; the desire to protect and expand their share of China's new prosperity gives peasants a material reason to respond favorably to the regime's argument that, above all else, China needs stability and order. But stagnating incomes, rapacious officials, and urban-rural inequalities have become the source of considerable discontent in many parts of coun-

tryside, which has sometimes erupted into violent protests. The relaxation of restraints on internal migration and widespread underemployment have created a "floating population" of more than 100 million former rural dwellers who seek better economic opportunities in the cities. These migrants could bring an element of instability to urban politics; they might also forge a link between city and countryside that, along with the expansion of telecommunications into the rural areas, may have the effect of broadening the political horizons of China's peasantry.

Economic transformation has planted the seeds of potential political change in China in other ways. New groups, including entrepreneurs, technocrats, and a more informed and consumer-oriented general public, may well become the basis for a more politically demanding *civil society. Similarly, the policy of opening China to the outside world, exemplified by the PRC's accession to the *World Trade Organization in 2000, may prove to be a double-edged sword from the viewpoint of Beijing's rulers. The country has been profitably integrated into the global economic system. But the opening policy makes the Chinese political system increasingly susceptible to external influences such as international human rights standards and the experiences of the tens of thousands of Chinese students, scholars, and officials who have traveled or studied abroad.

One of the biggest challenges facing China's post-Deng leadership is bolstering the severely tarnished *legitimacy of the Chinese Communist Party. Marxism seems of little relevance in the PRC other than serving as ideological garnish on the party's continuing claim to a monopoly over the formal political life of the nation. In its quest for popular support, the CCP has made strenuous efforts to portray itself as not only the architect of China's recent economic boom, but also as the sole guarantor of the domestic stability and international security needed to preserve and extend the country's growing prosperity.

The regime has also sought to enhance its legitimacy through blatant appeals to nationalism. The official media places considerable emphasis on the greatness and antiquity of Chinese culture, with the underlying message that it is time for the Chinese nation, under the party's leadership, to reclaim its rightful, central place in the global order. The reassertion of national pride and the redress of historical injustices were major themes in the propaganda and pageantry that accompanied the 1997 reversion of *Hong Kong to Chinese sovereignty after 150 years of British colonial rule. Some observers have expressed concern that such officially promoted nationalist sentiments could lead the PRC toward a more aggressive and even irredentist foreign policy. As evidence, they particularly point to Chinese military actions in the potentially oil-rich South China Sea, where the PRC's territorial claims conflict with those of several other nations, including Vietnam and the Philippines.

The PRC will undoubtedly be an important influence on an international system in which it occupies a rather anomalous position. By many measures (e.g., GNP per capital, level of technological development, structure of the economy), it is still very much a *Third World nation. In fact, the government in Beijing often proclaims itself to be the champion of Third World causes in *international organizations. By other measures (e.g., overall size of the economy, natural and human resources, military might), China is at least a potential superpower. In any case, the PRC is becoming an increasingly significant player in East Asian and world affairs. Whether the rise of China as a global power will have a stabilizing or destabilizing impact on the post–Cold War world order is one of the most debated and important questions about *international relations in the early twenty-first century.

(See also CONFUCIANISM; DEVELOPMENT AND UNDERDEVELOPMENT.)

Jonathan D. Spence, *The Search for Modern China* (New York, 1990). Roderick MacFarquhar, *The Politics of China 1949–1989* (New York, 1993). Marc Blecher, *China Against the Tides: Restructuring through Revolution, Radicalism, and Reform* (London, 1997). Andrew J. Nathan, *China's Transition* (New York, 1997). Alastair Iain Johnston and Robert S. Ross, *Engaging China: The Management of an Emerging Power* (New York, 1999). Maurice Meisner, *Mao's China and After: A History of the People's Republic*, 3d ed. (New York, 1999). Orville Schell and David Shambaugh, *The China Reader: The Reform Era* (New York, 1999). James C. F. Wang, *Contemporary Chinese Politics: An Introduction*, 6th ed. (Englewood Cliffs, N.J., 1999).

WILLIAM A. JOSEPH

CHINESE COMMUNIST PARTY. The Chinese Communist Party (CCP) is one of the last ruling communist parties in the world. Founded in 1921, the CCP gained power in 1949 and has ruled the People's Republic of *China since.

Before seizing national power, the CCP had fought an extensive guerrilla war against the Japanese (1937–1945) and later a civil war with the Kuomintang, or Nationalist Party (1945–1949). During this period, the CCP ruled a number of base areas with a total population of some 80 to 100 million people. This experience had a number of important consequences for post-1949 CCP rule. First, the CCP was able to form an alternative state structure in the base areas and use them as laboratories for policies for social and economic change. This is quite distinct from the Soviet experience and that of Eastern and Central Europe where most parties were imported from the Soviet Union after World War II. Second, the nature of the struggle and the fact that all senior party leaders were also military leaders has meant that the military has always been held in high esteem and has played an important part in the political process. The words of war and struggle dominate the vocabulary of the CCP. Further, when *Mao Zedong felt that the party had become corrupt in the early 1960s, he turned to the military as the repository of the virtues of plain living and struggle inherited from the revolutionary period. Third, to survive the Japanese invasion, the CCP had to use the tactic of a united front to appeal to a broad section of the population for support. This policy of class collaboration guided the initial years after 1949 and has formed the basis of policy since economic modernization became the key focus of party work from 1978 onward. Fourth, the CCP-led revolution was an indigenous one. Mao Zedong made it quite clear that the CCP was not fighting a war of liberation in order to become the "slaves of Moscow." The CCP was willing to ignore Soviet advice when it ran counter to national interests and to abandon the Soviet approach to development once its inadequacies and inapplicability to the Chinese situation became apparent. Last, the stress on organizational stability went hand in hand with the development of a cult around Mao Zedong as the supreme leader. Over-

reliance on the individual and the cavalier way in which formal structures have been treated hindered the process of institutionalization. Mao dominated politics to such an extent that it was impossible to oppose him publicly once he had made a decision. This, combined with the eradication of alternatives to the CCP rule, of competing social classes, and of intermediary organizations, meant that there was no effective feedback or opposition that could prevent policy disasters such as the excesses of the collectivization movement of the mid-1950s, the Great Leap Forward of the late 1950s, and the *Cultural Revolution launched in 1966. These policy disasters undermined credibility in the party and paved the way for the policies of economic modernization launched in the late 1970s.

In 1997, party membership numbered some 58 million (out of a population of over 1.2 billion), making it a large but still exclusive club. Membership criteria have changed over the years, reflecting shifts in ideology and recruitment policies. Currently, the stress is on recruiting better-educated members, rather than workers and peasants, to help oversee the policies of economic modernization. Over 70 percent of the Fifteenth Central Committee (elected in September 1997) have received a college education. Party membership is still popular with young people, especially college graduates. Twenty-six percent of all postgraduates are members and there are four party members for every 100 students—five times the 1990 level. However, the main reason for membership is that it is still beneficial for a good career. While much more social space and many more economic opportunities have opened up, the party is still the locus of political power, and few can achieve real political influence without membership and a record of political activism.

In theory, the party is organized in accordance with the principles of democratic centralism that subordinate the lower to the higher levels. The result is a hierarchical pattern with 3 million party organizations at the bottom based on work units or neighborhoods and the national bodies in Beijing at the top. Nominally, the supreme decision-making body is the National Party Congress, which meets once every five years. However, the formal power structure competes with individual *patron-client relationships where real power often lies. Before his death in 1997, *Deng Xiaoping had been the most important decision-maker in China as Mao had been before him. It remains to be seen whether the current general secretary, Jiang Zemin, can develop a more collective style of leadership or whether the internal CCP logic will force him to concentrate increasing power in his own hands.

The party is now presiding over a complex array of policies designed to develop a market-based economy combined with strong, centralized authoritarian rule. It supports de facto economic privatization with the private sector enjoying status equal to the formerly privileged state sector. It is removing responsibility for housing, medical insurance, and pensions away from the workplace to a mixture of private and public partnerships. These policies will revolutionize the relationship between the party and society and will profoundly undermine CCP capacity to control society as directly or as completely as in the past.

While the party no longer espouses *Marxism as a useful guide to action, it does adhere to Leninist principles for organizing society and has been very reluctant to relinquish control over newly emerging intermediary organizations. The party has been slow to come to terms with the social and political consequences of its economic reform program. The party has tried to shift legitimacy from its correct interpretation of ideology to one that is based more on economic competence and underpinned by appeals to nationalism and patriotism. However, previous economic failings have undermined broad-based legitimacy and, as many leaders know, legitimacy based solely on economic performance can erode very quickly.

There has been continued resistance to come to terms with the increasing diversity of society and its implications for party rule. With the party unwilling to redefine publicly its relationship to other organizations in society, to institutionalize the political process, and to offer a new social compact, much political activity now takes place outside the formal structures. To maintain its rule, the paramount task for the CCP will be to devise a political system that is not only an efficient managerial machine but also one that can accommodate the demands of an increasingly complex society.

(See also COMMUNIST PARTY STATES; GUERRILLA WARFARE.)

Tony Saich, "Much Ado About Nothing: Party Reform in the Eighties," in Gordon White, ed., *From Crisis to Crisis: The Chinese State in the Era of Economic Reform* (Armonk, N.Y., 1991). Tony Saich, *The Rise to Power of the Chinese Communist Party: Documents and Analysis* (Armonk, N.Y., 1996).

TONY SAICH

CHINESE REVOLUTION. At first glance, the Chinese Revolution looks like a younger sibling of the *Russian Revolution. It is true that the latter provided a revolutionary model to be followed, and that the nascent Chinese Communist movement was aided by its Russian counterpart. The ultimate victory of the Communists over their competitors within China does not imply, however, that the Chinese Revolution was merely a manifestation of an international movement inspired by Marxist *ideology. In a more fundamental sense, it was an indigenous *revolution with roots far back in the Chinese past.

External forces undoubtedly played a part in China's century of turmoil and revolutionary change. Beginning with the Opium War (1839–1842), Western powers compelled a secluded Chinese Empire to open several ports to foreign merchants and missionaries. As suggested by Japan's quick and successful response to the same challenge from the West, however, dramatic intrusion from abroad need not invariably lead to the kind of convulsive, painful, and protracted revolutionary process undergone by China between the mid-nineteenth and mid-twentieth centuries. Even before the West became a factor, the Chinese Empire was beset by internal troubles that by themselves might have brought about a traditional revolution in the form of a change of dynasty. When the last imperial dynasty was eventually overthrown in 1911, its fall resulted from the conjunction of growing external pressure and a host of long-unsolved and steadily accumulating domestic problems ranging from demographic imbalance and economic stagnation to administrative breakdown and growing assertiveness by autonomous social forces.

The 1911 revolution accomplished little beyond changing the form of the political system from an imperial to a republican one. The most obvious result was an accentuation of China's internal divisions and a further weakening of its ability to resist imperialist encroachments. For more than a decade, the country was so torn apart by the struggles of competing warlords that frustrated radical intellectuals deemed a political revolution like the one that had just overthrown the empire insufficient to solve China's ills. In their eyes, nothing less than a cultural revolution was needed to purge the Chinese people of some of their most ingrained habits and cherished values. In order to ensure the survival of the Chinese nation in a world dominated by an apparently more advanced civilization, they did not hesitate to repudiate Chinese cultural identity, and they relentlessly attacked *Confucianism as its symbol. Radical ideas found an outlet in the May Fourth Movement, named after an anti-imperialist student demonstration staged in Beijing on 4 May 1919.

The *Chinese Communist Party (CCP) was founded in 1921 in the wake of the May Fourth Movement. Following the orders of the Soviet-centered Comintern, the CCP merged with the main Chinese revolutionary party, the Kuomintang (KMT), led by the veteran revolutionary Sun Yat-sen (1866–1925); this alliance helped to promote the CCP from a tiny group of radical intellectuals into a mass movement able to foment labor strikes and urban insurrections in just a few years. Success came mostly in the wake of a new ave of anti-imperialist demonstrations. However, when the KMT-CCP United Front launched a military campaign in 1926 against old-style warlords and reunified the country in 1927–1928, the decisive victory belonged not to the CCP but to the KMT, the senior partner of the coalition. Chiang Kai-shek (1887–1975), the overall commander of the revolutionary armies, destroyed his one-time Communist allies before establishing his own personal rule over the country.

The Chinese Revolution thus was ushered into a new phase, one of protracted struggle between former revolutionary partners, between those who held that the revolution had been betrayed and those who claimed it had been won. Defeated and slaughtered in the cities, the Communists took refuge in the countryside. There they could agitate the poorer and much more numerous rural masses instead of the tiny urban proletariat who had been the main target of their mobilization efforts until 1927. Despite early success in establishing rural bases—by *Mao Zedong (1893–1976) in the southeast and by others elsewhere—the Communists proved no match for the armies of the KMT. The famous Long March (1934–1935) was at best a victorious retreat: victorious only in that the defeated Communist armies escaped annihilation and found a haven in the distant northwest. They might very well have been destroyed there if Japanese expansionism had not provided them with an opportunity to regroup and expand.

The Sino-Japanese War (1937–1945) was the single most decisive period in the building of the Communist victory. Playing the card of patriotic resistance against foreign invaders, the Communists established so-called "liberated areas," mostly in northern China. Within these areas they won over a peasant constituency, partly by shielding villagers from Japanese troops, party by undermining the influence of the traditional rural elite and distributing some of its possessions and revenues to the rural poor. By 1944–1945, solidly entrenched Communist areas, particularly Mao's base in Yanan, threatened a much-weakened central government. This government's military strength, support, and overall legitimacy had declined dramatically during the course of the war, as the KMT proved no more able to stand the test of war than had the tsarist government of Russia between 1914 and 1917.

Both the Russian and the Chinese communist revolutions therefore sprang from a world war. During the last phase of the Chinese Revolution (1946–1949), the CCP was able to parlay the advances it had already won thanks to World War II into further gains. In Manchuria, where most of the civil war was fought, the CCP implemented the same kind of rural mobilization policies that had succeeded elsewhere between 1937 and 1945. At first outnumbered by better-equipped armies, the CCP aptly exploited the poor command and steadily deteriorating morale of KMT forces. Hyperinflation accelerated the KMT's inability to cope with a protracted state of war. The Communist victory and the subsequent founding of the People's Republic of China on 1 October 1949 were a result of both the CCP's sweeping military successes and the internal crumbling of the KMT regime.

The timing and impact of the Japanese invasion of China and internal failings help explain the KMT's defeat. Efficient mass mobilization policies and clever military strategies and tactics, including guerrilla warfare, enabled the Communist challengers to exploit opportunities created by foreign aggression and indigenous weakness. The weakness of the KMT regime resulted largely from inherited problems. In fact, China's long-standing weakness may very well have been the fundamental cause of the Chinese Revolution.

In a sense, the revolution of 1949 grew out of the failure of the revolution of 1911. Latter-day Chinese revolutionaries—the Communists—added much of substance to the mostly nationalist, anti-imperialist program of their forerunners; they addressed social problems and eventually directed their attention to the plight of the rural as opposed to urban masses. Yet the often-heard characterization of the Chinese Revolution as a *peasant revolution requires at least two qualifications.

First, although northern Chinese peasants played a more decisive revolutionary role in the 1940s than that played by the Russian proletariat in 1917, in both cases a party of "professional revolutionaries" was firmly in charge. In China, agrarian reform was a means to an end, its goal to attract and organize enough peasants to win power. Whenever the imperatives of social revolution contradicted the requirements of military victory, the revolutionary elite regularly sacrificed the former to the latter. As for the rank and file, the peasant masses, only those villagers who happened to live in Communist-held areas, or more precisely some of those villagers (and not all of them willingly), rallied to the Communist side. Elsewhere peasants did not care or simply did not know about the revolution going on in their country. What limits the significance of the above qualification is that most revolutions are, after all, the work of a minority, and very few of them are accomplished for the sake of the poor majority—a fact illustrated in the Chinese case by the post-1949 gap between rural and urban incomes.

Second, although Chinese Communist leaders assigned special importance to both imperialism and peasant poverty as targets of their revolution, their discovery of the second was far from spontaneous. Only a tiny minority of those radical intellectuals who embraced communism in the early 1920s did so because they were moved by the sorry plight of the rural (or urban) masses. The social concerns and devotion to class struggle of most others, the huge majority of whom were essentially nationalist revolutionaries, were acquired later—or, more exactly, borrowed from the Leninist recipe for the conquest of power in a "backward" country.

While Lenin never hesitated to speak of "backward Russia," his Chinese disciples proved more reluctant to apply the epithet to their own country. They were certainly not unaware of China's backwardness; they had suffered from it and were anxious to overcome the basic conditions that prevented their country from succeeding in the international system. Even when publicly indicting imperialist *oppression*, many of them remained painfully conscious of the imperialist *challenge* as a model to imitate or emulate. Beyond the openly acknowledged goal of anti-imperialism, the revolutionary crusaders barely dissimulated their undeclared but more basic goal, namely, the modernization of a society lagging behind in a world that was rapidly moving ahead. In that sense, Mao's successors, who are no longer revolutionary, can be deemed more faithful in their overriding commitment to the modernization of China than Mao himself was.

(See also IMPERIALISM; LENINISM; MARXISM; NATIONALISM; TAIWAN.)

Lucien Bianco, *Origins of the Chinese Revolution, 1915–1949* (Stanford, Calif., 1971). John K. Fairbank, ed., *The Cambridge History of China*, Vol. 10: *Late Ch'ing, 1800–1911*, Part 1 (Cambridge, U.K., 1978). John K. Fairbank and Kwang-ching Liu, eds., *The Cambridge History of China*, Vol. 11: *Late Ch'ing, 1800–1911*, Part 2 (Cambridge, U.K., 1980). John K. Fairbank, ed., *The Cambridge History of China*, Vol. 12: *Republican China, 1912–1949*, Part 1 (Cambridge, U.K., 1983). John K. Fairbank and Albert Feuerwerker, eds., *The Cambridge History of China*, Vol. 13: *Republican China, 1912–1949*, Part 2 (Cambridge, U.K., 1986).

LUCIEN BIANCO

CHRISTIAN DEMOCRACY. A contemporary political movement with a substantial following in Europe and Latin America, Christian Democracy arose in the early twentieth century as a progressive alternative to the socioeconomic and political conservatism with which Roman Catholicism had been associated from the sixteenth through the nineteenth centuries. Most Christian Democratic parties were initially concerned with religious values and issues, but came to stress them less as time and *secularization proceeded apace. Today all parties embrace liberal democracy, and virtually all advocate a reform or welfare version of capitalism that provides for basic needs and for some worker participation in decision making. The German (Christlich-Demokratische Union/ Christlich-Soziale Union) and Italian (Democrazia Cristiana) are among the most successful of the European parties, while the Chilean, Venezuelan, and Salvadoran parties have been leading political forces in Latin America.

Most Christian Democratic parties set out to capture the middle or moderate conservative ground between ideologically defined parties of the Right and socialist Left. They hoped to supersede both by appealing to consciously Christian (Catholic and Protestant) constituents across a sociological spectrum. Their success in attracting business interests, middle-class elements, and non-Communist workers soon made them an "enlightened" alternative to the socialist left. Where they have come to power, whether alone or in coalition with others, it has generally been as a right-of-center force. This has been difficult for some party intellectuals and trade unionists to accept. In Germany and Italy, these groups have constituted a permanent, minority left wing within the party. Elsewhere, they have formed rival Catholic left parties (as in Chile) or joined forces with erstwhile leftist adversaries (as in France, El Salvador, and Venezuela).

Division and dissension among Christian Democrats during the 1960s, 1970s, and early 1980s were a consequence of their socially diverse followings, their lack of common sociological reading of historical experience, and the ease with which their social Christian principles could therefore be variously interpreted and applied. In countries (the Federal Republic of Germany and Italy) where sustained economic growth and prosperity provided them with an additional margin for error, such divisions caused little or no political damage. In other instances, however, economic decline fueled social and political polarization, forced parties to choose between right and left, and led to the alienation of important constituencies.

During the late 1980s, Christian Democratic movements and parties were political and electoral beneficiaries of the breakdown of the economies and political systems in Eastern and Central Europe. In Latin America, Christian Democracy's "third way" has also enjoyed a renaissance of sorts, thanks to a new willingness on the part of Marxists and other leftists to form alliances with "democratic" centrists and rightists as an alternative to continued *military rule, and to the imposition of neoliberal economic criteria by national governments and international financial institutions.

Christian Democratic parties coordinate with one another through loosely structured supranational mechanisms such as the International Union of Christian Democratic Parties, the (Latin) American Christian Democratic Organization, and a Christian Democratic caucus within the *European Parliament.

(See also RELIGION AND POLITICS; SOCIALISM AND SOCIAL DEMOCRACY.)

R. E. M. Irving, *The Christian Democratic Parties of Western Europe* (London, 1979). Michael Fleet, *The Rise and Fall of Chilean Christian Democracy* (Princeton, N.J., 1985). Gregory Baum and John Coleman, eds., *The Church and Christian Democracy* (Edinburgh, 1987).

MICHAEL FLEET

CHURCHILL, Winston. Winston Churchill was born in 1874 and died in 1965. After five years as a soldier and war correspondent, he entered the British Parliament in 1900 as a Conservative. Four years later he joined the Liberal Party, returning to the Conservatives twenty years later, and becoming Conservative Party leader in 1940, five months after he had been appointed prime minister of a national coalition government. This all-party administration, which he headed for five years, had been formed on the day of the German invasion of France, Belgium, and the Netherlands on 10 May 1940. He served a second time as prime minister, in peacetime, from 1951 to 1955.

Churchill's long career was often marked by controversy and dogged by political antagonism, for he was always outspoken and independent, expressing his views without prevarication; and his criticisms of others acquired all the more force thanks to his breadth of knowledge and his vivid, adept,

and penetrating language. The controversies were understandably many in a public life that spanned more than fifty years and saw him hold eight cabinet posts even before he became prime minister.

The range of Churchill's activities and experiences was extraordinary. He received his Army commission during the reign of Queen Victoria, fought in the Northwest Frontier province of India in 1897, took part in the cavalry charge at Omdurman in the Sudan in 1898, and was taken prisoner of war during the Boer War in South Africa in 1899. Strategy and tactics fascinated him and engaged his attention from his earliest days; he was also closely involved in the early development of aviation—learning to fly before World War I—and established the Royal Naval Air Service. He was an active participant in the inception of the tank. He was a pioneer in the advocacy and preparation of antiaircraft defense and in the evolution of aerial warfare. In the 1920s he foresaw the building of weapons of mass destruction, and in his last speech to Parliament, in 1955, he proposed using the existence of the hydrogen bomb and its deterrent power as the basis for world disarmament.

From his early years, Churchill had an uncanny understanding and vision of the future unfolding of events. His early military training and his natural inventiveness gave him great insight into the nature of *war and society. He was also someone whose personal courage, whether on the battlefields of empire at the turn of the century, during his mission to Antwerp to try to stiffen the resolve of its defenders in 1914, during his command of a battalion in the trenches on the western front in 1916, or during his dash to an Athens beset by civil war in 1944, was matched by a deep understanding of the horrors of war and the devastation of battle. "Much as war attracts my mind with its tremendous situations," he wrote to his wife Clementine from German army maneuvers in 1909, "I feel more deeply every year, and can measure the feeling here in the midst of arms, what vile and utter folly and barbarism it all is."

Both in his Liberal and Conservative years Churchill was a radical, a believer in the need for the state to take an active part, both by legislation and finance, in ensuring minimum standards of life, labor, and social well-being for all citizens. Among the areas of social reform in which he took a leading part both before and after World War I, including the drafting of substantial legislation, were prison reform, unemployment insurance, state-aided pensions for widows and orphans, a permanent arbitration mechanism for labor disputes, state assistance for those in search of employment, shorter hours of work, and improved conditions on the shop and factory floor. He was also an advocate of a national health service, of wider access to education, of the taxation of excess profits, and of profit sharing by employees. In his first public speech, in 1897, three years before he entered Parliament, he looked forward to the day when the laborer would become "a shareholder in the business in which he worked."

At times of national stress, Churchill was a persistent advocate of conciliation, even of coalition; he shunned the paths of division and unnecessary confrontation. In international affairs he consistently sought the settlement of the grievances of those who had been defeated and the building up of meaningful associations for the reconciliation of former enemies. After two world wars he argued in favor of maintaining the strength of the victors in order to redress the grievances of the vanquished and to preserve peace. In the 1920s and 1930s he was one of the leading advocates of collective security to deter war. In 1950 it was he who first used the word *summit* to refer to a meeting of the leaders of the Western and communist worlds, and subsequently he did his utmost to set up such meetings to end the dangerous confrontations of the *Cold War. Among the agreements that he negotiated with patience and understanding were the constitutional settlements in South Africa and Ireland and the war debt repayment schemes after World War I.

A perceptive, shrewd commentator on the events taking place around him, Churchill was always an advocate of bold, farsighted courses of action. The genesis of the British naval attack on the Dardanelles in 1915 was Churchill's determination to find a way to end the stalemate and bloodshed of the war of trenches and attrition in France; throughout the following years he begged the government not to embark on futile frontal assaults against the heavily fortified German trench line without first securing superiority, including air superiority. Between the wars, confronted by German rearmament, he insisted that only a well-armed Britain with superior air power to Germany's could deter Hitler from aggression; his warnings were mocked as alarmist and went largely unheeded.

Churchill had a complete and extraordinary faith in his own abilities and in his destiny. When he went to the western front in December 1915, with every possibility of being killed, he wrote to Clementine, "My conviction that the greatest of my work is still to be done is strong within me, and I ride reposefully along the gale." After nearly being killed by a German shell in March 1916 he wrote to his wife that, had he been killed, it would have been "a loss to the war-making power of Britain that no one will ever know or measure or mourn."

One of Churchill's greatest gifts, evident in several thousand public speeches as well as in his many broadcasts, was his ability to use his exceptional mastery of words and love of language to convey detailed arguments and essential truths; to inform, to convince, and to inspire. He was a person of great humor and warmth, of magnanimity; a consistent and lifelong liberal in outlook; someone often turned to by successive prime ministers between 1905 and 1929 for his skill as a conciliator. His dislike of unfairness, of victimization, and of bullying—whether at home or abroad—was the foundation stone of much of his thinking. His finest hour was the leadership of Britain when it was most isolated, most threatened, and most weak; when his own courage, determination, and belief in democracy became one with that of a beleaguered nation.

(See also POTSDAM CONFERENCE; WORLD WAR II.)

Randolph S. Churchill, *Winston S. Churchill*, vols. 1–2 (Boston, 1967–8). Martin Gilbert, *Winston S. Churchill*, vols. 3–8 (Boston, 1971–88). Martin Gilbert, *Churchill: A Life* (New York, 1991).

MARTIN GILBERT

CIA. See CENTRAL INTELLIGENCE AGENCY.

CITIZENSHIP. The term *citizenship*, meaning membership in a political community, comes to us from the classical Greek and Roman conception of man as a political being. Ancient citizenship was understood as the capacity to govern and to be governed. It implied the idea of equality before the law and active political participation, and its emergence is concomitant with the birth of *democracy. However, citizenship in the Greek democratic city-states was restricted to free and native-born men, and citizens only represented a minority of the population, even in Athens. Their participation in public life was only possible because of the existence of slaves, who were responsible for performing the main economic functions.

In Rome we can witness the beginning of a new dynamic. Although citizenship was still defined in terms of office holding, its extension during the empire, first to plebeians and then to conquered peoples, produced a much more heterogeneous body of citizens, and the term began to refer more to protection under the law than to active participation in its execution. Citizenship ceased to be identical with active participation in a political community and was reduced to a legal status. By edict of the emperor Caracalla in 212 C.E., citizenship was granted to the great majority of imperial subjects; only the very lowest classes and women were excluded.

After a long eclipse during the Middle Ages, the tradition of Greek and Roman republicanism was revived in the Italian republics of the Renaissance, finding its champion in Niccolò Machiavelli. It was also reformulated in England by James Harrington, John Milton, and other republicans in the course of the constitutional revolution of the seventeenth century. Later it traveled to the New World through the work of the neo-Harringtonians and was influential during the American Revolution.

The universalistic ideal of citizenship culminated in the French Revolution and the Declaration of the Rights of Man and Citizen. The main theoretical referent in this case is Jean-Jacques Rousseau, who in *The Social Contract* (1762) established the modern figure of the citizen by connecting it to the theory of consent. The citizen for Rousseau is a free and autonomous individual who is entitled to take part in making decisions that all are required to obey. Rousseau's conception of citizenship, which draws on both the classical republican tradition and on modern contractualism, attempts to link the republican conception of political community with the premises of individualism. Writing in the context of an emerging commercial society, Rousseau was aware of the tension between the common good and private interests, and saw in the dominance of organized group interests the main threat to the well-being of the body politic.

With the development of market relations and the growing hegemony of laissez-faire liberalism during the nineteenth century, the republican conception of the active citizen was displaced by a view of citizenship expressed in the language of natural *rights. The ideas of civic activity, public spiritedness, and political participation in a community of equals appeared as nostalgic relics to be discarded by most liberal writers who, following Benjamin Constant, declared that in order to preserve the "liberties of the moderns," it was necessary to renounce the "liberties of the ancients." Citizenship was reduced to a mere legal status, indicating the possession of rights that the individual holds against the *state. Defined in terms of rights, citizenship nevertheless played a very important and progressive role in shaping liberal democratic societies. In the case of Britain, for instance, T. H. Marshall charted a progression from civil to political and finally to social rights (*Citizenship and Social Class*, Cambridge, U.K., 1950). Obviously the situation is not the same in all countries. But there is no doubt that there is a strong connection between the institutions and practices of pluralistic liberal democracies and the liberal language of the citizen as a bearer of rights. Slowly, and through bitter struggles, it made possible the inclusion of women and racial or ethnic minorities into citizenship.

Today the liberal model of citizenship has gained a new momentum in countries where the main task is to establish the basic conditions for civil society and pluralistic democracy. However, it has increasingly been criticized in Western democracies for its individualistic bias, which is deemed responsible for the lack of cohesion and the destruction of common purpose and community values endemic in those societies. A school of "communitarians" has emerged who argue for the revival of the civic republican conception of citizenship with its strong emphasis on the notion of a public good, prior to and independent of individual desires and interests. Authors like Michael Sandel and Alasdair MacIntyre have taken issue with the work of John Rawls in order to criticize the liberal conception of the citizen and its view of the individual as someone who can have rights independently of the community to which she or he belongs. What is at stake in this debate is the possibility and desirability of a return to a tradition that many liberals see as premodern and incompatible with the *pluralism that is the novel characteristic of modern democracy. According to Isaiah Berlin, ideas about the "common good" today can only have totalitarian implications and are incompatible with the modern idea of liberty. Is it possible to combine democratic institutions with the sense of common purpose that premodern societies enjoyed? If politics in a modern democracy must accept division and conflict as unavoidable, what can be the status of a notion like the "common good"?

At the moment, one of the most discussed questions in many countries is how to establish a notion of citizenship that makes room for the increasingly multiethnic and multicultural character of the population. Such a problem has long existed in North America, but satisfactory solutions have yet to be found there as well. The difficulty seems to lie in the need to create unity without denying multiplicity. How might one combine an effective pluralism as far as cultural, linguistic, ethnic, religious, and other identities are concerned while constructing a common political identity around an allegiance to shared political principles? This is the contemporary challenge associated with citizenship for both communitarians and liberals.

(See also COMMUNITARIANISM; POLITICAL PARTICIPATION.)

Moses I. Finley, *Democracy Ancient and Modern* (New Brunswick, N.J., and London, 1973). Michael Sandel, ed., *Liberalism and Its Critics* (New York, 1984). Bryan S. Turner, *Citizenship and Capitalism* (London, 1986). Ralf Dahrendorf, *The Modern Social Conflict* (London, 1988).

CHANTAL MOUFFE

CIVIL DISOBEDIENCE. The open, deliberate, nonviolent breaking of a law, regulation, or order, including those of governments, courts, police, and military officials, is known as civil disobedience. Usually, the disobeyed command is seen to be illegitimate because of its content or origin. The command may also be believed to contradict a "higher" moral or religious principle. Disobedience of "illegitimate" laws may be practiced by individuals, small groups, or masses of people.

Civil disobedience may be practiced solely with the intent of refusing to participate in activities believed to be evil, without wider objectives. Or, it may be practiced as part of an organized campaign planned to achieve a specific objective, such as the repeal of racial segregation laws. Organized civil disobedience may have reformatory, revolutionary, or defensive objectives.

While the names of Socrates, Henry David Thoreau, Mohandas K. *Gandhi, and Martin Luther *King, Jr., are often best known in relation to civil disobedience, this method of nonviolent action has been widely practiced. These cases include American colonial resisters in 1766, London newspapers in 1768–1771 publishing prohibited reports of parliamentary debates, the breaking of the British Salt Laws in the 1930–1931 Indian independence satyagraha campaign, and the 1951 defiance campaign in South Africa in which *apartheid laws were deliberately broken to achieve their repeal.

Sometimes, however, certain commands of a strictly regulatory nature, seen to be morally neutral, may be disobeyed. This may occur when the disobedient group wishes strongly to protest a government policy against which it is difficult to find a clear point of resistance. Civil disobedience of morally neutral laws and regulations can also be practiced in an advanced stage of a strong nonviolent movement with revolutionary objectives. The aim is then to weaken further the government's control in order to hasten its full collapse. This stage was partially reached at certain points in the 1930–1931 Indian independence campaign. Gandhi regarded this action as at times morally justified but also as "a most dangerous weapon."

These types of civil disobedience are among nearly forty methods of political noncooperation. Some related but different methods of disobedience are withholding or withdrawal of allegiance, reluctant and slow compliance, nonobedience in absence of direct supervision, popular nonobedience, disguised disobedience, refusal of an assemblage or meeting to disperse, and noncooperation with conscription and deportation.

Issues prominent in the discussion of civil disobedience include: How does one determine when a law, order, etc., should be civilly disobeyed? Is civil disobedience justifiable within a liberal *democracy which provides opportunities to repeal morally offensive laws or policies? What are the distinctions between civil disobedience by individuals acting out of a personal moral decision and organized civil disobedience conducted by groups? Should established laws receive an assumption of obligation to obey them regardless of their content or purpose? Considerations include comparison of the consequences of civil disobedience with the consequences of passive obedience, and with the results of violence in the expression of strong dissent. In addition, discussions consider the issue of whether the willful breaking of law, albeit selectively and nonviolently, contributes to the indiscriminate breaking of laws, perpetration of violence, and social chaos. Finally, those concerned with the issues of civil disobedience consider how civil disobedience within a state relates to *international law.

(See also CIVIL RIGHTS MOVEMENT; NONVIOLENT ACTION; POLITICAL VIOLENCE; REVOLUTION.)

Henry David Thoreau, "On the Duty of Civil Disobedience," in *Walden and Other Writings of Henry David Thoreau* (New York, 1937), pp. 635–663. Paul Harris, ed., *Civil Disobedience* (Lanham, Md., 1989).

GENE SHARP

CIVIL RIGHTS MOVEMENT. The modern U.S. Civil Rights Movement was one of the most important freedom struggles of the twentieth century. As late as the 1950s, millions of African American citizens were oppressed and disenfranchised. This reality was especially shocking because it endured in a country believed to the world's leading democracy. White leaders promoted America as the shining model to be adopted by other countries wishing to break free from their past histories of human oppression.

The historic treatment of blacks in the United States stood in sharp contrast to the American image of democracy. In fact, *African Americans were forcibly transported to America as slaves. The institution of slavery lasted well over two centuries and produced the free slave labor that helped fuel the United States' enormous economic growth. Throughout the slave period, African Americans were officially defined as chattel, not human beings.

In both moral and economic terms, the U.S. Civil War (1861–1865) was fought over the issue of slavery. With the triumph of Union forces in 1865, the formal institution of slavery was defeated. For approximately a decade following the Civil War—the Reconstruction period—blacks were granted expanded *citizenship rights, such as freedom of movement, restricted access to the franchise, and equal access to employment. If this outcome had endured it would have erased a system of white supremacy and created a society based on principles of racial equality.

By the turn of the twentieth century it had become clear that white supremacy would be reinstituted. By the early 1900s, a formal system of racial segregation known as Jim Crow was hammered into place. It required that blacks and whites be segregated on the basis of race. The two races were not allowed to attend the same movie theaters; sit on the same side of a courtroom or be sworn in using the same Bible; occupy the same place on a public bus or train; or participate equally in the political process. Although the Jim Crow system was especially entrenched in the South, it was not limited to any region, and in many respects racial segregation was national in scope. Thus an 1896 *Supreme Court ruling, *Plessy* v. *Ferguson*, declared that racial segregation was constitutional, enshrining the blatantly discriminatory doctrine of separate-but-equal facilities. The national scope of Jim Crow was also evident in the U.S. military, where black soldiers served in racially segregated combat units until the post–World War II era.

By the 1950s, the overwhelming majority of southern blacks were disenfranchised. As a result, no blacks held any significant political offices in the region. Terror and violence, including lynching, were routinely used to keep blacks sub-

jugated. In the labor market only low-paying, undesirable jobs were usually available to African Americans. Under this arrangement white economic exploitation of blacks continued unabated. African Americans also experienced personal humiliation on a daily basis because racial segregation set them off from the rest of humanity and labeled them as an inferior race. Human dignity was stripped from African Americans: simple titles of respect such as "Mr." or "Mrs." were withheld, and even white youngsters held authority over all blacks, however elderly or eminent.

African Americans have consistently rebelled and protested against their subordination. These protests began during slavery and have endured over the succeeding generations. At times, resistance was collective and public, while at other times it remained less visible and more limited in scope. By the 1950s African Americans had a long, rich history of social protest to draw upon when confronting their oppressors. In short, the modern Civil Rights Movement was a part of the historic struggle for black liberation.

The modern Civil Rights Movement, which took root in the mid-1950s, was clearly one of the peaks of the historic black freedom struggle. This movement emerged in the Deep South, where black oppression was most intense and where the system of racial segregation was firmly entrenched. Given the depth of oppression and the power of the white opposition, why did such a powerful Civil Rights Movement erupt when it did?

The movement took off during this period for several reasons. First, by the 1950s large numbers of African Americans had migrated to southern cities. This *urbanization of the black masses provided them with new strength derived from tightly knit communities and dense, effective communication networks. Second, by the 1950s the National Association for the Advancement of Colored People (NAACP) had won successful legal battles against the Jim Crow system, especially in the 1954 Supreme Court decision *Brown* v. *Board of Education*, which overturned the 1896 *Plessy* v. *Ferguson* decision. The *Brown* ruling concluded that separate schooling based on race was unconstitutional. This ruling served to delegitimize the entire system of racial segregation and encouraged struggles for the implementation of court orders. It also generated massive white campaigns of resistance.

Finally, the international picture was changing in the late 1950s as African nations gained independence through anti-colonial struggles. African Americans identified with those struggles, which intensified their own thirst for freedom. Moreover, the context of *decolonization and *Cold War rivalry made the federal government susceptible to pressure from the Civil Rights Movement because America was determined to persuade these new African nations to model themselves after U.S. democracy, not the Soviet alternative. Racial oppression was an obstacle that stood in the path of harmonious relations between the United States and the new African nations. Thus, the federal government came under increased and sustained international pressure to support efforts to overthrow institutionalized racial segregation.

These factors created the fertile soil in which the modern Civil Rights Movement took root. By employing the strategy of mass, nonviolent, direct action, this movement galvanized widespread social protest in the streets and within oppressive institutions. For such a strategy to succeed, white communities, businesses, and institutions had to be disrupted. To do so, the leaders and organizers of the movement persuaded tens of thousands of African Americans to challenge their oppression by becoming involved in social protest.

The Civil Rights Movement succeeded in mobilizing massive nonviolent direct action. Innovative tactics included economic boycotts (beginning with the yearlong boycott of a bus company in Montgomery, Alabama, begun in December 1955 and led by Martin Luther *King, Jr.); sit-in demonstrations (started in February 1960 by black college students at a lunch counter in Greensboro, North Carolina); and mass marches (including a massive mobilization of whites and blacks in the August 1963 March on Washington, which culminated in King's "I have a dream" speech, and protest marches led by King that met with police violence in Selma, Alabama, in January 1965).

The goal of these protests was to overthrow the entire system of racial segregation and to empower African Americans by seizing the franchise. Southern elected officials utilized their governmental power and the resistance of the larger white community in a spirited (and often brutal) effort to defeat the Civil Rights Movement and to maintain legally enforced racial segregation. Participants of the Civil Rights Movement—many of them children and college students—were often beaten and brutalized by southern law enforcement officials, and thousands were arrested and jailed for their protest activities. Some leaders and participants—such as Medgar Evers, chair of the Mississippi state chapter of the NAACP in 1963, and three civil rights workers in Mississippi in 1964—were killed.

Nevertheless, an endless stream of highly visible confrontations in the streets, which contrasted the brutality and the inhumanity of the white segregationists with the dignity and resolve of black protesters, made the cause of black civil rights the major issue in the United States for over a decade during the 1950s and 1960s. The nation and its leaders were forced to decide publicly whether to grant African Americans their citizenship rights or to side with white segregationists who advocated racial superiority and the undemocratic subjugation of black people.

The movement could not be ignored. Eloquent leaders and their massive followings sustained the pressure on local elites and the federal government. Countless heroic figures inspired a massive following, among them: Rosa Parks, a dignified older woman and secretary for the local NAACP, who sparked the Montgomery bus boycott when she defied an order to move to the back; Martin Luther King, Jr., who emerged from the Montgomery bus boycott and the Southern Christian Leadership Conference (SCLC) to assume a position of preeminent moral leadership and national influence; James Forman, executive secretary of the more militant Student Nonviolent Coordinating Committee (SNCC), who was to raise questions about SCLC's and King's strategy; SNCC's leader, Stokely Carmichael (now Kwame Toure), who introduced the slogan "black power"; and Fannie Lou Hamer, daughter of a sharecropper who lived on a plantation, who went to a voter registration meeting run by Forman and other SNCC members, was arrested at the courthouse in Indianola, Mississippi, when she tried to register to vote, and then was beaten with a blackjack in prison.

These leading figures and thousands of movement partici-

pants articulated black suffering and the democratic aspirations of African Americans of every generation and circumstance. In addition, thousands of whites (students, lawyers, and other civil rights workers from all walks of life) were inspired to join the Civil Rights Movement. They participated in lunch-counter sit-ins, mass demonstrations, and campaigns such as the 1964 Mississippi Freedom Summer Project, a campaign that involved hundreds of volunteers in voter registration drives and the creation of "freedom schools." Some, like Andrew Goodman and Michael Schwerner, who were involved in the Freedom Summer campaign, and Viola Liuzzo, a Michigan homemaker shot by Klansmen after a rally in support of the march from Selma to Montgomery, lost their lives in the Civil Rights Movement and, in turn, helped inspire others.

Inevitable differences of ideology, leadership style, and approach emerged within the movement as the SCLC, SNCC, the Congress of Racial Equality (CORE), and other organizations reached different judgments about the value of *nonviolent action, the role of whites in the movement, and the influence of *Malcolm X. Whatever these controversies, the moral challenge and the widespread social disruption caused by the economic boycotts, the marches, the sit-ins, and other forms of nonviolent direct action, coupled with the international pressure, created an impasse in the nation that had to be resolved.

As a result, the Civil Rights Movement achieved several important legislative victories in *Congress. The landmark Civil Rights Act of 1964 outlawed discrimination in public accommodations on the basis of race, color, religion, or national origin; it granted authority to the attorney general to force the integration of schools through litigation; and it barred discrimination in employment practices on grounds of race, color, religion, national origin, or sex. The 1965 Voting Rights Act suspended the use of literacy tests, authorized the attorney general to challenge the constitutionality of poll taxes, and introduced procedures which provided for the appointment of examiners to ensure that all restrictions on black voter registration be ended. In short, it enfranchised the southern black population.

Beyond its historic overthrow of the Jim Crow regime and specific legislative relief, the Civil Rights Movement has affected U.S. politics in fundamental ways. The Civil Rights Movement demonstrated to the oppressed black community how such protest could be successful, and it made social protest respectable. The Civil Rights Movement also proved that at times significant *reform can occur through nonviolent action.

The significance of the Civil Rights Movement extends beyond the rights and freedoms of blacks. The movement also broadened the scope of politics and inspired diverse movements for citizenship rights and social justice in the United States and abroad. Before the Civil Rights Movement, many groups in U.S. society—women, Hispanics, Native Americans, the physically disabled, gays and lesbians, etc.—were oppressed but unaware of how to resist or galvanize support. The Civil Rights Movement provided a model of successful social protest and produced a host of new tactics. Moreover, the Civil Rights Movement had an influence on freedom struggles around the world. Participants in movements in Africa, Eastern Europe, the Middle East, Latin America, and

China have made it clear that they were inspired by and learned important lessons from the U.S. Civil Rights Movement.

For all its success and influences, however, the Civil Rights Movement did not solve all of America's racial problems. As the twentieth century closed, African Americans and many other nonwhite groups were still at the bottom of the social and economic order. These current conditions are exacerbated by a mean-spirited political climate in which the poor and oppressed are blamed for their own suffering and oppression. Because of the success of the Civil Rights Movement, a relatively large black middle class has emerged. At the same time over a third of the black community is trapped in poverty. Black Americans are disproportionately housed in the rapidly growing prison industry. Thus with the dawning of the new millennium some blacks find themselves experiencing the best of times while millions of others experience the worst of times. Poverty and inequality are also widespread outside the black community. Global poverty and suffering are equally evident. It may be that protest remains the only viable means to achieve greater empowerment. If this is the case, the Civil Rights Movement has left a rich legacy to inspire and inform future struggles.

(See also CIVIL DISOBEDIENCE; DISABILITY POLITICS; DU BOIS, W. E. B.; GAY AND LESBIAN POLITICS; HISPANIC AMERICANS; INEQUALITIES; RACE AND RACISM.)

Clayborne Carson, *In Struggle: SNCC and the Black Awakening of the 1960s* (Cambridge, Mass., 1981). Aldon Morris, *Origins of the Civil Rights Movement* (New York, 1984). David Garrow, *Bearing the Cross* (New York, 1986). Taylor Branch, *Parting the Waters* (New York, 1988). Doug McAdam, *Freedom Summer* (New York, 1988). Clayborne Carson, David J. Garrow, Gerald Gill, Vincent Harding, and Darlene Clark Hine, eds., *The Eyes on the Prize Civil Rights Reader* (New York, 1991). Azza Salama Layton, *International Politics and Civil Rights Policies in the United States, 1941–1960* (Cambridge, Mass., 2000).

ALDON MORRIS

CIVIL SOCIETY. For contemporary scholars, social activists, and development professionals, civil society is that collection of diverse *interest groups and social organizations that is strong enough to provide some autonomy and protection to individuals from the authoritarian and hegemonic tendencies of *states. Broadly, civil society underscores the importance of markets and liberal states to independent social life.

Since the 1970s, the concept of civil society has been used in diverse ways, reflecting its new popular appeal as an emancipatory ideal. The concept has helped to motivate and inspire democratic struggles under authoritarian regimes in eastern and central Europe, Asia, Africa, and Latin America. Scholarship on democratization, popular movements, *human rights, and community development in these regions has found the concept of civil society tremendously productive. Beyond academic scholarship, strengthening civil society has become a priority of thousands of *non-governmental organizations through the world and a pillar of the multibillion-dollar international development profession. Such conceptions of civil society trace their intellectual origins to Alexis de Tocqueville, whose 1835 classic *Democracy in America* emphasized the importance of independent associations to social life and to promoting democracy.

As a result of its recent popularity, the concept has become somewhat detached from its intellectual roots. The term civil society is now often used as an elaborate substitute for society, without any substantial difference in meaning. Sometimes, civil society is characterized as a society with rules for civility. While coherent definition and consistent use of a term cannot be, in itself, incorrect, some definitions of civil society do ignore the concept's rich history and conceal the implications of the original conception. To speak of the mobilization of civil society or the resolution of collective action problems within civil society, for example, is to mix conceptual metaphors in untenable ways. Social scientists and activists are now examining the ancestry of civil society more critically.

The origins of the concept lie in the Scottish Enlightenment (1740–1790). In the mid-eighteenth century, Francis Hutcheson, Adam Smith, David Hume, James Steuart, Adam Ferguson, and others began to regard the market less as a socially destructive force than as a cohesive element in modern society. Civil society was thought to be intimately related to commercial society. The conduct of business for profit was theorized to be an innocent occupation. Commerce was considered capable of pacifying political ambition and of thus promoting social virtue. "To what purpose is all the toil and bustle of this world?" Smith asked in the *Theory of Moral Sentiments* (1759). "To be observed, to be attended to, to be taken notice of with sympathy, complacency, and approbation." The original theorists of civil society considered market interactions to promote manners of civility.

The Scottish enlightenment conception of civil society, with its emphasis on manners and values in commercial society, is not identical to the Roman conception of *civilis societas*. The two conceptions share the notion that individuals may make and live as equals under laws that they themselves make (as citizens). However, Scottish Enlightenment thought considered commercial society, which classical societies did not experience, to be uniquely capable of promoting the manners of a civil society.

The institution of private property and the mechanisms for its protection are fundamental to civil society. Jean-Jacques Rousseau summarized this nicely. "The first person," he writes in *A Discourse on the Origins of Inequality* (1755), "who, having enclosed a plot of land, took it into his head to say this is *mine* and found people simple enough to believe him, was the true founder of civil society." In a similar way, Georg Wilhelm Friedrich Hegel's conception of civil society (*bürgerliche gesellschaft*) literally designates the commercially vital segment of a population, namely, traders, businesspeople, lawyers, and other professionals, who are afforded residence within the walls of fortified towns as the essence of civil society. Hegel regarded the market, or "the system of needs," together with public laws, the courts, the police, and corporations as the pillars of civil society, and civil society to be the ethical foundation of the state. John Locke's pre-Scottish enlightenment contract-based conception of civil society is often contrasted with Hegel's post-Scottish enlightenment conception. For Locke, civil society was equivalent to political society. For Hegel, in contrast, political society, and the state are made possibly by the development of civil society.

In contemporary usage, civil society is usually regarded as antithetic to the state. *Democracy and human rights activists prize civil society for its promise of independence, autonomy, and separation from the state. Nevertheless, it should be noted the state both protects and makes possible civil society. Important functions of the modern state are to protect private property and to produce patterns of expectation and behavior in society that promote a public order that specific governments can not easily alter. In this way, by promoting a political, economic, and social environment in which independent associations may form and operate, the state helps to create civil society.

(See also CITIZENSHIP; PLURALISM; SOCIAL CAPITAL.)

Goran Hyden, "Civil Society, Social Capital, and Development," *Studies in Comparative International Development* (Spring 1997). John Keane, *Civil Society: Old Images, New Visions* (Stanford, Calif., 1998).

CHRISTOPHER CANDLAND

CIVIL SOCIETY ORGANIZATIONS. See NON-GOVERNMENTAL ORGANIZATIONS.

CLASS AND POLITICS. See overleaf.

CLAUSEWITZ, Carl von. The first modern writer to develop a nondidactic theory of *war, Carl von Clausewitz (1780–1831) analyzed war as a permanent phenomenon of the human condition, with its own dynamic and timeless as well as changing elements. He entered the Prussian army at the age of twelve, and served as an infantry officer and in staff positions in the French Revolutionary and Napoleonic Wars. Between 1818 and 1830 he was director of the Berlin War Academy, during which time he wrote his major theoretical work, *On War*. He died before completing the extensive revisions he had planned.

Clausewitz believed that although war, like politics or art, was not a science, it could be studied scientifically. By combining historical research with the experience and study of contemporary wars, he created a broad evidentiary base to which he applied the analytic methods of German idealist philosophy. He developed his arguments dialectically and by making comparisons between past and present, which alone, he thought, made possible the discovery of universals. He tested these theoretical results against actual events, which called for further historical study. Not coincidentally, history rather than theory makes up the larger share of his writings.

According to Clausewitz, theory should identify the various elements (operational, tactical, etc.) of war, explain their function and interaction, and place war in its political context. Hypotheses and explanations must be logical, consistent, and above all realistic. Reality will always differ from its theoretical image, if only because reality includes imponderables. Theory must build chance, accidents, and emotions into its structure, but will never be truly comprehensive. Theory cannot provide laws for action, but by helping people think logically and realistically about war it might indirectly improve performance.

War is distinguished from other social activities by its element of large-scale, organized violence. Because violence is its defining property, the philosophically "ideal" conflict contains the highest degree of violence—absolute war. Not only are extremes of violence a logical necessity, war in the real world tends to approach the absolute as the result of technological development and of the dynamic process Clausewitz termed "escalation," in which each opponent is tempted to outdo the other.

The concept of absolute war, logically valid and supported by some historical evidence, helps us analyze all wars. But real wars have usually fallen short of the highest level of violence. This contradiction between theory and reality is partly explained by "friction," a concept Clausewitz developed to analyze chance, misunderstandings, and accidents in war. Its basic explanation, however, is found in an antithesis that Clausewitz joined to the thesis of absolute war. War is always influenced by forces external to it: by its political goals, and by the characteristics of the societies and governments in conflict. War is a continuation of policy by other means. If a particular war does not seek the opponent's annihilation but a lesser goal—defense of a border zone, for instance—then even theory does not demand the extreme. The concept of absolute war and the concept of war limited by friction, policy, and other factors, together define the dual nature of war.

It is a consequence of war's dual nature that a purely military evaluation of strategic or operational decisions is inappropriate. In a rational context, the kind and degree of violence should agree with the goal of policy, and the political implications of its use should be weighed.

These central tenets of Clausewitz's theory are supported by concepts such as friction, escalation, and "moral elements"—psychological characteristics of society, the armed forces, and the military leadership, which are difficult to analyze and quantify, but are of supreme importance. Lesser propositions address specifics of warfare, for instance the assertion that every attack loses impetus as it progresses.

Clausewitz wrote with great precision, but readers have often found his dialectic difficult to follow, or have mistaken the concept of absolute war as advocacy instead of a theoretical construct, which with its antithesis enables us to analyze the entire range of armed conflict. Despite many attempts, it has never been proved that his writings have seriously influenced the conduct of modern war. For instance, Germany's invasion of Belgium in 1914, regardless of the political consequences that were sure to follow, contradicts his warning against purely military decisions. His influence has been intellectual. *On War* is still read and discussed today because the work's concepts and formulations have proved to be an excellent introduction to the systematic, realistic study of war, past and present.

(See also FORCE, USE OF; STRATEGY.)

Carl von Clausewitz, *On War,* trans. and ed. Michael Howard and Peter Paret, rev. ed. (Princeton, N.J., 1984). Peter Paret, *Clausewitz and the State,* rev. ed. (Princeton, N.J., 1985). Carl von Clausewitz, *Historical and Political Writings,* trans. and ed. Peter Paret and Daniel Moran (Princeton, N.J., 1991).

PETER PARET

CLIENTALISM. See PATRON-CLIENT POLITICS.

CLINTON, Bill. It is probably the case that all presidents hope to "go down in history"; indeed, the goal of leaving behind a substantial "legacy" is generally regarded as an important influence on the behavior in their last years in office of that minority of modern presidents who have been lucky enough to serve for two full terms. William Jefferson Clinton need have no concern about whether or not his name will be

(cont. on p. 148)

CLASS AND POLITICS. The concept of class has had an erratic career in the contemporary analysis of politics. There was a time, not so long ago, when class played at best a marginal role in explanations of political phenomena. In the 1950s and early 1960s the dominant approach to politics was *pluralism. Political outcomes in democratic societies were viewed as resulting from the interplay of many crosscutting forces interacting in an environment of bargaining, voting, coalition building, and consensus formation. While some of the organized *interest groups may have been based in constituencies with a particular class character—most notably unions and business associations—nevertheless, such organizations were given no special analytical status by virtue of this.

From the late 1960s through the early 1980s, with the renaissance of the Marxist tradition in the social sciences, class suddenly moved to the core of many analyses of the *state and politics. Much discussion occurred over such things as the "class character" of state apparatuses and the importance of instrumental manipulation of state institutions by powerful class-based actors. Even among scholars whose theoretical perspective was not built around class, class was taken seriously and accorded an importance in the analysis of politics rarely found in the previous period.

While class analysis never became the dominant paradigm for the analysis of politics, it was a theoretical force to be reckoned with in the 1970s. Ironically, perhaps, in the course of the 1980s, as U.S. national politics took on a particularly blatant class character, the academic popularity of class analysis as a framework for understanding politics steadily declined. The center of gravity of critical work on the state shifted toward a variety of theoretical perspectives which explicitly distanced themselves from a preoccupation with class, in particular "state-centered" approaches to politics which emphasize the causal importance of the institutional properties of the state and the interests of state managers and cultural theories which place discourses and symbolic systems at the center of political analysis. While the class analysis of politics has by no means retreated to the marginal status it was accorded in the 1950s, it is no longer the center of debate the way it was in the 1970s and 1980s.

This is, therefore, a good time to take stock of the theoretical accomplishments and unresolved issues of the class analysis of politics. As a prologue to the discussion, in the next section we will briefly look at the concept of class itself. This will be followed in section 2 by an examination of three different kinds of mechanisms through which class can have an impact on politics. Using terminology adapted from the work of Robert Alford and Roger Friedland, I will refer to these as the *situational, institutional,* and *systemic* political effects of class. Section 3 will then briefly examine the problem of variability in the patterns of class effects on politics. The essay will then conclude in section 4 with a discussion of the problem of explanatory primacy of class relative to other causal processes.

The Concept of Class. The word "class" has been used to designate a variety of quite distinct theoretical concepts. In particular, it is important to distinguish between what are sometimes called *gradational* and *relational* class concepts. As

has often been noted, for many "class" is simply a way of talking about strata within the income distribution. The frequent references in contemporary U.S. politics to "middle-class taxpayers" is equivalent to "middle-income taxpayers." Classes are simply rungs on a ladder of inequalities. For others, particularly analysts working in the Marxian and Weberian theoretical traditions, the concept of class is not meant to designate a distributional *outcome* as such, but rather the nature of the underlying social relations which generate such outcomes. To speak of a person's class position is thus to identify that person's relationship to specific kinds of mechanisms which generate inequalities of income and power. In a relational class concept, capitalists and workers do not simply differ in the amount of income they acquire, but in the mechanism through which they acquire that income.

It is possible to deploy both gradational and relational concepts of class in the analysis of politics. Many people, for example, use a basically gradational concept of class to examine the different political attitudes and voting behaviors of the poor, the middle class, and the rich. However, most of the systematic work on class and politics has revolved around relational class concepts. There are two basic reasons for this: First, relational concepts are generally seen as designating more fundamental aspects of social structure than gradational concepts, since the relational concepts are anchored in the causal mechanisms which generate the gradational inequalities. To analyze the determinants of political phenomena in terms of relational class concepts is therefore to dig deeper into the causal process than to simply link politics to distributionally defined class categories. Second, relational class categories have the analytical advantage of generating categories of actors who live in real interactive social relations to each other. The "rich," "middle," and "poor" are arbitrary divisions on a continuum; the individuals defined by these categories may not systematically interact with each other in any particular way. Capitalists and workers, on the other hand, are inherently mutually interdependent. They are real categories whose respective interests are defined, at least in part, by the nature of the relations which bind them together. Building the concept of class around these relations, then, greatly facilitates the analysis of the formation of organized collectivities engaged in political conflict over material interests.

Adopting a relational perspective on class, of course, is only a point of departure. There are many ways of elaborating such a concept. In particular, much has been made of the distinction between the Marxian and Weberian traditions of class analysis. Weberians define classes primarily in terms of *market* relations, whereas Marxists define classes by the social relations of *production*. Why is this contrast of theoretical importance? After all, both Marxists and Weberians recognize capitalists and workers as the two fundamental classes of capitalist societies, and both define these classes in essentially the same way—capitalists are owners of the means of production who employ wage earners; workers are nonowners of the means of production who sell their labor power to capitalists. What difference does it make that Weberians define these classes by the exchange relation into which they enter, whereas Marxists emphasize the social relations of production?

First, the restriction of classes to market relations means, for Weberians, that classes only really exist in capitalist societies. The relationship between lords and serfs might be oppressive and the source of considerable conflict, but Weberians would not treat this as a class relation since it is structured around relations of personal dependence and domination, not market relations. Marxists, in contrast, see conflicts over the control of productive resources in both feudalism and *capitalism as instances of class struggle. This is not simply a nominal shift in labels, for it is part of the effort within *Marxism to construct a general theory of historical change built around class analysis. Aphorisms such as "class struggle is the motor of history" only make sense if the concept of "class" is built around the social relations of production rather than restricted to market relations.

Second, the elaboration of the concept of class in terms of production relations underwrites the linkage between class and exploitation that is central to Marxist theory. In the traditional Marxist account, exploitation occurs primarily within production itself, for it is in production that labor is actually performed and embodied in the social product. Exploitation, roughly, consists in the appropriation by one class of the "surplus labor" performed by another. While the exchange relation between workers and capitalists may create the *opportunity* for capitalists to exploit workers, it is only when the labor of workers is actually deployed in the labor process and the resulting products appropriated by capitalists that exploitation actually occurs. The characteristic lack of discussion of exploitation by Weberian class analysts thus, at least in part, reflects their restriction of the concept of class to the exchange relation.

While these differences between the Marxian and Weberian concept of class are important for the broader theory of society within which these class concepts are used, in practical terms for the analysis of capitalist society the actual descriptive class maps generated by scholars in the two traditions may not be so divergent. As already noted, both traditions see the capital-labor relation as defining the principal axis of class relations in capitalism. Furthermore, scholars in both traditions acknowledge the importance of a variety of social categories, loosely labeled the "new middle class(es)"—professionals, managers and executives, bureaucratic officials and perhaps highly educated white-collar employees—who do not fit neatly into the polarized class relation between capitalists and workers. There is little consensus either among Weberian or among Marxist scholars on precisely how these new middle classes should be conceptualized. As a result, particularly as Marxist accounts of these "middle class" categories have become more sophisticated, the line of demarcation between these two traditions has become somewhat less sharply drawn.

While Marxist and Weberian pictures of the class structure of capitalist society may not differ dramatically, their use of the concept of class in the analysis of political phenomena is generally sharply different. Weberians typically regard class as one among a variety of salient determinants of politics. In specific problems this means that class might assume considerable importance, but there is no general presumption that class is a more pervasive or powerful determinant of political

phenomena than other causal processes. Marxists, in contrast, characteristically give class a privileged status in the analysis. In the most orthodox treatments, class (and closely related concepts like "capitalism" or "mode of production") may become virtually the exclusive systematic explanatory principles, but in all Marxist accounts of politics class plays a central, if not necessarily all-encompassing, explanatory role. In the final section of this paper we will examine the problem of explanatory primacy for class. Before we engage that issue, however, we will examine the various ways in which Marxist class analysts see class shaping politics.

How Class Shapes Politics. Robert Alford and Roger Friedland, building on the analysis of Steven Lukes and others, have elaborated a tripartite typology of "levels of power" that will be useful in examining the causal role of class on politics: 1) *Situational* power refers to power relations of direct command and obedience between actors, as in Weber's celebrated definition of power as the ability of one actor to get another to do something even in the face of resistance. This is the characteristic form of power analyzed in various behavioral studies of power. 2) *Institutional* power refers to the characteristics of different institutional settings which shape the decision-making agenda in ways which serve the interests of particular groups. This is also referred to as "negative power" or the "second face of power" (see Bachrach and Baratz)—power which excludes certain alternatives from a decision-making agenda without, as in situational power, actually commanding a specific behavior. 3) *Systemic* power is perhaps the most difficult (and contentious) conceptually. It refers to the power to realize one's interests by virtue of the overall structure of a social system rather than by virtue of commanding the behavior of others or of controlling the agendas of specific organizations.

Alford and Friedland discuss this typology of power in an interesting way using a loose game theory metaphor: Systemic power is power embedded in the fundamental nature of the game itself; institutional power is power embodied in the specific rules of the game; and situational power is power deployed in specific moves within a given set of rules. When actors use specific resources strategically to accomplish their goals, they are exercising situational power. The procedural rules which govern how they use those resources reflect institutional power. And the nature of the social system which determines the range of possible rules and achievable goals reflects systemic power. There is thus a kind of cybernetic relationship among these levels of power: the system level imposes limits on the institutional level which imposes limits on actors' strategies at the situational level. Conflicts at the situational level, in turn, can modify the rules at the institutional level, which cumulatively can lead to the transformation of the system itself.

The class analysis of politics is implicated in each of these domains of power and politics. Although class theorists of politics do not explicitly frame their analyses in terms of these three levels of power, nevertheless the distinctions are implicit in many discussions.

Class and Situational Power. Much of the theoretical debate over the relative explanatory importance of class has occurred at the situational level of political analysis. Marxists (and non-Marxists heavily influenced by the Marxian tradition) typically argue that actors whose interests and resources are derived from their link to the class structure generally play the decisive role in actively shaping political conflicts and state policies. Sometimes the emphasis is on the strategic action of the dominant class, on the ability of capitalists to manipulate the state in their interests. Other times the emphasis is on the political effects of class struggle as such, in which case popular actions as well as ruling class machinations are seen as shaping state policies. In either case, class is seen as shaping politics through its effects on the behavioral interactions among political actors.

The theoretical reasoning behind such treatments of the class basis of situational power is fairly straightforward. Class structures, among other things, distribute resources which are useful in political struggles. In particular, in capitalist societies capitalists have two crucial resources available to them to be deployed politically: enormous financial resources and personal connections to people in positions of governmental authority. Through a wide variety of concrete mechanisms—financing politicians, political parties, and policy think tanks; financially controlling the main organs of the mass media; offering lucrative jobs to high-level political officials after they leave state employment; extensive lobbying—capitalists are in a position to use their wealth to directly shape the direction of state policies. When combined with the dense pattern of personal networks which give capitalists easy access to the sites of immediate political power, such use of financial resources gives the bourgeoisie vastly disproportionate direct leverage over politics.

Few theorists deny the empirical facts of the use of politically important resources in this way by members of the capitalist class in pursuit of their interests. What is often questioned is the general efficacy and coherence of such actions in sustaining the class interests of the bourgeoisie. Because individual capitalists are frequently preoccupied by their immediate, particularistic interests (e.g., in specific markets, technologies, or regulations), when they deploy their class-derived resources politically some scholars argue that they are unlikely to do so in ways which place the class interests of the bourgeoisie as a whole above their own particularistic interests. As Fred Block among others has noted, the capitalist class is often very divided politically, lacking a coherent vision and sense of priorities. Thus, even if capitalists try to manipulate politics in various ways, such manipulations often work against each other and do not generate a consistent set of policy outcomes.

The fact that capitalists have considerable power resources by virtue of their control over capital thus does not ensure a capacity to translate those resources into a coherent class direction of politics. What is more, in terms of situational power, capitalists are not the only actors with effective political resources. In particular, as Theda Skocpol, Anthony Giddens, and others have stressed, state managers—the top-level politicians and officials within state apparatuses—have direct control of considerable resources to pursue political objectives. Although in many instances the interests and objectives of state managers may be congruent with the interests of the capitalist class, this is not universally the case, and when overt conflicts between state managers and the bourgeoisie occur there is no inherent reason why capitalists will always prevail. Even more to the point, in many situations, because of the disorganization, myopia, and apathy of the capitalist class, state managers will have considerable room to initiate state policies independently of pressures from the capitalist class.

These kinds of arguments do not discredit the claim that class structures do shape both the interests of actors and the political resources they can deploy in struggles over situational power. However, the blanket claim that class-derived interests and power resources are always the most salient is called into question.

Class and Institutional Power. It was at least in part because of a recognition that at the level of situational power capitalists are not always present as the predominant active political actors that much class analysis of politics has centered around the problem of the institutional dimensions of power. The argument is basically this: The state should be viewed not simply as a state *in* capitalist society, but rather as a *capitalist* state. This implies that there are certain institutional properties of the very form of the state that can be treated as having a specific class character to them. The idea here is not simply that there are certain policies of the state which embody the interests of a specific class, but rather that the very structure of the apparatuses through which those policies are made embodies those class interests.

Claims about the class character of the institutional level of power involve what is sometimes called non-decision-making power or negative power. The basic argument was crisply laid out in an early essay by Claus Offe. Offe argued that the class character of the state was inscribed in a series of negative filter mechanisms which imparted a systematic class bias to state actions. "Class bias," in this context, means that the property in question tends to filter out state actions which would be inimical to the interests of the dominant class. The form of the state, in effect, systematically determines what does not happen rather than simply what does.

An example, emphasized by Claus Offe and Volker Ronge as well as by Göran Therborn, would be the institutional rules by which the capitalist state acquires financial resources—through taxation and borrowing from the privately produced surplus rather than through the state's direct appropriation of the surplus generated by its own productive activity. By restricting the state's access to funds in this way the state is rendered dependent upon capitalist production, and this in turn acts as a mechanism which filters out state policies which would seriously undermine the profitability of private accumulation. Or, to take another example, given considerable emphasis by Nicos Poulantzas (1973), the electoral rules of capitalist representative democracies (in which people cast votes as individual citizens within territorial units of representation rather than as members of functioning groups) have the effect of transforming people from members of a class into atomized individuals (the "juridical citizen"). This atomization, in turn, serves to filter out state policies that would only be viable if people were systematically organized into durable collectivities or associations. To the extent that this filter can be viewed as stabilizing capitalism and thus serving the basic interests of the capitalist class, then exclusive reliance on purely territorial, individualized voting can be viewed as having a class character.

This way of understanding the class character of an apparatus suggests a certain functionalist logic to the thesis that the state is a capitalist state: its form is capitalist insofar as these institutional features contribute to the reproduction of the interests of the capitalist class. This functional logic has been most systematically elaborated in Göran Therborn's *What Does the Ruling Class Do When It Rules?* Therborn stresses that the real analytical bite of the thesis that the state has a distinctive class character occurs when the state is analyzed comparatively, particularly across historical epochs. The class character of the state apparatus is a variable; state apparatuses corresponding to different class structures will have distinctively different properties which impart different class biases on state actions. If this "correspondence principle" is correct, then it should be possible to define the specific class properties of the feudal state, the capitalist state, and—perhaps—the socialist state. Take the example already cited of the mechanism through which the state acquires resources. In the capitalist state this occurs primarily through taxation, thus insuring the fiscal subordination of the state to private capital accumulation. In the feudal state revenues are acquired through the direct appropriation of surplus from the personal vassals of the king. And in the socialist state, state revenues are acquired through the appropriation of the surplus product of state enterprises. In each case, the argument goes, these class forms of revenue acquisition selectively filter out political practices which might threaten the existing class structure.

Many critics of the thesis that the state has a distinctive class character have argued that this claim implies a functionalist theory of the state. This accusation is certainly appropriate in some cases. In the early work on the state by Nicos Poulantzas (1973), for example, and even more in the work of Louis Althusser, there was very little room for genuinely contradictory elements in the state. The class properties of the capitalist state were explained by the functions they served for reproducing capitalism. The functional correspondence principle for identifying the class character of aspects of the state slid into a principle for explaining the properties of the state. This kind of functionalism, however, is not an inherent feature of the class analysis of the institutional level of political power. While the thesis that state apparatuses have a class character does follow a functional logic (i.e., what makes a given property have a given "class character" is its functional relation to the class structure), this does not necessarily imply a full-fledged functionalist theory of the state.

Class and Systemic Power. To say that capitalists have *situational* power is to say that they command a range of resources which they can deploy to get their way. To say that they have *institutional* power is to argue that various institutions are designed in such a way as to selectively exclude alternatives from the political agenda which are antithetical to their interests. To say that they have *systemic* power is to say that the logic of the social system itself affirms their in-terests quite apart from their conscious strategies and the internal organization of political apparatuses.

The idea that capitalists have such systemic power has been forcefully argued by Adam Przeworski, building on the work of Antonio *Gramsci. Przeworski argues that so long as capitalism is intact as a social order, all actors in the system have an interest in capitalists making a profit. What this means is that unless a group has the capacity to overthrow the system completely, then at least in terms of material interests even groups opposed to capitalism have an interest in sustaining capitalist accumulation and profitability.

This kind of system-level power has been recognized by many scholars, not just those working firmly within the Marxist tradition. Charles Lindblom's well-known study *Politics and Markets*, for example, is built around the problem of how the interests of capitalists are imposed on political institutions by the operation of markets even without any direct, instrumental manipulation of those institutions by individual capitalists. Indeed, this essential point, wrapped in quite different rhetoric, is also at the core of neoconservative supply-side economics arguments about the need to reduce government spending in order to spur economic growth.

There are two critical differences between Marxist treatments of this systemic level of analysis and most mainstream treatments. First, Marxists characterize these system-level constraints on politics as having a distinctive *class* character. Neoconservatives do not regard the private investment constraint on the state as an instance of "class power," because they regard markets as the "natural" form of economic interaction. The constraint comes from the universal laws of economics rooted in human nature. In contrast, the Marxist characterization of these constraints in class terms rests on the general claim that capitalism is a historically distinct form of economy.

The second important difference between Marxist and mainstream perspectives on the constraints capitalism imposes on the state is that most liberal and neoconservative analysts see this system-level logic as much less closely tied to the institutional and situational levels of analysis than do Marxists. Neoconservatives in particular grant the state considerably more autonomy to muck up the functioning of the capitalist economy than do Marxists. For neoconservatives, even though the political system is clearly dependent on the private economy for resources and growth, nevertheless politically motivated actors are quite capable of persisting in high levels of excessive state spending in spite of the economic constraints. The state, being pushed by ideological agendas of actors wielding situational power, can, through myopia, "kill the goose that lays the golden egg." Marxists tend to see state spending and state policies as less likely to deviate persistently from the functional requirements of capitalism because they see the levels of situational and institutional power as generally congruent with the level of systemic power. The structure of state apparatuses and the strategies of capitalists, therefore, generally prevent too much deviation from occurring. Neoconservatives, on the other hand, see the three levels of politics as having much greater potential for divergence. They believe that the democratic form of institutions and the excessive mobilization of popular forces systematically generates dysfunctional levels of state spending which are not necessarily corrected by the exercise of capitalist situational power or the negative feedback.

Variability in the Effects of Class on Politics. We have reviewed three clusters of mechanisms through which class shapes politics: the class-based access to resources which can be strategically deployed for political purposes; the institutionalization of certain class biases into the design of state apparatuses; and the way in which the operation of the system as a whole universalizes certain class interests. Frequently, in the more theoretical discussions of these mechanisms, the class character of these mechanisms is treated as largely invariant within a given kind of class society. Abstract discussions of "the capitalist state," for example, emphasize what all capitalist states have in common by virtue of being capitalist states. Relatively less attention has been given to the problem of variability. In many empirical contexts, however, the central issue is precisely the ways in which class effects concretely vary across cases. Let us look briefly at such variability in class effects at the situational, institutional, and systemic levels of political analysis.

One of the central themes of much Marxist historical research is the shifting "balance of class forces" between workers and capitalists (and sometimes other classes) in various kinds of social and political conflicts. Generally, expressions like "balance of forces" refer to the relative situational power of the contending organized collectivities—i.e., their relative capacity to actively pursue their interests in various political arenas. The task of an analysis of variability in the class character of situational power is thus to explain the social determinants of these varying capacities. Generally this involves invoking mechanisms at the institutional and systemic levels of analysis. Thus, for example, the enduring weakness of the U.S. working class within electoral politics has been explained by such institutional factors as the existence of a winner-take-all electoral system which undermines the viability of small parties, the lack of public financing of elections which enhances the political influence of financial contributors, and voter registration laws which make voter mobilization difficult, as well as such systemic factors as the location of U.S. capitalism in the world capitalist system. Each of these factors undermines the potential situational power of the working class within electoral politics. This enduring situational weakness, in turn, blocks the capacity of the popular forces to alter the institutional properties of the state in ways which would enhance their power. While in all capitalist societies it may be the case that capitalists have disproportionate situational power, capitalist societies can vary considerably in power of different subordinate groups relative to the bourgeoisie.

The same kind of variation is possible in terms of power embodied in the institutional properties of the state. In various ways, noncapitalist elements can be embodied in the institutional structure of capitalist states. Consider the example of workplace safety regulations. A variety of institutional forms can be established for implementing safety regulations. The conventional device in most capitalist states is to have a hierarchical bureaucratic agency responsible for such regulations with actual enforcement organized through official inspections, licensing requirements, and various other aspects of bureaucratic due process. An alternative structure would be to establish workplace occupational safety committees within factories controlled by employees with powers to monitor compliance and enforce regulations. Such administration procedures built around principles of what Joshua Cohen and Joel Rogers call "associational democracy" violate the class logic of the capitalist state by encouraging the collective organization rather than atomization of the affected people. To the extent that such noncapitalist elements can be incorporated into the institutional structure of the capitalist state, then the class character of those apparatuses can vary *even within capitalism.*

Finally, some theoretical work entertains the possibilities of variation in the class character of systemic power within capitalist societies. The essential issue here is whether the overall relationship between state and economy within capitalism can significantly modify the dynamics of the system itself. Do all instances of capitalism have fundamentally the same system logic simply by virtue of the private ownership of the means of production, or can this logic be significantly modified in various ways? Most Marxists have insisted that there is relatively little variation in such system logic across capitalisms, at least as it relates to the basic class character of system-level power. The transition from competitive to "monopoly" capitalism, for example, may greatly affect the *situational* power of different classes and fractions of classes, and it might even be reflected in changes in the class character of the institutional form of the state (for example, petit bourgeois elements in state apparatuses might disappear as capitalism advances). But the basic system-level class logic, Marxists have traditionally argued, remains organized around the interests of capital in both cases.

There has been some challenge to this view by scholars generally sympathetic to Marxian perspectives. Gøsta Esping-Andersen, for example, argues that differences in the forms of the *welfare state (which he refers to as conservative, liberal, and socialist welfare state regimes) can have a basic effect on the system logic of capitalism, creating different developmental tendencies and different matrices of interests for various classes.

Joel Rogers has forcefully argued a similar view with respect to the specific issue of industrial relations. He argues that there is an "inverse-J" relationship between the interests of capital and the degree of unionization of the working class. Increasing unionization hurts the interests of capitalists up to a certain point. Beyond that point, however, further increases in unionization are beneficial to capitalists, because they make possible higher levels of coordination and cooperation between labor and capital. This means that if, for example, the legal regime of industrial relations prevents unionization from passing the trough threshold in the curve (as, he argues, is the case in the United States), then unions will be constantly on the defensive as they confront the interests of capital, whereas if the legal order facilitates unionization moving beyond the trough (as in Sweden), then the system logic will sustain unionization. High unionization and low unionization capitalisms, therefore, embody qualitatively different system patterns of class power within what remains an overall capitalist framework.

Conclusion. Few scholars today would argue that class is irrelevant to the analysis of political phenomena, but there is much contention over how important class might be. The characteristic form of this debate is for the critic of class analysis to attack class reductionism, i.e., the thesis that political phenomena (state policies, institutional properties, political behavior, party strategies, etc.) can be fully explained by class-based causal processes. Defenders of class analysis, on the other hand, attack their critics for claiming that political phenomena are completely autonomous from class determinants. Both of these positions, when stated in this form, have no real defenders. Even relatively orthodox Marxists introduce many nonclass factors in their explanations of any given example of state policy and thus are not guilty of class reductionism; and even the most state-centered critic of class analysis admits that class relations play some role in shaping political outcomes.

The issue, then, is not really explanatory reductionism vs. absolute political autonomy, but rather the relative salience of different causal factors and how they fit together. A good example is the discussions of the development of the welfare state sparked by the work of Theda Skocpol and others advocating a "state-centered" approach to the study of politics. In an influential paper published in the mid-1980s, Ann Orloff and Skocpol argue that the specific temporal sequence of the introduction of social security laws in Britain, Canada, and the United States cannot be explained by economic or class factors. Rather, they argue, this sequence is primarily the result of causal processes located within the political realm itself, specifically the bureaucratic capacities of the state and the legacies of prior state policies.

The empirical arguments of Orloff and Skocpol are quite convincing given the specific way they have defined their object of explanation. But suppose there was a slight shift in the question. Instead of asking, "why was social security introduced in Britain before World War I, in Canada in the 1920s, and the United States in the 1930s?" suppose the question were, "why did no industrialized capitalist society have social security in the 1850s while all industrialized capitalist societies had such programs by the 1950s?" The nature of class relations and class conflicts in capitalism and the transformations of the capitalist economy would surely figure more prominently in the answer to this reformulated explanatory problem.

In general, then, the issue of causal primacy is sensitive to the precise formulation of what is to be explained *(explanandum)*. It is certainly implausible that class (or anything else) could be "the most important" cause of all political phenomena. For claims of causal primacy to have any force, therefore, it is essential that the domain of the explanations over which the claims are being made be well defined. Can we, then, specify the domain of *explananda* for which class is likely to be the most important causal factor? Implicit in most class analyses of politics are two very general hypotheses about the range of explanatory problems for which class analysis is likely to provide the most powerful explanations:

Hypothesis 1. The more coarse-grained and abstract the *explanandum*, the more likely it is that general systemic factors, such as class structure or the dynamics of capitalism, will play an important explanatory role. The more fine-grained and concrete the object of explanation, on the other hand, the more likely it is that relatively contingent causal processes—such as the specific legislative histories of different states or the detailed rules of electoral competition—will loom large in the explanation. All things being equal, therefore, the decision to examine relatively nuanced concrete variations in political outcomes across cases with broadly similar class structures is likely to reduce the salience of class relative to other causal processes.

Hypothesis 2. The more the reproduction of the class structure and the interests of dominant classes are directly implicated in the *explanandum*, the more likely it is that class factors—at the situational, institutional, and systemic levels—will constitute important causes in the explanation. This is not a tautology, for there is no logical reason why class mechanisms must be causally important for explaining class-relevant outcomes. Such a hypothesis also does not reject the possibility that causal processes unconnected to class might play a decisive role in specific instances. But it does argue that one should be surprised if class-based causal processes do not play a significant role in explaining political phenomena closely connected to the reproduction of class structures and the interests of dominant classes.

Taken together, these two hypotheses help specify the applicability of class to the analysis of politics.

(See also MARX, KARL; SOCIALISM AND SOCIAL DEMOCRACY; WEBER, MAX.)

Ralf Dahrendorf, *Class and Class Conflict in Industrial Societies* (Stanford, Calif., 1959). Ralph Miliband, *The State in Capitalist Society* (New York, 1969). Peter Bachrach and Morton S. Baratz, *Power and Poverty* (New York, 1970). Louis Althusser, *Lenin and Philosophy* (New York, 1971). Nicos Poulantzas, *Political Power and Social Classes* (London, 1973). Steven Lukes, *Power: A Radical View* (London, 1974). Claus Offe, "Structural Problems of the Capitalist State. Class Rule and the Political System. On the Selectiveness of Political Institutions," in Klaus Von Beyme, ed., *German Political Studies*, vol. 1 (London, 1974). Claus Offe and Volker Ronge, "Theses on the Theory of the State," *New German Critique* 6 (Fall 1975): 139–147. Nicos Poulantzas, *Classes in Contemporary Capitalism* (London, 1975). Charles Lindblom, *Politics and Markets* (New York, 1977). Göran Therborn, *What Does the Ruling Class Do When It Rules?* (London, 1978). Frank Parkin, *Marxist Class Theory: A Bourgeois Critique* (New York, 1979). Anthony Giddens, *A Contemporary Critique of Historical Materialism* (Berkeley, Calif., 1981). John Roemer, *A General Theory of Exploitation and Class* (Cambridge, Mass., 1982). Ann Orloff and Theda Skocpol, "Why Not Equal Equal Protection? Explaining the Politics of Public Social Spending in Britain, 1900–1911, and the United States, 1880s–1920" *American Sociological Review* 49, no. 6 (1984): 726–750. Robert Alford and Roger Friedland, *The Powers of Theory* (Cambridge, U.K., 1985). Peter Evans, Theda Skocpol, and Dieter Reuschmeyer, eds., *Bringing the State Back In* (Cambridge, U.K., 1985). Adam Przeworski, *Capitalism and Social Democracy* (Cambridge, U.K., 1985). Fred Block, *Revising State Theory: Essays in Politics and Post-industrialism* (Philadelphia, 1987). Gøsta Esping-Andersen, *The Three Worlds of Welfare Capitalism* (Princeton, N.J., 1990). Erik Olin Wright, *Class Counts* (Cambridge, U.K., 1997).

ERIK OLIN WRIGHT

CLASS AND POLITICS / ERIK OLIN WRIGHT

recalled once out of office. As only the second president to be impeached (though, in common with the first, Andrew, Johnson, acquitted by the Senate), Clinton's name will often be the right answer in television quizzes and college tests. It is probable that the reasons why Clinton was impeached will be sufficiently puzzling for future generations that, again as in the case of Andrew Johnson, a good essay question for students yet unborn will be to work out the reasons why. It is reasonable to suppose that Clinton would prefer his presidency to be remembered for more positive reasons, however, than his relationship with a White House staffer and in possibly committing perjury in attempting to conceal it. What was the significance of the Clinton presidency?

It is no disrespect to Clinton (and probably would not be seen by him as disrespectful) to say that a very important aspect of his presidency was political. Prior to Clinton's election in 1992, it had become fashionable to suggest that the Republicans had a "lock" on the presidency. The Republicans' successful use of "wedge" social issues and the reputation the Democrats had acquired as being too far from the mainstream suggested that the Republicans could extend their twelve-year grip on the White House. Clinton's success in defeating an incumbent president, George *Bush, who had led the United States and it allies to victory in the *Gulf War the year before the election, was startling. A slight downturn in the economy helped Clinton, though ironically the great boom of the 1990s had started before Bush left office. Yet Clinton's election strategy was regarded as "writing the playbook" on how center-left candidates could defeat their opponents who had enjoyed success in so many democracies in the 1980s. The Clinton campaign's use of polls and focus groups combined with adroit maneuvering on issues to steal the thunder of the right (as in Clinton's promise to "end welfare as we know it") provided a model that was closely observed and replicated by politicians in other countries such as Britain's leader of the Labour Party and prime minister, Tony *Blair. In the 1996 campaign, Clinton consolidated his position by developing the use of the tactic of "triangulation," positioning himself ideologically between the Republicans and the Congressional Democrats.

Even Clinton's political setbacks seemed to provide him with the opportunity to display political genius. The attempt to impeach and remove him from office after revelations about Clinton's sex life that seemed sordid and humiliating ended up costing the Republicans politically more than it cost him. The Democrats' loss of control of Congress in the 1994 elections seemed at first a repudiation of Clinton as well as of the Democratic Party, a humiliation that would strip away his ability to influence events. Yet in the six years that followed, Clinton displayed consummate political skill in handling the problems presented by "divided government." Although the Republican majority had arrived in Washington armed with a long list of legislation they intended to adopt in their "Contract with America," on only one issue, welfare reform, were the Republicans able to confront Clinton with the choice between displeasing his party by signing a bill into law or displeasing majority public opinion; even on this issue, Clinton, as noted above, had signaled his willingness to change existing policies. In general, however, Clinton succeeded in blocking most of the Contract with America and indeed often obliged the congressional Republican majorities

to accept liberal, even if small-scale, incremental policy initiatives that were popular with the public for fear that they would otherwise lose popularity and votes. Except in the year following the Republican capture of Congress, Clinton's legislative success score as compiled by the influential *Congressional Quarterly* (the percentage of votes in Congress on which the president takes a position and wins) was unusually high. In this, Clinton was aided by rhetorical skills that allowed him to take his case to the nation ("go public") with great success. Very few presidents have matched Clinton in his ability to enthuse voters both in person and via television. Clinton was also aided in his legislative maneuvering by continuous opinion polling and assiduous use of focus groups. Every State of the Union Address, for example, was tested in advance on focus groups as though it was a new product being test-marketed. All presidents have been concerned about public opinion, of course. However, presidents have generally distinguished the quest for office from governing. Clinton, however, made this concern so central in policy making that his presidency has been described as a "permanent campaign."

Clinton the politician will be regarded as a genius. His policy legacy is more in doubt partly because divided government, which prevailed for most of his administration, always obscures who is to be blamed or praised for a policy development. Clinton's supporters gave him great credit for the economic boom that lasted throughout his presidency, in particular because of his insistence in his 1993* budget (with no Republican support) on reducing federal deficits (which disappeared completely by the end of the century) rather than increasing spending on domestic programs. Yet the boom had begun under Bush, and others (notably the chairman of the Federal Reserve Board, Alan Greenspan) were also eager to claim credit which in any case might have been due to long-term influences such as technological change. Other significant policy initiatives such as welfare reform, ending deficits in the federal budget, and promoting the globalization of the U.S. economy through the securing congressional approval of the North American Free Trade Agreement *(NAFTA) and the creation of the *World Trade Organization (WTO) were the result of collaboration with Republicans as well as Democrats. Indeed, on trade issues, Clinton received more support from Republicans than from his own party. Only a few American presidents such as *Roosevelt during the *New Deal or *Johnson in the *Great Society period of the 1960s have had the privilege of leading a Congress controlled by their own party in making major policy changes. Clinton was not such a president. Yet those who lived through his presidency are likely to remember it as a golden era characterized not only by a strong economy but by major reductions (probably for reasons outside the president's control) in social problems such as crime and teenage pregnancy that had so concerned Americans for decades before Clinton entered the White House.

(See also PRESIDENCY, U.S.; TAXES AND TAXATION; WELFARE.)

Stephen Skowronek, *The Politics Presidents Make* (Cambridge, Mass., 1993). David Maraniss, *First in His Class: A Biography of Bill Clinton* (New York, 1995). Colin Campbell, *The U.S. Presidency in Crisis: A Comparative Perspective* (New York, 1998). Colin Campbell and Bert A. Rockman, eds., *The Clinton Legacy* (New York, 1999).

GRAHAM K. WILSON

CODETERMINATION is an institutional relationship between organized labor and business giving labor movements the right to participate with their employers in major decisions that jointly affect their firm and/or industry. Found in Northern Europe—including the Netherlands and Scandinavia, but most well known in the Federal Republic of Germany—codetermination (*Mitbestimmung* in German) allows representatives of workers and trade unions to obtain voting seats on the supervisory board of directors (*Aufsichtsrat*) of firms that have 2,000 or more employees.

Codetermination's roots lie in the guild structures of feudal Europe where handicraft traditions encouraged the transmission of worker skills in a master-journeyman-apprentice system that deeply embedded participatory traditions among skilled workers. Its modern form stems from worker participation movements during the Weimar Republic (1918–1933) when workers demanded increased rights in a newly democratic society. Curtailed by conservative governments in the 1920s, and cut short by the Nazis' suppression of independent worker representation, codetermination in its present form did not reappear until the formation of the Federal Republic of Germany in 1949.

German codetermination has two official forms, one for the coal and steel industries (*Montanmitbestimmung*) and one for all other industries. The former provides full parity for worker representatives in all decisions of the supervisory board (*Aufsichtsrat*), while the latter provides *nearly* full parity between worker and employer representatives, as a representatives of management always has the tie-breaking vote. Post–World War II roots of codetermination sprang from the anger of German workers toward the complicity of German industrialists with the Nazi war machine. This was especially true of the coal and steel barons, hence the full parity in those industries. Thus, after World War II, the idea of placing workers and union representatives on the boards of directors of these firms was seen by many as an opportunity to provide increased accountability to German capitalism.

The laws governing codetermination were first passed in the early 1950s and expanded in the 1970s and thus represent the powerful role of the trade unions in the politics of the postwar Federal Republic. They give the workers—and indirectly, their unions for those firms so organized—a form of institutionalized participation via membership on the supervisory board (*Aufsichtsrat*) of German firms. This participation, rather than making German firms uncompetitive, actually has had the opposite effect. Workers—and unions—can comprehend if not unilaterally determine corporate decisions regarding investment and the introduction of new technologies. Codetermination has allowed German workers a broader and deeper knowledge of the goals and strategies of the firms for which they work.

Codetermination has not been conflict-free in the Federal Republic. In 1976, at the time of the broadening of some of the unions' powers, the Constitutional Court ruled that worker representatives could never attain majority representation on the supervisory board. The court argued that such a provision could compromise private property in the Federal Republic. This ruling caused the unions to break away from a more structured process of consultation on macroeconomic policy—called concerted action—with the government and organized business. Despite this residual tension, however, codetermination has provided substantial benefits to German business, workers, and to the entire society.

The primary challenge that faced codetermination at the end of the twentieth century was its role in an increasingly integrated Europe. As a specifically German institutional structure, codetermination's role in European industrial relations—despite its tremendous advantages for fifty years in Germany—remained uncertain. Institutions seldom "travel well" from one country to another.

(See also LABOR MOVEMENT; SOCIAL MARKET ECONOMY.)

CHRISTOPHER S. ALLEN

COLD WAR. The term "Cold War" is used to describe the protracted conflict between the Soviet and Western worlds that, while falling short of "hot" war, nonetheless involved a comprehensive military, political, and ideological rivalry from the end of World War II to the early 1990s. It entered modern political vocabulary after World War II, as a description, popularized by the columnist Walter Lippmann, of the conflict between the Soviet and Western blocs. It was initially used to describe a historical period—the Cold War—that began with the breakdown of the wartime alliance in 1946–1947. Some writers saw an end to the Cold War in the 1950s, after the death of *Stalin; others saw its demise in the 1970s with *détente. The term "Second Cold War" was widely used to refer to the period after the collapse of détente in the late 1970s.

"Cold War" was, however, also used in a more analytic sense, not to denote a particular phase of East-West rivalry but rather to denote the very fact of the rivalry between the communist and capitalist systems itself, one that involved competition and confrontation but not all-out "hot" war. In this sense, the Cold War began not in 1945 but in 1917, with the accession of the Bolsheviks to power, and their proclamation of a worldwide challenge to capitalism, and continued until the late 1980s. The communist revolutionary challenge, and the Western response to it, were checked by a variety of factors—the fragmentation of the world into separate societies and states, the power of *nationalism, the fear of *nuclear weapons, the limits on the power of each side—but it nevertheless endured for more than seven decades. Whatever the periodicity or meaning adopted, most writers agreed that the Cold War, in the sense of a global rivalry between two competing and roughly equal blocs, ended, after *Gorbachev's accession to power in 1985, with the collapse of Soviet power and the end of the Soviet ideological challenge to the West.

The development of East-West rivalry was marked by a set of crises, in both Europe and the *Third World, and by an enduring competition in arms, especially nuclear weapons. Central as the *arms race was to Cold War, however, the latter comprised a broader strategic and political contest. After the end of World War II, Europe was soon divided by the "Iron Curtain" of communist border controls into the Soviet and Western blocs, which led to the Berlin blockade of 1948–1949 and to the formation, in 1949 and 1955, respectively, of the *North Atlantic Treaty Organization and the *Warsaw Treaty Organization. Further crises over Berlin followed in 1959 and 1961, and attempts by states under Soviet control to assert their independence were crushed by force—the German Democratic Republic (East Germany) in 1953, Hungary in 1956, Czechoslovakia in 1968, Poland in 1981. Yugoslavia, Albania, and Romania were able to evade Soviet domination but remained ruled by Communist parties until they, like the Soviet allies, were overwhelmed by the democratic revolutions of the late 1980s.

The rivalry of East and West was also fought out in the Third World. After the Azerbaidzhan crisis of March 1946, a dispute over Soviet reluctance to pull forces out of Iran that marked the first major dispute of the Cold War, there followed the *Chinese Revolution of 1949, the *Korean War of 1950–1953, the *Suez crisis of 1956, the Cuban Revolution of 1959 and, in its aftermath, the missile crisis of 1962, and the U.S. involvement in Vietnam of 1965–1973. In the latter part of the 1970s the collapse of détente and onset of the so-called Second Cold War was in part the result of U.S. concern at the advent to power of pro-Soviet revolutionary regimes in a dozen Third World states, notably South Vietnam, Afghanistan, Ethiopia, Mozambique, Angola, and Nicaragua.

The Second Cold War came after the lessening of tensions that was evident in the 1970s with the Strategic Arms Limitation Talks of 1972 and the *Helsinki Accords of thirty-three European nations, the United States, and Canada on European security in 1975. This amelioration had ended by the late 1970s and appeared dead when Soviet forces occupied Afghanistan in December 1979. The period after 1980 initially saw an intensification of East-West confrontation: an increased emphasis in the West on the arms race, with the deployment of intermediate-range cruise missiles in Europe and the Strategic Defense Initiative, and an encouragement by the United States of anticommunist guerrillas in Cambodia, Afghanistan, Angola, and Nicaragua.

In the Second Cold War the Soviet leadership appeared to have retreated behind the defensive positions of the earlier cold war, but from 1985 onwards, under Gorbachev's leadership, the Soviet Union made wide-ranging concessions that brought the earlier confrontation and the Cold War as a whole to an end. In 1988 the Soviet Union declared an end to military support for the Eastern European communist parties it had kept in power for forty years and in 1989 withdrew its forces from Afghanistan. In the same period it signed wide-ranging agreements on arms control and arms reduction with the United States, and abandoned its global ideological rivalry with the capitalist West. In November 1989 the opening of the Berlin Wall signaled the end of communist power in Eastern Europe. In December 1990 the Cold War was officially declared over at the Paris Organization for Security and Cooperative in Europe (OSCE) conference. In December 1991 the Soviet Union broke apart.

Writing on the Cold War has revolved around two broad questions. The first has been that of historical responsibility, of which side caused the cold wars of the late 1940s and late 1970s. Whereas earlier writings tended to polarize around a Western view that the Soviet Union was responsible and a Soviet view that the "imperialist" countries were to blame, a later school of "revisionist" Western writing stressed forms of U.S. responsibility. In the 1980s a "postrevisionist" school emerged, locating responsibility in both the Soviet and U.S. blocs, while, with the advent of glasnost in the Soviet Union after 1988, Soviet writers began for the first time to concede that the policies of Stalin and Brezhnev had contributed to exacerbating East-West tensions.

The second broad set of questions concern what the Cold War was and what the sources of the conflict were. Here four broad schools of explanation have emerged. The first, a traditional application of power politics, sees it as a continuation under new ideological guises of the kind of great power rivalry for empire, influence, and domination seen in earlier epochs. A second school stresses the cognitive and subjective factors, the degree of misperception involved in the failure of the two sides to maintain their wartime alliance and resolve subsequent disputes, and to extricate themselves from the reinforcing anxieties of the arms race. A third school views the Cold War as only apparently a rivalry between two blocs, and more as a means by which the dominant states within each bloc controlled and disciplined their own populations and clients, and by which those who stood to benefit from increased arms production and political anxiety promoted a mythical rivalry. Fourth, there are those who see the Cold War not primarily as a conflict between states or as a merely military rivalry but more as a conflict between two distinct, competing social and political systems, each committed to prevailing over the other at the global level. Despite its rapid and, in Europe, relatively bloodless end, the Cold War continues to exert a hold on world affairs. In Russia there is pervasive nostalgia for world stature, exacerbated by the economic collapse that has followed the end of Soviet centralization. In China a communist party still rules, amidst growing social and political pressures. Although communism as an alternative ideology is discredited, many of the tensions, economic and social, that produced it remain acute, as the breakdown of state control in a number of areas formerly ruled by communism has produced new civil and ethnic conflicts.

(See also ARMS CONTROL; CONTAINMENT; MARSHALL PLAN; PERESTROIKA; POTSDAM CONFERENCE; YALTA CONFERENCE.)

Fred Halliday, *The Making of the Second Cold War,* 2d ed. (London and New York, 1986). Raymond Garthoff, *Détente and Confrontation,* 2d ed. (Washington, D.C., 1994). John Lewis Gaddis, *We Now Know: Rethinking Cold War History* (Oxford, 1997).

FRED HALLIDAY

COLLECTIVIZATION. In the *Soviet Union and other countries under Marxist-Leninist rule, collectivization was a response to problems posed by agriculture for economic and social transformation. The ruling parties in these countries adopted rapid industrialization and transition to a socialist institutional order as their primary goals. After substantial debate in the 1920s, the question of the role of agriculture in the industrialization process was resolved in the Soviet Union in favor of an extractive approach. Under it, agriculture was to be a source of new recruits to the industrial labor force, of inexpensive food for the nonfarm population, and of raw materials for industry, while consuming as little as possible of the investment resources made available by this unequal transfer. However, further issues were raised by the question of the appropriate *institutional* model for agriculture under socialism as understood by the Soviets.

*Marx had viewed *peasants as a declining class and had focused most of his analysis of *capitalism and of its eventual demise on the conflict between the owners of industry and the industrial working class. Whereas the transformation of the latter actors into participants in a planned industrial economy under state ownership seemed a logical consequence of Marx's historical scheme, the prospects for any remaining tillers were unclear.

The fraction of the population still engaged in agriculture at the time of the *Russian Revolution in 1917, and in some countries coming under similar regimes in the years after World War II, was much larger than that in the northern European industrial societies that were Marx's primary referents. Cultivation in these countries was mainly on a small scale and by owner-operators or tenant farmers, not large-scale labor-hiring farms. Rather than attempt to transform these farms into state enterprises, the Communist leaders of the Soviet Union favored the establishment of "semisocialist" institutions called collective farms, in which output would be produced under joint management, with distribution of the net proceeds among participants in proportion to their labor contributions. A few such institutions were established on a voluntary basis following the Russian Revolution, and Soviet leader V. I. *Lenin advocated their gradual popularization through provision of state assistance and preference in commercial dealings. However, Joseph *Stalin opted for compulsory collectivization, a process that began in 1928 and was completed by 1937 despite resistance resulting in the slaughter of about half the country's livestock and an unknown number of human deaths by starvation. The institutions thus formed, called kolkhozy (singular kolkhoz), were subject to tight state controls in the forms of output targets, compulsory sales quotas, regulations on internal institutional structure, and intervention in the choice of officials.

The main economic difference between a collective farm and a state enterprise lay not in the degree of autonomy of the farm workers but rather in the fact that, unlike state employees, collective farmers were not paid guaranteed wages but had to survive on the net income produced by their unit. (A minimum wage for collective farmers was introduced in the Soviet Union in the 1960s.) Although destructive of lives and productive potential, the system allowed the state to eliminate open opposition in the countryside, to meet its targets for extracting output from agriculture, to induce a large labor transfer to the cities, and to avoid directly bearing agricultural risk by forcing the farmers to be residual income claimants.

In comparison with private farms, collective farms held income differentiation in check and allowed the nonfarm sector to obtain farm products without relying on the existence of a stratum of more successful commercial farmers and without having to offer the farmers economically attractive prices for their products. Turning the terms of trade against farmers required replacing market exchange by mandatory state procurement, the implementation of which was facilitated by the grouping of farmers into larger entities (the kolkhozy) over which officials could maintain effective control. The relatively large scale of the kolkhozy was also consistent with Marxist beliefs in the existence of economies of scale in agriculture and in the desirability of mechanization. However, partly to pacify farmer resistance and partly to rid the collective farms of the burden of producing labor-intensive products for which scale was clearly unimportant, collective farmers were permitted to maintain small private plots and to raise animals for meat, dairy products, and eggs.

The Soviet pattern was copied by other *Communist Party states, with the exception of Poland and Yugoslavia, the governments of which permitted perpetuation of private farms in the face of strong farmer resistance. Most of these countries

also established a certain number of state farms, organized along the lines of state factories. *China attempted to amalgamate its collective farms into still larger communes in 1958, but the move resulted in massive famine, and the system was reorganized in 1962 with small production teams as basic farm units. Between 1979 and 1983, China restored its households to the status of production units. China's communes and production brigades then became township and village governments that ran industrial enterprises and provided agricultural and other services to local residents. Dismantling of collective farms proceeded at different rates following the demise of Communism in Eastern Europe and the Soviet Union in 1989 and 1991. In many countries, most farmers remained within some type of cooperative structure as of the mid-1990s. Collective farms were widely viewed as having depressed agricultural performance by reducing production incentives. Chief culprits appear to have been internal egalitarianism, problems of supervision, and the role of the collectives as enforcers of the extractive policies of the state.

(See also COMMAND ECONOMY; COMMUNISM; RURAL DEVELOPMENT; SOCIALISM AND SOCIAL DEMOCRACY; STALINISM)

Alec Nove, *An Economic History of the U.S.S.R.* (Harmondsworth, U.K., 1969). Peter Nolan, *The Political Economy of Collective Farms: An Analysis of China's Post-Mao Rural Reforms* (Boulder, Colo., 1988). Louis Putterman, "Agricultural Producers' Cooperatives," in Pranab Bardhan, ed., *The Economic Theory of Agrarian Institutions* (Oxford, 1989), pp. 319–339.

LOUIS PUTTERMAN

COLOMBIA. Located in the northwestern corner of South America, Colombia is the third most populous country in Latin America (37 million people) and has the fifth largest economy. The country has a rugged topography, with three Andean mountain ranges traversing the western half, although the country's highest peaks are located off the Caribbean coast in the Sierra Nevada. South and east from the eastern plains are the scarcely populated Amazon territories. These geographical features have fostered regionalism and made national integration and state building difficult.

In 1830, some ten years after Gran Colombia gained its independence from Spain, Venezuela and Ecuador broke away (Panama gained its independence in 1903). By the 1850s, the country's two major political parties, the Partido Liberal and the Partido Conservador, were established. Their history includes periods of hegemonic one-party rule, civil wars, and coalition government. The parties often mobilized armed bands larger than the national army, indicating the weakness of the state and the military.

Numerous civil confrontations from 1851 to 1903 generated sectarian identification with the two parties. Liberals dominated national politics from 1863 to 1885, enacting anti-church reforms and federalist, secularist, and politically liberal constitutions. A centralizing reaction ultimately controlled by the Conservatives led to the 1886 Constitution, the basic text in effect until 1991, and reestablished church centrality. Conservatives controlled national politics until 1930, when the Great Depression and party divisions facilitated a Liberal victory.

Liberal President Alfonso López Pumarejo (1934–1938) enacted constitutional, fiscal, agrarian, and other reforms known as the "Revolution on the March." They helped the Liberals become the country's majority party by limiting church influence, expanding the urban electorate where the party was stronger, and increasing the party's support base within labor. However, intraparty divisions permitted a narrow Conservative victory in the 1946 presidential elections even as the Liberals retained congressional control. Local violence exploded into a national conflagration following the assassination of the populist Liberal leader Jorge Eliécer Gaitán in 1948. The country's oligarchic democracy ended as an undeclared civil war, *la violencia*, between adherents of the two parties took the lives of some 200,000 people and ushered in *military rule.

In 1957–1958, to facilitate a return to civilian rule and end partisan violence, leaders of the two parties agreed to join together in a Frente Nacional. Under the Frente Nacional agreement, the two parties shared equally in executive, legislative, and judicial posts; they also agreed that from 1958 to 1974 the presidency would alternate between the two parties.

The Frente Nacional coalition governments contributed to the country's transformation. Colombia became more urbanized and educated as the population doubled and the sectarian party identities that had justified coalition rule disappeared. However, regional party leaders and economic elites urged retention of coalition rule and efforts to open up the political system failed. During the 1970s, political turmoil and nonelectoral opposition in the form of labor protest, civic strikes, and guerrilla violence grew.

Since the early 1980s, Colombia has confronted increasingly more dramatic problems with political and criminal violence. Conservative President Belisario Betancur (1982–1986) sought ultimately unsuccessful peace agreements with the country's major guerrilla groups and enacted limited political *reforms. Violence further escalated as state authority was also challenged by drug trafficking groups. Liberal President Virgilio Barco (1986–1990) confronted terrorist activities by drug traffickers seeking to stop their extradition to the United States. Under Liberal President César Gaviria (1990–1994), some drug traffickers surrendered to authorities under plea-bargaining agreements, and accommodation was reached with a few guerrilla groups, principally the M-19 (Movement of the 19th of April of 1970). A democratizing constitution was also enacted in July 1991.

However, the country's situation deteriorated under Liberal President Ernesto Samper (1994–1998). Accused of accepting money from drug traffickers to help fund his election campaign, Samper's period in office was one of deteriorating relations with the United States and of a declining economy. His term also saw a further increase in the spiral of violence, increasingly carried out by actors independent of the state. The country's two major guerrilla groups, the Fuerzas Armadas Revolucionarias de Colombia (FARC), which controlled vast regions of the country where coca was cultivated, and the Ejército de Liberación Nacional (ELN), both grew stronger. And, increasingly, they confronted brutal paramilitary forces, which had complex ties with drug traffickers, conservative landowners, and elements of the state security forces. As many as a million internally displaced *refugees may have been generated by the continuing confrontations across these actors. Conservative President Andrés Pastrana (1998–) was ushered into office promising to seek peace, but had achieved little success by the middle of 2000.

Though Colombia has a long history of liberal constitutional government and a regime with many aspects of a political democracy, the country currently lacks a coherent state able to impose a democratic rule of law; thus, *political violence, targeted *assassinations and massacres, kidnaping, intimidation, and threats have continued with near-complete impunity.

The 1991 Constitution, however, removed all remnants of coalition government, provided for many citizen rights, and introduced electoral, participatory, and judicial reforms. It prohibited presidential reelection. Departmental governors, previously appointed, are now elected popularly, as mayors have been since 1988. It extended seats in Congress for representatives from indigenous and black communities, as well as extending to them special ethnic rights. Yet the Constitution did not address civil-military relations, maintaining intact a system of military justice accused of overlooking serious human rights abuses. In addition, no serious reform of the country's political party system was enacted. Thus, legislative seats are allocated by factional lists rather than official party lists, a procedure which has encouraged extreme factionalism and clientelism.

Especially at local levels, independent candidates and movements have been gaining importance in Colombia over the 1990s. However, since competitive presidential elections began anew in 1974, Partido Liberal factions have always obtained a congressional majority; candidates of the Liberal party have also won the presidency in all elections except in 1982 and 1998, when candidates emerging from the Partido Social Conservador won. After a truce was signed between the FARC and the Betancur administration in 1984, the FARC created a political party, the Unión Patriótica (UP), which increasingly came to overshadow the country's historic Partido Comunista de Colombia (PCC). Yet the UP confronted a campaign of extermination, with over 1,000 of its members assassinated between 1985 and 1991. In the early 1990s, the political movement formed by the M-19 once it lay down its arms had significant electoral success, but divisions and voter disaffection soon resulted in sharp electoral declines.

Colombia is a highly stratified society, and many, especially in rural areas, live in absolute poverty. Leading sectors of the economy are dominated by large economic conglomerates. Major business organizations seek regional balance and are well represented in the traditional parties. Organized labor tends to be strongest in the public sector, in petroleum and in manufacturing, though it represents a small percentage of the economically active population and is divided into competing confederations. Independent neighborhood associations, civil movements, and non-governmental organizations (NGOs) have grown as the links of traditional parties to societal groups have declined; over the late 1990s, many of these mobilized around peace and antiviolence campaigns. Historically strong, the influence of the *Roman Catholic Church—one of the most conservative on the continent—has been declining.

Until severe recession affected Colombia in the late 1990s, its economic record was steady though not spectacular. During the Frente Nacional period, coalition rule by two multiclass elitist parties inhibited radical policy shifts. In the 1970s, experiencing a strong coffee boom and an influx of foreign exchange due to marijuana and then cocaine exports, the country borrowed little from private commercial banks. Thus, the negative consequences of the debt crisis of the 1980s were felt less than in other Latin American countries. Responding to the globalization of the world economy and seeking increasing flows of foreign investment, the Gaviria administration implemented market-oriented reforms which were slowed under the subsequent Samper government. Average growth of 2.5 percent over the first part of the 1990s has been overshadowed by decade's end by severe recession, induced by low world prices for key exports such as oil, declines in investment flows, and high government deficits inherited from the Samper government, forcing the government to implement stabilization measures.

(See also DRUGS; GUERRILLA WARFARE; INTERNATIONAL DEBT.)

Jonathan Hartlyn, *The Politics of Coalition Rule in Colombia* (Cambridge, U.K., 1988). David Bushnell, *The Making of Modern Colombia: A Nation in Spite of Itself* (Berkeley, Calif., 1993). Francisco Leal Buitrago, ed., *Tras las huellas de la crisis* (Santafé de Bogotá, 1996).

JONATHAN HARTLYN

COLONIAL EMPIRES. This form of political organization, bringing a number of different cultures or tribes or nationalities under a superior central authority, has a history infinitely older than that of the nation-state. In modern times most empires were under European control, apart from the Chinese Empire (with origins in antiquity) and the ephemeral Japanese Empire. Modern empires have taken two main forms: the acquisition of territories overseas and their acquisition by landward expansion—although only the Russian Empire was in this latter category. The Portuguese and Spanish regarded their acquisitions as contributing to the greater glory of God. In more secular terms France invoked the *mission civilisatrice*; the United States appealed to Manifest Destiny; the pragmatic British spoke of the White Man's Burden. Each power insisted that empire building was, in part, unselfish, even noble. However, there was a tacit acceptance that empires contributed material benefits and also national prestige. This was the main reason why, after their defeat by Prussia in 1870, the French plunged into colonial adventures in Africa and Southeast Asia. For these conquests no solid economic motive could be adduced, but French esteem was enhanced: in the words of Lèon Gambetta, France had become a great power again.

How did the Europeans come to dominate Asia and Africa? They had acquired technology more advanced than those they came to conquer. Their ships were more maneuverable, they deployed greater firepower. Their military forces operated under stricter discipline: and this was the crucial factor— discipline, or systematic control—that enabled them to take on much greater numbers of opponents. They came to trade: first in luxury goods (spices, ivory, silks) previously monopolized by Arab and other commercial intermediaries, then in looking for markets for their own industrial products, and to exploit natural resources and cheap labor. There remained the intangible factor of national prestige, which led to the "scramble" for Africa and the "forward movement" in Southeast Asia.

This expansion was justified by pseudoscientific argument, grounded in a vulgarized version of Darwin, the "survival of the fittest." The principal authority on French colonial expansion, Paul Leroy-Beaulieu, noted in *De la colonisation chez les peuples modernes* that the world could be divided between the Western civilizations, others moving toward the same desti-

nation (principally Japan), a third category groping forward but unable to attain stability, hence (like India) necessitating a Western takeover—and then the major part of the world, containing "tribes barbarous and savage, addicted to conflict without end, knowing little of culture or technology." The West possessed the "right of intervention" in both of these latter cases.

Rivalry between Western colonial powers threatened, between 1890 and 1914, to develop into war on several occasions. However, the only open conflict was between Spain in its colonial twilight and the United States. This led to the cession of the Philippines and Puerto Rico from Spain to America. After World War I the German colonies were distributed among the victorious Allies as "mandates" (as were the Arab regions of the Ottoman empire). World War II saw the former Italian colonies in Africa placed under the British as "trust territories" before attaining independence. Similarly, the Pacific islands held by Japan were annexed by the United States: the Marianas were given self-government in 1986. Only Namibia remained under white rule until 1989 as a colonial fossil. Whereas colonies had previously been a symbol of world-class status, by the 1960s they symbolized backwardness. Portugal, the first European state to enter the colonial race, was nearly the last to leave, relinquishing its colonies only under pressure from the superpowers.

As an issue in the rivalries of the Great Powers, the colonies featured mainly in the period 1880–1914 when the Afro-Asian world was almost wholly under Western dominance. Between 1918 and 1939 two cases of expansion became international issues: the Italian takeover of Ethiopia and Japanese intervention in China. Both were raised in the League of Nations, which proved unable to influence the course of events. The UN was originally mainly a Western body, like the League of Nations, but from about 1960 it became a forum for the newly independent states protesting the remnants of colonialism, as in Dutch New Guinea and most persistently in Namibia, which South Africa continued to refuse to relinquish.

The heyday of the colonial empires was very brief, from about 1890 to 1950. Nevertheless, the legacy of Western colonialism (which some termed neocolonialism) could not be shaken off as rapidly as the formal colonial structure.

(See also DECOLONIZATION; IMPERIALISM.)

J. S. Furnivall, *Colonial Policy and Practice* (Cambridge, U.K., 1948). Rupert Emerson, *From Empire to Nation* (Cambridge, Mass., 1960). D. K. Fieldhouse, *The Colonial Empires: A Comparative Survey* (London, 1966). Hugh Tinker, *Men Who Overturned Empires* (Madison, Wis., 1987).

HUGH TINKER

COMMAND ECONOMY. During the Cold War, students of comparative economics were traditionally presented with two alternative systems for organizing economic activity: the market economy and the command economy. Unfortunately, this crude dichotomy drew attention away from hybrid forms of economic organization, such as the regulated economies of France and Japan, where state management was crucial to economic development.

The command economy is nevertheless a form of economic and political organization that can be conceptually distinguished from a market or regulated economy. In a command economy the state tries to attain as high a degree of control over economic activity as is practically feasible, based on state ownership of the means of production. Command economies were introduced by communist-led regimes in a bid to overcome their countries' perceived economic backwardness and "catch up" with the advanced industrial nations of the West. The apparent success of the Soviet model influenced many Third World countries, notably India, to adopt state planning in the 1950s, but these emulators did not achieve the degree of state control which was seen in the USSR or China.

The command economy cannot be understood in purely economic terms, since only regimes of a certain type—typically, *communist party states—sought that type of maximal economic control. There are no cases of a communist party staying in power without a command economy, and no clear cases of noncommunist regimes maintaining a command economy outside of wartime. Even in authoritarian or social democratic regimes with a high degree of state intervention, state employment is usually only about 25 percent of the labor force outside agriculture—while in command economies the state typically employs 90 percent or more of the nonagricultural labor force.

States with command economies differed in the degree of control they were able to establish. One can distinguish three broad categories: (1) the Stalinist command economy (Soviet Union 1929–1953, Albania 1945–1990, Eastern Europe 1948–1953, Cuba, and North Korea); (2) the "normal" command economy (Soviet Union 1953–1988, Eastern Europe 1953–1989); (3) the fragmented command economy (China since 1957, Yugoslavia 1964–1991). Almost all the command economies have gone through a Stalinist phase where the state tried to squeeze independent economic activity to a minimum, and then retreated when such policies proved counterproductive.

Most command economies (Poland and Yugoslavia being exceptions) introduced new forms of collective ownership in agriculture during their Stalinist phase, although China and Tanzania eventually broke up their collective farms and reverted to household agriculture. Some command economies tried to ban private enterprise in the service sector, while others (such as Hungary) tolerated some private service businesses.

The command economies developed a distinctive set of institutions for managing state-owned industry. A central planning board (Gosplan in the USSR) drew up a plan of output targets for the forthcoming year, measured in physical terms. These output targets along with input supplies were allocated to enterprises through the bureaucratic pyramid of industrial ministries.

The command economy relied upon a vast and cumbersome bureaucracy in which there were few incentives for efficiency and innovation. Labor and capital productivity was low, as was product quality and responsiveness to consumer demand. Firms faced what Hungarian economist Janos Kornai called a "soft budget constraint," meaning that there was little incentive for them to cut costs. A further disadvantage of the command economies was that they were relatively isolated from the international division of labor: foreign trade was about one-third the level one would have expected in a comparable market economy.

The main advantage of this system was that it enabled the state to mobilize resources from the rural sector, to hold down the wages of urban workers, and to concentrate the nation's efforts on the development of a few key strategic sectors. After a decade or two, however, the state found that it had exhausted the supply of underutilized labor, and had to try to shift from an extensive growth path (based on resource mobilization) toward intensive growth (based on more efficient use of existing resources). No command economy was able to make this transition and preserve its basic political and economic institutions intact.

China launched major economic reforms in 1978 which saw the return of semiprivate farming and the spread of private and municipal enterprise in industry. The Chinese economy grew by 8 percent per year over the next two decades, while the proportion of the economy controlled by the central state shrank to less than 10 percent.

At the end of the decade the command economy survived in only a handful of countries, such as the Democratic People's Republic of Korea (North Korea) and Cuba, but its legacy still cast a shadow over the post-socialist economies. In China, the state continued to subsidize the loss-making industries that it owned, while the economic boom had led to a large gap between the rich coastal provinces and the impoverished interior. Russia found it very difficult to make the transition from a highly centralized and militarized economy to a competitive market environment, and experienced an eight-year economic slump after the final collapse of central planning in 1991.

(See also POST-COMMUNISM.)

Jan S. Prybyla, *Market and Plan Under Socialism: The Bird in the Cage* (Stanford, Calif., 1987). Janos Kornai, *The Socialist System* (Princeton, N.J., 1992).

PETER RUTLAND

COMMON AGRICULTURAL POLICY. See EUROPEAN UNION.

COMMON MARKET. See EUROPEAN UNION.

COMMONWEALTH. The modern Commonwealth evolved from the British Empire. Addressing the desire of India, which had achieved independence in 1947 together with Pakistan, to remain in the Commonwealth while becoming a republic, Commonwealth prime ministers in 1949 devised a formula whereby allegiance to the Crown—hitherto the touchstone of membership of the British Commonwealth of Nations—could be replaced by recognition of the king (George VI) as the symbolic Head of the Commonwealth (without the adjective "British"). This facilitated transition, in the ensuing *decolonization process, from an empire to a multiracial, multicultural association of fifty-four sovereign and independent states, spread all over the globe, with a population today of one and a half billion; rich in its diversity; and linked not by treaty obligations but voluntarily and organically in their shared inheritance in language and in fundamental political values: democracy, human rights, independence of the judiciary, and the rule of law.

Biennial heads of government meetings ("CHOGMs"), noteworthy for their candor and informality, constitute the political core of the Commonwealth. Together with a network of ministerial and other meetings, CHOGMs establish priorities for the association's activities, fulfillment of which is primarily the responsibility of the Commonwealth Secretariat. The latter body was established in 1965 and is maintained at a modest level (310 staff, an annual assessed budget of £11 million, plus £22 million in voluntary contributions to various assistance programs). The main areas of work are the promotion of fundamental political values; *sustainable development, with emphasis on the problems faced by small states which compose a significantly higher proportion of total membership than is the case with the United Nations; and good governance and management.

The secretary-general, elected by the heads of government, has considerable scope both for personal diplomacy among member governments and on their behalf, as well as for influencing the work and priorities of the Commonwealth. Arnold Smith (1965–1975), a Canadian diplomat, successfully established both the independence and the competence of the Secretariat. Shridath Ramphal (1975–1990), former attorney-general and foreign minister of Guyana, was a world leader in the campaign against apartheid and in promoting international economic and development cooperation. Emeka Anyaoku (1990–2000), Nigerian diplomat and briefly foreign minister, has served the Commonwealth much of his working life. He has in particular championed the cause of democratically elected government and *human rights. The Durban CHOGM in November 1999 elected Don McKinnon, the New Zealand foreign minister, to succeed Anyaoku early in 2000.

The Commonwealth is very much an association of peoples as well as of governments. Non-governmental bodies and activities flourish, especially in the academic and professional field. Cooperation between governmental and non-governmental entities is close and relaxed. The recently created Commonwealth Business Council, a case in point, is a reflection of the emphasis, renewed by the Durban CHOGM, on meeting the challenges of globalization and seizing the opportunities it offers. The Commonwealth has been especially active on mitigation of the debt burden of poorer countries.

Lessening of the preoccupation with Southern African political affairs after the achievement of independence in Zimbabwe and Namibia, and the end of *apartheid in South Africa in the early 1990s, combined with the end of the *Cold War to permit clearer perception of the worldwide potential of the Commonwealth. Commonwealth principles were restated in the Harare Declaration of 1991. The declaration was given "teeth" by the Millbrook Action Programme adopted during the Auckland CHOGM in 1995. *Inter alia* it set up a Commonwealth Ministerial Action Group (CMAG) composed of eight foreign ministers, to deal with serious or persistent violations of the principles. Nigeria was suspended from membership in the wake of developments there. Following the restoration of civilian rule, it returned to the fold prior to the Durban CHOGM. Pakistan, in the light of the military coup the previous month, was suspended from Commonwealth councils. CMAG's mandate has been extended. This is an area which illustrates how the Commonwealth can act as a pilot fish for the United Nations, which it strongly supports.

The role as Head of the Commonwealth of Queen Elizabeth II, who came to the throne in 1952, has been much more than symbolic. Her personal commitment to, and knowledge of, the Commonwealth have been of great importance in smooth-ing the transition from empire to forward-looking and imaginative association. Although it may defy easy classification on conventional lines, the Commonwealth is demonstrably a phenomenon unique in history, and an international asset as well as a boon to its members.

The Report of the Commonwealth Secretary-General (biennial). Commonwealth Secretariat Web site, http://www. thecommonwealth.org.

PETER MARSHALL

COMMONWEALTH OF INDEPENDENT STATES. The Commonwealth of Independent States (CIS) is a twelve-member international organization established in December 1991 after negotiations to preserve the *Soviet Union failed. Originally founded by the presidents of the three Slavic republics of the USSR (Russia, Ukraine, and Belarus) at a meeting at Belovezhskoe Lake in Belarus, it was subsequently joined by Armenia, Azerbaijan, Kazakhstan, Kyrgyzstan, Moldova, Tajikistan, Turkmenistan, and Uzbekistan. In 1992 the Azerbaijani government of Abulfaz Elchibey withdrew, though Azerbaijan rejoined in 1993 after Elchibey was toppled and replaced by Heydar Aliev. Georgia originally refused to join, sending only observer delegations to Commonwealth meetings. But in 1993 Russian peacekeepers actively aided the advance of Abkhaz troops and an insurrection by supporters of Zviad Gamsakhurdia until the Georgian government agreed to become a CIS member. Russia then not only brokered a cease-fire between the Georgians and the Abkhaz, but also helped the government of Eduard Shevardnadze defeat its Zviadist opponents.

The CIS is governed by statutes adopted in January 1993. The organization seeks to foster cooperation predominantly in six spheres: economic, military, peacekeeping, border control, humanitarian and social issues, and coordination of foreign policies. Its chief institutions include a Council of Heads of State (the highest organ of the CIS), a Council of Heads of Government, an Interparliamentary Assembly, an Executive Secretariat (the permanent arm of the CIS, located in Minsk and consisting of 2,000 employees), and a series of committees focused on specific spheres of CIS activities. The CIS is coordinated by an executive secretary appointed by the Council of Heads of State. Ivan Korotchenya, a Belarusian technocrat, held the post from 1992 to 1998. He was replaced in 1998 by Russian oil and media tycoon Boris Berezovsky after accusations that the organization had fallen into disarray. A controversial figure, Berezovsky was expected to attempt to breathe new life into the organization, particularly its economic dimension.

Since its inception, the CIS has remained an organization in crisis. Among the broader reasons for this has been the perception that the CIS functions in part as a vehicle for extending Russian influence over the former Soviet republics, as well as the centrifugal attractions that pull these states away from Russia toward integration with Europe and the Middle East. Within Russia the creation of the CIS also remains a controversial issue, as many Russians blame Boris *Yeltsin for prematurely extinguishing the Soviet Union by creating the Commonwealth. Irrespective of how one views its relationship to Russia, there is generalized dissatisfaction over the way in which the CIS has operated. Early conflicts revolved around the division of former Soviet property, militaries, and debts. Territorial disputes plague a number of member states; indeed, Armenia and Azerbaijan fought a full-scale war over Nagorno-Karabagh. There is widespread discontent over the failure of the CIS to function effectively as an economic community. The economies of the post-Soviet states for the most part remain tightly linked. In September 1993 nine Commonwealth members agreed to establish an Economic Union (Georgia and Turkmenistan subsequently joined, though Ukraine entered only as an associated member). Yet the agreement remained largely on paper, and trade among CIS states continued to fall, declining by ten percent in 1997 alone. Subsequently, Russia, Belarus, Kazakstan, and Kyrgyzstan agreed to form a separate Customs Union; Central Asian states pursued separate plans for regional integration; and Georgia, Ukraine, Azerbaijan, and Moldova formed an informal bloc opposing greater economic or military consolidation within the CIS. Only in the sphere of air defense has there been significant military cooperation among CIS members. Each state has defined its own forms and degrees of participation, leading to considerable confusion within the CIS.

Russia has placed the CIS at the center of its *foreign policy strategy. Indeed, Boris Yeltsin declared 1998 "the year of the CIS" in an effort to revitalize the organization. Most observers believe, however, that the CIS is not likely to become an effective *international organization soon, and some have even predicted its imminent demise as conflicts among member states intensify.

Mark R. Beissinger, "The Deconstruction of the USSR and the Search for a Post-Soviet Community," *Problems of Communism* 40, no. 6 (November–December 1991): 27–35. Gail W. Lapidus, Victor Zaslavsky, and Philip Goldman, eds., *From Union to Commonwealth: Nationalism and Separatism in the Soviet Republics* (Cambridge, U.K., 1992).

MARK R. BEISSINGER

COMMUNICATIONS. See INFORMATION SOCIETY; MEDIA AND POLITICS.

COMMUNISM. The term "communism" originated among revolutionary societies in the Paris of the 1830s, where it combined two meanings. The first designated a political movement, of or on behalf of the working class, that was dedicated to the overthrow of emerging capitalist society. The second sense referred to the kind of society that such a movement wished to inaugurate. In the first sense communism was seen as an extreme and violent form of socialism, more fundamental in its approach to the abolition of private property than that advocated by socialists, who favored a relatively peaceful political stance and gradual social reform. This contrast finds its classic expression in the 1848 *Communist Manifesto* of *Marx and Engels.

In the latter half of the nineteenth century, however, the terms "socialism" and "communism" tended to be used virtually synonymously to designate the working-class movement as a whole. Most Marxist parties, including the two largest (in Germany and Austria), used the title "Social Democratic." The *Russian Revolution of 1917, the adoption by the Bolsheviks of the term "Communist" to describe their party, and, above all, the creation of the Third (Communist) International in 1921 gave the term a much more specific meaning. The aftermath of the Bolshevik revolution and the founding of the Third International involved the emergence of separate Communist parties sharply opposed to socialist or social democratic parties and advocating policies reminiscent of early European communists. These new Communist parties were organized, along Leninist "democratic centralist" lines, where power resided, formally as well as in practice, in the hands of a small Politburo. It was *Lenin, too, in his *State and Revolution*, who formalized the difference between communism and socialism as a project of social reorganization. Marx had already drawn a distinction between an immediately postrevolutionary society, in which reward would be according to merit, and a "higher stage of communist society" that would put into practice the famous slogan "from each according to his abilities, to each according to his needs." Lenin called the first of these societies "socialist" and the second "communist." Thus the parties of the Third International, although Communist, were running societies which were, as yet, only socialist.

With the consolidation of *Stalinism in the *Soviet Union, a third sense of "communism" emerged: a worldwide network of doctrinaire parties organized along authoritarian lines, propagating a worldview known as dialectical materialism and more or less completely subordinate to the political line laid down by the Communist Party of the Soviet Union (CPSU) through the operations of the Communist International. After the death of Stalin, this Communist movement entered a historical decline, the first serious symptom of which was the split between the Soviet and Chinese Communist parties in 1960, accompanied by the increasing unpopularity and difficulties of the Communist regimes in Eastern and Central Europe. In Western Europe, the long postwar boom and the lack of progress made by the Communist parties there led in the 1970s to the emergence of a trend known as Eurocommunism. The Eurocommunists, led by the Italian Communist Party, adopted a much more conciliatory attitude to parliamentary institutions and advocated what seemed to be *reforms rather than *revolution—to such an extent that the post-1917 distinction between socialism and communism as opposed political tendencies seemed to be disappearing.

The 1989 revolutions in Eastern and Central Europe and the collapse of communism in the Soviet Union marked the end of this decline of European communism and its reassimilation into the general socialist movement. The anti-Stalinist communist movement represented by Trotsky and his followers continues to exist but is numerically small and politically insignificant. The vanguard parties constructed along the Leninist model still operate in such places as China, Cuba, and South Africa, but their future seems far from assured. The two central ideas of Stalinist communism—the Leninist vanguard party and an economy planned by a centralized bureaucracy—have gone into terminal decline. However, communism in the very different sense of a more principled version of socialism, an aspiration to a society in which resources are divided primarily according to human need, is likely to have a future every bit as long as its past.

(See also CAPITALISM; CHINESE COMMUNIST PARTY; CLASS AND POLITICS; COMMAND ECONOMY; COMMUNIST PARTY STATES; LENINISM; MARXISM; NINETEEN EIGHTY-NINE; POST-COMMUNISM; SOCIALISM AND SOCIAL DEMOCRACY.)

Adam Westoby, *The Evolution of Communism* (New York, 1990). David McLellan, *Marxism after Marx*, 2d. ed. (New York, 1998.)

DAVID MCLELLAN

COMMUNIST PARTY STATES. When World War I broke out in 1914 there were no communist party states. For many years after the *Russian Revolution of 1917 there were only three, the *Soviet Union itself and two Asian outposts, Mongolia and Tuva; and as late as the end of World War II there were only five such states, located for the most part in Eastern Europe (Albania and Yugoslavia as well as the Soviet Union). Communist party states came subsequently into existence elsewhere in Europe (Bulgaria, Romania, Poland, Czechoslovakia, Hungary, and the German Democratic Republic [East Germany]), in Latin America (Cuba), and also in Asia (China, Vietnam, the Democratic People's Republic of Korea [North Korea], Laos, and Cambodia). By the late 1980s there were at least sixteen states that claimed allegiance to *Marxism-*Leninism and were ruled by communist parties, and these were known, in Soviet terminology, as the "world socialist system." A wider group of states, ruled by "vanguard" or "revolutionary-democratic" parties or movements, included Afghanistan, Angola, Congo (Brazzaville), Mozambique, Ethiopia, Madagascar, and Yemen. More broadly, a network of about 100 ruling or nonruling parties constituted what was known as the world communist movement.

Communist party states, however broadly defined, were never more than a small minority of the 150 or so states that were members of the United Nations. Their importance, however, was much greater than these limited numbers might have suggested. Communist-ruled states, for a start, accounted for about a third of the world's population and for more than 40 percent of the world's industrial production. Once the world's largest state, the Soviet Union was (until 1991) under communist rule, and communist rule has persisted in the world's most populous state, the People's Republic of *China. Communist party states constituted one of the world's main trading blocs, the Council for Mutual Economic Assistance, or Comecon (established in 1949), and one of the world's two major military alliances, the *Warsaw Treaty Organization, established for a period of thirty years in 1955 and extended for a further twenty in 1985 (both were dissolved in 1991 following the political changes in Eastern Europe). Above all, for the student of politics, communist party states have historically represented one of the most important and distinct types of political system, one that differentiated itself sharply from liberal *democracy and yet one that had a number of characteristics that differentiated it from other forms of authoritarian rule.

At least until the late 1980s, when a far-reaching process of systemic change began to affect them, communist party states could be defined in terms of four related characteristics. In the first place, all of the communist-ruled states based themselves on an official ideology, Marxism-Leninism, which was derived from the theories of Marx, Engels, Lenin, and (in China) *Mao Zedong, and which provided the vocabulary of politics in these states as well as the basis on which their rulers claimed to exercise authority. Second, the economy was largely or entirely in public ownership, in line with the Marxist doctrine that private ownership of productive resources

involved the exploitation of workers by those who employed them, and it was typically regulated through a machinery of central planning. The third distinguishing feature of communist party states was that they were ruled by a single or at least dominant communist party, within which power was highly centralized. And finally, the range of institutions which in Western democracies were more or less independent of the political authorities, such as the press, the trade unions, and the courts, came under the direct control of the party leadership at all levels.

The most important of these features was the presence of a Marxist-Leninist party at the center of public life, directing all aspects of the life of the society on the basis of a supposedly superior knowledge of the nature of social development conferred on it by the *ideology. This was what was known as the party's "leading role"; it derived most obviously from Lenin, particularly from his doctrine of the "vanguard party" set out in works such as *What Is to Be Done?* (1902). In this and other writings Lenin argued that *socialism would not come about through the automatic extension of trade union and other forms of working-class activism. What was necessary, for Lenin, was a theoretical understanding of the nature of such activity; and such an understanding would have to be brought to the workers "from the outside," by the educated intelligentsia—a notion that had obvious elitist potential. Lenin's views on party organization and structure were no less influential. For Lenin, as for the other Bolsheviks, the revolutionary party must be centralized and secretive; equally important, it should consist of "professional revolutionaries" whose occupation consisted largely or entirely of political activity.

Communist party states were periodically affected by patterns of reform or even radical change—such as in Czechoslovakia under Dubcek in 1968, when an attempt was made to construct a "socialism with a human face" that would have permitted a wide degree of political pluralism, or in Poland at the start of the 1980s, when a self-governing trade union called Solidarity secured a nationwide following; or in China during the Cultural Revolution, when Mao Zedong with the support of the army led a movement against "capitalist roaders" in the party itself. The processes of change that took place in the late 1980s and early 1990s were nonetheless unprecedented, as a series of contested elections and sometimes massive demonstrations led to the replacement of communist rule itself throughout most of the region.

The first noncommunist government for forty years was established in Poland in June 1989, after a newly legalized Solidarity had been allowed to take part and then to win almost all the seats in elections to the Polish parliament. Communists lost power later in the year in Hungary, East Germany, Romania, and Czechoslovakia, and in the year or so that followed in nearly all the countries in which their authority had formerly been unchallenged. By the late 1990s, communist rule remained in only a few countries, none of them in Europe: in Cuba (where Fidel *Castro insisted on communist orthodoxy), in China (where a student-led movement was brutally crushed at *Tiananmen Square in 1989), in North Korea (where Kim Il Sung, party leader from 1948 up to his death in 1994, was succeeded by his son), in Vietnam, and in Laos. Very substantial numbers, clearly, still lived under communist rule; but for most, this was the end of communism's "world tour, 1917–1989," even the "end of history" itself.

Scholars will debate the end of communist rule for a long time to come. The central problem, it might be argued, was the steadily falling rate of economic growth. Without economic growth, it was impossible to sustain the "social contract" between governments and their societies, a tacit bargain that involved the surrender of a range of political rights (such as the right to dismiss the government at elections) for a number of social and economic rights (such as guaranteed employment and housing). This, it appeared, had underpinned the communist party states in the 1960s and 1970s; but as growth rates began to falter, communist governments found it increasingly difficult to keep their side of the bargain. Most of the communist party states, in any case, had been sustained in the last resort by the USSR; and what was decisive in their case was not domestic developments, but the ending of the "Brezhnev doctrine" (under which Warsaw Pact troops would intervene if a communist government was in danger) and its replacement by what was dubbed the "Sinatra doctrine" (under which the East European states would be allowed to do it "their way").

Communist party states lasted longest where they were indigenous (as in Russia, or in China, Vietnam, or Cuba). All of them, however, had to find an accommodation with the rigors of the market and with domestic pressures for a degree of influence on the political process. And this meant that even where communists remained in power, the systems over which they presided had to change in ways that made them very different from the centrally planned and politically monopolistic states that had existed in the heyday of Soviet power.

(See also CHINESE COMMUNIST PARTY; COMMAND ECONOMY; COMMUNISM; POST-COMMUNISM; STALINISM.)

Leslie Holmes, *Politics in the Communist World* (Oxford, 1986). Ronald J. Hill, *Communist Politics under the Knife: Surgery or Autopsy?* (London, 1990). Stephen White et al., *Communist and Postcommunist Political Systems: An Introduction,* 3d ed. (London, 1990). J. F. Brown, *Surge to Freedom: The End of Communist Rule in Eastern Europe* (Durham, N.C., 1991).

STEPHEN WHITE

COMMUNITARIANISM is a social philosophy that maintains that societal formulations of the good are both needed and legitimate. Communitarianism is often contrasted with classical *liberalism, a philosophical position that holds each individual should formulate the good. Communitarians examine the ways shared conceptions of the good (values) are formed, transmitted, enforced, and justified. Hence their interest in communities (and moral dialogues within them), historically transmitted values and mores, and the societal units that transmit and enforce values such as the family, schools, and voluntary associations from social clubs to independent churches.

While laissez-faire conservatives and welfare liberals differ mainly with regard to the respective roles of the private sector and that of the state, communitarians are especially concerned with the third sector, that of *civil society. They pay special attention to the way social responsibilities are fostered by informal communal processes of persuasion and peer pressure.

While the term "communitarian" was coined only in the mid-nineteenth century, ideas that are communitarian in nature are to be found in the Old and New Testaments, Catholic theology (e.g., emphasis on the Church as community, and more recently on subsidiarity), and socialist doctrine (e.g., writings about the early commune and about workers' solidarity).

While all communitarians uphold the importance of the social realm, and in particular of community, they differ in the extent to which their conceptions are attentive to liberty and individual rights. Early communitarians such as Ferdinand Tönnies and Robert Nisbet stressed the importance of closely knit social fabric and authority. Asian communitarians are especially concerned about the values of social order. In the 1980s, Robert Bellah and his associates, Charles Taylor, Michael Sandel, and Michael Walzer criticized the excessive individualism of liberalism, America under President Reagan and Britain under Prime Minister Thatcher. Most recently, Alan Ehrenhalt's book *The Lost City: The Forgotten Virtues of Community in America* questioned the value of enhancing choice, achieved at the cost of maintaining community and authority.

In the 1990s, responsive communitarians such as Amitai Etzioni, Philip Selznick, William Galston, Mary Ann Glendon, and Jean Bethke Elshtain emphasized the need to balance commitment to the social good with respect for individual *rights, to reconcile the promotion of social virtue with liberty. They issued a platform endorsed by a wide range of leading Americans, published a quarterly (*The Responsive Community*), and formed a communitarian network. They have often been credited with having influenced leaders of different persuasions in a number of Western countries.

Responsive communitarians have developed several specific concepts and policies, drawing on their philosophy. They favor shoring up families, not traditional-authoritarian ones but peer marriages (in which mothers and fathers have equal rights and responsibilities). They fostered schools that provide character education rather than merely teach, but oppose religious indoctrinization. They developed notions of community justice, in which offenders, victims, and members of the community work together to find appropriate punishments and meaningful reconciliation. Responsive communitarians favored devolution of state power and the formation of communities of communities (within national societies and among nations), among many other policies.

Communitarian economics (or socioeconomics) replaces the assumptions of neoclassical economics with the premises that actors seek to both advance their self-interest and abide by their moral commitments; that actors often make nonrational choices; and that actors are individuals who are deeply affected (albeit not fully determined) by their communities rather than act as independent individuals.

Communitarian concepts have been gaining a following in response to excessive individualism in the West and a retreating from collectivism and authoritarianism in other parts of the world. They also serve as an antidote to religious fundamentalism. However, both as a social philosophy and as a public conception, it is a young discipline, so far not widely known nor followed.

(See also DEMOCRACY; NEW SOCIAL MOVEMENTS; PLURALISM.)

AMITAI ETZIONI

COMOROS. See INDIAN OCEAN REGION.

COMPARABLE WORTH. Pay equity, or comparable worth, is a reform strategy to reduce gender- and race-based wage discrimination, advocated since the mid-1970s, first in the United States, and then Canada, Britain, and other countries. Proponents argue that the wage gap between jobs held primarily by women and those held primarily by men (or by members of minority and majority groups) is caused by the undervaluation of women's jobs, which results from a long history of employers' and male workers' actions or beliefs that devalue women's skills. Comparable worth projects employ a technical strategy to eliminate this wage gap. Job evaluation, an established management tool, identifies the undervaluation and measures the amount of wage inequality by assessing levels of skill, complexity, responsibility, and adverse working conditions in various job classifications. Jobs with varying content, such as nursing and engineering, are evaluated according to these factors and given numerical scores, the wages of jobs with similar evaluation scores are compared, and inequity is identified when comparably scored jobs have different levels of pay. Implementation allocates wage increases to undervalued jobs.

Comparable worth is also a social movement that mobilizes for pay equity policies through legislation, collective bargaining, and litigation. In the United States, efforts have been primarily in state governments and jurisdictions. First used in the state of Washington in the early 1970s, the strategy spread rapidly thanks to the activities of women's organizations, labor unions, and feminist state legislators. The movement was assisted by a feasibility study published by the National Research Council in 1981 (Donald J. Treiman and Heidi I. Hartmann, *Women, Work, and Wages: Equal Pay for Jobs of Equal Value*, Committee on Occupational Classification and Analysis, Washington, D.C.). In 1998, a bill to establish pay equity policies at a national level was introduced in Congress. Internationally, the most comprehensive effort has been in Ontario, Canada, where Parliament passed a Pay Equity Act in 1987 covering employers in both private and public sectors. This act resulted in significant wage gains for women workers. However, after the Conservative Party came to power in 1995, funding for implementation was cut and the act was substantially weakened.

The predicted high cost of equity adjustments was a major argument against comparable worth. In spite of these predictions, pay equity adjustments have been inexpensive. Pay equity efforts increased in some countries in the late 1990s, particularly in Sweden and Norway. At the end of the twentieth century, the major issues were whether organizational downsizing and demands for flexibility undermine traditional job evaluation approaches. Pay equity supporters advocate a broad approach, including new forms of collective bargaining and measures to protect the gains already made.

(See also FEMINIZATION OF POVERTY; GENDER AND POLITICS; POLITICS.)

Joan Acker, *Doing Comparable Worth: Gender, Class, and Pay Equity* (Philadelphia, 1989). Heidi Hartmann and Stephanie Aaronson, *Pay Equity and Women's Wage Increases: Success in the States, a Model for the Nation* (Washington, D.C., 1994). Pat Armstrong and Mary Cornish, "Restructuring Pay Equity for a Restructured Work Force: Canadian Perspectives," *Gender, Work and Organization* 4, no. 2 (1997): 67–86. Deborah M. Figart and Peggy Kahn, *Contesting the Market: Pay Equity and the Politics of Economic Restructuring* (Detroit, 1997).

JOAN R. ACKER

COMPARATIVE POLITICS. See overleaf.

CONFUCIANISM. A system of ethics applicable to Chinese society, state, and culture, Confucianism was formulated by Confucius and his disciples and appeared primarily in *The Analects, The Great Learning, The Doctrine of the Mean,* and *The Book of Mencius* (known collectively as *The Four Books*). In some of these works, Confucius identified "five sets of relationships: [those] between the sovereign and ministers, father and son, husband and wife, elder and younger brothers, and between friends." He specified the ethical properties of some of these relationships as follows: "Father, kindness; son, filial piety; elder brother, goodness; younger brother, respect; husband, righteousness; wife, compliance; the sovereign, benevolence; ministers, loyalty." For more than 2,000 years, this system of ethics has been continuously and universally followed by the Chinese.

Confucian thought is characterized by a spirit of humanism, rationalism, and moralism. It is concerned with human relations, upholding *ren* (humanity or love) as its highest value; it relies on human experience—rather than any religious doctrine—to justify its beliefs; it emphasizes the regulation of all human conduct through ethical precepts. This spirit remained unchanged throughout Chinese history despite its frequent interactions with many other systems of thought, notably Legalism, *Buddhism, and Taoism.

In traditional *China, Confucianism exerted its influence primarily through two means. First, from 136 B.C.E. during the Western Han dynasty to the end of the Qing dynasty in 1911, Confucianism was accepted as the state orthodoxy by which the political conduct of all individuals, from the sovereign to the commoners, was regulated. Moreover, from 606 to 1905 C.E., most Chinese political and bureaucratic leaders were recruited through an examination system based in Confucianism.

Second, the Chinese have firmly accepted the Confucian belief in the perfectibility and educability of the common person. An ideal society could be realized, Confucius emphasized, because every individual was capable of acquiring virtues through self-cultivation, and the society should help individuals with this task by providing education to all. Confucian classics and their interpretations constituted the exclusive curricula in all Chinese private and state schools.

In contemporary times, Confucianism has been subject both to challenge and affirmation. In the early twentieth century, the Chinese New Culture movement argued that Confucian ethics were feudalistic in content and served the interests of monarchical absolutism; Confucianism was seen as responsible for the social and cultural stagnation of the nation. The *Chinese Communist Party, following this line of thought, has generally rejected Confucianism as being inimical to *Marxism-*Leninism, yet on occasion it has acknowledged, for reasons of expediency, certain progressive features of Confucianism, such as the emphasis on popular education and the application of a common set of ethics to all individuals.

Many scholars, both in China and overseas, have come to
(cont. on p. 166)

COMPARATIVE POLITICS. The term *comparative politics* refers to both a subject matter and a method of analysis. In principle, the two should complement each other; in practice, they frequently do not.

As a subject, comparative politics is the special field of teaching and research within the discipline of political science that is customarily devoted to "the politics of other countries or peoples." At least in the United States, its academic position has usually been somewhat marginal, flanked on the one side by U.S. politics (which are implicitly treated as incomparable) and, on the other, by *international relations (which are explicitly regarded as more consequential). Despite the number and variety of "other countries and peoples," vastly more political scientists are employed in studying the domestic politics and foreign relations of the United States.

The situation elsewhere used not to be very different. However, in recent years, teaching and research involving comparisons among European countries have increased significantly, and there are encouraging signs that a similar trend is emerging within Latin America and parts of Asia. For example, it has become almost inconceivable that a German, Italian, Dutch, or Spaniard would seriously attempt to understand his or her politics without at least some reference to the politics of neighboring states—if only because of the high levels of interdependence and joint policy-making embedded in the *European Community. Scholars from France and Britain may still be convinced, along with the Americans, of the uniqueness of their brand of politics, but that too may be waning. Only in these countries could one imagine that an introductory course in politics would refer just to the country in which it was being given.

As a method, comparative politics involves an analytical effort to exploit the similarities and differences between political units as a basis for developing "grounded theory," testing hypotheses, inferring causality, and producing reliable generalizations. As John Stuart Mill observed some 150 years ago, the practical difficulty of applying experimental techniques to political matters makes comparison of observed variance across "natural" units the most feasible—if still the second-best—technique for developing scientific knowledge in this field. Recourse to it is as old as political inquiry itself. Plato and, especially, Aristotle not only made systematic use of it but developed core concepts, typologies, and hypotheses that are still of great utility. As we shall see, the "fashion for comparison" has waxed and waned over the subsequent centuries, but the "urge to compare" has never completely disappeared.

If and when the subject and the method are successfully blended to produce reliable and cumulative generalizations across a wide range of settings, then comparative politics would cease being an exotic subfield and become virtually synonymous with the scientific study of politics. American politics would provide material for just another case; international relations would enrich our understanding of the broader contexts in which the cases are located. All systematic political inquiry—except for those few areas appropriate for controlled experimentation—would be explicitly or implicitly comparative.

Despite considerable effort by a distinguished group of scholars over the past four decades, such a synthesis is still on the distant horizon. As we shall see, there are some formidable obstacles to be overcome.

The Dependence on Theory and Concepts. "Comparativists" bear a double burden. Their topic demands that they produce useful information about foreign polities, but their method requires that they develop and apply analytical categories that are equivalent across the units they are examining. "Theory" is indispensable for establishing this comparability, but its tendency to rely on general and abstract concepts interferes with easy comprehension by nonspecialists and often generates understandings that are far removed from the explanations actors themselves use to describe and justify what they are doing.

Some original practitioners of the subdiscipline could afford to ignore this difficult issue. By confining their attention to those Euro-American polities with a common politico-cultural heritage and similar range of socioeconomic development, they could unselfconsciously rely on everyday labels and assumptions. James Bryce, A. Lawrence Lowell, and Woodrow Wilson are examples of learned scholars around the turn of the century who felt no need for elaborate and explicit conceptualization in going about their task of describing the institutions and norms of political life in Britain, the United States, and "the Continental Powers." To the extent that they had a theory, it was rooted in the comfortable assumption that eventually all countries would evolve toward a similar set of liberal democratic practices.

The Impact of Events. World War I, the Russian Revolution, and the rise of Fascist and National Socialist regimes during the 1920s and 1930s radically shattered this assumption of benevolent convergence. The range of variation within Europe in institutions, behaviors, and justifications increased with dramatic and tragic consequences. After World War II, when the Western European polities seemed to be returning to a common evolutionary path, the worldwide process of *decolonization and attendant struggles for national independence introduced new sources of diversity into the field. Indeed, the excitement that accompanied these changes—plus the policy needs for information coming from the U.S. government and the financial incentives for research coming from major foundations—produced a significant shift in the attention of comparativists away from the First World of Europe toward the "communizing nations" of the Second World and, especially, the "developing nations" of the Third World. Coping with this extraordinary increase in the number of units and the diversity of their situations demanded a major effort in explicit and elaborate theory-building. Much of this focused on the concept of "political development" and the search for "functional equivalences" beneath the bewildering variety of new institutions, practices, norms, and beliefs.

The "Golden Age." During the 1960s and 1970s, comparative politics became *the* major locus of theory-building within the discipline as a whole, and its innovations subsequently affected the more established fields of U.S. politics and international relations. Faced with explaining the "constitution" of the Soviet Union, "elections" in Albania, "parliaments" in Ghana, "professional associations" in Libya, "ministerial selection" in Sri Lanka, "federalism" in Argentina—not to mention "civil military relations" in Ecuador or "budgeting" in Zaire—one could not simply apply the usual labels without serious risk of distortion. The similarity in rhetoric hid an obvious absence of analogous behavior, intent, or consequence. But what could replace the old, comfortable rubrics? What makes a concept "transcultural" and "transportable"—hence, utilizable across polities of otherwise great diversity?

The answer to these questions led postwar comparativists to rely increasingly on general theory. Their first reaction was to postulate a universalistic characteristic of all polities, namely, their tendency to form systems whose components were interdependent and homeostatic. Then they defined the system components not as institutions but as functions, i.e., generic tasks that must be performed if the postulated equilibrium were to be reached and sustained. As these initially diverse systems were affected by a generic similar process, *modernization (i.e., economic development, urbanization, *secularization, literacy, industrialization, rationalization, bureaucratization, and so forth), the result would be *political development.

With these fundamental notions at hand (taken largely from social anthropology and biology, often via the sociology of Talcott Parsons), they courageously sallied forth not just to explain what was going on in an extraordinary diversity of settings, but also to create a new "universalistic" understanding of what politics was all about and why political development was bound to occur.

The results of this ambitious venture were mixed. Quantities of new and often very useful data were gathered about "exotic" places. Novel (or long-forgotten) aspects of *state-society relations such as clientelism and patrimonialism were opened up to inquiry. Sensitivity certainly grew with regard to the variety of ways in which political business could be conducted and institutions could be exploited. The exclusive emphasis on comparisons between "advanced polities" was irrevocably altered. Nevertheless, already by the early 1970s serious doubts about the paradigm had begun to arise, and by the 1980s the field had lost its unity of purpose. Complaints accumulated that the systemic functionalism was excessively abstract, weak in providing specific and researchable hypotheses, and incapable of orienting the collection of empirical data. Moreover, its Americocentric aspects became increasingly apparent. Equilibrium did not always set in. Functional tasks were not so nicely differentiated or performed so complementarily. Political systems on the "periphery" proved to be less autonomous and more subject to dependency and domination effects. Assumptions about the coherence and identity of "national" societies and their corresponding polities turned out to be overly optimistic. Traditional cultures were more varied and resilient than anticipated. They did not give way so easily to the "imperatives" of modernization. Autocracy rather than *democracy became the more probable outcome. Instead of the expected political development, something much more akin to political decay emerged in much of the Third World—and in the Second World of communism, a very different pattern of domination installed and consolidated itself.

The Reaction of Area Specialists. Meanwhile, the "American" promotion of comparative politics had spread to Europe. Practitioners there also tended to chafe at the limitations and assumptions of systemic functionalism, but for different reasons. European polities may have been manifestly more self-equilibrating than those of the Third World (after an initial decade of postwar uncertainty in some countries); however, the interdependence of components and, hence, the configuration of institutions often differed markedly from the paradigm case of the United States. Contrary to the prevalent view from America, it was not specialized performance of functions, overlapping cleavage patterns, broadly aggregative parties, and limited state interventions that could account for the relatively high degree of order that emerged. Also for Europeans, the flagrantly "ahistorical" nature of the general paradigm contradicted the abundant evidence for the persistent role of different historical residues, sequences, and trajectories in the region.

During the 1960s individual European scholars began to elaborate alternative models of political order and political change. Basically, they took the case they knew best (usually the one in which they lived and taught), summarized it, and generalized its characteristics to other settings. Stein Rokkan used his native Norway to produce an elaborate theory of historical cleavages and center-periphery relations; Giovanni Sartori analyzed the party system of Italy to challenge the American assumption of centrist-centripetal tendencies by showing how polarized-centrifugal patterns of competition could emerge; Gerhard Lehmbruch and Leonard Neidhart came up with models of *Proporz-* or *Pluralitäre-demokratie* to explain the special features of Swiss and Austrian politics; Arend Lijphart, Hans Daalder, and Val Lorwin exploited the cases of the Netherlands and Belgium to show how "segmented" rather than "overlapping *pluralism" could produce stability through a consociational form of democracy. While all the above were (at least initially) intended only to make sense out of the peculiar characteristics of continental European polities, Juan Linz abstracted the characteristics of what was a markedly deviant case in this context, Spain, and came up with the definition of a distinctive type, the authoritarian regime, that very quickly was picked up by scholars working on other parts of the world. Joseph Lapalombara's appropriation of *parentela* and *clientela* from the Italian political jargon to explain certain peculiarities of that country's interest in politics enjoyed a similar, if less successful, fate.

For Europeanists were not the only ones who resisted the universalistic appeal of systemic functionalism. From the start, specialists on such foreign areas as Latin America, Africa, Asia, and the Middle East regarded the pretensions of comparative politics with considerable skepticism. Their domain of expertise was being invaded by outsiders (some of whom, it must be admitted, did possess detailed knowledge of specific cultures, languages, and histories). The concepts being thrown at "their" societies seemed excessively abstract, insufficiently informative, and hardly value-neutral. Not only were the concepts biased toward the rational utilitarianism of Western societies, but they also seemed to justify various forms of policy intervention—not to say imperialist manipulation—by the already developed powers that were sponsoring and consuming comparative research.

In addition to the general culturally and historically based objections mentioned above, scholars working on and/or coming from these Third World countries began to develop alternative concepts and theories. The most significant of these focused on the international context within which politics was being conducted—particularly the unequal exchange between central and peripheral economies, owing to the differential historical development of a single world capitalist system. In a broader sense, it was argued that the conditions of late development and dependency upon external sources of demand, investment capital, ownership of enterprises, *elite values, and models of mass consumption altered the basic parameters of policy choice and led to different political outcomes. Guillermo O'Donnell drew the conclusion that, under these conditions of delayed, dependent development through import substitution, the most likely result would be not democracy but protracted bureaucratic authoritarian rule. This thesis produced a great deal of critical discussion and had an impact far beyond the South American

context from which it originated. A related conceptual innovation was the notion that *corporatism, not pluralism, was the most probable response in the realm of interest associations to such differences in patterns of development. This idea was very quickly diffused across national, regional, and cultural boundaries and, suitably reformulated, led to a major revision in the way that Europeans conceptualized their interest politics.

One group of area specialists paid little or no attention to all this ferment and controversy: those who worked on the Soviet Union, Eastern Europe, and China. With very few exceptions, they easily agreed that what was going on in their bailiwicks was incomparable and required a different approach. *Totalitarianism both provided an over-arching concept and served to justify a unique set of methods of observation and inference that could cope with its secretive and sinister nature. The static and isolated character of this subfield left its practitioners quite unprepared for explaining the remarkable (and unanticipated) changes that emerged during the late 1980s, and they have since been busy trying to join their long-lost comparativist colleagues.

The Proliferation of Methods, Levels, and Designs. If this dispersion of critiques and innovations were not enough, the subdiscipline of comparative politics has also been buffeted in recent decades by a proliferation of methods, levels, and designs. The original comparativists were scholars (all DWEMs: *Dead, White, European Men*—but not *Boring*) who worked alone, mainly used publicly available information about the public leaders and institutions of sovereign states in multiple settings (often mixed with a good deal of "itinerant wandering" and "participant observation"), and drew their conclusions based on prevailing standards of logic and inference (even if, occasionally, reaching unusual and counterintuitive conclusions). They made extensive use of typologies as simplifying devices to establish equivalences and differences. For example, Aristotle first separated Greek city-states into three descriptive categories: rule by one person, rule by a few people, and rule by all citizens, and then further divided them normatively into good and corrupt versions of each. Machiavelli relied heavily on the dichotomy between republican and princely government, Montesquieu on a trichotomy of republics, monarchies, and despotisms. Tocqueville broadened the focus to include private as well as public institutions, masterfully exploited the contrast between aristocratic and democratic societies, and offered the field a new *telos*, the ineluctable drive toward equality. Since these promising beginnings, the classification systems have multiplied and the thematic foci have shifted from one putative goal or end state to another—without producing much in the way of accumulated wisdom or conceptual convergence.

As mentioned above, comparativists have always supplemented "official" sources of information with a good deal of data gathering on their own. Through travel, personal experience in politics, and access to primary sources, as well as the reading of history, they have attempted to get beyond constitutional forms and legal categories to get at what "really" determines similarities and differences. Field research abroad for an extended period is still an obligatory *rite de passage* for all its practitioners.

The Behavioral Revolution. What is distinctive about recent practice is the reliance on new forms of data, new means of compilation, and new techniques of analysis. *Public opinion polling developed in the study of American politics and soon spread to comparative politics. The first efforts were relatively crude attempts to find out "if foreigners think like us," but with the spread of survey research facilities across the world and increasing sophistication in the conceptualization and translation of items, it became possible to design and execute multinational projects based on the attitudes of individuals. Gabriel Almond and Sidney Verba's *The Civic Culture* was a particularly ambitious "landmark" study that analyzed the opinions of mass publics in Britain, Italy, the Federal Republic of Germany (FRG), and Mexico. Since then, the volume of research on "comparative political behavior" has grown almost exponentially. Research is now conducted routinely on such items as voting preference, electoral turnout, citizen tolerance and subjective competence, confidence in institutions, modes of participation, salience of class and other bases of cleavage, party identification, difference in elite-mass values, etc., in a wide range of polities. It has even proved possible to study comparatively the emergence of new, allegedly postmaterialist, values and citizens' dispositions for engaging in "unconventional" political actions. Within the European Community, mass surveys covering all twelve member states are routinely conducted and reported in its *Eurobarometre* publications. Sizable collections of these attitudinal data have been assembled, such as the one at the Inter-University Consortium for Political and Social Research at the University of Michigan, or registered, for example, through the Data Information Service of the European Consortium for Political Research in Bergen, Norway, which allow researchers easy and inexpensive access for the purpose of secondary analysis.

The Appearance of Aggregate Data. But the explosion of sources and archives was not confined to surveys. With the independent development of national accounting systems and statistical services—and the growing availability of computers—scholars began to collect and manipulate large quantities of aggregate data. International organizations contributed to the standardization of many of these measures of national performance, and comparativists were soon adding indicators of their own. The publication of this information

in "handbooks" that covered virtually the entire universe of national states added a further stimulus. By now, machine-readable data sets on a wide range of subjects are available from commercial sources, and more will be available on CD-ROM disks.

The impact of this explosion of aggregate data has been at least as profound as that of survey data. It has permitted researchers for the first time to examine the full range of variance, "the universe," on a given subject. Previously, time, expense, and human limitations restricted the number of cases that a comparativist could deal with. These compilations have allowed analysts to bring the powerful tools of statistical estimation to bear and to incorporate many variables simultaneously in their analyses. The first efforts focused on relatively simple correlations such as that between "social mobilization and political *development" and "economic development and democracy." Subsequently, the scope of inquiry widened and the complexity of the models increased to tackle issues such as the political determinants of mass violence, industrial conflict, welfare policy, growth of state expenditures, social equality, "regime governability," and rebellion. The burgeoning field of comparative public policy owes a great deal to the stimulus of these new data sets and statistical techniques.

But these "gifts" have not been unmitigated blessings for comparativists. Much of the work ignored elementary problems of conceptual equivalence across units (not to mention empirical validity in the data); depended on crude inductive methods and *ex post facto* theorizing; neglected to measure concepts with adequate indicators; relied on static cross-sections and ignored time-dependent, dynamic relations; used statistical tools that were inappropriate for testing the postulated relationships; and failed to distinguish between correlation and causality. Nevertheless, the quality of both data and inference has improved consistently over time, and new techniques of statistical estimation are being introduced which should correct many of the analytical errors.

The Problem with Units. Both survey and aggregate data initially reinforced the already firmly entrenched tendency to use the nation-state as the exclusive unit of analysis for most comparative purposes. This was unfortunate for three reasons. 1) Most newly independent states had much less coherence and autonomy than did the established states of Europe, North America, and the "White *Commonwealth." This violated a basic assumption of the comparative method that the units should be equivalent in their capacity to act with regard to the properties being examined. 2) All comparisons are jeopardized by Galton's problem, namely, the possibility that the observations of a given variable are not "really" independent but caused by an underlying process of diffusion. With the "trade, investment, and communications revolution" that emerged during the postwar period, especially within certain, highly interdependent, regional contexts such as Western Europe, national states effectively lost their sovereign control over many policy processes. 3) The figures generated as national frequencies or averages often masked very substantial differences between unevenly developed regions and sectors within these countries. At times, this internal variation could be greater than that between the polities being compared. The national datum became an artifact of a nonexistent unit.

Growing sensitivity to these issues has resulted in several modifications of the method. Universal "samples" have been abandoned in favor of smaller and more homogeneous subsets of units. Some of these are geocultural areas, but many are based on new analytical categories that cut across these regions: "advanced industrial countries," "newly industrialized countries," and, perhaps, if the proper euphemism can be found, "really backward countries." Another trend is to exploit the infranational variation by comparing systematically the conditions and performances of *municipios, départements, provincias, regioni, Länder, estados autonómicos*, Soviet republics, etc. This approach began with U.S. states and cities, but now covers a wide range of polities where subunits have some significant degree of autonomy. Another strategy has been to focus on the meso-level of economic sectors. There is even an embryonic literature dealing comparatively with the emergent properties of supranational authorities and international organizations.

The Choice of Design. The classic format was for a scholar to study two or more units explicitly selected for their mix of common and contrasting features. Much of the production of comparativists, however, consists of "single country monographs" in which only one unit is ostensibly analyzed. The most famous and enduring of these is Tocqueville's *Democracy in America*. What accounts for its comparative status is both the way in which it is conceptualized, i.e., as a contrast between two types of societies, the democratic and the aristocratic, and the consistent, if often implicit, contrast which is made with an "absent" case, i.e., France. This case-study method has been used extensively in the postwar period, especially for dissertation research given the limited means at the disposal of young scholars. Not only have these monographs contributed heuristically to the eventual development of "grounded theory," examined critically "deviant cases," and served as "proving grounds" for new techniques, but they have also been replicated in other settings. It is important to remember that comparison is not just an event but a process. As such, it can involve the same scholar subsequently extending his or her coverage to other cases or other scholars picking up the original conceptualization and operationalization and applying them again.

The advent of aggregate data and, to a lesser extent, survey data encouraged a shift from "small N" strategies of single or paired cases to "large N" strategies which might even include the total relevant universe. Comparativists found themselves analyzing units whose language, culture, and history—even whose location—they did not know, simply because they were available in some data series of the United Nations Educational, Scientific and Cultural Organization or of the International Labor Organization. When the issues of incommensurability and unintelligibility became more salient, the enthusiasm for this design declined rapidly and researchers reverted to working on selected subsets of units where they were more familiar with the quality of the data and where they could bring more variables into the analysis—especially the effects of historical time, sequence, and memory.

Much intelligent discussion has focused on whether it is preferable, when comparing a small number of cases, to use a "most similar systems" design in which as many variables as possible can (putatively) be held constant, allowing only those under surveillance to vary—say, to study the impact of revenue windfalls on the party system by comparing Norway and Sweden—or a "most different system" design in which the effect of the same variable is traced by comparing two systems which otherwise have as little in common as possible—say, the impact of petroleum booms on Norway and Nigeria. Both have their generic advantages and disadvantages, and the choice hinges largely on whether one is seeking to maximize the specificity or the generalizability of one's findings.

One major limitation on the design of comparative research in the past has been definitively broken. Most studies were carried out by a single scholar, almost invariably an American or a European, working in relative isolation. With the increase in resources and the diffusion of competence in the social and political sciences around the globe, it has become possible to put together teams of scholars working on different countries from different disciplines. Originally, these were staffed, funded, conceptualized, and carried out almost exclusively by American academics—the Committee on Comparative Politics of the Social Science Research Council was the prototype—but this is now less likely to be the case. Most of the recently edited and multiauthored volumes cited in the bibliography of this essay were produced by collaborative efforts which were international in every aspect. Moreover, around the European Consortium for Political Research (ECPR) in Europe and the Consejo Latinoamericano de Ciencias Sociales (CLASCO) in Latin America, important new concentrations have formed to promote comparative research.

The State of the Art. It has been alleged that the personality of scholars tends to resemble the characteristics of the unit or units they study. If this were the case, most comparativists would risk schizophrenia as they are caught between the conflicting demands for providing specific and accurate information and searching for reliable and verifiable generalizations. Instead, they seem to have avoided such a collective pathology by vacillating over time between the two objectives—although individual practitioners have occasionally proved that it is possible to satisfy both simultaneously.

Their response to the postwar demand for a universalistic and relevant "science of politics" was initially enthusiastic and then increasingly skeptical. To the excesses of systemic functionalism, they reacted by stressing the specificities of culture, geographic location, economic exploitation, and social structure, while seeking to avoid excessive reliance on the idiosyncrasies of each case. The need for "history," "thick description," and "bringing the state back in" were among the slogans bandied about. Of course, some eminent students of comparative politics had long been speaking this sort of prose without knowing or proclaiming it. Even the more "mainstream" practitioners associated with development theory responded to the critiques. Samuel P. Huntington consistently stressed the longer-term cultural and institutional aspects of political change and arrived at much less sanguine conclusions about the likely outcome. The Social Science Research Council (SSRC) Committee on Comparative Politics in its later years turned its attention back toward Europe and recuperated a more historical perspective.

But comparative politics has not merely returned to its point of departure. Along the tortuous route, it picked up new concerns, new concepts, and a lot of new converts. It may have momentarily lost a clear sense of direction, but there are definite signs of movement, even of enthusiasm, among its contemporary practitioners. Few would question, however, that the subdiscipline is at an important crossroads.

Three challenges are looming on the horizon for comparativists: one to their theoretical foundations; one to their basic units of analysis; one to their subject matter. 1) The current fashion for rational choice and game-theoretic explanations raises the specter of a possible return to universalistic premises—based this time not on unconscious adjustment and functional equilibration at the macro level, but on stable solutions worked out through repeated exchanges between individual actors at the micro level. If completely successful, this approach would not only convert entire departments of political science into dependencies of neoclassical economics, but it would also wipe out the accumulated stock of comparativists' assumptions about the significance of cultural, institutional, and obligational factors. History would be reduced to the passage of time and the iteration of exchanges; institutions would be contingent on continuous calculation; preferences would be given rather than socially constructed; maximizing self-interest would be the only admissible norm. 2) Unprecedented increases in interdependence—through trade, investment, production, diffusion of images and tastes, spread of international

regimes and obligations, etc.—have greatly eroded the autonomy (not to mention the sovereignty) of the national states that have so far provided the subdiscipline with its principal units of observation and analysis. Galton's dilemma has run wild. In such a globalized context, no polity can choose and act independently. Will comparativists be able to shift their bases of inference, as well as their units of inquiry? Or will they be confined in the future to analyzing intertemporal and regional variations of a single "world system"? 3) The wave of democratization that has swept across the world since 1974 offers to comparativists the attractive prospect of once again being able to focus on a common topic. They looked on with dismay at the "praetorian politics" and "breakdown of democracy" in the 1960s and early 1970s; now they are turning their attention to the more heartening processes of "transition from authoritarian rule" and "consolidation of democracy." Whether this will trigger a resurgence in theoretical speculation about evolutionary convergence, or a greater conceptual sophistication about differences in the types of democracy that are emerging, remains to be seen. If the past is any guide, two things are certain: comparativists will divide into "generalizers" and "specifiers" in response to these issues, and the debate between them will contribute to keeping their subdiscipline lively, controversial, and consequential.

(See also AUTHORITARIANISM; BUREAUCRATIC AUTHORITARIANISM; COMMUNIST PARTY STATES; CONSOCIATIONAL DEMOCRACY; DEMOCRATIC TRANSITIONS; GAME THEORY; IMPORT-SUBSTITUTION INDUSTRIALIZATION; POLITICAL CULTURE; POLITICAL ECONOMY; POLITICAL PARTICIPATION; PUBLIC CHOICE THEORY.)

Carl Friedrich and Zbigniew Brzezinski, *Totalitarian Dictatorship and Autocracy* (New York, 1956). Gabriel Almond and James Coleman, eds., *The Politics of Developing Areas* (Princeton, N.J., 1960). Alexander Gerschenkron, *Economic Backwardness in Historical Perspective* (Cambridge, Mass., 1962). Gabriel Almond and Sidney Verba, *The Civic Culture* (Boston, 1963). Arthur Banks and Robert Textor, *A Cross-Polity Survey* (Ann Arbor, Mich., 1963). Bruce Russett et al., *World Handbook of Political and Social Indicators* (New Haven, Conn., 1964). Samuel Huntington, *Political Order in Changing Societies* (New Haven, Conn., 1968). Adam Przeworski and Henry Teune, *The Logic of Comparative Social Inquiry* (New York, 1970). Leonard Binder, ed., *Crises and Sequences in Political Development* (Princeton, N.J., 1971). Philippe C. Schmitter, "Still the Century of Corporatism?" in F. B. Pike and T. Stritch, eds., *The New Corporatism: Social-Political Structures in the Iberian World* (London, 1974). Charles Tilly, ed., *The Formation of National States in Western Europe* (Princeton, N.J., 1975). Juan Linz and Alfred Stepan, eds., *The Breakdown of Democratic Regimes*, 4 vols. (Baltimore, 1978). Fernando Henrique Cardoso and Enzo Falletto, *Dependency and Development in Latin America* (Berkeley and Los Angeles, 1979). Guillermo O'Donnell, Philippe C. Schmitter, and Laurence Whitehead, eds., *Transitions from Authoritarian Rule*, 4 vols. (Baltimore, 1986). Charles Ragin, *The Comparative Method* (Berkeley, Calif., 1987).

PHILIPPE C. SCHMITTER

the defense of Confucianism. Liang Sou-ming, Hsiung Shih-li, and Hsu Fu-kuan, for example, saw Confucianism as possessing certain transcendental qualities that characterized Chinese civilization, differentiating it from the world's other great civilizations. In the last three decades, a school of New Confucianism has emerged, with Mou Tsung-san, T'ang Chun-i, Tu Wei-ming, Thomas A. Metzger, and Yu Ying-shih as its leading advocates. They believe that the Confucian emphasis on *junzi* (the virtuous person) gives followers of Confucianism a common mission: to seek virtuous individuals, harmonious families, an orderly state, and a peaceful world. Some of these scholars have suggested that this mission has endowed modern Confucianism with a "transformative force" for social and economic changes—an idea opposite to Max *Weber's argument that Confucianism lacked an innate driving force for the betterment of life.

More recently, other scholars have suggested that Confucianism has contributed to the spectacular economic performance of the East Asian countries. In Japan, Taiwan, the Republic of Korea, Hong Kong, and Singapore, these scholars believe, the economic impact of Confucianism is manifested in the organizational characteristics of businesses, management-labor relations, the saving rate, and the strong emphasis on education. These conditions are linked to expanded foreign trade and investment opportunities as an explanation for why the Pacific Basin region has been the fastest-growing area of the world in economic terms over the last three decades.

In the 1980s Singapore proposed to incorporate Confucianism into school curricula and initiated Confucian-based social policies. Only a concern to maintain interethnic harmony among the Chinese, the Malays, and the Indians of the country persuaded the government to discontinue these efforts.

(See also NEWLY INDUSTRIALIZING ECONOMIES.)

H. G. Creel, *Confucius: The Man and the Myth* (New York, 1949). Hung-chao Tai, ed., *Confucianism and Economic Development: An Oriental Alternative?* (Washington, D.C., 1989).

HUNG-CHAO TAI

CONGO, DEMOCRATIC REPUBLIC OF THE. With a territory of 905,562 square miles (2,345,406 sq. km.), the Congo is the third largest country on the African continent. Since its creation as a territorial entity in 1885, the country has gone through four names: Congo Free State (1885–1908); Belgian Congo (1908–1960); Congo (1960–1971); and Zaire (1971–1997). The official designation as Democratic Republic of the Congo, to which the country returned in 1997, was originally adopted by a constitutional conference in 1964. The country should not be confused with the Congo Republic, formerly the colony of Middle Congo in French Equatorial Africa, whose capital, Brazzaville, lies on the other bank of the Congo River across from Kinshasa. As it became fashionable in the 1960s, it is easier to differentiate the two countries as "Congo-Kinshasa" and "Congo-Brazzaville."

The Congo's strategic location in the middle of Africa and its fabulous natural endowment of minerals and other resources unfortunately ensured that it would serve as a theater for the playing out of the economic and strategic interests of outsiders: the colonial powers during the Scramble for Africa; the superpowers during the Cold War; and neighboring African states in the post–Cold War era. In the face of this external threat, Congo's rulers resorted to both accommodation, by aligning themselves with some of the external interests, and resistance, by fighting off real or potential aggressors. In the process, they strove to acquire both a private fortune with which they could ensure personal rule and the absolute power needed to repress any internal opposition to their self-serving policies.

The most successful rulers in this regard were King Leopold II of the Belgians, founder and king-sovereign of the Congo Free State, and Mobutu Sésé Seko, who renamed the country "Zaire" in 1971 and ruled it as a private domain from 1965 to 1997. Leopold had acquired the Congo as a personal possession through skillful diplomacy and a judicious use of money and public relations. His brutal regime resulted in a calamitous loss of life of Holocaust proportions, with millions dying from forced labor, state-sponsored terrorism, and the resulting hunger and disease. The Belgian colonial system which succeeded him reduced the level of violence considerably, but remained a system of economic exploitation, political repression and cultural oppression, with limited benefits for the Congolese people. Taking over barely five years after independence, Mobutu merely reproduced the colonial model of exploitation and repression, his major innovation being the creation of a system of wealth accumulation benefiting hundreds of his relatives, cronies, and associates, both civilian and military, while the economic and social fabric of the country was disintegrating. His successor, Laurent-Désiré Kabila, spent his first three years in power basically following in Mobutu's footsteps, but with a new cast of domestic and external allies.

Decolonization and Mobutu's Second Republic (1960–1990). The Congo won its independence from Belgium on 30 June 1960. The Mouvement National Congolais (MNC) and its coalition of radical nationalist parties had captured a majority of seats in the Lower House of Parliament in the preindependence May elections. Patrice *Lumumba, the MNC leader, became the country's first prime minister, while Joseph Kasavubu, president of the Alliance des Bakongo (ABAKO), became the first ceremonial head of state.

This victory of a militantly nationalist leader with a strong national constituency was viewed as a major impediment to the Belgian neocolonialist strategy, particularly by its proponents in the business community, who hoped to preserve intact their economic dominance over the country's resources. Within two weeks of the independence proclamation, Prime Minister Lumumba was faced with both a mutiny by the army and a *secessionist movement in Katanga Province led by Moïse Tshombe, both revolts instigated by the Belgians and the second bankrolled by Belgian mining interests. The Katanga secession was actually announced on 11 July, one day after Belgium had deployed its own troops all over the Congo under the pretext of protecting European lives and property.

In the hopes of obtaining the evacuation of Belgian troops and white mercenaries, and thus ending the Katanga secession, Lumumba appealed to the United Nations Security Council to send a UN force to the Congo. However, the UN secretary-general, Dag Hammarskjöld, interpreted the UN mandate in accordance with the United States' Cold War imperative of preventing Soviet expansion in the Third World.

He emphasized the law-and-order functions of the UN force and placed greater value on the restoration of the economic and social infrastructure of the country than on confrontation with Tshombe and his Belgian backers. When Lumumba then requested and received aid from the Soviet Union in August, his removal from power under Western pressure and his eventual assassination on 17 January 1961 by his Congolese rivals with help and encouragement from Belgium and the U.S. Central Intelligence Agency (CIA) were all but ensured.

No sooner had the external patrons resolved the crisis of decolonization than the client state itself was plunged into a new and more severe crisis. The Western-backed government of Prime Minister Cyrille Adoula was faced with widespread popular resistance against the state because of its failure to satisfy the deepest aspirations of ordinary people for freedom and a better standard of living. The resistance began to manifest itself in January 1964 as popular insurrections for a "second independence" led by Pierre Mulele and other radical nationalists. The rebels were eventually defeated in 1965 by Prime Minister Tshombe's Katanga gendarmes, reinforced by white mercenaries, Belgian advisers, and U.S. logistical support. Parliamentary elections held the same year failed to produce a resolution of the leadership crisis among the moderates, as Kasavubu's newly designated prime minister, Evariste Kimba, was rejected on two separate attempts by a Parliament dominated by Tshombe's supporters and clients. Using this political impasse as a pretext and exploiting the Western powers' alarm at Kasavubu's overtures to African nationalists at the 1965 Accra summit of the Organization of African Unity (OAU), General Joseph-Désiré Mobutu, the army chief, carried out a *coup d'état on 24 November 1965, with the support of the CIA.

The Mobutu regime began as a military dictatorship with the entire army high command making up the junta. But it soon acquired all the characteristics of personal rule then found elsewhere in Africa: a one-party dictatorship under the authoritarian control of a single individual. Mobutu's power was so absolute that he could do anything his heart desired. An accomplished Machiavellian, he used his ill-gotten wealth and his powers of patronage to outfox potential opponents and to keep wavering officials in line. At the same time, he did not hesitate to use force when it could best serve his purposes. And he did so with such ferocity and regularity that gross violations of human rights, including assassinations, extrajudicial executions, massacres of unarmed civilians, and banishment to remote penal colonies, became one of the defining characteristics of the Mobutu regime.

Through frequent cabinet reshuffling and constant change of high-ranking officials, Mobutu gave as many people as possible the chance to enrich themselves, thereby developing a stake in the survival of the regime. A corrupt and degenerate ruling group, Mobutu's kleptocracy blocked economic growth and development by depriving the state of those essential means and resources required for satisfying the basic needs of the population. By privatizing the state itself, they succeeded not only in abolishing the distinction between public and personal property but also in destroying the country's economic infrastructure and social fabric.

The end of the Cold War removed the realpolitik rationale for Western support for the Mobutu regime and opened space for its internal opponents and foreign critics to intensify the struggle for democracy and human rights. A sustained drive in this regard had already been launched in 1980, when a group of thirteen members of Parliament, including Etienne Tshisekedi wa Mulumba, rebelled against the one-party system with a fifty-two-page letter to Mobutu demanding political reforms. The Group of Thirteen, as they became known, persevered through repeated jailing, harassment, and repression in defying Mobutu's laws against opposition parties by creating the Union pour la Démocratie et le Progrès Social (UDPS) in 1982. In the wake of prodemocracy agitation in Africa beginning with the October 1988 events in Algiers and the victories of the democracy movement in Eastern Europe, Mobutu decided to institute a process of "national consultation" in January 1990. Almost all of the 6,000 memoranda submitted as part of the consultation process called for radical political change. Prodded by this response and by pressure from his Western allies, Mobutu announced limited political reforms on 24 April 1990, including the end of one-party rule.

Political Developments since 1990. For all practical purposes, the Mobutu era ended in 1990, with the official demise of the Second Republic and the beginning of the transition to multiparty democracy. But the wily dictator was still hanging on to the helm of his sinking ship of state seven years later, when Laurent Kabila and his Rwandan backers dispatched him into exile on 17 May 1997. By the time the Sovereign National Conference voted to establish the political institutions of the transition on 4 August 1992, the Mobutu regime had been reduced to its bare essentials as a band of bloodthirsty thieves who survived by looting and thuggery. For regime diehards, all that seemed to matter was reliance on a few elite units of the military to maintain control over the mining and other revenue-generating parastatals, the central bank, customs office, and central tax office. Mobutu, the band's chief, was now afraid to set foot in the capital city, preferring instead to live in his Versailles-like palace at Gbadolite in the far north, on the border between the Congo and the Central African Republic. His was a government that could no longer govern, for lack of legitimacy at home and support abroad, and an administration that could no longer administer, given its lack of funds and the disenchantment of civil servants.

The result was a "catastrophic equilibrium," a situation in which the old order was dying but the new one was not yet born. The democratic opposition, the standard-bearer of the new order with the societal project of reestablishing the rule of law, failed in its historical mission of ushering in radical political change. At first, it succeeded in wrestling from Mobutu the right to hold a sovereign national conference, a kind of political reforms forum combining aspects of both a constitutional convention and a truth and reconciliation commission. In the Congo, the Conférence Nationale Souveraine (CNS) met from 8 August 1991 to 6 December 1992, though it was forcibly interrupted between January and April 1992. It was very successful in laying bare what had gone wrong with the country since 1960 and in chartering a new course for the future. Unfortunately, the resolutions of the CNS remained a dead letter because of three factors: the political immaturity of the opposition; Mobutu's resistance to change; and the lack of international support.

On top of all this came the genocide of 1994 in Rwanda. Approximately one million Hutu men, women, and children, including former government officials and the extremist In-terhamwe militia responsible for the genocide, settled in ref-ugee camps not far from the border with Rwanda. Hutu extremists used these internationally operated camps to re-group and launch raids into their country. In 1996, after two years in which the Mobutu regime and the international com-munity failed to do anything about this, the Tutsi-dominated government of Major General Paul Kagame intervened mili-tary to destroy the camps. With the help of troops from Uganda and Angola and the support of other countries, the Rwandans marched all the way to Kinshasa, where they put Kabila in power. During the seven-month war beginning in October 1996, the Mobutu military machine was shown to be nothing but a paper tiger. In August 1998, following Kabila's attempt to emancipate himself from the Rwandan tutelage, Rwanda and Uganda once again launched a military drive to change governments in Kinshasa. This time around they did not succeed, as Angola, Zimbabwe, and Namibia came to Ka-bila's rescue. The result was a widening war in Central Africa, with armies from at least eight states and a dozen of nonstate or rebel armies and militias. As the states involved on both sides of the war were actively engaged in looting the Congo's resources, the prospects for peace appeared remote, even after a UN *Security Council resolution of 4 February 2000 au-thorized, for the second time in forty years, the deployment of a UN force in the Congo.

(See also COLONIAL EMPIRES; DECOLONIZATION; FRANCO-PHONE AFRICA; GREAT LAKES REGION; RWANDAN GENOCIDE; UNITED NATIONS.)

Crawford Young and Thomas Turner, *The Rise and Decline of the Zairian State* (Madison, Wis., 1985). Adam Hochschild, *King Leopold's Ghost: A Story of Greed, Terror, and Heroism in Colonial Africa* (Boston and New York, 1998). Georges Nzongola-Ntalaja, *From Zaire to the Democratic Republic of the Congo* (Uppsala, Sweden, 1998). Herbert Weiss, *War and Peace in the Democratic Republic of the Congo* (Uppsala, Sweden, 2000).
GEORGES NZONGOLA-NTALAJA

CONGO, REPUBLIC OF. Originally known as the French colony of Middle Congo in French Equatorial Africa, the Re-public of Congo has a territory of 134,750 square miles (349,001 sq. km.) west of the Democratic Republic of the Congo, with which it is separated by the Congo River. Better known as Congo-Brazzaville to distinguish it from its giant neighbor, it has a total population of approximately 2,700,000 inhabitants. Although French is the official language, many other languages are spoken. Chief among them are Kikongo, Lari, Mboshi, and Lingala. Brazzaville (the capital), Pointe-Noire, Loubomo, Nkayi, Madingou, Sibiti, Djambala, Owando, Ouesso, and Impfondo are the major urban centers.

Since the advent of independence on 15 August 1960, the Congo has undergone serious political mood swings. Indeed, with Abbé Fulbert Youlou's conservative and neocolonial regime, the successive "socialist" regimes of Alphonse Massemba-Debat (1963–1968), Marien Ngouabi (1968–1970) and Denis Sassou-Nguesso (1977–1991), the transitional gov-ernment of André Milongo (1991–1992), and the ineffective government of Pascal Lissouba (1992–1997), even the best in-formed observer has the most difficult task in clearly deline-ating the nature of the political system in the Congo.

Before the civil war of the 1990s, the country was greatly marked by the rule of the *Parti Congolais du Travail* (PCT) un-der Ngouabi and Sassou-Nguesso, between 1969, the year the Congo became the first country in Africa to adopt *Marxism-*Leninism as state *ideology, and 1991, when the party-state regime was abolished at the National Conference. In theory, the PCT was a revolutionary workers' party guided by the principles of proletarian internationalism. The party's mission was to dismantle the colonial state and build a new social order, namely, a revolutionary people's democracy. The PCT's failure to eradicate the neocolonial state and to build an in-tegrated democratic society paved the way for the National conference in 1991, which laid the ground rules for the de-mocratization process.

The most tangible outcomes of the National Conference were the end of the PCT's political hegemony; the establish-ment of a transition government under the leadership of a World Bank technocrat, Andre Milongo, as prime minister; the legalization of multipartyism; and the liberalization and privatization of the economy. The transitional institutions, which included a provisional parliament known as the High Council of the Republic, paved the way for the presidential and legislative elections in 1992. Pascal Lissouba of the *Union Panafricaine pour la Démocratie Sociale* (UPADS) was elected president of the republic. Lissouba's election was to a great extent the triumph of the coalition between his party and the *Union pour la Renouveau Démocratique* (URD), it being an en-semble of many other political formations of which the PCT and Bernard Kolélas's *Mouvement Congolais pour la Démocratie et le Développement Intégral* (MCDDI) were the most prominent.

Dissatisfied with Lissouba, the coalition broke up a few months following its formation. New alignments emerged. Lissouba's UPADS and the URD remained in the government while Sassou-Nguesso's PCT and a number of minor parties formed the opposition under the umbrella of the *Forces Dé-mocratiques Unies* (FDU). Each one of major political forma-tions organized a militia and relied heavily on ethnic and regional loyalty. As it was, the tensions between the govern-ment and the opposition permeated every sphere of existence and societal living.

The democratization came to a halt in 1997, when the pres-idential election campaign was interrupted as fighting broke out between the army still loyal to Lissouba's government, and the militia of Sassou-Nguesso's coalition. In the end, Sassou-Nguesso's militia, locally known as the Cobras, tri-umphed over a divided army as well as over the Zoulous and the Ninjas, as the respective militias of Lissouba and Kolélas were called. The ouster of Lissouba and the return of Sassou-Nguesso to the presidency were a coup de grâce to the de-mocratization process.

On the economic front, the Congo entered the twenty-first century with virtually the same structural characteristics it inherited at independence in 1960. These consist of (1) a rural sector in which the majority of the population (80 percent) operates, and still overwhelmingly a subsistence economy; (2) a modern agricultural sector introduced by foreign capitalists during colonialism and that remains under their control; (3) a small industrial sector which in the main is limited to the extraction of raw materials, petroleum being its principal product; and (4) the banking and insurance sectors, which are also in foreign hands.

In theory, the Congo is a unitary republic. In fact, the country is divided along social class and ethnic, and regional lines. The overthrow of Pascal Lissouba, the use of militias and foreign armies—French and Angolan troops fought on behalf of Sassou-Nguesso—and the return of the latter to power have dashed all hope for democracy in this corner of Africa. As the new millennium began, the Ninjas of Bernard Kolelas were still fearlessly engaged in guerrilla warfare to destabilize and overthrow Sassou-Nguesso. It was the north versus the south all over again.

(See also FRANCOPHONE AFRICA.)

Samuel Decalo, *Historical Dictionary of Congo*, 2d ed. (Metuchen, N.J., 1996). John F. Clark and David E. Gardinier, eds., *Political Reform in Francophone Africa* (Boulder, Colo., 1997). Elikia M'Bokolo, "Comparisons and Contrasts in Equatorial Africa: Gabon, Congo and the Central African Republic," in David Birmingham and Phyllis M. Martin, eds., *History of Central Africa: The Contemporary Years since 1960* (London, 1998).

N. J. KU-NTIMA MAKIDI

CONGRESS, U.S. The U.S. Congress remains as distinctive a legislative body as it was when it first convened in the spring of 1789. Almost alone among the world's legislatures, it writes its own legislation and tries to monitor the vast governmental apparatus. Its powers, enumerated in the U.S. Constitution, are quite expansive. It has protected these powers largely by resorting to division of labor (creating standing committees and subcommittees) and by adding to its staff resources.

In reality there are two Congresses, not just one. By design and by historical experience, Congress is not only a lawmaking body; it is also an assembly of disparate representatives who owe primary allegiance to voters who are hundreds or even thousands of miles away from the nation's capital. These lawmaking and representative duties clash uneasily within the same institution.

Congress as a Representative Assembly. "All politics are local," remarked former House Speaker Thomas P. "Tip" O'Neill. Although national tides influence elections, congressional candidates, their voters, and often their issues and styles, are deeply rooted in local states and districts. States are represented equally in the Senate (two for each state). The 435 members of the House of Representatives represent separate districts based on population (the decennial census is held to apportion seats among states); the House also has four delegates and one resident commissioner from the District of Columbia and U.S. territories.

Formal constitutional requirements for office are few and simple: age (twenty-five years of age for the House, thirty for the Senate); citizenship (seven years for the House, nine for the Senate); and residency in the state from which the person is elected. But de facto rules favor candidates with longstanding, intimate ties to the state or district. Once elected, senators and representatives tend to be judged by voters more on their stewardship regarding local issues than on such national trends as economic cycles. Members are vulnerable to the charge of ignoring "home folks" or becoming overly fond of Washington life.

In most congressional elections, incumbents run for reelection, and they usually prevail. Since World War II, an average of 92 percent of all incumbent representatives and 75 percent of incumbent senators running for reelection have been

returned to office. Even in the early 1990s, in the midst of scandals and voter unrest, more members retired voluntarily (many under duress) than were actually defeated at the polls. Short of a major scandal or misstep, it is nearly impossible to topple a House incumbent—and nearly as difficult to dislodge a senator.

Incumbents have resources that ensure visibility and promote support: through speeches, statements, press releases, press coverage, newsletters and mailings, staff assistance, and constituency services. The average House member enjoys perquisites valued at well over a million dollars over a two-year term; senators' resources are valued at between $4 million and $7 million. And although incumbents need less money than do challengers, they receive more from outside sources that rightly view them as better investments than their opponents. Incumbents capture the lion's share of money given by political action committees (PACs) to congressional candidates. Many incumbents, in fact, finish their campaigns with a surplus.

Incumbent legislators fashion effective "home styles"—ways of projecting themselves and their records to constituents. Ingredients of their home styles include: a cultivated image of trust; plausible explanations of behavior in office; and shrewd use of the perquisites of office. Legislators' messages are conveyed through personal appearances, radio or television spots, press releases, and responses to constituents' requests for help ("casework").

Staff aides extend senators' and representatives' constituent outreach. About 12,000 people work in members' offices. Senators' staffs range in size from thirteen to seventy-one, depending on the state's population; the average is about thirty-six. Representatives' staffs average about seventeen. Constituent relations are their most time-consuming job. Members of Congress have from one to six local offices in key home-state locations; increasingly, casework and voter contacts are handled there.

Congress as Policy Maker: Committees and Parties. Congress has retained an active legislative role by delegating its workload to committees (and subcommittees) which write, revise, and oversee laws, programs, and agencies. Most bills and resolutions are referred to the relevant committee(s) of jurisdiction. It is very difficult, especially in the House, to bypass a committee that refuses to act on a measure. "Congressional government is committee government," wrote Woodrow Wilson (*Congressional Government*, 1885). "Congress in session is Congress on display, but Congress in committee is Congress at work."

House and Senate committee structures are complicated: the Senate has seventeen committees, and these have sixty-eight subcommittees; the House has nineteen committees with eighty-seven subcommittees. There are also four joint committees (with eight subcommittees), not to mention temporary panels, boards, and commissions.

Most standing committees are authorizing committees: They draft the substance of policies and oversee executive agencies' implementation of laws. There are also appropriations committees that draft bills empowering agencies to spend money for programs; revenue committees draft revenue bills to pay for the programs. In 1974 Congress created an elaborate internal budget process for setting guidelines (proposed by House and Senate budget committees) and regulating revenues and expenditures that are supposed to be followed by all committees; income and spending levels are brought into balance by reconciliation bills.

Committees normally exert decisive control over legislative proposals: Nine out of every ten measures referred to committee go no farther in the legislative process. Promising bills may be accorded staff research and public hearings—giving executive officials, lobbyists, and citizens a chance to speak publicly on the issue. If the bill has enough support, the committee will hold meetings to revise the text ("markups") and may eventually report the measure to the full chamber.

Each committee is a unique mixture of members, viewpoints, and decision-making styles. They differ in levels of conflict, partisanship, or public visibility. Many committees or subcommittees form ongoing alliances with executive agencies and relevant pressure groups, forming the so-called "iron triangles," or subgovernments, that dominate much routine domestic policy making.

Whereas committees provide expertise for legislating, the political parties manage the legislative process. The parties organize the two chambers, supply their leaders, shape the legislative agenda, and superintend the scheduling of business. Partisan control hinges on the size of the parties' ranks in the two bodies. The majority party (at least fifty-one senators or 218 representatives) organizes the respective houses; the party's size and unity determine how effective its control will be.

The House has a tradition of vigorous leadership. The Speaker combines the duties of presiding officer with those of party leader; historically, Speakers like Henry Clay (1811–1814, 1815–1820, 1823–1825), Thomas B. "Czar" Reed (1889–1890, 1895–1899), Joseph G. "Uncle Joe" Cannon (1903–1911), and Sam Rayburn (1940–1947, 1949–1953, 1955–1961) bent the unruly chamber to their will through procedural skills and the force of their personalities.

In the Senate, strong leadership is the exception rather than the rule. Not until the twentieth century did visible party leaders emerge; even then they were no match for powerful House Speakers. The conspicuous exception was Lyndon B. Johnson, who as majority leader (1955–1961) worked with the Senate's conservative clique to dominate the chamber as no leader has done before or since. Recent leaders have acted more as facilitators for individual senators' legislative goals and schedules.

Parties are the most stable and significant coalitions on Capitol Hill. Although party discipline is lax, party loyalty runs deep and is the leading determinant of voting in the two chambers. Indeed, party-line voting has been higher in recent years than at any time since the early twentieth century. Elected lawmakers are, in fact, more partisan than their constituents, whose declining party loyalties constitute a leading trend in contemporary U.S. politics.

At least four distinct periods, or eras, define the recent history of Congress. The first (roughly 1937–1964) was dominated by the conservative coalition of southern Democrats and conservative Republicans; the second was an era of liberal activism (1965–1978), marked by heavy Democratic majorities; the third was an era of fiscal restraint (1979–1994), characterized by a lagging economy and (except for 1993–1994) by divided government. The fourth period (1995–), although still unfolding, saw conservatives dominate the leg-

islative agenda, although party margins remained close and the late 1990s economic boom somewhat eased fiscal restraints.

Recent institutional and political trends define the characteristics of today's Congress. 1) Fewer measures are sponsored by individual senators and representatives. 2) Key policy decisions are packaged into huge "megabills," permitting lawmakers to combine their initiatives and escape adverse reactions to individual provisions. 3) Techniques of blame avoidance are employed to protect lawmakers from adverse effects of cutback policies. 4) Driven by growing party cohesion, party-line voting has reached modern-day highs on Capitol Hill. 5) Senate and (especially) House leadership is perceptibly stronger now than at any time since the 1910 revolt against Speaker Cannon. Today's leaders benefit not only from powers conferred by reform-era innovations of the 1960s and 1970s—for example, controls over legislative scheduling and, in the House, domination of the Rules Committee, they also respond to widespread expectations that they are the only people who can manage the legislative schedule.

"Americans are especially fond of running down their congressmen," observed Lord Bryce (*The American Commonwealth*, New York, 1888). Political pundits and humorists find in Congress's foibles ample material for ridicule. Serious scholarly and journalistic critics fault Congress for its disorder, inertia, and corruption. Congress gets only mediocre marks from the public at large. Public approval of the institution rises or falls with economic conditions, wars and crises, scandals, and waves of satisfaction or cynicism. Congressional approval also follows public approval of presidents.

In contrast, most individual senators and representatives are given high marks by their constituents. If voters think that elected officials as a class are rascals, they do not usually feel that way about their own elected officials. Nor do they show sustained eagerness to "throw the rascals out." Modern-day legislators tend to be handsomely rewarded at the polls, and to enjoy extended careers on Capitol Hill. This dichotomy is one more reminder of the "two Congresses" phenomenon: the dual character of the U.S. Congress as a collective maker of public policy and a collection of locally-oriented politicians.

(See also LEGISLATURE; POLITICAL ACTION COMMITTEE; POLITICAL PARTIES AND PARTY COMPETITION; PRESIDENCY, U.S.; UNITED STATES.)

Richard F. Fenno, Jr., *Home Style: House Members in Their Districts* (Boston, 1978). David W. Brady, *Critical Elections and Congressional Policy Making* (Stanford, Calif., 1988). Christopher J. Deering and Steven S. Smith, *Committees in Congress*, 3d ed. (Washington, D.C., 1997). C. Lawrence Evans and Walter J. Oleszek, *Congress Under Fire* (Boston, 1997). Gary C. Jacobson, *The Politics of Congressional Elections*, 4th ed. (New York, 1997). Roger H. Davidson and Walter J. Oleszek, *Congress and Its Members*, 6th ed. (Washington, D.C., 1998).

ROGER H. DAVIDSON

CONSERVATISM draws on basic human tendencies. People are often more concerned about current possessions than future possibilities. People are often attached to the old ways, just because they are the old ways. If it is conservative to heed such tendencies, conservatism is as old as politics.

But as a recognized banner in party competition, conservatism is less than 200 years old. There was no need for a conservative party until there came to be parties devoted to new creeds of progress or liberation. As a political designation, the term "conservative" seems to have originated in France, where it was embraced by moderate supporters of the Bourbon restoration in the 1820s. The term came into more general use a decade later, when it was taken up by the Tory Party in Britain.

As a reactive doctrine, conservatism has always been an ambiguous creed. The policy implications of the term have varied widely from one national and historical context to the next, depending on what policies conservatives set themselves to oppose. In the course of two centuries, "conservative" has meant as many different things as "liberal" or "progressive" or "socialist." In fact, by its nature, conservatism has been even more protean than its rivals.

As conservatives have generally championed national continuity against universalistic doctrines, they have been particularly resistant to justifying their positions as deductions from abstract principles. One of the earliest English literary references to conservatism is the disparaging remark of the young Disraeli that a "conservative government" is an "organized hypocrisy," invoking traditionalist rhetoric as it acquiesces to liberal measures.

Conservative parties or political forces have proved most enduring and effective, in fact, where ideological divisions were not too sharply defined. Conservatives have done well in party competition where, as in most English-speaking countries, they could accommodate the dominant liberal and democratic trends of the modern world without losing their core support. Historically, this sort of political maneuvering room was hard to secure in countries where religious divisions—or divisions rooted in the upheavals of the French Revolution—forced conservative advocates into narrow sectarian loyalties. Conversely, as ideological passions subsided in continental Europe, in the decades after the Second World War, avowedly conservative parties prospered in countries of Western Europe.

Three themes of conservative thought continue to have relevance to modern political disputes. First and perhaps most important is a resistance to utopian thinking. Modern technology, which has transformed so many aspects of daily life, encourages people to think that human nature itself can be transformed by social tinkering; conservatives insist on the political cautions and personal virtues of the past. A second theme, which follows in a way from the first, is a respect for authority and power—combined with a wary regard for their limits and their susceptibility to abuse. Conservatives have resisted the notion that enlightenment or self-interest, solidarity or *democracy will generate a spontaneous harmony among men, making recourse to force no longer necessary (or no longer recognizable as compulsion). Finally, conservatives have sought to defend particular practices and institutions—a traditional version of the family, a traditional sense of patriotic obligation, religious and moral standards. All these may be vital to a decent society, but are difficult to defend in a liberal framework that reduces all obligations to individual choice.

These attitudes do not necessarily lead conservatives to embrace free market policies. In the first part of the nineteenth century, all parties or groups called conservative opposed aspects of economic liberalization and supported particular constraints on trade. Many conservatives continued to embrace such stances—in the name of social harmony or national security or moral standards. Tensions between market-enthusiasts and social conservatives remain an endemic feature of conservative politics.

There are, however, deep affinities and historical connections between social conservatism and classical liberal views in economics. In the mid-eighteenth century, the Scottish philosopher David Hume derided the social contract theory of the Whigs and placed his central emphasis on "custom" and "sentiment." Yet if Hume ranks as one of the founding philosophers of conservatism, he was, at the same time, the mentor of Adam Smith, whose *Wealth of Nations* became the Bible of classical liberal economics. The great conservative thinker Edmund Burke was fulsome in his praise of Smith's work and Smith himself declared that Burke was the one man in England who thought as he did on economic questions.

By the mid-nineteenth century, the British Conservatives abandoned their historic position and committed themselves to support free trade. Conservative constituencies in many countries sought to make alliances with economic liberals (that is, classical liberals). In Canada and in some parts of Germany, in this same era, new parties actually called themselves "Liberal-Conservative" to emphasize the fusion of social conservative and economic liberal doctrines.

Since the late 1970s, "conservative parties" in Western democracies have often placed particular emphasis on reducing government controls and limiting government spending to foster private markets (a program often called "neoliberal"). In the following decade, U.S. President Ronald *Reagan and British Prime Minister Margaret *Thatcher exemplified this fusion of social conservative ideals with free market economics.

There are several trends of thought reinforcing this fusion. In the first place, much conservative opinion has been drawn to market competition as a means of enforcing an ethos of personal responsibility and self-discipline. A second point of convergence has been the fear that class-based appeals for the redistribution of wealth will weaken the state as much as the economy. Conservatives have also worried that a politics of pandering to interest groups would distract the attention of government from essential priorities and erode the underlying moral authority of government. Thatcher's program of *privatization and retrenchment thus appealed to many Tories as a way of strengthening the authority of the state in other areas. Finally, in the most theoretical terms, there is an evident affinity between liberal respect for market processes, responding to the diverse insights, circumstances, and priorities of vast numbers of individuals, and the conservative regard for traditions that embody the accumulated insights of generations. Both respect the discipline of constraints that are not dependent on any single, directing will.

It has long been argued that conservatives end up protecting the achievements of earlier reformers. At the end of the twentieth century, parties of the left in Western Europe and North America prospered by taking over the economic doctrines (and sometimes, also, the stern crime-control rhetoric) of conservatives. Conservative policies then seemed to prosper as conservative parties fell into disfavor with voters. But the modern world has a way of continually inspiring new ambitions to reconstruct social life. As long as these ambitions find their way into politics, there will be a place for conservative parties to resist wild impulses and to defend the good sense and solid virtues of steadier times.

(See also LIBERALISM; POLITICAL PARTIES AND PARTY COMPETITION.)

JEREMY A. RABKIN

CONSOCIATIONAL DEMOCRACY is found in several countries that are deeply divided into distinct religious, ethnic, racial, or regional segments. Its two principal and complementary characteristics are grand coalition and segmental autonomy: shared decision making by representatives of all significant segments with regard to matters of common concern and autonomous decision making by and for each separate segment on all other issues. Two additional characteristics are proportionality in political representation, civil service appointments, and the allocation of public funds, and the minority veto for the protection of vital minority interests. A possible variant of strict proportionality is deliberate minority overrepresentation. In all four respects, consociational democracy contrasts sharply with majority-rule democracy.

The first political theorist to use the term "consociation" was the early federalist thinker Johannes Althusius in his *Politica Methodice Digesta* (1603). It was revived by David E. Apter (*The Political Kingdom in Uganda*, Princeton, N.J., 1961) who, like Althusius, used it mainly to refer to a territorial-federal form of decentralized decision making. The first modern scholar to use the concept in the more specific sense given above—although he did not use the actual term—was the economist Sir Arthur Lewis (*Politics in West Africa*, London, 1965). Lewis also presented the first explicit argument that for deeply divided societies the consociational form of democracy is both more democratic and likely to be more effective than majority rule. From the late 1960s on, consociational theory has been developed and applied further by numerous political scientists, sociologists, and historians.

Examples of consociational democracy can be found all over the world. In Europe, it has established a largely successful record: in Switzerland since 1943; in Belgium after World War I and, with even better results, from 1970 on; in Austria from 1945 to 1966; in the Netherlands from 1917 to about 1967; and in Luxembourg during the same period of about half a century. Where, as in the last three cases, consociational democracy has declined or ended, the reason has not been that it failed but that it worked so well that it was no longer needed. Czechoslovakia was consociational from 1989 until its amicable partition in 1993. The 1998 agreement on *Northern Ireland envisioned a consociational government for this part of the United Kingdom.

In Africa, Asia, and Latin America, the record is mixed. India (since independence in 1947), Colombia (1958–1974), Malaysia (from 1955 on), and South Africa (since 1994) can be counted as largely successful examples. In Cyprus, the consociational experiment adopted upon independence in 1960 ended in civil war in 1963. The other cases are more ambiguous. Lebanon's consociational democracy collapsed in brutal civil strife in 1975, but it worked remarkably well for almost a third of a century (1943–1975) and was restored in 1989; moreover, the civil war was caused more by external forces than by weaknesses in the internal consociational system. Aruba's secession marked the end of consociationalism in the Netherlands Antilles (1950–1985), but secession was achieved by an entirely peaceful, negotiated process. Military rule came to Uruguay in 1973 and to Suriname in 1980, but by then the system of each—semi-consociational in Uruguay (1952–1967) and consociational in Suriname (1958–1973)—had already shifted to largely majoritarian patterns; hence in each case the failure was one of majority rule rather than consociationalism.

Pure consociationalism and pure majoritarianism are ideal types; actual political systems can be located along a range between the pure forms. Examples of countries in approximately the middle of the range, in addition to the Uruguayan case mentioned above, are Canada and Israel. Consociational practices can also be found in nondemocratic and predemocratic regimes, such as the United Province of Canada from 1840 to 1867 and Belgium after independence in 1830.

The comparative analysis of these cases has led to the formulation of several factors that are conducive to the establishment and maintenance of consociational democracy. The two most important of these are the absence of a majority segment and the absence of large socioeconomic inequalities. Others are segments of approximately equal size, a small population, foreign threats, countrywide loyalties that counteract segmental loyalties, and preexisting traditions of consensus.

Consociational democracy has made two important contributions to democratic theory. First, it challenges the traditional narrow equation of democracy with majority rule. Second, it extends the applicability of democracy to societies that were traditionally regarded as ill suited for democratic government.

Arend Lijphart, *Democracy in Plural Societies: A Comparative Exploration* (New Haven, Conn., 1977).

AREND LIJPHART

CONSTITUTION. The term "constitution" refers both to the institutions, practices, and principles that define and structure a system of government and to the written document that establishes or articulates such a system. Every *state has a constitution in the first sense and, since World War II, virtually every state—Britain, New Zealand, and Israel are among the exceptions—has a written constitution as well.

"Constitutionalism" denotes not merely the existence of either a written or an unwritten constitution, but a commitment to limited government. Some scholars argue that constitutions inherently limit government—either by regularizing the governmental process and thus prohibiting capricious action or by establishing policies or procedures that cannot be modified by ordinary legislative action. Others see limitation as the result of specific constitutional provisions, such as a bill of rights or the *separation of powers.

The exclusive focus on constitutions as a means of limiting governmental power is somewhat deceptive. Historically, constitutions have been made to empower states rather than to limit them. The first written constitutions were made during the American and French revolutions. These constitutions restructured governmental institutions, articulated political principles, and, in the case of the United States, proclaimed independence from colonial rule. In both France and the United States, written constitutions attempted to establish governments based on popular consent and respect for individual *rights.

These eighteenth-century French and American constitutions came to define the genre as a whole. Constitution-making was a recurrent feature of both nationalist and bourgeois revolutions in the nineteenth century. Coercion, as well as intellectual influence, spread the practice of writing constitutions. After World War II, colonial and occupying powers sometimes refused to relinquish sovereignty to indigenous peoples until "acceptable" constitutions were adopted. Now, a written constitution has become almost a prerequisite to international recognition for new nations. And, as the spate of constitution-making that followed the fall of the Berlin Wall suggests, writing a new constitution has become a conventional way of indicating major changes of regime.

A constitution constitutes a polity in a variety of ways. First, a constitution marks the existence of a polity that claims its own sphere of authority. This authority may be defined in terms of a particular region, particular people, and/or particular issues. Such authority need not be national. In federal systems, for example, each subnational government may have its own constitution.

Second, a constitution not only asserts that there *is* a polity, it also describes how that polity will be governed. Constitutions typically enumerate the institutions that comprise the state. Because institutional design affects both the distribution of political power and the making of governmental policy, the structure of the state is often hotly contested in debates over making or amending a constitution.

Finally, a constitution provides a vocabulary for politics. Both the identities one can claim and the claims one can make in the political sphere are, at least in part, constitutionally constructed. By privileging one set of identities over another, a constitution shapes political discourse. For example, because it restricts governmental discrimination based on race while allowing discrimination based on wealth, the U.S. Constitution encourages people to frame their grievances in terms of race rather than class. Even revolutionary politics may be articulated in terms of constitutional categories. Czechoslovakia's *Charter 77 movement chose to fight political repression by publicizing the state's violation of constitutional provisions. Members of the movement did not believe that the best form of government for Czechoslovakia would be one that implemented the guarantees of the existing constitution. But they knew that couching their criticisms in constitutional terms would give the movement the *legitimacy (both at home and abroad) that it would have lacked if it had attempted to challenge the constitutive principles of the regime more directly.

Constitutions are attempts to construct politics, both institutionally and rhetorically. To understand the significance of constitutions in *comparative politics, then, we have to look beyond the question of whether constitutions limit governmental power and investigate the variety of ways in which constitutions shape both the state and *political culture.

(See also Decolonization; Federalism.)

Giovanni Sartori, "Constitutionalism: A Preliminary Discussion," *American Political Science Review* 56 (1962): 853–864. Jon Elster and Rune Slagstad, *Constitutionalism and Democracy* (Cambridge, U.K., 1988). Stephen L. Elkin and Karol Edward Soltan, *A New Constitutionalism: Designing Political Institutions for a Good Society* (Chicago, 1993). Vivien Hart and Shannon C. Stimson, *Writing a National Identity: Political, Economic and Cultural Perspectives on the Written Constitution* (Manchester, U.K., 1993).

Suzette Hemberger

CONSTITUTIONAL MONARCHY. *Monarchy—literally "rule by one"—denotes a system of government in which the head of state ascends to his or her position by hereditary succession. (Examples have been recorded of elective monarchies, but no such arrangement has survived.) On accession the monarch may take any of a number of titles—usually that of king or queen, but in some cases emperor, prince, emir, or sultan. The distinction is often made between absolute and constitutional monarchies. Absolute monarchy is one in which the head of state is not constrained by provisions of the *constitution; constitutional monarchy is one in which the head of state is so constrained.

The basis of authority of absolute monarchies was essentially religious, and the nineteenth and early twentieth centuries witnessed the disappearance of most such monarchies as their claims to rule were variously contested. They were replaced by republican forms of government or, less commonly, by constitutional monarchies. In 1998, forty-three countries were ruled by monarchs, and of these all but seven were constitutional monarchies. Sixteen actually shared the same head of state—Queen Elizabeth II, head of state of the United Kingdom and of fifteen Commonwealth countries and British colonies. The largest single concentration of constitutional monarchies (ten) was in Western Europe. The characteristic feature of such monarchies is that policy-making resides with the elected government, the monarch fulfilling largely ceremonial and symbolic duties. Occasionally, though, the role of the monarch may be pivotal—for example, in breaking a constitutional deadlock or in attempting—either successfully, as in the case of King Juan Carlos I of Spain in 1981, or unsuccessfully, as in that of King Constantine II of Greece in 1967—to prevent a military *coup.

Vernon Bogdanor, *The Monarchy and the Constitution* (Oxford, 1995).

Philip Norton

CONTAINMENT. U.S. diplomat George F. *Kennan coined the term "containment" to describe the appropriate American strategy to counter the threat of Soviet expansionism in the aftermath of *World War II and the advent of the *Cold War. In February 1946, Kennan, then the relatively obscure chargé d'affaires in the Moscow embassy, was asked by the State Department for an "interpretive analysis" of Soviet intentions. Kennan's report on the evolving state of postwar relations between the *United States and the *Soviet Union arrived in Washington at a moment when Soviet pressures on Iran and Turkey were being viewed as an immediate threat to the global *balance of power. In recognition of his incisive cables from Moscow, Kennan was brought to Washington and asked to assume the directorship of the State Department's newly founded Policy Planning Staff. The initial public expression of Kennan's containment doctrine came in the July 1947 issue of *Foreign Affairs* in an article, published anonymously, on "The Sources of Soviet Conduct." Kennan advocated the adoption of a "long-term, patient but firm and vigilant" policy of "containment" to thwart Soviet expansionist tendencies. This would entail "the adroit and vigilant application of counter-force at a series of constantly shifting geographical and political points corresponding to the shifts and maneuvers of Soviet policy . . ." Kennan believed that the implementation of a containment policy would remain necessary until such time that the inherent contradictions of the Soviet Union's totalitarian system led to significant, if not profound, internal changes and a consequent moderation in Soviet external behavior.

Domestic critics of Kennan's relatively ambiguous counterforce strategy spanned the U.S. political spectrum. The most detailed and sustained critique of the "X" article came from the journalist Walter Lippmann, who argued that containment was a "strategic monstrosity" that would leave the United States responding indefinitely to probes whose timing and location would be determined by the Kremlin. Hailed as a grand new formula for U.S. foreign policy, the "X" article was perceived as the intellectual justification for the March 1947 *Truman Doctrine. This was denied by Kennan, who rejected the undifferentiated globalism suggested by the rhetoric of the Truman Doctrine. In his *Memoirs*, Kennan wrote that what he meant by "the containment of Soviet power was not the containment by military means of a military threat, but the political containment of a political threat."

The Berlin blockade, the Soviet Union's detonation of an atomic bomb, and the Chinese Communists' seizure of power in 1948–1949 reinforced the image of global confrontation and provided added impetus to the militarization of containment. A high-level policy review commissioned by the Truman administration in response to these events recommended the modernization and expansion of U.S. military capabilities. Following the outbreak of the *Korean War in June 1950, this document—NSC-68—provided a blueprint for the buildup of U.S. forces. The Korean conflict, which confirmed Kennan's prediction that the Soviet Union might use proxy forces for probes on the Eurasian periphery, marked the geographical extension of containment from Europe to Asia and beyond.

The *Eisenhower administration's desire to conduct a global containment strategy at lower economic cost led to a renewed emphasis on the U.S. nuclear deterrent and increased reliance on allies to provide conventional forces for local defense. In a January 1954 speech, Secretary of State John Foster Dulles advocated the threatened use of the United States' "massive retaliatory power" to deter Soviet expansionism. The press immediately seized upon the slogan of "massive retaliation" and portrayed it as a formula for turning every border skirmish into a nuclear showdown. Although prominent academic specialists argued for the continuing need for limited war capabilities, the Eisenhower administration maintained that its "New Look" strategy was a comprehensive approach in which *nuclear weapons, both strategic and tactical, were a complement to other policy instruments (such as alliances, covert operations, and negotiation).

President John *Kennedy, who assumed office in 1961 at a time when the *Third World was rapidly becoming the principal arena of superpower competition, favored decreased reliance on nuclear weapons for local defense. The expansion of conventional forces was a central component of his administration's move to a strategy of "flexible response" under which the United States sought to meet the Soviet challenge across the entire spectrum of threat, from guerrilla insurgency to thermonuclear war. The Kennedy administration placed greater emphasis on nonmilitary dimensions of containment (e.g., the use of economic assistance in the developing world), but did little, contrary to Kennan's long-standing recommen-dation, to exploit fissures within the Communist bloc (e.g., the Sino-Soviet rift).

The globalization of U.S. containment policy reached its zenith with the large-scale deployment of U.S. ground forces to *Vietnam following the 1964 Gulf of Tonkin incident. The *Johnson administration steadfastly contended that Vietnam was a symbol of U.S. resolve and that the failure to meet the Communist challenge there would undermine the credibility of American commitments elsewhere. Vietnam became a key test case of "flexible response." This strategy, which emphasized gradual escalation and the calibrated application of U.S. military power, was intended to demonstrate to the North Vietnamese that there was no alternative to a negotiated settlement. U.S. policy makers, however, underestimated the determination of an adversary who saw itself engaged not in limited, but total *war.

The *Nixon administration came to power in 1969 amid widespread public calls for a major retrenchment of U.S. overseas commitments as a consequence of the Vietnam debacle. Operating within this domestic context, President Richard Nixon and National Security Adviser Henry *Kissinger developed an approach to containment whose main element was a policy of *détente toward the Soviet Union. During the late 1970s, Soviet interventionist policies in the Third World, culminating in the 1979 invasion of *Afghanistan, undermined U.S. public support for détente and led to the *Reagan administration's return to a more militarized version of containment following the 1980 presidential election. The Reagan strategy featured a major rearmament program (including the Strategic Defense Initiative, or SDI) and support for antiCommunist insurgents in the Third World (e.g., the Afghan mujahidin).

In the mid-1980s, Soviet President Mikhail *Gorbachev, faced with intractable economic and social problems at home and a hostile external environment, initiated a sweeping internal reform program (i.e, *perestroika). These profound domestic changes were accompanied by correspondingly dramatic changes in Soviet external behavior (e.g., the 1988 decision to withdraw from Afghanistan and acquiescence to the collapse of Communist regimes in Eastern and Central Europe in 1989). In April 1989 testimony before the Senate Foreign Relations Committee, George Kennan, who had argued in his "X" article that profound Soviet domestic change (specifically the demise of a world-revolutionary ideology) would obviate the need for containment, stated that the Soviet Union "should now be regarded essentially as another great power, like other great powers . . ."

In the post-Soviet era, the ascendance of China as a great power in East Asia revived the issue of containment. U.S. officials, however, have eschewed the term because of its Cold War connotation and President *Clinton affirmed that U.S. policy toward China is one of engagement.

(See also DETERRENCE; VIETNAM WAR.)

"X" [George F. Kennan], "The Sources of Soviet Conduct," *Foreign Affairs* 25 (July 1947): 566–582. Adam B. Ulam, *The Rivals: America and Russia since World War II* (London, 1973). John Lewis Gaddis, *Strategies of Containment. A Critical Appraisal of Postwar American National Security Policy* (New York, 1982).

ROBERT S. LITWAK

COOK ISLANDS. See PACIFIC ISLANDS.

COOPERATION, INTERNATIONAL. See INTERNATIONAL COOPERATION.

CORPORATISM. Corporatism, or corporativism—the spelling varies by author, country, and period—is a distinctive way of organizing interests and influencing public policy. It has had an erratic history. As a practice, it is ancient. The Roman Republic had professional *collegia* with a distinctive public role; medieval city-states had elaborate systems of representation and self-government through monopolistic guilds. As a concept in the active vocabulary of political life or scholarly debate, however, it is of relatively recent origin. The first explicit references emerged in Europe during the latter third of the nineteenth century.

By some, corporatism was hailed as a novel and promising way for ensuring social harmony, even as a "third way" between *capitalism and *communism; by others, it has been roundly condemned as an illusory and reactionary effort to suppress political demands and impose authoritarian rule. It reached its greatest visibility under the *Estado Corporativo* of *Mussolini's Italy after 1928 and was much imitated by other autocratic regimes of the interwar period. With the defeat of *Fascism and *Nazism, the concept more or less disappeared from polite political discourse—except in Antonio Salazar's Portugal and Franco's Spain, where it remained on public display until their transitions to *democracy in the mid-1970s. Some of these "anachronistic" practices still characterize the interest politics of such countries as Argentina, Brazil, Greece, Indonesia, and Turkey.

In the mid-1970s, a group of scholars revived the concept to describe and explain certain puzzling features of advanced industrial democracies that could not be understood by the heretofore dominant paradigm, *pluralism. To differentiate the new variety from discredited previous experiences, these scholars usually added a prefix such as "liberal," "societal," or "neo-" to the corporatist root. Empirically, they drew special attention to developments during the late 1930s and the postwar period in a number of small European democracies and to the emerging properties in some of the larger ones, such as the Federal Republic of Germany (FRG) and Britain, that indicated a very different structure of organized *class, sectoral, and professional interests and a very different pattern of interaction with state agencies. From their diverse perspectives, these U.S., British, and German scholars began to identify an alternative model of state-society relations that was, nonetheless, compatible with democracy. The "corporatism debate" became the "growth industry" of the subsequent decade, especially in Western Europe.

Confusing Variety of Definitions. Given this checkered history, the concept of corporatism has been defined in many different ways. In the minds of some, it never managed to divest itself completely of its prior association with Fascism and authoritarian rule. Its practice has almost always been controversial. In contemporary politics, the term remains largely polemical—a label to be avoided even if one is practicing it, or something to accuse one's opponent of doing—despite the effort of many scholars to give it a more objective or, at least, less pejorative connotation.

Corporatism can be, and has been, defined as referring to a distinctive *ideology, variety of political culture, type of *state, form of economy, or even kind of society. The most productive usage has been to consider it as one of several possible arrangements through which interest associations can intermediate between their members (individuals, families, firms, groups of all kinds) and their interlocutors (especially agencies of the state with authority and other resources to satisfy their demands). When these associations are configured in a certain way or when they participate in decision making in a certain way, then it is appropriate to use the label *corporatist* to indicate their nature. It should be stressed that corporatism is not the only way to institutionalize such exchanges of influence. Except for the long-extinct practices of medieval cities and, more recently, those of the interwar autocracies, it has been relatively rare. Pluralism is a much more widespread "solution" to this problem among advanced industrial polities. Indeed, given its greater frequency and its allegedly strong link to forms of modern democracy, pluralism has enjoyed a virtual hegemony within the social sciences. Open advocates of corporatism in recent years have been few. Those who found some merit in its practices have often been compelled to disguise their advocacy behind other labels, such as "social partnership," "concertation," "coordinated market economy," or "societal bargaining." Even those who have merely studied it have labored under the accusation that they were promoting something intrinsically undemocratic.

Both pluralism and corporatism must involve themselves in two contrasting aspects of the political process: 1) they must communicate and transform member preferences into claims on others, especially public authorities; and 2) they must monitor and influence the subsequent behavior of their members with regard to realizing these claims. In the language of systems theory, intermediary associations have both input and output functions. In the language of political theory, they are simultaneously engaged in representation and control. An association that represents its members but cannot influence their subsequent behavior will be unlikely to command the attention of its interlocutors; conversely, one that only seeks to control behavior without reflecting member opinion risks being treated as a state agency and being rejected as illegitimate by those it claims to represent.

Behind the rival labels of pluralism and corporatism lie very different assumptions about how representation and control are mixed and embodied in associations. Figure 1 specifies the elements of the "pure" corporatist and the "pure" pluralist models. No existing polity exactly replicates the arrangement summarized in either column, although Austria comes closest to the former and the United States to the latter. Moreover, a good deal of research has demonstrated that within a given polity the configuration of organized interests may vary considerably across policy arenas and sectors. The same association may operate sequentially or simultaneously in a more pluralist or a more corporatist fashion as it interacts with different agencies or levels of government.

The right-hand column in Figure 1 summarizes the characteristics of a pure corporatist system with regard to both members and interlocutors. It begins with the input side of politics. Interests are organized into monopolistic units with nonoverlapping domains of representation, coordinated hierarchically by more encompassing "peak associations" and supported by involuntary contributions. In exchange for this,

Figure 1. Properties Distinguishing Pure Pluralist and Pure Corporatist Modes of Intermediation

I. REPRESENTATION (INPUT)

	PLURALIST	CORPORATIST
I. In relation to members	Multiple units	Monopolistic units
	Overlapping claims	Differentiated domains
	Autonomous interaction	Hierarchical coordination
	Voluntary adherence	Involuntary contribution
II. In relation to interlocutors	Mutual tolerance....................	Explicit recognition
	Opportunistic access.................	Structured incorporation
	Consultative role....................	Negotiative role
	Shifting alliances (log-rolling)	Stable compromises (package dealing)

II. CONTROL (OUTPUT)

	PLURALIST	CORPORATIST
I. In relation to members	Persuasive conviction.................	Interest indoctrination
	Leader prestige	Organizational authority
	Discriminate treatment	Coercive sanctions
	Selective goods	Monopolistic goods
II. In relation to interlocutors	Provision of information..............	Organization of compliance
	Irresponsibility for decisions	Co-responsibility for decisions
	Autonomous monitoring..............	Devolved implementation
	Mobilization of pressure	Withdrawal from concentration

the state grants explicit recognition to one association per category, incorporates that organization directly and reliably within the decision-making process, and negotiates its agreement with relevant measures. These usually involve comprehensive package deals across several issues. Seen from the output perspective, corporatist associations are actively engaged in defining and indoctrinating the interests of members and in exercising authority over the behavior of members, if necessary through the application of coercive sanctions and the withdrawal of services that members cannot do without, such as licenses, certifications, trademarks, etc. In return, the state receives the assured compliance of the entire category and devolves part of the responsibility for policy implementation upon the association.

Uneven Distribution of Cases. Much effort has been expended in labeling countries as more or less "corporatist." Less attention has been paid to specific sectors. The usual ordering places Austria, Sweden, Norway, Finland, and the Netherlands at the top; Denmark, Ireland, Switzerland, Belgium, and the FRG somewhere in the middle; Britain, France, and Italy further down in the category of "weak and unsuccessful" corporatisms; and the United States and Canada at the "pluralist" bottom of the list. Australia is an interesting case of a non-European country where "social contracting" between the state and peak associations has become a regular (if controversial) feature of its politics. Spain offers a fascinating example of how voluntary corporatist arrangements can be used to stabilize the transition from authoritarian rule to democracy. Japan has proven a very difficult country to classify along this continuum.

Ambiguity about Consequences. But what difference does it make if a country or sector is corporatist or pluralist? The relative "social peace" of Scandinavia, Switzerland, and Austria in the postwar era is one obvious consequence, but it takes considerable econometric work to tease out other probable socioeconomic effects. For example, analyses of data on

Organization for Economic Co-operation and Development (OECD) member states show significantly lower rates of inflation and unemployment in the more corporatist countries but not much difference in economic growth. For the 1960s and 1970s, comprehensive agreements between organized social classes and the state seemed to resolve a central dilemma of welfare capitalism: how to prevent full employment from generating inflation via union militancy. In such negotiations, workers could exchange short-term power advantage for long-term concessions in welfare and other policies. Macrocorporatism also offered a solution to growth-inhibiting "distributive coalitions." It shifted the calculus of interest to more encompassing organizations, thereby diminishing the likelihood of passing on the costs to others.

The consequences for politics have been more controversial. Although the finding that corporatist arrangements contribute to "governability" through greater citizen compliance and fiscal effectiveness seems widely accepted, the suspicion persists that they surreptitiously undermine democracy. Organizations replace persons as the principal participants; specialized professionals gain at the expense of citizen amateurs; direct functional channels of representation to state agencies displace territorially based legislative decision making; monopolies and privileged access are recognized at the expense of overlapping and competing associations; comprehensive national hierarchies diminish the autonomy of local and specialized organizations.

Nevertheless, one cannot deny that the most corporatist countries have also been stable democracies. Some of them, e.g., the Scandinavian polities, have even been in the forefront of experimentation with such measures as worker participation in management, open disclosure, ombudsman arrangements, public financing of parties, and so on. The spontaneous, voluntaristic, and autonomous features of pluralism may seem freer in principle, but in practice they reproduce greater inequality of access to power, especially across social classes. Corporatism evens out the distribution of resources across interest categories and guarantees formal parity in the decision-making process. The incorporation of associations in policy implementation seems to ensure greater responsiveness to group needs than the "arm's-length" relation separating the public and the private under pluralism. One may conclude that democracy is being transformed by modern corporatism (see P. C. Schmitter, "Democratic Theory and Neo-Corporatist Practice," *Social Research* 50, no. 4 [Winter 1983]: 885–928). Organizations are becoming citizens alongside individuals. Accountability and responsiveness are increasing, but at the expense of citizen participation and access for all groups. Competition is less interorganizational and more intraorganizational. Across advanced industrial societies, the pace of these changes is uneven; their acceptance is uncertain; their outcome by no means unequivocal—but all modern democracies are becoming more "interested," organized, and vicarious.

(See also AUTHORITARIANISM; CONSOCIATIONAL DEMOCRACY; INTEREST GROUPS; POLITICAL ECONOMY; POLITICAL PARTICIPATION.)

P. C. Schmitter, "Still the Century of Corporatism?" *Review of Politics* 36, no. 1 (1974): 85–131. P. C. Schmitter and G. Lehmbruch, eds., *Trends Toward Corporatist Intermediation* (Beverly Hills, Calif., and London, 1979). S. D. Berger, ed., *Organizing Interests in Western Europe: Pluralism, Corporatism, and the Transformation of Politics* (Cambridge, U.K., 1981). G. Lehmbruch and P. C. Schmitter, eds., *Patterns of Corporatist Policy-Making* (Beverly Hills, Calif., and London, 1982). J. H. Goldthorpe, ed., *Order and Conflict in Contemporary Capitalism: Studies in the Political Economy of Western European Nations* (Oxford, 1984).

PHILIPPE C. SCHMITTER

CORRUPTION. Few, if any, cultural or ethical traditions have lacked a concept of corruption, and no society has been completely free of the problem. The sources, justifications, and proper uses of power, and questions of virtue in communal life, have been major concerns for centuries. Most public discussion today focuses upon accountable government and honest political processes. At times, contemporary scholars have been reluctant to study corruption, as it is by definition a value-laden concept; many studies appeared in the 1960s and 1970s, but for two decades thereafter it received little attention. At century's end, however, corruption made a comeback as an analytical concept and public concern, particularly for those interested in democracy and economic development in a globalizing world.

Traditionally, "corruption" was often seen as an attribute of whole societies, or of their systems of rule. Thucydides, for example, saw corruption in the Athenians' decision to abandon principle and invade the island of Melos. The modern concept refers to the abuse of public roles or resources for private benefit, and thus commonly applies to specific actions or participants. But definitions have occasioned much debate, particularly when applied to changing societies: distinctions between "public" and "private" may be elusive, and corrupt benefits can be intangible or hard to distinguish from the legitimate results of politics. And what constitutes "abuse"? Laws or other formal rules are the most common standard, but they can lack *legitimacy and may say little about the social significance of an action. *Public opinion or the public interest are alternative standards, but may be too vague,

changeable, or relativistic, and can confuse the question of what corruption is with that of its effects. "Neoclassical" definitions treat corruption as a threat to core democratic values such as representation and deliberation. Principal-Agent-Client approaches define corruption in terms of interactions among top officials, functionaries, and members of the public.

Renewed interest in corruption has followed both a number of scandals in advanced as well as developing countries and major changes in the international system. The end of the Cold War and "late-twentieth-century" *democratic transitions deprived many corrupt regimes of their power and ideological camouflage and raised standards of governance higher. Global markets expose economies to intense scrutiny and competition for international investment and have ended the notion of corruption as an acceptable overhead cost of doing business in a country. International organizations such as the World Bank, the Organization for Economic Cooperation and Development (OECD), and the Organization of American States, which had long avoided the corruption issue, now regard it as a critical problem.

These trends have revived old debates and spurred new research. A generation ago, "functionalists" argued that corruption encourages economic growth by reducing bureaucratic delays, adapting inflexible policies, and creating informal market processes, and that it builds political links between leaders and followers. "Moralists" countered that corruption distorts politics and policy and diverts scarce resources. New data—including imaginative (if controversial) attempts at measurement—now strongly suggest that serious corruption harms economic growth, discourages foreign investment, and increases bureaucratic delays as officials contrive new ways to enrich themselves. It diverts expenditures from social services toward large projects, such as construction or arms deals, that offer major bribes. Rather than building democracy, corruption weakens political competition and preempts popular participation, enabling corrupt officials and their wealthy clients to exploit both state and people. Where people see corruption as inevitable, opposition to it will be weak.

Corruption is a problem, to one degree or another, in countries at all levels of development. Where it is most serious it is both the effect of, and a force sustaining, fundamental difficulties—a weak *civil society; impaired participation, competition, and institutions in politics and the economy; ethnic fragmentation; poor tax collection and an underpaid civil service; dependence upon outside investment or upon extractive industries such as oil or mining; or the influence of drug- or arms-dealers and organized crime. The list differs from country to country; but even if corrupt individuals are punished, without basic changes corruption will return.

Many unresolved issues drive current research. How did East Asia combine rapid growth with extensive corruption for three decades, while African corruption deepened instability and poverty? What role did corruption play in the Asian financial crisis that began in 1997? Conversely, can countries move toward markets and democracy without experiencing a surge of corruption? Do we need to distinguish among varieties, and is so-called "petty corruption" affecting ordinary citizens any less significant than high-level "grand corruption"? Is corruption linked to traditional values and practices such as *guanxi* (customs of reciprocity and exchange) in

China, or to ethnic and family networks in Asia and Africa? At all stages of democratization, how is corruption linked to political contributions? Are corrupt governments and economies less able to adapt in a global world?

Some of the most active developments have to do with reform. Powerful, well-funded anti-corruption agencies—many modeled on Hong Kong's Independent Commission Against Corruption—have been established in many countries. (Others have had much more difficulty mounting credible reforms.) Transparency International, an anticorruption organization based in Berlin and launched in 1993, now has chapters in over seventy countries. Thailand's new constitution is strongly oriented toward the prevention of corruption. The OECD nations and several others have negotiated a comprehensive antibribery treaty regulating the "supply side"—firms from wealthy nations that buy influence in developing countries—and ending the tax deductions long allowed by many affluent countries for bribes paid abroad. The Organization of American States is forging an anticorruption treaty for the Americas. Transparency International and the World Bank have helped the major forces of society to draw up "national integrity systems" in countries such as Tanzania.

There is no single best way to control corruption and no precise measure of progress toward that goal. Appropriate reforms will differ from one society to the next and will require long-term support. A thorough understanding of corruption will require continued research, but may yield both promising reforms and important insights into the new global system.

Arnold J. Heidenheimer, Michael Johnston, and Victor T. LeVine, eds., *Political Corruption: A Handbook* (New Brunswick, N.J., 1989). Kimberly Elliot, ed., *Corruption and the Global Economy* (Washington, D.C., 1997). Susan Rose-Ackerman, *Corruption and Government: Causes, Consequences, and Reform* (Cambridge, U.K., 1999).

MICHAEL JOHNSTON

COSTA RICA. Many Costa Ricans believe that they are victims of a geographical error. Costa Rica, according to this view, is a European nation that by mistake found itself located in Central America. There is a grain of truth to this idea because Costa Rica is so different from its neighbors. Central America has suffered from brutal military rule, political instability, economic underdevelopment, and extremes in the distribution of income, wealth, and land. Costa Rica, while having experienced all of these symptoms of political and economic underdevelopment, has done so to a far more limited extent than other countries in the region and has made considerable progress in overcoming all of them.

No single feature of Costa Rica sets it apart from the rest of Central America more than its system of political *democracy. Like its neighbors, Costa Rica was a colony of Spain until it was granted independence in 1821. Of all of the Spanish colonies in Central America, Costa Rica was probably the poorest and certainly the most isolated. This geographic isolation, however, may have proved to be an advantage because it seems to have helped to insulate the country from the politics of violence and military rule that came to dominate the rest of the region. Throughout the nineteenth century there was some domination by military strongmen, but at the same time, there were also signs of the growth of representative government.

It was not until the twentieth century, however, that the last vestiges of instability and authoritarian rule were fully overcome. With one brief exception, the first half of the century was characterized by elected, civilian governments dedicated to social and economic development. While the right to vote remained restricted to property-owning males, in 1925 the secret ballot was institutionalized, and in the years that followed an increasingly sophisticated voter-registration system was developed that has become the envy of even highly advanced industrialized nations. Perhaps the major turning point occurred in 1940 with the election to the presidency of Rafael Angel Calderón Guardia. Despite having been selected by the coffee-growing economic elite, once in office Calderón instituted a series of reforms that granted rights to workers (e.g., social security protection, minimum wages, eight-hour day). He proved to be a very popular president, but began to run into serious opposition from both the economic elite as well as sectors of the middle class when he formed an electoral alliance with the Costa Rican Communist Party in 1943. The alliance helped elect Calderón's handpicked candidate in the 1944 elections, but in the 1948 election, when Calderón ran again, he was defeated. The pro-Calderón legislature reacted by annulling the election, an act that enraged the populace and was the catalyst for a popular uprising led by José (Pepe) Figueres Ferrer. A brief but violent civil war erupted, thereby marring the tradition of domestic peace that had been developing. The rebels were victorious and under Figueres' guidance rewrote the constitution, which granted universal suffrage and other key rights and, perhaps most importantly, abolished the army. Unlike other victors in Latin American uprisings, Figueres voluntarily relinquished rule after holding dictatorial power for eighteen months. He successfully ran for election in 1953 under the banner of his newly established Partido de Liberación Nacional (PLN). In time, the PLN became institutionalized as the nation's best-organized, most electorally successful political party.

Since the 1948 Civil War, political stability and democracy have not been seriously threatened in Costa Rica. Every four years the PLN has competed against opposition forces, especially the Partido Unidad Social Cristiana, and has won more often than it has lost. It appears that the losses are more a function of the electorate's demand for "a new broom" to sweep out politicians who seem to have become corrupt or incapable than they are of any deep discontent about the way the system of government is run. There has emerged a broad consensus that democratic politics is desirable and that human and civil rights must be respected by those in power.

Political democracy has not protected Costa Rica from economic hardships, however. Although economic development was impressive throughout the 1950s, 1960s, and 1970s, with the emergence of modern infrastructure in the form of roads, a nationwide telephone system, and the widespread availability of health and education facilities, by the late 1970s the economic model of state-promoted development seemed to run out of steam. Beginning in the early 1980s a severe economic crisis developed: high inflation, unemployment, economic contraction, and the explosive growth of foreign debt. Costa Rica seemed to be slipping into the pattern experienced so often by its neighbors in the region. To some extent the economic crisis can be attributed to external factors, especially the destabilization of Central America resulting from the

Nicaraguan Revolution, the civil wars in El Salvador and Guatemala, and the breakdown of the Central American Common Market. But a large factor in the equation was that Costa Rica, with a total population of less than 3 million inhabitants, was not economically capable of financing the state-supported social services established since the 1940s.

The collapse of the economy was prevented by a large dose of foreign aid, most of it coming from the United States. This assistance enabled Costa Rica to begin a process of structural adjustment. The democratic nature of the system initially limited the capacity of the government to impose adjustment measures, such as the reform of the banking system, but as Costa Rica moved into the 1990s many of the reforms had been put in place. Economic growth and diversification continued as government spending was limited and the production of nontraditional exports was stimulated.

Costa Rica's traditional aloofness from events in Central America was affected as a result of the regional political and military crisis of the 1980s. President Oscar *Arias (1986–1990) played a major role in the efforts to negotiate a peace settlement in the region, for which he won the Nobel Prize. Once the peace process was well along, Central American leaders turned to the issue of restructuring the moribund Central American Common Market and creating durable regional institutions that would both help avoid international conflicts and stimulate regional economic growth. Many Costa Ricans, however, were reluctant to join this process for fear of being drawn into regional conflicts. Symptomatic of that fear was the reluctance of the Costa Rican legislative assembly to ratify the agreement to establish a Central American Parliament even after all of the other nations of the region had done so. The current challenge for Costa Rica is to maintain its democratic system while joining its neighbors in the search for sustained economic growth.

(See also U.S.–LATIN AMERICAN RELATIONS.)

Mitchell A. Seligson, *Peasants of Costa Rica and the Development of Agrarian Capitalism* (Madison, Wis., 1980). Lowell Gudmundson, *Costa Rica Before Coffee: Society and Economy on the Eve of the Export Boom* (Baton Rouge, La., 1986). Marc Edelman and Joanne Kenan, eds., *The Costa Rica Reader* (New York, 1989). Deborah J. Yashar, *Demanding Democracy: Reform and Reaction in Costa Rica and Guatemala, 1870s–1950s* (Stanford, Calif., 1997). John A. Booth, *Costa Rica: Quest for Democracy* (Boulder, Colo., 1998).

MITCHELL A. SELIGSON

CÔTE D'IVOIRE. Thirty-nine years of civilian rule over Côte d'Ivoire came to an abrupt halt when after a series of divisive political gaffes and rampant corruption the regime of Henri Konan Bedié, the nation's second president, was overthrown in a nonviolent and bloodless coup on 24 December 1999. General Robert Guei, who had served as the head of the joint chiefs of staff under Félix Houphouët-Boigny, assumed leadership of the military junta, named the Comité National de Salut Public (CNSP), and pledged his commitment to dialogue and a return ultimately to civilian rule. He selected a transition cabinet composed of military and civilians, the latter representing a cross-section of political parties, and proposed that a referendum be held to approve a new electoral code and constitution giving all Ivoirians an equal opportunity to participate in multiparty democracy.

Under the hegemony of the Parti Démocratique de la Côte d'Ivoire (PDCI), the multiethnic party that Houphouët founded in 1945 and led until his death in 1993, the territory had remained relatively stable. The fact that the PDCI had ably defended French political and economic interests in Côte d'Ivoire explains French support for the party leadership until recently—a commitment backed by financial support and an unassuming French military presence of about 500 French marines stationed at Port-Bouët, near the main airport. France did not intervene to maintain Bedié in office, though they have allowed him to take up residence there in exile. The groundwork for a close working relationship with France began when Houphouët represented Côte d'Ivoire in the 1945 First Constituent Assembly. Houphouët endeared himself to Africans throughout the French-speaking territories by initiating the Houphouët-Boigny Law abolishing forced labor in 1946. He extended his influence by founding the Rassemblement Démocratique Africain (RDA), an umbrella organization for political parties throughout francophone Africa. He held the minister of health porfolio for all of France in 1956. By referendum, in 1958, Côte d'Ivoire declined independence, in favor of semi-autonomy within the French Union, though full independence was granted, anyway, on 7 August 1960.

Under pressure from opposition groups and the international financial community (World Bank, International Monetary Fund, Paris Club), in addition to worldwide trends toward democratization, Houphouët was forced to implement constitutional provisions for a multiparty system (30 April 1990). The transformation of electoral politics came on the heels of the severe 1989 economic recession and the ensuing breakdown of the patron-client system. Côte d'Ivoire's liberal economy had been fueled by cash crop growing *peasants who had been guaranteed a minimum price for coffee and cocoa regardless of market fluctuations and whose productivity had placed Côte d'Ivoire among the world's top three producers of coffee, cocoa, and cotton. Other export crops include pineapples, oil palm, coconuts, timber, latex, and sugar. Petroleum production from two offshore wells was insufficient to alleviate strains on the budget or prevent the rescheduling of international debts. The "miracle" of Ivoirian economic development had disguised a weak industrial sector.

Under the one-party regime, national elections held at five-year intervals had confirmed into office the incumbent president and a single list of PDCI candidates for the National Assembly—a process justified as a means, according to Houphouët, to preserve unity within diversity. During the economic crisis, massive street demonstrations led by teachers, students, doctors, and workers in crucial sectors of energy and communications marked widespread dissatisfaction. They were disrupted by state police with a force that sometimes resulted in death; however, this repression did not match the level of violence used in several previous incidents (i.e., the Bogus Plot of 1963; the 1970 repression of the Parti Nationaliste (PANA) resulting in 3,000–4,000 deaths among the Bété in Gagnoa).

Among opposition parties that arose in the 1990 multiparty elections to challenge the PDCI, the frontrunners were the Front Populaire Ivoirien (FPI) and the Parti Ivoirien des Travailleurs (PIT), winning ten seats in the National Assembly. Laurent Gbagbo (FPI), the only candidate to oppose Houphouët in the presidential elections, won 18 percent of the vote. For the first time, a prime minister was selected, but not following the parliamentary model: Alassane Ouattara was merely appointed as an interministerial coordinator by Houphouët. Bedié, a former minister of finance and assembly member, was reelected to the presidency of the National Assembly where he maintained a privileged position as designated successor (a provision of the oft-amended Article 11 of the Constitution).

The formidable Rassemblement des Républicains (RDR) emerged as a multiethnic party and gained momentum with the selection of Ouattara as their presidential candidate for the 1995 elections. President Bedié blocked Ouattara's admission to candidacy by introducing an amendment to the electoral code requiring the birth of the presidential candidate and both parents in Côte d'Ivoire. Although Ouattara qualified, at independence his father was in the French colonial service in Upper Volta (Burkina Faso), lending Ouattara an appearance of non-Ivoirian origin during his youth and the early years of his professional career. (Journalists suffered severe repression and imprisonment when Bedié's origins were questioned.) Hence, the Republican Front, an RDR/FPI coalition, boycotted the 1995 presidential elections, but outdistanced other opposition party candidates for the National Assembly, the RDR picking up fourteen seats to the FPI's twelve.

By 1995, Bedié (though comfortably seated as an incumbent) in collaboration with the PDCI leadership began a rash of xenophobic propaganda resulting in the formulation of *Ivoirité*, an exclusionary ideology based on notions of birthright. Bedie's exclusionary tactics against Ouattara and the RDR split the nation geographically and along ethnic lines with Muslim peoples of the North heavily represented in the RDR. The historical north-south alliance between African planters and administrative elites (mostly Baulé) and the northern provincial chiefs (Malinké and Senufo), formed at the founding of the PDCI, was broken by Bedié's removal from office of several high-ranking civil servants of northern extraction and the incarceration of RDR leaders (Mrs. Henriette Dagri Diabaté, former minister of culture under Ouattara, and four parliamentarians). The November 1999 attacks by Krumen against Mossi migrant farmers in the western region had been linked to a state-sponsored anti-Burkinabe crusade to sour Ivoirians against a Ouattara candidacy. With Ouattara's resignation from his position as deputy managing director for Africa at the IMF and return to Côte d'Ivoire to prepare for the year 2000 elections, Bedié stepped up his repressive tactics and showed blatant disregard for the rule of law by using the Supreme Court to overturn a judge's approval of Ouattara's candidacy.

Religion and *ethnicity are still strong variables in political life. The three main religious branches are Christianity, 32 percent; Islam, 24 percent; and African traditional religions, 44 percent. There are over sixty ethnic groups, classified into four main linguistic divisions: Akan, 43 percent (Baulé, Agni), in the southeast; Kru, 17 percent (Bété, Guéré), in the southwest; Mandé, 27 percent (Malinké, Dan, Gouro), in the northwest; Voltaic, 13 percent (Senufo), in the northeast and central savannas. About 25 percent of the nearly 15 million inhabitants are foreigners, predominantly Mossi domestics and field laborers, followed by Africans from nearby states, French, and Lebanese. The Basilica of Our Lady of Peace, constructed in 1989, was symbolic of efforts by Houphouët to trace a line in the sand against a perceived threat of Islamic influence from the North.

(See also DEMOCRATIC TRANSITIONS; FRANCOPHONE AFRICA; RELIGION AND POLITICS.)

I. William Zartman and Christopher L. Delgado, eds., *The Political Economy of Ivory Coast* (New York, 1984). Robert E. Handloff, ed., *Côte d'Ivoire: A Country Study*, 3d ed. (Washington, D.C., 1991). Tessy D. Bakary, "Political Polarization over Governance in Côte d'Ivoire," in I. William Zartman, ed., *Governance as Conflict Management: Politics and Violence in West Africa* (Washington, D.C., 1997). Richard C. Crook, "Winning Coalitions and Ethno-regional Politics: The Failure of the Opposition in the 1990 and 1995 Elections in Côte d'Ivoire," *African Affairs* 96, no. 383 (1997): 215–42.

JEANNE MADDOX TOUNGARA

COUNTERINSURGENCY. While *guerrilla warfare has existed throughout history, modern insurgency emerged from the *Cold War and the *decolonization of the European empires in Asia and Africa. After the victory of *Mao Zedong's communist forces in China, most insurgent movements emulated the Maoist strategy of "people's war" which combined a leftist or communist ideology designed to mobilize the repressed segments of society, protracted guerrilla operations from rural bases, *terrorism, political warfare, and, when possible, foreign assistance. The Soviet Union, China, Cuba, and other communist nations often sponsored leftist insurgents as a form of proxy struggle against the West.

It took some time for states and their military forces to develop effective methods to defeat people's war. Counterinsurgency was difficult, in part, because it required governments to undertake fundamental political and economic reforms as well as military campaigns and law enforcement programs. Governments that treated counterinsurgency as a purely military problem usually failed. But even with an effective reform program, eradicating an insurgency was difficult so long as external sponsors were available.

Unfortunately, successful counterinsurgency usually required brutality and repression. Some states, like the United States in Vietnam, France in Algeria, and the white-dominated government in South Africa, met with battlefield success but political defeat as their publics eventually became unwilling to tolerate such actions. At times, governments that undertook the steps they felt were necessary for victory faced international pressure or isolation, in part because the insurgents attained some degree of international legitimacy as representatives of the downtrodden.

By the 1980s, rural people's war was still the dominant form of insurgency, but mutations had taken place. Decolonization was nearly complete so most insurgencies were internal struggles rather than wars of national liberation. In South America, some leftist rebels attempted an urban-based strategy relying heavily on terrorism, but met with little success. And, while insurgency and counterinsurgency remained methods of proxy conflict between the superpowers, Western-backed insurgents began to fight communist or pro-Soviet governments in places such as Angola, Nicaragua, and Afghanistan.

In the 1990s, more important changes took place. The demise of the Soviet Union cut off some of the sources of external sponsorship of insurgency. This forced many rebels to seek independent sources of funding and arms. In Latin America, leftist insurgents entered the narcotics trade. Diamond smuggling funded insurgents in Sierra Leone and Angola. In Sri Lanka, Northern Ireland, the Democratic Republic of the Congo, and Kosovo, insurgents used voluntary contributions as well as criminal activities. This made the law enforcement component of counterinsurgency very important.

By the mid-1990s, insurgency assumed an important ethnic dimension. In sub-Saharan Africa, Central Asia, South Asia, and the Balkans, states provided support or sanctuary to ethnically based insurgents as a means of proxy aggression against neighboring states. The Zapatista movement in Mexico introduced another change as it became the first "information age" insurgency, using a minimum of violence and relying instead on political activity, building a global support network with tools such as Internet Web pages and e-mail distribution lists.

Insurgency attempts to overthrow or pressure a government by taking advantage of the difficulty states face when undertaking repression, sustaining public support during a protracted conflict, or coordinating military, political, psychological, and economic activities. Future insurgents must do the same things, but are likely to find new, innovative strategies to replace Maoist people's war. States thus must develop new counters to them and do so in a way that does not isolate them from the global community since, in an era of globalization, pariah status spells economic and political disaster.

(See also ALGERIAN WAR OF INDEPENDENCE; NATIONAL LIBERATION MOVEMENTS; REVOLUTION; VIETNAM WAR.)

Steven Metz, *Counterinsurgency* (Carlisle Barracks, Pa., 1995).
STEVEN METZ

COUP D'ÉTAT. A nonconstitutional change of governmental leadership carried out with the use or threatened use of violence is known as a coup d'état. It has served historically in many African, Asian, and Latin American states as the major form of regime change. A coup d'état results in the formation of a governmental junta either dominated directly by the members of the armed services who seized political control or controlled indirectly by them through closely aligned civilians.

Explanations for coups d'etat fall into three broad schools: factors internal to armed forces (corporate and personal grievances); factors marking the environment of the political system as a whole; and international or extra-systemic factors. Corporate grievances include budget, policy autonomy, and potential threats to military identity resulting from the creation or expansion of paramilitary units. Personal grievances refer to concerns of individual officers who, for various reasons, are disaffected from the current national political and/or military leaders and who seek rectification by seizure of power and ouster of those in control. Environmental factors refer to domestic economic, political, and social settings. In general, certain levels of ethnic fragmentation, political mobilization, and violence have been correlated with coups. International factors include changes outside the domestic political and economic arena such as trends in world prices, direct or indirect encouragement of military intervention by

outside groups, and financial and technical assistance that enhances the political and coercive strength of armed forces.

The success of a coup d'état depends largely on surprise and total commitment of resources by the insurgents. In broad terms, planners of coups desire to displace the existing government as rapidly as possible. Planning of a coup d'état is confined to a small number of military officers. The risks of discovery and punishment preclude involvement of more than a handful of officers, themselves generally linked by ethnicity, rank, age, or other ties, until a few hours prior to execution. The new junta must seek some degree of popular legitimacy. As the overall levels of *modernization rise within societies, the obstacles to gaining such legitimacy seem to have increased, with consequent shifts in the major types of coups d'état.

Coups d'état can be classified into four groups: oligarchic, modernizing, radical, and guardian. Oligarchic coups are largely of historic interest. Characteristic particularly of nineteenth-century Latin America, they took place within preindustrial settings in which the officer corps showed little professionalization and levels of popular political awareness were minimal. Modernizing coups reflect increased professionalization of the officer corps and greater modernization of society. Such seizures of power are customarily led by military officers aware of the gap separating their societies from more developed ones, and ease the transition from traditional or oligarchic rule to rule by the urban middle classes and their allies. Radical coups introduce potentially revolutionary changes into society and place members of the armed forces into positions of unquestioned control. This intense politicization of the military, and the sweeping alterations undertaken in the distribution of power and resources, create widespread social tensions. The usual consequences have been either control falling into the hands of the military head of state and a reduction in the armed forces' direct political roles, or some form of military guardianship. Guardian coups occur in societies in which lower-class politicization has been encouraged and in which the armed forces have heritages of direct political involvement. Weaknesses of civilian governments, often manifested in uncontrolled violence or runaway inflation, encourage such military takeovers; on the other hand, traditions of professionalism within the officer corps and a distaste for politics among officers inhibit long-term exercise of power. The juntas develop close ties with middle-class and technocratic groups, occasionally leading to the emergence of *bureaucratic authoritarianism.

Disengagement of armed forces from direct political roles poses many problems. The usual impetus comes from divisions within the governing junta between hard-liners and soft-liners, the latter preferring to return to the barracks to reduce intramilitary tensions, the former pressing for intensification of the military's role. Such tensions also often lead to further coups d'état, thus continuing a cycle of "praetorian" politics. The rapid pace of liberalization and democratization in Latin America and in the former Soviet bloc during the 1980s and early 1990s and pressures against several African, Asian, and Middle Eastern military juntas, suggest, however, strengthened norms of governmental control over the armed forces.

(See also AUTHORITARIANISM; DEMOCRATIC TRANSITIONS;

MILITARISM; MILITARY RULE; POLITICAL VIOLENCE; REVOLUTION.)

Edward Luttwak, *Coup d'Etat: A Practical Handbook* (Cambridge, Mass., 1979). Claude E. Welch, Jr., *No Farewell to Arms? Military Disengagement from Politics in Africa and Latin America* (Boulder, Colo., 1987). S. E. Finer, *The Man on Horseback: The Role of the Military in Politics,* 2d ed. (Boulder, Colo., 1988).

CLAUDE E. WELCH, JR.

CRISIS. International crises punctuated the Cold War confrontation between the Soviet- and American-led blocs. Crises such as the Berlin blockade (1948), the outbreak of war in Korea (1950), the struggles over the islands of Quemoy and Matsu (1958), the Cuban missile crisis (1962), the uprising in Czechoslovakia (1968), and the shooting down of Korean Airlines flight 007 (1983) represented flashpoints that underscored the recurrent danger in that era of escalation to major—perhaps nuclear—*war. Even though the world has evolved beyond that superpower struggle, some fundamental qualities of crisis remain constant.

The term "crisis" comes from the Greek *krinein,* meaning to separate. In a critical medical condition a crisis is a turning point separating recovery from death. In an analogous manner crises in international politics are sometimes viewed as the turning point in a dispute leading either to peaceful resolution or escalation to war.

Scholarship on world politics has stipulated more specific meanings for crisis. Three alternative conceptualizations deserve attention. They represent not only definitional distinctions but also different levels of analysis and alternative theoretical and practical concerns. Important differences exist among systemic crises, confrontation crises, and decision-making crises.

*International systems consist of actors regularly interacting according to some structure that is maintained by norms, laws, or the distribution of capabilities. From the systemic perspective, a crisis is a powerful shock to the structure that holds the system together. Thus a systemic crisis threatens the stability of the international system and creates the possibility of destruction or a transformation. For example, the bipolar international system led by the opposing superpowers that prevailed after World War II experienced the shocks that led to the breakup of the Warsaw Treaty Organization and the collapse of the Soviet Union in the late 1980s and early 1990s. In effect, these crises terminated the existing bipolar international system.

When does a crisis lead to the destabilization of the international system? Some analysts suggest one kind of international system (e.g., multipolar vs. bipolar) is more susceptible to crises and the conditions under which they destabilize the system. Typically the conditions that trigger system crises have been wars or *revolutions that dramatically alter the power distribution among actors in international politics. In today's increasingly economically interdependent international system, other types of events (e.g., currency collapse or hyperinflation in key nations) may more frequently ignite future systemic crises. Because the financial and economic systems have become so interdependent, serious disruptions in a few countries have the potential of spreading throughout the entire global system. The financial crisis in Asia in the late 1990s posed exactly such a danger. In 1995, American policy makers anticipated that the debt crisis in Mexico could become contagious and therefore they provided substantial loans to reduce the difficulties in Mexico and to suppress its spread elsewhere.

Not all systemic crises need be dysfunctional for a system, particularly if leaders have the capacity to adapt and learn from the shocks. Leaders in systems or subsystems may actually use crises as a means of forcing member governments to take initiatives they otherwise might not take. The leadership of the European Union has repeatedly used deadline crises as a means of forcing member governments to take further integrative steps or risk collapse of that valued regional system, which produces beneficial results no party wishes to forgo. Thus the *Maastricht Treaty (1991) set deadlines by which participating countries had to fulfill requirements needed to adopt the common currency, the euro.

A second type of international crisis involves direct confrontation typically between two opposing parties. Whereas systemic crises concern the fate of the system as whole, crises between actors focus only on the consequences for the specific entities confronting one another. Confrontational crises are triggered when one actor initiates a major challenge to the position of another. After one party's challenge and the defiant response by the other, the fundamental dynamic involves bargaining—either directly or by tacit signaling. In the absence of successful negotiations, violent conflict follows. The 1982 Argentine challenge to British control of the Falkland Islands in the South Atlantic was immediately rejected by the Thatcher government. Negotiations failed and the brief Malvinas/Falklands War ensued. In the past, international confrontational crises involved opposing states, like Britain and Argentina. The post–Cold War era may witness greater diversity in the kind of parties engaged. Given the rising importance of nonstate actors in world affairs, the likelihood has increased that such crises might involve, for example, terrorists or multinational entities (e.g., World Bank, International Monetary Fund) or global corporations.

Specialists examining the confrontational crises frequently rely on one of two methods of inquiry—the theory of games or comparative case studies. Researchers applying *game theory generally address the conditions under which a stable solution to the crisis can be found. Case studies have focused on issues such as types of strategy, third-party intervention, and the conditions governing escalation. Regardless of the method, scholars and practitioners alike ask the same basic question: What bargaining strategies produce a successful outcome without escalation to greater violence or war?

In the third kind of crisis, the focus is within a single country or other political unit. Governmental or decision-making crises involve an event or other stimulus that poses a severe problem for the policy makers and possibly their constituents. Definitions of decision-making crises emphasize properties of the situation facing the policy makers. For example, a crisis can be viewed as the combination of high threat to basic goals of the policy makers, short time before the situation evolves in a manner undesired by them, and appearance as a surprise (i.e., a lack of expectation that the situation would occur). The attempted coup against Gorbachev in the Soviet Union (1991) came as a complete surprise, posed an enormous threat to his government, and offered only a short time before the plotters would be able to consolidate their control of the country if they were not stopped.

A basic question posed from the decision-making perspective is: What effects does a crisis have on the quality of decisions? What are the properties of government agencies or the characteristics of individual policy makers that enable them to manage crisis more or less effectively? Prescriptive studies seek to advance means to avoid crises or to manage them without severe consequences. Crisis management research establishes a standard for the quality of decisions (e.g., rationality, adaptation, avoidance of war) and then identifies circumstances in policy making that tend to deviate from that standard. Proposals for avoiding these crisis-induced difficulties are then recommended. For example, Irving Janis (*Victims of Groupthink*, Boston, 1972) contends that decision groups in crisis tend to engage in excessive concurrence seeking which erodes the quality of decisions. He proposes steps to reduce this concurrence-seeking behavior.

Occasionally, a crisis can evolve from one type to another. In October 1962, when the United States discovered that the Soviet Union was secretly placing nuclear missiles in Cuba, it was a decision-making crisis for the American government. Faced with extremely high threat, short time (before the missiles became operational), and surprise, could the American policy makers choose a wise course of action? Once the United States announced its intention to blockade Cuba in an attempt to force the withdrawal of the missiles, the crisis became a confrontation between the Soviet Union and the United States. Could the parties negotiate a solution without war? Then as the world learned of the missile crisis and the threat of war, the danger to the entire global system became apparent.

Although the threat of military crises remains, the contemporary interdependent world faces equally potentially dangerous crises from other directions such as economic instability or the rapid epidemic of a fatal disease.

Glenn Snyder and Paul Diesing, *Conflict Among Nations* (Princeton, N.J., 1977). Michael Brecher, Johanthan Wilkenfeld, and Sheila Moser, *Crises in the Twentieth Century*, 2 vols. (New York, 1988). Alexander L. George, ed., *Avoiding War: Problems of Crisis Management* (Boulder, Colo., 1991). Russel J. Leng, *Interstate Crisis Behavior, 1816–1980* (New York, 1993).

CHARLES F. HERMANN

CROATIA. An ancient South Slavic kingdom, sovereign from the ninth century to 1102, thereafter in dynastic union with Hungary (until 1918), ruled from 1527 to 1918 by the Austrian Habsburgs, modern Croatia—consisting of Croatia proper, Medjimurje, and most of Slavonia, Dalmatia, and Istria—was territorially fixed within the People's (later Socialist) Republic of Croatia, a federal republic of *Yugoslavia from 1945 to 1991. After losing all attributes of statehood and autonomy in the royal Yugoslav state (1918), Croatia became an autonomous banate of Yugoslavia (1939–1941) and then an Axis dependency (Independent State of Croatia, 1941–1945), but with significantly different borders.

In 1991, after a referendum on independence, the Republic of Croatia fought against the Yugoslav People's Army (JNA) and indigenous Serb militias, sponsored by the Milošević re-

gime in Serbia, to assert its newly proclaimed sovereignty, which was internationally recognized in 1992. Its population in 1991 was 4,784,265, of which Croats constituted 78 percent, Serbs 12.16 percent, and Yugoslavs 2.22 percent. The two main religious communities in 1991 were Catholics (76.5 percent) and Serbian Orthodox (11.1 percent). Meanwhile, the Serb population was significantly reduced, especially as a result of mass exodus and repression that accompanied the reconquest of Serb-controlled areas of northern Dalmatia, Lika, Kordun, Banija, and western Slavonia (Krajina in Serb usage) by the Croatian army (HV) in 1995; and the transfer, by the UN authorities, of eastern Slavonia, Baranja, and western Syrmium to Croatia in 1997. Similarly, Croat percentages were increased by the influx of refugees from Bosnia-Herzegovina and rump Yugoslavia (*Serbia and Montenegro). At the end of the 1990s Croatia was more nationally homogeneous than ever in its history.

Throughout the Yugoslav period Croatia was the bastion of opposition to centralism and Serbian hegemony. During the interwar period its politics were dominated by the Croat Peasant Party (HSS), which succeeded in effecting significant autonomy. The policies of the Axis-installed Ustaša (Insurgent) movement, besides its unconvincing show of independence and emulation of fascist models, were directed to anti-Serb violence, creating new obstacles to Croat-Serb coexistence. This led to Communist-led insurgency in which the Serbs massively participated. By 1945 Partisan operational units of Croatia numbered 100,740 fighters, of which Croats constituted 60.26 percent and Serbs 24.35 percent. The overrepresentation of Serbs in the Communist insurgency was translated into postwar influence, which, in turn, provoked Croat resentment and opposition, both inside and outside the ruling Communist Party (SKH).

In 1971, the movement for the affirmation of Croatia's statehood and financial independence, but also of limited political *pluralism and civil liberties, led by the reform wing of the SKH, the Matica Hrvatska cultural society, and the student movement at the University of Zagreb, was forcibly halted by *Tito. Most of the principals were expelled from the party and retired, but some, notably non-Communists, were tried and imprisoned. The consequences of 1971, especially the virtual criminalization of various aspects of Croat identity, hastened the collapse of political Yugoslavism. After the rise of Milošević's nationalist movement in Serbia and the East European "refolution," Croat Communists were obliged to agree to multiparty elections. Held in March and April of 1990, they were won by the populist party-movement Croatian Democratic Union (HDZ), led by Franjo Tudjman, a former JNA general, dissident historian, and political prisoner.

The HDZ and Tudjman personally shaped Croatia's course throughout the 1990s. They led Croatia from federal status to independence; established a strongly centralized political system in which the bicameral parliament (Sabor), the government, and the judiciary play secondary roles to the dominant presidential office; involved Croatia in the *Bosnian war and in attempts to carve up *Bosnia and Herzegovina (in agreement with Serbia), thereby courting international isolation; limited equal access to the public media; and carried out a kleptocratic privatization of state property. The authoritarian and nationalist regime, however, increasingly was challenged by the political opposition and human rights organizations. After Tudjman's death in December 1999 the opposition won parliamentary elections in January 2000 and formed a new six-party coalition government. Stipe Mesić, a candidate of the old anti-Tudjman opposition and the last president of federal Yugoslavia, was elected president of Croatia in February 2000. Croatia's prospects, including the end of its international isolation and the revival of its industry and tourism, have benefitted from the regime change.

(See also BALKANS; MACEDONIA, THE FORMER YUGOSLAV REPUBLIC OF; POST-COMMUNISM; SLOVENIA.)

Laura Silber and Allan Little, *The Death of Yugoslavia* (London, 1995). Marcus Tanner, *Croatia: A Nation Forged in War* (New Haven, Conn., and London, 1997).

IVO BANAC

CUBA, the largest island of the Caribbean, straddles the Gulf of Mexico and has historically been of enormous strategic importance for many countries. A colony of Spain from 1511 to 1898, it has also had a long and turbulent relationship with the United States.

Historical Background. Christopher Columbus discovered Cuba for Spain during his first voyage, on 27 October 1492. Diego Velázquez began permanent settlement in 1511, founding Baracoa on the northeastern coast. The island's limited gold deposits discouraged early settlement, but the colony became an important staging ground for the mainland exploration of Yucatán, Florida, and the Gulf Coast. In 1740 the Havana Company was formed to stimulate agricultural development by increasing the importation of slaves and regulating the export trade. The company was unsuccessful, selling fewer slaves in twenty-one years than the British sold during a ten-month occupation of Havana in 1762. Reforms by Charles III of Spain at this time further stimulated the development of the sugar industry.

Between 1763 and 1860 the island's population increased from less than 150,000 to more than 1.3 million. Slaves made the most dramatic growth, increasing from 39,000 in the 1770s to some 400,000 in the 1840s. In the nineteenth century Cuba imported more than 600,000 Africans, most of them after an Anglo-Spanish agreement to terminate the slave trade in 1820. The Cuban insistence on maintaining slavery and the slave trade raised considerable diplomatic controversy between Spain and Great Britain between 1817 and 1865.

The demands of sugar laborers, capital, machines, technical skills, and markets strained interracial relations, aggravated political and economic differences between metropolis and colony, and laid the foundation for the break with Spain in 1898. Spanish colonial administration had been corrupt, inefficient, and inflexible. The United States had shown a growing interest in the island and expeditions by U.S. filibusters won support in the United States, especially in the southern slave states. After the 1860s the United States tried many times to purchase the island.

Spain's failure to grant political autonomy, while increasing taxes, led to the outbreak of the first war of independence—the Ten Years' War (1868–1878)—which led to a military stalemate. The rich sugar producers of western Cuba and the vast majority of the slaves failed to rally to the nationalists, themselves divided over the questions of slavery, complete independence, or annexation to the United States. By 1895 the

political and economic crisis had grown more severe. U.S. investment had reached $50 million, and its annual trade with Cuba amounted to about $100 million. Cuban political organizations in exile were coordinated and mobilized by the poet and propagandist José *Martí, who died shortly after the outbreak of war on 24 February 1895.

By 1898 Spain had deployed more than 200,000 troops, both sides killed civilians and burned estates and towns, and commercial activity had virtually ceased. Stimulated, by the yellow press and a mysterious explosion aboard the USS *Maine* in Havana's harbor, the United States declared war on Spain on 25 April 1898. Hostilities ended in August when Spain signed a peace protocol in Washington. Cuban independence, granted by the Treaty of Paris (10 December 1898), began 1 January 1899 under U.S. occupation.

The military occupation restored normality. The Americans built a number of schools, roads, and bridges, they modernized Havana and deepened its harbor. But Americans were primarily interested in preparing the island for incorporation into the U.S. economic, cultural, and educational systems, not in fostering a free and independent state in Cuba.

The Cuban Republic, 1902–1958. The republican administration that began on 20 May 1902 under Tomás Estrada Palma faced difficulties both internally as well as from the dominant influence of the United States. Estrada Palma tried to retain power in the 1905 and 1906 elections, which were contested by the Liberals, leading to rebellion and a second U.S. occupation on 29 September 1906. U.S. Secretary of War William Howard Taft failed to resolve the dispute and Estrada Palma resigned. For the United States Charles Magoon administered a provisional government of Cuban civilians under the Cuban constitution. On 28 January 1909, Magoon handed over the government to the elected Liberal president, José Miguel Gómez.

The Gómez administration (1909–1913) set a pattern of graft, corruption, maladministration, fiscal irresponsibility, and social insensitivity, especially toward Afro-Cubans, that characterized Cuban politics until 1959. Some Afro-Cubans, led by Evaristo Estenoz and Pedro Ivonet, organized themselves to secure better jobs and more political patronage and to protest the ban on any political associations based exclusively on color and race. In 1912 government troops put down large demonstrations in Oriente. The pattern of political corruption was followed by Mario García Menocal (1913–1921), Alfredo Zayas (1912–1925), Gerardo Machado (1925–1933), Fulgencio Batista (through puppets 1934–1939 and himself 1940–1944 and 1952–1959), Ramón Grau San Martín (1944–1948), and Carlos Prío Socarrás (1948–1952). Machado and Batista (who overthrew Machado in 1933 with U.S. support), were the most notorious, holding power through coercion, assassination, and military action.

Beginning in the 1920s the income from sugar was augmented by an expanding tourist industry. Havana became especially attractive during the years of U.S. Prohibition (1919–1933). Yet the prosperity of the 1920s, 1940s, and 1950s enriched only a few Cubans. For the majority, poverty (especially in the countryside) and lack of public services were appalling. Unemployment and underemployment were rife, and wages were miserably low. Foreign interests controlled the economy, owning about 75 percent of the arable land, 90 percent of the essential services, and forty percent of the sugar production.

The collapse of Batistas regime on 1 January 1959 resulted as much from inherent institutional weakness as from the persistent challenges of Fidel *Castro's 26 July Movement (commemorating Castro's failed attack on the Moncada military fortress in Santiago on 26 July 1953) or from the Federation of University Students (later absorbed into the Young Communists Union), and other groups. Castro had been a candidate for the senate in the aborted elections of 1952. In 1955 Castro and some friends went to Mexico to prepare for the overthrow of Batista. An enlarged group, including the Argentinian revolutionary Ernesto (Che) *Guevara, landed in Cuba in December 1956 and was almost annihilated in its first attack. From the mountainous Sierra Maestra the survivors fought a two-year guerrilla campaign that capitalized on widespread disaffection with Batista.

The 26 July Movement had vague political plans, relatively insignificant support, and totally untested administrative skills. They quickly forged a devoted following from among poor *peasants, urban workers, youths, and the idealistic of all groups. The Communist Party of Cuba (PCC), dating to 1925, assumed a dominant political role, and the state modeled itself on the Soviet-bloc countries, becoming the first *communist party state in the Americas. The party remade itself in the 1960s and membership became highly selective, admitting less than five percent of the population.

Political Institutions. The PCC remains the only recognized political party. There is a directly elected National Assembly that meets formally twice per year, a Council of State, and a Council of Ministers. Local power is organized around neighborhood Committees for the Defense of the Revolution, 169 Municipal Councils, and a plethora of mass organizations. Nevertheless power is consolidated in the person of Fidel Castro through his multiple positions as first secretary of the Politburo, president of the Council of Ministers, and president of the Council of State.

The Cuban armed forces (Fuerzas Armadas Revolucionarias) have played an important role in government and society, especially since 1980. Created in the 1960s and led by Raúl Castro, Fidel's younger brother, the Cuban armed forces rank in the Americas only behind the United States and Brazil in size. Cuba spends more money on its armed forces on a per capita basis than any other country in the hemisphere. Until 1991 training and supplies came primarily from the Soviet Union, but more recently the armed forces have had to depend on local initiatives. Beside offering protection from external and internal threat, the armed forces have been deployed widely in Africa—especially in Angola, the Congo, and the Horn of Africa—and across the Caribbean, especially in Grenada and Guyana.

The Economy. By the end of the 1950s Cuba had developed one of the leading economies of Latin America. Nevertheless, the country was confronted by a number of major problems: a sugar monoculture (sugar accounted for four-fifths of total exports), a low rate of economic growth, a heavy dependence upon the United States for investment and trade, high rates of unemployment and underemployment, and significant inequalities between urban and rural areas, as well as among the various ethnic and racial groups.

When the revolutionary government took over in 1959, it set out to correct these problems through various means, the most significant being *collectivization of all means of production (except for about 9 percent of agricultural land); establishment of a centrally planned economy; emphasis on industrialization and the deemphasis of sugar production (both later reversed); formation of close economic ties with the Soviet Union; and development of social services, particularly in rural areas.

The measures taken achieved mixed results. The attempt to introduce central *planning (following the Soviet model of the 1950s) in 1961–1963 failed, in part, because of the lack of infrastructure and qualified personnel and because of overly ambitious goals. After a period of intense debate (1964–1966), the role of the central plan was reduced and emphasis placed on moral incentives (nonmonetary awards such as medals and titles, labor mobilization, and the development of the "new man" [1966–1970]). When this approach also failed to bring about the desired results, there was a return to Soviet-type central planning and the orthodox system of socialist incentives. Even as the Soviet Union began experimenting with market mechanisms in the mid-1980s, Cuban leaders rejected the possibility of altering the economy. The disintegration of communist governments throughout Europe and the breakup of the Soviet Union in 1991 caused the Cuban economy to go into free fall for a number of years. It recovered slowly after 1994 as a result of drastic reorganization and the introduction of new mixed public-private sector initiatives. In 1994 the U.S. dollar was introduced as legal tender and its ownership by individuals depenalized. The government also reopened nonstate food markets and encouraged private food production. Adjustment policies have been hard on the society, increasing unemployment, lowering labor productivity, sharply reducing general income, and exacerbating urban-rural inequities. Tourism and remittances from abroad rapidly surpassed sugar as contributors to the national income. The gradual reduction of the state roll in the overall economy has not alleviated diplomatic problems with foreign governments. The shooting down in 1996 of two small planes piloted by Cuban Americans challenging the island's airspace resulted in the passage of the Helms-Burton law by the United States that further restricted commercial relations between Cuba, the United States, and Third World countries. The successful visits in 1998 by Pope *John Paul II and the Canadian prime minister were undermined by ongoing repression. The passing of stringent laws against subversion in 1999 and the expansion of definitions of social delinquency have seriously eroded support in Canada, Spain, and Brazil, while the litigation over the rescue at sea of Elían González in 1999–2000 raised anew the complexities of U.S.-Cuban relations.

Foreign Policy. From the early 1960s Cuban *foreign policy was pragmatically designed to protect and perpetuate the Castro regime. But it has also manifested periods of idealism, especially in its support of several African governments and the regime of Salvador *Allende in Chile in the early 1970s. Principle rather than consistency has been the main feature of Cuban foreign policy. Cuba invests heavily in foreign aid, both of the civilian and the military type, although recently social programs have been emphasized. The implacable hostility with the United States did not prevent the two countries from establishing diplomatic missions in each other's capital cities to serve their common interests, or to meet periodically to discuss problems of mutual concern such as immigration and drug smuggling. Castro, in serving longer than any other leader in the world, has shown a remarkable ability over the years to respond creatively to new and challenging situations, although not always successfully.

(See also COLONIAL EMPIRES; GUERRILLA WARFARE; U.S. FOREIGN POLICY.)

Jorge I. Domínguez, *Cuba: Order and Revolution* (Cambridge, Mass., 1978). Carmelo Mesa-Lago, *Cuba in the 1970s: Pragmatism and Institutionalization* (Pittsburgh, 1978). Oscar Zanetti and Alejandro García, *Sugar and Railroads: A Cuban History, 1837–1959* (Chapel Hill, N.C., 1998). Marifeli Pérez-Stable, *The Cuban Revolution: Origins, Course and Legacy* (New York, 1999).

FRANKLIN W. KNIGHT

CUBAN MISSILE CRISIS. On 15 October 1962, American *intelligence discovered the first of six Soviet nuclear missile bases under construction in *Cuba. After a week of deliberation with a group of close advisers that would later become known as the Executive Committee of the National Security Council, or "ExComm," President John F. *Kennedy announced the discovery to the world in a televised address at 7:00 P.M. on 22 October. Stressing that the deployment had been undertaken secretly and in flagrant violation of his own warnings against such a move, Kennedy demanded that the missiles be withdrawn, and announced his intention to impose a naval "quarantine" on shipments of "offensive" weapons to Cuba. He warned Soviet Chairman Nikita *Khrushchev that any missile launched from Cuban territory against any nation of the Western Hemisphere would be considered an attack by the Soviet Union on the United States, requiring a full retaliatory response upon the Soviet Union. To back up his threat, Kennedy ordered a massive redeployment of forces to the Caribbean and placed the Strategic Air Command on heightened alert. Thus began the Cuban missile *crisis, widely regarded as the closest the world has yet come to nuclear war between the *superpowers.

Furious, Khrushchev immediately ordered construction at the missile sites accelerated, and denounced the quarantine as piracy—a flagrant interference with Soviet freedom of navigation and a gross violation of the Soviet Union's right to enter into military arrangements with friendly sovereign states. But by the time the quarantine took effect on the morning of Wednesday, 24 October—after a unanimous vote of support from the *Organization of American States—Khrushchev had ordered Soviet ships carrying suspect cargo not to challenge the U.S. blockade. An immediate confrontation on the high seas was thereby avoided. Still, for several days a settlement of the dispute eluded U.S. and Soviet diplomats. As the crisis dragged on, pressure began to build on both sides for more decisive action.

Neither Kennedy nor Khrushchev was prepared to risk nuclear war over the issue, and both became increasingly preoccupied with the danger that an accident or inadvertent military action might push them over the brink. An apparent break came on Friday, 26 October, when, in a long and emotional letter, Khrushchev vaguely offered to withdraw the missiles in return for a U.S. pledge not to invade Cuba. But in a letter received the following morning, Khrushchev seemed to back away from this position, offering instead to remove the missiles in return for the withdrawal of the fifteen U.S. Jupiter missiles from Turkey—obsolete medium-range nuclear missiles deployed under the aegis of the *North At-

lantic Treaty Organization (NATO). The ExComm as a whole argued strongly against such a deal on the grounds that it was politically unacceptable: it would be interpreted by the Soviets as evidence of U.S. weakness; it would be regarded as a betrayal of Turkey, a NATO ally, for whose benefit the Jupiters had been deployed; and it would be extremely unpopular domestically. The president decided to ignore Khrushchev's latest demand and "accept" his "offer" of 26 October.

As the ExComm deliberated on Saturday, 27 October, word reached the White House that an American U-2 reconnaissance plane had been shot down over Cuba, and that another had inadvertently strayed over Siberian airspace, narrowly avoiding a similar fate. At this point, Kennedy evidently resolved to bring the crisis to an end. Ignoring the ExComm's advice, he secretly instructed Secretary of State Dean Rusk to lay the groundwork for a contingency by which the secretary general of the UN would propose the Cuba-Turkey missile swap. Knowing this to be acceptable to Khrushchev, Kennedy therefore knew that it would provide a quick resolution to the crisis should events get out of hand. But Kennedy was saved from having to decide whether or not to execute his demarche by Khrushchev's sudden agreement on 28 October to withdraw the missiles from Cuba in return for a noninvasion pledge.

While Khrushchev's agreement proved to be the decisive break in the crisis, it did not immediately resolve the confrontation. Khrushchev had failed to consult Fidel *Castro on the matter, and Castro understandably felt betrayed by his Soviet patron. He therefore refused to allow UN inspectors to examine the missile sites to verify the withdrawal, forcing the U.S. Navy to make do by inspecting outbound Soviet ships from the air. Kennedy also insisted that the Soviets withdraw a handful of Il-28 light bombers, because these were believed to have a nuclear capability. But the Il-28s had been supplied to Cuba for coastal defense purposes wholly independent of the missile deployment, and it would take Khrushchev's special envoy, Anastas Mikoyan, a full three weeks to persuade Castro to comply. On 19 November, Castro finally relented, and on 21 November, Kennedy issued a proclamation terminating the quarantine.

Causes. The causes of the Cuban missile crisis continue to spark controversy. Evidence and testimony currently available indicate that Khrushchev decided on the deployment in the late spring of 1962, after a hasty and uncritical decision-making process involving only a small group of advisers. One of his main motivations seems to have been to deter a U.S. invasion of Cuba, which seemed inevitable to the Soviets and Cubans given the U.S. role in the *Bay of Pigs invasion the previous year, and in light of Operation Mongoose, the *Central Intelligence Agency's energetic covert campaign to topple the Castro regime. Another important goal was to counterbalance the United States' massive superiority in strategic *nuclear weapons, publicly revealed to the world by Deputy Secretary of Defense Roswell Gilpatric in an October 1961 speech exploding the myth of a "missile gap" favoring the Soviet Union. It is impossible to know which of these (if either) was the more important motivation—they were mutually reinforcing, and there is no evidence to suggest that Khrushchev asked the question of himself. A third and evidently subsidiary consideration was the desire to counterbalance the U.S. deployment of Jupiter missiles on the Soviet periphery, for reasons of prestige.

Conduct. The Cuban missile crisis is considered by many a classic case of prudent crisis management. Kennedy and Khrushchev managed to prevent the conflict from escalating while they sought and eventually found a solution satisfactory to both. They did so by avoiding irreversible steps, curtailing unwarranted bluster, and refraining from ultimatums. But others have criticized their handling of the crisis for being too timid or too bold. Kennedy's critics on the Right lament his unwillingness to seize the opportunity provided by the pretext of the Soviet deployment to deal decisively with Castro once and for all, while the United States enjoyed a massive advantage in strategic nuclear weapons and unquestioned local conventional superiority. His critics on the Left condemn his willingness to risk nuclear war merely to delay the inevitable—the vulnerability of the United States to Soviet nuclear weapons. Khrushchev's handling of the crisis has been largely criticized by hard-liners who condemn his willingness to yield to U.S. pressure. Others in the Soviet Union applaud his cautious handling of the situation and his willingness to compromise while condemning him for recklessly provoking the crisis in the first place.

Consequences. Almost paradoxically, the Cuban missile crisis was the immediate cause of a considerable improvement in U.S.-Soviet relations. A series of agreements intended to restrain the *arms race and improve crisis stability followed closely on its heels, of which perhaps the most important were the 1963 Limited Test Ban Treaty and Hot-Line Agreement. The crisis severely strained, but did not disrupt, Soviet-Cuban relations. Sources close to Kennedy insist that if he had won a second term as president, as seems likely given his popularity after the crisis itself, he would have ventured a reconciliation with Cuba. Kennedy's *assassination in November 1963 and his succession by Lyndon *Johnson, and Khrushchev's ouster in 1964 by Leonid Brezhnev, marked the end of their two countries' brief *détente, and forestalled any improvement in U.S.-Cuban relations. In a technical sense, the Cuban missile crisis was never fully resolved. No treaty was ever concluded governing the settlement, and the exchange of letters between Kennedy and Khrushchev formalizing the terms of their agreement has not been made public. It is questionable whether they contain the firm guarantees against an invasion of Cuba that the Soviet Union trumpeted publicly as Kennedy's major concession. Indeed, while in office, one U.S. president—Ronald *Reagan—publicly denied being bound by any such obligation. Nevertheless, the United States and the Soviet Union crafted and scrupulously followed a modus vivendi in which the purported terms on which the crisis was resolved played a pivotal role. The Soviet Union refrained from deploying military equipment with offensive capabilities to Cuba, and the United States acquiesced in a Communist-controlled Cuba with close ties to the Soviet Union. But even more importantly, the United States and the Soviet Union worked out rules of the road limiting provocative initiatives in areas each regarded as being within its sphere of vital interest. Thus the Cuban missile crisis performed the valuable service of helping to immunize against a similar event.

(See also LATIN AMERICAN REGIONAL ORGANIZATIONS; U.S.–LATIN AMERICAN RELATIONS.)

David L. Larson, ed., *The "Cuban Crisis" of 1962: Selected Documents, Chronology and Bibliography,* 2d ed. (Lanham, Md., 1986). Raymond L. Garthoff, *Reflections on the Cuban Missile Crisis,* rev. ed. (Washington, D.C., 1989). James G. Blight and David A. Welch, *On the Brink: Americans and Soviets Reexamine the Cuban Missile Crisis,* 2d ed. (New York, 1990).

DAVID A. WELCH

CUITO CUANAVALE. Between October 1987 and June 1988, in the fiercest conventional battles on African soil since Erwin Rommel was defeated at El Amien, the South African Defense Force (SADF) fought pitched tank and artillery battles with the Angolan army (FAPLA) and its Cuban supporters at Cuito Cuanavale. This small base at the confluence of two rivers, the Cuito and Cuanavale, located in southeastern *Angola, became important in the military history of Africa, for there the South African army, supposedly the best on the continent, was trapped with its tanks and artillery and held down more than 300 miles from its bases in *Namibia.

The South Africans had started the heavy military buildup from bases in Namibia in July 1987 and began the offensive in October. Failing to take Cuito Cuanavale with over 9,000 soldiers, even after announcing that it had done so, losing air superiority, and faced with mutinies among black troops and a high casualty rate among whites, the South Africans reached such a desperate situation that President Botha had to fly to the war zone when the operational command of the SADF broke down.

With Cuban reinforcements, the Angolans withstood major assaults on 23 January, 25 February, and 23 March. The South Africans were repulsed with heavy losses, and the Angolan and Cuban forces seized the military initiative. This initiative changed the military, political, and diplomatic balance in the region. After the coming to power of the Reagan administration in 1981 and the articulation of the principles of "constructive engagement," the SADF had become emboldened to embark on a massive destabilization of Southern Africa. This destabilization was in the form of a low-intensity *war in Mozambique and an open, conventional war in Angola. There was a counterinsurgency war against the Namibian peoples, and in South Africa itself the troops of the SADF occupied the African township. The SADF was overstretched and its offensive in Angola brought to the forefront the limitations of an army fighting without moral support at home and abroad.

The Cuban and Angolan forces were aligned with the African National Congress of *South Africa and the South West African Peoples Organization of Namibia. For the first time since 1981, the Angolan army was able to reoccupy the area adjacent to Namibia. So confident were the Angolans and Cubans that in the space of less than three months they built two airstrips to consolidate their recapture of the southern province of Cunene. Trapped by the rainy season, bogged down by the terrain, and encircled, the South Africans made one desperate attempt to break out on 27 June and were again defeated. One South African newspaper called the defeat "a crushing humiliation."

These episodes of war were followed by diplomatic initiatives that the South Africans had previously been able to block. After the 23 March reversals at Cuito Cuanavale, the South Africans started talks that culminated in the 22 December agreement on implementation of Resolution 435 of the

Security Council of the United Nations, laying the steps for the recovery of the independence of Namibia. A year later, in February 1990, the South African government released Nelson *Mandela and unbanned the African National Congress and the other liberation movements in South Africa.

The withdrawal of the SADF from Angola did not end the war. The army of UNITA continued fighting. There was a peace accord in 1991 leading to elections in September 1992. The party of UNITA lost the elections and returned to war. Twelve years after Cuito Cuanavale the Angolan society was still mired in warfare.

(See also SOUTHERN AFRICA.)

HORACE CAMPBELL

CULTURAL REVOLUTION. *China's Cultural Revolution (1966–1976), or "Great Proletarian Cultural Revolution" as it was formally called, was a movement launched by *Chinese Communist Party (CCP) chairman *Mao Zedong to stem what he perceived as the country's drift away from socialism and toward the "restoration of *capitalism." The campaign, which was euphorically described at its inception by its progenitors as "a great *revolution that touches people to their very souls" and which inspired radical students from Paris to Berkeley, is now regarded as having been a terrible catastrophe for the Chinese nation.

The origins of the Cultural Revolution can be traced to the mid-1950s when Mao first became seriously concerned about the path that China's socialist transition had taken in the years since the CCP had come to power in 1949. His anxieties about the bureaucratization of the party, ideological degeneration in society as a whole, and the glaring socioeconomic inequalities that had emerged as China modernized escalated through the early 1960s and propelled him to embark on a crusade to expunge the "revisionism" that he believed was contaminating the party and the nation.

Mao concluded that the source of China's political retrogression lay in the false and self-serving view of many of his party colleagues that class struggle ceased under socialism. On the contrary, the chairman concluded, the struggle between proletarian and bourgeois ideologies took on new, insidious forms even after the landlord and capitalist classes had been eliminated. The principal targets of Mao's ire were, on the one hand, party and government officials who he felt had become a "new class" divorced from the masses and, on the other, intellectuals who, in his view, were the repository of bourgeois and even feudal values.

Mao's decision to undertake the Cultural Revolution was strongly influenced by his analysis that the Soviet Union had already abandoned socialism for capitalism. The Cultural Revolution was also a power struggle in which Mao fought to recapture from his political rivals some of the authority and prestige that he had lost as a result of earlier policy failures. Furthermore, Mao saw the Cultural Revolution as an opportunity to forge a "generation of revolutionary successors" by preparing China's youth to inherit the mantle of those who had originally brought the CCP to power.

There was also a policy dimension to the Cultural Revolution: once those who were thought to be leading China down the "capitalist road" had been dislodged from power at all levels of society, a wide range of truly socialist institu-

tions and processes ("sprouts of communism") were to be put in place to give life to the vision of the Cultural Revolution. For example, elitism in education was to be replaced by schools with revamped, politicized curricula, mass-based administration, and advancement criteria that stressed good class background, political activism, and ideological correctness.

The complex and convoluted history of the Cultural Revolution can be roughly divided into three major phases. The mass phase (1966–1969) was dominated by the Red Guards, the more than 20 million high-school and college students who responded to Mao's call to "make revolution," and their often-vicious efforts to ferret out "class enemies" wherever they were suspected to lurk. During this stage, most of Mao's rivals in the top leadership were deposed, including China's president, Liu Shaoqi. The military phase (1969–1971) began after the People's Liberation Army had gained ascendancy in Chinese politics by suppressing, with Mao's approval, the anarchy of the Red Guards. It ended with the alleged coup attempt in September 1971 by Mao's disgruntled heir, Defense Minister Lin Biao, who had also been one of the Chairman's main allies in launching the Cultural Revolution. The succession phase (1972–1976) was an intense political and ideological tug-of-war between radical ideologies and veteran cadres over whether to continue or curtail the policies of the Cultural Revolution. Underlying this conflict was a bitter struggle over which group would control the succession to the two paramount leaders of the CCP, Chairman Mao and Premier Zhou Enlai, both of whom were in deteriorating health by the early 1970s. The decisive lot in this struggle was cast when the most prominent radicals (the "Gang of Four," which included Mao's widow, Jiang Qing) were preemptively arrested in October 1976, a month after the Chairman's death, by a coalition of more moderate leaders. The arrest of the Gang of Four is said to mark the official end of China's Cultural Revolution.

The Cultural Revolution is now referred to in China as the "decade of chaos" and is generally regarded as one of the bleakest periods in the country's modern history. The movement's ideals were betrayed at every turn by its destructive impulses. Hundreds of thousands, if not millions, of officials and intellectuals were physically and mentally persecuted. The much-vaunted initiatives that were to transform the nation often had disastrous consequences for China's education and cultural life. Economic development was disrupted by factional strife and misguided "ultraleftist" policies.

The market-oriented economic policies that China has followed since *Deng Xiaoping came to power in the late 1970s represent a thorough repudiation of everything the Cultural Revolution stood for. Nevertheless the memory of the movement still casts an ominous shadow over Chinese politics. Deng, who was purged during the Cultural Revolution as one of China's leading "capitalist roaders," and the other elderly leaders who made the decision to crush the *Tiananmen Square protests in June 1989 feared that, left unchecked, the demonstrations would snowball into Red Guard–like chaos. After Deng's death in 1997, his successors have continued to cite the experience of the Cultural Revolution as one of the reasons China cannot risk the disorder that democracy, by challenging Party authority, might bring to the country.

(See also IDEOLOGY; SOCIALISM AND SOCIAL DEMOCRACY.)

Roderick MacFarquhar, *The Origins of the Cultural Revolution*, 3 vols. (New York, 1974–1997). William A. Joseph, Christine P. W. Wong, and David Zweig, eds., *New Perspectives on the Cultural Revolution* (Cambridge, Mass., 1991). Michael Schoenhals, ed., *China's Cultural Revolution, 1966–1969: Not a Dinner Party* (Armonk, N.Y., 1999).

WILLIAM A. JOSEPH

CYPRUS. The modern state of Cyprus became independent in 1960 after eighty years of British colonial rule (1879–1959). Earlier it had been part of the Ottoman Empire, ruled by the *millet* system in which religious leaders, under the broad authority of the Ottoman administrators, exercised considerable autonomy in governing their coreligionists. The population was predominantly Eastern Orthodox Christian with a sizable Muslim minority, largely a result of migration during the centuries of Ottoman rule.

The imposition by the British of separate political and educational institutions for Greeks and Turks began the process of a shift in identity from religion to *ethnicity. Moreover the rise of nationalist movements and their respective terrorist bands—the National Organization of Cypriot Fighters (EOKA) for the Greeks and the Turkish Resistance Organization (TMT) for the Turks—reinforced segregation and enmity. During the 1950s the Greek Cypriot anticolonial movement for *enosis* (union) with Greece, spearheaded by the charismatic leader Archbishop Makarios, led to protracted negotiations among Britain, *Greece, and *Turkey, with the Cypriots in a subordinate role. The compromise was independence, but the terms of the new constitution structurally segregated the two communities while the treaty signed by the interested parties limited Cyprus's sovereignty.

Although a multiparty democracy, the state of Cyprus has fragmented, leaving the constitutional order inoperative. In 1960 two communal chambers, one Greek and one Turkish, were created and given broad policy-making powers, while the small minorities had to opt for membership in one of the two communities. The authority of the national government was limited, governmental positions were divided between Greeks and Turks with a Greek president and a Turkish vice president, each with the power of veto, and a separate majority vote of Greek and Turkish representatives in the national legislature was required for the passage of bills on crucial issues such as taxation and defense. As a consequence the government was stalemated, and President Makarios proposed majoritarian constitutional revisions, which led to ethnic violence.

The sequence of events that followed resulted in the de facto division of the island in 1974: The Turkish Cypriots rule the northern 30 percent of the island and the Greek Cypriot government controls the remainder. In the north, Turkish troops from the mainland remain, having first invaded in response to the overthrow of President Makarios by Greek Cypriot elements seeking union with Greece. Greek Cypriots fled south and Turkish Cypriots north, a "green line" was established demarking the two sectors, population movement between the sectors was prohibited, and a UN peacekeeping force was sent to maintain order. Interminable, inconclusive talks have taken place between the leaders of the two communities under the aegis of the UN secretary-general. In the intervening years the Greek Cypriot sector has prospered; the north remains largely agricultural as the Turkish Cypriot leadership settles the area with rural Turks from Turkey. Thanks to the emigration of Turkish Cypriots, the estimated 100,000 settlers from Turkey now nearly balance the remaining 105,000 indigenous Turkish Cypriots who remain. The number of Greek Cypriots is estimated to be 600,000.

For Greece and Turkey, Cyprus is one of the conflicting issue areas between them, while U.S. policy is set by its overall strategic interests in the region. Turkish Cypriots have declared themselves an independent state, the "Turkish Republic of Northern Cyprus," and have adopted several measures integrating themselves with Turkey (the only nation that has recognized their claim to sovereignty). Despite strong objections by the Turkish Cypriots and Turkey as well as the ambivalent stance of the United States, the European Union has taken up the issue of admitting Cyprus into its ranks. That move and the continuing involvement of the UN notwithstanding, it appears unlikely that the question of Cyprus's future will be settled anytime soon.

(See also NATIONALISM; RELIGION AND POLITICS.)

Vangelis Calotychos, ed. *Cyprus and Its People: Nation, Identity, and Experience in an Unimaginable Community* (Boulder, Colo., 1998).

ADAMANTIA POLLIS

CZECH REPUBLIC. The Czech Republic was established on 1 January 1993 after the peaceful dissolution of *Czechoslovakia. The country is a parliamentary democracy with a two-chamber legislature. The 200 members of the lower house are elected according to a system of proportional representation. The members of the upper chamber, the Senate, are elected by a majority system. There is an independent judiciary. Czech leaders have been more fortunate than many in the region because they have been able to link their efforts to recreate democracy to the interwar Czechoslovak republic, which maintained a democratic political system until the Germans invaded Bohemia and Moravia and dismembered the country in 1939.

The country's president is largely a symbolic figure whose powers were further reduced in 2000. However, Václav *Havel, who was elected president of Czechoslovakia in 1989 and became the Czech Republic's first president, exercised substantial influence due to his international reputation and moral stance as a leader of the former opposition and well-known playwright. From 1993 until 1998, the country was governed by a center-right coalition led by Vaclav Klaus. In 1997 the Czech Republic, which had been one of the most stable and prosperous of the post-communist countries, began to experience serious political and economic problems. Growing unemployment and concern about *corruption among political and economic leaders led to the victory of the Social Democrats in the 1998 elections. Unable to form a coalition with other parties, Social Democratic leaders formed a minority government which was able to rule only after the Social Democrats and main center-right party, the Civic Democratic Party, signed an opposition agreement.

As in other post-communist states, the political party system is still being formed. Parties are weak organizationally, and levels of party membership are very low. Partisan preferences fluctuate, and the party system itself is still in flux.

Those citizens who have benefited from the transition to the market, including those who are better educated, young, and live in urban areas, tend to vote for center-right parties. Those who have suffered most from the transition, including older voters, those with lower educational and skill levels, and those living in rural areas, tend to support center-left parties or the Communist Party. Former officials of the communist system, including members of the police and party apparatus, also support left-of-center groups. Far-right parties have generally not fared well in recent elections. The Republican Party, which seated deputies in the legislature after the elections held in 1990, 1992, and 1996, did not win enough votes to be represented in the legislature in the 1998 elections. There are a number of small ultraright and skinhead groups that draw support primarily from young unemployed males.

Most of the Czech Republic's approximately 10 million inhabitants are Czech. The Roma or gypsies are the largest minority. Many Roma have applied for asylum in Britain and other European countries. The *Council of Europe and other international bodies have criticized the Czech government discrimination against the Roma and sporadic violent acts and have called for stronger action to improve the situation. There are also small Slovak, German, Polish, Ukrainian, Russian, and Vietnamese minorities. Roman Catholicism is the largest religion; however many citizens do not consider themselves to be religious. There is also a strong Protestant tradition dating from the era of Jan Hus, an early reformer who was burned at the stake in 1415.

As the result of *privatization programs and the growth of new businesses after 1989, the economy is largely in private hands. Approximately 80 percent of those eligible participated in a program of coupon privatization. However, although this program had political benefits, it failed to bring about needed adjustments in the structure of the economy. Trade, which had been focused almost entirely on the Soviet Union and other socialist countries, was very quickly reoriented to the West after the fall of communism in 1989. The Czech Republic also attracted substantial amounts of foreign investment. Corruption and the lack of restructuring of the economy led to poor performance in the late 1990s. Unemployment, which remained between 3 and 4 percent through the mid 1990s, reached 9.8 percent in 1999. Coupled with disillusionment with the performance of political leaders and institutions, the decline in the economy led to social unrest and protests. It also led to growing support for the Communist Party and far-right movements.

Immediately after the end of communism in 1989, the leaders of what was then Czechoslovakia reasserted their country's independence on the international level. They negotiated the withdrawal of Soviet troops from their country and reestablished good relations with other Western countries. They also sought to restore Czechoslovakia to its rightful place as part of Europe by seeking to join European and Euro-Atlantic institutions. Leaders of the Czech Republic continued these policies after the dissolution of the federation. Czech officials took the lead in the movement to institutionalize and strengthen the Organization For Security and Cooperation in Europe. However, particularly after the dissolution of the Soviet Union in 1991, they placed main emphasis on NATO as a security system for Europe.

In March 1999, the Czech Republic became one of the first post-communist states to join the North Atlantic Treaty Organization. The country's leaders have also begun accession talks with the European Union (EU). In the late 1990s, EU leaders expressed concern about the state of the Czech Republic's preparations to enter the EU, and it appeared that the country's position among the frontrunners for membership was threatened. Actions to address EU concerns regarding policies toward the Roma, transparency in the economic realm, and other areas appear to have allayed these concerns.

Czech leaders, particularly President Havel, have emphasized their desire to play an active role in European and Euro-Atlantic institutions. The public and many political leaders opposed NATO actions in Kosovo in 1999. However, the country fulfilled its obligations as a new NATO member and sent a field hospital to the area. Czech troops also participate as peacekeepers. The Czech Republic also participates in a number of regional groupings, including the Visegrad group and the Central European Initiative.

(See also NINETEEN EIGHTY-NINE; POST-COMMUNISM; SLOVAKIA.)

Carol S. Leff, *The Czech and Slovak Republics: Nation Versus State* (Boulder, Colo., 1997). Sharon Wolchik, "Czechoslovakia," in Sabrina P. Ramet, ed., *Eastern Europe: Politics, Culture, and Society since 1939* (Bloomington, Ind. 1998), pp. 35–70.

SHARON WOLCHIK

CZECHOSLOVAKIA. Czechoslovakia was created as an independent state in 1918. The new state brought together groups that differed from each other in many respects. In contrast to the other states in the region, in Czechoslovakia, democracy survived until it was ended by outside forces.

Sudeten German dissatisfaction provided the pretext for Hitler's occupation of Czechoslovakia after the Munich agreement of 1938. The creation of the Slovak state under Hitler's tutelage in March 1939 and the Soviet Union's annexation of Subcarpathian Ruthene completed Czechoslovakia's dismemberment.

After World War II, Edvard Bene returned from exile to serve as president. In February 1948, the Communist Party provoked a political crisis that led to the formation of a communist-dominated government. All political forces not under the control of the Communist Party were banned. Industry was nationalized and agriculture was collectivized. Central economic planning and censorship were instituted. As the Stalinist system was consolidated, the political system increasingly relied on coercion to keep the population in line.

In the 1960s, declining economic performance, a new wave of reform in the Soviet Union, and increasing Slovak dissatisfaction led to the effort to create "Socialism with a Human Face," or the *Prague Spring. Under Alexander Dubcek, the party leadership began a process of political reform. After the effective end of censorship in March 1968, citizens pressed for more dramatic changes.

On 21 August 1968 the *Warsaw Treaty Organization (Warsaw Pact) invaded Czechoslovakia. Led by Gustáv Husák, the Communist Party restored censorship and tight political control. In 1977, *Charter 77 was formed, and it served as a focus for independent activity.

Mikhail *Gorbachev's policies initially had little impact in Czechoslovakia. However, despite the surface stability, the country experienced increasingly serious political and economic problems. In the last two years of communist rule, there was a marked increase in dissent. There were also important changes in the leadership of the Party.

When hundreds of thousands of Czech and Slovak citizens took to the streets after the brutal beating of peaceful student demonstrators by police on 17 November 1989, the communist system fell very quickly. The Communist Party leadership resigned, and in December Václav *Havel, the moral leader of the "Velvet Revolution," was elected president.

The new government took immediate steps to re-create democratic political institutions. Free elections were held in June and November 1990.

Czech and Slovak leaders had different views concerning the proper role of the federal and republic governments and economic reform. Although citizens in both parts of the country opposed the breakup of the state, their leaders negotiated the end of the federation. In January 1993 the federation was replaced by two separate states, the Czech Republic and the Slovak Republic.

(See also CENTRAL EUROPE; NINETEEN EIGHTY-NINE; STALINISM.)

Timothy G. Ash, *The Magic Lantern: The Revolution of '89 Witnessed in Warsaw, Budapest, Berlin, and Prague* (New York, 1990). Sharon L. Wolchik, *Czechoslovakia in Transition: Politics, Society, and Economics* (London, 1991).

SHARON L. WOLCHIK

D

DE GAULLE, Charles. See GAULLE, CHARLES DE.

DEBT CRISIS. See INTERNATIONAL DEBT.

DECOLONIZATION. The term *decolonization* is commonly defined as a change in *sovereignty, in which a *state recognizes the independence of a segment of the people formerly under its rule and their right to a government formed according to procedures determined by them. A new state acting under its own volition, free from the direct control of foreign actors, comes into existence as a part of the international community. In this sense, the separation of India and Ireland from Britain; of Zaire from Belgium; of Indonesia from the Netherlands; of Bangladesh from Pakistan are clear-cut examples of decolonization.

The difficulty with such a definition comes from the ambiguity inherent in the concept of sovereignty. Simply because a country is nominally independent does not mean that it is immune to foreign influence—at times to such an extent that it is part of an informal empire. Thus, until recently the countries of Eastern and *Central Europe were treated as sovereign by the international community while in fact the policies of the governments there were determined in most important respects by Moscow. In this sense, the events of 1989–1990 constituted the "decolonization" of this region every bit as much as, say, the independence of Algeria from France in 1962 can be covered by the term. Similarly, the United States has long enjoyed enormous influence in Central America. Yet if El Salvador may today be treated as a sovereign state, in all probability its government could not last a month without the backing of Washington. In a world of states with grossly unequal amounts of power, what constitutes sovereignty? In the 1960s, an African leader such as Kwame *Nkrumah of Ghana talked of "neocolonialism" as if decolonization were a flag-and-anthem ceremony signifying nothing more than the replacement of white bourgeois rule by a black bourgeoisie dedicated to the continued exploitation of the people allegedly given their independence.

If we agree that the concept of sovereignty is inherently ambiguous, we may more easily see decolonization in a broader, if less precise, light and use the term to refer not only to the independence of peoples once under formal imperial control but also to the increased independence of peoples never subjected directly to such rule. We may then see decolonization as related to such significant developments as the Young Turk movement in the Ottoman Empire at the turn of this century, to the Mexican Revolution of 1910, and to the rise of *nationalism and *communism in China. From this perspective, decolonization refers to the general process of nationalist uprising against European (including Soviet), U.S., and Japanese imperialism since about 1880, of which the story of the formal decolonization of European empires in Africa and Asia after 1945 is but one chapter (although often the only history included under the term).

If the definition of decolonization is no easy task, the elucidation of the forces that have created this process is an even more daunting challenge. On the one hand, each case is individual with its own specific character; on the other hand, decolonization is just as clearly a global phenomenon, linked historically to the character of the international political and economic system since about 1880, when a new round of European *imperialism began. To see developments during this period as a series of discrete case studies, each isolated by its own individual characteristics, would be to ignore the powerful worldwide trends that have molded local forces in terms that have a general identity.

The juxtaposition of specific cases of decolonization with the general process bearing this name can perhaps best be made by seeing the global process largely in terms of the dynamics of imperialism while analyzing decolonization in more local terms. In this sense, the history of modern decolonization is inextricably linked to that of modern imperialism.

Decolonization obviously refers to the inability or unwillingness of the previously powerful to continue to exercise their imperial rule. On the one hand, the imperialists could weaken themselves as occurred in the two world wars, which weakened Britain, France, Belgium, and the Netherlands. The rise of the United States and the Soviet Union as two self-proclaimed anti-imperialist superpowers after 1945 noticeably accelerated the process of European decolonization. On the other, the subject or weaker peoples were not assimilated or destroyed, and over time they developed a political capacity to ward off the imperialists. In countries as diverse as India and Vietnam the decisive development was the organization of powerful nationalist political movements whose first aim was to secure the independence of their countries and their effective sovereignty in world affairs. In the case of the end of the Soviet empire, similar distinctions between internal and international developments must be appreciated.

The character of these nationalist movements varied widely in terms of local conditions. In India, a national bourgeoisie dominated the Congress Party, headed by *Gandhi and *Nehru. In Vietnam, *Ho Chi Minh's Communist Party led the nationalist struggle. In Algeria, dispossessed Muslim peasants organized the Front de Libération Nationale and attacked French rule. In *Poland, workers and intellectuals joined *Solidarity and pledged to remove the Soviet-controlled Polish Communist Party from rule in Warsaw. In much of sub-Saharan Africa, by contrast, the Europeans prepared to leave power before it was actually demanded by well-organized nationalist groups. It is thus not surprising that the character of the particular local groups that took power during the decolonization process explains a good measure of the different experiences previously colonized peoples have had since independence. Just as very distinct interests, *ideologies, and organizations constituted the various nationalist movements, so the new governments have quite unique identities. Nevertheless, decolonization remains a general historical process, in good measure because the fortunes of imperialism are the stuff of which global history is made.

Given the variety of forces contributing to decolonization it is evident why no single theory can hope to explain more than a part of what occurred. Thus, the particular character of British, and later U.S., *hegemony over the *international system since about 1815 was of great significance. Both countries based their influence on an opposition to formal imperialism (even if they both engaged in it extensively) and the doctrine of free trade. By the twentieth century, the Anglo-Americans had decided that democratic government was the only legitimate form of state and that the claim of nationalist movements for independence was morally irrefutable. In sum, the international system dominated by London or Washington was relatively favorable to the growth of local nationalisms. An order primarily controlled by Germany, Japan, or the Soviet Union would presumably have made for a very different set of forces acting on the weaker peoples of the globe.

The structure of international politics played its role as well. A multipolar world promoted a scramble for colonies in the late nineteenth century, much as the rise of a bipolar world after 1945 brought powerful influences to favor the decolonization of the West European empires thereafter.

Yet another force influencing the character of decolonization was socioeconomic change among the previously colonized peoples. Technological development in the economically weaker regions tended to create urban cultures, new bureaucracies, and higher levels of education in a way that stimulated the rise of new political demands on the parts of colonial subjects. New forms of political organization there created a heightened sense of place and person—so giving rise not only to nationalism but to a tangible ability to engage in political expression. Just as political, military, economic, and cultural factors gave rise to imperialism, so too did changes in these various dimensions of social life lead eventually to decolonization.

The paradox of decolonization is that it has occurred in a century marked by a growing interdependence of nations. The resolution of the paradox of simultaneously increasing interdependence and independence among peoples at the end of the twentieth century may perhaps be found in concepts of *political development. As specific local functions increase in activity—as economic productivity increases, or as previously separated class or ethnic groups are brought into closer political contact—so too does the need arise for governing mechanisms designed to promote coherence and alleviate conflict. In this sense the increasing self-consciousness of distinct peoples can be understood as part of the very process of their growing interdependence. A heightened localism and a greater feeling of internationalism are therefore not necessarily contradictory developments but aspects of economic, cultural, and political life that are the result of more than two hundred years of development, beginning in the latter half of the eighteenth century, with the Industrial Revolution in Britain and the rise of nationalism concurrent with the French Revolution. Thus the study of decolonization obliges us at one and the same time to respect the vigor of local political forces, yet not to lose sight of the global changes of which they are a part.

(See also COLONIAL EMPIRES; NINETEEN EIGHTY-NINE.)

Tony Smith, ed., *The End of European Empire: Decolonization after World War II* (Lexington, Mass., 1975). Tony Smith, *The Pattern of Imperialism: The United States, Great Britain and the Late-Industrializing World since 1815* (Cambridge, U.K., 1981). Rudolf von Albertini, *Decolonization: The Administration and Future of the Colonies, 1919–1960*, 2d ed. (New York, 1982). Miles Kahler, *Decolonization in Britain and France: The Domestic Consequences of International Relations* (Princeton, N.J., 1984). Brian Lapping, *End of Empire* (New York, 1985). Stephen D. Krasner, "Sovereignty: An Institutional Perspective," *Comparative Political Studies* 21, no. 1 (April 1988).

TONY SMITH

DEFENSE. See SECURITY.

DEINDUSTRIALIZATION. The term *deindustrialization* came into vogue in the 1980s, to describe the loss of relatively high-paying factory jobs in advanced industrial nations. From the onset, there was confusion about what was being claimed, and about the appropriate government policies for remedying the presumed problem. While the "deindustrializers" fretted over the loss of these jobs, their critics argued that advanced nations were not really "deindustrializing" at all, since manufacturing output in the 1980s was not substantially lower, as a percentage of GNP, than it had been in previous decades. The reason for the decline in manufacturing employment, they said, was that manufacturers had become so productive that they now needed fewer workers. The shift from manufacturing to services within all advanced economies was an inevitable stage of development, much like the shift in the previous century from agriculture to manufacturing. The "deindustrializers" responded that, such explanations notwithstanding, well-paying manufacturing jobs were being replaced by low-paying service jobs, with the result that the United States was losing its middle class.

Most researchers have come to agree that the middle class is shrinking in the United States, although there is no consensus that "deindustrialization" is the culprit. Controlling for family size, geography, and other changes, the average income of the poorest fifth in the United States declined between 1977 and 1990 by about 9 percent, while the richest fifth became about 19 percent wealthier. That left the poorest fifth with 3.7 percent of the nation's total income in 1990, down from 5.5 percent twenty years before—the lowest portion they had received since 1954; and it left the richest fifth with a bit over half the nation's income—the highest portion ever recorded by the top 20 percent. The top 5 percent commanded 26 percent of the nation's income, another record. Some researchers, selecting different years and using different measurements, have found the divergence to be somewhat less pronounced than this, but they note the same trend.

Proposals for what to do about this widening gap are related to its presumed cause. The "deindustrializers" seek measures to preserve, protect, subsidize, or otherwise encourage the creation of well-paying manufacturing jobs that would supposedly restore middle-class incomes. Their critics—who attribute the divergence in incomes to factors such as the growth in single-parent, lower-income families, or the influx of young, unskilled, and inexperienced baby boomers and women into the work force—argue that such measures would be pointless. To the extent that the "deindustrializers" want to protect U.S. manufacturing jobs against foreign competition, moreover, critics contend that others would bear the burden of paying substantially higher prices for the goods they purchased, and that such policies also would invite foreign nations to bar American-made goods, resulting in losses for everyone.

The argument will continue to rage, but there is mounting evidence that the widening income gap is more related to changes in the global demand for labor than to changes in U.S. labor supply. Increases in the number of single-parent families, and in the number of baby-boomer and women job entrants, actually slowed after the late 1970s, just as the income gap in the United States began to widen precipitously. Moreover, other nations have experienced similarly diverging incomes, even without these demographic changes. This is not to suggest that the "deindustrializers" are entirely correct in attributing the widening gap to the loss of good manufacturing jobs, however. Other, broader trends are at work, involving services as well as manufacturing.

What has happened, it seems, is that national economies have become so integrated into a single global economy that labor supply and demand now operate worldwide. Highly skilled and talented workers in economically advanced nations confront an ever-larger world market for their services; thus the earnings of software engineers, lawyers, investment bankers, architects, management consultants, movie producers, and other professionals are on the rise. At the other extreme, unskilled workers—whether in traditional manufacturing industries or in services that are traded internationally, such as data processing—find themselves competing with a growing number of unskilled workers around the world, many of whom are eager to work for a fraction of the wages of unskilled workers in advanced nations. Thus are relatively unskilled workers in advanced industrial countries pushed into local service occupations where they must compete with labor-saving machinery, immigrants, and all the other unskilled workers who can no longer compete internationally. Their earnings are thus stagnating or declining.

The consequences for public policy are profound. The United States and other nations face three policy choices. They can attempt to preserve or protect older manufacturing jobs, or, alternatively, they can abdicate all responsibility to the magic of the global marketplace. Finally, industrialized nations may seek to enhance the capacities of their citizens to add value to the global economy, and thus command a higher standard of living from the world. Toward this end, they would increase expenditures on education, training, and infrastructure (roads, bridges, airports, and other forms of public capital), and on subsidies to global corporations that provide on-the-job training in advanced technologies.

(See also DEVELOPMENT AND UNDERDEVELOPMENT; FOREIGN WORKERS; FORDISM; POLITICAL ECONOMY; POSTINDUSTRIAL SOCIETY.)

Barry Bluestone and Bennett Harrison, *The Deindustrialization of America* (New York, 1982). Robert Z. Lawrence, *Can America Compete?* (Washington, D.C., 1984). Robert B. Reich, *The Work of Nations* (New York, 1991).

ROBERT B. REICH

DEMOCRACY. See overleaf.

DEMOCRACY, THE LIMITS OF LIBERAL. See page 201.

DEMOCRATIC TRANSITIONS. The democratic transitions of the 1980s replicated processes that had occurred in more isolated fashion in earlier decades. Indeed, Dankwart Rustow's seminal 1970 article "Transitions to Democracy: Towards a Dynamic Model" was published at a time when the predominant trend in the Third World was toward apparently entrenched forms of authoritarian rule: conservative military dictatorships in Latin America; one-party states often clothed with vaguely socialist rhetoric in most of Africa and parts of the Middle East; and *national liberation movements of communist inspiration in Southeast Asia. Rustow had worked on Turkey and Japan, and also drew on European experiences, and he broke with an earlier tradition that had explained the rise of democracy largely as a function of certain "social correlates" of *modernization—*urbanization, the spread of literacy, etc. Instead he directed attention toward the political conflicts and dynamic interactions through which a democratic compromise (or "pact") might emerge, and he suggested that democracies not forged in conflict might prove ephemeral. The essential insight of the "dynamic model" was that the conditions that precipitate a regime change are different from, and even contrast with, those strengthening the subsequent regime. Within this basic framework, a democratic transition begins when the outgoing authoritarian regime can no longer assure its continuity and ends when the incoming democratic regime has become securely established. During the intervening period of "transition" old political forces reemerge and new ones are constituted in a climate of uncertainty about their relative strengths and purposes. During a short period of intense political activity agreements are negotiated on the procedures that will govern competition for public office under the future democratic regime. The start and end points of a transition may be signaled by some highly visible watershed event, such as (1) the death or flight of a dictator, or the return of the military to their barracks, and (2) the holding of a "foundational" election, or the promulgation of a new constitution. In practice, however, not all democratizations have contained such unambiguous markers of the "transition" phase.

This perspective proved fruitful when interpreting the subsequent emergence and consolidation of democratic regimes in southern Europe—in Greece and Portugal in 1974, and in Spain two years later. All these three authoritarian regimes were the product of intense social and ideological conflict,

(cont. on p. 208)

DEMOCRACY. Recently, democracy seems to have scored a historic victory over alternative forms of governance. Nearly everyone today, whether of the *Left, Center, or *Right, claims adherence to democratic principles. Political regimes of all kinds throughout the world style themselves democracies—albeit that there may be vast differences between statement and execution. Democracy seems to bestow an aura of *legitimacy on modern political life: rules, laws, policies, and decisions appear justified when they are "democratic." This was not always so. The great majority of political thinkers from ancient Greece to the present day have been highly critical of the theory and practice of democracy. A uniform commitment to democracy is a very recent phenomenon.

The record contains little about democracy from ancient Greece to eighteenth-century Europe and North America. The widespread turn to democracy as a suitable form for organizing political life is less than a hundred years old. In addition, while many states today may be democratic, the history of their political institutions reveals the fragility and vulnerability of democratic arrangements. The remarkable difficulty of creating and sustaining democratic forms is illustrated by the flowering of Fascism and Nazism in twentieth-century Western Europe. Democracy has evolved in intensive social struggles and is frequently sacrificed in such struggles. This brief essay is about the idea of democracy, but in exploring the idea one cannot escape aspects of its history in theory and in practice. It will be evident that the concept of democracy and the nature of democratic arrangements are a fundamentally contested terrain.

The word "democracy" entered English in the sixteenth century from the French *démocratie*; the word is Greek in origin, having been derived from *dēmokratia*, the root meanings of which are *dēmos* (people) and *kratos* (rule). Democracy refers to a form of government in which, in contradistinction to monarchies and aristocracies, the people rule. It entails a state in which there is some form of political equality among the people. But to recognize this is not yet to say very much. For not only is the history of the idea of democracy marked by conflicting interpretations, but Greek, Roman, and Renaissance notions, among others, intermingle to produce ambiguous and inconsistent accounts of the key terms of democracy today: the nature of "rule," the connotation of "rule by," and the meaning of "the people."

Among the questions that require examination are: Who are "the people"? What constitutes a "people" entitled to rule themselves? What kind of participation is envisaged for them? How broadly or narrowly is the scope of rule to be construed? Is democracy a set of political institutions or a process? How does the size of a political community affect the nature and dynamics of democracy? Must the rules of "the people" be obeyed? What is the place of obligation and dissent? Under what circumstances, if any, are democracies entitled to resort to coercion of an element of "the people" or of those outside the sphere of legitimate rule?

Within the history of the clash of interpretations about these and related questions lies a deeply rooted struggle to determine whether democracy will mean some kind of popular *power (a form of life in which citizens are engaged in self-government and self-regulation) or an aid to decision making (a means to legitimate decisions of those voted into power from time to time). This basic struggle has given rise to three basic variants or models of democracy. First, there is direct or participatory democracy, a system of decision making about public affairs in which citizens are directly involved. This was the original type of democracy found in ancient Athens, among other places. Second, there is liberal or representative democracy, a system of rule embracing elected officers who undertake to represent the interests or views of citizens within the framework of the rule of law. Representative democracy means that decisions affecting a community are taken not by its members as a whole but by a group of people whom "the people" have elected for this purpose. In the arena of national politics, representative democracy takes the form of elections to congresses, parliaments, or similar national bodies and is associated with the system of government in countries as far afield as the United States, Britain, Germany, Japan, Australia, South Africa, Costa Rica, Senegal, and elsewhere. Third, there is a variant of democracy based on a one-party model (although some may doubt whether this is a form of democracy at all). Until recently, the Soviet Union, many East European societies, and some developing countries have been heavily influenced by this conception. The principle underlying one-party democracy is that a single party can be the legitimate expression of the overall will of the community. Voters choose among different candidates, putatively proposing divergent policies within an overall framework, not among different parties. The following expands on each of these models in turn. In the fifth century B.C.E., Athens emerged as the preeminent city-state, or *polis*, among many rival Greek powers; the development of democracy in Athens has been taken as a fundamental source of inspiration for modern Western political thought. The political ideals of Athens—equality among citizens, liberty, respect for the law, and justice—have shaped political thinking through the ages, although there are some central ideas (for instance, the modern liberal notion that human beings are individuals with rights) that notably cannot be traced directly to ancient thought.

The Athenian city-state did not differentiate between state and society, ruled as it was by citizen-governors. In ancient Athens citizens were at one and the same time subjects of state authority and the creators of public rules and regulations. The people (*dēmos*) engaged in legislative and judicial functions, for the Athenian concept of *citizenship entailed sharing in these functions, participating directly in the affairs of the state. Athenian democracy required a general commitment to the principle of civic virtue: dedication to the republican city-state and the subordination of private life to public affairs and the common good. The public and the private were intertwined. Citizens could only properly fulfill themselves and live honorably in and through the *polis*. Of course, who was to count as a citizen was a tightly restricted matter. Those who were excluded included women and a substantial slave population.

The Athenian city-state—eclipsed ultimately by the rise of empires, stronger states, and military regimes—shared features with republican Rome. Both were predominantly face-to-face societies, oral cultures, and both had elements of popular participation in governmental affairs and little, if any, centralized bureaucratic control. Both sought to foster a deep sense of public duty, a tradition of civic virtue or responsibility to the republic—to the distinctive matters of the public realm. In both polities, the claims of the state were given a unique priority over those of the individual citizen. However, if Athens was a democratic republic, contemporary scholarship generally affirms that Rome was by comparison an essentially oligarchic system. Despite this, it was Rome which, from antiquity, was to prove the most durable influence on the dissemination of notions of "active citizenship."

The meaning of the concept of "active citizenship in a republic" became a leading concern in the early Renaissance, especially in the city-states of Italy. Political thinkers of this period were critical of the Athenian formulation of this idea; shaped as their views were by Aristotle, one of the leading critics of Greek democracy, and by the centuries-long impact of republican Rome, they recast the classical republican tradition. While the concept of the *polis* remained central to the political theory of Italian cities, most notably in Florence, it was no longer regarded as a means to self-fulfillment. Emphasis continued to be placed on the importance of civic virtue but the latter was understood as highly fragile, subject particularly to corruption if dependent solely upon the political involvement of any one major grouping: the people, the aristocracy, or the monarchy. A constitution which could reflect and balance the interests of all leading political factions became an aspiration.

The core of the Renaissance political argument was that the freedom of a political community rested upon its accountability to no authority other than that of the community itself. Self-government is the basis of liberty, together with the right of citizens to participate—within a constitutional framework which creates distinct roles for leading social forces—in the government of their own common business. Freedom consists above all in the unhindered pursuit by citizens of their self-chosen ends. The highest political ideal is the civic freedom of an independent, self-governing republic.

In Renaissance republicanism, as well as in Greek democratic thought, a citizen was someone who participated in "giving judgment and holding office." Citizenship meant participation in public affairs. This definition is noteworthy because it suggests that theorists within these traditions would have found it hard to locate citizens in modern democracies, except perhaps as representatives or office holders. The limited scope in contemporary politics for the active involvement of citizens would have been regarded as most undemocratic. Yet the idea that human beings should be active citizens of a political order—citizens of their states—and not merely dutiful subjects of a ruler has had few advocates from the earliest human associations to the early Renaissance.

The eclipse in the West of the idea of the engaged citizen, one whose very being is affirmed in and through political action, is hard to explain fully. But it is clear enough that the antithesis of *Homo politicus* is the *Homo credens* of the Christian faith: the citizen who exercised active judgment was displaced by the true believer. Although it would be quite misleading to suggest that the rise of Christianity effectively banished secular considerations from the lives of rulers and ruled, it unquestionably shifted the source of authority and wisdom from this-worldly to otherworldly representatives. The Christian worldview transformed the rationale of political action from that of the *polis* or empire to a theological framework—to a preoccupation with how humans could live in communion with God. The Christian worldview insisted that the good lay in submission to God's will.

During the Middle Ages the integration of Christian Europe from the Eastern Atlantic seaboard to the Balkans came to depend on two theocratic authorities above all: the *Roman Catholic Church and the Holy Roman Empire. The entire fabric of medieval thought had to be challenged before the idea of democracy could reemerge. Not until the end of the sixteenth century did the nature and limits of political authority, law, *rights, and obedience become a preoccupation, from Italy to England, of European political thought. The Protestant Reformation, the most significant of all the developments that triggered new ways of thinking about political authority, did more than just challenge papal jurisdiction and authority across Europe; it raised the starkest questions about political obligation and obedience. Whether allegiance was owed to the Catholic Church, a Protestant ruler, or particular religious sects was not an issue easily resolved. The bitter struggles that spread across Europe during the last half of the sixteenth century, culminating in the Thirty Years' War in Germany, testified to the increasing divisiveness of religious belief. Competing religions, all seeking to secure for themselves the kinds of privileges claimed by the medieval church, had engendered a political crisis whose only solution would be to disconnect the powers of the *state from the duty of rulers to uphold a particular faith.

The impetus to reexamine the nature of the relationship between society and state was given added force by a growing awareness in Europe of the variety of possible social and political arrangements that followed in the wake of the discovery of the non-European world. The relationship between Europe and the "New World" and the nature of the rights (if any) of non-Europeans became a major focus of discussion. It sharpened the sense of a plurality of possible interpretations of political life. The direction these interpretations took was, of course, directly related to the context and traditions of particular countries: the changing nature of politics was experienced differently throughout the early modern period. But it is hard to overestimate the significance of the events and processes that ushered in a new era of political reflection, marked as it was by such dramatic occurrences as the English Revolution (1640–1688), the American Declaration of Independence (1776), and the French Revolution (1789).

Modern liberal and liberal democratic theory has constantly sought to justify the sovereign power of the state while at the same time justifying limits on that power. The history of this attempt since Thomas Hobbes (1588–1679) is the history of arguments to balance might and right, power and law, duties and rights. On the one hand, states must have a monopoly of coercive power in order to provide a secure basis on which trade, commerce, and family life can prosper. On the other hand, by granting the state a regulatory and coercive capability, political theorists were aware that they had accepted a force that could, and frequently did, deprive citizens of political and social freedoms.

Liberal democrats provided the key institutional innovation to try to overcome this dilemma—representative democracy. The liberal concern with reason, law, and freedom of choice could be upheld properly only by recognizing the political equality of all mature individuals. Such equality would ensure not only a secure social environment in which people would be free to pursue their private activities and interests, but also that the state would do what was best in the general and public interest—for example, pursue the greatest satisfaction of the greatest number. Thus, liberal democrats argued that the democratic constitutional state, linked to other key institutional mechanisms, above all the free market, resolved the problems of ensuring both authority and liberty.

Two classical statements of the new position can be found in the philosophy of James Madison (1751–1836) and in the works of two of the key figures of nineteenth-century English *liberalism: Jeremy Bentham (1748–1832) and James Mill (1773–1836). In their hands the theory of liberal democracy

received a most important elaboration: the governors must be held accountable to the governed through political mechanisms (the secret ballot, regular voting, competition between potential representatives, the struggle among factions) that alone can give citizens satisfactory means to choose, authorize, and control political decisions. And by these means, it was further contended, a balance could finally be obtained between might and right, authority and liberty. But who exactly was to count as a "citizen" or an "individual," and what his or her exact role was to be, remained either unclear or unsettled. Even in the work of James Mill's radical son, John Stuart Mill (1806–1873), ambiguities remained: the idea that all citizens should have equal weight in the political system remained outside his actual doctrine.

It was left by and large to the extensive and often violently repressed struggles of working-class, feminist, and radical activists in the nineteenth and twentieth centuries to achieve in some countries a genuinely universal suffrage. This achievement was to remain fragile in countries such as Germany, Italy, and Spain, and was in practice denied to some groups—for instance, many African Americans in the United States before the *civil rights movement in the 1950s and 1960s. Through these struggles the idea that citizenship rights should apply to all adults became slowly established; many of the arguments of the liberal democrats could be turned against existing institutions to reveal the extent to which the principle and aspirations of equal *political participation and equal human development remained unfulfilled. It was only with the actual achievement of citizenship for all adult men and women that liberal democracy took on its distinctively contemporary form: a cluster of rules permitting the broadest participation of the majority of citizens in the selection of representatives who alone can make political decisions (i.e., decisions affecting the whole of society).

The idea of democracy remains complex and contested. The liberal democratic tradition itself comprises a heterogeneous body of thought. However, the entire liberal democratic tradition stands apart from an alternative perspective—the theory of single-party democracy. It is worth saying something more about this, because it is associated with one of the key counterpoints to liberal democracy—the Marxist tradition.

The struggle of liberalism against tyranny and the struggle by liberal democrats for political equality represented, according to Karl *Marx (1818–1883) and Friedrich Engels (1820–1895), a major step forward in the history of human emancipation. But for them, and for the Marxist tradition more broadly, the great universal ideals of "liberty, equality and justice" could not be realized simply by the "free" struggle for votes in the political system and by the "free" struggle for profit in the marketplace. Advocates of the democratic state and the market economy present them as the only institutions under which liberty can be sustained and inequalities minimized. However, the Marxist critique suggests that, by virtue of its internal dynamics, the capitalist economy inevitably produces systematic inequality and massive restrictions on real freedom. Although each step toward formal political equality is an advance, its liberating potential is severely curtailed by inequalities of class.

In class societies the state cannot become the vehicle for the pursuit of the common good or public interest. Far from playing the role of emancipator, protective knight, umpire, or judge in the face of disorder, the agencies of the liberal representative state are meshed in the struggles of civil society. Marxists conceive of the state as an extension of civil society, reinforcing the social order for the enhancement of particular interests—in capitalist society, the long-run interests of the capitalist class. Marx and Engels contended that political emancipation is only a step toward human emancipation, that is, the complete democratization of society as well as the state. In their view, liberal democratic society fails when judged by its own principles—and to take these principles seriously is to become a communist.

Marx himself envisaged the replacement of the "machinery" of the liberal democratic state by a "commune structure": the smallest communities, which were to administer their own affairs, would elect delegates to larger administrative units (districts, towns); these in turn would elect candidates to still-larger areas of administration (the national delegation). This arrangement is known as the "pyramid" structure of direct democracy: all delegates are revocable, bound by the instructions of their constituency, and organized into a pyramid of directly elected committees. In the Marxist-Leninist model, this system of delegation is, in principle, complemented by a separate, but somewhat similar, system at the levels of the Communist Party. In practice, however, complementarity has meant party domination. It was only during the *Gorbachev era that a pyramid of councils, or soviets, from the central authority to those at local village and neighborhood level, were given anything more than a symbolic or ritualistic role.

What should be made of these various models of democracy today? The classical Athenian model, which developed in a tightly knit community, cannot be adapted to stretch across space and time. Its emergence in the context of city-states and under conditions of social exclusivity (no female participation, a slave economy, many other marginalized groups) was integral to its successful development. In contemporary circumstances, marked by a high degree of social, economic, and political differentiation, it is very hard to envisage how a democracy of this kind could succeed without drastic modification. The significance of these reflections is reinforced by examining the fate of the model of democracy

advocated by Marx, Engels, and their followers. The suitability of their model as an institutional arrangement that allows for mediation, negotiation, and compromise among struggling factions, groups, or movements does not stand up well under scrutiny, especially in its Marxist-Leninist variant. A system of institutions to promote discussion, debate, and competition among divergent views—a system encompassing the formation of movements, pressure groups, and/or political parties with leaderships to help press their cases—appears both necessary and desirable. Further, the political events in Central and Eastern Europe beginning in *1989 seem to provide remarkable confirmatory evidence of this.

Inevitably, then, one must recognize the importance of a number of fundamental liberal tenets concerning the centrality, in principle, of an impersonal structure of public power; of a constitution to help guarantee and protect rights; of a diversity of power centers within and outside the state; and of mechanisms to promote competition and debate among alternative political platforms. What this amounts to, among other things, is confirmation of the fundamental liberal notion that the separation of state from civil society must be an essential feature of any democratic political order. Conceptions of democracy that depend on the assumption that the state could ever replace civil society, or vice versa, must be treated with the utmost caution.

However, to make these points is not to affirm any one liberal democratic model as it stands. It is one thing to accept the arguments concerning the necessary protective, conflict-mediating, and redistributive functions of the democratic state; quite another to accept these as prescribed in the model of liberal democracy from Madison or Bentham onward. Advocates of liberal democracy have tended to be concerned, above all else, with the proper principles and procedures of democratic government. By focusing on government, they have deflected attention from a thorough examination of issues such as: formal rights vs. actual rights; commitments to treat citizens as free and equal vs. disparities of treatment in practice; concepts of the state as, in principle, an independent authority vs. involvements of the state in the reproduction of the inequalities of everyday life; notions of political parties as appropriate structures for bridging the gap between state and society vs. the array of power centers that are beyond reach of parties.

The implications of these points are profound. For democracy to flourish today it has to be reconceived as a double-sided phenomenon concerned, on the one hand, with the *reform of state power and, on the other hand, with the restructuring of civil society. This entails recognizing the indispensability of a process of "double democratization": the interdependent transformation of both state and civil society. Such a process must be premised on the acceptance of the principle that the division between state and civil society must be a central feature of democratic life, and on the notion that the power to make public decisions must be free of the illegitimate constraints imposed by the private flows of capital, as Marx foresaw. But, of course, to recognize the importance of both these points is to recognize the necessity of recasting substantially their traditional connotation.

If this leaves many questions open, it should not come as a surprise. The history of democratic theory and practice is coterminous with conflicts of interpretation and struggles for position—and this state of affairs is inevitable when politics is free of the constraints of authoritarianism in all its forms. Democratic politics is bound to the terrain of dispute and contestation. Democracy is an ingenious political arrangement for the articulation, expression, and mediation of difference. It is a testimony to the idea of democracy itself that the battle over its constitutive elements will, in all likelihood, continue.

One area where the battle will continue connects the idea of democracy to the larger framework of international affairs. The modern theory of the democratic state presupposes the idea of a "national community of fate"—a community that rightly governs itself and determines its own future. But national communities by no means exclusively program the actions, decisions, and policies of their governments, and governments by no means determine what is right or appropriate for their own citizens. For example, a decision to build a nuclear plant near the borders of a neighboring country is likely to be a decision taken without consulting those in the nearby country (or countries). Or the decision to permit the building of a chemical factory making toxic or other noxious substances may contribute to ecological damage which does not acknowledge national boundaries or frontiers. In a world of global interconnectedness—mediated by modern communication systems and information technology—there are pressing questions about the very future and viability of national democracies. Regional and global interconnectedness contests the traditional national resolutions of the key questions of democratic theory and practice.

Therefore, one ought not to be perplexed by increasing demands for, and attempts to realize, the extension of democratic forms and processes across territorial borders. Such a policy of democratization might begin, for example, in regions such as Europe—which recognizes the need for new, transnational collaborative institutions—by creating greater transparency in the key decision-making centers of the European Union and reducing the democratic deficit across all its major political bodies. Elsewhere it would entail restructuring the UN Security Council to give developing countries a significant voice in decision making; deepening the mechanisms of accountability of the leading international and transnational economic agencies; strengthening the enforcement capacity of *human rights regimes (socioeconomic as well as political); and creating, in due course, a new democratic UN second chamber. Such objectives point the way toward laying the foundations for forms of accountability at regional and global levels.

A political program of this type embodies elements of what I call a cosmopolitan conception of democracy. Faced with overlapping communities of fate—with, that is, a world in which the fortunes of individual political communities are increasingly bound together—citizens in the future will need to be citizens not only of their own communities, but also of the regions in which they live, and of the wider global order. They must be able to participate in diverse political communities—from cities and subnational regions to nation-states, regions, and wider global networks. It is clear that a process of disconnecting legitimate political authority from states and fixed borders has already begun as legitimate forms of governance are diffused "below," "above," and "alongside" the nation-state. But the cosmopolitan project is in favor of a radical extension of this process so long as it is circumscribed by a far-reaching commitment to democratic rights and duties.

Although the history and practice of democracy has been focused up until now on the idea of a specific locality (the city-state, the community, the nation-state), it is likely that in the future it will be centered on the international or global domain as well. There are no immediate solutions to the problems posed by global interconnectedness and its complex and often profoundly uneven effects—yet an important series of questions inescapably must be addressed. Certainly, one can find many good reasons for being optimistic about finding a path forward, and many good reasons for thinking that at this juncture democracy will face another critical test.

(See also CIVIL SOCIETY; CLASS AND POLITICS; COMMUNITARIANISM; CONSOCIATIONAL DEMOCRACY; INDUSTRIAL DEMOCRACY; INEQUALITIES; MARXISM; NINETEEN EIGHTY-NINE; PLURALISM; POLITICAL PARTIES AND PARTY COMPETITION; SOCIALISM AND SOCIAL DEMOCRACY.)

John Stuart Mill, *Considerations on Representative Government* (London, 1951). Karl Marx, *The Civil War in France* (Peking, 1970). John Pocock, *The Machiavellian Moment* (Princeton, N.J., 1975). Joseph A. Schumpeter, *Capitalism, Socialism and Democracy* (London, 1976). Aristotle, *The Politics* (Harmondsworth, U.K., 1981). Moses I. Finley, *Politics in the Ancient World* (Cambridge, U.K., 1983). John Keane, *Democracy and Civil Society* (London, 1988). Robert A. Dahl, *Democracy and Its Critics* (New Haven, Conn., 1989). Quentin Skinner, "The State," in Terence Ball, James Farr, and Russell L. Hanson, eds., *Political Innovation and Conceptional Change* (Cambridge, U.K., 1989). Patricia Springborg, *Western Republicanism and the Oriental Prince* (Cambridge, U.K., 1991). David Held, *Democracy and the Global Order* (Cambridge, U.K., 1995). David Held, *Models of Democracy*, 2d ed. (Cambridge, U.K., 1996).

DAVID HELD

THE LIMITS OF LIBERAL DEMOCRACY. In my book *The End of History and the Last Man* (1992), I argued that at the end of the twentieth century, there was no systematic alternative to liberal *democracy and a market-oriented economic system as the political and economic foundations for any economically advanced society. In order to defend this proposition, I need first to define what these terms mean, and what would constitute a systematic alternative.

A democracy is a regime based on the principle of popular *sovereignty, usually institutionalized through periodic, multiparty elections. A liberal regime is one in which a certain sphere of individual *rights are protected from the power of the *state—including the power of democratic majorities—through a rule of law. In a market-oriented economic system, the state protects private property rights, and provides primarily those public goods like defense, education, and certain welfare services that private markets cannot supply on their own. It is possible to have liberalism without democracy, as in the case of Wilhelmine Germany or *Hong Kong under British rule; it is possible to have democracy without liberalism, as in the case of *Iran under the ayatollahs; and it is possible to have a market-oriented economic system without either democracy or liberalism, as in the case of *Taiwan and the Republic of Korea (South Korea) in the early postwar period. The capitalist liberal democracy (which I will henceforth abbreviate CLD) that emerges at the "end of history" constitutes the union of all three—democracy, liberalism, and market economy—in a set of interlocking institutions.

It is important to note that this definition permits considerable variation in the specific ways in which these institutions are implemented, and specifically in the tradeoff that societies make between the twin governing principles of liberty and equality. All contemporary CLDs, for example, have *welfare states of varying size. These range, at the bottom end, from South Korea, which offers relatively modest social protections, to *Switzerland, the *United States, and *Japan, which cycle perhaps 40–45 percent of their GDPs through the state, to Scandinavian countries like *Sweden in which the state sector consumes upwards of 70 percent of GDP. Social protection can take many forms; Japan, for example, transfers relatively little income through welfare programs, but nonetheless provides protections for the livelihoods of lower-income people through an elaborate system of economic regulation. The United States, while famous for having a smaller and more recent welfare state than its European counterparts (it is the only country in this group lacking, for example, a comprehensive state-funded health-care system), nonetheless has a more progressive tax system. All of these countries, from Korea to Sweden, constitute CLDs. To argue for a systematic alternative requires the abolition of one of the three institutional pillars: the replacing of popular sovereignty with some other non-democratic principle of legitimate authority; the suspension of the core set of individual rights; or extremely severe constraints on the private ownership of property.

Why Capitalist Liberal Democracy? CLDs formally recognize the rights of individuals to own property, to speak, associate, practice religion, and finally to participate in the political process on an equal basis. The philosophical basis for this recognition of equal rights can be based, as in the contemporary libertarian thought of people like James Buchanan or Robert Nozick, on the sovereignty of individual preferences. Or it can based, as in the German idealist tradition, on the equal dignity of all human beings as moral agents. The sphere of equal recognition has grown over time; initially limited in many early CLDs to male property-owning members of the dominant ethnic or racial group, it has expanded over time to include all adult citizens.

While contemporary CLDs maintain welfare states of varying sizes to protect their citizens from certain social ills and to equalize incomes somewhat, they guarantee equality of opportunity and not substantive equality of outcomes, particularly with respect to economic status. There are several justifications for a system of limited government in which the state focuses more on equality of opportunity than equality of outcome, or on freedom over equality.

The first is undoubtedly economic. Liberal capitalist states, whether democratic or not, have compiled impressive records of long-term economic performance over those of the Right or Left in which governments have intervened heavily in economic matters, either to control commerce for national prestige or to promote social equality. The edifice of modern neoclassical economics has shown both theoretically and empirically why markets are more efficient allocators of resources than states in the case of private goods lacking significant externalities. Half a century ago, Ludwig von Mises and Friedrich Hayek suggested that the key failing of *command economies was their inability to deal with information, due to the local and tacit nature of much knowledge. This analysis has been amply borne out in the experience of real-world socialist economies. Moreover, it is likely that the advantages accruing to economies permitting a high degree of decentralized economic decision making increase over time as the complexity and technological intensity of economic life increases. Socialist states could plausibly organize industrial-era economic life; post-industrial or information societies, on the other hand, involve levels of complexity an order of magnitude or two higher, in which local knowledge dominates and where unintended consequences constantly emerge in ways that escape the ability of large, slow-moving state bureaucracies to anticipate.

A second critical advantage of a system of limited government with a secure rule of law is that it fosters generalized social trust and a self-organizing *civil society. Many highly centralized states from Imperial China to France and southern Italy have encouraged dependence on hierarchical sources of authority and a retreat into familism as a safe haven from predatory and capricious governments. This cultural pattern, once established, is very hard to eradicate and becomes a source of considerable political and social dysfunction over time.

The Critique from the Left. The chief accusation laid at the doorstep of CLD has been the economic and social inequality that it fosters or, more properly, fails to prevent. The workings of competitive markets necessarily create winners and losers; through no fault of their own, workers can lose their livelihoods because of a manager's poor investment decision, or because a commodity price drops in a distant market. *Globalization has added a new set of criticisms and sense of urgency to this classical critique from the Left: the ever-increasing mobility of capital compared to labor has had the effect of driving down wages worldwide. Low-skilled workers in the developed world have either seen their incomes fall, as in the United States, or else have become unemployed wards of the welfare state, as in Europe. This system might be justified if globalization led to development, but the financial crisis that developed in Asia, Russia, and other parts of the developing world in the late 1990s shows that the new global economy is dangerously unstable and in the long run an obstacle to development. Finally, it is argued that the global economy is profoundly undemocratic; in countries from Sweden to South Korea, social policies are designed not by democratic electorates but by faceless bureaucrats at the *International Monetary Fund or by an equally impersonal bond market.

There are several ways of answering these charges. Income inequality in the First World is a problem only from a national perspective. Every job destroyed in a developed country as a result of globalization reappears as several jobs in a *Third World nation, where workers in places like *Malaysia, *India, or *Vietnam are for the first time being given the opportunity to join the modern world. While it is true that they do not enjoy the same wages or social protections as workers in the First World, poor countries—whose chief comparative advantage is often their low labor costs—need to grow first before they can expand the kinds of social and environmental protections offered by rich ones. Jobs destroyed by the relentless advance of technology (a more important source of inequality than globalization for a country like the United States) show up as benefits to consumers in the form of lower prices, higher quality products, or increased opportunities for communications, leisure, and the like. Finally, it is by no means clear that the instability of the global economy that emerged at the end of the 1990s cannot be corrected through a variety of policy adjustments, such as a slowing down of the velocity of short-term capital flows. The Asian crisis of 1997–1998 was a setback, but did not erase the impressive record of closing the gap between Third and First World status for many of the region's countries within less than two generations.

Moreover, while economic inequality has been increasing in many developed countries, the nature of this inequality has been changing. As equality of opportunity and competition spread, inequality tends to be based less on ascriptive characteristics like inherited social class than on unequally distributed natural cognitive abilities or cultural and *social capital. A certain degree of economic inequality is related to differences in earnings over life cycles that are growing increasingly long. And inequality is greatly mitigated by social mobility, which remains high for relatively unequal societies like the United States, where a poor immigrant may easily see his children attend college.

A final defense of inequality in CLDs is prudential. While it is perfectly legitimate for states to seek to mitigate inequality through welfare policies, there is no known political or social model that can achieve full substantive equality at a tolerable political price, or without engendering unanticipated consequences that are much worse than the inequality that such policy sought to remedy in the first place. Social, ethnic, racial, and other groups vary tremendously with regard to cultural and social characteristics that determine their ultimate socioeconomic status, and their behavior cannot be easily manipulated by states. Simply transferring resources from one part of society to another does not engender self-sufficiency or dignity; indeed, it often creates moral hazard by encouraging the very behavior it was meant to ameliorate. The use of political power to correct economic inequalities in a democracy frequently opens the door to rent-seeking on the part of middle-class interest groups and voters who predominate in any democracy, and who tend to transfer resources from both the rich and poor to themselves. And in the extreme form of totalitarian dictatorship, the passion for equality has led to unspeakable crimes.

The Critique from the Right. There are two sorts of critiques of CLD that emanate from the Right. The first, a kinder, gentler version, is a communitarian one arguing that CLD tends to undermine itself by consuming the very cultural and social capital on which it is based. That is, CLD is based on a principle of individualism, formal law, and an agreement to keep the political and moral/religious communities separate. Over time, individualism undermines not only stifling social traditions inherited from the past, but also the social cohesion necessary to the functioning of any society. The Enlightenment sought to liberate human beings from the prejudice and orthodoxy of hierarchical religion; by this view, religion and cultural tradition continue to be necessary to support social order but are corroded by modern individualism.

The second, tougher critique was articulated most fully by Friedrich Nietzsche. Human beings, by his account, are born unequal with respect to talents and ambition, and moreover are made happy by hierarchy rather than equality; CLD commits a tremendous injustice by treating them as if they were equal. The bourgeois, egalitarian culture fostered by CLD produces conformity, mediocrity, and a narrowing of the horizons for ambition and greatness that was fostered by societies built on explicitly aristocratic principles. On this issue, the Left and Right sometimes join hands: both attack CLD for being philistine. Moral greatness, courage, artistic vision, and similar virtues are devalued in a commercial society that sees material wealth as the manifestation of success.

It is not clear that there is a full answer to either of these charges. But to the communitarian charge, one can argue that no real-world contemporary CLD has ever been devoid of culture; all have found ways of reconciling formal liberal rights with a preexisting set of cultural traditions, including religious ones. While there is a tension between the two, democracies have hardly collapsed in on themselves in the more than two hundred years since the American and French Revolutions. To the Nietzschean charge that CLD becomes the home for the Last Man, one can make a prudential argument that does not require us to endorse Nietzsche's preference for hierarchy. Human beings do indeed seek status and the recognition of their superior dignity; to hope to eliminate this deeply rooted instinct is as utopian as the socialist hope to make people altruistic towards the species as a whole. But the particular genius of CLD is to turn these instincts for hierarchy away from war, conquest, and violence, to economic competition in the marketplace, where it is socially productive, and to electoral competition within a democratic, constitutional framework. In contrast to traditional society, in which one could achieve status only as a warrior, priest, or bureaucrat, the dynamic, fluid, evolving economy and society in a contemporary CLD provides hundreds if not thousands of arenas for status competition. As Robert Frank (1985) suggests, small frogs in large ponds can easily choose different ponds in which their particular talents can loom larger. Whether the essentially bourgeois pursuits open to people in such a society will be sufficient to satisfy the competitive energies of the most ambitious natures is not clear, but the future stability and viability of capitalist liberal democracy may well ride on the answer.

Alternative Models. If we move from these abstract formulations to consider some alternative models, we find that most of them have key weaknesses. There are, empirically, a number of existing or historical alternatives to CLD that have abolished one of its three basic terms. These include, *inter alia*, a renewed form of *socialism; *fascism, or some other type of extreme *nationalism; theocracy, as in Iran after the Islamic revolution; and a kind of soft, paternalistic *authoritarianism that permits considerable economic freedom but no meaningful *political participation (Singapore, Malaysia, and Indonesia under Suharto were examples). There may be other systematic alternatives beyond these four, but together they constitute the majority of real-world cases. The issue is not whether they are viable or can exist in the modern world, since each today manifestly has real-world exemplars, but rather whether any of them will prove to be a superior social system and therefore potentially choice worthy on the part of people living in contemporary CLDs. The answer, it would appear, is no.

The collapse of the former Soviet Union and other *communist party-state countries has precluded, in my view, any return to a full-blooded form of centralized planning with severe constraints on private property. While ex-communists have returned to power in virtually all of the former communist world, few have advocated and none have been able to implement anything like a return to state takeover of the "commanding heights" of the economy. The failure of socialism is today perceived not simply as an economic but also a moral one. While there is clearly a craving for authority and political order in Russia and other former communist countries, there are also vivid memories of past tyranny that will make anything like restoration of communist rule very difficult.

Fascism, or an extreme nationalism based on ethnic or racial identity, appeared to be the direction in which many former communist countries were heading in the wake of the Soviet Union's collapse, as well as an alternative for many ethnically divided developing countries. In the early 1990s, there were fears that ethnic intolerance could spread to developed democracies such as France or *Germany, where anti-foreigner sentiment had led to the growth of fringe extremist parties like *Le Pen's *Front National* or the German *Republikaner* party. In retrospect, it would appear that fascism is primarily a disease of the transition out of communism, and has appeared as a realistic alternative primarily for countries that for various reasons have not been able to make either capitalist or democratic institutions work properly. Serbia today is hardly a model that anyone in the developed world would seek to imitate.

The same can be said for religious fundamentalism. While Islamic fundamentalism has proven stronger that liberal democracy in many parts of the Muslim world, its appeal is limited to those who are culturally Muslim to begin with. The appeal of Islamic fundamentalism seems to lie primarily in the failure of westernization and *modernization in certain Muslim societies; the appeal of this and other reactionary movements like Hindu fundamentalism in India is therefore self-limiting.

Regimes based on communism, fascism, or religious *fundamentalism all share a common problem: they have proven, for different reasons, to be incompatible with the highest levels of modern science and technology. That weakness is not shared by the fourth alternative, the kind of paternalistic authoritarianism practiced by a number of regimes in Asia. Unlike societies in the first three categories, Singapore, Malaysia, Indonesia, and the People's Republic of *China have proven to be capable of achieving extremely high rates of growth based on the acquisition of modern science and technology, and for that reason alone constitute the most plausible existing alternative to CLD.

The Asian economic crisis has, however, demonstrated one key weakness of the soft authoritarian model. This is not so much because these countries have fallen into hard economic times (there is no system that is not vulnerable to economic downturns), but rather because hard times revealed critical political weaknesses. Soft authoritarian regimes did not seek to base *legitimacy on indigenous cultural principles (e.g., *Confucianism); rather, they claimed legitimacy on the basis of their economic performance. This left them vulnerable when facing economic crisis; even for countries as culturally non-Western as Indonesia and Malaysia, there appears to be no alternative to democracy as a source of legitimacy when economic success no longer suffices. In the end it seems much more likely that Singapore and Malaysia will evolve along the democratic lines of Taiwan and South Korea rather than the reverse.

Beyond these four possibilities, we cannot know that some as yet undefined and unheard-of political or economic model will arise. Human history, while progressive overall, has been full of wrong turns and retrogressions. At the end of the twentieth century, however, one may question the likelihood of there being some obvious non-capitalist, non-liberal, non-democratic order that people simply haven't been imaginative enough to think up until now.

(See also CAPITALISM; DEVELOPMENT AND UNDERDEVELOPMENT; EQUALITY AND INEQUALITY; SOCIALISM AND SOCIAL DEMOCRACY.)

Friedrich A. Hayek, "The Use of Knowledge in Society," *American Economic Review* 35 (1945): 519–30. Ludwig Von Mises, *Socialism: An Economic and Sociological Analysis* (Indianapolis, 1981). Robert H. Frank, *Choosing the Right Pond: Human Behavior and the Quest for Status* (Oxford, 1985). Francis Fukuyama, *The End of History and the Last Man* (New York: 1992). John Gray, *Enlightenment's Wake: Politics and Culture at the Close of the Modern Age* (London and New York, 1995). Amitai Etzioni, *The New Golden Rule* (New York, 1997).

FRANCIS FUKUYAMA

THE LIMITS OF LIBERAL DEMOCRACY. Liberalism has a strong appeal. So much so that even critics of the way things are in supposedly liberal societies try to win favor by insisting on it. They want deep changes, to be sure. But these critics often insist that advancing liberal values should become a central project in any new order.

Such critics of liberal societies fail to go far enough. They need to submit the core values of liberal liberty and liberal equality to scrutiny. They have yet to ask if it isn't these values that have led to the poor state of affairs they would have us escape.

Liberty as Will. Liberal liberty loses a bit of its allure when one realizes that, whatever its philosophical disguises, it is a dispensation for agents to do what on their own they will to do. Crucial legal changes have been made in the interest of furthering liberal liberty. For it the English Poor Laws were amended in 1832, quickly making a labor market that left the most vulnerable without protection, and for it financial dealings were deregulated in the United States in the 1980s, bringing on a wave of failures of savings and loan companies for which the public paid dearly. Liberal equality also loses its allure on examination. It has been talked about as an ideal of generalized dignity, recognition, or concern that rules out discrimination and subordination. But looking closely, what we find is equal protection for willfulness. So it is equal protection for McDonald's to pay and for the cook to receive the wage they voluntarily settle on, whatever their differences in *power.

To be sure, liberalism has many guises. There is *laissez faire* liberalism, Kantian liberalism, welfare liberalism, Bill *Clinton–Tony *Blair third way liberalism, Wilhelm von Humboldt's liberalism, and Richard Rorty's liberalism. Liberal values are accented differently in each of them. There is, though, a common thread, which is what creates the difficulties that lead to a search for an alternative—one that promotes values associated with cooperation rather than volition.

That common thread is evident in the accounts given of liberty by the great liberals. For John Locke, in his *Second Treatise of Government* (1690), free individuals order their actions, possessions, and persons as they see fit. For John Stuart Mill, in his *On Liberty* (1859), freedom is pursuing our own good in our own way. And for Isaiah Berlin, in his *Four Essays on Liberty* (Oxford, 1969), political liberty is the area within which we can act unobstructed by others. In liberal thought, liberty is not to be the possession of a few but should pertain to all. If some did not have it, the will of others would override their wills. Not allowing this overriding introduces the theme of liberal equality. Equality imposes a proviso on liberal liberty to the effect that to have our way we do not bar the door to others' having their way unless perhaps in doing so liberty is on the whole enhanced. This proviso introduces a counterpoint to the liberal dispensation of will. For in determinations of where and how to limit unobstructed behavior, the question is no longer about the value of willing but about how to integrate distinct wills. Still, the function of liberal equality is not to restrict liberty but to enhance it, thus assuming liberty as the core value.

It is not obvious, though, when we are to say that in having our way we keep others from having theirs. Can we say that McDonald's keeps me from paying my car loan if, in a context of high unemployment, I agree to work for the low wage it offers? Under cover of a lack of consensus on whether or not my goal of keeping my car from repossession was obstructed, McDonald's enterprising spirit can surge ahead with impunity. Mill tried to deal with this problem by requiring that obstruction not be intentional, but this merely encourages an inhumane negligence by enterprises about the consequences of their activity.

Even if it were true that contracts made by the less powerful may sometimes not be free, liberalism gives the powerful a way of excusing themselves. They can say that, though the liberty of some is overridden, on the whole liberty is enhanced. Even admitting that McDonald's obstructs my effort to keep my car, it can claim that stopping its exploitation would not enhance liberty. Is this anything more than the corporate assumption that most restrictions of free enterprise are greater injuries to liberty than most restrictions of worker welfare? It is only under cover of this contested assumption about when liberty is enhanced that liberal practice can justify projects that without a doubt will interfere with what large numbers would otherwise do.

Limiting Liberty. Liberal practice has of course been checked at various times by specific limits on doing what an agent sees fit to do. Although *states were often targeted as the prime threat to the liberty of individuals, corporations have increasingly become a major target of popular campaigns in defense of liberty. Limits have thus been imposed on the liberty of both states and corporations. States were limited by the Fourteenth Amendment to the United States Constitution, which prohibits the states from taking away liberty or property without the due process of law. And corporations were limited by, among other things, occupational health and safety rules even where people were willing to contract for work without them.

Despite such limits, liberalism's history has been one of encouraging the projects of some despite their interference with what others would have done. Thus the will to empire, both territorial and economic, has been abetted by liberalism. Imperial military and economic savagery is supposed to have enhanced liberty. The will of the U.S. Treasury Department to open financial markets led in 1997–1998 to chaos in Southeast Asia. Low wages became even lower. But the liberty of *multinational corporations to profit from low wages was enhanced. Given the importance of these corporations in the global economy, the conclusion is spread about that their prosperity enhances liberty overall.

The objection is sure to be made that such liberal practices shouldn't reflect badly on liberal values. This misses the point that actual liberal practice is just what one would expect from adopting liberal values. Taken together, those values give a central place to liberty, equality's function being simply to enhance liberty. We have seen however that, in deciding when liberty is enhanced, liberalism is disposed to give more weight to the liberty of the larger projects of will undertaken by the powerful than to the liberty of the modest pursuits of ordinary life. Liberalism could weight matters differently only if it could erase the relevant power differences, which it could do only by going against the grain of its own view of liberty. This is why, in looking for a way to better our lot, values other than the liberal ones will need to provide the chief motivation.

In deciding what enhances liberty, shouldn't keeping liberal institutions healthy count for more than protecting multinationals? If anything is, these institutions seem to be the offspring of liberal values. Certainly representative *democracy, an uncensored press, equal opportunity, and an independent judiciary are worth keeping vigorous. But their relation to liberal values is at best indirect, since the ongoing struggles for developing these institutions have not been made for the sake of individual will. Instead, they have been carried out for the common goals of groups. Such goals include the economic improvement of all social sectors, the recognition of all as full citizens, and equality in health care and education. Workers, women, blacks, and gays have, along with their allies, fought for these goals and thereby expanded and strengthened those institutions. Their activity has then been directed at enhancing the ability to cooperate with others in an inclusive society rather than at giving greater scope to individual will. Being seated in a legislature and not having to be stereotyped in the press are signs of such inclusion.

Within the liberal tradition there is, though, a vested interest in having people believe that the spread of liberal values and practices was responsible for precisely such institutions of fairness. Whatever excuses one might make for liberals, they have a spotty record of support for these institutions. In striking down a New York law limiting the hours of bakery workers to sixty a week, the Supreme Court in *Lochner v New York* (1905) stood staunchly by the liberal principle that the liberty of contracting employers and employees is not to be interfered with. In this and other pro-employer decisions, the *Lochner* Court made clear it was anything but a judiciary independent of the employers. Today, unlimited financial contributions to U.S. politicians are defended on the ground that this kind of liberal willfulness is really political speech. The resulting political system fails to fit the basic democratic ideal of one vote per person. Equal opportunity also clashes with the liberal outlook. In *San Antonio School District v Rodriguez* (1973), the Supreme Court refused to reject a Texas financing plan that, in view of the role in it of local property taxes, led to schools in poorer districts getting less per student than schools in richer districts. The key here was the court's willingness to deny equal educational opportunity, affirming instead that it would be a first step toward allowing interference with wealth so as to attain economic equality. Liberal willfulness reaches a glorious high with the development of *international organizations—like the *World Trade Organization—that undercut national democracies with an elite rule by multinational corporations and national finance ministers. Because of continuing conflicts between liberal ideals and institutions of fairness, it promotes clarity to cease referring to the latter as liberal institutions. They emerged over liberal objections as lower orders in the society sought redress from liberal willfulness.

Liberalism has made concrete its general stricture against interference with a list of specific *rights. But in doing so it has had to borrow from massive struggles against absolutism, robber barons, the tabloid press, and racial exclusion. Included in the list are a right to freedom of thought and expression, a right to civil and political assembly, and a right to be governed by laws rather than arbitrarily. Despite the origin of these rights in struggles for common goals, liberalism conceives those protected by these rights as active centers of individual will. For it, rights form the framework for legitimate

volition, leaving the goods jointly aimed at by those struggles in second place. These rights are meant to give some order to the free-for-all among individuals pursuing their own goods.

However, introducing rights fails to do away with a problem faced above. In the liberal context of promoting liberty, the powerful will often decide that putting restrictions on liberty by enforcing rights is not in the interest of enhancing liberty. This is not to be passed off as a reflection in liberalism of a healthy conflict outside it between the powerful and the rest. It shows instead a weakness inside liberalism, which is revealed as giving only part-time protection to the less powerful. Liberalism's celebration of initiative, will, persisting through adversity, and going against the crowd makes ignoring rights plausible, weakening its claim to want the world to put a lock on initiative with rights that in recent centuries the less powerful have fought for. For there to be respect for rights they have fought for, the liberal context of promoting willfulness needs to be replaced with one that reflects the more congenial value of cooperation.

Liberalism wants to be all things to all people, ingratiating itself with the powerful by its talk of non-interference in what one wills and ingratiating itself with the less powerful by its talk of rights and spreading liberty. Just how difficult it is trying to have it both ways is evident when one considers that these rights were won in battles of the less powerful against the arbitrariness of the powerful. They were won in cooperative struggles for inclusion in certain social and political arrangements rather than in efforts of agents to press their will for their own advantage.

Welfare Liberalism. Many liberals feel the need to give a human face to liberalism. Tacking individual rights onto the liberal value of will failed to do this so long as the powerful could appeal to enhancing liberty as an excuse for overriding rights. So to give liberalism a human face, power differences themselves had to be addressed by some mechanism that would reduce inequality and poverty. To do this liberals wanting effective rights allied with the less powerful to create the institutions of welfare liberalism.

Liberal thinkers took up the task of refining notions of distributive justice that would give a fair value to civic and political rights. Thus John Rawls, in his *A Theory of Justice* (Cambridge, Mass., 1971), developed principles of justice that if applied would have eliminated important sources of inequality and poverty. What remained doubtful was whether the derivation of such principles could be carried out within the framework of liberalism. Rawls wanted his derivation to take place in a framework where individuals are mutually disinterested. So if he were successful, his welfarism would be a natural outgrowth of making a value of pursuing one's own good in one's own way. Over the years it has become evident to many readers of Rawls that his principles of justice sit uneasily in this liberal framework. Without being strongly motivated by more solidaristic values, agents will seek exit from projects aiming at greater equality, since many of them will reasonably believe they can be more successful on their own.

Richard Rorty, in his *Contingency, Irony, and Solidarity* (New York, 1989), has noted this conflict of liberty with justice and responded to it, not by attempting to unite them under the umbrella of liberalism but by redescribing them. He treats them as two incompatible liberal impulses, which, though not to be brought under one umbrella, are no longer in conflict.

One of them is the impulse to self-creation, which prescribes what we do with our aloneness. The other is the impulse to be decent and to provide welfare, which prescribes what we do with cruelty and suffering.

Self-creation here is only part of the traditional liberal liberty, since it is for Rorty only a private activity. It is related to the ideal of character building and individuality of the romantic liberal Wilhelm von Humboldt in his *The Sphere and Duties of Government* (London, 1854). However, for Rorty, as distinct from Humboldt, self-creation does not include the liberty to try out on the world the schemes developed in the course of self-creation. Rorty thereby significantly limits liberal liberty to act as one will in order to closet revolutionary thinkers in their studies since they are too dangerous to let loose on the world.

As a result, Rorty's other liberal impulse—to curb suffering—gets crippled from the outset. Without changes promoted by visionary thinking, capitalist democracy is the instrument Rorty leaves us to provide for amelioration and justice. But even unencumbered by the Cold War, capitalist democracy in the long boom beginning in 1992 has actually deepened suffering in the world. In sum, Rorty defuses the conflict in liberalism between liberty and justice only by privatizing liberty, leaving it with only a faint similarity to the more robust liberal liberty. More troublesome though is the result that Rorty thereby dilutes justice so that it must become compatible with capitalist democracy.

Toward Cooperation. Liberalism looks at social and political issues through the lens of liberal liberty. There is quite a different, and ultimately more sensible, lens—that of cooperation and its requirements. It is more sensible since we are all engaged in cooperative endeavors, some of which we don't dare imagine ourselves living without. With cooperative activity as the lens through which we consider improvements and innovations, the status of unobstructed volition is demoted to that of an instrument. In addition, with cooperation as the basic value, rights and justice will no longer seem extraneous, and hence easily ignored.

In giving importance to cooperation, there is no need to reject individual liberty; rather it comes to be seen as something that gains its importance within an overall context of cooperation. Liberal liberty is pernicious when it is picked out to be the lens through which we look at problems, since it is then brute, unconditioned, and commanding will. Moreover, it displaces cooperation when it is promoted as sufficient for everything citizens aspire for, as it was by former chair of the Council of Economic Advisers, Charles Schultze, in his *The Public Use of Private Interest* (Washington, D.C.; 1977). Neoliberals promote it today as a basis for prosperity and democracy, even though for the less powerful it tends to undercut both. However, where cooperation is respected and widespread, individual liberty operates, against a background of concern for others, to provide for reflection on the goals of cooperative projects and recuperation of the powers needed to engage in them. But in this role individual liberty no longer has the primacy that it had as liberal liberty.

Cooperation is a key to resolving a number of problems that liberals face. Where liberal liberty reigns, it is hard to avoid inequality and poverty and also hard to offer protection from the market by way of public goods. With cooperation as the basic motivating value, equality and public goods are less compromised and more stable.

Consider the issue of inequality first. A good start at equality is made by cooperative endeavor since it works by inclusion rather than exclusion. Cooperation of the sort relevant here—that between those who are related by some bond—involves sharing in an effort to realize a situation recognized as a good for all involved. The goal is inclusive in that it is a good for all involved. Also the shared effort, which may involve many distinct tasks and abilities, does not involve control over fundamental decisions exclusively by only a few of those involved. There is a distribution of control that spreads it widely enough so that nobody is given reason to feel they are only following orders. So cooperation is typically inclusive, both as to control and the goal. As such it tends toward equality in both resources and power.

In contrast, liberal liberty gives a wide berth for exclusion as a result of putting stress on doing what human persons or corporations want and on doing it in their own way. Getting ahead of others to wield more power, a company's making it to the market early with its products, having one's way in projects involving others—all of this has as a condition excluding or diminishing the satisfaction of others. The goals that mean the most give satisfaction that is singular, not common. One can, to be sure, want what is common, but then to the extent that others want it, one will need to cooperate with them in realizing it.

Cooperation is also the way toward the public goods many need for survival with dignity. The gap that liberal liberty permits between different groups threatens many with a lack of basic resources. Common goals in regard to education, information, health, transport, and security are proposed with the intention of getting agreement on public goods that would realize those goals. These public goods provide citizenship with a bedrock that is shared by rich and poor, black and white, elite, and common folk, native and immigrant. Without cooperation such public goods cannot be built and maintained. At certain times the more powerful may support public goods as a way of making the society as a whole responsible for costs they would otherwise have to bear alone. But the powerful would rather reduce their commitment by having the less powerful take even more responsibility for their own needs. The powerful prefer this since it enhances their liberty. In short, the cooperation needed to realize public goods is always threatened by the exit of the powerful. Privatization of public goods, partial or total, is one result of the threat the dominance of liberal liberty poses to cooperation.

From Liberty to Equality. An alternative to liberalism should provide greater assurance of equality. By lacking a reliable way to curb inequality, liberalism makes liberty effective for some but not all and makes cooperation unlikely where it is needed in social projects benefiting all. In searching for a more reliable basis for equality than liberalism, a culture of cooperation stands out due to its ability to enhance equality. Such a culture opens up a range of alternatives to liberalism that correspond to different forms of egalitarianism. Only some forms of egalitarianism may give a role to cooperatives in the familiar sense of worker-or consumer-owned enterprises. So in making cooperation a prime value, there is no intention to give a special place to cooperatives, whose ability to enhance cooperation and hence equality may be limited by competition among them.

In these alternatives to liberalism, cooperation is to be promoted at all levels, not just at the level of small groups and of the various sectors of enterprise. This broad emphasis on cooperation also lends itself to advancing common goals both in entire countries and in the world. Having a healthier society is felt everywhere as an urgent goal, to which the pursuit of global competitiveness and the invasion of for-profit medicine pose major obstacles. The goal of having sustainable environments is likewise a popular goal that is being blocked by the corporate frenzy to expand markets. Agitating for common goals, at whatever level, is mandatory, since they are the only feasible antidotes to the neglect of *basic needs.

Liberal neglect is not the only culprit; constant outbreaks of liberal barbarism must also be stopped. It is this barbarism that has created a race to the bottom, multiplying sweatshops where wages were already low and are now lower. It deliberately created markets for speculative capital that led to crises in which national currencies and standards of living plummeted. With effort and resources pouring into cooperative ways to meet basic human needs, there would be a reduction of liberal neglect and barbarism. Liberals would of course complain that serving those needs was interference with liberal liberty. In response, it can be noted that there would be an increase in the number of those who are advancing goals they have participated in setting.

The point of view of cooperation, which encourages forms of egalitarianism, is opposed not just to liberalism but as well to statism, which promotes state control of economic, social, and political activity. In a statist society, the state tries to act simply as one mighty individual whose will dominates its citizens. In contrast, cooperation comes from among the cooperators and not from a will imposed on them. This is why there can be no extended cooperation without participation in decisions. Where participation is absent, centers of control will develop which, under cover of pursuing common goals, actually advance their own power. This democratic feature of cooperation becomes a vital part of the egalitarianism that springs from cooperation. As was noted, liberalism's connection with democracy is more precarious in view of the struggle for control among wills trying to realize their own goods in their own way.

Liberals are not agreed about the role of such common goals. The more libertarian liberals, like Michael Oakeshott in his *On Human Conduct* (Oxford, 1975), think common goals are to play a role only within businesses and civic associations, whereas the attempt to have common goals in a society or a state works to limit freedom. In evaluating this view one needs to start with the undeniable fact that in today's urban, corporate, fragmented societies there has been a multiplication of needs for which self-reliance alone is of little help. Thus the conviction persists that for these needs to be satisfied there must be a broad collective effort. Such collective effort has proven successful in a variety of areas. Public health measures reduced drastically the incidence of infectious diseases. Social security for retirees reduced drastically the incidence of poverty among the elderly. Public anti-discrimination laws have drastically improved job access and pay for women and people of color.

However, the more welfare-oriented liberals, like Rawls in his *Political Liberalism* (New York, 1993), agree that at least some goods, which like the above are to be pursued by col-lective efforts, need to be agreed on prior to any discussion of justice. It is difficult to resist commenting that allowing some common goods to have this role leads away from liberalism. Liberal liberty can no longer remain the prime value if the cooperation needed for realizing such goods becomes the basis for the whole structure of liberal justice. It is apparent that liberal liberty has taken a secondary role from the moment that being just comes to depend on being in a context with certain social goods.

Just as there can be several varieties of liberalism, so too there are various directions in which the egalitarian view can be developed. Among others, there are social democratic and socialist directions, both of which can be expected to give cooperation first place over liberal liberty without in any way abandoning the later. The social democratic direction enhances well-being through a number of important cooperative projects—mostly public goods—whose existence curbs the realm of non-cooperative enterprise sufficiently so that cooperation becomes the basic social matrix. The existence of cooperative projects is then less precarious than in the matrix of liberal liberty. This direction has been explored by Karl Polanyi in his *The Great Transformation* (Boston, 1957).

A non-aggression pact between the regions of cooperation and liberal liberty becomes a needed part of taking the social democratic direction with the egalitarian view. Developing egalitarianism in the socialist direction is motivated, as suggested by Ralph Miliband in *Divided Societies* (Oxford, 1989), by the fragility of any such pact. The needed primacy of cooperation may fail as struggles for gain in the non-cooperative sector intensify, leading to a return to dominance of liberal liberty. *Socialism acts as a hedge against such fragility by restricting such struggles for gain even further. Based in the value of cooperation, it extends cooperation beyond the usual public goods to the major sectors of enterprise as well as to civic and political associations.

Whereas liberalism has been ascendant, triumphing over absolutism, *fascism, and *communism, the egalitarian options based on cooperation have, outside of relatively short periods, been part of an oppositional tradition. Liberalism has bounced back from depressions and wars of global proportions. It is nonetheless a system with a flaw in its very heart, since the protections it advances against overreaching are too weak to stop the drive of liberal will. This flaw continues to generate popular efforts to stop that overreaching—to stop the arrogance of *imperialism, the indifference to community, and the corruption of representatives. These popular efforts have had and continue to have a strongly participatory and cooperative character. As the price of liberal liberty becomes a heavier burden on the less powerful, their cooperative resistance to paying that price may well be the source of a widespread cooperative culture that will replace liberalism.

(See also CITIZENSHIP; COLONIAL EMPIRES; COMMUNITARIANISM; EQUALITY AND INEQUALITY; SOCIALISM AND SOCIAL DEMOCRACY; WELFARE STATES.)

John Dewey, *The Public and Its Problems* (1927) (Athens, Oh., 1980). Karl Marx, *The Civil War in France* (1871), in *Karl Marx/Frederick Engels: Collected Works*, vol. 22 (New York, 1986). Milton Fisk, *The State and Justice* (New York, 1989). Jürgen Habermas, *Between Facts and Norms*, trans. William Rehg (Cambridge, Mass., 1996). Michael J. Sandel, *Democracy's Discontent* (Cambridge, Mass., 1996).

MILTON FISK

and seemed set in a rigid mold of anticommunism, antiliberalism, and police repression that appeared impervious to the supposedly liberalizing effects of modernization. In all three cases bitter memories of earlier conflicts were invoked by the incumbents to justify repression, on the argument that any concessions would be seized on by a vengeful opposition seeking to reverse the verdict of history. The southern European transitions of the 1970s, however, revealed the extensive scope for compromise and democratic institution building once artificial restraints on political expression and negotiation were lifted. The trigger for democratic transition differed from country to country—in Greece the discredit arising from a military defeat by Turkey; in Portugal the demoralization and radicalization arising from a protracted stalemate in a colonial war; in Spain the death of *Franco. In all cases the fading of the *Cold War, the need to participate in a process of European integration premised on liberal capitalism, and the emergence of a new generation of politicians wishing to distance themselves from an archaic past, all contributed to subsequent processes of democratic consolidation.

These southern European precedents exerted a powerful influence over the Latin American transitions of the 1980s. Just as the *Spanish Civil War had contributed to ideological polarization in Latin America (with *Marxism and militant Catholicism as the two competing poles), the disappearance of the Salazar and Franco regimes and their replacement by modern and consensually-based political systems rather than by new upheavals, caused intransigents in Latin America to reconsider the scope for accommodation with their rivals. Other international factors also reinforced this tendency. The romance of the Cuban Revolution had faded (except perhaps in parts of Central America) and the "national security" reflex inspired by the threat of more Cubas had also run its course. Following Watergate and the Vietnam War the Carter administration took up the cause of *human rights, distancing itself from some of its most unsavory allies, notably in Argentina, Chile, Guatemala, and Uruguay. The evident failures of authoritarian politics—in Velasco's Peru, in Somoza's Nicaragua, and in Argentina after the *Malvinas/Falklands War—reinforced the demonstration effect coming from southern Europe. Nevertheless, more than an inchoate sympathy would be required to turn tentative, and often quite opportunistic, flirtations with *democracy into a continent-wide commitment to abide by the constraining rules of constitutional government. The democratic transitions of the 1980s took multiple routes and passed through a series of stages. In the beginning, the initiative was generally taken by liberalizing elements within the authoritarian ruling group. Perhaps influenced by external models, or perhaps simply seeking to buttress their own bargaining power within a regime conscious both of its strength and its social isolation, they advocated measures of *abertura*, or controlled liberalization, at least partly with the aim of dividing the opposition. But liberalizing measures tended to gather their own momentum as increased freedom of expression and organization led to the emergence of newly permitted organizations and demands. In due course, part of the political initiative would pass to these interests, which generally lacked the strength to bring down the existing order, but which could continually press for further extensions of the political realm. The "transition" process consisted of a series of improvisations under pressure, through which the composition and objectives of the authoritarian coalition were shifted toward cooperation and convergence with the more temperate elements of the opposition. "Liberalization" passed into "democratization" where this interaction resulted in an agreement (a "pact") to allow open contestation for public office, without a preordained victor. If the voters, rather than the incumbents, controlled the final outcome of this contestation, then the transition could be called democratic. Not all Latin American transitions took this form, however. In Central America, for example, the "transitions" to democracy of the 1980s and early 1990s were components of broader internationally supervised (or, in the case of Peru, imposed) political settlements. Democratization was part of "pacification," and its dynamics were constrained by the logic of the peace processes. In Brazil and Mexico extensive liberalization of the media and the party system preceded anything that could be called a "transition" to such an extent that analysts are hard pressed to identify the pivotal moment at which liberalization was superseded. (The 1988 Constitution is a plausible candidate for consideration in Brazil; the establishment of a trustworthy electoral agency in 1996 could be the best Mexican equivalent.) In Argentina and Bolivia there was no solid "pact," but rather a collapse of the military regime, which paved the way for a year or two of an uncontrolled transition. Despite all these complications, the outcome of the 1980s is remarkably clear. Almost all countries in Latin America have witnessed some form of transition to a broadly democratic (civilian constitutional) political regime. These regimes may not be fully consolidated (they often remain institutionally fragile and politically ineffective), but their medium-term prospects of survival are surprisingly good. On the whole the evidence from election turnout survey research and some data on social movements suggests that support for transitional democracies in southern Europe and Latin America is surprisingly broad. Support for the democratic regimes of Latin America may be more volatile than in the cases of the rather successful and consolidated democracies of southern Europe, but in most cases the basic constitutional framework is being preserved, and overt challenges to the formalities of a democratic regime are now rare.

The fading of the Cold War also witnessed a succession of democratic transitions in East Asia in the mid-1980s. The "people power" democratization of the Philippines following the ousting of dictator Ferdinand Marcos in 1986 seemed at first to validate those analysts who claimed that popular pressure from the streets could be more decisive than the pacts or maneuverings of political elites, but the euphoria soon faded, and Philippine democracy assumed a familiar top-down pattern, with disenchantment and demobilization at the base, while old-style politicking made its reappearance. The transition in South Korea was always more clearly controlled from above (the persistent security threat from the North ensured that the military would long retain council powers and leverage), but it too was accompanied by a short burst of popular participation and indeed radical activism, which soon faded. The clearest transition "from above" was the Kuomintang's decision, in Taiwan, to revoke martial law and allow competitive elections, before any obvious pressure from below had manifested itself. This proactive decision may have been influenced by the parallel developments in the Philippines and Korea, but also responded to a more specific political logic. By turning itself into a model democracy, Taiwan hoped to reenlist international support in its long-term rivalry with the Communist-ruled mainland. When Beijing stifled all possibility of a Chinese transition to democracy, in *Tiananmen Square in 1989, the Taiwanese gamble seemed likely to pay off.

With the collapse of the Soviet bloc at the end of the 1980s many countries of Eastern and Central Europe, and also in sub-Saharan Africa, have inaugurated their own processes of democratic transition. The Eastern and Central European "transitions" of 1989–1990 bear some intriguing resemblances to earlier southern European and Latin American processes, but the contrasts are sharp enough to raise the doubt that the use of prepackaged terminology could conflate the two distinct logics. The parallels work best for Poland and Hungary, where internally generated processes of liberalization and reform created some space for negotiation between weakening governments and resurgent oppositions. Poland's "roundtable" negotiations of spring 1989 fit surprisingly well within the framework of preexisting transition literature, and quite a few of the constitution-writing and election-inaugurating events of 1990 were entirely familiar in form. For example, Latin American debates over the relative merits of presidentialism and parliamentarism were taken up with a keen interest in various parts of Eastern and Central Europe. A striking similarity with southern Europe concerns the way in which prospective (or at least hoped-for) membership in the European Union may have stimulated a consensus favoring liberal forms of political organization linked with market-based economic reforms. Taking the ex-Soviet bloc as a whole and adopting a rather longer time horizon, however, these could prove relatively superficial resemblances that are overshadowed by more striking contrasts. The Eastern and Central European transformations all occurred very rapidly and were bunched together within a few months. The "contagion" effect was much more powerful and direct than elsewhere. Moreover, it can reasonably be argued that the dominant force at work was a Moscow-centered initiative (whether by decision or miscalculation) to dismantle the Soviet empire. The term "peaceful anticommunist revolutions" suggests itself as an alternative to the language of "democratic transitions." Some East European analysts prefer to speak of "triple transitions," from communism to democracy, but also from state control to market economy, and from East to West, all at the same time. Others argue that rather than "transition" it is more accurate to speak of "transformation." Such a shift in focus would have major implications for the subsequent outcomes. All other democratic transitions were directed against authoritarian regimes which fostered or sheltered certain minority capitalist interests, and the democratic opposition nominally embraced a range of anticapitalist or broadly "left-wing" orientations. For most East and Central Europeans, by contrast, capitalism was equated with liberty and anticapitalism with state monopolization of political and economic power. Both in ideological and in material terms the task of forging a "pluralist" political system was therefore quite different from elsewhere, especially in those parts of Eastern and Central Europe where the collapse of Soviet control also put national boundaries in question.

In Africa the collapse of the Soviet bloc and the conse-quent cessation of Cold War rivalries coincided with the decision of the South African regime to dismantle the formal structures of *apartheid and to seek a constitutional settlement to enfranchise the African majority. As externally promoted civil wars were steered toward more or less negotiated settlements, international pressure was brought to bear on sub-Saharan Africa's large array of one-party states. Put more cynically, Western donors no longer had much interest in providing further aid to client regimes whose corruption and mismanagement seemed inexpungible. The resulting Western demand for "democracy" could prove, in various cases, just an excuse for budget cutting. In the early 1990s, nearly a score of African states responded by lifting restraints on political opposition and convoking competitive elections. On the face of it, "transitions to democracy" swept through Africa almost as abruptly as through Eastern and Central Europe. But a decade later few of these African regimes remained in any sense democratic. Indeed many were riven by internal conflicts or even potentially international civil wars, confirming the old Rustow dictum that a securely established nation-state was a necessary precondition for durable democratization. The most populous sub-Saharan country, Nigeria, has repeatedly initiated democratic transitions that led to instability and fears of disintegration, and ended in reversal. By contrast the former white minority regime of South Africa possesses various advantages that *could* assist democratization—a diversified economy, a relatively better educational endowment (though provision is extremely unequal), some elements of efficient and impartial administration under some kind of rule of law. It is difficult to believe, however, that viable democracies will prove to be the norm in Africa as a whole, since for the most part national political communities are extremely fragile; patrimonial forms of administration dominate economic and political life; and the socioeconomic bases for institutional political bargaining are so weak and unstable.

In conclusion, the literature on democratic transitions that grew out of the Rustow analysis helped concentrate attention on the short-term dynamics of regime change, and on the crucial role of strategic interactions (and deflections) within political elites. This perspective worked best in southern Europe and South America, and could also be useful in East Asia. But it was not designed to deal with situations of state failure or disintegration (as in parts of Africa and the ex-Soviet bloc). It ignored international geopolitical considerations or changes of economic model. It has also been criticized for underestimating the importance of pressures from below and the demands of civil society. A more convincing criticism would be that it assumed a rather clear distinction between three stages—liberalization, transition, and consolidation—and postulated a short, intense interval during which all the main processes of regime change would be completed and assimilated into the consciousness of the key actors. A broad survey of worldwide experience would suggest that, on the contrary, democratization is often a protracted and fitful process, characterized by considerable inertia. As a consequence the neat "transition" phase may in practice be drawn out and dissolved into more ambiguous and unresolved processes of regime change.

(See also Authoritarianism; International Debt; Nineteen Eighty-Nine; One-Party System.)

Guillermo O'Donnell, Philippe Schmitter, and Laurence Whitehead, eds., *Transitions from Authoritarian Rule* (Baltimore, 1986). David Held, ed., *Prospects for Democracy: North, South, East, West* (Cambridge, U.K., 1992). John Higley and Richard Gunther, eds., *Elites and Democratic Consolidation in Latin America and Southern Europe* (Cambridge, U.K., 1992). Larry Diamond, *Developing Democracy: Toward Coalition* (Baltimore, 1999). Larry Diamond, Juan Linz, and Seymour Martin Lipset, eds., *Democracy in Developing Countries*, 2d ed. (Boulder, Colo., 1999). Juan Méndez, Guillermo O'Donnell, and Paulo Sérgio Pinheiro, eds., *The Un(Rule) of Law and the Underprivileged in Latin America* (South Bend, Ind., 1999).

LAURENCE WHITEHEAD

DENG Xiaoping, a revolutionary who saved *China from being consumed by its *revolution, was born 22 August 1904 in a village in Sichuan Province, eldest son in a distinguished landed family that had for three generations been a pillar of the community. His relationship to his father was respectful, and he joined the revolution in conformity with his family's progressive views. In the fall of 1920 Deng enrolled as a work-study student at the University of Lyon in France. Though he remained in France five years (acquiring a lasting taste for croissants and bridge), he later commented that he had not studied at all but worked as a laborer; in fact he spent much of his time in radical politics. In 1922 he joined the Chinese Socialist Youth League branch in France, and the French branch of the *Chinese Communist Party (CCP) upon its founding in 1924, where his intelligence and willingness to make himself indispensable in whatever capacity needed quickly brought him into the upper ranks of leadership. His role in publishing the local Party organ, *Red Light,* earned him the nickname "Docteur du Duplication," and he continued to write polemical articles even after becoming CYL chair. When local infighting with other Chinese political factions forced his departure in 1926, he spent half a year in Moscow before returning home to help Feng Yuxiang in Xian during Feng's brief flirtation with Marxism then joining the underground Party Center in Shanghai.

Deng worked mostly in Shanghai until urban Communist activity was effectively suppressed by Chiang Kai-shiks Nationalist in the early 1930s, interrupted by a brief stint as political commissar of the seventh Army in 1930–31. In 1932–33 he was criticized for political errors by a pro-Moscow party faction, a result of which in 1934 he lost all leadership posts, but gained the sympathy of *Mao Zedong, another victim of this purge. Deng worked with Mao during the latter's rise to power in the late 1930s and throughout the Sino-Japanese and civil wars. His most important contribution to the war effort was as political commissar of what became the Second Field Army, which inflicted a costly defeat on Japanese troops in August-October 1940 and waged the decisive Huai-Hai campaign that annihilated 550,000 Nationalist troops in southwest China in 1949. This provided Deng with his initial territorial base after the communist victory and the founding of the People's Republic of China (PRC). He served as political commissar of the Southwest Military and Administrative Commission in 1950–52, zealously implementing such central policies as *land reform. Beginning in 1952 he also became vice-premier of the PRC and in 1953 minister of finance and chair of the Central Economic Affairs Committee under Premier Zhou Enlai. By the mid-1950s he had shifted his base of operations almost entirely to the central level. In May 1954

he was first identified as secretary-general of the CCP Central Committee; in April 1955, he was elected to the Politburo, and in 1956 was elected youngest member of the newly established Standing Committee of the Politburo. "See that little man there?" Mao said, pointing to the 4'11" Deng during Khrushchev's 1954 visit to China. "He is highly intelligent and has a good future ahead of him."

Yet the loyalty of Mao's protégé was strictly professional. Deng joined a 1956 critique of the "cult of personality" and had reservations about many of Mao's policies and actions. He subtly distanced himself from Maoist policies during the aftermath of the disastrous Great Leap Forward (which Deng had initially supported). In the early 1960s Deng's secretariat helped implement such "revisionist" policies as the allocation of agricultural production quotas to individual *peasant households, gearing pay rates to productivity, meritocratization of the school system, and a deemphasis of class struggle in favor of economic recovery. Thus when Mao launched the *Cultural Revolution in 1966, Deng was ensnared in "errors" and soon became targeted as one of the "top Party persons in authority taking the capitalist road." Despite repeated self-criticisms, Deng thus endured his second (and most painful) fall, along with most other leading Party cadres of his generation. In addition to personal disgrace, one son (Pufang) was disabled by a suicide attempt during Red Guard interrogation, and Deng spent several years working under armed guard at a tractor factory.

Deng was however never expelled from the Party or criticized by name in the official press, and was permitted to submit additional self-criticisms, earning rehabilitation (as first vice premier) in 1973. Although Deng was useful to Mao in reorganizing the army after the most extreme phases of the Cultural Revolution, articulating China's worldview at the United Nations, and reviving industrial production, he soon fell into an alliance with the moderate premier, Zhou Enlai, who had incurred the ire of the Party's leading radicals (later "Gang of Four"). Deng helped draft an ambitious *modernization program that Zhou announced in January 1975 and which became a vehicle for freezing out the radicals' key policy-making positions. Promptly after delivering the funeral eulogy to Zhou in January 1976 Deng again came under media criticism for fostering a "reversal of correct verdicts" of the Cultural Revolution, and was dismissed from all posts (with Mao's concurrence) in April of that year. But in the aftermath of Mao's death in September and the arrest of the Gang of Four in October Hua Guofeng, was unable to resist pressure for Deng's rehabilitation. China's interim leader, after two self-criticisms, Deng reclaimed his old State and Party posts in July 1977. He lost no time outmaneuvering Hua to recapture the leadership agenda and in late 1978 introduced a new policy of "reform and opening to the outside world." This reform program was double-edged, aimed both at enhancing the efficiency of the economy and at undermining his political adversaries. Deng achieved his objectives over the next several years through a series of ingenious moves, including the wholesale rehabilitation of veteran cadres (followed by a rejuvenation campaign to encourage their retirement), an uncharacteristically liberal (and strictly pragmatic) attitude toward mass pro-democracy demonstrators, separating economics from politics, a repudiation of much of Mao's ideological legacy, and a public trial of the Gang of Four in early 1981.

Upon consolidating his hold on power in the early 1980s, Deng boldly promoted "socialism with Chinese characteristics." Communes were dissolved and replaced by family plots, markets proliferated in first rural then urban venues, and central financial controls devolved to local or factory levels. Reversing Mao's emphasis on China's "self-reliance," Deng opened the country to the outside world, inviting extensive trade and foreign investment; some 60,000 Chinese students were also allowed to study abroad, only half of whom returned. Repression of intellectuals was eased, only to be retightened at any sign of dissent. "Political structural reform" was endorsed but introduced with extreme caution so as not to threaten the party's monopoly on power. This created tension with China's increasingly open economy. When this culminated in a series of spontaneous mass protest in *Tiananmen Square in 1989, Deng ordered them crushed with brutal force. To the dismay of much of the world (including many colleagues), Deng consistently defended this act as absolutely necessary, advising heir apparent Jiang Zemin in 1991 that should future unrest occur, "They must immediately be suppressed! The later [the decision] the wider the unrest and the more difficult it is to restore order. . . ." Even after reaffirming his support for economic reform in 1992, Deng continued to reject further political liberalization. Deng Xiaoping died on 19 February 1997 at ninety-three, having been incapacitated by Parkinson's Disease for more than two years.

As leader of one of the world's largest and increasingly powerful countries during a pivotal reorientation of its developmental and strategic trajectories, Deng Xiaoping ranks among the most important political figures of the second half of the twentieth century. Apparently gruff and straightforward, the man actually abounded in ironies. Having spent his life in shrewd pursuit of political power, he steadfastly renounced the highest offices of the land when they were easily within his grasp, preferring to pull strings from behind the scenes. In terms of policy making Deng was extraordinarily flexible and informal: but when it came to policy implementation, he was bureaucratic and authoritarian. Deng was also a pragmatist who abandoned class struggle and the international crusade for socialist liberation; but he reacted harshly to any who challenged his own version of "Marxism-Leninism–Mao Zedong Thought." A decentralizer who gave unusual latitude to subordinates, he ruthlessly eliminated them if he disliked the policy outcomes. Despite leaving such unresolved contradictions for successors to sort out, Deng Xiaoping's achievements ensure him a place in modern Chinese history far exceeding his diminutive stature.

(See also SINO-AMERICAN RELATIONS.)

Deng Xiaoping, *Selected Works of Deng Xiaoping, 1975–1982* (Beijing, 1984). Deng Xiaoping, *Deng Xiaoping wenxuan*, 1938–1965 [Selected works], (Beijing, 1989). Deng Xiaoping, *Deng Xiaoping wenxuan* [Selected works], vol. 3 (Beijing, 1993). Deng Maomao, *Deng Xiaoping: My Father* (New York, 1995). David Shambaugh, ed., *Deng Xiaoping: Portrait of a Chinese Statesman* (Oxford, 1995).

LOWELL DITTMER

DENMARK. Danish democracy dates to the beginning of the twentieth century. The supremacy of the lower house and the right of its majority to form a government were established in 1901, and constitutional reform in 1915 completed the transition by universalizing suffrage and democratizing the upper house. The 1953 Constitution abolished the upper chamber entirely and Danish political institutions today fit the model of parliamentary government.

Danish politics are characterized by a multiparty system with strong and disciplined parties, frequent elections (on the average every two and a half years in the postwar period), an absence of single-party majorities (the last was before World War I), high voter participation (turnout has averaged over 80 percent since 1960), and stable coalition governments (until 1973). From the 1920s until the early 1970s, a five-party system framed by clear class divisions characterized Danish political competition. The Social Democrats predominated with an average vote of over 40 percent between 1929 and 1971; since 1932, the party has typically polled as many votes as the next two parties combined. Together the agrarian Liberals, Radical Liberals, and Conservatives averaged about 45 percent of the vote in this period. The Communist Party (CP), which had emerged from the Resistance with considerable working-class support, was replaced in Parliament by the Socialist People's Party (SPP) in 1960; the CP or SPP polled 5 percent to 10 percent between 1945 and 1971. The two-percent threshold for proportional representation permitted other groups to win seats, but, for half a century, the lines of partisan cleavage established by 1920 dominated the parliamentary landscape. Despite the multiparty system, Denmark enjoyed stable cabinet government because of the stability in party coalition patterns and the dominance of the Social Democratic–Radical Liberal alliance formed the foundation of Social Democrat dominance in government (thirty-three of forty years between 1929 and 1968) during this period.

This stable party system was shaken by the 1973 "earthquake election," which doubled the number of parties in Parliament from five to ten. One Danish voter in three cast a ballot for a party not represented in the previous Parliament. The most notable winner was the new, anti-tax Progress Party which ran second only to the Social Democrats. While the Progress Party's support has ebbed, fragmentation has persisted as eight to eleven parties have won seats in each subsequent election. Party fragmentation after 1973 has complicated cabinet formation and minority governments have been the rule. Subsequent Social Democratic–led governments and Conservative-led governments have governed effectively, however, and both have maintained the characteristic Danish *welfare state policies.

The foundation for the modern Danish welfare state was laid in the "red-green" agreement of 30 January 1933 between the Social Democratic–Radical Liberal cabinet of Social Democratic Prime Minister Thorvald Stauning (1873–1942) and the agrarian Liberal opposition. Successive Danish governments developed a complex system of transfer payments and social services to raise the level of those worst off and to maintain economic security for all. In the 1970s and 1980s, measures providing home assistance for the elderly and high-quality public day care for children eased women's entry into the labor market; women's labor force participation rates increased steadily from 44 percent in 1960 to 75 percent in 1985.

In the postwar period, policy making has increasingly become corporatist. Major interest organizations—labor, employers, and farmers—participate in policy deliberation and implementation. Indeed, these organizations have become so universal in membership and their policy involvement so significant that they constitute new channels of functional representation and democracy.

Despite the success of welfare measures in providing shared affluence (Danes have the highest living standard in the European Union), the period since the 1973–1974 oil price shock has been one of challenges: unemployment has remained stubbornly high; high tax rates have distorted economic behavior and undermined support for welfare policies; welfare spending has risen, partly because of rising take-up rates for some benefits, without improving actual welfare; and immigration has diminished the sense of social solidarity.

The Danes have been reluctant Europeans. Until Sweden and Finland joined the European Union (EV) in 1995, Denmark sought to keep one foot in Europe and the other in Nordic cooperation; the Danes saw themselves as a political—as well as geographical—bridge between *Scandinavia and the rest of Europe. Since Denmark joined the European Community in 1972, two-fifths to one-half of Danish voters have consistently opposed greater European integration, and Danes sent shock waves throughout the European Community in June 1992 by narrowly rejecting the *Maastricht Treaty designed to advance economic and monetary union and set the foundations for a common security policy. Danish voters subsequently ratified the bulk of the Maastricht Treaty in a second referendum in 1993, and approved the Amsterdam Treaty in 1998 by 55–45 margins. Yet Denmark was not among the eleven EU member states to join the euro zone when the single currency was introduced on 1, January 1999. Despite this considerable euro-skepticism, the Danish government has been prompt to adapt the national legislation to European standards. While nostalgia for the days when national policies were hammered out in Copenhagen is widely shared, most Danes—including many who consistently vote against greater European integration—recognize that Denmark, with little more than 5 million inhabitants, is simply too small to go it alone.

(See also CORPORATISM; ECONOMIC AND MONETARY UNION.)

Eric S. Einhorn and John Logue, *Modern Welfare States: Politics and Policies in Social Democratic Scandinavia* (New York, 1989). Kenneth E. Miller, *Denmark: A Troubled Welfare State* (Boulder, Colo., 1991).

JOHN LOGUE

DEPENDENCY. In the 1960s and 1970s, the originators of the dependency approach insisted that *Third World *development should be treated as a historically distinctive problem. They argued that diffusion of culture, technology, and resources from advanced industrial countries would not cause poor industrializing countries to replicate the developmental trajectories of Western Europe or the United States. In their view, industrializing in a global political economy already populated with industrial powers is a new kind of challenge, one that could not be analyzed in purely domestic terms or reduced to a reflection of structural change at the international level. Instead, the projects and struggles of local groups and classes interacted with constraints and opportunities generated by the global political economy to produce historically distinctive patterns of social, political, and economic change.

These assertions set practitioners of the dependency approach apart from earlier development theorists. *Modernization theorists saw the future of the Third World as shaped primarily by the global diffusion of the complex of "modern" values, attitudes, and social structures that prevailed in northwestern Europe and the United States. In this view the persistence of traditional local cultures was the principal obstacle to development. Neoclassical economists had a similar vision, except that they focused on entrepreneurship as the key value and the free market as the master institution. Marxists denied that the free market was the endpoint of the development, but still argued that the essence of change in the Third World lay in the diffusion of *capitalism. As long as the diffusion of global patterns was seen as the driving force of change, analysis naturally began with the dynamics of the metropole or "core" (the advanced industrial countries of Western Europe and the United States). Predictions regarding the future of the "periphery" (the poor nations of Asia, Africa, and Latin America) were essentially extrapolations from the experience of the core.

The idea of dependency emerged out of an intellectual tradition whose primary concern was to provide a convincing analysis of what was going on in the developing countries themselves. The cornerstone of the dependency literature was an essay produced by Fernando Henrique Cardoso, a Brazilian sociologist, and Enzo Faletto, a Chilean historian, in Santiago in the mid-1960s. Their essay had its roots in a long series of scholarly efforts by Latin Americans trying to understand why, after 200 years of pervasive political, economic, and cultural interchange with Europe and the United States, the degree of Latin America's "underdevelopment" vis-à-vis the advanced industrial countries had changed so little. Raúl *Prebisch and his colleagues working in Santiago for the UN *Economic Commission for Latin America and the Caribbean (ECLAC) had questioned the long-term benefits of pursuing comparative advantage by concentrating on the export of agricultural products and minerals. Celso Furtado, Caio Prado, Sergio Bagu, and others had dissected the historical connections between class structure and developmental trajectories. Florestan Fernandes, Pablo González Casanova, and Osvaldo Sunkel had examined the social and political implications of the local social structures that emerged from the long history of Latin America's interaction with the metropole. Cardoso and Faletto used the concept of dependency to recast and focus the debate. They offered a historical analysis of the transformations that had occurred in Latin America over the 150 years since the end of colonial rule and proposed that further efforts to analyze these transformations should use what they later came to call a "historical-structural" approach.

The historical-structural approach began the comprehensive analysis of economic and political actors reminiscent of classical political economy and set it in the context of a global system in which the fortunes of nations at different levels of development were bound together. It combined an analysis of the way in which relatively stable global structures conditioned the developmental possibilities of the various countries of Latin America with an appreciation of the way in which these structures had been transformed by historically specific conflicts and movements. Viewed through the lens of the historical-structural approach, the interweaving of interests across the divide that separates rich and poor countries cannot be reduced to a foreordained structural logic. The politics of development are full of contradictory combinations and unexpected twists and turns. Structures of domination meet with resistance from below. Those trying to maintain themselves in a position of dominance adopt new strategies that in turn yield unexpected opportunities for transformation. Social movements devise new definitions of what is politically possible and new organizational forms at the local level, while improvements in technology and communication make transnational mechanisms of control more effective. These contradictory trends do not just cancel each other out, they result in directions of change that could not have been spelled out in advance. Because they see development as historically open-ended, those who use the idea of dependency have, on the whole, preferred to think of it as a "methodology for the analysis of concrete situations of underdevelopment" rather than as a formal theory.

The dependency approach rejected the idea that the dynamics of diffusion drove the process of social change in Latin America, but it did not deny that the influence of the core was a critical force in shaping developments on the periphery of the world economy. The very term *dependency* highlights the extent to which the movement of economics and politics in poor countries is conditioned by a global economy dominated by others. Dependency flows from asymmetrical ties between nations, but it is not simply a relationship between countries. It involves an ensemble of ties among groups and classes both between and within nations. Groups and classes in the core have interests with respect to the course of development in the periphery. These resonate with the interests of some local groups and classes and conflict with those of others in ways that are contingent on historical circumstance.

Even during the period of "outward-oriented growth" in the late nineteenth century when all Latin American countries were relying on the export of primary products, there was variation. In countries where exports consisted primarily of minerals under the control of foreign capital, strategies of capital accumulation, political alliances, and possibilities for the emergence of local industry were different from those in countries where the production of agrarian exports was undertaken on locally-owned haciendas or latifundia. Such variation affected domestic responses to changes in the global economy. All the countries of Latin America were affected by the traumatic economic consequences of the Great Depression, but the growth of the nascent manufacturing sector was stimulated only in some of them. Once local manufacturing began to emerge, the situation became even more complicated. Landowners producing export crops in the periphery (Argentine cattle ranchers, for example) shared an interest in liberal trade agreements with exporters of industrial goods based in the core (Manchester textile merchants, for example). Local manufacturers whose interests were threatened by this local-foreign alliance sometimes turned to workers and middle-class groups in their search for political allies. The state apparatus became an arena of contestation. Later, when transnational corporations had been drawn into the process of local industrialization, local entrepreneurs suffered from their competition within the domestic market but were at the same time beneficiaries of the industrial societies that the transnationals were helping to create.

Although there is general agreement within the dependency tradition that prospects for development must be analyzed by looking at the interweaving of local interests and political strategies with those of groups and classes in the advanced industrial countries, there is a range of opinion with regard to developmental consequences. Early arguments seemed to imply that local agrarian and commercial interests allied with metropolitan manufacturers and foreign investors in extractive industries would be able to block industrialization in peripheral countries indefinitely. Even after it was clear that substantial industrialization was occurring in the countries of the periphery, some argued that powerful metropolitan interests would block the transfer to the periphery of full capacity to produce technologically innovative products and processes and that this would in turn force local industrialists to rely on wage-repressive strategies, undercutting the growth of domestic markets and the possibility for self-sustained growth. Others have focused on the possibility of an alliance of transnational and local capital constructed around a project of local industrialization. The "dependent development" that results from this sort of alliance may not carry with it the political and social consequences associated with industrialization in the core but, as cases like Brazil illustrate, it has produced substantial economic growth.

During the 1970s, the dependency approach gained adherents not just in Latin America but in North America and Europe as well. It provided the impetus for a rich outpouring of research, ranging from quantitative cross-national analyses of direct foreign investment (for example in the work of Volker Bornschier, Christopher Chase-Dunn, and Richard Rubinson) to detailed studies of the interplay of foreign and local actors in particular countries and sectors (as, for example, David Becker's work on copper mining in Peru or Gary Gereffi's study of the pharmaceutical industry). At the same time, the dependency approach was subject to a barrage of criticism. It was accused of focusing too much attention on the role of external ties and distracting attention from the dynamics of internal conflict and of not providing an adequate account of the dynamics of interaction between local and international groups and classes in other regions of the world, such as the newly industrializing countries of East Asia. Nonetheless, the dependency approach remained an important point of departure for cross-regional analyses, and Cardoso and Faletto's historical-structural methodology continued to serve as a guide for those working on the comparative study of development. At the dawn of the twenty-first century, the issues raised by the dependency approach remain as relevant as ever. International debt and its local consequences, the opening of domestic markets to new competition from imports, the return to an emphasis on outward-oriented growth all offer opportunities for the sort of analysis that Cardoso and Faletto proposed. Looking back over the decades since it emerged, dependency continues to stand out as one of the rare cases in which an approach generated primarily by scholars in the Third World subsequently came to have a pervasive influence on the perspectives of scholars working the core.

(See also CLASS AND POLITICS; IMPERIALISM; INTERNATIONAL POLITICAL ECONOMY; INTERNATIONAL SYSTEMS; MULTINATIONAL CORPORATIONS; NEWLY INDUSTRIALIZING ECONOMIES; POLITICAL DEVELOPMENT; TECHNOLOGY TRANSFER.)

Fernando Henrique Cardoso and Enzo Faletto, *Dependencia y Desarollo en América Latina* (Santiago, 1967); published in English as *Dependency and Development in Latin America* (Berkeley, Calif., 1979). Gabriel Palma, "Dependency: A Formal Theory of Development or a Methodology for the Analysis of Concrete Situations of Underdevelopment" *World Development* (1978): 881–894.

PETER B. EVANS

DEREGULATION. A wide-ranging deregulation of economic activity has been one of the notable developments of contemporary *political economy. For most of the twentieth century, the trend throughout the world had been toward more detailed and extensive regulation of business. Since the mid-1970s, however, most of the developed democracies have scaled down or abolished important regulatory programs. Many developing countries have followed suit. The *privatization of municipal services and state enterprises in the Western democracies and the liberalization of planned economies in Eastern and *Central Europe are evidence of deregulation during the last quarter of the twentieth century.

Politically, deregulation sometimes has resulted from economic or technological changes that led regulated industries to withdraw their support for regulation. In the United States the introduction of new forms of personal saving forced the banking industry to support the deregulation of deposit interest.

But for the most part deregulation has reflected intellectual and political developments. Academic economists had concluded by the 1960s that regulation of pricing and entry in multifirm industries was almost always unwarranted. By the mid-1970s, certain public attitudes were adding force to the economists' critique. These included anxiety about inflation, skepticism about the efficacy of government programs, and (especially in the United States) a moralistic anger about improper collusion between government and business. In addition, the globalization of the world economy has pushed many countries toward deregulation as a means of enhancing the competitiveness of their industries.

These forces promoted deregulation primarily in one class of regulatory programs—those that controlled entry or set production quotas or minimum prices in potentially competitive industries. Major industries that experienced deregulation include transportation (including railroads, trucking, airlines, intercity buses); financial services (banking, securities brokerage); communications (telephone equipment, long-distance service, broadcasting, cable television); agriculture (price supports, marketing orders); and many other industries and occupations. Although there were also efforts to reduce the cost or increase the efficiency of other regulatory programs (environmental protection, equal opportunity requirements, public utility regulation, and so on), these programs generally did not come under severe attack.

Support for deregulation has cut across political lines. In the United States, early sponsorship was provided by a liberal Democratic senator, Edward M. Kennedy, and a conservative Republican president, Gerald R. Ford. In Britain, deregulation was a central commitment of the conservative *Thatcher government. In France, broadcast deregulation was implemented by the socialist *Mitterrand government. The principal opposition generally came from regulated industries and their labor unions, which sought to preserve protection from competition. The ability to adopt deregulatory policy changes, therefore, typically depended on government's capacity to overcome pressure from narrow groups and act on behalf of widely shared interests. The scope and intensity of deregulation also reflected national dispositions toward market-oriented economic policies. The most wide-ranging deregulation occurred in the United States, Britain, and Australia; Canada, Italy, France, and Germany took more moderate steps toward deregulation; Japan, Denmark, and Austria adopted very limited measures. In the 1990s, the economic integration advanced by the European Union has led to wide-ranging deregulation among all the member countries.

For the most part, deregulation has delivered on its promise of economic benefits: lower rates and more flexible service in freight transportation, accelerated technological progress in communications, expanded entertainment and information services, lower average airfares, smaller commissions for the execution of stock transactions, and higher interest rates on savings deposits, among others. In a few cases, however, there have also been adverse consequences. These have included, in the United States, fare instability in the airline industry and, most important, the collapse of the savings and loan industry in the late 1980s. But even for those industries, there has been little support for reregulation.

The privatization of municipal services and state enterprises in the Western democracies and the liberalization of planned economies in Eastern and Central Europe are related manifestations of a worldwide pro-market trend in recent decades.

(See also PLANNING; THATCHERISM.)

Martha Derthick and Paul J. Quirk, *The Politics of Deregulation* (Washington, D.C., 1985). Kenneth Button and Dennis Swann, eds., *The Age of Regulatory Reform* (Oxford, 1989). Merilee S. Grindle, *Challenging the State: Crisis and Innovation in Latin America and Africa* (Cambridge, U.K., 1996).

PAUL J. QUIRK

DÉTENTE. Derived from the French verb "to slacken," détente denotes an easing of strained relations between states. In medieval French, a *destente* was the mechanism that tightened or loosened the tension of a crossbow string. Although the term has a long tradition in diplomatic parlance, its contemporary usage is identified primarily with the brief period of improved U.S.–Soviet relations during the 1970s. The chief architects of the *superpower détente were President Richard *Nixon and National Security Adviser Henry *Kissinger.

In his 1969 inaugural address, Nixon proclaimed an end to the "era of confrontation" with the *Soviet Union and the advent of an "era of negotiation." This move toward a less confrontational approach to relations with the Soviet Union came at a time of widespread public calls for a radical scaling down in U.S. overseas commitments following the Vietnam War. Operating within the constraints of this domestic political context, Nixon and Kissinger developed their détente policy as a realistic variation of George *Kennan's *containment doctrine. At the heart of this strategy was the concept of "linkage" under which the *United States sought to create a system of incentives and penalties to moderate Soviet behavior. Tangible economic benefits, such as *technology transfers or financial credits, were to be granted to promote more cooperative Soviet policies—for example, Moscow's assistance in resolving regional conflicts in Southeast Asia and the Middle East. The obverse, of course, was that such positive inducements would be withheld if the Soviet Union continued to pursue *Cold War policies. U.S. officials hoped that an expanding web of economic, political, and cultural relations between East and West would not only moderate Soviet external behavior but might also help foster a process of political liberalization within the Soviet Union itself. While acknowledging that the superpower relationship remained essentially competitive, Kissinger believed the long-term success of détente could lead to the creation of a new "structure of peace" and the end of the Cold War.

Détente diplomacy produced a range of bilateral accords, most notably on *arms control. The May 1972 summit meeting in Moscow between Nixon and Soviet leader Leonid Brezhnev yielded agreements on the limitation of strategic nuclear weapons (SALT I) and antiballistic missiles (ABM). In addition, a statement of "Basic Principles" was concluded that committed both sides to "exercise restraint" and eschew "efforts to obtain unilateral advantage at the expense of the other." These principles, likened by Nixon to a "road map," were to be a code of conduct regulating superpower behavior.

In practice, the implementation of the 1972 "Basic Principles" agreement was hindered by competing Soviet and U.S. conceptions of détente. If Nixon and Kissinger saw détente as a variation of containment, the Soviet leadership viewed it as an updated version of Nikita *Khrushchev's "peaceful coexistence" doctrine. Brezhnev asserted that while there was no alternative to détente in the nuclear age, it did not negate the Marxist tenets of international *class struggle. From Moscow's perspective, détente diplomacy offered mechanisms for keeping East-West competition within acceptable bounds to avert *war. The Soviets rejected the U.S. preference for linkage in favor of a compartmentalized approach in which arms control, regional conflicts, and economic relations were considered as discrete issues. In its efforts to impose its conception of détente on the Soviet Union, the U.S. administration found linkage difficult to achieve on issues where there existed a strong mutuality of superpower interest. During the *Angolan conflict of 1975–1976, for example, the Ford administration, despite Kissinger's warning that Soviet military assistance to one of the warring factions was incompatible with détente, did not suspend the SALT II negotiations given the powerful U.S. interest in completing a strategic arms limitation agreement.

An important milestone in détente diplomacy was the signing of the 1975 *Helsinki Accords by the thirty-five member states of the *Conference on Security and Cooperation in Europe (CSCE). Among its provisions, this agreement declared the inviolability of Europe's postwar borders and committed the signatories to the maintenance of fundamental *human rights. The Kremlin's failure to comply fully with the Helsinki Accords—notably, the continued suppression of political dissidents and Jewish activists—intensified public criticism of the U.S. administration's détente policy. This sentiment had been fueled in April 1975 by the humiliating defeat of the U.S.–backed regime in South Vietnam at the hands of Communist guerrilla forces supported by the Soviet Union. Conservative critics charged that détente had become a "one-way street" of U.S. economic and political concessions to the Moscow regime without any corresponding change in Soviet behavior. Under this domestic pressure, President Gerald Ford, who had succeeded Nixon in August 1974, was prompted to drop détente from his political lexicon in favor of the phrase "peace through strength" during the 1976 election campaign.

President Jimmy *Carter came to office in January 1977 with the avowed intention to continue his Republican predecessors' policy of détente toward the Soviet Union, albeit with greater assertiveness on the issue of Soviet human rights abuses. During the late 1970s, increased Soviet activism in the Third World (e.g., Angola, Ethiopia) was a major factor undermining superpower détente. This pattern of behavior culminated in the Soviet invasion of Afghanistan in December 1979—an act prompting Carter to withdraw the unratified SALT II treaty from Senate consideration. The Afghan invasion marked the end of the détente era and ushered in the return to a more militarized approach to containment under President Ronald *Reagan following the 1980 presidential election.

The Soviet–U.S. experience of the 1970s demonstrated that détente is a condition, not a structure, of *international relations. While the superpowers acknowledged a common interest in the prevention of nuclear war, both remained committed to the pursuit of unilateral advantage. The Nixon administration's hyperbolic rhetoric about a "structure of peace" created public expectations that détente marked the end of Cold War competition. The 1970s détente ultimately unraveled because the reality of political linkage made it impossible to isolate continued competition in the *Third World from other aspects of the superpower relationship, such as arms control.

The late 1980s did not witness the revival of the term *détente* during the improvement of Soviet–U.S. relations under Reagan and Soviet President Mikhail *Gorbachev. This stemmed not only from the desire to avoid unfavorable political connotations from the past; it also reflected the belief that profound Soviet societal changes—Kennan's key precondition for the end of the Cold War—might lead not to renewed détente but to a fundamental transformation in the structure of international relations.

(See also AMERICAN FOREIGN POLICY; INTERNATIONAL COOPERATION; SOVIET-AFGHANISTAN WAR; SOVIET FOREIGN POLICY; STRATEGIC ARMS LIMITATION TREATIES.)

Henry A. Kissinger, *White House Years* (Boston, 1979). Robert S. Litwak, *Détente and the Nixon Doctrine: American Foreign Policy and the Pursuit of Stability, 1969–1976* (Cambridge, U.K., 1984).

ROBERT S. LITWAK

DETERRENCE. Most simply, deterrence is dissuasion by means of threat. The term, with French roots, means "to frighten from." States try to deter one another from attacking, police try to deter criminals, and parents try to deter children from acts that may harm themselves or others. As an explicit policy, justified and guided by theory, the most developed form of deterrence originates in the *international relations of the nuclear era.

Elements of deterrence theory can be found in early writings on aerial warfare. For example, the mathematician F. W. Lanchester (*Aircraft in Warfare*, London, 1916) wrote: "The power of reprisal and the knowledge that the means of reprisal exists will ever be a far greater deterrent than any pseudo-legal contract." Its prominence, however, dates from the nuclear era, and especially U.S. efforts to deter perceived threats to itself and its allies by the Soviet Union and its allies. In 1946 Bernard Brodie published in *The Absolute Weapon* (New York) his famous statement which, without using the term deterrence, expressed the essence of subsequent policy: "Thus far the chief purpose of our military establishment has been to win wars. From now on its chief purpose must be to avert them."

U.S. Secretary of State John Foster Dulles articulated the policy as nuclear deterrence by threat of "massive" retaliation in 1954, when he declared an intent "to depend primarily upon a great capacity to retaliate instantly by means and at places of our own choosing." This threat was issued in response to the perceived continuing danger of Soviet aggression and to Americans, the unacceptable costs of meeting that "aggression" with large-scale conventional forces as had been done in the *Korean War. It represents an example of "extended" deterrence, wherein the deterrer wishes to prevent not a direct attack on itself but an attack on some third party (ally or neutral). Whereas the ability of a nuclear-armed superpower to deter a direct attack on itself was deemed to be high, extended deterrence—although practiced widely—has been thought to be more problematic, as the stakes to the deterrer were less and its willingness to use force therefore more in doubt.

In the emphasis on threat, deterrence is often distinguished from more general forms of persuasion, including those based principally on the offer of rewards. A more general theory of influence includes rewards, as do some deterrence theorists; nevertheless rewards are often neglected by such theorists. Moreover, as an exercise of dissuasion deterrence aims to prevent another party (typically an adversary) from taking certain actions, rather than to induce the adversary to undertake a particular action or to cease an action already under way. In strategic parlance the latter is often called compellence. Policies of deterrence and compellence both utilize coercion, but compellence typically is the more difficult as it demands an actual change in policy.

Deterrence is often conceptualized as a function of capability and will. That is, it is posited to succeed to the degree that the adversary perceives the deterrer as both able to inflict severe punishment and willing to do so—even perhaps at substantial cost to the deterrer. A deterrer may undertake various military or diplomatic actions to try to enhance an adversary's assessment of its capability and/or will. Deterrent threats may be expressed as a readiness to deny the adversary the ability to carry out or benefit from its action, as well as to punish the adversary (without necessarily denying it immediate benefits of the action). U.S. strategic nuclear deterrence policy typically has taken the latter form; Soviet policy took somewhat more often, the former.

A formulation emphasizing capability and will is embedded in rational deterrence theory, which assumes that the adversary will be able to make a well-informed means-end calculation of the damage which the deterrer can inflict and of the likelihood that the deterrer will actually carry out its threat. It thus forms part of a more general model of *rational choice based on expected utilities. A more general model, however, also includes terms for those incentives of the ad-

versary that are beyond ready manipulation by the deterrer; that is, it includes the adversary's subjective calculation of the likely costs and benefits not only of disregarding the deterrer's threat but also of those it may incur or forgo if it does allow itself to be deterred. These costs, in terms of missed opportunities or subsequent vulnerabilities, may be severe. The limited formulation of rational deterrence theory, by ignoring them, may give an erroneous prediction of behavior. For example, a leader faced with an internal political threat to power may be motivated to take risks internationally that would otherwise be deemed unacceptable.

Another limitation is simply that the adversary may not behave "rationally" even in the limited sense of rationality used here. Cognitive and social psychologists often challenge deterrence theory on its adequacy as an empirical predictor and therefore on its adequacy as a guide to policy formulation. Especially under conditions of severe crisis—surprise, finite decision time, and threat to major values perhaps magnified by deterrent threats—decision makers may make a very inadequate search for information and alternatives, may make very inaccurate estimates of the intentions or capabilities of the deterrer, and may even be unable to make ordered means-ends calculations of their own desired outcomes. Decision makers may be led, by their biases or "motivated misperceptions," to exaggerate their chances of success, especially if they are simultaneously faced with other threats to vital interests (e.g., such as internal political threats to power). Decisions taken by complex organizations lacking a strong leader may further deviate from the basic model of rationality as applied to the decisions of a single individual.

Academic scholarship has reached little consensus on the conditions and degree to which a theory of rational deterrence provides a reasonable explanation or prediction of behavior. Systematic empirical study of cases of extended deterrence indicates that it is more likely to succeed when the local balance of forces and the active and readily mobilizable balances of military force favor the deterrer (capability). Deterrence is also more likely to succeed when the deterrer's *crisis bargaining behavior is firm but flexible, and it has neither bullied nor appeased in a previous crisis (will, tempered by elements of reassurance as discussed below). These findings suggest that rational deterrence theory offers a useful guide to the interpretation of many cases; nevertheless there are many circumstances it does not adequately explain, and it is difficult to know in advance when its predictions will prove satisfactory.

Evaluation of the success of a deterrent threat is often difficult, as it requires an assessment of the adversary's prior intentions, and hence of the role of the threat in changing those intentions. It demands a counterfactual assessment of how an adversary would have acted in the absence of the deterrent threat. Decision makers' intentions are rarely known with certainty, either at the time of the threat or in their subsequent statements. Political decision-makers often have incentives to disguise the degree to which they may have allowed themselves to be dissuaded, or to expose their readiness to run great risks. Moreover, the manipulation of uncertainty, and thus of deception, is inherent in a deterrent situation. Both the deterrer and the adversary have incentives to appear more determined to fight than they really may be, and their intentions may change as they seem to gather more complete information on each other's incentives. Thus an observer may erroneously say deterrence has succeeded when the adversary in fact had little intention to attack (deterrence was really irrelevant) or may erroneously treat a retreat as evidence of an initial lack of resolve when in fact the adversary did probe the deterrer's apparent resolve and then changed its intentions (deterrence really did succeed).

The analytical and empirical problems may be most severe in situations of "general" rather than "immediate" deterrence, i.e., in which there is no crisis of explicit threat and counterthreat, but merely a long-term deterrent threat not matched with any overt military or political action by the adversary. Thus many Western observers often claimed that U.S. nuclear deterrence of Soviet attack on Western Europe succeeded, while Eastern or neutral observers questioned whether the Soviet Union ever had an intention to attack Europe that needed to be deterred by military threat.

Such considerations make it difficult to evaluate the success of U.S. massive retaliation policy in the 1950s, or to determine whether it was more successful than merely the threat of taking non-nuclear action might have been. Whereas the United States manifestly had the capability to inflict severe damage on the Soviet Union with *nuclear weapons, its willingness to do so remained in doubt, given the Soviet Union's emerging ability, in return, to inflict damage on the United States and/or its allies. The United States might have been perceived as more willing to take non-nuclear military actions that, although less punishing to the Soviet Union, also carried less danger of severe Soviet retaliation.

Doubts over the credibility of U.S. threats were inherent in the earliest policy formulations, and grew in subsequent years as Soviet capabilities grew. In the application to modem nuclear deterrence they came to illustrate a fundamental paradox of deterrence theory; the deterrer often is making a threat that would not be in its own interest actually to carry out. Policy attempts to grapple with this problem involved various statements about "graduated" or "flexible" response, leaving the adversary uncertain about what specific responses might be forthcoming to particular actions. As major powers have come to achieve relatively secure, invulnerable nuclear deterrent forces, the ability of other nuclear powers to make credible threats to use nuclear weapons against them has become more constrained, especially in situations of extended deterrence. Under these circumstances, however, mutual direct nuclear deterrence (sometimes called mutual assured destruction) is often regarded as relatively stable, except perhaps under conditions of crisis. Policies that attempt to deter by threatening to strike the adversary's "values" (loosely, its population centers) are often thought to be more stable than those directed toward the adversary's forces (specifically, its retaliatory capabilities), but in operational details the strategies and their likely consequences become highly complex. The moral dimensions of counter-population nuclear deterrence have come under intense scrutiny from proponents of the just-war tradition.

Uncertainty about intentions has been magnified by uncertainty about the deterring state's ability to completely control the use of force by its own military units; that is, by the possibility of unauthorized action by military commanders that would not necessarily be desired by the high-level leaders. Thus evolved some application of a strategy of the "threat that leaves something to chance."

Uncertainty may serve to undermine deterrence as well as to enhance it. Successful deterrence policies must combine threats with some measure of reassurance that dire consequences will not follow if the adversary does in fact abstain from an undesired action. A threat that leaves something to chance may help to deter the emergence of a political-military crisis, but should the crisis occur anyway, an adversary may feel compelled to make a "preemptive" strike if it fears that for one reason or another the deterrer may use force in any case. This, as well as the social-psychological conditions of crisis that may distort decision making, is why a policy of deterrence may become especially problematic in crises.

Policies of deterrence always entail some risk of failure—a potentially catastrophic failure when weapons of mass destruction are employed. In the post–Cold War era nuclear deterrence has come to be regarded as less necessary. The incentives of major powers to encroach on each other's territory or vital interests are reduced by the mutual rewards of cooperative relations under peacetime conditions. Efforts to abolish all nuclear weapons have gained greater credibility. The dangers of crisis instability are further reduced by various measures of arms reduction, information gathering, and communication. Nevertheless large numbers of nuclear weapons remain and policies of military deterrence are not entirely superseded.

(See also FORCE, USE OF; STRATEGY; SUPERPOWER; U.S. FOREIGN POLICY.)

Glenn H. Snyder, *Deterrence and Defense: Toward a Theory of National Security* (Princeton, N.J., 1961). Patrick M. Morgan, *Deterrence: A Conceptual Analysis*, 2d ed. (Beverly Hills, Calif., 1983). Bruce Russett, "Ethical Dilemmas of Nuclear Deterrence" *International Security* 8 (Spring 1984): 36–54. Paul K. Huth, *Extended Deterrence and the Prevention of War* (New Haven, Conn., 1988). Robert Jervis, *The Meaning of the Nuclear Revolution: Statecraft and the Prospect of Armageddon* (Ithaca, N.Y., 1988).

BRUCE RUSSETT

DEVELOPMENT AND UNDERDEVELOPMENT. See overleaf.

DICTATORSHIP. See AUTHORITARIANISM.

DIPLOMACY. Above and before all else, diplomacy is a system of communication between strangers. It is the formal means by which the self-identity of the sovereign *state is constituted and articulated through external relations with other states. Like the dialogue from which it is constructed, diplomacy requires and seeks to mediate otherness through the use of persuasion and *force, promises and threats, codes and symbols. It is also, according to the American humorist Will Rogers, "the art of saying 'Nice doggie' until you can find a rock."

The linguistic origins of diplomacy are fairly easy to ascertain, its historical beginnings less so. The word itself comes from the Greek verb *diploun*, referring to a folded document such as a tax receipt or passport. When these "diploma" be-
(cont. on p. 222)

DEVELOPMENT AND UNDERDEVELOPMENT. From its very beginning the science of economics has been preoccupied with economic development. But the theory of development as distinct from economic development came into vogue in the wake of World War II at the height of the nationalist movement in the *Third World. Third World countries embraced development in order to secure their independence from colonialism, to meet rising expectations of material betterment, and to become a going concern in the *international system. The West supported Third World aspirations to development in what was called "partnership in development." This support was apparently motivated by the need to maintain a presence in the Third World and to facilitate the fight against the spread of communism, which the West feared might get new impetus from the rapid industrialization of the Soviet Union. The earlier Western writings on development issues were interested in the problems of industrialization in Eastern and Southeastern Europe. Development theory emerged as a variant of a notable Western model of social transformation, *modernization theory. Modernization theory takes its point of departure from the evolutionary paradigm which dominated classical sociology. This paradigm extracted ideal characteristics of forms of society and posited a movement from lower ones to higher ones. The paradigms were also a theory of progress, which invariably represented the Western societies as the apex of historical evolution. For instance, Ferdinand Toënnies thought in terms of a movement from *gemeinschaft* to *gesellschaft*, Henry Maine from status to contract, Max *Weber from traditional forms of authority to the rational bureaucratic, and Emile Durkheim from mechanical to organic solidarity. As Westerners looked around for a way of making sense of the evolution of the Third World countries and relating them to their own experience and vision of the world, they fell back on the evolutionary theories of the past, using the terms of modernization to describe the movement of societies. They took for granted a theory of progress by which all societies are on a continuum moving from a state of backwardness to one of *modernity. In its most characteristic form, modernization theory posits an original state of underdevelopment characterized by, among other things, a low rate of economic growth which is amenable at least potentially to a change for the better, that is, development. This original state of backwardness is initially universal, but some countries in the West have managed to overcome it. Others would overcome it too. The spatial distribution of progress, however polarized it may appear to be at any point, is never static, but dynamic. By proximity and interaction, progress is diffused. Uneven development is essentially a transitional phenomenon which can be removed by creating certain favorable conditions within the underdeveloped regions and by ensuring the appropriate interactions between the underdeveloped regions and the developed ones. The evolutionary schema which modernization theory used to hang these ideas invariably made the desired end of societal evolution (modernity) the ideal characteristics of the West, so modernization could easily be construed as Westernization. The other side of this was the representation of premodern society as "backward," in an undesirable state of being or a "problem." There were specific disciplinary versions of modernization theory, and it was these disciplinary versions which were developed in the wake of the World War II for the comparison of the Third World societies that form the corpus of development theory. In economics one of the notable works of development theory was Rostow's *Stages of Economic Growth*. Rostow held that all societies evolve through five stages to self-sustaining economic growth: traditional society with a characteristically low level of technology and productivity; a transitional stage for satisfying the "preconditions" for change; the "takeoff" stage when structural constraints to industrialization have been removed and an entrepreneurial class has emerged; the drive to maturity when industrialization is well under way and the levels of technological development and productivity are high; and the society of high mass consumption when there is general abundance and society has moved beyond basic needs to the consumption of durable goods. A rather more sophisticated if less well known theory of economic growth is Alexander Gerschenkron's *Economic Backwardness in Historical Perspective*. Gerschenkron regards his stages of economic growth not so much as universal but as historical; he allows for the possibility of skipping stages and for multilinearity. The sociological development theories mainly restated the dichotomous evolutionary schema of classical sociology, such as Durkheim's mechanical and organic solidarity in *The Division of Labor in Society* and Weber's traditional and rational-bureaucratic authority in *Economy and Society*. One of the most influential classical sources of sociological theories of development was Talcott Parsons's *Social System*, which was famous for his pattern variables, a more complex version of the dichotomous schemes found in Durkheim and Toennies: particularism-universalism, ascription-achievement, and diffuseness-specificity. This was widely applied to societal development by theorists such as Edward Shils in *Political Development in New States* and Bert Hoselitz in *Theories of Economic Growth*. In political science the pioneering work of political development theory was *The Politics of Developing Areas*, edited by Gabriel Almond and James S. Coleman (1960). This study in comparative politics was highly suggestive of what became known as the developmental approach. Perhaps the best known work in the theory of *political development was Almond and Powell's *Comparative Politics: A Developmental Approach*. The work theorized that political systems are developed to the extent that they are characterized by structural differentiation, subsystem autonomy, and cultural *secularization. A more conventional stages approach was Organski's *Stages of Political Development*, which was much like a political science version of Rostow's *Stages of Economic Growth*. The theory of political development was treated in depth in the multivolume Princeton Series in Political Development, which was sponsored by the Committee on Comparative Politics of the Social Science Research Council of the United States.

Limitations. The development theories were at best heuristic devices. With minor exceptions they were too general and too vague to be taken seriously as scientific theories and paradigms even by the standards of the social sciences. Their major concepts could not be operationalized and their empirical referents were unclear; they could not be refuted or corroborated. They tended to be ahistorical because they assumed that the state of underdevelopment was initially universal; their teleologism distracted them from paying close attention to the realities on the ground in the developing societies. Finally they were too ethnocentric. They used evolutionary schema that made the desired end of social evolution the ideal characteristics of the West, which meant that in the final analysis development was confused with Westernization.

Marxism and Development. It is interesting to note that for all its concern with the emancipation of the oppressed and apparent appeal in the Third World, *Marxism does not have a theory of development. *Marx was not interested in the study of *capitalism in the less developed countries. He focused on the genesis of capitalism in Western Europe. To be sure, Marx understood capitalism to be a global phenomenon and treated it as such. Here and there, there are indications of the impact of the development of capitalism in less developed or preindustrial societies, notably in the *Communist Manifesto, Das Kapital,* and in the letters and articles for the *New York Herald Tribune* from 1853 to 1859. But these are passing references and not a treatment of the topic. This was by no means a matter of chance. There is a legacy of hostility and contempt for peasant societies in Marxism dating back to Marx himself. He considered peasants a reactionary force and peasant societies a drag on historical progress. The attitude to peasants in the *Communist Manifesto,* where peasants are referred to as barbarians, is typical. *Peasants and peasant societies were consigned to the role of objects of history whose fate was to be determined by what happened in the industrialized West. Peasant societies lacked internally generated dynamism, and there were no dialectics of development specific to them. This attitude did not encourage any serious study of the so-called backward societies or their development. It was assumed that while the impact of the globalization of capitalism was devastating for these societies, it was essentially progressive, the engine of their incorporation and development.

Underdevelopment. While development theory took underdevelopment for granted as an initially universal state and focused on explaining how development occurs, underdevelopment theory problematized underdevelopment as a historically constituted reality and concerned itself with theorizing its persistence.

Underdevelopment theory arose from two sources: theoretical debates within Marxism and the concrete development experience of Latin America. As we have seen, Marx had assumed the desirability and feasibility of capitalist development in the non-European countries and insisted that their development as part of the process of the globalization of capitalism would be no different from capitalist development in the West. But these assumptions had become a matter of

dispute within the Russian *Left. In particular the Narodniks disputed the view that capitalism was a desirable, feasible, or even a necessary option for preindustrial societies. The Narodniks saw in the Russian commune the possibility of a direct transition from a precapitalist mode of production to socialism. It was this debate that inspired *Lenin's great study, *The Development of Capitalism in Russia,* which came down on the side of orthodoxy. But that was not the end of the matter. The classic Marxist studies of *imperialism were to raise the questions of the progressive role of capitalism again and again. Unfortunately the questions were often obscured or deflated by more pressing issues which Marxist theorists had to deal with, namely, the revolution of 1905, the war, the collapse of international socialist solidarity, and the surprising ability of capitalism to increase real wages. But from the end of the 1950s the classical Marxist view was effectively challenged by a series of influential writings which argued that capitalist development in underdeveloped countries was neither feasible nor progressive. The first major work to break ground in this direction was Paul Baran's *Political Economy of Growth.* Baran argued that far from being an asset to progress, capitalism was, in prevailing conditions, inimical to it. The reactionary character of capitalism worldwide was particularly so in the underdeveloped countries, where it was incapable of developing the productive forces because of the opposition of the interests of capital in the developed countries:

. . . economic development in underdeveloped countries is profoundly inimical to the dominant interests in the advanced capitalist countries. Supplying many important raw materials to the industrialized countries, providing their corporations with vast profits and investment outlets, the backward world has always represented the indispensable hinterland of the highly developed capitalist West. Thus the ruling class in the United States (and elsewhere) is bitterly opposed to the industrialization of the so-called "source countries" and to the emergence of integrated processing economies in the colonial and semicolonial world. (Baran, pp. 11–12)

Latin American social scientists, notably *Prebisch, Cardoso, Sunkel, and Dos Santos, challenged the thesis that capitalism fosters development (the progressive thesis) and enunciated an alternative theory of underdevelopment; their particular version came to be known as *dependency theory because of its emphasis on the dominance of Western economies and the satellite status of Latin American economies. Initially the focal interest of the work done by the UN Economic Commission for Latin America (ECLA) under Prebisch was on international trade, particularly terms of trade. It opposed the classical standard theory of international trade developed from Smith and Ricardo through Heckshen, Ohlin, and Samuelson. ECLA argued that the world economy had been polarized into a center and a periphery. The former is characterized by a production structure which is homogeneous and diversified and the latter by a structure which is heterogeneous and specialized. The periphery is specialized in the sense that production is confined to a few primary commodities and to enclaves which have little or no linkages to the rest of the economy. It is heterogeneous on account of its dualism. Because of these features, the economies of the periphery cannot benefit much from the international division of labor and international trade. Low levels of productivity and unfavorable terms of trade add up to sustained unequal development. Building on the work of Baran and ECLA, André Gunder Frank came to represent the full development of dependency theory and to epitomize the left-wing challenge to the progressive thesis of classical Marxism. In his main work, *Capitalism and Underdevelopment in Latin America*, and through several writings, Frank developed his thesis that "underdevelopment as we know it today, and economic development as well, are the simultaneous and related products of the development on a world-scale and over a history of more than four centuries, at least, of a single integrated economic system: capitalism." He maintained that capitalisms at the center and the periphery are dynamically related and the dynamics produce development at both ends; the problem is that at the end of the periphery, what occurs is the development of underdevelopment. The underdevelopment of the periphery is a condition of the development of the center. Thus there is no way of eliminating underdevelopment at the periphery apart from delinking from capitalism. Another major contribution to underdevelopment theory, this time from Africa, came from Samir Amin. In numerous writings, particularly *Accumulation on a World Scale*, Samir Amin argued that the industrialized countries and the less developed countries are integrated in a manner which inhibits capitalism from performing its historical role of developing the productive forces in the underdeveloped countries. He asserted that from the beginning of the imperialistic period, the less developed countries were no longer capable of attaining autonomous self-sustaining growth, whatever their level of per capita output might be. One aspect of this state of affairs is that the periphery seeks development in competition with the center, which dominates it and distorts its structures, rendering them unsuitable for self-sustaining development. This competition leads to a distortion toward export activities, the choice of light industries and low technology, and toward tertiary activities, all of which transfer multiplier effects from the periphery to the center and block economic growth. Immanuel Wallerstein, whose monumental studies of the history of capitalism epitomize the world system perspective, contributed another very significant version of underdevelopment theory. In *The Capitalist World System* Wallerstein traced the major institutions of the modern world—classes, ethnic and national groups, households, and states—as effects of the development of the capitalist world system. He argued that the world system is unequal and that this is related to its capitalist character. The inequality resolves into a hierarchy of three kinds of *states or regions—the periphery, the semiperiphery, and the core—and the dynamics of economic forces, reinforced by the disparities of state power, ensures a steady flow of resources from the periphery to the core. Where a state or region is located in this hierarchic system is, for Wallerstein, essentially conjunctural, related to a number of contingent forces coming together in time and place. But once located it

tends to become fixed thanks to the operation of world market forces which not only accentuate the differences but also institutionalize them.

The Spread of Dependency Theory. Dependency theory was particularly influential in Latin America, whose historical experience played a major part in the invention of the theory. The empirical studies of international trade and the terms of trade in ECLA under the leadership of Prebisch led to doubts about the beneficial assumptions of the classical theory of international trade and later to suggestions about the differential effects of exchange in center and periphery. Through Prebisch, Furtado, Sunkel, Paz, Cardoso, Faletto, Dos Santos, and Marini, Latin America contributed more than any other region to the development of underdevelopment theory, in this case the dependency version. Through the ECLA and the radical movements the theory exerted considerable influence on government policies in the region. No wonder underdevelopment theory is largely associated with Latin America and regarded as Latin America's major contribution to the social sciences. Owing perhaps to geographical proximity, the rising radicalism in the Caribbean in the 1960s quickly adopted dependency theory. Some of the young scholars at the University of the West Indies were opposed to the ideas of the distinguished West Indian economist Arthur Lewis and were frustrated by his international and local influence. Lewis was not only a strong advocate of the crucial role of foreign capital, but his ideas ran in the direction of the neoclassical orthodoxies of the *International Monetary Fund (IMF)-type policy reform, such as devaluation, export promotion, and keeping wages low. Younger scholars, especially Owen Jefferson, Rex Nettleford, and Norman Girvan, used dependency theory to challenge him and to orient their own political practice. Academic radicalism in the Caribbean met and fused with the political and cultural radicalism of, for instance, the Rastafarian movement, the New World Group formed in Georgetown, Guyana, in 1962, the Black Power movement, and Michael Manley's Peoples National Party (PNP) of Jamaica. Thus Walter Rodney, a celebrated young historian from Guyana and a black nationalist, wrote one of the most famous treatises of underdevelopment theory, *How Europe Underdeveloped Africa;* Michael Manley, the leader of the PNP, was a scholar of some repute, and his book *The Politics of Change: A Jamaican Testament* took a dependency perspective. When Manley's PNP came to power, he took some of the dependency theorists into government with him. Owen Jefferson joined the Central Bank, Norman Girvan went into Planning, and Rex Nettleford became a special adviser to the prime minister. Manley himself quickly became a Third World leader and helped to spread underdevelopment theory in the Third World.

In Asia, underdevelopment theory in general, and the dependency approach in particular, was not so influential, but it has enjoyed a visible presence. It owed its development in India initially to the Indian Marxist intellectuals Dadobhai Naoroji and M. N. Roy. The development continued through the writings of a group of able theoreticians, especially Alavi and Banaji. Although it has a considerable presence in India, underdevelopment theory does not appear to have had the broad appeal and influence which it had in Latin America and the Caribbean. In Africa underdevelopment theory grew in three centers: the Institute for Economic Development and Planning (IDEP), which assumed a dependency orientation in the 1970s when it was headed by Samir Amin; the Council for the Development of Economic and Social Research (CODESRIA), the umbrella social science organization of Africa which, like IDEP, is based in Dakar, Senegal; and the University of Dar es Salaam's Faculty of Arts and Social Sciences, especially between 1966 to 1978. As in India, underdevelopment theory in Africa developed independently of Latin America. The social sciences were established very late in Africa, long after the nationalist movement was in full swing. So from the beginning the social sciences were impregnated with the values of the nationalist struggle against colonialism and imperialism. In these circumstances the dialectics of domination and satellization did not have to be invented; they were, so to speak, a matter of course. It is not surprising that one of the first major works by an African scholar on underdevelopment theory, *Social Science as Imperialism: The Theory of Political Development* (Ake), was a discourse on how Western social science constitutes the satellization and underdevelopment of Africa. Apart from Samir Amin, African scholars were self-absorbed; they did not take much interest in the Latin American debates or the debates on the Left in the West. They simply continued to develop the nationalist social science with its fixity on domination, satellization, and exploitation and evolved, in a natural progression, a corpus of underdevelopment theories which were more sensitive to issues of methodology and epistemology than the dependency literature of Latin America, but sharing rather similar political and policy commitments: Dan Nabudere, *The Political Economy of Imperialism*; I. Shivji, *The Silent Class Struggle in Tanzania*; Claude Ake, *Revolutionary Pressures in Africa* (1969); and others. Underdevelopment theory was very influential in policy circles in Africa—probably more so than in Latin America. This was due partly to the influence of CODESRIA on African social science and the African intelligentsia. Just as important was the influence of Dar es Salaam as a revolutionary capital of Africa from the mid-sixties. As the base of the Liberation Committee of the *Organization of African Unity (OAU), it was a gathering center for the leaders of the more radical nationalist and liberation movements from Angola, Mozambique, South Africa, Zimbabwe, Namibia—all of whom had their own home-grown theories of underdevelopment which emerged from their fixation on exploitative imperialism. At the same time all the leading theorists of underdevelopment theory in Africa except Amin were teaching at the University of Dar es Salaam. It was this group which founded the influential African Association for Political Science and the *African Journal of Political Economy*. Finally, underdevelopment theory was popularized by Julius *Nyerere, the president of Tanzania, and became part of the official *ideology in independent Mozambique and Angola. Not surprisingly the development

strategy which the OAU adopted in 1980—the Lagos Plan of Action—is heavily infused with the values and concepts of underdevelopment theory.

Criticisms of Underdevelopment Theory. It has been all but impossible to produce a scientific evaluation of underdevelopment theory. Its assumptions were so different from and so diametrically opposed to those of classical economics and modernization theory that it was not so much criticized as caricatured and dismissed. Much the same thing happened on the Left, where underdevelopment theories were also a frontal attack on the Marxist dogma of the desirability and feasibility of capitalism in the Third World. Also, both Western mainstream and left-wing social science appear to have rejected, on political grounds, the tendency of underdevelopment theory to hold the West responsible for the underdevelopment of the Third World. It is now common to proclaim that underdevelopment theory has been decisively refuted although just how this has been done is unclear, though not entirely implausible, given the performance of the Republic of Korea (South Korea), Thailand, Singapore, Taiwan, and the other *newly industrializing economies. What is clear is that underdevelopment theory is less influential today. It has been largely defeated—politically, not scientifically—by the collapse of the Soviet bloc, the Westernization of the former Soviet empire, and the renewed hegemonization of the market. More importantly, it has been largely defeated by the economic crisis of the Third World, which has forced many Third World countries to accept more dependence and adopt neoclassical solutions, notably the IMF-type structural adjustment programs, especially in Latin America and Africa. The paradox is that in its demise, underdevelopment theory is getting its most significant corroboration.

(See also COLONIAL EMPIRES; DECOLONIZATION; ECONOMIC COMMISSION FOR LATIN AMERICA AND THE CARIBBEAN; EQUALITY AND INEQUALITY; EXPORT-LED GROWTH; IMPORT-SUBSTITUTION INDUSTRIALIZATION; INTERNATIONAL DEBT; INTERNATIONAL SYSTEMS; NATIONALISM; NORTH-SOUTH RELATIONS; POLITICAL ECONOMY.)

Paul Baran, *The Political Economy of Growth* (New York, 1957). Bert Hoselitz et al., *Theories of Economics* (New York, 1960). Alexander Gerschenkron, *Economic Backwardness in Historical Perspective* (Cambridge, Mass., 1962). Edward Shils, *Political Development in the New States* (The Hague, 1962). Gabriel Almond and G. Bingham Powell, Jr., *Comparative Politics: A Developmental Approach* (Boston, 1966). André Gunder Frank, *Capitalism and Underdevelopment in Latin America* (New York, 1967). A. F. Organski, *The Stages of Political Development* (New York, 1967). Samir Amin, *Accumulation on a World Scale: A Critique of the Theory of Underdevelopment*, 2 vols. (New York, 1974). Issa G. Shivji, *Class Struggles in Tanzania* (London, 1976). Claude Ake, *Social Science as Imperialism: The Theory of Political Development* (Ibadan, 1979). Immanuel Wallerstein, *The Capitalist World Economy* (Cambridge, U.K., 1979). Dan Nabudere, *The Political Economy of Imperialism*, 2d ed. (London, 1980). Walter Rodney, *How Europe Underdeveloped Africa*, rev. ed. (Washington, D.C., 1982). Michael Manley, *The Politics of Change: A Jamaican Testament*, rev. ed. (Washington, D.C., 1990). W. W. Rostow, *The Stages of Economic Growth*, 3d ed. (New York, 1991).

CLAUDE AKE

gan to accumulate in state archives, specialists were needed to organize and conduct *res diplomatica,* or diplomatic affairs. Indeed, the "paper" origins of Western diplomacy coincide with the development of centralized empires requiring reliable communication with the periphery. From the early days of imperial Rome and the Holy See to the last days of the Holy Roman Empire, the figure who kept the keys to the diplomatic archives, that is, the *chancellor,* occupied a position of power comparable to the figureheads of empire.

It was not until late into the eighteenth century that the meaning of diplomacy was extended from the management of archives to the management of *international relations in general. The *Oxford English Dictionary* gives credit to Edmund Burke for first using the term in this modern sense in 1796. It could well be the case, however, that Burke cribbed this usage from his revolutionary rival Thomas Paine, who referred four years earlier in *The Rights of Man* (1792) to Benjamin Franklin as "not the diplomat of a Court, but of MAN." Obviously diplomacy, defined by the *OED* as "the management of international relations by negotiation," did not *begin* in 1792—unless, of course, one takes the pedantic view that it could *only* begin in 1792, the year in which the first nation-state emerged (France) and the word *international* itself was coined (by Jeremy Bentham).

Long before ambassadors were cloaked with the robes of *sovereignty (of king and queen, then nation-state), the earliest diplomats were thought to be the winged (of foot, then shoulder) representatives of the gods. The heralds of the Greek city-states operated under the protection of Hermes, the messenger of Zeus, as well as patron of travelers (and thieves). The *missi* ("messengers"), the proto-diplomats of the Carolingian Empire in the early Middle Ages, carried a caduceus as did Hermes, relying on the Holy and Roman aspect of the Empire for personal protection as they transmitted oaths of fealty, settled terms of disputes, and acted as the eyes and ears of Charlemagne and his successors. Well into the sixteenth century the mythological origins of diplomacy were cited for good effect. For instance, in *De Legationibus* (1584) the Italian jurist Alberico Gentili establishes the inviolability of envoys by tracing the origins of diplomacy back to God and His legates, the angels.

One should not, however, paint too hallowed a portrait of the first diplomats. The British ambassador Sir Henry Wotton failed to amuse King James when he remarked that "an ambassador is an honest man who is sent to lie abroad for the good of his country"; but he did provide an apt aphorism for the often conflicting duties of the diplomats of the period. Abraham de Wicquefort, who wrote one of the first manuals on diplomacy, *The Ambassador and His Functions* (1682), earned his diplomatic credentials in the service of Richelieu, Mazarin, and de Witt. He expressed the prevailing sentiments of the time when he defined the diplomat as "an honorable spy." Indeed, the rash of new treatises on diplomacy in the sixteenth and seventeenth century seemed intent on rescuing diplomacy from its Byzantine and Italianate origins—and less than pristine reputation. In these works (with over fifty written between 1430 and 1630) diplomacy is presented as a culture, in terms of a body of thought of how civilized behavior was to be propagated among "ideal ambassadors," and in terms of a body of individuals through which civilized behavior was to be reproduced in the fledgling institutions of a states-system.

The culmination of this textual civilizing process is François de Callières's *On the Manner of Negotiation with Princes* (1716). Drawing on his experience as an able negotiator for France, he acknowledges the rather low esteem in which diplomacy was held at the time, and proceeds to provide sound advice on how to redeem the profession. First and foremost of the diplomatic virtues should be honesty: although momentary advantage may be gained by deceit, "honest is the best policy . . . a lie always leaves in its wake a drop of poison." Second is civility, the art of dignified court behavior which was to be cultivated for the creation of a cosmopolitan diplomatic corps. And third is prudence, the necessary mix of intelligence, foresight, and flexibility in action that would allow the diplomat to best represent the interests of his prince.

The effort to capture the essence of diplomacy reaches its zenith in the classic text *Diplomacy* (1939) by the British diplomat and historian Sir Harold Nicolson. He modernizes de Callières by taking into account (and mildly regretting) the popularizing and often propagandizing effects of democracy and revolution on traditional diplomacy, while maintaining the classical belief that the "essence" of diplomacy is "common sense and charity applied to international relations." What Nicolson has in common with de Callières (as well as de Wicquefort and many other ex-diplomats who took up the pen) is that they were both serving governments at the apogee of imperial power, and understandably not too interested in looking too critically or deeply into alternative beginnings and future possibilities of diplomacy. The question must be asked, then, whether the dominant view of diplomacy as practical wisdom, working in combination with the expectation of reciprocal actions, was a moral prejudice of the European great powers.

There have been, after all, other diplomacies. In his book *The Beginnings of Diplomacy* (1950), Ragnar Numelin takes the reader on an ethnological voyage from Stone-Age Australia to pre–Columbian America to demonstrate that many of the fundamental practices of diplomacy predated modern Europe. Adam Watson, in *Diplomacy: The Dialogue Between States* (1982), is even more adept at identifying early diplomatic conventions of immunity, negotiation, and communication that were developed by Egyptians and Hittites, Greeks city-states and Hellenistic kingdoms, ancient China and India.

Yet the historical fact remains that the European model of diplomacy emerged triumphant. In *System of States* (1977) Martin Wight provides in erudite detail the history of how estrangement between Western Christendom and the Turks promoted the conferences and intercourse among the European powers which prefigured the establishment of a diplomatic system. In *Renaissance Diplomacy* (1955) Garrett Mattingly traces the development of the residential form of diplomacy among the five Italian city-states that eventually made its way into transalpine Europe. With the end of the Thirty Years' War (1618–1648)—and with it the threat of a universal monarchy under the Hapsburgs—the exchange of officially accredited agents, the establishment of permanent embassies, and the codification of a secular system of immunities became the standard form of diplomacy throughout Europe.

The golden age of diplomacy followed. From the eighteenth to the twentieth century a homogeneous yet cosmopolitan elite made up the diplomatic corps of Europe. They shared a common culture (aristocratic), a common language (French), and a common vision of order (*balance of power). World War I, however, brought revolutions, national democratic movements, and the first wave of anti-imperialism: the aristocratic veneer of the diplomatic corps began to wear thin. The "new diplomacy" of open negotiation and popular accountability, advocated if rarely practiced by Woodrow Wilson, Lenin, and Trotsky, left its mark on the consanguinity and conservatism of the *ancien régime*. The diplomatic corps, long an elite enclave, increasingly gave way to a meritocracy—taking into account, of course, the right schools, gender, and political affiliations. "Tact and intelligence," rather than the civil behavior of the court, is offered by Sir Ernest Satow in his *Guide to Diplomatic Practice* (London, 1922) as the proper qualification of the diplomat.

Not to be ignored, *imperialism played an important role in the spread and transformation of the diplomatic system. As great power politics expanded in an orderly if sometimes genocidal fashion into the Americas, Africa, and Asia, diplomacy went with it. Perhaps the most important artifact of the age of imperialism is the formation of a diplomatic culture, in the sense of a system of symbolic power and social codes that brings cohesiveness to the international society. Born of the European experience, the diplomatic culture found in the colonial encounter a new self-consciousness. Diplomacy was once again invoked as a civilizing process, but this time on a global scale in which a very large gap in development encouraged a unilateral form of diplomacy that to this day favors the West.

Diplomacy is now considered to be an essential international institution which provides the norms, protocols, and practices for the reconciliation of differences between sovereign states. The international relations scholar Hedley Bull believes that "the diplomatic profession itself is a custodian of the idea of international society," and he marvels at the integrating power of the diplomatic culture at a time when its elitist European underpinnings were coming under intense attack: "The remarkable willingness of states of all regions, cultures, persuasions and states of development to embrace often strange and archaic diplomatic procedures that arose in Europe in another age is today one of the few visible indications of universal acceptance of the idea of international society" (*Anarchical Society*, 1977).

Diplomacy remains, however, the institution by which states pursue their own particular interests. At the systemic level diplomacy might well seek to maintain an international order and general *peace. Yet that very order is often seen by individual states to be an obstacle to justice, or to the equitable distribution of wealth, or to the dissemination of a preferred ideology. Diplomacy's most difficult task continues to be the management of changes in relative power and ideological beliefs in the international system. One need not subscribe to a Machiavellian view of the world to find some truth in Frederick the Great's statement that diplomacy without power is like an orchestra without a score. When power and diplomacy fall out of kilter, diplomacy tends toward coercion, propaganda, and intervention. The dialogue of diplomacy then carries the threat of *war rather than the promise of peace.

In a time of rapid change in the states-system, what lies ahead for diplomacy? Many of the conditions which made diplomacy necessary and possible in the classical age of Europe still obtain. Strangers persist in the *international system. The bipolar estrangement of the *Cold War may have ended, and with it some of the worst excesses of "megaphone diplomacy," but disturbingly familiar sources of conflict have arisen in what once was the Soviet Union, the Balkans, Africa, and many other places where ethnic, religious, economic, and nationalist hostilities continue to surface. Indeed, as the number of powers increases, as power itself disperses and diffuses in the contemporary states system, and as diplomatic utterances multiply and speed up in the international communication web, one must ask whether the dialogue of diplomacy has become a cacophony. Global developments—from multilateral summitry to a transnational CNN—have diminished the independence and significance of the individual diplomat, whose home now more than ever is everywhere and nowhere.

Diplomacy as an institution endures, nevertheless. States continue to construct, confront, and sometimes cooperate with their alien others. As long as there is a need to communicate with strangers and to manage the movement of ideas, goods, people, and even armies across boundaries, there will be a need for diplomacy.

(See also FOREIGN POLICY; INFORMATION SOCIETY; INTERNATIONAL COOPERATION.)

Sir Ernest Satow, *Guide to Diplomatic Practice* (London, 1922). Sir Harold Nicolson, *Diplomacy* (Oxford, 1939). Hedley Bull, *The Anarchical Society: A Study of Order in World Politics* (London, 1977). Adam Watson, *Diplomacy: The Dialogue Between States* (London, 1982). François de Callières, *The Art of Diplomacy*, ed. M. A. Keens-Soper and Karl Schweizer (Leicester, 1983). James Der Derian, *On Diplomacy: A Genealogy of Western Estrangement* (Oxford, 1987).

JAMES DER DERIAN

DISABILITY POLITICS. People with disabilities typically occupy marginalized social and economic positions in contemporary societies. Among advanced industrial nations, one traditional focus of disability politics has followed from the assumption that disability connotes incapacity and socioeconomic dependence, an assumption rejected by many current advocates from the disability community as false, stigmatizing, and often self-fulfilling through the creation of policy and cultural disincentives to social participation. From this perspective, the primary role for disability politics has been to secure resources for public and nongovernmental programs providing cash benefits and rehabilitative services. Such political initiatives frequently emphasize the incapacity associated with disability and the moral blamelessness for their conditions of those who are unable to help themselves. At issue in such political discourse is often the moral entitlement of those who are "afflicted." Claims to public assistance of this sort are typically based on the contention that impairment is not the result of an individual's own choices and behavior, but rather random victimization, occupational injury, or, in the case of disabled veterans, national service. For example, many Western welfare states offer state pensions for people with disabilities considered unable to work.

Alternatively, a social model of disability conceptualizes disability as a social construction that is the result of interaction between physical or mental impairment and the social environment. In this model, disability politics takes far different forms, encompassing conflict over what social roles can appropriately be played by individuals who have disabilities, and how the state supports or restricts those roles through its policies on education, employment, public services, and participation in civic life. By characterizing the social isolation and enforced dependency of people with disabilities as the result of social choices rather than as the inevitable result of impairment, the social model suggests analogies between the social status of people with disabilities and other marginalized groups such as racial and ethnic minorities, women, or gays and lesbians. This approach to disability politics may generate disputes over civil rights, *political participation, and the role of individuals with disabilities and the organizations they create in shaping and controlling disability policy and services.

This alternative politics of disability builds on the perception that to have a disability does not prevent enjoyment of the activities of life typical for anyone else of a similar sex, age, or race in any society. Thus, the politics of disability in the First World has stressed goals of inclusive education, competitive employment, full political and social participation, and the use of public facilities and transportation. It insists upon the elimination of segregated, custodial services provided by the nondisabled for the purpose of keeping a separation between "normals" and the disabled/deviant/stigmatized individual. Those disabled people who identify with the disability rights movement and perceive themselves as members of a minority group would generally agree that social policy should change to incorporate people with disabilities into all phases of life on terms of equality, and would argue that the society, not the people with the disability, must change in order for this goal to be achieved.

Disability politics contends that the "difference" of disability need be no more shameful than any other form of human variation, and that society must reorganize its physical structures, social practices, and psychological attitudes to ensure that its members with disabilities can count on the equality of respect and the opportunity to develop their capabilities along with those who do not have disabilities. Disability politics grounded in a social model of the meaning of disability does not preclude recognizing the ways in which impairment can create particular needs for different means of accomplishing basic goals. Sign language interpretation, wheelchair-accessible homes and stores, publications available in formats usable by those who cannot read print, and workdays structured to allow for periods of rest would be part of any society that assumed the full humanity and capacity for contribution of members with impairments; and if the society were structured in this way, the impairment would no longer pose any obstacle to equality. Claims on health care resources or assistance services would be perceived as legitimate because the use of resources would permit attainment of the goals of respect and participation. As with other rights-based movements and forms of identity politics, demands for legislative and structural change are accompanied by efforts to change the views of those with disabilities themselves, who may have incorporated into their own views of their potential a perception that they were less capable than those without disabilities of enjoying a full life.

Having a disability, however, does not in itself lead to participation in collective political action. Disabilities are spread spatially and demographically across the general population, although many impairments are concentrated among those with the least economic, social, and political resources in their societies. Disability per se is not necessarily tied to a distinct social structure within most societies. While some disability advocates commonly refer to "the disability community," those who actively identify with this community may include only a small portion of the substantial number of people with disabilities in any society, particularly due to the stigma associated with disabilities. However, this stigma itself can contribute to the creation of a social group based on disability as common ties develop among people with disabilities. Disability also has become the basis for collective action in relation to its public policy function as a formal criterion of eligibility for the receipt of public benefits or special treatment. Once a shared identity is established, those defined as having a disability can become a distinct interest group which may become capable of mobilization.

In the past four decades, political activity by individuals with disabilities and organizations of disabled people has particularly increased, and much of that activity has been directed toward the goals of equal access, community integration, and independent living. Among the explanations that have been offered for this increase are emerging medical and assistive technologies that have supported independence for many people with disabilities, changing ideologies of treatment that have encouraged noninstitutional service strategies, and the models of other minority movements in the 1960s and 1970s that advocated for inclusion and social change. People with disabilities in many nations have formed organizations to represent the disability community and influence governmental bodies responsible for the enactment and implementation of public policy. Prominent examples include the British Council of Organizations of Disabled Peoples, the American Coalition of Citizens with Disabilities in the United States, and the Coalition of Citizens with Disabilities in Canada. Parallel to the formation of national coalitions has been the creation of cross-national coalitions including Disabled Peoples International (DPI), a cross-disability coalition of over 110 organizations from Europe, the Americas, Africa, and Asia, that has been particularly active in advocating for disability rights in international governmental and nongovernmental activities, and in supporting the development of organizations of people with disabilities around the world.

By the 1990s many appointed government officials responsible for making and enforcing government disability policies were recruited to their posts from such organizations of people with disabilities. The limited results of mainstream political activity have led many disability advocates to turn to more contentious political actions. Disability protestors have confronted public officials, blocked traffic, occupied public places and government offices, and been arrested. Such activities may increase in coming years, as the visibility of disability movements attracts greater numbers of adherents, and national and international networks of disability movement organizations provide greater support to collective political action.

(See also CIVIL DISOBEDIENCE; CIVIL RIGHTS MOVEMENT; INEQUALITIES; NEW SOCIAL MOVEMENTS; WELFARE STATE.)

Jerome E. Bickenbach, *Physical Disability and Social Policy* (Toronto, 1992). Jane Campbell and Mike Oliver, *Disability Politics* (London, 1996). James C. Charlton, *Nothing About Us Without Us: Disability Oppression and Empowerment* (Berkeley, Calif., 1997).

ADRIENNE ASCH
RICHARD SCOTCH

DISARMAMENT. An ancient ideal, disarmament—properly understood—is the near elimination of arms and military forces by one or more states, as opposed to *arms control in which weapons and forces continue to exist but are subjected to restraints on their number, nature, or use. What is referred to as partial or selective disarmament is really arms control, but the terms are often used interchangeably. Thus elimination of offensively oriented forces—an arms control measure—was the focus of the *League of Nations "disarmament" conference in 1932–1933, and the UN Special Session on Disarmament (1978) was devoted to arms control proposals.

Although disarmament can be imposed on the losing state after a *war (Japan in 1945) or adopted by a single state voluntarily (Costa Rica some years ago), it is mainly envisioned as a bilateral or multilateral endeavor. States can make parallel cuts on their own, and significant reductions sometimes occur this way—usually after a major war—but effective disarmament is normally felt to require formal treaties and elaborate inspection.

Disarmament is expected to contribute greatly to *peace by erasing the tools of war, easing interstate conflicts, and curbing the willingness or ability of governments to treat the threat or use of *force as legitimate. An additional objective is diverting resources from military preparations and war to other purposes.

One source of support for disarmament is pacifism; renunciation of the use of force, even in self-defense, makes possession of arms pointless. Another is the view, reinforced by *nuclear weapons, that the potential destructiveness of modern war exceeds tolerable limits in terms of sanity, morality, or any reasonable political objective.

Do arms cause wars? Disarmament supporters often assert that military capabilities encourage war by making it a constantly available option—otherwise using force would require rearming, a substantial undertaking. In an intense political conflict, disarmament would provide time for emotions to subside and for giving attention to other options. Supporters also contend that being armed brings participation in decision making by officials responsible for those capabilities, who are likely to urge or endorse the use of force as a proper and feasible recourse. The most influential view is that even forces intended solely for defense incite reciprocal fears of attack. The result is a *security dilemma—each state's individual pursuit of *security by arming adds to everyone's insecurity by inciting spirals of mistrust and arms racing that can culminate in war. Finally, supporters suggest that military capabilities provoke phenomena that promote the legitimacy of war, such as holding military forces and leaders in high esteem, celebrating past military achievements, dehumanizing enemies, and inciting intense feelings of *nationalism.

Opponents of disarmament contend that states have consistently been willing to carry political conflicts to lethal levels and to resort to force—their arming is the result, not the cause, of this. Hence even if disarmament were achieved, conflicts would eventually provoke rearming. Many opponents further assert that, in the nuclear age, the only reliable way to prevent war is *deterrence, i.e., disarmament would be disastrous. Usually added is the argument that in the anarchical *international system nothing prevents states from resorting to force and that states must therefore arm to protect themselves. Disarmament is thus impossible without transforming international politics (many disarmament supporters readily agree) through new institutions and processes for managing change, settling disputes, and policing agreements. This means either a supranational authority or concerted efforts of national governments motivated by a well-developed sense of global community and interdependent security. Either would entail prior political adjustments and agreements that are, say the critics, quite improbable in view of the entire history of international politics.

Governments ultimately side with the opponents, and disarmament has been of little significance. The League conference was soon followed by the military buildups leading to World War II. In 1961, under the rubric of "General and Complete Disarmament," the United States and the Soviet Union reached agreement on broad principles, and there was a flurry of popular and academic interest in disarmament. This had no discernible impact as each superpower soon initiated a large military buildup. The UN "disarmament decade" (the 1970s) coincided with unprecedented conventional arms transfers and the burgeoning of nuclear arsenals, followed by President Reagan's huge military buildup.

There have been some recent accomplishments. South Africa, Ukraine, Belarus, and Kazakhstan became the first states to give up nuclear weapons, while Argentina, Brazil, and the Democratic People's Republic of Korea (North Korea) have abandoned nuclear weapons development. There is renewed debate about seeking total nuclear disarmament, a cause endorsed by many scientists and eminent (retired) military leaders. The UN has conducted its first forcible disarmament, on weapons of mass destruction, in Iraq, and NATO pursued limited disarmament measures in Bosnia. The Land Mines Convention (1997) will eliminate millions of anti-personnel mines. However, despite revived interest in disarmament, alongside continued interest in civilian-based defense (via complete noncooperation and civil disobedience) as a substitute for arming, the outlook for general disarmament still remains bleak.

Richard J. Barnet and Richard A. Falk, eds., *Security in Disarmament* (Princeton, N.J., 1965). James E. Dougherty, *How to Think About Arms Control and Disarmament* (New York, 1973). Trevor N. Dupuy and Guy Hammerman, eds., *A Documentary History of Arms Control and Disarmament* (New York, 1973). *Report of the Canberra Commission on the Elimination of Nuclear Weapons* (Canberra, 1996). Joseph Rotblat, ed., *Nuclear Weapons: The Road to Zero* (Boulder, Colo., 1998).

PATRICK M. MORGAN

DISSENT, SOVIET. See SOVIET DISSENT.

DJIBOUTI. See FRANCOPHONE AFRICA; HORN OF AFRICA; INDIAN OCEAN REGION.

DOMINICA. See ENGLISH-SPEAKING CARIBBEAN.

DOMINICAN REPUBLIC. The Dominican Republic occupies the eastern two-thirds of the island of Hispaniola, which it shares with *Haiti. With approximately 8.1 million people, it has the second-largest population in the Caribbean.

Initial independence from Spain in 1821 lasted only a few months owing to an invasion from Haiti, which occupied the country until 1844. Fear of renewed invasion led Dominicans to seek protection, chiefly from France, Spain, and the United States. Historically, the government revolved largely around *caudillo* strongmen and their intrigues involving foreign powers; Spain reannexed the country from 1861 to 1865. External debt, political instability, and U.S. involvement in Dominican affairs expanded in the last half of the nineteenth century. Upheaval followed the assassination of Ulíses Heureaux in 1899, ending a seventeen-year reign. By 1907, the United States controlled Dominican customs and became the country's sole foreign creditor. The country fell under direct U.S. military occupation from 1916 to 1924. Improvements in transportation and communications and particularly the formation of a constabulary force under the occupation facilitated the rise to power six years later of Rafael Leónidas Trujillo Molina (1930–1961).

Trujillo's regime involved personal rule, large-scale corruption, arbitrary decisions combined with attention to legal forms, and ruthless violence (including a 1937 massacre of some 12,000 Haitians in the border area). These were juxtaposed with the forging of national integration, the establishment of state institutions, reduction in the extent of direct control by foreigners, and the beginnings of industrialization, however distorted. In the wake of the 1959 *Cuban Revolution, intervention by the United States and sanctions by the Organization of American States preceded and followed Trujillo's assassination on 30 May 1961. These actions helped prevent family members from continuing in power. Democratic elections in 1962 were won by Juan Bosch and his Partido Revolucionario Dominicano (PRD).

*Democracy, however, was not to come easily. Bosch was overthrown by conservative forces only seven months after assuming office. The discovery of a civil-military conspiracy to try to bring him back to power led in April 1965 to U.S. intervention out of an exaggerated fear of a "second Cuba." Joaquín Balaguer, the former Trujillo puppet president, easily defeated a dispirited Bosch in elections held in 1966. Disillusioned with liberal democracy, Bosch left the PRD in 1973 to found a more radical, disciplined, cadre-style Partido de la Liberación Dominicana (PLD). Balaguer gained reelection with overt military pressure against his opposition in 1970 and 1974. However, in 1978 Balaguer was forced to accept electoral defeat to a more moderate PRD; domestic and international pressure was important in blocking a coup in the making. Following the inauguration of the PRD government, a purge of top military officers occurred; with additional forced retirements over time, the fear of military coups in the country has diminished significantly. The PRD won again in 1982, but economic crisis, charges of corruption, and increased strength by Bosch and his PLD facilitated a victory by Balaguer and his Partido Reformista Social Cristiano (PRSC) in 1986. In 1990, the two octogenarians, Balaguer and Bosch, were the primary contenders; with Bosch claiming fraud, Balaguer won by a narrow plurality. An equally narrow victory by Balaguer in 1994 over José Francisco Peña Gó-

mez of the PRD was facilitated by well-documented allegations of fraud; the ensuing crisis forced Balaguer to agree both to shorten his term in office to two years and not to run for the presidency in 1996. In that year, Leonel Fernández of the PLD defeated Peña Gómez of the PRD in the second round of the presidential elections with support from Balaguer and the PRSC. In 2000, Hipolito Mejía of the PRD won the presidential elections.

The country's current constitution dates from November 1966, amended in August 1994. It grants extensive powers to the president, who is elected for a four-year term and following the 1994 reform cannot be reelected immediately. Senators, deputies, mayors, and members of municipal councils are also elected for four-year terms. Due to the 1994 reform, they are now elected halfway through the president's term. The Chamber of Deputies has 149 representatives elected by proportional representation. The Senate has thirty members, one from each province. It names members of the Central Election Board, responsible for overseeing elections, and the Board is also dependent on the executive for the disbursement of funds. Both of these issues have often fueled charges of partisanship and fraud. Since 1994, the Supreme Court is named by a Council of the Magistrature with representation from all three branches of government; the Supreme Court, in turn, names all other judges. This change is gradually improving the quality and the image of the judiciary. The country has limited civil service legislation, and government patronage and jobs play major roles in the elections.

The ability of the country's three major parties to monopolize voter support relied primarily on the charisma and strong leadership of Balaguer (PRSC), Bosch (PLD) until his retirement in 1995, and Peña Gómez (PRD) until his death in 1998. As of mid-2000, only the PRSC had not yet made the transition from tight control by its aging traditional leader, even as it experienced historically low levels of voter support in the 1996 and 1998 elections. It recovered only slightly in 2000 when Balaguer was again the party's candidate. The PRD has been strongest among urban, lower-class voters and the PRSC in rural areas, and among conservative Catholic, female, and older voters. The PLD has competed with both parties for votes (especially replacing the PRSC over the late 1990s), building a base in urban and eastern sugar-growing regions of the country.

The Dominican Republic is a highly stratified society, with extensive poverty. Economic crisis, public sector deficits, and government policy decisions led to further declines in the provision of health, education, and utility services, until the mid-1990s. Extensive migration, both to Dominican cities and abroad, has resulted; urbanization has increased from 35 percent of the population in 1960 to 67 percent in 1997, while approximately 10 percent of Dominicans live overseas, particularly in the United States. At the same time, Haitian migration into the country is extensive, and Haitian labor is exploited in the sugar fields, in other agricultural areas, and in construction.

The strongest interest groups reflect business interests, as organized labor is weak and divided. In recent years neighborhood associations have played prominent roles in civic strikes. The Roman Catholic Church has sought to play a mediating role in political and economic crises and faces a growing challenge from the increased presence of Protestant and evangelical churches, which now represent some 10 to 25 percent of the country's population.

Although historically the economy has revolved around sugar, it experienced a reorientation in the 1980s. In the late 1960s and early 1970s, the country's high growth rates were stimulated by economic aid, public sector construction, and *import-substitution industrialization. During the 1970s and 1980s, oil price increases and the sharp decline in world sugar markets caused economic problems, which were exacerbated by the debt buildup of the late 1970s. In the 1990s, and into the current decade, the Dominican Republic's relatively high growth rate has depended upon foreign exchange generated by tourism, light assembly manufacturing, free trade zones, and remittances and investment capital from overseas Dominicans.

(See also INTERNATIONAL DEBT; INTERNATIONAL MIGRATION.)

Howard Wiarda, *Dictatorship, Development, and Disintegration: Politics and Social Change in the Dominican Republic*, 3 vols. (Ann Arbor, Mich., 1975). Frank Moya Pons, *The Dominican Republic: A National History* (New Rochelle, N.Y., 1995). Jonathan Hartlyn, *The Struggle for Democratic Politics in the Dominican Republic* (Chapel Hill, N.C., 1998).

JONATHAN HARTLYN

DOMINO THEORY. The domino theory is most familiar as one of the principal justifications for the *Vietnam War. The term itself traces to a 1954 press conference in which President Dwight D. *Eisenhower explained the strategic importance of Vietnam to the United States in terms of "a row of dominoes set up; you knock over the first one and what will happen to the last one is the certainty that it will go over very quickly . . . the loss of Indochina, of Burma, of Thailand, of the Peninsula [Malaysia] and Indonesia following . . . Japan, Formosa, the Philippines and to the southward; it moves in to threaten Australia and New Zealand. . . . So the possible consequences of the loss are just incalculable to the free world."

Every president from Eisenhower to Gerald Ford based his commitment to Vietnam in large part on the domino theory. The same was true for U.S. commitments in many other parts of the *Third World, in particular in Central America in the 1980s. Unless the Nicaraguan *Sandinistas were removed, the *Reagan administration warned, all the nations of Central America would tumble, U.S. credibility around the world would be weakened, and even "the last domino"—the United States itself—would be threatened by Soviet and Cuban bases as well as by masses of refugees fleeing across U.S. borders.

Critics of such commitments, however, rejected the foreboding chain of events forecast by the falling dominoes metaphor, and thus questioned whether the interests at stake justified both the scope and types of commitments that were made. In Southeast Asia, for example, they argued that the eventual fall of both South Vietnam and Cambodia was less a substantiation of the domino theory than a highly destructive self-fulfilling prophecy.

With the waning of the *Cold War, the domino theory has lost its traditional centrality to debates over U.S. foreign policy. Somewhat ironically, though, the revolutions that swept Eastern and *Central Europe in 1989 might be seen as the domino theory in reverse: the rebellion against *communism in one country did help foment rebellion against communism in the other countries, and the old communist regimes fell one on top of the other.

(See also AMERICAN FOREIGN POLICY; DETERRENCE; NINETEEN EIGHTY-NINE.)

John Lewis Gaddis, *Strategies of Containment* (New York, 1982). Bruce W. Jentleson, "American Commitments in the Third World: Theory vs. Practice" *International Organization* 41 (Autumn 1987): 667–704.

BRUCE W. JENTLESON

DRUGS. Humans have used mood-altering substances for therapeutic and social purposes since ancient times. Opium figured in Greek pharmacological texts over 2,000 years ago and the spread of opium-poppy cultivation eastward from Greece and Mesopotamia surely must have been greeted as a great advance in alleviating pain and suffering. In the nineteenth century, however, two factors made drugs move from medical miracle to cause for international conflict, pitting the modern capitalist industrial world against preindustrial societies. First, industrializing Europe and North America intensified their colonial and commercial reach into other continents and, second, modern industrial chemistry converted the comparatively weak raw material of coca and opium into the powerful and extraordinarily lucrative derivatives of cocaine and heroin.

In the Opium Wars (1839–42 and 1856–60), the first major international conflicts over drugs, the British, in a very different role from that of the industrial nations today, defeated the Chinese, who had banned the nonmedicinal use of opium in 1729, and forced them to permit British merchants and their U.S. junior partners to import and sell British-grown Indian opium. The British goal was commercial, to rectify a major trade deficit created by imports into Britain of Chinese tea, silks, and handicrafts. To reduce their new opium-based trade deficit, the Chinese permitted massive domestic production. By 1906, China produced over 35,000 tons of nonmedicinal opium annually, 85 percent of the world total, and had 13.5 million addicts.

Late in the century, the United States and Britain reversed their roles, moving from defenders of opium traders to moralistic crusaders against drug use and trade. They secured a regime of conventions and treaties banning the traffic and the result can be measured in the decline of world opium production to 7,700 tons in 1934, of which China produced 83 percent, and to 1,000 tons by 1970.

With governments now officially controlling or banning nonmedicinal opium and heroin while addicted users still provided a market, the cultivation, processing, transportation, and distribution quickly shifted into the hands of criminal enterprises. Indeed, international trafficking of heroin and cocaine, as well as amphetamines and other synthetic drugs, can best be understood as driven by the market factors of supply and demand. If demand for such products remains high while prohibition reduces supply, it raises the price and, hence, the incentive to traffickers. Contrary to claims that drug trafficking is purely demand-driven, however, entrepreneurial drug traffickers and dealers also creatively work the supply side, as when Colombian cartel members pioneered cocaine shipments by the planeload.

For significant drug supplies to reach users in a trading system which criminalizes their sale or possession, cultivation, refining, transport, and marketing systems necessarily develop complex clandestine financial, logistical, and political support networks. Cultivation of drug crops, like legal agriculture, requires credit between planting and harvest: and international trade in drugs, like other international commerce, needs the guarantee of bankers between consignment and delivery. Small shipments travel in myriad ways, but for large shipments, the transportation itself must be carefully organized, often requiring the collaboration of shipping or airline personnel and of customs or patrol agents. Traffickers combine threats, violence, and lucrative payoffs to develop very effective political cover from production to ultimate consumption as graphically conveyed by the "option" offered authorities by Latin American traffickers: Silver or lead?

International conflict, especially where intelligence agencies play major roles as they did in the Cold War, facilitates this evasion of accountability, for intelligence agencies are by definition unaccountable, and can justify in the name of national security their collaboration with traffickers in exchange for information, contacts, and financial or transport services. U.S. intelligence, especially through the *Central Intelligence Agency (CIA), provided support and cover for the Mafia and the Corsican underworld as they organized heroin shipments via Marseille after World War II; for a massive expansion of opium production under Chinese Nationalist military control in northern Burma after the Chinese Revolution; for sustaining a secret army in Laos during the Vietnam War with the revenues from opium cultivation and heroin production, including transport of the opium on CIA-owned aircraft and financing through banks that handled accounts for the covert activities of the agency; for anti-Soviet guerrilla fighters in the Afghan civil war to fund themselves, so that the Golden Crescent of Southwest Asia surpassed the opium output of the Golden Triangle of Southeast Asia; for cocaine traffickers to ship their product to the United States during the Contra war allegedly in planes the Reagan administration was using for arms shipments; and for CIA-collaborator Manuel Noriega in Panama to protect the principal banking institutions that laundered funds and guaranteed shipments for the cocaine cartels.

Migration and conflict, particularly civil wars that disrupt societies and economies but do not disrupt international commerce, facilitate trafficking. They generate major population movements and the tightly-knit refugee or immigrant communities that often provide the necessary financial, logistical, and political cover. Trafficking by Chinese Chiu Chao syndicates in Asia; Chinese, Sicilians, Cubans, and Colombians at various times in the United States; and Russians and Kosovar Albanians more recently in Europe all illustrate this dynamic.

Drugs have a corrosive influence on almost every form of human activity. They not only corrupt individuals and weaken the bonds of family and community, but the vast resources they generate, estimated at $400 billion in 1998, give rise to criminal organizations that challenge and erode state legitimacy and sovereignty while increasing violence and abuse by both civilians and police authorities. Since cocaine became a major export from Colombia, violent crime has multiplied, so that the 31,808 homicides in 1997 topped the world charts with a homicide rate of 84 per 100,000. Armed ideological or nationalist political movements are not immune

from corruption, for when they seek to fund themselves through direct involvement in the traffic, it is not long before the extraordinary resources set leaders and factions against one another and destroy the legitimacy and viability of the movement, as occurred among Shan nationalist in Burma. Consider the hopes raised by Brazil's gradual redemocratization in the 1970s and 1980s, when vibrant democratic social movements offered for the first time the promise of autonomous political participation and real policy benefits for Rio's shantytown dwellers. By the early 1990s cocaine traffickers based there, seeking to control authorities that might permit police raids, took over or suffocated these movements.

Proposed solutions range from punitive prohibition, focused principally on eliminating supply; to the public-health or harm-reduction approach, emphasizing prevention and treatment to control demand; to libertarian legalization. The experience of the last thirty years shows that simple prohibition does not work, for it perversely but consistently increases the value of drugs, violent criminality, and supply. And prohibition of weaker drugs fosters a transition to stronger, more dangerous drugs. Acceptance of the logic of this dynamic defines the Dutch public-health approach of decriminalizing marijuana while emphasizing prevention and treatment for harder drugs. Rejection of this logic led the United States to pressure Jamaica, Colombia, and Mexico to eradicate marijuana in the 1980s, after which Colombian cocaine production soared, and marijuana networks in Jamaica and Mexico quickly adapted their infrastructure to ship cocaine to the United States. When Pakistani President Mohammad Zia ul-Haq banned alcohol in 1979, just as Afghan rebels next door were expanding opium production, he triggered a wave of hard-drug use that by 2000 had created an estimated 1.5 million Pakistani heroin addicts plus 2 million opium and hashish addicts.

The international regime from the turn of the century to 1970 did not end drug trafficking but reduced it significantly. U.S. policy since then has contributed to the traffic's revival, both through covert intelligence activities and through an unwillingness to recognize the problem as shared by all nations and therefore solvable only through a collaborative international regime. Instead, U.S. foreign policy has held other countries responsible for American drug addiction, a charge the producing countries, untroubled until the 1980s by significant addiction, rejected. Since then, however, producing countries have also suffered major addiction and criminality. There is now a worldwide consensus that drug trafficking poses a threat to individual, national, and international security, but no consensus on solutions.

The United States consistently opts for tough law-and-order policies, imposed unilaterally even if negotiated bilaterally, rather than working collaboratively through international institutions. U.S. aid programs stress military solutions, including crop spraying with toxic defoliants, armed assaults on suspected producers or dealers, and extradition of traffickers for trial in the United States. When Colombia, for example, reluctantly accepts such aid, it erodes the legitimacy of the elected government, gives sanction to a military with a record of extensive human rights abuses, and undermines the very institutions necessary to address the problem. Colombian political leaders naturally resist or resort to partial compliance, because such an imposed regime places far greater sacrifices on the institutions and citizens of Colombia, who bear the environmental consequences of defoliation, the human rights abuses of the military and right-wing paramilitaries, and the generalized criminal violence, that on U.S. citizens and institutions. In debates over a proposed $1.3 billion aid package to Colombia in 1999 and 2000, U.S. officials made clear that they were unwilling to let funds for crop eradication and development be distributed in rebel-controlled areas, even though the Colombian government considers drug control, political reconciliation with armed leftist rebels, and legal restraints on paramilitary human-rights abusers to be integral parts of a tripartite strategy which, if dismembered, cannot succeed.

Internationally, the revitalized United Nations Drug Control Programme could provide the institutional base for a credible, legitimate international regime where costs and benefits would be shared among participants. It recognizes that crop substitution must be accompanied by socioeconomic development. This agency is handicapped, however, because its funding is voluntary and contributors may earmark their donations for specific programs. U.S. contributions have been relatively limited, and not earmarked for crop substitution with development, so the international regime remains skewed toward punitive prohibition. This suggests that drug trafficking will continue to be a major threat to individual, national, and international security.

(See also DEMOCRATIC TRANSITIONS; U.S.–CENTRAL AMERICAN RELATIONS.)

Alfred W. McCoy, *The Politics of Heroin: CIA Complicity in the Global Drug Trade* (Brooklyn, N.Y., 1991). Bruce M. Bagley and Juan G. Taktlian, "Dope and Dogma: Explaining the Failure of U.S.-Latin American Drug Policies," in Jonathan Hartlyn, Lars Schoultz, and Augusto Varnas, eds., *The United States and Latin America in the 1990: Beyond the Cold War* (Chapel Hill, N.C. 1992), pp. 214–234. Eva Bertram, Morris Blachman, Kenneth Sharpe, and Peter Andreas, *Drug War Polities: The Price of Denial* (Berkeley, Calif., 1996). Elizabeth Leeds, "Cocaine and Parallel Politics in the Brazilian Urban Periphery: Constraints on Local-Level Democratization" *Latin American Research Review* 31, no. 3 (1996): 47–83. Ronald D. Renard, *The Burmese Connection: Illegal Drugs and the Making of the Golden Triangle* (Boulder, Colo., 1996). Sewall H. Menzel, *Cocaine Original: Implementing the U.S. Anti-Drug Policy in the North Andes—Colombia* (Lanham, Md., 1997).

KENNETH PAUL ERICKSON

DU BOIS, W. E. B. Born in Great Barrington, Massachusetts, on 23 February 1868, William Edward Burghardt Du Bois died in Accra, Ghana, on 27 August 1963, on the eve of the March on Washington. His mother, Mary Silvina Burghardt, was a domestic whose family had lived in the Berkshire Hills since the early eighteenth century. Alfred Du Bois, the father he never knew, was an itinerant mulatto barber of French-Haitian extraction. Du Bois attended Fisk University in Nashville, Tennessee, from which he graduated in 1888, after three years. Further scholarship assistance permitted him to attend Harvard College, where he earned a second bachelor of arts degree in philosophy in 1890. In 1895, Du Bois was awarded a doctorate of philosophy in history, the first African American to achieve this distinction at Harvard. His dissertation, "The Suppression of the African Slave Trade to the United States of America," was selected as the first monograph of the influential Harvard Historical Series (1896). After completing course work for the doctorate, Du Bois pursued two

years of graduate work in economics at the University of Berlin (1892–1894). Unable to secure a position at a major American research university in the United States, Du Bois taught assorted subjects at Wilberforce University (Ohio). There were several tentative offers from Booker T. Washington of a professorship at Tuskegee Institute (Alabama) during the period when Du Bois held positions at the University of Pennsylvania (1896–1897) and Atlanta University (from 1898). Although he had applauded Washington's famous 1895 racial compromise address at the Atlanta and Cotton States Exposition, Du Bois rapidly evolved into an opponent of what he eventually termed the "Tuskegee Machine." The years 1900 to 1910 saw Du Bois achieve worldwide recognition for his scholarship (*The Philadelphia Negro*, 1899; the eighteen Atlanta University Studies publications) while simultaneously assuming the role of civil rights militant and propagandist. Publication of his most famous work, *The Souls of Black Folk* (1903), in which Du Bois repeated remarks first made in London in 1900—that the "problem of the 20th century is the problem of the color line"—decisively established his leadership role. In 1905, he was a principal organizer of the Niagara Movement (comprising African Americans Du Bois memorably dubbed the "Talented Tenth"). In 1910, with a group of white progressives outraged by increasing antiblack violence in the urban North, Du Bois became cofounder of the National Association for the Advancement of Colored People (NAACP). His fiery, opinionated editorship of *The Crisis* (1910–1934) propelled the monthly NAACP magazine to a circulation of 100,000 by 1919. Scholarship was not neglected, however: his publications included the biography *John Brown* (1909) and the interpretive histories *The Negro* (1915), *The Gift of Black Folk* (1924), and *Africa* (1930). Two novels, *The Quest of the Silver Fleece* (1911) and *Dark Princess* (1928), and a collection of essays, *Darkwater* (1920), significantly influenced the arts and letters movement of the 1920s (the Harlem Renaissance and its analogues) as well as the Black Aesthetic of the 1960s. Du Bois's espousal of a socialist scheme for separate racial development led to his resignation from the NAACP in 1934 and return to Atlanta University. *Black Reconstruction* (1936), his most important monograph, and the founding of the scholarly journal *Phylon*, as well as the abortive attempt to obtain foundation financing for *The Encyclopedia of the Negro*, were the main undertakings of that period. Du Bois returned to the NAACP after his enforced retirement from Atlanta University at age 75 and promptly embroiled himself in the Progressive Party controversy, supporting Henry Wallace in defiance of NAACP policy. Invited to depart again, Du Bois joined Paul Robeson's Council on African Affairs, participated in the 1949 Cultural and Scientific Conference for World Peace at the Waldorf-Astoria Hotel, became an officer of the Justice Department-disapproved Peace Information Center in 1950, and ran a vigorous campaign for the U.S. Senate from New York on the American Labor Party ticket. At age 83, he was indicted and unsuccessfully tried by the Justice Department under the Foreign Agents Registration Act. Du Bois's interesting account of the "Second Red Scare" appeared in the 1952 book, *In Battle for Peace*. In 1958, Du Bois's passport was restored. Accompanied by his second wife, the novelist and musicologist Shirley Graham, he traveled widely in the Soviet Union and China. His recommendation to Premier Nikita *Khrushchev to create the Institute of African Studies in the Academy of Sciences was quickly implemented. The Lenin Prize was awarded in 1959. On 1 October 1961 (in honor of the Russian Revolution), Du Bois joined the American Communist Party, stating that "capitalism cannot reform itself." The Du Boises departed for Ghana immediately, where he spent his remaining years at work on the *Encyclopaedia Africana,* a project supported by the *Nkrumah government. He was given a state funeral, and is buried in Accra.

(See also AFRICAN AMERICANS; CIVIL RIGHTS MOVEMENT; RACE AND RACISM; SOCIALISM AND SOCIAL DEMOCRACY.)

Julius Lester, ed., *The Seventh Son: The Thought and Writings of W. E. B. Du Bois,* 2 vols. (New York, 1971). Arnold Rampersad, *The Art and Imagination of W. E. B. Du Bois* (Cambridge, Mass., 1976). Joseph P. DeMarco, *The Social Thought of W. E. B. Du Bois* (Lanham, Md., 1983). Manning Marable, *W. E. B. Du Bois: Black Radical Democrat* (Boston, 1986).

DAVID LEVERING LEWIS

E

EAST GERMANY. See GERMAN DEMOCRATIC REPUBLIC.

EAST TIMOR. See INDONESIA; TIMOR.

EASTERN EUROPE. See CENTRAL EUROPE.

ECOLOGY. See ENVIRONMENTALISM; GREEN PARTIES.

ECONOMIC AND MONETARY UNION (EMU) was agreed in the *Maastricht Treaty (negotiated in 1991, ratified in 1993). EMU actually began, after a staged transition period, on 1 January 1999, when then the exchange rates of eleven of fifteen members of the European Union (EU) were locked together and tied to the value of the euro, EMU's new single currency; at the same time an independent European Central Bank (ECB)—governed by a board composed of a president, vice president, and four others, appointed by the member states for nonrenewable terms of up to eight years—took over responsibility for monetary and exchange rate policy for all EMU members. The new single currency, the euro, which started as a financial market and accounting currency, is to become the public single currency at the beginning of 2002, replacing the national currencies of all EMU members.

EMU first appeared on the agenda in 1969, after the initial, "Common Market" stage of European integration had been implemented. The leaders of the then six EU member states commissioned the Werner Report (1970, after Pierre Werner, prime minister of Luxembourg) which set out three stages of transition to EMU, scheduled for completion in 1980. These plans were shelved, however, during the economic troubles of the 1970s. Instead, in 1978 the French and the Germans, eager to stabilize exchange rates, created the European Monetary System (EMS). EMS was built around an Exchange Rate Mechanism (ERM) in which each member currency (all EU member states belonged to EMS, but only those who so desired participated in the ERM) varied around the others within agreed "bands" of fluctuation.

The EMS/ERM, initially a compromise between French and German interests, played an important role in the coming of EMU. When the French Socialist government in 1983 had to choose between ambitious domestic reforms and continuing participation in ERM, it reconsidered its policies and turned toward renewing European integration. Then in 1985 a re-energized European Commission, led by Jacques Delors and backed by French President *Mitterrand and German Chancellor *Kohl, proposed the "1992" program to "complete the Single Market." This bold change sparked movement toward EMU, which was a logical step that could render the new single market irreversible.

Behind the preliminary "Delors Report" on EMU (1989) was complicated bargaining. The French desired EMU both to further European integration and gain some of the control over European monetary policy which, under EMS, the Germans and their Bundesbank had acquired. The Germans, lukewarm about EMU but willing to proceed as a way of furthering European integration after *German unification, wanted to retain this control. The Maastricht Treaty addressed most German concerns. EMU would involve an ECB, at the center of a system of European national central banks, statutorily dedicated to price stability. The ECB's independence from politics was modeled on that of the German Bundesbank. National central banks had to become similarly independent before a member state could be eligible for EMU. Eligibility was further limited by five "convergence criteria" that were designed to ensure the strength of the new single currency and to rein in the more profligate member states of the EU (Italy in particular). The inflation levels and interest rates of candidates had to be close to an average of the three best records in the EU. Annual budget deficits had to be lower than 3 percent and cumulative debt less than 60 percent of GDP. Finally, currencies had to have been in the EMS-ERM "narrow band" for at least two years. These criteria confirmed that there would be a two-speed Europe in monetary policy.

Maastricht established a staged transition to EMU. The first stage was deemed already to have begun in 1990 with the liberation of capital movement inside the EU. Stage two began in 1994 with the creation of the European Monetary Institute (EMI) to monitor convergence. Stage three might have begun as early as January 1997 had a majority of member states been eligible; it would begin in January 1999, no matter how many had qualified, with membership decided in May 1998 on the basis of 1997 statistics.

Smooth passage through these stages was difficult in the rocky economic circumstances of the mid-1990s. The Germans, worried about a weak single currency, insisted in 1996 on a "stability and growth pact" to continue stringent convergence criteria beyond the beginning of EMU, and so the pact was incorporated into the Amsterdam Treaty in 1997. Heroic efforts on the part of EU members, including Italy and Spain, to meet the convergence criteria followed, and by May 1998 eleven member states had qualified for EMU. The UK and Denmark having opted out at Maastricht, only Sweden, which decided not to join, and Greece, which had not qualified, were outside the "Euro-11."

The launching of EMU on 1 January 1999 was a success. The first president of the ECB was Wim Duisenberg, a Dutchman. Fears that the new Central Bank would be overly rigid quickly dissipated and the ECB's first year was characterized by relatively accommodating policies. These led to a rapid decline in the value of the euro vs. the U.S. dollar, facilitating European exports and growth. Fears that EMU would accentuate the EU's problem of high unemployment were also eased. Other concerns would take time to assuage, however. How long could a weak euro persist? What would happen if a region or economic sector suffered an unexpected economic shock? Under EMU, given the relative lack of automatic stabilizers and EU fiscal federalism together with Europe's low level of labor mobility, either wages or social benefits would have to decline—an unappealing prospect, politically. What would happen if the ECB pursued monetary policies disapproved by a majority of member states? The situation whereby monetary policy was "federalized" and macroeconomic policy remained national was potentially explosive. EMU was designed to create much more open and flexible financial markets in Europe, and this presaged great changes for countries in which capital was supplied to firms outside market arrangements. In short, EMU was likely to face major challenges in the years to come.

(See also FINANCE, INTERNATIONAL.)

European Union, *Treaty on European Union* (Luxembourg, 1992). Peter Ludlow, *The Making of the European Monetary System* (Oxford, 1982). Tommaso Padoa-Schioppa, *The Road to Monetary Union in Europe* (Oxford, 1994). Loukas Tsoukalis, *The New European Economy*, 2d ed. (Oxford, 1993). Peter Kenen, *Economic and Monetary Union in Europe: Making Maastricht Work* (Cambridge, 1995). Jean Quatremer and Thomas Klau, *Ces Hommes qui ont fait l'euro* (Paris, 1999).

GEORGE ROSS

ECONOMIC COMMISSION FOR AFRICA. Created by the *United Nations General Assembly in 1958, the Economic Commission for Africa (ECA) currently serves fifty-three countries. As with its European, Asian, and Latin American counterparts, the ECA's responsibility has evolved from postwar reconstruction to economic cooperation and development.

Member states provide policy guidance, while the annual meetings of ministers responsible for economic/social *development and *planning from these countries constitute the highest legislative organ of the commission. But the ECA's work program is also strongly influenced by the UN secretariat in New York which provides most (97 percent) of the organization's $100 million annual budget and appoints the ECA's executive secretary.

In 1997, the ECA secretariat had a total staff strength of six hundred, about a third of whom are professionals, the rest being support staff. Most of these staff are in the headquarters in the organization's headquarters in Addis Ababa although in 1997 the incumbent executive secretary, K. Y. Amoako, moved 25 percent of ECA staff to the five subregional development centers (SRDCs), to ensure program follow-through at regional and national levels.

The ECA can claim at least six major achievements or roles. First, the creation of regional institutions for promoting development and cooperation among African states. These institutions include the *African Development Bank (ADB), the *Economic Community for West African States (ECOWAS) and some forty other such institutions which it still supports.

Second, the ECA has encouraged economic integration, including the signing by all the African states of the Abuja Treaty for an African Economic Community with a joint secretariat provided by the ECA, the *Organization of African Unity (OAU) and ADB. Third, it functions as a think tank for responding to domestic and international challenges confronting the region. It published the *Lagos Plan of Action* (1980), although it is more famous for its *African Alternative Framework to Structural Adjudgement Programmes for Socioeconomic Recovery and Transformation* (1989). It organized a regional conference of African entrepreneurs, governments, and donors on reviving private sector investment (1996) and another on gender (1998). Fourth, usually in collaboration with the OAU, the ECA advocates policies on African development prospects, which have led to initiatives such as the Africa's Priority Programme for Economic Recovery (APPER), 1985, the United Nations Programme for Action for Africa's Economic Recovery and Development 1986–1990 (UN-PAAERD), and the United Nations System-wide Special Initiative on Africa (1995) for which ECA chairs implementation with UNDP (United Nations Development Programme).

A fifth role for the ECA is as adviser to African states on strategic development issues. Its five substantive programs areas (economic and social policy analysis, food security, information management, regional cooperation, and development management) and the Women's Center provide advice to member states on request.

Finally, the ECA is a clearinghouse of information on African development—it publishes several bulletins on development issues, including reports on the economic and social situation in Africa, and has a well-stocked library on African development. It is helping African countries develop their electronic information infrastructure.

In spite of its achievements, the ECA faces a number of problems that affect its effectiveness as a development agency. Firstly, its work program is determined exclusively by national governments, sidelining other institutional actors critical to improving African governance and development. Secondly, like other UN organizations, the ECA is bedeviled with a large bureaucracy most of which already has lifetime contracts. Most of bureaucrats got their jobs by politics rather than professional criteria, and the agency relies more and more on consultants for discharging most essentials activities. ECA shares this problem with the rest of the UN system and spends almost 90 percent its budget on staffing costs. Finally, declining UN resources will most likely make radical rationalization of the bewildering array of UN organizations on African development mandatory.

(See also FOOD POLITICS; GENDER AND POLITICS; INFORMATION TECHNOLOGY.)

United Nations Economic Commission for Africa, *Serving Africa Better: Strategic Directions for the Economic Commission for Africa* (Addis Ababa, 1996).

BAMIDELE OLOWA

ECONOMIC COMMISSION FOR LATIN AMERICA AND THE CARIBBEAN. The Economic Commission for Latin America and the Caribbean (ECLAC) was founded by the UN in 1948 in order to coordinate policies for the promotion of economic development in the Latin American countries. The Caribbean joined in 1984, so that now the thirty-three countries of the region are full members, as are the United States,

Canada, France, the Netherlands, Portugal, Spain, and the United Kingdom. The function of ECLAC, often known by its Spanish acronym CEPAL, is to research regional and national economic problems and provide expert advice on the formulation of economic strategy. The Latin American Institute for Economic and Social Planning (ILPES) was founded by ECLAC in 1962 to provide training and advisory services. Both ECLAC and ILPES are located in Santiago de Chile.

The influence of ECLAC on public policy making in Latin America is mainly exercised through its contribution to regional discourse on industrialization, trade, and poverty issues in the form of an economic doctrine known as "structuralism." This doctrine holds that markets are embedded in historically specific institutional structures which constitute markets, leading to supply rigidities, response lags, and demand disequilibria at both national and international levels. These factors in turn determine both the nature of economic adjustment to external shock and the appropriate form of public intervention. The ECLAC *Economic Survey*, published annually since 1948, is the authoritative source regarding economic and social trends and issues in the region, combining rigorous statistical analysis with independent policy evaluation. The commission also publishes influential studies on topics such as regional trade integration, industrial development, external debt, and poverty reduction. The ECLAC staff and associated experts present their personal views in the journal *Cepal Review*, published three times a year.

Since its foundation, ECLAC has led a more active and independent life than its counterparts in other regions such as the Economic Commission for Africa or the Economic and Social Commission for Asia and the Pacific. This reflects both a strong local tradition of heterodox thought on economic development and the nationalist sentiments of Latin American states, which have led in turn to a tradition of confrontation with Washington which is unusual for UN institutions. Internationally, ECLAC has an affinity of outlook with the *United Nations Conference on Trade and Development (UNCTAD) and the *International Labor Organization (ILO) and has recently engaged in a productive dialogue with the *Inter-American Development Bank (IDB). Within Latin America, ECLAC significantly influenced the establishment of several regional organizations: the Andean Pact, the Central American Common Market (CACM), and the Sistema Económico Latinoamericano (SELA). Arising from its views on public economic intervention, domestic market protection, and social resource allocation, ECLAC has often entered into conflict with the *World Bank and the *International Monetary Fund (IMF) on issues such as trade liberalization and macroeconomic management.

The considerable influence of ECLAC in the region was originally derived from its articulation of a critical approach to the problems of late industrialization and disadvantageous trade relations established by its first executive secretary, Raúl *Prebisch. This structuralist doctrine was subsequently extended to encompass problems of technology transfer, agrarian reform, inflation, and employment; as such it expressed the thought of the leading Latin American economists of the postwar decades. It had a major influence throughout the region in the 1950s and 1960s, not only on state bureaucracies but also on universities, trade unions, business groups, and even liberation theology. Structuralist doctrine then became a

key element of the international debate on *Third World underdevelopment—although its misuse in "dependency" and "world system" theories eventually undermined the commission's reputation. Chile under Allende, Peru under Velasco, and Mexico under Echevarría implemented structuralist ideas in their radical economic experiments in economic strategy: their subsequent collapse further discredited this approach.

The 1980s were thus a difficult time for ECLAC, as monetarism and liberalization became the dominant economic doctrines in the region and the debt crisis made official confrontation with Washington somewhat costly. This decline of influence was exacerbated by the growing predominance of neoclassical economists in Latin American universities and policy agencies. Nonetheless, ECLAC continued to produce important work on debt negotiation, structural adjustment, technology transfer, regional integration, and the causes of poverty. Structuralist doctrine was also central to the design of a redistributive economic strategy in Nicaragua under the Sandinistas and in the repeated attempts at heterodox monetary stabilization in Brazil.

ECLAC has gradually regained its regional influence during the 1990s as the costs of economic liberalization became clear in terms of both social inequality and macroeconomic instability. The establishment of new regional trade arrangements—the North American Free Trade Agreement (*NAFTA), the Southern Common Market (MERCOSUR), and the planned Free Trade Area of the Americas (FTAA)—restored impetus to debates on industrialization strategy and policy coordination. Widespread concern over persistent poverty and environmental degradation legitimized the ECLAC focus on public action to improve income distribution and achieve sustainable development. The experience of volatile capital flows made the need for active macroeconomic policy and prudential market regulation evident. The inclusion in mainstream economics of concepts of market failure, endogenous growth, and institutional interaction also makes the structuralist approach more acceptable. In consequence, ECLAC now has the opportunity to regain its original initiative in Latin American economic debate—and through this to underpin democratic discourse in the region.

(See also DEVELOPMENT AND UNDERDEVELOPMENT; IMPORT-SUBSTITUTION INDUSTRIALIZATION; LAND REFORM; LATIN AMERICAN AND CARIBBEAN REGIONAL ORGANIZATIONS; LIBERALISM VS. ALTERNATIVE MODELS; REGIONAL DEVELOPMENT BANKS.)

Raúl Prebisch, "Five Stages in My Thinking on Development," in G. Meier and D. Seers, eds., *Pioneers in Development* (New York, 1984). ECLAC, *Policies to Improve Linkages with the Global Economy* (Santiago, 1995). ECLAC, *The Equity Gap: Latin America, the Caribbean and the Social Summit* (Santiago, 1997).

E. V. K. FITZGERALD

ECONOMIC COMMUNITY OF WEST AFRICAN STATES.

The Economic Community of West African States (ECOWAS) was established on 28 May 1975 in Lagos, Nigeria, with the principal objective of promoting cooperation and development in virtually all fields of economic activity among its sixteen member states, enhancing their bargaining power in international negotiations to enable the West African countries to present themselves as larger, more attractive investment partners to the outside world, and contributing to the progress and development of the African continent. ECOWAS is perhaps the most visible, and certainly the most studied, of the current experiments in regional integration in sub-Saharan Africa.

Since its inception, ECOWAS has had more than twenty-four ordinary and extraordinary summit meetings of the Authority of Heads of State and Government. With 210 million inhabitants, a surface area of 6.7 million square kilometers, and immense human, natural, and mineral resources, West Africa has all the ingredients for successful integration and rapid development. Despite these advantages, ECOWAS has not made much progress toward the goal of creating a common market among its member states and of fostering collective economic self-reliance among these countries.

The Community is, however, not without some impressive accomplishments in terms of its impact on West African citizens, its significant interventions to maintain regional peace and security, as well as political and diplomatic benefits derived from its annual meetings. ECOWAS is the first major economic grouping in Africa whose member countries have abolished entry visas in order to ease movement of Community citizens within the subregion. Also in progress is the institution of the ECOWAS travel certificate, ECOWAS traveler's checks, and the harmonized immigration and emigration form. A Community-wide insurance scheme is in place for ECOWAS citizens and a telecommunications project, financed by the ECOWAS Fund, has resulted in improved communications among member states. All this, together with the construction of interstate roads, will enable ECOWAS to make great strides toward provision of the regional infrastructures needed to stimulate trade and investments.

The most impressive success recorded by ECOWAS is with respect to the maintenance of regional peace and security. The decision of the heads of state of the West African countries to launch the ECOWAS Ceasefire Monitoring Group (ECOMOG) operation in Liberia (August 1990), and subsequently, in Sierra Leone (1997–1999) and Guinea-Bissau (1998), represents an attempt by the ECOWAS to employ peacekeeping operations as part of its approach to finding a peaceful solution to the crises in the subregion in line with the practice already established by the United Nations. The ECOWAS decision marked a strategic turn in the international approach to the management of internal crises. ECOMOG is the first real attempt by African countries to solve an African conflict. It has earned international respect for Africa by striving to return Liberia, Sierra Leone, and Guinea Bissau to normalcy. The United Nations *Security Council, the *Organization of African Unity (OAU), and the *Nonaligned Movement have highly commended ECOWAS for its untiring efforts to restore peace, security, and stability in Liberia.

Two other benefits, both political, derive from ECOWAS's annual meetings. One is the exposure heads of state receive in their own media and in the media of other West African states from participating in a meeting with a large number of other heads of state. But probably more important are the opportunities offered by these annual meetings for the political leadership of West Africa to deal with regional issues of importance to them that could not easily be dealt with in the much larger annual meetings of the OAU or at the bilateral level. In this regard, ECOWAS appears to be becoming a re-

gional diplomatic or political organization, and this evolution may sustain it even in the face of its failure to realize its formal goals of economic integration. Closely related to this is the establishment of the ECOWAS Mechanism for Conflict Prevention, Management, and Resolution Peace-keeping and Security, together with a Regional Observation and Monitoring Center, as well as a Mediation and Security Council to meet the challenges of managing full-scale conflicts and internal crises in the West African subregion.

Significantly, too, ECOWAS maintains a cooperation network with other regional organizations and with international groupings of non-ECOWAS member states. Today, more than fifteen international organizations have relations with ECOWAS. It has deepened cooperation not only with such intergovernmental organizations in West Africa as the West African Economic and Monetary Union and the Permanent Inter-State Committee for Drought in the Sahel but also with the European Union, the World Bank, the Commonwealth, the OPEC Fund, the United Nations Development Program, the United Nations Economic Commission for Africa, and a number of international institutions. ECOWAS also constitutes one of the major building blocks of the African Economic Community. Consequently, it is working in close collaboration with the OAU to facilitate the realization of the objectives of the all-important Pan-African Economic Community. In addition, bilateral cooperation efforts have been established with France, Belgium, Japan, and Italy. Cooperation with such *non-governmental organizations (NGOs) as the Konrad Adenauer Foundation has greatly assisted the Community in implementing some of its programs. Above all, ECOWAS has been granted observer status in several organizations, including the World Bank.

However, the challenges confronting ECOWAS are daunting. They include consolidation of democracy and pluralism in West Africa, consolidation of regional peace and security, strong and sustained commitment of the political leadership to the goals of regionalism, greater involvement of the private sector in Community programs, popularization of ECOWAS activities and programs, and speeding up the process of regional integration that would enable the Community to effectively respond to the challenges of the emerging world of trading blocs, rapid changes in technology, liberalization of world trade, and the *globalization of world production.

Looking beyond the year 2000, the future of ECOWAS may depend on the setting up of the Community Parliament and the Court of Justice, establishment of a West African economic and monetary union, and the emergence of a regional hegemony with the will and the resources to promote regionalism. A politically stable and prosperous *Nigeria could play that role in West Africa. The fast track approach adopted by Nigeria and Ghana in December 2000 to accelerate the integration process of ECOWAS was a significant step toward integration.

Uka Ezenwe, *ECOWAS and the Economic Integration of West Africa* (London, 1983). S. K. B. Asante, *Regionalism and Africa's Development: Expectations, Reality, and Challenges* (London, 1997). Real Lavergne, ed., *Regional Integration and Cooperation in West Africa: A Multidimensional Perspective* (Ottawa, 1997).

S. K. B. ASANTE

ECONOMIC PLANNING. See PLANNING.

ECONOMIC POLICY COORDINATION. See POLICY CO-ORDINATION, ECONOMIC.

ECONOMICS. See INTERNATIONAL POLITICAL ECONOMY; POLITICAL ECONOMY.

ECUADOR. Politics in modern Ecuador continues to be shaped by its unique geography and by enduring social and economic legacies since its independence in 1830. Lying on the equator in South America, Ecuador's distinctive terrain includes tropical coast, Andean highlands, and part of the Amazonian basin. Economic power has been centered in the port of Guayaquil and the export-oriented coastal plantations, political power in the highland capital of Quito. In contrast to the dynamic coastal economy, the highlands have been characterized by a traditional hacienda system that kept much of Ecuador's indigenous population, 30 percent of their inhabitants, outside the political system. These legacies have led to chronic interregional conflicts, weak political institutions, and fluctuation between democracy and military rule.

For most of the twentieth century, Ecuador remained economically dependent on primary agricultural exports, first coffee and cacao and then bananas and shrimp. Limited industrialization inhibited the growth of the working and middle classes and consequently political parties to represent them. However, the discovery of oil in the Amazon in the early 1970s combined with a reformist military government (1972–1979) changed the path of Ecuador's political development. State control over the oil industry lessened the state's dependence on agricultural export earnings and traditional elite domination. Using oil resources, the military rapidly expanded the size and scope of the state, stimulated industrial development, and initiated agrarian reform.

Although the military's policies accelerated widespread socioeconomic and political change, the regime lacked the political institutions to harness the resulting rural and urban mobilization. Ecuador became the first country in South America to return to democracy in 1979. In contrast to earlier democratic periods, the new 1979 constitution granted universal suffrage for the first time by extending the vote to illiterate, thus enfranchising much of the indigenous population.

These positive political developments were offset by the global debt crisis in 1982. Ecuador's oil wealth did not reduce its economic vulnerability to the world market. A decline in oil prices in the 1980s pushed the country into recession. Since that time, Ecuador's democratic governments have been engaged in a precarious balancing act, juggling international demands for economic austerity with domestic calls for increasing public economic and social investment. The government's ability to organize and implement coherent policy and reform has been undermined by intense conflicts between presidents and Congress (often motivated on the basis of regional affiliation) and exacerbated by a fragmented and personalistic party system. Economic growth was further eroded by an intermittent border war with Peru in 1994–1995.

Since 1996, Ecuador has experienced a dramatic period of political and economic instability. There were five presidents in the span of four years and a continuing deterioration of the economy. The proposed dollarization of the country prompted a short-lived coup in January 2000. Increasing popular frustration with weak democratic institutions, particularly on the part of the indigenous movement, led to a renewed interest in military intervention and nondemocratic alternatives. At the outset of the twenty-first century Ecuador faced a dual challenge: to rebuild the economy and to create an effective system of democratic governance with limited resources to do so.

(See also DEMOCRATIC TRANSITIONS; INTERNATIONAL DEBT.)

Corkill and Cubit, *Ecuador: Fragile Democracy* (London, 1988). Anita Isaacs, *Military Rule and Transition in Ecuador, 1972–1992* (Pittsburgh, 1993).

MONIQUE SEGARRA

EGYPT. In the early nineteenth century, Egypt was formed as a centralized state out of a province of the Ottoman Empire. The new state promoted agriculture and modern industry, and expanded its empire abroad from the Sudan to Syria. In 1839, however, European states intervened to reestablish nominal Ottoman authority, forcing Egypt to disarm itself and remove restrictions on the penetration of European commerce and capital.

The building of the Suez Canal and a modern transport and irrigation network during the 1850s and 1860s accelerated Egypt's incorporation into the European world economy, principally as a producer of raw cotton. Export agriculture concentrated landownership in the hands of a Turkish-speaking elite and produced a new stratum of European and Levantine financiers and merchants tied to powerful European banks. In 1881 a reformist movement attempted to replace absolutist rule subservient to European creditors with parliamentary government, but within a year British troops invaded Egypt and reestablished a client regime.

Britain's colonial rule lasted until Egyptian independence in 1922, which followed a second nationalist revolt in 1919. Egypt became a *constitutional monarchy, although the British retained their military presence, control of Egyptian foreign policy, and considerable influence over domestic affairs. In 1936 Britain withdrew its troops to the Suez Canal zone, but the economic hardships of World War II and Egypt's defeat in the Palestine war of 1948–1949 led to violent popular protest against the British presence and the incompetence of the monarchy. In 1952, army officers led by Gamal Abdel *Nasser seized power, abolished the monarchy, and negotiated Britain's withdrawal from Suez.

Today, Egypt is a constitutional republic, ruled by a president who is nominated to a six-year renewable term of office by the People's Assembly and approved by the electorate. The president appoints the prime minister and other members of the government, lays down the general policies of the state, issues decrees with the force of law, declares states of emergency and war, and is the supreme head of the armed forces and the police. The judiciary is protected by the constitution from political interference and in practice has maintained significant independence, to the extent that the regime has been forced to evade its powers by the almost continuous use of martial law and military courts.

Following the 1952 coup Egypt became a *one-party system. The new regime suppressed existing parties and replaced them with the Liberation Rally, which was renamed the Arab Socialist Union (ASU) in 1962 and organized in communities and workplaces as an agency of popular political mobilization. The ASU leadership weakened after the death of President Nasser in 1970 and after conservative forces reasserted themselves under his successor, Anwar *Sadat. In 1976 Sadat permitted rival political organizations to form, first as platforms within the ASU and from 1978 as separate parties.

The ASU itself became the National Democratic Party, remaining the ruling political party. Closely linked to the government and the state-controlled media and security forces, it has been assured of large electoral majorities. Left-leaning intellectuals and Nasserists organized the National Progressive Unionist Party, whose support was strong among industrial workers and whose criticisms prompted the regime to establish the religious-nationalist Socialist Labor Party as a more loyal opposition. The center-right New Wafd, successor to the popular pre-1952 nationalist party, emerged as the most influential opposition party.

Communist, Nasserist, and Islamic political parties continue to be banned, and labor unions, an important force before 1952, remain under government control. However, the Muslim Brotherhood, a mass political movement formed in 1929 and suppressed after 1954, was allowed to reorganize semi-legally in the 1970s as an alternative to the Left. After the assassination of President Sadat in 1981 by members of a militant Islamic cell, the Brotherhood was also seen as an alternative to religious extremism. Its program of social and cultural conservatism is supported by powerful elements in the state, including parts of the judiciary, and by the religious establishment. Its members have won People's Assembly seats under the name of other parties and dominate elections to many professional organization. Under Sadat's successor, Hosni Mubarak, opposition newspapers were allowed more freedom. Since the state bans the holding of public meetings, the press provides the only public forum for criticism of government policy. But its efforts in the late 1990s to expose financial corruption, especially in the presidential family, led to new restrictions reestablishing the limits to political dissent.

Support for the regime lies among landowners; the upper ranks of the bureaucracy and the armed forces; and a burgeoning class of entrepreneurs and property speculators, some controlling large, family-based conglomerates. These groups benefited from the regime's earlier policies of land reform, industrialization, and military growth and remain dependent on the state for protected markets, contracts, and commissions.

Half the country's population is now urban, concentrated in the two major cities of Cairo and Alexandria. Although the industrial workforce is more than a million strong, most of the urban population is employed in the service sector. The rural population remains predominantly agricultural, but despite reform measures land is still concentrated in a few hands. In 1987, 48 percent of farmland was held in farms of more than five acres, the maximum size of a family farm, by the top 10 percent of landholders. This stratum holds political power in the countryside.

Egypt's population is largely Muslim, with Christians estimated at 10 percent. During the colonial period, parts of the Christian community prospered as intermediaries for European capital and political power, but since the 1950s their position of relative privilege has declined. This has contributed to Christian-Muslim animosity and sometimes violence, especially in areas where the Islamic movement is strong.

Women in Egypt benefited from the emergence of a feminist movement early in the twentieth century, in the context of the nationalist struggle. After 1952 they gained the right to vote and to stand for election as well as wider access to education and employment. As education moved them into the workplace, many women adopted a modern form of veiling, with motives ranging from piety and political activism to dealing with the discomforts of a male-dominated public space. At the same time, the wider growth of the Islamic movement carried with it a reassertion of the male prerogatives weakened by these economic and social changes.

The Nasser regime undertook a program of state-controlled capitalist development labeled "Arab socialism." The 1952 agrarian reforms dispossessed the small landed aristocracy and guaranteed the security of tenant farmers. The regime initially sought international investment, but when the United States refused to finance the keystone of its development program, the Aswan High Dam, the state was forced into a more active economic role. The Suez Canal was nationalized, and after the abortive Suez invasion by Britain, France, and Israel in 1956, the regime Egyptianized European banks and enterprises. Egyptian business elites and landowners prospered but were unwilling to invest in rapid industrialization to promote wider prosperity and reduce pressure from the left, which was subject to growing repression.

In the 1960s the military regime moved against the power of private Egyptian capital, nationalizing banks, major companies, and industries, and passed laws giving workers shares of profits, a minimum wage, and free health care and education. Five-year *planning focused on a program of *import-substitution industrialization in iron and steel, aluminum, chemicals, and other heavy industry, and efforts were made to extend the land reform. Egypt's defeat in the June 1967 Arab-Israeli war weakened the regime, however, and enabled the emergent bureaucratic and military elite, together with large landowners and the urban bourgeoisie, to resist further reform.

The Sadat regime reflected these interests. The 1974 economic "opening" (*infitah) encouraged foreign investment in collaboration with local capital, but the boom occurred in construction, property speculation, consumer imports, tourism, and other services, rather than renewed industrial growth. By the mid-1990s services accounted for 60 percent of the country's GDP, while industry and agriculture contributed only 20 percent each. Oil exports, Suez Canal tolls, tourism, and the remittances of millions of men who went to work in the Gulf became the major sources of foreign income, all of them highly volatile.

Unable to promote self-sustaining growth or further redistribution, the regime preserved social order through the 1980s by subsidizing the cost of food and other necessities. This was financed by borrowing from abroad, including subsidized U.S. loans and grain sales on a scale that exceeded U.S. aid to all the rest of Africa combined. Together with extensive purchases of U.S. arms, these loans drew the government heavily into debt. Although part of the debt was later forgiven, the collapse of oil prices after 1985 forced the government to seek IMF aid to refinance its obligations. In exchange, in 1991 and 1996 Egypt accepted IMF economic programs that cut social spending and price controls, began the privatization or liquidation of state enterprises, and opened the country more fully to private foreign investment and trade. By the late 1990s the reforms had stabilized inflation, the currency, and the fiscal balance, but deregulated prices had caused havoc in agriculture and in textiles, Egypt's major industry, and export growth was lagging behind the surge in imports. There was a speculation boom in property and in the revived Cairo stock exchange, but the level of long-term investment and job creation remained low. The state abandoned its lingering commitment to redistribution of wealth and revoked many of the economic rights won in the Nasser period, in particular rent controls and the security of tenant farmers against eviction.

Egyptians live with high unemployment and declining access to adequate housing, nutrition, health care, and education. The population grew from 40 million in 1980 to 60 million in 1998, although family planning programs have now slowed the annual growth rate to under 2 percent, among the lowest in Africa and the Middle East. With public protest forbidden, popular opposition to determining social conditions and growing inequality continues to be channeled by the moral and organizational resources of Islamic associations, some of them clandestine and violent. In 1992 the Islamic Group (al-gama'a al-islamiyya) launched a terror campaign in Cairo and the south, targeting foreign tourism as a mainstay of the economy and a symbol of Egypt's corruption by the West. The state suppressed the group at the cost of many hundreds of lives. Anxious for the support of less subversive Islamic activists, however, the regime was unwilling to halt a persistent, occasionally violent campaign against prominent Egyptian secularists and used the threat of destabilization to refuse the demand of opposition parties and human rights groups for effective democratic rights.

Egypt's economic and military dependence on the United States since the mid-1970s has reduced its international role. Until oil wealth financed the growth of Saudi Arabia and Iraq, Egypt was the predominant Arab power and a leader in wider anti-imperialist coalitions such as the *Nonaligned Movement and the *Organization of African Unity. Israel's unsuccessful 1956 Suez invasion affirmed Nasser's leadership of a populist *Arab nationalism, and was followed in 1958 by political union with Syria to form the short-lived United Arab Republic. The United States opposed Arab nationalism, which threatened its more oligarchic Arab allies, forcing Egypt and other populist states to depend increasingly on the Soviet Union. In 1967 Israel again invaded Egypt, this time with U.S. support, after Israeli-Syrian clashes had led Egypt to reimpose its pre-1956 blockade of Israeli shipping in the Gulf of Aqaba. In response to a humiliating defeat, Egypt began realigning itself to gain U.S. support. The October 1973 war forced Israel into military disengagement talks. Sadat's November 1977 trip to Jerusalem led to the 1979 Camp David peace accords by which Israel withdrew in stages from Egyptian territory and promised some form of autonomy to the Palestinians in the West Bank and Gaza Strip.

The other Arab states opposed a peace treaty that left Israel holding the West Bank and Gaza under military occupation, and broke diplomatic relations with Cairo. Egypt's formal isolation lasted a decade, interrupting aid from the Gulf states and increasing Cairo's dependence on Washington. The *Iran-Iraq War (1980–1988), however, drew Egypt closer to Saudi Arabia and Jordan in joint support of Iraq, and after the war ties with Syria and Libya were remade. Egypt's participation in the *Gulf War (1991) strengthened the regime's position at home and in Washington. After the 1993 Oslo Agreement giving the Palestinians in Israeli-occupied territories limited self-rule, Egypt was unable to push Israel or the United States to support full Palestinian statehood. The United States, in turn, continued to support the Egyptian state and its refusal to extend political freedoms at home.

(See also ARAB-ISRAELI CONFLICT; COLONIAL EMPIRES; DECOLONIZATION; FOREIGN WORKERS; INTERNATIONAL MIGRATION; ISLAM; NASSERISM; NATIONALIZATION; SUEZ CRISIS.)

Anouar Abdel Malek, *Egypt: Military Society* (New York, 1968). Robert Springborg, *Mubarak's Egypt* (Boulder, Colo., 1989). Arlene MacLeod, *Accommodating Protest: Working Women, the New Veiling, and Change in Cairo* (New Haven, Conn., 1991). P. J. Vatikiotis, *The History of Modern Egypt from Muhammed Ali to Mubarak* (Baltimore, 1991). Gregory Starrett, *Putting Islam to Work: Education, Politics, and Religious Transformation in Egypt* (Berkeley, Calif., 1998).

TIMOTHY MITCHELL

EISENHOWER DOCTRINE. On 5 January 1957, U.S. President Dwight D. *Eisenhower delivered a major *foreign policy address in which he asked Congress to authorize the use of armed *force to aid any country requesting help "against overt armed aggression from any nation controlled by international communism." On 9 March, the lawmakers ratified what is known as the Eisenhower Doctrine, a rationale for U.S. intervention directed primarily at the *Middle East, where radical nationalist opposition to the West had sharpened in the aftermath of the *Suez Crisis. The Eisenhower Doctrine affirmed U.S. determination to become the leading power in the region. Eisenhower had just blocked a military campaign by Britain and France, the former colonial powers, who, along with Israel, hoped to recapture the nationalized Suez Canal and overthrow Egypt's president *Nasser. The U.S. president now made it clear that the *United States itself reserved the right to intervene in this oil-rich zone if it perceived its vital interests threatened. The Eisenhower Doctrine was in some sense a continuation of the *Truman Doctrine of ten years earlier (March 1947), which had provided U.S. military aid to Turkey and Greece to block any extension of Soviet influence into the Mediterranean and the Middle East. The Eisenhower Doctrine reflected the same *Cold War imperatives, but it was broader, aimed in large measure at containing radical *nationalism. Washington identified radical nationalism with the Soviet Union for three main reasons. First, it considered nationalist demands for control over resources like oil to be the practical equivalent of *communism in terms of interfering with corporate control and access. U.S. oil companies were consolidating their interests in the region at the time, and Washington wanted to make it clear that it would combat nationalizations or other interference in these highly profitable enterprises. Second, radical nationalists had rejected a proposed anti-Soviet military alliance, known as the Baghdad Pact, and they had taken a leading role in the emerging movement of "nonalignment." Secretary of State John Foster Dulles believed that countries who refused to be allies were virtual enemies, and he viewed nonalignment as thinly disguised support for communism. Third, radical nationalist regimes in Egypt and Syria had recently established direct military and economic relations with Moscow. In fact, such steps had been less ideological than pragmatic, and the regimes domestically were anticommunist. But Washington was inclined to see these governments as extremely vulnerable to Soviet "penetration" and subversion, if not as functional Soviet allies. The Eisenhower Doctrine, then, was a means to hold these governments in check, to pressure them toward accommodation, and to sanction direct military *intervention if absolutely necessary. Eisenhower's proclamation coincided with a visit to Washington by King Saud of Saudi Arabia, whom the United States wanted to build up as a conservative regional ally and counterweight to Egypt's Nasser. In fact, the U.S. government invoked the Eisenhower Doctrine only twice, and never in circumstances of external aggression. In April 1957, Washington sent emergency aid to Jordan and moved the Sixth Fleet to the eastern Mediterranean to support King Hussein, whose throne had been threatened by an abortive military coup. And in July 1958, U.S. Marines landed in Lebanon to defend the Lebanese government of Camille Chamoun in the midst of a civil war and in the wake of a nationalist military coup in Iraq. Soviet involvement was absent in both cases, as U.S. policymakers were well aware. After the Eisenhower administration left office in January 1961, the U.S. government no longer invoked the doctrine. The new Kennedy administration sought greater accommodation with nationalists in the Middle East. Later in the decade, the Nixon Doctrine expressed a policy of relying on regional surrogates (like Iran and Israel in the Middle East) to protect and advance U.S. interests. But in 1980, the *Carter Doctrine returned to the idea of direct U.S. military intervention—now focused on the oil-rich Persian Gulf and Arabian Peninsula area. That doctrine, and the military preparations it called into being, laid the groundwork for the massive intervention of U.S. forces in the *Gulf War of 1991.

(See also ARAB NATIONALISM; CONTAINMENT; NASSERISM; NONALIGNED MOVEMENT.)

Alan Dowty, *Middle East Crisis: US Decision-Making in 1958, 1970, and 1973*, pt. I (Berkeley, Calif., 1984). Douglas Little, "Cold War and Covert Action: The United States and Syria, 1945–1958" *The Middle East Journal* 44, no. 1 (Winter 1990).

JOE STORK

EISENHOWER, Dwight D. Born in Denison, Texas, on 14 October 1890, Dwight D. Eisenhower was the son of a section hand on the railroad. The family moved to Abilene, Kansas, in 1891; there he grew up and graduated from high school in 1911. He won an appointment to the U.S. Military Academy at West Point, from which he graduated, and received a commission as a second lieutenant in the U.S. Army. His army career was marked by slow promotion and high praise from his superiors, one of whom was General Douglas MacArthur.

In December 1941, Chief of Staff George C. Marshall brought Lieutenant Colonel Eisenhower to Washington, gave him a temporary promotion to major general, and put him in charge of the Operations Division of the War Department. In June 1942, Marshall sent Eisenhower to England to take command of the European Anglo-American invasion of North Africa; in May 1943, he forced the surrender of the German-Italian military units in Africa; in July, he commanded the

Anglo-American invasion of Sicily; in September, forces under his command invaded Italy at Salerno. In December 1943, President Franklin *Roosevelt selected him to command Operation Overlord, the invasion of France in Normandy.

In June 1944, Eisenhower launched the assault. By late August, his troops liberated France from the Germans. In December, his forces met and hurled back the last great German offensive of the war, in Belgium, known as the Battle of the Bulge. In March 1945, British, U.S., and Canadian troops crossed the Rhine River and overran Germany. On 7 May 1945, at his headquarters in Reims, France, Eisenhower presided over the unconditional surrender of Germany.

Eisenhower emerged from *World War II as the most successful and famous general in the world. He was also immensely popular personally. A political career seemed natural and inevitable. In 1948, Democrats and Republicans alike wanted to nominate him for the *presidency, but he declared that a professional soldier ought not get involved in partisan politics. He retired as chief of staff and took the position of president of Columbia University.

In 1951, at President Harry *Truman's request, he left Columbia to become the first Supreme Allied Commander, Europe, head of the military arm of the *North Atlantic Treaty Organization (NATO). The Republicans, desperate after losing five presidential elections in a row, were eager to nominate him in 1952. Party leaders convinced him that if he did not run, Senator Robert Taft would be the Republican nominee; Taft was an isolationist who had voted against NATO, and would pull the United States out of NATO if he became president. If the Democrats won, the leaders predicted it would be the end of the two-party system and the beginning of *socialism in the United States. To avert such calamities, Eisenhower reluctantly agreed to accept the nomination.

He won a landslide victory over Democratic nominee Adlai Stevenson in 1952, and again for reelection in 1956. As president, he was extremely popular. Partly this was a result of his sunny disposition, his big grin, his "there's nothing to worry about" manner, his ability to project himself as "just plain folks." Mainly, however, his popularity was a product of his policies.

He was a political conservative who always sought the middle of the road. His philosophy was that the extremes on any political debate were always wrong. He wanted a balanced budget, but not at the expense of the social programs created by the *New Deal Democrats in the 1930s. He was a moderate on civil rights, willing to enforce the law as laid down by the Supreme Court in *Brown v. Topeka* (1954) but unwilling to move aggressively to integrate the schools. He wanted to eliminate communist influence in the schools and in government, but was opposed to the methods used by Senator Joseph *McCarthy.

Eisenhower was a great builder. More schools were built during his administration than any other (they were, admittedly, necessary because of the baby boom). The St. Lawrence Seaway was one of his achievements. His proudest boast was that he initiated and carried through the Interstate Highway System, the greatest public works project in history.

He was a general who hated war. He ended the *Korean War with an armistice six months after taking office, and entered no others, in a decade in which the *Cold War was at its most dangerous. Nearly all his advisers wanted him to save the French position in *Vietnam in 1954, but he refused to commit U.S. troops. War with China seemed all but certain on three occasions during his presidency, but he always managed to find a peaceful solution.

In 1955, he went to Geneva for a summit with Nikita *Khrushchev, the first time a U.S. president met with a Soviet leader since the end of World War II, to establish a system of peaceful coexistence. Eisenhower held down the costs and dangers of the *arms race through the 1950s in a way that no one else could have done. Both political parties demanded more defense spending, especially after the Soviets launched the first satellite, Sputnik, in 1957, but Eisenhower consistently held that building more weapons would not create more security, and that a balanced budget was more important than defense spending. Eisenhower was no reformer. Except for his appointment of Earl Warren as chief justice, black Americans had little to thank him for; neither did women, or the poor, or other minorities. He opposed McCarthy's witch-hunting methods, but did almost nothing personally to stop the senator. Nor was he a risk-taker. The counterpoint to his success in achieving and maintaining peace was his failure to "roll back" *communism in Central and Eastern Europe (as he had promised to do in the 1952 campaign), or to stop the spread of communism to Vietnam and Cuba. To his critics, he appeared to be a do-nothing president, content to "stand pat" and preside over a rich, happy, self-satisfied nation. He left his party vulnerable to Senator John F. *Kennedy's 1960 presidential campaign charges that he had allowed the nation to "fall behind" the Soviets. Eisenhower gave the nation eight years of peace and prosperity, a claim no other president in the twentieth century could make. In 1961, he retired to his farm in Gettysburg, Pennsylvania. He died on 28 March 1969. He was survived by his wife Mamie and his son John.

(See also AMERICAN FOREIGN POLICY; CIVIL RIGHTS MOVEMENT; EISENHOWER DOCTRINE.)

Dwight D. Eisenhower, *Crusade in Europe* (New York, 1948). Dwight D. Eisenhower, *The White House Years*, 2 vols. (Garden City, N.Y., 1962–1963). Stephen E. Ambrose, *Eisenhower: Soldier and President* (New York, 1990).

STEPHEN E. AMBROSE

EL SALVADOR. The smallest Latin American country (5.8 million inhabitants as of 1999), El Salvador achieved independence from Spain in 1821 as part of a confederation of Central American states that endured until 1839. After independence weak governments commanded few resources and were vulnerable to the ambitions of neighboring states and local caudillos. Lack of access to the Caribbean meant economic isolation, which began to end when the Panama Railroad linked the oceans in 1855. Coffee gradually replaced indigo, the traditional colonial crop, as the main export, and provided the resources and the impetus for the consolidation of the state. The needs of the coffee industry transformed economic institutions: colonial-era corporate forms of land tenure were eliminated and a banking system was created. Educated elites were the main beneficiaries of this process. Self-described liberal politicians belonging to this group, in power after 1870, accelerated economic reforms by exercising firm control over the labor force and the political system. Elections were controlled through a clientelistic system based on the influence of landowners who thus wielded considerable power.

The Great Depression strained the system by creating widespread unemployment. In 1932, a peasant rebellion with ethnic connotations and some communist support exploded in the western provinces where most Indians (then 20 percent of the population) lived. The new military government of General Maximiliano Hernández Martínez (1882–1966) responded with massive repression that claimed more than 10,000 lives, many of them Indian. This event, known as the *Matanza*, sanctioned army rule in the eyes of the oligarchy and bound both groups together. Military governments sought to legitimize themselves through rigged elections and periods of flexibility until 1979.

After World War II governments tried to industrialize the country through import substitution and the creation of the Central American Common Market in 1954. These efforts succeeded in increasing the share of industry to one-fifth of GNP by 1970. Industrialization and the expansion of export agriculture concentrated capital and land ownership. A brief war erupted in 1969 when increasing numbers of displaced Salvadoran peasants migrated to Honduras and competed for land. Hondurans already resented El Salvador for benefiting disproportionately from the Common Market, which was virtually destroyed by the war.

With social tensions increasing, reformers within the political system advocated land redistribution. They were frustrated by recalcitrant landowners. The oligarchy strengthened links with an army that stepped up its counterinsurgency role. The Organización Democrática Nacionalista (ORDEN), a paramilitary organization, was created to identify and suppress "communist agitators." As *human rights violations became widespread, left-wing activists demanding radical redistribution of wealth and power began to organize labor actions in the late 1960s; guerrilla organizations were formed starting in 1970. Christian activism increased political awareness among land-deprived peasants. Church groups were radicalized after becoming targets of paramilitary groups.

By 1979 *political violence was widespread. The success of the Nicaraguan Revolution seemed an opportunity to some, a dire warning to others, and a call to action to many. Young military officers in alliance with reformist civilians organized a coup d'état in October, a last-ditch effort to introduce reforms and deflect demands for revolutionary change. The new leaders were unable to control powerful army officers and human right violations continued unabated. Hopes for a moderate solution dissipated after the murder of Monsignor Oscar Arnulfo Romero (1917–1980), the archbishop of San Salvador, whose powerful denunciations of human rights violations had enraged the right wing. Civil war started in 1981 with an offensive by a recently formed coalition of five guerrilla organizations, the Frente Farabundo Martí para la Liberación Nacional (FMLN), named after a communist leader of the 1932 *Matanza*.

The United States saw the conflict as a chapter of the Cold War. From 1981 to 1992 it spent more than $4 billion to prop up civilian regimes and promote elections, while financing the rapid expansion of a powerful army resistant to civilian control. The United States considered the army indispensable to defeating the guerrillas and thus was unable to end the army's human rights violations. In 1989 a guerrilla offensive in the capital persuaded both sides of the impossibility of prevailing militarily, while the fall of the Berlin Wall softened

U.S. opposition to a negotiated solution. A UN-brokered negotiation between the government and the FMLN culminated in the Peace Accords of January 1992. The conflict claimed more than 70,000 lives and generated massive migrations; an estimated 1.2 million Salvadorans are now living in the United States as a result.

The 1992 Peace Accords restructured the army and police, strengthened the independence of the Supreme Court, demobilized the guerrillas, and established a Truth Commission to investigate human rights violations. Since 1992 elections have been free and fair, the army has lost considerable influence, the branches of government have shown signs of independence, and public debate is vigorous.

The FMLN became a political party as part of the Accords, while the most conservative elements of Salvadoran society organized around the Alianza Republicana Nacionalista (ARENA), a party founded in 1981 by Major Roberto D'Abuisson (1943–1992), a charismatic former military officer implicated by the 1993 Truth Commission in the murder of Archbishop Romero. Both parties dominate contemporary politics. The FMLN has made substantial progress in municipal and legislative elections, but ARENA has won three consecutive presidential elections. The need to appeal to a broad spectrum of voters has moderated both parties and made the government more responsive to the population. The challenges are great: extremely high crime rates, income inequality, widespread poverty, and environmental degradation.

ARENA governments have diminished the role of the state in the economy by privatizing banks and utilities, lowering tariffs, and following cautious monetary policies. They have also promoted public education. Peace has brought rapid economic growth after years of depressed demand as well as the stimulus of remittances from Salvadorans abroad, currently the most important source of foreign exchange. Industry, still one-fifth of the economy, now has a significant *maquila* sector, part of the globalization of the economy which is proceeding apace.

(See also GUERRILLA WARFARE; IMPORT-SUBSTITUTION INDUSTRIALIZATION; U.S.–LATIN AMERICAN RELATIONS.)

Thomas Anderson, *Matanza: El Salvador's Communist Revolt of 1932* (Lincoln, Neb., 1971). William H. Durham, *Scarcity and Survival in Central America* (Stanford, Calif., 1979). Tommy Sue Montgomery, *Revolution in El Salvador* (Boulder, Colo., 1982). Héctor Lindo-Fuentes, *Weak Foundations: The Economy of El Salvador in the Nineteenth Century, 1821–1898* (Berkeley, Calif., 1990). James Dunkerley, *The Pacification of Central America* (London, 1994).

HÉCTOR LINDO-FUENTES

ELECTIONS AND VOTING BEHAVIOR. Over the past two centuries, electoral institutions have come to play a role in the governmental structures and political processes of most nations. The forms that these institutions take, and the precise role that they play, however, vary enormously from place to place and over time. The most fundamental dimension on which national electoral systems vary is the opportunity for opposition within the formal electoral framework. Democratic electoral processes permit opposing forces to depose and replace current officeholders. What could be called authoritarian electoral systems, by contrast, do not permit the electoral defeat of those in power and serve primarily as instruments of mass mobilization and legitimation for the regime.

The Emergence of Democratic Elections. In general, democratic electoral systems are most likely to evolve and persist in societies where politically relevant resources, including the capacity to employ armed force or violence, are distributed relatively widely outside the control of the central government. Generally, electoral processes are introduced when governments face economic difficulties, military demands, or internal political challenges that require them to seek popular support and to create formal channels of participation and opposition. Few ruling groups, however, are anxious to see these channels effectively used by their political foes. At some point in every nation's electoral history, incumbent *elites have sought to use military force to suppress their electoral opponents.

But military force is by no means the only important factor. Where other politically relevant resources and skills, such as wealth, education, communications, and organization, are relatively widely diffused and outside the state's control, the likelihood that incumbent elites can successfully eliminate their opponents is lessened. It is for this very reason that economic development, as Seymour Martin Lipset and others have shown (*Political Man*, New York, 1963), was historically conducive to the evolution of democratic electoral institutions.

Voter Mobilization. In most nations, contending forces have sought to make use of a variety of different appeals to link themselves to popular followings. The most effective and durable appeals are those based on voters' class, religious, or ethnic identifications and regional attachments. Whether and how any particular social group or stratum will participate in electoral politics, however, cannot be directly inferred from some characteristic of the group itself. The relative political significance of race, class, religion, and so forth depends in large measure on when, how, on what basis, and by whom a group is electorally mobilized.

For example, in the United States in the early twentieth century the Republicans mobilized northeastern workers partly on the basis of their religious and ethnic affiliations. In the 1930s, however, by sponsoring welfare, economic, and labor programs, Franklin D. *Roosevelt was able to bring most of these same voters into the Democratic Party on the basis of their class identification. Thus, it is not surprising that in a variety of national and historical settings, individuals with very similar social origins and life conditions have been mobilized by political forces that differed substantially from one another in aims and methods. For example, as Martin Shefter observes ("Party and Patronage: Germany, England and Italy" *Politics and Society* 7, no. 4 [1977]: 403–451), southern Italian peasants who migrated to northern Italian cities were recruited by Socialist and, later, Communist parties while their cousins who migrated to American cities became the mainstays of conservative patronage machines. Conversely, individuals with very different social characteristics have been mobilized by the same or similar parties. For example, conservative parties in all the Western democracies have been able to use patriotic and ethnic appeals to recruit large numbers of working-class voters to stand alongside their middle-class compatriots.

Contemporary American Political Patterns. In the United States today, the two major political parties have mobilized substantially different segments of the mass electorate. The Democrats have a strong base among unionized workers, *African Americans, and individuals working in the public and not-for-profit sectors of the economy. To maintain the allegiance of members of these groups, the Democratic Party generally advocates enlargement of the public sector, expansion of federal social spending, programs designed to serve the interests of organized labor, and policies aimed at furthering the cause of civil rights. The Republican Party, by contrast, has built a powerful base in the business community, among more affluent Americans, and among social and religious conservatives. To maintain their upscale base of support, Republicans generally advocate lowering taxes, reducing the scope of federal regulation of business activities, and limiting social and welfare spending. To appeal to religious conservatives, the Republican Party has adopted a position of opposition to abortion and support for prayer in the public schools.

In recent decades, neither the Democrats nor the Republicans have been able to score a decisive victory in the electoral arena. Between 1968 and 1992, the Republicans generally maintained control of the White House while Democrats held majorities in both houses of Congress. In 1992 and 1996, Democrat Bill *Clinton won election to the presidency. After 1994, however, the Republicans were able to control both houses of Congress. Their inability to achieve decisive electoral success has encouraged politicians from both parties to attempt to use the news media and the courts to defeat opponents they could not fully overcome at the polls. Thus, during the *Nixon and *Reagan presidencies, Democrats made much of media revelations of wrongdoing in the White House, and initiated investigations that led to the ouster of Richard Nixon in the Watergate affair and to the weakening of the Reagan presidency in the Iran-Contra scandals. In a similar vein, Republicans made use of media relations of possible scandals in the Clinton White House to justify congressional investigations and the appointment of a special prosecutor to look into allegations of financial and personal misconduct on the part of President Clinton leading, eventually, to Clinton's impeachment. Used as political tools, revelations and investigations erode the significance of national electoral politics by allowing groups that were unable to prevail in the electoral arena to overturn the electorate's verdict. This practice hardly seems consistent with the theory of democratic politics.

Elections and Popular Influence. The evolution and persistence of democratic electoral institutions can substantially alter the relationship between citizens and the *state. In particular, democratic electoral processes can transform the relationship between popular influence and state power. Even in the absence of elections or formal mechanisms for their expression, citizens' wishes almost always have some impact upon governments' conduct. Even the most autocratic regime must, at the very least, concern itself with popular disorder.

In the absence, however, of formal mechanisms for its expression, popular influence tends to be inversely related to governmental power. So long as they command military forces and an administrative apparatus sufficiently powerful to compel popular obedience and deal with threats to their rule, governments can afford a measure of indifference to popular pressure. If, on the other hand, the state's military and administrative institutions are too weak, then those in power are likely to become more concerned with citizens' needs and preferences. The advent of the democratic election, however, meant that even when governments possessed the military and administrative capacity to compel obedience, popular influence was no longer necessarily reduced. Popular influence and state power could coexist.

At the same time that they potentially strengthen popular influence over governments' conduct, elections also serve as important institutions of governance. Elections are among the principal mechanisms through which contemporary states regulate mass political action and strengthen their own power and authority. First, elections socialize political activity. Elections make how, when, where, and which citizens take part in political life a matter of public policy rather than simply a matter of individual choice, transforming what might otherwise consist of sporadic, citizen-initiated acts into a routine public function. This helps to preserve governments' stability by containing and channeling away potentially more dangerous or disruptive forms of political activity. Second, elections can bolster governments' power and authority. The opportunity to participate in elections can help to persuade citizens that the government is responsive to their needs and wishes and can help to persuade citizens to obey, to pay taxes, to accept military service, and so on.

Finally, to the extent that elections take the place of other, more spontaneous forms of popular *political participation, they allow incumbent elites an opportunity to regulate popular intervention into policy-making processes. Thus, those in power often seek, through election laws, to regulate the composition of the electorate in order to diminish the weight of groups they deem to be undesirable. Historically, nearly everywhere electoral laws denied participation on the basis of gender and frequently on racial or ethnic-nationalist grounds. During the nineteenth century, property requirements and weighted voting schemes were employed throughout Europe. In the United States, today, unusually cumbersome registration requirements help to inhibit voting by the poor and uneducated.

Similarly, regimes may undertake to manipulate the translation of voters' choices into electoral outcomes through regulation of the criteria for victory (i.e., the selection of majority, plurality, or proportional voting systems) and through the organization of electoral districts (gerrymandering). In general, majority and plurality voting systems create higher thresholds for legislative representation than do proportional systems; as a result, they are generally preferred by more established forces. In nineteenth-century Europe, entrenched conservative parties usually preferred majority and plurality voting systems to reduce the representation of emerging working-class groups. However, as working-class parties gained in strength and threatened to win electoral majorities, conservative groups came to see *proportional representation as a barrier against socialism. By the same token, many ruling groups have attempted to insulate some institutions and policy-making processes from electoral control by limiting the impact of elections on the composition of the government and administration. The most obvious forms of insulation are the confinement of popular election to only some governmental agencies, various modes of indirect election, and lengthy tenure in office for elected officials.

Democratic elections are a regulated and constrained form of popular intervention into governmental processes. Indeed, often elections are introduced or the suffrage expanded because spontaneous forms of mass political action threaten to have too great an impact on governments' actions. Walter Lippmann once observed that "new numbers were enfranchised because they had power, and giving them the vote was the least disturbing way of letting them exercise their power" (Clinton Rossiter and James Lare, eds., *The Essential Lippmann*, New York, 1965). Over time, the vote can provide the "least disturbing way" of allowing ordinary people to exercise power because elections can formally delimit mass influence that rulers are unable forcibly to contain.

(See also CITIZENSHIP; CLASS AND POLITICS; DEMOCRACY; ETHNICITY; POLITICAL BUSINESS CYCLE; POLITICAL PARTIES AND PARTY COMPETITION; POLITICAL REALIGNMENT; RELIGION AND POLITICS.)

Angus Campbell, Philip E. Converse, Warren E. Miller, and Donald E. Stokes, *The American Voter* (New York, 1960). Robert A. Dahl, ed., *Political Oppositions in Western Democracies* (New Haven, Conn., 1966). Seymour Martin Lipset and Stein Rokkan, eds., *Party Systems and Voter Alignments: Cross-National Perspectives* (New York, 1967). Bernard Grofman and Arend Lijphart, eds., *Electoral Laws and Their Political Consequences* (New York, 1986). Kay Schlozman and Sidney Verloa, *Voice and Equality* (Cambridge, Mass., 1995). Benjamin Ginsberg and Martin Shefter, *Politics by Other Means* (New York, 1999).

BENJAMIN GINSBERG

ELITES. The term *political elites* has different uses. Elites are leaders who perform important roles in the governance of society; they make the important decisions or have influence in decisions at the national and local levels of government. There are many types of elites—presidents or prime ministers, parliamentary deputies, judges, administrators, political activists. There are elites who hold no formal position at all: policy specialists, campaign consultants, and political financiers, for example. Elites have been the subject of much writing, from Plato to the present. Many controversies have developed about their characteristics and their functions. Two conflicting positions have been argued: (1) elites do play, and should play, a dominant role in operating political systems, with the public having only a minimal or subordinate role, perhaps only in the periodic election of leaders; (2) elites do share, and should share, power with their publics if they are to survive, be effective and responsive, and if we are to realize the goal of a democratically based political order. Which of these two positions is valid?

In terms of social and economic background, political elites are unrepresentative of the public. For example, over 80 percent of the national elites of the United States and Western *democracies have a university education, compared with 20 percent or less of the adult populations (although higher in the United States). Elites are much more likely to have learned about politics in their families than is true of the public. Because of social class status and family exposure, they have much better chances to enter political careers. Hence there is a social bias in elite selection. However, considerable opportunity exists for those with lesser education and those from working-class families to become active in politics at the local level and to take positions in local government. From 40 percent to 60 percent of city elites in Western democracies do not have a university education, and 40 percent come from working-class families.

Many paths to political elite status exist. Political parties are important recruiters, as are civic groups, labor unions, and business associations. Such groups are often the channels to political careers. In them elites develop an interest in politics, as well as experience, and undergo a process of screening and grooming for political positions. Each community and each country constitutes a special context, or elite culture, within which this grooming takes place.

Political elites vary greatly in their beliefs. In one study of the national elites of six countries, it was found that 23 percent favored extensive governmental control over the economy, 19 percent favored very minimal control, and the remainder took differing intermediate positions. The values of elites also differ. When these same elites were asked what their value priorities were for the future, 35 percent mentioned social justice and equality, 30 percent mentioned economic security or economic welfare, and the remainder had a mixture of responses. Elites are not homogeneous. Indeed, research demonstrates the pluralism of elites and their heterogeneity in social backgrounds, interests, attitudes, and values. There is no unified power elite or ruling class that runs cities or nations in democratic societies.

The study of elites deals with their performance, that is, their impact on policy, on voters, and on change or stability in the system. The new leadership that emerges after elections can, and often will, change the direction of public policy. Thus, elections can have consequences. Similarly, parties, through their activists, can affect election outcomes if they mobilize their vote. New elites can change, even revolutionize, societies in liberal or reactionary directions, as the sweeping changes in Eastern and Central Europe attest.

A major question is, Under what conditions can elites be made more responsive to the public? We know that political activism through community groups results in closer linkage of elites' views to public views. We know that the defeat of elites at the polls can produce policy change. We also know, however, that voter turnout is often low (particularly in the United States) and that citizen apathy is high. We also know elites are very entrenched—for example, over 90 percent of incumbent U.S. congressional representatives are regularly victorious in elections. But research has also shown that the possibility of defeat can make leaders more responsive and that electoral competition therefore is crucial. Thus neither the model of elite dominance nor the model of citizen control over elites represents complete reality. Both models are useful. Elites exercise *power, but they are also constrained by the potential, and actual, power of political organizations, public opinion, and mass protests.

(See also POLITICAL PARTICIPATION; POLITICAL PARTIES AND PARTY COMPETITION.)

Joel D. Aberbach, Robert D. Putnam, and Bert A. Rockman, *Bureaucrats and Politicians in Western Democracies* (Cambridge, Mass., 1981). Samuel J. Eldersveld, *Political Elites in Modern Societies: Empirical Research and Democratic Theory* (Ann Arbor, Mich., 1989).

SAMUEL J. ELDERSVELD

EMPIRE. See IMPERIALISM.

EMPIRES, COLONIAL. See COLONIAL EMPIRES.

ENGLISH-SPEAKING CARIBBEAN. The English-speaking Caribbean (sometimes known as the "Commonwealth Caribbean") includes twelve independent countries and six dependent territories. The former are Antigua and Barbuda, The Bahamas, Barbados, Belize (on the Central American mainland), Dominica, *Grenada, *Guyana (on the South American mainland), *Jamaica, Saint Kitts/Nevis (known also as Saint Christopher/Nevis), Saint Lucia, Saint Vincent and the Grenadines, and *Trinidad and Tobago. The dependencies are Bermuda, British Virgin Islands, Cayman Islands, Anguilla, Turks and Caicos Islands, and Montserrat. All are past or current British colonies.

Together the English-speaking territories (including the dependent states) have a population of about 5.9 million, varying from 2.5 million in Jamaica and 1.3 million in Trinidad and Tobago down to only 42,800 in St. Kitts/Nevis. The smallest dependent territory, Montserrat, had 10,400 people in 1995. However, the island was devastated by a volcanic eruption in mid-1995, forcing all but a few thousand residents to flee abroad.

After a period of representative rule based on a limited franchise, the English-speaking Caribbean territories became Crown Colonies with nominated or mixed nominated-elected legislatures. Minor reforms were instituted over time, but it was not until social disturbances swept the region in the late 1930s that political parties were allowed and universal suffrage was introduced. The growth of *nationalism and the effects of World War II led to increasing pressures on the British who proposed a West Indies federation as a prelude to independence. A federation was duly instituted in 1958, comprising all the territories except The Bahamas, Belize, and Guyana. However, federal negotiations bogged down on issues of finances and taxation, location of the capital, distribution of powers, and labor mobility. As a result, the two largest countries, Jamaica and Trinidad and Tobago, pulled out of the federation in 1962, opting instead for immediate independence.

In 1966 Barbados sought and attained its independence, leaving the status of the seven smaller islands of the eastern Caribbean uncertain. Since they were considered to be too small to go it alone, Britain devised a new constitutional status for them termed "Associated Statehood." This allowed them to be self-governing in all but their external affairs and defense. Eventually, world acceptance of the imperative of *decolonization, even for very small states, facilitated the independence of these eastern Caribbean states. Grenada became independent in 1974, after a period of turmoil attributable to widespread concern about independence under the autocratic Sir Eric Gairy; Dominica gained its independence in 1978; St. Lucia and St. Vincent in 1979; Antigua and Barbuda in 1981; and St. Kitts/Nevis in 1983. Of the English-speaking countries that did not participate in the federation, a decision on Guyana's independence was delayed by ethnic and political unrest linked to heightened hostility between the dominant Indo-centric party and its Afro-centric rival. Independence was eventually achieved in 1966, two years after the introduction of an electoral system of proportional representation that brought the African-based People's National Congress (PNC) to power. The Bahamas became independent peacefully in 1974. Belize's independence was delayed by a long-standing claim by Guatemala to Belize's entire territory, but was finally achieved in 1981 under British "security guarantees."

The English-speaking Caribbean states inherited certain political institutions and norms from *Britain that gave them a reputation for democracy and stability. These included two-party dominant systems, parliamentary democracy, cabinet government, bicameral legislatures, constitutional monarchy (with the monarchy represented by a governor-general), and a commitment to general elections every five years. Over time, most of these institutional and constitutional norms have been modified either by design or happenstance. Democracy in the region has been highly personalistic, with strong leaders and their parties remaining in power for several terms of office, largely due to the power of patronage. However, this began to change in the late 1980s, when political confidence was eroded by the decline of the region's economy resulting from oil price increases, trade difficulties, and heavy debt service burdens. To deal with the economic decline, governments bowed to international financial institutions and imposed structural adjustment programs. Later, in keeping with the emergence of a global regime of liberalization, free trade and open economy policies, abandoned in the nationalist 1970s, were reintroduced. Coupled with the natural demise of the postcolonial nationalist leaders, the new economic imperatives have led to the emergence of younger pragmatic leaders with tentative holds on power that are easily eroded by ineffective economic performance.

Moreover, despite the English-speaking Caribbean's reputation for stability, various sources of societal and political tensions can be identified. Ethnic tensions between Indians and Africans in Guyana and in Trinidad and Tobago have been reflected in racially-based politics and patronage. In Guyana the Afro-centric PNC kept a repressive hold on power until 1992 when Dr. Cheddi Jagan became president at the head of an Indo-centered coalition. In Trinidad and Tobago, the Afro-based People's National Movement (PNM) also managed to keep power until 1995 when the Indian-based United National Congress (UNC) came to power in coalition with a small Tobago-dominated party. In other areas, the rise of a postcolonial generation concerned about neocolonialism and distributive justice was largely responsible for widespread antigovernment "Black Power" disturbances in Trinidad and Tobago in 1970. The same phenomenon engendered the rise of left-wing parties throughout the region and effected the rise to power of the socialist Michael Manley in Jamaica in 1972 and the New Jewel Movement in Grenada in 1979. The latter regime dissolved into factions in 1983 and was removed by a U.S. invasion supported by the Eastern Caribbean states, Barbados, and Jamaica. Other incidents that have belied the region's reputation for stability include mercenary-led coup attempts against the Barbados and Dominican governments in the 1970s, secession threats and prison disturbances in Union Island (St. Vincent) in the 1970s and 1990s, secession threats by Nevis in the 1990s (Anguilla, once federated with St. Kitts and Nevis, seceded successfully in 1967, returning to colonial status), and drug trafficking and refugee problems. Perhaps the most unusual event was the attack in 1990 by a group of Islamic militants on the sitting parliament in Trinidad and Tobago. The prime minister and other parliamentarians were brutalized and the capital was the scene of heavy rioting.

The countries of the English-speaking Caribbean, with the exception of Guyana, are classified by the World Bank as middle-income and high-income countries. This designation, which makes them ineligible for Official Development Assistance and for assistance from the World Bank–affiliated International Development Association, belies the structural problems experienced by these economies. Small size has made it difficult to achieve economies of scale. The countries are still mainly primary producers: of minerals and fuels (oil in the case of Trinidad and Tobago, bauxite in Jamaica and Guyana); sugar (especially Jamaica, Barbados, Trinidad and Tobago, Guyana, and St. Kitts); bananas (primarily Dominica, St. Lucia, St. Vincent, and also Grenada and Jamaica); cocoa and spices (Grenada); and citrus products (Belize). All are also in varying degrees dependent on tourism. Industry is generally light industry and assembly operations (particularly important in Barbados). Trinidad and Tobago is the most heavily industrialized with investments in steel, natural gas, ammonia and urea, methanol, and petrochemicals.

Per capita GDP for the region in 1995 ranged from US$18,497 in the British Virgin Islands and $12,436 for The Bahamas to $830 for Guyana. Most countries fall in the $2,000 to $7,000 range. Both the Cayman Islands and The Bahamas are tax havens specializing in financial services, in addition to tourism. Many other islands depend on offshore operations, both industry and banking.

Like all primary producers, the countries of the English-speaking Caribbean are highly vulnerable to fluctuations in world market prices. This problem is compounded by the small size of their markets. One of the ways in which they have tried to overcome the limits of size has been through regional integration. The Caribbean Free Trade Area (Carifta) was initiated in 1968 and in 1973 it became the Caribbean Community and Common Market (Caricom). Members committed themselves to removing tariff barriers, establishing a common external tariff, harmonizing fiscal incentives to investment, coordinating foreign policy, and strengthening functional linkages. All the independent English-speaking countries plus Montserrat eventually joined Caricom, although The Bahamas opted to join the Community only, not the Common Market. Initially, intraregional trade expanded under integration, but in the 1970s Caricom almost collapsed as a result of quarrels over the unequal distribution of benefits, balance-of-power problems caused by the increase in oil prices, and ideological polarization between socialist Jamaica, Guyana, and Grenada and the conservative states of the Eastern Caribbean.

After the U.S. intervention in Grenada in 1983, Caricom leaders moved to heal rifts. In 1992, a West Indian Commission (WIC), established by the leaders to suggest future directions for Caricom, published an influential report calling for deeper and wider integration. The commission's proposals were offered against the backdrop of increasing globalization, widespread global endorsement of economic and political liberalization, and the end of the Cold War which left the Caribbean states somewhat marginalized, no longer able to exercise leverage as Cold War allies of the United States. In view of these difficulties, the WIC's call for deeper and wider in-

tegration was seen as a way to increase the region's bargaining leverage as well as improve its weakening trade position. Caricom governments therefore responded by establishing formal trade agreements with Venezuela and Colombia, the Southern Cone Common Market (Mercosur), and the Andean Common Market (ANCOM). Moreover, Caricom played a key role in the creation in 1994 of the Association of Caribbean States (ACS), a potential free trade arrangement that united the Caricom states with members of the Central American Integration System (SICA), the Dominican Republic, and Cuba. Dependent Caribbean states participate as associated members. At the same time, Caricom expanded to include non-English-speaking Suriname in 1994 and, in 1997, newly democratizing Haiti. In addition, a commission was established in 1993 to explore areas of collaboration between Caricom and Cuba.

Under liberalization, Caribbean countries have been faced with the probability of elimination of the preferential treatment they have received from the United States since 1983 (under the Caribbean Basin Initiative, CBI), from Canada since 1986 (under CARIBCAN), and from Europe since 1975 (under the *Lomé Convention). In the 1990s Caribbean banana producers lost a bid to maintain their dominant position on the European market in the face of pressures from Central American countries. Other problems for the region have stemmed from the creation of the North American Free Trade Agreement (NAFTA) in 1992 joining the United States, Canada, and Mexico. NAFTA has led to the diversion of trade and investment from the Caribbean to Mexico. The Caribbean's response has been to seek "NAFTA parity," that is, equal treatment with Mexico for a finite period of time. However, the U.S. Congress has been reluctant to grant this, and negotiations for Caribbean entry into NAFTA (either on a state-by-state basis or collectively) have for the same reason also been put on hold. On the other hand, in 1994 the United States joined the Latin American nations in committing to establish a Free Trade Area of the Americas (FTAA) by the year 2005. While the larger Caribbean states which had expressed a desire to join NAFTA have embraced the concept of hemispheric free trade, the smaller Caricom countries have been more reluctant, given their lack of trade competitiveness.

The Eastern Caribbean states, though members of Caricom, have inherited strong habits of collaboration dating from the period of Associated Statehood. The community they formed was named the Organization of Eastern Caribbean States (OECS) in 1981. The Eastern Caribbean Common Market, the economic arm of the OECS, is tightly integrated, including monetary integration. However, a movement to integrate these countries politically has not been successful. The OECS also adheres to a security mechanism, the Regional Security System, which is a by-product of the intervention in Grenada. Barbados and Jamaica are members as well, and Trinidad and Tobago collaborates in various security exercises.

Because of their geographical proximity to the United States, the Caribbean countries have established close economic, political, and security links with this superpower. Except for a few of the smaller countries which trade mainly with Europe, the United States is by far the main market for Caribbean exports. All countries import heavily from the United States, with smaller levels of imports from Japan and

Canada. U.S. political influence over Caricom countries has been exercised, in the post–Cold War era, primarily in the arena of narcotics trafficking. The United States has signed a number of agreements with Caricom countries, including so-called "Shiprider" agreements which allow U.S. ships to intercept drug suspects in territorial waters. The threat of decertification (which allows the United States to freeze aid to countries not complying with drug collaboration policies) has been a major influencing factor.

The English-speaking Caribbean countries participate in a number of international organizations, including the UN and the *Organization of American States. Except for St. Vincent and St. Kitts, they are members of the Nonaligned Movement, in which Guyana has been particularly active. A major concern of the 1990s is the issue of sustainable development. The region was active in the formation of the Alliance of Small Island States (AOSIS) at the UN, a group with particular concerns about such issues as rising sea levels, ozone layer depletion, tourism-related development, and issues of market size. The UN held a special summit to address these issues in Barbados in 1994 and has incorporated these concerns in its comprehensive agenda on economic and social issues.

(See also COMMONWEALTH; DRUGS; ECONOMIC COMMISSION FOR LATIN AMERICA AND THE CARIBBEAN; LATIN AMERICAN REGIONAL ORGANIZATIONS.)

Anthony T. Bryan, ed., *The Caribbean: New Dynamics in Trade and Political Economy* (Miami, 1995). Jacqueline Anne Braveboy-Wagner and Dennis J. Gayle, eds., *Caribbean Public Policy: Regional, Cultural, and Socioeconomic Issues for the Twenty-first Century* (Boulder, Colo., 1997).

JACQUELINE ANNE BRAVEBOY-WAGNER

ENTITLEMENTS. Social protections and benefits that a state owes to is citizens are known as entitlements. In the most general sense, entitlements are akin to social *rights, in which a government promises to ensure its citizens access to various goods and services, such as minimum income, housing, health care, or employment. The notion of entitlements became particularly important in the welfare states created by advanced industrial societies after World War II.

The use of the term "entitlement" varies across nations. In most Western European nations, entitlement expresses a general political commitment by the state to provide social benefits. In the United States, entitlement has taken on a more specific meaning. Reflecting the importance of legal mechanisms in U.S. policy making and the absence of a tradition of social rights, entitlements have been enumerated in detail and defined as legal claims in the United States. This way of defining entitlements grew out of the legal movements of the 1960s that sought to define social policy benefits as a form of property. Although the Supreme Court has declined to endorse formally this view of policy, in practice courts have struck down numerous administrative barriers that reduced access to social benefits and have guaranteed clients the right to appeal decisions altering the benefits.

This legal defense of access to social policy benefits has been accompanied by an increasingly detailed description of the components of an entitlement in the United States. The value of itemizing entitlements in this way is debated among theorists of the welfare state. American liberals, who tend to favor this approach, argue that it ensures access to social ben-

efits. Critics, such as the British social theorist Richard Titmuss, charge that the "fragmentation of entitlement" removes needed discretion and deprives beneficiaries of choice (Brian Abel-Smith and Kay Titmuss, eds., *Selected Writings of Richard Titmuss: The Philosophy of Welfare,* London, 1987). At the same time, critics fear that itemizing entitlements creates a ceiling defining the maximum level of benefits.

Entitlements have been the subject of considerable contention in U.S. budgetary politics since the 1970s. Because the benefits of entitlement programs must be made available to all who are eligible for them, the costs of these policies are difficult to control. As administrative barriers fell and new programs were established, expenditures for entitlement programs expanded rapidly from 1965 to 1974. When the American economy stagnated in the 1970s and deficits soared in the 1980s, government officials expressed strong concern about the uncontrollable nature of spending for entitlement programs, which comprised nearly half the national budget by the 1990s. But entitlement programs, which include *Social Security and Medicare, remained politically popular because the broad majority of American families relied on them. This popularity made politicians reluctant to cut these programs.

During the early years of the Clinton administration, the Bipartisan Commission on Entitlement and Tax Reform was created to consider how the costs of entitlements could be contained. Although the commission drew substantial attention to the growth of entitlement programs, political divisions blocked any action and a declining budget deficit eventually reduced the salience of the issue. The single most significant change in entitlements occurred in 1996, when Congress voted to abolish Aid to Families with Dependent Children (AFDC), the entitlement program serving poor families. In its place, Congress created a new program in which benefits are subject to time limits and to various conditions set by the state and federal governments. The abolition of AFDC reflected the political weakness of programs that provide assistance to the nonworking poor in the United States rather than a substantial challenge to the concept of entitlements. Entitlements remain popular as the key social programs that serve the American middle class.

(See also ENTITLEMENTS, THE FUTURE OF; MEDICARE AND MEDICAID; TAXES AND TAXATION.)

R. Kent Weaver, "Controlling Entitlements," in John E. Chubb and Paul E. Peterson, eds., *The New Direction in American Politics* (Washington, D.C., 1985), pp. 307–341.

MARGARET WEIR

ENTITLEMENTS, THE FUTURE OF. See overleaf.

ENVIRONMENTALISM. See page 253.

EQUAL RIGHTS AMENDMENT. In 1923, three years after women won the suffrage in the United States, the first Equal Rights Amendment (ERA) to the Constitution of the United States was introduced in the U.S. *Congress. Its primary proponents were the professional and upper-middle-class suffragist militants of the National Women's Party. The amendment was opposed by "social feminists," Progressives, and union leaders, who, in the absence of a strong labor movement in

(cont. on p. 256)

THE FUTURE OF ENTITLEMENTS. Americans have for more than three decades experienced a stunning decline of trust in their government, especially their federal government. Yet the programs that account for most of the federal government's budget—Social Security pensions, Medicare, and defense—are among those governmental activities Americans overwhelmingly support. In short, Americans have a conflicted view—diminished expectations for what government can accomplish generally and high regard for those social insurance programs that cushion the retirement and medical needs of America's elderly (and disabled).

How can that be? While explaining the decline in trust involves a mix of long- and short-term factors, one culprit is a persistent strain of media-amplified complaints about the performance of American social policy. Critics paint an unflattering portrait of American social policy—particularly Lyndon Johnson's so-called *Great Society programs—as a failed enterprise: unaffordable, unmanageable, and undesirable. This view is both factually questionable and interpretively misleading, but it is regularly distributed. Factually, the programs most Americans think undesirable—Aid to Families with Dependent Children is the leading example—are the least significant fiscally, have always been frugally funded, and have now been "reformed" out of existence. Interpretively, critics have lumped these small controversial programs together with major social insurance programs—of which Social Security pensions and Medicare are the major budget items—as part of an "entitlements crisis" that threatens to destroy America's future.

This is the background to the 1990s debate over the future of entitlements, a debate that was made all the more salient when the Clinton administration and the Republican-controlled Congress agreed to a balanced budget package in the summer of 1997. Budget-balancing meant facing fiscal facts. That in turn meant dealing with the popular entitlement programs, not the easily attacked programs for groups of despised poor people. It also meant dealing with them against a backdrop of presumed governmental incompetence.

As we argue in *America's Misunderstood Welfare State*, it is simply not true that American social programs have been subject to uncontrolled growth or unresponsive to straitened economic circumstances. It is not the case that our social welfare budget is unaffordable, either in the sense that Americans are unwilling to pay for it or because it is driving the country to economic ruin. It is demonstrably untrue that the Great Society initiatives of the 1960s exacerbated the very problems they were meant to address. Finally, it is simply wrongheaded to claim that the programs on which we spend most of our social welfare dollars—Social Security pensions and Medicare—are unpopular, unneeded, or fraudulent. Understanding those programs—and rejecting the exaggerated alarm about them—is one way to address the "future of entitlements." We begin with Social Security pensions and then take up the Medicare debate.

Although "entitlements" encompass a variety of issues, we focus on Social Security pensions and Medicare because they embody "entitlements" in two ways. First, a budgetary expression, entitlements are simply programs whose outlays are not subject to annual appropriations limits. Instead, once eligibility criteria are satisfied, the government is obliged to finance benefits or forced to change legislation. So understood, entitlements include everything from Medicare to Medicaid, food stamps to Social Security, as well as enormous "tax expenditures" for housing subsidies, child care, retirement savings, and employment-based health care benefits. Second, a cultural category, entitlements suggest deservingness. The idea is that the benefits received are rightly given, with obligations felt by the giver and no stigma felt by the beneficiary. Under either understanding our largest social insurance programs, Social Security pensions and Medicare, easily qualify.

The Case for Social Security Pensions. The most often heard claim is that Social Security is unaffordable and will not be sustainable in the future. Debates over Social Security pensions are generally presented as a response to fiscal crisis. It goes something like this: As the baby boomers age, the number of beneficiaries double. With real wage indexing, benefits double again, producing a $400 billion per year increase in Social Security obligations. These increases cannot be managed without raising taxes drastically. The claim is that taxes would have to be raised 50 percent—from 12.4 to 18 percent of payroll—or Social Security benefits would have to be cut 40 percent in order to remain solvent. By 2012 the deficits will begin and annual Social Security deficits will be $100 billion per year, skyrocketing to more than $200 billion per year by 2032. Most critics do not question whether the Social Security program is worth keeping. Rather, they claim to care only about how it should be financed. The old system of pay-as-you-go, they say, is broke. The new solution—put "compound interest to work" on individual investment accounts—will let the "market" fix the problem of affordability.

Beneath the surface of the technical debate about Social Security's tax rates, benefit schedules, and long-term financial future is a deep ideological divide between defenders and opponents of social insurance. Defenders, like us, see necessary adjustments as a natural and inevitable evolution of a prized public institution. Opponents see these occasions as opportunities for radical revision—times for convincing Americans, especially the young, that social insurance pensions are an unfair, unsustainable sham. Extrapolating short-term trends into the indefinite future, they portray Social Security pensions as uncertain promises, unlikely to be fulfilled and requiring a strong dose of market medicine to put things right. They use the demographic certainty of an older population to make the unwarranted claims that the United States will not be able to pay its Social Security bill without draconian tax increases or massive benefit reductions.

This kind of forecasting of a fearful state of affairs twenty to fifty years ahead is what we have termed "future dread." The problem with future dread is this. Any trend, extrapolated far enough into the future, is likely to produce a state of affairs no one would like. (We suspect that an extrapolation of recent incarceration rates into the late twenty-first century would suggest that most Americans will then be in jail.) But projections are not predictions: They depend for their plausibility on the validity of their assumptions. And mostly they assume that nothing else changes while the projected trend continues.

For example, while it is true that the ratio of workers to retirees is projected to fall from about 3 to 1 down to 2 to 1, it is not the case that the number of Americans dependent on the workforce will sharply increase over the next several decades. The composition will change, but the increase in older Americans will be balanced in part by decreases in the number of children Americans will be raising. In fact, the overall dependency ratio is projected to be about the same in 2060 as it was in 1960.

Indeed, many demographic and economic factors may mitigate the dire predictions of the "entitlement hawks." The birth rate has recently turned up and could, with increased immigration, expand the twenty-first-century workforce. If not, wage rates and FICA tax receipts should go up very sharply as firms compete to attract a smaller workforce. But our point is not that countervailing trends will solve all of our problems. It is rather that "the problem" is not what it seems from simple projections combined with an assumption that public policy will remain the same to produce fiscal crises.

Indeed, if plausible ameliorative actions are taken into account, there is nothing that could responsibly be called a fiscal crisis in Social Security pensions. The problems that exist are manageable in scale, and the remedies are so affordable that if no one had mentioned them they could probably have been implemented without many noticing the changes. Robert M. Ball, former commissioner of Social Security in both Democratic and Republican administrations, has, for example, proposed reducing the projected seventy-five-year deficit with six moderate adjustments in pension formulas coupled with a new investment strategy.

Remedy	Reduction in deficit
1. Extension of coverage to new hires in excluded state and local government positions	−0.22%
2. Increase in length of computation period for determining benefits	−0.28%
3. Change in taxation of benefit	−0.62%
4. Correction of consumer price index	−0.29%
5. Interaction among the proposals	+0.04%
6. Investment by independent board of small proportion of revenues in stocks	−0.82%

As Ball observes, the system today is accruing substantial surpluses, and total income will exceed outlays until about the year 2020. Thereafter, Social Security reserves must be retired to pay current benefits that exceed the level of current taxes. Some adjustments need to be made in benefit levels, taxation levels, or trust fund earnings, so that Social Security's retirement program can pay all its bills thirty-five years from now. The simple fact, however, is that not only can something very close to the present system be financed, financing it is not very hard. The Ball plan closes the projected gap in future funding without tax increases and with extremely modest changes in current benefit levels. Other options exist to do the same thing. The point is that "future dread" is being used to distort the scale of the financing problems of Social Security and to render plausible radical, ideologically driven alternatives such as massive "privatization" of the Social Security system.

Most critics want to privatize pensions because they do not trust the government, because they believe the American people do not trust the government, or because of concerns that Social Security depresses savings rates. They argue that Americans prefer market risk to political risk and that individual citizens, not a government agency, should control investment decisions. They oppose solutions such as Ball's proposal to invest some of the Social Security reserves in the equity markets because the government cannot be trusted to invest in the private capital markets without meddling with them as well. None of these arguments is persuasive.

Even assuming that some portion of Social Security taxes is to be invested in equities rather than Treasury bonds (as is currently done), workers would not, on average, be better off investing individually for retirement than having those investments made through Social Security. The administrative costs of individual investing are much higher than for collective investment. Moreover, individual investing exposes beneficiaries directly to temporal fluctuations in the financial markets. Moving to mandatory individual accounts will, therefore, make many worse off. Indeed, if individual investors are exposed to the thrills and spills of the stock market via individual accounts, Social Security ceases to provide social insurance. There is no reason, other than ideological antipathy to government money management, for Americans to prefer individual investment to the Ball plan for collective assumption of stock market risk. (A defined benefit program promises future pension levels independent of momentary stock market levels; it spreads the risk of fluctuations over many cohorts and thus insulates individuals from most market risk.)

There are, however, obvious reasons for private money managers to prefer "privatization" in an individual accounts form. But the argument about government "meddling" in capital markets is not compelling. Indeed, one of the great success stories of American public policy since the 1930s has been the maintenance of confidence in financial markets by massive governmental "meddling" in the form of regulation. To be sure, direct investment carries political risks. But investing Social Security funds in equity securities need not roil capital markets, so long as investments are limited to broad "index" funds, these funds are managed solely in the interest of beneficiaries, and government is a passive shareholder. (This is precisely the case for pension funds covering government workers now.)

Moreover, there are clear political risks in the private accounts alternative. The greatest is that Congress will be compelled to allow access to the money for nonretirement purposes as it has done repeatedly with individual retirement accounts. If that occurs, many individual accounts may simply not be there when retirement age arrives.

In addition, there is the standard "wastefulness" argment against relying on Social Security pooling as the major government instrument of retirement pensions: the claim that every dollar of government money would reduce poverty more efficiently among the retired and disabled if it were "means-tested." This argument ignores what gives political support and stability to a social policy, and operates under the illusion that means-tested programs fare well over time. They do not, and that constitutes an additional risk to economic security.

All of these arguments can be swept aside, of course, by reverting to the more general claim that all entitlements are undesirable public commitments. This argument is hard to take seriously. Poll after poll has established that Americans support the principles of social insurance, but fear for its future. Limiting the individual risk of inadequate income in old age hardly seems like a bad idea in a market economy. Concern about the affordability of popular entitlements is what animates American discussion, not doubts about their desirability in principle.

Amidst the predictions of doom and gloom and proposals for radical revision we need to return to Social Security's original purposes and to recognize the extent of its successes. Social Security was designed to prevent old age from becoming synonymous with impoverishment. And it was to accomplish that goal in a nonstigmatizing way. Social Security pensions are a pooled retirement arrangement. You pay in when you are working and receive from those who are working when you retire. So far it has an extraordinary record of success. The American Social Security system protects workers against inflation risks, bankruptcy risks, and market risks. It has been running for more than sixty years without ever missing a payment. Poverty in old age has not been vanquished, but the elderly are now poor less often than is the population as a whole. Social Security entitlements have thus provided a firm base for retirement security.

In short, America has constructed a collective worker-contributor, not an individualized saver-investor version of retirement security. The "every boat on its own" ethos of the market economy is tempered by the "everybody in the same boat" ethos of social insurance. Social insurance represents a social ideal of economic security, one guaranteeing a sense of deservingness and individual dignity through participation while working in a cooperative social enterprise. Rather than a "safety net" for those who "fail," social insurance entitlements provide a solid platform upon which all can build their future economic security.

This social ideal has intended and desirable political consequences. It produces an us/us rather than a we/them political dynamic. The question is not what "we" (the affluent) should do for "them" (the impoverished). Rather, it is how we should manage the risks of economic misfortune that will befall some of us at any one time and threaten all of us over the course of our lifetimes. This perspective both stabilizes the politics of particular programs and dampens the fires of class conflict that might otherwise destabilize the political order more generally.

It is from this perspective that we view the "future dread"

syndrome as so destructive. If a crisis is declared every time even a modest adjustment in Social Security is needed, the cumulative effect is a corrosive sense that we cannot manage our collective affairs. This misleading rhetoric inflames those who oppose the system while rendering its defenders resistant to adjustment of any type. That combination is a bad political bargain. It produces diminished psychological security even as the provision of economic security has been maintained. This was not the promise of Social Security, and it should not be its future.

The Case for Medicare. Charges of undesirability, unaffordability, and ungovernability are unpersuasive in medical care as well. But these claims, unlike those about Social Security pensions, raise more genuine worries about Medicare's fiscal future. A somewhat longer view reveals, however, that these projections present a puzzle, rather than a crisis. For most of Medicare's history, its expenditures grew about as rapidly as outlays in the private medical economy. Since 1993, Medicare's expenditures have grown at a more rapid rate than the private medical economy. And it is this atypical feature—a more rapid rate of inflation in Medicare rather than the other way around—that, in combination with projected early deficits in the Medicare Trust Fund, set off another round of debates (which includes the notion of *privatization).

The necessary background to the contemporary Medicare debate is this. The program's early implementation stressed accommodation to the medical world of the 1960s. Its objective was to keep the economic burden of illness from overwhelming the aged or their children. It was assumed then that incorporating all the elderly into the wonders of American medicine was the welcome task at hand. Thirty years later, the setting is radically different. The difficulties of Medicare are those of an American medicine that has many troubles. In the world of American private health insurance, cost control has now arrived with a vengeance. Medicare became unsettled and will remain so unless we accept that limiting Medicare expenditures need not mean eviscerating, or even radically transforming, the program. The price of cost control will undeniably have to be borne, but that burden should be borne, as social insurance would prescribe, proportionately.

Costs have indeed risen in Medicare, and it is important to pay attention to the rate of increase in outlays. But one should not be deluded into thinking that it is all because of technology and aging of the society, two of the most common explanations. Between 1983 and 1993, Medicare expenditures rose less rapidly than the rest of the medical economy. They did so in part because of bargaining over price on the physician side and through the diagnosis-related payment for hospitals. But in the last two and a half years, Medicare has been rising at about 10 percent per year when the rest of the medical economy has been rising between 3 to 5 percent per year. We need to worry about that, but not under the guise of thinking that there is something called a "trust fund" that is going to become insolvent. Cost escalation is not a necessary feature of the Medicare program. It is a consequence of particular techniques of monitoring and reimbursement.

Critics (and some defenders) continue to use the language of insolvency to describe Medicare's future, a dreaded one in which the program's "trust fund" will literally run out of money. However, the U.S. government has a feature that no private household has, which is that if it is not going to have the funds available in some year in the future, it can change the benefits and it can change the revenues. Congress can increase the taxes that finance Medicare, if it has the will. Likewise, it can reduce the benefits and reimbursement provisions of the program. Or it can do some of both. Channeling the fiscal consequences through something called a "trust fund" changes nothing in the real political economy.

It is important to understand that Medicare can be adjusted in ways that fully preserve the national commitment to health insurance for America's elderly and disabled. One place to start is the reduction of the growing gap between the benefits Medicare offers and the obvious needs of its beneficiaries. What Medicare pays for should be widened to include the burdens of chronic illness. Widening the benefits package does not mean that total expenditures must rise proportionately. Expenditures represent the volume of services times their prices. Many other nations have not only universal coverage and wider benefits than Medicare, but spend less per capita than we do for their elderly. Canadians, for example, are able to do this because they pay their medical providers less, spend less on administration, and use expensive technology less often.

Medicare's financing also could use some overhauling. Raising payroll taxes will have to be part of the answer. For some this is simply ruled out of current discussion, a good example of fearfulness defeating evidence. The breadth of public support of Medicare suggests it is possible to mobilize popular opinion in favor of tax increases where the problem is clearly defined and the justification convincingly offered.

Some tout the forms of privatization as the "solution" to Medicare's problems. One is a broad proposal for Medical Savings Accounts ("MSAs"). Instead of participating in group insurance at the place of employment or paying the health insurance portion of FICA taxes, Americans would be required to contribute (tax free) to MSAs to cover their medical needs. The consequence will be to transform medical care as an aspect of social insurance into a highly segmented system: private insurance for the relatively well-off; welfare medicine for everyone else. The second "privatization" approach retains social insurance coverage for the elderly, but attempts to save money by having private managed care plans compete for Medicare's patients. This alternative poses no direct threat to social insurance. Rather, the worrisome question is whether managed care can save money and deliver decent medical care at the same time to the elderly—or anyone else.

We need debate over how Medicare should be improved. What we do not need is debate that scares the country about its future by disseminating false claims about Medicare's unaffordability. It would indeed be a "crisis" if the legitimate health costs of our aged and disabled were unaffordable. And it is true that a pattern of health expenditures increasing at twice the rate of national income growth is unsustainable over the long run. But there is no reason to believe we must tolerate this future.

What is really important is to get medical care inflation under control. People who say our elderly and our aging society is unaffordable, and partake in "future dread" sessions, about a society that has 18 to 19 percent of its population over sixty-five, ought to reflect on the present day in Sweden, Norway, Finland, and Germany. These countries already have proportions of the population over sixty-five equal to the proportion we anticipate in the year 2020. They spend between 8.5 percent and 9.5 percent of their gross national product on medical care, and we spend between 14 to 15 percent of our GNP right now. This suggests that the problem is not aging, but the rapid increase in the American medical care sector's cost more generally.

Conclusion. The continued vitality of America's version of social insurance is uncertain as we begin the twenty-first century. Contemporary debate goes beyond responsible tinkering to fundamental restructuring. A wider range of critics—conservative figures joining libertarians and neoliberals—are complaining about the "excesses" and worrisome future of entitlements. With monetary support from the financial services industry, the fears of the future are buttressed by those with the most obvious pecuniary stakes in a sharply curtailed public retirement program, as well as restructuring the Medicare and disability programs. To counter these ideological and economic interests will require the mobilization of ordinary Americans. And that will not happen without rediscovering why social insurance arguments made sense in the first place, and by clarifying the crucial difference between abandoning universal programs and adapting them to changing demographic and economic circumstances.

Imagine for a moment this country without social insurance entitlements, where working Americans have to bear the burden of supporting their aged parents, where everyone risks financial disaster from corporate downsizing, the vagaries of the business cycle, the whims of the global market, incapacity from sudden illness, and their parents' catastrophic medical costs. Its likely politics would oscillate between attempts to entrench the status quo by regulation—tariffs, plant closing laws, job guarantees, employer mandates, and the like—and bitter contests over who amongst the poor are sufficiently "deserving" to get aid.

It is hard to imagine how American workers would be brought to accept the desirability of an ever-changeable market with flexible and modest legal constraints. Those without protection who ended up seeking public financial assistance in their time of need would be an undeserving "other." They would become the Americans who, by participating (and failing) in a truly free market, became a "drag on the economy." Without social insurance the most reasonable scenario is the collapse of any strong sense of national, social solidarity, fueled by the contentious interest-group politics of economic regulation. It would not be a society most Americans would want.

(See also POPULATION POLICY; TAXES AND TAXATION.)

Marilyn Moon, *Medicare: Now and in the Future* (Washington, D.C., 1996). Jacob Hacker, *The Road to Nowhere* (Princeton, N.J., 1997). Eric R. Kingson and James H. Shulz, eds., *Social Security in the 21st Century* (New York, 1997). Michael J. Graetz and Jerry L. Mashaw, *True Security: Rethinking American Social Insurance* (New Haven, 1999). Theodore R. Marmor, *The Politics of Medicare*, 2d ed. (New York, 2000).

THEODORE R. MARMOR
JERRY L. MASHAW

THE FUTURE OF ENTITLEMENTS. A demographic iceberg looms ahead in the future of the largest and most affluent economies of the world—the challenge of global aging. What is visible above the waterline is the unprecedented growth in the ratio of elderly to working-age people. What lurks beneath the surface are the wrenching fiscal and economic costs that threaten to bankrupt even the greatest of powers. To date, the developed countries have accumulated roughly $70 trillion in unfunded liabilities for pension and health-care benefits—an unsustainable lien on the future six times greater than their official public debt.

The central policy issue is not whether the developed countries will change course, but how and when. Will they do so sooner, when they still have time to control their destiny? Or later, in the midst of economic crisis and political upheaval?

Timely *reform will not be easy. Voters have become habituated to pay-as-you-go systems that bank every generation's future retirement on the next generation's resources, rather like a giant Ponzi scheme. The most direct reform approach—simply cutting public retirement benefits—would impose widespread hardship on working-class households that have few alternative means of support. Any reform approach, moreover, must overcome widespread public denial. People find it hard to believe that a system that worked wonderfully for their parents (who signed up early) will not do nearly as well for their kids (who are signing up late). In Europe, where the "*welfare state" is more expansive, the public regards generous unfunded pensions as the very cornerstone of social democracy. In the United States, the problem is not so much a habit of welfare-state dependence as the peculiar American notion that every citizen has personally earned and therefore is "entitled" to whatever benefits government happens to have promised.

A successful reform approach must therefore go beyond mere fiscal sacrifice and offer a positive vision of a society that cares for its future. It must prepare society to meet the needs of a burgeoning number of elders without overburdening the economy or overtaxing the young. While restraining pay-as-you-go promises, it must encourage (even require) people to prepare alternative means of support. We must, in other words, adopt an entirely new paradigm of aging that is affordable and sustainable in a rapidly graying world.

Collapsed Assumptions. During the early post–World War II decades, the developed world greatly expanded public pension and health-care benefits for retirees. At the time, this expansion seemed affordable. The number of retirees was relatively small, the cost of health care was modest, and rapid growth in the workforce, economy, and tax base was expected to continue indefinitely. Since the mid-1970s, all of these conditions and assumptions have collapsed.

Consider longevity. When U.S. *Social Security was founded in 1935, the typical U.S. worker at age sixty-five could expect to live another 11.9 years. By the year 2040, that worker is projected to live another 19.6 years. If the normal retirement age had been "indexed" to longevity since 1935, he or she would today have to wait until age seventy-three to receive full benefits and tomorrow even longer. In reality, workers throughout the developed world have been retiring earlier, not later—further expanding the number of retired beneficiaries while depleting the number of working taxpayers. In Western Europe, most workers are eligible for full public retirement benefits at age sixty. Over the last twenty-five years, the employed share of men aged sixty to sixty-four has dropped from 70 to 32 percent in Germany, and from 67 to 22 percent in France.

Meanwhile, the fertility rate of the developed world (that is, the number of lifetime births per woman) has entered an unprecedented decline. In the early 1960s, that fertility rate was 2.7. Today, it has fallen to 1.6, far beneath the 2.1 "replacement rate" needed merely to maintain a fixed population from one generation to the next. So steep is the fertility decline that continental Europe and Japan are on track to lose two-thirds of their current population before the end of the twenty-first century. In nearly every developed country, with the possible exception of the United States, the working-age population (aged fifteen to sixty-four) will start shrinking no later than the 2020s. Combined with lower rates of productivity growth, this expected work-force shrinkage has radically reduced official projections of real growth in future worker payroll, which normally constitutes the tax base supporting today's pay-as-you-go retirement systems.

The U.S. state of Florida is well known for its vast number of elderly people (aged sixty-five and over), making up nearly 19 percent of the population. What is less well known is that today's Florida is a demographic benchmark that every developed nation will soon pass. Italy will pass it as early as 2003, followed by Japan (in 2005) and Germany (in 2006). France and Britain will pass present-day Florida a decade later, around 2016. The United States and Canada will pass it in 2021 and 2023. The delay is largely due to large postwar baby booms, which are now slowing—but will later accelerate—the aging of their populations.

A standard indicator of the social cost of aging is the ratio of working-age people to elderly people. As recently as 1960, this ratio was 6.8 to 1 in the developed world. Today, it has fallen to 4.5 to 1. By the year 2030, it is projected by the Organisation for Economic Co-operation and Development (OECD) to fall to 2.5 to 1. This figure, stunning as it is, may be optimistic, since it assumes that fertility rates will rebound from today's low levels and that longevity will grow more slowly in the future than it has in the past. In any case, it understates the seriousness of the challenge because it does not reflect the trend toward earlier retirement. The actual ratio of contributing workers to retired (or disabled) pensioners is much lower—and has been dropping much faster. It has already dropped to 3.0 in the developed world, and is projected by the International Monetary Fund to drop to 1.5 by 2030. In some European countries, it is projected to drop beneath 1.0.

Unsustainable Projections. Graying means paying. Between 1995 and 2030, according to the OECD, the average bill for public pensions in the developed world will grow by over 4 percent of GDP. In nations that have the most generous pension systems or are aging the most rapidly—for example, Japan and the countries of continental Europe—the extra cost will amount to over 6 percent of GDP, or over 15 percent of worker payroll. In the United States, the extra cost will be less, about 2.5 percent of GDP. Britain and Australia face no significant cost growth—in part due to their modest pension benefits formulas and to new personally owned savings programs that allow future public benefits to shrink as a share of average wages.

Yet pensions are not the only public costs that rise as populations age. Public health benefits could turn out to be an even bigger burden. Not only are health costs rising faster than GDP for everyone, but the elderly consume three to five times more health-care services per capita than younger people. Moreover, the older elders are, the more they consume (especially long-term care). And it is precisely the population of the oldest old that will be growing the fastest—a phenomenon demographers call the "aging of the aged."

Stir these multipliers together, and the likely cost trend is explosive. If health-care spending per capita grows just 1 percent faster per year than the average wage, public health benefits would rise by 6 percent of the typical developed country's GDP between 1995 and 2030. And this is a conservative assumption. In the United States, where per-capita Medicare outlays have historically risen 4 percent faster per year than the average wage, the growth will probably be much greater. America's insatiable appetite for high-tech medicine is thus likely to overwhelm any advantage it derives from the relatively modest cost of its public pensions. None of these calculations, moreover, includes new government initiatives (already under consideration in several countries) to cover rising out-of-pocket spending on long-term care by elders and their families.

All told, the cost of public retirement benefits—pensions and health care—is on track to rise by between 9 and 16 percent of GDP in most of the developed countries. This vast increase is three to five times what the United States currently spends on national defense. It also represents an extra 25 to 40 percent taken out of every worker's taxable wages—in countries where total payroll tax rates often exceed 40 percent already.

The massive fiscal challenge of global aging leaves the developed world no easy options. Deficit financing will not work. Government borrowing to pay for projected pension deficits alone would, by the 2030s, consume all the savings of the developed world. Cutting other public spending will not work. So great is the projected growth in retirement benefits that many governments could eliminate all nonbenefit spending (from defense and infrastructure to police and schools) and still run deficits by the 2020s. Raising taxes will not work. Most developed countries are now at or beyond their threshold of efficient taxation—and many European leaders warn that higher tax rates will slow the economy more than raise new revenue. This is particularly true for payroll taxes in economies where high structural unemployment can be attributed in part to the high cost of labor.

Toward a New Paradigm. The developed countries need to move toward a whole new paradigm of aging, one that is every bit as revolutionary as the demographic transformation they are entering. The objective of this new paradigm is to make aging both more secure for older generations and less burdensome for younger generations. It can be implemented through policy reforms that can be grouped into six basic strategies, each promising huge fiscal and economic payoffs.

First, reduce elder dependency by encouraging later retirement, longer work lives, and lower barriers to elder employment. Governments everywhere, especially in continental Europe, could generate enormous savings without lowering elder living standards by raising the eligibility age for public pensions.

Second, increase the size of today's economy (and tax base) by encouraging more work from the nonelderly—either by getting working-age citizens to work more or by increasing the inflow of working-age immigrants. Nations with low rates of immigration (for example, Japan) or with high labor costs and high unemployment (for example, Germany) would be well advised to consider this "American" strategy.

Third, increase the size of tomorrow's economy (and tax base) by raising more numerous and productive children, so that the cost burden is spread over a larger and more affluent rising generation. The Scandinavian and French traditions of generous public funding for pronatal incentives and investment in children is likely to spread to other countries—in part, in response to worries about population decline.

Fourth, reduce the fiscal cost of elder dependency by stressing filial obligation—that is, by increasing the willingness of tomorrow's grown children, however numerous or productive they are, to support their own elderly parents through informal and familial channels. Societies in which the extended family is weakest, elder poverty is highest, and long-term care costs are rising the fastest (for example, the United States) have much to learn from "Confucian" societies such as Japan, where most elders still live with their adult children.

Fifth, reduce the fiscal cost of elder dependency by targeting benefits on the basis of financial need. Though Australia is now the only developed country where all public pension benefits are means-tested, many other countries may eventually turn to this "floor of protection" strategy.

Sixth, reduce the fiscal and economic cost of elder dependency by requiring people to provide in advance for their own old-age dependency—by saving and investing more of their income during their work lives. Britain and Australia (along with Chile and Singapore) are showing the developed world that there are many different ways to move toward funded retirement savings.

All of these strategies will stir up controversy, and no one yet knows which will be widely implemented—or where. For the United States, I have long advocated gradually raising the Social Security retirement age to seventy (and indexing it to longevity thereafter) and subjecting all federal benefits to an "affluence test" for households above the median income. I am also attracted to reforms that require individuals to provide for their own retirement through some form of mandatory and funded savings program. This strategy does most to overcome one of the biggest economic challenges of an aging society, which is how to sustain adequate rates of national savings and investment. It offers individuals the most retirement and income flexibility in a future in which, quite frankly, no one knows how long people may live or how high health expenses may rise. It guarantees the most security and the highest return to contributing workers, while freeing up government resources for a more generous floor of protection. Above all, it is the only strategy that does not impose direct (tax) or indirect (economic and familial) burdens on future generations.

Rising Above Ideology. I believe global aging will become the transcendent political and economic issue of the twenty-first century. By the year 2030, some developed countries may exceed a median age of fifty-five, twenty years older than the oldest median age (thirty-five) of any country on earth as recently as 1970. Nearly half of the adult population of today's developed countries and perhaps two thirds of the voters will be at or beyond today's eligibility age for publicly financed retirement. So we have to ask: When that time comes, who will be doing the work, paying the taxes, saving for the future, and raising the next generation?

Indeed, the coming demographic transformation raises fundamental questions about the future of the developed world. How will this transformation restructure the economy, as many nations with shrinking work forces experience a long-term stagnation (or even decline) in their real GDP? How will it affect global financial markets and regional economic unions like the *Economic and Monetary Union, as different nations respond to the aging challenge with widely diverging benefit reforms and fiscal policies? How will it reshuffle the ethics of life and death, as medical progress acknowledges limited resources? How will it transform attitudes toward

progress and posterity, as youth becomes less numerous and influential? How will it affect the geopolitics of the next century, and particularly the capacity of the great powers to maintain their security commitments, as today's global divide between rich and poor nations is redefined as a divide between old and young nations?

At issue is whether the world's great powers can respond to a silent and slow-motion crisis. Global aging will be a test. Some say that democracies can focus only on this year's emergency—a problem known, in American circles, as the "Pearl Harbor" syndrome. Others say that political gridlock on global aging is due to declining confidence in government. Voters know something has to be done, but do not trust politicians to act in their long-term interests or to distribute the short-term sacrifices fairly. Without that trust, voters cling to the retirement status quo, however unsustainable.

One thing is certain: Before taking effective action, leaders must rise above ideology and engage the practical realities. The left will have to stop defending the expansion of retirement benefits as the cornerstone of progressive government, and realize that they are fast pushing all future-oriented spending out of public budgets. The right will have to move beyond a program of mere fiscal restraint, and offer a coherent blueprint for how society intends to care for tomorrow's vast number of elder dependents. Both sides will have to resist the power of the organized elderly, who favor the status quo over what most elders personally care about—their grandchildren's future. Otherwise, the developed world may eventually witness a socially destructive "war between generations" over the use of public resources.

Amid the partisan crossfire, citizens can easily forget that they share a common destiny. To make timely reform possible, every special interest must join a new coalition on behalf of our common destiny. Unless we embrace a new paradigm of aging, many of our highest hopes for the future will be sacrificed.

(See also POPULATION POLICY; SOCIALISM AND SOCIAL DEMOCRACY; TAXES AND TAXATION.)

C. Eugene Steuerle and Jon M. Bakija, *Retooling Social Security for the Twenty-first Century: Right and Wrong Approaches to Reform* (Washington, D.C., 1994). World Bank, *Averting the Old Age Crisis: Policies to Protect the Old and Promote Growth* (New York, 1994). International Monetary Fund, *Aging Populations and Public Pension Schemes*, Occasional Paper no. 147 (Washington, D.C., 1996). Organisation for Economic Co-operation and Development, *Ageing in OECD Countries: A Critical Policy Challenge*, Social Policy Studies, no. 20 (Paris, 1996). Watson Wyatt Worldwide, *From Baby Boom to Elder Boom: Providing Health Care for an Aging Population* (Washington, D.C., 1996). Alan Auerbach, Laurence J. Kotlikoff, and Willi Leibritz, eds., *Generational Accounting Around the World* (Chicago, 1999). Peter G. Peterson, *Gray Dawn: How the Coming Age Wave Is About to Transform America and the World* (New York, 1999). United Nations, *Long-range World Population Projections: Based and the 1998 Revision* (New York, 1999).

PETER G. PETERSON

ENVIRONMENTALISM. This essay highlights the conceptual foundations, traces new developments, and highlights new directions in the relationship between environmentalism and politics. Current developments in the environmental domain will likely pave the way for further adjustments in this relationship as the international community begins to develop a more fully integrated view of interactions between natural and social systems and between social relations and life-supporting properties. As we begin the first decade of the twenty-first century, not only are the traditional ideas and practices built on the separation of social and natural systems increasingly challenged, but earlier conceptions of environmentalism are also being revised significantly. This essay reviews the recent thinking and attendant consequences on environmental politics for the international community of the twenty-first century.

As originally conceived, environmentalism assumed three meanings, buttressed by three views, each with different sources, content, and consequences. They all share a view of humanity as integral to nature, of nature as empowering humans, and of the relationship between both as uneasy at best, if not threatening to the integrity and viability of nature and hence of humans. The essence of this shared view is the need for restoring a symbiotic relationship between humans and nature which, by necessity, requires fundamental alterations in human behavior and in the characteristics of social life. The first definition of environmentalism is one of *conceptual* orientation: ideas of nature, ecological balances, and ecological growth as central to the survival of the human species. The second definition of environmentalism is one of *process* which stresses how humans influence and alter nature and, in the domain of the economic and the political, how this influence is detrimental to social relations, both national and international. The third definition of environmentalism is a *political* program, ideology, and plan of action at all levels of social aggregation.

Each of these definitions of environmentalism invokes powerful contentions and differences of views, which illuminate the underlying strains between humans and their natural habitats but have also impeded the development of a sufficiently cohesive shared understanding such that effective political action can be identified, pursued, and implemented.

These contentions are in turn shaped and driven by the power and motivation of different actors and groups with both direct and indirect interests in the outcomes of deliberations over the definition of environmentalism. A sort of expanded and enhanced political participation on environmental issues is emerging across the world involving interactions among individuals, including scientists, public officials, conservationists, and industrialists, organized groups, cross-boundary entities, *international organizations, and supranational interests. The environmental cliché of the 1990s—"think local, act global"—reflects both the scale and scope of emerging contentions. At issue is both national and international control over environmental ideas, objectives, and policies in the twenty-first century.

The essence of environmentalism as a concept is a view of humans as part of nature, not as separate from it, a view of humans as symbiotic with nature, not as adversaries. This concept has important analytical implications: it calls for an integrated conception of life on earth that addresses the coherence of environmental and social processes. It seeks an explanation of the interdependence among all elements necessary for life. It addresses the vulnerabilities and susceptibilities of life-sustaining properties as humans press their claims on nature. From these, two premises are generated: one, the activity and reality of ecological balance in contrast to the inertness and passivity of "nature"; and two, the integrationist and planetary view of the human/nature interaction where micro/macro linkages, feedback effects, delays, uncertainties, resiliences, and surprises operate to shape eventual outcomes at all levels and in different time frames.

From these views and premises there emerge two boundary conditions: the "smallest" unit of action and the "largest" entity. In the context of this interpretive essay, from a social science perspective, we posit the bounds at one end to be set by individuals in their natural environments and at the other by planetary properties and characteristics. For conceptual purposes, the bounding issue then forces a delineation of the properties of the "smallest" and "largest" entity and of indicators, measures, and linkages.

Among the properties of the "smallest" unit, the individual in a household, environmentalism suggests that human beings are trapped in a fundamental paradox: (1) every implementation of knowledge and skills results in a degradation of resource(s) from a "more usable" to a "less usable" form with consequent production of (sometimes toxic) wastes; (2) technology itself requires resources—energy of some kind and other materials; the more "modern" the knowledge and skills, moreover, the greater has been the amount and range of energy and other resources required; and also (3) the more "advanced" the technology, the greater has been the amount and range of resources that people have believed they needed above and beyond the basic necessities to which they were accustomed. This means that overall environmental degradation increases with population growth and is further multiplied by technological advancement but that outcomes vary through time according to the relative and usually changing levels of the three master variables. The underlying premise is that, combined with existing levels and growth rates of population, however, each new increment of technological development has tended to multiply the production of carbon dioxide and other agents of environmental degradation. The ultimate challenge is to find ways of decoupling the connection between economic activity and environmental degradation.

Key properties at the planetary level remain significant in the evolving understandings of environmentalism. First, while the basic biogeochemical characteristics of environmental change are generally understood, there remain major uncertainties about the feedback effects on both the physical and social processes. Second, environmental as well as social processes operate along multiple, unequal, and sometimes overlapping time horizons. Variability in time increments complicates assessments of the underlying processes. Fundamentally the long lead times in both social and environmental processes—and the separation of "cause" and "consequences"—themselves amount to major sources of uncertainty. Third, there are a host of related uncertainties associated with these intertemporal effects. In particular, there are crucial intergenerational impacts of environmental change whereby future generations incur the environmental costs of the actions of past and present generations, which reflect the complexities associated with long lead times. Fourth are the irreversibilities. It may well be that some patterns of environmental alterations cannot be "undone," nor can the underlying sources be eliminated either wholly or in part at least not within the frame of historical rather than geological time. Finally, unevenness in both the sources of environmental disturbances as well as in the consequences raise concerns for about international equity. Not all countries contribute the same way to the global balances, nor are they affected uniformly, which further constrains the development of international responses to environmental problems.

These features characterize some crucial uncertainties associated with global environmental change. Because human activities are incremental in historical time and therefore minuscule in geological time, they confound analytical assessments of complex feedback, time horizon, and differentials in sources and in consequences. Together these factors bear on the political issues concerning the environment and on the policy responses of the international community to them. Central to all three meanings are evolving understandings about processes interconnecting humans and social systems.

In retrospect, we now appreciate that the initial understanding of environmentalism discussed above represented a nascent perceptive, one that increasingly took shape in the latter decades of the twentieth century. This initial view can be referred to as "old" environmentalism, in contrast to the "new" environmentalism that takes account of recent specifications adjustments, and modification.

In substantive terms, new environmentalism is defined by three interacting sets of emergent features. The first relates to the impact of *globalization on environmentalism, and the globalization of environmentalism itself. These are distinctive processes, but their interactions reinforce their pervasiveness. The second pertains to the changing status of environmentalism in the context of policy priorities, nationally and internationally. This involves a shift is from lesser to greater legitimization, and from less to more common resort to legal instruments for framing and enforcing environmental norms and values. Jointly these represent the legitimization of environmentalism and its increasing relevance to policy domains. The third feature characterizing the new environmentalism derives from the other two, namely, its institutionalization. Closely connected to legitimization, the institutionalization represents the behavioral aspects and the society-wide manifestations of environmental considerations. It also refers to the routinization of ways in which environmentalism is incorporated in a variety of social interactions.

The globalization of environmentalism is clearly a matter of *scale*, keeping in mind the implied linkages across levels, from the local to the global, and between terrestrial and atmospheric domains. Legitimization is a matter of *status*. Ideas and behaviors that are not legitimized are, for all practical purposes, beyond the pale of public policy. For effective action—in theory or in practice—legitimacy is always a necessary, and sometimes even a sufficient, precursor. The growing legitimacy of environmentalism reflects new awareness of the sanctity of life supporting properties and the salience of ecological resilience for social viability. Institutionalization can be regarded as reflecting the *scope* of social penetration. By institutionalizing responses to environmental considerations, a society enhances prospects for sustained responses. In the best case, institutionalization guarantees routinization and hence a form of permanence. In fact, weaknesses in the institutionalization and its supporting capacities are all factors that account for the discrepancy between principle and practice in environmentalism.

Central to the new environmentalism is recognition of the dependence of social systems on the "health" of natural systems and the growing intersection between environmental issues and *sustainable development. This recognition is evidenced in both policy and popular circles, and to varying degrees and extent, in the scientific community. It has also led to a serious reconsideration of boundary conditions differentiating the two types of systems, and the environmental versus the sustainability domains. At the same time, it has become apparent in some academic quarters that the traditional modes of analyzing economic performance and political objectives—in both theoretical and empirical terms—continue to be profoundly flawed in their explicit exclusion of both environmental and sustainability considerations.

The new environmentalism, building on the old conceptions, appears to be generating a record of efforts toward adjustments extending beyond basic attention to environmental matters. There are several bases for this inference. These include (1) the impact of national and international learning as reflected in increasing attention to reporting, methods of accounting, and formulation of socioeconomic models encompassing both environmental and developmental features; (2) apparent institutional developments at both global and national levels designed to transform concepts into action, most notably in international environmental agreements, evolving international law on sustainable development, and new attention to sanctions in response to environmental damage; (3) continued politicization of environmental issues at all levels; and (4) the impact of new actors and agencies in the environmental domain, along with the paradox of power potentials due to weakness.

None of these alone is definitive, and none is without inherent problems and contradictions, But jointly they provide evidence for the new environmentalism, which reinforces a growing appreciation worldwide of the interdependence of humans and nature, and the connectivities among communities, ecological zones, and political jurisdictions.

The evolution of environmental problem solving may be construed as a process of learning. International and national decision makers have gradually come to accept a broader, interdependent, symbiotic, and holistic conception of the environmental system for their pollution control efforts and have adapted their policies accordingly. Still, most arrangements remained remedial rather than preventative, coordinating policies to regulate emissions rather than addressing the underlying conditions (sources) that give rise to emissions. In this connection, international directives to ensure national reporting of environmental measures may generate transparency effects that themselves create pressures for action.

All of this is buttressed by the changing characteristics of international agreement over the past decade and the gradual evolution of international environmental law and *international law pertaining to sustainable development. By the end of the twentieth century, more than 140 multilateral environmental treaties had been concluded. In this process, precedents were being set in place to shape a new treaty-making process. The establishment of framework agreements has provided the basis for consensus on more specific and more binding efforts. Binding agreements are now in place with respect to marine pollution, acid rain, a regional seas program, and, of course, the ozone layer. This type of treaty making is quite different from formal agreements in other areas salient to the international community, such as arms control, where great attention to detail defines the general approach from the outset. This mode of treaty making also creates a political constituency for environmentalism. It is more flexible and allows for agreement on more effective results. Equally important is the fact that environmental treaties have accomplished two contradictory goals: a reaffirmation of sovereign national rights and a reaffirmation of international constraints on national activities.

At both the national and the global levels, there is an emergent awareness of the security dilemma inherent in the fact that actions usually considered normal and legitimate could be detrimental to the environment or harbor environmentally threatening consequences. Policies and behaviors are, to some extent, increasingly being scrutinized for the implicit environmental costs. And even national environmental institutions, such as the U.S. Environmental Protection Agency (EPA), are beginning to connect environmental factors to matters of national security, and security agencies are considering the threats due to environmental degradation.

The proliferation of new actors in world politics—including environmental actors—and new forms of cross-border, transnational linkages have as an underlying cause the transnational networks sharing a modicum of technical consensus about environmental degradation. The consequence of these trends includes a notable diffusion of responsibility for dealing with environmental issues. This process has created an emerging constituency for global environmental protection at the international level. Some organizations are located in the state; others transcend territorial boundaries; still others have supranational status. Moreover, when individuals affiliated with such groups are in the government, their primary attachment tends to be their scientific causal beliefs rather than their role positions, and in turn they are likely to use their political power to promote their environmental concerns.

Environmental rationality in international decision making may alter the significance of power differentials between actors. This change may benefit the weaker parties, such as nongovernmental organizations, as it gives them greater influence over decision making and an enhanced ability to add issues that concern them to international negotiations. Though the form of policy making for environmental protection is being transformed, but structure of international relations from which such environmental problems originate remains basically unchanged. There are major differences, even contradictions, in the imperatives or priorities of decision-making and governance at the national, international, and global levels. From the perspective of national decision-making, the problem is managing internal pressures and transformations due to changes in population, resources, and technology, Policy-making procedures are gradually being set in place by many nations in response to the challenges posed by environmental changes. For example, domestic ecological conditions are gradually being incorporated into the decision-making process, and economic, strategic, and domestic policies may no longer easily be pursued without regard for cross-border and global environmental ramifications. In other words, states appear to recognize the practical bounds of *sovereignty when it comes to environmental matters.

From the perspective of the *international system, the global management of national environmental changes may generate dislocating effects or create costs to be borne by others. The pattern of organized international institutional responses to national environmental issues often influences the range of acceptable policies domestically. Involvement by nation-states with international organizations generally entails explicit demands from those organizations for state adjustments and policy changes. When states are confronted with resource scarcity and pressure for making resource allocation decisions, they sometimes use force internally to constrain domestic demand and limit political dissent. If resource bases and environmental conditions continue to deteriorate, countries may respond in ways that could adversely affect not only the internal population/resource balances but also relations with neighbors and with the international community. In the years ahead, considerations such as these may render sustainable development a core premise of evolving international law. In sum, the "new" environmentalism incorporates the principles of legitimacy, universality, equity, and participation.

Nazli Choucri, ed., *Global Accord: Environmental Challenges and International Responses* (Cambridge, Mass., 1993). Winfried Lang, ed., *Sustainable Development and International Law* (London, 1995). Robert S. Chen, W. Christopher Lenhardt, and Kara F. Alkire, eds., *Consequences of Environmental Change—Political, Economic, Social*. Proceedings of the Environmental Flash Points Workshop (Washington, D.C., 1997). Helge Ole Bergesen, Georg Parmann, and Øystein B. Thommenssen, eds., *Yearbook of International Co-Operation on Environment and Development 1999/2000* (Lysaké, Norway 1999). Nazli Choucri, "The Political Logic of Sustainability, in Egon Becker and Thomas Jahn, eds., *Sustainability and the Social Sciences* (New York, 1999).

Nazli Choucri

the United States, were trying to institute protections for at least women workers—special protections that would have had to be dropped or extended to men by an ERA's requirement of formal equality.

By the 1960s, a number of professional associations and both political parties supported the ERA; however, Democratic President John *Kennedy's Commission on the Status of Women concluded that such a "constitutional amendment need not now be sought." One year later, opponents of the Civil Rights Act added "sex" as a protected category to the proposed act, hoping to induce some representatives to vote against it. But the act passed as amended. By 1970, the federal Equal Employment Opportunity Commission had interpreted the 1964 act to forbid precisely the special protections for women (in most cases extending the protections to men) that had made the unions oppose the ERA.

In 1970, therefore, the Pittsburgh chapter of the newly formed National Organization for Women (NOW) took direct action to promote the ERA, which NOW had given first place on its Bill of Rights for Women. After two years of controversy, the ERA passed the House of Representatives with a vote of 354 to 23, and the Senate with a vote of 84 to 8. The amendment's substantive clause read: "Equality of rights under the law shall not be denied or abridged by the United States or by any State on account of sex."

The ERA then went immediately to the states, Hawaii ratifying on 22 March 1972, the day the Senate passed the amendment. Twenty-nine more states ratified in 1972 and early 1973, the earliest with unanimous or nearly unanimous votes. By 1973, however, the opposition had begun to organize, led by Phyllis Schlafly, a maverick from the right wing of the Republican Party. A skilled political entrepreneur, Schlafly tied the ERA to homemakers' fears of the changes entailed by the growing number of women in the paid labor force, the increasing number of divorces, and other larger social changes that had emerged along with the growing women's liberation movement in the United States. She tied the ERA as well to conservative and mainstream legislators' anger at the *Supreme Court's liberal decisions, and to state legislators' fears of losing control over most issues regarding women, which the U.S. federal system allocates primarily to the states. Five more states ratified in 1974, 1975, and 1977. None ratified after 1977 despite the triumph of ERA proponents in 1978 in getting Congress to extend the original 1979 deadline to 1982. On 30 June, the final deadline for ratifying the ERA passed, with only thirty-five of the required thirty-eight states having ratified.

In *public opinion polls, a majority of the U.S. public (57 percent in the "average" survey) always supported the ERA. Men were as likely to support it as women, the working class as likely as the middle class, blacks somewhat more than whites, and Catholics somewhat more than Protestants. Fundamentalists, frequent churchgoers, parents with large families, older people, and rural residents tended to oppose the amendment. The amendment lost because it came to be linked with abortion (the Supreme Court decision of *Roe v. Wade had legalized abortion in 1973) and could be portrayed as dividing women (homemakers versus women in the paid labor force). Its proponents failed to meet objections that the amendment would force changes that most Americans disapproved (e.g., drafting women for combat in the armed forces). It stopped being a nonpartisan issue (the right wing came to power in the Republican Party with the candidacy of Ronald Reagan and withdrew the ERA from its platform), and it had to be ratified by states with fewer than 15 percent women legislators (in the unratified states 79 percent of the women legislators but only 39 percent of the men favored the amendment).

Although feminists criticized it for detracting from other causes, in the long run the struggle for the ERA helped build the prestige and budget of NOW (the budget rose from $700,000 in 1977 to $8.5 million in 1982), making the organization the strongest independent feminist organization in the world and putting it in a position to demand successfully that the Democratic Party run a woman for vice president of the United States in the 1986 election. The ERA struggle also helped build the feminist movement in the United States to the point at which by 1989 one out of three women in the United States was reporting to poll takers that she considered herself a "feminist"—about the same percentage as considered themselves Democrats or Republicans.

Argentina (1853) and Iran (1907) were the first countries to guarantee in their constitutions equality for "all inhabitants," including women. After 1945, when the UN Charter affirmed the "equal rights of men and women," many of the world's nations adopted similar clauses in their constitutions. In 1982, the Charter of Rights in Canada's new constitution guaranteed "the right to the equal protection and equal benefit of the law without discrimination and, in particular, without discrimination based on . . . sex," generating litigation under that clause that has greatly extended women's rights. The impact of each of these constitutional clauses, including the "equal protection" clause of the U.S. constitution, which now governs legislation affecting women in the absence of an ERA, must be judged by the policy decisions reached under it.

(See also FEDERALISM; FEMINISM; FEMINIZATION OF POVERTY; GENDER AND POLITICS; GENDER GAP.)

Janet K. Boles, *The Politics of the Equal Rights Amendment: Conflict and the Decision Process* (New York, 1979). Mary Frances Berry, *Why ERA Failed* (Bloomington, Ind., 1986). Jane Mansbridge, *Why We Lost the ERA* (Chicago, 1986).

JANE J. MANSBRIDGE

EQUALITY AND INEQUALITY. See overleaf.

EQUATORIAL GUINEA. The political history of Equatorial Guinea is one of continuous oppression and repression of the people by the Spanish during the colonial period since the eighteenth century, and following independence, on 12 October 1968, at the hands of two unscrupulous African dictators. Bordered by Cameroon and Gabon, Equatorial Guinea is hard to spot on the map. One of the tiniest countries in Africa, on the west coast, Equatorial Guinea is made up of the islands of Bioko, Annobon, Corisco, and Elobeys on the Atlantic Ocean, and Río Muni, inland, altogether measuring some 10,000 square miles (26,000 sq. km.) of surface. It is inhabited by about 500,000 people, mostly Fang (who constitute about 90 percent of the population of Rio Muni), the few Kombe, Balenque, and Bujeba, as well as the dwindling Bubi, descendants of slaves. Equatorial Guinea is predominantly a
(cont. on p. 261)

EQUALITY AND INEQUALITY. The politics of the world today are beset by tensions arising from inequality. Whether it be within a country or between countries or both, the privileges and valuables enjoyed by some have provoked conflicts, violent or nonviolent, with those who are, or who feel themselves to be, less favored. These privileges and valuables—which may relate to prestige, respect, power, or wealth and income—are often distributed according to race, gender, religion, or culture. In 1990, inequality was cited as a basis for conflicts in nations as diverse as South Africa, the Soviet Union, the United States, and India. Unequal women's rights were of particular political concern in Africa and the Muslim world. Unequal income among countries is a major source of global tensions. Inequality is especially important for understanding the ferment in the Middle East where the oil wealth of some, coupled with state-sanctioned racial and religious privileges, saturate the popular outlook, providing the ever-present foundation for political and violent struggle.

Indeed, inequality, actual or perceived, is, throughout the world, the greatest motivating force in politics. The emphasis here is on *inequality* rather than *equality* simply because equality, literally, is not to be found outside of the world of mathematics. It means identity. When people cry out for equality, they are actually demanding equality with respect to some particular thing or things. They may not express their demands in terms of "equality." They merely demand *more,* or they may seek legislative or administrative action that they believe will give them more, of something they desire, whether it be an economic or a psychic good. But most of the time they have their eyes on how others in their reference group, or in other categories not far removed in status or monetary income, are faring. It is relative rather than absolute equality that they are seeking.

No doubt this proposition about inequality could be contested. It might be claimed that persons, above all, seek power, whether it be the *power accruing to a ruler or "power to the people." But they generally desire power either to gain more than they have (perhaps material things, perhaps recognition) or to preserve what they already possess. It is some perceived equality or inequality that they wish to maintain or obtain.

True, this is not always the case. People may seek "more" of something not to attain equality, either generally or with regard to those who have more of that commodity than they do, but because they enjoy excelling, being, if possible, "number one." In short, it is superiority (a special kind of inequality), rather than equality, that they are striving for.

Another possible claimant for priority as a political motivating force is liberty. After all, it was the modern demand for liberty (the overthrow of existing authorities) that, in succeeding, led to relatively greater equality, especially of political power—and this process is ongoing. Those who demand more money claim that without it they are deprived of effective liberty (to supply their needs and satisfy their desires). But in every society some have more effective liberty than others, and this inequality is a major source of discontent that finds expression in politics.

None of this constitutes proof of the proposition that either resentment of inequality or the desire to attain it is the primary motivating force in the world of politics. That statement is not capable of proof or disproof. But it seems beyond rational doubt that it is one of the small number of candidates to be the mainspring of politics. Whether it be the world of *states, a state of tribes, racial or ethnic groups, or indeed any group, even the family, questions of sharing (whether of power, rank, prestige, income, wealth, welfare, well-being, or whatever) are bound to arise—sharing in what proportions and in proportion to what? The examination of the agenda of almost any legislative body will give abundant support to this proposition.

It is not that all of us are out to maximize only our own personal goods. Many seek and pursue a common good and the good of others; probably most of us do so much of the time, especially when our own good is not too much endangered; but, in a world of scarcity, even a society of altruists would be divided over the relative priority to be given to various goods and over who were the most deserving. In any case, that is a problem more remote than need be considered here.

The demand to minimize inequality seems to have been on the rise for a long while. Alexis de Tocqueville, over a century and a half ago (in his monumental *Democracy in America* [New York, 1945], vol. 1, p. 6), declared that "the gradual development of the principle of equality is a providential fact. It has all the chief characteristics of such a fact. It is universal, it is lasting, it constantly eludes all human interference, and all events as well as all men contribute to its progress." As monarchies, dictatorships, even oligarchies gradually are replaced by some form of government that is at least struggling to become democratic, we have all become aware of Tocqueville's prescience. The movement toward democracy and the advance of the principle of equality in other aspects of social life have not been without setbacks, nor will they be in the future. These may be severe and far from brief, but the overall direction of change seems undeniable. Even dictatorial regimes claim to be essentially democratic, and they do indeed partake of some of the characteristics of *democracy. In general, the responsiveness of government to the views of citizens increases unabated. Slavery has been virtually abolished. *Apartheid is slowly dying. Greater equality in political rights and economic conditions flow from these developments.

This trend toward greater equality is by no means confined to the spread of political democracy; it appears to characterize all hierarchical structures, public or private—even the military, although probably least evident there. The flattening of social pyramids is observable in all walks of life. What has become of the family patriarch? Committee chairpersons no longer enjoy the predominant position once occupied by chairmen. The same tendency, in varying degrees and by no means universally, is observable in business organizations. Where the spread of equality began, whether in the social or the political realm, is of no consequence, for, in the United States especially, it has become so ingrained in society generally that it is bound to be reflected in politics more narrowly defined. In some parts of the world it may take centuries for this episodic movement, enduring many reversals, to reach a stage comparable to that of the industrial democracies.

As "natural law" tended to be superseded by "natural rights," and the latter in turn by "*human rights" (rights that are the same and equal for all persons), the individual gained in stature and in dignity. "Subjects" became "citizens," and citizens had rights that must be respected. The crumbling of dictatorial power in the Soviet Union and other communist regimes owes much to their adherence to the *Helsinki Accords. This clarion call for human rights and, even more importantly, this authorization to monitor nations with respect to their observance of these rights provided *legitimacy for demands that could previously be ignored.

The concept of *rights, although unknown to the ancient world, is far from new. What is at least modern is the contention that, with respect to many of the most critical rights, all persons are equal. This proposition is enunciated in the Universal Declaration of Human Rights, and the implementation of these rights is reduced to *treaty form in a series of covenants of various rights subscribed to by most of the nations of the world. Equality of the races and of the sexes have become continuing battlegrounds. "Equality" is today a "virtue word." Like "justice" or "love," no one is against it; but people may mean different things by it.

It is not only individuals who assert equal rights, a fact that leads to problems. From the early days of *international law, at least from the time of *Grotius, sovereign states have been held to possess equal rights, a claim that leads to difficulties. The *League of Nations foundered on the obvious issue: should the tiniest legally independent principality, such as Monaco, have a vote of equal weight to those of states hundreds of times larger, more populous, more powerful, and wealthier than it? The unsupportable nature of this claim was recognized, in a rough sort of way, when the UN was brought into being. The Security Council of the UN, its only organ that can make legally binding decisions, is composed of but a handful of its total membership. This might not be incompatible with the equality principle if all members of the council were elected in a way that provided equal power to each of the member states; but this is not the case. A small number (five) of the council members are "permanent." They cannot be replaced, nor is provision made for adding to their number. Moreover, the permanent and nonpermanent members are not created equal: each of the permanent members has an absolute veto over all substantive actions of the council.

In yet another way the UN charter runs into difficulties with the equality principle. How does it accord with the rights of individuals? If the vote of a state of 10 million is to count the same as that of a country with a population of 200 million, what becomes of the equal rights of citizens? Here it would appear that the ideas of the equality of humankind and that of states are in head-on conflict. The U.S. Constitution, in the case of the Senate, provides an example of the same problem, rendered less serious in a unit as politically homogeneous as is the United States as compared with the UN.

The case of *international organizations only casts in larger form a more fundamental problem that theories of human equality have always encountered. It is simply this: given that human beings cannot be identical, in what respects can they be equal? Even when it is a single element, such as income or wealth, serious difficulties arise, as has been noted above. When it comes to the ethical validity of competing claims, the problem becomes much more difficult. Aristotle cast it in terms of "numerical" versus "proportionate" equality. If, for instance, it is income that is in question, numerical equality would be achieved if every person or household received exactly the same amount. Proportionate equality would mean that income would be distributed in proportion to merit. But what is merit? Need, capability, work, production, ability to do what the public is willing to pay for (as in the cases of football players and film stars)? The list is long and the problem of selection is daunting. The difficulty is further complicated if we ask the question, What should count as income? Money only, or psychic income, or all that contributes to happiness? Further, should the comparison be made at a given point in time, or longitudinally, looking at the experience of a person through his or her lifetime? And what about generational equity? How much should youth be taxed for the benefit of the elderly? It is easy to see why Aristotle concluded that the "passion for equality" is "at the root of sedition"; and why we are considering the proposition originally enunciated.

It is also apparent that the quarrels over absolute equality and relative equality challenge Tocqueville's thesis regarding the onward march of equality, as though it were a simple, unambiguous goal. No society is truly egalitarian. *Elites are omnipresent; but in many countries elites have changed in three important respects: degree of power, privilege, or status; unity; and continuity. For instance, the British elite today (whether measured in terms of political power, economic domination, or social *class) by no means has influence comparable to its eighteenth-century counterpart. This, in no small measure, reflects the decline of deference, itself the effect of numerous factors, such as the growth of the bourgeoisie at the expense of the landed aristocracy, the development of the professional and skilled classes, and the enlarged electorate following electoral reforms. Japan stands out as a country in which an elite has maintained a dominant position for a long time, in spite of striking technological development; but even there signs of its declining power are evident. The significance of elites also depends greatly upon their unity. The power of an elite united by common interests and lifestyle is likely to be much greater than that of one that is highly dispersed among such elements as big business, scientists, the military, union leaders, and so on. Finally, what about continuity? To what extent are elites able to pass along their privileges to their descendants? It is notable that in highly industrialized countries mobility is much greater than in societies where agriculture predominates: a fact that interferes with the continuity of elites.

Another pertinent aspect of inequality is its distribution. The importance of a large middle class as a protection against *revolution has long been recognized. In a healthy society the inequalities, whether of political or of economic power, pose much less of a threat to stability if they are virtually continuous from the lowest to the highest category and if the gap between rich and poor, between powerful and powerless, is mediated by a large and easily permeable middle class. The very fact that "middle class" is today so much more difficult to define and identify than was the "bourgeoisie" even in Marx's day, is testimony to its diversity, its lack of homogeneity. While this feature makes for difficulty in obtaining consensus, by the same token it blurs the distinction between elites and masses, with its threat of either exploitation or revolution. Those at the bottom can see the possibility of step-by-step improvement, especially for their children.

If to economic differences one adds ethnic, linguistic, racial, or gender inequalities, the case obviously becomes much more complicated. Just how complicated and resistant to broad generalization the matter can be is illustrated by the Canadian case. In Quebec, the French-speaking population a decade or so ago was economically less well-off than the English-speaking minority and, rightly or wrongly, perceived themselves to be discriminated against. A strong separatist movement developed, although it did not succeed and the threat of secession subsided. Today, however, in spite of the fact that many of the more well-to-do English-speaking people have left the province and many of the French-speaking ones enjoy an improved position both economically and socially, the move for separation has once more become a federation-threatening force. In this case, at least, it appears that economic differentials, while not insignificant, are not necessarily determinant. Matters of culture, including a common language, and of race (especially exemplified in the United States) may be even more important than economic inequalities. And, even without regard to their relative importance, inequalities are cumulative in their effect. One person's grievance about unequal treatment arising out of cultural differences may combine with another person's grievance attributable to economic inequality, contributing cumulatively to discontent.

We have spoken of a trend toward equality, then shown how that leads to a discussion of kinds of equality, especially numerical and proportionate, which, as some would see it, is really a matter of equality versus inequality, and thence have been led to consideration of related political issues. Now let us turn to another aspect of the problem, one that is introduced by the concept of equality of opportunity. It will become apparent that it, too, leads directly to many of the central issues of politics and of public policy.

"Equality of opportunity" is easily seized upon as a phrase well designed to capture at once the virtues of equality and of liberty. Liberty without opportunity would come close to

being a contradiction in terms, and equality without opportunity sounds like the equality of slaves or prisoners. It might be said that the phrase marries equality and liberty; but divorce, as will appear, is by no means impossible. The importance of this concept and its value are great, but so are its pitfalls. How to provide all with equal opportunities? If it is taken to mean only that no laws shall bar anyone from pursuing legitimate goals to the best of her or his abilities, few would disagree. But also few would find it sufficient. What about bars imposed by lack of education, prejudice, inadequate home background? What, indeed, about differences in income as effective limits to the exercise of liberty? Some would go further and say, What about genetic handicaps, mental or physical? Many steps have already been taken in the United States and elsewhere along the lines that these remarks suggest. For instance, in the United States conditions largely associated with race are addressed by such programs as Head Start, Upward Bound, and affirmative action. The latter in particular, especially when it leads to the requirement of racial quotas, has led to serious political dispute.

Pushed to its logical conclusion, the concept of equality of opportunity would seem to demand the prohibition of all bars to the freedom of migration from country to country, the abolition of inheritance and, indeed, of the family itself. Probably few would wish to go that far even if (improbably) all this could be done without drastically reducing the standard of living. An even greater problem: at what point must opportunities be equal? Throughout life? Even these few lines are probably enough to demonstrate that the ideal of equality of opportunity, splendid starting point for discussion as it may be, is no more than a beginning. Even the brief analysis above shows how it leads, step by step, to virtual equality of condition, something that could not be attained or maintained without great intrusions on liberty. Hence the "divorce" referred to above of liberty from equality. Indeed, this tension between equality and liberty largely accounts for the fact that quarrels over the ideal of equality comprise the mainspring of politics and the source of the major dilemmas of public policy, as neoconservatives insist on the priority of individual liberty and U.S. liberals and European social democrats press for greater equality.

The subject of equality of opportunity does, however, invite consideration of another topic that is both virtually endless and yet too relevant to our topic to be avoided: the market. Communist societies worldwide, which sought to minimize unjust inequalities by instituting state control of both production and distribution, were driven to attempt to move to a market system. They discovered that in practice state control did not eliminate great economic inequalities, did produce great political inequality (at the expense of liberty), and vastly decreased total production; but the postcommunist societies that have emerged are finding the transition extremely difficult.

Use of a market system, giving individual liberty priority over equality in the distribution of both capital goods and consumer goods, both in theory and practice, has a strong claim to being more efficient than central *planning and control. It increases the size of the pie that is to be distributed, so that it is possible for the economically worst off to be better off than they would be under a more egalitarian system that suffers from greater scarcity. This advantage may be more assured if appropriate steps are taken to place a floor under impoverishment. Without the latter, the market system leads to gross economic inequalities, which in turn may translate into political inequalities. Both of these are widely seen as unjust; when they become intolerably so, they are answered by governmental regulations of the market or by systems that are mixtures of private and public enterprise, "mixed economies." Moreover, relying as it must upon competition, upon individual self-interest, the market tends to encourage greed and exploitation, and to discourage the social aspect of human nature, altruism, and fellow-feeling, which it is the aim of *socialism and *communism to encourage, and on which to an important degree the political stability of all modern states depends. Here again regulatory measures are called for.

Can the market system be so modified and regulated as to escape the worst of its bad tendencies? Most of the nations of the world, especially those that are substantially industrialized, are constantly wrestling with this problem. It is not one to which a single solution is likely to be found.

The second, related question has to do with human nature. Is it fixed or can it be altered? If the latter, how and how much? Can human self-interest be so qualified as to make human sympathy, altruism, fellow-feeling, or commitment to certain ideas of justice prevail to the extent that what might be a golden mean, an optimum mixture of free markets and political controls (the latter including redistributive taxation), would cease to be so, even though other relevant conditions remained the same? The record of past and present strongly suggests that human nature is ambivalent between self-seeking and benevolence, and, within certain limits, is likely to remain so for the foreseeable future, even despite heroic attempts to produce radical change.

By no means are all of the inequalities that prevail under a market system attributable to the market, however. The evidence seems conclusive that the largest part of inequalities arises out of family background; whether by nature, nurture, genes, training, or example, personal success is largely determined during the first five years of life. By this time one's mental and physical abilities, energy level, propensity to save, and other important factors have already been firmly implanted, subject in most cases to only relatively minor modification, as has been well documented by Sir Henry Phelps Brown in *The Inequality of Pay* (London, 1977).

Are we then condemned to remain in a vicious circle, with underclass breeding underclass? Such a grim outlook is not justified, for two reasons. First, even minor modifications in distribution through regulation and public policy initiatives can be pyramided in succeeding generations and, in time, result in not insignificant improvements in equality of opportunity. Second, the evidence refutes the notion that the underclass syndrome is ironclad. If it were, we would have a

caste system, whereas in reality we have quite considerable class mobility, a fact that we owe in important degree to the phenomenon of genetic combinations and permutations, as well as to pure luck after birth. These factors can and should be supplemented by improved schooling, especially in the early years, directed precisely toward overcoming the handicaps produced by an inferior home environment. This would be costly, involving a large amount of one-on-one instruction, and progress would be painfully slow, but it would eventuate in a more productive society, even paying for itself financially in the long run.

As for the international scene, I must venture into a more speculative realm. By now we are all familiar with the term *multinational*. IBM is a prime example; it operates worldwide, but it is a U.S. firm. What, though, of Visa International, which, Alvin Toffler tells us (*PowerShift*, New York, 1990), "is owned by 21,000 financial institutions in 187 countries and territories," while "its governing board and regional boards are set up to prevent any one nation having 51 percent of the votes" (p. 460). The significance of this development for present purposes is that the nation-state is thereby weakened as an independent entity. Power is dispersed. *Imperialism and neocolonialism are upstaged. If guerrillas or even hostile nations threaten such entities, to whom will they turn for help? Possibly to an enlarged and renamed UN, where it is no longer one-nation, one-vote, but where such entities as a truly *World Bank unite with other global entities to share power on an equal footing.

The world of two great superpowers may never be repeated. Change, perhaps ever more rapid, will certainly continue. It will be accompanied by turmoil and probably by violence. One can envisage a world in which Europe, America (the Western Hemisphere?), and Asia (Africa?), along with such transnational entities as those suggested above, are the players: even one in which the players operate on less unequal terms than they do today and whose constituents likewise share power more equally than is now the case. But by this point we surely have moved at least into the twenty-second century, and must recognize that a starkly different scenario might be quite possible—equally possible?

(See also Citizenship; Conservatism; Ethnicity; Gender and Politics; Liberalism; Modernity; Race and Racism; Social Mobility; United Nations; Welfare State.)

R. H. Tawney, *Equality* (New York, 1931). J. Roland Pennock and John W. Chapman, eds., NOMOS IX, *Equality* (New York, 1967). J. Roland Pennock, *Democratic Political Theory*, chap. 1 (Princeton, N.J., 1979). Amy Gutmann, *Liberal Democracy* (Cambridge, U.K., 1980). Douglas Rae et al., *Equalities* (Cambridge, Mass., 1981). Giovanni Sartori, *The Theory of Democracy Revisited*, chap. 12 (Chatham, N.J., 1987). Lloyd L. Weinreb, *National Law and Justice* (Cambridge, Mass., 1987). Ian Shapiro and Grant Reeher, eds., *Power, Inequality, and Democratic Politics* (Boulder, Colo., 1988). J. Roland Pennock, "Normative Political Theory," in *Annual Review of Political Science*, vol. 3, ed. Samuel Long (Norwood, N.J., 1990). Peter Weston, *Speaking of Equality* (Princeton, N.J., 1990).

J. Roland Pennock

rural country but very Chistianized. Ninety percent of the population claim to be Roman Catholic, the remainder identifying themselves as religious traditionalists.

Located in Africa's equatorial rainforest, Equatorial Guinea is endowed with very few natural crops, except for cocoa, the country's major export commodity, and, most recently, oil, which has sustained the current dictator's oppressive regime, providing the country with a per capita income of over $500 a year, one of the highest in sub-Saharan Africa. Cameroon, Spain, and France are the major trading partners, to the extent that Spanish and French are the country's official languages. Since 1970, Equatorial Guinea has been a member of the Central African Franc Zone, using the franc as its monetary unit.

The first oppressive regime started immediately after independence when Francisco Macias Nguema, a Fang from the Esaungu clan, took the reins of power from the Spanish. As in most of colonial Africa, Equatorial Guinea entered the era of independence amid the euphoria of the multiparty system, which elected Nguema as its first president. Again, as in most of postcolonial Africa, by 1970, the new president had declared the country a single-party system under his Partido Unico Nacional de los Trabajadores (PUNT), initiating one of the four most brutal regimes Africa has ever seen, along with Jean-Baptiste Bukassa's in Central African Republic, Idi Amin's in Uganda, and Mariam Mengistu's in Ethiopia.

Nguema instituted a reign of terror resulting in assassinations, murders, tortures, and arrests of both educated and noneducated Equato-Guineans, accused of opposing the regime or of plotting to overthrow it. Criticized by humanitarian organizations, such as Amnesty International, and even by other African regimes, the persecution of perceived opponents continued unabated until Nguema's violent overthrow by his own nephew, National Guard Lieut.-Col. Teodoro Obiang Nguema, on 3 August 1979. Captured, Macias Nguema was tried and executed on 29 September 1979. Thus began a military rule that, under the trappings of democratic reforms, has one way or the other remained, into the new millennium, one of Africa's most oppressive regimes.

Obiang Nguema ruled through his hand-picked Supreme Military Council until 1981, when he finally appointed a civilian administration, followed by a bogus August 1982 constitution that appointed him president for a seven-year term. A year later, he personally appointed his own legislative assembly of forty-one members for a term of five years. Meanwhile, although executions were not as frequent as during the previous regime, Obiang was notorious for the torture and arrests of opposition members, interspersed with releases, amnesties, and personal pardons. Just as during his uncle's rule, thousands of Equato-Guineans lived abroad in exile, some having formed their own political parties to oppose the Malabo regime. Emulating his uncle, Obiang Nguema created his own party, the Partido Democratico da Guine Equatorial (PDGE) in 1986 and used the pseudo-party to be elected president by an open ballot in 1989, allegedly, capturing 99 percent of the vote cast by fewer than half of the registered voters.

Harassed by the international community and overwhelmed by the strength of the movement toward democratic reforms during the early 1990s, Obiang Nguema accepted the principle of multiparty democracy, and appointed a transition government (but of only members of his party), in January 1992, and bestowed amnesty upon all opponents of the regime both at home and abroad. This was followed, in June, by the recognition of the first opposition parties, such as the Uniao Popular and the Partido Liberal. The subsequent coalition of opposing parties into the Plataforma de Oposicion Conjunta, in September 1992, did not deter the president, who continued his practice of arrests and prison terms for anyone criticizing or demonstrating against his administration.

Scholars have debated which of the two Nguemas was more brutal than the other and more responsible for the violation of human rights in Equatorial Guinea. They agree, however, that Obiang Nguema, before executing his uncle in 1979, had participated in most major murder and torture activities of Macias Nguema's regime. Unfortunately, whatever he did in the country, it was clearly known by Spain, France, Gabon (which helped him execute his plan), and Morocco. The latter has provided him with security and protection by well-trained Moroccan guards.

R. Fegley, *Equatorial Guinea: An African Tragedy* (New York, 1989). Ibrahim Sundiata, *Equatorial Guinea: Colonialism, State Terror, and the Search for Stability* (Boulder, Colo., 1990). Max Liniger-Goumaz, *Who's who de la dictature de Guinee Equatoriale: Les Nguemistes, 1979–1993* (Geneva, 1993).

MARIO J. AZEVEDO

ERITREA. The borders of present-day Eritrea were first drawn during Italian colonization (1889–1941). After three decades of war with Ethiopia, its last colonizer, Eritrea achieved independence in May 1991 with the military victory of the Eritrean People's Liberation Front (EPLF), and became a UN member in 1993.

Eritrea encompasses an area of 46,774 square miles (121,144 sq. km.). The country's temperate highlands are inhabited by settled farming communities, the lowland regions of the Red Sea coast and the western areas by, for the most part, nomadic herders; the total population, comprising nine ethnic groups and evenly divided between Christians and Muslims, is estimated to be 4 million. A history of religious tolerance and cultural autonomy has cemented national unity, but a socioeconomic gap remains between town and country and between the sexes. Closing this gap has been the centerpiece of government policy as evidenced by investment programs and activities in regard to education, health, and infrastructure in the rural areas as well as affirmative action measures in favor of women such as reserved seats in legislative bodies. Party cadres, joined by students and national military service cadets, reach out to the people in planting trees and building roads, schools, clinics, and irrigation dams. In these efforts, self-reliance is the principal policy orientation.

The EPLF, renamed the People's Front for Democracy and Justice (PFDJ) in 1994, has been the governing party, led by President Isaias Afwerki. On 23 May 1997, following three years of public debate, a constituent assembly ratified a draft constitution that provides, among other things, for an executive president elected by, and accountable to, parliament; an independent judiciary; and a bill of rights. During the constitutional debates, concerns were repeatedly expressed mainly centered on three issues: government accountability, the need for a multiparty system, and economic policy, including the government's role in the economy. Government accountability and competitive parties are guaranteed in the constitution. But, in the absence of an organized opposition, the PFDJ is expected to rule for the foreseeable future. As to economic policy, rapid economic growth is the governing priority, and the PFDJ considers a multiparty system to be a luxury that a war-ravaged country like Eritrea cannot afford. Critics respond with cautionary tales of the corruption of African *one-party systems, governments which promised an era of plenty on the condition that people exchange liberty for bread. The critics argue that bread and liberty are not mutually exclusive, that democracy and development should go hand in hand.

The debate continues unresolved, with echoes of the "developmental state" reverberating in the corridors of power, and Singapore extolled as a model. The market ideology of an export-oriented economy has replaced earlier ideas of planned economy, provoking concerns about the market preempting national values, including those enshrined in the Constitution, such as *democracy, stability, social justice, *human rights, and communal solidarity. If Eritrea follows the path of Singapore, the question is: Do the conditions that vaulted Singapore to a first-class economy apply to Eritrea today? Can Eritrea's economy—agriculture, livestock, light industry—be the basis for a "takeoff"? To Eritrean policy makers, human-power development, discipline, and hard work are what count in the global economy. To that end, educational and administrative policies and practices have been redefined. Meanwhile, the government has pinned hopes on marine resources, tourism, and minerals, including offshore oil, which are expected to draw foreign investments and provide employment and a better life for a war-weary people.

These projections are based on an assumption of lasting peace and stability. But Eritrea has more than once fallen victim to geography and global politics—as in 1950 when, owing to U.S. strategic considerations, it was yoked to Ethiopia by UN resolution. Reflecting on Eritrea's misfortune, an Italian wit once remarked, "Eritrea chose the wrong colonizer"—that is, Italy. He might have added, "and the wrong neighborhood"—the Red Sea and Ethiopia. Ironically, U.S. policy makers propounded the fateful 1950 resolution in the interest of securing peace in a region that would shortly be engulfed by war. The irony of history repeated itself more recently in an armed clash between erstwhile allies—the new Eritrean and Ethiopian governments. That conflict confirmed Eritrea's decision, at independence, to keep half of its guerrilla forces, supported by reserves, as the backbone of its national defense.

(See also ETHIOPIA; HORN OF AFRICA; IGAD; POLITICAL PARTIES AND PARTY COMPETITION.)

Alberto Pollera, *The Native Peoples of Eritrea* (Lawrenceville, N.J., 1999). Gebre H. Tesfagiorgis, ed., *Emergent Eritrea: Challenges of Economic Development* (Trenton, N.J., 1993). Ruth Iyob, *The Eritrean Struggle for Independence: Domination, Resistance, and Nationalism, 1941–1993* (Cambridge, U.K., 1995).

BEREKET HABTE SELASSIE

ERITREAN WAR OF INDEPENDENCE. Fought since 1961, the war in Eritrea would have earned the dubious distinction of beating Vietnam's record as the longest *war in the modern world, had it not ended in May 1991. Why this war, and how did the Eritreans manage to wage it for so long?

*Clausewitz's dictum that war is the continuation of politics by other means applies in the Eritrean case with tragic poignancy. The politics of Eritrean self-determination from British occupation (1941–1952; following Italian colonial rule, 1889–1941) and subsequently from Ethiopian encroachment came to a head in 1961–1962.

With its defeat in World War II, Italy relinquished its legal right to its colonies in a treaty signed in 1947, under which the Four Powers (France, the United Kingdom, the United States, and the Soviet Union) would dispose of the former Italian colonies by agreement, failing which they would submit the matter to the United Nations General Assembly. Libya's and Somalia's cases were determined without much ado at the UN; Eritrea proved to be difficult, principally because of Emperor *Haile Selassie's interest in acquiring it and U.S. strategic and geopolitical interest in the Red Sea region. The convergence of these two interests and the dominant U.S. position sealed the fate of Eritrean self-determination.

Instead of gaining independence, as demanded by the majority of its inhabitants, Eritrea was joined with *Ethiopia in a lopsided federation under "the Sovereignty of the Ethiopian Crown." It was lopsided because it lacked a basic principle of *federalism: a neutral arbiter between the Eritrean entity and Ethiopia. It was also imposed by a U.S.–engineered resolution instead of by a freely expressed referendum as practiced in other cases of self-determination of colonized peoples. Moreover, the emperor's government began encroaching on Eritrean autonomy soon after the federation came into force in 1952. Eritrean protests were ignored by the UN, which bore responsibility for the integrity of the federation. Finally, emboldened by the impunity with which he had violated the UN arrangement, Emperor Haile Selassie abolished the federation in 1962.

A year earlier, in September 1961, the Eritrean Liberation Front (ELF) declared armed struggle, galvanizing a disappointed nation. By 1970, when the Eritrean People's Liberation Front (EPLF) was established, the Eritrean War had become Haile Selassie's principal preoccupation. Indeed, it was a major cause for his demise four years later. His successors adopted his policy of a military solution to the "Eritrean problem," vowing to "liquidate the secessionist rebels." Sixteen years later, Haile Selassie's successors, who had increased their armed forces eightfold, to 250,000, not only failed in their objective, but also lost ground. The EPLF defeated the Ethiopian army on 24 May 1991 and, following a UN-observed referendum in April 1993, it formed a government.

The essence of the Eritrean case is that it represents denied *decolonization, not a secession. It is analogous to those of Namibia and Western Sahara. Ethiopian diplomacy, backed first by the United States (1953–1976), then by the Soviet Union, miscast it as a secession, thus turning Africa opinion against Eritrean independence. Military victories by the EPLF and a reappraisal of the basis of Eritrean claims then began to sway international opinion in favor of Eritrean independence.

Despite the incalculable cost, the Eritreans have proved that a nation determined to win its rightful place in the family of nations is capable of surviving overwhelming odds. The Eritreans, led by the EPLF, triumphed against a much bigger Ethiopian army that was backed by external powers. The primary source of this triumph was the support of the population which sacrificed life and property for its cause. The second was the nature of the guerrilla army, its experience, its resilience and tenacity, its adeptness at the use of weapons, and its knowledge and mastery of the terrain. Its creation of a disciplined organization and impressive social infrastructure, notably in education and health, helped secure and maintain very wide popular support.

The end of the war in Eritrea was followed by an agreement reached between the EPLF and the transitional government of Ethiopia to a peaceful settlement of the Eritrean question through a referendum.

(See also DECOLONIZATION; ETHIOPIA; GUERRILLA WARFARE; HORN OF AFRICA.)

Bereket Habte Selassie, *Eritrea and the United Nations and Other Essays* (Trenton, N.J., 1989). Georges Nzongola-Ntalaja, ed., *Conflict in the Horn of Africa* (Atlanta, 1991).

BEREKET HABTE SELASSIE

ESTONIA. See BALTIC STATES.

ETHIOPIA. The historical antecedents of Ethiopia are found in the Christian kingdom of Abyssinia, whose own history links it to the Axumite empire that flourished in the northern part of the Ethiopian plateau in ancient times. The emergence of the modern state begins in the reign of Menelik II, the Abyssinian ruler who not only repelled an Italian invasion in 1896 and spared his country the experience of colonialism but also expanded his domain prodigiously through conquest and gave the state, henceforth called Ethiopia, its present borders. Unlike Abyssinia, Ethiopia was a heterogeneous empire impossible to rule through the feudal Abyssinian political system. Consequently, a process of modernization was launched by *Haile Selassie, who became regent in 1917, king in 1928, and emperor in 1930; he ruled Ethiopia until he was overthrown in 1974. Under him, the power of the Abyssinian aristocracy was broken, the governmental process was centralized, the state was reinforced with bureaucratic, military, and security apparatuses, and Haile Selassie ruled as an absolute monarch in a state where conventional political life had not yet appeared.

Nevertheless, powerful forces opposed to the regime emerged among dissident ethnic groups and social classes. Dissidence grew among groups that had been forcibly incorporated into the state by Menelik's expansion. Opposition also mounted among the Eritreans in the former Italian colony, who had been deprived of self-government by Haile Selassie when he dismantled a federal scheme that had linked *Eritrea with Ethiopia from 1952 to 1962. Generally such groups inhabited the arid lowland periphery of Ethiopia where no sign of development had appeared, and many were Muslim pastoralists, ignored and alienated by a state dependent on cultivation and ruled by Christians. Denied normal political outlets, some of these groups were driven to armed rebellion beginning in the early 1960s.

Dissidence bred also among the new social groups spawned by the system of modern education installed in the 1940s and by the process of economic change that began the following decade. The intelligentsia was alienated by its exclusion from power and the domination of the economy by foreign capital, which limited the scope for native enterprise. Ethiopia's nascent working class was alien-

ated by the regime's collusion with foreign employers to reduce labor costs, which resulted in harsh exploitation. Dissidence also affected the junior army officer corps, whose members shared the outlook of the intelligentsia, and the soldiers who bore the burden of fighting against oppositional guerrilla movements in various parts of the country. The regime's most militant opponents were the students from the university and secondary schools. Having espoused Marxism as their ideological guide, they succeeded in making it the only credible political alternative to the *ancien régime*.

A devastating *famine in 1972–1974 that was largely ignored by the government galvanized the dissident social groups into simultaneous, albeit uncoordinated, action that caused the collapse of the imperial regime in 1974. A group of 112 junior and noncommissioned officers and plain soldiers representing units of the military establishment seized power. Influenced by the radicalism of the intelligentsia and wishing to secure its support, this group, known as the Dergue (Committee), itself espoused Marxism, and decreed a series of basic socioeconomic reforms that revolutionized Ethiopian society. Among these were the nationalization of rural land and its distribution equally among working peasants, the nationalization of industry, finance, large-scale trade, and other sectors of the economy, and the nationalization of urban land and extra housing. The reforms effectively wiped out the economic base of the old ruling class.

The Dergue's espousal of Marxism did not appease the radicals who demanded civilian rule and attacked the regime, provoking a violent reaction that claimed many victims and effectively silenced all opposition to military rule from that quarter. However, armed opposition from dissident ethnic and regional groups proliferated and became a serious threat to both the regime and the state. The Eritrean rebels nearly overran their province in 1977, and Somali irredentism provoked an invasion from neighboring *Somalia the same year. A new movement sprang up in the northern Abyssinian province of Tigray, an impoverished, desiccated land, tormented by drought and famine. Yet another movement claimed to represent the Oromo, Ethiopia's most populous group. The goals of these movements ranged from secession and independence in the case of Eritrea, to secession and union with Somalia in the case of the Somali living in Ethiopia, to regional self-rule for Tigray.

The Dergue's response to this manifold challenge was devoid of political substance. Instead, it increased the size of the military establishment tenfold and fought civil wars on several fronts. The regime's ideology and reforms alienated the United States, heretofore Ethiopia's chief patron and provider of military aid. Its place was eagerly taken by the Soviet Union, which provided the weaponry needed. While war raged, Ethiopia's economy stagnated, but its population grew at the rate of 3 percent per year and exceeded 42 million in 1984, when the first census was taken. Food production hardly kept up, and the country faced a serious problem of food insufficiency. When drought revisited northern and eastern Ethiopia in the early 1980s, a severe famine ensued, claiming lives by the hundreds of thousands and making the country a ward of international charity. Ten years after it came to power, the military regime headed by Colonel Mengistu Haile Mariam sought to institutionalize itself by creating political structures based superficially on the Soviet model. A constitution adopted in 1987 sought to address the problem of ethnic and regional dissidence by providing self-government to some ethnic and regional groups, although it defined Ethiopia as a unitary state.

The offer was not taken seriously by the rebels, who went on the offensive in the late 1980s encouraged by the dramatic changes in the international scene and the suspension of Soviet military aid to the Ethiopian regime. A sustained drive southwards by the Tigray Peoples Liberation Front (TPLF) caused the collapse of the Dergue in May 1991. The Eritrean Peoples Liberation Front (EPLF) took control of Eritrea and formalized the region's independence through a referendum held two years later. Ethiopia came under the rule of the Ethiopian People's Revolutionary Democratic Front (EPRDF), a coalition of ethnic political factions cobbled together and controlled by the TPLF.

In the political vacuum that ensued after the collapse of military rule, the new regime was able to impose its own design for the reform of the Ethiopian state. A national (ethnic) movement itself, the TPLF was an advocate of the principle of national self-determination, and it proceeded to make it the basic principle for constitutional, political, and administrative reform. Ethiopia has over eighty national (ethnic) groups, and they were all encouraged to form political organizations to represent them. A federal scheme was created with national (ethnic) groups as its constituent units; the country was divided into ethnically defined regions which, according to the constitution adopted in 1995, enjoy broad autonomy, including the right to use ethnic languages in education and as the medium of official communication.

Political recognition of *ethnicity was proclaimed the foundation of democratic rule in Ethiopia; a bold departure from prevailing practice elsewhere in Africa. A plethora of ethnic political parties competed in a series of local, regional, and national elections and constitutional referenda in the first half of the 1990s, giving the impression of broad participation and open competition for political power. This impression was marred by the fact that all these contests were won by the EPRDF, and parties not affiliated with it were not able to gain a foothold at any level. The latter claimed the scheme was designed to enable the TPLF, which formally represents an ethnic constituency composing less than 10 percent of Ethiopia's population, to control the entire state. Most of the opposition groups boycotted the last round of elections, charging the regime headed by TPLF leader Meles Zenawi with a variety of abuses of civil and political rights. More ominously, Islamic fundamentalist groups in the Somali region and the secessionist Oromo Liberation Front declared war on the EPRDF. As the twenty-first century began, the Ethiopian state was again embattled with violent opposition at home and involved in a border war with Erithea.

(See also ERITREAN WAR OF INDEPENDENCE; FOOD POLITICS; HORN OF AFRICA; INTERGOVERNMENTAL AUTHORITY FOR DEVELOPMENT; SECESSIONIST MOVEMENTS.)

John Markakis, *National and Class Conflict in the Horn of Africa* (Cambridge, U.K., 1987). Christopher Clapham, *Transformation and Continuity in Revolutionary Ethiopia* (Cambridge, U.K., 1988). Edmond J. Keller, *Revolutionary Ethiopia* (Bloomington, Ind., 1988). Andargachew Tiruneh, *The Ethiopian Revolution, 1974–1987* (Cambridge, 1993)

JOHN MARKAKIS

ETHNICITY. See overleaf.

EUROPEAN COURT OF JUSTICE. The legal order of the European Community (EC) is founded on an international treaty, the Treaty of Rome, which came into force in 1958 and which has been subsequently amended, most notably by the Single European Act, with effect from 1987; the *Maastricht Treaty (1993); and the Treaty of Amsterdam (1999). To this extent, the EC legal order corresponds to patterns which are familiar under public *international law governing treaties. Such conflation of EC and public international law is nonetheless apt to mislead. The frequent assertion that EC law, despite this background, is of a novel, indeed unique, character owes its basis primarily to the remarkably dynamic and imaginative contribution of the European Court of Justice. Based in Luxembourg and currently comprising fifteen judges, one per member state, the Court insisted in the early 1960s on the key constitutional principles of the supremacy of EC law—that it should override national law in the event of conflict—and its direct effect—that it should be capable of invocation by private parties before national courts of the member states. Even these notions were not unknown in public international law, but the Court, even in its early rulings, packaged them in the language of "a new legal order," signifying its determination to establish a distinctive character for EC law.

The Court has gone so far as to describe the treaty as having established a "constitutional legal order based on the rule of law" which serves radically to distance the system from its public international law roots. The Court's label reflects the way in which EC law has deeply penetrated the fabrics of national legal orders. The pronouncements of the European Court are endowed with real practical effect by the consistent readiness of national courts to absorb the view from Luxembourg and to apply it with fidelity. In this way, a judicial partnership operative at national and transnational level developed, within which the system of supervision of member states acting in violation of EC law was rendered immeasurably superior to one dependent on the intervention of the European Commission alone.

State courts also act as guardians of legal rights deriving from EC law. This collaboration between courts in Europe is enhanced by the preliminary reference procedure found in the treaty, which permits (and in some circumstances requires) national courts to refer questions about the interpretation and validity of Community law to the European Court. This cuts a fertile channel between national and EC level and locates the European Court in a powerful position to ensure the uniform development of the EC legal order. Developments during the 1990s suggested rumblings of discontent among some national judiciaries about perceived overexpansionism by the institutions of the EC, including the Court, and it seems likely that the expression of such anxieties will generate an intensification of the European
(cont. on p. 268)

ETHNICITY. A phenomenon associated with contact between cultural-lingustic communal groups within societies, ethnicity is characterized by cultural prejudice and social discrimination. Underlying these characteristics are the feelings of pride in the in-group, common consciousness and identity of the group, and the exclusiveness of its members. It is a phenomenon linked directly or indirectly to forms of affiliation and identification built around ties of real or putative kinship.

In reality ethnicity is a very complex phenomenon and, like other social phenomena, it is subject to change. Its form, place, and role in society may alter. Its links with other social phenomena such as politics, religion, and class relations may change, posing new questions. In fact, ethnicity hardly exists in a pure form. It is always closely associated with political, juridical, religious, and other social views and forms of interaction, which constitute important ingredients of the ethnic phenomenon. Hence ethnicity sometimes finds expression in political domination, economic exploitation, and psychological oppression.

The nature, intensity, and forms of expression of ethnicity are determined by various factors. These include the size and location of the various linguistic-cultural groups in the society; the strength and cohesion of their leaderships; the courage, determination, and nature of the underprivileged classes; the degree of foreign influence in the society; the nature, persuasiveness, and power of the dominant ideology; the prevailing social customs, tradition, and culture of the various linguistic groups; and the form of government of the society. Other factors include historical patterns of relations between different cultural groups, the level of development of the groups, the socioeconomic context in which the groups make contact, and the pattern of group migration to the place of contact. Thus ethnicity varies from place to place depending on the existence and significance of these factors and combinations of them. It is found in both developed and underdeveloped countries, in societies with differing ideologies, and in societies with different historical-cultural backgrounds.

Potentially, ethnicity embodies both positive and negative elements. On the positive side it involves an appreciation of one's own social roots in a community and cultural group without necessarily disparaging other groups. As a reference phenomenon it provides a material as well as an emotional support network for individuals in society. This function is particularly important as the society becomes more complex, massified, bureaucratized, impersonal, and alienating. It fosters a sense of belonging as part of an intermediate level of social relations between the individual and society. Thus ethnicity may serve as an adaptive mechanism which enables the individual to adjust successfully to the increasing alienation of mass societies. It enables the individual to overcome the socioeconomic insecurity consequent on divisive competition in market-oriented societies. In this regard, ethnicity binds individuals together, gives them internal cohesion, encourages them to provide for each other's security, and promotes their sense of identity and, therefore, their sense of direction. Ethnicity offers a personal solution to the generic problems of exploitation and oppression.

On the other hand, the negative aspects of ethnicity make it problematic for social harmony in multicultural societies. It embodies passionate symbolic and apprehensive aspects, which promotes violent conflict. The *genocide in Rwanda and Bosnia-Herzegovina and the politicide in Somalia, Croatia, and Kosovo underline a unique and ugly character of ethnicity, namely, its all-consuming, violent intensity. Ethnicity produces ethnic identity that like all primary identities crystallizes the self holistically. Its claims are totalistic because ethnicity presumes to articulate all signifying practices, and to encapsulate the whole way of life of the members of the ethnic group. Therefore, ethnic conflict is necessarily intense because those involved in it are inclined to believe that they are defending their whole way of life. The aggressive and murderous militiaman may believe that his very existence is threatened by the perceived injury to his ethnic group.

In another respect, ethnicity promotes hostility and violence. Within the in-group, and especially during competitions with out-groups, hostility among members is usually met with a united hostile front by all the other members through the process of socialization. If necessary, it is forcibly suppressed. But the internal restraints against hostility are relaxed at times of interethnic rivalry, which stresses ethnic group security and economic well-being. Such relaxation permits hostility toward the out-group. The in-group accepts violence as a legitimate mode of keeping the outsiders in their place.

Two types of violence are associated with ethnicity: direct and indirect violence. In the former case, the group or government imposing frustration and inciting the hostility is identified and made the object of the violent response. In indirect violence, however, the real cause of the response is not the victim of hostility. The violent response cannot be appropriately directed because of the remoteness, vagueness, ambiguity, or danger associated with the target. The aggrieved ethnic group finds a substitute on which it displaces the hostility. Often however, direct and indirect victimization coincides when the cause of direct violence is the traditional target of indirect violence. This coincidence exacerbates interethnic hostility.

Thus ethnicity causes adverse effects on the peace, harmony, and integration of national societies. These negative effects are reflected in the political instability which has plagued a number of multiethnic societies around the world and which contributed with dramatic effect to the breakup of the Soviet Union, Czechoslovakia, and Yugoslavia, the disintegration of the Somali state, the protracted bloodletting in Lebanon, and to endemic political tensions in countries such as Northern Ireland, Uganda, Spain, Cameroon, Sri Lanka, Sudan, Canada, Nigeria, and Belgium, to name a few. The negative effects of ethnicity overshadow the positive effects because they are usually more dramatic and have graver consequences for the survival of the nation-state concerned. This explains why a great deal of effort is put in combating ethnicity inspite of its positive aspects. However, an effective struggle against ethnicity must be based on an adequate understanding of the phenomenon.

The Emergence of Ethnicity. Attempts to understand ethnicity fail when they conceive of it in self-explanatory manner; when they place emphasis on ethnicity as an epiphenomenon with very little account taken of its substratum. Analysts often believe that interests arising from the various ethnic identities differ from one another because of the differences among the ethnic groups. Hardly any thought is given to how and why individuals embrace ethnic identity in the first place, the origin of the ethnic group interest, and the similarity in both interests and characteristics across various ethnic groups. There is clear evidence of interethnic harmony in spite of interethnic differences.

On the other hand, it is becoming increasingly clear that ethnicity emerges as a result of pervasive anxiety associated with very rapid changes and structural transformations, the consequent rupture of traditional solidarities, the forcible transformation of cultures, the oppressive homogenization of cultures, and the emergence of a pervasive sense of losing control of one's affairs even in the case of the most powerful actors. In reaction to the threat thus posed, ethnicity emerges and intensifies as individuals embrace primary identities such as ethnic identity. This preference for primary identities arises from the generalized and cultural nature of the threat, which demands nothing but the crystallization of the self holistically. This is precisely what primary identities do.

State violence is the critical element in the consummation of this threat. In the absence of a democratic culture, state violence is used to force through rapid structural changes in the processes of state building and development. This violence is often not provoked. It occurs in the routine business of projecting power to realize vested interests and sustain domination.

It usually does not arise from articulated and perceived differences between the state and its victims. The differences emerge ex post facto from the coercive unilateralism of the state. Eventually a competitive opposition arises ex post facto from the blatant abuse of power in a process in which the reckless projection of power accumulates a critical mass of desperate enemies.

Ethnicity emerges, persists, and intensifies where there is a conjuncture of physical insecurity, arising from state repression, and socioeconomic insecurity, arising from the failure of state socioeconomic policies. It is remarkable for ethnicity and ethnic conflict that these two conflict-prone activities, state repression and the failure of socioeconomic policies, are simultaneously and widely occurring in Africa. And they are doing so within the context of an international environment which is extremely threatening to Africa, and an African domestic situation in which the constant failure of collective endeavors, as well as intensifying poverty and inequality, immensely compound and confound the rigors of existence. Such circumstances in Africa and elsewhere in the world render people edgy, aggressive, and available for mobilization into violent social movements, including ethnic movements. The resultant emergence and intensification of ethnicity renders violent ethnic conflicts highly probable.

The conjuncture of state building and development has given rise in various parts of the world to massive population shifts, created new notions of *citizenship, fundamentally altered the structures of economic opportunity, unleashed a dynamic of class formation at the urban and rural levels, and reshaped the perception, goals, and methods of political and economic actors. The centralization of state power through *one-party system regimes, authoritarian communist rule, military dictatorship, and even authoritarian multiparty regime, the persistence of a zero-sum competition to monopolize, that power, the intensification of the depth of corruption and primitive accumulation, massive changes in the agrarian sector, the intensification of the processes of class formation and consolidation, and reliance on coercion rather than legitimacy to hold the people together are causing anxiety and cultural threat to the population.

This is reinforced by developments in international relations. *Globalization is bringing everyone in the world into closer proximity, shrinking everything into one small intimate space to be fought over incessantly. It has created a highly charged competitive economic environment that causes a great deal of anxiety even for the winners. Such anxiety is further compounded by the increasing openness of boundaries, which exposes everyone, everywhere, to the unblinking view and judgment of a global society. Shrinking physical space, increasing proximity, and enforced intimacy cause tension and anxiety by crowding people into even smaller space with all their differences and mutual suspicions intact. Even when it tries to induce common values, as, for example, through the global market, globalization does not reduce the tension; if anything, it increases tension by inducing convergence on the same values and focusing demand on the same scarce resources.

The conjuncture of these internal and external environments is increasing ethnicity as well as ethnic consciousness, and consequently these processes foster a tendency toward the decomposition of the nation-state into linguistic, religious, and ethnic components. This decomposition is reflected in the dismemberment of the Soviet Union, Czechoslovakia, Ethiopia, Somalia, and the Comoros. The ruptures, tension, and uncertainties generated by this conjuncture nurture an orientational upheaval, which the abstract universalism of civil identity in the nation-state cannot contain. This upheaval elicits particularistic but holistic cultural identities including ethnic identity. As is clearly illustrated by Yugoslavia and Somalia, these identity switches tend to be associated with violent implosions.

Thus when we focus on state violence as the fundamental cause of ethnicity, some of the established knowledge of ethnic conflict and the means of ethnic conflict resolution are no longer useful. It is no longer possible to confuse the symptoms such as ethnicity, religion, and nationality, which are manipulated by politicians and activists, with the fundamental causes of conflict, especially elite strategies of power, the enormous premium on the control of the state, the arrogant use of state power, the immensity of this power, its proneness to misuse and abuse, and its lack of neutrality in social struggles. The focus of analysis and understanding shifts from cleavages such as ethnic, religious, and linguistic differences to such issues as political *legitimacy, governance, *human rights, citizenship, armaments, and arms trade.

Resolving the Ethnic Problem. Various policies have been implemented to solve the problem of ethnicity but without success. They include separate development for the various groups, with as little contact with other groups as possible. It is reflected in the colonial policy of "Sabongari" in northern Nigeria by which not only the southerners but also the northern migrants were forced to live apart from the local population. In *apartheid South Africa it took the form of the "Bantustan" policy, in Zimbabwe and South Africa the policy of "townships" by which Africans lived separately from whites in designated black townships. In the rest of colonial Africa whites lived in "European quarters" far away from the African residential areas. Another colonial policy was indirect rule, which permitted each ethnic group to sustain its particular heritage within an administrative unit of its own.

Other policies include the centralization of state power in a unitary form of government in order to be able to contain the centrifugal forces of ethnicity. The one-part-system follows a similar logic, seeking to shift emphasis away from ethnicity onto more integrative national issues than the multiparty system which exerts very little control over party programs, policies, and mobilization activities. *Federalism is another policy. Through the decentralization and devolution of state power to ethnic groups it hopes to dilute ethnicity and fashion a cohesive society.

Secession has been tried as a solution to ethnicity in many countries of the world. It demands separate statehood for an ethnic group that feels oppressed within the boundaries of its original state. Similar to secession, irredentism is a declaration of the failure to manage ethnicity within an existing state. An ethnic group within the state then demands to be united with its kith and kin in a neighboring state. Both secession and irredentism often involve violence because forces which control the original state and insist on its sovereignty and territorial integrity usually oppose their demands.

However, the most common response to ethnicity has been the group of policies associated with "ethnic arithmetic," "ethnic balancing," "federal character," and power sharing. Its guiding light is the representation of various ethnic groups and subgroups in the decision-making process of government. In South Africa it found an acclaimed expression in the power-sharing arrangement that attended the 1994 post-apartheid elections. But sometimes the system of proportional electoral representation is also used to diffuse ethnic tension by ensuring adequate political representation for the various ethnic groups. At other times regulatory policies are employed such as the imposition of a two-party system in Nigeria by the Babangida military dictatorship. The object is to keep ethnicity away from public view. Finally, symbolic policies seek to diffuse ethnicity by integrating ethnic groups in common endeavors, through the conceptualization and pursuit of common concerns. Examples include "Ujamaa" in Tanzania, "Harambee" in Kenya, and "Ethiopia Tikdem" (Ethiopia First) in Ethiopia under Mengistu.

These policies have so far failed to contain ethnicity. This is because their single-minded emphasis on the differences among ethnic groups as the critical explanatory variable of ethnicity neglects the fundamental role of the undemocratic state in galvanizing these differences into hostile activities. If the undemocratic state is responsible for the ethnicity that breeds ethnic violence, then the solution to ethnicity must start with a thoroughgoing democratization of the state. The objective of this democratization should not be limited to that of liberal *democracy, much less that of its variant, multiparty democracy. Instead, it must be a form of democracy which links the political and economic needs of the people, a social democracy that views economic regression as the other side of political regression. As a form of democracy that is motivated by the people's yearnings for popular empowerment, it must emphasize concrete and social *rights rather than abstract political rights.

Driven by the social base of the society, this democracy of popular empowerment will find unique institutional forms in accordance with the historical conditions of the people. It will entail decision-making power over and above the formal consent of electoral choice. It will go beyond individualism to cooperation, beyond having consent taken to actually giving it, beyond seeking freedom in competition and cultural alienation to finding solidarity and cultural fulfillment. As a democracy that expresses the historical conditions of the people, it will recognize and reflect cultural pluralism. As such it will have to recognize nationalities, subnationalities, ethnic groups, and communities as social formations that express the desire for freedom and self-realization, and grant them rights to cultural expression and political and economic participation. How this will be concretized will vary from state to state in accordance with variations in the balance of forces in the struggle for democracy.

In general, however, such a democracy should guarantee the rights of the members of each ethnic group to be secure in their lives and property, as well as secure from arbitrary arrest and punishment, and for them to enjoy equal opportunity in real terms in trade, business, employment, education, the enjoyment of social amenities, and in the growth of their peculiar culture. It should encourage the recognition of the equal rights of all ethnic groups and discourage ethnic privileges and nepotism.

Thus ethnicity can only be attenuated by the consistent application of democratic principles, norms, values, and procedures in socioeconomic and political life. Only a policy that is based on clear, consistent, and democratic principle is realistic in the search for solutions to ethnic problems. Such a policy must appraise each concrete ethnic demand from the perspective of removing all inequality, all privileges, and all exclusiveness. Democracy is vital for interethnic harmony.

(See also BOSNIAN WAR; CLASS AND POLITICS; KOSOVO WAR; MULTICULTURALISM; NATIONALISM; POLITICAL VIOLENCE; RACE AND RACISM; RELIGION AND POLITICS; SECESSIONIST MOVEMENTS.)

A. Mafeje, "The Ideology of Tribalism" *Journal of Modern African Studies* 9, no. 2 (1977): 253–262. D. Horowitz, *Ethnic Groups in Conflict* (Berkeley, Calif., 1985). J. V. Montville, ed., *Conflict and Peacemaking in Multiethnic Societies* (Lexington, Mass., 1990). P. Van de Berghe, *State Violence and Ethnicity* (Niwot, Colo., 1990). T. R. Gurr, *Minorities at Risk: A Global View of Ethnopolitics* (Washington D.C., 1993). H. Glickman, ed., *Ethnic Conflict and Democratization in Africa* (Atlanta, 1995). O. Nnoli, *Ethnicity and Development in Nigeria* (Aldershot, U.K., 1995). R. Stevenhagen, *Ethnic Conflict and the Nation-State* (London, 1996).

OKWUDIBA NNOLI

Court's desire to work with, rather than to confront, its allies in the national courts. The Court's future role close to the center of the process of European integration seems assured. One example of its persisting vigor is found in the Amsterdam Treaty, which extended its jurisdiction part of the way into the non-EC pillars of the EU from which it had been almost wholly excluded by the Maastricht Treaty.

(See also EUROPEAN UNION; INTERNATIONAL COURT OF JUSTICE.)

Renaud Dehousse, *The European Court of Justice* (Basingstoke, U.K., 1998).

STEVEN WEATHERILL

EUROPEAN PARLIAMENT. See EUROPEAN UNION.

EUROPEAN UNION. The European Union (EU) is the most recent name for the organizations of European integration which began after *World War II. After centuries of conflict, culminating in the murderous first half of the twentieth century, Europe was clearly in need of a new beginning. A unique postwar setting provided the context. The defeat of the Axis powers left Europe broke, destroyed, vulnerable, divided, and occupied militarily. The power of the United States in the *Cold War and Europe's need to reconstruct created new incentives for Western European nations to commit to democracy and reconsider their relationships.

The First Period. The first step came in 1950, when Jean *Monnet persuaded French Foreign Minister Robert Schuman to propose a "common market" in the coal and steel industries in response to American insistence on rehabilitating Germany. The result was the European Coal and Steel Community (ECSC), established in 1952, with the six members—France, Germany, Italy, Belgium, the Netherlands, and Luxembourg—who would later form the European Economic Community (EEC). The British, determined to sustain the *Commonwealth, stayed out. Institutionally the ECSC had a "High Authority" of appointed officials with considerable supranational power, checked mainly by a council of ministers from the member states.

The momentum established by ECSC was momentarily broken when ratification of a European Defense Community, designed as way of responding to American insistence on German rearmament, was rejected by the French parliament in 1954. New talks eventuated in 1957 in the Treaties of Rome that founded the European Economic Community (EEC, a suggestion that originated among the small Benelux countries) and Euratom (a European atomic energy agency). The EEC treaty, signed by the ECSC six, announced great ambitions for the creation of a unified Europe flowing from the integration of economic activities. The British, yet again, abstained from participating.

The Rome Treaties outlined a first period in which EEC members would establish a customs-free internal market zone surrounded by a single external tariff with other common policy areas, including a Common Agricultural Policy (CAP) designed to promote agricultural modernization—something upon which the French insisted. These matters were to be run from Brussels, designated as the EEC's administrative center, by an appointed supranational commission which was as-

signed the jobs of proposing and implementing legislation and enforcing the treaties. The new EEC's institutional structure, which resembled that of the ECSC, had a legislative arm to vote commission proposals up or down in the form of a Council of Ministers from member states. Provisions were also made for a *European Court of Justice (ECJ) in Luxembourg to build up a body of European law binding on member states through adjudication and litigation. Finally, there was a weak parliamentary assembly whose members were appointed by member state governments.

The goals for the first period were reached even earlier than the treaty itself had envisaged, but not without difficulties. The British, having failed to persuade the EEC's original six to sign less ambitious arrangements for a free trade zone, then founded a European Free Trade Area (EFTA) in 1960 to compete with the EEC. EFTA, which eschewed the supranational goals of the EEC, enrolled Austria, Denmark, Norway, Sweden, Portugal, and Switzerland (with Finland and Iceland joining later). Then when the EEC quickly gathered strength, which the British had not expected, the United Kingdom applied to join. French President De *Gaulle vetoed their application in 1963, however, and again in 1966, denouncing the British as insufficiently "European" and too closely tied to the United States.

Behind this were French convictions about what the EEC should be. In geopolitical terms, de Gaulle wanted it to become a "third force" in international affairs, an international pole between the two Cold War superpowers. He also sought to ensure French power within an EEC through insistence upon intergovernmental, not supranational, methods. Thus when European Commission President Walter Hallstein proposed budgetary steps which de Gaulle perceived as overly supranational there followed a major confrontation over European governance, leading to a withdrawal of France—the "empty chair" crisis—from participation in the Council of Ministers for six months in 1965. The Rome Treaty had projected eventual Council of Ministers decision making by a "qualified majority" of votes (with votes weighted to reflect the size of member states). French obduracy led to the 1966 "Luxembourg Compromise" in which any member state could veto a proposal that it judged inimical to its basic interests. For the next two decades the EEC was de facto intergovernmental and advances to supranationality were blocked.

The intergovernmentalist equilibrium struck at this point reflected deeper realities. The EEC was a "Common Market" between separate national economies. EEC member states, for the most part, were pursuing national economic strategies. The EEC provided them new outlets for trade, gave them some protection from the outside world, in particular from a United States pressing constantly for further trade liberalization, and a painless way of modernizing agriculture through the CAP. Further supranationalization might have deprived EEC member states of the economic tools to steer their national economies.

Crises. De Gaulle's resignation in 1969 allowed a burst of new energy. The European Parliament gained new budgetary powers, plans were drawn up for "economic and monetary union" (the Werner Report of 1970), an EEC-wide social policy, and a more ambitious regional development policy. Moreover, there was a first enlargement involving four ex-EFTA members—United Kingdom, Ireland, Denmark, and Portugal (there might have been five, but the Norwegians voted against in a referendum). Any British illusions that that EFTA would be a rival to the EEC had clearly faded, but lack of British enthusiasm for EEC supranationalism persisted.

The new energy did not produce as much as might have been anticipated. The EEC's economic situation had changed abruptly in the mid-1970s. Chronic inflation in EEC member states was compounded by the oil shocks of 1973 and 1979 and was accompanied by rising unemployment. The U.S. abandonment of the Bretton Woods international monetary system fed international currency instability which threatened the Common Market. The most significant problems, however, flowed from the divergent economic choices of EEC members in response to these new economic challenges. One symptom was the rise in nontariff barriers in intra-EEC trade. Finally, integrating the new members was difficult, particularly because the British, having struck a bad bargain to enter, obstinately demanded renegotiation. Prime Minister *Thatcher, elected in 1979, thus insisted stridently upon a rebate of part of the United Kingdom's financial contribution as a prerequisite for any significant new EEC decisions, blocking the Brussels machinery.

As Japan and the Asian "tigers" became new economic competitors and the United States started the massive technological shift permitted by innovations in electronics, European economic growth stagnated and unemployment rose. Another indication of the EEC's difficulties was that most initiatives in the 1970s resulted from bilateral talks between heads of state and government rather than the new European institutions. Monetary instability threatened the entire Common Market, for example, but it took close collaboration between German Chancellor Schmidt and French President Giscard d'Estaing to found a new European Monetary System (EMS). In EMS the currencies of countries choosing to belong to the "exchange rate mechanism" (ERM) were kept within "bands" of variation around a specific valuation formulae, but not all EEC members belonged to the ERM. Nonetheless EMS and monetary integration were central to subsequent developments. In these years the French president also formalized biannual summits of heads of state and government—later called European Councils—which became the source of strategic guidance to other European institutions and introduced further high-level intergovernmentalism into the EU system. The final major innovation was the beginning of direct election to the European Parliament in 1979, a step toward grounding the parliament's credibility in response to growing criticism about the "democratic deficit" of European institutions.

The Great Renewal. The early 1980s were a low point. Member states could not agree on much of anything, and as "Europessimism" spread unresolved problems piled up. A major recession began in 1979, stretching well into the 1980s. After elections brought the Left to power in 1981, the French tried to respond to this with a new program of national economic voluntarism and redistributive reform which was at odds with the policies of other EEC members. The monetary effects of this had come to threaten the existence of EMS by 1983. In response, rather than deal a potentially fatal blow to European integration French President *Mitterrand reversed

French policies. EMS survived while the French joined others in adopting tough policies to combat inflation. The French choice was as much for Europe as it was for a changed economic policy. With new policy convergence it was possible to settle many of the big issues on the EU's table. A solution was quickly brokered for the "British check" problem, stalled negotiations about Spanish and Portuguese membership were regenerated, leading to accession in 1986, and a new commission and commission president, Jacques Delors, were appointed.

The Delors Commission set immediately to work with a white paper to "complete the Single Market" by the end of 1992. The paper set out several hundred measures to make a single integrated European economy out of the interconnected national economies in the Common Market. Agreement on this was facilitated by desires for market liberalization among major EU members, including the British. Thus a multilateral Intergovernmental Conference (IGC) was quickly convened to change existing EU treaties to facilitate implementation of the "1992" program, concluding in the Single European Act (SEA, ratified in 1987). The SEA, the first in a series of revisions to the European "constitution" (i.e., its treaties), brought "qualified majority" voting on Single Market programs, amending powers to the parliament, new environmental policies, more coordinated European research and development programs, regional redistribution, and social policy. Rapid action occurred in all of these areas. More ambitious research and development goals were set and more funding provided. The "structural funds" for regional development were doubled in the five-year period as a result of the 1987 "Delors package" on budgetary matters, and doubled again in the early 1990s. A "social charter" proposing a wide range of new European social policy initiatives, tabled in 1989, was implemented in the 1990s in a comprehensive "Action Program."

The next large step was *Economic and Monetary Union (EMU). The Delors Report on EMU was approved in 1989 and two new IGCs were scheduled to begin in later 1990. The first was to adapt existing treaties for EMU and the second, a German suggestion, was to discuss "political union" focusing on democratic accountability and responsibility, the powers of the European Parliament in particular, plus foreign policy cooperation. The *Maastricht Treaty on European Union, ratified in 1993, was the result, setting out daring new priorities. EU member states agreed to pool sovereignty over monetary policy in an independent European Central Bank (ECB) committed to price stability and a single European currency, later named the euro, by 1999. Maastricht also set the EU toward establishing a Common Foreign and Security Policy (CSFP), common policies in matters of justice and home affairs, and greatly increased the powers of the European parliament by allowing "codecision" with the Council of Ministers.

Another IGC, to review the workings of Maastricht, produced the Amsterdam Treaty. Signed in 1997, it further extended and simplified "codecision," added new clauses on social policy, modified procedures for the CFSP, moved parts of Maastricht's intergovernmental "third pillar" on justice and home affairs into the Community "first pillar," and inserted new provisions on flexible participation by member states in EU matters. A fourth IGC began in 1999 to focus upon adapting EU institutions in the light of pending enlargement. Such an accumulation of multilateral conferences to rewrite the EU treaty base was no accident. Europe is clearly engaged in a major constitution-writing exercise that will stretch well into the next millennium.

Europe in the New Millennium. European integration is one of the great political success stories of the second half of the twentieth century. There has been lasting peace in the EU area, no small accomplishment in itself. European nations have pooled major dimensions of their sovereignty and tied their destinies together. In the economic realm there has been extensive, and quite unique, federalization. There is a genuine single market and market regulation, a single monetary policy, and a single currency. In other important areas, taxation and social policy, member states retain substantial powers. The "mix" seems to work. The EU has become a magnet and beacon for aspiring new democracies, and the Union's achievements to this point are impressive indeed. Three formerly authoritarian countries, Spain, Portugal, and Greece, have modernized and consolidated democratic polities with EU help and inspiration. Ireland, another new member, has been changed economically and socially beyond recognition. The EU has managed its complex ally–rival relationships with the United States with skill. EU institutions, initially experimental and repeatedly remodeled, have done their jobs.

The agenda for the new century is nonetheless challenging. The EU has pledged to enlarge its membership to qualified formerly communist nations of Central and Eastern Europe, and the Union could well double its membership by 2010. This will make Europe the single largest market in the world in GDP terms, but it presents new challenges. As earlier, EU enlargement is not simply the extension of economic arrangements. The union also must bear responsibility for laying solid foundations for thriving democratic societies. The institutional structures of the union will have to be scrutinized anew to maximize their contributions to a democratic future, in the midst of persistent discontent about a "democratic deficit" and indications of flagging public support. The EU's economy needs to incorporate the innovations of the "information society," to grow and to alleviate unacceptable levels of unemployment. Some of the adjustments to make this happen will be painful. The population of EU member states is aging, creating new and unprecedented strains on national social programs and budgets. Coping is primarily a national matter, but the EU will have a significant coordinating role. Finally, the EU, which is rapidly becoming a political union, is also an actor of growing importance in international affairs, almost despite itself. Does the EU really want to have a focused foreign and defense policy? The CFSP has begun to pick up momentum, in part in response to the weaknesses revealed in the crises of Bosnia and Kosovo. How strong is Europe's political will in this area? Can Europe become a more serious partner of the United States through NATO, and what will this do to transatlantic relations? The euro is fast establishing the EU as a monetary and financial rival to the United States, creating more challenges for transatlantic relations. The EU success story may continue into the new millennium, but only if European energy to do so can be sustained.

(See also ROME, TREATY OF.)

Francois Duchne, *Jean Monnet* (New York, 1994). Stanley Hoffmann, *The European Sisyphus* (Boulder, Colo., 1994). Timothy Bainbridge, *The Penguin Companion to European Union*, 2d ed. (London, 1998). Desmond Dinan, *Ever Closer Union*, 2d ed. (Boulder, Colo., 1999). Andrew Moravosik, *The Choice for Europe* (Ithaca, N.Y., 1999). J. H. H. Weiler, *The Constitution of Europe* (Cambridge, U.K., 1999).

GEORGE ROSS

EXPORT-LED GROWTH. Classical and neoclassical economists have consistently emphasized the gains from international trade. Adam Smith argued that trade provided a "vent" for surplus productive capacity, and David Ricardo's model of comparative advantage showed the gains from economic specialization. Trade was also held to have a number of dynamic effects, contributing to growth in the long run. Export industries could be the leading sector in the economy, growing more rapidly than other sectors and thereby serving as an "engine" of growth.

The first theory of export-led growth emerged from studies of the economic history of the land-abundant "countries of recent settlement," particularly Canada, Australia, and Argentina. This "staple" theory held that the discovery of a primary product in which a country has comparative advantage would have a number of positive effects on the exporting country: attracting capital inflows and labor; establishing linkages with other sectors; inducing innovation, increases in productivity, and infrastructural development; opening the economy to the transfer of technology and skills; and contributing to higher levels of capital accumulation.

Critics argued that these beneficial mechanisms had not operated for a majority of developing countries. Export-led growth did not create dynamic linkages within the economy, in part because foreign ownership of export activities, such as mining or plantation agriculture, resulted in a transfer of profits out of the exporting country. The expected dynamic effects of trade also depended on the product being exported. Learning, technological innovation, and linkages were considered more likely in manufacturing than in agriculture or mining.

Second, an export orientation exposed developing countries to adverse international shocks and increased their dependence on the international system. Declining terms of trade for tropical products were held to perpetuate or even increase international economic inequality. In the short run, dependence on exports exposed countries to price volatility, which was particularly damaging in countries specialized in one or a narrow range of export products. Finally, dependence on exports created possible political vulnerabilities because more powerful developed-country importers could manipulate trade relations as a means of exercising political influence.

These arguments were not without merit, and helped explain why some countries had not benefited from trade to the expected extent. Moreover, they had a profound political and ideological influence in the *Third World, providing the justification for the pursuit of *import-substitution industrialization through protectionist trade policies. These arguments also provided the rationale for political efforts in the 1970s to institutionalize a New International Economic Order (NIEO) that would offset the disadvantages of export dependence through trade preferences and international commodity agreements.

Yet as general propositions, the critical arguments did not hold up well. The applicability of the staple theory was admittedly limited, but agricultural exports had contributed to growth in some circumstances. The commodity boom and oil price increases of the early 1970s showed that international price trends could favor producers of primary products and that developing countries could rewrite investment contracts to their advantage. The establishment of linkages through the processing of tropical products was also not ruled out. Nor were countries as vulnerable to short-run price fluctuations as had been thought; the critical issue was how to design mechanisms for smoothing the financial and fiscal impact of price fluctuations.

Through the 1960s, the debate about export-led growth centered almost exclusively on the advantages and disadvantages of trade in traditional tropical products: foodstuffs, agricultural raw materials, and ores, minerals, and metals. Yet by the mid-1960s, a number of developing countries began to expand their exports of manufactured products, setting in motion a new round of debate about trade policy.

These countries fell into two groups. In the first were large Latin American countries that had industrialized through import-substituting policies, including Argentina, Brazil, and Mexico. In response to *balance of payments problems, these countries sought to expand their exports of manufactured goods. The policies used to accomplish this objective included exchange rate devaluation, selective import liberalization for exporters, subsidies and tax rebates, and incentives for foreign firms to expand their exports. Some countries, such as Brazil, were successful in diversifying their export structures, not only in light, labor-intensive manufactures but in intermediate and processed raw materials.

In general, however, these policy reforms did not result in a shift toward an export-led growth model. Incentives remained biased toward import-substituting activities, and export-promotion policies were applied inconsistently. Although there was some increase in trade, these economies remained relatively closed and did not generate adequate foreign exchange through exports to service their mounting external debt.

The second group of countries were the East Asian newly industrializing countries (NICs): the Republic of Korea (South Korea), Taiwan, Hong Kong, and Singapore. These countries developed dynamic export sectors beginning in the 1960s. The transition to an export orientation varied somewhat from country to country. Hong Kong and Singapore were historically entrepôt economies, dominated by commerce and service industries. When export growth began in the 1950s in Hong Kong, it came mainly from textile and apparel firms that had fled the Communist revolution in China. In Singapore, by contrast, the export takeoff did not begin until the late 1960s and was almost completely dependent on export-oriented foreign firms.

Korea and Taiwan both had developed fledgling manufacturing sectors during the period of Japanese occupation and through import-substituting policies in the 1950s. Both countries undertook important policy reforms in the early 1960s that marked a change of strategy, including exchange rate devaluations, selective import liberalization, efforts to attract foreign direct investment, as well as other government supports to exporters.

Despite their differences, these four countries shared a number of common features. All were resource-poor countries with relatively abundant supplies of well-educated labor. All exploited their comparative advantage in light, labor-intensive manufactures. But over time, they gradually diversified into technology-, skill-, and even capital-intensive goods in response to rising labor costs, international competitive pressures, and growing protection in their advanced country markets. All depended heavily on the U.S. market. Most significantly, all grew extremely rapidly and managed to do so while maintaining relatively egalitarian distributions of income.

The success of East Asian NICs has generated a number of important controversies. The most central one concerns the role of policy in their rapid economic growth. Neoclassical economists have stressed the pursuit of market-oriented policy reforms and a stable macroeconomic environment as the most important sources of growth. The export takeoff followed changes of trade policy in South Korea and Taiwan, generating a virtuous cycle from higher exports to higher savings and investment, technological innovation and learning, and higher growth.

The critique of the neoclassical position has come from a diverse group of political scientists, economists, and sociologists who place greater emphasis on the institutional setting. They have underlined that export-led growth was not a function of the market alone but was accompanied in Korea, Taiwan, and Singapore by a variety of state interventions, including continuing state ownership of industry, trade protection in a number of sectors, subsidies, and the development of substantial trade bureaucracies to monitor performance and provide information to exporters. Moreover, incentives to investment were as important as incentives to export. Second, all shared a number of particular political features that facilitated the transition to export-oriented policies, including weak or repressed labor movements, weak leftist parties, strong "developmentalist" bureaucracies, and authoritarian political leaderships.

A second controversy surrounds the role of foreign direct investment and globalization in NIC growth and exports. Critics contended that the new export-led growth models based on manufactures resulted in dual economies just as the old export-led growth had, with export enclaves dominated by foreign firms. Lowered transport costs allowed multinational corporations to transfer the labor-intensive portion of the production chain "offshore" to low-wage countries. This "new international division of labor" had minimal effects in terms of technology transfer or linkages with the domestic economy. In fact, with the exception of Singapore, export-led growth in East Asia has not been the result of foreign investment but of domestic firms, and the share of foreign firms in total exports has fallen. Moreover, foreign investment has contributed to indigenous technological capabilities.

A third controversy concerns the revival of export pessimism. Skeptics have argued that the East Asian NICs grew rapidly because of buoyant international conditions. When world trade growth slows and more and more developing countries expand their exports, export-led growth may be less viable or profitable than it was in the past. The export-oriented NICs have also been the major targets of the "new protectionism."

Critics of the new export pessimism have responded by noting that the NICs have generally been able to circumvent protectionist restrictions through industrial upgrading. For example, the East Asian NICs have continued to export textiles and apparel by focusing on high-quality niches, while simultaneously shifting to more capital- and technology-intensive goods, such as autos South (Korea) and computer peripherals (Taiwan and Singapore).

By the end of the 1980s, there were substantial pressures on most developing and socialist countries to expand their exports, including large debt burdens, the declining availability of commercial lending, and the inefficiencies associated with import-substituting and autarkic models of development. A wave of trade reform and export promotion swept the Third World, and a new tier of exporters emerged in Southeast Asia, Latin America, and Eastern Europe.

The Asian financial crisis of 1997–1998 generated fresh controversy about the sources of East Asia's export dynamism and whether it was sustainable. However, the crisis only blunted East Asia's export capabilities in the short run and ultimately reinforced the need for increased foreign investment and outward-oriented trade strategy.

(See also DEVELOPMENT AND UNDERDEVELOPMENT; NEWLY INDUSTRIALIZING ECONOMIES; PROTECTION.)

Bela Balassa, *The Newly Industrializing Countries in the World Economy* (New York, 1981). David Yoffie, *Power and Protectionism: Strategies of the Newly Industrializing Countries* (New York, 1983). Stephan Haggard, *Pathways from the Periphery: The Politics of Growth in the Newly Industrializing Countries* (Ithaca, N.Y., 1990). Dan Rodrik, "Getting Interventions Right: How South Korea and Taiwan Grew Rich" *Economic Policy* 20 (April 1995): 55–107.

STEPHAN HAGGARD

F

FALKLANDS WAR. See Malvinas/Falklands War.

FAMINE. A famine is a sudden and localized increase in human death caused physically by inadequate consumption of food. Famines tend to come and go quickly. In this regard they differ from chronic undernutrition, a condition that affects many more people on a continuous basis. The Food and Agriculture Organization (FAO) of the United Nations estimates that more than 800 million people worldwide are now suffering from chronic undernutrition. Chronic malnutrition is usually a reflection of material poverty, landlessness, or low social status. The malnourished suffer from impaired health, reduced physical strength, diminished mental alertness, and high rates of infant mortality. Famine affects many fewer people, but it can be a more dramatic condition, because it brings a sudden and often quite concentrated increase in adult as well as infant mortality.

Three distinct schools of thought dominate the contemporary study of famine. The first approach links famine to a physical decline in food availability, from natural disasters such as drought or crop disease. Impacts of drought on regional food availability can be severe. In 1991–92, grain yields in the ten states of the *Southern African Development Community (SADC) were only 56 percent of normal due to scant rainfall, and regional stockpiles were inadequate to cover the shortage. Cereal production fell by 60 percent in Malawi and Swaziland, and by more than 70 percent in Namibia and Zimbabwe, placing 17–20 million people at risk of starvation.

Criticism of this Food Availability Decline (FAD) approach has been offered by Amartya Sen, who argues from historical evidence—especially from the Great Bengal Famine of 1943—that mass starvation can take place even when the total quantity of food available within a country has not declined. Sen argued that "entitlement" to food was more important than physical availability, and that when food entitlements are based on exchanges of labor for wages to purchase food, essential entitlements can be taken away even when food is abundant, simply by an adverse shift in the price of food relative to the price or availability of wage labor. Sen's approach provided a powerful explanation for why in many famines some starve (e.g., landless laborers) while others in the same district or village do not. Sen's approach also helps explain why starvations were largely avoided in the SADC drought of 1991–92. On that occasion international relief agencies were able to replace normal food entitlements by more than doubling their shipments of food aid to the region.

A third approach looks to political malfunction, beyond both natural disasters and adverse market shifts. This approach notices that the most devastating famines of the twentieth century were brought on either by warfare or by state policies weak in political accountability to the rural poor.

International warfare was a prominent source of famine during the first half of the twentieth century, most conspicuously during the German blockade of Leningrad in 1941–42, when more than 600,000 people died of starvation. More recently, internal warfare has dominated as a cause of famine in sub-Saharan Africa. Among the most affected countries have been Somalia, Sudan, Ethiopia, and Mozambique. When internal war breaks out, armies or militia bands will steal or destroy food crops and food shipments, including relief shipments. Farming activities will be interrupted, as physical insecurity pushes people off the land, or reduces the incentive to plant crops (for fear that they will be stolen or destroyed). Countries experiencing conflict in Africa on average have produced 12.4 percent less food per capita in war years than in peacetime. Large numbers of rural people become internally displaced, separated from their normal food entitlements, and often beyond the reach of international relief. Where internal war is not under way (as in the 1991–92 SADC case), food aid to drought stricken regions can be highly effective in preventing famine. Where violent conflict is taking place (as in southern Sudan in 1986–88, or in Somalia in 1991–92) international relief often cannot reach those at risk, and starvation among displaced people cannot be avoided. Over the past thirty years, 7 million Africans have died fighting, perhaps 6 million more have been made international refugees, and 16 million more have been internally displaced.

Scholars agree that violent conflict can lead to hunger, but they do not yet agree on whether hunger leads to violent conflict. Most efforts to attribute recent violent conflicts in regions such as Africa to hunger (or to other kinds of resource scarcity) have failed to give parallel attention to the many more obvious explanations that are available to explain violent conflict in Africa—such as poorly drawn postcolonial boundaries or ethnic competition for control of the state.

Threats from violent conflict notwithstanding, state policies lacking in political accountability to the rural poor were the most devastating cause of famine throughout the twentieth century. In the Soviet Union in 1932–34, at least 6 million excess deaths occurred in Ukraine as a result of Stalin's forced collectivization and food extraction policies. In the People's Republic of China in 1959–62, Mao Zedong's Great Leap Forward policy led to a massive famine, with over 15 million excess deaths due to disrupted production and excessive state procurements from the countryside. Amartya Sen later contrasted this Chinese calamity to an avoidance of famine in India in 1965–66, when the monsoon rains failed two years in a row. Sen inferred that press freedom and democracy helped, in India, to pressure government officials into a timely response. Lack of press freedom and democracy helps, in this regard, to explain the last significant famine of the twentieth century, the one that struck the Democratic People's Republic of Korea (North Korea) after 1995.

(See also DEVELOPMENT AND UNDERDEVELOPMENT; EQUALITY AND INEQUALITY; FOOD POLITICS.)

Amartya Sen, *Poverty and Famines: An Essay on Entitlement and Deprivation* (Oxford, 1981). Robert Conquest, *Harvest of Sorrow: Soviet Collectivization and the Terror-Famine* (New York, 1986). Francis M. Deng and Larry Minear, *The Challenges of Famine Relief* (Washington, D.C., 1992). Jean Dreze, Amartya Sen, and Athar Hussain, *The Political Economy of Hunger* (Oxford, 1995).

ROB PAARLBERG

FANON, Frantz. Frantz Fanon was born in Martinique, French Antilles, in 1925 and died in 1961. After his initial education in Martinique, he studied medicine in France, graduating in 1951 and specializing in psychiatry. He practiced psychotherapy in France and was later posted in 1953 to Bilda, Algeria, where he resigned his appointment in 1956 to join forces with the Algerian revolutionary movement to end French colonial rule in Algeria, Front de Liberation Nationale (FLN).

Fanon's major political writings, notably *Black Skin, White Masks* and *Wretched of the Earth*, which had a major, electrifying impact on the politics of black liberation movements in the African diaspora in the 1960s and 1970s and on African liberation movements, continue to be relevant to African and international politics today because of their radical, revisionist adaptation of existentialism, Jung's psychoanalytic theory, and *Marxism to the analysis of race relations and to the effect of *imperialism on African and *Third World politics and development. Racism, violence, colonialism—including internal colonialism, freedom, human rights: these are contemporary global problems, threatening the prospects for world order. They are central themes and concerns in Fanon's political writings, reflecting his concern for the human condition. His relevance to contemporary world politics is reflected in the following ethico-practical issues he raised in his political theory: the commitment and responsibility of the intellectual, the legitimacy of political authority, and the alienating and anomic impact of certain types of political structures on the individual.

There is a timeless force to his analysis of the human predicament in colonial and postcolonial Africa and to his almost prophetic insights into the nature of postcolonial African politics, situated within the context of imperialism as a global phenomenon. Three important areas underscore his continuing relevance.

First, there is his conception of theory as an ethico-culturally grounded, practical, policy-oriented activity, indispensable to the construction of viable political systems, especially in Africa, and the Third World generally. Second, his dialectical analysis of the relationship between racism and imperialism provides insights into the sociology of race relations in plural societies, and the ideology of racial domination and of the role (physical, psychological, and structural) of violence in sustaining that domination. This analysis also provides his moral justification of violence, based on his theory of the economy of violence, as necessary to terminate racial domination and replace it with reciprocity and mutuality. Third, he brought a pioneering class analysis, especially the notions of contradictions and dialectics, as opposed to the mainstream emphasis on *pluralism and structural functionalism in expatriate Africanist social science scholarship, to bear on African politics. As a result, his analysis pointed, with remarkable prescience, to a process of political decay, corruption, economic mismanagement, militarization of politics, and descent into *authoritarianism in postcolonial Africa. Beyond this, Fanon's contribution was in positing a central place and role not only for culture in the development process in Africa but also for *Pan-Africanism as a force for continental unity and development.

(See also COLONIAL EMPIRES; DECOLONIZATION; DEVELOPMENT AND UNDERDEVELOPMENT; RACE AND RACISM.)

Emmanuel Hansen, *Frantz Fanon: Social and Political Thought* (Columbus, Ohio 1977). L. Adele Jinadu, *Fanon: In Search of the African Revolution* (London, 1986).

L. ADELE JINADU

FASCISM. The term *fascism* was first used to identify the political system by which Italy was ruled from 1922 to 1945. It now also refers to a prototype of *totalitarianism and is applied to variations of political systems thought to parallel the Italian model.

The term derives from the Italian *fascio*, a perfectly ordinary word with no more sinister meaning than "bundle," "weight," "group," or "grouping." When used in a political context, the English equivalent would be *league, alliance,* or *union;* the German might be *Bund.*

Contemporaries found fascism difficult to define. Scholars have not fared better: too often they have agreed to use the term without agreeing on what it means. Depending on their viewpoint, scholars have traced fascism's origins to such varied sources as Plato's *Republic,* to Romantic radicals like Rousseau, to conservative philosophers who idealized a strong *state like Fichte and Carlyle, Hegel and Nietzsche. Other scholars have identified protofascist regimes ranging from the French Revolutionary Terror to Napoleon III's Second Empire.

These precedents are useful to indicate that fascism was a unique blend of earlier *ideologies and institutions. Nevertheless, fascism was essentially a creature of *World War I, a response to the revolutionary changes which that conflict brought to European politics, culture, and society. The term came into use at that time, and the two decades between World War I and *World War II have often been described as the "era of fascism." With the defeat of the fascist regimes in World War II, fascism has apparently disappeared as a major political phenomenon, a threat to the international order. Yet, given the right crisis, fascism, or at least fascist-style regimes, could once again emerge.

Fascism has been difficult to define in part because its ideology varied so widely. It was often easier to understand what fascism was against than what it stood for. Fatherland, flag and country, old-fashioned patriotism against the threats of internationalism and the Bolshevik menace constituted the core of fascism's appeal. This fanatic "blood-and-soil" *nationalism was often transmuted into racism, ranging from a generic ethnic pride to a violent, biological racism and *antisemitism, as in the case of Nazi Germany. Fascist ideology also included a romantic, antirational allure, an appeal to the emotions, to a quasi-religious longing for a mystic union of peoples and their prophetic leader. In reaction to the utilitarian liberal state, fascism revived aspirations toward the normative or "ethical state." According to this view, the community existed not simply as a practical convenience but in order to fulfill the individual's ethical and moral potential.

How people perceived these themes depended on the eye of the beholder. Conservatives viewed fascism as a bulwark against Bolshevism or as a middle way between a worn-out liberal capitalism and the communist horror. Radicals viewed fascism as a genuinely revolutionary ideology that would sweep away discredited ideals and institutions and replace them with a new, disciplined, cohesive society.

If fascism is difficult to define as an ideal, it is no easier to delimit in practice. In defining fascism, it is useful to recall the movement's genesis. Fascism originated in Italy after the end of World War I and scored its first big success with *Mussolini's "March on Rome" in 1922. In Italy, fascism was primarily a response to the crisis of the liberal state's political institutions. The Italian prototype spawned wide variations. Every major European country developed at least a fascist party or movement. José Antonio Primo de Rivera's Falangists in Spain, Corneliu Codreanu's Legion of the Archangel Michael in Romania, Action Française and the Croix de Feu in France, Leon Degrelle's Rexists in Belgium, Oswald Mosley's British Union of Fascists in England, Ferencz Szalasi's Arrow Cross movement in Hungary, all claimed to find inspiration in fascism. They drew on the Italian model, or, as often in Eastern Europe, on the Nazis, or a combination of both. Movements or parties, however, did not always blossom into full-blown regimes. In some cases, as in Romania and Hungary, fascism came to power only under the aegis of the World War II Nazi occupation.

Looming as the dominant model after 1933 was the example of Nazi Germany. But the extreme violence, brutality, and racism of the Nazi regime set it apart, and scholars today are still uncertain whether to include the Nazi example under the general rubric of fascism. How little the fascist regimes had in common became evident when Italy and Germany attempted to create a bloc of fascist powers with the Axis (1936) and then contracted a formal *alliance with the Pact of Steel (1939). The union proved to be notoriously awkward and quickly foundered during World War II. Thus, rather than a generic "fascism," it would be more accurate to speak of "fascist-style regimes."

Nevertheless, within wide national variations, fascist states had certain characteristics and aspirations in common. In their political systems, they created police states, *one-party systems led by a charismatic dictator. Their economic systems aimed to develop some form of national *socialism. The government was to play an active role in controlling the economy, but unlike Marxian socialism, the state was not to take over the means of production. Fascist socialism was directed at the interests of the nation, not a particular *class. Fascism also aspired to some form of the corporativist (or corporatist) state. The antagonism between labor and capital, fostered under the liberal state, was to be bridged in the form of corporations. Through these guildlike structures, labor and capital were to find common ground in developing their particular economic sector. Economic interest would sub-

merge or supersede class interest. In *foreign policy, fascist regimes were unabashedly expansionist and imperialist. Mussolini revived Italy's vision of African colonial empire. *Hitler's Third Reich aspired to a great Volkisch empire in Poland, Russia, and the Ukraine. Hungarian fascists dreamed of dominating the Danube basin; Spanish Falangists coveted African possessions and perhaps even hoped to reannex Portugal.

Given its many forms in ideology and practice, interpretations of fascism have also varied widely. Historically, four major interpretations can be distinguished: fascism as the crisis of the liberal state, as *totalitarianism, as the radical right, as a revolt against *modernity.

In the 1920s and 1930s, many contemporaries quite naturally viewed fascism as a crisis of the old liberal system. Liberal political values and institutions had failed. In their place, fascism surfaced: a series of brutal, barbaric, violent dictatorships, led by charismatic tyrants, bereft of ideas or plans for the future. Communists, in particular, viewed fascism as a last, desperate authoritarian phase of capitalism. But such interpretations ignored the genuine mass appeal of fascism and minimized the fascist vision, no matter how confused, of a disciplined, cohesive society.

A second major interpretation, popular during the Cold War, saw fascism as totalitarianism. Proponents of this view were deeply influenced by the apparent identity of fascism, in its last stages, with communism. The Nazi-Soviet Pact of 1939, combined with the disclosures of *Stalin's purges and mass murders and postwar revelations of the *Holocaust, suggested that fascists and communists were cut from the same cloth.

A cornerstone of this interpretation is the importance of terror and the repressive apparatus of the modern state. Certainly fascism was a prototype of the modern totalitarian state—in the words of Mussolini, "Everything within the state, nothing outside the state, nothing against the state." Fascism aspired to total control over its citizens, leaving them with no island of privacy. With the aid of twentieth-century mass media, fascist states could reach and control their citizenry in a way that earlier regimes could not. Yet there were wide variations in the repressive powers and the totalitarian reach of fascist or fascist-style regimes. The control of a Mussolini or a *Franco was never comparable to that of Hitler or Stalin.

The equation of fascism and *communism also minimizes the ideological differences and the social and institutional bases of fascist and communist regimes. In its crudeness and violence, fascist ideology cannot be easily compared with the sophistication of *Marxism. Nor were the social and institutional bases of fascist and communist societies comparable. Fascist regimes protected middle-class interests and preserved and compromised with traditional institutions like the church and the military far more than the communists did. Mussolini signed the Lateran Pacts and protected Italian big business. Stalin repressed the church and murdered kulaks.

In the 1960s, a third major interpretation of fascism as "a radicalism of the right," as traditional conservative ideas pushed to an extreme, emerged. Fascism as totalitarianism emphasized the novelty of fascism; fascism as a "radicalism of the right" emphasized its continuities with the past. Such an interpretation, however, lays too much stress on political ideology. Moreover, such a view, with its accent on the "conservative" or "reactionary" aspects of fascism, ignores the genuinely revolutionary and innovative goals to which fascists often aspired.

With a lessening of the *Cold War and increasing stability in international relations, fascism has been viewed as "a revolt against modernity," a protest against the pace of social and cultural change wrought by rapid industrialization. Such an interpretation focuses less on political systems than on paths to social development. In this view, fascism appears as one of several possible routes, together with liberal *capitalism and socialism, to modern society. Fascist regimes mobilized and disciplined societies to transform themselves far more rapidly than would have been the case under a laissez-faire system. Under fascism, however, direction came "from above" in such a way as to avoid upsetting the social structure.

In perspective, however, the transformation under fascist regimes appears to have been ambivalent and often superficial. Fascist regimes froze or retarded development more than they sped it up. Italy's transformation into the West's fourth major industrial power occurred during the postwar decades after the fall of fascism. Germany was already a modern, industrialized society when the Nazis came to power, and some scholars have argued that Nazism was in fact a reaction to *modernization, a desire to return to a simpler preindustrial past.

World War II totally discredited fascism as an ideology with mass appeal. These days the term applies to anything from right-wing terrorist groups in Italy to *Third World military dictatorships, from ordinary police to motorcycle gangs. Most commonly, the term is used as a label for Third World military dictatorships ranging from the latest juntas in Africa or Latin America to Saddam *Hussein's Iraq. Following the events of 1989 and the end of Soviet influence in Eastern Europe and the Balkans, fascist-style movements and popular outbursts have surfaced in these regions. Observers have commented that if democratic regimes do not develop there, fascist-style regimes might arise. They would feed on the conflicting nationalisms in the area, and they might be spearheaded by the military. Even if such regimes were to emerge, however, it appears unlikely that they would pose a threat to the international order in the way that the fascism of the interwar period, led by Nazi Germany, precipitated the crisis of World War II.

Thus fascism is probably more dormant than dead. Old-style fascism of the interwar period is unlikely to reemerge. Nevertheless, the fascist ideology appeals to our deepest longings for community, for solidarity, for safety in the face of a seething world. Scenarios that might bring forth fascist-style regimes in Europe or the United States are not difficult to imagine. What if the tide of immigrant workers and refugees from the Third World appeared to overwhelm Europe or the United States? What if the *AIDS epidemic continues to spread uncontrollably? What if a stock market crash set off a worldwide economic panic? Any such prolonged *crisis might condition people to respond to fascist-style appeals: ultranationalism, revolutionary fever, antirationalism, a mystic faith in a strong leader. Future fascisms, like the earlier ones, would vary with local political traditions and circumstances. With the development of mass media and computers

such future fascist regimes would have new totalitarian capacities.

(See also AUTHORITARIANISM; CORPORATISM; IMPERIALISM; MILITARY RULE; POLITICAL VIOLENCE; RACE AND RACISM; TERRORISM.)

Eugen Weber, *Varieties of Fascism* (New York, 1964). Ernst Nolte, *Three Faces of Fascism* (New York, 1966). S. J. Woolf, ed., *European Fascism* (New York, 1969). Walter Laqueur, ed., *Fascism: A Reader's Guide, Analyses, Interpretations, Bibliography* (Berkeley, Calif., 1976). Stanley G. Payne, *Fascism: Comparison and Definition* (Madison, Wis., 1980).

CLAUDIO G. SEGRÈ

FEDERALISM. Modern federalism, according to British political scientist K. C. Wheare (*Federal Government*, 4th ed., New York, 1964), was invented in Philadelphia, Pennsylvania, 200 years ago by the authors of the U.S. Constitution. Until then, a federal country had been seen as a league or club of member states. Under the U.S. Constitution, each citizen is a citizen of two governments, national and state.

There is general agreement among experts that a functioning federal system, composed of a number of regional governments, must have a democratic and pluralist political system that provides opportunities for access and participation by citizens at both the national and state levels. Otherwise, the idea of self-expression by the regional component governments would not be meaningful. (The term *state* is used for various regional entities—states, provinces, republics, cantons, *Länder*—in this article.) Most experts also agree that an effective federal form needs to operate under a written *constitution that stipulates the responsibilities of the central and state governments, the role of the states in the amendatory process, and the rights of *citizenship.

Advocates of federalism see it as a way to protect against central tyranny, increase citizen participation, encourage innovation (the states as "laboratories"), and strengthen community identity and values. Opponents of the federal form criticize its slowness to respond to new challenges, its perceived inability to take advantage of technological advances, and the allegedly cumbersome nature of its governmental decision-making and implementation processes.

The basic objective of federalism is to reconcile unity and diversity. In particular, federalism has been adopted in various forms by many nations as a way to balance the interests of different ethnic and language groups, although this was not the purpose of the founders of U.S. federalism, in some cases where former colonies covering a large territory with a vast unsettled frontier were joined together. The Swiss federation, founded in 1848, has twenty-three cantons (the equivalent of states in the United States). For over 100 years, it has balanced the interests of three major ethnic and language groups (German, French, and Italian). Federalism in India and Canada likewise seeks to reconcile the interests of different ethnic and language groups, although the tensions in these countries have at various times caused serious problems for the federalism bargain.

Among political scientists, there are debates about the nature of federalism. One school stresses the amorphous nature of federalism and its operational complexity. U.S. political scientist Morton Grodzins, a leading exponent of this position, likened modern federalism to a marble cake (rather than a layer cake) characterized by constantly shifting, swirling patterns of functions, finances, and administrative arrangements. Some members of the Grodzins school describe federalism as inevitably progressing toward a centralized governmental system. According to this view, federalism is, in effect, a way station to unitary government.

A second school highlights the distinctive role of regional governments in federal systems, however designated—states, provinces, republics, cantons, *Länder*. Some members of this second school view federalism as cyclical in nature, noting that the role of states tends to increase in some periods and contract in others. Generally speaking, the role of the central government tends to expand in liberal periods (that is, periods in which progovernmental views are strong) and to contract in conservative periods (in which, in turn, the role of the states expands).

Many nations have attempted to institute a federal form, sometimes copying the actual wording of the U.S. Constitution. Often, however, they either have not carried out the intent or have tried to do so but were unable to establish or maintain a federal form. The Caribbean Federation and the East African Federation are examples of failed federations. The Soviet Union was federal in its formal constitution but not in actual behavior; it has now been replaced by a far looser association, which includes the Russian federation consisting of twelve republics. The emergence of a unified market among the member nations of the *European Union (EU) raises the interesting prospect of a movement toward a federal system in Europe.

A useful way to view the federal bargain is to focus on major aspects of the role of state governments including, for example, (1) the political and constitutional aspect of the federal relationship, referring to the powers of the states to determine, organize, and control their own legal and electoral systems; (2) their fiscal role, referring to the way in which, and the degree to which, the states can set and levy their own taxes; (3) the programmatic dimension of federalism, referring to the functional areas of governmental activity over which the states have sole or predominant responsibility; (4) the role of state governments in the policy-setting process of the central government (for example, in the upper house of the legislature); and (5) the role of the states in determining the form, functions, and finances of local units of government.

Countries currently and frequently classified as federal are Australia, Canada, Brazil, the Federal Republic of Germany, India, Malaysia, Nigeria, Russia, Switzerland, and the United States.

(See also CONSOCIATIONAL DEMOCRACY; PLURALISM; POLITICAL PARTICIPATION.)

Thomas J. Anton, *American Federalism and Public Policy* (Philadelphia, 1989). Richard P. Nathan and Margaret M. Balmaceda, "Comparing Federal Systems of Government," in Robert J. Bennett, ed., *Decentralization, Local Governments and Markets: Towards a Post-Welfare Agenda* (Oxford, 1990).

RICHARD P. NATHAN

FEDERATED STATES OF MICRONESIA. See PACIFIC ISLANDS.

FEMINISM. The term "feminism" refers to various theories and movements that critique male bias, examine issues of female subordination, and seek to find ways to eliminate gender inequity. Feminism is not simply a list of women's issues or synonymous with the constituency of women. Rather, feminism is a transformative perspective that women or men can adopt by looking specifically at any situation or issue in terms of how it affects women and by examining critically how the social construction of gender affects the issue in question. The activity this constitutes varies by context, time, and place; as the leading *Third World women's organization, Development Alternatives with Women for a New Era (DAWN) states: "There is and must be a diversity of feminisms, responsive, to the different needs and concerns of different women, and defined by them for themselves. This diversity builds on a common opposition to gender oppression and hierarchy which, however, is only the first step in articulating and acting upon a political agenda" (Gita Sen and Caren Grown, *Development, Crisis, and Alternative Visions: Third World Women's Perspectives*, Stavanger, Norway, 1985, p. 13).

Over the past three decades, a vast number of projects and treatises have developed around the world that address how gender constructs and constricts daily life, reflecting the vitality of current exploration of the implications of feminism for all societies. Gender is increasingly recognized as a central category for understanding politics that has policy implications in most areas and affects men as well as women. As feminism is examined in relation to various fields, it transforms the way knowledge is constructed and how we conceive of society and politics.

Development of Feminism. Individuals and groups in different historical eras have opposed female subordination and sought to fashion a better life for women. But the concept of a modern women's movement took shape in the nineteenth century, and use of the term "feminism" to describe such activity began in Europe at the end of that century. Late-nineteenth-century and early-twentieth-century women's movements tended to focus primarily on education, individual political and legal *rights (including voting and property rights in the West and participation in independence struggles in the South), or on women's special needs as mothers or as keepers of society's virtue.

Contemporary Western feminism began its theoretical revival with the 1949 publication of *The Second Sex* by Simone de Beauvoir. She challenged the secondary "other" status of women in a society that assumed men as the subject and maleness as the norm. De Beauvoir asserted that women are made subordinate by *patriarchy, not born that way naturally. The activist resurgence of feminism in the West came with the 1960s black rights, national liberation, antiwar, and student movements.

This resurgence had two major strands: women's rights and women's liberation. Women's rights (sometimes called liberal feminism) emphasizes the demand for equality of women with men in the mainstream of society. Based on the tradition of liberal *democracy, it seeks equal opportunity for women as individuals with rights to be obtained through legislation, rational enlightenment, and reform.

Women's liberation arose primarily among women in New *Left movements who fought for equality in "the revolution" and sought women's freedom from mainstream patriarchal structures. This strand spawned various feminisms offering radical interpretations of women's oppression and what is necessary for liberation: socialist, radical, lesbian, cultural, and women of color feminism have been the most visible.

Socialist feminism, stronger in Europe and Australia than in the United States, has many variations depending on which Left traditions it draws on. It fuses these theories by bringing gender perspectives to Marxist analysis, asking new questions that alter, not abandon, the framework's emphasis on class. Radical feminism, asserting the primacy of sex/gender as categories of analysis, views relations between the sexes as political—a concept pioneered by Kate Millett's *Sexual Politics* in 1969. Recognizing sexuality as central to women's oppression, it concentrates on issues involving the control of women's bodies such as reproduction, heterosexuality, and sexual violence. Lesbian feminism is both a movement for the rights of lesbians and a theory analyzing heterosexism (compulsory heterosexuality) and how it maintains gender roles adding to the oppression of all women. Cultural feminism as a theory posits the importance (and some claim superiority) of women's different nature and values; but the term sometimes refers more to women's art, music, spirituality, and other cultural forms.

These broad categories describe the evolution of contemporary Western feminism in relation to the century's dominant political theories, but feminist developments have moved beyond such boundaries. Feminism has spawned specialized fields that draw on all these theories. Discussion increasingly focuses on identity politics and the question of differences between women as well as between women and men. In the 1980s and 1990s, movements and writing from the Third World and by women of color in the West have significantly influenced feminist development, resulting in more attention to the intersection of gender with other factors such as race, class, sexuality, age, culture, *geography, and religion.

Global Feminism. Feminists have been active in Asia, Africa, Latin America, and the Middle East at different points in the nineteenth and twentieth centuries prior to today's movements. According to Kumari Jaywardena's study of twelve Eastern countries (*Feminism and Nationalism in the Third World,* New Delhi, 1986), movements for women's emancipation and *political participation took place within a context of nationalist struggles "aimed at achieving political independence, asserting a national identity, and modernizing society." In Latin America, early-twentieth-century feminists focused primarily on gaining the vote and on women's education.

Contemporary feminism in the Third World got a boost from the UN International Women's Year in 1975 and the Decade for Women, 1976–1985. The UN decade's theme, "Equality, Development, and Peace," reflected Western emphasis on equality, Third World preoccupation with development, and the Eastern bloc's focus on peace. Going into the decade, most women's advocates in Africa and Asia linked improvement in women's status to bringing them into economic development, while Latin American and Caribbean feminists focused on enhancing women's participation in movements for change and viewed imperialism and class as primary causes of female poverty and subordination.

The UN decade created a global dialogue that gave space

and legitimacy to exploring women's lives and provided a context for women's projects in developing countries. As women in many parts of the world encountered multiple obstacles to their empowerment, more turned to feminism to interpret the web of gender, race, class, and cultural biases women face. The UN has held four world conferences on women (Mexico City, 1975; Copenhagen, 1980; Nairobi, 1985; and Beijing, 1995)—all accompanied by nongovernmental forums, which enabled women to make global connections, as did the 1977 Tribunal on Crimes Against Women in Brussels and many subsequent independent women's global initiatives. The Mexico City and Copenhagen conferences saw considerable conflict between Western and Third World women, especially over what are "women's issues," but they still provided common ground for learning from each other.

By 1985, many women were moving beyond previous divisions and making connections between demands for equality, development, and peace. More Third World women had become feminist, finding a need to act autonomously and seeing the key role of gender in issues like poverty, violence, and reproductive health. Many Western feminists came to understand better the importance of race, class, and economic development in shaping women's oppression. Feminists who had struggled to establish certain "women's issues" such as equal pay and reproductive rights as serious public policy matters saw the need to broaden feminism and assert that all issues concern women. Thus the Nairobi conferences, attended by over 15,000, were characterized by more constructive dialogue demonstrating that out of the ferment of the decade, global feminism was emerging.

The decade between the Nairobi and Beijing world conferences saw rapid growth in women's regional and global networking. This approach was used both to exchange experiences and to influence the ever-increasing globalization that was affecting more women's lives. By the time of the 1995 Beijing World Conference on Women, feminist networks had successfully brought gender onto the agenda at other UN world conferences (The '92 Earth Summit in Rio, the '93 Human Rights Conference in Vienna, the '94 Cairo Population Conference, and the '95 Social Summit in Copenhagen). Women were increasingly viewed as a global force. This led the Beijing conference and accompanying forum to be the largest UN gathering to date with over 50,000 people attending and considerable world attention focused on the debates that raged there over gender and other issues raised by feminists from around the world.

There are of course many differences among women, and priorities vary between groups, but commonality exists among feminists on broad goals, such as those articulated by the International Workshop on Feminist Ideology and Structures sponsored by the Asian and Pacific Centre for Women and Development, Bangkok, 1979: "1.) Freedom from oppression for women involves not only equity, but also the right of women to freedom of choice, and the power to control their own lives within and outside of the home . . . The removal of all forms of inequity and oppression through the creation of a more just social and economic order, nationally and internationally, a process that involves women in national liberation struggles and as active participants in national development plans."

Global feminism means not only that activity is occurring around the world but also that women in each setting are connected by global forces. Further, it calls for a holistic approach which understands that domination by gender is linked to domination based on other differences and that sociopolitical and economic issues such as poverty, militarism, and sexism are interrelated.

Global feminism has not produced large international organizations but is characterized by networking and clearinghouses for information sharing and coordinating strategies. Both multipurpose and specialized groups organize global campaigns, monitor the UN and other international institutions, conduct trainings, serve as resource centers, and publish a wide array of publications as well as network electronically to provide a web of interconnections among groups and individuals. Many global networks and events focus on topics like health, women's studies, reproductive rights, and development; others are area-specific, like the Women Living Under Muslim Laws International Solidarity Network or the Latin American and Caribbean Health Network. Solidarity and strategies for feminist action globally are built around concrete issues. This work is based on respecting diversity of needs and approaches in each locale while recognizing common concerns, like violence, which take different cultural forms but disrupt women's lives everywhere.

Feminism often emerges out of national independence or social change movements, but usually becomes autonomous in order to develop theory and action that is not submerged by other interests and can articulate women's perspectives more forcefully. Women in many places are now addressing the need to transform basic social concepts such as development and democracy from feminist perspectives and are interacting with other movements to do so. For example, Latin American feminists call for extending democracy to the private sphere, rallying around a Chilean slogan coined in the struggle against dictatorship: "Democracia en el país y en la casa" (democracy in the country and in the home). Ecofeminists analyze connections between treatment of the earth and of women and contribute gendered analysis to environmental movements that question society's attitudes toward industry, science, and nature.

One of the major challenges of feminism in the 1990s has been to a male-biased and limited concept of human rights. Demanding that "women's rights are human rights," this global women's movement has sought to incorporate women's realities into the concepts and practices of human rights, transforming and making that community more inclusive in the process. This effort, like others bringing feminist analysis to global concepts and institutions, seeks to utilize women's perspectives as a basis for generating new, more democratic and more effective approaches to change. Feminism's promise then is both to improve women's lives and to seek a better future for the human race and for the planet.

(See also CLASS AND POLITICS; DEVELOPMENT AND UNDER-DEVELOPMENT; EQUALITY AND INEQUALITY; FEMINIST THEORY; GAY AND LESBIAN POLITICS; GENDER AND POLITICS; IDEOLOGY; IMPERIALISM; MARXISM; NEW SOCIAL MOVEMENTS; NON-GOVERNMENTAL ORGANIZATIONS, RACE AND RACISM; REPRODUCTIVE POLITICS; SOCIALISM AND SOCIAL DEMOCRACY; WOMEN AND DEVELOPMENT.)

Center for Women's Global Leadership, ed., *Gender Violence and Women's Human Rights in Africa* (New Brunswick, N.J., 1994). Rebecca Cook, ed., *Human Rights of Women: National and International Perspectives* (Philadelphia, 1994). Sonia Correa with Rebecca Reichmann, *Population and Reproductive Rights: Feminist Perspectives from the South* (Barbados, 1994). Amrita Basu, ed., *The Challenge of Local Feminisms: Women's Movements in Global Perspective* (Oxford, 1995). M. Jacqui Alexander and Chandra Talpade Mohanty, eds., *Feminist Genealogies, Colonial Legacies, Democratic Futures* (London, 1996). Eva Friedlander, ed., *Look at the World Through Women's Eyes: China NGO Forum Proceedings* New York, 1996). Mahnaz Afkhami and Erika Friedl, *Muslim Women and the Politics of Participation: Implementing the Beijing Platform* (Bethesda, Md., 1998).

CHARLOTTE BUNCH

FEMINIST THEORY. Western feminist theory locates and names *power as it defines the lives of women in the home and in the market (as mothers, daughters, sisters, wives, and lovers) and the ways they bring their gender along with them from the home to the market and back again. At its best feminist theory reinvents the way we think about power itself because it directs us to the politics of sex. It requires that we reimagine the relationship between the personal and political realms of life; the public and the private; the family and the economy; the domestic and the waged spheres of work. In its more limited scope it is a corrective to a "generalized" viewing of political theory that presumes the male standard as the referent.

Feminist theory examines and critiques the relations of power that are defined in and through the sex/gender system that "unnaturally" differentiates women from men. The feminist viewing of this problematic system of power, which privileges men while denying women legal and political equality and sexual freedom, has shifted over time. Different theorists of feminism reflect the changing times, histories, and varied conceptions of women's power and oppression.

Western feminist theory first developed in eighteenth-century England both as a critique and extension of bourgeois democratic rights. Mary Wollstonecraft argued in *A Vindication of the Rights of Woman* (1792) that women had the same capacity for rationality as men and therefore should be included in ongoing societal changes. She very specifically argued for women's right to an education. There were many variations of this liberal equal *rights theme that called for women's rights to be similar to men's in terms of property, contracts, etc. The articulation of liberal *feminism—which both endorsed the discourse of *liberalism and indicted it for its exclusion of women—was the center of Western feminist theory through the early twentieth century.

Modern Western feminist theory emerged in 1970 via its roots in this earlier liberal feminism, its roots in the *civil rights movement of the 1960s, and its embrace and critique of New *Left politics. Feminist theory, through the 1970s, was articulated by a series of critical dialogues between feminism, liberalism, and radically leftist and Marxist theory. As such, the naming of feminist theory is done through "other" political identities: socialist feminists define the problem for women as the system of capitalism and its intersections with *patriarchy and/or male privilege; radical feminists theorize the system of patriarchy as the central problem of women's domination; radical lesbian feminists focus on the problem of heterosexuality as the pivotal core of women's oppression; anarcha-feminists highlight the problem of structure within the systems of *capitalism and patriarchy. By the late 1970s black and *Third World feminisms emerged as a critique of the white privilege inherent in feminist theory itself.

Contemporary Western feminist theory in the 1980s moved beyond the dialogues that sought to differentiate feminisms from each other and instead began to articulate a more pluralized notion of feminism at its core. Feminist theory emerged with an understanding of gender and its sexual class structure that cuts through the differences of race and economic class while recognizing its semiautonomous political status. There is no uncontested agreement about how the various systems of oppression intersect with the gender system. But feminist theory has mapped and charted patriarchal privilege as a key political/power relation to be threaded through these other systems of power.

Theory always develops in dialogue with other theory and with the particular historical and political contexts of the moment. Whereas feminist theory in the 1970s established its epistemological identity through multiple constructions of patriarchal privilege, the contemporary period is one of cross-dialogue and critique of the various feminisms themselves. The focus of the 1970s was on Western society and its structural barriers toward women. The focus of the 1980s for feminist theory was a critique of feminism itself and the ways it reproduces aspects of a racist and patriarchal society. In the 1990s this dialogue continues with a specific focus on the concept of difference. This is in large part due to the influence of women of color within feminist theory, in part due to a dialogue with postmodernist and French feminist theory, and in part a reaction to the neoconservative antifeminist discourse that dominates the U.S. state and policy arenas.

Feminist theory has always had to contend with the "problem" of difference, particularly women's supposed difference from men. This notion of difference focuses on women as homogeneous; as though they all are alike, and different from men in the same way. In reaction, liberal feminism takes the stance that women are not different from men, that they are the same, or more similar than different. Cultural feminism, often also termed "essentialism," argues that women are different and the difference is positive, i.e., women are more caring, less competitive, more likely to be peaceful. Women of color take the concern with difference in other directions and demand a recognition of racial and economic class diversity as a starting point for any discussion about similarities and variations among "women" considered both as a group by itself *and* as distinct from men. These developments, some of which have been farther developed by *postmodernism, continue to keep feminist theory open to new invention and theorization.

There is no one feminist theory, but this is different from saying that feminism has a problematic theoretical status. Rather, it means that there are a variety of ways to theorize the key institutions and relations of patriarchy. There are various interpretations of the institution of motherhood (the conflation of bearing and rearing children and domestic labor) as distinguished from biological motherhood; the dichotomization of public and private life and the personal from the political; and the intersections of patriarchy, economic class, racism, and heterosexism. As a result feminist theory theorizes

women's lives in the ways they interact with the relations of power. Because systems of power are always shifting and being reconstituted, feminist theory must continually redefine itself from the multiple sites of women's oppression. Hopefully this creates the possibility of using feminist theory to change and reconstruct systems of power.

(See also ANARCHISM; CLASS AND CLASS POLITICS; GAY AND LESBIAN POLITICS; GENDER AND POLITICS; MARXISM; RACE AND RACISM; REPRODUCTIVE POLITICS; WOMEN AND DEVELOPMENT.)

Shulamith Firestone, *The Dialectic of Sex* (New York, 1970). Kate Millett, *Sexual Politics* (Garden City, N.Y., 1970). Juliet Mitchell, *Woman's Estate* (New York, 1971). Ti-Grace Atkinson, *Amazon Odyssey* (New York, 1974). Adrienne Rich, *Of Woman Born* (New York, 1976). Zillah Eisenstein, *The Radical Future of Liberal Feminism* (New York, 1981). Gloria T. Hull, Patricia Bell Scott, and Barbara Smith, eds., *All the Women Are White, All the Blacks Are Men, But Some of Us Are Brave* (New York, 1982). Catharine A. MacKinnon, *Feminism Unmodified* (Cambridge, Mass., 1987). Hazel Carby, *Reconstructing Womanhood: The Emergence of the Afro-American Woman Novelist* (New York, 1987). Linda Nicholson, *Feminism/Postmodernism* (New York, 1990).

ZILLAH EISENSTEIN

FEMINIZATION OF POVERTY. The term "feminization of poverty" came into use in the late 1970s as an expression encapsulating the phenomenon of women's increasing presence among the ranks of the poor. U.S. sociologist Diana Pearce coined the phrase in 1978 and the popular media began to mention it by the early 1980s. In 1981, the President's National Advisory Council on Economic Opportunity made the prediction that "all other things being equal, if the proportion of the poor in female headed families were to continue to increase at the same rate as it did from 1967 to 1978, the poverty population would be composed solely of women and their children by the year 2000." This prognosis was widely mentioned in discussions of domestic policy during the 1984 presidential election. By 1990, the feminization of poverty was commonly cited whenever poverty and gender were discussed together.

Although there are analytic problems with the term, its popularity served the important purpose of bringing the particularities of women's poverty to political attention. There are two major reasons why women in most societies have been historically and are currently vulnerable to poverty. First, women's access to breadwinner's wages, and the social benefits accruing to them, have been limited by cultural expectations, discrimination, and employment and educational segregation. Second, most cultures have assigned women the bulk of society's unpaid caregiving work: child care, care for elderly and infirm family members, and general family maintenance duties. Such nurturing obligations compete for women's time and attention when they enter the waged labor market, and yield the label "dependence" when they are supported economically by the paid employment of husbands, by government transfer payments, or by private charity.

Several social changes of the late twentieth century have caused women's long-standing poverty to represent an increasing proportion of the entire poverty population, increasing from 50 percent of all poor adults in the United States in 1960 to 62 percent by 1995. Most important has been that the growing acceptability of women's participation in the labor market has contributed to a dramatic rise in the numbers of two-parent families with both adults employed outside the home. Consequently, more two-parent families have been able to escape poverty status—even as the related overall lessening of the "family wage" has left families or households with only one wage earner more vulnerable to poverty. At the same time, a complex set of social forces, including the increased cultural tolerance of divorce and the expansion of social welfare benefits, has led to a dramatic increase in the number of divorced and never-married mothers: in the United States families headed by women have doubled in proportion to all families over the past thirty years. In addition, gender differences in longevity within the expanding elderly segment of the population mean that more older women live longer as singles and are therefore in greater jeopardy of poverty.

Taken together, these trends yield a poverty population in most Western industrial nations that is increasingly composed of single women and their children. Policy advocates, politicians, and feminists have viewed this situation with alarm and have called for a wide array of responses aimed at both changing the nature of the problem and responding directly to the needs of poor women and their families. The most widespread political responses have been two-pronged. On the one hand, there has been a call among mainstream politicians and policy advocates for more public support for "family-friendly" policies to promote greater self-sufficiency for women who face problems finding jobs with adequate wages in the labor market (e.g., child care subsidies, child support assurance, earned income tax credits, paid family leave). On the other hand, the more significant policy response has been to overhaul systems of the income maintenance supports that have historically been targeted toward single mothers. Especially in English-speaking nations, and most profoundly in the United States, "*welfare reform" has been proposed as the solution to women's pauperization, at least, if not to the problem of women's poverty itself.

In the United States, since the 1980s, wide political support grew for the idea that women's poverty was sustained, if not caused, by the existence of a welfare system that offered an entitlement to income without a mandate that all adults (single-parent mothers as well as all fathers and most married mothers) must rely on private employment and not government subsidies as their primary source of income. In 1988, the Family Support Act altered the national welfare system that had been established as part of the Social Security Act of 1935 so that the basic federal family income subsidy (Aid to Families with Dependent Children, AFDC) was linked much more closely to employment. This was accomplished primarily through inclusion of mandated work requirements as well as permission for a host of state options mandating that women participate in work, training, or community service activities in exchange for support. From 1989 until 1996, heated policy debates occurred in Congress, and in state legislatures, over the future direction of "welfare reform."

As the research and debates continued, the policy focus shifted away from creating an overt response to the feminization of poverty, or even to the existence of poverty itself. Instead the goal for many became, in President Clinton's 1992 campaign phrase, to "end welfare as we know it." The passage, after rancorous debate, but finally with significant bi-partisan support, of the Personal Responsibility and Work Opportunity Reconciliation Act (PRWORA) in August 1996 was the culmination of this debate. Among other things, this important piece of legislation "devolved" responsibility for income maintenance to the states—replacing AFDC as a federal entitlement with the Temporary Assistance to Needy Families (TANF) Program, available through a federal block grant structure. PRWORA mandated a five-year time limit for receipt of federal income subsidies to families headed by able-bodied adults and linked provision of federal funding to work participation among increasing numbers of recipients. There was a deemphasis on *education and training, and an explicit approach of "work first," whereby welfare recipients should be helped, and pushed, into employment as a condition for receipt of child care, training, and other subsidies. There were provisions aimed at reducing teen pregnancy and "illegitimacy" rates.

From 1995 through 1998, welfare rolls in the United States began a dramatic decline, of over 30 percent in many states. Many, including President Clinton, have seen this drop as an indication that state and federal welfare reform is working. Others have pointed out that, despite low unemployment rates, family poverty is not decreasing but is increasing or holding steady, and that a decline in welfare participation may increase children's poverty. For a range of reasons, women's poverty, as such, commands little public attention except in terms of providing the transitional child care, transportation, employment, and health care subsidies that are required to move people from "welfare to work."

Other countries, especially English-speaking nations, have begun to consider proposals for reforming their income maintenance programs along the U.S. model—again with the stated goal of reducing "welfare dependence," not necessarily women's poverty. Indeed, by the end of the twentieth century the "feminization of poverty" may well have become a historical term useful for crystallizing the debates of the 1980s, and still descriptive of the problems facing single mothers, but anachronistic in relation to ongoing policy debates in the United States and other industrial nations.

(See also FEMINISM; GENDER AND POLITICS; WELFARE STATE.)

Diane Dujon and Ann Withorn, eds., *For Crying Out Loud: Women's Poverty in the United States* (Boston, 1996). Randy Albelda and Chris Tilly, *Glass Ceilings and Bottomless Pits: Women's Work, Women's Poverty* (Boston, 1997). Katherine Edin and Laura Lein, *Making Ends Meet: How Single Mothers Survive Welfare and Low Wage Work* (New York, 1997).
ANN WITHORN

FIJI. See PACIFIC ISLANDS.

FILIBUSTER. The filibuster in the U.S. Senate is an informal term describing extended debate. On most legislation, the Senate's rules do not limit debate. As long as a senator seeks recognition to speak, or a senator continues to speak, debate cannot be limited. By filibustering, senators attempt to prevent a vote on a measure or amendment.

The term "filibuster" was adopted to describe extended debate in the mid-nineteenth century. The term was imported from the then popular Spanish word *filibustero* used to describe pirates and marauders who plundered the Spanish West Indies and other parts of the Americas. The term came to be used to describe a rebellious technique for disrupting Senate action.

Between 1806 and 1917, the Senate had no rule that allowed a motion to limit debate and cause a vote. In 1917, the Senate adopted Rule 22, which allowed two-thirds of senators present and voting to invoke cloture. In 1949, the rule was amended to raise the threshold to two-thirds of all elected senators and to allow cloture on procedural motions, except motions to consider changes in Senate rules. In 1959, the rule was amended again to reduce the threshold to two-thirds of senators present and voting and to allow cloture on measures related to Senate rules. In 1975, the threshold was reduced to three-fifths of all elected senators, except for measures related to Senate rules, which continued to be subject to the two-thirds present and voting threshold.

In the late twentieth and early twenty-first century, filibusters and threatened filibusters have become more common. They are used by minorities to block legislation and to gain bargaining leverage with majorities.

(See also CONGRESS, U.S.)

Franklin L. Burdette, *Filibustering in the Senate* (Princeton, N.J., 1940). Sarah A. Binder and Steven S. Smith, *Politics or Principle: Filibustering in the United States Senate* (Washington, D.C., 1997).

                                                    STEVEN S. SMITH

FINANCE, INTERNATIONAL. International finance refers to monetary transactions across political borders, usually involving the exchange of currencies. Because different economies use different currencies, basic transactions such as trade, loans, and asset sales are more risky and complicated when conducted internationally.

Arrangements for setting exchange rates are the core of the international monetary system. At one extreme, nations can fix (or "peg") the price of their currency relative to others. In the late nineteenth century, for example, most currencies were convertible into gold, effectively fixing their exchange rates. The result was a predictable environment for international transactions with a strong anti-inflationary bias. But it was also an environment that gave national monetary authorities little autonomy or discretion. At the other extreme, currency rates can be determined each day in the marketplace. They fluctuate (or "float") as supply and demand varies among currency traders, importers, and exporters. Monetary authorities may still intervene, either to dampen short-term volatility or to influence the long-term direction of rates (so-called managed floating), but they are not committed to either fixed rates or to specified target zones. Such floating rates pose uncertainties for traders and investors, but they give monetary authorities wide scope to determine national policies.

All these varied monetary arrangements have been tried since World War II. As the war drew to a close, the United States and Great Britain organized a multilateral conference to reconstruct the world financial system. Meeting at Bretton Woods, New Hampshire, in 1944, they devised a new system of fixed exchange rates. Though nominally based on gold, the Bretton Woods system was actually based on the one currency that was widely accepted for exchange and reserve purposes: the U.S. dollar. Reconstruction proved slower than anticipated, and most European currencies did not become fully convertible until the late 1950s. But once established, the Bretton Woods system of pegged rates lasted for more than a decade, providing a stable framework for trade and investment among the world's major economies.

The central principle of this system was its stable exchange rates. Rates varied only within narrow bands. Larger changes were permitted only to cope with fundamental balance-of-payments problems. The *International Monetary Fund (established at Bretton Woods) monitored the system and provided short-term resources to help states hold their currencies within these bands. A crucial element of the arrangements was the informal U. S. pledge to redeem dollars for gold at $35 per ounce. Foreign central banks relied on that pledge and held dollars as well as gold to settle their balance of payments shortfalls. This "dollar-exchange" system of pegged rates permitted world trade to grow steadily on a base of expanding dollar reserves.

There were, however, fundamental difficulties in implementing the system. One overriding worry was how to earn enough hard currency to overcome the "dollar shortage" of the 1940s and 1950s. Economist Robert Triffin peered further ahead and saw that the real crisis would not be too few dollars but too many (Triffin, *Gold and the Dollar Crisis*, New Haven, Conn., 1960). As dollars slowly accumulated in foreign central banks, they would eventually exceed U.S. gold holdings. When that happened, the U.S. pledge to redeem dollars for gold would become untenable and the system itself unstable. Triffin's point and its implications were soon acknowledged by experts, but the structural problems were never solved.

The Bretton Woods arrangements suffered another fundamental problem that festered through the 1960s: its uneven impact on balance of payment adjustment. While deficit countries faced clear pressures to deflate in order to maintain exchange rates, surplus countries such as Germany did not face similar constraints and were not forced to revalue. The dollar, linchpin of the system, also faced mounting difficulties. Although the United States had unique advantages as the creator of dollar reserves, it had no effective way to depreciate a currency that was becoming increasingly overvalued.

The strong dollar profoundly affected America's role in the world economy. It stimulated vast increases in U.S. foreign investment, which became a contentious issue in Western Europe, especially in France. At home, it damaged exports and encouraged imports, hurting all traded-good industries. America's international deficits were growing, and the Bretton Woods system offered no clear avenue to limit them. Unlike other deficit countries, the United States could simply fund its shortfall by printing the world's reserve currency, and it did so. Private speculators added to the pressures to realign exchange rates. With capital markets now closely linked, they could move large sums into stronger currencies, such as the deutsche mark, instantly and at low risk.

The Bretton Woods system finally collapsed in August 1971 when France and the Federal Republic of Germany (West Germany) began converting their burgeoning dollar reserves into gold, forcing the United States to abandon its convertibility pledge. Efforts to restore a fixed-rate system using new parities (the 1971 Smithsonian Agreement) ultimately failed. By default, the world's major currencies began floating. (Less developed economies continued to peg their exchange rates to one or two large trading partners.)

This unplanned system has persisted for three decades, combining floating rates and ad hoc intervention by monetary authorities. The major economic powers have sometimes intervened jointly, as they did after the 1985 Plaza Agreement and the 1987 Louvre Accord. The aim of this informal (and often short-lived) cooperation is to manage the crucial nexus of the dollar, yen, and deutsche mark.

Since the breakdown of Bretton Woods, the only sustained institutional effort to control exchange rates has been a regional one in Europe. Beginning in 1972, the European Community, led by France and Germany, sought to facilitate trade and investment by narrowing their regional currency movements. Their cooperation was formalized in 1979 against the backdrop of continued dollar instability. The stated goal was to create "a zone of monetary stability in Europe." Not only has the European Monetary System succeeded. Its leading members actually managed to create a usable common currency (the euro) and an independent monetary authority (the European Central Bank), all complementing the larger process of European integration.

Outside of western Europe, central banks have found it extremely difficult to manage exchange rates. Private financial markets now determine currency rates on a day-to-day basis. To affect these rates directly, central banks buy and sell foreign exchange in the markets. They hope to shift private agents' expectations and thus the composition of their currency portfolios. It is a difficult task and often an unsuccessful one, made more difficult by traders' ability to move vast sums of short-term capital electronically across borders. These private markets dwarf the scale of intervention by monetary authorities, even joint intervention, and proved to be a major source of instability during the Asian financial crisis of the late 1990s.

Ironically, private currency markets are so large partly because floating rates are so volatile. To control their exposure to currency movements, multinational corporations hedge with foreign-exchange contracts and use international capital markets to match longer-term assets and liabilities in multiple currencies. The result is a vast international market for short-term capital, a market that dwarfs the underlying transactions of importers, exporters, and long-term investors.

The growth of these interdependent markets for capital and foreign exchange represents an important shift in international financial structure. The world's largest capital market, the London-based Euromarket, is now an essentially unregulated one. Along with other "offshore" banking centers, it eliminates many of the costs and constraints of domestic banking.

The offshore markets began in the early 1960s, fostered by U.S. restrictions on interest rates and a tax on foreign borrowing. Major U.S. banks responded by allowing their London subsidiaries to accept deposits and grant loans denominated in dollars. The Euromarkets grew rapidly because of their cost advantages for large-scale depositors and borrowers. They benefited from low regulatory overhead and intense competition among international banks. These offshore markets, from London to Hong Kong, became centers of global finance,

increasing the pressures to deregulate national financial markets in western Europe, Japan, and North America.

The Euromarket's largest participants are multinational firms, but the most controversial are Third World states. Their borrowing started in the early 1970s, aimed at sustaining rapid growth without dependence on direct foreign investment. Debts grew dramatically after the oil shock of 1973–74, funded, ironically, by bank deposits from oil-producing states ("petrodollar recycling"). Lending standards seemed relaxed, at least in retrospect, but commercial credits were still limited to larger economies in Latin America and Asia, plus a few states with rich natural resources. Weaker economies, such as those of sub-Saharan Africa, had to rely on aid donors.

Banking syndicates made their loans on standard commercial terms, usually five to ten years, with principal due at the conclusion. Interest rates were recalculated periodically to reflect the banks' cost of funds. Profits came from initial fees and negotiated "spreads" above the interest costs.

These arrangements marked a substantial change from foreign lending practices over the past 150 years. Earlier loans were mostly bonds, sold by banking houses to individual investors. Defaults were not uncommon, but they generally harmed bondholders and not the banking system. The quality of Euromarket loans, on the other hand, directly affects the solvency of large banks. National monetary authorities are thus drawn into foreign loan problems and their renegotiation.

After a second oil shock in the early 1980s, these loan problems proliferated. The world economy contracted and commodity prices fell sharply. Real interest rates soared and remained high. As a result, debt burdens rose while debt-servicing capacity plummeted. In August 1982, Mexico announced its inability to meet current debts. It was soon followed by most other major debtors among the developing countries, including Brazil, Argentina, and Venezuela.

The debt crisis was initially understood as a short-term emergency, requiring an infusion of liquidity and a sharp contraction of imports. The banks moved to reschedule immediate obligations, but offered no debt forgiveness. Before any rescheduling, they insisted that debtors agree to austerity programs supervised by the International Monetary Fund.

Perceptions of the debt crisis gradually changed as it persisted through the 1980s and early 1990s. Debtors paid a high price in political instability, forgone income, and lower future productivity, but without returning to creditworthiness. Commercial banks, export-credit agencies, and aid donors finally began to set aside major loan-loss reserves and to write down their impaired credits. Official U.S. policies were also changing. The initial focus had been almost exclusively on the banking system's stability. That remains important. But beginning in 1985, the United States also began to promote structural adjustment and economic growth as longer-term solutions. The Baker Plan, developed under Treasury Secretary James Baker, was underfunded and unsuccessful, but it did signal a policy shift. The 1989 Brady Plan, also from the Treasury, went further and encouraged commercial debt relief. Even so, the largest debtors continue to face heavy payments and find it difficult to attract voluntary lending. With credit markets so tight, a number of less developed countries have changed their approach to international finance. They have reversed their long-standing opposition to multinational firms and invited new equity investments.

Some poorer states in Africa and Asia have been unable to attract either new loans or significant foreign investment. Unable to meet their current interest payments, they have been forced to reschedule debts and seek large-scale relief from private creditors and aid donors.

(See also ECONOMIC AND MONETARY UNION; INTERDEPENDENCE, ECONOMIC; INTERNATIONAL DEBT; INTERNATIONAL POLITICAL ECONOMY.)

Charles Lipson, *Standing Guard: Protecting Foreign Capital in the Nineteenth and Twentieth Centuries* (Berkeley, Calif., 1985). Miles Kahler, ed., *The Politics of International Debt* (Ithaca, N.Y., 1986). Jeffrey D. Sachs, *Developing Country Debt and Economic Performance* (Chicago, 1989). Barry Eichengreen, *Globalizing Capital: A History of the International Monetary System* (Princeton, N.J., 1996).

CHARLES LIPSON

FINLAND. Located on the Baltic Sea between Sweden and Russia, Finland has seen its historical development being profoundly affected, both internally and internationally, by each neighbor in turn. In size, political system, institutions, and social structure, however, Finland is a Scandinavian country. Although geographically the country straddles the border between East and West, Finland, with its *parliamentary democracy, multiparty system, and market economy, possesses the central features of West European societies.

From the Middle Ages until 1809 Finland formed part of the Swedish kingdom. Absorbed by the Russian empire as a result of the war of 1808–1909, the country became an autonomous grand duchy with the Russian tsar as grand duke, operating under the Swedish legal system. This arrangement lasted until 6 December 1917, when Finland was able to gain its independence from a Russia weakened by revolution and civil war.

Another prerequisite for the gaining of independence, however, was that economic conditions had developed rapidly during the closing years of the nineteenth century. Owing to extensive forests and the greatly increased demand worldwide for paper products, toward the end of the nineteenth century Finland was quickly drawn into the world economy.

The rapid integration of Finnish farmers into the capitalist economy also explains why landowning *peasants came to represent a crucial nation-building force in Finnish society. For example, independent peasants made up the core of the victorious White army during the civil war of 1918, defeating the Reds at the same time the Reds were defeating the Whites in Russia.

During World War II Finland fought two wars against the Soviet Union, was for a time a cobelligerent with Germany, and made a separate truce with the Soviet Union in September 1944. Finland was never occupied by foreign forces, and it maintained its system of market economy and parliamentary system throughout. It was, however, condemned to pay heavy war reparations.

Due partly to the vicinity of the Soviet Union and partly to the very rapid change from an agrarian to an industrial society during the first two decades after World War II, Finland was a very conflict-ridden society. Cabinets were short-lived, industrial strikes were common, and the Communist Party was in the 1950s and 1960s supported by almost a quarter of the electorate. From the early 1970s onward the social conditions improved rapidly, and Finland adopted institutional arrangements typical of the Scandinavian *welfare state. Communist support dwindled rapidly, and by the 1990s had almost disappeared. After the 1995 elections, the Conservatives and the Social Democrats formed the two dominant parties in a coalition government, undoubtedly reflecting the dominance of an urbanized middle class. At the same time, the Finnish economy has modernized greatly and has been at the forefront in the application of new manufacturing and information technologies.

In 1995 Finland became a member of the *European Union. In 1998 the parliament voted to join the *Economic and Monetary Union (EMU) and participate in the single currency initiative. Finland has become well represented in several of the important bodies of the EU, and the country has generally given strong support to European integration. Simultaneously, the traditional cooperation with the Nordic countries, in particular with Sweden, has continued, especially in the fields of education, social policy, and economic affairs.

(See also SCANDINAVIA.)

Risto Alapuro, *State and Revolution in Finland* (Berkeley, Calif., 1988). Max Engman and David Kirby, eds., *Finland: People, Nation, State* (London, 1989). Synnove Vuori and Pekka Yla-Anttila, *Industrial Transformation in Finland: From Factory Driven to Technology Based Growth* (Helsinki, 1992). Pekka Kosonen and Per Kongshoj Madsen, eds., *Convergence or Divergence: Welfare States Facing the European Integration* (Brussels, 1994). Teija Tiilikainen, *Europe and Finland: Defining the Political Identity of Finland in Western Europe* (Abo, Finland, 1997). Mikko Kautto et al., eds., *Nordic Social Policy: Changing Welfare States* (New York, 1999).

ERIK ALLARDT

FOOD POLITICS. The politics of food and agriculture can vary dramatically from country to country, depending most of all on the level of industrial development. Governments in nonindustrial developing countries have tended to tax rural agricultural producers and to subsidize urban consumers. By contrast, governments in industrial countries tend to subsidize rural producers and tax urban food consumers. When nations undergo rapid industrial development, they tend to switch the bias in their food and agricultural policies accordingly. In this century, Japan, Taiwan, and the Republic of Korea (South Korea) have all switched from taxing farmers and subsidizing consumers to taxing consumers and subsidizing farmers.

Why these divergent policy patterns? The tendency of nonindustrial countries to subsidize food consumers is a part of what Michael Lipton has called "urban bias" (*Why Poor People Stay Poor*, Cambridge, Mass., 1977). The political sources of urban bias have included (1) a pro-industry, anti-agriculture bias among elites in postcolonial developing countries (likewise among Marxist-Leninist *elites in centrally planned societies); (2) the political disorganization and low social status of remote rural villagers in most developing countries; and (3) the political threat to regime survival that can be presented by urban food consumers, rich and poor alike. These consumers in developing countries are especially sensitive to food prices because a relatively larger share of their total income tends to be spent on food purchases (often nearly 50 percent).

The policies of taxing farmers and subsidizing consumers

has frequently gone wrong in the developing world, especially in those countries that have been *command economies. Where implicit taxes on farmers have been steepest—for example, in much of sub-Saharan Africa, and also historically in the Soviet Union—food production failed to keep pace with either population growth or demands for dietary enrichment. In most African countries, food crop production has declined on a per capita basis since independence. It is popular to blame this adverse trend on cash cropping, but in most of Africa nonfood cash crop production per capita has actually declined more rapidly than food crop production.

In order to keep food consumption increasing in these circumstances, the supply gap must be made up through commercial or food aid imports. To ensure low food prices in urban areas, developing country governments have also been obliged to spend beyond their means on direct consumer food subsidies. When these governments subsequently try to cut back on these food subsidies (often a condition for obtaining new lending from the *International Monetary Fund), they have found themselves politically challenged in the streets by rioting mobs.

The contrasting tendency of governments in wealthy industrial countries to provide generous subsidies to rural food producers (rather than to urban food consumers) is attributable to (1) the price support demands that farmers in rich countries make when personal income growth in the agricultural sector begins to lag behind rapidly growing income in the industrial sector, and (2) the willingness of urban consumers to accept these price support demands, both because their share of personal income spent on food shrinks with affluence and because productivity growth in the farming sector (owing to the mechanization of production, increased chemical fertilizer use, and the adoption of high-yield *green revolution seed varieties) results in lower real commodity prices for consumers even when price supports are factored in. It also becomes more affordable for rich industrialized countries to subsidize farmers because the total number of farmers in such countries will be shrinking. Over the last thirty years, the number of full-time farmers in Japan, for example, has declined by 70 percent. As this process has continued in the most advanced industrial countries, political disputes over farm subsidies have become less divisive than new issues such as consumer food safety, biotechnology, animal rights, and farm chemical use.

Still, if commodity prices in rich countries are set too high above market-clearing levels (as in the *European Union, under the Common Agricultural Policy), the result can be a burdensome surplus of high-priced farm products hard to dispose of except through food aid, export credits, or wasteful and costly export subsidies. The use of such export subsidies can bring industrial country governments into direct trade conflicts with each other. Efforts in the *World Trade Organization (WTO) to negotiate away rich country import restrictions and export subsidies often meet resistance because food trade measures are impossible to disentangle from domestic price supports, which farm lobbies may consider nonnegotiable.

One of the most controversial aspects of the international politics of food has been the question of "food power"—the hypothetical international power advantage enjoyed by food-exporting nations over food-importing nations. Political leaders in some food-importing countries have at times argued for the importance of "food self-sufficiency" so as to reduce the vulnerability associated with import dependence.

This hypothetical vulnerability to food power has seldom been tested, mostly because food-exporting nations are constrained by domestic producers from withholding commercial exports. On those occasions when "food power" has been attempted, the exporter's advantage has not been confirmed. In 1980–1981, when the United States imposed a partial grain embargo on the Soviet Union following the Soviet invasion of Afghanistan, the Soviet Union had little trouble finding alternative grain suppliers in Argentina, Australia, Canada, and the European Community. Total Soviet grain imports actually increased during the period that the U.S. embargo was in place. In 1990, following the Iraqi invasion of Kuwait, a comprehensive economic embargo was imposed on Iraq by the UN Security Council, but it excluded food and medicine exports on humanitarian grounds. So long as rich countries continue to subsidize food production, international markets are likely to remain—in most years—a setting in which buyers rather than sellers enjoy a political and commercial advantage.

(See also LAND REFORM; RURAL DEVELOPMENT; TAXES AND TAXATION.)

Kym Anderson and Yujiro Hayami, *The Political Economy of Agricultural Protection* (Sydney, 1986). Amartya Sen, *Poverty and Famines: An Essay on Entitlement and Deprivation* (Oxford, 1981). David Orden, Robert Paarlberg, and Terry Roe, *Policy Reform in American Agriculture: Analysis and Prognosis* (Chicago, 1999).

ROBERT PAARLBERG

FORCE, USE OF. *International relations are often described as being *anarchic*—that is, there is no central authority in world politics, much less one with the power necessary to ensure order and prevent the use of force among *states. Unlike activities *within* a state's borders that normally are subject to the authority of the state enforced by its government agencies, the relations *among* states are not subject to any external governance or enforcing authority. There is no authority in international relations superior to that claimed by any single sovereign state. Indeed, states claim by virtue of their *sovereignty, which is recognized formally by other sovereign states, not only the right to exercise complete authority over matters on territory within their jurisdiction but also the *right* to be independent or autonomous in relation to other states in the formulation and execution of *foreign policy.

Although there is no enforcing authority in international relations, there are internationally recognized rules and norms for state behavior, some of which have acquired the force of law. The 1928 Pact of Paris, or Kellogg-Briand Treaty, outlawed *war "as an instrument of policy" and called exclusively for "pacific means" for dealing with "all disputes or conflicts" among states. Nevertheless, states continued to use force in their relations with other states during the 1930s, even if only in self-defense. The *United Nations Charter (1945) asserts that states "shall settle their disputes by peaceful means" (Article 3) and that they "shall refrain in their international relations from the threat or use of force against the territorial integrity or political independence of any state" (Article 4). At the same time, however, Article 51 describes self-defense against an attack for states acting individually or collectively as an "inherent right." Moreover, it provided for a collective security machinery under the UN Security Council (UNSC) with authority to impose *sanctions and take other measures including the use of force. (By contrast, the earlier *League of Nations, which was established after World War I, had authority to impose economic sanctions against an aggressor but lacked authority to use force.)

In practice, exercise of this authority by the UNSC has proven difficult in the absence of consensus among the great powers or permanent members of the Security Council, any one of which can exercise a veto and thus block collective UN action. The Soviet Union did not vote (and thus did not exercise its veto) in the UNSC's authorization in 1950 for a collective response to the invasion of the Republic of Korea (South Korea); however, the UN was blocked from taking so central a role in many subsequent situations when some members sought a similar response. For a time, the UN General Assembly tried to assume this role under "Uniting for Peace" resolutions. Even this rather weak mechanism fell into disuse in the 1960s when an expanded UN membership was less prone to support such action. Although peacekeeping eventually became a significant UN contribution to conflict management in the Middle East, Africa, Cyprus, Korea, and elsewhere, the absence of consensus among the permanent UNSC members precluded the UN from using its collective security machinery as originally intended. By contrast, UN actions in 1990 and 1991 to redress Iraq's aggression against Kuwait were a demonstration of how a consensus among the great powers and other states can make collective and effective UN action possible.

Subsequent years have been marked by a continuation of armed intervention by outside states acting for humanitarian purposes in countries torn by civil strife as in Somalia, Haiti, central Africa, and the Balkans in Europe. Although *international law customarily prohibits intervention in the domestic affairs of other sovereign states (unless requested by the legitimate government of the state subject to such intervention), broad language in the UN Charter does authorize using force under UNSC auspices in response to a contingency endangering international peace and security (Chapter VII, particularly Article 42). Consistent with long-standing individual and multilateral relief efforts in natural disasters, intervention for humanitarian purposes also reflects a growing human-rights consensus that not only prescribes under international law certain civil or political, social, and economic rights but also prohibits certain acts defined as *war crimes, *genocide, and other crimes against peace and humanity. Nevertheless, as with other uses of force, armed intervention also has very real human and material costs. The expected net effect on the human condition stands as a humanitarian criterion for limiting use of force in such circumstances—whether or not to intervene with armed forces and, if so, how to conduct such interventions so as to minimize or reduce the adverse consequences of such actions.

One approach to maintaining order in an anarchic international system of states is agreed rules or norms that are followed by states typically because it is in their enlightened self-interest to do so. Rules or norms concerning the use of force that may have the binding or obligatory character of international law are those that have become established by formal agreement (treaties or covenants), have come into being through customary practice, conform to generally accepted principles, or have been established through the interpretations or writings of jurists such as those on the *International Court of Justice (ICJ). Beyond resort to the ICJ, imposition of sanctions, or other nonlethal methods, when states choose to use force aggressively, thus violating international law, there frequently is no remedy for the victimized state or states except the use of force in self-defense or collective self-defense. In this sense, then, the world remains a self-help system of relations among states.

International law concerning war draws heavily from the just war doctrine in Western political thought. One finds this concern about justice and war in Cicero but developed further over the centuries by Augustine, Aquinas, Gentilis, Victoria, Suarez, and others. The writings of *Grotius on war and those who would follow him gave legal character to what previously had been moral doctrine concerning right conduct in war (*jus in bello*) and the right to use force or go to war in the first place (*jus ad bellum*).

As they have evolved over the centuries, the principles of "just war" may be summarized today as including the following: (1) there must be a *just cause* (such as self-defense against an aggressor); (2) decisions to go to war and conduct the war are to be made by *legitimate authority*; (3) *proportionality* must be observed between means and ends in going to war and in conducting the war; (4) there must be some chance of success in attaining legitimate objectives through resort to the use of force; (5) the use of force should be a last resort after efforts to use peaceful means have been exhausted; (6) weapons immoral in themselves (indiscriminate weapons or those causing needless suffering) must not be used; and (7) decisions on going to war and how the war is to be conducted should be taken with the right intention—an important provision because any abstract set of principles can be misused by the unprincipled to "justify" actions taken for illegal or immoral purposes.

In contrast to a purely pacifistic position, whether on religious or secular grounds, that would renounce any use of force, the just war doctrine attempts to set limits on resort to (and actual use of) force in international relations. There has been considerable debate on the present-day applicability of just war principles, given the presence of nuclear and other weapons of mass destruction. The morality of threats to use mass-destructive force, even if the intent is to deter or effectively preclude such wars, has been hotly disputed. Most concede, however, that just war principles remain relevant at least in relation to smaller-scale wars. Indeed, the overall intent in just war thinking about conduct in war is to moderate or limit the death (particularly of noncombatants) and destruction that would occur in the absence of such rules.

Short of hostilities, the threat of force—"saber rattling" or what has been referred to more formally as "coercive diplomacy" or "compellence"—may be employed to influence the behavior or compel actions by other states. Alertness and readiness levels may be increased, reserves mobilized, standing forces redeployed to new locations, or other actions may be taken to signal to an adversary both the capability and the resolve to use force. Even though no forces or weapons may engage in actual hostile fire, the threat to do so may be understood nevertheless as equivalent to a use of force. In coercive diplomacy the attempt is to induce actions or changes in the actual behavior of other states. *Deterrence policies, by contrast, are somewhat more passive; the effort is to deliver a credible threat that there will be a response to include the use of force if certain actions are taken by another state or group of states. Threats to use force can thus be considered a use of force even if no hostilities actually take place. However passive, the mere presence of military forces postured to defend a country and thus dissuade a would-be aggressor is a use of force.

Efforts have been undertaken in recent years to inhibit the use of force through arms reductions (of "conventional" or non-nuclear forces and nuclear, chemical, biological, and any other mass-destructive categories of weaponry) and through establishing various confidence- and security-building measures. Thus, notifications in advance of military exercises and provision for observers from other countries attempt to reduce the likelihood that these events will be misperceived as having hostile intent. In an effort to reduce the threat or risk of war or lesser uses of force considerable attention also has been paid to the numbers, types, and peacetime stationing and readiness of forces.

Notwithstanding all of these efforts, resort to the use of force by states remains part of international relations. Some have sought to delegitimize war as an instrument of state policy by changing over time the attitude toward war by leadership elites or masses of peoples. Nevertheless, the use of force persists. Indeed, in an anarchic world that lacks central authority with the power to enforce international law and global norms, there are few obstacles to a state's use of force other than the threat or actual use of countervailing force by other states.

(See also ANARCHY; ARMS CONTROL; GULF WAR; HUMANITARIAN INTERVENTION; KOREAN WAR; NUCLEAR WEAPONS.)

Kenneth N. Waltz, *Man, the State, and War* (New York, 1959). Robert J. Art and Kenneth N. Waltz, eds., *The Use of Force: Military Power and International Politics*, 5th ed. (New York, 1971, 1999). Michael Walzer, *Just and Unjust Wars* (New York, 1977, 1992). Geoffrey Best, *War and Law Since 1945* (Oxford, 1994).

PAUL R. VIOTTI

FORDISM. A remarkable fusion of incremental technological change and radical social innovation, a synthesis first achieved in the Ford Company's Highland Park plant immediately prior to World War I, established Fordism as a world-historical force with the stunning immediacy of a natural upheaval. The chasm that separated traditional craft methods of automobile manufacture from the new Fordist mass production system appeared almost without warning, although the fault lines which coalesced to produce it often traced their origins a considerable distance into the past. Evolutionary improvements to established practice in component manufacturability, product design, equipment specialization, materials flow, work coordination, and business organization had already expanded annual output of Ford's Model T automobile more than thirty-fold in the five years before the moving assembly line was introduced in 1912–1913. With even more fundamental changes in the social organization of production accompanying the imposition of line-paced continuous manufacture, labor time for constructing each automobile was further reduced from 12.5 hours only a few months earlier to just ninety minutes.

Ford's system not only revolutionized automobile production (within a few years, Ford had captured 55 percent of the U.S. auto market) but, in successfully applying mass production methods to so complex an object, it established a universal logic of industrial production, portending fundamental transformation in many areas of manufacturing and the potential historical regression of societies unable to deploy the new techniques effectively. Its economic and cultural implications were so vast that, even at its inception, contemporaries recognized that Fordism laid claim to defining the epoch.

Thus freighted with historical significance, it is inevitable that Fordism should become interpretively overburdened. In stark contrast with its most famous product, a single model appealing to a range of desires ("available in any color a customer wants so long as it is black"), Fordism is in fact a broad term masquerading as a singular concept. Some equate it with the scientific fragmentation of tasks and specialized division of labor characteristic of Taylorism. For others, Fordism is synonymous with the assembly line. Somewhat more inclusively, Fordism is identified with mass production, the use of specialized machinery and semiskilled labor to manufacture standardized products in large volumes. Fordism has also been conceptualized as an "accumulation regime," a growth path governed by positive feedback loops connecting mass production and mass consumption. At the other end of the spectrum, Fordism achieves a meaning as nebulous as it is all-encompassing when it is understood as definitive of American culture or, still more broadly, as the essence of a particular stage in the development of industrial civilization. The contemporary catchphrase intended to suggest its eclipse—post-Fordism—suffers from a similar problem of diverse and often noncommunicating applications.

Fordism proper involved a refinement and synthesis of disparate, if intersecting, trends within the realm of production method and industrial organization, that is, something rather more than a single element of the production process and rather less than a totalistic cultural form.

The essential precondition for the possibility of Fordist mass production was the practical manufacture of precisely interchangeable parts first accomplished in small arms production under the auspices of the U.S. Ordnance Department and diffusing to the fabrication of sewing machines, agricultural equipment, bicycles, and, eventually, automobiles. The very idea of exactly duplicated components eliminated the craft worker's raison d'être, the ability to create a wide variety of different products or models and to provide experience-based solutions to fabrication problems. Ford pushed this idea to its limit: "There cannot be much hand work or fitting if you are going to accomplish great things."

With parts interchangeability, tasks and processes can be disconnected from each other (and from the same worker) and, thus decomposed, they can be reordered in new configurations. As a consequence, substantial experimentation in task rationalization had already occurred in Ford's plants independently of F. W. Taylor's application of the "armory system's" norms of precise measurement and exact replication to the practice of human labor itself. The central tenets of Taylorism—the analytical decomposition, separation, and standardization of movements and tasks to their smallest efficient scope; functional specialization or the assignment of discrete tasks to distinct workers; scientific selection of the work force; a clear division of labor between the tasks of conception and execution—were all manifest in Fordist production. Yet Fordism and Taylorism were quite divergent in that Taylor's system focused on individual conformity to objective task requirements whereas Ford was far more concerned with the coordination of tasks or posts and the flow of work between them.

The constant refinement of parts interchangeability, machine specialization, and work standardization compelled engineering concern for the systemic integration of machine operations, materials circulation, the distribution of labor, and work organization. Constant, if pragmatic, exploration of integrative techniques and practices culminated in the moving assembly line and the concomitant organization of large-scale manufacture as an integrated, continuous flow, a genuine social innovation.

This same preoccupation led Ford also to build on tendencies toward vertical integration already advanced in other industrial sectors. The "visible hand" of industrial organization was pushed to its logical conclusion at Ford's gigantic River Rouge complex which constituted a virtually self-contained manufacturing system, from the production of raw materials to shipping of the finished product, at a single location. The final step in this extensive nesting process—the integration of discrete work stages into a coherent manufacturing process and of the manufacturing process into a sequentially coordinated production system—was to link the production system directly with the economy as a whole. This connection was established through Ford's distinctive concern to cheapen final product price as opposed to sustaining high-price monopolistic market control, a strategy that presupposed a combination of mass production and mass consumption.

Despite its extraordinary achievements, the inherent rigidity of the supply-driven Fordist system rendered it rapidly obsolete: in less than two decades, Ford's market share declined from three-fifths to less than one-fifth as the company was bested by more flexible rivals. Ford's commitment to specialization was so rigorous and its production system so tightly interdependent that significant engineering improvements (battery-powered ignition, electric starters, shock absorbers) could not be accommodated. Model redesigns were resisted as long as possible and the coordination of sales levels and output became increasingly difficult. When substantive model overhauls occurred, as with the replacement of the fifteen-year-old Model T with the Model A, they required long-term plant closures and equipment scrapping and retooling on a massive scale. High levels of vertical integration proved counterproductive when declines in demand increased unit costs more rapidly for Ford than for its competitors. Henry Ford's propensity for maintaining personal leadership of the firm further reduced organizational responsiveness and innovative capabilities. The impact of employment security and high wages on workers was undermined by the constant acceleration of the assembly line, the only possible Fordist response to deteriorating competitiveness.

Far from monolithically defining industrial society in general or even particular national economies, Fordism remained one logic of production among others: indeed, imperial conceptualizations of Fordism have left largely unexplored its relationship to, and integral dependence on, non-Fordist sectors of the economy. Insofar as Fordism diffused beyond the United States, it was modified substantially by existing institutional structures and industrial cultures. It is not clear that skill-based manufacturing in Germany or Japanese forms of collaborative manufacturing owe much to Fordism at all. The growth of mass consumption certainly preceded the advent of Fordism, and rapid advances in national income levels, such as those occurring in postwar Europe, owe as much to factors like urbanization and the conversion of traditional sectors to capitalist techniques as to national adaptations of Fordist practice.

In this context, the question of "post-Fordism" also seems quite misplaced. To the extent that mass production was not defined by Fordism alone, the reality of post-Fordism long preceded its conceptual formulation. On the other hand, to the degree that post-Fordism denotes the end of of mass production, it neglects the continuing salience of Fordist principles in the movement toward more flexible forms of manufacturing. These include large-scale organization and economies of scale, the capital cost constraints inherent in flexible automation, and the ability of mass production firms to achieve greater flexibility, as in contemporary forms of modular production (the achievement of high levels of product customization on the basis of extensive component and subassembly standardization), through simultaneous refinement and transcendence of Fordist techniques.

(See also DEINDUSTRIALIZATION; POLITICAL ECONOMY.)

H. Arnold and F. Faurote, *Ford Methods and Ford Shops* (New York, 1915). D. Hounshell, *From the American System to Mass Production, 1800–1932* (Baltimore, 1984). C. Maier, *In Search of Stability: Explorations in Historical Political Economy* (Cambridge, U.K., 1987). Bob Jessop, "Fordism and Post-Fordism: A Critical Reformulation," in A. J. Scott and M. Storper, eds., *Pathways to Industrialization and Regional Development in the 1990s* (Boston, 1992).

RICHARD GORDON

FOREIGN AID. In the second half of the twentieth century, foreign aid became an integral part of *international relations throughout the world. The origins of foreign assistance programs are often said to date back to the *Marshall Plan, which involved large-scale and extended financial support by the United States to a number of West European countries that were recovering from the Second World War. Almost fifteen years later, in 1961, foreign aid became formally institutionalized with the establishment of the Development Assistance Committee (DAC) of the *Organization for Economic Cooperation and Development (OECD). The DAC provides guidelines and monitors foreign aid given by OECD members. The DAC also provided a generally accepted definition: financial programs qualify as Official Development Assistance (ODA) if they are primarily intended to promote economic development, if at least 25 percent of the program consists of grants (gifts), and if loans are extended at below-market interest rates.

Not all foreign assistance programs qualify as ODA. Most importantly, since the early 1950s, many foreign aid programs have been of a military nature. Such programs ranged from the exchange of military advisers to the sales of arms below world market prices or the provision of loans and grants to purchase military equipment from the donor. Obviously, in such cases, the main purpose was not economic development. For most donors, development aid and security aid have generally been handled by different governmental departments and agencies and they have been accounted for under different rubrics in the government's budget.

Aid donors may be individual countries, intergovernmental organizations, or private agencies. Multilateral organizations include the UN, the World Bank, and regional development banks. Examples of private aid organizations are Oxfam (U.K.) and Save the Children (U.S.A.). Bilateral aid (between individual countries) presently accounts for about 70 percent of all aid flows. The three biggest donors in absolute numbers in the late 1990s were Japan, France, and the United States. In relative terms (aid as a percentage of GNP), the three largest donors were Denmark, Norway, and the Netherlands. The three biggest recipient countries in absolute numbers were Israel, Indonesia, and China.

The purpose and meaning of foreign aid are not nearly as straightforward as they may seem to the casual observer, and they are disputed in the scholarly literature. The general public perceives foreign aid as a means to promoting development and prosperity. This is the motive most frequently articulated by donor and recipient governments, often in sincerity. But a whole range of other motives can be identified as well and sometimes they effectively crowd out the agenda.

Apart from "altruistic" motivations, at least two reasons for aid giving are identified in the literature. First, as indicated above, certain countries give aid for reasons related to their political and strategic interests. Sometimes, aid serves to facilitate the military presence of the donor in the recipient country (for example, the lease of a military base). It may also serve to provide the recipient country with the military power to deter threats from other countries or from domestic rebel forces. Much of the aid donated by the United States and the Soviet Union during the *Cold War can be explained on those grounds. Second, aid is sometimes given for reasons relating to commercial reasons. The best example of this is so-called tied aid: financial assistance is provided on the condition that the recipient uses the funds to purchase goods from the donor. Japan has frequently been criticized for such programs, though it was quite common among most donors.

Recipient governments, too, are not always exclusively motivated by considerations of economic development. Their relationship to the donor may be driven by external or internal security considerations. For example, Soviet aid to Eastern and Central European countries during the Cold War played a critical role in the domestic stabilization of unpopular regimes, even if the declared purpose of such aid programs was to deter external threats. Similarly, U.S. aid to a country such as Zaire, said to serve development and security interests, effectively financed and legitimized a dictatorship and stalled development for many years.

It is often quite difficult to distinguish between all these different motivations. The first reason is that the declared purpose of aid can be misleading. The second is that aid can serve multiple purposes simultaneously for both donors and recipients. In addition, no matter what the official aim of a particular aid program, there are almost always political implications. At the very least, by giving and receiving aid the donor and recipient countries legitimize each other—an important symbolic transaction in international relations. In more practical terms, aid tends to result in some leverage for the donor country—even if sometimes this leverage turns out to be less than expected.

The foreign aid regime is best understood as an extension of the prevailing international order at large. For most of the second half of the twentieth century, foreign aid reflected the Cold War order. From an ideological perspective, foreign aid was primarily given by the United States and the Soviet Union and their (more or less) affluent allies in an effort to apply their model of development to less developed countries. *Capitalism and socialism provided competing models of development and different visions of *modernity, but they shared a fundamental belief in progress and social engineering. As such, development aid in general is clearly a product of the modernist era.

But the Cold War was not all about ideology. From the perspective of realpolitik, foreign aid was primarily given to bring the recipient country into the sphere of influence of the donor(s) or to keep it from straying to the opposite side. While the superpowers and their allies had a clear strategic agenda, many recipient governments exploited the Cold War to further their own interests. Egypt, in the 1970s, is possibly one of the best examples of a country that applied this strategy with considerable success.

Since the ending of the Cold War and the reorganization of the international political order, foreign aid has undergone major changes. The most immediate and dramatic impact became visible in countries that had been highly dependent on aid from the superpowers and that were subsequently dubbed "Cold War orphans" (examples include Cuba and Zaire). Obviously, all aid from the former East bloc disappeared. But military and development aid given by Western countries has also declined markedly.

Between 1985 and 1997, ODA by all major donor countries dropped from .35 percent of their combined GNP to .22 percent of their combined GNP. The decrease has been most dramatic in the United States, where it dropped from .24 percent to .08 percent. During most of the Cold War, the United States was by far the largest foreign aid donor, but since the end of the Cold War, Japan's aid budget has almost consistently exceeded that of the United States. Indirectly, the end of the Cold War allowed for the emergence of "aid fatigue" among donor countries (especially the United States) and for mounting criticism of allegedly unsuccessful long-term structural development programs (especially in South Asia and sub-Saharan Africa). Many donors have shifted priority from long-term structural development programs to short-term projects that aim at crisis control (for example, refugee resettlement, disaster relief, land mine removal).

The ending of the Cold War coincided with the ideological victory of *liberalism. In its wake, donors have slashed aid budgets on the assumption that trade policies are more effective in stimulating development than is aid. Further, since there are no longer two competing models of development, but only one, aspiring recipients have no choice but to declare adherence to an ideology of translational liberalism. This ideology is sometimes referred to as the "Washington consensus," whose proponents include the United States government and major international organizations such as the International Monetary Fund and the World Bank. The result has been the emergence of a new and prominent type of recipient: countries that are "in transition" to becoming free market democracies. In this new foreign aid regime, there is thus a premium on "good governance" as defined in the discourses of translational liberalism. But all that does not mean that politics and security do not continue to matter, especially for the world's only remaining superpower. At the turn of the century, the biggest recipients of United States foreign aid were Israel, Egypt, and Russia.

(See also DEVELOPMENT AND UNDERDEVELOPMENT.)

David H. Lumsdaine, *Moral Vision in International Politics: The Foreign Aid Regime, 1949–1989* (Princeton, N.J., 1993). Robert Cassen et al., *Does Aid Work?* 2d ed. (Oxford, 1994). Steven Hook, *National Interest and Foreign Aid* (Boulder, Colo., 1995). Richard Grant and Jan Nijman, eds., *The Global Crisis in Foreign Aid* (Syracuse, N.Y., 1998).

JAN NIJMAN

FOREIGN INVESTMENT. See FINANCE, INTERNATIONAL; MULTINATIONAL CORPORATIONS.

FOREIGN POLICY. The term "foreign policy" is a nineteenth-century expansion of the idea of "policy," which had been in use since Chaucer to denote a government's conduct of affairs. The phrase "foreign affairs" was increasingly common from the seventeenth century, as the growing volume of state business began to compel a clearer organizational distinction between home and abroad in the secretariats of royal households. But the idea of a coherent set of positions towards the outside world, or a "foreign policy," seems to have been a product of the bureaucracy and systematization of the industrial age.

For modern observers, foreign policy is at once a phenomenon, a concept, and a major area of study. No definition can do full justice to all three of these aspects of the term, but it is still possible to establish a starting point from which the arguments about interpretation can develop. For there are almost as many views of foreign policy as there are different schools of thought on international relations, or types of political ideology in the world.

Foreign policy, then, can be characterized as the sum of official external relations conducted by an independent actor (usually a state) in *international relations. Such a definition is short enough to be of practical use, while retaining sufficient flexibility to incorporate the changes that have occurred and continue to occur in the nature of modern international politics. To take the components of the definition: "international relations" refers to the web of transactions across state boundaries by all kinds of groups and individuals, and "external relations" to the same activities from the point of view of these actors as they move outside their own society into dealings with others. Neither is restricted to "politics" in the narrow sense, as almost any act can be political if it relates to fundamental issues like the distribution of power or the setting of social values and priorities. On the other hand relations must be "official" to qualify as foreign policy because otherwise all transactions could be included and there would be no inherent sense of agency or purposive action, which is what the term "policy" always implies. In this sense all external relations conducted by the legitimate officeholders of the entity express and contribute to foreign policy: defense ministers, foreign trade ministers, and environment ministers

may be almost as involved as their colleagues in charge of the diplomatic service. To the extent that senior bureaucrats also take part directly in high-level international transactions, they too will be conducting foreign policy, although their margin of maneuver will vary enormously from state to state and issue to issue. At the extremes, bureaucratic and political competition sometimes means that a state is running several foreign policies simultaneously.

The "sum" of external relations is important because although we talk properly about a country's specific foreign policy towards this state or that, the use of the term *tout court* must always be holistic—it represents the entire package of actions and attitudes towards the outside world. Lastly, it is important to define foreign policy as issuing from "independent actors" rather than the more conventional restrictive definition, so as to avoid chaining ourselves to the state in an era when it is evident both that foreign and domestic policy often blur into each other, and that non-state actors are major participants in international relations. So although it has to be admitted that the great majority of foreign policies belong to states, which still monopolize the business of global politics, there is no intrinsic reason why other actors, such as churches or political groups, which transcend on a transnational basis much of the control theoretically exercised by states, should not be deemed to have "foreign" policies. For they, like nation-states, naturally distinguish between their internal character and the international system. We may need to qualify their actions as "private foreign policies," but they can be analyzed in ways not dissimilar to states.

Most non-state entities, however, have neither the reach nor the motivation to go beyond mere external relations into foreign policy proper. The average sporting federation or municipality can rarely defy government-to-government structures. While some companies, regions, and governments-in-exile do have the resources to achieve a high profile in international politics it is particular entities, like the African National Congress or the Anglican Church, rather than whole categories that qualify as foreign policy actors.

Economic *interdependence has increased the number of transnational entities and their opportunities for independent action, although here too variable patterns of development and liberalization make it a more patchy process than is often assumed. While there may be relatively few enterprises capable of challenging states frontally, as Rupert Murdoch's News International has done, many others have complicated the foreign policies of governments. The disputes over extraterritoriality, for example, between the European Union and the United States, only arise because of the existence of companies that operate internationally, and in the first instance on the basis of the market, regardless of national security policies.

Governments have also had to contend increasingly with international *non-governmental organizations as participants capable themselves of shaping international politics. Although nominally based in one country, organizations like Amnesty International, Greenpeace, and Médecins sans Frontières have increasingly taken on a transnational quality and operate on the basis of specified values unrelated to those of any particular national interest. For their part governments do not stand on the sidelines observing. They have developed ways of coping with such actors, and of using them. As a result, both foreign policy and international politics are more subtle and complicated processes than in the Cold War era.

The literature that has burgeoned on foreign policy since 1960 provides us with the means to understand both the underlying forces which shape a country's foreign policy, and the evolution of the phenomenon itself. This literature constitutes what is now a major subarea of international relations, known variously as foreign policy analysis (FPA) or comparative foreign policy (CFP). It takes the micro, or actor-perspective on international relations, as opposed to the macro, or system-perspective in which patterns are identified without going into the motivations of the actors who produce them. Views differ on what can be achieved at the micro level of analysis. The CFP school, which became well established in the United States, has preferred a behavioral methodology, and has operated on the assumption that it should be possible to generalize about the behavior of states and foreign policies, as classes of phenomena, once sufficient data has been generated by rigorously scientific methods. This positivist approach did not catch on in most European or Commonwealth universities, or in the more traditionalist American faculties. There are also now signs that after the expenditure of considerable effort, money, and ingenuity, some of the main proponents of the school have come to realize its limitations. Quite apart from the general debate about positivism, foreign policy is an insufficiently discrete phenomenon to be able to bear the weight of extensive cross-cultural comparisons and generalizations.

This is to say that because foreign policy as an activity is not sharply different from other kinds of public policy, it cannot generate an exclusive theory of behavior to fit it; also, that the variations over countries and time periods are large enough to enforce damaging qualifications on attempts to derive general laws. More than a wholly distinctive universe of human behavior, foreign policy represents an arena in which various forms of explanation may be brought together, enabling us to say a great deal about the nature of foreign policy, its making, its interaction with domestic politics, and its place in our understanding of international politics as a whole.

This more eclectic approach, which has established itself as the most fruitful way to study foreign policy, employs the dialectical approach of critically testing generalizations and case studies against each other. It uses theory without being enslaved to it, in the sense of concentrating on what are known as "middle-range theories." At one end of the spectrum this means rigorously constructed hypotheses about closely defined particular aspects of foreign policy (or "structured empiricism" in Michael Brecher's words), of which the best example is Brecher's own work on decisions under conditions of crisis. At the other end of the same scale of middle-range theories are sets of insights, more loosely organized but not less valuable for that, on such matters as the tendency of decision makers to lean on historical analogies, or the impact of geopolitical and other environmental constraints on choice. In the middle is a good deal of impressive work on the domestic sources of foreign policy, perception and misperception, bureaucratic politics, and the problems attending the notion of rational conduct in the context of foreign policy. The dominant position of *rational choice approaches in political

science has failed to catch on in foreign policy analysis for this very reason: the limitations of the "rational actor" model had been fully exposed by the mid-1970s.

The comparative spirit informs most of this writing, even if a tendency towards the case-study method sometimes obscures that fact. Indeed, the foreign policy characteristics of certain types and groups of states have attracted a good deal of attention from those wishing to link the study of foreign policy making to the broader patterns of international relations. Small states, middle-range powers, developing countries, Islamic states, and west European states all fall into this category. In this sense "comparative foreign policy" is often conducted along traditionalist lines and is not to be associated exclusively with the behavioral school referred to above.

The study of foreign policy has thus evolved over more than thirty years. Despite continuing differences over methodology and scope, it deals in essence with the content of policy on the one hand and the process of foreign policy making on the other. Most often, however, it focuses on the interactions between the two, starting from the premise that what is done will be partially determined by how it is done, and allowing for the possibility of human beings asserting their existential rights to choice, even in the most constricted circumstances. Moreover the environments in which action takes place are to be regarded as crucial but not given; the interplay of domestic and international factors is an endlessly varied and elastic process.

For the most part the contemporary analysis of foreign policy has been driven by a dispassionate desire to open up previously neglected questions. But the spirit of scientific inquiry should not be allowed to obscure the points of connection between the concerns of policy analysis with rationality and perception, and that long-standing normative approach which dwells on such subjects as the extent to which law or morality should affect diplomacy, and the tension between short-term and long-term considerations in foreign policy. Realism, with its black-boxing of the state and its reductionist emphasis on interests as the basis of foreign policy, cannot match foreign policy analysis in this respect as a meeting place for the empirical and philosophical aspects of states' activities towards each other. Indeed, recent poststructuralist work on discourse and identity has tended to argue that no such distinction can be made; the very concept of "foreign" policy is constituted in its familiar way as the result of a dominant discourse which should be deconstructed so as to reveal its narrowing assumptions about both identity and values. Poststructuralists have revived theoretical interest in foreign policy by examining language and the various worldviews thereby revealed.

Yet the study of foreign policy still faces an important challenge for the future. For the very need to define foreign policy broadly enough so as to cater to a wider range of actions than those encompassed by traditional diplomacy, shows how it is becoming difficult to distinguish the aspects of public policy which are directed towards foreigners from those which are primarily in the domestic domain. The problems of migration and criminality which are high on the "new" agenda of post–Cold War international politics require, by definition, strategies which are both internally and externally directed. If such a distinction becomes increasingly unsustainable, the study of foreign policy will merge with that of *comparative politics to form a new, broader focus on the politics and policies of states (or whatever systems for mobilizing decisions may replace states) within the complex web of global interdependence. The disappearance of foreign policy that this would represent, however, is still many decades into the future. Even then the concept would probably need reinventing under another name, given the inherent tendency of human collectivities to perceive inside as different from outside. Whenever foreign policy seems on the point of losing its contemporary relevance, it has the habit of bouncing back to the center of our concerns, whoever and wherever we are.

James N. Rosenau, *The Scientific Study of Foreign Policy*, 2d ed. (London, 1980). Yaacov Y. I. Vertzberger, *The World in Their Minds: Information Processing, Cognition and Perception in Foreign Policy Decision Making* (Stanford, Calif., 1990). Alexander George, *Bridging the Gap: Theory and Practice in Foreign Policy* (Washington, D.C., 1993). David Campbell, *Writing Security: United States Foreign Policy and the Politics of Identity*, rev. ed. (Minneapolis, 1998).

CHRISTOPHER HILL

FOREIGN WORKERS. The explosion in the number of persons working outside of their home country since 1945 is the inevitable product of the relentless globalization of the world economy and the evolution of an international labor market. Although every region has been affected—in 1998, for instance, a large majority of workers in the Gulf states were aliens—the advanced industrial countries have especially benefited from and borne the unique political and social costs of post–World War II labor migration. Of the tens of millions of foreign workers in the world, more than half reside in the OECD countries. Foreign workers compose more than 6 percent of the labor force of France, 9 percent of Germany, 9 percent of the United States, 10 percent of Austria, and 19 percent of Canada and Switzerland. In Australia, which has had both a large temporary and permanent foreign worker program, aliens compose 24 percent of the total labor force.

The initial catalyst for the mass migration of foreign workers from the developing to the advanced industrial societies was the economic boom generated within the latter countries between 1945 and 1969, a period of unprecedented economic expansion that precipitated acute labor shortages and rigid labor markets. To remedy these problems and to sustain economic growth, private employers and governments recruited foreign workers from the Third World and Eastern Europe. Their efforts were unambiguously successful. During the duration of the boom, economic growth, an abundant labor supply, and productivity gains were strongly correlated in the advanced industrial countries.

Although many governments, and particularly those in Western Europe, have attempted to curtail new labor immigration since the general economic downturn of the early 1970s, they cannot conjure away through a simple shift in state immigration policy the structural dependence of their economies on foreign workers. Nor can they eradicate the push factors impelling workers from the less developed and the economically liberalizing countries to emigrate in search of employment. In the first instance, foreign labor has come to fulfill an indispensable role in the domestic economies of the OECD countries by providing a highly flexible, inexpen-

sive, and malleable workforce that is almost as essential to fostering economic growth and prosperity during the recent period of high native unemployment as it was during an earlier era of full employment. In the second instance, the revolutionary economic, political, and social upheavals visited upon Asia, Eastern Europe, Latin America, and other regions since the early 1980s have swelled the ranks of foreign workers seeking access to the labor markets of the industrial societies.

After significantly expanding during the 1980s and early 1990s, the overall flow of immigrants into the OECD countries has begun to stabilize. However, a number of factors are currently operating that will indefinitely sustain relatively high levels of international labor migration. First, despite high overall unemployment rates, shortages of skilled and highly skilled workers persist within many OECD countries. Second, the inexorable demographic ageing of First World populations creates economic incentives for governments in the advanced industrial societies to tolerate some labor immigration. Third, whatever the intentions of governments and private employers, increasing income differentials between the most and the least developed countries, high unemployment in the developing and newly liberalizing economies, internecine ethnic strife, and the continuing outbreak of civil and regional wars inevitably increase the availability of mobile foreign labor. And fourth, ever faster and cheaper modes of transportation and the easier transmission of economic information facilitate the movement of workers across national borders.

Yet another factor facilitating the migration of labor, the establishment of a regional space within which workers may move relatively freely, pertains almost exclusively to the completion of the single market within the *European Union during the 1990s. Approximately 5 percent of the EU's 370 million residents currently live outside of their country of citizenship. However, for a variety of cultural, structural, and political reasons, less than 2 percent of the EU labor force, or 2.5 million persons, are intra-EU migrants, a number that is dwarfed by the 13 million non-EU citizens legally residing within the EU. The planned eastward expansion of the European Union after 2002 combined with the continued impact of the aforementioned global forces on general labor migration trends will continue yielding an abundant, perhaps an overabundant, supply of foreign workers within the EU. The challenge for EU policy makers will be to manage the social and political tensions generated by these conditions within the context of high unemployment and projections of only modest employment growth.

(See also GLOBALIZATION; INTERNATIONAL MIGRATION; INTERNATIONAL POLITICAL ECONOMY; LABOR MOVEMENT; NORTH-SOUTH RELATIONS, RACE AND RACISM.)

Stephen Castles and Mark J. Miller, *The Age of Migration* (New York, 1993). Nigel Harris, *The New Untouchables: Immigration and the New World Worker* (New York, 1995).

ANTHONY M. MESSINA

FOUCAULT, Michel. Having taken his degrees in philosophy and psychology and taught in Sweden, Poland, the Federal Republic of Germany, and Tunisia, Michel Foucault (1926–1984) finally, in 1970, occupied a chair in the history of systems of thought in France's most prestigious institution of higher learning, the Collège de France. During the 1960s, Foucault's work was associated with structuralism and antipsychiatry, but he denied kinship with either group. In the 1970s and 1980s he was known in the United States as a poststructuralist, and again he was unhappy with the designation. He acknowledged an affinity with the work of Gilles Deleuze for both political and philosophical similarities. Politically he participated in the Groupe Information Prisons (GIP) and was active in various causes, such as gay rights, *feminism, and anticolonialism, that emerged in the wake of *May 1968 and the *New Left. As an intellectual with a concern for the victims of domination he may be compared to Voltaire and Jean-Paul Sartre. But he strove to redefine the stance of the intellectual in important ways.

Foucault's writings may be characterized as "post-Marxist" in the sense that he attempted to develop strategies of interpretation that define mechanisms of domination outside the workplace, or, better, outside the category of the mode of production. Each of his books addresses a historical topic or field, discovering how that realm of experience was colonized or controlled by hierarchical apparatuses. These domains are madness in *Madness and Civilization* (1961), medicine in *The Birth of the Clinic* (1963), the human sciences in *The Order of Things* (1966), punishment in *Discipline and Punish* (1975), and sexuality in *The History of Sexuality* (1976–1984). He also wrote a treatise on his methodology, *The Archaeology of Knowledge* (1969). In addition Foucault wrote important books on art, especially on René Magritte (*This Is Not a Pipe* [1973]) and on Raymond Roussel (*Death and the Labyrinth* [1963]). Finally, important articles and interviews have been collected in Donald Bouchard, ed., *Language and Counter-Memory, Practice* (1977); Colin Gordon, *Power/Knowledge* (1980); and Lawrence Kritzman, *Foucault: Politics, Philosophy, Culture* (1988).

Much of this work betrays the influence of Friedrich Nietzsche: Foucault follows a genealogical paradigm, one that searches backward in history for a point of difference and, once locating that, deploys that difference as a critical lever for the analytical critique of the phenomenon in the modern period. This principle is opposed to all forms of evolutionism that trace the rise and development of a phenomenon that culminates in the present. Foucault also looks for the interplay of discourse and practice in the topic, rather than assuming a split between opinion and action. The specific combination of discourse and practice that he identifies he calls a "technology of *power" or "microphysics of power." He treats these configurations as mechanisms of power that have positive effects of constituting subjects or individuals rather than negative effects of restricting or constraining their action. Taken together, these innovations construct a model for a new kind of cultural history, a history that is neither intellectual nor social but a startling combination of them. Foucault's historical paradigm, which connects very well with certain new directions in the history of women and minority groups and in *feminist theory and anticolonialism, offers a new departure for critical studies in the social sciences.

The salient theme of Foucault's work is the critique of the Cartesian subject, the autonomous, rational individual. He attempts to show how the Cartesian individual is a faulty starting point for theory and politics, how it is a historical phenomenon that requires investigation, not affirmation. He has been most concerned to examine the forms of rationality generated in a culture characterized by this sort of subject-position. In this sense his work intersects that of Teresa de Lauretis in *Technologies of Gender* (Bloomington, Ind., 1987), and also bears a resemblance to the sociology of Max *Weber and to those such as Georg Lukács and the Frankfurt School whose work elaborates his study of instrumental rationality and bureaucracy. But Foucault's position deviates from theirs in the degree that it reflects upon the configuration of the author in scientific studies and refuses to allow the author a privileged stance of objectivity or authority. Thus Foucault rejects what he calls "the universal intellectual," someone whose scientific work affords a position of authority either as objectivity or within a movement of emancipation. Instead he proposes a category of "the specific intellectual," one whose discourse may be taken up by those seeking to protest domination but which derives its power only from within defined institutional and historical contexts.

(See also MARXISM; MODERNITY; POSTMODERNISM.)

Mark Poster, *Foucault, Marxism and History* (New York, 1974). Hubert Dreyfus and Paul Rabinow, *Michel Foucault: Beyond Structuralism and Hermeneutics* (Chicago, 1982).

MARK POSTER

FRANCE. Modern France is a product of centuries of historical sedimentation. French, theretofore regarded as a debased form of Latin, became the official language in 1539, in the reign of François I. Under the seventeenth-century royal absolutism of Louis XIV, *Colbertiste* (after Jean-Baptiste Colbert, Louis's chief minister) state-led patterns of economic development were firmly set out, Catholicism universalized at the expense of France's Protestants, and France's ambitious international role defined. The revolution of 1789 added new layers, prefiguring subsequent debates over the *monarchy, desirable forms of political representation, and more radical proposals for a centralized Jacobin *democracy. Henceforth an image of revolutionary upheaval would be deeply imprinted on France's collective memory. Finally, in the revolution and its Napoleonic aftermath, France—then Europe's largest nation with a population of 28 million—reconfigured its imperialist international vocation.

Modernization. Nineteenth-century France had extraordinary difficulty in making constitutional choices. There were thus episodic alternations of monarchy and revolutionary crisis (1830, 1848, 1871) until the foundation of the Third Republic, modern France's hardiest constitutional arrangement, which lasted from 1871 to World War II. Dramatic political cleavages persisted. Republican France struggled against Catholic and rural France through centralizing programs of public education to endow every young French person with uniform tools for *citizenship. Monarchists and the antirepublican nationalists who slowly replaced them struck back in the Dreyfus affair of the 1890s. (Dreyfus, a Jewish officer unjustly accused of treason, became the center of an intense struggle between reactionaries and republicans.) When the *labor movement emerged it, too, was ideologically riven between moderate and revolutionary wings. The early Third Republic also reformulated French imperialism into a system of protectionist walls sheltering mother country and colonies from serious competitors.

World War I began another half-century of political turbulence in which disagreements about constitutional forms overlapped, and were slowly changed by, modernization. The Great War cost the nation a substantial minority of its male population and brought new divisive ideological themes. The *Left, growing in importance as industrialization progressed, split between Socialists and pro-Soviet Communists. The labor movement would thus be marked by factional infighting that both weakened it and strongly politicized French industrial relations. Third Republic institutions, built on social "stalemate" between the rural, provincial world of the nineteenth century and more dynamic urban capitalism, made important choices extremely difficult to make. In addition, politically conservative and socially paternalistic capitalists would not seek common ground with radicalized labor interests. The result, fed by the Great Depression and a newly ominous international context, was growing delegitimation of the republic itself. Reformist Popular Front governments after 1936 were unable to survive long enough to institute needed reforms. Divided, France was quite unable to confront the rise of *fascism elsewhere in Europe and the shock of the first modern experience of Left government precipitated much of the *Right toward antirepublicanism.

Defeat by the Germans in June 1940 led to political capitulation and the authoritarian, backward-looking Vichy regime of Marshal Pétain, supported by much of the traditional French Right. In the name of patriotism Vichy compromised with the Nazis, in particular in the treatment of Jews. France's modernizing elements found their way into the resistance movement that emerged. The discredit of the Right and the commitment of the Resistance opened the brief post-Liberation period after November 1944 to a wide range of reforms. Extensive nationalizations endowed the state with new power over the direction of France's economy. France's *welfare state was greatly expanded. A caste of modernizing technocrats, symbolized by Jean *Monnet and his *planning commission, sought to use new state leverage for a rejuvenated Colbertisme and its success distinguished France's postwar development trajectory from those of other European societies.

Post-Liberation governments did less well at building new political institutions. Disputes between General Charles de *Gaulle, Resistance leader and first postwar prime minister, and the Left over the place of the executive led in 1946 to de Gaulle's angry resignation and denunciation of an emerging "regime of the parties." The constitution of the new Fourth Republic—barely approved by the electorate—made the National Assembly the seat of all power in which majority coalitions, made volatile by a new voting system of proportional representation, became even more changeable in the Cold War after 1947. France's alignment on the U.S. side forced the Communists, with 25 percent of the electorate, into quasi-permanent isolation. Governments had thenceforth to be constructed from among Center-Left and Center-Right groups who rarely agreed. In consequence the Fourth Republic drifted rightward, finally to be taken hostage by forces determined to preserve French colonialism. From 1946 until 1958 there was bloody, costly, and divisive warfare, first in Indochina and then in Algeria.

Despite political confusion, socioeconomic modernization proceeded apace. French elites were central in the founding of the European Coal and Steel Community in 1951 and in the 1957 Treaty of Rome founding the European Economic Community (EEC). The economy grew healthily, but the Fourth Republic did not live to reap the fruits. A quasi-coup in May 1958 brought Charles de Gaulle to power. The new presidentialist Constitution of the Fifth Republic adopted by referendum in September 1958 greatly increased the power of the executive. The president, elected independently of Parliament (indirectly, to begin with, and then by direct universal suffrage after 1962), could appoint and dismiss the prime minister and the government, dissolve the National Assembly, call referenda under certain circumstances, and speak for the country in international affairs. Governments, very dependent on the president, were themselves strengthened against the Parliament by provisions which allowed them to control the National Assembly's agenda, making it difficult for governmental legislation to be defeated.

When President de Gaulle ended the *Algerian War, and France's imperial era, in June 1962, a quest for a new world role began. De Gaulle, fortified by the autonomy granted by France's new nuclear force de dissuasion, took distance from the United States in Europe and the *North Atlantic Treaty Organization in relations with the Soviet Union and the Third World and in financial policy. Europe was newly central to French concerns and there de Gaulle promoted the implementation of a customs-free Common Market, while insisting that the EEC take on an intergovernmental cast—a Europe des patries—and vetoing Britain's membership on the grounds that the British were not sufficiently European.

The Gaullist 1960s were the culminating point of the "thirty glorious years" of economic growth in which France was transformed from the most rural of all advanced societies, reconstructed its cities, watched television and bought new cars, and began to send its youth to universities in unprecedented numbers. The energetic state-dirigiste programs contained in France's periodic "indicative" economic plans helped these processes forward. Quite as important, the end of a protectionist empire-oriented economic outlook led France to turn to the new EEC. The growth-producing effects of increased intra-European trade helped France prosper.

Decomposition-Reconfiguration. The social complications of economic success ended de Gaulle's brilliant career, however. Inept handling of massive protests by students and workers in the May–June 1968 "events" led to his resignation in April 1969. His presidential successors until 1981, Georges Pompidou (elected in 1969, died in office in 1974) and Valéry Giscard d'Estaing (from 1974 to 1981), were obliged to temper conservative proclivities with new concern for social policy, in part because the French Left was demonstrating new political vitality. The dramatic change in economic circumstances after the first oil shock in the mid-1970s complicated the situation. In the new policy stalemate which followed, growth declined, inflation rose rapidly, and unemployment, which had been very low in the boom years, shot up.

The Left came to power when Socialist leader François *Mitterrand defeated Giscard d'Estaing in the 1981 presidential elections. In its first two years after 1981, the Mitterrand presidency mounted a Colbertiste project of massive nationalizations, state economic planning, and dirigiste industrial policy. It also legislated important reforms to give workers and unions more power in the workplace and a degree of governmental decentralization. The project led straight to an impasse, however, as inflation rose, imports flooded the domestic market, and the franc weakened. By 1983 Mitterrand and the Socialists had to begin a cultural and policy revolution, committing to austerity, deregulatory economic restructuring, and a more open and mixed economy. Deflation and the maintenance of a strong franc—*monetarism, in fact—drove macroeconomic policy thereafter. One consequence was that unemployment rose dramatically—to 12 percent of the labor force in the mid-1990s. As the Socialists shifted, the Communists declined and the Right changed as well. The rise of the xenophobic Front National (FN, which won nearly 11 percent of the vote in the 1984 Europarliamentary elections) placed the moderate Right, which had already lost its sense of political project, in a difficult situation. It would have difficulty winning without co-opting the extreme Right yet was unlikely to win if it did.

Modesty at the Millennium. By the mid-1990s, France was in uncharted waters. The political formulae that had underlain both Left and Right in the postwar period had disintegrated. When the Mitterrand era ended in cronyism, corruption, and policy aimlessness, the Socialists had again to reconstruct their image and practices, which they did quite successfully. The party's new leader, Lionel Jospin, barely lost the presidency in 1995 and two years later became prime minister at the head of a "rainbow" Left coalition. The Socialists' new identity involved an austere quest for international competitiveness within a liberalizing European Union accompanied by domestic reformism "with a human face" to preserve the welfare state, redistribute work (through the thirty-five-hour week), and promote new forms of social solidarity. The Right was less successful. Jacques Chirac won the presidency in 1995, after two years of new cohabitation between Mitterrand and Chirac's forces in 1993–1995, then lost his parliamentary majority to the Left in 1997, causing the Right's crisis and divisiveness to deepen.

In this unsettled new context the Constitution of the Fifth Republic revealed a different face. There had been an unspoken assumption until the mid-1980s that the political influence of the presidency would automatically produce a parliamentary majority in support of presidential policies. The method chosen by de Gaulle after 1958 for parliamentary elections—single-member constituencies with a runoff in the event no majority emerged at the first round—was designed to promote this. Yet the Constitution also contained the possibility of a president from one side of the political spectrum and a parliamentary majority from the opposition, a circumstance that could severely limit the enhanced executive power which de Gaulle, its creator, had meant to build into the new order. From 1986 to 1988, 1993 to 1995, and from 1997 into the new millennium France thus experimented with "cohabitation."

The economic shift begun in the 1980s was enduring, partly underlying the changing political landscape. Enhanced market internationalization, particularly through the European Union, a restructuring of production, and rapid technological change changed French outlooks. Nationalist *Colbertisme* retreated, French elites gave increased attention to the market, and politicians, particularly on the Left, abandoned anticapitalist dreams about "revolutionary" transformation.

By the 1990s France's new place in the world had also become clearer. France's nostalgia for great power status gave way to focused effort to influence the course of European development through the *European Union. France took the lead to relaunch European integration, beginning with the post-1985 program to complete the European Single Market. The *Maastricht Treaty, ratified in 1993, committed the EU to Economic and Monetary Union (EMU) and the euro, another largely French initiative. EMU came into being, after a staged transition, in 1999 when monetary policy sovereignty for EMU members, including France, was transferred to an independent and supranational European Central Bank. Following a Franco-German initiative Maastricht also proposed the construction of a Common European Foreign and Defense Policy (CFSP). Little happened initially, but Europe's failures in confronting violence in the Balkans, changes in the EU Treaty at Amsterdam in 1997, the post–Cold War reconfiguration of French and other EU member states' defense postures, and British-French rapprochement (in the St. Malo declaration of 1998) eventually placed new crisis management planning and action on the EU's table. Initial focus was on building a European defense force to complement NATO as a limited "European pillar" with specific tasks. For France, which had resisted full incorporation into NATO and sought greater European autonomy from the United States from the 1960s, this was a huge change.

At the millennium France had come almost full circle. In the early modern period it had been a founding, and imperious, member of the quarrelsome universe of European nation-states that then exploded in the murderous first half of the twentieth century. Throughout most of the second half of this century France had sought a distinctive national model for development and an independent presence on the world stage. In the 1980s and 1990s, however, the nationalist, statist, internationally ambitious, and proudly autonomous France became something very new. Thus for the first part of the twenty-first century France's fate would be tightly tied to that of a uniting Europe which itself was growing to cover a vast portion of the entire European continent. Politically, France was bound by agreements to delegate significant dimensions of its sovereignty to the EU. Its remaining powers, particularly those in fiscal and social policy, were important, but their use was constrained by the broader European and global context. In economic terms, France would rise or fall on its success in the broader, increasingly integrated, European economy, itself subject to the stresses of *globalization. After centuries of universalist ambition, France finally recognized its *interdependence with others. Its influence will remain considerable in this new world, however, particularly if it is able to regenerate its economy, confront unemployment, reconfigure its social programs, and continue its commitment to democracy.

(See also COLONIAL EMPIRES; DECOLONIZATION; GAULLISM; MAY 1968; SOCIALISM AND SOCIAL DEMOCRACY.)

Stanley Hoffmann et al., *In Search of France* (Cambridge, Mass., 1963). Peter A. Hall, *Governing the Economy: The Politics of State Intervention in Britain and France* (New York, 1986). George Ross, Stanley Hoffmann, and Sylvia Malzacher, *The Mitterrand Experiment* (New York, 1987). Pierre Favier and Michel Martin-Roland, *La Décennie Mitterrand*, 4 vols. (Paris, 1990–1999). Peter A. Hall, Jack Hayward, and Howard Machin, eds., *Developments in French Politics* (New York, 1994). George Ross, *Jacques Delors and European Integration* (Oxford, 1995).

GEORGE ROSS

FRANCO, Francisco. Born in El Ferrol, a port town in the province of La Coruña, on 4 December 1892, Francisco Franco Bahamonde was the son of a lower-middle-class family. He was the youngest of three brothers, short in stature, with delicate features and a soft, somewhat shrill, voice. At the age of fifteen he enlisted in the Toledo Military Academy, where the decisive features of his character took shape. There, he identified with the frustrations of the Spanish army, which was torn between a mystic belief in its destiny—to save *Spain from the inefficiency of its politicians—and the humiliation suffered during the war against the United States in 1898. At the age of seventeen Franco was made an officer and volunteered to serve in Morocco; this was the best means toward quick promotion.

Franco joined the Spanish Foreign Legion in 1920. In 1923 he married Carmen Polo, the daughter of a wealthy businessman. She instilled in his life bourgeois order and Catholic piety. At the age of thirty-three he was promoted to colonel, and it was then (February 1925) that he took command of the Foreign Legion. One year later he became the youngest general in Europe, and in 1928 he was appointed head of the Zaragoza Military Academy.

The coming of the Second Republic, following the April 1931 elections, curbed Franco's military career. But in 1933, when the conservative Right took over the government of the republic, Franco returned to active service and within a year was promoted to major general. His staunch loyalty to the conservative forces of the republic was revealed when he was called to quell the Asturian miners' rebellion in October 1934. His services were rewarded in May 1935 when he was appointed Army head of staff.

Thanks to his military prestige and notable political skill, which enabled him to obtain military aid from both *Hitler and *Mussolini, Franco became head of the conservative forces, rebelling against the Republic on 18 July 1936. On 1 November of that same year he was elected head of state of Nationalist Spain and generalissimo of its armies, but General Franco's rebel regime needed three long years of civil war to gain control of the whole nation. During *World War II the new nationalist regime was saved thanks to Franco's astute *diplomacy; he knew how to support the cause of the Axis powers without taking on irreversible military or diplomatic commitments.

Franco's regime started as a military dictatorship but later adopted a civil structure, reflecting its middle-class social base. On 19 April 1937 the Falange (the Spanish fascist party) merged with other right-wing political forces and became the regime's official political party, known as the Movimiento. Unlike Nazism and *fascism, "Francoism" was not based on a revolutionary party of the masses nor on a patriotic youth movement, but on conservative forces such as the army, the church, and the *caudillo* (leader). In other words, before the regime began to rely on economic prosperity and the seductions of a consumer society—a policy that, from the 1960s onward, would create a gradually unsustainable tension between *development and *modernization on the one hand and political *authoritarianism on the other—it rested on the traditional forces of Spanish society. Until the late 1950s, the social foundations of Francoism were the large landowners of the south, the Castilian middle-class peasantry, the new bourgeoisie that had sprung up in the shadow of the black market, and the bureaucracy of a country of "red tape" and hierarchies.

Ideology and the party never played a central role in Francoism; the party was an instrument of the government, not the other way round. The structure of Franco's governments was always flexible owing both to his practice of adapting his policies to changing conditions—provided that such "adaptation" would not undermine political authority—and his insistence on constantly restructuring the balance of forces within his conservative coalition. The army and the church—the latter providing the main ideological cement of Franco's regime—were the pillars that sustained the unity of the new Spain. Although a negative facet of the regime was that it excluded those who did not share the ideals of Franco's crusade against *parliamentary democracy and *liberalism, a positive facet of the regime was that it channeled conservative interests into evolutionary forms.

Francoism was more than just the personal rule of a dictator, although it was not a completely totalitarian regime, either. Juan Linz defined Franco's government as an institutionalized authoritarian system, that is, a political system with limited political *pluralism, devoid of a coherent or clearly defined ideology.

Franco's regime received very little international backing until 1953, when it managed to break its diplomatic isolation thanks to the concordat with the Holy See and a cooperation treaty with the United States. Until then, the regime was able to ignore any reactions that its domestic policy might provoke in Europe; it even managed to profit politically from international hostility. Franco reacted to this hostility toward his regime by presenting it to the Spanish people, who closed ranks around him as a manifestation of the supposed international conspiracy against Spain.

Franco was head of state and prime minister until 1973, and carried out official duties such as presiding over important cabinet meetings and receiving ambassadors. He was head of the Movimiento—Spain's only political organization—and generalissimo, supreme commander of all the armed forces.

Franco died on 20 November 1975, connected to an array of sophisticated medical devices, and with Saint Teresa's arm at his side and the cloak of the Virgin on his bed. His death was symbolic of the Spain he had ruled: a modern, industrial nation and consumer society obsessed by the relics of a traditional Catholic state.

(See also ROMAN CATHOLIC CHURCH; SPANISH CIVIL WAR.)

Stanley Payne, *Franco's Spain* (London, 1968). Edouard de Blaye, *Franco and the Politics of Spain* (Harmondsworth, U.K., 1976). Paul Preston, ed., *Spain in Crisis: The Evolution and Decline of the Franco Regime* (Hassocks, U.K., 1976). José Amodia, *Franco's Political Legacy: From Fascism to Facade Democracy* (London, 1977). Raymond Carr and Juan Pablo Fusi, *España, de la dictadura a la democracia* (Barcelona, 1979).

SHLOMO BEN-AMI

FRANCOPHONE AFRICA. Comprising the sub-Saharan nations for which French is the language of government, all of which were colonies of France or Belgium, Francophone Africa consists of seventeen countries that form a contiguous bloc in West and Central Africa; to them may be added Malagasy and the Comoros of the Indian Ocean, and Djibouti on the Horn of Africa.

Francophone Africa includes nearly half the area of sub-Saharan Africa, and its population of more than 150 million is one-third of the sub-Saharan African total. Congo-Kinshasa, with some 40 million inhabitants, is the largest and most populous country of the group; Cameroun, Malagasay Republic, and Côte d'Ivoire follow with just over 10 million each. In West Africa, *Islam is the dominant religion, though Christianity and local religions are important in Côte d'Ivoire, Togo, and Benin. In Central Africa and Madagascar, Christianity is dominant, with Catholics outnumbering Protestants.

These political units were formed through European conquest in the period 1880–1920. *France organized most of its conquests into two large federations: French West Africa was formed in 1905 with its capital in Dakar; French Equatorial Africa was formed in 1910 with its capital in Brazzaville. French Madagascar had a separate government general. Congo-Kinshasa had its origin in the Congo Independent State, founded by King Leopold II of Belgium in 1885; it became the Belgian Congo in 1908. The conquest of German colonies during World War I led to creation of additional Francophone territories, French Togo and Cameroon, and Belgian Ruanda-Urundi, under mandate from the League of Nations and then the UN. Independence came to almost all of Francophone Africa in 1960: Guinea gained independence in 1958; Rwanda, Burundi, the Comoros, and Djibouti later.

The term *Francophone Africa* came into usage in the years after independence, when it was no longer appropriate to refer to *French Africa*. Thereafter, the tenuous unity of the francophone countries was reinforced by political and cultural developments. Most obvious among these was the emergent role of France as neocolonial power, providing economic, military, and technical aid, and linking the Francophone nations in a series of international groupings, starting with the *Organisation Commune Africaine et Malagache*, founded in 1960.

In addition to the French presence, some African factors serve to sustain the identity of Francophone Africa. Use of the French language in Africa expanded greatly with the growth of public education after independence. The elites of the Francophone countries are united by a common cosmopolitan culture, based on the French system of higher education and reaffirmed by such institutions as the news magazine *Jeune Afrique* and the Libreville-based radio station, Africa No. 1. Further, the commonality of the Francophone states serves them, in continental politics, as a counterweight to the relative power and wealth of such English-speaking states as Nigeria, Kenya, Zimbabwe, and, ultimately, South Africa. The Francophone countries participate actively in the *Organization of African Unity.

The former French colonies of West and Central Africa are all members of the franc zone, with the *Communauté Financière Africaine* (CFA) franc pegged at 0.01 French franc. This hard-currency status has given these countries monetary stability, though it has not prevented devaluation, as with the 50 percent devaluation of the CFA franc in 1994. Congo-Kinshasa, Rwanda, Burundi, and Madagascar have autonomous currencies, as did Mali and Guinea before they rejoined the franc zone.

*Structural adjustment programs of the *International Monetary Fund have influenced virtually every Francophone African country, but particularly Congo-Kinshasa and Côte d'Ivoire, which have the largest debts. These programs caused the launching of *privatization campaigns by most governments, most notably by those which had followed socialist policies. For Francophone Africa, more so than Anglophone Africa, expansion of the state sector of the economy was an inheritance from the colonial era.

Soviet influence in Francophone Africa rose with the emergence of radical regimes—first in Guinea and Mali in the 1960s, and during the 1970s in Madagascar, Benin, and Congo-Brazzaville. More significantly, the United States developed very close relations with President Mobutu Sese Seko of Zaire and with Félix Houphouët-Boigny of Côte d'Ivoire, and exercised influence over African *international relations through those ties.

French influence in Africa was limited for a time by the rise of radical regimes, but in the 1980s France regained influence in all its ex-colonies, and grew to influence in the ex-Belgian colonies; Soviet influence with the socialist regimes declined accordingly. The French president meets annually with African heads of state. In 1986 France acted on the proposal of Leopold Sedar Senghor of Senegal for creation of an organization of Francophone states. The new organization included Zaire, Rwanda, and Burundi; it also included the former French North African colonies of Morocco and Tunisia, but not Algeria; and it included Egypt, Seychelles, and Mauritius, which were British colonies, but where French is spoken widely. Within the Francophone organization, Belgium, Canada, and Switzerland have challenged France as donors of aid to African, Asian, and Pacific countries.

France has also been deeply involved in military supply and assistance in Africa, and has intervened militarily in Chad, Gabon, Central African Republic, and the Comoros. French interests in Europe, however, progressively limited the depth of military commitment to Africa.

Francophone Africa participated fully in the 1989–1990 wave of democratization movements. In Benin a movement for multiparty democracy, at virtually the same time as those in eastern Europe, swept away the one-party state, especially through the National Conference of February 1990.

From that point a four-year political struggle unfolded throughout Francophone Africa, based on two competing strategies. The strategy of *civil society*, using a script drawn from Benin, sought to create wider political participation through demands for the holding of national conferences. The protests were led by academic, professional, and bureaucratic figures, but with strong resonance among organized women, students, and peasants. The countervailing strategy of *the power*, based on the successful tactics of Félix Houphouët-Boigny in Côte d'Ivoire, sought to maintain the established political order through holding of strategically timed party congresses, and local and national elections.

By the end of 1993, new regimes had taken power, mostly through elections, in Benin, Congo, Mali, Central African Republic, Niger, Madagascar, Burundi, and Chad. Old regimes held on to power in Côte d'Ivoire, Gabon, Cameroon, Togo, Burkina Faso, Mauritania, Zaire, Rwanda, and Guinea.

Violence and warfare gained the upper hand in events from 1994, as democratization movements in Rwanda and Burundi took a disastrous turn. In Burundi, assassination of the elected president in 1993 provoked waves of killings. The assassination of the presidents of both countries in an April 1994 plane crash unleashed a campaign of genocidal murder against

Rwandans identified as Hutu. The big powers first ignored the killings, then sent in UN forces. Meanwhile the Rwandan Patriotic Front (RPF), based on Tutsi exiles in Uganda, gained control of Rwanda, and its victory sent refugees flooding into Zaire. In 1996, RPF forces gave support to a hurriedly assembled coalition in Zaire which, using a strategy of insurrection, was able to succeed where civil society had failed, and overthrew the Mobutu regime. In May 1997 Laurent Kabila proclaimed himself president in Kinshasa, and renamed the country Democratic Republic of Congo. Domestic and international conflicts, thus connected, soon drew all the countries of Central Africa into a balance of power struggle.

At the turn of the millennium, Francophone Africa remained in significant political turmoil, especially in strife-torn Central Africa. Nonetheless, the role of popular political expression and participation had grown substantially. Thus in Senegal, Abdoulaye Wade, who had several times contested the presidency, finally defeated Abdou Diouf in the election of 2000.

(See also AFRICAN REGIONAL ORGANIZATIONS; COLONIAL EMPIRES; DECOLONIZATION; FOREIGN AID.)

Colin Legum, ed., *Africa Contemporary Record* (New York, annual to 1988). Patrick Manning, *Francophone: Sub-Saharan Africa, 1880–1985*, 2d ed. (Cambridge, U.K., 1998).

PATRICK MANNING

FUNDAMENTALISM is a deep and total commitment to religious belief, involving a return to supposed fundamentals, away from doctrinal compromises with modern social and political life. The term is used to describe a wide range of political and religious phenomena, including Protestant denominations, Jewish groups, Buddhist movements, Hindu political parties, and Islamic governments.

The term has its origins in U.S. religious history. In the early twentieth century, fundamentalism arose as a U.S. Protestant movement, guided by the doctrine of complete faith in the five *fundamentals*—the absolute truth of the Bible, the virgin birth of Jesus, the supernatural atonement, the physical resurrection of Jesus, and the authenticity of the Gospel miracles. A variety of Protestant groups have been described as fundamentalist because of their adherence to these (or similar) fundamental principles. Fundamentalism has been a significant political force in the United States since the 1920s.

Recently, fundamentalism has come to have a broader meaning and it has been increasingly seen as a global phenomenon—movements analogous to those in the United States having appeared in many countries and regions. Though the concept is somewhat problematic outside the context of U.S. Christianity, the term is now very widely used, both in the popular news media and in scholarly literature. It denotes a variety of movements worldwide, both religious and religio-political.

The historical process of *secularization provides a background for all discussions of fundamentalism. Societies and individuals have moved away from the dominance of religious institutions and ideas. Religion and state have been separated, and religious-based laws and prohibitions have been abolished. Fundamentalism rejects this secularization process and seeks to reverse it.

Fundamentalism takes so many forms, in so many different religious and cultural traditions, that generalizations can be only approximate. Fundamentalist *ideology typically centers on the following four beliefs: (1) that there is one set of religious teachings that contains the fundamental, basic, and essential truth about humanity and the deities, (2) that this truth is opposed by forces of evil, which must be vigorously fought, and (3) that this truth must be followed according to unchangeable traditions; and (4) that those who espouse this ideology have a special relationship with the deities.

Fundamentalists are commonly individuals who feel threatened by *urbanization, industrialization, and modern secular values. Their ideology may have little substantial social or political consequences as long as it remains within the religious realm and is limited to a relatively small group. Typically, fundamentalist beliefs are tied to political *conservatism, *authoritarianism, and prejudice. Fundamentalist ideology thus reflects a hostile confrontation with modern society. The fundamentalist strategy not only rejects any accommodation, but also contains a utopian vision for reconstructing society.

The messianic or apocalyptic dreams of many religious groups include the idea of political domination of a state (or even the world) by their membership. Believers may take such dreams seriously, and the fantasy of future greatness and domination can compensate for their current deprivation. In some cases, adherents translate messianic dreams into plans for political action. The ideology of fundamentalism then becomes a political ideology embodied in a substantial political movement, which may gain mass support or even political power.

By contrast to secularization, which calls for the separation of religion and politics, fundamentalism looks to the resacralization of politics and the politicization of religion. Fundamentalism rejects *modernity, though it does not necessarily reject modern technology. It opposes the modern ideals of individualism, voluntarism, *pluralism, free speech, and the equality of women.

Fundamentalist movements often present a telling critique of late capitalist society, which they portray as being composed of alienated, atomistic, selfish individuals, engaged in the obsessive pursuit of pleasure without heed for its consequences for others (or even for themselves). Fundamentalist ideologies share a critique of modernity and its consequences—materialism, selfishness, tolerance for uncontrolled sexualities, decline of family ties, and urban crime.

This cultural aspect accounts for some of the breadth of the fundamentalist appeal. The deprivations and stresses of modernity, be they economic, psychological, or cultural, feed fundamentalist movements, as the crisis of global capitalism is felt in center and periphery nation-states. As a solution to alienation and dislocation, fundamentalism prescribes a commitment to gender role, family, and community. A rhetoric of "family values" and patriarchal authority can be heard in fundamentalist doctrine from Oklahoma to Tehran. The fundamentalist ideology everywhere appears as collectivist and communalist—individual rights are seen as secondary to the interests of the community. Fundamentalists call for reversing the historical course of secularization and modernity, and recreating a premodern (or precolonial), idealized past.

Fundamentalism thrives in conditions of economic and social crisis. In countries of the periphery in particular, fundamentalism has often arisen where secular, authoritarian governments have held power and failed. In these circumstances, fundamentalism arises as an alternative project, and its anti-modern ideology assumes wide appeal because of its similarity to the ideology of anti-imperialism and the hostility to Western domination. In some cases, ironically, fundamentalism has been supported and manipulated by foreign countries in their efforts to influence local or regional politics. This was very clear in Afghanistan, where the Islamic guerrilla movements fighting against the Soviet occupation in the 1980s were funded and trained by the United States, with support from Pakistan and Saudi Arabia. Conservative governments have also promoted fundamentalist political groups as a counterweight to left oppositions, as was the case in Egypt under Sadat in the 1970s.

Fundamentalist ideology has much to say about the lives of women and reproductive rights. Fundamentalist movements are usually opposed to contraception and in favor of modest dress and the overall subordination of women. Fundamentalist regimes have often issued dress codes and laws about the segregation of the sexes in public. They also typically limit women's involvement in public life, their freedom of movement, and their legal rights. Male superiority and privilege is formally embodied in the law. Yet fundamentalist movements have attracted much support from women, whose domestic role is especially threatened by market relations and extreme individualism.

Political fundamentalism rejects liberal *democracy and proposes an elite ruling class, made up of religious leaders or leaders sanctioned by the religious authority. Fundamentalist regimes are authoritarian because a religious state must follow the religious authority invested in the clergy, who alone can interpret the scriptures. Some may describe this as totalitarian, because religious law is applied to all aspects of life.

Fundamentalism is inclined to suppress the rights of other religious or secular forces in society and even to organize violence against them. In India, Hindu fundamentalist movements have attacked Muslims and burned mosques. In Israel, Jewish fundamentalists have demanded religious-based laws and practices (closing down all public transportation on the sabbath, for example) and some have violently attacked Palestinians. In the United States, fundamentalists have demanded religious prayers in public schools and some have been involved in killing doctors practicing abortions.

Fundamentalism as a religio-political ideology can be found all over the world. As a significant political movement aspiring to create a religious state it can be found in about thirty nations, but as a dominant power it exists in very few countries. We find the label applied to Christian groups with political influence in Southern Africa and Latin America, to Mormons in the United States, and to Buddhists in South Asia. Sinhala-Buddhist fundamentalism in Sri Lanka, inspired by a vision of the Sinhala as the curators of Buddhism, is a factor in the protracted and bloody conflict between Sinhalese and Tamils. Another example of Buddhist fundamentalism, the Dalai Lama, represents a vision of a feudal Tibetan state ruled by the clergy.

Many important fundamentalist movements and even several fundamentalist regimes are to be found in the Islamic world, a vast region from Indonesia and Malaysia at one end, to Algeria and Morocco at the other, and from the so-called Islamic republics of the former USSR to West Africa, especially Nigeria. In some of these countries, fundamentalists' attempts to make their version of Islam binding on the whole population have led to serious conflicts. Afghanistan, Algeria, and Egypt are three cases where fundamentalists gained wide followings and their bids for power led to extreme violence. Each one of these countries suffered from deep economic and social crises and from failed authoritarian secular regimes.

Have fundamentalist movements and regimes, which seek to reverse secularization and to create a resacralization of politics, succeeded in their goal? In a few cases, and in the short term, the anwer may be yes. But over the longer term, most evidence suggests they have not succeeded. Even where fundamentalism appears to have triumphed, as in Iran, its success has been transitory and based on a population still deeply religious and not yet secularized. As the Iran case shows, even when a fundamentalist clergy control political power for twenty years (1980–2000), they cannot hold back secularizing trends. Eventually the Iranian population opted for a more open and tolerant kind of politics, pushing religion back toward a more restricted or private sphere.

Fundamentalism may not be as potent a force as some thought in the 1980s, but it remains an important religious, social, and political phenomenon. In a world of wrenching change and uncertainty, millions of people will continue to turn to fundamentalist movements in their search for a more secure and morally grounded social order.

(See also GENDER AND POLITICS; RELIGION AND POLITICS.)

Martin E. Marty, ed., *The Fundamentalisms Project*, 5 vols. (Chicago, 1991–1995). Benjamin Beit-Hallahmi and Michael Argyle, *The Psychology of Religious Experience, Belief, and Behaviour* (London, 1997). Lawrence Davidson, *Islamic Fundamentalism* (Westport, Conn., 1998).

BENJAMIN BEIT-HALLAHMI

G

GABON. A heavily forested country created by France in western equatorial Africa between the 1840s and 1880s, Gabon achieved national independence on 13 August 1960. Its constitutions of 21 February 1961 and 26 March 1991 established a presidential form of government within a democratic republic. The attempts of the first president, Léon Mba (1902–1967), to gain control of the National Assembly through the establishment of a single political party provoked the coup of 17–20 February 1964 by young military officers.

French military intervention restored Mba to power and eliminated his opponents from public life. Intervention allowed Mba to install a dictatorship which he transferred to his chosen successor, Omar Bongo (b. 1935). Bongo, supported by the French government and French interests doing business in Gabon, was able to establish a single party, the Parti Démocratique Gabonais (PDG), on 12 March 1968. The PDG executive replaced the National Assembly as the source of legislation. As head of the PDG, state, and government, Bongo practiced a clientism or patrimonialism that offered members of the French-educated elite (numbering about 2,000) well-paying positions in government and administration. Those who refused his terms for incorporation into the ruling class became exiles; internal critics met death. The unprecedented expansion of petroleum revenues from the early 1970s gave Bongo and the ruling class unexpected opportunities for increased power and personal enrichment.

The petroleum-based economy transformed Gabon in other ways. It led to the neglect of food crops and to the emptying of the countryside where the bulk of the one million Gabonese had previously lived. Given the low rate of population growth, 20,000 Europeans provided most of the technical and managerial skills for the economy while 100,000 Africans from other countries predominated as petty retailers, local transporters, and unskilled laborers. But the oil boom and related activities gave rise to a larger wage-earning class, thereby increasing the influence of socioeconomic factors in a politics hitherto shaped more by ethnic, regional, and religious factors.

The Bongo regime built the Transgabonese Railway from Owendo on the Gabon Estuary to Franceville in the Upper Ogooué River Valley in order further to develop manganese, uranium, timber, and other resources of the interior. It improved health and education for the ordinary citizen. But its extravagance, wastefulness, and corruption contributed to a severe financial crisis in the late 1980s when world demand and prices for petroleum declined. The austerity measures taken to deal with this crisis contributed to a popular upheaval in early 1990. Bongo defused the crisis by restoring a multiparty system and permitting freer exercise of civil liberties. Thanks to electoral fraud, repression, and French assistance, the PDG went on to win the National Assembly elections of September–October 1990 and December 1996 as well as the presidential elections of 1993 and 1998, thereby retaining its grip on power. Since early 1997, however, the two main opposition parties have controlled the municipal governments of Libreville and Port-Gentil.

James F. Barnes, *Gabon: Beyond the Colonial Legacy* (Boulder, Colo., 1992). David E. Gardinier, *Gabon* (Oxford, 1992). David E. Gardinier, *Historical Dictionary of Gabon* (Metuchen, N. J., 1994). Douglas A. Yates, *The Rentier State in Africa: Oil Rent Dependency and Neocolonialism in the Republic of Gabon* (Trenton, N.J., 1996).

DAVID E. GARDINIER

GAMBIA. The Republic of the Gambia is approximately 4,000 square miles (10,500 sq. km.) in area and has a population of about 1,000,000. It became an independent country on 18 February 1965. The first Europeans to visit the area were the Portuguese who arrived in the mid-fifteenth century. They were later replaced by the French and British. In 1900 the British brought the country under one imperial roof. For the next sixty-five years the Gambia witnessed constitutional changes which gradually gave the franchise to the peoples of the former colony (Banjul) and the former protectorate (the hinterland). Political parties emerged in the early 1950s. Between 1951 and 1962 the arena was dominated by the People's Progressive Party (PPP) of Dr. D. K. Jawara and the United Party (UP) of the Gambian lawyer Pierre Sarr Njie. Because of the polarization between the urban politicians of the capital city of Banjul and their rural counterparts, "a green revolution took place," according to Gambia scholar Arnold Hughes. The capturing of political power by the PPP changed the political landscape of the country.

When the Gambia became independent, it inherited a Westminister model of government from the British. There was a Parliament with thirty-two representatives drawn from single district constituencies and four chiefs elected by their peers. A judiciary patterned after that of Britain facilitated the administration of justice, while a bureaucracy built during colonial rule became the instrument of administration for the political class that captured power at the time of *decolonization. The Gambia underwent a constitutional change in 1970, after a referendum approved the adoption of a republican constitution that replaced the office of prime minister with that of the presidency.

Between 1970 and 1994 the Republic witnessed seven major events. The first was the abortive coup of July 1981; the second was the 1982 decision of the Gambia and *Senegal to form the confederation of Senegambia; the third was the breakup of the confederacy in 1989, following a row between the two countries over the question of rotational leadership of the confederation. The fourth major event was the 22 July 1994 coup d'état which brought Lt. Col. Yaya Jammeh to power. This second interference with the democratic process has changed the entire political landscape. The fifth major event was the bloody and aborted countercoup which resulted in numerous deaths; the sixth was the development of internal rivalry within the ruling junta and the jailing of Vice President Sana Sabally and Minister of Interior Sadibou Hydara. The seventh major event—the capitulation of the military to both internal and external pressures for early return to civilian rule—has resulted in the civilianization of the regime and the emergence of a multiparty system dominated by President Jammeh's party.

Since independence, the Gambia has developed a number of diplomatic relations with other states in the African and international arenas. Being a small country with limited resources, the Gambia has a small diplomatic service with embassies in London, Brussels, Paris, Washington, Freetown, Riyadh, and Lagos. The country is a member of the Organization of African Unity (OAU), the Commonwealth, the Organization of Islamic Conference (OIC), the UN, and the Economic Community of West African States (ECOWAS).

Arnold Hughes, "From Green Uprising to National Reconciliation: The People's Progressive Party in the Gambia," *Canadian Journal of African Studies* 9, no. 1 (1975). Abdoulaye Saine, "The Coup d'État in the Gambia, 1994: The End of the First Republic," *Armed Forces and Society* 23, no. 1 (Fall 1996).

SULAYMAN S. NYANG

GAME THEORY. A branch of mathematics, game theory is used to analyze competitive situations whose outcomes depend not only on one's own choices, and perhaps chance, but also on the choices made by other parties, or "players." Because the outcome of a game is dependent on what *all* players do, each player tries to anticipate the choices of other players in order to determine its own best choice. How these interdependent strategic calculations are made is the subject of the theory.

Game theory was created in practically one stroke with the publication of *Theory of Games and Economic Behavior* (Princeton, N.J., 1944; 3d ed., 1953) by the mathematician John von Neumann and the economist Oskar Morgenstern. This was a monumental intellectual achievement and has given rise to scores of books and thousands of articles in a variety of fields.

The theory has several major divisions, the following being the most important:

- 2-person versus *n*-person: the 2-person theory deals with the optimal strategic choices of two players, whereas the *n*-person theory mostly concerns what coalitions, or subsets of players, will form and be stable, and what constitute reasonable payments to their members.
- zero-sum versus nonzero-sum: the payoffs to all players sum to zero (or some other constant) at each outcome in zero-sum (or constant-sum) games but not in nonzero-sum games, wherein the sums are variable; zero-sum games are games of total conflict, in which what one player gains the others lose, whereas nonzero-sum games permit the players to gain or lose simultaneously.

- cooperative versus noncooperative: cooperative games are those in which players can make binding and enforceable agreements, whereas noncooperative games may or may not allow for communication among the players but generally assume that any agreement reached is in equilibrium—that is, it is rational for a player not to violate it if other players do not, because the violator would be worse off, or at least not better off, if it did.

Games can be described by several different forms, the three most common being: 1) *extensive (game tree)*—indicates sequences of choices that players (and possibly chance, according to nature or some random device) can make, with payoffs defined at the end of each sequence of choices; 2) *normal/strategic (payoff matrix)*—indicates strategies, or complete plans contingent on other players' choices, for each player, with payoffs defined at the intersection of each set of strategies in a matrix; 3) *characteristic function*—indicates values that all possible coalitions (subsets) of players can ensure for their members, whatever the other players do. These different game forms, or representations, give less and less detailed information about a game—with the sequences in form 1 dropped from form 2, and the strategies to implement particular outcomes in form 2 dropped from form 3—to highlight different aspects of a strategic situation.

Common to all areas of game theory is the assumption that players are rational: they have goals, can rank outcomes (or, more stringently, attach utilities, or values, to them), and choose better over worse outcomes. Complications arise from the fact that there is generally no straightforwardly best strategy for a player because of the interdependency of player choices. (Games in which there is only one player are sometimes called "games against nature" and are the subject of decision theory.)

A game is sometimes defined as the sum total of its rules. Common parlor games, like chess or poker, have well-specified rules and are generally zero-sum games, making cooperation with the other player(s) unproductive. Poker differs from chess in being not only an *n*-person game (although only two players can play it) but also a game of incomplete information, because the players do not have full knowledge of each other's hands, which depend in part on chance.

The rules of most real-life games are equivocal; indeed, the "game" may be about the rules to be used (or abrogated). Thus, international politics is considered to be quite anarchistic, though there is certainly some constancy in the way conflicts develop and may, or may not, be resolved. Arms races, for instance, are almost always nonzero-sum games in which two competitors can benefit if they reach some agreement on limiting weapons, but such agreements are often hard to verify or enforce and, consequently, may be unstable.

With the diminution of the superpower conflict, interest has focused on whether a new "*balance of power"—reminiscent of the political juggling acts of European countries in the nineteenth and early twentieth century—may emerge in different regions or even worldwide. Game theory offers tools for studying the stability of new alignments, including those that might develop on issues of *political economy.

Consider, for example, the General Agreement on Tariffs and Trade (GATT) and its later incarnation, the *World Trade Organization (WTO), whose durability is now being tested by regional trading agreements that have sprung up among countries in the Americas, Europe, and Asia. The rationality of supporting WTO or joining a regional trading bloc is very much a strategic question that can be illuminated by game theory. Game theory also provides insight into how the domestic politics of a country impinges on its foreign policy, and vice versa, which has led to a renewed interest in the interconnections between these two levels of politics.

Other applications of game theory have been made to strategic voting in committees and elections, the formation and disintegration of parliamentary coalitions, and the distribution of power in weighted voting bodies. For example, the voting weights of members of the *European Union Council of Ministers, and its decision rule for taking action (e.g., simple majority or qualified majority), have been studied with an eye to making the body both representative of individual members' interests and capable of taking collective action. In sum, game theory can be used both to analyze existing strategic situations and to shed light on new situations that might arise were there a change in the rules, the preferences of the players, or the information available to them.

(See also INTERDEPENDENCE; PUBLIC CHOICE THEORY; RATIONAL CHOICE; STRATEGY.)

Steven J. Brams and D. Marc Kilgour, *Game Theory and National Security* (New York, 1988). George Tsebelis, *Nested Games: Rational Choice in Comparative Politics* (Berkeley, Calif., 1990). James D. Morrow, *Game Theory for Political Scientists* (Princeton, N.J., 1994).

STEVEN J. BRAMS

GANDHI, Indira. One of modern *India's important political leaders, Indira Gandhi was born in 1917. She was the daughter of Jawaharlal *Nehru. Born to politics, she took an intermittent part in the nationalist movement, headed by Mohandas *Gandhi and her father. After India gained independence, she became president of the Congress Party during 1959–1960. She subsequently served as a cabinet minister from 1964 to 1966 and eventually became prime minister of India in 1966. She remained India's prime minister until 1977, when her Congress Party suffered defeat at the elections. She regained the office of prime minister in the 1980 parliamentary elections and retained that office until her *assassination in 1984.

Indira Gandhi's political legacy is ambiguous. The proximity of her reign, moreover, makes an overall assessment difficult. On the economic front, she continued the policies of previous Congress governments, emphasizing self-reliance, capital-intensive industrialization, an inward-looking trade policy, and a large role for the public sector. India's industrial performance during these years was, at best, sluggish. Where she did make changes, they tended to be ideologically disparate. On the one hand, she nationalized the banking industry. Conversely, she pushed the *green revolution and a turn to commercial agriculture, leading India toward self-sufficiency in food. After regaining power in 1980, she also attempted to liberalize India's economy and to relax state controls.

Where Indira Gandhi left an indelible mark was in the field of politics. She introduced a genuinely populist style to Indian politics and sought to address the issue of poverty through public sector programs. Her slogan *Garibi Hatao* (Out with Poverty) set a viable strategy for electoral mobilization. The populist tone also helped lay out a political agenda to which all her opponents had to respond.

Indira Gandhi had little success in actually alleviating poverty. Her efforts were constrained by a lack of resources on the one hand and a reluctance and inability to engage in such structural reforms as land redistribution on the other. Nevertheless, her style of leadership deeply affected the nature of India's political system. She centralized decision making and created a personalized regime that bypassed the institutions of both party and state. This weakened India's political institutions—such as the Parliament, *federalism, and the Congress Party—and diminished the country's capacity to resolve political conflicts without violence.

Indira Gandhi was both a cause and a consequence of India's growing political problems. By the late 1960s, social and economic changes had considerably weakened the regional elites on which Congress under Nehru had relied. Indira Gandhi sought to salvage Congress's political position by creating a personalistic and populist rule. Her style, however, also weakened the principal political institutions of India. Pressed by growing political opposition, she declared a state of emergency in 1975, which led to a two-year period of authoritarian rule. She did, however, call—and ultimately lose—a general election in 1977.

During the 1980s, she increasingly turned to religious and ethnic issues to mobilize the electorate. An important consequence of this approach was the exacerbation of a religious-based secessionist movement in India's northwestern state of Punjab. Growing turmoil in that state led her to order a major army operation in 1984 against the Sikhs (a religious minority) and eventually resulted in her assassination.

In foreign relations, Indira Gandhi kept India on the path of nonalignment, and she became chairperson of that movement in 1982. She was, on balance, more sympathetic to the Soviet Union, and Indo-U.S. relations during her reign remained strained. Indira Gandhi also played a decisive role in the 1971 war with *Pakistan that led to the creation of *Bangladesh.

(See also NONALIGNED MOVEMENT; RELIGION AND POLITICS.)

Inder Malhotra, *Indira Gandhi: A Personal and Political Biography* (London, 1989).

PRATAP MEHTA
ATUL KOHLI

GANDHI, Mohandas. On 2 October 1869 at Porbandar, a small town in what was then one of the princely states in Kathiawar in Gujarat, *India, Mohandas Karamchand Gandhi was born to a family that belonged to the Vaishya (trading) community and were Vaishnavas of the Vallabhacharya Hindu tradition. Jainism was strong in Gujarat, and Gandhi was accustomed to an atmosphere that combined both the devotional and the ascetic tempers. Thanks to his father, who was a high government official first in Porbandar and then in Rajkot, he was no less used to regarding moral and political questions as interrelated. He was married to Easturba Makanji in 1882 when both were thirteen years old. From 1889 to 1891 he studied law in London. During that period he became friendly with vegetarians and theosophists and familiarized himself with the *Bhagavadgita*, Edwin Arnold's *The Light of*

Asia, and the New Testament. Unable to establish himself as a lawyer on his return to India, in 1893 he accepted an assignment as legal adviser to Dada Abdullah & Company in Durban, South Africa, remaining in that country until 1914.

During those twenty-one years his interests extended from those of his mainly Muslim merchant clientele to the general cause of the Indian immigrants in South Africa, more particularly the cause of the indentured laborers. In the course of his work at this stage he used the following techniques: the amicable settlement of disputes whenever possible, various means of rousing *public opinion (constitutional agitation in law courts, petitions, journalistic campaigns, deputations to Parliament), and the new strategy of nonviolent resistance known as *satyagraha* (literally "grasp of truth"). In South Africa Gandhi was not a full-time politician, as he continued to earn his living as a lawyer and, moreover, organized two model communities, called Tolstoy Farm and Phoenix Settlement. It was during his South Africa days that he developed his belief in an across-the-board approach, combining socio-economic, ethico-religious, and political concerns. He suspended his nonviolent campaign for Indian civil rights during the Boer War of 1899–1902 and the Zulu rebellion of 1906–1907, organizing an ambulance corps for noncombatant duties. This signified two new steps in his political thinking, namely, that resisters should not take advantage of an enemy's predicament and that those who claim rights should be prepared to undertake duties. By 1914 his efforts in South Africa were largely successful, and his attention shifted to India, with which he had been in touch over the years through periodic visits and contacts.

From 1915 on he gradually acquired the status of a national leader in India's struggle against British rule. Politically he was different both from the moderates, who believed in constitutional methods, and from extremists or terrorists, who were willing to resort to violence. Gandhi's role as a political figure includes his building up of the Indian National Congress (which was already in existence at the time) as the main vehicle of the independence movement, the organizing of a mass movement beyond the control of the party, and the nurturing of a network of voluntary institutions that would serve both as a training ground for volunteers and as a nucleus of the new society that he believed would come into existence when independence came.

His own life history—which ended with his assassination by a Hindu fanatic on 30 January 1948—is scarcely distinguishable from his involvement in the political and other events that took place in his country at the same time. A series of *satyagraha* campaigns of varying scales showed that nonviolent resistance could be effective against injustice and in resolving conflicts and could be used as a tool in the fight for national liberation. The first campaign on Indian soil was in Champaran in Bihar in 1917. It was carried out by Indian cultivators against the British indigo factory owners. The campaign was notable for the fact-finding engaged in by Gandhi and his associates, the bringing in of volunteers from other parts of India, and the beginning of "constructive work" in the village, the last of these being regarded by him as an indispensable part of any *satyagraha* campaign. In Ahmedabad in 1918 Gandhi entered into a labor dispute in which textile workers confronted an enlightened family of mill own-

ers, the Sarabhais. It was Gandhi's first experience with India's industrial proletariat. The conflict in the Kheda district in the Bombay Presidency the same year was yet again of a different kind: between the peasants and the local administration. The method resorted to was a no-tax campaign.

The next stage of Gandhi's political career had as its target the repeal of the Rowlett Act, which continued wartime measures to put down political violence. Such measures were indubitably repressive in peacetime. The campaign took the form of a strike; but sporadic violence broke out, and crowds were fired on in Jallianwala Bagh in April 1919. The combined effect of the killing of innocent people on Baisakhi festival day and Gandhi's sympathy with Indian Muslim support for pan-Islamic efforts were major factors leading to the noncooperation movement against the British, proposed by Gandhi and adopted by the Indian National Congress in a special session in September 1920. The movement involved the boycott of educational institutions and the founding of parallel ones, the adoption of *swadeshi* (homemade goods, including *khadi* or homespun cloth), and the boycott of legislative councils and courts. The moral component of this political attempt to paralyze the administration was the shedding of fear of the rulers and a self-purification that aimed at the promotion of Hindu-Muslim unity, the removal of untouchability, abstention from alcohol, and the purging from Indian society of forced labor and other evils. However, the involvement of congress workers in a violent incident at Chauri Chaura in 1922 led Gandhi to suspend the plan to embark on massive civil disobedience. Gandhi believed that all political activity must be peaceful and that the outbreak of violence was a sign that the people were not yet ready for mass action.

As a political educator Gandhi sought to channel the energies of ordinary people in constructive ways so that neither anger aroused by local grievances nor the innate explosive force of *nationalism would lead to violence. He continued to negotiate with the British government and to lead the nationalist movement even when he was in jail. He resigned from the Congress Party in 1934 but remained the chief figure on the Indian political scene. The civil disobedience movement he launched in 1930 to protest the Salt Laws showed once again his flair for symbolic acts. Gandhi's combination of negotiation, courting arrest, direct action, and constructive work provided a new form of political activity at a time when constitutionalists, socialists, and extremists were each advocating different lines of action. His tutelage of Congress Party workers was always fraught with difficulty because those who believed that politics could be moralized were in a minority. India attained freedom at the end of World War II, and the partition of the country went through despite Gandhi's own wishes. Having encouraged the Congress Working Committee to come to its own decisions, he felt unable to use his personal influence to achieve a different end. Instead, in an attempt to bring about peace, he visited parts of the country where sectarian violence had broken out. The goal of *swaraj* (self-rule) would not be attained as long as conflict remained.

Gandhi's key concepts of *satyagraha* (nonviolent resistance), *swadeshi* (homemade goods), and *swaraj* (self-rule) have become part of the political vocabulary of the twentieth century. Of these it was the first that captured the imaginations of leaders such as Martin Luther *King, Jr., and Nelson *Mandela. His "oceanic circle" metaphor for the relationship between the individual and collectivities, with the individual firmly at the center, provided a nonhierarchical model for a changed society. If there was a touch of propheticism in his political style, this was balanced by his practical sense in giving importance to the restructuring of socioeconomic affairs. Some of Gandhi's ideas became incorporated into Indian state policy, including constitutional safeguards for the scheduled castes (formerly known as "untouchables") and the promotion of cottage industries.

(See also DECOLONIZATION; HINDUISM; ISLAM; NEHRU, JAWAHARLAL; NONVIOLENT ACTION.)

MARGARET CHATTERJEE

GANGS. The term "gang" has generally been used to identify a grouping of individuals involved in some type of antisocial behavior. To use the term so loosely, however, presents an inaccurate picture of gangs and their actual relationship with other people or institutions in society. Sociologically, gangs have been and continue to be collectives of individuals who are associated with each other through some formal organizational structure, and who are involved in both legal and illegal activities. It is precisely because of their organizational dimension (leadership structure and codes regulating behavior) and illegal activities that historically the term became synonymous with "Mob," "Syndicate," and Mafia. While the term "gang" has been used interchangeably with each of these terms, since the 1950s it has been used to identify groups whose membership is composed primarily of adolescents or young adults.

In regard to their social basis, gangs display two general characteristics. First, they are composed of individuals from low-income families. In essence, gangs represent an organizational response by those from low-income backgrounds to secure the material possessions that they lack. Second, gangs are generally, although not exclusively, composed of adolescents or young adults. One significant demographic development since the 1970s has been that the age level of gangs has steadily risen, with increasing numbers of individuals thirty years of age or older participating in them.

Politically, gangs have been used throughout the world by a wide variety of political actors as resources to achieve their goals. The political use of gangs has assumed a number of forms. First, in many countries, and especially in the United States, gangs have been used by politicians (or political parties) to assist in the mobilization of voters. To this end gangs help to disseminate information, transport individuals to the polls for election, and pressure individuals to support the political position they have been solicited to proselytize—assuming some of the duties, in other words, once handled by urban political machines. In effect, the gang is simply an independent organization for hire on an ad hoc basis. However, elsewhere, particularly in the Third World, gangs have been directly integrated into the various political machine organizations. Because *political machines are more salient in many of these countries, the gang becomes an enduring element within that organizational form.

Second, in countries like El Salvador, Mexico, and Argentina, gangs have been used by individual politicians and governments alike to help enforce desired policies and/or suppress opposition. While the use of gangs to eliminate political opponents by intimidation or murder is mostly a Third World phenomenon, it has also occurred in the United States (the El Rukns gang in Chicago, for example) and South Africa.

Third, gangs may act as an unofficial arm of the state or, conversely, a countervailing force against a particular form of state action. At times gangs serve as a local police force, at others as a guardian against police harassment. In low-income communities throughout the world, and among middle-income communities primarily in the Third World, gangs provide protection that the police either cannot (for lack of efficiency or power) or will not (for personal or class interests) provide. Cases in which gangs deter police abuse have occurred to a limited degree in the United States but are more widespread in low-income communities of the Third World. However, such gangs are also able to, and often do, impose an alternative form of tyranny on the individuals within their control.

Fourth, politicians and government officials have used gangs symbolically as part of a strategy to achieve a particular political objective. In this regard, gangs are depicted as an impending physical, social, or economic threat to the larger community and must, it is argued, be effectively deterred. Such appeals have been used throughout the United States and have been generally successful in winning support for a particular candidate, policy, or program.

Finally, various political insurgency groups—for example, in Nicaragua, El Salvador, Vietnam, South Africa, and the United States—have actively recruited gangs for their military operations. In such cases, gangs are seen as having both the skills to perform violent acts and the advantage of being familiar with the social and physical geography that is being contested. However, while they may be active in insurgency groups, gangs lack the organizational capacity and the ideological will to become central actors in the establishment of a social movement. They are essentially organizations whose goals are limited to maintaining the organization and maximizing the benefits of its members, rather than organizations possessing a broad social vision.

In conclusion, then, gangs arise in response to a particular economic situation and as such are primarily economic, not political, organizations. Nonetheless, despite the fact that gangs are rarely pivotal actors in the political arena, they can and do influence the political dynamics within the local communities where they are active.

(See also POLITICAL VIOLENCE.)

Martín Sánchez Jankowski, *Islands in the Street: Gangs and American Urban Society* (Berkeley, Calif., 1991). Felix Padilla, *The Gang as an American Enterprise* (New Brunswick, N.J., 1992). Ko-Lin Chin, *Chinatown Gangs: Extortion, Enterprise, and Ethnicity* (New York, 1996). Kayleen Hazelhurst and Careon Hazelhurst, eds., *Gangs and Youth Subcultures: International Explorations* (New Brunswick, N.J., 1998).

MARTÍN SÁNCHEZ JANKOWSKI

GATT. See WORLD TRADE ORGANIZATION.

GAULLE, Charles de. The French military and political leader Charles de Gaulle was born in Lille on 22 November 1890 and educated in Paris. His father came from an old family of soldiers, lawyers, and writers belonging to the small nobility, his mother from a bourgeois small business family; both were ardent Catholics and monarchists. The third of five children, Charles decided early to become a soldier, and at 15 wrote an essay in which he saw himself saving France from defeat as military commander against Germany. After graduating from the military school of Saint-Cyr, he served in the regiment of Colonel Philippe Pétain. Wounded in *World War I, he spent almost two-and-a-half years in captivity in Germany. After taking part in the defense of Warsaw against the Russians in 1920, he returned to France, married Yvonne Vendroux, lectured at the Ecole de Guerre, served on Marshal Pétain's staff, and wrote several books, including a study of the causes of Germany's defeat (among which the abdication of civilian control over the military was crucial) and the *Edge of the Sword*, an essay on leadership that was also a self-portrait. In the 1930s, he became the champion of the idea of a motorized, professional army capable of offensive action. Despite his efforts, and those of his political mentor Paul Reynaud, the cult of the defensive prevailed in a tired nation, and his warnings were disregarded even after *World War II began.

After fighting with some success as the commander of an armored division, he served briefly in Reynaud's last cabinet of the Third Republic in June 1940, and decided not to accept defeat. When Marshal Pétain replaced Reynaud and called for an armistice, de Gaulle flew to London and, on 18 June 1940, at the BBC, called on the French to continue to fight and to join him. Few did, but he obtained Winston *Churchill's help, and despite many setbacks, difficult relations with the British, and Franklin D. *Roosevelt's hostility, he set up what was in effect a French government in exile and succeeded in obtaining the support of the parties and movements of the Resistance in occupied France. He organized, from London and Algiers, the restoration of the republican state in France, and was greeted with enthusiasm as liberator by the French in the summer of 1944.

As head of the provisional government of the republic, he soon ran into conflicts with the old and new political parties over a variety of issues, and particularly over their preference for a parliamentary system they would dominate. He resigned in January 1946, hoping to be called back soon. He had to wait for twelve-and-a-half years, during which the Fourth Republic staggered from crisis to crisis. He set up the Rassemblement du Peuple Français (RPF) against it in 1947. Its program was intensely anticommunist, nationalist in foreign and colonial affairs, and sought "association" as a third way between *capitalism and *socialism in social affairs. The RPF had a very successful start but soon got bogged down and divided, and de Gaulle retired to his country home at Colombey-les-deux-Eglises, where he wrote his *War Memoirs*. The settlers' revolt in Algiers in May 1958, however, provided him with the opportunity to return to active politics; receiving a legally valid delegation of power from the dying Fourth Republic, he was able to create the constitutional system, centered on a strong presidency, he had advocated openly since 1946.

As president of the Fifth Republic from January 1959 on, he undertook the painful liquidation of the *Algerian War of Independence, leading to Algerian independence in 1962. He had to overcome two military rebellions in Algiers, and to proceed in stages, leaning on French support through refer-

endums. After a failed *assassination attempt, he called again for a referendum on a constitutional amendment in October 1962 so as to ensure the popular election of the president, and won. He embarked on a domestic policy of economic *modernization and on a grandiose *foreign policy aimed at providing French military autonomy through the development of a nuclear strike force, at turning the European Economic Community into a "Europe of states," and at reducing the influence of the superpowers in the world. This led him to challenge the United States repeatedly (he converted French dollar reserves into gold and took France out of the military-political structure of the *North Atlantic Treaty Organization) and to initiate a policy of *détente toward the Soviet Union. His authority was seriously weakened by the students' revolt and workers' strike in *May 1968, but he prevailed at the end of the month, after having "disappeared" for a day. However, when he staked his power once more on the success of a referendum (on regional decentralization and a reform of the Senate), he lost and resigned on 27 April 1969. He again retired to Colombey and worked on his new memoirs; these were left unfinished when he died of a stroke on 9 November 1970.

De Gaulle was the most important French political leader since Napoleon. To many of his compatriots, this intransigent defender of French grandeur saved the honor of the nation during World War II and restored its institutions and status. Although his role as founder and leader of the Fifth Republic was more controversial, his ambitious if often unsuccessful diplomatic activism, his extraordinary dramatic sense—demonstrated in his press conferences, TV speeches, journeys at home and abroad, and many public ceremonies—his mastery of the French language, and his success in establishing a regime that was strong without being dictatorial—a novelty in French history—earned him the admiration even of many of his opponents. His vision of a Europe "from the Atlantic to the Urals," with a reunited Germany, seemed utopian in the 1960s but turned out to have been prophetic in 1989. His main legacy is a constitutional system that has proved to be far more flexible than many observers had believed and that has erased the image of a weak executive, parliamentary division, and party impotence which the two previous republics had created.

De Gaulle disdained dogmas and believed in the exploitation of circumstances. He knew how to adapt: his colonial policies were prudent during World War II, far more rigid in 1945, and reactionary in the days of the RPF, but he became a worldwide champion of national self-determination in the Fifth Republic, just as he became the champion of reconciliation with the Federal Republic of Germany even though he had tried to impose a repressive policy after the defeat of *Hitler in 1945. He knew the necessity and merits of *international cooperation, but the two fixed stars in his constellation were his will to preserve French independence and grandeur (thus excluding any possibility of a supranational Europe) and his insistence on strong executive leadership appealing to national unity and the common good above factions and interests. In this respect, he appears to have (finally) synthesized the different and conflicting traditions of the Old Regime, plebiscitarian leadership, Jacobin republicanism, and *parliamentary democracy. He reminded the French of the greatness of their past, appealed both to the classical and to the romantic "families of thought," and owed much of his prestige to his literary gifts and intellectual incisiveness—another traditional source of political authority in France. But in his policies he also prepared the French for the future, and while realizing that France was no longer a superpower, refused to accept mediocrity and passivity. Twenty years after his death, his greatness is recognized by almost all the French, even if it is perhaps more a source of nostalgia and less an inspiration than he had hoped.

(See also EUROPEAN UNION; GAULLISM; GERMAN UNIFICATION.)

Stanley Hoffmann and Inge Hoffmann, *de Gaulle artiste de la politique* (Paris, 1973); English version in Stanley Hoffmann, *Decline or Renewal? France since the 30s*, New York, 1974). *De Gaulle et le service de l'Etat* (Paris, 1977). Bernard Ledwidge, *de Gaulle* (London, 1982). Jean Lacouture, *de Gaulle*, 3 vols. (Paris, 1984–1986; English abridged version of vol. 1, London, 1990). Pierre-Louis Blanc, *de Gaulle au soir de sa vie* (Paris, 1990).

STANLEY HOFFMANN

GAULLISM. In contemporary French history, the term *Gaullism* has had three distinct meanings. From 1940 to 1945, during *World War II, the term designated the attitude of those who, rejecting the armistice signed with Germany by Marshal Pétain in June 1940, rejoined General Charles de *Gaulle in order to put *France back in the war on the side of the Allies. Between 1946 and 1958, Gaullism was a form of opposition to the Fourth Republic, whose unstable parliamentary regime was challenged in favor of institutions whose keystone would be a president of the republic with preeminent constitutional powers. Finally, in the third period, Gaullism was nothing other than the support given to the general's own politics after he returned to power in 1958 and served as president of the newly formed Fifth Republic from 1959 until his resignation in 1969. Since then the term has been used in reference to those who declared themselves his heirs. By reference to these three periods, one may attempt to define Gaullism.

In examining the evidence, one must conclude that Gaullism is neither a doctrine nor a political *ideology. No text defines its content; it tends neither to the *Left nor *Right. Considering its historical progression, it is a pragmatic exercise of power that is neither free from contradictions nor of concessions to momentary necessity, even if the imperious word of the general gives to the practice of Gaullism the allure of a program that seems profound and fully realized.

A Strong State. Flexibility aside, Gaullism relies on a fundamental principle on which everything else follows: the "certain idea of France," which opens de Gaulle's *War Memoirs*. France appeared to him to be an indomitable entity, a "person" with whom a mystical dialogue was maintained throughout history. The goal of Gaullism, therefore, is to give precedence to its interests, to ensure that the voice is heard, to make it respected, and to assure its survival.

To achieve this aim, according to de Gaulle, it is first necessary that France become strong from within; parties are attacked as representing divisive interests and the French people are urged to regroup, to overcome their partisan quarrels within a larger unity. The historical heritage of the country is accepted in its entirety, the monarchy of the Old Regime that built France no less than the revolution that led it to dominate Europe. To remain worthy of its past, the nation must endow

itself with a powerful *state. By affirming in 1946 the necessity of resting the institutions of the state on a strong executive, de Gaulle flew in the face of the "republican tradition," according to which power must reside chiefly in the elected assembly made up of representatives of the sovereign nation. In addition, his desires to establish authority by direct universal vote; to speak to the country over the heads of the parliamentarians via radio broadcasts, press conferences, and trips to the provinces; and to elicit direct voter input via referendums were perceived by republicans as proof of a tendency toward dictatorial power. It took his resignation following the negative referendum of April 1969 to show that his lofty respect for *democracy was more than a mere rhetorical ploy.

Gaullists assume that a strong France must be based on a strong economy and a stable society; they believe that France can play a role in the world only if it possesses economic and financial means. From the Gaullists' perspective, it is the imperative of the state, as guardian of the national interest, to give impetus to economic growth and to guide it. Liberal opinion is accepted if it promises more efficiency than planning. As for social justice, so long as its natural distrust of big business can be allayed, it is less a matter of doctrine than a means of upholding stability. To put an end to *class struggle, Gaullists hope to make use of participation, a nineteenth-century concept of which the general spoke frequently, but which he allowed his associates to ignore.

Vision of the World. If the aim of Gaullism is a strong France, this is above all in order to give it the power to strongly influence the world's future. According to de Gaulle, history consists of the rivalry between nations struggling to realize their own ambitions. To enable France to fulfill its international role, the first imperative was to overcome the factors that restrict its latitude internationally—for example, by freeing it, through *decolonization, "of constraints, henceforth without counterpart, imposed on it by the empire." It was no less important that it assure itself of ways to guarantee its national independence without resorting to allies whose interests might not coincide with those of France. This imperative required an independent nuclear capability whose realization was relentlessly pursued despite obstacles and criticism.

In short, from a Gaullist perspective, France could not hope to play a world role if it remained a slave of its U.S. ally. Refusing a bipolar world bequeathed, in their view, by the *Yalta Conference, Gaullists sought *alliances founded on partnership and equality, refusing to acknowledge any system of protection by the *superpowers. For France, placed in the U.S. orbit, this conception would lead to its distancing itself from the military policies of the *North Atlantic Treaty Organization and to its rejection of the technical and economic domination of overseas interests exemplified by the control exerted by U.S. investors and the controversial role of the U.S. dollar in the international monetary system. Nevertheless, regaining national independence did not enable France, a middle-ranked power, to determine the destiny of the planet. To counterbalance the two superpowers, Gaullism counted on Europe, conceived not as a supernational entity but rather as a confederation of sovereign states whose members engage in common policy, autonomous from the superpowers, and significantly politically influenced by France. But all attempts to create such confederation failed in the face of the desire of the other European powers to remain closely allied to the United States.

Heritage. Gaullism has had a profound influence on the history of the Fifth Republic after de Gaulle. President Georges Pompidou, from 1969 to 1974, referred explicitly to "continuity" with regard to the Gaullist way of doing things. Thereafter, those political parties that are heirs to Gaullism—the Union des Démocrates Pour la République (UDR) until 1976, and later the Rassemblement Pour la République (RPR)—wished to remain faithful to the inspiration of the general. Above all, throughout the 1980s, Gaullism became an integral part of the national heritage. Thus Gaullism has contributed to a consensus that, since 1984, has been establishing itself in a country whose *political culture was, until then, made up of divisions and relentless antagonisms.

The institutions founded by de Gaulle and consolidated by Pompidou are no longer the focus of political controversy. Presidential domination, so decried at the time of its inception, has been reinforced by all of the general's successors, including the socialist François *Mitterrand. The policy of national independence founded on an independent nuclear military capability has achieved consensus. As for Gaullist *foreign policy, since 1969 it has become the guiding force of French *international relations, even if presidents since de Gaulle have expressed it in more flexible terms.

It is no exaggeration to say that Gaullism has molded postwar France. At the same time, considering that the essence of Gaullist ideas are now accepted by everyone, those who wish to be the legitimate heirs of de Gaulle (e.g., Jacques Chirac of the RPR) now have an identity crisis. It is difficult for them to distinguish themselves from other political perspectives.

Gaullism for Export? Does Gaullism, a tempered *nationalism adapted to the late twentieth century, have any significance beyond the borders of France? It has often been poorly understood and pejoratively judged, as foreign observers and French adversaries of Gaullism have emphasized the appearances (monarchical attitudes, abrupt words, harsh statements) over the realities. It is undeniable, however, that Gaullism has identified a number of real problems that have aggravated international affairs for many years and that continue to do so: the dysfunction of the international monetary system, the problems of the *Third World, the dominance of the superpowers, the dangers of hegemonic powers, and the continuing strength of national sentiment. All in all, it appears unfair to liken Gaullists to national leaders such as Amintore Fanfani in Italy who are determined to advance the parochial interests of their countries in the international community, for none has exceeded de Gaulle himself in promoting the conditions designed to accomplish his objectives or in understanding the consequences of those objectives. Gaullism appears to be a peculiarly French phenomenon, without doubt the quintessential French political phenomenon of the twentieth century.

(See also EUROPEAN UNION.)

Jean Charlot, *Le gaullisme* (Paris, 1970). Jean Touchard, *Le gaullisme 1940–1969* (Paris, 1978). Jean Charlot, *Le gaullisme d'opposition 1946–1958* (Paris, 1983). Serge Berstein, *La France de l'expansion I: La République gaullienne 1958–1969*, Nouvelle histoire de la France contemporaine, No. 17 (Paris, 1989).

SERGE BERSTEIN

GAY AND LESBIAN POLITICS. Within every age, culture, nation, and people in the world, women have loved women and men have loved men. Social contexts and constructs differ, as do interpretations and assumptions. Lifestyles differ, and the question of identity has varied responses. But (some) women emotionally and physically love women and (some) men emotionally and physically love men. In short or prolonged periods of their lives. Secretly or openly. They always have, and they always will.

Legal Progress. More than a century ago, in 1897, the Scientific Humanitarian Committee in Germany tried to prove scientifically that homosexuality was a biological phenomenon. Homosexuality (or uranism as it was then called) should be seen as a God-given variation of nature, argued scientific leaders such as C. H. Ulrichs, M. Hirschfeld, and (in the Netherlands) J. A. Schorer. Together with progressive thinkers, artists, and industrialists they fought against laws criminalizing homosexual behavior (successfully in Norway). A fairly open European lesbian and gay subculture (Berlin, Paris) led to decriminalization discussions in many countries. Poland passed a new penal code in 1932 fixing the age of consent for heterosexual and homosexual acts equally at the age of fifteen.

A century later the battle for decriminalization still continues. The famous Stonewall riots in New York City on 28 June 1968 were the start of gay men fighting back against physical assaults by police forces who knew themselves to be supported by a legal context where anal and oral sex between persons of the same sex was a crime (in all U.S. states until 1961). The Stonewall riots became a symbol of the right to self-determination which is today celebrated at Lesbian and Gay Pride marches and festivals all over the world. "Coming out of the closet" or living an open lesbian or gay lifestyle at work and among family and friends has become much more common. In the last two decades decriminalization of lesbian and gays has been successfully fought for in more than thirty countries such as New Zealand (1986), South Africa, Ecuador, and Fiji (1998), and Chile and Romania (1999).

South Africa since 1998 has had the most progressive antidiscrimination laws in the world. Although women have married women and men have married men in ceremonies all over the world, full legal marriage status will be achieved for the first time in the Netherlands in 2001—and adoption of children from previous marriages, artificial insemination, etc., will be possible. But the adoption of children from other countries will not be possible, as the international political community is not considered ripe for it.

Social Ups and Downs. Much lesbian and gay "her" and "his" tory in Greek, Roman, Hindu, Buddhist, and African communities is slowly being researched and uncovered. Open lesbian and gay life thrives in periods of economic prosperity and political/social respect for diversity. The European subculture "bubble" burst in the 1930s when Nazis in Germany sent 7,000 gays a year to jails and, later, concentration camps. Estimates of lesbians and gays who died in World War II vary from 20,000 to 80,000. Gay men had to wear a pink triangle; many lesbians were categorized with prostitutes as antisocial elements and were made to wear a black triangle. In the 1980s Dutch lesbians and gays collected funds and political support for the Pink Triangle Monument in Amsterdam to draw attention to this forgotten group of Nazi victims—who have yet to receive apologies or compensation for their suffering.

In Western/Northern countries the political ideology of many lesbian and gay groups which emerged in the 1970s was relatively straightforward: lesbians and gays should be able to live openly and freely and not be discriminated against—in law, jobs, or social context. Discussions about the origins of homosexual or bisexual orientation (biological, childhood, social) continue, but most lesbians and gays consider these debates irrelevant or absurd. Lesbian *feminism took political ideology beyond the equal rights issue into the basic assumptions of male and female gender roles as a social construct. Lesbian separatists choose to spend their love and energy in a women's context only—privately or professionally. Such thinking about "a space of our own" was transformed in the 1980s and '90s into lesbian/feminists being actively and openly involved at United Nations Conferences on Women (Nairobi 1985, Beijing 1995) regarding a wide variety of issues such as women against violence, working toward a human rights–based approach to individual lifestyle choices, and for the improvement of the (socially, economically, and politically marginalized) position of lesbians and gays in many countries.

The *AIDS crisis has had a profound effect on the gay community. Many leaders were lost, but the movement rallied. Organized voluntary or paid support such as "buddy systems" has had a general effect on health services. In many countries where (homo)sexuality was a taboo topic, AIDS/HIV prevention programs have had a broader social effect. In some countries (e.g., Latin America) sexual choices became part of a public and political debate, often with popular support from people and groups at all levels of society and in disregard of the dominant Roman Catholic Church. The lesbian and gay community took responsibility and has been cooperating fully with health and education services—and has received extensive government funding, often for the first time. At the same time the AIDS/HIV crisis has also negatively affected the image of gay people—and has certainly absorbed a huge amount of energy. Even in continents where AIDS is predominantly a heterosexual illness (Africa), the link with homosexuality remains, complicating prevention efforts. Discrimination against homosexuality has increased once more—even in a country like the Netherlands, known for its liberal and progressive attitudes, coming out as a teacher at schools or in small country villages is a problem. At the same time there are many heartrending stories of how (small) communities have rallied around a gay teacher or doctor suffering from AIDS. Within families AIDS has forced the issue of sexual diversity such as bisexuality out in the open. Even within the Catholic Church an open discussion has started about the (large) number of priests who are afflicted with the AIDS/HIV virus—thus forcing a discussion about the theory and practice of celibacy.

For lesbians an increasingly important topic has been the right to have and to legally take responsibility for children. Artificial insemination (self-help or through medical services) has allowed lesbians to set up a variety of parenting situations. Fatherhood is sometimes anonymous; at other times the known and at times gay father is actively involved in the parenting. As family law in most countries is totally based on the monogamous heterosexual model, lesbian mothers have had great difficulty in adopting each other's children and in arranging parental rights in conflict situations. Sometimes the biological father who has not been involved in the day-to-day parenting is granted more rights by the "straight" legal system than the nonbiological mother who has brought up a child from birth.

The wider issue here is that social and legal systems are lagging behind the reality of a wide diversity of lifestyles. In many ways the lesbian and gay community has taken the lead in making individualized choices in how to style their private lives, living together or apart, showing long-term emotional and physical commitment without necessarily taking on all the trappings of life in marriage. In the economically strong industrialized world but also in higher and educated classes in Latin America, African, and Asian countries these choices offer new lifestyle options for both gays and heterosexuals. The buying power of childless gays has been discovered in a growing range of gay businesses—and commercials from Asia to Latin America show that camp humor can now be used to sell products. Obviously as the power of "pink bucks" increases, so does the political power of a growing group of lesbian and gay voters who demand respect for diversity from local and national governments.

Within professions the level of openness of lesbian and gay lifestyles differs hugely. Generally speaking, in professions that historically have been closed communities, where women also have had great difficulties in being accepted on an equal footing (such as the military, the church), lesbians and gays are still facing serious oppression from daily discrimination to full-fledged human rights issues. Amnesty International finally took up lesbian and gay cases in 1990 after a decade of discussions and much lobbying by members of the International Lesbian and Gay Association (ILGA) around the world.

Lesbian and Gay Politics Around the World. The last two decades of the twentieth century saw an enormous increase of lesbian and gay organizations around the world. In Latin America and Caribbean countries some 400 such organizations exist, in Africa and Asia up to 150 each. In eastern Europe more than 100 lesbian and gay organizations have emerged in the last decade. In Western countries these numbers most likely reach above 10,000. These figures do not take into account a growing lesbian and gay Internet community. This presents heretofore unknown opportunities: for instance, in China the first book about lesbian lifestyles is being written and will be printed and distributed by the state publisher. This will occur at a time when gays and lesbians still face severe social and political oppression in China.

The ILGA has been the main international activist forum since 1978. It has more than 350 members from eighty countries. It now has five regional branches, and in the last decade ILGA has held conferences in Mexico, Brazil, and South Africa. It was granted United Nations ECOSOC status in 1994, but this was suspended one month later under pressure from the U.S. conservative lobby, which claimed that the ILGA was an umbrella organization for pedophile groups. The ILGA went through a painful process of proving itself "clean" in the wake of these charges. The UN suspension has not been lifted. The ILGA is still mainly run on voluntary resources, and apart from work on political lobbying toward decriminalization, AIDS campaigns, etc., it is a fairly loose network of lesbian and gay political activists. Interestingly, the biggest international event for lesbians and gays has been the Gay

Games, which have now been held five times, the largest one being in Amsterdam in 1998 (100,000 participants).

Lesbian and gay organizations around the world are still mainly emancipation movements. They have mostly not professionalized and not become significantly involved in international solidarity and human rights work. Although it is recognized (even at UN level) that lesbians and gays live and love in every country in the world, they still need to keep their identity and lifestyle fiercely secret. Development organizations have seldom supported lesbian or gay groups as human rights organizations. The joint United Nations Program on AIDS (UNAIDS) demands to work with groups that have no connection with ILGA because of the UN suspension.

The existing Latin American, African, and Asian networks (partly formed by lesbians and gays, partly by lesbian feminists) are finding it very difficult to shift the main male and Western orientation of global thinking about gay issues, their perspective on the AIDS issue, and their diversity practices.

The hope for the twenty-first century is that *globalization and the opportunities opened up by the Internet will increase the human rights and daily space for the millions of lesbians and gays around the world who continue to live secret, marginalized, and persecuted lives.

(See also GENDER AND POLITICS; NEW SOCIAL MOVEMENTS.)

SYLVIA BORREN
REBECA SEVILLA

GENDER AND POLITICS. See overleaf.

GENDER GAP. The gender gap refers to a growing divergence in attitudes and behavior between men and women, primarily related to candidate selection and approval and partisan preference. In the United States, women voters are more Democratic and less conservative than men, creating a widening gap as white male voters have defected to the Republican Party. The gap has remained remarkably consistent during the past sixteen years, with between 53 and 58 percent of women voting Democratic each year, in congressional and presidential races. In the United States, gender differences in political evaluations were first noticed and widely discussed in the 1980 presidential election campaign, and have persisted ever since. In that year, it first became evident that while men supported Ronald Reagan by a large majority, women split their vote more evenly between the Democratic and Republican candidates. Other gender-based differences, including voter turnout, partisan identification, and assessment of presidential effectiveness, have also been observed. With regard to partisan identification, the Democrats have a higher level of support among women. This preference has manifested itself in congressional and statewide elections, as well as the presidential contests. Another dimension of the gap involves support by women for female candidates if their nomination is accompanied by policy commitments that incorporate or emphasize women's concerns.

Perhaps even more important than the gender gap has been the so-called "marital gap." This phenomenon reflects distinctive voting patterns among married and single political participants. The marital gap is greatest between married men and single women. Another dimension of the gap that has been identified is that dividing working or "independent" women from housewives; differences among them on some issues are as great as differences between men and women.

Origins of the gender gap are to be found in greater liberalism among women. Women are more likely than men to favor a greater role for government in social service provision and to support policies that aid the disadvantaged, including social programs for the poor, elderly, and disabled. Women are also more likely to endorse a reduced military and more environmental protection. While there are some gender-based differences regarding specifically feminist issues such as support for the Equal Rights Amendment, the women's movement, and children's concerns, on the whole, support for so-called "women's issues" does not differentiate male and female voters. However, there is no consensus regarding the sources of gender-based political behavior. Some argue for a female perspective based on economic self-interest, contending that women's increased dependence on the state for welfare and employment accounts for gender-based political differences between men and women. Others support the view that women's roles as wives and mothers have given them a more humanitarian political perspective. For other analysts, the women's movement helped to reinforce and articulate the notion that women's interests are fundamentally different from those of men. This trend accelerated as more women identified with their gender and came to appreciate its political significance. Growing awareness of politics as important and the linkages created by group membership and identification brought about by the expansion of *feminism and the women's movement thus helped to create the gender gap.

Outside of the United States, a cross-national perspective reveals some similar trends with regard to the gender gap and women's political behavior. Evidence from Canada, Sweden, Norway, France, and Britain shows a modest, if less marked and documented, trend related to gender-based attitudes and voting, pointing to a turn away from support for parties of the Right in some instances. In Britain, in particular, a "gender-generation" gap has emerged, as women under thirty favored the Labour Party in large numbers in the late 1990s. Gender-based policy attitudes provide evidence of potential gaps concerning such issues as nuclear energy, unemployment, and defense, as well as women's concerns. The extent to which a more left-wing or liberal women's vote becomes operational may depend on the willingness of parties to stress relevant issues related to gender gap concerns and the capacity of gender-based movements to mobilize women for electoral purposes.

(See also ELECTIONS AND VOTING BEHAVIOR; FEMINIZATION OF POVERTY; GENDER AND POLITICS; NEW SOCIAL MOVEMENTS; REPRODUCTIVE POLITICS.)

Carol Mueller, ed., *The Politics of the Gender Gap: The Social Construction of Political Influence* (Berkeley, Calif., 1988). Robert Darcy, Susan Welch, and Janet Clark, *Women, Elections, and Representation* (Lincoln, Nebr., 1994). Richard Seltzer, Jody Newman, and Melissa Voorhees Leighton, *Sex as a Political Variable* (Boulder, Colo., 1997).

JOYCE GELB

GENERAL AGREEMENT ON TARIFFS AND TRADE. See WORLD TRADE ORGANIZATION.

(cont. on p. 316)

GENDER AND POLITICS. During the 1990–1991 Persian Gulf crisis many people learned for the first time that Kuwaiti women had organized a suffrage movement. This news joggled conventional minds. For Muslim women, especially those in the conservative states surrounding the oil-rich gulf, typically were imagined to be secluded, banned from the public arena. Yet here were Kuwaiti women calling their own rallies, building alliances with men in the prodemocracy movement, organizing resistance against the Iraqi invaders, and holding exile strategy sessions in London. This new information about Kuwaiti women's suffrage campaign forced many outside observers not only to reimagine Muslim women but to rethink Kuwaiti politics and perhaps the entire political landscape of the Persian Gulf crisis. Ten years later, Kuwaiti feminists still were campaigning for the right to vote. Now the country had an openly contentious legislature, but in December 1999, men calling themselves liberals in the all-male legislature saw standing up to the state's autocratic emir as more important than voting for women's suffrage. When the emir proposed a bill according Kuwaiti women the right to vote, enough liberal male legislators joined with conservative lawmakers to defeat the emir's bill, thus leaving women disenfranchised at the start of the new millennium.

Movements to demand the vote have been the most visible site of women in politics. For many, it is the only time they take women's impact on politics seriously. It is also one of the few moments when men's presumptions about their own place in politics—as men—are thrown into sharp relief. The spotlight, however, usually is turned on women suffragists only in the final phase of their campaign, when the men in power are being forced to revise their ideas about *political participation, when glasses are raised (by some) upon women's victory. Then the stage of gendered political drama goes dark, to be lit up again only briefly when the "first woman" is elected to parliament or chosen to head a national party or is tapped for prime minister. This sort of superficial coverage ignores the ripple effects that women's struggle to vote sends through the whole political system. It also overlooks the ways that women's suffrage campaigning challenges men's lives, in the state and in the home. Kuwaiti women, like their suffragist predecessors in Finland, the Philippines, the United States, and Mexico, know that one of the reasons so many men—and not a few women—object to women being allowed to vote is that granting such a right will alter ideas not only about what it means to be "womanly" in Kuwaiti society but what it means to be "manly" as well. More is, and always has been, at stake than merely the ballot box.

For "gender and politics" is never just about women; it is about the ways in which relations between women and men shape public power. Maybe it is more useful to think of the topic as "the gendering of politics," that is, the processes by which public life is infused with presumptions about what it means to be a woman and what it means to be a man. Every time the definition of "femininity" is changed—for instance, by women insisting that "woman voter" is not an oxymoron—the meaning of "masculinity" must be reconsidered as well. Once women can vote on the same terms as men, to be manly no longer can be deemed coterminous with exercising public responsibility. Individual men indeed may still be con-

sidered responsible public actors, but that mantle of political seriousness will have to be earned; it no longer simply comes with the hormonal territory. Therefore, when women win the vote, powerful character attributes such as "mature," "adult," "rational," and "serious" will lose at least some of their masculinized undertones. Not all, however: if women are allowed into the voting booth but are kept out of the legislature, cabinet, treasury, and the war room, masculinity's special relationship to those valued human qualities may survive. And, as a consequence, the state itself will continue to be intimately related to masculinity, giving men a privileged relationship to any government that they will be reluctant to surrender.

One has only to look at the collective portrait of the thirty-four heads of government gathered in Paris in November 1990 to sign the historic Charter of Paris for the New Europe. The gathering marked the end of the Cold War. Newspaper headlines heralded the meeting as the "end of an era." But a reader with any gender consciousness could not help but be struck by not what was new but what was persistent. The ceremonial photograph was full of men in dark suits. One had to squint to find the two women among the thirty-four heads of government: Gro Brundtland, prime minister of Norway, and Margaret Thatcher, prime minister of Britain. If the historic photograph had been taken just two days later, Gro Brundtland would have been the lone woman head of government; Margaret Thatcher had by then resigned, and all three contestants for her job were men. Decades after most of these societies had accorded women full *citizenship, the most serious and powerful posts in public life remained masculinized, that is, defined in such a way that women were not considered fit to hold them. The post–Cold War era might have dawned, but it was with an old gender formula still in place. As of early 2000, there was not a single woman head of government in all of the NATO and European Union countries. But the view from the top of the political pyramid can be deceiving. On the rungs just below there were gender rumblings. Britain's governing Labour Party had a record number of women on its parliamentary benches. France's ruling Socialist Party had undergone an internal gender revolution. Even the patriarchal French conservative Gaullist party had selected its first woman leader, Michèle Alliot-Marie.

Gender refers to the meanings we assign to being a woman or being a man. Since the eighteenth century, feminists, scholars, and activists together have taken up the task of revealing just how much of political life has been built on presumptions about femininity and masculinity. While often resistant, many people have found it easier to acknowledge that political institutions and ideas have been constructed out of ideas about race and about social class than to admit that ideas about gender have been just as crucial. One reason for this analytical stubbornness may be that ideas about what it means to be manly or feminine strike very close to individuals' own sense of identity, and few people want to admit that their personal identities might rest on manipulations of political power. Furthermore, to accept this *feminist theory about how political life works would mean acknowledging that seemingly personal relations between women and men—including the most intimate emotional and sexual relations—do not occur in a protected private sphere; rather, according to feminist analysis, these relationships among friends, lovers, and relatives

311

are seen to be building blocks of the wider public sphere and thus fraught with power and *ideology. Given the cost of this intellectual leap, perhaps it is not surprising that most political observers prefer to talk of class and race while ignoring gender. These acts of ignoring gender produce incomplete, often misleading political commentary: for instance, an inadequate explanation for the staying power of Serbia's authoritarian regime; an unreliable analysis of the causes of Rwanda's 1994 genocidal violence.

Feminists are not advocating the linkage between public power and private relationships. They simply are pulling back the curtain on a reality they believe has been denied because that denial serves to privilege masculinity in political affairs. In showing how politics has been gendered, they are revealing two realities of political life: first, anyone or any group seeking to control public affairs will try to control private spheres of human activity as well; second, consequently, most conventional explanations of how governments work have grossly understated the amount of power operating in politics. These two assertions are the radical elaborations of the now-familiar feminist analytical assertion, "The personal is political," a concept whose meaning has changed with the changing dynamics of *patriarchy.

The term "patriarchy" harks back to relationships controlled by a certain kind of fatherhood, a male parenting whose authority over children and adult women in the household derives from presumptions that adult men are more rational, more capable of looking after the well-being of the other members, and thus better suited to speak on their behalf to the outside world. In eighteenth-century France and nineteenth-century China, this model of fathering was considered a microcosm of the entire political system: as the patriarchal father's authority was over his wife and children, so the monarch's authority was over his subjects. Thus these monarchies have a vital stake in preserving patriarchal family relations; they were thought to be essential to the maintenance of the larger political order. Although today that analogy has been subverted in most countries by the spread of republican notions of popular sovereignty, patriarchal principles nonetheless have proved adaptable and persistent.

Any country's political system is patriarchal insofar as it depends on the existence of three conditions. First, a patriarchy is a kind of social or political order in which people who are feminine—women, and in many societies, gay men—are thought to be naturally, automatically, inevitably best suited to certain tasks (listening, caring, weeding, providing sexual services, hauling water, assembling microchips), while people who are masculine—"real" men—are thought naturally inclined to perform other tasks (talking, exploring, strategizing, plowing, welding, fighting). In other words, a patriarchal society rests on a gender division of labor. In their *Divided Britain* (London, 1989), for example, Ray Hudson and Allan Williams provide evidence to support their assertion that Britain remains patriarchal. They note that in 1984, within British Rail, then one of the largest government-owned enterprises, men constituted 589 of the 591 senior managers and 20,201 of the 20,201 track repair workers. The British civil service's reliance on the gender division of labor was no less remarkable: in 1987, women made up 76 percent of the low-level administrative assistants, but a mere 4 percent of the personnel in the elite grades that included the influential permanent secretaries and directors.

Second, a patriarchy is a social or political order in which the things that masculine people do are deemed of greater social value—more "productive," more "serious," more "skilled"—than the things that feminine people do. Thus the woman who weeds is less likely to be talked to by the UN agricultural development officer than the man who plows; the woman who cares for children is less likely to be called as a witness before a legislative committee than the man who calculates the cost of childcare. Third, and this makes clear the centrality of power to patriarchy, in a society that has remained patriarchal the people who perform the allegedly more valued, masculine tasks are deemed to have the responsibility of looking after, protecting, and controlling the people who perform the less valued, feminine tasks.

That is, a patriarchal polity is more than a gender division of labor arranged hierarchically. A patriarchy is a system designed for the control of one sector of society over another. Thus, women's demand for meaningful participation in the political arena chips away at all three legs of the patriarchal structure: the gender division of labor becomes disturbingly blurred; the accompanying political and social hierarchy wobbles; the exercisers of patriarchal control lose their confidence.

In doing so, women's campaigns—campaigns for the vote, education, equal pay, and senior policy posts; against dowry burnings and trafficking in women; for land titles; for divorce and abortion rights; against domestic violence; for criminalization of marital rape—reveal how and why so many political regimes and the state structures supporting them have become so invested in patriarchy. Any country's political system rests on patriarchy insofar as any one of these campaigns are imagined by senior and mid-level officials to be a threat to "social order." To make sense of the often entrenched, even violent resistance to women's rights, one has to understand that patriarchy has its benefits not only for individual men, but for entire governmental systems. Many commentators have been slow to admit that the state has a profound stake in women weeding and men plowing, that the state is invested in men's pleasure being able to define heterosexual sex, that the state benefits from the feminization of the home and the masculinization of reason. It has been easier for these conventional commentators to think of political systems resting solely on skewed—ungendered—distributions of capital and weaponry.

But there is abundant evidence now that regimes and the states beneath them in fact have taken deliberate steps to sustain a sort of hierarchical gendered division of labor that provides them with cheapened, often completely unpaid, women's productive labor. This is most blatantly visible in the Third World export processing zones (EPZs) established with international agency assistance and local government public services and tax breaks. On average these state-fostered light industry factory zones depend on a labor force that is 70 percent female precisely because both the factory owners and the government's officials believe that women will accept lower wages, thus allowing products from the EPZs to compete more effectively on the international market. If ideas about femininity were turned upside down, if all men were expected to perform hours of unpaid child care, if women's paid work were considered as important to those women as men's paid work were to men, the local regimes, foreign and local corporate managers, and their international agency backers would have to surrender one of their chief means of sustaining domestic political stability and international economic order. The 1997–99 Asian economic crisis exposed—for those who were paying attention—just how reliant most local regimes and their international underwriters are on patriarchal role expectations. Thus the masculinized government of the Republic of Korea (South Korea) in 1997–98 pressured thousands of South Korean women—women whose low-paid work had fueled the earlier Korean economic miracle—to voluntarily give up their industrial jobs, to assign their top priority to the unpaid work of bolstering the plummeting self-confidence of their newly laid-off husbands.

Feminist researchers are providing impressive evidence that governments deploy gendered resources in order to pressure women to have the high—or low—numbers of children officials think are needed for state security. This was exposed in the intense debates sparked by the 1993 United Nations Conference on Population and Development. International women's organizing produced major concessions from government and the UN. National identity itself has been built out of notions of women's subordination to men: women's "traditional" seclusion in the home or "traditional" identities as self-sacrificing mothers have been turned by governmental officials and their nationalist supporters into essential elements that glue the "nation" together. If women rejected these roles and values, nationalists in countries as otherwise dissimilar as Iraq, the United States, Russia, Poland, Israel, and Singapore appear to believe, this fragile creature, the nation, would fall apart and the state in turn quickly would lose its *legitimacy: without "motherhood," the nation-state would deteriorate into a mere state.

The sites to watch in order to determine whether any particular regime in the world is taking active steps to shore up its patriarchal foundations are not always the most visible or newsworthy. In fact, if a country's president, its cabinet, or even its national legislature has to take decisive action to secure the three legs of patriarchy, it is probably a signal that patriarchal relationships between women and men are in jeopardy. Given the unnaturalness of so many aspects of a patriarchal order, it is usually fraught with instability and filled with daily struggle, though that struggle—of women in abusive marriages, of women workers coping with the double burden of job and home responsibilities, of women politicians trying to overcome sexism in party nomination processes—is often imagined as outside the arena of "real politics" and thus not taken into account by those assessing the dynamics of power in any political system. But the final stages of any women's campaign, while dramatic and thus impossible for even the most gender-unconscious commentator to overlook, are not necessarily the most representative of patriarchy at work. Rather, the sites to monitor are more mundane: lower courts, housing authorities, race relations boards, public hospitals, tourism and immigration offices, secondary schools, land reform tribunals, police stations, welfare departments, military field commands.

In the early twenty-first century, one must add to this list of political sites those institutions that operate outside state boundaries: the World Trade Organization, the World Bank, the Commission of the European Communities, the International Monetary Fund, the UN Development Program, the UN High Commission for Refugees, the North Atlantic Treaty Organization, the Organization of African States, the South Pacific Forum, the Hague and Arusha UN War Crimes Tribunals, and the Conference on Security and Cooperation in Europe. In their everyday operations these supranational authorities also are making decisions which either weaken or prop up patriarchal pillars of today's gendered politics. Their decisions are nearly always gendered—sometimes in their motivations, sometimes in their consequences, sometimes in both.

For example, the UN High Commission for Refugees (UNHCR) must constantly decide in the administration of any of its camps—in East Timor, Pakistan, Lebanon, Somalia, or the Congo—whether to empower women or to sustain masculinized authority. Although women and their dependent children constitute at least 70 percent of all current refugees, it is usually male refugees within the camps who presume to have authority, often using it to strengthen men's militias, while preventing women from gaining access to UN literacy classes. In the last decade, women acting in humanitarian and human rights groups have formed alliances both to reveal how political the UNHCR's gendered policies are and to change them. Similarly, women activists have created international pressure groups to lobby the WTO, the EU, and the World Bank.

On the other hand, patriarchal relationships between men and women do benefit specific men, not simply governments. It is for this reason that many political institutions and movements claiming to be in opposition to the current regime may in practice support that regime's efforts to sustain sexual divisions of labor and gendered inequalities. Business associations harshly critical of a socialist regime's policies on investment or welfare may nonetheless share with that regime the assumption that men, not women, are the natural participants in business-government bargaining sessions. Male leaders of leftist parties may seize every chance to point out the failings of the current conservative government and yet be no less defensive in the face of women's charges that all the country's political parties, left, center, and right, operate as if they were men's clubs. It is because patriarchal beliefs about masculinity and femininity benefit both individual men and a masculinized state that the specifically patriarchal character of any given government is so hard to discern—or transform.

Thus when women in any country do manage to gain some genuine influence in any sector of the opposition, it becomes significant: it serves to highlight the specifically patriarchal foundations of the government in power and perhaps even the state as a whole. For example, even in her brief 1980s tenure as the leader of the Japan Socialist Party, Takako Doi was able to draw groundbreaking media attention to the long-entrenched Liberal Democratic Party's all-male senior leadership's belief that it could continue to rule without nominating women candidates for seats in the lower house of the Diet. Likewise, in 1999's national parliamentary elections New Zealand's voters produced a historic "first" that shed new light on the masculinized norms of party politics worldwide. In November 1999, New Zealand voters brought into the prime minister's office Helen Clark, leader of the Labour Party. She replaced as prime minister another woman, Jenny Shipley of the Conservative Party. Neither Clark nor Shipley was the widow or daughter of a former prime minister.

In the 1980s, observers in a number of countries began to note an occasional patterned difference between women's voting and men's voting; they called it the "*gender gap." The belief that men and women are always likely to cast their ballots differently, regardless of their variations in regional interests, their generational experiences, or their economic circumstance, in fact is not all that new. Mexican and French male political leaders who claimed to espouse revolutionary republican principles nonetheless blocked female suffrage for decades because they were convinced that women in these two Catholic countries would be more prone than men to vote for conservative candidates backed by their local priests. Still, the gender gap is different. It is not presumed to dictate differences between men and women political participants on all issues as a result of biologically ingrained feminine conservatism. Rather, where it has appeared in recent years, this electoral gender gap has been tied less to specific candidates than to their parties' platforms and to the particular issues that have gained saliency in the electoral campaign.

Thus, for example, in the United States during the 1980s the national Republican Party began to rely on its popularity among white men. Men of color and women of all racial groups became less inclined than white men to vote for Republican presidential candidates. This gendered—and racial—voting pattern in turn began to shape partisan policy decisions. In 1990, two years into his administration, President George Bush vetoed a congressionally passed civil rights bill that would have strengthened minority and women's rights in employment. The National Public Radio correspondent Nina Totenberg reported ("All Things Considered," 25 October 1990) that the president made this decision at least in part because his White House advisers, with one eye on the voting booth, sought to solidify President Bush's support among his most solid constituency, white male voters. In the 2000 U.S. presidential and congressional electoral contests, Democratic strategists tried to keep their disproportionate support among women voters, while Republican strategists debated how to narrow the gender gap without alienating their male loyalists.

The concept of the gender gap, however, is not just a tool used by strategists and policy makers to determine the costs and rewards of one policy option over another. Polls that show a marked difference between women's and men's voting or policy preferences, if widely publicized, can strengthen or weaken the women's movement in that country. If women can see that, despite their racial and class differences, as women, they collectively hold views on taxes, abortion, child care, or war that are quite distinct from those held by most men in their society, there is a greater likelihood that they can imagine organizing politically as women. Thus Molly Yard, then head of the largest U.S. feminist organization, the National Organization for Women, was heartened when polls were published in November 1990 showing that women's attitudes toward military operations in the Persian Gulf were strikingly different from those of men. This had not always been true. During the Vietnam War, when the women's movement was still in its infancy, polls showed almost no differ-

ence in U.S. women's and men's attitudes toward the war. But twenty years later one of the reasons that George Bush's presidential advisers were so eager to bolster his support among white males in October of 1990 was that the polls showed his popularity slipping because of the drawn-out nature of the Persian Gulf crisis. It was especially women voters who were telling pollsters that they disapproved of the president's policies toward Iraq. In one poll, when men and women were asked whether they would support a U.S. invasion of Iraq, the gap yawned to 25 percent: 73 percent of women were opposed, compared with just 48 percent of men.

Women's differences with men over questions of military policy have provoked analytical and strategic discussion in countries as socially and politically dissimilar as 2000's Russia, Liberia, Serbia, and Sri Lanka, where women have organized all-women's groups to press their governments' male officials to take more energetic steps to end civil wars and their accompanying military violence. Earlier, in 1980s Argentina, Chile, and Britain, women developed feminist strategies to confront what they believed were patriarchal causes of *militarism. Are women by nature less violent than men? Is this international prominence of women in *peace movements to be explained hormonally? Women themselves disagree. However, as the understanding of the subtle processes of constructing masculinity and femininity becomes more sophisticated, there is waning confidence in essentialist explanations. Scholars instead are pointing to childhood socialization differences in many cultures that encourage little girls to resort to talking, listening, and compromise as ways to resolve conflict while those same cultures encourage little boys to see outcomes in terms of clear-cut victories and losses. Other scholars have investigated gendered socialization differences among adults. For instance, male national security intellectuals have been shown to have adopted forms of language that allow them to distance their feelings from the destructive formulas they are designing; similarly, military officials have not presumed that twenty-year-old men are natural soldiers and thus deliberately have employed rewards and punishments to instill those attitudes in new recruits. At the same time, investigations into the militaristic attitudes of some women, including prominent political figures such as Margaret Thatcher and Indira Gandhi, make it clear that antiwar attitudes are the product of socialization and experience, not genetic makeup. That is, those attitudes are not biological; they are gendered. If women do express notably less enthusiasm for their government's military solutions to conflicts, the reasons lie in the ways they have been taught to be feminine in their cultures.

This of course makes it difficult to critique societies' patriarchal ideologies: should the antimilitaristic attitudes be thrown out with the patriarchy that fosters such gendered differences in attitude and perspective? Many have rejected this as a false choice. It is necessary instead to deconstruct ideas that have been packaged monolithically as "femininity." Those ideas that are socially valuable, feminist antimilitarists argue, should be perpetuated; they should be taught to men as well as to women; no woman who espouses such an attitude should be marginalized in public affairs for being "naive"; no man who promotes such an idea should have his manliness questioned; no man who rejects such antimilitaristic ideas should be considered the model of masculinity and thus treated as if he were the standard-bearer of public responsibility.

Demilitarization and democratization have provided settings in Eastern and Central Europe, Latin America, Africa, and Asia for monitoring the gendered implications of political change. If militarization does privilege not just men but conventional masculine values in many cultures, then steps taken toward demilitarization should provide a more serious public hearing for people, usually women, espousing nonmasculinist ideas. If patriarchy thrives on hierarchical pyramids of authority, then democratization should open doors to women's wider political participation. The limited evidence suggests that the relationships may be more complicated.

In Chile, the overthrow of the military junta led by General Augusto Pinochet was in no small measure due to women's organizing all-women's campaigns during the 1980s. As Chilean anthropologist Ximena Bunster has described in her articles on women and *torture and the politics of Chilean military wives (in June Nash and Helen Safa, eds., *Women and Change in Latin America,* Hadley, Mass., 1986; in Eva Isaksson, ed., *Women and the Military,* New York, 1988), the Pinochet regime's hold over public life was profoundly gendered, and thus the loosening of that grip would have to be gendered. However, despite women's self-conscious reconstructing of femininity as part of their antijunta and *human rights campaigns, it proved difficult to turn the eventual demilitarization movement into a genuinely antipatriarchal movement. The civilian men leading the prodemocracy political parties, while opposing the military rule, still had a stake in defining electoral politics in masculinist terms. As a result, although women have gained new bureaucratic footholds in the new government and have became more mobilized within both the leading center and left parties, the post-Pinochet governments remained overwhelmingly male. Chile, in 2000, was the only Latin American country whose laws totally banned divorce.

Likewise the historic democratization of Eastern and Central Europe in the early 1990s, which brought with it the end of the Cold War militarization of Europe, had very mixed results for women's relationships both to men and to the state. Communist regimes in Eastern and Central Europe, like their Soviet model, had made the emancipation of women a pillar of their political legitimation. In practice, although women did gain paid jobs, social security, and reproductive rights, this emancipation did not mean the demasculinization of Soviet or Eastern and Central European politics. Rather, it meant that women gained access to the waged labor force while still being treated as the primary caretakers of men and children in the home. The "double burden" was as crucial as state ownership of industry to the post-1945 political systems of Czechoslovakia, Poland, the German Democratic Republic, and Hungary. Yet the collapse of these Communist systems in the face of popular pressure during 1989 did not translate into the demasculinization of politics. If Eastern and Central Europe's newly elected officials encouraged women to see in the market economies a chance to lighten their double burdens without confronting men by exchanging full-time jobs for part-time jobs, then the transition to a free market form of democratic polity may encourage women's further withdrawal from the political arena. If, in addition, as is especially evident in Poland, the rejection of Soviet-backed Communist regimes is fueled by a *nationalism rooted in presumptions about women's patriotic motherhood, then democratization is likely to be accompanied by state policies aimed at reducing women's reproductive rights.

Drusilla Menaker reported (*Boston Globe,* 2 December 1990) that a survey by the Inter-Parliamentary Council in Geneva showed that in every one of the legislatures in the former Soviet bloc women lost seats in the first post-Communist open elections. Women comprised 12 percent of the Polish parliament after the popular elections, compared with 20 percent when the Communist Party chose all the candidates; in Hungary women's representation dropped from 21 percent to 7 percent; Bulgaria's postdemocratization parliament was only 3.5 percent women, a fall from the earlier 21 percent; Czechoslovakia's was down to 6 percent from 29.5 percent. The newly unified German parliament replicated the same masculinist pattern, celebrating its debut with less than 10 percent women representatives. In the Soviet Union the more openly elected Congress of People's Deputies, the flagship of glasnost politics, in 1990 included just 15 percent women. It is not that the legislatures under the formerly Communist systems had political power; they did not. But it appears that once the legislative arms of these now-democratized states have gained meaningful influence, women have been marginalized by men eager to dominate the newly influential legislative bodies and newly legitimate political party organizations.

These developments in Latin America and Eastern and Central Europe reflect broader patterns in gendered politics today. First, states may undergo seemingly radical changes in their left-right associations and yet remain dependent on patriarchal concepts of masculine and feminine roles in those states. Second, genuine alterations in gendered political systems will not come until men's relationships to women in the allegedly "private" spheres of domestic life are deemed serious political objectives. Those movements that have the greatest chance of demasculinizing political life, consequently, are those in which women's diverse experiences of power are taken seriously as the basis of both political theorizing and strategizing; they are those in which at the same time all men's stake in maintaining the three legs of patriarchal society is openly acknowledged.

(See also CLASS AND POLITICS; FEMINISM; FEMINIZATION OF POVERTY; GAY AND LESBIAN POLITICS; GLOBALIZATION; GULF WAR; NEW SOCIAL MOVEMENTS; RACE AND RACISM; REPRODUCTIVE POLITICS; WOMEN AND DEVELOPMENT.)

Kumari Jayawardena, *Feminism and Nationalism* (London, 1986). Mariann Githens, Pippa Norris, and Joni Lovenduski, *Different Roles, Different Voices: Women and Politics in the United States and Europe* (New York and London, 1994). Joni Seager, *The State of Women in the World: An International Atlas* (London and New York, 1997). Rita Arditti, *Searching for Life: Grandmothers of the Plaza de Mayo* (Berkeley, Calif., 1999). Hanna Herzog, *Gendering Politics: Women in Israel* (Ann Arbor, Mich., 1999). Valerie Sperling, *Women's Organizing in Contemporary Russia* (London and New York, 1999). Mary Ann Tetrault, "Sex and Violence: Social Reactions to Economic Restructuring in Kuwait," *International Feminist Journal of Politics* 1, no. 2 (September 1999): 237–255. Cynthia Enloe, *Maneuvers: The International Politics of Militarizing Women's Lives* (Berkeley, Calif., 2000).

CYNTHIA H. ENLOE

GENOCIDE. Despite the fact that genocide, i.e., the use of deliberate measures taken with the intent to physically destroy a racial, ethnic, religious, or other similar group, has taken place throughout history, it was only recently that such atrocious practices became a matter of specific and explicit prohibition by *international law. Today, however, it is universally recognized that genocide is the gravest international crime and the most dangerous violation of *human rights and that the international community is morally and politically responsible to take steps to prevent its occurrence and to punish persons responsible for crimes amounting to genocide.

Such recognition arose in response to a number of episodes of genocide during the first half of this century, in particular the Nazi *Holocaust during *World War II. The genocidal policies of *Hitler's Germany stand above all comparisons because they were a part of a carefully calculated plan to systematically annihilate particular nations, races, religions, and political groups.

The tragedy of the Nazi holocaust led a Polish jurist, Raphael Lemkin, to coin the word *genocide* from the Greek word *genos* (race, people) and the Latin *caedere* (to kill) and to begin action aimed at the international prohibition of genocide, which would in turn provide the necessary international legal basis for action against this crime. One result of this initiative was the Convention on the Prevention and Punishment of the Crime of Genocide, which was adopted unanimously by the UN General Assembly on 9 December 1948 (UN Treaty Series, vol. 78, p. 278) and which entered into force on 12 January 1951. The convention was subsequently ratified or acceded to by more than 100 states, and it is now universally accepted that prohibition of the crime of genocide as defined in that convention belongs to peremptory norms (*ius cogens*) of international law.

In the terms of the convention "genocide means any of the following acts committed with the intent to destroy, in whole or in part, a national, ethnical, racial or religious group, such as (a) Killing members of the group; (b) Causing serious bodily or mental harm to members of the group; (c) Deliberately inflicting on the group conditions of life calculated to bring about its physical destruction in whole or in part; (d) Imposing measures intended to prevent births within the group; (e) Forcibly transferring children of the group to another group." Punishment for acts of genocide and associated acts such as complicity in genocide, whether committed in time of peace or in time of war, applies to "constitutionally responsible rulers, public officials or private individuals." The contracting parties to the convention are obliged to enact legislation that makes genocide a crime within their territories and to provide effective penalties for persons guilty of genocide or of associated acts. Persons charged with any of these acts shall be tried "by a competent tribunal of the State in the territory of which the act was committed, or by such international tribunal as may have jurisdiction. . . ."

The provisions relating to the question of jurisdiction reflect the major deficiency of the convention and, indeed, of the entire international legal system in regard to prosecution of international crimes: the absence of compulsory international criminal jurisdiction. In the case of genocide this problem poses particular difficulties. The crime of genocide can hardly be committed without at least indirect involvement of a government, and it is unlikely that such a government would bring before the court individuals directly responsible for such crimes. The only real solution to this problem would be the establishment of an international tribunal with an appropriate jurisdiction in criminal matters relating to international crimes such as genocide. The idea of an international criminal court with the competence to try persons responsible for genocide and other crimes of comparable magnitude gained strong support in the 1990s, at the time of genocides against the Bosnian Muslims and, later, the Tutsis in Rwanda. Two ad hoc criminal tribunals were established by the UN Security Council. Simultaneously, the drafting of the Statute of the International Criminal Court with a general jurisdiction was accelerated. In 1998 the UN General Assembly convened a diplomatic conference in Rome which adopted the Statute of the International Criminal Court. The Court's jurisdiction (limited to the most serious crimes of concern to the international community) includes the crime of genocide as defined in the 1948 Convention. The Statute of the Court will enter into force as an international treaty binding for its state parties following the necessary sixty ratifications. The process of ratification is expected to take a number of years.

Furthermore, recent experience has thrown into relief the fact that genocide is not merely an internal affair of state and that the UN has the moral and legal right to intervene.

(See also WAR CRIMES.)

Raphael Lemkin, *Axis Rule in Occupied Europe* (Washington, D.C., 1944). Leo Kuper, *The Prevention of Genocide* (New Haven, Conn., 1985).
DANILO TÜRK

GEOPOLITICS. Originally coined by the Swede Rudolf Kjellen in 1899, geopolitics was popularized in the early twentieth century by the British geographer Halford Mackinder as part of his effort to promote the field of geography as an aid to British statecraft. It was intended to signify the impact of geographical factors such as the spatial disposition of the continents and oceans and the distribution of natural and human resources upon international politics at a time when the whole world was finally available for state territorial and economic expansion.

During the 1920s and 1930s Mackinder's formal model of a Eurasian "heartland" rising to global dominance if not checked by cohesive reaction from the encircling "outer or insular crescent" was adopted by certain Nazi apologists to justify Germany's expansionism. In German *Geopolitik* the heartland model was added to concepts of movable frontiers, autarky, *Lebensraum* (living space or room to expand), and *Panideen* (pan-ideas such as PanAmericanism, as expressed in the *Monroe Doctrine in the United States). Some of these ideas were directly inspired by the writing of the German geographer Friedrich Ratzel on the "laws of the spatial growth of states." There is still controversy over whether German *Geopolitik* directly influenced Nazi policies.

In the aftermath of *World War II the term fell into disuse, especially among professional geographers, because of its association with Nazi policies and ideas of environmental determinism from which geographers were in retreat. Formal geopolitical models, especially Mackinder's heartland model, continued to appear in geography textbooks, and some academics made "adjustments" by allowing for changes in military technology (airpower, nuclear weapons, etc.) and changes in regional "ecology" resulting from the disintegration of the European colonial empires. However, in the absence of much explicit continuity with the prewar period geopolitics acquired two new meanings: 1) as a synonym for geostrategy in the pursuit of particular diplomatic and military goals and 2) as the equivalent of political geography, in the sense of areal variation in political phenomena at all scales, including the global.

The more classical usage returned to prominence in U.S. debates over international politics in the late 1970s and early 1980s. Interest groups such as the Committee on the Present Danger and ideological elements strong in the first *Reagan administration argued that the United States must redouble its efforts at "containing" the Soviet Union after the détente and "idealism" of the United States following the *Vietnam War. They used explicit geopolitical language about the "domino effect" of revolutions in Central America, Soviet desire for warm-water ports and oil deposits in the Middle East, and the key role of the U.S. Navy in denying the world's sea-lanes to the Soviet Union. From this perspective the United States and the Soviet Union were seen as successor states to, respectively, Britain's nineteenth-century maritime empire and French and German attempts to assemble an overwhelming "continental bloc."

In this context some geographers began to question whether geopolitics, in the sense of the geographical ordering of the world into a hierarchy of "strategic regions," "spheres of influence," "buffer zones," and "strategic locations," existed in *foreign policy only when the term was used in reference to formal geopolitical models (such as Mackinder's). Rather, geopolitics could be viewed as any discourse about geographically defined interests including particular models privileging fixed geographical "facts" about the world. From this point of view geopolitics did not disappear after World War II or when moral rhetoric replaced *Realpolitik* in the pronouncements of politicians. It is implicit in the practice of foreign policy.

In line with this dynamic conception of geopolitics, as the world political economy changes the criteria used for ordering the world geographically change. Currently, economic rather than military-territorial considerations are becoming more central to discussions about geopolitics in the United States and the Pacific Basin is challenging Europe as the highest-priority region for U.S. policymakers. But older themes from the height of U.S.–Soviet competition in the 1950s persist even as their real-world basis is undermined. Geopolitical discourse can lag behind the world it purports to explain.

Since the nineteenth century the geopolitics of, first, Britain, and, second, the United States, have been hegemonic at the global scale because of the dominant position of these states. Other states could either consent or pose a challenge. In this century a succession of challenges, both global (for example, Nazi Germany and Japan in the 1930s and 1940s; the Soviet Union during the *Cold War) and regional (for example, Gaullist France in Europe; India in South Asia; Iran and Iraq in the Middle East), have been made to the global status quo but as yet without international success.

(See also Domino Theory.)

John Agnew and Stuart Corbridge, "The New Geopolitics: The Dynamics of Geopolitical Disorder," in Ronald J. Johnston and Peter J. Taylor, eds., *A World in Crisis? Geographical Perspectives*, 2d ed. (Oxford, 1989), pp. 266–288. Simon Dalby, "American Security Discourse: The Persistence of Geopolitics" *Political Geography Quarterly* 9 (April 1990): 171–188.

John A. Agnew

GEORGIA. A former Soviet republic, Georgia declared its independence from the Soviet Union on 9 April 1991 and adopted its current constitution in 1995. This constitution established a semi-presidential republic; The president acts both as the head of state and the head of government. The Georgian executive dominates the weaker parliament and federal court. Georgia boasts a mixed electoral system, utilizing both proportional representation multimember districts and first-past-the-post single-member districts for parliamentary elections. Georgia has a multiparty system, although most parties do not overcome the 7 percent threshold for parliamentary representation.

In the October 1999 parliamentary election, three parties (out of thirty-five) gained representation. President Eduard Shevardnadze's Georgia's Union of Citizens party won the majority of seats. Georgia's Revival, led by Aslan Abashidze, and Industry Will Save Georgia formed the opposition. In April 2000, Eduard Shevardnadze won presidential reelection with 80 percent of the vote. However, international election observers criticized some electoral practices and Shevardnadze's opponents disputed the result.

Indeed, throughout its period of independent statehood, Georgia has experienced an uneasy democratic transition. The first democratically elected president of Georgia was Zviad Gamsakhurdia, elected just after independence in May 1991. In 1992, Defense Minister Tenghiz Kitovani and paramilitary leader Djaba Ioseliani ousted Gamsakhurdia from the leadership. Ioseliani and Kitovani invited former Soviet Foreign Minister (and former Georgian Communist Party First Secretary) Eduard Shevardnadze to govern Georgia. In 1992, the Georgian army, which supported Kitovani, battled opposition groups favoring Gamsakhurdia. Although Gamsakhurdia died in 1992, his supporters remain opposed to the Shevardnadze government and have maintained a strong antigovernment presence in Georgia.

Since its independence, the Georgian government has faced difficulties maintaining territorial control and legitimacy. Upon the dissolution of the Soviet Union, two regions declared their independence: the northwestern region of Abkhazia and the northern region of South Ossetia. The Georgian army, as well as several paramilitary groups, fought active wars with rebels in both regions. The wars displaced people in both regions, most significantly in Abkhazia. Over 500,000 Georgian refugees fled Abkhazia, many moving into hotels in major cities. Their repatriation remains a crucial issue for any peace settlement.

At the end of 1993, Georgia joined the *Commonwealth of Independent States, inviting CIS peacekeepers (mostly Russians) to help stabilize the Abkhaz and Ossetian regions. At the time of writing, neither the Abkhaz nor the Ossetian conflicts have been resolved. Although South Ossetia is repairing relations with the Georgian government in Tbilisi, Russian troops still monitor the region. While there has been no formal peace settlement, Abkhazia remains essentially independent of Georgian governance.

With international monetary aid and private investment, the Georgian economy grew during 1995–1996, but faltered during the Russian economic crisis of 1997. Georgia has not yet recovered and has been plagued with high unemployment. Shevardnadze's economic policy has sought to recreate Georgia's place on the "Silk Route," specifically providing passage for Caspian oil from Azerbaijan to Turkey, as well as continued relations with the West. Shevardnadze's opponents, particularly Abashidze, have argued against this emphasis, contending that Georgia should focus on its relations with Russia. In either case, most Georgians consider good relations with their neighbors essential for prosperity.

(See also POST-COMMUNISM.)

Radio Free Europe/Radio Liberty, *Transcaucasus/Central Asia Newsline,* November 1, 1999. On-Line Resource. URL: *http://www.rferl.org/newsline/1999/11/011199.html* Antadze, Ia, "Parliamentary Elections in Georgia." *The Kartvelologist: Journal of Georgian Studies* 6 (Spring 2000): 47–56.

JULIE GEORGE

GERMAN DEMOCRATIC REPUBLIC. The German Democratic Republic (GDR)—also known as East Germany—was created in the Soviet-occupied zone after World War II as a separate German state next to the Federal Republic of *Germany (FRG). Founded on 7 October 1949, the GDR (population 16 million) ceased to exist on 3 October 1990, upon its unification with the FRG (which until then had also been known as West Germany) following the peaceful revolution of fall 1989. Thus the political history of the GDR can be divided into three periods: the formative stage in the postwar years, the four decades of communist rule, and the transition period beginning with the peaceful revolution.

After the defeat of Nazism, the wartime Allies determined the political restructuring of Germany in accordance with the Potsdam Agreement of 1945 in their respective zones. The Soviet military administration allowed the rebuilding of political parties and unions, favoring, however, the Kommunistische Partei Deutschlands (KPD). In April 1946, the larger party on the Left, the Sozialdemokratische Partei Deuschlands (SPD), was pressed into merging with the KPD to form the Sozialistische Einheitspartei Deutschlands (SED). The new party became a mechanism for the communists to control the political process. The distance between the occupation zones widened during the *Cold War, and the division of Germany led to the formation of the GDR as a *communist party state with a centrally planned economy.

Even though four other political parties existed—the Christlich-Demokratische Union (CDU), the Demokratische Bauernpartei Deutschlands (DBD), the Liberal-Demokratische Partei Deutschlands (LDPD), and the National-Demokratische Partei Deutschlands (NDPD)—the SED kept tight control of all other so-called bloc parties that were part of the Nationale Front. Elections to the parliament were held every four years, allowing only one unified list. A fixed distribution of seats among the political parties and other organizations, such as the Freier Deutscher Gewerkschaftsbund (FDGB), the Youth Organization, and the Women's Federation, was prearranged before the elections.

Political decision making was highly concentrated and centralized. In 1952, the *Länder,* or states, were abolished, allowing the central government in the capital, East Berlin, to control and administer policies uniformly in the entire country. The most important body politically was the Communist Party, with power concentrated in the politburo of the SED (first secretary, 1951–1971: Walter Ulbricht; 1971–1989: Erich Honecker). The SED became one of the most tightly controlled and organized communist parties in the Soviet bloc. In 1988 it had 2.1 million members. Based on a *nomenklatura* system, all key positions in the state administration, the economy, education, the media, and the military were controlled by the party. Even the judiciary was dependent on SED directives and policies, neglecting opportunities to claim individual rights while favoring state power and control. The powerful secret police, the *Stasi (Staatssicherheit)* or state security, monitored and controlled the population, keeping files on over 6 million people. Before the collapse of communist rule it had some 106,000 employees; additionally, between 1.6 and 2 million citizens were unpaid "informers" for the regime.

Economic policies in the GDR were molded largely upon those of the Soviet Union. Production targets were set by five-year plans and economic planning was directed by the politburo. More than 85 percent of the GDR's economy was run by nationalized enterprises, agriculture was collectivized, and even small-scale industries, crafts, and services were almost entirely socialized. Unlike the Soviet Union, however, the GDR could draw upon its fairly advanced industrial as well as human resources. Under the Honecker regime, the development of microelectronics and other new technologies was aggressively promoted, but results were modest. To enhance political legitimacy the SED also introduced social policies in the 1970s, including a housing program and benefits for mothers.

The SED firmly rejected the reform ideas proposed by the Soviet Communist Party leader Mikhail *Gorbachev in 1985–1986. As conditions in the *international political economy became increasingly unfavorable for the *command economies in Eastern and *Central Europe and the Soviet Union—leading to declining growth rates, deterioration of the standard of living, increasing pollution, and foreign debts—the GDR withstood the squeeze longer than other countries in the region, largely owing to favorable trade conditions and economic relations with the Federal Republic.

Mass migration of East Germans to the West through the open border between Hungary and Austria in the fall of 1989 led to mounting popular pressure and increased oppositional activity including the forming of the Neues Forum in September 1989, the refounding of the SPD, and actions by small civil rights, women's, and environmentalist groups, some of which had existed for some years, mostly under the shelter of the Protestant Church. Almost 2 percent of the population emigrated to the Federal Republic in the second half of 1989. Mass demonstrations in Leipzig, Berlin, Dresden, and other cities under the slogan "We are the people" led to hectic leadership change in the SED. The dramatic and unexpected opening of the Berlin Wall on 9 November 1989 accelerated the collapse of the communist regime. Only a few weeks later, the party was forced to give up its "leading role," agree to roundtable negotiations with oppositional groups, and schedule free elections. But insufficient attempts were made to abolish the power of the secret police and to reform the economy.

The first and last free elections to the GDR parliament, the *Volkskammer*, which took place on 18 March 1990, were a mandate for quick unification with the Federal Republic. Supported by West German Chancellor Helmut *Kohl, the CDU-led Alliance for Germany, which had called for quick unification, won 48 percent of the vote; the SPD, which had favored a slower, more cautious approach to unification, received 21 percent; the Partei des Demokratischen Sozialismus (PDS), successor to the SED, received 16 percent; while the civil groups that had helped carry out the peaceful revolution were clearly marginalized. The GDR government moved to accomplish unification as quickly as possible. After the currency union that introduced the West German deutsche mark into the GDR on 1 July 1990, the GDR parliament decided to join the Federal Republic by accession under Article 23 of the West German Basic Law, and reunification occurred on 3 October 1990.

Given the lack of reliable empirical data, it is difficult to assess to what extent citizens in the GDR had developed identification with and support for their state. Orientation toward the Federal Republic had always been a powerful underlying pattern of popular attitudes, and the attempt of the SED regime to foster identification with a "socialist nation" has clearly failed. However, for years to come significant political cultural differences between citizens in the west and the east of Germany will prevail as the challenges of reducing structural inequalities and fostering a sense that "we are one nation" continue.

(See also COMMUNISM; ENVIRONMENTALISM; GERMAN UNIFICATION; NINETEEN EIGHTY-NINE; INTERNATIONAL MIGRATION; POTSDAM CONFERENCE; POLITICAL CULTURE.)

James McAdams, *East Germany and the West: Surviving Détente* (New York, 1985). Marilyn Rueschemeyer and Christiane Lemke, eds., *The Quality of Life in the German Democratic Republic: Changes and Developments in a State Socialist Society* (New York, 1989). Elizabeth Pond, *After the Wall: American Policy Toward Germany* (New York, 1990.)

CHRISTIANE LEMKE

GERMAN UNIFICATION came as a surprise. Feelings were mixed about achieving it, even among Germans themselves. Bismarck's Germany seemed to have been too big for the European state system and unstable internally. The Nazi regime was often seen as only a monstrous caricature of the repression at home and adventurism abroad feared to be inherent in any unified German state. By contrast, the western Federal Republic of *Germany, or FRG (West Germany), was a manageable partner for France in a European confederation and a particularly faithful ally for the United States in the *North Atlantic Treaty Organization (NATO). Without the eastern regions, the Federal Republic achieved an internal political and cultural balance that made it a model of democratic civility. Meanwhile, the *German Democratic Republic, or GDR (East Germany), appeared to encapsulate the more repugnant traits of both *communism and the old imperial authoritarianism.

Officially, however, the Federal Republic awaited unification and welcomed refugees as citizens. But other policies suggested a different view. In the early *Cold War, the Federal Republic chose a posture of unremitting hostility toward the East German state. Any unification would be on the West's own terms. Democracy, capitalism, and a Western orientation had clear priority. As wary coexistence stabilized, the Federal Republic began to imagine more intimate relations—perhaps leading to some confederal structure. But a single state was thought unlikely in the foreseeable future, both because the Soviet Union would not permit it and because the GDR would be strong enough to reject it. Unification could be achieved only as "two states in one nation," the formula popularized by Willy Brandt in the 1970s. Meanwhile, the Federal Republic would continue as the principal U.S. ally in NATO and France's principal partner in the European Community (EC).

It was changing Soviet policy that permitted Germany's sudden unification. With the Soviet leader Mikhail *Gorbachev dedicating himself to reform and a "common European home," Soviet force was no longer ready to buttress the communist regime in East Germany. Unification grew imminently possible. The United States blessed it and no other Western power could forestall it.

In October 1989, huge demonstrations forced the communist leader Erich Honecker to resign. East Germans had begun streaming to the West in the late spring. Its authority slipping away, the communist government began dismantling the Berlin Wall on 9 November 1989. As the flow continued, the Federal Republic, welcoming refugees with automatic *citizenship and economic aid, faced enormous disruption. Nothing would resolve the situation, it was widely argued, short of complete unification. Chancellor Helmut *Kohl's coalition of his own party, the Christlich-Demokratische Union (CDU), the Bavarian Christlich-Soziale Union (CSU), and Foreign Minister Genscher's Freie Demokratische Partei (FDP) gradually came to favor rapid absorption of the GDR. The Sozialdemokratische Partei Deutschlands (SPD) opposition inclined toward delay and confederation with East Germany. By February 1990, it was agreed that negotiations for the new Germany would take place in a "two-plus-four" format, which meant bilateral German talks in parallel with collective talks adding Britain, France, the Soviet Union, and the United States.

Hopes for avoiding a reborn single Germany lay with the GDR. If it could reform rapidly enough to gain legitimacy from its own population, unification could be confederal. The GDR scheduled elections for 18 March. The principal contenders proved to be the well-financed affiliates of the West German parties rather than either the indigenous reformist coalition or the reconstituted communist party, transformed into the Partei des Demokratischen Sozialismus (PDS). The East German CDU won a near majority (48.1 percent) and headed a coalition pledged to entering the Federal Republic. By early May, the two German states reached final arrangements for a currency union—on terms generous to holders of eastern marks. Economic union took place on 1 July. A formal treaty, signed on 31 August, set the terms for unification. The GDR would be dismantled into five *Länder* (states), which would accede to the Federal Republic under Article 23 of its

Basic Law. Both parliaments ratified the treaty on 20 September, and unification occurred on 3 October.

The two-plus-four talks resolved Germany's international status. The new Federal Republic was to continue the formal relationships of the old. Gorbachev and Kohl met in the Soviet Union and confirmed that the Federal Republic would remain in NATO, and that Soviet troops would leave Germany by 1994. The Federal Republic would permit no foreign troops in the old East German territory, continue to renounce biological, chemical, and nuclear weapons, and cut its army to 370,000. On 12 September in Moscow, a final settlement ended the special rights and responsibilities of the Four Powers and guaranteed the Older-Neisse border between Poland and Germany.

At a Conference for Security and Cooperation in Europe (CSCE) summit in Paris opening on 19 November 1990, member states signed a treaty limiting conventional forces in Europe, formally proclaimed the end of Europe's military and economic division, and affirmed Europe's adherence to democratic freedoms and *human rights. The new Germany also reaffirmed its links to the EC and to continuing European integration.

In December, the first all-German federal elections gave Chancellor Kohl's CDU/CSU 44 percent of the vote. Genscher's FDP was also a big winner—with 11 percent. The SPD, whose leader, Oskar Lafontaine, had campaigned for a confederal structure, took only 33.5 percent. The Kohl coalition had triumphed on all sides. The Federal Republic had swallowed the GDR. Germany was once more a single state, despite all the misgivings. This new Germany was mostly free from the trammels of the postwar system, and the Federal Republic seemed, more than ever, Europe's leading power.

Celebration was brief. The Kohl government seriously understated the immediate costs of absorbing the GDR. Rapid economic union collapsed much of East Germany's uncompetitive economy, further burdened by an acute environmental mess. Private business was diffident about providing new capital. Unemployment in the five new *Länder* reached frightening levels. Heavy new welfare and pension costs helped push the general government financial balance from a small West German surplus in 1989 to a combined deficit that reached 3.3 percent of nominal GDP by 1991. The Bundesbank resisted monetizing the deficit and interest rates jumped to record levels as early as 1989. By February 1991, the chancellor, despite election promises, asked for a large tax increase.

By 1997, the German government had transferred one trillion deutsche marks to the East and relief was not yet in sight. General government net financial liabilities jumped from 20.7 percent of GDP in 1990 to over 50 percent by 1998. Meanwhile, the German current account turned negative from 1991 to 1998.

Germany's unification greatly affected general European economic and political history. At the close of 1991, the *Maastricht Treaty (ratified in 1993), which renamed the EC the *European Union (EU), sought to compensate for the disruptive effects by intensifying Europe's integration. An *Economic and Monetary Union (EMU) and a Common Foreign and Security Policy (CFSP) were slated to follow. Meanwhile, German interest rates helped to precipitate a European currency crisis in 1992. A difficult period of European monetary instability threatened to undermine the common market itself. In 1998, after several years of fractious negotiations, Germany, France, and nine other EU nations adhered to an EMU with a common currency (the euro), scheduled to be in everyday use by 2002. Renouncing the deutsche mark was unwelcome to many Germans, but was thought necessary to bind a bigger Germany to its neighbors. And given the new Germany's regional burdens, shedding the deutsche mark would arguably help its international competitiveness. Meanwhile, united Germany was gradually being pushed to accept a greater security role.

German internal politics were also changed. Absorbing the GDR created a new social and economic profile and different political and cultural balances. Chancellor Kohl's triumphal popularity in the federal elections of 1990 obscured the changes. But by 1994 the Kohl coalition returned with only a small majority in the Bundestag and soon lost control of the Bundesrat, a situation that blocked the reforms widely thought necessary to sustain German economic competitiveness. The eastern electorate returned to the left, including the rejuvenated communists (PDS). In the 1998 federal elections, eastern votes contributed heavily to Chancellor Kohl's defeat, after a record sixteen years in power. A triumphant SPD, led by Gerhard *Schröder, formed a fractious coalition government with the environmentalist party, Bündnis '90/Die Grünen (the Greens). Within a few months, the new coalition had lost its majority in the Bundesrat. It was not clear that postwar Germany's stable party system or capacity to sustain strong coalition governments should any longer be taken for granted. Meanwhile, the eastern *Länder* continued to lag behind. Overall German growth was tepid and unemployment remained at record levels. Unification was continuing to weigh significantly upon national and European history.

(See also NINETEEN EIGHTY-NINE.)

Elizabeth Pond, *Beyond the Wall: Germany's Road to Unification* (Washington, D.C., 1993). Konrad Jarausch, *The Rush to German Unity* (New York, 1994). Condoleeza Rice and Philip Zelikow, *Germany Unified and Europe Transformed: A Study in Statecraft* (Cambridge, Mass., 1995).

DAVID CALLEO

GERMANY, FEDERAL REPUBLIC OF. A key player has emerged once again on the international stage in the twentieth century's closing years. The Federal Republic of Germany (FRG), which celebrated its fiftieth anniversary in 1999, has assumed important political responsibilities in European and world affairs. The government's assertion of political power came just at a time when its operations shifted from the former sleepy capital of Bonn to bustling cosmopolitan Berlin. By then nine years had elapsed since the *German Democratic Republic (GDR) had acceded to the FRG in October 1990. As a consequence the country's political and economic strength increased. Government leaders felt that they could not shirk duties and obligations, military included, expected of powerful states. In 1999, when the Kosovo crisis in the former Yugoslavia erupted, the German government, under its NATO obligations, committed units of its air force to combat operations for the first time since World War II.

History. To understand these shifts in power, a brief glance back into history is necessary. Before 1871 Germany consisted of numerous rival principalities and fiefdoms. In 1871 Kaiser William I and Chancellor Otto von Bismarck formed the Second Reich. The governing authoritarian elites, consisting of the Prussian landed nobility (the Junkers), the bureaucracy, and the military, had no intention of allowing a democratic system to flourish that might challenge their rule. In the next decades Germany became a powerful economic and military state.

Germany's power did not prevent its political collapse and military defeat at the end of World War I. Thereupon social democratic leaders formed a republic, whose democratic constitution, adopted at Weimar in 1919, provided for a parliamentary system and guaranteed individual rights. The Weimar governments, however, could not establish a strong base in the face of the Great Depression of 1929, which led to massive unemployment among workers. Many now voted for the Nazis, who became the strongest party in 1932. On 30 January 1933, President Paul von Hindenburg appointed Adolf *Hitler chancellor, thereby dooming the Weimar Republic.

Hitler, promising to give jobs to the workers and to restore the country's reputation, gained the support of the population. He established a totalitarian regime, banned the opposition parties and trade unions, and controlled the media. He instituted a system of terror against all opponents and eventually against Jews, leading to their emigration or annihilation in the Holocaust. Hitler's armies invaded Poland on 1 September 1939, which led to World War II and, in 1945, to Germany's military collapse.

The victorious Allied powers—the United States, Britain, France, and the Soviet Union—carved up Germany into four occupation zones and gave much of eastern Germany to Poland. In the zones, they began a denazification, demilitarization, and reeducation program. In their zones, the Soviets imposed a communist and the Western Allies a liberal capitalist system. From 1947 on the *Cold War between them torpedoed any hope that an all-German government could be formed.

In 1949, two rival states emerged on the territory of the former German Reich. On 21 September, the Western Allies terminated military government in their zones, allowing the creation of the FRG. The new democratic government operated in Bonn under a provisional constitution, the Basic Law, which the constituent state (*Land*) assemblies had approved earlier. In the eastern zone, Soviet authorities on 7 October created the GDR, with East Berlin as its capital. Political power lay in the hands of the communist-dominated Socialist Unity Party (SED). Party cadres occupied all top posts in the ministries, the army, and the collectivized economy.

For forty years, the two states coexisted uneasily, having abandoned hope for reunification. But once Hungary, in line with a liberalization process in the Soviet Union and Poland, opened its Austrian border to East Germans, the GDR population began its own peaceful revolution against the oppressive regime in late 1989. On 9 November GDR officials opened the border to West Berlin and West Germany, which led to the emergence of a democratic system. On 3 October 1990, the GDR acceded to the FRG, thereby creating a united Germany.

The Bases of Politics. The new Germany borders the North Sea and the Baltic, and has common frontiers with Denmark, the Netherlands, Belgium, Luxembourg, France, Switzerland,

Austria, the Czech Republic, and Poland. It is 357,000 square kilometers in size, an area slightly smaller, in comparison, than Montana. Germany's chief natural resources are iron ore, bituminous coal and lignite, potash, timber, lignite, natural gas, salt, and nickel. Its agricultural crops are wheat, potatoes, sugar beets, barley, grapes, and cheese. Its strong export-oriented industries—engineering, automobile manufacturing, electronics, and chemicals—make it the third largest industrial nation, outranked only by the United States and Japan. Yet the German economic growth rate has slowed down since 1990 and it is no longer considered the economic model in the international arena. The government has provided massive financial support to modernize the east German economy and to retrain workers, thereby increasing the national debt. Some German firms have relocated parts of their operations to eastern Europe where wage costs are lower. To ensure a strong currency and keep inflation low, interest rates are kept moderately high. The country is plagued by a persistent unemployment rate of 4 million workers, or 10 percent of the labor force, reaching nearly 20 percent in the former GDR. Lowering taxes has not produced a revival of the economy. CDU/CSU and SPD-led governments have introduced reform packages that would reduce the level of social spending, but, facing the gauntlet of diverse interest groups, have made only modest changes.

Germany's population totals 82 million, of whom 15.4 million live in eastern Germany. Nearly a third of the FRG population resides in cities of over 100,000. Non-Germans, including Turks, Italians, Greeks, Poles, and refugees from the former Yugoslavia, comprise nearly 9 percent of the total. The population is 35 percent Protestant, 34 percent Roman Catholic, 1.7 percent Muslim, and 29.3 percent unaffiliated or espousing other religions. Germany's population is aging as a result of a low birth rate, one of the lowest in the world. According to specialists' projections, by the year 2040 the population will have declined significantly, unless immigration is liberalized. By then the number of youth under twenty years will total only 15 percent (currently 22 percent) and those over sixty years will jump to 37 percent (currently 21 percent).

Political Institutions. The Federal Republic has evolved into a stable and strong democracy, the first in Germany's history. The Basic Law's architects opted for a parliamentary system, in which the chancellor and members of Parliament are the key actors. The country's president is the ceremonial head of state and has limited political powers, such as dissolving the Bundestag if there is a deadlock between it and the executive. The president is expected to remain nonpartisan while in office.

The chancellor wields executive authority, guides governmental policy, and mediates disputes between cabinet ministers. If policy differences between a minister and the chancellor cannot be bridged, the chancellor can request a minister to resign or the minister may decide to resign. Major cabinet turnovers have been rare, although chancellors occasionally have reshuffled their cabinets, shifting a minister from one post to another. To stabilize the political system and prevent the frequent changes of chancellors characteristic of the Weimar regime, the Basic Law stipulates that if the opposition party (or parties) in the Bundestag votes to oust a chancellor because of fundamental policy differences or other causes, it must first agree on a successor. This process, called a constructive vote of no confidence, has prevented the Weimar practice of ousting a chancellor without agreeing on a successor.

The Parliament consists of two houses, the Bundesrat (Upper House), representing the constituent states (*Länder*), and the Bundestag (Lower House), the people. Members of the two houses debate policy issues, mediate and integrate interest group claims, legislate, control the budget, and challenge the government. The Bundesrat's sixty-nine members, appointed by the *Länder* cabinets, must approve federal legislation and administer decrees affecting the *Länder*. In instances of discord between the two chambers, a mediation committee will seek to reconcile differences.

The 669 Bundestag deputies are elected for a four-year term. Their number will be reduced to 598 in 2002 to make the legislative body more manageable. (Prior to Germany's unification in 1990, the number was fixed at 496.) The deputies are elected on the basis of a mixture of proportional representation and the Anglo-Saxon single-member district system. To gain Bundestag representation, a party must obtain a minimum of 5 percent of the national vote or win three seats in the districts. The provision was designed to prevent the political instability of the Weimar period when too many clashing minor parties held Reichstag seats.

The current party system is in a state of flux. The conservative Christian Democratic Union (CDU) and its Bavarian affiliate, the Christian Social Union (CSU), and the left centrist Social Democratic Party (SPD) have been the rotating national governing parties in West Germany from 1949 to 1990 and since then in united Germany. The CDU, rocked by financial scandals in 1999, can no longer expect to receive automatic backing from its faithful supporters. Indeed, supporters of all parties have identified less with them, have opposed some of their policies, or have become disillusioned by unfulfilled promises. As a consequence, many former supporters have refrained from voting, have switched from one major party to the other, or have cast their vote for a minor party. Some minor parties—the market-oriented Free Democratic Party (FDP), the environmentalist Greens, and the leftist Party of Democratic Socialism (PDS), the successor party to the GDR Socialist Unity Party—have seats in the Bundestag. Others, such as three right-wing parties (the Republicans, the National Democratic Party, and the German People's Union), whose leaders have made xenophobic speeches, have never received enough votes to be in the Bundestag and to challenge regime governance. They have, however, gained seats in a few state legislatures and in the European Parliament. Should these parties intend to subvert the democratic basic order, the Constitutional Court can declare them unconstitutional.

The German political culture has changed over the decades. Student, peace, ecology, and feminist movements have had an impact on the FRG's political system from the late 1960s to the 1980s. In the 1990s, most eastern and western Germans support the democratic system but a psychological divide between them continues to frustrate the politicians' aspirations for unity. Neo-Nazi groups and skinheads have committed numerous acts of violence against foreigners. A minority of ordinary German citizens hold an anti-immigration senti-

ment; 5 million of them signed CDU/CSU-sponsored initiative petitions in 1999 against a SPD-Greens government bill that if successful would have granted dual citizenship to many foreigners living in Germany. Parliament enacted a more restrictive law instead.

External Relations. Germany's role in the international order has increased in the 1990s. Regardless of whether a conservative CDU/CSU-FDP coalition or, since 1998, an KSPD-Greens coalition is in power, the government, with its armed forces strength of 338,000, has been a loyal member of NATO. It has called for a strengthened United Nations and for admission of East/Central European states into the European Union (EU) if the additional financial burdens on EU member states can be met. It has supported the creation of the European Economic and Monetary Union and the supranational single currency, the euro. In the dynamic globalization process, German governments have not dared to limit the activities of powerful German-owned multinational companies. The policy makers know that any controls or unfavorable taxation policies might mean the transfer of plants to lower-wage countries, which in turn would lead to higher domestic unemployment and a sluggish economy.

German governments, regardless of political coloration, have pursued domestic and foreign policies that indicate accord on most basic principles. Their attempt to strengthen cooperation and coordinate trade and fiscal policies among EU states has made headway, but not yet for EU's foreign and military policies. The German governments, despite political, economic, and social obstacles at home and abroad, have succeeded in maintaining a vibrant democratic system over the decades of the country's existence. Unless a major economic crisis erupts, the system can expect to continue satisfying the needs of most of the country's population.

(See also GERMAN UNIFICATION; GREEN PARTIES; KOHL, HELMUT; KOSOVO WAR; SCHRÖDER, GERHAUD.)

Gerard Braunthal, *Parties and Politics in Modern Germany* (Boulder, Colo., 1996). David P. Conradt, *The German Polity*, 6th ed. (New York, 1996). Andrei S. Markovits and Simon Reich, *The German Predicament: Memory and Power in the New Europe* (Ithaca, N.Y., 1997). Clay Clemens and William E. Paterson, eds., *The Kohl Chancellorship* (London, 1998). Mary N. Hampton and Christian Søe, eds., *Between Bonn and Berlin: German Politics Adrift?* (Lanham, Md., 1999). Peter H. Merkl, ed., *The Federal Republic of Germany at Fifty: The End of a Century of Turmoil* (Houndmills, U.K., 1999).

GERARD BRAUNTHAL

GHANA. Although its relatively small size 92,099 square miles (238,536 sq. km.), has belied its role in African political development over the last ninety years, Ghana was in the forefront of the anticolonial struggle. In the postcolonial era, Ghana has gone from being a bastion against neocolonialism to becoming a showpiece for international finance.

The First Republic (1957–1966) was notable for two reasons. First, it had a decidedly Pan-Africanist and anticolonial posture. Ghana under Kwame *Nkrumah was placed at the service of nationalist and liberation movements, and it became the refuge for people of African descent.

Second, it made attempts at economic development financed by local reserves, building a credible social and economic infrastructural base. Unfortunately, the regime was limited in its ability to sustain genuine development, becoming heavily dependent on external sources. Even as it proclaimed a socialist state in 1960, it was relying on these sources for half of its development funds. Socialism implied a determining role for the state: Ninety percent of total public revenues was invested in newly created state enterprises whose direct beneficiaries were an alliance of party activists, businesspeople, and bureaucrats. Investment in the public good resulted in a culture in which public service became an opportunity for wealth accumulation.

No other regime, with the possible exception of the present one, has come close to matching the potential and promise of the Nkrumah era. In 1966, the National Liberation Council (NLC), an army-police alliance, overthrew Nkrumah. It opened up the economy to vigorous external influence. The predominant role of the state was curtailed through the sale of public enterprises to foreign and local private concerns.

The NLC installed a new civilian government in 1969 after organizing an election significant for its prohibition of ideas and people associated with Nkrumah and his party, the Convention People's Party (CPP). This government, headed by Prime Minister Kofi Busia, followed the policies of the NLC, especially in its efforts to stop a mounting external debt. To do this, the regime found itself implementing policies largely dictated from external sources. In its foreign policy, it adopted a policy of dialogue with apartheid South Africa that alienated supporters at home and abroad. Unable to deal with balance of payment problems, high unemployment, labor disputes, high prices of goods, and low export prices, the regime succumbed to the armed forces in 1972.

Since its foray into active politics, the Ghanaian military has become highly politicized and protective of its corporate interests. Indeed, since 1972, it has remained the prime mover behind state power. Its 10,600 members (9,000 army, 800 navy, and 800 air force) enjoy generous government expenditure, ranked fifth behind education, public services, economic services, and health.

During its rule between 1972 and 1979, under General I. K. Acheampong (1931–1979), the military reached its nadir, mismanaging the economy and alienating almost all segments of the society. In this sense it had performed much like its predecessors. Not by accident, the lower ranks and junior officers took steps to "discipline" their superior officers, assuming state power in 1979 and again in 1981. In the interim, a civilian government headed by Dr. H. Limann (1934–1998) also succeeded in incurring the wrath of Ghanaians with its inability to govern.

Perhaps the most significant point regarding the military was its ability to spawn a quasi-revolution, both within its ranks and among Ghanaians—a populist uprising that has had revolutionary tendencies. The Provisional National Defense Council (PNDC) assumed power in December 1981 under Flight Lieutenant Jerry John Rawlings (b. 1947). For most of the 1980s, the government attempted to create conditions for necessary changes in the economy. Initially, the Rawlings government was populist, open, and determined to demystify government and politics—indeed, it had as members two military men (a junior officer and a noncommissioned officer), a priest, a factory worker, and a university student. It encouraged people and workers to organize themselves and held the view that achieving economic progress entailed a policy of self-reliance and national control of resources.

Initiating change while seeking a semblance of socioeconomic sanity proved to be a daunting task. First, the PNDC faced the real problem of managing a neocolonial, dependent economy. Second, it had divisions within its ranks and serious opposition from entrenched local and external interests. Third, between 1982 and 1984 Ghana experienced a prolonged, severe drought and extensive bush fires that at times wiped out large quantities of food and export produce.

In 1983, the PNDC reached an agreement with the international financial community on an Economic Recovery Program/Structural Adjustment Program (ERP/SAP). It has had mixed results, with positive macro-level economic performance. However, the severest impact of the ERP/SAP has been on the large majority of Ghanaians: declining wages, high inflation, deteriorating health care, fewer jobs, and increasing privatization of the economy. Indeed, ERP/SAP has meant even more reliance on external resources for development than ever before.

In 1992, the Rawlings-led PNDC gave way to the Rawlings-led National Democratic Congress (NDC) in a controversial election ushering in Ghana's Fourth Republic. Effectively, the NDC is a carryover from the PNDC. In 1996, the NDC and Rawlings won a second term in a much more credible election which demonstrated the extent to which they built a well-oiled machine, perhaps the first of its kind in Ghanaian history.

The political process is relatively open, with many political parties, an active opposition in Parliament, an ebullient press, and a proliferation of radio stations. There have been regular local government elections, and hopes are high that Ghana will continue to enjoy some stability in the foreseeable future.

(See also SOCIALISM AND SOCIAL DEMOCRACY.)

K. B. Dickson, *A Historical Geography of Ghana* (Cambridge, U.K., 1969). Geoffrey Kay, ed., *The Political Economy of Colonialism in Ghana: A Collection of Documents and Statistics, 1900–1960* (Cambridge, U.K., 1972). Adu Boahen, *Ghana: Evolution and Change in the Nineteenth and Twentieth Centuries* (London, 1975). Rhoda Howard, *Colonialism and Underdevelopment in Ghana* (New York, 1978). J. H. Frimpong-Ansah, *The Vampire State in Africa: The Political Economy of Decline in Ghana* (Trenton, N.J., 1992).

AKWASI P. OSEI

GLASNOST. See GORBACHEV, MIKHAIL; PERESTROIKA; SOVIET UNION.

GLOBALIZATION. See overleaf.

GOLD STANDARD. More a myth than a working monetary system for the international economy, the gold standard has to be understood as a declaration of faith in an ideal world rather than an accurate description of monetary relations between states before *World War I. For two centuries, most liberal economists have advocated the adoption of some system that would provide stable money for the world market economy. Most of them have extolled the virtues of the gold standard as the theoretical model for such a system. Its supposed automaticity, divorcing monetary management from political interference by governments, and thus depoliticizing economic policy making, was what has always particularly recommended it to them.

(cont. on p. 328)

GLOBALIZATION can be conceived as a process (or set of processes) which embodies a transformation in the spatial organization of social relations and transactions, expressed in transcontinental or interregional flows and networks of activity, interaction, and power (see Held and McGrew, et al., 1999). It is characterized by four types of changes. First, it involves a *stretching* of social, political, and economic activities across frontiers, regions and continents. Second, it is marked by the *intensification*, or the growing magnitude, of interconnectedness and flows of trade, investment, finance, migration, and culture. Third, it can be linked to a *speeding up* of global interactions and processes, as the development of worldwide systems of transport and communication increases the *velocity* of the diffusion of ideas, goods, information, capital, and people. And, fourth, the growing *extensity, intensity*, and *velocity* of global interactions can be associated with their deepening *impact* such that the effects of distant events can be highly significant elsewhere and specific local developments can come to have considerable global consequences. In this sense, the boundaries between domestic matters and global affairs become increasingly fluid. Globalization, in short, can be thought of as the widening, intensifying, speeding up, and growing impact of worldwide interconnectedness.

Three broad accounts of the nature and meaning of globalization can be identified, referred to here as the hyperglobalist, the skeptical, and the transformationalist views. These define the conceptual space of the current intensive debate about globalization.

The Hyperglobalists. What distinguishes the present era from the past, argue the hyperglobalists, is the existence of a single global economy transcending and integrating the world's major economic regions (see, for instance, Ohmae, 1990). In variously referring to "manic capitalism," "turbo-capitalism," or "supra-territorial capitalism," these globalists seek to capture the qualitative shift occurring in the spatial organization and dynamics of a new global capitalist formation. Inscribed in the dynamics of this new global capitalism is, they argue, an irresistible imperative toward the denationalization of strategic economic activities. Today it is global finance and corporate capital, rather than states, which exercise decisive influence over the organization, location, and distribution of economic power and wealth.

Since the authority of states is territorially bound, global markets can escape effective political regulation. In this borderless economy, states have no option other than to accommodate global market forces. Moreover, the existing multilateral institutions of global economic surveillance, especially the *Group of 7 (G7), *International Monetary Fund (IMF) World Bank and *World Trade Organization (WTO) largely function to nurture this nascent "global market civilization."

In this "runaway world," nation *states are becoming "transitional modes of economic organization and regulation" since they can no longer effectively manage or regulate their own national economies. Economic globalization spells the end of the *welfare state and social democracy. In effect, the hyperglobalists hold, the autonomy and sovereignty of nation-states have been eclipsed by contemporary processes of economic globalization.

The Skeptics. By comparison the skeptical position is much more cautious about the revolutionary character of globalization (see, for example, Hirst and Thompson, 1999). While generally recognizing that recent decades have witnessed a considerable intensification of international *interdependence, the skeptical interpretation disputes its novelty. By comparison with the *belle époque* of 1890–1914, the intensity of contemporary global interdependence is considerably exaggerated. Moreover, the spatially concentrated nature of actual patterns of economic interdependence suggest that globalization is primarily a phenomenon largely confined to the major OECD states. Further, these states have been the very architects of a more open liberal international economy. Dismissing the idea of a unified global economy, the skeptical position concludes that the world is breaking up into several major economic and political blocs, within which very different forms of *capitalism continue to flourish. The emphasis upon footloose capital and a new global capitalist order is overstated as is the decline of the welfare state. Rather than a new world order, the post–Cold War global system has witnessed a return to old-style *geopolitics and neoimperialism, through which the most powerful states and social forces have consolidated their global dominance. In presuming the novelty of the present, so the skeptical position suggests, the hyperglobalists ignore the continued primacy of national power and sovereignty.

What is to be made of these accounts? Are we on the edge of a global shift—a fundamental shakeout of world order? Or is the narrative of globalization simply mere rhetoric? Is a productive synthesis between these two positions possible?

An Intermediate Way: The Transformationalist Analysis. To begin with, it is crucial to acknowledge that globalization does not simply denote a shift in the extensity or scale of social relations and activity. Much more significantly, argue the transformationalists, it also involves the spatial reorganization and rearticulation of economic, political, military, and cultural power (see Held and McGrew et al., 1999). The current debate about globalization ought primarily to be about the question of power: its modalities, instrumentalities, organization, and distribution. Globalization can thus be understood as involving a shift or transformation in the scale of human social organization that extends the reach of power relations across the world's major regions and continents. It implies a world in which developments in one region can come to shape the life chances of communities in distant parts of the globe. Highly uneven in its embrace and impact, it divides as it integrates. Globalization may mean a shrinking world for some but for the majority it creates a distancing or profound disembedding of power relations. As the East Asian crisis of 1997–1998 demonstrated, key sites of global power can be quite literally oceans apart from the subjects and communities whose future they determine.

Globalization too has to be understood as a multidimensional process which is not reducible to an economic logic and which has differential impacts across the world's regions and upon individual states. Nor is it a novel process but rather has a long history—from the age of premodern empire building to the contemporary era of corporate empires. Of course, its contemporary articulation has many unique and distinctive attributes—not least amongst them near real time communication.

Historically, globalization has always been and remains a vigorously contested process—from the struggles against slavery and the movements for national independence to the more recent global protest against the WTO's millennium trade round. Indeed, it can be argued that across many domains—from the cultural to the technological—globalization has contributed to a remarkable politicization of social life while also creating new modalities and institutional arenas through which its imperatives are contested. Such developments are most in evidence with respect to economic and political globalization.

Economic Globalization. Contemporary patterns of economic globalization have been strongly associated with a reframing of the relationship between states and markets. Although the global economy as a single entity is by no means as highly integrated as the most robust national economies, the trends point unambiguously toward intensifying integration within and across regions. Patterns of contemporary economic globalization have woven strong and enduring webs across the world's major regions such that their economic fate is intimately connected. Levels of interregional trade are largely unprecedented while the form which trade takes has changed considerably. Despite the fact there is a tendency to exaggerate the power of global financial markets, ignoring the centrality of states to sustaining their effective operation especially in times of crisis, there is much compelling evidence to suggest that contemporary financial globalization is a market, rather than a state, driven phenomenon. Reinforced by financial liberalization, the accompanying shift toward markets and private financial institutions as the "authoritative actors" in the global financial system poses serious questions about the nature of state power and economic sovereignty.

Alongside financial integration, the operations of *multinational corporations integrate national and local economies into global and regional production networks. Under these conditions, national economies no longer function as autonomous systems of wealth creation since national borders are no longer significant barriers to the conduct and organization of economic activity. The distinction between domestic economic activity and worldwide economic activity, as the range of products in any superstore will confirm, is becoming increasingly difficult to sustain.

Central to the organization of this new global capitalist order is the multinational corporation. In 1999 there were over 60,000 MNCs worldwide with 500,000 foreign subsidiaries, selling \$9.5 trillion of goods and services across the globe. Today transnational production considerably exceeds the level of global exports and has become the primary means for selling goods and services abroad. Multinational corporations now account, according to some estimates, for at least 20 percent of world production and 70 percent of world trade. It is global corporate capital, rather than states, which exercises decisive influence over the organization, location, and distribution of economic power and resources in the contemporary global economy.

Contemporary patterns of economic globalization have been accompanied by a new global division of labor brought about, in part, by the activities of multinationals themselves. Developing countries are being reordered into clear winners and losers, as the experience of the East Asian tiger economies shows. Such restructuring is, moreover, replicated within countries, both North and South, as communities and particular locales closely integrated into global production networks reap significant rewards while the rest struggle on its margins. Economic globalization has brought with it an increasingly unified world for elites—national, regional, and global—but divided nations and communities as the global workforce is segmented, within rich and poor countries alike, into winners and losers.

Furthermore, the globalization of economic activity exceeds the regulatory reach of national governments while, at the same time, existing multilateral institutions of global economic governance have limited authority because states, still jealously guarding their national *sovereignty, refuse to cede these institutions substantial power. Under such conditions, global markets may effectively escape political regulation. For the most part, the governance structures of the global economy operate principally to nurture and reproduce the forces of economic globalization while also serving to discipline and streamline this nascent "global market civilization." Yet, in some contexts, these governance structures may carve out considerable autonomy from the dictates of global capital and/or the G7 states. Hence, multilateral institutions have become increasingly important sites through which economic globalization is contested, by weaker states and by the agencies of transnational civil society. The G7 states and representatives of global capital have found themselves on many occasions at odds with collective decisions or rule making. Moreover, the political dynamics of multilateral institutions tend to mediate great power control, for instance through consensual modes of decision making, such that they are never merely tools of dominant states and particular social groupings.

Alongside these global institutions, there also exist a parallel set of regional bodies, from APEC to the EU, which represent an additional attempt to shift the terms of engagement with global market forces. Within the interstices of this system operate the social groups of an emerging transnational *civil society, from the International Chamber of Commerce to the Jubilee 2000 campaign, seeking to promote, or to contest and bring to account the agencies of economic globalization. Economic globalization has been accompanied by a significant internationalization of political authority associated with a corresponding globalization of political activity.

Political Globalization. Two fundamental transformations have shaped the constitution of contemporary political life. The first of these involved the development of territorially based political communities—modern nation-states. The second more recent transformation has by no means replaced the first in all respects, but it has led to a break in the exclusive link between geography and political power. It can be illustrated by a number of developments.

In the first instance, there has been an institutionalization of a fragile system of multilayered global and regional governance. At the beginning of the twentieth century there were thirty-seven intergovernmental organizations (IGOs). By the close of the century, nearly 300 were delivering important global or regional collective goods. This multilateral system institutionalizes a process of political coordination among governments, intergovernmental and transnational agencies—public and private—designed to realize common purposes or collective goods through making or implementing global or transnational rules, and managing transborder problems, e.g., the WTO. Of course, it is scarred by enormous inequalities of power, and remains a product of the inter-state system. But it has, nevertheless, created the infrastructure of a global polity and new arenas through which globalization itself is promoted contested, or regulated. It has also instigated new forms of multilateral, regional, and transnational politics.

A remarkable transnationalization of political activity has been associated with this internationalization of the state. In 1909 there were 371 officially recognized international *nongovernmental organizations (INGOs), by 2000 there were approximately 25,000 (including the International Chamber of Commerce, the International Confederation of Free Trade Unions and Greenpeace International). These include a proliferation of associations, social movements, advocacy networks—from the womens' movement to Nazis on the Internet—and citizens groups mobilizing, organizing, and exercising people power across national boundaries. This explosion of "citizen diplomacy" creates the basis of communities of interest or association which span national borders, with the purpose of advancing mutual goals or bringing governments and the formal institutions of global governance to account for their activities. Whether it constitutes the infrastructure of a translational civil society remains open to debate.

There has, moreover, been an important change in the scope and content of international law. Twentieth-century forms of *international law—from the law governing war to that concerning crimes against humanity, environmental is-

sues, and *human rights—have created the basis of an emerging framework of "cosmopolitan law," law which circumscribes and delimits the political power of individual states. In principle, states are no longer able to treat their citizens as they think fit. Although, in practice, many states still violate these standards, nearly all now accept general duties of protection and provision, as well as of restraint, in their own practices and procedures. This internalization or nationalization of international law has been evident in other areas too. There has, for instance, been an explosive growth of private international and commercial law. These developments have encouraged what some legal scholars refer to as a shift from a monistic conception to a polycentric conception of legal sovereignty.

As governments and their citizens have become embedded in more expansive networks and layers of regional and global governance, they have become subject to new loci of authority above, below, and alongside the state. Indeed, the form and intensity of contemporary political globalization poses a profound challenge to the Westphalian "states as containers" view of political life. In particular, political space and political community are no longer coterminous with national territory, and national governments can no longer be regarded as the sole masters of their own or their citizens' fate. But this does not mean that national governments or national sovereignty have been eclipsed by the forces of political globalization; The state is not in decline, as many hyperglobalists suggest.

Globalization and the Transformation of Political Community. Contemporary globalization is associated with a transformation of state power as the roles and functions of states are rearticulated, reconstituted, and reembedded at the intersection of globalizing and regionalizing networks and systems. The metaphors of the loss, diminution, or erosion of state power can misrepresent this reconfiguration. For while globalization is engendering, for instance, a reconfiguration of state-market relations in the economic domain, states and international public authorities are deeply implicated in this very process. Economic globalization by no means necessarily translates into a diminution of state power; rather, it is transforming the conditions under which state power is exercised. Moreover, in other domains, such as the environmental, states have adopted a more activist posture while in the political domain they have been central to the explosive growth and institutionalization of regional and global governance. These are not developments which can be explained convincingly through the language of the decline, erosion or loss of state power. For such metaphors (mistakenly) presume that state power was much greater in previous epochs. On almost every conceivable measure, states, especially in the developed world, are far more powerful than their antecedents. So too are the demands placed upon them. The apparent simultaneous weakening and expansion in the power of states under conditions of contemporary globalization is symptomatic of an underlying structural transformation. This is nowhere so evident as in respect of state sovereignty and autonomy, which constitute the very ideological foundations of the modern state.

There are many good reasons for doubting the theoretical and empirical basis of claims that states are being eclipsed by contemporary patterns of globalization. We would emphasize that while regional and global interaction networks are strengthening, they have multiple and variable impacts across diverse locales.

Neither the sovereignty nor the autonomy of states are simply diminished by such processes. Indeed, any assessment of the cumulative impacts of globalization must acknowledge their highly differentiated character since it is not experienced uniformly by all states. Globalization is by no means a homogenizing force. The impact of globalization is mediated significantly by a state's position in global political, military, and economic hierarchies; its domestic economic and political structures; the institutional pattern of domestic politics; and specific government as well as societal strategies for contesting, managing, or ameliorating globalizing imperatives. The ongoing transformation of the Westphalian regime of sovereignty and autonomy has differential consequences for different states.

While for many hyperglobalizers contemporary globalization is associated with new limits to politics and the erosion of state power, the transformationalist argument developed here is critical of such political fatalism. For contemporary globalization has not only triggered and encouraged a significant politicization of a growing array of issue-areas, but has also been accompanied by an extraordinary growth of institutionalized arenas and networks of political mobilization, surveillance, decision-making, and regulatory activity which transcend national political jurisdictions. This has expanded enormously the capacity for, and scope of, political activity and the exercise of political authority. Neither the hyperglobalists nor the skeptics provide the proper conceptual resources to grasp this. Globalization does not prefigure the "end of politics," nor the simple persistence of old state ways; instead, it signals the continuation of politics by new means. Yet, this is not to overlook the profound intellectual, institutional, and normative challenges which it presents to the organization of modern political communities.

Political communities are in the process of being transformed. At the heart of this lies a growth in transborder political issues and problems which erode clear-cut distinctions between domestic and foreign affairs, internal political issues and external questions, the sovereign concerns of the nation-state, and international considerations. In nearly all major areas of public policy, the enmeshment of national political communities in regional and global processes involves them in intensive issues of transboundary coordination and regulation. Political space for the development and pursuit of effective government and the accountability of political power is no longer coterminous with a delimited national territory. The growth of transboundary problems creates "overlapping communities of fate"—that is, a state of affairs in which the fortune and prospects of individual political communities are increasingly bound together. Political communities are locked into a diversity of processes and structures which range in and through them, linking and fragmenting them into complex constellations. National governments by no means simply determine what is right or appropriate exclusively for their own citizens.

This condition is most apparent in Europe, where the development of the European Union has created intensive discussion about the future of national sovereignty and autonomy. But the issues are important not just for Europe and the West, but for countries in other parts of the world, for example, Japan and the Republic of Korea (South Korea). These countries must recognize new emerging problems, for instance, problems concerning *AIDS, migration, and new challenges to peace, security, and economic prosperity, which spill over the boundaries of nation-states. There are emerging overlapping communities of fate generating common problems within and across the East Asian region.

Political communities today are no longer discrete worlds. Growing enmeshment in regional and global orders and the proliferation of transborder problems has created a plurality of diverse and overlapping collectivites which span borders binding together directly and indirectly the fates of communities in different locations and regions of the globe. In this context the articulation of the public good is pried away from its embeddedness in the bounded political community: it is being reconfigured in the context of global, regional, and transnational orders. The contemporary world is no longer "a world of closed communities with mutually impenetrable ways of thought, self-sufficient economies and ideally sovereign states" (O'Neill, 1991, p. 282). This is not to assert that territorial political communities are becoming obsolete but, rather, to recognize that they are nested within global, regional, and transnational communities of fate, identity, association, and solidarity. Political community today is being transformed to accord with a world of "ruptured boundaries."

(See also DEVELOPMENT AND UNDERDEVELOPMENT; ENVIRONMENTALISM; FINANCE, INTERNATIONAL; INFORMATION TECHNOLOGY; INTERNATIONAL MIGRATION; INTERNATIONAL POLITICAL ECONOMY.)

K. Ohmae, *The Borderless World* (London, 1990). O. O'Neill, "Transnational justice" in D. Held, ed., *Political Theory Today* (Cambridge, U.K., 1991). D. Held, A. McGrew, D. Goldblatt, and J. Perraton, *Global Transformations: Politics, Economics and Culture* (Cambridge, U.K., 1991). P. Hirst and G. Thompson, *Globalization in Question*, 2d ed. (Cambridge, U.K., 1999).

DAVID HELD
ANTHONY McGREW

The key features of a gold standard system were, first, that the central banks of countries considered to be party to the system were pledged freely to buy and sell gold (and only gold) at a fixed price in terms of the home currency; and second, that private residents in such countries were legally entitled to possess gold and to export and import it freely. Fixed exchange rates resulted from the use of gold as the common *numéraire* of international transactions, in which the prices of different national currencies were expressed. Differences that might develop from time to time in the market values of these currencies, reflecting for example unequal rates of inflation, would result in—and be automatically corrected by—either inflows or outflows of gold. Adjustment was supposed to work by the impact of such gold flows on the monetary base of the country, either expanding or contracting the money supply and thus influencing the general price level. It was a system, in short, that (if theory were applied in practice) would allow the general preference for national political autonomy for the state to be reconciled with the preference of ruling classes of the industrial countries for an open, efficient market economy aided by a minimum degree of monetary stability.

In practice, an approximation to such a system only prevailed from the 1870s to the outbreak of war in 1914. (Some would argue for an even shorter heyday, of two decades from the early 1890s—only slightly longer than the duration of the working Bretton Woods system, from 1958 to 1971.) Even then, for good political reasons and to preserve the coherence of civil society and the stability of the state, governments resisted the deflationary imperatives of adjustment under the gold standard. Especially in later years, they used their reserves of foreign exchange to finance deficits, prudently conserving gold as the ultimate war chest for national security in an increasingly unstable political system.

Moreover, the vaunted stability of this golden age of international monetary relations rested on, first, the relatively immobile real value of gold as compared with silver; and second, on the stability of the value of the British pound sterling in terms of gold from 1817 to 1914. This stability, in turn, was maintained thanks to a British statute—the Bank Charter Act of 1844—that limited severely the power of government to expand the money supply and thus to finance deficit spending. The system also may be said to have rested on a third factor, the involuntary compliance of peripheral developing countries, who needed the capital provided by the core, with its uneven availability and price—a kind of dependence also experienced by indebted developing countries in the 1980s.

(See also FINANCE, INTERNATIONAL; INTERDEPENDENCE; INTERNATIONAL POLITICAL ECONOMY.)

R. Triffin, *The Evolution of the International Monetary System* (Princeton, N.J., 1964). M. De Cecco, *Money and Empire* (Oxford, 1982; reprint London, 1987).

SUSAN STRANGE

GORBACHEV, Mikhail. The leader of the *Soviet Union from 11 March 1985 until 25 December 1991 and the initiator of the most far-reaching *reforms in Soviet history, Mikhail Sergeevich Gorbachev was born into a peasant family in the village of Privolnoe in the Stavropol region of southern Russia on 2 March 1931. He had to combine work in the fields with study at school during and after World War II; it was the award of the Order of Red Banner of Labor for his achievements as an agricultural worker in 1949, together with scholastic success, that made possible his admission to the Law Faculty of Moscow University in 1950.

Gorbachev made the most of this unusual opportunity for a boy from a peasant family. He was active in the Law Faculty Komsomol organization and he graduated with distinction in 1955. It was at the university in 1951 that he met his wife, Raisa Maksimovna Titorenko, a student in the Philosophical Faculty; they were married in 1953. Their exceptionally close relationship ended with the death of Raisa in 1999.

Having obtained a law degree, Gorbachev returned to his native Stavropol region and embarked on a political career, first in the Komsomol apparatus and later as a Communist Party official. (He had joined the party in 1952, the year before *Stalin's death.) By 1966—just four years after moving from the Komsomol apparatus to the party organization—Gorbachev was party first secretary in the city of Stavropol, and by 1970 he had become the first secretary of the regional party committee *(kraikom)*, a post which led to entry to the Central Committee of the Communist Party of the Soviet Union (CPSU) in 1971.

Gorbachev was in charge of one of Russia's most important grain-growing areas and, as such, maintained his links with a former first secretary of that region, Fedor Kulakov, who was the secretary responsible for agriculture within the party leadership in Moscow. It was, however, Kulakov's sudden death in 1978 that led to Gorbachev's being brought to Moscow to take over agricultural administration. By 1980 Gorbachev was a full member of the Politburo as well as a secretary of the Central Committee, a combination of posts which made him a potentially powerful figure.

Gorbachev supported Yury Andropov as successor to Leonid Brezhnev in 1982, and during Andropov's leadership Gorbachev's responsibilities were widened. However, the backlash against Andropov's disciplinarian and anticorruption crackdown led the Politburo selectorate on Andropov's death to opt for a return to a safer and more predictable leadership style, choosing Brezhnev's ally of long standing, Konstantin Chernenko, in preference to his younger and much better qualified rival, Mikhail Gorbachev.

Chernenko's death in March 1985, only thirteen months after he succeeded Andropov, meant that Gorbachev's wait was over, and just a week after his fifty-fourth birthday he became general secretary of the Central Committee of the Soviet Communist Party and leader of his country. Although the choice of Gorbachev was anathema to some of the old guard, his nomination got through the Politburo and was endorsed by the Central Committee within twenty-four hours of Chernenko's death.

What followed was one of the most dramatic periods of change in Russian as well as Soviet history, culminating in the demise of the Communist system and the disintegration of the Soviet state. Gorbachev put radical political and economic reform on the Soviet agenda, quickly signaling his intentions by his political appointments. By promoting Eduard Shevardnadze to full membership of the Politburo and appointing him foreign minister in succession to Andrei Gromyko in the summer of 1985 and by bringing Aleksandr Yakovlev into the Secretariat of the Central Committee and the

Politburo, Gorbachev demonstrated his own readiness to embrace what became known as the "new political thinking" on both foreign and domestic policy.

By 1990 Gorbachev's international diplomacy had earned him the Nobel Peace Prize after relations with the United States and Western Europe had been put on a new, cooperative footing, and the Soviet Union had accepted the political autonomy of the countries of Eastern and Central Europe and even the unification of Germany within the North Atlantic Treaty Organization (NATO) and the European Community (EC). Whereas Gorbachev had hoped initially to see reformed Communist regimes in Eastern and Central Europe, he made the crucial decision to abandon the "Brezhnev doctrine" and accept free elections, which, in turn, meant accepting noncommunist systems in what had formerly been called "the Soviet bloc."

Domestically, there was also a contrast between Gorbachev's reform initiatives—which were remarkably bold in the Soviet context—and some of their unintended consequences. The latter included interethnic violence, large-scale independence movements in almost half of the Soviet Union's fifteen republics, and the threat of the breakup of the multinational Soviet state (which became a reality in the aftermath of the failed coup of August 1991).

Soon after he became general secretary, Gorbachev began the process of replacing conservative Communists in the leadership and of promoting both political and economic reform. His personal telephone call in December 1986 to Andrei Sakharov, who had been exiled to the provincial city of Gorky (now restored to its old name of Nizhny Novgorod) by the Brezhnev leadership in 1980, symbolized a new willingness to tolerate the expression of dissident opinions. Gorbachev's policy of glasnost led to the gradual publication of numerous books previously taboo, including some—such as *Solzhenitsyn's *Gulag Archipelago* and Orwell's *Nineteen Eighty-Four* and *Animal Farm*—which called into question the foundations of the Soviet system.

The term "*perestroika," which Gorbachev had introduced at the outset of his general secretaryship, came to signify the comprehensive reform of the Soviet political and economic system. Radical reform was placed on the political agenda by Gorbachev at important Central Committee meetings in January and June 1987 and at the Nineteenth Conference of the Communist Party in 1988. In 1989 competitive elections for a new Soviet legislature—the Congress of People's Deputies of the USSR (which elected an inner body, the Supreme Soviet)—took place, and this representative assembly became one in which criticism could be voiced and the executive could no longer rely on getting its every proposal accepted.

Gorbachev was a proponent of competitive elections, but initially he aimed at a one-party *pluralism in which electoral choice would be linked to democratization of the Communist Party and the legitimation of different opinion groupings and regional interests within it. It was only in early 1990 that he publicly accepted the need to legalize the creation of other political parties and to take the reference to the "leading role" of the Communist Party out of Article 6 of the Soviet Constitution. When elections were held in the various Soviet republics in 1990, several of them produced non-Communist majorities. Most troubling for Gorbachev was the choice of Boris *Yeltsin in May 1990 as chairman of the Supreme Soviet of the Russian Republic. Yeltsin, who left the Communist Party in July of the same year, had become a more popular politician within *Russia than Gorbachev himself, whose domestic prestige was by this time significantly lower than his international standing.

Faced by mounting problems, Gorbachev attempted in 1990 to increase his personal power not within the Communist Party, whose institutions (including that of the Politburo) he downgraded, but in a new state presidency. In March 1990 he became the Soviet Union's first *president* and later in the year acquired the power to rule by decree. Those reformers who supported these moves hoped that Gorbachev would now be able to take more resolute steps toward the introduction of a market economy, which he had embraced in principle but which was extraordinarily difficult to introduce in practice. He was criticized, however, both by those who feared a return to capitalism and by radicals who felt that he was moving too slowly with economic reform.

After a period of half a year during the winter of 1990–91 in which he made significant concessions to those who were pressing for a more conservative approach to the Soviet Union's economic and interethnic problems, Gorbachev established a new *modus vivendi* with the more radical proponents of change, including those from a majority of the Soviet republics, when he initiated a series of "nine-plus-one" meetings in April 1991. This involved an effort to agree on a new union treaty with the nine republics willing to remain in a renewed and decentralized Soviet federation. Over the next few months he took steps also to mend fences with Yeltsin, who had acquired substantially increased power and authority through his election as president of the Russian Republic in June 1991. By this time Gorbachev could speak for the Soviet Union only after a prior process of negotiation and accommodation with the leaders of the major Soviet republics.

The draft Union Treaty which emerged from the protracted negotiations between Gorbachev and a majority of republican leaders, including Yeltsin, not only devolved a great deal of federal power to the republics but came close to creating a confederation. It was, above all, to preempt this further diminution of central power that the leaders of the Soviet army, government, KGB, Ministry of Interior, and military industry joined forces in an attempted coup which began on 18 August 1991 when Gorbachev was put under house arrest in his holiday home on the Crimean coast. The coup was over by the evening of 21 August. Widespread resistance in Moscow, led by Boris Yeltsin in the Russian White House, played a crucial part in the defeat of the putschists, but just as important was the refusal of Gorbachev to have any truck with the coup leaders. This deprived the putschists of a constitutional fig-leaf to cover their seizure of power.

For Gorbachev the coup was the beginning of the end of the main part of his political career. Insofar as it accelerated the breakup of the Soviet Union, it naturally called into question its presidency. Gorbachev, weakened by the fact that he had himself appointed the senior politicians and officials who in August 1991 betrayed him, strove to preserve a renewed union and warned of the dangers ahead if the Soviet Union split into fifteen separate states (with the prospect of further interethnic conflict and fissiparous movements to follow). Nevertheless, a Ukrainian referendum vote for independence on 1 December 1991 was followed by a meeting on 8 December of the presidents of Russia, Ukraine, and Belarus at which they declared that the Soviet Union was "ceasing its existence" and at which they announced they would be establishing a *Commonwealth of Independent States. On 25 December 1991 Gorbachev made a televised speech, announcing his resignation as president of the Soviet Union, and on the same day he handed over his functions as commander-in-chief of the armed forces (and control over nuclear weapons) to Yeltsin. By the end of the month, the Soviet Union had formally ceased to exist.

In the perspective of Russian and Soviet history, Gorbachev must be counted a great reformer. The system he inherited, however, required comprehensive transformation rather than mere reform. Gorbachev increasingly recognized this, but he had to take account of powerful conservative interests as well as of radical centrifugal tendencies. Moreover, the dual challenge of democratization and marketization in the face of growing and competing nationalisms and of "left"-"right" ideological polarization made the task of a transition leader in the Soviet Union far more daunting than in any other European country. Given the national tensions that had been suppressed for so long, it is far from clear that any leader could have accomplished the enormously difficult task of combining democratization of the system with preservation of the union.

Domestically, for better or worse (and mostly for better), Gorbachev's impact on Russian history has been immense. Internationally, he did more than anyone else to end the *Cold War by allowing the East European states to regain their national independence and by breaking with Soviet traditional foreign policy. Since leaving office Gorbachev has headed his own think tank in Moscow. From an essentially social democratic position he has been a trenchant critic both of the Yeltsin administration and of the Russian Communist Party.

(See also COMMUNIST PARTY STATES; POST-COMMUNISM.)

Archie Brown, *The Gorbachev Factor* (Oxford, 1996). Mikhail Gorbachev, *Memoirs* (New York, 1996).

ARCHIE BROWN

GRAMEEN BANK. Begun in 1976 by Professor Mohammad Yunus as an experiment in small-scale lending to the poor in Bangladesh, the Grameen Bank has become one of the premier institutions in the international development field. In the process it overturned some major hard-won truths in development theory; it has also become the pathbreaker and principal standard setter in establishing the new field of microcredit, inspiring emulators in many countries, including a number in the United States.

The overturned wisdom came from efforts to promote Third World agricultural production through credit systems. Gradually and painfully it became clear after decades of international donor investment that subsidized credit almost invariably failed, as bigger farmers, having the most collateral in the form of their land, would get the largest loans and would also become the worst defaulters. Yunus started his experiment believing that he could make very small loans to poor people without requiring collateral and could preclude default by focusing on the need for timely repayment. In succeeding, he showed that credit programs for the poor are not doomed to fail.

Supported by international donors, the bank grew rapidly and by the late 1990s included over 2 million members and more than US$2 billion in loans cumulatively granted. It has continued to operate through very small loans (average size: US$160) and it enjoys a repayment rate of more than 97 percent. The bank covers more than half of the country's 68,000 villages, thus remaining largely rural in a country where more than 80 percent of its 120 million people still live in the countryside. The most acclaimed single fact about the bank is that some 95 percent of the members are women, a formidable achievement in a country that is overwhelmingly Muslim and in which *purdah* (female seclusion) remains an important cultural institution.

The bank's success rests on several factors. First, the borrowers are organized into groups of five, screened by gender and class (no member can own more than half an acre of land). Second, continuous emphasis on discipline ensures that loans are a group responsibility rather than an individual one, that members participate in highly structured weekly meetings, and that they repay their loans on time—each aspect facilitated by an emphasis on public transparency throughout all activities. Third, loans are made at commercial rates, thus discouraging the free riders and defaulters who invaded and plagued earlier programs; but even commercial rates are much more reasonable to the borrowers than traditional moneylender rates, so the program attracts borrowers. Fourth, the program assumes that borrowers have the skills needed to engage in independent economic activity such as rice processing, poultry production, or petty trading, and so need no further training, lack of capital, in other words, is the only real constraint for them. Finally, the Grameen Bank has accompanied its lending program with a human resource investment effort largely aimed at female adult literacy.

Critics have noted that the bank's steady expansion has constituted perhaps as much a problem as a success, in that incentive to repay loans hinges too much on rolling them over into larger loans (thus encouraging the borrowers to get too far in debt). Others question how much poor women have actually been empowered to manage their future. But in promoting economic self-sufficiency among its borrowers, the bank has proven very successful.

(See also DEVELOPMENT AND UNDERDEVELOPMENT; WOMEN AND DEVELOPMENT.)

Helen Todd, *Women at the Center: Grameen Bank Borrowers after One Decade* (Boulder, Colo., 1996).

HARRY W. BLAIR

GRAMSCI, Antonio. Although born in 1891 into the family of a seamstress and a minor Sardinian civil servant on the periphery of Italian society, by 1924 Antonio Gramsci had moved to the center of Italian political life as a leader of the Communist Party and of the democratic opposition to *fascism. Jailed in 1926 by *Mussolini's government, Gramsci spent ten years in prison and died in 1937, soon after his release. But his writings throughout that decade, collected as the *Prison Notebooks*, ensured that his influence on Italian, European, and world politics would continue to grow. In them Gramsci developed an original and nuanced Marxist theory of society and political change that has had significant impact on political practice and on both Marxist and non-Marxist scholarship.

Gramsci's turn toward an intellectual life was influenced by a crippling accident he suffered as a boy. Scholarly accomplishments allowed him to escape a backward rural society that persecuted him as a hunchback. Yet Gramsci always defended the interests of the rural masses along with those of industrial workers. He became a socialist journalist soon after entering the university in Turin in 1911. Turin was then the Italian hub of the second industrial revolution, a center of assembly-line, mass production industries. Throughout the period of Italian labor militancy that lasted through World War I, Gramsci championed the spontaneous factory council movement, fearing however that the councils' insufficient political realism and their disunity would make them ultimately ineffectual.

Gramsci was impressed by the success of the *Communist Party of the Soviet Union and, in 1921, helped found its Italian counterpart. He worked for the Comintern in Moscow for two years, until May 1924, when he returned to Italy as a leader of the parliamentary opposition to the Fascist government. Mussolini signaled the end of his toleration of that opposition two years later when, ignoring parliamentary immunity, he had Gramsci and other Communist leaders arrested.

Despite the privations of prison, Gramsci was able to keep his mind active. He received books from the Cambridge economist Piero Sraffa, and the two corresponded—albeit obliquely and somewhat haphazardly—through Gramsci's sister-in-law. Gramsci, like Sraffa (who worked with the Cambridge Keynesians and who never treated *Marx's economics as dogma), was an open-minded and creative thinker. Gramsci's prison writings reevaluated the social "superstructures"—politics, law, culture, religion, art, and science—which had been given little systematic attention in contemporary Marxist theorizing owing to its focus on the determining role of the "economic base." Using a similar architectural metaphor, Gramsci emphasized the importance of the superstructures. He suggested that they were like a building's walls, windows, doors, and staircases, built upon the economic base and forming with it a "historical bloc," which had to be understood in its entirety.

Gramsci saw the political activity of different social classes as directed toward establishing, maintaining, or undermining particular historical blocs. The establishment and maintenance of a historical bloc represents the "supremacy" of a *class, which involves both force and consent. Opposing social forces must be dominated, but supremacy cannot be achieved without "*hegemony," noncoercive leadership over a coalition of allied social forces. To establish hegemony, a class must sacrifice some of its narrow, often purely material goods in order to serve some of its allies' interests.

Gramsci understood hegemony as being established within "civil society," by which he meant the realm of voluntary social action, the realm in which collective identities are formed. In societies with effective parliamentary systems, where the realm of civil society is extensive, Gramsci saw the role of the socialist movement as waging a "war of position," unifying social forces that could oppose *capitalism (thus forestalling the divide-and-conquer tactics of the capitalists) and disputing mystifications offered to suggest a unity of interests between capitalists and the masses. Gramsci saw communist parties in advanced capitalist societies as contributing to the general political role played by progressive "intellectuals" at any time of social change. Intellectuals help form collective identities; they help overcome the limits of our "common sense," our everyday beliefs. Gramsci argued that the usual problem with the common sense of the masses is not a "false consciousness," or a deep belief in the mystifications that promote an exploitative society, but a "contradictory consciousness," an incoherent mix of beliefs, that contains the germ of the coherent, self-reflective "good sense" that should guide a socialist and democratic society.

Gramsci's ideas influenced the Eurocommunist movement in Western Europe after World War II. They also have had an impact on activists in the *Third World, especially when they have tried to define the proper role for progressive, often Westernized intellectuals in the movements against colonialism and neocolonialism. Gramsci's work has also had an impact on more academic studies of society. In sociology, in some parts of the world, he has joined the canon of masters that includes Marx and *Weber. His theories have guided studies of the historical sociology of individual *states, the role of culture in social change, and the role of the peasantry in industrial societies, among other topics. Recently Gramsci's political theory has had a significant impact on the study of *international relations, primarily because his central concepts focus on a process of statecraft and do not require scholars to treat all juridical nation-states as fundamentally similar. For example, Gramsci's theory allows us to consider *decolonization and the extension of legal sovereignty as a control structure, a means of maintaining the hegemony of the ruling classes in the advanced industrialized states.

(See also EUROCOMMUNISM; MARXISM; PEASANTS; SOCIALISM AND SOCIAL DEMOCRACY.)

Anne Showstack Sassoon, ed., *Approaches to Gramsci* (London, 1982). David Forgacs, ed., *An Antonio Gramsci Reader: Selected Writings, 1916–1935* (London, 1988).

CRAIG N. MURPHY

GREAT BRITAIN. See BRITAIN.

GREAT LAKES REGION. No region of the African continent has known as much political strife, loss of life, and social dislocation during the last forty years as the Great Lakes Region. This is a region whose name is derived from the system of lakes and tributaries draining the central section of the Great Rift Valley of Africa. The great lakes in the system, some of which were named after European monarchs by the first white men to see them, are Victoria, Albert, Edward, Kivu, Tanganyika, Mweru, and Malawi. Lake Victoria is the second largest lake in the world and the largest in Africa, while Tanganyika is the second largest in Africa and the fifth largest in the world. Geographically, the region can be said to comprise nine countries: Congo (DRC), *Uganda, Kenya, *Rwanda, *Burundi, *Tanzania, Zambia, Malawi, and Mozambique. However, the label "Great Lakes Region" is conventionally restricted to the core of the region, whose members are Congo, Uganda, Rwanda, Burundi, and Tanzania. With Lakes Victoria and Albert being the sources of the White Nile—while Ethiopia's Lake Tana is the source of the Blue Nile—the countries of the core have a major stake in the larger political economy and geopolitics of the Nile River Basin.

Together, these five countries constitute an area of 1,383,299 square miles (3,582,746 sq. km.), representing 12 percent of the African landmass. They have a population of approximately 124 million people, or 15.5 percent of the estimated total population of Africa in 2000, about 800 million. Most of the inhabitants speak Bantu languages, and Kiswahili, the national language of Tanzania, is also a lingua franca throughout the region.

The high level of cultural integration and informal economic transactions in the region has been superseded by political and social cleavages, which have caused a lot of turmoil since 1959. Even before the Congo, Rwanda, and Burundi were freed from Belgian rule in 1960 for the first and 1962 for the last two, ethnic identity construction and mobilization, encouraged by the colonialists, were already wrecking havoc in these three countries. In Rwanda, the Hutu-Tutsi conflict took a dramatic turn for the worst in 1959, when the Tutsi-dominated monarchy was overthrown and thousands of Tutsi fled into exile in neighboring countries to escape massacres at the hands of the Hutu majority. In Burundi, it was the Tutsi minority that assumed an oppressive role, the first major result of political and social intolerance there being the 1972 *genocide against the Hutu. As neighboring countries, Uganda, Congo, and Tanzania became the major recipients of refugees from the Hutu-Tutsi conflict in Rwanda and Burundi.

While Tanzania and Uganda respectively achieved independence from Britain in 1961 and 1962 in an orderly fashion, the crisis of *decolonization in the Belgian Congo also affected the region in an adverse manner. Its sequels, particularly the eastern Congo rebellions of 1964–65, included a guerrilla base in the mountains overlooking Lake Tanganyika in which Ernesto *Che Guevara and a Cuban expeditionary force spent nearly seven months in 1965. They were there, in the context of the *Cold War, to provide technical assistance to Congolese revolutionaries, including Laurent Kabila, who were fighting against the Western-backed government in Kinshasa. Revolutionaries from Burundi were also in the camp, acquiring skills for their own struggle on the other side of the lake. Tanzania made it possible for Cuba, China, Egypt, and other socialist or nonaligned countries to send assistance to the Congolese guerrillas.

As the most politically stable country in the region, Tanzania has not only welcomed thousands of refugees from the other four countries, it has also provided sanctuary to political exiles from the Congo and Uganda. In 1979, Tanzania became the first country in Africa to help overthrow a tyrannical regime in another sovereign country. In the process of repulsing Ugandan troops, which had invaded northwestern Tanzania, the Tanzanian army marched all the way to Kampala, Uganda's capital, where it helped Ugandan dissidents get rid of the murderous Idi Amin regime. It remained in Uganda until 1981, to assist in what was then believed to be a transition to a democratically elected government. When the transition failed to materialize, guerrilla leader Yoweri Museveni went back to the bush with young fighters, nearly a quarter of whom were children of Rwandan Tutsi refugees, to wage a successful armed struggle against the Milton Obote and Tito Okello regimes. Museveni took over on 25 January

1986, and he has governed Uganda since then under a "movement regime" or what he prefers to call a "no-party democracy." In reality, it is a single-party regime under the National Resistance Movement, the political arm of his guerrilla organization, the National Resistance Army (NRA).

Having helped Museveni come to power in Rwanda, NRA deputy commander Fred Rwigyema and NRA acting chief of military intelligence Paul Kagame were to lead their next military adventure in 1990, this time in a drive to conquer their native Rwanda, as leaders of the Rwandese Patriotic Front (RPF) and its military arm, the Rwandese Patriotic Army (RPA). The Hutu dominated regime of Major General Juvénal Habyarimana had, since coming to power through a coup d'état in 1973, refused to allow Tutsi refugees to return home. The military confrontation between the RPF and the Habyarimana regime ended in a stalemate. The *Organization of African Unity (OAU) and regional states succeeded in having the two sign a peace agreement in 1993 at Arusha, Tanzania. This included a power sharing arrangement by which the regime, the RPF and moderate Hutu leaders were to take part in a transitional government likely to lead the country to a new political dispensation, with democratic rights for all of its citizens.

The Arusha Accords were never implemented, partly because of the lack of mutual confidence between the belligerents, and mostly because of resistance by Hutu extremists, who were committed to "Hutu Power" at all costs. Given the basically identical ethnic makeup in Rwanda and Burundi, significant developments in one country have a major impact in the other. Thus, the murder in October 1993 of Melchior Ndadaye, the first democratically elected president of Burundi and a Hutu, by the Tutsi dominated army there, reinforced the feelings of Hutu extremists in Rwanda, who felt that the Tutsi couldn't be trusted.

The downing of President Habyarimana's plane as it was about to land at the Kigali airport on 4 April 1994 unleashed one of the major instances of genocide in the twentieth century. In three months, between 800,000 and 1 million people were killed. Most of them were Tutsi, although Hutu moderates were also targeted. The killing squads consisted of units of the Forces Armées Rwandaises (FAR); the extremist Hutu militia known as Interahamwe, or "those who work together," and ordinary citizens, who joined the frenzy either voluntarily or through official coercion and peer pressure. The international community did nothing to prevent the genocide, despite ample warnings, nor to stop it once it was unleashed. Only the victory of the RPA, which took over Kigali in July 1994, ended the genocide.

Over 2 million Hutu fled Rwanda, with over 1 million, including the extremists and their administrative and military apparatus, settling in UN *refugee camps across the border around the Congolese cities of Goma, Bukavu, and Uvira. For two years, Congolese authorities and the international community did nothing to stop these genociders from making incursions into Rwanda to fight the newly established regime. In October 1996, the Kagame regime in Kigali launched a military drive to destroy the camps and, with them, the bases of the ex-FAR and Interahamwe in the Congo. The drive was so successful that Uganda, Angola, and other African states joined it in a generalized offensive to end the corrupt and discredited regime of Mobutu Sese Seko, who had been in power in the Congo since 1965. To find a Congolese who could serve as window dressing for the offensive, the anti-Mobutu coalition picked Kabila, the former guerrilla chief who had become a gold and ivory smuggler, as leader of an instant Congolese liberation front. On 17 May 1997, Rwandan troops and their Congolese auxiliaries took over Kinshasa, and Kabila proclaimed himself president and changed the country's name from Zaire back to its original name of Congo.

A year later, in August 1998, Rwanda and Uganda invaded the Congo for the second time, in an effort to remove Kabila from power and replace him with a leader more likely to advance their strategic and economic interests in northeastern Congo. While they gave as rationale for their action the use of Congolese territory for military purposes by Rwandan and Ugandan rebel groups, the Museveni and Kagame regimes were actually part of a wider strategy to partition the Congo and loot its rich natural resources. As Kabila's mentors, the governments of Rwanda and Uganda were actually involved in managing the Congo's security apparatus. Until July 1998, the commander in chief of the new Congolese army was Major James Kabareebe, a RPA officer who had grown up in Uganda. As Kabila sought to emancipate himself from foreign tutelage to build up his own popularity as a national leader, he became dispensable.

From the perspective of political economy, the underlying causes of the regional war that began in August 1998 were the decay of the Congolese state under the weight of Mobutu's thirty-year kleptocracy, and the longstanding envy of external powers, including poor neighboring states like Uganda, Rwanda, and Burundi, vis-à-vis Congo's rich array of natural resources. The invasion of the Congo by these Lilliputian states would have been unthinkable under normal circumstances, with a responsible government and functioning state institutions. With the rapid disintegration of the Mobutu regime under the weight of the democracy movement since January 1988 and its loss of unconditional Western support in the post–Cold War era, a normal state had been replaced by Mafia-type organizations led by Mobutu's own generals. For these organizations, chaos was preferable to order for purposes of maximizing their wealth. Museveni and Kagame took advantage of this situation and moved in to fill the vacuum created by the disintegration of the Mobutu regime. They came to fish in troubled waters, with the hope of extracting as much wealth as they could in the form of Congo's gold, diamonds, timber, coffee, tea, and rare metals.

Unwilling to see these little states impose their will on the Congo and monopolize control over its resources, Angola, Zimbabwe, Namibia and, for a while, Chad, also intervened militarily on Kabila's side. Thus began the first major regional war of postcolonial Africa, involving armies from at least nine states and a dozen of rebel armies and militia groups. Given the large number of belligerents and the interests at stake, it is a war that none of the two sides—the anti-Kabila alliance of Rwanda, Uganda, Burundi, and Congolese rebels as well as the pro-Kabila group involving Angola, Zimbabwe, and Namibia—can win militarily, and one that is difficult to resolve peacefully. Mediation efforts by the *Southern African Development Community (SADC), the OAU, and the UN have so far succeeded in obtaining a cease-fire agreement, but the region is still far away from achieving peace. In fact, last-

ing *peace and *security are unlikely unless the other four countries in the region follow Tanzania's example in putting in place an inclusive government based on free and fair elections and multiparty competition. The persistence of personal rule in Uganda, Rwanda, and the Congo, and the continuing civil war in Burundi do not offer good prospects for the transition to democracy, as well as for peace and security.

(See also CONGO, DEMOCRATIC REPUBLIC OF; DEMOCRATIC TRANSITIONS; RWANDAN GENOCIDE.)

Georges Nzongola-Ntalaja, *From Zaire to the Democratic Republic of the Congo* (Uppsala, Sweden, 1998). Didier Goyvaerts, ed., *Conflict and Ethnicity in Central Africa* (Tokyo, 2000). Herbert Weiss, *War and Peace in the Democratic Republic of the Congo* (Uppsala, Sweden, 2000).

GEORGES NZONGOLA-NTALAJA

GREAT SOCIETY. The Great Society is the name that President Lyndon Baines *Johnson gave to the outpouring of social and economic policies enacted in the United States during the 1960s. New initiatives increased the federal government's role in the domains of health care for the poor and elderly, education, and low-income housing. These policies were complemented by Keynesian macroeconomic management to promote full employment; civil rights measures to ensure equal opportunity for *African Americans; and a highly visible "War on Poverty," which sought to end poverty in the United States.

The Great Society represented a completion of many initiatives first contemplated in the 1930s during the *New Deal. With it, the U.S. federal government took a role in promoting the social welfare of its citizens akin to that assumed by many European nations immediately after World War II. However, the Great Society featured distinctly American approaches to social policy and remained less far-reaching than most European *welfare states. The programs inaugurated during the Great Society sought to promote equal opportunity rather than to redistribute income or to guarantee social rights.

A variety of economic, political, and social factors created a favorable environment for social *reform in the 1960s. Postwar growth had boosted the U.S. economy, but "pockets of poverty" continued to exist in areas left behind by industrial transformation. Some groups were more economically vulnerable than others: the elderly and African Americans had particularly high rates of poverty as the United States entered the 1960s. Although the decade began with a sluggish economy, by the mid-1960s, unprecedented prosperity allowed the federal government to increase spending on social programs without raising taxes. As James T. Patterson (*America's Struggle Against Poverty, 1900–1980,* Cambridge, Mass., 1981) has noted, this secure economic climate took the sting out of increased public spending; social reform could be accomplished without redistributing wealth.

Politics, too, moved in directions favorable to social reform in the 1960s. Since the 1950s, congressional Democrats had been pressing for action on a range of social policy issues including education, health care, and unemployment. And, after a decade of struggle, the southern *civil rights movement succeeded in drawing national attention to the exclusion of African Americans from the economic prosperity and political rights enjoyed by the majority of whites.

The shock of President John F. *Kennedy's *assassination in 1963 finally jolted Congress into action. The unfulfilled promise of the Kennedy administration, which had vowed to get the country "moving again," provided renewed impetus for reformers. When combined with President Johnson's considerable legislative skill, these circumstances made Congress more amenable to social legislation than it had been in several decades. This predilection to increase the federal role in ensuring social welfare was strongly reinforced in 1964, when Americans elected the most liberal Congress since 1936.

Many of the Great Society programs had been on the nation's agenda for decades. The Medicaid and Medicare programs, which established health insurance for the poor and the elderly respectively, represented a compromise that established a federal role in ensuring the nation's health but fell short of the national health insurance proposed since the 1930s. The panoply of low-income housing programs enacted in the late 1960s and the establishment of a Department of Housing and Urban Development in 1965 extended federal activity in the field of housing beyond the small public housing programs authorized in the 1930s. The Keynesian tax cut enacted in 1964, which aimed to stimulate the economy and reduce unemployment, represented the triumph of an economic strategy first tried in 1938.

Other initiatives reflected concerns that had grown during the 1950s. Support for federal aid to education, traditionally the province of states and localities, mounted as localities struggled to accommodate the explosive demands on public education created by the postwar baby boom and as concern about the different capacities of local governments grew. Although federal aid to education actually increased by very little during the 1960s, the acknowledgment of a federal role in funding public education represented a new departure. A second new area of federal activism was civil rights. In 1964, the Civil Rights Act outlawed discrimination in public facilities, ending over a half century of legally sanctioned racial segregation in the South. The Voting Rights Act passed a year later sought to ensure black political rights and laid the foundation for the conquest of political power by a generation of black politicians in the following decade.

The newest and most visible element of the Great Society was the War on Poverty. Although many of the components of the attack on poverty were not new, the effort to package them into a concerted effort to end poverty was novel. The charter legislation for the War on Poverty, the Economic Opportunity Act of 1964, created programs for youth job training, public service employment for youth, a volunteer national services corps, and a new Office of Equal Opportunity, operating out of the Executive Office of the President. The most innovative aspect of the War on Poverty were community action agencies, which were established in localities across the country to administer the new programs with the "maximum feasible participation" of the poor. In creating these agencies, the federal government bypassed state and city government to establish the first direct relationship between community groups and the federal government.

Despite its flamboyant rhetoric, the War on Poverty did not commit the federal government to major spending to reduce poverty; its greatest gains were in promoting black political empowerment. Although the War on Poverty was officially race-neutral, in practice it focused on urban minorities. Local black communities seized on community action programs to challenge the exclusionary practices of local governments and

service bureaucracies. As black riots spread across urban America in the 1960s, the federal government used community action agencies to funnel resources into these troubled communities.

The social reform launched by the Great Society lost its momentum in the late 1960s as spending on the *Vietnam War limited funds for domestic social purposes. Equally important was dwindling support for the War on Poverty in the wake of urban rioting. Although federal social spending would rise under the Nixon administration, the emphasis on federal activity and the focus on the poor that characterized the War on Poverty diminished in the 1970s. And, as inflation and unemployment grew in the 1970s, confidence that government could solve economic and social problems declined.

The Great Society left an uneven institutional legacy. Some of the policy innovations of the 1960s have survived over a decade of conservative administrations: the federal government continues to help finance health care for the poor and elderly and provides modest aid to education. Many of the neighborhood community organizations created by the community action programs still deliver social services to poor neighborhoods. Some of the programs pioneered in the War on Poverty, including early childhood education provided by Head Start, have survived attempts to eliminate them. But the programs that have survived, particularly those aimed at the poor, are poorly funded and struggle for resources. Other policy innovations, including most of the job training and employment efforts of the Great Society, have been abandoned altogether.

The intellectual and policy legacy of the Great Society remains hotly contested. Liberal supporters point to successes in reducing poverty levels and call for extensions of many programs including health care, job training, and education. Critics from the Left blame the limited focus of the Great Society for its failure to sustain political support and call for broader policies that can appeal to both the middle class and the poor. Conservatives, by contrast, argue that the social policies of the 1960s distorted the work incentives of the poor and are consequently responsible for the growth of an urban *underclass dependent on government subsidies.

The central vision of the Great Society, that federal government should provide equal opportunity for all citizens, unraveled as funds grew tight and new policies proved unable to sustain public support. But, because of its bold ambitions, the Great Society will continue to provide the touchstone for future debates about social policy in the United States.

(See also KEYNESIANISM; POLITICAL PARTICIPATION.)

Henry J. Aaron, *Politics and the Professors: The Great Society in Perspective* (Washington, D.C., 1978). James T. Patterson, *America's Struggle Against Poverty, 1900–1980* (Cambridge, Mass., 1981). Allen J. Matusow, *The Unraveling of America: A History of Liberalism in the 1960s* (New York, 1984).

MARGARET WEIR

GREECE. In 1829 Greece became an independent, sovereign state after a seven-year nationalist war to gain independence from Ottoman rule. But its sovereignty was limited. Three "protecting powers"—Britain, France, and Russia—imposed a foreign absolute monarchy and restricted Greece's autonomy.

The current boundaries of Greece—from Crete to the southern tip of the Balkan peninsula to Macedonia, along with the majority of the Aegean, Dodecanese, and Ionian islands—were finalized at the end of World War II with the addition of the island of Rhodes. Its population has increased from approximately 750,000 in 1830 to 10 million in the late 1990s, largely owing to territorial expansion and partly to the refugee influx from Asia Minor after the 1920s population exchange with *Turkey.

Although ancient Greece was seen by the West as the cradle of *democracy, its subsequent historical experience was the spiritual religiosity of Byzantium followed by incorporation into the Ottoman Empire. Greek society was not influenced by the Enlightenment and the socioeconomic transformations in the West during the seventeenth and eighteenth centuries. As a consequence of its historical legacy, its traditional culture, and the imposition of a foreign authoritarian regime at the time of independence, the foundations of *liberalism and democracy in modern Greece have been shaky. Military intervention and military coups, *authoritarianism, and dependence on a foreign patron have punctuated its history. The underlying principles of a liberal democratic polity, individual *rights and liberties, have not been integral to its *political culture. The state has been perceived as the communal, organic embodiment of the Greek nation. Even in periods of democratic regimes, restrictions have existed on the exercise of rights.

Prior to World War II Greece was ruled by the dictator Ioannis Metaxas (1936–1940), who modeled his reign on European *fascism. Italian and German occupation during the war was succeeded by a devastating civil war (1945–1950), prompting the *Truman Doctrine for the defense of Greece and Turkey against communism and the Soviet Union. After the defeat of the guerrilla forces, an authoritarian, repressive regime, albeit within a parliamentary framework, was established in 1950. Power was lodged in the military, the monarchy, and the United States, the latter being instrumental, if not decisive, in the selection of Greece's political leadership. By the early 1960s social discontent was widespread, demands for democratization were mounting, and the ruling oligarchy felt threatened, while Greece's policy on *Cyprus antagonized the United States. In response a military coup was executed in 1967 by colonels active in a paramilitary organization and supported by Greece's patron, the United States. Seven years of repressive military rule under the slogan "Greece for Christian Greeks" collapsed in 1974 as a result of the fiasco of an attempted coup against President Makarios of Cyprus.

In 1975 a new Greek constitution reestablished a parliamentary system, a far more democratic one than in the past. The powers of the president (elected by the legislature) were diminished and transferred to the prime minister by a 1986 constitutional amendment. A perennially contentious issue is the independence of the judiciary. Although constitutionally independent, Greece's two highest courts, the Council of State (administrative) and the Supreme Court (civil and criminal), tend to be politicized.

Politics in Greece are clientelist, lacking until recently significant class, ideological, or programmatic conflict, except among the Left. The multiparty system that took form after 1975 witnessed the rise of the newly organized Panhellenic Socialist Movement (PASOK) led by Andreas Papandreou. Campaigning on anti-Americanism, his anti-junta credentials,

*populism, and democratic socialism (more participatory and less corporatist than social democracy), Papandreou and PASOK won a resounding electoral victory in 1981. The political landscape changed—PASOK replaced the traditional center; the electoral support of the traditional Left declined; smaller Marxist parties, appealing primarily to intellectuals, were formed; and the traditional Right, renamed New Democracy, espoused neoliberalism. Simultaneously, both an environmental and a women's movement appeared, challenging the traditional parameters of Greek politics. A neofascist party has little support, although it gained ground in 1998. Once in power, while maintaining populism, Papandreou modified or reversed his stance on numerous issues, and clientelist politics became his hallmark. Opposition to Greece's membership in the European Community (EC) dissolved, anti-Americanism remained a rhetorical device, U.S. base agreements were renegotiated, and domestic reforms were minimal. Legislation on women's rights was the most significant reform. In 1989, under a cloud of major financial scandals, PASOK lost the elections, but it returned to power in 1993. Upon Papandreou's death in 1996, he was replaced by Costas Simitis, a technocrat and a modernizer.

Throughout its modern history Greece has been a peripheral or semiperipheral state. It has been a political client of one or another great power, and an economic dependency of the more advanced economies of the West. Dependent on foreign loans for financing its external debt, for meeting budget deficits, and for aid in industrialization, it has failed to industrialize. Unemployment and underemployment have been perennial problems that have been alleviated only by emigration from Greece, the latest large exodus being that of the "guest workers" to western Europe during the 1960s and early 1970s. (The late 1990s, however, witnessed an influx of immigrants.) Despite an ideological commitment to capitalism, the public sector has been vast, while the small industrial and manufacturing sector is heavily government-controlled or state-owned. In 1997 the prime minister embarked on a major program of privatization, budget austerity, and a host of fiscal measures designed to meet the requirements of the *Maastricht Treaty and make Greece eligible for participation in the single currency initiative. Thanks to the highly bureaucratized nature of the Greek state, the middle class is largely composed of public sector employees who in turn are members of powerful trade unions, and the latter reacted with massive strikes and demonstrations against Simitis's liberalization policies, which include moves to introduce labor flexibility. Greece was admitted to the EMU in June of 2000.

The Greek Orthodox Church and the military have been powerful political institutions in Greece. The military has had a history of intervention, at times in alliance with a political faction, at times, as in 1967, on its own. In the aftermath of the military junta's brutal rule, its ignominious action against the president of Cyprus, and its subsequent disintegration, there appears to have been a "return to the barracks" and a restoration of civilian control. By contrast, the church, financed largely by the state, remains powerful, partly because legally Eastern Orthodoxy is the established religion in Greece, partly because it is a critical component of Greek nationality. The church suffered a major defeat in 2000, however, when the government eliminated religious affiliation from citizens' identity cards.

Membership in the EC (1981) was initially sought for political reasons to protect against resurgence of military rule, and later as a vehicle for grants from the structural funds and subsidies from the common agricultural policy. Greece has had little foreign investment, but moves toward greater economic integration have resulted in significant European buyouts of the few successful Greek enterprises. Despite economic benefits, Greek policy is ambivalent with regard to moves for greater integration. Intensely nationalistic, Greeks are reluctant to lose sovereignty or delegate authority to community organs, particularly as the EC moves toward greater political integration. Nevertheless, the Simitis government is committed to the Europeanization of Greece and its political and economic integration into the EU. It has dropped its initial opposition to Turkish membership in the EU and remains supportive of membership for Cyprus.

While the Greek political leadership struggles domestically with recurrent pressures for modernization and development of its society and economy, foreign policy remains a major concern. Greece has been a member of NATO since 1952 and has been an ally of the United States. Its principal foreign policy issue has been relations with Turkey. Conflict over the continental shelf, over territorial waters, over the Turkish minority in Greece and the Greek minority in Turkey, and over Cyprus (populated by Greeks and Turks) has been ongoing, and the issues remain unresolved. With the collapse of communism in Eastern Europe and particularly the breakup of Yugoslavia, new foreign policy issues have come to the fore. *Macedonia (formerly part of Yugoslavia), in particular, inflamed nationalist passions: Greeks argue that the name usurped Greek history and the legacy of Alexander the Great. Greece supports greater economic cooperation among the Balkan states while politically it is inclined toward Serbia.

(See also DEMOCRATIC TRANSITIONS; FOREIGN WORKERS; MILITARY RULE; PATRON-CLIENT POLITICS; SOCIALISM AND SOCIAL DEMOCRACY.)

Richard Clogg and George Yannopoulos, eds., *Greece under Military Rule* (New York, 1972). T. S. Kariotis, ed., *The Greek Socialist Experiment: Papandreou's Greece, 1981–1989* (New York, 1992). Kevin Featherstone and Kostas Ifantis, eds., *Greece in a Changing Europe* (Manchester, 1996).
ADAMANTIA POLLIS

GREEN PARTIES are a recent development in the politics of advanced societies, building on environmentalist concerns about the impact of economic growth. The political breakthrough came only in the late 1960s when citizen-based movements challenged the prevailing growth strategy and opposed both the peaceful and military uses of nuclear energy. Over some three decades, *new social movements gave rise to political parties promoting an alternative *political economy, a radically different way of organizing society. Events played their part: serious accidents at Three Mile Island (1979), the Seveso spillage of toxic chemicals (1983), and, most notably, the meltdown of the Chernobyl reactor in 1986.

The most electorally successful Green parties are those of Western Europe, though the picture is variable: they are less effective in the new Mediterranean democracies (Spain, Portugal, Greece), whereas ideological disputation and quarrels over strategy have debilitated some parties (in Denmark, Norway, and the Netherlands) more than others, allowing New Left parties to represent green issues.

Green movements in East/Central Europe (the Danube Circle in Hungary, Bündnis '90 in the former GDR or East Germany, Ekoglasnost and the Green Party of Bulgaria) played a key role in the overthrow of communist regimes, with Greens winning seats in the national legislatures in Romania, Slovakia, and Bulgaria, though the political agenda of these transitional societies is principally about accelerating growth and stabilizing democracy. *Postmaterialism is salient in North America, but finds its organized expression in *nongovernmental organizations and issue-specific campaigning groups. Ecology has experienced some electoral success in Australia and New Zealand. And, though green social movements are active in some developing countries, notably in India, politics there is driven by familiar materialist and nation-building goals.

The Greens' impact is uneven, even in political systems culturally disposed to postmaterial issues. Clearly, political opportunity structures play a part in facilitating electoral success. Green or, for that matter, other small niche parties are more likely to win national representation in elections conducted on the proportionality principle, and better able to operate where there is public financing for parties and availability of free election broadcasting time. These political opportunity structures have assisted Green Party development in most of continental Europe, with the most effective Green parties in Germany, France, Sweden, Belgium, Austria, Switzerland, Luxembourg, Ireland, and Finland. The consistently poor showing of the British Green Party owes much to an electoral system that heavily discriminates against minor parties.

Ideology. There is no uniform green *ideology. Conflict over ideology, the meaning of greening as between pure green or "deep ecology" (nature before humanity) and a red-green or homocentric tendency, occurs in every Green party, though with differential effect. Green ideology is eclectic, a synthesis of conservative and radical instincts: nostalgia for antimodernist and spiritual values, a dialectic between libertarian individualism tending to *anarchism and altogether more collectivist preferences. There is, however, a green leitmotif, an unremitting critique of the political economy of advanced societies, ideological preferences that locate Green parties outside the conventional left-right axis of party politics. This ideological singularity enhances the Greens' appeal to its main support base, a distinctive constituency of the younger, better-educated and the morally engaged who are disaffected with the "old" productionist politics.

There is more to this discourse than incremental tinkering with public policy, conserving finite natural resources, challenging productionist values, replacing the wantonness of private enterprise or the short-termism of mainstream public policy with a novel strategy of "*sustainable development," utilizing fiscal and other policy instruments—both punitive and as incentives—to discourage pollution. Green parties also aspire to far-reaching changes in individual lifestyles: a reduction, indeed a major shift, in consumption patterns, conservation of scarce resources, use of alternative technologies, reorganization of working practices, changes in gender relations, and, not least, instilling by example new social values, aspirations, and moral conduct. These are internationalist movements, looking beyond narrow geopolitical boundaries, with a holistic outlook rooted in universal values. Accordingly, the ecology crises faced by particular societies are identified as local expressions of a global crisis requiring the remedy of worldwide peace and supranational cooperation. This weltanschauung has facilitated ad hoc, issue-based cooperation between Green parties and ecological pressure groups: notably, Greenpeace and Friends of the Earth. The mismatch between the large numbers of citizens who subscribe to environmental concerns and the comparatively small numbers who either join or vote for Green parties is a paradox of Green politics everywhere; a conundrum that has rather more to do with the logics of national party politics than it has with the nonsalience of ecologism in contemporary societies.

Organization: The Democracy Predicament. Greens take democracy seriously, and as such experience difficulty organizing grass-roots movements into effective party organizations. Green parties face predicaments familiar to all radical parties: how to build an electoral base in mainstream politics, provoking conflict between fundamentalists who prefer principles to power and pragmatists who seek power in order to implement principles. Party fundamentalists are held accountable to rank-and-file activists, policy deliberations are openly conducted, management of party affairs is transparent, and control of party personnel is shared between regional or local parties and a national parliamentary leadership, usually within federated structures that only loosely coordinate the activities of semiautonomous grassroots members. Some parties have undertaken organizational reforms to facilitate a parliamentary role, though not to the exclusion of the grass roots from party councils. Even parliamentary leadership is exercised collectively, with power balanced between ideological factions, usually with a gender parity.

Invariably, there is tension between those preferring an inchoate movement to a formal party status. The outcome is usually a compromise, a movement-party model, but this makes for difficulties in conducting effective electoral politics. Confusion over official policy is a hindrance, as are disorganized election campaigns and a reluctance to identify a singular leadership. Many Green parties are handicapped by a public image of incompetence, even among voters otherwise sympathetic to radical ideas, or by apparent indifference to the demands of modern election campaigns. These problems likewise affect the role of Green parties in government, inasmuch as Green ministers must liaise with activists and keep faith with party doctrine, thus constraining freedom of maneuver and inclining other parties to discount them as partners of last resort in coalition negotiations.

Strategy: The Radical Dilemma. Green parties face another persistent dilemma: whether or not to cash in on a modest parliamentary presence by joining coalitions led by mainstream parties, usually from the social democratic left, in exchange for a handful of cabinet seats.

If the 1980s was the decade of the democracy predicament, the 1990s saw many Green parties confronting the strategy dilemma, some with more internal turmoil than others. A trend is apparent in events. Wherever the vagaries of coalition arithmetic have presented Green parties with the prospect of sharing power, pragmatists, led by Green parliamentarians, have convinced reticent rank-and-file members to seize the opportunity—though not in most cases without a febrile debate about the costs of compromising political integrity. This was most notable in Germany, where in 1997 Die Grünen/

Bündnis '90 joined the SDP-led coalition and immediately sparked a bitter dispute as the parliamentary leadership became associated with government backtracking on "promised" nuclear reactor closures and the NATO bombardment of Serbia. There was rather less controversy when Greens joined social democratic coalitions in Italy (1994), Finland (1995, and again in 1999), France (1997), Sweden (1999), and Belgium (1999).

By and large, Green pragmatists have resolved the radical dilemma, much as socialist parties did a generation earlier, by trading a modicum of power over public policy for those unavoidable compromises implied in Max *Weber's apt metaphor about boring through "the hard boards of politics."

Futures. Skeptics predicted the demise of Green parties, seeing them merely as the irresponsible moralizing of a privileged generation of youthful idealists with the time, money, and intellectual capacity to think the worst of a capitalism that provided material surpluses to finance reflective radicalism in its academies. This was always a caricature of a movement driven by more pressing matters than intellectual self-indulgence. The modern world is bewildering, complex, and dangerous, and a growing number of citizens are concerned about current economic and social priorities. And though a postmaterial mood is still exceptional, political ecology cannot be dismissed as merely eccentric.

And, whereas support for Green parties has fluctuated in relation to the health of the economy—higher during periods of prosperity, tailing off during cyclical recessions, when minds are concentrated on threats to material well-being—there is nothing unexceptional about this inverse equation. Nor does it indicate the obsolescence of political parties focused on reconciling aspirations for a comfortable life with enlightened stewardship of a fragile planet of finite resources. Indeed, the response of governments at the global level, increasingly interfacing with the green lobby to confront the challenges of climate change, greenhouse gases, damage to the ozone layer, the pollution potential of China's emergence as an industrial powerhouse, and the immense cleanup costs of former communist states, underlines a changing public policy agenda, and points to shifts in the public mind-set that place green issues at the very center of international and domestic politics alike. Green parties occupy a distinctive political space; they are almost certainly here to stay.

(See also CHERNOBYL NUCLEAR ACCIDENT; ENVIRONMENTALISM.)

A. Bramwell, *Ecology in the Twentieth Century* (1989). S. Kamieniecki, ed., *Environmental Politics in the International Arena* (1993). R. Dalton, *The Green Rainbow: Environmental Groups in Western Europe* (1994). B. Doherty and M. de Geus, *Democracy and Green Political Thought* (1996). M. O'Neill, *Green Parties and Political Change in Contemporary Europe: New Politics, Old Predicaments* (1997).

MICHAEL O'NEILL

GREEN REVOLUTION. The term "green revolution," as coined in 1968, refers to the introduction and adoption of high-yielding varieties of wheat and rice—two of the three most important crops in the world—in the less developed nations in Asia and, to a lesser extent, in Latin America and Africa. These varieties were generally developed by the International Maize and Wheat Improvement Center (CIMMYT) in Mexico and the International Rice Research Institute

(IRRI) in the Philippines in cooperation with national agricultural research programs. They were usually short or semidwarf in growth habit, and responded to fertilization without lodging or falling over.

By the 1982–83 crop year, about 61 percent of the wheat area in the noncommunist developing nations and nearly 42 percent of the rice area were planted with these varieties. Additional areas were also planted in the communist nations of Asia, especially the People's Republic of China (which largely developed its own high-yielding varieties of rice). All told, the high-yielding varieties spread more widely and more quickly than any other technological innovation in the history of agriculture in the developing nations. The process still continues, though at a slower rate.

This green revolution, along with the adoption of improved production practices, has brought about increased productivity, and this has led to significant changes—generally quite positive—in the countries and regions where the new varieties have been adopted. The economic and social changes have been relatively well monitored. Political effects have not been so closely studied and remain somewhat more speculative. The economic and social impacts have, however, undoubtedly influenced political issues.

The principal immediate effect of the high-yielding varieties is to increase grain production. The result is that more food is produced at lower cost per unit than would otherwise be the case. This means that farmers, especially early adopters, receive higher incomes. Consumers—rural and urban—are able to buy more food at lower cost; low-income consumers, who spend a large percentage of their income on food, particularly benefit. Employment of farm workers is often expanded. The direct and indirect increases in incomes in turn have multiplier effects among merchants and others in the local community and in the region. More general economic growth is stimulated.

The benefits are, however, not always shared equally among producers. And some groups—especially farmers and regions that are late to adopt the technology or unable to do so—may actually be disadvantaged as expanded production elsewhere brings prices down. But the extent of this disadvantage in some areas may be moderated by shifts in the labor force and by changes in production patterns.

Views of the economic and social effects of the green revolution have shifted over time. At first, there was concern that the new technology would primarily be adopted by larger and wealthier farmers and that this would widen class differences in the countryside. But the reality has been rather different: The highly divisible biological technology embodied in the high-yielding varieties has proved to be quite accessible to smaller farmers and has been widely adopted by them, although sometimes at a slower pace. Government policies, social structure, and the degree of development of infrastructure also influence the rate of adoption and the distribution of benefits.

The generally widespread and equitable adoption of the high-yielding varieties of wheat and rice has also changed perceptions of their political effects. In the early years of the green revolution, especially in the early 1970s, there was substantial concern about political destabilization—that the green revolution would turn red. This has not turned out to be the case; if anything, the green revolution may well have lessened the potential for revolutionary change.

One political problem originates at the country level but emerges in the international arena: a much more nationalistic view toward plant genetic resources, especially on the part of developing countries. Whereas these resources were once seen as the "heritage of mankind," they are now viewed more as a commodity with potential commercial value. The growing exercise of intellectual property rights by national and multinational firms has reinforced this attitude. Thus, the maintenance of genebanks and the international flow of plant genetic resources—the basis for the green revolution—may be much more difficult in the future.

Other problems also have a political origin. First, public concern about the health and environmental aspects of biotechnology (in particular, genetically modified organisms), while strongest in developing countries, may flow over into developing countries and inhibit the development of technologies that would be of great value in meeting their present and future food needs. Secondly, at the other end of the spectrum, public indifference about funding of public research for and in developing countries threatens to undercut the basis for future green revolutions. The private sector has much to offer, but principally for more advanced and affluent regions.

Whether green revolutions in developing nations will come to be merely a piece of history or an important part of our future depends to an unprecedented degree on how political factors play out in the opening years of the twenty-first century.

(See also DEVELOPMENT AND UNDERDEVELOPMENT; FOOD POLITICS; LAND REFORM; RURAL DEVELOPMENT; SUSTAINABLE DEVELOPMENT.)

Michael Lipton with Richard Longhurst, *New Seeds and Poor People* (Baltimore, 1989). Gordon Conway, *The Doubly Green Revolution: Food for All in the Twenty-First Century* (London, 1997).

DANA G. DALRYMPLE

GRENADA. The most southerly of the Windward Island chain of West Indian islands, Grenada is part of the *English-speaking Caribbean. It controls two Grenadine islands, Carriacou and Petit Martinique. Its area is about 130 square feet (345 sq. km.). Its population of 97,500 (1995) is relatively homogeneous: 90 percent of African origin, with a white or mixed minority and a small number of Portuguese and East Indian descendants. Grenada is perhaps most known internationally for its Cold War role as the scene of a dramatic U.S. invasion in 1983.

The island was a pawn in the colonial rivalry between France and Britain until it was ceded to Britain in 1763. It became a British Crown Colony in 1877, with a limited representative system that was slowly liberalized as the Crown came under pressure from local and regional labor activists. After World War II, universal adult suffrage was introduced and a party system was developed.

In 1950 Eric Gairy, a populist leader who had been a labor organizer among West Indian oil workers in Aruba, formed the Grenada United Labor Party (GULP) and quickly gained a strong following among the rural proletariat. In contrast, the Grenada National Party (GNP), formed in 1953, attracted support from the middle and upper classes. Except for a few brief intervals, GULP dominated Grenada's politics from the first general elections in 1951 through independence in 1974, until it was dislodged by a coup in 1979. Although Gairy initially championed the cause of the masses, his extended tenure was marked by strong personalist government, widespread patronage, and corruption.

In 1973 the New Jewel Movement (NJM) was formed. NJM sought to tap the discontent of the young and unemployed and the energies of some elements of the middle class. By independence, NJM was supported by a broad cross-section of the community that had resorted to demonstrations against the prospect of a Gairy regime. With the arrival of independence NJM became part of the parliamentary opposition. In 1979 NJM leaders staged the English-speaking Caribbean's first successful coup. The People's Revolutionary Government (PRG) was led by the relatively young, middle-class Maurice Bishop who implemented a socialist "people's democracy" with a mixed economy.

The regime's close links with Cuba and the Eastern Bloc, its relatively high level of militarization, alleged human rights violations, and refusal to schedule elections, all alarmed the United States and Grenada's eastern Caribbean neighbors. In 1983, a dispute between governmental factions resulted in the execution of the prime minister and some members of his cabinet, as well as the death of many civilians. The eastern Caribbean countries formally requested U.S. *intervention and, with Barbados and Jamaica, lent military support. The resulting invasion restored order, but at the cost of many Grenadian lives as well as a few deaths among Cuban and U.S. military personnel.

The PRG had replaced Grenada's parliamentary democracy with collective government represented by a Political Bureau supported by parish councils. In 1984, parliamentary government was restored, but the former two-party system was replaced by multiparty democracy that resulted in unstable coalition government. A somewhat more stable system was returned in 1995 when the New National Party (NNP) won a majority (8 out of 15) in the House of Assembly.

Grenada's economy is dependent on export of cocoa, nutmeg, and assorted spices. Its GDP per capita in 1995 was US$2,721. Small-scale agriculture has been the backbone of the economy, with some light industry, mainly handicraft and garment production.

In addition, various governments have sought to improve agro-industry and fishery production, but success has been limited. As is the case in most of the Caribbean, tourism is an important source of revenue for Grenada, although the island's performance in this highly competitive area has been variable. Expectations of major economic development, linked to perceived increased U.S. attention after the 1983 invasion, were not borne out. Indeed, although the country did receive increased U.S. aid, only a few major investments in light industry materialized. Meanwhile, the agricultural sector has also been plagued by declines in production attributable primarily to insufficient incentives and to crop disease.

The focus of Grenada's external affairs is on the regional arena. Grenada has supported the widening and deepening of the Caribbean Community and Common Market (Caricom) in the interest of expanding its own small market and increasing its economic competitiveness. It also belongs to the smaller Eastern Caribbean Common Market. Grenada is a member of the Organization of Eastern Caribbean States and has supported the idea of political union among the Windward Islands, although a consensus with the other islands has not been achieved. Relations with Cuba, broken in the aftermath of the U.S. intervention, have been restored and revitalized. Grenada is a member of the Association of Caribbean States (ACS), the Organization of American States, the UN, the Commonwealth, and the Nonaligned Movement. (See also U.S.–LATIN AMERICAN RELATIONS.)

Jacqueline Braveboy-Wagner, *The Caribbean in World Affairs: Foreign Policies of the English-speaking Caribbean* (Boulder, Colo., 1989). Jorge Heine, ed., *A Revolution Aborted: The Lessons of Grenada* (Pittsburgh, 1990).
JACQUELINE ANNE BRAVEBOY-WAGNER

GROTIUS, Hugo. Huig de Groot (Hugo Grotius is the Latinized version of his name, used in his major works) is most widely remembered as a leading intellectual figure of the seventeenth century and an important writer on *international law and *international relations. Grotius was born in 1583 at Delft in the United Provinces of the Netherlands or Dutch Republic. His early career was marked by an astonishing range of achievement. A child prodigy, he entered the University of Leiden at age 11. When he visited Paris at the age of 15 he was acclaimed by King Henri IV as "the miracle of Holland." In 1599 he was admitted to the bar of The Hague, and in 1607 he was appointed to the high legal office of advocate-fiscal of Holland.

Already the author of several volumes on the history of the Dutch Republic, which was a new and in many ways insecure state, in 1609 he published his first legal work, *Mare Liberum.* This classic exposition of the freedom of the seas defended the activities of the Dutch East India Company when threatened by the Spanish and Portuguese empires.

In 1613 Grotius was appointed pensionary of Rotterdam—a more important post than its name might suggest. However, within five years his political career in Holland came to an end. Like many in Holland, he had coupled his Protestantism with support for toleration both at home and abroad. In 1618 Prince Maurice, the commander of the Dutch Republic's armies, imposed a more militant and less tolerant regime on Holland. Grotius's patron, Johan van Oldenbarnevelt, was arrested and executed, while Grotius himself was sentenced to life imprisonment. In 1621 he made a celebrated escape from the castle of Loevestein in a chest of books.

He was in exile for almost all the rest of his life—mainly in Paris, where he spent two ten-year periods. In the first, sustained by a small pension from the king and by literary earnings, he wrote and published (in 1625) *De Jure Belli ac Pacis* (On the Law of War and Peace)—his major, and last, work in the field of international law. He also dreamed of a triumphant return to Holland, but when he did go back, in 1631–1632, he could not resume his previous career in Dutch politics. He had once more to flee abroad, and from 1634 to 1644 was again in Paris, this time in the important post of Swedish ambassador at the French court. He had been appointed by the Swedish chancellor, Axel Oxenstierna, and when in 1644 Oxenstierna's influence temporarily declined,

Grotius was recalled to Sweden and relieved of his post. The following year, on his way back to Paris, Grotius was shipwrecked in the Baltic, and died two days later at Rostock.

Grotius wrote many books, including poetry, translations, and studies on theological and historical topics. He is most remembered today for *De Jure Belli ac Pacis*, which addresses perennial problems of international relations: justifications for *war and military intervention; restraints in war; the *legitimacy or otherwise of rebellion; the treatment of the vanquished after a war.

Grotius has often been seen as the "father of international law." This description points to his achievement as a systematic writer who drew together strands from an eclectic variety of sources of law. His work had a special significance because, in his day, the society of independent sovereign states was beginning to emerge in its modern form—a development symbolized three years after his death by the 1648 Peace of Westphalia. Grotius provided a guide to the operations of this new system of sovereign states. However, he cannot properly be seen as the begetter of international law. Not only did his writing draw heavily on classical writers, and on recent predecessors such as Alberico Gentili (1552–1608), but also the very idea that international law—deriving as it does from long tradition, and from the interests and practices of states—can have a single "father" is doubtful.

Grotius is associated with a "Grotian" tradition of thought about international relations—one that accepts the *sovereignty of *states, and even their right in certain circumstances to wage war, but at the same time stresses the existence of shared values and the necessity of international rules. A lawyer who took fully into account the practice of states, his thinking had considerable influence in many countries long after his death and provided the basis for a flexible tradition of thought about international law and relations, capable of being adapted to a variety of conditions and causes.

Hugo Grotius, *De Jure Belli ac Pacis Libri Tres* (1625), translated by Francis W. Kelsey (Oxford, 1925). Hedley Bull, Benedict Kingsbury, and Adam Roberts, eds., *Hugo Grotius and International Relations* (Oxford, 1990).

ADAM ROBERTS

GROUP OF SEVEN. The term "Group of 7"(G7) refers to two different, closely interrelated processes of high-level economic *diplomacy among the most powerful capitalist nations (United States, Japan, Germany, Britain, France, Italy, Canada, plus the president of the European Union), and between them and the rest of the world. The first, involving heads of state, their staffs, and key ministers, was established in 1975 and expanded in 1994 to admit post-communist Russia to some discussions on political matters. In 1998 the Birmingham Summit saw fuller Russian participation, giving birth to the "G8." The Russian role, however, is marginal on fundamental economic matters.

The second forum, the major focus of this essay, is the ongoing process of meetings and communication between finance ministers and central bankers of the summit nations, plus the Managing Director of the *International Monetary Fund (IMF). These deal with macroeconomic and related questions involved in G7 attempts to manage the global economic order. This "G7" forum was formalized at the Tokyo Summit of 1986. It is occasionally supplemented by involvement of other ministries, for example, to deal with microeconomic issues such as unemployment and trade, and links between economic development and the environment.

Since the first leaders' summit, agendas have become less "economic," and increasingly political, including East-West security, the Middle East, responses to the invasion of Afghanistan, changes in China, Eastern and Central Europe, and the former USSR, human rights, regional security, and arms control. The G7/G8 leaders' process has spawned follow-up ministerial forums held annually: the "Quadrilateral" meetings on trade between the European Union, the United States, Canada, and Japan (they began in 1982), foreign ministers' meetings (1984), environment (1992), employment (1994), crime/terrorism (1995), plus meetings on assistance to Russia (1993); Ukraine (1994); the global *information society (1995); crime (1997); and energy (1998). In some cases this involved setting up task forces to oversee G7 initiatives, e.g. on money laundering, nuclear safety, and transnational organized crime.

The "economic" G7 process is much more intensive and ongoing than the others, since it involves three or four formal meetings annually of finance ministers and central bankers, as well as informal meetings. Similar meetings have sometimes only involved the United States and Japan (G2); these two and Germany (G3 meetings have all been informal and unreported, although with the European Economic and Monetary Union in 2001 the G3 may replace the G7 as the official forum). The formal meetings are often for public (market) consumption and only reflect a small part of the continual communication and occasionally coordination and synchronization of intervention in the markets. In the 1990s, G7 meetings discussed the organization of financial transfers to pay for U.S. and British expenditures in the *Gulf War, strategy toward Soviet debt; economic and political restructuring of the former East Bloc; regulatory frameworks for the financial sector; lending programs to create a more attractive "investment climate" and "good governance" in the *Third World; trade and investment liberalization; balance of payments and fiscal problems; unemployment; fighting corruption; and the liberalization of electronic commerce.

The wider setting of the G7 process includes international economic organizations such as the Organization for Economic Cooperation and Development (G24), the *World Bank, IMF, and the Bank for International Settlements in Basel. It also involves think tanks, research institutes, and private organizations which combine perspectives from the private sector (especially financial forums such as the Group of 30), the academy, and officialdom with those of politicians. Taken together, these processes are designed to steer markets and underpin the financial stability of the system (for example, through developing common standards of capital adequacy and prudential practice for banks and other firms providing financial services and products). The summits and the G7 are indicative of a gradual process of "the internationalization of the state" and *civil society in the making of economic policy.

The G7 process has proven to be controversial. Its main limitations relate to the differences in economic and strategic priorities among its members (especially between the United States of America and Germany, the leader of the European Union's regionalization process) and the ad hoc nature of its responses to a changing global political economy. Attempts to promote coordinated macroeconomic policy, control exchange rate fluctuations, manage huge trade imbalances, or to apply prudential regulation of banking have met with minimal success. This has meant, at best, an incomplete internationalization of political authority, and at worst, a sense of political paralysis among the G7. Crucial in this equation were changed economic conditions, notably massive, almost instantaneous flows of private mobile capital in globally integrated, round-the-clock financial markets.

Following the Reaganite period of "benign neglect" of the world economy, the early to mid-1980s saw a G7 coordinated, IMF-led intervention to prevent the Third World debt crisis from triggering a global financial collapse. In 1987 G7 authorities pumped liquidity into the system to prevent the stock market crash from triggering a major global recession (as had occurred following the Wall Street crash of 1929). In the 1990s, however, the G7 seemed important in the face of not only slower growth, but also a rapidly deteriorating world economy. While footloose capital flows searched for speculative gains and safe havens in the midst of economic turbulence, global unemployment (massively underestimated in official figures) intensified. The main victims of cascading financial crises were the vulnerable and the poor. In many respects this situation was exacerbated by G7 policies which stressed liberalization and macroeconomic stabilization (austerity policies) as a condition of assistance. Moreover, since the Mexican peso crisis of 1994–1995, larger and larger amounts of public money have been expended in bailouts of private banks and investors. This process was channeled through the IMF, acting under the aegis of the G7 (but with the U.S. Treasury especially influential). The Halifax Summit communiqué of 1995 sought to "avoid future Mexicos" through enhanced IMF surveillance and resources. Nevertheless, by 1998 contagion effects of the massive Asian financial crisis (involving several "new Mexicos," including Russia) and the long Japanese economic slump reverberated throughout the world.

While at the end of the twentieth century, G7 cooperation apparently intensified (in the sense of the frequency of meetings), world economic instability had increased. It was thus legitimate to pose the question: were the forms of knowledge and the methods used by the G7 leaders to understand, interpret, and steer the brave new world of liberalized global capitalism adequate to the task? And if not, what were the alternatives to the G7 in the twenty-first century?

(See also FINANCE, INTERNATIONAL; INTERNATIONAL CO-OPERATION; INTERNATIONAL DEBT; INTERNATIONAL POLITICAL ECONOMY; NORTH-SOUTH RELATIONS; POLICY COORDINATION, ECONOMIC.)

R. Putnam and N. Bayne, *Hanging Together: The Seven-Power Summits* (London, 1987). Y. Funabashi, *Managing the Dollar: From Plaza to the Louvre* (Washington, D.C., 1988). S. Gill, "Global Finance, Monetary Policy, and Co-operation among the G7, 1944–92," in P. Cerny, ed., *Finance and World Politics* (Aldershot, Haats, U.K., 1993), pp. 86–113. C. F. Bergsten and C. Randall Henning, *Global Economic Leadership and the Group of Seven* (Washington, D.C., 1996).

STEPHEN GILL

GROUP OF 77. See NORTH-SOUTH RELATIONS; UNITED NATIONS CONFERENCE ON TRADE AND DEVELOPMENT.

GUATEMALA. The most populous Central American country, with a population of over 11 million (60 percent of which is Mayan Indian). Guatemala has had a particularly turbulent history. The extreme polarization of Guatemala's social structure stems largely from the compounding of class with ethnic divisions.

The Spanish Conquest, a violent clash of two socioeconomic systems and two cultures, forcibly "integrated" Guatemala's Indians into "Western civilization." The conquest also integrated Guatemala into an expanding capitalist world market that determined the colony's production priorities and systematically channeled its surplus to foreign economic *elites. This dependent relationship left internal legacies that have endured far longer than colonial status itself: agricultural mono-export (at the expense of food production), concentration of landholding in the hands of a small minority, and forced Indian labor as the underpinning of the entire socioeconomic structure.

Independence in 1821 brought little change in the internal structures, although it began a diversification of Guatemala's external contacts, replacing the Spanish monopoly with Britain, and later Germany and the United States. Within Guatemala, power alternated between Liberals and Conservatives until the Liberal "Revolution" of 1871. The triumph of the Liberals, who ruled with an iron hand until 1944, coincided with the rise of coffee as the dominant export at the same time, three U.S. corporations (most notably the United Fruit Company) began monopolistic operations there. These developments greatly intensified the concentration of land as well as the levels of coercion applied to the subjugated Indian labor force, with the army becoming the principal labor mobilizer and enforcer. This period also saw considerable expansion of U.S. influence over internal Guatemalan affairs, in alliance with the local landed oligarchy.

Under the weight of the crises caused by the world depression of the 1930s, the old neocolonial order finally cracked in 1944, when a broad-based coalition of middle- and working-class groups overthrew Liberal dictator Jorge Ubico. Thus began the Revolution of 1944–1954, the only genuinely democratic experience in Guatemala's entire history. The *revolution—under the governments of Juan José Arévalo (1945–1950) and Jacobo Arbenz (1951–1954)—guaranteed basic democratic liberties (including free elections), abolished forced labor, granted minimum wages and basic rights for workers and *peasants, and increased social welfare and equality. In addition, the revolutionary governments modernized and diversified Guatemalan capitalism, encouraging the growth of national enterprises and regulating foreign investment. Most significant was Arbenz's agrarian reform, which distributed land to over 100,000 peasant families.

Coming on top of other nationalistic moves by Arbenz, the expropriation of some United Fruit land prompted an angry response from the U.S. government. The United States charged Guatemala with serving as a "beachhead for Soviet expansion" in the Western Hemisphere, despite the adherence of the Arbenz government to the principles of capitalist economic development and democracy. The *Central Intelligence Agency organized the overthrow of the Arbenz government in June 1954 and installed in its place a pro-U.S. counterrevolutionary regime. This regime immediately reversed the democratic and progressive legislation of the revolution and unleashed wide-scale repression.

The legacy of the revolution and its violent end was to

compound the social polarization already characteristic of Guatemala. Nevertheless, the counterrevolution was unable to literally "reverse history" because the same underlying structural dynamics and contradictions continued to develop. The Guatemalan economy, like that of all Central America, enjoyed a thirty-year period (1950–1980) of growth based on the expansion of agricultural exports. But even *export-led growth generated turmoil because of extreme inequities in resource distribution. For example, in the 1970s, the diversification of exports brought significant new land expropriations (from peasants) and concentrations (largely in the hands of army generals using their control over the state to accumulate wealth); this impoverishment stemming from land concentration intensified geometrically.

The land crisis in Guatemala was compounded in the 1980s when pressures emanating from the world economy hit Central America as severely as the depression of the 1930s. As a consequence of this combination of domestic and international factors, the Guatemalan economy contracted during the 1980s; inflation and unemployment reached unprecedented proportions and purchasing power plummeted. As of the late 1980s, over 87 percent of the population lived below the poverty line, over two-thirds in "extreme poverty" (unable to afford a basic minimum diet). On numerous welfare indicators, Guatemala's record was the worst in the hemisphere, particularly for Mayas and women.

Politically, post-1954 Guatemala was ruled primarily by military regimes; and even during the periods of civilian government, 1966–1970 and after 1985, the army dominated politics from behind the scenes. But these hard-line regimes faced constant challenges, as Guatemala underwent a thirty-six-year civil war (1960–1996), Latin America's longest and bloodiest. The first wave of leftist guerrilla insurgency, during the 1960s, was centered in the eastern region, and although small, it was contained only after a major counterinsurgency effort, organized and financed by the United States. This first "dirty war" cost the lives of over 8,000 civilians and introduced to Latin America the phenomena of semiofficial death squads and "disappearances" of civilian opposition leaders.

Defeated temporarily in 1968, the insurgents reorganized and reinitiated their struggle in the 1970s, in the western indigenous highlands. The active involvement of up to half a million Mayas in the uprising of the late 1970s and early 1980s was without precedent, and this remarkable "awakening" in the indigenous highlands threatened the army's century-old domination over rural Guatemala. The army's "scorched earth" methods in smashing the insurgency left over 440 villages totally destroyed, some 150,000 civilians dead, and over a million uprooted and displaced. Subsequently the army militarized the entire Guatemalan countryside in order to prevent any future uprisings. But despite these very harsh means of controlling the population, by the late 1980s, Guatemala's rulers faced renewed activity by the insurgents (now united in the Unidad Revolucionaria Nacional Guatemalteca, URNG).

Even as the war continued, all major players in Guatemala and the United States recognized the need to establish formal civilian rule. The 1985 election brought to power the first civilian president in twenty years, but that government did very little to control the army or address the country's underlying problems. In the 1990 election, abstention was extremely high, and no real opposition parties were permitted. By 1991, peace talks between the government and the URNG had begun, reflecting a national consensus that Guatemala could not be truly democratized until the civil war was ended through substantive political negotiations, rather than a military victory by either side.

Even after the United Nations became the moderator in 1994, final peace accords were not signed until 29 December 1996. On paper, the accords promised historic and far-reaching changes, particularly in demilitarizing and democratizing the country and recognizing new rights for the indigenous majority. But even as participatory spaces expanded significantly, the struggles to gain governmental compliance with and implementation of the peace accords as well as to eliminate Guatemala's structural inequalities continued into the twenty-first century.

(See also GUERRILLA WARFARE; LAND REFORM.)

Carol A. Smith, ed., *Guatemalan Indians and the State, 1540–1988* (Austin, Tex., 1990). Piero Gleijeses, *Shattered Hope: The Guatemalan Revolution and the United States, 1944–1954* (Princeton, N.J., 1991). Susanne Jonas, *The Battle for Guatemala: Rebels, Death Squads and U.S. Power* (Boulder, Colo., 1991). Ricardo Falla, *Massacres in the Jungle: Ixcán, Guatemala, 1975–1982* (Boulder, Colo., 1992). Kay Warren, *Indigenous Movements and Their Critics* (Princeton, N.J., 1998). Susanne Jonas, *Of Centaurs and Doves: Guatemala's Peace Process* (Boulder, Colo., 2000).

SUSANNE JONAS

GUERRILLA WARFARE. A method utilized by small, mobile units to harass, weaken, demoralize, and combat larger conventional forces, guerrilla warfare antedates modern history. References to irregular forces appear in the Hittite *Anastas Papyrus* of the fifteenth century B.C.E.; in ancient Chinese military writings; in biblical stories depicting Jewish resistance to Syrian forces; in Roman military history against North Africans, Iberians, Germans, and Gauls; and in medieval accounts of ethnic, religious, and dynastic *wars. There is no major part of the world in which some sort of guerrilla warfare has not been utilized by the weak against the strong, by resistance forces against foreign invaders, by technically or numerically inferior armies against better-equipped, larger, or more powerful forces.

No single theater of operations or mode of combat defines guerrilla warfare. Historically, guerrilla fighters operated in rural areas, forests, mountains, and deserts. As the world's population concentrated more in cities in the nineteenth and twentieth centuries, urban guerrilla warfare became more common. Indicative of this was the publication in 1966 of the Uruguayan Abraham Guillen's *Strategy of the Urban Guerrilla*. Guillen's work synthesized the consensus of revolutionary writers on guerrilla warfare by the 1960s: "In a war of liberation, final victory is not military but political; the victorious side will destroy the enemy's morale and outlast the enemy in a war of attrition."

At times guerrilla warfare varies little in appearance from banditry; at other times it involves a relatively large number of light infantry units operating independently but in communication with one another or even with conventional forces. Typical operations involve surprise attacks and ambush; destruction of enemy supplies; cutting of transportation and communication links; attacks on advance units or stragglers; assassinations of political leaders, military officers, and police; and hostage taking. Guerrilla units often live off the land, attempt to make allies and intelligence assets of local populations, or may even be local residents who carry out guerrilla raids and then return to their lives as peasants or workers. Sanctuary in neighboring countries sometimes makes guerrillas even more effective. Examples include Greek guerrilla bases in Albania, Yugoslavia, and Bulgaria (1946–1949); Vietnamese sanctuaries in Cambodia and Laos (1950–1970); Nicaraguan contra camps in Honduras and Costa Rica (1980s); and Afghan rebel retreats in Pakistan (1980s).

Civil wars, insurgencies, and independence movements often include elements of guerrilla warfare; American independence struggles against the British in the late eighteenth century, Haitian liberation from France (1804), and the independence movements in Spanish America (1810–1825) all found irregular forces combating regular armies. Guerrilla forces often obtain support from conventional forces, whether domestic or foreign, engaged in combat against common enemies.

The term "guerrilla" warfare was popularized in modern military history by the actions of Spanish irregulars resisting Napoleon's invasion of the Iberian peninsula in 1807. Hit-and-run attacks by small Spanish units supported with matériel and advisers by British and Portuguese conventional forces introduced the *guerrilla*, or "little war," into the military lexicon. (The word was formed by adding the diminutive suffix to the Spanish word for war, *guerra*.)

In the nineteenth century, guerrilla warfare played a role in a number of European conflicts, including the Greek War of Independence (1821–1827) and the Italian *Risorgimento* (1848–1871). European colonialism in Asia and Africa induced guerrilla resistance from Burma to New Zealand and South Africa. British, French, Italian, and Portuguese armies faced periodic guerrilla struggles throughout their imperial domains.

Twentieth-century writing on guerrilla warfare has paid increasing attention to its political significance. T. E. Lawrence (*The Seven Pillars of Wisdom,* 1935) is often credited with the first theoretical contribution to understanding guerrilla warfare not as a military tactic supporting conventional military operations but as a *political* movement utilizing irregular warfare as a tactic. After World War I and the success of the Russian revolutionaries (1917), Marxist-Leninist theorists also incorporated doctrine concerning guerrilla warfare into their writings. Lenin introduced the concept of "protracted revolutionary war"; Trotsky and Stalin also accepted partisan warfare as an instrument of revolutionary struggle, providing a doctrinal foundation for Soviet assistance to *national liberation movements later in the century.

In China (1930s and 1940s) *Mao Zedong systematized and attempted to universalize the method of rural guerrilla warfare, blending classical Chinese military writings, Marxist-Leninist doctrine, and the experiences of Chinese resistance and civil war. Relying heavily on Mao and the experience of Vietnamese resistance against the Japanese and French, the Vietnamese General Vo Nguyen Giap sought to extend the international revolutionary appeal of guerrilla warfare as "people's war" in *People's War, People's Army* (1962): "Guerrillas rely upon heroic spirit to triumph over modern weapons, avoiding the enemy when he is stronger, and attacking him when he is the weaker."

Guerrilla warfare as a technique, however, is as useful to counterrevolutionary forces, ethnic and religious minorities, nationalists, or brigands as it is to revolutionaries. Likewise it may be used as an instrument of foreign policy by nations supporting irregular forces for their own policy objectives. Examples include Cuban support for guerrillas throughout Latin America in the 1960s and early 1970s; U.S. support for Afghan Muslim irregulars and Nicaraguan contras (1980s); East German support for Chilean resistance fighters (1970s, 1980s); and South African support for Angolan guerrilla forces (1970s–1990s).

Guerrilla warfare frustrates conventional armies by making "victory" impossible in the traditional sense. Because guerrillas attack in small numbers, by surprise or ambush, and disappear into the surrounding countryside or towns, it is extremely difficult to achieve military success, that is, destruction of enemy forces. Inability to distinguish between guerrilla fighters and local populations generates tension between military personnel and civilians. The desire for intelligence concerning guerrilla organization, operations, and location frequently leads conventional forces to adopt repressive measures that alienate noncombatants. Historically these measures have included interrogation by *torture, collective punishment of populations where guerrilla activity or presence is suspected, concentration of populations into "protected zones" in the hope of denying resources to guerrillas, forcing local populations to join in combat against guerrillas, and requisitioning supplies or animals from peasant populations.

Twentieth-century *counterinsurgency techniques became somewhat more sophisticated as a result of the lessons learned from a number of guerrilla wars, for example, the British experience in the South African campaigns against the Boers (1899–1902), in Ireland against the Irish Republican Army (1919–1921), against African insurgents such as the Mau Mau in Kenya (1952), and in Malaya and Cyprus (1950s). French conflicts in Algeria and Indochina (1952–1954) as well as the U.S. experience in Vietnam (1960s–1970s) and widespread guerrilla wars in Latin America (1960s–1980s) also contributed to modern counterinsurgency methods. These experiences have led to a growing awareness of the political as well as military dimension of guerrilla warfare.

Nevertheless, some revolutionaries, nationalists, and opponents of incumbent regimes around the globe continued to utilize guerrilla warfare into the late 1990s and early twenty-first century. The Revolutionary Armed Forces of Colombia (FARC), Sendero Luminoso (Shining Path), Tupac Amaru in Peru, the New People's Army and Muslim insurgents in the Philippines, radical pro-Palestinian groups in the Middle East, the Zapatistas in Mexico, the Polisario Front in the western Sahara, and liberation fighters in Chechnya, Russia, exemplify the widespread and persisting challenge of guerrilla movements in the contemporary world.

(See also ALGERIAN WAR OF INDEPENDENCE; CHINESE REVOLUTION; DECOLONIZATION; GUEVARA, ERNESTO.)

Brian Loveman and Thomas Davies, *Che Guevara on Guerrilla Warfare,* 3d ed. (Wilmington, Del., 1997). Ian F. W. Beckett, *Encyclopedia of Guerrilla Warfare* (Santa Barbara, Calif., 1999).

BRIAN LOVEMAN

GUEST WORKERS. See FOREIGN WORKERS.

GUEVARA, Ernesto. With the victory over Cuban dictator Fulgencio Batista in 1959, Ernesto ("Che") Guevara became the symbol of revolutionary *guerrilla warfare against the old order in Latin America. An advocate of armed struggle to overturn capitalism and create *socialism in the *Third World, Guevara's portrait on millions of posters and banners served notice of the revolutionary challenge represented by the *Cuban Revolution to Latin American regimes and to the foreign policy of the United States.

Ernesto Guevara was born 14 June 1928 in Rosario, Argentina, the descendant of two old and respected Argentine families. His parents early rejected the conventions of Argentine society and adopted a near bohemian lifestyle, thereby providing Ernesto with a liberal political ambience enjoyed by few youth of his social class. That advantage was offset, however, by the fact that Guevara was stricken early with the asthma that was to debilitate him throughout his life and severely affect his activities as adventurer and guerrilla warrior, particularly in 1967 in Bolivia.

While still in medical school, Guevara traveled widely in South America, and, when he finished, he embarked on the odyssey that was to shape his life and that of the world around him. He was in Guatemala in 1954 when the U.S.-orchestrated coup ousted the government of Jacobo Arbenz Guzmán. After the victory of the Central Intelligence Agency-trained forces in Guatemala, he went to Mexico where he joined a band of young, revolutionary exiles from Peru and *Cuba.

Led by Fidel *Castro, the rebels sailed to Cuba on the ship *Granma* in December 1956. The Cuban Revolution had begun. During the struggle against Batista, Guevara served both as a military commander and as doctor, but it was as the former that he became renowned in the early 1960s. Guevara served in a series of posts, including a disastrous tenure as minister of industry (1961–1965). In 1965, he dropped from public view, and was widely reported to be leading guerrilla movements all over the Third World (Africa, Southeast Asia, etc.). In his famous treatise *Guerrilla Warfare* (1960), Guevara had argued forcefully that revolutionary guerrilla warfare would be successful only in those countries where a "Caribbean-type dictatorship" was present. Later he modified that thesis several times until, in 1966, in a speech to the Tricontinental Congress in Havana, he called for the creation of "many Vietnams" to confront the United States and the rest of the imperialist West. That his initial thesis was the most correct was proved tragically in the Bolivian fiasco of 1966–1967 where he and his followers were captured or killed. Guevara was taken alive, but killed by his captors.

Guevara's political career after Batista's defeat might lead one to conclude that he had failed miserably. But to dismiss Guevara in that way is to miss the true significance of his life and work. His was a call to action, a call to the youth of Latin America to rise up and throw off the shackles of the ages. Even more important, however, was his promise of ultimate victory to those who kept the faith and persevered in their revolutionary tasks and fervor. His life and his message served as the inspiration and motivating force behind the guerrilla movements that sprang up all over Latin America in the 1960s and 1970s. That inspiration and example also served to galvanize the United States into altering seriously its military posture in the hemisphere, and it pushed the Soviet Union into military, political, and economic positions in Latin America that it would have preferred greatly to avoid. (See also REVOLUTION.)

John Gerassi, ed., *Venceremos: The Speeches and Writings of Ernesto Che Guevara* (London, 1968). Rolando E. Bonachea and Nelson P. Valdés, *Che: Selected Works of Ernesto Guevara* (Cambridge, Mass., 1969). Donald C. Hodges, *The Legacy of Che Guevara* (London, 1977).

THOMAS M. DAVIES, JR.
BRIAN LOVEMAN

GUINEA. Located on the coast of West Africa, Guinea, a former French colony, became independent in 1958. Guinea was able to preserve its freedom and national sovereignty for twenty-six years under President Ahmed Sékou Touré, by playing off the West against the East. The Parti Démocratique de Guinée (PDG), led by Sékou Touré, spearheaded the struggle for national liberation and was instrumental in the social, political, and cultural development of postcolonial Guinea, despite the pressures from France and its Western allies. Because of its rejection of the membership of the French Community, Guinea was ostracized and denied economic and technical assistance, in the French Community, Guinea was ostracized and denied economic and technical assistance, in addition to the withdrawal of all French civil servants. In reaction, Guinea turned to the East but limited the communist influence by adapting its economic policies and its ideology to the needs and possibilities of the postcolonial situation. From 1958 to 1964, the PDG encouraged and supported the active participation of all social groups in the process of making decisions. It addressed the social injustices and inequalities from the past, through state-organized agricultural cooperatives and subsidized small industries, the abolition of polygamy, the suppression of ethnocentric and regionalist associations, and the struggle against nepotism and gender discrimination in education and work.

After 1964, influenced by the exacerbation of the tensions between the privileged groups (traders, plantation owners, lawyers, and teachers) and its supporters (peasants, workers, women, and youths), the PDG initiated the dictatorship of the "class of the people" against the "class of the enemies of the people." This was the beginning of Sékou Touré's personal rule. As a matter of fact, from 1964 on, the PDG controlled every aspect of the society. Exiled Guineans and their allies in Africa and the West made many attempts to overthrow Sékou Touré and his government in the 1970s. The PDG used these attacks to substantiate its allegations of plotting, and indirectly justify the decisions to purge the party and the state of Sékou Touré's enemies and explain away the deepening of the social and economic crises. In 1982, responding to the overwhelming economic crisis of the late 1970s, Guinea reconciled with France. As a result, Sékou Touré introduced radical reforms to promote individual initiative and free enterprise. These new liberal ideas influenced the ideology of the PDG and dictated a new capitalist approach to the postcolonial economic problems. President Sékou Touré died unexpectedly, in March 1984.

Two weeks after Sékou Touré's death, a successful military coup transformed the political landscape of Guinea. The constitution was abolished and the PDG was banned and replaced by a military junta, the Conseil Militaire de Redressement National (CMRN). A military dictatorship was established, with Lansana Conté, a general from the Susu ethnic group, as CMRN chairman and president of the Republic. He inherited all of Sékou Touré's dictatorial powers, including the political control of the state and the use of presidential decrees to nominate government officials. A military-dominated council of ministers and a majority of military officers turned provincial governors ran the government and the four major provinces respectively. Nepotism and corruption soon led to popular discontent, an attempted coup d'état in July 1985, and the subsequent physical liquidation of a considerable number of the prominent elites of the Mandenka ethnic group. Pursuing Sékou Touré's early initiative with the Western financial institutions, the military leaders turned to the World Bank (WB) and the International Monetary Fund (IMF) and gradually accepted all of the conditions laid down for economic recovery. This led to new reforms, with the appointment of a large number of civilian officials to the cabinet.

A new constitution was adopted in 1991 and a multiparty system was introduced. Thirty-nine political parties were created, the majority of which were ethnically based. In the two elections held respectively in 1993 and 1998, President Lansana Conté emerged as the winner. During these elections, President Conté's party, the Parti d'Unité et du Progrès (PUP) was closely competing with four major opposition parties: Rassemblement du Peuple de Guinée (RPG); Unité pour la Nouvelle Republique (UNR); Parti Republican Populaire (PRP); and Parti Démocratique de Guinée-Ahmed Sékou Touré (PDGAST), the renewed PDG. The opposition parties are now united through a coalition, the Coordination Démocratique (Codem). There has been a rebirth of freedom of expression, with the publication of numerous newspapers and magazines of different tendencies. However, the government still controls the national radio and television stations, and the Conté regime remains authoritarian and brutal.

In the economy, small industries have been privatized and all of the state subsidized welfare programs have been abandoned and replaced by ill-functioning *non-governmental organizations (NGO), financed by the external donors. The private sector is being promoted through the removal of state controls over prices, trade, and the exchange rate. Consequently, the state is losing its powers to regulate the economy and can no longer protect workers, peasants, women, and youths. As a result, hundreds of thousands of workers have lost their jobs and there are almost no job opportunities for even the educated youths. Wages are still very low, and they are not adjusted to the inflation-ridden new market economy. The number of discontented people is growing proportionately to the current hardships. However, compared to the other West African societies, Guinea has been able to contain its social contradictions by resisting the policies of the World Bank and International Monetary Fund, which emphasize the market against the political, social, and cultural factors. Its leaders are very active in the *Economic Community of West African States (ECOWAS). How long will the people continue to accept the present economic hardships? If unchecked, the present economic crisis may lead to a deeper political instability and unpredictable social upheavals.

(See also FRANCOPHONE AFRICA; PRIVATIZATION.)

Thomas E. O'Toole, *Historical Dictionary of Guinea (Republic of Guinea/ Conakry)*, 2d ed., African Historical Dictionaries, no. 16 (Metuchen, N.J., 1987). Patrick Manning, *Francophone Sub-Saharan Africa, 1880–1985*, 2d ed. (Cambridge, U.K., 1998).

MOHAMED SAIDOU N'DAOU

GUINEA-BISSAU. One of Africa's smallest countries, Guinea-Bissau has experienced one of the most turbulent political developments on the continent since its independence from Portugal on 10 September 1974. Comprising a population of about one million during the late 1990s, made up mainly of five ethnic groups, namely, the Balante (32 percent), the Fulani (22 percent), the Mandyako (14.5 percent), the Mende or Mandingo (13 percent), and the Pepel (7 percent), Guinea-Bissau is an amalgam of several isolated islands and the archipelago of Bijagos (eighteen islands), and a small inland portion that, put together, account for the country's total surface area of 13,948 square miles. The population is predominantly Muslim (about 46 percent), and 14.4 percent Catholic, the remainder being religious traditionalists or Protestants.

One of the poorest sixteen countries in the world, this former Portuguese colony has few natural resources to provide an acceptable living standard to its population. Cashew nuts, peanuts, rice, millet, palm kernels, and sorghum help sustain the population, which is often visited by recurrent and devastating Sahelian droughts. Lack of know-how, premature nationalization of resources, such as land and private enterprise, and forcible establishment of collective farms to conform to the dictates of "scientific socialism," which the government adopted following independence, led Guinea-Bissau to the brink of economic disaster. The situation, aggravated by the resentment of Guineans over the predominance of Cape Verdian leadership, resulted in the first coup d'état against President Luís Cabral, half-brother of Amílcar Cabral, the nationalist who founded the Partido Africano de Indpendência da Guiné e Cabo Verde (PAIGC) in 1956. Cabral declared a guerrilla offensive against the Portuguese in 1963, capturing two thirds of the country by 1972. Unfortunately, he was assassinated by Portuguese agents in January 1973. Yet the war continued until April 1974, when the Portuguese abandoned their wars in Africa following the overthrow of Premier Marcello Caetano's government by young officers in Lisbon. Portugal recognized Guinea-Bissau's independence on 10 September 1974, even though many countries had already extended their diplomatic recognition to the colony's unilateral declaration of independence the previous year.

In 1980 a split occurred between Cape Verdians and Guineans, which resulted in the approval of two separate constitutions and the overthrow of Luís Cabral by Prime Minister Bernardo Nino Vieira in November. Vieira subsequently ruled Guinea-Bissau through a Revolutionary Council that was almost entirely military, still maintaining the one-party structure adopted at independence. The forcible removal of Cabral and the regime's autocratic nature, manifested in arrests and executions of opponents of the government, resulted in widespread discontent within the country. This was exacerbated by Guinea-Bissau's poverty and mismanagement of its economy, which led to constant labor strikes during the 1980s, forcing the government to accept, in 1983, a structural adjustment program that devalued the Guinean peso by 40 percent.

In October 1990, a national conference of 350 delegates, representing all walks of life, gathered in Bissau to recommend constitutional democratic reforms. Supported by the PAIGC in 1991, Vieira announced that all reforms would be completed by 1993, that socialism would be replaced by a free market economy, and that the single-party system would be over. Thus, in 1992, a Multi-Party Commission of Transition commenced its constitutional work that would introduce meaningful democratic changes in the country.

However, the endless arrests of opponents, in the army, the government, and at large, continued to the point of almost derailing the move toward a multiparty system. Presidential and legislative elections took place on 3–4 January 1994, with eight presidential candidates and 1,136 candidates for the National Assembly running. Following a second round of a president run-off on 7 August 1994, Vieira defeated his opponent, Kumba Yalla, by a vote margin of 52.03 percent to 47.97 percent. He then appointed Manuel Saturnino as prime minister. In the National Assembly elections, the PAIGC captured 62 of 100 seats, thus gaining a clear majority. Over a dozen parties participated in the new democratic process.

However, Vieira's election did not guarantee political stability. Guinea's admission into the monetary Central African Franc zone in 1997, which displeased many Guineans, alleged Guinea-Bissau military assistance to Senegalese Casamance secessionists, which elicited air strikes by the Senegalese Armed Forces on Guinea-Bissau territory; and a maritime border dispute with Guinea-Conakry created unprecedented political unrest in the tiny republic. Economic hardship brought about a four-day strike of public sector employees in August 1997, and forced the government to raise salaries by 50 percent. In May 1998 Vieira was renominated PAIGC president, but, in June, he was overthrown by the military under the leadership of General Ansumane Mane. Despite the involvement of 1,300 Senegalese and 400 Guinean troops, the government was unable to regain control. Mediation by ECOWAS and the Lusophone community failed to resolve the crisis, and General Mane prevailed in 1999. He organized elections that were won by the veteran opposition leader Kumba Yalla.

(See also LUSOPHONE AFRICA.)

R. A. Lobban and P. Mendy, *Historical Dictionary of Guinea-Bissau* (Lanham, Md., 1997). C. S. Proenca, *Os efeitos da politica de estabilizacao e ajustamento estrutural no bem-estar das familias urbanas: O caso de Bissau, 1986–1993* (Lisbon, 1998).

MARIO J. AZEVEDO

GULF STATES. Before 1971, Bahrain, Qatar, and the seven smaller Arab Gulf emirates—Abu Dhabi, Dubai, Sharjah, Ras al-Khaimah, Fujairah, Umm al-Qaiwain, and Ajman—were all protectorates of Britain, which provided political advisers to each ruling family and overall supervision by a Resident based in the Gulf. Oman enjoyed nominal independence, although British advisers continually intervened in the country's internal affairs to prop up the ruler of the port of Muscat in his struggles with tribal confederations of the interior.

Bahrain and Dubai remained important commercial centers into the 1920s and 1930s, while Sharjah served as headquarters for British military forces in the area during the 1940s and 1950s. Internal politics in each emirate consisted largely of jockeying between the ruling family and prominent merchants for control over the local economy, centered around the harvesting and distribution of pearls. In Dubai, wealthy merchants forced the ruler to recognize a consultative council in 1938, although he disbanded it after only five months. In Bahrain, the beginnings of oil production in the 1930s and the construction of a large-scale oil refinery on the islands created a relatively large and vocal working class, whose leaders joined with discontented tradespeople to form a series of nationalist movements in the 1950s. Omani politics remained insulated from the effects of popular mobilization in neighboring principalities during the 1930s and 1940s.

Throughout the region, the coming of oil reinforced the position of the ruling families and their British-run administrations, providing them with resources to use in suppressing or co-opting their domestic opponents. Abu Dhabi's vast oil revenues and its ruler's willingness to spend them on economic and social projects in the six smaller emirates to the north provided the basis for the formation of the United Arab Emirates (UAE) at the start of 1972, following Britain's withdrawal from the Gulf. Beginning in the 1960s, oil monies provided the ruler of Oman with the means to achieve both the unification of the coastal enclaves of Muscat and Salalah with the country's tribal hinterland and the suppression of the rebellion in the southern province of Dhofar, bringing an unprecedented degree of stability to Omani politics.

Bahrain, refused a preeminent role in a larger federation of Arab Gulf states, opted to stand alone, becoming independent in August 1971. The ruler, Shaikh 'Isa bin Sulman Al Khalifah, became head of state, while the heir apparent, his son Shaikh Hamad, became minister of defense and Shaikh Isa's brother, Shaikh Khalifah bin Sulman, took the office of prime minister. Close relatives of the ruler have continued to occupy the most important posts in the cabinet, joined by a limited number of Western-educated notables drawn from the established rich merchant community. The size and scope of the central administration grew throughout the 1970s, as the state initiated industrial projects, promulgated labor laws, and expanded health and other social welfare services. The 1980s saw a burgeoning of the country's armed forces, with major air and naval bases constructed on the islands according to plans drawn up by the U.S. Army Corps of Engineers and sizable weapons purchases from U.S arms manufacturers.

Trade unionists orchestrated a wave of strikes in Bahrain's larger industrial enterprises in early 1974, prompting severe repression on the part of state security forces. In the wake of these strikes, hard-liners within the ruling family pushed through a new security law that authorized the ministry of the interior to arrest and imprison anyone suspected of "endangering or . . . planning to endanger the security of the state or disturb public order."

With the suppression of the trade union movement, the most serious challenges to the regime have come from Bahrain's heterogeneous Islamist movement. The more moderate or reformist wing of this movement, consisting of such organizations as the Sunni Society for Social Reform and the Shi'i Party of the Call to Islam, advocates limits on state intervention in social and religious affairs; the more radical or militant wing, including the Islamic Action Organization and the Iranian-sponsored Islamic Front for the Liberation of Bahrain, calls for the overthrow of the existing political and social order, by violence if necessary. Mass demonstrations organized by Shi'i militants broke out repeatedly during 1979–1980. In December 1981, the authorities announced that they had broken up a plot by a group of militants having ties to the Islamic Front to assassinate the ruler and take over key government buildings.

Bahrain's Islamist movement revived after the 1990–1991 *Gulf Crisis, when the government refused to recognize petitions demanding the reinstatement of the National Assembly. Shi'i preachers appealed to the population to support the drive to recall Parliament and criticized the authorities for failing to combat unemployment among Bahraini citizens. Their efforts mobilized not only the general public but also such previously apolitical forces as the members of local religious societies (husainiyyahs) and women in outlying villages. Growing Shi'i activism led to clashes between protesters and the police throughout 1994. By the last months of 1995, political agitation had turned into outbursts of arson and sabotage. Luxury hotels, state-affiliated commercial and industrial establishments, and cafes catering to expatriate laborers were all attacked during the course of 1996.

Qatar also remained outside the Arab Gulf federation and became independent in September 1971. Five months later, the prime minister and de facto ruler, Shaikh Khalifah bin Hamad Al Thani, deposed his cousin and took the title of emir with the overt support of neighboring Saudi Arabia. Factional skirmishing between relatives of the deposed ruler and the new emir continued to shape the country's internal politics, and led to a proliferation of high government posts as a way of mollifying discontented senior shaikhs. Declining oil revenues after 1986 heightened disaffection both within the ruling family and among the general population. In January 1992, representatives of fifty prominent Qatari families petitioned the ruler to set up an elected national council as a means of "guaranteeing an effective participation of the people" in public policy making. The emir flatly refused to acknowledge the petition, and those who had signed the document found themselves subject to harassment by the police. The heir apparent, Shaikh Hamad bin Khalifah, deposed his father to become ruler in June 1995.

Abu Dhabi, Dubai, Sharjah, Fujairah, Umm al-Qaiwain, and Ajman merged to form the UAE in July 1971. The ruler of Abu Dhabi, Shaikh Zayyid bin Sultan Al Nuhayyan, became president of the federation, while the ruler of Dubai, Shaikh Rashid bin Maktum, became vice president. When Ras al-Khaimah finally joined the UAE in February 1972, a Supreme Federal Council consisting of the seven rulers was established with authority to elect the president and vice president, ratify federal legislation, and draw up the federal budget. The Supreme Federal Council also approves the appointment of a federal prime minister nominated by the president; the president and prime minister then select the members of a Council of Ministers charged with formulating and implementing laws for the federation as a whole. A representative Federal National Council meets to debate issues confronting the union, but this body has no power to initiate legislation. The federal bureaucracy is funded primarily by Abu Dhabi and is staffed largely by nationals from Dubai and Sharjah, along with considerable numbers of Arab expatriates. The line demarcating federal administration from individual emirate administrations remains fuzzy despite the dissolution of most emirate cabinets soon after independence.

Each emirate has a history of factionalism among prominent shaikhs within its respective ruling family. Shaikh Zayyid of Abu Dhabi deposed his brother Shaikh Shakhbut to become ruler in 1966, naming a close relative of Shaikh Shakhbut UAE minister of the interior as a way of keeping accounts balanced. The ruler of Sharjah was assassinated in 1972 by one of his cousins, who had previously been ousted by the British; the Supreme Federal Council stepped in to appoint the ruler's son, Shaikh Sultan bin Muhammad, to succeed his father. In June 1987, Shaikh Sultan's brother attempted to seize control of the emirate. This putsch was defeated only when the Supreme Federal Council nominated Shaikh Sultan's rival as Sharjah's heir apparent. Dubai, on the other hand, carried out a more peaceful transition in leadership following the death of Shaikh Rashid in September 1990, partly owing to the integration of the ruling family into the local commercial elite.

What little opposition there has been to the regimes that constitute the UAE has come from groups impatient with the pace of change in the federation. State employees in the poorer northern emirates struck in May 1981 over the government's failure to peg salaries to the cost of living; students at the federal university in al-Ain have periodically demonstrated and boycotted classes to protest the prohibition against forming a student union and to demand that greater control over university administration be given to UAE nationals. A series of isolated bombings in Dubai and Abu Dhabi during the early 1980s prompted local security services to tighten restrictions on and surveillance of foreign nationals, particularly Palestinians, residing in the country.

In Oman, eighty-five years of continual conflict between tribal forces loyal to the Ibadi imamate centered in the valleys and plains of the interior and townspeople subject to the sultan in the port city of Muscat came to an end with Sultan Said bin Taimur's reconquest of the hinterlands around the capital and the resignation of the imam in December 1955. The former imam almost immediately joined his brother in soliciting support from Omani laborers working in Saudi Arabia for an antisultanate organization, the Oman Revolutionary Movement. Armed members of this organization landed along the northern coast in June 1957 and, after pushing the sultan's armed forces out of the area, were in turn defeated by British troops and aircraft seconded to the ruler.

Five years later, discontented inhabitants of the southern province of Dhofar began raiding oil company and military installations around the town of Salalah. These guerrillas held a congress in June 1965 and issued a manifesto calling for the province's independence from the central government in Muscat. More radical activists took control of a second congress in September 1968, renamed the movement the Popular Front for the Liberation of the Occupied Arab Gulf, and adopted an explicitly anti-imperialist platform. This new organization initiated a campaign of armed struggle against government officials and troops throughout Dhofar, with the assistance of the People's Republic of China, the Soviet Union, and Iraq. Early victories sparked the formation of a companion movement in the north, which carried out unsuccessful attacks on two garrisons in the summer of 1970. The formation of this second organization prompted critics of the sultan within the regime to encourage his son, Qabus, to seize control of the country.

Immediately after taking power, Sultan Qabus adopted a dual policy of granting amnesty to any dissidents who would surrender to the central government and complementing military moves against the Popular Front with development projects in the districts from which it drew its support. This combination put Popular Front activists on the defensive, and a series of government victories on the battlefield during 1972–1973 forced the guerrillas to retreat to the most desolate areas of the south. State forces overran the Front's remaining strongholds during the summer and fall of 1974, and by the end of 1976 the sultan was able to claim that order had been fully restored in Dhofar.

In November 1980, Sultan Qabus ordered a ministerial committee to consider ways to broaden the process of formal consultation within policy-making circles. The committee's deliberations resulted in a set of decrees creating an appointed State Consultative Council the following October. The sultan presided over the first session of the new council in early November. This body was granted no legislative powers; its mandate was limited to advising the ruler on proposed laws, and its meetings were held in secret.

At the height of the Gulf crisis of 1990–1991, Sultan Qabus announced that an elected Omani Consultative Council would replace the State Consultative Council. In actuality, caucuses of provincial notables meet periodically to draw up lists of candidates that are vetted by the deputy prime minister for legal affairs before being presented to the sultan, who appoints council members from the individuals named on the lists. Dissatisfaction with this procedure contributed to the appearance of a clandestine Islamist movement in 1994 that attracted support from professionals and well-to-do businesspeople in the larger cities.

(See also DECOLONIZATION; ISLAM; MIDDLE EAST; RELIGION AND POLITICS.)

John Duke Anthony, *Arab States of the Lower Gulf: People, Politics, Petroleum* (Washington, D.C., 1975). Calvin H. Allen, *Oman: The Modernization of the Sultanate* (Boulder, Colo., 1987). Fred H. Lawson, *Bahrain: The Modernization of Autocracy* (Boulder, Colo., 1989). Jill Crystal, *Oil and Politics in the Gulf: Rulers and Merchants in Kuwait and Qatar* (Cambridge, U.K., 1995).

FRED H. LAWSON

GULF WAR. The Gulf War, fought between *Iraq and a military coalition led by the United States, lasted just forty-three days—from 17 January through 27 February 1991. Coalition forces launched the war in response to Iraqi leader Saddam *Hussein's invasion and annexation of the small, oil-rich state of *Kuwait on 2 August 1991.

The United States and Britain demanded Iraq's withdrawal, and they obtained a strong international consensus, reflected in a series of UN *Security Council resolutions. Resolution 660, adopted unanimously within twenty-four hours of the invasion, called for the immediate and unconditional withdrawal of Iraqi forces. Resolution 661 of 6 August imposed severe economic *sanctions against Iraq. And eventually, Resolution 678 of 29 November authorized the use of *force against Iraq.

Although the United States obtained UN backing, it chose to act militarily and diplomatically with considerable autonomy. Claiming an imminent threat to the *security of *Saudi Arabia and the Persian Gulf oil-producing region, the U.S. administration of President George *Bush rushed U.S. naval and ground units to the Gulf on 7 August, bypassing possible formation of a UN multinational force. Britain (and later, France) contributed contingents, as did Egypt, Syria, Saudi Arabia, and a number of other Gulf states; several other states in Europe and Asia contributed naval, medical, or other ancillary units. By the time the war began, however, U.S. forces accounted for about three-quarters of the combat personnel and an even higher proportion of heavy weapons, aircraft, and naval ships.

In the months leading up to the military conflict, intense diplomatic activity—by UN Secretary-General Javier Pérez de Cuéllar, French President François Mitterrand, Soviet President Mikhael Gorbachev, and others—sought to obtain Iraq's withdrawal from Kuwait before a 15 January deadline specified in UN Resolution 678. Iraqi leader Saddam Hussein proposed to link his settlement of the crisis to the withdrawal of Israel from the territories it occupied. Amid mixed signals from Baghdad, efforts to find a diplomatic formula for Iraqi withdrawal were rejected by the United States and its allies, who affirmed that Iraqi withdrawal was not negotiable.

At an early stage, the United States moved toward a military resolution of the conflict. On 8 November, President Bush deployed 200,000 additional troops, moving the coalition forces from a defensive to an offensive posture. And on 18 November, U.S. officials stated that "neutralization" of Iraq's military and nuclear capacity had become additional objectives beyond Iraqi withdrawal from Kuwait.

By the time hostilities broke out, the United States and its coalition partners had assembled more than 750,000 military personnel, 1,200 high-performance aircraft, 300 naval vessels including eight aircraft carriers, and 1,800 tanks. Many of these forces and weapons, drawn from Western Europe, would not have been available had not the *Cold War ended and the Soviet Union given its high-profile accord to the *war plans of its former enemies.

In the combat theater, coalition forces faced approximately 400,000 Iraqi troops, armed with relatively advanced Western and Soviet arms acquired during the long and bloody *Iran-Iraq War (1980–1988). The Iraqi army was not a particularly high quality fighting force, however, and its strategic reserves were extremely weak compared to those of the United States and its coalition partners.

The coalition campaign began with a forty-day air war. Intense, round-the-clock bombing destroyed not only military targets but also much of Iraq's civilian infrastructure, including power plants and factories. The war ended with a brief and devastating four-day ground campaign. As Iraqi forces retreated, they were exposed to lethal air and ground attacks.

To obtain a cease-fire and armistice, Iraq was forced to agree to all relevant Security Council resolutions, including renunciation of all claims to Kuwait and agreement to pay heavy reparations for the damage done in Kuwait. Soon thereafter, the Bush administration announced that it was seeking to oust Saddam Hussein. The UN imposed stringent conditions on the lifting of sanctions, and Iraq refused to comply. There followed much additional suffering in Iraq because of abortive antigovernment uprisings and UN general trade sanctions that devastated the Iraqi economy for many years after the war's end.

The war was very costly. In addition to the great physical destruction suffered by Iraq and Kuwait, coalition direct expenses (including social-aid packages) have been estimated at well over $150 billion. The United States was unable and unwilling to bear more than a small share of these costs, so it obtained financing from various partners, especially Kuwait and Saudi Arabia. The Saudis' conservative estimate of their total war-related expenses was $54 billion; Kuwait spent at least $25 billion (and probably far more); Japan and Germany contributed about $10–20 billion each; and Britain, France, the United States, and some small Gulf states accounted for most of the remainder of the outlays.

Though the war resulted in fewer than 500 casualties among coalition forces, Iraqi military casualties have been estimated at 50,000–100,000, while civilian casualties are thought to have reached at least 10,000, mostly due to the air war. In addition, casualties due to the civil war within Iraq are believed to have reached 50,000.

The crisis also led to massive displacement of people. At least half a million fled from Kuwait, including many *foreign workers who lost homes, savings, and livelihood. Iraq also expelled 1–2 million Egyptians and other foreign workers; Saudi Arabia expelled as many as 1 million Yemeni workers because Yemen refused to support the coalition. And after the postwar Iraqi uprisings, approximately 2 million people were displaced. Altogether, 4–5 million people migrated within an eight-month period, one of the largest population movements in recent history.

The war had a very serious environmental impact. The Iraqis released large quantities of crude oil into the Persian Gulf, destroying fish and wildlife on a vast scale. They also set fire to most of the Kuwaiti oil wells before withdrawing from the emirate. Coalition bombing, which struck nuclear and chemical weapons installations, also caused serious environmental damage. Coalition bombing may also have contributed to the release of oil into the Persian Gulf, while the coalition air and ground campaign left lethal radioactive powder from depleted uranium shells in a wide area of military operations.

The coalition move toward war was opposed by a substantial segment of *public opinion in most of the involved countries. In the United States, Congress was narrowly divided on the issue and antiwar demonstrations took place in many cities. In France, Defense Minister Jean-Pierre Chevènement resigned. And in many countries throughout the world there were large and sometimes violent public protests. Once the war was under way, the U.S. government and most of its Western partners were able to rally domestic public support, thanks in part to careful management of mass-media coverage, but worldwide there remained broad opposition. Debate continues as to whether the war was necessary to accomplish Iraqi withdrawal from Kuwait and why the United States went to war with a regime it had armed and supported until just before the crisis.

The war was the first major military conflict in the post–Cold War period. As such, the Soviet Union played only a secondary role in the crisis and in general tended to support the United States. The United States emerged from the war as the undisputed leader of the global political and military system.

(See also Diplomacy; International Migration; Refugees; United Nations.)

Phyllis Bennis and Michel Moushabeck, *Beyond the Storm: A Gulf Crisis Reader* (New York, 1991). John Bulloch and Harvey Morris, *Saddam's War: The Origins of the Kuwait Conflict and the International Response* (London, 1991). Theodore Draper, "The Gulf War Reconsidered," *New York Review of Books*, 16 January 1992, 46–53. Theodore Draper, "The True History of the Gulf War," *New York Review of Books*, 30 January 1992, 38–45. Dilip Hiro, *Desert Shield to Desert Storm* (New York, 1992).
— JAMES A. PAUL

GUYANA. A former British colony which gained independence in 1966, Guyana was governed from December 1964 to October 1992 by the socialist People's National Congress (PNC). The PNC was replaced that year by the People's Progressive Party with a civic component (PPP/Civic) led by Dr. Cheddi Jagan, the PPP's founder. He died suddenly in April 1997 and his widow, Janet Jagan, led the PPP/Civic to a second electoral win in December of that year. The major parties remain the mainly black PNC and the predominantly East Indian PPP/Civic. Individuals of Indian descent comprise 51 percent of a population of approximately three-quarters of a million and blacks 38.3 percent. Those of Portuguese and other European origins, Chinese, and native Amerindians make up the remainder of the Guyanese population.

Upon winning the presidency in 1992, Dr. Cheddi Jagan embraced centrist economic policies, accepting structural adjustment programs and other neoliberal policies. These were a continuation of the PNC's policies during its last two years in office, and they promoted foreign investment in joint ventures with the state via privatization of state-owned industries and services. Some social welfare programs were also expanded or initiated. Institutional infrastructure was weak, but the government's policies attracted support from multilateral sources including the International Monetary Fund (IMF), the World Bank, and the Inter-American Development Bank (IDB), as well as the United States, Britain, Canada, and some Third World countries.

The 1997 elections that brought Janet Jagan to power were challenged by the PNC, which claimed that the elections were rigged. Independent foreign agencies and human rights organizations all declared the elections "free and fair," as did a specially convened Caribbean Community (Caricom) audit team. An agreement by the PNC, led by ex-president Desmond Hoyte, to cooperate with the new government was brokered by Caribbean leaders at their 1998 summit in St. Lucia. However, matters have significantly deteriorated since then. Mrs. Jagan has been pilloried by the PNC for being a white American even though she has lived in Guyana for over fifty years as a naturalized citizen, and tensions between blacks and East Indians increased, raising the specter of the racial riots of the early 1960s. Blacks charge widespread discrimination by East Indians in government and the private sector. There are also claims by East Indians that blacks attack them because of prejudice.

The professionalism of the police and the Guyana Defense Force (GDF) has prevented violence on a large scale. The police, however, have been accused of excessive use of force upon occasion. Racial animosities have contributed to political instability and a climate inhospitable to local and foreign investment. The current government's focus is on pursuit of sustainable development by boosting production in gold mining and forestry along with the traditional exports of bauxite, sugar, and rice. But economic growth is marginal, and civil discourse between the government and the opposition has been marred by incendiary rhetoric, which has undermined progress toward greater democracy.

In foreign policy, Guyana continues to be moderately pro–Third World in its bilateral relations and in support of multilateral issues such as environmental cooperation at the United Nations (UN), in the Nonaligned Movement (NAM), and in the Organization of American States (OAS). Given the country's political instability and weakening economy, its leadership role in Caricom has greatly diminished. In recent years Guyana has also become a player in the export of illegal drugs to the Caribbean and the United States. Corruption is rife as people at all levels seek to cash in on this lucrative trade. Despite ongoing cooperation among Guyana, other Caribbean countries, and the United States to lessen and ultimately to stop the trade, the prognosis for success is not encouraging.

Percy H. Hintzen, *The Costs of Regime Survival: Racial Mobilization, Elite Domination, and the Control of the State in Guyana and Trinidad* (Cambridge, U.K., 1989). Ralph R. Premdas, "Guyana: Ethnic Politics and the Erosion of Human Rights and Democratic Governance," in *Democracy in the Caribbean: Myths and Realities* (Westport, Conn., 1994).

FESTUS L. BROTHERSON, JR.

H

HAILE SELASSIE. Emperor Haile Selassie liked to compare himself to the Roman Emperor Justinian. He considered his revised constitution of 1955 and the European-inspired codes of law that he promulgated in *Ethiopia in the late 1950s and early 1960s as prime achievements. He did not take kindly to criticism of these laws and the *constitution.

The 1955 constitution promised cabinet and parliamentary government with an independent judiciary as guardian of a Bill of Rights. At the same time it proclaimed the sanctity of the emperor's person and the paramountcy of his power. In short, the emperor was a traditional ruler with modern pretensions. The tension between his modernizing agenda, with its wrenching demands, and the resistance of traditional concepts and vested interests marked his fifty-eight-year rule, first as regent (1916–1930), then as emperor until his fall in 1974.

Schooled at a French Catholic mission, Haile Selassie began his career as a young governor of his father's province of Harar, where he had been born in 1892. Harar was a prized governorate among Emperor Menelik's newly conquered territories, and was thus entrusted to Ras Mekonnen, Haile Selassie's father and Menelik's trusted cousin. From his youth in Harar, Haile Selassie (then called Tafari) acquired the empire mentality together with an appetite for business, the result of his European contacts. These contacts also eventually helped him to garner support in his bid for the imperial throne. In 1916 he overthrew Lij Yasu, Emperor Menelik's chosen successor, installed Menelik's daughter, Zewditu, as figurehead queen, and began his long rule at the age of 26.

Upon Zewditu's death in 1930, he ascended the throne under the name Haile Selassie. A year later he promulgated a "modern" constitution to undergird the reforms which he had initiated, undermining the power of the regional potentates. The main reforms concerned the introduction of a national army, taxation, and a paid central bureaucracy.

Haile Selassie attained world renown by events beyond his control. In 1936 *Mussolini's Fascist forces invaded Ethiopia, sending the emperor into exile. His memorable appeal for help at the *League of Nations fell on deaf ears, but received wide coverage, thus starting his career as a world figure of great fascination. Four years later Mussolini's alliance with Hitler came as a boon, enabling the emperor to return home with British and Allied assistance.

Five years of Italian rule left him with an impressive infrastructure and fledgling industrial and commercial enterprises. The emperor lost no time in exploiting these legacies to his benefit and to those of his loyal followers. Meanwhile he also acquired Eritrea with the help of U.S. *diplomacy. His imperial appetite overreached itself, however, when in 1962 he unilaterally abolished the UN-arranged federation of Eritrea with Ethiopia. There is a historical irony: in annexing Eritrea, the emperor flouted the very international law to which he appealed when his own country was invaded. The *Eritrean War of Independence began then and would haunt him to his last days, as it has haunted his successors.

His *modernization programs had also spawned new social forces with the attendant tensions and demands. An abortive coup in 1960 led by the head of his bodyguards broke the ice, ushering in an era of protests and clandestine movements. The emperor ignored these developments, finding refuge in international affairs. In 1963 he hosted the founding meeting of the *Organization of African Unity (OAU), becoming its first chairman. It was to be a short-lived glory.

In 1974 he was overthrown by the armed forces which his modernization created. He died in 1975 under mysterious circumstances. His epitaph might read: "Despite his stature and achievements, few mourned him."

Margery F. Perham, *The Government of Ethiopia,* 2d ed. (London, 1969). Christopher Clapham, *Haile Selassie's Government* (London, 1969).

BEREKET HABTE SELASSIE

HAITI. The poorest country in the Western Hemisphere, Haiti has also been burdened with a political history of oppressive dictatorships and instability. Sharing the Caribbean island of Hispaniola with the Dominican Republic, the country has a population of 7.2 million people, two-thirds of whom live in rural areas. Per capita income is less than $300 per year and the adult literacy rate is only 45 percent.

Formerly a colony of France, Haiti achieved its independence in 1804 after the only successful slave revolution in modern history. Between independence and the U.S. occupation in 1915, Haiti was ruled by an alliance of merchants and the military. The occupation, partly to counter rising German influence in the country, lasted until 1934; while it improved Haiti's infrastructure, it also exacerbated many structural problems such as economic and administrative centralization, monocrop exports, fiscal weakness, and poverty. Moreover, the new military force created by the United States ruled the country until 1957 when François "Papa Doc" Duvalier was elected president.

Duvalier quickly centralized power through the use of violence against his opponents, principally at the hands of the infamous *tontons macoutes.* In 1964 Duvalier declared himself "President for Life"; on his death in 1971, his son Jean-Claude "Baby Doc" inherited the position. A less skilled politician governing in more difficult economic times, Jean-Claude Duvalier was clearly not competent to rule. A growing popular movement for democracy compelled the United States to withdraw support for Jean-Claude, who fled to exile in France in 1986.

The provisional governments between 1986 and 1990 were unstable and violent, unable or unwilling to oversee significant change. The presidential election of 1990 saw victory go to Father Jean-Bertrand Aristide, a Catholic priest and champion of the desperately poor majority. Recipient of over two-thirds of the popular vote, Aristide spent barely half a year in office; he fled to Venezuela on 1 October 1991 following a military *coup d'etat, and later went to the United States. His brief presidency contributed to increased polarization in Haiti, as Aristide tried to implement changes to benefit the majority of the population. He tried to reform the military and proposed social welfare and agrarian policies that conflicted with the interests of the landowners and privileged urban elites. These policies, plus others that were perceived as threatening by the military, led to the coup.

In previous years, Aristide's overthrow would have been applauded or, at the very least, ignored in Washington and many Latin American capitals. In the post–Cold War era and the era of new democracies, however, Aristide's counterparts saw his ouster as potentially undermining their own positions. Thus, the Organization of American States and the United Nations, backed by the U.S. and European governments, took the lead in attempting to negotiate Aristide's return. It took three years and a U.S.–led military intervention, however, to oust the military and return Aristide to the presidency, with fewer powers. Constitutionally barred from a second consecutive term of office, Aristide was succeeded to the presidency in the December 1995 elections by his former prime minister, René Préval.

The Préval government faces daunting challenges. The old military has been dismantled, but violence by former members and paramilitary death squads, drug trafficking, and corruption by public officials are impediments to stability. The most critical problem, however, is the fissure between the impoverished majority and the small wealthy and powerful urban elite. This division, along with the lack of a viable productive economy, dependency on imports and foreign aid for basic necessities, and unmet expectations aroused by the transition to democracy, poses the greatest challenge to the Préval government and his successors.

(See also U.S.–LATIN AMERICAN RELATIONS.)

Amy Wilentz, *The Rainy Season: Haiti Since Duvalier* (London, 1989). Simon M. Fass, *Political Economy in Haiti: The Drama of Survival* (New Brunswick, N.J., 1990). Alex Dupuy, *Haiti in the New World Order: The Limits of the Democratic Revolution* (Boulder, Colo., 1997).

ALEX DUPUY

HAMMARSKJÖLD, Dag. Best-known for his achievements as UN secretary-general, Dag Hammarskjöld was born in Jönköping, Sweden, on 29 July 1905 and died at Ndola, Northern Rhodesia, on 18 September 1961. Son of a former prime minister of Sweden and educated at Uppsala and Stockholm universities, he entered public service, becoming under-secretary of the Swedish Ministry of Finance and chair of the governors of the Bank of Sweden in 1935 and secretary-general of the Swedish Foreign Office in 1949. From 1953 until his death in 1961 he served as UN secretary-general.

Hammarskjöld was an intellectual of wide-ranging interest.

He was a distinguished economist, diplomat, lawyer, and administrator, and was also passionately interested in art and literature. He chaired the Nobel Literature Prize Committee of the Swedish Academy and translated a number of difficult literary works—*Anabase* by Saint-John Perse and *Antiphon* by Djuna Barnes, for example—into Swedish.

Taking over a UN debilitated by the *Cold War, the *Korean War, and the Joseph McCarthy era in the United States, Hammarskjöld rapidly gained the confidence of governments and restored the morale of the international civil service, and his use of the secretary-generalship to engage in active but quiet personal diplomacy transformed the position from a predominantly administrative one into an important political and diplomatic resource. Among his many achievements were the release of the U.S. prisoners in China in 1955; his work in defusing the *Suez Crisis of 1956 and in setting up the first UN peacekeeping force; his successful management of the 1958 Lebanese crisis; and the UN's activities in the Congo, in the course of which he met his death in a plane crash.

Hammarskjöld developed the secretary-general's diplomatic and mediating role, the doctrines of UN "presences" and "good offices" in conflict areas, and the now well-recognized technique of peacekeeping. He was indefatigable in defending the independence and integrity of the secretary-generalship and of the UN Secretariat. He was extraordinarily courageous in standing up for the principles of the UN Charter with powers both great and small. This approach did not endear him to some powerful leaders, and he ended his life disowned and vilified both by Nikita *Khrushchev and Charles de *Gaulle. By others, however, he was greatly respected and admired.

Hammarskjöld was a highly articulate and imaginative man who wrote most of his own statements and speeches. These have stood the test of time remarkably well and are increasingly referred to as classic expressions of international principle and practice. He believed that, through a process of creating precedents and case law, the UN would be gradually transformed from an *institutional* mechanism into a *constitutional* instrument recognized and respected by all nations. He worked tirelessly to give practical shape to this vision.

Hammarskjöld is perhaps best remembered as a courageous and visionary international leader and a master of multilateral *diplomacy. His posthumously published notebook, *Markings*, is a unique record of the inner life of a public figure.

(See also CONGO CRISIS; UNITED NATIONS.)

BRIAN URQUHART

HAVEL, Václav. Czech playwright, longtime champion of *human rights, and former president of the Czech and Slovak Federative Republic, Václav Havel was born on 5 October 1936 in Prague of well-to-do parents, Václav M. Havel and Boena Vavreková Havlová. As the result of communist educational policies that discriminated against children of the former bourgeoisie, he was forced to finish high school through night courses while working as a laboratory assistant. Denied admission to university study, Havel studied briefly at a technological university and eventually completed his studies as an external student at the theater department of the Academy of Arts. After completing his military service, he worked as a stagehand at the ABC Theater. He soon moved to the Theater on the Balustrade, and there played an important role in the innovative developments that took place in the small theaters of Prague in the 1960s. Havel's early plays, *The Garden Party* (1963), *The Memorandum* (1967), and *The Increased Difficulty of Concentration* (1968), established his reputation as the leading exponent of the theater of the absurd in *Czechoslovakia. Active in the circle of young writers involved in the journal *Tvá* in the mid-1960s, Havel also worked for change in the official Writers' Union in 1968, during the *Prague Spring.

Although he was forbidden to take any part in public life after the end of the reform period, Havel continued to write. The authorities did not allow his work to be published or performed in Czechoslovakia during the period of political orthodoxy that followed the Soviet invasion of Czechoslovakia in August 1968. Nonetheless his plays, including *The Conspirators* (1971), *The Beggar's Opera* (1972), *The Mountain Hotel* (1974), *Audience and Private View* (1975), *Protest* (1978), *Largo Desolato* (1984), *Temptation* (1985), and *Slum Clearance* (1988), and books, including *Living in Truth* 1987) and *Letters to Olga* (1988), received widespread acclaim abroad. In 1969, he was awarded the Austrian State Prize for European Literature. His activities in defense of human rights led to further honors, including the Jan Palach Prize, the Erasmus Prize, the Olof Palme Prize, and the Frankfurt Book Fair Peace Prize.

Havel was one of the founders of the *Charter 77 movement and the Committee for the Defense of the Unjustly Persecuted (VONS). Arrested numerous times for his independent activities, he was placed under house arrest from 1977 to 1979. In 1979, he was sentenced to four-and-a-half years in prison for alleged antistate activities. Released in March 1983, Havel continued to be a tireless champion of human rights and an advocate of "living in truth." In early 1989, as the result of his participation in the commemoration of the 1969 suicide of Czech student Jan Palach, Havel was once again imprisoned for several months.

Havel was the leading force behind the creation of the Civic Forum, the organization that arose to lead the mass protests that overthrew the communist regime in November 1989. He quickly emerged as the leader of the revolution and the symbol of his country's hopes for democracy and the future. His selection as president of Czechoslovakia by a Parliament still dominated by communists in December 1989 capped the victory of the "Velvet Revolution." Havel was reelected as president by the Federal Assembly after the June 1990 elections.

As the result of his steadfast refusal to compromise with the communist regime, Havel exercised an authority that went far beyond the powers of his office. Clearly the dominant political figure in Czechoslovakia in the early postcommunist period, his presidency was characterized by an attempt to infuse morality into day-to-day politics. Together with Jiří Dienstbier, the dissident colleague who became his foreign minister, Havel pursued a high-profile strategy designed to reassert Czechoslovakia's independence in foreign policy and reclaim its place among European nations. After negotiating the withdrawal of Soviet troops from Czechoslovakia, the country's new leader reestablished Czechoslovakia's traditionally warm relations with the United States and took important steps to rejoin Europe. Czechoslovakia's acceptance as a member of the Council of Europe, the interest and aid offered Czechoslovakia by other democratic states,

the country's acceptance as a member of NATO in March 1999, and progress in accession talks with the EU, all attest to the success of these efforts. After the breakup of the federation in 1993, Havel was elected to two terms as president of the *Czech Republic.

(See also NINETEEN EIGHTY-NINE.)

Jan Vladislav, ed., *Václav Havel, or Living in Truth* (London, 1986). Václav Havel, *Disturbing the Peace* (New York, 1990). Eda Kriseova, *Václav Havel: The Authorized Biography* (New York, 1993).

SHARON L. WOLCHIK

HAYA DE LA TORRE, Víctor Raúl. Born in Trujillo, Peru, in 1895, Haya studied at the Universities of Trujillo, San Marcos, London, and Oxford. During his student's days in Lima, he helped to obtain the eight-hour workday, founded the People's Universities and led a 1923 protest against the attempt by President Augusto B. Leguía (1863–1932) to dedicate Peru to the Scared Heart. Shortly afterward he was jailed and deported.

During his first exile (1923–31), Haya assisted Julio Antonio Mella (1900–29) in founding the José Martí People's University in Havana and worked for José Vasconcelos (1882– 1959), Mexican secretary of education. At the University of Mexico, Haya raised the Indoamerican flag at a public event considered the founding ceremony of APRA (American People's Revolutionary Party). Afterward, he visited the Soviet Union, attended the 1927 International Congress of Anti-Imperialists, lectured in France, the United States, Mexico, and Central America, and widely published his views.

The Peruvian Aprista Party (PAP), founded in September 1930 after the overthrow of President Leguía, elected Haya its presidential candidate for the 1931 elections. After electoral irregularities, his main rival, General Luis M. Sánchez Cerro (1889–1933), was proclaimed winner. The new government unleashed a reign of terror against the PAP. Haya was placed in solitary confinement, but his life was saved by petitions from several Latin American congresses and world-renowned personalities. He was freed after Sánchez Cerro was assassinated in 1933. Following a few months' truce while General Oscar R. Benavides (1876–1945) consolidated himself in power, Haya went into hiding again to lead his party's underground struggle for the next twelve years. As the PAP was barred from having his own presidential candidate, Haya helped form a National Democratic Front and elect José Luis Bustamante y Rivero in 1945. In October 1948 the PAP was outlawed once more and Haya complied with his party's directive to seek asylum in the Colombian Embassy in Lima. For five years, the authoritarian government of General Manuel A. Odría (1907–74) refused to grant him safe conduct, and Haya's residence in the embassy became a *cause célèbre* in international law. Under international pressure, Haya was permitted to leave Peru in 1954 and spent the following seven years as an exile in Europe.

Haya won the 1962 presidential election, but the Electoral Board declared his candidacy a few thousand votes short of the minimum 33 percent required. In 1978 Haya was elected a member of the Constituent Assembly with the highest preferential votes. Thus, he presided over the assembly and signed the 1979 constitution before dying of lung cancer on 15 August of that year.

Haya's international fame rests on his leadership of APRA, from whose ideology and basic program other democratic parties in Latin America borrowed extensively. Haya's platform of fundamental *reforms and his books advocating the social democratic transformation of Peru and promotion of a United States of Indoamerica were attacked as extremist and utopian by conservatives and as centrist and reformist by Stalinists. The day Haya died, the governments of Peru and Venezuela declared a day of national mourning in recognition of his great influence on contemporary hemispheric politics. Two million people, about 30 percent of the voting population of the country, observed his funeral procession.

(See also SOCIALISM AND SOCIAL DEMOCRACY.)

Robert J. Alexander, ed., *Aprismo: The Ideas and Doctrines of Victor Raúl Haya de la Torre* (Kent, Ohio, 1973). Luis Alberto Sánchez, *Haya de la Torre y el APRA*, 2d ed. (Lima, 1980). Eugenio Chang-Rodríguez and Ronald G. Hellman, *APRA and the Democratic Challenge in Peru* (New York, 1988). Luis Alva Castro, ed., *Haya de la Torre y la integración indoamericana* (Lima, 1996).

EUGENIO CHANG-RODRÍGUEZ

HEALTH CARE. See WELFARE STATE.

HEGEMONY. The term *hegemony* was found in *Thucydides classical Realist *History of the Peloponnesian Wars* (fifth century B.C.E.). The major reconceptualization is attributed to Antonio *Gramsci (1891–1937) in his *Prison Notebooks*, and helps to explain the relationships between *power, stability, and order in *international relations (IR). The concept is used in such debates as the question of U.S. hegemonic decline. Other historical instances of hegemony include Britain in the nineteenth century and the Soviet Union in the communist world between 1945 and 1989.

To understand hegemony, it useful to know Robert Cox's (in Robert O. Keohane, *Neo-Realism and Its Critics* [New York, 1986]) distinction between "critical" and "problem-solving" theories: The former seek to reveal the social basis of power and potential for transformation of world orders; the latter accept the order largely as it is, developing formulas to manage it.

Critical Theories. Classical Realists (e.g., Machiavelli, E. H. Carr) and Historical Materialists (e.g., Fernand Braudel, Robert W. Cox) identify hegemony as a balance of forces under specific historical conditions. Thus each has a historicist epistemology, but with different ontologies of IR, with Classical *Realism's based upon regional or global orders (e.g., the relations between ancient Greek city-states and others in the Levant and North Africa). Marxist ontology is a social totality, its major elements being social forces and social structures (frequently categorized into modes of production, such as feudalism and capitalism). Both approaches stress the dynamics of power, production, and the *state in given orders.

Nonetheless, each perspective defines hegemony with regard to different conceptions of agency. For Classical Realism this is a dominant state (e.g., Athens; Rome; Britain; the United States) exerting hegemony over others (respectively: other Greek city-states in the fifth century B.C.E.; the Roman Empire, at least in its Byzantine form, up to its collapse in 1453; the British Empire and Continental Europe in the nineteenth century; the "free world" after 1945). The counterparts in *Marxism are social classes or historical blocs, drawn from

one or a combination of states. In both approaches, the ruling classes or *elites exercise hegemony and leadership by articulating and synthesizing conceptions of general interests, so that their material power is embedded in, and strengthened by, political consent.

Gramscian approaches stress the crucial role of ideas in the achievement of hegemony, which occurs when the worldview, social principles and practices, and intellectual and moral leadership of the ruling group are so internalized by subordinates that the order in which hegemony is exercised appears natural or inevitable. Hegemony thus configures the "limits of the possible" as they are conceived by different groups and classes in a civilization or political order. Hegemony can be said to be achieved in a negative sense when no credible alternative has emerged to challenge the prevailing order, that is, when no strong counterhegemonic tendencies or movements have begun to materialize. A hegemonic international order would be achieved when the major institutions and forms of organization—economic, social, and political—as well as the key values of the leading elements in the dominant state(s) become models for emulation in subordinate states (Cox, 1987). In the case of post-1945 capitalism, the patterns of emulation are stronger in the developed states than in the less developed. In the former, liberal *democracy and rule by consent generally characterize political life, with economic policy subordinated to the needs of capital. Hegemony is thus embedded in the ideas, institutions, and practices of a system which formally separates politics, economics, and state from civil society. Nevertheless, the quality and intensity of hegemony change over time, within and across states and world orders.

Problem-Solving Theory. Neorealism (see Keohane, 1986) has emerged recently as a problem-solving theory to establish a conceptualization of system dynamics and the techniques for the reproduction of the existing order. Using a positivist epistemology, and incorporating aspects of Liberal Institutionalism, it develops a utilitarian calculus of states' costs and benefits as an apparatus to help manage IR. The ontology is an *international system, constituted mainly by interactions of states (or governments) and markets (individuals, firms).

More specifically, the conceptualization of interstate relations is based upon Hobbes's reading of Thucydides' *History* (which he translated). States are assumed to behave like Hobbesian egoistic individualists, as if in a state of nature (or international *anarchy) in a struggle of all against all for survival. Rational constraints are placed on this struggle through the *balance of power or hegemonic domination. However, if hegemony declines or the balance of power changes, international conflict may rise, after a period of relative equilibrium.

By contrast with Marxism, Neorealists assume a basic structural continuity in IR, despite cycles of changing power balances, or rise and decline of empires or hegemonies. The best-selling book by Paul Kennedy, *The Rise and Fall of the Great Powers* (New York, 1987), symbolized the widespread recognition of U.S. decline, and of the idea of cycles of rising and declining hegemony, and a transition to a posthegemonic era. Moreover, U.S. writers have frequently associated hegemony with international economic order, openness, and postwar prosperity.

American concerns come together in the hybrid liberal/Neorealist theory of hegemonic stability (THS), which states that hegemony is a necessary but not sufficient condition for the creation of an open economic order. However, in the absence of hegemony, international *public goods (e.g., international *security, global macroeconomic stability) and international *regimes (e.g., in trade, money) may be undersupplied. Thus in the 1930s the world economy had no hegemon both willing and able to act as lender of last resort, provide a market for distress goods, and steer the global macroeconomy. Also the United States was the biggest economic power, but a second-rank military power (Kindleberger, 1973). Given that most applications of THS in the post-1945 era assume U.S. decline, they conclude that "after hegemony" (Keohane, 1984) there may be tendencies toward economic closure, disorder, and conflict, unless states cooperate rationally. Other powerful nations should be willing to share burdens of collective management and leadership, in their "enlightened self-interest."

Comparison of Perspectives and Conclusion. Various conceptualizations of hegemony and world order can be identified. Each sees the question of hegemony differently.

Since for Classical Realists morality is subordinate to power, hegemony is simply the acceptable face of dominance, and it declines when other states have sufficient power to challenge it. Repercussions of hegemonic decline depend upon the specific historical conditions which surround it, which today involve the breakup of the Soviet Union and the collapse of the ability of Russia or other Soviet successor states to act as a global counterweight to U.S. power. This implies not a decline but an increase in U.S. dominance in the security structure.

For Gramscians, the issue is not U.S. power as such, more the balance of social forces which constitute a given world order, its dynamics and propensity to change. Nevertheless, U.S. behavior appears less and less based on the articulation of universal interests and consent, more on unilateral applications of U.S. economic and military force: this change is bound up with the decline in the hegemonic appeal of postwar international arrangements. This approach suggests that cumulative and conjunctive changes have served to transform the conditions of existence of the post-1945 world order. Thus the hegemonic structures associated with the Pax Americana may be eroding, at both domestic and international levels, creating a "crisis of hegemony" (Gill, 1990). New world order possibilities can be hegemonic or nonhegemonic, progressive (emancipatory, peaceful, democratic, and based upon recognition and acceptance of civilizational differences) or regressive (based on dominance, force, violence).

By contrast, Neorealism's concept of international structure is individualistic and akin to the liberal economic concept of market structure. The practical problem is analogous to managing a shift from stable, monopolistic power relations (duopolistic in the security regime) to the more unstable relations of oligopolistic competition (among the leading states). Liberal, "regime" variants of the THS suggest that improvements in interstate cooperation and collective management can offset the effects of declining hegemony by reducing transaction costs and uncertainties, and by increasing information flows, predictability, and flexibility. *International cooperation is thus a second-best solution to the problem of international

order in a system which might otherwise tend toward damaging competition and rivalry.

The THS is thus a "problem-solving" theory. It combines with rational choice and analysis, *game theory, and liberal functionalism to clarify the conditions under which public goods and political order are created and maintained under conditions of (ascending or declining) hegemony. Both Classical Realism and Historical Materialism develop "critical" theories in that they identify the nature of and conditions for hegemony, highlight the inequalities and subordinations of a given order, and indicate counterhegemonic forces perhaps latent in the historical situation.

(See also CLASS AND POLITICS; FORCE, USE OF; INTERNATIONAL POLITICAL ECONOMY; LIBERALISM; PUBLIC CHOICE THEORY.)

Charles P. Kindleberger, *The World in Depression, 1929–39* (Berkeley, Calif., 1973). Robert O. Keohane, *After Hegemony: Co-operation and Discord in the World Political Economy* (Princeton, N.J., 1984). Robert W. Cox, *Production, Power and World Order: Social Forces in the Making of History* (New York, 1987). Stephen Gill, *American Hegemony and the Trilateral Commission* (Cambridge, U.K., 1990).

STEPHEN GILL

HELSINKI ACCORDS. The Helsinki Accords of 1975 are a diplomatic agreement among thirty-five states that exerted significant influence on its communist signatories in the field of *human rights. The Accords are an example of a continuing political process that generated important results despite different initial expectations. They also exemplify the internationalization of human rights issues.

In the 1950s and 1960s the Soviet Union, seeking to legitimate its geopolitical position in Europe, repeatedly called for a European security conference. Broadened, according to conditions set by the Western European states, to include discussions on human rights and economic issues and to include the United States and Canada as participants, such a conference was first held in 1972. The resulting Helsinki Accord (officially the Final Act of the Helsinki Meeting of the *Conference on Security and Cooperation in Europe), which was signed by all European and North American states except Albania, pledged the signatories to certain security, economic, and human rights principles.

The Soviet Union and its allies published the text in full, as called for by the agreement itself, and accepted a series of review or follow-up conferences. Publication combined with review had the effect of spotlighting Soviet and East European human rights practices, which the parties had agreed were proper subjects for international scrutiny. In response to publication and dissemination of the Accord, especially in the Soviet Union and Czechoslovakia, Helsinki monitoring groups sprang up, demanding that their governments implement the principles—which included "the right of the individual to know and act upon" human rights—contained in the Accord. Monitoring groups were ruthlessly crushed in these two states in particular. This accelerated attention to Eastern violations of rights.

Initial Western emphasis on human rights and humanitarian principles, which made up Basket Three (Basket One comprised *security issues, Basket Two economic ones), was the product of West European rather than U.S. *diplomacy. In the mid-1970s U.S. foreign policy, as greatly influenced by Henry

*Kissinger, regarded human rights as basically an internal matter of states and a sentimental impediment to "realistic" geostrategy. Kissinger and others were skeptical about what came to be called the Helsinki process, fearing that the Soviet Union would achieve the legitimization of its control over Eastern Europe without having to give anything significant in return. Hence the United States, like the Soviet Union, only reluctantly agreed to the terms of Basket Three.

By 1977, at the first review conference in Belgrade, the United States assumed the leadership of the Western states in focusing on human rights. The Soviet Union, while reacting strongly to the U.S.-led criticisms, did not abandon the Helsinki process, since the 1975 agreement had been proclaimed by Moscow as one of the great achievements of the Brezhnev era. Moreover, the Soviets were reluctant to abandon Basket One's security principles, even as they came under attack for their violations of human rights in Basket Three. In subsequent review conferences and more specialized follow-up meetings, the West—with increasing unity—continued to devote attention to Eastern violations of Basket Three principles. In return, Eastern states reversed their argument that specific criticisms were an interference in domestic affairs, and began to criticize Western violations of social and economic rights.

The West directed their comments to two audiences: the governments of the Eastern states and those individuals dissenting from prevailing practices in Soviet-bloc states. Both audiences were affected by the Helsinki process. Interviews with released dissidents made clear that they were morally sustained by developments in the Helsinki process, as reported by the Western media and other channels of communication. And although some governmental changes could be traced to Helsinki pressures prior to 1985, after that date and the rise of Mikhail *Gorbachev in the Soviet Union, it was clear that Moscow increasingly accepted the human rights and humanitarian principles of Basket Three. After the Eastern and Central European political revolutions of 1989, Basket Three principles helped to provide standards of behavior for the reform regimes. In 1990 a Helsinki follow-up meeting in Copenhagen unanimously endorsed the ideas of political pluralism, multiparty *democracy, an independent judiciary, separation of the state from political parties, and special protection for minorities.

The Helsinki Accords led to an institutionalized process of diplomacy without a formal organization. The Helsinki process had no charter, no budget, no secretariat. Despite the lack of clear law and organization, the Accords as diplomatic instrument played a major role in East-West relations by helping to transform Stalinist states into states that respected internationally recognized human rights. Later, after the *Cold War, the process allowed the development of an East-West security apparatus in the Organization for Security and Cooperation in Europe, which has conducted peacekeeping operations in parts of the former Soviet Union and created the first codes of conduct for soldiers involved in peacekeeping.

(See also SOVIET–EAST EUROPEAN RELATIONS; SOVIET FOREIGN POLICY; U.S. FOREIGN POLICY.)

A. Bloed and P. Van Dijk, eds., Essays on Human Rights in the Helsinki Process (Dordrecht, 1985). Jonathan Luxmoore, The Helsinki Agreement: Dialogue or Delusion, Institute for European Defence and Strategic Studies, Occasional Paper no. 20 (London, 1986). Vojtech Mastny, ed., Helsinki, Human Rights, and European Security (Durham, N.C., 1986).

DAVID P. FORSYTHE

HINDUISM. The word *hindu* derives from *sindhu* (*Indus* in the Greek transliteration), the name of the great river of the northwest of the South Asian subcontinent, a region still known as Sindh. It is found in ancient Greek writings and refers to the natives of northern India. The terms *India* and its Persian counterpart *Hindustan* designate the territory around the Indus. In the usage of Muslims who settled in the region, "Hindu" came to refer to the non-Muslim population. (The official Indian term for *India today—Bharat—does not bear reference to this history.)

Hinduism, the modern Western term for the majority religion in India, is not a religion in the Semitic sense, that is, based on prophetic revelation, sacred scripture, monotheism, and ecclesiastical organization. The Indian term that comes closest to "religion" is *dharma*, which might be glossed as "socio-religious order." "Hinduism" can best be defined as a set of ideas and practices of the upper, so-called twice-born castes that are based on the interpretation of the ancient Vedas and auxiliary textual traditions by Brahman priests. In addition, a multiplicity of religious movements and centers have arisen over time that are only partly integrated with Brahmanical discourse and practice.

The expansion of Western colonial power in South Asia spawned a number of movements that responded to the challenge of both Christianity and *modernity by formulating a unified Hinduism. In the late nineteenth century these movements developed into forms of religious *nationalism. The notion of "Hindu nation" must be regarded in terms of the comparable notion of "Muslim nation" that led to the founding of Pakistan or to that of a "Sikh nation." Nationalists on the Indian subcontinent tend to construe shared religion as the basis of the nation-state, and the most powerful political movement in India in the 1980s and 1990s endeavored to find common ground for the establishment of a Hinduism that will serve as the national religion. This common ground consists of a limited set of issues, such as conversion, protection of the sacred cow, or the rebuilding of sacred sites destroyed in periods of Muslim conquest. Such issues create a fragile unity among the majority that depends on strong antagonism toward minorities such as Christians and Muslims. Christian missionaries are protrayed as the "dark forces" behind separatist movements in tribal areas. Muslims are portrayed as "secret agents" for Pakistan.

The influence of Hindu nationalism on Hindu-Muslim relations has important implications for the development of international relations between India and Pakistan. This is especially true for the contested region of Kashmir and is exemplified by the testing of nuclear bombs in 1998 by the Indian government, led by Hindu nationalists, and the quick response by the Pakistani government.

(See also RELIGION AND POLITICS.)

Peter van der Veer, Religious Nationalism: Hindus and Muslims in India (Berkeley, Calif., 1994).

PETER VAN DER VEER

HIROHITO. Showa Emperor Hirohito, the 124th in the world's oldest surviving *monarchy, according to legend, was born Taisho Emperor Yoshihito's and Empress Kujo Setsuko's eldest son on 29 April 1901. Known as Prince Michi in his childhood, he was brought up from infancy as *Japan's future sovereign ruler and commander in chief of its armed forces. At the age of ten, he was appointed an officer of the Imperial Army and Navy, as provided in the Imperial Family Members Status Ordinance. He became crown prince in 1916, and Japan's first crown prince ever to go abroad in 1921 when he visited Europe. In that same year, he was named prince regent to assist his ailing father. In 1924, he married Princess Kuni, or Nagako, and succeeded Taisho Emperor upon the latter's death. He formally ascended the Chrysanthemum Throne in November 1928.

Under modern Japan's first *constitution promulgated in 1889, Hirohito was, like his grandfather Meiji and his father, not only Japan's sovereign ruler but also a god in human guise, as most Japanese either believed or pretended to believe. Hirohito himself probably did not believe himself to be divine, but he probably did believe that he descended from gods. In the wake of Japan's defeat in *World War II, he publicly renounced his divinity in January 1946. Under Japan's new constitution drafted by U.S. lawyers and promulgated in November 1946, Hirohito lost his status as Japan's sovereign and became merely its "symbol." He escaped trial by the Tokyo International War Crimes Tribunal, thanks to General Douglas MacArthur's goodwill and favorable testimony by wartime leaders, especially General Tojo Hideki, absolving the emperor of any personal responsibility for the *war and wartime atrocities. In his later life, Hirohito made history by visiting Europe in 1972 and the United States in 1975.

Hirohito's role in Japanese politics before and during World War II, especially his involvement in preparations for and conduct of the war itself, remains controversial. All agree that his personal intervention was a critical factor in the Japanese government's decision to surrender to the Allies in August 1945. Opinion is divided, however, on Hirohito's responsibility for the initiation of the war in 1941 and wartime Japanese conduct. Most Japanese and many non-Japanese authors believe that he was a gentle-mannered, peace-loving, and liberal person who was manipulated by his war-mongering civilian and, especially, military advisers and was kept in the dark on details of the war preparation and execution. A few authors hold him responsible for the beginning and execution, as well as the ending, of the war.

Historical records made public in recent years, especially Hirohito's own testimony heard and recorded by a group of his closest confidants on the eve of the *war crimes trial in 1946 and published in late 1990 and early 1991, tend to support the minority view. These records reveal that the emperor was fully informed of and consulted about every important detail concerning the preparation for and execution of World War II, as well as the war against China that preceded it. Moreover, they indicate that he routinely and authoritatively intervened in decisions not only on broad policy issues but also on specific and detailed operational and personnel problems. The records also show that Hirohito supported the continuation of the war until about June 1945 and that his subsequent decision to support Japan's unconditional surrender was based almost exclusively on his concern to save Japan's throne, rather than its people or territory, from certain and total destruction.

Hirohito survived the war by more than four decades before he died in January 1989. An emotional national wake and mourning followed. His role in World War II notwithstanding, he retained the loyalty and devotion of his erstwhile subjects until the very end.

Edward Behr, *Hirohito: Behind the Myth* (London and New York, 1990). Akira Yamada, *Shōwa tennō no sensō shidō* [The Showa emperor's wartime leadership] (Tokyo, 1990). Hidenari Terasaki and Mariko Terasaki Miller, *Showa tenno dokuhakuroku, Terasaki Hidenari goyogakari nikki* [The Showa emperor's monologue and the diary of the emperor's aide Terasaki Hidenari] (Tokyo, 1991).

Haruhiro Fukui

HIROSHIMA. The Japanese city of Hiroshima is known throughout the world as the site of the first atomic attack. On the morning of 6 August 1945 a U.S. B-29 bomber, *Enola Gay*, dropped an atomic bomb on Hiroshima from a height of about 580 meters (1,900 feet). The most authoritative Japanese study concludes that the bomb killed 118,661 persons, left another 30,524 severely injured, with a further 48,606 slightly injured. Of the inhabitants of Hiroshima at the time, 118,613 were reported to have avoided injury. The city was devastated by the attack but was completely rebuilt in the years following *World War II.

A second atomic bomb was dropped on the city of Nagasaki late in the morning of 9 August 1945, causing heavy damage and casualties. The most careful estimates conclude that 73,884 were killed and more than 75,000 injured in the attack on Nagasaki.

Japan had been making peace overtures in various foreign capitals prior to the atomic attacks, but it began to offer formal surrender immediately after the second attack, as early as 10 August. By 15 August, Japan's offer to surrender was accepted by the Allies. Japanese authorities had been promised that the emperor would not be charged with any responsibility for the *war and that the emperor system could continue to operate even during the period of U.S. military occupation.

Mention of Hiroshima represents for people everywhere the dawn of the nuclear age. It is associated in the political imagination with the use of a weapon of mass destruction as a tactic in warfare, and it is understood to signify massive human suffering.

At the time of the attacks, few in the United States or elsewhere raised questions about the propriety of *nuclear weapons. The atomic bombs were perceived as weapons of unsurpassed potency. President Harry *Truman and his close advisers justified the use of atomic bombs at the time by arguing that the alternative would have been an invasion of the main Japanese islands, costing upwards of 1 million American lives. Disclosures over the years, including intelligence estimates in 1945, suggest a far smaller number, and generally anticipated Japanese surrender before the invasion was scheduled to have taken place. Moreover, it is clear that wartime leaders such as Truman and Winston *Churchill, both of whom defended the use of the bomb against Japan, were aware of the apocalyptic implications of atomic weaponry.

After more than four decades the Hiroshima decision remains controversial and hotly debated. Some scholars have argued that the overriding reason for the use of the atomic bomb against Japan was to exert diplomatic leverage on the Soviet Union in the postwar world, or to end the war quickly before Soviet military involvement would give Moscow a greater voice in postwar Pacific peace arrangements.

In subsequent decades Hiroshima has served as a central symbol for *peace movements around the world. More conservative political elements, those committed to strategic roles for nuclear weapons, tend not to look back closely at Hiroshima, except possibly to reanalyze the bureaucratic milieu of the decision. In contrast, those who have objected to the reliance on nuclear weapons in the post-1945 world seek to consider the effects on Hiroshima in the most concrete possible manner, by listening to the voices of the survivors, by detailing the forms of physical and psychological damage, and by invoking images of mass death and suffering.

In 1963, a Japanese court, assisted by three *international law experts, decided the *Shimoda* case involving several survivors. The Tokyo District Court decided that the atomic attacks violated international law, judging the bombs to be indiscriminate weapons used against civilians.

The decision to attack Hiroshima with an atomic bomb has become, if anything, more controversial with the passage of time. Nothing conclusive has yet been established. Recent academic writing has tended to favor the view that the official claim of saving lives was, at best, an exaggeration, while the revisionist claim of seeking diplomatic leverage over the Soviet Union was at least partially correct.

Hiroshima remains a powerful symbol of the catastrophic implications of the nuclear age. The Japanese experience of atomic war, despite greater casualties taken during the fire bomb attacks on Tokyo and the much greater destructiveness of subsequent hydrogen bomb technology, has been responsible for what is sometimes called "a nuclear allergy." Japan has legislated against any use, development, or possession of nuclear weapons. Some critics of Japanese *security policy suggest that such a posture is hypocritical, as Japan has welcomed "the nuclear umbrella" provided by the United States throughout the *Cold War period.

As long as there will be students of international politics, debates about Hiroshima will persist: Was it necessary? Did it really shorten the war? Did it make political leaders and the public aware of the great menace of war in the nuclear age? Should we morally condemn Hiroshima? Should we regard the use of atomic bombs against Hiroshima as a crime of state?

Social science cannot hope to answer these questions definitively, and yet the study of the decision and its effects remains valuable. It brings us closer to the realities of the nuclear age than any other single event, and enables us to clarify for the future our moral and legal attitudes toward relying upon weapons of mass destruction for purposes of either *deterrence or combat.

Gregg Herken, *The Winning Weapon: The Atomic Bomb in the Cold War, 1945–1950* (New York, 1980). *Hiroshima and Nagasaki: The Physical, Medical, and Social Effects of the Atomic Bombings,* Report of the Committee for the Compilation of Materials on Damage Caused by the Atomic Bombs in Hiroshima and Nagasaki (New York, 1981).

RICHARD FALK

HISPANIC AMERICANS. Latinos, or Hispanic Americans, constitute the second-largest and most rapidly growing distinctive ethnic group in the *United States. The impact that this group has had on domestic and international affairs in the United States is substantial and promises to be even more significant in the future. While sharing close ties based on Spanish heritage and language, Hispanic Americans are of diverse national backgrounds, originating not only from the Iberian Peninsula but from most of the nations of the Western Hemisphere, including the Caribbean and Central and South America. The umbrella terms *Hispanics* and *Latinos* are used to designate this extremely heterogeneous group comprising more than 28 million people of more than twenty national origins in the United States. In 1996 this included about 18 million Mexican Americans, 3.1 million Puerto Ricans, 1.1 million Cuban Americans, 4 million from other nations in Central and South America, and 2 million "others."

History. Hispanics, particularly Mexican/Spanish Americans, have been one of the longest-established ethnic groups in the United States. Explorers representing Spain made several contacts with the New World in the late fifteenth and early sixteenth centuries, and a number of colonial settlements were established in what would later become the United States, primarily in Florida (St. Augustine), New Mexico (Santa Fe), California, and Texas. Through its war with Mexico, the United States gained vast new territories in the mid-nineteenth century, including much of what is now Texas, New Mexico, Arizona, Nevada, California, Colorado, and Utah. *International migration from Mexico to the United States, more accurately described as a continuous ebb and flow across a 2,000-mile border, has persisted to the present day. One major wave of migration occurred in the early 1900s when largely unskilled peasant immigrants entered the United States from Mexico. Immigration to the United States has continued as economically depressed Mexicans seek to improve their economic condition. The official policy of the United States has at times encouraged this source of labor and at other times, primarily during economic difficulty, has discouraged it, even "repatriating" Mexicans. Major deportations occurred during the depression of the 1920s and the recession of the 1950s.

Puerto Ricans have been citizens of the United States since the Jones Act of 1917. The island of Puerto Rico has been a U.S. Commonwealth since 1952, and Puerto Ricans possess almost all legal privileges of U.S. citizenship. Puerto Ricans continue to make frequent trips between the island and the major cities of the northeastern United States, especially New York, particularly since the advent of regular air travel between the island and the eastern seaboard in the 1950s.

Relatively few Cubans lived in the United States until the Cuban revolution and the coming to power of Fidel Castro in 1959. Subsequently, a large number of Cuban refugees, including many middle- and upper-class professionals, entered the United States, settling mainly in south Florida. Subsequent waves of immigration occurred in 1965 and again in 1980, when Castro expelled the "Marielitos," a group that was of substantially lower economic and social status compared with those that had preceded it.

The other 4 million or so Hispanic Americans have various histories. Migrations to and from the United States from other countries of Central and South America have varied depending on the political and economic situations in their home countries and the fluctuating policies of the United States. In the late 1970s and 1980s there was a tremendous increase in the number of political refugees fleeing the turmoil in the countries of El Salvador, the Dominican Republic, Guatemala, and Panama.

Demographics. The social and economic characteristics of Hispanic Americans are difficult to describe because of the great diversity that is often concealed by summary statistics. The Hispanic population represents about 11 percent of total U.S. population and is growing very rapidly. In fact, one of the most significant demographic characteristics of Latinos is that their numbers are growing many times faster than the rest of the nation. The Hispanic population grew 53 percent between 1980 and 1990 and another 27 percent between 1990 and 1996. Almost half the growth was due to immigration. Although increasingly dispersed, Hispanics are concentrated in certain regions of the country, with Mexican Americans primarily in the Southwest, Puerto Ricans in the urban centers of the Northeast, and Cubans concentrated mostly in Florida.

Latinos are significantly younger than the general population of the United States, averaging twenty-five years of age as against thirty-four for the population in general. Socioeconomically, Hispanics are among the most depressed of all U.S. ethnic groups. In 1996, about 30 percent of Hispanic families fell below the poverty line; the figure was less than 10 percent among non-Hispanics.

The level of educational attainment among Hispanics improved only slightly during the past two decades and remains below the level of non-Hispanics. The proportion of non-Hispanics who have completed four years or more of college was 29 percent in 1996—three times as high as that of Hispanics. At the precollegiate level, the situation is worse; only 53 percent of Hispanics twenty-five years or older have completed four years of high school compared to 85 percent of non-Hispanics.

Political Situation. In addition to being socioeconomically disadvantaged, Latinos as a group are underrepresented in U.S. politics. For example, in 1998, there were no Hispanic U.S. senators and only eighteen Hispanic members of the U.S. House of Representatives. Of all the elected public official positions in the country only about 1 percent were held by Hispanics. In general, Latinos are registered to vote in lower percentages, participate in the electoral process less frequently, discuss politics and public affairs less, and make fewer campaign contributions than do other Americans. One reason for this comparative lack of participation in the political process is the youthfulness of the population. Young people generally are less political. Another is that about 40 percent of the Hispanic population are noncitizens who are ineligible for formal participation. Hispanics have had relatively weak political organizational bases, especially at the national level. One reason for the problem in developing a national base has been the difficulty of reconciling differences among various national origin and regional groups. No unifying national leadership of recognizable stature has emerged.

Because of their concentration and diversity, it is most likely that Hispanics will be most successful in politics at the grassroots level. Latinos have made some impressive strides on the local and state levels, particularly since the beginning of the 1960s. Hispanics have been crucial to the victories of mayors in several large cities and are being elected in significantly growing numbers to city councils, school boards, and state legislatures. Effective local organizing, including get-out-the-vote campaigns and legal challenges to minority vote dilution practices, have produced significant gains. The courts have ordered redistricting and bilingual election materials.

Major efforts to increase Latino naturalization and registration are being made by such organizations as the National Association of Latino Elected Officials and the Southwest Voter Registration and Education Project. These massive efforts have resulted in Latino voter registration rates remaining at roughly the same level from 1984 through 1996. The actual rate of voting among Latinos also has remained remarkably constant over the past several general elections. The rate has remained several percentage points below that of the non-Hispanic electorate, but this is notable given the rapidly increasingly large numbers of this new electorate.

Numbers are still very important in U.S. politics, and the rapidly expanding potential Latino electorate has caught the attention of candidates, political parties, and public officials. The gains in the numbers of Latinos registered and voting have not gone unnoticed. In the 1996 general election, Latinos significantly increased their voting numbers over their 1992 turnout (by 16 percent), while the turnout for the total population decreased by 8 percent. The result was that Latino voters made up 5 percent of the total voters in 1996, an increase over the 4 percent of 1988 and 1992.

Much of the future success of Hispanics gaining proportionate political influence will be the result of the politics of coalition. The coalitions may form among the various Latino groupings as well as with non-Latino groups that share at least part of a common political agenda. It is most probable that such coalitions will be issue-based. The primary issue for coalitions is improving the socioeconomic conditions (incomes, jobs, and education) of the less well-off. After that, two issues seem to be of particular importance to Latinos. The first is immigration. Migration back and forth between most Hispanic countries and the United States has been fairly continuous throughout U.S. history, but the 1980s and 1990s have brought unprecedented numbers of immigrants from Latin America. In 1996 over 40 percent of the foreign-born population was Hispanic. It is estimated that about one million legal and illegal immigrants enter the United States each year, and of those about 40 to 50 percent come from Central and South America and the Caribbean. Concern over immigration and its effects on the United States and over the plight of the immigrants themselves has fueled intense domestic debate and has become a point of discussion between the United States and its neighbors to the south. It is possible that immigration-related politics is actually displacing civil rights issues as the major focus of Latino politics. Another domestic issue of great relevance to Hispanics is that of language policies. This generally focuses on the preservation of the Spanish language and includes controversies over bilingual education and "official English." Actions and statements perceived to be attacks on the Spanish language, as well as on immigrants, have catalyzed political mobilization by many native-born Hispanics who see these challenges as attacks on them and their culture.

Perhaps the most fundamental situation around which Latinos unite is their perceived treatment by members of the core American culture. Throughout history, Hispanics have been discriminated against simply on account of their distinctive ethnicity. For many years there existed policies and practices that resulted in the separation of Hispanics from non-Hispanics in schools as well as overt discrimination in employment and politics. Although eliminated in many of its more blatant forms, discrimination persists and in fact may be on the upswing. After the gains of the *civil rights movement and some corresponding improvement in the well-being of many Hispanics, some forms of benign neglect and even attempts to undo developments of the 1960s and 1970s have resulted in partial regression in the areas of affirmative action and equity.

The heightened importance of immigration, its effects on public education, the economy, Latino income and education, and the related challenges to language policies and affirmative action programs have been added to the continuing rallying point of antidiscrimination to ensure a heightened role for Latinos in U.S. politics for the foreseeable future.

International Politics. Hispanic Americans are particularly well situated to play an important role in world politics, particularly in the Western Hemisphere. Most of the people of the Western Hemisphere are Spanish-speaking, and Hispanic Americans who share the cultural characteristics of both their mother countries and the United States can play a singularly significant role in bridging the gap between the United States and the countries of Latin America.

As U.S. foreign relations based on the Cold War fades, attention may well be redirected toward the Third World, including Asia, Africa, and Latin America. As countries in Latin America develop into more industrialized and modern democracies, they can benefit greatly from cooperation with the United States. Reciprocally, the United States needs to be an integral partner in the Pan-American community, treating its neighbors with respect and concern.

Likewise, Latinos in the United States, if increasingly brought into the political system, not only can be valuable intermediaries in this nation's dealings with the countries of the Western Hemisphere but also can provide an ever-growing pool of as yet untapped talent and human resources to American society itself.

(See also CONGRESS, U.S.; ELECTIONS AND VOTING BEHAVIOR; ETHNICITY; MULTICULTURALISM; POLITICAL PARTICIPATION; RACE AND RACISM; U.S.–LATIN AMERICAN RELATIONS.)

Matt S. Meier and Feliciano Rivera, *Dictionary of Mexican American History* (Westport, Conn., 1981). Joan Moore and Harry Pachon, *Hispanics in the United States* (Englewood Cliffs, N.J., 1985). Frank Bean and Marta Tienda, *The Hispanic Population of the United States* (New York, 1987). Rodolfo O. de la Garza, Louis DeSipio, F. Chris Garcia, John A. Garcia, and Angelo Falcon, *Latino Voices: Mexican, Puerto Rican, and Cuban Perspectives on American Politics* (Boulder, Colo., 1992). Rodney E. Hero, *Latinos and the U.S. Political System: Two-Tiered Pluralism* (Philadelphia, 1992). Earl Shorris. *Latinos: A Biography of the People* (New York, 1992). Geoffrey Fox, *The Hispanic Nation: Culture, Politics, and the Constructing of Identity* (Secaucus, N.J., 1996). F. Chris Garcia, *Pursuing Power: Latinos and the Political System* (Notre Dame, Ind., 1997).

F. CHRIS GARCIA

HITLER, Adolf. Probably no leader in world history has been so despised, adulated, and feared as Adolf Hitler. His responsibility for endless human suffering and vast numbers of deaths is rivaled only by *Stalin. During the twelve years of the Third Reich his charismatic sway enthralled millions of Germans who listened raptly to his words and followed his leadership to the very end. At the height of his power in 1942 he dominated almost all of Europe and western Russia while his armies and Schutzstaffel (SS) units moved from conquest to conquest. To the present time he is virtually the only historical figure whose malignant notoriety has not been subject to significant revisionist interpretations.

The meteoric rise of Adolf Hitler presents an exception to Newton's principle that no effect can be greater than its cause. He was a man who came out of nowhere. Until the age of thirty he showed no evidence of superior talents, no disciplined work habits, and no capacity for stable relationships. He had little education and few coherent ideas. Before he came to power in 1933, most dismissed him as an eccentric nonentity or an unreliable extremist. Finally, he was not even a German.

Hitler was born in 1889 at Braunau am Inn in Austria. The son of an Austrian customs official, Alois Schickelgruber Hitler, and his third wife, Klara, who came from a peasant background, Hitler was a sullen, rebellious child. The early conflicts with his authoritarian father were soothed by his indulgent mother. When she died of cancer in 1908 he lost an anchor in the stormy seas of his adolescence. By that time he had already abandoned the Catholic church and any pretensions to middle-class respectability.

From 1907 to 1913 he lived a vagrant life in Vienna. Rejected twice by the Academy of Fine Arts, he drifted aimlessly, taking odd jobs and hawking his own sketches on streets and in taverns. Although he claimed impoverishment, it was really self-imposed; he received orphan's benefits from the state and could have lived comfortably if he had wished.

During this period Hitler picked up his basic political ideas, most of them from the seamy netherworld of lower-class Vienna. They included crackpot Aryan racism with a fanatic preoccupation with "purity of blood," a stereotypical *anti-semitism set forth in violent sexual imagery, and a polyglot list of enemies: *Marxism, *capitalism, *democracy, pacifism, the stock exchange, and the press. Suffusing all of these ideas was the dream of a Greater *Germany.

After moving to Munich in 1913, he found himself surprised and elated by the outbreak of World War I in 1914. Without delay he joined a Bavarian infantry regiment and served at the front as a message runner. He demonstrated personal courage in battle and was awarded the Iron Cross–First Class, relatively rare for a lance corporal. Twice wounded, the last time temporarily blinded in a mustard gas attack, he was evacuated to a military hospital near Berlin. There he learned the terrible news of Germany's defeat and of revolutions breaking out everywhere. He vowed vengeance and claimed voices called him to rescue Germany from the treasonous grasp of Jews and Bolsheviks. In what he called "the most momentous decision of my life," he resolved "to become a politician."

In the summer of 1919, while still in the army, Hitler was assigned to report on some smaller political groups in Munich. One of these, soon to be renamed the Nationalsozialistische Deutsche Arbeiterpartei (NSDAP), he joined, and soon became its chairman. By November 1921 he led a movement of 3,000 members and began to exhibit remarkable political gifts, especially in the arts of party organization, the selection of political lieutenants, propaganda symbol manipulation, and public speech making.

From the very beginning, Hitler sensed the need to form

organizational structures to help the movement expand. Quickly he established units of the brown-shirted Sturmabteilung (SA) and a blackshirted bodyguard battalion, the SS. He also set up many other entities—district offices, newspapers, publishing houses, speakers' schools—all to promote the Nazi message. To lead these units he found the "right people": the war veteran Hermann Göring; a disgruntled intellectual, Joseph Goebbels; and the fanatic Heinrich Himmler. All had in common a personal devotion to Hitler and a lust for power.

Also at an early date Hitler recognized the power of symbols, myths, and rituals to reinforce belief in Nazism and to forge bonds of affiliation to the party. For example, the swastika, the "Heil Hitler" greeting, SS uniform regalia, and party rallies were deliberately introduced by Hitler to stimulate the convictions of true believers. Finally, Hitler's impassioned oratory was crucial to his propaganda triumphs. Hitler often extolled the superiority of the spoken over the written word. His carefully rehearsed speeches, sometimes lasting two hours, were masterful dramatizations of Nazi myths. Amplified by recently invented electrical loudspeaker systems and further extended by radio broadcasts, Hitler's voice began to be heard throughout the country.

In November 1923, at the high point of a disastrous inflation, Hitler attempted the overthrow of the Bavarian government in Munich, but it was poorly planned and was a complete failure. Police bullets stopped his marching columns, sixteen party members were killed, and Hitler was arrested. At his trial for high treason he, typically, denounced the judges and said "the eternal court of history" would set him free.

Convicted by the court, he served only nine months of his five-year sentence. In prison he turned adversity into advantage by writing his first and only major book, *Mein Kampf (My Struggle)*. This sprawling work—two volumes of turgid prose called by critics of his party "Mein Krampf" ("My Cramp")—was a mishmash of convoluted ideas. One chapter gave away his secrets for effective propaganda: "Keep the message simple"; "Repeat it and repeat it again"; "Don't admit doubts or qualifications"; "Always attack"; "Know that the biggest untruths will be believed."

The years 1925 to 1929 were lean ones for Hitler and the Nazi Party. With the introduction of a new currency after the 1923 inflation, the economy recovered and advanced rapidly. Political democracy at home seemed assured. Abroad, Germany was welcomed into the *League of Nations as a good neighbor. Hitler was left with few "fighting issues."

Nevertheless, he and his political lieutenants acted "as if" Germany still had enemies and the Nazis would soon come to power. Abandoning the illegal *putsch*, he decreed street violence, vicious propaganda, and tireless electioneering to subvert the Weimar democracy. Some radical followers demanded more socialism in the party platform. Other Nazis, looking for the financial support of industrialists, were more conservative. As always Hitler was a master of such contradictions. He claimed Nazism rose above the *Left and *Right. "We are for Germany," he cried.

By 1928 the Nazis had won only twelve seats out of 491 in the Reichstag. But their fortunes changed dramatically in the 1930 election. After the worldwide economic depression had hit Germany with particular severity—ultimately unemployment reached 32 percent—the Nazis attained 107 seats in the Reichstag. Money now streamed into the party treasury from big business seeking insurance from the Nazis and from the middle classes hoping for the defeat of *socialism and *communism.

In 1932 Hitler officially acquired German citizenship and ran for president. Although he lost to Field Marshal von Hindenburg, he was now a national figure. In the next-to-last free election in Weimar, Germany, the Nazi Party gained 37.4 percent of the vote, becoming by far the largest party in the Reichstag. A confident Hitler began a series of "power plays" with nationalists, conservative industrialists, and the military. After months of intrigues, a reluctant von Hindenburg finally appointed "the Bohemian corporal" chancellor of Germany on 30 January 1933. It was a triumphant moment for Hitler; the man from nowhere had at last become someone.

With astonishing energy Hitler moved to consolidate and expand his power. He used the Reichstag fire of 27 February 1933 as an excuse to intimidate his political opponents and suspend civil liberties. The Nazis gained in the quasi-free 5 March 1933 elections, but their 44.5 percent plurality still fell short of the hoped-for majority. So Hitler engineered an "enabling act" to give him dictatorial powers for the next four years. He used this authority immediately to "coordinate" many German institutions; this meant the elimination of unreliable opponents and Jews and the conversion of institutions into Nazi organs. One by one, venerable, proudly independent German institutions succumbed. In 1934, Hitler carried out a "blood purge" against unruly SA leaders who had pressed for a "second, more radical, revolution." After the murder of top SA leaders, the regular army and SS acquired new influence and Hitler created a new post for himself, *Führer* (Leader). Only the churches remained relatively independent of Nazi control.

The next years of the Third Reich at peace witnessed an extensive transformation of German society. Unemployment disappeared. The economy expanded. Wages increased, and cheap consumer goods filled stores. Part of the reason for the boom was Hitler's rearmament of Germany; war contracts brought jobs and artificial prosperity.

Most Germans felt pride in their country and its leader. Hitler ordered the construction of new public buildings, workers' housing developments, and *Autobahnen* (highways)—actually planned before 1933. He orchestrated the Berlin Olympics of 1936 into a great propaganda triumph. And the trains were running on time—of course they always had in Germany, but Hitler took credit for everything.

But black clouds also darkened these "achievements." With Hitler's approval, Jewish shops were boycotted, books by Jewish authors were burned, and political opponents and Jews were sent off to concentration camps such as Dachau. The Nürnberg Laws of 1935 defined what constituted Jewishness and denied Jews citizenship. In the 1938 *Kristallnacht* (Night of Broken Glass), Nazi gangs smashed synagogues and Jewish stores. Most Jews, of course, were loyal, productive citizens of Germany; they posed no conceivable threat. In fact Jews in Germany in 1933 comprised less than one percent of the population.

Germany's *foreign policy preoccupied Hitler more and

more in the 1930s. It was as if, having subdued Germany's domestic institutions, Hitler now searched for new worlds beyond Germany's borders to conquer. He found them in Germany's neighbors, and one by one they too fell before his *diplomacy by intimidation. Later on he used his armies.

As early as 1933 it was clear that Hitler would refuse to allow Germany to become a normal European power. In that year he withdrew Germany from the League of Nations. He reintroduced military conscription in 1934 and reoccupied the Rhineland in 1936. The next year, in a secret meeting with his general, Hitler outlined a vast plan for the subjugation of Europe and the Soviet Union. Having annexed Austria and Czechoslovakia, he began *World War II by an unprovoked attack against Poland in 1939.

Thereafter, German armies trampled through Denmark, Norway, the Low Countries, France, the Balkans, and finally the Soviet Union. Only Britain held out as a belligerent. The turn of the tide took place in two decisive battles: the defeat of Germany at El Alamein in North Africa in 1942, and the surrender of the German Sixth Army at Stalingrad two months later. The fiction of German invincibility had been dissolved. Hitler now called for the total mobilization of the German people to win the war, but it was too late. Hitler's promised "secret weapons" never materialized. Soviet armies entered Germany from the east and the remaining Allied armies invaded from the west.

Deep in his Berlin bunker, Hitler directed his war, sometimes deploying nonexistent armies. He cursed his fate, Germany's enemies, especially Jews, and the German people, who had proved unworthy. After marrying, Hitler and Eva Braun committed suicide together on 30 April 1945.

After the war the full extent of Hitler's depravity became known. More than one hundred Nazi concentration camps dotted the map of Europe. Even more horrifying were the mass extermination camps in Poland, where countless millions of Jews, Slavs, prisoners of war, Gypsies, and homosexuals were gassed. The names of these "death factories" have become emblems of Nazi barbarism: Auschwitz, Belzec, Chelmno, Majdanek, Sobibor, and Treblinka.

Why does Hitler continue to fascinate the contemporary mind? Perhaps his monomaniacal charismatic leadership presents challenges to conventional categories of rational political analysis. Other controversies swirl around Hitler's career. Did Hitler believe in his ideas or was he a cynical opportunist? (It would be a dangerous mistake to deny that he was a fanatic, true believer.) Were there limits to Hitler's power in Nazi Germany? (Without doubt there were many limits, often not recognized.) Was Hitler a great military leader? (He had an exceptional memory for tactical detail, and he had great gifts in planning strategic attacks. He was less strong in retreats.) Why did he commit so many mistakes in World War II, such as the needless declaration of war against the United States in 1941? (More often than not his *ideology and *psychology blinded him to reality.) Was the Final Solution intended by Hitler from the early days or did it grow out of functional decisions made during the war? (Most Hitler biographers take the intentionalist side over the functionalist in the debate.) Was Hitler insane? (No, but psychiatrists have diagnosed Hitler after his death as a "borderline personality" with strong paranoid tendencies intensified by monorchidism.)

It is well to admit that interpretations of Hitler's career necessarily serve diverse political ends and constituencies. Some Marxist historians have downplayed Hitler's importance and ascribed to him the role of puppet in the hands of monopoly capitalists. Other historians have seen him as the direct descendant of Martin Luther and Otto von Bismarck, or as "the gutter come to power." Today it is difficult to conceive the historical fact of Nazism without the leadership of Adolf Hitler or the enthrallment of millions of Germans without his spellbinding presence.

(See also Fascism; German Democratic Republic; Germany, Federal Republic of; Holocaust; War Crimes.)

Adolf Hitler, *Mein Kampf*, trans. Ralph Manheim (Cambridge, Mass., 1943). Alan Bullock, *Hitler: A Study in Tyranny*, rev. ed. (New York, 1964). J. P. Stern, *Hitler: The Fuehrer and the People* (Berkeley, Calif., 1975). Robert Waite, *The Psychopathic God: Adolf Hitler* (New York, 1977). Eberhard Jaeckel, *Hitler's World View: A Blueprint for Power* (Cambridge, Mass., 1981). Ian Kershaw, *Hitler* (New York, 1991).

RICHARD M. HUNT

HO Chi Minh. The Vietnamese revolutionary Ho Chi Minh (1890–1969) is one of the most controversial figures of the twentieth century. To some he was a patriotic figure who led his people to victory over the combined forces of French colonialism and U.S. *imperialism. To others he was a hardbitten agent of international *communism who betrayed the cause of Vietnamese *nationalism in the interests of Moscow.

Ho Chi Minh (whose real name was Nguyen Tat Thanh) was born the son of a minor imperial official in central *Vietnam in 1890. From his father he learned to resent French colonial rule over his country, and in 1911 he accepted employment with a French steamship line in order to learn the secret of Western success at its source.

In 1917 Ho Chi Minh arrived in Paris. Taking the name Nguyen Ai Quoc (Nguyen the Patriot), he became involved in nationalist activities and addressed a petition to the victorious Allied powers, meeting at Versailles to frame the post–World War I order, demanding independence for his country. In 1920 he became a founding member of the French Communist Party and three years later was called to Moscow, where he was trained as an agent by the Communist International and sent to south China with instructions to form the first Marxist revolutionary organization in French Indochina.

In 1930, under Ho's direction, a formal Indochinese Communist Party (ICP) was created. One year later he was arrested in Hong Kong on suspicion of revolutionary activities, and after a short stay in prison returned to Moscow, where he remained for five years, reportedly recovering from illness. In 1938 he returned to south China. After serving two years with Chinese Communist military units, he established contact with leading elements of the party inside Vietnam just as his country was coming under Japanese military occupation.

In May 1941 the party, now again under his leadership, formed a broad national front called the League for the Independence of Vietnam, or Vietminh, to struggle for national independence at the end of the Pacific war. In the so-called August Revolution, launched at the moment of Japanese surrender to the Allies in the summer of 1945, the Vietminh seized power in North Vietnam and declared the formation of an independent Democratic Republic of Vietnam (DRV).

Nguyen Ai Quoc, now taking the name Ho Chi Minh, was named president. But the French reoccupied the south, and when efforts to reach a compromise settlement failed, the Franco-Vietminh conflict broke out in December 1946.

In 1954, the French government agreed to a negotiated settlement, the Geneva Accords. The agreement divided Vietnam into two temporary administrative zones, with the DRV in the north and anticommunist forces in the south. Ho had played an active role in persuading his colleagues to accept a compromise.

Ho Chi Minh remained president of the DRV until his death in 1969. In the north, he promoted efforts to create a fully socialist society along Marxist-Leninist lines. Land was collectivized and the urban sector was placed under state ownership. At first, he hoped to complete reunification with the south by peaceful means, but national elections called for by the Geneva Accords did not take place, and in 1959 the DRV decided to resume a strategy of revolutionary war. Ho sought to mobilize international support for the Vietnamese cause by attempting to mediate the Sino-Soviet dispute, but had little success. Six years after his death, however, all of Vietnam was under communist rule.

In his long career as a revolutionary and as president of his country, Ho Chi Minh was both an active leader of his party and a symbol of the Vietnamese struggle for independence and national unity. His genial temperament, simple habits, and collegial style earned him the respect of his adversaries as well as the devotion of many of his compatriots. Although his writings do not display the intellectual grasp of a *Lenin or a *Mao Zedong, his sense of timing was superb and in his actions he displayed a profound sense of history and strategy.

Was he primarily a nationalist or a communist? That may remain forever a matter of speculation. It is clear that he was motivated from childhood by a desire to create a free and prosperous Vietnam. On the other hand, he had a lifelong hatred for colonial oppression and there is no reason to doubt his deep commitment to the Marxist vision of a future communist utopia. Undoubtedly, in his own mind he was both revolutionary and patriot, as communist doctrine and practice, suitably revised to meet local conditions, provided him with a framework to realize his goal of a peaceful, independent, and democratic Vietnam.

(See also DECOLONIZATION; REVOLUTION; VIETNAM WAR.)

Jean Lacouture, *Ho Chi Minh: A Political Biography,* trans. by Peter Wiles (New York, 1968). Ho Chi Minh, *Selected Writings* (Hanoi, 1977).

WILLIAM J. DUIKER

HOLLAND. See NETHERLANDS.

HOLOCAUST. The term *Holocaust* is widely used when referring to the project of physical annihilation of the "Jewish race," conceived and administered by Nazi Germany in the course of *World War II. A special name was felt necessary for the atrocity perpetrated against the Jews (the only other ethnic group which was to share their fate under Nazi rule were the Romany or Gypsies), for it differed from the much more common cases of *genocide in that it was not aimed at the incapacitation and enslavement of a conquered population nor was it an outburst of communal hostility exacerbated by war conditions. Rather, the Nazi campaign to exterminate the Jews was the product of a planned, designed, and monitored long-term operation calculated to destroy the marked category to the last man, woman, and child. Thanks to the military defeat of Germany, the project of the Holocaust was not implemented in full; by common estimates, however, up to 6 million European Jews perished during its operation.

The chronicle of the Holocaust was subjected after the war to meticulous historical research and has now been documented in great detail. Even so, efforts to explain the event continue unabated. Scholars agree that, both in its conception and its implementation, the Holocaust escapes understanding; its occurrence in the very center of the civilized world, and in the middle of a century that believed itself to exemplify the ultimate triumph of modern rationalism over cruelty and savage passions, seems to contradict the logic of the civilizing process assumed to guide the development of recent centuries.

As to the course the Holocaust actually took, historians are divided into the intentionalist and functionalist schools. Intentionalists believe that total destruction of the "Jewish race" was envisaged by *Hitler and his immediate entourage from the first moment of their struggle for power and certainly from the very beginning of Nazi rule. Steps leading logically to the "final solution" were taken systematically well before the outbreak of war, yet the last act had to wait until the war provided the necessary cover for deeds that otherwise would have aroused moral outcry and active resistance. Functionalists, on the other hand, maintain (without denying the crucial role played by Hitler's anti-Jewish obsession) that Hitler entertained a very general idea of "getting rid of the Jews" and making Germany *Judenrein* ("Jew-clean")—the rest being an outcome of the unplanned and unanticipated twists of political/military conditions and of the inner operational logic of the state, party, and martial bureaucracies that undertook the implementation of Hitler's will. According to this view, the practice of the "final solution"—the organized murder of the entire Jewish population with the help of specially formed *Einsatzgruppen* ("task units"), gas chambers, and crematoria—arose gradually, as German military victories stretched far and wide the boundaries of the "Thousand-Year Reich," thus rendering increasingly impractical the initially planned forced expulsion of Jews from German territory.

However important—and however unlikely—is the resolution of this hotly debated issue, the task of explaining the Holocaust splits into two partly separate questions. First, why was the destruction of the Jews willed in the first place—or, to put it another way, why were the Jews selected as the targets for destruction? Second, how could the mass murder, once conceived, be perpetrated, given that its implementation needed the cooperation of hundreds of thousands of experts and functionaries (regardless of their personal feelings toward the Jews), and at least the passive consent and nonresistance of the millions of witnesses and bystanders?

As to the first question, long-established Judeophobia, inherited by modern Europe from the millennium of Christendom, is the most common answer. It had its roots in the charge of betrayal and murder of Christ; it was institutionalized in premodern Christian Europe through the practice of exclusion and repetitive assaults against Jewish populations. It was given new content and promoted through new arguments in the context of a rapidly modernizing Europe, when multifarious yet widespread anxieties born of uncertainty brought about by social change were targeted at the purported morbid influence of Jews recently let out of the ghettos, or explained away with the help of theories of Jewish conspiracy. In a Europe struggling to impose new reassuring certainties, Jews were cast as the epitome of chaos and ambiguity and the ultimate source of the most painfully felt afflictions of the modern condition. In accordance with the new, scientific stance, the anti-Jewish charge was shifted from Judaism to Jewishness, from the wrong and dangerous faith the Jews preached to the biologically determined hereditary traits of the race that could not be rectified by reeducation or religious conversion. The old Judeophobia took the form of modern *anti-Semitism. It was not difficult, therefore, to seek in the baneful traits and sinister deeds of the Jews an explanation for the agonies that befell most of the German nation once the challenges of modernization were topped by the misery of the loss of World War I. It was not difficult, either, to decide that only a physical estrangement, not another missionary, assimilative effort, would put an end to the corrosive impact of the Jews.

In the memorable phrase of Hannah *Arendt, "Anti-Semitism explains perhaps the choice of the victims, but not the nature of the crime" called the Holocaust. The second question, therefore, confronts the interpreter with greater difficulty than the first. The mass murder of the Jews was not an outcome of a momentary outburst of crowd passion but of a long-term, systematic activity that involved meticulous planning, careful division of labor, and the cooperation of "ordinary" institutions and businesses normally engaged in such neutral operations as running the railway network, designing trucks, developing new chemicals, or building houses. As in all complex operations in which partial tasks must be closely correlated so that they combine in the fulfillment of the overall purpose, the Holocaust required neutralization of all personal motives that could interfere with the master plan: Its success could not be made dependent on such imponderable and unmanageable factors as the emotions and personal beliefs of the actors—for instance, the intensity of Jew-hatred in each of the hundreds of thousands of participants. Its undisturbed performance also had to be made secure from all "outside" interference—for instance, opinions of the laity who might be critical of the plan and the methods used to fulfill it.

Unlike traditional pogroms, the Holocaust was therefore a thoroughly modern operation that availed itself lavishly of the advantages offered not only by the technological equipment that modern industry alone is capable of delivering, but also by the impersonal, efficient logic of modern bureaucracy. The Holocaust was a form of genocide conceivable solely under the conditions of *modernity; by the same token, it revealed the awesome murderous potential created with the advent of modern civilization with its advanced technology and methodology of scientific management. The unholy alliance between the Holocaust and modernity expressed itself also in the unprecedentedly grandiose scale of the enterprise, and above all in its functionality. The Holocaust was conceived and executed as part of a total project toward the construction of a "new order." Jews had to be destroyed because they did not fit into the vision of an artificially designed "better society" (envisaged in the *ideology of National Socialism as a

racially clean society, catering to the superior values and historical destiny of the German race). This ambition was itself thoroughly modern and would be unthinkable if not for the modern concern to "remake the world," to bring it into "harmony" with whatever has been defined as the needs of the people for whom the new order is to be built. In this respect, the Holocaust must be classified among other attempts to annihilate whole categories of population in the name of constructing a pure and harmonious society—for instance, the mass murder of "hostile classes" on the territory of the Soviet state in the course of constructing the "classless" communist society.

The availability of technical and managerial resources developed in the advanced stage of modern civilization to societies still struggling with modernizing problems and the attendant psychic anxieties and social tensions made the Holocaust and similar mass crimes possible. This condition is propitious to the spread of chiliastic totalitarian ideologies and totalitarian rule, tantamount to a unique condensation of power by the state and a unique freedom of action for the rulers of the state. The former condition places in the hands of state rulers means of destruction of unprecedented magnitude, allowing them to exploit the condensation of power and freedom from constraint for the pursuit of grandiose social engineering schemes which more often than not involve the thorough "remaking" of the population insofar as it is deemed unsuitable for the perfect society about to be constructed.

The conditions that made the Holocaust possible in Germany more than half a century ago—the coincidence of modern technology and vision on the one hand and the tensions characteristic of the process of modernization on the other— persist today in many parts of the globe. Therefore, it cannot be assumed that the Holocaust has been in contemporary history a unique event never to be repeated. The exploration of the roots of Holocaust-type phenomena and the conditions under which their recurrence may be prevented therefore figures prominently among current social scientific and political concerns.

(See also NUREMBERG TRIALS; TOTALITARIANISM.)

George A. Kren and Leon Rappoport, *The Holocaust and the Crisis of Human Behavior* (New York, 1980). Leo Kuper, *Genocide: Its Political Use in the Twentieth Century* (New Haven, Conn., 1981). Raoul Hilberg, *The Destruction of European Jews*, 3 vols. (New York, 1983). Michael R. Marrus, *The Holocaust in History* (London, 1987). Richard L. Rubenstein and John Roth, *Approaches to Auschwitz* (San Francisco, 1987). Zygmunt Bauman, *Modernity and the Holocaust* (Ithaca, N.Y., 1989)

ZYGMUNT BAUMAN

HONDURAS. The population of Honduras is about 5 million and is largely mestizo; there are small concentrations of African Americans in the North Coast areas as well as in the Bay Islands. Although Roman Catholicism is the dominant religion, Protestantism has made important inroads in recent years. The country's capital is Tegucigalpa, which has a population of about 800,000. San Pedro Sula, located in the steamy North Coast area, has a population that has ballooned to about 500,000 in recent years. It is the economic heart of the country, producing almost 40 percent of its national product.

The Honduran economy is heavily dependent on the production of agricultural exports. Bananas and coffee account for about one-half of export income. Industrial production lags far behind other Central American countries and government expectations of economic growth based on an increased number of assembly plants (*maquilas*) have not been realized. Indeed, the latter have come under international criticism for exploitation of workers, particularly women and children. The national currency has been under severe stress because of capital flight, government deficit financing, and a high value relative to the U.S. dollar. Just under 50 percent of the population still lives in the countryside, where there is serious pressure for *land reform. Conditions in the country were worsened in late October 1998 by the devastating impact of Hurricane Mitch, which killed hundreds of Hondurans and destroyed 85,000 homes and 70 percent of its transportation infrastructure. While international response was substantial, charges of government inefficiency and corruption in distributing the aid led some donors to hire their own construction companies and work directly with non-governmental organizations, which assumed major roles in organizing reconstruction. As a result the latter have substantially increased their capacity to influence government.

Another important political actor in Honduras is labor. The formal organization of Honduras's *labor movement dates from 1954 and the successful strike of workers on the country's foreign-owned North Coast banana plantations. The Honduras Workers' Confederation (CTH) is the country's most important and powerful labor organization. Bringing together workers from banana, public sector, and peasant unions, the CTH has periodically taken a major leadership role in the promotion of political change in Honduras. A Christian-based General Confederation of Workers (CGT) emerged during the early 1960s during a period of intense rural mobilization. A Marxist-oriented Federation of Honduras Workers (FUTH) represents public utility and beverage workers' unions.

Despite the quite significant role of labor confederations, political life in Honduras has been dominated by civilian caudillos and military strongmen. Following nearly twenty years of military rule between 1960 and 1980, a civilian government was elected in 1980. Since then, there have been five other democratically elected presidents. In practice, the executive branch has primacy in the country's decision making. A unicameral legislature has gradually expanded its role but still is subordinate to the president and the military. The country's system of justice is controlled by its Supreme Court, whose nine justices are appointed for four years coinciding with the presidential term. A National Electoral Council administers the country's elections and voting census. However, the politicized nature of the organization has traditionally made it the focal point of intense partisan activity during each electoral campaign.

Honduras has one of the oldest party systems in Latin America. Both the National and Liberal parties trace their antecedents to the late 1800s. The former tended to be a conservative, promilitary party during much of the post–World War II period. The Liberal Party was more oriented toward lower classes and given to social reform efforts. By the mid-1980s, however, the platforms of two parties were similar in orientation. Personalistic conflict within both parties is heavy and usually divisive; their constituencies are cross-class in nature, although the National Party tends to draw more heavily on rural voters. Two other parties have regularly contested power during the last three decades, but neither the Christian Democratic nor the Innovation and Unity parties have provided serious challenges to the National and Liberal parties.

Honduras's key location in the middle of Central America gives it a strategic importance in diplomatic and economic matters. In the 1980s, the country was a key ally of the United States in its efforts to undercut the Sandinista government in Nicaragua and the guerrillas in El Salvador. More recently such issues as obtaining greater access to the U.S. market and investment, controlling the transshipment of drugs to North America, and increased illegal immigration to the United States have become priorities in bilateral relations. None will be resolved easily.

(See also MAQUILADORAS; U.S.–CENTRAL AMERICAN RELATIONS; U.S.–LATIN AMERICAN RELATIONS.)

Mark B. Rosenberg and Philip L. Shepherd, eds., *Honduras Confronts Its Future* (Boulder, Colo., 1986).

MARK B. ROSENBERG

HONG KONG. A British colony from 1841 to 30 June 1997, Hong Kong reverted to Chinese sovereignty as a Special Administrative Region (SAR) of the People's Republic of China (PRC) on 1 July 1997. The British domain had been established in three phases: in 1842 Hong Kong island was ceded to Britain in perpetuity, as was Kowloon peninsula in 1860; and in 1989 a ninety-nine-year lease was signed on the New Territories, which accounted for 92 percent of the domain's total land area of 1,095 square kilometers. Located at the estuary of the Pearl River in southern *China; Hong Kong is a highly urbanized community of 6.8 million, of whom over 95 percent are ethnic Chinese.

From the mid-nineteenth century to 1949, Hong Kong was an outpost of Western penetration into the Chinese market and a major service and transport center for the China coast, Southeast Asia, and trans-Pacific trade. The 1949 Chinese Communist revolution and the 1950 Korean War UN embargo greatly curtailed the colony's China trade and forced it to industrialize. Light manufacturing flourished from the 1950s until the 1970s when Chinese economic reform revived Hong Kong's entrepôt functions. Since then, with much of its manufacturing facilities relocated to South China, Hong Kong has become a world financial and communication hub for the Chinese and Asian markets. Hong Kong's GDP per capita was US $26,115 in 1997, with nearly 80 percent of its total workforce of 3.2 million in the service sector and only 11 percent in manufacturing, which accounted for less than 10 percent of GDP.

Until 1985, the people of Hong Kong enjoyed social and economic freedoms but no democracy under British colonial rule. The governor was always a British official dispatched from London who in turn appointed all members of the Executive and Legislative Councils. British expatriates monopolized the upper echelons of the civil service until the late 1980s. Operating under the British common-law legal system, the colonial regime practiced limited government—low taxation, balanced budget, lax economic regulations, and minimal social expenditures—behind a laissez-faire façade which in fact favored big business, especially British interests.

In 1982, the PRC and Britain entered into secret negotiations—from which the people of Hong Kong themselves were excluded—regarding the future of Hong Kong. Signed on 19 December 1984, the Sino-British Joint Declaration stipulated that the colony would be returned to China in 1997; China, in turn, promised that Hong Kong SAR would retain "a high degree of autonomy," and that its capitalist economy, social freedoms, and legal system would remain unchanged for fifty years according to the "one country, two systems" formula. The accord also specified the selection of the SAR chief executive and legislature by elections. Differences on the exact meaning of such "elections" were to color Hong Kong politics during the transitional years 1984–1997.

In 1985 in a first, the British incorporated twenty-four indirectly elected "functional constituency" seats into the sixty-member legislature. Further advance toward direct elections was stalled until 1991 by the need of "convergence" with the PRC's Hong Kong Basic Law, the SAR's mini-constitution, which was promulgated in April 1990. The *Tiananmen Square incident of 4 June 1989 had a decisive impact on the finalization of the Basic Law, which was tightened to ban any future Hong Kong "subversion" against the PRC central government and placed strict limits on directly elected components of the SAR legislature at least until 2007. The historic 1991 Hong Kong legislative elections included eighteen universal suffrage, directly elected seats. Seventeen of these were captured by the pro-democratic camp, which gained two thirds of the popular vote with a voter turnout rate of nearly 40 percent. All pro-Beijing candidates were defeated.

In mid-1992, the arrival of the last British governor, Chris Patten, and his reform proposal for the 1995 elections signaled a change in British policy from appeasement to confrontation with China over Hong Kong. The Patten reform enlarging the democratic franchise was condemned by Beijing, which retaliated by invalidating the "through train" agreement under which the 1995 legislature elected under British rule would serve until 1999, two years into the SAR era. In June 1993 Beijing preemptively set up a shadow government organ as "the second stove" to take charge of SAR preparatory work without British cooperation.

The September 1995 elections drew a turnout rate of 36 percent to choose twenty directly elected members and thirty indirectly elected functional seats, plus ten electoral college seats. The democratic camp took 64 percent of the popular vote and a total of twenty-nine seats. The pro-Beijing camp performed poorly. On 11 December 1996 the Beijing-appointed 400-member SAR Selection Committee chose Beijing's preferred candidate, C. H. Tung, a Shanghai-born tycoon, as the first SAR chief executive. Ten days later, the committee created a pro-Beijing, business-oriented "SAR provisional legislature" to replace the one elected in 1995. The lack of legitimacy was evident in the fact that Selection Committee members themselves claimed fifty one of the sixty provisional legislature seats.

At midnight, 30 June 1997, Hong Kong was retroceded to PRC sovereignty, an event witnessed by millions around the world via a televised Sino-British ceremony in Hong Kong. Right after the departure of the British delegation, the PRC top leadership swore in C. H. Tung and the senior SAR officials as well as the "SAR provisional legislature," thus fulfilling Beijing's threat to undo the Patten reforms.

Under domestic Hong Kong and international pressure and because the "SAR provisional legislature" had no justification under the Basic Law, elections were held to elect the first SAR Legislative Council on 24 May 1998. An unexpectedly high voter turnout rate of over 53.3 percent (1.5 million) helped to secure the return of the democratic camp, which gained twenty out of sixty seats and two thirds of the popular vote even in the face of deliberately distorted electoral rules enacted by the "provisional legislature."

Beijing so far has refrained from overt and direct interference in the SAR internal administration. The PRC authorities control only the SAR's foreign affairs and defense (as symbolized by the 8,000 Chinese troops in Hong Kong). Thus there may be grounds for optimism that the "one country, two systems" principle as codified in the Basic Law will be respected. However, damage was done by the "SAR provisional legislature" in collusion with the executive-led SAR government in rolling back civil liberties and human rights legislation in their first months in office. Such regressive measures, carried out by a system lacking checks and balances and accountability, do not augur well for the prosperity and stability of Hong Kong as a free and democratic society under PRC sovereignty. It would also affect Beijing's cherished goals for reunification with Taiwan and its relations with Hong Kong's many global partners, especially the Western industrial democracies.

Ming K. Chan, ed., *Precarious Balance: Hong Kong Between China and Britain, 1842–1992* (Armonk, N.Y., 1994). Michael Yahuda, *Hong Kong: China's Challenge* (London, 1996). Ming K. Chan, ed., *The Challenge of Hong Kong's Reintegration with China* (Hong Kong, 1997).

MING K. CHAN

HORN OF AFRICA. Associated with *war and famine in recent years, the Horn of Africa is a strategically located and potentially rich region. Lying astride the northwest Indian Ocean and the Red Sea, across the oil-rich Arabian peninsula and the Persian Gulf region, it has been a crossroads of history between Africa and Asia.

The combined effect of history and geography is reflected in the region's demographic makeup, culture, national identities, and religion. Its close proximity to the cradles of Christianity and *Islam facilitated the early spread of these two religions, which acted as centralizing and harmonizing factors, and at times as causes of conflict. They have both left an indelible mark on the life and peoples of the region.

More recently, European colonial rule left its mark on the region, notably in the realm of governance, the capitalist market economy, and in the colonially fixed boundaries which cross ethno/linguistic lines and define the national/state identity of the five countries of the region—Sudan, Eritrea, Ethiopia, Djibouti, and Somalia.

The postcolonial political economy of the region, as of much of Africa, is a study in squandered resources and missed opportunities caused by disastrous policies and politics. Failed development models, which were externally oriented and urban-biased, mostly inspired by external sources of finance, have left the populations burdened with huge debts. That in turn has conditioned the policies and behaviors of the governments, leaving the people worse off. The region's economic potential—both human and material—thus remains largely unrealized.

Sudan and Ethiopia were once considered the breadbaskets for the region and beyond, but have become basket cases. Somalia and Eritrea have marine and other resources that have been barely touched. And Djibouti's deep-sea, natural harbor could make it the Hong Kong of the region. The region as a whole not only can be self-sufficient but can produce surplus for export in livestock, dairy products, fruits and vegetables, oil seeds, gum arabic, cotton, coffee, oil, copper, and other resources. This potential can be realized only if present policies are changed in favor of self-sustainable development strategies which can engage the optimal participation of the populations and which benefit the majority, not just narrowly based urban elites. Moreover, changes in policies will require drastic changes in politics.

As things stand, faulty development policies have been exacerbated by disastrous politics. The latter may be summed up as the politics of domination and exclusion which have engendered conflicts drawing foreign intervention and a massive flow of costly arms into the region. The militarization of the region, and its consequent brutalization of society, have had a destabilizing effect.

Political instability has characterized the region against a grim background of economic stagnation, social unrest, and ethnic cleavage. Until recently, only Djibouti has been relatively stable. Its relative stability can be attributed largely to the wisdom of its leadership, which maintained a fair balance in governance between its two ethnic groups—the Issa Somalis and the Afars—and which stayed neutral in the Ethiopian–Somali conflict over the Ogaden. Recent events are raising questions about Djibouti's stability, as some Afars have revolted on the grounds of what they claim to be an Issa domination of the state. Djibouti adopted a French-style presidential system upon gaining independence in 1977, after over a century of French rule.

In contrast, Somalia began with a Westminster-type parliamentary government in 1960. However, Somali politics proved to be clannish and fractious, precipitating a military coup in 1969 led by Siad Barre. The military regime established one-party rule with "scientific socialism" as its guiding ideology. The promised healing and unifying quality of this ideology was short-lived, overwhelmed as it was by clan politics. Somalia remains a nation in search of a state. Meanwhile, the northern part broke away but is yet to gain international recognition.

In Ethiopia, Emperor *Haile Selassie's "modernizing" monarchy was overthrown by a radical military group which, under Mengistu's leadership, imposed a Soviet-style one-party rule on the country. *Marxism-*Leninism was written into the 1984 constitution as guide and arbiter of politics and society, with suffocating effect. The overthrow of both the Siad and Mengistu regimes in 1991 raised hopes of *democracy, equal rights, and self-determination. The struggle for these ends continues.

In Sudan, a civilian parliamentary government, to which the departing British transferred power in 1956, was overthrown two years later by a military takeover. Since then civilian and military governments have exchanged power four times. The civilian side of the equation has been dominated by the Umma, a sectarian party, continually challenged by another sectarian party, which facilitated military intervention. The current military regime is backed by a new religious party, the National Islamic Front, which insists on the application of *Shari'a (Islamic law) in all Sudan. Hence the continued rebellion in the south.

The politics of exclusion plays out in the region with variations on a theme, that is, domination by one group, whether on an ethnic, sectarian, fractional, or regional basis. Thus in Sudan, the south (mostly Christian) is excluded from power. In Ethiopia the central Amhara group dominated the country to the exclusion of the Oromo and others until 1991. Rebellions by the southern Sudanese and the Oromo can be explained in terms of the politics of exclusion. In Somalia also, the rebellion and secession of the northern Somalis was caused by their exclusion from power and allegations of economic discrimination of their region in favor of the south.

Eritrea's case is unique: it was a case of denied *decolonization. The limited autonomy that was imposed on the Eritreans under a UN-arranged federation with Ethiopia was abolished by Emperor Haile Selassie in 1962, provoking the armed struggle which ended in Eritrean victory in May 1991. Following a referendum to be held in April 1993 under international observation, the Eritreans are seeking to build an independent, democratic nation-state. The end of the war in Eritrea and the overthrow of the Mengistu regime in Ethiopia were followed by a conference held in Addis Ababa on 1–5 July 1991 which issued a charter with a framework for the principles of self-determination, democracy, and mutual accommodation.

The above-listed conflicts, in addition to the strategic location of the region, have drawn foreign interventions—from the two superpowers, which changed clients as it suited them, to the Israelis, the Cubans, and other surrogates of the superpowers. The end of the Cold War seemed to augur well for a peaceful resolution of the costly wars in the Horn of Africa. Unfortunately, the war continues in the Sudan, Eritrea and Ethiopia went to war in May–June 1998, and Somalia is still a nation in search of a unified state.

(See also COLONIAL EMPIRES; DEVELOPMENT AND UNDERDEVELOPMENT; ERITREAN WAR OF INDEPENDENCE; ETHNICITY; FOOD POLITICS; INTERNATIONAL DEBT; MILITARISM; MODERNIZATION; ONE-PARTY SYSTEM; RELIGION AND POLITICS.)

Bereket Habte Selassie, *Conflict and Intervention in the Horn of Africa* (New York, 1980). Georges Nzongola-Ntalaja, ed., *Conflict in the Horn of Africa* (Atlanta, 1991). Francis Deng, *War of Visions: Conflict of Identities in the Sudan* (Washington D.C., 1996). Hussein Mohammad Adam and Richard Ford, eds., *Mending Rips in the Sky: Options for Somali Communities in the 21st Century* (Lawrenceville, N.J., 1997).

BEREKET HABTE SELASSIE

HOUSING. See WELFARE STATE.

HUMAN DEVELOPMENT INDEX. The annual *Human Development Reports* of the *United Nations Development Programme (UNDP) have presented the Human Development Index (HDI) since 1990. A single index is useful in focusing attention on an alternative to Gross National Product (GNP) for measuring and comparing national development. It has considerable political appeal. It has a stronger impact on the mind, draws public attention more powerfully than a long list of many indicators, combined with a qualitative discussion. The strongest analytical argument in its favor is that it shows up the inadequacies of other indexes. It directs our attention away from material goods to the social sectors: nutrition, education, and health. But it should always be remembered that human development is a much richer concept than what can be caught in any index, whether GNP or HDI.

The HDI comprises (1) the logarithm of GDP per head, calculated at the real purchasing power, not at exchange rates, up to the international poverty line (in reports subsequent to the first of 1990, this was modified in various ways); (2) literacy rates and, since the 1991 report, mean years of schooling; and (3) life expectancy at birth. These disparate items are brought to a common denominator by counting the distance between the best and the worst performers and thereby achieving a ranking of countries. Critics have said that not only are the weights of the three components arbitrary but also what is excluded and what is included.

One of the drawbacks of average income per head is that it is an average that can conceal great inequalities. But, it may be objected, the components of the HDI, namely life expectancy and literacy, are also averages. They can conceal vast discrepancies between males and females, rich and poor, urban and rural residents, different ethnic or religious groups. The HDI has in fact been illuminatingly disaggregated by gender, region, and ethnic groups for a few countries for which data were available. The HDI has also been adjusted for gender disparities. This procedure makes a considerable difference to the rankings of countries.

The HDI does not include measures of other aspects of human development such as leisure, security, justice, freedom, human rights, and self-respect. It would be possible to register a high HDI in a zoo or even a well-run prison. And, although at low incomes illness often leads to death, the HDI has no independent indicator of morbidity, absence of which is surely one of the most basic needs. Life can be nasty, brutish, and long.

(See also DEVELOPMENT AND UNDERDEVELOPMENT; INEQUALITIES; LANGUAGE POLICY.)

Human Development Reports 1990–1998, for the United Nations Development Programme (Oxford). See especially the technical notes. Paul Streeten, "Human Development: The Debate about the Index" *International Social Science Journal* 47, no. 1 (March 1995): 25–37.

PAUL STREETEN

HUMAN RIGHTS. Human rights do not emerge exclusively from Western philosophical and political principles. The cultures of every world region contain important references to principles and standards of behavior in human relations. Amartya Sen tells of the Indian emperor Ashoka in the third century B.C.E. whose political inscriptions favored tolerance and individual freedom, both as part of state policy and in relations of different people to each other. The domain of toleration, Ashoka argued, must include everybody without exception.

According to Hans-Peter Gasser, the first humanitarian legal rules are often found in major literary works of the culture (for example the Indian epic *Mahâbhârata*), in religious books (such as the *Bible* or the *Quran*), or in rules on the art of war (the rules of *Manu* or the Japanese code of behavior, the *bushido*).

For the language of *rights, as opposed to the values of freedom, respect, and tolerance, we must refer to the revolutionary texts of the eighteenth century. The American Declaration of Independence in 1776 claimed as self-evident truths "that all men are created equal; that they are endowed by their Creator with certain unalienable rights; that among these are life, liberty and the pursuit of happiness." In 1789 the French Declaration on the Rights of Man and the Citizen included a catalog of rights and emphasized the rights of citizens to participate in the formation of law.

The authors of the American and French declarations wanted to protect individual rights against arbitrary rule. They believed in natural law, human reason, and universal order and believed rights to be the property of persons capable of exercising rational choice—which excluded women, nonwhites, and slaves.

By contrast, under our modern definition, human rights are *universal*, a term introduced during the final drafting of the Universal Declaration of Human Rights, to emphasize that it was not just the new member states of the *United Nations who had to respect these rights. Since then, the concept of human rights has attained increasingly broad support and is now firmly established under international law. Universality in this context also means that human rights apply to everyone—by virtue of their humanity—everywhere, and at all times.

The international human rights revolution is relatively recent. Latin American states sought to enforce human rights through the International Conferences of American States (first held in 1890) and the Central American Court of Justice (1908–1918). In the 1920s and 1930s, the League of Nations and the International Labour Organization made some headway on protection for national minorities and labor standards, though they did not tackle human rights as such. The Charter of the United Nations, adopted in 1945, committed the new world organization to promote "universal respect for, and observance of, human rights and fundamental freedoms." A number of non-governmental organizations and Latin American countries pushed hard for a stronger charter reference to human rights and reminded the major powers of promises made during World War II.

Immediately following the war, the victors prosecuted individuals responsible for wartime human rights violations, convincing them of war crimes and crimes against humanity in the International Military Tribunal at Nuremberg and the International Military Tribunal for the Far East in Tokyo. The UN General Assembly affirmed the findings of both tribunals, and by 1950 the movement toward a permanent International Criminal Court had already begun.

On 10 December 1948, the UN General Assembly proclaimed the Universal Declaration of Human Rights, a document that sets out philosophical foundations of rights, including their universality and equality of application. The declaration establishes a broad range of civil and political rights, including freedom of assembly, freedom of thought and expression, and the right to participate in government. The declaration also proclaims that social and economic rights are indispensable, including the right to education, the right to work, and the right to participate in the cultural life of the community.

The declaration allows limits on human rights, but only when determined by law, to protect the right of others and to meet the "the just requirements of morality, public order and the general welfare in a democratic society." A debate has arisen over whether the human rights message should be tempered by reference to responsibilities, and how to reflect the fact that some societies, in particular Asian societies, are said to value respect for authority, family, and community over individual freedoms. However, no state now formally questions the commitments contained in the Universal Declaration.

A major *Cold War controversy between the Socialist states and the West marked the declaration's final adoption. The Socialist bloc argued, among other things, that civil and political rights should be limited so as to prevent the return of Fascism. These states were unable to achieve their aims in the final wording of the declaration and eventually abstained in the General Assembly vote, along with Saudi Arabia and South Africa.

The language of the declaration contrasts strikingly with the political conditions at the time of its adoption. The peoples under colonial domination had no place in the drafting process, nor were they immediately the beneficiaries of these new rights. Yet the declaration boldly asserted in its preamble that "it is essential, if man is not to be compelled to have recourse, as a last resort, to rebellion against tyranny and oppression, that human rights should be protected by the rule of law."

Over the years, new additions and perspectives have broadened the human rights catalog. Treaties such as the African Charter of Human and Peoples' Rights of 1981 and the Arab Charter on Human Rights (1994) reflect postcolonial thinking and add elements not included in the Universal Declaration. Furthermore, the UN has broadened the list of rights through a series of resolutions—on independence for colonial countries and peoples, on the right to *self-determination, on natural resources, on the new international economic order, and on the right to development. These resolution have addressed some of the questions of inequality between states and the fundamental structural problems of the international order. It has been pointed out that the Universal Declaration is clearly not "exhaustive but only exemplary" of the human rights and fundamental freedoms mentioned in the UN Charter.

Translated into over 200 languages, the Universal Declaration has had a huge influence in spreading the philosophy of human rights and in inspiring legal texts and decisions. Peoples and individuals around the world have often invoked it when demanding respect for their rights. Several constitutions have taken its provisions as the basis for a bill of rights; and national and international courts have subsequently invoked the declaration in their judgments.

Soon after the UN adopted the Universal Declaration, disagreement arose over whether economic and social rights gave rise to the same obligations as civil and political rights. The West pointed to the lack of political freedom in the Socialist countries, insisting that civil and political rights had to be given priority. The Socialist bloc responded by championing economic equality and social benefits for all, charging that that the West lacked respect for economic rights. In spite of these battles, the General Assembly adopted three new instruments on 16 December 1966: the International Covenant on Economic, Social and Cultural Rights, the International Covenant on Civil and Political Rights, and the Optional Protocol, which provides for individual complaints about violations of the civil covenant. Together with the Universal Declaration of Human Rights these three treaties make up what is often known as "The International Bill of Rights."

The Cold War antagonists continued their disagreement as to what the UN should do to ensure respect for this Bill of Rights. Each side accused the other of human rights violations, but both sides seemed content to avoid concrete action. State representatives at the United Nations put their energy into a welter of resolution writing and treaty making. Even before the Universal Declaration, the General Assembly had adopted the Convention on the Prevention and Punishment of the Crime of *Genocide. The General Assembly subsequently adopted a range of treaties and conventions on Racial Discrimination, *Apartheid, *Torture, the Rights of the Child, Discrimination against Women, and the Rights of Migrant Workers. This international legislation became part of an impressive legal framework, monitored by expert bodies at the UN. In addition regional commissions and courts established by the Organization of American States, the Council of Europe, and the Organization of African Unity monitor compliance with the relevant regional treaties.

Countries worldwide have now started to embed human rights in their legal systems. The Universal Declaration and the international treaties have often become part of the law of the land through increasing references in national constitutions and legislation. Many countries have enacted greater human rights protection than demanded by the Universal Declaration, as for example the South African Constitution of 1996. The explosion of national human rights institutions around the world has transformed the politics of human rights from political rhetoric into an instrument for changing the lives of people everywhere.

As rights have become more truly universal, scholars have been interested in discovering the deep cultural connections among societies, to understand the rights enunciated in the international documents in terms of familiar local cultural traditions rather than alien law-making process.

The second World Conference on Human Rights, held in Vienna in 1993, brought together representatives from 171 states and also thousands of human rights activists and representatives of rights organizations from all over the world. Many were surprised at the diversity of the numerous participants. A movement had mushroomed. The governments reaffirmed their commitment to the Universal Declaration and set out a program of action. The also called for a UN high commissioner for human rights (a post created later that year by the General Assembly).

The conference showed strains in the world of human rights. There was a legitimacy crisis over who could speak in the interests of the people whose rights were being debated. The clamor from human rights organizations shocked many governments. Women also unsettled the conference by demanding that their rights be recognized and insisting that delegates consider questions of violence against women, rape during armed conflict, and systematic practices that disadvantage women. While new divisions arose, old ones diminished. Former Cold War antagonists abandoned their fight over the priority for different types of rights. The conference even reaffirmed the right to development (championed by developing countries and opposed by the United States) as "a universal and inalienable right and an integral part of fundamental human rights."

Two main concluding observations seem pertinent. First, governments do not now insist on a so-called *domaine réservé* excluded from human rights scrutiny. States have agreed in the Vienna World Conference and at the UN General Assembly that "the promotion and protection of all human rights is a legitimate concern of the international community." States which are singled out for criticism of their human rights record are nowadays less likely to appeal to the blanket defense that such criticism is "an interference in internal affairs," and more likely to point to the dubious records of the accusers, or the selectivity involved in choosing to highlight the issue in question. In fact, human rights law now sometimes even requires states to exert criminal jurisdiction over individuals accused of international crimes (such as torture) committed in other countries. And in July 1998 a conference in Rome adopted a statute for an International Criminal Court with jurisdiction over war crimes, genocide, and crimes against humanity, to come into force as soon as sixty countries ratify.

Second, human rights protection is now no longer seen as an end in itself, but rather as an integral part of other international goals such as maintaining peace and security, preventing refugee flows and protecting returning refugees, promoting international development, fighting against corruption, establishing a fair trading regime, and moving toward regional integration. Efforts to protect human rights have come a long way since the proclamations and declarations that launched the idea. Not only have human rights organizations sprung up in all regions of the world and at all levels (local, regional, and international) but human rights have become a rallying cry for civil society and opposition groups. Many now use human rights as a yardstick for considering the legitimacy of governments. The human rights message helped trigger the transformation to democracy in parts of Latin America and in Central and Eastern Europe. However, considerable concern remains.

In the post–Cold War world, the weapons trade has fueled violent conflicts in all regions of the world. Globalized markets and competition for foreign investment have forced governments to reduce social protections and ignore their commitment to human rights. These shifts have alerted many human rights groups to new implications for the enjoyment of human rights. Attention is now turning to large corporations, the international financial institutions, the international trade and investment regimes, and the power of regional organizations. Nevertheless, there is a determination to ensure that states and governments are held accountable for failing to live up to their international obligations.

We care about rights because we care about each other. The language of human rights obligations is the simplest way to express that sense of sympathy and outrage. Concerned citizens will continue to demand change as long as the inherent dignity of any human being remains threatened, unprotected, and unrealized.

(See also NUREMBERG TRIALS; REPRODUCTIVE RIGHTS.)

Theo van Boven, "General Course on Human Rights," vol. 4, bk. 2, *Collected Courses of the Academy of European Law* (1993), 1–106. Henry Steiner and Philip Alston, *International Human Rights in Context* (Oxford, 1996). Andrew Clapham; "Mainstreaming Human Rights at the United Nations—Challenge for the First High Commissioner for Human Rights," vol. 7, bk. 2, *Collected Courses of the Academy of European Law* (1999), 159–234. Raija Hanski and Markku Suksi, eds., *An Introduction to the International Protection of Human Rights* (Åbo, Finland, 1999). Paul Lauren, *The Evolution of International Human Rights: Visions Seen* (Philadelphia, 1999). Johannes Morsink, *The Universal Declaration of Human Rights Origins, Drafting, and Intent* (Philadelphia, 1999). Peter Van Ness, ed., *Debating Human Rights* (London, 1999). D. P. Forsythe, *Human Rights in International Relations* (Cambridge, U.K., 2000).

ANDREW CLAPHAM

HUMANITARIAN INTERVENTION. See overleaf.

HUNGARY. After emerging in the late Middle Ages as a major European power, Hungary came under the domination of the Ottoman and Habsburg Empires. The roots of the modern state lie in the national revival movement of the early nineteenth century. The *revolution of 1848 secured autonomy in a new, liberal constitution, only to be crushed by Austrian and Russian arms. The Austro-Hungarian Compromise of 1867 granted Hungary self-government, albeit with joint administration of foreign affairs, defense, and finance. The bicameral legislature consisted of an upper house of civil and religious notables and a lower house elected on the basis of a limited, property-linked suffrage. In a predominantly agrarian society, the *peasantry enjoyed no direct political representation. The conservative ruling elite divided mainly over the merits of qualified autonomy and warded off the challenges of democratic socialism and bourgeois *liberalism with measured reforms and industrial development.

The defeat of Austria-Hungary in *World War I unleashed disintegrative ethnonational pressures. Barely half of Hungary's population was ethnically Magyar, and initially liberal nationalities laws had given way to more assimilative policies that fed separatist tendencies. Faced with Allied demands for territorial concessions, an embryonic liberal regime headed by Count Mihály Károlyi surrendered power to a Communist–Social Democrat directorate that styled Hungary a republic of councils. This "dictatorship of the proletariat," led by the Communist Béla Kun, attempted for four months in 1919 to impose Leninist revolution and then collapsed.

With the restoration of the old constitution in 1920, Hungary became a fully independent kingdom, the actual head of state being Admiral Miklós Horthy. The impartial rule of law generally prevailed, and the franchise was initially extended to two-thirds of the adult population, then trimmed again; only the Communist Party was proscribed. Until 1944 a variable coalition known as the governing party ruled Hungary. The dominant political values were irredentist *nationalism, inspired by the Treaty of Trianon, which reduced the country's territory and population by two-thirds, and a conservatism hostile not only to left and right radicalism but to bourgeois liberalism as well. The political opposition encompassed the Social Democrats, who however had agreed to limit their activity; a populist movement that focused on the needs of the peasantry; and, in the late 1930s, right-wing radicals, including the fascist Arrow Cross party. The government enacted a limited *land reform and social welfare measures and labored to surmount the economic consequences of territorial truncation and the depression; industrialization received a boost from the expansion of German economic influence.

(cont. on p. 375)

HUMANITARIAN INTERVENTION refers to a range of unilateral or collective actions taken by the international community to provide assistance to the population of a target state experiencing unacceptable and persistent levels of human suffering caused by natural disasters, deliberate government policy, or state collapse. Humanitarian intervention is unique and is easily distinguishable from other types of intervention discussed below because it includes moral considerations in the framing of a state or group of states' response to events taking place outside its borders; it places humanitarian concerns above most other concerns—often defined in terms of national security interests—which drive the foreign policy of sovereign states. Also, to classify an intervention as "humanitarian" is to ascribe to it greater moral and legal importance, making it easier to justify politically before an electorate, especially when considerable public expenditures are involved.

Historically, there have been two traditions of state intervention: intervention to preserve the balance of power and intervention to assert internationally accepted values. The former was associated with the foreign policy interests of great powers. Thus, for example, the foreign policies of Britain in the nineteenth century and the United States in the twentieth century have included strong interventionist components. The second tradition, intervention to assert internationally accepted values, never established or claimed that the first form was problematic because such values reflected Western views.

The current debate about humanitarian intervention reflects important changes that have occurred in international relations since the end of the Cold War. A unique feature of this period of intense superpower rivalry was the division of the world along ideological lines between the United States and the former Soviet Union. These countries enforced a level of hegemonic stability that temporarily suppressed potentially destructive conflicts in their respective areas of influence.

Conflicts did arise during the Cold War and some of them triggered external intervention. However, many of these conflicts—such as in Afghanistan, Angola, El Salvador, and Nicaragua—were primarily proxy wars which occurred at the periphery of the system. Since they were relatively few, they did not constitute major threats to the international system. Also, by avoiding direct and simultaneous involvement in these proxy wars, the superpowers reduced the risk of escalation, possibly involving nuclear weapons, which might threaten the overall stability of the system.

The end of the Cold War and the collapse of the Soviet Union resulted in fundamental changes in the structure and internal balance of the international system. The predictable nature of superpower relations within a bipolar international system gave way to a more unstable interaction both between and within states. This has produced various international crises of dimensions not seen since the end of World War II. Indeed, a peculiar feature of the emerging international system in the immediate aftermath of the Cold War is the increasing number and ferocity of intrastate conflicts. Such conflicts—triggered primarily by ethnic, nationalistic, or religious tensions—are associated with increasing occurrences of governmental breakdown, disputed sovereignty, and state collapse. These conflicts are also the primary cause of most complex emergencies, often involving unspeakable atrocities and widespread human suffering, that have confronted the international community in the last decade. Prominent features of these crises include *war crimes and an extensive repertoire of crimes against humanity like *genocide, ethnic cleansing, rape, and the displacement of large segments of the population through deliberate starvation.

As mentioned before, humanitarian intervention is one of several mechanisms available to the international community to alleviate such human suffering and, in some cases, prevent the deaths of millions of innocent people, particularly in situations when the state or organized elements within it deliberately slaughter or starve large segments of the population for political ends. Humanitarian intervention is also critical in situations where the government of a target state is unable to meet the *basic needs of its population effectively due to fragmented political authority, economic collapse, or civil war.

Besides humanitarian intervention, other types of responses are available to the international community including political, economic, and military interventions. Since most relations between states are peaceful, most of the political and economic interactions between states are mutually beneficial, i.e., designed to maximize each state's foreign policy objectives. Nevertheless, political and economic intervention can also be used for hostile purposes. Hostile political and economic interventions often involve the adoption of unilateral or collective measures aimed at changing the behavior of a target state. In an increasingly interdependent world, the isolation resulting from the imposition of political or economic sanctions is often sufficiently painful to compel a target state to change its domestic and international policies. In cases when political and economic *sanctions prove inadequate to force compliance to accepted international norms of state behavior, military interventions are carried out to impose a new regime in a target state.

Political Aspects. The doctrine of humanitarian intervention has experienced a dramatic revival with the end of the Cold War. Humanitarian intervention is now seen as a legitimate instrument available to the international community which can be used to help people caught in complex emergencies. In such cases—especially when the target state is unable to meet the basic needs of the population—the international community has stepped in to alleviate human suffering. Yet the political and legal justifications of humanitarian intervention still generate considerable debate especially at a time when the realignment of global political forces and increasing awareness of the crucial link between *human rights and international peace have emboldened major powers into taking a more interventionist posture.

The objectives of humanitarian intervention vary according to the foreign policy objectives of the major players. Occasionally, when *famine—resulting in large-scale internal displacement of populations—is the most visible consequence of a complex emergency, intervention takes the form of deliveries of food, medical supplies, drinking water, and other basic needs. Occasionally, such international efforts escalate into programs to manage "tent cities" of up to hundreds of thousands of people.

Given the variety of foreign policy interests of the major international powers, recent experiences in humanitarian intervention have exhibited a considerable degree of selectivity. International responses to complex emergencies tend to be faster in states deemed strategically important either because of their geographical position or due to the existence of important natural resources like oil. In the absence of important strategic interests for the major powers, only the international media can draw enough attention to justify intervention. The media's role in this context is critical since it is the conduit through which the Western public obtains information about complex emergencies occurring abroad. The images transmitted through television, in particular, often condition both public willingness to support action and government views regarding the relative importance of a specific emergency. Still, media coverage, however objective it may be, does not treat all emergencies adequately. Some emergencies receive the bulk of attention while others are mostly ignored. The tragic case of Rwanda in 1994, where approximately one million minority Tutsi were slaughtered by organized elements of the majority Hutu, illustrates the consequences of Western selectivity.

Although the criteria used by the international community to decide where humanitarian intervention may or may not take place remain unclear and subjective, reflecting the political interests of the major powers, current practice suggests that some specific violations are now considered so abhorrent that they will prompt near-universal demands for intervention. These include mass slaughter of the population by the state, extermination through starvation or the withholding of basic human services, forced exodus, occupation, and the denial of the right to self-determination.

Ultimately, beyond the immediate goal of alleviating human suffering, humanitarian intervention seeks to address some of the underlying causes of these emergencies. Increasingly, therefore, the long-term objectives of humanitarian intervention involve creating the foundations for rebuilding the target state along democratic lines.

The relationship between democratic rule, human rights, and international peace has long been accepted. Western liberal democracies, in particular, recognize that democratic rule is a necessary condition for the upholding of other human rights. The right to participate in government—minimally in the form of free adult universal suffrage as the best approximation to actual political consent and true representativeness—is not only a very important human right in itself, it is also instrumental to the enjoyment of other fundamental rights. This is why major human rights conventions include the right to political participation and the principle of democratic rule is part of the wider body of international law. However, beyond upholding human rights, democracies are inherently peaceful in the sense that they rarely go to war against each other. Therefore, democratic rule is consonant with the ideal of lasting world *peace. Ironically, to achieve this goal, military force is often used. It should not come as a surprise, therefore, that many contemporary humanitarian interventions include a military component.

Military-Security Aspects. A crucial prerequisite for humanitarian intervention to succeed is the existence of a secure environment, even if rudimentary and restricted to a small area, in the target state. Thus, in cases when widespread human suffering is the result of armed conflict or state collapse, humanitarian intervention must include a military component.

The military component of such operations often involves one or a combination of several elements including the dispatch of ground combat troops with the authority to engage combatants interfering in relief efforts or causing anarchy in the society, the use of air and naval forces to enforce no-fly zones or sea blockades to protect relief efforts from attack by hostile forces, and the provision of military logistical support for the delivery of relief supplies. Without such military presence to reestablish a modicum of security, if not stability in affected areas, humanitarian intervention is highly problematic as aid workers and the humanitarian assistance they bring become easy targets. Thus, particularly since the end of the Cold War, humanitarian intervention involving a strong military component has taken place when the international community, especially the West, determines that a state is no longer capable of fulfilling its obligations to citizens.

The increasing acceptability of the use of military power in humanitarian interventions raises fundamental issues regarding international relations in the post–Cold War era. Foremost among them, as mentioned before, is the issue of selectivity of Western countries. With the end of the Cold War and the reduced political power of developing countries, the West is now consolidating the political gains resulting from the collapse of the Soviet Union and the rejection of communism in most parts of the world. This involves translating political into economic gains to continue strengthening capitalist economic systems. Consequently, important constituencies of the electorate in Western countries are increasingly vociferous in their demands that humanitarian interventions be restricted to places where major interests are at stake. Thus, for most Western countries at the end of the twentieth century, intervention—whether political, economic, military, or humanitarian—must also fulfill clearly defined foreign policy objectives. When no benefits can be anticipated, the UN is seen as the best instrument to alleviate suffering around the world. But this ignores an important point. The UN—unlike the major powers such as the United States, which have the political and military capacity to intervene unilaterally in the post–Cold War era—is seriously constrained by many critical factors. At the political level, UN intervention still requires a consensus among member states in the Security Council. In addition, major financial constraints have forced the UN to reconsider many of its traditional roles in international affairs. Moreover, the lack of a standing UN military force severely limits its capacity to intervene in complex emergencies. However, beyond the political and military aspects of humanitarian intervention are critical legal issues. What are the international legal foundations of humanitarian intervention?

Legal Aspects. The end of the Cold War set in motion profound and irreversible changes in international relations. Although a clear power structure to replace the defunct bipolarity is yet to appear, the contours of the emerging order suggest that it will rest on both traditional notions of power and shared universal values emphasizing the supremacy of human beings over states. This change reflects the recognition that the rights of peoples and individuals around the world cannot be trampled by the state which governs them. This notion of an international system resting on the observance of certain minimum social and political conditions, where those states which transgress may be severely sanctioned, is quickly becoming a guiding principle in global politics. In this context, a major implication for international relations concerns the responses by the international community to major violations of universal values.

In recent times, the most common and controversial response to gross violations of human rights has been humanitarian intervention. The controversy generated by this preferred response is not surprising since it goes to the heart of the sovereignty vs. humanity debate in international politics and *international law. At a deeper level, this tension reflects considerable anxiety and suspicion among developing countries concerning a new and more formidable form of domination, this time executed with the legitimating stamp of the UN, that will serve to promote essentially Western values and aspirations to the detriment of weaker states' *sovereignty.

The current Westphalian system of international relations that emerged in the mid-seventeenth century rested squarely on state sovereignty. This principle recognizes states as exercising supreme authority within their internationally recognized borders. Thus, for more than three centuries, governments throughout the world could manage their internal affairs as they saw fit, even when domestic policies clashed with or violated prevailing international values.

Although states are not ready to impose limits on their sovereignty, the emerging international consensus adds an element of elasticity and porosity to this concept. For example, for many states, human rights issues are no longer regarded as residing exclusively within domestic jurisdictions. Consequently, human rights problems associated with complex emergencies are now seen to affect the entire international system not only because they involve unacceptable levels of human suffering but also because they may represent a threat to peace and security beyond a state's borders. Given this increasing sense of interconnectedness, the international community—especially the major Western powers—has been willing to carry out humanitarian interventions even in the absence of approval by the sovereign state or authorities claiming control over disputed areas of a target state.

The legal foundation for this reformulation of the principle of state sovereignty can be found in a substantial body of international law concerning human rights. It is also supported by long-standing political and philosophical ideas about government and popular accountability. In recent times, the power of television and other media has reinforced these legal and political-philosophical foundations. By transmitting shocking images of inhumane behavior and human suffering around the globe, the media have contributed to the elevation of human rights concerns from the legal cellars to the very top of the international political agenda.

Human rights are now an integral part of both conventional and customary international law. They aim to protect individuals, groups, minorities, or entire peoples. Some core human rights—such as the right to life, to physical integrity and the absence of torture or degrading treatment, to freedom of conscience, religion, and thought, to equality before the law and to fair treatment by the law, nondiscrimination, etc.—are now irrevocably part of international *jus cogens*, i.e., part of the body of peremptory international law from which no derogations are permitted. These rights have been enshrined in general human rights conventions like the 1966 Covenants and other documents, notably the Universal Declaration of

Human Rights. Furthermore, various other human rights treaties concerning specific issues including slavery, genocide, racial discrimination, gender discrimination, apartheid, torture, and other inhumane treatment have been adopted by most members of the international community. Similarly, the Geneva Conventions and Protocols are the cornerstones of the laws of armed conflict which aim to maintain universal principles of humanity during armed conflict.

Besides human rights law and the law of war, a new global consensus is emerging about the principle of international solidarity in the face of natural or man-made disasters within states. This principle implies that, in times of distress reaching beyond a target state's ability to respond successfully, all members of the international community with the means to assist have a duty to do so. This principle also stresses a corresponding obligation on the part of the target state to use such assistance effectively. In circumstances of governmental incapacity or state breakdown, humanitarian intervention may be necessary to help the affected population even without consent by the target state or the effective authorities in disputed areas.

The end of the Cold War and the disappearance of the ideological divide between East and West provide a unique opportunity for the universal implementation of fundamental human rights principles both in times of peace and in conditions of internal or international conflict. Not surprisingly, the outdated principle of noninterference in the internal affairs of sovereign states has been an important casualty of this new era in *international relations. The principle of noninterference evolved to protect the territorial integrity and political independence of states. However, since recent gross violations of human rights which triggered large-scale humanitarian intervention have occurred in places where the territorial integrity and the political independence of the target state are under threat or collapsing primarily due to internal forces, noninterference can no longer be used as a credible justification for inaction.

The fulfillment of human rights and related humanitarian obligations are now seen as having benefits extending beyond the individual or groups for whose protection they have been created. All members of the international community have a legitimate interest in their implementation both within and outside their borders. When a member state fails to meet such human rights obligations, other states have the right to complain publicly or through diplomatic channels. Indeed, the implementation mechanisms of most international human rights agreements allow states to launch formal complaints against any violator. Such complaints may result in international condemnation. However, in some cases, persistent violations may trigger unilateral or multilateral action like Tan-

zania's intervention in Uganda in 1978–79; Vietnam's intervention in Cambodia in 1979; the West African states' intervention in Liberia in 1990; the U.S.-led interventions in northern Iraq in 1991, Somalia in 1992–93, and Haiti in 1994; French-led intervention in Rwanda in 1994; and the UN's intervention in Bosnia in 1995.

These examples suggest that international shock in the face of human suffering triggers demands for humanitarian intervention even when it erodes traditionally recognized principles of sovereignty and noninterference in the internal affairs of sovereign states. Humanitarian intervention has become an essential feature of the post–Cold War world order.

Conclusion. The end of the Cold War has revealed that some of the main attributes of states are quite problematic. The image of strength and stability often associated with the member states of the international community has often been little more than an illusion. In the absence of major powers willing to perform de facto or quasi-trusteeship functions, many states have collapsed under severe domestic pressures. One of the most important consequences of governmental breakdown and state collapse has been the occurrence of complex emergencies demanding international humanitarian intervention to avoid major human catastrophes. This, in turn, has encouraged considerable debate about some of the major principles of international relations and international law. Currently, the internal affairs of independent states are no longer seen as inviolable especially when unacceptable human suffering of a large segment of the population is involved.

The removal of the constraints imposed by the Cold War has facilitated the emergence of an international consensus regarding the legal, political, and moral basis for international measures to alleviate human suffering around the world. Humanitarian intervention has become an effective and positive form of intervention in international relations.

(See also BOSNIAN WAR; INTERNATIONAL LAW; RWANDAN GENOCIDE; UNITED NATIONS.)

John Harriss, ed., *The Politics of Humanitarian Intervention* (New York, 1995). Richard Falk, "The Complexities of Humanitarian Intervention: A New World Order Challenge" *Michigan Journal of International Law* 17 (1996): 491–513. Stanley Hoffmann, ed., *The Ethics and Politics of Humanitarian Intervention* (Notre Dame, Ind., 1996). Sean D. Murphy, *Humanitarian Intervention* (Philadelphia, 1996). Oliver Ramsbotham and Tom Woodhouse, *Humanitarian Intervention in Contemporary Conflict* (Cambridge, Mass., 1996). John Charvet, "The Idea of State Sovereignty and the Right of Humanitarian Intervention" *International Political Science Review* 18 (1997): 39–48. Bhikhu Parekh, "Rethinking Humanitarian Intervention" *International Political Science Review* 18 (1997): 49–69. Fernando Teson, "Collective Humanitarian Intervention" *Michigan Journal of International Law* 17 (1996): 323–371.

ASSIS V. MALAQUIAS

Hungary adhered to the Axis to win the return of some territory at the expense of Czechoslovakia in 1938 and of Romania in 1940. Its participation in the war against the Soviet Union was so grudging that in 1944 Germany occupied the country and imposed an Arrow Cross dictatorship. At year's end, a provisional government of former opposition parties and Communists was created under Soviet auspices.

The political climate in economically devastated Hungary favored moderate change, and a thorough land reform was effected. The Communists nevertheless won barely 17 percent of the vote in the relatively free elections of November 1945. The center-right Smallholder Party emerged as the principal non-Communist force, winning a clear majority, but at Soviet insistence a coalition government was formed. A democratic constitution adopted in 1946 styled Hungary a republic with a sovereign unicameral parliament; the Paris Peace Treaty restored the prewar borders. Communist subversion and agitation gradually incapacitated the democratic majority. On *Stalin's instructions, the Communists in 1948 forcibly absorbed the Social Democrats into the Hungarian Workers' Party and set course for revolutionary change.

The party, dominated by Mátyás Rákosi and a few other former émigrés, imposed *Stalinism on Hungary. The goal of building socialism was enshrined in a new Soviet-type constitution, and all state institutions and mass organizations were subordinated to the party. Initially, the party won some support from the poorer social strata and some intellectuals with its promise of equality, social justice, and *modernization. All political opposition was suppressed, and the party itself underwent massive purges. To the extent that the new system had enjoyed some popular *legitimacy, this was soon dissipated by the brutality of the dictatorship, a decline in the standard of living, and suppression of nationalism in favor of Sovietization.

After Stalin's death, Rákosi was compelled to share power with a reformer, Imre Nagy, who pursued a more balanced economic strategy while alleviating rule by terror. This "New Course" was soon halted by Rákosi, but "revisionism" gained ground among party intellectuals. Khrushchev's de-Stalinization and the revolution in Poland galvanized Hungarians to challenge their ruler in October 1956. Over a period of two weeks, a multiparty government formed under Nagy's premiership promised to restore democracy and a mixed economy and, apprehending Soviet military intervention, renounced the *Warsaw Treaty Organization (Warsaw Pact) and proclaimed Hungary's neutrality.

The revolution was crushed by armed force, and Communist dictatorship reimposed, under the renamed Hungarian Socialist Workers' Party headed by János Kádár. Kádár's immediate task was to rebuild the party and complete the *collectivization of agriculture. This accomplished, in the 1960s he adopted a conciliatory "alliance policy" that relaxed political and social discrimination in access to higher education and official posts and led in 1968 to the adoption of a "New Economic Mechanism." The latter aimed to revive Hungary's faltering economy by introducing some elements of the market. The greatest progress was made in agriculture, where investment and self-management greatly improved productivity. A more tolerant cultural policy and the introduction of multiple candidacies in parliamentary elections (still controlled by the Patriotic People's Front, a party appendage) were other concessions by a regime in quest of legitimacy.

The reform was halted in the mid-1970s as a consequence of Soviet and domestic conservative pressures, then was relaunched with new decentralizing measures and concessions to small-scale private enterprise. Despite partial reforms and Western loans, a declining growth rate and mounting foreign debt precipitated an economic crisis in the mid-1980s. Political dissent, meanwhile, spread among intellectuals and within the party itself.

*Gorbachev's willingness to loosen Soviet *hegemony unleashed a quiet revolution in Hungary. In May 1988 a reformist party leadership dumped Kádár and set course for controlled democratization and a marketized economy. Opposition groups pressed for more radical change, and the demoralized party rapidly lost its grip. In October 1989 party reformers created the avowedly social democratic Hungarian Socialist Party, and the constitution was amended to style Hungary a simple republic (rather than "people's republic"), guarantee full political and civil rights, and allow for free elections.

Successive elections produced orderly changes in government, with the center-right prevailing in 1990, the center-left in 1994, and the center-right again in 1998. Continuity has marked both domestic and foreign policy. The domestic priority was to institute market economy; sweeping privatization has drawn foreign investment on a scale unmatched in the region.

The main foreign policy priorities are integration with Europe and guarantees of cultural rights for Hungarian minorities in the neighboring states, notably Romania and Slovakia. Although Budapest concluded bilateral accords with the host states, some of the minorities remain a source of discord. Hungary backed Western initiatives in the former Yugoslavia and, in 1999, earned membership in the North Atlantic Treaty Organization (NATO). Hungary is also in the first group of Central European countries to be considered for membership in the European Union.

These domestic and foreign policy priorities enjoy broad popular support; the changes of government have been due largely to discontent with the social costs of transition to a market economy. In terms of European integration and security, Hungary has become a factor for stability.

(See also CENTRAL EUROPE; COMMUNIST PARTY STATES; NINETEEN EIGHTY-NINE; PERESTROIKA; SOCIALISM AND SOCIAL DEMOCRACY.)

Bennett Kovrig, *Communism in Hungary from Kun to Kadar* (Stanford, Calif., 1979). Andrew C. Janos, *The Politics of Backwardness in Hungary, 1825–1945* (Princeton, N.J., 1982). Ivan Volgyes, *Hungary: A Nation of Contradictions* (Boulder, Colo., 1982).

BENNETT KOVRIG

HUSSEIN, Saddam. Saddam Hussein seems to have been introduced to violence at an early age. Born in 1937 into a family of peasant cultivators near Takrit, a small country town on the Tigris about a hundred miles from Baghdad, he was brought up by his mother and stepfather. In the official hagiographies, Saddam Hussein is "credited" with three, possibly four, killings before his attempt to assassinate President 'Abd al-Karim Qasim in October 1959.

After primary school in Takrit, he was sent to Baghdad in the early 1950s to continue his education. *Iraq was then ruled by a pro-Western oligarchy; all opposition parties were proscribed, and political life, dominated by the Communists, was effectively driven underground. In 1955, attracted by *Arab nationalism, Saddam Hussein joined the Iraqi Ba'th Party, which then had about 300 members.

In the immediate aftermath of the revolution which overthrew the ancien régime in July 1958, the Communists enjoyed a brief period of ascendancy, but they were bitterly opposed by the pan-Arabists (Nasserists and Ba'thists), who, together with conservative and religious forces, felt threatened by the Communists' potential radicalism and the apparent favor they enjoyed from the revolutionary government. In October 1959 Saddam Hussein and a group of Ba'thist conspirators tried to assassinate the president, 'Abd al-Karim Qasim. Qasim was wounded but survived, and Saddam Hussein fled to Egypt, where he stayed until a Ba'thist-Nasserist coup overthrew Qasim in February 1963. On his return he became a protégé of the Ba'th's Syrian founder, Michel 'Aflaq, who put him in charge of the civilian wing of the Iraqi party in 1964. He was also linked, by family ties, to a number of Ba'thist army officers, most notably General Ahmad Hasan al-Bakr, who had served as prime minister for a few months in 1963.

In 1968 another coup brought the Ba'th back to power and al-Bakr to the presidency. Saddam Hussein ensured that the party consolidated its grip on the state machinery and the armed forces by appointing trusted individuals to top posts in the army and by putting himself in charge of the country's internal security services. By 1969, at the age of thirty-two, he had become assistant secretary-general of the Ba'th Party and vice president of Iraq. Through the 1970s he gradually consolidated his power through his alliance with al-Bakr and by placing his friends and relatives from Takrit in key positions in the various internal security services and the Republican Guard.

The Ba'th's apparently progressive orientation convinced the Soviet Union to conclude a treaty of friendship in 1972 and later to encourage the Iraqi Communist Party to join it in a National Patriotic Front. Soviet expertise enabled Iraq to develop its unexploited southern oilfields, and the Iraq Petroleum Company was nationalized, which gave the government—now equivalent to "Saddam Hussein and his entourage"—full control over the country's substantial oil revenues. The alliance with the Communists gave him a vital breathing space in his attempt to muzzle his most persistent opponents, the Kurds. The Kurdish movement was defeated in 1975 as a result of an agreement with the shah of Iran, under which the shah undertook to close the Iranian borders to the Kurdish guerrillas. After that the alliance with the Communists was no longer necessary, and a ruthless campaign was initiated against them. By the mid-1980s most Iraqi intellectuals, and almost all Iraqi leftists, had either been killed, imprisoned, or forced into exile.

In July 1979 Saddam Hussein took over the presidency from al-Bakr, demonstrating the extent of his power a few days later by turning against some of his closest former allies within the Ba'th party. A "plot" was discovered in which a number of members of the ruling Revolutionary Command Council (RCC) were implicated. Those found guilty were executed, with great publicity, by Saddam Hussein and the surviving members of the RCC in person.

Barely a year after having consolidated his power within Iraq, Saddam Hussein made a bid for regional leadership by launching an invasion of the newly constituted Islamic Republic of Iran. He identified himself closely with the war, which he named Qadisiyat Saddam, a reference to the Arab defeat of the Iranians in the first decades of Islam. After initial successes, Iraqi forces were driven back by the Iranians, but the war continued for eight years. Iran's eventual demoralization and defeat owed a great deal to the willingness of both the United States and the USSR to supply Iraq with arms, intelligence, and military training. Saddam Hussein used chemical weapons against Iranian forces—as he was to do against the Kurds in March 1988—and ordered several hundred thousand Iraqi Shi'is deported to Iran on the grounds that they were "really" Iranians and thus enemies of the Iraqi state.

During and after the war with Iran, a highly developed personality cult evolved. Enormous pictures of the "Great Leader" were visible everywhere and buildings, monuments, and suburbs were named after him. Although it was difficult to represent the deadlock at the end of the war with Iran as a victory, Saddam Hussein managed to do so. Huge monuments commemorating the war were commissioned, the most well-known being a metal sculpture forming an arch out of swords held in two hands, the latter cast from molds taken from the president's own wrists.

During the middle and latter 1980s the Kurdish population had taken advantage of the war to create virtually independent enclaves in northern Iraq. In 1988 Saddam Hussein undertook a vast pacification campaign against them, known as the *Anfal*, in the course of which at least 100,000 Kurds were murdered and buried in mass graves near the Iraqi-Saudi border. The regime's grosser *human rights violations occasioned only verbal condemnation from the West, since many Western countries had either advanced huge sums to Iraq or were hoping for rich pickings from postwar reconstruction.

In August 1990, in another bid for regional supremacy, Saddam Hussein invaded *Kuwait. A multinational force under UN auspices and U.S. leadership was dispatched to Saudi Arabia. In mid-November Iraq was given until 15 January 1991 to withdraw from Kuwait, and although various efforts were made to find a diplomatic solution, Saddam Hussein proved adamant. In January and February 1991 coalition bombing devastated Iraq's infrastructure, and in the last days of February the allies launched a ground offensive. After five days Iraq agreed to a cease-fire, and Iraqi troops began a disorderly and chaotic retreat from Kuwait.

Shi'i and Kurdish uprisings followed the war. Although the "rebels" initially gained control of large areas, units of the Republican Guard responded with exceptional brutality and were quickly able to gain the upper hand both in southern Iraq and in Kurdistan. A mass exodus of Kurds to the Iraqi-Turkish and Iraqi-Iranian borders began, and by the end of April there were about 2.5 million refugees, both Kurds and southerners.

There has been a long period of stalemate since the end of the *Gulf War. The UN-imposed sanctions have remained in place, causing great suffering to the people of Iraq but evoking little but indifference from its leader. In addition, the unity of the anti-Iraq coalition has become strained with the passage of time. An oil-for-food agreement, which, if adopted earlier, might have alleviated much of the severe malnutrition and infant mortality the country has experienced, was eventually accepted by the regime in 1996. A series of confrontations and crises was occasioned by Saddam Hussein's attempts to hinder the activities of UNSCOM (United Nations Special Commission on Iraq) inspection teams, stationed in Iraq to seek out and destroy Iraq's weapons of mass destruction. In December 1998, British and American forces launched a four-day bombing campaign against Iraq to force the regime to comply with UNSCOM's wishes, and rather more unrealistically, to try to hasten its overthrow. Neither objective was realized.

It is clear that Saddam Hussein's clannish power base is inherently fragile. On the other hand, his monopoly of the means of coercion, the fragmentation of the opposition, the absence of any serious rivals, and, perhaps most important, the fear on the part of his neighbors and of the West of the chaos that might follow his downfall, all assist him to stay in power. It is ironic to recall that in the 1980s, when Iraq's relations with the West were extremely cordial, it was fashionable to assert that Saddam Hussein's programs of modernization and development were creating a new kind of national consensus in Iraq. In fact, the arbitrary and lawless nature of his regime has been a prime factor in ensuring the persistence and revival of "primordial" loyalties to tribe, clan, region, sect, and family. The policies he has pursued have acted as the principal causes of the reproduction and hardening of division, rather than contributing to its demise.

(See also IRAN-IRAQ WAR; KURDISTAN.)

Samir al-Khalil, *The Republic of Fear: The Politics of Modern Iraq* (London, 1989). Efraim Karsh and Inari Rautsi, *Saddam Hussein: A Political Biography*, 2d ed. (London, 1997). Amatzia Baram, *Building Towards Crisis: Saddam Husayn's Strategy for Survival* (Washington, D.C., 1998). Marion Farouk-Sluglett and Peter Sluglett, *Iraq since 1958: From Revolution to Dictatorship*, 3d ed. (London, 1999). Charles Tripp, *A Political History of Iraq* (Cambridge, 2000).

MARION FAROUK-SLUGLETT
PETER SLUGLETT

I

IBN-KHALDUN. Born in Tunis in times of great political turmoil, Ibn-Khaldun (1332–1406) served variously as political adviser, prime minister, and judge in several North African states and Muslim Spain. In later life he settled in Cairo, where he taught at al-Azhar and was appointed Grand Malaki Judge. The great passion of his later years was writing a "universal history" whereby he sought to explain the chaotic politics of his day by discovering general causes for the rise and decline of *states. His introduction, in English translation *The Mugaddima*, sets forth a theory of history and society together with a method, his "science of culture."

Best known is his notion of the dynamic of new states and political movements, which he calls *asabiyya* or (social) solidarity. It arises in simple societies where economies of necessity produce an ethos of community. Political institutions are rudimentary: the leadership of the most able and respected. As the society grows, subgroups appear, loyalties become divided, and the subgroup with the strongest solidarity becomes dominant. Chieftainship turns into kingship. The king consolidates his power through force. Natural solidarity disappears and decline begins.

Decline leads ultimately to the disintegration of state and civilization if not checked by the appearance of a new group with solidarity. Such a new group is unlikely to rise within the state, however. Rather, a less advanced people with rising solidarity typically takes over the state and changes its manner of life—albeit temporarily. Eventually they also will generate the same processes which led to the decline of the state they conquered.

Although the notion of *asabiyya* is a prominent part of Ibn-Khaldun's explanation of social and political change, it does not begin to indicate the extraordinary character of his writings, which Toynbee described as "undoubtedly the greatest work of its kind that has ever yet been created by any mind in any time or place."

Ibn-Khaldun anticipated critical themes in modern political thought. He turned from considering how things ought to be to studying states and societies as they "really are" a full century and a half before Machiavelli. He located the vital force of human behavior and thus society in passions, not reason, two centuries before Hobbes. Only after four centuries did another philosophy of history appear, with Hegel, and even then not based on material-empirical reality. Although Ibn-Khaldun's theory of history was grounded in material reality, he did not find it necessary to disavow either political philosophy or religion. His thought thus represents a unique instance in the transition from classical to modern theory, and it continues to influence contemporary political and social theory in the Middle East.

Mugaddimat Ibn Khaldun (Prolégomènes D'Ebn Khaldoun), 3 vols. Paris, 1858). Ibn Khaldun, *The Mugaddimah: An Introduction to History*, trans. Franz Rosenthal, Bollingen Series XLIII, 3 vols. (Princeton, N.J., 1958; edited and abridged by N. J. Dawood, 1969). Muhsin Mahdi, *Ibn Khaldun's Philosophy of History: A Study in the Philosophic Foundations of the Science of Culture* (Chicago, 1964).

ENID HILL

ICELAND. An island in the North Atlantic between Norway and Greenland, Iceland has an ethnically homogeneous population of 250,000. It is a member of the UN, the North Atlantic Treaty Organization, the Organization for Economic Cooperation and Development, the European Free Trade Association (EFTA), and a range of Nordic institutions. Its economy is integrated into the European Union's (EU) single market through the European Economic Area (EEA) agreement (together with Norway). It is a *parliamentary democracy and has a constitutional president and a Lutheran Protestant state church. Iceland was under the control of Norway from 1262 to 1523, and then under that of Denmark. In 1845, its Parliament was reestablished as an advisory council to the Danish king. Limited home rule was granted in 1874, limited parliamentarism in 1904, and full sovereignty (except in foreign policy matters) in 1918. In the nineteenth century, the Icelandic elite emulated Danish politics and culture. But the old language was not displaced, and as part of the independence struggle language was purified and Icelandic culture and institutions revived. Iceland declared neutrality in *World War II, but was occupied by British troops in 1940, replaced by U.S. troops in 1941. In the postwar security structure, the Keflavik airport, near Reykjavik, the capital, was a point of strategic importance. U.S. use of the base was granted in a bilateral agreement (1951). The U.S. presence gave rise to protests from the left.

The most important party in the postwar period has been the Independence Party, which has received on average 40 percent of the vote. It is a right-wing party, with support from most employers, but also from all other classes. The Progressive Party has its main base in provincial regions, principally agricultural and fishing villages. On the left is the Social Democratic Party (founded in 1946, along with the Federation of Labor). A split in the 1930s produced a Communist Party which in 1958 asserted its independence from Moscow, being absorbed into the socialist People's Alliance, which was established as a party in 1968. A Women's List has held parliamentary seats since 1983.

Iceland is entirely dependent on exports of fish, especially cod. Still, its per capita income is as high as that of the other Nordic countries. There are special provisions for fish exports in the trade agreements with the EU. Most industries are linked to the fisheries (processing, shipyards), but Iceland also exports aluminum. The state and the cooperative movement have been heavily involved in the fisheries sector. Most savings were allocated through state banks, and there was no stock exchange. However, during the 1980s, *privatization and liberalization changed this. Trawler owners, fishermen (whose income is determined by sharecropping arrangements), and fish processing firms are crucial social forces.

Economic policies created a devaluation–high inflation cycle, with double-digit inflation since 1972 (reaching a peak of 83 percent in 1983). The labor market is very tight, with a high employment rate and long working hours. Unemployment was never above one percent in the 1970s. Union membership is a condition for employment. Indexation used to be a main focus in the negotiation of collective agreements: in hard times (low fish prices, lack of foreign currencies), indexation was modified; as conditions improved, large-scale strike activity restored full indexation. In the late 1980s, this pattern of adjustment was changed, and through the 1990s, a low-inflation, hard-currency approach prevailed, giving rise to real adjustments implying periodically higher unemployment rates.

A *law of the sea *regime is crucial for Iceland. In 1950–1952, Iceland unilaterally extended its national fishing zone to four nautical miles, escaping European embargoes by exporting processed fish to the United States and the Soviet Union. Iceland has always supported UN efforts to secure an international law of the seas. UN conferences in 1958, 1960, and 1974–1975 produced majorities, but no resolutions on extended national controls over fish resources. Iceland made extensions anyway, to twelve nautical miles in 1958–1960, fifty nautical miles in 1972 (declared unilaterally, with reference to resource depletion), and 200 nautical miles in 1974–1975. On each occasion Britain sent warships. The 1958 dispute was settled in the International Court of Justice. But the 1970s saw two "cod wars": small coast guard vessels would cut the trawls of British trawlers, narrowly escaping larger British navy vessels. No lives were lost. A settlement was reached in 1976. The Icelandic fishing fleet has been modernized since the 1970s, and now consists of technologically sophisticated freezer trawlers which also traverse distant, international waters in search of that one crucial resource: fish.

(See also SCANDINAVIA.)

Stefán Olafsson, *Modernization and Social Stratification in Iceland* (Reykjavik, 1991). Gudmundur Halfdanarson, *Historical Dictionary of Iceland* (London, 1997).

LARS MJØSET

IDEALISM. In the context of *international relations, idealism refers to the body of thought that regards fundamental reform of the system of international relations to be both essential and possible. Idealists treat the sovereign independence of *states as a basic cause of *war and its attendant misery. Over centuries they have proposed plans for *international law and organization that would, as Immanuel Kant put it in 1784, cause states to "abandon" their "lawless state of savagery and enter a federation of peoples in which every state could expect to derive its security and rights . . . from a united power and the law-governed decisions of a united will" (*Idea for a Universal History with a Cosmopolitan Purpose*, in Hans Reiss, ed., *Kant's Political Writings*, Cambridge, U.K., 1970).

In Kant's version, idealism expressed a kind of tragic optimism about international relations. After centuries of ever-more-destructive wars, people would finally come to realize "what reason could have suggested to them even without so many sad experiences": that the independence of states must give way to an effective *international organization capable of enforcing genuine *peace. Liberals of the nineteenth century like Jeremy Bentham or John Stuart Mill had a more sanguine view of international reform. As international trade spread, so too would *international law and functional international organization; nationalistic sovereign states would come to be seen as irrelevant and atavistic.

*World War I shattered this painless view of international progress but also created the *League of Nations. Supporters of Woodrow Wilson's vision for the League sought to rally *public opinion around the cause of international organization because they believed it to be the only way to prevent another war. Idealism as term of description came into wide use in the 1920s, as scholars and publicists like G. Lowes Dickinson, Alfred Zimmern, and James T. Shotwell indefatigably urged nations to forsake "their illusions, their cupidity and their pride" in order to build the League of Nations into "a working machine for peace" (Dickinson, *The International Anarchy, 1904–1914*, London, 1925, p. 37). These thinkers shared a belief in the essential goodness of human nature, the primacy of ideas and education, and in the ultimate *power of an aroused world public opinion. The Kellogg-Briand Pact of 1928 outlawing war "as an instrument of national policy" began as an idealist initiative (from James T. Shotwell in New York) and was emblematic of idealist hopes for international reform.

The events of the 1930s were widely interpreted as discrediting the approach of idealism, though, perhaps ironically, idealists like Zimmern or Arnold Toynbee implacably opposed the British policy of appeasement, whereas the "realist" E. H. Carr provided arguments in support of Chamberlain's policy at Munich. After *World War II, idealism did not so much die as migrate to U.S. liberal supporters of the UN. In the early postwar period, a debate between "realists" and "idealists" occurred among intellectuals as the United States settled into the *Cold War with the Soviet Union. Idealists tended to argue for more negotiations and wished to base *American foreign policy on the moral ground of international law and the UN; realists denounced idealism's naïveté and urged a policy based on the national interest defined in terms of power. Echoes of this debate can be heard in disagreements about nuclear *deterrence and intervention in external conflicts. Idealism has always claimed to speak for higher human aspiration and the possibility of peace; more recently it has also embraced the cause of global *environmentalism.

(See also INTERNATIONAL COOPERATION; REALISM; RIGHTS; SECURITY; UNITED NATIONS.)

Sissela Bok, *A Strategy for Peace: Human Values and the Threat of War* (New York, 1990). Terry Nardin and David Mapel, eds., *Traditions of International Ethics* (Cambridge, U.K., 1992).

MICHAEL JOSEPH SMITH

IDEOLOGY. The term *ideology* was coined in the late eighteenth century by the French philosopher Destutt de Tracy (1754–1836). A wealthy and educated nobleman who was strongly influenced by the European Enlightenment, de Tracy sought to develop a new discipline that would be concerned with the systematic analysis of ideas and sensations. It was this discipline that he described as *ideology*—literally, the science of ideas. He believed that this discipline would enable human nature to be understood and hence would enable the social and political order to be rearranged in accordance with the needs and aspirations of human beings. The early project of ideology was thus a natural development of certain themes characteristic of the Enlightenment, such as the capacity of human beings to understand and control the world through systematic, scientific analysis.

In the early nineteenth century, the meaning of the term *ideology* was transformed in complicated ways. This transformation began when the French emperor, Napoleon Bonaparte, turned against Destutt de Tracy and his associates, whom he described as *idéologues*. Napoleon condemned ideology as a vague and abstract doctrine that would confuse people and undermine the rule of law. As his military campaigns ran into difficulties and his position weakened both at home and abroad, Napoleon's attacks on ideology became more sweeping and vehement. Many kinds of religious and philosophical thought were condemned as ideology. Thus the meaning of the term began to change: *ideology* ceased to refer only to the science of ideas and began to refer also to the ideas themselves, that is, to a body of ideas that were alleged to be erroneous and divorced from the practical realities of political life.

The term was further transformed by *Marx and Engels. In their writings the term acquired a new status as a critical tool and as an integral component of a new theoretical system. But Marx and Engels did not use the term in a clear and consistent way. In *The German Ideology*, written in 1845–1846 but left unpublished, Marx and Engels criticized the views of the so-called "Young Hegelians" such as Ludwig Feuerbach, Bruno Bauer, and Max Stirner. In characterizing the views of these thinkers as "the German ideology," Marx and Engels were following, very broadly, Napoleon's use of the term: the work of the Young Hegelians was the equivalent, in the relatively backward social and political conditions of early nineteenth-century Germany, of the doctrines of de Tracy and his associates. The views of the Young Hegelians were ideological in the sense that they were entirely abstract and unconnected with the material conditions of social and political life.

In other writings Marx laid the foundations for a somewhat different and more innovative notion of ideology. He suggested that, in societies divided into classes, ideas may play an important role in articulating the conflicting aims and interests of different social classes. Ideas may also shape the ways in which individuals perceive the social world and their positions within it, thereby affecting the course of social and political change. In the works where Marx analyzed these phenomena in some detail—such as *The Eighteenth Brumaire of Louis Bonaparte* (1852)—he rarely used the term *ideology*, speaking instead of *ruling ideas, fixed ideas*, etc. But this aspect of Marx's work served as an inspiration for subsequent authors and helped to redefine the nature and scope of ideology.

In the course of the twentieth century there has been a proliferation of writings on ideology, and the term has been used in many different ways. One can draw a broad distinction between two different conceptions of ideology that are prevalent in the literature today. In the first place, some social and political analysts use the term *ideology* to refer to any system of thought or belief that animates social or political action: this is what may be described as the neutral conception of ideology. According to this conception, ideologies are discrete and relatively coherent systems of thought or belief, and the task confronting the analyst is to delineate these systems and describe their main features. (See, for example, Martin Seliger, *Ideology and Politics*.) This line of inquiry is exemplified by the tendency to think of ideologies in terms of "isms"—*conservatism, *liberalism, *socialism, *communism, *fascism, Nazism, etc. Most modern political regimes and parties, as well as social and political movements (e.g., the women's movement, the green movement), are characterized by ideologies in this sense. The capacity of such organizations or movements to mobilize support and secure some form of *legitimacy depends on a continuous process of producing and renewing their respective systems of thought or belief.

This use of the term can be distinguished from a second usage, which may be described as the critical conception of ideology. Unlike the neutral conception, the critical conception implies that the phenomena characterized as ideology are misleading, illusory, or one-sided; the very characterization of something as ideology carries with it an implicit criticism or condemnation. Hence the analysis of ideology is, on this account, inseparable from the critique of ideology. There is considerable disagreement within the literature about exactly how the critical conception of ideology should be understood. Some theorists regard ideologies as sets of ideas about the social world that are in some sense "false" or illusory, whereas other theorists prefer to think in terms of the interrelations between symbolism and *power. An example of the latter approach is the proposal to conceptualize ideology as the ways in which symbolic forms serve, in particular circumstances, to establish and sustain relations of domination. (See John B. Thompson, *Ideology and Modern Culture*.)

One advantage of the critical conception of ideology is that it enables the analyst to broaden the domain of analysis. Although the institutions of organized political power are an important site of ideology, it is also appropriate to consider the ways in which meaning is mobilized by other institutions and in other spheres of social life. The mass media are particularly important in this regard. Among the first authors to study the mass media as a source of ideology in modern societies were the early "critical theorists" linked to the Frankfurt Institute for Social Research. These theorists, including Max Horkheimer (1895–1971) and Theodor Adorno (1903–1969), were interested in the development of the entertainment industry—or "culture industry," as they called it—in the late nineteenth and early twentieth centuries. Writing in the 1930s and 1940s, they argued that this industry has given rise to a new form of ideology in modern societies. By producing large quantities of standardized and stereotyped cultural goods (popular films, magazines, books, etc.), the culture industry was providing individuals with imaginary avenues of escape from the harsh realities of social life and was weakening their capacity to think in a critical and autonomous way. Horkheimer and Adorno suggested that these developments, among others, had rendered individuals more vulnerable to the rhetoric of Nazism and fascism. (See Max Horkheimer and Theodor W. Adorno, "The Culture Industry.")

Other authors have also been concerned with emphasizing the importance of ideology in shaping or forming the individual or subject. Ideology is viewed by some social thinkers as a principal mechanism of socialization: through the diffusion of ideology, individuals acquire a sense of themselves as subjects and acquire the skills and attitudes necessary for the reproduction of the social order. An example of this approach is the work of the French Marxist Louis Althusser. Although Althusser's work has been influential, it has also been sharply criticized for failing to provide, among other things, a satisfactory conception of the human subject.

The concept of ideology is a highly contested notion, and there is no general consensus today concerning the most appropriate way to define the term. Nevertheless, many commentators would agree that the study of ideology is an indispensable part of social and political analysis. Political systems, social and political movements, and relations of power and domination are always interwoven in complex ways with ideas, beliefs, and symbolic forms of various kinds. Power is rarely exercised without some kind of symbolic attribute or support. It is this aspect of power, and of social and political life more generally, that has come to define the distinctive province of the study of ideology.

(See also CLASS AND POLITICS; INFORMATION SOCIETY; PSYCHOLOGY AND POLITICS; PUBLIC OPINION.)

Louis Althusser, "Ideology and Ideological State Apparatuses," in *Lenin and Philosophy and Other Essays*, trans. B. Brewster (London, 1971), pp. 121–173. Max Horkheimer and Theodor W. Adorno, "The Culture Industry," in *Dialectic of Enlightenment*, trans. J. Cumming (New York, 1972), pp. 120–167. Martin Seliger, *Ideology and Politics* (London, 1976). Jorge Larrain, *The Concept of Ideology* (London, 1979). John B. Thompson, *Ideology and Modern Culture* (Cambridge, U.K., 1990).

JOHN B. THOMPSON

IMF. See INTERNATIONAL MONETARY FUND.

IMMIGRATION. See INTERNATIONAL MIGRATION.

IMPERIALISM. The term *imperialism* was originally used as an invective against the expansionist policy of Napoleon I, and a little later against the expansionist policy of Britain. The rhetorical use of this term continues today, appearing frequently in the discourse of *Third World nationalist and Marxist-Leninist leaders. But, like many other political terms, it is a scientifically valid concept, useful in explaining various phenomena in contemporary society.

The pioneer in formulating the scientific concept of imperialism was an English economist, J. A. Hobson (1858–1940), who published *Imperialism: A Study* in 1902, a seminal work for future research on this phenomenon. Hobson's study focused on late-nineteenth-century imperialism, which could be distinguished from previous forms of imperialism in two ways: the existence of several empires in competition with one another, and the predominance of finance capital over mercantile capital.

In his examination of imperialist expansion, Hobson attached particular significance to the competition between empires. He also tried to show that imperialist policies favored financial speculation over production and market expansion. On these and other points, Hobson opposed the followers of Joseph Chamberlain (1830–1886), a famous entrepreneur from Birmingham, who advanced the doctrine of "commercial imperialism," and the supposed advantages it would bring about for English workers. Hobson rejected the notion that imperialism could bring advantages to either workers or capitalists in metropolitan countries. Marxist authors, however, reject Hobson's "reformist" proposal that imperialist expansion be replaced by internal market expansion, through an increase in workers' wages and services that would increase effective demand.

The impossibility of resolving, through *reform, the contradictions created by imperialist expansion, lies at the base of the theories of imperialism elaborated by Rudolf Hilferding (1877–1941), Rosa Luxemburg (1871–1919), and V. I. *Lenin (1870–1924). In 1910 Hilferding published *Finance Capital: A Study of the Latest Phase in Capitalist Development*, in which he agreed with Hobson that imperialist competition led inevitably to violence. Hilferding highlighted the use of violence in the creation of a wage labor force in the colonies. At the same time, he rejected as impossible the reformist proposal to expand internal markets through wage increases, pointing out that such an alternative would necessarily reduce profits. Noting the dominant role of finance capital and the concentration of capital under monopoly ownership of an oligarchy, Hilferding concluded that this extreme polarization of wealth under imperialism presaged the "last stage" of the fight between the bourgeoisie and the proletariat. Once most of the means of production were concentrated in a few hands, the expropriation of the "capitalist oligarchy" would give rise to *socialism—without the need to expropriate the minor and middling entrepreneurs. Hilferding thus linked the fight against imperialism to the fight for socialism, and the fight for political power to the fight for economic power. The relationship between imperialism and national oppression was acknowledged, but subordinated to a *class analysis and the class struggle.

Rosa Luxemburg also viewed imperialism as "the last stage in the historical race of *capitalism." Proceeding from a Marxist class analysis, she described the crucial role played by the unequal exchange between imperialist (capitalist) and colonized (procapitalist) countries in the accumulation of capital. In *The Accumulation of Capital*, she also emphasized the historical role played by *militarism in capital accumulation, and pioneered the study of the relationship among political domination, military occupation, and external debt. Moreover, in addition to describing how militarism is used to ensure the conditions of accumulation (through the subjection of colonies, as a weapon in the competitive struggle between capitalist countries, etc.), Luxemburg argued that militarism "is a preeminent means for the realization of surplus value; it is in itself a province of accumulation," which would later form the basis of the "*military-industrial complex" of the great empires.

In *Imperialism, the Highest Stage of Capitalism*, Lenin began his discussion of imperialism by asking what he called "the main question": "whether it is possible to reform the basis of imperialism, whether to go forward to the accentuation and deepening of the antagonisms which it engenders, or backwards towards allaying these antagonisms." He rejected the possibility of reforming capitalism of its imperialist tendencies, insisting that imperialism was the inevitable "highest stage" of capitalism, which could only be defeated by *revolution. "Imperialism," wrote Lenin, "is capitalism in that stage of development in which the dominance of monopolies and finance capital has established itself; in which the export of capital has acquired pronounced importance; in which the division of all territories of the globe has been completed."

Lenin criticized Kautsky for his theory of "ultra-imperialism," pointing out that it was merely a restatement of Hobson's theory of "inter-imperialism." He accused Kautsky of obscuring the true nature of imperialism by implying that "a union of world imperialism, and not struggle amongst imperialisms," was possible, and that "a phase when war shall cease under capitalism" would come. Lenin also took Kautsky to task for his belief that "the rule of finance capital lessens the unevenness and contradictions in world economy," insisting that, "in reality, it *increases* them" (italics in original). Further on he added: "Monopolies, oligarchy, the striving for domination instead of the striving for liberty, the exploitation of an increasing number of small or weak nations by an extremely small group of the richest or most powerful nations—all these have given birth to those distinctive characteristics of imperialism which compel us to define it as a parasitic or decaying capitalism."

This last statement turned out to be historically incorrect; as for the others, they were not particularly original. According to Georg Lukács, "Lenin's contribution to the understanding of imperialism was more tactical than theoretical: in other words, Lenin connected the struggle against capitalism to the struggle against imperialism, the struggle for national self-determination to the struggle of the proletariat for state power. His theory of anti-capitalist politics and anti-imperialist politics left a mark on a whole epoch" (*Lenin: A Study on the Unity of His Thought*, Boston, 1971). Lenin influenced the strategy of Marxist-Leninist states, which declared themselves anti-imperialist from a class standpoint. He also had a direct or indirect influence on those nationalists who lacked a class analysis. He proposed joining revolutionary civil war to anticolonial war, and the war of the proletariat (constituted as a hegemonic class) to war for national liberation. Fighting against imperialism was equivalent to fighting against monopoly capital, even to fighting for socialism. This was the legacy passed on from *Stalin to Palmiro Togliatti, from *Mao Zedong to *Ho Chi Minh to Fidel *Castro.

The crisis of a whole epoch, and of *Marxism-*Leninism as a theory and practice useful for understanding imperialism and waging the struggle against it, became evident from 1985 onward in Lenin's own country, where it began to be supplanted by *perestroika. In his speech of 2 November 1987, Mikhail *Gorbachev raised what he called "some tough questions." "Given the current stage of world development," Gorbachev asked, "is it possible to influence the nature of imperialism and block its most dangerous manifestations? . . . Can capitalism get rid of militarism and function and develop in the economic sphere without it? . . . Can the capitalist system do without neo-colonialism, which is currently one of the essential factors to its survival?" (*October and Perestroika: The Revolution Continues*, Moscow, 1987, p. 62). Gorbachev's questions would have been inconceivable in the era of Marxist-Leninist orthodoxy, when everybody relied on the answer Lenin himself had given to what he called "the main question." Most damaging of all to the Leninist legacy, the official revelation of contradictions encountered by the Soviet Union included a profound self-criticism concerning the policy of enforcing the hegemony of "state socialism" over neighboring countries as well as within its own borders. Those policies had been labeled as imperialist by Western ideologues. The *Truman administration used these policies to justify the so-called *containment of Soviet "expansionism" or "imperialism," but in Marxist-Leninist circles, the labeling of the Soviet Union as "imperialist" was officially understood as a "class response" of the bourgeoisie bent on spreading lies in order to fan the flames of the *Cold War.

However, the leadership of the People's Republic of *China waged a campaign against the Soviet Union, accusing it of being "social-imperialist." This term had been used by Lenin to attack the leaders of the German Social Democratic Party, "justly called," according to Lenin, "social-imperialist, that is, socialist in words and imperialists in deeds" (Lenin, *Imperialism*, ch. 9). Chinese propagandists defined the characteristics of Soviet "social imperialism" based on the presumed policy of the Soviet Union to compete with the United States for world *hegemony. They also pointed to the Soviet domination and exploitation of Eastern and *Central Europe and *Third World countries, as well as to their behavior toward the nationalities and ethnic groups of Central Asia within the borders of the Soviet Union. Chinese criticism denounced a series of Soviet policies as presumably identical to those of any modern imperialist state, particularly those of the United States. Chinese rhetoric, loaded with metaphors, examples, and distinctive epithets (such as "revisionist renegade coterie," used to designate the Soviet leadership) obscured what was objectively true about this denunciation.

The resemblance between imperialist and "social-imperialist" policies was remarkable. The insulting character of the criticism, however, prevented some from delving more deeply into the controversy. Nevertheless, the Chinese theory of social imperialism and the struggle against it was limited by its lack of a class analysis, although it claimed to be Marxist-Leninist. Failing to take into account the fundamental class differences between the Soviet Union and the United States, the Chinese equated the "imperialism" of the Soviet Union with the imperialism of the United States. The Chinese analysis thus broke the "Leninist" link between imperialist exploitation and capitalist exploitation. "Imperialism" thus became a class-neutral term and lost explanatory precision.

The denunciation of the main policies of "social imperialism" amounted to a sort of enumerative definition. Among the characteristics were the following: "socialist economic integration," used by the Soviet Union as an instrument of "social imperialism"; an "international division of labor" that furthered "social-imperialist" domination; "economic organizations" or *multinational corporations that dominated by virtue of their control over finance, services, products, and cheap manual labor; irrational exploitation of the natural resources of the dominated countries; "uneven trade" with them; military agreements such as the *Warsaw Treaty Organization (Warsaw Pact) with Soviet lines of command;

military integration depending on other armies; control of weapons production by the hegemonic country; enforcement of extraterritorial rights by the Soviet Union; hiring advisers and experts to handle arms and logistics; use of military maneuvers to apply pressure (for instance, in the Balkan countries); punishment of unsubmissive governments by deferral of payments and other aid and through actions to destabilize them; surprise invasions such as that of Czechoslovakia in 1968; long-standing governments of occupation; the ability to launch not only defensive but offensive strikes around the world, but particularly in Central Europe. The Chinese, in their denunciations, adopted the classic language of imperialism, speaking of Soviet "neocolonialist policy" and of the Eastern European countries' "dependency"; of "exploitation" and domination as part of a plot to replace a "defeated imperialism" with a rising one.

The link between imperialism and monopoly capitalism was no longer the essence of the problem for those calling themselves Marxist-Leninists. The "crisis" in the theory of imperialism mirrored the defeat of the Leninist project in general, mired as it was in the bureaucratization of "state socialism."

The end of the Western *colonial empires gave rise to ideological interpretations of the "end of imperialism" similar to those written recently about the "end of history." Bill Warren's *Imperialism: Pioneer of Capitalism* (London, 1980) stands out in this regard. His lack of rigor in the use of statistics and Marxist texts does not deprive Warren's work of a certain importance: he sets up a dialectic by which the defeat of Marxist-Leninist and nationalist struggles supposedly corresponds to that stage in the development of capitalism where, as a result of imperialism, it has become a "supranational" system, thus rendering national working-class struggles unnecessary. Warren contends that global capitalism would not have existed without imperialism, and that socialism is impossible without the previous global extension of capitalism. But he also insists that the historical phenomenon of imperialism ended once the underdeveloped countries were incorporated into the capitalist system. This notion of a return to classic, premonopoly capitalism, however, is as inaccurate as his central thesis that dependent nation-states have ceased being a necessary feature of the capitalist system. Warren's theses tend to deny the importance of the problem of imperialism. In that sense they correspond to a relatively older tradition which admitted the existence of imperialism or discussed its demise, without acknowledging the importance to capitalism of specifically imperialist exploitation.

Authors such as John Strachey (*The End of Empire*, 1959) advanced the opinion that following World War II imperialism was no longer necessary, given the increase in the standard of living in the metropole. Others such as Michael Barratt Brown (*After Imperialism*, 1963) have contended that the prosperity of countries like Britain no longer depended on colonial ventures, which ceased to have macroeconomic significance. For these authors, such historical and social demarcation of imperialism is important in defining the phenomenon. For instance, according to Brown, the "colonial tribute to the great powers" corresponds to an extremely low percentage, which he calculates as 3.3 percent of the GNP of Britain. His calculation, however, does not take into account the fact that imperialism or "colonial tribute" is a *social rela-*

tion, which retains enormous significance for both the monopoly enterprises and "tributary nations." Authors such as Hamza Alavi have even gone so far as to say that, beginning in the 1960s, the "new" imperialism no longer used the exportation of capital as a means for "exploiting cheap labour overseas," but confined itself to the expansion of production in metropolitan markets and to the control of world markets ("Imperialism Old and New," *Socialist Register*, 1964). On the contrary, as Paul Sweezy has demonstrated, beginning in the 1960s, the "multinational corporations moved their manufacturing facilities to lower-wage countries" ("Imperialism in the 1990s," *Monthly Review*, October 1989).

The fact that Lenin's prediction that imperialism would be "the eve of socialist revolution" has not been proved correct does not imply that the phenomenon of imperialism—the hegemony of monopoly capital and capitalist nation-states—has ended. Nor has the struggle of workers and peoples in the dominated countries against domination and exploitation ended. On the contrary, there is every indication that the phenomenon of imperialism not only persists in the midst of recent, world-historic changes, but has intensified the control that the great powers exercise over the so-called Third World and the so-called socialist countries.

Among the recent changes in imperialist exploitation, Harry Magdoff has emphasized 1) "The integration of military production with the dominant industrial sectors"; 2) "the rising importance of the multi-national corporations which drive towards worldwide control of the most profitable and newest industries in both the periphery and advanced countries"; and 3) "the priority of the interests of military-multinational industry in the affairs of the State" ("Imperialism: A Historical Survey," *Monthly Review*, May 1972). In other words, the structures and subsystems of exploitation are changing, but the phenomenon has not abated.

In the article quoted above, Paul Sweezy raised the possibility that some "additional empires," such as the Soviet Union and/or China, would share domination of the world market with the United States–Canada, Western European, and Japanese blocs. He went so far as to say that this new collegiate imperialism or imperialist club does not seem to contain "the seed of a violent confrontation." His theses are similar to those of superimperialism, but they may have a greater validity today, as the focus of antagonism shifts from East-West to North-South. The policies of the economic superpowers may result in a more or less lasting distribution of the world's markets and resources among them. This distribution arrangement might be founded on 1) a relative disarmament; 2) financial, monetary, and commercial agreements on a world scale; and 3) measures leading to a more or less unequal redistribution of GNP in the world, and between the North and the South. But this resolution of imperialism's contradictions may be circumvented by other features of late-twentieth-century imperialism which are not easily overcome.

The transfer of "surplus" from the "periphery" to the "center" increased considerably during the 1970s and 1980s, even as neoliberal policies have stressed the effects of disaccumulation and underconsumption of the dependent world as a result of unequal terms of trade, expansion of transnational corporations, and external debt. The apparent victory of capitalism over the Eastern bloc and over the nationalist governments of the South has taken place at the same time as the exploitation of the periphery by world capitalism has intensified. Many studies carried out by international organizations (especially the UN, Food and Agricultural Organization, *International Labor Organization, *World Health Organization, *World Bank, and *International Monetary Fund) present data on capital transfers and declines in standards of living in the countries of the periphery which indicate that the imperialist exploitation and domination of these countries is more thorough than ever.

Many researchers have studied this worldwide phenomenon, focusing on the economic, social, political, and cultural relations of the "center" to the "periphery," of the "metropole" to the "dependent" countries, considering the world as a "system." Among these researchers—of differing ideological and intellectual tendencies, Marxist and structuralist—some stand out for their theoretical and analytical contributions: Paul Baran, Fernando Henrique Cardoso, André Gunder-Frank, Samir Amin, Arrighi Emmanuel, and Immanuel Wallerstein. In their analyses, the imperialist countries appear as a subset, closely articulated to the periphery through transnational corporations and associated dependent bourgeoisies. The *development problems of the periphery assume more importance in their definition of imperialism. Some of the authors, such as Anouar Abdel Malek, approach the phenomenon of imperialism as a dialectic between domination and liberation, as a struggle between dominant states and national movements, where politics, technology, and war occupy the foreground.

(See also NORTH-SOUTH RELATIONS.)

PABLO GONZÁLES CASANOVA

IMPORT-SUBSTITUTION INDUSTRIALIZATION. The term *import substitution* (IS) has two related, yet distinct, meanings. First, it refers to the economic process through which local production displaces, or substitutes for, previously imported goods. This process may be triggered by changes in domestic demand or transport costs that make local production profitable or by the interruption of imports as a result of war, embargo, or depression.

The term *import substitution* is also used to refer to policy interventions, particularly trade restrictions, that have the effect of stimulating local industrialization at the expense of imports. These policies may also arise initially as a result of external economic shocks. For example, governments often respond to *balance-of-payments crises by restricting trade to conserve foreign exchange. Although these restrictions may not have the intention of increasing the profitability of domestic manufactures, they can have that effect.

IS has also been a more self-conscious component of nationalist economic thinking. IS policies have been adopted by developing countries throughout modern history. To develop an indigenous industrial base required protection against the superior competitive position of more advanced countries. Protection of local manufacturing activities was central to British mercantilism in the seventeenth and eighteenth centuries and was advocated by Alexander Hamilton in the United States in his famous *Report on Manufactures*. Soviet economic thinking consistently championed autarky and self-reliance in international economic relations. This idea exerted a powerful influence in other socialist countries, for example

in Eastern Europe, which quickly sought to replicate the entire range of basic industries. Soviet thinking had influence in interwar Turkey and postindependence India as well.

In the postwar period, the justification for import substitution was most highly developed in Latin America, where the Great Depression of the 1930s and two world wars stimulated industrial development in the larger countries, especially Argentina, Brazil, and Mexico. Later, the smaller countries of South and Central America and those of Africa also pursued IS policies as the process of development became inextricably associated with industrialization.

Political leaders and local entrepreneurs feared that local industries would be undermined or impeded by foreign competition. This fear was coupled with substantial pessimism about export prospects. It was believed that a secular decline in the terms of trade would result in "immiserizing growth" for the developing world if it continued to specialize in traditional raw material exports. These ideas were most forcefully argued by Raúl *Prebisch and the UN *Economic Commission for Latin America.

The pursuit of IS usually progressed through several phases, although they necessarily overlapped to some extent. In the first phase, protection was extended to producers of light manufactures, such as textiles, apparel, and food processing. These ventures could be carried out by local entrepreneurs because they involved relatively standardized technologies, were not particularly capital-intensive, and could draw on pools of relatively unskilled labor. At some point, however, the domestic market for these goods became saturated. At this juncture, policymakers faced difficult choices about which new sectors should be emphasized. Consumer durables and intermediate and capital goods production were typically more demanding of capital, technology, and skilled labor, factors in which most developing countries were deficient.

The decision to pursue "secondary" IS in these sectors had important implications for the ownership patterns of IS industries. In the first phase of IS, domestic entrepreneurs gained and thus were likely to support IS policies. In the secondary phase of IS, however, state-owned and foreign firms usually played a larger role. Intermediate goods production, particularly in steel and oil refining, was typically carried out by state-owned enterprises. A number of larger Latin American countries became important sources for IS foreign investment in sectors such as chemicals, automobiles, and linked industries such as glass and rubber that were beyond the technological reach of local firms.

As early as the mid-1960s, criticisms of IS industrialization began to appear, particularly among neoclassical economists. First, the protection of domestic industry increased the profitability of the manufacturing sector at the expense of agriculture. This had a number of undesirable implications, favoring the city over the countryside, accelerating rural-to-urban migration, and contributing to an unequal distribution of income. By distorting the allocation of resources, IS introduced tremendous inefficiencies, favoring high-cost sectors in which the country had no comparative advantage.

A second line of criticism concerned the penetration of foreign firms and the role of foreign capital more generally. Although IS was designed to increase self-reliance, in many cases it resulted in greater dependence on foreign firms. These firms occupied powerful positions in highly oligopolistic industries and engaged in a number of practices that were seen as detrimental, including the introduction of inappropriate technologies, production processes, and products. In the 1970s, the forward momentum of industrial deepening was sustained in many countries through extensive foreign borrowing. In the 1980s, governments found themselves saddled with the external debt not only of state-owned enterprises but of inefficient private firms in IS sectors.

A third line of criticism concerned export performance. High levels of protection and overvalued exchange rates designed to reduce the costs of importing capital goods and machinery had the effect of discouraging exports. Countries pursuing IS faced recurrent balance-of-payments problems, often solved in the short run by reliance on more protection.

Finally, there were a number of political criticisms of IS. From the *Left, it was argued that the pattern of secondary IS tended to support an elite consumption profile, particularly by emphasizing the production of costly consumer durables such as automobiles. Instead of emphasizing the deepening of the industrial base through secondary IS, according to this view, it would be preferable to widen the domestic market by improving the distribution of income and focusing production on widely consumed basic goods. From the *Right, it was argued that the institution of protection and various subsidies to industry resulted not only in inefficiencies but in a corruption of political life: entrepreneurs concentrated on securing privileges, or "rent-seeking," rather than on productive activities, and the initiation of trade restrictions necessarily gave rise to black markets in goods and foreign exchange.

These criticisms were often indiscriminate, attributing all problems of development to misguided industrial policies. Some IS industries were relatively efficient or had the potential to become so. This was evident in the fact that many, if not most, industries in the advanced industrial states began initially as IS industries, with trade liberalization and the development of exports coming later. This was even true of the export-oriented East Asian economies: Japan, the Republic of Korea, and Taiwan. All three developed their manufacturing base through a subtle combination of protectionist policies, subsidies, and aggressive promotion of exports. Although they managed to avoid the excesses of IS in other developing countries, they were by no means wholly liberal in their trade policies.

Nonetheless, IS as a general strategy came under increasing pressure in the 1980s. Many countries came to recognize the cumulative inefficiencies and costs associated with IS. The withdrawal of international lending associated with the *debt crisis made capital-intensive investments less viable and increased the importance of developing export industries in order to earn foreign exchange. The rapidity of technological change in major industries such as electronics made "self-reliance" a more costly and complicated goal and made it imperative that developing countries maintain close links with world markets.

The pressures to abandon IS were also political. The international financial institutions, including the *World Bank and the *International Monetary Fund, pressed vigorously for trade liberalization. The United States also launched a more aggressive policy in the mid-1980s by placing greater emphasis on opening markets abroad through the threat of retaliation. Major targets of this campaign were the relatively de-

veloped newly industrializing countries that had maintained high levels of protection, including Brazil, India, and even export-oriented Korea.

This combination of domestic and international factors has led to several sharp reversals of import-substituting policies. Mexico, Chile, and Turkey provide three important examples, as do the countries of Eastern and Central Europe. Yet it is unlikely that IS will be abandoned altogether. The adjustment costs of moving toward a new strategy are potentially high for both workers and capitalists and thus are likely to meet domestic political resistance. A more likely outcome is the evolution of more mixed industrial strategies that combine elements of protection and support for domestic industry with greater emphasis on exports and the development of international competitiveness.

(See also DEVELOPMENT AND UNDERDEVELOPMENT; EXPORT-LED GROWTH; NEWLY INDUSTRIALIZING ECONOMIES.)

Raúl Prebisch, *The Economic Development of Latin America and its Principal Problems* (New York, 1950). Raymond Vernon, "International Investment and International Trade in the Product Cycle" *Quarterly Journal of Economics* 80 (May 1966): 190–207. Albert Hirschman, "The Political Economy of Import-Substituting Industrialization in Latin America," in Albert Hirschman, *A Bias for Hope* (New Haven, Conn., 1971), pp. 85–123. Gerald Meier and Dudley Seers, eds., *Pioneers in Development* (New York, 1984).

STEPHAN HAGGARD

INDIA. The Republic of India, the world's largest democracy, emerged from under British colonial rule as a sovereign nation-state in 1947. Its present constitution, adopted on 26 January 1950, provides for a Westminster-style parliamentary form of government in a federal union that currently consists of twenty-five states and seven centrally administered union territories. The constitution was a culmination of a process of evolution toward representative government that began under the British.

The constitution formally vests all executive powers of the government in the president, who is the head of the state. The president, however, exercises power, with only rare exceptions, upon the advice of the prime minister and the Council of Ministers with whom real power rests.

The president is elected for a five-year term by an electoral college consisting of elected members of both the bicameral parliament and the state legislatures. The upper house of parliament, the Rajya Sabha (House of the State) consists of members who are elected for six-year terms by an electoral college made up members of the state legislative assemblies. The lower house, the Lok Sabha (House of the People), is the supreme legislative body in India and consists of 542 members who are directly elected for a five-year term according to a single-member-district system in which the individual with the highest tally of votes wins the seat. The prime minister is elected by the parliamentary members of the majority party in the Lok Sabha. The conventions of cabinet government are used and the prime minister and the cabinet are collectively responsible to Parliament and must retain the confidence of the majority of the members of the Lok Sabha.

An analogous structure of government exists in each of the states. Each state has a governor, who is appointed by the president for a five-year term, and a popularly elected legislature, which may be bicameral or unicameral and is elected for five years. The leader of the majority party in the legislature is elected chief minister, who, with his or her cabinet colleagues, is responsible to the legislature and must command the confidence of a majority of the members. Although the constitution is federal, it provides for strong unitary features, including the ultimate power of the center to control and take over direct administration of the states under those conditions it deems fit.

The constitution also provides for an independent judiciary. The powers of the Indian Supreme Court are comparable to those of the Supreme Court of the United States and include broad original and appellate jurisdiction and the right to judge the constitutional validity of the laws passed by parliament. The courts have been important institutions in the political system. The relative balance of parliamentary sovereignty and judicial review is imprecisely defined and is being constantly negotiated and contested. During the last decade the Court has become increasingly more independent and assertive in the exercise of its powers.

The Indian armed forces, numbering some 4 million, remain largely apolitical, professional, and firmly under civilian control. The command and control of India's nuclear weapons program also remain under civilian control. The Indian army is, however, often relied upon to deal with domestic law and order problems in areas of insurgency or during riots.

Economy. India's economic record has been mixed. After independence, it pursued a development strategy aimed at self reliance through import substition and capital-intensive industrialization. Until the early 1990s India had a mixed economy with the state sector dominating the industrial sectors, both by direct ownership and a system of controls regulating private enterprise. Between 1950 and 1980 the economy grew at a modest rate of 3–4 percent a year. Since 1985 the growth rate has averaged 6–7 percent.

In 1991, India's development strategy underwent a profound change. A vast array of domestic investment licensing and trade controls were abolished, tariffs were reduced, direct foreign investment and portfolio investment were permitted, and partial privatization of the public sector enterprises is under way. Trade and financial services liberalization have integrated India into the global economy to an unprecedented degree. Although some capital controls remain in place, this trend is likely to continue. The next big challenge in the process of liberalization is likely to be the liberalization of the agricultural sector and the further privatization of state-owned enterprises.

In the agricultural sector, still India's dominant sector, the *green revolution has ushered in gains in productivity. But despite steady growth, India's failures on the human development front remain unconscionable. Forty percent of the population remains in chronic poverty; per capita income is approximately $400; life expectancy is fifty-four years and literacy 64 percent. The paradox of India is that it at the same time possess a sophisticated scientific, technical, and financial infrastructure and is one of the leading centers of information technology and software.

The most serious challenges facing the economy are the size of the government's fiscal deficit. While India's external debt is of serviceable proportions, its internal debt is very high. Government deficits have led to a reduction in infrastructure and capital investment on the one hand and virtual stagna-

tion in the social services sector like health and education on the other.

Politics and Society. India has sustained a contentious but vibrant democratic process amidst great odds. It is an immensely politicized society. Since independence there have been thirteen general elections; four in the last decade. Both voter turnouts and anti-incumbency have been steadily on the rise. With the exception of a brief suspension of the democratic process between 1975 and 1977 when Indira *Gandhi declared a state of emergency, India has had an open and free democratic process. Independent bodies like the Election Commission have ensured that elections are free and fair.

The political process in India can best be understood through changes in the party system. The Indian National Congress dominated India's politics until 1990 retaining power in all but the 1977 and 1989 elections. Although Congress returned to power in 1991, it has been steadily declining since. What has emerged in the wake of the decline of the Congress is an extremely fragmented party system. Since 1989 alone India has had six prime ministers; since 1995 all its governments have been coalitions of at least a dozen parties and this trend is likely to continue. But there has been a good deal of policy continuity and institutional stability amidst high turnover of governments.

The Indian National Congress, or now just the Congress, was created in 1885 as an organization of anglicized, Western-educated elites. During the 1920s, under the leadership of Mohandas *Gandhi, it was transformed from an elite political organization into a mass nationalist movement that incorporated a wide array of social groups. This forced upon the Congress the delicate tasks of balancing and reconciling contradictory interests. The Congress in the process developed an accommodating ideology and diffuse organization that eschewed *class conflict.

From 1967 onward, when Indira Gandhi took power, Congress' capacity to negotiate social conflict has been systematically eroded. The increasing mobilization of new groups considerably diminished the capacity of those intermediaries and local notables on whom Congress had relied. And the ideological center of Indian politics has shifted considerably: State-led industrialization has given way to a freer market. And the Hindu nationalist Bharatiya Janata Party (Indian People's Party) has been attempting to redefine India's national identity along Hindu majoritarian lines. The last decade has also seen the remarkable political rise of the backward and scheduled castes, who now wield political power in most states. Indian democracy has become more representative and contentious at the same time.

The Bharatiya Janata Party, which now heads India's coalition government, champions Hindu *nationalism. The party gets somewhere between 22 and 27 percent of the popular vote. In 1992 it spearheaded a movement that led to the demolition of the Babari Mosque in Ayodhya (a site it claims is the birthplace of the Hindu god Ram). Since then, the imperatives of electoral politics and coalition formation have compelled the party to downplay its nationalist agenda. But it is widely regarded as hostile to India's minorities, in particular Muslims and Christians. Although on economic issues that party has moved away from its nationalist agenda, it continues to remain a source of anxiety for minorities.

Since independence, both central and state governments

have pursued policies of positive discrimination for India's lowest strata, namely, the scheduled castes and tribes. In 1990, a decision by India's national government to expand preferential treatment to include other backward castes became a volatile issue in Indian politics. Caste still remains, at least at the state level, a significant axis of political mobilization. The BJP has traditionally been an upper-caste party, although it is slowly gaining ground among the backward and scheduled castes. However, the fragmentation of the electorate on caste lines is likely to make it very difficult for any political party to acquire the kind of dominance Congress had from 1950 to 1985. Caste politics is likely to remain contentious, especially in North India.

India's linguistic, regional, ethnic, and religious diversities are prodigious and have generated important obstacles to nation building. India has some forty-six officially listed other tongues, seventeen of which have achieved the status of recognized languages. Hindi is spoken by the largest number of people, though this group fails to add up to a majority. Over time, the political system has evolved complex compromises in the face of such diversity and related protest over language issues, most notably in the state of Tamil Nadu in 1963 and Punjab in the late 1960s. The compromises now provide for the joint use of Hindi and English in parliamentary proceedings, the use of Hindi as a language of communication between the center and Hindi speaking states, and the use of English between the center and the non-Hindi speaking states. Adequate provisions also exist for the teaching of other languages in various states. The States Reorganization Act of 1956 and the subsequent amendments in 1960 and 1966 also brought the boundaries of the southern states in conformity with traditional linguistic regions. The principal political grievances that arise out of the language issue seem to have been resolved. There are proposals pending to break up three large North Indian States of Madhya Pradesh, Uttar Pradesh, and Bihar into smaller units.

In India, democratic incorporation has been very successful at coping with demands for regional autonomy. The reorganization of states has, however, failed to accommodate aspirations for self-determination in states such as Kashmir, Assam, and in the northeast. These states, along with Punjab, have experienced long and often violent struggles, directed against the center. While the movement in Punjab has been, through a combination of force and political maneuvering, dissipated, the other states are likely to continue to experience a good deal of political violence. The situation in Kashmir, India's only Muslim majority state, is likely to remain unresolved for some time to come. Kashmir not only has a strong movement seeking independence from India; it is also claimed by *Pakistan.

The prospects for Indian politics seem to suggest increasing politicization of social cleavages. As demands grow and such institutions as political parties remain weak, the body politic is likely to be characterized by intermittent political violence. India's democracy is however, unlikely to crumble. Democratic aspirations run deep, the economy is steady, and the institutions of the state remain strong. However, these institutions are unlikely to be very effective at alleviating India's unconscionable poverty and its human costs; nor are they likely to do away with all the violence that the contest over India's national identity has generated in the last decade. Indian democracy will remain a paradoxical combination of unyielding self assertion and human deprivation.

Foreign Policy. India's foreign policy was persistently governed by a belief in alignments, although during the *Cold War it was somewhat closer to the Soviet Union. Since Independence, India's relations with its neighbors, Pakistan and China, have been especially strained and embittered. Armed conflict with Pakistan over the long-standing territorial dispute over Jammu and Kashmir resulted in the division of the state into Pakistan-held and Indian-held sectors. There was renewed armed conflict in 1965 and again in 1971 when, following a political crisis in East Pakistan, Indian intervention led to the creation of *Bangladesh. Both sides are involved in a low-level war of attrition over Kashmir.

Both India and Pakistan conducted nuclear tests in 1996 and are now openly declared nuclear powers. The threat of an arms race on the subcontinent is very strong, although fiscal imperatives in both countries are likely to slow it down.

India also has an outstanding territorial dispute with China involving 14,500 square miles (37,500 sq. km.) of territory in the Aksai Chin area of Kashmir and 36,000 square miles (93,250 sq. km.) of territory in Arunachal Pradesh. The dispute escalated into a military conflict in 1962 and relations have been strained since. India is likely to continue to seek an independent foreign policy, although its increasing incorporation into the global economy is likely to push it toward better relation with the United States.

(See also HINDUISM; IMPORT-SUBSTITUTION INDUSTRIALIZATION; NEHRU, JAWAHARLAL; NONALIGNED MOVEMENT.)

Francine Frankel and M. S. A. Rao, eds., *Dominance and State Power in Modern India: Decline of a Social Order*, 2 vols. (Delhi, 1989, 1990). Paul Brass, *The Politics of India since Independence* (Cambridge, 1990). Atul Kohli, *Democracy and Discontent: India's Growing Crisis of Governability* (New York, 1991). Christophe Jafferlot, *The Hindu Nationalist Movement in India* (London, 1996). Sunil Khilnani, *The Idea of India* (London, 1997). Jeffery Sachs, Nirupam Bajpai, and Ashutosh Varshney, eds., *India's Economic Reforms* (Delhi, 1999).

PRATAP MEHTA

INDIAN OCEAN REGION. The islands of the western Indian Ocean—Comoros, Maldives, Mauritius, Réunion, and Seychelles—have much in common, yet each is different in many ways. They share many economic, social, historical, political, geographical, and geophysical characteristics. Until quite recently they were all isolated, in the backwater of the international political arena, and were colonies or dependencies of either France or Britain. Except for Réunion, which is an Overseas Department of France, they achieved their independence in the 1960s and 1970s: Comoros in 1975, Maldives in 1965, Mauritius in 1968, and Seychelles in 1976.

The histories of the islands vary. For example, Maldives had great social and economic influences from South Asia. The other islands were uninhabited until the colonization by Western powers during the eighteenth and nineteenth centuries. With British and French rule came indentured workers from India and Africa to supply labor for the plantation/agricultural systems which were established to serve the growing markets of industrializing Europe. The main emphasis was placed on cash crop production of sugarcane, coconuts, palm oil, and tea. These colonial ties—linguistic, religious, and especially economic—formed the cultural and social heritage for these islands at independence. Ethnic cleavages and resulting frictions from ruled-ruler relationships (of imported African and Indian labor and imported European supervisors) have left their mark on many of the states. Cash crops have resulted in each state's being an "international price taker" with very little control over its economic destiny. Instead of building mechanisms and infrastructure for self-sufficiency, these islands were forced to continue to rely on food imports as well as high levels of other imported consumer goods.

Each of the island states is small by international comparisons, and none is larger than 965 square miles (2,500 sq. km.). For example, the Maldives group is less than 115 square miles (300 sq. km.) in total area. Agriculture has little room for expansion and development, and in some islands lack of fresh water is an economic as well as a social problem. Their natural resource bases are very small. There are some mineral resources (including offshore oil), but thus far no state in the region has benefited significantly from fuel or nonfuel minerals.

In terms of population these states are also quite small. Seychelles, with a population of only 78,000, is one of the world's smallest mini-states. Maldives has a population of 280,000, Comoros has nearly 400,000, Réunion has over half a million, and Mauritius, the largest, has about 1 million. Populations are rising rapidly, and unemployment is a problem in all the states. Nevertheless, the average population growth rate is below the less developed country average. Population pressures have increased for virtually every state during the past generation. Mauritius, fortunately, has a more diverse economic base to support increasing and more densely populated areas, while Maldives' resource base is low. For Maldives, population density has been and will remain a serious development problem. The other states, particularly Comoros and Seychelles, have found their density problems worsening, especially since the amount of good land in these two states is quite small, both in relative and absolute terms. Comoros and Maldives are very poor by international standards and are classified as least developed countries (LDCs) by the UN. Réunion, Seychelles, and Mauritius have moved into "middle-income" status.

Organizations and Political Change. The political structures of these island states vary. Nonetheless, despite somewhat authoritarian rule in the 1970s and 1980s, they have, in general, moved to democracy during the 1990s. All the countries are members of the Commonwealth (although France still controls Réunion and a part of Comoros).

Mauritius is a multiparty democracy, and for many years was one of the region's few democracies. The government is headed by a president who appoints a prime minister and a council of ministers. The Legislative Assembly is composed of sixty-two elected members and eight members appointed by the attorney-general. Politics in Mauritius has generally been open. President Uteem was first elected in 1992 and reelected in 1997.

Seychelles' government is headed by a president who is head of state, head of government, and commander of the armed forces. The National Assembly is composed of thirty-three elected members. After a coup in 1977 the president was empowered to rule by decree. During the 1970s and 1980s there were several coup attempts, but the country moved to democracy in 1993. The current president, France René, was reelected in 1993.

Comoros is also a federal Islamic republic. The president is both head of state and head of government and is directly elected for six-year terms and appoints a prime minister. The country's recent political history has been turbulent, with several coups and coup attempts. The nation has become much more open in the past ten years, and the last election (in 1996) saw fifteen candidates vie for the office. Nonetheless, the island's political structure is complicated by Mayotte (physically a part of the Comoran archipelago), which decided to remain a part of France when the rest of the islands declared independence in 1975. Mayotte is administered by France as an Overseas Collective Territory. The territory sends one delegate to the National Assembly and to the Senate in Paris.

Maldives's government is led by a president who is head of state and commander of the armed forces. The president is elected by popular vote and appoints eight of the forty-eight-member elected cabinet. There are elections every five years, but the current president, Maumoon Gayoom, first elected in 1983, was elected to his fifth term in 1998.

Réunion is an Overseas Department of France and as such is administered as an integral part of the Republic. Five representatives are sent to the French National Assembly and three to the Senate. The island is run by a general council, composed of forty-four elected members. While there is some movement favoring independence from France, the vast majority of people want to retain the status quo. Elections have been contested by about a dozen political parties.

Output and the Economy. All of the islands share most of the economic problems associated with small island states in general. These problems include relatively and absolutely small populations, absence of economies of scale, limited opportunities for employment or development, and isolation from world markets. With open economies dependent on the world economic system, they suffer from primary production of one or two agricultural products which are subject to severe price fluctuations, and over which they have little if any control. There is little industrial activity or development. Subsistence activities, either farming or fishing, are widespread in most of the states. Of these states, only Réunion and Mauritius have economies where less than 90 percent of the population is engaged in those subsistence activities. Trade has continued to be geared principally with the industrialized countries and with Britain and France in particular. Generally, the former British colony of Seychelles has tended to maintain stronger trade ties with Britain, while Comoros and Réunion have retained stronger links with France. Maldives never had particularly strong ties with Britain, and Mauritius (originally ruled by France) has had more of a balance in its trade partner mix.

Because of their relatively diversified natural resource bases, diversified economic sectors, and well-developed human and physical infrastructures, Mauritius and Réunion have good long-term economic prospects. For the short and medium term, however, both will have problems. Mauritius will have to maintain its competitiveness with South Asia in cheap manufactured textile exports, keep its import levels down, and diversify further from agricultural production. Mauritius could benefit from increased tourism in the region. Réunion continues to hide its severe structural economic problems by its reliance on French budgetary assistance. Its industries are inefficient and will have to modernize. Because of its relatively high education levels and large amounts of foreign (i.e., French) investment, however, the economic prospects for Réunion are bright. For the short term, however, France will have to deal with some unemployment and rising consumer expectations in Réunion. Neither Maldives nor Seychelles has many natural resources; nevertheless, if they can maintain economic and political stability they should have fair to good long-term economic prospects owing in large part to their tourism sectors. For Maldives, the short and medium terms appear about the same as the long term. It must continue to receive Official Development Assistance to keep its economy viable, yet the country will gain increasing foreign exchange from increased tourism. Comoros has the lowest level of natural resources in the region. Its prospects for both the medium and long term are not bright. Most of its economy is geared toward the subsistence sector, and what little modern sector activities exist are export-oriented with little local value added. There appears little likelihood of increased tourism in the islands. Until it settles its territorial dispute with France, it cannot be assured of continued and sizable French economic assistance.

International and Regional Political Affairs. Britain had a strategic monopoly over the area from the end of the nineteenth century until World War II. However, Japan's defeat of the British fleet in the Pacific in 1942 essentially ended that hegemony. After the war Britain did not have the desire or the ability to reassert its dominance. Rather, it was engaged in withdrawing its military forces worldwide. Following World War II France continued its modest-sized military presence, and in 1947 the United States set up a tiny task force based in Bahrain. The Soviet Union did not yet have a fleet capable of operating so far from its home bases. During the 1960s interest in the region gradually began to increase as Britain began preparations for granting independence to its remaining colonies or possessions in the area. The United States and Britain made several agreements for the use of former British colonial possessions, including Diego Garcia. In 1965 Britain formed the British Indian Ocean Territory (BIOT) from several small islands in the Chagos archipelago. Resettlement of the native populations to Mauritius has been a sore point between the regional "progressive" states and Britain ever since. These states claim that Britain did not adequately compensate the people it removed. By the mid-1970s the United States had begun to establish a naval communications and an air base on Diego Garcia, and its Seventh Fleet was authorized to extend well into the western Indian Ocean. A landmark was reached in 1967 when Britain announced its strategy of force withdrawal "east of Suez" by 1971. It was then that the United States and the Soviet Union began to jockey for position in the region. The Soviets began to regularly deploy a small but growing military fleet, and also began to engage in more economic activities, principally fishing. During this period the French maintained and even increased their presence in the region, becoming stronger militarily than the United States, the Soviet Union, or Britain. France operated from bases in Réunion and Comoros. France has remained committed to maintaining a strong presence and wants to protect its economic and political interests, especially in Mayotte and Réunion.

As the oil crisis of the 1970s intensified, many planners in the West began to reassess the area's strategic value because of the large amount of oil which passes through the region. More than 90 percent of Japan's oil, for example, passes through (or near) Maldives. When the Suez Canal was closed during the 1967 Middle East War, the shipping lanes around South Africa's Cape of Good Hope became more important as the major alternative route. About 50 percent of Western Europe's oil passes around the Cape. Comoros, Mauritius, and Seychelles lie directly within those sea lanes; that route retained its importance even after the reopening of the canal because increased ship sizes (particularly oil tankers known as very large cargo carriers, or VLCC, and ultralarge cargo carriers, or ULCC) made passage through the Suez Canal impossible. Tensions have remained high in the Middle East during the past two decades: armed conflict occurred between a number of nearby states including Somalia-Ethiopia, Iran-Iraq, and Iraq-Kuwait. During the early 1980s the United States established its Rapid Deployment Joint Task Force and signed access agreements with a number of nearby African littoral states. In 1971 the UN's General Assembly passed a resolution declaring the Indian Ocean a "zone of peace," with a vote of 61 to 0 (with 55 abstentions—from all permanent members of the Security Council except China). Since the end of the Cold War, the countries in the area have looked more toward regional economic cooperation. The Indian Ocean Commission was established in 1982 to help develop tuna fishing (a major resource for all the states), regional tourism, and environmental protection. In 1997 a new organization—the Indian Ocean Rim Association for Regional Cooperation (IORARC)—was established with a broader membership and goals, including improving trade, investment, science, technology, and tourism.

(See also DECOLONIZATION; DEMOCRATIC TRANSITIONS; ETHNICITY; FOREIGN MILITARY BASES; FRANCOPHONE AFRICA; MADAGASCAR; SUEZ CRISIS.)

André Scherer, *La Réunion* (Paris, 1980). F. M. Bunge, ed., *Indian Ocean: Five Island Countries* (Washington, D.C., 1983). R. Cohen, *African Islands and Enclaves* (London, 1983). Ashok Kapur, *The Indian Ocean: Regional and International Power Politics* (New York, 1983). Larry Bowman, *Mauritius: Diversity and Democracy in the Indian Ocean* (Boulder, Colo., 1991).
DONALD L. SPARKS

INDONESIA. Strategically located between the Indian and Pacific Oceans, Indonesia extends 3,200 miles (5,100 km.) west to east, equal to the distance from Seattle to Washington, D.C., or Ireland to Azerbaijan. In 2000 an estimated 216 million people lived on some 6,000 Indonesian islands, making it the world's fourth most populous country.

In Asia only India is culturally more diverse. Hundreds of distinct indigenous languages are spoken in the archipelago. No country has more Muslims, who constitute nearly 90 percent of the whole of Indonesia's population. The remainder include Buddhists, Hindus, Catholics, and Protestants. All of these labels conceal variations in practice and piety.

One island, Java, is the homeland of the largest ethnic group, the Javanese, who form roughly half the country's population. The other half spans a congeries of smaller groups, the largest of which are the Sundanese, who also call Java home. Java is the demographic, socioeconomic, and political heartland of Indonesia, its infrastructure and opportunities having made it a magnet for the ethnic minorities that people the "outer islands." On Java stand Indonesia's three most populous cities, including the capital, Jakarta, with its estimated 10 million inhabitants. The outer islands are rich in natural resources—oil, gas, timber, minerals—much of whose value in revenues from exports has been transferred to Java. This imbalance has long stimulated resentment on the periphery against the central government in Jakarta.

The effort to keep Indonesia together has benefited from the cross-cutting character of cultural and class cleavages and the unifying effects of national language and nationalist success. Heartland and periphery alike are multiethnic and multireligious. With exceptions to be noted below, ethnicity, religion, residence, occupation, and wealth have tended not to coincide. Overlapping identities and statuses have restrained the potential for violence that can arise when such differences coincide.

National unity has also been served by aspects of history and language. Had the Dutch not created and maintained the Netherlands Indies as a single colony, there would have been no such encompassing political space for Indonesians to inherit. The national language of Indonesia is not the mother tongue of a major ethnic group, but a neutral and egalitarian lingua franca. The 1945–49 revolution against Dutch efforts to recolonize the archipelago after World War II forged a "1945 generation" of Indonesian leaders who shared the experience of struggling for the "one country, one people, one language" to which Indonesian patriots had sworn fealty in 1928.

Following its achievement of de jure independence as a unitary republic in 1950, Indonesia underwent rule by two presidents, Sukarno (1945–1968) and Suharto (1968–1998), and three regimes: "parliamentary democracy" in 1950–57, "guided democracy" in 1959–65, and "Pancasila democracy" in 1968–1998, with periods of transition in between.

*Parliamentary democracy brought freedoms of expression and association, a multiparty system, and reasonably free and fair elections organized nationally in 1955 and locally in 1957. But these features also stimulated political instability: revolving-door cabinets, a stalemated constituent assembly, and regional resistance to centralized rule from Jakarta. Mutual suspicions simmered among anticommunist officers, political Muslims, minority Christians, secular nationalists, and a communist party heartened by its growing electoral strength. Outer-island rebellions, partisan deadlock, military intervention, and Sukarno's growing impatience with what he derided as "fifty-percent-plus-one" democracy all interacted to doom this first regime.

The "guided democracy" that Sukarno imposed in 1959 was more guided than it was democratic. No further elections were held; press freedom was curtailed; allegedly disloyal parties were banned. Sukarno's obsession with national unity, including his effort to transcend the rivalry of "nationalism, religion, and communism" through ideological fusion, ruled out open political competition. The farther leftward his anti-imperialist rhetoric carried him, the more alarmed anticommunist officers and Muslims became. The Indonesian Communist Party (PKI) meanwhile had become the largest nonruling Marxist-Leninist party in the world, with influence not only in society and culture but in certain units of the armed forces as well. In October 1965 junior officers with links to the PKI assassinated six anticommunist commanders of the army.

Blamed, rightly or wrongly, on the PKI, these killings were used by a Javanese Muslim army general named Soeharto, the officers who sided with him, and militant Muslims, among other anticommunists, as a license to ban communism and arrest or slaughter its adherents. Hundreds of thousands may have died in the resulting pogrom. Reversing the anti-Western direction of Sukarno's regime, General Suharto established a "New Order" that underwrote with military force and foreign support a series of initiatives in political engineering and physical development that yielded unprecedented political stability and economic growth.

In Indonesia over the quarter-century from 1969 to 1994, annual gains in per capita GDP averaged a remarkable 4.8 percent. Judged against the records of other developing economies, the distribution of income did not become significantly more unequal. By and large, the macroeconomic policies pursued by Soeharto's trusted civilian technocrats worked well. In the 1970s, revenues from oil and gas were reinvested in agriculture. In the 1980s, falling world prices for hydrocarbons were treated as an incentive to help reduce the economy's dependence on primary exports by encouraging labor-intensive manufacturing and services.

This third regime called itself "Pancasila democracy." The name appropriated the five principles (panca sila) of Indonesian identity that Sukarno had enunciated on the eve of the revolution of 1945: monotheism, humanitarianism, unity, democracy, and justice. Neither democracy nor justice figured in Jakarta's invasion and annexation of East *Timor in 1975–76. By 1985 all social or political organizations in the enlarged country were required to subscribe to Pancasila.

The army was the backbone of this regime. Active or retired military officers occupied key national, provincial, and local offices to secure the nation against subversion by what they saw as atheistic communists and Westernized liberals on the left and fanatic Muslims on the right. If the communists were believed to have violently betrayed the nation in 1965, the liberals were charged with wanting to trade "Pancasila democracy" for a naively procedural politics that could reopen the ideological wounds of the 1950s and 1960s. Politically assertive Muslims were accused of wanting to replace the explicitly religious but nonconfessional New Order with an intolerantly Islamic state. In this context, Suharto's autocratic "Pancasila democracy" could be termed a regime of the "extreme center."

Every five years since the 1970s, a People's Representative Council (DPR) and a larger People's Consultative Assembly (MPR), respectively, approved the government's development plans and reacclaimed Suharto president. According to rules that favored the regime, elections to these bodies were held in 1971, 1977, 1982, 1987, 1992, and 1997. Competing in the last five of these contests were the regime's own ostensibly non-party vehicle, Functional Groups (Golkar), based in the bureaucracy but extending into industry, agriculture, and services; the Development Unity Party (PPP), an attempt to fuse and domesticate Islamic political parties; and the Indonesian Democracy Party (PDI), an umbrella for nationalist and Christian parties. Golkar won all six of these polls; its majorities varied from roughly two fifths to three fourths of the national vote. But for the regime, these were occasions for insurance and display more than tests of political survival. Many of the seats in the DPR and most of those in the MPR were filled through official approval, not electoral choice.

In July 1997, a sudden drop in the value of Thailand's currency precipitated a monetary crisis in Southeast Asia. Hardest hit was Indonesia. Many of its firms and banks had contracted huge debts in dollars on the expectation that the loans could be converted to Indonesian rupiahs, invested in risky deals in booming local markets, and serviced or repaid by reconverting to dollars a portion of the resulting profits. The spreading realization that these plans were unsustainable quickly capsized the rupiah. The currency's losses—from 2,500 rupiahs to the U.S. dollar in mid-1997 to 8,500 in mid-2000, with plunges to depths as low as 17,000 in between—triggered capital flight massive enough to bankrupt much of the economy. In 1998, Indonesia's per capita GDP shrank 16.2 percent.

As urban poverty and joblessness rose, so did unrest. By ruining Suharto's technocratic-authoritarian formula for success—legitimation by economic performance, stability through political constraint—the economic crisis and concomitant *political violence scuttled his regime. In Jakarta in May 1998, spiraling demonstrations, the fatal shooting of student protesters by security forces, rising energy prices, citywide riots, and defections from his own cabinet led Suharto to resign in favor of his vice president, B. J. Habibie.

Habibie's presidency lasted until October 1999. His chief achievement was to facilitate his country's second transition to democracy since the failed experiment of the 1950s. New freedoms of expression and association bred hundreds of newspapers, websites, activist groups, and political parties. Legislative institutions at national, provincial, and district levels were democratized in June 1999 when most of their members were chosen in competitive elections. The quotas that Suharto had reserved for the military were reduced to single-digit percentages of all seats in these newly elected bodies. Laws were adopted to limit presidential terms, protect civil liberties, and decentralize power to the regions. Habibie allowed the people of East Timor to vote against continued association with Indonesia, which most of them did in free and fair balloting organized by the United Nations in August 1999.

As in 1955, the 1999 election fragmented political authority. The Indonesian Democracy Party of Struggle, an offshoot of the PDI, came in first with some 34 percent of the popular vote, followed by Golkar, the Revival of the Nation Party (PKB), the PPP, and the National Mandate Party (PAN), in that order. Golkar and PAN leaders were chosen to chair, respectively, the DPR and the MPR. On 21 October 1999, by a narrow margin, the latter body elected PKB founder Abdurrahman Wahid to become Indonesia's fourth president, with PDIP chief Megawati Sukarnoputri (Sukarno's daughter) as his vice president. The MPR also cancelled its previous ratification of the annexation of East Timor, leaving that territory to evolve with UN help toward independence.

Deeply Islamist parties did not fare well in the 1999 elections in Indonesia. Nor did a new left arise to replace the still banned PKI. Revelations of military complicity in atrocities around the archipelago brought the prestige of the armed forces to an all-time low. The tripolar suspicions and hatreds

that had swallowed regimes in the 1950s and 1960s seemed to have been overcome.

But the events of 1998–99 also elevated representation above coherence. By opening the floodgates of public criticism, dispersing authority outward and downward, and giving all major contenders some stake in Wahid's government, democratizing reforms slowed the policy process at a time when multiple emergencies demanded quick policy responses. Wahid himself contributed to his difficulties through erratic behavior and a failure to focus from the start on economic reform, not to mention the adult-onset blindness that left him reliant on what some argued was a narrowing set of close confidantes.

By mid-2000, fears spread for the survival not only of Indonesia's nascent democracy but of the nation-state itself. Of particular concern were four exceptions to the pattern of cross-cutting identifications that had long helped stabilize the country. Unlike their co-citizens, Indonesians of Chinese descent are mostly Christian, urban, and commercial—and enjoy, on average, greater wealth as well. Shaken by economic collapse and targeted by mobs in Jakarta in May 1998, many of the better-off in this minority transferred their funds and families safely outside the country—hurting the ability of the economy to recover from the Asian financial crisis. The slowness of that recovery—zero economic growth in 1999 and only marginal improvement anticipated in 2000—in turn stimulated centrifugal activity at the distinctive extreme opposite ends of the archipelago, in devoutly Islamic Aceh to the west and Christianized Papua (Irian Jaya) to the east.

By 1998, in the eastern province of Maluku, where Muslim communities were additionally distinguished by residence, occupation, and to an extent ethnicity as well, Muslim migrants and political changes seen as favoring Muslims had begun to alienate local Christians. In January 1999 in Maluku's capital a minor altercation at a transport terminal escalated into bloodshed. In Aceh, by mid-2000, a shaky peace had been announced between independence forces and Jakarta. In Papua a people's congress had affirmed the territory's independence, but had not taken up arms and still wished to negotiate its conflict with Jakarta. In Maluku, where enemies were local, the killing went on.

Indonesia did not seem on the verge of complete disintegration. But one could question the capacity of central elites to meet such a daunting triple challenge: to revitalize their country's economy while strengthening its democracy and retaining its periphery, all at the same time.

(See also DEMOCRATIC TRANSITIONS; ISLAM.)

Richard W. Baker, M. Hadi Soesastro, J. Kristiadi, and Douglas E. Ramage, eds., *Indonesia: The Challenge of Change* (Singapore, 1999). Donald K. Emmerson, ed., *Indonesia beyond Suharto: Polity, Economy, Society, Transition* (Armonk, N.Y., 1999). Adam Schawrz, *A Nation in Waiting: Indonesia's Search for Stability*, rev. ed. (Boulder, Colo., 2000).

DONALD K. EMMERSON

INDUSTRIAL DEMOCRACY. The meanings of the term *industrial democracy* have varied in complex ways over the course of more than a century since the term began to be used widely, and this has reflected the capacities of different industrial actors to appropriate democratic discourses to their own interests. In the United States of the late nineteenth and early twentieth centuries, for instance, industrial democracy was propagated by employers as a way of introducing worker voice (and sometimes a share in profits), but on terms controlled by the employers themselves. This version stressed trust and cooperation rather than conflict, and was often explicitly directed at keeping unions out. In the 1920s, employers referred to works councils and employee representation plans as industrial democracy, while unions saw them as little more than company unions. During World War I some union leaders saw joint (or tripartite) management of certain firms and industries as a form of industrial democracy, and Sidney Hillman of the Amalgamated Clothing Workers even managed to articulate a blend of this with the more informal traditions of workers' control from below. The success of the Congress of Industrial Organizations (CIO) in the 1930s decisively shifted the favored uses of the term within the *labor movement to the unions' bargained share of participation in determining job classifications and their distribution within an accepted framework of scientific management. Only with the crisis of mass production in more recent years have some union leaders begun to link industrial democracy to direct participation in the work process and joint union-management projects to reorganize it, but even here the terms used by unions and managers alike—*involvement* and *participation*—have carried a much weaker connotation of citizen *rights than does *democracy.*

In Europe there have been similar variations in the meanings of industrial democracy, although the much more militant and often revolutionary movements on the shop floor in the early part of the century produced decidedly more syndicalist conceptions. The British industrial relations theorist Hugh Clegg argued in an influential work (*A New Approach to Industrial Democracy*, Oxford, 1960) against joint consultation schemes and held that only collective bargaining by unions independent of management and the state could produce genuine industrial democracy. Direct participation in management could even jeopardize the union's capacity to represent worker interests. The Industrial Democracy in Europe Research Group's cross-national study (*Industrial Democracy in Europe*, Oxford, 1981), while also highlighting the importance of formalized bargaining and union mobilization, is much more positive about the outcomes of joint consultation and codetermination, and finds legislation to have been one of the most important factors in expanding worker influence and involvement over the preceding decades.

Labor movements in Sweden and Norway have been most successful in appropriating a rights discourse of industrial democracy both to counter managerial attempts to dominate work reform and to enrich the meaning of the concept itself. The pathbreaking sociotechnical systems theory of work redesign of Fred Emery and Eric Trist of the Tavistock Institute in London introduced an analysis of the labor process itself into the vocabulary of industrial democracy via the Norwegian Industrial Democracy Project of the 1960s. The unions in both countries developed ambitious legislative programs for industrial democracy that were realized under Social Democratic governments in the 1970s. New laws mandated greater representation of unions on boards of directors and greater powers of shop stewards on the shop floor. An innovative approach to health and safety regulation was incorporated into work environment laws that mandated union participation and local initiative rather than expert-dominated and rule-based strategies. Worker participation in the design of new technologies has been facilitated by laws mandating that employers share information and bargain over design and implementation, and unions have begun to develop their own perspectives and collective resources (data stewards, technology consultants, study circles) to democratize this process. Unions in service sectors have developed innovative ways of incorporating consumer and client voice into the technology and work design process, thus enriching meanings even further in the direction of postindustrial democracy. And the participation of women workers in some of these projects has begun to transform what was previously an almost exclusively male discourse. The self-management of time, fostered by rights to flexible working time options and publicly financed leave policies (e.g., job sharing, parental and educational leaves), further enriches the discourse of industrial democracy with feminist and postindustrial themes.

(See also FEMINISM; POSTINDUSTRIAL SOCIETY; SOCIALISM AND SOCIAL DEMOCRACY; WORKERS' CONTROL.)

Carmen Sirianni, ed., *Worker Participation and the Politics of Reform* (Philadelphia, 1987).

CARMEN SIRIANNI

INDUSTRIALIZATION. See MODERNIZATION; URBANIZATION.

INEQUALITY. See EQUALITY AND INEQUALITY.

INFITAH. The *infitah* that blossomed in *Egypt in the early 1970s meant the "opening up" of Egyptian society to the nonsocialist world. This entailed an opening to foreign capital and a shift toward a more market-based economic system, with fewer planning constraints than had been imposed on the economy under President Gamal Abdel *Nasser from 1954 to 1970. It also entailed an opening to the West via Egypt's peace agreement with Israel, which was brokered by the United States and facilitated by a U.S. commitment to massive amounts of economic and military aid to Egypt. And, third, *infitah* promised an opening by President Anwar *Sadat and his successor, Hosni Mubarak, to parliamentary democracy.

Tunisia had quietly adopted similar reforms at about the same time as Egypt, but by the late 1980s, the policies of *infitah* had spread throughout the Arab world. The impetus for this shift came from disillusionment with poorly designed domestic economic programs (e.g., *import-substitution industrialization) in the face of the decline of oil-based income in the region. For example, labor migration from the poorer countries to the oil-rich was reversed and contributed to rising unemployment in the home countries, a problem for which the home governments had no solution.

The resulting shortages of foreign exchange, *balance of payments deficits, and mounting debt and debt-service problems led many Arab countries, including Morocco, Tunisia, Algeria, Egypt, the Sudan, Jordan, Syria, the Yemens, and Iraq, to turn to the *International Monetary Fund for support and to impose the requisite economic austerity programs on their countries. The subsequent IMF- and *World Bank–supervised economic restructuring programs promoted production for export and further enhanced opportunities for foreign capital investment. Emphasis shifted from public to private ownership and production, while public welfare programs contracted.

Rising social costs like inequality and unemployment, as well as the reduction of public services and subsidies, led to outspoken criticism of the governments undertaking restructuring. In an attempt to win over the citizenry to the new regime and to reestablish their credibility, governments turned increasingly to parliamentary democracy, the political face of *infitah*.

(See also INTERNATIONAL MIGRATION.)

Henri Barkey, ed., *The Politics of Economic Reform in the Middle East* (New York, 1992). Alan Richards and John Waterbury, "The Checkered Course of Economic Reform," in *A Political Economy of the Middle East*, 2d ed. (Boulder, Colo., 1996), pp. 222–50.

KAREN PFEIFER

INFORMATION SOCIETY. Throughout the twentieth century, the economic system of the United States has evolved toward the production and distribution of information and away from the production and distribution of material goods.

In the first decades of the twentieth century, organizational experts mastered the secrets of running large corporations and governments. They did so by inventing a system dependent on communications technologies and bureaucratic techniques, in order to ensure the smooth and timely flow of information among staffs, departments, and decision makers. When successfully implemented, these advances allowed institutions to grow to unprecedented sizes. The rise of big government, with its threat to the privacy of citizens and potential for controlling their lives, represents the best-known political consequence of this wave of the information revolution. As Winston Smith discovered in George Orwell's classic *1984*, government's capacity for domination depends on sophisticated communications systems. But in comparison with Orwell's Oceania, government today appears less monolithic and omnipotent. Moreover, journalists have actively documented government abuses of communications technology, so that Orwell's warning appears less shocking to contemporary citizens who are naturally skeptical of government's intentions.

Integration and Fragmentation. Increasing recognition, in the years following World War II, of the commercial value of information intensified a transformation of the U.S. economy that had been under way throughout most of the twentieth century. In the early 1960s, the economic exchange of information probably accounted for 30 percent of the GNP, and by the 1990s approached 50 percent. In a significant way, the modern U.S. economy spends its resources producing and distributing information. Where early-twentieth-century workers sold the labor of their hands in fields and in factories, late-twentieth-century workers mostly sell the labor of their brains. Approximately half of all workers in the United States hold occupations in the information sector, and similar tendencies can be observed for countries such as Britain, Germany, Japan, and Singapore.

Early studies of the information society emphasized new developments apparently leading to a *postindustrial society.

However, many scholars now see the information society as deeply rooted in the historic growth of *capitalism and in the expansion of industrialization. Accordingly, the information society may be seen as a continuation of the social forces that forged industrial capitalism in the United States. The shift from agriculture, to industrial, to information work took place well before World War II. In other words, changes in the economy and in the labor force that led to the information society were well under way before the computer revolution.

The steady evolution of an information environment revolves around media, information technologies, and information work. In the United States, capitalism allowed for an unplanned proliferation of commercial communication channels. These many channels structure private life and become major sources of personal participation in the political process. Certainly, in the United States, people's view of national politics and issues is almost totally constrained by the commercial media. Moreover, in those countries where a significant portion of adults labor as information workers, they may develop a heightened sensitivity to information, and to the value of information, leading to a perception of the democratic process as an information process. Thus, the products of capitalism and the realities of information work may converge in powerful ways to create new attitudes toward political life.

Because the television networks are profit-making organizations, they must adhere to the calculus of commercial news production. The networks minimize costs by maintaining news crews in the largest U.S. cities where, they reason, news stories are most likely to occur. In addition, they seek out scheduled events that can be planned into the day's production decisions. For its part, government speaks the language of big media by crafting messages to conform to the constraints of televised news production.

However, one countercurrent is visible. The mass communication of political news seems to be changing in response to the proliferation of cable systems throughout the United States, resulting in departures from network news practice. Cable News Network (CNN), for example, offers foreign news organizations the opportunity to present news stories directly to U.S. audiences. The availability of political news produced according to different cultural assumptions challenges some of the journalistic conventions created by the networks. Moreover, because of its reciprocation policy, CNN has reached viewers in numerous countries including the former Soviet Union. If CNN is ultimately successful, it will integrate the world news market into an information system dominated by a few giant suppliers, CNN among them. At the same time, CNN may lead the way to a television marketplace of diversity closer to that enjoyed by magazine readers.

Because marketing strategy dictates that successful vendors identify discrete market segments and package their product to appeal to the characteristics of one or more segments, the media environment is characterized by a host of programmers, advertisers, publishers, editors, announcers—and a few politicians—competing for the attention of the targeted segments. Contrary to the nation-as-community image depicted during election years, the audience presents a highly fragmented appearance to the message producer. Moreover, commercial messages dominate the media environment, in quantity and quality. They contribute to the formation of a consumer culture of great power, precisely because individuals derive from it their knowledge of the world beyond their own personal experience. Indeed, most adults in the United States spend as many hours with media as they do at work, while their children spend more hours watching television than attending school. These patterns appear to extend to other industrial countries as well. For the individual in the information society, information overload generated by consumer culture requires coping skills of the highest order.

The pervasiveness of messages delivered by big media establishes a daily environment of information overload. Not only must citizens be alert to the occasional political message, but they also contend with the obstacle of sheer volume when they choose to speak out. With few exceptions, political discourse never takes center stage. The forms of commercial media define the audience's expectations and have come to dominate political communication. Neither commercial nor political messages stress the interrelationship among issues that underlies the political agenda. From the perception of the audience, the media environment appears as a rush of discrete products. In other words, the media encourage individuals to approach the political agenda as a lineup of unconnected issues.

When citizens take action, mobilization around a local issue forms a kind of community of communication. Landlords in Santa Monica, California, circulated videotapes showing prorent control members of the city council in an unfavorable light and won the next election. Websites and listserv urge visitors to take positions on political issues and offer information on how to make oneself heard. In New Jersey, opponents of a tax hike used a multitude of media including local call-in radio stations to air grievances and attract attention to a growing tax revolt. In Eastern and Central Europe, individuals defied governments' control over television by using homemade satellite dishes to receive foreign programming. Solidarity kept its movement alive in Poland by producing video documentaries with its message distributed for viewing on videocassette recorders.

Nor is political communication outside established avenues limited to the industrialized countries. Followers of the Ayatollah *Khomeini delivered his message by distributing hundreds of thousands of audiocassettes and created a movement against the Shah of Iran. During the democracy movement in spring 1989, dissenting Chinese students maintained contact with the outside world by communicating on many of the 30,000 fax machines available through private businesses. In Latin America, localized media have played critical roles in establishing the legitimacy of every group seeking to control government. For example, during the Cuban Revolution, *Radio Rebelde*, a portable radio station hidden in the mountains of Oriente Province, kept the voice of Castro alive, demonstrating the seriousness of his claim to the leadership of the country. Similar low-power stations in Guatemala, El Salvador, and Nicaragua have supported rebel groups' efforts to win the support of the people. What is certain is that politically motivated people will utilize whatever information technologies they can access, no matter how complex the technology, no matter how underdeveloped the country.

Politics and Information. The tendency toward big news organizations and integrated information markets dominated by a few corporations continues to emerge along with frag-

mented media environments and communities of communication exploiting small media for political purposes. Integration and fragmentation represent two sides of the same need—to communicate in order to exercise power. However, although the tendency is easily documented, the consequences are not. Concern for the consequences of integration prompted a coalition of developing nations to challenge U.S. dominance of world media markets as constituting cultural domination and a threat to the national sovereignty of those nations where U.S. firms controlled large shares of media markets. From the mid-1970s, UN agencies became arenas for opposing U.S. policies. The *Mass Media Draft Declaration* (UNESCO, 1976), the *Interim Report of the Commission on Communication Problems* (UNESCO, 1978), and the *MacBride Commission Report* (Paris, 1980) argued that the hegemonic nature of U.S. capitalism threatened small nations. The United States, with occasional European support, countered that the dominant role played by the United States in the integration of world-media markets resulted from the natural workings of the international marketplace for information. Increased polarization and conflict in the 1980s led to U.S. withdrawal from UNESCO. While neither side disputed the facts with respect to integration, they quarrelled over differing interpretations of the consequences. No similar debate concerning the consequences of fragmentation has yet taken place, and only recently have social observers begun to analyze the repercussions of fragmentation.

(See also CENSORSHIP; ELECTIONS AND VOTING BEHAVIOR; INFORMATION TECHNOLOGY; MEDIA AND POLITICS; PSYCHOLOGY AND POLITICS; PUBLIC OPINION; TIANANMEN SQUARE.)

Eileen R. Meehan, "Towards a Third Vision of an Information Society" *Media, Culture and Society* 6 (July 1984): 257–271. Neil Postman, *Amusing Ourselves to Death: Public Discourse in the Age of Show Business* (New York, 1985). Jorge R. Schement and Leah A. Lievrouw, "A Third Vision: Capitalism and the Industrial Origins of the Information Society," in Jorge R. Schement and Leah Lievrouw, eds., *Competing Visions, Complex Realities: Social Aspects of the Information Society* (Norwood, N.J., 1988), pp. 33–45. Robert M. Entman, *Democracy Without Citizens: Media and the Decay of American Politics* (New York, 1989). Terry Curtis, "The Information Society: A Computer-Generated Caste System?" in Vincent Mosco, ed., *The Political Economy of Information* (Madison, Wis., 1990), pp. 95–107.

JORGE REINA SCHEMENT

INFORMATION TECHNOLOGY. As the world prepared for the twenty-first century, electronic media—particularly computers and satellites in space—altered the nature of mass media organizations, world news, and traditional government internal information controls. Because one satellite can cover a third of the globe, its messages and images ignore national boundaries and thus radically alter the historic balance of power between nation–states and media corporations. Media entrepreneurs, like individuals, can operate outside of their national home bases in relative independence of governmental control.

Two additional developments have altered government-versus-corporation relations. Increasingly, a single, large multinational media corporation can control the entire communications system from creation of content to distribution and delivery to home or office. It does this by ownership of newspapers, magazines, radio, television, books, motion pictures, videocassettes, production facilities for all these media, as well as national and international distribution networks and control of the telephone or satellite dish that brings media material into individual homes. The other change is digital techniques that permit conversion of material from one form into a different one, like a motion picture into a videocassette playable into individual homes or over a television station.

Media power and profit have encouraged large firms to acquire as many different media as possible under each major firm's control. Thus, for example, at the turn of the century, a German firm, Bertelsmann, controlled 10 percent of all world publishing in the English language. Similarly, News Corporation, an Australian firm owned by an American, Rupert Murdoch, became a major media producer worldwide, including in the United States. Major American firms like Disney, AOL Time Warner, Viacom, and General Electric, Britain's BBC, and Japan's Sony became worldwide creators and distributors of a wide spectrum of media products from daily news to computerized games, receivable from Siberia to South Africa.

As a result, societies under authoritarian rule have become less able to control corporate and private information transmissions. In 1989, for example, despite strict internal controls by the People's Republic of China, students with fax machines spread instant news of slaughter in Beijing's *Tiananmen Square of hundreds of citizens demanding more democratic freedoms. Nevertheless, the utility for economic growth of such new media has been so indispensable to China's commerce and industry that devices for the distribution of information like taxes have been permitted to increase almost 100 times since the Tiananmen Square Suppression.

International regulation of global communications has consisted largely of adoption of desired general principles and purely technical standards. The United Nations Declaration of Freedom of Information calls for "free flow of information within countries and across frontiers." Attempts to achieve technical compatibility of the world's communication systems are made by the International Telecommunications Union, which meets every four or five years. Within most countries governmental communications and utilities commissions create and monitor the rules for each country's domestic broadcasting and popular media. In the United States the Constitution forbids official control over printed matter, but permits broadcast regulation.

Numerous *non-governmental organizations operate on national and world scales to lobby for legislation that would promote their ends. In the United States, for example, a Center for Media Education monitors national legislation to press for what it sees as more salutary public needs in television. A Cultural Environment Movement, started in the United States, presses globally against gratuitous violence and inadequate presentation of education in commercial television. Similar citizen efforts appear periodically in other nations as well.

(See also Censorship; Information Society; Media and Politics; Public Opinion.)

Ben H. Bagdikian

INTELLIGENCE. Although spying is as old as humankind—by the seventeenth century in England, "King Charles's cavalry" was a euphemism for money, distributed secretly to purchase influence—peacetime national intelligence services developed out of military staff functions only in the twentieth century. The rise of global communications and the end of the *Cold War upended the world of intelligence: U.S. intelligence had become accustomed to a world of one main target, the Soviet Union, few consumers, and too little information, most of which came from its own secret systems and was therefore regarded as reliable. Now, it is a world of many targets, many consumers, and vast amounts of information, most of it unreliable.

The classic task for foreign intelligence comprises two parts: collecting information and analyzing it and putting it together to see what it means. The collection comes in many forms. Foreigners provide "human intelligence," or HUMINT, secretly to intelligence officers abroad (or openly to diplomats). Signals intelligence, or SIGINT, is the intercepting of communications or other signals of interest; and imagery intelligence, or IMINT, comes from satellites or aircraft taking pictures or radar and infrared images of the ground. These sources were the stock-in-trade of Cold War intelligence. Now, fewer countries around the world are closed societies and the Web and other information sources can be tapped openly—what intelligence calls "open source."

Still, collection by satellites and other so-called national technical means consumes the bulk of the $28 billion or so annual budget of the U.S. intelligence agencies—together referred to as the "intelligence community." The collecting of secrets is done by a variety of agencies: the National Reconnaissance Office builds and operates satellites, the National Security Agency collects SIGINT, the recently created National Imagery and Mapping Agency combined the nation's imagery operations, and the CIA's Directorate of Operations conducts espionage. On the open side, State Department officers and military attachés report from foreign countries and the Foreign Broadcast Information Service openly monitors foreign media.

The task of analysis is dominated by the CIA's Directorate of Intelligence, though the Defense Intelligence Agency provides analysis of military issues, the State Department has its own small Bureau of Intelligence and Research, and there are still smaller groups of more specialized analysts scattered throughout the U.S. government. Most of these analysts work in Washington, not abroad. More professorial than conspiratorial, they sift through the piles of information, both secret and not.

Centralizing intelligence function, especially analysis, in the *Central Intelligence Agency was a legacy of Pearl Harbor, given the perception that the army, navy, and State Department operating separately were unable to sort out warning signals of the impending Japanese attack and alert senior officials of government. Intelligence is more centralized in the U.S. government than in almost any other.

The CIA's Directorate of Operations is the secret intelligence service for the United States, usually called the clandestine service, and it is the counterpart of Israel's Mossad, Britain's MI6, or the foreign operations of the KGB during the Soviet period. When abroad the service's officers work under "cover," usually the "light cover" of a U.S. embassy. Ostensibly they are diplomats and thus enjoy diplomatic immunity from prosecution in the countries to which they are accredited.

Few CIA officers are "spies" in the sense of popular novels; indeed, most of those novels are not about spying, or espionage, at all but rather about counterespionage. The "spying" typically is done by foreigners employed or managed by CIA officers, that is, foreign "assets" who are "run" by their CIA "case officers." These assets are lured to betray their countries for varying combinations of belief and greed. The most famous U.S. spy in the Soviet Union, Col. Oleg Penkovskiy, was a "walk-in" who simply offered to work for the CIA.

Besides conducting espionage, CIA officers abroad seek to protect U.S. institutions from penetration by foreign intelligence services, which is "counterintelligence," a task once described by James Angleton, longtime head of CIA counterintelligence, as "a wilderness of mirrors." In one well-known case from the 1960s, a Soviet defector was kept under virtual house arrest for three years while U.S. intelligence agencies argued about whether he was real or a Soviet "plant."

At home, the Federal Bureau of Investigation (FBI) is charged with both counterintelligence and managing foreign spies while they are in the United States, as diplomats for instance. In its domestic intelligence—as distinct from its law enforcement—the FBI is the counterpart of Britain's M15 or the domestic operations of the KGB. The division of responsibility between the FBI and the CIA, which is barred from domestic spying, has made for awkward relations between the two from time to time. For instance, it took the two seven years to ferret out Aldrich Ames, the CIA officer who was a Soviet "mole" and whose information on CIA operations in the Soviet Union enabled Moscow to identify and execute at least ten U.S. spies. In an effort to do better, in 1995 a National Counterintelligence Center was created, to be jointly run by the two agencies.

The third, and most controversial, task of foreign intelligence is covert action, or actively trying to influence, in secret, the politics of foreign nations. The 1947 U.S. National Security Act authorized the CIA to "perform such other functions and duties related to intelligence affecting the national security as the National Security Council may from time to time direct"— vague language for the formal authorization covert action.

With the end of the Cold War, covert action wound down. In the 1960s, though, the CIA's secret war in Laos, not so much secret as unacknowledged, consumed several million dollars a day, and in the 1980s the CIA provided as much as a half billion dollars a year to the rebels in Afghanistan who were resisting Soviet control of their country. Short of these large paramilitary operations, CIA political operations have attempted to sway foreign elections or other political outcomes by secretly providing money or other assistance to political parties, trade unions, and other groups. The CIA's success in the Italian elections of 1948 set a pattern that was later repeated in Chile and other countries.

When these secret operations became public, they stirred debate, especially between the President and Congress. Debate over the Chile operation was part of the backdrop for the nation's first congressional investigation of intelligence in the 1970s, which led to the creation of formal intelligence oversight committees in both houses of Congress and to more regular procedures for informing Congress of covert actions. When the *Reagan administration was accused of circumventing those procedures a decade later, in selling arms to revolutionary Iran in return for releasing U.S. hostages, then using the proceeds to fund Nicaraguan "contras" fighting the Marxist government of their country, another scandal and investigation ensued.

With the end of the Cold War and the revolution in information, however, the task confronting intelligence is less how to manage secret operations than how to add value through open ones. Most of the world is not closed but open; it does not have to be spied upon but can be openly observed. Secrets are still useful in pursuing terrorists or understanding the military power of the remaining closed states, but so much more information is available openly. In these circumstances, not just the United States but also other countries face questions about the role of espionage and about the value of existing intelligence capacity in a changed world. Is intelligence to be in the business of secrets or the business of information? If the latter, then does it become the nation's designated scanner of the Internet?

In the United States, the big technical collection agencies have turned their spy satellites from their original purpose, keeping tabs on the Soviet Union, to a newer mission, providing support to U.S. and allied warfighters by letting them know the location of enemy forces. Technology has improved to the point that images or signals can be transmitted to commanders in a matter of minutes, even seconds. Yet the process raises a host of questions. Is intelligence returning to its pre–Cold War mission as primarily military? What about other national purposes? The support to war fighters also foreshadowed another sea change in the world of intelligence, for the consumers of that intelligence were not just Americans but other countries involved in the military operations as well. How can intelligence, that most "national" of functions, be used to build broad international coalitions to maintain international *peace and *security?

(See also Diplomacy; Terrorism.)

Sherman Kent, *Strategic Intelligence for American World Policy* (Princeton, N.J., 1948, 1965). John Ranelagh, *The Agency: The Rise and Decline of the CIA* (New York, 1986). Mark M. Lowenthal, *U.S. Intelligence: Evolution and Anatomy* (Westport, Conn., 1992). Commission on the Role and Capabilities of the United States Intelligence Community (called the "Aspin-Brown Commission" after its two chairmen), *Preparing for the Twenty-First Century* (Washington, D.C., 1996). Michael Herman, *Intelligence Power in Peace and War* (Cambridge, U.K., 1996).

GREGORY F. TREVERTON

INTER-AMERICAN DEVELOPMENT BANK. The 1959 Charter of the Inter-American Development Bank (IDB) created the world's first regional multilateral lending institution. The IDB is an inter-American financial institution designed to promote the economic and social *development of its Latin American constituents. It has forty-six members; it included twenty-five of the thirty-three sovereign states in Latin America and the Caribbean, the United States, Canada, and nineteen nonregional members. Unlike the *World Bank and the *International Monetary Fund, the borrowing nations have a majority of the votes in the IDB (53.9 percent); the United States, with 34.5 percent, is the biggest shareholder.

The IDB has played key roles in economic and social development programs sponsored by the *Organization of American States (OAS), beginning with a plan adopted in 1960 and subsequently articulated as the Alliance for Progress. The bank has traditionally provided two types of loans:

loans from the "ordinary capital account" for productive and infrastructural projects (with near-commercial interest rates and fifteen- to twenty-five-year maturities) and loans from the Fund for Special Operations (FSO) to finance social development projects (with one- to four-percent interest rates and maturities of thirty to forty years). During its first thirty years of operation, from 1961 through 1990, the IDB approved US$47 billion of loans to Latin American and Caribbean nations. About three-quarters were from the ordinary capital account and one-quarter from the FSO.

The issue of U.S. predominance in IDB lending decisions has been constantly debated. The IDB Board of Directors approves loans from the ordinary capital account by simple majority. FSO loans, however, require a two-thirds majority, with voting power weighted according to the relative size of a member's contribution. While U.S. voting power in the FSO declined with the introduction of new member capital contributions, especially after 1976, many Latin Americans continued to complain that the system allowed the United States to impose its preferred development models on the region, which, they said, did not necessarily apply to their needs.

This conflict reached crisis proportions in the 1980s during the negotiations over the seventh replenishment of the IDB's capital. The *Reagan administration insisted that Latin American members give up their right to approve loans with their simple majority of votes. The basic issue was the U.S. contention that the borrower-controlled IDB had failed to attach sufficiently tough conditionality on its loans. After a three-year dispute, an agreement was reached in 1988 to allow nonborrowing members to delay loans for up to a year. Other changes will reduce the IDB bureaucracy and extend its activities to policy-based lending, similar to the World Bank's sectoral loans. In return, the United States agreed to the replenishment, which almost doubled the bank's lending capacity to US$22.5 billion between 1990 and 1993.

(See also AFRICAN DEVELOPMENT BANK; ASIAN DEVELOPMENT BANK; U.S.–LATIN AMERICAN RELATIONS.)

Sidney Dell, *The Inter-American Development Bank* (New York, 1972). Samantha Sparks, "The IDB Prepares for the 1990s" *Overseas Development Council Policy Focus,* No. 1 (1989).

G. POPE ATKINS

INTERDEPENDENCE. The term *interdependence* refers to the mutual dependency of state interests. Isolated, independent states are not affected by what other states do or by what happens to the *international system as a whole. In contrast, interdependent states are affected directly (either positively or negatively) by the national policy of one or more of their number. Thus opponents in *war are highly negatively interdependent (if one wins, the other loses) whereas essential trading partners are positively interdependent (they both gain from trade).

Interdependence can vary in symmetry, degree, and type. Some interdependent relationships are likely to produce cooperation, others conflict.

1. *Symmetry*—Symmetric interdependence means mutual dependence and equality in the relationship. Asymmetric interdependence suggests that one is more dependent on the other than the other is on the one. The second party, then, is in a position to manipulate the dependence of the first. Kenneth Waltz contends that great (or super) powers benefit from the dependence of others on themselves, but are not themselves similarly constrained. Waltz believes that high interdependence is a force for conflict because nations wish to resume full independence and untrammeled sovereignty free from foreign control. Most other analysts argue that high interdependence (of positive, trading ties, for instance) is a potential force for cooperation, as nations come to accept and benefit from that relationship. In Latin America and the Third World, generally, many have come to believe that asymmetric interdependence or dependence on First World capital and markets is a factor causing conflict between the North and the South. Some go so far as to label it "structural imperialism." From this standpoint, a more positive linkage between North and South awaits greater symmetry in the relationship.

2. *Degree*—Interdependence can refer to linkages that are important or only peripheral. It is sometimes said that "vulnerability" interdependence represents a "tie that is costly to break," while "sensitivity" interdependence denotes a tie which either party can easily cast aside. This is because the service or good which a lesser interdependence provides can be obtained elsewhere. These terms, however, are influenced by trends in the international political-economic system. A country with abundant oil reserves (like the United States in the 1950s) may have only a "sensitivity" interdependence with Middle Eastern oil producers. As those reserves are depleted, however, sensitivity yields to "vulnerability" interdependence with foreign suppliers of oil. A country with a small percentage of foreign trade relative to its GNP may have only a modest need for the imports of others and place little emphasis upon its own exports. As its imports increase, however, and trade rises as a fraction of GNP, export markets overseas may become a matter of vulnerability interdependence: they are essential to maintain a strong balance of payments.

3. *Type*—Interdependence will vary with the nature of the international "game" that is being played, as illustrated below.

In Figure 1 (Prisoners' Dilemma game) the pattern of interdependence (suggested by payoffs in the game) is conflictual. Although both parties would be better off if each played "cooperate," each thinks: "If the other plays 'cooperate' and I 'defect,' I do better still." Thus, each "defects" and cooperation is lost. In Figure 1 each player has a dominant strategy of playing "defect" because it gains (4 or 2) if it defects as opposed to (3 or 1) if it cooperates.

In Figure 2 (Chicken), there is no dominant strategy given that the outcomes of "cooperate" (3 or 2) are of the same

Figure 1. Prisoners' Dilemma

	Cooperate	Defect
Cooperate	3, 3	1, 4
Defect	4, 1	2, 2

value as the outcomes of "defect" (4 or 1). Everything in this game is contingent: it depends on what the other player does. If one is sure the other will play defect, it is in one's interest to cooperate (yielding 2, 4). If, on the other hand, one thinks the other will cooperate, then one's interest is to defect (and derive the 4, 2 payoff). In this case, cooperation is contingent; it may or may not emerge.

Figure 2. Chicken

	Cooperate	Defect
Cooperate	3, 3	2, 4
Defect	4, 2	1, 1

In Figure 3 (Assurance II), however, the interdependent relation is much more benign. In this game the incentive to cooperate is overwhelming and the (4, 4) outcome is achieved. (Each party derives [4 or 3] from a strategy of cooperation and only [2 or 1] from a choice of defection.)

Figure 3. Assurance II

	Cooperate	Defect
Cooperate	4, 4	2, 3
Defect	3, 2	1, 1

These three games are characteristic of different aspects of international politics. The second game, Chicken, is frequently claimed to apply to superpower crisis relations. In the 1962 *Cuban missile crisis, for instance, Secretary of State Dean Rusk was reported to have asserted: "We were eyeball to eyeball and the other guy just blinked." Fearing that the United States might resort to force, the Soviets backed down. More recent information suggests that President John F. Kennedy was equally aware of the dangers of a clash (the 1, 1) payoff and was also ready to make significant concessions to avoid that outcome. In superpower relations mutual defection is likely to be very unfavorable and, indeed, catastrophic to both sides.

In trade negotiations or *arms control talks, the Prisoners' Dilemma frequently applies. Under conditions of pure rationality, this condition should always lead to disagreement. In fact, it has not always done so. Studies show that people playing Prisoners' Dilemma against one another eventually work out an agreement on the (3, 3) (cooperative) payoff. Tit-for-tat strategies can contribute to this outcome. Among allies, the Assurance II game typically holds: that is, each side considers its own best payoff to lie where the other partner also benefits. To conclude from these three illustrations: in the

most general sense interdependence is neutral; whether it is cooperative or conflictual depends upon the nature of the situation and of the particular game that is being played.

In recent years Harold Kelley and John Thibaut have tried to decompose interdependent game matrices into different components. Without trying to illustrate this complex process here, one should observe that Kelley and Thibaut find three different dimensions in such games: reflexive control, fate control, and behavior control. Reflexive control refers to that amount of the payoff that A can guarantee, no matter what B does. Fate control refers to A's ability to control the payoffs that B gets. Behavior control refers to the amount of the payoff that is dependent upon joint action by A and B. One may hypothesize that in a nuclear deterrent relationship, countries can guarantee an unfavorable outcome for the other state, but they cannot guarantee a favorable outcome for themselves: that is, fate control is very high and reflexive control very low. In trading relationships among countries (usually typified by a Prisoners' Dilemma game), fate control also dominates all other dimensions of the matrix. It is only as one proceeds to coordination games that behavior control becomes dominant, as illustrated by Figure 4 (the Coordination game). Fate control and reflexive control are both zero. The achievement of favorable payoffs for both sides depends entirely on coordinating their responses. Such games are involved in driving on the right-hand side of the street and not, for instance, on the sidewalk. Membership in institutions may also facilitate the development of coordination games. Institutional members are more likely to coordinate on certain courses of action because of procedural regularities, precedent, and the frequency of interaction in an institutional setting.

Figure 4. The Coordination Game

	Strategy 1	Strategy 2
Strategy 1	4, 4	0, 0
Strategy 2	0, 0	4, 4

Since 1945 the international system has become more "interdependent" in the sense of there being a greater "connectedness" among nations. What one nation does now, for good or ill, directly impinges on another. This does not mean, however, that positive interdependence or *international cooperation has grown in equal proportion. Any such development depends in turn on the type, degree, and symmetry of interdependence. It appears that symmetry may be increasing as the result of the transformation of a previously bipolar system into one more multipolar in character. The process of economic development has enabled a number of less developed states to become new industrial countries. At the same time, the relative economic lead of the United States, Europe, and even Japan is declining, while the growth rates and competitiveness of China and a number of Pacific Region countries (at least until 1997) has been increasing. Under these circumstances, the amount of symmetry in international economic relations will also increase. The acceptance of interdependence has also risen in that military alternatives to enmeshment in an interdependent economic system are progressively less attractive. Because of institutional development and greater interaction, Prisoners' Dilemma games have to some degree been transformed into cooperative ones. At the same time the world is far from achieving the status of an Assurance game or a game of Pure Coordination. Conflictual interdependence, as evidenced in the Persian Gulf and wars in central Africa, is still quite high.

(See also DEPENDENCY; DETERRENCE; GAME THEORY; INTERNATIONAL POLITICAL ECONOMY; NORTH-SOUTH RELATIONS.)

Johan Galtung, "A Structural Theory of Imperialism," *Journal of Peace Research* (1970). Kenneth Waltz, "The Myth of Interdependence," in C. P Kindleberger, ed., *The International Corporation* (Cambridge, Mass., 1970). Richard Rosecrance and Arthur Stein, "Interdependence: Myth or Reality," *World Politics* (1973). Robert Keohane and Joseph S. Nye, *Power and Interdependence* (Boston, 1977). Harold Kelley and John W. Thibaut, *Interpersonal Relations: A Theory of Interdependence* (New York, 1978). Herman Schwartz, *Dominions and Dependency* (Ithaca, N.Y., 1990). Arthur Stein, *Why Nations Cooperate* (Ithaca, N.Y., 1991)

RICHARD ROSECRANCE

INTEREST GROUPS. Once the political community grows beyond the manageable dimensions of the town meeting, some kind of representative mechanisms become essential to *democracy. Among the various links between the individual and political institutions are interest groups. This category includes organizations of many kinds—among them unions, business and professional associations, consumer and environmental groups, and groups concerned about political issues ranging from abortion to speed limits to public funding of religious schools. Interest groups are fundamental to the politics of every functioning contemporary democracy; indeed, it is difficult to imagine democracy on a national scale without them.

The boundaries between interest groups and other politically relevant social collectivities are not completely distinct. Interest groups resemble political parties in many of their activities—for example, campaigning for candidates, making campaign contributions, screening appointments for public office, and formulating policy alternatives. Unlike political parties, however, they do not nominate candidates to campaign under their name for the purpose of running the government. Interest groups can be differentiated from social movements by their greater degree of formal organization. However, many social movements—for example, the women's movement in the United States—encompass not only informal groups and individual sympathizers but formal associations as well. Because many of the private organizations that get involved in politics—most notably, corporations—do not have members in the ordinary sense, many students of politics substitute the term "organized interests" for "interests groups."

Almost inevitably, all interest groups perform certain functions: They provide information to public officials to assist in designing sound policy; they seek to persuade policy makers to pursue a preferred course of action, an activity that may be difficult to distinguish in practice from the attempt to inform; they communicate with members—keeping them apprised as to what the government is doing, educating them about the political process, and cultivating support.

In spite of the similarities in their role as intermediaries in a two-way process of communication, there are substantial differences among interest groups within any particular democracy as well as enormous diversity across democracies with respect to the nature of organized interest politics. The groups in any single democracy vary considerably in terms of their size, their level of resources, the number and kinds of issues they embrace, and the proportion of the potential constituency they can claim to represent as members or sympathizers. Furthermore, they differ in the extent to which they concentrate solely upon the political or combine political and nonpolitical means of promoting the interests of the organization and its members. In addition, they differ in the extent to which they function as insiders or outsiders—utilizing traditional, low-profile means of achieving political influence or adopting more public tactics of mobilization and protest—and are accepted as legitimate by public officials.

Across democracies there are substantial differences in the nature of interest group politics—differences that reflect differences in the nature and relative importance of their formal political institutions, the number, strength, ideological distinctiveness, and competitiveness of their political parties, and their political traditions and political culture. There is wide variation simply in both the number of groups and the proportion of citizens who are members of any group at all; in the Scandinavian countries, where most employees belong to some kind of union or professional association, it is much higher than in, for example, Italy. There are also differences in the relative difficulty faced by emergent interests in getting organized and entering the political fray; the nature and number of the axes of political cleavage encompassed in organized interest politics; the degree to which interest representation is highly aggregated or fragmented in either functional or geographical terms; and the extent to which interest groups have a monopoly on the organization of a particular constituency. In addition, there are marked differences in terms of the relative strength of organizations representing different kinds of interests—in particular, in the vigor of the opposition provided by organized labor and citizens' groups concerned about consumer and environmental issues to traditionally powerful business organizations.

Democracies vary with respect to not only which interest groups get involved but also how interest groups get involved in politics. Democracies differ in the extent to which interest groups cooperate as well as compete and in the strength of their links to like-minded political parties; for example, British trade unions traditionally had a much closer relationship to the Labour Party than their American counterparts have ever had to the Democrats. Furthermore, democracies differ in terms of the mix of techniques ordinarily employed by interest groups—for example, in the emphasis placed on protests or on direct mail communications with members. In addition, democracies differ in both the overall strength of interest groups and the relationships between interest groups and government.

Some political scientists have suggested that there are two basic patterns of organized interest interaction with the state, neocorporatist and pluralist. According to the neocorporatist model—approximated most closely by Sweden, Austria, and

Switzerland—mechanisms providing for equal representation of individuals on a geographical basis are supplemented by mechanisms providing for functional representation of organized interests—ordinarily by a relatively limited number of peak associations. Such organizations are recognized and licensed by the state and attain a regularized role in policy making through delegations of administrative power or participation on public councils or committees. Important government decisions are made only after consultation with major economic interests, most notably, workers, employers, and farmers.

In contrast, according to the pluralist model interest groups are much more numerous—less highly aggregated and organized around multiple bases of political conflict—and much more autonomous. Pluralist interest group politics, approximated most closely by the United States, is relatively permeable to the entry of new groups, and groups arise and get involved in politics at their own initiative, rather than at the behest of the state. In a politics of *pluralism, interest groups have greater freedom in choosing which political battles to fight in which political arenas. Typically, those battles involve shifting, issue-specific coalitions taking sides on issues of narrower, more limited import.

It is essential to recognize that these alternative models, which have generated considerable scholarly discussion and some controversy, are ideal types. No polity actually conforms to either model and many countries—for example, France where a strong, centralized state has meant comparative weakness for interest groups or Japan where regular consultation between business and government more or less excludes labor—evidence a pattern that is neither pluralist nor corporatist nor anything in between. Furthermore, in most countries no single pattern obtains for the making of policy in all issue areas: The formulation of foreign policy, for example, is less likely to entail regularized bargaining with interest groups than the making of agricultural policy.

Recent decades have witnessed two important developments in interest group politics. First is the emergence of interest representation at the European Union. Although group activity in Brussels often arises within individual EU nations, many of the groups involved are European-level rather than national organizations. In addition, there has been an advocacy explosion in democracies everywhere with—in a pluralist fashion—more concerns being represented by more groups. In particular, supplementing traditional economic groups representing business, farmers, and workers is a growing number of citizens' groups concerned about an array of issues including nuclear proliferation, the environment, immigration, and the rights of gays, women, and ethnic minorities. How these developments will alter interest group politics is not yet clear. Nonetheless, private associational life will surely remain essential to the functioning of democracies around the world.

(See also CONSOCIATIONAL DEMOCRACY; CORPORATISM; ELECTIONS AND VOTING BEHAVIOR; LABOR MOVEMENT; NEW SOCIAL MOVEMENTS; POLITICAL PARTIES AND PARTY COMPETITION.)

Kay Lehman Schlozman and John T. Tierney, *Organized Interests and American Democracy* (New York, 1986). John P. Heinz, Edward O. Laumann, Robert L. Nelson, and Robert H. Salisbury, *The Hollow Core: Private Interests in National Policy Making* (Cambridge, Mass., 1993). Sonia Mazey and Jeremy Richardson, *Lobbying in the European Community* (Oxford, 1993). Clive C. Thomas, ed., *First World Interest Groups: A Comparative Perspective* (Westport, Conn., 1993).

KAY LEHMAN SCHLOZMAN

INTERGOVERNMENTAL AUTHORITY ON DEVELOPMENT. Formerly known as the Intergovernmental Authority on Drought and Development (IGADD), the Intergovernmental Authority on Development (IGAD) was established in January 1986 with the aim of combating drought and desertification. Its founding members were Djibouti, Ethiopia, Kenya, Somalia, the Sudan, and Uganda. A seventh member, Eritrea, joined in September 1993. The organization's headquarters is in Djibouti.

From 1986 until 1996 IGADD possessed neither the organizational resources nor the basic infrastructure needed to coordinate the efforts of member countries to cope with the consequences of famine, drought, and underdevelopment. These weaknesses were exacerbated by conflicts within and between member countries. Uganda emerged from decades of dictatorship under the Amin and Obote regimes. Ethiopia engaged in a thirty-year war against Eritrean nationalists; the war ended in 1991, but a border war erupted between the two countries in 1998. In the Sudan the north-south conflict has festered for decades, and the country has emerged as Africa's renascent theocracy under the combined leadership of a military junta and the National Islamic Front. Somalia imploded, adding anarchy and warlordism to the existing crises of drought and famine in the south, while its northern region has seceded to establish the "Somaliland Republic." Only Djibouti and Kenya remained relatively stable despite mounting opposition to incumbent regimes.

In 1995, IGADD leaders held an extraordinary meeting in Addis Ababa and resolved to restructure the organization and draft a new charter. On 21 March 1996, the organization was renamed IGAD, and its mandate expanded to include the attainment of collective self-reliance, peace, and security in the subregion. IGAD's organizational structure borrows heavily from the *Organization of African Unity (OAU). Its main organs are the Assembly of Heads of State and Government, the Council of Ministers, the Committee of Ambassadors, and a Secretariat. The new charter mandated the harmonization of trade, customs, transport, and communications to ensure free movement of goods, services, and people. The new mandate included the management and resolution of interstate and intrastate conflicts which had posed barriers to sustainable development in the past.

IGAD's expanded mandate addressing political and economic problems of the subregion has led to increased interaction with the OAU, the United Nations, the European Union, and the Common Market for Eastern and Southern Africa. As a mediator of conflicts involving member states IGAD has organized fora for Somali factions to discuss the conditions for peace. It successfully pursued dialogue which resulted in the recognition of the right of the people of southern Sudan to self-determination and continues to play a major role in attempting to resolve the civil war in the Sudan. It also joined the UN and the OAU in efforts to promote dialogue between Ethiopia and Eritrea following the eruption of their border war in 1998.

IGAD, in its second decade of existence, has demonstrated an increased effectiveness in addressing the barriers to the subregion's development. Successful implementation of its objectives will depend on member states' continued commitment to dialogue and joint economic ventures as the foundation for a peaceful, stable, and prosperous regional network.

(See also HORN OF AFRICA.)

Fredrik Soderbaum, *Handbook of Regional Organizations in Africa* (Uppsala, 1996).

RUTH IYOB

INTERNAL COLONIALISM. The term *internal colonialism* has had two somewhat different connotations in the literature. It was initially employed in the late nineteenth century by Russian populists to describe the exploitation of peasants by urban classes. Later, Antonio *Gramsci, V. I. *Lenin, Evgeny Preobrazhensky, and Nikolai *Bukharin used it to characterize the persisting economic underdevelopment of certain Russian and Italian regions. In this connotation, internal colonialism is a process of unequal exchange between the territories of a given state that occurs either as a result of the free play of market forces or of economic policies of the central state that have (intended or unintended) distributional consequences for regions. This conception of internal colonialism is primarily found among economists of *development; the first quantitative model of it was Mihail Maniolescu's, which was inspired by the marked contrast between urban wealth and rural poverty in Depression-era Romania. A second model was developed by Hans Singer and Celso Furtado, after a study of the extensive regional disparities in post-World War II *Brazil (Love, 1989).

Since the 1960s, however, the term has tended to be reserved for regions that are simultaneously economically disadvantaged *and* culturally distinct. The impetus for the new emphasis on culture came from the Mexican sociologists Pablo Gonzáles Casanova and Rodolf Stavenhagen, who observed that the poorest territories in Latin America tended to be those largely inhabited by people adhering to cultural practices that were granted low status by the rulers of the central state.

Even so, this concept was more useful for descriptive than explanatory purposes until it was applied explicitly to the relationship between England and the Celtic and/or nonconformist territories of Wales, Scotland, and Ireland from the sixteenth through the twentieth centuries. This was the first demonstration that internal colonialism (of any variety) could be found in the industrialized heartland—indeed in a state which spawned both the industrial revolution and the doctrine of free trade. Instead of coming to resemble the English core economically in the wake of market diffusion and industrialization, Wales, Scotland, and Ireland tended to develop specialized export economies; instead of assimilating to the core culturally and politically, the inhabitants of these peripheral regions maintained separate cultural and political traditions and often supported nationalist political movements.

Internal colonialism is considered responsible for the establishment of a cultural division of labor, which is a principal determinant of *peripheral nationalism. The cultural division of labor is a social structure that reserves high-status jobs for members of the core culture, or those capable of assimilating to it, relegating all others to lower rungs in the occupational hierarchy. This theory has been applied to historical and contemporary cases of peripheral nationalism in *Canada, *Finland, *France, Alaska, *New Zealand, and other societies, although no systematic empirical review of these studies has yet appeared. The best comparative assessment of the internal colonial theory of peripheral nationalism is Charles C. Ragin's study of ethnic political mobilization in thirteen Western European societies, which concludes that it is applicable to a large number of cases of peripheral nationalism in these societies, but not to all of them.

(See also BRITAIN; NATIONALISM; SECESSIONIST MOVEMENTS.)

Michael Hechter, *Internal Colonialism: The Celtic Fringe in British National Development, 1536–1966* (Berkeley, Calif., and London, 1975). Charles C. Ragin, *The Comparative Method: Moving Beyond Qualitative and Quantitative Strategies* (Berkeley, Calif., 1987). Joseph L. Love, "Modeling Internal Colonialism: History and Prospect" *World Development* 17, no. 6 (June 1989): 905–922.

MICHAEL HECHTER

INTERNATIONAL BANK FOR RECONSTRUCTION AND DEVELOPMENT. See WORLD BANK.

INTERNATIONAL COOPERATION. The issue of international cooperation provides a unifying theme in the study of national *security and *international political economy. International cooperation refers to the mutual adjustment of government policies through a process of policy coordination. Cooperation must be distinguished from harmony, a situation in which unilateral pursuit of self-interest automatically facilitates the ability of others to achieve their goals (Robert O. Keohane, *After Hegemony*, Princeton, N.J., 1984). Thus, cooperation does not require that states confront no conflicts of interest, but addresses how they might be able to overcome these conflicts to their mutual benefit.

This understanding of international cooperation reflects the predominance of the "realist" paradigm in the study of *international relations. Realists, focusing on the anarchic nature of the *international system and the intensity of insecurity fostered by anarchy, argued that these factors presented formidable obstacles to cooperation among states. Labeling authors who focused on the international pursuit of common goals and the role of *international law in constraining conflict "idealists," the realists made a coherent case for the persistence of discord among states.

In recent years, a response to these realist arguments has been mounted by a group of theorists known as neoliberals. Accepting core realist assumptions such as the central role of self-interested, rational states and the condition of anarchy in the *international system, neoliberals argue that, under certain conditions, international cooperation may nevertheless occur. Their analysis begins by addressing collective action problems, i.e., situations in which unilateral, self-interested state action leads to outcomes that leave all actors dissatisfied. These outcomes are suboptimal in the sense that alternatives exist that would benefit all actors, hurting none. National trade policies are commonly used as an example: while all states would prefer a system of free trade to one with high levels of *protection, each has an individual incentive to impose restrictions on trade. Myopic pursuit of self-interest thus leaves all states dissatisfied.

Neoliberals argue that far-sighted governments will search for mechanisms that allow them to cooperate to overcome dilemmas of collective action. Thus, they describe a path to international cooperation that does not require assumptions of altruism or self-abnegation on the part of individual states. Instead, cooperation allows egoistic, rational states to better achieve their policy objectives. In this world, cooperation is unstable because each government faces temptations and domestic pressures to "cheat" or unilaterally change its policies to the detriment of others and its own temporary advantage. For neoliberals, cooperation needs to be explained rather than assumed.

Following this reasoning, and drawing on the insights of economists and others studying problems of strategic interaction, theorists have identified a series of factors that will facilitate international cooperation. Although idiosyncratic factors may weigh heavily in some historical cases, three factors should encourage cooperation in general: the existence of common interests, the participation of a small number of actors, and a long shadow of the future.

Cooperation will not occur unless states perceive some common interest in cooperation. Common and conflicting interests often exist side by side in international politics, so that governments see benefits from cooperation but find it difficult to take the risk of pursuing these mutual benefits. Both the constraints of state survival in a self-help system and the pressures of domestic politics may push governments away from risky cooperative endeavors even if the potential advantages of such endeavors are large. However, the larger the degree of common interest, and the smaller the degree of conflicting interest, the more likely it becomes that governments will find a way to overcome these difficulties.

A second factor conducive to international cooperation is the involvement of a small number of actors. When the number of states involved in an issue area is large, negotiating mutually acceptable agreements and monitoring compliance with such agreements become more difficult. Thus, cooperation is often easier when only a few states need to coordinate their policies to achieve superior outcomes. Small numbers make negotiations less cumbersome, increase the ability of actors to recognize and understand one another's preferences, and make identification and punishment of those breaking cooperative arrangements less problematic.

Third, neoliberals argue that a long "shadow of the future" encourages international cooperation. The more states value future benefits relative to immediate gains, the more willing they will be to take the chance of cooperating today. A state with a short-run perspective will behave myopically, only considering the immediate costs and benefits of its actions, and thus will be tempted to cheat on cooperative agreements. However, such behavior can become costly in the long run, as a myopic state will develop a reputation for unreliability. Thus, a state that cares about the future will be more willing to forgo immediate gains in order to gain future benefits from cooperation.

In what kinds of situations are these three factors—common interests, small numbers, and a long shadow of the future—increased? Theorists have focused on two elements that

facilitate cooperation. First, a common explanation of cooperation is "hegemonic stability theory." This theory posits that cooperation requires one dominant state to provide the necessary conditions. Thus, the international system is stabilized during periods when one state, such as Britain or the United States, plays a leadership role. Eras without a hegemony, such as the 1930s or, some suggest, the 1980s, see an upswing in the level of uncooperative state behavior.

A second explanation of cooperation relies on the impact that international institutions can have on state behavior. Because institutions increase the level of information available to states, create dense patterns of issue linkages, and encourage their members to think about the future, they tend to create the conditions necessary for the emergence of cooperation. Such institutions often include formal organizations, such as the *European Union, but can also take the form of less formal arrangements, such as the *World Trade Organization.

(See also HEGEMONY; LIBERALISM; REALISM; REGIME.)

Robert Axelrod, *The Evolution of Cooperation* (New York, 1984). Kenneth A. Oye, ed., *Cooperation Under Anarchy* (Princeton, N.J., 1986).

LISA L. MARTIN

INTERNATIONAL COURT OF JUSTICE. The possibility of substituting law for force in *international relations is not new, and rests heavily on the availability of reliable mechanisms for resolving international disputes effectively. The main obstacle to such an approach has been the preference by many governments for the greater flexibility of *diplomacy. As well, the modern idea that a sovereign state should not restrict its discretion in relation to conflict resolution also inhibits recourse to judicial modes of settlement.

World War I pushed forward the process of committing states to third-party adjudication. Several influential U.S. lawyers ardently believed that establishing courts was virtually equivalent to creating a world peace system. A world court was a minor part of the vision of a reformed international order as championed by Woodrow Wilson. In 1921 the Permanent Court of International Justice was established as an independent international body, with some connections to the *League of Nations. This court decided thirty-two cases (as well as delivered twenty-seven advisory opinions) during its eighteen years of existence, but none touched the major war-threatening issues of the era between the two great wars of the century.

The United States never became a party to this first institutional embodiment of a world court. Participation was successfully resisted by the same political forces that opposed U.S. membership in the League of Nations. At the same time, support for the world court project continued to grow, particularly in the United States. The experience of World War II strengthened these internationalist forces sufficiently so that in the subsequent *peace process the United States became a leading member of the UN and an active participant in the revised version of the World Court, now formally named the International Court of Justice (ICJ).

Despite these steps forward, the existence of an adjudicative alternative to diplomacy and *war remains marginal and contested. The U.S. government's attitude toward adjudication at the global level is ambivalent, at best, suggesting the persistence of opposing ideas about the place of judicial set-tlement and law in international relations. The idea of en-trusting important disputes, especially in the area of peace and *security, to the ICJ came to be widely regarded in influ-ential circles as "legalistic" and naïve, being incompatible with the actualities of international politics.

Another problematic side of the ICJ arises from its unrep-resentative character. Each of the five permanent members of the *Security Council is assured one of the fifteen judges, with the remaining ten selected by electoral process involving the main organs of the United Nations.

The ICJ is the main judicial arm of the UN, its role being set forth in Articles 92–96 of the UN Charter. It is located in The Hague, and is available to states seeking a judicial reso-lution of disputes in accordance with *international law. The ICJ can also be used by the organs of the UN to render "ad-visory opinions," clarifying points of international law that arise during their operations. Unlike judgments in disputes between states, advisory opinions provide authoritative ren-derings of international law, but they are without binding ef-fect except in relation to the body that put the legal question before the World Court but even then only for the occasion.

Considering that the ICJ has been in existence far more than fifty years, its caseload is rather light. This reveals a reluctance by most governments to use this method of dispute settle-ment rather than an absence of intergovernmental contro-versy regarding legal rights and duties.

Although adjudication is infrequent, there are a wide range of issues that have been brought to the World Court over the years. The spectrum includes boundary delimitation, use of force, diplomatic relations, hostage-taking, right of asylum, maritime issues, and economic rights. The advisory opinion role of the ICJ has often touched upon important controver-sies such as the financial obligations of UN members and the rights of South Africa to extend apartheid to the administered territory of South-West Africa (now Namibia). In 1996 the ICJ issued an advisory opinion in response to a request from the General Assembly on the legality of nuclear weapons. The decision was notable in several respects, but especially for the extent to which the majority of judges cast doubt upon the legality of nuclear weapons. Also, the fifteen judges unan-imously agreed that the existing nuclear weapons states have a legal duty in good faith to pursue nuclear disarmament. Through 1999 the ICJ had issued sixty-nine judgments and twenty-four advisory opinions.

Although all UN members are entitled to use of the court, none can be required to do so without an additional expres-sion of consent. Many important international treaties contain a provision agreeing to submit a dispute to the ICJ in the event that cannot be resolved by diplomacy. In general, states are reluctant to lose control over their policy options. This is partly due to an atavistic sense that it represents a denial of *sovereignty to accept the authority of an international insti-tution on matters of vital state interests. The compulsory dispute-settlement procedures of the *World Trade Organi-zation suggest a notable sovereignty-cutting trend in the area of international trade, but it is doubtful that this trend will encourage an expansion of ICJ authority.

States seem unlikely to make use of the World Court in big cases even in the likelihood of success. In addition, major states committed to a course of policy are not often willing to change course in the face of an adverse judicial decision. Moreover, the UN is not in a position to implement such a decision in the face of defiance, especially if the loser is a major state. At the same time, even a nonimplemented deci-sion can sometimes make a contribution in the struggle for public opinion and in strengthening the diplomatic position for claims being made by the winning side.

Recent experience suggests that there are two possible di-rections for the development of a more effective World Court. The first is to restrict the activity of the court to technical areas such as clarifying minor *boundary disputes or allocating shares of the continental shelf. In these settings the court has demonstrated its competence and states seem willing to re-spect the outcome even if it goes against their claims. There is less emphasis on winning and more on stabilizing a rela-tionship. The second direction would be to encourage more states to consent to resolve their disputes before the court by agreeing in advance to accept compulsory jurisdiction, and then to increase pressure for compliance. The United States and Britain seem to prefer, at this point, the first direction, whereas the countries of the South seem more inclined to move in the second direction.

The growing importance of functional issues, and the de-cline of ideological controversy regarding the content of in-ternational law, may support an expanding role for the World Court in the years ahead.

(See also EUROPEAN COURT OF JUSTICE; FORCE, USE OF; UNITED NATIONS.)

Hersch Lauterpacht, *The Development of International Law by the Inter-national Court* (London, 1958). R. P. Anand, *Studies in International Ad-judication* (Delhi, 1969). Shabtai Rosenne, *The Law and Practice of the International Court*, 2d ed., 2 vols. (Leyden, Netherlands, 1985). Richard Falk, *Reviving the World Court* (Charlottesville, Va., 1986). Thomas J. Bodie, *Politics and the Emergence of an Activist International Court of Jus-tice* (Westport, Conn., 1995).

RICHARD FALK

INTERNATIONAL DEBT. International lending is a subset of international investment, and has long been a prominent feature of world economic and political affairs. Cross-border debts have been important to economic activity in many nations and have frequently given rise to domestic and inter-national political conflict.

The economic principles of international lending are rela-tively straightforward. Loans across national borders nor-mally respond to differences in rates of return: capital flows from where it is plentiful (and interest rates low) to where it is scarce (and interest rates high). From the standpoint of the investor, this difference in rates of return makes foreign lend-ing attractive. However, these higher rates also reflect the generally greater risk of foreign as compared to domestic bor-rowers. If the foreign debtor refuses to service its debt, the creditor has fewer ways of collecting than domestically—es-pecially if the foreign debtor is a national government, for creditors cannot foreclose on a sovereign state. In return for accepting a higher degree of risk, foreign lenders demand a higher interest rate (risk premium).

From the standpoint of borrowing nations, such as the United States in the nineteenth century or most developing countries in the twentieth century, foreign loans have several interrelated effects. First, they increase the local supply of capital, allowing national investment to exceed savings. Second, they increase the supply of foreign currency, allowing national imports to exceed exports. Third, inasmuch as they are extended to governments, they increase the financial resources of the public sector, allowing the government to spend more than it takes in.

Foreign loans generally make economic sense to the borrower if they serve directly or indirectly to increase national output and ability to export (or to produce previously imported goods). To repay foreign lenders eventually, the country must use loans to contribute to economic growth and the country's earnings of foreign currencies. This process can be indirect, but sooner or later loans must increase growth if they are to justify themselves. For example, borrowing might allow the government to increase spending on transportation infrastructure that is not directly productive, and does not directly increase exports, but that allows private economic agents to increase output and exports (perhaps by opening new agricultural or mining regions).

In addition to the underlying economic relationship, international debt has important institutional features. Typically, a large proportion of international loans is made to governments: from the standpoint of a foreign lender, national governments are generally better credit risks than are national firms, which are themselves in any event subordinate to government control. Before 1965, most long-term loans were made in the form of bond flotations; since then, bank lending has also been important. In either instance the number of creditor financial institutions (investment or commercial banks) is generally small. International loan markets are often characterized by credit rationing, in which some countries are unable to borrow at any interest rate. This is due, among other things, to the fact that the ability of creditors to enforce contractual compliance on foreign governments is very limited in the absence of a binding judicial system such as undergirds domestic financial relations. And, for reasons that are controversial, international lending tends to go in waves or cycles of boom and bust: a ten- or twenty-year period of easy money is followed by an equivalent period of little lending.

The political implications of international debt are generally clearest when debt must be serviced (i.e., interest payments made and principal repaid). At this point the favorable economic effects of capital inflow are reversed. The country must save more than it invests in order to send capital abroad; it must export more than it imports in order to send foreign currencies abroad; and its government must bring in more than it spends. These three adjustments can be painful, especially if they have to be undertaken rapidly.

The two most prominent modern experiences with international lending were in the interwar period and since 1970. In the 1920s, U.S. and British capital markets lent heavily to semi-industrial countries in Central, Eastern, and Southern Europe and in Latin America. When the Great Depression of the 1930s hit and prices of these countries' exports plunged, most of them defaulted on their debts amid great domestic and international political turmoil. Since 1970, international banks and investors have lent hundreds of billions of dollars to developing countries. Such countries as Brazil, Mexico, and the Republic of Korea (South Korea) grew very rapidly at least in part because of the availability of ample foreign finance.

This lending was interrupted in the early 1980s, when interest rates rose dramatically amid a generalized recession. As a result, many debtors did not make payments, once more amid domestic and international political turmoil. Most of Latin America, indeed, spent the 1980s mired in recession, inflation, and political conflict as the debt burden exacted an enormous socioeconomic and political toll. The resumption of lending in the 1990s was also punctuated by crises in Mexico and East Asia.

The international politics of international debt are dominated by the complexity of enforcing property rights, such as the creditor's contractual right to debt service payments, across national borders and against sovereign governments. Creditors have tried many ways to induce compliance by debtors. One is military force: in the pre–World War II era military intervention by home governments of creditors, up to and including direct colonialism, sometimes served to enforce contracts (although whether debt problems were important causes of such intervention is controversial). China, Egypt, and the Caribbean are among the regions in which foreign military interference was associated with foreign lending. Another is the formation of clubs or committees of a country's creditors, which can collaborate to use such economic threats as a cutoff of future loans or trade credits to bring pressure to bear. A third way, common over the past twenty-five years, is to rely on an international organization such as the *International Monetary Fund to monitor and attempt to enforce loan contracts.

In the final analysis, however, the absence of an international bankruptcy court means that resolution of debt problems depends on the interaction of the two sides. When debt comes due, debtors wish to pay as little as possible, while creditors want as much as possible. Debtors threaten to reduce or halt debt service payments. Creditors threaten to seize assets the debtor may have overseas (the national airline's airplanes, bank deposits), or to exclude the debtor from future borrowing, or to retaliate by other means; sometimes they offer new loans or other side payments as an incentive for the debtor to honor past obligations.

Careful studies have found that over the very long run (decades or more) and on average, debt problems are bargained out to where the final rate of return on the loan, taking into account unpaid interest and principal, ends up being roughly equivalent to the return on domestic financial assets. This is evidence that in the final analysis international loan markets are relatively efficient, in that risk premiums charged to borrowers that may default tend on average to reflect the actual probability of default.

Hostilities between debtors and creditors can affect broader political relations among nations, and are sometimes blamed for wars both small and global. In the 1930s, the heavy economic burden of foreign debts contributed to the rise of highly nationalistic, often fascistic, movements in Central, Eastern, and Southern Europe, and to the resentment of these countries and their populations toward the creditor nations of Western Europe and North America. The debt crisis of the

1980s exacerbated North-South political tensions, as many in the developing world felt that they were suffering solely to line the coffers of international banks.

In addition to international conflict over the distribution of costs and benefits involved in international lending, there are many analogous domestic disputes. There is no guarantee that those within a borrowing nation who benefit from foreign loans are the ones who will be asked to sacrifice to repay them. Foreign finance can go to reduce borrowing costs to industry, for example, while the resources to service this debt can be extracted from agriculture. Such domestic distributional patterns are sure to give rise to political struggles.

Just as foreign borrowing tends to increase the domestic supply of capital and foreign exchange, making loans and imports cheaper, the need to service debt reduces this supply, making loans and imports more expensive. By the same token, inasmuch as foreign borrowing by the government allowed it to provide more services with lower taxes, servicing debt requires a curtailment of public services and increased taxes. Those who had, during borrowing, come to rely on inexpensive loans and imports, and on government services, can be expected to protest the reversal, as can those required to pay higher taxes.

The requirements of foreign debt service can impose severe burdens on debtor societies. The need to raise funds for service of the foreign debt is often associated with domestic depressions, severe unemployment, and spiraling inflation. Debt problems were factors in the dismal economic performance of Latin America in the 1980s and Southeast Asia in the 1990s. Issues related to the foreign debt have been central to political turmoil, the collapse of authoritarian regimes, and pressures to undertake politically difficult economic reforms.

The domestic and international politics of foreign debt interact. In a country burdened with costly debt service payments, those economic interest groups hardest hit by the impact of these payments clamor for the government to take a tougher stance against its creditors—to shift some of the burden onto foreigners. Such demands are countered by other domestic economic interest groups who may rely on their ties with overseas markets or who are concerned about the precedent set by government disregard for private property rights. At the same time, creditors press the debtor government for prompt and full debt service payments with whatever means they have at their disposal.

In the midst of a full-fledged debt crisis, such as those involving many semi-industrial countries in the 1930s and the 1980s, a swirling spiral of domestic and international political conflict can cause great political and economic instability. International debt issues exacerbated domestic and international conflict during the Great Depression, while the debt crisis of the 1980s also saw major changes in domestic politics and foreign policies throughout the developing world.

Foreign loans can be important contributors to economic development. However, international debt is inherently political, and frequently conflictual. Economic and political factors interact to determine whether foreign debt will be an unproblematic contribution to national development or the cause of major domestic and international political strife.

(See also FINANCE, INTERNATIONAL; INTERNATIONAL POLITICAL ECONOMY; NEWLY INDUSTRIALIZING ECONOMIES; NORTH-SOUTH RELATIONS.)

Jeffrey Sachs, ed., *Developing Country Debt and Economic Performance* (Chicago, 1989). Barbara Stallings and Robert Kaufman, eds., *Debt and Democracy in Latin America* (Boulder, Colo., 1989). William R. Cline, *International Debt Reexamined* (Washington, D.C., 1995).

JEFFRY A. FRIEDEN

INTERNATIONAL FINANCE. See FINANCE, INTERNATIONAL.

INTERNATIONAL LABOR ORGANIZATION. The International Labor Organization (ILO) has been a specialized agency of the UN system since 1946. It was founded at the end of the World War I as an independent adjunct to the *League of Nations, both with headquarters in Geneva. The ILO subsumed the International Labor Office, established at the turn of the century to promote what was called then "international labor legislation," and intergovernmental agreements on welfare standards for industrial labor, such as the eight-hour day and restrictions on child labor.

In late nineteenth-century Europe, the movement for international labor legislation argued that governments enforcing benign working conditions would be at a competitive disadvantage vis-à-vis those allowing unchecked labor exploitation. However, if global agreement on improving working conditions could be achieved, any economic disadvantage to more progressive nations would vanish.

The ILO's organization recognizes that the initial impetus for improving labor standards will come first from labor groups and then from industries and states where high standards already have been won. Delegations to the ILO, unlike those to any other major intergovernmental organization, include representatives of national associations of labor unions and of employers. The employers' associations often overrepresent advanced industries in which labor conditions tend to be better. Member governments do not have to adhere to ILO standards, but international benchmarks help domestic interest groups and states with more advanced labor standards to make demands upon laggards.

ILO standard setting was important in the interwar years but become less central during the *Cold War. The tripartite system of representation broke down: Communist bloc states sent seemingly unitary delegations, and noncommunist labor representatives united with their governments to isolate the Soviet Union and its allies. Under the leadership of the United States, the ILO advocated the American system of collective bargaining. However, promotion of the U.S. model of resolving disputes between workers and employers was not the same as upgrading of labor standards to the highest followed anywhere in the world, the original ILO goal.

As the importance of the ILO's original activities diminished, its secretariat took on new functions. It expanded activities in the *Third World, providing technical assistance on employment promotion and human resources to African, Asian, and Latin American governments. Since the 1970s, the ILO has become a leader in debates about development strategy by funding and promoting much of the original research that supported strategies aimed at fulfilling basic human needs.

During the 1990s, Cold War problems faded, but neoliberal policies of deregulation, promoted by the rich countries, undermined the ILO's efforts to expand labor regulation to an increasingly globalized labor market. Toward the end of the decade, however, a worldwide movement to promote "core labor standards" strengthened the ILO and gave it a more important voice in the system of global economic and social policy.

(See also DEVELOPMENT AND UNDERDEVELOPMENT; LABOR MOVEMENT; UNITED NATIONS.)

Carol R. Lubin and Anne Winslow, *Social Justice for Women: The International Labor Organization* (Durham, N.C., 1990). Nicolas Valticos, *International Labour Law* (The Hague, 1995). International Labour Office, *Report of the Director-General: Decent Work* (Geneva, 1999).

CRAIG N. MURPHY

INTERNATIONAL LAW. See overleaf.

INTERNATIONAL MIGRATION entails not merely physical relocation, but a change of jurisdiction from one state to another and eventually also a change in membership from one political community to another. Both aspects of the process, emigration and immigration, therefore elicit considerable public concern and provoke political contention within and between countries.

A basic determinant of contemporary international movement is the dramatic inequality of social and economic conditions in a world whose farthest corners have been reached by market forces and that is more integrated than ever before. Although individuals usually prefer to work close to their homes, economic necessity may drive them to move about within their country or beyond. Information about conditions abroad is universally available, and the declining cost of long-distance transportation affords mobility to many of the inhabitants of even the poorest countries. Employment opportunities become available as employers in the richer countries seek to lower their costs by hiring less demanding *foreign workers who can also be more easily disposed of; immigrants also fill jobs shunned as too dirty or too dangerous, and often undertake small businesses that are of little interest to larger investors. Demographic projections suggest a continued expansion of the supply of potential migrants independently of demand, as many less developed countries will remain unable to provide jobs for their large and growing generations.

However, people do not move for economic reasons alone. Approximately half of today's international migrants are *refugees, driven out of their country by outright persecution at the hand of the government or some other agent, or by life-threatening violence. The bulk of them originate from the developing world, especially Asia and Africa, as well as from post-Communist Eurasia, notably ex-Yugoslavia and the ex-Soviet Union. These forced movements occur mostly as a by-product of processes that generated waves of refugees in Europe in earlier times, notably attempts to create unified new states in culturally diverse regions, and confrontations between dominant and subordinate classes in agrarian societies marked by extreme inequality and ruled by authoritarian governments. Refugees are also produced by "failed states" that become cockpits for battling warlords. Such conflicts often elicit intervention by outside powers, resulting in an expansion in their scope and duration. They tend to be more destructive today because both governments and their opponents have access to cheap rapid-fire weapons; furthermore, protracted violence in poor and densely populated countries may occasion severe food shortages and health crises, which also generate more population displacements. From the 1970s onward, the developing world was engulfed in an unprecedented refugee crisis; although most of the displaced remained in their region of origin, some were invited to resettle in the United States and other Western countries (notably Vietnamese and Cubans), while others entered into the worldwide migratory stream and sought asylum in the West as well.

However, these economic and political conditions determine only potential movements because states intervene to control exit and entry. In earlier times, under conditions of population scarcity and political absolutism, most states sought to prevent the loss of valuable subjects by imposing severe sanctions against their departure. From the late eighteenth century onward, however, recognition of the right of individuals to leave their country (and to return freely) became the hallmark of liberal regimes, in keeping with the doctrine that membership rests on consent. Adoption of a permissive stance on exit was facilitated by soaring population growth and the industrial revolution, which occasioned what came to be viewed as a burdensome surplus of uprooted poor. Under the new conditions, emigration turned from a problem into a solution. Twentieth-century authoritarian states adopted the exit stance of their absolutist predecessors; but thanks to their greater police capacity, they were able to close their borders even more tightly: the Berlin Wall erected in 1961 became a symbol of this policy. One of the most immediately perceptible by-products of the political liberalization of the Warsaw Treaty Organization (Warsaw Pact) countries in the late 1980s was the opening of their borders. However, this did not lead to a massive outpouring of emigrants because of restrictions the states to which people might go maintain on entry.

Most states maintain severely restrictive immigration policies, with the major exception of the United States and other overseas republics or dominions from the late eighteenth to the early twentieth century, when they eagerly sought settlers to fill the land and workers to develop their economies. Control over the inward movement of strangers was deemed by the founders of *international law to constitute a fundamental attribute of *sovereignty on grounds of *security, since in its absence an invading army might merely walk in. Under prevailing world conditions, completely open borders would lead to a gradual worldwide equalization of wages; hence another major function of immigration control is to preserve the advantageous conditions the better-off countries have achieved. Most political theorists also believe that no political community can function without a limit on membership, which today is denoted by citizenship; and some theorists as well as much of the general public believe that the sudden broadening of a country's cultural heterogeneity is problematic for national unity. In this perspective, control of entry constitutes but the first of a broad array of mechanisms for enforcing political boundaries, which encompasses also conditions for acquiring citizenship by way of naturalization.

For these reasons, restrictive immigration policies remain the norm among the affluent democracies today, and provide a sharp contrast with the liberalization of the international movement of capital, goods, and information. However, most

(cont. on p. 412)

INTERNATIONAL LAW refers to the body of legal standards, procedures, and institutions governing the interaction of sovereign *states. One main purpose has been to orient and channel the *foreign policy of states so as to further relationships of coexistence and cooperation. To this end international law (1) delimits the sphere of internal authority of every member of the community of states (each state has exclusive jurisdiction within its territory, particularly over matters not covered by international law); (2) organizes forms of cooperation (mainly through intergovernmental organizations such as the UN, military alliances, economic institutions, etc.); and (3) sets the main goals to be pursued by states (*peace, respect for *human rights as well as the rights of peoples to *self-determination) and accordingly prohibits what is contrary to those goals (aggression, large-scale violations of human rights, war crimes, crimes against humanity, and forcible denial of the right of peoples to self-determination).

A second dimension to international law is now evident—even if it has not been recognized as international law strictly speaking. International law has developed outside the realm of cooperation and coexistence in the realm of foreign policy; international law has now permeated national legal orders; it has become the law of the land normally giving rise to rights and obligations at the national level. Trade and investment regimes have developed with a corpus of principles, rules, and procedures which operate at a transnational level outside the interstate discourse. Even if the rules owe their origin to international texts agreed in cooperation they take effect in the national legal orders with coercive effect.

The third and most recent dimension of international law relates to the development of a global legal order capable of imposing respect for international law. We might characterize this as a trend gradually moving beyond horizontal interstate cooperation and coexistence in foreign affairs into the field of growing coercion authorized by a centralized organ. The 1990s saw the Security Council authorize the use of force in response to violations of international law and in order to provide humanitarian assistance. The council also established two international criminal tribunals: for the former Yugoslavia and for Rwanda. Furthermore, mandatory sanctions were imposed in response to various situations, sometimes with questionable effectiveness, but nevertheless with considerable effect. Such coercive measures suggest that the concept of global law enforcement of international law is now more real that theoretical, although it is limited to the realm of threats to international peace and security, and even in this realm it proves to be selective.

Principles of International Law. International law has been primarily concerned with the behavior of states. States are considered the principal actors on the international scene. They are aggregates of individuals dominated by an apparatus which exercises authority over them. State goals are quite distinct from the goals of each individual or group. Yet states are no longer free to act in ways which deny the rights of peoples, individuals, or groups. International law places constraints on how states can act.

Second, normally responsibility for violations of the rules governing the behavior of states does not fall upon the transgressing official but is attributed to the group to which he or she belongs (the state community). Here we are confronted with a striking deviation from domestic legal systems. In do-

mestic systems we are accustomed to the notion of individual responsibility: the individual who commits a tort or any other breach of law shall suffer in consequence; the transgressor must either make good the damage or—in the case of crime—is liable to a criminal penalty. There are, however, exceptions, one of which is "vicarious responsibility," when the law provides that someone bear responsibility for actions performed by another person with whom the former has special ties (for example, a parent is legally responsible for damage caused by his or her children); sometimes legal entity is held responsible for the acts performed by one of its representatives on behalf of the entity group (as in the civil liability of corporations).

In the international legal system these exceptions (collective responsibility) become the rule. If a state official breaks international law (as when a military commander orders his or her pilots to intrude upon the airspace of a neighboring state, or a national court disregards an international treaty granting certain rights to foreigners, or a police officer infringes upon diplomatic immunity by arresting or maltreating a diplomat), the wronged state may take action against the whole community to which the state representative belongs, even though the community has neither carried out nor ordered the infraction. For instance, the state which has become the victim of the internationally unlawful act can claim the payment of a sum of money (to be paid by the offending state's treasury) or resort to reprisals damaging the other state's interests rather than those of the actual authors of the offense (for example, the freezing of assets, the suspension of a commercial treaty, and so on).

Third, while in domestic legal orders the three main functions typical of any legal system (lawmaking, adjudication, and law enforcement) are entrusted to central organs acting on behalf of the whole community (parliaments, courts, and law enforcement officers), in the international community such authority is fragmented and diffuse. As a consequence, organizational rules are at an embryonic stage. The machinery that exists for discharging the three functions relies heavily on the states that it is supposed to be controlling. Normally it is for states to create and change law, to settle disputes, and to impel compliance with the law. This decentralized system allows for states to take certain proportionate countermeasures as a measure of self-help. Nevertheless there is increasing resort by states to the jurisdiction of the *International Court of Justice and other international tribunals for the settlement of disputes. The judgments of these tribunals have considerably enriched the texture of international law and increased its relevance for states as principles are developed and rules are applied in concrete situations.

Historical Evolution of International Law. The origin of the international community in its present structure and configuration is usually traced back to the Peace of Westphalia (1648) which concluded the Thirty Years' War. Indeed, it is about this time that the decline of two preexisting structures of power (the Catholic Church and the Holy Roman Empire) became final, and the international community took the form of a set of independent entities (sovereign states), each equal to each other and no longer subject to any superior authority. The subsequent evolution of the international legal community can be divided into two basic periods: from 1648 to World War I, and from World War I to the present day.

408

In the first period, the community was conceived as comprising a relatively small number of subjects, all "Western" and relatively homogeneous. Until the end of the nineteenth century, the dominant members of this international community had a common ideological and religious background and shared a common socioeconomic outlook: they espoused a market economy and took a capitalist approach. In addition, there were no international political organizations designed to harmonize the actions of the states and establish permanent links of cooperation among them. Nor were there legal restrictions imposed on the use of *force, with the consequence that the bulk of legal rules (for example, those protecting territorial *sovereignty and political independence) were respected only by powerful states and only when this did not run counter to their own interests. It follows that international legal standards afforded a protection which was provisional and precarious, which is why lesser states so often resorted to treaties of alliance and promoted a *balance of power between stronger states. Lastly, we can say that responsibility for internationally wrongful acts was a "private affair" involving only the offending and victim states. For the other states in this international community breaches of international standards of behavior were something extraneous, in which they were not allowed to meddle. There was no common interest in compliance with the law. Only those states directly and immediately injured by a wrongful act were entitled to take the remedial steps provided by law.

After 1917, this international community began to lose its homogeneity as a result of the founding of the Soviet Union, and in the 1960s and 1970s numerous new African and Asian states emerged from colonization. For a time the new international community was split into three main segments (Western, socialist, and the developing countries), each with a distinct socioeconomic philosophy, a fairly clear ideology, and different political motivations. Another characteristic of the twentieth century was the mushrooming of *international organizations which, without dethroning sovereign states, have come to play a significant role not only as meeting points for states but also as mechanisms for exercising leverage on individual states. Among these organizations are those with a political mandate: at the world level the United Nations; at the regional level, the Organization of American States, the Council of Europe, the European Union, the Organization for Security and Cooperation in Europe, the Arab League, and the Organization of African Unity (to mention only a few). An important role is also played by specialized bodies working in the fields of labor relations (the International Labor Organization), economic relations (the World Bank and the International Monetary Fund as well as the regional development banks), health (the World Health Organization), culture (the United Nations Educational, Scientific and Cultural Organization), the peaceful use of atomic energy (the International Atomic Energy Agency), and trade (the World Trade Organization).

Other salient traits of the present community are the imposition of sweeping legal restrictions on the resort to the military force and even economic coercion. A last distinguishing trait of the present pattern is that certain values have been recognized by states who have decided to give these values legal relevance and significance: peace, self-determination of peoples, and the protection of human dignity from outrageous manifestations of cruelty such as *genocide, racial discrimination (in particular *apartheid), slavery, *torture, and other large-scale or gross violations of *human rights. One of the consequences of the international recognition of this set of values is that their violation is no longer the "private business" of the offending state and the victim, but amounts to a "public affair" involving the whole international community; any member state can step in and raise legitimate concern about respect for international law, even though it has not suffered direct injury from the wrongful act. Furthermore, at least with respect to some of those values (torture, the prohibition of crimes against humanity, in particular genocide), international rules now provide for the personal criminal responsibility of the state officials who engage in such prohibited acts, in addition, of course, to the traditional state responsibility which will be triggered where the acts of the individual can be attributed to the state.

All these developments in the world community have not, however, been so revolutionary as to obliterate the traditional interstate model of the international community. As a result, two different patterns in law, one traditional, the other modern, currently live side by side. The new legal institutions that have developed since World War I (and with greater intensity since 1945) have not uprooted or supplanted the old framework; rather, they appear to have been superimposed on it, even though their main purpose is to attenuate the most conspicuous deficiencies of the old one (unrestricted resort to the use of force, no scrutiny of how a state treats its own nationals, and an absence of multilateral institutional arrangements for the enforcement of the international rule of law).

In *The Anarchical Society: A Study of Order in World Politics* (New York, 1977), Hedley Bull drew the distinction between what he considered the three competing traditions of thought put forward throughout the history of modern states: the Hobbesian, or realist, tradition, "which views international politics as a state of war"; the Grotian, or internationalist, conception, which emphasizes the element of cooperation and regulated interaction among sovereign states; and the Kantian, or universalist, outlook, "which sees at work in international politics a potential community of mankind," and lays stress on the element of "transnational solidarity." Applying Bull's framework, it is difficult to avoid the conclusion that in its first stage of development the international community was shaped according to the pattern of Hobbesian and Grotian traditions. The "new" international legal institutions, however, appear to be largely patterned on the "Kantian" model of thought, trying to mitigate the most striking defects of the old system by introducing certain improvements such as the creation of international organizations and the placing of sweeping restraints on the use of force. In particular, the new "setting" has endeavored to attenuate the shortcomings of the decentralization of the three legal functions (lawmaking, adjudication, and law enforcement) referred to above. Indeed the new coercive powers executed by the Security Council in the context of the use of force, the prosecution of international crimes, and the imposition of sanctions can best be explained by reference to this emerging Kantian model of a cosmopolitan polity. Nevertheless, much decision-making power remains with states, even when international organizations act.

The Effectiveness of International Law. International legal standards play a significant role in the world community. Since every sovereign state needs to communicate day to day with other states, even the most powerful states, such as the United States, cannot estrange themselves from international interaction but need to maintain a certain degree of association. They require such association to protect their nationals living abroad, sell their goods to other states, buy the commodities they need, enter into agreements providing for the stationing of troops in foreign countries, and to attempt to influence the policies of other nations through international institutions. Even more compelling are the reasons for middle-sized and smaller states to engage in international relations under international law and to deal with other countries. For example, their economic and commercial needs may be more dependent on other states and they may even need to create agencies that can provide defensive "umbrellas" in the case of aggression by other states. All of these multiple relations need a medium through which they can be effected. International law plays precisely this role. In spite of its weaknesses and inadequacies, this body of law discharges the important task of providing a channel through which international relations are effected with relative ease. In turn, this body of law contributes to making states "system—conscious," in Stanley Hoffmann's terminology (*The State of War: Essays in the Theory and Practice of International Politics* [New York, 1965], p. 91), that is, "aware of the existence and structure of the whole" and by and large cooperative within the framework of preestablished patterns of behavior.

Commentators are fond of highlighting the fact that the private interests of states often override wider public concern for compliance with international law, and that international tribunals seem only to play a minor role in the enforcement of international law. Nevertheless, the enormous number of treaties that all states enter into, and the number of *international organizations through which they cooperate, should constitute sufficient evidence that sovereign states take international law into account on a daily basis. This is especially so in areas where *reciprocity plays a role: diplomatic and consular relations, commercial and economic dealings, protection of nationals abroad, safeguarding of investment in other countries, etc. On careful analysis, it often becomes clear that enforcement procedures turn out to be less defective than is normally claimed. On the whole, it can be said that even in those areas where it is more difficult to induce states to abide by international law (military and strategic relations, particularly when states' vital interests are at stake), many states proceed with great caution and will seek to stay within the bounds of the international rules for a number of reasons: the pressure that can be exercised on the delinquent party within the UN system; public opinion reacts badly to disregard for international law; the need to be seen as reliable and not to damage good relations in the economic, commercial, and political fields.

Nevertheless, it cannot be denied that the present body of international rules suffers from three major flaws. First, it has been almost always unable to impose sweeping and effective physical restraints on military violence whenever a state feels that its interests are better safeguarded by resort to force. International legal standards (and the international institution which should, in principle, safeguard international peace and collective security, the UN Security Council) have often played only a minor role in preventing that state from taking such a step. However, the Security Council's authorization of the use of force in the 1990s suggests that there is increasing readiness to respond to threats to international peace and security through the use of force with an intention to uphold the international rule of law. The new paradox is that some new initiatives to uphold the rule of law may themselves breach international law where they are unauthorized or fail to respect the laws of armed conflict (think of NATO's reaction to gross breaches of human rights in Kosovo). Second, there is no permanent institution for *disarmament: only those states that freely subject themselves to armament limitations restrain themselves in this area; other states retain almost unqualified freedom and Article 26 of the UN Charter (which gives the Security Council responsibility for proposing a system for the regulation of armaments) remains a dead letter. However, since the end of the Cold War the Security Council has imposed a number of arms embargoes on countries posing a threat to international peace and security and Iraq had a disarmament and weapons inspection regime imposed on it by the Security Council in the wake of its invasion of Kuwait in 1991. Third, the UN for fifty years primarily pursued the goal of what Johan Galtung ("Peace," in David L. Sills, ed., *International Encyclopedia of the Social Sciences*, vol. 2 [New York, 1968], p. 487) calls "negative peace," i.e., the absence of armed conflict, while attaching lesser importance to "positive peace," i.e., the introduction of international social justice. (And, in addition, even in the field of "negative peace," it has turned out to be defective especially with regard to internal armed conflicts.) In the twenty-first century it is much more likely that international organizations, and the states which are their members, will give greater priority to aspects of positive peace: reduction of poverty and disease, minority rights protection, economic development, and education. This is because there is increasing recognition that action in these spheres is perhaps the only way to prevent outbreaks of conflict and disorder.

Of course, these three flaws should not be attributed to international law as such, but to the lack of political will of the key states in the international community. Had they the political will to do away with those weaknesses the present state of legal affairs would change.

International Law as the Vanishing Point of Law. In 1952 Sir Hersch Lauterpacht wrote that "international law is the vanishing point of law" ("The Problem of the Revision of the Law of War," in *29 British Year Book of International Law* [London, 1952], p. 382). There is some truth in this proposition. International legal rules have weak structural underpinnings (i.e., no authoritative bodies regularly producing law, few compulsory procedures for settling legal disputes, and selective enforcement of the law through political bodies such as the Security Council). International law is therefore bound to seem like a weak legal system whenever international rules do not coincide with converging state interests.

But it is precisely these features of international rules which make inquiry into this body of law particularly enlightening for anyone interested in legal systems and international relations. International legal rules closely reflect the constellation of state interests. They are not accompanied by those technicalities so often found in municipal law. This latter body of law, being highly sophisticated—as a result of the existence of independent legislatures, executives, and judiciaries—often conceals the real relationship between the sociopolitical constellation and the legal framework—the metalegal context and its legal reflection. Too many mediations, subtleties, and legal mechanisms tend to obscure the fact that legal rules and procedures are in the final analysis designed to safeguard certain interests, to promote the specific goals of social groups, or to strike a balance among the competing or conflicting interests of those groups. International law, by contrast, easily reveals the relationship between socioeconomic or political interests and the agreed legal rules and highlights the possibility of normative frameworks even in the absence of formally agreed legal standards. This is one of the principal reasons why this branch of law has been such a rich area of study for scholars interested in jurisprudence, legal theory, and the sociology of law.

Future Prospects. Three factors are likely to heighten the role of international legal institutions in the world community. First, the tremendous tensions created by the existence of weaponry capable of destroying the earth several times over have increased the value of existing international legal machinery for facilitating negotiation and agreement. Permanent international fora such as the Geneva Conference on Disarmament and the Security Council will play a crucial role in checking the possibility of the acquisition and use of weapons of mass destruction. The Security Council's investigatory and monitoring activities in Iraq over nearly ten years have created an important, if controversial, precedent. A second trend is the development of powerful centrifugal forces within nation-states. Minorities are becoming more and more vocal; ethnic groups throughout the world vociferously claim respect for their identity as well as for a measure of autonomy, and even international status; peoples are claiming the right to self-determination which can take the form of a demand for independence through secession but may also involve demands for inclusion in government. Civil society organizations representing widely divergent causes are branching out across the international community and setting up their own international networks which in turn have strengthened the reach and impact of international law. These and other collectivities tend to disrupt the fabric of nation-states and the interstate international legal order. They have introduced into the world community a less state-centered approach which in the long run will transform the present framework of international relations. Existing international institutions can serve a very important purpose by channeling and responding to these centrifugal forces; they can make room for peaceful integration by accommodating competing demands within an orderly framework—without, however, doing away completely with the interstate structure at the hub of the world community.

A third phenomenon should be emphasized: attention to international crime and *terrorism has led to increased cooperation and spawned new branches of international law. The causes of terrorism are of course multifarious and often difficult to grasp. One contributing factor is certainly the existence of authoritarian structures within many states, not to mention profound social and economic inequalities among states. Yet another factor is the progressive fragmentation of the various centers of power in the international community and the corresponding proliferation of poles of interest. The international community is no longer crystallized into a few great blocs, each dominated by one Great Power, well able to control any centrifugal tendency. Because the Great Powers, which together could have dominated the world, have for many years found it difficult to reach agreement, the international community has now split into many centers of power of varying size, each with a modicum of authority; these centers sometimes protect and aid private groups in other state communities. Another important factor is the inability of the international community in its organized forms (especially the UN) to offer an adequate response to requests for greater international justice, and to the need for preventive mechanisms to defuse economic and social conflicts both at the national and transnational levels. It is evident that terrorism, far from disrupting the legal and organizational structures of the world community, has prompted states to step up their mutual cooperation on criminal matters and devise mechanisms based on common interest, designed both to prevent terrorist groups from attacking innocent civilians or state officials, and, in case such attacks are carried out, to arrest the culprits and bring them to justice. Treaties which demand that states either extradite or prosecute those accused of terrorism committed outside their territory have multiplied and are now copied in fields such as money laundering, corruption, and drug trafficking.

In contrast to the three aforementioned trends, a tendency exists in the international community which might, in the very long run, erode the role of international institutions and law: regionalization. It is common knowledge that regional (economic or political) institutions have been created in various areas of the world (e.g., the European Union, the North American Free Trade Agreement). The reasons behind the drive toward setting up these institutions are obvious: within areas where states tend to share common political values, economic outlooks, and cultural backgrounds, it is much easier to achieve integration (at the political, economic, and normative and institutional levels) than in the world community at large. However, it seems more likely that regional bodies will not supplant world organizations but rather will constitute the building blocks for the progressive, if slow, construction of more adequate world institutions and legal rules than the present ones.

(See also DIPLOMACY; GROTIUS, HUGO; INTERNATIONAL COOPERATION; REALISM; SOVEREIGNTY; UNITED NATIONS.)

Wolfgang Friedman, *The Changing Structures of International Law* (London, 1964). Richard A. Falk, *The Status of Law in International Society* (Princeton, N.J., 1970). Eduardo Jiménez de Aréchage, "International Law in the Last Third of a Century" *Hague Recueil* 159, no. 1 (1978). Antonio Cassese, *International Law in a Divided World* (Oxford, 1986). Richard A. Falk, *Revitalizing International Law* (Ames, Iowa, 1989). Thomas M. Franck, *The Power of Legitimacy among Nations* (New York, 1990). Antonio Cassese, "Violence, War and the Rule of Law in the International Community," in D. Held, ed., *Political Theory Today* (Cambridge, U.K., 1991), p. 255. Rosalyn Higgins, *Problems and Process: International Law and How We Use It* (Oxford, 1994). Ian Brownlie, *Principles of Public International Law*, 5th ed. (Oxford, 1998).

ANTONIO CASSESE
ANDREW CLAPHAM

of them do provide for the admission of limited numbers in specific categories which include the close relatives of citizens and legal residents; foreigners who have an ancestral link to the receiving country; persons who qualify as refugees and have no other place to go; and individuals with desirable skills, often for only a limited period of time. Overall, the overseas democracies (United States, Canada, Australia, New Zealand) maintain a somewhat more open door than the other industrialized states (Europe and Japan); but whereas the United States attributes the largest share of admissions on the basis of family reunion, reflecting the weight of ethnic groups close to the immigrant experience in its political process, the others allocate admissions on the basis of an elaborate "point" system in which economic considerations are more prominent. Most European countries recruited large numbers of temporary foreign workers during the boom years 1950–1973 and reluctantly allowed them to stay on permanently afterward; although they have sought to minimize new immigration, most of them recognize an obligation to permit residents to bring in family members. A few states have adopted explicit "laws of return" providing for the admission of people who qualify as nationals on the basis of ancestry; prominent examples are Israel with respect to those who qualify as Jews, and Germany with respect to the descendants of German emigrant settlers in eastern Europe and Russia.

The immigration policies of advanced industrial societies also tend to display a cyclical pattern of relative openness and restriction, shaped by fluctuating labor demand, which is itself increasingly determined by the dynamics of the *international political economy, as well as by a more general sense of confidence or insecurity in the future. These policies are interactive, in that the actions of any important receiver alter the situation faced by all others; and this tends to exacerbate the restrictionist trend in hard times. The most recent cycle was launched by the post–World War II boom; by the early 1970s, the foreign-born constituted about 7 percent of the population of the Western industrial world as a whole, with the singular exception of Japan, and a much larger proportion of its labor force. The restrictionist phase was triggered by the downturn of the 1970s and compounded by the escalating refugee crisis. Economic recovery in the 1990s and the prospect of aging populations has revived the call for both skilled and unskilled temporary foreign workers in a number of affluent industrial societies, notably the United States and Germany.

However, the immigration door is not easily slammed shut. Once flows have come into being, they tend to be self-sustaining because the networks that have been constituted facilitate additional movement; and liberal democracies are constrained from resorting to the draconian measures necessary to effectively close borders. Hence immigration continues to take place in hard times, often exacerbating "nativist" or xenophobic movements and parties. As barriers against ordinary immigration proliferated, some migrants tried their luck by filing an asylum claim; hence existing mechanisms for processing applications were rapidly overwhelmed, and the appearance of large numbers of questionable refugees further fueled xenophobic fires. This has led to a tightening of procedures, with deleterious consequences for some genuine refugees. In Europe, anti-immigrant sentiment focuses on the alleged unassimilability of Muslims; in the United States, on the formation of a Hispanic subculture and the alleged threat this might pose to national unity.

With only a handful of states still preventing their citizens from leaving, international migration today is being regulated mainly by the states to which people seek admission. As immigration policy worldwide is in the restrictive phase of the cycle, the gap between potential and actual migration has grown to huge proportions, resulting in the perception of an immigration crisis in the making. Although this sense of crisis has abated somewhat in the United States, it persists in Western Europe. Yet concurrently, barriers to movement are being lowered within the affluent segment of the world. In particular, the European Union has steadily dismantled its internal borders, affording to the citizens of its member states the possibility of living and working in any other state. This has the effect of transforming international migration into internal migration. If and when completed, this process would be tantamount to the creation of a rudimentary European citizenship and constitute a major transformation of the region's political organization.

(See also DEVELOPMENT AND UNDERDEVELOPMENT; EQUALITY AND INEQUALITY; GLOBALIZATION; HUMAN RIGHTS; MULTICULTURALISM; NINETEEN EIGHTY-NINE.)

Aristide R. Zolberg, Astri Suhrke, and Sergio Aguayo, *Escape from Violence: Conflict and the Refugee Crisis in the Developing World* (New York, 1989). Stephen Castles and Mark J. Miller, *The Age of Migration: International Population Movements in the Modern World* (New York, 1993). Wayne A. Cornelius, Philip L. Martin, and James F. Hollifield, *Controlling Immigration: A Global Perspective* (Stanford, 1994). Myron Weiner, *The Global Migration Crisis: Challenge to States and to Human Rights* (New York, 1995). Noah M. J. Pickus, ed., *Immigration and Citizenship in the Twenty-First Century* (Lanham, Md., 1998).

ARISTIDE R. ZOLBERG

INTERNATIONAL MONETARY FUND. The International Monetary Fund (IMF) is a central pillar of the postwar economic order established at the Bretton Woods Conference of 1944. It was designed to oversee the global rules governing money in general and adherence to orderly currency relations among the industrial countries in particular. It also was intended to be a lender of last resort for rich and poor countries alike. But the world for which the IMF was created has long ceased to exist and the IMF has found itself thrust into roles that were neither planned nor expected. Its primary mission has become to minister prescriptions to financially distressed economies, especially among the developing countries. In the process, it has acquired immense influence over the economic destinies of many countries. It also has acquired a reputation as an unrelenting disciplinarian whose programs and policies produce economic austerity, social unrest, and political instability. In its proclivity for becoming enmeshed in controversy, the IMF indeed is without peer among *international organizations. According to one claim, the *IMF has overthrown more governments than *Marx and Lenin combined.

Origins. The creation of the IMF reflected a reaction against the beggar-thy-neighbor practices such as currency restrictions and competitive devaluations that hobbled the world economy in the interwar period. It also represented the triumph of *Keynesianism, which called for greater activism by the state to maintain growth and employment and to cushion the domestic economy against external dislocations. The IMF's articles of agreement call on it to provide its members "the opportunity to correct maladjustments in their *balance of payments without resorting to measures destructive of national or international prosperity." It was enjoined, therefore, to dedicate itself to reducing the duration and intensity of upsets in international payments. Toward these ends, Britain, represented at Bretton Woods by none other than John Maynard Keynes, pushed for rules that would place the burden of adjustment to payments imbalances on surplus as well as deficit countries. Britain also argued for relatively automatic and generous access to a sizeable volume of liquidity. These demands, which would be voiced repeatedly by developing countries in subsequent decades, were resisted by the *United States, then the largest creditor state and the one with decisive influence over the essential elements of the monetary *regime. Although it became the first global agency to perform such a role, the IMF was endowed with only a modest amount of resources, to be used for short-term lending to countries running temporary payment problems. Access to these resources by any member was to be limited by a quota and, beyond a minimal threshold, governed by policy conditions, a principle that is now referred to as "conditionality."

To avert both the rigidities of the gold standard and the turbulence of the experiments with floating rates in the 1920s and 1930s, the architects of the monetary regime decided on relative exchange stability. Each member of the IMF was required to establish a par value for its currency defined in terms of gold. These fixed exchange rates could be altered to correct a "fundamental disequilibrium" (a term never precisely defined), but only upon consultation with and approval of the IMF. The Fund, in effect, was made the locus of the collective management of exchange rates. The code of behavior it was assigned to uphold also required liberal rules for international payments: Members were to dismantle multiple exchange rates and discriminatory currency arrangements and, after a transitional period, to adopt convertibility for current account transactions.

Evolving Roles in the World Economy. The early years of the IMF are forgettable. As the enormity of the task of postwar recovery became apparent, the IMF was relegated to the sidelines. The United States, rather than the IMF, emerged as the primary source of financing for Western Europe. Moreover, the IMF could do little to induce countries to eliminate currency restrictions—the transition to convertibility was not completed by the major European countries until 1958, and by Japan not until 1964. However, by the end of the 1950s the IMF started to emerge from the cold. It became a focal point of international monetary collaboration. It also came to occupy a central position in external assistance for balance of payments financing and began to exercise, in more credible fashion, its authority to supervise the exchange practices of its members.

In the 1960s worries about a future liquidity shortage led to efforts to provide an alternative to what had become the primary form of global money, the U.S. dollar. These efforts led to the creation in 1969 by the IMF of the world's first artificial reserve asset, Special Drawing Rights (SDRs), to be allocated to members in proportion to their quotas in the Fund. By then, however, the world faced a problem of excessive liquidity, due to the outflow of dollars brought about by the large external deficits of the United States. The regime of pegged exchange rates the IMF had been charged with overseeing came under considerable strain and finally collapsed on 15 August 1971 when the United States suspended convertibility of the dollar into gold. The IMF was eclipsed in both the initial but abortive attempts to reform the old regime and in the ensuing struggle to build a successor regime that would give the United States greater freedom of maneuver. That successor, formally sanctioned in the 1978 second amendment of the IMF articles of agreement, legalized what had evolved since 1973: floating exchange rates. The choice of exchange systems was left up to the discretion of each member. The IMF was asked to exercise "firm surveillance" over exchange rate policies, but was given few binding rules to enforce this function, let alone any means of shaping the policies of the dominant economies.

In the 1970s, the IMF's role in balance of payments financing was undermined as well. The international capital markets assumed the task of recycling the massive surpluses of the *Organization of Petroleum Exporting Countries (OPEC), thereby becoming for the first time in the postwar years the principal instrument of lending for sovereign borrowers. Developed and developing countries alike, seeking to escape the strictures associated with conditional financing from the IMF, turned to private banks with alacrity. The industrial countries, which traditionally accounted for the bulk of IMF's lending, ceased to be borrowers altogether before the end of the decade. On the other hand, most of the developing countries that turned to the Fund for conditional lending were ones that were not sufficiently creditworthy to qualify for commercial finance. For an organization that already had been stripped of many of its functions in the monetary regime, the prospect of marginalization was very real. The IMF responded by expanding access to its resources, granting multiyear loans to allow longer periods for adjustment, and also by relaxing its conditionality provisions. However, the venture in liberalized lending was short-lived as the IMF, bowing to pressures from the *Reagan administration, reverted to its standard posture.

The predicament of the IMF at the beginning of the 1980s was captured by the title of a survey in *The Economist* (26 September 1981): "Ministry without Portfolio." From an institutional standpoint, the declaration by Mexico in August 1982 that it was unable to service its external debt was a windfall. The IMF was called upon to assist in mounting a rescue operation that would be repeated as many other developing countries, beset by a convergence of external economic shocks and prolonged fiscal mismanagement, followed Mexico into bankruptcy. The IMF became the pivot in the strategy for managing the debt crisis. The rescheduling of not only official but also private debt was made contingent on the negotiation of an adjustment program with the IMF. For a while, the agency even was able to use its muscle to press commercial banks to extend new financing to debtor states. At the same time, however, it emphasized the sanctity of existing obligations and insisted that the debtors maintain full and timely servicing of their bank debts. Otherwise, recalcitrants were to be denied access to its own credits. The Fund tipped the balance of bargaining power away from the debtors, so much so that it incurred the charge that it was serving as a collection agency for the banks.

The IMF was instrumental in defusing one of the most severe threats to the stability of the postwar international financial system. Its intervention helped to avert a rash of defaults and moratoria, a rupture in relations between creditor and debtor states, and a collapse by any of the major banks. However, the debt crisis also revealed the limits of the influence of the IMF. Its presence was not enough to induce the banks to continue with "concerted"—i.e., involuntary—lending. Instead, the banks gradually reduced their exposure in developing countries and soon went into wholesale retreat. Nor did the measures orchestrated through the IMF enhance the debtors' capabilities for a quick resumption of growth or return to creditworthiness. On the contrary, to service their debts most debtors had to undergo a wrenching adjustment, strangling imports, slashing investment and consumption, and thereby shrinking their economies. For Latin America, as for sub-Saharan Africa, the 1980s became the "lost decade" of development.

All in all, the task of managing the debt crisis posed a mixed blessing for the IMF. On the one hand, it checked the institution's slide toward obsolescence. On the other hand, it dragged the IMF into numerous controversies from which it, like the debtors, could not readily disengage. While the IMF was critical in containing the debt crisis, it did not succeed in resolving it. Unwittingly, by providing the organizational infrastructure for policies of muddling through, it even may have prolonged it. Only toward the end of the decade, as the strategy of debt restructuring began to unravel, was the IMF enlisted to offer financial support for debt reduction. Even then, however, the IMF ventured into financing debt reduction schemes with caution, given fears of the transfer of risk from private creditors. The travails of debtor states also left the IMF with a worry of a yet more immediate and personal nature: as it began the 1990s, arrears to its coffers approached a record $5 billion. By then, the IMF had become transformed from a temporary to a permanent source of financing for many countries, a role far removed from its original mandate in the world economy. Yet ironically, during most of the 1980s, as claims on its loans fell due, the IMF took more resources out of the *Third World than it put in, thereby itself becoming a net drain for debtor states. The Fund had evolved into the executor of a bargain that struck many of these states as improbable: policy reforms with conditions that were stiffening in return for external support that was dwindling.

The 1990s proved to be even more tumultuous for the IMF. The decade saw the IMF insinuate itself more intrusively and more forcefully in the process of economic reform in borrowing countries. It pushed, often with messianic ardor, the agenda of liberalization codified in the "Washington Consensus" and extended its traditional involvement in macroeconomic policy and behavior to issues of "good governance," including increasing transparency and accountability, reducing public sector *corruption, promoting the rule of law, and securing property rights. In words and in deeds, it emphasized the virtues of untrammeled financial markets, both national and global, and pushed its members to dismantle controls on capital movements. The decade also saw a substantial expansion in the IMF's volume of lending to developing countries, facilitated by several major increases in its funding and borrowing resources. By 2000, it had lending programs in more than 50 countries. Having taken the lead in integrating into the world economy the former *communist party-

states of Eastern and Central Europe, the IMF was designated as the instrument for guiding the transition of the countries that emerged from the breakup of the Soviet Union. This mission, which entailed nothing less than a transformation from socialist *command economy to market-based *capitalism, left the organization with an extremely checkered record. While it can plausibly claim to have contributed to the achievement of an irreversible transformation in the economies of Hungary and Poland, its experiences in the most important of the "transition economies," Russia, were little short of disastrous. What was dubbed as "the rescue of the century" turned into an embarrassment. The IMF persisted with the delivery of sizeable financing packages to the *Yeltsin regime in the late 1990s even after it became clear the regime had reneged on its commitments to the Fund and even when, by its own accounts, it discovered it had been lied to by the Russian central bank. Nor did the IMF reverse course in Russia after it witnessed the plunder of the state by the "oligarchs" through the *privatization of oil and gas companies, or after the government defaulted on its obligations to foreign bondholders.

However, no episode in the IMF's history left it with so many scars as did its handling of the Asian financial crisis of 1997–99. The eruption of the crisis was unsettling in itself as it occurred in countries whose economic fundamentals had been certified by the IMF as basically sound. Among them were the overachievers of the Third World, the IMF's own star pupils who had followed many of the nostrums about "market-friendly" policies, including its prescriptions for freedom of capital inflows and outflows, and who had become the darlings of "emerging market" investment managers. As the panic in financial markets that began in Thailand spread to Indonesia and the Republic of Korea (South Korea) (and yet later to Russia and Brazil), the IMF stepped in to contain the contagion. It assembled rescue packages of a scale that dwarfed anything it had attempted in the past—well over $100 billion for the first three of these countries alone. The magnitude of these resources, which were used mainly to repay foreign creditors, was matched by the scope of the policy changes it extracted in return. The IMF imposed its classical deflationary prescriptions such as increases in interest rates and reductions in public spending. These measures were draconian and helped to plunge the economies into recession, driving businesses into bankruptcy, and creating widespread unemployment. The economic dislocations also sparked political and social unrest which, in at least one country, Indonesia under Suharto, paved the way for regime collapse. In addition, the IMF seized on the occasion to push for a variety of reforms to curb "crony capitalism": in South Korea, to loosen the links between the state and the *chaebols* (conglomerates); in Indonesia, to dissolve agricultural monopolies. The prescriptions drew fire from many sources, including the *World Bank. The austerity measures, in particular, were widely seen as inappropriate for economies that did not fit the mold of the reckless or the insolvent cases commonly confronted by the IMF: None of the countries at the epicenter of the crisis was suffering from a major bout of inflation or a runaway fiscal deficit; the debt problems each of them faced was that of the private, not public, sector; and, moreover, all of them had unusually high savings rates. The IMF's own postmortems on the crisis admit that some its actions may have added fuel to the fire. Its insistence on the closure of sixteen troubled banks in Indonesia, for example, is seen as having helped to trigger a full-scale banking panic, sending depositors to withdraw their funds even form sound financial institutions and accelerating the plunge of the rupiah.

The Asian financial crisis provided a stark reminder to all the actors, not the least to the IMF itself, of the costs and risks associated with the financial *globalization it had championed. The crisis raised fresh doubts about the capacity of the IMF to cope with the effects of a sudden exodus of foreign private capital from a developing country, a novel shock that was first encountered, albeit in less virulent form, in the Mexican peso crisis of 1994–95. The Asian financial crisis also raised to the fore a question that is likely to be asked with increasing frequency in the years ahead: is the IMF, as presently constituted, a necessity or an obstacle in a task as daunting as the management of international economic turbulence?

Organizational and Financial Structure. The IMF has been aptly compared to a credit union: every member makes a contribution to a pool of funds and can then draw on them when the need arises. Central to its operation is the quota assigned to each member country. Quotas determine the size of a member's financial contribution, known as a subscription; its voting power in the IMF's decision making bodies; the "access limits" or amounts it is entitled to borrow; and its share of SDR allocations. The size of individual quotas, in turn, is determined by a complex formula that measures each country's relative weight in the world economy, and by political bargaining. Quotas are adjusted periodically, typically as part of agreements on boosting the IMF's capital base. These have been increasingly protracted and contentious exercises as they as they entail not only fresh outlays of funds but also potential changes in pecking orders.

The stratification of power among states has been one of overwhelming continuity: the IMF has remained the preserve of the powerful and the affluent even as its membership, 182 strong by 2000, has expanded to include virtually every country. The most notable changes have consisted of reshuffling within an existing hierarchy—specifically the Group of 5 (the United States, Germany, Japan, Britain, and France)—rather than the emergence of a new hierarchy. Even in the formal attributes of power, the United States continues to command a preponderance. Thus, while its voting share has declined from more than one-third to less than one-fifth, the United States still has more than enough votes to prevent a change in the structure of the organization or in the distribution of quotas, two decisions that require a majority of 85 percent. A variety of other decisions require a majority of 70 percent. These super majorities, which have become more pronounced as the ranks of developing countries in the Fund have grown, effectively preclude actions that violate the preferences of the industrial countries.

While voting shares are fought over zealously, the prevailing practice has been not to resort to voting. Decisions typically are adopted by consensus. Moreover, on numerous policy issues, including the design of lending programs, the staff of the agency enjoys substantial autonomy. The staff, numbering close to 3,000, is headed by the managing director who, as part of a convention that balances the consignment of the presidency of the World Bank as an American fiefdom, is a European national. But even in the appointment of the latter the United States has a de facto veto, as it demonstrated

in 1999 during the tortuous selection of a successor to Michel Camdessus. There has been one exception to the exclusivity of the North in the inner circle: Saudi Arabia. It has been co-opted by virtue of becoming a major supplier of borrowed resources, which, after subscriptions, are the primary source of the Fund's liquid assets. Along with the Group of 5 countries, Saudi Arabia, China, and Russia each has its own seat on the twenty-four-member board of executive directors, who are responsible for overseeing the day-to-day business of the organization. The other sixteen directors are elected as representatives of motley country groupings. The majority of countries, therefore, have no direct representation in the organization. The executive directors formally derive their authority from the board of governors, the supreme policy-making organ, composed of ministers of finance or heads of central banks of each member, who meet once a year.

The IMF has crafted a complex amalgam of procedures and mechanisms to govern access to its lending resources. This access is expressed in terms of tranches, each equivalent to 25 percent of a country's quota. The first of these, the so-called "reserve tranche," can be withdrawn automatically, much like a demand deposit. The next, the first of four "credit tranches," also is available with minimal conditions. Access to the next three, referred to as the "upper credit" tranches, is more demanding as it is conditional on the conclusion of a stabilization program with the IMF. Early in its history, the IMF developed the "standby arrangement" as its main vehicle of conditional financing. The arrangement authorizes a country experiencing balance of payments difficulties to draw, in installments, a line of credit, subject to adherence to measures stipulated in the stabilization program. The loans have a short-term focus, typically of one year, and are repayable within three to five years, a period that in some cases can be extended up to ten years.

Over the years, the IMF has adapted its financing modalities in an effort to cope with altered circumstances. In 1963, it set up the Compensatory Financing Facility (CFF) to help countries, especially primary producers, experiencing shortfalls in export earnings for reasons beyond their control. In 1969, it created a Buffer Stock Financing Facility to allow members to contribute to schemes designed to stabilize prices of individual commodities. These two facilities established the precedent for increasing access to financing beyond the limits set by credit tranches. In 1981, the CFF was expanded to assist countries facing payment difficulties brought about by higher cereal import costs. The scope of the CFF was broadened yet again in 1988 when it was replaced by the Compensatory and Contingency Financing Facility (CCFF), a mechanism intended to cover additional external shocks such as higher world interest rates.

Other, more temporary, facilities have been devised in response to economic contingencies. In the wake of the first oil shock, two one-year oil facilities were installed in 1974 and 1975 to provide additional financing to both developed and developing countries. Of greater durability is the Extended Fund Facility (EFF), introduced in 1974 to provide balance of payments support for longer periods than those under traditional standbys. EFF loans are intended to support medium-term programs, generally running over three years, and are repayable over a maximum of ten years. In establishing the EFF, the IMF acknowledged the principle that the payment problems of many developing countries are "structural" in nature and, hence, that they require longer periods of adjustment. That same principle is embodied in the Structural Adjustment Facility (SAF) and in the Enhanced Structural Adjustment Facility (ESAF). Both facilities, created in the 1980s, have been geared toward adjustment programs with longer horizons. The programs are drawn up in negotiations with both the IMF and the World Bank. Compared to most IMF loans, which are at market terms, SAF and ESAF credits were made extraordinarily concessional, carrying annual interest charges of only 0.5 percent. The borrowers have been without exception the poorest countries. The ESAF became the primary vehicle for lending to these countries and the preoccupation with poverty became yet more explicit when it later was renamed the Poverty Reduction and Growth Facility (PRGF).

The financial contagions of the 1990s paved the way for the creation of additional financing structures under the control of the IMF. In 1997, a Supplemental Reserve Facility (SRF) was established to provide short-term assistance to countries struck by a sudden and disruptive loss of market confidence. The SRF is targeted at countries in the throes of a crisis that poses a systemic threat. By contrast, the Contingency Credit Line (CCL), founded in 1999, is designed to forestall such a crisis by offering a commitment of support in advance to a prequalifying country. Both facilities pose an amalgam of incentives and disincentives to borrowers and creditors alike. That the IMF would be designated for managing such initiatives is indicative of the importance its powerful shareholders continue to attach to the institution.

The 1990s also saw a further recasting of the IMF's financing modalities. All along, the Fund had selectively loosened the links between quota size and borrowing ceilings in order to allow countries expanded access to its resources. The links were severed altogether with the Asian financial crisis: the rescue package for South Korea, for instance, was almost twenty times its quota.

The IMF Under Assault. The IMF has been subjected to a mounting barrage of criticism in recent decades. From the halls of Congress to the boardrooms of Wall Street, from eminent economists on the right to equally eminent ones on the left, from *human rights activists to labor group protestors— the voices demanding that the IMF be leashed or shut down altogether have grown more numerous and more strident. The IMF is accused of being a power unto itself, unhampered by external restraints on its behavior, and unaccountable for the costs of its flawed policies. It is accused of trampling on national *sovereignty, perpetuating a new *imperialism by imposing Western economic and cultural values, subverting democratic processes in economically beleaguered countries, while cloaking its own decisions in a mantle of secrecy. It is accused of creating moral hazard by encouraging, through expectations of the prospect of publicly supported bailouts, private lenders and investors to engage in excessive risk taking and government authorities in borrowing countries to undertake imprudent economic policies. It is accused of being a tool of the advanced industrial countries, relentlessly pursuing the dominant economic orthodoxy of the day, while harboring a myopic view of political and social realities in developing countries and turning a blind eye on the hardships produced by its demands. For many of the latter countries,

the decision to turn to the IMF is an act of desperation and the negotiations with it an exercise in brinkmanship. To them the Fund has become a lender of last resort in literal and ironical sense.

Of all the failings for which the IMF has been castigated, its conditionality policies and practices have been paramount. The issue has become more intractable and pronounced in recent decades as its low-conditionality lending has all but vanished. Indeed, by the 1980s, Keynes' warnings about the danger of the IMF becoming a "grandmotherly" organization had been amply realized. Conditionality affects every major facet of a stabilization or *structural adjustment program a borrower is expected to undertake in return for a loan. It is formalized in a letter of intent to the IMF and codified in a set of "performance criteria" expressed in quantitative ceilings and targets. Compliance with these conditions is the test for continued access to the loan; a breach, on the other hand, normally triggers its suspension, an eventuality that often leads to a new round of negotiations over a new program. While there are variations from case to case, there is remarkable continuity in the contents. The standard measures—often branded as the "bitter medicine"—consist of limitations on credit expansion, reductions in government spending, restriction on public sector wages and employment, increases in taxes or user fees, and devaluation of the national currency. The focus, therefore, is preponderantly on demand restraint. The IMF's foray into structural adjustment has entailed a concern with objectives that go beyond stabilizing balance of payments. Hence, Fund programs have increasingly incorporated supply side measures such as trade liberalization and financial reform. But such measures, intended to improve economic efficiency and expand productive capacity, are a complement to, not a substitute for, macroeconomic stabilization. The same applies to the building of social safety nets and other measures designed to mitigate the effects of austerity. Such measures also do not usually comprise the core of conditionality.

At least five major lines of criticism have been leveled against IMF conditionality. First, critics accuse the IMF of applying simplistic, largely monetarist, diagnoses of and prescriptions for the problems facing developing countries. Operationally, they hold, its policies tend to assume that the causes of balance of payments problems are a function of government mismanagement and profligacy; consequently, the Fund downplays both the external origins of payment disturbances and the structural rigidities of developing economies. Secondly, and relatedly, they charge it with making a fetish of instruments that often are misguided or perverse. For example, it has been shown, in settings where exports cannot be increased quickly, devaluation can produce recessionary and inflationary outcomes with no benefits to the balance of payments. Thirdly, the Fund is castigated for insisting on large and swift changes in policy. Instead of more gradual and flexible adjustments, it has shown a strong penchant for shock treatments that, to many, amount to overkill, destabilizing countries both economically and politically. Fourthly, the IMF is criticized for resorting to a spurious precision in devising performance criteria. Targets and ceilings tend to be set rigidly, and in pinpoint fashion, even though the analytical foundations may be wobbly. Yet a fifth contention is that the IMF has neglected the distributional implications of its lending policies. In particular, it is taken to task for doing little to cushion the impact on the poorer segments of the population who are most likely to be hurt by higher prices for staples, cutbacks in health spending, and other hardships that commonly accompany stabilization and adjustment programs.

Few elements of this indictment are wanting in substantiation. In words and in deeds, the IMF provides daily grist for the mill of its critics. For many, the spectacle of IMF president Michel Camdessus standing with arms folded in January 1998 as he watched and embattled Indonesian President Suharto sign the agreements that would hasten his downfall will remain an enduring testimony to the imperiousness of the IMF. For others, the IMF's persistent exhortations about the removal of restrictions on capital flows, even in countries lacking the necessary regulatory and monitoring safeguards, are emblematic of its abundant capacity for policy malpractice. However, these indictments frequently overlook more complex realities. Many of the IMF's actions and inactions reflect the conflicting pressures to which the organization has been subjected. To wit, the IMF has faced competing demands from different quarters for widening and narrowing the scope of surveillance and conditionality on issues of poverty alleviation, income distribution, human rights, and environmental protection. It is largely at the behest of its most powerful shareholders that it began to tackle these issues. It is this dominant coalition of *Group of 7 countries that has determined and continues to determine what the IMF can and cannot do. And it is to these same countries that many of its failings are ultimately ascribable, such as its inability to pursue a countercyclical lending policy in the 1980s when developing countries faced the worst economic crisis since the Great Depression, or its failure to make much headway in providing relief for the poorest debtors under the so-called Initiative for Heavily Indebted Poor Countries (HIPC), which it launched with the World Bank in 1996. That the burden of adjustment continues to be borne by the economically distressed countries, or that private investors and lenders are able to deflect pressures to be "bailed in" during financial crises, also are not limitations for which the IMF is itself responsible.

Unsurprisingly, a good deal of the behavior of the IMF has been a response to the dictates of its most powerful paymaster, the United States. For example, it was under pressure from the Treasury Department and the White House that the IMF mounted the successive lending packages to Russia in the 1990s. IMF officials had few illusions about their ability to alter the economic landscape of Russia after the collapse of *communism. They were more than a little skeptical about the intentions of Russian authorities to adhere to their reform pledges to the Fund. The likelihood that any financial resources the IMF marshalled would be misused did not escape them, either. However, as was the case with the assistance it was asked to give in earlier decades to the regime of Ferdinand *Marcos in the Philippines or that of Mobutu Sese Seko of Zaire, the IMF had little choice but to accommodate the interests of Western powers, particularly the United States, in Russia.

Some of the controversies that have mired the IMF are inevitable. Countries typically approach the IMF much like a patient on a stretcher—after a crisis has erupted, after a currency has plunged, after deficits have soared, after reserves have been depleted, after banks have failed, after capital has taken flight, or after the threshold of default has been crossed. In such circumstances rarely is there a pain-free cure that will allow the patient to quickly stand on his own feet again. However, in such circumstances the presence of the IMF also can serve as a convenient scapegoat for less than popular reforms. Revealingly, while most Indonesians and Koreans were inclined to cast the IMF as the villain during the Asian contagion, some saw it as a savior, forcing through a necessary, long overdue, reform agenda that would not have been enacted otherwise.

In addition, the IMF has been more flexible in its thinking and behavior than its detractors would allow. Its notions of what is preferable and what is feasible in the realm of economic policy-making has continued to evolve. Its conceptions of development has been considerably more eclectic than the presumed fixation with *monetarism would suggest. It has evinced growing concern with questions of political sustainability and distributive consequences. It has also become less doctrinaire in its application of conditionality, paying heed to policy changes that are likely to allow for growth and judging progress not merely by numerical targets but also by qualitative criteria. A chastened IMF, having acknowledged that some of its policies caused more harm than good, has tempered some of its strictures after the Asian financial crisis: it has conceded that liberalization is not an unqualified blessing and that some countries may stand to gain by imposing controls on capital outflows or taxes on capital inflows. It has relaxed its longstanding proscriptions against budget deficits; it also has abandoned its taboo against lending to countries that have defaulted on external obligations. It even has swallowed some of its own prescriptions for financial transparency: the IMF now routinely publishes on its website (http://www.imf.org) letters of intent and policy framework papers once treated as matters of high secrecy.

To a large extent, such adaptations constitute an exercise in damage control. They do not resolve the crisis of credibility facing the IMF. The managers of the IMF have been acutely mindful of the mismatch between its authority and its *legitimacy. The poor track record of the IMF's lending programs—the institution's foremost product—remains a glaring reminder of the limits of the reach of the IMF. A wealth of studies, including some conducted by the agency itself, have arrived at a similar finding: the record of compliance in Fund programs is weak and has grown weaker over time. In the majority of developing countries, failure of implementation has been the norm. Moreover, the economic performance of countries that do adhere to the performance criteria has not been dramatically different from that of countries that do not. And its vaunted power notwithstanding, the IMF's ability to influence the implementation of adjustment programs has been marginal despite the fact that most developing countries have faced a dearth of alternatives to the IMF.

Prospects. Long before the IMF reached its fiftieth birthday in 1994, it was a markedly different institution from the one founded at Bretton Woods. In its relations with the developed countries, it was but a shadow of its past self. It had been reduced to a helpless bystander in the process of macroeconomic coordination among the Group of 7. These leading industrial powers showed little enthusiasm about engaging the IMF in the deals they struck with each other on monetary and fiscal policies. Over these countries, the Fund's surveillance function is dead and is destined to remain so as long as they do not need to turn to it as supplicants. For the foreseeable future, the prospect of the IMF becoming a global central bank—once the hope of some, the fear of others—also is remote at best.

In the developing countries, the IMF continues to act as the guardian of economic orthodoxy, even though it often finds itself preempted in that role by its twin across the street, the World Bank. It is likely to remain the certifier of economic rectitude, providing the seal of approval that other actors have come to demand before lending to or investing in most developing countries. However, the Fund is also likely to have to contend with a growing number of recalcitrants, among whom Malaysia during the Asian crisis may be the forerunner, who have the wherewithal and the determination not to turn to it for help in economic restructuring.

The IMF will also face greater demands for its own restructuring. The advent of a new century saw a flurry of initiatives for reforming the IMF; at the same time, the IMF found itself at the center of a host of proposals for reforming the "international financial architecture." There was a widely shared sense that the IMF had become overextended and overburdened and, hence, that it needed to return to its original mandate and concentrate on preventing and mitigating financial crises, especially liquidity and banking crises, leaving such tasks as reducing poverty to the World Bank. There was a robust consensus on the need for the IMF to disengage from the enterprise of long-term and repeated lending, especially to countries able to attract private capital. There also was substantial agreement on the need to limit the scope and the depth of conditionality. While many of the reform blueprints called for reducing the mission of the IMF, others went in the opposite direction and called for expanding its purview, making it a focal point, for example, on codes of principles for corporate governance and in international consultations among financial regulators. On the other hand, with the return of stability to financial markets at the end of the 1990s, the more ambitious elements in the agenda to redesign the international financial system—such as the formation of an international bankruptcy mechanism to handle workouts between creditors and debtors, or the creation of a full-fledged international lender of last resort—dissipated quietly but quickly, as did the likelihood of major changes in the political governance of the IMF itself.

The reality is that the leading powers in the world economy have too much of a stake in existing arrangements to show much appetite for reinventing the IMF or for charting a new Bretton Woods. For these actors, the IMF remains a preferred instrument for coping with financial crises. Hence, while the schemes for alternatives proliferate, the prospects are for incremental tinkering rather than wholesale restructuring. The prospects also tend to favor ad hoc, case-by-case treatment of financial crises through existing channels rather than generalized solutions through new instrumentalities and new modalities. Consequently, there have been few serious efforts to alter the burdens of adjustment in payments, currency, debt, or banking crises. The stakes of the powerful are also likely to ensure that in the decades immediately ahead the IMF will continue to occupy the position of *primus inter pares* in the hierarchy of international financial institutions. But that po-

sition will not resolve the larger issues affecting the role of the IMF in a world in which the globalization of financial markets has increased the vulnerability of countries to external disturbances that can be transmitted virulently by private actors over which it has no control. Nor will it settle the yet larger question of its role in international economic governance in the twenty-first century.

(See also DEVELOPMENT AND UNDERDEVELOPMENT; FINANCE, INTERNATIONAL; INTERNATIONAL DEBT; INTERNATIONAL POLITICAL ECONOMY; NORTH-SOUTH RELATIONS.)

Richard N. Gardner, *Sterling-Dollar Diplomacy in Current Perspective* (New York, 1980). John Williamson, ed., *IMF Conditionality* (Washington, D.C., 1989). Tony Killick, ed., *The Quest for Economic Stabilization: The IMF and the Third World* (New York, 1984). Catherine Gwin et. al., *The International Monetary Fund in a Multipolar World: Pulling Together* (Washington, D.C. 1989). Bretton Woods Commission, *Bretton Woods: Looking to the Future* (Washington, D.C., 1994). Graham Bird, *IMF Lending to Developing Countries: Issues and Evidence* (London, 1995). Richard H.R. Harper, *Inside the IMF: An Ethnography of Documents, Technology and Organisational Action* (San Diego, 1998). Barry J. Eichengreen, *Toward a New Financial Architecture: A Practical Post-Asia Agenda* (Washington, D.C., 1999).

DON BABAI

INTERNATIONAL ORGANIZATIONS. One marked change in *international relations over the past century has been the dramatic increase in the number of international organizations. The advent of intergovernmental organizations (IGOs) is often traced to the founding of the International Telegraph Union in 1865 although there was a small number of limited membership bodies before that date. In 1909 there were only thirty-seven IGOs and 176 international nongovernmental organizations (NGOs); the respective figures today are around 400 and 5,000. There has also been a tremendous increase in the number of congresses and conferences that IGOs sponsor. In the middle of the nineteenth century there were about two to three such meetings a year; today there are close to 4,000 annually.

International organizations are particularly important in international relations because they generally constitute the central decision-making components of international *regimes and influence the development of these regimes. International regimes are systems of norms and rules in particular issue areas that regulate state behavior and decision making. Without the permanent decision-making institutions of international organizations the growth of *international cooperation to manage international *interdependence would be greatly curtailed.

There are four main types of voting arrangements (or requirements for the approval of decisions) in international organizations: unanimity, majority rule, selective majorities, and weighted voting. Throughout most of the nineteenth century IGOs had a voting rule of unanimity; that is, the support of all member states was required for the passage of resolutions. In the latter part of the nineteenth century some organizations began to pass recommendations by qualified majorities (usually two-thirds of the membership). In the twentieth century more organizations have been allowed to pass recommendations by majority votes, but states also have accepted selective-majority or weighted-voting formulas for legally binding resolutions. These formulas have specified that certain powerful states must give their consent to organizational decisions and/or that states' votes in the organizations should be weighted according to their importance in the issue area. For example, the UN Security Council requires that the five permanent members support or do not vote against a resolution, and the *International Monetary Fund (IMF) and *World Bank distribute votes largely according to states' financial contributions and require different majorities depending on the importance of the issues. In other words, power realities are integrated into the decision-making formulas of IGOs when their decisions are binding on member states.

There are four key functions or roles of IGOs in the development of international regimes: the facilitation of agreements, the altering of states' and nongovernmental actors' influence in the formation and implementation of regimes, the promotion of compliance with regime rules, and the legitimation of particular ideologies or international practices.

A central function of international organizations is that they facilitate the development of regimes and particular cooperative activities. Without permanent headquarters and secretariats and regularly scheduled meetings it would be very difficult for states to collaborate to the extent that they do. States could, of course, organize ad hoc meetings to deal with particular problems, but there certainly would not be the volume of meetings and accords that there are as a result of the presence of permanent organizations.

A second function of international organizations is that they alter the distribution of influence in international decision making and hence the nature of acceptable regimes. IGOs provide the large number of small and weak states with the opportunity to use their voting power to secure accords they could not ordinarily achieve. Since the 1960s most of these states have been developing or *Third World countries, and they have used their ability to pass and/or block resolutions to extract concessions from the developed world. Overall the process of coalition building to secure adequate backing for regimes or specific resolutions is now an integral part of international politics. Another notable feature of the decision-making process in many international organizations is the prominence of secretariat personnel. They are often the source of technical information, and they sometimes act in a mediatory capacity.

A third role concerns international organizations' promotion of compliance with accords, and these activities can be divided into explicit and implicit roles. The explicit roles concern the gathering of information on the compliance of states and nongovernmental actors with agreements and the settlement of disputes over the terms of the accords. In some organizations there are permanent dispute settlement institutions and/or procedures for the creation of dispute settlement bodies. International organizations sometimes apply *sanctions against states that do not comply with regime rules or organizational decisions (an example being the UN Security Council), but on the whole the application of sanctions and enforcement activities are left to the informal coordination of policies among member states.

International organizations sometimes perform an implicit role in the promotion of compliance—largely through the regulation of problems that must be managed for a particular regime to be politically acceptable. That is to say, states will be predisposed to violate regimes governing certain aspects of an issue area if other regimes are not created to manage other aspects. An example is what a number of international organizations have done to support the existence of free-access jurisdictional regimes for the oceans, airspace, and outer *space. They have established regulatory systems to prevent damages to the parties involved and to third parties while operating in the three nonterrestrial areas. Without such regulatory arrangements states would extend their jurisdictions into these regions in order to control damages to themselves and others.

International organizations also legitimate particular international practices and ideologies. This particular function is one that has been highlighted by neo-Marxist writers concerned with relations between developed and developing countries, but it is not confined to them. A frequently heard argument is that international organizations under the sway of the developed capitalist powers utilize their control of financial resources and information flows to legitimate particular domestic and international economic practices. In the words of Antonio *Gramsci, they promote "ideological *hegemony."

Proponents of the three major theoretical traditions in international relations (*realism, *liberalism, and neo-Marxism) have different perspectives on these four roles and on the significance of international organizations in global politics. Realists are rather pessimistic about prospects for significant international collaboration and do not attribute to international organizations any significant influence on international regimes. At most they might see such organizations as rather weak facilitators of agreements on regimes and of the most powerful states' hegemony in international relations.

Neo-Marxists for the most part share this perspective on the lack of importance of international organizations in global politics in that they see the hegemony of the most powerful capitalist powers as the central feature of global politics. However, some neo-Marxists are more likely than realists to stress the role of international organizations in facilitating (or legitimating) the hegemony of the most powerful countries—in their case, the dominance of the capitalist powers (the core) over the weaker developing states (the periphery). After the states in the periphery overthrow the hegemony of the core states, some neo-Marxists would probably project an expanded role for international organizations built on common interests among most peoples, but they do not predict such a development in the short run.

Those scholars who are most receptive to attributing important roles to international organizations are liberals. While liberals as a group differ in some important ways, they see international organizations as important in leading states to understand mutualities of interest, to acquire new values, and to learn the benefits of cooperation. Liberals also regard international organizations as important facilitators of the predominance of certain *ideologies—particularly economic liberalism and internationalism. In their view many international organizations that have been created in the post-1945 era (for example, the IMF and World Bank) have had significant impacts on the institutionalization of liberal economic and political values in international regimes.

(See also INTERNATIONAL POLITICAL ECONOMY; LAW OF THE SEA; NORTH-SOUTH RELATIONS; UNITED NATIONS.)

Inis L. Claude, Jr., *Swords into Plowshares: The Problems and Progress of International Organization*, 4th ed. (New York, 1970). Stephen D. Krasner, *International Regimes* (Ithaca, N.Y., 1983). Harold K. Jacobson, *Networks of Interdependence: International Organizations and the Global Political System*, 2d ed. (New York, 1984). Ernst B. Haas, *When Knowledge Is Power: Three Models of Change in International Organizations* (Berkeley, Calif., 1990).

MARK W. ZACHER

INTERNATIONAL POLITICAL ECONOMY. Concerned with the political determinants of international economic relations, international political economy tries to answer such questions as: How have changes in the international distribution of power among *states affected the degree of openness in the international trading system? Do the domestic political economies of some states allow them to compete more effectively in international markets? Is the relative poverty of the *Third World better explained by indigenous conditions in individual countries or by some attribute of the international economic system? When can international economic ties among states be used for political leverage?

Some History. During the 1950s and 1960s *international relations as a field of study and a matter of public policy was concerned primarily with *security. The *Cold War dominated the interest of scholars and the attention of policymakers. International economic issues were a secondary concern. Between East and West economic transactions were highly politicized and tightly controlled. Among the countries of the West economic disputes were muted. The rules of the game and the patterns of international economic transactions were taken as given. There were only a few isolated scholars working on questions related to the political determinants of international economic relations.

Attention devoted to international political economy increased dramatically after 1970 for several reasons, some intellectual and academic, others related to political events. For the United States, things began to go awry. The U.S. balance of payments deficit increased in the late 1960s under the burden of the *Great Society and the *Vietnam War. The deficit prompted the *Nixon administration to initiate a chain of events that destroyed the postwar international monetary system based on the 1944 Bretton Woods Agreements. The U.S. decision first to suspend gold payments in August 1971, and ultimately to accept a system of flexible exchange rates, made it evident that international economic relations involved political choices and not just technical calculations. The quadrupling of oil prices in 1973–1974 drove home the fact that the United States was inextricably involved in a world economy which it could neither isolate itself from nor unilaterally control.

Attention to international political economy was further reinforced by academic developments. The old agenda of international politics had become exhausted. The study of international organization had not moved beyond an arid formality practiced by specialists in *international law. Economics as an academic discipline increasingly came to emphasize mathematical modeling as opposed to the study of specific empirical developments.

Hence, many developments—the *Organization of Petroleum Exporting Countries (OPEC) and the rise of oil prices, the collapse of the Bretton Woods monetary system, the demands of the Third World for a *New International Economic Order—were not being investigated by either political scientists or economists. This academic gap was a major incentive for the development of international political economy as a distinct field of study. There is no consensus about how developments in international political economy should be explained. Analysts have pointed to the international distribution of power, the importance of mutual self-interest, class interests, and domestic political structures as explanations for outcomes in the world economy. The four major theoretical approaches to the field have been *realism, *liberalism, *Marxism, and domestic politics.

Realism. Realism makes the following basic assumptions: 1) The constituting actors in the *international system are sovereign states. 2) The international system is in a state of anarchy: there is no accepted political authority; states engage in self-help. 3) States must be primarily concerned with their own security and therefore with relative rather than absolute standing. A state must have the power to, at a minimum, protect its territorial and political integrity. 4) States are rational unified actors. Domestic politics, individual irrationality, or organizational failures have only a marginal impact on policies and outcomes.

The explanatory variable for realism is the distribution of power among states; for instance, *hegemony in which there is one dominant state, bipolarity in which there are two dominant states, or multipolarity in which there are several states of about equal power.

The evidence that realists utilize requires operationalizing the power of states by, for instance, looking at the size of armies, aggregate economic output, or the ability to make credible threats and offer rewards to other states.

The basic claim of realism is that given a particular distribution of power among states it is possible to explain both the characteristics of the system and the behavior of individual states. Realism makes no effort to probe the domestic determinants of foreign policy; what counts is state power and external constraints.

The most prominent argument derived from a realist perspective is the theory of hegemonic stability. Hegemonic stability asserts that a stable open international economic system is most likely when there is a hegemonic distribution of power; that is, when there is one state that is much more influential than any of the others. With regard to trade a hegemon is likely to favor openness because such a trading *regime would increase its economic well-being and economic growth, and provide it with more political leverage. A hegemonic power would also have the resources to entice or coerce other states into participating in an open regime, and to provide the system with collective goods such as financial resources to prevent a collapse of the banking system. International openness has been associated with two periods when there was an economic hegemon—Britain during the last part of the nineteenth century and the United States during the last half of the twentieth century.

Liberalism. The basic assumptions of liberalism are the following: 1) There are a multiplicity of actors in the international system. These include multinational corporations, international organizations, foundations, and terrorists as well as states. 2) These actors are rational and calculating but they pursue a multiplicity of different objectives. Different actors have different power capabilities in different areas. 3) *International relations and especially international political economy both offer opportunities for everyone to gain at the same time. Actors are more concerned with their absolute well-being than with their relative position vis-à-vis others.

The explanatory variable for liberalism is the configuration of interests and capabilities associated with a given issue area.

The evidence that is needed for a liberal perspective involves specifying the relevant actors (states, multinationals, etc.), assessing their resources, and stipulating their objectives.

Liberalism is the international analogue to pluralist analyses of the domestic polity. There are many different actors with different interests. There are opportunities for cross-cutting cleavages. A liberal analysis suggests more of a tendency to system stability than is the case for realism because there are more opportunities to cut deals. Actors are not simply involved in a zero-sum game to maximize their own relative power.

The most important development for a liberal perspective is the growth of *interdependence. As transportation and communications costs have declined, international economic transactions—trade, finance, *technology transfer—have increased dramatically. The benefits of an open world economy have increased. More and more actors have a stake in a stable international economic order.

The most important recent development in the area of international political economy, cooperation theory, is a hybrid between realist and liberal approaches. It is realist in its assumption of unified rational actors but liberal in its assumption of a non-zero-sum world in which absolute gains are more important than relative position. For cooperation theory the basic problem is to resolve collective action problems in which individual choice leads to suboptimal outcomes; for instance, no one state wants to act as a lender of last resort in a financial crisis, but the absence of a lender of last resort could leave every state worse off.

The most important statement of the theory of cooperation in the literature that is explicitly directed to the study of international political economy is Robert Keohane's *After Hegemony* (1984), which argues that cooperation is possible even without a hegemonic state if institutions can overcome problems of market failure. By providing more information, establishing mechanisms for monitoring, and generating shared expectations institutions can create an environment in which interstate cooperation is possible even without a single dominant leader.

Marxism. Marxism makes the following basic assumptions: 1) The basic actors in the social system are classes defined by their relationship to the means of production. 2) In international relations the interests of classes are manifest in the policies of states and other actors.

The explanatory argument for Marxism delineates the way in which capitalism generates inherent contradictions—a declining rate of profit, underconsumption, and a growing tension between the socialization of labor and the continued private concentration of ownership and political power—and the efforts of capitalist states to overcome these contradictions. For *foreign policy this implies that capitalist states must be imperialistic because they need to maximize the opportunities for foreign investment, access to new sources of raw materials, and the use of cheap foreign labor. *Capitalism is inherently a system of exploitation and, in the international system, this implies that the wealthy capitalist core will exploit the Third World periphery.

The evidence utilized by Marxist perspectives involves the concentration of economic power and the sociopolitical characteristics of economic systems.

Marxist analysis of the international political economy has concentrated on the relations between the rich and the poor areas of the world. The most prominent exemplar of this approach has been *dependency theory, which maintained that both the wealth of the capitalist core countries and the poverty of the Third World periphery was a function of the exploitative mechanisms of the world capitalist system. Capitalist states used foreign aid and military assistance to keep conservative regimes in power. Multinational corporations used their privileged access to external markets to prevent the development of technologically advanced production in the periphery. Raw materials companies despoiled the natural resources of less developed countries.

Developments in the 1980s, not only the collapse of the communist system in Eastern Europe but, more important, the economic success of some Third World countries, raised very serious questions about the empirical validity of dependency theory. If Taiwan and the Republic of Korea (South Korea), which were economically backward areas in the 1950s, could develop so spectacularly in the 1970s and 1980s, could capitalism be seen as an inherently exploitative system? As variation in the performance of Third World states increased over time, dependency theory, with its focus on the world capitalist system as opposed to the indigenous characteristics of individual states, became more problematic.

Domestic Politics. The final theoretical focus of international political economy has been the relationship between domestic political structures and the international system. One of the striking successes of international political economy as a field of study is that it has integrated international relations and *comparative politics, fields that were much more distinct before 1970. There are two important lines of inquiry. The first examines the impact of the international system on domestic political structures. The second investigates how variations in domestic political structures affect foreign economic policies and outcomes.

There is no dominant argument about the impact of the international system on domestic political structures. The works of Peter Katzenstein and Ronald Rogowski are illustrative. In *Small States in the World Economy* (1985), Katzenstein argues that the development of what he calls democratic corporatism in the small European countries (Austria, Sweden, Switzerland, Denmark, the Netherlands, Norway, and Belgium) reflects their heavy involvement in the international economy. In democratic corporatist polities distinctions between state and society are blurred and all important groups are incorporated into political decision making. Such inclusive political institutions are needed to lessen the risk of internecine quarrels that would be economically disastrous because they would preclude swift adjustment to rapidly changing external conditions.

Ronald Rogowski in *Commerce and Coalitions* (1989) shows

how changes in the international opportunity for trade can have a dramatic impact on the power of domestic groups within a given political system. More trade strengthens the position of abundant factors of production and weakens that of scarce factors. For instance, in a country with an abundance of labor but a scarcity of capital and land, new trading opportunities would be beneficial for workers but harmful to the interests of the holders of capital and land because production would shift toward labor-intensive activities and away from capital-intensive and land-intensive activities.

The second line of inquiry relating domestic political structures and the international economic system examines the ways in which different domestic structures affect foreign economic policies. One prominent example of this kind of approach distinguishes between weak and strong states. In weak states political power is fragmented among many institutions—the legislature, public bureaucracies, private pressure groups. It is difficult to formulate a coherent foreign economic policy. The United States is the most obvious example. In polities with strong states power is concentrated in the hands of a small number of actors in the executive branch who can set policy and secure, through coercion or incentives, the support of major groups in civil society. Japan is the illustrative case.

In sum, international political economy has been concerned with developments in the world system that are only likely to become more important in the years to come. International trade and financial flows, which have always been important, are becoming even more salient for the well-being of individual states and their citizens. Because of their saliency, decisions about international economic policy will not be left to the private sector or to faceless technocrats; they will be a matter of concern for political leaders and their constituencies. The challenge of international political economy is how best to understand these concerns and the behaviors and outcomes that they generate.

(See also CLASS; FINANCE, INTERNATIONAL; INTERNATIONAL COOPERATION; INTERNATIONAL ORGANIZATIONS; PLURALISM.)

Charles P. Kindleberger, *The World in Depression* (Berkeley, Calif., 1973). Immanuel Wallerstein, *The Modern World System* (New York, 1974). Peter A. Gourevitch, "Second Image Reversed: The International Sources of Domestic Politics" *International Organization* 32 (Autumn 1978): 881–912. Stephen D. Krasner, ed., *International Regimes* (Ithaca, N.Y., 1983). Richard Rosecrance, *The Rise of the Trading State* (New York, 1985). Robert Gilpin, *The Political Economy of International Relations* (Princeton, N.J., 1988).

STEPHEN D. KRASNER

INTERNATIONAL PUBLIC FINANCE. Finance—the transfer and management of liquid resources—has two dimensions: private and public. Of the two, private is the more developed, both as a discipline and field of activity, spanning both the state and the international arena. This reflects its greater risks, potential profits, and volume of flows. Public finance is also well developed, but until recently only at the level of the state and smaller political entities. The term "finance" originated with the Old French *finer* (to end or settle, applied to indebtedness) and crept into other Romance languages as a Gallicism and into English via the Middle English *finance*. Both private and public finance evolved in parallel,

and in line with the development of economies and political systems, through the stage of the nation-state. But whereas national public financing flourished with expenditures for war and other concerns of state, public expenditures lagged far behind private outlays in the international arena until World War II.

The postwar growth of *globalization and of international *regimes and public institutions has catapulted the importance of international public finance. *Organization for Economic Co-operation and Development (OECD) data indicate that official development finance (ODF) from 1990 to 1998 fluctuated between 21 and 63 percent of total net resource flows from country-to-country development assistance and multilateral agencies to aid recipients, excluding the use of *International Monetary Fund (IMF) credit, interest payments by aid recipients, the administrative costs of intergovernmental institutions—the beginnings of international public administration—and other public international expenditures. The first use of the term "international public finance," and its treatment as a theory and discipline, was made in 1992 in Ruben P. Mendez's *International Public Finance: A New Perspective on Global Relations* (New York, 1992). Further work has since been carried out, especially in the theory of global public goods, in its development as part of the academic curricula of public economics and international relations, and in policy discussions in international public fora.

Public finance, which may also be defined as the economics of the public sector, is concerned primarily with the correction of market failures to improve economic efficiency. This applies to both the national and international levels. Free-riding by individuals and firms acting in their immediate self-interest is paralleled in the international community by the free-riding of constituent governments acting in their "national interest." Global public goods, such as peace and security (the international analogue of national defense, and of law and order), a safeguarded ozone layer, and *international law, rules, and standards, are not provided by the private sector and therefore need public sector intervention through the *United Nations. The market similarly will not reduce international negative externalities, such as the emission of chlorofluorocarbons or marine oil pollution, nor will it promote positive externalities, such as are generated by rain forests or vaccinations. These are the subject of the Montreal Protocol on Substances That Deplete the Ozone Layer, global environmental agreements, and the *World Health Organization. The *World Trade Organization tries to correct competitive breakdowns in international trade, the *World Bank complements incomplete private capital markets for less developed countries, and the IMF provides a type of balance-of-payments insurance not available from the private sector. The IMF and informal mechanisms like the *Group of 7 try to perform a coordinating and stabilizing function, albeit very selectively. The International Development Association (IDA) and other multilateral aid programs perform another function of public finance, income redistribution, although it is minuscule compared with intranational redistribution.

International public finance is obviously needed and functioning, although it is much less active than finance within states. This is due partly to the fact that financing the needed activities depends almost entirely on voluntary contributions, there being no true system of global taxation, user charges, or fiscal and monetary policy. It is also due to inadequate political will and the absence of a world government. It is clear, however, that the problems and issues that call for public finance in states have international analogues and require strong action—if not by a world government, by the international public sector. The international public institutions that constitute the sector are growing in importance, and the governments and citizens of states are becoming more aware of the urgency of public action in the international economic arena, and of international institutional and financial reform.

(See also INTERNATIONAL FINANCE; INTERNATIONAL POLITICAL ECONOMY.)

Charles P. Kindleberger, "International Public Goods Without World Government," *American Economic Review* 6, no. 1 (March 1986). Ruben P. Mendez, "The Provision and Financing of Universal Public Goods," in Meghnad Desai and Paul Redfern, eds., *Global Governance and Economics of the World Order* (London, 1995).

RUBEN P. MENDEZ

INTERNATIONAL RELATIONS. See overleaf.

INTERNATIONAL SYSTEMS. In a 1947 Princeton speech General George C. Marshall doubted "whether a man can think with full wisdom and with deep convictions regarding certain of the basic issues of today who has not at least reviewed in his mind the period of the Peloponnesian War and the fall of Athens"; he probably had in mind *Thucydides'* time-defying claim to have written his history not for momentary popularity, but "for all time." Indeed, Thucydides wished to discover an exact knowledge of the past "which (human nature being what it is) will, at some time or other and in much the same ways, be repeated in the future."

Definitions and Cautions. Although Thucydides would not have used the term, contemporary scholars would attribute the regularities that made such fruitful comparisons possible to the systematicity of *international relations, meaning, in Thucydides' case, the regularized connections between the component units of the Greek-cum-Persian international system, and vis-à-vis its external environment. In the contemporary sense, real international systems consist of the major units of international life, their regularized relationships with each other, and vis-à-vis their internal and external environments.

In the case when the component units are sovereign *states, Martin Wight (*Systems of States*, Leicester, U.K., 1977) characterizes these defining relationships as of four sorts: messengers, including heralds, ambassadors, resident agents, spies, and hostages; conferences and international institutions; a common language (presumably including the cultural and diplomatic meanings that make linguistic communication possible); and trade and commerce, which he argues have been of special importance in the development of state systems. To this may be added the regularities of human-environmental interchanges, among which can be distinguished technological/resource, biochemical/ecological, and cosmological aspects.

Some of the most interesting international systems have not been state systems. Asian and African civilizations and the pre-Columbian Americas have produced a number of hierarchically structured suzerain systems of considerable longevity. Medieval Europe witnessed a complex of interpenetrating transnational political and religious hierarchies within which a variety of local nonsovereign political entities found their place.

As even this brief listing of variant international systems suggests, several cautions are in order with respect to Thucydides' oft-cited search for timeless (and universally valid) truths. Perhaps the better analogical ideal for students of international systems is neither Ptolemy's nor Kepler's nor Newton's nor Einstein's laws of planetary motion, but the kinds of developmental historical processes that have led to the supersession of one of these theoretical accounts by another in human scientific understanding. Then again, such cumulative, developmental thinking may be too modernist or optimistic. More realistic alternative historical accounts of international systems might look like histories of dynasties or families, living in different contexts. Think of the rise and disintegration of empires or civilizations, or the transition from limited *balance of power equilibria to global hegemonic systems, themselves subject to ecological overextension and exhaustion.

Second, any feminist might legitimately raise the question whether the abstractly inclined men that George Marshall had in mind, and the extremely masculine political world of the Greeks and Persians that Thucydides studied, exhausted the possibilities of human nature. Even Giambattista Vico, a politically conservative Catholic writer of the eighteenth century, doubted that human nature was constant. Like Aristotle, he thought of human institutions as humanly, and thus variably, constructed; and he included the culturally, socially, and historically shaped features of human personalities and institutions within this realm of the variably constructed and changeable.

Third, Martin Wight has cautioned against using supposedly "timeless" (and universally valid) systematicity assumptions as a way of equating historically distinct international systems. Contrasting the modern European balance of power system with Thucydides' era, he argues: "If Thucydides does not provide [a theory of the balance of power], it is because the Greeks did not possess one. Just as they had no diplomatic system and no public international law, so they had no sense of an equilibrium of power being the foundation and as it were the constitution of international society" (Wight, 1977, p. 66).

So modern men and women can be said to be socialized into possibly different internationalized relevant roles, political identifications, beliefs, and feelings than medieval ones; and "postmodern" media/terrorist world politics can be described as made by actors, many of which eighteenth-century European diplomats would have difficulty recognizing. Whether the new players are more civilized and knowledgeable is debatable. At least the historicity of international relationships—the fact that their past is embedded in current, internationally shared memories, definitions, and practices—suggests that both continuity and innovation are informed possibilities in the international arena.

Because systematicity may involve historicity—as in the way states learned, evolved, or developed commonly recognized ways of balancing the power of a state threatening to

(cont. on p. 428)

INTERNATIONAL RELATIONS. A generic concept for a vast array of activities, ideas, and goods that do or can cross national boundaries, international relations (IR) embraces social, cultural, economic, and political exchanges that occur in ad hoc as well as institutionalized contexts. Because communication and transportation technologies continue, relentlessly, to lower the barriers and shrink the distances that separate cultures, societies, economies, and *states, fewer and fewer realms of experience remain outside the domain of IR.

For some researchers the broad array of IR phenomena is viewed as the basis of a "field." A few even see it as the paramount discipline because its scope extends across the globe and because its concerns embrace every dimension of human experience. For a preponderance of those who examined IR, however, its vast empirical domain is regarded as too broad for any one discipline, let alone any one investigator, to probe in its entirety. The facets of individual and collective behavior relevant to any IR problem, it is argued, are too numerous and too diverse for the development of coherent theories and methodologies necessary to the disciplined procedures that comprise a recognizable and viable field.

Whether or not one considers IR a separate field, inquiries into its dynamics might be expected to be profoundly interdisciplinary, with scholars joined in collaborative efforts to unravel the complexities of particular problems, countries, regions, institutions, or processes. Such synthesizing of expertise, however, is more the exception than the rule. Most inquiries into IR tend to be narrowly confined to work in a single discipline. Rarely do these separate endeavors converge. Rather, the practitioners in each discipline tend to hold constant the variables that tap the skills of their disciplines.

This account of a fragmented "nonfield" describes only part of the intellectual framework that has evolved in international studies. A more salient characteristic is that most students of the subject are political scientists and most inquiries focus on one or another political aspect of IR. The number of sociologists, anthropologists, psychologists, economists, and historians who specialize in international exchanges is small, both within each of their disciplines and within international studies itself. Professional societies such as the International Studies Association have long sought to develop a multidisciplinary membership, but their efforts have largely been in vain.

So predominant are political scientists, in fact, that the domain of IR is often referred to as "international politics." For all practical purposes, this term and IR have become virtually synonymous. Indeed, this terminological ambiguity also extends to labels such as "world politics," "international studies," and "foreign affairs."

Fragmentation and Dominance. However problematic the fragmentation of IR and its dominance by political scientists, this skewed state of affairs can be readily explained. One reason for it is that the most developed of the social sciences, especially economics and psychology, are so preoccupied with and confident of their paradigms that their practitioners are disinclined to engage in collaborative work with colleagues in the less developed sciences. Such an attitude is

further reinforced by a reward structure wherein advancement tends to go to those who make a mark through disciplinary research rather than to those who engage in interdisciplinary or multidisciplinary inquiry.

Another source of the fragmented state of IR studies is a continuing tendency toward specialization in the various disciplines, a narrowing of foci such that investigators become expert at delving deeply but not broadly into their subject matter. The result is that they are unlikely to encounter interdisciplinary problems.

But perhaps the prime reason for the skewed state of the nonfield is to be found not in the structure of disciplines but in the structures of IR itself and, especially, in the long-term standing tendencies of these structures to collapse into destructive *wars. Historically the activities of international actors have been neither subject to a central authority nor governed by widely shared norms. Thus IR does not offer the underlying substantive coherence on which most of the social sciences are founded. Sociology has long derived minimal coherence from the presence of all—encompassing entities called societies, which tend to be national in scope and which, as such, serve to coordinate the hierarchies, value consensuses, habitual practices, policy goals, and institutional arrangements that evolve under their auspices. Likewise, leaving aside for the moment the subfield of international economics, the discipline of economics has maintained coherence by focusing predominantly on economies that are national in scale and that, as such, have managed the practices and institutions whereby markets are created, investments generated, trade flows sustained, and the labor force trained and employed. Much of political science, too, has been organized around a national entity, the polity or the state, which has the sovereign authority to maintain order, provide justice, protect territory, conduct *foreign policy, and otherwise enhance the general welfare.

IR does not fit these disciplinary boundaries. No international or world society subsumes national societies and infuses coherence into the subject. No international or world government exercises authority over national states. The global economy does control national markets to a considerable extent, but these controls vary from one country or situation to another. Thus, if there is any aspect of IR about which the diverse approaches to the subject fully agree, it is that the systemic properties of IR are best characterized as anarchical—that is, there are no centralized institutions capable of prevailing over any or all international actors. The *anarchy of IR does not amount to sheer disarray because the cooperative and patterned interactions of the actors that do possess authority have resulted in the evolution of international structures. Nevertheless, it is an anarchical system in the sense that an overarching global authority has yet to evolve which coherently links its components into a common system of rule.

It is hardly surprising, therefore, that the analysts who gravitate toward the study of IR have been primarily those relatively few political scientists inclined to gear their disciplinary skills toward the phenomena in which bargaining, coercion, and other techniques of statecraft are used either to maintain cooperation and balance or to sustain conflict and wage war in the absence of an overall authority. Through both default and intellectual concern, in other words, IR has been skewed by the predominance of political scientists who are either not put off by the anarchical nature of IR or who are drawn to the subject by predispositions to explain and avert the devastating effects of war.

The Impact of Change. These characteristics of international studies are now showing signs of transformation because the patterns of boundary-crossing activities that comprise IR began to change profoundly in recent years. Not only have the arrangements for managing international affairs that emerged after World War II—the *Cold War era—come to an end, but the dynamics that underlie the prevailing arrangements appear to be undergoing significant alterations.

In the first place, because of the ways in which diverse technologies have rendered social life ever more complex and interdependent, the repercussions of the boundary-crossing activities that comprise IR are no longer confined to contiguous relationships or even regional affairs. Rather, their reach has become global: Intended or not, virtually any interaction that transgresses national boundaries can today precipitate ripple effects everywhere in the world. Second, and no less important, these activities are no longer restricted to nation-states. A wide range of "nonstate" actors—some transnational, others subnational—now engage in these activities in such a way as to have significant consequences for the course of events and the structures of world affairs. Third, the greater density of actors and the greater complexity of their interactions have resulted in a declining utility of military force and an increased preoccupation with the economic dimensions of global life. War is by no means an obsolete instrument of policy, but the ability to achieve goals through threatening or resorting to coercive means has lessened and, accordingly, so has the attractiveness of military action. Fourth, the globalization of IR, the proliferation of its actors, the delegitimation of war, and a host of other dynamics have weakened the competence of national governments, heightened the coherence of subnational governments, expanded the readiness of citizens to join in collective action, and thus brought about authority crises in many parts of the world, sometimes relocating authority either "upwards" in the direction of transnational entities or "downwards" toward subnational collectivities.

All these changes have had the cumulative effect of eroding and obscuring the boundaries that separate countries, that differentiate domestic from foreign affairs, and that distinguish economics from politics. Strictly speaking, in other words, IR as "inter-nation" relations has increasingly become a misnomer. It may not be long, in fact, before the aforementioned terminological ambiguity yields to a new, more accurate set of overall labels such as "transnational relations" or "global affairs."

Among the more obvious indicators of the transformations at work in IR is the emergence of *international political economy (IPE) as a specialized field of inquiry and the advent of international regimes as a concept employed by many investigators. Although still very much the focus of political scientists rather than of collaborative work between them and economists, IPE has mushroomed since the 1970s as the prime subfield of international studies.

The substantive foci, concepts, and problems of IPE are too diverse, however, to constitute a separate discipline. Like IR, IPE consists of congeries of research interests and theoretical foci that do not derive from a common framework and, indeed, are often contradictory. They share only a concern for the overlap of economic and political dynamics in one or another situation.

Similarly, the turn away from military affairs and toward *political economy has heightened an awareness that international actors can be as cooperative in their relationships as they are potentially conflictual. Given the absence of an overarching global authority structure, this awareness has led to the evolution of neoliberalism as a theoretical perspective, which focuses on the question of how and why sovereign states and autonomous nonstate actors manage to cooperate sufficiently to move toward their goals and avoid breakdowns in their relationships. In response to this question, the concept of international *regime has emerged to fill the conceptual gap. Most fully set forth in *International Regimes*, edited by Stephen D. Krasner (Ithaca, N.Y., 1983), an international regime is conceived to consist of shared norms, rules, principles, and procedures to which all the actors in a particular issue area subscribe, either tacitly or explicitly, sufficiently to maximize cooperation and minimize conflict in that issue area. Hence, for example, the IR literature is filled with research on the "oil regime," the "monetary regime," the "whaling regime," and so on through all the issues that crowd the global agenda.

Diverse Approaches and Theories. It must quickly be noted that some, perhaps many, IR analysts do not agree with the foregoing discussion of the impact of change. Yes, they concur, the Cold War has ended and the present is in many ways considerably different from the past in IR. But, asserts this line of reasoning, the changes involve shifts within the interstate system that has prevailed for four centuries, not transformations of that system. States may be somewhat weaker and other types of actors may have expanded their capacities, but states still retain their sovereign rights and can still resort to coercive techniques to enforce their will. Consequently, all the changes of recent decades, although not trivial, are occurring in a constant context. The state-centric, anarchical system, this argument concludes, is still functioning as it always has.

Those who stress continuity over change in world politics tend to share a realist, neorealist, or neoliberal approach to the subject. All these perspectives view history as demonstrating the appropriateness of states as the most encompassing entity capable of maintaining the coherence of societies, protecting the borders of countries, and advancing the collective interests of its citizens. This perspective thus regards states as durable, as capable of resisting any changes that might undermine their core interests. Unlike neorealists and neoliberals, realists presume that the core interests of different states are antithetical to one another and that, accordingly, states endlessly seek to enhance their power in order to serve their national interests. Despite the absence of an overarching global authority, the pursuit of conflictual interests by states is not seen by realists to result necessarily in a war of all against all. War does sometimes occur, but realism posits the conflicts among states as tending toward equilibrium as states shift their *alliance relationships to maintain the balance of power whenever its coherence is threatened.

Although both the neorealist and neoliberal perspectives emphasize the durability of states and their reliance on power to serve their national interests, they differ in that the former stresses the relative gains to be had through international cooperation while the latter focuses on absolute gains. Both perspectives differ from realism by virtue of a lesser concern with the diplomatic, military, and strategic sources that sustain or alter the *balance of power and a greater preoccupation with the socioeconomic and political dynamics that enable states to overcome their differences and accommodate each other. Most neorealists and neoliberals therefore tend to be students of IPE and to see utility in the regime concept as a means for explaining the adaptability of states and the interstate system. Indeed, it is probably the case that neorealism and neoliberalism are presently the most widely shared perspectives in international studies.

More accurately, these perspectives appeal widely to IR analysts in the United States and Europe. Students of the subject in the developing world are much less concerned with identifying and specifying the overall perspective or paradigm within which they conduct their inquiries. Preoccupied with the dire plight of their country and region, investigators of the developing world tend to eschew theory, to be highly pragmatic, and to focus on policy problems. To the extent that some students of IR in the developing world have turned their attention, at least in the 1960s and 1970s, to tracing and explaining overall patterns, they have tended to be attracted to *dependency theory, a perspective that posits the developing world as historically exploited by the rich industrial nations of the Northern Hemisphere. Put differently, neorealism and neoliberalism are the most widely held IR perspectives because the study of IR is undertaken mostly in the West and, especially, in the United States.

But a quick review of the history and present status of IR studies in the West clearly reveals that *realism, neorealism, and neoliberalism are not the only perspectives that organize and sustain teaching and research. Realism was not the first broad approach to IR studies that enjoyed wide acceptance. Previously, during the period between the first and second world wars, *idealism was the dominant perspective. Stimulated by Woodrow Wilson's call for effective international institutions and "open covenants openly arrived at," IR specialists devoted the interwar decades mostly to probing issues of *international law and morality, an effort which was idealist in the sense that questions of power and its utilization tended to be ignored, as if the ascendancy of international organizations and law would be sufficient to prevent war and inappropriate, amoral exercises of power. When Hitler exercised German power, ignored the constraints of international law and morality, and overran Europe, the ground was laid for the realist perspective to replace idealism as a basis for grasping and researching world politics. Munich—where Britain and France acceded to German demands in 1938, hoping to achieve "peace in our time"—became a symbol of the failure of idealism and a spur to framing a "realistic" approach to the challenges of world politics. World War II could have been averted, the realists claimed, if France and Britain had not let their ideals distort their calculations of national interest and had told Hitler they would contest Germany on the battlefield rather than yield to his demands.

Anticipated by E. H. Carr in *The 20 Years' Crisis, 1919–1939* (London, 1939) and subsequently elaborated compellingly by Hans J. Morgenthau in successive editions of his postwar text *Politics Among Nations* (New York, 1972), realism became the dominant approach to IR in the late 1940s and 1950s. It also served as the prime intellectual foundation for the perceptions of the threats and the framing of the policies that came to be called the Cold War. Indeed, echoes of Hitler and Munich reverberated powerfully through the first post–Cold War crisis as much of the world engaged in collective action to contest Iraq's conquest of Kuwait in 1990.

With the introduction of scientific methods into the social sciences late in the 1950s, some IR analysts were emboldened to question the adequacy of realism and its core assumption that all states conduct themselves similarly in the international arena. The state is not an abstraction, they argued, but rather consists of identifiable decision makers who respond to a variety of internal as well as external stimuli when they define their interests and exercise their power. And because states are dissimilar in their structures, histories, and capabilities, this reasoning emphasized, their officials are bound to vary in their conduct of foreign relations. These reactions to realism thus gave rise to the behavioralist approach to IR, which predominated throughout the 1960s and into the 1970s. To grasp world politics, the behavioralists contended, it is necessary to uncover the patterns whereby the duly constituted decision makers of states perceive the world, respond to challenges, frame problems, and ultimately make the choices embodied in their foreign policies. But the recognition of these patterns involved more than reflection and judicious historical inquiry for the behavioralists. They asserted that better methodologies, those used by scientists, were available to differentiate between recurring patterns and deviant cases in world politics, that through systematic quantification of the relevant variables it was possible to probe beneath the abstractions around which the realist perspective was organized.

For a variety of reasons, the promises of behavioralism were not fulfilled before doubts about its utility set in. Like realism, it too yielded its predominant position. By the 1980s, with the ever-greater *interdependence of world affairs and the continuing shift toward a global economy, the neorealist and neoliberal perspectives took hold, as did pluralist and transnational approaches that stressed the importance of nonstate actors and the diversity of the processes through which international affairs unfold. In addition, while Marxist and neo-Marxist formulations diminished with the end of the Cold War, other approaches emerged to organize the work of IR in Europe and elsewhere. Critical theory, rational choice, and game theoretical perspectives were especially compelling to a number of analysts. Fewer were attracted to poststructural and postmodern philosophies as a means of understanding the "subtexts" of IR.

Still another recent perspective, the "postinternational," developed by the present author in *Turbulence in World Politics* (Princeton, N.J., 1990) and elaborated further in *Along the Domestic-Foreign Frontier* (Cambridge, U.K., 1997), posits world politics as bifurcated into two prime structures. According to this view, states in the interstate system are active primarily in the diplomatic-political-military arena; diverse nonstate actors, meanwhile, are seen as forming a "multicentric" system that processes mainly socioeconomic issues. These two broad systems of world politics are conceived to be essentially independent of each other even as they are also competitive and interactive. More importantly, the bifurcated structure of IR is viewed as especially conducive to the management of the tensions between change and continuity that are so acute in the present era: Whereas the state-centric system is seen as well suited to coping with the persistent and pervasive pressures for conducting world politics along long-established lines, the multicentric system is regarded as capable of absorbing the dynamics whereby authority is undergoing relocation in both upward and downward directions.

The most recent development in the IR field is that of "constructivism." Less a theory than an approach derived from sociological perspectives, constructivism has won increasing numbers of adherents largely because it presumes that the identities and interests of states are socially constructed rather than inherent in their geopolitical circumstances. Thus, unlike the "neo" approaches, constructivism focuses on ideas, norms, and culture as well as on how macro actors are fashioned or limited by the conceptions of them held by the micro actors of which they are comprised. A succinct evaluation of constructivism, its potentials and problems, can be found in Jeffrey T. Checkel's "The Constructivist Turn in International Relations Theory" (*World Politics* 50, no. 2 [January 1998]: 324–48).

This account of the recent history of IR studies may leave the impression that the several shifts to new perspectives occurred easily. Such was not the case. As documented by K. J. Holsti in *The Dividing Discipline: Hegemony and Diversity in International Theory* (Boston, 1985), the shifts were the focus of intense debates and an escalated rhetoric about the proper paths to international "truth." This was especially the case when the behavioralists began to challenge the realists: As can be seen in the compendium of essays edited by Klaus Knorr and James N. Rosenau (*Contending Approaches to International Politics*, Princeton, N.J., 1969), each side was capable of viewing the other as misguided regarding the philosophical premises and research methodologies most suited to discerning, measuring, and assessing the underlying dynamics of world politics. Symposia edited by Robert O. Keohane (*Neorealism and Its Critics*, New York, 1986) and David A. Baldwin (*Neorealism and Neoliberalism: The Contemporary Debate*, New York, 1993) reveal that the neorealist and neoliberal perspectives also evoked considerable controversy over their premises and potentials as an overall guide to inquiry.

On the other hand, it is perhaps a measure of maturation in the study of IR that more recently both the foci and intensity of such debates have changed. Where the controversies once raged around methodological and epistemological issues, today analysts argue mostly about substance—about whether international regimes are in fact operative, about whether the hegemonic leadership of the United States has undergone decline, about whether another country is likely to surface as the hegemon of the twenty-first century, about the extent to which states and the interstate system are undergoing transformation almost as if a live and let-live attitude has set in with respect to theoretical and methodological questions. Even the substantive debates appear to be conducted within the context of a shared tolerance, a readiness to acknowledge that there are no simple answers, that IR has become extraordinarily complex, and that therefore understanding is best advanced through a variety of approaches.

Notwithstanding the climate of tolerance that presently marks inquiry into IR, as of the 1990s, with competing perspectives continuing to anchor the work of analysts in different parts of the world, the study of the subject is as fragmented as world politics itself. Whether the end of the Cold War, the decline of superpowers, the upward and downward relocation of authority, the weakening and yet continued viability of states, and the unrelenting pace of change will lead to a convergence around fewer approaches remains to be seen. The history and complexity of IR, however, make it seem very doubtful that any single conception of the dynamics of global politics will come to unify the study and teaching of global affairs.

(See also GULF WAR; INTERNATIONAL SYSTEMS; LIBERALISM; MARXISM; MULTINATIONAL CORPORATIONS; NONGOVERNMENTAL ORGANIZATION PLURALISM; POSTMODERNISM.)

Richard C. Snyder, H. W. Bruck, and Burton Sapin, eds., *Foreign Policy Decision-Making: An Approach to the Study of International Politics* (New York, 1962). Hedley Bull, *The Anarchical Society. A Study of Order in World Politics* (New York, 1977). Kenneth N. Waltz, *Theory of International Politics* (Reading, Mass, 1979). Robert O. Keohane, *After Hegemony: Cooperation and Discord in the World Political Economy* (Princeton, N.J., 1984). Immanuel Wallerstein, *The Politics of the World-Economy: The States, the Movements, and the Civilizations* (Cambridge, U.K., 1984). Robert Gilpin, *The Political Economy of International Relations* (Princeton, N.J., 1987). James Der Derian and Michael J. Shapiro, eds., *International/Intertextual Relations: Postmodern Readings of World Politics* (Lexington, Mass., 1989). James N. Rosenau and Ernst-Otto Czempiel, eds., *Governance Without Government: Order and Change in World Politics* (Cambridge, U.K., 1992). Barry Bugan, Charles James, and Richard Little, eds., *The Logic of Anarchy: Neorealism to Structural Realism* (New York, 1993). John Gerard Ruggie, *Constructing the World Polity: Essays on International Institutionalization* (London, 1998).

JAMES N. ROSENAU

become hegemonic—it is necessary to add to our conception of international systems a discussion of their historical constitution, reformation, and dissolution processes. International systems may be said to be constituted by the norms, the principles, or the practices engendering and/or embodying these norms or principles. Just as Thucydides saw human nature as constitutive of the distinctive member units and their interrelationships with each other and their environments, so John Ruggie has characterized the early modern state system in terms of an emergent, postmedieval clustering of quasi-mechanical time-space descriptions, territoriality, private property, and sovereignty relationships.

Ruggie, Richard Ashley, Robert Cox, and others have recently joined a debate with Kenneth Waltz, Robert Gilpin, and other "neorealists" about how naturalistically or historically to approach the constitutive processes of international political systems. Thus scholarly discussions of contemporary international relations have joined worldwide discussions of the nature of, and prospects for, modern and postmodern forms of international life.

Alternative Perspectives on the Contemporary International System. With these conceptual distinctions and cautions in mind, one can still make some useful claims about contemporary, past, or future international systems. We shall contrast political-military, economic, and ecological systemic conceptions.

Together, the actions of the European powers, their subjects, and their "significant others" have created, sustained, and modified the institutions of the Westphalia state system. These have included: a) the balance of power (a practice of flexible state realignments against a potentially preeminent power, first formally recognized in the Treaty of Utrecht of 1713); b) a hierarchy of power relations and realms (the Peace of Cateau-Cambrésis, 1559, treated violent conflicts over resources and territories in the peripheral West Indies as separable from wars in a more central European zone, which suggests redescribing such power hierarchies as *imperialism, when seen from peripheral perspectives); and c) the collective security practices of Great Power conflict management, particularly the regularization of postwar outcomes through diplomatic conference (such as the 1518 Treaty of London between the pope, the Holy Roman Emperor, and the kings of France, Spain, and England). Such conferences were often identified with the Concert of Europe in the nineteenth century, and the *League of Nations and the UN in the twentieth century.

Although subjects were normally treated as obligated to follow the laws of their sovereign, a pattern of diplomatic immunity and extraterritoriality for embassies has evolved in the European state system; this was the historical basis for official Western revulsion at the holding of embassy personnel by revolutionary Iranian students in 1979–1981.

Issues of environmental degradation were generally not recognized as worthy of international action before the twentieth century, but scientific and technical knowledge facilitating the "conquest of nature" was avidly pursued and fairly widely shared by the scientific establishment of those times.

A number of transformations in the modern, European state system have been associated with the contemporary era, usually seen as starting somewhere in the twentieth century. Thus it has been argued that the contemporary world has entered an era of world politics, globalizing the balance of power and transcending the European origins of the interstate system. In that process, the traditional concept of a "Great Power" has continued to have meaning when defined in terms of significant *nuclear weapons delivery capabilities, but newer, sometimes conflicting notions of economic "powers" or "*superpowers" also exist.

Others have argued that the Westphalian system of territorially sovereign nation-states is being even more radically transcended. Somehow, the equal and absolute juridical and territorial sovereignty of each nation-state seems a unit-constituting principle out of phase with a world of "superpowers" and "satellites," *multinational corporations with budgets greater than many states' GNPs, UN peacekeeping forces, *International Monetary Fund loan conditions, and UN development programs. And there is the quite remarkable contemporary growth of supranational institutions in, and associated with, the *European Community. Moreover, many postcolonial states, whose state governments' territorial and juridical sovereignty has been buttressed politically and legally by UN membership, have failed to supersede the transnational or subnational political importance of ethnic groupings whose origins preceded the colonial period.

In the post-1945 period, ideological "East vs. West" politics became highly visible, where both a "capitalist vs. communist" ideological reading and a "United States plus allies vs. the Soviet Union plus allies" geopolitical meaning were intended. East vs. West *Cold War geopolitics forcefully divided Germany, Europe, and Korea in the late 1940s. Similar arrangements later, and temporarily, were imposed by the Great Powers on Vietnam in the 1968 Geneva Conference. But with the end of the Cold War and the breakup of the Soviet Union, "North vs. South" politics became more prominent.

"North-South" or "core-periphery" geopolitical language can also be associated either with the original European Great Power system or with the globalized East-West system of the Cold War era, or the emerging post–Cold War, multipolar arrangement—in which Japan, the United States, and an increasingly united Western Europe are playing important leadership roles.

The exclusion of the People's Republic of China from representation in the UN Security Council for nearly twenty-five years after it consolidated power over mainland China, as well as its identification with other less developed *Third World states, called into question its early acceptance as a Great Power in the "core" of the world's political system. But the ambiguous status of the People's Republic of China for much of the Cold War period supports the more general claim that the less developed and often newly independent states of the global South have been precariously autonomous, with their juridical sovereignty not being matched by a unified, widely accepted, integrated and self-steering polity. With postrevolutionary China and perhaps postindependence India as important, partial exceptions, most "Southern" or Third World states have experienced considerable economic penetration. *Dependency and asymmetric interdependence have been a reality among many pro-Western export-oriented states in regions of the world identified as economic "peripheries" or "semiperipheries."

Quite a number of related arguments have concerned the contest for political and economic *hegemony within the increasingly globalized balance of power system. Hegemonic competition may produce temporary periods of bipolar or multipolar stability, but both historical and simulational studies have suggested a cyclical (but irregular) movement toward long, bloody, hegemonic wars. Holland in the seventeenth century, Britain in the nineteenth, and the United States in the twentieth century have emerged as world hegemons consequent upon victory in such wars. This interpretation had been considerably strengthened—and given a challenging economic interpretation as endemic to the growth and decay dynamics of the capitalist world economy—by the early Kondratiev-inspired literature on long waves of economic growth and (war-exacerbated) inflation, followed by periods of relative stagnation.

Just as total *war involving total weapons, world-wide conflicts, and totalitarian states have created the most important challenge to the international state system in the twentieth century, so it might be hypothesized that the next century will face its greatest challenges from the worldwide drive to achieve living standards comparable to those of contemporary industrial and postindustrial societies, and the enormous cultural and environmental stresses associated with such modernistic striving. Not only will North-South politics become more important, the ecological consequences of energy and resource intensive forms of industrial development will be felt around the globe.

Perhaps the most startling confirmation of the existence of hard-to-transcend limits to growth of worldwide industrial society has been the discovery of polar ozone holes and the apparent reality of global warming. World system dynamics not completely unlike those surmised by *Ibn-Khaldūn, Jay Forrester, and Fernand Braudel are increasingly recognized as real. The international system is being transformed into an environmentally reactive world system which must be lived with, rather than simply dominated.

(See also DIPLOMACY; INTERNATIONAL LAW; INTERNATIONAL POLITICAL ECONOMY; MODERNITY; NORTH-SOUTH RELATIONS; POSTMODERNISM; REALISM; UNITED NATIONS.)

Morton Kaplan, *System and Process in International Politics* (New York, 1957). Ibn Khaldun, *The Mugaddimah: An Introduction to History* (Princeton, N.J., 1969). Hedley Bull, *The Anarchical Society* (New York, 1977). Sam Cole, *Global Models and the International Economic Order* (New York, 1977). Martin Wight, *Systems of States* (Leicester, U.K., 1977). James Der Derian, *On Diplomacy: A Genealogy of Western Estrangement* (Oxford, 1982). Fernand Braudel, *Civilization and Capitalism, 15th–18th Century* 3 vols. (New York, 1981–1984). Thucydides, *The Peloponnesian War* (Harmondsworth, U.K., 1983). Robert Keohane, ed., *Neorealism and its Critics* (New York, 1986). Joshua Goldstein, *Long Cycles: Prosperity and War in the Modern Age* (New Haven, Conn., 1988). Thomas Cusack and Michael Stoll, *Exploring Realpolitik: Probing International Relations Theory with Computer Simulation* (Boulder, Colo., 1990).

HAYWARD R. ALKER, JR.

INTERVENTION is most commonly understood to mean the use of military force by one country to interfere in the internal affairs of another country, although it connotes more generally the element of coercion or imposition in relations among states and may include political interference, economic *sanctions, covert operations, and even cultural domination. The principle of nonintervention, resting on the prior principle of sovereignty and tracing back to the seventeenth century Treaties of Westphalia, has been a cornerstone of contemporary international relations, and the practice of intervention has therefore not generally been considered legitimate. Article 2(4) of the UN charter prohibits the threat or the use of force between states, and other international legal conventions enshrine the principle of noninterference in the internal affairs of states.

Nonetheless, intervention was a systematic feature of the post–World War II international order, especially as practiced by core states in the *Third World. Major Western interventions took place in Indochina, the Middle East, Central America and the Caribbean, Africa, and elsewhere. The *Cold War dynamics of confrontation and competition drove much intervention in this period. The Soviet Union as well carried out numerous interventions as part of its foreign policy, including in Hungary, Czechoslovakia, and Afghanistan.

The legalistic paradigm in international affairs focuses on the formal principles of *sovereignty and nonintervention while the realist tradition emphasizes interstate competition. In contrast, critical *political economy approaches link interventionism to theories of *imperialism, arguing that the impulse to intervene is grounded in the asymmetric structure of the international system itself. Powerful countries and alliances of countries intervene to preserve existing asymmetries in power and wealth, to defend Great Power *hegemony, and to suppress the aspirations of weaker nations for greater economic autonomy or political independence. Intervention in this view is an expression of global class conflict, often undertaken to secure access by core states and their multinational corporations to economic resources and investment opportunities.

However, the transformation of world politics with the end of the Cold War and the process of *globalization appear to be changing the ways in which scholars and policy makers perceive intervention. The emerging "conventional wisdom" holds that further internationalization of society places greater limitations on national sovereignty and legitimates collective "*humanitarian" interventions. Humanitarian and peacekeeping operations, democracy promotion, defense of *human rights, multilateral military campaigns, and actions against international drug trafficking have been carried out with increasing frequency since the end of the Cold War under UN aegis and other multilateral venues. The 1991 Gulf War, carried out by a U.S.–led force under the UN umbrella in the name of collective security, was followed by UN-sponsored "humanitarian" intervention in Somalia, the dispatching of international peacekeeping forces to Haiti, Cambodia, East Timor, and elsewhere, the military campaign organized by NATO to expel Serbian forces from Kosovo in the former Yugoslavia, and a battery of programs in Iraq following the Gulf War, ranging from economic sanctions to stationing UN "monitoring" and "humanitarian" missions in Iraqi territory.

These new modalities of intervention certainly suggest the rise of collective political authority in the global system, but they have generated sharp polemics. Critical analyses challenge the conventional interpretation of the new interventionism with the claim that it represents a shift in the mechanisms of control, and even new forms of colonialism, by an increasingly unified transnational elite intent on maintaining structures of domination and suppressing demands for a more thoroughgoing democratization of the emergent global capitalist order.

(See also INTERNATIONAL LAW; MILITARISM; REALISM.)

Peter J. Schraeder, ed., *Intervention in the 1990s* (Boulder, Colo., 1992). Thomas G. Weiss, ed., *Collective Security in a Changing World* (Boulder, Colo., 1993). James Mayall, ed., *The New Interventionism* (New York, 1996). William I. Robinson, *Promoting Polyarchy: Globalization, U.S. Intervention, and Hegemony* (Cambridge, U.K., 1996).

WILLIAM I. ROBINSON

INTIFADA. Twenty years after the West Bank, Gaza Strip, and East Jerusalem were occupied in the war of June 1967, they were shaken by a spontaneous popular upheaval which surprised the Israeli authorities, the *Palestine Liberation Organization (PLO), and most other parties to the conflict. The intifada (the Arabic word means "uprising") of the 2 million Palestinians of these areas, which began on 9 December 1987, significantly changed the scope and dimensions of the *Arab-Israeli conflict. Specifically, it restored the primacy of the conflict's Palestinian-Israeli aspect, which was for many years eclipsed by the related one involving Israel and neighboring Arab states.

During the first four years of the intifada, more than 1,000 Palestinians, over 250 of them children sixteen years of age and younger, were killed by the Israeli occupation authorities, and approximately 120,000 wounded. In that same period, 16,000 were administratively detained (i.e., imprisoned without trial) for periods of six months or more, and tens of thousands of others jailed after trial by military courts. In consequence of this dramatic upsurge in the conflict, which was the subject of intense international media attention, the intifada imposed itself, and the conflict between Palestinians and Israelis, on the consciousness of the United States and Europe, Israel, and the Arab world. This was all the more significant since in the years preceding the uprising, the Palestinian aspect of the conflict had faded from international awareness.

Following the outbreak of the intifada, and in large measure because of it, important changes took place in the policies of many of the actors involved in the conflict. One of the first and most striking changes was Jordan's abdication of its responsibility for the West Bank in July 1988. In November 1988, at the 19th Palestinian National Council held in Algiers, the PLO launched a peace initiative based on an explicit acceptance of the legitimacy of the 1947 partition of Palestine which had created the state of Israel, and called for a peaceful settlement between a Palestinian state in the West Bank and Gaza Strip and Israel to be based on UN Security Council *Resolution 242. Soon afterwards, PLO leader Yasir *Arafat explicitly accepted the existence of the state of Israel, renounced terrorism, and accepted 242, thereby meeting U.S. conditions for a dialogue with the United States, which began in December of the same year.

In the United States, *public opinion and media coverage for the first time became sympathetic to the Palestinians and critical of Israeli practices in a sustained fashion. This was instrumental in persuading the Reagan administration to start a dialogue with the PLO (it was broken off eighteen months later) and in provoking the first muted criticisms of the level of U.S. aid to Israel in Congress and elsewhere. Owing in part to these shifts in public opinion, the Bush administration

brought the Palestinians into the negotiations with Israel which began at Madrid in 1991 and led to the 1993 Oslo accords; it initially insisted, however, that Israel retain veto power over any Palestinian chosen to negotiate with it, thus excluding the PLO.

In Israel, the impact of the intifada was felt economically and in a variety of other ways. Thinking in Israeli strategic and policy-making circles was deeply influenced by it, as evidenced by the Jaffee Center report *The West Bank and Gaza: Israel's Options for Peace* (Tel Aviv, 1989), the first authoritative statement to weigh the possibility of a Palestinian state in the occupied territories. The impact of the intifada on Israeli opinion contributed to the Shamir government's opening talks with the Palestinians in 1991, and was a factor in inducing the Labor government of Yitzhak Rabin which succeeded it in 1992 to negotiate directly with the PLO and to sign the Oslo accords giving Palestinians limited self-government in parts of the occupied West Bank and Gaza Strip.

In spite of all these and other important effects of the intifada, after several years of sacrifices (the intifada petered out in 1991 in the wake of the *Gulf War), many Palestinians felt that they had little to show for their efforts against Israeli occupation. A new grassroots leadership drawn from a younger generation had emerged in the occupied territories, linked to the PLO and with deep indigenous roots and strong popular support. This leadership had succeeded for a time in defining the Palestinian agenda and in giving Palestinians a sense of purpose and pride, as local committees established themselves as the leading force in communities throughout the West Bank and Gaza Strip. But in spite of all the changes wrought by the intifada, the Israeli government was able to resist the very limited pressures exerted on it by the United States and the rest of the world to move toward a negotiated compromise settlement of the conflict.

One of the consequences of the intense frustration among Palestinians caused by the failure of the intifada and of the negotiations which followed to produce a peaceful settlement with Israel was an increase in violence against Israeli civilian targets, which had decreased markedly during the first thirty months of the intifada. Another consequence was an apparent growth in the influence in the occupied territories of Islamic factions such as Hamas and the Islamic Jihad, which expressed hostility toward negotiated settlement as advocated by the PLO and characterized the conflict in absolute, uncompromising religious terms.

The intifada thus succeeded in changing, perhaps irrevocably, the outlines of the conflict between Palestinians and Israelis, and had significant impact on world public opinion. However, both the intifada and the negotiations it produced failed to impel the Israeli government to withdraw fully from the Palestinian territories occupied in 1967 or to accept the creation there of a Palestinian state, which were the goals for which it was originally launched.

Zachary Lockman and Joel Beinin, eds., *Intifada: The Palestinian Uprising Against Israeli Occupation* (Boston, 1989). Ze'ev Schiff and Ehud Ya'ari, *Intifada: The Palestinian Uprising—Israel's Third Front* (New York, 1989). Roger Heacock and Jamal Nassar, eds., *Intifada: Palestine at a Crossroads* (New York, 1990). Don Peretz, *Intifada: The Palestinian Uprising* (New York, 1990).

RASHID I. KHALIDI

INVESTMENT FOREIGN. See FINANCE, INTERNATIONAL; MULTINATIONAL CORPORATIONS.

IRAN. A relatively large country (636,000 square miles; 1,648,000 sq. km.) in Southwest Asia, Iran's twentieth-century political history was strongly affected by international rivalry for influence over its oil resources. Prior to World War I, the principal foreign threat came from neighboring Tsarist Russia and the British Empire, each interfering in Iran's domestic politics to promote friendly governments. Foreign intervention dramatically declined between 1921 and 1939 when Moscow was preoccupied with creating the Soviet Union and London perceived few threats to its expanding oil interests in southwestern Iran. Although Iran acted more independently in this period, its economy became more integrated into the international market system. The outbreak of World War II revived foreign interest in the country's policies and resources, culminating in a joint Anglo-Soviet invasion in August 1941.

These persistent foreign interventions prompted intense debates within Iran over the most effective means of securing the country's independence and led to the emergence of two major political currents: secular and religious *nationalism. Secular nationalists, mostly political activists educated in Europe, North America, or, after 1930, Iran's secularized public education system, generally believed their country could successfully confront Europeans by adopting Western political institutions, economic programs, and social policies. In contrast, the religious nationalists believed imitation of the West reinforced the country's dependence and so they advocated a return to traditional cultural values, especially those of Shi'i *Islam, the religion of 90 percent of the population. Despite their different perspectives, both secular and religious nationalists viewed the country's shahs (kings) as compromising with foreign powers in order to maintain royal autocracy. Consequently, secular and religious groups sometimes cooperated to restrict the shah's powers, most notably in the 1905–1907 Constitutional Revolution. More typically, shahs exploited conflicts among secular and religious nationalists to enhance royal prerogatives.

The Pahlavi dynasty (ruled 1926–1979) generally tried to co-opt the secular nationalists by promoting many economic and social reform policies they advocated. These programs initiated the industrialization and urbanization processes that significantly transformed Iranian society, especially after rising oil prices dramatically increased state revenues. The government's diverse development projects supported a large bureaucracy, a national army, and internal security forces—institutions that greatly strengthened the central government. The secular nationalists favorably referred to all reforms as *modernization. Nevertheless, because the first Pahlavi shah (ruled 1926–1941) used his power to rule as a dictator, he failed to develop a political support base among secular nationalists. His social policies, such as secularizing the educational and legal systems, generally antagonized the religious nationalists and cost him support among the clergy as well.

Following World War II, Iran became one of the earliest scenes of the emerging Cold War struggle between the West and the Soviet bloc, as each sought to incorporate the country within its alliance system. Iran's efforts to pursue a neutral foreign policy ended in August 1953 when an American- and British-supported military coup d'état overthrew Prime Minister Mohammad Mosadeq, who had forced the shah, Mohammad Reza (ruled 1941–1979), to reign as a constitutional monarch. Subsequently, the shah consolidated a royal dictatorship while cultivating close ties with the United States. The shah's policies alienated both secular and religious nationalists, who began gradually to cooperate in opposing his rule. In 1978, several groups formed a broad-based religious-secular coalition under the charismatic leadership of the exiled clergyman Ayatollah Ruhollah *Khomeini. This coalition mobilized Iranians in cities and towns throughout the country to participate in mass anti-shah demonstrations. A popular revolutionary movement grew rapidly, demoralizing the extensive security forces; by February 1979, the movement had overthrown the monarchy and established a republic. The new government terminated Iran's long-standing alliance with the United States and began to chart a neutral course vis-à-vis the superpowers.

The secular-religious coalition began to dissolve soon after the initial success of the revolution. The various secular parties faced a serious disadvantage in the postrevolutionary political contest because they appealed primarily to college students and professionals, a small, urban elite in a society where 80 percent of adults had not completed high school. The religious parties appealed more broadly to shopkeepers and artisans in the urban bazaars, lower-ranking civil servants, industrial workers, and peasants. In general, the religious nationalists successfully portrayed the secularists as Westernized "liberals" who had lost touch with their Islamic cultural roots and wished to create a "democratic" republic that would be un-Islamic and ultimately as dependent upon the West as had been the shah's regime. Through their control of revolutionary organizations that assumed judicial and security functions, the religious nationalists effectively intimidated their secular rivals. Significantly, those religious groups affiliated with Khomeini capitalized on his nationwide popularity to draft a constitution, approved in a December 1979 referendum, that vested ultimate political authority in a senior Shi'i theologian, or *faqih,* who has broad powers to appoint the chief military and judicial authorities. The constitution designated Khomeini the first *faqih* and provided that his successors be chosen by a special assembly of high-ranking clergy.

The constitution also stipulates that the head of government is an elected president who serves a four-year term and may be reelected once. The president appoints the cabinet, but each minister must be approved by the legislature. The president also selects several vice presidents, one of whom serves as the de facto prime minister. The constitution preserves the national assembly, or Majlis, that was first created in 1906. In its "Islamicized" version, the Majlis is a single-chamber body of 270 members who are elected every four years. The Majlis is independent of the executive, which has no power to dissolve it. A unique institution, known as the Council of Guardians, reviews all Majlis legislation and has authority to veto any laws that do not conform to Shi'i Islamic principles. The judiciary is independent of both the executive and the Majlis. The chief judicial authorities must be clergy with advanced training in the codices of Shi'i Islamic law.

Despite the personal popularity of Khomeini, there was significant opposition to the notion of the Shi'i clergy having any special authority to rule in an Islamic government.

The Mojahedin-e Khalq, a prerevolutionary clandestine organization that developed into a mass political movement after 1979, actually launched a major nationwide uprising in June 1981. The regime crushed the rebellion with a reign of terror that lasted for eighteen months; at least 13,000 Iranians, 90 percent of whom were political dissidents, were killed in this conflict. Since 1981 the leadership of the Mojahedin and also various secular opposition parties has been based outside of the country.

The Islamic republic inherited an economically and socially diverse society. Although the government did not alter the primarily capitalist nature of the economic system, one of its aims has been to distribute wealth from oil revenues more equitably. The country's 70,000 villages, where 38 percent of the total 62 million population resides, have been the beneficiaries of major development programs that have provided them with roads, electricity, piped water, primary schools, and health clinics. Price support policies for agricultural commodities and interest-free credit to finance crop production helped transfer more money to rural areas. The regime's policies have been less successful in ameliorating living conditions for the urban poor. City population has increased an average of 4 percent annually since the revolution because of high migration from the villages. Tehran, the capital and one of Asia's largest and most congested cities, has failed to resolve problems associated with its pollution, inadequate water and sewerage systems, and inefficient and poorly maintained public transportation services. Four other cities with populations over one million, Mashhad in the northeast, Isfahan on the central plateau, Tabriz in the northwest, and Shiraz in the south, face similar problems, albeit on a smaller scale.

Disagreement over economic policy opened ideological rifts among Iran's ruling elite. During the first decade of the Islamic Republic, the clergy's preoccupation with foreign policy goals not only deflected its attention from the domestic economy but also helped to maintain its political unity. Initially, consensus focused on the twin objectives of ending the deposed monarchy's de facto alliance with the United States and presenting Iran as a model of *Third World independence from Western political, economic, and cultural domination. Iraq's September 1980 invasion of Iran enabled the clergy to mobilize popular support around the national cause of defending the country against foreign aggression. The end of hostilities in August 1988 paved the way for refocusing policy concerns onto long-neglected economic matters. More pragmatic political leaders argued that the government's failure to promote economic growth threatened the revolution's future. They used both the Majlis and the press as forums to present their perspective: past policies stressing economic self-sufficiency had contributed to the economic recession; and Iran must abandon its isolationism and cooperate with Western nations in order to obtain resources for creating a just, Islamic society at home. Such views alarmed the conservatives, who argued that extensive diplomatic ties and commercial relations, especially foreign loans and investments, would make Iran dependent upon Western countries, compromise the aims of the revolution, and ultimately undermine the very legitimacy of the Islamic Republic.

The pragmatists' emphasis on programs designed to alleviate immediate economic difficulties had broad appeal. In-

creasingly, they began to focus on issues of personal freedoms, arguing that economic progress and civil liberties are linked. An articulate advocate of this view, Mohammad Khatami, was elected president in 1997 following a campaign that stressed the need to create a "civil society" in which individual economic and political rights are protected by transparent laws. Khatami's vision is opposed by conservatives, who argue that average citizens are not qualified to make morally correct political decisions and therefore must be guided by clergy with specialized knowledge of religious texts which reveal God's plan for an Islamic society. Such conservatives occupy powerful positions in the legislative and judicial branches of government and try to block Khatami's efforts to expand civil liberties.

(See also IRAN-IRAQ WAR; IRANIAN REVOLUTION; RELIGION AND POLITICS; SECULARIZATION.)

Nikki Keddie, *Roots of Revolution* (New Haven, Conn., 1981). Nikki Keddie and Eric Hoogland, eds., *The Iranian Revolution and the Islamic Republic* (Syracuse, N.Y., 1986). Ervand Abrahamian, *Khomeinism* (Berkeley, Calif., 1993). Asghar Schirazi, *The Constitution of Iran: Politics and the State in the Islamic Republic* (London, 1997).

ERIC HOOGLAND

IRAN-IRAQ WAR. In September 1980, *Iraq launched full scale air and ground attacks across the 730-mile (1,170-km.) border it shares with *Iran, initiating a *war that raged intermittently until a cease-fire was declared in August 1988. This protracted contest—the longest conventional interstate war of the twentieth century—recalled the infantry trench warfare of World War I, while its later phases incorporated modern ballistic missile technology to attack cities and economic targets. Some 367,000 Iraqis and Iranians were killed and more than 700,000 wounded, by conservative Western estimates, and the war devastated both economies.

The ostensible causes of the Iran-Iraq War (sometimes referred to as the Gulf War of 1980–1988) included disputed borders and rights to a vital waterway, the Shatt al-Arab. Fundamentally at issue was the question of regional *hegemony. On one level this was the latest episode in a history of contention for regional power between Iran and Iraq. At another level, it pitted the revolutionary Islamism of the new regime in Tehran against the Arab nationalist dictatorship in Baghdad, now backed by most of the major powers.

The outbreak of full-scale armed conflict between the two states was preceded by a series of border clashes, and by Tehran's appeals to Iraq's Shi'i Muslims (about 55 percent of the population) to follow Iran's revolutionary example and overthrow the secular tyranny of President Saddam *Hussein. This campaign included sabotage bombings in Baghdad and at least one attempt to assassinate a major Iraqi government official. Baghdad, for its part, escalated hostilities in order to take advantage of the postrevolutionary disarray in Iranian society, especially in the armed forces, and Iran's international isolation, particularly its estrangement from the United States. Its immediate pretext and goal was to overturn the 1975 Algiers agreement, signed by Saddam Hussein and the shah of Iran, which ratified Iranian demands for sharing sovereignty over the Shatt al-Arab in return for ending Iranian support of Kurdish insurgents in northern Iraq.

Iraq's initial incursion captured some 6,000–8,000 square miles (15,000–21,000 sq. km.) of Iran's oil-rich and Arab-populated Khuzestan province, destroying several cities and numerous towns, but failed to inflict any decisive defeat on Iran's forces. The contest was mainly waged by ground forces, though the opening weeks of the war saw both countries' air forces engaged as well.

After the first six months, by March 1981, Iranian forces had rallied to prevent further Iraqi advances. A second phase of the war began in mid-1982, when Iran took the offensive to push Iraq out of most of the Iranian territory it had occupied and, a year later, carried the ground war into Iraqi territory. The war settled into a pattern of stalemate, as year after year Iran launched seasonal "final offensives" which never successfully broke through Iraqi defenses. This second phase coincided with the emergence of a new regional dimension, as the Iran-Iraq war became an Iranian-Arab war. Iraq secured the financial and political support of Saudi Arabia, Kuwait, and other oil-rich Arab states of the gulf, as well as political and limited military support from Jordan and Egypt. The goal of preventing an Iraqi defeat was also shared by the major powers. The Soviet Union, which had cut off arms shipments to Iraq at the beginning of the war, resumed its role as Iraq's major military supplier; France supplied sophisticated warplanes and missile systems; the United States provided important agricultural shipments and credits.

From the outset, both combatants targeted one another's oil export facilities. Iraqi facilities were closer to the war zone, and thus effectively closed early in the conflict. Iraq's vulnerability was compounded when Syria, in 1982, supported Iran by closing off Iraq's pipeline outlet across Syria to the Mediterranean. This left a pipeline through Turkey as Iraq's only oil export outlet until late in the war, when new pipelines through Saudi Arabia were opened. A third phase, the "tanker war," began in early 1984, when Iraq used French-supplied jets and missiles to interdict Iranian oil exports. Baghdad's aim was to employ technological superiority to break the Iranian siege on the ground. Because Iraqi oil exports by tanker were already closed down, Iran could retaliate only by attacking the shipping of Iraq's allies, Kuwait and Saudi Arabia, risking Western intervention to impose a cease-fire that would appear to favor Iraq.

Something like this scenario finally occurred by early 1987, when the United States responded to Kuwaiti requests for protection of its tankers by dispatching a naval force that grew to some fifty warships. This corresponded with the fourth and final phase of the war. Iran's last, unsuccessful "final offensive" of January-February 1987 was followed by a series of successful Iraqi campaigns to recover lost territory. The combination of Iraqi ground victories and a series of naval clashes with U.S. forces in the gulf, culminating in the destruction of an Iranian airliner that killed 291 civilians, persuaded Iran to accept UN Security Council Resolution 598 which established a cease-fire more or less on Iraqi terms. Negotiations toward a final settlement proceeded in a desultory fashion until the fall of 1990. Then Iraq, in the context of confrontation with the United States following Baghdad's invasion of Kuwait, accepted Iran's terms for settlement based on the status quo ante—namely, the 1975 Algiers accord.

Several dimensions to this conflict deserve mention. The first is the extent to which this was an "oil war." Without access to oil revenues—their own and in the case of Iraq those of its Arab allies—neither country could have sustained a war of this scope, intensity, and duration. The conflict, moreover, grew out of the *Iranian Revolution, itself profoundly shaped by Iran's oil-based political economy, and both countries had experienced oil-motivated overt and covert interventions by the United States and other powers, interventions that also directly influenced the outcome of this conflict.

A second notable aspect is the durability of the postcolonial nation-state. Iranian appeals to Shi'i coreligionists had no more impact on Iraqi morale or loyalty than did Iraq's efforts to enlist the ethnically Arab population of southern Iran. National rather than sectarian or ethnic solidarities prevailed.

Finally, in many ways the Iran-Iraq War linked the Iranian Revolution of 1978–1979 to the 1991 *Gulf War, the regional confrontation that followed Iraq's invasion of Kuwait in August 1990. Iraq emerged with its economy exhausted and its political ambitions frustrated, but its military much stronger and more cohesive. Kuwait provided both the provocations and the pretexts for Baghdad to make a new bid for regional hegemony. The war had also facilitated the extension of U.S. military forces in the region, both the important naval combat experience of 1987–1988 and, more significantly, the construction of sophisticated bases and ports in Saudi Arabia, without which the deployment of half of U.S. combat forces worldwide to the gulf in the fall of 1990 would have been impossible.

(See also ISLAM; KHOMEINI, RUHOLLAH; KURDISTAN.)

"The Strange War in the Gulf" *MERIP Reports* 125/126 (July–September 1984). Dilip Hiro, *The Longest War: The Iran-Iraq Military Conflict* (New York, 1991).

JOE STORK

IRANIAN REVOLUTION. The Iranian Revolution of 1978–1979 was one of the most momentous and unique events of the postwar epoch: it challenged the established distribution of power in much of the *Middle East and the Islamic world and provided major international conflicts with the United States and *Iran's neighbor, *Iraq. The *revolution itself began in 1978, at a time when the shah, or Persian king, had been in apparent control for twenty-five years and had used the substantial oil revenues that Iran had been earning in the 1970s to build up his country's economy and international importance. By September 1978 the shah's government was confronted with widespread protests, involving millions of people, in the major cities of Iran. Although the first protests had been led by secular opponents of the regime, leadership had quickly passed to the Islamic clergy under the leadership of Ayatollah *Khomeini, in exile since 1964.

By January 1979 the shah was forced to flee. Khomeini returned to Iran on 1 February and after a brief armed uprising against the remnants of the shah's army on 11–12 February, he took power. Within weeks he had proclaimed the establishment of the Islamic Republic of Iran, and proceeded to transform the political, social, educational, and cultural life of the country to meet what he regarded as Islamic principles.

Power lay in the hands of the leading clergy and the networks of Islamic committees set up throughout the country. The ministries of state and the armed forces were subjected to clerical control. Opposition to Khomeini's regime continued for several years and led to armed clashes with opponents of the clergy, both left-wing guerrillas in the cities and Kurdish insurgents in the western mountains.

Khomeini proclaimed a policy of militant neutrality, under the slogan "Neither East nor West," and appealed to the Islamic and other oppressed peoples of the world to rise up against their rulers. In many parts of the Islamic world, in particular, underground and opposition groups looked to Iran for support and example against governments seen as secular or tied to the West. Iranian influence was especially strong amongst Shi'a in Lebanon.

Two conflicts in particular came to dominate Iranian foreign policy. The first was with the United States and began on 5 November 1979 when a group of Islamic militants, proclaiming themselves to be students following the Imam's line, seized the staff and buildings of the U.S. embassy in Tehran. The Iranian government swung behind these militants and made a series of demands, including the handing over of the shah, then in the United States, and the return of his wealth. The United States froze all Iranian assets and, unsuccessfully, attempted military action to free the hostages. In January 1981, the hostages were released in return for a financial settlement of U.S.-Iranian claims and counterclaims.

The second major conflict came in September 1980 when Iraq, angered by Iranian calls for the overthrow of the Ba'thist regime in Baghdad, invaded Iran in the hope of toppling the Khomeini government. In the ensuing war, in which over a million people are said to have died, neither side was able to prevail over the other or to overthrow the other's government. In 1987 U.S. and other Western navies, anxious about Iranian influence, entered the war on Iraq's side, and in August 1988 Iran finally accepted a UN Security Council resolution on a cease-fire.

The Iranian Revolution was the first successful upheaval of modern times to justify itself in religious terms and to be led by the clergy. More than any other revolution, it rejected modern ideas of progress, democracy, and material well-being. At the same time it was distinct from most *Third World revolutions in taking place in cities and in involving relatively little armed conflict. Some analyses stress the particular power of radical Islamic *ideology, others the appeals of ideological returns to the past, and others the particular conflict between the shah's state, sustained by oil-based modernization, and society.

(See also IRAN-IRAQ WAR; ISLAM; RELIGION AND POLITICS.)

Nikki Keddie, *Roots of Revolution: An Interpretive History of Modern Iran* (New Haven, Conn., and London, 1981). Ervand Abrahamian, *Iran Between Two Revolutions* (Princeton, N.J., 1982). Shaul Bakhash, *The Reign of the Ayatollahs* (London and New York, 1985). Gary Sick, *All Fall Down* (New Haven, Conn., and London, 1985).

FRED HALLIDAY

IRAQ. The modern state of Iraq was created in 1920, as part of the peace settlement following World War I. The victorious Allies divided the Arab provinces of the former Ottoman Empire between them, and Britain, which had been in occupation of the provinces of Basra and Baghdad for most of the war and Mosul by the end of the war, was appointed mandatory power under the new system of international trusteeship established by the *League of Nations.

Although parts of the country had been united under a single government at various times in the past, the entity which emerged in 1920 had had no previous independent existence as a nation-state. Britain imported a king, Faisal, son of Sharif Hussein of Mecca, and endowed Iraq with a constitution and a bicameral legislature. The mandate, a form of indirect rule where Arab ministers and officials were closely supervised by British advisers whose advice had to be taken, came to an end in 1932, when Iraq was admitted to the League of Nations as an independent state. By this time Britain had secured Iraq's present northern boundary, had made sure that the concession for oil exploration and exploitation was given to the Iraq Petroleum Company, a conglomerate of British, Dutch, French and American oil interests, and had generally tried to create a social base for the monarchy by confirming "suitable" tribal leaders in full possession of what had previously been the customary holdings of "their" tribes. In addition, Britain retained military bases in Iraq and generally continued to exercise strong political and economic influence.

For much of the period between the end of the mandate in 1932 and the *revolution of 1958, the country was torn by profound political and socioeconomic tensions. First, the concentration of wealth and power in a few hands, and the concentration of economic activity in the cities, caused a flood of rural-to-urban migration, particularly to the capital, mostly on the part of sharecroppers escaping lives of extreme deprivation on the large estates of the rural south. Their presence in the cities, usually in poor squatter settlements on the outskirts, served to inflame the economic and social tensions already present.

Second, the profoundly unrepresentative nature of the government, and the close association of many of its leading figures with Britain, meant that its policies were out of step with the aspirations of most of the population. The opposition included liberal democrats, Arab nationalists, Kurdish nationalists, and communists, the latter having emerged after World War II as the largest and most influential political force in the country.

The revolution of July 1958, although widely supported, took the form of a military coup, led by a group of disaffected military officers who had no ties to any particular political party but were committed to national independence, nonalignment in the *Cold War, and a gamut of social, economic and political reforms. However, within weeks of the revolution, political differences began to surface between the communists, the Kurds, and the pan-Arab nationalists, both Nasserist and Ba'thist.

With their roots in the shantytowns, the emerging labor movement, and the new professional middle classes, the communists continued to be the principal political force in the country immediately after the revolution, but their position was ambivalent. They supported the president, Brigadier 'Abd al-Karim Qasim, partly because of his progressive social and economic policies—apart from his housing and welfare programs, Law 80 of 1961 was the first legislation enacted to restrict the activities of foreign oil companies in any Arab country—and partly because they did not believe that external and internal forces would permit them to remain in power even if they were to succeed in seizing it.

In addition, like Qasim, the communists were opposed to the Arab nationalists' demand that Iraq should join the United Arab Republic of Egypt and Syria (UAR). Given President Gamal Abdel *Nasser's known antipathy to political parties, they considered joining the UAR as tantamount to agreeing to a ban, or at least to tight restrictions, on their activities. As a result, "unity" (*wahda*), both for and against, became the main rallying point in the struggle between right- and left-wing forces, which only ended with Qasim's overthrow in 1963.

The second political force, the Kurdish national movement, although fragmented, was dominated by the *Kurdistan Democratic Party and its leader, Mulla Mustafa Barzani, who died in exile in 1979. Although many Kurds have migrated to the cities, they originate in the mountainous north and northeast of Iraq, and form some 20 percent of the total Iraqi population of some 20 million (1994 estimate). Most Iraqi Kurdish politicians and parties have sought some form of regional or local autonomy within Iraq, but armed Kurdish organizations and political groupings have been in conflict with the authorities in Baghdad since the inauguration of the state in 1920, largely because of the authorities' refusal to countenance such aspirations.

The party with the greatest long-term success in postrevolutionary Iraq has been the Ba'th. Although the Ba'thists never attracted the level of mass support commanded by the communists, they eventually succeeded in taking power and maintaining it in their hands by a combination of skillful organization and an alliance with key military officers. Together with the Nasserists they organized a military coup against Qasim and the Left in February 1963, but were edged out of government by their partners after eight months. These months saw some of the most terrible violence hitherto experienced in the postwar *Middle East, directed against the communists and the Left. After five years in the wilderness the Ba'th engineered another coup in July 1968.

Ba'thism is a variety of pan-Arab nationalism, based on the premise that there is a single Arab nation, which has been divided artificially, first by the Ottomans, and subsequently by European and American *imperialism, and *Zionism. Once the Arabs are liberated and united, it is believed, social conflicts within and between particular states (or "regions of the Arab nation") will subside. Ba'thism has three central aspirations: unity, freedom, and socialism. Unity refers to the unity of the Arab nation, freedom to freedom from imperialism and Zionism, and socialism to a general aspiration towards state-directed economic development supported by a mixed economy.

After its rise to power, the Ba'th leadership attempted to legitimate its rule in these very general terms, and the party expanded into an organization with several million members. Since it had less than 1,000 members at the peak of its influence in 1960–1963, the party in the form it assumed in the early 1970s was created *after* its advent to power. The National Patriotic Front—an alliance between the Ba'th and the communists concluded a year after the *nationalization of oil in 1972—continued to exist on paper long after it had become completely redundant; in practice no political opposition was tolerated after 1976. The leadership developed several wellequipped security services to repress real and potential opposition, from the Kurds, from the left, and, increasingly in the middle 1970s, from Shi'i political groups and parties.

Although there is a National Assembly and a Revolutionary Command Council, neither institution has any independent authority, and real power has been almost exclusively in the hands of one man since the early 1980s. In the course of the 1970s and 1980s, Saddam *Hussein, who became president in 1979, concentrated power more and more in his own person, his immediate family, and his closest associates, and developed an elaborate cult of personality around himself.

A number of factors assisted in bringing this about. In the first place, the huge increase in oil revenues since 1973, shortly after the nationalization of oil, naturally went straight into the hands of the state, which had already become equivalent to "Saddam Hussein and his circle." Second, these same revenues made Iraq, with its relatively large population, a major market for Western and Japanese products, including consumer goods, industrial and infrastructural projects, and military hardware; the buildup of the latter in the 1970s and 1980s was instrumental in Saddam Hussein's decision first to attack Iran and subsequently to annex *Kuwait.

In addition, the great apprehension aroused in the West, the Soviet Union, and much of the Arab world by the establishment of the Islamic Republic of Iran meant that Saddam Hussein was able to attract virtually unquestioning support from most of the rest of the world for more than a decade. The war against Iran, launched in September 1980 and lasting just under eight years, was a disaster for both sides; some 400,000 were killed and 750,000 wounded, with almost incalculable costs of infrastructural damage and losses both in oil revenue and GNP. Some two years later, Iraq invaded Kuwait.

By almost any reckoning, this was an extraordinarily foolhardy act. Various motives have been put forward—for instance, that Kuwait was "demanding" repayment of the substantial loans it had made to Iraq during the *Iran-Iraq war, that Iraq was in desperate need of foreign exchange, and that Kuwait, along with some other Gulf states, was flooding the international market with cheap oil to an extent which was gravely impeding Iraq's chances of economic recovery. Given that Kuwait was in no position to force Iraq to repay, that Iraq was spending huge sums on armaments and prestige reconstruction projects, and that a binding OPEC agreement on oil prices had been reached six days before the invasion, none of these reasons seems particularly convincing.

Reaction to the invasion was swift. In the five months between the invasion itself and the beginning of the *Gulf War in January 1991, an array of forces from Bangladesh, Britain, Egypt, France, Morocco, Pakistan, Saudi Arabia, Syria, and the United States mustered in Saudi Arabia, backed by UN resolutions and the moral support of the European Community, Japan, and the former states of the Warsaw Treaty Organization. A sanctions regime was imposed which remains in force at the time of writing.

According to one observer, the invasion and the war (that is, the period between 2 August 1990 and 27 February 1991) resulted in at least 100,000 military and civilian deaths and some 300,000 wounded. As many as 2.5 million people (including foreigners working in Iraq and Kuwait) were displaced; over $170 billion in property and infrastructural damage was caused in Iraq, perhaps $60 billion worth in Kuwait, excluding the environmental effects of the firing of Kuwaiti oil wells.

A few days after the war ended, risings against the regime broke out in southern Iraq and in Kurdistan. Although the "rebels" gained control of large areas between the end of February and the beginning of March, units of the Republican Guard were soon able to gain the upper hand in Basra, Najaf, and Karbala, where they carried out indiscriminate executions. At the end of March, Iraqi helicopters and troops launched raids on Kirkuk and other Kurdish cities. A mass exodus of Kurds to the Iraqi/Turkish and Iraqi/Iranian borders began; by the end of April there were about 2.5 million refugees, both Kurds and southerners. The Kurds fled largely because they feared a repetition of the regime's bombing of Halabja in March 1988 with chemical weapons, which had killed more than 5,000 people. In April 1991, Britain and the United States set up a military exclusion zone in the Kurdish area north of latitude 36° N. Over time this arrangement facilitated the emergence of a de facto Kurdish autonomous area with its own government and national assembly.

In December 1992, the United States decided to enforce a second air exclusion zone over southern Iraq (south of latitude 32° N), in a largely unsuccessful attempt to halt the drainage and forcible evacuation of the marshlands, which had provided natural cover for opponents of the regime. There were air attacks against targets in Iraq in January 1993, following Iraqi incursions into Kuwait, and U.S. bombers destroyed Iraqi intelligence headquarters in Baghdad some six months later.

Throughout the 1990s there were a number of attempts by the Iraqi government and some of its friends and neighbors (notably Turkey, France, and the Commonwealth of Independent States) to persuade the UN Security Council to lift sanctions, but faced with the threat of a U.S. veto, and also by compelling evidence of persistent Iraqi noncompliance on matters related to chemical and biological weapons, the sanctions remained in place. In 1996 Iraq eventually accepted UN Resolution 985, which allowed it to sell a limited amount of oil to pay for the import of food, medicine, and pipeline spare parts; the amount involved was almost trebled (to $10.5 million per annum) in February 1998.

A referendum in October 1995 gave Saddam Hussein a not entirely unexpected 99.96 percent of the vote, but it is impossible to obtain a clear picture of the internal situation. Coup attempts, each generally followed by massive reprisals, were reported in January, February, and June 1992, in September and November 1993, March, May, and June 1995, and June and December 1996. There were reports of mutinies in the Republican Guard in the spring and summer of 1995, as well as a number of high-level defections, perhaps most notably the flight of two of Saddam Hussein's daughters to Jordan with their husbands in July 1995.

One of the sons-in-law, General Hussein Kamil Majid, had previously been minister of defense, and was thus able to give his debriefers in Amman crucial information on Iraqi nonconventional weapons. In an act of quite extraordinary folly, the two sons-in-law returned to Iraq in February 1996, where they were immediately shot by other family members, presumably at the instigation of their father-in-law. One consequence of this—in spite of his having been seriously wounded in an assassination attempt in December 1996—was the rise in importance and responsibility of Saddam Hussein's ferocious older son, 'Udayy.

Nevertheless, while the coups and defections indicated Saddam Hussein's increasing isolation, there was no evidence that the regime was crumbling. It was almost impossible for any opposition to organize within Iraq, and the effectiveness of the externally based Iraqi National Council was greatly reduced by the long-standing divisions and mistrust within Kurdish ranks—leading to bitter interfactional fighting in 1994 and 1995.

Since the end of the Gulf War, there have been a number of standoffs between the regime and the UNSCOM (United Nations Special Commission on Iraq) inspection teams, stationed in Iraq to seek out and destroy weapons of mass destruction, culminating in December 1998 when the U.S. and British air forces bombed Baghdad for four days. Since then, UNSCOM has not returned to Iraq. It is difficult to predict how long this stalemate will continue, but it is clear that no lasting progress toward peace and stability in Iraq can be made while Saddam Hussein remains at the helm, and equally clear that the regime's continuation in power ultimately serves no one's interest but its own.

Hanna Batatu, *The Old Social Classes and the Revolutionary Movements of Iraq: A Study of Iraq's Old Landed Classes and Its Communists, Ba'thists, and Free Officers* (Princeton, N.J., 1978). Samir al-Khalil, *The Republic of Fear: The Politics of Modern Iraq* (London, 1989). Amatzia Baram, *Building Towards Crisis: Saddam Husayn's Strategy for Survival* (Washington, D.C., 1998). Marion Farouk-Sluglett and Peter Sluglett, *Iraq Since 1958: From Revolution to Dictatorship*, 3d ed. (London, 1999). Charles Tripp, *A Political History of Iraq* (Cambridge, U.K., 2000).

MARION FAROUK-SLUGLETT
PETER SLUGLETT

IRELAND. As a small state on the edge of Western Europe, Ireland (population 3.7 million) has tended to be particularly preoccupied with its external environment. In the past the dominant feature in that environment was Britain and the dominant issue was political autonomy. From the 1950s on, however, as Ireland became more and more involved with the wider world, the issues became as much economic as political.

Political History and Institutions. The Act of Union of 1800 abolished such limited elements of devolved government as Ireland, or rather its "ascendancy" class, had enjoyed in the late eighteenth century. In the course of the nineteenth century, gradual democratization politicized and institutionalized the fundamental cleavage between Ireland and England, between north and south Ireland, between unionist and nationalist, and, although the lines of conflict were not entirely coterminous, between Protestant and Catholic. Following a short, sharp guerrilla struggle (kindled by the 1916 Easter Rising but waged in earnest from 1919 to 1921), secession from the United Kingdom was achieved in the Anglo-Irish Treaty of 1921, the six northeastern counties being given the right to opt out of this settlement, a right that was promptly exercised (see *Northern Ireland). From the point of view of the secessionists, the achievement was partial. This was not just because of the "loss" of the northeast; the settlement was also limited by various constitutional ties with the British monarchy and by concessions in regard to the use of naval facilities. All of this ensured that the issue of relations with the former imperial power continued to dominate the politics of the new state. At the outset this issue was a highly divisive one that caused a brief but bloody civil war (1922–1923) between pro- and anti-treatyites. This division then became the basis of the cleavage between the two main political parties, which, after some changes in nomenclature, emerged in their present forms (Fine Gael [pro-treaty] and Fianna Fáil [anti-treaty]). In any event, it is clear in retrospect that there was little potential for the development of any other cleavage. Secession had produced a remarkably homogeneous society—95 percent Catholic, predominantly agrarian with a significant *land reform program already completed, and with a tiny industrial proletariat. The limited scope for the emergence of a capital-labor conflict was symbolized and reinforced by the Labour Party's decision not to contest the 1918 election and has been reflected in Labour's persistent minority status in the party system ever since. The declining salience of the moderate nationalist versus strong nationalist (pro-treaty-versus-anti-treaty) cleavage from the 1960s on did not lead to the realignment of the party system on the basis of any alternative cleavage but to two competing catchall parties with residual differences on the nationalist issue. Apart from the Labour Party, other minor parties have appeared from time to time; the current crop includes the center-right Progressive Democrats and the Green Party.

That democracy was successfully established despite the turbulent period of armed independence struggle and civil war was due in part to an aspect of the British legacy—a democratic political culture and a set of state institutions (bureaucratic, judicial, and parliamentary) that were either inherited or copied from the former colonial power. The 1922 Constitution did contain some institutional innovations, including judicial review, proportional representation, and provision for referendums. A new constitution was enacted under Fianna Fáil in 1937, but the new features were mainly political and ideological rather than institutional. In the last three decades of the twentieth century, a changing Ireland had to undertake a series of referendums to dismantle this constitutionalized ideological inheritance—the "special position" of the *Roman Catholic Church (removed in 1972), the prohibition of divorce (removed at the second attempt in 1995), and the (suspended) claim to jurisdiction over the territory of Northern Ireland (removed pursuant to the Belfast Agreement in 1998). Running counter to these liberalizing developments, in 1983 the electorate inserted an apparently absolute ban on abortion into the constitution. This provision was circumscribed by a Supreme Court judgment in early 1992, but an attempt to revise the clause in question in order to deal with problems arising from the Supreme Court judgment was defeated in a referendum later the same year. The issue was thereby thrown back into the lap of the legislature but, given the deep cleavage in Irish society on the issue of abortion, another referendum seems likely.

The Economy. From the early 1930s on, economic and industrial strategy were outrightly protectionist. The failure of that policy, as manifested in severe economic crises and mass emigration, led to a dramatic U-turn in 1958 and to the adoption of a policy of *export-led growth, free trade, and the encouragement of foreign investment. The initial results of this new strategy were encouraging, but the high hopes of the 1960s, buoyed by an expectation of an era of economic progress that was to be ushered in by EC membership in 1973, ran foul of the oil crises of the 1970s. The response of successive governments was to shore up living standards by increasing public spending. Because of their particular history, the major political parties lacked fixed ideological anchorage

on such issues. As a result, they competed at the spending end rather than from opposite ends of the spend-save spectrum. This approach was particularly evident in the Fianna Fáil election manifesto of 1977. The result was that the national debt/GNP ratio rose by nearly 90 percent between 1973 and 1986. Stringent corrective measures were finally undertaken by Fianna Fáil after the 1987 election. The government's recovery strategy was aided by support from the main opposition party and was buttressed by corporatist-style national pay and policy agreements that have since then been renewed on a regular basis. The fiscal and economic criteria set for participation in the *Economic and Monetary Union reinforced the new policy approach. (Despite the obvious difficulties occasioned by the country's level of trade with Britain, Ireland was, from the outset, a committed supporter of EMU.) While the influence of particular causes is difficult to determine and while the long-term prospects for the "Celtic tiger" remain a matter of debate, what is unmistakable is the transformation in the Irish economy indicated by sustained growth rates and falling unemployment. Equally unmistakable are the attendant problems of labor shortages, infrastructural bottlenecks, and threatening inflation.

Foreign Policy. If Irish economic policy can be seen as a process of adaptation to the forces of *globalization, Irish foreign policy can also be seen as traversing a path from isolation to involvement. Neutrality in World War II was part and parcel of the preoccupation with the relationship with Britain and with the issue of sovereignty. A policy of neutrality continued to be pursued in the postwar period, manifesting itself in Ireland's independent activist posture in the UN in the 1950s and 1960s. The minimal definition of neutrality policy is noninvolvement in military alliances; the maximal definition aspires to total independence in foreign policy. Despite the urging of the maximalists, Ireland never became directly involved with the Nonaligned Movement, nor did it develop particularly close relations with the other European neutrals. With EC accession in 1973, neutrality was explicitly recognized as conditional, the condition that would trigger change being the achievement of a full European political union with its own defense competence. In the early 1980s, however, neutrality received a boost by being linked in popular attitudes with a rejection of the new Cold War. In turn, at the end of the 1980s, some of the assumptions associated with the concept of neutrality were put in question by the collapse of communism and by the end of the Cold War. Ireland's emphasis on neutrality had retarded the development of European political cooperation in the 1980s by keeping military aspects out of discussions of security cooperation. The *Maastricht Treaty, ratified in 1993, signaled an end to the exclusion of the defense dimension, though special allowance for Ireland's position is made in the treaty's reference to not prejudicing "the specific character of the security and defence policy of certain member states." In Ireland's case this specific character boils down to not joining a military alliance. This position did not prevent Ireland from joining the NATO-led Partnership for Peace (PfP) in 1999; the formal "presentation document" involved in this step stated that "Ireland's decision to participate in PfP is in full accordance with Ireland's policy of military neutrality, which has always been pursued in tandem with full and active support for collective security, based in international law." Nor has neutrality prevented Ireland from participating in the evolving structures of European security and defense policy. In this context, the constant refrain has been that this is about conflict prevention and about humanitarian, rescue, peacekeeping, and crisis management tasks (referred to as the Petersberg tasks) and is not about creating a European army.

The evolution of European security policy is but one of several areas in which membership in the *European Union is placing more demands on Irish policy. Economic success has meant that only about half the country now qualifies for structural funds. Such funds will in any event be considerably squeezed as the Union enlarges. The prospect of enlargement also puts Ireland and other small member states on the defensive in regard to the share-out of positions and power in the Union's decision-making institutions. In short, the need to adapt to membership in the Union is not something that is confined to the early stages of membership but something that continues and will continue to confront both Irish policymakers and the Irish public.

Northern Ireland and Anglo-Irish Relations. By the mid-1960s, the shift away from narrow nationalist preoccupations was becoming evident in a new flexibility in relations with Northern Ireland. This nascent revisionism was severely tested by the recrudescence of violence in Northern Ireland in 1969. However, Irish policy did not revert to irredentism, though there were some pressures in that direction. Rather it became largely a matter of coping and crisis management, the Sunningdale Agreement being the only moment in the early years of the "troubles" when a more strategic approach flourished but all too briefly. A return to a longer-term joint approach by the Irish and British governments was mooted in 1980 and, after prolonged and difficult negotiations, was institutionalized in the Anglo-Irish Agreement of 1985. This centered on starting a process designed to lead to agreed structures for the internal government of Northern Ireland, to structures that would take account of the all-Ireland dimension of the problem, and to the ending of paramilitary violence. While agreement between the parties and factions in Northern Ireland has been the key to the often precarious peace process, both the Irish government and the Irish electorate have played important roles, the former acting as mediator and guarantor of nationalist interests and the latter providing overwhelming popular endorsement of the Belfast Agreement in the referendum of May 1998.

Ireland has wrestled with the imperative of national independence in a world in which boundaries are more and more permeable in economic, political, and cultural terms. Cultural identity, which in the past was highly salient, inward-looking, and a source of gnawing self-doubt, is probably now more taken for granted, more open, and more secure. Considerable internal or domestic problems continue to exist and, in an era of globalization, tackling many of them cannot be separated from an appropriate strategy for dealing with the external environment. Both politically and economically, and in the Anglo-Irish, European, and international contexts, this strategy is now geared toward making the best of limited sovereignty by positively cultivating interdependence.

J. J. Lee, *Ireland 1912–1985: Politics and Society* (Cambridge, U.K., 1989). Patrick Keatinge, *European Security: Ireland's Choices* (Dublin, 1996). Anthony Leddin and Brendan Walsh, *The Macroeconomy of Ireland*, 4th ed. (Dublin, 1998). John Coakley and Michael Gallagher, eds., *Politics in the Republic of Ireland*, 3d ed. (London, 1999).

RICHARD SINNOTT

ISLAM. Western views of Islam are structured predominantly by political and cultural antagonisms. Rivalry between Islamic and Christian powers in Europe and the Mediterranean in the medieval period, later political and economic competition with the Ottoman Empire, anticolonial nationalist movements in Muslim countries, and the contemporary emergence of oil-rich sheikhs and the radicals of Khomeinist Iran have contributed in the West to a powerful sense of "Islam" as a unitary and usually corrupt and malignant force. Together with racist stereotypes of "the Turk" and "the Arab," and more recently "the Shi'i fanatic-terrorist," such notions lead to a view of Islam as a politically unified, all-encompassing motive and framework for action. These images and assumptions are false and impede understanding.

The Prophet Muhammad (d. 632 C.E.) believed that in the Quran he was delivering a direct message from God in the Arabic language but addressed to pagans, Jews, and Christians alike. He is regarded as the last of the Prophets and the Traditions, or Hadith, of his words and practice are also central Islamic texts. Membership in the community of Muslims, the *umma*, is in principle open to whoever submits to God, the meaning of *Islam*.

The language of prayer and scripture is Arabic, but most Muslims today are in fact non-Arab. In Asia there are majority or significant communities in Afghanistan, Pakistan, India, Bangladesh, Malaysia, and Indonesia, with minorities in the southern Philippines, the successor states of Soviet Central Asia, and western China; in Africa, major populations are found in the West and Saharan zones from Senegal through northern Nigeria to the Sudan, with an important presence in Tanzania and down the East African coast. The principal modern imperial Muslim power was the Turkish Ottoman Empire, which ended with its defeat in World War I. And one of the most important revolutions of the second half of the twentieth century has been in Iran, where Muslim clerics and Ayatollah Ruhollah *Khomeini's interpretation of Islamic power emerged as dominant. Changes and tensions within Iranian society and the clerical groups, and the growing importance of open elections in Iran (won convincingly, in February 2000, by the "reformers"), show how complex the new patterns of Islamic politics can be.

"Islam" should therefore be thought of in terms of historical, political, and social diversity. It is certainly neither an exclusively Arab phenomenon nor a monolithic unity. Religious forces interact with other factors, whether social, cultural, or economic, in varied ways and by no means always in a major role. There is no centralized religious hierarchy to assert worldwide spiritual or political leadership.

All Muslims are required to perform the five pillars of Islam: a) the profession of faith, the *shehadah*, that "there is no God but Allah and Muhammad is his Prophet"; b) the five daily prayers, which may be made in any place but at particular set times (Friday is the day of the communal prayer when sermons are delivered at the major mosques, frequently with a state-backed message; as centers for social gatherings, mosques also act as local political, propaganda, and information points, especially if the government obstructs other public gatherings); c) payment of the *zakat*, or alms tax; d) fasting from dawn to dusk during the holy month of Ramadan; and e) making the *hajj*, the pilgrimage to Mecca, at least once in a lifetime if circumstances permit. Observance varies widely between and within social groups. So does the role of the state. Some, such as Saudi Arabia since its inception, Nimeiri's regime in the Sudan (particularly from 1983 until his fall in 1985), Zia al Haqq's dictatorship in Pakistan (1977–1989), and the Islamic Republic of Iran, seek to identify the state with religious controls, especially on women's dress and social roles, as the most public symbol of collective purity. Libya follows Colonel Muammar *Qaddafi's much-disputed interpretations. Other governments try to appropriate religious observance as national projects, as with Malaysian state supervision of the pilgrimage. Attempts to produce an Islamic banking system (without taking interest, which is forbidden) have so far been of only limited success in the context of a capitalist world economy.

The nature of authority over the *umma* has been an issue since the Prophet's death. Though ideally community and the Islamic order are one, in practice divisions between state and religious considerations have always occurred. Rulers made competing claims to leadership. Jurists differed over legal interpretations in the *Shari'a*, the Islamic law. The Quran can be cited to support disparate policies.

Disputes arose over who should become the *khalifa*, or deputy ruling the community. Those who became known as Sunnis (i.e., those taking the *sunna* or path of the Prophet), the vast majority of the world's Muslim population, accept the right to rule of the first four "rightly guided" caliphs and the Ummayad and Abbasid dynasties after them (661–1258). Caliphs were to be accepted as protectors and agents of the shari'a. Rulers, however unjust, tend to be acknowledged by Sunni jurists as having temporal power over the *umma*, although other elements of a society may rise against oppression. Sunni jurists have great respect for the doctrine of the consensus of those best qualified to make judgment in the community, the notion of *ijma*.

Shi'i Muslims, on the other hand, believe that the Prophet's son-in-law Ali, fourth of the rightly guided caliphs, was chosen by Muhammad as his successor as Imam, or leader, of the community and that Ali's descendants should rightfully have been at the head of the *umma*. (*Shi'a* refers to being the "party" of Ali.) The majority Shi'i view is that the twelfth imam in line from Ali became "hidden" (he vanished in 873 C.E.) and that he will finally return to establish justice on earth. They particularly venerate Ali and one of his sons, the Imam Hussein, who in 681 was killed at the battle of Kerbela in Iraq. His martyrdom is ritually remembered every year and may become a powerful political symbol of the unjustly persecuted Shi'a in times of crisis. At other times a more quietist practice accommodating to worldly powers may prevail.

By far the majority in Iran, Shi'a also constitute just over half of the Iraqi population, where a specifically Shi'i politics has not emerged. It has in the Lebanese "confessional" system, where Shi'a are the largest such category. But they divided in the Lebanese wars (which began in 1976) into rival Amal and more radical Iranian-backed Hizbollah groupings. The dynasty ruling the Yemen under an imam until its overthrow in 1962 represented a different branch of Shi'a, the Zeydi. There are other relatively small groups of Shi'a in eastern Saudi Arabia, India, and East Africa.

Forms of authority and their relations to politics are various under Islam. Families known as the *ashraf* or *sadat* claiming descent from the Prophet and therefore a particular holiness and legitimacy frequently have local political relevance. In Morocco such descent is important in the position of the monarch. In the Kuwaiti crisis of 1990, King Hussein of Jordan referred to his family's sherifian status and President Saddam *Hussein produced a holy genealogy for himself and a call for *jihad. Responses to such claims vary from acceptance to derision.

Sufi orders, or mystical brotherhoods, include members from many strata in society owing loyalty to sheikhs who might have politically important roles. In Algeria such groups often led resistance to the French in rural areas in the nineteenth century. The Sanusi order of Libya gave a focus to the struggle against Italian colonialism, forming the state of modern Libya and becoming an independent monarchy under British tutelage in 1951, before being displaced by Colonel Qaddafi's idiosyncratic blend of "Islamic socialism" in 1969. The Muridiya of Senegal still have an important national and economic position. But Sufi groups were often too divided for political action and were attacked by nationalist, modernists, and radicals of all hues as doctrinally suspect, un-Islamic, and backward. More recently, some conservative regimes have encouraged them, as President Anwar *Sadat did in Egypt in the 1970s, to support a more quietist and apolitical Islam against Islamic and secular radicalism.

The learned men and jurists, the *'ulema*, have reproduced the Islamic traditions in educational and legal fields, though they have lost their monopoly to modern state apparatuses. Reformists among them stressing a return to a pure Islam and the role of individual legal interpretation played an important role from the late eighteenth century on. They formulated Islamic responses to the challenge of Western power and claims to scientific truth and superiority, but sought "progress" and the modernizing of religious institutions.

In the Arab world, Africa, India, and Indonesia, this trend had a great influence on nationalist ideology and politics. The idea of an Algerian nation owed much to the teaching of the Association of Reformist Ulema led by Ben Badis and founded in 1931 under the inspiration of Egyptian reformism. Modern Nigerian Islam and politics were profoundly influenced by the Usman dan Fodio movement of the early nineteenth century. The creation of Pakistan in 1947 under the leadership of Jinnah and the Muslim League is a major example of political significance, and the continuing importance of the Muhammidiyah Association (founded in 1912) in Indonesia shows the social and welfare significance of such reformist movements.

Reformist *'ulema* tended to become subordinated to more secular, liberal, and urban-based nationalist movements in the nationalist struggles of the twentieth century and to be politically sidelined by the newly independent states, as happened in Algeria, Egypt, and most radically of all in Turkey under Kemal *Atatürk.

Traditionalist *'ulema* opposed them, distrusting their support of individual interpretation in the shari'a, their alleged openness to the West, and their concern for change. In Saudi Arabia, with dynastic rule and a strict interpretation of Islamic law, the 'ulema play a larger role than in any other Sunni state. The revival of the Ulema movement in Indonesia (the Nahdat al Ulama, mainly rural and based in eastern and central Java among the powerful teachers of peasantry or religious boarding schools) grew into an important opposition to the modernists. In the presidential elections of late 1999, however, the head of this movement, Abdurrahman Wahid (known also as Gus Dur), was elected president of a democratic Indonesia after the downfall of the previous military dictatorship of Suharto. Wahid took office consistently preaching tolerance, pluralism, and a separation of politics and religion, a more "modernist" position than some of the modernists themselves espoused.

In general, the Sunni traditionalist 'ulema too have been forced into subservience to the state. Iranian Shi'i mullahs, on the other hand, had a historically stronger position and preserved greater social and economic autonomy through their schools, universities, religious endowments, and links with the bazaar. This played a key part in their emergence under the Ayatollah Khomeini as the dominant force in the revolution, together with their capacity to carry the street and urban masses with them in a populist call for social justice. The foundation of an Islamic republic under the "Guardianship of the Jurist" represents a novel attempt to provide a model of what an Islamic state should be.

Modern radical Islamic movements have often attacked popular Sufism, the 'ulema, and regimes alike as corrupt, calling for resistance to "non-Islamic" practices and the influence of foreign powers. They seek to make society an Islamic order based on the Quran and the law on the model of the Prophet's first community of believers in Medina. The Muslim Brothers of Egypt, founded in 1928 among new urban classes, are the leading Sunni example. They were brutally suppressed under Nasser in 1954 and 1965 but occupy a leading oppositional role in the Egyptian National Assembly under Mubarak. This trend became politically important in the 1980s in Algeria, Tunisia, Jordan, and wings of the Palestinian movement, often in the cities and among students and young people. The Muslim Brotherhood has been suppressed in Syria (particularly in Hama in 1982). All groups operate in a framework of the nation-state and modern party organization.

More extreme and sectarian groups now declare that Muslim society must be entirely re-created from the beginning by jihad as there is no true Islam save that of the group members, everyone else being in a "state of ignorance" (jahiliya). Such a group assassinated President Sadat of Egypt in 1981.

Hostility to "capitalism" and "socialism," the call for a return to communal existence, "authenticity," and the pursuit of social justice and welfare are powerful utopian appeals precisely because they are shorn of political and practical details. In a context of severe economic problems, the disappointments of independence, the growth of bureaucracies, party, military, and security apparatuses with their surveillance and patronage networks, and the attempt to close off any space for opposition, the language of divine truth can become the only publicly available powerful weapon against the corruption of princes. Disparate oil wealth, massive economic problems, Palestinian-Israeli conflict, and the lack of power in the world system as the "South" seems yet more subjugated to the "North" have created fertile ground for

such movements since the 1960s, and their attraction is likely to remain strong.

(See also RELIGION AND POLITICS.)

Hamid Enayat, *Modern Islamic Political Thought* (London, 1982). Edward Mortimer, *Faith and Power: The Politics of Islam* (New York, 1982). Michael Gilsenan, *Recognizing Islam* (London, 1982 and 1990; New York, 1983). James P. Piscatori, ed., *Islam in the Political Process* (Cambridge, U.K., 1983). Edmund Burke III and Ira M. Lapidus, eds., *Islam, Politics, and Social Movements* (Berkeley, Calif., 1988). John L. Esposito, ed., *Islam in Asia: Religion, Politics, and Society* (Oxford, 1988). Sami Zubaida, *Islam, the People, and the State* (London, 1988).

MICHAEL GILSENAN

ISOLATIONISM. The term *isolationism* denotes a country's determination to avoid unwanted foreign involvements and the power to compel others to respect that intention. In practice the internal and external *foreign policy environment of the United States permitted an isolationist policy only under uniquely favorable circumstances. U.S. isolationism was never a mere response to geographic factors or a thoughtless preoccupation with internal concerns or self-sufficient pursuits. The United States was never a hermit nation; its isolationism was predominantly military and political, not commercial or intellectual. From its beginning the United States faced the recurrent demands for protection of its commercial and trading interests, the pressures of democratic ideologues to involve the country wherever freedom and self-determination seemed to be at stake, and the necessity to curtail or eliminate competing centers of power in the Western Hemisphere or threats to the *balance of power in Europe. The Founders demanded the freedom of action that would enable the nation, in George Washington's words, to choose "peace or war, as our interests, guided by justice, shall counsel." Together these external pressures permitted little isolation, whether in mind or action, from the major trends and events in world politics. From its founding, the United States became involved in every European war that ventured onto the Atlantic.

Behind the isolationism of the Founders was the conviction that the United States would render itself more harm than good by meddling in external affairs that were not its direct concern. Policy, so defined, governed the conduct of nations generally. U.S. noninvolvement in the political and military affairs of Europe in the nineteenth century resulted from the continent's fundamental stability. The perennial *security of the United States from European encroachment in the absence of costly defense measures created the illusion that such security flowed, not from the European equilibrium or British naval dominance of the Atlantic, but from the great ocean itself. For many in the United States, security became synonymous with separation from the politics of Europe under the assumption that no European development could endanger the United States. What began to change after 1900 was the increasing frequency of trends and events that seemed to challenge the country's ever-expanding interests. Writers and intellectuals who demanded U.S. responses to perceived threats from abroad seldom advocated more than moral strictures or reliance on international agencies. Interwar isolationists still presumed that German power and expansionism could not endanger the security of the United States if properly defended with air and naval power. By the late 1930s U.S. isolationism assumed an Asia-first cast; leading isolationists who opposed any involvement in European affairs from 1939 to 1941 revealed no restraint in their demands for an uncompromising posture toward Japanese expansion in the Far East.

After Pearl Harbor some historians accused the isolationists of poor judgment, sympathy for fascism, even denying the United States the policies required to prevent war. A determined, if ineffectual, isolationism reappeared in opposition to the *Cold War involvements in Europe from the *Truman Doctrine to the *North Atlantic Treaty Organization, as well as in the determination of some Republicans, in their response to the China, Indochina, and Korea issues, to return *U.S. foreign policy to an Asia-first orientation. Only later amid the globalist policies of the Cold War did many historians and analysts begin to judge that the isolationists of the 1930s were not totally wrong in their efforts to constrain the country's burgeoning commitments that led eventually to a two-front U.S. war during World War II. But isolationism cannot describe the preferences of those in the United States who, since midcentury, have favored a more limited definition of national interests and thus a more restricted use of force than that demanded by concepts of global danger and responsibility.

Selig Adler, *The Isolationist Impulse: Its Twentieth-Century Reaction* (New York, 1957). Manfred Jonas, *Isolationism in America, 1935–1941* (Ithaca, N.Y., 1966).

NORMAN A. GRAEBNER

ISRAEL. The Israeli state, from a comparative perspective, belongs to the category of immigrant-settler nation-states, based on a frontier society that has never finalized its social and geographical boundaries. On 14 May 1948, Israel declared its independence, following a UN resolution dividing the former British colonial state of Palestine into a Jewish and an Arab state. Israeli leaders affirmed that the new state belonged to all the Jewish people, but not necessarily to its citizens, and invited immigration by Jews worldwide.

Israel's founders began to settle in Palestine in the 1880s, joining a small Jewish population already resident there. Jewish immigrants, inspired by *Zionism and escaping from *anti-Semitism, came in increasing numbers, mainly from Eastern Europe. They built a polity, called the yishuv, creating many social and political institutions and developing a new national language (modern Hebrew), culture, and nationalism. However, their goals and interests clashed with those of the local Arab population, causing intercommunal and interethnic conflict throughout the British colonial period (1917–1948).

The *Holocaust in Europe and the changing immigration policy of the United States greatly increased Jewish migration to Palestine and strengthened support for the state-building project among the Western Jewish diaspora and among Western public opinion generally. The new state, led by David *Ben-Gurion, won rapid diplomatic recognition from both the United States and the Soviet Union.

But Arab residents of Palestine and many surrounding Arab states remained opposed. The day after Israel's declaration of independence, units of Arab armies entered Palestine and joined Arab irregular forces in an effort to prevent the establishment of the new state. Israel soon prevailed, and armistices signed with neighboring states in 1949 gave Israel control over a territory about 30 percent larger than that allocated by the UN partition plan. During hostilities, some 700,000 Arabs were uprooted from their homeland and became *refugees.

The social, political, and economic institutions of the yishuv proved resilient and enduring after 1948, but the Jewish homeland nevertheless changed profoundly. Ben-Gurion and his colleagues set up a strong state, and the population grew rapidly with the arrival of Jews from Europe and from Muslim countries in Asia and North Africa. Immigrants doubled the Jewish population from 650,000 to 1.4 million between 1948 and 1951. By 1998, Israel's population had reached nearly 6 million. Immigration of Jews from the former Soviet Union, especially strong after 1989, increased Israel's population in the 1990s by about 1 million.

Although modified since 1996 by direct election of the prime minister, Israel is considered a *parliamentary democracy with a *cabinet government accountable to a single-chamber legislature elected by *proportional representation. However, Israeli democracy is severely limited by several constitutional anomalies, rooted in the inability of the legislature, the judicial system, and the political culture to distinguish between nationalism and religion. Thus, the whole sphere of personal status laws (marriage, divorce, etc.) and even the right to belong to the Jewish nationality are outside the jurisdiction of civil courts and are under the authority of religious (Halachic) laws and the jurisdiction of rabbinical courts, which are highly discriminatory against women and homosexuals. The Law of Return—one of Israel's primary basic laws (which substitute for a formal constitution)—and several other laws, considered "affirmative action" in favor of the persecuted Jewish nation, in effect discriminate against Israel's Arab citizens.

In 1996, Israel instituted a two-ballot electoral system, with one ballot being used for the post of prime minister and the other for party lists, not necessarily identical with the parties of the candidates for prime minister, to be represented in the legislature. This hybrid system encourages an even more multiparty system than the previous system and promotes many different opinions in Israel's legislature, known as the Knesset. From the foundation of the state until 1977, the Labor Party and its direct predecessors dominated political life. The party's power rested on its control of key institutions of the yishuv, especially the Histadrut, the central trade union, with its large network of social services, health care facilities, and agricultural and industrial enterprises. Under Labor's influence, Israel's economy and social policy came to be heavily dominated by government institutions, along a social-democratic model.

During the 1970s, however, Labor lost its political preeminence. Some attribute this change to disillusionment among the country's elite with Labor's performance, especially in national defense. The 1977 general election marked the end of the party's long stay in power. For the next fifteen years, the right-wing Likud bloc governed at the head of its own coalition or in a "national unity" coalition with

Labor. Likud's first prime minister, Menachem Begin, won the Nobel Peace Prize jointly with Egypt's president, Anwar *Sadat, in recognition of the peace agreement of 1979 between the two countries. Later Yitzhak Rabin, Shimon Peres, and Yasir *Arafat shared the same prize in the wake of the Israeli-Palestinian accords. Likud was unwilling, however, to grant further "land for peace" concessions. Likud was narrowly defeated in the elections of June 1992; the Labor government that replaced it embarked on a new course, particularly with respect to recognizing the right of the Palestinian people to self-determination. In September 1993 a Declaration of Principles was signed by the government of Israel and the *Palestine Liberation Organization. An agreement of September 1995 further called for a gradual transfer of authority and territories of the occupied West Bank and Gaza Strip to a Palestinian National Authority ("autonomy"), without specifying the final status and scope of this newly created political entity. On 29 October 1994 a peace treaty was signed with a second Arab state, the Hashemite Kingdom of Jordan.

However, the implementation of the agreements with the Palestinians aroused a highly emotional controversy among the Jewish-Israeli public that culminated in the *assassination of Prime Minister Rabin by a national-religious zealot on 4 November 1995. In an election held on 29 May 1996, a right-wing national-religious coalition, headed by directly elected prime minister Benjamin *Netanyahu, was returned to power. Despite declarations that Netanyahu's government would honor the previous government's international commitments, the rapprochement process with the Palestinians was halted. In an additional election held on 17 May 1999 the candidate of Labor, Ehud Barak, defeated Netanyahu with a great margin (57 percent). The fragmentation and weakening of the party system continued, and the established government was based on an unstable and internally divided coalition.

Israeli society has been deeply affected by the *Arab-Israeli conflict and especially by the series of wars that Israel has fought with various Arab countries—in 1948, 1956, 1967, 1973, and 1982. Israeli political culture has been colored to a certain degree by militarism: In addition to conventional wars, Israel throughout its history had had to deal with manifestations of Palestinian *guerrilla warfare—a situation that intensified in late 1987 with the outbreak of the *intifada, a revolt by Palestinians of the occupied territories against twenty years of Israeli rule, and one whose ultimate goal was Palestinian statehood. Israel has prevailed in these conflicts thanks to its powerful military and security system, but the Israeli public has nonetheless felt embattled in a hostile region, a feeling that was accentuated in 1991 when Israeli was exposed to Iraqi missile attacks during the *Gulf War.

In the 1990s, Israel's conventional military strength was among the world's most imposing—a standing army of 130,000 backed by an elaborate reserve system of 500,000, and armed with very sophisticated weaponry. External sources also refer to Israel as a regional nuclear power, and Israel refused to sign the international nuclear nonproliferation treaty. Though effective, Israel's defense system has been a burden on the economy. Defense expenditures—about 30 percent of GNP on average—are very high, and compulsory draft and annual reserve duty impose other substantial material and social costs.

Israel has built an advanced industrial economy that is strong in a number of high-technology fields, especially electronics, software, and medical and military equipment. Rapid development of the economy was spurred by the high level of education and technical competence of Israel's immigrants as well as by heavy state spending and large amounts of external capital. Major sources of external capital include reparations from the Federal Republic of Germany, contributions from Jews in the diaspora, funds brought in by immigrants, and—especially since the early 1970s—aid from the United States.

The government not only plays a leading role in the Israeli economy; it is also the country's largest civilian employer and owner of 93 percent of the land. The state and public bureaucracy and armed forces, and the firms that they directly or indirectly control within the state, are also very large employers. Voices in favor of *privatization or economic restructuring have emerged in both Likud and the Labor Party since the 1980s. Since then, the Histadrut and its firms and institutions have been slowly privatized and dismantled both by the Labor and Likud governments. This included Koor Industries, Israel's largest corporate employer, with interests ranging from steel and cement to salad oil. During the 1980s, however, there were growing doubts in Israel about the effectiveness and the future economic viability of these institutions. The Histadrut, as well as the government, gradually gave up their industrial and commercial holdings. The Histadrut began reshaping itself as a pure trade union. A bank-shares crisis in 1983, collapse of the stock market, and hyperinflation in the early 1980s underscored the economic problems. In addition, the shortage of water remains a difficult economic and development issue for Israel.

Within Israel, political conflicts reflect a number of important social cleavages. The deepest cleavage is between Israel's Jewish and Arab citizens. The latter, numbering about 1 million in the late 1990s, or 20 percent of the population, face a variety of legal and social discriminations and barriers to economic and professional advancement. Most Arabs define themselves both as Palestinians and as loyal citizens of Israel, but they tend to feel that their future is uncertain and their rights unprotected in a state which defines itself as belonging to the whole of the Jewish people and not to its citizens.

Another important cleavage is between Israel's Ashkenazim, or European Jews, and the approximately equal number of "Oriental" Jews who have come from countries in the Middle East and North Africa. The former hold most of the top posts in business, politics, the military, and the professions, while the latter are heavily represented among occupations with lower pay and prestige. Many Oriental Jews feel that they face prejudice and discrimination and that their culture and heritage are not sufficiently respected. Their resentment has been effectively mobilized by Likud and other right-wing forces, but also by an ethnic-religious community-based party, "Sephardic Torah Guardians" (Shas). The immigrants from the former Soviet Union have also established a successful ethnic party.

Israel also faces conflict over the role of the Jewish religion in the life of Israeli society. Though its active adherents number less than a fifth of the Jewish population, Orthodox Judaism has considerably influenced public policy. Orthodox religious courts govern all Jewish marriage and divorce, for example, and the state subsidizes Orthodox religious schools. Beginning in the 1970s, religious parties held the balance in the Knesset between the right- and left-wing blocs, so their influence grew further, much to the dismay of many secular Jews.

The issue of the occupied territories has been a key political division in Israel since 1967, one that has carried over into the debate over the final status of the "autonomy" granted to Palestinians following the 1993, 1995, and 1999 accords. The debate over territories also involves questions about the boundaries and nature of Israel, as well as the future status of about 180,000 Jewish settlers in the occupied territories. Hard-liners and messianic religious-nationalists lay claim to the whole "Land of Israel," referring to biblical, historical rights as well as security concerns. Some of them even talk of "transfer"—a policy to remove Palestinians from the land, to make it exclusively Jewish. The "doves" place more emphasis on compromise over territory and promotion of a democratic, secular, civil state and society, in which all citizens are equal. Territorial issues are also the focus of much extraparliamentary politics. Gush Emunim, a religious millenarian movement, leads the drive to settle the territories, while its secular opponents like Peace Now agitate for withdrawal and territorial compromise.

The Arab-Israeli conflict has dominated Israeli foreign relations. After 1967, Israel developed a particularly close alliance with the United States. Israel has also had close relations with important states in Western Europe, including Britain, France, and Germany. These ties enabled Israel to maintain its economic and military strength, and they paved the way for privileged trade relations since the 1980s: a free-trade link to the United States and status as a special trading partner with the European Union.

After the June War of 1967, Israel faced diplomatic isolation from the Soviet bloc and many countries in the Third World, and it encountered hostility at the UN and in many world gatherings. That isolation began to ease in the late 1980s, particularly as the Cold War ended; in 1991 the Soviet Union restored diplomatic relations and the Soviet successor states followed suit. In the Middle East, however, Israel to date has established diplomatic relations with only two Arab countries—Egypt and Jordan.

Peace talks began in the fall of 1991 between Israel and its Arab neighbors, opening up a possibility of regional peace—especially after the treaty with the Palestinians—including possible accords on disarmament, water, environmental protection, and joint efforts for trade and development. Any such agreements would require lengthy talks and extensive concessions on the part of both Israel and its negotiating partners.

(See also INTERNATIONAL MIGRATION; RELIGION AND POLITICS.)

Dan Horowitz and Moshe Lissak, *Origins of the Israeli Polity* (Chicago, 1978). Ian Lustick, *Arabs in a Jewish State* (Austin, Tex., 1980). Shmuel N. Eisenstadt, *The Transformation of Israeli Society* (London, 1985). Baruch Kimmerling, *Israeli State and Society: Boundaries and Frontiers* (Albany, N.Y., 1989). Baruch Kimmerling, "Patterns of Militarism in Israel," *European Journal of Sociology* 2 (1993): 1–28. Michael N. Barnett, ed., *Israel in Comparative Perspectives: Challenging the Conventional Wisdom* (Albany, N.Y., 1996). Asher Arian and Michal Shamir, *Election in Israel—1996* (Albany, N.Y., 1998).

BARUCH KIMMERLING

ITALY. A nation-state since 1861, Italy has so far experienced three different regimes and since 1992 has been undergoing a difficult and complex politico-institutional transition. It was a constitutional monarchy with limited, but increasing political participation until 1922, when it fell under Fascist rule. From 1922 until 1943 *Mussolini instituted an authoritarian regime that led the country towards some socioeconomic *modernization at the price of suppression of civil and political rights and ultimately at the cost of a disastrous war in alliance with Nazi Germany. The Resistance struggle against German occupation of Italy and the Fascist puppet regime produced the seeds of a democratic revival. The monarchy was abolished through a referendum in 1946 and a republic with a parliamentary form of government was created. A constituent assembly drafted a constitution that was very progressive with respect to civil, political, and social rights, but rather traditional with respect to the structures of the state. For fear of the reemergence of authoritarian rulers, a weak executive was shaped, a parliament composed of two chambers with the same functions and the same powers was constructed, and proportional representation was utilized for all elected assemblies (except small local governments). All these institutional arrangements created the opportunities for consociational agreements between Christian Democratic–controlled governments and a powerful Communist opposition, unable for international reasons to become a real alternative. Since then all Italian governments have been unstable multiparty coalitions. From 1945 until 1981 all prime ministers were representatives of the Christian Democratic Party (DC). Between 1981 and the beginning of the present transition with the collapse of the Christian Democratic Party in 1993, there were only three non-DC prime ministers (the Republican Giovanni Spadolini, and the Socialists Bettino Craxi and Giuliano Amato).

A diversified party enjoying wide interclass political support and backed by the powerful *Roman Catholic Church, the business community, and, for lack of a better alternative, U.S. administrations, the DC provided both Italy's underlying political stability and, due to its internal factionalization, the tensions leading to frequent short-term instabilities. With the stability of political coalitions since the birth of the Italian Republic in 1946, the stability of governmental personnel, despite more than fifty governments, and even the stability of policies, governmental instability represented a sort of safety valve for a political system without alternation. Changes in the relative strength of DC factions were largely responsible for governmental instability, allowing some turnover in governmental personnel and, correspondingly, in the many patronage positions dispensed by the government.

Economic reconstruction and the subsequent economic miracle of the late 1950s and 1960s were achieved thanks to a shrewd, though probably unplanned, combination of two elements: unregulated social change and a mixed economy. The sociopolitical climate created by the DC produced an individualistic mobilization of the Italian population, accompanied by mass migrations from the south to the north, from the agricultural sector to the industrial and tertiary sectors, and from rural areas to large towns. Moreover, for patronage purposes the DC both inflated the public administration and expanded the public sector of the economy, notably through the Istituto per la Ricostruzione Industriale (IRI), which helped it keep tight control over the banking system. Until 1976, the radio and television system was also fully state controlled.

So long as resources kept growing, this strategy allowed the DC to enlarge and consolidate its power base. Because of its real and perceived subordination to the Soviet Union, the Communist Party (PCI) was not considered a legitimate or credible claimant to governmental power. However, the PCI did play the role of a legitimate opposition, gathering votes of protest and for change. At the beginning of the 1970s a series of political, cultural, and socioeconomic changes threatened the continuation of DC rule. The process of disengagement of the PCI from the Soviet Union was finalized by its criticism of the Soviet intervention in Czechoslovakia and acceptance of the *North Atlantic Treaty Organization. At the same time, the Socialists were no longer willing to accept a subordinate role in DC-led coalitions and openly advocated a leftist alliance. The student movement and renewed militancy of industrial workers indicated the need for profound changes in the nature of social relations and the distribution of social power. In a national referendum on the law allowing divorce, a sizable majority voted to sustain this law. Catholic cultural dominance was defeated for the first time, even though the Church remained an influential actor on the sociopolitical scene. Finally, a long period of economic difficulties began, largely attributed to DC mismanagement of the economy, excessive party patronage in the public sector, a hypertrophied and inefficient public administration, and a crisis over the form of government as shaped by the DC (the so-called material constitution).

By no means deprived of its electoral support (oscillating between 33 and 39 percent) and never abandoned by the Church, the Italian business community, or the United States, the DC withstood the crisis of the 1970s thanks also to divisions within the *Left. The controversial PCI strategy of historic compromise was never shared by the Socialist Party (PSI) and produced disorientation among leftist groups even leading to the emergence of terrorist movements. In the meantime, the shrinking, the diversification, and the fragmentation of the working class seemed to go hand in hand with the fragmentation of the political spectrum. Always divided into three competing factions—the largest, the Confederazione Generale Italiana dei Lavoratori (CGIL), dominated by the PCI, but also including the PSI; the second largest, the Confederazione Italiana Sindacati Lavoratori (CISL), closely tied to the DC; the third, the Unione Italiana del Lavoro (UIL), led by the PSI but also including the Social Democratic Party (PSDI) and the Republican Party (PRI)—the unions pursued a strategy of centralization and wage flattening. In response, industrial cadres and shopfloor management challenged union policies and created their own unofficial organizations, and workers' groups in specific sectors (for instance, the railway system and state schools) gave birth to special bodies for representation and bargaining called Cobas (grassroots committees). All this severely hampered the official union movement and the Left while making it more difficult to formulate coherent governmental policies. Divisions within the union movement also allowed the curtailment of the indexation system, which linked wages to inflation, by decree of Prime Minister Bettino Craxi in 1984. In addition, the improvement of economic conditions, almost a new boom toward the end of the 1980s, further reduced the power of the unions. Unemployment, especially among young southerners, was mitigated by various welfare measures. Increasingly, the developed regions of the north came into conflict with the central government over issues of distribution and power.

The unsolved politico-institutional crisis that plagued Italy throughout the 1990s was triggered by the fall of the Berlin Wall in November 1989. Immediately, the PCI decided to change its name, transforming itself into the Democratic Party of the Left (PDS). More important, especially in the north, many voters for the various centrist parties, the DC included, no longer felt motivated to support those parties and their coalitions as a bulwark against a now-nonexistent Communist threat. Several among these northern voters looked for territorial representation as offered by the emerging Lombard League, now called the Northern League. Moreover, the decline in political and electoral strength of the traditional governing parties meant that they could no longer prevent through parliamentary votes the judiciary from investigating their corrupt practices. Systemic *corruption, the product of the lack of alternation in the government and the consequent feeling of impunity, was exposed by the judges of the far-reaching Clean Hands (*Mani Pulite*) investigation. By 1994, all the secretaries of the five-party coalition (*pentapartito*) that had dominated Italian politics up to 1992 had been indicted. Last, though by no means least, the dissatisfaction of voters with institutional and electoral arrangements that not only made governmental alternation almost impossible, but sharply limited political accountability, has translated into three national referendums. In June 1991, in April 1993, and, again, in April 1999, defying the wishes of all governing parties, voters indicated their strong preference for a plurality system.

The March 1994 elections were the first to be held according to an electoral system that allocates three-fourths of the parliamentary seats through a plurality formula in single-member constituencies and one-fourth through proportional representation. Not a single party of the First Republic survived the momentous change. While not all entirely new, the parties winning seats in parliament had significantly transformed themselves and changed their names and organizations. The newest of them all was Forza Italia, an ad hoc political movement created by the media tycoon Silvio Berlusconi in answer to the distinct possibility that the Left, led by the PDS, might win the national elections. Thanks to an exceptionally contradictory coalition between his Forza Italia and the anti-southern and laissez-faire Northern League in the north and between Forza Italia and the former neo-fascist, statist, and largely southern-based Alleanza Nazionale in the south, Berlusconi obtained a majority of parliamentary seats and was appointed prime minister. In less than eight months all contradictions exploded and Berlusconi's government was replaced by a nonpolitical government of professionals. In new elections, held in April 1996, a diversified and heterogeneous coalition called the Olive Tree (Ulivo), including the PDS, former Christian Democrats (now Popolari), the Greens, and a few socialists, and supported by unreconstructed Communists (Rifondazione Comunista), defeated the so-called Polo delle Libertà led by Berlusconi. Now advocating the secession of the north, dubbed Padania (i.e., the Po River Valley), the Northern League ran alone and did surprisingly well.

The major task of the Ulivo government, led by Romano Prodi, former chairman of the IRI, consisted in meeting the criteria defined by the Maastricht Treaty for Italy's participation in the European Monetary Union. Although generally loyal and convinced Europeans, all Italian decision makers were used to playing a passive role on the European as well as the global scene. Totally subservient to U.S. policies during the Cold War, Italian governments seemed now to be unable to exploit their newly acquired foreign policy discretion except, to a limited extent, in the Mediterranean area and in commercial dealings with central and eastern European countries. Understandably, the first prerequisite of any successful Italian foreign policy remains Italy's presence among the most important European states. Through a rigorous economic policy, some lucky circumstances, and the awareness of the Italian people that the challenge was indeed historic, Prodi's government considerably trimmed the state's deficit, significantly reduced the inflation rate, and gradually cut interest rates so that by May 1998 Italy had succeeded in figuring among the partners of the process of European monetary unification. Nevertheless, the second prerequisite for any successful participation in the processes of European integration—a modern constitution and effective political institutions—has not yet been achieved.

As the twenty-first century began, the Italian economic system appeared in good shape. The unemployment rate remains relatively high, but Italy is not an outlier in the European context. The *welfare state is being slowly downsized, though more decisive reforms may be needed. Two factors militate against quick adjustments. First of all, the party system does not appear in the least to have stabilized. Indeed, an ongoing process of minor changes, aggregations, and disaggregations has not yet produced lasting realignments; the head of the opposition, Silvio Berlusconi, is a defendant in several trials for fraudulent budgets and illegal financing of political parties; and the two major coalitions, the Polo delle Libertà on the center-right and the Ulivo on the center-left, appear constantly challenged respectively by the Northern League and by Rifondazione Comunista. On 9 October 1998, Rifondazione split on a crucial vote denying confidence in Prodi's government, thus provoking his resignation. The new prime minister, Massimo D'Alema, a former Communist, leads a very heterogeneous coalition constructed on the ashes of the Ulivo. Second, the August 1993 reforms of the electoral system have not been followed by similar reforms of other institutions. The government remains weak; Parliament continues to be slow and cumbersome in its functioning; local governments do not have enough political and fiscal autonomy; and the public administration is still unresponsive and inefficient except for a few happy islands such as the Treasury and the Bank of Italy. Moreover, there has been prolonged and bitter debate over the new rules of the game.

As long as streamlined rules are not drafted and accepted by all Italian political actors and governmental and parliamentary institutions are not reformed in such a way as to provide both political stability and decision-making efficacy, the Italian political system is bound to remain vulnerable to many unforeseen challenges. The stability of the past, at times bordering on immobilism and stagnation, has been replaced by mobility and change, by economic revival and political uncertainty. The Second Republic, however, has not yet taken root.

(See also CHRISTIAN DEMOCRACY; CONSOCIATIONAL DEMOCRACY; ECONOMIC AND MONETARY UNION; RELIGION AND POLITICS.)

Paul Ginsborg, *A History of Contemporary Italy: Society and Politics, 1943–1988* (Harmondsworth, U.K., 1991). David Hine, *Governing Italy: The Politics of Bargained Pluralism* (Oxford, 1993). Patrick McCarthy, *The Crisis of the Italian State: From the Origins of the Cold War to the Fall of Berlusconi* (New York, 1995). Martin J. Bull, *Contemporary Italy: A Research Guide* (Westport, Conn., 1996). Stephen Gundle and Simon Parker, eds., *The New Italian Republic: From the Fall of the Berlin Wall to Berlusconi* (London, 1996). Vittorio Bufacchi and Simon Burgess, *Italy Since 1989: Events and Interpretations* (London, 1988).

GIANFRANCO PASQUINO

IVORY COAST. See CÔTE D'IVOIRE.

J

JAMAICA. An island nation in the western Caribbean, Jamaica, with 2.5 million inhabitants, is the most populous of the former British West Indian colonies. The economy is very trade dependent; the country imports over 60 percent of what it consumes. The principal economic activities and primary sources of foreign exchange are bauxite mining and alumina production, tourism, and sugar and banana exports. The value of earnings of the illegal marijuana crop, although disputed, is also undoubtedly significant. In 1990–1995, per capita GDP was somewhat over U.S.$1,700. Over 90 percent of the population is of African or mixed African and European descent. Color is closely related to *class, the lower classes being black, the upper classes largely white, and the middle classes black or brown. Jamaicans are predominantly Christians with the Anglican, Roman Catholic, and Presbyterian Churches being the principal denominations. The indigenous Rastafari religion also has a large following especially in the urban lower classes. Independent since 1962, Jamaica is a *parliamentary democracy fashioned after the British Westminster-Whitehall model. The security forces are comparatively small and have complied with the doctrine of civilian supremacy. The two major parties, the People's National Party (PNP) and the Jamaica Labour Party (JLP), alternated in government between 1944 and 1997, with each party serving two consecutive terms and then losing at the polls in bids for a third term.

The nationalist movement emerged out of the West Indies–wide labor unrest of the 1930s. The labor rebellion did much to convince the British to initiate the process of *decolonization, which began with the first election with universal suffrage in 1944 and continued with the gradual introduction of self-government in the 1940s and 1950s. The break between the PNP, led by Norman Manley, and the major trade union, whose leader, Alexander Bustamante, formed his own party, the JLP, in 1943, set the pattern of modern politics. It is a highly competitive two-party system, each party having a union base and cross-class electoral support. Initially the parties differed; the PNP had a Fabian socialist position, and the JLP had a populist one. The PNP had a strong base in the middle classes, and the JLP in the lower classes. These differences gave way to both ideological and sociological convergence of the parties in the 1950s. Both parties pursued a strategy of industrialization based on foreign investment, primarily in bauxite and alumina. Tourism was another significant growth sector, also heavily based on foreign investment. This strategy resulted in significant economic growth in the 1950s and 1960s, but also a large trade deficit, a highly import-dependent manufacturing sector, growing unemployment, and great income inequality.

After coming to power in 1972 the PNP revived its commitment to democratic socialism and embarked on a reform process that included expansion of state control over crucial sectors of the economy, improvement of health and educational services, increases in income levels of the lower classes, political mobilization, and a turn in foreign policy toward nonalignment. This led to a class realignment in the 1976 elections, won by the PNP, with the upper and middle classes moving toward the JLP and the lower classes toward the PNP.

In the 1970s Jamaica's Prime Minister Michael Manley took a leadership role in Third World politics. The PNP's nonaligned policy, particularly its close relations with Cuba, resulted in sharply deteriorating relations with the United States. Domestically, the relationship to the transnational bauxite/aluminum companies underwent a significant change; the Jamaican state acquired a stake in the local operations of these companies and strengthened its own capacity for research and management in the industry. A *balance of payments crisis forced the government to accept *International Monetary Fund (IMF) agreements in 1977 and 1978, and the ensuing deterioration of popular living standards led to the defeat of the PNP in the 1980 elections. The election campaign was characterized by unprecedented levels of violence, with over 500 people losing their lives in political warfare.

At the outset, the JLP government under the leadership of Edward Seaga quickly established warm relations with the United States and committed itself to a free-market, export-oriented path of development, signing on to a *World Bank structural adjustment loan. Other than deregulating imports, cutting public spending, and privatizing a small number of public enterprises, however, the government did not greatly reduce the state's role in the economy. In the important bauxite-alumina sector, the government increased its role in ownership and marketed a growing share of alumina and bauxite to parties other than the four North American multinationals, which had accounted for all of Jamaica's bauxite-alumina exports prior to the PNP government's 1974 initiative. The JLP government contracted significant amounts of official development loans, and by the mid-1980s debt service consumed half of export earnings. Tourism made a spectacular recovery in the 1980s, and production in export platforms increased significantly. But the bauxite industry declined in the early 1980s, and growth in other sectors remained sluggish.

These problems stimulated several rounds of devaluations, which drastically cut living standards and undermined the government's support, leading to a victory of the PNP in the 1989 elections. Owing in part to the PNP's shift to the center and in part to the constraints of IMF agreements, the new

PNP government's policies differed little from those of its predecessor. In fact, the PNP government accelerated the divestment of state enterprises and deregulation of the economy. The 1990s have been characterized by conservative fiscal management, reduction of inflation and the debt-service ratio, moderate growth in exports, but very low overall economic growth and high open unemployment. Nevertheless, there was a slight reduction in poverty in the first half of the 1990s, and in the election of December 1997 the PNP won an unprecedented third term.

(See also ENGLISH-SPEAKING CARIBBEAN, NONALIGNED MOVEMENT; POLITICAL VIOLENCE; SOCIALISM AND SOCIAL DEMOCRACY; STRUCTURAL ADJUSTMENT PROGRAM.)

Trevor Munroe, *The Politics of Constitutional Decolonization: Jamaica, 1944–1962* (Mona, Jamaica, 1972). Evelyne Huber Stephens and John D. Stephens, *Democratic Socialism in Jamaica: The Political Movement and Social Transformation in Dependent Capitalism* (Princeton, N.J., 1986). Patsy Lewis, ed., *Jamaica: Preparing for the Twenty-first Century* (Kingston, 1994). Anthony Payne, *Politics in Jamaica* (Boston, 1994).

JOHN D. STEPHENS
EVELYNE HUBER STEPHENS

JAMES, C. L. R. Born in *Trinidad, West Indies, Cyril Lionel Robert James (1901–1989) attended Queen's Royal College (QRC), a local high school, where he taught for a few years after he graduated. He also wrote for *Trinidad* and *The Beacon*, two Trinidadian magazines, before he migrated to England in 1932. Later that year, James published *The Life of Captain Cipriani*, and began to write on cricket for the *Manchester Guardian*. In England James became involved in the Independent Labour Party and later joined the Trotskyist movement, out of which came *World Revolution, 1917–1936* (1937). In 1936 James published *Minty Alley*, his only novel, which he had brought with him from Trinidad. Before leaving London to do political work in the United States in 1938, James published *Black Jacobins*, a major analysis of the Haitian Revolution and one of the works by which he is best remembered. In England, James also completed two other major intellectual feats: he translated Boris Souvarine's *Stalin* (1939) from French to English and, with the assistance of Ria Stone, translated Karl *Marx's *Economic and Philosophical Manuscripts of 1844*, the first time that this work was translated into English.

In the United States, James continued his work in the socialist movement. In 1939, he met with Leon *Trotsky in Mexico to discuss "the Negro Question," as the political problems of African Americans were labeled at that time. Until 1953 when he was deported to the United Kingdom during the McCarthy trials, James worked to organize the sharecroppers in the South. Together with Raya Dunayevskaya, James formed the Johnson-Forest Tendency (pseudonyms for James and Dunayevskaya, respectively) after breaking with Trotsky's interpretation of *Marxism in 1940. In the United States James authored a number of works. Among them were *The Invading Socialist Society* (1947), an analysis of the mass movement toward new forms of social organization; *Notes on the Dialectics* (1948), an examination of Hegelian dialectics and its application to the proletarian struggle; *State Capitalism and World Revolution* (1950), "the theoretical summation of the work of the Johnson-Forest Tendency"; and *Mariners, Renegades and Castaways* (1953), an examination of Herman Melville's fiction, which he wrote while he was incarcerated on

Ellis Island. In this, his American period, James also began a potentially important work, *Notes on American Civilization*, which Anna Grimshaw published in summary form as *The Struggle for Happiness*. His abrupt departure from the United States prevented him from completing this work.

Returning to England, James picked up where he had left off. In the wake of the Hungarian Revolution, together with Grace Lee and Pierre Chaulieu, he wrote *Facing Reality* (1958). In 1958, James returned to Trinidad where he worked with Eric Williams, his former student at QRC and colleague in London in the 1930s, to develop the People's National Movement (PNM), the nationalist party of the country. In Trinidad, James edited *The Nation*, the weekly organ of the PNM, which carried forward the struggle for national independence. After spending two years in Trinidad, James ended his association with the PNM, later formed the Workers and Farmers Party, contested the 1965 general elections, and lost. In that Trinidad period James published the very important *Modern Politics* (1960), a brief discussion of the development of *democracy, and *Beyond a Boundary* (1963), a seminal work that documents the manner in which the dominant culture disseminates its values through sports.

After leaving Trinidad, James kept on writing and working. In 1977, he completed *Nkrumah and the Ghana Revolution* and returned to the United States in the 1970s where he taught at Federal City College, in Washington, D.C., for a number of years. After his teaching stint in Washington, James returned to London where he died in 1989. James was buried in Tunapuna, Trinidad, his birthplace. In the latter period of his life, James returned to Trinidad occasionally, lectured, and wrote a number of pamphlets, among the more important of which was *Walter Rodney and the Question of Power* (1983). In many ways, James remained a Renaissance person. In his long life, he wrote about history, politics, culture, music, philosophy, and sports. To the end of his days, he was a supreme lover of cricket; a compilation of his many articles on the game is contained in *Cricket* (1986).

James's importance lay in his creative application of Marxist principles to the struggle for liberty that took place in the world in which he lived, particularly in the *Third World. He proudly proclaimed himself a Marxist and believed that eventually socialism would triumph. He did not believe in what he called the "state socialism" of the Soviet Union nor in the bureaucracy of Eastern Europe as they existed until recently. As he noted in *Facing Reality*:

The whole world today lives in the shadow of the state power. This state power is an ever-present self-perpetuating body over and above society. It transforms the human personality into a mass of economic needs to be satisfied by decimal points of economic progress. It robs everyone of initiative and clogs the free development of society. This state power, by whatever name it is called, One-Party or Welfare State, destroys all pretense of government *by* the people, *of* the people. All that remains is government *for* the people.

James always believed in the power of the working people and their capacity to organize themselves for their own liberation. To him, the alternative was clear: *socialism or barbarism. He remained optimistic about the eventual triumph of socialism and welcomed the emergence of *Solidarity in Poland. He also believed in the creativity of the masses. "Any cook can govern," he argued, and he saw in the everyday activities of ordinary people the seeds of a new socialist society. This is one reason why he was interested in all new forms of social organization and popular cultural forms such as the U.S. cinema industry of the 1950s or the calypso movement in Trinidad and Tobago. James's legacy remains his belief in the working people and their capacity eventually to triumph.

(See also ENGLISH-SPEAKING CARIBBEAN.)

C. L. R. James, *Black Jacobins* (New York, 1963). C. L. R. James, *Notes on Dialectics* (Westport, Conn., 1980). Paul Buhle, *The Artist as Revolutionary* (London, 1988).

SELWYN R. CUDJOE

JAPAN. Modern Japan was born in the mid-nineteenth century, like most other nations in Asia, Africa, and Latin America, out of unexpected and unwelcome contact with Western powers. Even though it escaped direct physical conquest and colonial rule by a Western power, Japan's encounter with the West had far-reaching effects on a nation that had lived in deliberate isolation for two and a half centuries. It triggered an immediate revolution, known as the Meiji Restoration, and led to a radical transformation of the nation's entire political order and social system. The fervently nationalist leaders of the new government believed their primary mission to be the preservation and consolidation of Japan's political independence in a world dominated by predatory Western powers. That mission called for the creation of modern armed forces equal to the Western powers', and that, in turn, called for the development of a modern industrial economy.

This mission was largely accomplished by the turn of the century when the Japanese economy, while still predominantly agricultural, had a thriving light-industry sector. By the first decade of the twentieth century, a world-class ship-building industry had emerged and railroads crisscrossed the island empire. By the second decade of the century, Japan was building not only all its locomotives but all its naval cruisers as well. By then, it had fought and won wars against China and Russia and grown into the third-largest naval power, surpassed only by the United States and Britain.

Democracy and Authoritarian Reaction in Prewar Japan. Pre-*World War II Japan experienced much more than just the rapid industrialization of its economy and the rise of its military power. The direct contact with the West led to exposure to a broad range of modern ideas and *ideologies as well as to modern weapons and industrial economy. As a result, the cultural preferences and ideological beliefs of the Japanese people became considerably more diverse than previously. Moreover, as a part of its frantic drive to modernize Japan and catch up with the Western powers, the Meiji government promptly established a national system of compulsory elementary and voluntary middle-school education. Universities and colleges, many with American and European professors on their faculty, soon followed.

The imported Western ideologies gave rise to political movements and organizations. By the mid-1870s, "freedom and people's rights movements" were formed in various parts of the country and began to campaign vigorously for the establishment of a Western-style parliament. By the early 1880s, political parties emerged and some government leaders themselves began to propose introduction of a constitutional and parliamentary form of government. In 1889, a constitution,

modeled on Prussia's, was promulgated, and the next year the first session of the bicameral parliament—known as the Imperial Diet and composed of a House of Representatives of elected members and a House of Peers of hereditary and appointed members—was convened. Two decades later, in the wake of World War I, the parliamentary system appeared successfully established; during the decade known as Taisho Democracy, not only did a succession of party-based governments rule the nation but also democratic theory prevailed in academia, the popular press espoused liberal ideas, and a variety of interest groups and social movements were formed, from Marxian-inspired labor and *peasant unions to Japan's first feminist organization.

The rise of political parties and the antigovernment mass movement provoked the oligarchic and authoritarian government to tighten its control of public opinion through the propagation of Confucian and *Shinto dogmas, especially absolute deference and loyalty to the emperor. The government also used a "thought police" to suppress antigovernment and antimilitary ideas and movements. A number of laws setting limits to the freedoms of citizens were enacted, culminating in the promulgation in 1925 of a Peace Preservation Law that banned all organizations opposed to Japan's "polity," or the rule by the emperor and his confidants.

Meanwhile, the military expanded its power and influence both at home and abroad. In the early 1930s, as the Japanese economy was mired in a prolonged recession and public disaffection with the civilian government's apparent inability to cope with the situation mounted, the military embarked on a series of attempts to take over the government by force. Within a decade, the military had achieved most of its objectives: Japan had signed a military alliance treaty with Nazi Germany and Fascist Italy, vastly expanded the unprovoked war against China, enacted a national mobilization law, and, finally, led Japan into a suicidal war with the United States.

Within half a year of its highly successful surprise attack on Pearl Harbor in December 1941, Japan began to lose one major naval battle after another in the Pacific. By the middle of 1945, it was evident that Japan had lost the war. Tokyo and other major Japanese cities had been subjected to increasingly frequent and devastating air raids by Allied bombers, Japan's southernmost island, Okinawa, had been landed upon and occupied by Allied troops, and, above all, two major cities, Hiroshima and Nagasaki, had become the first sites of nuclear holocaust in human history. Japan surrendered to the Allied powers on 15 August 1945, and came under their occupation for the next seven years.

Japan Demilitarized and Democratized. The occupation forces under the direction of the Supreme Commander for the Allied Powers (SCAP), General Douglas MacArthur, set out to achieve two basic goals, the demilitarization and democratization of the country. Accordingly, the Japanese government released all political prisoners, repealed the Peace Preservation Law, abolished the thought police and all other oppressive institutions, enfranchised women, recognized labor unions, liberalized education, and democratized the economy. Reforms were undertaken also in education, local government, the civil service, antitrust law, civil and criminal codes, and, above all, the constitution itself.

As a result of these reforms, especially the enactment of a

new, radically democratic, and uniquely pacifist constitution authored by U.S. lawyers, Japan was reborn into a virtually new nation. Its sovereign was no longer the emperor but the Japanese people; the people's fundamental human rights were unconditionally and permanently guaranteed; and, above all, Japan as a nation renounced, in Article Nine of its new constitution, its own right to maintain any form of military power or to engage in acts of war to settle international disputes. In the meantime, Japan's top wartime leaders, with the conspicuous exception of the emperor, were arrested, twenty-five of them were tried by an international military tribunal established, and seven of them were subsequently sentenced to death and sixteen to imprisonment for life for their "crimes against humanity." Some 200,000 others were removed from public office on grounds of their wartime collaboration with the military.

The postwar reforms also helped, directly or indirectly, the rise in political power and influence of the reformed Diet, political parties, and a variety of special interest groups. By the end of 1945, the prewar political parties, which had been defunct during the war, had reemerged and new ones formed, followed by employer associations, farm organizations, and labor unions. The last became the main source of electoral and financial support for the socialist parties, while the organized employers and farmers constituted two of the most important pillars of support for the conservative parties, especially the Liberals and Democrats who merged into the Liberal-Democratic Party (LDP) in 1955.

The occupation-sponsored demilitarization of Japan, however, was neither as thorough nor as successful as it might have been if not for a dramatic change in U.S. policy in response to the exigencies of the looming *Cold War. By mid-1947, the priority of the occupation policy shifted to the economic rehabilitation and political stabilization, rather than complete demilitarization and democratization, of Japan. Japan was given a new role as a major ally of the United States in the struggle against international *communism. Following the outbreak of the *Korean War in mid-1950, a 75,000-strong Police Reserve Force was created at SCAP's order. By 1954 this outfit had evolved into a full-fledged military force of three services, known as the Self-Defense Forces (SDF). As the Cold War unfolded, the de facto rearmament of Japan proceeded at a slow but steady pace until, by the end of the 1980s, the SDF had become one of the best-equipped armed forces in the world.

The democratization program also suffered some setbacks. The substantial decentralization of political power and control accomplished under the initial occupation policy was reversed to some extent after the end of the occupation, especially in the areas of police and educational administration. The municipal police units created during the occupation to counterbalance the centralized power of the national police were absorbed by the latter in 1954, in the name of efficiency and economy. For similar reasons, the popular election of local education board members initiated in 1948 was abolished in 1956 and replaced by appointment by heads of local government.

*Democracy in postwar Japan may also be said to have suffered from the virtual monopoly of government power by the conservatives and, after 1955, by a single conservative party, the LDP. Except briefly during the occupation period and for a little over two years from mid-1993 to early 1996, the conservatives have dominated the Diet at the expense of the splintered opposition. Moreover, politics in postwar Japan in general and elections in particular have been as often and as seriously tainted by corruption as in prewar Japan.

Under the 1947 Japanese constitution, the party that controls the nation's legislative branch also controls its executive branch. This is because the prime minister must be a member of and elected by the Diet, and he or she in turn appoints all other members of the cabinet. Moreover, the majority of those cabinet members must be current Diet members. In practice, nearly all cabinet members appointed since 1947 have been Diet members affiliated with the ruling party.

The judiciary enjoys, in principle, complete decision-making autonomy and freedom. However, all judges, except the chief judge, of the Supreme Court are appointed by the cabinet, the chief judge is designated by the cabinet for nominal appointment by the emperor, and judges of all other courts—i.e., higher, district, family, and summary courts—are designated by the Supreme Court and appointed by the cabinet. The executive branch is thus in a position to exercise some, if not strong, influence on the constitution and operations of the judiciary.

Like its prewar antecedent, Japan's postwar Diet is bicameral and consists of a House of Representatives and a House of Councillors. Whereas, however, members of the prewar House of Peers were either hereditary or appointed by the emperor, all members of the postwar House of Councillors are, like those of the House of Representatives, popularly elected. Between the two houses, the House of Representatives is the larger (currently 500 seats) and more powerful than the House of Councillors (252 seats). If the two houses fail to agree on a budget bill or the ratification of an international treaty, the decision by the House of Representatives prevails; any other type of bill that has been passed by the House of Representatives but defeated in the House of Councillors becomes law if passed again by the House of Representatives with the concurrence of two thirds or more of its members.

Under the new election laws enacted in 1994, 300 of the 500 House of Representatives members are elected from single-member districts and the remaining 200 from eleven much larger districts by the method of proportional representation. The majority (152) of the 252 House of Councillors members are elected from multimember districts, as had all House of Representatives members been until the 1994 change of the system. Under such a system, known as the Single Non-Transferable Vote (SNTV) system, two or more candidates of the same party often run against each other, as well as against candidates of rival parties. Indistinguishable by ideology or policy, these candidates tend to compete on the basis of highly personal services to their constituents. Such services usually involve the use of money. In the case of LDP candidates, a substantial portion of the money is provided by intraparty factions rather than by the party's official treasury. SNTV thus encourages factionalism in the party. As of the late 1990s, there were five entrenched factions in the LDP. While not directly concerned with or involved in intraparty debates and decision making on policy issues, these groups are deeply interested and involved in the distribution not only of political money but also of all important party posts and, by virtue of the LDP's control of both the legislative and executive branches of government, Diet committee chairmanships, cabinet portfolios, and several scores of subcabinet administrative posts. They compete with special ferocity over the selection of the LDP president who is virtually guaranteed the office of Japan's prime minister.

Over the years, the regime of de facto one-party rule has also given rise to a number of competing coalitions of LDP Diet members, senior civil servants, and leaders of special interest groups, each formed within a particular policy area such as agriculture, construction, telecommunications, defense, and so on. In many cases these coalitions have become so entrenched and influential that they are de facto subgovernments. These subgovernments are the main actors in Japan's rampant pork barrel and "money politics," and contribute to the political scandals that frequently rock the nation.

Japan's Rise and Fall as an Economic Superpower. Postwar Japan achieved more unambiguous success in the area of economic development. When the occupation forces landed in Japan in the fall of 1945, the nation was on the verge of total economic collapse. Well over 10 million people were jobless in the face of savage inflation. In the next few years, a succession of Japanese governments tried hard, but in vain, to overcome the economic crisis. The devastating inflation finally began to be brought under control by a set of draconian belt-tightening measures taken upon the advice of a Detroit banker and special adviser to SCAP, Joseph M. Dodge. These measures helped kill the inflation, but only at the price of a spate of business failures and increased unemployment. It was the unexpected boom brought by the Korean War that solved Japan's unemployment problem and put an end to its protracted postwar economic woes.

The special procurement boom of the Korean War period paved the way for a series of long booms beginning in the mid-1950s. Driven by the still-fresh memory of poverty and hunger among its citizens and led by thriving export trade, the Japanese economy grew thereafter at a rapid and consistent pace unparalleled among advanced industrial nations, until it became the second-largest market economy in the world by the end of the 1960s. In the next two decades, Japan became the world's leading producer and exporter of increasingly sophisticated industrial goods, from ships to color televisions, machine tools, automobiles, and semiconductors. By the early 1990s, it was the world's largest creditor nation and donor of economic aid.

The Japanese "miracle" owed a great deal to the undervalued yen under the fixed-exchange-rate regime introduced in 1949 and to the availability of relatively inexpensive raw materials, especially oil from the Middle East. As a result, the Japanese economy experienced a severe shock in the early 1970s when U.S. President Richard *Nixon announced a New Economic Policy, including the suspension of the dollar's convertibility and de facto abandonment of the fixed-exchange-rate regime. The yen's value relative to the dollar's soared thereafter; between 1971 and 1991, the yen gained by more than 60 percent against the dollar. This change caused considerable hardships among export-dependent Japanese busi-

nesses, driving many small businesses to bankruptcy. The 1973 energy crisis compounded the problem and caused Japan's annual economic growth rate to dip below zero for the first time since the early postwar years.

The exchange rate realignment and the oil crisis of the early 1970s thus led the Japanese economy out of the period of extraordinarily high growth rates into one of more moderate but still respectable rates through the 1980s. In the latter half of the 1980s, a speculative boom driven by policy-induced low interest rates produced a period of ephemeral exuberance, dubbed a "bubble economy." This was followed by a protracted recession that reduced the annual growth rates to nearly zero percent, the lowest level among the advanced industrial nations. The problem was aggravated by a financial and banking crisis—another by-product product of the bubble economy—in the late 1990s. By the last decade of the twentieth century, Japan had thus fallen from the status of an economic superpower, although it remained a leading economic power.

Japan had also become a significant potential military power with one of the best-equipped armed forces in the world. It had become, however, neither a military superpower nor a militarist power. Its defense budget, very large as it was in absolute dollar terms, amounted to only about 1 percent of Japan's $5 trillion (1995 figure) gross national product, by far the lowest ratio not only among the advanced industrial nations but even in comparison to most developing nations. The SDF's arsenal included neither nuclear weapons nor long-range bombers, nor was it likely to include either in the foreseeable future.

The state of the SDF accurately reflected the prevailing pacifist mood of a Japanese public still haunted by memories of wartime and early postwar hardships and deprivations. Japanese public opinion had accepted the SDF only very slowly and grudgingly, and the succession of conservative governments had by and large stayed within the bounds of the antimilitary public opinion. The SDF's mission was thus officially explained as strictly defensive, as barring operations abroad, and, above all, as requiring no offensive, especially nuclear, weapons.

Following the 1979 Soviet invasion of Afghanistan, the restrictions on the SDF's mission and operational scope were slightly relaxed in the name of more equitable burden-sharing with the United States. The Japanese government undertook to defend the sea-lanes vital to its own self-defense within 1,000 nautical miles of its territory, permitted SDF units to participate in multinational joint military exercises, and committed slightly more than 1 percent of GNP to defense. The changes were, however, more cosmetic than substantial, and postwar Japan's fundamental commitment to a nonmilitary path to prosperity and glory remained intact.

Postwar Japan and the World. Much as before World War II, Japan developed the closest economic and political relationship with the United States and nations in East Asia. Its relations with nations in other regions of the world gradually expanded, but remained far less vital.

The timing and manner of Japan's postwar "return" to individual East Asian nations were dictated mainly by the history of Japan's colonial rule and wartime occupation and the imperatives of the Cold War. The intense anti-Japanese feeling among Korean leaders and people nurtured during the half-century of brutal Japanese rule prevented normalization of Japan's diplomatic relations with the Republic of Korea (South Korea) until 1965. Relations with the Democratic People's Republic of Korea (North Korea) remain yet to be normalized.

During the Korean War Japan signed a peace treaty with the Nationalist Chinese government in Taiwan, rather than with the government of the People's Republic of China in Beijing. The existence of that treaty and internal political instability in mainland China, as well as the continuing Cold War, delayed normalization of Japan's relations with the People's Republic until 1972 and the formal signing of a peace treaty until 1978.

Postwar Japan reestablished political and economic relations with many Southeast Asian nations via reparations payments. In accordance with a provision in the 1951 Peace Treaty, Japan paid the bulk of these reparations in the form of technical services in the construction of power stations, roads, bridges, port facilities, irrigation systems, factories, and so on. This particular manner of its reentry into Southeast Asia helped Japan establish a predominant economic position in the region in the next few years. The recipients of Japan's postwar reparations rapidly shifted the main sources of their imports, foreign investments, and economic aid from their former colonial masters to Japan. By the 1980s, Japan had thus not only "returned" to East Asia but had become the leading trading partner, investor, and aid donor for most nations in the region. Japan's economic relations with Australia, New Zealand, and other Pacific island nations also expanded rapidly in the 1970s and 1980s.

Japan's expanding presence initially made many people in the region, especially in China, both Koreas, Malaysia, Singapore, and the Philippines, concerned about its long-term political and strategic implications. By the 1980s, however, much of the concern about Japanese political control had dissipated and been replaced by a nearly single-minded demand for infusion of more Japanese capital and technology into local economies and better access to Japanese markets for local exports. Despite its own economic difficulties, Japan remained the leading economic power in the region and, to a somewhat lesser extent, in the world, as the twentieth century drew to its close.

(See also CONFUCIANISM; FINANCE, INTERNATIONAL; HIROHITO; MILITARISM; PACIFIC REGION; PROTECTION; WAR CRIMES.)

Kent E. Calder, *Crisis and Compensation: Public Policy and Political Stability in Japan, 1949–1986* (Princeton, N.J., 1988). Gary D. Allinson and Yasunori Sone, eds., *Political Dynamics in Contemporary Japan* (Ithaca, N.Y., 1993). Hitoshi Abe, Muneyuki Shindo, and Sadafumi Kawato, *The Government and Politics of Japan*, trans. James White (Tokyo, 1994). Richard J. Samuels, *"Rich Nation, Strong Army": National Security and the Technological Transformation of Japan* (Ithaca, N.Y., 1994). David M. O'Brien, with Yasuo Ohkoshi, *To Dream of Dreams: Religious Freedom and Constitutional Politics in Postwar Japan* (Honolulu, 1996). Masaru Kohno, *Japan's Postwar Party Politics* (Princeton, N.J., 1997). Gerald Curtis, *The Logic of Japanese Politics: Leaders, Institutions, and the Limits of Change* (New York, 1999). John W. Dower, *Embracing Defeat: Japan in the Wake of World War II* (New York, 1999). Louis Hayes, *Introduction to Japanese Politics*, 3d ed. (Armonk, N.Y., 2000).

HARUHIRO FUKUI

JAPAN-U.S. RELATIONS. Historically, Japan-U.S. relations have followed a regular fifty-year cycle, alternating between cooperative and antagonistic phases. The first antagonistic phase occurred when U.S. foreign policy became outwardly aggressive, coinciding with Japan's rising nationalism, more recently, Japan-U.S. relations have unravelled with the United States' embracing of China and slighting of Japan. The first cooperative phase began in 1853, in the midst of Anglo-American competition for Chinese trade, when President Millard Fillmore, backed by the four "Black Ships" of the U.S. Navy, forced feudal Japan out of its 230-year self-imposed isolation. (The United States wanted Japan to provide coaling stations for American ships in the new age of steamships. To this date, the Japanese use "Black Ships" as a metaphor for unwanted external pressures.) This first phase ended around 1905, when President Theodore Roosevelt mediated the peace treaty concluding the Russo-Japanese War. By this time the United States had become increasingly concerned about potential competition with Japan for Pacific *hegemony. In 1903, President Roosevelt prophetically declared, "the United States will tolerate no other 'top dog' in the Pacific region. If Japan wants to be the top dog, she must be beaten."

After World War I, each nation became progressively more xenophobic. In 1924, the United States banned Japanese immigration, viewing Japan through the racist paradigm of the "Yellow Peril." Across the Pacific, militarist Japan adopted an equally racist paradigm of the "Anglo-Saxon–Jewish" conspiracy against Japan. In the late 1930s, Japanese politics became totalitarian after a forty-year experiment with *constitutional monarchy. By 1940, alarmed by the aggressive behavior of the Axis powers—Germany, Japan, and Italy—in Europe, Africa, and Asia, the United States abandoned the policy of *isolationism which had been adopted after World War I and which had led to a rupture in Japan-U.S. relations. Japan attacked Pearl Harbor on 7 December 1941 and pulled the United States into *World War II. The war ended in Japan's defeat on 14 August 1945. However, Pearl Harbor has been etched ever since in America's deep-seated distrust of Japan. Every time Japan-U.S. relations sour, Americans dredge up the Pearl Harbor paradigm while the Japanese fall back on the Black Ships paradigm, straining their relations.

Under the relatively benign policies of the U.S. occupation forces in Japan after World War II, the second cooperative phase of Japan-U.S. relations began. This was a throwback to the late nineteenth century when Japan began to modernize. The United States helped Japan's democratic forces carry out long-overdue social, political, economic, and educational reform. The U.S. occupation also broke up the tight, hierarchical controls of family-owned industrial combines (*zaibatsu*) like Mitsui, Mitsubishi, and Sumitomo, over their member corporations. These moves paved the way for more dynamic, flexible strategic alliances (*keiretsu*) of managerially independent firms. They facilitated Japan's economic recovery in the 1950s and rapid economic growth in the 1960s.

In the late 1940s, the *Cold War split the U.S.-led West from the Soviet-led East. Under the *Truman Doctrine, the United States helped revive Japan and the Federal Republic of Germany (West Germany) as new members of the Western bloc, a part of the American effort to contain the spread of communism.

Although Japan regained political independence in 1951, the U.S.-Japan Mutual Security Treaty entrusted the United States with the responsibility for Japan's external security. Japan's preoccupation with economic interests at home and abroad matched the emerging "Pax Americana" of U.S. hegemony after World War II. In the late 1950s, the United States included Japan and West Germany in the economic order associated with Pax Americana. With freer access to the markets, raw materials, capital, and technology of the United States and other countries of the West, Japan achieved its rapid postwar economic growth of the 1960s. However, Pax Americana had produced the following fundamental changes in the world order, sowing the currently seeds of their antagonistic mutual relations.

First, by the 1980s, Pax Americana's *geopolitics had been replaced by a world of geoeconomics. Technological and economic strength became the main determinant of a nation's security. Military spending had become an economic and technological burden on the United States, while the deterioration of public education and social infrastructure like transportation had weakened its economic and national security. In an era when technological innovations for civilian use often determined advancements in defense technology, the United States had become increasingly dependent on Japan even for such defense-related technology as microelectronics. By the mid-1980s, the decline of the U.S. economy and technology vis-à-vis Japan triggered a more aggressive U.S. foreign policy toward Japan.

Second, from the mid-1970s to the 1980s, many U.S. manufacturing firms, seeking to reduce wage costs, moved their factories to places in East and Southeast Asia other than Japan. American management's disdain of workers and engineers accelerated the loss of manufacturing skills and bases in the United States. The loss of higher-paying jobs in nondefense manufacturing industries gave rise to chronic trade deficits and economic and technological nationalism in the United States. The United States began to restrict Japanese imports and to demand that Japan set aside a U.S.-dictated market share for American goods and services. As the United States mistakenly blamed Japan's alleged import restrictions for America's economic and social problems, Japan-U.S. relations became strained. In addition, the United States became dependent on Japanese loans to finance mounting budget deficits, aggravating American policy makers' unwanted sense of dependency on Japan.

Japan's economic and technological rise enabled it to sell more value-added goods and services to the United States. In the 1970s, the United States accounted for 20 to 25 percent of total Japanese exports; in the 1980s, the figure reached 35 percent. The rising value of the Japanese yen against the U.S. dollar and U.S. restrictions on Japanese imports combined to spur direct Japanese investments in the United States throughout the 1980s. By 1990, Japan's cumulative direct investment in the United States passed $110 billion, employing over one million Americans. From electronics, automobiles, steel, and machine tools to telecommunications, U.S. nondefense manufacturing industries were revitalized with massive infusions of Japanese capital, technology, and management know-how. However, the American public did not see Japan's renewed dependence on the U.S. market as beneficial to America's hegemony in the world. The American

mass media frequently whipped up the American Pearl Harbor paradigm, employing oft-repeated war metaphors in headlines like "Japan's Surprise Invasion of Hollywood" to refer to Sony's purchase of Columbia Pictures.

Third, the so-called Pacific Basin Club—Australia, New Zealand, China (including Hong Kong), the Republic of Korea (South Korea), Taiwan, Japan, and the seven nations of the *Association of Southeast Asian Nations (ASEAN)—began to trade and invest more and more among themselves. By the end of the 1980s, Japan replaced the United States as the leading trade and investment partner of the other Pacific Basin nations.

Fourth, by the early 1990s, the disintegration of the Soviet Union and the end of the Cold War reduced the Soviet threat in the Pacific. This challenged the basis of the U.S.-Japan Mutual Security Treaty that had made Japan a political and military ward of the United States for almost forty years. At the same time, the Soviet threat had forced the two countries to contain their economic rivalry in order not to weaken their alliance against the Soviet Union. Once the Soviet threat subsided, the Japanese public viewed the U.S. military bases and their control over Japan as having overstayed their welcome. In the United States since the collapse of the Berlin Wall in 1989, American public opinion has increasingly soured against Japan, which was perceived as the only remaining threat to the U.S. hegemony in the Asia-Pacific region. America's distrust of Japan has remained strong even after the United States and Japan traded their places of economic power after 1991.

As a consequence of these developments, "Contain Japan" or "Japan Bashing" thinking came to dominate the U.S. view of Japan. Fifty years after the end of World War II, Japan-U.S. relations once again entered an antagonistic phase due to their economic rivalry in the Asia-Pacific region. In Japan, neonationalist sentiment surfaced, encouraged by Japan's rising influence in the Pacific. This ideological turnabout was fueled by a generational change in Japan. Japanese who had no direct experience of the benign policies of the U.S. occupation were moving into leadership positions in business, government, and political circles. Japan-U.S. relations drifted further apart as Japan's economic bubble burst in 1991 and the country was gripped by serious political and economic paralysis. The Japanese public's fear for their future fueled the rising influence of the nationalists who distrusted the United States.

In the period after 1991, Japanese banks hoped to grow out of their bad debts by expanding their reckless lending particularly to South Korea, Hong Kong, Thailand, Malaysia, and Indonesia. Easy money from Japan created these Asian countries' own economic boom which finally burst in the fall of 1997, triggering the widespread implosions of the Japanese and other Asian economies, dubbed the "Asian Contagion." The Asian Contagion threatened the U.S. economy and even the advent of a worldwide great depression. The United States blamed Japan for the Asian Contagion and pressured Japan into bailing out other Asian economies including China and carrying out banking and other economic reforms. Japan's slow response led the Clinton administration to mistakenly embrace China as the "Future of Asia" and spurn Japan as if Japan were a totalitarian state and China a democratic and free-market reformer. In reality, Japanese, not Chinese, technology and capital will continue to be needed by the world.

The present situation calls for grand bargaining in order to mend unravelling Japan-U.S. relations. Without such cooperation, the world will be unable to cope with the global problems of the twenty-first century. No nation can go it alone in coping with major political and economic disruptions in the global era in which capital, technology, and information move at the speed of light through the World Wide Web. The world is threatened by a likely collapse of Russian economy and polity, Chinese and North Korean expansionism, Middle East and West Asian instabilities, massive population explosions, and the continued destruction of the natural environment worldwide.

How can the two economic powers of the world rise to the occasion? The logical first step would be for them to stop blaming each other for their own economic and political problems at home and to abandon their bilateral micromanagement of U.S.-Japan trade and investment. Instead, the two nations should cooperate and let the World Trade Organization adjudicate their trade and investment disputes. Japan and the United States need to transform the U.S.-Japan Mutual Security Treaty from a Cold War tool into a political framework in the Pacific Age. It should be in the interest of both nations to work in unison to nudge China and North Korea toward political and economic coexistence with the other Asia-Pacific nations.

(See also DEINDUSTRIALIZATION; INFORMATION TECHNOLOGY; PACIFIC RIM; U.S. FOREIGN POLICY.)

Yoshi Tsurumi, "U.S.-Japanese Relations: From Brinkmanship to Statemanship" *World Policy Journal* VII, no. 1 (Winter 1989–1990). Donald Calman, *The Origin and Nature of Japanese Imperialism* (New York, 1992). Michael Schaller, *Altered States: The United States and Japan Since the Occupation* (New York, 1997). Walter LaFeber, *The Clash: US-Japanese Relations throughout History* (New York, 1998).

YOSHI TSURUMI

JIHAD. Originally the doctrine of struggle against unbelievers for the expansion and protection of the Muslim community, jihad is closely linked with *hijra* or emigration from non-Muslim society. According to the doctrine, the sins of a person making jihad are remitted and death "on the path of God" is martyrdom which secures immediate entry to paradise. Scholars also have spoken of "the greater jihad" as the internal struggle against one's own sinful tendencies or as the personal struggle for the good against what is forbidden.

Jihad is a collective duty, but women, minors, and the sick are among categories legally excluded. It is also a personal duty, though not one of the five pillars of Islam. Shi'i teach that jihad can only be under the leadership of the Imam, whereas Sunnis accept the proclamation of even an unjust ruler. Most believe jihad cannot be declared against fellow Muslims, though Ayatollah Ruhollah *Khomeini did so against the rulers of Iraq in the *Iran-Iraq War.

In the colonial period, wars against external forces were often regarded as jihad: for example, by the Sanusi religious order who proclaimed it against the Italians in Libya in 1912, and by the Mahdi in the Sudan against the British and the Egyptians (1881–1885). More recently, guerrillas fighting the Russian occupation of Afghanistan in the 1980s saw themselves as mujahidin, as did certain groups opposed to

the shah of Iran in the 1970s, and who later opposed the Ayatollah Khomeini.

Many authorities consider that if Muslims live in a society ruled by non-Muslims but are not under threat and can perform their ritual duties, then jihad is not obligatory. States are not constantly at war, and good relations and treaties with non-Muslim powers are permissible. This is most relevant in the modern period when many Muslims in Africa, Asia, and Europe live in nation-states that are neither under Muslim rulers nor, where the ruler is a Muslim, under the *shari'a.

Modern reformers, facing a world dominated by non-Muslim powers in which Muslims live with members of other communities in many distinct nation-states with their own secular interests, have emphasized the moral nature of jihad. They see military jihad only as defensive against oppression. Nationalist movements most often stressed the homeland rather than the Muslim community, even if they made *nationalism a quasi-sacred cause and used jihad rhetorically when they thought it opportune. Modernists such as President Bourguiba of Tunisia tried to appropriate the concept as meaning the struggle for national development.

Islamic radical movements scorn such interpretations and stress *Islam as an expansionist world order. Jihad is again a fundamental duty and active struggle for the global application of the shari'a. They also seek to "purify" Muslim societies of "corrupt" and "tyrannical" Muslim rulers, used by some in justification of the assassination of President *Sadat of Egypt in 1981.

The identification of sacred duty with violence or national wars is made in many political systems and states. Muslims *qua* Muslims are no more bellicose than followers of any creed, religious or otherwise. Jihad has been used in some Western writings to justify the view that all Muslims are aggressive fanatics, but this claim says more about Western views of others than about the behavior of Muslims, and is false.

(See also ARAB NATIONALISM; RELIGION AND POLITICS; SECULARIZATION.)

Rudolph Peters, *Islam and Colonialism: The Doctrine of Jihad in Modern History*, Mouton Religion and Society Series, no. 20 (The Hague, 1979).

MICHAEL GILSENAN

JOHN PAUL II. The pope elected by the College of Cardinals on 16 October 1978 was an unexpected choice, Karol Wojtyla, archbishop of Krakow, Poland. The first Polish pope, he chose to be known as John Paul II. His election followed the thirty-three-day reign of John Paul, whose brief passage had highlighted not only his gift for communication and simplicity but also the need for a successor of strong intellect and robust health. Cardinal Wojtyla was known for the active part he had taken in the Vatican Council and in synods, and for his numerous journeys outside Poland.

Poland is a country strongly anchored in its fidelity to Rome, yet the pope's Slavic origins made him familiar with the spiritual and theological traditions of Eastern Christendom. Eastern Europe has always been a site of exchange and synthesis between different cultural traditions, while each of its nations has vigorously upheld its own. The origins and personal talents of John Paul II incline him to responsibilities of worldwide scale.

Born in 1920, he was compelled to join the workforce during the war, while a seminarian. He was ordained in 1946 and was a professor of moral theology at the Catholic University in Lublin and chaplain to the students; he became an auxiliary bishop in 1958, then archbishop of Krakow in 1964, and a cardinal in 1967. He therefore has an intimate knowledge of the complexities that underlie the relationships between Catholics, Jews, and Protestants in Poland, which have been complicated by the years of Nazi and then communist rule. Like all Polish bishops he has had to contend with the communist regime. In his fight for his faith as well as for *human rights he has experienced contacts with a profoundly Christian people, as well as a political environment which was indifferent or hostile to religion.

As pope, in all his speeches, writings, and exchanges, he has strongly affirmed that the fight for social justice and human dignity is an intrinsic part of the spreading of the Gospel. It is through man that the Church accomplishes its mission. This certainty rests on the faith in Man's greatness as an image of God, and therefore on the conscious belief in a human dignity to be defended against all possible forms of dehumanization. This has led the pope to speak out against all attacks on human life be they in the private domain, such as* abortion or euthanasia, or in a more public one, concerning, for instance, forms of economic or political tyranny.

Pope John Paul II expounds the demands of Christian living according to the teachings of the *Vatican II Council in the language of his audience. He was not impeded by the Iron Curtain (which disappeared only in 1989, not without his contribution), nor by opposition, nor by danger—he has been the target of at least three known assassination attempts. In the first ten years of his papacy he had already visited seventy-four countries, in every continent; ten years later his ninety first trip led him to the Holy Land and Jerusalem, suggesting to the world by word and by deed what strong will, good faith, and leadership are all about. His prayer asking forgiveness to God for the offenses of Catholics during the World War II touched many, including Israeli Jews and those of the diaspora. During this trip he also asked for more understanding among those living in the Holy Land while pleading for justice and the realization of a homeland for the Palestinians.

Some within the *Roman Catholic Church feel ill at ease with the pope's strong personality. Indeed, John Paul II has undertaken to instill a new vigor in the Church, in the spirit of the Vatican II Council; he obviously wishes to quicken the faith of the members of the churches he visits. At the same time, the visibility imparted to the Church by the crowds which rally round him, constitutes, to his mind, a means to oppose the grasping *secularization which deadens the sense of the sacred. In an even broader sense, confronted with the enormous risks of human degradation inherent in a society dominated by the materialistic exigencies of technology and economics, he undertakes to muster the ethical forces to give humanity the first and ultimate importance. "We must be convinced of the priority of ethics over technique, of the primacy of man upon things, of the precedence of mind upon matter" (from John Paul II's speech at UNESCO, 2 June 1980.)

This itinerant mission is one of the salient features of the Church as personified by the pope and makes it difficult to classify John Paul II in a traditional category. In his doctrinal and above all his moral teachings, he is rather traditional and concedes nothing to the evolution of sexual and conjugal mores in a modern civilization. However, his statements concerning public life—whether about economics, politics, or society—and his opening to other religions identify him as resolutely progressive.

John Paul II is also a seeker after truth, who looks back on history, reads it anew, and at times finds new significance in major historical events. He preaches repentance and forgiveness. The Galileo sentence must be reconsidered in the light of modern though; so must the Crusades, the Inquisition, and the Church's attitude towards the Jews: the Church's responsibility must be acknowledged. During the Jubilee year 2000 he multiplied the occasions on which this responsibility was stated and forgiveness asked, with a high point in March 2000 during his trip to the Holy Land.

John Paul II is strongly committed to ecumenism: he wishes for a rapprochement with the Orthodox Church. To foster an interreligious dialogue he encourages contacts with non-Christian religions. When in Morocco in 1985 he spoke to a crowd of young Muslims, an unprecedented event in the history of the papacy. In 1986 he gathered sixty-three leaders of the world's religions at Assisi and led them in a prayer for peace. This meeting created a precedent that was to be repeated regularly. He always urges his listeners to open their minds and hearts; concurrently he systematically opposes all forms of "integrism" in the Church—i.e., a refusal of the Vatican II spirit—and in the world.

John Paul II's lifelong political commitment is marked by his ceaseless fight against Marxism and the communist system. In 1978 he traveled to Poland to commemorate Saint Stanislas's martyrdom. In a communist land he demanded the right to freedom and self-determination. Later he defended and met with its leader, Lech Walesa. He has had considerable influence on the evolution of the political and social situation in Poland and the other Eastern European countries, perhaps contributing to the demise of communism. He also met with Gorbachev in 1989 just before the dismantling of the USSR. Timing seems to have always been his gift, with the pope giving a nudge to situations which were ripe for change.

In South America he has confronted the proponents of the *liberation theology, whose political commitment is strong. His attitude, decidedly hostile at first, was eventually tempered with greater understanding for the pastoral urgencies. Nevertheless he remains firmly opposed to the political commitment of the movement, which uses the analytical tools of Marxists. According to the pope, one must never confuse religion and politics. On the contrary, he pleads for the right to life and human dignity in all its forms.

The pope is much interested in Lebanon and concerned by the threats to the Christian community, including the traditional divisions that have Christians fighting among themselves. He sees Christianity as a barrier against integrism coming from Islamic rites and traditions.

In his quest to spread the Gospel to the young people of the world, John Paul II created the World Youth Days: these occur on a national level each year and on an international level every two years. On these days the pope invites the youth of the world to come and meet him, giving him an occasion to spread the word of Jesus Christ in terms of liberty, love, and respect for human life. Buenos Aires, Santiago de

Compostela, Częstochowa, Denver, Manila, and Paris have already hosted this event; another was scheduled to be held in Rome in August 2000. At the last two events, the crowds numbered in the millions.

By means of repentance the and reexamination of history, John Paul II has strengthened Catholicism. He has been able to confront in a neverending dialogue the challenges of *Islam, of integrism, of nationalism, he who was the advocate of the Polish nation.

(See also RELIGION AND POLITICS.)

HENRI MADELIN

JOHNSON, Lyndon Baines. Born on 27 August 1908 on a farm in the Texas Hill Country near the village of Stonewall, Lyndon Baines Johnson was the eldest of five children. His father, Sam Ealy Johnson, had served in the Texas legislature, and young Lyndon grew up in an atmosphere that emphasized politics and public affairs. Lyndon's mother, Rebekah Baines Johnson, encouraged her son's ambition and sense of striving. In 1913 the Johnsons moved to nearby Johnson City. Young Lyndon was educated in local schools in the area and graduated from high school in Johnson City in 1924.

During the next several years, Lyndon tried various jobs in California and Texas without success. In 1927 he entered Southwest Texas State Teachers College in San Marcos. A history and social science major, he was active in campus politics. He earned his elementary school teacher's certificate in 1928 and for one year was a principal and teacher at Cotulla in south Texas. His work with the destitute Hispanic students there had an important effect on his attitude toward poverty and the role of government.

Johnson received his B.S. degree in 1930. He had already taken part in several political campaigns. Late in 1931 he became the secretary to a member of Congress, Richard M. Kleberg of Texas. During the four years he held the position he gained valuable contacts in Washington. In 1934 he met and married Claudia Alta ("Lady Bird") Taylor, daughter of a prosperous planter and storeowner in Marshall, Texas. Two daughters were born to the Johnsons during the 1940s. Lady Bird Johnson proved to be an effective political partner. Her business acumen was an important element in the success of the radio and television stations that the Johnsons acquired in Austin during the 1940s and 1950s.

Johnson's first important political position was as director of the National Youth Administration (NYA) in Texas from 1935 to 1937. He established a system of roadside parks to put young Texans to work and quietly fostered the participation of *African Americans in some NYA programs. When the incumbent member for the Tenth Congressional District died in 1937, Johnson entered the race as a devoted supporter of Franklin D. *Roosevelt and the *New Deal. He spent eleven years in the House of Representatives and became intimately familiar with the legislative process. He was a follower of the programs and policies of Franklin D. Roosevelt and a close ally of Majority Leader (later Speaker) Sam Rayburn. He was the chair of the Democratic Congressional Campaign Committee in 1940 and helped the Democrats retain control of the House. In 1941 he ran for the Senate from Texas, but was narrowly defeated in a special election.

Upon the outbreak of World War II in December 1941, Johnson entered the Navy as a lieutenant commander. He saw combat during an inspection tour of the South Pacific in 1942. He left the Navy in response to President Roosevelt's directive that members of Congress should remain in Washington. Johnson made another race for the Senate in 1948 against the popular former governor, Coke Stevenson. Texas had lost its earlier affection for the New Deal and Johnson stressed his own *conservatism in the election. The runoff primary in August 1948 was very close. Amid charges of ballot box stuffing and other fraudulent practices, Johnson was declared the Democratic nominee only after extended legal battles. He easily defeated his Republican opponent in the general election.

Johnson was an effective senator who mastered the organization and rules of the upper house. His Democratic colleagues elected him majority whip within three years, and in 1953 he was chosen to be minority leader—the youngest such leader in the history of the Senate. Johnson won a second term in 1954. The Democrats regained control of Congress that same year, and in January 1955 he became the majority leader.

In his rush to power, Johnson had neglected his health. During the early summer of 1955, he had a severe heart attack. He returned to his duties in the Senate in late 1955. He pursued a strategy of bipartisan cooperation with the Republican administration of Dwight D. *Eisenhower. As majority leader Johnson was instrumental in the passage of civil rights acts (the first in more than eighty years) in 1957 and 1960. He also played a large role in establishing the National Aeronautics and Space Administration (NASA).

Johnson wanted to be president throughout the 1950s. Power in the Senate did not mean that he could win delegate votes from the Democratic Party or surmount his party's reluctance to name a southerner as its national candidate. After his nomination campaign against John F. *Kennedy failed, Johnson agreed to become the vice-presidential candidate in 1960. Johnson campaigned hard across the South, and his ability to put Texas and other southern states in the Democratic column helped Kennedy gain a narrow victory.

The vice-presidential years from 1961 to 1963 were hard on Johnson. He carried out the assignments he received from Kennedy, including chairing the National Aeronautics and Space Council and the President's Committee on Equal Opportunity. Johnson resented the absence of any real power, and he was angered at the slights he received from the people around Kennedy.

Kennedy's *assassination in November 1963 brought Johnson to the *presidency in tragic circumstances. He conducted himself during the transition in a manner that reassured the nation and set his administration on a constructive course. The new president was particularly skilled with Congress, and he persuaded lawmakers to pass much of the stalled Kennedy legislative program. During the spring of 1964 Johnson set forth his domestic objectives, termed the *Great Society. He wanted to use the affirmative power of government to establish programs that would end poverty and racial discrimination. Congress readily approved his requests to increase foreign aid, reduce taxes, and pass conservation legislation.

The centerpiece of Johnson's achievements in this early phase of his presidency was the Civil Rights Act of 1964. The new law outlawed segregation in public accommodations and pursued fair employment practices. Johnson's administration was identified, more directly than that of any previous president, with the aspirations of African Americans. Another major domestic goal was the "war on poverty" that led to a food stamp system, a Job Corps for unemployed youth, and community action programs to deal with the local needs of poor Americans. The Office of Economic Opportunity directed these Great Society initiatives.

In foreign policy, Johnson inherited the commitment that Kennedy had made to the preservation of South Vietnam. He decided in late 1963 not to withdraw from Southeast Asia. During 1964, the Tonkin Gulf incident of August and the resulting Tonkin Gulf Resolution from Congress reflected popular support for Johnson's policy of cautious commitment to the future of *Vietnam. Johnson used his moderation in foreign affairs to win an overwhelming electoral victory over his conservative Republican opponent, Senator Barry M. Goldwater of Arizona, in the 1964 presidential election.

With his popular mandate, Johnson pressed for the enactment of Great Society legislation during 1965–1966. Laws to deal with education, conservation, health care, immigration, and poverty poured out of Congress. The Voting Rights Act of 1965 safeguarded African-American voting rights and expanded black participation in southern politics. By the end of 1965, however, the momentum of the Great Society had slowed because of conservative opposition to the liberal programs and eroding public support for the *Vietnam War.

Johnson faced mounting foreign policy problems. A military intervention in the *Dominican Republic in 1965 produced congressional criticism. More important, escalation of the war in Vietnam during the summer through a bombing campaign and the full-scale combat role for U.S. troops led to popular protests in the United States. Antiwar demonstrators focused on Johnson and made it difficult for him to travel around the country. Social unrest at home compounded the president's difficulties. Riots with racial overtones began in 1965 and continued in major cities during the remainder of his presidency. The political skills that had taken Johnson to the White House proved of little help as his popularity declined.

The war in Vietnam seemed stalemated as 1967 ended. The Tet offensive in February 1968 was a defeat for North Vietnam militarily but a blow to Johnson's weakened standing at home. Faced with political challenges from Eugene McCarthy and Robert Kennedy in the Democratic Party, Johnson also worried about his own health if he ran again. On 31 March 1968, he announced that he was limiting the bombing of North Vietnam and was seeking negotiations. In a political surprise, he also announced that he would not be a candidate for reelection. Johnson left office on 20 January 1969 and died on 22 January 1973.

Unfriendly biographers have depicted Johnson as driven only by a lust for power. His personality could be abrasive and his methods were often crude. Nonetheless, Johnson was also a liberal nationalist who was impelled to improve the lives of Americans generally. Despite his foreign policy failure in Vietnam, Lyndon Johnson was one of the most important presidents of the period after World War II. His ambitious Great Society symbolized the expansive policies of U.S. *liberalism. The reaction to this program laid the basis for the conservative trend that followed him. The war in Vietnam called into question the ability of the *United States to exert its influence where it chose in the world. Johnson's broad concept of presidential power came under criticism because of the excesses of his White House years. Lyndon Johnson had tried to be a great president and achieved some impressive results. He also demonstrated the limits of the government and the presidency to produce social change and to pursue an activist foreign policy.

(See also AMERICAN FOREIGN POLICY; CIVIL RIGHTS MOVEMENT.)

Lyndon Baines Johnson, *The Vantage Point: Perspectives of the Presidency, 1963–1969* (New York, 1971). Vaughn Davis Bornet, *The Presidency of Lyndon B. Johnson* (Lawrence, Kans., 1983). Robert Dallek, *Lone Star Rising: Lyndon Johnson and His Times, 1908–1960* (New York, 1991).
                                                    LEWIS L. GOULD

JORDAN. The state of Jordan came into being after World War I, when Britain and France imposed their rule over lands of the defeated Ottoman Empire. In 1920, the British government took formal control of the territory as part of its Palestine Mandate. Soon afterwards, on 15 May 1923, the British accorded separate status to the territories east of the Jordan River, recognizing them as the Emirate of Transjordan and affirming Prince Abdullah, son of the Sherif Hussein of Mecca, as ruler.

Abdullah's family, the Hashemites, had sought to create a united Arab kingdom after the war, a project blocked by the British and French. Abdullah thus partly symbolized the movement for Arab unity and independence. Ironically, however, because of Transjordan's scant resources and small population, Abdullah remained heavily reliant on Britain for more than three decades. During that time, the British effectively controlled the country's army and finances, and British advisers virtually ran the government.

In 1946, Britain granted formal independence, the name of the country was changed to Jordan, and Abdullah took the title of king. In 1948, when *Israel was created, the Jordanian army joined in the ensuing *Arab-Israeli conflict, taking control of the Old City of Jerusalem and a substantial block of *Palestine to the west of the Jordan River—an area generally known as the West Bank. Four hundred thousand Palestinian refugees entered Jordanian-controlled territory during the hostilities; afterwards, unable to return to their homes in the new Jewish state, they became long-term residents, the majority in squalid *refugee camps. When King Abdullah formally annexed the West Bank to his kingdom in 1950, he assumed rule over this explosive social and political situation.

Dependent on British and the West for financial and political support, Abdullah agreed to pursue a policy of nonbelligerency with Israel, the powerful new neighbor to the west, and sought to impose his authority over the Palestinians. This created many difficulties in an era of growing Arab and Palestinian nationalism and led to Abdullah's death in Jerusalem at the hands of a Palestinian assassin on 20 July 1951. Abdullah's son Talal succeeded his father but reigned only briefly. His son Hussein then assumed the throne in 1953 at the age of seventeen. Hussein identified himself with *Arab nationalism, but he nonetheless maintained a close alliance with Britain and later the United States. Through the years, he survived radical nationalist opposition to his rule—an opposition that found one important base in the kingdom's Palestinian population and that drew support from various Arab regimes such as *Egypt, *Syria, and *Iraq.

The early years of Hussein's rule were particularly stormy. In 1955, he bowed to popular pressure and refused to join the Baghdad Pact, a short-lived regional security group organized by Britain and the United States. Then, in 1956, parliamentary elections resulted in an outspokenly nationalist Parliament. Under pressure from the new government, the king dismissed General John Glubb, the British chief of staff of Jordan's army, and not long after annulled the British-Jordanian Treaty.

In spite of these early accommodations, Hussein eventually affirmed his rule and his alliance with the West, at the expense of political freedoms. In April 1957, Washington sent emergency economic and military assistance to Hussein and moved the Sixth Fleet to the eastern Mediterranean in response to an abortive military coup. Shortly thereafter, the king purged the government of nationalists and banned all political parties except the Muslim Brotherhood—a ban that was to remain in force for over thirty years. Freedom of expression was substantially curtailed at this time as well. In the West Bank, where many Palestinians questioned the *legitimacy of Jordanian rule, repression was particularly harsh.

The political balance in the kingdom shifted with the June War of 1967, when Israeli forces quickly defeated the royal army, capturing Jerusalem and the entire West Bank. More than 200,000 Palestinian refugees fled across the Jordan River during and immediately after the war. In dozens of camps, a Palestinian guerrilla movement took form, launching raids across the new border and touching off Israeli reprisals. When commandos of the *Palestine Liberation Organization (PLO) challenged the authority of the Jordanian government, the king cracked down with his army in September 1970.

Though Israel occupied the West Bank, the Jordanian government continued to exercise considerable authority in the territory, paying the salaries of teachers and civil servants and competing with the PLO and other political forces for legitimacy. But after the October War of 1973, the increasingly powerful PLO won the support of all other Arab states based on its claim to represent Palestinians. The emerging idea of an independent Palestinian state in the Israeli-occupied territories dealt another blow to King Hussein's claim to sovereignty over the Palestinians and their territory. The king responded by suspending parliament in 1974; the body would remain suspended for over ten years.

Jordan enjoyed an economic boom for over a decade after the 1973 war, thanks largely to soaring oil prices. Although the country was not an oil producer, it obtained large aid grants from oil-rich Gulf states, took in substantial remittances from Jordanians and Palestinians working in the Gulf oil economies, and profited from its role as a regional trade and financial center. When oil prices began to decline in the early 1980s, Jordan's economy found a new source of profits: its role as major transshipper for *Iraq during the *Iran-Iraq War. Prosperity muted political problems for a time. Thousands flooded into Amman from the countryside to participate in the boom, swelling the population of the capital to about 1.3 million—or nearly half the country's population—by 1985.

The Palestine question remained at the center of the kingdom's political agenda during the 1980s. Discussions between the king and the PLO led to temporary accords in 1985 for a Palestinian-Jordanian negotiating strategy and an eventual joint confederation, a formula responsive to pressures from the United States and Israel. This formula never won full support within the PLO, however, and in August of 1988, after the *intifada in the Occupied Territories, the king publicly relinquished responsibility for the West Bank in favor of the PLO, losing much of his remaining leverage over the territories.

Meanwhile, tension at home was rising as the Jordanian economy faltered. The end of the Iran-Iraq War had removed the last big economic prop. A series of price increases on government-subsidized necessities in April 1989 set off anti-government riots that swept the south, traditional bedrock of Hashemite rule. The king sought to rebuild his authority by offering a program of broad political liberalization—curbing the security forces, restoring Parliament, and calling parliamentary general elections for the first time in more than twenty years.

The elections, held in November 1989, resulted in a victory for the Muslim Brotherhood, which won a third of the eighty-seat parliament. The king managed to integrate Islamic representatives into the government, however, without a major shift in the political system.

The *Gulf War of 1990–1991 revealed the kingdom's continued political and economic vulnerability. Throughout the crisis, King Hussein refused to join the anti-Iraq coalition, losing Jordan's large economic aid from the Gulf oil producers and the United States. The Jordanian economy was also swamped by 300,000 refugees—mostly Jordanians and Palestinians—who had fled or been deported from Kuwait and the Gulf states.

By 1992, much of the crucial aid flow had been restored (now from the Federal Republic of Germany and Japan), but the government of King Hussein continued to face serious problems. Most ominous was the possibility of continued conflict over the Palestine question, leading potentially to expulsion of more refugees from Israel or even another regional war.

Economic problems and Islamic fundamentalism also challenged the monarchy. Under these difficult circumstances, the king sought to build consensus around the throne by promising broader democratization. In June 1991 he rallied all political forces of the country behind a new "National Charter," proposing substantially enlarged pluralism, including a legalized multiparty system and the repeal of martial law, which had been in effect since 1967.

When the PLO and Israel signed an agreement in 1993, King Hussein felt free to negotiate his own deal with his powerful neighbor. The 1994 Jordanian-Israeli Peace Treaty not only declared an end to hostilities but proposed a partnership between the two states. Soon afterwards, the king reversed his policy on Iraq and adopted a hostile position towards Iraqi President Saddam Hussein. Jordanian national consensus fell apart, as a broad range of opposition parties rejected normalized ties with Israel and opposed the government's support for U.S. policies towards Iraq.

Opposition continued to grow, though there was no direct challenge to Hashemite rule. Governments struggled to curb dissent, restricting political and press freedoms. The growing opposition reflected economic difficulties, as well as conflicts between the government and Jordan's Palestinian population. Between 1991 and 1999, eight different cabinets tried without success to restore consensus.

In 1999, King Hussein died of cancer after forty-six years on the throne. The population mourned his death as the end of a familiar era. In his final days, Hussein bypassed his brother Hassan, long seen as heir to the throne, naming instead his son Abdullah, a young army officer who had been educated in the United States.

Under King Abdullah, the government liberalized Jordan's economy by privatizing public enterprises, enacting new copyright laws, and removing trade barriers, but much of the population remained in poverty and economic growth was disappointingly slow. Abdullah cracked down on the Islamic resistance movement Hamas, long a source of friction with Israel, and he successfully reconciled Jordan with estranged Arab leaders in the Gulf and Syria.

Jordan will continue its economic liberalization drive and remain closely tied to Washington. But opposition could explode if the economy fails to take off. Jordan's future also depends on a stable settlement between Israel and its neighbors, especially the Palestinians. Abdullah's heavy reliance on the feared Intelligence Department in an increasingly open economy suggests that the future of the political system will be sorely tested.

(See also BALFOUR DECLARATION; ZIONISM.)

P. J. Vatikiotis, *Politics and the Military in Jordan* (London, 1967). Naseer Aruri, *Jordan: A Study in Political Development* (The Hague, 1972). Peter Gubser, *Jordan: Crossroads of Middle Eastern Events* (London, 1983). Rodney Wilson, *Politics and the Economy in Jordan* (London, 1991).

LAMIS ANDONI

JUDICIAL REVIEW. The power of certain courts to invalidate laws or actions of governmental officials as unconstitutional is known as judicial review. In federal nation-states, such review applies both to state and national legislation. While a theory of judicial review was intimated in English law, most notably in Lord Chief Justice Edward Coke's decision in *Dr. Bonham's Case* (1610), judicial review of national legislation is usually traced to the *United States and especially to Chief Justice John Marshall's decision in *Marbury* v. *Madison* (1803). In denying Marbury's request for relief, Marshall ruled that the law under which Marbury appeared before the U.S. *Supreme Court violated the Constitution.

The U.S. Constitution of 1787 does not actually state the power of judicial review, but it has been accepted since 1803 and has been copied by many other nations, especially those liberated by the Allies and victims of the dictatorial excesses that led to World War II. Judicial review is consistent with the idea of a written *constitution, expressing the consent of the people, superior to ordinary acts of legislation, and unchangeable by ordinary legislative means. Accepting *parliamentary sovereignty and with no rigid constitution, Britain has no judicial review although a fair number of Britain's onetime colonies are among the approximately sixty-five nations that now do. Most such nations specifically state this power in their constitutions. In federal systems, where it is especially common, judicial review provides a peaceful means of resolving conflicts between the national government and the

sovereign subunits. Judicial review also helps settle disputes among branches of the national government in systems employing *separation of powers.

The U.S. model of judicial review is "diffuse," enabling courts at all levels to exercise such review, albeit only in genuine "cases or controversies" where parties have established "standing." In such cases, trial court judgments may be reviewed by appellate tribunals, with the Supreme Court having final judgment. Countries with such systems—often with common-law backgrounds—include a number of Latin American nations as well as Greece, Australia, Canada, Japan, India, Pakistan, Burma, and most Scandinavian nations. Germany, France, Spain, Italy, and other countries—often with civil-law traditions—have a more "concentrated" mode of review that follows the Austrian example where a specific court or courts, sometimes separate from the regular judicial system, resolve constitutional questions. Some such nations have more relaxed requirements for standing than do American courts, even permitting advisory opinions. In the United States, the president appoints judges with the advice and consent of the Senate, and their service is contingent on good behavior. Nations where concentrated judicial review is exercised are more likely to vest appointments in the legislative branch and have fixed terms and/or mandatory retirement ages. Some nations, Portugal, Switzerland, and a number of Latin American countries, for example, have "mixed" systems blending elements of the concentrated and diffuse models.

Although positively linked to governmental stability and to free political systems with competitive political parties, judicial review may, as in the United States, pit the judgments of unelected magistrates serving for life against those of the people's representatives elected for fixed terms. U.S. courts, like others, have developed various maxims by which to defer or bypass controversial political issues, especially in the realm of foreign affairs where the need for quick action is often incompatible with judicial second-guessing and where constitutional limitations may be particularly difficult to define. U.S. courts also favor political and equal protection rights over others, modifying an earlier preference for property rights.

Even in countries like the United States where judicial review is firmly established, disputes arise as to how freely such review should be exercised. "Interpretivists" and advocates of judicial restraint believe courts should void only legislation which clearly violates the constitutional text. "Noninterpretivists" advocate judicial activism to remedy perceived injustices in society even where such rulings proceed from natural-law principles or the spirit and/or structure of the constitution rather than from a specific text. Judicial activists also downplay *stare decisis* (respect for precedent), preferring to remedy perceived judicial errors. In the United States, judicial decisions can be overturned only by the courts themselves or through the difficult constitutional amending process. In countries with such rigid constitutions, courts are sometimes urged to initiate changes, the line between alterations through amendment and changes through judicial interpretation often being a particularly fine one.

Allan R. Brewer-Carías, *Judicial Review in Comparative Law* (Cambridge, U.K., 1989).

JOHN R. VILE

JUNE WAR OF 1967. See ARAB-ISRAELI CONFLICT.

K

KAMPUCHEA. See CAMBODIA.

KAZAKHSTAN. See CENTRAL ASIA.

KEMALISM. The name given to the *ideology that evolved during the 1920s and 1930s under the auspices of the Turkish national movement led by Kemal *Atatürk, the origins of Kemalism are to be found in the policies of the Young Turks who attempted to modernize and create a sovereign multinational empire. The Kemalists, freed of the imperial burden by the defeat of the Ottoman Empire, emphasized *nationalism. Influenced by the ideas of the French Revolution, they sought to create the "new Turk" (and the new *Turkey) to replace the "Ottoman." Because Turkish society lacked a developed, modern *class structure with a bourgeoisie and a working class, Kemalism adopted corporatist *populism, emphasizing the classless nature of Turkish society. Kemalism saw conflict only between the old, defeated ruling class and "the people" or "the nation," defined in terms similar to the French "nation" of 1789.

In the 1920s, Kemalism left the initiative for economic development to the private sector. But the failure of the wealthy classes to invest in economic *development, the onset of the world economic crisis in the West, which discredited *capitalism and *democracy, and the success of the Soviet and Italian experiments encouraged the Kemalists to use the state to engineer society. The full-blown ideology of Kemalism, in which the state and party became dominant in all spheres of life, was adopted by the ruling People's Republican Party (RPP) in 1931. The party defined the new Turkey as nationalist, republican, populist, secular, statist, and revolutionary. These "six arrows" became the guiding principles of the nation and were incorporated into the Constitution in 1937.

The ideological challenge of Italian *fascism forced the Kemalists to give a new twist to their ideology. Responding to Italian claims that their movement was fascist, Kemalists took the position of anticolonialists and argued that fascism was a variety of *imperialism. They claimed that Kemalism was an appropriate ideology for precapitalist societies struggling for their independence and striving for nationhood, whereas fascism was suitable only for semicapitalist societies in crisis. Here we find the first inklings of the "Third Worldism" which made Kemalism popular among *national liberation movements in Asia and Africa, a model for Reza Shah in contemporary Iran, and, later, *Nasser in Egypt.

At home Kemalism successfully mobilized Turkish society to promote socioeconomic development, although on a highly authoritarian basis. But its very success made it redundant after 1945. Its policies produced new classes which demanded the right to organize independently of the state and a bourgeoisie that insisted on a mixed economy. Once Kemalism gave way to multiparty politics in 1945, militant *secularism disappeared. Though all parties, especially the RPP, continued to profess their loyalty to Kemalism, it steadily dissolved as a coherent ideology and practice, although it became a useful weapon used by the establishment against ideological challenges from the left. The armed forces set themselves up as the guardians of Kemalism after the coup of 1960. But even they paid only lip service to its ideals. Since then, as *Nasserism and other similar radical nationalist ideologies have weakened, Kemalism as a coherent system has lost its capacity to inspire. But its emphasis on secularism, egalitarianism, and nationalism still defines goals which many Turks aspire to.

Ali Kazancigil and Ergun Özbudun, eds., *Atatürk: Founder of a Modern State* (London, 1981). Jacob Landau, ed., *Atatürk and the Modernization of Turkey* (Boulder, Colo., 1984). Feroz Ahmad, *The Making of Modern Turkey* (London, 1992).

FEROZ AHMAD

KENNAN, George. Born in 1904, he was the epitome of the public figure, George Kennan's contributions to both international relations and scholarship have had an effect on the world and how people think about it. His career has embraced four distinct fields: diplomacy, foreign policy-making, historical scholarship, and political criticism.

His diplomatic career began in 1926, a year after he graduated from Princeton University, with his appointment to the U.S. Foreign Service. He rose rapidly through the ranks and performed duties in key overseas posts, including Berlin, Moscow, Prague, and Vienna. Trained as one of a handful of U.S. specialists on the *Soviet Union, Kennan was stationed in Moscow during much of the 1930s and between 1944 and 1946. His sure command of the Russian language and knowledge of the country's history, politics, and economy earned him the admiration of ambassadors under whom he worked in Moscow: William Bullitt (1933–1936), Joseph Davies (1936–1938), and W. Averell Harriman (1943–1946). While serving as the embassy's chargé d'affaires in 1946, Kennan composed the "Long Telegram," a seminal *Cold War document that helped alert President Harry S. *Truman's administration to ideological and security problems then posed by the Soviet Union. Kennan twice held ambassadorships: in 1952 to the Soviet Union, which ended unceremoniously when Joseph Stalin's government declared him persona non grata, and in 1961–1963 to Yugoslavia.

During the Cold War years 1946–1950, Kennan was a prominent policymaker in Washington. In this period he wrote the so-called "X Article," which appeared in July 1947 in the influential journal *Foreign Affairs*. In this article Kennan elaborated upon themes from the Long Telegram, and advocated measures to check and frustrate Soviet international ambitions: the *containment policy. The most controversial passage from the X Article, and the one whose meaning scholars have long disputed, was ambiguous even by Kennan's own later admission. He asserted: "...the Soviet pressure against the free institutions of the Western world is something that can be contained by the adroit arid vigilant application of counter-force at a series of constantly shifting geographical and political points, corresponding to the shifts and maneuvers of Soviet policy."

However unclear the intentions of the X Article, government papers that he wrote at the time make plain that Kennan wanted containment to rely primarily on economic and political programs, and only secondarily on military strategies. The militarization of containment policy, exemplified by the founding of the *North Atlantic Treaty Organization and the acceleration of the nuclear arms race, seemed excessive and dangerous to him. As director of the State Department's Policy Planning Staff in 1947–1949, he was able to promote his preferred version of *American foreign policy through crucial work on the *Marshall Plan and attempts to rehabilitate postwar Japan. His dissatisfaction with the increasing military orientation of U.S. foreign policy under secretaries of state Dean *Acheson and John Foster Dulles helped lead to his resignation from the Foreign Service in 1953.

Kennan then joined the history faculty at the Institute for Advanced Study at Princeton and began a scholarly career that he interrupted only once—to represent the United States in Yugoslavia. Until his retirement in 1974 (and subsequent status as professor emeritus), Kennan wrote a number of important books analyzing such topics as early Soviet-U.S. relations, U.S. diplomacy, and the origins of World War I.

Kennan has not only distinguished himself as a man of belles lettres since the mid-1950s—twice he was awarded the Pulitzer Prize—but he has also won the attention of many statesmen and members of the politically literate public as a commentator on contemporary international affairs. His written statements, lectures, and expert testimony before congressional hearings have touched on a number of significant issues. These have included Soviet-U.S. disengagement from Europe, the folly of American involvement in Vietnam, the dangers of unbridled arms race, the need for accommodation with the Soviet Union, and the desirability of multilateral cooperation to solve global environmental problems.

Kennan has never developed a systematic political philosophy. But implicit in his pronouncements and recommendations over the course of more than six decades are a set of underlying assumptions that, taken together, constitute a theory of politics. This blends elements of realpolitik with ideas ultimately traceable to conservative thinker Edmund Burke and theologian Reinhold Niebuhr. At the core of Kennan's conception is a preoccupation with the continuity and intrinsic value of human civilizations and history. For him the United States must recognize that international problems are properly understood when viewed in historical context and that successful foreign policy requires taking the long view of both problems and solutions; to cultivate a world environment that will contain or prevent large-scale warfare, U.S.

policymakers and citizens must also appreciate that their adversaries do not have a monopoly on evil but have a role to play within a vast scheme of history and ultimate purpose.

(See also DIPLOMACY; TRUMAN DOCTRINE.)

Geroge Kennan, *Memoirs: 1925–1950* (Boston, 1967). George Kennan, *Memoirs: 1950–1963* (Boston, 1972). George Kennan, *Sketches From a Life* (New York, 1989).

DAVID MAYERS

KENNEDY, John Fitzgerald. The thirty-fifth president of the United States, John Fitzgerald Kennedy was born on 29 May 1917 in Brookline, Massachusetts. His father, Joseph Kennedy, was a hard-driving businessman who instilled in his sons a passion for power and achievement. Joseph Kennedy served President Franklin *Roosevelt in several capacities, most notably as ambassador to Britain in the years before World War II. John F. Kennedy fought in the Pacific in that war, and, shortly after his return to civilian life, won a seat in the House of Representatives in 1946. Elected senator from Massachusetts in 1952, Kennedy began to eye a still-higher office. A successful run in the primaries brought him the Democratic Party presidential nomination in 1960. Defeating the Republican candidate, Vice President Richard *Nixon, Kennedy became the youngest person and the first Catholic ever to be elected to the presidency.

Kennedy was determined to be an activist president. The centerpiece of his domestic policy was economic growth. Convinced that the American economy was lagging behind its potential, Kennedy proposed to stimulate the economy with taxation policies designed to foster greater investment by business and consumption by individuals. The resulting economic growth, he believed, would produce a shared abundance, ending conflicts between business and labor over the distribution of wealth. Kennedy's chief problem in economic policy was to persuade suspicious business elites that he genuinely wanted a partnership with them. Courting the business community throughout his presidency, he succeeded in inducing the investment to make the American economy grow faster. Higher rates of growth were, however, accompanied by an increase in economic inequality, since the prosperous were the biggest winners from Kennedy's policies.

The social policy initiatives of the Kennedy administration were squarely in the *New Deal tradition. Kennedy was unsuccessful on the two most controversial issues: Federal aid to education was killed in the House, especially due to resistance from Catholic Democrats unhappy with the exclusion of parochial schools, and medical care for the aged under *Social Security died in the Senate after a vigorous campaign of opposition from the American Medical Association. He won smaller legislative victories on the minimum wage, aid to depressed areas, and construction funds for higher education. Before Kennedy's death, planning had begun for an anti-poverty program, an initiative that Lyndon *Johnson would transform into the War on Poverty in 1964.

During Kennedy's presidency, the *civil rights movement by black Americans gained increasing momentum. Kennedy was caught between the moral and political force of the civil rights movement and the congressional bastions of the white South in his own Democratic Party. Hoping to hold the support of both blacks and white southerners, Kennedy approached civil rights conflicts cautiously and sometimes reluctantly during his first two years in office. In 1963, however, civil rights demonstrations led by Dr. Martin Luther *King, Jr., in Birmingham, Alabama, created such a dramatic and explosive confrontation that Kennedy was compelled to take stronger action. Appearing on television, the president told the nation that equal treatment for black Americans was a moral issue. He also proposed major new civil rights legislation, which was passed by Congress after his death.

Kennedy's paramount concern as president was *foreign policy. Upon assuming the presidential office, he proclaimed that the *Cold War had entered a critical stage. "Each day," he said in his first State of the Union Address, "we draw nearer the hour of maximum danger. . . ." In Kennedy's grim analysis, a United States that had drifted dangerously under the previous administration now faced a global offensive from an increasingly aggressive Soviet Union. Acting on the basis of this analysis, Kennedy urged upon Congress a massive buildup of U.S. military forces at all levels.

"The hour of maximum danger" was soon upon Kennedy. In the summer of 1961, the United States confronted the Soviet Union over the divided city of Berlin. Opposing Soviet Premier Nikita Khrushchev's effort to break the long-standing impasse over Berlin on Soviet terms, Kennedy announced a new military buildup and employed martial rhetoric to summon U.S. citizens to a new test of their resolve. Although the confrontation ended inconclusively after the Communists constructed the Berlin Wall, it had awakened fears of war between the two superpowers.

Those fears returned a year later, in much greater magnitude, in the *Cuban missile crisis. In October 1962, when the United States discovered that the Soviet Union had secretly deployed medium-range nuclear missiles on the island of Cuba, Kennedy and his advisers debated the proper U.S. response. Rejecting suggestions that the missiles might have been placed in Cuba to deter an invasion by the United States or to rectify an imbalance in strategic weaponry that left the Soviets far behind the United States, the president interpreted the Soviet move as the supreme test of U.S. will. Demanding that the Soviets withdraw their missiles, Kennedy began a naval quarantine of Cuba and, through diplomatic channels, warned of further military action. The gravest nuclear crisis of the postwar era ended when Khrushchev acceded to Kennedy's demands and pulled out the missiles in exchange for a U.S. pledge not to invade Cuba. Sobered by this frightening confrontation, the United States and the Soviet Union negotiated a limited nuclear test ban treaty in 1963.

For Kennedy, the challenge of communism had to be met in every corner of the globe. Part of Kennedy's strategy to deny the Third World to communism involved modernization efforts and attempts to secure friendly regimes, as exemplified by his Alliance for Progress in Latin America. The U.S. policy of providing financial assistance and promoting internal reforms and stronger police and military forces was intended to help Third World nations through the turbulence that might foster the growth of insurgent movements. Where armed struggles by guerrilla forces threatened pro-U.S. regimes, the nation-building strategy relied on counterinsurgency warfare. Vietnam became the test case for the Kennedy administration's counterinsurgency approach. Although Kennedy was skeptical about the situation in Vietnam, he deep-

ened American involvement there in an effort to prove that U.S. power could master any challenge.

Kennedy was assassinated in Dallas, Texas, on 22 November 1963. Popular during his presidency, he became a revered national hero after his tragic death. In retrospect, his brief administration was the apex of postwar U.S. globalism. Kennedy vigorously asserted the power and pride of a nation enthused by its preeminent role in the world. It would be left to his successors to confront the limits to U.S. power that Kennedy had not acknowledged.

(See also ASSASSINATION; BAY OF PIGS INVASION; NUCLEAR WEAPONS; PRESIDENCY, U.S.; U.S. FOREIGN POLICY; VIETNAM WAR.)

Thomas G. Paterson, ed., *Kennedy's Quest for Victory: American Foreign Policy, 1961–1963* (New York, 1989). James N. Giglio, *The Presidency of John F. Kennedy* (Lawrence, Kans., 1991).

BRUCE MIKUFF

KENYA. The Republic of Kenya lies on the equator in East Africa astride the Rift Valley and flanking the Indian Ocean; its land area is 220,624 square miles (571,416 sq. km.). Kenya has a population of approximately 30.3 million with a 1.5 percent annual growth rate (estimates as of 2000). Comprising this population are more than forty ethnic groups, the main ones being the Kikuyu, the Luhya, the Luo, the Kalenjini, and the Kamba. Accompanying the Africans are the numerically smaller Asian, European, and Arab populations.

The various African groups migrated into the area long before the advent of colonialism. Groups such as the Maasai lived pastoral nomadic lives on the rangelands of Kenya while others such as the Kikuyu settled on the fertile cropland of the central forest regions and took up sedentary agriculture.

The area came under the suzerainty of the Imperial British East Africa Company in 1888 when the company received a royal charter to administer the territory. The British government took over formal administrative responsibilities in June 1895. The British colonial administration built a railroad between Mombasa and Lake Victoria and subsequently leased vast amounts of land to white settlers: the belief being that only under settler control could the territory be developed economically. The leases dispossessed many Africans of their traditional lands and provided the seeds for future social unrest.

The land loss hit the Kikuyu the hardest, and in their desperation they sent a representative, Jomo Kenyatta, to London to lobby for their land. In this way the Kikuyu came into the forefront of the independence struggle. The land question was never resolved to the satisfaction of the Africans. Between 1952 and 1956, the Kikuyu, under an underground movement known as the Kenya Land Freedom Army, waged an ill-fated guerrilla war against the British—the Mau Mau rebellion. (The origin of the term *Mau Mau* remains obscure. It was probably a derogatory expression coined by white settlers.) The African fighters were defeated militarily; however, the British decided to relinquish control of the colony.

Britain granted Kenya independence in December 1963 under the Majimbo constitution. A federal-type system was put in place to protect the smallest tribes: the effective power of the central government was reduced in favor of the regions.

Jomo Kenyatta became the first prime minister of independent Kenya under the Kenya African National Union (KANU). As leader, he wanted to replace the Majimbo constitution with one that put more power in the hands of the national government while also destroying the opposition party, the Kenya African Democratic Union (KADU).

Both of Kenyatta's goals were accomplished in 1964. KADU dissolved itself "in the interest of Kenya" and the leaders were absorbed into KANU. On 12 December of the same year, Kenya officially became a republic with Kenyatta as president, reestablishing the central administration of the colonial authorities and helping to strengthen a tempered Kikuyu dominance. An attempt to upset the one-party state in May 1966 by a radical faction of the KANU, the Kenyan People's Union (KPU), was halted when the state intervened in political processes and finally declared the KPU illegal.

In general, under Kenyatta, politics were dominated by factionalism that essentially amounted to Kikuyu versus non-Kikuyu, for tribal links were the basis for patronage and the Kikuyu dominated in economic terms. Kenyatta seemed able to rise above this by his assumption of the role of Mzee—"the father of the nation"—and by the suppression of dissent. He retained power until his death in 1978.

Upon Kenyatta's death, Vice President Daniel arap Moi peacefully and constitutionally succeeded to the presidential office. His tenure in office has been marked by the de facto one-party state becoming de jure in June 1982 when KANU was made the sole legal party and by increasing repression following the attempted coup by the Kenyan Air Force. By 1988, Moi amassed enough influence to push through other constitutional amendments. The secret ballot was abolished in primary elections, with voters required to line up in public behind pictures of candidates. In addition, the length of time a suspect could be held was increased from twenty-four hours to fourteen days, and the independence of the judiciary was undermined when the amendment separating the judiciary and executive branches was repealed.

The stirrings of discontent which began with Moi's actions in the 1980s erupted into a larger movement for democracy in the 1990s. Encouraged by changes across Eastern Europe, clergy, lawyers, students, and opposition politicians began to debate openly the merits of a multiparty system. Moi declared the debates unconstitutional and illegal and ordered all discussion to end. One cabinet minister even urged cutting off the fingers of those who raised two as a symbol for the two-party system. The influential *Nairobi Law Monthly*, one of the few voices of opposition, was banned and its editor jailed.

Protest took on a new form, involving segments of the population previously not expressing public opposition to the Moi/KANU regime. As a result, Moi became more antagonistic toward aid donors, particularly the United States and Norway, who urged the government to improve *human rights conditions in the country. In November 1991, a consortium of donors assembled by the *World Bank in Paris finally decided to suspend aid to the Kenyan government for six months unless President Moi allowed multiparty elections. Three weeks later, President Moi legalized opposition politics in the country, opening the way for elections in 1992.

Kenya held elections in 1992 and in 1997, neither of which led to substantive changes. Phenomenal levels of corruption, including media manipulation, opposition discrediting, harassment of pro-democracy activists, and financial disparities between parties, pervaded both elections in favor of the ruling KANU. Those in power have maintained an uneven playing field in order to control the state and the economic spoils that the international community has readily bestowed since so-called democratization, thereby perpetuating an authoritarian-like regime that uncannily resembles its colonial predecessor.

Kenya followed in colonial footsteps in its economic policy as well. The 1965 document "African Socialism and Its Application to Planning in Kenya" established the economic foundations—capitalism, free enterprise, and controlled state participation in the economy. Despite attempts to industrialize, the Kenyan economy is dominated by agricultural production and the sale of cash crops, coffee, and tea being the most important, on the international market. Kenya sustains a flourishing tourist trade as well. There is a significant amount of manufacturing.

Kenya has pursued several cooperative economic ventures with other East African countries. In June 1967, Kenya, Uganda, and Tanzania signed the treaty establishing the East African Community (EAC) to provide closer integration in economic matters. However, Kenya was the main beneficiary of the intraregional trade because it was more developed than the other partners. The EAC disbanded in February 1977 because of growing conflict over unequal gains as well as political rift between the three heads of state: Kenyatta, Idi Amin, and Julius *Nyerere. Since 1995, the governments of Kenya, Uganda, and Tanzania have been collaborating to revive the EAC. Kenya has been a member of the Common Market for Eastern and Southern Africa (COMESA), a regional body of Eastern and Southern African states, since 1978.

Internationally, Kenya maintains a pro-Western foreign policy. Although it sustains ties to Britain, Kenya has developed closer ties with the United States. One of Kenya's main security concerns has been the threat of Somali irredentist activity in its northeastern territory; it has signed several cooperative agreements with Ethiopia, which is similarly threatened. Kenya is a member of the UN and its specialized and related agencies while also belonging to the *Nonaligned Movement and the *Organization of African Unity.

(See also COLONIAL EMPIRES; DECOLONIZATION; GUERRILLA WARFARE; ONE-PARTY SYSTEMS.)

Colin Leys, *Underdevelopment in Kenya: The Political Economy of Neocolonialism* (Berkeley, Calif., 1974). Gavin Kitching, *Class and Economic Change in Kenya: The Making of an African Petite Bourgeoisie* (New Haven, Conn., 1980). David Throup, *Multi-Party Politics in Kenya: The Kenyatta and Moi States and the Triumph of the System in the 1992 Election* (Athens, Ohio, 1998).

FANTU CHERU

KEYNESIANISM. The term *Keynesianism* owes its origins to the thought of John Maynard Keynes (1883–1946), a prolific British economist whose most influential work was *The General Theory of Employment, Interest, and Money*, first published in 1936. Keynes's doctrine was at once a denunciation of the then-orthodox view that a modern economy, left to its own devices, would naturally tend to adjust to an operational level at "full employment," an analytic account of the way the economic system might instead be "stuck" at an underemployment equilibrium, and a prescription of the policy interventions needed to stimulate a depressed economy. The crucial argument of *The General Theory* rested on the claim that aggregate demand (primarily the sum of spending by the public on consumer goods, by producers on investment goods, and by governments) was the fundamental determinant of levels of national income and employment. In Keynes's view, aggregate demand during the years of the Great Depression was indeed deficient; hence, the remedy for the distresses of that time should be sought through measures to spur total spending. Monetary policy—directed toward reductions in interest rates to encourage investment spending—could play a role in this strategy, but its effectiveness was held to be limited. Far greater impact was expected from an activist fiscal policy in which governments would add to total demand by running deliberate deficits, particularly by adding to their outlays for public works. Keynes's analysis provided a theoretical rationale for the enlargement of government's role in the management of the economy—and it represented a clear and direct challenge to the long-standing view that the test of a government's "fiscal responsibility" was a balanced budget. Besides calling for a reorientation in conventional thinking about the scope and form of government intervention, *The General Theory* also called for a reorientation in formal economic theory. The subsequent development of "macroeconomics"—in which the aggregative behavior of such magnitudes as saving, investment, consumption, etc., are the focus of attention—is built on the foundations of Keynes's doctrine. Keynes was overly aggressive in his own claims for the "revolutionary" character of his findings. Others had arrived independently at similar conclusions, particularly with respect to the conduct of economic policy. Keynes succeeded, however, in introducing a novel technical vocabulary which captured the imagination of a budding generation of professional economists. Not only did this theoretical system seem to offer solutions to urgent practical problems presented by the Great Depression, it also provided a framework within which an intellectually exciting range of empirical investigations could proceed.

As originally constructed, the Keynesian "model" was intended to address the issue of persistent mass unemployment. Initially, however, its direct impact on the formulation of economic policy was slight. In *Britain, treasury officials were not notably sympathetic to Keynes's recommendations on remedies for unemployment. In the United States, his arguments had a mixed reception. President Franklin D. *Roosevelt did indeed reorient his administration's economic strategy in 1938 when he called for a deliberate program of deficit spending: although his administration had recorded deficits in each of its preceding years, the president had always insisted that balanced budgets remained his goal. This shift represented an intellectual conversion, but it is not clear that the analysis provided by *The General Theory* was decisive in bringing it about. The arguments which persuaded the president to rethink the role of an activist fiscal policy were packaged by aides who had already developed an analysis of changes in the "net contribution of government to spending" to account for the totally unanticipated downturn in the U.S. economy in 1937 (which occurred at a time when the economy was still well below its capacity). A number of the *New Deal economists were, however, delighted to invoke the authority of Keynes to reinforce positions they had reached on their own. Even so, by 1940—when "Keynesianism" had been well assimilated into official U.S. thinking—it still came through with an American accent. The central message, as read by Lauchlin Currie, the economic adviser to the president, was that aggregate demand management in the United States should focus on producing a "high consumption–low saving" economy. This could be accomplished through more aggressive programs of progressive taxation and transfer payments to those at the lower end of the income distribution. Thus, it was argued, the "social objectives of the New Deal" could be reconciled with "sound [i.e., Americanized 'Keynesian'] economics." Deficit financing of public works—which had figured so prominently in Keynes's own policy prescriptions—was downplayed.

The "Keynesian" way of thinking came into its own in World War II. Shortly after the outbreak of hostilities, Keynes produced a pamphlet entitled *How to Pay for the War*. This was an application of the Keynesian apparatus of aggregative analysis to a problem quite different from the one it was originally designed to deal with. In wartime, the objective of demand management was to suppress private consumption and investment spending in the interests of releasing resources for military mobilization and to constrain upward pressures on prices. In both Britain and the United States, the tools provided by the Keynesian model proved to be invaluable in organizing the thinking of policymakers around the potential size of the "inflationary gap," with attention to measures necessary to contain it (i.e., some combination of increased taxes and borrowing from the public to drain off excessive purchasing power, direct controls over consumer prices, restrictions on access to materials normally used in private capital formation, etc.).

The "Keynesian" perspective further left its mark on planning for the postwar economic order. At the international level, the architecture of the Bretton Woods agreements—in which Keynes participated personally as a British delegate—owed much to his influence. The fruit of this work was the creation of two new institutions—the *International Monetary Fund (IMF) and the International Bank for Reconstruction and Development. Their purpose was to create a climate favorable to expansion of international trade and investment in which individual countries could also pursue "full employment" policies at home. The rigidities of the *gold standard—the rules of which implied that countries experiencing balance-of-payments difficulties should curtail domestic demand—were rejected. Instead, a debtor country could seek accommodation from the lending facilities of the IMF to cover its trade and payments deficits. In principle, the adjustments needed to correct its international accounts could be accomplished without resorting to domestic deflation. This amounted to an extension of the Keynesian conception of aggregate demand management from the national to the international scene.

The Keynesian style of thinking also inspired the approach of a number of governments to the management of domestic economic affairs after World War II. Consensus was readily reached on one proposition: that a reversion to depression conditions was intolerable and unacceptable. Keynes's disciples were confident that his teachings could ensure a different—and much happier—result. This approach found its way into the blueprint for postwar Britain produced in the Beveridge Report *Full Employment in a Free Society* (published in 1944) and into the macroeconomic strategies pursued by the postwar Labour government. Keynesians in the United States were instrumental in promoting the Employment Act of 1946. Their original aspirations—contained in the initial versions of this bill—did not survive congressional scrutiny. They had hoped to enact legislation that would create a fiscal authority (staffed by economic experts of the "correct" persuasion) with discretionary powers to alter tax rates and government spending programs in light of the requirements of economic stabilization. This grand vision was frustrated: indeed there was a touch of naïveté in the expectation that elected officials would delegate the jurisdiction over spending and taxing to faceless "experts," however insistently the latter might assert their competence as "scientists." Even in watered-down form, the Employment Act was a victory of sorts. It put the U.S. government formally on record as responsible for maintaining "maximum levels of employment, income, and purchasing power." (The language of "full employment," however, had been struck.) In addition, it created a three-member Council of Economic Advisers within the Executive Office of the President. The council was charged only with the preparation of reports on the state of the economy and had no operational responsibilities. Nevertheless, it was expected that the "new economics" would henceforth have a hearing at the pinnacle of power.

In the 1950s, Keynesian doctrine was more widely dispersed. In Britain and the United States, it became the centerpiece of mainstream academic teaching. Not surprisingly, its absorption in countries cut off from Anglo-Saxon intellectual developments during the war—particularly Germany and Japan—came later and was never complete. The rallying cry of "full employment," however, was one that no government dependent on support from the electorate could afford to ignore. And whether it chose to endorse a Keynesian route toward that goal or not, the insistence of Keynesians that the goal was attainable meant that the message commanded attention. In many countries, Keynesianism—which, in its early iterations, had often been regarded as dangerously interventionist—came to be regarded as essentially conservative in the sense that its approach to aggregate demand management promised to stabilize a "mixed economy" and thus to undercut support for more radical structural changes in the economic system.

The 1960s in the United States witnessed a much-heralded "laboratory test" of applied Keynesianism in peacetime. The Kennedy administration's Council of Economic Advisers—composed of academic Keynesians and chaired by Walter Heller—successfully orchestrated a tax cut to attack unemployment and to raise the economic growth rate at a time when the federal budget was in deficit. The early results went according to expectation, and confidence in the ability of Keynesians to "fine-tune" the economy to a noninflationary full-employment track reached its all-time high. Keynesianism fared less well in the 1970s, even though a conservative U.S. president—Richard M. *Nixon—proclaimed that "we are all Keynesians now." The stagflation of those years—in which unemployment coexisted with rising inflation rates—was a reality that could not be readily explained within the framework of the Keynesian model. Indeed, in the eyes of critics of

Keynesianism, the very application of this doctrine was responsible for much of the discomfort in the world economy. According to such diagnoses, the "Keynesian era"—the end of which was now trumpeted—had led governments to lower their guard against inflation because of excessive concern for the evils of unemployment. In addition, the preoccupation of Keynesians with sufficient aggregate demand, it was alleged, had given too much emphasis to expanding consumption and too little to the encouragement of saving. The result was inadequate capital formation and declining productivity growth.

This disenchantment with Keynesianism provided a propitious environment within which alternative approaches to economic analysis and political management could flourish. The doctrine of *monetarism then took on fresh vitality with its claim that size of the money supply was the force driving the performance of the economy. Its advocates maintained that governments had been misled by the fiscal "fine tuners" and that a stable climate for noninflationary growth could be achieved only when central banks disciplined themselves to restrain expansion of the money supply to preannounced targets. Automaticity, not discretion, in policy-making should now be the order of the day. Few governments were immune from this shift in the tide—and certainly not those of Britain and the United States where the supremacy of Keynesianism had once seemed secure.

Change also occurred in the conduct of international economic affairs: the fixed exchange rate feature of the Bretton Woods system was swept away in favor of a regime of floating rates in which the international value of national currencies would be determined by the allegedly impersonal forces of the marketplace.

Keynesianism as a political rallying point was dealt yet another blow by the electoral triumphs of Ronald *Reagan in the 1980s. In their rhetoric at least, the "supply-siders" of Reaganomics were determined to undo the "demand side" economics of Keynesianism.

Since the 1970s, Keynesianism may have lost much of its luster. But even its critics have paid it the ultimate tribute: they have defined their own positions in reaction to the doctrines associated with Keynesianism.

(See also BALANCE OF PAYMENTS; FINANCE, INTERNATIONAL; INTERNATIONAL POLITICAL ECONOMY; POLITICAL ECONOMY.)

Donald Winch, *Economics and Policy: A Historical Study* (London, 1969). John Maynard Keynes, *The Collected Writings of John Maynard Keynes*, 31 vols. (London, 1971–1989). David N. Worswick and James Trevithick, eds., *Keynes and the Modern World* (Cambridge, U.K., 1984). Peter A. Hall, ed., *The Political Power of Economic Ideas: Keynesianism across Nations* (Princeton, N.J., 1989). Mary O. Furner and Barry Supple, eds., *The State and Economic Knowledge: The American and British Experiences* (New York, 1990). Herbert Stein, *The Fiscal Revolution in America*, rev. ed. (Washington, D.C., 1990).

WILLIAM J. BARBER

KHOMEINI, Ruhollah. Ruhollah Musavi Khomeini (1902–1989), the most important leader of the *Iranian Revolution, was born in the small town of Khomein, located in central *Iran about 180 miles (290 kilometers) south of Tehran. Both his grandfather and father were Shi'i Islamic clergy. Because his father was killed while Khomeini was an infant, he was raised by an uncle, who provided him an early religious education. In 1918, Khomeini went to the nearby city of Arak to study in the seminary set up by the renowned theologian Ayatollah Abdol-Karim Haeri-Yazdi. In 1922, after Haeri-Yazdi had been invited to establish a major theological center in Qom, Khomeini moved there to continue advanced religious studies. After his mentor's death in 1936, Khomeini was recognized as one of Qom's religious scholars and taught in the prestigious Fayziyeh seminary.

Khomeini first acquired national prominence in 1944 with the publication of a book that attacked secular policies during the reign of Reza Shah (1926–1941). Although Khomeini raised the idea of an Islamic government in this early work, it would be another twenty-five years before his concept of rule by the clergy was fully developed. Two years after this book appeared, Khomeini became closely associated with Ayatollah Borujerdi, then regarded as the most distinguished cleric in the Shi'i world. Because Borujerdi opposed the clergy's participation in politics, Khomeini refrained from political activity, even during the turbulent National Front era (1949–1953), when some of his clerical colleagues were politically involved. Borujerdi's death in 1961, at a time when no single cleric was regarded as his equal, provided an opportunity for Khomeini to emerge as one of several contenders for Borujerdi's position as paramount Shi'i theologian while simultaneously obviating any need to show deference to the views of a senior religious figure.

Within two years, Khomeini had acquired a reputation as a senior cleric who was not afraid to criticize the government's domestic and foreign policies as contrary to Islamic principles. Khomeini's antigovernment sermons led to his arrest in June 1963, an incident that sparked several days of mass protests throughout the country which were forcibly suppressed with thousands of casualties. Khomeini refused to remain silent following his April 1964 release from prison, his opposition sermons focusing on legislation granting diplomatic immunity to U.S. military personnel in Iran. Khomeini's outspokenness led to his second arrest in November 1964, but this time the government sent him into exile to Turkey; a year later, Iraq permitted him to settle in the Shi'i pilgrimage and theological city of Najaf.

Khomeini and his supporters never forgot the violent events of 1963 and commemorated them annually, each year gaining more adherents to their cause, which by the early 1970s had become the overthrow of the shah's regime. During his thirteen-year stay in Najaf, Khomeini elaborated his theory of Islamic government. His original contribution to Shi'i political theory is *velayat-e faqih*, or rule by the clergy. Khomeini argued that the twelve saintly successors and descendants of the Prophet Muhammad transferred their political authority (*velayat*) to the Shi'i clergy, in particular to those trained in Islamic jurisprudence (*faqih*). Monarchies and other forms of government that fail to defer to the clergy are illegitimate, and pious Muslims are obligated to overthrow them.

Khomeini's views on Islamic government gained broad appeal throughout the 1970s as the shah became more authoritarian and his foreign policies more aligned with those of the United States. Former students and political dissidents visited the increasingly revered ayatollah in exile and smuggled back into Iran cassettes of his sermons denouncing the shah's government. Khomeini acquired a charisma that derived from his reputation for honesty, moral rectitude, ascetic lifestyle, reli-

gious knowledge, and uncompromising opposition to the shah's dictatorship. The January 1978 forcible suppression of pro-Khomeini protests in Qom touched off a cycle of demonstrations that spread throughout the country and mobilized millions of people by the end of the year. The increasing momentum of the mass popular movement demoralized the security forces; the shah fled the country in January 1979, and his regime was soon toppled.

Following his own triumphal return to Iran in February 1979, Khomeini supervised the creation of an Islamic republic as the country's preeminent *faqih*. The success of the *revolution in Iran inspired Islamic-based political opposition movements in other Middle Eastern countries and led to confrontation with the United States and the war with secular Iraq (1980–1988). Thus, during the last ten years of his life, Khomeini was as much preoccupied with foreign relations as he was with efforts to institutionalize clerical rule in Iran. His style of rule generally was to refrain from direct involvement in the day-to-day affairs of government, preferring to serve as arbiter of the differing political perspectives among the clergy.

(See also IRAN-IRAQ WAR; ISLAM; RELIGION AND POLITICS.)

Hamid Algar, ed. and trans., *Islam and Revolution: Writings and Declarations of Imam Khomeini* (Berkeley, Calif., 1981). Shaul Bakhash, *The Reign of the Ayatollahs: Iran and the Islamic Revolution* (New York, 1984).
ERIC HOOGLUND

KING, Martin Luther, Jr. For many Americans, Martin Luther King, Jr., epitomizes the black freedom struggle in the United States during the 1950s and 1960s. Born in Atlanta, Georgia, on 15 January 1929, King was the second of three children of Martin Luther King, Sr., a prominent Baptist minister, and Alberta Williams King, a teacher in the city's Jim Crow (segregated black) schools. His early years were spent in the relative security of a middle-class family environment. Following his graduation in 1948 from Morehouse College in Atlanta, King abandoned a youthful notion of pursuing a career in medicine or law and, instead, enrolled at Crozer Theological Seminary in Chester, Pennsylvania. While at Crozer, he developed a fascination with the philosophy of Mohandas *Gandhi, who successfully employed passive resistance and civil disobedience (*satyagraha*) in his campaign to break the grip of British imperialism in India. King earned a bachelor of divinity degree in 1951. He continued his education at Boston University's Graduate School of Theology and received a Ph.D. in systemic theology in 1955. In Boston, he met Coretta Scott, whom he married in 1953. The union would produce four children.

In 1954, while completing his doctoral dissertation, King accepted a call to pastor the prestigious Dexter Avenue Baptist Church in Montgomery, Alabama. His return to the South placed him in the midst of a confluence of events that would push the young minister into the national spotlight. On 1 December 1955, Rosa Parks, a black seamstress, was arrested for refusing to relinquish her seat on a crowded city bus to a white man. This incident sparked a boycott of the city's bus lines by members of Montgomery's black community. Although initially reluctant to become directly involved in the proposed boycott, King eventually acceded to the request of his friend, the Reverend Ralph Abernathy, and Montgomery's most outspoken black activist, E. D. Nixon, that he assume the presidency of the Montgomery Improvement Association (MIA), an organization formed to sustain the protest. Under the auspices of the MIA, King directed a yearlong campaign which employed the strategy of nonviolent direct action to challenge the local bus segregation ordinance. The boycott ended in 1956 when the *Supreme Court upheld a federal appellate court order striking down bus segregation in Montgomery. As leader of the successful boycott, King found himself catapulted to national prominence. Capitalizing on the momentum generated by this victory, he organized the Southern Christian Leadership Conference (SCLC) in 1957. This organization, based in Atlanta, became the institutional center for King's civil rights activities for the next decade.

Although King neither directed nor participated in most of the nonviolent direct action protests of the early 1960s, his leadership at demonstrations in Alabama and Washington, D.C., focused national attention on the depth and persistence of racism in the South. In 1963, nonviolent efforts to eliminate segregation in Birmingham, Alabama, produced few immediate results, but the brutal assaults by local police on peaceful demonstrators under King's direction left searing images in the public mind. Responding to criticism from fellow clergy following his arrest in Birmingham, King penned "Letter from Birmingham Jail," in which he eloquently proclaimed the moral imperative of resisting unjust laws. In August of the same year, King participated in the historic March on Washington, organized to protest racial inequality in the United States and to promote federal civil rights legislation. Addressing the assembled throng from the steps of the Lincoln Memorial, King galvanized the audience with his "I Have a Dream" speech, which evoked his vision of a future America freed from the psychic scars of racism. King's role in this mass demonstration probably assured both his selection as *Time* magazine's "Man of the Year" for 1963 and his receipt of the 1964 Nobel Peace Prize. Further, King's influence on the *Kennedy and (following Kennedy's *assassination) *Johnson administrations was instrumental in securing passage of the landmark Civil Rights Act of 1964. Turning his attention in 1965 to the political powerlessness of black southerners, King organized a march from Selma, Alabama, to the state capitol in Montgomery to demand the vote for disenfranchised black Alabamans. This event provided impetus for passage by Congress of the Voting Rights Act of 1965.

Despite his victories, King faced numerous challenges to his leadership. Many younger black activists complained that the strategy of nonviolent direct action had outlived its usefulness. They denounced King as too conservative and too willing to compromise with whites in positions of power. The new slogan of the day was "Black Power," a concept that King viewed as counterproductive to his dream of interracial harmony and peace. Others criticized him for ignoring the economic problems confronting millions of *African Americans, many of whom lived in desperate conditions in the major cities of the North and West. When he turned his attention to racial problems outside the South, as in Chicago in 1966, King often faced angry receptions by blacks and whites. Moreover, in 1967, King's public opposition to the United States' involvement in the *Vietnam War deprived him of further support from the Johnson administration. Finally, King endured unrelenting attempts to discredit his leadership by

J. Edgar Hoover, director of the Federal Bureau of Investigation. Nevertheless, he forged ahead with a plan to conduct a "Poor People's March" to Washington for the purpose of emphasizing the economic plight of many blacks in the United States. In the spring of 1968, he traveled to Memphis, Tennessee, to lend his support to garbage collectors in that city who were striking for higher wages and improved working conditions. Here King was assassinated on 4 April, as he stood talking with friends on the balcony of a local motel.

In contrast to widespread attempts at apotheosis in the years immediately following his death, recent students of the *Civil Rights Movement have characterized Martin Luther King, Jr., as simply one among many men and women whose actions fueled the black protest movement. In fact, some scholars have argued persuasively that King's leadership was not essential to the success of the struggle for racial equality. King's legacy to the sociopolitical fabric of the United States, however, is substantial. According to historian August Meier, by emphasizing the power of redemptive love, King effectively played upon the guilt of many whites in the United States in order to increase their awareness of the needs and aspirations of the nation's African-American population. He forced the nation to respond to the existing contradiction between the ideal of the American dream and the reality of an obdurate system of caste that promoted racial inequality. He advanced the cause of freedom through his advocacy of nonviolent protest and his powerfully articulated vision of a color-blind nation. Martin Luther King, Jr., then, among the many leaders of the black freedom struggle, became for both blacks and whites in the United States a symbol of the concept of racial and social harmony.

(See also CIVIL DISOBEDIENCE; MALCOLM X; NONVIOLENT ACTION; RACE AND RACISM.)

August Meier, "On the Role of Martin Luther King" *New Politics* 4 (Winter 1965): 52–59. David Garrow, *Bearing the Cross: Martin Luther King, Jr., and the Southern Christian Leadership Conference* (New York, 1986). Clayborne Carson, "Martin Luther King, Jr.: Charismatic Leadership in a Mass Struggle" *Journal of American History* 74 (September 1987): 448–454.

JAMES M. SORELLE

KIRGHIZSTAN. See CENTRAL ASIA.

KIRIBATI (GILBERTS). See PACIFIC ISLANDS.

KISSINGER, Henry. Few leaders have had as much influence on U.S. *foreign policy over as long a period of time as Henry Kissinger. Since the mid-1950s, Kissinger has helped shape the way people in the United States think about global politics through his eight books and innumerable articles, interviews, and public statements. He played a major role in American foreign policy by serving as adviser for national security affairs during President Richard *Nixon's first term (1969–1972), and as secretary of state in Nixon's aborted second term and the presidency of Gerald Ford (1973–1977).

Although Kissinger has achieved international recognition, many in the United States regard him ambivalently. They see his allusions to tragedy in history, his emphasis on power in international relations, and his esteem for leaders such as Prince Metternich of Austria, Otto von Bismarck of Germany, and Charles de *Gaulle of France as evidence of his European cast of mind.

Kissinger's achievements, including his 1973 Nobel Peace Prize, gain added significance when contrasted with the events of his early life. His birth in May 1923 to an Orthodox Jewish family in Fürth, Germany, coincided with the rise of Nazism in German politics. Many interpret his emphasis on order and limits as a reaction to the chaos of his youth. Kissinger's family fled Germany in 1938 for the United States.

Following his wartime service in the U.S. Army, Kissinger enrolled at Harvard University in 1947. His undergraduate thesis, "The Meaning of History"—an idiosyncratic treatment of the philosophies of history of the English historian Arnold Toynbee, the German historian Oswald Spengler, and the German philosopher Immanuel Kant—provides a key to much of his later thinking. Kissinger completed his doctoral program in the Department of Government in 1954. He remained at Harvard, teaching and writing about international politics, for almost fifteen years.

Kissinger is linked with other realist scholars of international politics who achieved prominence in the United States after World War II, such as George *Kennan, Hans Morgenthau, and Reinhold Niebuhr. In contrast to the "legalistic-moralistic approach to international problems" (George Kennan, American Diplomacy: 1900–1950, Chicago, 1951), the realists regard conflict as inherent in the state system and emphasize the *balance of power as the primary means of maintaining order. Kissinger's doctoral dissertation concerning the Congress of Vienna, later published as A World Restored: Metternich, Castlereagh and the Problems of Peace, 1812–1822 (Boston, 1957), presents a similar worldview. The balance of power and what Kissinger refers to as *legitimacy—i.e., acceptance of the existing order by the major powers—are its principal elements.

Throughout the 1950s and 1960s, Kissinger established his reputation as a scholar of international politics. His strength was his ability to synthesize political and military patterns of thought in novel forms. During this period, his affiliation with the Rockefeller Brothers Fund and the Council on Foreign Relations exposed him to the nation's business and government elites. His association with Governor Nelson Rockefeller of New York contributed to his own rise to power.

Kissinger's first book, Nuclear Weapons and Foreign Policy, New York, 1957), challenged the Eisenhower administration's reliance on massive nuclear retaliation to deter aggression. Kissinger believed this strategy left the United States paralyzed in the face of ambiguous challenges from Communist powers—no single one of which was worth an all-out war. In an eclectic work, The Necessity for Choice (New York, 1961), Kissinger continued to address U.S. defense policy, but he also dealt with the U.S. style in diplomatic negotiations, political evolution in the Soviet Union and the emerging nations, and the role of the intellectual in policy-making. The book provided a trenchant criticism of *American foreign policy. Kissinger's thinking on U.S.-European relations, including his description of the growing structural problems in the Atlantic Alliance, is presented in The Troubled Partnership (New York, 1965).

The Nixon-Kissinger years marked a period of fundamental transition in the U.S. role in world affairs. The Nixon administration's four "state of the world" messages (1970–1973),

prepared under Kissinger's direction, defined this transition and provided a new conceptual basis for American foreign policy. Kissinger emphasized that the *Cold War era of rigid blocs had ended. An evolving balance among five major powers—China, Japan, the Soviet Union, the United States, and Western Europe—now dominated international life.

This perception of a new global order underlies Kissinger's actions as diplomat and policy architect as well as his portrayal of events in his memoirs White House Years (Boston, 1979) and Years of Upheaval (Boston, 1982). Kissinger's secret opening to China in July 1971 set the stage for more normal relations with Beijing and gave the United States added flexibility in a new triangular relationship with China and the Soviet Union. In place of the United States' economic and political dominance of Western Europe and Japan, Kissinger called for an era of partnership in which each would act more in its own interests. He supported relative strategic parity with the Soviet Union instead of military superiority.

Kissinger sought stability in political dealings with the Soviet Union. He was the major proponent of *détente—a policy that tried to transform U.S.-Soviet relations by emphasizing restraint and the negotiation of differences. The Strategic Arms Limitation Talks (SALT), in which Kissinger played an important role, were the centerpiece of détente.

Kissinger also helped define and implement the Nixon Doctrine—a doctrine that substituted for the postwar policy of *containment. No longer would the United States serve as the world's police force; rather, its allies and other regional powers would be encouraged to take responsibility for their own security. The Nixon Doctrine provided the basis for Kissinger's negotiation of the end of U.S. involvement in the *Vietnam War.

The 1960s and 1970s marked the passage of the United States from its post-World War II dominance of world affairs and the international economy to a more equal status with other countries. Kissinger's approach to global politics urged the nation to recognize the need for a transition between those two eras, as well as a sense of its own limits. This is his principal legacy as scholar, diplomat, and foreign policy strategist.

(See also DIPLOMACY; REALISM; STRATEGIC ARMS LIMITATION TREATIES.)

Stephen R. Graubard, Kissinger: Portrait of a Mind (New York, 1973). Peter Dickson, Henry Kissinger and the Meaning of History (Cambridge, 1978). Gregory D. Cleva, Henry Kissinger and the American Approach to Foreign Policy (Lewisburg, Pa., 1989).

GREGORY CLEVA

KOHL, Helmut. Helmut Kohl, chancellor of *Germany from 1982 until 1998, was born in 1930 in Ludwigshafen in what is now the state of Rhineland-Palatinate. Kohl was only a teenager at the conclusion of World War II in 1945. A career politician, Kohl was active in the Christian Democratic Party (CDU) in his home state, serving in many elected and appointed positions during the 1950s and 1960s for his moderately right-wing party. He was first elected to the position of minister-president of Rhineland-Palatinate in 1969 and served until 1976. In 1976 he was the chancellor-candidate of the CDU and its sister party the Bavarian-based Christian Social Union (CSU) against the center-left coalition of the left-wing Social Democratic Party (SPD) and the small, centrist Free

Democratic Party (FDP). Kohl lost that election to the Social Democrat Helmut Schmidt but retained his party's leadership.

In October 1982 when the FDP decided to end its coalition with the SPD in favor of joining forces with the CDU-CSU, Kohl became chancellor by virtue of his party leadership of the CDU. In order to ratify this change with the voters, Kohl's new coalition government called early elections in the winter of 1983 and the CDU-CSU-FDP achieved a strong majority position. Kohl was subsequently reelected in 1987, 1990, and 1994, thus becoming the longest-serving postwar chancellor. Had he been reelected in the 1998 election, he would have served longer as chancellor than Otto von Bismarck, the founder of modern Germany in 1871.

During his first term of office (1983–87) Kohl was sometimes compared to Margaret Thatcher and Ronald Reagan, who had also displaced center-left parties (in 1979 and 1980, respectively) to win their country's executive offices. At first, Kohl suffered badly in comparison to Thatcher and Reagan, especially since—unlike previous chancellors Helmut Schmidt and Willy Brandt—Kohl spoke only German and seemed provincial unlike the urbane and cosmopolitan Brandt and Schmidt. Eschewing sharp ideological rhetoric, however, Kohl relied on a more pragmatic approach to leadership which drew on his long experience in party politics in the Federal Republic. Kohl had great electoral success but his moderate policies did not sharply turn German politics in a rightward direction during his sixteen years in office.

During Kohl's first term there were no major changes in direction and few significant policy innovations. Some observers predicted that Kohl would either lose the 1987 election or face a challenge from within his own party grouping by having a competing opponent as chancellor-candidate. However Kohl's political skills within his party—he reportedly knew the name of every Christian Democratic mayor in the country—and institutional skills within his center-right coalition enabled him to both fend off internal opponents and defeat the SPD and the other party of the German left, the Greens, in the 1987 elections.

Kohl was helped in his three successive reelection efforts by the lack of effective opposition from the SPD and the Greens. He also benefited from his early embracing of European unity in the Single European Market which forged increased economic and political unity in the 1990s. Acting more on pragmatic than ideological grounds, Kohl's endorsement of a more unified Europe helped solidify Germany's position among its neighbors. This proved particularly important given Germany's aggressive posture toward other European countries during World War I and World War II.

Despite the favorable short-term factor (the 1987 election) and the favorable long-term factor (European unity), Kohl faced increasing criticism during the late 1980s and seemed quite indecisive. A right-wing party (the Republikaner) won representation in several regional elections in the winter and spring of 1989 as it sought to question German-Polish borders (the Oder-Neisse line) which had been fixed in several post–World War II treaties.

Kohl's extrication from these political troubles came with the surprising East German quest for freedom in the fall of 1989. Rather than playing on old ideological rhetoric from the Cold War, Kohl and his center-right coalition embraced the rapid process of dissolution of the former *German Democratic Republic (GDR) as communist East Germany was called. Acting quickly and pragmatically, Kohl took his political opponents on both the left and right by surprise. By the spring of 1990, when events proceeded so rapidly in the GDR that demands for freedom were being surpassed by demands for unification of the two Germanies, Kohl quickly positioned himself as the "chancellor for Germany." He also instituted a currency reform which—against the wishes of Karl Otto Pöhl, the leader of the Bundesbank (Federal Reserve Bank)—gave most favorable exchange rates to citizens of the former GDR.

Kohl's optimistic and enthusiastic endorsement for a unification process that promised to avoid hardship for former GDR residents resulted in electoral gains for the CDU-CSU-FDP coalition in regional voting in the former GDR prior to unification. It also carried over after formal *German unification in October of 1990 to electoral victories for his coalition in subsequent regional elections, as well as the Bundestag (parliamentary lower house) federal elections—the first all-German elections since 1933—in December of 1990. Thus, in the space of a few short years, Kohl's image by the beginning of his second term (1990–1994) was transformed from that of an unexciting career politician to the most significant political figure in Germany since Konrad Adenauer, the first chancellor of the FRG.

Within two years of the 1990 election, however, the euphoria of unification had given way to the reality of the full dimensions of its costs. In retrospect, many observers felt that Kohl had too cavalierly underestimated the material and social expenditure of such a huge undertaking. Having promised eastern Germans that their lives would be better, he was forced to concede that the process of transition would take many years of hardship. He also promised western German voters that no new taxes would be necessary to pay for the massive rebuilding costs, a promise he was also forced to rescind within a year of the 1990 elections. Kohl's CDU soon suffered sharp losses in regional elections, the most surprising of which was the SDP's victory in Kohl's home state of Rhineland-Palatinate for the first time in the post–World War II period.

The losses of state elections by the CDU in the early 1990s meant that the SPD opposition attained control of a majority of the sixteen state governments which, under the German political system, gave the SPD control of the upper house of the German legislature, the Bundesrat. The upper house has considerable constitutional powers, as it must accede to all laws passed in the Bundestag, which meant that Kohl's political power diminished after losing control of the upper house. Consequently, Kohl's last term (1994–1998) offered few policy innovations and the CDU-led government was unable to produce major reforms of the tax, pension, or employee-relations systems. More significantly, the economic imbalance between the relatively prosperous western Germany and the poorer eastern Länder persisted.

In retrospect, Kohl's clearheaded pragmatism proved effective for Germany and Europe at two pivotal historic moments: German unification and the birth of the *European Union. However, political exhaustion after sixteen years in power and the failure to solve stubborn domestic problems such as unemployment and the lagging resuscitation of the eastern German states proved his undoing. On 27 September

1998, Kohl and the CDU-CSU suffered a crushing electoral defeat to the SPD's Gerhard *Schröder, as the CDU suffered its biggest losses in the five eastern *Länder*. Shortly after the 1998 election, Kohl announced that he would step down as party leader.

CHRISTOPHER ALLEN

KOREA, DEMOCRATIC PEOPLE'S REPUBLIC OF. The Democratic People's Republic of Korea (DPRK), or North Korea, is a singular and puzzling nation that resists easy description. Because its leadership is secretive and unyielding to foreign attention, many basic facts about the country are unknown. Thus pundits are able to project stereotypes onto it, such as a Stalinist attempt at creating "1984"; a socialist "basket case"; a Confucian/Communist monarchy; Che Guevara's idea of what Cuba should eventually look like. In the late 1990s it was the poster child for two new images: a rogue terrorist state, according to the United States and some of its allies, and a "failed state" that could not feed its own people and faced massive famine. In the night of our ignorance, North Korea confirms all stereotypes.

The DPRK was established on 9 September 1948. Emerging within the bowels of Russian Red Army occupation after World War II, it thus took its administrative and industrial structure from Soviet models. Kim Il Sung (1912–1994) and most of the top leadership, however, had been anti-Japanese guerrillas in northeast China in the 1930s; thus Soviet influence mingled with two other experiences: the resistance to Japanese colonialism (slogans in the DPRK still exhort citizens to "live in the way of the anti-Japanese guerrillas") and that of Chinese communism. These two influences help explain DPRK domestic and foreign policy: Maoism competed with Soviet doctrines and gave the regime an internal "mass politics" emphasis, while externally the DPRK has based its strategy on close relations and backing from China, while tilting toward Moscow from time to time for tactical reasons. In the 1960s and 1970s the DPRK also sought to be an exemplary postcolonial *Third World nation. The demise of the Soviet Union in 1991, however, deprived North Korea of both strategic and economic support, making it more dependent on China than ever, and forced the leadership to break out of its isolation and develop better relations with the United States and with the Republic of *Korea (South Korea).

Foreign influences, while significant, have been less important than the indigenous political culture. The DPRK has been unique among *Communist Party States for its top-down leader principle and its corporatist organizational doctrine. This is a tightly held, total politics, with undoubted repressive capacity and many political victims—some reports suggest up to 100,000 people may be held in prisons and reform-through-labor camps. In city, town, and village there is Kim Il Sung; everywhere there is Kim Il Sung. Born on 15 April 1912 and the only top leader the country had from its founding until his death by heart attack in July 1994, no leader in the twentieth century stamped a nation with his presence like Kim. He was then and remains today the father figure of a family/nation, a body politic, which is expected to return fealty to him. This pattern of "socialism in one family" is the heritage of Korea's long history of Confucian statecraft, yielding a kind of socialist *corporatism which appeals to a people with a strong extended family system, high consciousness of

lineage, and deeply inbred patriarchal norms. North Korea often impresses foreigners precisely by its cultural conservatism. The 1972 DPRK constitution (the second since 1948) defined the family as the core unit of society. Furthermore, marriages are still arranged in the North, family themes are exalted in the arts, and the regime has never sought to break up the family unit. Therefore it was entirely predictable that when Kim died his eldest son, Kim Jong Il, would take over the leadership.

After Kim's death North Korea was visited with two years of flood (1995 and 1996), a summer of drought (1997), and a resulting *famine that has claimed or threatened the lives of two million people. This is a textbook example of the calamities that are supposed to attend the end of the Confucian dynastic cycle. Kim Jong Il waited out the traditional three-year mourning period for the first son of the king before assuming his father's titles: he became secretary of the Korean Worker's Party (KWP) in 1997 and inherited the position of maximum leader at the fiftieth anniversary of the regime's founding on 9 September 1998. At the turn of the new century he appeared to have fully consolidated his leadership, and with much external aid and no more catastrophic weather, harvests began to return to pre-1995 levels.

The country is ruled by the KWP, designated a "mass party of a new type" ever since its inception in 1946. Among Communist regimes Korea long had the highest percentage of the population enrolled in the party, fluctuating between 12 and 14 percent. The Korean revolution, far from polarizing the population exclusively into good and bad classes, pursued an inclusive, all-encompassing mass politics. The Koreans have envisioned their society as a mass, the gathered-together "people," rather than a class-based and class-divided society. The reigning doctrine, known as *Juche*, is defined as self-reliance and independence in politics, economics, defense, and ideology. It first emerged in 1955 as P'yongyang drew away from Moscow, and then appeared full-blown in the mid-1960s as Kim sought a stance independent of both Moscow and Beijing. It might best be translated as, "put Korean things first, always"—a type of nationalism. The North Koreans also adapted typical postcolonial Third World policies to their indigenous political culture and to Soviet-style socialism: an economic program of rapid industrialization through multiyear plans; Lenin's notion of national liberation; Stalin's autarky of socialism in one country. The DPRK's desire for autarky fit Korea's "Hermit Kingdom" past, and represented a kind of closure from the world economy after decades of opening under Japanese imperial auspices.

North Korea was once the supreme example in the postcolonial developing world of conscious withdrawal from the capitalist world economy—but withdrawal *for* development, withdrawal with development. Until the 1980s its growth rates were generally high: not just in industry, which might be expected given Japanese industrialization of northern Korea, but also in agriculture. According to a published Central Intelligence Agency report, North Korea's per capita GNP was the same as South Korea's in 1976. It probably kept pace through to 1983, in part because of South Korea's 6 percent loss of GNP in 1980. The DPRK's total production of electricity, coal, fertilizer, machine tools, and steel was comparable to or higher than South Korean totals in the early 1980s, in spite of its population being half that of the South. Since the mid-1980s, however, the DPRK's industrial economy has foundered badly, beset by obsolescent technologies, energy bottlenecks, declining foreign aid, and bad central management. The South has forged far ahead of it; indeed, by the late 1990s the DPRK's industrial economy was nearly moribund—energized only by joint ventures with South Korean firms such as Hyundai and Daewoo.

The world in the twenty-first century seems more inhospitable to P'yongyang's policies than at any point since 1948. Yet this cloistered regime faced the death of its founding leader and remained stable; it also played a masterful diplomatic game after its support from the Soviet bloc ended. By deploying its graphite nuclear reactor and its long-range missiles as bargaining chips it got one agreement after another out of the United States, often involving significant U.S. concessions. For more than a decade many observers have expected the regime simply to collapse; but predictions based on the idea that the regime draws deeply from the well of Korean tradition and anticolonial nationalism, and will therefore have staying power in the post–Cold War world, have been correct so far. In the late 1990s the DPRK began slowly to open itself to the outside world, with a new free-export zone and a variety of joint ventures. The process accelerated with a diplomatic flurry in 2000 that opened relations with Italy, Australia, and other advanced industrial countries culminating in a dramatic summit in P'yongyang between the presidents of North and South Korea. The historic meeting produced an agreement intended to advance peace and reconciliation between the two Koreas and held the promise of reducing North Korea's isolation. But, despite these overtures, P'yongyang still has not departed from the long-standing policies of corporatist politics and heavy-industry-first economics at home and attempts at self-reliance abroad that have characterized the DPRK and limit the prospects of fundamental regime change.

(See also KOREAN WAR.)

Bruce Cumings, *Korea's Place in the Sun* (New York, 1997). Nicholas Eberstadt, *The End of North Korea* (Washington, D.C., 1999). Helen Louise Hunter, *Kim Il-song's North Korea* (New York, 1999).
BRUCE CUMINGS

KOREA, REPUBLIC OF. Occupying the southern half of a peninsula that juts from continental Asia toward Japan, the Republic of Korea (South Korea), despite its meager territory, is not a small country by other measures. In 1998 the Republic of Korea had a population of 47 million, and a Gross Domestic Product that in 1997 made it the eleventh largest economy in the world. In terms of the economy, however, it is the speed of its growth, and not the sheer size, that has commanded world's attention on Korea. South Korea has been a developmental *wunderkind* of the late twentieth century, growing at a rate almost unsurpassed in the world. This would not have been anticipated when Korea became independent in 1945 or throughout the 1950s when South Korea was an economic basket case sustained by the *United States. The rapid pace of development has contributed to political instability, however, and exacerbated Korea's tendency toward *authoritarianism, up until 1988, when arbitrary rule gave way to *democracy and feisty parliamentary politics.

Korea has had a long tradition of centralized bureaucracy,

and many observers believe that this goes a long way to explain the Korean propensity toward authoritarianism and state-centrism. But culture and history may not be sufficient to explain the turbulence of Korea's modern politics. In reality, the agrarian bureaucracy of the Yi dynasty (1392–1910), which preceded Korea's entry into the international system, was not quite as strong as it was believed to be. The state ostensibly dominated the society, but it was in fact the landed aristocratic families that kept the state at bay and perpetuated local power for centuries. This pattern was broken when *Japan colonized Korea in 1910, substituting a brutal and modern state for a decaying agrarian bureaucracy. Korea had suffered some 900 invasions in its 2,000 years of recorded history, being the focus of Chinese, Japanese, and Russian competition in Northeast Asia; but it was the Japanese annexation of Korea that left an indelible mark on modern South Korean politics.

From 1910 to 1945, Japan created in Korea a web of modern, centralized bureaucracies modeled after the Meiji bureaucracies (which were themselves modeled after Prussia's), and this ended up serving as the basis of South Korea's administrative structure after its independence in 1945. The Japanese colonial government also intervened extensively in the economy, in order to exploit its colony more efficiently and, later, to mobilize for the Pacific War. The government was also proactive in supporting the Japanese conglomerates (the *zaibatsu*) who took risks by investing and expanding markets in colonies. In return for this, the conglomerates complied with and supported government policies. This pattern of state interventionism and state-business business collaboration finds some resonance today in the practices of the South Korean political economy. In any event, the result of the Japanese colonial policy was a paradox. It spurred economic growth but immiserated the populace, increased agrarian output but also increased tenancy, and created an industrial structure that was an appendage of Japan's interests.

When Japan surrendered to the Allied forces in 1945, a country that had been unified for thirteen centuries was divided at the thirty-eighth parallel, with the Soviet Union occupying the north (and then turning it over to Kim Il Sung) and the United States occupying the south until 1948, when the Republic of Korea was founded. This division was a calamity. It separated families, and attempts to unify the country ended up in the *Korean War (1950–1953) involving the *United Nations and *China, and costing more than two million Korean lives, as well as American and Chinese lives. The war also perpetuated deadly politics in both North and South Korea, leading to ruthless repression of political dissent in the name of national security. The successive wave of democratization in South Korea since 1987 has changed all that, and President Kim Dae Jung's engagement policy toward the *Democratic People's Republic of Korea in the north has eased the hostility between the two Koreas somewhat. But true reconciliation between the two Koreas remains a long way off.

The ravages of colonialism and war were devastating to the Republic of Korea, and the recovery was slow, painful, and costly. In the 1950s, the United States poured close to $1 billion a year in military and economic aid into the Syngman Rhee regime (1948–1960) in order to sustain, in the end, a very modest growth. The generous aid was instead siphoned off to reinforce a formidable state structure that included a very large bureaucracy and a dominating police and military. It also subsidized large industrialists, who in turn helped Rhee win elections.

The long-awaited economic growth finally happened in the mid-1960s, resulting from a combination of factors: a vigorous U.S. foreign economic policy that liberalized the economic regime in Korea and emphasized *export-led growth; rapprochement with Japan, which provided more developmental aid; Korea's participation in and windfall gains from the *Vietnam War; and, finally, the emergence of a regime that was capable of harnessing these opportunities into sustained economic development.

General Park Chung Hee, who ruled the Republic of Korea for nearly two decades from 1961 to 1979, was an anticommunist and modernizer. In those years the Republic of Korea was molded in his image, and also in the image of what Washington desired from its client—a bulwark of anticommunism that was also a shining example of a vibrant, modern, capitalist economy. This garrison state had little room for liberal democracy, and Park, after an experiment with limited parliamentary democracy in the 1960s, put an end to it by 1972. Through bureaucratic authoritarian measures known as the *Yushin*, he was made president for life, and the parliament became a rubber stamp; opposition parties were dissolved, their leaders sent either into exile or jail; dissenters, including students, intellectuals, and workers, were muzzled and terrorized; and the entire society was paramilitarized, equipped with one of the world's largest standing armies and a vast civilian reserve force. The tension created by the terror finally snapped in 1979, when, amid a growing economic crisis, workers, students, and common people poured into the streets of South Korea, and Park Chung Hee was assassinated by his own security police chief in what was probably a bungled coup attempt.

The exit of Park Chung Hee provided no relief for those who had hoped for democracy. In less than a month of Park's assassination, a young officer named Chun Doo Hwan seized power within the military in a *coup d'état in which several high officers were killed. Chun had been a favorite of Park's, had commanded Korean troops in the Vietnam War, and was head of the powerful Army Security Command at the time of the assassination. In protest against the tightening grip of Chun, who now had himself made head of the Korean Central Intelligence Agency (KCIA), students and common people protested in ways unprecedented since 1960. This led to martial law, which then touched off province-wide rebellion in the southwest, centered in the provincial capital of Kwangju, leaving at least 200 civilians dead. Chun violently put down the rebellion and went on to become president of the republic, but he never transcended his role in the bloodletting in Kwangju. The Kwangju massacre remains a deep wound in the Korean body politic.

In the first half of the 1980s, a new team of U.S.-educated economic managers succeeded in opening up the economy, doing away with the *import-substitution policies of the 1970s, liberalizing imports, dismantling subsidies for exports and specific industries, privatizing banks, and developing a vibrant equity market. But the political system remained fundamentally authoritarian, the emergence of new political elites and new political parties notwithstanding. In 1987 Chun sought to have the ruling party ratify Roh Tae Woo, his close friend, as his chosen successor, and this triggered massive urban demonstration throughout Korea. The world was riveted to television broadcasts showing chaos at the site of the coming 1988 Summer Olympics. Suddenly Roh Tae Woo announced direct elections for the presidency, for a single five-year term, and lifted previous restrictions on most political activities. He challenged the opposition, which failed to seize the opportunity that had been so long in coming.

When the elections came in December 1987, Kim Dae Jung and the other major opposition figure, Kim Young Sam, were unable to agree on a single candidate to challenge the incumbents. They renamed their parties and ran separately, splitting the opposition vote (totaling 53 percent) and thus allowing Roh to stay in power with 37 percent of the votes cast. They compounded the blunder in the 1988 assembly elections, splitting 101 seats between them while the ruling party got only eighty-six. The opposition parties in the Republic of Korea have not transcended their past as clientelist groupings around one strong leader. Nonetheless, the election of 1987 ushered in a period of significant political liberalization, including greater freedom of press and assembly and the restoration of the civil rights of former detainees.

In 1990 Kim Young Sam joined with the ruling group to form yet another new party, the Democratic Liberal Party, molded in the image of Japan's Liberal Democratic Party. The ruling groups thus hoped to emulate the longevity and stability of Japan's one-party rule, and for a while it seemed to work. In December 1992, Kim Young Sam was instituted as the first civilian president in nearly thirty years, and in an unprecedented move, proceeded to put former military dictators on trial on charges of corruption and sedition, thus to confront South Korea's authoritarian past. Kim Young Sam's achievement in deepening the democratic process in Korea was overshadowed, however, by a series of financial scandals involving his own son, and by an international financial contagion that spread from Southeast Asia and ended up eroding investor confidence in Korea, as well. In December 1977 South Korea signed a $58 billion IMF package, including loans from the International Monetary Fund, the World Bank, and the Asian Development Bank; in return Korea agreed to accelerate the opening of its financial and equity markets to foreign investment and to reform and restructure its financial and corporate sectors to increase transparency and accountability.

The worst financial crisis in South Korea's history coincided with yet another presidential election, one that brought Kim Dae Jung—a long-time opposition politician, political prisoner, and a human rights activist—to power. One of his main concerns in his five-year term that began in December 1997 is to restructure the economy, especially the heavily-indebted corporate sector. But it is his other concern, the relationship with North Korea, that may prove to be his lasting legacy.

The administration of Kim Dae Jung has pushed its policy toward North Korea, which is called the "sunshine policy," or the "engagement policy," and which means the use of the private sector to encourage peaceful exchange, involving trade, tourism, and investment in special economic zones in North Korea. This policy marks a fundamental shift toward the North, for under this formulation, the Republic of Korea has forsworn any intent to undermine or absorb the North and has pursued increased official and unofficial North-South contact. This policy, in conjunction with the four-party talks involving the United States, China, and North and South Korea to establish a permanent peace regime that would replace the 1953 military armistice, offers the best chance to date of maintaining stability in the Korean peninsula. The United States has also offered North Korea the promise of lifting sanctions and normalizing relations, in return for ending its nuclear weapons and long range missile related programs.

(See also BUREAUCRATIC AUTHORITARIANISM; COLONIAL EMPIRES; DEMOCRATIC TRANSITIONS; IMPORT-SUBSTITUTION INDUSTRIALIZATION; NEWLY INDUSTRIALIZING ECONOMIES.)

Jung-en Woo, *Race to the Swift: State and Finance in Korean Industrialization* (New York, 1991). Bruce Cumings, *Korea's Place in the Sun* (New York, 1997). Don Oberdorfer, *The Two Koreas* (New York, 1997).

MEREDITH WOO-CUMINGS

KOREAN WAR. The Korean War has been subject to frequent reinterpretation since it was fought in the early 1950s. For president Harry S *Truman, Korea was a "police action" which began on 25 June 1950 when North Korean forces backed by the Soviet Union launched a full-scale, unprovoked invasion across the thirty-eighth parallel, to which the United States responded by invoking United Nations sanctions and leading some sixteen nations into battle. The war ended on 27 July 1953 when an armistice was signed at Pánmunjom, thus reestablishing the status quo ante.

By the 1960s Westerners had renamed it "the limited *war," a conflict different from the world wars in being less than a total war and in being shaped by political decisions taken in Washington. The most noteable of these was the Truman-MacArthur controversy, with Truman seeking to limit the conflict to the Korean peninsula, while General Douglas MacArthur sought to extend the war to China. According to this interpretation Korea was a success for Truman's *containment policy, but a failure for MacArthur—a stalemate yielding "a substitute for victory."

The *Vietnam War influenced another revision of meaning of the Korean conflict, which scholars in the 1970s increasingly came to see as a civil war in which revolutionary nationalism confronted a status quo–oriented United States. Even the dates of the war changed. Its origins were pushed back into Korea's colonial experience with Japan when the military leaderships of both North and South Korea were formed (northerners had been anti-Japanese guerrillas, while the high command of the South Korean Army had fought with Japan), and to political and guerrilla conflicts in 1945–49 and small border wars in 1949–50. There was a corresponding deemphasis on the "start" of the conventional fighting in June 1950 and a significant spreading of responsibility for the coming of the war.

By the 1980s, however, Korea was "the forgotten war." Books and documentaries by that title proliferated, and the war entered an ambiguous realm: not World War II, but not quite Vietnam either, falling somewhere between the stools, more a question mark than a known quantity. Korean War veterans also protested their exclusion from the American popular memory. This was also a decade when new light was shed on the war, as scholars exploited reams of newly declassified documents. Most historians now questioned the conventional assumption that Joseph *Stalin launched the war

for his own purposes or in concert with Kim Il Sung; rather, the assault in June 1950 was Kim Il Sung's idea, with perhaps more Chinese than Soviet support. The direct U.S. role in suppressing left-wing politics in the South during its military occupation (1945–48) was definitively proved. Captured Korean documents showed that the origins of the North Korean regime were much more complex than had been thought, with significant indigenous and Chinese influence in addition to the Soviet role. Both Korean sides were also deeply implicated in the border fighting that ensued from May through December 1949. New materials further showed that the U.S. decision to march into North Korea was taken by Harry Truman, not Douglas MacArthur, under a frank "rollback" doctrine. Truman also thought long and hard about extending the war to China and sacked MacArthur in April 1951 mainly because he wanted a reliable commander in place should that happen. The Truman administration also attempted to use atomic diplomacy to settle the war as early as 1951, whereas this had been thought to be President Dwight D. *Eisenhower's strategy only in 1953.

New materials on the Chinese entry into the war in October 1950 show how difficult this decision was, with *Mao Zedong taking the lead. They also show a combined North Korean–Chinese strategy to lure United Nations forces deep into the interior of Korea after the famous amphibious landing at Inch'on in order to stretch supply lines and gain time for a dramatic reversal on the battlefield. That reversal came as 1950 turned into 1951, when Sino-Korean forces drove UN troops back below the thirty-eighth parallel and again captured Seoul. But General Matthew Ridgway organized a successful defense that stabilized the front well south of the thirty-eighth parallel. UN forces then resumed the offensive, retaking Seoul and reestablishing a Korea divided roughly along that same line. The war could have ended here, but it continued through two years of difficult peace negotiations.

The 1990s brought new interpretations of the Korean War, based on newly declassified Soviet documentation. These materials show more involvement by Stalin than most scholars had thought in the outbreak of conventional war in June 1950, although his involvement was ambiguous and wavering. Kim Il Sung held several secret meetings with Stalin and Mao in early 1950, hoping to gain their backing for an assault on the South. Stalin was reluctant and worried, but ultimately supportive. The full record of Kim's discussions with Mao remains secret, but Beijing was also supportive, particularly because Kim had been a member of the Chinese Communist Party in the 1930s and had many Chinese allies from that period. Ultimately, though, the dominant impetus for taking the existing conflict to the level of conventional war was from North Korea.

All these are Western views. For Koreans in North and South, the likelihood of war came with the division of the ancient integrity of the Korean nation, through the unilateral action of U.S. officials in mid-August 1945, to which Stalin quickly acquiesced. For the South it was a just war to recover "lost territories" in the North and to resist Soviet and Chinese expansion. For the North it was a just war to resist U.S. imperialism and reunify the homeland. For Koreans and some 37,000 American soldiers stationed in South Korea, the war continues today through a "cold peace" held only by the armistice, and with a hot war an ever-present possibility, given that more than a million soldiers still confront each other along the demilitarized zone. But in June 2000 the leaders of South and North Korea met for the first time since the country was divided, and the southern leader, long-time dissident Kim Dae Jung, has stated his determination to bring a final end to the Korean War before he leaves office in 2003.

Eventually the Korean War will be understood as one of the most destructive and one of the most important wars of the twentieth century. Perhaps as many as 4 million Koreans died, three-quarters of them civilians (Japan lost 2.3 million people in the Pacific War). The Korean War gave Japan's war recovery and industrialization a dynamic economic boost, which some have likened to "Japan's Marshall Plan." In the aftermath of the war, two Korean states competed toe-to-toe in economic development, turning both of them into modern industrial nations. Finally, it was this war and not World War II that established a far-flung American base structure abroad and a national security state at home, as defense spending nearly quadrupled in the last six months of 1950, reaching a peak of $500 billion (in current dollars) that was never reached again during the Cold War. Today Koreans continue to seek reconciliation and eventual reunification of their torn nation, and Americans deal with a massive and expensive military-industrial complex that has lost its raison d'être, but continues apace as the primary American legacy of the Korean War.

(See also KOREA, DEMOCRATIC PEOPLE'S REPUBLIC OF; KOREA, REPUBLIC OF; UNITED NATIONS; U.S. FOREIGN POLICY.)

Bruce Cumings, *The Origins of the Korean War*, 2 vols. (Princeton, N.J., 1981, 1990). Rosemary Foot, *The Wrong War: American Policy and the Dimensions of the Korean Conflict, 1950–1953* (Ithaca, N.Y., 1985). Chen Jian, *China's Road to the Korean War* (New York, 1994). William Stueck, *The Korean War: An International History* (Princeton, N.J., 1995).

BRUCE CUMINGS

KOSOVO WAR. The *North Atlantic Treaty Organization's 1999 conflict with *Yugoslavia has been called a "virtual war" for its reliance on remote, high-tech weaponry, particularly air strikes against Serb targets in support of the Kosovo Albanians whose lightly armed fighters served as a surrogate for NATO ground forces. But in other ways as well, the seventy-eight-day Kosovo War became a surrogate or test case for international issues whose gravity far exceeds the direct geopolitical significance of Kosovo itself, one of the poorest and remotest corners in Europe.

These issues, which continue to vex the West just as they complicate relations with Russia and China, include the following: When does humanitarian crisis justify intervention in a sovereign state? What is the role of the *United Nations, that of its Security Council in sanctioning intervention and its peacekeepers in enforcing a settlement? What are an expanded NATO's responsibilities for European security, and what will be the division of leadership duties and military capabilities between the United States and European members? Finally, what can be done to prevent ethnic conflict, and can viable multiethnic states be rebuilt once such conflict has occurred? The latter sets Kosovo somewhat apart from the earlier wars of Yugoslavia's collapse. For, much more than the conflicts in *Slovenia, *Croatia, and Bosnia, the Serbian and Albanian sides in Kosovo were divided by deep cultural, linguistic, and historic differences. Theirs was, much more than

the politically motivated conflicts in other Yugoslav republics, indeed based to a considerable extent on "ancient hatreds."

Both Albanians and Serbs claim to be the original inhabitants of Kosovo, a region tucked between Montenegro, *Macedonia, and *Albania proper in the southwest of modern-day Serbia. While the records of antiquity are inconclusive, it is known that the region fell under Serbian domination in medieval times as the Nemanja dynasty expanded its kingdom from its original base to the north. While the Orthodox Serbs built churches and monasteries in the region, religion did not become a central feature of the Serb-Albanian rivalry in Kosovo until the rise of the Ottoman Empire. Many more Albanians than Serbs converted to Islam for the privileges this brought (though a large number of Albanians embraced Christianity, especially Catholicism). Still, just as some Serbian leaders cooperated with the Turks for local political advantage, so too did some Albanians fight against them regardless of their common faith. This complexity was seen in the 1389 battle of Kosovo Polje (Kosovo field), where Serb and Albanian forces were found on both sides in what was later recorded in Serbian nationalist mythology as a doomed but glorious stand against the advance of Islam.

Pressure on Kosovo Serbs increased during the Ottoman centuries, particularly after their support of an Austrian offensive that followed the Turks' defeat at Vienna (1683) and their subsequent victory at "the second Battle of Kosovo" (1689). Again, some Albanians too joined the Austrians in fighting the Turks, but did not suffer the broad reprisals that Serbs did, many thousands of whom now fled the region together with their Orthodox Patriarch. While the Albanians now constituted a majority in Kosovo, and a small elite prospered under the Sultan's administration, most Kosovo Albanians—like Kosovo Serbs—were poor peasants. And even the elite grew uneasy as the subsequent weakening of the Ottoman system was paralleled by the strengthening of national movements among the empire's other subject peoples, principally Serbs and Greeks. Albanians suffered reprisals in those areas where Serb power grew, but as yet the Albanians lacked a national movement, or a national church, to unite them.

It was at this time—in the mid-to-late nineteenth century—that events occurred which hardened the modern Serb-Albanian enmity. These included various massacres that, though often occasioned by the interference of the Great Powers (chiefly Turkey and Russia, in their war of 1876–77), further poisoned relations between the two peoples. They also included the rise of nationalist ideologies that, as in the case of Serb intellectuals' canonization of the Kosovo legend and demonization of the Albanians, were notable for their tendentiousness and chauvinism. Belatedly a pan-Albanian movement also was launched with the founding of the League of Prizren (a city in south-central Kosovo) in 1878. Significantly, in contrast to the overwhelmingly Orthodox Serbs, the Albanian movement was notable for its secular character and the role played by an influential Catholic minority; as was noted frequently then and since, "The religion of the Albanians is Albanianism." Still, in political terms, this was no substitute for a strong, established state and powerful foreign patrons, both of which the Serbs had and the Albanians lacked.

When the Ottomans were defeated in the First Balkan War

(1911), Serbia swiftly conquered Kosovo and took horrific revenge against the Albanians. The tide turned in World War I, with Austria's initial success in the Balkans and Albanian reprisals against the Serbs. And it turned once again with the defeat of the Central Powers and Serbian recovery of Kosovo. In just a decade, tens of thousands had died on both sides, and hundreds of thousands had been displaced—many never to return. The new Yugoslav state, while pledging to observe minority rights, forcefully encouraged Albanians to leave Kosovo (for Turkey, or for the new Albanian state) while launching a program of Serb "recolonization."

This pattern would be repeated in World War II, with massacres, expulsions, and the eventual reimposition of Serbian hegemony following the Axis defeat. This time it was the Germans and (specifically in Kosovo) Italians who invaded. For Albanians, the Italian occupation was milder than Serbian rule of the interwar period and, importantly, united Kosovo with Albania proper. And though nowhere so barbaric as that of the German puppet regime in Croatia (the Ustaše), the war years saw the flight of some 100,000 Serbs from Kosovo. Largely passive during the war, Albanian resistance grew with the coming of the Serb-dominated Partisans led by Josip *Tito, and an uprising that began in late 1944 was not fully suppressed until 1952. And again, as with the Serb-led Yugoslavia that emerged from World War I, the Serb-dominated Yugoslavia (now socialist) that emerged from World War II began with a vicious crackdown on its Albanian population.

In its early, Stalinist phase, *Tito's regime—largely through the policies of Serbian interior minister Alexander Ranković—dealt extremely harshly with Kosovo. Mass arrests, beatings, and staged show trials cracked down on Yugoslavia's restive Albanians. But there were opposition movements: some advocated outright independence, some sought union with Albania proper, and some demanded full republic status for Kosovo (instead of a fictitious "autonomy" within the Serbian republic). While the latter was never granted—despite an Albanian population comparable to that of the Slovenes, who had their own republic—Tito decided to loosen the centralized control that was provoking resistance in other regions as well. Ranković was dismissed in 1966, and in 1968 a series of concessions were granted—real administrative autonomy for Kosovo, elevation of Albanian language and culture, a new university in Pristina—later enshrined in the Yugoslav constitution of 1974.

But while angering Serb nationalists, the concessions did not address two trends that were exacerbating Kosovo's problems. One was demographic, a higher Albanian birthrate that, in tandem with a steady exodus of Serbs, saw the latter fall from nearly 30 percent of Kosovo's population (in 1948) to less than 15 percent (by 1981). The second was economic, Kosovo's lag behind the rest of Yugoslavia, with shortages and unemployment only sharpening Serb-Albanian rivalry. Serbs' anger grew at the discrimination they increasingly felt, a cause that some Serb nationalists took up with charges of "*genocide" (resulting from the supposedly political motivation behind the high Albanian birthrate) and "treason" (on the part of a complacent Communist Party). Kosovo Albanians' resentment simmered too, for despite their ostensible autonomy, economic and social problems still grew while only an Albanian nomenklatura (party elite) prospered. These problems boiled over soon after Tito's death, in 1981, when massive protests provoked imposition of martial law.

As elsewhere in Eastern Europe, it was probably inevitable that nationalist ideologies would emerge to compete for popular loyalties with the collapse of communism. And, as in the USSR, it was also likely that such ideologies would present an irresistible vehicle for ambitious politicians to gain power as a troubled multiethnic state tottered. What was not inevitable was the rise of a particular leader—in this case, Serbia's Slobodan Milošević—who would so boldly inflame nationalist passions and so readily resort to war in order to advance his goals. Milošević began down this path in 1987, when he first openly and chauvinistically embraced the cause of the Kosovo Serbs, issuing a challenge not just to the Albanians, but to all the Serbs' "enemies." In 1988, employing mass rallies and staged demonstrations, he purged his rivals and became unchallenged leader of Serbia. In 1989, he threatened force to engineer an end to Kosovo's autonomy and fired thousands of Albanians from their jobs, replacing them with Serbs. Slovenes, Croats, and other non-Serbs watched aghast as his media inflamed Serbian nationalism while he maneuvered to replace federal Yugoslavia with a Serb-dominated state. In 1990 this fueled Croat, Slovene, and Bosnian nationalism and doomed efforts to find interrepublician compromise. By 1991, as newly elected Slovene and Croat governments moved toward secession, Serbia prepared for war.

Clashes in Slovenia were brief as Milošević decided, since the republic was home to few Serbs, to cede its independence. But the wars in Croatia (1991) and Bosnia (1992–1995) were exceedingly bloody as Serb communities there—backed by the Yugoslav army and various paramilitary formations—carved out large territories for union with Serbia by means of brutal "ethnic cleansing." Kosovo remained quiescent at this time, though the Albanians pointed out the obvious contradiction in Milošević's logic: if Serb minorities had the right to secede rather than live under the new Croatian or Bosnian states, then why didn't Kosovar Albanians have the same right? But with no chance of armed opposition, and their cause ignored abroad, Albanians chose passive resistance. In 1992, an underground ballot elected a president of the unofficial "Kosovo Republic," Ibrahim Rugova, who supported withdrawal from Serb-dominated public life. Under Rugova's Democratic League of Kosovo (LDK), Albanians constructed a parallel system of education, health care, and local administration. Staffed by the thousands earlier fired from such jobs in now Serb-run institutions, and supported by unofficial taxation as well as remittances from abroad, this policy also saw the rise of a vigorous private economy as the Serbian-dominated public sector deteriorated.

But by the late 1990s, two developments helped end Rugova's experiment. One was the West's failure to address Kosovo's plight, especially its exclusion from the 1995 Dayton Accords (and the easing of sanctions against Serbia) that halted the war in Bosnia. Second was the 1997 crumbling of state authority in Albania proper, a development that facilitated ties between Kosovo Albanians and their kin abroad, including a vigorous traffic in arms. In 1998, the Kosovo Liberation Army (KLA), a small and shadowy group that had engaged in sporadic acts of violence since 1996, launched a concerted campaign of anti-Serbian terror. Kidnappings and killings of police officials brought a brutal Serbian response, with entire families slain and whole villages destroyed in reprisal. The funerals of Albanian dead—often women and children—became rallying points for Kosovars frustrated with the passivity of Rugova's LDK and lured by the call to arms of such as Hashim Thaçi (a KLA military leader) and Adem Demaçi (a longtime dissident and KLA political spokesman).

Under Western pressure, the Serb counteroffensive briefly waned in the spring of 1998 but then resumed with even greater fury (and effectiveness) in the summer. Once "liberated" areas of Kosovo, such as Drenica, were pacified, while news came of new massacres in Serb operations against such Albanian strongholds as Orahovac and Dečani. With some 100,000 Albanians taking refuge outside Kosovo, and another 200,000 internally displaced, fears grew that winter could see widespread death from starvation or the elements among those hiding in the mountains and forests. NATO began preparations for military action while U.S. diplomat Richard Holbrooke (the chief architect of Dayton) brokered an October compromise that saw Milošević agree to cease military operations, admit Western observers, prepare fair elections, and restore genuine autonomy. In the event, neither the Albanian nor Serbian sides substantially changed course. KLA attacks continued, and the Serbs responded with increasingly brutal reprisals. A "last straw" came in January 1999, with the massacre of some forty-five Albanians at Račak, an act that galvanized Western opinion and set the stage for emergency peace talks held at Rambouillet, near Paris, in February and March. While the Albanian delegates resisted Western proposals that promised anything less than a near-term referendum on full independence, the Serbian side resisted even more stubbornly provisions that included a large deployment of NATO peacekeepers. In the end, the Kosovo Albanians signed on to the plan that Milošević, despite an eleventh-hour visit from Holbrooke, rejected. NATO bombing of Serb targets began on 24 March.

NATO's decision had perhaps as much to do with maintaining its credibility—following many broken promises by Milošević—as it did with defending Kosovo's long-suffering Albanians. In the latter it was a dismal failure as the outbreak of war permitted Milošević to abandon all restraint and launch a terror campaign that rapidly uprooted nearly all of Kosovo's remaining Albanians. Expecting Milošević to capitulate within a few days, another Western mistake was U.S. President Clinton's early assurance that ground troops would not be introduced. For his part, Milošević underestimated NATO's determination to prevail, particularly as its fiftieth anniversary celebrations approached. He also underestimated the West's ability to handle the huge refugee outflows, some 850,000 Kosovo Albanians streaming into Macedonia, Montenegro, and Albania. In hindsight, evidence that Milošević had long prepared a "final solution" to the Albanian problem seems clear: a new flow of Serbian forces into Kosovo even before Rambouillet, a purge of any but the hardest-line military leaders, and an intensification of ethnic cleansing even before the war began (some 25,000 Albanians driven out in just the week prior to Rambouillet's collapse).

As the war continued through April and into May, strikes on roads, bridges, oil refineries, and power plants inflicted enormous damage on the Serbian economy. A debate over the designation of military versus civilian installations—and the cost in civilian casualties—was heightened with the accidental destruction of a crowded passenger train and the intentional bombing of the Serbian Television building. Another accidental strike (against the Chinese embassy in Belgrade) seriously damaged Washington's relations with Beijing. Ties with Moscow had already soured as Russia strongly opposed any interference in Yugoslavia without Security Council approval. While such a resolution would surely have been vetoed, and so was never introduced, the Security Council did indirectly endorse the campaign by voting down a resolution (supported by both Russia and China, highly sensitive to interference in their treatment of Chechen and Tibetan minorities) condemning NATO's action. Though anti-Western fury in Moscow was great, and it would take almost a year before NATO-Russia ties were normalized, it was also Russia that played a key role in the war's resolution. With the bombing well into its third month and no sign of yielding on either side, Russian envoy Victor Chernomyrdin in early June helped persuade Milošević to accept (with only slight changes) the West's original terms for a settlement.

The reasons for Serbia's capitulation remained unclear. Early NATO boasts of having crippled the Serbian military turned out to be much exaggerated; rather than destroying 50 percent of Serbian armor, for example, decoys and deception kept the toll well below 20 percent and most Serbian forces left Kosovo intact. Such revelations, like those after the 1991 *Gulf War, renewed debate over the efficacy of modern airpower, particularly when employed at long range in a conflict marked by distinctly premodern, close-range brutality. It appears rather that Milošević yielded due to the crippling of Serbia's civilian economy, a strategy raising grave humanitarian and legal questions. While the Hague Tribunal (having recently indicted Milošević) dismissed Yugoslav charges that NATO was guilty of war crimes, Amnesty International concluded the opposite. Estimates of Serb civilian deaths range from 500 to 5,000 (the latter a Yugoslav government claim) while up to 10,000 Albanians were killed or are still missing.

Another political-military issue heightened by the Kosovo War was Europe's continuing inability to meet its decade-old goal of forging a Common Defense and Security Policy (CDSP), to act decisively in a crisis absent U.S. leadership. American dominance continues in modern military capabilities as well, highlighted by the fact that while providing significant airpower and personnel in the Kosovo War, Europe was almost entirely reliant on the United States for high-tech munitions, advanced command and control, and timely intelligence. In the words of German foreign minister Joschka Fischer, "The Kosovo War was mainly an experience of Europe's own insufficiency and weakness." To redress these weaknesses, European leaders subsequently announced plans for a 60,000-strong rapid reaction force capable of timely intervention in a future Kosovo-style crisis. For their part, while welcoming the Europeans' goal of greater defense self-sufficiency, American officials also express ambivalence should it result in a weakening of the U.S.-led NATO alliance. In any case, the difficult budgetary and organizational reforms required to ease Europe's military inferiority remain mostly in the early, planning stages.

Beyond Europe, the Kosovo War's implications for international relations are also ambiguous. While many initially hailed (or criticized) a new era in which state sovereignty would be subordinate to humanitarian concerns, enthusiasm for (or fears of) a new interventionism quickly waned. Even U.S. secretary of state Madleine Albright, who argued strongest for military action against Milošević, cautioned that not only could the United States not serve as "the world's policeman," but that potential future interventions would be weighed on "a case-by-case basis," with traditional national interests a key consideration. Such was the lesson of East *Timor, a mission soon after the Kosovo War, where an Australian-led force intervened to halt Indonesian military reprisals against a secessionist Timorese minority. Rather than the harbinger of a new era of global *humanitarian intervention, an overwhelmingly Asian-Pacific coalition acted when its regional security interests were threatened.

This reality (occasioning charges of hypocrisy or racism by those concerned with Africa's numerous humanitarian crises, but easing tensions with Russia and China) has also to do with the unforeseen difficulties of postwar reconstruction and reconciliation in Kosovo. Over 40,000 KFOR (Kosovo Force) troops oversaw the return and resettlement of some one million Albanian *refugees. But this has been their only real success, for KFOR (*together with nearly 4,000 international police) has been unable to halt a pattern of revenge killings and intimidation that has taken over 500 lives and driven some 150,000 Serbs out of Kosovo. Another 100,000 Serbs remain, vastly outnumbered by the nearly 2 million Albanians who overwhelmingly support full independence for Kosovo. Still legally part of Serbia, Kosovo is currently a de facto international protectorate for which partition (with a majority of Serbs concentrated in the city of Mitrovica, near the border with Serbia in the north) is the most likely long-term prospect. Though largely demilitarized into a civilian Kosovo Protection Force, some KLA elements continue to plan for insurrection (and maintain arms caches) aimed at full independence, while others have established lucrative black market and protection rackets that stymie the efforts of UNMIK (the U.N. Interim Mission in Kosovo) to establish a secure, law-governed society. As for the other Western goal, that of reestablishing a multiethnic society, the prospects of that appear almost nil.

Recalling the unrest of the early 1980s, it was often noted that "the wars of Yugoslavia's collapse began in Kosovo, and they will end in Kosovo." Given the region's continuing instability, and the continued difficulty merely of coordinating American and European objectives, much less those of the West with China and Russia, the accuracy of even this gloomy presentiment remains to be proven.

(See also BOSNIA AND HERZEGOVINA; BOSNIAN WAR; U.S. FOREIGN POLICY.)

Amnesty International, Kosovo: The Evidence (London, 1998). Noel Malcolm, Kosovo: A Short History (New York, 1999). Ivo H. Daalder and Michael E. O'Hanlon, Winning Ugly: NATO's War to Save Kosovo (Washington, D.C., 2000). Tim Judah, Kosovo: War and Revenge (New Haven, Conn., 2000).

ROBERT D. ENGLISH

KU KLUX KLAN. The Ku Klux Klan has been a loosely connected succession of racial terrorist societies in the United States. The name came from the Greek *kyklos,* meaning "circle," to which was added the alliterative word "klan." In general terms, there have been five periods of Klan history: Reconstruction, the national Klan of the 1920s, post–World War II rebirth, late '70s revival, and the turn toward the Radical Right in the '80s and '90s, which Klansmen call the "Fifth Era." Variously the Klan has been a counterrevolutionary, a vigilante, a moral enforcer, a nativist, an anti-Catholic, an antisemite, a fraternal lodge, a moneymaker, a resistance movement, and a status society for Southern poor-boy politics and resentments. Unvaryingly, it has stood for white supremacy.

First organized as a social club in Pulaski, Tennessee (1866), it spread quickly as a means of controlling black people freed by the Civil War. Most active outside the plantation "black belt" areas, the Klan and like groups such as the Knights of the White Camellia spread across the South. Through intimidation and murder, the Klan sought to drive black people out of politics, overturn the new Reconstruction state governments, control black labor, and restore black subordination. Members came from all levels of white male society, led initially by local elites. Former Confederate Cavalry General Nathan Bedford Forrest was its first Grand Wizard. Its murders ran into many hundreds and the victims of its beatings and other intimidations numbered in the thousands. By the time the federal Enforcement and Ku Klux Klan Acts of 1870–1871, federal troops, and trials closed it down, the Klan had basically accomplished its goals.

D. W. Griffith's epic 1915 motion picture *The Birth of a Nation* based on Thomas Dixon's 1905 racist novel *The Clansman,* helped produce a revival. Organized as a social lodge, the Klan spread rapidly after World War I as the defender of Protestant morality against social change. Created by Colonel William J. Simmons and ruled during most of the 1920s and 1930s by Hiram Wesley Evans, it became the great fraternal lodge of the 1920s for white, native-born, Protestant men and women. Prohibition and anti-Catholicism were added to white supremacist beliefs shared with a majority of Americans. Most of the Klan violence was in the South and Southwest, but the Klan drew support in the North and West and helped elect more than twenty governors and U.S. senators, from Maine to California. Inept leadership, internal conflict and corruption, immorality and violence discredited the Klan, which declined rapidly in the later 1920s. It lingered on locally in the Southeast and died during World War II.

Revived after World War II, it splintered into small competing units, hostile to organized labor, and unable to prevent desegregation in the South, despite church burnings, beatings, bombing, and murder. Klansmen assaulted the 1961 "Freedom" bus riders in Alabama and offered murderous resistance to the civil rights movement in Mississippi. The murder of the three summer volunteers in Philadelphia, Mississippi (1964), forced President Lyndon *Johnson to use a reluctant Federal Bureau of Investigation (FBI) against the Klan. The murder of Viola Liuzzo after the Selma to Montgomery March in Alabama (1965) helped him push through the 1965 Voting Rights law. The FBI undertook secret illegal harassment of the Klan (COUNTERINTELPRO), federal juries sent Klansmen to jail under the Reconstruction-era anti-Klan Acts and a new 1968 civil rights protection law (18 U.S.C. 245), and eventually state juries began to convict. In 1977, the man whose bomb killed four young girls in the 1963 Birmingham 16th Street Baptist Church, went to jail.

At the end of the 1970s, a minor Klan revival appealed to a blue collar constituency that blamed job uncertainty on affirmative action and government favoritism to *African Americans. In the 1980s Alabama lawyer Morris Dees emerged as a powerful Klan opponent. Attacking Klan pocketbooks, his Southern Poverty Law Center (SPLC) won large damage payments for victims' families by suing Klans for the actions of their members. Klans pushed recruitment of prison inmates and young street-violent skinheads, and a young former neo-Nazi and Klan leader, David Duke, was elected to the Louisiana legislature and drew wide support for U.S. Senate (1990) and governor (1991) by manipulating issues of race and government welfare programs. Leaders rise briefly. Klans split. There are no new ideas, plans, unity, resources, or prestige, but with less than 5,000 members and needing police protection from assault by counterdemonstrators, fragmentary Klans persist in more than half of the states. They are fueled by racial rage and paranoia, sustained by the Internet, Willis Carto's *Spotlight*, *The Turner Diaries*, and Christian Identity religion, increasingly involved with the fiercely antisemitic Radical Right and its paramilitary militants. Responding to growing racial harassment and violence, Congress passed a Hate Crimes Statistics Act (1990), and many states have added penalties for bias-related crimes. At century's end, Klan hate crimes, increasing in reported number, were the actions of "loose cannon" Klansmen rather than planned acts of organizational *terrorism.

(See also ANTISEMITISM; CIVIL RIGHTS MOVEMENT; RACE AND RACISM; RIGHT.)

Allen Trelease, *White Terror: The Ku Klux Klan Conspiracy and Southern Reconstruction* (New York, 1971). David Chalmers, *Hooded Americanism: The History of the Ku Klux Klan* (Durham, N.C., 1987). Shawn Lay, ed., *The Invisible Empire in the West: Toward a New Historical Appraisal of the Ku Klux Klan in the 1920s* (Urbana, Ill., 1992). For current Klan Information, consult Southern Poverty Law Center (Montgomery, Ala.), Center for Democratic Renewal (Atlanta, Ga.), and the Anti-Defamation League of B'nai B'rith (New York).

DAVID CHALMERS

KURDISTAN. The name given to the homeland of the Kurds, a Muslim people numbering approximately 20 to 25 million, Kurdistan comprises most of eastern and southeastern Turkey, northern Iraq, parts of northwestern Iran, and small slices of northeastern and northwestern Syria. In all these states, Kurdistan has long been a peripheral and relatively underdeveloped area. Its most important natural resource is oil; the chief wells are near Kirkuk and Khaniqin, both in present-day Iraq and of essential importance to that country. Kurdistan is also well endowed with that other, increasingly scarce resource, water: it is here that the Euphrates and the Tigris, as well as their major tributaries, have their origins.

Most of Kurdistan is very mountainous; animal husbandry and small-scale agriculture are the major economic activities, with smuggling a third major source of income in the border zones. There are also a few large and fertile plains, such as those of Arbil in Iraq and Diyarbakir in Turkey, where large-scale capitalist agriculture is practiced. The mechanization of agriculture, starting in the 1950s, led to rapid urbanization. The towns in and near Kurdistan, traditionally centers of crafts and trade, offer little industrial employment. Many migrants therefore moved on to cites or to areas of labor-intensive agriculture elsewhere in their country of residence or abroad.

There are no reliable counts of the Kurds (or other ethnic groups) in any of these countries, and only very rough estimates are possible. Turkey has the largest Kurdish population, numbering between 8 and 13 million (out of a total population of 66 million). Then follow Iran, with 4.5 to 7 million Kurds (out of 65 million), and Iraq, where the Kurds, at over 4 million, make up around a fifth of the population. Well over a million Kurds live in Syria (out of 17 million), while Kurdish enclaves in the Transcaucasian republics add up to over a half million. Numerous Kurds, perhaps as many as 30 to 40 percent, now live outside Kurdistan proper, as a result of deportations, labor migration, or flight.

The Kurdish ethnic identity is not based on unity of language or religion. The southern and northern Kurdish dialects (known as Sorani and Kurmanji, respectively) are not mutually intelligible, while there are also several million speakers of more distantly related Zaza (in Turkey) and Gurani (in Iraq and Iran). These languages belong to the Iranian family and are therefore unrelated to Turkish or Arabic, although they contain numerous loanwords from them.

Most Kurds are Sunni Muslims, but a significant minority in Turkey belong to the heterodox Alevi sect, while smaller numbers adhere to other syncretistic sects, Yezidi and Ahl-i Haqq; the southern fringes of Kurdistan, meanwhile, are home to considerable numbers of Twelver Shi'a. In spite of this linguistic and religious diversity, there is a widespread awareness among all these groups of belonging to a larger common entity, and all have at times taken part in Kurdish nationalist rebellions. This is not to say that there has ever been a united Kurdish movement; division by personal, tribal, regional, and sectarian rivalries has been the rule rather than the exception. The geopolitical situation has moreover made the Kurds vulnerable to manipulation by outside powers. Iran and Syria have supported Kurdish parties active in Iraq and Turkey, while Iraq has supported the Iranian Kurdish parties.

Kurdish *nationalism first emerged among members of the educated elite around the turn of the twentieth century but did not develop into a mass movement until the 1960s, appearing first in Iraq. Qassem's left-wing military coup (1958) raised Kurdish expectations of more equal participation in the state: when these were frustrated, Kurdish leader Mulla Mustafa Barzani took to the mountains and initiated a guerrilla war. As this was dragged on, it politicized Kurdish society, inviting increasingly wider participation throughout Iraqi Kurdistan. The guerrilla warfare contributed to the fall of several governments and resulted in 1970 in a peace agreement promising autonomy as well as Kurdish participation in the central government. When the government failed to implement the agreement in full, fighting flared up again in 1974–1975, when the Kurds received considerable Iranian support and secret U.S. and Israeli aid. During the *Iran-Iraq War, 1980–1988, the Iraqi Kurds once again were supported by and cooperated with Iran, without any lasting gains and at great human cost. More than half of Iraqi Kurdish villages were razed, their inhabitants deported to other parts of the country, resettled in new towns and concentration camps, or, as occurred in 1988 on a large scale, summarily executed. In the final offensives against the Kurds that year, known by the code name of "Anfal," Iraq repeatedly used chemical arms against guerrilla positions and villages in the guerrilla-controlled districts. These attacks were followed by systematic deportations of the population, after which vast numbers of men—perhaps as many as 100,000—were carried off to the south and summarily executed.

Iraq's defeat in the *Gulf War of 1991 provoked a massive uprising of the Iraqi Kurds. Iraq's suppression of this rebellion caused the displacement of almost two million Kurds and led to an international intervention. The United States and its allies created a "safe haven" in northern Iraq and extended protection against Iraqi air raids. With tacit allied consent, Kurdish militia forces extended the area of the safe haven further southeast, including more Kurdish-inhabited districts (but not oil-rich Kirkuk and Khaniqin), into what gradually became a semi-independent Kurdish entity. In 1992 the Kurds held elections for a regional parliament and established a regional government, composed of the two major Kurdish parties. Relations between these partners rapidly deteriorated due to conflicts over control and scarce resources, leading to serious fighting between them—beginning in 1994 and continuing intermittently until 1998—and to a division of the region between the two parties, each now running its own regional government. U.S. efforts to impose a peace on the Kurds and thereby strengthen the anti-Saddam coalition were only moderately successful.

The long struggle of Iraq's Kurds has also had an impact on Kurds in neighboring countries and strengthened their nationalism. In Iran there had been, in the aftermath of World War II, a short-lived independent Kurdish republic centered around Mahabad. The central government, however, soon reasserted its authority and defeated the republic. Thereafter, the shah effectively suppressed all Kurdish political aspirations. In the year of the Iranian Revolution (1978–1979), however, Kurdish nationalism proved capable of mobilizing large masses; the demand for some form of autonomy, put forward by Kurdish leaders, appeared to be almost universally endorsed. As the Shi'i character of the new regime became increasingly apparent, this demand only grew stronger. Government attempts to reimpose central authority led to protracted guerrilla warfare, the Kurdish fighters initially operating from bases in Iran, and later from bases close to the Iraqi border. By the mid-1980s, the Kurdish resistance was reduced from a mass movement to a number of guerrilla bands carrying out hit-and-run raids. Iran's assassination of the most prominent Kurdish leaders—Ghassemlou was killed while negotiating with Iranian officials in Vienna in 1989—fatally weakened the Kurdish resistance. In the 1990s, there was a notable upsurge of Kurdish cultural activities, made possible by the changing climate in Iran. The Iranian reform movement found strong support among Kurds, who hoped to make ethnic rights part of the wider reform agenda.

In Turkey, where the very existence of the Kurds has long been denied, Kurdish demands were initially limited to recognition of the Kurdish language and culture and appeals for economic development of the Kurdish provinces. During the 1970s a new Kurdish awareness, first arising among the Kurds living in Turkey's large cities, spread across Kurdistan and developed into a rapidly radicalizing nationalism, including talk of independence. Kurdish parties and organizations, though illegal, brought entire districts more or less under their control. The Turkish military coup of 1980, fol-lowed by large-scale operations in the Kurdish provinces, cut short most of this Kurdish movement and ushered in a new period of forced assimilation. The military was challenged by the radical and extremely violent Workers Party of Kurdistan (PKK), which started a guerrilla war in 1984 and has since forced Turkish public opinion to admit, for the first time in history, that the country's Kurdish problem cannot be defined out of existence. Grassroots support for the PKK reached its peak in the early 1990s, but its efforts to make a transition from guerrilla struggle to legal politics and mass mobilization were largely unsuccessful as a result of effective repression. Much of the countryside was evacuated and thousands of villages were destroyed, cutting the guerrillas off from the population; a succession of legal pro-Kurdish parties were banned, and death squads decimated Kurdish civil society. In 1999, the PKK leader, Abdullah Öcalan, was captured and sentenced to death. The PKK renounced the armed struggle but maintained a significant force under arms in camps in Iraqi Kurdistan. Repeated Turkish military invasions in northern Iraq have failed to dislodge the PKK there.

(See also ARAB NATIONALISM; ETHNICITY; GUERRILLA WARFARE; INTERNATIONAL MIGRATION; KEMALISM.)

Martin van Bruinessen, *Agha, Shaikh and State: The Social and Political Structures of Kurdistan*, rev. ed. (London, 1992). Human Rights Watch/Middle East, *Iraq's Crime of Genocide: The Anfal Campaign against the Kurds* (New Haven, Conn., 1995). David McDowall, *A Modern History of the Kurds* (London, 1996).

MARTIN VAN BRUINESSEN

KUWAIT. Kuwait was founded in the early 1700s by an alliance of tribes that migrated from central Arabia to the northern Gulf. One extended family, the Al-Sabah, soon captured a predominant position in local politics; by the end of the eighteenth century, senior Al-Sabah sheikhs regularly succeeded one another as leaders of the community. Each ruler's power nevertheless remained severely limited by the rich merchants who provided goods and revenues vital to the Kuwaiti economy. Influential merchant families punished overly capricious or exploitative rulers by emigrating to other Gulf ports. Furthermore, Kuwait's rulers faced challenges throughout the nineteenth century from Ottoman governors based in Basra who wished to annex the town, as well as from the Al-Sa'ud's attempts to extend its control along the Gulf littoral and British efforts to reorganize regional trade. In 1899, Sheikh Mubarak bin Sabah signed a treaty with the British Political Resident in the Gulf binding "himself, his heirs and successors not to cede, sell, lease, mortgage, or give for occupation or for any other purpose any portion of his territory to the Government or subjects of any other Power without the previous consent of His Majesty's Government."

British backing, along with the oil revenues that began flowing into the central treasury in the years after World War II, enabled the Al-Sabah to consolidate its hold over Kuwaiti politics at the expense of the merchant community. During the 1950s, Sheikh Abdullah bin Salim eased the commercial elite out of a variety of administrative and consultative posts in the government. In return, the Al-Sabah earmarked funds for improvements to the port, expanded the national health and education systems, and subsidized the purchase and development of unused land around Kuwaiti citizens. Such programs created a wide range of mutual interests between the ruling family and the commercial elite, while dampening popular enthusiasm for *Arab nationalism.

With the end of the British protectorate in June 1961, the Kuwaiti regime promulgated a constitution that provided for a fifty-member elected National Assembly and a council of ministers appointed by the ruler (emir), who was also empowered to select the prime minister, dismiss the Assembly, and rule by decree whenever it was out of session. Parliamentary politics during the 1960s largely pitted a bloc of liberal nationalist deputies critical of the regime's pro-Western foreign policy and restrictive labor regulations against bedouin allies of the ruling family and a smaller number of representatives of the country's Shi'i minority. Government attempts to encourage parliamentary agitation in support of the *nationalization of the Kuwait Oil Company set the stage for hotly contested elections in 1975, which resulted in victory for a number of vocal opponents of the regime's economic and social policies. When it became evident in the late summer of 1976 that the critics enjoyed widespread support among poorer citizens and the press, the emir dismissed the National Assembly and introduced a more stringent press law.

Kuwait's indigenous Shi'i community responded to the *Iranian Revolution of 1978–1979 by organizing a series of mass meetings and demonstrations. The authorities countered by deporting a prominent Shi'i cleric with close ties to the Islamic Republic and expelling a large number of politically suspect expatriates. They then resurrected the National Assembly as a way of rallying support for the regime among Kuwaiti citizens. But the elections of February 1981 gave Sunni Islamists enough seats to dictate the agenda governing Assembly debates over the next four years, while Shi'i militants launched a wave of bombings and hijackings in an attempt to undermine the authority of the Al-Sabah. The ruling family turned to liberal nationalist and bedouin candidates as allies in the 1985 balloting, but the new Nasserist deputies soon joined forces with the Islamist opposition, and in July 1986 the cabinet asked the emir once again to dismiss the National Assembly on the grounds that its divisiveness threatened national security at a time when the *Iran-Iraq War was moving closer to the country's borders.

After the Assembly was dissolved, the ruling family and its rich merchant allies made greater use of the armed forces and security services to suppress the local Islamist movement. Shi'i military and police commanders were cashiered; Shi'i religious rituals and celebrations were increasingly circumscribed; surveillance was stepped up in Shi'i districts; and many longtime residents of the Kuwaiti Shi'a were deported to Iran. These policies drove the regime into closer collaboration with Iraq and the states of the Gulf Cooperation Council, and particularly enhanced ties between the Kuwaiti and Saudi security services. Militants loyal to the Islamic Republic responded by escalating their attacks against government offices and petroleum installations, at the same time that Iranian forces began targeting Kuwaiti oil tankers traversing the Gulf. The conjunction of these internal and external attacks caused government oil revenues to plummet, dramatically increasing the state's budget deficit. Consequently, the Kuwaiti leadership abandoned its traditional neutrality vis-à-vis the great powers and invited both the Soviet Union and the United States to escort its tankers past Iranian territory. This step aroused strong criticism in the local press, prompting the interior minister to announce in August 1987 that the government would refuse to grant bases to U.S. forces operating in the Gulf under any circumstances.

Throughout the winter and spring of 1990, prominent Kuwaitis called for the restoration of the National Assembly, petitioning the emir to abide by the terms of the 1962 Constitution and hold new elections. The ruler riposted by announcing the creation of a seventy-five-member National Council, one-third of whom would be appointed and charged with amending the rules governing parliamentary action and debate. Leaders of the former National Assembly immediately rejected this proposal and pledged to boycott elections to the new body; seven notable pro-Parliament activists were arrested in early May. The elections held the following month evidenced neither the enthusiastic popular participation desired by the regime nor the general abstention urged by the opposition. Confronted with domestic unrest and falling world oil prices, the government stepped up petroleum production as a way of paying for its economic and social programs. This move provoked threats from Iraq, whose leadership blamed their own economic troubles on Kuwait's failure to abide by the oil production quotas mandated by the *Organization of Petroleum Exporting Countries (OPEC). When negotiations between Kuwaiti and Iraqi officials collapsed at the end of July, the Iraqi army overran Kuwait.

In the aftermath of the Iraqi invasion, the prime minister hinted on several occasions that an elected Assembly would be restored as soon as the Al-Sabah regained control of Kuwait. He told a group of Kuwaiti notables in mid-October that "the people of Kuwait can only be rewarded for their trust and loyalty by further trust," and that women, who were ineligible to vote in earlier elections, could expect to "play a greater role in liberated Kuwait." Reformers welcomed these remarks but expressed concern over intimations from other cabinet members that martial law would be imposed on the country during the initial period following an Iraqi withdrawal. When the Al-Sabah returned to Kuwait in March 1991, a state of emergency was indeed declared, and the cabinet appointed in mid-April included no critics of the government. Parliamentary elections in October 1992 resulted in victory for an unprecedented number of Islamists and liberal reformers, who joined forces to castigate the government for both its handling of the crisis with Iraq and its management of oil and investment policy. The adoption of a bill mandating segregation between the genders on the campus of Kuwait University by 2001 tarnished the liberals, who lost out in the October 1996 balloting to representatives of tribes loyal to the ruling family.

(See also GULF STATES; GULF WAR; ISLAM; NASSERISM; SAUDI ARABIA.)

Jacqueline S. Ismael, *Kuwait: Social Change in Historical Perspective* (Syracuse, N.Y., 1982). Jill Crystal, *Oil and Politics in the Gulf: Rulers and Merchants in Kuwait and Qatar* (Cambridge, U.K., 1995).

FRED H. LAWSON

KYRGYZSTAN. See CENTRAL ASIA.

L

LABOR MOVEMENT. The term "labor movement" points in two directions. In its "union" sense it refers to efforts by wage workers in industrial societies to pursue collectively their interests at the workplace and in the labor market. Even when engaged in the most mundane of these concerns, however, unions have consistently run up against legal, ideological, and policy barriers which only self-conscious political organization, usually through labor-based parties, could confront. Labor movements, writ large, have thus acted in both market and political arenas. They have also traditionally constituted the major source of opposition to unrestrained free-market *capitalism.

The idea of individuals selling themselves on an open labor market at going market price is historically constructed, as are the legal prerogatives contained in notions of private property and contract, upon which this idea is premised. The rise and success of capitalism in Europe and elsewhere happened to workers with historical memories in which the effects of markets were limited by guilds, concepts such as "just prices," and notions of communal solidarity. The marketization of human life and labor which the new order brought was thus hard to accept. It was quite natural, therefore, for early wage workers to organize themselves to resist the full effect of capitalist labor markets. It was quite as natural for capitalists, armed with self-justifying liberal economic theories, to try and prevent them doing so successfully.

From the beginning collective actions by workers, often involving strikes, challenged employers not only on essential issues of remuneration, working conditions (including the length of the working day), and control over the organization of work, but also on issues of recognition of workers' rights to organize into unions. These attempts to confront the effects of capitalism attracted the attention of rebellious intellectuals. A persistent pattern of alliance was thus established between workers, their unions, and such intellectuals, who often gave theoretical voice to working-class concerns. In the nineteenth century, when neither the permanence nor the basic structures of market-based capitalist societies were clear, this alliance produced a wide range of creative reflection about alternative, and more humane, ways of organizing society, inspired by the writings of Robert Owen, Fourier, Blanqui, Bakunin, Lassalle, *Marx, Engels, and others. Various conceptualizations of socialism, which would become the characteristic *ideology of the labor movement, came from this alliance.

The labor movements which emerged from the crucible of capitalist industrialization varied between and within countries. The pattern and rate of industrialization and the ways in which it mobilized labor were critical factors creating different mixes of different types of workers. The political settings in which industrialization occurred, particularly whether workers were granted the vote or not, were also very important. The outcomes, clear by the early twentieth century, were national labor movements with generally similar concerns, but with great differences about how to approach these concerns. Specific movements might be united or divided, more or less centralized, dominated by craft or industrial unions, politically moderate or radical, or even apolitical in different ways—radical, anarcho-syndicalist in some parts of Europe, or "Gompersist" in the United States.

The nationalist fervor of World War I dashed hopes that labor movements would become an international "resistance front" to capitalism. Labor's terrain was clearly national. Nonetheless the development of a vision of capitalist society as structured into classes in which the working class was the central hope for progressive change was widespread, supported by libraries of intellectual argumentation. Most national labor movements, given *democracy and advancing industrialism, thus settled down in a quest to protect workers in the market and humanize capitalist societies through reformist political action, usually through social democratic parties.

In most cases, labor movements elaborated a multidimensional program. There should be fully institutionalized collective bargaining in the labor market and trade union rights in the workplace. Politically, capitalism should be democratized, often through public ownership of industry, increased state intervention and steering of the economy, plus the elaboration of a wide range of social policies to moderate harsh market outcomes. Most of these changes were to be achieved by the resolute use of national states to regulate and supplement the market.

There were important exceptions to this. Certain labor movements, the U.S. case being the most prominent, eschewed explicit party strategies to achieve their goals. In addition, large parts of the revolutionary branch of the labor movement affiliated with the Communist Third International following the 1917 Russian Revolution. This step involved the subordination of national movements to an international strategy coordinated, and very quickly, by Moscow. The Soviet Union's pursuit of brutal Stalinist economic modernization and "socialism in one country" beginning in the later 1920s transformed Soviet unions themselves into instruments for supplying docile labor for purposes decided by the party and bureaucratic center (a model exported to Eastern and Central Europe after 1945). Communist labor movements elsewhere then found themselves obliged to expend most of their resources in very costly efforts to support Soviet international purposes. The fundamental cleavages between Communists and Social Democrats internationally and within societies, particularly in Latin Europe, damaged labor movements almost everywhere.

The record of labor movement success in the interwar period was spotty. In a number of places, often following pitched battles—as in the Congress of Industrial Organizations campaign in the United States and the Popular Front in France—partial victories, particularly on the bargaining front, were achieved. But the devastating effects of the Great Depression of the 1930s in terms of unemployment and disrupted lives made labor action difficult. Moreover, the Social Democratic program, however reformist it had become, still struck fear into the hearts of the propertied and the conservative. Thus little was won in the political arena except in Scandinavia and, in very different ways, in *Roosevelt's *New Deal in the United States, where no Social Democratic Party existed. In societies where democracy itself had been but precariously established, antidemocratic opposition to labor gains, as in Weimar Germany, post-1918 Italy, and 1930s Spain, helped Nazism, Italian *Fascism, and other illiberal movements to come to power, subsequently to destroy labor movement autonomy and abolish labor parties.

The three decades after World War II, in contrast, were the high point of the labor movement's history. The progress of "Fordist" mass-production industry was favorable for union organization and collective bargaining success—"webs of rules" were woven in the workplace which consecrated worker and union rights, particularly in the area of job security, and avenues of appeal. The immediate aftermath of the war also coincided with a simultaneous advance of political democracy and pro-labor voting in a number of societies. In the flurry of reformism which followed, the *welfare state was greatly extended and instruments for broad state intervention in the economy were elaborated.

Many labor movements substantially and felicitously modified their programs in response to the Great Depression and wartime experiences. Labor thus embraced a vision of the "mixed economy." Private corporations, themselves willing to accept labor presence at firm level, pursued profits in a context of enhanced state economic steering of a Keynesian type to moderate the business cycle and achieve stable growth and full employment. The long postwar expansion transformed societies and individual lives, allowing the acquisition of a wide range of new consumer goods, extensive redistribution of profits into high wages, and, through taxation, social services such as health care, pensions, and education. In many places Social Democratic ideas about economic management and trade union ideas about the contractual organization of workplace life became hegemonic, and where unions, Socialist parties, and capitalist firms were able to strike harmonious "neocorporatist" arrangements, such as in Sweden and Austria, great advances were possible. For the first time it seemed that the benefits of a capitalist market system could be obtained without the worst of its costs.

The contemporary period, beginning with the two oil shocks of the 1970s and the widespread turn of governments to deflationary *monetarism in the 1980s, has brought a swift end to postwar trends. The internationalization of economic development has undercut the national premises of earlier approaches and moved the entire planet toward a single market for labor, products, and financial capital. There has also been a decisive shift to free market liberal and deregulatory economic ideologies according to which unions are sources of "rigidity" and state involvement in economies a major cause of inefficiency.

In this new context, governments, even Social Democratic ones with ties to union movements, have had to pursue more restrictive economic management, placing highest priority on a quest for international competitiveness for their national firms. Redistributing and achieving full employment have become secondary. From the point of view of firms, the capacity to change technologies, the organization of production, and product offerings rapidly in response to accelerated market fluctuations has become paramount. Given these new priorities of "flexibilization" firms have moved to decentralize collective bargaining, individualize its content, and, often, avoid dealing with unions altogether. This has undercut earlier trade union strength in the workplace and made it more difficult for unions to aggregate local concerns into a broader "labor movement" vision. Rising unemployment has also greatly weakened unions in both their market and political capacities.

These unfavorable policy and market movements coincide with important sociological changes. The share of "classical" industrial workers in national work forces has declined in the face of the growing importance of new middle-strata administrative and "intellectual" workers, female labor-market participation, and *underclass labor-market sectors often occupied by deprived minorities. The place of labor has thus been relativized. Simultaneously there have arisen new types of political expression among salaried new middle strata and the intelligentsia which have deprived the labor movement of allies, particularly among the intellectuals whose earlier help had been important.

At the millennium there seems but slim hope that the old labor movement can be reconstituted on new ground. The market capacities, mobilizational resources, and memberships of union movements have declined almost everywhere. Even where unions remain important, nowhere do they retain their earlier status. Where once they had been widely perceived as the core of progressive social and political projects, now more often than not they are regarded as *interest groups like any other. Social Democratic parties have attenuated their connections with unions and older outlooks in order to make new appeals to nonlabor constituents. Ideas about class and class conflict have disappeared from political discourses. Much of the earlier policy repertory of trade unions and labor parties has been jettisoned.

Labor movements became profoundly "nationalized" in the twentieth century. In the twenty-first century, as new areas of the planet enter the international economy, they must create international labor market and political ties. This will not be easy, since there exist profound conflicts of interest between prosperous workers in wealthy societies and poorer, less secure workers in developing areas. New approaches are needed. Labor movements still constitute the single largest associational groupings in most market societies, but their situation has changed dramatically. Labor has always had to respond to the challenges presented by expanding and changing markets. Responding to contemporary *globalization looks to be the most daunting such challenge in labor's history.

(See also AMERICAN FEDERATION OF LABOR AND CONGRESS OF INDUSTRIAL ORGANIZATIONS; CLASS AND CLASS POLITICS; CORPORATISM; FORDISM; NEW SOCIAL MOVEMENTS; SOCIALISM AND SOCIAL DEMOCRACY.)

Selig Perlman, *A Theory of the Labor Movement* (New York, 1928). David Brody, *Workers in Industrial America* (New York, 1980). Peter Lange, Maurizio Vannicelli, and George Ross, *Unions, Crisis and Change: French and Italian Unions in the Political Economy* (London, 1982). Richard Freeman and James Medoff, *What Do Unions Do?* (New York, 1984). Peter Gourevitch, Andrew Martin, and George Ross, *Unions and Crisis: Sweden, West Germany and the UK* (London, 1984). Gary Marks, *Unions in Politics* (Princeton, N.J., 1989). Frances Fox Piven, ed., *Labor Parties in Postindustrial Societies* (New York and Oxford, 1992). Anthony Ferner and Richard Hyman, *Industrial Relations in the New Europe* (Oxford, 1998). Andrew Martin and George Ross, eds., *The Brave New World of European Labor* (New York and Oxford, 1999).

GEORGE ROSS

LAND REFORM. The central idea of land reform—reflected in the rallying cry "land to the tiller"—is that the state will acquire agricultural land from landlords and plantation owners and transfer it to tenant farmers, agricultural laborers, and others who are landless. Land reform has been a highly important political and economic process during this century, with major land reforms carried out by at least twenty-five countries. Some of these reforms have followed communist *revolutions (as in the Soviet Union, the People's Republic of China, Cuba, and Vietnam); some have followed noncommunist revolutions (as in Mexico and Bolivia); and some have come in nonrevolutionary settings, such as the immediate postwar land reforms carried out with U.S. support by Japan, Taiwan, and the Republic of Korea (South Korea).

More recently, parallel problems of state divestiture and decollectivization of land that had been collectivized have loomed large for "second generation" land reforms in formerly (or still) communist countries, including Russia and China.

In the developing countries, land is still the principal source of livelihood, security, and status for a majority of the population, with six families out of ten engaged in agriculture. In a number of these countries, the issue of land ownership still looms large: over half a billion of the world's poorest and most powerless people still make their living from land they do not own. The more classic problem of insecure tenants and ill-paid agricultural laborers is still found in a score of countries, including India, Pakistan, Bangladesh, the Philippines, Indonesia, most of Central America, Brazil, Egypt, and South Africa. Such landlessness underlies a number of persisting problems. Farmers with insecure tenure and poor remuneration lack incentive to make long-term improvements to the land. Because of their low productivity and lack of purchasing power, the village economy stagnates. Aggrieved, landless *peasants have, moreover, provided rank-and-file support for a series of bloody twentieth-century revolutions, whose direct toll has been more than five million lives.

Landlessness is also related to high birthrates. Landless people face an insecure old age, for as their physical powers decline they are likely to be evicted from land they do not own. Many of their children die of hunger or disease, and female children have little prospect for schooling or jobs in the stagnant village economy. Where children are the only old-age security, these factors encourage bearing many children to ensure that some will survive to care for the parents. Finally, landlessness is implicated in both excessive urbanization and large-scale deforestation and erosion, as rootless and desperate people flee their traditional villages. Many parallel problems—especially low productivity, poverty, and disempowerment—once confronted the workers on collective farms. By far the largest of these state farming systems, that of China, was successfully broken up into small family farms in the early 1980s, but about 100 million people still live on collective farms in Russia and elsewhere.

Successful land-reform programs can reverse these processes:

- They provide aggrieved peasants an alternative to revolutionary violence (and also can be acceptable to many landlords, if accompanied by reasonable compensation for their land). Simultaneously, they help lay the groundwork for evolutionary democratic change as peasants endowed with increased security, status, and power within the village—freed from the "power domain" of the landlord, or the collective's director—participate with increasing effectiveness in the political life of their community and in voicing demands on the central government.
- They sharply increase agricultural productivity, as peasants assured of long-term rights to individual land holdings introduce irrigation and other capital improvements. Such prosperous small farmers become, in turn, the buyers of a wide range of locally produced goods and services (brick houses, clothes, radios, health care, and schooling), helping to create many new nonagricultural jobs. Indeed, ex-landlords can invest their compensation in the new enterprises.
- With increased prosperity and better nutrition, health care, and schooling, the stage is set for the "demographic transition": a steep decline in infant and child death rates is followed by an even larger decline in the number of births. Taiwan and South Korea, a generation after land reform, have achieved low infant mortality and birth rates comparable to those of the United States.
- Meanwhile, secure on their own land, families are far less likely to part for the city or push desperately onto marginal forest lands.

Yet the industrial democracies have supported land reforms only sporadically. Sometimes a crisis situation (South Vietnam in 1970, El Salvador in 1980) has galvanized tardy U.S. support as an alternative to radical revolution. A default solution is then to focus on industrial development, pretending that agriculture and the rural poor can be ignored. At other times (Russia and South Africa in the 1990s) support for land reform has not been matched with adequate foreign aid, and even where there have been enough resources (Egypt in the 1990s) bureaucracies have been reluctant to weigh in on the controversial issue of redistributive land reform.

(See also COLLECTIVIZATION; DEMOCRATIC TRANSITIONS; DEVELOPMENT AND UNDERDEVELOPMENT; ENVIRONMENTAL-ISM; FOOD POLITICS; POPULATION POLICY; RURAL DEVELOPMENT; WOMEN AND DEVELOPMENT.)

Roy L. Prosterman and Jeffrey M. Riedinger, *Land Reform and Democratic Development* (Baltimore, 1987). Gene Wunderlich, ed., *Agricultural Landownership in Transitional Economics* (Lanham, MD., 1995).

ROY L. PROSTERMAN

LANGUAGE POLICY. Like all other public policy making, language policy, defined as government choices of language form and function, is the result of perception of problems and the organization of interests with demands for government action. Supporters believe that communication problems of classes, ethnic groups, newly independent states, genders, age categories, or regions can be resolved by a language policy such as a mass literacy campaign, bilingual or immersion language education, officialization of one or more languages, translations, and symbolic recognition as a national language. Ideologies of liberation, equality, social change, *democracy, nationalism, *pluralism or group-based diversity and revolution transform demands to solve narrowly defined communication problems into a program to change the society and political system.

In democracies, well-organized minority groups have demanded language policies which would add new functions for their languages. In response to Spanish speakers' interests the U.S. Congress passed the Bilingual Education Act of 1968, thus adding a new function—medium of instruction—for Spanish. Canada implemented French-English bilingual services through the Official Languages Act of 1967 in response to French speakers' demands; Catalan became an official language in a democratic post-Franco Spain.

Countries which achieved political independence this century have had a somewhat different agenda; they have used language to consolidate new national identities and to facilitate access to power and wealth by groups previously excluded because they did not speak or read the official colonial language. Tanzania's government officialized Swahili, meaning that it became the medium for written government business and education; Israel chose Hebrew rather than English; Hindi is co-official in India with English; Egypt, Morocco and Algeria chose Arabic rather than English or French; Officialization of Latvian in the newly independent Latvia excluded Russian in private enterprise as well as in government communication.

No matter what the regime or the historical moment, language policy cannot succeed without language planning, systematic implementation of authoritative choices over time. Planning of any kind requires the appointment of government agents, annual budget requests to support their innovations, evaluation and active support by the interest groups who wanted the policy in the first place. The Académie Française, the Academy for the Hebrew Language in Israel, the Office de la Langue Française in Quebec, the Turkish Language Society, the Office of Bilingual Education and Minority Languages Affairs, created in 1974 by the U.S. Congress, are among the almost 150 language planning agencies in the world.

Legislators, judges, and heads of state enunciate a choice of language function and leave implementation to planners.

When Indonesia's leaders chose Bahasa as their official language—a choice of function—the planners took charge of the modernization of the lexicon or vocabulary and the standardization of spelling—choices of form—in order that the language could serve its new communication functions. Depending on how much authority the government gives them, the planners can control the use of language by printers, the media, government publications, and by private enterprise (contracts and advertising, for example). All these choices have political and economic consequences.

One consequence is a change in the pattern of development and modernization. Mustafa Kemal, the founder of modern Turkey, used language policy to further his ideal of a modern and secular nation. After deciding that spoken Turkish would serve as the basis of the written official language, he changed its form by ordering the adoption of the Latin or Roman script in place of the previously used Arabic script; he insisted on lexical borrowings from German, French and English instead of Arabic. His purpose was to draw a unified Turkey closer to western Europe as a way to modernize and to secularize the society.

Language policy can also help change patterns of participation in power, wealth and status: officialization of a previously unrecognized language spoken by the masses such as Bengali in Bangladesh should open up the political system to the uneducated, i.e., those who cannot read and speak English or Urdu. It should facilitate access to jobs which no longer require skill in a foreign language; and it gives prestige to popular culture by publicly recognizing the dignity of its medium of expression. Planners in Norway, Tamil Nadu in India, and Greece developed the spoken language as a standard or tried to bring the literary and spoken languages together to facilitate communication by the less educated masses. Such a language policy promotes democracy and *social mobility.

Language policy can also serve international political goals. The best-known movement has been Francophonie, a network of educational institutions, professional organizations, government officials, and literary groups directed by French-speaking elites in France, Quebec, Belgium, Senegal, Lebanon, Haiti, and elsewhere. They cooperate to maintain and diffuse a standard international French while facilitating economic and political cooperation among states using French.

Not everyone accepts language policies and plans, and conflict may be the result. Promotion of Sinhala in Sri Lanka, starting in 1956 with the "Official Language Act," sparked the revolt of the Tamil minority which feared loss of jobs, power and prestige. Shortly after Algeria excluded both French and Berber from public life in July 1998 the Kabylia or Berber-speaking area erupted in violence. Russian speakers in the Baltic states of Estonia, Latvia, and Lithuania, accustomed to the best jobs and prestige during the days of the USSR, have reacted strongly to the imposition of new official languages. After thirty years of bilingual education in California opponents convinced voters to support Proposition 227 in 1998, thus ending mandatory teaching in languages other than English.

Any government policy responding to well-organized interests can spark a reaction and an opposition. Since language also evolves organically and due to the innovations of great writers or "language strategists," as Brian Weinstein has written in *The Civic Tongue* (New York, 1983), a case may be made against language policy. However, because democracies try to solve the problems of their societies, language policy will always be one of their potential resources.

(See also ETHNICITY; PUBLIC POLICY.)

Robert L. Cooper, *Language Planning and Social Change* (Cambridge, U.K., 1989). Brian Weinstein, ed., *Language Policy and Political Development* (Norwood, N.J., 1990). Bernard Spolsky, *Sociolinguistics.* Oxford Introductions to Language Study (Oxford, U.K., 1998).

BRIAN WEINSTEIN

LAOS. The Lao People's Democratic Republic (LPDR) was proclaimed on 2 December 1975, thus putting an end to the 600-year-old monarchy. This landlocked nation of 3.5 million people, sandwiched between China to the north, Burma and Thailand to the west, Cambodia to the south, and Vietnam to the east, was proclaimed a French protectorate in 1893. It regained its independence sixty years later, only to be torn by a drawn-out civil war pitting the Pathet Lao, a Marxist revolutionary movement, against the Royal Lao government. The victorious Pathet Lao established an orthodox, Marxist-Leninist, *communist party state directed by the Lao People's Revolutionary Party (LPRP). Up to an estimated 90 percent of the small, educated middle class not undergoing political reeducation subsequently fled the country.

Under the terms of the constitution promulgated in August 1991, political power remains the monopoly of the governing party. At the apex stands the Political Bureau of the Central Committee, which is elected by and answerable to the Party Congress. Delegates to both organs reflect regional and ethnic divisions, which, more than class or ideology, determine political outcomes.

The 1991 Constitution enhanced the powers of both the state president and the National Assembly, the supreme popularly elected legislature, which meets twice a year during its five-year term. The prime minister is appointed by the state president, but the government, which consists of some twenty ministries and state committees with ministry status, is answerable to the National Assembly. Considerable overlap exists between the top echelons of the party and government, which makes any clear definition of party-state relations an impossibility. Of the mass organizations that play a significant political role, the most important is the Lao Front for National Construction. Although Laos is still predominantly a Buddhist country, the Lao United Buddhists Association exerts virtually no political influence.

Regionalism in Laos results in a larger degree of political and economic decentralization than is usual in a communist party state. This is exacerbated by divisions between over sixty ethnically distinct "nationalities," grouped into the politically and culturally dominant lowland Lao and their upland Tai cousins (66 percent of the population); the mountain-dwelling hill tribes, who broadly supported the revolutionary movement (22 percent); and the opium-growing Hmong (Meo), most of whom opposed it (12 percent). Whereas the political influence of the hill tribes is strong in the more mountainous, poorer provinces, they are underrepresented in the central government and upper echelons of the party.

Political change has occurred since 1975 as a result of both internal and external pressures, including poor economic performance, the inability of the socialist bloc to meet Lao requirements for aid and investment, and improved relations within the region. Anticommunist insurgents now pose no threat to the survival of the regime.

Following Pathet Lao seizure of power, the small industrial sector was nationalized, the market for goods and services closely regulated, and a program of agricultural *collectivization initiated. Stiffening peasant opposition and plummeting production forced suspension of *collectivization in 1979. Relaxation of orthodox socialist policies followed as the government launched the country's first five-year plan (in January 1981). Although plan targets remained unmet, economic performance did improve sufficiently for moderates within the LPRP to push for further reforms during the second five-year plan. Since 1988, Laos has actively solicited foreign, particularly Thai, investment in timber, manufacturing, power generation, and tourism, while reprivatizing a number of nationalized enterprises.

The wartime dependence of the Pathet Lao on Vietnamese communist support continued after 1975 with the signing of a twenty-five-year Treaty of Friendship and Cooperation. Though relations with Vietnam remain close, the Treaty is unlikely to be renewed as in July 1997 both countries joined the Association of Southeast Asian Nations (ASEAN).

With the collapse of the Soviet Union, Laos has received *foreign aid mainly from Japan, Sweden, Australia, and France. Relations have also much improved with Thailand, China, and the United States. Thus, Laos has reverted to something approaching its traditional role in mainland Southeast Asia—an impoverished buffer state between Thailand and Vietnam concerned to obtain maximum levels of economic aid from any country willing to assist.

(See also BUDDHISM; COMMAND ECONOMY; VIETNAM WAR.)

Martin Stuart-Fox, *Buddhist Kingdom, Marxist State: The Making of Modern Laos* (Bangkok, 1996). Martin Stuart-Fox, *A History of Laos* (Cambridge, U.K., 1997). Grant Evans, *The Politics of Ritual and Remembrance: Laos since 1975* (Chiang Mai, Thailand, 1998).

MARTIN STUART-FOX

LATIN AMERICAN AND CARIBBEAN REGIONAL ORGANIZATIONS. Two main types of Latin American and Caribbean regional organizations have evolved: those promoting economic integration and those purporting to coordinate regional responses to particular problems. Among the former, the most important organizations have been the Latin American Free Trade Association (which evolved into the present Latin American Integration Association, LAIA), the Andean Group, the Central American Common Market (CACM), the Caribbean Community (CARICOM), the Organization of Eastern Caribbean States (OECS), the Common Market of the South (MERCOSUR), and the Association of Eastern Caribbean States (ACS). The latter include the Latin American Economic System (SELA) and the Rio Group, the most significant of a number of entities.

After World War II, regional integration was largely stimulated by the UN *Economic Commission for Latin America and the Caribbean, which saw regional or subregional integration as a way to resolve the problems of small markets. Organizations began to be formed in the 1960s that initially enjoyed some success in eliminating tariff barriers and increasing the volume of trade, but a number of problems worked against integration as envisioned by their charters. Common difficulties stemmed from disparities in the nature of differing national economies. The benefits of increased trade and industrial growth were not shared equally by member states, and competing interests of the large, medium, and small economies inhibited mutually satisfactory equalization policies. The planned distribution of industrial production was particularly unsuccessful. Other problems occurred when products imported from other members were more expensive than, or inferior in quality to, similar products formerly imported from outside the region. In addition, national rivalries, long-standing boundary and territorial disputes, and changing governments with opposing policy orientations complicated cooperation.

Latin American and Caribbean integration has also been marked by recent positive elements on which future developments may be based. A more cooperative intra–Latin American climate, and specific support for integration measures, was created by the departure of military regimes and redemocratization in much of the region in the 1980s. The concept of economic integration was expanded to the entire continent in June 1990, when President George *Bush proposed his Enterprise for the Americas Initiative, to be followed by the North American Free Trade Agreement (*NAFTA), which went into effect in January 1994. The hemispheric movement, however, moved slowly over the next five years.

Although the second type of Latin American regional organizations—those designed to coordinate regional response—also began in the 1960s, they increased in importance after the mid-1970s and took on new significance with the end of the Cold War. They have been largely based on the assumption that Latin American states will be more influential in the *international system if they adopt common positions and a united stance toward the rest of the world. Such efforts were seen as a parallel to economic integration; in the 1980s, they increasingly discussed prospects for some kind of political integration as well. The first transregional endeavor came in 1964 when most Latin American states joined the Special Latin American Coordinating Committee (CECLA). Although no formal agreement was signed or organizational apparatus created, CECLA periodically convened as a regional caucusing group before the *United Nations Conference on Trade and Development (UNCTAD) or other international meetings.

CECLA was superseded as the Latin American regional caucus by the Latin American Economic System (SELA), as part of the latter's broader agenda. In 1975, twenty-three states signed a charter establishing SELA, with a permanent secretariat located in Caracas; three new Caribbean states later joined. SELA's organizational structure is simple: a council of ministers meets at least once annually, with the power to appoint ad hoc action committees; and a permanent secretariat provides operational support and conducts staff studies. SELA has been active in a number of areas. It urge supports economic integration although it is not an integration scheme itself and does not propose to be one. It has put forward proposals to resolve the debt crisis, and it has done many studies on trade relations and capital flows between Latin America and the United States, Europe, and Japan.

Attempts to mediate conflicts in Central America led to a new and important multipurpose regional association that extended its agenda to include a number of seminal international issues. In December 1986, the foreign ministers of the eight countries involved in the Contadora and Support Group states met in Rio de Janeiro and adopted a declaration creating the Permanent Mechanism of Consultation and Political Coordination, known as the Rio Group and, for a time, as the Group of Eight (until the membership expanded). The declaration said that, based on their previous experience of joint action in the Contadora process, they had decided to strengthen and systematize their political coordination through regular consultation on topics of common interest. The declaration provided for regular meetings of foreign ministers. In addition, annual summit meetings of heads of state were begun in November 1987, and regular conferences of finance ministers were instituted in December 1988. In June 1988, representatives from SELA, the Inter-American Development Bank, the UN Economic Commission for Latin America and the Caribbean, and the Latin American Integration Association were invited to participate in the foreign ministers' meetings. By the mid-1990s the group's membership consisted of almost all of the sovereign Latin American and Caribbean states.

Rio Group purposes have evolved to include efforts (1) to strengthen Latin American democracy through sustained economic and social development and regional cooperation and integration; (2) to continue discussion of all aspects of the Central American crisis and to reiterate support for the peace plan initiated by President Oscar *Arias of Costa Rica known as the Esquipulas agreements (until that process was completed); (3) to prefer negotiated agreements with external creditors over a collective moratorium or "debtors' cartel" and to suggest specific measures; (4) to call attention to the problem of an unstable international financial system and the need to create a free and fair international trading system; (5) to work toward a Latin American common market, with full awareness to reform existing integration schemes; (6) to cooperate for disarmament and scientific, technical, cultural, and educational interchange, and to deal jointly with problems of clandestine arms trade, *terrorism, drug trafficking, and environmental degradation; and (7) to promote discussions with other nations and intergovernmental organizations in a climate of goodwill (of particular interest was the formal institution of an annual meeting of Rio Group and European Union foreign ministers).

(See also DEMOCRATIC TRANSITIONS; ENVIRONMENTALISM; INTERNATIONAL DEBT.)

Sidney Weintraub, ed., "Free Trade in the Western Hemisphere," *Annals of the American Academy of Political and Social Science* 526 (March 1993). G. Pope Atkins, "Latin American Integration and Association," chap. 7 in *Latin American and the Caribbean in the International System,* 4th ed. (Boulder, Colo., 1999).

G. POPE ATKINS

LATIN AMERICAN FREE TRADE ASSOCIATION. See LATIN AMERICAN AND CARIBBEAN REGIONAL ORGANIZATIONS.

LATINOS. See HISPANIC AMERICANS.

LATVIA. See BALTIC STATES.

LAW OF THE SEA. Humans have long used the oceans for transportation, resources extraction, recreation, and dumping; only in the last few years has their full biological and climatological significance begun to be appreciated. The law of the sea, the treaty-based and customary international rules regulating marine activities and apportioning supervisory authority over ocean users, reflects a balancing of the interests of maritime and coastal states and of the different groups of ocean users.

The "traditional law of the sea," developed primarily among the European powers in the seventeenth through nineteenth centuries, secured this balance by dividing the oceans into two zones. The waters and seabed within three nautical miles of shore formed the territorial sea, where coastal state authority was limited only by foreign ships' right of innocent passage. Beyond that limit lay the high seas, equally open to the ships of all states for navigation, fishing, and fighting. These rules remained stable as long as fish, then the main exploitable ocean resource, remained plentiful enough to be treated as a common pool resource open to all. Since navigation also flourished best under an open access rule and fishers and navigators could easily accommodate one another, ocean users had few conflicts; the main concern was balancing coastal state concerns for security against seaborne attack with mariners' desire to range the seas at will.

By the mid-twentieth century, increasing exploitation of ocean resources was straining the balance of interests supporting the traditional rules. Larger fishing fleets equipped with improved gear caused notable depletion of fish stocks in many areas. By 1940 it was possible to exploit oil and gas deposits lying in the subsoil under shallow waters, and in succeeding decades wells spread to the edges of the continental margin and into areas of severe conditions like the North Sea. By 1965 new mining technology inspired expectations of exploiting the "manganese nodules" and metallic crusts of the deep ocean floor. Increased interest in the coasts and oceans as recreational sites and the growing awareness of environmental matters developing in nearly all countries during the 1970s added protecting the marine environment to the long list of ocean issues.

The politics of ocean issues also became more complex. The League of Nations and then the United Nations altered the lawmaking process by institutionalizing the practices of multilateral conference diplomacy. These gave the increasing number of small coastal states additional weight in the negotiating process and made it harder for the great powers to guide the law of the sea's evolution among themselves. Individuals and firms engaged in ocean resource exploitation became increasingly powerful lobbies in favor of extending national control over portions of the ocean even in some of the traditional maritime states. Owners of offshore oil or gas platforms believed that only governments could provide the strong protection of property rights they needed to make their large investments in fixed assets while local fishing communities faced with new competition from distant water fleets wanted their rivals kept away from the stocks they fished. Shipping and naval circles thus faced far stronger competition for influence over maritime policy than ever before.

The mid-twentieth-century international negotiations, whether bilateral controversies over particular coastal states' efforts to assert control over fishing and other resource exploitation or the partly successful First (1958), abortive Second (1960), and extended Third (1973–1982) UN Conferences on the Law of the Sea, produced a fundamental reordering of the law of the sea. The binary division into territorial sea under almost complete coastal state control and high seas used by all under supervision by their flag state was replaced by a more complex set of zones with different mixes of coastal and flag state authority. The process began in the mid- to late 1940s when Venezuela, the United Kingdom, and the United States claimed jurisdiction over continental shelf mineral and hydrocarbon exploitation and some Latin American states then claimed control over all fishing within 200 miles of shore. The continental shelf claims did not impinge much on navigation or fishing, and were emulated by so many states that coastal state control over continental shelf resources was customary law by 1958. The fisheries claims were hotly contested because they appeared to threaten not only traditional fishing practices but also navigation, oceanographic research, and naval mobility.

The results of the First UN Conference foreshadowed the general direction of development by consolidating one and accepting two new zonal concepts. Though insisting that stocks further out should be managed by international commissions including both coastal and fishing states, the major maritime powers did accept exclusive fishing zones extending no more than twelve nautical miles from shore. Participants acknowledged the new concerns created by widespread private possession of fast motor vessels in agreeing that coastal states should have the right to enforce customs, fiscal, immigration, and sanitary regulations anywhere within twelve miles of shore. Yet the thorny issue of whether the territorial sea should be extended that far, or the three- to twelve-mile belt covered by the concept of a contiguous zone limiting control to those purposes, went unresolved in 1958 and 1960.

The Third UN Conference agreed to divide the oceans into six main zones. Four permit varying degrees of coastal state control over ocean uses: territorial seas extending twelve nautical miles from shore, contiguous zones extending an additional twelve miles, exclusive economic zones (EEZs) entailing jurisdiction over resource exploitation in the water column as far as 200 nautical miles from shore, and continental shelves extending at least 200 miles but up to 350 where the geological continental margin is broader. Expansion of the territorial sea was accompanied by some assurances for navigators, including a new regime of transit passage in straits that would otherwise be closed. Acceptance of the EEZ allowed coastal states to assert exclusive rights over fish stocks, triggering a major reallocation of fishing rights because some 90 percent of world fish catch was taken in these areas. In sum, authority to decide many ocean resource issues was given to individual coastal states.

Deep seabed and high seas resource issues have taken longer to resolve. The deep seabed discussions began with Malta's 1967 proposal to treat that area as the "common heritage of mankind" and became an extended South-North confrontation over the terms and powers of the projected International Seabed Authority (ISA). *Third World governments, seeking a precedent for organizing the world economy on an intergovernmental rather than a market basis as much as direct material benefits, wanted mining monopolized by a strong ISA operating under one state–one vote, simple majority decision-making rules. Industrial state opposition forced a retreat to qualified majorities giving them a veto over major decisions and a "parallel system" allowing state-owned or private firms licensed by the ISA to do half of the mining. Continued opposition, particularly from the United States, and additional Third World concessions inspired by the receding of prospects for profitable seabed mining and a shift towards more market-oriented economic policies, led to additional changes of ISA decision rules and mining guidelines in the 1994 Agreement on Seabed Mining. Continuing disputes about high seas fishing, affecting stocks subject to catch limits inside an adjacent EEZ, inspired efforts to win agreement from flag states that they would not allow their fleets to undermine conservation programs.

Though formal acceptance of the 1982 Convention was delayed until November 1994 by the seabed mining impasse, many of its provisions were followed so widely that they became customary law. Entry into force means that the other parts, including the innovative dispute resolution clauses, now bind the approximately 100 signatories. However, the 1982 Convention marks only the start of the process of revising the law of the sea to meet contemporary needs. More than two-thirds of the world's population lives within 100 kilometers of a coastline, straining the oceans' potential as recreation site and waste dump. With continuing overcapacity in fishing, more than half of the world's major fish stocks are depleted or at the edge of depletion and fish farming is becoming an ever more important source of food for the world's growing population. Greater awareness of how seriously land runoff, atmospheric pollution, and ocean activities affect the seas has led to demands for tighter restrictions on and greater action against polluters. Interstate disputes over remote island groups newly valuable as the basis for asserting control over hydrocarbons or fishing grounds have led to armed incidents. In all these areas the law of the sea requires and is receiving additional elaboration.

(See also ENVIRONMENTALISM; INTERNATIONAL LAW; NORTH-SOUTH RELATIONS.)

D. H. Cushing, *Population Production and Regulation in the Sea* (Cambridge U.K., 1995). Michael Weber and Judith Gradwohl, *The Wealth of Oceans* (1995). Lawrence Juda, *International Law and Ocean Use Management* (London and New York, 1996).

M. J. PETERSON

LE PEN, Jean-Marie. Jean-Marie Le Pen was born on 28 June 1928 in La Trinité-sur-Mer in Brittany, a fishing and farming region in northwest *France. After graduating from a Jesuit high school, Le Pen enrolled in the Paris Law Faculty in 1947. In 1953, he joined the Foreign Legion serving in France's colonies in Indochina as editor of the Legion's journal and, in 1956–1957, in *Algeria as an intelligence officer. In January 1956, running as a Poujadist, the twenty-seven-year-old Le Pen became the youngest deputy in the French National Assembly and earned a reputation as one of its foremost orators. He lost his seat in 1962. In a life devoted almost entirely to politics, he held national office for only six years.

During the 1950s and 1960s, the French extreme *right was nostalgic for the collaborationist and authoritarian Vichy regime of *World War II and violently opposed to granting Algeria its independence. Its political doctrine was characterized by *anti-Semitism, racism, and a deep-seated hostility to

*parliamentary democracy. However, Le Pen realized that these ideas were inappropriate to changed political circumstances. The ability of the Fifth Republic to withstand the tensions of the *Algerian War of Independence and to survive President Charles de *Gaulle's 1969 resignation from office demonstrated enormous popular support for democracy and the futility of extreme right attacks on the Republic. During the famous *May 1968 nationwide strike, the success of middle-class Parisian students in using dramatic slogans to spread their antiauthoritarian message to all classes of the French population demonstrated to Le Pen that success in politics was not determined exclusively by numbers, but by one's ability to win what was later called the "vocabulary battle." And continuing revelations about the active role that Vichy had played in the early 1940s by sending Jews to German concentration camps made overt expressions of anti-Semitism a political liability.

But the various factions of the extreme right seemed unaware of these changes in French political culture, and they continued during the 1960s to indulge their penchant for extremist doctrine, street fighting, and violent demonstrations. Le Pen worked against this, endeavoring to convince extreme right leaders that the route to electoral success lay in adopting a pacific image and playing by the rules of the democratic game. October 1972 saw his efforts crowned with success with the establishment of the National Front (NF) and his election as president of the new organization. However, it was not until the NF ran an anti-immigrant campaign in 1983 and elected four city councillors in the small city of Dreux that the party caught national attention. From that point on, the Front began to win between 10 and 15 percent of the vote in French and European elections. Le Pen himself won 14.4 percent of the vote in the 1988 presidential election, and 15 percent, or 4.5 million votes, in the 1995 presidential election.

Le Pen's success in the 1980s and 1990s was due to a number of factors. Le Pen argued that reducing the number of immigrants would cut down on unemployment, crime, and other social problems. By immigrants, Le Pen meant Arab North African as well as black African workers, many of whom had flocked to France from its former colonies in the 1950s and from Algeria after it achieved independence in 1962. While a minority of Front supporters were motivated by xenophobia and racism, others turned to the party because they agreed with Le Pen's linking immigration to unemployment. Still others supported the Front out of disgust with government corruption scandals in the 1980s and 1990s. Le Pen also posed as the only politician who "said out loud what everyone thinks," calling for immigrants to be excluded from France's generous public housing and welfare system. Finally, he ensured continued support from diehard extreme rightists by regularly making coded anti-Semitic remarks, such as his notorious assertion that the German gas chambers were only a "detail" of World War II.

Le Pen's accomplishment was to create a major political party out of disparate extreme right elements and to focus public attention on France's immigration policy. Indeed, by the 1990s, the mainstream parties reacted to the Front's anti-immigrant message by imposing tighter controls on immigration, implementing fast-track procedures to deport illegal immigrants, and increasing the number of police and security personnel. Elsewhere in Europe, and especially in Germany, extreme right parties borrowed Le Pen's anti-immigrant arguments and slogans to use in their own election campaigns. And extreme right parties everywhere copied Le Pen's style of couching anti-Semitic, racist, and antiparliamentary messages in a coded, allusive, and ambiguous language.

However, in January 1997, Le Pen's greatest achievement, the unification of the extreme right under the banner of the National Front, fell apart. Tired of Le Pen's autocratic party rule, critical of Le Pen's refusal to moderate the party's public image or to establish links with the mainstream right, Bruno Mégret, the Front's second-in-command, led a large number of party members and leaders out of the NF and established a competing organization, the National Front-National Movement. Today, there are in France two National Fronts; one led by Le Pen, the other by Mégret.

The result of the split has been to call into question Le Pen's life's work. Although his domination of the original National Front is, for now at least, uncontested, Le Pen's days as the dominant figure on the French extreme right are numbered. He is over seventy years old, his charisma has been tarnished by his tendency toward verbal and, occasionally, physical violence, and his leadership will be severely tested by the challenge from the breakaway faction led by Mégret. Only history will decide whether Le Pen's legacy will be the rebirth of a viable political party of the extreme right or a political movement which, torn apart by quarreling and factionalization, spirals downward toward ineffectiveness.

(See also DECOLONIZATION; INTERNATIONAL MIGRATION; RACE AND RACISM.)

Jonathan Marcus, *The National Front and French Politics* (London, 1995). Harvey G. Simmons, *The French National Front* (Boulder, Colo., 1996).

HARVEY G. SIMMONS

LEAGUE OF NATIONS. The covenant of the League of Nations, the first permanent international organization charged with the task of preserving international *peace and *security, was drafted during the Paris Peace Conference in 1919, primarily under the influence of President Woodrow Wilson of the United States, Robert Cecil of Great Britain, and the French diplomat Léon Bourgeois. The core of the new covenant was Article 10, under which the members agreed to preserve each other's territorial integrity and political independence against external aggression. Articles 11 through 16 defined procedures for resolving international conflicts. All states were obligated to submit their conflicts to arbitration, judicial settlement, or to the League Council which could investigate, conciliate, and recommend terms of settlement. If the council unanimously recommended a course of action or terms of settlement, the parties could not subsequently use armed force. If there was no unanimity, then the parties could go to *war following a three-month cooling-off period. In the event that a state used armed force contrary to the procedures and prohibitions contained in the covenant, member states were obliged to employ economic *sanctions. The league could only recommend military sanctions.

The League of Nations comprised an assembly, to which all members belonged, and a council of permanent members (initially Britain, France, Italy, and Japan) and four (expanded to eleven by 1936) non-Great Powers elected for set terms by the assembly. The assembly in 1920 established the Permanent Court of International Justice, a legal body to which certain kinds of disputes could be referred for decision or advisory opinions.

The U.S. Senate did not approve the Treaty of Versailles, in which the covenant was embedded, so the United States remained outside the organization. Germany was admitted as a permanent member of the council in 1926, and the Soviet Union in 1934. In 1935, Japan and Germany withdrew from the organization. Throughout most of its history, the league contained no more than four of the seven Great Powers.

The League of Nations broke radically from eighteenth-century and nineteenth-century international practices. The idea of mutual guarantees and the statement (Article 11) that any use of armed force was a matter of concern to all members contravened the old principle of neutrality. The covenant also undermined the principle of a sovereign's right to employ force. War was not outlawed, but its legitimacy became highly circumscribed. Finally, the league inaugurated the idea of collective economic sanctions.

The league was unable to take effective measures against Japanese, Italian, German, and Soviet aggression between 1931 and 1939. It could deal with situations where the parties to a conflict generally wanted to avoid war, and where the obligations under Article 10 were taken seriously. The aggressive powers of the late 1930s had purposes that were fundamentally incompatible with the core ideas in the covenant.

Despite these shortcomings, the league's organs did consider sixty-six disputes and conflicts between 1920 and 1939. Twenty were referred to other agencies. Eleven cases involved conquest contrary to league principles and procedures. But in the remaining thirty-five cases (76 percent), league procedures, recommendations, and decisions resulted in compromise outcomes. This level of achievement is substantially higher than the record of the UN since 1945. The organization employed plebiscites, mediation, conciliation, and fact-finding to fashion settlements in conflicts among its members. Economic sanctions collectively employed against Italy for its attack on Ethiopia in 1935–1936 were the first on behalf of the international community, and they almost worked.

The League of Nations also supervised the fast-growing network of private transactions between societies. It established or incorporated bureaus and committees dealing with disease, communications, traffic in arms, slavery, drugs, and conditions and protection of labor, women, and children. The specialized agencies collected statistics, disseminated information, sponsored conferences, and placed pressure on governments to observe international conventions or upgrade their domestic legislation on these issues. The league organized a mandates system, under which Imperial Germany's overseas colonies were administered by some of the *World War I victors. The mandatory powers were held responsible for promoting "the well-being and development" of the local populations. The league had a right to monitor the performance of this "trust." The covenant implied that the ultimate goal of the tutelary relationship was to educate the colonial peoples to political independence.

Governments and league officials debated during *World War II whether to reform the league or to launch a new international organization. The United States and the Soviet Union decided the debate in favor of creating a new *United Nations. Although some league committees continued to function during the war, in the security field the league ceased to operate in 1941. It was formally disbanded in April 1946.

(See also FORCE, USE OF; INTERNATIONAL LAW.)

Alfred Zimmern, *The League of Nations and the Rule of Law* (London, 1936). F. P. Walters, *History of the League of Nations*, 2 vols. (London, 1952).

KALEVI J. HOLSTI

LEBANON. During four centuries of Ottoman rule (1516–1918), the term "Lebanon" referred to a vaguely defined region centered on the Mount Lebanon range, near the eastern Mediterranean coast. The region's main inhabitants were Maronite Christians, as well as adherents of an offshoot of Islam known as Druze.

After World War I, France gained control of the area. In 1920, it created the state of Lebanon, with today's boundaries, by adding to Mount Lebanon various adjacent regions, inhabited mainly by Sunni and Shii Muslims and by various Christian groups, notably Greek Orthodox and Greek Catholics.

France ruled Lebanon through a system known as "confessionalism," which posts religious seats in parliament, cabinet offices, and civil service on the basis of religious affiliation. This colonial system gave preeminence to the Maronites, Lebanon's largest single religious community at that time, who had long-standing religious and economic ties to France. The system ensured that the country's various Christian communities (then a majority of the population) controlled the political system, disadvantaging the Muslims.

The Lebanese increasingly opposed French rule and, overcoming their sectarian differences, fought together against the colonial power. In 1943, on the eve of independence, the leaders of the various communities negotiated an informal National Pact. It continued the confessional system and guaranteed a Christian majority in Parliament, even though Muslims accounted for a growing proportion of the population and were probably already in the majority. In spite of the favored position of the Christians, and especially the Maronites, Muslim elites had a place in the new system too. The pact gave the presidency and the top army command to Maronites, but the prime minister was to be a Sunni, the chief of staff a Druze, and the speaker of the parliament a Shii. In the civil service and army commands, Christians were assured a majority, but Muslims had posts as well. Though Lebanon was independent, not merged with Syria as many Muslims preferred, the pact affirmed that Lebanon would orient itself toward the Arab world.

During the 1950s under conservative pro-Western governments, Lebanon became the commercial capital, banking center, and playground of the Arab world. However, the political system came under increasing strain, as the largely Christian elite amassed great wealth, while blocking basic social reforms like public education, health care, and housing for the predominantly Muslim poor. Rich conservatives insisted on low taxes, ensuring a weak, underfunded central government. With few national institutions, many Lebanese identified more with their religious communities than with the nation as a whole.

In 1958, when President Camille Chamoun endorsed the *Eisenhower Doctrine, refused demands for reform, rigged parliamentary elections, and won an unconstitutional second term, the country exploded into civil war. *Nasser's Egypt supported left-wing and Arab nationalist rebels, while right-wing Maronite militias backed Chamoun. At Chamoun's request, U.S. military forces intervened. Eventually, the factions negotiated a settlement whereby General Fouad Chehab, the popular army chief who had stayed out of the fighting, assumed the presidency.

Chehab used his popular support and his control of the powerful security apparatus to promote social reform. He strengthened the educational system, built roads, and spurred economic development, giving priority to manufacturing over services. Most importantly, he tried to build a sense of Lebanese national identity that transcended sectarian loyalties. But neither Chehab nor his successor was able to break the power of the traditional sectarian politicians or significantly undermine the confessional system.

During the 1960s, the Lebanese economy boomed, especially financial services. By mid-decade, Lebanon had more bank deposits per capita than any country in the world. While bankers prospered, much of the countryside was transformed from small holdings into large commercial farms, driving thousands of peasants off the land and into the burgeoning slums of Beirut and other cities. A rising tide of protest against class disparities and inadequate social services strengthened left-wing forces, who demanded fundamental reform and called for a nonsectarian *democracy. Conservatives, especially the Maronite parties, rejected reform, and their militias prepared to fight against what they saw as foreign-inspired radical threats to the social order.

In 1970 the *Palestine Liberation Organization (PLO), driven out of Jordan, established its headquarters in Beirut and expanded its guerrilla bases in the south, near the Israeli border. The PLO found its main support among the 300,000 Palestinian refugees who lived without *citizenship rights in Lebanon, but it also enjoyed sympathy from many Lebanese who supported the Palestinian cause and saw it as a force for social change in Lebanon and the Arab world. Conservative Lebanese, however, viewed the autonomous armed Palestinian presence as an affront to Lebanon's sovereignty, a threat which exposed Lebanon to Israeli attack; they also perceived the PLO as a supporter of the Lebanese reformists.

In April 1975, tensions finally exploded into full-scale *civil war between a largely Muslim and Druze coalition demanding reform and a predominantly Maronite alliance rejecting change and insisting that the Lebanese army clamp down on the Palestinians. As fighting intensified, the army broke up along sectarian lines, tax revenues dried up, and the Lebanese government nearly ceased to function. The PLO, which initially sought to avoid involvement, soon entered the civil war on the side of the reformist forces.

In the summer of 1976, Syrian military units, acting nominally as Arab League–sponsored peacekeepers, entered Lebanon in force. Seeking to prevent a victory of the reformist-PLO bloc, they threw their support initially to the Maronite militias. Later, consolidating their role as arbiter of the conflict, the Syrians shifted sides.

Syrian forces soon occupied more than half of Lebanese territory, gaining a growing leverage over the government and over most institutions of Lebanese society, including the economy and the press. Civil war continued, punctuated by innumerable truces and lulls. Religious-sectarian animosities increasingly displaced ideological quarrels as the driving force of the conflict. All sides perpetrated atrocities against noncombatants, including massacres, *torture, car bombs, and hostage taking. Gangs lacking any political program soon set up neighborhood protection rackets; meanwhile, foreign governments gave money, arms, and support to various Lebanese factions. By late 1976, the end of the first phase of the civil war, some 30,000 Lebanese and Palestinians had been killed, 60,000 wounded, and at least 300,000 displaced from their homes. Many neighborhoods, towns, villages, and refugee camps were badly damaged or destroyed.

The militias partitioned Lebanon into exclusive religious enclaves and took charge of local administration, collecting taxes, providing social services, and operating ports. For the first time, the country's impoverished Shia built their own political and military force, demanding a political role commensurate with their new status as Lebanon's largest community. In the Syrian-controlled Beqaa Valley, farmers grew hashish and opium as staple export crops. Many Lebanese came to have an economic interest in the strife. All attempts to end the civil war failed.

From the earliest days of the fighting, *Israel had developed close ties with Maronite militias. In March 1978 Israeli forces invaded south Lebanon up to the Litani River; soon withdrawing, they left a Lebanese-manned "South Lebanon Army" under their control in a ten mile wide "security zone" adjacent to the border. In June 1982 Israel again invaded Lebanon. This time its forces, along with Maronite militias, besieged Beirut in an effort to annihilate PLO headquarters and destroy the powerful Palestinian combat units assembled to defend the city. After two months of intense Israeli bombardment and heavy civilian casualties, PLO leaders and fighters withdrew under a U.S.-brokered cease-fire.

With Israeli forces controlling much of the southern half of the country, a pro-Israel Lebanese government sought to reestablish central authority. U.S. land and naval forces lent their support to the postwar government and intervened directly in the continuing intercommunal fighting. The new government failed to gain control, however, and a violent Syrian-backed Lebanese resistance compelled the United States to withdraw its forces in 1983 and Israel to pull its troops back to the border zone in 1985. Intercommunal fighting continued fitfully, with occasional upsurges of intense violence. Syrian forces remained in control of large areas in the north and east, and Syria gained overwhelming influence over the political scene, including domination over the ineffective but still symbolically important central government.

Military stalemate, the collapse of Lebanon's economy, and growing war weariness opened the way for the United States and Saudi Arabia to broker an agreement in October 1989, known as the Taif Accords. This agreement, reached by members of the Lebanese Parliament, amended the 1943 National Pact by giving Muslims equal parliamentary representation and by strengthening the powers of the prime minister. But otherwise the confessional system remained intact. With U.S. support, Syrian forces eventually crushed opposition to the accords and imposed a cease-fire among the combatants. A new pro-Syrian government began to disarm the militias and broaden its authority to include much of the country, though

Israel continued to control the border region and launched military actions against the Lebanese resistance in the south.

In 1992, Rafiq Hariri, a fabulously rich businessman, was named prime minister. Many hoped he would lead Lebanon to a new era of prosperity and organize the rebuilding of war-ravaged Beirut. His government lowered taxes and privatized public services, steps that pleased the wealthy but led to declining government revenue and a steep rise in official debt. The government could not respond to the country's huge needs for postwar reconstruction and social programs, and by the late 1990s nearly half of government revenue was devoted to servicing the national debt.

A real estate boom, centering on luxury buildings and land speculation, fed inflation, while the rest of the economy made little progress. Rocked by corruption scandals, the government lost its popular support and reacted harshly to discontent and protest. General Emile Lahoud, head of the army since 1989, was elected president in October 1998. One month later, Hariri finally resigned and an old-style politician, Salim al-Hoss, formed a new government. The new government organized Lebanon's first country-wide local elections in thirty-five years and it moved to ease tight restrictions on the press and public gatherings.

Meantime, in the South, Hizbollah guerrillas waged constant war on the occupying Israeli forces and their Lebanese proxies. Israel struck back with military attacks and bombing raids, often against civilian targets, including Lebanon's electricity grid. In May 2000, Israel finally withdrew its forces. But *Syria continued to maintain a large military presence in the country.

Efforts to put Lebanon back together have been slow and sectarian identities and loyalties remain powerful. But a new regime in Syria, and the possibility of regional peace agreements, open up important new possibilities. Still, Lebanon's fractured society and its weak government offer only moderate prospects of overcoming the legacies of the civil war, building a viable economy and achieving fully independent statehood.

(See also ARAB-ISRAELI CONFLICT; ARAB NATIONALISM; POLITICAL VIOLENCE.)

Walid Khalidi, *Conflict and Violence in Lebanon* (Cambridge, Mass., 1979). Jonathan C. Randal, *Going All the Way: Christian Warlords, Israeli Adventurers and the War in Lebanon* (New York, 1983). Helena Cobban, *The Making of Modern Lebanon* (London, 1985). Tabitha Petran, *The Struggle over Lebanon* (New York, 1987). Kamal Salibi, *A House of Many Mansions* (London, 1988). Carole Dagher, *Bring Down the Walls: Lebanon's Post-War Challenge* (New York, 2000). Farid El-Khazen, *The Breakdown of the State in Lebanon* (Cambridge, Mass., 2000).

JAMES A. PAUL

LEFT. As a political term, the *Left* derives from the practice of the French revolutionary parliament, where "radical" representatives sat to the left of the presiding officer's chair, while "conservatives" sat to the *right. Since the French Revolution the Left has been associated with demands for greater popular sovereignty and democratic control over political, social, and economic life. The Left has been identified with the belief that democratic movements are capable of transforming social institutions in a manner that improves the human condition. Conservatives, on the other hand, warn of the "perverse," unintended consequences of social change (or "social engineering") and praise the "prescriptive" wisdom of long-standing institutional and cultural practices.

In the nineteenth century the European Left consisted of an unstable coalition between an emergent working class and middle-class "radical" anticlerics who fought for universal suffrage and elimination of established state religions. Middle-class radicals largely rejected the demands of socialist parties for greater popular control over the capitalist economy. After World War II, the mainstream Right in industrial democracies accepted the Left's demand for universal political suffrage. But conservatives caution that *democracy should only extend to popular selection of competing elites whose rule is essential to any complex society.

The modern Right also contends that economic redistribution and state regulation promote inefficiency and a restriction of liberty. In contrast, the Left holds that the equal worth of liberty can only be guaranteed by universal, public provision of basic human needs such as education, health care, and child care. In addition, the Left believes that popular participation in workplace governance increases productivity, as does public expenditure on infrastructure, research and development, and job training. In sum, while the Right holds that equality and liberty inherently stand in tension, the Left believes that the two values are synergistic.

The Left has been severely divided over the requisite means to achieve the end of extending popular sovereignty to all social institutions. Since the *Russian Revolution, communists have argued that without the leadership of a revolutionary vanguard party the working class by itself would only demand incremental reforms of *capitalism. In addition, communists contended that only *nationalization of industry and a centrally planned economy could achieve rapid industrialization and economic efficiency. But in industrial democracies whose working class fought for universal suffrage and civil liberties, the majority of the Left has advocated parliamentary and gradualist strategies for democratization.

Western European social democratic, labor, and socialist parties were also divided over whether democratization was best achieved by humanizing capitalism or striving for *workers' control of production. After World War II most West European social democratic parties, as well as liberals in the United States, embraced a mixed capitalist, Keynesian *welfare state as the institutional means by which to achieve social justice. But in the 1960s the student *New Left, as well as militant sectors of the trade unions, argued that only participatory democracy could alleviate workplace alienation. Many in the Left sought a "third way," a democratic *socialism which rejected both corporate dominance of the welfare state and the bureaucratic domination of the inefficient *command economies of Eastern Europe.

The Left's renewed interest in decentralized, democratized authority drew upon anarchist, syndicalist, and feminist traditions long ignored by most communists and social democrats. The economic stagnation and restructuring of the 1980s, however, both weakened the traditional trade union core of the Western Left and thwarted this search for a third way. As the crisis of a Keynesian welfare state identified with social democracy engendered a conservative upsurge in most Western polities, the Left found itself reduced to fighting defensive battles in support of the very welfare state reforms it had only recently hoped to move beyond.

This crisis of the welfare state, combined with the collapse of authoritarian *communism in Central and Eastern Europe and the failure of Soviet-style economies to achieve equitable and efficient development in the *Third World, has contributed to a (perhaps temporary) demoralization of the international Left. (Capitalist development in the Third World has also abjectly failed to serve popular needs, though the highly statist, "planned" capitalisms of East Asia are often, ironically, cited by the Right as examples of "free-market miracles.") Authoritarian communism's repression of independent life in civil society sensitized the Left to the central role in a free society of social movements independent of state and party control. In addition, most leftists now recognize that movements for emancipation often organize around nonclass identities such as *race and *gender. In light of the failures of command economies, most leftists now recognize that the market and regulated competition are useful mechanisms for coordinating the activities of decentralized, efficient firms. But the Left continues to advocate for worker participation in firm management, as well as for state regulation of economic activity through fiscal, monetary, and industrial policy. While such social and ideological transformations will influence the nature of a twenty-first century Left, its core values are likely to remain the democratization of political, economic, and cultural life.

(See also ANARCHISM; CONSERVATISM; FEMINISM; IDEOLOGY; KEYNESIANISM; LABOR MOVEMENT; LIBERALISM; NEW RIGHT; NEW SOCIAL MOVEMENTS; REVOLUTION.)

David Caute, *The Left in Europe Since 1789* (New York, 1966). Michael Harrington, *Socialism: Past and Future* (New York, 1989).

JOSEPH M. SCHWARTZ

LEGISLATURE. Although legislatures exist in virtually every nation, they vary greatly in their power and stability. The U.S. *Congress and the Brazilian Chamber of Deputies are both legislatures, but the former has played a central and enduring role in the U.S. policy-making process while the latter has had a variable, but at most marginal, impact on policy decisions made by others. But what defines both of these institutions and what separates them from those institutions that are not legislatures is a set of essentially democratic characteristics that govern their membership and operation.

Simply put, legislators are elected by a larger public to which they are formally responsible and in whose interests they are presumed to act. In this role, they articulate the concerns of constituents, political parties, and *interest groups, and they intercede with bureaucrats on behalf of those whom they represent. No special training or expertise is required for membership in the legislature, each member possesses equal voting power, and decisions are taken publicly and by majority vote.

Thus, the legislature stands at the confluence between democratic theory and democratic practice; indeed it is often regarded as the most visible indicator of a nation's commitment to democracy. It is no accident that the trend away from authoritarianism and toward democracy that went forward in Eastern and Central Europe, East Asia, and Latin America during the early 1990s involved in each nation a more prominent role for legislative institutions.

If these democratic characteristics unite legislatures, they are distinguished from each other, first, by their role in policy making which, in turn, is connected with their constitutional relationship with the executive branch and, second, by their capacity to survive from year to year.

Although all legislatures are involved in making *public policy, some legislatures play a more salient role than others. The U.S. Congress initiates and determines the details of public policies affecting every economic, social, and international question on the nation's agenda. The Japanese Diet, in comparison, debates and occasionally modifies proposals the essentials of which have been decided by business, government, and party leaders. In one-party states such as Singapore, all the legislature does is approve, with minimal discussion, a small number of decisions made by the executive.

The relative policy-making power of the legislature and the executive is determined by both constitutional and partisan factors. In parliamentary systems, the executive is both selected and removable by the legislature, but the locus of power in the system depends upon whether or not the executive's party commands a strong, disciplined majority in the legislature. If it does, which has generally been the case in Britain, then the legislature's role will be less important. If it does not, which has generally been the case in Italy, the legislature's role will be more prominent.

In presidential systems characterized by an independently elected and nonremovable executive, the role of the legislature varies. The U.S. Congress has been quite prominent even when the president's party has controlled a legislative majority. In both Russia, where the president has not had a dependable legislative majority, and in Kenya, where the president's party has been in control, the parliament has played a generally subordinate role to the president.

Finally, some legislatures are more vulnerable than others to attacks on their existence and prerogatives. In the United States and Great Britain, the policy-making role of the legislature has remained unaltered in its constitutional design for centuries. In Argentina and Thailand, military coups have produced frequent changes in the prominence, membership, and structure of the legislature. And in Eastern and Central Europe, the power and prominence of the legislature fluctuates as these nations struggle to institutionalize more democratic political systems.

(See also PARLIAMENTARY DEMOCRACY; POLITICAL PARTIES AND PARTY COMPETITION.)

Gary W. Copeland and Samuel C. Patterson, eds., *Parliaments of the Modern World* (Ann Arbor; Mich., 1994).

MICHAEL L. MEZEY

LEGITIMACY. The concept of *legitimacy* refers to a political order's worthiness to be recognized. Because the reasons offered in support of an order can differ—the preservation of customary forms of social life, the continuity of a legally recognized dynasty, the maintenance of peace and security, the promotion of general welfare, etc.—one can also speak of different conceptions of legitimacy according to the kind of reason given. Even the general definition may be controversial, however, since it restricts the term to political orders and ties the concept to the idea of providing grounds (rather than simply equating legitimacy with the de facto acceptance of a political order by its citizens).

Legitimus, like the related *legalis*, derives from the Latin *lex* (law), and in its early usage in Roman jurisprudence no clear distinction is drawn between the legitimacy and legality of a regime: an *imperium legitimum* or *potestas legitimus* designated rule according to law in contrast to arbitrary rule or tyranny. Under the influence of Christian thought, in medieval jurisprudence the concept of legitimacy also remained closely tied to the ideas of natural law and a normatively ordered cosmos. With the rise of absolutism in the sixteenth century, the idea of a secular justification of political power spread rapidly (see Jean Bodin, *The Six Books of the Commonwealth* [1576], Cambridge, Mass., 1962), and under the subsequent influence of social contract theory and Enlightenment thought the concept was gradually democratized and aligned with the idea of popular sovereignty: "Sovereignty resides with the people, the only legitimate source of power" (Simonde de Sismondi, *Observations générales sur le gouvernement actuel*, Paris, 1815). With the "legitimist" disputes between the ultramonarchists and constitutional monarchists (Charles de Talleyrand) over the restoration of the Bourbon dynasty in France, the concept finally entered into the mainstream of political discourse.

At the beginning of this century, Max *Weber's distinction between the traditional, charismatic, and rational-legal forms of legitimate domination paved the way for a sociological conception of legitimacy (*Economy and Society,* Berkeley, Calif., 1978). His definition of legitimacy as "belief in the legality of enacted rules" contributed to the development of legal positivism and the decline of the classical connection between legitimacy and substantive values or worldviews. Weber's position has recently been advocated in an extreme form by the systems theorist Niklas Luhmann, whose defense gave rise to an influential debate in the 1970s with the critical theorist Jürgen Habermas.

If the concept of legitimacy is not severed from the need to provide reasons and narrowly reduced to the question of the *state's capacity to generate belief in its legitimacy, several distinct types of legitimation can still be identified. Substantive theories assume there is a normative natural order that provides a measure for the legitimacy of a political order. Only regimes whose policies conform to this "good old law" are worthy of recognition. The liberal-minimalist model, by contrast, rejects the idea that legitimacy must involve reference to substantive values in this manner. Legitimacy depends rather on the state's ability to maintain peace, under the rule of law, between individuals and groups who hold widely divergent and even conflicting conceptions about the ultimate value of life. This conception, which can be traced back at least to Benjamin Constant (1767–1830), construes legitimacy as a modus vivendi in which an expanded interpretation of religious toleration replaces the search for substantive moral truth. A third model, which may be called discursive or democratic-proceduralist, has its roots in Rousseau and Kant and has recently been defended by Habermas. Legitimacy is understood in terms of the counterfactual ideal ("regulative idea") of an agreement between free and equal citizens, and the task becomes that of designing political institutions to reflect that ideal while also leaving them open to ongoing criticism in light of it. Although it does not presuppose the idea of a normative natural order, this model sees legitimacy as relying on more than a modus vivendi. Finally, one can identify a "postmodern" model in which the search for universal legitimating grounds is abandoned in favor of a return to narrative traditions. The idea is not to present a general account of legitimation based on an appeal to universal "reason" but to practice more immanent and local forms of critique under the banner of plurality and innovation. Whether this approach, which can be found in the works of Jean-François Lyotard, Jacques Derrida, and Michel *Foucault, constitutes a distinct alternative remains to be seen. Much depends, of course, on the actual ability of one or another of the alternatives to respond successfully to the dilemmas of legitimacy in increasingly interdependent yet functionally differentiated and multicultural societies.

(See also CITIZENSHIP; POSTMODERNISM; SOVEREIGNTY.)

William Connolly, ed., *Legitimacy and the State* (New York, 1984). Athanasios Moulakis, ed., *Legitimacy/Légitimité* (New York, 1986). John Rawls, *Political Liberalism* (New York, 1993). Jürgen Habermas, *Between Facts and Norms* (Cambridge, U.K., 1996).

KENNETH BAYNES

LENIN, Vladimir Ilich. The Russian thinker and political leader Vladimir Ilich Lenin articulated the primacy of political will in an age of total *war. Yet his political *ideology, *Leninism, promised an ultimate end to politics after a period of continuous warfare among classes and nations. Heir to the ideas of many, including *Marx and *Clausewitz, Lenin saw politics as the continuation of war by other means. Politics, not economics, was the fundamental agent of historical change. But at the end of history lay true victory and peace, namely, the annihilation of all enemies and therefore of all politics. To build *socialism was to eliminate class struggle by eliminating all social classes but one, the proletariat.

Lenin's main political contribution was the theory of the omniscient vanguard party, made up not of workers, but of professional revolutionaries and intellectuals, the class from which he came and which he despised. Trained as a lawyer, Lenin denied the rule of law in favor of a higher apocalyptic historicism, dialectical materialism, an ideology of absolute truth understood correctly only by Lenin and his party.

Lenin adapted the economic theories of Marx and Engels to support the primacy of politics as a form of class war in which consciously organized individual wills could overcome the spontaneous forces of history. A continuous reviser of Marxist ideas to suit Russian political conditions, Lenin claimed an orthodoxy superior to his revisionist rivals, right and left. His Manichaean worldview divided friends and light from enemies and darkness. His metapolitics depended on the violent ultimate triumph of a single social class, the proletariat, over its historically doomed enemy, the bourgeoisie. In the end Lenin's own elusive personality dissolved into a militant political ideology.

"V. I. Lenin" was one of many revolutionary pseudonyms used by Vladimir Ilich Ulyanov to publish under the censorship conditions of imperial Russia. Born 22 April 1870 (10 April, old style) in the Volga River town of Simbirsk, Lenin was the fourth of six children of a superintendent of schools and member of the hereditary nobility, Ilya Ulyanov. In 1887, Lenin's older brother, Aleksandr, was executed for his role in a plot to kill Tsar Aleksandr III.

After graduating from the law faculty of the University of Kazan in 1891, Lenin converted to *Marxism and engaged in the typical career of a professional revolutionary—arrest, prison, and political exile. He spent the years 1900–1917 in Munich, Paris, Geneva, Cracow, and Zurich as a radical journalist and leader of the Bolshevik faction of the Russian Social Democratic Workers' Party (RSDWP, founded 1898). In April 1917, after the collapse of the Imperial government during World War I, Lenin returned to Petrograd with hundreds of other political exiles transported by the German government to foment revolution. He masterminded the successful Bolshevik seizure of power in November 1917 and led the new Soviet government as chair of the Council of People's Commissars (Sovnarkom). After suffering a stroke in May 1922, Lenin died in Moscow on 21 January 1924. The father of the *Russian Revolution, and his wife, Nadezhda Krupskaya, left no children.

Lenin's political career began with the peasant-centered revolutionary conspiracy of Russian *populism in the 1880s and, after his brother's death, shifted from terrorism to Marxism. From Russian thinkers such as P. I. Pestel and P. N. Tkachev, Lenin inherited the Jacobin notion of a political seizure of power from above as the key to revolution. The scientistic, historicist, materialist, and economic ideas of Marx, combined with Russian populism, formed the basis of his emerging "Leninism" around 1900, expressed in the RSDWP journal *Iskra (The Spark)*, of which Lenin was an editor.

As a Bolshevik after the RSDWP split of 1903, Lenin favored both legal participation in the Russian parliament (Duma) and illegal underground activity, mainly strikes and bank robberies. In 1907–1912, he nearly lost control of Bolshevism to rivals impressed with the concurrent rise of antiparliamentary syndicalism and trade unionism in Western Europe. In 1917, Lenin sharply opposed the liberal democratic provisional government and, with *Trotsky and others, called for a seizure of power in the name of the soviets, or workers' councils, as the prelude to world revolution and a classless society without state power. He then successfully defended Soviet rule during a bloody civil war (1918–1921) and created the organs of a new state.

Lenin's influence on domestic politics in the *Soviet Union derived from his political will, personal charisma, and ideology, not the offices he held. He founded both the Communist Party of the Soviet Union (CPSU) and the Soviet Union, with its single-party political system and democratic centralist hierarchy of power. He originated the principles of antifactionalism, purge, and the banning of all opposition parties (after disbanding the freely elected constituent assembly in January 1918), on which *Stalin would later build his totalitarian police state. His voluminous writings became scripture defining the party line and the correct view of history. Lenin died, but Leninism survived, in his ideology and in the Red Square mausoleum, as a cult designed by rival Bolshevik "god builders" who viewed socialism as a surrogate religion for the masses.

Lenin's overall role in the political history of the Soviet Union was perhaps greater in death than in life. Leninist ideology defined the terms of political discourse and struggle for succession among Trotsky, Bukharin, Zinoviev, and Stalin in the 1920s. Stalin, Khrushchev, and Brezhnev all claimed Lenin's mantle. Leninism defined correct party policy against the ideological enemies of dogmatism, revisionism, and opportunism. It became the political language of the mass mobilization, industrialization, and militarization of Soviet society.

Beginning in the 1890s, Lenin in his writings revised Marxist theory to fit Russian conditions, borrowing ideas and using them as political weapons. In *The Development of Capitalism in Russia* (1899), he argued that industrialization made Russia ripe for proletarian revolution. In this, Lenin was more Marxist than Marx, who had observed the revolutionary potential of the Russian peasant commune in the 1870s. In *What Is to Be Done?* (1902), titled after the populist novel by his idol, N. G. Chernyshevsky, Lenin argued for the primacy of political organization and discipline over worker spontaneity and trade unionism. He expanded his authoritarian notion of democratic centralism in *One Step Forward, Two Steps Back* (1904) and defended absolute materialist truth against relativism and idealism in *Materialism and Empirio-Criticism* (1909). In *Imperialism* (1916), Lenin blamed finance capital for World War I and predicted inevitable international civil war.

During the summer of 1917, Lenin argued in *State and Revolution* for a necessary, but temporary, dictatorship of the proletariat, to be succeeded at some undefined future time by (in Engels's words) the "withering away of the state." Finally, in *Left-Wing Communism: A Childhood Disease* (1920), Lenin renewed his pre-1914 assault on European syndicalism for its direct action and worker spontaneity. Lenin's ideas were rarely original. They constituted a form of political warfare appropriate to the conditions of the day and were enormously influential both in the Soviet Union and abroad.

Lenin played a central role in the 1917 Revolution and the formation of the Soviet Union (1922). He turned the Bolsheviks from cooperation with, to hostility toward, the provisional government. His letters and articles prodded the Bolshevik central committee to seize power in November. He wrote the decrees on land reform and peace with the Central Powers that engineered short-term peasant support for an urban revolution and led to the Treaty of Brest-Litovsk (1918). He oversaw Soviet victory over the White Armies during the Russian Civil War and a "breathing-space" New Economic Policy (1921–1928) that allowed limited capitalism to develop (whether this was a strategy or a tactic is still debated), and later served as an economic reform model for Khrushchev and *Gorbachev. Lenin's deathbed testament warned against the growth of excessive state and party bureaucracy and a centralization of political power, which, in fact, simply extended his own ideas and which, because of illness, he was powerless to halt.

Lenin was also the most important figure in the Soviet experience of a violent attempt to achieve the transition from capitalism through socialism to communism. For years, Soviet historians and Western critics saw Leninism as identical with Bolshevism and as the logical ancestor of Stalinism. More recently, Leninism has been recognized as distinct from both pre-1917 Bolshevism and post-1929 *Stalinism. Yet the opening of the Soviet archives after the collapse of the Soviet Union in 1991 has supported earlier views of Lenin as a ruthless, brutal, misanthropic dictator who relied on Stalin for establishing policies and had no respect for Trotsky. Newly published documents show that Lenin consistently advocated the use of force, disdained humanity, hated the *peasantry, and opposed the New Economic Policy. Genealogical research indicates that Lenin came from mixed Russian, Kalmyk,

Jewish, German, and Swedish stock, and that he and his family were registered in Simbirsk Province as nobility in 1886. In 1918, Lenin dismissed western reports of the massacre of the Romanov family of Nicholas II as capitalist lies. In 1920, Lenin launched his armies into Poland in the optimistic hope of starting a European revolution. His rhetoric from the civil war period was violent; he issued explicit orders to hang rich peasants and to shoot recalcitrant priests and rich landowners. He also threatened to burn the city of Baku to the ground. Post-Soviet archival revelations tend to support the traditional view that Lenin was the architect of Stalinist *totalitarianism.

Lenin's significance outside the Soviet Union has generally followed success or failure by foreign communist parties in their own countries. Lenin was a well-known and thorny figure in international socialist politics under the Second International (1887–1914). His clarion call to turn World War I into a civil war became the basis of the Comintern, or Third International, founded in Moscow in 1919. The Comintern, through its links with communist parties in other countries, became a parallel arm of Soviet foreign policy and its Council of Foreign Affairs. His writings, published in nearly every language, became international guidelines for world revolution. But Leninism remains only one variant of Marxism, whose appeal to intellectuals has generally been more analytical and critical than action-oriented. Lenin spawned no intellectual tradition in the manner of Marx or Freud, aside from a political ideological orthodoxy institutionalized in his own country.

Despite his cult status in the Soviet Union, especially in the 1920s and 1960s, Lenin ironically stands for the sacrifice of self to ideology. His revolution liberated individuals only for a one-man dictatorship that suppressed individual freedom in expectation of a future classless, stateless society. Revolution in the name of the people produced one-party rule in the name of a social class, the proletariat. The dream of international revolution gave way to the reality of Stalin's "socialism in one country," the Soviet Union. National liberation ultimately meant Soviet empire. Economic compromise led to a planned, command economy of state power, not consumer demand.

The genius of Lenin lay in his political ideology. He recognized that the most effective ideological myth of revolution is one that claims absolute, not relative, truth. But in the multipolar world of global interconnections and high technology, Leninism ultimately failed to provide either political liberation or the material benefits so often promised and postponed. His legacy, an ideological empire, has now collapsed.

(See also CLASS AND POLITICS; COMMUNIST PARTY STATES; RUSSIA.)

Nina Tumarkin, *Lenin Lives! The Lenin Cult in Soviet Russia* (Cambridge, Mass., 1983). Robert C. Williams, *The Other Bolsheviks: Lenin and his Critics, 1901–1914* (Bloomington, Ind., 1986). Philip Pomper, *Lenin, Trotsky, and Stalin: The Intelligentsia and Power* (New York, 1990). Richard Pipes, ed., *The Unknown Lenin: From the Secret Archive* (New Haven, Conn., 1996).

ROBERT C. WILLIAMS

LENINISM. At its first major congress the Marxist movement that had begun to form in the Russian Empire during the last one or two decades of the nineteenth century split into two factions, Mensheviks and Bolsheviks, that came to disagree about revolutionary strategy, tactics, and organization. In the Bolshevik faction Vladimir *Lenin eventually emerged as the sole acknowledged leader, and after his death the legacy of ideas and practices that he left was given the name *Leninism*. This legacy is a unique blend of orthodox *Marxism, as accepted in Social Democratic parties around the turn of the century, with elements specific to Russian revolutionary populism. It is by no means unambiguous or internally consistent; but some general statements can nonetheless he made about it. Leninism offers prescriptions on two problems: first, how to bring about a proletarian *revolution in a country like Russia, and, second, how to govern the country once such a revolution has occurred.

Revolutionary Strategy. Like all Russian Marxists, Lenin took it for granted that a Russian revolution would have to come in two stages: the first, or bourgeois, revolution designed to replace the tsarist system with a bourgeois democratic one, and only the second revolution aimed to usher in a proletarian dictatorship leading to *socialism and *communism. For the initial revolution, he argued, the Marxist movement and the proletariat supposedly represented by it would need allies because the working class alone was too small. Lenin's program for the "democratic" revolution therefore sought to appeal to the peasantry and to Russia's national minorities.

Moreover, Leninism incorporates a thorough reexamination of the Marxist model of *capitalism. Instead of treating capitalism as the system prevailing in the most developed countries, Leninism sees it as a global system, called *imperialism; and in this global system all underdeveloped nations are regarded as potential allies in the revolutionary struggle, while the proletariat of the imperialist nations tends to be written off, superprofits having bribed it into acquiescence. At the same time, Leninism insists that in all political alliances the proletariat should play the leading role.

The Party. Leninism sharply distinguishes between two elements of the Marxist movement—the working class, which reacts against the exploitation of labor in uninformed, "spontaneous" fashion, and the small group of bourgeois intellectuals who join the movement because Marxist theory has made them "conscious." Both consciousness and spontaneity are essential driving forces of revolution. Spontaneity means that the exploited masses will be mobilized for revolutionary action, while consciousness is needed to guide this rebellion into political effectiveness. Leninism regards itself as the science of revolution making and therefore insists on the hegemony of consciousness over spontaneity: unguided revolutionary action will be futile and must be prevented because the working class by itself cannot be expected to understand its own interests.

Consciousness must be institutionalized in the party, which should function as the command center or general staff of the revolution. It should be a small organization recruiting only those who, armed with scientific knowledge (i.e., Marxist theory), will become professionals in revolution making. Like other organizations based on professional expertise, it should be organized according to principles of bureaucratic rationality, although Leninism stresses the importance of the authoritarian command structure and of strict discipline much more than the Weberian model does. Because the elitism of

this arrangement runs counter to strong democratic traditions in the socialist movement, Leninism seeks to combine authoritarian and democratic principles in a form of party governance called democratic centralism. But in practice the centralist tendencies have always overwhelmed the democratic and participatory ones.

Nevertheless, this *elite party seeks to mobilize the masses. For this purpose it develops two means—organization and propaganda. To organize the masses it creates a vast network of auxiliary organizations modeled on those developed earlier by the German Social Democratic Party, and educational activity is divided into long-range indoctrination ("propaganda") and short-term arousal ("agitation"). According to Lenin, one of the most effective means of mobilizing the masses for revolutionary action is the heroic deed: once conditions have ripened for revolution, a small beginning anywhere will serve as the spark that will set off a general political conflagration. In 1917 he was confident that a communist revolution in Russia would serve as the beginning of an all-European proletarian revolution; and on the basis of this expectation he defended his party's seizure of power.

Tsarist rule had been overthrown in February/March 1917. The left-of-center parties that tried to rule the country afterwards faced overwhelming problems that they were unwilling or unable to solve quickly. Impatient and angry, large masses of the poor supported the only party that promised quick and drastic solutions—the Bolsheviks; and thus by endorsing the utopian expectations and the bitter resentment of the Russian underclass, Lenin led his party to power.

The Soviet State. The Soviet state established in 1917 went through several distinct phases employing different policies and institutions. Yet certain principles remained more or less constant; they make up the Leninist pattern of government. Chief among them are the extension of democratic centralism over the entire system of government; the priority of economic growth; the cultural revolution; and the willingness to apply terror.

Leninist theory demands that the masses be drawn into participation in public life. For this purpose the Communist Party creates a vast network of mass organizations and associations. For the administration of the country, the relevant organization is the system of soviets (councils). At the same time, central control over this entire system is exercised by the Party, which regards itself as the repository of the genuine national interest and as the organization of the most enlightened citizens. The Party assures its control through a variety of methods, but ultimately through terror, i.e., through the threat of indiscriminate and unlimited violence against anyone suspected of dissenting from the Party's will. Readiness to apply terror is an acknowledged principle of Leninism. The first priority of the Leninist state is the task of economic construction and reconstruction, for its ultimate goal, genuine communism, presupposes an affluent industrial society. One of the auxiliary tasks in this connection is a "cultural revolution," designed to transform a people steeped in traditional peasant culture and religion into literate, sophisticated city dwellers who know how to handle modern technology.

In its relations with the outside world, the Leninist state from its very beginning followed two mutually exclusive aims. One of them was the pursuit of the national interests of the Soviet state through fostering fruitful relations with governments of the capitalist countries. The other aim was to promote revolutions that would overthrow these capitalist governments. Pursuing both aims at one and the same time promoted chronic failure in both.

Stalinism. After Joseph *Stalin became the single most powerful leader of the Soviet Union and of international communism, his interpretation of Lenin's heritage became the orthodox version of Leninism. In this interpretation, Leninism demanded a commitment of the nation's total material and human resources to a crash program of industrialization, so that Leninism became entrepreneurship of a primitive but powerful sort. An essential element of this program was the imposition of a new serfdom on the peasantry by forcing them into collective farms. The control over the nation's organizational and associational life was extended into all areas of human activity, including science, the arts, and entertainment. In every field of endeavor, orthodoxies were strictly enforced through censorship. Meanwhile the revolutionary terror endorsed by Lenin was institutionalized in the practice of prophylactic justice, through a system of police supervision and punishment designed to eliminate *potential* offenders and dissenters, including potential challengers high in the Party, the government, and other elites.

Leninism in its Stalinist version took pride in eliminating unemployment and in providing cheap housing, free medical care, free education, and similar social services. But it also rejected egalitarianism and endorsed a system of social stratification based on the value of a person's services to the state. It continued to declare the working class to be the leading class of Soviet society, but in reality allowed the workers to remain exploited by a managerial class.

By the mid-1930s, Stalin declared dogmatically that *socialism had been achieved, even though full communism was still in the very distant future. Thus his version of Leninism effectively eliminated the ideals and dreams in the name of which the revolution had been made—*Stalinism implied the withering away of utopia.

Alternatives to Stalinism. The Stalinist version of Leninism, which officially came to be called Marxism-Leninism, was challenged by many leaders within the Bolshevik movement. Nikolai *Bukharin, who was alert to the links between economic centralization and unchecked political power, advocated a policy of slower economic growth that would permit a gentler and more democratic political system. Aleksandr A. Bogdanov and others, criticizing the Party's exclusive attention to problems of economic growth and political control, suggested that it should also develop the cultural and spiritual aspects of the transition from capitalism to socialism. Leaders of the Workers' opposition interpreted Leninism in an anarcho-syndicalist spirit, demanding *workers' control of industry and grass-roots democracy through the unions and the soviets. Aleksandra M. Kollontai and other Bolshevik feminists sought to combine revolutionary Marxism with the demands for women's liberation, including liberation from conventional sexual morality.

Lev D. *Trotsky's ideas do not constitute an alternative to Stalinism. Instead, they were its precursors: Trotsky must be recognized as a major pioneer of Stalinism, although it probably required a Stalin type to put his ideas into practice.

Leninism Worldwide. As long as the *Soviet Union was the only country governed by a Leninist party, its Stalinist dogma was acknowledged by all other communist parties as orthodox Leninism, although splinter parties analogous to the oppositions in the Soviet Union formed in many countries. When communist parties came to power in Eastern Europe in the wake of World War II, many of their leaders expected to apply Leninism in a more democratic and humane manner but were forced to adopt the strict Stalinist version. Nonetheless, reformers in the Eastern and Central European parties and also in the Soviet Union eventually repudiated Stalinism, appealing to neglected aspects of Lenin's heritage.

The Yugoslav party, excommunicated by Stalin, developed its own, Titoist version of reform Leninism. In China and Indochina, the revolutionary strategies of *Mao Zedong and *Ho Chi Minh led to a very different interpretation of Leninism, and so did the ideas and practices of Latin American communists. *Eurocommunism in Western Europe gave Leninism a rather social democratic interpretation, while in some African countries ruled by parties that called themselves Marxist-Leninist, Leninism meant little more than a commitment to revolutionary anticolonialism, economic planning, and government by a single party.

The collapse of communist regimes in Eastern and Central Europe as well as the dissolution of the Soviet Union have produced a crisis for Leninism, the outcome of which is uncertain. The people who ousted ruling communist parties from power have also removed statues and posters of the once-idolized Lenin, and some of them now repudiate every idea and every word once associated with him. In time, some parts of this heritage, especially his theory of imperialism, may, of course, come to be appreciated again.

(See also COMMUNIST PARTY STATES; PEASANTS.)

Herbert Marcuse, *Soviet Marxism: A Critical Analysis* (New York, 1958). Leonard B. Schapiro, *The Communist Party of the Soviet Union* (New York, 1960). Alfred G. Meyer, *Communism*, 4th ed. (New York, 1984). Alfred G. Meyer, *Leninism* (Boulder, Colo., and London, 1986).

ALFRED G. MEYER

LESOTHO. See SOUTHERN AFRICA.

LIBERALISM. A protean doctrine with views on matters as diverse as epistemology and *international relations, liberalism has been interpreted in different ways throughout history. As a minimal definition we can say that liberalism considers individuals the seat of moral value and each individual as of equal worth. Hence, the individual should be free to choose his or her own ends in life. Liberalism may be morally neutral in regard to the ends people choose for themselves, but it is not morally neutral in its view that such individual choice is desirable and must be safeguarded from unwarranted interference from the *state. Liberalism is a view of the world, an *ideology, and to adopt it is to take a stand.

This essay has three parts. It begins by distinguishing and examining the principal strands of thought within the liberal enterprise as a whole. The second part is concerned with the history of liberalism, considering both liberal institutions and liberal doctrine. The final part of the essay analyzes liberalism in postwar Europe—in both its geopolitical and domestic influences—and considers the stability of the advanced core of liberalism as well as the possibility of liberalization elsewhere.

The Philosophical Underpinnings. There have been two principal concerns within liberalism. One has centered on epistemology or claims about human knowledge; the second concern has been liberalism's relationship to *capitalism.

The key figures within the epistemological tradition are the Scottish philosopher David Hume (1711–1776) and his German counterpart Immanuel Kant (1724–1804). What is most striking about Hume's thought and that of British empiricism is its simplicity. Human beings can only build up a picture of the world, in his view, by means of their senses, for nothing exists except sensation. The trouble with this position is that it led Hume to something like despair: if we have only our senses, it is impossible to guarantee the reality of the external world, the regularity of nature, and even causation itself. While Kant did not try to disprove Hume, he sought to restore a sense of order by arguing that our minds could only approach reality by means of regular causal principles. Moreover, he sought to guarantee the special status of humanity by arguing that reason is not simply, as Hume has it, "a slave to the passions."

These two views are important for liberalism insofar as Kantianism underwrites British empiricism in an absolutely necessary way. In its utilitarian guise, empiricism was open to the objection that the general happiness of a group of ten people might be increased if, say, the bodily parts of one healthy member were shared out to the other nine incapacitated members. Of course, the British empiricists inhabited a society in which great respect was shown to individuals, and they did not themselves recommend such policies of dismemberment. Nonetheless, the Kantian position gives the firmest possible base for treating all human beings as ends rather than as means. Additionally, both views share the same enemies. Both mount attacks against superstition and authority, and individuals are left as masters of their fate.

If empiricism and Kantianism remain unsettling in the ways in which they diminish our certainty, the best-known defense of liberalism bravely seeks to make a virtue of necessity by praising doubt. As nobody can be completely sure of anything, the English philosopher John Stuart Mill (1806–1873) argued, it is vital that every opinion have a hearing—so that the best idea, in the light of current evidence, can win out. This striking view has implications for political life: if individuality of view is encouraged, a common culture of literacy and tolerance is crucial to sustain ordered debate. This opens the specter of relativism, of liberalism as but one option. That liberalism has to justify itself against its rivals tends to shift attention from pure doctrine to the efficacy of its social institutions in comparison to those of its rivals. With Scottish economist Adam Smith (1723–1790), liberalism turned to less lofty concerns and forged an enduring association with capitalism and the vitality—and political consequences—of wealth creating markets.

A great novelty of Smith within the tradition of Western thought lies in his preference for wealth over virtue, that is, a society of abundance rather than a frugal one designed to encourage moral virtue. The basic justification was simple and democratic: The standard of life of normal people would be enhanced. But a more important issue was involved. The making of money, about which Smith had few illusions, had served historically in Europe as a counterbalance to the pursuit of *power, the former being a calm rather than a violent passion, and it remained the best guarantee of decent politics. Smith endorsed capitalism as a means to his ultimate value—control of arbitrary rule, a premise that has remained a touchstone of liberalism.

The Rise and Fall of Liberalism. Intellectual doctrines are often codifications of social practices which may, in turn, have an impact on social life. This observation most certainly applies to liberalism, and we need first to examine in turn the social bases that support liberalism before then turning to an analysis of its loss of hegemony in late-nineteenth-century Europe.

Comparative historians agree that the uniqueness of the West lies in the fact that power was held in many sets of hands. Whereas a Chinese empire had a settled status order (which distinctively sought to control the destabilizing forces of capitalism), Europe was much more varied. The Christian Church provided a certain unity for Europe as a whole, and within that shell there was constant restlessness created by competition between states and in the market and complicated interactions between political and economic forces. The character of the whole can be seen in the calling of parliaments—institutions unique to the West—in which nobles, church, and burghers (and peasants in the Swedish case) voted kings special funds, habitually for the conduct of war. The absence of a single center made experiments possible. One example was the autonomy allowed city-states in Flanders and in northern Italy. The "materialist" fact of centers in which the burgher was king ensured a demand for technology, without which European intellectual and social progress would have been impossible.

If this social portfolio provided a baseline of *pluralism, a very long and varied set of events translated favorable circumstances into a liberal world. European pluralism prevented the triumph of any party in long wars of religion, and the crucial liberal doctrine of tolerance accordingly slowly struggled to the fore. The diversity of the system was such that restrictions imposed in one locale could not prevent advances elsewhere, and these later had, on pain of extinction, to be imitated by laggards. Particularly crucial in this respect was, as Barrington Moore has demonstrated, the slow conversion of the English aristocracy to commercial agriculture—a development which ruled out for Europe as a whole the creation of nonplural absolutist power systems. When England triumphed over France in the Napoleonic Wars, it seemed that liberalism would be triumphant.

But in the 1870s the English model—by that time insisting as much on free trade as on retrenchment and reform—came under widespread assault. Intellectually, counter-Enlightenment ideas accused liberalism either of providing insufficient support for the self or of standing in the way of true individuality, contradictory charges which, nevertheless, could blend into a single positive ideology. The charges have some validity, but the critics of liberalism suffer from more serious problems. Intellectually, they construe society as an abstraction hovering over the individual with potentially unconstrained powers. More importantly, the historical record has demonstrated that the worship of society in a form glorifying instinctualism—including the "will to power"—was most significantly realized at the Nuremberg rallies. It may be that individuality is not, as John Stuart Mill believed, easy. But to achieve individuality, through struggle and with some personal costs, seems far less expensive socially than any alternative.

Did liberalism fall apart instead for institutional reasons? The key Marxist charge in this connection is that liberal society suffers from class conflict. It is indeed true that a revolutionary working class played a significant role in the *Russian Revolution of 1917, and the German workers had as their agent a political party with distinctive socialist goals. But what can now be seen clearly is that working-class militancy was by no means uniform within capitalist society: it was effectively absent in the United States, nearly absent in England, and strongly present only in the classical model in Germany and, most militant of all, in czarist Russia. Militancy resulted from autocratic and authoritarian old regimes seeking to exclude workers through antisocialist legislation of various sorts: Where workers were free to organize under a liberal state, they naturally did not fight politically against the state that had given them *citizenship, but fought industrially, in the workplace, in order to achieve better pay and conditions from capitalists. Differently put, liberalism disperses conflict throughout society, whereas the concentration of power tends to focus it. Insofar as some nation-states became politically unstable in the late nineteenth century, it was less because they were capitalist than because they were not yet liberal.

The same essential point applies to a second institutional failing held to follow from the relations of liberalism to capitalism, this time concerning liberalism or openness in international trade. It is indeed true that several states sought to protect their own producers from the world market at the end of the nineteenth century, and that this did lead to increased international trade rivalry. But such rivalry did not in itself lead to armed conflict. If we are to understand the origins of World War I—as we must, because it (in combination with World War II, which was occasioned by the social forces unleashed in World War I) created the world in which we now live—it is necessary to comprehend the nature of the German state, whose backing for Austria was the crucial determinant of war in 1914. What is crucial is that Wilhelmine Germany ended up with two policies: one directed worldwide, supported by intellectuals, the excluded middle class, some heavy industrialists, and Social Democrats, and another directed eastward, favored by the army and the traditional landed upper class. The presence of two policies meant that Germany alienated every major state and thereby brought on itself a coalition that led to its greatest fear—that of having to fight on two fronts. How was such a blunder possible? The German state was a court: Whoever had the ear of the kaiser was influential—the trouble was that the kaiser, without a Bismarck, listened to many and did not ensure that a single grand strategy was put into place. Again, it was the absence of liberalism—in the sense here of cabinet government and parliamentary control—rather than the presence of capitalism which caused disaster.

Liberalism Triumphant? At the end of the twentieth century, some polemicists claimed that liberalism was—and would remain—triumphant. There is an uncomfortable amount of hubris involved in that claim. Liberalism spread in the heart of the advanced world less because of any inevitability than because the Anglo-Saxon power triumphed, none too easily, in two world wars. Equally, *decolonization, which has removed the illiberal character of European rule abroad, has not led, as hoped, to the spread of liberalism.

Instead, the perceived need to centralize power to speed development has increased authoritarian and dictatorial rule. We need to make distinctions in order to establish the ways in which liberalism is more and less solidly in place at the start of the twentieth century in comparison with the start of the nineteenth.

The most famous argument asserting the primacy of liberalism was that made at the end of the 1950s proclaiming "an end to ideology." This assertion was both disingenuous and unhelpful in hiding the fact that liberalism is itself an ideology needing to be defended as such. However, there was then and is now much truth to the basic contention that the great ideologies of the twentieth century, from the fascist *Right to the Marxist *Left, have been massively discredited by historical events. The defense of the people against fear as well as the ability of liberal and capitalist societies to provide affluence for citizens in the prosperous core sustain liberalism's appeals. This is not to say that everyone accepts this state of affairs. Ideological hostility toward the soulless world of liberalism remains on the part of many intellectuals. More significantly, capitalism raises profound issues of *equality and inequality in global terms, even as the reach of liberalism beyond the wealthy core remains in doubt.

The core of liberal society has prospered to an extraordinary degree in the years since 1945. U.S. dominance of capitalist society as a whole led to the reconstruction of the Federal Republic of Germany and Japan and to a very wide acceptance of a historic class compromise. Liberalism in the international order has fostered multilateral free trade and *globalization. In recent years, fears that trade rivalries between capitalist states—notably among Europe, Japan, and the United States—may destabilize international relations have grown and with them efforts to harmonize relations through the creation of the *World Trade Organization, in itself an expression of liberalism in the guise of free trade.

An important question of the age facing liberals concerns the fate of advanced but authoritarian regimes. Can regimes which industrialized by concentrating power, that is, which suffered "revolutions from above," make a successful transition to liberal *democracy? In Eastern and Central Europe, there is no doubt but that the Soviet model collapsed both because of external capitalist pressure and because of internal pressures exerted by ever more important educated labor. The states involved have faced a double and simultaneous transition, to capitalism and to democracy, and prospects for successful double transitions in post-communist societies seem even bleaker in the first years of the new century than they did a decade earlier.

The fact that authoritarian capitalist regimes, in contrast, face a single transition to democracy gives them better prospects. But here, too, the result is likely to be variable. Latin American states have historically mobilized populations, and this can make the self-control required while decompressing an authoritarian regime difficult to achieve; faced additionally with debt, such states may continue to oscillate between demonstration and *military rule. The prospects in East Asia have looked comparatively better, although the economic crisis that erupted in 1997 revealed both the diversity of outcomes and the challenges that lie ahead for the *newly industrializing economies to consolidate their *democratic transitions.

The single most vital question facing liberals is, however,

quite different. Many societies are not developing at present, and some look likely never to develop: They suffer from massive population increases, a lack of natural resources, corrupt bureaucracies, disastrous epidemics, and, in striking instances, ecological catastrophe. That this is so, of course, offends the most utilitarian aspect of liberalism, that is, the desire to feed people; it rules out key questions of liberal political rule almost completely. An examination of the world economy—in terms of resource, trade, and capital flows—decisively demonstrates that the advanced world does not depend upon most such states, and this explains why they are increasingly ignored. This cannot but worry liberals. The misery of much of the world remains a threat as much as a disgrace to the liberal heartland; it is also a threat that must be confronted if liberalism is to survive.

(See also AUTHORITARIANISM; CONSERVATISM; DEVELOPMENT AND UNDERDEVELOPMENT; GEOPOLITICS; POST-COMMUNISM; SOCIALISM AND SOCIAL DEMOCRACY.)

Barrington Moore, *Social Origins of Dictatorship and Democracy* (Boston, 1966). Robert Paul Wolff, *The Poverty of Liberalism* (Boston, 1968). Isaiah Berlin, *Four Essays on Liberty* (Oxford, 1969). Albert Hirschmann, *The Passions and the Interests: Political Arguments for Capitalism Before Its Triumph* (Princeton, N.J., 1977). Michael Howard, *War and the Liberal Conscience* (Oxford, 1978). Michael Sandel, *Liberalism and the Limits of Justice* (Cambridge, U.K., 1982). Michael Doyle, "Kant, Liberal Legacies, and Foreign Affairs," *Philosophy and Public Affairs* 12, nos. 3 and 4 (1983). Quentin Skinner, "The Idea of Negative Liberty: Philosophical and Historical Perspectives," in R. Rorty, J. B. Schneewood, and Q. Skinner, eds., *Philosophy in History: Essays on the Historiography of Philosophy* (Cambridge, U.K., 1984). John A. Hall, *Liberalism: Politics, Ideology, and the Market* (Chapel Hill, N.C., 1988). Nancy Rosenblum, *Liberalism and the Moral Life* (Cambridge, Mass., 1989). José Merquior, *Liberalism: Old and New* (Boston, 1991).

JOHN A. HALL

LIBERATION THEOLOGY. A new current in Christian theology, mainly in Latin America, that first emerged in the 1960s, liberation theology argues that a central element in the message of the Bible is the special duty of the believing Christian to work for the liberation of the poor and oppressed in history. It also criticizes earlier theological writing and teaching as excessively abstract and too supportive of existing power structures.

The description of liberation theology given by the movement's founder, Gustavo Gutiérrez, as "critical reflection on Christian praxis in the light of the Word," contains three important elements in what is claimed to be a new way of doing theology—it is critical of the status quo, it is committed to action by and for the poor, and it is biblically based. In their original formulations, the writings of the liberation theologians emphasized the need for a new hermeneutic, developed out of the experience of the poor. They argued that the insights of social science should be used to identify the causes of oppression and the ways in which they can be removed. In keeping with the views of many Latin American social scientists of the time, the principal cause of Latin American poverty and oppression was seen to be "dependent *capitalism," and the remedy the socialization of the private ownership of the means of production. However, from the outset there was also a commitment to the promotion of "Christian base communities" among the poor in order to enable them to apply biblical insights to their situation of oppression. Lib-

eration theology therefore is both a method of doing theology and an analysis of the social situation of the poor that combines elements of Marxist-influenced *socialism and of grass-roots *populism.

The emergence of liberation theology is rooted in the changes in worldwide Catholicism in the 1960s and the experience of Latin American Christians. The Second Vatican Council (1962–1965) brought the Latin American bishops to Rome for several months each year over a period of four years, and its effort to modernize the church culminated in the adoption of "The Pastoral Constitution on the Church in the Modern World" (*Gaudium et Spes*), which opened the church to other religions and points of view, including those of atheism and *Marxism. In Latin America the challenge of the *Cuban Revolution and the pressures for reform promoted by the Alliance for Progress created a ferment among intellectuals and students that led to an increasingly revolutionary outlook. When the former Catholic chaplain at the National University of Bogotá, Camilo Torres, joined a Marxist guerrilla movement in 1966 and was killed in a confrontation with the Colombian military, many Christians debated the morality of his commitment to *revolution. By 1968 when the Conferencia Episcopal Latinoamerican (CELAM) met at Medellín, Colombia, there was a significant group that considered the situation of the poor in Latin America to be an urgent concern for the church. In the Medellín documents, the bishops called on the church to give "effective preference to the poorest and most needy sectors" and described the situation in many parts of Latin America as one of "injustice that can be called institutionalized violence . . . violating fundamental rights," warning that "the temptation to violence is surfacing in Latin America."

Gustavo Gutiérrez, a Peruvian priest trained in Europe, was an advisor to the bishops and probably wrote the words quoted above. Armed with the legitimation derived from the bishops' statements, he argued that Latin America needed a social revolution and that violence might be required to liberate the poor. In *A Theology of Liberation*, the 1971 book that was the founding document of the movement, Gutiérrez identified as the cause of Latin American underdevelopment the domination of the major capitalist countries, especially the United States. He argued that the class struggle was a central fact and neutrality impossible and called upon the church to recognize that loving one's enemies requires recognizing those enemies and the necessity of combatting them. The *class struggle was based on the "dichotomy of capital and labor and the exploitation of man by man" and the solution was social ownership of the means of production.

This revolution was not to be carried out by a Leninist revolutionary elite. Rather, the poor and the oppressed were to be agents of their own liberation through the grass-roots base communities that had already been organized in Brazil and endorsed by the Medellín meeting. Gutiérrez's writings thus combined both structuralist anticapitalism and populist communitarianism and linked both to biblical themes, especially the verse from Isaiah 61 quoted by Christ in Luke 4 when he says that he has come "to preach the good news to the poor (and) to liberate those who are oppressed."

The publication of the Gutiérrez book coincided with a heightening of revolutionary ferment in Latin America. In Chile, the election of Salvador *Allende, a Marxist socialist with the support of one and later two left Christian groups, seemed to typify the kind of cooperation between Marxists and Christians that liberation theology recommended. Other writers such as the Brazilian Hugo Assmann and the Argentinian José Miguez Bonino argued more strongly than Gutiérrez that socialist revolution was the only option for Christians, and the Christians for Socialism movement held a continent-wide meeting in Chile in April 1972. In *The Liberation of Theology*, Juan Luis Segundo of Uruguay endorsed the use of a "hermeneutics of suspicion" to unmask the ideological content of most theological writings.

The movement grew after the overthrow of elected governments in countries such as Chile and Uruguay in the mid-1970s, and it began to receive attention in Europe and the United States. An effort was made by more conservative church leaders to root out the liberation theologians from the CELAM bureaucracy and educational programs, but they demonstrated their influence at the next CELAM meeting in Puebla, Mexico, in 1979. Most of them were not invited to the conference, but operating from outside the meeting they prepared position papers that influenced the content of the Final Document of the Conference, which endorsed "the preferential option for the poor" and declared that "the Church has a duty to proclaim the liberation of millions of human beings among whom are many of the Church's own children." The document also attacked the "free market economy," which makes it possible for small groups, "often tied to foreign interests," to make large profits "while the vast majority of the people suffer."

Yet the bishops did not accept the liberationist position uncritically. Following statements made at the conference opening by *John Paul II, who had been made pope only three months before, the bishops warned of "the risk of ideologization run by theological reflection when it is based on a praxis that has recourse to Marxist analysis," and they denounced the "re-reading of the Gospel on the basis of a political option" involving "a strategic alliance between the Church and Marxism." The meeting also endorsed the Christian base communities but warned against "the theories of the People's Church, born of the people in opposition to the official or institutional church."

The warnings came none too soon, for five months later, on 19 July 1979, a popular uprising headed by the Frente Sandinista de Liberación Nacional (FSLN) ended the forty-year rule of the Somoza family in Nicaragua. In October 1979 a reformist coup in El Salvador overthrew the conservative military, initiating a period of revolutionary upheaval that plunged the country into civil war the following year.

In both countries liberation theology played a role. In Nicaragua it had inspired leading Catholic priests, intellectuals, and students to ally themselves with the *Sandinista movement, despite its known Marxist orientation, because they viewed the alliance as an exercise of the preferential option for the poor. Similarly in El Salvador, when the Frente Farabundo Martí de Liberación Nacional (FMLN) began *guerrilla warfare in 1980, leading Catholic intellectuals and the left wing of the Salvadoran Christian Democratic Party joined the Frente Democrático Revolucionario (FDR), which allied itself with the FMLN. In both countries, the base community movement had also taken on a clearly political character, and in Nicaragua the new Sandinista government supported the "church of the poor" that opposed Archbishop (later Cardinal) Miguel Obando y Bravo when he criticized the Sandinista government. It is possible to exaggerate the direct political influence of liberation theology in Latin America, but in small countries such as those in Central America, which are unstable and uncertain of their future, the conversion of a relatively small group of students, intellectuals, and labor and peasant leaders to the liberationist approach had a significant influence on their *political development. Fidel *Castro himself recognized this in a set of interviews he gave to a Brazilian liberation theologian in support of the establishment of long-term alliances between Marxists and progressive Christians.

In the 1980s the Vatican's Congregation for the Doctrine of the Faith, headed by Cardinal Josef Ratzinger, began to criticize liberation theology. The Brazilian Franciscan, Leonardo Boff, was summoned to Rome in 1984 to explain statements critical of the hierarchy in his book *Church, Charism and Power*, and despite widespread support in Brazil he was ordered to observe "penitential silence" for a year. In the same year the Vatican issued the first of two instructions on liberation theology, warning against the "risks of deviation damaging to the faith and Christian living . . . that are brought about by certain forms of liberation theology which use, in an insufficiently critical manner, concepts borrowed from various currents of Marxist thought," among them "a biblical hermeneutic marked by rationalism" and "a partisan conception of truth."

In 1986, a second Instruction on the subject took a more positive attitude toward aspects of liberationist thought, especially the base communities, "if they really live in unity with the universal church," and theological reflection based on experience, if it is done "in the light of the experience of the church itself." It also admitted that armed struggle might be legitimate "as a last resort to put an end to an obvious and prolonged tyranny" but warned that it could also be "a cause of new forms of slavery." Shortly after the second Instruction was issued, the pope wrote a letter to Brazilian bishops, many of whom had long been supporters of liberation theology, in which he described liberation theology as "not only timely but useful and necessary" provided that it is developed "in full fidelity to church doctrine, attentive to the preferential, but not excluding or exclusive, love for the poor."

The papal statement was a recognition that liberation theology had wide support in Latin America, and that, purged of its Marxist elements, it could be an important way to reach the poor and the oppressed. Leading liberation theologians such as Gustavo Gutiérrez had already moved in their writings in a more spiritual and communitarian direction, abandoning the earlier calls for revolution. Leonardo Boff had accepted his (temporary) silencing, saying that "I would rather walk with the church than walk alone," and insisting on his orthodoxy on central doctrines such as the Eucharist, the Trinity, and devotion to the Virgin Mary.

In the 1980s elected civilian governments took office in nearly every Latin American country, following a decade of repression in which the hideous violations of *human rights under military regimes had given the Catholic *Left a new appreciation of the values of the "bourgeois" *democracy that they had earlier denounced. As the dreams of an alternative model of socialism perished in the upheavals of Eastern and

*Central Europe and the electoral defeat of the Sandinistas, the liberation theologians, like much of the rest of the Latin American Left, gave renewed attention to the need for developing effective grass-roots organizations that could express the needs of the poor and oppressed through democratic institutions. The continuing influence of the movement was affirmed in Brazil in the late 1980s, when mayoral elections in several important cities saw victory go to products of the base community movement, and again in Haiti in 1990, with the landslide victory of Father Jean-Bertrand Aristide in the country's presidential election.

Why did liberation theology show so much more staying power than other comparable movements of the 1960s? One reason may be its proponents' insistence on remaining within the Catholic church (there are some Protestant liberation theologians such as José Miguez Bonino and Rubem Alves, but the overwhelming majority are Catholic), linking their political and economic radicalism with a continuing reliance on the Bible and traditional theological symbols and (reinterpreted) doctrines. Another reason may be that their core teaching, the special concern of Christianity with the poor and oppressed in opposition to the status quo, represented central—but often ignored—elements of the biblical message. Critics may attack the liberationists' flirtations with Marxism and their naïveté about the operation of national and international economics, but an approach that takes account of the radical implications of the Christian message and that is willing to learn, as liberation theology has done, from the experience of the poor and oppressed will have a continuing vitality and appeal.

(See also DEVELOPMENT AND UNDERDEVELOPMENT; RELIGION AND POLITICS; REVOLUTION; ROMAN CATHOLIC CHURCH; VATICAN II.)

Michael Novak, *Will It Liberate? Questions about Liberation Theology* (New York, 1986). Phillip Berryman, *Liberation Theology* (New York, 1987). Arthur F. McGovern, *Liberation Theology and its Critics: Toward an Assessment* (Maryknoll, N.Y., 1989). Paul E. Sigmund, *Liberation Theology at the Crossroads: Democracy or Revolution?* (New York, 1990).

PAUL E. SIGMUND

LIBERIA. By 1867, approximately 20,000 blacks from the United States had colonized this sub-Saharan country based on the American model. Since then Liberia, once a symbol of liberty for freed slaves, has gradually been transformed into one of the most underdeveloped nations in the *Third World. This phenomenon is largely attributed to the deterioration of a political economy structured on the institutionalization of privilege as determined by one's *ethnicity.

Participation in the early government and economic enterprises was confined to the American black elite. Economic activity was based in Monrovia, the capital, for fear that extension into the hinterland would threaten the hegemony of the Americo-Liberians. The signing of a loan agreement between the Firestone Corporation and the government of Liberia in 1927 marked the beginning of American financial supervision and resulted in an influx of investors scrambling for Liberia's cheap and abundant natural resources. By the turn of the century *multinational corporations (MNCs), which enjoyed minimal taxes and maximum repatriation, had practically depleted the major export earnings of iron ore, rubber, and cocoa. These companies, whose investments totaled U.S.$425 million as of 1980, began to seek buyers for

their concerns and pulled out of the country, because of political instability and dwindling natural resources. The revenue generated from these MNCs had benefited only 5 to 10 percent of Liberians. Increases in GNP were unaccompanied by infrastructural development.

The decline in Liberia's economic system is intertwined with the inconsistencies of its political system. The origins of the governing unit stem from the freed slaves who sought to realize their freedom by adopting and exaggerating Western values and even assumed the role of masters in their new country. A family dynasty evolved and dominated the political sphere well into the period of African nationalism in the 1960s, when the contradictions of the Liberian elite were revealed. Historically, the Americo-Liberian government silenced the rumblings of discontent which the indigenous population expressed over resident taxes, increasing rice prices, erosion of local autonomy, and the failure to extend privileges. Fiscal mismanagement and nepotism during the administration of William Tubman (1944–1971), followed by destabilization under William Tolbert (1971–1980), led to military rule. In spite of human rights violations under the military regime of Samuel Doe (1980–1990), the United States extended over $50 million to sustain his ten-year tenure.

The civil war that ensued in 1990 as a result of opposition to Doe's oppressive rule devastated the physical and social infrastructure of the country. Over half of the 2.5 million Liberians were killed or became refugees in surrounding countries and abroad. Ethnically based warlords vied for dominance during the seven years of the war. At the outset, it was hoped that the United States would intervene in what was historically a virtual American protectorate, but the U.S. policy of "benign neglect" toward African peoples prevailed.

A significant aspect of the Liberian civil war was the involvement of a regional organization in seeking to resolve it militarily and politically. The *Economic Community of West African States (ECOWAS), a grouping of sixteen predominantly authoritarian governments dominated by *Nigeria, established a peacekeeping force, the Economic Community Monitoring Group (ECOMOG), to contain and end the conflict militarily, while diplomatic efforts were made to help Liberian factions reach a political settlement. After twelve failed peace accords, a final agreement was reached in 1996 for resolving the conflict through democratic elections.

Charles Taylor, the most powerful of the warlords, was elected president by a war-weary and beleaguered population. As part of a power-sharing formula meant to promote peace and national unity, the new government includes leaders from all the major warring factions. As they begin to enjoy the material benefits of power, it is evident that the average Liberian bore the brunt of a senseless bloodbath for the economic gain of a few. Even with elections and a free press, the road to genuine democracy will continue to be long and arduous in Liberia.

(See also ECONOMIC COMMUNITY OF WEST AFRICAN STATES.)

Yekutiel Gershoni, *Black Colonialism: The Americo-Liberian Scramble for the Hinterland* (Boulder, Colo., 1985). Edward Lama Wonkeryor, *Liberia Military Dictatorship: A Fiasco Revolution* (Chicago, 1985). J. Gus Liebenow, *Liberia: The Quest for Democracy* (Bloomington, Ind., 1987). Clement Adibe, "The Liberian Conflict and the ECOWAS–UN Partnership," *Third World Quarterly* 18, no. 3 (1997).

Z. S. IFE WILLIAMS

LIBERTARIANISM. Although sometimes used broadly to refer to a strong concern about liberty irrespective of other political views, the term "libertarianism" is more narrowly applied (especially in the United States) to a political-cum-intellectual movement that revives and develops classical or European *liberalism. Libertarians espouse the principles of private property, consent, and contract. In economic terms these principles imply a free market; but not all issues are properly cast in terms of markets. Libertarians emphasize that "spontaneous" social order can function beneficently based on the legal principles they favor. They share a moral repugnance to central *planning or regulation by government, which they deem to involve coercion. They typically favor a noninterventionist *foreign policy, not least because of the link between war, the growth of the state, and the loss of domestic freedoms. Some libertarians take their opposition to the state to the point of anarchism.

Contemporary libertarianism, however, is complex. It might be understood as consisting of three loosely interrelated strands. First, there is the academic revival of classical liberalism after World War II. Friedrich Hayek, Milton Friedman, and Ronald Coase played a key role. Other important influences were James Buchanan and Gordon Tullock's public choice critique of a "benevolent despot" model of government and of "rent seeking," as, well as the work of many other market-oriented economists; Richard Posners and Henry Manne's work in "law and economics" and Richard Epstein's constitutional jurisprudence; Robert Nozick's *rights-based *Anarchy, State, and Utopia* and the contractarianism of Buchanan; and Thomas Szasz's critique of psychiatry and the "therapeutic state."

Second, there is a strongly individualistic current in U.S. culture, which has been reinforced from a variety of intellectual sources. The typical libertarian's views in the United States have a pedigree that runs variously through later Scholastic thought, the Levellers, John Locke, Thomas Paine, Thomas Jefferson, early French liberalism, Jacksonian social theory, the Manchester liberalism of Cobden and Bright, Herbert Spencer, and Benjamin Tucker. In the twentieth century some important influences are H. L. Mencken, Albert J. Nock, "old Right" isolationism, Ludwig von Mises and "Austrian" free market economics, the novelist and philosopher Ayn Rand, and the polymath Murray Rothbard. Rothbard was notable for offering a "package" of property rights (including self-ownership) and nonaggression against others as a foundation for libertarian ethical, social, and political thought.

Third, there is a more explicitly political libertarian movement. This draws upon a wide diversity of individualistic and nonstatist currents in U.S. life, from opposition to the *Vietnam War and the military draft, through tax resistance and the cause of "hard" money, to the often religiously inspired home schooling movement, and those who wish to end the involvement of government in the control of consensual crime. The Libertarian Party, founded in 1971, is the third largest U.S. political party and has run presidential candidates since 1972.

In the United States there is also an important network of libertarian policy or ideas-related organizations of which the Cato Institute is the most prominent. Internationally, libertarianism has made its impact through the influence of academic work and an international network of market-oriented public policy institutes. Ideas from such institutes—notably about *privatization and *deregulation—have been adopted by governments of a variety of complexions. Politically, libertarianism is sometimes confused with modern, market-oriented *conservatism. But libertarians typically differ sharply from conservatives regarding foreign policy and issues such as the legalization of drugs and prostitution.

(See also Public Choice Theory.)

David Boaz, *Libertarianism: A Primer* (New York, 1997). David Boaz, ed., *The Libertarian Reader* (New York, 1997). A useful starting point for information on all aspects of libertarianism is www.free-market.com.

JEREMY SHEARMUR

LIBYA. A desert country in North Africa, Libya emerged as an independent state in 1951. The territory had been seized by Italy shortly before World War I and forged into a single colony during long military campaigns against local tribes between 1911 and 1927.

Over 100,000 Italians came to settle in Libya as part of a Fascist policy of "demographic colonization." The *Mussolini regime, which proudly spoke of Libya as Italy's *Quarta Sponda* or "Fourth Shore," spent 1.8 billion lira to build roads and other infrastructure to strengthen its hold on the colony.

When Allied forces defeated the Axis armies in North Africa in 1942, British and Free French forces occupied Libya, and Italy's colonial control came to an end. Between 1942 and 1951, British military administrations controlled Tripolitania and Cyrenaica, while France controlled the Fezzan.

The new state, created as a monarchy at British insistence, was placed under the rule of the religious leader Idris al-Sanusi, a pro-British figure who had lived in exile in Egypt since 1923. At the time of independence, Libya was one of the world's poorest nations. Mostly desert, with only 2 percent of its territory arable, Libya's major exports were esparto grass and scrap iron from its World War II battlefields. The new state had to depend on foreign aid from Europe and the United States and to accept, in return, foreign military bases on its soil and a foreign policy that espoused Western interests in the region.

Though Libya had a small population of just 1.1 million, it was not politically coherent or socially homogeneous. The urban mercantile classes of the two major cities—Tripoli and Benghazi—shared in the wider culture of Egypt and the Middle East, while the major tribes of Cyrenaica were still extremely narrow in their outlook: bound to the Sanusi religious order and the monarchy which was based on it.

Many Libyans were very poor and resented their government's subservience to the West. This bred political radicalism, especially among the youth who were increasingly influenced by the radical *Arab nationalism of neighboring Nasserist Egypt.

On 1 September 1969, a group of junior officers overthrew the monarchy; their leader was a young signals captain, Muammar *Qaddafi. The new Revolutionary Command Council was dominated by Qaddafi who, along with many of his comrades, came from the hitherto insignificant region of Sirtica. The new regime soon revealed the strong influence of *Nasserism.

For the next decade, the new political system was in constant evolution, as it changed from radical Arab nationalism tinged with *Islam to the idiosyncratic system of the *jamahiriyah* ("state of the masses"), as outlined in Qaddafi's political treatise, the *Green Book*. During the 1970s, the regime attempted to create a popular power base and to eradicate irredentist support for the previous system among rural populations and in Cyrenaica. In doing so, however, it also alienated large sections of Libyan society.

In 1969 and 1970, in the wake of two failed coup attempts and consequent trials, the royalists went into exile. In April 1973, the Libyan "cultural revolution," proclaimed at Zuwara, forced out the intellectuals and media personalities. In August 1975, a failed army coup led to arrests and executions of young officers who had originally been part of the regime's support base. In September 1976, business and commercial groups began to leave, as "popular sovereignty" and the *jamahiriyah* were proclaimed to be the basis of Libya's Constitution and the economy was effectively nationalized. In 1977, the Islamic religious establishment and the Qaddafi regime disagreed violently over the role of Islam in the *jamahiriyah*. By 1980, therefore, there was considerable opposition to the regime, both at home and abroad, as domestic political reform was pushed ahead.

The *jamahiri* system expresses the concept of "direct popular democracy" and bans political parties as special interest groups that threaten the common purpose of the "people's authority"—Libyan society overall. All Libyans are members of one of the 2,150 Basic Popular Congresses (BPCs) through residential location or professional affiliation. The congresses discuss all local, regional, national, and international policy issues and mandate delegates to the General People's Congress (GPC), which is the equivalent of a parliament and usually meets twice a year, in March and September. The GPC elects the members of the General Popular Committee (cabinet) in which the members, the secretaries (ministers), have specific responsibilities for secretariats (ministries). Local administrative and executive responsibilities devolve into Local Popular Committees, appointed by the BPCs but linked to the appropriate secretariat, which carry out day-to-day administration.

The individual political commitment required by such a system—in which Qaddafi and his close associates have no formal role—was so great that it rapidly fell into decay. In 1978, therefore, the leader created the Revolutionary Committee movement, directly responsible to him and designed to galvanize and control the popular committee system and the armed forces. The Revolutionary Committees also became an instrument of repression and *terrorism when, after February 1980, they were instructed to "eliminate the stray dogs of the revolution," a policy which resulted in a diplomatic breach with Britain in May 1984. Its members were essentially young activists and regime supporters who now also occupy important formal governmental positions. Until the mid-1990s, however, real power resided in a third, informal level of national political structure, in which members of the tribes to which the leadership belongs—the Warfalla, the Maghara, and, particularly, the Qadhafa—occupy all crucial positions in the administration, economy, and security system. Now Colonel Qaddafi's own family dominates the power structure as his sons come of age.

This domestic radicalism was largely made possible by Libya's massive oil revenues, which reached US$22 billion by 1980, before declining steadily during the 1980s to around US$8 billion today. The revenues paid for development, consumer imports (Libya imports 65 percent of the food its 4-million-strong population consumes), arms (US$14 billion to the Soviet Union alone), and a radical foreign policy based on anti-imperialism and *populism, with support for national liberation movements in the Middle East and Africa, such as the *Palestine Liberation Organization, the Front de Libé'ration Nationale (FROLINAT) in Chad, or the Polisario Front in Western Sahara. Its apparent support for international terrorism and for Iran during the *Iran-Iraq War earned it Western hostility, exemplified by U.S. military attacks in August 1981 and March–April 1986, and isolation in the Middle East and Africa, particularly after defeat by Chad in a border war in March 1987.

Since 1987, Libya has attempted to recover from its diplomatic isolation. It joined the Maghreb Arab Union, alongside Tunisia, Algeria, Morocco, and Mauritania, in February 1989, and has dramatically improved relations with Egypt, Sudan, and Chad. Relations with European states, except Britain, also improved at the end of the 1980s, although the United States has maintained an economic blockade since 1986. Libya also cautiously supported the U.S.–led multinational coalition against Iraq in early 1991, despite considerable domestic opposition. However, U.S., British, and French claims of Libyan responsibility for terrorist attacks on aircraft (Pan Am Flight 103 over the Scottish town of Lockerbie in December 1988 and a UTA DC-10 flight over Niger in September 1989) have ensured that international hostility to the Qaddafi regime endures, despite internal liberalization. In response the Libyan leader has sought to renew his ties with Egypt and, during 1998, attempted to construct a Sahelian and Saharan confederation under Libyan leadership. It was only with the agreement on the Lockerbie issue between Britain and Libya in April 1999 that international hostility began to abate. Under the agreement, the two persons accused of responsibility for the destruction of Pan Am Flight 103 were transferred to the Hague for trial under a tribunal set up under Scottish law. United Nations sanctions were suspended, although the United States maintained its sanctions in force.

E. G. H. Joffé and K. S. McLachlan, eds., *Social and Economic Development in Libya* (Wisbech, U.K., 1981). John Wright, *Libya: A Modern History* (London, 1982). René Lemarchand, ed., *The Green and the Black: Qadafhi's Policies in Africa* (Bloomington, Ind., 1988).

GEORGE JOFFÉ

LIECHTENSTEIN. See SMALL STATES AND TERRITORIES.

LITERACY. See LANGUAGE POLICY.

LITHUANIA. See BALTIC STATES.

LOANS, FOREIGN. See INTERNATIONAL DEBT.

LOMÉ CONVENTION/COTONOU AGREEMENT. Association between Africa and Europe became formalized in 1958, when France's African colonies were granted preferential trade, aid and investment status under Part IV of the Treaty of Rome. Upon attaining independence in 1960, eighteen (later nineteen) African and Malagasy Associated States renegotiated the association status with the six member states of the European Community (EC, later the *European Union, or EU). Since 1963, the association or "partnership" has been governed by the two Yaoundé Conventions (Yaoundé I, 1964–1969 and Yaoundé II, 1971–1975), the Lomé Convention (1975–2000), and the Cotonou Agreement (beginning June 2000).

Britain's entry into the EC in January 1973 required that the original agreement, which involved only *Francophone African states, be broadened to include its African, Caribbean, and Pacific (ACP) partners within the *Commonwealth. Following protracted negotiations, the first Lomé Convention was signed on 29 February 1975 between the nine EC member states and forty-six ACP states.

The Lomé Convention/Cotonou Agreement is a legally binding contractual agreement based on partnership, reciprocity, and equal benefits between the EU and the ACP states in the areas of trade, commodities, minerals, aid, and agricultural and industrial development. The Lomé I Convention (1975–1980) has been renegotiated and renewed four times and was followed by the Lomé II (1980–1985), Lomé III (1985–1990), and Lomé IV (1990–2000) conventions, and by the Cotonou Agreement (2000–2020).

The institutional framework of ACP-EU cooperation includes the Council of Ministers, the Committee of Ambassadors, and the Joint Assembly. The Council of Ministers, whose decisions are binding, is the major decision-making organ of the Lomé Convention; it is composed of representatives of the EU Council of Ministers (plus one delegate of the EU Commission) and of representatives of the ACP governments, and meets annually. The Committee of Ambassadors, which monitors the implementation of the Convention, is composed of representatives of each EU member state (plus a representative of the EU Commission) and of representatives of each ACP state; it meets twice a year. The Joint Assembly acts in a purely consultative capacity and is composed of members of the European Parliament and ACP members of parliament.

In the area of trade, the prevailing rule is that of free and non-reciprocal access to the EU market of almost all ACP export products, abolition of all quantitative restrictions, and gradual elimination of non-tariff barriers (NTBs). Excluded from this rule are products subject to the EU's Common Agricultural Policy (such as beef, veal, and dairy products), as well as products falling under a special trade regime (such as bananas, sugar, rum, and textiles). Because of these restrictions and the EU's restrictive definition of rules of origin, resort to safeguard clauses and to a broad range of NTBs, the African ACP exporters' share of the EU market shrank from 6.7 percent to 3 percent between 1975 and 2000. In the area of commodities, the system of stabilization of export earnings (Stabex) provides financial compensation to ACP countries in the event that fluctuations in the price or quantity of any of forty-nine stipulated products lead to sharply reduced export earnings. Since its creation, the Stabex system has been dysfunctional in many ways: limited product coverage (restricted to unprocessed commodities); a complex and unfavorable method of calculation for transfer entitlement; extreme beneficiary country and product concentration; and insufficient financial allocation. Similarly, in the area of minerals, the system of stabilization of mineral exports (Sysmin) is designed to maintain the production capacity of the ACP countries' mining sectors at a viable level and is activated when these countries experience a 10 percent fall in production and/or export capacity as a result of exceptional events.

The main instrument of ACP-EU cooperation is the aid program, or "financial and technical cooperation." This program includes grants by the European Development Fund (EDF) and loans by the European Investment Bank (EIB) aimed at financing national and regional development programs and projects in the areas of infrastructure, agriculture, industry, energy, and mining. Among the major problems of financial and technical cooperation are: insufficient financial endowment (particularly with regard to the increased number of ACP states and rate of inflation), administrative and procedural problems, and a predominantly "colonial" sectoral distribution of aid (with 80 percent of total aid allocated to infrastructure and commodity production support). Under Lomé V, the extended 9th EDF—endowed with 13.5 billion euros for the period 2000 to 2005—is designed to help ACP producers diversify their production and exports and to deepen the various regional integration processes. Other areas of ACP-EU cooperation include the environment, agricultural cooperation, food security and rural development, development of fisheries, industrial development and cooperation, development of services (tourism, transport, communications, and informatics), cultural and social cooperation, structural adjustment support, and regional cooperation.

In April 1997 South Africa became a "quasi-member" of the Lomé Convention—with access to the EDF resources—and the seventy-first ACP state. In October 1999 the EU and South Africa concluded a separate *Trade, Development and Cooperation Agreement*. In February 2000 an ACP-EU agreement on the extension of the Lomé Convention was reached. This agreement provides for an eight-year transition period (and twelve-year implementation period) during which market access of ACP products into the EU will continue under the current arrangement, and new negotiations on trade and economic arrangements with the EU shall be negotiated and concluded. Lomé V, signed in May 2000, as well as the Africa-EU summit of Cairo, Egypt (3–4 April 2000) signaled a new determination on the part of ACP, African, and European leaders to transcend economic development issues in order to give their cooperation a distinctly political dimension, including concern for democracy, good governance, human rights, and the rule of law.

A quarter-century of Lomé regime (1975–2000) has not succeeded in significantly altering the ACP states' traditional trade and aid patterns, and in launching them decisively on the path to self-sustained development. In a changing international economic environment characterized by the end of the *Cold War, globalization, the establishment of a new international trade regime managed by the *World Trade Organization (WTO), the broadening of the EU, and the gradual erosion of trade preferences, the ACP states are becoming increasingly marginalized. Indeed, the post-Lomé era occurs within the context of a new world economic order premised on the end of the preferential trade policies on which the ACP-EU agreements are based. Given these structural constraints, does the Lomé regime really have a future? The Lomé Convention has not been able to prevent the further marginalization of the ACP (notably African) states. Furthermore, the goals of Lomé—elimination of poverty, promotion of self-sustainable development and of democratic governance—have not been achieved, in part because geo-strategic and economic interests have prevailed over developmental concerns. Ultimately, the post–Cold War situation calls for an end of the preferential, non-reciprocal Lomé relationship and the eventual discontinuation of the Lomé regime.

(See also INTERNATIONAL POLITICAL ECONOMY; NORTH-SOUTH RELATIONS.)

John Ravenhill, *Collective Clientelism: The Lomé Conventions and North South Relations* (New York, 1985). I. William Zartman, ed., *Europe and Africa: The New Phase* (Boulder, Colo., 1992). Robert Kappel, *European Development Cooperation with Africa: The Future of Lomé* (Leipzig, 1996). Guy Martin, "The EU and Africa: The Lomé Convention into the 21st Century," in G. Martin, *Africa in World Politics: A Pan-African Perspective* (Trenton, N.J., 2001).

GUY MARTIN

LUMUMBA, Patrice. Born in Katako-Kombe, *Zaire, on 2 July 1925, Patrice Lumumba was an autodidact. He began his career in the colonial postal service in 1954 before joining the Kinshasa-based BRACONGO brewery company as a sales manager. Meanwhile, he became a member of various native *elite circles and, later, cofounded and chaired the nationalist party Mouvement National Congolais (MNC). From then on he was a full-time politician, attending conferences such as the All African People's Conference in Accra, Ghana, in 1958, organizing political rallies, and participating as the MNC chief delegate to the Round-Table Conference on Zaire's Independence in Belgium.

After the MNC's victory in the national elections, Lumumba was invested prime minister and minister of defense of the coalition government to run the country at independence on 30 June 1960. Three months later, Lumumba faced the first constitutional crisis in a conflict opposing him to the head of state, Joseph Kasavubu, which prompted an attempt by Mobutu, then a colonel and the army's chief of staff, to neutralize both parties. Later, Mobutu ordered Lumumba's arrest, imprisonment, and transfer to the Katanga (now Shaba) province where he was summarily executed on 17 January 1961. He was thirty-five.

Lumumba was a controversial person. While his friends admired him as a nationalist leader, his enemies simply considered him a communist, a demagogue, and a dangerous man. Lumumba's posthumous book *Congo, My Country*, however, portrays a gradually maturing politician whose ideas and experience changed as he faced new challenges and met new people.

Lumumba's closest friends and advisers divide his political life into three phases. During the first phase, Lumumba, like most *évolués*—the colonially created group of Zairian elite—believed in the "Belgian civilizing mission" in Zaire and wanted to achieve a constructive synthesis between Western and African values. The second phase began shortly before Zaire's independence. Disappointed by the Belgian reluctance to grant equal rights, Lumumba began to shift toward an increasingly nationalist position. He was then inspired by such radical African leaders as Kwame *Nkrumah of Ghana, Sékou Touré of Guinea, and Gamal Abdel *Nasser of Egypt. The last phase started at independence and ended with his assassination two hundred days later. During that time, Lumumba had become "a lonely man in power." Though democratically elected, he had to face numerous obstacles from internal rivals and major Western democracies. Among the latter were the Eisenhower administration in the United States and most European interests in Zaire.

It is hard to predict what Zaire would have been had Lumumba been able to consolidate his power. However, it is certain that his nationalist ideal, his struggle to keep his country unified, strong, and prosperous, his anticolonial and non-aligned stance, and his position in favor of a united Africa had a strong appeal throughout Africa and beyond. Lumumba's political philosophy still resonates in Zaire today.

(See also CONGO CRISIS; DECOLONIZATION; NATIONALISM.)

Patrice Lumumba, *Congo, My Country* (London, 1962). Thomas Kanza, *The Rise and Fall of Patrice Lumumba: Conflict in the Congo* (London, 1978).

MUSIFIKY MWANASALI

LUSOPHONE AFRICA. Lusophone Africa comprises about 30 million people in the five former Portuguese colonies in Africa—Angola, Mozambique, Guinea-Bissau, Cape Verde, and São Tomé e Príncipe—whose official language has remained Portuguese. Having undergone very similar brutal and archaic colonial experiences, the five newly independent countries have developed similar political ideologies and structures that have fostered a sense of community that is surpassed only by the former French colonies. This commonality of philosophy and past experiences has been reinforced by the recently (1996) created Comunidade de Paises de Lingua Portuguesa (CPLP), or the Community of Countries of the Portuguese Language, which includes *Portugal and Brazil.

Even though the Portuguese carried out considerable trade with their incipient colonies, sent sailors, priests, and adventurous settlers who mingled with the Africans, adopted African cultural traditions, and lived off the land as *sertanejos*, *prazeros*, or *lancados*, they grew tired of the little benefit they derived from Africa prior to the beginning of the twentieth century. Slavery had become a lucrative enterprise from the sixteenth century on, but the Portuguese Crown officially abolished the slave trade during the 1870s. However, as the scramble for Africa intensified during the 1880s, Portugal felt threatened and did all it could to preserve its empire both at the Berlin Conference (1884–1885) and thereafter, signing favorable treaties with France, Britain, Belgium, and even the Union of South Africa during the 1890s.

To protect and develop its empire, Portugal introduced the concessionaire system within its colonies, which bestowed monopolistic privileges of land and mineral and agricultural resources upon certain companies such as the Mozambique Company in Mozambique. These companies were usually foreign-owned, even though a Portuguese residing in Lisbon or in the colony might be the president. It was during this time that taxation, forced labor, and forced recruitment for the army and the police were introduced. As the colonial system entrenched itself, Africans were forced to grow certain cash crops such as cotton, rice, tobacco in Angola and Mozambique, sugar cane in São Tomé e Príncipe, and peanuts and bananas in Cape Verde and Guinea-Bissau.

The brutal colonial policies were reinforced under Prime

Minister Antonio de Oliveira Salazar, who abolished foreign companies in the 1930s, but saw the overseas empire primarily as a source of wealth for continental Portugal. The old Portuguese tendency of assimilating the conquered populations continued, but only on paper. Assimilation entitled an African to all privileges, rights, and responsibilities of a Portuguese citizen, but it often required conversion to Catholicism, adoption of the Portuguese language and culture, and the ability to read and write. This policy, which benefited less than 5 percent of the population of the colonies combined, created a dual system of assimilated or "civilized" and indigenas or noncivilized. Those Africans under the *sistema do indigenato* had no rights whatsoever, and their land could be expropriated by any white settler, the government, a company, and, at times, by an assimilated African.

Governed by hardly democratic regimes over the centuries and by an open dictatorship following the establishment of the Estado Novo (1928–1968), Portugal attempted to stifle any nationalist manifestation in its colonial empire. Thus, when the French and the British allowed the formation of parties in their colonies during the post–World War II era, the Portuguese steadfastly opposed the trend and claimed that there were politicians elected in the colonies that represented Africans' interests in the Portuguese parliament, the Cortes, or the Assembleia Nacional. Repression increased in the Portuguese colonies when aspirations for independence mobilized the African masses during the late 1950s and early 1960s. Portugal claimed, most emphatically after 1951, that the colonies were Portuguese provinces and therefore an integral part of continental Portugal, all brought together under a united, multiracial empire, speaking the same language and enjoying the same rights and privileges. Thus, political arrests, imprisonment, torture, murder and assassination, mysterious disappearances, forced internment, and exile, mainly to São Tomé e Príncipe or Cape Verde, became the norm prior to independence.

Portuguese determination to stifle by force any colonial movement toward independence and refusal to negotiate with the nationalist leaders compelled the Africans to embark on guerrilla warfare to dislodge at all cost the colonial state. Thus, the Frente de Libertacao de Mocambique or Mocambique Liberation Front (FRELIMO) of Dr. Eduardo Mondlane, educated in the United States, declared war on the Portuguese colonial government in Mozambique and initiated a guerrilla offensive in September 1964. The Angolan nationalist movements, the Movimento Popular da Independencia de Angola (MPLA) under Agostinho Neto, the National Front for the Liberation of Angola (FNLA), under Holden Roberto, and the Uniao Nacional da Independencia Total de Angola (UNITA), under Dr. Jonas Savimbi, initiated their guerrilla warfare against Portugal in 1961–1966, although sporadic violent activities had been carried out in and around Luanda, Angola's capital, as early as 1956, eliciting violent reprisals from the Portuguese troops.

In Guinea-Bissau and Cape Verde, Amilcar *Cabral organized the Partido Africano da Independencia da Guiné and Cabo Verde (PAIGC) and initiated an armed struggle against the Portuguese in 1963. São Tomé e Príncipe remained on the sidelines but the sentiments of its people were in unison with those of their fellow nationalists in the other Portuguese colonies. The Comite de Libertacao de São Tomé e Príncipe was founded in 1960, changing to the Movimento de Liberatacao de São Tomé e Príncipe (MLSTP) in 1972. It never saw combat, however.

The Portuguese government gathered some 150,000 relatively well-equipped troops to fight in the three rebel colonies (there was no fighting in Cape Verde, since the leaders, who assumed prominent control of the PAIGC, decided to join the Guineans and fight on Guinea-Bissau territory). Although no credible casualty figures have been floated around regarding the three liberation wars either on the Portuguese or the African side, they must have been in the thousands. The mounting casualties suffered by the Portuguese army led a group of young officers, calling themselves the Movimento das Forcas Armadas, to overthrow in April 1974 the government of Marcello Caetano, who had succeeded Antonio de Oliveria Salazar as prime minister in Lisbon in 1968.

As a reaction against a brutal colonial system that only war was able to eliminate and the underdeveloped, backward state of the colonies, immersed in a capitalist model that was intrinsically a part of nineteenth- and twentieth-century *capitalism, the new nationalist leaders rejected capitalism and opted for Marxism-Leninism, which they called socialism. Under socialism, private property would be severely curtailed, private institutions (schools, hospitals, law firms, banks, and other businesses) would be nationalized; religious "superstition" and ignorance wiped out; government-controlled shops, cooperatives, and collective villages and farms would be run and controlled by the state; and the government would run and control large land enterprises, such as farms, left behind by panic-stricken Portuguese colonialists who abandoned the new independent country.

Politically, the new countries would be under a one-party state, and the former guerrilla front would institute a system of "centralized democracy," where the masses would vote from the local cells to the district, provincial, and national precincts. The presidential candidate would be selected by the party sitting in congress, while the people would be represented by a people's assembly, people's courts, appeals courts, and a supreme court (whose judges would be presidential appointees) to constitute a judiciary in tune with the grass roots, even though traditional authorities were to be removed immediately and their influence in the countryside eliminated. In the process, any opposition was seen as reactionary and demonstrating the pernicious tendencies of the despised bourgeoisie. Peasants and workers or the proletariat were the preferred classes.

Thus, as a consequence of unwise policies, the lack of experience, external interference, and the tendency toward political autocracy and oligarchy prevalent in most of Africa following independence, each Portuguese colony either experienced another period of civil violence or war, as has been the case of Angola, Mozambique, and Guinea-Bissau, or crippling political instability, as happened in Cape Verde and São Tomé e Príncipe prior to the mid-1990s.

In Angola, immediately after independence in 1975, UNITA, assisted by apartheid South Africa and by the United States and Zambia, and the MPLA, during the Cold War enjoying relatively massive assistance from the Soviet Union and Cuba, were embroiled in a fratricidal war that continued into the twenty-first century. This occurred despite cease-fires and multiparty elections in 1992 that kept in power the incumbent party, the MPLA, and its president, Eduardo dos Santos.

In Mozambique, the Mozambique National Resistance, first under Andre Matsangaissa and then under Afonso Dhlakama, with financial and military support from Southern Rhodesia (until 1980) and South Africa thereafter, waged a war that virtually destroyed the country, as FRELIMO vowed to fight on. Fortunately, the two sides, under the auspices of the Italian government and the Catholic Church, signed a peace accord in 1992 which led to multiparty democratic elections in 1994 and 1999. Both ended in an apparent victory of the ruling party, FRELIMO.

Of the fighting colonies, Guinea-Bissau was the most promising, in view of the united front it forged against the Portuguese, the high popular determination of the struggle, and the political and diplomatic shrewdness it showed. Five years after independence, however, in November 1980, the unification process broke loose, and Cape Verde and Guinea-Bissau were at each other's throats. Party affiliation was broken up, and in November 1981 a coup d'état occurred, overthrowing Luiz Cabral as Guinea-Bissau's first president, replaced by Bernardo Nino Vieira.

In São Tomé e Príncipe, Angolan troops had to be brought in in March 1978, when a serious coup attempt was rumored, and several prominent leaders and government officials were arrested. As a Marxist state, São Tomé e Príncipe received considerable assistance from the Soviet Union and Cuba. In August 1990, the government finally allowed a referendum, making the country a multiparty state, which led to presidential elections in March 1991. Miguel Trovoada, an independent candidate, won the presidency, after the ruling party had lost the National Assembly elections in January 1991. A major coup d'état by the army, on 15 August 1995, failed to remove Trovoada permanently, following mediation by Angola, which had threatened to cut off financial assistance. In 1996 Trovoada once again won the presidency and continued to preside over a poor country, whose economy is based almost solely on cocoa exports. Threatened by a collapsing economy, São Tomé e Príncipe began abandoning its Marxist programs, joined the International Monetary Fund and the World Bank in 1977, and slowly liberalized the economy. In 1986, a three-year restructuring program was introduced by the IMF, leading to several demonstrations and workers' strikes. Yet, in 1996, further austerity measures were enacted, but, eventually, São Tomé e Príncipe was lax in implementing the measures, forcing the IMF to declare, in 1997, that the country did not deserve a debt cancellation.

Angola and Mozambique, although relatively rich in natural resources—Angola has oil and diamonds, for example—saw their reliance on the Soviet Union and Cuba weakening and joined the International Monetary Fund and the World Bank also in 1987 and 1988, and eventually accepted structural adjustment programs that remained in effect as recently as 1996, with mixed economic results, at best. Cape Verde announced the end of a single-party system in September 1990. National Assembly and presidential elections were held in January and February 1991, respectively, resulting in a double defeat for the ruling Partido Africano de Independencia de Cabo Verde (PAICV), and a victory for the Movimento

para a Democracia (MPD), led by the country's newly elected president, Manuel Mascarenhas, who was subsequently re-elected in 1996. Despite its meager economic resources (banana exports, livestock, and fishing), Cape Verde's economy has done well without the restructuring programs that are mandated by the International Monetary Fund or the World Bank.

There is no doubt that the Portuguese legacy has had a unique impact on the former colonies of Angola, Mozambique, Guinea-Bissau, Cape Verde, and São Tomé e Príncipe. The policy of assimilation, to which the five colonies were subjected, was a double sword that retarded the resurgence of a strong nationalist movement and forced them eventually to wage a guerrilla war that brought independence fifteen years after most of the British, French, and Belgian colonies had achieved theirs in 1960. All five new countries experienced governance problems immediately following independence, partly because of leadership intransigence and autocratic propensities, as has been the case in most of Africa, except that here, autocracy led to civil wars (in Angola, Mozambique, and Guinea-Bissau), coup d'états (in Guinea-Bissau), extreme political bickering (in Cape Verde and São Tomé e Príncipe), and political chaos well into the late 1990s.

All five former colonies, rejecting Portugal's extreme capitalist imperialism, adopted a Marxist ideology that proved unwise during the 1980s with the collapse of their centralized economies, the West's refusal to provide economic assistance, and the fall of the Soviet Union. Except for Cape Verde, all four remaining Lusophone countries have done poorly in economic terms, despite assistance from the International Monetary Fund and the World Bank once they abandoned the tenets of an extreme socialist philosophy.

Finally, although all five Lusophone African countries abandoned the single-party system in favor of a multiparty system during the early 1990s, the political situation was still intimidating to the opposition in early 2000, and violations of human rights have occurred. So, as the former Portuguese colonies entered the twenty-first century, Angola was still in total political disarray, the outcome of which is everyone's guess, and the others were limping politically and economically. Mozambique, in addition, had suffered a severe setback caused by heavy floods in early 2000.

(See also COLONIAL EMPIRES; DECOLONIZATION; DEMOCRATIC TRANSITIONS; MARXISM.)

James Duffy, *Portuguese Africa* (Cambridge, Mass., 1961). Alfredo H. Willensky, *Trends in Portuguese Overseas Legislation for Africa* (Braga, 1971). William Minter, *Portuguese Africa and the West* (Harmondsworth, England, 1972). Neil Bruce, *Portugal: The Last Empire* (New York, 1975). Armando Castro, *O sistema colonial portugues em Africa (meados do seculo XX)* (Lisbon, 1978). David Birmingham, *Frontline Nationalism in Angola and Mozambique* (Trenton, N.J., 1992). Mustapha Dhada, *Warriors at Work: How Guinea-Bissau Was Really Set Free* (Niwot, Colo., 1993). Phyllis Peres, *Transculturation and Resistance in Lusophone African Narrative* (Gainesville, Fla., 1997).

MARIO J. AZEVEDO

LUXEMBOURG. The Grand Duchy of Luxembourg, which is a relatively recent entity (its title dates back to 1315, its current boundaries and independence to 1839, and the accession of the House of Nassau-Weilburg to 1890), has preserved from its more distant past a culture marked by its dual Romano-Germanic roots and by a strong attachment to Catholicism despite the upheaval caused by the Reformation. With a population of some 430,000 inhabitants, it is today the smallest member state of the *European Union (EU) and of the North Atlantic Treaty Organization (NATO).

History has not been kind to Luxembourg, whose existence has been called into question repeatedly by international crises. This was particularly the case after the German occupation during World War I and the brutal Germanization at the hands of the Nazi regime between 1940 and 1944, when the Grand Duchess Charlotte and the government supported the Allies. After World War II, the Grand Duchy became an active participant in the process of forming economic and political union within Europe. As early as 1944, it joined with Belgium and the Netherlands to found an economic union (Benelux).

Modern metallurgy was the vector of the Industrial Revolution in Luxembourg. The iron and steel industry, initially dominated by family businesses, graduated to limited companies and then large industrial groups (Aciéries Réunies de Burbach-Eich-Dudelange [ARBED]). The iron and steel industry halted traditional emigration flows and then stimulated immigration, first of Italians and then of Portuguese. Consequently, the worldwide crisis in the steel sector in the 1970s hit the country extremely hard. All economic and social structures rested on this basic industry, and the very existence of the country was affected. A tripartite committee consisting of the ARBED management, the government, and the trade unions (the "Luxembourg model") coordinated orderly cutbacks, and *modernization was achieved without recourse to dismissals of redundant employees.

The Luxembourg economy, which was the only one in the European Union to survive the crisis without significant unemployment, enjoys the highest per capita income in the EU, with a stable and prosperous economy marked by steady growth, low inflation, and low unemployment. Luxembourg is the headquarters for one of the major European telecommunications groups, the Compagnie Luxembourgeoise de Télédiffusion (CLT). It is also a leading financial market: banking services account for a growing share of the economy, as growth in the financial sector has easily compensated for decline in steel.

Luxembourg, which has a monetary union with Belgium (the Belgo-Luxembourg Economic Union), is a free exchange area for European currencies with no form of credit control. Although there is a great deal of concern about the effects of *Economic and Monetary Union (EMU) with its free movement of capital and potential tax harmonization within the

EU, the Grand Duchy is counting on the country's calm labor situation and political stability to attract foreign investors.

Luxembourg is a *constitutional monarchy and a *parliamentary democracy. Universal suffrage for men and women was introduced in 1919. The political parties still bear the traces of the ideological struggles from which they emerged. The Chreüstlech-Sozial Volkspartei (CSV), the Letzeburger Sozialistesch Arbechterpartei (LSAP), and the liberals of the Demokratesch Partei (DP) are the traditional groups. In addition, Luxembourg has an effective Green Party, Dei Greng Alternativ (GAP). The green movement, although divided and not so strong as in Germany, for example, enjoys parliamentary representation, and benefits from the concern of the general public about the French Cattenom nuclear power plant, built near the Luxembourg border.

Coalition governments are the rule. With two brief exceptions—in 1925 and in 1974–1979, when a liberal socialist government was led by Gaston Thorn—the CSV has led the government in coalition with either the LSAP or the DP. Since the 1984 elections, when Pierre Werner gave up his post of prime minister to Jacques Santer (his favored successor in the CSV), a Christian-Socialist coalition, which regained public support in the 1989 elections, has formed the Luxembourg government. Jean-Claude Juncker has served as prime minister since 1995.

On 19 June 1990, Luxembourg, Belgium, the Netherlands, France, and the Federal Republic of Germany signed the Schengen Convention, which is intended to abolish border controls for individuals between the five countries. But paradoxically, although the Grand Duchy was one of the pioneers of European unification, the single market is a source of concern to Luxembourg because it threatens its status as a tax haven. In a more positive vein, however, Luxembourg benefits in both economic and geopolitical terms from the presence of several significant European Union institutions, including the Commission, the Court of Justice, and the general Secretariat of the European Parliament. The EU institutions, particularly the Court of Justice, add a further element to Luxembourg's character as a European melting pot. The Grand Duchy has, nevertheless, held on to its heritage and has built harmonious labor relations and a tradition of political consensus that it considers a model for its European neighbors.

Gilbert Trausch, *Le Luxembourg à l'époque contemporaine* (Luxembourg, 1981).

MATEO ALALUF

M

MAASTRICHT TREATY. The Maastricht Treaty (officially the Treaty on European Union; so called after the small Dutch town where final talks were held in 1991) brought substantial changes to the Treaties of Rome (1957) and the Single European Act (SEA, 1986), in particular so as to facilitate the beginning of *Economic and Monetary Union (EMU). It also brought commitment to a Common Foreign and Security Policy (CFSP), common justice and home affairs policies, and enhanced powers for the European Parliament. Finally, it changed the official name of "Europe" from the European Community (EC) to the *European Union (EU).

Maastricht was the logical culmination of processes begun in the 1950s. The Treaty of Rome (1957), signed by six continental countries, created a European customs-free zone behind a common external tariff accompanied by a number of common policies (particularly in agriculture). When these national economic models were challenged in the 1970s by economic change, there followed a difficult decade. Integration was revived after 1985 when the European Commission proposed to "complete the Single Market" by the end of 1992. The SEA (ratified in 1987) changed the EU Treaties to facilitate this, particularly to allow "qualified majority" voting in the Council of Ministers on Single Market programs, give new amending power to the Parliament, and create new regional development and social policies. Final movement to Maastricht started in 1989 with the "Delors Report" on EMU. EU members then decided to hold a new Intergovernmental Conference (IGC) to make EMU possible. The Germans insisted on a second, parallel IGC on "political union," in particular to expand the power of Parliament and enhance foreign policy cooperation. Both began in December 1990.

In the EMU talks a number of big issues were resolved. Speaking for the poorer EU states, the Spanish vowed to block everything if there were no provisions for new regional aid for EMU, resulting in a new "Cohesion Fund." British opposition was neutralized by allowing the British to opt out of EMU without preventing anyone else from joining (the Danes were also allowed to opt out). The Germans, lukewarm about EMU, insisted upon stringent policy "convergence criteria" for EMU membership to ensure that economically profligate countries—Italy in the first instance—were kept out until their houses were in order. Maastricht thus set convergence targets for budget deficits (3 percent of GDP), longer-term debt (60 percent of GDP), inflation, interest rates, and currency stability (tied to best results across the EU). The French also wanted an "economic government" to set the Community economic policy, but the Germans refused. The Germans also succeeding in assuring the complete independence of the proposed ECB, which was to be dedicated to price stability.

The final big issue was timing. The Delors Report had proposed a three-stage progression, already begun in 1990 when controls on capital movement were eliminated within the Single Market. Stage 2, which the report set for 1994, would have created the ECB to "apprentice" for final EMU, but the Germans, facing the costs of unification, wanted to slow things down. Stage 2 became a "European Monetary Institute" to monitor convergence. Passage to the third stage, when currencies would be locked together and the new ECB would prepare to introduce the euro, was left vague until the last minute. Then a compromise proposed by France and backed strongly by Italy was accepted. EMU would happen in January 1997 in the event that a majority of states were eligible. If this did not come to pass, there would then be a fixed date, 1 January 1999, when EMU would happen no matter how many were eligible. This compromise ensured that EMU would actually take place.

The second IGC on "political union" was less tidy. Ambitions, again largely French, for coordinating EU foreign and defense policies ran up against member state disunity in the uncertain moment after the end of the Cold War. Solemn language about a European Common Foreign and Security Policy (CFSP) was very tentative. Member states might decide on general areas of concern and on joint actions within these areas, but the rules for decision making made it very difficult for Europe to act at all, let alone in time to have an effect. On "justice and home affairs," directions were set to extend the "Schengen" arrangements intended to eliminate ordered controls. A "Europol" for coordinating police information and action would be created to offset the security problems of the abolition of internal borders, minimal standards for EU citizenship were set out, and common approaches to immigration policy and political asylum were envisaged. These proposals, like those for CFSP, were really declarations of intent.

The most tangible products of the political union IGC were increases in the powers of the European Parliament. Up to Maastricht, the Council of Ministers was the EU's real "legislator," voting on commission proposals. The SEA allowed the parliament to propose amendments but withheld final decision power. The new treaty allowed the Parliament to "co-decide" with the council on a range of issues. This change, meant to remedy the "democratic deficit" and enhance the EU's public credibility, was unfortunately embedded in opaque decision procedures. The parliament also acquired the right to vote proposed commission presidents up or down.

The negotiations raised fundamental questions about the EU's overall "architecture." Federalists advocated a "tree" model—a central community "trunk" connected to different "branches." Confederalists proposed a "temple" with three separate pillars joined by a common preamble. The temple model prevailed and the policy areas closest to the heart of remaining member state sovereignty, the CFSP (the second pillar), and "justice and home affairs" (the third) became separate entities. The "community," focusing primarily on economic integration, was the first pillar.

This institutional equilibrium was unstable, however. The temple formula established that certain policy areas, better suited to community approaches, became intergovernmental, in particular in justice and home affairs. Moreover, Maastricht left unresolved a number of important issues. The negotiators thus called for yet another IGC in 1996, leading to the 1997 Amsterdam Treaty. In the meantime, however, Maastricht proved unpopular with European public opinion, partly because of Europe's new economic difficulties. The Danes voted against ratifying the treaty in June 1992 (later reversing themselves after Denmark had been granted a number of special exemptions) and the French barely approved it three months later. Opinion polls elsewhere indicated widespread anxiety about integration, in particular about EMU. Leaders held steady nonetheless, and Maastricht was implemented, culminating in the beginning of EMU in 1999.

(See also ROME, TREATY OF.)

European Union, *Treaty on European Union* (Luxembourg, 1992). Charles Grant, *Delors: Inside the House That Jacques Built* (London, 1994). George Ross, *Jacques Delors and European Integration* (Oxford, 1995). Andrew Moravcsik, *The Choice for Europe* (Ithaca, N.Y. 1998).

GEORGE ROSS

MACAO. See HONG KONG; SMALL STATES AND TERRITORIES.

MACEDONIA, THE FORMER YUGOSLAV REPUBLIC OF.
The modern Macedonian state is formed from one of communist *Yugoslavia's six constituent republics where the Macedonians were recognized as a distinct people. Previously the interwar Yugoslav state had viewed them as Serbs. They were until very recently viewed as ethnic Bulgarians by *Bulgaria, which has historically claimed the territory. Independence followed the peaceful withdrawal of the Yugoslav army in 1991. However, *Greece, which gained the Aegean part of geographic Macedonia after the Balkan Wars of 1912–13, claims sole possession of the name "Macedonia" and vetoed international acceptance of the new state under that name. The state was finally accepted into the United Nations in April 1993 under the above temporary name.

In the census of 1994 out of the total population of 1,936,877 there were: 1,288,330 Macedonians (66.5%); 442,914 Albanians (22.9%); 77,252 Turks (4%); 43,732 Roma (Gypsies); (2.3%); 38,620 (2%) Serbs; 15,315 "Muslims" (0.8%); 8,467 Vlachs (0.4%); and 22,607 others (1.2%). The numbers remain controversial with, for example, the Albanians claiming far higher figures. The Macedonians are Orthodox Christian by belief while the Albanians are predominantly Sunni Muslim (with some Roman Catholics), the Turks wholly Sunni Muslim, and the Roma both Muslim and Christian.

Macedonia is a democratic republic with a 120-seat parliament and a directly elected president. The main political cleavages center on continuity from previous communist structures opposed to new political forces, and the interethnic question with ethnic Albanians voting overwhelmingly for their own parties and many wanting autonomy for western Macedonia (where they make substantial majorities) and even union with Kosovo and Albania. Despite severe initial problems including economic blockades by Greece, the economy survived and the currency stabilized. Macedonia is strategically placed at the heart of the *Balkans, although its armed forces remain very small. It is a member of the Council of Europe and looks toward membership of the European Union.

(See also BOSNIA AND HERZEGOVINA; CROATIA; KOSOVO WAR; POST-COMMUNISM; SERBIA AND MONTENEGRO; SLOVENIA.)

Hugh Poulton, *Who Are the Macedonians?* (London, 1995).

HUGH POULTON

MADAGASCAR. The Republic of Madagascar, located some 220 miles (350 km.) east of Mozambique, has a population of about 14 million. Despite a relatively diversified resource base in comparison with many African countries, Madagascar is still one of the world's poorest countries: Perhaps three-fourths of the population lives on a per capita income of less than US$50. Consumer welfare has been declining almost continuously since independence, and food consumption per head has generally declined.

Madagascar became a French protectorate in 1890 and gained autonomy in the French Union in 1958. Madagascar made a peaceful transition to independence in 1960 under its president, Philbert Tsiranana. By the early 1970s there was growing dissatisfaction with the conservative and somewhat authoritarian Tsiranana regime. After a series of strikes and riots in the capital, Antananarivo, Tsiranana turned over the government to the armed forces. By 1975 political unrest and a mutiny by the police in the capital led to another change of government led by Lieutenant Commander Didier Ratsiraka. Following his major policy statement, the Charter of the Malagasy Socialist Revolution, Ratsiraka nationalized the banks, mines, oil refinery, and shipping company, and closed the U.S. satellite tracking station. He continued with a military-style government.

Social and political unrest grew in the late 1970s, again due primarily to economic concerns, this time in the drought-stricken rural areas. Riots followed in 1981. The radical Ratsiraka regime began to eliminate organized dissent during this period. After the president announced his intent to run for a second term of office, Madagascar experienced increased social and economic unrest. Food shortages again sparked riots in the rural areas, mostly in southern Madagascar in the late 1980s. After riots again broke out in the capital, the government suppressed virtually all opposition. In 1989 Ratsiraka was elected to a third term in a somewhat fair election, at least compared with the previous two. By 1990, and after considerable domestic and international pressures, Madagascar officially allowed other parties to contest elections and generally engage in political debate. Elections were held in 1992; a French-trained medical doctor, Albert Zafy, won the presidency after several runoff elections the next year, ending Ratsiraka's seventeen years of dictatorship. Zafy was impeached in 1996, and Ratsiraka returned to power. Madagascar's new constitution contains only a few checks on the power of the executive.

Madagascar's economic situation remains troubled. During

the 1980s the GNP per capita declined by about 3.4 percent annually, with a current GNP per capita of perhaps US$200. Madagascar's population has more than doubled since 1950, and was estimated at 16 million in the year 2000. Probably half of the population is under twenty years old. Almost three-fourths of the working population is engaged in agriculture, most at the subsistence level, although this percentage has declined slightly in recent years. Agriculture is the country's largest source of foreign exchange (as much as 80 percent of the total). Agriculture declined in the 1970s and 1980s due to inappropriate government agricultural policies, droughts, and four cyclones. Rice is the most important food crop; in fact, Madagascar has the highest per capita consumption of rice in the world.

After three decades of state intervention and economic decline, Madagascar began to liberalize its economic policies in the mid-1980s. In 1986, it launched a new investment code, which encouraged private foreign and domestic investment. The Malagasy franc has been devalued, and the government has successfully negotiated agreements with its major official and private creditors at the London Club and the *Paris Club. The government also began to close a few state-run enterprises which were running at a loss. In 1996 the *International Monetary Fund approved a $118 million Enhanced Structural Adjustment Facility. This was the first agreement with the IMF since 1991. In 1997 the *World Bank approved a $70 million Structural Adjustment Credit.

Madagascar's foreign policy has undergone significant changes of direction. Madagascar's initial foreign policy after independence was conservative, and it gave the West (particularly France) virtually uncritical support. It broke with France over only a few issues, such as maintaining diplomatic recognition of Taiwan. It withdrew from the Franc Zone in 1973. Ratsiraka's cornerstone policy was the "Indian Ocean Zone of Peace" initiative, supporting nonalignment and a demilitarization of the area. Madagascar moved closer to the Soviet Union, and generally supported the Eastern bloc in the UN and other international fora. Nevertheless, Madagascar did not grant naval rights to the Soviets at the major port, Diégo-Suarez. Madagascar now is a member of the Indian Ocean Commission, the Common Market for Eastern and Southern Africa (COMESA), the Nonaligned Movement, and the Organization of African Unity. It maintains an "all-points" diplomatic relations strategy, which includes official relations with Israel, North and South Korea, Taiwan, the People's Republic of China, and Iran.

(See also INDIAN OCEAN REGION; INTERNATIONAL DEBT.)

Maureen Covell, *Madagascar: Politics, Economics, and Society* (London, 1987). H. Brandt and M. Brown, *Madagascar* (Oxford, 1993). P. M. Allen, *Madagascar: Conflicts of Authority in the Great Island* (Boulder, Colo., 1995).

DONALD L. SPARKS

MAGHREB. The term "Maghreb," an Arabic word signifying "the place where the sun sets," denotes the western part of the Arab world. The word has most commonly been applied to that region of North Africa which came under French colonial authority in the nineteenth and early twentieth centuries, namely, *Algeria, *Tunisia, and *Morocco. In the modern era, however, geopolitics and economics have contributed to an expanded notion of the region that includes the states of *Libya and *Mauritania as well as the contested territory of *Western Sahara. Covering some 2.3 million square miles (5.96 million sq. km.) with a population of about 75 million people, the region has defined some common institutions under the 1989 Treaty of Marrakech but has yet to achieve any significant degree of political or economic integration.

A historic crossroads through which Romans, Arabs, Ottomans, and Europeans passed, the modern Maghreb is most marked by a common language, Arabic, and a common religion, *Islam. Its economy was essentially agrarian until the discovery of oil and natural gas in Algeria and Libya in the 1950s. The idea that the states of the Maghreb ought to form some kind of regional grouping took shape after World War II under the aegis of the nationalist movements of that era. Even prior to Algerian independence, representatives of three political parties—Istiqlal of Morocco, Tunisia's Neo-Destour, and the Algerian Front and Liberation Nationale—held a conference in Tangier, Morocco, in April 1958 at which they adopted a resolution calling for a federal union among the three states. Yet frictions over borders and regime types prevented any rapid implementation of the Tangier declaration. On the contrary, Morocco and Algeria, whose cooperation is clearly essential to any form of regional integration, fought a brief border war in 1963 just one year after Algeria acquired independence.

In 1964, Tunisia, whose constitution commits the country to support efforts toward the formation of a "Greater Maghreb," organized another meeting of the three states plus Libya. They formed an organ called the Permanent Consultative Committee of the Maghreb which met intermittently until 1975 in an effort to sponsor increased trade, coordination of economic policy, and harmonization of the four states' relations with the European common market. Trade within the region, however, did not increase significantly: By the end of the 1980s, it represented only 3 percent of the total trade. While the lack of economic complementarity was clearly an obstacle to functional cooperation, political tensions much amplified by the dispute between Morocco and Algeria over Western Sahara also blocked progress toward creation of a regional bloc.

Worldwide forces of *globalization and economic integration pushed the states of North Africa toward a new effort of regional cooperation in the late 1980s. The steady progress of Western Europe toward a fully integrated economy disrupted long-standing patterns of trade that had been established during the colonial era and had persisted well beyond it. Declining oil revenues also dealt a severe blow to the region's rentier states. Another factor prompting the governments to expand their mutual cooperation was the rise of Islamist movements challenging the postcolonial regimes. Third, regional cooperation appeared in the late 1980s to be a possible path toward resolution of the conflict regarding Western Sahara. These three factors prompted the heads of state of Algeria, Libya, Mauritania, Morocco, and Tunisia to found the Union du Maghreb Arabe (UMA) in February 1989.

The Treaty of Marrakech instituting the union invokes the bonds of history, religion, and language as "ties of fraternity" upon which to build cooperation in the domains of diplomacy, defense, economic development, and cultural matters. The treaty stipulates that the heads of state should meet every six months, serving in turn as chair of the union's Presidential

Council. Headquarters for the organization were subsequently established in Rabat, the capital of Morocco, under the direction of a Tunisian diplomat who was appointed secretary-general. While the secretariat was mandated to draw up practical plans for economic integration, progress toward regional unity depended primarily upon the will of the five heads of state. Conditions of political instability, particularly in Algeria, have rendered such cooperation at the summit extremely problematic since the formation of the UMA. Moreover the failure to achieve an amicable settlement of the Western Saharan issue hobbled the organization. In December 1995, Morocco called for a suspension of the organization's activities, largely because Algeria continued to support the Sahrawi nationalists seeking a referendum on the status of Western Sahara.

The euphoria surrounding the proclamation of the UMA faded away as the member-states accorded priority to their individual national interests. Morocco, committed to the annexation of Western Sahara, pursued a policy of closer relations with the European Union than with its partners in the UMA. Algeria, the potential core state of any regional union, gave primacy to the internal problems posed by the armed Islamic opposition during the 1990s. Libya, isolated by international sanctions, and Mauritania, geographically and economically marginal, were not in a position to knit the region more tightly together. Only Tunisia, whose President Zine el-Abidine Ben Ali perceived significant economic and diplomatic benefits for his country through greater regional integration, tried seriously to resuscitate the moribund UMA in the late 1990s.

The Maghreb is a strategically significant zone whose political stability and foreign policy behavior affect Mediterranean Europe, sub-Saharan Africa, and the Middle East. In terms of population and resources, it is a key link in any chain of African economic integration. The states of North Africa have often assumed leadership roles in Arab and African affairs, more often individually than collectively, however. Like other regions of the world, the Maghreb was subject in the late 1980s to a resurgence of civil society—including Islamist movements—that challenged the generally authoritarian political order. The leaders sought to respond in part by creating the UMA as an instrument of relegitimization to be achieved through greater economic and political cooperation. Yet having failed to construct strong regional institutions, the states of North Africa have fallen short of the vision of "brotherly" unity that its intellectuals have long espoused.

Bassma Kodmani-Darwis and May Chartouni-Dubarry, eds., *Maghreb: Les Années de transition* (Paris, 1990). Dirk Vandewalle, ed., *North Africa: Development and Reform in a Changing Global Economy* (New York, 1996). Yahia Zoubir, ed., *North Africa in Transition: State, Society, and Economic Transformation in the 1990s* (Gainesville, Fla., 1999).

ROBERT A. MORTIMER

MALAWI. A small landlocked country in southeast Africa, Malawi has a population of 10 million and a per capita income of US$160, making it one of the poorest countries in the world. Agriculture is the chief economic activity, accounting for 90 percent of export earnings. Its timely debt repayments and implementation of Western economic prescriptions enable Malawi to receive modest sums of foreign aid from Western governments, Japan, and multilateral lending agencies.

An estimated 35 percent of the population observe African traditional beliefs, 50 percent are Christian, and 15 percent Muslim. English is the official language, while Chewa, one of about a dozen local languages, is the national language.

Britain declared the country a protectorate in 1891 under the name British Central Africa, but renamed it Nyasaland in 1907. In 1915 John Chilembwe, an American-educated preacher, fomented a rebellion in which three whites and forty blacks were killed. This marked the beginning of the nationalist struggle. In 1944 Africans formed the Nyasaland African Congress (NAC) to press for economic and social reforms, but not independence. That changed, however, when white settlers in Southern Rhodesia (now Zimbabwe), Northern Rhodesia (Zambia), and Nyasaland, with the endorsement of Britain, formed the Federation of Rhodesia and Nyasaland in 1953. The NAC quickly opposed it, fearing that the federation would further subjugate blacks under white rule, and seized the opportunity to demand secession and independence. Opposition increased when Hastings Kamuzu Banda, a physician and strong critic of the federation, arrived in the country in 1958, after forty years in the United States, Britain, and Ghana, to lead the struggle.

On 6 July 1964 the country became an independent state under the name Malawi, with Banda as prime minister. Three months later a cabinet crisis over internal and external policies led the prime minister to dismiss three ministers; three others resigned in sympathy. In 1965 Henry Chipembere, former minister of education, led an unsuccessful coup attempt and subsequently escaped to the United States. In 1966 the country became a republic, with Banda as president. In 1967 Yatuta Chisiza, former minister of home affairs, was killed while leading a guerrilla insurgency into the country. These failed coups strengthened Banda's dictatorial rule, and in 1971 he became president-for-life. During his rule, all parliamentary representatives had to be members of the single ruling Malawi Congress Party, and internal policies were enforced mainly through the Young Pioneers, a paramilitary group. Although tensions existed between the army and the group, the president defused them by playing the politics of tribalism and regionalism, often targeting northerners as the source of the nation's problems. But in 1993 the army, in a firefight, destroyed the Young Pioneers, and so clipped the president's authority.

By then, Banda was also being pressured by students and workers, as well as by international lending agencies, to implement democratic reforms in the wake of the fall of communism in the former Soviet Union and the creation of multiparty democracy in apartheid South Africa and other African countries. In May 1994, in Malawi's first multiparty presidential elections in thirty years, Banda lost to Bakili Muluzi, leader of the United Democratic Front (UDF).

Under President Muluzi, Malawi has experienced relative democracy, including a promising free press, but its economy has suffered severely due to loss of revenues from tobacco, the major cash crop, and charges of rampant corruption among senior officials. Muluzi was reelected president in May 1999. With the holding of free and fair elections for a second time, Malawi seemed embarked on consolidating democracy.

Africa Watch Report, *Where Silence Rules: The Suppression of Dissent in Malawi* (New York, 1990). *Guy C. Z. Mhone*, ed., *Malawi at the Crossroads: The Post-Colonial Political Economy* (Harare, Zimbabwe, 1992).

WALUSAKO A. MWALILINO

MALAYSIA. Comprising Peninsular Malaysia, previously known as Malaya, which lies at the southeastern tip of the Asian continental landmass, and Sabah and Sarawak, which occupy the northwestern flank of the island of Borneo, to the east of Peninsular Malaysia, Malaysia has a population of about 23 million, of which about four fifths is in Peninsular Malaysia. The indigenous Muslim-Malay community constitutes about three fifths of the population on the peninsula, with ethnic Chinese accounting for a quarter and ethnic Indians for less than a tenth. In Sabah and Sarawak, however, while the Chinese proportion is roughly the same, there are few Indians, and Muslim Malays are a minority. Instead, other non-Muslim indigenous minorities predominate.

The boundaries of Malaysia today have existed since 9 August 1965, when the island republic of *Singapore seceded from the federation created less than two years before. The eleven states of the earlier Federation of Malaya gained independence from Britain on 31 August 1957. On 16 September 1963, Singapore and the Borneo states of Sabah (previously North Borneo) and Sarawak merged with Malaya to form Malaysia.

After centuries of presumably Hindu Malay rule, a Muslim maritime empire based in Malacca was established in the early fifteenth century. In 1511, Malacca was captured by the Portuguese, before falling into Dutch hands in 1641. The British East India Company colonized Penang in 1786 and Singapore in 1819, and gained control of Malacca with the Napoleonic Wars in Europe. The division of Southeast Asia into broad European spheres of influence dates back to the Anglo-Dutch Treaty of 1824 in which can be found the origins of contemporary boundaries between Indonesia and Malaysia.

Sarawak came under the control of the Brooke family while the North Borneo Chartered Company gained control of Sabah in the middle of the nineteenth century. Colonization of the peninsular hinterland, fueled initially by the British desire to control tin mining, began in 1874 and was completed before the outbreak of World War I.

Varied British administrative arrangements continued in Peninsular Malaysia until the Japanese invasion in late 1941. After the Japanese occupation, the British unsuccessfully tried to introduce a Malayan Union arrangement in 1946 after an initial period of British Military Administration (BMA). In 1948, the Federation of Malaya arrangement emerged instead and, in 1955, the first elections were held for a federal legislature in anticipation of independence in 1957.

Although Malaya, as the world's leading exporter of tin and rubber, had long been Britain's most lucrative colony, pressures from a communist-led insurgency, militant labor organizations, and other nationalist groups, in addition to the new postwar international situation, ensured formal independence from the British, with a continuing heavy British imprint on postcolonial government and political institutions.

Malaysia is a constitutional monarchy in which nine of thirteen states have hereditary rulers (sultans) dating back to the colonial era, claiming legitimacy from the precolonial period. Since 1957, these rulers have taken turns serving as king for five-year terms. The remaining states have constitutional governors appointed for renewable five-year terms.

At the federal level, there is a bicameral parliament comprising the Dewan Rakyat (Lower House) and the Dewan Negara (Senate). The Dewan Rakyat consists of elected members of parliament from 193 heavily gerrymandered constituencies greatly varying in size, both geographically and demographically, with the registered voting population in the largest constituencies more than six times that in the smallest constituency. Members of the Senate are nominated by the federal and state governments. The states have elected legislative assemblies, except for the Federal Territory of Kuala Lumpur, the national capital. Municipal elections, largely won by opposition parties, have been discontinued since the mid-1960s.

The executive is led by the prime minister, who invariably has also been president of the United Malays National Organisation (UMNO), which has dominated the Alliance and, then, the National Front ruling coalition. Except for Sabah (1985–1994), Sarawak, Penang, Kelantan, and Trengganu, the state governments have also been led by UMNO leaders chosen by the UMNO national president. Except for the Kelantan (1959–1978 and since 1990) and Trengganu (briefly in the late 1950s and since 1999) governments, led by the Islamic Party (Parti Islam SeMalaysia, or PAS), all other state governments have belonged to the national ruling coalition dominated by UMNO.

The first prime minister, Tunku Abdul Rahman, led Malaya to independence on 31 August 1957 and formed Malaysia in September 1963. He retired in 1970 after the ruling Alliance secured only 45 percent of the popular vote in the May 1969 third general elections. His successor, Abdul Razak, expanded and renamed the ruling coalition after increasing government intervention including affirmative action in favor of ethnic Malays ostensibly to improve interethnic relations. After his untimely death in early 1976, he was succeeded by his brother-in-law Hussein Onn, who retired in mid-1981 in favor of Mahathir Mohamad.

Mahathir has made his mark on the country as a visionary modernizer, not averse to abuse of his considerable powers. His leadership has been marked by Islamization, emulation of Japan and the East Asian *newly industrializing economies, pro-business *corporatism, heavy industry promotion, *privatization, attempts to accelerate industrialization, and technological progress, as well as strong nationalist and Third Worldist rhetoric accompanied by pragmatic economic policies. In late 1999, he secured a fifth electoral mandate despite considerable popular, especially Malay, criticism of his regime's alleged corruption, cronyism, nepotism, and betrayal of Islamic values.

Public administration has been dominated by the civil service inherited from the British colonial period, although there has been considerable Americanization since the mid-1960s. There are also professional services linked to some ministries and government departments as well as state civil services. Formally independent of the federal and state governments are various statutory bodies.

Malaysia has enjoyed fairly rapid economic growth since independence, especially throughout much of the 1970s and from the late 1980s until 1997 when it was severely affected by the Asian financial crisis. However, the economic wealth of the country has been rather unevenly distributed along class, ethnic, and regional lines, which has led to ethnic and regional discontent and political mobilization, as well as to various policies ostensibly designed to ameliorate these inequalities. Post-election race riots in May 1969 opened the way to some political realignment and the introduction of the New Economic Policy (NEP) in 1971, which aimed to create the socioeconomic conditions for national unity—defined primarily in terms of improved Malay/non-Malay relations—by reducing poverty and enhancing the economic position of Malays in order to reduce interethnic differences.

With the weakening of the communist-led insurgency in the mid-1950s and the repression of the parliamentary Left in the mid-1960s, there has been virtually no ideologically inspired politics to challenge ethnic political mobilization. Class-based and other social movements are rather weak, especially in the face of overriding ethnic divisions. Instead, support for and opposition to the government have both been largely channeled through ethnic mobilization. Since the 1970s, the opposition has centered around the ethnic Chinese–based Democratic Action Party (DAP) and the ethnic Malay–based Islamic Party (PAS), except for a brief period when the latter joined the ruling coalition in the mid-1970s. Despite significant poverty reduction and improvement of the Malay economic condition, implementation of the NEP has exacerbated rather than reduced interethnic tensions. Uneven regional development has heightened regional resentment toward the federal government, especially in Sabah and Sarawak.

The Malay-dominated armed forces have not threatened political stability, and are unlikely to do so, at least as long as Malay political dominance remains unchallenged. However, since the peace treaty with the communist-led insurgents in December 1989, the traditional concern of the army and the police with communist subversion has declined.

U.S. influence has grown, especially since the mid-1960s. Malaysia has supported important Third World initiatives since the 1960s (e.g., Chinese entry into the UN, the call for the New International Economic Order, and sanctions against the governments of Israel and South Africa).

The Mahathir government since the early 1980s has raised Malaysia's profile in international forums such as the UN, the Commonwealth, the Nonaligned Movement, the Muslim world, the Association of Southeast Asian Nations, and Asia Pacific Economic Cooperation.

Harold Crouch, *Government and Society in Malaysia* (Ithaca, N.Y., 1996). E. T. Gomez and K. S. Jomo, *Malaysia's Political Economy*, 2d ed. (Cambridge, U.K., 1999).

JOMO KWAME SUNDARAM

MALCOLM X. More than a generation after his death, Malcolm X remains one of the most controversial black figures of the twentieth century. He was born in Omaha, Nebraska, on 19 May 1925, the seventh of eleven children. His father, Earl Little, was reportedly an enthusiastic supporter of Marcus Garvey's United Negro Improvement Association. Malcolm Little attended school in East Lansing, Michigan, but dropped out in the eighth grade when his family moved to Boston. Involvement in criminal activities in Roxbury and Harlem resulted in 1946 in a ten-year prison sentence for burglary and larceny. Prison was a transforming experience for Malcolm. While serving his sentence he was introduced by his younger brother Reginald to the Lost-Found Nation of Islam (known popularly as the Black Muslims) led by the Honorable Elijah Muhammad. Malcolm became a devout supporter of the Nation and changed his surname to X to symbolize his trans-

formation into an "ex-smoker, ex-drinker, ex-Christian, ex-slave." In prison, he also embarked upon a process of self-education. Beginning by copying words out of a dictionary, he progressed to reading works on history, philosophy, and anthropology.

After being paroled in 1952, Malcolm became an eloquent member of the Nation of Islam, whose doctrines suggested that the white race was on the verge of being destroyed by God and that Elijah Muhammad would lead the black race to safety in a separate state. Malcolm founded mosques in Boston, Philadelphia, and Harlem and started the newspaper *Muhammad Speaks*. He was soon elevated to the position of national spokesman and awarded Mosque Number 7 in Harlem, the second most important mosque of the Nation of Islam. Courteous and soft-spoken in private, Malcolm proved to be a fiery and provocative public speaker. In spite (or perhaps because) of his message that all white people were "devils" and the satisfaction he took in stories of white suffering, many young whites as well as blacks responded sympathetically to his apocalyptic language, and he was frequently invited to speak before predominantly white audiences. Malcolm was extremely critical of black leaders. He denounced integration, the nonviolent philosophy of Martin Luther *King Jr., and the more traditional *civil rights movement, which he characterized as a "mealy-mouth, wait-in, beg-in, plead-in, kind of action." Instead, Malcolm defended the legitimacy of violent reaction by blacks against their common white oppressor and against racial injustice. Although in the last months of his life he made overtures of friendship to mainstream civil rights leaders, many continued until his death to be wary of him.

In 1963, a rupture developed between him and Elijah Muhammad, allegedly because of Malcolm's remark that President John F. *Kennedy's *assassination in November of that year was a case of "chickens coming home to roost." Malcolm left the Nation of Islam in 1964 and founded his own organizations, the first of which was the Muslim Mosque, Inc. He made a pilgrimage to Mecca in 1964, followed by travels later that year to the *Middle East and Africa, where he was warmly received. As a result of his pilgrimage, he renounced his allegiance to the Nation of Islam and converted to orthodox *Islam. He adopted the Muslim name El-Hajj Malik El Shabazz and denounced Elijah Muhammad as a "racist" and "faker." In 1965, he founded the Organization of Afro-American Unity. Malcolm was assassinated while giving a speech at the Audubon Ballroom in Harlem on 21 February 1965. Three Black Muslims were convicted of his murder in March 1966. More than a decade later, one of them gave sworn testimony confirming that Malcolm had been assassinated by the Nation of Islam, although the Nation has continued to deny involvement in his death.

Malcolm's *Autobiography*, written with his cooperation by Alex Haley (author of *Roots*), appeared nine months after Malcolm's death. The book was instrumental in transforming Malcolm X in the public imagination from demagogue to the foremost spokesman of radical black nationalism, referred to generally as the "Black Power movement." Fascination with Malcolm X's life and thought continues, and by the early 1990s he had become an icon in American cultural life. A movie of his life was completed by the director Spike Lee in 1992.

(See also AFRICAN AMERICANS; NONVIOLENT ACTION; RACE AND RACISM.)

Alex Haley and Malcolm X, *The Autobiography of Malcolm X* (New York, 1973). Louis A. DeCaro, *On the Side of My People: A Religious Life of Malcolm X* (New York: New York University Press, 1996). Michael E. Dyson, *Making Malcolm: The Myth and Meaning of Malcolm X* (New York: Oxford University Press, 1995).

ROWENA OLEGARIO

MALDIVES. See INDIAN OCEAN REGION.

MALI. The Republic of Mali (formerly French Sudan) is a Sahelian, landlocked former French colony in West Africa with a land area of approximately 475,000 square miles (1.24 million km.) and a population estimated at 10.6 million in 1998. During that year, GNP stood at US$2.6 billion, while GNP per capita was $250. The capital city is Bamako, and *Islam is the dominant religion.

Mali gained independence from France on 20 June 1960 as the Mali Federation (Senegal and Mali). The federation broke up on 20 August 1960, and on 22 September 1960 the dominant party, the *Union Soudanaise-Rassemblement Démocratique Africain* (US-RDA), led by Modibo Kéïta, opted for socialism. As leader of the US-RDA and the country's first president, Kéïta set about to nationalize the economy through the development of state enterprises and the creation of a national currency, the Mali franc; to tighten the party's and the administration's control over the polity and civil society; and to launch a non aligned, Pan-African foreign policy, with close ties to the Soviet Union and other Eastern bloc countries, notably Cuba and China.

Mali was soon confronted with serious political, economic, and social difficulties, partly due to the West's latent hostility toward its ideology and policies. The February 1967 monetary agreement with France brought the country back into the Franc zone. Capitalizing on deep-seated popular discontent owing to economic problems, political repression, and the excesses of the party's militia, a military *coup d'état toppled the Kéïta regime on 19 November 1968. Fourteen junior army officers ruled through the *Comité Militaire de Libération Nationale* (CMLN), led by a young lieutenant, Moussa Traoré, who became the country's second head of state. From 19 November 1968 until 2 June 1974, the CMLN government ruled by decree, further liberalizing the economy and polity while continuing the US-RDA's non-aligned foreign policy. The constitutional referendum of June 1974 and the creation in March 1979 of a new party, the *Union Démocratique du Peuple Malien* (UDPM), contributed to the institutional legitimization of *military rule. The June 1979 legislative and presidential elections, followed by the dissolution of the CMLN, confirmed the UDPM's and Moussa Traoré's dominance over the Malian political system.

Opposition to the increasingly authoritarian, corrupt, and nepotic rule of the Traoré clan coalesced around disgruntled "Modibist" bureaucrats and a faction of the army (soldiers and mid-ranking officers) who felt excluded from Traoré's kleptocratic system. The mounting political and social malaise finally culminated in an open and bloody confrontation between frustrated youths (mostly schoolchildren) and the army. Acting on behalf of senior army officers, Lt.-Colonel Amadou Toumani Touré intervened to stop the bloodshed

(there were over 200 deaths), toppled the Traoré regime, and assumed power on 26 March 1991. Touré immediately set up a *Conseil de Réconciliation Nationale* (CRN), which appointed a broad based *Comité de Transition pour le Salut du Peuple* (CTSP) as a government of transition from military-authoritarian to civilian-democratic rule. A National Conference (29 July–14 August 1991), which brought together forty-eight parties and some 700 associations, adopted new political rules and institutions, notably a new electoral code, new party statutes, and a new constitution. This popular and sovereign assembly also established the agenda and 1992 schedule for *democratic transition: first a constitutional referendum (12 January); then municipal (19 January); legislative (22 March and 5 April), and presidential elections (12 and 26 April). Of forty-eight political parties and movements initially registered, only four emerged from the electoral process: the *Alliance pour la Démocratie au Mali* (Adema), led by Alpha Oumar Konaré; the *Comité National d'Initiative Démocratique* (CNID), led by Mountaga Tall; a revamped US-RDA split into two rival factions led by Tiéoulé Konaté and Baba Haïdara, respectively; and the former UDPM with a new label.

On 26 April 1992, Alpha Oumar Konaré of Adema won the presidential elections over challenger Tiéoulé Konaté and eight other candidates. As a result of the presidential elections of 16 May 1997, Konaré was re-elected with 84.3 percent of the vote. On 13 April 1997, Mali held a first round of legislative elections, but the results were annulled by the Constitutional Court. New legislative elections in which Adema won 130 out of the 147 seats in the National Assembly took place on 20 July and 3 August 1997. A first round of municipal elections was held on 21 June 1998 in which Adema won sixteen of the nineteen contested municipalities (out of a total of 701). Regrouped under the banner of the *Collectif des partis politiques d'opposition* (Coppo), the radical opposition parties boycotted the whole electoral process, refused to acknowledge the results, and called for civil disobedience. Following violent protest resulting in the death of one army officer, the main opposition leaders were briefly detained in August 1999. The government eventually managed to resolve the political crisis by convening a "National Forum on Mali's political and institutional problems" in January 1999. An attempt at national political reconciliation, the Forum brought together 600 participants and aimed at reviewing a number of key constitutional and legal provisions, including the constitutional law, the electoral law, the charter of the political parties, the statute of the opposition, and the law on the media. In October 1999, the government launched a major anti-corruption campaign designed to expose and sanction all cases of financial fraud and embezzlement in the public service. In its third report, published in April 2000, the anti-corruption commission identified over fifty such cases for adjudication. On 14 February 2000, prime minister Ibrahim Boubacar Kéïta (who is also president of the Adema) resigned and was replaced by Mandé Sidibé. The government put together by Sidibé on 21 February 2000 included seven members of Adema, as well as representatives of the moderate opposition and civil society (regrouped in the *Convergence nationale pour la démocratie et le progrès*/CNDP), but excluded the radical opposition. The resignation enabled Kéïta, the official Adema candidate to the succession of Konaré, whose term of office expires in 2002, to reinforce his control over the party and prepare for the next presidential election. Kéïta's main opponent in this race will most likely be Amadou Toumani Touré, who so ably presided over Mali's democratic transition (1991–1992).

The challenges facing the Adema regime are daunting. Nine years after its creation, the party, renamed *Alliance pour la Démocratie au Mali-Parti Africain pour la Solidarité et la Justice* (Adema-PASJ), is plagued by factional conflict. Reinvigorated by its electoral victories in the successive presidential, legislative, and municipal elections, Adema-PASJ is definitely a political force to reckon with, though not quite the broad based mass party that it aspires to be. Indeed, Adema-PASJ is progressively evolving into a single party (or "party-state") characterized by confusion between the political and administrative spheres and hegemonic control over the county's political life. Furthermore, mounting social unrest characterized by sporadic student and civil servant strikes could easily be transformed into political capital by a unified opposition coalescing around vibrant civil society organizations. It remains to be seen whether the campaign for the 2002 presidential election will offer the opposition an opportunity to rally and prevent this dangerous slide into *authoritarianism.

(See also FRANCOPHONE AFRICA; SOCIALISM AND SOCIAL DEMOCRACY.)

Cheick Oumar Diarrah, *Le Mali de Modibo Kéta* (Paris, 1986). Joseph-Roger de Benoist, *Le Mali* (Paris, 1989). Pascal J. Imperato, *Mali: A Search for Direction* (Boulder, Colo., 1989). C. O. Diarrah, *Mali: Bilan d'une Gestion Désastreuse* (Paris, 1990). C. O. Diarrah, *Vers la IIIème République du Mali* (Paris, 1991). C. O. Diarrah, *Le Défi démocratique au Mali* (Paris, 1996). Cerdes, *Le processus démocratique malien de 1960 à nos jours* (Bamako, 1997).

GUY MARTIN

MALTA. See SMALL STATES AND TERRITORIES.

MALVINAS/FALKLANDS WAR. The Malvinas/Falklands War (2 April–14 June 1982) was the world's first major naval missile conflict and presaged the emergence of the new post-Cold War era in pitting an emerging *Third World country against an established European power.

The dispute centered on issues common since World War II: a long-held claim of territorial rights by a developing country lodged against an excolonial power. The Argentine military junta—in an effort to distract its public from concern with the "dirty war," in which 15,000–30,000 Argentine civilians were killed or "disappeared," and from the economic failures of the military regime—made a nationalist appeal to recover the islands 300 miles off their coast. This territory had been lost to *Britain in the nineteenth century.

The British, led by Conservative Prime Minister Margaret *Thatcher, couched the dispute with *Argentina in terms of the right of self-determination on the part of the ethnically British Falkland Islanders. The British government, too, used the conflict as a unifying national issue in the midst of economic hardships resulting from conservative fiscal and economic policies.

*War erupted as the result of a series of miscalculations and the influence of the United States. Argentina claims that the United States intimated that it would not interfere with Argentine assertions of sovereignty over the islands. Subsequent U.S. assistance to Britain, in the form of *intelligence and ma-

terial support, are viewed as a betrayal by Argentines and other Latin Americans who expected, at best, a demonstration of hemispheric unity against a European interloper or, at worst, neutrality. The Argentines judge the U.S. role as critical, asserting that combat would not have broken out had Britain not had U.S. assurances. The *Organization of American States and Latin America in general supported Argentina, but U.S. influence thwarted any attempts at concrete action. The British expected assistance from the United States to liberate the oppressed Falklanders from a brutal military regime. The *European Community generally sided with Britain. France embargoed exports of arms to Argentina, which severely limited Argentine military capability.

The role of the UN was minimal. Negotiations over the status of the islands had been ongoing for decades; the failure to make progress in those negotiations is cited by Argentines as the motivation for military action.

The war progressed rapidly with continual British successes based upon their naval and ground force superiority, although the Argentine air forces inflicted heavy damage to British ships. Some five weeks of fighting in and around the islands resulted in the complete surrender and capture of all Argentine forces, which were then repatriated immediately through Uruguay. The British military commitment to the *security of the islands increased, presenting some problems for the British commitment to *North Atlantic Treaty Organization security forces, but those have been mitigated by the thaw in the *Cold War occurring in 1989–1990. The Argentine junta collapsed, leading to the longest continual civilian rule in Argentina since 1930, but the *sovereignty issue of the islands is still a sensitive one in Argentina. The end of hostilities was not recognized until the inauguration of President Carlos Saùl Menem in 1989.

(See also U.S.–LATIN AMERICAN RELATIONS.)

Rubén E. Moro, *The History of the South Atlantic Conflict: The War for the Malvinas* (New York, 1989).

BLAIR P. TURNER

MANDELA, NELSON. Born in Qunu, Transkei, on 18 July 1918, Nelson Rolihlahla Mandela was descended from the Thembu royal lineage. Suspended from Fort Hare University in 1940 for leading a student strike, he traveled to Johannesburg, working initially as a compound police officer before beginning legal studies. Joining the African National Congress (ANC) in 1942, Mandela helped to establish the Youth League, a group determined to recast the ANC's temperate philosophy in the mold of a militant, racially exclusive *nationalism. In 1949, the league persuaded the ANC to adopt its program of action. By 1951, however, Mandela's friendships with Indian activists and white communists prompted him to revise his conviction that African nationalists should not cooperate across race lines. That year Mandela helped plan a "defiance campaign" against "unjust laws." Appointed "volunteer-in-chief," Mandela was among the first to be arrested. Throughout the decade, as the ANC's deputy president, Mandela played a major role as an ANC strategist. In 1952 he founded an attorney's partnership with his comrade Oliver Tambo. He married twice, the second time in 1958 to Nomzamo Winifred Madikizela.

Following the 1960 Sharpeville massacre, Mandela was detained five months and the ANC was outlawed. In 1961, elected secretary of a National Action Council, he led a nationwide general strike on 29–31 May. In October he helped form a sabotage organization, Umkhonto we Sizwe (Spear of the Nation). Mandela left *South Africa in January 1961 to tour the continent seeking financial and military support. He returned in July 1962 and was arrested on 5 August. Imprisoned for incitement, he was convicted again after the capture of other Umkhonto leaders. Mandela received a life sentence on 11 June 1964. During nearly three decades of imprisonment Mandela succeeded in maintaining his authority over successive generations of convicted activists, uniting the loyalties of different strands of black resistance behind the ANC. Beginning in 1985, a series of meetings with government leaders initiated by Mandela helped to persuade the authorities to begin constitutional negotiations with the ANC. On 11 February 1990 Mandela was unconditionally released. As ANC president from 1991, his leadership was crucial in curbing the expectations of his organization's often unruly following and instilling the discipline required for a "pacted" democratization. He was co-winner with President F. W. de Klerk of the Nobel Prize in 1993; after the ANC's electoral victory in 1994 he served as South African president from 1994 to 1999. The Mandela government succeeded in reforming public finance, widening the scope of welfare programs, and encouraging economic revival. Mandela's personal achievements included symbolic acts of reconciliation with the Afrikaner minority and defense of constitutional values. Divorced in 1995, he married Graca Machel in 1998. Remaining active after his retirement from public office, in 2000 he became chair of the Burundi peace talks.

Nelson Mandela contributed significantly to the ANC's ideological formation during its development as a popular movement in the 1950s. He was a powerful proponent of the multiracial "Congress Alliance." Though influenced by *Marxism, he maintained an admiration for British *parliamentary democracy as well as supporting an ideal of a classless society modeled on precolonial institutions. Despite his advocacy of working-class mobilization, Mandela fostered his social connections with the rural aristocracy, skillfully balancing different exhortations to the various constituencies within the ANC's popular following. After 1960, his personal courage and theatrical style were vital in retaining for the ANC the adherence of rank-and-file militants. He pioneered the ANC's transformation to a clandestine insurgent body and led its second metamorphosis into an electorally oriented political party. His speech from the dock in 1964 enhanced his stature as, in the words of the London *Times, "a colossus of African nationalism." Four decades later, he remains Africa's most internationally influential statesman.

Nelson Mandela, *Long Walk to Freedom* (London, 1993). Martin Meredith, *Nelson Mandela: A Biography* (London, 1997). Anthony Sampson, *Mandela: The Authorised Biography* (London, 1999).

TOM LODGE

MAO ZEDONG. By all reasonable standards of historical judgment, Mao Zedong must be counted among the half-dozen most important political actors in modern world history. Mao was the acknowledged leader of the greatest and most popular of modern revolutions. And almost unique among revolutionary leaders, he remained the dominant figure in the postrevolutionary regime for more than a quarter of a century, presiding over the beginnings of the modern industrial transformation of the world's most populous land. Certainly no one influenced more profoundly, for better or for worse, the lives of more people than did Mao Zedong by virtue of his person, his power, his policies, and his thought.

The son of a rich *peasant, Mao Zedong was born in the village of Shaoshan in Hunan province on 26 December 1893. During his early years, the old imperial Chinese order was rapidly disintegrating, radical reformist and revolutionary movements were rising, and newly introduced Western ideas and ideologies were undermining faith in traditional values and beliefs. Although the young Mao became well versed in classical Chinese texts and retained a strong attachment to certain aspects of tradition (especially historical novels and poetry), he soon became caught up in the radical political and iconoclastic intellectual currents that swept Chinese cities in the years preceding and following the Revolution of 1911 that overthrew the imperial system. As a student at the middle and normal schools in the provincial capital of Changsha during the years 1913–1918, Mao eagerly assimilated a broad range of Western ideas, briefly pursued a career as a teacher, and embarked upon his lifelong career as a political organizer, establishing the "New People's Study Society," one of the more important of the local groups that were to prove so politically and ideologically instrumental in the making of the radical May Fourth Movement of 1919. In Changsha, Mao became involved with *New Youth* magazine, that extraordinarily influential westernizing and iconoclastic journal of the new intelligentsia that molded the ideas of a whole generation of modern Chinese political and intellectual leaders. It was in *New Youth* that Mao's first published article appeared in 1917, "A Study of Physical Culture," which combined an ardent Chinese *nationalism with a no less ardent rejection of traditional Chinese culture—in this instance an attack on the Confucian separation between mental and manual labor. It was a uniquely modern Chinese combination of nationalism and cultural iconoclasm that very much reflected the radical spirit of the times and one that was to remain a prominent feature of the Maoist vision.

In late 1918, Mao Zedong left Changsha for Beijing. Beijing University had then become the center of radical Chinese intellectual and political life. Under the influence of radical intellectuals and their activist student followers, Mao became increasingly politicized. Even though he was unable to enroll as a regular student, he worked as an assistant librarian at the university and was first introduced to Marxist theory in the winter of 1918–19 as a member of a loosely organized Marxist study group. But Mao did not become an immediate convert to *Marxism. He later described his ideas at the time as a "curious mixture" of Western *liberalism, democratic reformism, and utopian socialism or anarchism. It was only after his return to Changsha in the summer of 1919, under the influence of the increasingly radical and fiercely nationalistic currents then rising in *China, that Mao began to be attracted to the political message of the *Russian Revolution and its accompanying Leninist version of Marxism.

Yet Marxian influences are by no means apparent in Mao's prolific writings and frenetic political activities during the winter of 1919–20. Rather, what is most clearly evident is a powerful populist strain that celebrates the organic unity and inherent revolutionary potential of the Chinese people. Also celebrated, again in typically populist fashion, was a belief in the advantages of backwardness. Although the Chinese people had been oppressed and made impotent for "thousands of years," Mao wrote in his main treatise of the period entitled "The Great Union of the Popular Masses," this historic backwardness promised great political advantages for the future—for, as he confidently put it, "that which has accumulated for a long time will surely burst forth quickly." These populist-type beliefs were to remain enduring characteristics of the Maoist mentality, profoundly influencing Mao's reception and reinterpretation of Marxism.

Mao Zedong's actual conversion to Marxism, according to his own testimony, occurred only in the summer of 1920, following discussions with one of his political mentors in Shanghai. He then plunged into organizational activities, working to establish a labor union for miners in his native province of Hunan and organizing a small Communist group in Changsha, one of several such local groups in various parts of the country (and among Chinese students studying abroad) which coalesced into the *Chinese Communist Party. Mao was one of the thirteen delegates who attended the party's founding congress, secretly convened in Shanghai in July 1921.

During the first, urban-based phase of the party's history (1921–1927), and especially during the period of the Soviet-fashioned Communist-Nationalist anti-warlord alliance (1924–1927), Mao's populist proclivities increasingly drew him from the cities to the countryside—and from the proletariat to the peasantry. Mao was not the only, nor the first, Chinese Communist to discover the revolutionary potentialities of the peasantry, but he did of course prove to be the most important. During the years 1925–1927, he devoted the greater portion of his prodigious energies to detailed investigations of rural socioeconomic conditions, to the organization of peasant associations, and (under Nationalist auspices) to the training of a peasant organizational cadre. Mao's populist impulses found their fullest expression near the end of this period in his famous "Report on an Investigation of the Peasant Movement in Hunan," published early in 1927. Here, in what is perhaps the most pristine expression of what later came to be known as "Maoism," the young Mao celebrated the spontaneity of peasant revolt, an elemental force that he described as a tornado and a hurricane, one "so extraordinarily swift and violent that no power, however great, will be able to suppress it." Mao not only looked to the peasantry as the popular base of the *Chinese Revolution; he also attributed to peasants themselves all those elements of revolutionary creativity and standards of political judgment that orthodox Marxist-Leninists reserved for the Communist Party. For Mao, it was not the party that was to judge the revolutionary capacities of the peasantry, but rather peasants who were to judge the revolutionary sufficiency of the party. Throughout, the document emphasized, in most non-Leninist fashion, the creative revolutionary works that the peasants were accomplishing on their own and expressed hostility to all external organizational restraints.

The "Hunan Report," so heretical from an orthodox Marxist-Leninist point of view, no doubt would have earned Mao his expulsion from the Chinese Communist Party had it not been for the collapse of the Communist-Nationalist alliance just weeks after the publication of the document. It was in early April 1927 that Chiang Kai-shek turned his army to the task of destroying the Communists and their urban-based mass organizations. The relatively few Communists who survived the counterrevolutionary carnage were driven from the cities and sought refuge in the more remote areas of the countryside. The tie between the Communist Party and the urban working class was severed and was to remain broken until 1949. The confinement of the *revolution to the rural areas was the essential condition that permitted Mao's political ascendancy in the Communist Party and the emergence of "Maoism" as the dominant Chinese version of Marxism.

The rise of Mao Zedong to party leadership in the mid-1930s was accomplished only after a long and bitter struggle against a Moscow-supported faction of Chinese Communists—and in direct defiance of *Stalin. During the entire Stalinist era of the world Communist movement, Mao was the only leader of a Communist party to achieve leadership without the blessings of the Soviet dictator. The Chinese party's de facto independence of Moscow sowed one of the seeds of the later Sino-Soviet dispute. The Yanan era (1935–1945)—so called after the area in remote northwest China where the Communists established a base area to escape annihilation by Chiang Kai-shek's Nationalist forces—was the heroic and decisive phase in the history of the Chinese Communist revolution—and it was undoubtedly Mao's finest hour as a revolutionary leader and military strategist. Under Mao's leadership and through a combination of popular nationalist and social revolutionary programs, the Chinese Communists won enormous popular support, especially among the peasantry of north China, the essential basis for their eventual victory over the Nationalists. During the Yanan era the distinctive Chinese variant of Marxism-Leninism (canonized as "Mao Zedong Thought") crystallized as a formal body of doctrine. It was an ideology marked by powerful nationalist, populist, and voluntaristic impulses that greatly modified the inherited corpus of Marxist-Leninist theory. Indeed, "Maoism" implicitly defined itself, in large measure, by its *departures* from the main premises of Marxist theory. It was a doctrine that rejected the Marxist orthodoxy that capitalism is a necessary and progressive phase in historical development and thus the essential prerequisite for socialism. Accordingly, Maoism rejected the Marxist faith in the industrial proletariat as the necessary bearer of the new society, instead looking to the peasantry as the truly creative revolutionary class in the modern world. Further, Maoism inverted the Marxist conception of the relationship between town and countryside in the making of modern history, rejecting the Marxist and Leninist assumption that the city is the source and site of sociohistorical progress. And reflecting the lack of any real Marxist faith in objective laws of historical development, Maoism placed a decisive emphasis on the role of human will and consciousness in molding social reality.

Such were some of the essential intellectual and ideological preconditions for the Maoist-led Chinese Revolution, which took the historically unprecedented form of harnessing the revolutionary energies of the peasantry in the countryside to "surround and overwhelm" the conservative cities. That unique revolutionary process, with a now-semisacred Mao Zedong as its unquestioned leader, culminated in 1949 when the Red Army defeated the numerically superior armies of Chiang Kai-shek's Nationalists—and peasant soldiers victoriously marched into the cities to "liberate" an urban working class that had been mostly politically passive since the defeats of 1927. On the basis of that victory, the People's Republic of China was formally established on 1 October 1949, unifying China after a century of disintegration and humiliation. In 1949 Mao stood high atop the Gate of Heavenly Peace ("Tiananmen"), appearing as both national liberator and socialist prophet.

Mao Zedong dominated the history of the People's Republic for more than a quarter of a century, until his death in September 1976, just as he had dominated the history of the rural-based revolution that had produced the new *communist party-state. Much of what is unique and distinctive about both the general pattern and the specific events of China's turbulent postrevolutionary history must be credited to—or blamed upon—the leadership of Mao Zedong. Rarely in world history has an entire historical era been so deeply stamped by the personality of a single individual.

In considering the thought and policies of Mao Zedong over "the Mao era" (1949–1976), one is struck by several enduring themes. First, it is a period animated by the notion of "permanent revolution." Although the Maoist theory of permanent (later "continuous") revolution was not explicitly set forth as part of "Mao Zedong Thought" until 1958, the essential components of the notion were present from the outset— an impatience with history that expressed itself in an ambivalent attitude toward the Marxist assumption that socialism presupposed *capitalism; a burning determination to pass through the Marxian-defined "stages" of history in the most rapid possible fashion; an ardent faith that people armed with the proper will and spirit can mold social reality in accordance with the dictates of their consciousness, regardless of the material circumstances in which they find themselves, and indeed a tendency to extol the advantages of backwardness as such for the advancement of socialism. The latter notion was to find its most extreme expression in Mao's celebration of the alleged Chinese virtues of being "poor and blank."

This utopian impulse to escape the burdens of history manifested itself in the brevity of the "bourgeois" or "New Democratic" phase of the history of the People's Republic, essentially terminated at the end of 1952 with the proclamation of the beginning of the period of "the transition to socialism." It further revealed itself in the 1955–1956 campaign to collective agriculture, accomplished in little more than a year. And it found its most fulsome expression in the disastrous Great Leap Forward campaign of 1958–1960, whose utopian *ideology envisioned a spiritually mobilized populace simultaneously bringing about the full-scale *modernization of China *and* its transition from socialism to *communism within a few short decades.

A populist modification of *Leninism is another strikingly pervasive feature of Mao Zedong's postrevolutionary theory and practice, one manifestation of which was a continuous tension between the person and persona of Mao, on the one hand, and the institution of the Chinese Communist Party, on the other. The tension originated with the "Hunan Report" of 1927 when Mao drew a sharp dichotomy between the revolutionary spontaneity of the peasant masses and the conservative restraints that political parties (and intellectuals) attempted to impose upon them. A similar dichotomy reappears after 1949, with Mao presenting himself not simply as the chairman of the Communist Party but also as the embodiment of the popular will struggling against the conservatism of an increasingly bureaucraticized party apparatus. This tension between Mao the leader and the institution he led dramatically revealed itself in July 1955 when Mao personally overrode the collective decisions of the party leadership and appealed directly to "the people" in launching the accelerated campaign for agricultural collectivization. It is also apparent in the "Hundred Flowers" campaign of 1956–1957 when Mao encouraged nonparty intellectuals to criticize the Communist Party from without. And the tension culminated in the *Cultural Revolution, which began (but did not end) with the extraordinary Maoist call for the masses to rebel against the authority of the party and its organizations.

Perhaps the most distinguishing feature of the postrevolutionary Mao Zedong was his historically unique (if ultimately unsuccessful) attempt to reconcile the means of modern economic development with the ends of socialism. Rejecting the inherited Stalinist orthodoxy that the combination of rapid industrialization with state ownership of the means of production would more or less automatically guarantee ever higher stages of socialism and eventually communism, Mao emphasized that the continuous socialist transformation of human beings and their social relations was essential if the process of modern economic development were to have a socialist outcome. This social radicalism was responsible, in part, for the adventures of the Great Leap and the Cultural Revolution—and Mao Zedong must bear the historical and moral responsibility for the enormous toll of death and suffering that resulted from these extraordinary events, however unintended those results may have been. But Maoist social radicalism also served to forestall the fully Stalinist institutionalization of the postrevolutionary order in China and perhaps served to keep alive, among some, the hope for the eventual realization of the ultimate socialist goals that the revolution promised. It certainly kept the postrevolutionary order in flux, providing Mao's successors, including *Deng Xiaoping, with considerable flexibility for charting a new course of development.

The conventional view of the Mao era is that Mao Zedong sacrificed modern economic development to "ideological purity" in a vain and costly quest for some sort of socialist utopia. Yet the actual historical record of the era suggests that Mao was more successful as an economic modernizer than as a builder of socialism. Over the Mao period (1949–1976), China was transformed from a primarily agrarian nation to a relatively industrialized one, the ratio of the value of industrial production to total production increasing from 30 to 72 percent. From 1952 (when industrial output was restored to its highest prewar levels) until the close of the Mao era, Chinese industry grew at an average annual rate of 11 percent, the most rapid pace of industrialization achieved by any major nation (developed or developing) during that time. Indeed, Maoist industrialization, however crude the process was in many respects, compares favorably with comparable decades in the industrialization of Germany, Japan, and the Soviet Union, hitherto generally regarded as the three most successful cases of modernization among major "latecomers" on the world industrial scene.

Rapid industrialization during the Mao period exacted enormous human and social costs, as had been the case with other late-industrializing countries, and most of the costs were borne by the peasantry. Agricultural production barely kept pace with population growth, and living standards in both town and countryside largely stagnated after 1957 as the state extracted most of the surplus product to finance the development of heavy industry. Yet although the blunders, deficiencies, inequalities, and imbalances that marked and marred the process were many and grave, future historians nevertheless will record the Mao era as the time when the basic foundations for China's modern industrialism were laid.

Far more questionable than Mao's status as a modernizer is his reputation as the creator of a socialist society. For what is most strikingly absent in both Maoist theory and practice is the elemental Marxist principle that socialism must be a system whereby the immediate producers themselves democratically control the products and conditions of their labor. In the Maoist system, by contrast, the control of labor and its fruits was left in the hands of an ever larger and more alien bureaucratic apparatus. Mao, to be sure, repeatedly conducted antibureaucratic campaigns, and there is no reason to doubt the genuineness of his antipathy to bureaucracy. But from those campaigns, he time and again failed to devise any viable means of popular democratic control over the powerful bureaucratic apparatus over which he uneasily presided. And if Mao broke, at least in some significant ways, with the Stalinist strategy of socioeconomic development, in the political realm the Maoist regime retained essentially Stalinist methods of bureaucratic rule and consistently suppressed all forms of intellectual and political dissent in Stalinist fashion. The Mao era was thus marked by a deep incongruity between its progressive socioeconomic accomplishments and its retrogressive political features, an incongruity that precluded any genuine socialist reorganization of Chinese society.

The Mao era in the history of the People's Republic was one of the most turbulent periods in modern world history, and it remains one of the most controversial. When the political passions engendered by the era have subsided, most future historians will likely evaluate Mao Zedong much in the fashion in which he is now ideologically portrayed by his successors in Beijing. First and foremost, Mao will be lauded as modern China's greatest nationalist, the leader of a revolution whose enduring achievement was to bring national unification and independence to the world's most populous land—after a century of repeated internal political failures and grave external impingements. Mao will also be seen as a great modernizer who, despite monumental postrevolutionary blunders, presided over the initial modern industrial transformation of one of the world's most economically backward lands, inaugurating a lengthy process destined eventually to make China a great world power. Ultimately, Mao Zedong's role as a pioneer of socialism will receive less attention and will appear far more problematic than his legacy as a nationalist modernizer.

(See also CLASS AND POLITICS; DEVELOPMENT AND UNDER-DEVELOPMENT; COLLECTIVIZATION; POPULISM; SINO-AMERICAN RELATIONS; SOCIALISM AND SOCIAL DEMOCRACY; STALINISM; ZHOU ENLAI.)

Benjamin I. Schwartz, *Chinese Communism and the Rise of Mao* (Cambridge, Mass., 1958). Mao Tse-Tung [Mao Zedong], *Selected Works of Mao Tse-Tung*, 5 vols. (Beijing, 1967–1977). Ross Terrill, *Mao: A Biography*, 2d ed. (Stanford, 2000). Maurice Meisner, *Marxism, Maoism, and Utopianism: Eight Essays* (Madison, Wis., 1982). Stuart Schram, *The Thought of Mao Tse-Tung* (Cambridge, U.K., 1989). Jonathan Spence, *Mao Zedong* (New York, 1999).

MAURICE MEISNER

MAQUILADORAS. The term *maquila*—first used to designate the grain retained by peasants as compensation for their work in medieval Spain—was extended in the 1970s to export-oriented plants operating in less developed countries as subsidiaries or subcontractors of transnational corporations. In the same way that tillers transform wheat into flour, maquiladoras process raw materials and components into finished or semifinished goods that are then sold in world markets. In the late 1960s, the term was applied to factories along Mexico's northern border. At present, it is broadly used to name operations in more than 175 export-processing zones (EPZs) spread across fifty countries, mostly in Asia, Latin America, and the Caribbean.

Maquiladoras reflect the growing integration of the world economy. Starting in the 1960s, companies in advanced industrial nations began to relocate manufacturing operations to EPZs where wages were comparatively low and political conditions hospitable. Export-processing zones first grew throughout the so-called Asian Tigers: South Korea, Taiwan, Hong Kong, and Singapore. Mexico's maquiladora program—the largest of its kind anywhere in the world—expanded during the 1970s at the same time that Malaysia, Indonesia, and, eventually, Vietnam opened their doors to similar kinds of production. In the 1980s, the Dominican Republic and other points in the Caribbean were swept by the export-processing trend. At the beginning of the new millennium even countries formerly under the influence of the now-dismembered Soviet Union—Croatia, Latvia, Romania, Russia—boast export-processing zones.

Mexico's maquiladora program illustrates some of the factors that have led to the diffusion of export-led industrialization. Unemployment and popular discontent followed the termination, in 1964, of the Bracero program—a bilateral agreement that had allowed the entry of Mexican agricultural workers into the United States since 1942. By attracting foreign investment in the maquiladora sector, the Mexican government, in partnership with local entrepreneurs, sought to create new jobs while reducing political strife and facilitating technological transfer. Maquiladoras proliferated in border cities like Ciudad Juárez, Tijuana, and Matamoros whose proximity to the United States held geographical advantages. The program was sustained by governmental stimuli that included customs-law changes authorizing the temporary entry of raw materials, machinery, and components for assembly. Foreign ownership restrictions of Mexican factories were waived to stimulate investment. Mexican maquiladoras became a blueprint for the North American Free Trade Agreement (*NAFTA) implemented in 1994.

The expansion of the Mexican maquiladora program has

been impressive. In 1968 there were scarcely 100 plants scattered along Mexico's northern border, which employed 5,000 workers; by 1998 the number of factories had grown to nearly 3,000 and the number of workers to more than a million. The principal sectors of production continue to be electronics, textiles and apparel, and transportation equipment. Together those branches employ nearly 74 percent of all maquiladora workers. Two-thirds—approximately 655,000—are in border cities, although increasing numbers of plants are now located in the interior. About half of Mexico's manufactured exports are over 44 percent of its total exports are derived from the maquiladora industry. Since 1985 maquiladoras have represented the fastest-growing segment of the Mexican economy, recently surpassing tourism and petroleum-related activities as a source of foreign exchange.

The program has always had critics. Despite their rapid growth, maquiladoras employ only 8 percent of Mexico's labor force and the majority of workers are women between 16 and twenty-five years of age, a particularly vulnerable segment of the labor force. Maquiladoras have been denounced as sweatshops that do not afford most workers seniority, benefits, safe working conditions, or adequate wages. Moreover, maquiladoras have not always created significant linkages with domestic economies or fulfilled hopes of technological transfer. Finally, many observers point to the environmental dangers associated with types of production such as electronics. Despite these objections, maquiladoras continue to be seen by governments in less developed countries as one of the few viable means to create jobs and to integrate national economies into the world's system of production.

(See also GLOBALIZATION; MULTINATIONAL CORPORATIONS; U.S.–CENTRAL AMERICAN RELATIONS; U.S.–LATIN AMERICAN RELATIONS; WOMEN AND DEVELOPMENT.)

M. Patricia Fernández-Kelly, *For We Are Sold, I and My People: Women and Industry in Mexico's Frontier* (Albany, N.Y., 1983). Susan Tiano, "Maquiladora Women: A New Category of Workers?" in Kathryn Ward, ed., *Women Workers and Global Restructuring* (Ithaca, N.Y., 1990). Altha J. Cravey, *Women and Work in Mexico's Maquiladoras* (New York, 1998). Lucinda Vargas, "The Maquiladora industry in Historical Perspective" *Business Frontier* [publication of the El Paso Branch of the Federal Reserve Bank of Dallas], 4 (1998).

PATRICIA FERNÁNDEZ-KELLY

MARCOS, Ferdinand. Born on 11 September 1917 in Sarrat, Ilocos Norte, the *Philippines, Ferdinand E. Marcos rose to prominence to become the most controversial Philippine president in the country's history. The only president to win re-election, he extended his second four-year term by invoking the emergency provisions of the Philippine constitution and stayed another fourteen years in power. At the time of his fall in February 1986, he had ruled the country for half of its post-independence years. Five presidents shared the first half before him.

Accused of the 1935 murder of his father's political rival, Marcos became a celebrity for having handled his own defense, taking and passing the bar examinations during the trial, and winning his acquittal in 1939. During World War II, he became an anti-Japanese guerrilla fighter. His claim to be the most decorated Filipino soldier was based largely on undocumented wartime feats.

He began his meteoric rise to political power by winning the congressional seat in his home province; he would become senator, senate president, and, finally, Philippine president in 1965. In the meantime, in 1954, he had married a poor relation of the prominent Romualdez clan, the young and beautiful Imelda Romualdez.

Marcos was a consummate politician—bright, energetic, and ruthless. During his presidential campaign in 1965, for example, he commissioned Hartzell Spence to write his biography. *For Every Tear a Victory* (New York, 1964), focusing on the candidate's wartime feats and medals, was a brilliant political tool in a country much taken by heroes. Marcos later used this image to forge a partnership with the military in governing the Philippines under his authoritarian rule.

His twenty-year presidency saw the Philippines transformed from an "Asian showcase for democracy" with economic growth second only to Japan's in 1966 to a conjugal dictatorship of plunder and economic devastation in partnership with his wife, Imelda. He built more infrastructure than all other Philippine presidents combined. He reoriented Philippine foreign policy by normalizing relations with socialist countries, improving relations with the United States, and strengthening links with Asian neighbors through membership in the Association of Southeast Asian Nations.

During his second term in office he initially sought to shift to parliamentary democracy through a new constitution, but this effort was aborted when he imposed martial law in September 1972. Martial law caused the systematic destruction of democratic political institutions, the rise of the military, the plunder of the economy, the escalation of communist insurgency and Muslim separatism, and mounting poverty and violence.

His trusted associate, General Fabian C. Ver, chief of staff of the military, was suspected of leading the conspiracy to assassinate Marcos's principal political rival, former Senator Benigno ("Ninoy") Aquino, on 21 August 1983. The assassination triggered massive protests against Marcos, culminating in his peaceful overthrow on 22–25 February 1986. He fled to Hawaii and remained in exile until his death on 28 September 1989.

His legacy of plunder and violence continued to haunt the country he claimed to have loved dearly. Imelda Marcos was remembered for excessive extravagance, ostentatious living, and indecent display of wealth. Nevertheless, regionalism, the culture of forgiveness, and a sense of gratitude among some Filipinos enabled the Marcos family to return to the Philippines, where Imelda and her two older children won positions in local and congressional elections. They are in large measure part of the return of cronyism in the Philippines that has taken place under President Joseph "Erap" Estrad, who was elected in 1999. Much abhorred by the wider public, they are unlikely to win national elections in the foreseeable future.

Raymond T. Bonner, *Waltzing with a Dictator: The Marcoses and the Making of American Policy* (New York, 1987). Belinda A. Aquino, *The Politics of Plunder: The Philippines Under Marcos* (Quezon City, 1987).

CAROLINA G. HERNANDEZ

MARIÁTEGUI, José Carlos. José Carlos Mariátegui was Latin America's most original and important socialist thinker. Although his work was centered on *Peru, it transcended the boundaries of that country and came to be studied throughout the continent. Indeed, the Argentine social critic José Aricó has called Mariátegui's magnum opus, *The Seven Interpretive Essays of Peruvian Reality,* the only significant theoretical work produced by Latin American *Marxism. In addition to journalism and theoretical essays, Mariátegui's activities included the organization of Peru's General Confederation of Workers and the Socialist Party.

Mariátegui was born into a humble family in Moquegua, Peru, on 14 June 1894. He had only a primary education and, at the age of fourteen, took his first job with a Lima newspaper. Moreover, he had continual health problems, owing to a childhood knee injury that led to several unsuccessful operations. Later an infection necessitated the amputation of his good leg. He died on 16 April 1930, at the age of thirty-five.

In 1919, Mariátegui founded the journal *La Razón,* which was critical of the Peruvian government. When the journal was shut down, Mariátegui was sent abroad, ostensibly with a scholarship. In Europe, and particularly in Italy, he began his autodidactic education in Marxism through the Italian historicist perspective; at the same time, he acquired great familiarity with contemporary bourgeois culture. Having married a woman "and some ideas" (as he put it), he returned to Lima in 1923 and began his task of analyzing Peruvian society and building a *socialism that was "neither an imitation nor a copy." In this task, Mariátegui came into growing conflict with another young leftist leader, Victor Raúl *Haya de la Torre.

His efforts resulted in the publication of *Amauta,* a vanguard theoretical journal on Peruvian issues; *Labor,* a workers' newspaper; and *The Seven Essays.* In terms of political practice, he founded the Socialist Party during the second half of 1928. For Mariátegui, use of the name *socialist* rather than *communist,* as well as the controversy his nonorthodox ideas would provoke at the conference of Latin American communist parties in Buenos Aires in 1929, were an expression of creative Marxism. The latter had to be based on concrete conditions within Peruvian society and as part of an effort oriented toward the consolidation of a vigorous workers' movement, the vanguard of the *revolution.

In his many works, Mariátegui emphasized that what characterized Peruvian society was its colonial heritage, racial heterogeneity, and incipient *capitalism. The racial heterogeneity of its predominant Indian population, far from being a disadvantage, provided two important political tools to transform Peruvian reality. First were the Indian communities which, according to Mariátegui, represented a concrete possibility for agrarian socialism in Peru. Second was the Andean tradition, which constituted an important component of Peruvian social consciousness and a mechanism for promoting the political mobilization of the popular classes. These ideas continue to have a following today, and several parties in Peru claim to be inheritors of Mariátegui's tradition.

Jesús Chavarría, *José Carlos Mariátegui and the Rise of Modern Peru, 1890–1930* (Albuquerque, N. Mex., 1979). José Aricó, *Mariátegui y los Origines del Marxismo Latinoamericano,* 2d ed. (Mexico City, 1980).

HERACLIO BONILLA

MARSHALL ISLANDS. See PACIFIC ISLANDS.

MARSHALL PLAN. Proclaimed by Secretary of State George Marshall at Harvard University on 5 June 1947, the Marshall Plan was the largest and most successful program of foreign assistance ever undertaken by the U.S. government. The harsh European winter of 1946–47 convinced Washington that interim aid programs had failed to achieve economic recovery. The British withdrawal from the eastern Mediterranean, which led to the *Truman Doctrine on 12 March 1947, also signaled the weakness of Western Europe. The failure of the Moscow Conference in April 1947 to reach agreement on German reparations encouraged the search for a new policy. As Marshall put it, "the patient is sinking while the doctors deliberate."

Marshall's speech offered U.S. funding for a cooperative European recovery program. The secretary of state set forth certain conditions, including the need for a high degree of inter-European cooperation and the inclusion of Germany. Although his advisers expected rejection, Marshall even invited the Soviet Union to participate, arguing that "our policy is directed not against any country or doctrine but against hunger, poverty, desperation, and chaos." But he added that "its purpose should be the revival of a working economy in the world so as to permit the emergence of political and social conditions in which free institutions can exist."

British Foreign Secretary Ernest Bevin quickly seized upon Marshall's offer and called for a European conference in Paris. Although he sent a large delegation, Soviet leader Joseph *Stalin ordered them to walk out of the meeting, refusing to accede to the American demand for disclosure of economic information and arguing the plan was incompatible with the Soviet system of central *planning. Stalin had concluded that the Marshall Plan was designed to build a hostile Western bloc and attempt to detach Eastern Europe from Soviet control. The Soviets pressured Poland and especially Czechoslovakia to abandon the conference, and later in the year Stalin created the Cominform to control the East European parties and a new trading organization, the Council of Mutual Economic Assistance (COMECON), for Eastern Europe. The *Cold War division of Europe was defined by the Soviet rejection of the Marshall Plan.

The sixteen countries which remained at the Paris conference agreed to form the Committee on European Economic Cooperation (CEEC), to prepare a report on European economic capacities and requirements, and to devise a four-year program for economic recovery. At U.S. insistence, they included the Western zones of Germany, a critical step in the reintegration of Germany into Europe. The CEEC's program aimed to increase agricultural production to prewar levels and to push industrial production even higher. It also called for the elimination of the "dollar gap" through an increase in European exports, and for the creation of an organization to foster economic cooperation, what became the Organization for European Economic Cooperation (OEEC). The final goals of the CEEC were the creation of internal financial stability and a curb on inflation. Though the Europeans estimated their financial need at US$22 billion, this figure was later scaled back to US$17 billion.

The debate in Congress was a bitter one, with supporters such as former isolationist Arthur Vandenberg pitted against an opposition led by Senator Robert Taft. To build support among the public, a group of influential private citizens organized the Committee for the Marshall Plan to Aid European Recovery. The Communist seizure of power in

Czechoslovakia in February 1948 spurred final passage of the plan. The Marshall Plan became part of the *containment strategy against the Soviet Union, even though Congress still prohibited the use of assistance to purchase military supplies.

The Economic Cooperation Administration (ECA), the organization which administered the Marshall Plan, did not "control" the Western European economies, though it did exert U.S. influence over the use of assistance. Aid most often took the form of food and raw materials, which the European governments would sell to their citizens. The money from these sales, called counterpart funds, remained in the local currency in a special account. These funds were then used for special projects or investments agreed on between the United States and the recipient country. Britain used the assistance to retire some of its debt, while France channeled funds into the Monnet Plan for the modernization of its infrastructure. The Germans eliminated production bottlenecks within their economy and supported the isolated city of Berlin.

Between 1948 and 1951, Congress authorized more than US$13 billion for the European Recovery Program. In its initial years of operation, Marshall Plan assistance amounted to approximately 10 percent of the annual federal budget. After the outbreak of the *Korean War in June 1950, the United States authorized the use of Marshall Plan assistance to provide for the rearmament of Western Europe. At the end of 1951 this change in emphasis became official as the ECA became the Mutual Security Administration.

The most striking legacy of the Marshall Plan—and the testament to its success—is how often it is still invoked as an analogy to contemporary problems. There have been calls for Marshall Plans to assist Eastern and Central Europe's and Russia's transition to market economies, to rescue the Asian economies from the crisis of 1997, and to promote development in the Balkans after the war in Kosovo. However, with the passage of time historians have tended to emphasize the extraordinarily unique conditions and circumstances that allowed for the Marshall Plan's success. Western Europe already had the skilled labor force, infrastructure, and governing institutions in place. It needed dollars, and the overwhelming economic strength of the United States in 1947 meant it could provide those dollars without causing undue sacrifice for Americans. Under the Marshall Plan, Western Europe's aggregate GNP increased 32 percent, agricultural production jumped 11 percent over prewar levels, and industrial output exceeded 1938 levels by 40 percent. Although the dollar gap did not disappear, inflation and unemployment decreased, and the plan successfully promoted European political stability under democratic institutions. European cooperation increased through organizations such as the European Payments Union and the European Coal and Steel Community, and the *European Union and currency union of today can also be considered legacies of the Marshall Plan. A final legacy of the plan was the division of Europe until 1989, breaking the traditional trading patterns between Eastern and Western Europe, and binding the Western European countries in closer political and economic relationships with the United States.

(See also FOREIGN AID; NINETEEN EIGHTY-NINE; U.S. FOREIGN POLICY.)

Alan Milward, *The Reconstruction of Western Europe* (Berkeley, Calif., and Los Angeles, 1984). Michael Hogan, *The Marshall Plan America, Britain, and the Reconstruction of Western Europe* (New York, 1987). Charles S. Maier and Gunter Bischof, eds., *The Marshall Plan and Germany* (New York, 1991). David Reynolds, ed., *The Origins of the Cold War in Europe: International Perspectives* (New Haven, Conn., 1994).

THOMAS ALAN SCHWARTZ

MARTÍ, José. To *Cuba and Spanish America, José Martí is considered to be the precursor of Cuba's political independence as well as the prophetic voice of the deep transformations that would occur in Cuba a century after his birth. Martí was born in Havana on 28 January 1853 into a humble Spanish family. He owed his humanist and patriotic tendencies to his mentor, Rafael María de Mendive. Imprisoned on 21 October 1869, Martí was deported to Spain on 15 January 1871, when a letter condemning those who defended the Spanish cause was discovered in his possession. In Spain, he studied law and philosophy. He also traveled in France, Mexico, and Guatemala. Upon his return to Cuba in 1878, he again pronounced himself against the colonial status of the island. Deported to Spain once again, he left shortly thereafter for New York, where he remained from 1881 to 1895.

In the United States, Martí's activities were fundamentally centered around journalism, disseminated throughout the continent, as well as the writing of poetry and a novel. At the same time, his long stay in the United States convinced him of the idiosyncrasy of "European America" and of the risks that it represented to Latin America. His knowledge and authority on the matter were increasingly geared toward promoting the definitive independence of Cuba, definitive not only vis-à-vis colonial Spain but also against neocolonial domination by the United States.

The product of his work in favor of the liberation of the island, *Bases del Partido Revolucionario Cubano*, was approved by the party on 5 January 1892. It declared that the party was founded to achieve "the complete independence of the island of Cuba" and "to encourage and assist with the independence of Puerto Rico." In addition, Martí contributed to the organization of the Cuban exiles and the creation of a military expeditionary force. At the end, he himself was involved in the military activities until his death in combat on 19 May 1895.

His premonitions about new threats menacing the American continent were expressed in the vibrant pages he wrote 10 January 1891, under the title *Nuestra América*, for the second Pan-American Congress, convened under U.S. initiative. In them, he prophetically cautioned about "the disdain of the formidable neighbor, which unknowingly is the major danger to our America."

Christopher Abel and Nissa Torrents, eds., *José Martí, Revolutionary Democrat* (Durham, N.C., 1986).

HERACLIO BONILLA

MARTIAL LAW. See MILITARY RULE.

MARX, Karl. Born in Trier, Germany, in 1818, Karl Marx saw his intended careers in university teaching and journalism frustrated by political suppression, and he moved to France and then Belgium. After the failure of the 1848 *revolutions (in which he took an active part), Marx settled in London in 1849. It was here that he produced his major works on political economy, including *Das Kapital*. He died in 1883.

Of all the nineteenth-century versions of socialism, it is Marx's that has proved intellectually the most influential and politically the most powerful. Drawing on the diverse traditions of German classical philosophy (G. W. F. Hegel), French utopian socialism, and Anglo-Scottish political economy (Adam Smith and David Ricardo), Marx's ideas centered around what he called his materialist conception of history. This allotted a central role throughout history to the development of the forces of production, which, together with their concomitant relations of production, formed a kind of economic base that determined the political and ideological superstructure of society. Whereas in the past the forces of production had been in the hands of successive minority classes, Marx believed that economic *development in his own time, and particularly deepening crises of *capitalism, meant the imminence of the conquest of the productive forces by the majority of society, who would be able to inaugurate a system of common ownership. Marx's theories are at their strongest in analytical/critical aspects, particularly in dealing with historical topics such as the transition from feudalism to capitalism or the role of the *state in contemporary capitalist society. With the life of neo-liberalism and the collapse of *communism, it is in his analysis of the economics and *ideology of capitalist societies that Marx continues to be most relevant. In outlining a theory for future revolutions, however, Marx was less successful: he extrapolated too readily from contemporary trends, and his own theory precluded any detailed account of how, politically and economically, a future socialist society might be organized.

Marx's ideas first came to world attention through the triumph of *Lenin and the Bolshevik Party in 1917—although it is worth remembering that two of the central tenets of *Leninism, the vanguard role of the party and the doctrine of *imperialism, are not to be found in Marx. With the emergence of *Stalinism, the ideas of Marx became transformed into an ossified and barren ideological system. In recent decades, the fuller publication of Marx's writings (and especially his earlier works) has revealed a more philosophical and humanist side to his theories. This aspect has been prominent in "Western" *Marxism, which has developed a thoroughgoing critique of capitalist society. In the Third World Marx's ideas appear, usually modified by Lenin, as an ideology of *modernization calculated to appeal to elites. To date at least, attempts to put Marx's ideas into practice have not met with long-term success. To reverse one of his best-known aphorisms: he (and his followers) have been better at interpreting the world than at changing it.

(See also LIBERALISM; SOCIALISM AND SOCIAL DEMOCRACY.)

David McLellan, *Karl Marx: His Life and Thought* (New York, 1974). Saul Padover, *Karl Marx: An Intimate Biography* (New York, 1978).

DAVID MCLELLAN

MASS MEDIA. See INFORMATION SOCIETY.

MARXISM. See overleaf.

MAURITANIA. The Islamic Republic of Mauritania occupies a large area of the Sahara Desert and a portion of the Atlantic coast of West Africa. Due to the remoteness of the territory, Mauritania was one of the last areas of the African continent to be effectively colonized. The French, who ruled the country from 1903 until independence in 1960, never really gained effective administrative control until the 1920s. The population, of approximately 2.5 million people, is almost entirely Muslim.

The Mauritanian economy is very narrowly based. During the 1960s, the "modern" economy was dominated by iron ore and, to a lesser extent, copper mining. These minerals were exploited almost entirely by foreign-owned mining consortia. The mining activities generated significant state revenue, although they did little to diversify the economy. Offshore fisheries (some of the richest in the world) were dominated by foreign fishing fleets, and these too contributed almost nothing to local development. The Mauritanian government made feeble efforts to establish industry during the 1960s, and especially the 1970s, but these efforts were poorly planned and, ultimately, unsuccessful. Agriculture was neglected throughout this period, and desertification gradually reduced arable land.

Economic conditions worsened significantly during the 1970s. First, a worldwide decline in the prices of Mauritania's mineral exports caused a substantial, and unexpected, drop in revenues. The accumulated foreign debt (US$2 billion in 1992) became largely unpayable. Second, a drought devastated the countryside, destroying much of the cattle herd and the livelihood of a large segment of the population. Destitute herders converged on the already crowded urban areas and generated extremely rapid urbanization, especially in and around the capital city, Nouakchott. Third, Mauritania participated in a protracted war in the Western Sahara region during the period 1975–78, which absorbed scarce economic resources.

All these problems exacerbated long-standing ethnic and regional tensions. Essentially, the country is divided between the northern Arabic-speaking peoples and several southern groups, mainly Wolofs and Peuls. The northerners account for about two-thirds of the population, and they have traditionally dominated national politics. With their political dominance, the northerners have attempted to Arabize the country and to promote Arabic, at the expense of French, in the educational system. The southerners, more oriented toward the French language, have resisted these efforts, leading to periodic riots and uprisings.

From the time of independence in 1960 until 1978, the country was ruled by Moktar Ould Daddah, under the official Parti du Peuple Mauritanien. During most of this period, the country functioned as a one-party state. The growing economic dislocations gradually discredited the Daddah regime, and it was overthrown in 1978. A succession of military councils ruled from 1978 until 1991, when a new constitution was adopted and military rule officially came to an end. The military leader, Colonel Maawiya Ould Sid'Ahmed Taya, was elected president in 1992 and then reelected in 1997. Despite this nominal democratization, the political system retains authoritarian qualities. Serious human rights abuses—including arrest without trial; torture and execution of political prisoners; and persecution of Wolof and Peul political groups—have continued to occur. The practice of *haratine* slavery, while officially outlawed, continues to be practiced in at least certain regions. With the assistance of the *International Mon-

(cont. on p. 533)

MARXISM. Predictions about the course of humanity have never been treated kindly by the "real movement of history." Yet seldom in that history has a writing been so prescient as the 150-year-old *Manifesto of the Communist Party.* Much of the document reads better today than when it was written. That two young Germans in their late twenties could have such foresight about today's world in the confines of a forty-two-page essay written near the beginning of their forty-year collaboration suggests that other insights await those who are willing to reread Karl Marx and Frederick Engels. The two have a lot to say about today's world, particularly about its oppressed majority for whom their perspective was intended, and to those who seek an alternative to this reality.

When, in the late 1990s, the "Asian" economic crisis threatened global repercussions on the scale of the Great Depression, it became apparent that the campaign to confine Marx and Engels to the dustbin of history in the wake of the implosion of the Soviet Union in 1989 was at best premature. Never has *Stalinism, the political current that exercised such a powerful hold on how they were read for more than seven decades, been so discredited as it is today. Thus, it is possible to approach Marxism with a freshness that very few have had the opportunity to do so until now. Revisiting Marx and Engels makes clear that much that was done in the name of Marxism (or Marxism-*Leninism) over the course of the last seventy years throughout the world had little to do with their actual program.

The Material Basis of Oppression. Why would a government deny its citizens such basic liberties as freedom of the press and free speech? What explains why *peasants and the poorer layers of society are routinely disadvantaged in the political process? Why are the wealthy privileged? These were exactly the questions for which the young Marx sought answers, working as a cub reporter for a liberal daily in Rhineland, Germany, in 1842–43. Marx saw the need to return to Hegel, the intellectual mentor of his generation, one who had drawn on the insights of the liberal economists James Steuart and Adam Smith to produce the best that Western thought had to offer on political theory and *political economy. Standing on Hegel's shoulders, Marx recognized the inadequacies of this most brilliant of minds, especially his disdain for "true *democracy." It was precisely the quest to realize "true democracy—the sovereignty of the people," that motivated Marx to begin his lifelong inquiry into political economy.

His inquiries pointed to the emergence and role of private property in societal evolution, a development that reached its logical conclusions with the coming of the capitalist mode of production in the second half of the eighteenth century. Along with the alienation of individuals from one another, or the erosion of community, came the commodification of all of society including most of all human labor. Every facet of life becomes a commodity to be bought, sold, or rented, be it politics, news, medical services, and the academy in advanced capitalist countries, or the human genome or internal organs of people living in underdeveloped countries. At the same time, it is *capitalism, in its campaign to create and conquer markets everywhere, that makes the objective reality of a global human community a conscious possibility for the first time.

If Marx and Engels only lived to see early capitalism, they did have the advantage to witness the transition from a precapitalist to the capitalist mode of production. From such a vantage point, and by contrasting capitalism with previous systems, they could see its essence more clearly than those who were later locked in its embrace and who were, thus, more prone to treat capitalism as natural. They didn't mince words about its origins. The "real movement of history"—the basis for their newfound "materialist conception of history"— as opposed to, for example, the rationales of religious doctrines, was unambiguous about the millions whose lives were lost in capitalism's birth: slaves from Africa, aborigines in the Americas, and peasants in Europe. As Marx's *Capital* graphically puts it, "Capital comes [into the world] dripping from head to toe, from every pore, with blood and dirt."

The unprecedented increase in wealth *and* poverty was one of the most striking aspects of this new system of production for those who lived through its arrival. The inequalities of previous class societies, i.e., those based on private property, began to pale in comparison—a tendency that has accelerated as witnessed by developments in the United States over the course of the last two decades. And for the first time these inequalities took on a global character from which the phenomenon of underdevelopment derives today. Their most thorough treatment of how this emerged was the case of Ireland.

England's subjugation of its oldest colony took on a qualitatively different character with the coming of industrial capitalism. First, the colonial state insured that the nascent industrial developments in the colony would be nipped in the bud so as not to compete with the metropole. Second, the 1846–47 famine, which was as much a creation of the colonial state as a product of nature, was used as a means to clear the land of people and replace them with pasture in order to serve the food needs of the metropole. Last, a portion of Ireland's "surplus" population could then be used as cheap labor in the metropole, with the further advantage of dividing workers in England on the basis of national and religious origins. Thus, Marx and Engels provided the first detailed analysis of a process that would be generalized throughout the world.

The key to Marx and Engels' contribution to democratic theory and practice was their insistence on the incompatibility between private property, together with the inevitable inequalities that it generates, and democracy. Although they were not the first to see this, they were the first to provide an explanation based on their historical materialist perspective, what they called a "scientific" as opposed to, again, for example, a religious explanation. Quite early they concluded that only with the elimination of private property could democracy be realized—a view that was widely held in the workers' movement of their day. Thus, the necessity of not just a political but a social revolution. As to which social layer to look to for leading that revolution, the logic of their analysis and the actuality of their era led them to the industrial working class, the "modern proletariat"—the first oppressed class in history that has not only the interest but the capability to overthrow class society. Only with the working class in power—the "dictatorship of the proletariat"—could class exploitation be ended and, thus, "true democracy" instituted.

The 1848–1849 *revolutions that swept Europe taught them to see the upheavals in global terms. By the end of 1848, they had concluded that the fate of the German revolution was linked to the successful outcome of a worldwide revolutionary process that combined national liberation, antifeudal and anticapitalist struggles "waged in Canada as in Italy, in East Indies as in Prussia, in Africa as on the Danube" (*Marx-Engels Collected Works*, 1975–, vol. 8, p. 215)—challenging, thus, the oft-alleged Eurocentrism of Marx and Engels.

Their research allowed them to strengthen this judgment two years later in their analysis of developments in the United States. "The most important thing to have occurred [in the United States], more important even than the [1848] February Revolution, is the discovery of the California gold-mines. . . . [As a result] the center of gravity of world commerce . . . is now the southern half of the North American peninsula . . . the Pacific Ocean will have the same role as the Atlantic has now and the Mediterranean had in antiquity" (*Collected Works*, vol. 10, pp. 265–66). Capital's fears about the global impact of the clouds only recently hanging over Asia and the Pacific, the new "center" of world capitalism, testify once again to their prescience. As for Europe's place in this new scenario, Marx rendered a judgment in 1857. While a socialist revolution might begin in "this little corner of the earth," it could easily be crushed since capitalism was "still in the ascendant over a far greater area" (*Collected Works*, vol. 40, p. 347). The success of the European revolution, henceforth, was inextricably linked to the revolutionary process elsewhere—an insight that rings even truer today.

Though having barely existed for "one hundred years," capitalism, as the *Manifesto* acknowledges, "has created more massive and more colossal productive forces than have all preceding generations together." But therein lies its Achilles' heel. Such a productive machine "is like the sorcerer who is no longer able to control the powers of the nether world whom he has called up by his spells." Unlike any previous economic system capitalism suffers from "the epidemic of over-production . . . too much means of subsistence, too much industry, too much commerce." It is precisely this feature that

leads to periodic "crises." Marx's later discovery of the tendency for the average profit rate to decline was crucial in explaining overproduction. Too many unprofitable goods and services is the basis of today's deflationary spiral, threatening another worldwide downturn. The lack of any controls for such developments, owing fundamentally to the private property basis of capitalism, is exactly what the actions of the International Monetary Fund (IMF) and its sponsors have revealed in the inadequacy of their responses to the Asian crisis of 1997.

The *Manifesto* argues further that capital can only solve its crises by either destroying "a mass of productive forces"—the Second World War as the solution to the Great Depression and the basis for the postwar boom would be such an example—or by conquering "new markets and by the more thorough exploitation of the old ones." That virtually all capitalists today, especially since the worldwide capitalist downturn of 1974–75—a classic example of a crisis of overproduction—must constantly search for new markets and, at the same time, squeeze more labor from their existing workforces is again testimony to the power of Marx and Engels's analysis.

Capital's need for a "more thorough exploitation" of labor means that workers will increasingly be at the center of world politics, as events around the globe have already shown. Capital and the governments that do its bidding seek to dismantle the post–World War II "social pacts" in the name of rationalization, competitiveness, or IMF conditionalities. Workers from Europe to Asia, from Africa to the Americas, have begun to mobilize in numbers not seen since the end of the war. What is especially characteristic of these mobilizations is their increasingly diverse composition owing to the *globalization of labor, the natural by-product of the globalization of capital. Labor is far more multinational, multiracial, and multigendered than what was true in Marx and Engels's time, a development that would not have surprised them. The national and racial similarity between the strikers in France's massive work stoppage in December 1995 and the players in its World Soccer Cup triumph in 1998 is not coincidental.

"What Is to Be Done?" With their new perspective Marx and Engels sought immediately to link up with Europe's proletariat. Owing to the strengths of their arguments and active efforts to make their case they were eventually successful. The most politically advanced of these workers invited them to lead their organization—renamed at their urging the League of Communists—and to write a program for it, the *Manifesto*. Published on the eve of the 1848 revolutions, it sought to persuade communists who had tended to function in a conspiratorial fashion to end their sectarian stance toward the working class and to see themselves as the most conscious layer of the proletariat.

Contrary to the usual portraits of them as just theorists, Marx and Engels were active organizers—consistent with

Marx's *Theses on Feuerbach*. While workers were the revolutionary class, they had to be won to a communist program that required conscious and active leadership. On the basis of the League experience and earlier organizing efforts, they formulated organizational views that remained with them to the end, many of which became part of V. I. *Lenin's arsenal.

One of the things that clearly distinguished them from other self-styled socialists and communists within the workers' movement was their view that the fight for communism was intimately linked with the fight for political democracy. Responding in 1892 to the charge—one that still continues until today—that he and Marx ignored democratic forms of governance, Engels countered: "Marx and I, for forty years, repeated ad nauseam that for us the democratic republic is the only political form in which the struggle between the working class and the capitalist class can first be universalized and then culminate in the decisive victory of the proletariat" (*Collected Works*, vol. 27, p. 271). For many a twentieth-century would-be Marxist this advice was either unavailable or ignored with all the tragic consequences.

Very much related to the democratic struggle was the necessity to support the national liberation efforts of oppressed peoples, such as the Irish and Polish, another way in which the "sovereignty of the people" could be realized. While it is true that Marx and Engels never formulated a full-blown theory about nationalism, they left revolutionary socialists a rich record, based on their extensive activities, on how to approach the issue—one that served as a basis for Lenin's detailed treatment of the "national question." Thus, the claim that they ignored nationalism is simply not borne out by the record.

But what about the related charge that they misjudged the hold of nationalism? Doesn't history, especially since 1989, show that the *Manifesto* at least overestimated the cosmopolitanizing effects of capitalism? This claim misses the point that the document is first and foremost a political statement, a call to action. "The Workingmen have no country" is a call to workers to not let national differences be an obstacle to their unity rather than a denial of the existence of such differences. This applies as well to settings where capitalist property relations were either eliminated or severely curtailed as in the former Yugoslavia. After nearly a decade of slaughter in which workers, differentiated by religion, language, and national origin, have paid the highest price, isn't it appropriate to call on them to recognize that what they have in common is more important than what they share with the warlords who pose as their leaders? To win workers to such a perspective would of course require the kind of activist leadership that Marx and Engels brought to the national as well as other questions.

The main political lesson that Marx and Engels distilled from the 1848–49 revolutions was the necessity of independent working-class political action. The liberal bourgeoisie had unmistakably demonstrated that it couldn't be counted on to institute political democracy let alone the social program that workers demanded. This didn't mean, however, that workers should do it alone. To the contrary, the revolutionary upheavals had convinced them of the correctness of their strategy of the "people's alliance," the alliance they fought to forge between workers, peasants, and the urban middle classes. At the heart of this coalition was the alliance of the first two classes led by workers.

When a new revolutionary era opened in the early 1860s, Marx saw this as the opportunity to implement the lessons of 1848. Under his leadership, the International Working Men's Association (IWMA), founded in 1864, made independent working-class political action a reality for the first time in European politics. Critical of trade unions for having "kept too much aloof from the general social and political movements"—what Lenin would later call in his *What Is to Be Done?* (1902) the problem of "economism"—he led the fight, through the organization, to convince unions to "learn to act deliberately as organizing centers of the working class in the broad interests of its *complete emancipation*"—in other words, to think socially and act politically. Marx's efforts, with Engels's crucial assistance, and against the opposition of currents in the workers' movement that dismissed political action like the anarchists, laid the basis for what would eventually be the mass workers' parties of Europe, for example, the present-day Socialists and Social Democrats, respectively, in France and Germany.

Contrary, therefore, to received wisdom, Marx and Engels made a decisive contribution to the democratic breakthrough at the beginning of the twentieth century. In particular, the mass working-class parties that they helped to bring into being were crucial in extending the suffrage to socially excluded groups like women and the poor. Their contribution was not inadvertent but purposive owing to their program and activism. As they would have expected, the role of the working class in the democratic breakthrough continues to resonate. The *democratic transition under way in South Africa exemplifies this fact.

One of the most enduring myths about Marx and Engels is that they intended their perspective for only the most advanced capitalist countries. Related to this is the claim that they disparaged or at best ignored the peasantry. The latter myth is fueled in part by the way that the *Manifesto* deals with the peasantry and an inadequate reading of Marx's *Eighteenth Brumaire of Louis Bonaparte*. Their ceaseless efforts, however, to implement the worker-peasant alliance simply give lie to this claim. More important is that from about 1870 onward they prioritized developments in Russia, an underdeveloped and overwhelmingly peasant country. Equally important is that revolutionaries and radicalizing youth in Russia—especially after the publication of *Capital* in Russian in

1872, the first in any other language—had no doubt about the applicability of Marxist program to their circumstances.

In declaring as they did in 1882 that "Russia forms the vanguard of revolutionary action in Europe" they did not assume that socialist transformation was on the immediate agenda in an underdeveloped country like Russia. Rather the transition would begin there through the democratic revolution but could only be consummated if it spread to a more advanced capitalist country, particularly Germany, where the material prerequisites for such a transformation existed. Socialist Germany could then assist Russia in its transition. Between the Russian Revolution in October 1917 and the failure of German socialists to take power in 1923—coming on the heels of two previous failed attempts—this seemed like a real possibility. That socialist transformation could begin in the underdeveloped world but had to extend to advanced capitalist countries to be successful is more relevant today than ever. Evidence continues to mount that the post–World War II Third World revolutionary process, often in the name of "Marxism," may have reached an impasse that can only be resolved in the advanced capitalist world.

From the very first, Marx and Engels differentiated themselves from the utopian socialists and their blueprints for the future by emphasizing that "communism is not a doctrine but a *movement*; it proceeds not from principles but from *facts*" (*Collected Works*, vol. 6, p. 303). They only once saw the need to provide an addendum to the *Manifesto*, to enrich its theory on the basis of the facts of the first workers' revolution, the Paris Commune in 1871. The insurrection taught that "the working class cannot simply lay hold of the ready-made state machinery, and wield it for its own purposes." The disappointment of workers with rule by Social Democratic parties provides—admittedly in a negative way—evidence for this conclusion.

By far the most powerful myth about Marx and Engels is that Stalinism is the necessary product of their thought and practice. What would they have thought of this phenomenon? The quick answer is that Stalinism confirmed their basic view that socialism can't be built on the backs of the working class. But perhaps the best response to this question comes from Lev *Trotsky (1879–1940), a leader of the Russian Revolution who offered the most convincing explanation within a Marxist framework. Trotsky's thesis was that Stalinism constituted a counterrevolution in which the bureaucracy usurped political power that had momentarily been in the hands of Russia's workers and peasants after October 1917. The failure of the revolution to spread westward was the necessary political condition for this overturn. At the same time, the counterrevolution was fundamentally political rather than social—it did not lead to the restoration of capitalist property relations that had been overthrown in 1917–18. However, the substitution of the "dictatorship of the bureaucracy" for the "dictatorship of the proletariat" meant that socialism could not be constructed in the Soviet Union. For Trotsky, as well as Marx and Engels, the overthrow of capitalism was never equated with the construction of socialism. The latter required conscious leadership which hindsight makes clear was no longer available in the Soviet Union by the end of the 1930s.

The relative ease with which the Stalinist edifice began to crumble after 1989 caught most observers off-guard. For decades, non-Marxist and some "intellectual Marxist" analysts had held that the totalitarian hegemony of Stalinism was virtually impregnable. Trotsky, whose most systematic presentation of his views is in his 1936 book *The Revolution Betrayed*, had better foresight. He argued that the Stalinist regime in the Soviet Union was an ephemeral phenomenon, as it proved to be. Also, the emphasis that he placed on the centrality of property relations in social revolutions—again in the tradition of Marx and Engels—goes a long way toward explaining the difficulty global capital has had in the former Stalinist states, especially Russia, in reintroducing capitalism. To do so would require not just a political but a social revolution.

The only state leadership in the world today that unabashedly raises the banner of Marxism resides in Havana. Whether the Cuban Revolution is the last gasp of an earlier development or the harbinger of a new era of socialist revolutions will be decided by the real movement of history. Global capitalism ensures what Marx and Engels could only anticipate: a world in which most producers are wage workers and, thus, subject to the same destabilizing forces inherent in its mode of production. Far from certain is whether there will be those workers and their allies—sufficient in numbers, consciousness, and will to see this as an opportunity to make the final lines of the Manifesto a reality for the first time: "The Proletarians have nothing to lose but their chains. They have a world to win." What is especially different about today's world is that those who are inspired by this vision have a much better chance of finding the real Marx than the millions miseducated for almost seven decades by the once-hegemonic Stalinist apparatus in all its demoralizing and deadly incarnations.

(See also ANARCHISM; CLASS AND POLITICS; COMMUNISM; COLONIALISM; DEVELOPMENT AND UNDERDEVELOPMENT; EQUALITY AND INEQUALITY; NINETEEN EIGHTY-NINE; SOCIALISM AND SOCIAL DEMOCRACY.)

Hal Draper, *Karl Marx's Theory of Revolution*, 4 vols. (New York 1977–1990). Alan Gilbert, *Marx's Politics* (Boulder, Colo., 1989). Michael Levin, *Marx, Engels, and Liberal Democracy* (New York, 1989). John Ehrenberg, *The Dictatorship of the Proletariat* (New York, 1992). August Nimtz, Jr., *Marx and Engels: Their Contribution to the Democratic Breakthrough* (Albany, N.Y., 2000).

AUGUST H. NIMTZ, JR.

etary Fund, Mauritania has embarked on a substantial economic restructuring program, which devalued the national currency, the *ouguiva*, and reduced restrictions on foreign investment. Agriculture, previously neglected, has received augmented financial support, mostly through foreign aid. Additional resources have also been invested in the fisheries sector. This restructuring program has produced ambiguous results: In recent years, there has been some modest economic growth, although research by Mohameden Ould-Mey raises concerns about the equity impact of these programs.

(See also FRANCOPHONE AFRICA.)

Mohameden Ould-Mey, *Global Restructuring and Peripheral States: The Carrot and the Stick in Mauritania* (Lanham, Md., 1996).

DAVID N. GIBBS

MAURITIUS. See INDIAN OCEAN REGION.

MAY 1968. The term *May 1968* should be understood in two ways, literally and metaphorically. The "events of May," as the French called them, were first of all a cluster of large-scale social protests which shook the very foundations of French politics. At the same time, undoubtedly because of its amplitude, May 1968 became the symbolic nexus of an international contagion of student and new middle strata protests which marked the later 1960s and which in retrospect can be seen to have permanently changed the course of politics in most advanced industrial societies.

The "events of May" began early that month with a gigantic student protest against the regime of General Charles de *Gaulle. The roots of unrest lay in the *modernization over which de Gaulle's Fifth Republic had presided and the difficulties which it had posed for French society and the French polity. Rapid economic growth, urbanization, consumerization, occupational and life-style changes came together with an unprecedented demographic boom to destabilize traditional French ways. Social discomfort in the earlier 1960s was contained by the charismatic Gaullist regime. Despite this, given its largely traditionalist social base and the benevolent *authoritarianism of its leader, the regime had limited capacities for understanding the new social concerns which modernization brought.

It was no surprise that the student and intellectual world provided the spark for explosion. Inept efforts to update the French educational system—expansion of university teaching without adequate budgets, poor and alienating facilities, and incompetent reflection about curricular organization and change—fed student and intellectual malaise. France's student milieus were traditionally prone to agitation and, moreover, had already been touched by the burgeoning international movement of protest against the *Vietnam War. The "events" themselves were provoked directly by a march, led by Daniel Cohn-Bendit ("Danny the Red"), from the Nanterre campus in suburban Paris to the Latin Quarter to protest against plans to bring student anti-Vietnam activists to trial.

After the marchers had held a rally in the Sorbonne courtyard, police moved in brutally for mass arrests. The interaction was prototypical. The authorities believed that a show of force would intimidate the student movement. Militant student leaders, acting in deliberately provocative ways, were quite as convinced that such repression, given the depth of

student discontent, would provoke a mass movement. Barricades were thus repeatedly erected in the Latin Quarter. Pitched battles between excited students and ferocious-looking riot police occurred, replete with barrages of paving stones answered with tear gas. The student leaders proved the better strategists. In short order the totality of Paris's very large student population was mobilized while the movement spread through the provinces. An intense week of startling confrontation between government and students, broadcast live on French radio and television, polarized French adult society.

The ideological content of the student movement was an interesting combination of anarchistic "new culture" slogans—"bring imagination to power," for example—and the strident *Marxism and Third Worldism which led to the ritual singing of "l'Internationale" after big rallies. Indeed, the real objects of the student movement were difficult to discern. Some wanted to reform the educational system. Others wanted to strengthen opposition to the Gaullist regime. Still others, and probably the majority, thought that they were engaged in revolution. The social base of the movement was "new-middle-class youth" in profound intergenerational conflict on the cusp of France's modernization. Movement leadership, in contrast, was largely drawn from a preexisting universe of student leftist groups perpetually seeking out "masses" to direct.

On 11 May, after a week of student protest, French union leaderships called for a one-day strike of solidarity with the students in an effort to warn the Gaullist government away from its course of repression. This strike, meant to be brief, precipitated a decentralized brushfire among workers all over the country. Three days later France was completely shut down by a national strike movement which, at its peak, encompassed virtually the entire French working *class, perhaps the largest single strike in the history of modern societies. The workers sought redress for an entirely different set of grievances from the students', largely in the area of industrial relations (wages, employment security, union rights), to which the Gaullist regime and French employers had proved unwilling to respond over the years.

The contiguity of student and strike movements came very close to destabilizing France. When General de Gaulle, appreciated for a decade as a consummate political strategist, was unable to prevent the situation from deteriorating, French elites prepared for dramatic political changes. A solution was finally proposed by Prime Minister Georges Pompidou based on dividing students from workers by negotiating an end to the strike and then calling new legislative elections. After nearly a month of *Sturm und Drang*, the strike was finally settled. The student movement, which had itself degenerated toward utopian extremism, then began to wane as the impending elections led political elites back into tried-and-true campaign paths. In the heat of general social panic which May 1968 promoted, General de Gaulle's electoral coalition won a sweeping victory.

De Gaulle's career was nonetheless fatally compromised by May 1968. He ultimately resigned in April 1969. The course of French economic and social life was likewise profoundly changed by the "events." The strike settlement was costly, contributing to inflation and currency devaluations and ultimately to the economic difficulties which overtook France in the 1970s. The course of French social policy was changed after May in more generous and less authoritarian directions as well. Student leftists, convinced that *revolution was on the way, followed a course of exhausting agitation which wore them down by the early 1970s. Gathering its own strength in the aftermath of the "events," the French Left began to move decisively toward its 1980s successes, eventually providing a legitimate home for many of the May movement's more able leaders.

The symbolic role of May 1968 is quite as important. May in Paris was the most spectacular and eloquent moment of the broader parade of student upheaval of the 1960s. Because it had brought a major European society, if not to the verge of revolution, at least to an advanced stage of disorder, it was seen as a model for what student protest might achieve and a confirmation for the most committed student activists that they were a new vanguard of fundamental social change. At virtually the same moment the anti-Vietnam mobilization in the United States was reaching its peak—obliging President Lyndon *Johnson to renounce any attempt at reelection. With student activism paralyzing major campuses, rebellions against conscription and discipline in the armed services growing, and unprecedented violence marking public life, it looked as if American society were disintegrating. Likewise German students mobilized dramatically in the streets of Berlin and Frankfurt and the "*Prague Spring" pursued its tragic course in Czechoslovakia amid a tide of smaller movements almost everywhere in advanced societies. In the aftermath of the events in Paris, Italian students and workers initiated the long "Hot Autumn" which was to loom so large over Italian politics in the 1970s.

It would take some time for the deeper meaning of this international wave of protest, with the French May at its symbolic center, to become clear. In effect, the content of progressive politics in advanced societies was changing dramatically. Older, labor-centered political patterns would henceforth be challenged, and have to share their political space on the Left with the newer issues and ways of organizing characteristic of the educationally credentialed new middle strata, particularly those engaged in public-sector and "helping" professional occupational roles. A new feminism, "green" ecology movements, and other such mobilizations would come to share the Left political stage with and complicate the lives of social democratic and other older Left formations.

(See also GAULLISM; NEW LEFT; NEW SOCIAL MOVEMENTS; POSTMATERIALISM.)

Alain Touraine, *The May Movement: Revolt and Reform* (New York, 1971). George Ross, *Workers and Communists in France*, ch. 10 (Berkeley, Calif., 1982). Jacques Capdevielle and René Mouriaux, *Mai 68: L'entre-deux de la modernité* (Paris, 1988). David Hanley and Anne Kerr, eds., *May '68: Coming of Age* (London, 1989). Sidney Tarrow, *Democracy and Disorder: Protest and Politics in Italy, 1965–1975* (Oxford, 1989).

GEORGE ROSS

McCARTHYISM. The term *McCarthyism* was invented in late March 1950 by *Washington Post* cartoonist Herbert Block (Herblock). It referred to tactics employed by Republican Senator Joseph R. McCarthy of Wisconsin, who for some two months had been rocketing to international fame by charging that subversives in the federal government were influencing and setting national policy. The term rapidly became used to iden-

tify methods used by advocates of the Second Red Scare (1948–1957), who made reckless personal charges of Communist and pro-Communist activities for the sake of political, psychological, and economic profit.

Postwar frustrations, especially associated with Soviet aggression in Western Europe, were largely responsible for the emergence of McCarthyism. Several politicians in the elections of 1946 learned that voters could be influenced by charges that their opponents were "soft" on the "Reds." But claims of Communists in high places began to appear in many areas of American life. In 1947, for example, the House Committee on Un-American Activities held widely publicized hearings on disloyalty in the film industry.

The 1948 presidential election saw the Democratic incumbent Harry S. *Truman record a stunning upset victory over the Republican Thomas Dewey. In the aftermath many Republicans became convinced that future victories could best be achieved by claiming that Democrats, especially liberals within the party, were aiding the Communist cause. Soon such events as the Judith Coplon case (in which a Department of Justice employee was arrested as a Soviet spy), the Communist takeover of China, the Soviet Union's unexpected development of the atomic bomb, and the sensational perjury conviction of the liberal Alger Hiss (which many interpreted as a vindication of charges that he had been a Red spy), persuaded many in the United States that something was definitely wrong in Washington.

Joe McCarthy entered the picture in February 1950, charging—without evidence—that there were 205 Communists in the State Department. The allegations grew more widespread, eventually resulting in the persecution and firing of people in all walks of life. The Second Red Scare, with the flamboyant, publicity-conscious McCarthy as its leader, was under way. Republicans eagerly—and successfully—employed McCarthyism in the elections of 1950 and 1952, culminating in the 1952 presidential race, won by Dwight *Eisenhower with the aid of McCarthy (a man he personally despised) and his supporters.

McCarthy quickly became a thorn in the side of the new administration by attacking Republicans, army leaders, and even the president himself. His shrill charges of subversive activity led to the televised Army-McCarthy hearings in 1954, in which McCarthy claimed unconvincingly that the military was riddled with Reds. In front of millions of viewers, McCarthy revealed himself to be an irresponsible bully. He was censured by the Senate later that year for offensive conduct toward colleagues.

Still, McCarthyism continued, in the nation's churches, libraries, schools, mass media, governmental bodies, and elsewhere. It began to fade in 1956, when Eisenhower easily won reelection, and it was buried the following year by the United States Supreme Court in several decisions including *Watkins v. United States* and *Jencks v. United States*.

The Second Red Scare directly affected only a small minority of Americans, and few people, pollsters reported, considered the issue of major importance. Still, McCarthyism clearly had some negative impact on *American foreign policy, politics, the media, and intellectual freedom, and McCarthyism as a term denoting a politically motivated witch-hunt to discredit ideological opponents has remained in the lexicon of U.S. politics.

(See also COLD WAR; COMMUNISM.)

Thomas C. Reeves, *The Life and Times of Joe McCarthy: A Biography* (New York, 1982). Thomas C. Reeves, ed., *McCarthyism*, 3d ed. (Malabar, Fla., 1989). Richard M. Fried, *Nightmare in Red: The McCarthy Era in Perspective* (New York, 1990).

THOMAS C. REEVES

MEDIA AND POLITICS. See overleaf.

MEDICARE AND MEDICAID. Government efforts in the United States to expand access to health care are unique among industrialized countries. In Britain, the government provides a comprehensive range of medical services to the entire population. By contrast, Canada and the United States, which share similar legal and cultural traditions, maintain private provision of health services even while pursuing quite different incremental approaches to health care reform. Canada expanded coverage by health service: universal government insurance for hospital care in the late 1950s and physician services in the late 1960s. Canadian patients continue to have a free choice of private health care providers; most hospitals are private or voluntary, nonprofit organizations and many physicians choose private, independent practices.

By contrast, the United States expanded government insurance by selected population groups. Medicare and Medicaid expanded coverage to the elderly, the disabled, and the poor. The programs provided money to a limited segment of the population to purchase from private providers a limited range of services. The result is that Britain, Canada, and other industrialized countries guarantee universal access to medical care; the United States alone among advanced industrialized nations lacks universal health insurance.

Medicare and Medicaid consumed just over $300 billion in 1997 or about 4 percent of gross domestic product. Medicare costs the federal government about three times as much as Medicaid.

Medicare provides medical insurance for a clearly defined set of services to the elderly and disabled who have contributed to the *Social Security system. Medicare's Part A, financed largely through payroll taxes, covers in-hospital care; the program's Part B covers doctors' fees and other outpatient services and is financed by a premium and general tax revenues, which cover about three-quarters of its costs. In addition to requiring its beneficiaries to pay a variety of charges for its covered services, Medicare does not cover a variety of medical expenses such as pharmaceutical drugs and extended nursing home care. (Over 80 percent of private health plans offer a more generous package of benefits.)

Medicaid covers the medical care of *welfare recipients and the "medically indigent"—those who fail to qualify for public assistance but lack the income to cover necessary medical expenses. The federal government uses general tax revenues to offer matching funds to local governments and state governments, who control (in quite different ways) its benefits, eligibility requirements, and administration.

The most striking reforms of government health program in the second half of the 1990s involve converting Medicare from a program that covers all services on a stipulated menu to a program that pays recipients a defined sum toward the purchase of a private insurance policy. The goals of this transition from a "defined benefit" to a "defined contribution" program are to give Medicare recipients the financial incentive to seek low-cost insurance policies (they have to bear the cost of premiums that exceed the government payment) and to reduce the government's financial risks. Critics have warned that encouraging economic competition among health insurers for Medicare recipients will result in lower quality of care as health plans reduce costs in order to offer still lower premiums.

(See also GREAT SOCIETY; WELFARE STATE.)

Theodore Marmor, Jerry Mashaw, and Philip Harvey, *America's Misunderstood Welfare State* (New York, 1990). Lawrence Jacobs, *Health of Nations: Public Opinion and the Making of American and British Health Policy* (Ithaca, N.Y., 1993).

LAWRENCE R. JACOBS

MERCANTILISM. The early mercantilist writers of the sixteenth and seventeenth centuries never thought of themselves as such. The term was largely unknown until, in the *The Wealth of Nations* (1776), Adam Smith criticized the mercantile system for its obsession with precious metals as the source of all wealth. His attack was largely confined to the commercial policies that flowed from this view, but later liberal economists have widened their understanding of mercantilism to include any government interference in the market of which they disapprove. In the nineteenth century, Friedrich List and the German historical school of political economists viewed mercantilism more favorably, arguing that active government management of the economy was an essential instrument of nation- and *state-building. Despite the intellectual dominance that liberal economics achieved during the twentieth century, most governments have continued to follow their advice.

The mercantile system was a product of the emergence of the early modern state with its centralized administration and standing army. Mercantilist policies varied from country to country, but their principal objectives were similar: to maximize the power of the sovereign and the well-being of his or her subjects. Under mercantilism power and wealth were synonyms not opposites.

These objectives were pursued within an intellectual climate which had two background features. The first was the belief that the state could only prosper by prevailing over its enemies: it had to be in a position to fight and win *wars. Since wars had to be paid for, governments needed a war chest, particularly as their tax base was narrow and financial credit in short supply. The second feature was the belief to which Adam Smith took such fierce objection, that wealth was fixed, residing in a finite stock of gold and silver. This zero-sum assumption meant that in any exchange, what one side gained, the other lost. It lay behind the export bounties and import prohibitions, the competition for bullion and colonies, and the mercantile wars of the early modern period. Indeed, mercantilism may be regarded as the economic dimension of the system of European power politics which developed after the signing of the Treaty of Westphalia in 1648.

The mercantilist worldview led to a preoccupation with *security and control in monetary and commercial relations between states. In monetary affairs a surplus was regarded as of paramount importance. Since wealth resided in money, a deficit meant impoverishment. A hoard of bullion was also necessary to fill the war chest, a consideration which weighed

(cont. on p. 540)

MEDIA AND POLITICS. In contemporary discourse, the word "media" has multiple meanings. In one construction, media, the plural of medium, are the channels through which information is transmitted to an audience. In this sense, we speak of the medium of television or of print. The word is used in a second sense as well. In this definition, "the media" is a synonym for the press or reporters, the agents who are the custodians of the narratives that pass through the channel of the media in the form of news in its various forms.

The first sense of the word was central to an important decision of the U.S. Supreme Court which held that the candidates have an affirmative right of access to the broadcast media. The ruling, handed down in July 1981, was the result of a challenge by the Carter campaign to network denial of the right to purchase thirty minutes of prime time in December 1979. Writing for the Court, Justice Warren Burger argued that "it is of particular importance that candidates have the opportunity to make their views known so that the electorate can intelligently evaluate the candidates' personal qualities and their positions on vital public issues before choosing among them on election day" (*CBS Inc.* v. *FCC*, 453 U.S. 367, 1981).

The second sense was at play in the court decree on printing of the Pentagon Papers. When the Nixon administration went to court to try to stop the *New York Times* and the *Washington Post* from publishing them, Justice Black wrote for the majority that

the Government's power to censor the press was abolished so that the press would remain forever free to censure the Government. The press was protected so that it could bare the secrets of government and inform the people. Only a free and unrestrained press can effectively expose deception in government. And paramount among the responsibilities of a free press is the duty to prevent any part of the government from deceiving the people and sending them off to distant lands to die of foreign fevers and foreign shot and shell.

In other words, Black found that the two newspapers were doing "precisely that which the Founders hoped and trusted they would do" (*New York Times Co.* v. *United States*, 403 U.S. 713, 717, 1971). This decision was rendered in the face of the Nixon administration's argument that publication would cause "the death of soldiers, the destruction of alliances, the greatly increased difficulty of negotiation with our enemies, [and] the inability of our diplomats to negotiate."

Just as the Nixon administration found the Court decision on the Pentagon Papers problematic, so too some find the protections afforded broadcast political speech troublesome. For example, J. B. Stoner, a politician running for state office in Georgia in 1972, paid to air an ad that said in part that "the main reason why niggers want integration is because niggers want our white women." The National Association for the Advancement of Colored People (NAACP) protested

and asked the Federal Communications Commission (FCC) to ban further airing. The FCC refused on the grounds that only a clear and present danger of imminent violence would justify tampering with a political commercial. The ruling was justified by the guarantee of free speech even for claims that are abhorrent ("FCC Won't Back Racist Ad in South," *New York Times*, 4 August 1972, p. 37). Independent presidential candidate Barry Commoner was also not stopped in 1980 from airing an ad that contained a word barred from entertainment programming: *bullshit*. Also, in 1972, presidential candidate Ellen McCormick was permitted to air an ad showing aborted fetuses that would not have been permitted to air had it not been considered protected political speech.

At one level, the media serve as a go-between, carrying the candidates' arguments to a larger audience than they could reach solely through interpersonal communication. On another, the media act as critical observers, examining politicians' records and proposals, and constructing narratives that help citizens make sense of the political world. In our focus on the second definition of media, we sometimes forget that some of the more important moments of our national life are a function of the existence of media as a channel. In the past four and a half decades, the number of nationally broadcast speeches by presidential candidates has dropped dramatically. A form that was once a staple of general elections has now all but disappeared from television although it survives in the form of the five-minute Saturday radio address by the president and response from a person from the opposing party. But where the public could come to know the party nominees through their nationally televised addresses in the 1950s, the 1960 campaign introduced a form that now constitutes the most watched event of the fall presidential season: the presidential debate. Although reporters have played some role, whether that of panelists or moderator, in each of the presidential general election debates, the bulk of the speaking time is the candidates'.

Debates are opportunities for politicians to distinguish their positions on issues by answering substantive questions about them. They are also a time for voters to compare the candidates. The media perform several roles in presidential general election debates by airing them live, covering them as news stories, and often providing the journalists who serve as questioners.

Taken together, the seven presidential elections containing debates have shown that they reinforce voters' perceptions more often than altering them, teach voters both about the candidates' positions on issues and character, and forecast the issue agenda of the future presidents as well as their communicative competence and habits of mind. However, postdebate press reports can alter the public's sense of who "won" and "lost" a debate and focus viewers and readers on tactical assessments rather than on a debate's substance.

Research since the first debates of 1960 has revealed fairly consistently that debates do not usually change votes. When change does occur, it is usually among those who were leaning to but not strongly committed to their candidate and those experiencing cross-pressures. In most elections, this is a small population; polling data suggest that most voters have usually decided how to vote before the first debate airs (Kathleen Hall Jamieson and Christopher Adasiewicz, "Debates in the United States," *Televised Election Debates: An International Comparison*, London, 1998).

The news media can distort the electoral process in the way they cover the campaign in general and the debates in particular. By forecasting that there will be little to learn from debates and by stressing the staged nature of the events, reporters and pundits discourage viewership. By sidestepping a discussion of the candidates' similarities and differences on issues for post-debate speculation about who won or lost, who looked more presidential, and about supposed decisive moments, particularly gaffes, reporters diminish the likelihood that viewers will move what they learned from the debate from short-to long-term memory.

The way the press frames a campaign may influence the decision-making process of voters as well. Framing refers to selecting and emphasizing some aspects of a story over others. One of the most problematic tendencies of the press is its focus on the strategy, or horse-race, aspects of campaigns rather than the issues being discussed. On average, studies show that about two-thirds of news articles about campaigns frame the news in terms of who is winning and losing instead of reporting and examining candidates' claims. A national survey on voters and media done by the Media Studies Center/Roper Center in September 1996 found 46 percent of respondents reporting that the media were paying too little attention to issues and 50 percent saying that there was too much attention being given to who's ahead and behind. The result is that campaigns end up being covered like sports or wars, with game and battle metaphors used to describe candidates and events. Candidates with good electoral prospects are "front-runners" while others are "long-shots"; politicians who are aggressive in a debate "came out with both guns blazing," and "hit a home run" or "scored a touchdown" if they "win" the debate and failed to "land a Hail Mary pass" or to "land a knockout blow" if they "lose."

The behind-the-scenes activities of politicians and their advisers become more important in such news stories than what the candidates are actually saying. For example, news reports are more likely to say that a candidate spoke at an auto factory in Detroit because she was courting the union vote than to describe what the candidate said and to examine her past record and comments about labor issues.

Polls are events only in the sense that they are created by the media and private organizations that conduct them, yet they are featured prominently in the coverage of electoral campaigns, either as aspects of larger stories or as the basis of entire reports. When they are about who is winning and who is losing at any given moment, polls lend themselves naturally to strategy frames. Poll-dominated news stories discourage reporting on candidates' proposals and instead lead to analyses of the politicians' plan to win.

The strategy frame focuses on conflicts between a front-runner and an opponent. As a result, in every presidential general election since 1960 reliance on news reports for information about the campaign would lead one to conclude that it contained a far higher level of attack than was in fact the case (Jamieson, Paul Waldman, and James Devitt, "Mapping the Discourse of the 1996 US Presidential General Election," *Media Culture and Society* 20 [1998]: 323–338).

While strategy is an integral part of any campaign, overemphasizing this aspect of the electoral process at the expense of substantive discussion of issues and candidates' claims has undesirable effects on the way voters think about the political process (Joseph N. Cappella and Jamieson, *Spiral of Cynicism: The Press and the Public Good*, New York, 1997). People who read and watched news stories that focused on the strategy behind a mayoral race were more likely to make cynical judgments about the candidates and the election than were those exposed to stories that focused on candidates' stands.

Both strategy and issue frames increase political learning in audiences, especially in print news. In other words, reading about politics, regardless of the frame employed, teaches people something about a campaign. The question is, what does it teach? There are important differences between strategy and issue frames, particularly in television news. In the Cappella and Jamieson study, after a week's news audiences in both strategy and issue conditions were shown the same video of a debate among mayoral candidates. Those who had been exposed to broadcast and print strategy stories learned more strategy information from that debate, while those who watched and read stories focusing on issues learned more about candidates' positions. Print news appears to have a smaller effect on political learning than does broadcast news.

Strategy stories extend beyond campaigns to dominate other types of political news, such as that involving public policy matters. About two-thirds of stories about the 1994 health care reform debate in the United States used a strategy frame, a percent similar to election coverage. As in campaign coverage, strategy frames activated cynical evaluations of the public policy process in audiences. Although the health care reform debate involved a lengthy discussion featuring various philosophies about how best to provide health coverage to the uninsured, news stories focused predominantly on winners and losers, as well as on the motives of the key figures in the debate. As in the study of the mayoral race, audiences exposed to strategy stories about the health care debate were more likely to make cynical judgments after seeing a substantive videotaped discussion on the topic than were people exposed to issue-based stories. In this study, however, issue stories also activated cynicism. Importantly, those who read either kind were as poorly informed about the substance of the health care reform debate as were those in the control who read a single article on health care reform. The reporters' focus on conflict minimized the likelihood that readers would understand the nature of the competing plans. Instead those in the study developed a generalized sense that the system was failing.

The news media's tendency to focus on strategy rather than substance in political reporting has a problematic effect on the way audiences think and learn about campaigns and policy debates. Strategically framed news highlights the self-interested motivations of the individual actors in the political process. By doing so, it leads people to focus on the negative, individuating aspects of politics rather than on more substantive concerns, and to then make negative attributions about both politicians and the political process.

While the way the news media frame a public policy discussion can affect the way the public thinks about politics, merely choosing to report on some policy matters and not others can influence the importance people attach to issues. Scholars call this "agenda setting," a reference to the way media encourage people to think about some issues merely by covering them more than others. Agenda setting posits both that the media tell us what to think about and also what not to think about. During the 1988 campaign, for example, neither the demise of the Soviet Union nor the savings and loan collapse became matters of candidate and public concern in large part because neither was a focus of press attention.

Many scholars have found strong correlations between the topics most frequently covered in the press and the issues people tell pollsters they think are the most important. For example, crime is covered more often than foreign policy; correspondingly, most people rank crime as one of the more important issues while foreign policy barely registers on the public opinion radar (at least in times of peace). In an important study of the 1968 campaign, McCombs and Shaw (1972) determined that the topics stressed in the press were very highly correlated with those the public thought were important.

It is not clear from survey-based agenda setting research, however, whether the media cause public agendas or whether there is another explanation. It could be that media and the public share agendas because some issues are more pressing than others, or because elites give these issues more attention. Time series analysis has strengthened the claim that reporting in the media is in fact producing the agenda setting effect.

Media attention to certain issues can also have an effect on policy makers. In a study of public policy issues in Congress,

Martin Linsky found (*Impact: How the Press Affects Federal Policymaking*, New York, 1986) that the press exercised a greater effect on the *process* of policy making than the *content* of policy, speeding up decision making and, especially with negative coverage, pushing that decision making to higher levels of bureaucratic officials. In presidential politics, Michael Delli Carpini argues that the relationship between media coverage and governing is built simultaneously on conflict and cooperation and is increasingly institutionalized ("Critical Symbiosis—Three Themes on President-Press Relations," *Media Studies Journal* [Spring 1994]: 185–197). For example, reporters covering the president are based in a pressroom at the White House, where they file stories based on regular press conferences and press releases from the executive branch. Recognizing the importance of controlling the issue agenda, congressional leaders as well as White House occupants manipulate both the topics and the frames offered the press; reporters respond with increased wariness about those in power.

When the press focuses on some issues, these not only tend to become the most important in the minds of audiences, they may determine the subjects on which the public evaluates politicians. This effect, known as priming, suggests that if the press focuses on the economy, the public will judge policy makers based on their evaluations of the economy rather than on an issue that is covered less frequently. Thus, if a person thought the economy was in poor shape, she would tend to have an unfavorable opinion of the president. Priming does not predict whether the evaluation would be negative or positive, however, but simply that the ones that receive the most coverage will be the issues on which a politician is judged.

Media can then set the agenda, prime, and frame. The extent to which they are able to do so is a function of the political and media climate. For example, as the Gulf War experience shows, one reason approval ratings for the president climb during the buildup to a war is that other elite policy makers such as members of Congress (wherein rests, after all, the constitutional authority to declare war) are hesitant to criticize the president for fear of being perceived as unpatriotic or as usurping the president's prerogative to determine foreign policy. The result is a one-sided media environment in which the president can define the crisis. Communication research has consistently shown that the media are most powerful in influencing public opinion when they present a one-sided message that comes from an influential source and conforms to a cultural or social norm, such as a need to rally in times of national crisis.

The public climate can also minimize the president's control of the agenda. When elite opinion—which could include both policy makers and the media—begins to coalesce around an opposing viewpoint, the two-sided tendencies of news will expose the public to counterarguments it may find persuasive. Public opinion can also turn when the media present negative evaluations of how the president (or any other policy maker) is handling a matter defined as a "crisis."

These factors played out during the course of the Vietnam conflict. When President Lyndon Johnson made a de facto declaration of war against North Vietnam following the Gulf of Tonkin "incident," few in Congress opposed his call for action. The public supported the Vietnam War in the beginning, but that support began to ebb as elite opinion leaders began questioning American involvement and media reports began providing evidence contrary to claims by the president and the military that the war was being won.

When it comes to coverage of political scandals, media influence on public opinion is less certain. The Monica Lewinsky scandal is illustrative. If the theories apply, the amount of coverage as well as its salacious nature should have produced priming and agenda setting. Instead, President Bill Clinton's job approval ratings recovered quickly from an initial drop and remained high even after a nationally televised speech in August 1998 in which he admitted he had misled the country about the affair.

Why didn't media preoccupation with the scandal have an effect on public assessments of Clinton's handling of the job of president, and why didn't it displace other issues in the public assessment of the problems facing the country? There appear to be two related explanations. Tracing the relationship between media coverage of the scandal and public approval ratings of the president, John Zaller argues that "bottom line" politics, meaning peace and prosperity, matter more to public judgment of a president than does media coverage of personal character ("Monica Lewinsky's Contribution to Political Science," *PS: Political Science and Politics* [June 1998]: 182–189). Zaller shows, for example, that Clinton's approval ratings climbed several points after the State of the Union speech in which he trumpeted a series of accomplishments ranging from a strong economy to a balanced budget. Zaller argues that the public made an assessment that the president's personal peccadilloes mattered less than his ability to maintain national and economic security.

Another explanation of the media's inability to set the public agenda in the Lewinsky scandal is that people make a distinction between the public and personal lives of politicians, a distinction that the press doesn't necessarily grant. An examination of opinion polls from the first several months of the discussion shows that the public consistently drew a line between personal sexual behavior and conduct in office in evaluating Clinton (Jamieson and Sean Aday, "When Is Presidential Behavior Public and When Is It Private?" *Presidential Studies Quarterly*, 1998). Polls showed that people saw adultery as a private matter with majorities reporting they would be willing to look the other way if he lied about an affair under oath. But strong majorities said the president would lose their support if he encouraged others to lie under

oath or participated in a conspiracy to hide illegal behavior. So while the press framed the story in large part as a sexual matter, the public appeared to draw the line at more job-related offenses. This is consistent with Zaller's argument that people are able to focus on substantive issues in a scandal despite the tenor of media coverage.

While coverage of the scandal may have had a limited effect on Clinton's job approval ratings, it still had the potential to affect the political process. In the Lewinsky case, Clinton's support among congressional Democrats suffered following his public admission that he misled people about the affair. In addition, it energized congressional Republicans who appeared ready to make the president's behavior an issue in policy debates and in mid-term elections. This could have had the effect of minimizing Clinton's ability to push legislation through Congress.

As a channel and a gatekeeper, the media play an important role in the political process. They provide the information citizens need to make evaluations of their elected representatives, and they can act as a channel between citizens and politicians. The press also acts as a check on government abuses by investigating and exposing the misuse of power. At the same time, the way the media cover politics can be problematic. The tendency to utilize strategy rather than issue frames when reporting on campaigns and policy debates prevents the dissemination of substantive information and activates cynical judgments in audiences. By covering some issues more than others, the media also set the agenda for the public and for policy makers. In addition to this agenda setting effect, the media may prime audiences to evaluate politicians on frequently covered issues rather than less frequently reported ones. The press has similar effects on the public and on policy in times of crisis, fostering consensus when opposing viewpoints are scarce, but playing a role in turning public opinion by publishing negative evaluations of the way political leaders are handling the crisis.

(See also CENSORSHIP; ELECTIONS AND VOTING BEHAVIOR; INFORMATION TECHNOLOGY; PRESIDENCY, U.S.; PUBLIC OPINION; PUBLIC POLICY; SUPREME COURT OF THE UNITED STATES.)

Maxwell McCombs and Donald Shaw, "The Agenda Setting Function of News Media," *Public Opinion Quarterly* (1972): 176–185. Michael B. Grossman and Martha J. Kumar, *Portraying the President: The White House and the News Media* (Baltimore, 1981). R. L. Behr and Shanto Iyengar, "Television News, Real-World Cues, and Changes in the Public Agenda" *Public Opinion Quarterly* (1985): 38–57. Shanto Iyengar and Donald Kinder, *News That Matters: Television and American Opinion* (Chicago, 1987). J. G. Geer, "The Effects of Presidential Debates on the Electorate's Preference for the Candidates" *American Politics Quarterly* 16, no. 4 (1988): 486–501. W. Lance Bennett and David L. Paletz, eds., *Taken by Storm: The Media, Public Opinion, and U.S. Foreign Policy in the Gulf War* (Chicago, 1994).

KATHLEEN HALL JAMIESON
SEAN ADAY

heavily on governments which often relied on mercenaries to fight their wars. The logical absurdity of all governments seeking a surplus at the same time was not perceived as a problem: within a zero-sum world, there had to be winners and losers. There was no difference, in principle, between the acquisition of territory through conquest and the acquisition of bullion as the result of an act of piracy on the high seas.

In commercial relations, the same "realist" logic applied. It led to protectionist attitudes toward foreign trade. Thus, for example, Johann Joachim Becher wrote: "It is always better to sell goods to others than to buy goods from others, for the former brings a certain advantage, and the latter inevitable damage." Hence, governments attempted to keep foreign goods out, a practice which was also good for local employment, and to subsidize the export of manufactures. Foreign trade was strictly controlled through the provision of royal charters, as a means of raising revenue. And since control was important, some mercantilist writers urged buying only from your own customers, i.e., bilateralism.

In his historical survey (*Mercantilism*, London, 1955), Eli Heckscher suggests that two events, the Boston Tea Party and the publication of *The Wealth of Nations*, doomed mercantilism as a social order. By the beginning of the nineteenth century it was no longer respectable to advocate practices in which there was no distinction between legitimate trade and plunder. Moreover, David Ricardo's *Theory of Comparative Advantage* undermined the conception of political economy as a zero-sum set of relations, while *imperialism and capitalist development led to the emergence of a global economy and an increasingly complex international division of labor. The liberal challenge to mercantilism, based on the advantages of relatively open foreign trade rather than economic *nationalism, was thus advanced on both practical and intellectual grounds. At first sight it was enormously successful. Yet, the fact that international society consisted of competitive sovereign states (not of individual profit maximizers) ensured the survival of many mercantilist policies. In the late twentieth century, these still provide the basis of national solutions (or attempted solutions) to the problems of *interdependence.

The ends of economic nationalism—the protection of the interests and welfare of the community—are not the same as those of mercantilism—the power and wealth of the sovereign state—but the means used to pursue these ends are often similar. In *The Closed Commercial State* (1800) Johann Fichte described in detail the principles on which a completely self-sufficient, autarkic national community should be based. These included the planning of production, investment, and employment and a total prohibition of foreign trade. Since states vary in their resource endowments, success required military expansion until the nation reached its "natural frontiers," at which point there would be no further need for either trade or war. Fichte's vision is the prototype of aggressive economic nationalism. Few governments have been tempted to follow his prescriptions, although his ideas probably influenced the economic policies of the Third Reich toward Eastern Europe during the 1930s. Between 1960 and 1980, many *Third World governments attempted to industrialize through *import-substitution policies. However, the postwar *international system offered few opportunities for territorial expansion, and none has pursued self-sufficiency with anything approaching the rigor envisaged by Fichte.

Throughout the twentieth century, a milder version of economic nationalism has established itself as the norm, even infiltrating the liberal international institutions (*International Monetary Fund, International Bank for Reconstruction and Development, and *General Agreement on Tariffs and Trade) which were established after World War II. This milder version, in which the right of governments to give preference to their own nationals is implicitly acknowledged, draws heavily on the legacy of mercantilism.

The early mercantilists had no conception of the business cycle. The final proof that the international division of labor could not safely be ignored came with the Great Depression of the 1930s: business failure and mass unemployment were transmitted from country to country in the manner of an epidemic. The cure which governments adopted was to fall back on a range of mercantilist measures for promoting exports and inhibiting imports, e.g., high tariffs, import quotas, export subsidies, currency manipulation.

After 1945 an attempt was made to insure against a repetition of these "beggar your neighbor" policies on the grounds that they had failed to bring about economic recovery and had contributed to the poisoning of political relations in Europe and the drift to war. Despite significant progress in trade liberalization under the General Agreement on Tariffs and Trade, it has not proved possible to abolish protectionism altogether. In the 1970s and 1980s there was a sharp increase in the use of export subsidies, voluntary export restraint, and organized marketing agreements, all neo-mercantilist measures. During the 1980s and early 1990s, many governments attempted to reduce their direct involvement in the market, but so long as their electoral fortunes depend largely upon the performance of the economy, it is doubtful whether democratic states can abandon mercantilist policies altogether.

(See also CAPITALISM; PROTECTION; REALISM.)

Friedrich List, *The National System of Political Economy* (New York, 1841, reprinted 1904). Jacob Viner, "Power versus Plenty as Objectives of Foreign Policy in the Seventeenth and Eighteenth Centuries" *World Politics* 1, no. 1 (October 1948): 1–29. Eric Roll, *A History of Economic Thought* (London, 1961). David Baldwin, *Economic Statecraft* (Princeton, N.J., 1985). Robert Gilpin, *The Political Economy of International Relations* (Princeton, N.J., 1987). James Mayall, *Nationalism and International Society* (Cambridge, U.K., 1990).

JAMES MAYALL

MERCENARIES. White mercenaries played major roles in conflicts in weak African states from 1960 onward. Until 1990, the characteristic pattern was the hiring of one or more specialists in unconventional warfare to act as officers, then recruiting individuals to serve as troops. The mercenary force assembled to defend the secession of the Congo's mineral-rich Katanga province was the prototype; many veterans of the Congo served in other African wars.

After 1990, mercenary activity involved security firms, some of which participated in mining enterprises as well as guarding them. The prototype was Executive Outcomes, based in South African and drawing upon veterans of that country's counterinsurgency forces.

Mercenaries appeared in the former Belgian Congo in 1960. The officers and noncommissioned officers of the *gendarmerie* or army of secessionist Katanga were regular Belgian army personnel, but mercenaries were recruited in Belgium by the security police.

To reduce dependence upon Belgium, Katanga sought additional white mercenaries from Rhodesia, South Africa, and France. The English-speakers formed a separate unit under Colonel Mike Hoare of South Africa. Major Roger Faulques of France led the anti-UN fight. When the UN ended the secession in 1963, French mercenary Bob Denard and former Belgian settler Jean Schramme led a hundred mercenaries and several thousand African *gendarmes* into Angola, where other Katangans joined them.

In 1964, with supporters of Patrice *Lumumba controlling half the Congo, former Katanga leader Moïse Tshombe returned from exile to head the central government. He summoned Schramme and 8,000 "Katangans" and gave Hoare the job of forming a white mercenary force. A motorized column headed by Hoare's men was nearing the Lumumbist capital of Kisangani when Belgian paratroops dropped from U.S. planes to seize the city and rescue white hostages.

General Joseph Mobutu's coup of November 1965 was motivated in part by his desire to prevent President Joseph Kasavubu from dismissing the mercenaries before the Lumumbists were defeated. Mercenaries then played key roles in two efforts to restore Tshombe to power.

Mercenaries played minor roles on both sides in the Nigeria-Biafra war. Mercenaries and arms for Biafra were arranged by Jacques Foccart, secretary-general for African affairs at the French presidency.

In 1975, Denard helped Ali Soilih overthrow President Ahmed Abdallah of the Comoros, just months after the archipelago gained its independence from France. In 1978, Denard invaded the islands and reinstalled Abdallah. When François Mitterrand vowed to rid the Comoros of the mercenaries in 1981, Denard apparently won South African support. In 1989 South Africa and France agreed that Denard and his men should leave and a show of French military force forced them out.

White mercenaries also served as ground forces in Sudan and Angola, and as *coup d'état strike forces in Guinea, Equatorial Guinea, Benin, Togo, and the Seychelles, not always successfully.

In the 1990s, Executive Outcomes provided security to mining operations in Angola and Sierra Leone. In 1997, an attempt was made to export the Executive Outcomes model to Australasia. Papua New Guinea Prime Minister Julius Chan signed a contract with London-based Sandlines International, a firm associated with Executive Outcomes, to suppress the secessionist movement on mineral-rich Bougainville island. The arrival of about seventy mercenaries, mostly South Africans, provoked strong reactions both domestically and internationally. Brigadier General Jerry Singirok, commander of the armed forces, demanded that Chan resign and was himself dismissed, which led to a mutiny by troops loyal to Singirok. A judicial inquiry cleared Chan of corruption charges in connection with the contract, but he was defeated in elections. Australia, expressing concern about the destabilizing effect mercenaries could have in the Pacific region, announced that it would sign an international convention banning the recruitment, use, financing, or training of mercenaries.

In 1996–1997, Mobutu hired Serbs and other Europeans to combat the invasion headed by Laurent Kabila. Mobutu reportedly approved a plan with South Africans operating under the name Stability Control Agencies (Stabilco), but his regime collapsed before more than a handful of the South Africans could begin work.

Before and after the end of the Cold War, both the strategic location of certain states and the presence of important minerals attracted mercenaries. Gerry S. Thomas's attempt to distinguish mercenaries from other operatives by three negative characteristics—including lack of support from their own government—is called into question by these cases, since the United States, South Africa, France, and Belgium all recruited and financed mercenaries, including their own citizens.

(See also DECOLONIZATION; INDIAN OCEAN REGION; MILITARISM.)

Gerry S. Thomas, *Mercenary Troops in Modern Africa* (Boulder, Colo., 1984). Elizabeth Rubin, "An Army of One's Own," *Harper's*, February 1997. William Reno, *Warlord Politics and African States* (Boulder, Colo., 1998).

THOMAS TURNER

MEXICO. The twentieth-century Mexican political system grew directly out of the experiences and goals of the Mexican Revolution, 1910–1920. The latter included agrarian reform, workers' guarantees, state control of subsoil resources, a more equitable society, and economic *nationalism. Although these objectives have not been fully realized, they established a framework of reference for all political contenders from that point forward. Reinstitutionalization was accomplished, largely, in the period between 1920 and 1940.

The system that emerged was highly centralized, characterized by strong presidentialism and a one-party state. The Partido Revolucionario Institucional (PRI) dominated the electoral system and the bureaucracy from the 1930s using its patronage to control labor unions and rural organizations, and limiting access to political power. However, after a massacre of striking students by government forces in 1968, public pressure led to a slow liberalization of the political process. Over the subsequent three decades, opposition parties and dissident voices were more in evidence. In July 2000 seven decades of PRI domination ended with the election of Vicente Fox Quesada of the center-right Partido de Accion Nacional (PAN).

The Mexican Revolution. The Mexican Revolution (1910–1920) grew out of discontent with the government of Porfirio Díaz (1876–1911). Díaz had come to power via what claimed to be a liberalizing movement with the motto, "Effective suffrage, no reelection." However, Díaz disregarded the no-reelection pledge and remained in power for thirty-five years with only a brief hiatus when one of his supporters occupied the presidency from 1880 to 1884. Enormous dispossessions of land from indigenous and other rural communities led to burgeoning agrarian unrest, while the growing middle class found its access to power and prosperity blocked by Díaz supporters and by increasing U.S. investment, especially in the northern tier of states. Even some economic elites found their upward political mobility blocked. The revolution which resulted was characterized by cross-class alliances, even within factions. After Díaz had been driven from the country, differences in revolutionary interests, along with factional disputes, led to major splits and continued violence. Eventually

Constitutionalists, united under Venustiano Carranza, prevailed over forces led by Pancho Villa and Emiliano Zapata. Both factions contained members from all economic groups. The Constitutional Congress of 1917 was a highly contested gathering which nevertheless was able to articulate the major goals of the revolution and to establish them as a consensual framework for measuring future governments' success or failure.

Institutionalization, 1920–1940. During his presidency (1917–1920), Carranza took measures to reestablish control over Mexico's oil fields, but made few attempts to implement the social goals of the revolution. He even began to take lands expropriated by revolutionary forces and to return them to their original owners. Only with the presidency of Alvaro Obregón (1920–1924) did land reform begin in earnest; Obregón also ordered the Department of Labor to oversee workers' rights. Advances in both areas were necessary in order to consolidate mass support for the centralizing government. Violent challenges from unsuccessful factions and even from within the winning coalition were common. When Obregón chose fellow Sonoran Plutarco Elías Calles to succeed him, another former associate and Sonoran, Adolfo de la Huerta, rebelled, uniting the opposition, including a large number of military officers and disappointed revolutionaries. The failure of the delahuertista movement successfully weeded out the strongest potential opposition, most notably within the military. Although there were subsequent rebellions, the military was largely brought under central government control. In fact, by 1940, the Mexican military was securely subordinated to the civilian state.

Obregón's government also began to move against foreign, particularly U.S., control of Mexican oil. At this time, Mexico was the second largest producer of oil in the world, just as oil was becoming the major energy source for both industrial and military purposes. Although limited by a need for foreign capital, the Mexican government successfully negotiated the Bucareli agreements of 1923 with the United States. This agreement provided that holders of subsoil rights who had invested in these properties prior to the Constitution of 1917 could maintain control of these resources. At the same time, the United States recognized that the Mexican state had ultimate rights over the subsoil. During subsequent administrations, Mexico continued to undercut the position of foreign oil companies, leading to the expropriation of almost all foreign holdings in the Mexican oil fields under President Lázaro Cárdenas in 1938. This move was extremely important in establishing the economic nationalism so important as a revolutionary goal.

Lázaro *Cárdenas, president from 1934 to 1940, also made significant strides in realizing the social goals of the revolution. *Land reform was a particular priority. Cárdenas was able to make many formerly provisional land distributions legally definitive, and he added new ones for a total of approximately 50 million acres. Federal expenditure for education soared, and government teachers poured into the countryside, encouraging support for the revolution and the centralized state. He also promoted the reorganization of the Mexican labor movement under Vincent Lombardo Toledano and his Confederación de Trabajadores de México. Although the labor movement would go through future permutations, it was closely allied to the Mexican state.

The Official Party. An important factor in the development of the Mexican political system was the establishment of a political party designed to unite revolutionary factions. The first step was taken after the assassination of presidential candidate Obregón, who was running for a second term in 1928. President Plutarco Elías Calles quickly organized a broad-based political party, the Partido Nacional Revolucionario (PNR), to ensure the continuation of political order. The party has changed names several times and is currently known as the Partido Revolucionario Institucional. It has been almost completely symbiotic with the Mexican state, has subsumed most labor and campesino (rural peasant) organizations, and has exercised enormous powers of patronage.

The Mexican Presidency. The presidency, since the Mexican Revolution, has been the most important and by far the most powerful institution within the Mexican state as well as within the PRI. The president has been the center of authority, the arbiter between power contenders, and the guardian of the principles of the revolution. The president has operated not only as the head of government, but also of the official party. The holder of this office has often used it to resolve political issues, without resorting to the legal system or to legislative bodies. This intervention has extended, as recently as the 1990s, to overturning state and local elections. Several early presidents were actual participants in the revolution, while later presidents were drawn from the elite in the PRI. However, in the 1980s and 1990s, the presidency was increasingly occupied by technocrats, usually with training in economics, who has risen through the ranks of the federal bureaucracy. These men had few ties to the popular classes, had not formerly been elected to office, and lacked grassroots party experience. Moreover, they have distanced themselves from the hallowed goals of the Mexican Revolution. Carlos Salinas (1988–1994), for example, declared land reform dead in Mexico and significantly changed the agrarian laws.

Since Obregón named Calles as his choice for the 1924 elections, the president has chosen the next official party candidate. In early 2000, President Ernesto Zedillo responded to popular demands for a more open process and instituted primary elections within the PRI. However, the president's power and influence led to the nomination of his favored candidate, Francisco Labastida Ochoa, who lost in the July 2000 elections.

The 1968 Massacre. The government of President Gustavo Díaz Ordaz (1964–1970), in the process of readying the Mexican capital for the Olympic games in 1968, overreacted in August of that year to relatively minor student disturbances by unleashing a paramilitary force. The repression stimulated protests at the National University (UNAM), leading eventually to a national student strike. In mid-September, troops were sent in to seize the UNAM campus, inflaming the situation still further. Student organizers responded by calling for a rally in the Plaza de Tres Culturas in the district of Tlaltelolco, an area surrounded by middle-class apartment buildings. The government responded on 2 October 1968 by sending in army and police units accompanied by tanks and armored vehicles. When demonstrators refused to disperse, gunfire erupted. Students, bystanders, and residents returning home were caught in the crossfire. Many fled into the apartments, where they were pursued by government agents. Although the official death count was forty-three, most observers believe that between three and four hundred were killed. The legacy of this brutal action was an insistent questioning of the nature of the political system and of the legacy of the Mexican Revolution. In 1999–2000 new student protests resulted in the shutting down of UNAM for months until the government used force to reopen the campus.

Liberalization and the Growth of the Opposition. By the mid-1970s, some leaders within the PRI believed that the image of the party and the political system could be improved by making opposition participation more feasible. Electoral reforms followed, culminating in the establishment of an independent Federal Electoral Institute (IFE), the allotment of government money to eight contending parties for campaign purposes, a Congress in which 300 of the deputies are elected by relative majority in individual congressional districts and 200 more according to proportional representation for each party as measured by the percentage of the total vote. In the 1997 elections, the combined opposition won control of 262 of the 500 seats, the first time that the PRI had not had an absolute majority in the Chamber of Deputies.

The two major opposition parties are the National Action Party, established in 1939, and the Democratic Revolutionary Party, which came into being in 1988 after the presidential election of that year. The PAN has generally been more ideologically conservative that the PRI and has been regarded as allied to business and the Catholic Church. The PRD is based on a small group of leftist parties and disaffections from the PRI, most notably that of Cuauhtémoc Cárdenas, son of the enormously popular 1930s president Lázaro Cárdenas.

The Elections of 1988, 1994, and 1997. The 1988 presidential election was another watershed for Mexican politics. The PRI candidate, Carlos Salinas, was yet another technocrat; the PAN fielded a businessman, Manuel Clouthier, while Cuauhtémoc Cárdenas was the candidate of a leftist populist coalition known as the Front for National Reconstruction (FDN). Although official tallies indicated that Cárdenas received only 31 percent of the vote, many Mexicans believed that he had actually defeated Salinas, who officially garnered 51 percent. Clouthier was third with 17 percent, consistent with previous PAN performance in presidential elections. The campaign period was conflictual: several journalists and a prominent Cárdenas campaign organizer were murdered.

The 1994 presidential election campaign began in troubling circumstances. On 1 January 1994, the Zapatista Army of National Liberation began an uprising in the largely indigenous southern state of Chiapas; two months later, PRI candidate Luis Donaldo Colosio was assassinated during a campaign appearance in a poor neighborhood in Tijuana. The Colosio murder has never been satisfactorily solved, attributed by rumor variously to drug interests, conservative members of the PRI, or the opposition. These incidents seem to have worked in favor of the PRI, as Mexicans expressed enormous concern about instability and violence. Election turnout was very high: 78 percent of registered voters—an unprecedented number. PRI candidate Ernesto Zedillo received 51 percent of the vote, a result recognized by most Mexicans as credible. The PAN total increased to 26 percent, while the PRD dropped to 17 percent.

In July 2000 the PAN's candidate, Vicente Fox Quesada, garnered 43 percent of the vote, the PRI's Francisco Labastida Ochoa 36 percent, and the PRD's Cuauhtémoc Cárdenas first

17 percent. Vincent Fox Quesada promised a peaceful democratic transition with special attention being paid to economic growth, eliminating corruption, ducahorial reform, and negotiating trade and immigration issues with the United States.

Women in Politics. Significant changes in the role of women in Mexican politics have been taking place in recent decades. Although most women have been in the less influential branches of government, particularly the legislative, in recent years women have enjoyed some important elected and appointed posts. Mexico City's mayor in 2000, Rosario Robles Berlanga, who took over when Cárdenas resigned to run for president, has enjoyed great popularity. Moreover, PRI president Zedillo had two women in his cabinet, Foreign Minister Rosario Green and Environmental Minister Julia Carabias.

The United States and Mexico. The relationship between the two countries has been relatively peaceful since the establishment of NAFTA in 1994. Trade between the two countries has increased significantly since then. Two other major issues remain: the illegal drug trade and oil production. The fact that 80 percent of the illegal *drugs coming into the United States are routed through Mexico and by U.S. perception that the drug trade is having a major corrupting influence on the Mexican government have led to considerable concern in the U.S. Congress, although no trade sanctions have been imposed.

Oil has also been an issue. Although Mexico is not a member of OPEC, in March 1999, faced with oil prices per barrel of about $10, its government reached an agreement with Saudi Arabia and Venezuela to cut back production. By early 2000, prices had almost tripled, and gas at the pump in the United States had reached an average of $1.42 a gallon. These increases led to clamor in the U.S. Congress for President Clinton to pressure Mexico to expand production. Mexico, again in conjunction with Saudi Arabia and Venezuela, agreed to do so in March 2000.

Political Prospects. As Mexico moved into the twenty-first century, certain trends were apparent. First of all, the domination of the PRI ended. Although the party continued to exercise enormous influence, Mexico is no longer a one-party state. The system is also opening up to participation by women. NAFTA oil agreements, migration, tourism, and cooperative endeavors suggest an ever more intimate relationship between the United States and Mexico in the future.

Roderic Ai Camp, *Political Recruitment across Two Centuries: Mexico, 1884–1991* (Austin, 1995). Linda B. Hall, *Oil, Banks, and Politics: The United States and Postrevolutionary Mexico, 1917–1924* (Austin, 1995). Victoria Rodríguez, ed., *Women's Participation in Mexican Political Life* (Austin, 1998). Friedrich E. Schuler, *Mexico between Hitler and Roosevelt: Mexican Foreign Relations in the Age of Lázaro Cárdenas, 1934–1940* (Albuquerque, 1998). Hector Aguilar Camin and Lorenzo Meyer, *In the Shadow of the Mexican Revolution: Contemporary Mexican History, 1910–1989* (Austin, 1999). Roderic Ai Camp, *Politics in Mexico: The Decline of Authoritarianism* (New York, 1999).

LINDA HALL

MICRONESIA, FEDERATED STATES OF. See PACIFIC ISLANDS.

MIDDLE EAST. The region of the world comprising Egypt, the Arabian Peninsula, and the states of the Fertile Crescent

(Syria, Lebanon, Israel, Jordan, and Iraq) is known as the Middle East. It is also frequently said to include the Arab states of North Africa, as well as Turkey and Iran. In this larger sense, the region covers about 10 percent of the earth's land surface and supports about 5 percent of the world population.

The name Middle East has a recent origin. For many centuries, European geographers used the term "Near East." During World War II, the British designated their military headquarters in the region as the "Middle East Command." Thereafter, the term "Middle East" came into general usage, and today this Eurocentric term remains the name of choice for both scientific and popular discourse, not only in the West but also in the region itself.

The Middle East is not a concept rooted in physical geography. Natural boundaries do not mark it off unequivocally from other areas of habitation such as Africa and Central Asia. Rather, the Middle East takes meaning from human history, geopolitics, culture, and *political economy. Though alternative regional conceptions exist for some of the same territories—among them the Arab world, the Islamic world, and the Mediterranean basin—the Middle East has proved in recent times to be the most useful and enduring analytical framework.

The Middle East enjoys great historical and cultural unity—even more so, perhaps, than Europe. Most of its lands were ruled for over four centuries by a single state—the Ottoman Empire—and in the eight previous centuries Arab-Islamic empires often held sway. As a result, the overwhelming majority of the population adheres to *Islam, and Arabic is spoken as the vernacular in most countries while it is honored as the language of religion in most of the remainder. Architecture, arts, and even cuisine have a marked similarity throughout the region.

A long history of competition and conflict with Europe defines the region. For over ten centuries, powerful Middle Eastern states clashed with European military forces and generally held the upper hand. As recently as 1683, an army from the Middle East nearly conquered Vienna. These conflicts, often considered in the West as a clash of Christianity with Islam, pitted neighboring civilizations and empires against one another and often had economic roots. The long competition did much to form the states, institutions, and consciousness of the modern world.

In the past two centuries, and especially the past hundred years, the *balance of power shifted radically. European states came to dominate the Middle East economically and militarily and for a time ruled it directly through colonies and protectorates. Since World War II, the United States has supplanted Europe as the dominant power in the region. Though no colonies remain, the peoples of the region are inclined to resent their subordinate status and look back with wonder at an earlier age. In Europe and North America, on the other hand, the region is often portrayed as a dangerous, inhospitable place, marked by violence, corruption, fanaticism, and voluptuousness. Such ideas of history, of Self and of Other, are central to the notion of the Middle East.

Many relatively weak nation-states now divide the region. Created by European colonial powers, these states are often bitter rivals and their conflicts fuel regional instability—much as did the intense rivalries of European states. More than two dozen border wars since 1945, including five major conflicts

between Arab states and Israel, have involved all but four of the region's twenty-two states, and most border claims remain unsettled. Under these circumstances, political movements seeking greater regional unity have achieved little progress, and neither Pan-Arabism nor Pan-Islamism have borne fruit. The *Arab League and the Islamic Conference Organization seek to establish closer ties between their member states, but they have gained little power. Efforts in recent years to promote regional ties through trade pacts have also been largely unsuccessful, and less than 5 percent of all Middle East trade is intraregional.

The Middle East is the world's most arid region, with desert covering more than half of its land surface. Heavy human use over a very long period and shifting climate have led to the steady spread of deserts and the destruction of human and animal habitats. Aridity has concentrated the rapidly growing population and created serious problems of agricultural development; the Middle East imports by far the highest proportion of food of any world region, and some large countries like Egypt import over half of all their basic foodstuffs.

Since irrigated agriculture is in wide and growing use in the Middle East, competition for scarce ground and river water has created a number of sharp interstate conflicts. Turkey, Syria, and Iraq dispute the use of the waters of the Tigris and Euphrates river systems; Israel and its neighbors quarrel over underground aquifers and claims to the Jordan River system; while Egypt, Sudan, and Ethiopia differ over the Nile.

The geopolitical importance of the Middle East in today's world partly results from its location on the major trade routes between Europe and Asia. The Suez Canal is the most important such corridor, linking the Mediterranean and the Red Sea and accounting for 14 percent of world trade. Other vital seaways include the Turkish Straits, the Strait of Hormuz at the mouth of the Persian Gulf, and the Bab al-Mandeb at the southern entrance to the Red Sea.

Even more important than transportation looms the role of the Middle East as an oil producer whose output fuels the industrial economies of Europe and Japan. Ten regional countries are major producers, and some, such as Saudi Arabia and Kuwait, have amassed great wealth through export earnings. Recent figures show the region accounting for 36 percent of the world's crude oil production and about 9 percent of the world's refined product. With a large proportion of the world's petroleum reserves—about 70 percent by most estimates—the region will produce the majority of the world's oil in just a few decades. Oil production in the Middle East, far less costly than elsewhere in the world, has been enormously profitable. Military and economic control of the region is therefore considered a key to global power.

The heavy concentration of oil resources in the Middle East has sharpened international rivalry and wars in the past century and has led to political instability and conflict in the Middle East itself. Oil revenues, which have enriched the treasuries of unpopular regimes, are also believed to have strengthened the tendency toward authoritarian governments in a region where even partially democratic political systems are rare. Most regimes have spent heavily on military forces. The Middle East consequently imports more arms than any other region of the world and accounts for some 25 percent of world trade in major weapons.

Located on Europe's periphery, the Middle East will probably be drawn increasingly toward the *European Union and incorporated into the European trading network in the twenty-first century. Israel, Turkey, and the states of North Africa are furthest along this path. Expanded European direct investment is also likely in the near future. The influence of Western culture and lifestyles can be expected to increase as well, especially as international television programming and Internet access become more available across the region.

Will the Middle East become absorbed into Europe or will it move to affirm its own regional economy and culture? Regionwide, Islamic movements signal a strong popular resistance to Europeanization. But whether the peoples and states of the Middle East will build common structures to affirm their mutual identity remains to be seen.

(See also ARAB-ISRAELI CONFLICT; ARAB NATIONALISM; CO-LONIAL EMPIRES; DECOLONIZATION; EISENHOWER DOCTRINE; ORGANIZATION OF PETROLEUM EXPORTING COUNTRIES; RELIGION AND POLITICS; SUEZ CRISIS.)

Charles Isawi, *An Economic History of the Middle East and North Africa* (New York, 1982). Alasdair Drysdale and Gerald Blake, *The Middle East and North Africa: A Political Geography* (New York, 1985). Gerald Blake, John Dewdney, and Jonathan Mitchell, *The Cambridge Atlas of the Middle East and North Africa* (Cambridge, U.K., 1987). Deborah J. Gerner, *Understanding the Contemporary Middle East* (Boulder, Colo., 2000).

JAMES A. PAUL

MILITARISM is usually defined as the excessive or illegitimate influence of military institutions, policies, and values on civil society. From the very beginning, the term has been used primarily in a pejorative sense—to paint as abnormal a nation or society in which the military leadership exercises inordinate control over national life—although some effort has been made in recent years to invest the concept with greater analytical precision. Even so, the term is generally reserved for regimes that engage in autocratic or atavistic displays of military power, as in the saturation of urban neighborhoods with armed guards (to deter unwanted political activity) or the ready use of *force to resolve international disputes.

The label of militarism was first used in the late nineteenth century in Europe to characterize the imperial pretensions of Emperor Napoléon III (ruler of France, 1852–1870) and the efforts of the Prussian Junkers to fashion a powerful, military-dominated German state. Similarly, in the interwar years, the term was commonly used to describe and deprecate the Fascist regimes in Italy, Germany, Spain, and Japan. More recently, in the postwar period, the term has been used by critics of governments of both East and West who have opposed the massive U.S. and Soviet investment in nuclear and non-nuclear forces.

In all of these cases, the term has been used to castigate what is seen as the encroachment of a nation's military sector onto the civilian sphere. The implication is that there is a natural boundary or divide between the legitimate functions of the military—that is, defense of the nation in times of *war and appropriate training in times of *peace—and all other human activities. When that boundary is crossed, when the military usurps any of the roles normally ascribed to civilian institutions, then a process or condition of militarism is said to exist.

This interpretation of militarism was given its fullest expression in the 1938 classic *A History of Militarism*, by the German-American historian Alfred Vagts. "Militarism," Vagts wrote, "has connoted a domination of the military over the civilian, an undue preponderance of military demands, and emphasis on military considerations, spirits, ideals, and scales of value, in the life of states."

A similar perspective was advanced in the post–World War II period by Marek Thee of the International Peace Research Institute in Oslo. Militarism begins "with the abuse of the military of its legitimate function and its encroachment on political affairs," he wrote in 1980. As this process proceeds, "the military tends to usurp roles and prerogatives in society which go beyond democratic legitimacy, intervening in internal [affairs] and imposing its will in external affairs." Thee and his colleagues saw evidence of this process in the *Cold War behavior of the two superpowers, entailing the creation of a vast *military-industrial complex devoted to the development and production of ever more sophisticated weapons, and a propensity for overt or covert intervention in regional *Third World conflicts.

This interpretation of militarism was also extended during the Cold War to the analysis of military-dominated regimes in the Third World. For many observers, the tendency of Third World military elites to overthrow civilian governments and to exercise authoritarian control over civil institutions was a deplorable expression of classical militarism. "In the Third World particularly," Ruth Leger Sivard wrote in 1989, "the intrusion of military authority into the political arena has been a fast-growing exercise." In *World Military and Social Expenditures* (13th ed., Washington, D.C., 1989) she reported that 64 Third World countries (out of a total of 120) were ruled by "military-controlled governments," wherein senior military officers occupied key government positions and the state security forces possessed extrajudicial powers under martial law decree. These forces were often aided in these efforts, either directly or indirectly, by the military or *intelligence agencies of the two Cold War superpowers.

Militarism, then, has generally been seen as entailing an aberrant or atavistic use of military force. In contrast to this interpretation, a number of social scientists have attempted to develop an alternative understanding of militarism, one that views the expanded role of the military as a natural consequence of state formation in the modern world. As states evolve, they argue, there is a natural tendency of state authorities—whether military or civilian—to seek the concentration of political and economic power in the central government's hands, often by constructing civilian institutions on hierarchical military models and/or by involving military elites (which often possess technical and bureaucratic skills not available elsewhere) in the management of state-run agencies and enterprises. Hence, in this analysis, there can be no clear-cut boundary between the military and civilian sectors of society, as each is routinely interpenetrated by the other.

Adherents to this perspective tend to prefer the term "militarization" to militarism, as the former bears less risk of inviting a normative impulse into the analysis of these phenomena. Whereas militarism has tended to be seen "as something exceptional, archaic, or even exogenous to modern society," John R. Gillis wrote in 1989, "militarization carries no such evolutionary presuppositions." Rather, militarization is a process that can be detected in all modern states, whether or not they exhibit the overt displays of military force associated with Hitler's Third Reich and Mussolini's Italy.

The debate over militarism abated somewhat following the end of the Cold War, as the U.S.-Soviet military competition drew to a close and many states—especially in Europe—reduced both the size of their armed forces and the proportion of national funds devoted to military purposes. From a high of $1.3 trillion in 1987, total world military spending dropped to $1.1 trillion in 1991 and to $840 million in 1994 (in constant 1994 dollars), a decline over seven years of 36 percent. Even more significant, the proportion of central government expenditures devoted to military purposes on a global basis dropped from 18.3 percent to around 10 percent over this same period. With the revival of civilian governments in Latin America and parts of Africa, moreover, the number of Third World states ruled by military regimes experienced a sharp decline.

The post–Cold War reduction in armed strength and military spending was not universal, however. In some areas, the military remains a significant factor in domestic political affairs and in many cases has increased its access to government funds and resources. The People's Liberation Army (PLA) of China, for instance, has intervened on several occasions (most notably in *Tiananmen Square in 1989) to suppress popular movements for democracy, and continues to exercise significant influence over national policies; in Turkey, the military-controlled Supreme National Security Council used its extraordinary powers in 1997 to remove a democratically elected government formed by the Islamic-oriented Welfare Party. In both India and Pakistan, the military's quest for enhanced weaponry has led to the development and testing of *nuclear weapons and the accelerated acquisition of conventional arms. These, and a number of similar developments in other countries, have prompted fresh concerns about the effects of militarism.

Of particular concern to analysts has been the reproduction of many aspects of classical militarism at the substate level, as reflected in the rise of ethnic militias, separatist forces, and local warlords. These forces have emerged as significant actors in many of the countries that have experienced state collapse and/or the outbreak of ethnic warfare (as, for example, in Angola, Bosnia, Chechnya, Congo, Liberia, Rwanda, Sierra Leone, Somalia, Sri Lanka, and Sudan). Typically, this has entailed the threat or use of violence to subdue the local population or to drive off members of opposing ethnic and religious groups (the process known as "ethnic cleansing"). As noted by Barry R. Posen in an important 1993 essay, this has resulted in the outbreak of military rivalries *within* states that are similar, in many respects, to the rivalries that often develop *between* states.

(See also FOREIGN MILITARY BASES; MILITARY RULE.)

Alfred Vagts, *A History of Militarism* (London, 1938; New York, 1959 and 1967). John J. Johnson, ed., *The Role of the Military in Underdeveloped Countries* (Princeton, N.J., 1962). Adam Yarmolinsky, *The Military Establishment: Its Impact on a Society* (New York, 1971). Asbjørn Eide and Marek Thee, eds., *Problems of Contemporary Militarism* (London, 1980). John R. Gillis, ed., *The Militarization of the Western World* (New Brunswick, N.J., 1989). Barry R. Posen, "The Security Dilemma and Ethnic Conflict," *Survival* 35, no. 1 (Spring 1993): 27–47. William Reno, *Warlord Politics and African States* (Boulder, Colo., 1998).

MICHAEL T. KLARE

MILITARY OCCUPATION. See FOREIGN MILITARY BASES.

MILITARY RULE. Armed forces have been influential actors in the countries of Asia, Africa, Latin America, and the *Middle East since World War II. Some *Third World countries under military rule are not "new." Ethiopia, Thailand, and Latin American countries were independent states long before 1945. Many countries in these areas hardly can be called "developing" ones either. In not a few, per capita income has stagnated or declined in recent decades. Thus we cannot take for granted that armed forces come to prominence in new states or in developing ones. Indeed, military forces have been significant actors in ancient Rome and in the empires that have grown up and disintegrated in Asia and the Middle East. What should interest us is how civil-military relations change over time within countries or differ from country to country at similar periods of history.

Armed forces have comparative advantages in moving people and material by virtue of their logistical abilities. They are usually, but not always, relatively well-armed compared to other groups in society. This brings us to the distinction between the official and regular military forces of the state and bands of warring people, guerrillas, local police, and other organizations of force. These organizations may well compete with regular military forces; they may sometimes be heavily armed. Insurgents can become organized into regularized armed forces, as occurred during the Chinese and Vietnamese anticolonial and civil wars.

Also, the official armed forces may vary from huge armies with highly specialized service branches—India and China, for example, each have a million or more soldiers under arms—to the small, largely infantry units of some African countries. An armed force may expand very rapidly, as the Nigerian army did during the Nigerian Civil War when it grew from 10,000 to over 250,000 between 1968 and 1970.

It is striking, however, that in many non-Western states, both large and small, militaries play a powerful role in the politics of their countries. In the industrial countries of the West such as the United States and France, militaries are important interest groups, take significant shares of government budgets, and may have veto power over crucial public issues. In 1958–1960, in the aftermath of the *Algerian War of Independence, the French military posed a challenge to continued civilian rule. Military rule, however, in contrast to military influence, has been rare in the countries of Western and Eastern Europe since 1945.

Military rule may be defined by the fact that the head of state achieves a ruling position by virtue of a place in the military chain of command. True, junior officers may come to power. In Africa especially it has not been unknown for junior and even noncommissioned officers to seize power, as exemplified by Captain Marien Ngouabi's ascendancy in Congo-Brazzaville (1968), Sergeant Samuel Doe's *coup d'état in Liberia (1980), and Flight Lieutenant Jerry Rawlings's coup in Ghana (1979).

The military establishment itself may be highly fragmented, and an officer or noncommissioned officer may stage a coup as much against a segment of the army as against civilians. This pattern characterized Idi Amin's 1971 coup in Uganda and also occurred periodically in postwar Argentina. Moreover, it is a mistake to think that militaries rule without civilian allies. In fact, civilians often may try to provoke military takeovers in order to bolster their class or ethnic positions. The military coup of 1964 in Brazil is a case in point where business groups feared the growing *populism of civilian elites and growing working-class activism.

In the Middle East and in Africa, one ethnic group may act against others through military coups. Thus, for example, the prominence of Shii officers has been striking in Syria under Hafiz Al-Assad since 1970. Coups and countercoups in Nigeria have had critical ethnic components.

To talk then of *the* military is something of a misnomer. Armed forces are split by service branch, ethnic group, rank, and often class background. It is a matter of empirical investigation as to how cohesive are military organizations. Similarly, it is a matter of empirical study to find out how professionalized are armed forces and whether or not they are distinctive corporate bodies marked off from civilians by education, training, and socialization processes. Militaries usually have specific codes, uniforms, and training, and their officers go to special academies. But whether this training and recruitment makes them cohesive and distinctive by attitude or policy preference as compared to civilians is an open question.

It is not always easy to decide whether a particular leader maintains power by virtue of place in the chain of command or the support of the armed forces. *Mao Zedong rose to power in China by forging the *Chinese Communist Party and leading a broad revolution, but during the *Cultural Revolution in the late 1960s and 1970s he came to rely on particular military units as well as components of the Communist Party and students. Both Gamal Abdel *Nasser and Anwar *Sadat tried to civilianize their leadership in Egypt in the 1960s and 1970s. Both were military figures, but they used civilian parties and interest groups to maintain their power and to give them freedom from their own militaries. Yet military support was critical to their continued rule.

The social science literature on coups and military rule has established few generalizations that we can put forward with great confidence with respect to why and when military coups take place or what are the consequences of military rule in terms of policy preferences and development outcomes. Coups have occurred in nations large and small, have been carried out by armies large and small. Clearly, however, it is difficult to stage a junior officer coup in a large army—Pakistan's, for example.

Within Asia, Africa, Latin America, and the Middle East, few countries have escaped at least some period of military rule. India has been one. But India does not have a relatively high per capita income even within developing countries. It has a tradition of British civilian supremacy—but so do many former British colonies. Nor has the Congress Party in India proved to be highly institutionalized and coherent over the last two decades.

It is not true that militaries are more likely to be "modernizers" or more successful in bringing about economic development than are civilian counterparts. Indeed, both the case study literature on military rule and cross-national aggregate data work that has utilized statistics to test hypotheses show us that there is as much differentiation within the category of military rule as there is between military and civilian regimes. Personal leadership has been important to the evolution of specific patterns of military rule. As within civilian regimes, the class and ethnic composition of society has been a powerful factor within military rule.

If militaries have not been associated typically with higher growth rates or particular patterns of economic development, they frequently have tried to curtail *political participation by parties and interest groups only to find that they need allies in civilian society in order to extend their influence beyond the barracks or the statehouse. Sometimes these allies have been civilians with a bent for revolution, as in Ethiopia after 1975 or Peru during the early period of the Velasco-Alvarado regime (1968–1975). Often they have been elites with status quo tendencies, as in Brazil, Paraguay, or Pakistan.

Looking at *foreign policy outcomes, we do not find that military regimes align themselves in clear-cut ways. The Argentine military came to grief after its failed invasion of the Malvinas/Falklands, as did the Greek colonels after their Cyprus fiasco. But military regimes have not proved to be more aggressive or nationalistic than civilian ones.

Idiosyncratic leaders such as Idi Amin in Uganda have destroyed their own militaries in order to stay in power. Others, such as General Evren in Turkey (1980–1983), have tried to guide their countries back to civilian rule.

One relatively understudied phenomenon is that of transitions from military rule. Chile, Argentina, Uruguay, and Brazil, among other Latin American countries, reverted to civilian rule in the late 1980s. A number of African countries have had oscillating periods of military and civilian rule, Ghana and Nigeria in particular. Where the armed forces have carried out bloody repression of civilians, as in Argentina and Chile, civilian rule is more difficult to achieve and to sustain, for the officers insist on protection against prosecution. Frequently, as in Brazil and Argentina, the armed forces have left civilians with large debt burdens and bloated state enterprises. The policies of expanding the state sector have not been unique to military regimes, but these regimes have been especially closed off from broad public scrutiny and accountability.

(See also Democratic Transitions; Development and Underdevelopment; Militarism.)

Gavin Kennedy, *The Military in the Third World* (New York, 1974). Amos Perlmutter, *The Military and Politics in Modern Times* (New Haven, Conn., 1977). Henry Bienen, *Armies and Parties of Africa* (New York, 1978). Alain Rouquie, *The Military and the State in Latin America* (Berkeley, Calif., 1987).

Henry S. Bienen

MILITARY-INDUSTRIAL COMPLEX. For nations in the industrial era, national defense has meant an industrialized defense and therefore a defense industry. In the United States the defense industry includes corporations that produce for the civilian market as well as the military one, but its core consists of firms whose primary customers are the military services. The defense industry needs the military services; it was brought into being by military contracts during World War II, and it has been sustained in the half-century since by military contracts. The military services, in turn, need the defense industry. The industrial firms put political pressure on Congress and the Executive to maintain defense spending and the budgets of the military services. This mutual, symbiotic relationship between military services and industrial corporations has given rise to the concept of the military-industrial complex (MIC). The phrase itself was first used by President Dwight *Eisenhower in January 1961 in his Farewell Address: "In the councils of government, we must guard against the acquisition of unwarranted influence, whether sought or unsought, by the military-industrial complex. The potential for the disastrous rise of misplaced power exists and will persist." Having commanded the allied armies in World War II and having institutionalized U.S. peacetime military spending during his presidency, Eisenhower was the highest possible authority on the topic. His phrase described a reality that had only come into being during his own administration.

In the United States, the MIC is composed on the military side by the services—the air force, navy, army, and marines. On the industry side it is composed of about two dozen corporations. The largest of these defense contractors are those engaged in the production of aircraft and missiles; in the 1990s, most of these merged into three large groupings: Boeing-McDonnell Douglas, Lockheed-Martin, and Northrop-Grumman.

A crucial link in the MIC are the elected political officials, especially those who sit on the congressional committees dealing with the armed services and who vote the authorizations and appropriations for weapons systems. They benefit from having weapons contracts given to firms in their districts or states, and they both pressure and support the military in the awarding of these contracts. Some observers consider the congressional committees to be as important to the process as the military services and the defense corporations and speak of the three elements as an "iron triangle."

Over the years, critics of the MIC have charged it with causing several distortions, or worse, in public policy: 1) higher defense budgets than have been reasonable or necessary (e.g., aggravating the arms race with the Soviet Union from the late 1940s to the late 1980s); 2) within the general defense budget, procurement of destabilizing or inappropriate weapons systems (e.g., strategic bombers and ballistic missiles, where cruise missiles could accomplish the same ends with less risk and less expense); 3) within a particular weapons system, inefficient production because of "waste, fraud, and abuse," resulting in fewer weapons at greater cost; 4) the weakening of the non-defense industrial base of the United States (e.g., making it in the 1970s–1980s less capable of competing in the world market for civilian products, especially against Japan and Germany, whose own defense industries were quite small).

The United States has the most well-known and well-examined MIC, but one can be found in other countries as well. It was particularly important in the Soviet Union. Some analysts think that the entire Soviet economy from Stalin to Brezhnev was a vast military-industrial complex. The Soviet military industry—the "metal-eaters" in Khrushchev's words—was the only part of the Soviet economy that seemed to work, and it provided a model for the rest of the society. But over the long run, the expense of maintaining it (between 15 and 20 percent of Soviet GNP) drove the Soviet Union into economic decline, political upheaval, the collapse of the Warsaw Pact, and finally the dissolution of the Soviet Union itself. In the diminished economy of Russia, the military industry still looms large.

France and Britain also have substantial defense industries. Their greatest impact on world politics probably comes from their dependence on large-scale exports to Third World countries. And since the 1980s, other countries, including China, Israel, and Brazil, have entered into the international arms trade with their own MICs.

Military needs helped foster industrial and technological innovation, including Eli Whitney's development in 1798 of the mass production process for U.S. army muskets. For almost two centuries thereafter, military needs helped bring new industries into being (e.g., chemicals, aviation, computers, and semiconductors), and during the *Cold War military spending helped to stabilize the overall level of U.S. economic activity (in what has been called military *Keynesianism). Yet military spending also diminished the capacity of some U.S. industries to compete in the world market. The two halves of the complex, the military and the industrial, have always been a dynamic and unstable equilibrium. There have been times when the real threat to a nation's industry seemed to come not so much from another nation's military, but from its own.

(See also MILITARISM; SECURITY.)

Gregory Michael Hooks, *Forging the Military-Industrial Complex: World War II's Battle of the Potomac* (Urbana, Illinois, 1991). Ann Markusen et.al., *The Rise of the Gunbelt: The Military Remapping of Industrial America* (New York, 1991). Ethan B. Kapstein, *The Political Economy of National Security: A Global Perspective* (Columbia, S.C., 1992). John L. Bois, *Buying for Armageddon: Business, Society, and Military Spending since the Cuban Missile Crisis* (New Brunswick, N.J., 1994).

JAMES KURTH

MINI-STATES. See SMALL STATES AND TERRITORIES.

MINORITIES. See RACE AND RACISM.

MITTERRAND, François. In 1964, six years after Charles de*Gaulle's return to power as leader of *France, an opposition politician wrote a fiery pamphlet, *Le Coup d'Etat permanent*, denouncing de Gaulle for overthrowing the Fourth Republic and creating a republic and powerful presidential office tailored to de Gaulle's own personality. Ironically, this same politician waged an unceasing and ultimately successful battle to replace de Gaulle as France's president. François Mitterrand finally was elected in 1981 and occupied the Elysée (the presidential palace) for fourteen years, longer than any French president in history. Yet, in part because he changed so often during his long political career, it is difficult to characterize the Mitterrand legacy.

Mitterrand was born 26 October 1916 in the village of Jarnac, in Charente, a conservative and prosperous agricultural region in southwest France. The family was quite affluent and solidly anchored on the right of the political spectrum. Mitterrand attended Catholic boarding school. Like many talented middle-class provincial students, he pursued higher education in Paris. During his student days, he remained quite conservative, for example, joining the Croix de Feu, one of the far right paramilitary organizations that flourished in France in the 1930s. Although, after he moved toward the socialist side of the political spectrum, his conservative past was no secret, revelations toward the end of his presidency about the full extent of his far right connections produced a political bombshell.

During World War II, Mitterrand began the break with conservative orthodoxy that resulted in his becoming France's most influential Socialist politician. However, his political evolution was slower and less complete than he later proclaimed. In 1938, he was drafted into the French army and, after war began, was wounded (and decorated). He was captured by the invading Nazi forces and, while in prison camp, was influenced by the ideas and social commitment of fellow prisoners from the left, secular (laïque) political tradition—the major rival in France to the conservative Catholic milieu.

Mitterrand escaped from prison in 1941 and for two years led a double life: he was an administrator in the puppet Vichy government—and was decorated by the regime for his service; yet, at the same time, he forged identity papers for members of the Resistance. Following the Nazi invasion of unoccupied France in 1942 and the abolition of the Vichy regime, and for the remainder of the war, Mitterrand displayed great courage and skill in organizing former prisoners of war for Resistance activity.

Mitterrand's first meeting with de Gaulle occurred at this time. Conflicting ambition and policy differences separated the two men, and the rivalry that developed lasted until de Gaulle's death in 1970. After the Liberation of Paris in 1944, when de Gaulle refused to offer the independent young Mitterrand a ministerial position in the newly created provisional government, Mitterrand broke openly with de Gaulle. In 1946, after one electoral defeat, he was elected to the National Assembly in the Fourth Republic; he occupied elected office for most of the following half century.

Mitterrand proved a brilliant tactician in the intricate parliamentary maneuvers of the Fourth Republic. At the ripe age of thirty-one, he was appointed to a junior cabinet post, and he later occupied ministerial positions with responsibility for overseas colonies, interior, and justice. In general, Mitterrand espoused the orthodox political beliefs of the time: his reputation derived from a talent for political maneuver, not vision.

Mitterrand's political career was abruptly checked when de Gaulle regained power in 1958 and created the constitutional framework of the Fifth Republic. Mitterrand was among the few Fourth Republic politicians who displayed total opposition to de Gaulle, on the grounds that de Gaulle had violated constitutional procedures and republican traditions. As a result, his former image as a political operator was replaced by that of a principled leader. He now applied his formidable tactical skills to rebuilding the divided Socialist Party—which he joined in 1971—and the alliance he promoted between the Socialist Party and the Communist Party, the other major opposition on the *Left, represented a powerful alternative to the incumbent conservative coalition.

Yet, as the 1981 presidential election approached, Mitterrand seemed the perennial outsider—and loser—following more than two decades in opposition and defeats in two presidential elections. However, thanks to the economic stagnation of the 1970s (for which the conservative governing coalition was blamed) and the conservatives' political divisions and exhaustion, Mitterrand defeated President Valéry Giscard d'Estaing, who was running for reelection in 1981. Mitterrand swept in a large Socialist majority on his coattails

in parliamentary elections following his own election. After twenty-three years, the opposition gained control of the Fifth Republic, and Mitterrand and his allies enjoyed an extraordinary opportunity to reshape France.

There were many policy shifts during Mitterrand's fourteen-year term as president. In his first years in office, between 1981 and 1983, Mitterrand's Socialist government sponsored a whirlwind series of reforms, including decentralization of the state, liberalization of the judicial system, and restructuring industrial relations, the economy, and media. The most controversial change was a sweeping program of nationalization, which put thirteen of France's twenty largest industrial firms and virtually all banks and insurance companies under direct public control. Mitterrand was the principal architect of the new course, and firmly controlled the government and the Socialist parliamentary majority. The Socialist reforms helped modernize rigid bureaucracies, political institutions, and policies. However, with the exception of the nationalization measures, the reforms were a pale version of those already implemented by Scandinavian and German Social Democratic governments.

The reformist phase abruptly ended in 1983, when economic and political difficulties forced Mitterrand to moderate the earlier course and adopt austerity measures. The "right turn" of 1983 was a regime-defining moment, and signified the Left's abandonment of audacious reformist ambitious. Mitterrand's personal standing in the mid-1980s fell to record lows. However, paradoxically, his fortunes began to rise when he was forced to share power with the conservative parliamentary majority that was elected in 1986 and governed until 1988—a situation referred to as cohabitation. Outmaneuvering conservative prime minister Jacques Chirac during cohabitation and in the 1988 presidential elections, Mitterrand was triumphantly reelected president in 1988 and sponsored new parliamentary elections which returned the Socialists to power. So began a new phase of united Socialist rule—which in turn ended in 1993 when, as a result of rising unemployment and economic recession, the Right regained control of the National Assembly. Mitterrand's major initiative during this period was to cooperate with German chancellor Helmut *Kohl in strengthening European integration, notably by establishing a timetable for launching the euro, the common European currency.

The last phase of Mitterrand's presidency, following the Socialist Party's overwhelming defeat in the 1993 parliamentary elections and the return of cohabitation, and running through the end of his presidential term in 1995, was marred by illness, revelations about unsavory associations in his past, as well as political scandals involving his close political allies. A series of journalistic investigations revealed that Mitterrand's associations with the Far Right were closer than he had acknowledged—and had secretly continued long after World War II. (For example, Mitterrand admitted that after the war he had been a close friend of René Bousquet, the Vichy regime's director-general of police, and he entertained Bousquet at his Paris apartment as late as 1983.) Mitterrand died of cancer less than a year after leaving office.

Mitterrand can be credited with three major accomplishments as president. First, he demonstrated that the Left was able to govern in a responsible, capable fashion. Second, he helped reduce political divisions in France and assured political and institutional stability. Third, his leadership enabled France to remain a major political and economic force within the world—ranking fourth or fifth by many economic measures. In particular, his leadership was vital in promoting European political, economic, and monetary integration. However, his legacy was tarnished by charges of opportunism, deception, and scandal. Although he will be remembered as a towering figure of twentieth-century French history, his record will remain the object of intense debate.

(See also Economic and Monetary Union; European Union; Socialism and Social Democracy.)

Wayne Northcutt, *Mitterrand: A Political Biography* (New York, 1991). Alistair Cole, *François Mitterrand: A Study in Political Leadership* (London, 1994). Pierre Péan, *Une Jeunesse française: François Mitterrand, 1934–1947* (Paris, 1994). Franz-Olivier Giesbert, *François Mitterrand: Une vie* (Paris, 1996). Julius W. Friend, *The Long Presidency: France in the Mitterrand Years, 1981–1995* (Boulder, Colo., 1998).

MARK KESSELMAN

MODERNITY. See overleaf.

MODERNIZATION. The term *modernization* became prominent in the social sciences and in more general discourse in the years following World War II. Increasing attention was then being paid to the possibility that the so-called underdeveloped societies of the *Third World might attain levels of development—whether economic, social, or political— hitherto associated only with modern industrial societies. The studies of modernization that emerged in this period entailed a far-reaching shift in basic orientation compared with earlier, "classical" sociological approaches. Instead of stressing the specificity of European civilization and attempting to explain why *modernity developed only in the West, the postwar studies of modernization assumed that the development of modernity constituted the apogee of the evolutionary potential of humanity in general, the kernels of which are in principle to be found in most societies. These studies evaluated societies according to several indices of modernization and attempted to explain what societal factors facilitate or impede their development and the consequent emergence of a modern social order.

The most important types of such indices included sociodemographic, structural, cultural, and psychological characteristics. Among the major sociodemographic indices were *urbanization, industrialization, levels of *literacy and education, as well as openness to modern modes of communication. Structural characteristics were identified as a high degree of role specialization and differentiation; the availability of resources not committed to fixed ascriptive groups (such as kinship or territoriality); the predominance of achievement criteria rather than ascription in the allocation of the major social roles; and the development of and differentiation between large-scale, diverse, and functionally specific organizations, on the one hand, and more informal interest-based groups, on the other.

Culturally, the process of modernization was said to involve a growing differentiation of the major arenas of cultural activity such as religion, philosophy, and education; the development of specialized intellectual and cultural roles; the spread of education and communications; and wider mass participation in the cultural arena. Finally, on the individual level, modernization was seen as giving rise to a new cultural-psychological outlook characterized by greater ego flexibility; the ability to adjust to wider societal horizons; a broadening of the spheres of interest; growing potential empathy toward other people and situations; and more emphasis on self-advancement and mobility.

In most of these studies modern and traditional societies were depicted as juxtaposed. Traditional societies were defined as basically restrictive and limited, whereas modern societies were seen as much more expansive and able to cope with a continually widening range of problems in their internal and external environments alike. Societies on the move from traditional to modern were designated as transitional.

Behind these theories there loomed a vision of the inevitability of progress toward modernity, toward the development of a universal modern civilization, and toward the convergence of industrial societies. Most of these theories implicitly took for granted that the Western European and U.S. experiences constituted the major paradigm of modern society and civilization. The institutional and ideological developments in the contemporary world, however, have not upheld this vision. The great institutional variability of different modern and modernizing societies—not only among the transitional but also among the more developed societies such as the United States, Western Europe, and Japan— became more and more apparent, giving rise by the late 1960s to new models of modernization.

Two major approaches to the problem may be identified. The first approach stressed the importance of the traditions of different societies for understanding the variability of modern or modernizing societies; this approach negated the dichotomy between modern and traditional societies and their dynamics. The second approach emphasized international factors, especially the global capitalist system, as the major explanatory variables in the process of modernization.

These approaches have certainly pointed to some important influences on the dynamics of modernization. They are not able, however, to explain all the patterns of change which have been taking place in different traditional and transitional societies in the contemporary world. These approaches have not faced squarely the problem of how different patterns of change arise in response to the sociodemographic, structural, and ideological aspects of modernization enumerated above. Accordingly, some of the assumptions of these approaches need reappraisal as did those of the initial model of modernization.

The starting point of such a reappraisal is the historical fact that modernization, or rather modernity in its basic institutional and cultural aspects, crystallized first in the West—in Europe and in the United States—from the sixteenth century on. This modernization then expanded by economic, military, political, and ideological means throughout the world and created a series of continually changing world systems. The original institutional formations and cultural contours of modernity as they developed in the West were closely related to the capitalist economy and civilization, which were characterized by the bureaucratization of different aspects of social life, a secular worldview, and the development of a distinctive cultural orientation toward modernity. This orientation em-

(cont. on p. 555)

MODERNITY. The word *modern* entered the center of West European intellectual debate in the seventeenth century (although it had been sporadically used as far back as the fifth century); ostensibly, it meant no more than "current" or "of recent origin." And yet the context of its appearance and fast-growing popularity suggest a deeper than merely technical meaning: the quality of "being of recent origin," being newly created, had suddenly become a matter of acute interest, apparently acquiring a thoroughly novel significance. That significance derived from changing values, which now, unlike in previous centuries, favored the new over the old, denied authority to the past, and approved of irreverence to tradition and readiness to innovate, to "go where no man dared to go before." From the moment of its triumphant entry into public discourse, the idea of the modern tended to recast the old as antiquated, obsolete, out of date, about to be (deservedly) sunk into oblivion and replaced.

The idea of the modern reappeared in the seventeenth century as a militant concept, as the focus of contention in the so-called "Quarrel of Ancients and Moderns" that lasted in France and England for almost a century. Arts and literature served as the initial battleground: after the spectacular achievements of scientists like Newton and Descartes, with the Royal Society in England and more diffuse but no less influential *sociétés de pense*, in France valiantly promoting the unprecedented excellence of new science and philosophy, the question had to be asked sooner or later whether this upward movement was the lot of science alone or of all human endeavors—particularly of creations like painting and poetry. The Ancients (like Nicolas Boileau and Jean de La Fontaine in France, Sir William Temple and Jonathan Swift in Britain) defended the long-standing conviction that the peak of human achievement had been reached in Greek and Roman antiquity and that the inevitably inferior products of later generations could attempt no more than to struggle in vain to approximate its perfection. Earlier, such propositions were voiced routinely, seen as trivially true, and aroused no dissent. Now, however, inspired by the astonishing discoveries of the new science, opposing views began to spread and gain in popularity. The holders of the traditional views were redubbed Ancients—a concept, for the Moderns, tinged with contempt and derision. Charles Perrault and Bernard de Fontenelle were among the most pugnacious and vociferous advocates of the modern, daring attitude, which would draw its confidence from the belief that, as in science, so in all other fields of spiritual creation, the new may be better (truer, more useful, more right, more beautiful) than the old; that the potency of human reason and skill is unlimited; and that therefore human history has been and will forever remain a relentless march upward and forward.

The Quarrel was never conclusively resolved to everybody's satisfaction (a century later the Romantic movement resuscitated the ideas that the Moderns strove to put to rest once for all); it just fizzled out, as the philosophical edge of the issue was blunted by the rapid pace of practical cultural change. In retrospect, however, the Quarrel may be better appreciated as the condensed expression of a revolution taking place in the European mentality; of the new feeling of self-reliance and self-assurance, readiness to seek and try unorthodox solutions to any current trouble and worry, belief in the ascending tendency of human history and growing trust in the capacity of human reason. In the nineteenth century, the emergent mentality itself came to be described as modern, and the dominance of such mentality came to be seen as one of the crucial symptoms of the new age of modernity.

Modernity may be best described as the age marked by constant change—but an age aware of being so marked; an age that views its own legal forms, its material and spiritual creations, its knowledge and convictions as temporary, to be held "until further notice" and eventually disqualified and replaced by new and better ones. In other words, modernity is an era conscious of its historicity. Human institutions are viewed as self-created and amenable to improvement; they can be retained only if they justify themselves in the face of the stringent demands of reason—and if they fail the test, they are bound to be scrapped. The substitution of new designs for old will be a progressive move, a new step up the ascending line of human development.

Progress is, essentially, a human accomplishment. It consists in applying human reason (rationalizing) to the task of making the world better geared to serve human needs. Whatever is seen as a human need, as a condition of agreeable life, is accorded unqualified priority over all other considerations: the nonhuman part of the world (nature) is of itself meaningless, and any meaning it may be given can derive only from the human uses to which it is put. Designing an artificial, rational order of the human habitat is not an arbitrary choice; it is a necessity, an unavoidable human condition, for to be habitable the world must be made fit for the satisfaction of human needs through science-assisted technology. Science and its technological applications are therefore the principal sources and instruments of political, social, cultural, and moral progress. They are both the expression and the vehicle of human ascendancy over nature.

To modern Europe, conscious of its own historicity, styles of life and institutions that differed from those it currently approved were merely steps leading to its own, superior condition—survivals of its own past. Other cultures were seen as forms temporarily arrested in their development, and in this "frozen" state retarded. This belief gave modern Europe its characteristic self-confidence as a carrier of historical destiny, a collective missionary with the duty to spread the gospel of reason and to convert the rest of the world to its own faith and form of life. In case of resistance, the objects of prospective conversion could only be viewed as primitive, as victims of superstition and ignorance, whose authority (and particularly the ability to decide what was best for them) reason denied in advance. The modern period in European history (and the history of countries that underwent early the process of Europeanization) was therefore an age of proselytism, one marked by colonization of the non-European world and by repeated cultural crusades aimed at the regional, ethnic, or class-bound traditions within European societies themselves.

The modern *state was invested with functions never contemplated by premodern rulers. It had to impose a unified order on vast territories heretofore regulated by a variety of local traditions; by the same token, it had to make the creation and maintenance of social order a matter of deliberation, conscious design, monitoring, and daily management, rather than limit itself to the observance of traditional customs and privileges. (It had, one might say, to assume a gardener's, rather than a gamekeeper's, stance toward the society.)

The new tasks involved standardization of law and legal institutions across the state; unification, and often direct administration, of the process of popular education; and securing the priority of unified legal discipline over all other, particularistic loyalties. It is for this reason that modern states engaged in the process of nation building, having assumed the form of nation-states rather than dynastic realms. They promoted national unity over ethnic differentiation, deployed *nationalism in the service of state authority, and adopted the promotion of national interests as the criterion and purpose of state policies. It is for the same reason that the modern state rejects and devalues traditional entitlements to rule (such as the longevity of rights) and charismatic rule (which is grounded on peculiar—and superior—personal qualities of a given ruler), demanding discipline to its own commands solely on formal, legal grounds: that is, referring to the fact that the commands have been issued by duly appointed incumbents of offices entitled to make rulings related to the given area.

By all historical standards, modernity (often referred to as "modern civilization," to locate it as a distinct type of social organization and culture among other civilizations, ancient, medieval, or contemporary) has been a remarkable success. It has come closer than any other known civilization to the status of genuine universality. It seems to be on the way to becoming the first global civilization in history. The states of the modern world may be politically and ideologically divided and even locked in mutual conflict, but they all agree on the superiority of the modern way of running human affairs and use modern methods and implements to assert themselves and pursue their ends. The modern form of life seems to have no serious competitors left among the forms it displaced; it has succeeded, moreover, in confronting its own difficulties and "developmental problems" in a way that strengthens the ascendancy of the worldview and pragmatic stance that are its own most characteristic traits. Thus modernity is usually described as the ultimate form of historical development. Inherently dynamic, modern civilization yet retains its own identity. It is capable of continuous creativity rather than, like other civilizations, ossifying and losing the capacity of creative adjustment to new challenges. With its arrival, the world has been split into a modern part and the rest, confronted with the challenge of *modernization.

Most theoretical models of modernity select inner dynamism and the capacity for change and self-improvement as the central characteristics and the ultimate sources of modernity's worldwide ascendancy and attractiveness. They also agree that to explain that dynamism is the most important task—and duty—of any theory of modernity. Beginning with the early nineteenth century, most analysts sought the secret of modern dynamism in the emancipation of human action from the shackles of custom, tradition, and communal obligations and in its subjection solely to the criteria of efficient task performance. In Karl *Marx's picturesque expression, "everything solid melts into air, everything sacred is profaned": once the authority of tradition has been sapped and denied, nothing can prevent human courage from setting ever more ambitious tasks and designing ever more effective ways of performing them. It is the match between means and ends that now decides which course of action is to be chosen. As the U.S. social theorist Talcott Parsons put it (elaborating on the ideas of the nineteenth-century German sociologist Ferdinand Toünnies), in modern times the traditional ways of assessing actors and their actions have been reversed. Action is now judged "out of context," independently of the sociocultural setting in which it takes place and the social standing of its human objects—solely according to the universal rules of adequacy and efficiency. By contrast, actors are judged by their specific performances relevant to the task at hand, not by their general qualities. What truly counts is what is being done and how, not by whom and why. Selection of action is freed from all criteria—personal loyalties, political commitments, and moral norms, for example—that are irrelevant to the pursuit of the task at hand.

Division and separation are indeed constant themes in the theoretical discourse of modernity. The German sociologist Max *Weber proposed that the separation of business from household was the constitutive act of modern economy. Thanks to that separation, business decisions were emancipated from the pressure of moral obligations and personal commitments that guide family life. In still more general terms, the significance of separation was elaborated on by Immanuel Kant. In reference to his division between pure reason, practical reason, and judgment, many theorists of modernity (notably Juürgen Habermas in Germany and Ernest Gellner in Britain) consider the separation and mutual autonomy of the discourses of truth, moral norms, and aesthetic judgment (setting apart the spheres of science, ethics, and arts) as the most distinctive and decisive feature of modern mentality and practice. Beginning with Adam Smith, division of labor and splitting of complex functions into smaller and more manageable tasks has been seen as the most conspicuous factor of modern efficiency and productivity. Emile Durkheim, a French sociologist of the early 1900s, saw in the progressive, ever more minute division of labor the substance and the motive force of all aspects of historical development. The more complex is the division of labor, the simpler and more straightforward are separated functions; therefore they may be better mastered and more efficiently performed by specialists, who can now concentrate fully on effective means of "problem resolution." Expertise becomes a trademark of modern economy, science, art, and politics alike.

All fields of modern life, as Weber insisted, tend to become progressively rationalized. Action is rational (in the instrumental sense) insofar as it is oriented toward a clearly conceived and well-defined end, and thereafter based on the calculation of relative efficiency of alternative means to achieve it. Rational action is guided by motives and purposes, amenable in principle to conscious scrutiny and correction, and not determined by forces of which the actor is unaware or over which he or she has no control. Rational action splits the context of performance into ends and means and is guided solely by the effort to match the second against the first. Action is rational (again, in the instrumental sense) insofar as it consists in such decision-making and choice, even if a specific choice made by a given actor here and now is not the best conceivable or is even downright mistaken. Indeed, most choices stop short of the ideal. Means may be miscalculated because of inadequate or erroneous knowledge. Moreover, task-oriented activity is seldom free from interference by "impure" factors, irrational insofar as they are irrelevant to the task at hand—like the actor's uncontrolled habits and traditional loyalties, affections that get in the way, or commitment to values that interfere with the efficient performance of the given task. Rationality is therefore a tendency rather than the accomplished reality of modernity; a continuous, though by and large inconclusive, trend discernible in all fields of social life. For instance, according to Weber, the rule-governed, task-subordinated, impersonally acting organization, subjected to a meticulous division of functions, strict hierarchy of command, and scrupulous matching of personal skills of incumbents to the objective requirements of office, is the specifically modern, rational form of government.

The other side of rationalism is, of course, the taming or suppression of everything irrational—everything that interferes with the work of reason and detracts from the pragmatic effectivity of action. This irrational element in human behavior is called passion, which has been construed as the major obstacle on the road to the rule of reason. Modern civilization is prominent as much for its suppression of passions as for its promotion of the rationality of human conduct. More than in any other sphere, rational organization of society consists in controlling, defusing, incapacitating, or channeling away human instinctual drives and predispositions. A thorough analysis of this other, dramatic face of modernity is associated first and foremost with the work of Sigmund Freud. According to Freud, modern civilization substitutes the "reality principle" for the "pleasure principle"—the first being the necessary condition of peaceful, secure coexistence, the second being a natural predisposition of humans that clashes with the first. In practical terms, this substitution means constraint: pursuit of happiness is trimmed and limited by the consideration of what it is possible to achieve without paying costs too excessive to conceive of the effort as worthwhile. Partial security is obtained in exchange for at least part of the individual's freedom. Adequately civilized behavior is marked by self-constraint; society, so to speak, "leaves a garrison in a conquered city" in the form of the socially trained individual conscience that prompts the individual to suppress such urges as may fall in conflict with the socially approved norms.

In his study of the modern condition—entitled *Civilization and Its Discontents*—Freud theorizes that modern civilization inevitably breeds discontent and resistance, and that its perpetuation thus involves an element of mental or physical coercion. The picture of modernity that emerges from Freud's analysis is far from peaceful and benign. The rule of reason has psychologically traumatic consequences. From the individual's point of view, it cannot be an unambiguous blessing, as it leaves quite a considerable part of human needs downgraded, unattended, or starved. This is why reason's rule is continuously resented and can never be complete; it will go on prompting rebellion against itself. Again and again, people pressed to abide by the cool and unemotional rules of calculation of costs and effects will rally instead to the defense of suppressed affections, natural urges, and the immediacy of human contact.

Another rendition of the inner contradiction and ambiguous impact of civilization (and modern civilization in particular) can be found in Friedrich Nietzsche's concept of a spontaneous and instinctual "Dionysian" rebellion as a constant, only barely tamed threat, ever again boosted by the "Apollonian" effort to construct a logical, rational, and harmonious world order. This theme, in its Freudian-Nietzschean rendition, is directly or implicitly present in virtually all of the numerous critiques of modernity as an ambitious, but in many respects abortive, project aimed at overall rationalization of social organization and individual human behavior. Two types of critique are particularly prominent. One (undertaken by the "mass politics" theoreticians inspired, in somewhat different ways, by the "elite" theory of Vilfredo Pareto, the concept of the "revolt of the masses" popularized by José Ortega y Gasset, and the "iron law of oligarchy" articulated by Robert Michels) points out that, contrary to rationalistic rhetoric, modern conditions promote a blatantly irrational, heavily aestheticized mass politics that hinders rather than promotes rational choice. Another (mainly associated with the Frankfurt School tradition of critical theory, established by the work of Theodor Adorno and Max Horkheimer, but going back for many of its ideas to the early twentieth-century German sociologist Georg Simmel) uncovers the irreparable conflict between the drive to rationalize supra-individual institutional structures and the promise to render individual decisions amenable to free rational choice.

All in all, resistance to rationalization has been as prominent a mark of modernity as has rationalization itself. The history of modernity is punctuated by criticisms of its excesses or even of the vanity or evil of its motives and historic ambitions. For every intellectual expression of enthusiasm for the breathtaking vistas opened by modern science, technological expertise, and political expediency, there has been a protest against the "drying up" of individuality and genuinely human affectivity. Against the modern promise of a human species empowered in its struggle to make the world more hospitable, critics have hastened to point out that even if the species as a whole gains in freedom, its individual members do not; they are denied true choice, having been "functionalized" and transformed into "cogs in the machine." Against the utility of reason-guided problem solving, the critics have defended the values of individuality, the indivisible whole, and the all-too-human right to be different, erratic, and altogether irrational. Beginning with the Romantic poetry of the early nineteenth century, through decadence, the militantly "modernistic" avant-garde of the early twentieth century, dadaism, surrealism, and up to present-day postmodern culture (which proclaims normlessness the only cultural norm and calls for resistance to all authority, declining even to supply a foundation for its own practice)—the modern rationalization drive has been accompanied by a stridently oppositional culture bent on the defense of individual freedom and emotional experience. Cultural rebellion against the reality of society, a virtually constant antagonism between social and political practices and advanced cultural creation, whether in philosophy, art, or literature, has been thus far a most astonishing—and apparently permanent—feature of modernity.

An explanation of this paradox is sought in the specifically modern structure of daily life and individual experience. The most salient attribute of the latter is its fragmentariness; cast into the densely packed urban environment and bound to spend most of his or her life among strangers, the individual finds its difficult, perhaps impossible, to integrate experience into a meaningful whole. Within the horizon drawn by individual experience, time seems to split into unconnected events and space into unrelated spots. If there is a bond of mutual dependence that unites them into a cohesive totality—such a link eludes the individual observer, facing but brief and spatially limited episodes of the drama. Modern experience, it was first pointed out by the French poet and critic Charles Baudelaire, is a sighting of a fleeting moment. To be in tune with modern experience, art ought to represent the world as fragmentary and transitory—as a collection of "fleeting moments."

As Georg Simmel indicated, the characteristic feature of modern experience is the lack of coordination and communication between civilization as total cultural product and the snippets of cultural achievement that individuals are capable of assimilating and using as the building material in constructing their own identities. The sum total of cultural products far exceeds individual absorptive capacity. This fact, on the one hand, frees cultural creation from its bonds with daily life and permits thereby an infinite specialization and infinite expansion within each specialized field (hence the logarithmic acceleration in the growth of science, technology, and the arts, which exacerbates still further the original conflict); on the other hand, however, it leaves to individuals the awesome task of patching together "meaningful lives" out of the subjectively meaningless splinters of other, unknown or invisible totalities. While performing this task, individuals must be able to compare the incomparable and combine elements that apparently do not belong together; for this they need a strategy that, so to speak, "imposes" comparability between wildly discrepant experiences, and thus allows them to make choices while neglecting the qualitative differences between the objects of choice. Hence the intellect (capacity for abstract, formal thinking) and money are simultaneously inevitably products and indispensable instruments of life under modern conditions. Both address themselves solely to the quantitative aspects of experienced phenomena, and downplay their qualitative characteristics.

These and related characteristics of human habitat have persisted throughout the modern era, constantly gathering force. They continue to mark present-day Western and Westernized societies and continue to spread into areas of the globe until recently seen as "traditional" or "premodern." Nonetheless, some observers suggest that modernity in its classic form has run its course and has been replaced, or is about to be replaced, by another sociocultural formation, which they call postmodernity. Descriptions of this allegedly new formation (meant to demonstrate its novelty and qualitative distinction from modernity) do not differ on the whole from the above description of the modern condition. There is, however, one significant difference on which the assertions about the "end of modernity" and the advent of postmodernity tend to found their credibility: if throughout the modern era the "messiness," ambivalence, spontaneity, and uncertainty inherent in social and individual life were seen as temporary irritants, to be eventually overcome by the rationalizing tendency, they are now seen as unavoidable and ineradicable—and not necessarily irritants. It now has been accepted that historical processes have no specific end or direction; that pluralism of values and forms of life is here to stay; and that the centers of political power, most notably state governments, have lost both the resources and the ambitions that characterize the "gardening stance." The all-inclusive designs of "rational society" and global social-engineering schemes and cultural crusades that backed them seem to have fallen into disrepute and have been all but abandoned. The recent collapse of the communist command economies and all-regulating states has provided a most spectacular display of this tendency.

(See also POSTMODERNISM.)

Krishan Kumar, *Prophecy and Progress: The Sociology of Industrial and Post-Industrial Society* (Harmondsworth, U.K., 1978). Zygmunt Bauman, *Legislators and Interpreters: On Modernity, Postmodernity, and Intellectuals* (Cambridge, U.K., 1987). Juürgen Habermas, *The Philosophical Discourse of Modernity* (Cambridge, U.K., 1987). John F. Rundell, *Origins of Modernity: The Origins of Modern Social Theory from Kant to Hegel to Marx* (Cambridge, U.K., 1987). David Harvey, *The Condition of Postmodernity* (Oxford, 1989). Anthony Giddens, *Consequences of Modernity* (Cambridge, U.K., 1990). Agnes Heller, *Can Modernity Survive?* (Cambridge, U.K., 1990). Bryan S. Turner, ed., *Theories of Modernity and Postmodernity* (London, 1990).

ZYGMUNT BAUMAN

phasizes a scientific outlook (including the radical tendency to critique the world), individual autonomy and emancipation, an ideology of equality, and a conception of society as an object of active construction by conscious human action.

The construction of modern society gave rise in the West, especially in Europe, to nation-states and class societies and to a strong emphasis on economic development. The expansion of modernity beyond Europe gave rise to the development of different types of modern societies and to a great variety of institutional constellations, as well as of cultural orientations toward modernity. This variety indicates the necessity to go beyond some of the assumptions of the initial studies of modernization, without however forgetting that such variety developed out of the interaction between the institutional forces and ideological premises of the first examples of modernity as developed in the West and the various societies on which they impinged.

The varieties of modernization suggest that different aspects of the process such as industrialization, urbanization, and political modernization are not necessarily interlinked. Furthermore, such variability can be seen not only, or even mainly, in different institutional patterns but in the combination of these with the different cultural contours of modernity. Such programs may entail different interpretations of many of the basic premises of modern civilization: the nature of equality; the extent of participation by wider social sectors in various aspects of public life; the relative importance of economic development in the panorama of human goals; the balance between productive and distributive economic priorities; the construction of new symbols and collective identities; and negative or positive attitudes toward modernity in general and to the West in particular.

These different orientations toward modernity were shaped by the continuous interaction between the "point of entry" of any society into the modern *international system and specific aspects of the society's traditional order, including the social, political, and economic formations already existing in these societies, the basic values of these civilizations, and the patterns of authority, hierarchy, and equality that prevailed in them. These varieties of modernization were the product of actions by elites and major counterelites, protest movements, and the overall historical experience of social change in these societies.

The multiplicity of types of modern societies does not negate the obvious fact that, in many central aspects of their institutional forms, such as occupational patterns and industrial structures, or in the organization of education and cities, very strong convergences are apparent in different modern societies. These convergences have indeed generated common problems. However, the means of coping with these problems differ greatly among nations, which again reflects how these different modern societies have been shaped by their specific institutional development and cultural contours and by their historical experiences.

(See also DEVELOPMENT AND UNDERDEVELOPMENT; POLITICAL CULTURE; POLITICAL DEVELOPMENT; SECULARIZATION; WEBER, MAX.)

S. N. Eisenstadt, *Modernization, Protest, and Change* (Englewood Cliffs, N.J., 1966). S. N. Eisenstadt, *Tradition, Change, and Modernity* (New York, 1973). A. Inkeles and D. H. Smith, *Becoming Modern: Individual Change in Six Developing Countries* (Cambridge, Mass., 1974).

S. N. EISENSTADT

MOLDOVA. The Republic of Moldova is a relatively small country (approximately 13,000 sq. mi. [33,670 sq. km.] and a population of approximately 4.3 million) in southeastern Europe, bordered by Ukraine and Romania. Its population is ethnically mixed: Romanian speakers (64.5%), Ukrainians (13.8%), Russians (13%), Bulgarians (2.0%), the Turkic-origin Gagauz community (3.5%).

Formerly a republic of the USSR, Moldova became independent on 27 August 1991. Four competitive national elections have been held since independence; for the president of the republic in 1991 and 1996, and for Parliament in February 1994 and once again in March 1998. Each of these elections was scrutinized by foreign observers and found to be free and fair.

On independence, Moldova's sovereignty was challenged by two active separatist efforts, one on the left bank of the Dniestr (the "Dniestr Republic"), and another in southern Moldova, (the "Gagauz Republic"). While the Gagauz crisis was successfully ended in 1995, the Transdniestrian secession remains unresolved.

Under the constitution enacted in 1994, the head of state of Moldova is the president of the republic. He is charged with guaranteeing the independence and unity of the republic, and overseeing public authorities. The president may be impeached by vote of two thirds of the total number of deputies elected to Parliament. His case is then heard by the Supreme Court of Justice. The president names the prime minister following consultation with Parliament. Once chosen by the president, the prime minister selects a government and establishes a program which is then submitted to Parliament for a vote of confidence. Parliament is given the power to dismiss the government or an individual member through a vote of no confidence by a majority vote.

Moldova has a unicameral legislature (the Parliament) made up of 104 deputies elected to four-year terms by means of direct universal vote. The Parliament passes laws, may call for referendum, and exercises control over the executive as called for in the constitution. The Moldovan judicial system consists a Supreme Court of Justice, a Court of Appeals, subordinate tribunals, the Superior Council of the Magistracy, the Procuracy, and a Constitutional Court. The Constitutional Court is comprised of nine deputies, three chosen by the president and six by the Parliament. It is the sole authority with constitutional jurisdiction in the republic.

Legislators in Moldova are elected through a proportional representation closed list system, with a 4-percent threshold for participation. Unlike the vast majority of proportional representation systems, Moldova adopted a single national electoral district. The president is chosen for a four-year term through a two-round popular election, with a requirement that more than 50 percent of the vote must be gained for victory in the first round. If no candidate achieves such a majority, a runoff between the top two candidates determines the outcome in the second round.

The transition from Soviet socialism to a capitalist economy has produced serious instability. While substantial privatization has occurred in the second half of the 1990s, especially in the agricultural sector, the role of the state in economic activity remains strong. The breakdown of the former Soviet system and the loss of Moldova's traditional markets, combined with the weak development of private enterprise, have resulted in loss of production, very high levels of unemployment, and sharp declines in consumption.

(See also POST-COMMUNISM.)

William E. Crowther, "The Politics of Democratization in Postcommunist Moldova," in Karen Dawisha and Bruce Parrott, eds., *Democratic Changes and Authoritarian Reactions in Russia, Ukraine, Belarus, and Moldova* (London, 1997), pp. 282–329. Charles King, *The Moldovans: Romania, Russia, and the Politics of Culture* (Stanford, Calif., 1999).

WILLIAM E. CROWTHER

MONETARISM. The concept of monetarism was initially devised to describe a school of economic thought that emphasizes the impact of the money supply on the rate of inflation and economic output, and it is now widely used to describe the economic policies of governments that have been influenced by this school of thought.

The term *monetarism* was introduced in 1968 by the economist Karl Brunner to describe an approach to economics then being developed by economists in the United States, notably at the Federal Reserve Bank of St. Louis and the University of Chicago, where Milton Friedman did much to popularize the doctrine. It built upon the quantity theory of money, initially used by the classical economists, and formalized by Irving Fischer in 1926, to suggest that the price level varied directly with the amount of money in circulation, and it was subsequently extended by rational expectations theorists who argued that activist macroeconomic policy was likely to be ineffective because its impact would already be discounted by highly rational actors in the private economy.

From a political perspective, monetarism was most significant as a challenge to *Keynesianism, the doctrine that dominated economic policy-making in the capitalist world for thirty years after World War II. The two doctrines were based on quite different views of the economy. Whereas Keynesians saw the private economy as fundamentally unstable and in need of active macroeconomic management, monetarists regarded the private economy as inherently stable and government policy as likely to be destabilizing. Whereas Keynesians believed that an active fiscal policy could reduce the level of unemployment, monetarists argued that the "natural" rate of unemployment was fixed by structural imperfections in the labor market and relatively impervious to macroeconomic manipulation over the long run. While Keynesians argued that inflation was often generated by excess aggregate demand or wage militancy that might be addressed by an incomes policy (statutory or voluntary wage and price restraint), monetarists argued that the rate of inflation could be controlled best by the establishment of fixed targets for the rate of growth of the money supply.

Accordingly, monetarists tended to depreciate the effectiveness of fiscal policy, associated with changes in the budget balance, in favor of a focus on monetary policy. They opposed "discretionary" macroeconomic management in favor of a policy based on relatively fixed "rules." They preferred to use the rate of growth of the money supply, rather than the level of interest rates, as a monetary target. Where Keynesians emphasized government action to reduce unemployment, mone-

tarists gave highest priority to reducing inflation. Although the views of individual monetarists varied on important points of detail, they tended to be ranged against Keynesians along these general lines, and their views were underpinned by a fundamentally different model of the economy that gave prominence to monetary variables.

In the political sphere, monetarism became an important doctrine during the 1970s largely as a consequence of two economic developments. First, rates of inflation began to rise more rapidly in the industrialized world from the end of the 1960s. Second, unemployment began to increase along with inflation during the 1970s. These developments called traditional Keynesian analyses into question. As political attention shifted to the problem of inflation, monetarist doctrines acquired more prominence because they were directly oriented to inflation, whereas Keynesian doctrines had initially been devised to explain unemployment. Moreover, Keynesian explanations for inflation turned heavily on the Phillips curve, which postulated an inverse correlation between the level of unemployment and the rate of inflation. That analysis seemed unpersuasive after 1974 when both variables began to rise simultaneously in many nations. As a result, initially contentious monetarist arguments about the importance of the rate of growth of the money supply and the limited effectiveness of fiscal policy were gradually incorporated into the analyses of mainstream economists during the 1970s and 1980s.

However, the political popularity of monetarist doctrine during the 1970s and 1980s was also a response to broader political developments. Many governments initially responded to rising rates of inflation with efforts to secure wage and price controls. These efforts drew politicians into protracted negotiations with trade unions and employers about complex distributional issues on which it was difficult to secure a consensus, and the compression of wage differentials that often accompanied income policies generated resentment among the workforce. Such neocorporatist efforts strained the political authority of many governments, especially in nations such as Italy and Britain, where it was difficult to mobilize consent among decentralized union movements. Thus, a monetarist approach that promised to reduce inflation without any need for an incomes policy began to seem increasingly attractive to many politicians and voters.

Monetarist doctrines also had a special appeal for conservative politicians because they provided a new rationale for policies that conservatives had long espoused, including reducing public spending and taxation, limiting state intervention and the power of trade unions in order to reinforce the role of market mechanisms in the allocation of resources, and renouncing the responsibility of governments for unemployment. Thus, monetarist arguments began to figure prominently in the market-oriented programs that conservative politicians promulgated during the 1970s and 1980s.

The impact of monetarist economics was greatest in Britain, where it was embraced by a small group of Conservative politicians led by Margaret *Thatcher, who became the leader of the party in 1975 and imposed many monetarist tenets on the government after she became prime minister in 1979. Largely as a result of her influence, monetarism is seen in Britain not just as an economic doctrine but also as a political doctrine closely associated with her efforts to give priority to reducing inflation rather than unemployment, to reduce the role of the state in the economy by privatizing many public enterprises, to limit the power of the trade unions in politics and the labor market, to reduce income taxes on higher incomes as well as public spending, and to make the control of the monetary aggregates the central target of macroeconomic policy. Paradoxically, the last of these efforts and the one most central to monetarist economic doctrine has been the least successful. By the end of the 1980s, the exchange rate and the level of interest rates had become more important targets of British policy, as the authorities found it exceedingly difficult to attain monetary targets.

Elsewhere in the world, monetarist doctrine has had the most influence on central banks and monetary authorities, who now tend to monitor and target the rate of growth of the money supply on the grounds that it feeds directly into the rate of inflation. Under its chair, Paul Volcker, the U.S. Federal Reserve Bank publicly embraced this approach in 1979. However, monetarist ideas have also contributed to a widespread view among economic policy-makers that the effectiveness of active fiscal policy against unemployment may be distinctly limited and that budget deficits should thus be avoided. Therefore, monetarism is closely associated with the collapse of the Keynesian consensus in the 1970s and the resurgence of conservative economics since the 1980s.

(See also CONSERVATISM; CORPORATISM; LABOR MOVEMENT; POLITICAL ECONOMY; TAXES AND TAXATION.)

Keith Cuthbertson, *Macroeconomic Policy: The New Cambridge, Keynesian, and Monetarist Controversies* (London, 1979). John T. Woolley, *Monetary Politics: The Federal Reserve and the Politics of Monetary Policy* (Cambridge, U.K., 1984). Peter Riddell, *The Thatcher Government*, 2d ed. (London, 1985).

PETER A. HALL

MONGOLIA. The heartland of the empire of Genghis Khan (1162–1227 C.E.) and his successors, Mongolia (1924–92, Mongolian People's Republic) is a landlocked country of 600,000 square miles (1.5 million sq. km.) and approximately 2.4 million people lying between Russia and China. The princes of northern (Outer) Mongolia submitted to Manchu (Qing) rule in 1691. Following the republican revolution in China in 1911, the Manchu governor left Outer Mongolia, which declared its independence. The *Bogd Gegeen*, or spiritual leader of Mongolia's Lamaists, was proclaimed khan of Mongolia on 16 December, and the country's religious center, Urga, became the capital.

Two underground nationalist revolutionary groups formed in 1919 and joined forces in June 1920 as the Mongolian People's Party (MPP). Northern Mongolia was occupied by anti-Bolshevik "White" Russian forces in October 1920, and the MPP developed its activities in the Siberian towns of Irkutsk and Kyakhta. Mongolian revolutionary troops crossed the border at Kyakhta on 18 March 1921 and with the help of the Soviet Red Army defeated the "Whites" and entered Urga on 6 July. A people's government under the limited monarchy of the *Bogd Gegeen* was proclaimed on 11 July, now celebrated as National Day.

After the death of the *Bogd Gegeen* in 1924, a national assembly, or Great Hural, was held to endorse a republican constitution. The third congress of the MPP in 1924 adopted *Lenin's formula for "bypassing capitalism" with Soviet help and proclaimed itself the ruling party, adopting the name

Mongolian People's Revolutionary Party (MPRP). The capital was renamed Ulan Bator (Red Hero). Political extremism and purging of leaders in the 1920s and 1930s and the ruthless destruction of Lamaism left the country devastated. Thousands of innocent people fell victim to the "personality cult" of "Mongolia's Stalin," Horloogiyn Choybalsan (1895–1952). Mongolia had entered a long period of political isolation, having treaty relations only with Soviet Russia and with Tannu-Tuva (part of Outer Mongolia until 1911 and absorbed into the USSR in 1944). When Japanese forces attacked Mongolia in 1939, Soviet troops helped force them back. In World War II, Mongolia fought a brief campaign against Japanese forces in northern China in 1945.

Following the Yalta agreement of 1945, Mongolians voted overwhelmingly for independence in a plebiscite, which the Republic of China recognized. On Choybalsan's death in 1952, Yumjaagiyn Tsedenbal became premier and then, in 1974, chairman of the presidium of the People's Great Hural (head of state). Until his illness and removal from power in 1984, Tsedenbal had been concurrently MPRP general secretary for some forty years. Mongolia's traditional livestock economy had changed little, but *collectivization was completed in the 1950s. Grain-producing state farms enabled Mongolia to become self-sufficient in wheat in most years. Coal mining was developed for electric power generation, and the railway line across Mongolia linking Siberia and northern China was completed. The pressures of the Sino-Soviet dispute and the Chinese *Cultural Revolution in the 1960s encouraged the Soviet leadership to invest more heavily in Mongolia's economy and defense. Mongolia joined the Council for Mutual Economic Assistance (COMECON) in 1962. The number of Soviet technicians working in Mongolia grew rapidly. Soviet army and air force units were stationed in Mongolia. It was not until the restoration of Soviet and Mongolian relations with China at the end of the 1980s that the Soviet units began to leave.

As Soviet *perestroika and *glasnost* swept the communist world, the MPRP, challenged by the vigorous development of alternative political movements, was forced in 1990 to renew its own leadership, surrender its role as the only legal party, and participate in the country's first-ever free elections. In the new People's Great Hural elected in July 1990, however, the MPRP received 85 percent (375) of the 430 seats while the Mongolian Democratic Party (MDP) received only 4 percent of the seats (16). The first session of the People's Great Hural elected Punsalmaagiyn Ochirbat (MPRP) to the new post of president of Mongolia and appointed the State Little Hural (standing legislature) with proportional representation of political parties.

A new Mongolian Constitution, adopted by the People's Great Hural on 13 January 1992, enshrined the Mongolian people's human rights, including ownership of land and other property. Elections to a new, single-chamber seventy-six-seat national assembly, the Mongolian Great Hural, were called for June 1992. The MPRP, which won seventy-one seats, formed a new government headed by Prime Minister Puntsagiyn Jasray.

In the 1996 general elections the MPRP finally lost power, taking only twenty-five seats in the Great Hural against the fifty won by the Democratic Alliance (DA), a coalition of the National-Democratic and Social-Democratic parties. The new prime minister, Mendsayhany Enhsayhan, and his cabinet were approved by the Great Hural but were not members of it. In the 1997 presidential elections Natsagiyn Bagabandi, the MPRP leader, defeated the incumbent President Punsalmaagiyn Ochirbat, standing for the DA. In May 1998 Enhsayhan was replaced as prime minister by DA leader Tsahiagiyn Elbegdorj, and a new cabinet was formed from among Great Hural members. Elbegdorj lost a vote of confidence in July, and the new DA prime minister, Janlavyn Narantsatsralt, was appointed only in December 1998. However, Narantsatsralt resigned in July 1999 and was replaced by Rinchinyamyn Amarjargal. In December 1999 the Mongolian Great Hural rejected a presidential veto and passed the first amendments to the 1992 Constitution. When routine general elections were called for July 2, 2000, the MPRP was leading the polls.

(See also COMMUNIST PARTY STATES.)

Alan J. K. Sanders, *The People's Republic of Mongolia: A General Reference Guide* (Oxford, 1968). Alan J. K. Sanders, *Mongolia: Politics, Economics and Society* (London, 1987). Ole Bruun and Ole Odgaard, *Mongolia in Transition* (Richmond, U.K. 1996). Alan J. K. Sanders, *Historical Dictionary of Mongolia* (Lanham, Md., 1996).

ALAN J. K. SANDERS

MONNET, Jean. Born in Cognac, in the southwest of France, Jean Monnet (1888–1979) did not attend a university, instead entering the family cognac business at an early age. During World War I, he persuaded the French government to organize a joint executive commission with Britain to coordinate nautical transportation of provisions and war material. Monnet served as deputy secretary-general of the *League of Nations between 1920 and 1923, and went on to pursue international business activities with large American firms.

During World War II, Monnet presided over a French and British coordinating committee, formed for the purpose of purchasing war materiel. He became a trusted adviser to President Franklin *Roosevelt in the launching of the program which would make the United States the "Arsenal of Democracy."

In 1945, Monnet was appointed head of the French Commissariat du Plan by General Charles de *Gaulle. He directed the establishment of the first French plan (for modernization and equipment). In 1950, he proposed to Robert Schuman, the French minister of foreign affairs, the basis for a new policy regarding the Federal Republic of Germany. The policy was founded on principles of equality of rights and European integration. It was adopted by the French government and made public on 9 May 1950 (the Monnet-Schuman Declaration). The policy was the foundation for the European Coal and Steel Community (ECSC) and the European Defense Community (EDC), presented by the French government in October 1950 for the purpose of placing the rearmament of Germany in a European context.

After the rejection of the EDC by the French National Assembly in August 1954, Monnet retired from public service, but he remained active as a private citizen in discussions and negotiations which led to the March 1957 conclusion of the *Rome Treaties (concerning the European Economic Community or Common Market and the European Atomic Energy Community or Euratom). In an "Action Committee for the United States of Europe" (October 1955), he brought together the leaders of the democratic parties and independent trade unions of the six member countries of the ECSC. Until 1973, when Monnet withdrew from public life, the committee would defend the principles of European integration, would demand the expansion of the Communities to include Britain, and would support the work of European integration.

Drawing on his extensive network of personal relationships with leaders on both sides of the Atlantic, Monnet exerted an extraordinary influence during the decisive postwar years. In this he was aided by his capacity to imagine or identify new, clear, and attainable ideals, by the force of his belief in contacts at the highest level, and, finally, by his absolute lack of self-interest, as evident in his refusal of every office and public honor. The fixed principles of the Monnet-Schuman Declaration continue to guide the functioning and development of the European Community: equality of the rights of all participants, transfer of powers to independent institutions, the establishment of a European judicial system, and democratic control by a parliamentary assembly.

(See also EUROPEAN COURT OF JUSTICE; EUROPEAN UNION; PLANNING.)

Jean Monnet, *Memoirs* (New York, 1978). Douglas Brinkley and Clifford Hackett, eds., *Jean Monnet: The Path to European Unity* (New York, 1991).

EMILE NOEÜL

MONROE DOCTRINE. What came to be known as the Monroe Doctrine originated in President James Monroe's message to Congress on 2 December 1823. The enduring element of Monroe's statement was a warning to Europeans to keep "hands off" the Western Hemisphere and not to extend further their control in the Americas. The message articulated ideas already well established in U.S. foreign policy. The idea of geographic, political, economic, and social separation of the New World from the Old, with the Americas having distinct interests, dated from before U.S. independence; it complemented ingrained *isolationism. Monroe echoed these sentiments, in the specific context of perceived threats from Russia, France, and Spain, when he said that the political system of Europe was essentially different from that of America; and that the United States would consider any attempt by them to extend their system to any portions of the Western Hemisphere, or to control the newly independent Latin American countries, as dangerous to U.S. *peace and safety and "the manifestation of an unfriendly disposition towards the United States." Monroe assured Europe of U.S. reciprocity by promising that the United States would not interfere in its internal concerns. Unilateralism was indicated by the rejection of a prior British proposal for a joint declaration and by rebuffing subsequent Latin American suggestions for formal alliance against Europe.

Monroe's declaration was largely ignored as a policy guide during most of the nineteenth century, a period of U.S. military weakness and domestic preoccupations. A number of European military and other interventions, and even colonizations in Latin America, brought little response.

By the end of the nineteenth century, with the U.S. rise to great power status, the Monroe Doctrine had become the "cornerstone" of U.S. foreign policy. "Corollaries" appeared that further defined the doctrinal content. The broadest extension was the Roosevelt Corollary of 1904. President Theodore Roosevelt said that "chronic wrongdoing" or "impotence" in the Americas might force the United States, because of its adherence to the Monroe Doctrine, "to the exercise of an international police power." The United States invoked the Roosevelt Corollary for the next quarter-century in order to preempt European intervention and to justify U.S. *imperialism and coercive instruments. U.S. military intervention and occupation, formal protectorates, and increasing economic domination, all in the circum-Caribbean, were inspired by geopolitical thinking regarding the Panama Canal. Latin Americans, even those not directly the targets of U.S. coercion, vigorously protested violations of their sovereignty and advocated nonintervention as an international legal principle.

The United States went through a series of steps that transformed the unilateral Monroe Doctrine into a multilateral inter-American policy of nonintervention and mutual *security. President Herbert Hoover's Under Secretary of State, J. Reuben Clark, wrote a memorandum in 1928 that was made public in 1930 dissociating the Roosevelt Corollary from the Monroe Doctrine. President Franklin D. *Roosevelt adhered to inter-American treaties in 1933 and 1936 that prohibited any intervention "directly or indirectly, and for whatever reason, in the internal or external affairs of the parties," a principle notably reaffirmed in the Charter of the *Organization of American States (1948) and the Inter-American Treaty of Reciprocal Assistance (*Rio Treaty, 1947).

During the *Cold War doubt was cast on the extent to which the United States truly considered the Monroe Doctrine to have been multilateralized and intervention made illegal. The Monroe Doctrine was referred to as the justification for the overthrow of the Guatemalan government (1954), the Bay of Pigs adventure (1961), and the Dominican Republic invasion (1965). In response to assertions by Soviet Premier Nikita *Khrushchev that the Monroe Doctrine was dead, the Department of State proclaimed that its principles were "as valid today as they were in 1823."

In the 1980s and 1990s, by contrast, the doctrine was rarely referred to regarding Central American conflict and was not used to justify the U.S. invasions of Grenada and Panama. The retirement of the Soviet Union from hemispheric affairs and its subsequent dissolution, plus the lack of other external threats, made the Monroe Doctrine irrelevant in the post-Cold War era.

(See also GEOPOLITICS; INTERVENTION; U.S. FOREIGN POLICY; U.S.–LATIN AMERICAN RELATIONS.)

Dexter Perkins, *The Monroe Doctrine, 1823–1826, 1826–1867*, and *1867–1907*, 3 vols. (Cambridge, Mass., 1927; Baltimore, 1933 and 1937). Dexter Perkins, *A History of the Monroe Doctrine* (Boston, 1963). Ernest R. May, *The Making of the Monroe Doctrine* (Cambridge, Mass., 1975).

G. POPE ATKINS

MOROCCO. Known in Arabic as *al-Maghrib*, Morocco is the most westerly Arab country. Located in the northwest of the African continent, it is only 10 miles across the Strait of Gibraltar from Spain, with which it shared a common kingdom and culture for many centuries.

Morocco is today a *constitutional monarchy, among just three monarchical political systems in Africa. The king plays a very strong role in politics, though there is a lively multiparty political system and an active and moderately independent civil society. Morocco aspires to closer economic and political ties to Europe, but it is plagued by deep poverty and riven by social unrest. After the death of longtime ruler King Hassan II in 1999, the new monarch, Mohammed VI, remains the center of a conservative, corrupt, and often repressive political system.

For many centuries, sultans ruled Morocco from the ancient capitals of Fez and Marrakesh. But in 1912, French troops seized most of the territory, while Spanish forces took control of a zone along the northern coast.

Both powers installed protectorates, ruled nominally by the sultan but closely controlled by a European administration. The French authorities installed a modern network of transportation and communication, light industries, and mechanized and irrigated farms. Casablanca, a small fishing village, became the country's largest city and its foremost port and financial center. From the new capital of Rabat, the French constructed a strong, highly centralized state which imposed a harsh domestic order and enforced a new legal system. Though the half million European settlers lived well, most Moroccans faced deep poverty and discrimination.

In the 1940s an anticolonial movement gathered strength, led by the Istiqlal Party under the leadership of Allal al-Fassi. Sultan Muhammad ben Youssef cautiously supported the movement. By the mid-1950s, the French finally decided to withdraw, and Spain soon followed suit. The country attained a united independence in 1956.

Unlike most postcolonial states, Morocco's victorious independence movement did not assume direct power. The sultan, who crowned himself King Muhammad V in 1957, kept the upper hand, drawing on his personal prestige and the support he enjoyed from foreign backers and from conservative leaders in the Moroccan countryside. Internal disputes weakened the Istiqlal Party and a breakaway group soon formed the Union Nationale des Forces Populaires (UNFP) in 1959, and called for extensive *land reform and socialist initiatives to overcome poverty and bolster lagging economic development.

Many of Morocco's urban poor and intellectuals, opponents of the monarchy and advocates of a united North Africa, rallied to the UNFP. The French, fighting a military campaign against independence in neighboring Algeria, provided aid and advisers which bolstered the king against his radical nationalist opposition. In early 1960, only five months after the party was founded, police rounded up most UNFP leaders, claiming evidence of a plot. Many were tortured and eventually sentenced to prison, although little credible evidence was presented against them.

In February 1961, Muhammed V died and his son succeeded as Hassan II. Hassan pardoned the UNFP prisoners and eventually promulgated a constitution in December 1962. The constitution placed few restraints on the monarchy, however, and extensive official fraud marred the subsequent elections. In July, police arrested most UNFP leaders; confessions extracted under torture led to another dubious trail. Some, including leader Mehdi Ben Barka, fled into exile.

Morocco inherited many public enterprises from the colonial period, especially the large and profitable state phosphate-mining company. To these the government added fresh investments in chemicals, light industry, trade, and tourism. Though the regime was conservative and laissez-faire, it ironically built a heavily state-controlled economy. In the private sector, the king himself was the richest and largest investor, who built a portfolio of holdings throughout the economy.

Nearly half Morocco's population continued to face dire poverty; many lived in urban shantytowns; almost three-quarters were illiterate. A small middle class of professionals and civil servants lived modestly. By contrast, the king enjoyed fabulous luxury in ten palaces, while courtiers and ministers enriched themselves on unchecked corruption.

With political parties weakened, spontaneous mass protest racked Morocco's cities. In March 1965, when the government announced austerity measures, Casablanca exploded in riots, and Rabat and Fez soon followed. Special security forces crushed the uprisings, leaving at least a thousand casualties. Soon the king dissolved parliament and declared a state of emergency that continued for the next five years. In October, UNFP leader Ben Barka was kidnapped on the streets of Paris by agents of the King's secret police and never reappeared.

Having depended on the military to crush the left, the monarchy soon faced a threat from the armed forces themselves. In July 1971, high army officers launched a nearly successful coup on the king's birthday. Then, in August 1972, Moroccan air force jets tried unsuccessfully to shoot down the royal passenger plane. The king sent many of the military rebels to the firing squad and jailed others in a notorious underground political prison.

Often described as a thousand-year-old institution, the Moroccan monarchy is best understood as a recent recreation. Though the king is "Commander of the Faithful" and seems the incarnation of an ancient oriental despot, he runs a strong, modern state with an efficient police and propaganda apparatus. Hassan II ruled for thirty-seven years. A staunch ally of the West in regional as well as international politics, King Hassan enjoyed the solid support of France and the United States. Both powers gave generous aid, as well as military and security assistance.

In 1975, king and opposition found themselves united. A desert colony to the south, ruled by Spain, had long been considered by nationalists as a part of Morocco. As Spain's hold on this phosphate-rich territory weakened, the king led 350,000 Moroccans across the border in a "Green March" to claim the land. The following year, Spain signed over its colony. In response, residents of annexed *Western Sahara formed a liberation movement called Polisario and, with aid from Algeria, began to fight Moroccan forces, demanding independence. War costs deepened Morocco's economic problems for more than a decade and the future of the territory remains uncertain.

Real wages fell sharply in Morocco and a serious drought drove thousands off the land and into the cities. Meanwhile, the *International Monetary Fund pressed for austerity. When the government raised prices on necessities, trade unions called a general strike. In June 1981, the poor of Casablanca rose in protest, and fighting in the city raged for four days until special units of the army finally crushed the last pockets of resistance. In January 1984, a second wave of riots swept the country, leading to another harsh counterattack by security forces, with hundreds of casualties. A third wave of protests broke out in the northern cities of Fez and Tangier in December 1990, leaving fifty dead and thousand of casualties.

During the 1980s, as in other countries of the region, Islamic groups emerged as a major political force. Flourishing in urban slums and attracting a following in universities and even in the army, the Islamists called for a purified Islamic politics, and some played a leading role in the riots. The king angrily accused Islamists of being pawns of foreign enemies and the police implacably hunted them down. Some disappeared, while others languished in frightful prisons. Many Islamist publications were closed and their organizations banned.

By the end of the 1990s, Morocco's population reached nearly 30 million, more than three times the number at independence. Casablanca, fed by rural migrants, became one of Africa's largest cities. Economic troubles, worsened by nearly US$19 billion in foreign debts, plagued the country, even though wealthy patrons like Saudi Arabia and Kuwait offered aid. Responding to pressures from creditors, the royal government had privatized dozens of state enterprises and introduced new measures of austerity. More than 60 percent of the population remained illiterate.

Through a combination of repression and cooptation, the palace kept the Islamic movement largely within the confines of the legal political opposition. To enhance his Islamic credentials, the king built the world's largest and most lavish mosque on the shore at Casablanca. Rather than invite Islamists into the government, though, King Hassan offered the post of prime minister in 1998 to Abderrahman Youssefi, a long-exiled leader of the biggest party of the left, the Union Socialiste des Forces Populaires. But the new socialist premier headed a cabinet of seven different parties, in which palace loyalists held the key ministries of defense, foreign affairs, and interior. The longtime chief of royal repression, Interior Minister Driss Basri, remained at his post.

In July 1999 King Hassan died. Though some had wondered whether the monarchy would survive the passing of the old ruler, Hassan's son Mohammed VI succeeded to the throne in a seamless transition. The new king made a number of gestures towards a more open political system by arranging for the return of famous exiles and dismissing the feared Basri. He soon asserted royal domination, though, and the Youssefi government had little room for independence or innovation.

The royal system continues to combine repression with nominally democratic institutions. Opposition newspapers criticize the government, *human rights committees function, elections allow a modicum of public discussion, and parliament occasionally holds a serious debate. But the king rules, and individual Moroccans enjoy scant ability to influence affairs of state.

(See also COLONIAL EMPIRES; DECOLONIZATION; DEVELOPMENT AND UNDERDEVELOPMENT; ISLAM.)

David Seddon, *Moroccan Peasants* (Folkestone, U.K., 1981). Tony Hodges, *Western Sahara: Roots of a Desert War* (Westport, Conn., 1983). I. William Zartman, *The Political Economy of Morocco* (New York, 1987). Gilles Perrault, *Notre Ami le Roi* (Paris, 1990). Henry Munson Jr., *Religion and Power in Morocco* (New Haven, 1993). John P. Entelis, *Culture and Counterculture in Moroccan Politics* (Lanham, Md., 1996). Abdellah Hammoudi, *Master and Disciple: The Cultural Foundations of Moroccan Authoritarianism* (Chicago, 1997).

JAMES A. PAUL

MOZAMBIQUE. Mozambique is a former Portuguese colony that achieved its independence in June 1975. Claimed by Portugal as its overseas territory since Vasco da Gama set foot on its soil in 1498, Mozambique has experienced diverse political circumstances that have set it apart both from its counterparts in the Lusophone community of nations and the rest of Africa. The country has one of the fastest population growth rates in the world, close to 4 percent a year, and is home for some 15,700,000 people, made up of eleven distinct major ethnic groups and several smaller ones, namely, the Tonga (about 3 million), Rhonga, Nguni, Swazi, Atewe, Manhica, Ndau, Chope, Maconde, Makua, Ajaua, Maravi, Tawara, Nyungwe, Swahili, and Indians. Religion has been a contentious issue in the country, as the government has attempted to play one group against the other, recently favoring the Muslims and Protestants over the Catholics. Even though figures presented by the West claim that 5 million Mozambicans (32 percent) are Christians, virtually all Catholic, and 4 million are Muslim (25 percent), the government has claimed that the Muslims constitute the largest number, followed by Catholics, traditionalists, and a few Hindus.

Until 1951 Mozambique was considered to be a colony of Portugal, and, as such, without any political rights, although the official policy of the Crown, as early as the sixteenth century, remained assimilation, which required that the African be able to read and write, speak Portuguese, and have employment. Being a Catholic and monogamous was virtually a condition sine qua non for achieving the assimilated status, which bestowed upon the newly assimilated African all the rights, privileges, and responsibilities of a metropolitan Portuguese citizen. Even on the eve of independence, the number of assimilated Africans was negligible, hardly higher than 1 percent of the population. As a result of the nationalist movements that spread over Africa, Portugal declared Mozambique a province of Portugal in 1951.

During the nineteenth century and following Antonio de Oliveira Salazar's ascent to power as prime minister of Portugal in 1930 and the enactment of the constitution of 1933, Africans were legally divided into assimilated, or civilized, and indigenes, or noncivilized. The indigenes not only had no political rights, but they also had no rights of any kind, paid taxes, were subjected to forced labor, and could lose their land through expropriation by the colonial government, settler companies, and individual Portuguese or assimilated Africans. Therefore, while the assimilated African was relegated to second-class citizenship, the indigene was stripped of his humanity. Yet although artificially and effectively divided politically and socially, Mozambicans had one thing in common: they longed for political freedom. Political discontent was expressed through writings (e.g., poetry), the formation of associations, such as the Associacao Negrofila de Mocambique, and strikes, as happened in the docks of Lourenco Marques (now Maputo) during the 1930s and 1950s. Manifestations of discontent continued even when Mozambique was declared a province of Portugal in 1951 and all Africans assimilated or made citizens during the 1961–1964 period.

Three Mozambique liberation movements met in Dar-es-Salaam, Tanzania, in 1962, with the intended objective of uniting in a common front against the Portuguese in Mozambique, namely, the Uniao Nacional Africana de Mocambique Independente (UNAMI), founded by Mozambican exiles in Malawi in 1961; the Uniao Democratica Nacional de Mocambique (UDENAMO), founded in Rhodesia in 1960;

and the Uniao National Africana de Mocambique (MANU), created in Mombasa, Kenya, in 1961. Out of the talks emerged the Front for the Liberation of Mozambique (FRELIMO) on 25 June 1962. Several other small fronts, such as the Comite Revolucionario de Mocambique (COREMO) emerged during the 1960s, but none could rival FRELIMO, whose leadership was entrusted to Dr. Eduardo Mondlane, a U.S. educated anthropologist, with Urias Simango as vice president. The liberation war was declared on 25 September 1964.

The centralized nature of FRELIMO, made up mostly of Marxists and Leninists trained in the Soviet Union and Algeria, presaged how the front would govern if Mozambique were to become independent. A small nucleus of the so-called trained cadres (Marcelino dos Santos, the ideologue; Samora Machel, later to become the first president of Mozambique; Joaquim Chissano, named by the Central Committee as the second president of Mozambique after Machel's death in an airplane crash in 1986), and a few others made all the front's decisions. Intransigence, dogmatism, and insecurity created a persistent aura of suspicion, violence, and infighting that resulted in a number of unexplained defections from the front and the deaths of leading members such as Mondlane in 1969, Silverio Nungu, and Filipe Magaia during the 1970s.

FRELIMO expected a long war against the Portuguese government but was pleasantly surprised when the Portuguese army in Lisbon overthrew the government of Premier Marcello Caetano in April 1974 and handed over power to the front, following one year of governmental transition, on 25 June 1975. FRELIMO called the new country the Mozambique People's Republic. Without the benefit of a popular election, Machel became the president of the new Marxist republic. In 1977 FRELIMO nationalized all property and the country's resources, and abolished all private institutions. In reality, the country was ruled by a nondemocratic oligarchy, although FRELIMO called its rule democratic centralism. No parties were allowed in Mozambique, and participation in government was contingent upon one's membership in the centralizing party. The Church was persecuted, and flagrant abuses of human rights, allegedly perpetrated by the government and vigilante groups, euphemistically known as "*dinamizadores*," or "dynamizers," were documented by Amnesty International.

The establishment of a Marxist regime in the country, the purging of war veterans, the failure of the new state-owned farms, the imposition of collective villages, and the creation of reeducation camps led to widespread discontent. Helped by then (Southern) Rhodesia and, later, South Africa, the Mozambique National Resistance (RENAMO) emerged in 1977. Mozambique not only had closed its border with Rhodesia in compliance with the U.N. sanctions in 1976, but had also allowed Zimbabwean and South African nationalists to establish guerrilla bases against the two Southern African white regimes on its soil.

The war between RENAMO and FRELIMO did not end until 4 October 1992, when the two signed a peace agreement brokered by the Italian government, the Catholic Church, and the governments of Zimbabwe and Kenya. As a result of the agreement, RENAMO was recognized as a political party, in preparation for the first multiparty presidential and National Assembly elections, which were eventually scheduled for October 1994. The new constitution guaranteed all freedoms and limited presidential incumbence to three five-year terms. The name of the country was officially changed to the Republic of Mozambique, while the economy would be based on the forces of the free market rather than on the socialist or Marxist model. In addition, the rebel and the Mozambique armed forces were equally fused as one national army. To ensure fairness, both the national elections and the demobilization of the soldiers were done under UN supervision, known as the UN Operation in Mozambique (ONUMOZ). Besides FRELIMO and RENAMO, several other parties registered to participate in the elections, including the Partido Nacional Democratico, the Partido Nacional de Mocambique, and the Partido Africano de Mocambique, which formed a weak electoral coalition called the Uniao Democratica (UD).

Afonso Dhlakama, leader of RENAMO, reluctantly acknowledged and accepted the results of the elections, which gave him 33.73 percent of the vote, 53.20 percent having gone to Joaquim Chissano. In the National Assembly contest, FRELIMO garnered 129 seats to 112 for RENAMO and 9 for the UD. Out of a population of some 15 million, 6.1 million had registered to vote, of whom 80 percent actually went to the polls on 27–29 October 1994. While the relations between RENAMO and FRELIMO remained tumultuous in the period between the first and the second elections, which occurred in early December 1999, the country's masses focused on reconciliation and rebuilding their lives shattered by a war that destroyed perhaps one third of the country's infrastructure. However, the rancor between FRELIMO and the other fifteen parties was clear when the opposition boycotted the 30 June 1988 municipal elections, which attracted a voter turnout of only 14.6 percent in the twenty-three cities and ten towns selected for the experiment.

The elections of 1999, however, were the most contentious and threatened to unravel the tenuous working relations that had developed between RENAMO and FRELIMO over the previous five years. Voting was heavy in every province, and RENAMO, supported by some newspapers, had declared itself the winner in both the presidential and the National Assembly elections. Yet, the National Election Commission, which took more than two weeks to count and announce the results, fueling the speculation about attempts to "fix" the ballots in favor of the ruling party, announced that FRELIMO had won both contests. Paradoxically, the opposition, in this case RENAMO, the only other party allowed to run for the presidency, had won a majority of the votes in the country's six most populous provinces—Zambezia, Niassa, Tete, Manica, Sofala, and Nampula—while Cabo Delgado, Maputo, Inhambane, Gaza, Xai-Xai, and the city of Maputo voted for Chissano and FRELIMO. A pandemonium ensued. RENAMO refused to accept the electoral results and took the case to the Supreme Court. As expected, the Court, still working in close alliance with the state and the Electoral Commission, declared that, despite minor irregularities, the elections had been free and fair and that therefore they could not be overturned.

RENAMO threatened to transfer its headquarters to Beira (from Maputo), with the rumored ominous prospect that it might attempt to establish its own government. FRELIMO, in turn, threatened to anull the party altogether and govern the country alone. The international community, eager to see stability in the country and promote investment, sided with the ruling party and supported the claim that the elections had indeed been fair. As a result, at the beginning of February 2000, RENAMO announced that it had transferred part of its headquarters to Beira where it has some of its strongest supporting constituencies. The government stood steadfast in its threat to declare RENAMO illegal. Lawyers from both sides were deeply involved in the dispute as the new millennium advanced.

(See also DECOLONIZATION; GUERRILLA WARFARE; LUSOPHONE AFRICA; MARXISM.)

Mario J. Azevedo, *Historical Dictionary of Mozambique* (Metuchen, N.J., 1991). William Finnegan, *A Complicated War: The Harrowing of Mozambique* (Los Angeles, 1992). Daniel Jouaneau, *Le Mozambique* (Paris, 1995).

MARIO AZEVEDO

MULTICULTURALISM. The term "multiculturalism" emerged in the 1960s and 1970s in countries like Canada and Australia, and, to a lesser extent, Britain and the United States. The policy focus was often initially on schooling and the children of Asian/black/Hispanic post/neocolonial immigrants, and multiculturalism meant the extension of the school, both in terms of curriculum and as an institution, to include features such as "mother-tongue" teaching, non-Christian religions and holidays, halal food, and Asian dress. From such a starting point, the perspective can develop to meeting such cultural requirements in other or even all social spheres and the empowering of marginalized groups. In Canada and Australia, however, the focus was much wider. From the start multiculturalism included, for example, constitutional and land issues and has been about the definition of the nation. This was partly because these countries had a continuous and recent history of ethnic communities created by migration, usually from different parts of Europe; because there were unresolved legal questions to do with the entitlements and status of indigenous people in those countries; and, in the case of Canada, because there was the further issue of the rise of a nationalist and secessionist movement in French-speaking Quebec. Hence, the term "multiculturalism" in these countries came to mean, and now means throughout the English-speaking world and beyond, the political accommodation by the state and/or a dominant group of all minority cultures defined by reference to race or *ethnicity. The term is sometimes also used to encompass groups by reference to nationality, aboriginality, or religion, but as these groups tend to make larger claims, they usually resist having their claims reduced to those of immigrants.

Nevertheless, even today, both in theoretical and policy discourses, multiculturalism means different things in different places. In North America it can encompass discrete groups with territorial claims, such as the Native Peoples and the Quebecois (Kymlicka, 1995). In Europe, groups with such claims, like the Slovaks and the Scots, are thought of as nations, and multiculturalism refers to a post-immigration urban melange. While in North America, language-based ethnicity is seen as the major political challenge, in Western Europe, the conjunction of the terms "immigration" and "culture" now nearly always invokes the large, newly-settled Muslim populations. Sometimes, usually in the United States, political terms such as multiculturalism and "rainbow coalition" are meant to include all groups marked by "difference" and historic exclusion such as women and gays (Young, 1990).

The latter meaning derives from the fact that the ethnic assertiveness associated with multiculturalism has been part of a wider political current of "identity" politics which first germinated in the 1960s and which transformed the idea of equality as sameness to equality as difference. Black power, feminist, and gay pride movements challenged the ideal of equality as assimilation and contended that "a positive self-definition of group difference is in fact more liberatory" (Young, 1990, p. 157). Indeed, the attack on color-blind, culture-neutral political concepts such as equality and citizenship, with the critique that ethnicity and culture cannot be confined to some so-called private sphere but shape political and opportunity structures in all societies, is one of the most fundamental claims made by multiculturalism and the politics of difference. It is the theoretical basis for the conclusion that allegedly "neutral" liberal democracies are part of a hegemonic culture that systematically de-ethnicizes or marginalizes minorities. Hence, the claim that minority cultures, norms, and symbols have as much right as their hegemonic counterparts to state provision and to be in the public space, to be "recognized" as groups and not just as culturally neutered individuals.

The African American search for dignity has contributed much to this politics, which has shifted attention from socioeconomic disadvantage, arguably where their need is greatest. It has inadvertently promoted identities based on indigeneity, language, religion, and suppressed nationhood, none of which properly address the identity concerns of *African Americans. Nathan Glazer has indeed argued that there is no prospect of multiculturalism in the United States; the processes of assimilation are doing their work with non-European immigrants, as they have done with their European predecessors (although Spanish has emerged as a major second language in parts of the United States). The group that will not melt in, because American society lacks the determination to combat racism, are not the bearers of new cultures but the African Americans (Glazer, 1997). In Glazer's view, "multiculturalism" in the United States means no more than "we lack the will to overcome the black-white divide."

On this reading it is no surprise that multiculturalism in the United States seems to be confined to the field of education and, uniquely, to higher education, where passion is expended on arguments about the curriculum in the humanities ("the canon"), punctilious avoidance of disrespect ("political correctness"), and anxiety about the ethnicization of student dorms ("balkanization"). Academic argument has, however, no less than popular feeling been important in the formulation of multiculturalism, with the study of colonial societies and political theory being the disciplines that have most forged the terms of analysis. The ideas of cultural difference and cultural group have historically been central to anthropology and other related disciplines focused on "primitive" and non-European societies. The arrival in the metropolitan centers of peoples studied by scholars from these disciplines has made the latter experts on migrants and their cultural needs. They also enabled critics from previously colonized societies, often themselves immigrants to the "North," to challenge the expert and other representations of the culturally subordinated. These intellectual developments have been as influenced by the collapse of Marxism as by postcolonial migrations. The failure of the economic "material base" ex-

planations of the cultural "superstructure," as the social sciences took what has been described as "the cultural turn," turning from the study of economic to cultural structures, has given birth to a series of successor or "postmodern" or postcolonial approaches under the rubric "cultural studies" (Said, 1978; Hall, 2000).

The prominence of political theory in multiculturalism is also to be partly understood in terms of the internal dynamic within the discipline. Rawls's *Theory of Justice* (1971) is the founding text in the modern revival of normative Anglo-American political theory. It promised a philosophically grounded, systematic answer to questions of distributive justice in societies, such as the contemporary United States, which were assumed to be characterized by a value *pluralism. Subsequent debate, including Rawls's reformulation of his own position, focused not on Rawls's conclusions about distribution but his assumptions about rationality and value pluralism. The generation of political theorists following Rawls thus have come to define their questions more in terms of the nature of community and minority rights than in terms of distributive justice, no less than their social theory peers defined it in terms of difference and identity rather than class conflict. In each case the intellectual framework lent itself to multiculturalism, even when the term itself was not favored.

One of the most fundamental divisions among scholars concerns the validity of "cultural groups" as a point of reference for multiculturalism. The dominant view in sociocultural studies asserts that talk of groups necessarily overlooks internal differences, including hierarchies, gender inequality, and dissent, and insists that culture is always fluid and subject to varied influences, mixtures, and change. To think otherwise is to "essentialize" groups such as blacks, Muslims, Asians, and so on. Political theorists, on the other hand, continue to think of cultural groups as sociopolitical actors who may bear rights and have needs that need to be institutionally accommodated. This approach challenges the view of culture as intrinsically hybridic and primarily expressive by putting moral communities at the center of a definition of "culture" (Parekh, 2000). Empirical studies in Britain suggest that both these views have some substance. While many young people, from majority and minority backgrounds, do not wish to be defined by a singular ethnicity but wish to actively mix and share several heritages, there is simultaneously development of distinct communities, usually ethno-religious and sometimes seeking corporate representation. The emergence of religious, most specifically, Muslim political mobilization has led some to argue that religion is a feature of plural societies that is uniquely legitimate to confine to the private sphere.

Multiculturalism has had a much less popular reception in mainland Europe. Its prospect has sometimes led to extreme nationalist parties winning control of some towns and cities, a significant share of the national poll, and sometimes even a share in the national government, as in the case of the Freedom Party in Austria. Anti-multiculturalism is, however, not confined to extremist parties, nor even to those of the Right. In France, where intellectual objections to multiculturalism have been most developed, multiculturalism is opposed across the political spectrum, for it is thought to be incompatible with a conception of a "transcendent" or "universal" citizenship which demands that all "particular" identities, such as those of race, ethnicity, and gender, which promote part of the republic against the good of the whole, be confined to private life. The implosion of Yugoslavia, with its "ethnic cleansing," marks the most extreme reaction to multinational statehood and plural societies and the political status of historic minorities, including the Roma (gypsies), remains conflictual thoroughout the territories of the former Austro-Hungarian, Ottoman, and Russian empires. Many post-colonized states in Asia and Africa are experiencing ethnonationalist and seccessionist movements, and some, such as India, Malaysia, and Indonesia, are also struggling with nonterritorial multiculturalism.

The political accommodation of ethnic or national minorities, then, is a major contemporary phenomenon across the world, filling some of the space that accommodation of the working classes occupied during most of the twentieth century. Viewed this way, multiculturalism constitutes powerful, if diverse, intellectual challenges in several parts of the humanities and social sciences, with profound political ramifications.

(See also CLASS AND POLITICS; GAY AND LESBIAN POLITICS; GENDER AND POLITICS; INEQUALITIES; INTERNATIONAL MIGRATION; NATIONALISM; RACE AND RACISM; RELIGION AND POLITICS.)

E. Said, *Orientalism* (London, 1978). I. M. Young, *Justice and the Politics of Difference* (Princeton, N.J., 1990). W. Kymlicka, *Multicultural Citizenship: A Liberal Theory of Minority Rights* (Oxford, 1995). N. Glazer, *We Are All Multiculturalists Now* (Cambridge, Mass., 1997). S. Hall, "The Multi-cultural Question" in B. Hesse, ed., *Un-Settled Multiculturalisms* (London, 2000). B. Parekh, *Rethinking Multiculturalism: Cultural Diversity and Political Theory* (Cambridge, Mass., 2000).

TARIQ MODOOD

MULTINATIONAL CORPORATIONS. The multinational corporation (MNC) exists to shift resources globally in an efficient manner consistent with creating value and maximizing wealth for its owners. The central economic concerns of nation-states are to create full employment and an equitable distribution of wealth for its citizens. These institutional goals are sometimes in concert and sometimes in conflict. When corporations shift resources into a nation-state the attendant impact may include the growth of employment and the growth of the middle class. However, outflow of resources will most often result in just the opposite outcome. Corporate shifts in resources are also related to issues as significant and diverse as environmental protection, industrial and scientific innovation, global distributions of wealth, state autonomy, corporate autonomy, national development, regional integration, *globalization, and even campaign financing. In order to compete for these resources within the global market in the last decade, states have often offered free rein and numerous incentives to multinationals. Critics who see these initiatives as working to benefit MNCs at the expense of the national interest and some constituent populations have referred to growing corporate influence as the "dark side" of globalization.

In order to fully understand the domestic political tensions generated by MNCs it is useful to understand how the internationalization of a corporation through the creation of a network of affiliates creates wealth. We therefore first turn to theories dealing with trade, internalization of knowledge, the product cycle, and firm- and country-specific advantages.

When a firm decides to enter a foreign market it may do so by various means. In a world of perfect markets all international business would be done through free trade. Products would be imported and exported in accord with the efficiencies dictated by the law of comparative advantage. However, barriers to free trade and other market imperfections have resulted in the growth of MNCs. As a result, the internal markets within MNCs provide many of the efficiencies lost through impediments to free trade. The placement of an affiliate production facility in a host country eliminates any tariff burden placed by that host upon trade. Similar location advantages such as lower labor costs are obvious as well. However, the advantages associated with the internalization of MNC knowledge require clarification and discussion.

If one defines any firm-specific advantage in information, management, or technology as knowledge, knowledge is a difficult product to price. The difficulty in pricing knowledge is that it is only an intermediate and intangible product involved in the development, production, or sales of the final product. It is not exactly clear how much value it contributes to the final result. Companies also have difficulties protecting their firm-specific competencies because the knowledge that underlies the competencies cannot be sold unless the buyer has the opportunity to investigate thoroughly the value of the knowledge. However, once the buyer has made this investigation, they have received a substantial amount of the benefit without paying any of the costs. The solution to this problem is found in confining the use of this proprietary knowledge generated by the firm-specific investments to the internal market of the MNC within a network of its affiliates.

This same question of knowledge protection is also central to the product cycle of MNCs made known through the work of the late Raymond Vernon. In Vernon's early work (1971), entrepreneurs develop new products first in the home markets of MNCs in response to the needs generated by that market. Development and distribution of this new product involves a steep learning curve and careful coordination of the design, manufacturing, and marketing divisions of the firm. The product is therefore manufactured for the home market first. It is only after the product becomes established in the home market and potential or actual demand develops in foreign markets that the product is then exported. Indeed, some firms actually export limited quantities to test whether the demand in these markets will justify horizontal foreign direct investment (FDI), which refers to a company engaged in an activity setting up operations in another country to perform a similar activity. The MNC will have an initial advantage over firms that may begin production in foreign markets since some or all of the initial development costs will have been recovered. In addition, production costs will be lower in the first mover MNC as learning curves will have shortened with experience. These firm-specific advantages help MNC affiliates overcome advantages of local firms that stem from their familiarity with the culture, politics, language, and human resource practices of the host country.

It is at this stage that the knowledge question emerges in context. If the product knowledge could be licensed to a local concern, the MNC could limit risk and the cost of new production facilities. However, since the firm's product knowledge cannot be protected through licensing, this too drives the horizontal FDI solution. Eventually, the innovative product matures into a standardized product and most production moves from the country of origin to offshore sites. Since there is little issue of new learning in the mature production phase, firms already deployed in these settings remain there, or move to settings with even cheaper production costs, in order to provide the most competitive prices to consumers while also maximizing profits to the firm. This final stage of production may therefore entirely eliminate production of the product in the home market, along with most of the jobs that are related to this product.

MNCs involved in the manufacture of complex and innovative products are led to horizontal FDI because of knowledge protection and production costs. But resource locations and market forces move MNCs involved in extraction to vertical FDI, or setting up operations in another country in order to extract a raw material that is then sent to the home or a third country for processing before it is sold. Although oil and mining companies in an earlier era limited explorations to their national markets while having their governments preclude foreign firms from doing the same, modern extraction efforts have become global in scope. This is because there is only a fixed amount of oil and nonrenewable mineral resources available to these firms, and they have to be willing to extract them from any site around the world in order to deny them to their competitors. Thus MNCs will guarantee the supply of raw materials for the firm's refined finished products and the maintenance of sufficiently large volume to experience competitive economies of scale and scope. However, the competition between these few extraction companies and the economic needs of the states containing these resources have led to environmental, labor, and other issues related to extraction. Indeed, since some states have not had the financial or technological resources to extract these resources efficiently, they have relied upon corporate resources to extract oil or minerals so that they could advance their own revenues. As a result, states are sometimes lax in regulating the MNCs in order to secure their favors. Indeed, in many instances in both production and in resource extraction, states have been accused of a "race to the bottom" in providing MNCs with profitable conditions at the expense of environmental, labor, and revenue enhancing policies.

The ongoing tension between state interests and corporate interests may be seen not only from the concerns of labor and environmental activists in dealing with this "race to the bottom," but also in terms of corporate arrangements that may diminish in value after foreign investment has been in place for some time. What Vernon referred to as the "obsolescing bargain" is marked by a shift in the bargaining positions of governments and foreign firms after the foreign investor has been fully committed through the investment of considerable time and money. The benefits derived from foreign investment itself can change the economic landscape by providing new capital, international standards, and information to increasingly informed domestic elites. These new entrepreneurs, often with ties to government officials, may then be equipped to take over the management of the foreign concern. Foreign-owned utilities like phone companies and power plants, which may well become monopolies, seem onerous to state authorities precisely because of their strategic centrality and their corporate insulation from direct government control. In such situations, corporate needs for rate in-

creases, since they are carried directly to the consumer, are gauged by the state by standards of mass political acceptability rather than by standards of legitimate corporate expenses. MNCs will often accede to these political currents rather than risk their larger investment.

The conditions that marked the "obsolescing bargain" led to a wave of government-directed expropriations of U.S.- and European-based multinationals in developing countries during the 1970s. However, increasingly common policy directions toward *privatization of government corporations in the 1980s, and the fall of communism, have reduced threats of government-led expropriations. In addition, the deregulation of international investment capital in the 1990s offered foreign corporations some additional bargaining credibility in any counterthreat of relocating their resources. Since host governments would regret the loss of revenue, corporate officers would prefer not to absorb substantial moving costs, and international shareholders could become averse to funding corporations with serial political liabilities, MNCs have shown increased awareness of the need to appear as benign corporate citizens in their host countries.

The two-edged manner in which the deregulation of global capital has come to offer MNCs additional locational mobility while also serving as a check on corporate business practices brings us to the matter of regulating MNCs in the current era of globalization. This is an era marked not only by the international deregulation of finance capital and financial services, but also by markedly decreasing costs in information processing, telecommunications, and transportation. Corporations may now move beyond simple replication of their home production facilities in host countries and actually segment parts of the global production process to states with local production advantages. Thus, design and finance of a new product may come from one country, assembly from another, advertising and marketing from yet another, and local customization from several other regional sites. Software development may similarly move around the world, following the sun, as one set of developers hands off their day's work to their colleagues who are beginning their workdays at other points on the production chain. The system is therefore remarkably efficient and ordered with respect to using resources for the maximization of corporate profit. In doing so, it has also created a wide range of new facilities and employment opportunities in previously remote corners of the world. However, all of this may come with costs and contradictions in dealing with issues of income equity, social justice, environmental protection, and cultural identity. The good news is that many of those who would address these issues, including concerned *non-governmental organizations (NGOs), intergovernmental organizations (IGOs), individuals, national agencies, and even MNC corporate responsibility leaders, also have affordable access to global telecommunications and information processing. In the post–Cold War system, the economic marketplace and the marketplace of ideas are free to draw from the same well and give back to the same constituent populations.

It is notable that as the tight bipolar system of the Cold War was receding and the MNC was growing international scholars came to realize that the nation-state as the primary autonomous political actor in the *international system was giving way to a range of competing actors operating with linkages unrealized by the realist model. Theorists such as Robert Keohane and Joseph Nye (1977) realized early the meaning of new interdependencies between states. In their analysis of a state's relations to another state, the vulnerability of one state's domestic market to the other's clearly had political linkages that could extend beyond market considerations. Moreover, they found that the markets of major trading partners were becoming increasingly sensitive to the actions of others and hence interdependent at a level previously unknown. Similarly, various substate interests including coalitions of NGOs, like-minded bureaucratic colleagues across states, and similarly minded domestic political interest groups facilitated these interdependencies. Robert Rothstein's work of about the same period (1979) focuses upon regulatory regimes drawn from state or substate interests that, while very effective, really came to exist outside of the usual diplomatic alliance conventions or intergovernmental organization apparatus. The much later work of James Rosenau (1990), which arrived on the scene at the very beginning of globalization, also took note of the spontaneous and diverse coalitions he called "cascades" that formed around issues in the face of international turmoil and increasing political openness. The theme of coalitions of diverse international actors forming in order to resolve far-reaching global issues has been one that has grown with the rise of new international actors and with the changes that have given rise to the political economy of globalization.

The current environment of the MNC in the era of globalization is thus one of emergent alliances and coalitions across a broad array of actors. Firms may well need to form alliances with other firms because of the rising development costs of new technologies or because of the increasingly global scale and scope of their business. Government leaders or bureaucracies may set aside regulatory efforts in order to encourage investment or, conversely, form coalitions with NGOs, IGOs, domestic constituencies, international labor, or even progressive segments of international capital to impose and diffuse regulatory regimes in the public interest. These policy coalitions addressing so-called "dark side" issues of globalization may also be initiated by any of the grass-roots members of these coalitions. The main thing is that coalitions addressing issues of unequal distribution, job training, the environment, and other potential evils now have the electronic resources to coalesce, organize, and advance their interests. If this seems to be a reformulation of democratic pluralism in the global market this should hardly be surprising. The major authors of the General Agreement on Tariffs and Trade (GATT) and the Bretton Woods agreements that gave rise to the current international economic structure were deeply committed to notions of pluralism. They sought to guarantee fairness through regulation from above via a series of international efforts. One such effort, the International Trade Organization, which contained provisions for regulating the prices of commodities, preserving the autonomy of developing country governments, and providing for international adjudication of complaints against firms, was defeated by corporate interests. Only the GATT provisions emerged from these efforts. Subsequent efforts in the UN, in regions, in industries, and in bilateral agreements have yielded relatively little fruit, but have at least addressed issues of labor conditions in the apparel industry, corporate taxes in multiple jurisdictions, opening the banking and telecommunications industries, and increasing transparency in corporate accounting practices.

While many of these top-down agreements addressed mass-based interests, even more seemed directed to improving the growth and access of corporate interests around the world. It would appear to be up to the coalitions from below to address more mass-based issues and help to codify and implement such policy measures within the UN, the European Union, and other international organizations with regulatory machinery.

(See also DEVELOPMENT AND UNDERDEVELOPMENT; ENVIRONMENTALISM; EQUALITY AND INEQUALITY; FINANCE, INTERNATIONAL; INFORMATION TECHNOLOGY; WORLD TRADE ORGANIZATION.)

Raymond Vernon, *Sovereignty at Bay: The Multinational Spread of U.S. Enterprises* (New York, 1971). Robert O. Keohane and Joseph S. Nye, *Power and Interdependence* (Boston, 1977). Robert L. Rothstein, *Global Bargaining: UNCTAD and the Quest for a New International Economic Order* (Princeton, N.J., 1979). Alan M. Rugman, Donald J. Lecraw, and Laurence D. Booth, *International Business* (New York, 1985). James N. Rosenau, *Turbulence in World Politics: A Theory of Change and Continuity* (Princeton, N.J., 1990). Raymond Vernon, *In the Hurricane's Eye: The Troubled Prospects of Multinational Enterprises* (Cambridge, Mass., 1998). Sarah Anderson and John Cavanagh with Thea Lee and the Institute for Policy Studies, *A Guide to the Global Economy* (New York, 1999). Thomas L. Friedman, *The Lexus and the Olive Tree* (New York, 1999). Aseem Prakesh and Jeffrey Hart, eds., *Globalization and Governance* (London, 1999).

LAWRENCE C. KATZENSTEIN
STEFANIE LENWAY

MUNICH CONFERENCE. See WORLD WAR II.

MUSSOLINI, Benito. The founder and leader of Italian *fascism and the first successful European fascist dictator, Benito Mussolini served as prime minister of *Italy from 1922 to 1943. Mussolini (born in Predappio, 29 July 1883) was from the Romagna, a region known for its political radicalism. His father was an anticlerical, Socialist blacksmith, his mother a schoolteacher. Pugnacious, restless, and surly, the young Mussolini obtained a certificate as an elementary school teacher in 1902 and then spent nearly a decade as an itinerant teacher, journalist, and Socialist agitator in Switzerland, Austria, and Italy. In 1910 he began living with Rachele Guidi, whom he married in 1915; she bore him five children. The oldest daughter, Edda, eventually married Galeazzo Ciano, who became Mussolini's foreign minister in 1936.

The future Duce (Leader) of fascism and reviver of Italy's colonial ambitions began his political career as a revolutionary Socialist opposed to Italy's colonial war against Libya in 1911. His first major opportunity as a radical politician and journalist came in 1912 when he was appointed editor of the Partito Socialista Italiano newspaper *Avanti*. When *World War I broke out, at first he advocated neutrality for Italy, then reversed himself and called for intervention on the Entente side. For this the party expelled him, and in November 1914 he launched his own newspaper, *Il Popolo d'Italia*, which later became the organ of the Fascist movement. He served briefly in the army until he was wounded in 1917.

On 23 March 1919, in Milan, Mussolini and a politically heterogenous collection of war veterans and radicals founded the revolutionary, nationalist Fasci di Combattimento ("Fighting Leagues"). In the 1919 national elections the Fascists did poorly. Mussolini capitalized on middle-class fears of a socialist revolution during the "Red Biennium" (1919–1920) and on the struggle of big landowners and industrialists in the Po Valley to beat back resurgent socialist labor organizations. This latter conflict spawned the notorious Blackshirt squads that carried on province-wide civil wars against socialists, communists, liberals, and Catholics. Mussolini's great triumph—a sign of his formidable political skills—came in October 1922. Backed by nothing more than his unruly, poorly armed Blackshirts, he threatened to "march on Rome." His bluff worked, and King Victor Emmanuel III invited Mussolini to form a coalition government (28 October 1922). Fascist violence, however, continued. Public outrage in 1924 over the murder of Socialist deputy Giacomo Matteotti by Blackshirt thugs nearly toppled the Fascist government. Mussolini counterattacked and declared a dictatorship in January 1925.

Mussolini had no clearly defined program. In practice, he continued many projects and policies initiated by his Liberal predecessors. Despite the bombastic propaganda that accompanied them, his social programs of land reclamation, economic self-sufficiency, and population growth were largely failures. Among his most popular and enduring legacies were the 1929 Lateran Pacts with the Vatican.

Always the journalist, picturing the morning's headlines, Mussolini in the 1930s initiated an aggressive foreign policy. This included colonial expansion, with the conquest of Ethiopia (1935–1936) and the annexation of Albania (1939), and intervention on the Fascist side in the *Spanish Civil War (1936–1938). Mussolini's fatal mistake was to abandon Italy's traditional role as a balancing power between blocs and to commit himself to Nazi Germany by the Rome-Berlin Axis (1936) and the Pact of Steel (May 1939). In June 1940, with the fall of France, Mussolini, anticipating a short war, intervened on the side of his German ally in *World War II. A series of military defeats led to a no-confidence vote at a meeting of the Grand Council, the supreme Fascist decision-making body, on 25 July 1943. The following day Mussolini was deposed by the king and placed under arrest. He was rescued by the Germans, and in October 1943 was placed in charge of the puppet Italian Social Republic, headquartered at Salò on Lake Garda, until the German collapse in April 1945. Then, with his mistress, Claretta Petacci, the aging and beaten dictator attempted to flee into Switzerland. Italian partisans captured the couple, who were summarily executed on 28 April at Giulino di Mezzegra near Lake Como. The bodies were strung up by the heels and exposed to the public in Milan's Piazzale Loreto.

Within the Italian political tradition, Mussolini's regime was unprecedented for its violence, its repression of civil liberties, and its aspirations to create a totalitarian state. Nevertheless, Mussolini's regime also recalled a long tradition of Machiavellian princes and petty tyrants, as well as the chain of powerful prime ministers, from Camillo Cavour and Francesco Crispi to Giovanni Giolitti, who ruled Liberal Italy.

Mussolini's regime has often been dismissed as a superficial one that left relatively few marks on Italian political life. Since the fall of fascism, Italy has unquestionably developed a strong democratic political system with a new constitution, a multiparty system, women's suffrage, and strong safeguards against political centralizaion. Nevertheless, aspects of Fascist legislation, including the Lateran Pacts, were incorporated wholesale into the Italian constitution of 1948. Traces of the corporativist (or corporatist) state are evident in the national structure of the Italian labor movement, in provisions regarding nationwide collective bargaining. Other influences include the persistence of state-owned and state-controlled public and semipublic enterprises like the Istituto per la Ricostruzione Industriale (IRI).

On the international level, until he fell under *Hitler's shadow in the late 1930s, Mussolini represented the prototype of the successful fascist dictator. The Duce was probably more typical of the classical fascism of the 1920s and 1930s than were Hitler and Nazism. In a world still reeling from the revolutionary effects of World War I, Mussolini appealed as a strong leader with an air of quasi-military efficiency about him, a man who could make the trains run on time even in a backward nation such as Italy. His slogans and programs appeared to offer a middle way between the extremes of communism and a discredited liberal capitalism. Aspects of the corporativist state were imitated in Spain and elsewhere. His theatrical oratorical style served as a model to aspiring politicians ranging from Argentina's Juan *Perón to Egypt's Anwar *Sadat.

(See also AUTHORITARIANISM; CORPORATISM; TOTALITARIANISM; VATICAN CITY STATE.)

Ivone Kirkpatrick, *Mussolini* (New York, 1964). Renzo De Felice, *Mussolini*, 7 vols. to date (Turin, 1965–). Denis Mack Smith, *Mussolini* (New York, 1982).

CLAUDIO G. SEGRÈ

MYANMAR [BURMA]. A junta, the State Peace and Development Council (SPDC), replaced the State Law and Order Restoration Council (SLORC) on 15 November 1997. A faction of retired field commanders from the narcotics-growing regions were shunted into an advisory group, but little else changed. The SPDC replaced retiring General Than Shwe with General Maung Aye, but retained navy and air force generals as well as the intelligence chief, Lt. General Khin Nyunt, and a dozen other senior officers. The SPDC bases its authority on the 1974 constitution written to serve General Ne Win, who managed the government after his 1962 coup through an ersatz socialist democracy until he resigned in June 1988 as the bloody democracy uprising gathered strength. Economic privatization modeled on the Chinese experience has since become official policy.

Myanmar is wedged between India and China, giant civilizations that have variously influenced Burma since antiquity; for example, spoken Burmese is related to a family of languages in western China, whereas the written script was introduced by monks from south India. Ethnic Burmans migrated from western China over a millennium ago and today Burma has about 50 million people, two-thirds of whom are Burmans; Shans are part of the Tai peoples in Yunnan, Thailand, and Laos; the Karen number several million and are Burma's largest indigenous minority; others include Arakanese, Kachins, Chin, Mon, Palaung, Karenni, Wa, Lisu, Lahu, Akha, and dozens of smaller tribes. They constitute three linguistic families, Tibeto-Burman, Mon-Khmer, and Tai, although today Burmese is written and spoken by most.

Minorities inhabit the hills surrounding the central plain and the delta regions of the Irrawaddy and Salween. Many Chinese and Indians live in the larger cities, and to the west, in Arakan, some 300,000 Muslims share the language and culture of Bangladesh. Perhaps 3 million Burmese, mostly Karens, Kachins, Chins, and Lisu, are Christians who accept animistic rituals like the Burmans, who are mostly Theravada Buddhists.

Parliamentary democracy was introduced by the British through local elections in the 1920s, followed by national elections the 1930s. At independence Premier U Nu was elected and remained in power until 1962, but for a two-year hiatus. Various civil-military cabinets ruled until the 1988 coup, which lost any facade of legitimacy after 1990 when the National League for Democracy (NLD) swept the election with 80 percent of the elected candidates.

That election turned on the oratory of *Aung San Suu Kyi who, after two decades abroad, had returned in 1988 to care for her dying mother. She drew the electorate together as no one had since her father's death. While he was only thirty-two when assassinated, he had already negotiated independence from Britain; more importantly, minority leaders trusted him because he promised to honor their request for political autonomy within the Union of Burma. By evoking her father's memory, Aung San Suu Kyi became an overnight political force. The junta could not ignore her and they saw her as a threat, believing that if she gained power Burma would turn into warring fiefdoms, a country splintered like Yugoslavia and Afghanistan. Her inexperience and pledge to rule nonviolently seemed quixotic to them. Burmans tend to view minorities as natural enemies, and a reverse contempt is often shared by minorities for the Burmans. Beyond ethnicity, Burma also suffered from massive bombing during World War II and decades of ideological struggle led by the Burma Communist Party (BCP) thereafter. The BCP waxed and waned until it self-destructed in 1989, victim of complicated ethnic politics, although its demise was precipitated when China stopped giving assistance.

Until the Burma Socialist Peoples Party (BSPP) collapsed, Burma's economic development was staged in four-year plans formulated by government economists and socialist politicians. Actual production statistics were always doubtful. Political development was measured by membership in parties—a million Burmese joined the Anti-Fascist People's Freedom League [AFPEL] in the 1950s; the BSPP had 1.5 million members in the 1970s. And within two years, Aung San Suu Kyi's NLD had recruited a half-million members, even after support became dangerous.

The rhetoric of free enterprise replaced socialism in the 1990s as SLORC and its SPDC successor welcomed foreign investors to exploit Burma's abundant natural resources. They charged large license and lease fees which rebuilt depleted foreign exchange reserves, acquired new military and medical supplies for the army, and stabilized their political position. SLORC encouraged joint ventures in the hospitality industry, while foreign energy corporations invested millions exploring for gas and petroleum. Also, between 1992 and 1996 the country enjoyed some tranquillity as Lt. General Khin Nyunt negotiated cease-fires with the insurgents and led the investment effort. But by the end of the decade only a natural gas pipeline into Thailand came to fruition, while tourism was far behind expectations. Most investors were waiting for resolution of Burma's political strife.

Tranquility was short-lived because of shortfalls in farm production. While goods appeared in the markets, few could afford them as floods and natural disasters struck. Ongoing human rights abuses and suppression of the NLD opposition continued and warfare with the Karen National Union and a separatist Shan army spilled into Thailand. Over 100,000 Burmese sought refuge. Sanctions by the United States and its allies further crippled Burma's economy, already disrupted by corruption and mismanagement exacerbated by the 1997 Asian currency crisis.

The narcotics trade complicates Burmese politics. By the 1980s opium had become a financial pillar for several insurgent armies as well as elements of the Burmese military. None of these profits are reported as part of Burma's national product, nor do the substantial repatriated earnings of tens of thousands of Burmese working abroad. Their work is often illegal—sex trade, narcotics, and slave labor contracts.

Burma joined the Association of Southeast Asian Nations (ASEAN) in 1997 after years of isolation. Foreign assistance, given in abundance during the democracy period of 1948–62, had declined until Chinese military and economic aid constituted the largest source of outside help. Burma suffered enormously from its isolation; it desperately needs financial, management, and technical help.

Burma's infrastructure is crumbling, the education system deteriorates, the universities were closed for most of the 1990s and reopened only in mid-2000. The people's welfare declines, despite a gloss of sparkling new buildings and highways along the tourist trail and the affluence of a military-civilian elite. The divisive ethnicity, corruption and mismanagement, the narcotics trade, and political repression are likely to cause this beautiful country's instability to continue, even if the military and the NLD reach some power-sharing accommodation.

(See also BUDDHISM; MILITARY RULE.)

Michael Aung Thwin, *Pagan: The Origins of Modern Burma* (Honolulu, 1985). Mya Than and J. L. H. Tan, eds., *Myanmar Dilemmas and Options* (Singapore, 1990). Aung San Suu Kyi, *Freedom from Fear* (New York and London, 1991).

JOHN H. BADGLEY

N

NAFTA. The North American Free Trade Agreement (NAFTA) committed the United States, Mexico, and Canada to eliminate tariffs and other barriers to the free flow of goods, services, and capital. It imposed strict and sweeping disciplines on policies in areas such as investment, protection of intellectual property, and financial services, and it created mechanisms for resolving disputes between the signatory states as well as between states and private investors. NAFTA was designed to limit the ability of the public sector to regulate or control private firms. For example, a key principle of the NAFTA is national treatment: all foreign firms must be accorded the same treatment as national firms.

NAFTA deepens the preexisting Canada–United States Free Trade Agreement (FTA), implemented in 1989. The initiative came from President Carlos Salinas de Gortari (1988–1994) of Mexico, who sought to consolidate sweeping domestic economic reforms and ensure that Mexico remained a strategically important location for investment by firms seeking to enhance their international competitiveness in a globalized marketplace. U.S. President George *Bush (1988–1992) welcomed Salinas's initiative and pursued negotiations in order to lock in Mexico's market-friendly reforms, as well as to apply pressure on countries involved in negotiating the Uruguay Round of GATT. Canada initially wavered over whether to join NAFTA, but Prime Minister Brian Mulroney (1984–1993) decided to participate in the talks in order to ensure no erosion of Canadian preferential access to the U.S. market.

The main text of NAFTA was negotiated over a period of fourteen months between June 1991 and August 1992. Subsequently, following the electoral defeat of the Republicans and the election of Bill *Clinton, supplemental accords on labor and the environment were negotiated between February and August 1993. In November 1993, the deal was ratified by the U.S. Congress and became law on 1 January 1994.

The NAFTA negotiations brought together countries of different sizes, levels of development, and domestic institutions. Although asymmetries of power and wealth among the three nations did not inhibit the negotiation of a formal accord, these differences critically shaped the process and outcome. The United States was able to use the promise of access to its large and wealthy market to extract concessions from Mexico that would have been unimaginable only a few years earlier, when Mexico was promoting domestic industries with highly protective tariffs and subsidies. Mexico was, however, willing to undertake, unilaterally, many of the concessions it offered in the course of the negotiations because, under President Salinas, Mexico had shifted away from protectionism and state intervention to a model of growth based on open markets and a reduced role of the state. Canadian negotiators, having already concluded an FTA with the United States, had an attractive alternative to NAFTA, and they stubbornly refused to make concessions that would leave Canada, in their judgment, worse off than under the FTA.

Mexico's highly centralized and vertical political system, and its lack of checks and balances, made it harder for Mexican negotiators to resist U.S. demands by pointing to domestic constraints, which is a well-established bargaining technique used by U.S. negotiators. Although Mexico developed a mechanism for consultation with the private sector, domestic lobbies were less well institutionalized in Mexico. By contrast, the U.S. negotiators resisted any changes demanded by Mexico or Canada that would require bringing NAFTA before hostile committees in the House of Representatives or Senate, or that would provoke the opposition of domestic regulators; they also insisted that the demands of domestic lobbies be met so that a supportive coalition could be built to lobby for congressional ratification to NAFTA. The agreement provides a compelling example of how divided government can be a bargaining asset in international negotiations.

NAFTA benefits corporations seeking to rationalize production on a continental scale. For auto producers it eliminates tariffs, domestic content, and trade balancing requirements. It gives Mexico generous quotas in textiles in return for rules of origin that protect U.S. producers. Even agriculture is liberalized across the board over a period of fifteen years. In financial services, U.S. banks can establish 100 percent foreign-owned subsidiaries in Mexico, and over time they are allowed to buy increasing shares of Mexican financial operations. Dispute resolution panels, created in the FTA to review antidumping actions and ensure they are consistent with national law, are extended to Mexico under NAFTA. A dramatic, and controversial, innovation is in the investment chapter where private firms can directly challenge governments in court when their policies violate the principles of nondiscrimination and national treatment.

(See also PROTECTION; WORLD TRADE ORGANIZATION.)

Gary Clyde Hufbauer and Jeffrey J. Schott, *NAFTA: An Assessment* (Washington, D.C., 1993). Frederick W. Mayer, *Interpreting NAFTA: The Science and Art of Political Analysis* (New York, 1998). Carol Wise, ed., *The Post-NAFTA Political Economy: Mexico and the Western Hemisphere* (University Park, Pa., 1998).

MAXWELL A. CAMERON

NAMIBIA. The southwest African territory of Namibia gained its independence on 21 March 1990, following a twenty-four-year war of liberation led by the South-West Africa People's Organization (SWAPO). Sam Nujoma, the leader of SWAPO, was inaugurated as the first president of Namibia.

The new government is a nonracial, unitary democracy with a progressive bill of rights included in its constitution. Executive power is vested in a cabinet headed by a president who is head of state and commander in chief. The president is elected by direct universal suffrage to a five-year term. Legislative authority is possessed by a seventy-two member National Assembly and a National Council consisting of two representatives from each region. An independent judiciary is headed by a Supreme Court. Women are accorded equal rights under the constitution, and capital punishment is prohibited. An ombudsman has power to investigate the government.

Germany took Namibia in 1883 following a series of treaties by F. A. E. Lüderitz. Germany's control over "South-West Africa" (SWA) was recognized by other major powers at the Berlin Conference of 1884–1885. When German authorities met violent resistance from the Namibian people, Germany responded by pursuing a genocidal campaign against the Herero and the Nama. Between 1904 and 1906, the Herero were reduced from about 70,000 to 15,000. More than half of the 20,000 Nama also were eliminated.

With World War I, Britain ordered its South African dominion to seize SWA. In 1915 this mission was achieved. In 1919, upon the termination of the war, the League of Nations set up a mandate system allowing former German colonies to be administered by mandatory states. South Africa was appointed the mandatory over SWA.

Following World War II, the UN assumed the responsibilities of the League, and a trusteeship system superseded the mandate system. South Africa was the only mandatory not to join the trusteeship system, arguing that the UN lacked the authority to supervise League mandates. South African proposals to annex SWA were rejected by the UN in 1946.

In 1966, the UN General Assembly voted to terminate South Africa's mandate for Namibia on the grounds of maladministration, and SWAPO (founded in 1957 as the Ovamboland People's Congress) began military actions against South African Defense Forces in Namibia.

In June 1971, the *International Court of Justice ruled that South Africa's continued occupation of Namibia was a violation of *international law. Members of the UN also were obligated to refrain from any acts supporting South Africa's administration in the territory.

In January 1988, the United States began negotiations with Angola and Cuba to implement a "linkage" policy that tied Namibian independence to the removal of Cuban troops from Angola. South Africa agreed in March 1988 to join these talks. In May 1988, South Africa suffered a major military defeat at Cuito Cuanavale, Angola, at the combined hands of Cuba, Angola, and SWAPO. South Africa agreed to a formal ceasefire on 8 August. On 22 December 1988 a formal treaty was signed by South Africa, Angola, and Cuba at UN headquarters, providing for independence elections in Namibia and the evacuation of all Cuban troops from Angola by July 1991.

The UN Transitional Assistance Group (UNTAG) assumed a supervisory presence in Namibia on 1 April 1989, and began repatriating over 40,000 Namibian exiles. Independence elections were held from 6 to 11 November 1989. SWAPO won the election with 58 percent of the vote. The Democratic Turnhalle Alliance (DTA) received 27 percent, and eight other parties shared the remainder of the vote. Support for SWAPO was broad-based, but was especially solid in the northern war zones. The DTA had a strong showing among whites, Hereros, Bushmen, and other groups that had collaborated with South African authorities.

Namibia is an expansive country (318,261 sq. mi.; 824,292 sq. km.), about twice the size of California, but possessing a population of only about 1.7 million. Most of the infrastructure of the country is sandwiched between the Namib Desert along the Atlantic coast and the Kalahari Desert, which straddles the Botswana border. Windhoek is the capital and largest city with a population of about 130,000. Walvis Bay, Namibia's principal port, possesses a population in excess of 20,000.

Namibia is a relatively prosperous country, possessing a GDP per capita income of US$3,700. It is among the top twenty mining countries in the world; mining accounts for the largest part of the GDP and earns about 75 percent of total export revenue. The most important mines are the diamond concerns at Oranjemund, considered the richest gem diamond source in the world. These mines are controlled by Namdeb, a partnership between De Beers and the government. The Rossing uranium mine is one of the largest uranium mines in the world. The Tsumeb base metal mine, once Africa's largest producer of lead and zinc, has been nearly depleted, and operations were placed in provisional liquidation in 1998. Namibia also possesses a rich offshore fishing industry and a karakul fur industry.

Although SWAPO had professed socialist goals as a liberation movement, the newly independent government has administered a mixed economy and did not nationalize mines or other major sectors of the economy. The country is economically dependent on South Africa and is a member of the South African Customs Union. The Namibian dollar is the official currency. Namibia is a member of the *Southern African Development Community (SADC), which fosters regional economic cooperation. Namibia joined other SADC states in contributing troops in 1998 to assist the Democratic Republic of Congo in fending off a rebellion aimed at toppling that government.

Namibia established close relations with South Africa following the latter country's transition to a multi-racial democracy in 1994. The Trans-Kalahari Highway, linking Namibia with the Witwatersrand area of South Africa, was completed in 1998. The Trans-Caprivi Highway promises to facilitate closer relations with Zambia and Zimbabwe.

Relations with Botswana have been tenuous due to a boundary dispute over islands in the Chobe River. The World Court ruled in December 1999 that these islands belonged to Botswana. Namibia also expressed concerns when Botswana harbored Caprivi refugees following a failed secessionist attempt in 1999.

Subsequent elections in December 1999 increased SWAPO's representation in the National Assembly to 76 percent. While peace and stability have come to Namibia, state debt has continued to grow. Taxation on personal and corporate income increased in the late 1990s, as did the general sales tax on goods. Namibia's free press has criticized the government for corruption and maladministration. The Namibian constitution required that the president retire following the completion of his second term in 2000, but Sam Nujoma was elected to a third term with 77 percent of the vote.

(See also SOUTHERN AFRICA.)

Tore Linne Eriksen, *The Political Economy of Namibia: An Annotated, Critical Bibliography* (Oslo, 1989). *The Namibian* (http://www.namibian.com.na).

ALLAN D. COOPER

NASSER, Gamal Abdel. Born 15 January 1918 in the upper Egyptian village of Bani Murr, Gamal Abdel Nasser (Jamāl ʿAbd al-Nāʿsir) was educated mainly in Alexandria and Cairo. His father was a postal clerk. In November 1935, while a student at Cairo's al-Nahda School, known for its nationalist activism, Nasser was wounded by British soldiers during a demonstration demanding restoration of the constitution. He subsequently flirted with many political organizations and ideologies without committing himself fully to any of them, although he briefly joined the quasi-fascist Young Egypt.

In March 1937, Nasser enrolled in the Military Academy, opened to middle-class boys as a result of the Anglo-Egyptian treaty of 1936. There, and at his first posting in upper Egypt, he made friends with ʿAbd al-Hakim ʿAmir, Zakariya Muhyi al-Din, and Anwar* Sadat—all future leaders of the Free Officers organization. Like many of Egypt's educated youths, these young officers had been radicalized by the failure of the leading nationalist party, the Wafd, to end the British military occupation of Egypt, and they were dismayed by Egypt's ineffective parliamentary democracy and its weak response to Egypt's economic and political crisis. Nasser and the others were particularly offended when British tanks surrounded ʿAbdin Palace on 4 February 1942 and forced King Faruq to install a Wafd government.

In 1943, Nasser became an instructor in the Military Academy, a post that enabled him to make contacts with future officers. Later, while commanding a battalion in the Arab-Israeli War of 1948–1949, his unit was encircled and besieged at Faluja. Like other nationalist officers serving on the same front, Nasser viewed this experience as a metaphor for Egypt's corrupt and inequitable internal regime, which he saw as the fundamental cause for the defeat. He was outraged by the lack of an adequate military plan, the political manipulation of the army by the palace, and reports that members of King Faruq's entourage had sold faulty weapons to the army.

Because the civilian nationalist opposition was too weak and disunited to take action, Nasser recruited discontented junior officers into the Free Officers organization—a disciplined and cohesive group that set as its goal the overthrow of the regime. The officers had only a vague program of national reform, influenced by the demands for social justice adopted by the post–World War II nationalist movement. On 23 July 1952 they executed a nearly bloodless coup and formed a Revolutionary Command Council (RCC) headed by General Muhammad Naguib. Three days later they deposed King Faruq.

On 9 September 1952 the RCC proclaimed a *land reform that limited agricultural holdings, regulated rents, and promised to distribute land to poor peasants. The economic goals of the land reform—stimulating industrial development and providing land for the landless—were incompletely realized, but it symbolized a break with the old regime and curtailed the power of its dominant class, the large cotton growers allied with the monarchy and the British. The RCC also raised the minimum wage, encouraged the formation of trade unions, and enhanced job security, though it also imposed corporatist control over the labor movement and prevented independent political action by workers. In 1953 the regime banned the old political parties and abolished the monarchy.

Though it dismantled parliamentary democracy and limited political expression, the military regime won genuine popular support. In 1954, Nasser consolidated his personal power by eliminating Naguib from the government. He then successfully concluded a treaty with Britain in October of the same year, securing the evacuation of British troops from the Suez Canal Zone by June 1956. The popularity of the new regime—due in no small measure to Nasser's political style and personal charisma, which made common people feel they had a stake in politics—extended beyond Egypt to the entire Arab world.

Nasser became a symbol of independence and resistance to European colonialism and *imperialism. He assumed leadership of the pan-Arab national movement and achieved international prominence as a pioneer in the *nonaligned movement of Asian and African states. His dramatic *nationalization of the Suez Canal on 23 July 1956, his support for Palestinian grievances against Israel, and his acquisition of arms from Czechoslovakia led to the *Suez Crisis. On 29 October 1956 Britain, France, and Israel attacked Egypt and sought to overthrow his regime. Despite Egypt's military defeat, the attackers were forced to withdraw and Nasser emerged a hero. The war prompted the regime to nationalize all enterprises owned by foreign nationals in Egypt, a precursor to more extensive nationalizations in 1961 and 1962, as well as other populist redistributive economic measures known as Arab socialism.

Nasser's rhetoric intensified as his pan-Arab commitments increased after 1956, yet he avoided military confrontations with Israel. In May 1967, Syrian criticism of his passive response to Israeli raids on Syria and Jordan convinced Nasser to mobilize his army and blockade the Straits of Tiran. In response, Israel launched a preemptive strike and devastatingly defeated Egypt, Syria, and Jordan. Nasser resigned in the face of the defeat, but millions of Egyptians came out into the streets and persuaded him to stay on.

Nasser died on 28 September 1970. At his death, Israel still occupied Egyptian territory captured in the June War of 1967, and a deepening crisis gripped the economy. Military and economic failure described the limits of Nasser's efforts to assert Egyptian independence and highlighted the undemocratic aspects of his regime, which had become increasingly repressive in the late 1960s.

(See also ARAB-ISRAELI CONFLICT; ARAB NATIONALISM; MILITARY RULE; NASSERISM.)

Jean Lacouture, *Nasser* (New York, 1973). P. J. Vatikiotis, *Nasser and His Generation* (London, 1978). Joel Gordon, *Nasser's Blessed Movement: Egypt's Free Officers and the July Revolution* (New York, 1992).

JOEL BEININ

NASSERISM. A radical nationalist political movement, Nasserism is associated with the regime of Egyptian President Gamal Abdel *Nasser (1952–1970). Nasserists saw their movement as an anti-imperialist challenge to continuing European political and economic influence in the *Middle East in the postcolonial era and to the interests of large landholders who were regarded as obstacles to industrial development because of their collaboration with European interests. At the same time, Nasserism opposed Marxian conceptions of * class struggle and the revolutionary transformation of society. From the mid-1950s to 1967, Nasserism acquired a wide following in the Arab world as Nasser's personal charisma, militant *Arab nationalism, and skillful maneuvering between the two *Cold War great power blocs inspired enthusiastic popular support throughout the region. Nasserism has many similarities with Peronism in Latin America and with other varieties of radical, secular nationalism in the Middle East.

Nasserism was not a well-articulated philosophy developed before Nasser and the Free Officers seized power in the *coup d'état of 23 July 1952. Its two seminal texts—Nasser's *Philosophy of the Revolution* (1954) and the Egyptian National Charter (1962)—were composed after the actions they justify were substantially completed. The Free Officers had no previously existing social base of support outside the army; and despite the initial popularity of the new regime, it was undemocratic and did not tolerate collective action initiated by grass-roots activists. Its successive single parties—the Liberation Rally, the National Union, and the Arab Socialist Union—were bureaucratic, hierarchical organizations.

Nasserism gained great influence outside *Egypt because Nasser's anti-imperialist foreign policy established him as the dominant political figure in the Arab world. After signing a treaty in 1954 stipulating that the last British troops would leave Egypt by June 1956, thus ending an occupation begun in 1882, Nasser refused to join the anti-Soviet Baghdad Pact because it might have required Egypt to permit foreign troops on its soil once again. In April 1955, Nasser further angered the West by attending the Conference of Asian and African States in Bandung, Indonesia, where he emerged as a leading exponent of nonalignment and positive neutralism.

Because of Egypt's independent foreign policy orientation, the United States refused Nasser's requests to purchase arms. Egypt's ignominious defeat in the Arab-Israeli War of 1948–1949, its inability to thwart raids into its territory launched by Israel in reprisal for violations of its borders, and the regime's dependence on support of the army made military modernization an urgent matter. Hence, in September 1955, Egypt announced it would purchase weapons from Czechoslovakia. In retaliation, the United States and Britain withdrew their offers to assist in financing the construction of the Aswan High Dam—a critical economic development project. In response, on 23 July 1956, Nasser announced that Egypt would nationalize the Suez Canal and finance construction of the dam with the canal transit fees. An electrified Arab world rallied to Egypt's support.

*Nationalization of the Suez Canal and Egypt's support for the Algerian Front de Libération Nationale led Britain, France, and Israel to launch a joint attack against Egypt on 29 October 1956. The ensuing Suez-Sinai War ended in military defeat for Egypt, resulting in Israeli occupation of the Sinai Peninsula and the Gaza Strip. But Israel's withdrawal, under pressure from both the United States and the Soviet Union, gave a political victory to Nasser, who was hailed as the defiant hero of anti-*imperialism, anti-Zionism, and Arab nationalism.

Forces inspired by Nasser's actions were active in Syria, Lebanon, Jordan, Iraq, and the Arab Gulf states, although they were not politically or organizationally united. The election of a nationalist government in Jordan and the ouster of Glubb Pasha in 1956–1957, the unification of Egypt and Syria in the United Arab Republic (UAR) in 1958, the civil war in Lebanon in 1958, and the deposition of the Hashemite monarchy in Iraq in 1958 were all expressions of the radical nationalist upsurge in the Arab world that, inspired by Nasser's example, threatened pro-Western rulers and interests. However, despite the popularity of the slogan, Arab unity was not realized. Syria left the UAR following a military coup in 1961, motivated in part by opposition to the nationalization of banks and other large-scale enterprises that initiated the policies of Arab socialism.

The Ba'th Party, which also advocated Arab unity and socialism, saw itself as the natural organizational vehicle for Nasserism. But unity talks with Egypt held after the Ba'th came to power in Syria and Iraq in 1963 failed. Nasser refused to accept the ideological tutelage of the Ba'th; so despite the similarity between their views, the Ba'th and Nasser were rivals for the leadership of the radical pan-Arab movement of the 1960s.

The Movement of Arab Nationalists (MAN), a pan-Arab party founded by Palestinians after 1948 with branches in several Arab countries, looked to Nasser for leadership until the mid-1960s. The Palestinian MAN members eventually formed the Popular Front for the Liberation of Palestine and its splinter, the Democratic Front for the Liberation of Palestine—component organizations of the *Palestine Liberation Organization. The MAN branch in Aden became a key element in the National Liberation Front that expelled the British and established the People's Democratic Republic of South Yemen in 1967. Omani members launched a guerrilla war based in Dhofar province against the sultan of Oman that was crushed after the shah of Iran intervened in 1973.

Other political forces influenced by Nasser include: Kamal Junblat's Popular Socialist Party in Lebanon; the Murabitun, a Sunni militia active during the Lebanese civil war; and al-Ard, a movement of Palestinian Arab citizens of Israel in the late 1950s and early 1960s. When Muammar *Qaddafi executed his coup d'état ousting the king of Libya in 1969, he regarded Nasser as his model.

The demise of the UAR, the failure of the 1963 unity talks, Egypt's costly and indecisive intervention on the republican side in the Yemeni civil war (1962–1967), an economic crisis in Egypt beginning in 1965, and Israel's overwhelming victory in the June 1967 war diminished the mass appeal of Nasserism and other varieties of secular Arab nationalism. Many of Nasser's policies were reversed by his successor, Anwar *Sadat. His legacy in Egypt is claimed by small opposition groups—elements of the National Progressive Unionist Party and a Nasserist party.

(See also Arab-Israeli Conflict; Nonaligned Movement; Perón, Juan Domingo; Suez Crisis; Zionism.)

Malcolm Kerr, *The Arab Cold War: Gamal 'Abd al-Nasir and his Rivals*, 3d ed. (London, 1971). Jean Lacouture, *Nasser* (New York, 1973).

JOEL BEININ

NATIONAL LIBERATION MOVEMENTS. Political organizations dedicated to the pursuit of political independence from foreign domination, economic independence, social revolution in an anticapitalist direction, and a cultural revolution to remove the influence of previously dominant external forces and to substitute an indigenous culture in their place are known as national liberation movements. The concept conflates *class struggle with national identity and self-determination by embracing the notion of "the oppressed nation" present in Leninist theory.

The principal targets of these movements have been the colonial powers. Yet as the process of *decolonization has approached completion, movements struggling to remove what they perceive to be exploitative and alien regimes within sovereign states (e.g., the Sendero Luminoso in Peru or the *African National Congress in South Africa) or to detach components of a sovereign state's territory (e.g., the Eritrean People's Liberation Front in Ethiopia) from control by the center have gained prominence.

The process of national liberation may be peaceful or violent, although self-styled liberation movements tend to adopt armed struggle and *guerrilla warfare as means of attaining their objectives. Generally, these are only one part of a larger strategy for gaining power, involving the mobilization of social classes and groups previously outside national politics. This includes not only programs of political education but also the establishment of a broad array of socioeconomic and political organizations (trade unions, students' and women's organizations, and *peasant associations) tied to the liberation movement.

Although in theory such efforts expand considerably the social bases of politics, practice suggests that participation is limited in scope by the resistance of traditional populations to inclusion in politics. The substance of this participation is also limited by the hierarchical organization of liberation movements, the frequently personalistic nature of leadership, the claim of such movements to be the sole legitimate representatives of their peoples, and by their lack of tolerance toward alternative political organizations and programs. These characteristics leave little space for pluralism in the politics of opposition to colonial rule and—if these movements attain power—in the political activity of the states they rule. In this sense, despite their stated objectives, national liberation movements have tended to be vehicles for the replacement of external elites with internal ones who use their position in much the same way as their predecessors, to appropriate resources from the people they rule.

The principal focus of liberation movements is the acquisition of state power. Yet because the enemy—*imperialism—is seen in critical respects to be an international phenomenon, these movements generally also conceive themselves to be participants in a universal struggle against political and economic oppression. As such, they have sought to develop international links among themselves and with states and groups who share their interest in weakening the hold of the West over the *Third World. Their struggles, consequently, frequently became entangled in the broader global competition between the United States and the Soviet Union and the blocs these powers represented. Struggles for national liberation became important vehicles for expansion of the Soviet role in the Third World. However, the deeply nationalistic inclinations of the leaderships of these movements, the frequent disparity between their concrete national and regional interests, and the global agenda of the Soviet Union greatly constrained the Soviet capacity to build and sustain influence in this fashion. The recent deemphasis on global class struggle and universal bipolar competition in *Soviet foreign policy during the Gorbachev era, followed by the dissolution of the Soviet Union, weakened the link between struggles for national liberation and global politics.

(See also COLONIAL EMPIRES; LENINISM; NATIONALISM; REVOLUTION.)

S. NEIL MACFARLANE

NATIONALISM. See overleaf.

NATIONALIZATION. Two distinct types of government policies may be referred to by the term *nationalization*. The first is public ownership: the state's possession and control of private property, particularly in key industries. The British Labour government asserted such control in the late 1940s and early 1950s when it nationalized the coal, gas, electricity, steel, and transport industries. French Socialists pursued similar policies in the early 1980s and offered a similar rationale: greater income equality, rationalized production, and greater state control over economic *planning. In Britain, many of the same industries were reprivatized in the 1980s, under Conservative Prime Minister Margaret *Thatcher. Thatcher not only stressed the costs and inefficiency of state control (also important issues to the French Socialists, who quickly abandoned their nationalization plans after an initial foray into banking and steel), but also her opposition in principle to such public ownership, even in cases of natural monopolies.

Nationalization can also refer more specifically to the seizure of *foreign* assets and their transfer to local ownership, usually to state firms. Such indigenization policies were pursued extensively in Latin America, Africa, and the Middle East in the 1960s and 1970s. They were focused largely in raw materials and extractive industries, in countries that were highly dependent on export earnings from those industries. The most vulnerable sectors, according to Raymond Vernon, were those that had already developed standardized products and processes, but where foreign investors had not yet adapted to their weaker bargaining position with host countries. The largest expropriations came in oil exporting countries, which replaced foreign oil companies with state-owned enterprises in production and refining. Foreign firms still had significant advantages in exploration, transport, and marketing and used them to maintain a major international role. Indeed, nationalized firms have continued to rely on them for final sales and sometimes for operations and management.

Nationalization is a sharply contested political process. At stake is control over the local economy and, more broadly, control over the direction of economic development and the role of foreign capital. It has been a focal point for economic controversy between rich and poor nations throughout the twentieth century. Foreign property was nationalized after political transformations in Mexico (1917), the Soviet Union (1917), Turkey (1923), Chile (1970), and Iran (1951, 1979), among others. These new governments had widely differing ideologies, but all stressed some form of economic

(cont. on p. 579)

NATIONALISM. The history of the study of nationalism is closely intertwined with the history of its subject. When the forty-two founding members of the *League of Nations assembled in 1920, they inaugurated an era in which the nation became the only internationally legitimate *state form. The sudden appearance, out of the debris of the Habsburg, Hohenzollern, and Romanov empires, of many new nation-states in Central and Eastern Europe, all basing their sovereignties on ancient identities, immediately attracted the attention of comparative historians. It was the achievement of Carlton Hayes (New York, 1931) and Hans Kohn (New York, 1944) to show conclusively that, in spite of these claims to antiquity, nationalism was a late-eighteenth-century creation, and that exactly this *modernity was one reason for its recent spread to Asia and Africa. With different emphases, both argued that nationalism owed its origins to a *secularization of political thought generated by the Renaissance and the Enlightenment, to the egalitarian implications of *liberalism, and to the conceptions of republicanism and *citizenship popularized by the upheavals of the American and French revolutions.

After World War II the study of nationalism went into general eclipse. In Europe, nationalism seemed profoundly discredited by its association with Nazism, *fascism, and *anti-Semitism. In Eastern Europe, most of the new states of 1920 had fallen under Moscow-controlled communist regimes at least formally committed to the concept of proletarian internationalism. In a battered Western Europe under U.S. domination, institutions were being initiated that would lead to a putatively supranational *European Union. Hence, although anticolonial nationalist movements were gaining ever-greater impetus in Asia and Africa, it was tempting to regard them as signs of these regions' backwardness, and to believe that nationalism was in the process of being historically superseded in civilized Europe.

In the 1970s, however, against most expectations, an explosion of new nationalisms broke out in Western Europe—above all Scottish and Welsh in Britain, Flemish in Belgium, Breton and Corsican in France, Basque and Catalan in Spain. In the late 1970s, wars broke out between the communist regimes of China, Vietnam, and Cambodia. During the 1980s, revived nationalisms were breaking up Stalin's East European empire. At the start of the 1990s, Yugoslavia had disintegrated, and the Union of Soviet Socialist Republics had divided into an uncertain Commonwealth of Independent States, as the heterogeneous populations once "united" by tsars and Bolsheviks moved rapidly toward separate independences. Still more puzzling was the fact that while the membership of the UN continued to rise—by 1991 it had four times the membership of the League of Nations of 1921—transnational corporations and electronic communications were creating a planetary economic system more intricately unified than ever before in history.

These extraordinary developments encouraged, in the 1980s, a scarcely less extraordinary proliferation of theoretically innovative and comparative studies of nationalism. Two basic assumptions held by the pioneers of the interwar years were, from differing perspectives, generally discarded. First was the idea that, at least in any simple way, nationalism represented a "stage" in some steady evolutionary march, as suggested by both liberal and Marxist theory. For violent Basque nationalism, arising in the most advanced industrial zone of Spain, appeared exactly contemporaneous with violent Tamil nationalism in agrarian northern Ceylon. Second was the conception that nationalism was primarily an *ideology—a political and philosophical creed analogous to liberalism or conservatism—a conception that had been nourished by the writings of nineteenth-century intellectuals and politicians such as Giuseppe Mazzini, Jules Michelet, Simón Bolivar, and Sun Yat-Sen. By the 1980s, these texts had become period pieces of demonstrable intellectual shallowness.

The search for a more profound understanding of nationalism was guided by an awareness of its modernity and of its astonishingly rapid spread across the entire globe through dozens of different cultures, social orders, and political-economic systems. In this search two general tendencies have become plain, one emphasizing political and economic change, the other stressing transformations of technology and culture (or consciousness). Miroslav Hroch's meticulous, cross-national analyses (Prague, 1968; Cambridge, 1985) of the rise and development of nationalism in Central and Eastern Europe pioneered the close sociological study of the different types of regional *elites, professional groups, and economic interests that took up nationalism and led nationalist movements in three distinct, successive stages: apolitical, romantic folklorizing, propagandizing of literate publics, and organizing of mass movements. Hroch's geographical frame and sociological perspective were subsequently widened by thinkers such as Tom Nairn in *The Break-Up of Britain* (London, 1977), who tied the spread of nationalism directly to the "uneven *development" characteristic of the global onrush of industrial *capitalism. Just as weak and backward states attempted to protect themselves from external economic domination by erecting high tariffs around local industries, so groups whose interests and status were being undermined by powerful metropoles promoted nationalism among available masses in order to build political-cultural walls, behind which they could defend and enhance their power. Nationalism's putative exclusivism, its emphasis on unique cultures, literatures, histories, and languages—and its absence of intellectual depth—made it an ideal instrument for building the vertical, cross-class alliances that such threatened elites most urgently required.

At the same time, other scholars began to explore the puzzling availability of mass publics for nationalist propagandizing. Why were so many very ordinary people willing to lay down their lives for nations of whom their grandparents had never heard? Generally speaking, provisional answers came from two directions. On the one hand, Ernest Gellner (Oxford, 1983), among others, explained this new availability in terms of the dislocations caused by modern industrial society, and by the development of new, highly centralized and standardized institutions of indoctrination, some of them agencies of the state, others of the mass market. Industrialism destroyed traditional, often face-to-face, rural communities and drove millions of people into wholly strange factories and urban slums. That same industrialism imposed an immense mechanical discipline—working hours, production rates, quality controls, transportation schedules, and so forth—unintelligible for all traditional cultures. Almost simultaneously came the modern state, with its program of standardized, hierarchical public education for everyone within its reach, and the mass market in communications (first books, then newspapers, radio, and television), which together appeared to make sense of modern life and to create the illusion of vast new "citizen" communities

Gellner's somewhat functionalist approach to the appearance of nationalism did not directly explain either its emotional appeal or its attachment to a seemingly fabricated antiquity. Accordingly, other scholars, most notably Anthony Smith (especially New York, 1983; Oxford, 1986) and John Armstrong (Chapel Hill, N.C., 1982), turned to the religious, cultural, and political antecedents of nationalism—those earlier sentiments, memories, local attachments, and identities—which were, so to speak, the bricks out of which Nairn's protectionist walls were eventually to be constructed.

All these studies have their own important contributions to make to any considered understanding of what is certainly the single most powerful political force of modern times. The early work of Hayes and Kohn showed that the peculiarly limited, but conceptually egalitarian, notion of the nation could not come into existence without the intellectual overthrow of two long-standing, fundamental axioms of political life and human history. The first was that all societies were naturally ordered as hierarchies under sovereigns whose right to rule was divinely prescribed and sanctioned. The second was that human beings were, at bottom, members of vast religious collectivities, divinely directed and inspired, whose ultimate mission was to encompass the entire population of the planet. History began with the First Man, and would end with a Last Day. By the end of the eighteenth century, divine monarchy was beginning a meteoric collapse, while the territorial stretch of the great world religions had stabilized, after centuries of conflict, into something close to their present limited extents. Meanwhile, divine, cosmological time was being rapidly undermined, initially in Europe, by the new sciences of geology and astronomy, and by capitalism's mass production of chronometers and clocks, as well as dated newspapers and magazines, inaugurating the mass acceptance of what the philosopher Walter Benjamin called "homogenous, empty time." Meanwhile, space was coming to be envisioned in a wholly new way, exemplified by the mass-produced Mercatorian map, which viewed the world, as it were from God's vantage point, as a flat plane whose most important markings, first longitude and latitude, then political boundaries, were impossible to see, on the ground, in everyday experience. To these deep changes *liberalism and republicanism gave a political cast, invoking collectivities of bounded, mapped extent, and ruled by popular, no longer divine, consent.

Out of these changes emerged, between 1776 and 1830, the first substantial plurality of nation-states—not in Europe but in the Americas. The approaches of Hroch and Nairn suggest why nationalism was born first in the New World rather than the Old. Capitalism, chronometry, and shipbuilding technology had made possible, in the eighteenth century especially, the unprecedented transportation of millions of Europeans, fully aware of themselves as transoceanic migrants, to a huge, rich region thousands of miles away from Europe. Here were born Nairn's first "peripheries," Anglo-Saxon and Iberian creoles, who shared religion, language, customs, laws, and post-Renaissance worldviews with their respective metropoles, but who were devastatingly subordinated to them as mere "Americans" and "colonists." Here too were born, already in the seventeenth century, apolitical antiquarians who sought to connect Aztec Moctezuma with conquistador Cortés, Incan Atahualpa with the God-sent pirate Francisco Pizarro. After them came, as Hroch's model suggested, angry, elite political propagandists, whose life chances and worldviews were shaped by the contours of their peripheralization. Spanish or Anglo-Saxon they might in every way be, but they were barred from metropolitan careers, and confined within metropole-defined administrative units—the Thirteen Colonies, Brazil, Mexico, or Venezuela. Intensifying economic and political domination by the Bourbon monarchy in Spain and the Hanoverian in England drew creole planters, merchants, and professional elites into the propagandists' embrace. The North American slogan "no taxation without representation" expressed, in exemplary fashion, the emerging nationalist coalition. Soon after came social (and military) mobilizations made possible by the spread of the newspaper and other products of print capitalism, and by extraordinary political inventions such as José de San Martín's baptizing of Quechua-speaking Andeans as "Peruvians." By the 1820s, if not earlier, an international model of the nation-state was in place, which, over the next century and a half, spread, through print and school, all over the world.

Between roughly 1820 and 1920, the Old World became the next stage for nationalist movements. Initially, the French Revolution provided a powerful impetus in this direction, but first with Napoléon Bonaparte's assumption of an emperorship ruling most of continental Europe, and then the victory of the imperial Holy Alliance in 1815, monarchies remained the norm in Europe until the firm establishment of the Third Republic in France in 1871 in the wake of Louis Napoléon's crushing defeat by Bismarck's armies. Europe's monarchs, however, presided over realms which, built up over centuries by war and dynastic marriages, inevitably included communities speaking completely different languages and preserving widely divergent cultures and historical traditions. Close ties of royal kinship made it possible for Hohenzollerns to rule in Prussia and Romania, and Wittelsbachs in Bavaria and Greece; Queen Victoria was related to every significant royal house in Europe. Yet, at the same time, the long decline of Latin as the trans-European language of civilization had brought all monarchies to adopt one or other vernacular—English, Castilian, German—as a unifying language of administration and power.

Under these circumstances, language came to serve in Europe, in the manner the Atlantic had earlier done for the Americas, as a profoundly peripheralizing force. Intensifying this force were three intertwined agencies of change. Industrialism's uneven spread produced historically unprecedented economic inequalities and huge population movements, as well as regional and cultural disparities, within each monarchical realm. The standardization, centralization, and proliferation of the state's activities brought traditionally quite isolated, self-contained communities into far closer, and often disagreeable, contact with one another. Along with military conscription, modern education had, as Gellner acutely argued, the most profound impact. For this state-sponsored education had an almost wholly novel character. It was fully standardized, it was minutely stratified, it used a single vernacular at its higher levels, and, in a way that classical education had scarcely been, it was functionally geared to the realm's economic and workforce needs. Increasingly, people were being differentially trained for jobs rather than educated to be civilized human beings.

Most significant of all, the rapid expansion of literacy and the development of mass newspaper readerships brought new, mediated, political communities into being; for while Sicilians and Venetians might not comprehend each other's speech, they had been made capable of simultaneously reading standardized, mass-produced printed Italian. These mediated, or imagined, communities were often very large, but they were necessarily limited to those capable of direct or indirect access to each printed language, and their stretch almost never coincided with the boundaries of Europe's dynastic realms. In this fashion, printed languages, tied as they were (actually or potentially) to occupationally orientated educational systems, and to the inmost mechanisms of industrial life, became available as strong "tariff walls" behind which emerging imagined communities could hunker down for protection and advancement. (Unsurprisingly, it was therefore always the privileged "metropolitans" who came last to nationalism—Germans in Austria-Hungary, English in the United Kingdom, Turks in the Ottoman Empire.) Thanks in part to the models provided by revolutionary France and the Americas, these communities envisioned themselves as popular, and usually republican, in opposition to dynasties which had no obvious nationality and whose *legitimacy was essentially based on preindustrial notions.

For the same kinds of structural reasons, nationalisms finally emerged in an Asia and an Africa subjected in the course of the nineteenth century to European *imperialism's military power, capitalist penetration, industrial civilization, and administrative and educational modernization. Just how important this conjuncture was can be seen from the history of the most ancient of Europe's Asian colonies. By the end of the sixteenth century Spaniards already controlled most of what is today the Philippines, but Philippine nationalism only appeared three centuries later. By the mid-seventeenth century, the Dutch dominated the Indonesian archipelago, but Indonesian nationalism was born only at the start of the twentieth. Everywhere the historical timing of nationalism's birth was tightly synchronized with the appearance of vernacular newspapers, job-market education, industrial production and consumption, mass migration by railway, steamship, and motor vehicle, and the spread of clock time and Mercator space.

Yet the Asian and African nationalist movements, developing after those in the Americas and Europe, and in various ways learning from them, had their own special characteristics. As in the New World, their early languages were those of the metropole, though these languages were secondary linguae francae rather than mother-tongues. In a manner similarly reminiscent of the Americas, the movements took the administrative units, into which the caprices of rival imperialisms had bound them, as the natural territorial stretch of the nation-states they were dreaming into existence—even where, as was usually the case, these territories bore no relationship to the domains of precolonial polities. But their attachments were no longer primarily secured by the bureaucratic and geographical limits set by the imperial center on the careers of their elites. For the age of mechanical reproduction brought the logoized map of the colony into classrooms, railway stations, magazines, and proliferating government offices. On the other hand, unlike the independence movements in the Americas, they were able to take advantage, early in the twentieth century, of all those organizational means for mass mobilization (centralized political parties, trade unions, peasant leagues, women's associations, etc.) which Europe had invented in the course of the nineteenth century. They benefited, additionally, from the fact even the metropoles were increasingly defining themselves in national terms, such that a League of Empires became unthinkable, and the House of Hanover belatedly nationalized itself as House of Windsor.

While the investigations led by Hayes, Kohn, Hroch, Nairn, and Gellner signally deepened and widened understandings of the historical sociology and *political economy of nationalism, they did not really explain the passions it aroused, the sacrifices it evoked, or the sense of antiquity which it so surprisingly conjured up. In this regard, the studies of Anthony Smith, J. A. Armstrong, and an array of cultural historians and historically minded anthropologists made powerful contributions by investigating the antecedents of nationalism and the processes whereby "ethnicities" and what are now often called "identity politics" have emerged, especially in advanced industrial societies.

In its earliest manifestations in the Americas, nationalism had already shown a double face. The Declaration of Independence in 1776 made no mention of "America," Christopher Columbus, or the Pilgrim Fathers, and San Martín's Peruvianization of Incan peasants moved them into a limitless future rather than toward an immemorial past. But both invoked a kind of homeland of *patria* to which a loyalty was due on the basis of settled residence, landscape, and daily interaction: *nosotros americanos*, as Mexican patriots became accustomed to say. Contributing to this "identity" (which was both more and less than nationalism) was the proto-racist disdain of the metropoles, who often regarded the creoles as irremediably contaminated by their extra-European birth. If they did not conceal black or "Indian" ancestries, as surely many did, the very air of the American environment, its climate, flora, and fauna were felt to produce a natural and fatal degeneration. Argentina, Venezuela, Peru—it made no difference: a creole was a creole, an identity rather than a nationality. In the course of the nineteenth century, as secularization, historicism, and print civilization grew steadily more powerful, these seeds developed intertangled vines.

It is likely that secularization played the most profound role, particularly in its unwitting encouragement of self-conscious, ideological racism. The conquistadors had justified their barbarous depredations by a Christianizing mission. Pious Jesuits, devoting themselves to the spiritual care of African slaves, could still view themselves as instruments of redemption. An idea that the ultimate core of each human being was a soul—God-given, genderless, classless, raceless, ageless—still prevailed. But as the soul gradually withered away, it was replaced by a variety of intramundane essences shaped above all by racism and sexism. It still made sense to fierce Catholic, sixteenth-century Iberian rulers to convert (forcibly) their Jewish and Muslim subjects to Christianity. By the enlightened nineteenth century, however, true anti-Semitism had been born: a Jew was genetically a Jew, no matter what his or her beliefs, place of birth, gender, or political loyalty. Women were turned into "eternal woman," no longer eternal souls temporarily garbed in female flesh. From there it was but a step to the secular biologization of culture, traditions, language, and memory into excluded/exclusive "identities" for which nationalism's open-armed acceptance of "naturalization" was less and less possible.

Historicism, allied with print capitalism, made scarcely less important contributions. No better instance is afforded than the generous-minded, French nationalist historian Jules Michelet (1798–1874), who was possibly the first major European intellectual to claim to speak on behalf of the dead, precisely because they could not know what their lives really meant. In his conception, millions of "French" people (who did not know of themselves as such) had for hundreds of years labored (without understanding their mission), speaking languages which were often not French, to make possible the French Revolution and the liberation of the modern world. Confronted all over the France he knew with visible residues of ancient polities, religions, and languages, and, as a classically trained historian with access to documentary records stretching back 2,000 years, Michelet could only unify them, outside God's time, by an eternal France. Out of Michelet came the possibility of reading Peking Man as Chinese, the builders of Stonehenge as British, and the ancient Mayans as Mexicans. That this possibility soon became virtually a necessity was the result of three factors: 1) the physical presence in every zone of the world of multifarious relics of the past; 2) the immense, easily available documentation of a thousand pasts that print capitalizm brought to the huge new reading publics; 3) a new inaccessibility to those pasts caused precisely by the revolutionary transformations engendered by industrialism, secularization, and nationalism itself. In the face of a suddenly

577

remote prenationalist past, the nationalist was like the adult faced with his or her own baby photographs: the evidence seemed to imply an identity with someone unrecognizable and unremembered. Out of this forgetting/remembering came a historicized essentialism (as it were, an eternal Germanness or German "identity") first put in service to nationalism, but later fully available for the construction of "ethnicity" and "ethnic identity"—outside history. Hence, in due course, the Irish-American who lives in the United States speaks no Gaelic, knows no Irish literature, wears no Irish clothes, and plays no Irish sports, but who, with an ethnicized Catholicism at his back, feels firmly Irish.

Contemporary anthropological studies show these processes at work today in even the most remote corners of the globe. The children of illiterate tribal parents (who lived by oral folk memory, practiced subsistence agriculture or nomadic hunting, and were connected by unmediated kinship networks) are sucked into schools, put into uniforms, sent into factories, hauled into offices, and invited into cinemas. As *Marx poignantly wrote: "All that is solid melts into air"— except that the parents may still be there, and the tribal group is inscribed ethnically in the national history textbooks.

Even *communism, which in its heroic early days believed that it was historically superseding nationalism—under the banner of proletarian internationalism—found that it was up against a force too deeply rooted in modern living to be overcome. *Lenin's Soviet Union did not regard itself a national polity, and for decades it commanded the loyalty of millions living beyond its borders. But after 1945, a plethora of new communist states came into existence, nationally defined, if under various degrees of Soviet influence. In 1978–1979, the communist states of China, Vietnam, and Cambodia went militarily at each other's throats. Today, once-Communist Yugoslavia has disintegrated in bloody interethnic fighting, and the Soviet Union has ceased to exist. It seems unlikely that twenty years hence the territory now ruled by the Chinese Communist Party, heir of the Ch'ing emperors, will be united under a single *sovereignty.

It is possible, in fact, that the very way in which the early communist rulers attempted to solve "the national question" will prove to have exacerbated the contemporary crises. For they relied primarily on the secular power of communism's social doctrines and revolutionary global mission at the ideological level, and the organizational might of communist parties and their militaries and polices at the administrative-political level, while leaving, or even creating, imagined shells for latent "identity politics." Uzbekistan, Slovenia, Macedonia, and Azerbaijan, for example, remained formal units into which such states were territorially segmented, while their respective inhabitants were allowed no genuine political autonomy as such. A powerless Ukraine and an impotent Belarus even had token seats in the UN. At the same time, so-called nationalities (which one might read as "ethnic groups") were even, up to a point, encouraged to build museums, organize folk dance troupes, and publish traditional literatures, just so long as no political claims were made on such bases. But once the engine of the administered economy seized up, once trust in, and fear of, communist leaders declined, and confidence in the promised future decayed, the shells came quickly to be filled by a frustrated sense of nationalism that was often warped by forcibly ethnicized pasts. An "administrative Georgia," demarcated by Moscow and full of all kinds of peoples, including ethnicized Georgians, has become, almost in a flash, a territory from which all those unable to prove three generations of "biological" Georgian ancestors are being violently expelled. Georgians in this imagining are the polar opposite of San Martín's Peruvians.

Even in Western Europe, comparable processes seem to be at work. Witness the nervousness arising from an impending integration which, because it threatens real sovereignties, has the potential to "ethnicize" what are now still nations. Even less than the Soviet Union does a European Union correspond to the deep-rooted imaginings of nationalism. From a Georgianized Germany and a Belarusanized Britain little that is amiable can be expected. The irony of the present condition is that the world is today unified, at one level, by a capitalism more fluid and transnational than ever before, and that it is this unification that makes the republican sovereignty of the citizen nation so necessary.

See also DECOLONIZATION; EQUALITY AND INEQUALITY; ETHNICITY; RACE AND RACISM; RELIGION AND POLITICS.)

Aira Kemiläiren, *Nationalism: Problems Concerning the Word, the Concept and Classification* (Jyvaskyla, 1964). Elie Kedourie, ed., *Nationalism in Asia and Africa* (New York, 1970). Hugh Seton-Watson, *Nations and States* (Boulder, Colo., 1977). John A. Armstrong, *Nations before Nationalism* (Chapel Hill, N.C., 1982). John Breuilly, *Nationalism and the State* (Manchester, U.K., 1982). Donald Horowitz, *Ethnic Groups in Conflict* (Berkeley, Calif., 1985). Partha Chatterjee, *Nationalist Thought and the Colonial World: A Derivative Discourse* (London, 1986). Ernest Gellner, *Nations and Nationalism* (Oxford, 1986). Anthony Smith, *The Ethnic Origins of Nations* (Oxford, 1986). Homi Bhabha, ed., *Nation and Narration* (London, 1990). Eric Hobsbawm, *Nations and Nationalism since 1788* (Cambridge, U.K., 1990). Leah Greenfield, *Nationalism: Five Roads to Modernity* (Cambridge, Mass., 1992). John Hutchinson and Anthony D. Smith, eds., *Nationalism* (Oxford, 1994). Gopal Balakrishnan, ed., *Mapping the Nation* (London, 1996). Montserrat Guibernau, *Nationalisms: The Nation-State and Nationalism in the Twentieth Century* (Cambridge, U.K., 1996.

BENEDICT R. O'GORMAN ANDERSON

*nationalism and all seized some foreign assets as part of their program. Capital-exporting states not only opposed the expropriations as such, they typically regarded them as part of a broader and more objectionable socialist movement. They responded with diplomatic protests and sometimes with economic *sanctions and force (both overt and covert). Multinational firms added their own important sanctions, especially in oligopolistic industries such as oil, where producers could isolate economic nationalists from world markets.

Compensation has often been a central issue in these disputes because investors are usually offered little or no payment. Host states generally claim their rights as sovereign powers to determine what payment, if any, is due to foreign investors. Multinational firms and their home states respond by citing traditional international legal standards, which require full and immediate compensation in hard currency. This controversy reached its apex in the 1970s, when many less developed states expropriated major foreign investments with little compensation. The same states, holding a majority in the UN General Assembly, passed a series of resolutions asserting their "National Sovereignty over Natural Resources." By the late 1970s, the spread of these nationalizations had effectively changed their political meaning. Earlier, in postrevolutionary Mexico, in Ataturk's Turkey and Mossadegh's Iran, both the state and investors considered nationalization part of a wider attack on foreign capital and an assertion of socialized state control of the economy. In the 1970s, by contrast, nationalizations by member states of the *Organization of Petroleum Exporting Countries, such as those by Saudi Arabia and Venezuela, were understood by all participants as relatively narrow business disputes, fully consistent with foreign investment in other sectors.

The worst of these disputes have now subsided. One reason is that virtually all older foreign concessions in raw materials have been nationalized. Vulnerable firms, recognizing the changed environment, have abandoned their outmoded strategy of stiff political resistance, a strategy that relied on support from their home government and corporate allies. Instead, they have developed new, more flexible arrangements for working with state-owned firms, as well as a sharper concern for political risks. State-owned firms have also recognized the economic importance of sustaining these international commercial ties to ensure marketing and technological skills. Joint ventures, management contracts, and long-term trade partnerships have all proliferated, in part because they diminish the political risks of foreign investment. Moreover, new investments are typically concentrated in less vulnerable sectors, particularly manufacturing and service industries, which are difficult to operate effectively as nationalized industries. Major political goals of indigenization, such as local employment and export growth, are now likely to be pursued through regulatory policies rather than by blunt threats of expropriation.

The long debt crisis in Latin America and Africa has also changed political attitudes toward foreign investment and lessened the threat of nationalization. In the 1970s, foreign capital was readily available as loans to larger economies among the less developed countries (LDCs). After 1982, when Mexico effectively declared itself insolvent, these voluntary financial flows stopped to nearly all LDC borrowers. Facing severe balance-of-payments pressures, major debtors such as Mexico slowly reversed their long-standing policies restricting foreign ownership and actively encouraged direct investments by multinational firms. The rhetoric of sovereign rights, public ownership, and indigenous control—so prominent in the 1960s and 1970s in mobilizing nationalist support for expropriations—was largely abandoned.

(See also FINANCE, INTERNATIONAL; FORCE, USE OF; INTERNATIONAL DEBT; MULTINATIONAL CORPORATIONS; PRIVATIZATION.)

Stephen J. Kobrin, "Expropriation as an Attempt to Control Foreign Firms in LDCs: Trends from 1960 to 1979" *International Studies Quarterly* 28 (September 1984): 329–348. Charles Lipson, *Standing Guard: Protecting Foreign Capital in the Nineteenth and Twentieth Centuries* (Berkeley, Calif., 1985).

CHARLES LIPSON

NATIVE AMERICANS. When Europeans first settled in America north of the Rio Grande, the Native American (or American Indian) population, estimated at from 3 to 7 million persons, was divided into several hundred distinct, culturally diverse groups, or tribes. Indigenous political organization varied, from formalized hierarchical structures within clearly bounded groups to loose and informal associations of villages or bands.

Most European colonial powers eventually recognized Indian groups as having some degree of *sovereignty over the lands they occupied. In subsequent years, they and, later, the United States used a combination of diplomacy, purchase, guile, and warfare to force Indian nations to give up their lands. Beginning late in the eighteenth century, land dispossession usually was formalized in *treaties signed between the United States and Indian nations. These treaties typically specified not only land cessions but increasing degrees of U.S. control over tribes' external affairs and, eventually, their internal affairs as well.

Land dispossession was accompanied by a precipitous drop in aboriginal numbers owing to warfare, economic collapse, and, in particular, European-introduced diseases. By 1900, the indigenous population of what is now the lower forty-eight states had dropped below 300,000.

By then, most remaining Native Americans had been confined on reservations—lands typically unwanted by whites and reserved to the tribes by treaty, legislation, or executive agreement. A side effect of treaty making and the reservation system was the institutionalization of once relatively fluid Indian group boundaries, laying in place the political framework that has designated contemporary tribes as the primary political actors in Indian affairs.

Today these reservation lands, held in trust for tribes by the federal government, are all that remain of the original Native American land base. Indian numbers, on the other hand, have recovered dramatically. The 1990 U.S. census counted nearly 2 million Native Americans, widely distributed across the country.

At least some degree of Native American political power also has been reestablished. In 1924, Congress affirmed that Indians born within the territorial limits of the United States were citizens. While some jurisdictions opposed Indian voting well past mid-century, Indians' right to vote in federal, state, and other elections was largely secure by the 1950s. In

1934, responding to persistent reservation poverty and the communitarian and progressive ideals of some leading *New Deal figures, Congress passed the Indian Reorganization Act (IRA). Among other things, this legislation gave formal recognition to tribal governments and encouraged their formation. While the powers of these governments were severely limited, by legitimizing them and opening the political arena to them, the IRA helped initiate a long process of Native American political resurgence.

In subsequent decades, a wide assortment of Indian groups—not only tribes but pan-Indian organizations and single-issue constituencies—mobilized in pursuit of Native American political agendas, airing long-standing grievances over lands and *rights. One factor that significantly advanced this development was the gradual emergence of a politicized supratribal identity. Beginning in the 1940s, as growing numbers of Indians spent time in multitribal urban communities, reservation-based tribes came to recognize that their survival depended in part on cooperative effort. A generalized Indian identity increasingly appeared in Indian politics, representing a disposition to act not only on tribal but on supratribal terms, providing a basis for collective action on a larger scale.

At the same time, as Native Americans began to move into the mainstream of the larger society, migrating off the reservations to urban areas, and as that society made greater inroads on the reservations, new cleavages began to emerge within Indian communities. Following both cultural and class lines and overlaying aboriginal tribal differences, these cleavages complicated both tribal and supratribal politics. Nonetheless, Native Americans have managed to retain a substantial consensus over their broadest political goals, which emphasize a recurrent theme: the preservation of the politically sovereign, culturally distinct, land-based tribal communities that the original treaties guaranteed but that the United States repeatedly has tried to undermine. Much of the internal debate has had to do with the desired nature of those communities, the best ways to preserve them, and the distribution of economic and political benefits within them.

By the mid-1960s, these various factors had come together in a diffuse but growing Native American political movement directed at the reassertion of Indian control over Indian communities, lands, and lives. As the claims of the disadvantaged penetrated the political arena in these years, Indian claims were heard as well, while Indian resources—including increased education, growing organizational networks, federal funds from the War on Poverty, and a willingness to engage in confrontational political action—gave those claims political teeth. Over the next decade and a half Native Americans seized the political initiative in Indian affairs, using litigation, protests, and assertions of tribal rights and powers to reverse the pattern of the previous two centuries.

Partly in response to this activism, in 1975 Congress passed the Indian Self-Determination and Education Assistance Act, which, along with other legislation and subsequent court decisions, placed enlarged power over their own affairs in the hands of Indian nations. Since 1980, much Native American political action reflects the efforts of newly empowered tribal governments to initiate their own programs of economic and social renewal and to solidify their political gains.

Despite these gains, American Indians continue to face widespread poverty and remain subject to the will of Congress and the often-unpredictable decisions of the judicial branch. At the start of the new century, Indian nations again are struggling to protect their sovereign powers. Many of their battles are over resources and treaty-based entitlements. Non-Indian constituencies have organized to gain access to Indian-controlled resources such as water, fish, and minerals, and to limit certain tribal economic activities such as gaming, where a few Indian nations have been wildly successful. There are recurrent efforts in Congress, the courts, and the public to abrogate the treaties that form the basis of Native American–U.S. relations, to undermine tribal sovereignty, and to force Indians to integrate as individuals into the economic and political mainstream. Many Indians have chosen, on their own, just such integration: Today urban Indians significantly outnumber the reservation population. But even in the cities, most Native Americans remain fierce defenders of treaty rights, sovereignty, and the remaining land base.

Native Americans today occupy a unique political position in the United States, rooted in a treaty-based relationship that sets them apart from all other groups in American life. The preservation of that relationship and tribal sovereignty within it remains at the heart of Native American politics.

(See also ETHNICITY; NEW SOCIAL MOVEMENTS.)

Charles F. Wilkinson, *American Indians, Time, and the Law* (New Haven, Conn., 1987). Stephen Cornell, *The Return of the Native: American Indian Political Resurgence* (New York, 1988). Sharon O'Brien, *American Indian Tribal Governments* (Norman, Okla., 1989). Vine Deloria, Jr., and Clifford M. Lytle, *The Nations Within: The Past and Future of American Indian Sovereignty,* 2d ed. (New York, 1998).

STEPHEN CORNELL

NATO. See NORTH ATLANTIC TREATY ORGANIZATION.

NAURU. See PACIFIC ISLANDS.

NAZISM. See FASCISM; HITLER, ADOLF.

NEHRU, Jawaharlal. One of modern *India's great political leaders, Jawaharlal Nehru (1889–1964) was prominent during India's nationalist movement against British *colonialism, and, although he differed from Mohandas *Gandhi on important political matters, he was Gandhi's designated political heir. Nehru was president of India's premier political organization, the Congress Party, several times and was actively involved in the negotiations over independence and the partition of India. He became the first prime minister of independent India in 1947 and remained in that office until his death in 1964.

Nehru was a political leader of international standing. His main achievement was to give the Congress, India's ruling party, a modernizing coherence that helped set India on a firm path of secular *democracy and self-sufficient economic *development. The three planks of his political outlook for India were economic *planning, social *reform, and a nonaligned foreign policy.

Nehru was a self-proclaimed socialist. As an architect of Indian development, he steered India toward adopting a mixed economy with a large public sector and considerable state control of the private sector. Moreover, he favored heavy industry aimed at buttressing India's self-reliance. Although the economic impact of this strategy was mixed, there is no doubt that India during Nehru's reign achieved industrialization with considerable depth. He also attempted land redistribution with the hope of boosting India's agricultural production. Here his efforts met with little success. An overriding commitment to democracy meant a strong respect for fundamental *rights, including the right to private property, and this, in turn, often took precedence over such ambitious economic reforms as land redistribution.

Even though modern India was born amid religious strife, Nehru's strong commitment to a secular India helped India's minorities feel secure. In retrospect, it is clear that Nehru's success on this front, as on other fronts, was partial. Perhaps he assumed, too readily, that tolerance for minorities and social reform would result simply from the extension of the franchise. The result was that there remained an unbridgeable gap between his ideas and the religious and cultural aspirations of the groups in the society that he presided over, one that he could not quite overcome. Although Nehru's own example and charisma contributed to temporary political success, his death did not leave behind strong institutions to carry out his agenda.

In foreign policy, Nehru was a founder of the worldwide *Nonaligned Movement. He also laid down the basic tenets of Indian foreign policy that helped put India on the world map as a leading developing country. Nevertheless, in spite of considerable successes, he could not resolve India's border disputes with China and Pakistan. War with China in 1962 and the failure to find a lasting solution to the dispute with Pakistan over Kashmir are debits in Nehru's foreign policy record.

(See also MODERNIZATION; NATIONALISM; SOCIALISM AND SOCIAL DEMOCRACY.)

S. Gopal, *Jawaharlal Nehru: A Biography*, 3 vols. (London, 1975–1984). M. J. Akbar, *Nehru: The Making of India* (New York, 1985).

PRATAP MEHTA
ATUL KOHLI

NEPAL is a landlocked country situated between China and India. Its topography is dominated by the high mountains and hills of the Himalayas, except for a narrow area along its southern flank bordering India. This geographical orientation to the south has tied Nepal (population 21 million) to India in many respects.

Nepal's modern history has been shaped by geography, the colonial legacies of South Asia, and its own quest for national identity. That quest became intense following the conquest of Kathmandu Valley by the Gorkhali King Prithvi Narayan Shah—the founder of modern Nepal—in 1768. Taking note of Nepal's difficult geopolitical location between China and India, Prithvi Narayan advised his successors not to get too close to either one, in order to avoid domination. Internally his rule was inspired by a Hindu religious ethos and a brand of military chivalry that together would come to dominate the political culture of Nepal. A rigid caste hierarchy characterized the post-Shah political structure and social relations.

The Shah rule was supplanted by the Rana family oligarchy after a violent coup in 1846. For 104 years, the Shah kings were relegated to the background and were treated as figureheads until they were restored by a successful anti-Rana movement launched jointly by the Nepali people and the king with the support of India. The rise of monarchy in 1951, along with the declining influence of political parties, retarded the evolution of democracy. In December 1960, King Mahendra not only dismissed the elected government headed by the Nepali Congress (NC) but also ended multiparty democracy, which he denounced as divisive and antinational in character.

Masking personalized rule in the garb of a native political model, Mahendra banned all parties. Despite extensive state-sponsored efforts to make the new system workable, it proved unable to attract widespread support for the regime. As a result, all major political groups remained an active source of opposition. The changing international environment of the late 1980s was also crucial in promoting Nepal's democratic movement. The regime was isolated both internally and internationally, causing disquiet among the ruling circles. King Birendra finally announced the end of the partyless system after the movement reached its climax on 8 April 1990.

Nepal is now governed under a democratic constitution prepared by a commission over a period of three months. One of the successes of the democratic experiment has been the participation of various Communist groups that were otherwise opposed to the multiparty parliamentary system. Many powerful leftist groups had joined the democracy movement initiated by the NC and subsequently had been inducted into the interim government that was in place until the election of May 1991. The NC and the Communist Party of Nepal (Unified Marxist-Leninist) later became, respectively, the ruling and the recognized opposition parties in the 205-member House of Representatives.

Nepal has witnessed a series of coalition governments since the 1994 midterm elections. The Communists led by the CPN (UML) were given the opportunity to rule the country after the NC was unable to muster a majority in the House. The CPN (UML)'s minority Communist government was initially supported by both the Communist and non-Communist parties, including the NC, and lasted nine months until it was ousted by the combined anti-Communist opposition parties within Parliament.

The nature of party alignment varied after the collapse of the minority government. All parties in Parliament scrambled to find new partners regardless of ideology and background. The movement coalition—the NC and the CPN (UML)—joined hands with the Pancha Party, which had been formed by supporters of the former regime after the restoration of multiparty system. Power-hungry and unstable, the parties involved in making and breaking governments failed to live up to the expectations of the people. They sought to survive by any means, and political defections and party splits became a common phenomenon in democratic Nepal. Ideological differences were no barrier to entering coalition governments.

The short democratic exercise in Nepal has been characterized by both positive and negative trends. People are now better qualified to evaluate the parties and leaders and to hold them responsible when their performance lags. Widespread frustration is at the same time construed by some antidemocratic elements as a failure of the system and has encouraged them to try to reverse the process. But most Nepalese people know that absolute monarchy is no longer an alternative to democracy, nor are they prepared to support the violent movement intensified by the underground Maoist Communists. People want only efficient and accountable governance based on popular mandate.

LOK RAJ BARAL

NETHERLANDS. A stable democracy located in northwestern Europe, with 15 million people, the Netherlands is the most populous of the smaller democracies. Its location in the Rhine Delta makes the Netherlands highly dependent on trade with Germany and other members of the European Union.

Although formally a *constitutional monarchy, the dominant traits are parliamentary government and a unitary system. Except for cabinet formations, the monarch's role is largely symbolic. Cabinets are responsible to a multiparty parliament, and coalition government is the norm. The prime minister (minister president) leads but does not dominate the cabinet. Cabinet ministers are often experts in their own fields and enjoy considerable autonomy within their departments. Cities and provinces elect councils and assemblies, but mayors and provincial governors are appointed (in consultation with local leaders) by the Crown.

Elections must be held every four years. The Dutch system of *proportional representation effectively treats the entire country as a single national constituency; parties with as little as 1/150th of the national vote can secure a seat in Parliament. However, although as many as fourteen parties have been represented in the lower house (Second Chamber), the contemporary party system is dominated by four parties. Labor (PvdA), the Christian Democratic Appeal (CDA), and the Liberals (VVD) have roots in nineteenth-century class and religious divisions, while Democrats '66 (D'66) originated in protest against elite bargaining and cooperation. A fifth party, Green Left (GL), is an amalgam of smaller parties to the left of the Labor Party. Heir to social-democratic traditions, the Labor Party has tempered its earlier advocacy of a fairer distribution of wealth, knowledge, and power and defense of the welfare state with acceptance of budgetary restraints. The Christian Democratic Appeal is a centrist force formed by the 1980 merger of the Catholic and two Protestant parties: the CDA and its predecessors were represented in every cabinet from 1918 to 1994. Except on moral issues, the Liberals are on the right, generally favoring more market and less state intervention. However, the party has eschewed extreme Thatcherite positions. Democrats '66 characterizes itself as a progressive force, favoring greater popular control (for example, direct election of mayors) and a pragmatic approach to politics.

Once sharply defined by the articulation of Calvinist, Catholic, and Socialist "pillars" (cradle-to-grave networks of religious or ideologically based organizations), the class and religious base of party support is increasingly blurred. Although the Christian Democrats derive their core support from regular church attenders, the party casts its electoral appeal not in terms of religiosity but rather its ability to govern. The active cadres of the Labor Party and a portion of their electoral support come not from the working but from the middle classes. Liberals and Democrats '66 also draw support from the secular middle classes, as does Green Left.

Proportional representation and persistent multipartyism have ensured that no single party has a majority. Cabinets emerge from protracted negotiations that determine not only the composition but also the policies of the government. Forming a cabinet takes at least two to three months. Negotiations are overseen by the monarch, who may appoint one or more "informateurs" to seek out a basis for a majority government, but once established, cabinets frequently last a full four-year term. Parliamentary support is not automatic. Parliamentary parties are disciplined and cohesive but retain the freedom to criticize the government and demand changes in policy.

Cabinet and Parliament are at the apex of the policy process, but not the only actors involved in it. Governments draw on independent experts and try, not always successfully, to enlist the support of organized interests. Ministries often maintain formal and informal contacts with *interest groups, and the government meets regularly with trade unions and employers' associations, organized in the Foundation of Labor, a bipartite organization, and the Social and Economic Council (SER), a formal advisory organ made up of representatives of trade union federations, employers' associations, and independent experts appointed by the Crown. Both were intimately involved in the formulation and implementation of statutory incomes policies in the 1950s and 1960s. Although these two corporatist structures lost prestige in the 1970s, both are key arenas for discussions among trade unions, employers, and government.

Both the Social and Economic Council and Foundation of Labor lost influence when social partners were unable to conclude central wage accords in the 1970s. A 1982 Foundation of Labor agreement was a turning point: confronted with massive unemployment and a threat of renewed wage regulation, trade unions and employers agreed to reopen existing contracts and eliminate automatic wage indexation in exchange for the possible creation of part-time jobs. Although advisory and nonbinding, the 1982 agreement was followed in sectoral negotiations and provided a template for future cooperation. Nonbinding agreements facilitated the creation of part-time jobs and provided a foundation for the Dutch "economic miracle" in the 1990s. Nevertheless, the extent of cooperation should not be overstated. Agreement between trade union federations and employers' associations was difficult to achieve and was often reached only under the threat of government intervention. Nevertheless, cooperation and consensus are touted as the basis of the Dutch "model."

The margins open to Dutch policy makers are not wide: constraints come both from domestic interests and the openness of the economy. The Dutch have responded by moderating wages and endorsing European integration. One of the original six members of the European Economic Community, the Netherlands has been a strong and consistent supporter of economic and political integration. Dutch monetary policies have presaged European monetary union: the guilder has been tied to the Deutschmark since the early 1970s, and the Netherlands Bank uses its considerable autonomy to shadow German policy. Faced with growing deficits and massive unemployment, the Dutch began trimming public sector expenditures in 1982, preparing themselves for the Maastricht criteria for monetary union well before these were broached. Supporters of a wider and deeper European Union, the Dutch also favor deregulation, freer world trade, and a social Europe.

The Netherlands has been classified as a *consociational democracy, a corporatist system, and more recently as a consensual democracy. None of these labels describes the contemporary Dutch system accurately. Characterization of the Netherlands as a consociational democracy, held together by the deliberate efforts of political elites to reach compromises, stems from the segmentation of Dutch society into distinct pillars or subcultures and the apparent absence of crosscutting ties among them. Consociational interpretations overstate both the severity of conflicts and the role which political elites may have played in ameliorating them and apply only to the Netherlands between 1918 and 1967. Since then, both the scope and impact of pillarization and the extent of elite accommodation have receded. Corporatist approaches emphasize regular consultations with trade unions and employers' associations but overstate the extent to which social partners determine policy. Trade unions and employers were intimately involved in shaping and administering the income policies central to the postwar industrialization of the Netherlands, but since the 1960s there has been little agreement on key issues. Governments have been more than willing to proceed with policies opposed by either employers (the mid-1970s) or, since then, the trade unions. Of the three labels, consensual democracy is the most appropriate, but only if we take this not to mean a system characterized by consensus but rather one in which consensus is sought but not always achieved.

(See also CHRISTIAN DEMOCRACY; CORPORATISM; MAASTRICHT TREATY; SOCIALISM AND SOCIAL DEMOCRACY.)

Hans Daalder and Galen A. Irwin, eds., *Politics in the Netherlands: How Much Change?* (London, 1989). Ken Gladdish, *Governing from the Center: Politics and Policy-making in the Netherlands* (DeKalb, Ill., 1991). Jelle Visser and Anton Hemerijck, '*A Dutch Miracle': Job Growth, Welfare Reform, and Corporatism in the Netherlands* (Amsterdam, 1997).

STEVEN B. WOLINETZ

NEUTRALITY. See FORCE, USE OF.

NEW DEAL. Franklin *Roosevelt promised "a new deal for the American people" in his speech accepting the 1932 Democratic nomination for president. The phrase survived as a name for his twelve-year presidency and, more specifically, for his administration's considerable domestic achievements. Eclectic, experimental, the New Deal defies easy classification. Many of its programs were stillborn; many others were failures. But some endured and made the New Deal the single most important episode in the shaping of the United States in the twentieth century.

The "First New Deal." The domestic policies of the Roosevelt presidency passed through three distinct phases. It took office at the lowest moment of the Great Depression and moved immediately to stabilize the economy. In its first year, the administration produced a major reform of the floundering U.S. banking system (which included federal insurance of bank deposits); a new federal agency to regulate the financial markets (the Securities and Exchange Commission); an ambitious experiment in flood control and regional planning (the Tennessee Valley Authority); and a federal program to protect farmers from fluctuating crop prices (the Agricultural Adjustment Administration). All these efforts survived, in one form or another, to become enduring parts of the federal government.

Other early New Deal efforts were less lasting. Federal relief agencies—all of them explicitly temporary—funneled assistance to the nation's estimated 15–25 million unemployed. More ambitious was the National Industrial Recovery Act (NIRA). It included a guarantee to workers of the right to bargain collectively through unions and a major new public works program. But its centerpiece was the National Recovery Administration (NRA), whose mission was to create a harmonious, vaguely corporatist economic order in which capital, labor, and government would cooperate to stabilize prices, wages, and production. By 1935, when the *Supreme Court invalidated the NRA, it was already a political and economic failure.

The "Second New Deal." By the spring of 1935, the New Deal faced new demands. The Depression continued. The trade union movement, invigorated by the collective bargaining provisions of the NIRA, pressed for new *reform legislation. Dissident politicians on the *Right and the *Left attacked the administration and, some believed, threatened Roosevelt's reelection. The administration responded with a new set of initiatives, frequently labeled the "Second New Deal."

Some of the most celebrated efforts of the Second New Deal were, like many of those in 1933, ultimately transitory: a major new work relief program, the Works Progress Administration; a highly publicized assault on utilities monopolies; a dramatic (if largely symbolic) effort to raise taxes on the wealthy. But the most enduring measures were the National Labor Relations Act (NLRA; better known as the Wagner Act) and the Social Security Act. The NLRA restored the collective bargaining protections that the now-invalidated NIRA had created in 1933, but added vital new enforcement mechanisms (most importantly the National Labor Relations Board) to ensure compliance by employers. Over the next several years, it contributed to successful unionization drives in the largest American industries. The Social Security Act established the framework of the modern U.S. *welfare state. It created two important social insurance programs: old age pensions and unemployment insurance, which offered potential support to most Americans. It also offered welfare benefits to more narrowly defined "categories" of people: the handicapped, the elderly poor, and dependent children. In doing so, it established a lasting and generally invidious distinction between federal "insurance" and "welfare" (public assistance) mechanisms.

The "Third New Deal." Roosevelt's landslide reelection in 1936 emboldened him to try to consolidate his own power within the federal government with a series of efforts some historians have labeled the "Third New Deal." But despite the apparent mandate, Roosevelt's second term was much less successful than his first. He proposed to reorganize the federal bureaucracy in ways that would enhance presidential power, but the plan floundered in the face of powerful opposition from congressional conservatives who charged him with wanting to create a "dictatorship." More important, the president tried to halt the succession of defeats his programs were suffering in the Supreme Court. He asked *Congress to allow him to appoint additional justices, and thus expand the Court's membership, to shift its ideological balance in his favor. The proposal ultimately failed in Congress. Before it did, however, two of the existing justices (almost surely in response to the "court-packing" threat) began voting to uphold New Deal measures, hence creating an effective liberal majority.

The most significant policy initiative of Roosevelt's second term was his response to the serious recession that began in the fall of 1937. The new crisis was at least partially a result of a premature effort in 1937 to balance the budget by reducing federal spending on relief. In the spring of 1938, the government announced a major new drive to investigate and police monopolies, which many liberals accused of having caused the recession. Of more lasting importance, it reversed its budget decisions of the previous year and launched a $5 billion spending program whose purpose was to stimulate economic activity by increasing mass purchasing power. Never before had the government made such explicit use of its fiscal powers to stabilize the business cycle. This approach to managing the economy would soon become known as *Keynesianism and would establish a lasting, if always controversial, place in public policy. Later that year, the administration won approval for the Fair Labor Standards Act, which established a national minimum wage and set limits on hours of work. This was the last major domestic achievement of the New Deal. By early 1939, the government was beginning to turn its attention to the growing international crisis that would soon draw the United States into war and that would ultimately do what the New Deal itself was never able to accomplish: restore prosperity to the U.S. economy.

Legacies of the New Deal. The New Deal had a lasting impact on both government and politics. It contributed to the mobilization and organization of new economic groups—most notably farmers and industrial workers—who would henceforth play a major role in shaping public policy. The Roosevelt administration also established the outlines (and the limits) of the modern U.S. federal commitment to social provision. It expanded the regulatory functions of the state and, at the same time, ensured that capitalists would retain most of their traditional prerogatives. It produced a major *political realignment in party politics and a new Democratic coalition (often called the *New Deal coalition) large enough to dominate U.S. politics for nearly forty years. Not least, the Roosevelt administration also created a set of ideas, known as "New Deal *liberalism," that survived for more than a generation as the basis of reform experiments.

(See also CORPORATISM.)

Arthur M. Schlesinger, Jr., *The Age of Roosevelt*, 3 vols. (Boston, 1957–1960). William E. Leuchtenburg, *Franklin D. Roosevelt and the New Deal* (New York, 1963). Ellis Hawley, *The New Deal and the Problem of Monopoly* (Princeton, N.J., 1966). Anthony Badger, *The New Deal* (New York, 1988). Steve Fraser and Gary Gerstle, eds., *The Rise and Fall of the New Deal Order* (Princeton, N.J., 1988).

ALAN BRINKLEY

NEW LEFT. The New Left in the United States was a movement of self-understood radicals, mostly students, in the 1960s. Larger and more diffuse than any distinct organizations, it aimed to galvanize a more general radical movement. Most of the central figures were in their twenties during that decade, and were born during or just before World War II;

most of the rank and file were born after the war and were part of the so-called baby boom, which filled the expanding colleges and universities. Although the central figures began as student activists, the New Left grew into an intellectual tendency that included academics, principally in the social sciences and humanities; professionals (doctors, lawyers, social workers, etc.) who shared its concern for the rights of helpless and victimized people; and other radicals.

Two single-issue movements activated the New Left: 1) The *civil rights movement, beginning with the Montgomery bus boycott (1955–1956) and accelerating with student sit-ins and freedom rides (1960–1961), which stirred not only black students but white supporters in the North as well as the South; and 2) the movement against *nuclear weapons (1959–1963). Many of the original New Left activists were children of the Communist-dominated Old Left, and most of the others came from the homes of *New Deal liberals. Most shared the values of their parents but believed in direct action for change. They perceived the Old Left as having been fatally weakened both by *McCarthyism and Khrushchev's 1956 revelations about Stalin's crimes. They thought conventional *liberalism had been compromised by its commitment to the *Cold War. Many were stirred by the *Cuban Revolution (1958–1959) and by the cultural dissidence of the beat writers (principally Jack Kerouac and Allen Ginsberg).

Seeking intellectual coherence, student activists borrowed the term *New Left* from British intellectuals (including E. P. Thompson and Raymond Williams) who had left the Communist Party and helped form the Campaign for Nuclear Disarmament (1957). Unlike the Britons, most of the U.S. New Left were not Marxists. They disdained what the influential U.S. sociologist C. Wright Mills called "the labor metaphysic" and hoped to find other social constituencies with the social weight and commitment to transform society in an egalitarian and democratic direction. Hopeful about the prospects for radical politics under a liberal administration, they still, like the British, looked for a radical alternative to what they saw as staid or deadlocked party politics.

The foremost statement of New Left principles was the Port Huron Statement of Students for a Democratic Society (SDS), named after the town in Michigan that was the site of the group's first convention (1962). Most of the programs recommended by the Port Huron Statement and subsequent papers were staples of New Deal and social democratic traditions: the abolition of poverty, the elimination of racial segregation, the end of the Cold War, nuclear disarmament, the reform of universities in a democratic direction. But the main idea of the Port Huron Statement was "participatory democracy": direct participation in the decisions that affect people's lives. SDS insisted that anticommunism had been tainted by McCarthyism; they stood instead for anti-anticommunism.

From 1965 on, the main force that swelled the New Left was the *Vietnam War. Gathering strength, the New Left spun off a movement against the war, and in the popular mind became principally identified with that movement. SDS, which had nine chapters and some 600 members in 1963, grew to some 300 chapters and 100,000 members in 1969. National demonstrations against the war grew from 25,000 people (April 1965) to 500,000 (November 1969). As the war escalated, the New Left (or what increasingly called itself "the movement") became not only larger but more militant.

During this time, however, the core of New Left organizers came to regard themselves as more than a protest movement. They increasingly saw themselves as committed to a radical transformation with an antiauthoritarian spirit. Pragmatic, many were reluctant to call themselves "socialist" or "anarchist"; they borrowed elements from both traditions, as well as from liberalism. Toward that end, they experimented with community organizing among the poor; with projects in student-centered education; with attempts to radicalize factory workers. But their principal base was the university campuses. Best represented among elite universities in the early 1960s, their class base moved progressively downward by the early 1970s. By 1970, demonstrations against the draft, against military education, against corporate recruiters, against disciplinary rules, and in favor of ethnic studies departments took place on hundreds of campuses.

In the course of the decade, the New Left came to see itself as part of a worldwide movement of radical youth. New Left groups sprang up throughout Western Europe and Canada, usually also based on campuses, and militantly opposed to the Vietnam War—but only in the United States did the movement of ethnic minorities play such a large part in the the overall movement. In 1968, the New Left felt an affinity with Czechoslovakia's *Prague Spring, with the student revolutionaries of France and the Federal Republic of Germany, and with the radical students massacred by government troops in Mexico. By the end of the decade, however, its most intense identifications were with revolutionaries of the Third World, especially Vietnam.

By 1967, most of the New Left had moved (in the words of its own slogan) "from protest to resistance." Many, observing the massive disaffection of college-educated youth—as signaled in drug use, popular music, hippie clothing, long hair, and so forth—came to feel that a radical transformation of the society was necessary, although they had little conception of a new order. By 1968, they saw institutions from university administrations to the Democratic Party as hopelessly oppressive.

In this setting, and in the context of an intensifying war, by 1969, a significant portion of the New Left considered itself revolutionary. As a growing number of students expressed opposition to the war, SDS was torn apart by a fight between two revolutionary factions, and disappeared.

In the early 1970s and continuing throughout the decade, New Left activists pursued radical politics by other means. Some moved into the left wing of the Democratic Party and were able to achieve local influence, though not national power or organization. Some tried to apply principles of radical democracy in their professional activities. Some transferred their passions into movements that extended some of the principles of the New Left—mainly the women's, gay, and environmental movements. Some, having "burned out," retired from public life and devoted themselves to private pursuits.

The New Left's impact is not simple. It helped end racial segregation and the Vietnam War, spawned important subsequent movements, contributed to antiauthoritarian tendencies throughout the society, left strong influences in the acad-

emy, and helped undermine the culture of the Cold War. But its excesses—along with the erosion of *liberalism—helped break apart the Democratic Party and to fuel the post-1960s *Right.

(See also LEFT; MAY 1968; NEW RIGHT; NEW SOCIAL MOVEMENTS; POLITICAL PARTICIPATION; SOCIALISM AND SOCIAL DEMOCRACY.)

Massimo Teodori, ed., *The New Left: A Documentary History* (Indianapolis, 1971). Kirkpatrick Sale, *SDS* (New York, 1973). Todd Gitlin, *The Sixties: Years of Hope, Days of Rage* (New York, 1987). James Miller, *"Democracy Is in the Streets": From Port Huron to the Siege of Chicago* (New York, 1987).

TODD GITLIN

NEW RIGHT. The term *New Right* has gained usage since the mid-1970s in a number of advanced industrial democracies, especially the United States and Britain. In both these countries advocates of New Right arguments had been active since the early 1960s, but it was in the wake of the 1973–1974 economic crisis and the electoral success of Ronald *Reagan (1980) and Margaret *Thatcher (1979) that the term became commonplace.

Meaning. The term *New Right* refers to a range of conservative and liberal ideas including principally a commitment to individual freedom and the primacy of the free market in preference to *state policies. These fundamentals become the basis for policies such as privatizing the public sector, deregulation, reducing the *welfare state, monetarist macroeconomic measures, and, in some cases, a conservative moralism.

These principles give rise to two different approaches to politics. The first includes those who advocate traditional liberal values of personal freedom (defined negatively as protection from state intrusion), market processes, and minimal government. In this view, individuals are the most important units within society and their capacities must be maximized. Such liberal New Right theorists believe that political and economic freedoms are the most important values that can be realized in the polity and that they are best attained in that polity which confines itself to providing a legal framework and certain *public goods (infrastructure). The writings of F. A. Hayek, particularly *The Road to Serfdom* (London, 1944) and *The Constitution of Liberty* (London, 1960), and Milton Friedman's *Capitalism and Freedom* (Chicago, 1962) are influential statements of these principles.

The second New Right approach promotes the conservative values of inequality, social hierarchy, traditional moralism, and, in some cases, a strong state. Proponents of this position believe that many aspects of the welfare state have encouraged a breakdown of traditional values such as commitments to the family and religion, and undesirable social behavior such as bearing children outside of marriage. Exponents of these views include George Gilder in *Wealth and Poverty* (New York, 1981) and Roger Scruton in *The Meaning of Conservatism* (London, 1980).

Origins. The ideas of New Right theorists and activists are not especially new, enjoying a lineage with preindustrial conservative beliefs and nineteenth-century liberalism. However, such ideas were displaced from the political agenda of Western industrial democracies during the first three decades following World War II as social democrats captured the political initiative. Returning these ideas to the center of political debate became the self-proclaimed task of a number of interest groups and activists.

In Britain, the founding in 1957 of the Institute of Economic Affairs (IEA) was the key event. Through its publications (notably the Hobart and Occasional Papers series) and sponsorship of conferences, this organization served as a conduit promoting the arguments of the *Right in economic and social policy. The IEA also introduced the basic tenets of *public choice theory to British policymakers and politicians, including the claim that bureaucracies are inefficient because bureaucrats are self-interested maximizers (William Niskanen, *Bureaucracy: Servant or Master?* London, 1973) and that politicians relying on Keynesian demand management have an inherent tendency to run budget deficits (James Buchanan et al., *The Economics of Politics,* London, 1978). The IEA was joined in the 1970s by the Adam Smith Institute and the Centre for Policy Studies. In the mid-1970s, these groups won influential supporters within the Conservative Party and enjoyed direct access to policymakers after the 1979 electoral success of the Tories led by Margaret Thatcher.

In the United States, the *National Review,* founded in 1955 and edited by William F. Buckley, Jr., served as a key forum for the promulgation of conservative views opposed to the mainstream liberalism associated with the presidential administrations of the 1960s and 1970s. Opposition to the "liberal consensus"—the U.S. counterpart of the European social democratic consensus—was organized through the pages of Buckley's periodical, the editor's right-wing credentials having been established in *God and Man at Yale* (Chicago, 1955), an attack on collectivism and atheism (coincidentally the concerns of New Right liberals and conservatives respectively). Many of these ideas influenced the 1964 Republican presidential candidate Barry Goldwater, whose resounding defeat by President Lyndon Johnson seemed to augur poorly for the Right. But the success of Ronald Reagan in delivering a televised speech on Goldwater's behalf proved a glimpse of the future.

From the mid-1970s, the New Right in the United States enjoyed a revival parallel to that in Britain. Conservative intellectuals publishing in the *National Review* were joined by disillusioned radicals, notably Irving Kristol and Norman Podhoretz; self-proclaimed New Right conservative organizations including Howard Phillips's Conservative Caucus and Paul Weyrich's Committee for the Survival of a Free Congress and think tanks such as the Heritage Foundation proliferated and gained influence. In 1981 Richard Viguerie published *The New Right: We're Ready to Lead* (Falls Church, Va., 1981) and with his colleagues began to use direct-mail technology to raise funds and disseminate ideas. The religious Right, represented most vocally by Jerry Falwell's Moral Majority, was sympathetic with the aims of intellectual and populist conservatives. Together these groups—intellectual conservatives, New Right and religious activists—provided an important part of the groundwork for Ronald Reagan's successful presidential candidacy in 1980.

Significance. New Right ideas have had considerable influence on public policy in Western democracies. Monetarist policy has been widely accepted as the key instrument for defeating inflation, although, as recent British trends illustrate, the policies implemented have varied in success. The policy of reducing the public sector through privatization and deregulation has become a general one. Many Western democracies have engaged in extensive privatization programs, and this strategy has extended to the new democracies of Eastern and Central Europe.

The New Right has had considerable significance in redefining the political agenda in Western democracies and in displacing social democracy. As a consequence, the market has gained wide acceptance as an appropriate mechanism for resolving social and economic problems. The New Right has capitalized on a disillusionment with national economic planning and an acceptance of the important role of incentives in stimulating economic growth. Both the Labour Party in Britain and the Democrats in the United States have been placed on the defensive by the spread of these arguments and have been forced to revise their own programs. With the collapse of state *planning systems in Eastern and *Central Europe and the widespread adoption of privatization policy, New Right ideas have in important ways achieved dominance in the intellectual arguments informing public policy in Western democracies since the 1980s. This dominance is, of course, vulnerable to political change, and the growing problems of the new market-based economies in the postcommunist societies of Europe may raise important questions for the New Right.

(See also CONSERVATISM; LIBERALISM; MONETARISM; NEW LEFT; SOCIALISM AND SOCIAL DEMOCRACY.)

Kevin Phillips, *Post-Conservative America: People, Politics and Ideology in a Time of Crisis* (New York, 1982). Gillian Peele, *Revival and Reaction: The Right in Contemporary America* (Oxford, 1984). David G. Green, *The New Conservatism: The Counter Revolution in Political, Economic and Social Thought* (New York, 1987). Desmond S. King, *The New Right: Politics, Markets and Citizenship* (Chicago, 1987).

DESMOND KING

NEW SOCIAL MOVEMENTS. A flowering of new groups concerned with *environmentalism, women's rights, peace, consumerism, and other new issues has transformed the politics of advanced industrial societies. These new social movements (NSMs) are now important and contentious actors in the political process of most democracies, and similar political forces are growing in the emerging democracies of Eastern Europe and the Pacific region. These movements and their organizational representatives translate the public's changing values and issue interests into a potential political force, challenging the influence of established *interest groups (such as unions and business associations), and altering the political agendas and political style of contemporary democracies.

Although NSMs take a variety of forms, they share a common political *ideology that challenges the prevailing social goals and political style of Western industrial democracies. This alternative political ideology is especially strong among European movements, although the same themes appear in muted form among American groups. Environmentalists emphasize the theme of a sustainable society and economy as the underlying premise of environmental action, and the women's movement stresses the dual goals of reshaping social norms about the role of women in society and equalizing life chances between men and women. These distinct interests are bridged by a common political identity that emphasizes the quality of life for individuals, whether it is the quality of the natural environment, the protection of *human rights, or peace in an insecure world. These groups also share certain libertarian themes: Individuals must control society rather than the reverse, and personal fulfillment and self-expression should be maximized.

One of the most significant contributions of NSMs has been at this ideological level. NSMs are not just interest groups; they have also sought to reshape public discourse and consciousness. Environmental thinking has reshaped how we think about our relationship to nature, just as the women's movement has reshaped gender relations. The creation of new political frameworks, and the introduction of these frameworks into politics, have been the major influences of these movements. These are movements of identity as well as interests.

The structure and style of the political groups spawned by these social movements also reflect their challenging ideology. For example, the popular base of these groups differs from earlier progressive movements, such as the *labor movement or agrarian movement. The participants in NSMs are not drawn from the underprivileged of society, but from young, better-educated, middle-class citizens who share the postmaterial values of NSMs. Participants are recruited into political activity by their own values and their ties to alternative political organizations, and there is a substantial overlap between the activists and supporters of the various movements. In terms of their numbers, membership in NSM organizations now exceeds formal political party membership for most Western democracies. While there is substantial support for these same issues in Eastern and Central Europe and the developing nations in Asia, actual participation in NSMs in these nations is much more limited.

One of the distinctive characteristics of NSMs is the variety of organizational forms they have spawned. Many movement organizations are large, complex bureaucracies, such as the Sierra Club or the National Organization for Women in the United States; others are small elitist organizations or activist foundations, such as Friends of the Earth. The innovative aspect of these movements is the creation of new organizational structures that stress decentralizations and participatory decision making and which sharply contrast to the hierarchic and bureaucratic tendencies of most economic interest groups. This alternative organizational style is most visible in locally based citizen action groups or local branches of national organizations; similar tendencies can be observed, however, even in larger NSMs. The women's movement in several European states is skeptical of an institutionalized women's lobby that might dominate the movement, and similar antiorganizational tendencies are apparent among opponents of nuclear power. These movements are also distinguished by their development of multinational interest groups—such as Greenpeace, World Wide Fund for Nature (WWF), or Friends of the Earth—that create an international basis for political action.

Another feature of NSMs is their expansion of the accepted methods of political action to include protests, spectacular actions, and other forms of unconventional activity. Because of their own values and status as a challenging group, NSMs place a greater reliance on unconventional political activities to mobilize their potential supporters and exert public pressure on the political establishment: Environmental activists add dyes to industrial discharges to demonstrate the reach of pollution; peace groups assemble a human chain connecting military installations; and women's groups organize large demonstrations on issues such as abortion rights. Early scholarship stressed only the unconventional nature of NSMs, but the practical demands of politics also involve these groups in established channels of interest group influence. As participants in the political process, NSM organizations also advocate changes in this process. NSMs have criticized traditional patterns of decision making and pressed for more direct citizen input into policy making and policy administration.

One clear example of the new political options created by NSM is the emergence of new green political parties in recent years. NSMs often assisted in the formation of the new *green parties that emerged in the 1980s. Green parties now hold seats in many Western European national parliaments as well as the European Parliament, and nascent green parties are forming in the emerging democracies of Eastern and Central Europe. These parties' alternative ideology, decentralized structure, and participatory style are a sharp contrast to the established political parties in these nations. Green parties epitomize the alternative values of the movement, and they differ so markedly from the established parties that they are sometimes described as the "anti-party parties."

The overall significance of NSMs is perhaps best illustrated by how political systems are responding to their challenges. These movements have produced broadscale reforms in the policies of contemporary political systems. Nearly all democratic states now acknowledge the importance of the environmental issue, and most have responded with sincere efforts at policy reform. Global environmental problems—such as depletion of the ozone, disposal of toxic wastes, and acid rain—are creating a new international environmental awareness. Similarly, the changes in the role of women in Western societies and the implementation of new legislation to protect women's rights have reshaped contemporary societies and social relations. Significant and ongoing administrative reforms in Europe, Japan, and the United States are increasing the citizens' role within the political process. Thus, these movements have not created a new political order, but they have renewed the democratic process of advanced industrial societies.

(See also FEMINISM; GAY AND LESBIAN POLITICS; GENDER AND POLITICS; PEACE MOVEMENT; POLITICAL PARTICIPATION; POSTMATERALISM; REPRODUCTIVE POLITICS.)

Russell Dalton, *The Green Rainbow: Environmental Interest Groups in Western Europe* (New Haven, Conn., 1994). Enrique Laraña et al., *New Social Movements* (Philadelphia, 1994). Sidney Tarrow, *Power in Movement* (Ithaca N.Y., 1994). Doug McAdam et al., *Comparative Perspectives on Social Movements* (Cambridge, U.K., 1996). Thomas Rochon, *Culture Moves* (Princeton, 1998).

RUSSELL J. DALTON

NEW ZEALAND. Situated in the South Pacific, midway between South America and Southeast Asia, part of the circum-Pacific volcanic "rim of fire," New Zealand is a former British settlement colony, now an independent state. The population of some 3.7 million people is predominantly of British extraction, although approximately 15 percent is made up of indigenous Polynesians—the Maori—and a further 5.6 percent of other Pacific Islanders.

Constitutionally, the British monarch—in her capacity as queen of New Zealand—is still head of state in New Zealand, although this is largely a formal position today, with the royal powers largely devolving upon the governor-general as the monarch's representative. As befits the country's evolution from colony through dominion status to independent state, since 1930 the governor-general has been appointed on the advice of New Zealand ministers, and since 1967 governors-general have all been New Zealand–born. More recently, although still a minority concern, there has been a steady growth of interest in republicanism.

As the original inhabitants of the country, the Maori occupy a special position under the terms of the Treaty of Waitangi (1840), which formally ceded sovereignty to the British Crown. In return, the Crown (in the European version of the treaty) confirmed and guaranteed to the chiefs and tribes the full exclusive and undisturbed possession of their "Lands and Estates, Forests, Fisheries" so long as they wished to retain them, in addition to granting them "all the Rights and Privileges of British Subjects."

For much of New Zealand's history—and particularly following the Land Wars of the 1860s—the Treaty of Waitangi was largely ignored by successive New Zealand governments, but from the 1970s onward it has been central to attempts to forge a new and more equitable arrangement between *pakehas* (New Zealanders of European descent) and Maori.

Dating from 1854, the New Zealand Parliament enjoys a record of constitutional continuity second only to the U.S. Congress in the *Pacific region. With a centralized Westminster-type cabinet system, no formal constitution, and very cohesive political parties, New Zealand has a parliament that has been unicameral since 1950. At the 1996 general election, it changed from a simple plurality electoral system to *proportional representation. A "Bill of Rights" was passed in 1990, but this is an ordinary statute rather than supreme law. This merely requires that the attorney general provide a certificate with the introduction of any measure that contravenes it. In the 1996 general election, the change was made from simple plurality to a Mixed Member Proportional electoral system (MMP).

Instead of the normal legal constitutional safeguards, heavy emphasis is placed on triennial general elections along with pragmatic devices and arrangements such as an ombudsman; an independent broadcasting authority; a race relations conciliator; the Waitangi Tribunal (set up in 1975 to consider claims made by the Maori people under the Treaty of Waitangi); an Official Information Act; and the courts. New Zealand follows the common law tradition of the United Kingdom with its own hierarchy of courts comprising district courts, high court, and court of appeal. In constitutional matters the courts are largely limited to the doctrine of *ultra vires*, judging whether a government agency has exceeded the powers granted to it under statute or regulation, although in recent times the courts have been given increasing responsibility for deciding a growing number of issues arising under the aegis of the Treaty of Waitangi.

The formal executive of the country is the Executive Council, made up of two or more cabinet ministers and normally presided over by the governor-general. The practical decision-taking center, however, is the cabinet, usually consisting of some twenty ministers of cabinet rank and supplemented by four to six noncabinet ministers. Emphasis is placed on both collective responsibility and collective decision-taking, and ministers often hold multiple portfolios.

In New Zealand, consideration of the executive cannot be divorced from the role of the parliamentary party caucuses, which represent an important part of the collective decision-taking process. In the case of the Labour Party, cabinet members are elected by and from the parliamentary party caucus, and most important cabinet decisions are deemed to require caucus endorsement. The National Party, too, makes extensive, if less formal, use of its caucus. Both parties require their parliamentary leaders to be elected or reendorsed by caucus every three years.

A wide range of interest groups represent capital, labor, environmental interests, peace groups, etc. Several of these groups have had close links with the Labour Party, and a number of trade unions are directly affiliated to it. Third and minor parties rarely flourished under the simple plurality electoral system, but the introduction of an electoral system similar to that of the Federal Republic of Germany, combining proportional representation and single member districts, has led to a greater probability of coalition governments and thus an enhanced status for third parties.

Socioeconomic and urban-rural differences are the predominant social cleavages. Class is important but has always been a much less pronounced factor than in Britain, and, in common with many other countries, class-based voting has declined in the second half of the twentieth century. At the same time, considerations of gender, and particularly of race, have risen sharply. Religion has not played an important role in New Zealand politics.

Similarly, a shift has taken place in economic policies from those of a predominantly Keynesian complexion to a market-liberal stance with a heavy emphasis on user payment and the selling off of state enterprises. A rapidly developing free market with Australia, under the provisions of the Australia–New Zealand Closer Economic Relations Trade Agreement 1983 (CER), is projected to result in a single economic (but not political) entity.

New Zealand was unusual in building up what was a relatively affluent welfare state upon a predominantly agricultural base. There are limited natural resources (gold, coal, oil, and natural gas). As a temperate agriculture producer, New Zealand was severely disadvantaged by Britain's accession to the European Community (even despite useful transitional arrangements). Trade has been diversified extensively. In 1950, for example, 66 percent of New Zealand exports were sent to Britain. Britain now ranks fourth as an export market, following Australia, Japan, and the United States.

A small state with total armed forces of under 10,000, New Zealand was a loyal ally of both Britain and the United States until the prohibition of the visits of nuclear-armed and nuclear-powered ships led to the formal suspension of the ANZUS alliance by the United States in 1986. New Zealand was a founding member of the UN in 1945, and has played an active role in peacekeeping from Korea to Bosnia as well as in the specialized agencies. Increasingly, New Zealand has played an important role in environmental matters, ranging from protection of the ozone layer to the prohibition of whaling and drift-net fishing. The latter is a reflection, in part, of its growing involvement with the communities and interests of the smaller islands of the South Pacific.

(See also ANZUS TREATY.)

Keith Jackson and Alan McRobie, *Historical Dictionary of New Zealand* (Lanham, Md., 1996). Geoffrey Palmer and Matthew Palmer, *Bridled Power*, 3d ed. (Auckland, 1997). *New Zealand Official Yearbook*, Department of Statistics (Auckland 1998).

KEITH JACKSON

NEWLY INDUSTRIALIZING ECONOMIES. The terms "newly industrializing economies" (NIEs) or "newly industrializing countries" (NICs) first appeared in the late 1970s to refer to a small group of developing countries that had been successful not only in industrializing rapidly but in expanding their exports of manufactured products. These countries fell into two groups. Several large countries in Latin America that had industrialized through high levels of tariff protection, particularly Mexico, Brazil, and Argentina, began at various points to promote exports of nontraditional products. The Latin American NICs did develop more diversified export structures that included labor-intensive light manufactures and even some intermediate and capital goods, but export-promotion policies were not always vigorously pursued and did not generate adequate foreign exchange to service rising external debt.

The term "NIEs" was often used to refer exclusively to a second group of East Asian countries: the Republic of Korea (South Korea), Taiwan, Hong Kong, and Singapore. Korea and Taiwan industrialized in the 1950s through import-substitution, and Singapore and Hong Kong were initially commercial entrepôts. The transition to *export-led growth was somewhat different in the four cases, but there are important similarities in their growth paths. All initially exploited their comparative advantage in light, labor-intensive manufactures, gradually diversifying into technology-, skill-, and even capital-intensive goods. All depended heavily on the U.S. market and attempted to attract export-oriented foreign direct investment.

The emergence of the NIEs raised several important policy and political questions. The East Asian NIEs appeared to pursue a more market-oriented development strategy than other developing countries. Because of their rapid and relatively egalitarian growth, they were held up by development economists and the international financial institutions as models of success. Yet there is substantial debate about how market-oriented the East Asian NIEs really are. Hong Kong never departed from a strong commitment to laissez-faire policies, but export-oriented industrialization in Korea and Taiwan involved a substantial degree of state intervention, such as continued protection and subsidies, as well as market-oriented reforms. Moreover, economic reform efforts in these countries were led by strong, authoritarian governments. These conditions cast some doubt on whether their experiences could be replicated elsewhere. Nonetheless, a "second tier" of countries attempted similar export-oriented growth strategies in the 1980s with some success. These countries included Thailand, Malaysia, and Turkey, and the NIE label was extended to them as well.

The second policy issue surrounding the emergence of the NIEs concerns trade. The rapid growth of manufactured exports from these countries, particularly the East Asian NIEs, created severe competitive pressures and contributed to adjustment problems in a range of mature industries in the advanced industrial states including textiles and apparel, footwear, and consumer electronics. As a result, the NIEs have been major targets of the so-called "new protectionism" in Europe and the United States: nontariff barriers designed to restrict trade with particular countries in particular products. In the 1980s, the larger NIEs also came under increasing pressures to liberalize their own markets and to "graduate" by giving up their developing-country status with reference to a number of preferences.

In 1997–98, a number of the Asian NIEs experienced a severe financial crisis; Korea, Indonesia, and Thailand were the most seriously affected. Although the crisis was partly the result of external factors, including a withdrawal of foreign lending, it also reflected deep-seated weaknesses in the NIEs' financial systems and corporate governance. The crisis resulted in a new round of economic reforms to increase foreign investment and liberalize trade and thus reinforced their outward orientation.

(See also DEVELOPMENT AND UNDERDEVELOPMENT; INTERNATIONAL POLITICAL ECONOMY; PACIFIC REGION; PROTECTION.)

Stephan Haggard, *Pathways from the Periphery: The Politics of Growth in the Newly Industrializing Countries* (Ithaca, N.Y., 1990). Morris Goldstein, *The Asian Financial Crisis: Causes, Cures and Systemic Implications* (Washington, D.C., 1998).

STEPHAN HAGGARD

NGOS. See NON-GOVERNMENTAL ORGANIZATIONS.

NICARAGUA. Strategically located across the Mesoamerican isthmus and with waterways that facilitate transisthmian transit, Nicaragua has often held geopolitical significance greater than its size and population (around 4.5 million in 1998) would suggest. The prospect of an interoceanic canal across Nicaragua generated attention in the nineteenth century and encouraged repeated external interventions. Although independence came in 1823, the creation and modernization of a nation-state continued into the last decade of the twentieth century as the Nicaraguan Revolution (1979–1990) ended and civilian democracy began. Despite periods of relative stability (1857–1893, 1936–1977), conflict between Liberal and Conservative elites was often violent. Nicaraguans repeatedly experienced (and sometimes sought) external intervention that intensified local conflict. When Liberals invited U.S. filibusterer William Walker into a partisan squabble in 1856, he seized the entire country and triggered a regional war. The United States in 1911 installed a Conservative regime to protect the U.S. monopoly over the Panama Canal, then occupied Nicaragua (1912–1925) to contain Liberal rebellion. Liberal revolt again brought U.S. occupation from 1927 to 1933 when U.S. marines and the U.S.-trained Nicaraguan National Guard fought the anti-imperialist guerrilla Augusto Sandino.

National Guard commander Anastasio Somoza García seized power in 1936 and used the Guard, the Partido Liberal Nacionalista (PLN), and U.S. aid to rule Nicaragua until his assassination in 1956. Power passed to his sons Luis (1956–1967) and the more repressive Anastasio Somoza Debayle (1967–1979). The dictatorial dynasty promoted rapid economic *modernization characterized by corruption, increased economic inequality, and deterioration of the PLN and Conservative parties. Spiraling repression eventually deepened opposition, spawned a revolutionary coalition headed by the Frente Sandinista de Liberación Nacional (FSLN), and caused widespread popular insurrection that toppled the regime in 1979.

The revolutionary government (1979–1990) expanded the state, reorganized government, developed a new constitution (1987), and held clean elections (1984, 1990). Economic reorganization, property confiscations, and the hostility of the United States and the Catholic Church helped polarize revolutionary Nicaragua and contributed economic decline, counterrevolutionary opposition (the contras), and a decade of civil war. FSLN National Directorate member Daniel Ortega Saavedra, elected president in 1984, lost the 1990 election to the United Nicaraguan Opposition (UNO—a multiparty coalition) and transferred power to Violeta Barrios de Chamorro. Out of power, the FSLN retained widespread electoral support, a large legislative bloc, and ties to labor and the military.

Nicaragua's party system, state, and political economy reflect its turbulent political history. The Conservative and Liberal (later PLN) parties arose out of regional/ideological conflicts before independence and became loose, nonideological, personalistic movements among the nation's agrarian bourgeoisie. Conservative dominance (1857–1893) was broken by rising middle sector support for the Liberals. Conservative collaboration with the U.S. occupation after 1912 and later with the Somozas further undermined the party. The Somozas' PLN lost credibility, splintered, and eventually declined. Liberal and Conservative splinter groups persisted throughout the *revolution, and several joined the victorious UNO coalition. The Liberals recovered in 1996, electing Arnoldo Alemán Lacayo president on the Alianza Liberal (AL) coalition ticket.

The FSLN, founded in 1961 by Marxist-Leninists who had quit the (communist) Partido Socialista Nicaragüense, struggled as a guerrilla movement until 1978, then emerged as leader of the anti-Somoza coalition. Upon victory, the FSLN marginalized its allies, took over the state for eleven years, created a party-based military, and broadened and consolidated its popular base. As president of Nicaragua (1984–1990) and party head (1990s), Daniel Ortega increasingly dominated the FSLN despite losing presidential bids in 1990 and 1996. Key intellectuals and leaders left the FSLN, and funding and mass organizations dwindled in the mid-1990s as debates over ideology, strategy, organization, and various scandals undermined the party's prestige. Small parties multiplied after 1979; there were more than twenty in 1990 and more than forty by the 1996 election. In 1996 the AL reunited many Liberal factions to win the election.

During the 1980s the contras, strongly backed by the United States, raised 18,000 troops to fight the revolution. Consisting of ex-National Guard, Miskito indigenes, peasants, and even Sandinistas, the contras failed militarily but provoked economic damage and prompted Sandinista power abuses that contributed to the FSLN's electoral defeat in 1990. Contra political parties fared poorly in the 1990 and 1996 elections.

State institutions reflect Nicaragua's dramatic political evolution. The Somozas expanded the state but also captured and corrupted it, especially the Central Bank and National Guard. The Sandinista revolution reorganized and greatly expanded government services, economic regulation and management, and the military and police. With special emergency powers and an FSLN majority during the 1980s, President Ortega overshadowed the unicameral National Assembly. During the Chamorro and Alemán administrations (1990–1996 and 1996–2001, respectively) constitutional reform weakened the executive and strengthened the Assembly, while neoliberal economic reforms sharply shrank the public sector. The regular judiciary, corrupted by the Somozas, was politicized during the revolution. The Supreme Court, however, has gained independence from other governmental branches during the 1990s.

The National Guard, a combined military/police force with 14,000 troops at its peak, collapsed in 1979 and was replaced with the FSLN-dominated Ejército Popular Sandinista (EPS) and Policía Sandinista (PS). The EPS and PS were national institutions but also partisan—commanded by top Sandinistas, ideologically trained, protective of the revolution, and with Soviet-bloc assistance and advice. The EPS and its conscripted militia grew to over 100,000 troops organized for counterinsurgency at the peak of the contra war, but decreased rapidly after 1990 to 12,000 troops. The Chamorro government enacted a new Military Code, renamed the army (the Ejército Nicaragüense), civilianized and renamed the police (Policía Nacional), and retired longtime army chief and FSLN leader Humberto Ortega Saavedra. Army loyalty to civilian rulers and officers' partisanship remained concerns of post-1990 governments.

A country burdened by enduring social cleavages, Nicaragua is divided between its fertile, volcanic Pacific littoral (approximately a third of the territory) with 90 percent of the population and the wet Atlantic lowlands. The Pacific populace is fairly ethnically and culturally homogeneous (Spanish-speaking, Catholic, and mestizo) and dominates national life. The Atlantic zone's people, mostly Protestants, include English-speaking blacks and 100,000 indigenes. The Atlantic peoples generally resent politicoeconomic incursions from the Pacific. Such resentment fed the Miskitos' armed resistance to the revolution in the 1980s and prompted a regional autonomy law in the late 1980s. Nicaragua underwent a major surge of religious fervor (1970s–1990s) that affected politics both among nominal Catholics (probably 80 percent) and Protestants—divided among many fast-growing largely evangelical denominations. An important Catholic minority, the "peoples' church," supported the Sandinista revolution, while the more conservative Catholic church majority and hierarchy opposed it.

Nicaragua has historically exported coffee, cotton, and beef/hides; owners of the large farms supplying these products constituted much of the political elite. The agroexport bourgeoisie diversified into other crops and manufacturing in the 1960s under the Central American Common Market (CACM). Divisions within the bourgeoisie and eroding popular living conditions stimulated the 1979 insurrection. In the 1980s deteriorating terms of trade, the CACM's collapse, capital flight, the contra war, a U.S. economic embargo, and revolutionary policy devastated the economy. Agriculture and manufacturing declined rapidly; much of the population turned to informal services to survive. This process eventually undermined the revolution by alienating voters of all classes.

The Chamorro government's draconian neoliberal *structural adjustment program contained inflation and restored fiscal order, but further deepened poverty and left 1996 gross domestic product per capita at only half that of 1970. Modest growth by the late 1990s held some promise, but political factors appeared likely to restrain economic recovery. Eventual stabilization of the postrevolutionary polity will likely require both tolerance by voters and a long-elusive consensus upon democratic rules among fragmented politicoeconomic elites. While power passed smoothly from incumbents to challengers in the democratic elections of 1990 and 1996, the weak economy could endanger future political stability, especially given intense Sandinista/anti-Sandinista cleavages and Nicaragua's violent political tradition.

Throughout the twentieth century the United States has powerfully influenced Nicaragua, first with its occupations, then by supporting the Somozas, and most recently with its implacable hostility toward the Sandinista Revolution. Soviet/Cuban aid helped shore up the revolution, especially during the mid-1980s. Nicaragua was thus a major focus of East-West tension throughout the 1980s, but this ended with the Cold War's demise.

Although Nicaragua's neighbors expressed nervousness about the revolution and several cooperated with U.S. anti-Sandinista policies, other Latin American powers generally opposed U.S. intervention and sought to contain it. Eventually, Central American presidents negotiated a regional peace process (1987–1990) under which the contra war ended. The 1990 election—observed by the United Nations, Organization of American States, and others at Nicaragua's behest—ended Sandinista rule and thus reduced conflict among Nicaragua, its isthmian neighbors, other Latin American nations, and the United States. Since 1990, U.S. policy toward Nicaragua has promoted neoliberal economic reforms, resolution of property disputes arising from the revolution, institution building, and containment of FSLN influence within the polity.

(See also GUERRILLA WARFARE; U.S.–LATIN AMERICAN RELATIONS.)

John A. Booth, *The End and the Beginning: The Nicaraguan Revolution* (Boulder, Colo., 1985). Ralph Lee Woodward, Jr., *Central America: A Nation Divided* (New York, 1985). Thomas W. Walker, ed., *Reagan Versus the Sandinistas: The Undeclared War* (Boulder, Colo., 1987). James Dunkerley, *Power in the Isthmus: A Political History of Modern Central America* (London, 1988). John A. Booth and Thomas W. Walker, *Understanding Central America* (Boulder, Colo., 1993). Dario Moreno, *The Struggle for Peace in Central America* (Gainesville, Fla., 1994). Rose J. Spalding, *Capitalists and Revolution in Nicaragua: Opposition and Accommodation* (Chapel Hill, N.C., 1994). Thomas W. Walker, ed., *Nicaragua Without Illusions: Regime Transition and Structural Adjustment in the 1990s* (Wilmington, Del., 1997).

JOHN A. BOOTH

NIGER. With a population of more than 8 million and a land area of 490,350 square miles (1.27 million sq. km.), Niger is the largest country in West Africa but one of the least densely populated. Poor resources, unstable and declining prices for uranium exports, severe periodic drought, and foreign debt stand in the way of economic prosperity and provide the backdrop for developments in recent post-independence politics.

The themes dominating politics since independence in 1960 include military intervention; curbs on civil liberties; protests by students and by labor unions representing civil servants, teachers, and employees of parastatals; arrests of political opposition members and union leaders; the search for political stability through multiparty politics; ethnic tension between the Djerma and the Hausa; and rebellion by the Tuareg.

A 1974 military coup, led by Col. (later Maj. Gen.) Senyi Kountche, ousted Hamani Diori, president of Niger's first republic. A tentative political opening occurred between 1978 and 1987 with the appointment of a provisional parliament and constituent assembly, the release of several political detainees, the gradual incorporation of civilians into the cabinet, and the adoption by plebiscite of a national charter. With the death of Kountche in 1987, political reform, accompanied by political instability, accelerated. Niger's second republic was installed with Kountche's successor, Brig. Ali Saibou, the sole candidate, winning nearly 100 percent of the vote and with a legislative assembly elected from a single list of candidates.

Over several months in 1991, a national conference, consisting of delegates representing political and professional organizations, civil servants, and women's and students' groups, established a provisional government with an interim legislature and wrote a new constitution. Army mutinies and strikes by civil servants over salary arrears dominated events during 1991 and 1992. In December 1992, the new constitution was adopted by referendum, and in February 1993, elections were held for a new national assembly. Niger's third republic was installed with a government led by a coalition of parties opposed to the dominant (and military-backed) party, the Mouvement National pour une Société de Développement (MNSD). Financial crisis continued to plague the government, which faced protests from public sector employees over salary arrears and from students over grants arrears. The 50 percent devaluation of the CFA in January 1994 exacerbated the crisis and increased the intensity of strike action and civilian clashes with security forces. The breakup of the opposition coalition led to a change in prime ministers, the dissolution of the national assembly, renewed labor and student protest, and the election of a new national assembly in early 1995. This time, the MNSD won the majority of seats but the new government became paralyzed by a constitutional struggle for power between the president and the prime minister, who represented opposing party forces.

In January 1996, the military again seized power to put an end to political instability and pledged to return the country to civilian rule within a year. Domestic and international pressure brought about an even faster turnaround for the military leader, Col. (later Brig.-Gen.) Ibrahim Bare Mainassara. By midyear, a new constitution was approved by referendum, political parties were unbanned, and the state of emergency declared at the time of the coup was lifted. Mainassara defeated (and also arrested) three opponents in a presidential election in May and was installed as the president of Niger's fourth republic. Subsequent elections for a new national assembly were boycotted by a coalition of opposition parties. Efforts at national reconciliation continued through 1998.

During the 1980s and 1990s, the various governments of Niger had to deal with a rebellion by Tuaregs displaced by drought. Returning from Libya and Algeria, and unhappy with relief and resettlement efforts, Tuareg guerrillas attacked government installations and suffered fierce counterattacks from government forces. Negotiations with rebel leaders began in 1992 over resettlement, regional autonomy, and the integration of Tuareg into the national military and civil service. A speedy settlement has been hampered by the splintering of the Tuareg into more than ten groupings, a number of which refuse to accept terms negotiated by rival groups. By early 1998, an agreement over most issues had been worked out with most factions, but sporadic clashes between splinter groups and government forces continued.

Robert B. Charlick, *Niger: Personal Rule and Survival in the Sahel* (Boulder, Colo., 1990). *Africa South of the Sahara* (London, 1998).

BEVERLY GRIER

NIGERIA. Nigeria, Africa's biggest country with a population of over 100 million people, and located in the West African subregion, was formally established in 1914 under British colonial rule. It was in that year that the protectorates of Northern and Southern Nigeria, as well as the Colony of Lagos, were amalgamated to create one country with a unified administrative structure. It achieved independence from Britain in 1960 initially as a Westminster-type parliamentary democracy led by a prime minister as head of government and a governor-general representing the queen of England as head of state. In 1963, however, the country severed constitutional links with Britain and became a republic, with the office of the governor-general transformed into a nonexecutive president. By 1979 the Westminster parliamentary system had been completely abandoned in favor of an American-type presidential system.

By far one of Africa's most heterogeneous countries, it is generally reckoned that Nigeria has some 250 distinct ethnic groups, although the Hausa, the Igbo, and the Yoruba constitute the three largest groups, each with some 20 million people. Other large ethnic groups include the Ibibio, the Ijaw, the Kanuri, the Nupe, and the Tiv. All of Nigeria's ethnic groups boast a very long precolonial history, with many already organized into elaborate state systems prior to the arrival of the forces of British colonialism and the creation of the modern nation-state. The country's population is also reckoned to be roughly evenly divided between followers of Christianity and Islam, with the latter mainly concentrated in the north of the country and the former in the south. There is, however, also a significant number of Nigerians who have stuck with their traditional religious and belief systems. Furthermore, syncretism is widespread.

The broad coincidence of religion with *ethnicity and geography—the Hausa in northern Nigeria are predominantly Muslim, the Igbo in the east predominantly Christian, and the Yoruba in the west are roughly divided between the two religions—has tended to give a strong ethnoreligious and regional character to politics in the country. Managing ethnoreligious diversity has, therefore, been one of the biggest problems of political governance in Nigeria, accounting, in part, for the recurring instability that has wracked the country since independence and which resulted first in prolonged

*military rule from January 1966 to October 1979 and December 1983 to May 1999, and then in a bloody civil war that ran from 1967 to 1970 following the decision of the Igbo to secede from the federation.

The civil war is reckoned to have cost the country at least a million lives and although the country emerged from it with its territorial integrity intact, ethnoreligious conflicts have continued to be a regular feature of Nigerian politics, consuming all parts of the country and assuming a level of greater intensity in the context of the steep economic decline and intense military *authoritarianism of the 1980s and 1990s. These crises have translated into renewed ethnoreligious challenges to the Nigerian nation-state, challenges which have entailed efforts at subverting the secular status of the federation, as is evidenced, for example, by formal and informal bids at the extension of the Sharia beyond civil matters into the penal code.

And yet, politics in Nigeria is not all about ethnoreligious bickering. The postindependence period has witnessed the rapid formation of a middle class of professionals in the public and private sectors, as well as an urban working class whose ranks have grown with the expansion of commercial and industrial activities in the country. Thanks to these classes, a tradition of vibrant national-territorial and secular associational life was quickly established in the country, giving a nonparochial dimension to national politics and enabling policy issues to be debated and canvassed on the basis of ideological dispositions and cross-cutting concerns with the advancement of national unity, social justice, and economic development.

Since the amalgamation of 1914, Nigeria has had a series of constitutions designed to take cognizance of the changing political circumstances of the country. Apart from the Lugardian Constitution of 1914 itself, the colonial period witnessed the promulgation of four other constitutions, namely, the Clifford Constitution of 1922, the Richards Constitution of 1946, the Macpherson Constitution of 1951, and the Independence Constitution of 1960. Since 1960 the country has had five constitutions. Following the postindependence decision to replace the queen as head of state, the 1963 Republican Constitution was promulgated. This was followed with the 1979 constitution that marked the end of thirteen years of military rule and the birth of the Second Republic (1979–1983). Following the overthrow of the Second Republic by the military, a renewed effort was made to provide a fresh constitutional basis for the restoration of elected government, and this culminated in the 1989 constitution which was to serve as a framework for the Third Republic.

That republic was not, however, fully inaugurated as the incumbent military president, General Ibrahim Babangida, was extremely reluctant to give up power and, in his bid to sit tight, transformed the transition to civil program which he had initiated into a cat-and-mouse game that resulted in the repeated postponement of the terminal date for military rule and, ultimately, the annulment of the 12 June 1993 presidential elections. The 1989 constitution was abandoned after this and a new military regime, headed by General Sani Abacha, produced yet another constitution, the 1995 constitution, that was reportedly adopted by the ruling junta but was never made public amid another self-succession effort by Abacha. That effort ended with Abacha's sudden death in June 1998;

his replacement, General Abdulsalami Abubakar, amended the 1995 constitution to produce the new 1999 constitution on the basis of which Nigeria was finally returned to elected government in May 1999 to mark the birth of the Fourth Republic.

Prolonged exposure to direct political governance has taken a huge toll on the professionalism and *esprit de corps* of the Nigerian Armed Forces made up of the army, the navy, and the air force. From initially being a coherent and mobile force respected for its early peacekeeping role in Africa, the military was gradually reduced into an instrument for the illegal seizure of political power and the advancement of the personal interests of incumbent commanders. By the time the Fourth Republic was inaugurated, the military was already severely discredited as a national institution; it was also wracked by internal divisions, which are just beginning to be redressed through a program of training and reorientation aimed at restoring professionalism and discipline within the framework of elected civilian political control.

The Fourth Republic consists of three tiers of government: federal, state, and local. At the federal level, government consists of the executive, headed by an executive president who operates with the assistance of a vice president and a council of ministers; the National Assembly, consisting of the Senate, which is the upper chamber, and a House of Representatives; and the judiciary, made up of federal high courts, courts of appeal, and the Supreme Court. It is a constitutional requirement that appointments into the executive arm of government should reflect the diversity of the country. Each of the thirty-six states of the federation is represented equally in the Senate by three elected senators; the federal capital territory of Abuja has one elected senator. All states are also represented in the House of Representatives, although here, emphasis is put on population in the delineation of constituency boundaries and the determination of the number of elected representatives per state.

At the state level, the executive arm is headed by an elected governor; the legislature, known as the State House of Assembly, by a speaker; and the state judiciary, consisting of magistrate, customary, high, and (in the northern states) Sharia courts, is headed by the chief judge. Local governments, numbering 774, consist of elected councilors led by a popularly elected chairman. The size of the various state houses of assembly and the number of local government councilors provided for depend on the population of the geographical area which they cover. Playing an advisory role at the federal level is the Council of State, made up of all surviving former heads of state, the incumbent president and his deputy, and the governors of the thirty-six states that make up the federation.

Elections are decided on a first-past-the-post basis and are supervised by the Independent National Electoral Commission (INEC), which also has responsibility for registering political parties. Politics in the Fourth Republic is formally organized around three registered political parties, namely, the People's Democratic Party, which is presently the ruling party at the federal level; the All Peoples Party; and the Alliance for Democracy. To qualify for registration, parties are expected to have offices and membership spread across the country. But equally significant on the national political terrain are a host of associations and trade unions mostly concentrated in urban centers across the country.

Although at independence Nigeria was predominantly an agrarian economy, with cocoa, groundnuts, cotton, hides and skin, sisal, and palm produce accounting for the bulk of its exports, by the early 1970s this changed dramatically, following the increased significance of oil in the country's export and revenue profile. This shift occurred on the back of the OPEC oil price revolution of 1973 and resulted in oil accounting for over 90 percent of export receipts. The massive revenue boom, which accrued to the country, enabled the government to undertake major investments in education, health, national transportation, telecommunications, and energy and power sectors; it also served as the context for corruption to flourish as public office holders, as well as local and foreign contractors and businesspeople, enriched themselves at the expense of the Nigerian public.

The fact that post–civil war revenue allocation has been distributed on the basis of a formula which works in favor of the federal government at the expense of the other tiers of government, and which does not provide for ample allocations to the communities from which export income is derived, has been a sore point in contemporary Nigerian federalism. The revenue allocation question has been transformed into a major political issue by the increased centralization of national-territorial administration, a by-product of prolonged military rule, the concentration of power in the presidency, and the perceived lopsided nature of appointments and opportunities. It is this concern that lies at the heart of the turmoil in the Niger Delta region of the country, the center of oil and gas exploration and production, and which underpins the rebirth of the competing ethnic, religious, and regional identities that dominate political discussions in the country. Many are convinced that, in spite of the existence of an elected National Assembly, the country needs to convene a sovereign national conference to negotiate a basis for the continued unity of the country.

Demographic weight and oil wealth enabled Nigerian leaders to project the country as a leading voice in African and developing-country affairs; since the early 1970s, Africa has been defined as the centerpiece of its foreign policy. Active participation in African diplomacy has seen the commitment of resources to the national liberation effort in Southern Africa, regional cooperation and integration in West Africa, and peacekeeping/enforcement activities in Chad, Liberia, and Sierra Leone.

(See also COLONIAL EMPIRES; DECOLONIZATION; DEMOCRATIC TRANSITIONS.)

Okwudiba Nnoli, *Ethnic Politics in Nigeria* (Enugu, Nigeria, 1980). Billy J. Dudley, *An Introduction to Nigerian Government and Politics* (London, 1982). Adebayo Olukoshi, *The Politics of Structural Adjustment in Nigeria* (London, 1993). Attahiru Jega, *Identity Transformation and Identity Politics under Structural Adjustment in Nigeria* (Uppsala, Sweden, 2000).
ADEBAYO O. OLUKOSHI

NINETEEN EIGHTY-NINE. As the year began in January 1989, the general consensus in the West was that *communism would maintain its hold over Eastern and *Central Europe and the Soviet Union well into the twenty-first century. Perhaps the most prominent proponent of this analysis was the former U.S. ambassador to the United Nations, Jeane Kirkpatrick, who advanced the thesis that communist societies were immune to change from within because of their rulers' success in atomizing citizens from one another. In the view of Kirkpatrick and her cothinkers, authoritarian societies such as Pinochet's Chile could be transformed because they allowed room for action independent of the state, but such autonomous activity was virtually impossible under totalitarian communism.

Yet by December 1989, Poland had held partially free elections in June in which the *Solidarity opposition won all but one of the contested seats; Hungary's communist leaders had conceded the right to completely free elections, which would take place in March of the following year; and the hard-line rulers of Czechoslovakia had resigned, with the Communist Party pledging to give up its monopoly on political power. The breathtaking changes of 1989 were symbolized by the fact that the Czech former dissident Václav *Havel, imprisoned for nine years under the old regime, became Czechoslovakia's new president.

Collapse was contagious: Demonstrations in the German Democratic Republic (GDR, or East Germany), which had begun in the fall of 1989, grew larger and larger, while tens of thousands of East Germans poured out of the GDR, allowed in September by the still-communist Hungarian government to escape through their country. Budapest's willingness to grant passage to fleeing East Germans marked the end of the perverse solidarity of the East bloc communist leaders, who had for decades helped keep their shared social system in place by forcing each other's citizens to return to their native countries if they were caught trying to leave. On 7 November, the infamous Berlin Wall separating East and West Germany fell, as GDR leaders tried desperately to conciliate their restive population with the concession of freedom to travel to the West. But to no avail—the days of communist leaders in East Germany were clearly numbered, though their final ouster did not take place until the following year. Finally, as 1989 drew to a close, Romania's Nicolae Ceaușescu, the most repressive of East European communist leaders, was overthrown in December.

In October 1989, Soviet foreign minister Eduard Shevardnadze had announced the Soviet Union's new policy of nonintervention in Eastern Europe, the so-called Sinatra doctrine (taken from the lyrics, "I did it my way," of a Frank Sinatra song). While at first it was unclear whether the Soviets meant what they said, it soon became apparent that they were serious, which effectively pulled the rug out from under the East German regime of Erich Honecker and Miloš Jakeš's Czechoslovak communist government.

The precise Soviet motives for adopting this new hands-off policy are still unknown. However, it is highly unlikely that Mikhail *Gorbachev and other leaders of the Soviet Union believed that they were setting in motion a process that would culminate in the collapse of communist leaderships throughout Eastern Europe, not only in the countries mentioned above, but within months in Albania and Bulgaria as well. It is even more unlikely that Soviet leaders deliberately set about to depose the Communist Party leadership of the Soviet Union itself.

Gorbachev's decision not to intervene in Eastern Europe was no doubt motivated by the hope that conservative, old-line leaderships would be replaced by communist reformers who could act flexibly enough to keep the system intact. Likewise, he probably hoped that within the Soviet Union a mod-

ernized and liberalized communist system could survive. Yet by August 1991, with the failure of the hard-line coup attempt in Moscow, the communist system was finished in the countries of the old Soviet bloc. Only in Cuba, North Korea, Vietnam, and Laos did communism survive, albeit in some cases in increasingly attenuated form.

After the Euphoria. The collapse of communism in Central and Eastern Europe and the Soviet Union was greeted with euphoria by millions around the world. But the elation soon dissipated as it became evident that the new democracies of the former Soviet bloc faced massive problems and widespread discontent.

The sources of discontent were both economic and political. People had hoped that the end of the old system would bring relief from the economic crisis of the communist system, which had been unable to deliver consumer goods at anything comparable to Western levels. Moreover, the vast majority of people had hoped not only for political liberties but also to be rid of the entrenched communist elites. But the new post-communist leaders adopted radical "free-market" programs, which meant "shock therapy" austerity measures for the bulk of the population in the old Soviet bloc. At the same time, the old communist privileged class, the so-called nomenklatura, often managed to retain its prerogatives—either by holding on to its previous ministerial or management positions, or by manipulating the *privatization process so that they themselves became the new owners of property. This process was so typical that it became known widely as "spontaneous privatization" or "nomenklatura embourgeoisement."

For the most part, Western analysts believe that shock therapy is a necessary, if painful, requirement for destroying the old communist system, while Western-led international financial institutions such as the *International Monetary Fund (IMF) and the *World Bank have made the adoption of rapid privatization and radical austerity measures a precondition for Western aid, debt forgiveness, or debt rescheduling. This Western stance has reinforced the conviction of most of the first wave of post-communist leaders of Central and Eastern Europe and the Soviet Union that state intervention in the economy is harmful, and that state ownership of enterprises is intrinsically inefficient.

Unfortunately, the social cost of the transformation process has been extremely high. Unemployment soared in all the countries of the region. Meanwhile, the cost of energy and consumer goods rapidly increased as post-communist governments in Eastern Europe and the former Soviet Union freed prices, slashed subsidies, and held down wage levels. To make matters worse, domestic industry was severely weakened by the rush of Western imports that followed the abolition of import controls; meanwhile, in an effort to protect farmers and industries at home, Western governments maintained high levels of *protection against lower-priced goods from the East.

The proponents of shock therapy, led by its foremost advocate, Jeffrey Sachs of Harvard University, argued that it was the only way to raise living standards and strengthen democracy in ex-communist countries. After the initial "shock," a strong surge in trade was supposed to occur, bringing living standards up to Western European levels. All the countries adopting shock therapy experienced prolonged economic crisis and mass impoverishment, although the depth of the crisis varied from country to country. In none, however, did living standards approach those of Western Europe during the first decade after 1989. And in all the former communist nations of Europe, economic misery fueled the growth of authoritarian nationalist political currents.

The crisis was deepest in Russia, where the government of Boris *Yeltsin launched a radical shock therapy program in 1991. The vast majority of the population experienced great hardships. Savings were wiped out by hyperinflation in 1992. Pensions and wages went unpaid for months at a time. Large parts of the population were reduced to living by barter and promissory notes. There was widespread malnutrition and a profound health crisis—an increase in typhoid, diphtheria, tuberculosis, deaths from stress-related diseases, and the rates of murder and suicide. Overall life expectancy declined sharply, especially for Russian males. Popular anger largely took the form of demoralization and political apathy, but some of it was channeled in the direction of growing xenophobia and disillusionment with democracy, which the "reformers" had succeeded in identifying with free market capitalism.

Shock therapy was supposed to create the institutional conditions for foreign investment, which Sachs and others saw as key to the economic revival of the former Soviet bloc. But those countries that adopted the policy have attracted little foreign investment. Critics of the policy saw it as a Western-imposed plan for social engineering that was, at best, misguided, and, at worst, a deliberate attempt to subordinate Eastern Europe and the former Soviet Union to Western economic and political power. Shock therapy aimed at breaking up the old Soviet-dominated Council for Mutual Economic Assistance (COMECON) region as an interdependent unit and substituting a "hub and spokes" system, in which the West would be the hub and the former communist states the spokes. Both negative incentives (threatening to withhold IMF loans, for example) and positive encouragements were used to elicit cooperation from the target states. The chief positive incentive has been the offer of membership in the European Union. Candidates for membership—there were five by the end of the 1990s: Poland, the Czech Republic, Hungary, Slovenia, and Estonia—had to reduce government regulation of business and liberalize prices, trade, and capital flows to qualify.

The United States feared that the revolutions of 1989 might lead to the creation of a pan-European economic and security structure like that proposed by François Mitterrand in 1990—a European confederation stretching "from the Atlantic to the Urals"—which might eclipse, the *North Atlantic Treaty Organization (NATO) and thus sideline U.S. power in Europe. Shock therapy's hub and spokes design, therefore, fit into the U.S. preference for excluding Russia from Europe and absorbing most of Eastern Europe into NATO, a policy that was also supported by Britain. Thus, the disappearance of the Warsaw Treaty Organization (Warsaw Pact), while seeming to deprive NATO of its raison d'être, actually gave it a new lease on life. In 1999, Poland, Hungary, and the Czech Republic joined NATO. The United States also used NATO to organize Western intervention in the crises spawned by the breakup of Yugoslavia.

Overt *nationalism has been on the rise throughout the region since the changes of 1989. In part this was inevitable, given the pent-up popular resentment against the artificial multinationalism of many of the communist states. Far from eradicating traditional national feelings, the domination by the "center" in countries like communist Yugoslavia or the former Soviet Union added new dimensions to old animosities. Moreover, the harsh economic and social conditions that followed the revolutions of 1989–90 intensified the inevitable conflicts.

The growth of nationalism and xenophobia left few areas of Europe's former communist zone untouched and, in some cases, produced an extraordinary level of violence. Yugoslavia fell apart in 1991 as the non-Serb republics declared their independence in response to the virulent Serb chauvinism of Slobodan Milošević. Milošević, in turn, engineered savage military assaults on, first, Croatia and then Bosnia. The brutal war in Bosnia ended with the Dayton Accords in 1995, which divided the republic along ethnic lines; meanwhile, the war allowed Croatian president Franjo Tudjman, with Western acquiescence, to expel virtually the entirety of that country's Serbian minority. Throughout the 1990s, the mainly Albanian population of the Serbian province of Kosovo was subjected to severe repression; finally, an armed revolt of Kosovar Albanians and massive "ethnic cleansing" by Milošević's forces led to a brief war by NATO against Serbia in 1999. The Russian government under Yeltsin and his successor, Vladimir Putin, made war on the Chechens, who sought their independence. Tensions between the Czechs and Slovaks, fed in part by popular discontent with the shock therapy program of prime minister Václav Klaus, caused the breakup of the Czechoslovak federation at the end of 1992 and the creation of two new nations, Slovakia and the Czech Republic. There was discrimination against, and sometimes physical attacks on, minorities in many countries. Restrictive citizenship laws in Latvia and Estonia disenfranchised those countries' large Russian minorities. But intolerance was harshest toward the Roma, or Gypsies, at least eight million of whom live in Eastern Europe. Particularly in Slovakia and Romania, where they comprise 10 and 8 percent of the population, respectively, the Roma found their situation considerably worse than it had been under communism, with strict social segregation and no protection against violence, including attacks by the police.

The social frustrations that mounted in the aftermath of 1989 also encouraged a witch-hunting atmosphere toward any individuals suspected of responsibility for the oppression of the communist years. Economic and social insecurity fostered widespread popular resentment as people searched for scapegoats to explain their hardships. Moreover, many members of the old elite had been allowed to slip comfortably into positions of power and privilege under the new order. One reason the new leaders permitted this to happen was because they felt they needed the expertise of these old figures; another reason was that they desperately hoped to avoid risking the open social conflict that they feared would accompany a strong challenge to the prerogatives of the communist elite.

However, a high price had to be paid for routinely granting the old figures of power new positions of authority. *Human rights groups like the U.S.-based Helsinki Watch, which had played a critical role in monitoring human rights violations of communist regimes, expressed growing concern in the 1990s about such post-communist practices as the uncritical use of old police files to determine if individuals in Central and Eastern Europe had been guilty of collaborating with the secret police, with no opportunity for accused individuals to challenge the contents or confront their accusers. Yet much of the population, exasperated by the growth of stark new inequalities and by the fact that communist bureaucrats were rising to the top regardless of their past roles, had little patience with civil libertarians who called for due process in deciding the culpability of former communists.

At the same time, however, in most of the countries of the former Soviet bloc, the old communist parties, now renamed "socialist," experienced a resurgence. The economic hardships produced by shock therapy promoted anger toward the centrist and conservative parties that, in most cases, initiated these policies and even a certain nostalgia for the relative security of communism, with its full employment and low-cost public services. Ex-Communist parties actually came to power at various times in Hungary, Poland, Bulgaria, and Lithuania, and they became important oppositional forces in the Czech Republic and Slovenia; they never really lost power in Romania and Serbia. In Germany, the Communists, renamed the Party of Democratic Socialism, were strong in the former GDR. In opposition, the ex-Communist parties acted as the voice of protest against privatization and high unemployment, but in power—apart from Romania and Serbia—they pursued policies that differed little from those of the other major parties.

The Future of Postcommunist Societies. Democracy is fragile throughout Central and Eastern Europe and the former Soviet Union. In part this is because of the weakness of civic opposition movements in the communist years. Those who contended that communism was impervious to change from below because of its success in preventing the emergence of democratic movements overstated their case—witness the Hungarian Revolution of 1956, Czechoslovakia's 1968 *Prague Spring, the courageous Soviet dissidents, the Polish Solidarity movement of the 1980s, and the dramatic events of 1989.

Yet it was difficult to organize popular movements under communism, especially movements with any longevity and social depth. When the collapse of 1989 came, therefore, in most instances much of the population was newly involved in public life, with very little experience in democratic debate or participation. This legacy of the past contributed to the difficulty of building viable democratic institutions in Central and Eastern Europe and the former Soviet Union after the fall of communism.

The democratic initiatives that blossomed throughout the region in 1989–90 were an important, albeit frail, source of future civic vitality. If the West can be both generous and flexible toward Central and Eastern Europe and the former Soviet Union; if it can encourage an experimental and socially sensitive approach to building post-communist society; then it can help foster the economic conditions under which these tender initiatives can survive and flourish.

(See also COMMONWEALTH OF INDEPENDENT STATES; COMMUNIST PARTY STATES; DEMOCRATIC TRANSITIONS; HELSINKI ACCORDS; PERESTROIKA; POST-COMMUNISM.)

Timothy Garton Ash, *The Uses of Adversity* (New York, 1989). Joanne Landy, "Politics and the Economy: What's to Come in the USSR?" *Social Policy* 22, no. 2 (Fall 1991): 17–31. Ivo Banac, *Eastern Europe in Revolution* (Ithaca, N.Y., 1992). John Feffer, *Shock Waves: Eastern Europe After the Revolutions* (Boston, 1992). Peter Gowan, "Neo-Liberal Theory and Practice for Eastern Europe" *New Left Review*, no. 213 (September–October 1995).

THOMAS L. HARRISON

NIXON, Richard Milhous. The thirty-seventh president of the United States, Richard Milhous Nixon (1913–1994) remains the most durable yet polarizing American political figure of the second half of the twentieth century. He helped to launch the *Cold War that he also helped to end. He typified the McCarthy era that he also helped to restrain. The man whose early career gave him the nickname "Tricky" eludes a final judgment.

Born of Ulster-Irish parents who had become Quakers, he grew up in Southern California, where his family had an adequate income, for which it nonetheless did conscious scrambling. In the town and at the college named after the Quaker poet John Greenleaf Whittier, Nixon was an industrious and successful student, debater, and amateur actor. He studied law at Duke University (1934–1937) on a scholarship; applied, unsuccessfully, for employment with the Federal Bureau of Investigation; and entered a law firm back in Whittier. In 1942, Nixon joined the war effort as a Washington bureaucrat (in the Office of Emergency Management). But after six months at this job he volunteered for the navy, which sent him to the South Pacific as a supply officer.

The year he was mustered out of the navy (1946), he ran the first of two vitriolic campaigns in California that established his reputation as a man always on the attack. In 1946, he defeated a popular incumbent, Jerry Voorhis, in a contest for the U.S. House of Representatives. The campaign was among the first to make an opponent's relation to communism the issue—Nixon alleged that Voorhis had ties with a Communist-influenced union (the CIO).

After an unchallenged reelection to his House seat in 1948, Nixon waged another ferocious campaign, this time against Helen Gahagan Douglas for the Senate, helping further to define Cold War electioneering (his campaign literature called Douglas a "pink lady," the name of a faddish cocktail). During his second term in the House, Nixon had been the most active member of the Committee on Un-American Activities in the investigation of Alger Hiss on a charge of espionage. Earlier in 1950, Hiss was convicted of perjury in his answers to that charge. This sent Nixon into the election year as the hero of anti-Communists; but he already was, and would forever be, a villain for those who believed that Hiss had been destroyed by the falsehoods of his accuser, Whittaker Chambers.

The year of the Hiss conviction and the Helen Douglas campaign was also the year when Senator Joseph McCarthy of Wisconsin began his melodramatic denunciation of Communists in government. By 1952, Dwight *Eisenhower chose the young Senator Nixon as his running mate, hoping to bring Taft Republicans of the Right into alliance with the Eastern branch of the party led by Eisenhower's promoter, Thomas Dewey. Nixon was expected to address the concerns and control the excesses of the McCarthyites.

During the Campaign, however, allegations about a "secret" Nixon campaign fund (an essentially innocent arrangement) made the Eisenhower team consider dropping him from the ticket. In a desperate bid to be retained, Nixon went on national television to make an emotional revelation of his financial status. The speech is called "the Checkers speech" after the dog he itemized among his belongings. The reaction to this speech forced Eisenhower reluctantly to embrace a man he still distrusted. In the self-abasements of the Checkers broadcast, Nixon revealed a knack for prevailing by being violated. As one of the world's aggrieved, he would know how to mobilize resentments.

As vice president, Nixon was more active than his predecessors in that office—discreetly so after Eisenhower's heart attack and later stroke. In his travels, Nixon was vilified by mobs in Latin America and by Nikita *Krushchev in Moscow—to his political betterment at home. Nixon lost the presidency in 1960 by the closest margin in the history of the presidential elections. Popular myth ascribes his loss to a poor showing in the first televised debate with his opponent, John F. *Kennedy. But Nixon blamed his loss on Eisenhower's unwillingness to manipulate the economy at election time—a mistake Nixon would not repeat in 1972.

Sent back to California by his defeat, Nixon ran a halfhearted and feckless race for governor, and gave a bitter "last press conference" after the loss that seemed to end his political career. His leaving California, his political base, to practice corporate law in New York seemed to confirm his demise. Yet, by an extraordinary political resurrection, Nixon forged a role for himself as party veteran, campaign adviser, and fund-raiser. He stayed loyal to the party during its disastrous defeat under Barry Goldwater in 1964, winning back conservatives who had grown cool to him during his service under Eisenhower (and who were looking with admiration to a new conservative star, Ronald *Reagan).

Nixon began his effort toward the 1968 Republican nomination as an apparent underdog to Michigan governor George Romney; but he defeated Romney, and fended off a last-minute bid by Reagan to lead the Republican Party against an incumbent vice president (Hubert Humphrey) who was even more crippled by dependence on his own president, Lyndon *Johnson, than Nixon had been in 1960.

By choosing the aggressive Spiro T. Agnew as his running mate, Nixon kept many conservatives from drifting toward the third-party candidacy of Governor George Wallace of Alabama. Although Nixon beat Humphrey only by a plurality (43.4 percent to Humphrey's 42.7), the combined vote for Nixon-Agnew and for Wallace and his running mate, Air Force General Curtis LeMay, came to 57 percent—a clear repudiation of the Johnson administration.

As president, Nixon was experimental in domestic affairs, although not insistent on the innovative programs he sponsored (e.g., the Family Assistance Plan). Yet Nixon's interest in domestic programs was dutiful. His enthusiasm and best skills were reserved for foreign policy. With great ingenuity he maneuvered toward goals he was not previously suspected of (or credited with) cherishing—normalized ties with the People's Republic of China, the easing of tensions (*détente) with the Soviet Union, and *arms control agreements (SALT I signed, SALT II negotiated). He used unorthodox methods in working for these accomplishments—secrecy, "back channel" communications outside customary diplomatic conduits, and the practical displacement of his secretary of state (William Rogers) by an all-purpose personal emissary (National Security Council aide Henry *Kissinger).

A right-wing revolt against these moves was contained by Nixon's prolongation of the *Vietnam War. Many conservatives, angered by the "sellout" of Taiwan and the limitation of nuclear weapons, were unwilling to desert a president while the Left was demonstrating against him in the streets. Nixon tried to turn the war over to South Vietnamese forces ("Vietnamization"), but had to support those forces' faltering efforts with ancillary technological interventions—the secret bombings of Cambodia (1969), followed by an open "incursion" into Cambodia (1970), ever-heavier bombing of North Vietnam's cities, followed by the mining of Haiphong's harbor (1972). Working for a peace "with honor" (i.e., without open abandonment of South Vietnamese allies), in 1969 Nixon rejected terms little worse (and far better enforceable) than he had to settle for in 1973—after 20,000 more American deaths and proportionally graver casualties to both sides in Vietnam itself. When the South Vietnamese regime fell after U.S. withdrawal, Nixon blamed that on congressional unwillingness to resume the bombing and negotiating cycles.

The great domestic priority for Nixon was his own reelection. Determined not to repeat Eisenhower's mistake of facing an election with poor inflation and employment figures, he timed the 1971 imposition of wage and price controls (an abomination in the eyes of his early supporters) to bring about a spurt of renewal in 1972. He even wanted to replace Spiro Agnew on his 1972 election ticket with the wage and price manager, Secretary of the Treasury John Connally. Taking no chances on the election, Nixon arranged for the political surveillance and covert activities that led to a break-in at Democratic headquarters in the *Watergate Hotel and to the chain of revelations and attempted cover-ups that resulted in his resignation after a landslide reelection in 1972.

Although ready to abandon ideological consistency himself, Nixon managed to heat the ideological temperature around him in ways that will confuse all judgments made on him into the foreseeable future. Those who had admired him were dismayed at his reversals on subjects like China, détente, and arms control. These things were, in turn, his finest achievements in the eyes of his natural opponents who could not, despite these good works, forgive him his years of redbaiting, his conduct of the Vietnam War, and his attempts at the suppression of dissent. He survived by keeping all sides off balance—which makes it hard for a consensus to be reached among people so often inspired and disgusted by his acts (often in swift succession). Yet, just as Nixon worked at his own political resurrection after the electoral defeats of 1960 and 1962, he spent his years after resigning office in a strenuous and partly successful attempt to rehabilitate his reputation. Denied control over his own presidential papers after his attempt to alter and suppress the record during the Watergate crisis, he nonetheless raised the money to build his own library in Yorba Linda, California, to whose opening Presidents Ford, Reagan, and Bush came in a kind of ritual of Republican reinstatement. Never fully able to cast off the specter of Watergate, he died in New York City in 1994. Nixon will, no doubt, be respected but not liked, in death as in life; but always he will fascinate.

(See also McCARTHYISM; POLITICAL BUSINESS CYCLE; PRESIDENCY, U.S.; STRATEGIC ARMS LIMITATION TREATIES.)

Richard Nixon, *Six Crises* (Garden City, N.Y., 1962). Garry Wills, *Nixon Agonistes* (Boston, 1970). Richard Nixon, *RN: The Memoirs of Richard Nixon* (New York, 1978). Stephen E. Ambrose, *Nixon, Volume I: The Education of a Politician* (New York, 1987). Stephen E. Ambrose, *Nixon, Volume II: The Triumph of a Politician, 1962–1972* (New York, 1989). Herbert S. Parmet, *Richard Nixon and His America* (Boston, 1990).

GARRY WILLS

NKRUMAH, Kwame. In the course of a career that spanned four decades, and that saw him assuming, variously, the roles of intellectual, anticolonial fighter, pan-Africanist, nationalist, socialist, diplomat, and prime minister and president of *Ghana, Kwame Nkrumah distinguished himself as one of the greatest leaders of the twentieth century.

The humble circumstances of his birth in 1909, in a Ghanaian village, contributed to his acute consciousness of, and lifelong struggle against, colonialism and exploitation. He was educated in Ghana and the United States. While in the United States, he became involved in the fight for *African Americans and in Marcus Garvey's movement; he helped Paul Robeson, W. E. B. *Du Bois, and the Council on African Affairs to promote African decolonization and self-determination as well.

Moving to London in 1945, he became co-organizer of the Pan-African Congress of 1945, from where he helped plan the subsequent anticolonial nationalist struggles in Africa and elsewhere. Later, in 1958, as the head of newly independent Ghana and torchbearer of African emancipation, he organized two historic conferences: the Conference of Independent African Nations and an All-African People's Conference. Ghana, under Nkrumah, became the training ground for anticolonial struggle and African unity, in accordance with his belief in the "oneness of Africans" and the "total liberation of the continent."

Ghana owes much of its significance to the force of Nkrumah's personality and intellect. Forming the largest mass organization in Ghana's history, the Convention People's Party (CPP), in 1949, he led Ghana to independence in 1957, opposed by the middle-class professionals and intelligentsia who felt he had usurped their right to succeed the colonialists.

In the first few years of Nkrumah's rule, Ghana was relatively prosperous mainly thanks to its healthy export earnings and to Nkrumah's decision to invest in the social and economic infrastructure of the country—education, industrial projects, health clinics, factories, and housing. Nkrumah's preoccupation with the "political kingdom," however, came at the expense of a full-fledged socioeconomic revolution: before long, the realities of managing a neocolonial entity took hold. The CPP became a shell of itself; state institutions—among them the army, police, and civil service—retained their colonial character; more important, the economic structures in place before independence remained intact.

Steering Ghana in these times proved difficult. Nkrumah's political opponents became bolder and stronger, twice attempting his assassination. He, in turn, became more repressive—detaining without trial, and eventually creating a one-party state. The once-representative CPP became a vehicle for crude wealth accumulation and repression. It constructed a personality cult around "the redeemer" and "the leader who never dies." Coupled with the perils of dealing in an increasingly hostile external economic environment, an impasse was inevitable. Even though the armed forces, with external help, overthrew his regime in February 1966, Nkrumah continued to cast a long shadow over Ghanaian politics until his death in 1972.

One of Nkrumah's legacies is as a theoretician of the African *revolution. In ten books and numerous pamphlets, he laid out the historical, philosophical, theoretical, analytical, and prescriptive foundations of the struggle for liberation in Africa. He concretized the notion of the triple heritage of modern Africa: traditional, Islamic, and European.

Ultimately, his most enduring legacy for Africa's future will be his exemplary life of commitment and struggle. He was a patriot grappling with questions of emancipation, dependence, neocolonialism, and the creation of a genuine social revolution. His life is instructive in the seeming contradictions between his words and deeds, as an avowed anticolonialist yet managing a neocolonial economy, and for his ideological shifts dictated by specific historical circumstances. Throughout his life, however, Kwame Nkrumah remained the truest servant of genuine African unity.

(See also AFRICAN SOCIALISM; DECOLONIZATION; NATIONALISM; PAN-AFRICANISM.)

George Padmore, *Pan-Africanism or Communism?* (London, 1955). Basil Davidson, *Black Star: A View of the Life and Times of Kwame Nkrumah* (London, 1973). Erica Powell, *Private Secretary (Female)/Gold Coast* (New York, 1984).

AKWASI P. OSEI

NON-GOVERNMENTAL ORGANIZATIONS. Organizations like Oxfam, Greenpeace, *Amnesty International, and thousands of others serve the public on a national and international scale. Known variously as "private voluntary organizations," "civil society organizations," and "citizen associations," they are increasingly called "NGOs," an acronym that stands for "non-governmental organizations." The *United Nations system uses this term to distinguish representatives of these agencies from those of governments. While many NGOs dislike the term, it has come into wide use, because the UN system is the main focus of international rule-making and policy formulation in the fields where most NGOs operate.

Charitable and community organizations, separate from the state, have existed in many historical settings, but NGOs are primarily a modern phenomenon. With the extension of *citizenship rights in Europe and the Americas in the eighteenth and nineteenth centuries, people founded increasing numbers of these organizations, as instruments to meet community needs, defend interests, or promote new policies. The French writer Alexis de Toqueville emphasized the importance of what he called "political associations" as institutions of *democracy, uniquely numerous and influential in the United States at the time of his famous visit in 1831. New legal rules for private corporations, emerging at this same time, provided modern juridical authority for the organizations and increased their defenses against state interference.

The antislavery movement, founded in England in the late 18th century, gave rise to many such organizations and eventually led to the World Anti-Slavery Convention (1840), a milestone gathering to coordinate the work of citizen organizations on an international basis. The World Alliance of

YMCAs was founded soon after, in 1855, and the International Committee for the Red Cross came into being in 1863. During the nineteenth century, independent associations of this kind addressed many issues, including women's rights, the condition of the poor, alcohol abuse, and municipal reform. Trade unions emerged as a leading force in the NGO movement later in the century.

Today, NGOs address every conceivable issue and they operate in virtually every part of the globe. Though international NGO activity has grown steadily, most NGOs operate within a single country and frequently they function within a purely local setting. Some, such as legal assistance organizations, mainly provide services. Some, such as chambers of commerce, concern themselves with narrowly defined interests. And some, such as neighborhood associations, promote civic beautification, or community improvement. But many important NGOs, such as those working for *human rights and social justice, campaign for broad ideals.

At the international level, thousands of organizations are active. According to one estimate, some 25,000 now qualify as international NGOs (with programs and affiliates in a number of countries)—up from less than 400 a century ago. Amnesty International, for example, has more than a million members and it has affiliates or networks in over ninety countries and territories. Its London-based International Secretariat has a staff of over 300 which carries out research, coordinates worldwide lobbying, and maintains an impressive presence at many international conferences and institutions.

Political scientists often refer to NGOs as "pressure groups" or "lobby groups," but this concept does not do justice to these organizations and their broad public influence. In the 1980s, the term *"civil society" came into fashion, but it proved too broad and amorphous. For this reason, a cross-disciplinary speciality emerged in the 1990s focusing on NGOs and their role in society. Scholars working in this area have noted that NGOs can command great legitimacy, sometimes more than national authorities. An opinion poll in Germany, for example, found that considerably more respondents said they trusted the NGO Greenpeace than the German Federal government. NGOs create *"public goods," needed by citizens, that are not ordinarily created in the for-profit marketplace. Economists sometimes refer to NGOs and the broader, nonprofit part of the economy as the "Third Sector," to distinguish it from government and private business. In some large countries, this sector accounts for millions of jobs and billions of dollars of economic activity.

NGOs are often seen as synonymous with nonprofits, but a distinction between the two is useful. Nonprofits include a very wide range of organizations, including museums, universities, and hospitals, that focus on services and rarely (if ever) engage in advocacy. By contrast, NGOs always have an important advocacy mission.

In the field of *international relations, scholars now speak of NGOs as "non-state actors" (a category that can also include transnational corporations). This term suggests NGOs' emerging influence in the international policy arena where previously only states played a significant role. Though NGOs have few formal powers over international decision making, they have many accomplishments to their credit. In recent years, they have successfully promoted new environmental agreements, greatly strengthened women's rights, and won important *arms control and disarmament measures. NGOs have also improved the rights and well-being of children, the disabled, the poor, and indigenous peoples. Some analysts believe that these successes resulted from increasing globalization and the pressure of ordinary citizens to control and regulate the world beyond the nation state.

NGO work on the environment led to the adoption of the Montreal Protocol on Substances Depleting the Ozone Layer in 1987. The International Campaign to Ban Land Mines, an NGO coalition, was prime mover in the Mine Ban Treaty of 1997. The Coalition for an International Criminal Court was indispensable to the adoption of the 1998 Treaty of Rome, and another NGO mobilization forced governments to abandon secret negotiations for the Multilateral Agreement on Investments in 1998. In the late 1990s, the NGO Working Group on the *Security Council emerged as an important interlocutor of the UN's most powerful body, while the Jubilee 2000 Campaign changed thinking and policy on poor countries' debt. At the same time, an increasingly influential international NGO campaign demanded more just economic policies from the *World Trade Organization, the *International Monetary Fund, and the *World Bank. These recent NGO victories have often been due to effective use of the Internet, enabling rapid mobilization of global constituencies.

NGOs operate with many different methods and goals. Some act alone while others work in coalitions. Some organize noisy protests and demonstrations, while others prefer sober education or quiet diplomacy. Some "name and shame" those in power who abuse citizen rights, while others work closely with the authorities. Some simplify the issues for broad public campaigns, while others produce detailed studies to inform policy makers.

NGO action can be analyzed on three different levels: micropolicy, macropolicy, and norm-setting. Some NGO campaigns combine all three. For example, the World Court Project, a network of NGOs opposed to *nuclear weapons, successfully brought a landmark case to the World Court in 1996 on the legality of nuclear weapons. Getting the Court to accept the case was a victory in the arena of micropolicy, but the larger campaign goal included macropolicy (changing governments' strategic reliance on nuclear weapons) and norm-setting (persuading the public that nuclear weapons are immoral and a threat to real security).

Governments and international organizations at times find NGOs a nuisance or even threatening to their interests. But officials, nonetheless, look to NGOs for innovative ideas and information. Officials also grudgingly recognize that consultation with (and support from) NGOs gives their public decisions more credibility. Former Secretary General Boutros Ghali affirmed that NGOs "are an indispensable part of the legitimacy" of the United Nations, while his successor Kofi Annan has said that NGOs are "the conscience of humanity."

NGOs are very diverse and by no means are all equally laudable. In addition to organizations dealing with human rights, environmental protection, and humanitarian assistance, there are NGOs representing industry associations like soap and chemicals, narrowly zealous religious organizations, and advocates of obscure causes like Esperanto and space colonization. While some NGOs are fiercely independent, others are known as the creatures of governments, businesses, or even criminal interests. Some have hundreds of thousands of members around the world while others speak for only a handful of people. Some have large central secretariats and some are very decentralized. With such diversity, generalizing about NGOs can be difficult.

Recently, the number of NGOs has been growing rapidly. Thousands of NGOs have sprung up in such diverse countries as France, Bangladesh, the Philippines, and Chile. Many observers see these trends as signs of increasing *pluralism and democracy, because authoritarian and paternalistic governments have either outlawed independent NGOs or confronted them with severe administrative hurdles and harassment. Large numbers of NGOs certainly help to reflect a complex and diverse social reality and represent a rich variety of citizens' needs and concerns that governments, on their own, could scarcely identify or accommodate.

As NGOs take an increasingly important role in political life, some critics are concerned that NGOs speak in many different and conflicting voices that can fragment and weaken political action. Often, there are many competing NGOs in the same policy field and their mutual contest for influence can undercut political effectiveness. Many respected NGOs work hard to overcome this narrowness by operating in close partnership with others. Some NGOs themselves specialize in coalition building. InterAction, for instance, serves as the umbrella for dozens of humanitarian organizations in the United States.

Even the most democratic governments subject NGOs to some type of control, such as registration and financial oversight. *International organizations like the UN require officially accredited NGOs to pass through a review process to determine which are legitimate partners. Thanks partly to these controls and to the ethos of public service in the NGO community, NGOs are not often accused of *corruption, breaches of the law, gross failure to live up to their mandate, or other serious abuses. Compared with the frequent scandals of corruption and abuse of authority by officials of nation states, NGOs appear as relatively virtuous.

Nonetheless, some accuse NGOs of being structurally undemocratic and unaccountable. Elected government officials often defend themselves against NGO criticism by pointing out that NGO leaders are not elected. Though it is true that NGO leaders do not stand for election, they are held accountable by boards of directors, membership bodies, and other constituencies. They also must win voluntary financial support each year from members and donors and cannot rely on legally enforced taxation as governments do.

Financing. Large international NGOs may have operational budgets in the tens of millions of dollars, though most NGO budgets are considerably smaller. Compared to corporations and governments that count their annual revenue in multiple billions, even the largest NGO budgets are very small indeed.

NGOs are usually financed by a combination of sources. Traditionally, membership dues have provided the main source, but today, NGOs tap many other sources including grants or contracts from governments and international institutions, fees for services, profits from sales of goods, and funding from private foundations, corporations, and wealthy individuals.

Increasingly, relief and development NGOs like CARE and Oxfam receive large grants from governments' international assistance programs. In the 1990s, the UN High Commis-

sioner for Refugees expressed alarm that governments were increasingly channeling funds for humanitarian assistance to their own national NGOs rather than to multilateral agencies. The agencies were losing their capacity to coordinate relief in large-scale emergencies, as dozens of NGOs appeared on the scene.

By 1994, *European Union funding of NGOs had risen to about US$1 billion. According to UN staffer Antonio Donini, public grants represented 1.5 percent of NGO income in 1970 and 35 percent in 1988. Such grants probably accounted for more than 40 percent of NGO income by the end of the century. This trend inevitably exposes NGOs to pressure from governments and limits their capacity to act independently.

When NGOs take money from businesses, big foundations, and rich individuals, such hefty grants can likewise create relations of influence and potentially lead NGOs away from their mandate to serve the broader public. Increasingly, also, NGOs sell products or services, just like a private company. The American Association of Retired Persons (AARP) is an extreme example of this tendency. In 1996 it had US$3.8 billion in gross revenue for supplemental health insurance and nine mutual funds with US$13.7 billion in assets. To many observers, this looks more like a financial services company than an NGO. Thousands of other hard-pressed NGOs worldwide have taken the business path—selling credit cards, Internet services, travel tours, and key rings, while charging for services they once provided free.

Diplomatic Role. Though NGOs have long operated internationally, their role in the sphere of official diplomacy was relatively restricted until after World War II. NGOs won their right to a voice at the United Nations by heavy lobbying during the wartime negotiations (1943–45). Their rights were eventually guaranteed by Article 71 of the UN Charter and affirmed by many subsequent decisions. By 2000, about 2,500 NGOs had consultative status with the UN and many thousands more had official arrangements with other organs in the UN system and other intergovernmental bodies.

The Earth Summit in Rio, in 1992, set the pace for intense NGO participation in world conferences, with 17,000 NGO representatives participating in the NGO parallel forum and 1,400 directly involved in the intergovernmental negotiations. NGOs helped make the conference a success, claimed an important place in the conference declaration, and played a key role in developing post-conference institutions, like the Commission on *Sustainable Development. Three years later, the Fourth World Conference on Women, in September 1995, attracted an astonishing 35,000 NGO representatives to Beijing to the parallel forum and 2,600 to the intergovernmental negotiations.

NGOs have been most effective when they work together in coalitions, pooling their resources and coordinating their lobbying efforts. There are important NGO networks on the environment and on international economic policy that allow NGOs to coordinate their actions in many countries and at international conferences and negotiations. Third World Network, based in Malaysia, is an especially active example that addresses a very broad range of policy issues. There are national networks like the Philippine-based Freedom from Debt Coalition and the German NGO Network on Environment and Development. And there are regional networks like ARENA, the Asian Regional Exchange for New Initiatives, or the Continental Network of Indigenous Women of the Americas, or AFRODAD, the African Debt and Development Network. In 1995, an international consultation of NGO networks concluded that: "Business and government are organized at the international level. There is a growing need to articulate countervailing visions . . . In the long run, we have to invent the infrastructure so citizens can participate effectively in the democratic management of the global system. Over the next decade, NGOs and their networks are one of the important precursors of an accountable global civil society."

As discussions continue about democracy and accountability in global decision making, it becomes increasingly clear that NGOs have a vital role to play. *Globalization has created both cross-border issues that NGOs address and cross-border communities of interest that NGOs represent. National governments cannot do either task as effectively or as legitimately. In the globalizing world of the twenty-first century, NGOs will have a growing international calling.

(See also ENVIRONMENTALISM; INTERNATIONAL DEBT.)

Thomas Princen and Matthias Finger, *Environmental NGOs in World Politics* (London, 1994). Paul J. Nelson, *The World Bank and NGOs: The Limits of Apolitical Development* (New York, 1995). Thomas G. Weiss & Leon Gordenker (eds.), *NGOs, the UN & Global Governance* (Boulder, 1996). Peter Willetts, *"The Conscience of the World:" The Influence of Non-Governmental Organisations in the U.N. System* (London, 1996). Global Policy Forum, *NGOs and the United Nations* (New York, 1999).

JAMES A. PAUL

NONALIGNED MOVEMENT. The Nonaligned Movement (NAM) is an international social movement of small and middle-sized states whose principles, collective identity, strategies, and organization seek to establish a more equitable and peaceful world order. It began with twenty-five states, mostly former colonies, in Belgrade in 1961. In a postcolonial era characterized by East-West conflict and the nuclear arms race, new states in Africa, Asia, the Caribbean, Latin America, and Europe struggled against being drawn into superpower alliances of the Cold War led by the United States and the former USSR, and formed the NAM to preserve their political and economic independence, change the world system, and influence global matters.

Nonalignment is an integral part of the *foreign policy of NAM members. Its principles include a commitment to peace and disarmament, especially an end to militarization and nuclear weapons; economic equality, particularly through restructuring international economic and political orders that exploit the South to benefit the North; cultural equality, including an end to Western cultural imperialism and a reorganization of the world information and communications system that supports it; and multilateral decision making on global matters through support of the UN.

The NAM is a relatively new type of political formation—an international, state-centered, nonhierarchical, dynamic coalition of members with different political, economic, social, and religious systems. It has a flexible organization and meets in different regions and at the UN. The most important are foreign ministers' meetings and summits of heads of state at which nonaligned policy statements are prepared for action within the UN system. The chair of the NAM is rotated, as well, and decisions are made by consensus.

From its first summit to its eleventh in 1995, the NAM has grown to 113 states representing more than half the world's population. Summit meetings respond to current international crises and make recommendations for resolving long-standing issues. The 1961 Belgrade summit sought peace and the prevention of a nuclear holocaust that could result from East-West tensions. Support for *decolonization and *national liberation movements was the focus of the second and third summits, in Cairo (1964) and Lusaka (1970). The Algiers summit (1973), with its call for a New International Economic Order, was a watershed. In their analysis of how the arms race increased global economic disparities, the nonaligned called for disarmament and linked it to the transfer of resources for development.

The NAM increased its membership and institutionalization through its fifth, sixth, and seventh summits (Colombo, 1976; Havana, 1979; New Delhi, 1983). Its support for decolonization contributed to many newly independent states choosing nonaligned status. This was also a period of destabilization, as it dealt with regional conflicts in the *Third World and efforts by the West to thwart nonaligned activities through military interventions and withdrawal of economic assistance. At Harare (1986), its eighth summit, the NAM focused on defending the right of the peoples of southern Africa to achieve self-determination outside an East-West framework, calling again for the independence of *Namibia and the end of apartheid, both of which have been achieved.

At its ninth and tenth summits, the NAM deftly made the transition to a post–Cold War world—another watershed. In Belgrade (1989), it sought a more constructive discourse with the West as the Cold War drew to a close, but expressed fear of new regional conflicts and the persistence of North-South inequities. The Jakarta summit (1992) made development and the eradication of poverty a global priority, reiterating the Algiers focus, and called for a new multilateralism, including greater North-South cooperation. The eleventh summit, in Cartagena (1995), elaborated the NAM's new orientation. It promoted national development that focused on services for people and noted the effects of such global issues as the degradation of the environment and illicit drug trafficking on development. It also pursued the North-South dialogues and increased democratization of the UN, such as reforming the Security Council, to better address economic inequities.

The NAM has accomplished many objectives. It contributed to the end of the Cold War through continual emphasis on the futility of the arms race and the relationship between disarmament and development. It initiated UN Disarmament Conferences, supported North-South dialogues, and devised action programs for a New International Economic Order. It has advanced the end of all forms of colonialism, especially in its pursuit of a UN settlement of Namibian independence and its efforts to resolve Middle East tensions, including the recognition of the rights of Palestinians. Other actions include the return of cultural artifacts to countries of origin, the rights and welfare of youth and women, the protection of the global environment, the formation of a new international information order, and more.

The NAM will have to respond to a new world situation. With the end of the Cold War, greater attention can be given to eliminating regional conflicts. Religious and ethnic conflicts within states and between states need to be resolved. North-South disparities replace East-West tensions as the central focus of inequities among states and regions and pose different problems and solutions. The UN remains a center of multilateral decision making for the NAM, but faces many challenges to restructure itself. Disarmament efforts took a new turn with India's and Pakistan's nuclear testing in 1998. The "Asian economic crisis" has worldwide ramifications and political and economic dimensions. The destruction of the environment and its impact on development is a global issue as developing countries industrialize. Numerous social issues need attention, including the situation of children, the advancement of women, and the persistence of racism. The NAM has proved adaptive to changes over the decades as it asserts the vision and role of small and middle-sized developing states in reshaping the world order. Its principles and practices contribute to a new theory of *international relations.

(See also INTERNATIONAL SYSTEMS NORTH-SOUTH; RELATIONS.)

A. W. Singham and Shirley Hune, *Non-alignment in an Age of Alignments* (London and Westport, Conn., 1986). *Cartagena 95: Basic Documents* (Cartagena, 1995). Renu Srivastava, *India and the Nonaligned Summits* (New Delhi, 1995).

SHIRLEY HUNE

NONPROLIFERATION, NUCLEAR. India's nuclear tests in May 1998, followed by Pakistan's nuclear detonations a few days later, reverberated throughout the international nonproliferation *regime. Since the end of the *Cold War, this regime had come under new strains, but had managed to limit the spread of *nuclear weapons, as it had during the previous four and a half decades.

Since the end of World War II, only the United States (1945), the Soviet Union (1949), Britain (1952), France (1960), and China (1964) had successfully tested nuclear weapons. India had exploded a so-called peaceful nuclear device in 1974, while Pakistan (until May 1998) and Israel were widely suspected of maintaining "bombs in the basement." The nuclear club, while larger than preferable, was far smaller than many had predicted. The major reason was the strength of the international nonproliferation regime that has developed since the 1950s. This regime includes a number of legal arrangements between and among the nuclear weapons states (NWSs) and non-nuclear weapons states (NNWSs). The 1968 Non-Proliferation Treaty (NPT) is widely viewed as the centerpiece of the regime. Under the NPT, which has 186 members (all countries except India, Pakistan, Israel, and Cuba), the NNWSs promise to refrain from acquiring nuclear arms in return for unfettered access to nuclear technology for peaceful purposes and a reduction in the nuclear arsenals of the NWSs. The treaty thus attempts to codify the somewhat artificial distinction between peaceful and military uses of nuclear technology. In 1995, its members decided to extend the NPT indefinitely, subject to periodic review conferences to determine whether the NWSs were abiding by their pledges to disarm.

Other important pillars of the regime are *international organizations and agreements that make it difficult for states to misappropriate nuclear technology: the Vienna-based International Atomic Energy Agency (IAEA), which applies safeguard mechanisms to nuclear activities; the 1963 Partial Test Ban Treaty, which prohibits member-states from testing nuclear devices in the atmosphere, in outer *space, and underwater; the 1967 Treaty of Tlatelolco, which makes all of Latin America a nuclear-weapons-free zone; and the Nuclear Suppliers Group, a collection of over thirty countries that have agreed not to transfer particularly sensitive nuclear technology to NNWSs that do not adhere to the NPT and IAEA safeguard agreements. Further, many countries have independently come to understand that a nuclear arsenal would be detrimental to their domestic policy objectives by requiring the diversion of scarce economic and scientific resources; foreign policy objectives would be harmed, as well, by aggravating relations with neighbors, allies, adversaries, and international lenders.

To be sure, a handful of countries have not accepted the underlying premise of the nonproliferation regime, namely, that the spread of nuclear weapons is destabilizing to regional and international security. Rather, these countries regard these weapons as a prized scientific and engineering accomplishment, evidence of modernity, a source of status and political influence, and a means to deter and intimidate adversaries.

Still, the nuclear tests by India and Pakistan ran counter to some encouraging nonproliferation developments in recent years. The newly independent states of the former Soviet Union returned to Russia the nuclear weapons they inherited that were stationed on their territory and took steps, with international assistance, to ensure that their nuclear materials were accounted for and under proper physical protection (although the transfer of nuclear technology, especially to Iran, continued to arouse concern). Both Russia and the United States were also slowly coming to grips with safely disposing of nuclear weapons material from their dismantled nuclear arsenals.

Suspected nuclear weapons programs had also been thwarted, at least temporarily. The Democratic People's Republic of Korea agreed to freeze and eventually dismantle its national nuclear program, including its plutonium production plant, in a 1994 "Agreed Framework" deal with the United States. Iraq's nuclear ambitions were exposed by the *Gulf War; the United Nations subsequently established a Special Commission (UNSCOM) and empowered it to destroy, remove, or render harmless Baghdad's nuclear (as well as chemical, biological, and ballistic missile) activities. However, due to Iraq's refusal to cooperate with UNSCOM and disagreements among the permanent members of the UN Security Council over continuing sanctions on Iraq, UNSCOM was replaced in April 2000 with the UN Monitoring, Verification and Inspection Commission (UNMVIC). It is unclear whether this new entity will be any more effective in getting Iraq to comply with its international obligations to disarm.

At the international level, the Comprehensive Test Ban Treaty (CTBT) was opened for signature in 1996; although over 145 countries have signed it, it will not come into force until it is ratified by at least all forty-four countries that possess nuclear reactors. The U.S. Senate's refusal in October 1999 to consent to ratification of the CTBT dealt a blow to this multilateral effort to curtail the spread of nuclear weapons. Recent efforts have also concentrated on a missile material cutoff treaty, which would cap (but not eliminate) the production of nuclear weapons materials.

Do the Indian and Pakistani tests announce the start of a new global nuclear *arms race? Or are they the last spasms of an anachronistic technology that has been outpaced by global markets and the new information superhighway? The answer may depend on how the international community responds to the actions of Delhi and Islamabad. Will it simply acquiesce to the reality of a nuclear South Asia by seeking a new accommodation with the latest members of the nuclear club? Or will it take steps to reinforce the nonproliferation regime that has served the cause of regional and international stability so well for the past fifty years?

The answers to these questions may turn on another factor—the push for national missile defense (NMD) by the United States. In the late 1990s NMD evolved from a purely domestic issue concerning budgetary and technological questions to a global debate focusing on arms control strategy and proliferation considerations. Critics claim NMD would upset the existing strategic balance by forcing other countries to increase their nuclear arsenals in order to pierce the defensive shield; it would also spell the end of the Anti-Ballistic Missile (ABM) Treaty, which has formed the basis of superpower deterrence and strategic stability for almost thirty years. Advocates argue that a strategic posture based on defense rather than the threat of nuclear retaliation is more moral; also, nothing should dissuade the U.S. Government from protecting its population. Some advocates of NMD also express a willingness to share the defensive technology with other countries to overcome their concerns. How the United States handles this issue will significantly influence prospects for nonproliferation.

(See also ARMS CONTROL.)

Scott D. Sagan and Kenneth N. Waltz, *The Spread of Nuclear Weapons: A Debate* (New York, 1995). Rodney Jones, ed., *Tracking Nuclear Proliferation 1998* (Washington, D.C., 1998). Jospeh Cirincione, ed., *Repairing the Regime: Preventing the Spread of Weapons of Mass Destruction* (New York, 2000).

MITCHELL B. REISS

NONVIOLENT ACTION. A general technique of sociopolitical action applied by people and institutions through the use of symbolic protest, noncooperation, and nonviolent intervention, nonviolent action may also be called "nonviolent struggle" or "nonviolent sanctions." Since the 1986 struggle against the *Marcos dictatorship in the Philippines, this technique is frequently called "people power."

Role of Power. Nonviolent action is an application of a very simple truth: people do not always do what they are told to do, and sometimes they do that which has been forbidden. This technique is thus rooted more in human stubbornness than in a belief in turning the other cheek. When people refuse their cooperation, withhold their help, and persist in their disobedience and defiance, they are denying their opponents the basic human assistance and cooperation which any government or hierarchical system requires. If they do this collectively through their established independent social institutions or newly improvised groupings for a sufficient period of time, the power of that government or hierarchical system will weaken and potentially dissolve. The basic political principle underlying nonviolent action is that hierarchical systems and all governments, including dictatorships, are able to function only to the degree that they receive the submission and cooperation of the people and institutions within them—whether that assistance is freely given or induced by fear.

A Technique of Conflict. Nonviolent action is a way to conduct conflict. It is a response to the problem of how to act effectively in politics, especially how to wield *power. In this technique, however, people and institutions apply societal pressures other than physical violence. Nonviolent action may involve: (1) acts of omission—that is, people may refuse to perform acts which they usually perform, are expected by custom to perform, or are required by law to perform; (2) acts of commission—that is, people may perform acts which they do not usually perform, are not expected by custom to perform, or are forbidden to perform; or (3) a combination of acts of omission and commission.

Methods of Struggle. Three broad classes of methods are included in the technique. (1) Where the nonviolent group uses largely symbolic actions intended to help persuade the opponents or someone else, or to express the group's disapproval and dissent, the behavior may be called nonviolent protest and persuasion. Marches, parades, and vigils are among the methods of this class. (2) Where the nonviolent group acts largely by withdrawal or the withholding of assistance, submission, and cooperation, its behavior may be described as noncooperation. This class contains three subclasses: social noncooperation (such as social boycotts or ostracism), economic noncooperation (including many types of economic boycotts and labor strikes), and political noncooperation (among them noncooperation with government units, *civil disobedience, mutiny, and severance of diplomatic relations). (3) Where the nonviolent group acts largely by direct intervention, its acts may be referred to as nonviolent intervention (disrupting usual routines psychologically, socially, economically, politically, or physically). The methods in this class include sit-ins, hunger strikes, nonviolent obstruction, nonviolent invasion, and parallel government. Some of the more visible manifestations of people power, such as blocking tanks, fall into this class.

Often in this technique people use their usual roles in the social system as means of direct resistance. This occurs, for example, when factory workers refuse to continue working because of a grievance, or when judges refuse to enforce the illegitimate orders of putschists. The impact of noncooperation will be influenced by the type or extent of the group's usual participation in the normal functioning of the system. The application of noncooperation by key groups and the use of multiple methods of nonviolent struggle have the potential to slow, halt, paralyze, or even disintegrate the institution or political system against which it is employed.

Such defiance will not be welcomed by the opponents, and they may apply extreme violent repression in attempts to force a resumption of passive submission and cooperation. That will not necessarily succeed, however. Nonviolent struggle has been demonstrated to be capable of operating successfully under such harsh repressive conditions.

Indeed, at times the use of extreme violence against disciplined nonviolent struggle may contribute to the success of the resisting population. Through a process of "political jujitsu," violent repression sometimes drives more people to join in the resistance, alienates some usual supporters of the opponents sufficiently that they, too, protest and resist, and causes third parties to oppose the opponent group and support the nonviolent struggle group.

Mechanisms of Change. The nonviolent technique has its own requirements for effectiveness. These include sound strategy, wisely chosen tactics and methods, persistent action despite repression, and nonviolent discipline. Physical violence, or the threat of it, is excluded in nonviolent action, for it disrupts the general dynamics of this type of conflict.

The technique possesses special mechanisms of change which must be implemented if a given struggle is to succeed. When successful, nonviolent action achieves results through one of four broad mechanisms of change or some combination of them. (1) In conversion, the opponents come around to a new point of view in which they positively accept the nonviolent actionists' aims. (2) In accommodation, the opponents choose to compromise and grant some of the resisters' objectives, adjusting to the new situation produced by the conflict but without changing their viewpoint. (3) Where nonviolent coercion operates, change is achieved against the opponents' will and without their agreement because they have lost control. Nevertheless, the opponents still retain their institutional positions and hold to their original opinions. However, the sources of their power have been so undercut by the nonviolent means that they no longer are able to deny the objectives of the nonviolent actionists. (4) Finally, in disintegration, the opponents' sources of power are so completely removed that the whole system or government simply falls apart. This occurred, for example, with the communist regimes in the German Democratic Republic (East Germany) and Czechoslovakia in 1989.

"War without Violence." Nonviolent action is so different from milder peaceful responses to conflicts (such as conciliation, arbitration, and negotiation) that several writers have pointed to certain similarities of nonviolent action to military warfare. Nonviolent action is also a means of combat. It, too, involves the matching of forces and the waging of "battles," requires wise strategy and tactics, and demands of its "soldiers" courage, discipline, and sacrifice. The degree of bravery required, however, is no greater than that required by military means, and the casualty rates in nonviolent struggles repeatedly appear to be very much lower than those in comparable violent conflicts.

The Choice of Nonviolent Struggle. Nonviolent action has been overwhelmingly applied by groups that would have been willing to use violence in other circumstances. In most cases the choice to employ the nonviolent means has been made out of pragmatic considerations. These include assessments of the resisters' objectives and resources, the nature of the conflict, and the strengths and weaknesses of the opponents. Such action has seemed to be the obvious way to pursue certain objectives. In many cases nonviolent struggle has been consciously chosen because optional violent forms of action were seen in advance to be ineffective or unrealistic, or because violence had already been used and failed.

Nonviolent struggle has sometimes been practiced widely even when the rhetoric of resistance has been "armed struggle"—as was the case in South Africa in the 1970s and 1980s with the widespread use of school boycotts, rent strikes, and demonstrative funerals. A similar situation occurred in some European antifascist resistance movements during World War II that used such forms as strikes, civil disobedience, and symbolic protests, although they supported the Allied military efforts.

Much more rarely, nonviolent means have been chosen over violence for religious or ethical reasons, or at times because of a mixture of normative and practical motives. In some cases, even when pragmatic political considerations were dominant in the choice of nonviolent struggle, the movement has taken on certain religious or ethical overtones. This was the case in the campaigns of the Indian National Congress for independence from Britain in the 1920s, 1930s, and 1940s. Those struggles, often under *Gandhi's leadership, and also the civil rights campaigns in the 1950s and 1960s in the Deep South of the United States, under the leadership of Martin Luther *King, Jr., and others, are very important, but they are not historically typical. In most cases, elements of religious or ethical nonviolence are much weaker or absent, and charismatic leaders are not present.

Scholarly Study and Preconceptions. Nonviolent action has in recent decades been subjected to the beginnings of research and analysis by social scientists. As a result, it is now clear that some common assumptions about this technique and various preconceptions about its requirements and limitations are not valid. As late as the 1960s, for example, it was sometimes assumed that nonviolent struggle in politics had been an innovation made by Gandhi. It is now clear, however, that nonviolent struggle has been widely practiced throughout history in all parts of the world.

The belief that nonviolent action usually requires much more time to produce success than does violence is not accurate. As with violence, the length of nonviolent struggles varies widely. In some cases, success has even come within days or weeks, as in the nonviolent revolutions against the military dictatorships of El Salvador and Guatemala in 1944 or in the noncooperation and defiance of the August 1991 coup in the Soviet Union.

Contrary to the view that nonviolent action can occur or succeed only under democracies, much nonviolent struggle has been practiced, sometimes successfully, against oppressive systems and extreme dictatorships. For example, nonviolent resistance was used with varying degrees of effectiveness during the Nazi occupations of Norway, Denmark, and the Netherlands. Nonviolent struggle even at times played a significant role in saving Jews from the *Holocaust, as in Berlin, Bulgaria, and Denmark. In communist-ruled Eastern European countries, nonviolent struggle was widely practiced, beginning in 1953 in East Germany, then in both Poland and Hungary in 1956. Czech and Slovak resistance to the 1968 Soviet-led invasion was a powerful case of improvised nonviolent struggle used for national defense which held off the Soviet objective of a hard-line regime for eight months. The successful ten-year struggle of *Solidarity in Poland (1980–1990) exemplified the ability of people to carry on nonviolent resistance under the harsh conditions of martial law. In 1989–1990 nonviolent struggle contributed significantly to the collapse of communist rule throughout Eastern and Central Europe.

Surprisingly, the preconception that this technique can operate only when both parties share common ethical norms, such as the Judeo-Christian heritage, still surfaces from time to time. Much contrary evidence exists, however. Nonviolent struggle has been widely practiced in diverse cultures of the world, including its use by Muslims, atheists, Hindus, Buddhists, Marxists, and people of other persuasions. Scholarship on nonviolent struggle has also clearly separated the technique of nonviolent action from belief systems espousing ethical or religious "principled nonviolence" or "pacifism"—of which there are various types. Some groups of believers in "nonviolence" still view the nonviolent technique and moral or religious belief systems as necessarily closely tied. Some such believers even reject nonviolent action. Belief systems espousing ethical and religious nonviolence are clearly distinct phenomena from nonviolent action. Although nonviolent action is usually extraconstitutional (that is, it does not rely upon established institutional procedures of the state), it is possible to incorporate the technique into constitutional government at various points, and even to use it to defend an established government against attack.

Civilian-Based Defense. Since 1964, serious explorations have been made into the potential of a refined, developed, and prepared use of the nonviolent technique for national defense, against both internal *coups d'état and foreign aggression. This policy is usually now called "civilian-based defense." It aims to block domestic usurpers or foreign aggressors from establishing illegitimate rule over the attacked society.

Opinions differ among policy makers and strategists of this policy as to its proper role in a country's defense preparations. Increasingly, the disagreements are not about whether civilian-based resistance options have a role, but rather about what role that should be, and how large a role they are capable of playing. In 1986, the Swedish Parliament unanimously added such a "nonmilitary resistance" component to its overwhelmingly military "total defense" policy. Switzerland and Austria have similar components, officially at least. In 1991 the writings about civilian-based defense influenced the Lithuanian, Latvian, and Estonian defenses against attempted coups aimed to depose the independence-minded governments of those countries.

Increased Knowledge and Practice. Knowledge about the nature, requirements, and strategic principles of the nonviolent technique is increasing and spreading at the same time that the practice and visibility of nonviolent action are expanding. This technique is now widely recognized as a potentially powerful alternative to violence for groups engaged in acute conflicts. The development of research and policy studies on this technique itself marks a significant new stage in the historical development of the technique.

(See also CIVIL RIGHTS MOVEMENT; NINETEEN EIGHTY-NINE; PEACE; PEACE MOVEMENT; POLITICAL VIOLENCE; PRAGUE SPRING; REVOLUTION.)

Gene Sharp, *The Politics of Nonviolent Action* (Boston, 1973). Peter Ackerman and Christopher Kruegler, *Strategic Nonviolent Conflict* (Westport, Conn., 1994). Ronald McCarthy and Gene Sharp, eds., *Nonviolent Action: A Research Guide* (New York, 1997).

GENE SHARP

NORTH AMERICAN FREE TRADE AGREEMENT. See NAFTA.

NORTH ATLANTIC TREATY ORGANIZATION. Founded in 1949, the North Atlantic Treaty Organization (NATO) has played a collective defense role for its member allied states. The geographic scope of NATO was specified in Article 6 of the North Atlantic Treaty as including "the territory of any of the Parties in Europe or North America" as well as any "islands under the jurisdiction of any of the Parties in the North Atlantic area north of the Tropic of Cancer." In the event of attack upon any NATO member or "on the forces, vessels, or aircraft of any of the Parties" when operating in or over "the Mediterranean Sea" or elsewhere in "the North Atlantic area," *alliance members are committed under Article 5 of the same treaty to "assist the Party or Parties so attacked." More specifically, each member is pledged "individually, and in concert with the other Parties," to take "such action as it deems necessary" for restoring and maintaining "the security of the North Atlantic area." Such action may include "the use of armed force," although this is not a necessary response.

Beyond the collective-defense role of the NATO alliance, Article 2 identifies a much broader purpose. Alliance members are to pursue "further development of peaceful and friendly international relations by strengthening their free institutions, by bringing about a better understanding of the principles upon which these institutions are founded, and by promoting conditions of stability and well-being." Moreover, NATO countries "will seek to eliminate conflict in their economic policies and will encourage economic collaboration between any or all of them." From the start, NATO was understood to be more than just a military alliance.

NATO came into existence soon after the beginning of the *Cold War. Direct military response to Soviet closure of access routes to Berlin in the form of an airlift of supplies to the beleaguered city (1948–1949), *Marshall Plan aid to help rebuild the economies of Western European states (beginning in 1947), the *Truman Doctrine (announced on 12 March 1947) by which the United States pledged "to support free peoples who are resisting attempted subjugation by armed minorities, or by outside pressure," and formation of the *Council of Europe, the Western European Union (WEU), and NATO were among the Western responses to the changed international environment. NATO soon became an essential part of a new European security order that aimed to contain the Soviet Union and curb any expansionist tendencies it might have, to anchor in the West what would become the Federal Republic of Germany (FRG), and to assure U.S. commitment to the defense of Western Europe.

The charter members of NATO were the members of the WEU (Belgium, France, Luxembourg, the Netherlands, and the United Kingdom) plus Canada, Denmark, Iceland, Italy, Norway, Portugal, and the United States. Later accessions, bringing membership to its current nineteen, were Greece and Turkey (1952), the FRG (1955), Spain (1982), and three former *Warsaw Treaty Organization Warsaw Pact members—the Czech Republic, Hungary, and Poland (1999). NATO's post–Cold War Partnership for Peace reaches out to a diversity of nonmember states in the North Atlantic area to include both former Warsaw Pact members, former Soviet republics, and neutral or nonaligned states—Albania, Armenia, Austria, Azerbaijan, Belarus, Bulgaria, Estonia, Finland, Georgia, Kazakstan, Kyrgyzstan, Latvia, Lithuania, Macedonia, Moldova, Romania, Russia, Slovakia, Slovenia, Sweden, Switzerland, Tajikistan, Turkmenistan, Ukraine, and Uzbekistan.

In 1966, claiming independent control of its military forces as a national prerogative, France withdrew from the alliance's integrated military command structure; however, it retained its membership in NATO and remained a full participant in the North Atlantic Council. Military-to-military, bilateral coordination by France with other NATO members, including the United States, increased substantially during the 1980s with joint planning and exercises conducted outside of the NATO structure. France also continued to participate in the WEU (which had added the FRG and Italy as members in 1954), but the organization maintained a low profile until the 1980s when it came to be seen as a useful complement to NATO (or by some as a potential substitute for NATO). A new role for the WEU emerged in the early 1990s as it assumed the task of coordinating European participation with the United States and Canada outside of the NATO area. Out-of-area NATO commitments had long been controversial within the alliance; the WEU merely provided an alternative forum for managing this issue. Following decisions taken in 1991 and 1992, the WEU has also served as agent on defense matters for the European Union and steps have been under way since 1999 to integrate WEU functions within the European Union itself.

Another difficult issue for NATO has been persistent conflict between two alliance members, Greece and Turkey. Following the crisis over Cyprus in 1974, considerable progress was made under NATO auspices in managing, though not resolving, conflict between the two. Indeed, peaceful management of Greek-Turkish conflict is seen by some as a most important NATO success story.

Resource constraints and economic competition among the NATO allies in arms production and sales have produced tensions within the alliance. Feeling that it has borne a disproportionate share of NATO defense costs, the United States for many years repeatedly called for greater burden sharing—an irritant to European allies who argued that many of their contributions were overlooked in the U.S. calculus. Acquisition of weaponry for use by NATO allies has also been highly charged politically, given its implications for industrial competitiveness within the alliance. Joint production and licensing arrangements with offset payments are among the measures that have been adopted to manage this issue. Rationalization, standardization, and interoperability (RSI) also became goals for a more efficient allocation of resource by the NATO allies. As a practical matter, however, it has been extremely difficult to agree upon rationalization—a national division of labor among the allies—or standardization and interoperability of weapons, ammunition, and spare parts.

NATO's military strategy in the 1950s and 1960s was heavily reliant on the threat of massive nuclear retaliation as response to aggressions, conventional or nuclear, by the Soviet Union and its Warsaw Pact allies. In 1967, NATO strategy shifted formally to flexible response, a posture that allowed for conventional *war-fighting options while still retaining a nuclear first-use option should that be deemed necessary. Forward defense—not trading space (particularly German territory) for time in any kind of planned, strategic retreat—was also an important element of the new NATO strategy. Both flexible response and forward defense were intended only as part of a *deterrence posture aimed at avoiding warfare al-

together. In addition to deterrence and the purely military aspects of security, the 1967 Harmel Report recognized the continuing importance of diplomatic efforts to reduce tensions and create stable international relations conducive to maintaining peace. As such, deterrence and *détente were seen as complementary approaches to security in the North Atlantic area.

The twin military-diplomatic track to security was also reflected in a 1979 decision to respond with a two-track approach to Soviet deployments of a new category of intermediate-range ballistic missiles. *Arms control negotiations were to be undertaken at the same time that NATO prepared to deploy its own ballistic and cruise missiles. Although NATO began missile deployments in 1983, the two-track approach did succeed in 1987 when the United States and the Soviet Union agreed to eliminate all intermediate-range ballistic missiles from their inventories. Throughout these negotiations, the NATO allies consulted regularly as they have done in other arms control talks—strategic arms limitation talks (SALT) in the 1970s, strategic arms reduction talks (START) beginning in the 1980s, mutual and balanced force reductions (MBFR) conducted between 1973 and 1989, and conventional forces and confidence-and security-building measures in the 1980s and 1990s. The latter negotiations resulted in agreement on substantial reductions and ceilings with respect to conventional forces, while providing for an extensive regime of notifications of exercises and troop movements and mutual inspections. Significantly, these negotiations were conducted under the auspices of the Conference on Security and Cooperation in Europe (CSCE).

Reduction of the risk of war in Europe through arms control and confidence building has led to a major reassessment of NATO strategy and NATO's relation to other international organizations associated with European security. NATO's London Declaration (1990) made it clear that changed circumstances had made reduced reliance on *nuclear weapons possible. Emphasis was also placed on the enduring political and economic aspects of collaboration among the NATO allies as elaborated in Article 2 of the North Atlantic Treaty, suggesting a reduced emphasis on "the purely military aspects" of the alliance.

Since the 1990s, NATO's headquarters in Brussels and its military command headquarters in Mons, Belgium, have undertaken major restructuring of military forces consistent with the new post–Cold War environment. At the same time, however, collective uses of force under NATO auspices—bombing campaigns and ground-force deployments, the latter primarily for peacekeeping purposes—have been conducted in the former Yugoslavia alongside civil efforts by UN agencies, the Organization for Security and Cooperation in Europe (OSCE), and various *non-governmental organizations (NGOs). Given tensions among alliance members with different perspectives, coordinating such activities proved difficult. U.S. reluctance in future decades to play as large a role in European security matters may lead to a different role for NATO as other alternatives are developed. Nevertheless, all-European alternatives to reliance on NATO—the WEU or a new defense arm of the *European Union—do not yet enjoy the infrastructure, forces, and institutional development that NATO has achieved in more than half a century of its existence.

(See also CONTAINMENT; SECURITY; STRATEGIC ARMS LIMITATION TREATIES.)

William T. R. Fox and Annette Fox, *Nato and the Range of American Choice* (New York and London, 1967). George Liska, *Nations in Alliance: The Limits of Interdependence* (Baltimore, 1968). Douglas J. Murray and Paul R. Viotti, eds., *The Defense Policies of Nations: A Comparative Study* (Baltimore, 1982, 1989). *The North Atlantic Treaty Organization: Facts and Figures* and *The NATO Handbook*, Brussels, NATO Information Service, various editions.

PAUL R. VIOTTI

NORTH KOREA. See KOREA, DEMOCRATIC PEOPLE'S REPUBLIC OF.

NORTH-SOUTH RELATIONS. Most analysts use the term "North South relations" to refer to the multilateral aspect of relations between developed and developing countries, which have gone through major transformations over the last four decades. Initially, as the developing countries achieved independence and began to act as a group on international issues, there was great optimism about the future of the North-South relationship. The oil crisis and the economic turbulence of the 1970s and after marked a second and far more controversial stage of the relationship. Confrontation became the norm, implicit beliefs about a long-term harmony of interests between the two sides were challenged, and many analysts were pessimistic that a viable relationship could be established. A third stage of the relationship began to emerge during the 1980s as the oil crisis waned, the debt crisis gained in force, supporters of market approaches became dominant among developed (and some developing) countries, and political and economic problems—domestically and internationally—continued to grow. For many developing countries the 1970s and 1980s were lost decades for development. Sharply increased resource transfers became even more imperative. Whether the confrontational North-South relationship of the past can now be replaced by a more cooperative relationship is unclear, but there are only limited grounds for optimism. In any case, these three stages, while overlapping to some extent, have largely defined the nature of the North-South relationship, an evolutionary relationship that is in part autonomous and in part a reflection of wider trends and developments in *international systems.

Why was there so much optimism in the early stage of North-South relations? One reason was that in developed and developing countries, political and intellectual elites tended to assume that economic development would be relatively easy, that political independence would ensure economic independence, and that relations between the two sides would be contentious in the short run but mutually beneficial in the long run. The developing countries would rapidly industrialize through import substitution and thus end dependence on raw materials exports whose terms of trade were declining. And what worked for the developed countries in the past would also work for the developing countries. For a while, until the oil crisis that began in 1973, the record of economic and political performance seemed to justify the optimism, although that record was greatly facilitated by extraordinarily high rates of growth in the world economy.

The second stage of North-South relations was dominated by the ascent of the *Organization of Petroleum Exporting Countries (OPEC), an unsettled world economy, and a major challenge by the *Third World—led by the Group of 77, its negotiating entity in the UN system—to establish a New International Economic Order (NIEO). OPEC's success in sharply raising oil prices energized the Third World, changing perceptions about relative power and the prospects for changing the international order. If other commodity producers could not emulate OPEC, because oil was indeed "different," it was at least hoped that the tacit threat of the oil weapon would induce the developed countries to make important concessions. But the OPEC "threat" was never implemented, largely because the main OPEC countries did not have much interest in undermining a system from which they were earning substantial benefits, and the developed countries could thus safely respond with a policy of delay and passive resistance. The developed countries also believed that the NIEO proposals were ideologically hostile to the liberal order they had created and in many cases economically unsound (even, in some instances, in terms of helping the Third World). Because the developing countries needed help quickly and because their effective power was largely limited to setting institutional agendas and passing resolutions—which could be ignored by the developed countries—the strategy of delay succeeded. But this meant that *both* sides lost an opportunity to negotiate useful changes.

The leadership of the Group of 77 clearly overestimated how much the configuration of power had changed in its favor and persisted in a strategy of confrontation, of demanding acceptance of new principles before discussing specific proposals, well past the point where confrontation had any chance of success. Still, because it was an article of faith in the Third World that unity was its only weapon (apart from the illusion that OPEC would sacrifice its own interests for the rest of the Third World), and because unity could be unraveled by compromises that did not promise benefits to all, the leadership was sharply constrained in its ability to alter negotiating strategies. Moreover, most of the Third World needed greatly increased international support not only to deal with the effects of rising import prices for oil, food, and manufactured goods, but also to deal with the growing domestic problems created by failures in political and economic development. This too made compromise difficult because only the presumed benefits of massive change seemed to promise enough additional resources to the Third World. Thus compromise was resisted and the Group of 77 continued to pursue a strategy that would have been appropriate only if underlying power relationships had in fact altered significantly and if in fact the postwar economic system was facing the "beginning of the end."

The second stage of North-South relations ended badly for the Third World. The arrival of power in several developed countries of conservative administrations that were even more hostile to the antimarket proposals in the NIEO, a continued decline in economic performance in most developing countries that undermined unity and forced an emphasis on immediate coping strategies, and the arrival of an era of interdependence that seemed only to promise increased dependence for developing countries marked the end of this difficult and confrontational period in North-South relations. If, however, we think of the South not merely as a coalition of the weak that won few benefits but also as an international social movement, responding to change and seeking to direct it in favorable ways, perhaps the balance sheet is not as bleak. The Third World did force consideration of its problems and perspectives, it did have some of its ideas and proposals incorporated into the mainstream discussion of the issues, and it did perhaps increase awareness of proper negotiating strategies and of both the limits and the possibilities of group bargaining. Debt, for example, began to be treated as a development issue rather than a liquidity problem; the industrialized countries recognized the need for special programs to help the least developed countries; and issues such as trade, finance, and industrial development were linked in discussions, rather than treated as separate topics. But the South did not achieve the NIEO, which was largely a rhetorical goal.

The third stage of North-South relations has been, and is, dominated by a sense of crisis, even despair. The "descent" of OPEC, the aftereffects of the debt crisis, trade conflicts, the rise of protectionism, and instability in the world monetary system are among the factors that have contributed to the sense of crisis. Some parts of the Third World, especially in East and Southeast Asia, did reasonably well over the past decade, but financial turmoil in those regions starting in 1997 may mean that the Asian "miracle" was fragile and that movements toward democratization will be undermined. Other parts of the Third World, especially in Africa, have been barely able to cope, forced to cut imports, to impose austerity policies, and to become even more dependent on external resource transfers.

In these circumstances, common action by the Group of 77 in the multilateral arena has become even more problematic because splits within the coalition have become more salient, the ability to remain unified behind long-term restructuring goals has diminished, and the emphasis has turned to short-term coping strategies. The growing emphasis on market approaches, reflecting both pressures from the developed countries and the manifest failures of nonmarket approaches, has also undermined the ideological coherence of the NIEO policies. "Coalitions of sentiment," as in the past, are being replaced by shifting and perhaps unstable "coalitions of interests." Perhaps the creation of the *World Trade Organization and the increasing number of developing countries who are accepting its norms and principles will generate more long-run prosperity, but the transition to the market will be rocky and the trading system itself may become increasingly conflictual.

There are also other secular trends that are generating ominous forecasts about the prospects for much of the Third World. The most profound of these trends concerns escalating deterioration as a result of linked crises from population growth rates, declining agricultural productivity, water shortages, and environmental decay. In addition, the amount of raw materials in manufactured products has continued to decline, injuring prospects for the many raw materials exporters in the Third World. Even the highly successful newly industrializing countries (NICs), whose prosperity rested initially on exporting labor-intensive manufactured goods, may suffer as labor costs become an increasingly smaller component of the final cost of manufacturers. This trend will also make it even more difficult for other countries to emulate the success of the NICs.

As Third World states are increasingly differentiated by their ability to cope, as multiple pressures and rising demands compel an emphasis on nationalistic, short-run responses, and as the developed countries turn away from the Third World and offer primarily lectures about the market, will North-South disappear as a central axis of concern? A definitive answer is impossible because North-South is not autonomous and is dependent on developments in the world economy and on domestic performance. Much also depends on ideological interpretation as conservative realists, free market advocates, liberal reformers, and radical theorists all bring their own perspectives to past, present, and future. Given the complexity of the issues, the wide diversity within the Third World, and the absence of a general theory of North-South, the lack of consensus is not surprising.

North-South will surely continue to exist in a formal sense as multilateral negotiations continue and as the problems besetting the Third World require some degree of *International cooperation for resolution. But it is likely to be most salient only on issues where the Third World is genuinely united, issues such as institutional reform and increased resource transfers. The "grand strategy" of confrontation is unlikely to be revived as the world order is transformed by trends and developments that neither side foresaw or clearly comprehends. North-South's greatest weakness has been insufficient concern with domestic linkages, a point of importance because international policies create opportunities that can be grasped only by states pursuing appropriate domestic policies. Only if these linkages are understood will North-South become an arena for the pursuit of mutual benefits rather than one of confrontation or compensation for failed domestic policies.

(See also DEVELOPMENT AND UNDERDEVELOPMENT; IMPORT-SUBSTITUTION INDUSTRIALIZATION; INTERNATIONAL DEBT; INTERNATIONAL POLITICAL ECONOMY; LOMÉ CONVENTION; NEWLY INDUSTRIALIZING ECONOMIES; NINETEEN EIGHTY-NINE.)

Robert L. Rothstein, *The Weak in the World of the Strong* (New York, 1977). Stephen D. Krasner, *Structural Conflict—The Third World Against Global Liberalism* (Berkeley, Calif., 1985). Robert L. Rothstein, "The Limits and Possibilities of Weak Theory: Interpreting North-South," *Journal of International Affairs* 44, no. 1 (Spring/Summer 1990): 159–181.

ROBERT L. ROTHSTEIN

NORTH YEMEN. See YEMEN.

NORTHERN IRELAND. A constituent part of the United Kingdom, Northern Ireland's political legitimacy has been contested by Irish nationalists since the 1920 partition of Ireland. Sectarianism and *nationalism have intersected throughout the modern history of this region, nourished by the coincidence between religious and political allegiances. Although devolution of the British state and the pathbreaking 1998 "Good Friday" agreement to form a power-sharing government suggest reforms of historical proportion, Northern Ireland society remains deeply divided along ethno-religious lines.

At the opening of the twentieth century, the northeast of Ireland was the major locale for internal opposition to constitutional efforts at home rule and to the Irish nationalist republican movement. The execution of republican leaders after the failed Easter Rebellion of 1916 thrust much of Catholic

Ireland into the nationalist camp, but segments of the more industrialized sectors and especially the descendants of Protestant settler colonialists in the northeast saw little economic advantage to independence and feared a loss of civil and religious liberties should the independence movement succeed. Partition under the 1920 Government of Ireland Act conceded the power of Unionist opposition to independence. The establishment of an independent Republic of Ireland with a constitution laying claim to its lost northern counties and asserting a special role for the Roman Catholic Church further underscored the need for Protestant unity and control. In the face of perceived external threat and internal disloyalty to the state, the Unionist Party fostered Protestant solidarity across class lines.

From 1920 to 1972, Stormont, the seat of local government, exercised relatively autonomous authority over the internal affairs of the region. Westminster retained control only of fiscal and treaty powers. Throughout this period, Protestants, who constituted about two thirds of the populace of Northern Ireland, dominated Stormont through the Unionist Party; Catholics, with about one third of the populace, generally supported reintegration with the predominantly Catholic Republic of *Ireland through the Nationalist Party. The Irish Republican movement (Sinn Fein) and its military wings have been almost entirely Catholic.

During the course of devolved rule, the leadership of the Ulster Unionist Party warded off internal conflicts among Protestants and effective opposition by nationalist Catholics. Unionists adopted electoral mechanisms designed to reduce flexibility in voter choice and favor Protestant votes (e.g., single-member constituencies, gerrymandered boundaries, and plurality rules); provided an official proportion of seats on the Ulster Unionist Council to delegates selected by the Protestant fraternal Orange Order; and gave preferential treatment to Protestants in public housing, works, and employment. Unionists exercised control over regime opponents through repressive legislation such as an infamous Special Powers Act that permitted arrest and suspension of civil liberties to anyone suspected of nationalist activities and through a three-tiered constabulary that virtually armed the entire Protestant male adult populace. In the face of such sectarian rule, the Nationalist Party frequently boycotted elections.

The political and socioeconomic bases of Protestant unity and Catholic opposition to this regime were eroded by developments in post–World War II Britain, especially the growing welfare state, the expansion of multinational capitalism, and the declining power of Ulster's industry. In this context of Britain's more active role in Ulster's internal affairs, a civil rights movement developed in the mid-1960s. Through sit-ins and marches, a coalition of Catholic professionals, university students, trade union activists, liberal Protestants, Labour members of Parliament, and supporters of the Irish Republican Army (IRA) directly challenged the system of political patronage and discrimination. A Social Democratic Labour Party (SDLP) was formed to press the nationalist and civil rights case in government. But the civil rights coalition was short-lived. The charismatic Reverend Ian Paisley founded the Democratic Unionist Party to mobilize loyalist Protestants against reform and to limit any government concessions to Catholics. Ethnic conflict escalated as loyalists resisted civil

rights marches and culminated in the emergence of a Provisional Irish Republican Army to defend Catholic neighborhoods, the dispatch of British troops throughout the province, and ultimately, in 1972, the introduction of direct rule by Westminster. The protracted ethnic antagonisms and suspicions were strengthened by British restrictions on civil liberties and human rights. For the next several decades, political and paramilitary opposition to power-sharing proposals was strong among both loyalists and republicans.

The "Troubles" have taken an enormous toll on the region. During the 1980s and 1990s, staple industries declined significantly and average unemployment exceeded 20 percent. Industrial decline and unemployment were felt sharply in both Protestant and Catholic working-class communities where paramilitaries found their base. Antidiscrimination policies and increased funding of nongovernmental associations fostered the development of a Catholic new middle class who largely supported the moderate nationalism of the Social Democratic Labour Party. At the same time, political alienation in working-class Catholic areas was especially profound, particularly after the death of republican prisoners in a 1981 hunger strike. In the wake of the strike, Sinn Fein, the political wing of the Provisional Irish Republican Army, ran candidates for the first time in Northern Ireland's history—its strategy of the "bullet and the ballot" appeared to successfully challenge the SDLP and spurred the governments of Britain and Ireland to push forward a process for negotiated settlement that would involve all political parties of the conflict in Northern Ireland. These efforts resulted in an Anglo-Irish Agreement (AIA) in 1985 which guaranteed that there would be no change in the status of Northern Ireland without the consent of the majority of the people in the region. Should such a majority approve the establishment of a united Ireland, both governments agreed to support such legislation in their parliaments. Unionist opposition to the AIA surfaced quickly, shaped in part by a fear of secret deals with Sinn Fein and in part by a recognition that demographic changes might produce a Catholic majority within a generation. But the agreement set the stage for a peace process that brought about republican and loyalist cease-fire, a Joint Declaration for Peace in 1995, and an elected Forum for peace talks, as well as official Joint Party talks.

In the face of vociferous opposition from many loyalists and republicans and substantial breaks in the cease-fires (including the massive 1996 bombing of Canary Wharf in London by the IRA), the peace process proceeded, with the active engagement of the American government, under the leadership of former U.S. Senate Majority Leader George Mitchell. In April 1998, the "Good Friday" agreement was signed, laying the basis for the establishment of a consociational form of government. The agreement affirms that so long as a majority of the citizens of Northern Ireland agree, the union will be maintained; it also affirms Nationalist aspirations for closer ties with the Republic through the establishment of a North-South Ministerial Council and other cross-border bodies. Finally, the agreement proposes the inclusion of a Civic Forum that would provide an arena for the participation of a broad segment of civil society, including trade unionist and voluntary and community groups, in politics. Notwithstanding strong divisions in the unionist community, the agreement secured majority support in both Northern Ireland

(71 percent) and the Republic (95 percent) in a referendum held in May 1998, and all political parties contested elections for the new Northern Ireland Assembly. A complex system for weighting votes insured that nearly all parties, including the small cross-communal Northern Ireland Women's Coalition, as well as one of the two parties associated with Protestant paramilitaries, the Progressive Unionist Party, secured seats in the new assembly. Despite the success of the referendum and the political prestige accorded First Minister David Trimble of the Ulster Unionist Party and Seamus Mallon of the Social Democratic Labour Party for their efforts to form a power-sharing government, the implementation of the agreement has been problematic. An anti-agreement republican group calling itself the Real IRA was responsible for the most extensive violence in the history of the "Troubles," a bombing in Omagh which killed twenty-nine people in August 1998. And loyalist opponents have also tried to sabotage the agreement through violence. Loyalist and republican paramilitaries retain massive amounts of weapons and explosives and, in light of continued sectarian outbreaks, it is not surprising that efforts to form a government nearly foundered on the issue of decommissioning. In July 1999, the Ulster Unionist Party refused to participate in the formation of the Executive with Sinn Fein, without a formal commitment to hand weapons over to the independent commission monitoring the process. The political stalemate was broken only in late 1999 when Mitchell's brokerage secured a formal statement from Sinn Fein, acknowledging a commitment to decommissioning and a contingent agreement on the part of the Unionist Party to go forward.

Despite the agreement on power-sharing, Northern Ireland remains an ethnically segregated and politically divided society. Although much research indicates that the two populations share common attitudes toward business, social class, family, and sexuality, there are important social and cultural practices that reinforce division. Educational and residential segregation, religious insulation, different leisure activities, and distinct voluntary associations all reinforce the sense of separate confessional identities and political values. The decades of the "Troubles" have exacerbated the extent of segregation and ethnic antagonism, most often evident during the summer marching season when the Protestant loyalist associations celebrate their religious heritage, ethno-national identity, and the Union with parades and communal gatherings. Often routed through Catholic neighborhoods, the parades have triggered violence, fueled interethnic antagonism, and become a major point of political contention. Policing is also a major point of contention, as the constabulary are predominantly Protestant and there is deep suspicion of criminal justice procedures among Catholics.

The impacts of British devolution and of the European Union on the future of Northern Ireland are uncertain. Under the devolution scheme, local governments will take over the administration of policies and distribution of funds for training, jobs, health, and education. The new Northern Ireland Assembly will face significant concern for communal parity in distribution of funds and implementation of policies. Although the European Union has contributed substantial funding to community groups and economic development initiatives that cross communal lines, the outcomes of these efforts to foster peace and reconciliation activities remain unclear.

And the EU's funding of regional languages and cultural projects may also foster greater ethno-political competition in Northern Ireland where concerns with ethnic parity are particularly acute. Devolution and the EU may support the peace process or may unwittingly foster greater ethno-regional politics.

Brendan O'Leary and John McGarry, *The Politics of Antagonism* (London, 1993). Joseph Ruane and Jennifer Todd, *The Dynamics of Conflict in Northern Ireland* (Cambridge, U.K., 1996). Cathall McCall, *Identity in Northern Ireland: Communities, Politics and Change* (New York, 1999).

KATHERINE O'SULLIVAN SEE

NORWAY. A small West European state of about 4 million inhabitants, Norway is relatively homogeneous both in terms of ethnicity (except for a Lapp population of 40,000 in the north) and religion (88 percent of the population are members of the Lutheran state church). Norway has a very long coastline facing the North Atlantic. Its most sensitive border is with Russia in the far North, close to the Kola Peninsula, which contains the former Soviet Union's largest concentration of marine forces. In the Cold War era, the northern part of the country was of crucial strategic importance as the northern flank of the NATO alliance, of which Norway has been a member since 1949.

A very poor and backward society in the early modern period, Norway has experienced considerable economic transformation since the mid-nineteenth century. Despite heavy dependence on the international economy, Norway avoided the pattern of underdevelopment often fostered by such dependence and became one of the world's richest countries per capita in the postwar period. Fish and timber were traditional export staples. Historically a seafaring nation, its merchant marine achieved success of international proportions. At the turn of the century, cheap energy could be generated by Norwegian waterfalls, and a sector of energy-intensive chemical industry (e.g., aluminum) became the new cornerstone of the economic structure. In the late 1960s, another energy source—oil—was discovered on the continental shelf west of Norway.

An independent Norwegian state existed in medieval times, but from 1523 to 1814 Norway was a Danish colony. There was no indigenous aristocracy. In 1814 Norway was granted home rule in a union with *Sweden, an arrangement that lasted until 1905. The cabinet consisted exclusively of civil servants, supported by sections of the countryside, bureaucracy, and business interests. In the national assembly (Stortinget), the opposition consisted of rural groups—the 1814 constitution had enfranchised all farmers—with important support among the urban intelligentsia. These groups became the Conservative (Høyre) and Liberal (Venstre) parties, respectively. The Liberals led the struggle for parliamentary government (1884) and together with the Labor Party (Det Norske Arbeiderpartiet, founded in 1887) secured universal suffrage for men in 1898 and for women in 1913. As industrialization spread in the early twentieth century, parties relating to special interests split from the Liberals: an Agrarian Party (Senterpartiet, 1920) and a Christian Party (Kristelig Folkeparti, 1933) supported by lay Protestant countercultures and those opposed to alcohol consumption. The bourgeoisie increasingly supported the Conservatives while the labor movement remained strong and unified. After some turbulence in the 1920s and the formation of a small Communist Party, Labor embarked on a reformist strategy. In 1961, an independent neutralist Socialist People's Party, or Sosialistisk Folkeparti (SF), broke away from Labor. Still, the basic structure of Norwegian postwar politics consists of a homogeneous social democratic Left facing a fragmented nonsocialist bloc. Labor was in power for nearly thirty years (1935–1965), except for united front governments during the German occupation of 1940–1945). Since then, collaborative governments of nonsocialist parties (the latest one 1997–2000) have alternated with Labor governments, but some emphasis on economic *planning and the institutional *welfare state has always persisted.

Norway has a mixed economy, with little direct state ownership of industry. Until the 1980s, the financial system was thoroughly regulated, with state banks providing a large share of total credit. Many traits of the Norwegian social structure—no indigenous aristocracy, a historically weak bourgeoisie, strong state, united *labor movement, small-scale owner-occupied farming—have bolstered equality as a basic norm. The social partners (workers, employers, farmers, and fishermen) have been organized in centralized bodies, and incomes policies have been consensual, although since the late 1970s, separate confederations for academics and white collar workers have challenged the traditional trade union confederation (Landsorganisasjonen).

The oil wells of the North Sea made Norway the largest oil exporter outside of *OPEC and, as a result, the Norwegian business cycle is heavily influenced by oil prices. Unemployment was low until the late 1980s. The oil price slump in 1985 created severe adjustment problems. Financial deregulation was implemented, causing a transitional financial crash in the late 1980s. Politics has become more volatile. In 1973, a right-wing populist tax-revolt party (the Fremskrittspartiet, or Progress Party) emerged. This, as well as a reorganized left-wing party, the Socialist Left Party, or Sosialistisk Venstreparti (SV), have gained support in the late 1980s, at the expense of Labor and the Conservatives. Norwegian governments twice negotiated the terms of entry into the European Union (1972, 1994), but in each of the ensuing referenda, voters came out narrowly against membership. As a signatory to the European Economic Area (EEA) agreement, however, Norway has been fully integrated into the EU's single market since 1994. This implies that Norwegian legislation includes all EU directives relating to the single market, despite the fact that Norway is not represented at all in the EU decision-making process. Norway's influence in Brussels is only indirect (in technical committees), through certain EEA institutions, and through informal diplomacy. This peculiarly asymmetric kind of integration so far has not created big problems, but that is partly due to implicit recognition by the EU Commission that Norwegian national interests in sensitive areas such as oil and gas must not be challenged.

(See also SCANDINAVIA; SOCIALISM AND SOCIAL DEMOCRACY.)

Stein Rokkan, "Norway: Numerical Democracy and Corporate Pluralism," in Robert Dahl, ed., *Political Oppositions in Western Democracies* (New Haven, Conn., 1966), 70–115. Jan Fagerberg, Adne Cappelen, Lars Mjøset, Rune Skarstein, "The Decline of Social-Democratic State Capitalism in Norway" *New Left Review* 181 (May–June 1990): 60–94.

LARS MJØSET

NUCLEAR WEAPONS. The first atomic weapons, including the two dropped on *Hiroshima and Nagasaki in 1945, derived their energy from fission, the splitting of atomic nuclei. Modern nuclear weapons, however, are based on fusion, the joining together of atomic nuclei at extremely high temperatures, the heat for which is created by an initial fission reaction. The subsequent chain reaction creates an enormous release of energy, causing massive destruction through the combined effects of heat, fire, shock, and wind. High levels of radiation are the by-product of the uranium and plutonium used in the fusion reaction.

The actual nuclear device, which can be the size of a small piece of luggage, is contained within a casing called a warhead. Strategic nuclear weapons are divided into four categories, according to the way in which the warhead is delivered to its target: intercontinental ballistic missiles (ICBMs), which carry the warhead into space and release it on a trajectory toward its target; submarine-launched ballistic missiles (SLBMs), which work in the same way, but are launched from submarines instead of land; bombers, which carry the warhead to its target; and cruise missiles, which reach their targets by air, flying a preprogrammed route close to the ground. In principle, however, a nuclear device can reach its target by virtually any means, including automobiles and even parcel post. Nuclear weapons have also been adapted to many other weapons systems, including artillery shells, land mines, short-range missiles, surface-to-air missiles, and depth charges.

Distribution. The vast majority of nuclear weapons are in the hands of the five nations known to possess them: the United States, Russia, China, France, and Britain (who, not coincidentally, are also the five permanent members of the UN Security Council). A portion of the formerly Soviet nuclear arsenal remained on Ukraine soil in the aftermath of the dissolution of the Soviet Union. In addition, several other nations are now assumed to possess nuclear weapons. India, which first exploded a "peaceful nuclear device" in 1974, may have a small arsenal of nuclear weapons intended for Pakistan, which has vigorously pursued the development of its own nuclear weapons. In 1989, an Israeli technician confirmed that Israel has built as many as several hundred nuclear weapons as weapons of last resort in the ongoing Middle East conflict. Other nations which are suspected to be developing nuclear weapons include Iraq and Libya. With the possible exception of Israel's, these arsenals are much outweighed by those of China, France, and Britain, each of which has many hundreds of weapons. Their arsenals, in turn, are dwarfed by those of the superpowers, who maintain many thousands of weapons in their so-called "tactical" arsenals, while reserving many thousands more for their "strategic" arsenals.

In 1968, international negotiators concluded the Nuclear Non-Proliferation Treaty (NPT), intended to halt the spread of nuclear weapons to other countries and to create an international *regime for the development and oversight of peaceful nuclear technologies. By 1987, more than 100 nations had ratified the treaty or had agreed to abide by its safeguards. But that treaty has only a twenty-five-year life span. Any extension or renewal is not automatic, but must be renegotiated.

Deterrence between the Superpowers. The awesome destructive power of nuclear weapons has fundamentally transformed military strategy and the nature of *war in general. For the first time in the history of warfare, the destructiveness of the means of war far outweighs most ends for which a global nuclear war could be undertaken.

While the United States possessed an overwhelming nuclear superiority throughout the late 1940s and 1950s, by 1960 the Soviet Union had built a nuclear stockpile large enough to guarantee that any nuclear attack upon it could be met with a significant nuclear retaliation. In the years following, the Soviets added to their arsenal, reaching rough parity with the United States by the late 1960s. This novel balance gave rise to the theory of "mutual assured destruction" (MAD). The MAD theory holds that, if both nations have the ability to destroy each other's society, neither will use nuclear weapons for fear of bringing devastation upon itself. Under the conditions of MAD, the purpose of continuing to maintain nuclear weapons is to deter an attack by the other.

Policymakers, defense officials, and experts have long disagreed over what constitutes a credible threat to retaliate, and what level of destruction against the attacker must be "assured" in order for deterrence to be stable. At one extreme, some have argued that the guaranteed destruction of not more than a few major urban centers is a sufficient deterrent against attack. According to this view, a small number of nuclear weapons with a very high certainty of reaching their targets is all that is needed for *security. At the other extreme, some have asserted that a nation must be able to respond at a higher level of violence than its opponent, whatever its opponent's level is, for *deterrence to be guaranteed.

Deterrence, by its nature, is a highly symbolic process: it requires both parties to convince each other that they have the strength and the will to respond to threats against their vital interests. Deterrence has placed a high premium on demonstrations of resolve. During the *Cuban Missile Crisis of 1962, for example, both the United States and the Soviet Union felt that a symbolic defeat would undermine the credibility of their nuclear deterrent, to the detriment of their overall security and influence. During this crisis and others of the *Cold War, there were moments at which the commitment of national resolve was at least as important as the prima facie issues themselves.

One critique of MAD is its failure to provide a motive for retaliation: if a nation's society has been obliterated, what rational motive—other than sheer revenge—would prompt decisionmakers to launch the massive retaliation guaranteed by MAD? If a nation has ceased to exist, what national interest can it pursue by launching a retaliatory strike? Many have responded that even the slightest probability of retaliation is sufficient to deter attack—given the colossal stakes, any potential aggressor must fear that the victim will act out of revenge. But others have felt that decision makers need options other than massive retaliation after a nuclear attack. In order for deterrence to be convincing, they argue, a country which has been attacked must still be able to respond with selective, punitive retaliations. If the attacked country retains the ability to engage in cycles of increasing violence, an aggressor will not feel that it can gain a decisive advantage with a massive, sudden first strike. This argument became especially prominent in the United States in the late 1970s, and led to an emphasis on weapons and strategies for protracted nuclear warfare (often called "warfighting").

MAD had the effect of "wiring together" the security of the two superpowers, for they both relied upon the stability of deterrence to ensure their security. Thus, paradoxically, any attempt by one country to gain an absolute advantage might actually diminish its own overall security by undermining deterrence. The less stable the nuclear balance, the more precarious the situation was for both sides, even for the country favored by the imbalance.

The recognition of this interdependence led the United States and the Soviet Union to seek ways in which to ensure stability. Through *arms control, the superpowers sought to maintain an essential parity of nuclear forces and to limit the deployment of some especially destabilizing weapons systems (the Anti-Ballistic Missile Treaty, for example, limited national defenses against nuclear missiles). The two countries also negotiated an extensive array of "confidence and security-building measures" designed to facilitate communications in a crisis, prevent misunderstandings, and safeguard against accidental launches.

Utility of Nuclear Weapons. The enormous destructiveness of nuclear weapons, plus the absence of any kind of effective defense against them, gives them unique qualities. Three situations are worth distinguishing: wars between nations possessing them in quantity, wars between nations having only a few, and wars between a nation that has them and one that does not. Consider the dramatic third possibility first. A nation possessing nuclear weapons in quantity that fights a war against one that does not possess them could, in principle, win that war absolutely and almost instantly, by using a portion of its nuclear arsenal.

Such a war has not been witnessed, however. In substantial measure it has not, because there also is a strong, worldwide "taboo" against any nuclear use. The Soviet Union did not use nuclear weapons in Afghanistan and the United States did not use them in Vietnam or Iraq. It is true that in the first two cases, an additional reason why the nuclear power eschewed their use was some fear of a reaction by the other superpower. But at least equally important was a fear of incurring universal ignominy by using weapons that are generally feared as hideous and hyperviolent, and that, to many people, even carry some air of the magical. The United States could not even consider the global consequences of using nuclear weapons against Iraq in the *Gulf War, even though the Soviets would have taken no immediate military action in response.

Any war between two nations that both possess nuclear weapons in quantity would carry consequences so colossal that anything like full-scale use would mean the annihilation of them both, and enormous damage to others as well. Between the United States and the Soviet Union such a war would have produced global environmental damage so profound that there is doubt whether humanity would have survived. Between heavily armed superpowers, however, the enormous inhibition of MAD came into play and, paradoxically, nuclear weapons had relatively little value. It is worth noting that, in the future, wars might become imaginable between other nations having substantial nuclear arsenals

(China and India? Israel and Iraq? China and the independent Russian Republic?). Such twenty-first-century possibilities have not yet been much considered.

The remaining case is war between nations that have only a few nuclear weapons. At present, many specialists would predict that this is the least unlikely case in the coming decades. (At the time of this writing, a nuclear war between India and Pakistan is seen by some as perhaps the most worrisome possibility.) One reason why this case seems the least unlikely is that the temptation may be great to strike against a weak enemy. If the other side has only a few weapons, and especially if those weapons are relatively vulnerable to attack, the desire may be great to remove a terrible danger by direct action.

Nuclear Weapons and the Cold War. Our chief experience, to date, of what nuclear weapons mean has been the East-West Cold War (roughly 1947–1989). Future generations may come to see that as a special case. For some fifteen years, one side in that Cold War was enormously superior to the other in nuclear capabilities, and through much of that time could have readily attacked and defeated the other, but forebore to do so primarily because of its own values. Subsequently, the other side also deployed nuclear weapons in quantity and made them relatively secure from attack. Thereby it created the situation of MAD, which, while uncomfortable, is one of the less dangerous nuclear configurations possible.

In the Cold War, the United States explicitly extended its nuclear deterrent guarantee to Western Europe, via the *North Atlantic Treaty Organization (NATO), and the Soviet Union effectively extended it to Eastern Europe, via the *Warsaw Treaty Organization (Warsaw Pact). Western Europe also received significant protection by the development of first British and then French nuclear weapons. While it is impossible to be sure, many specialists believe that Cold War nuclear deterrence went a long way toward preventing the outbreak of World War III in Europe, despite some intense East-West crises there. It has been otherwise rare for two great military alliances, in intense mutual competition, to avoid war. In this sense nuclear weapons surely promoted peace and stability during these decades. However, it can be argued that East and West, essentially stymied in Europe, turned to the Third World to play out their competition and thereby caused, or at least enlarged, Third World conflicts beyond what they otherwise might have been. It also can be well argued that we are indebted to a substantial factor of good luck in having so far avoided an accidental (or "inadvertent") nuclear war, caused by computer malfunction or human error.

Nuclear Weapons in the Twenty-First Century. With the passing of the Cold War, humanity's experience of nuclear weapons and their meaning may turn to other regions. Some specialists fear that the twenty-first century may witness one or more Third World nuclear wars, a concern that has deepened with the testing of nuclear weapons by India and Pakistan. Such wars would not only be locally devastating but also would cause worldwide ecological damage, perhaps severe damage. In the coming decades, much may depend on whether the "taboo" against the actual use of nuclear weapons is strengthened or weakened. It could be strengthened by a renewed Nuclear Non-Proliferation Treaty, prospects for which would be improved if Israel moves to a formal recognition of its status as a nuclear power. Further arms reductions by the existing nuclear powers would also strengthen the prohibition. But U.S.-Russian tensions over arms control have increased with new American interest in developing a missile defense system, as have fears that it might set off an arms race between China, India, and Pakistan. Worse still, the taboo could be gravely weakened if, after many decades of no actual use of nuclear weapons, they then are used, in the Third World or elsewhere. Especially it would be weakened if the first such fresh use was followed by a second, a third, and so forth. If the first aroused an intense worldwide revulsion, the world might thereafter move strongly toward nuclear disarmament and strict nonproliferation. But if the first was followed by a second nuclear use, and then by more, one of the grimmest of all possible futures might come into being—a world in which the use of nuclear weapons in warfare came to seem "normal."

(See also ARMS RACE; RULES OF WAR.)

Donna Gregory, *The Nuclear Predicament: A Sourcebook* (New York, 1986). Herbert M. Levine and David Carlton, *The Nuclear Arms Debate* (New York, 1986). Richard Smoke, *National Security and the Nuclear Dilemma: An Introduction to the American Experience*, 2d ed. (New York, 1987). Philip Bobbitt, Lawrence Freedman, and Gregory F. Treverton, eds., *U.S. Nuclear Strategy: A Reader* (New York, 1989).

RICHARD SMOKE

NUREMBERG TRIALS. The Nazi and Japanese atrocities of *World War II were without precedent in modern times. Since 1941, Allied leaders repeatedly warned the Axis powers that war criminals would be brought to trial. A United Nations War Crimes Commission was created in 1943, and the Soviets held sporadic *war crimes trials even while hostilities were going on. Naturally, however, the most highly placed individuals could not be apprehended and indicted prior to the unconditional surrender of Germany and Japan in 1945.

The principal trial of German war criminals following the war was held in Nuremberg, Germany, before an international military tribunal that had been established in the 1945 London Agreement for the Prosecution and Punishment of the Major War Criminals of the European Axis. The tribunal consisted of four judges and four alternates from the contracting states: the United States, the Soviet Union, Britain, and France.

Twenty-four defendants, headed by Hermann Göring, were indicted. Of these, one (Robert Ley) committed suicide before the trial commenced, and the proceedings against another (Gustav Krupp) were indefinitely suspended owing to his senile degeneration. One of the remaining twenty-two (Martin Bormann) was tried *in absentia*. The Indictment also sought to declare as criminal seven groups and organizations.

The Nuremberg trial began in November 1945. After hundreds of sessions, in which many witnesses were heard and thousands of documents submitted, the tribunal delivered judgment on 30 September–1 October 1946. In all, nineteen defendants were convicted and three (Hans Fritzsche, Hjalmar Schacht, and Franz von Papen) acquitted. The sentences were death in twelve instances (Bormann [*in absentia*], Hans Frank, Wilhelm Frick, Göring [who managed to commit suicide before execution], Alfred Jodl, Ernst Kaltenbrunner, Wilhelm Keitel, Alfred Rosenberg, Fritz Sauckel, Arthur Seyss-Inquart, Julius Streicher, and Joachim von Ribbentrop), life imprisonment in three (Walter Funk, Rudolf Hess, and Erich Raeder), and imprisonment for a fixed number of years in four (Karl Dönitz, Albert Speer, Konstantin von Neurath, and Baldur von Schirach). Of the seven groups, four (the SS, the SD, the Gestapo, and the Leadership Corps of the Nazi Party) were declared criminal organizations. The Soviet judge dissented from the acquittals of the three defendants and two of the three organizations, as well as from Rudolf Hess's life sentence.

The Nuremberg trial was conducted in a manifestly fair manner which impressed all impartial observers. The records of the proceedings, including the documentation of the Nazi atrocities, were published in a series of forty-two volumes. The irrefutable evidence of unprecedented horrors speaks for itself after more than half a century.

Although proceedings against ordinary war criminals have many antecedents, the Nuremberg trial is the first to have been held before an international penal court. Moreover, the indictment (based on the Charter of the Tribunal, annexed to the London Agreement) went beyond traditional war crimes, and encompassed also crimes against peace and crimes against humanity.

The "Nuremberg principles" have been consistently endorsed by the international community, although for several decades the endorsement was more abstract than real. In the 1990s, in the wake of atrocities in the former Yugoslavia and in Rwanda, two new *ad hoc* international penal tribunals were set up. Moreover, in 1998, a statute for a permanent International Criminal Court was adopted by a United Nations diplomatic conference convened in Rome. In all three instances, the Nuremberg precedent is overtly followed in many important respects.

As the recent texts indicate, several innovative dimensions of the Nuremberg trial have acquired an unassailable position in contemporary *international law. Thus, there are no lingering doubts about the validity of the concept of crimes against humanity. Moreover, attempts by international offenders to elude criminal responsibility by relying on attribution of their acts to the state or an obedience to superior orders are doomed to failure.

The Nuremberg trial has gained wide recognition as a watershed event. It has firmly embedded the principle of personal accountability for violations of international criminal law. Offenders, however highly placed in the government or in the military hierarchy, are liable to trial and punishment by an international penal tribunal.

(See also HOLOCAUST; WAR CRIMES TRIBUNAL.)

Robert E. Conot, *Justice at Nuremberg* (Cambridge, U.K., 1983).

YORAM DINSTEIN

NYERERE, Julius. Mwalimu Julius Kambarage Nyerere was born in Butiama in the Lake Victoria region of Tanganyika in 1922. He was educated at Catholic missionary schools and from 1943 to 1945 attended Makerere University in Kampala, Uganda. While he was a student in Kampala, Nyerere came into contact with nationalist leaders from Kenya and Uganda who were at that time creating the organizational and personal linkages among those who opposed British colonialism.

He was exposed to the ideas of Fabian socialism after World War II when he studied at Edinburgh University in Scotland. Nyerere graduated from the university in 1952 and returned to East Africa.

Between 1949 and 1955, there were worker protests in all the territories of East Africa with general strikes, peasant uprisings, and other forms of protest. The resistance to colonialism took a violent form in Kenya after the formation of the Land and Freedom Army (called Mau Mau by the British). In Tanganyika, a small organization called the Tanganyika African Association (TAA) had agitated for self-rule since the 1920s, and after the worker protest, became the leading nationalist organization. Nyerere, who had returned to become a secondary-school teacher, had joined the TAA and emerged as the most articulate spokesperson for independence. He was elected president of the TAA in 1953. By 1954, the organization had widened and deepened its membership and became a registered political party called the Tanganyikan African National Union (TANU). In the contemporary history of *Tanzania, 7 July is designated Saba Saba, meaning the seventh day of the seventh month. This was the day that TANU was officially launched.

Nyerere was the first chairperson of TANU and remained the leader of this party throughout its existence. In 1977 TANU was united with the principal political party in Zanzibar, the Afro Shirazi party, to form the Chama Cha Mapinduzi (CCM), or Revolutionary Party. Nyerere was elected the first chairperson of the party at its first congress in 1977 and was reelected at the two subsequent congresses in 1982 and 1987. He retired as the leader of the party in 1990.

Julius Nyerere and the party led Tanganyika out of colonialism to become an independent nation on 9 December 1961, and Nyerere became the first prime minister. After the Zanzibar Revolution of January 1964, Tanganyika and Zanzibar joined together on 26 April 1964 to form the United Republic of Tanzania. Nyerere was the executive president of the Union. The Arusha Declaration of 1967 promulgated the ideas of socialism, self-reliance, and education for self-reliance. These principles emanated from the philosophy of Nyerere that was called "Ujamaa," or familihood. Nyerere's vision of socialism and of an original African contribution to humanity was based on the reconstruction and regeneration of the village community as the basis of community and political life.

Nyerere was called Mwalimu (teacher) both by the citizens of Tanzania and by those in the Organization of African Unity (OAU) who recognized his contribution to the decolonization of Africa. In 1964, the OAU designated Dar es Salaam as the headquarters of the OAU Liberation Committee. It was from Dar es Salaam that all of the movements that were fighting against colonialism operated. After the fall of Portuguese fascism and the independence of Mozambique in 1975, the loose consultations between Botswana, Tanzania, Zambia, and Mozambique were formalized with the creation of the Frontline States (FLS). The FLS included Botswana, Angola, Mozambique, Tanzania, Zambia, and Zimbabwe. The collaboration between those fighting to end white minority rule in Africa elicited hostile responses from the Western world and those leaders in Africa such as Mobutu Sese Seko and Idi Amin who were dictatorial. In 1978, the Ugandan army of Idi Amin attacked Tanzania, and Nyerere took the decision that the Tanzanian army should not only repulse the Ugandan forces from Tanzanian territory but also remove Idi Amin from power.

Under the leadership of Nyerere, Tanzania achieved significant gains in terms of social policy in relation to the delivery of social services, and by the time Nyerere stepped down as president in 1985, Tanzania had one of the highest literacy rates in Africa. Nyerere was a leading critic of the neoliberal prescriptions of the International Monetary Fund and the World Bank. He became the chairperson of the South-South Commission, an international commission to promote trade and economic cooperation between the countries of the exploited world. Nyerere was opposed to *genocide and genocidal violence. He was one of the few African leaders to speak out against the genocide in Rwanda in 1994. Toward the end of the 1990s, Nyerere dedicated himself to finding an end to the genocidal violence in Burundi. He was the facilitator of the peace talks that were held in Arusha to find a lasting solution to the intercommunal violence in that country. He founded the Nyerere foundation for Peace and Development to move Africa from warfare and militarism to peace and reconstruction. Nyerere died in London on 14 October 1999.

HORACE CAMPBELL

O

OCCUPATION, MILITARY. See FOREIGN MILITARY BASES.

OCEANIA. See PACIFIC ISLANDS.

OCTOBER WAR OF 1973. See ARAB-ISRAELI CONFLICT.

OMAN. See GULF STATES.

ONE-PARTY SYSTEM. The term "one-party system" (sometimes referred to as "one-party state") includes, at its broadest, two rather different types of regimes. In the Marxist-Leninist or "vanguard" party state, the party is distinguished by its restricted membership, highly structured internal organization, commitment to a Leninist *ideology, and direct supervision of the organs of state power. The second type of single-party state, considered here, has a mass rather than elite membership and is generally rather weakly organized, with a variable level of ideological commitment, and exists alongside government organs rather than directly controlling them.

The origins of this type of one-party system lie in anticolonial nationalism and state consolidation in newly independent states; though characteristic of "nationalist movements" the world over, its classic location has been in tropical Africa. In several cases, including Malawi and Tanganyika (Tanzania), nationalism resulted in the formation of an overwhelmingly dominant movement which faced no appreciable internal opposition. At independence, a single party then monopolized political activity, regarding itself as the authentic expression of a new national identity. In others, such as Ghana or Zambia, where two or more viable parties existed at independence, a single party was deliberately created by the government in order to restrict opposition and to prevent the articulation of divisions that it regarded as dangerous to the stability of a new and often artificial state. This unity was sometimes achieved by the straightforward suppression of rival parties, but more often by inducing opposition leaders to join the governing party through the offer of ministerial portfolios. Sometimes, as with Congress in India or the Partido Revolucionaro Institucional (PRI) in Mexico, a dominant party still permitted opposition parties to exist.

These differences were reflected both in ideologies of one-party rule and in the ways in which such parties actually operated. All one-party systems shared an emphasis on the unity of the party, which in turn was taken to represent the unity of the nation, and on the dominant role of the party leader, who was rapidly elevated to the role of executive president; in some cases, as in Malawi, he became president for life. Party ideologies reflected the personality of the leader, but owed much to Jean-Jacques Rousseau's ideal of the general will. In the eyes of its most articulate defender, Julius *Nyerere of Tanzania, the one-party system was greatly superior to the divisive struggles of rival parties. He derisively compared a multiparty system to a sterile game of football, whereas the single party was likened to a "two-way all-weather road" through which popular wishes could be conveyed to the government, and government policies transmitted to the people. In some cases, such as Guinea and Mali, the insistence on unity and condemnation of enemies of party and nation at times approached paranoia.

Efforts were sometimes made to achieve a measure of internal party democracy. In Tanzania, party elections were held in which two candidates, each carefully scrutinized and approved, competed for popular approval. In Kenya, where the party was the vehicle for a level of factional competition that would not have been tolerated in Tanzania, any number of candidates could stand for election to parliament. Sometimes, as with Kwame *Nkrumah's Convention People's Party (CPP) in Ghana, candidates were simply selected from the center and declared elected unopposed. Even where internal party competition was recognized, however, this was not allowed to challenge the position of the leader, and became instead a vehicle for fractional conflict over patronage. The one-party system thus was ultimately irreconcilable with popular debate or choice over either national leadership or basic party policies.

The actual policies followed by one-party regimes have varied widely. They have often been associated with "populist socialist" development strategies, in which the state took over the reins of the economy and sought to use the government, aided by popular mobilization through the party, to promote rapid economic growth. In states such as Côte d'Ivoire, Kenya, and Malawi, however, one-party rule accompanied explicitly capitalist development policies. One of Africa's most distinctive single parties, the True Whig Party (TWP) of Liberia, served as the vehicle for a capitalist oligarchy dominated by the immigrant Americo-Liberian segment of the population. The success of one-party systems has varied likewise. In Ghana the party, atrophied by the absence of popular participation, decayed to a point at which it could readily be toppled by a military coup. In Guinea, the one-party system lasted as long as its founder, Sékou Touré, and was overthrown immediately after his death. On the other hand, one-party regimes in Côte d'Ivoire, Kenya, Malawi, Tanzania, and Zambia lasted for over a quarter of a century; the Liberian TWP, ousted in 1980, had by that time enjoyed more than a century of uninterrupted rule.

One-party regimes suffered a heavy blow from the end of the Cold War, which revealed the hollowness of their claims to represent a united nation, and deprived them of the tacit support which they had often received from external patrons. Throughout Africa, one-party constitutions were rapidly revised to permit multiparty competition. Leaders including Kenneth Kaunda in Zambia and Hastings Banda in Malawi were voted out of office in the resulting elections, though in some countries, such as Côte d'Ivoire and Tanzania, the former single party succeeded in retaining power. Elsewhere, however, new national independence movements replicated the conditions under which single-party systems had previously arisen. Eritrea, where the victorious Eritrean People's Liberation Front (EPLF) became the ruling party under the name of the People's Front for Democracy and Justice, was a classic case, while several of the newly independent Asian former Soviet republics, including Kazakhstan, Turkmenistan, and Uzbekistan, became one-party states in all but name. Only under conditions of exceptional national unity, however, such as those sometimes accompanying *decolonization, can the one-party system realize its stated goal of representing popular aspirations. The lack of accountability within such a system renders it inherently liable to corruption, and the creation of a genuinely participatory political structure must inevitably result in its demise.

(See also AUTHORITARIANISM; COMMUNIST PARTY STATES; LENINISM; MILITARY RULE; POST-COMMUNISM.)

Gwendolen Carter, ed., *African One-Party States* (Ithaca, N.Y., 1962). Immanuel Wallerstein, "The Decline of the Party in Single Party African States," Joseph LaPalombara and Myron Weiner, eds., *Political Parties and Political Development* (Princeton, N.J., 1966). Aristide Zolberg, *Creating Political Order: The Party-States of West Africa* (Chicago, 1966). Ian Bremmer and Ray Taras, eds., *New States, New Politics: Building the Post-Soviet Nations* (Cambridge, U.K., 1997).

CHRISTOPHER CLAPHAM

OPEC. See ORGANIZATION OF PETROLEUM EXPORTING COUNTRIES.

ORGANIZATION FOR ECONOMIC CO-OPERATION AND DEVELOPMENT. The Organization for Economic Cooperation and Development (OECD) was founded in 1961 as successor to the Organization for European Economic Cooperation, the agency that had distributed *Marshall Plan funds in Western Europe. The OECD is governed by a Council of Ambassadors; however, most of its work is carried out by the Secretariat at its Paris headquarters or within committees and working groups that employ professionals throughout the industrialized world. Compared with international organizations such as the European Union and the United Nation, the OECD has few ties to the public in member countries. The only *non-governmental organizations granted consultative status are the Business and Industry Advisory Committee to the OECD (BIAC) as the representative of business, and the Trade Union Advisory Committee to the OECD (TUAC) as the representative of labor.

When the OECD began, it was envisioned in part as continuing the Marshall Plan, with developed countries joining the United States as donors and with states in the developing world to be the recipients. This has remained one of the major tasks of the organization. Its Development Assistance Committee (DAC) serves as a coordinating mechanism among donor countries. Within it, donors make pledges to each other about the levels of support they will provide to developing nations, and donors share information on their development activities. Building on this role, the OECD has become a caucusing group within UN agencies like the United Nations Conference on Trade and Development, where relations between more industrialized and less industrialized economies are discussed. The organization is sometimes referred to as a "club of the rich," and in negotiating forums, OECD membership is often considered synonymous with "the North" facing the *Third World caucus, the Group of 77, "the South."

The conflict between North and South over development assistance and the structure of the world economy brought about a major innovation within the OECD. In the 1973–1975 oil crisis, the apparent influence of the *Organization of Petroleum Exporting Countries over the world price of oil led OECD members to create the International Energy Agency (IEA) to coordinate national stockpiles of oil and intervene in world markets when price increases threaten.

Third World critics point to the IEA and argue that the OECD has evolved away from its founding purpose into an agency concerned exclusively with members' interest in trade promotion and financial market deregulation. It is certainly true that now most OECD activity, both of the secretariat and of various working groups, involves studying how economic cooperation among its members can be increased. The organization mainly studies individual OECD economies or sectors across all the industrialized countries. The expertise of the OECD staff and the organization's status as one of a few forums that include all rich countries has given the OECD a role in preparing for the annual economic summits of the *Group of 7, an innovation in statecraft which also began after the first oil crisis.

The OECD became the focus of worldwide protests over the proposed Multilateral Agreement on Investments (MAI), a new regime to extend the rights of investors and limit the regulatory capacity of states over foreign investments. Although the agreement had far-reaching implications, negotiations (which began under OECD auspices in 1995) took place in secret. Not even parliaments of the OECD member countries were consulted. Information about the process leaked out and eventually the negotiating document became public in 1998. News reports quoted *World Trade Organization Director General Renato Ruggiero as describing the MAI as the "constitution for a single global economy." As public opposition grew and protests spread, organized largely by e-mail and the world wide web, governments backed away and negotiations were eventually suspended. This became known as "the first victory of the Internet guerrillas."

As of 2000, the OECD had twenty-nine members, about one sixth of the world's countries (with about the same proportion of the world's population). Of the original twenty founding members, all but Canada and the United States were located in Europe. During the 1960s and 1970s, four new members joined, including Japan, Australia, and New Zealand in the Asia-Pacific Region. After a pause of more than twenty years, the organization admitted five new members in the 1990s—two newly-industrialized countries (Mexico and the Republic of Korea) and three former communist countries (the Czech Republic, Hungary, and Poland).

(See also DEVELOPMENT AND UNDERDEVELOPMENT; NORTH-SOUTH RELATIONS.)

Miriam Camps, *"First World" Relationships: The Role of the OECD* (New York, 1975). Andrew Jackson and Matthew Sanger, *Dismantling Democracy: the Multilateral Agreement on Investments (MAI) and its Impact* (Ottawa, 1998). Michael J. Artis and Massimiliano Marcellino, *Fiscal Forecasting: the Role of the IMF, OECD and EC* (Florence, 1999).

CRAIG N. MURPHY

ORGANIZATION FOR SECURITY AND COOPERATION IN EUROPE. See HELSINKI ACCORDS.

ORGANIZATION OF AFRICAN UNITY. The Organization

of African Unity (OAU) was established in May 1963 amid much pomp and ceremony, at a time when the Pan-Africanist idea of continental unity was popular and during a period of momentous changes in international relations. The end of the European colonial era and the rise of the *Nonaligned Movement of *Third World countries occurred against a backdrop of a divided world of East-West rivalry for global control. Conceived as a harmonizing center of nations, the UN had instead become an ideological battleground between East and West with the emergence of blocs in which the Third World began to play a significant role.

Two basic points must be made regarding the UN and the OAU as *international organizations. First, the UN is a microcosm of the world's state system, reflecting the interests of world governments. Governments, not people, are represented at the UN. The same is true of the OAU—it represents African governments, not peoples. Second, the modern African state system was shaped by colonial history: What became national boundaries were fixed by European rulers and crosscut ethnic lines in almost all cases.

At the second OAU summit in Cairo in 1964, African leaders accepted these boundaries over the objection of the Pan-Africanist minority voice led by Ghana's Kwame *Nkrumah. The latter advocated a "United States of Africa" that would transcend the colonial (and precolonial) legacy and transform the fragmented state system. Nkrumah contended that the postcolonial state system would be politically divisive and economically wasteful, a contention that proved to be prophetic. The tension between this Pan-Africanist idea and the fragmented state system is implicit in the compromise solution embedded in the OAU Charter, Article II of which advocates "the promotion of solidarity and cooperation" among African states as well as for the defense of their sovereignty and territorial integrity.

The OAU is clearly a creature of compromise which bridged the gap between a hitherto ideologically and geographically divided continent. This was no mean achievement. But, as a creature of compromise, the OAU tended to be all things to all governments, and its resolutions by and large have been ineffectual. Controversial issues have been continually postponed for fear of a split in the organization. The OAU thus has failed to exert moral authority to censure errant leaders or governments, even those engaged in grave violations of *human rights, such as Idi Amin of Uganda, Mengistu of Ethiopia, and Siad Barre of Somalia. The Banjul Charter (African Charter on Human and Peoples' Rights) adopted in 1986 is yet to be enforced, although its adoption is expected to exert moral pressure and help in the development of African human rights law.

On the credit side, the OAU can justly boast of some suc-

cessful mediations of conflicts. The first such mediation concerned a territorial dispute between Algeria and Morocco. It was followed by other efforts in the Congo in the mid-1960s and in Nigeria in the late 1960s. In all cases the issues were clear-cut and the debates focused and coherent. The "OAU principles" of sovereignty and territorial integrity were applied with clarity and consistency.

Regarding Southern Africa and the *decolonization of the former Portuguese territories, the OAU's role was admirable as well. The establishment of the liberation committee, the channeling of financial, material, and military aid to the liberation fighters of those territories, as well as the diplomatic campaigns conducted in support of their respective causes have been among the organization's best achievements.

The OAU fell far short of its stated objectives and periodic rhetorical commitments when it concerned the settlement of more complex interstate and intrastate conflicts. Its inability (or unwillingness) to mediate between Ethiopia and Somalia, or to confront the challenges posed by the developments in Eritrea and southern Sudan, are among its signal failures. On the other hand, it occasionally met challenges head-on, as it did, for example, in the Chad dispute by seating the Habré delegation to the exclusion of the Goukouni delegation in 1987. Again the divisive question of Western Sahara ended in the admission of the Sahrawi Arab Democratic Republic to OAU membership. That decision cost the OAU Morocco's membership, underscoring the risks which have caused the OAU to postpone the resolution of contentious issues for fear of a split.

The OAU's failure to apply a vigorous political will in search of lasting solutions to some of Africa's problems must be viewed in a larger historical perspective. To begin with, there is the fragmented postcolonial state system. Then there is the troubled economy, declining and distorted; there are political unrest, war, and famine, all of which have undermined Africa's confidence and dampened the earlier enthusiasm. In each state, perceived national or domestic needs have dictated harmful policy options, including costly militarization. Such conditions do not foster bold moves in the settlement of disputes, but instead induce caution and inaction.

Nevertheless, some bold resolutions and plans of action have been adopted by the OAU. The Lagos Plan of Action of April 1980 is one such measure in the economic arena, together with the use of the UN *Economic Commission for Africa in working out alternative strategies for Africa's economic development. The OAU serves as the Secretariat for the African Economic Community under the Abuja Treaty. In the political sphere, the use of the *Economic Community of West African States in the resolution of the Liberian conflict in 1991 was another example of how regional and subregional organizations might be used for economic and political objectives. In the realm of human rights, the OAU's adoption of the African Charter on Human and Peoples' Rights is another example of this promise and potential. More recently, the OAU has been engaged in election monitoring and in devising mechanisms for conflict prevention, management, and resolution.

However, the gap between promise and performance is too wide for comfort. And in view of the prevailing international economic and legal order which does not favor developing nations, the Pan-Africanist aspiration of political unity, economic prosperity, and social progress remains a distant dream at best. In that context, it can be fairly said that the resolutions and plans of action will remain dead letters for the foreseeable future.

In sum, the OAU has played a useful role in Africa's liberation and in the settlement of some conflicts, but the failures far outweigh the successes. The OAU is a financially weak institution whose members cannot be compelled to pay their dues. In order to obviate the problem of finance caused by delinquency in dues payment by member governments, the OAU has passed a resolution which denies voting rights to members with unpaid dues. The resolution also imposes moral sanctions of a sort by calling for the publication of a list of delinquent members. The OAU Committee on Contributions has done a commendable job in thus improving the organization's financial situation.

Perhaps the current winds of democratic change will help foster a proper reappraisal and reorientation of policy and action to reflect the popular will. The central drama of Africa in the early twenty-first century will be seen in the response to this dilemma, and in this critical mission the OAU has a historic responsibility.

(See also INTERNATIONAL SYSTEMS; PAN-AFRICANISM.)

Zdenek Cervenka, *The Unfinished Quest for Unity in Africa and the OAU* (New York, 1977). Yassin El-Ayouty and William Zartman, eds., *The OAU after Twenty Years* (New York, 1984). G. O. Olusanya, "Reflections on the First Twenty-five Years of the OAU" *Nigerian Journal of International Affairs* 14, no. 1 (1988): 67–72.

BEREKET HABTE SELASSIE

ORGANIZATION OF AMERICAN STATES. The Organization of American States (OAS) is the preeminent institution in the Inter-American System of multilateral, multipurpose cooperation among the western hemispheric states. The system traces its formal beginnings to 1889 through an uninterrupted series of international conferences and organizational development. Today the overall system is largely (but not exclusively) institutionalized in the OAS and the *Inter-American Development Bank; the Inter-American Treaty of Reciprocal Assistance (*Rio Treaty) is available but has been moribund since the early 1980s. These whites are coordinated but have separate existences under their own conventions, as well as overlapping but distinct membership.

The charter of the OAS was agreed upon in 1948 to serve as the basic constitution for western hemispheric regional organization and to coordinate various organs and agencies. The OAS charter has been substantially amended on three occasions, by protocols approved in 1967, 1985, and 1993, which went into force in 1970, 1988, and 1996, respectively; a formal amendment regarding democratic processes in the member states, signed in 1992, went into force in 1997.

In 1991, the OAS achieved universal regional membership of the thirty-five sovereign American states. Charter members in 1948 were the United States and the then-twenty Latin American states. Beginning in 1962, former British Caribbean dependencies gained independence and joined the OAS. Belize and Guyana, in accordance with original charter provisions, were not allowed to become members because of unsettled boundary disputes with member states Guatemala

and Venezuela, respectively; but the 1985 charter amendments dropped the membership-denial provision, and Belize and Guyana both joined in 1991. Suriname, a former colony of the Netherlands, was incorporated in 1975. Canada accepted membership in the OAS in 1990. Cuba technically remains a member, but multilateral sanctions imposed in 1962 denied "participation" to the *Castro government. The OAS has invited representatives from nonhemispheric states, the Holy See, and the UN to attend its meetings as permanent observers; as of 1998, forty-one entities had formal observer status.

The general purposes of the OAS have involved mutual security (coordinated with Rio Treaty procedures), economic cooperation and development (partly in concert with the Inter-American Development Bank), nonintervention and sovereign equality, peaceful settlement of disputes, representative democracy and *human rights, countering drug traffic, and protecting the environment. The various member states assign them different priorities and levels of commitment.

From the end of World War II to the mid-1960s, the United States primarily pursued mutual security goals in the Cold War context and sought to convert the OAS into an "anti-Communist alliance." Latin Americans urged their own economic preoccupations, as well as the nonintervention principle as the institutional sine qua non. Interests temporarily converged under what came to be known as the Alliance for Progress when, from about 1959 to 1965, U.S. policies linked developmentalism to a definition of security that took into account economic and social progress. From the mid-1960s to 1979, the United States did not perceive serious security threats in Latin America, and its interest in economic development declined; it did, however, address the issues of human rights. Latin Americans expressed dissatisfaction with U.S. regional dominance and insistence on an anti-Communist alliance, and resentments over U.S. trade and aid restrictions, intransigence on the Cuban issue, and violation of treaty-based pledges of nonintervention with unilateral coercive actions in Cuba, the Dominican Republic, and Chile.

The charter amendments of 1967 emphasized Latin American concerns by strengthening and broadening OAS economic and social functions; political and security purposes were somewhat deemphasized as a consequence, although no treaty changes were made. Economic development activities were expanded, continuing into the 1980s, but the United States remained unwilling to commit significant resources to developmental programs. The most positive area of activity in the 1970s, continuing into the 1980s, was the reinforcement of human rights organization within the OAS. The American Convention on Human Rights, agreed to in 1969, went into effect in 1978 for the ratifying states; it expanded the authority of the Inter-American Commission on Human Rights and established the Inter-American Court of Human Rights.

During the decade after 1979, the importance of the OAS declined even further. The United States pursued its Central American policies with only peripheral reference to the OAS, and Latin Americans, in turn, went outside the system to make their most important multilateral peace proposals (the Contadora initiative and the peace plan, initiated by President Oscar *Arias of Costa Rica, known as "Esquipulas II"). The United States invaded Grenada in October 1983, entirely ignoring the OAS charter. The OAS is only one of several forums, and not the most important, for dealing with the external debt crisis.

In the late 1980s, and as inter-American cooperation progressed in the post–Cold War era, interest grew in resuscitating the OAS. Security issues involving threats from nonhemispheric entities were nonexistent, although a number of intraregional situations remained problematical. The promotion of democracy and free trade were declared the overarching purposes, within which the pressing common problems, such as numerous economic questions, immigration and refugee policies, drug traffic, human rights, and environmental concerns, were dealt with. Long-standing inter-American tensions seemed to be transcended by an evolving consensus that hemispheric relations were best approached within established institutions designed to emphasize compatible interests and accommodate differences.

(See also INTERNATIONAL DEBT; LATIN AMERICAN AND CARIBBEAN REGIONAL ORGANIZATIONS; U.S.–LATIN AMERICAN RELATIONS.)

O. Carlos Stoetzer, *The Organization of American States*, 2d ed. (Westport, Conn., 1993). G. Pope Atkins, *Encyclopedia of the Inter-American System* (Westport, Conn., 1997).

G. POPE ATKINS

ORGANIZATION OF PETROLEUM EXPORTING COUNTRIES. The Organization of Petroleum Exporting Countries (OPEC) was established in September 1960 by Venezuela, Saudi Arabia, Iran, Iraq, and Kuwait. Other countries which qualified for membership and joined later were Qatar (1961), Indonesia and Libya (1962), Abu Dhabi (1967, later transferred to the United Arab Emirates, 1974), Algeria (1969), Nigeria (1971), Ecuador (1973), and Gabon (1975). Ecuador and Gabon withdrew in 1992.

The concept of an oil producers' organization began to take form at the first Arab Petroleum Congress in Cairo in 1959, and in the months following, Pérez Alfonzo of Venezuela and Abdullah Tariki of Saudi Arabia worked toward its realization. Pérez Alfonzo's vision was for controlled use (conservation) of oil through a mechanism of production sharing (cartelization) by the main oil producers; in national terms this would simultaneously have upgraded the value of Venezuelan oil against the competition of lower-cost Middle East oil. Tariki was an Arab nationalist who saw an oil alliance with Pérez Alfonzo as a means to greater Arab strength and to the development of political change in Saudi Arabia. Their success in creating OPEC was due partly to the timing of Arab political developments in 1959–1960, and partly to an increasingly competitive oil market. The catalyst was the decision by the oil companies to reduce the posted price of Middle Eastern crude oils. This was precisely the trigger that Pérez Alfonzo was waiting for. Because of its direct effect on government revenues from oil, the price reduction was decisive in bringing Iran into the new organization.

For ten years OPEC achieved little in terms of its original underlying objectives, which were to improve its share of revenue from oil and ultimately to gain control over its natural resources. Production sharing, the vision of Pérez Alfonzo, was never acceptable to Iran nor, in spite of Tariki, to Saudi Arabia. Negotiations with the companies for improved terms were slow and only marginally effective.

During these first ten years, however, OPEC laid the groundwork for its later success; in the first place it gained experience on how to negotiate with the companies and how to present itself to a wider, often skeptical, audience; second, it obtained widespread practical, if never legal, acceptance of the principle that the law of changing circumstances applied to the concession contracts between oil-producing countries and the oil companies; and, third, in Resolution XV1.90 of June 1968, it agreed to a series of policy objectives for the organization.

OPEC's high noon was the period 1970–1973 when, from a position of market strength and political confidence, it negotiated with the oil companies new terms relating to revenue (split of profit and "rent") and to ownership ("participation"). Milestones were the Teheran and Tripoli agreements on price (1971) and the Riyadh agreement on participation (1972). The first phase of OPEC's activity ended in October 1973 when, in the euphoria of the Arab-Israeli war, OPEC doubled the oil price by its own decision, dismissing the oil companies from the negotiating table. This was quickly followed by a further doubling of price at a meeting in December in Teheran, taking advantage of the Arab oil embargo and production cutbacks that had also been imposed in October. It was followed with pressure for majority participation in the oil concessions, which the companies, even if they wished, were by now unable to resist. OPEC's original objective, to control its own oil resources, was thus achieved.

This success, however, had an important implication for OPEC; because it had, in effect, arrogated to itself the unilateral responsibility for oil price management, its relevance as an international organization was greatly enhanced—the more so, given that member countries of the *Organization for Economic Co-operation and Development (OECD) saw themselves challenged by a threat not only to their energy security but also to their *balance of payments and to the international monetary system. One result was the creation of the International Energy Agency within OECD.

Although OPEC had a high media profile, after 1973 it soon became apparent that its influence in international political terms was far less than it had at first seemed; nor did it in practice even have the ability to manage the oil market, although its members amassed vast revenues in the process.

In reality, the member countries of OPEC had no common objectives. Their different political attitudes, systems, and interests were such that even agreement on how to set or pursue an oil price objective was beyond their capability. In the context of international politics, the objectives of, for instance, Iran, Saudi Arabia, Iraq, Algeria, and Venezuela were too much at variance to admit to any workable consensus. This was proved by the weakness of OPEC's summit declaration (Algiers, 1975), by the failure of the Conference on International Economic Cooperation (CIEC) or, as it was commonly known, the North/South Dialogue (1977), and by OPEC's inability to create a long-term strategy (1979). As for price management, in the years 1973–1979 the bitter arguments (often publicly expressed by Amuzegar of Iran and Yamani of Saudi Arabia) between the countries seeking higher prices and those preferring lower prices were only resolved by the unilateral use of its oil swing production capability by Saudi Arabia, with occasional additional support from Kuwait and Abu Dhabi. OPEC was frequently credited with the oil price increases of 1973 and, after the *Iranian Revolution and the outbreak of the *Iran-Iraq War, with the increases of 1979–1980, when the price of oil again increased more than twofold, from US$12.50 to more than US$30 per barrel. In reality, OPEC in both cases followed a market that was violently affected by external events; it then tried to use the new and higher price level created by those events as a base from which to operate, irrespective of subsequent changes in market conditions. In the 1970s, the result was to maintain nominal prices during a time of continuous high inflation (so that much of the initial increase was lost in real terms); in the 1980s, the result was a price collapse as conservation policies and economic recession slashed OECD demand for oil. OPEC efforts to maintain prices in this period would have collapsed even more quickly if the production capacity of Iran and Iraq had not been drastically reduced by the effects of the war between them.

From 1982, OPEC's efforts to maintain price levels by running itself as a cartel and setting production quotas for each member (thus meeting the original production-sharing objective of Pérez Alfonzo) failed. OPEC had no capacity to apply *sanctions against, or otherwise to police, members who broke the quota agreements they had undertaken. Moreover, the basic mistrust that existed between members (with Iran and Iraq at war with each other for eight years and Iraq subsequently invading Kuwait) and the diverse political and economic interests of member countries combined to erode OPEC's ability to set prices.

The 1990s were destructive to OPEC. Only Saudi Arabia, Iraq, Kuwait, and Venezuela had a meaningful capacity to expand their oil production; OPEC market power was weakened by the continuing development of non-OPEC oil and by the spread of alternatives, in particular gas; and its influence weakened by the commoditization of oil and the widespread use of the futures market. More fundamentally, OPEC members were, one by one, responding to the attractions of liberalization as their revenues fell and their investment needs rose; the only countries whose commitment to the institution of OPEC remained recognizably consistent throughout were those members which most needed it for political cover, Saudi Arabia and Kuwait.

(See also ARAB-ISRAELI CONFLICT; ARAB NATIONALISM; FINANCE, INTERNATIONAL; INTERNATIONAL ORGANIZATIONS; INTERNATIONAL POLITICAL ECONOMY; NORTH-SOUTH RELATIONS.)

Fadhil J. al-Chalabi, *OPEC and the International Oil Industry: A Changing Structure* (Oxford, 1980). Ian Seymour, *OPEC: Instrument of Change* (London, 1980). Pierre Terzian, *OPEC: The Inside Story* (London, 1985). Robert Mabro, ed., *OPEC and the World Market: The Genesis of the 1986 Price Crisis,* Oxford Institute for Energy Studies (Oxford, 1986). Ian Skeet, *OPEC: 25 Years of Prices and Politics* (Cambridge, U.K., 1988). Robert Mabro, *OPEC Behavior 1960–98: A Review of the Literature* (Journal of Energy Literature 4, no. 1, 1998, Oxford Institute for Energy Studies).

IAN SKEET

OSTPOLITIK. In its generic form, Ostpolitik comprised the Federal Republic of *Germany's (FRG) political relationships with its East European neighbors and the Soviet Union. Ow-

ing to the Federal Republic's location in the middle of the European continent and its hegemonic dominance over the area often referred to as *Mitteleuropa,* Germany's Ostpolitik assumed paramount importance for countries that remain beyond its immediate purview. For West Europeans and North Americans, too, Germany's Ostpolitik, though often welcomed, persistently caused some anxiety emanating from the fear and suspicion that Germany's (potentially excessive) rapprochement with the East would be forged at substantial cost to West European security. Developments such as Otto von Bismarck's finely honed balancing act between East and West *(Schaukelpolitik),* the conciliatory strategy vis-à-vis the Soviet Union via the Rapallo Treaty of 1922, and the Hitler-Stalin Pact of 1939, have given Ostpolitik a dubious reputation in certain Western quarters. It was precisely a consequence of this ambivalent legacy that the pejorative term "Genscherism" became commonplace in Western capitals during the late 1980s, denoting to its users yet another suspiciously cozy arrangement between an influential German politician (in this case the Federal Republic's foreign minister Hans-Dietrich Genscher) and the Soviet elite.

On a more positive note and more specifically, Ostpolitik stands for Willy Brandt's concrete measures to have the post-1945 European order fully accepted by the Germans and their neighbors, thereby making the Federal Republic one of the prime movers toward European reconciliation and global détente. Accompanied by a generally hostile attitude toward Eastern Europe and the Soviet Union among most West Germans, the 1950s and 1960s witnessed Konrad Adenauer's first initiative toward making Germany an integral member of the family of European nations by irretrievably anchoring the Federal Republic in Western Europe and the Atlantic Alliance. These measures comprised what subsequently came to be known as Westpolitik.

The second step in this conciliatory and integrative process—Ostpolitik—was taken by the Brandt-led Social-Liberal (Sozialdemokratische Partei Deutschlands-Freie Demokratische Partei) coalition in the early 1970s via extensive treaties between the Federal Republic and its Eastern and Central European neighbors, notably Poland, Czechoslovakia, the Soviet Union, and the *German Democratic Republic (GDR). Concretely, Brandt's Ostpolitik included specific moves in three distinct areas: (1) With regard to the Soviet Union, the Federal Republic pledged to increase its economic relations with that country and exchanged declarations of the nonuse of force. (2) With regard to Eastern European countries, the Federal Republic signed a similar agreement with Poland, which included German recognition of the Oder-Neisse line as Poland's permanent western border with Germany. Treaties with other East European countries, followed by international recognition of the GDR and the entry of both German states into the UN and other international bodies, completed the East European segment of Ostpolitik. (3) The most tangible and far-reaching aspects of Ostpolitik involved relations between the FRG and the GDR. A treaty between West Germany and East Germany established "special relations" between the "two states in Germany." Thus, for the first time, the FRG officially recognized the de facto existence of another German state. Above all, the treaty between the two German states called explicitly for an array of concrete measures to improve human relations between East and West Germans on a daily level. (4) Lastly, the so-called quadripartite agreement secured the status of West Berlin.

In short, Willy Brandt's Ostpolitik was nothing short of an unequivocal recognition of Germany's—indeed Europe's—postwar reality. As such, it represented a decisive, although long overdue, step in Germany's lengthy and arduous process of coming to terms with its National Socialist past. Only in this context do the bitter controversies surrounding Ostpolitik in the West German debate of the early 1970s make sense. Ostpolitik's ultimate triumph must be seen in the fact that through its normalization of East-West relations it contributed to an atmosphere of openness that ultimately destroyed the East's Stalinist dictatorships and thereby rendered Ostpolitik itself obsolete.

(See also GERMAN UNIFICATION.)

William E. Griffith, *The Ostpolitik of the Federal Republic of Germany* (Cambridge, Mass., 1978). Helmut Kistler, *Die Ostpolitik der Bundesrepublik Deutschland 1966–1973* (Bonn, 1982). Peter Bender, *Neue Ostpolitik: Vom Mauerbau zum Moskauer Vertrag* (Munich, 1986). Wolfram F. Hanrieder, *Germany, America, Europe: Forty Years of German Foreign Policy* (New Haven, Conn., 1989).

ANDREI S. MARKOVITS

OUTER SPACE. See SPACE.

P

PACIFIC REGION. Vigorous expansion in trade, investment, and other economic ties in the East Asian and Pacific economy have been critically important to the region's extraordinary growth in the second half of the twentieth century. Despite the financial crisis in 1997–1998, and average growth of only 1 percent a year in Japan through the 1990s, the medium- to longer-term growth trajectory is for faster-than-average world growth in the developing economies of East Asia in the first half of the twenty-first century.

East Asia's production in the four decades after 1960 grew from less than one quarter of North America's to rough equality with that of North America and more than one quarter of the world's. During this period, East Asia was a main source of dynamism in international and, especially, long-distance trade. It became the most important source of world savings—larger than North America or Europe—and overwhelmingly the largest source of surplus savings for international investment.

In the period from the mid-1960s to the late 1990s, the share of the Pacific (here including East Asia, North America, and Australasia) in world trade grew from around 30 percent to around 45 percent. East Asian and Pacific countries transact 73 percent of their trade with each other. In 1965 intraregional trade was less than 50 percent of Pacific trade. In that year, more than half of intraregional trade in the Pacific was with North America; by 1999, the largest proportion was with East Asian and Western Pacific countries. The proportion of intraregional trade in the Pacific now exceeds that in the European Union; in 1999, intraregional trade amounted to 71 percent of Europe's total trade.

The process of East Asian and Pacific economic integration intensified as Japanese and other East Asian corporations followed in the last decade of the twentieth century the pattern of overseas expansion set by U.S. multinationals and private investors in the 1950s and 1960s. China became the largest developing-country recipient of foreign investment in the 1990s and the second-largest destination for foreign investment in the world.

In the 1990s there was a large increase in short-term capital inflow into East Asian developing economies as banks and institutional investors were attracted by the experience of sustained growth in these economies, in excess of 8 percent in the decade to 1995. The remarkable boom ended in 1997 with sharp depreciation of regional currencies, a collapse in asset markets (real estate and stock prices), and a sharp decline in growth. Thailand, Indonesia, Korea, Malaysia, and Hong Kong were the worst-affected economies, the first three requiring international financial support and intervention by the International Monetary Fund (IMF) to stabilize their currencies and financial markets. The crisis was a product of weaknesses in foreign exchange and macroeconomic policy management and inadequacies in the regulation and supervision of financial markets as well as structural problems in the relationships between business and governments. These problems have encouraged extensive programs of economic reform (in part under IMF-imposed restructuring programs) and, in Indonesia, led to the demise of the Soeharto regime and the institution of democratic parliamentary elections.

Through the crisis, China continued to grow at around 7 percent a year. And, by 1999, all the crisis-affected economies except Indonesia were recovering strongly. The underlying conditions supporting faster-than-average long-term growth (high savings, strong education, open trade, open investment) remain in place, and the competitive strength of many of these economies has been enhanced by reforms put in place in response to the crisis.

Japan's economic stagnation continued through the last years of the twentieth century, a consequence of financial sector weakness, prolongation of overdue corporate restructuring, and mismanagement of macroeconomic policies. Japan's medium- to longer-term growth will be lower in the twenty-first century, even with a resumption of strong productivity growth, because of the shrinking work force and, later, declining population.

North America and Australasia enjoyed a period of remarkably strong and sustained growth while East Asia languished in the late 1990s. This was the result of exceptional productivity growth, a wave of investment associated with the new technologies, and policies that captured the advantages of a period of cheap capital, as investors retreated from "emerging" markets in East Asia and elsewhere.

The shift in the world's economic center of gravity toward East Asia and the Pacific brought with it huge changes in the international economic and geopolitical systems, as well as in the analytic and ideological prisms through which people all over the world came to view reality. These developments were of particular importance in the conduct of international trade and economic diplomacy. East Asian economies, coming from different starting points, committed to programs of trade and investment liberalization and came, through active participation in the Uruguay Round of trade negotiations, to play a more important role in international trade diplomacy.

China's *modernization and opening produced rapid trade and industrial transformation and unprecedented growth of real incomes. The economy was transformed from a predominantly centrally planned system to a largely market system in the 1980s and 1990s. At the beginning of the 1980s China's role in world trade was relatively unimportant; by 1999, it was the fourth-largest trading nation in the world (if Hong Kong's trade is included with the trade of the mainland net of trade between Hong Kong and China). In late 1999, China and the United States settled on the terms of China's accession to the World Trade Organization (WTO) and set the scene for regularizing most-favored-nation trading status for China in U.S. market.

Despite the growth of intraregional trade, Pacific countries have not moved to form a European-style economic union or a discriminatory trading bloc. Such a development is inimical to the long-term interests of the region, which is critically reliant upon rapid trade transformation and global market access. The political, economic, and cultural diversity in the region militates against such arrangements within the Pacific, except on a subregional basis—as within North America, between Australia and New Zealand, and among the ASEAN group of countries. The overarching framework for regional cooperation is the *Asia Pacific Economic Cooperation (APEC) forum, which was established in 1989.

The increasing share of intraregional trade in East Asia itself and the shocks of the East Asian crisis nonetheless encouraged East Asian countries to begin to contemplate new arrangements for subregional cooperation exclusive to East Asia. A number of subregional trade agreements have since been put on the agenda, and Japan has advocated the formation of an Asian Monetary Fund and regional currency arrangements. Yet East Asia's international economic policy priorities continue to be served predominantly through global institutions, and the rise of China, in particular, will increasingly have to be accommodated within global arrangements.

(See also GEOPOLITICS; GLOBALIZATION; STRUCTURAL ADJUSTMENT PROGRAM.)

Peter Drysdale, ed., *Reform and Recovery: The Role of the State and Economic Enterprise in East Asia* (London and New York, 2000).

PETER D. DRYSDALE

PAKISTAN. In 1947, at the moment of the British withdrawal from South Asia, a movement orchestrated by the All-India Muslim League under Mohammad Ali Jinnah led to the emergence of Pakistan out of the predominantly Muslim northwestern and eastern extremities of the subcontinent. Although it was intended as a homeland for Muslims, less than three quarters of the Muslims at the time of *India's partition became citizens of Pakistan. Bounded by the Himalayas in the north and the Arabian sea in the south, the Islamic Republic of Pakistan borders India, Iran, and China, while a strip of Afghan territory separates it from the Central Asian republics. Marked by lofty mountain ranges, plateaus, and lush green plains, the rich variations of Pakistan's physical geography are mirrored by the cultural diversities of its people.

Since independence Pakistan has striven to reconcile its Islamic identity with the imperatives of a modern state structure. Despite a religious bond, Pakistan's constituent units are characterized by linguistic, cultural, and economic disparities. Pakistan's socioeconomic heterogeneities and the ensuing political cleavages have forced the adoption of half a dozen constitutional frameworks—parliamentary and presidential—based on *federalism. Yet the suspension of representative government for more than twenty-five years since independence fashioned a state structure more unitary than federal in form. Seven years before Pakistan's first military intervention in 1958, the military and the civil bureaucracy had established their dominance within the state structure. The shift in the balance of power from elected to nonelected institutions saw *military rule under General Ayub Khan (1958–1969) and General Yahya Khan (1969–1971), the "populist" era of Zulfikar Ali Bhutto (1971–1977), and the military regime of General Zia-ul-Haq (1977–1988). Even with the restoration of parliamentary democracy after 1988, Pakistan was unable to shake off the political and socioeconomic legacies of *authoritarianism, paving the way for another military intervention in October of 1999.

In the absence of well-organized political parties, the clash between a centralized administrative structure and a regionally differentiated Pakistani society has strengthened provincial sentiments, confounding the task of forging an exclusively Islamic identity. Long-standing structural imbalances within the state, polity, and economy, not the lack of a coherent religious ideology, have been at the root of Pakistan's domestic instabilities. The breakaway of Bangladesh (formerly East Pakistan) in 1971 was simply the most dramatic manifestation of the problems involved in basing national identity on religion alone. There have been continuing tensions in Pakistan's western provinces where the distribution of political power and economic resources privilege the majority province of the Punjab, which also dominates the military and the civil bureaucracy. Of the minority provinces, the North-West Frontier Province has been relatively successful in staking a claim to state power and economic resources. The sense of alienation in Sind and Baluchistan, as well as among linguistic minorities within them, has been sharpened by the prolonged suspension of representative government and selective political mobilization under direct or quasimilitary rule.

Regional and international strategic requirements have exacerbated Pakistan's domestic dilemmas. Relations with India have been strained by memories of partition, two wars over Kashmir, and a third resulting in the dismemberment of Pakistan with the creation of *Bangladesh. Fears of India's hegemonic ambitions and unsettled borders with Afghanistan have seen the diversion of scarce financial resources into the defense effort and the ascendancy of a mainly Punjabi military establishment to the commanding heights of the state. By manipulating their connections with the centers of the *international system in London and Washington, senior state officials during the Cold War era sought to raise a viable shield of regional defense and to tip the domestic balance against elected institutions. Membership in the Southeast Asia Treaty Organization (SEATO) and the Baghdad Pact entitled Pakistan to U.S. military and economic aid. The benefits of association with the United States eventually bore fruit once the Soviets invaded Afghanistan in December 1979. Washington set aside reservations about Pakistan's nuclear program, rewarding Zia-ul-Haq's military regime with billions of dollars of aid for supporting the Afghan resistance movement.

Western assistance in the 1980s spawned a parallel arms and drugs economy. The presence of three million Afghan refugees together with the suspension of democracy and selective disbursement of state patronage fueled social conflict, especially in Sind where unemployed youth armed with sophisticated weapons waged war against rival linguistic communities. The grafting of military officers into top positions within the state structure gave them privileged access to key sectors of the economy. Efforts to stretch the networks of political collaboration brought segments of the dominant socioeconomic strata—landlords and emergent commercial and industrial groups—within the state's orbit of patronage.

During the longest period of military rule in Pakistan's history (1977–1988) the political system became even more subservient to the nonelected institutions of the state. Political parties were banned and support was extended to local notables acceptable to the military-bureaucratic establishment. Massive infusions of funds swayed voting patterns, reliance on clan-based ties diluted party programs, and the brazen use of state power ensured the success of favored candidates. The monetization of politics and concerns with local development issues meant greater dependence of politicians on the state apparatus. Vast sums of money were distributed to assembly members elected on a nonparty basis in 1985 along with imprudent loans to the regime's supporters. The return to party-based democracy in 1988 accentuated the trend with grave implications for the fiscal health of the state. With debt reservicing charges outstripping revenue receipts and regional tensions foreclosing cuts in the defense budget, the state exchequer has been unable to redistribute resources more equitably between the center and the provinces or between the Punjabi and the non-Punjabi provinces.

Despite four general elections between 1988 and 1997, the transition to democracy was thwarted by persisting imbalances within the state structure, growing political polarization, paralyzing external and domestic debts, and overall economic stagnation. Since the 1985 constitution aimed at perpetuating quasimilitary rule, three presidents could dismiss four elected governments and assemblies in less than a decade. Both the elected governments of Benazir Bhutto's Pakistan People's Party (1988–1990 and 1993–1996) and Mian Nawaz Sharif's Pakistan Muslim League (1990–1993) were ousted on charges of corruption and maladministration. After winning a two-thirds' parliamentary majority in 1997, Nawaz Sharif pushed through a constitutional amendment stripping the president of powers to dismiss elected governments and assemblies. Curbing presidential powers without strengthening the parliament or the judiciary increased the likelihood of a military intervention.

Instead of redressing the imbalances within the state structure, Sharif concentrated on bolstering his personal power. The quest proved elusive given the state's chronic financial crisis and a rising graph of political and sectarian violence. In May 1998, an economically precariously placed Pakistan matched India's nuclear explosions, provoking American-led international sanctions. In an ill-fated move Sharif endorsed the army's decision to take control of the Kargil heights in Kashmir, only to buckle under American pressure and call for a unilateral withdrawal to stave off a war with India. The closing months of the twentieth century saw the prime minister trying to restore his sagging political fortunes by replacing the chief of the army staff with his own appointee. In a country where political processes have remained subject to the imperatives of an inequitable state structure, it provided the army high command with the pretext to intervene yet again as the final arbiter of Pakistan's destiny.

(See also DEMOCRATIC TRANSITIONS; INTERNATIONAL DEBT; ISLAM; NUCLEAR WEAPONS.)

H. Gardezi and Jamil Rashid, eds., *Pakistan: The Roots of Dictatorship* (London, 1983). H. A. Rizvi, *The Military and Politics in Pakistan, 1947–86* (Lahore, 1986). Omar Noman, *The Political Economy of Pakistan, 1947–85* (New York, 1988). Ayesha Jalal, *The State of Martial Rule: The Origins of Pakistan's Political Economy of Defense* (Cambridge, U.K., 1990; Lahore, 1999). Ayesha Jalal, *Democracy and Authoritarianism in South Asia: A Comparative and Historical Perspective* (Cambridge, U.K., 1995). Ian Talbot, *Pakistan: A Modern History* (London, 1998).

AYESHA JALAL

PALESTINE. In the twentieth century, the region known as Palestine has been a field of intense conflict between peoples who have laid claim to it as their national home on grounds of long residence and historic and religious associations. Prior to the development of national states in the region after World War I, "Palestine" was not a separate political entity, but the name had long been in use. It was the name of a Roman province, and in the tenth century Arab geographers referred to "Filastin" (the Arabic name for Palestine) as one of the provinces for Syria. From the fifteenth century until World War I, Palestine formed part of the Ottoman Empire, and changing provincial boundaries blurred its separate status. However, for adherents of the three main monotheistic religions—*Islam, Judaism, and Christianity—"Palestine" remained the locus of holy sites of great significance: Jerusalem (al-Quds), Hebron (Khalil), Bethlehem, and Nazareth, to name only a few.

By the end of the Ottoman period (1914) the inhabitants of Palestine numbered approximately 650,000, the vast majority of whom were Arabs. Some 10 percent of the Arabs were Christians and the rest Muslims; in addition there was a Jewish population of approximately 75,000. About three-quarters of the Arab population were settled cultivators. Only about 5 percent of the total population were nomadic pastoralists (bedouin).

The development of a separate and distinctive Palestinian identity was a consequence of two major historical developments which began in the late nineteenth century. The first was the growth of European economic, political, and military intervention in the *Middle East. This culminated after World War I in the division of the Middle East into spheres of control among the major European powers, primarily Britain and France, with Palestine falling under a League of Nations mandate assigned to Britain. Arab nationalist and pan-Arabist movements had grown in response to Western intervention in the nineteenth century. With the drawing of new national boundaries under the post–World War I treaties, these *nationalisms took more specific forms.

A second cultural factor in the development of a separate Palestinian nationalism was the Zionist movement, which sought to establish a "national home" for the Jews in Palestine under the aegis of British rule. Jewish settlement had begun during the late Ottoman period on a small scale, but the National Home policy agreed to by the British administration explicitly facilitated immigration, settlement, and the acquisition of land in Palestine, and separate Zionist institutions. *Zionism aimed to create a Jewish homeland in Palestine, and therefore of its nature was unable to accommodate the demands and aspirations of the Arab population. The Jewish population grew, mainly through immigration, from 11 percent of the total in 1922 to 30 percent of the total population of 1,739,624 in 1944.

Prior to the period of British Mandate rule (1922–1948), Palestine's Arab inhabitants defined themselves mainly according to local, regional, and religious or family allegiances. While these continued to be important, the rise of *Arab nationalism had influenced some members of the Palestinian elite. However, it was the sense of threat generated by the new Jewish settler movement sponsored by the British that gradually created a new consciousness in the Arab inhabitants of their identity as Palestinians.

In the first years of the Mandate many looked to a union with Syria to bring about an end to the National Home project and British rule. As this hope faded, the Arab elites sought to change British policy through negotiation and appeals to Islamic solidarity in the Arab region to defend the holy places. By the 1930s the economic pressures created by Jewish settlement and land buying increasingly impinged on the lives of the majority of the Palestinian population. The nature of nationalist protest began to change as the strategies and self-interested infighting of the elites were challenged by new tendencies: among the intelligentsia by a more radical secular nationalism; and among the poor and dispossessed by a radical and redemptive Islam embodied in the movement of Shaikh al-Qassam, killed by the British in 1935. His attempted uprising and death were one of the triggers for the full-scale Palestinian uprising which took place from 1936 to 1939, against the Zionist movement and against British rule, crushed only by the use of massive force.

The 1940s found the popular Palestinian nationalist movement which had taken shape in the 1930s in ruins. The traditional leadership tried to reassert its position, but its status and effectiveness were diminished. In contrast, the Zionist movement, despite its own internal rifts, had consolidated its position over the decade since 1936. The *Holocaust had united world Jewry behind Zionism and had created moral support in the West for a Jewish homeland. Greatly increased Jewish immigration to Palestine had also shifted the demographic balance of forces. The 1947 UN plan for the partition of Palestine into separate Jewish and Arab states was rejected by the Palestinians and the Arab world who refused to truncate Arab Palestine or to recognize a separate Jewish state. The ensuring impasse resulted in virtual civil war. The British prepared to pull out while the Zionists sought to gain control of as much territory as possible, including land beyond that assigned to them in the partition plan.

The war of 1948–1949, in which the forces of the newly declared state of *Israel defeated Palestinian forces as well as armies sent from neighboring Arab states, resulted in the obliteration of "Palestine" as a state. The state of Israel occupied a large part of the territory with the remainder held by *Jordan (the West Bank) and *Egypt (the Gaza Strip). Of the Palestinian Arab population, some 700,000, fleeing the fighting, had been barred from returning to their homes, or expelled beyond the boundaries of the new Jewish state by Israeli forces. Those who had fled were scattered in the West Bank, in the Gaza Strip, and in surrounding Arab countries, mainly Lebanon, Syria, and Jordan. Only a tiny percentage of the refugees were ever permitted to return to their homes inside Israel. In 1950 some 160,000 Palestinians remained under Israeli rule. During the June War of 1967, the map was again revised, with the Israeli occupation of all Jerusalem, the West Bank, the Gaza Strip, and the Golan Heights. Thus virtually the entire area of Palestine came under Israeli rule.

From 1949, Palestine became an idea, and Palestinian national identity took on a distinctive form, based on the loss of a homeland and the longing to return. The experience of dispossession, or of living under Israeli rule, has varied according to class, location, and circumstances. Divisions and resentments have developed over the years between social layers within the exiled community in Jordan and Lebanon. The squalor of the refugee camps has contrasted with the relative affluence, if not security, of middle-class urban dwellers. Differences arose between those who have established themselves in the Gulf or the United States and all others; and between those living under Israeli rule and those outside. Yet in times of crisis all are drawn together by the sense of identity through dispossession and by the insecurity of the stateless.

The *Palestine Liberation Organization (PLO) has embodied both this aspiration for a return to Palestine and the sense of loss. Its appeal has been both to a secular nationalism— the right of the Palestinians to their own land and *self-determination—and also at times to the idea of reclaiming Palestine's Islamic holy places, especially Jerusalem. The idea of the Palestinian "revolution" is a common reference point. *Revolution* here is a broad term connoting a redemptive nationalist struggle, not necessarily a class struggle. Islamic groups have placed much stronger emphasis on the liberation of the holy places, *jihad, and an Islamic Palestine. These groups have not, however, exercised a decisive influence on the direction of the movement.

The Israelis contributed to this sense of identity by their efforts to deny the Palestinians any cultural memory or political identity. For many years Israelis denied the very existence of "Palestinians" as a category distinct from "Arabs" and with a legitimate claim to identity and self-determination. This denial took the form of censorship, political repression, and control over education. Palestinian citizens of Israel have lived the constant contradiction between the Israeli denial of their specific identity and history and its refusal to accord them equal treatment as citizens. The marginality, in the course of several generations, has reinforced rather than diminished a sense of Palestinian identity in the younger generation. In the occupied territories, attempts to repress political and cultural identity have similarly proved counterproductive. The *intifada, coming after twenty years of occupation, is clear evidence of the growth and consolidation, despite internal disputes, of national feeling in the territories.

The geographical definition of Palestine has been based on the boundaries under the British Mandate, but since the 1970s an increasing number of Palestinians have been willing to accept the idea of a Palestinian state "on a part of Palestine," thus allowing for the continued existence of an Israeli state. This position was embodied in the PLO's 1988 declaration of an independent state, followed by the explicit recognition of the Israeli state. This strategy envisages a Palestinian state based in the occupied West Bank and Gaza Strip.

However, several crucial questions remain. The first regards the status of Jerusalem, which contains sites holy to Islam, Judaism, and Christianity and is claimed by both Palestinians and Israelis. Second, the geographical discontinuity of such a Palestinian state would create strategic and economic problems. Third, after over twenty years of Israeli occupation, the economies of the territories have been made highly dependent on the Israeli economy. This dependence, whether on Israel or other neighboring states, would be difficult to break. Finally, there remains the question of what proportion of over 4 million Palestinians such a state could accommodate.

During the 1990s, major changes occurred in Palestinian perceptions of their future. Attitudes among the younger generation in the West Bank and Gaza Strip had been altered by the experience of the intifada. The initiation of negotiations with Israel, beginning with the Madrid peace conference, led to increased activity among Islamist groups, in particular Hamas, which gained support at the expense of secular nationalists and leftists especially in the Gaza Strip but also in the West Bank. Hamas opposed the idea of a Palestinian state on only a part of historic Palestine and began attacking Israeli targets.

The Oslo peace process, initiated in 1993, had not, as of mid-2000, resulted in agreement on the key "final status" issues: the borders of a new Palestinian state, the future status of Jerusalem, the future of Israeli settlements on occupied territory, and the future of Palestinian refugees in the diaspora. Yet it has resulted in several major shifts that are unlikely to be reversed. The creation of the Palestinian Authority (PA), under President Yassir *Arafat, is likely to become the government of a Palestinian state, however inadequate this proves to be in regard to the key issues outlined above.

The enthusiasm which greeted the formation of the PA in 1994 has waned, as progress in the peace talks stalled and the PA presided over a faltering democratic process and declining economic conditions, caused mainly by the constraints on movement imposed by Israel on security grounds. The PA, under pressure to crush serious resistance, especially by Islamists, has developed an overblown and unaccountable security apparatus. Although some progress has been made in establishing administrative structure, cronyism and corruption have been a frequent subject of complaint. Tensions persist between PLO cadres who arrived from "outside" and the political elites in the West Bank and Gaza, especially those who are not Fatah supporters. However, leftist nationalist groups have not so far succeeded in forging policies or alliances which seriously challenge the dominance of Fatah in the governing structures.

The Palestinian state as envisaged under a final agreement emerging from the Oslo process is likely to be narrowly defined and geographically fragmented. Such an outcome will raise serious questions for the future and identities of those Palestinians left outside it, if a right of return is not realized. The most vulnerable and alienated refugee community is that in Lebanon, the second largest in the diaspora.

Palestinian nationalism has had a shifting relationship to Arab nationalism and pan-Arabism. Palestinians have invoked Arab nationalism and unity to help reclaim the territory of Palestine. However, in the last two decades Pales-

tinians have expressed increasing bitterness that while the liberation of Palestine has served as a slogan to sustain pan-Arabism, the Arab states have provided only limited support to the Palestinian cause.

(See also ARAB-ISRAELI CONFLICT; RELIGION AND POLITICS; UNITED NATIONS.)

Gershon Shafir, *Land, Labor and the Origins of the Israeli-Palestinian Conflict* (Cambridge, U.K., 1969). Rosemary Sayigh, *Palestinians, from Peasants to Revolutionaries* (London, 1979). Edward Said, *The Question of Palestine* (London, 1980). Nels Johnson, *Islam and the Politics of Meaning in Palestinian Nationalism* (London, 1982).

SARAH GRAHAM-BROWN

PALESTINE LIBERATION ORGANIZATION. The Palestine Liberation Organization (PLO) was formed by the Arab summit conference in January 1964 in order to contain and channel renewed *nationalism among the Palestinians, displaced by *Israel's foundation in 1948. The 422-member Palestine National Council (PNC), the PLO's policy-making parliament, first convened in Jerusalem in May 1964. The PNC elected a fifteen-member Executive Committee, which elected as chair the veteran diplomat Ahmad al-Shuqayri. The PNC endorsed a National Charter that sought to restore *Palestine to Arab rule and formed the Palestine Liberation Army (PLA), whose units were attached to the armed forces of Egypt, Syria, and Iraq.

When Israel defeated those armies in June War of 1967, their leaders and the PLO officials were discredited. The lawyer Yahya Hammudah replaced Shuqayri as chair in December 1967. The Palestinian guerrilla movements, which had remained aloof from the PLO, swelled in size after they withstood Israel's attack on Karameh, Jordan, in March 1968. Yasir *Arafat, head of Fatah, the largest group, was elected chair at the fifth PNC (February 1969), at which more than half the members came from guerrilla forces. Fatah, formed in 1958, called for the establishment of a "democratic, non-sectarian Palestine state in which all groups will have equal rights and obligations irrespective of race, color and creed."

The PLO charter, amended at the fourth PNC (July 1968), reflected the guerrillas' emphasis on popularly-based armed struggle, rejected *Zionism and the partition of Palestine, termed Judaism "a religion . . . not an independent nationality" (Article 20), and called for "the total liberation of Palestine" (Article 21). The charter upheld Arab unity, but emphasized that just as the PLO would "not interfere in the internal affairs of any Arab state" (Article 27), it would also "reject all forms of intervention, trusteeship and subordination" (Article 28) by Arab governments. The charter could only be amended by a two-thirds vote of the total membership of the PNC, at a special session.

Arafat not only led Fatah but also, as PLO chair, commanded the PLA units. He formed the Palestinian Armed Struggle Command (PASC) in 1969 as a police force to maintain order in refugee camps in Jordan and Lebanon. By June 1970 the Unified Command of the guerrilla groups included Fatah, the largest group; the Popular Front for the Liberation of Palestine (PFLP), founded by Dr. George Habash in December 1967; the Popular Front-General Command (PF-GC), whose leader Ahmad Jabril broke away from PFLP in 1968; the Democratic Front for the Liberation of Palestine (DFLP), whose Jordanian head, Naif Hawatmeh, left the PFLP in February 1969; the Syrian-sponsored Saiqa, formed in 1968; and the Iraqi-sponsored Arab Liberation Front (ALF), formed in January 1969. The PLO provided an umbrella for the diverse groups, which often worked at cross-purposes. Fatah focused on freeing Palestine from Israeli rule and sought amicable relations with Arab governments. In contrast, the PFLP and DFLP worked to overthrow conservative Arab regimes prior to liberating Palestine. Saiqa and the ALF were controlled by rival branches of the Ba`th Party, which emphasized Arab unity rather than Palestinian nationalism. They also differed on tactics: Fatah, Saiqa, and the DFLP denounced the PFLP and PF-GC for hijacking foreign airplanes in 1969–1970.

Disagreements with Arab host governments crystallized in mid-1970 when Egypt and Jordan accepted a U.S.-mediated cease-fire with Israel. In September 1970 Jordan's King Hussein used the occasion of the PFLP's landing hijacked planes on Jordanian soil to launch a military showdown with the PLO, accusing it of seeking to overthrow his government. All the guerrilla units were forced out of Jordan by late 1971. They regrouped in Lebanon, where the Cairo Agreement (November 1969) regulated their presence in the refugee camps and along the border with Israel.

The PLO established a complex institutional structure in Lebanon, which included hospitals and clinics run by the Palestine Red Crescent Society, handicrafts and light industries, and planning and research centers. Such affiliated organizations as the unions of workers, engineers, writers, journalists, teachers, students, and women ran activities throughout the *Middle East. The Palestine National Fund handled fundraising and disbursement.

Palestinian despair in the early 1970s after the defeat in Jordan was signaled by desperate attacks by Black September commandos, including the *assassination of Jordan's prime minister in Cairo in November 1971 and the kidnapping and murder of Israeli athletes at the Olympic Games in Munich in September 1972. Nonetheless, PLO leaders began to revise their political objectives. The eleventh PNC (January 1973) secretly resolved to form a Palestine National Front in the Israeli-occupied West Bank and Gaza Strip, which would work politically to end Israeli rule in those parts of Palestine. Following the October War (1973), the twelfth PNC (June-July 1974) advocated the establishment of an "independent combatant national authority . . . over every part of Palestinian territory that is liberated." (Even though the PNC rejected a permanent *peace with Israel, the PFLP viewed the resolution as tantamount to accepting Israel's existence and withdrew from the Executive Committee of the PLO, remaining only on the intermediate-level Central Council.)

The PLO's standing in the Arab world was consolidated in October 1974 when the Arab summit at Rabat affirmed "the right of the Palestinian people to establish an independent national authority under the command of the Palestine Liberation Organization, the sole legitimate representative of the Palestinian people, in any Palestinian territory that is liberated." The PLO's international role was enhanced in November 1974 when, following Arafat's address to the UN General Assembly, the PLO secured observer status at the UN. Furthermore, pro-PLO candidates swept the West Bank municipal council elections in 1976 and the thirteenth PNC (March 1977) stressed the Palestinians' "right to establish their inde-

pendent national state on their own land." By then, Fatah had paramount influence within the PLO, since the PFLP had failed to mobilize other groups behind its Rejection Front and Saiqa had virtually collapsed in the wake of Syrian-supported attacks on Palestinians during the initial phase of the Lebanese civil war.

The PLO's strategic shift from the goal of reclaiming all Palestine to the goal of forming a state alongside Israel failed to have the intended diplomatic impact. It was sidetracked first by Egyptian President Anwar *Sadat's bilateral negotiations with Israel, which culminated in the March 1979 peace treaty, and then by the Israeli invasion of Lebanon in June 1982. The Egyptian-Israeli accord provided for a transitional period of self-rule on the West Bank and Gaza Strip that excluded the PLO and downplayed the prospects of Palestinian statehood. The Israeli invasion, designed to destroy the PLO's military and political infrastructure in Lebanon, was complemented by Israel's dismantling the municipalities on the West Bank and Gaza Strip. During the sixty-seven-day Israeli siege and aerial bombardment of Beirut, Arafat negotiated the withdrawal of Palestinian forces from the Lebanese capital. In August 1982, he moved the PLO headquarters to Tunis. Palestinians living in refugee camps near Beirut, no longer protected by PLO forces, suffered vengeful attacks by Israeli-protected Lebanese Forces the next month.

The PLO seemed severely weakened by the Israeli invasion, especially when several Fatah officers denounced Arafat in 1983, decrying the evacuation and calling for renewed combat with Israel. Syria hosted not only those dissidents but also the leaders of the PFLP, DFLP, and PF-GC. Nonetheless, Arafat reinvigorated his diplomatic efforts and formed a counterweight with his erstwhile antagonists Egypt and Jordan. The seventeenth PNC (November 1984), held in Amman, enabled Arafat to join King Hussein in February 1985 in calling for a confederation of Jordan and a Palestinian state on the West Bank and Gaza Strip. However, the PLO appeared to weaken and fragment further when Washington did not respond to the joint initiative, Israel bombed the PLO headquarters in Tunis in October 1985, dissident Palestinians launched terrorist attacks in late 1985, and King Hussein renounced the accord in February 1986. Despite these tensions, Arafat reconsolidated the movement at the eighteenth PNC (April 1987, Algiers). Despite Syrian opposition, the PFLP and DFLP resumed their seats on the Executive Committee, the Palestine Communist Party gained a seat for the first time, and only the numerically insignificant dissident Fatah and PF-GC remained outside the PLO's fold. The PLO was thus well positioned to respond to the popular *intifada ("shaking off") that swept the West Bank and Gaza Strip beginning in December 1987. The Unified National Leadership of the Uprising contains the major groups within the PLO, and it helped propel the PLO to endorse the establishment of an independent Palestinian state at the nineteenth PNC (November 1988, Algiers). That PNC endorsed, for the first time, both the UN General Assembly's partition plan of 1947 and UN Security Council *Resolution 242 of November 1967, and called for "*security and peace for every state in the region." The next month Arafat explicitly recognized Israel's right to exist as a Jewish state and underlined the PNC's renunciation of *terrorism. The Central Council elected Arafat president of Palestine in April 1989.

The PLO was transformed by events of the early 1990s. The 1991 *Gulf War witnessed the defeat of a lynchpin of Arab radicalism, Iraq, as well as the erosion of Saudi and Kuwaiti support for the PLO as a result of Arafat's pro-Iraqi stance. Israel also used the war as an opportunity to crush the intifada. Second, the decline of the Soviet Union weakened a major source of the PLO's diplomatic assistance. As a result, the PLO decided to support the American-led Arab-Israeli peace process initiated at the Madrid peace conference of October 1991. Bilateral negotiations between Israelis and Palestinian negotiators acting on behalf of the PLO later commenced, but achieved little progress.

In August 1993, Israel and the PLO shocked the world when it was revealed that each side had been involved in unprecedented secret negotiations in Norway designed to forge a peaceful end to decades of conflict. The result was a series of agreements signed in the 1990s that led to an Israeli withdrawal from parts of the West Bank and Gaza and to the creation of a PLO-led proto-state called the Palestinian Authority (PA). As the peace process led to the solidification of the PA and the movement toward some form of Palestinian statehood, the PLO essentially had become virtually extinct as a functioning entity by early 2000.

(See also ARAB-ISRAELI CONFLICT; GUERRILLA WARFARE; NATIONAL LIBERATION MOVEMENTS; REFUGEES.)

William Quandt, Fuad Jabber, and Ann Mosely Lesch, *The Politics of Palestinian Nationalism* (Berkeley, Calif., 1973). Bard O'Neill, *Armed Struggle in Palestine* (Boulder, Colo., 1978). Aryeh Yodfat, *PLO Strategy and Politics* (New York, 1981). Helena Cobban, *The Palestine Liberation Organization* (New York, 1984). Alain Gresh, *The PLO* (London, 1986). Rashid Khalidi, *Under Siege: PLO Decisionmaking during the 1982 War* (New York, 1986). Shaul Mishal, *The PLO under Arafat* (New Haven, Conn., 1986). Emile Sahliyeh, *The PLO after the Lebanon War* (Boulder, Colo., 1986). David Makofvsky, *Making Peace with the PLO* (Boulder, Colo., 1996). Yezid Sayigh, *Armed Struggle and the Search for State: The Palestinian National Movement, 1949–1993* (Oxford, 1997). Avraham Sela and Moshe Ma'oz, eds., *The PLO and Israel: From Armed Conflict to Political Solution, 1964–1994* (New York, 1997).

ANN M. LESCH

PAN-AFRICANISM. The Pan-African Movement has been the principal agency for the self-definition of the African People in the twentieth century. This movement has been manifest both at the subjective level of race consciousness and the objective level in relation to its organizational forms. These are more widely known, with the written record focusing on the seven Pan-African Congresses held between 1900 and 1994. In institutional terms, the *Organization of African Unity is the most concrete manifestation of Pan-African aspirations. The Pan-African Movement has gone through many stages in the last century and for this brief analysis five main stages will be highlighted.

Stage 1. Pan-Africanism and the quest for self-definition arose out of the concrete realities of the partition of Africa and the massive violence, destruction, *genocide, and division that arose at the end of the nineteenth century and the rise of racism and racial violence in the United States. The small intelligentsia in the African diaspora were the main spokespersons for the ideas of African independence and dignity. At the popular level the opposition to domination took cultural and religious forms such as the rise of the Rastafari move-

ment in Jamaica, the Kimbanguist movement in the Congo, Ethiopianism, and other social movements such as the Garvey movement. Scholars such as W. E. B *Du Bois convened international meetings called Pan-African Congresses, which sought to bring together those with the agenda to liberate Africa from colonialism and to end lynching and segregation in the United States. There were five congresses between 1900 and 1945. The 1945 meeting brought together leaders such as DuBois, Kwame *Nkrumah, George Padmore, and Jomo Kenyatta.

Pan-Africanism from below was manifest in the consciousness of ordinary Africans, and inspired the largest mass movement of the century on both sides of the Atlantic in the form of the Universal Negro Improvement Association (UNIA). Marcus Garvey, the UNIA president, was born in Jamaica and migrated to the United States in the period of World War I. Garveyism took root in the U.S. where the ideas of African redemption found a fertile base in a society that was struggling against the *Ku Klux Klan and those extremist groups for which lynching was a Saturday night outing. The UNIA had branches in all parts of the world, with its newspaper, the *Negro World*, acting as the voice of the Pan-African movement in the period of the Harlem Renaissance.

The rise of *fascism under Hitler and Mussolini and the ideas of white supremacy were to be a major challenge for all of humanity. The Italian invasion of Abyssinia in 1935 was another moment when the Pan-African consciousness of Africans rose to become a force in international politics. The failure of the *League of Nations to respond to the atrocities of the Italians led Africans to warn of the dangers of fascism and world war. In this sense the global Pan-African movement was a major force of the antifascist movement, as many *African Americans volunteered to fight on Ethiopia's side. In this period of fascism and war, Pan-African scholars and intellectuals such as Du Bois, Padmore, C. L. R. *James, Aimé Césaire, and Richard Wright articulated the ideas of liberation and redemption. In the French-speaking territories, Negritude was another variant of Pan-Africanism.

Stage 2. The period of the struggle for *self-determination and independence, in which the intellectual leaders of the Fifth Pan African Congress in Manchester like Nkrumah and Kenyatta became actively involved, is usually referred to as the nationalist phase of Pan-Africanism. The nationalist movement embraced the idea that independence was to be the basis for the regeneration and reconstruction of Africa. Cheik Anta Diop of Senegal, Frantz *Fanon of Martinique, and Amilcar Cabral of Guinea-Bissau were among those who made outstanding contributions to Pan-Africanism by linking the Pan-African project to the *decolonization of the mind. Fanon as a psychiatrist traced mental illness to colonial rule and linked the transformation of the health and sanity of the people to national liberation and African unity. Diop used the contributions of the Egyptian civilizations to affirm the cultural and linguistic unity of Africa as a basis of Pan-Africanism. And Cabral emphasized the role of national culture as a weapon of liberation. Walter Rodney and Julius *Nyerere were also among the noted intellectuals who defined the Pan-African agenda in the twentieth century.

The idea of Pan-African responsibility in the national liberation struggle was best articulated by Ghana's Kwame Nkrumah, in the credo that the independence of one part of

Africa would be meaningless until all of Africa was liberated from colonial rule and white minority domination such as apartheid. In 1958, one year after the independence of Ghana, Nkrumah convened the first All African Peoples Conference. It was at this meeting that members of the embryonic *Civil Rights Movement of the United States came into contact with the mass movements that were fighting in Africa such as the Algerian and Kenyan struggles for independence. It was also at this meeting that Patrice Lumumba was introduced to the wider Pan-African community. The struggles over the independence of the Congo were to be a major test for the international Pan-African movement.

Stage 3. The Organization of African Unity was formed in May 1963 as a compromise between those who wanted full mobilization to counter Belgian and French incursions in the Congo and those countries that wanted appeasement with imperialism. This compromise between the Monrovia and Casablanca groups of Pan-Africanists led to the formalization of Pan-Africanism with the emergence of a number of *international organizations in the telecommunications, information, medical, health, sports, and other sectors. The Pan African News Agency and the All African Nations Cup (in soccer) are two of the Pan-African institutions that are most well known to Africans at home and abroad.

In 1964 the OAU created the Liberation Committee with the mandate to support militarily, politically, and diplomatically those countries still under *apartheid and colonial rule. In effect the struggle against apartheid was to become the principal reference point for Pan-Africanism after the Soweto revolt of 1976. Despite the cooperation in relation to apartheid, OAU member states undermined one of the principal credos of Pan-Africanism, through the clause of noninterference in the internal affairs of sovereign states. This restriction protected dictators and ensured that the organization did not intervene to stop *genocide in Burundi in 1972 and was incapacitated when the massive genocide took place in Rwanda in 1994.

Pan-Africanism was at all times a blend of *nationalism and internationalism. In the twentieth century the Civil Rights Movement in the United States acted as a beacon for this internationalism. And it is through this movement that solidarity with African struggles worldwide was articulated in the positive messages of *Malcolm X, Martin Luther *King, Jr., Angela Davis, and Kwame Ture (formerly Stokely Carmichael), the principal leaders of the movement, and by writers such as Lorraine Hansberry and James Baldwin. African American singers were also representatives of this movement, and their message of "respect" and black pride were communicated widely throughout the world.

Bob Marley, the Rastafarian cultural leader, was another notable Pan-African spokesperson of the century, who wanted to transcend racial divisions with a universal message of African unity, love, peace, and human emancipation. Africans and non-Africans alike embraced his music and ideas, and his message of Pan-African emancipation was an inspiration to all of humanity. The Rastafari movement was an expression of Pan-Africanism from the grassroots and could be distinguished from the Pan-Africanism of states as manifest in the OAU. It was this vibrant Pan-Africanism from below that transcended states, which is manifest in the declarations of the sixth and seventh Pan African Congresses,

held respectively in Dar es Salaam, Tanzania, in 1974 and in Kampala, Uganda, in 1994. In spite of attempts to turn them into miniature OAU gatherings, these meetings did bring out new voices and new visions for the future of Africa.

Stage 4. Most forceful among these voices were those of African women, who declared that the Pan-Africanism of the formal leadership was androcentric and patriarchal. While some organizations such as the Pan-Africanist Congress of Azania still held to the all class nationalism of the *decolonization period, in the main the youth, women, and independent cultural artists sought new avenues to express Pan-African ideals. The rise of dictators and military leaders who plunged the continent into war set back the goals of continental unity by many decades. By the end of the century there were more than twenty-eight wars in Africa and the militarism at the level of the struggle for power was having a negative effect on all aspects of social life. There was even in the midst of this carnage the call for the implementation of the African Charter on Human and Peoples Rights. This Charter had been adopted in the seventies and had become a rallying point for human rights activists all over Africa. The coming to power of Nelson *Mandela in South Africa in 1994 created a new momentum for democracy and human rights, and the moral leadership of Mandela provided a breath of fresh air in the sea of dictators such as those found in Kenya, Nigeria, Togo, and Sudan.

Stage 5. By the end of the century African women had emerged with a new definition of Pan-Africanism that emphasized the humanity of Africans and not simply the independence of states. At the seventh Pan-African Congress in Kampala, the women who were present formed the Pan-African Women's Liberation Organization (PAWLO). The struggles against violence, warfare, destruction, and violation had taken the Pan-African discussion to a new level. In the process there was a sharp distinction between the Pan-Africanism of the leaders and that of ordinary people. The challenge of the *HIV/AIDS pandemic had required a new leadership, and the old slogans of unity and independence were inadequate to inspire the movement to defend the livelihood of Africans.

In May 1999, a meeting of Pan-African Women in Zanzibar proposed a peace agenda, including far-reaching demands for an end to militarism and arms purchases, and the need for peaceful resolutions of the wars then raging in Africa. These women noted the impact of globalization on human reproduction in Africa and made far-reaching recommendations for the mobilization of Africa's resources for African renewal. The women's call for peace was very different in tone and content from the call of Thabo Mbeki, the new President of South Africa, for an African Renaissance. This was critiqued as another importation of the ideas of the European Enlightenment. However, the very differences of opinion over the African Renaissance reflected the search for a redefinition of Pan-Africanism for the twenty-first century.

In the midst of all the negative developments, there was a renewed call for realizing Nkrumah's dream of a "United States of Africa," with regional economic groupings such as the Economic Community of *West African States (ECOWAS) and the *Southern African Development Community (SADEC) to serve as building blocks for an African economic community under the 1991 Abuja Treaty. At the 36th Summit of the OAU held in Togo from 10–12 July 2000, African leaders took cognizance of the reality of economic integration through informal crossborder channels together with the challenges of globalization, and adopted a continental unity plan initially proposed by Libyan leader Muammar Khadafi, which calls for the establishment of an African Union on the model of the European Union in 2001.

(See also AFRICAN REGIONAL ORGANIZATIONS; COLONIAL EMPIRES; DEVELOPMENT AND UNDERDEVELOPMENT; RACE AND RACISM; RWANDAN GENOCIDE.)

Horace Campbell, *Pan-Africanism* (Toronto, 1975). *Declaration of the Delegates and Participants at the 7th Pan African Congress* (Kampala, Uganda, 1994).

HORACE CAMPBELL

PANAMA. Geography is destiny on the isthmus between North and South America, where the Pacific and Atlantic oceans are separated by a strip of land only fifty miles wide. Political developments since the Spanish Conquest have been marked by an ongoing struggle for access to and control over the transit route—whether the gold, silver, and slave routes using mules or dugout canoes until 1739; the first transcontinental railroad, completed in 1855; the French canal effort of the 1880s; or the U.S.-built Panama Canal since 1903.

As a result, an urban commercial elite developed and predominated both in the economic and political realms, as opposed to a rural-based oligarchy as in most Latin American countries. Alliances and conflicts with other groups, national or foreign, in this century have largely revolved around access to the Canal Zone, a process that intensified in the late 1980s, in anticipation of the year 2000 and the return of full control of the canal and surrounding land to Panama. The period was marked by the invasion by the United States in December 1989 to replace a military government with statist and populist leanings with one that was friendly to the United States and favored a privatized and deregulated economy.

Much of Panama's economic activity traditionally centered on the transit zone—through servicing the civilian and military inhabitants of the Canal Zone and the highly paid Panamanians employed there, in addition to providing some ancillary services to canal users—or on the banana export industry near the western frontier. During the 1970s the government promoted diversification of Panama's international services, based on the establishment of an international banking center, taking advantage of the circulation of the U.S. dollar in Panama, and expansion of the Colón Free Zone, the world's largest free zone after Hong Kong. Along with other countries in Central America, Panama also became a *drug transshipment point, an activity that sporadically enjoyed official protection.

By 1988, Panama's 2.3 million inhabitants had a per capita income of over US$2,000, although they suffered one of the worst income distributions in Latin America. The expansion of the public sector through heavy borrowing in the 1970s helped contribute to 80 percent literacy rates and a decline in infant mortality to under thirty per thousand. Nearly half the population lives in the metropolitan area, in the Panama-Colón corridor.

Panama has a presidential form of government, under which elections for president and the Legislative Assembly are held every five years. Smooth transitions have been the exception, however, and since Panama's independence from Colombia in 1903, most presidents have been ousted before completing their term.

Political parties were banned for ten years following the October 1968 military coup against President Arnulfo Arias, Panama's most famous politician, who was first elected president in 1940 and reputedly won every election in which he ran through 1984. His espousal of support for the Axis powers during World War II ensured his swift removal, as the Panama Canal and the Canal Zone were vital elements in the allied war effort.

General Omar Torrijos Herrera emerged as leader of the Revolutionary Process, as it was known, from 1969 until his death in an airplane crash in 1981. Under his leadership a new constitution was approved in 1972, providing for elections to a National Assembly of 505 representatives from municipal subdistricts and for a much-enhanced role for local councils. As a result, sectors that had been largely excluded from the political process—peasants, Indians, women, and organized labor—were incorporated directly, albeit under the tutelage of the military. In this period Panama took on a larger role regionally and engaged in negotiations with the United States to take control of the Panama Canal in 2000. Through the Contadora group, Panama promoted a Latin American stance toward Central American problems in the 1980s.

Torrijos's chief of intelligence, Manuel Antonio Noriega, became commander in 1983 of the Defense Forces, increasingly taking a more political role. In 1984 the government candidate won by a suspiciously small margin, only to be ousted by Noriega a year later, and in 1989 the elections were annulled when it became obvious the opposition had a two-to-one victory.

Noriega's long association with the U.S. government, including the *Central Intelligence Agency since the mid-1960s and the Drug Enforcement Agency in the 1970s and 1980s, made him an unlikely figure to lead a genuine nationalist movement when relations with the United States deteriorated in mid-1987. His command of psychological operations gave him control with maximum use of fear and minimal violence. The U.S. invasion of Panama in December 1989 that ousted Noriega was welcomed locally, despite the more than 550 deaths and widespread destruction and looting that resulted.

The political forces in power in the post-invasion period had in common a favorable attitude toward U.S. policy, anticommunism, and dislike of the military. While some were interested in recovering access and privileges denied to them since 1968, commercial sectors that had benefited from the 1970s expansion of Panama's role as an international service entrepôt proposed dismantling all restrictions to free trade.

Organized labor, deliberately courted and favored by Torrijos in a labor code that guaranteed job stability and minimum wages, was weakened by the high unemployment rate resulting from *sanctions imposed by the United States in its efforts to remove Noriega. Public-sector employees were similarly demoralized by fiscal austerity and political manipulation. Other social forces and popular movements were co-opted or repressed during the period of military government, leading to their demobilization and fragmentation.

The 1994 elections were closely fought and considered to be the cleanest in Panama's history, thanks to a widespread desire for a new democratic culture fostered by the Catholic Church's Justice and Peace Commission that successfully negotiated an Ethical Electoral Pact between the seven competing parties and their respective presidential candidates. The winning candidate, however, Ernesto Pérez Balladares, had only 31 percent of the votes cast, returning Noriega's and Torrijos's political party, the Partido Revolucionario Democrático (PRD), to power, and showing the electoral folly of a fragmented opposition.

The government speeded up the implementation of structural reforms proposed by the multilateral development banks, privatizing state enterprises including ports and the telephone service and removing tariff protection for agriculture and industry, in line with requirements for Panama's entry to the World Trade Organization. The main challenges now facing Panama's incipient democracy are the successful transition to Panamanian management of the Panama Canal, productive use of the former military bases on the banks of the Panama Canal, incorporation of the marginalized urban population that suffers one of the highest urban unemployment rates in Latin America 16 percent in 1998), and key political decisions on constitutional reform proposals that include the possibility of reelection of an incumbent president. Security challenges include containing the overflow of Colombia's political problems into the vulnerable Darien province, controlling drug flows through Panamanian territory, and maintaining domestic peace and international neutrality without a local military or the presence of U.S. troops on Panamanian soil.

(See also INTERVENTION; MILITARY RULE; PANAMA CANAL TREATY; U.S.–LATIN AMERICAN RELATIONS.)

Steve C. Ropp, *Panamanian Politics: From Guarded Nation to National Guard* (New York, 1982). George Priestley, *Military Government and Popular Participation in Panama: The Torrijos Regime, 1968–1975* (Boulder, Colo., 1986). Tom Barry and John Lindsay-Poland, *Inside Panama: The Essential Guide to Its Politics, Economy, Society and Environment* (Albuquerque, N. Mex., 1995). Luis Murillo, *The Noriega Mess: The Drugs, the Canal and Why America Invaded* (Berkeley, Calif., 1995).

CHARLOTTE ELTON

PANAMA CANAL TREATY. The Panama Canal Treaties were signed by U.S. President Jimmy *Carter and Panama's chief of government Omar Torrijos on 7 September 1977 at the Organization of American States. The main Panama Canal Treaty abrogated the 1903 Hay-Bunau-Varilla Treaty and mandated that the United States gradually turn over to Panama responsibility for the administration, operation, and defense of the canal until the year 2000—when Panama would have complete jurisdiction and operational authority over the canal. The Treaty on the Permanent Neutrality of the Panama Canal granted to both the United States and Panama acting together or, if necessary, unilaterally, the right to defend the canal after the year 2000. The Neutrality Treaty was ratified by the U.S. Senate on 16 March 1978 and the Canal Treaty on 18 April, both by the same vote, 68–32.

Panama was a province of Colombia when the latter rejected a treaty with the United States to build a canal. The Panamanians, who frequently rebelled against Colombian rule, accurately judged that the United States would not come to Colombia's aid, as it had in the past, if the Panamanians rebelled. On 3 November 1903, Panama declared its independence. Within two weeks, the United States recognized Panama, and Secretary of State John Hay signed a treaty with Philippe Bunau-Varilla, an enterprising French citizen with interests in Panama, who had just been appointed by Panamanian leaders as their Minister Plenipotentiary to the United States. The treaty ceded "rights, power, and authority" to the United States to exercise jurisdiction as "if it were sovereign" over a zone ten miles wide—"in perpetuity"—and to construct, operate, and defend a canal.

Panamanians protested the treaty's provisions, but only after riots killed twenty-four people near the canal in 1964 did the United States begin to negotiate seriously the repeal of the 1903 treaty. Negotiations dragged on for thirteen years because U.S. presidents were sensitive to the political cost of "giving away" the canal. By 1977, the Panamanian "patience machine," in Torrijos's pungent phrase, "was running out of gas," and Carter judged that the greatest threat to the canal would be U.S. failure to negotiate new treaties. In addition, a number of Latin American presidents informed Carter that good relationships between the United States and their countries would depend on the United States negotiating such treaties.

Because polls showed that the canal transfer was very unpopular, Carter had to undertake a massive educational effort. The treaties were approved by a single vote in the United States and a close vote in Panama. The treaties were implemented very slowly because of the hostile relationship between the Reagan and Bush administrations and General Manuel Antonio Noriega in the 1980s. After Noriega's fall in 1989, Panamanian responsibility for the operation of the canal proceeded smoothly, although the reverted properties were transferred slowly. The final transfer of the Canal took place on 31 December 1999. Despite last minute fears and the absence of the U.S. President and Secretary of State from the ceremony, the transfer was successful.

(See also U.S.–LATIN AMERICAN RELATIONS.)

David McCullough, *The Path between the Seas: The Creation of the Panama Canal, 1870–1914* (New York, 1977). William J. Jordan, *Panama Odyssey* (Austin, Tex., 1984). George D. Moffett III, *The Limits of Victory: The Ratification of the Panama Canal Treaties* (Ithaca, N.Y., 1985). Mark Falcoff, *Panama's Canal* (Washington, D.C., 1989).

ROBERT A. PASTOR

PAN-ARABISM. See ARAB NATIONALISM.

PAPAL STATES. See VATICAN CITY STATE.

PAPUA NEW GUINEA. See PACIFIC ISLANDS.

PARAGUAY. A distinct society has developed in this landlocked country devoid of significant natural resources. In the early decades after independence (1811), Paraguay resembled its neighbors with dictatorial leaders vying for power, frequently resulting in civil war. Its divergence from its neighbors was cemented by a devastating war with Argentina, Brazil, and Uruguay (the War of the Triple Alliance, 1865–1870) which witnessed the loss of over fifty percent of Paraguay's population. Paraguay's population of 4.8 million is one of the most homogeneous in Latin America. More than 90 percent of the population is of mixed descent and most speak Guarani as well as Spanish. One-half of the population still lives in rural areas. Paraguay's location between Brazil, Argentina, and Bolivia made it a natural spot for contraband, which continues to be a key economic activity in an economy with a per capita GDP of $2,100.

While developing two well-established political parties, Colorados and Liberals, Paraguay's political system in the twentieth century continued to be characterized by instability with a victory against Bolivia in the Chaco War (1932–1935) bolstering the legitimacy of the armed forces. Stability would come with a coup by General Alfredo Stroessner in May 1954. Stroessner would go on to be elected to eight terms as president. He frequently ruled under constitutional state of siege provisions, but his real power derived from the successful marriage of the Colorado Party, the armed forces, and key members of the business elite. His thirty-four-year reign saw Paraguay become increasingly isolated from the world community and even from its neighbors.

With massive *foreign aid and the impetus provided by the construction of the Itaipu hydroelectric project, Paraguay enjoyed significant growth during the 1970s. But the 1980s proved a decade of debt and recession (as it did throughout Latin America) and attempts by Stroessner to keep a stranglehold on the Colorado Party led to a split, which resulted in serious opposition to his continued domination.

Stroessner's rule came to an end on 2 February 1989, when he was forced into exile by General Andrés Rodríguez (1989–1993). While no democrat, Rodríguez did increase political freedom but did nothing to curtail corruption. Bowing to both internal and external pressure, the general stepped down from office, handpicking as his successor Juan Carlos Wasmosy, a wealthy engineer.

Wasmosy's presidency (1993–1998) was characterized by weakness and indecisiveness, especially in the face of a challenge from General Lino Oviedo whose own presidential ambitions led to an attempted barracks revolt in April 1996. When Oviedo received the Colorado Party's nomination in September 1997, the party was badly split. The May 1998 elections resulted in a clear and relatively clean victory for the ruling party despite its internal divisions. Raul Cubas Grau, standing in for Lino Oviedo (who was in prison for insurrection and was barred from running by the Supreme Court), received some fifty-four percent of the vote against some forty-three percent for an opposition coalition, the Alianza Democrática, led by perennial candidate Domingo Laino of the Partido Liberal Radical Auténtico. Thus the Colorado Party will continue its decades-old rule, but with more internal division than ever, and with a key authoritarian figure waiting in the wings.

(See also MILITARY RULE.)

Carlos A. Miranda, *The Stroessner Era* (Boulder, Colo., 1990). Peter Lambert and Andrew Nickson, eds., *The Transition to Democracy in Paraguay* (New York, 1997).

MARTIN WEINSTEIN

PARASTATALS. Public enterprises formed in order to enhance the economic and social health of a nation, parastatals come into being through a variety of means and circumstances.

Ownership Typology and Revenue Sources. Public enterprises vary considerably in their rationale and function. They may differ in methods of incorporation, in their relationship to the central administrative structure, their source of capital funds, and the degree of management independence. Public enterprises, therefore, run the gamut between governmental departments and privately owned and controlled nonprofit and for profit organizations. They are engaged in a whole spectrum of economic activities including agriculture, mining, construction, manufacturing, utilities, commerce, transportation systems, and financial and other services. In mixed economies, they compete with the domestic private producers for market share and may often be fully or partially exempt from tariffs for importing capital goods and raw materials.

Bearing in mind the variety of ideas and forms of state enterprises, a parastatal or public enterprise (the terms are used interchangeably) is an organization which:

- is owned by public authorities to the extent of 50 percent or more;
- is under the top managerial control of the owning public authorities, such as public control, including, *inter alia*, the right to appoint top management and to formulate critical policy decisions;
- is established for the achievement of a defined set of public purposes, which may be multidimensional in character;
- is engaged in activities of a business character;
- is consequently placed under a system of public accountability; and
- involves the basic idea of investment and returns and services.

This delineation excludes non-profit-making institutions which are purely concerned with providing social services such as fire departments, government relief organizations, public hospitals, regulatory bodies, and state organizations that have no economic or commercial functions but which, nonetheless, often are referred to as state enterprises.

Through monetary and fiscal policy and deficit financing, governments of industrialized countries can induce growth, increase employment, and affect interest rates and foreign exchange parity. They can also stimulate demand for their goods through *foreign aid to developing nations, and thus increase exports. Developing countries generally do not have such abilities, and if they wish to increase employment or induce growth, governments must engage in the production of goods and services via parastatals.

State ownership and control often involves projects with large capital outlays that may not be profitable. Such projects, therefore, may not appeal to the private investor. However, industries that provide vital products and services, including steel plants, fertilizer factories, and manufacturing plants, may have to be established by the government with no regard to their profitability. Such state enterprises are established with a conscious choice for security and self-reliance over profit, and the desire to control the major part of the national economy.

With goals as ambitious as these, there is a built-in tension between profitability and the social benefits parastatals contribute to the nation as a whole. When the public enterprises do not make a profit and require continued subsidies from

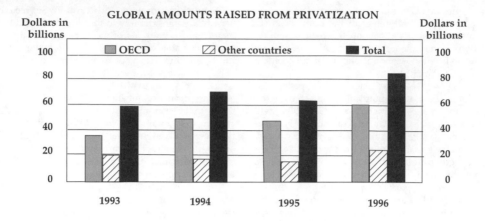

the government to stay afloat, they become a target of criticism by those who question the validity of their social objectives.

A wealthy nation may transfer the ownership of its largest oil producers, utilities, and manufacturing concerns into public hands for ideological reasons, while a new, poorer nation may be forced to take control of its vital interests soon after becoming independent. In the latter case, the absence of an established entrepreneurial class necessitates government involvement. Parastatals have also been created out of privately owned enterprises in financial peril. To risk their complete failure could mean serious damage to the national economy. To avoid this, they are taken over by the government. For example, the Philippine government nationalized major firms owned by former associates of Ferdinand Marcos because they failed to repay government-guaranteed loans. However, recent political developments have tended toward the divestiture of public enterprises to private ownership. With the functional decline of the ideological divide, a discussion of parastatals can no longer presuppose the existence of public enterprises as part of the paradigm of socialist economies.

Witness the 1988 decision of China's Communist party chief Zhao Ziyang to sell stock in China's state enterprises to bolster performance and profitability. What is remarkable about this shift is that China is the last bastion of socialist government in the world, Cuba notwithstanding. As revealed by the OECD trend analysis (see above), privatization is increasing on a global scale in terms of financial transactions across a range of sectors.

In struggling for an answer to the question, Are parastatals a success?, scholars can find as many examples of parastatals that make a financial and social contribution as those that have fallen short of their objectives. However, increasingly the question is neither about the ideological basis nor the functionality of parastatals but, instead, the financial feasibility and viability of *privatization. The international banks (*International Monetary Fund and *World Bank) that have made loans to developing nations since World War II are now making evidence of privatization efforts a condition for aid. However this strong inclination to phase out parastatals begs a basic question concerning the ultimate rationale behind privatization efforts. Is privatization simply an alternative means for rationalizing the public sector, or is it instead a means toward the introduction of an ideological paradigm shift? The IMF's campaigns to encourage the sale of parastatals and the general deregulation of economies has continued unchecked by concerns for regional conditions and capacities for extensive privatization. On the strength of IMF advice and consensus, the Mexican government, in the late 1990s, implemented policies to liberalize trade and deregulate their economy as well as privatizing parastatals (Nadal, 1997). However, without adequate financing and investment structures, the Mexican economy leaned on capital inflows as a crutch to support its skyrocketing current-account deficit. Eventually the value of the peso swooned and Mexico tumbled into economic depression. If parastatals continue to be proscribed by leading economic advisors, certain structural requirements for privatization must be met, including:

• political stability,
• historical mode of public change (legislated vs. decreed changes),
• financing and investment structure availability,
• openness of financial markets,
• presence of an indigenous entrepreneurial class,
• public sector support,
• governmental administrative oversight, and
• infrastructure (social, institutional, and physical).

While the degree to which each individual structural factor may either negatively or positively impact upon privatization certainly varies, it is important that countries considering privatization programs realize that many of these factors work in concert with one another. There must be a strong political commitment and support for privatization programs. Additionally, the privatization programs must be pragmatic and creative in approach, designed to exploit a country's specific opportunities for development. As Pfeffermann (1988) observed, parastatals cannot be arbitrarily privatized because the transaction costs associated with the privatization process can be even more burdensome than restructuring the enterprise to more efficient management practices. The institutional reform that the New Zealand government undertook in the mid-1980s is very instructive. Under the weight of a severe economic crisis (Campos and Pradhan, 1996), the government created radical institutional reforms that sought to completely redefine the role of government. The government established the State-Owned Enterprise Act of 1986, followed by the State Sector Act of 1988, the Public Finance Act of 1989, and the Fiscal Responsibility Act of 1993. The State-Owned Enterprise Act took the government out of production and provision of services that the private sector could just as well provide competitively. The State Sector Act reformed the civil service system. The Public Finance Act provided transparency and changed the accounting system of the nation by introducing an accrual accounting system. The Fiscal Responsibility Act not only introduced transparency and accountability, but also implemented fiscal discipline through full and frequent disclosure of aggregate fiscal information. These changes in concert have made it possible to transform the role of government in the provision of public goods and services.

The Debate Continues. The question of whether the superiority of the private sector performance is a given is debated endlessly in part because the debate is often confounded by unstated ideological assumptions. The assumptions are about the efficacy and the merits of private ownership and government sponsored enterprises. In a comparative study, Nayar (1991) contrasted the profitability and contribution to development of public and private aluminum and steel companies in India (for the period 1958–1988), and found that the private enterprise sector performed better. He also found that private firms were equally effective in backward-area development and meeting obligations to employees in terms of housing, benefits, and wages. In addition, he observed that the private sector's capacity utilization was superior to that of public enterprises. Nayar attributes the superior performance of private enterprises to property rights theory, which holds that the nature of ownership is the critical determinant of performance. In contrast, Israel (1991), among others, favors state intervention in the marketplace but wants a more fluid relationship between state and private sector enterprises. He argues that government should be an effective enabler and negotiator, and should put itself in a position to maximize public and private market potentials. Past government policy toward the private sector was inconsistent in Israel's view, as it ignored the problem of small business while yielding to pressures from the larger ones. In the meantime, Israel observes that government policies, especially in developing countries, have saddled public enterprises with an excessive number of often contradictory economic, political, and social objectives, making their effective management practically impossible.

The new role for the government that Israel advances, as negotiator and entrepreneur between the public and private sectors, seems to provide an optimal strategy for development that is rich with potential. In other words, the unnecessary dichotomization, and hence polarization, of public and private sector enterprises' activities, a grievance committed by many proponents of either sector, is not helpful to society. What may be helpful and productive, at this historical juncture, is an efficiency-oriented and less politicized public policy that will provide an interface and appropriate linkages between government enterprises and private businesses.

(See also NATIONALIZATION; PROTECTION.)

R. Fabrikant, "Developing Country State Enterprises: Performance and Control," *Columbia Journal of Transactional Law* 15 (1976): 40–56. R. Millward, "The Comparative Performance of Public and Private Ownership," in Lord Hall of Ipsden, ed., *The Mixed Economy* (New York, 1982), pp. 83–84. P. Dunleavy, "Explaining the Privatization Boom (in Britain): Public Choice versus Radical Approaches," *Public Administration* (Spring 1986): 13–34. Y. Aharoni, *The Evolution and Management of State Owned Enterprise* (Hagerstown, Md., 1987). G. Pfeffermann, "Private Business in Developing Countries—Improved Prospects," Discussion Paper Number 1, International Finance Corporation (1988): 13–20. R. C. Moe, "Privatization from a Public Management Perspective," CRS Report for Congress (March 1989). A. Israel, "The Changing Role of the State in Development," *Finance and Development* 28, no. 6 (June 1991): 41–43. B. R. Nayar, "Property Rights Theory and Government Efficiency: The Evidence from India's Public Sector," *Development Policy Review* 9, no. 2 (1991): 131–150. Organization for Economic Cooperation and Development, "Financial Market Trends," no. 64, June 1996. E. Campos and S. Pradhan, "Budgetary Institutions and Expenditure Outcomes," *Policy Research Working Paper*, World Bank (September 1996). A. Nadal, "The Micro-Economic Impact of IMF Structural Adjustment Policies in Mexico," *On the Wrong Track: A Summary*

Assessment of IMF Interventions in Selected Countries (1997), www.igc.org/dgap/.

BERHANU MENGISTU

PARIS CLUB. The Paris Club is not a club. It is a grouping of creditor governments which meets periodically to negotiate a rescheduling of debts owed them by individual debtor governments. These debts include export credits and guarantees and concessional loans. A debtor government will ask for a meeting of the Paris Club when it is unable to service fully its external public debt. A debtor is normally required by creditor governments to have negotiated a stabilization agreement with the *International Monetary Fund (IMF) before a Paris Club meeting takes place. Creditors are reluctant to agree to reschedule debts without some evidence that debtor governments are implementing economic reforms aimed at improving their future abilities to service their debts.

Paris Club meetings are normally chaired by an official of the French treasury, and staff work for those meetings is usually provided by the IMF. Debtor governments participating in Paris Club negotiations are almost wholly drawn from the developing world, though in the 1990s, a number of former socialist bloc countries, including the Russian Federation, have rescheduled their debts through the Paris Club. Creditor governments participating in a Paris Club meeting typically include those of Western Europe, North America, and Japan. Participation by creditor governments varies according to which government's debt is being rescheduled. Private banks and other commercial lenders do not participate in Paris Club negotiations. (They usually renegotiate their credits through the "London Club.") However, they are expected to provide debtors with terms comparable to those negotiated at the Paris Club.

The Paris Club first met in 1956 to reschedule the debt of Argentina. Until the end of the 1970s, it was involved primarily in rescheduling the debts of Latin American governments. By the late 1970s, African debtors began to seek Paris Club reschedulings in increasing numbers. Between 1980 and 1998, seventy-three countries had Paris Club agreements; many of them had multiple agreements (with Senegal holding the record at twelve). The largest regional grouping seeking debt reschedulings was African, with thirty-three countries seeking relief.

Since the 1980s, the terms of Paris Club reschedulings for the poorest countries have become progressively more favorable. By 1996, under the "Naples terms" (agreed to at the *Group of 7 meeting in Naples, Italy, in 1994), eligible highly indebted, poor countries (HIPC) could negotiate rescheduling terms of either the flow of debt repayments or the stock of total debt owed other governments which would reduce up to two-thirds of the present value of the debt. These arrangements typically were applied against export credits; most governments had canceled some or all of the concessional loans owed them by poor countries.

In 1995, the *World Bank, other multilateral creditors, and creditor governments agreed to a further arrangement for restructuring the debt of eligible HIPC. The aim of this initiative would be to reduce the debt of these countries to levels they could reasonably be expected to service. The debt reduction would include for the first time debt owed multilateral banks like the World Bank. Countries would first reschedule the flow of their bilateral debts (i.e., what they owe annually in debt servicing) under the auspices of the Paris Club on Naples terms. If after three years of "good performance" in economic management, a government still required further debt reduction to reach a sustainable debt burden, it would then negotiate its stock of bilateral debt in the Paris Club on terms that would reduce its net present value by up to 80 percent. Where necessary, these arrangements would be supplemented by others involving increased financial support from multilateral banks or other measures by those institutions to reduce the debt. The cumbersomeness and time-consuming nature of these new arrangements for the forty-one eligible HIPC have resulted in only six countries benefiting from them by mid-1998.

(See also DEVELOPMENT AND UNDERDEVELOPMENT; FINANCE, INTERNATIONAL; INTERNATIONAL DEBT; INTERNATIONAL POLITICAL ECONOMY.)

Thomas Calleghy, "Globalization and Marginalization: Debt and the International Underclass" *Current History* 96, no. 613 (November 1997).

CAROL LANCASTER

PARLIAMENTARY DEMOCRACY. Occasionally given a broad definition, parliamentary democracy connotes any form of representative *democracy, thus distinguishing it from forms of plebiscitary and direct democracies. In its narrower and more precise definition, it is a particular form of representative government: essentially, a democratic system in which government is drawn from and is regularly answerable to the elected national assembly. Commonly the executive is subject to dismissal on political grounds (as distinct from removal by impeachment) by that assembly. The concept itself has its origins in the nineteenth century, when the notion of democracy became allied with a parliamentary form of government.

The juxtaposition of the two words is significant. *Democracy* serves to distinguish the form of government from one-party and other states in which the national assembly—although it may formally constitute an elected parliament—is not elected on the basis of a free choice between candidates. *Parliamentary* distinguishes the form of government from that in which the executive is elected separately from the legislature (presidential government), a dichotomy well recognized by Bagehot. Some states, such as France, have a hybrid system, with an elected executive but with ministers drawn from, and dependent for support on, the national assembly. Parliamentary democracy is a feature of West European states and, increasingly, of a number of post-Communist European states. It is also a feature of "old" *Commonwealth nations, notably Canada, Australia, India, and New Zealand. It is less prevalent in Africa, South America, the Middle East, and the Far East.

(See also PARLIAMENTARY SOVEREIGNTY.)

Walter Bagehot, *The English Constitution* (1867, reprinted London, 1963).

PHILIP NORTON

PARLIAMENTARY SOVEREIGNTY. With its origins in England, parliamentary sovereignty, in its English application, constitutes a judicially self-imposed doctrine under which the courts apply without challenge on grounds of being contrary to the provisions of the *constitution, all measures being passed by the Queen-in-Parliament. The doctrine was variously asserted by legal scholars before the late seventeenth century, but it was confirmed as a judicial rule by the Glorious Revolution of 1688. (Common lawyers allied themselves with Parliament in contending that the king must be subject to the law of Parliament, and that if the king must be so subject, then so too must be his subjects, including the courts.) The doctrine was given its most authoritative articulation in the nineteenth century by A. V. Dicey, Vinerian Professor of English Law at Oxford University. According to Dicey, the doctrine had three elements: 1) Parliament has the right to make or unmake any law whatever; 2) No person or body is recognized by the law of England as having a right to override or set aside the legislation of Parliament; and 3) The right or power of Parliament extends to every part of the Queen's dominions.

The definitions and scope of the doctrine have been variously challenged. To what extent can Parliament "unmake" acts conferring independence? Formally it could, and courts in Britain would apply such legislation, but in practice it would be unenforceable. The doctrine has limited use outside the United Kingdom, most *Commonwealth countries—often federal states—being subject to written constitutions and *judicial review.

(See also DEMOCRACY; FEDERALISM; PARLIAMENTARY DEMOCRACY.)

A. W. Bradley, "The Sovereignty of Parliament—in Perpetuity?" in Jeffrey Jowell and Dawn Oliver, eds., *The Changing Constitution* (Oxford, 1985), pp. 23–47. Philip Norton, "The Glorious Revolution of 1688 and 1689: Its Continuing Relevance" *Parliamentary Affairs* 42, no. 2 (April 1989): 135–147.

PHILIP NORTON

PATRIARCHY. Throughout its long history, the term *patriarchy* has denoted male authority in various contexts, notably religion, politics, and the family. In modern political thought in the West, the concept has lent itself to the debate about political *power and *legitimacy. For example, in *Patriarcha*, written in the seventeenth century by Sir Robert Filmer, paternal authority, monarchical privilege, and divine power were equated. Filmer was refuted by John Locke in his *Two Treatises of Government;* however, Locke's rejection of patriarchal domination in the public realm did not extend to the private realm of the family, a distinction that has been interpreted as an influential articulation of the emerging relationships between *capitalism, bourgeois male *citizenship, and the subjugation of women.

More recently, the sociologist Max *Weber used *patriarchy* to describe the form of social organization in which the father not only stood at the head of the kinship network but also controlled its economy. However, the most familiar and extensive usage of the term today emerges from *feminist theory in the West. Although earlier feminists, such as Virginia Woolf, had used the term, Kate Millett gave the concept its contemporary currency in her theoretical analysis of patriarchy, *Sexual Politics* (New York, 1970). Millett defined patriarchy as a gendered system of social control that pervaded all aspects of human existence, including politics, industry, the military, education, philosophy, art, literature, and civilization itself. This analysis enabled an expansion of traditional notions of politics to include the hitherto "private" spheres of love, sexuality, marriage, and children. The family was politicized as the foundation of patriarchal power. Millett argued that perceived differences between the sexes (women are passive and nurturing; men are active and ambitious) maintained the normative familial structure of a heterosexual male-headed household, in which the woman's primary tasks of childbearing and childrearing "naturally" constrained her free and equal participation in society. In the family, males and females were socialized into sex roles, thereby ensuring general complicity in inequality as well as the transmission of patriarchal ideology across generations. The longevity of this system of male dominance was aided by its methods of surveillance and rewards, which coerced or seduced women into accepting their secondary status. While Millett's theory acknowledged the violence of class and race, it insisted that patriarchy was more enduring, more comprehensive, more uniform, and therefore antecedent and more fundamental to understanding other forms of injustice.

The transhistorical universality of gender oppression suggested by this analysis has been problematic for feminist theory. Its assumption of similar structures of social domination in vastly different societies across millennia is undermined by the notion of a historically specific, context-bound, social construction of key concepts such as "power," "woman," "family," and "the state." Furthermore, women's experience of their sexual roles, social status, and economic options has varied widely depending on the material and ideological conditions of the time. Socialist feminists, among others, have called for a refinement of the concept of patriarchy to acknowledge the specific forms, characteristics, and boundaries within a mode of production. Consequently, the collaboration between sexual hierarchy and *class structure in the formation of patriarchy under capitalism has received extensive treatment, replacing an essentialist conception of patriarchy with a complex set of mutually constitutive, socially constructed relations of power. However, the notion of patriarchy remains limited as long as the complicated relationships between a plurality of human characteristics and social experiences such as gender, class, race and *ethnicity, nationality, and colonial experience, are muted in favor of one dominating concept, such as gender.

For women outside the intellectual mainstream from which these theoretical analyses of patriarchy have emerged, the struggle to translate conceptual understanding into political activism is particularly acute. Nonwhite and non-Western feminists are challenged by the many intersecting strands of oppression in their daily lives. On the one hand, these women are aware of the problematic gender relations within their communities. On the other hand, they feel compelled to unite with their menfolk against commonly experienced discrimination, such as racism, in the larger society. In addition, the global expansion of capitalism and Western neocolonialism has elicited nationalist or cultural nativist responses from the *Third World that, for the moment of resistance, suggest a solidarity between genders that transcends patriarchal relations. For example, the tendency of Western feminists to condemn out of hand certain unfamiliar practices, such as arranged marriages and veiling, has prompted counterallegations of cultural insensitivity, arrogance, and racism from Third World women. To eliminate patriarchy, the feminist consensus calls for a redefinition of social practices, a transformation of assumptions about social reality, and an overturning of existing structures of domination.

(See also EQUALITY AND INEQUALITY; FEMINISM; GENDER AND POLITICS; RACE AND RACISM; WOMEN AND DEVELOPMENT.)

Zillah R. Eisenstein, ed., *Capitalist Patriarchy and the Case for Socialist Feminism* (New York, 1979). Heather Eisenstein, *Contemporary Feminist Thought* (London, 1984). Sonia Kruks, Rayna Rapp, and Marilyn B. Young, *Promissory Notes: Women in the Transition to Socialism* (New York, 1989). Kumkum Sangari and Sudesh Vaid, eds., *Recasting Women: Essays in Colonial History* (New Delhi, 1989). Chandra Talpade Mohanty, Ann Russo, and Lourdes Torres, eds., *Third World Women and the Politics of Feminism* (Bloomington, Ind., 1991).

ARATI RAO

PATRON-CLIENT POLITICS. The foundation of patron-client politics rests on an exchange between actors of unequal power and status: the more powerful, or patron, offers protection and access to scarce resources such as land or jobs to the client; the client in turn provides support and services such as labor or votes for the patron. Political structures based on such exchanges were first described by anthropologists studying Mediterranean societies, and persist in organizations such as the Mafia; but patron-client politics exists in a wide variety of systems, spread across the globe. The "*political machines" of American cities such as Chicago under Mayor Richard Daley provide an example, as do the party systems of many Third World states in which local political bosses such as landlords or traditional chiefs trade the votes of their subordinate peasantry for favors received from the central government. Patron-client relations readily infiltrate apparently bureaucratic organizations, such as the *Communist Party of the Soviet Union during the period it dominated Soviet society, in which powerful leaders sought to place their own personal supporters in key posts.

Despite variations in setting, patron-client systems are guided by a common logic. They arise in hierarchical societies, where individuals and groups compete at each level of the hierarchy, but where there is scope for collaboration between those at different levels. Marxists often criticize such collaboration for obscuring the "real" conflict between classes; but clientelism arises in situations where class politics is inappropriate, not because class differences and exploitation are absent (quite the contrary), but because they are so entrenched that it is rational to work within them. The link between patron and client is often expressed in terms of personal obligations (such as godparenthood) or communal solidarity: *ethnicity in its myriad forms provides a powerful vehicle for clientelism because it reinforces cross-class linkages as a basis for political action. Underlying it all, however, is an eminently rational struggle for control of political and economic resources that can also cut across ethnic barriers when the logic of competition requires. Patron-client links thus provide a flexible and effective tool, the persistence of which is not surprising. They extend into international relations, where the inequality of states, and their mutual need for protection and support, mirror the conditions in which they flourish in domestic politics. The patron state provides military protection or economic aid, in exchange for which the client state offers diplomatic support or economic opportunities. Such links, which readily involve personal relationships between national leaders, likewise cut across the unequal economic relations between industrial and underdeveloped states.

Clientelism nonetheless suffers crippling defects. It is inherently inefficient because it is geared to meeting particularistic rather than universal goals; jobs or development projects are allocated by patronage criteria rather than by qualification or need. It emphasizes distribution rather than production and is often parasitic on the productive economy. It erodes any appeal to common values while encouraging ethnic conflict and often leading to a pervasive cynicism. Such political stability as it provides depends more on buying the support of key groups than on establishing any basis for *legitimacy. Ultimately it must be seen as a barrier to *political development, even though its usefulness ensures that elements of clientelism persist even in the most sophisticated political systems.

(See also DEVELOPMENT AND UNDERDEVELOPMENT; MODERNIZATION; PEASANTS.)

S. N. Eisenstadt and Rene Lemarchand, eds., *Political Clientelism, Patronage and Development* (Beverly Hills and London, 1981).

CHRISTOPHER CLAPHAM

PEACE. The term *peace* can be interpreted narrowly as the absence of warfare, i.e., organized violence, between groups defined by country, nation (culture, *ethnicity), *race, *class, or *ideology. International or external peace is the absence of external wars: inter-country, inter-state, or international (in the sense of intercultural). Social or internal peace is the absence of internal wars: ethnic, racial, class, or ideological groups challenging the central government, or such groups challenging each other. As central governance came late in human history, so did *war among and against governments. Conclusion: many wars are avoidable, many types of peace are achievable.

This concept of peace is carried by the Latin *pax*, related to pact, as in *pacta sunt servanda*, "treaties must be observed." The implicit theory that peace is a contractual, conscious, and mutually agreed upon relationship is the source of the Western *international law tradition.

Another Roman legacy is *si vis pacem, para bellum*, "if you want peace, prepare for war." This constitutes another strand in mainstream Western peace theory: peace through *deterrence of any potential aggressor, countering the aggressor with the deployment of military force. Mainstream occidental thought about peace has changed little during the past 2,000 years, apart from oriental elements during the Middle Ages.

Broader definitions of peace usually include the concept of *pax*, but extend it by asking, "What type of violence?," "Violence by whom?," and "Peace with whom?" The first question leads to a distinction between violence to the body and violence to the mind and spirit. An example of the latter is life under the threat of extermination in a war in which weapons of mass destruction are used (e.g., a nuclear war), extending the definition of peace to absence of war and the *threat* of war. The problem with offensive deterrence is that the same capability can be used to attack even if the motivation is defensive. Some argue that this is the best that can be hoped for.

The second question tries to identify the actor capable of

inflicting damage and motivated to do so. Consider, however, the case when no such actor exists, yet harm is being done. Thus, 40,000 children die daily from avoidable causes such as malnutrition. To the extent that these deaths are not war-related, they occur under conditions of peace as narrowly conceived. Instead they can be attributed to structural violence, built into the structure within and between countries, and not necessarily intended by anybody. Twice as many children die annually from structural violence as there were people killed annually in the direct violence of World War II.

Structural violence differs from institutionalized direct violence that is perpetrated to vindicate honor or to revenge (vendetta), and from institutional violence linked to particular social institutions. Concretely, structural violence takes the form of economic exploitation and/or political repression in intra-country and inter-country class relations. In imperialist structures the two come together, with exploitation and repression so heavy that life expectancy in the periphery of the periphery countries is less than one-half of that at the top. Another form is violence to nature.

Structural violence may also be institutionalized, that is, deeply rooted and protected against reduction and elimination by countervailing social forces. The "military-bureaucratic-corporate-intelligentsia" complex, instrumental in modern warfare and in direct violence against any *revolution, violent or nonviolent, benefits from that protection.

Both direct and structural violence may be internalized, that is, cultural violence may be used to legitimate the exercise of violence, direct or structural, by one group against another. Examples include appeals to "chosen peoples" and "superior races." The notion of male gender superiority has been used to legitimate gender violence of both varieties—killing of unborn females, infanticide, circumcision, incest, family violence, rape, and widow-burning—in addition to exploitation and repression.

In comparison with the Roman *pax*, the Greek *eirene*, the Hebrew *shalom*, and the Arab *salām* seem to approach "peace with justice," including an absence of direct and structural violence. The question is which part has priority.

The third question—"peace with whom?"—is answered in new ways further east, by the Hindi *shanti* and *ahimsa*, also usually translated as "peace." *Shanti* means "inner peace," peace with oneself, with no part of body-mind-spirit doing violence to other parts. *Shanti* can be seen as complementing the occidental focus on "outer peace," and as a necessary condition for "outer peace." *Ahimsa* means "no-harm," including to self (inner peace) and nature, bringing in the ecological dimension missing in the Occident (an exception being Saint Francis of Assisi). *Ahimsa* was the peace concept used by the leading peace practitioner of our times, M. K. *Gandhi, as the basis for nonviolent struggle, *satyagraha*, against such structural violence as racism, caste, and gender, industrialism and colonialism/imperialism, and as an alternative to communal, social, and international direct violence. Gandhi also tried to create an ecumenical peace culture, providing the most complete answer so far to the problem of achieving peace in a very broad sense by peaceful means. Aspects of his approach were taken up by the *civil rights movement in the United States (especially by Martin Luther *King, Jr.) and by the European dissident and peace movements in their struggle for a nonviolent end to the *Cold War in 1989.

Still further east the Chinese *ho p'ing/p'ing ho* and the Japanese *heiwa/wahei* point to inner, social, and international harmony; they complement the concepts of outer and inner peace, seeing harmony between the international, social, and personal spheres as a necessary condition for all of them to come true.

Coming full circle, we return to the narrow *pax*, well institutionalized and internalized in the Occident. Missing in that concept is attention to structural violence, inner peace, nonviolence, and harmony between the spheres of the human condition. But the concept of peace is open, like freedom and justice, with no culture having any monopoly on its definition. We have to draw on the human experience as a whole, not only on one gender, in one generation, in one corner of the world. All are aspects of a more universal concept of peace not yet defined.

(See also ETHNICITY; FORCE, USE OF; GENDER AND POLITICS; IMPERIALISM; INTERNATIONAL COOPERATION; PEACE MOVEMENT; POLITICAL VIOLENCE.)

A. C. Bouquet and K. S. Murty, *Studies in the Problems of Peace* (Bombay, 1960). Takeshi Ishida, "Beyond Traditional Concepts of Peace in Different Cultures" *Journal of Peace Research* 6, no. 2 (1969): 133–145. Johan Galtung, "Cultural Violence" *Journal of Peace Research* 27, no. 3 (1990): 291–305.

JOHAN GALTUNG

PEACE CORPS. The purpose of the U.S. Peace Corps, as stated in Executive Order 10924 signed by President John F. *Kennedy on 1 March 1961, was to "be responsible for the training and service abroad of men and women of the United States in new programs of assistance to nations and areas of the world." Such a charge placed the agency firmly within the established tradition of participatory development aid programs such as the British VSO (Volunteers in Service Overseas) and realized earlier proposals proffered by Rep. Henry Reuss of Wisconsin under the Point Four Plan.

The distinctive ethos of the organization emphasized the volunteers' status as invited residents of their host nations, fully subject to local restraints of custom and law. Benefits for American culture were envisioned from the creation of a cadre of people possessing firsthand knowledge of world development problems and possibilities who would educate citizens back home about their countries of service and make the United States more flexible in adapting to rapidly shifting geopolitical realities.

The Peace Corps idea triggered diverse reactions. Domestic political opposition to the proposal ranged from a virtually unanimous resolution against it by the Daughters of the American Revolution to former president Eisenhower's characterization of it as "a juvenile experiment." The response of the international community was encouraging, if guarded, given the fact that teams of Soviet technical advisers were already active in many *Third World nations.

Following his appointment as interim director in 1961, R. Sargent Shriver participated in congressional hearings on the viability of the Peace Corps as a continuing federal program and undertook a goodwill tour to prospective African and Asian host nations. Specific invitations for Peace Corps members were issued by presidents Kwame Nkrumah of Ghana and Julius Nyerere of Tanganyika (Tanzania), creating the now-traditional image of the Peace Corps volunteer living in a village setting among the people and speaking the local language.

The unique nature of Peace Corps service gave all volunteers a dual political identity that made them potentially vulnerable to manipulation. Their behavior, atypical of U.S. government representatives abroad, also exposed them to charges of being agents provocateurs. Some people assumed no Americans would willingly contribute two years of their lives to help another nation unless as a cover for espionage. Such attitudes reflected the larger patterns of Cold War thought and the role played by covert action. Although persistent intermittent rumors of Peace Corps links to the Central Intelligence Agency have surfaced over the four decades since its inception, no proof of this claim has ever been adduced. Volunteers could also be used in pursuing certain local political agendas. Perhaps the best example of this was the total expulsion of Peace Corps workers from Bolivia in 1971 on charges of conducting sterilization and birth control programs and spreading drug addiction in the guise of health care. Paradoxically, this openness to challenge and question provided a heretofore absent channel for cross-cultural communication and a mechanism for questioning stereotypes on both sides. It was this quality that President George Bush viewed as crucial in agreeing to send the Peace Corps to the restored democracies of Poland, Hungary, and Czechoslovakia in the early 1990s.

The legacy of Peace Corps service for the United States has been substantial, with alumni heading bodies such as Amnesty International and the Agency for International Development and contributing to virtually every field and profession. In 1986, the formation of the National Council of Returned Peace Corps Volunteers (later the National Peace Corps Association) served notice that the agency's influence would continue to be felt on both the international scene and in the field of American social change.

(See also AMERICAN FOREIGN POLICY; POPULATION POLICY.)

Robert B. Marks Ridinger, *The Peace Corps: An Annotated Bibliography* (Boston, 1989). Karen Schwarz, *What You Can Do for Your Country: An Oral History of the Peace Corps* (New York, 1991).

ROBERT B. MARKS RIDINGER

PEACE MOVEMENT. In the twentieth century the European continent has been the site of a repeated cycle of *arms races and *war scares. Each of these cycles has produced peace movements that seek a reduction of international tensions. The armament drives that preceded each of the two world wars produced vigorous movements particularly in the smaller European countries, where many hoped to avoid being drawn into big-power rivalries.

Peace movements between the wars were largely pacifist, seeking disarmament and an avoidance of international entanglements. The experience of World War II and the new realities created by the *Cold War and by nuclear *deterrence have made obsolete the idea of pacifist withdrawal from the international system. As a result, postwar peace movements have abandoned pacifism as a central aspect of their beliefs. But postwar peace movements have continued to flourish when international tensions have grown and when new types of armaments—especially *nuclear weapons—have been introduced.

Both of these conditions were met in the early 1980s. The immediate trigger for the peace movements that swept Europe at that time was the decision by the *North Atlantic Treaty Organization (NATO) in 1979 to deploy 572 Pershing II and cruise missiles in five NATO countries. This decision was made at a point when relations between the United States and the Soviet Union were as tense as they had been in twenty years. Twenty-eight percent of a sample of Europeans, and fifty percent of those who considered themselves members of the peace movement, went so far as to say that "we are heading directly toward world war" (*Eurobarometer 21: Political Cleavages in the European Community*, Brussels, April 1984). The peace movement that swept Western Europe as a result of these tensions was the largest political movement in Europe in this century. During the month of October 1983 alone, over 3 million people demonstrated in the cities of Western Europe against NATO's plans for new nuclear weapons.

Despite this great size, the protest tactics characteristic of political movements have been notoriously ineffective in altering public policies. One of the few concrete peace movement successes before World War II occurred in 1923 in the Netherlands, when a governmental plan to modernize the Dutch fleet led to a gathering in Amsterdam of a then unheard-of 80,000 demonstrators, followed by a petition campaign that gathered over one million signatures (twenty percent of the entire population) within a period of three weeks. Thanks to pressure from the opposition Social Democratic Workers Party, and from the socialist and Catholic wings of the trade union movement, the Dutch Parliament rejected the plan for a new naval fleet by a single vote.

The much larger peace movement of the early 1980s was not able to claim such success. Of the five countries that agreed in 1979 to accept the Pershing II and cruise missiles, all confirmed their commitment to deployment between 1983 and 1985 despite the massive demonstrations and petition campaigns during those years. It would be going too far to say that the peace movement had no policy impact. The Dutch government, for example, twice delayed its final decision on the new missiles, and the Belgians agreed to accept their forty-eight cruise missiles only in several stages. Yet the peace movement failed to attain its main objective, which was to prevent the nuclear modernization envisaged by NATO in 1979. Although cruise and Pershing II missiles were eventually removed from Europe under the provisions of the Intermediate-Range Nuclear Forces (INF) Treaty of 1988, peace movement pressure was only an indirect factor in obtaining the INF agreement.

The greater immediate impact of the peace movement was on domestic political alignments within the various West European countries. Social democratic parties in several countries were converted from support for the missile deployment to opposition. Because social democratic parties were not in power in the early 1980s, their opposition to the missiles proved fruitless. Yet the peace movement did manage to reawaken the more radical wing of the European social democratic parties as well as to revive the traditions of political activism in many churches and trade unions.

The greatest medium-term impact of the peace movement was to open a debate about nuclear weapons policy, which until then had been largely the province of a small group of experts, NATO officials, and top military and civilian leaders. The original plan to modernize NATO's intermediate-range nuclear forces in 1979 took shape in NATO's Nuclear Planning Committee and in a series of meetings of NATO foreign and defense ministers. When the British Parliament debated the INF plan in 1980, it was the first debate on nuclear weapons in fifteen years in the House of Commons. Across Europe, the subject of nuclear strategy went from being a technical issue to a political issue. Policies that had long been taken for granted were now being questioned, and alternatives were being proposed where it was once believed that none existed. The ability of the peace movements to demonstrate widespread public interest in the subject of nuclear weapons gave parliaments an incentive to become more aggressive in demanding a role in *security policy.

The impact of this change in the political process on nuclear and security issues has become clear only in the 1990s, nearly a decade after the height of the peace movement mobilization. The democratization of the countries of Eastern and Central Europe and the dissolution of the *Warsaw Treaty Organization (Warsaw Pact) and of the Soviet Union have created an environment in which a fundamental rethinking of the ways and means of European security is needed. Two results of these changes are the absence of a threat from the East and much less U.S. involvement in European security. A Europe no longer divided between East and West is experiencing intensified, sometimes violent ethnic and nationalist conflict. It also faces new problems of defining the nature of potential threats to European security, and of developing international structures of alliance and cooperation that will respond to those threats.

Initially, the question of alternative means of guaranteeing security was addressed only by those within peace movements and within such allied organizations as peace research institutes. It is remarkable today how much their ideas have now been brought into the mainstream of European debate. Collective security arrangements that bridge the entire European continent, defensive deterrence strategies, and the problems of converting military production into nonmilitary forms of productive capacity are all issues that were placed on the agenda within the peace movement but dismissed by others as unrealistic. It is still far from certain what form post–Cold War security arrangements in Europe (or elsewhere) will take, and how effective they may be in the face of ethnic-nationalist conflicts in regions as disparate as Central Africa and eastern Europe, but it is clear that the ideas developed within peace movement circles will be important in structuring that debate.

(See also ARMS CONTROL; NEW SOCIAL MOVEMENTS; SOCIALISM AND SOCIAL DEMOCRACY.)

Diana Johnstone, *The Politics of Euromissiles* (London, 1984). Ulrike Wasmuht, *Friedensbewegungen der 80er Jahre* (Giessen, Germany, 1987). Thomas Rochon, *Mobilizing for Peace* (Princeton, N.J., 1988).

THOMAS R. ROCHON

PEACEKEEPING. See HUMANITARIAN INTERVENTION.

PEASANTS have often been defined as low-status cultivators who are trapped in a double bind of material poverty and political marginality. Like other venerable definitions in the social sciences, this one has advantages and very real limitations. Its signal merit has been to focus our attention on the fact that peasants labor in a subsistence economy that is typically precarious and subject to predation by powerful *elites. As a result, peasants share in otherwise diverse cultural and historical contexts share a common vulnerability to natural and human-made disaster that constrains peasant strategies in the direction of an emphasis on subsistence security and family survival. As many scholars have shown, the logic of peasant society cannot be easily translated into the more familiar categories of urban, industrial life.

However, the notion that the common predicaments of peasant societies imply a homogeneous peasant class has become increasingly difficult to maintain in the face of a growing scholarly literature focused on the empirical dynamics of power and production in small-scale rural societies. Without always being explicit, scholarship suggests that the people we call peasants manifest extraordinary diversity and complexity in property rights, economic hierarchies, and relations to the forces and means of production. In this sense, peasants are quite unlike capitalists or proletarians, whose economic location and forms of stratification show how much more commonality and coherence than the almost lush diversity of peasant societies. Indeed, as the otherwise quite distinctive work of political scientists such as Samuel Popkin, James C. Scott, and Joel Migdal implies, class is much less significant as a basis for understanding peasant life than are convergent peasant political institutions and survival strategies rooted in the logic of subsistence cultivation. Seen from this perspective, peasants can no longer be understood as merely as subordinate class of backward marginals without history or politics. Instead, peasants have increasingly come to be understood as historical actors whose collective responses to nature and elite demands have significantly affected the transition to the modern world.

Political scientists have made substantial contribution to the rediscovery of the peasant as a historical agent, and the remainder of this essay focuses on a synthetic overview of the empirical findings of their work. Those findings will be discussed under the three headings of localism, political invisibility, and the strategic flexibility of custom.

Localism refers to the universal tendency of peasants to define their primary collective interests and collective political action in terms of highly localized, small-scale territorial groups. Usually confined to a hamlet, village, or group of related villages, these microgroups are the most important organizations of peasant life, and the institutional arrangements they contain are central to rural politics, economic production and exchange, and ritual and religious practice. Similarly, when peasants engage in collective action, whether in moments of revolt or during more routine resistance, the goal of their project is usually the defense of the autonomy of local institutions against the claims of outside elites. Conversely, however, peasants rarely organize at national or even regional levels, and most large-scale peasant movements can be understood as temporary alliances of local communities that in the end will return to their component villages and localities. Even the spectacular events of the French, Russian, and Mexican *revolutions might best be interpreted as tremendous explosions of rural localism that drew their energy from an attempt by ordinary rural people to strengthen local cohesion and local control of subsistence resources. In this sense, the ubiquitous elite enemies of peasants, absentee landlords and tax collectors, are not so much class enemies as intrusive and unwanted outsiders who threaten the precarious equilibrium of local practices.

The intense localism of peasant life used to be understood as resulting from the blinding effects of false consciousness, unthinking traditionalism, and the general inability of peasant classes to act in a properly "class" (i.e., national, large-scale) fashion. However, much recent research indicates that this interpretation is unacceptable, for it denies the very real dependence of peasants on local institutions for whatever margin of wealth, status, and power they possess. Networks of neighbors and neighboring kin are the primary determinants of peasant well-being, and their help or hostility can mean the differences between disaster and comfortable survival. As a result, peasant localism is a "rational" adaptation strategy to a world in which large-scale, translocal institutions are either unavailable or unreliable as the basis for peasant welfare. This means that rural localism is unlikely to disappear until peasants are effectively integrated as citizens into national governments that are capable of underwriting rural welfare and that are responsive to popular demands. It can be argued that this process has thus far occurred only in the advanced industrial nations, and it is unlikely that even postrevolutionary regimes like that of the People's Republic of *China have eliminated the salience and structural causes of peasant localism.

Although localism is the most important institutional characteristic of peasant societies, it is closely linked to what is best described as a politics of invisibility. Generations of field researchers have remarked on the reticence of peasants to speak openly and objectively about the ways in which they arrange their lives. This suspicion of outsiders is a rational response to a situation in which outsiders are typically trouble, especially when they make demands on scarce community resources. However, public reticence can also be seen as part of a broader strategy of disguising, or rendering invisible to outsiders, key dimensions of their lives. For example, it is often the case that the formal institutions of local government prescribed by central elites are less important to peasants than informal, customary means of decision making that are ignored or unknown by central bureaucrats. Similarly, peasants try to conceal the size of their harvests, the extent of their fields, and even the meaning of ritual events. All of this must be understood as an attempt to create a barrier to the penetration of local institutions by potentially predatory elites. As James C. Scott argues, this sort of camouflage is vital if peasants are to retain a sufficient degree of local autonomy to meet the pressures of a subsistence-driven environment. Moreover, by creating a network of institutions and resources that are invisible from the outside, peasants are able to construct a stable routine protected from the arbitrary interference of national states and their agents. Naturally, the extent of this invisibility varies across time and among societies, but the degree to which peasants actively conceal themselves is an important marker of the difference between peasant institutions and the visible politics of mass publics and *public opinion characteristic of industrial democracies.

The final important way in which peasant survival strategies intersect with peasant political institutions has to do with the subtle interplay between custom and peasant politics. It is a commonplace that peasants adhere tenaciously to customary norms governing everything from kinship and inheritance to work routines and community celebrations. To outsiders, the depth and persistence of such customs underscore peasant traditionalism and conservatism, particularly because rural customary codes change only slowly and incrementally in response to shifting constellations of opportunities and interests. Yet as political scientists have come increasingly to realize, peasant custom should not be seen solely as an index of conservatism or a brake on innovation. Instead rural custom must be understood as a strategic response to an unpredictable environment in which customary codes help to provide order and meaning in a disordered world. In addition, peasant custom is flexible in the sense that peasants are able and willing to renegotiate custom in reaction to changing incentives. For example, kinship practices that once favored partible inheritance may be collectively reformulated to favor primogeniture in response to shrinking land allotments and population growth. Once again, it is important to keep in mind that this strategic flexibility of custom is only possible because peasants are involved in local institutional networks that allow for collective deliberation and political redefinition of traditional norms and values. Custom is, in fact, one more resource that peasants have available in their enactment of strategies of subsistence and survival.

Current research continues the traditions of analysis sketched above with few modifications. What is still needed, however, is a more thorough comparative analysis of cases outside Europe, Asia, and Latin America, especially so that work on Africa can be incorporated in comparative empirical theory.

(See also Class and Politics; Green Revolution; Land Reform; Patron-Client Politics; Rural Development.)

Joel Migdal, *Peasants, Politics, and Revolution* (Princeton, N.J., 1975). James C. Scott, *The Moral Economy of the Peasant* (New Haven, Conn., 1976). Samuel Popkin, *The Rational Peasant: The Economy of Rural Society in Vietnam* (Berkeley, Calif., 1979). James C. Scott, *Weapons of the Weak: Everyday Forms of Peasant Resistance* (New Haven, Conn., 1985). Victor Magagna, *Communities of Green: Rural Rebellion in Comparative Perspective* (Ithaca, N.Y., 1991).

VICTOR V. MAGAGNA

PEOPLE'S REPUBLIC OF CHINA. See China.

PERESTROIKA. In its Soviet definition, perestroika ("restructuring") involved the "deep, revolutionary renewal of all aspects of the life of Soviet society, providing socialism with the most modern forms of organization, and disclosing to the fullest extent possible its qualities in all respects: economic, sociopolitical and ideological" (*Kratkii politicheskii slovar'*, Moscow, 1989). Although the term had been used by *Stalin and earlier Soviet leaders, it became most closely associated with the attempt—in the end, an unsuccessful one—to renew and reinvigorate socialism that was advanced by the *Gorbachev leadership in the *Soviet Union between 1985 and 1991.

At the outset of his administration Mikhail Gorbachev's objectives were still fairly obscure, even at leading levels of the party. Gorbachev, unlike his main rivals for the leadership, had not addressed a party congress, and he had still (in

March 1985) no published collection of writings to his name. He had made only a few visits abroad, to Canada in 1983 and to Britain in late 1984, on both occasions as the head of a delegation of Soviet parliamentarians. There were, however, several indications, in his biography and known policy positions, that his administration would be rather more than a continuation of those of his predecessors. Gorbachev was a relatively young leader, just fifty-four on his election, too young to have fought in the war or to have known the worst of *Stalinism; he was unusually well educated, with a law degree from Moscow University; and he was known to be open-minded, particularly by his university contemporaries.

There were also some clues in Gorbachev's speeches before his accession that his leadership would be an innovative one. The clearest indication of this was a lengthy speech to an *ideology conference in December 1984, not published in full at the time, in which the future general secretary made positive references to self-management and to social justice (in effect, an attack on the corruption of the later Brezhnev years) and called for the further development of socialist *democracy and glasnost ("openness") in the media and public life. There were further clues in Gorbachev's speech at the local elections in February 1985, made at a time when Konstantin Chernenko's illness was already well known. Gorbachev defined the Soviet system as a form of rule "of the workers for the workers," and called for the party "again and again to check its political course against the rich experience of the people." These and other speeches made it clear that a Gorbachev administration would continue the reforms of its predecessors but also place them within a broader framework of political and moral regeneration.

Of all the policies that were promoted by the new leadership after March 1985, glasnost was probably the most distinctive. Glasnost did not mean an unqualified freedom of the press or the right to information; nor was it original to Gorbachev. It did, however, reflect the new general secretary's belief that without a greater awareness of the real state of affairs and of the considerations that had led to particular decisions, there would be no willingness on the part of the Soviet people to commit themselves to the program of perestroika. "The better people are informed," Gorbachev told the Central Committee meeting that elected him, "the more consciously they act, the more actively they support the party, its plans and programmatic objectives." This led to more open treatment of social problems such as drugs, prostitution, and crime. It also led to a more honest consideration of the Soviet past, including the repression of the 1930s and the corruption of the Brezhnev era.

The "democratization" of Soviet political life was a further part of perestroika. The political system established by the October revolution, Gorbachev told the Nineteenth Party Conference in 1988, had undergone "serious deformations," leading to the development of a "command-administrative system" that had become the main obstacle to perestroika. A limited experiment in electoral choice had taken place in June 1987; the Party Conference approved a more far-reaching "radical reform" of Soviet political life, and this led to a related series of constitutional changes in late 1988. These included an entirely new electoral law, on the basis of which the national elections in March 1989 were conducted on a largely competitive basis, and the establishment of a working parliament (the Supreme Soviet) elected by a larger and popularly elected assembly called the Congress of People's Deputies. Attempts were also made to democratize the operation of the Communist Party itself through competitive ballots for leading positions, greater information about all aspects of the party's activity, and (in the rules that were adopted at the Twenty-eighth Congress in 1990) greater respect for the rights of minorities.

Together with these changes, for Gorbachev, there had to be a "radical reform" of the Soviet economy. Levels of growth had been steadily declining since at least the 1950s, and by the late 1970s they had reached the lowest levels in Soviet peacetime history. Indeed, as Gorbachev pointed out in early 1988, if the sale of alcoholic drink and of Soviet oil on world markets were excluded, there had been no real growth in the Soviet economy for the previous fifteen years. Radical reform, as Gorbachev explained to the Party Congress in 1986 and to a Central Committee plenum the following year, involved a set of related measures. One of the most important was a greater degree of decentralization of economic management, leaving the state to set broad parameters but allowing factories and farms a much greater degree of operational autonomy. Retail and wholesale prices would gradually be reformed so as to eliminate indiscriminate subsidies, and enterprises that failed to pay their way might be liquidated. These objectives were gradually broadened to encompass a more far-reaching program of "destatification" and limited forms of private ownership as part of a transition to a "regulated market economy." (The attempt to combine these rather different principles led, in the event, to a fall in national income of four percent in 1990, and of fifteen percent in 1991.)

Despite a series of reforms of this kind, the nature and consequences of perestroika remained somewhat obscure. What, for a start, was its relationship to "socialism" and the longer-term objective of transition to a wholly communist society? Nikita *Khrushchev had promised that the Soviet Union would construct a society of such a kind by 1980 in the Party Program that was adopted under his guidance in 1961. His successors swiftly dropped that commitment and began to describe the Soviet Union, from the early 1970s, as a "developed socialist society," whose evolution into a fully communist one was a matter for an unspecified point in the fairly distant future. Leonid Brezhnev's successors in turn made clear that the Soviet Union was at the very beginning of the stage of developed socialism, and that its further evolution would require a "whole historical epoch." Gorbachev's original objective, as he explained it to the Central Committee that elected him, was the "acceleration of socioeconomic development and the perfection of all aspects of Soviet life." This soon developed into a larger view of a "new image" of socialism, one that (as Gorbachev explained to the Party Conference in 1988) would be free of the abuses of the Soviet past and open to the contribution that had been made by the social and religious thought of other nations.

Gorbachev set out his thinking at greater length in an important article, "The Socialist Idea and Revolutionary Perestroika," which appeared in *Pravda* in November 1989. Drawing on a series of speeches over earlier weeks, the Soviet leader insisted there could be no detailed blueprint of the kind of society he and his colleagues wished to construct, nor would it come about quickly. Perestroika, rather, would be a lengthy stage in the historical development of socialism, "probably extending into the twenty-first century." It would, however, avoid both the "bureaucratic deformations" of the Soviet past and the gross inequalities of *capitalism. It would draw upon the experience of other countries, including social democratic parties in Western Europe. It would be a "genuinely democratic and self-governing social organism." And it would involve the greatest possible degree of cooperation between East and West to resolve their common problems, in line with the "new thinking" on international problems that had been a hallmark of his administration.

The Twenty-eighth Party Congress in July 1990 advanced these rather general guidelines with a "Programmatic Declaration," discussed in draft earlier in the year, which was intended to set out the party's intentions for the short and medium term. It indicated that the "essence of perestroika" was a transition from an "authoritarian, bureaucratic system to a society of humane, democratic socialism." However difficult, this was the "only way of securing a worthwhile life and realizing the [Soviet Union's] material and spiritual potential." A society of this kind would be one in which the "purpose of social development" was human development. There would be "diverse forms of property and management," and the sole source of political power would be the "sovereign will of the people." A society of this kind, finally, would "consistently work for peaceful and equal cooperation among nations."

Perestroika had consistently been clearer in its condemnation of the abuses of the past than in its specification of a Soviet future, and by the end of the Gorbachev era any such vision had a relatively limited appeal to a population whose actual experience was one of shortages, rising prices, and social inequalities. Indeed quite different interpretations could be offered of the whole project of perestroika. For an influential group of critics within the party, for instance, perestroika reflected the undue influence of a group of academic economists infected by "market euphoria." For critics of this kind, well represented in the Central Committee, collective forms of property were to remain dominant, glasnost was not to be exploited by "demagogues," and ordinary workers were to be protected from any move toward the market. For another group of critics, most of whom had left the party by 1990, and many of whom were to join with Boris *Yeltsin in leading post-Soviet *Russia, perestroika was much too limited in its objectives. Rather than "democratization," they wanted democracy; the party, they thought, should limit itself to a purely parliamentary function, and they insisted on the full "de-ideologization" of Soviet public life.

Perestroika could also be placed within the broader perspective of communist reform. It was, in this sense, one of a series of attempts that had been made to find a "middle way" between capitalism and the Stalinist form of socialism, one that respected individual rights but at the same time avoided the social inequalities that were associated with the market. There were many similarities, for instance, between Gorbachev's perestroika and the *Prague Spring of 1968, when reformers led by Alexander Dubček had sought to develop a "socialism with a human face." There were some similarities with developments in the Soviet Union itself in the 1920s, when a form of mixed economy had developed and a rea-

sonably wide range of opinion had been reflected in the official media. By the early 1990s, however, no convincing "third way" had been found: the countries of Eastern and Central Europe, and then Russia, had mostly opted for capitalism and liberal democracy, and at least one of those that remained under communist rule (China) had been compelled to maintain its position by wholesale repression. Perestroika, launched to reinvigorate socialism, was in the end a stage in the collapse of communist rule; glasnost allowed its shortcomings to be discussed openly, and democratization allowed its opponents to make a successful challenge through elections that for the first time allowed electors to make their own choices.

(See also COMMUNISM; COMMUNIST PARTY STATES; NINETEEN EIGHTY-NINE; POST-COMMUNISM.)

Mikhail Gorbachev, *Perestroika* (New York and London, 1987). Richard Sakwa, *Gorbachev and His Reforms* (London, 1990). Stephen White, *After Gorbachev*, 4th ed. (Cambridge, U.K., and New York, 1994). Archie Brown, *The Gorbachev Factor* (Oxford, 1996).

STEPHEN WHITE

PERÓN, María Eva Duarte de. Better known as Evita, María Eva Duarte de Perón was the wife of Juan Domingo *Perón during his first term as president of *Argentina (1946–1952) and one of the most influential women in Latin American history. Born on 17 May 1919 in a hamlet of Buenos Aires province, she was the fifth illegitimate child of Juana Ibarguren and Juan Duarte. At fifteen, having completed her primary schooling, she left for Buenos Aires to pursue an acting career. She began playing silent parts on the stage, but by the early 1940s, Eva Duarte was a starlet who earned her living doing radio soap operas while waiting for her big role in a film. Her life began to change when she met Colonel Perón, head of the Labor Secretariat and soon-to-be minister of war as well as vice president. To the dismay of his fellow officers and Argentina's social and political elite, she openly became his mistress.

The transformation of the dark-haired actress into the fiery, blond, charismatic leader of the *descamisados* ("shirtless ones") was a slow process that began after the dramatic events of 17 October 1945, when thousands of workers gathered in Buenos Aires to demand the release of the imprisoned Perón. Contrary to the accepted belief, Evita neither helped to organize nor participated in the workers' demonstration—though she tried to obtain a writ of habeas corpus for Perón's release. Perón wrote her a loving letter from jail: he was concerned for her well-being and safety and promised to marry her. Indeed, on 21 October, in a quiet civil ceremony, Eva Duarte became the wife of Perón.

Shortly after the wedding, Perón began his campaign for the presidency. Though Evita could not vote because she was a woman, and as such was expected to remain in the background, she accompanied Perón in his tours of the provinces, took part in strategy meetings, stood by him waving to the enthusiastic crowds, and even addressed a women's rally in Buenos Aires.

Her interest in politics and her influence increased decisively after Perón took office in June 1946. She began to meet daily with workers' delegations, union leaders, and officials of the Secretariat of the Labor Confederation, thus continuing the work that Perón did as secretary of labor. She frequently addressed Perón's supporters on his behalf and proved to be a rousing speaker. After a triumphant European tour which she undertook without Perón, she returned in time to urge the passage of a law granting women the vote.

Evita was never formally part of Perón's government, though she tried unsuccessfully to be the Peronist vice-presidential candidate in the 1951 elections. She was officially only Argentina's First Lady, but she was a one-woman propaganda ministry for Perón and his trusted liaison with labor. She was also president of the Eva Perón Foundation, a well-endowed social welfare organization. She used the foundation funds to build hospitals, schools, youth hostels, and low-income housing, and to buy thousands of goods that she distributed to the needy. In addition, she was president of the women's branch of the Peronist Party, which helped to reelect Perón in 1951 with an overwhelming female vote.

Evita's death from cancer on 26 July 1952 undermined the stability of Peronism. She was a crucial component of that political structure and irreplaceable—as Perón soon realized when his economic policies began to strain his relationship with the *descamisados*. On the other hand, her death transformed her into a powerful myth that became essential for the survival of Peronism after Perón's ouster in 1955 and, despite the repression of successive military dictatorships, its return to power in 1973 along with Perón's own reelection that same year.

Julie M. Taylor, *Eva Perón: The Myth of a Woman* (Chicago, 1979). Marysa Navarro, *Evita* (Buenos Aires, 1981).

MARYSA NAVARRO-ARANGUREN

PERÓN, Juan Domingo. The most important and controversial political leader of twentieth-century *Argentina, Juan Domingo Perón sharply divided Argentines during and after his lifetime over the issues of distribution of income and political power. In historical retrospect, he may be seen as a leader who wanted to extend to the lower classes the standard of living and the political enfranchisement that Hipólito Yrigoyen and the Unión Cívica Radical had brought to the Argentine middle classes earlier in the century. One of the few South American leaders to be known throughout the world, Perón championed a "Third Force" in world politics and encouraged wider *political participation by Argentine women.

For the first five decades of his life, Perón showed little indication of his future accomplishments. Instead, he followed a rather typical military career. Born to a middle-class family in 1895, he graduated in 1913 from the Colegio Militar. After rising to the rank of lieutenant colonel, he studied mountain warfare techniques with the Italian Alpine troops in 1939 and 1940, having an opportunity personally to evaluate Italian, German, and Spanish *fascism while in Europe. In 1943, as a colonel, Perón worked with a group of officers to depose the incumbent government and share in collective power for two years. He headed the new Secretariat of Labor and Social Security, working to expand the size and influence of labor unions and to make their members loyal to him personally. Perón went on to become minister of war and vice president before other officers, sensing his expanding authority, deposed him in October 1945.

Perón's true assumption of power came on 17 October 1945 when a vast crowd of workers and other supporters assembled in the Plaza de Mayo in Buenos Aires, demanding his release from imprisonment on Martín García Island. Once released, Perón addressed the cheering crowd from the balcony of the Casa Rosada, where he would give a series of famous speeches in years to come.

In 1946, Perón was elected to the Argentine presidency in one of the freest elections in Argentine history; he was elected to a second term in 1951. A military coup in 1955 deposed him, sending him into exile first in Paraguay and ultimately in Madrid. For many years, historians and political leaders in Argentina tried to write Perón off as a has-been, but this ultimately proved impossible. In 1973, he returned triumphantly to Argentina and to the presidency after eighteen years in exile.

The basis for Perón's power was the Justicialista (Peronist) Party. Multiclass in nature, ranging over the ideological spectrum from far right to far left, it was an archetypal example of *populism. Peronism has been able to count consistently on support from ten percent of the upper classes and seventy percent of the lower classes. Perón built fierce and durable loyalty for the movement during his first presidency, during which he increased the proportion of national wealth going to the working class very substantially. By 1955, however, the real wages of many workers had fallen back to the levels of the 1940s, because economic growth was not strong enough to support the higher wage levels. More important than economic gains, members of the working class and trade unions had achieved a sense of political consciousness and economic entitlement that made them combative participants in Argentine politics for decades to come.

Juan Perón also had high ambitions in international politics. Quite accurately, he predicted that if the countries of Latin America did not join together, they would remain weak and put upon by more powerful nations. Often credited with originating the concept of the *Third World, Perón after 1945 dreamed of a coalition of states allied to neither the Soviet Union nor the United States. Argentine yearning for leadership of this movement appears in one of the most common Peronist slogans: *Ni yanqui, ni marxista—peronista* (Neither Yankee, nor Marxist—Peronist).

Much of Perón's popularity can be attributed to his fiery second wife, María Eva Duarte de *Perón ("Evita"). Evita campaigned for him in the 1946 election and later became the symbol of Peronism through her charismatic oratory and her advocacy of social welfare as president of the Fundación Eva Perón. Her death from cancer in 1952 was a major blow to Perón in political as well as personal terms. While in exile in Spain, he married María Estela Martínez ("Isabel"). When Perón returned to the presidency in 1973, she became his vice president and succeeded him after his death in office in 1974. Isabel, in turn, was overthrown by the military in 1976.

In perspective, the range of Perón's influence remains striking. Peronist President Carlos Menem reversed the traditional economic policies of Perón, working to privatize state enterprises and to encourage citizens' economic self-reliance rather than their dependency on the state, saying that Perón's policies were for the 1940s and 1950s but that another era had come to Argentina in the 1990s. Nevertheless, Menem carefully copies much of the personal lifestyle of General Perón, his mentor and role model. Even those who find Perón's policies dated and fallible continue to evoke his memory as a political symbol of the full enfranchisement of the working class.

Frederick C. Turner and José Enrique Miguens, eds., *Juan Perón and the Reshaping of Argentina* (Pittsburgh, 1983). Juan Domingo Perón, *Obras Completas*, Fermín Chaves, series ed. (Buenos Aires, in process).

FREDERICK C. TURNER

PERSIAN GULF. See GULF STATES.

PERSIAN GULF WAR. See GULF WAR.

PERU. Politics in twentieth-century Peru have been shaped in many ways by nineteenth-century events: reluctant independence in the 1820s, military rulers almost exclusively until the 1870s, and economic ruin with the loss of the War of the Pacific (1879–1883) to Chile. Democratic forms have rarely prevailed for very long; the limited liberal democracy established between 1895 and 1919 is to date Peru's most extended period of elected civilian rule.

The major political conflict from the 1930s through the 1960s was between the country's first mass-based political party, the Alianza Popular Revolucionaria Americana (APRA), and the army. APRA represented the middle class and newly organizing agricultural and industrial workers, while the military, at least until 1962, protected the interests of established elites. However, a historic shift in Peruvian politics began with a military coup d'état in 1968. Led by a now reformist army and commander in chief, General Juan Velasco Alvarado (1968–1975), the regime tried to transform Peru.

Most notable were a major agrarian reform, the rapid expansion of unions and the legalization of a Marxist union confederation, and a threefold expansion in the size and scope of government through private company nationalizations and a much expanded range of public programs. Unfortunately, the military government's reforms far exceeded the country's capacity, contributing to increased inflation, repeated debt crises, and chronic economic stagnation. A 1975 consolidating coup led by General Francisco Morales Bermúdez (1975–1980) slowed reform and eventually committed an increasingly harassed armed forces to the restoration of civilian rule.

Under a new constitution (1979), Peru returned to democracy with the politically exhausted military's blessing. The May 1980 national elections were the country's first in seventeen years and the first ever under universal adult suffrage. With successive national (1985 and 1990) and local (November 1980, 1983, 1986, and 1989) elections, Peru experienced its most extended democratic period (1980–1992) in over sixty years. Proportional representation ensured multiple party access to Congress and municipal councils, contributing to one of the most diverse array of parties among the Latin American democracies of the 1980s.

The Izquierda Unida (IU) coalition, largely Marxist, included six parties and was Peru's second largest at both the national and local levels for most of the decade. Indeed, as late as 1988 IU appeared poised to win the presidency in 1990. A rancorous split, however, led to multiple candidates who captured only 11 percent of that presidential vote between them. This fragmentation of the Left continued through the 1990s.

APRA, which came to straddle the center of the Peruvian political spectrum, gained 37 percent of the 1978 Constituent Assembly before dividing after the death in 1979 of party founder Victor Raúl Haya de la Torre and seeing its support fall significantly in the 1980 elections. Under Alan García, APRA regained its reformist dynamism and captured the presidency in 1985, with 53 percent of the vote and a majority in both houses. The dramatic failure of García's policies, however, meant that APRA was repudiated in the 1990 elections, and it has yet to recover.

The center-right coalition of Fernando Belaúnde Terry's Acción Popular (AP) and Luis Bedoya Reyes's Partido Popular Cristiano (PPC) went from victor in 1980 to vanquished in 1985 to leading contender status again by 1989, with the entrance into politics of novelist Mario Vargas Llosa and his Movimiento Libertad. As the Frente Democrático (FREDEMO) with Vargas Llosa as its standard bearer, the Right took more mayoralties in the November 1989 municipal elections than any other party or coalition. Up until a month before the 1990 elections, Vargas Llosa appeared poised for victory. But after a surprise loss to upstart Alberto Fujimori (1990–), Vargas Llosa left Peru and the FREDEMO coalition broke apart.

Although in 1980 and 1985 the parties of the victorious presidential candidates won a majority in both houses as well as the first plurality in the next municipal elections, neither Belaúnde (1980–1985; also president 1963–1968) and AP nor García (1985–1990) and APRA were able to implement policies that responded effectively to popular demands. In fact, each administration completed its term with Peru substantially worse off. Were it not for the large "informal" sector (about forty percent of the urban population generating almost half of Peru's goods and services) and the "illegal" sector (until the mid-1990s, Peru's Upper Huallaga Valley produced some 60 percent of the coca leaf used in the manufacture of cocaine, employed about 300,000 people, and generated over US$1 billion in foreign exchange annually), Peru would have been economically prostrate. Surprisingly, however, most of the population remained committed to democracy and demonstrated their discontent through the election of different parties.

Nevertheless, economic crisis played into the hands of Latin America's most radical guerrilla movement, Sendero Luminoso (SL), begun in the 1960s as one more Marxist faction at the University of Huamanga in the isolated and predominantly Indian department of Ayacucho. In 1980, this now extreme Maoist movement declared a "people's war" at the very moment Peru returned to democracy. During the 1980s political violence accounted for over 16,000 casualties and $15 billion in damages to a $28 billion economy. By 1990, when over 4,000 were killed, political violence had become generalized.

Almost no one predicted the "Fujimori tidal wave" in the 1990 elections. His support grew from one percent in a public opinion poll the first week of March to 24 percent in the first round of the presidential elections in April to 57 percent in the June runoff against Vargas Llosa. Alberto Fujimori and his Cambio 90 party, formed less than six months before the election, came to be seen as a popular alternative to the over-confident Right. Once in office, however, the new president surprised many with a series of controversial moves which ended hyperinflation (from 7,650 percent in 1990 to 3 percent in 1999), restored net economic growth by 1994 (averaging almost 5 percent annually through 1999), began to reduce extreme poverty (from 26 percent in 1991 to 15 percent by mid-1998), and underwent SL (from 4,300 casualties in 1990 to less than 200 by 1999).

However, a dynamic if flawed democracy was sacrificed in the process. In April 1992, President Fujimori suspended congress, the judiciary, and the constitution in a self-administered coup, or *autogolpe*, with the support of the armed forces. Although formal democratic processes were subsequently restored after intense international pressure under a new 1993 constitution, many of the changes introduced are seen as limiting in various ways the development of a truly democratic system.

Among them are electoral rules facilitating the proliferation of new political groups to weaken and divide the opposition and the establishment of a single national electoral district that eliminates department (state) level representation. They also included a complex ballot in the 1995 elections that invalidated over 4 million of the 9 million votes for congress and gave the president's political grouping a majority in congress with only nineteen percent of the total vote. In the flush of his own reelection with 64 percent of the valid vote, President Fujimori proclaimed a "direct democracy, without parties or intermediaries," got his compliant congressional majority to vote a general amnesty for human rights violations, some egregious, and concentrated power in the office of the presidency, with over 30 percent of the national budget.

Fujimori further consolidated personal control by securing passage of multiple electoral law and other adjustments, some unconstitutional. The most notable allowed for yet another reelection, removed judges who opposed his reelection, stacked with supporters the Junta Nacional de Elecciones (JNE), gave the intelligence services greater powers, revoked the citizenship of a television station owner who broadcast damaging information on government wiretapping of prominent Peruvians, and selectively harassed public officials and journalists who took stands against such initiatives.

In spite of these political machinations which have led many to characterize the Fujimori government as authoritarian rather than democratic, the president remains popular, especially outside of Lima. He is credited with restoring peace and security, ending hyperinflation, generating sustained economic growth, and reversing the spread of endemic poverty. A network of government agencies now provides significant resources for restoring Peru's infrastructure devastated by the SL guerrillas. In a program attracting worldwide attention, his government has targeted Peru's 200 poorest districts and has spent over $1 billion since 1991 on such community development projects as potable water, lunches and utensils for schoolchildren, latrines, irrigation, and electrification.

Significantly, the political opposition remains weak and divided, although by July 1998 its members were able to gather more than the 1.2 million signatures required by the constitution to force a referendum on whether the president should be allowed to run for a third term in April 2000. In yet another egregious political machination, however, Fujimori supporters in congress unconstitutionally thwarted this popular initiative on a dubious technicality. In spite of this and other manipulations designed to assure the president's victory in the April 2000 elections, he came up just short of the 50 percent required to win in the first round, and was forced into a runoff with the second place candidate. His opponent in the second round was to be Alejandro Toledo, a U.S.-educated economist without prior political experience. However, a week before the vote Toledo withdrew, charging that conditions would not allow a free and fair election. Thus President Fujimori's third term began under a cloud of domestic and international opprobrium, and was likely to limit his chances for continued success.

In foreign policy, Peru has shifted over the course of the decade from the strong Third World position, often anti-American, pursued since the 1960s. With the adoption of a liberal market-oriented model in 1990 as the cornerstone of its strategy of economic stabilization and growth, the government has emphasized improved relations with the International Financial Institutions (IFIs) and private foreign banks, companies, and investors. Such efforts have paid off with Peru's full international economic reinsertion by 1994 and significant infusions of foreign capital (some $8 billion). Overall, relations with the United States have also improved after decades of tension, especially in counterdrug initiatives, trade and investment, and debt reduction (including a Brady Plan in 1997 forgiving some $9.2 billion of the $23 billion foreign debt). Between 1995 and 1997, Peru received more government-to-government economic assistance from the United States than any other Latin American country (about $225 million per year, or 25 percent of total assistance dispensed). Concerns remained, however, over democracy and human rights issues.

The worst flare-up ever of a 175-year-old border dispute between Peru and Ecuador in January–March 1995 (with 700–800 casualties and a direct cost of over $500 million) produced serious and sustained efforts to find a definitive solution under the 1942 Rio Protocol with the assistance of guarantor countries (Brazil, Argentina, Chile, and the United States) success was finally achieved in October 1998 after personal diplomacy by the Peruvian and Ecuadoran presidents. The dramatic hostage crisis provoked by guerrilla group Movimiento Revolucionario Tupac Amaru (MRTA), with its occupation of the Japanese ambassador's residence between December 1996 and April 1997, captured worldwide attention. A Peruvian military operation which resulted in fourteen guerrillas being killed and all but one of the forty-two hostages freed, produced no lasting damage to the close Peru-Japan ties forged since Japanese-Peruvian Alberto Fujimori's first election in 1990.

(See also DEMOCRATIC TRANSITIONS; GUERRILLA WARFARE; U.S.-LATIN AMERICAN RELATIONS.)

David Scott Palmer, ed., *Shining Path of Peru*, 2d ed. (New York, 1994). Orin Starn, Carlos Iván Degregori, and Robin Kirk, eds., *The Peru Reader* (Durham, N.C., 1995). Maxwell A. Cameron and Philip Mauceri, eds., *The Peruvian Labyrinth: The Polity, Society, and Economy* (University Park, Penn., 1997).

DAVID SCOTT PALMER

PHILIPPINES. The Philippines is an archipelago of 7,100 islands, islets, and atolls located southeast of the Asian mainland. It straddles the South China Sea and the Pacific Ocean and serves as a gateway to the international straits linking Northeast and Southeast Asia to the Indian Ocean and the Middle East. Its strategic location has made it a prize asset in U.S. global strategy since the turn of the twentieth century. Covering nearly 115,300 square miles (300,000 sq. km.), Philippine land territory sprawls over some 500,000 square miles (1.3 million sq. km.) of oceanic waters and has a population of 75 million (1999). The islands are grouped into Luzon in the north, the Visayas in the center, and Mindanao in the south. The country's premier city, Manila, which is located on Luzon Island, is its political, economic, and education center.

The Filipinos are a blend of Malay, Chinese, Spanish, and American heritages, reflecting their long history of racial mixing through trade and colonialism. The islands were "discovered" by Ferdinand Magellan on 16 March 1521; Spain consolidated its rule in 1571 upon the acknowledgment of Spanish sovereignty by the local chiefs of Manila. Spain created in the Philippines a centralized political structure bringing under the Spanish Crown independent Malay kingdoms and indigenous tribes already trading with Chinese merchants. Its defeat in the Spanish-American War (1896–1898) led to the imposition of rule by the United States after a bloody war (1898–1902) against the Filipinos, erstwhile U.S. allies, who fought in vain to retain their independence.

These successive colonialisms produced the modern Filipino, mixed in race, primarily Roman Catholic in religion (85 percent), conversant in English and in at least one of their eighty-eight distinct languages and dialects. Filipinos share the liberal democratic values of the West but remain burdened by socioeconomic structures shaped by colonialism, which enable the rich minority to dominate the poor majority.

Social Bases of Politics. The social bases of politics were laid out during the country's colonial history when powerful local elites were coopted by the Spaniards. In return, they were afforded the privilege and opportunity to amass land-based wealth. In some cases, their wealth came from marriage with rich but low-status Chinese merchants. They produced a class of leaders wielding both economic and political power who led the nineteenth-century reform movement seeking liberalization in the colony within the context of Spanish rule, who fought U.S. colonialism, rewon independence, and have ruled the country since then. The national hero, Jose Rizal, and first Philippine president under the U.S. rule, Manuel L. Quezon, as well as subsequent presidents, including Ferdinand E. *Marcos and Corazon ("Cory") C. *Aquino, were among their members.

The major ethnolinguistic groups that have shaped politics in the Philippines were the Tagalogs, Ilocanos, and Pampangans of Luzon, the Cebuanos of the Visayas, and the Muslim Maranaos and Tausugs of Mindanao. Close to the seat of power in Manila, Tagalogs have exerted the greatest political influence dating back to the nineteenth-century reformists and their revolutionary successors. They succeeded in making Tagalog the basis of a national language called "Filipino" at a time when Cebuano-speakers constituted the majority; by 1990 it was the language understood by most Filipinos.

Ethnolinguistic distinctions and consequent regionalism were reinforced by geographical fragmentation, posing physical difficulties for easy travel and communication. They contributed to a perception of Manila-based, Tagalog-dominated "colonialism" by other groups. Nevertheless, ethnolinguistic rivalry has not erupted into large-scale violence except in two cases: Muslim separatism in Mindanao and the autonomy movement of ethnic communities in the Cordillera Mountains. Regional autonomy for these two groups is recognized in the 1987 Constitution.

Religion is a not central political issue, even in Muslim separatism whose real cause is socioeconomic-political domination of the Muslim minority by the Christian majority. Be that as it may, all Philippine presidents have been Roman Catholics except Fidel Ramos (1992–1998), who is Protestant.

Philippine politics demands alliance making across the three island groups. Hence, presidential candidates from Luzon are careful to have vice-presidential running mates from either the Visayas or Mindanao, and vice versa. Sometimes, marriages of politicians are contracted with this regional complementation in mind.

The politicization of the intelligentsia, farmers, and laborers since the 1930s led to the emergence of left-leaning organizations centering initially on the Soviet-oriented Philippine Communist Party and the Hukbong Mapagpalaya Laban sa Hapon (an anti-Japanese guerrilla group known as the Huks). An ideological split spawned the Beijing-oriented Communist Party of the Philippines and its armed wing, the New People's Army (CPP/NPA), in the late 1960s, which is still conducting an active insurgency against the government.

The Political System. *Authoritarianism and *democracy provide the experiential and ideological backdrop of the political system. The authoritarianism of traditional culture was reinforced by repressive colonial structures and processes including those under wartime Japanese rule. However, Philippine encounters with Western liberal ideas through the nineteenth-century reformists and its actual experience with U.S. democracy (1902–1942, 1946–1972, 1986 onward) shaped modern Filipino political orientation. The experience under Marcos after he declared martial law in 1972 made authoritarianism unpalatable to the majority. Hence, redemocratization under Aquino followed the fall of Marcos in the "People Power Revolt" of 22–25 February 1986 and was sustained under the subsequent presidencies of Ramos (1992–1998) and Joseph "Erap" Estrada (1998–2004).

The 1987 Constitution restored a presidential-style democratic government operating under separation of powers and checks and balances. The bicameral legislature consists of a twenty-four-member Senate elected nationwide and a 250-member House of Representatives largely elected through single-member constituencies. To secure the representation of minority groups, some seats were filled through a party-list system. Terms of office are six years for senators, three years for House members.

The president, who heads the executive branch, serves for a single six-year term. Executive powers are severely constrained, especially emergency powers including declaration of martial law, to prevent a repeat of authoritarian rule. Executive appointments require confirmation by the Commission on Appointments for heads of executive departments, ambassadors, and chiefs of mission, as well as military promotions from the rank of colonel or navy captain and up.

Personality-oriented political parties have dominated Philippine politics. Until 1972 the Nacionalista (NP) and Liberal

(LP) parties were the major organizations. Since then many groups have emerged, such as Marcos's New Society Movement, the "Pro-Cory" Philippine Democratic Coalition, the Laban Party, Ramos's Lakas-NUCD, and Estrada's LAMMP. Parties and groups have very little ideological distinction, except for left-wing ones.

The erosion of military professionalism during the Marcos era fractionalized and politicized the officer corps. Military coups led by reform-oriented officers and those loyal to Marcos became a major threat to political stability between 1986 and 1989. In May 1992 former defense secretary Fidel Ramos was elected president to succeed Aquino in a largely peaceful multiparty election. His policy of reconciliation and unconditional amnesty led to the end of military rebellion.

Socioeconomic Policies. Both *import-substitution industrialization and *export-led growth have been tried as strategies for economic development. Neither seems to have worked as basic structural problems traceable to inequitable wealth distribution have not been addressed. Various agrarian reform programs have not been implemented fully owing to landlord opposition in and out of Congress. An international debt burden of US$46.4 billion in 1999 tied up some 40 percent of the national budget in debt service, diverting resources from development needs such as building job-creating enterprises for some 750,000 new entrants annually to the labor force.

The population of the Philippines, growing at 2.3 percent annually during 1990–1995, reached 75 million by 1999. The influential Catholic Church remained opposed to a population program endorsing artificial birth control measures. A related problem is the incidence of poverty, which stood at 40 percent in 1999.

Internal Conflict. Social unrest since the conclusion of World War II has diverted national resources and energies from the task of nation building and economic development. The domination of the economy and the polity by the governing elite has prevented fundamental social restructuring, an essential component of moderating social conflict.

Consequently, the Philippines remained threatened by a communist insurgency amid the global collapse of communism and long after most of Southeast Asia had neutralized this internal threat. Ethnic conflicts also remained unresolved because fear of exacerbating ethnic differences has prevented effective decentralization and power sharing, measures that could have allayed ethnic minorities' fear of Christian domination and assured their participation in forging a single nation out of the country's multiethnic society. Muslim secessionism continues despite the grant of local autonomy and a 1996 peace accord between the Ramos government and the Moro National Liberation Front (MNLF). In early 2000, internal war once more erupted in Muslim Mindanao, led this time by MNLF's fundamentalist breakaway faction, the Moro Islamic Liberation Front.

Foreign Policy and International Relations. Bilateral relations with the United States, centered around the agreement that allowed American military bases in the Philippines, were transformed during 1991 by a series of events which culminated in its termination. These relations remained difficult until the conclusion in 1999 of the Visiting Forces Agreement governing American military personnel in the Philippines. Oil imports and labor exports, at times the country's highest in-

come producer, make relations with labor-importing countries in the Middle East as well as Japan, South Korea, and Taiwan crucial. The most serious foreign policy challenge, however, stems from the South China Sea disputes where creeping occupation of contested territories by China, Malaysia, and Vietnam has raised tension since the late 1990s. Hence, a combination of international pressures and internal conflicts is likely to challenge the building of the Philippine nation into the early twenty-first century.

(See also COLONIAL EMPIRES; DEMOCRATIC TRANSITIONS; INTERNATIONAL DEBT.)

Daniel B. Schirmer and Stephen R. Shalom, eds., *The Philippines Reader: A History of Colonialism, Dictatorship and Resistance* (Boston, 1987). Stanley Karnow, *In Our Image: America's Empire in the Philippines* (New York, 1989). Amando Doronila, *The State, Economic Transformation, and Political Change in the Philippines, 1946–1972* (New York, 1992). W. Scott Thompson and Wilfrido V. Villacoarta, eds., *The Philippine Road to NIChood* (Manila, 1996). Felipe B. Miranda, ed., *Democratization: Philippine Perspectives* (Quezon City, 1997). David G. Timberman, ed., *The Philippines: New Directions in Domestic Policy and Foreign Relations* (Singapore, 1998). David Steinberg, *The Philippines: A Singular and Plural Place*, 4th ed. (Boulder, Colo., 2000).

CAROLINA G. HERNANDEZ

PINOCHET, Augusto. As the president who ended four decades of electoral *democracy and state expansion in *Chile, Augusto Pinochet Ugarte installed an unusually personalistic and durable authoritarian regime along with a market-driven economy. He saw his mission as ridding Chile of Marxist parties and excessive government intervention in the economy.

Pinochet was born in the port city of Valparaiso on 25 November 1915. He graduated from military school in 1939 and from the War Academy in 1952. In the latter institution, he subsequently taught geopolitics and military geography. He rose through the ranks until becoming commander-in-chief of the Army in 1973 during the climactic crises of the elected socialist government of Marxist Salvador *Allende Gossens. Pinochet led the junta that seized power on 11 September and thereafter ruled for seventeen years.

During his first three years in office, Pinochet alienated international opinion with massive *human rights violations. He shut down all democratic institutions. The security forces imprisoned, tortured, murdered, or exiled thousands of Chileans, especially members of leftist parties and labor unions.

Pinochet reversed not only Chile's democratic traditions but also its statist industrial and social welfare policies. He quickly returned to former owners their lands and factories expropriated under Allende. In 1975 he implemented a monetarist "shock treatment" to lower the triple-digit inflation unleashed by Allende. Advised by the technocratic "Chicago Boys" (so called because of their ties to the Economics Department at the University of Chicago), Pinochet then instituted Latin America's most drastic conversion to a neoliberal, free-market system. He moved decisively to liberalize trade, promote nontraditional exports, slash government spending, privatize public enterprises, reduce social services, and weaken labor unions. During 1976–1981, the results included high levels of growth, export diversification, stable prices and exchange rates, foreign indebtedness, *deindustrialization, regressive income concentration, and unemployment.

In the glow of his economic "miracle" in 1980, Pinochet

institutionalized his rule through a controlled plebiscite to approve an authoritarian constitution. That charter kept him in the presidency until 1988, when another plebiscite offered him the opportunity for eight more years in office. In 1981–1982, however, an international recession and debt crisis capsized the economy. By 1983, protests against the dictatorship by social organizations and the banned political parties convulsed the country.

Despite mounting domestic and foreign opposition, Pinochet revived the economy by 1985 and retained power. He barely survived an assassination attempt by leftist guerrillas in 1986. Then in the 1988 plebiscite his candidacy was defeated by a coalition of seventeen centrist and leftist parties in favor of a full return to representative democracy. Those same parties, prevailing over candidates sympathetic to Pinochet in the subsequent presidential and congressional elections of 1989, took office in 1990.

Grudgingly but peacefully, Pinochet transferred the presidential sash to his opponents. He claimed that his mission to bring health to the policy and economy had been completed. At the same time, he remained commander of the Army. Most Chileans hailed the end of his harsh regime, but a minority continued to revere Pinochet as the strongman who had saved the country from Marxism and economic mismanagement.

Quite unexpectedly in late 1998 while on a visit to Britain, General Pinochet was arrested and held for extradiction to Spain to stand trial for crimes against humanity. After ruling that Pinochet was immune from arrest because he had been head of state at the time of the crimes, the Law Lords reversed the original decision and the general was held in custody until 16 February 2000. He was released at that time on the basis of mental incapacity to assist in his own defense. Upon his return to Chile, however, he was faced with more than seventy-five criminal lawsuits alleging responsibility for gross violations of human rights. The inauguration of the Socialist Ricardo Lagos as President shortly after Pinochet's return (11 March 2000) led to increasing expectations that the General would eventually be called to account. The Pinochet case is widely regarded as reflecting a growing international consensus that human rights law transcends claims of national *sovereignty in cases involving crimes against humanity.

(See also AUTHORITARIANISM; INTERNATIONAL DEBT; INTERNATIONAL LAW; MILITARY RULE; MONETARISM.)

Genaro Afriagada, *Pinochet: The Politics of Power* (Boston, 1988).

PAUL W. DRAKE

PLANNING. Most human beings, whether individually or in association with others, prepare to affect the future. In other words, they plan. With the evolution of high-technology industrialism, competing planners have invented many separate planning methods, each with its own respected jargon, literature, interest groups, and high priests. Some make special efforts to coordinate the specialists and guide results. All are involved—despite frequent protestations to the contrary—in efforts to get, keep, and use some degree of *power or influence.

Much of the important planning in life has always taken place on a relatively small scale. Thus, parents may plan for the number and timing of children, students for learning certain subjects and preparing for future careers, and teachers for improving a curriculum or writing books. Managers of police departments, fire departments, and hospitals plan the deployment of their usually scarce resources. On a larger scale, governments plan to promote economic growth, to direct growth in particular sectors, and to cushion the effects of the business cycle. Government planning emerged in response to discontent with the effects of market competition in which governments only facilitated private transactions. During the twentieth century, planning has taken two distinct forms, central command and democratic planning.

Market Competition and Government. One of the great successes of industrial civilization has been the maturation of government-supported competitive markets. Over the centuries, small urban spaces for the display of goods by farmers and artisans have become part of national and transnational markets for the exchange of goods and services, including specialized facilities for labor, land, and finance. This maturation took place largely as the result of government policies in Western Europe and North America during the eighteenth and nineteenth centuries. On the one hand, as celebrated in the vast literature of laissez-faire, governments withdrew (often reluctantly) from various forms of state monopoly and control of private activities. On the other hand, as Karl Polanyi explains, governments took on the responsibility of "enormous increase in continuous, organized and controlled intervention" (*The Great Transformation*, New York, 1957). This has involved public action to protect private property, build police and military forces, create money and banking systems, regulate weights and measures, and maintain judicial machinery for enforcing contracts. Governments also enlarge opportunities for business investment by providing infrastructures of roads, water supply, public health and education, and by developing foreign policies that support business operations abroad.

With these supports, private companies can plan ahead for greater profits, market penetration, technological advance, and political influence. Vigorous efforts throughout an enterprise may be promoted through both fear of failure and the expectation of the greater rewards that can flow from success. This often leads to higher quality of output, an improved range of goods or services, and increased efficiency. Through mass production and reduced costs and profits per unit, companies may not only earn larger total profits but also facilitate long-term growth in the volume of goods and services available to a society. In seeking mainly his own gain, as Adam Smith observes with regard to an individual employing "his capital in support of domestic industry" (not industry as a whole), he may thus promote public interests that were "no part of his intention" (*The Wealth of Nations* [1776], New York, 1937, p. 423).

But as Robert Burns put it, "The best laid schemes o' mice an' men gang aft a-gley." Going astray may result from imperfect information, serious error, changing conditions, or being outsmarted by rivals. Successful planning may impose unforeseen damages upon employees, consumers, or the environment; these are rarely reflected in a firm's accounts. The healthy effects of market competition may be offset by mergers, cartels, or price leadership understandings, most of which are legitimated or tolerated by government. Such arrangements tend to concentrate economic and political power, keep or push selected prices up, or manufacture shortages by setting ceilings on production. In periods of seriously short supply, unregulated competition can lead to dangerous outbreaks of hoarding, speculation, profiteering, and political unrest.

In preindustrial or industrializing societies, competitive markets have enlarged the opportunities for businesspeople and landowners to live longer and accumulate more wealth. But aggregate growth of income and population has often been associated with an enormous growth in the number of poor people with few expectations of escaping absolute or relative deprivation. Low-paid jobs, joblessness, and massive underemployment provide too little of the purchasing power needed for profitable investment to meet domestic needs. The most disastrous by-products of competitive markets have been the sharp economic fluctuations of the "capitalist business cycle," and the political turbulence resulting therefrom, during problems which have been moderated but not eliminated by greater expansion of government intervention and coordination.

Central Command. One response to the ravages of competitive *capitalism was centralized government planning. During the period from Francis Bacon to Saint-Simon (seventeenth to eighteenth centuries), the idea of unlimited progress through science-based central command became an article of faith among West European *elites. With rationality as their guide, redesigned governments would construct ideal societies. In this spirit, socialists promised that national control of economic affairs would end exploitation and promote economic justice. Poverty, colonialism, and *war would be replaced by prosperity, independence, and *peace. Revolutionary socialists argued that with the forceful expropriation of private property, the immense productive forces of technology, once freed from the fetters imposed by capitalism, would operate "in accordance with a common plan" (Karl Marx, *The Communist Manifesto*). Humankind could then gradually pass from scarcity to abundance, and the history of human freedom would begin. Evolutionary socialists disagreed. They campaigned instead for *welfare state reforms, which were slowly legitimated as an alternative to the specter (usually exaggerated) of violent *revolution. These reforms helped make market operations more productive, allowed increases in living standards, and, by alleviating poverty, joblessness, and urban decay, undermined support for revolutionary movements in developed societies.

In 1917, when the Bolsheviks seized power in Russia, they had no idea how to run an economy "in accordance with a common plan." At first, *Lenin thought that capitalism had reduced management to "the extraordinary simple operations—which any literate person can perform—of checking and recording, knowledge of the four rules of arithmetic, and issuing receipts" (*State and Revolution*, 1917). Later, he introduced "war *communism" modeled largely on German central planning during World War I. He then sponsored a state-led scientific management program avowedly based on U.S. corporate principles of promoting labor discipline and productivity. A dominant slogan was "American technique plus Soviet power." By the time that "American technique" was already oriented toward decentralization, *Stalin's Five-Year Plans were devised on the principle of running the economy like One Big Company—but with more concentration at the top than capitalist companies usually attempted. The Stalin-

ists and their successors rivaled (some would say exceeded) anticommunist fascist regimes in concentrating political power, suppressing opposition, and building an empire. They counterbalanced the incompetence and corruption of their central bureaucracies with remarkably efficient mind control and public relations. They won international prestige for having abolished unemployment (allegedly), helping defeat the fascist Axis in World War II, supporting many anticolonial movements, and opposing *apartheid in South Africa. Although this was no part of their original intention, the Stalinists and their successors produced enough literate people, scientists, intellectuals, and artists to help dismantle the empire and fragment the system of central command.

Democratic Planning. In the West, the worldwide capitalist depression of 1929–1939 was so deep and long that it shook faith in laissez-faire *ideologies and led to greater expansion of government intervention and coordination. In 1939, as World War II began in Europe, many people saw that it was the war, far more than welfare-state planners, that would conquer the Great Depression. In the name of "winning the peace," postwar planning became a widespread activity. Books, conferences, "think tank" seminars, and government reports offered a plethora of ideas on both transitional reconversion and longer-term policies. Under the banner of planning for full employment, many governments accepted the responsibility of preventing another general mass depression. In the United States, a loose policy guidance system (abjuring the dangerous word *planning* was set up under the Employment Act of 1946. In France, "indicative planners" brought business and labor leaders together to set national goals; these were then backed up by government credit policies. The Federal Republic of Germany, Japan, Switzerland, and Scandinavian countries went still further in getting business, banking, and labor elites together to promote overall growth and help tame "the business cycle."

Procedurally, democratic planners tend to follow John Dewey's earlier concept of "a continuously planning society" instead of one with fixed blueprints ("The Economic Basis of the New Society," *Intelligence in the Modern World,* New York, 1939). In diverse ways, they combine fiscal and monetary policy with government interventions on behalf of managed competition, a strategy advocated by Eugene V. Rostow for the United States (*Planning for Freedom*, New Haven, Conn., 1960). *Cold War military spending (the importance of which was exaggerated by radicals and denied by conservative economists) has also been a factor. Thus in countries of constitutional capitalism, downturns, now labeled "recessions," have been relatively short and mild. Mass depression has been confined to ethnic ghettoes and areas hit by plant closings, declining basic industries, or farm failures. In developing countries, the record is much more mixed. When national economic growth has occurred, it has often been accompanied by large-scale underemployment and inflation.

During the Cold War, the sustained tension between the United States and the Soviet Union seemed permanent. Thus, planning to "win the peace" rarely occurred. With the surprisingly sudden collapse of the Soviet empire in 1991, no government seemed prepared for either short-term conversion or longer-term growth. For the new regimes in former communist countries, the transition to welfare state capitalism has proved enormously difficult. *Privatization measures have placed former state properties under the control of former state oligarchs. Laissez-faire ideologies have diverted attention from the government activities and the intermediary organizations of civil society without which competitive markets cannot mature. Nowhere in the world does central command wither away easily. In countries of high-technology capitalism, conversion of military industries to peacetime pursuits is particularly difficult under conditions of slow-growth stagnation or recession. In poor countries, development planners can no longer play one side of the Cold War against the other. Throughout the world, planners have begun to debate alternative approaches to a truly global *political economy.

The most intensive planning takes place at the higher levels of transnational corporations and such agencies as the *International Monetary Fund and *World Bank. The relevance of these efforts to the fulfillment of basic *rights and fundamental freedoms will long be a matter of debate. Truly democratic planning requires painful—although far from revolutionary—changes in the culture and power structure not only of government and political parties, but also of families, schools, workplaces, and organized religion. Major shifts would be essential within developing countries as well as in their relations with more industrialized societies. Yet any resulting release of intelligence and moral commitment would inevitably be resisted by the elites, technocrats, bureaucrats, and patriarchalists who regard democracy as too precious to be wasted on the many.

(See also COMMAND ECONOMY; INTERNATIONAL POLITICAL ECONOMY; REFORM; SOCIALISM AND SOCIAL DEMOCRACY.)

Mary Parker Follett, "Individualism in a Planned Society," *Dynamic Administration* (London, 1932). Donald N. Michael, *On Learning to Plan and Planning to Learn* (San Francisco, 1973). Otis Graham, Jr., *Toward a Planned Society* (New York, 1976). Charles E. Lindblom, *Politics and Markets* (New York, 1977). Bertram Gross and Kusum Singh, "Planning under Freedom," in Barry Checkoway, ed., *Strategic Perspectives in Planning Practice* (Lexington, Ky., 1986). Melville Branch, *Planning: Universal Process* (New York, 1990). United Nations Development Programme, *Human Development Report* (New York, 1990).

BERTRAM GROSS

PLO. See PALESTINE LIBERATION ORGANIZATION.

PLURALISM. The term "pluralism" was created in legal studies and political science in the early twentieth century to designate theories that strongly emphasized the importance of human associations other than the *state. Previously, in its general though rarely employed usage in English, the world simply meant, as the *Oxford English Dictionary* defines it, "the character of being plural." It had been used more specifically in England since the fourteenth century to refer to the ecclesiastical practice according to which a single clergyman of the Church of England held more than one position with a life-time income attached. After the work of the American philosopher William James (1842–1910), in the United States it was also applied to philosophical theories that recognized more than one ultimate principle, as in morals or ethics, for example. In the mid-twentieth century social scientists sometimes applied the term to countries that were divided into fairly distinct racial, ethnic, tribal, religious, or linguistic groups, as in some of the newly emerging countries in Africa.

In political science and law, however, pluralism came to be attached to theoretical and empirical work that stressed the role played in politics by associations, organizations, and groups that were relatively independent of the state and one another, such as trade unions, business firms, religious organizations, political parties, and many others. Typically, pluralist work in this sense was both descriptive and prescriptive, empirical and normative. From a pluralist perspective, a diversity of fairly independent associations like these is not only a fact (at least in democratic countries) but also desirable. However, neither pluralist writers nor their critics always sharply distinguished their empirical descriptions from their evaluations. Consequently it is not always clear whether their statements about pluralism are meant to be purely descriptive and explanatory, or judgments about the desirability of the state of affairs described, or both.

In legal and political theory, pluralist writers have always contended with critics who advanced diametrically opposing views. Drawing broadly on a standard definition of "monism" as a theory asserting that reality consists of a single element, the opposing views can conveniently be described as "monistic."

The work to which the term "pluralism" was first explicitly attached arose during the first two decades of the twentieth century in opposition to widely prevalent legal doctrines asserting that the state is uniquely "sovereign." In this context, "sovereign" meant that all other associations within the limits of a state were entirely subject to its supreme authority. Among the best known advocates of an alternative view, which can be called legal pluralism, were Léon Duguit, whose principal works appeared in France between 1911 and 1913, and Harold Laski in England, who not only translated Duguit but also mounted his own attack on the idea of state *sovereignty. Legal pluralists like Duguit and Laski contended that the monistic view of the state as "sovereign" was empirically false in countries like France and Britain where, for example, the state simply lacked the authority to suppress crucial associations such as religious organizations, trade unions, and the like. Moreover, they insisted, no state that attempted to achieve absolute internal sovereignty would be morally justifiable.

In their attack on state sovereignty, legal pluralists echoed earlier views—Greek, Roman, and medieval—that had also emphasized the actual and proper existence of associations within a political society. By contrast, later conceptions of state sovereignty advanced by Jean Bodin (1530–1596), Thomas Hobbes (1588–1679), John Austin (1790–1859), and others stressed the overwhelming primacy of the state. Even the French Revolution, Duguit argued, had merely substituted the sovereignty of the nation for that of the monarch, thereby creating a myth that thereafter gained hold widely throughout Europe. The myth, Duguit contended, implied not only an exact correspondence between state and nation but also the suppression in the national territory of all groups exercising independent authority: churches, business firms, and trade unions, for example, and, in federal systems, cantons, provinces, and states. Both implications, he pointed out, were denied by the facts of actual social and political life in many countries—not least in countries with vigorous municipal governments and federal structures. Some legal pluralists, including Duguit, not only insisted on the rightful independence of associations other than the state but went even further, contending that the state was simply one association among many, neither more important nor necessarily more powerful (in all circumstances) than others.

In the 1920s, legal pluralism acquired a substantial number of intellectual supporters, including, in addition to Laski, A. D. Lindsay, Ernest Barker, J. N. Figgis, and G. D. H. Cole in Britain. During the next decade, however, interest in legal pluralism greatly declined, and thereafter it almost disappeared in both Britain and the United States. Critics argued that legal pluralists had overstated their case, misrepresenting the prevailing doctrines of sovereignty and exaggerating the relative strength and importance of associations in comparison with the state. Laski himself became a Marxist. The Great Depression of the 1930s and World War II lent greater credibility to the belief that strong central governments were necessary for general well-being, and even for the survival of democratic systems and national independence. However, the decisive blow to legal pluralism probably came from the rise of authoritarian and totalitarian ideas and systems in the Soviet Union, Germany, Italy, Austria, and Spain. These systems demonstrated that a highly centralized authoritarian state could virtually eradicate autonomous associations, and certainly could deny them a significant place in social, economic, and political life. Thus while pluralism in associational life might be desirable, and was a basic characteristic of liberal and constitutional political systems, authoritarian regimes demonstrated that it was definitely not an inherent feature of all modern political systems.

From the mid-1950s to the mid-1960s, pluralism reappeared in the view that a fundamental constituent of modern democratic orders is the existence of associations that are relatively independent of one another and of the state. This perspective (which we might call democratic pluralism) explicitly countered the older monistic argument, strongly endorsed by Jean-Jacques Rousseau in *The Social Contract* (1762), that associations were undesirable because they expressed interests narrower than the general good. Democratic pluralism had been foreshadowed by, among many others, Alexis de Tocqueville, who in his famous *Democracy in America* (1835–1842) implicitly rejected Rousseau's monistic view and contended instead that a rich associational life was essential to democracy.

With its federal system, separation of powers, relatively decentralized political parties, and multiplicity of groups and associations, the United States provided a setting that was unusually supportive of pluralist interpretations. In 1908 A. F. Bentley set out a theory of politics that focused on the primacy of small groups; in 1929 E. Pendleton Herring described the role of group interests in the U.S. Congress; the perspectives of Bentley and Herring on the importance of groups in U.S. political life were systematically developed and documented by David Truman in a highly influential work in 1951. The general thrust of these approaches was opposition to the common belief, espoused not only by Rousseau but by many others, that for groups to advance their group interests was necessarily inimical to the public good.

However, in the 1950s and 1960s this form of pluralism came under attack by many who drew on older monistic theories arguing that even in ostensibly democratic systems political systems were actually dominated by a relatively unified ruling class or elite. To writers like Vilfredo Pareto, Gaetano Mosca, and Robert Michels, a ruling class was an inherent condition of social life and organization. To others, who were mainly but by no means exclusively Marxists, a ruling class was an inevitable consequence of capitalism and would vanish with its disappearance. In contrast, democratic pluralists contended that although serious inequalities in political resources prevented full political *equality among citizens, careful empirical studies of local and national governments in democratic countries failed to show that political life was dominated by an identifiable ruling class. On the contrary, empirical work demonstrated that public policies and decisions were often significantly influenced by different groups with different and even conflicting interests and objectives. Because of the *rights and opportunities guaranteed in democratic systems, and the advantages that associations provided their adherents, democratic pluralists contended that a multiplicity of relatively independent associations was inevitable in a democratic system. What is more, like Tocqueville they argued that associations were a positive benefit to democracy: They served to educate citizens in political life, strengthened them in their relations with the state, helped to insure that no single interest would regularly prevail on all important issues, and, by providing information, discussion, negotiation, and compromise, even helped to make public decisions more rational and more acceptable than they would otherwise be.

Antipluralists contended in turn that pluralist accounts neglected the effects, in practice, of democratic pluralism. Some critics insisted that pluralists described only a facade, behind which existed the reality of monistic rule by capitalists or business *elites. Even if the ruling elite did not always control specific decisions, they said, it indirectly maintained its domination by preventing matters adverse to its interests from being placed on the agenda of the official decision makers. The elite, antipluralists argued, also manipulated public opinion, creating a circularity in beliefs running from the elite to the public to elected officials.

While rejecting these claims, democratic pluralists agreed that social and political pluralism was not, by itself, a guarantee that democratic values were adequately achieved. Social pluralism, they said, was necessary to democracy; it was not sufficient. In some cases, associations might even tend to stabilize inequalities, deform civic consciousness by exaggerating group interests, distort the public agenda, and alienate some control over decisions from the general public to the groups themselves. Yet because social pluralism is necessary, inevitable, and desirable in a democratic order, associations cannot be destroyed without destroying democracy itself. As with individuals, so with associations: Independence or autonomy, though necessary to a good life, also creates opportunities for individuals to do harm. Like individuals, associations ought to possess some autonomy, and at the same time ways should be found to eliminate or reduce the harm they might cause. How best to achieve a desirable balance between autonomy and control is, then, a fundamental problem of pluralist democracy.

Democratic countries meet this problem in different ways, as became clear with the advance of comparative studies. Research on different democratic countries soon revealed that the critiques of democratic pluralists by antipluralists in the

United States were focused, more narrowly than they usually made clear, on the particular defects and achievements of democracy in the United States. Studies of other countries showed that although all democratic countries were fundamentally pluralist, they might vary greatly in their specific patterns of cleavages and the relative strength of associations in different spheres. At one extreme, in the United States the relative absence of class-based political organizations, the decentralized nature and comparative weakness of national trade unions, the persistence of cross-cutting cleavages, and other factors gave its pluralism a rather decentralized form. At the other extreme were democratic countries where national bargaining between employers and unions that included most of the labor force typically led to agreements supported by the government, and carried out by legislation if need be. This "corporatist" variant of democratic pluralism, so unlike the pluralist patterns in Britain and the United States, existed for many years not only in Sweden but in some form in the other Scandinavian countries, the Netherlands, the Federal Republic of Germany, and Austria as well. Because of historical and societal factors, then, democratic pluralism can take a variety of concrete forms.

Both in theory and practice, during the last decades of the century pluralism appeared to have entered into a new and considerably more complex phase. On the one hand, with the decline and breakdown of Communist Party regimes, particularly in Eastern and Central Europe and the Soviet Union, the desirability of pluralism became a rallying cry for opponents of the theory and practice of authoritarian rule. Like legal and democratic pluralists earlier, antiauthoritarian advocates of pluralism insisted on the need for independent associations in political, social, and economic life. Drawing on the older vocabulary of Hegel and Marx, they saw pluralism as an essential ingredient of *civil society, which in turn was essential to democracy and human rights. These antiauthoritarian pluralists could be understood as offering an amalgam of both legal and democratic pluralism.

Liberalization and democratization in these countries soon revealed the fundamental problem of democratic pluralism mentioned above. Through their newly formed associations many people gained an influence and a degree of freedom in political life they had hitherto been denied. At the same time, the interests and goals advanced by some groups were seen by others as clearly harmful. Thus the introduction of pluralism brought with it the need to confront the inescapable dilemmas of pluralist democracy.

Meanwhile in many of the older democratic countries, older patterns of pluralism were somewhat altered by a marked increase in what was sometimes called "identity politics." Many people who believed themselves to be subject to arbitrary discrimination or injury because of, among others, their race, ethnicity, language, country of origin, region, gender, or sexual orientation and others became more politically active and formed associations. Discussion of the benefits, harms, and political importance of pluralism gained greater intensity and a new content. In particular, sharp debate turned on the question whether cultural diversity—*multiculturalism—should be deliberately limited or on the contrary systematically protected and encouraged. In any case, some writers argued, because of immigration and changes in attitudes, a significant increase in cultural diversity, whether desirable or undesirable, was inevitable in most democratic countries.

Thus controversies over pluralism as fact and value seems likely to persist indefinitely, together with the inescapable dilemmas resulting from pluralism in a democratic society.

(See also CLASS AND POLITICS; CONSOCIATIONAL DEMOCRACY; CORPORATISM; FEDERALISM; INTEREST GROUPS; NEW SOCIAL MOVEMENTS.)

Harold Laski, *Problems of Sovereignty* (New Haven, Conn., 1917). Léon Duguit, *Law in the Modern State* (New York, 1919). David B. Truman, *The Governmental Process* (New York, 1951). Robert A. Dahl, *Who Governs?* (New Haven, Conn., 1961). William E. Connolly, ed., *The Bias of Pluralism* (New York, 1971). Peter Hardi, "Why Do Communist Parties Advocate Pluralism?" *World Politics* 32 (July 1980): 531–552. Robert Dahl, *Dilemmas of Pluralist Democracy: Autonomy vs. Control* (New Haven, Conn., 1982). John W. Chapman and Ian Shapiro, eds., *Democratic Community* (New York, 1993). Seyla Benhabib, ed., *Democracy and Difference* (Princeton, N.J., 1996). Gary Jacobsohn and Susan Dunn, *Diversity and Citizenship* (Lanham, Md., 1996). Eva Etzioni-Halevy, *Classes and Elites in Democracy and Democratization* (New York, 1997).

ROBERT A. DAHL

POL POT. Cambodian political leader, secretary of the central committee of the Cambodian Communist Party, and prime minister of Democratic Kampuchea (1976–1979)—was born in 1925 (as Saloth Sar) to a prosperous peasant family in central *Cambodia in the French colonial era. Raised by relatives in the capital, Phnom Penh, and educated there, he earned a scholarship in 1949 to study electronics in France. In 1952 he joined the French Communist Party. Returning home in 1953 he became a schoolteacher and worked in secret as a Communist. In 1963 he was named secretary of the Cambodian party's central committee and took refuge in the countryside from the police. In 1965–1966 he visited North Vietnam and China; after being criticized in Hanoi and praised in Beijing he became a Maoist. In 1968, while still in hiding, he inaugurated armed struggle against Cambodia's ruler, Prince Sihanouk, and when Sihanouk was overthrown in a pro-American coup in 1970 Saloth Sar, aided by Vietnam, led his followers, the Khmer Rouge, into a civil war. With victory in 1975 the Khmer Rouge emptied Cambodia's towns, abolished money, courts, and markets, collectivized private property, and set everyone to work as agricultural laborers. In 1976 Saloth Sar changed his name to Pol Pot and became prime minister, while keeping his past identity and the existence of the Communist Party a secret. His harsh, utopian policies, clumsily modeled on those in Maoist China, led to hundreds of thousands of deaths from starvation, untreated diseases, overwork, and executions. Pol Pot, like Stalin, blamed failures on "enemies" in the party who were arrested by the thousands and killed. In 1977 Pol Pot made a state visit to China, brought the Communist Party into the open, and declared war on Vietnam. As the war went badly, he attempted to open Cambodia to the outside world while intensifying purges inside the party. In January 1979 his regime was driven from power by a Vietnamese invasion. Pol Pot spent the next eighteen years in camps along the Thai-Cambodian border, commanding a formidable guerrilla force and dreaming of resuming power. His faction, with substantial support from China and Thailand and tacit support from the United States, was the only government in exile to hold a seat in the

UN. The Khmer Rouge signed the Paris Peace Accords in Cambodia in 1991, but boycotted the UN-sponsored elections two years later. By 1995–1997 the movement was rife with factionalism after Pol Pot attempted to reintroduce the harsh policies that he believed had led to his victory in 1975. Placed in custody by his colleagues in 1997, he died of heart failure in April 1998. Many who knew him have praised his revolutionary zeal, his deceptively smooth manner, his apparent sincerity, and his skill at presiding over small groups. His place in history is assured. At least 1.5 million Cambodians, or one in seven, perished between 1975 and 1979, making the Cambodian revolution on a per capita basis the most murderous in a century of revolutions.

(See also VIETNAM WAR.)

Ben Kiernan, *The Pol Pot Regime* (New Haven, Conn., 1995). David Chandler, *Brother Number One: A Political Biography of Pol Pot*, 2d ed. (Boulder, Colo., 1999).

DAVID CHANDLER

POLAND. For the first time since it emerged in 1918 as an independent country after over 120 years of partition, Poland has good reason to possess a secure sense of independence and sovereignty. Its 1999 inclusion in the *North Atlantic Treaty Organization (NATO) and the launching of negotiations on entry into the European Union, scheduled to take place as early as 2003, provide the best *security and economic guarantees for a stable future in the club of liberal market democracies.

Polish internal politics have seen eight prime ministers in office between 1989 and 1998, and the divide between ex-Communists and the legatees of *Solidarity remains as great as ever, with added strains emerging within the inherently unstable semipresidential system of government. Nevertheless Poland has sustained an enviable level of economic growth of six percent per year, is down to single-figure inflation accompanied by falling unemployment that is now below average EU levels, and has held its budget deficit to a respectable 1–2 percent. A vibrant private sector coupled with an impressive foreign direct investment of over US$20 billion has pushed Poland to the forefront of the transition countries.

Poland still faces the politically as well as economically daunting task of restructuring its massive steel and mining industries, not to mention its highly fragmented and outdated agricultural sector. Nevertheless the bulk of the population appears to have embraced modern consumerism (and attendant personal indebtedness) after the uniform drabness of *communism. Half a million new cars are sold annually, and Poles are shopping in modern supermarkets and adopting a new lifestyle, including modern forms of leisure and exotic foreign travel.

Solidarity, which grew out of the 1970s independent trade union movement and arrived dramatically on the world stage in August 1980, has been transformed from a mass social movement of 10 million members to become part trade union and part political party, one that serves as the political vehicle for right-wing and center parties opposed to the continued influence of ex-communists in Polish politics. For its part, the main postcommunist party, after having sat on the opposite side of the negotiating table in 1980, has sought to play down its past and build an image as a social democratic party oriented toward a well-managed, capitalist but caring future. Each side has tasted power and in turn been removed by the ballot box, which has helped to cut down the number of political parties and introduce something of a clearer left-right divide. However, the overriding image is of the two main groupings confronting each other across fault lines created in the past, while the nation as a whole hurries along to a future of personal affluence and belated *modernity.

Any "rearview mirror" account of postwar Polish history would reveal that, in Poland's case, the yoke of communist rule was relatively light, but that the sociopolitical and cultural legacies of the period have been hard to shake off. Among these legacies are, on the one hand, the endemic corruption, clientelism, and scandals that taint the democratic political leaders and, on the other, the powerful influence of the Catholic Church.

More successful than that of many East-Central European counterparts, Poland's brand of communism led to steady economic growth (and a US$40 billion foreign debt by the end of 1979), urbanization, and increased upward social mobility for a largely rural-based population. Universal literacy gave birth to a million-strong active intelligentsia, which, in alliance with the increasingly disgruntled and put-upon workers, contributed to the system's eventual downfall, a process that is already receding from the collective memory.

It is perhaps no surprise that the crucial years 1956 and 1968—years of worker and student opposition, respectively—are even more distant to the youthful Polish population than the bloody workers' riots sparked off by meat price rises of 1970 on the northern seaboard or the occupation of the Gdańsk shipyard in July 1980. The 1980s saw Poland's communists engaged in the ever more fruitless tasks of half-hearted economic reform allied to democratic experiments aimed at sharing the hitherto unquestioned power of the Communist Party (Polish United Workers' Party, or PUWP). This culminated in their biggest gamble, the Roundtable Agreement of 5 April 1989, where the participants negotiated what was in effect the end of communist rule.

The semifree elections of June 1989 to the so-called Contract Parliament—in which the PUWP risked only one-third of the seats and lost all those—were quickly followed by the immediate effects of stabilization policies which dissipated much of the euphoria of newfound freedoms. Thus a surprised Solidarity found itself in power alongside an equally uneasy president, General Wojciech Jaruzelski, the author of martial law and now the joint overseer with Lech *Wałęsa of Poland's extrication from communism and Soviet domination and the beginning of a new chapter of Polish politics.

It was perhaps inevitable that the government of Tadeusz Mazowiecki would suffer a rapid erosion of political support as it not only tackled the tasks of economic stabilization and political democratization but also faced internal dissension and fragmentation. Inflation of 78.6 percent in January 1990 alone led to draconian measures that resulted in a steep fall in production of 24.2 percent for that year accompanied by mass unemployment and drastic cuts in living standards.

The nineteen months of the Mazowiecki government were marked by the desire to see Soviet troops depart from Polish soil as well as delicate policies regarding the aspirations toward independence of Poland's immediate neighbors such as Lithuania and Ukraine. Membership in NATO was at this time unthinkable. It was only the meeting of the presidents of Poland, Hungary, and Czechoslovakia at Višegard in February 1991 which would initiate a process of lukewarm regional cooperation on a common road out of the *Warsaw Treaty Organization (Warsaw Pact) and COMECON and the first steps toward Europe and NATO.

Stopgap changes to the Stalin-era Constitution and far-reaching local government reforms ran alongside the collapse of the PUWP and its emergence as the SdRP (later to lead the successful twenty-eight-group parliamentary front—the SLD), the winding up and verification of the Security Service (SB), and the controversy over the "thick line" which Mazowiecki wished to draw under the chapter of Poland's communist past. An unwillingness or inability to apply a Czech or Hungarian solution to the unresolved question of lustration legislation has meant that the problem of "collaboration" has exercised all subsequent parliaments. These issues as well as Mazowiecki's independence from his "kingmaker" Wałęsa drive a wedge between Solidarity's secular, liberal, and outward-looking moderates and the radicals who continue to be more nationalist, church-oriented, and outspokenly anti-communist. Wałęsa's successful presidential campaign of late 1990 further exposed these divisions within Solidarity.

In 1991 Poland's first fully democratic elections saw twenty-four parties gain seats in the Sejm (parliament) and further fragmented the Solidarity camp. While continuing recession contributed to the declining legitimacy of the political class, new divisions of public opinion emerged after the Church sought to fill the normative gap left by the collapse of the official ideology of Marxism-Leninism. Conflicts over religious education in schools and crucifixes on walls, the reappropriation of Church property ahead of any general legislation on restitution, and the vexed question of abortion rights created a host of acrimonious and divisive issues.

The six- and eight-month-long minority right-wing governments which followed the 1991 elections reflected the fragmented nature of party politics in the Sejm of 1991–1993, a situation which appeared to suit the president. At the root of the instability was the exclusion from the formation of a government of the two largest parties in the Sejm. The pariah status of the ex-communist SLD (13.04 percent of the seats) and the unpopularity of the UD of Geremek and Mazowiecki (13.48 percent of the seats) continue to fragment politics in Poland.

Thus the governments which emerged from the political brokering of minority groupings known as the Five or the Seven were hostages to fortune. However, they also proved to be their own worst enemies. The first government of Jan Olszewski was never to Wałęsa's liking and fell by his hand when it sought to play the "secret files" card, naming the president himself as a former collaborator. The government of Hannah Suchocka that followed finally allowed in the UD, although from the outset it was locked in bitter strife with its main coalition partner, the nationalist-Catholic ZChN. It was able to push through mass privatization and other reforms but was brought down in an atmosphere of strikes and religious controversy by a single vote in a no-confidence motion proposed by Solidarity itself.

The September 1993 general election ushered in a coalition of the SLD and PSL, inheritors of the official ruling parties of the communist period. The all-too-overt intervention of the

Church coupled with disenchantment with the bickering Solidarity leadership led to a largely negative vote for the post-communists. The main Catholic grouping obtained 6.37 percent of the popular vote but as a coalition failed to find a seat in the parliament, and some 34.6 percent of the electorate who had voted for the right were left without a voice in the Sejm. This circumstance was more than adequately addressed in the 1997 elections when the disparate right-wing forces were marshaled into a powerful alliance under Solidarity's AWS.

The intervening four years of rule by the coalition of the SLD and the peasant PSL, first under their leader Waldemar Pawlak and then Jozef Oleksy and Wlodzimierz Cimoszewicz, produced little in the way of challenging legislation, and much-needed further economic and social welfare reform was left on hold. Energies were spent in bringing all the major areas of economic and sociocultural activity under control, a task made easier as the country began an unbroken run of economic recovery as the earlier policies of "shock therapy" began to pay dividends. Wałęsa's unsuccessful attempt at re-election in 1995 saw the end of cohabitation (in which the president may be from a different party than the governing majority of the Sejm) and the almost total hegemony of the postcommunists.

Although the new president, Alexander Kwaśniewski, promised to be a president of all the people, he did little to obstruct the parties in power. It was only after the September 1997 general elections brought the forces of Solidarity back to government that the inherent difficulties of cohabitation under the new Polish constitution, which had been adopted by referendum earlier in the year, became apparent. The new government under Jerzy Buzek of the AWS in coalition with the UW of Geremek and Balcerowicz did not command the three-fifths parliamentary vote required to overturn a presidential veto. Poland faced an increasing risk of political stalemate. Important bills such as those completing Poland's administrative decentralization and utilities privatization, as well as those specifying civilian control over the military or cutting back on the mining and steel industries, were subject to tactical struggles with critical policy issues held hostage to partisan politics.

At the same time Poland faces tough negotiations on accession to the *European Union that have the one advantage of as yet being above party politics, although not immune to disputes from within the government itself. How long this bipartisan line survives when transitional conditions in such areas as agriculture, the free movement of persons, and access to property rights are spelled out remains to be seen. For the time being anti-EU and nationalist voices remain confined to Radio Maria, which does not reflect Church opinion but nonetheless has a large audience.

Concerns over the state of Poland's security services appear to have been allayed, and preparations for NATO membership are well on course with a majority of members, including the United States, having already voted in favor of its expansion. Most significantly, on the basis of a meeting in June 1998 with the Polish president, the Russian leadership appears to have acquiesced in Poland's membership. With the increased sensitivity of the Baltic Sea countries to regional security and given its well-established relationships with Lithuania and Ukraine, Poland will have a pivotal role to play along most axes of European politics.

(See also DEMOCRATIC TRANSITIONS; JOHN PAUL II; NINE-
TEEN EIGHTY-NINE; RELIGION AND POLITICS; ROMAN CATHO-
LIC CHURCH; TRUTH AND RECONCILIATION COMMISSION.)

Antoni Dudek, *Pierwsze Lata III Rzeczypospolitej* (Kraków, 1997). An-
drzej Antoszewski and Ryszard Herbut, eds., *Polityka W Polsce W latach
90: Wybrane Problemy* (Wrocław, 1998).

GEORGE KOLANKIEWICZ

POLICY COORDINATION, ECONOMIC. Increasing economic interdependence has enabled unprecedented growth in
the value of trade and unimagined efficiency in the ability of
financial markets to capitalize on potential gains anywhere in
the world. But it is now virtually impossible for any country
to insulate itself from significant economic events or decisions
in other nations. Governments have long understood the strategic nature of international economic policy, and self-
defeating cycles of retaliation as occurred with protectionist
tariffs in the 1930s are infrequent. But modern interdependence adds two complications: at least for the major economies, domestic policies as well as explicitly international ones
must be undertaken with an eye to their impact on others;
and the contagiousness of financial crises, producing adverse
impacts on the virtuous as well as the guilty, can often be
contained in a timely way only by coordinated action. Countries have addressed these developments by seeking to coordinate their policies to manage or avoid market failures or
to provide *public goods. Economic policy coordination refers
to any commitment involving national governments in which
the parties agree to undertake some action intended to better
their common economic welfare, but that would not have
been undertaken on strict short-term, self-interest maximizing
grounds.

Because collective action circumscribes national policy discretion, it implicates not only international strategic calculations but also domestic political constraints. It is useful to
distinguish among three categories of economic policy coordination, in terms of the magnitude of the economic challenge
and the ambitiousness of the political bargain: managing crises, providing information, and establishing a currency area.

Crisis management has been the most visible goal. A few
widely publicized successes at joint actions by the major economies generated great initial optimism, including the 1967
agreement among the United States, Germany, and Japan to
reduce interest rates, the 1978 bargain trading German and
Japanese domestic stimulus for U.S. oil price deregulation,
and the 1985 Plaza agreement on dollar depreciation. It was
thought that the annual economic summits would orchestrate
international stabilization, but this has proven impractical. At
the same time, the worry in the theoretical literature about
enforcement and uncertainty as obstacles to coordination has
proven to be exaggerated: free riding on others' collective efforts has not been frequent, and the absence of a consensual
causal model of the international economy has slowed but
not stymied reciprocity. Although receiving little publicity in
the 1990s, a great deal of crisis-management consultation goes
on among major central bankers and finance ministers, and
elite journalists and economists participate in an "invisible
college," generating policy options and articulating the case
for (and against) coordinated commitments. The Asian financial crisis of 1998, for instance, reinvigorated concern about

the developing role of lender of last resort, particularly being
free from resistance from Japan and the United States to expanding domestic demand in order to strengthen the Asian
economics export sector. The challenge of gaining political
support, in either country, for such coordinated action shows
the political difficulty, even when the costs of inaction are
prominent.

The provision of information or common standards can often be accomplished through existing institutions, but it typically faces opposition in the domestic political arena. Reliable
information about the domestic financial system and the solvency of banks and firms is essential to efficient capital markets. Following crashes in Latin America in the 1980s, the
international financial community set up a system for banks
in the major economies to report their lending country by
country to the Bank for International Settlements. The Asian
financial crisis showed that this system has not worked: for
instance, private companies in Korea and Indonesia had
much larger foreign currency debts than anyone had estimated, and lax regulation by the Ministry of Finance allowed
Japanese banks to keep huge losses off their books. The effect
of widespread fraudulent accounting and financial practices
on international transactions can only be corrected by an independent third party with the ability to certify good practice,
and such an agency would rest on a coordinated undertaking
by governments. Similar problems of standard setting arise
with antitrust regulation, where the need is to create common
rules for reviewing cross-border mergers. In this category, the
gain to the international economy from uniform rules is obvious, but imposing such standards will often pit the government against the most powerful and best-organized of
domestic interests.

These two categories of policy coordination—managing crises and disseminating common standards—often appear as
top-down flows of knowledge and rules from center (the IMF,
World Bank, or U.S. Treasury) to periphery. Although such a
hierarchical arrangement is one route to coordination, its
avoidance of politics does not guarantee better outcomes.
Many would argue that the Asian financial crisis and Russia's
economic calamity show a certain hubris on the part of the
IMF and others. Surrounded by organizational cultures that
foster secrecy and that narrow consultation, international
lenders have made policy mistakes that could have been
avoided by a more inclusive and public deliberative process.

The third and most ambitious form of economic coordination involves the parties in a more equal and participatory
process. The goal of establishing a monetary union or free
trading area brings to the fore the necessary interplay between economics and politics, as the recent history of the
*European Union shows. The tradeoff is essentially between
reduced transaction costs with a single currency or lower customs barriers, and diminished national sovereignty over interest rates, exchange rates, or tariffs as policy instruments.
The dislocation is small if member countries are similar in
productivity and prices, and if wages are flexible and labor
mobile in response to demand shifts. But these conditions do
not describe the European economies, and the *Maastricht
Treaty's conditions for entry into the EU have posed a huge
economic challenge. Moreover, many of the member nations
have met the deficit, debt, and inflation targets only by inducing high levels of unemployment. The prospect of sus-

tained unemployment, and corresponding pressure on social service expenditures, will heighten domestic political conflict over the value of membership. In the longer run, if a European Central Bank is to implement effective monetary policy and exercise the taxing and redistribution power needed to compensate for national and regional disparities, history suggests that political union will be essential to stable fiscal centralization.

Since the 1980s, the exchange of information and successful coordination to meet various financial crises has built familiarity with the issues and trust among major participants. At the same time, the experience has highlighted the inappropriateness of focusing on the narrowly economic, and the tendency of international agencies and abstract theoretical models to overlook essential local variation. The political difficulties—especially the need for more inclusive consultation—suggest that economic policy coordination faces many of the same problems that have bedeviled North-South coordination over standards for environmental protection or working conditions.

(See also Economic and Monetary Union; Globalization; International Political Economy; North–South Relations.)

Richard N. Cooper, Barry Eichengreen, Gerald Holtham, Robert D. Putnam, and C. Randall Henning, *Can Nations Agree?* (Washington, D.C., 1989). David McKay, *Rush to Union: Understanding the European Federal Bargain* (London and New York, 1996). Martin Feldstein, "The Political Economy of the European Economic and Monetary Union: Political Sources of an Economic Liability" *Journal of Economic Perspectives* 11 (1997): 23–42.

M. Stephen Weatherford

POLITICAL ACTION COMMITTEE. A political committee organized by a corporation, labor union, trade association, professional, agrarian, ideological, or issue group to support candidates for elective office and, by inference, to defeat others is called a political action committee (PAC). PACs raise funds for their activities by seeking voluntary contributions, which are pooled together into larger, more meaningful amounts and then contributed to favored candidates or political party committees. PACs are a uniquely U.S. phenomenon, although labor unions and business federations exist elsewhere.

The number of PACs climbed sharply after the 1974 amendments to the Federal Election Campaign Act imposed contribution limitations on congressional candidates. The act not only diminished the potential for big givers but also put emphasis on seeking out larger numbers of smaller contributors, a process effectively achieved through group efforts. Thus PACs are mediating structures legitimized by law. They act as an institutionalized outreach by providing a process to gather contributions systematically through groups of like-minded persons for whom issues are a cohering element in their political activity.

The growth of PACs has been helped along by the dramatic shift from neighborhood politics to nationalized socioeconomic and *interest group politics. Corporations and labor unions, for example, are socioeconomic units replacing geographic wards and precincts. The workplace and vocational specialty have come to attract the loyalty of politically active citizens, replacing loyalties once enjoyed by political parties.

PACs are better able to adapt to these changes than are political parties because PACs can focus on single issues or give priority to emerging issues and still survive with limited but devoted constituents, whereas parties rely on broad-based consensus. The issue orientation of PACs leads a few to make independent expenditures, a form of parallel campaigning without the collaboration of the candidate favored.

As PACs have gained influence, they have become increasingly the object of criticism. Poll data indicate that a majority of U.S. citizens feel that too much money is spent on elections, and that those with money to spend have too much influence over government. Critics suggest that contributions give PACs undue influence over election results; that PACs favor incumbents and thereby decrease the competitiveness of election campaigns (67 percent of all PAC contributions in the 1995–1996 election cycle went to incumbents, and the percentage that incumbents received is even greater when PAC gifts to open-seat candidates are subtracted from the total amount); that PAC sponsors enjoy extraordinary access to officeholders and exert decisive influence on legislative decisions, making it difficult for lawmakers to represent the interests of the public as a whole. Some critics further argue that PAC contributions are inherently corrupt, serving as legalized bribery of candidates for public offices. Most critics, however, contend that election finance reform should move in the direction of restraining, not abolishing, PACs, because prohibitions would raise questions of constitutionality.

However, there is one common understanding among PAC supporters and detractors: that PAC growth has been substantial (about 4,000 are registered with the Federal Election Commission and that PACs will remain controversial as long as they continue to be a major supplier of campaign funds.

(See also Congress, U.S.; Elections and Voting Behavior; Political Parties and Party Competition.)

Herbert E. Alexander

POLITICAL BUSINESS CYCLE. The term "political business cycle" refers to the efforts of politicians to manipulate the timing and outcome of phases in the business cycle. Because policy makers, such as the president, are held accountable by voters for inflation, unemployment, and economic growth, they have an incentive to influence these outcomes if they wish to remain in office. Theories of the business cycle call attention to the key role played by *political* motivations in economic policy making.

The typical political business cycle model, initially put forward by William Nordhaus and Edward Tufte, focuses on the desire of incumbent elected officials in democracies to be reelected. The government does this by taking advantage of lags between the implementation of fiscal (i.e., budgetary) and monetary policies and their effects on the economy. Essentially, in the months preceding an election, governments can be expected to pursue policies that stimulate economic activity, thus increasing real disposable income and decreasing unemployment. Voters reward the incumbents with reelection, because they decide for whom to vote based upon recent economic performance rather than what might happen in the future. Because the inflationary consequences of such a policy show up only after the election, governments are then able to pursue policies that restrain economic activity. When inflation is brought under control, the government can then return to an expansionary policy in time for the next election. Other political business cycles point to the importance of which economic classes are in control of the government. Governments controlled by parties of the left are said to be more concerned with reducing unemployment than inflation, while center-right parties tend to have the reverse preferences.

Rigorous analyses have repeatedly revealed scant evidence for the notion that preelection upswings are the rule rather than the exception. Initial political business cycle research focused on outcomes (e.g., unemployment), which governments influence only indirectly, ignoring shifts in the level of policy instruments (such as fiscal and monetary aggregates) that governments directly control. When variations in the latter have been examined, almost no support for the political business cycle has been found. The model's assumption of an unsophisticated electorate and strategic politicians has been criticized as an oversimplified abstraction without much support in fact. The models assume a degree of knowledge about, and control over, policies and outcomes that make it possible for policy makers to induce greater popular support. It is doubtful, however, that the state of economic knowledge and the political system's capacity are sufficient to produce precisely timed and carefully gauged outcomes. Such models also focus exclusively on short-term macroeconomic policies while ignoring other kinds of policies (e.g., regulations, tax expenditures) that affect the economy over the longer term. Yet another criticism is that the theory of political business cycles assumes that policy is driven by a simple, singular compulsion on the part of policy makers to get reelected. It ignores the importance of international actors, organized interests, and governmental institutions and policy makers' own conceptions of what constitutes "good" economic policy.

(See also ELECTIONS AND VOTING BEHAVIOR; POLITICAL ECONOMY; PUBLIC OPINION; PUBLIC POLICY.)

William D. Nordhaus, "The Political Business Cycle," *Review of Economic Studies* 42 (April 1975): 169–190. Edward R. Tufte, *Political Control of the Economy* (Princeton, N.J., 1978). M. Stephen Weatherford, "Political Business Cycles and the Process of Economic Policymaking," *American Politics Quarterly* 16 (January 1988): 99–136.

GARY MUCCIARONI

POLITICAL CULTURE. Involving both the ideals and the operating norms of a political system, political culture includes subjective attitudes and sentiments as well as objective symbols and creeds that together govern political behavior and give structure and order to the political process. Nations generally have both elite and mass political cultures, along with further subcultures that are rooted in regional, occupational, class, ethnic, and other differences.

Classical political theorists starting with Plato and Aristotle and continuing through Montesquieu, Rousseau, and Tocqueville all recognized the importance of custom, tradition, mores, and religious practices for explaining political differences. However, the formalizing of the concept of political culture had to await the convergence after World War II of three intellectual currents: advances in anthropology involving psychocultural theories; innovations in the technology of sample surveys, which made possible the quantification of attitudinal differences; and the emergence of area studies, which globalized the social sciences while preserving an appreciation of cultural differences. The adoption of the concept of culture, one of the most powerful in the social sciences, radically changed the study of political behavior. The political values of individuals and societies are no longer to be seen as mere random congeries of opinion but can be analyzed as having coherent patterns, based on psychologically identifiable human characteristics. Thus, political science is able to exploit important advances in psychology, anthropology, and sociology.

Political culture became an established concept in political science largely as the result of the impact of Gabriel A. Almond and Sidney Verba's classic study, *The Civic Culture* (Boston, 1963). Almond had earlier stimulated interest in the concept with his seminal article, "Comparative Political Systems" *Journal of Politics* 18, no. 1 [August 1956]: 391–409), in which he observed that "every political system is embedded in a particular pattern of orientation to political action."

Political culture soon became a widely accepted concept, but there has been considerable variation in both method and focus in its study. The utilization of rigorous sample surveys was initiated by Almond and Verba (1963), repeated in their book *The Civic Culture Revisited* (Boston, 1986), and carried on in many other important works since then. A second common approach has focused more on the socialization processes that are critical in both forming and transmitting political cultures. A third approach looks at historical traditions with special emphasis on continuities and changes during the modernization process. Finally, there are case studies that generally deal with significant theoretical or policy issues, such as the extent to which cultures can be changed by conscious policies or by the operations of specific institutions, such as the mass media.

Although there has been increasing appreciation of the merits of the different approaches and a noticeable retreat from the more extreme conceptual and methodological positions, there has been no decline in lively debates about the concept of political culture. Possibly the most fundamental of these debates has been over the issue of explaining political change in light of the presumed durability of cultures. In the late 1960s and early 1970s political culture was attacked as a conservative, if not reactionary, abomination. It was believed by some that *Mao Zedong, Fidel *Castro, and other revolutionary leaders had successfully changed the thinking of the masses in their respective countries, and therefore that the presumed constraints of culture represented merely the hegemonic domination of the feudal and bourgeois classes, which the arrival of the revolution would shatter. By the mid-1980s, however, it was apparent that communist claims about producing revolutionary "new human beings" was largely propagandistic pretension and that people in all the socialist countries have by and large continued to manifest their national cultures. Also, as the 1960s have receded into history, there is greater appreciation that the disorders of the 1960s in American life associated with the *Vietnam War and the *Civil Rights movement represented not revolutionary changes in American political culture but the playing out of what Samuel Huntington has called the "disharmonies" inherent in the "American creed," which has always contained contradictions and dilemmas as a result of conflicting ideals (*American Politics: The Promise of Disharmony*, Cambridge, Mass., 1981).

The problem of change has also been raised from the opposite ideological perspective by rational choice theorists who insist that calculations of self-interest are generally stronger than cultural predispositions. Samuel Popkin (*The Rational Peasant*, Berkeley, Calif., 1979) and Robert Bates (*Rural Responses to Industrialization*, New Haven, Conn., 1976), for example, have shown that peasants in Third World countries will change their behavior in response to positive incentives. Aaron Wildavsky ("Choosing Preferences by Constructing Institutions: A Culture Theory of Preference Formation" *American Political Science Review* 81, no.1 [March 1987]: 3–21) has argued, however, that the preferences on which decisions are based are the products of cultural learning, and hence the way people interpret their self-interest is rooted in culture.

Closely related to the rational choice argument is the challenge to political culture theory of those who stress the importance of stuctures in determining behavior. According to advocates of the "bring back the *state" school, attitudes and values are unimportant; it is the basic institutions of state and society that are decisive in shaping national development. Such institutions, including class structures, are, in their view, the prime norms of history that shape cultures. It is not clear, however, that causation goes only in one direction. Perhaps a sounder view is that culture and structure are closely interrelated, that each affects the other, and that it is impossible to decide which is more important.

By the late 1980s there was a significant revival of interest in political culture. The crisis of the communist states raised speculations not only about the reasons why national cultures were not homogenized under Marxist-Leninist rule, but also posed questions about the relative prospects for democratic development among the once-authoritarian systems.

The revival of interest in culture was also spurred by the conspicuously different patterns of development among *Third World countries. The pronounced successes of the newly industrializing economies with Confucian traditions as contrasted to the continuing stagnation of other less-developed countries caused scholars to reexamine the relationship of culture to economic development. Thus the study of *political economy that began with an emphasis on rationalistic policy analysis increasingly returned to the type of culture and society issues first explored by Max *Weber, Emile Durkheim, and Talcott Parsons. Political culture also came to play a large role in the study of advanced industrial nations because, as Ronald Inglehart points out, when countries become more affluent, issues of cultural values tend to replace basic necessities as the focus of political life.

The 1990s saw sustained interest in the relevance of cultural factors because political agendas worldwide stressed *human rights, the rule of law, and "transitions to *democracy." In asking questions about the attitudes and values basic to democratic politics, contemporary political scientists were returning to the central questions that Almond and Verba confronted in *The Civic Culture* at the beginning of systematic research into political culture.

(See also CLASS AND POLITICS; DEMOCRATIC TRANSITIONS; POLITICAL DEVELOPMENT; POSTMATERIALISM.)

Lucian W. Pye and Sidney Verba, eds., *Political Culture and Political Development* (Princeton, N.J., 1965). Sidney Verba, *Elites and the Idea of Equality* (Cambridge, Mass., 1988). Ronald Inglehart, *Changing Culture* (Princeton, N.J., 1989).

LUCIAN W. PYE

POLITICAL DEVELOPMENT. The study of stages of change in the structure of government is known as political development. The basic notion is that human society and government become more complex over time, passing through successive stages. (For example, these stages might be called hunting and gathering, agrarian, and industrial—to give but one possible nomenclature.) Corresponding to changes in social or economic structure are changes in political organization. Although different theories of change may posit the importance of various factors in accounting for development, whatever the proposed sequence of stages and their underlying dynamic, the outcome of all the various conceptions of political development is that political organization varies in degrees of complexity and that the history of the species shows a tendency toward increased complexity.

A hypothetical sequence of stages may serve as an example of how this thinking works. At a first stage, a group coheres thanks to family bonds, religious consensus, and the leadership of an individual of outstanding capabilities. Nothing that resembles a government or *state exists as an institution apart from the group. Politics, or the social application of *power, is vested in the group or a specific individual. At a second stage, the diffused power of the group or of the single leader gives way to the rule of families or clans. A group of individuals now share in power, deciding among themselves how decisions are made and applied for the entire collectivity. At a still-later stage, family rule becomes more institutionalized in kingships with the help of bureaucracies—of which military, finance, courts, and religion are the most crucial. Here the ability to write is often seen as basic to a more advanced political form. Finally, in the current era, party systems appear, governmental functions proliferate, and the general population becomes politically more participatory.

What should be apparent from such an outline is that political development is related to stages of the increased complexity of the state, what is sometimes called the "institutionalization" of government. Different writers discuss the character of this complexity in their own ways, but what their definitions all have in common is the notion that the state becomes more varied in the functions it performs, more open to acquiring new roles in relation to society, and either more responsive to the variety of groups in society or more able to control their behavior directly. Corresponding to this increased complexity of functions, states acquire increased coherence. Institutions formed on the basis of regularized procedures tend to replace the dictates of personal preference or the interests of special groups, and the state as an entity acquires a formal role to such an extent that one can speak of the consolidation of the rule of law.

It must be understood that descriptions such as the foregoing are ideal types that correspond to historical reality only generally. No particular state ever corresponds perfectly to its ideal type, that is, to a schematic definition of its character of the kind provided here. Nevertheless, thinking of the state as evolving in its structure in correspondence with changes occurring in the economic and social dimensions of group life is the essence of conceptualizing the character of political development.

However necessary it may be to see the reality of political development, its actual definition is sometimes a contentious matter because of teleological meanings often ascribed to the term. When development is studied teleologically, the presumption is that there is an evolutionary design to the character of social change such that some forms of government proceed automatically and necessarily from others. Yet critics make three telling observations concerning any such supposition.

First, history shows that apparently more advanced stages of political development may suddenly be surpassed by seemingly more backward forms. For example, the more decentralized and feudal regimes of Britain and Japan proved better able to industrialize than the more centralized governments of France and China, yet the latter appear to have been more complex politically. Thus, as time passes, there may be "advantages to backwardness," such that an apparently more primitive form of political organization demonstrates a better ability to adapt to new historical conditions.

Second, the concept of political development may be ethnocentric when it imputes a linear form of development to history. For example, the suggestion by some writers that the future of agrarian societies today will be an imitation of the character already assumed by industrial, democratic Western countries and Japan is a problematic notion. Nevertheless, the idea that all polities might eventually "converge" as democratic governments resurfaced in the 1990s in the aftermath of the cold war given the triumph at the end of the century of liberal democracy over its fascist and communist rivals. The implicit assumption that somehow a more developed polity is also morally superior is especially debatable. The practice of slavery, for example, was a condition often imposed by more politically developed peoples on those less fortunate or powerful than themselves and may scarcely be thought to represent a morally superior form of behavior. In short, less developed states today are not inherently inferior morally to those more developed, and their future may be distinctively different from what the West has achieved.

Finally, while some states today may well be more developed than others, there is no final stage where development will stop. We need only think of the anarchy of international relations and the distance humans still have to go to achieve some modicum of institutionalized international government to see this point clearly. Those polities that congratulate themselves today on being "modern" or "developed" may appear primitive indeed to later observers. Is there a final point at which development will cease? There are those today who speak of liberal *democracy, for example, as if it will become the universal form of government after which nothing more advanced can be imagined. However, given the continuing anarchy in *international relations, it is hard to believe that the work of political development will not continue to confront us. Here the contemporary example of the integration of the *European Union (EU) serves as an inspiration to many of the way a collection of different peoples with a fratricidal past can evolve political institutions in common that may eventually result in their full integration. This case apart, the prospects for world government seem dim indeed.

Aside from these debates over the nature of political de-

velopment, yet another reason the term presents difficulties is that no easy measurement is available to indicate how developed a polity is. By contrast, the concept of economic development is readily apparent: one may look either at the size of the GNP or the sectoral distribution of productivity and from these indices establish a relative ranking of a country's economic level. Yet given the considerations mentioned above, one must be cautious when asserting firm distinctions about relative levels of political development. Because the actual path of political development may vary so much from country to country, with a seemingly "advanced" country beginning to stagnate while a seemingly "backward" polity leaps forward, and because its features are less easily amenable to statistical measure, the level of development of the state is far less easy to ascertain than the level of economic development. Finally, although states at similar stages of development may in many ways resemble one another, there may be important differences among them as well, reflecting either their inherited political traditions or the expression of unique political forces that will give an individual stamp to the state in question. Which is more "developed" will then be an idle question.

Is development reversible? Of course it is; one need only think of the history of the Roman Empire. Nevertheless, the literature tends to deal with stages as if, once achieved, they represent gains in the character of the state such that disintegration to a lower form of political organization is unlikely although not impossible. Students of political development therefore must be aware that the process may stagnate or reverse.

The question of why development occurs has stimulated a vast literature. Marxists see a dynamic of history in the forces of technology, leading societies to have higher and higher divisions of labor economically that call forth more advanced political structures. Other writers point to the forces of war or to the power of ideologies as giving birth to more complex forms of the state, which then in turn stimulate changes in the socioeconomic forces over which they rule. A blend of these various approaches is probably the most fruitful way to think about development, although on occasion one or another of the various theories may have superior insights into how economic, social, and political complexity increase and thus what we commonly refer to as development occurs.

The notion of political development is essential to the study of history. Yet both its causes and its very definition remain hobbled by serious debates that must be engaged, for the topic cannot be dismissed.

(See also DEVELOPMENT AND UNDERDEVELOPMENT; MARXISM; MODERNIZATION; POLITICAL ECONOMY.)

Barrington Moore, Jr., *The Social Origins of Dictatorship and Democracy* (Boston, 1966). Samuel Huntington, *Political Order in Changing Societies* (New Haven, Conn., 1968). Leonard Binder et al., *Crises and Sequences in Political Development* (Princeton, N.J., 1971). Myron Weiner and Samuel P. Huntington, eds., *Understanding Political Development* (Boston, 1987). Francis Fukuyama, *The End of History and the Last Man* (New York, 1992). Lucian Pye, *Aspects of Political Development* (Boston, 1996).
TONY SMITH

POLITICAL ECONOMY. The discipline termed political economy examines the relationship of individuals to society, the economy, and the *state. Having begun as an integrated field of moral, economic, and political inquiry, it has subsequently fragmented into the study of the economy as an autonomous system, the application of rational individualist reasoning to all aspects of society, and the debate over policy problems with an economic dimension.

Origins of the Concept—A Unified Theory. Emerging in the eighteenth century, political economy drew on the individualism of Hobbes and Locke, the pragmatism of Machiavelli, and the empiricism of Bacon. Its theorists desanctified social discourse. They thought of governments and all human institutions as instruments, as devices formed by human beings to solve problems, as "efficient institutions," not as divine creations nor the accretion of tradition. Political and social institutions were akin to machines: if broken, they were to be fixed, using standards of empiricism, pragmatism, and utility.

Political economy stressed purposive action by goal-seeking individuals. Adam Smith and David Ricardo used it to theorize about the market economy and to attack mercantilist policies. James Mill and Jeremy Bentham used it to integrate representative government with the calculus of utilitarianism, equating good policy with the aggregation of individual preferences: "the greatest good for the greatest number." Political economists wrote about everything: morals, prisons, freedom, wealth, art, goodness, virtue, constitutions, leadership, war, and peace. Over time, however, the concept of political economy fragmented into discrete components so varied that contemporary users of the label do not necessarily communicate with or know anything about each other. Still, we may identify two large limbs on the tree of political economy, each stressing a different postulate of the founders: one branch focuses on the postulate of individual rationality, the other on the postulate of interconnectedness, or the interaction between economics and other forces.

The Postulate of Individual Rationality. Methodological individualism can be applied to any branch of human behavior (or nonhuman, for that matter). In this approach, social analysis requires a secure "micro" foundation on individuals having a coherent goal (the maximization of welfare) and the capacity for ends-means calculations in pursuit of that goal. Preference functions are taken as given and human nature is held constant. What varies are incentives. Variance in human behavior derives from the rewards or punishments induced by alternative institutional arrangements.

These assumptions have led to various branches of work. At its most abstract, modern economics behaves like mathematics, drawing out the implications of a few key axioms as a deductive body of thought without any particular real-world reference. The ideas are tested solely by their internal logic, valued for beauty, elegance, coherence. In the more applied form, propositions about the economy are derived from theory and confronted with data from actual economies. The empirical debates have to do with such topics as *monetarism, *Keynesianism, inflation, market structure, rational expectations, and efficient institutions.

By and large, contemporary economics has been self-contained. It has not been interested in examining the influence upon economic behavior of variables that lie outside its logic: values, culture, history, politics, ideology. Prestige in research has gone to theory and to econometrics. Expertise

specific to countries, historical periods, companies, and policy has had low prestige, as evidenced by the Nobel Prizes or appointments at leading universities. In recent years, however, applied topics and noneconomic influences on economic behavior have gained new favor as objects of theoretical attention.

Economic reasoning, the presumption of optimizing behavior by individuals, has been applied to many topics in fields other than economics. Social choice, public choice, and rational choice are all labels used for these efforts. Mancur Olson's *The Logic of Collective Action* (Cambridge, Mass., 1963) explores the obstacles to cooperative behavior which arise in the pursuit of public goods, when people are able to "free ride" by getting a benefit without exerting any effort to get it. In studying the organization of the modern firm, Oliver Williamson examines how "principals," those with power, delegate authority to their "agents" to obtain desired goals; see his *Markets and Hierarchies* (New York, 1975) and *The Economic Institutions of Capitalism* (New York and London, 1985). Several social scientists interpret the structure of the federal bureaucracy in the United States as the solution by legislators of their own principal-agency problem, that of creating institutions which carry out the imperatives legislators face in getting reelected (see Mathew McCubbins, Roger Noll, and Barry Weingast, "Structure and Process, Politics and Policy: Administrative Arrangements and the Political Control of Agencies," *Virginia Law Review* (March 1989): 431–482.). Sam Popkin, in *The Rational Peasant* (Berkeley, Calif., 1979), and James Scott, in *The Moral Economy of the Peasant* (New Haven, Conn., 1976), explore the rationality and moral reasoning of peasants. In *Taking Chances* (Berkeley, Calif., 1975), Kristin Luker examines why teenagers fail to use contraception even when they know the consequences.

The Postulate of Interconnectedness. This approach rejects the autonomy and self-sufficiency of neoclassical economics. The economy is seen as a societal output. Economic performance derives from political choices, social organization, culture, circumstances, history. The economy is constructed, not somehow natural. Tocqueville, *Marx, Saint-Simon, Comte, Durkheim, and *Weber worked in this integrated manner in the nineteenth century, as did Talcott Parsons in the twentieth century.

Contemporary social science links positivist research techniques to these kinds of systemic questions in modern political economy. In *The Affluent Worker in the Class Structure* (London, 1969), John Goldthorpe and David Lockwood examine how prosperity affects the political behavior of the working class in capitalist society. In *The Second Industrial Divide* (New York, 1984), Charles Sabel and Michael Piore show the ways in which ethnicity, family, and religion facilitate a distinctive form of efficient capitalist economic organization, often known as the "Italian model." With his book *British Factory/Japanese Factory* (Berkeley, Calif., 1990), Ronald Dore brought the study of Japan into a broader framework of comparative capitalism. In *Dualism and Discontinuity* (Cambridge, U.K., 1980), Suzanne Berger explores the politics that favors small-scale enterprises in capitalist economies. In *National Diversity and Global Capitalism* (Ithaca, N.Y., 1996), Berger and Dore explore the debate over *globalization—do market forces compel convergence or reward efficient differentiation?

Policy Debates. These differing intellectual approaches to the relationship between politics and economics are reflected in policy debates:

a) The role of public policy in shaping market efficiency. The analytic separation of market and society entails a quarrel over the role of the state and public policy in producing growth and efficiency. The minimalist view sees least as best; the state need only be a "night watchman," keeping peace, preventing crime, allowing an autonomous economy to function. By contrast, the "developmental state view" sees the market as requiring substantial provision of public goods, that is, items whose diffuse benefits fail to elicit enough private rewards to be provided by the market. These include education, research, public health, physical infrastructure, and uniform standards. Advocates of industrial policy argue that state policy can contribute to efficiency in the strategic promotion of selected industries. Theorists of regulation explore policies concerning market and firm structure to consider efficient institutions.

The policy disputes involve both highly advanced industrial economies and those at early stages of development. They arise from disagreement over the past, as well as the present. The minimalists claim that economic growth occurs when prices are right, a condition best achieved with little state action, for which they offer British and U.S. growth as proof. State intervention leads to "rent-seeking," an extraction of wealth by officials who contribute nothing to efficiency, or to interest group distortion of policy, favoring efficient sectors over potentially efficient ones (urban residents, for example, using political control to keep down food prices, thereby preventing farmers from earning income through exports).

The state activists dispute this interpretation of the U.S. and British past, noting state promotion of canal and railroad building and other infrastructure, and cite Alexander Hamilton and Adam Smith as advocates of this approach. They cite Germany and Japan as examples of state "involved" growth, a model now being taken up by the East Asian *newly industrializing economies (NIEs), particularly the Republic of Korea (South Korea), Taiwan, Hong Kong, and Singapore. The minimalists dispute this interpretation of those countries. Economists would see this as an argument over the volume and quality of public goods the state needs to supply; political scientists would see this as an argument over the political circumstances that produce growth-promoting policies, be they activist or minimalist; sociologists would see this as an argument about the determination of collective goals and social structures needed to sustain growth.

On the side of the minimalist state view lie a good portion of the economics profession and some economists located in places such as the *World Bank and the *International Monetary Fund (IMF), who have urged extensive privatization and expenditure cuts to developing countries. On the side of the developmental state view can be found many political scientists, sociologists, and some heterodox economists, including Robert Wade (*Governing the Market*, Princeton, N.J., 1990) and Stephan Haggard (*Pathways from the Periphery*, Ithaca, N.Y., 1990). In the 1980s the success of Japan seemed to favor the activists. In the 1990s, the decline of Japan and the success of the American model tilted the balance toward the minimalists. The Asian financial crisis of 1997 provoked a sharp debate, still continuing, about the capacity of developmental states to surmount "crony capitalism," the adequacy of orthodox models of financial adjustment, and the role of international agencies in domestic policy.

b) Foreign economic policy. How should a nation relate to the international economy? The neoclassical argument hinges on free trade: the optimal policy for a country is to have open borders. This view has been challenged since the nineteenth century by conservative nationalists as well as by political radicals. Nationalists sought self-sufficiency and political military strength, radicals social transformation; neither thought that these goals could be reached by free trade within a capitalist economy. In their view, the market would act to favor those already strong, the first industrializers.

The debate continues for developing countries. Critics of dominance by the advanced industrial countries argued that the free market traps developing countries in a subordinate role in the international division of labor. In the Latin American view, the solution to the problem lay in state-directed* import substitution industrialization (ISI) strategies. A few countries in East Asia opted for export-oriented industrialization (ESI) strategies instead: state intervention was extensive, but oriented toward promoting industries that would produce goods for export rather than toward replacing imports. In the event, ESI countries have developed more rapidly than those that chose ISI.

There is still much discussion regarding the political economy of development. The United States and international advisers have pressed governments to privatize, deregulate, and open their borders. Japan and some European advisers have argued that states need to invest in education, encourage research, and subsidize key growth industries. In the meantime, intellectual barriers that isolated regions of the world within specialized subfields have been surmounted. Comparisons between Latin America and Asia are now common. Similarly, there is comparison of deregulation in statist economies and transition problems in the former communist countries. Economic development has been revived as a field of economics; comparative political economy flourishes.

The advanced countries, meanwhile, have witnessed a revival of long-standing political tensions over the proper response to growing international trade. Can countries go their own way on domestic social services and economic policies, or does competition force convergence? The empirical side of this debate gives rise to research about the actual record of policy and outcomes. It largely finds that considerable differences remain in economic policy (the trade-offs among growth, equality, and stability) and in outcomes. (See Thorbert Iverson, *Contested Economic Institutions: The Politics of Macroeconomics and Wage Bargaining in Advanced Democracies*, Cambridge, U.K., forthcoming.)

Trade requires international agreements that set forth the rules by which it will be conducted. The United States influenced those rules in 1945, but it then accounted for 50 percent of world GNP; although it is still the world's most dynamic economy, that figure is now closer to 20 percent. The world is economically multipolar. Can rules be established in the absence of a dominant power, a hegemon? In Europe economic integration has gone remarkably far, encompassing not only the integrated trade market and the concordance of regulatory standards but monetary union as well. In global terms, the shift from the General Agreement on Tariffs and Trade to the *World Trade Organization testifies to a desire for stronger dispute resolution mechanisms, and thus for more free trade.

While countries have liberalized trade, disputes remain. Agricultural subsidies in the advanced industrial world harm the developing countries, for whom food exports would be a major instrument for launching a successful export-oriented growth strategy, propounded, indeed, by the very countries urging privatization and market strategies. Nontariff barriers remain potent and the subject of tension among the United States, Japan, and Europe. Regulation extends the debate over "improper" barriers to trade to include many aspects of society traditionally not on the international bargaining table. The United States and European countries accuse Japan of excluding products and investment through these instruments (leading to the "Structural Impediments Initiative"). Japan claims that the *keiretsu* and other forms of organization are simply efficient market instruments which are available to any country, and are therefore not valid elements of international regulation or dispute. Within countries, trade continues to generate political conflict over the degree of economic liberalization and the social support needed to manage the transitions involved. The political economy of trade and international economic relations is a highly developed area of research integrating economics and politics. Important works include Barry Eichengreen, *Golden Fetters: The Gold Standard and the Great Depression, 1919–1939* (New York, 1992), Beth Simmons, *Who Adjusts? Domestic Sources of Foreign Economic Policy During the Interwar Years, 1924–1939* (Princeton, N.J., 1994), Ronald Rogowski's *Commerce and Coalitions* (Princeton, N.J., 1989), and articles by Michael Hiscox in the journal *International Organization* (1999 and 2000).

Another arena of research explores the causes of efforts to remove central banks from political influence and the consequences of these steps.

c) Equality, social mobility, environment. A third category of policy disputes in political economy concerns the attainment of goals other than growth and efficiency. Arguments are made on behalf of equality of income, opportunity, and participation in public life; over notions of social justice, health, safety, housing, security, a safety "net" for each citizen; over the role of leisure, culture, and individual fulfillment; over gender, ethnicity, race, and other elements of social relationships; over environmental quality and preservation of resources; and finally, over values of national power, domination, attainment, glory, autonomy, and security. All of these goals have an economic component. At a minimum they involve resources and the allocation of resources. They involve the use of politics to interact with the economy in order to attain these goals. The political economy tradition approaches these questions with a set of distinctive tools. It asks cost-benefit questions and considers incentives, markets, and institutions. It proposes solutions that take account of collective action problems, monitoring, "agency," delegation of authority. It examines values, culture, and community in the context of institutions and interests. It is willing to put a price on pollution, for example, or on a type of medical operation, or on disease prevention, and to ask, "How much is saving a

life worth?"—an approach which often enrages analysts not trained in this tradition.

The Field Today. Some students of political economy are interested in economics but not politics; as "pure economists" they study the properties of a model. Some are interested in politics but not economics; they study economic reasoning applied to political institutions. Still others explore the elements of interactive systems, as economics and economic reasoning interact with other social systems and influences. *Caveat lector.*

Readers can find trends in contemporary writing that evoke something of the historical linkage among morality, politics, economic reality, and economic reasoning with which political economy began more than two centuries ago. Jon Elster in *Ulysses and the Sirens* (Cambridge, U.K., 1984), *The Cement of Society* (Cambridge, U.K. 1989), and *Solomonic Judgements* (Cambridge, U.K., 1989) pushes at the bounds of rationality by looking at a wide range of individual "moral" dilemmas. The connection between rationality and culture has been re-forged in explorations of the interaction of norms and institutions; norms provide mechanisms of coordination and interaction that resolve problems of multiple equilibria. Values and affective ties help structure action in many areas of life from international relations to dispute resolution in small communities. See, for example, Peter Katzenstein, *The Culture of National Security: Norms and Identity in World Politics* (New York, 1996), and Robert Ellickson, *Order without Law: How Neighbors Settle Disputes* (Cambridge, Mass., 1991). Amartya Sen in *The Political Economy of Hunger* (Oxford, 1990) and *Women, Technology, and Sexual Division* (New York, 1985) examines the moral and political economy of famines and the treatment of women in developing countries. Barrington Moore in *Social Origins of Dictatorship and Democracy* (Boston, 1966) and Perry Anderson in *Origins of the Absolutist State* (London, 1974) probe the interconnections among economic polity, institutions, and political development. Albert O. Hirschman, in addition to his pioneering contributions to the study of economic development in *The Strategy of Economic Development* (Boulder, Colo., 1988), proposed in *Exit, Voice, and Loyalty* (Cambridge, Mass., 1970) analytic tools for understanding the effects of how people express dissatisfaction. Hirschman has also become a historian of political economy through such work as *The Passions and the Interests* (Princeton, N.J., 1977), which examines changing attitudes toward the political consequences of market society.

In the hands of theorists such as these, political economy evokes the power and forcefulness of its ancestors.

(See also DEVELOPMENT AND UNDERDEVELOPMENT; EQUALITY AND INEQUALITY; EXPORT-LED GROWTH; INTERNATIONAL POLITICAL ECONOMY; RATIONAL CHOICE.)

PETER GOUREVITCH

POLITICAL MACHINE. Political machines are organizations dedicated to mobilizing votes or demobilizing opposition for the purpose of winning elections and the spoils of office. They practice machine politics, in which material inducements such as jobs are exchanged for the votes of low-skilled citizens, lucrative contracts for projects including trolley systems and housing construction are exchanged for financial support from the entrepreneurial class, and favors in the administration of law that range from a fixed traffic ticket to changes in zoning ordinances are exchanged for votes. That electoral defeat may terminate these material benefits produces a high reliability for the organization, hence the name "machine." By making electoral appeals on the basis of ethnicity and slating members of subordinated groups to political offices, machine politicians mixed material incentives with the intangible incentives of ethnic pride.

The classic urban political machine in the United States was dominated by the nineteenth-century Irish; when they subsequently occupied the bottom rungs of the employment queue, immigrant Poles, Jews, and Italians practiced machine politics. Machines advanced the political inclusion of these groups; however, emphasis on ethnicity did much to dampen class consciousness in the United States. It appears that African Americans and Latinos will succeed in adapting this institution to the twenty-first century.

In their most mature and rare form, machines become synonymous with centralized control of a political party organization and electoral domination; more frequently, they are factions of a party or another sociopolitical organization. Machines may compete against other machines or be opposed by reformers who typically call for a more issues-based and less materially corrupt politics.

Because of declines in immigration, the rise of merit-based hiring, the social policies of the *New Deal (1932) and Great Society (1964), racial disharmony between urban white ethnics and minorities of color, and anti-corruption reforms, the death of the political machine as an institution of urban America has been reported many times. Certainly these factors and others have weakened or killed machines in particular cities but others have adapted and flourished. The functions of the machine account for the adaptability and survival of this institution. Candidates at the federal, state, and local levels continue to see machine politics as an effective tool for organizing and mobilizing votes. Local leaders continue to see them as an effective means for delivering services and coordinating the diffuse activities of mayors, city councils, and bureaucracies. Cities continue to attract poorer residents who, in awareness of the material incentives that the machine organization can offer, willingly vote for the candidates of the organization. Cities continue to spend huge sums of money on projects that allow politicians a range of discretion in the awarding of contracts, and urban politicians continue to devise strategies to subvert merit-based employment and to add discretion to the distribution systems for urban services. The term "pinstripe patronage" has been coined to describe the awarding of lucrative city bond work to legal and financial firms that consequently become major campaign contributors to individual politicians and party organizations.

(See also PATRON-CLIENT POLITICS; POLITICAL PARTICIPATION.)

Raymond Wolfinger, "Why Political Machines Have Not Withered Away and Other Revisionist Thoughts" *Journal of Politics* 34 (May 1972): 365–398.

RICHARD A. KEISER

POLITICAL PARTICIPATION. The concept of *political participation* covers an extraordinary range of activity. Consider these images:

- *Tiananmen Square, Beijing, June 1989: tens of thousands of people, mostly young, peacefully but with intense commitment risk their lives to influence the leaders of the largest nation on earth to alter the rules of the political game;
- A committee of Sri Lankan rice farmers meets with irrigation officials to determine the timing of water release and review their respective responsibilities for supervising water use;
- A citizen of Kansas City argues with a police officer over a traffic ticket.

Despite their obvious contrasts, these scenarios share a core theme that constitutes a definition of political participation: action by private citizens seeking to influence governmental decisions. As the examples suggest, political participation can take the form of individual, small group, or mass action. It may be narrowly self-interested or breathtakingly self-sacrificing, sporadic or sustained, spontaneous or highly organized, cooperative or confrontational, legal or illegal, peaceful or violent. Participants may seek to influence policies or their implementation, to retain or change the decision makers, or (more rarely) to defend or alter the institutions and rules of the political game.

A great deal of political participation is rational problem-solving behavior. People vote, campaign, lobby, demonstrate, strike, or riot because they think that the government can solve some individual or group problems. Participation entails costs: at a minimum, participants spend time, money, and other resources; at a maximum, they may risk losing their jobs, their liberty, or even their lives. Who participates, through what modes, and for what goals therefore will reflect people's perceptions regarding:

- relevance: can the government help with the problem? (The answer is especially clear if the government is viewed as a major source of the problem, for example, by imposing burdensome regulations.)
- efficacy: are the authorities likely to respond positively?
- alternative means: given the specific problem and the expected government reactions, are the benefits of participation higher or its costs lower than available alternatives like aid from other sources, individual or group self-help, or waiting for others to take political initiative?

Mancur Olson (*The Logic of Collective Action*, Cambridge, Mass., 1965) argues that this last option, free-riding, is a formidable impediment to collective action of many types. Albert O. Hirschman (*Exit, Voice, and Loyalty*, Cambridge, Mass., 1970) adds "exit" as another alternative to "voice" or political action: the individual's best course may be to change occupation or neighborhood, or even to migrate abroad.

The rational self-interest perspective is powerful, but it deals inadequately with much political participation. "Other-regarding values" such as civic duty or group loyalties often affect voting levels. Protest ranging from antiwar or pro-ecology "green" demonstrations to popular uprisings against oppressive regimes are prompted less by calculated self-interest than by passionate commitment to values such as civil liberties, group self-determination, or long-run global welfare, and often also by rage against injustice and corruption.

Key issues regarding political participation are the determinants of varying levels and modes, the implications thereof for trends in participation, and the consequences for individuals, groups, and nations. The focus here is on fairly conventional participation in ordinary times, leaving discussion of mass movements and *revolution to other entries.

Determinants. Surveys in many countries demonstrate that better-educated and higher-status individuals are more likely to be politically active, especially for modes of participation that are more demanding and complex than voting. Virtually everywhere men tend to be more active than women, even after controlling for other factors such as education. People in middle age brackets are usually more active than youths or the elderly.

Organizational membership, identification with ethnic, regional, or religious groups in culturally diverse nations, and rural and small town residence all encourage participation, independent of (and often outweighing) the effects of individual traits. Strong identification with an organization or group may make political action seem more relevant or effective. Moreover, group loyalty (and fear of group disapproval of free-riding) heightens the incentive to participate. *Ethnicity has proved a particularly potent base for political participation in many ethnically diverse societies. Religion is a powerful mobilizing force not only in the Middle East and Latin America but also elsewhere, as in Ireland, Poland, and Korea. Class has proved less crucial in most of the world than many theorists expected. Political traditions and institutions powerfully shape levels and modes of participation. Voting is an obvious example: between the extremes of compulsory voting and no elections are all shades of ease or difficulty in registering and voting. National or local laws and traditions may similarly facilitate or obstruct lobbying, contacting, and demonstrating, for all citizens or for particular groups.

Political circumstances swell or diminish participation. Closely contested elections or highly charged issues (for example, abortion in the United States) prompt previously passive citizens to vote, lobby, or demonstrate.

Trends. In the 1950s and 1960s, it was widely assumed that broadening political participation was an integral aspect of *modernization. Participation would increase naturally as education spread, communications improved, voluntary associations proliferated, and expanding government activity offered more benefits and imposed more regulation. As authoritarian governments took power in the late 1960s and 1970s in much of Africa, Asia, and Latin America, many political scientists discarded the earlier assumptions. But the unprecedented wave of popular pressure for more open political systems in the late 1980s suggests that the older analysis was not wrong, but partial: broad social trends, such as the spread of education and access to mass media, do strengthen the impetus for political participation in the long run. But elite goals and strategies usually powerfully constrain short-run options.

Moreover, patterns of participation change over time in particular countries, and some types of participation may decline. The secular fall in voting rates in the United States, for example, has been the focus of considerable concern. Since different modes of participation vary fairly independently, reduced voting need not imply reduced overall participation, but the trend nevertheless affects how the political system works.

Consequences. The turn or return to more open political systems in the 1990s lent urgency to the question of consequences of broad-based or expanding participation. Classic liberal and conservative theories offer multiple—and conflicting—assumptions on the issue. Liberal theory sees widespread participation as crucial to responsive and responsible government. Citizen involvement and a sense of shared responsibility in public choices will raise levels of information, moderate claims on government, and increase legitimacy and stability, it is argued. A stronger voice for ordinary people enhances equality. Opportunity to hear diverse views and gain fuller information on local conditions and popular priorities improves the design and efficiency of public programs. More stable and efficient government enhances economic growth. Conservative critics have long challenged these assumptions, questioning the capacity of ordinary citizens to grasp the complexities of public affairs, to perceive their own long-term interests, and to compromise in the larger public interest. Indeed, they argue, widespread participation is likely to harden positions, escalate demands, intensify conflicts, and thereby threaten both stability and minorities' rights. Mass pressures may also result in paralysis or in conflicting and unsustainable policies.

Remarkably little research has seriously tested these competing visions. Much of the research on consequences, moreover, is weakened by using voting rates or indices of *democracy as proxies for the broader concept of participation. Efforts to link expanded participation rates to increased income equality across nations show little relationship. That outcome is not surprising, because relatively privileged groups, especially urban middle classes, are nearly always more active political participants than the very poor. Similarly, evidence on links between participation (or democratic forms of government) and rates of economic growth is inconclusive.

Assessing the effects of participation on stability poses special problems, because most measures of stability include indices of protest and *political violence, yet these are also modes of participation. Obviously not only the amount but also the modes and goals of participation bear on stability. In ethnically divided nations mass participation may well be disintegrative. But it is possible to structure political parties and other institutions to cut across cleavages and reduce their destabilizing effects. The impact of participation on legitimacy and stability also is strongly affected by popular expectations relative to governmental resources and capacity. Participation is far too diverse a concept to permit easy generalizations. Some theorists have suggested the notion of an "optimum" level of participation that encourages governments to be responsive yet permits them to act consistently and decisively. But the idea of "optimum level" offers little practical guidance. As growing numbers of nations are affected by the global pressures for democratization, each confronts complex interactions and some painful trade-offs between rapidly expanding participation, stable and effective government, economic revitalization, and equity. And all face formidable challenges to design institutions such as electoral laws or relations between legislature and executive that will channel participation constructively.

(See also CIVIL SOCIETY; CLASS AND POLITICS; CONSERVATISM; DEMOCRATIC TRANSITIONS; ELECTIONS AND VOTING BE-

HAVIOR; INTEREST GROUPS; LIBERALISM; NEW SOCIAL MOVE-
MENTS; PLURALISM; POLITICAL PARTIES AND PARTY
COMPETITION; RATIONAL CHOICE; RELIGION AND POLITICS;
REPRODUCTIVE POLITICS; SOCIAL CAPITAL.)

Samuel P. Huntington and Joan M. Nelson, *No Easy Choice: Political Participation in Developing Countries* (Cambridge, Mass., 1976). Sidney Verba, Norman Nie, and Jae-on Kim, *Participation and Political Equality: A Seven-Nation Comparison* (Cambridge, U.K., 1978). Norris, Pippa, ed. *Critical Citizens: Global Support for Democratic Government* (New York, 1999). Margaret Conway, *Political Participation in the United States* (Washington, D.C., 2000).

JOAN M. NELSON

POLITICAL PARTIES AND PARTY COMPETITION. See overleaf.

POLITICAL REALIGNMENT.

Political realignments are cyclical, sharp, comprehensive, and durable shifts in voter and elite behavior due to some profound shock to the polity (such as a massive economic downturn as occurred in the United States after 1929). Such shocks energize new issues, mobilize voters to come to the polls in greatly increased numbers, and cause some to change their previous political allegiances. That reaction usually occurs not in one election alone, but over several in succession.

For much of U.S. history, the major political parties have benefited from a remarkable partisan stability among voters—a rock-like support expressed at the polls in election after election and which allowed one of the parties to win most contests in an era and thus dominate government policy. These long periods of stability have been abruptly interrupted five times, beginning in elections in 1800, 1828, 1854, 1894, and 1932. In each case, as old issues lost their force and new pressures emerged, a particular calamity—the depression after 1929, for example—unleashed forces strong enough to overturn and then realign the elements comprising the political world.

Realignments are followed by a new period of political stability. Before a realignment, the electorate behaves predictably. Once it has ended, voters do so again, in their new configuration, with a new majority party controlling the government and enacting, in its turn, its policy agenda. Thus, in the United States, after 1932, the Democrats dominated the national government for a generation and enacted a range of unprecedented legislation. Similarly, in Britain, after the realigning election of 1945, the Labour Party, in a similar situation, successfully passed a new legislative program of its own design.

Realignments have thus clarified politics, marked precise dividing points between different eras, and supplied a critical dynamic for peaceful change within political systems. But in recent years, changes in the external environment of politics linked to broad economic and social transformations of society—the growth of a more educated, less readily mobilized population, and the increased power of the media, especially television, in shaping political attitudes, for example—have led to increasingly volatile popular voting and no further realignments. Since the 1960s, election outcomes in the United States, Britain, and in much of Western Europe have reflected fluctuating short-term forces such as the unusual attractiveness of a particular candidate, or the impact of a dramatic

episode such as an incident of racial violence during an election, rather than stable, deeply imbedded partisan loyalties. This voter dealignment from parties has significantly altered the rules of the game. Confusion and fragmentation reign as voters wander from candidate to candidate and from one party to the other in successive elections. In the United States, there have been few clear policy mandates. Government has been divided between Republicans and Democrats with neither able to control the policy arena in a sustained way. In Britain, the growth of nationalist parties in Wales and especially Scotland and the proliferation of center parties counterposed to both Labour and Conservative have vastly complicated politics and made electoral behavior less predictable. More generally in Western Europe, the development of *new social movements, the growth of xenophobic and neofascist parties, and the vitality of environmental issues and *green parties have vastly complicated elections and voting behavior.

This volatile voter pattern, and consequent decline in the realignment dynamic, has provoked questions as to whether these political systems any longer have the ability to relieve pressure on them and redirect government in a peaceful manner. Some are less bleak in their assessment, believing that many elements have realigned over the past generation in both the United States and Europe, albeit without the clarity of the consistent patterns in popular voting characteristic of the party-dominant eras of national politics.

(See also ELECTIONS AND VOTING BEHAVIOR; POLITICAL PARTIES AND PARTY COMPETITION.)

Walter Dean Burnham, *Critical Elections and the Mainsprings of American Politics* (New York, 1970). Bruce A. Campbell and Richard J. Trilling, eds., *Realignment in American Politics: Toward a Theory* (Austin, Tex., 1980).

JOEL H. SILBEY

POLITICAL SCIENCE. See page 674.

POLITICAL VIOLENCE.

Scholars have used the phrase "political violence" since the 1960s to refer to the use or threat of physical harm by groups involved in domestic political conflicts. Initially it was an inclusive term for all disruptive forms of internal opposition to governments, including political *terrorism and *assassinations, antigovernment riots and demonstrations, rebellions, and revolutionary warfare, also known as "civil violence." Later its usage expanded to include governments' acts of repression and violence against their own citizens, also known as "state violence."

Some peace researchers have criticized the narrow conception of political violence as physical injury, arguing that deprivation and social injustice also are forms of violence that they label "structural violence." Almost all conflict and peace researchers would agree that these three aspects of political violence are closely linked: structural violence is a major cause of civil violence, while state violence is both a common response to civil violence and a stimulus to intensified opposition.

Measures of various aspects of political violence have been used to compare civil conflict across regions and over time. Data for the 1950–1980 period show that Western and most Third World democracies have widespread protest but little rebellion or state violence and few conflict deaths. By con-

(cont. on p. 677)

POLITICAL PARTIES AND PARTY COMPETITION.

Although political parties play key roles in organizing the politics of the world, finding a definition that captures all of them while distinguishing them from other groups is a difficult task. As we shall see, parties take different forms under different kinds of political systems, and their degree of importance varies greatly, from nation to nation, from party to party, and from time to time. They may be of any size and any (or no) ideological persuasion. They may appeal only to the most narrow segment of the electorate, or assume the form of a "catch-all party," which tries to do what its name implies. Their internal organization may be democratic or authoritarian. Because they are networks, composed of individuals who enter and leave more or less at will, their boundaries are constantly shifting. They use a wide range of campaign techniques. Sometimes they control the work of government, singly or in coalition with one another, and sometimes they have no effective control even over their own elected representatives. The general public may hold them in admiration or contempt, or an ambivalent blend of both. They perform important functions—structuring the vote, recruiting leaders, organizing and carrying out political campaigns, and formulating (and sometimes carrying out) programs of government—yet interest groups, the media, and independent candidates often perform these same functions as well or better.

What, then, is a political party? The one safe definition is: parties are political organizations that nominate candidates for public office under their own names. This definition does not tell very much about parties and their infinite variety, but it applies to all parties and only to parties. (When an interest group runs a candidate for office under its own name, it becomes, at least temporarily, a political party, and when a political organization consistently fails to nominate candidates, it ceases to be a party.)

The Origins of Parties. As the nation-state gained *power and permanence in Europe beginning in the fifteenth century, that power became ever more centralized in the hands of monarchs. Since even the most autocratic leaders require a certain measure of advice and consent, monarchs commonly set up advisory councils composed of the higher and more trusted members of the nobility and the clergy. These councils, precursory legislatures, steadily gained in power, and eventually became elected legislatures, although at first the franchise was limited to a very narrow elite. Within these bodies, groups, commonly called "factions," formed around key leaders or families to struggle for their control. Such groups were the progenitors of parties.

True parties did not appear until the nineteenth century. The expansion of suffrage in such nations as France, Britain, and the United States forced those who sought election to parliament—or, in the United States, to Congress and the presidency—to seek support outside the government in order to win reelection to it. External organizations were created and gradually assumed lives of their own, independent of those who had established them. At this point, the modern political party had been born.

Once those in office saw the need for parties to keep them in office, those not in office began to see parties as a possible way to get there. Organization bred counterorganization, and by the end of the nineteenth century the mass membership party was born, a kind of party composed (at least at first) of outsiders rather than insiders, and depending less on the personal wealth and "natural aristocracy" of its leaders than on the force of numbers, good organization, and an effective system for collecting dues.

In the earliest days of party politics, new parties tended to form around the structured cleavages of the time: rural vs. urban, church vs. state, center vs. periphery, employers vs. workers (Lipset and Rokkan, 1967). The parties thus formed—and the electorates that gave them their support—tended to endure even when the cleavages themselves weakened or disappeared (Lipset and Rokkan, 1967; Stefano Bartolini and Peter Mair, *Identity, Competition and Electoral Availability*, Cambridge, U.K., 1990).

Today, however, although Labor parties still exist and often take power (Piven, 1992), new parties are less likely to be based on social cleavages, such as class or religion, and even ethnic parties are usually small and incapable of taking power. Parties today have a variety of origins. Some, such as green parties fighting for better protection of the environment, stem from differences of opinion on contemporary issues. Others grow out of disagreements among *elites that matter little to a general public more concerned with the struggle for survival—the multitude of new parties in Eastern and Central Europe after the fall of communism offered many examples of this kind of party (Lawson, Rommele, and Karasimeonov, 1999). Yet others form in response to the ambitions and resources of their leaders, in a raw quest for power, as in the republics of the former Soviet Union.

Such origins are unlikely to lead to parties as stable as their predecessors. However, the older parties are themselves changing rapidly, even when the names remain the same. Such change is especially apparent in the larger catch-all parties, such as the major British and American parties, which constantly seek to redesign their coalitions to meet the shifting interests of potential majorities, but the formerly stable parties of multiparty regimes have also often been forced to adjust or cede power to new organizations (Kay Lawson and Peter Merkl, eds., *When Parties Fail*, Princeton, N.J., 1988).

A nation's electoral system is another factor that helps to determine what kind of parties a nation will have—and how many of them there will be (Arend Lijphart, *Electoral Systems and Party Systems*, Oxford, 1994). Where nations are divided for election purposes into single-member districts and all it takes to win is a plurality of the vote, smaller parties tend to drop out and a two- or three-party system is likely to evolve. Where the districts are larger and multimember, with each party represented according to its strength (the system known as proportional representation), smaller parties are motivated to keep contesting, and a multiparty system is more likely (Duverger, 1959). Single-member districts with runoff elections, as in France, fall in between: the supporters of the smaller parties can use the electoral process and the bargaining power of their votes on the second round to win important concessions, but the control of public office remains in the hands of the major parties.

The Organization of Parties. Key questions regarding how parties are organized include how democratic the party is, what rewards it provides its most active members, how factional or cohesive it is, and where exactly it begins and ends—its *boundaries* (Katz and Mair, 1994; Lawson, 1994).

Internal party democracy is impossible, according to Roberto Michels, who proclaimed the "Iron Law of Oligarchy": every organization, including political parties, is ruled by a narrow few. Organizations must have speed and efficiency to be effective, members are lazy and hero-worshipping, and leaders always become certain of their own indispensability; these three factors make oligarchical rule inevitable, even when parties are formed by persons strongly committed to democratic procedures (*Political Parties*, New York, 1959; first English version 1915).

Others agree. Samuel Eldersveld (*Political Parties. Behavioral Analysis*, New York, 1964) has argued that U.S. parties are characterized by *stratarchy*: layers of oligarchies consisting of the independent fiefdoms of machine politics loosely connected to equally elite-controlled state and national organizations. (Never mind that David Mayhew demonstrated more recently that only thirteen states ever really had machines worthy of the name in his *Placing Parties in American Politics*, Princeton, N.J., 1986.) Others have found the same phenomenon in parties throughout the world; despite the important role parties play in democracies (Arthur Lipow, *Political Parties and Democracy*, London, 1996), they themselves rarely observe the rules of democratic governance.

Even if parties are almost always commanded by a few, the relationships party activists have with those few vary greatly, and depend on what rewards the party seeks for itself and for its followers. Newer parties may offer their active members the chance to take part in formulating programs and choosing candidates, as well as working for electoral victory. Older and more established parties tend to be more pragmatic, seeking the rewards of power for their own sake and offering activists a share of the patronage that will become available with success. The demands of the modern campaign mean that parties everywhere rely less on traditional activists, and more on donors who give generously in return for special access or specific promises of aid for their causes or companies. Key members of the party organization thus become its leaders, experts, and donors, not its rank and file activists.

Another question regarding party organization is the extent, durability, and institutionalization of factions. As V. O. Key, Jr., demonstrated in his classic study, *Southern Politics* (New York, 1949), the more secure a party's hold on power, the more likely it is to be riven by faction. The Japanese Liberal Democratic Party and the Italian Christian Democratic Party (until its downfall) are the two examples most often cited outside the United States, but any large, relatively successful party may exhibit such divisions. Factions in pragmatic American parties tend to be transient and variable; those in more programmatic organizations, such as European Socialist parties, are normally longer-lived and better institutionalized.

Another characteristic of the party as organization is its lack of fixed boundaries. Unlike most other organizations, parties can never quite say who or what they are. Frank Sorauf pointed out in *Party Politics in America* (Boston, 1984) that a party is always supplemented by "the party in the electorate" (non-activist voting supporters) and "the party in government" (its elected representatives). Mildred Schwartz shows (in *The Party Network*, Madison, Wis., 1990) how shifting and indeterminate the nature of that supplement can be. The ever-varying activities of members, elected representatives, interest group representatives, and major campaign donors make any party less a fixed entity than an ever-changing *network*.

Parties at Work. The work of political parties in authoritarian systems is relatively simple: normally placed in office by a combination of military and demagogic power, ruling parties in such systems try to keep their supporters in line (sometimes coercively, sometimes clientelistically, usually with a combination of stick and carrot) and to carry out the work of government as directed by other agents with greater power (the military, the demagogue and his personal entourage, sometimes a combination of both). They are the shield of power and its instrument. The domination of parties by others in such regimes is not changed merely by the creation of an apparently competitive multiparty system. Clever autocrats in Peru, the Sudan, and Uganda (among others) have found ways to maintain themselves firmly in power while permitting minor parties to form; military control reigns over multiparty regimes as it did over single-party systems in Ecuador, El Salvador, and Paraguay (among others). Counting the number of parties no longer is sufficient to identify the nature of a regime.

The work of parties in democratic systems can also be simply stated—they must place their representatives in the elective positions of government and try to run that government according to the plans they made before achieving office—but such work is, as we note below, much more difficult to carry out.

Parties in Campaigns. In authoritarian systems, campaigns and elections are heavily controlled. Parties may work hard to drum up enthusiastic response, but the outcome is rarely in doubt and when surprises occur, further coups d'état are usually in the offing.

In democratic systems, the nature of the political campaign has come full circle. The earliest campaigns were created by candidates, not parties; so are many of today's. Mass communications technology has not only made it easier to reach the electorate but has also placed greater emphasis on the personal characteristics of the candidates, a phenomenon that empowers candidates at the expense of their parties.

In the United States this has come to mean more reliance by candidates on their own organizations and less on the parties, whose labels are wrested from them via hard-fought primary battles, after which the winners conduct the general election contest, using but not relying exclusively on whatever aid the parties can provide. In Europe, where campaign costs are reduced by public funding, normally funneled through the parties, and by the provision of free media time, candidates are less likely to separate themselves so thoroughly from their parties: rather than replace them, strong candidates take them over (examples include Jacques Chirac and the Rassemblement pour la République in France, Tony Blair and the Labour Party in Britain). In such cases, the party remains a powerful force, but is at the beck and call of its currently most powerful candidate.

The tactics of modern campaigns, whether conducted by party or candidate or both, have changed dramatically, and this development also affects the parties, placing ever greater power in the hands of their hired experts. Trained political consultants develop computerized lists for every purpose, gather poll data, and target audiences for the receipt of appropriate messages by television, radio, telephone, or mail. They train candidates (and their surrogates, such as family members or running mates) to perform well in all the new tasks of campaigning. Above all, if campaign costs are not limited by law and/or covered by public financing, they raise the funds to pay for all these activities, including their own salaries (Gary W. Selnow, *High-Tech Campaigns: Computer Technology in Political Communication,* Westport, Conn., 1994). This new style of campaigning appeared first in the United States, but parties throughout the modern world are rapidly being forced to face the same demands.

Parties in Government. The role parties play in government also varies from system to system. With some simplification, we may say that the key differences are whether the system is authoritarian or democratic; if democratic, whether the constitutional system is presidential or parliamentary; and if par-liamentary, whether there are many parties or few and the relative strength of each.

In authoritarian systems, where the general population takes little or no part in collective decision-making, the ruling elite often employs a party to organize its control. Subordinate but significant careers are made by joining that party, by becoming a candidate (certain of victory in a single-party system), and by carrying out the mandates of its leaders in the offices of government. In such systems, the role of the party man or woman in government has been largely indistinguishable from that of obedient bureaucrat.

Parties play a stronger role in government in the world's democracies, particularly those with a parliamentary system. A presidential system, in which the chief executive has powers independent of the legislature, poses difficult problems for parties seeking to govern. Directly elected presidents are former candidates who have succeeded in dominating their parties and winning election in the largest possible single-member district, the nation at large. Such an accomplishment is seldom conducive to humility, or to accepting the restraints of party discipline. Once in office, presidents commonly use the power of their mandates to reinterpret their parties' programs as they wish. They are more likely to be limited by the strength of the partisan opposition, especially when it controls the legislature, than by the disapproval of their fellow partisans. Furthermore, even when government is not divided in presidential systems, the willingness of the legislators of the president's party to use their power to restrain the chief executive in the name of the party's program is likely to depend on the extent of their own commitment to that program, the party's control over their chances for renomination to candidacy in winnable constituencies, and the party's ability to provide them with campaign funding. In the United States, the first is uncertain and the second is all but eliminated by the combination of primary elections and the high rate of incumbency reelection (normally 98 or 99 percent). The parties do provide significant campaign funding, but this alone cannot guarantee a high measure of compliance with the party's program when the president has other priorities to pursue.

A democratic parliamentary system provides a much stronger arena for political parties determined to carry out their programs, especially when one party is able to win a majority of the seats in the lower house. In such a system "parliament is sovereign" and the majority party is the party that rules. Yet even then the party *qua* party may be hardpressed to take a directing role in governmental affairs. The party ostensibly in power is limited by the tendency of that power to concentrate first in the hands of its own elected leadership, particularly the prime minister, and secondly in those of civil servants who know only too well how to circumvent the election-driven demands of probably transient politicians.

A party may temporarily wrest power back by changing its leadership, as the Conservatives did in the United Kingdom in 1990, but victory is likely to be short-lived if the new leader comes to feel sure of popular backing for the party's continued dominance: the Ironic Law of parliamentary party politics is that the greater the party's electoral success, the weaker it itself will be vis-à-vis its leadership.

Parliamentary elections do not always produce a majority for a single party, particularly if a system of proportional representation is used (see above). Although proportional representation has the important advantage of permitting each party to win seats much more proportionate to its strength in the electorate than is possible in winner-take-all systems, it can also sometimes give small parties a greater share of power (though not of seats) than would seem warranted. Forming a majority coalition may require compromises with small parties either of the center or the political fringe (Ian Budge and Hans Keman, *Parties and Democracy: Coalition Formation and Government Functioning in Twenty States*, Oxford, 1990, and Michael Laver and Norman Schofield, *Multiparty Government: The Politics of Coalition in Europe*, Oxford, 1990). Such results have led many parliamentary systems (Germany and Italy, for example) to adopt mixed electoral systems, awarding a certain share of seats in the legislature on the basis of plurality election (thereby strengthening the likelihood of a strong majority), and the rest on the basis of proportional representation (thereby ensuring the presence of minor parties that have won at least a certain percentage—usually five percent—of the vote).

The role of parties in government is slowly moving beyond the nation-state. Although parties have been quintessentially national in origin and practice, international processes of regionalization and globalization are having their effect: when power calls, parties listen and respond. John Gaffney (ed., *Political Parties and the European Union*, London, 1996) and Simon Hix and Christopher Lord (1997) have begun to document the slow but steady movement of party politics into the governance of the European Union.

Decline and Continuity. Originating in faction, thriving on contention, checked by constitutional and statutory law as well as by the strength of opposing forces, taken over by candidates contemptuous of their paltry offerings, and betrayed by the weakness and/or corruption of their own leadership, parties have found it difficult not only to govern as they have promised, but to maintain a credible role of any kind in modern polities. Public opinion polls show a greater disdain for parties and party politicians than ever before, while voters seem never to have been less willing to state a party affiliation or, having stated one, to vote consistently.

Nevertheless, the answer to whether or not parties are in decline is not a simple one. There is, for one thing, some evidence that the decline may have bottomed out, as rates of affiliation and evaluation scores tend to stabilize. More significantly, the parties themselves continue to function regardless of popular discontent with their performance. Old parties refuse to die, although names, tactics, and even ideologies may all be changed. Renascent subnationalism and increasing global interdependence serve not to stymie but rather to stimulate the creation of new parties, as new nations, or nations new to democracy, automatically channel their battles over policy, ideology, and the very shape of government into the parties they hasten to create, and transnational parties are formed to match the larger boundaries of supranationalism. Nothing seems to stop the parties; they endure and even prosper.

What accounts for the durability of the political party? Perhaps the same thing that accounts for its variability. If human beings are to live at all comfortably, some form of association to which all cede a share of their personal sovereignty is required. Yet the very institutionalization of government is a process that cuts it off from the common man and woman and makes of it something alien, threatening, distant, strange. Some way must be found to reach out to government, to keep it in touch with the rest of us, even, in democracies, to make it do our bidding. Some way must be found for those in government to reach out to us, to let us know what they have been doing and why, and to get from us expressions of support that permit them to count on our compliance. Parties are the organizations we have invented for those purposes. We disdain them and misuse them, we allow others to use them as instruments of corruption and tyranny, we try to ignore them and we pretend their day is over. Yet nevertheless, again and again, we find we cannot do without them. If we did not have political parties, we would no doubt invent them tomorrow.

(See also AUTHORITARIANISM; CHRISTIAN DEMOCRACY; DEMOCRACY; ELECTIONS AND VOTING BEHAVIOR; PARLIAMENTARY DEMOCRACY; POLITICAL MACHINE; POLITICAL PARTICIPATION.)

Maurice Duverger, *Political Parties* (New York, 1959). Seymour Lipset and Stein Rokkan, eds., *Party Systems and Voter Alignments* (New York, 1967). Frances Fox Piven, *Labor Parties in Postindustrial Societies* (New York, 1992). Richard S. Katz and Peter Mair, eds., *How Parties Organize: Change and Adaptation in Party Organizations in Western Democracies* (London, 1994). Kay Lawson, ed., *How Political Parties Work: Perspectives from Within* (Westport, Conn., 1994). Alan Ware, *Political Parties and Party Systems* (Oxford, 1996). Simon Hix and Christopher Lord, *Political Parties in the European Union* (1997). Piero Ignazi and Colette Ysmal, eds., *The Organization of Political Parties in Southern Europe* (Westport, Conn., 1998). Kay Lawson, Andrea Rommele, and Georgi Karasimeonov, eds., *Cleavages, Parties, and Voters: Studies from Bulgaria, the Czech Republic, Hungary, Poland, and Romania* (Westport, Conn., 1999).

KAY LAWSON

POLITICAL SCIENCE. Political science is an academic discipline that focuses on the study of government and politics, broadly defined. Its concerns include the formal organization and operations of governments, the clash of power and values that is politics, and the processes of authoritative decision making and the administration of public policies. The discipline embraces both normative theories about the nature of justice, freedom, and good governance, and the empirical study of actual institutions and practices. At its most fundamental level political science can be said to be the study of power and the distribution of values in societies and among nations. In the famous words of Harold D. Lasswell, a founder of the modern discipline, political science is the study of "Who gets what, when, and how."

Political science has deep roots in classical Western civilization, going back to the ancient Greeks. Plato's *Republic* was the earliest deductive work in political philosophy that addressed the question of what constitutes an ideal government, and Aristotle's *Politics* was the first inductive study of types of political systems. The philosophical tradition of political theory was further advanced during the Middle Ages by St. Augustine and St. Thomas Aquinas, and then by Machiavelli and Hobbes during the Renaissance, and Locke and Rousseau with the Enlightenment. In Europe the break from speculative political philosophy came in the nineteenth century with legal institutional studies and the emerging of political sociology, as in the works of Jeremy Bentham, John Stuart Mill, Karl *Marx, Emile Durkheim, and Max *Weber.

It was, however, in the United States that political science took on its modern form as a discipline concerned with the "scientific" study of politics. It was in American universities, and particularly at the University of Chicago in the 1930s and 1940s, that the discipline adopted rigorous methods in both concept formation and quantitative testing. In striving to become more scientific the discipline sharpened the distinction between fact and value, between what is and what ought to be, between objective analysis of cause and effect, on the one hand, and what should be preferred as most desirable, on the other hand. In this process of becoming systematically empirical, political science opened its doors to welcome the concepts, theories, methods, and findings of the other social sciences. It took, for example, from sociology survey research methods for measuring attitudes and *public opinion, from psychology knowledge about individual and group behavior, from anthropology the concept of culture, and from economics theories for *political economy and *rational choice theory. This development, which is usually referred to as the "behavioral revolution," gave to political science a distinctive American stamp, not only because the American political scene was the overwhelming object of study, but also because the dramatic growth of political science took place in the United States, with the result that now nearly ninety percent of all political scientists are either Americans or American trained.

The behavioral revolution created divisions within the discipline between those practitioners inclined toward the social sciences and those tending to the humanities, such as history and philosophy. By the mid-twentieth century the discipline was beginning to fragment into numerous distinct subfields, and it was losing its core base that political theory and philosophy once provided. For a time the key subfields were political philosophy, methodology, American politics, public administration, *comparative politics, *international relations, and political economy. There has, however, been an explosion of subfields, driven by both subject matter and methods of analysis. In part the discipline has been pulled in new directions because of newsworthy developments. Thus, for example, the emergence of the new states of the Third World produced the subfield of *political development; the Cold War and nuclear weapons generated defense studies and arms control; problems in the advanced industrial societies led to specialization on *welfare issues. But subfields also emerged out of intellectual developments as, for example, the adoption of concepts from psychology spurred political psychology, anthropology stimulated the study of *political cultures, and microeconomics inspired formal theory and the rational choice approach. Further diversity came about when what had once been contained in the field of American politics was expanded to take on a comparative perspective. The result was the emergence of such subfields as political party systems, comparative legislative behavior, *federalism, polling, and elections. The American Political Science Association, the professional organization of the discipline, now uses ninety-nine specialization designations for classifying its members, and its annual meetings are organized according to forty-four divisions representing different specializations.

Although the process of fragmentation has created something of an identity problem for the discipline, it is also a sign of intellectual vitality. The discipline has experienced sustained growth even as there have been rises and falls in the popularity of different subfields, so that today there are 127 Ph.D. training programs in political science in American universities. Most people trained in political science seek careers as professors in the discipline, but many others go on to government service or work at research centers and foundations, or become consultants and advisors.

Behind all of the diversity, political scientists generally share a common interest in politics, which means an interest in both individual and collective behavior with respect to the play of power and decision making. Indeed, almost all forms of political analysis are based on implicit or explicit assumptions about human nature, on the one hand, and the operations of society, on the other. This means that all political analysis must incorporate, with varying degrees of sophistication, both psychological and sociological concepts. It uses psychological concepts when the need is to understand the actions and attitudes of individuals, whether as leaders or followers and citizens. Sociological concepts are needed for explaining collective behavior, whether that of small groups or the nation-state, or even the international system as a whole.

The behavioral approach was based on a logical positivistic philosophy of science, which was strongly empirical and in which the unit of analysis was the actions of human agents, making decisions to advance their values. The focus of analysis is thus on the clash of interests, and on the fact that power is always a critical factor in politics. In this perspective, the tradition of analyzing historical developments in terms of impersonal social, economic, or political "forces" had to be refined and made more precise by recognizing that in theory there must always be some particular individuals involved in any historical process. There was thus a break from the legalistic tradition of analyzing institutions, such as the state, as abstractions. The behavioral approach sought to look behind the formal institutions and identify what the particular actors were doing. Thus for example, instead of stopping with the identification of the theoretical ideals of *democracy, the approach focused on the role of parties and interest groups and the cross-pressures that politicians constantly experience.

The behavioral movement was exceptionally fruitful in advancing knowledge about American voting behavior. The main theories about voting practices were developed at the University of Michigan's Survey Research Center. Initially the studies focused on finding correlations between voting patterns and such demographic and sociological variables as age, socioeconomic class, sex, religion, and *ethnicity. Increasingly it became necessary to introduce more psychological and political considerations, such as party identification, belief systems, and issue orientations. In time, however, it became apparent that by going to the extreme in trying to measure the motivations and the psychological predispositions of individuals, researchers were collecting more information than went into actual voting behavior. The result has been a return to a greater appreciation of the role of institutions, such as political parties, in constricting choice and thus giving concentrated focus to voting decisions. People can only vote in response to the issues raised by the candidates and the parties, and not according to all that go into their psychological makeup and belief systems.

This retreat from extreme behavioralism also took place in the development of structural-functionalism as a method of comparing political systems. The emergence of over 100 new states after World War II and the ending of Western colonialism created a major problem for the discipline because most of the new entities lacked the stable institutions of government common to the more established states. There was also often a large gap between form and substance in power arrangements. One major theoretical approach for meeting this challenge was the creation of an analytically abstract functional model of what constitutes a political system. It was posited that all political systems by definition are composed of a particular set of interacting functions, which can be performed in different ways and by different structures or institutions. The functions ranged from socializing people into the political culture, articulating interests, formulating rules, and dispensing justice. Systems could thus be compared according to how and by whom each function was being carried out. Thus, in some systems the lawmaking function might be performed by an elected legislature, in another by the leadership of the single party that monopolized power, and in still another by a council of elders or a hereditary ruler.

Since the structural-functional model of a political system was developed to meet the problems posed by the emerging new nations, the approach was usually associated with modernization theory that sought to contrast traditional and modern systems. It was assumed that there was a range of "modern" ways for performing the functions that were different from "traditional" practices. Political development thus involved the institutionalization of increasingly specialized structures for performing the functions. One of the advantages of the functional model was that it highlighted the fact that although in theory it might be possible to contrast sharply "modern" and "traditional" categories, in actual practice even the most traditional system usually had some "modern" forms and practices, and modern systems generally have some elements of the "traditional."

By the 1980s there was a further retreat from extreme behavioralism with the "bring back the state" movement and the development of what was called "new institutionalism." This development focused on the impact that state authority can have on historical processes of political development. At the same time another significant and related innovation was the rise of rational choice and formal theory. This was an approach which took as its model microeconomic theory and asserted that the political actions of individuals and institutions could best be analyzed by presuming that they would always seek to maximize their self-interest in competition with the interests of others. The rational choice school did gain great favor in the discipline, but over time it became apparent that political behavior cannot generally be simplified to the degree that market operations can be in economics. Rather in political science it is necessary to identify the sources and character of preferences and to note how strongly different values are held. Political behavior is not limited to the domain of rationality but is sensitive to cultural differences and the play of emotions.

A persistent problem in making political science more scientific has been that for many questions there are not enough examples or cases to make statistically significant analysis. This has been an especially troublesome problem for comparative politics, given the limited number of countries, especially when they are divided according to any useful typology. Much of the best work on many areas of the world has been done by area specialists who are not centrally concerned with more general comparative theory building. Some comparativists have, however, sought to overcome this problem by showing how single case studies can be formulated so as to test more general hypotheses, and thereby provide significant generalizations and hypotheses that can be tested in future case studies involving other countries.

Possibly the most serious obstacle to advancing the scientific character of political science has been the tradition of rewarding novelty and not the testing of hypotheses suggested by others. There has consequently been little accumulation of findings, as is basic to the growth of any science, but instead there has been a constant race to produce new "paradigms." In subfield after subfield progress in testing any particular theory or model is quickly abandoned as attention is diverted to new formulations. Thus instead of an accumulation of knowledge, progress in the discipline has been marked by shifting fads and fashions.

Political science, like most of the social sciences, went through a phase of radical self-criticism during the 1960s in which critics charged that the discipline's stance of "scientific objectivity" was in fact an ideological mask that implicitly, and maybe intentionally, advanced the interests of the status quo and, by extension, the interests of the United States. With the collapse of the Soviet Union and of communism more generally, this criticism was abated and replaced by a rise in interest in problems of transitions to democracy. The traditional interest of political philosophy in the ideals and practices of democracy had to be expanded to include more dynamic theories about the processes for building democracies. Much research went into exploring the relationship of democracy to economic conditions and institutions. It was often hard for some scholars to separate factual analysis from ideological preferences when it came to the question of the relationship of democracy to free market economies. In a related development the failure of political science to foresee the sudden end of the Cold War and the demise of the Soviet empire raised troublesome questions about the quality of international relations theories and accuracy of what had been presumed to have been solid knowledge about world politics.

In the late 1990s there was also a rise in interest about the political consequences of economic *globalization and the information and communications revolutions. The state was seen as coming increasingly under siege from international forces that set limits on domestic policy choices. At the same time, however, the state was being challenged internally by the emergence of ethnic and other forms of identity politics, such as multiculturalism in the United States and fundamentalist religious movements in some other countries. These domestic developments challenged a common assumption in much of political science that the movement of history toward democracy would also produce more secular and rationally oriented societies. Within the discipline there was also a new debate over whether the advanced industrial societies might not be evolving toward a postmaterialistic form of politics. Survey researchers were discovering that in these societies people were less concerned about the traditional political issues relating to material well-being and were becoming more identified with cultural issues, such as abortion, sexual orientation, the environment, and human rights.

A final fundamental division among political scientists is that between those who engage in applied policy research and those who follow more theoretical interests; a difference comparable to that between applied science, or engineering, and pure science. Although both approaches share a great deal of basic knowledge, there are some significant differences. Political scientists with policy interests must employ what has been called manipulative analysis; that is, they must concentrate on variables that policy makers can readily influence by their actions. They will seek to explain the likely consequences of different policy choices and to warn those in responsible positions of impending developments that should be guarded against. In contrast, those engaged in more academic research will center their analyses on the more constant and enduring factors that constitute the defining parameters of the problem under study. Although less concerned with immediate policy issues, such research does provide the underpinning knowledge that will be useful for subsequent applied work.

This relationship between applied and more academic research points to the basic fact that the creative force within the discipline of political science is the interaction between real world developments and academic advances in theory and methodology. The discipline thus has no set boundaries, but rather it is in a constant state of scientific growth and change, even as it also strives to preserve the best of humanistic knowledge.

(See also CLASS AND POLITICS; MODERNIZATION; POLITICAL PARTIES AND PARTY COMPETITION; RELIGION AND POLITICS.)

Gabriel A. Almond, *A Discipline Divided* (Newbury Park, Calif., 1990). Ada Finifter, ed., *The State of Discipline II* (Washington, D.C., 1993). Herbert Weisberg, ed., *Political Science: The Science of Politics* (New York, 1986).

LUCIAN W. PYE

trast, the autocratic regimes of Africa, Asia, and the Middle East tend to have high levels of state violence, rebellion, and many conflict deaths. Until the late 1980s the socialist states were largely successful in inhibiting both protest and rebellion. On the rare occasions when domestic resistance did occur it was suppressed with intense state violence, as happened in Hungary in 1956 and China in 1989. After elected governments were established in Eastern Europe and the Soviet successor states their patterns of political conflict and violence increasingly resembled those of the more turbulent Western democracies. Deadly spirals of rebellion and repression took place in the former Yugoslavia and the Caucasus, but in most post-communist states protest became far more common than violent rebellion and repression.

The most deadly types of political violence are civil wars and government-sponsored campaigns of mass murder. Since World War II more than fifty episodes of genocide and politicide (political mass murder) have occurred, for example in Tibet (1959), Guatemala (1966–1984), and Rwanda (1994). Most victims have been unarmed civilian members of ethnic and religious groups, classes, or political parties that were targeted for elimination by authorities. During the last half of the twentieth century far more people, many of them women and children, have died in civil wars and mass murder than were killed in all international wars in that era. In 1998, 86 armed conflicts with more than 100 fatalities per year were being fought within states. In the sixteen most serious of these civil wars more than 80,000 people died; since these wars began, their cumulative fatalities were about 5 million.

Serious international repercussions often follow from political violence. Most of the world's 21 million refugees and asylum seekers in 1999 were fleeing from civil wars and politicides. Political violence also provokes military *intervention. During the Cold War the United States provided military support or combat units for governments or rebels in eighteen civil wars, the Soviet Union in fourteen. In East Bengal (1971), Cambodia (1977), Uganda (1968), and Liberia (1990–1996) episodes of mass murder triggered military intervention by neighboring countries or regional alliances. Because of the potentially destabilizing effects of political violence the major powers, regional organizations, and the UN have given increasing attention to mediation and peacekeeping in civil conflict situations. Perhaps as a result, by the late 1990s more civil wars were being settled and globally the numbers of fatalities and refugees had begun to decline.

(See also REVOLUTION.)

Carnegie Commission on Preventing Deadly Conflict, *Preventing Deadly Conflict: Final Report with Executive Summary* (New York, 1997). Peter Wallensteen and Margarita Sollenberg, "Armed Conflicts, Conflict Termination and Peace Agreements, 1989–1996." *Journal of Peace Research* 34, no. 3 (1997): 339–358. *World Conflict Map 1996*, Interdisciplinary Research Program on Causes of Human Rights Violations, Leiden University (Leiden, 1997).

TED ROBERT GURR

POPULATION POLICY. A population policy aims to act on one or more of the major demographic variables—fertility, mortality, and migration—to influence the rate of growth, size, distribution, or composition of a human population or subpopulation. Interventions under a population policy consciously seek to address demographic objectives, including measures to affect marriage and childbearing, nutrition and health, rural and urban development, and internal or external migration. Demographic objectives are themselves generally linked with larger collective goals such as economic growth, improved social welfare and quality of life, and environmental protection. This definition of population policy would exclude a policy that has unintended demographic consequences. Because health and migration traditionally have been accepted spheres of government involvement even without explicit demographic objectives, population policy as it emerged in the mid-twentieth century most often refers to measures designed to influence birth rates and therefore the size and growth rate of a population.

As far back as Plato, the social implications of changes in population size and growth rates have captured the attention of intellectuals in both the Western and non-Western worlds. Much of the debate has revolved around propositions such as those advanced by Thomas Robert Malthus in *An Essay on the Principle of Population* (1798). Malthus contended that population growth inevitably outstrips the land and resources available to support additional people. Although Malthus himself did not advocate interventions other than individual "moral restraint," his intellectual descendants have used variations of his argument in advocating for policies to limit fertility. In a direct challenge to Malthus, Karl *Marx argued in *Das Kapital* (1883) that the emergence of a surplus labor force, and, hence, "overpopulation," was a consequence of the capitalist mode of production. Other social thinkers, economists, and eugenicists prior to World War II expressed concerns about population trends. These concerns tended to stay out of the forefront of public attention, however, due to the slow pace of population change and the relative infeasibility of policy interventions.

It was not until the 1940s, when death rates in developing countries were declining rapidly in response to improved nutrition and health conditions, that the idea of public policies to induce a corresponding decline in birth rates gained many adherents. In 1952, newly independent India was the first country to adopt a national population policy explicitly aimed at reducing fertility through the promotion of family planning. Other Asian countries, such as Pakistan and the Republic of Korea (South Korea), were among the first to follow India's example in the 1960s in the belief that they could thereby improve their economic prospects. The trend soon took hold, and as of 1994, governments from eighty-three countries, representing every region of the developing world, reported to the UN that they have policies to lower fertility levels in their countries.

Explanations for the widespread adoption of population policies in recent decades include growing knowledge of population trends in all societies through periodic censuses and demographic analyses; the dominance of ideologies of state intervention in the economy and the institutionalization of development planning; improvements in contraceptive technologies, especially since the early 1960s; and, in most countries, the weakening influence of religious opposition to family planning. International cooperation involving the United Nations Population Fund (UNFPA), other parts of the UN system, development aid agencies, and private organizations has also played a critical role in assisting many developing countries to initiate population policies and programs. After 1965, the government of the United States became the leading supporter of this cooperation, although increasingly joined by other donors, developing countries, and, since 1990, countries of Eastern Europe and the former Soviet Union. U.S. support has essentially been maintained over the past three decades, while sensitive to changing leadership in the executive branch and Congress as well as to the influences of domestic groups concerned with family planning, abortion, women's health, and the environment.

National policies built around active promotion of family planning have been shown to have contributed significantly to fertility declines in a number of countries, including Mexico, Thailand, and Indonesia. In still other countries where family planning programs have been active, including Bangladesh, Kenya, and Egypt, relatively high levels of contraceptive use have now been achieved nationwide. As a result, population growth rates in these countries have moderated. Yet growth rates exceeding 2 percent annually remain typical of most developing countries, and globally, about 80 million people are added to the total population each year. The country with the strongest fertility reduction policy is the People's Republic of China. Most analysts agree that the policy explains much of the dramatic decline observed in birth rates in China since the early 1970s. In 1978, the government announced a "one-child policy," which has been at times rigorously enforced. Exceptions to the policy are permitted, although accusations of *human rights violations continue.

Many countries have been reexamining their population policies since the International Conference on Population and Development (ICPD), a global UN conference held in Cairo in 1994. Responding to an unprecedented mobilization of non-governmental organizations (NGOs) at ICPD, especially women's NGOs, governments determined that population policies should start with respect for the individual and be free of discrimination, coercion, and violence. The ICPD Program of Action called for a comprehensive approach to global population stabilization, focusing on universal access to family planning and other reproductive health services. The comprehensive approach included efforts to educate women and achieve gender equality and to address a wide range of sustainable development goals, including reducing the high levels of consumption in developed countries.

In India, following ICPD, quantitative fertility targets, once a central feature of the national family planning program, have been dropped. India and other countries have also broadened their family planning efforts to encompass other reproductive health needs of women. A number of countries are giving greater attention to male participation in reproductive health as well as to young people ages ten to twenty-four, who now constitute one-third of the world's population. Community-based approaches focusing on women's empowerment are increasing. Beyond the impact of ICPD, trends in many countries toward more mixed economies, democratization, and decentralization of government also place new constraints on formal national population policies—although these trends may indirectly contribute to fertility decline.

On the other side of the equation, policies to raise birth rates were adopted even before the end of World War II by some countries in Europe, including the Soviet Union, Germany under the Nazis, France, and Sweden. In Western Europe, family allowances and other benefits have been designed primarily as welfare measures, with pronatalist objectives ambiguous or absent, and with little long-term impact on fertility. In Eastern and Central Europe, in addition to positive incentives to raise fertility, some governments have restricted access to contraception and abortion. These measures were carried to their harshest extreme in Romania from the late 1960s until the communist party state was overthrown in 1989.

Currently, pressures for more pronatalist policies in some countries of Europe and the former Soviet Union are stimulated by fears about the consequences of sustained fertility rates significantly below replacement levels, including population aging and declining population size. Overall, twenty-one governments reported to the UN in 1994 that they have policies to raise fertility. Another twenty-nine governments have policies under which they actively seek to maintain current fertility rates.

On the international level, alignments on population policy no longer follow East-West or North-South splits, as in earlier periods. Consensus exists on policies to facilitate universal access to contraception. However, among countries dominated by conservative Catholic or Islamic religious outlooks, strong opposition remains to key elements of post-ICPD population policies, including gender equality, responses to unsafe abortion, and other aspects of sexual and reproductive health. These unresolved issues, together with the continued momentum of population growth, ensure that population policies will remain controversial in world politics for the foreseeable future.

(See also DEVELOPMENT AND UNDERDEVELOPMENT; NORTH-SOUTH RELATIONS; REPRODUCTIVE POLITICS; WOMEN AND DEVELOPMENT.)

Gunnar Myrdal, *Asian Drama: An Inquiry into the Poverty of Nations*, 3 vols. (New York, 1968). Jason L. Finkle and C. Alison McIntosh, eds., *The New Politics of Population: Conflict and Consensus in Family Planning* (New York, 1994). Laurie Ann Mazur, ed., *Beyond the Numbers: A Reader on Population, Consumption, and the Environment* (Washington, D.C., 1994).

BARBARA B. CRANE

POPULISM. Populist movements claim to represent the people as a whole: sometimes the entire nation, sometimes the majority of the people. They often begin as movements of protest against parties which they see as entrenched defenders of the existing social order; if successful, they themselves end as parties. Radical versions of populism, sometimes right-wing, sometimes left, seek to represent and mobilize the poor or the underprivileged masses, though rural radical populists have often made common cause with what they see as their counterpart in the cities, organized labor.

Other populist movements, however, particularly agrarian-based ones, have mistrusted established parties of the Left, viewing them as defenders of the interests of organized urban workers only. Hostile to the city, these movements celebrate farmer or "peasant" values.

Yet other populist movements claim to represent a majority distributed across all social classes and other divisions. Finally, at its very loosest, the term has been applied to any political leader or movement able to mobilize support on a wide scale, for instance Margaret *Thatcher or Ronald *Reagan.

Historically, the term "populism" was used in the United States in the 1890s to describe the People's Party, the most powerful in a series of similar movements, such as the Grangers of the 1870s and 1880s, which sought to represent the interests of small farmers, especially in the West. Between 1860 and 1890, this sector nearly tripled in size. But their lives were governed by the industrialized East, which controlled the commodity markets, the prices that farmers had to pay for agricultural inputs, the banks they depended on for credit, the agencies that stored the grain, the grain exchanges that purchased it, and the railroads that transported it. The protracted depression of the last decades of the century drove farmers into politics: To them, the two major established political parties, the Democrats and the Republicans, between them, put the power of the state at the disposal of the dominant economic interest groups. In the 1892 presidential election, the People's Party polled a million votes. Four years later, in order to appeal to nonfarmers, the party platform was widened to include another populist theme pioneered by movements like the Greenbackers—monetary reform. The addition of "free silver" to its program brought the People's Party candidate in the 1896 presidential election, William Jennings Bryan, to within half a million votes of victory.

The second major movement to which the label "populist" has been applied was the *narodnichestvo* of tsarist Russia. This was not a movement of the peasantry so much as a movement about the peasantry, primarily on the part of intellectuals fired with the idealistic belief that the heart of Russian culture was the village, whose central institution was the communitarian system of landholding. Though capitalist relations were beginning to penetrate the countryside, the *Narodniki* believed not only that this process could be halted but that a new social order based on the egalitarian principles embodied in the village community could be brought into being at the level of the state as a whole. This *ideology, being anticapitalist, was unacceptable to those who, like Stolypin, were striving to bring into being a large new class of entrepreneurial peasants who would establish a solid base for capitalism in the countryside. It was equally unacceptable to *Lenin, who considered that capitalism was already well established in the countryside. The proletarianization of ex-peasants would inevitably lead them to ally themselves with the urban workers. In 1874, large numbers of young city intellectuals "went to the people," only to meet with incomprehension, mistrust, and even betrayal to the police. But in the years following World War I, the ideas of the *Narodniki* became a significant political force in several countries of Eastern Europe (Bulgaria, Poland, Romania) and peasant parties even came to power.

The dual hostility of populists to both capitalist "Big Business" and to "scientific" socialism also emerged in two movements in adjoining farming provinces of Canada between the two world wars. Both were responses to the depression of the 1930s, but the Cooperative Commonwealth Federation (CCF), which controlled the province of Saskatchewan until the post–World War II epoch, and Social Credit, in Alberta, were very different in orientation. The CCF not only brought grain-storage and agricultural supplies under provincial *parastatal agencies, but also organized insurance, transport, and much of general retail trade on a cooperative basis. Social Credit, by contrast, saw the solution to the province's problems in

the monetary nostrums of Major Douglas. Again, whereas Getúlio *Vargas of Brazil developed themes borrowed from Italian fascist *corporatism, in Argentina the much more radical Peronist movement—which still persists to this day—was based on organizing the mass of the poor urban workers into powerful trade unons. Their claim to represent the common people was expressed in Evita *Perón's idealization of the *descamisados*, the "shirtless ones."

By the 1960s, when nearly a score of new countries came into existence in black Africa, many observers saw resemblances between the ideologies of some of the new "single parties" and the older classical nineteenth-century and earlier twentieth-century populisms. These parties claimed to embody an authentic Africanness, a cultural distinctiveness rooted in village culture that had only been interrupted during the colonial era. The towns implanted by Europeans, the divisions between one African people and another fostered by colonialist policies of divide and rule through emphasizing tribal differences, and the Marxist conception of social class were all denounced as Western distortions. Instead, the populist parties in power dedicated themselves to "nation building," a modern restatement of a postulated traditional egalitarianism and solidarity of the village.

In the immediate euphoria of the post-independence period, these parties commanded widespread popularity. But as that power was used to eliminate opposition at all levels, and, in the case of Tanzania, to enforce *collectivization of the villages overnight, popular support withered. People now saw populist ideology simply as rhetoric disguising the monopolization of power by a new class which ruled because it controlled the political apparatus of the state.

Those disillusioned with populism have often shifted to a more class-based radicalism or, more commonly, to an ethnic-based opposition. Yet the populist ideal of a society run in the interests of the common people retains its appeal to a wide range of people.

(See also AUTHORITARIANISM; CLASS AND POLITICS; NEW SOCIAL MOVEMENTS; ONE-PARTY SYSTEM; PERÓN, JUAN DOMINGO.)

Ghita Ionescu and Ernest Gellner, eds., *Populism: Its Meanings and National Characteristics* (London, 1969). Margaret Canovan, *Populism* (London, 1981).

PETER WORSLEY

PORTUGAL. Having emerged in the twelfth century, Portugal is among the oldest polities in Europe. The Atlantic archipelagos of the Azores and Madeira were colonized in the fifteenth century, a prelude to 500 years of multicontinental imperialism. Mainland and islands cover 35,550 square miles (approx. 92,092 sq. km.), with a resident population in 1997 of 9,944,750.

Liberal constitutionalism was introduced in the 1820s and a centralized, French-style administrative system in the 1830s under the Braganza dynasty, which was overthrown on 5 October 1910. The First Republic suffered from political instability that encouraged military interventions, culminating in the movement of 28 May 1926, which inaugurated a military dictatorship. In 1932 the Catholic economics professor and finance minister António de Oliveira Salazar (1889–1970) was appointed prime minister, a position he held until incapacitated in 1968. In 1933 he introduced the "New State," an authoritarian corporative political system that had the support of Republican and Monarchist conservatives and Catholics offended by the anticlericalism of the preceding regime, which had separated church and state in 1911. Salazar kept Portugal neutral during World War II and seemingly liberalized his regime after 1945, but elections were rigged and his supporters filled the National Assembly.

Nationalist revolts broke out in the Overseas Provinces of *Angola, *Guinea, and *Mozambique in 1961–1964. The strain of these colonial struggles was the main preoccupation of Salazar's successor, Marcello Caetano (1906–1980). He attempted political liberalization without success and he was overthrown by the Movimento das Forças Armadas (MFA) on 25 April 1974. This coup ushered in seventeen months of semirevolutionary turmoil. The first postcoup president, General António de Spínola, tried to reassert authority but was forced to resign on 30 September 1974. Government was then dominated by the radical MFA, which engaged in rapid *decolonization. On 11 March 1975 a countercoup by Spínola failed and was followed by large-scale state confiscation of private banks and large companies as well as land occupations in the south.

After elections for a constituent assembly (25 April 1975) resulted in victory for the Partido Socialista (PS) of Mário Soares, the MFA split into revolutionary, pro-Communist, and anti-Communist factions. The climax of this revolutionary process came on 25 November 1975 when a revolutionary coup was foiled. The new constitutional regime formally began in July 1976. The Portuguese transition from dictatorship to democracy was tortuous and sui generis, though contemporaneous with that in Greece and preceding that in Spain.

The constitution of 2 April 1976 instituted a democratic system in which the powers of the prime minister and single-chamber legislature (Assembly of the Republic), elected for a four-year term by citizens over eighteen by proportional representation, are balanced by those of the president, elected every five years by direct universal suffrage. General António Ramalho Eanes, operational commander of the antirevolutionary forces on 25 November 1975, was elected in 1976 and 1980. Soares, the first civilian president for sixty years, was elected in 1986 and reelected in 1991. Another Socialist, Jorge Sampaio, was elected in 1996.

The constitutional text of 1976, influenced by the MFA, committed Portugal to making the transition to socialism and proclaimed the nationalizations and agrarian reform of 1975 irreversible. It also made the military the constitutional watchdog and allowed politico-administrative autonomy for the Azores and Madeira. The revision of 1982 ended the military's political role, replacing the Council of the Revolution by a civilian constitutional court. The second revision, in 1989, removed the commitments to socialism and the irreversibility of *nationalizations, thus sanctioning the extensive reprivatization program of Aníbal Cavaco Silva (Social Democrat prime minister 1985–95), continued by his PS successor António Guterres. Another constitutional revision in 1997 introduced referendums, the first, on abortion, being held in 1998.

Since 1976, Portugal has enjoyed stability of regime, although there were ten changes of government, caused by constitutional bickering and party rivalries, between 1976 and 1985. Greater governmental stability was achieved when the Partido Social Democrata (PSD) won absolute majorities in 1987 and 1991 and the minority PS government elected in 1995 retained its popularity.

The two strongest parties are the PS, a democratic socialist party founded by Soares in 1973, and the PSD, founded as the Partido Popular Democrático in 1974, which has generally been liberal-reformist in orientation but joined the European People's Party in 1996. Parties in decline are the Partido Comunista Português (PCP), founded in 1921, backbone of opposition to Salazar and traditionally strong among the shrinking proletariat, and the Centro Democrático Social/ Partido Popular (CDS/PP), originally a conservative Christian Democrat party founded in 1974 but which went through a populist Euroskeptic phase from 1992 to 1998.

The rate of unemployment has been among the lowest in Western Europe since the 1970s and was seven percent in 1997, but the rate of inflation, peaking at 30 percent in 1983, fell to two percent in 1998. Portugal is dependent on imports for over four-fifths of its energy. An unfavorable trade balance is offset by tourism (over 23 million foreign visitors in 1995) and emigrants' remittances. Portugal's GDP was approximately US$100 billion in 1995, with the $10,060 per capita rate representing a rise from 50 to 70 percent of her European partners' average in a decade.

Portugal, a founding member of the European Free Trade Association in 1960, opted for a fully West European political future when, despite Communist opposition, it applied in 1977 to join the European Community (EC), of which it became the eleventh member in 1986. Membership has vastly stimulated trade with Spain (now its main trading partner but previously negligible), led to greatly increased foreign investment, and secured significant development aid from the Community's structural funds, equivalent to four percent of GDP a year, which have helped transform the country. In 1996 12 percent of the work force was employed in agriculture and fisheries (27 percent in 1985) and 57 percent in services (40 percent in 1985).

Portugal has been a full participant in the European integration process, joining the Western European Union (1988) and participating in peacekeeping in Bosnia, adhering to the Schengen Accord (1991) on reducing border controls, and signing the 1992 *Maastricht Treaty of European Union (EU) and the Amsterdam treaty of 1997. In 1998 Portugal, in part thanks to privatization receipts paying off debt, achieved the criteria for joining the single European currency.

Portugal was a founding member of the North Atlantic Treaty Organization in 1949 and is particularly valued therein for its possession of the Azores, with a U.S. base at Lajes (on Terceira). The Portuguese military, 217,000 strong in 1975 at the end of the colonial wars, had been reduced to 55,000 by 1997.

The Portuguese remain proud of their imperial and cultural achievements, seen in the current attempt to create a community of Lusophone countries with Brazil and its former African possessions. Portugal administered the territory of Macao until its return to China on 20 December 1999, and successfully mobilized EU and other international support for East Timor (its former colony invaded by Indonesia in 1975), culminating in that territory's independence in 1999.

(See also ANGOLAN CONFLICT; COLONIAL EMPIRES; DEMO-CRATIC TRANSITION; MILITARY RULE; PRIVITIZATION; SOCIAL-ISM AND SOCIAL DEMOCRACY.)

R. A. H. Robinson, *Contemporary Portugal: A History* (London, 1979). Scott B. MacDonald, *European Destiny, Atlantic Transformations: Portuguese Foreign Policy under the Second Republic, 1974–1992* (New Brunswick, N.J., 1993). Thomas Bruneau, ed., *Political Parties and Democracy in Portugal: Organizations, Elections, and Public Opinion* (Boulder, Colo., 1997). José M. Magone, *European Portugal: The Difficult Road to Sustainable Democracy* (Basingstoke, U.K., 1997).

RICHARD A. H. ROBINSON

POST-COMMUNISM. Just as *communist party states had identified a distinct group of political systems, so too post-communism has come into general use to identify a group of states that share a number of important characteristics that arise from their experience of communist rule but which are not established democracies.

Post-communism identified such states negatively, by what they were not rather than by what they were; and it was a term that did not find favor in the post-communist countries themselves, which were generally anxious to emphasize their newly acquired democratic institutions and their (generally) shared European heritage. But as the twenty-first century opened, scholars of comparative politics continued to regard it as the least unsatisfactory term to identify a group of systems that could still be helpfully considered within the context of their origins in communist rule.

Although they were far from uniform, communist party states shared a number of important characteristics that in turn exercised some influence on the process of democratic transition and on the post-communist systems that replaced them. Most obviously, communist rule had meant an economy that was largely or entirely in public or at least nonprivate ownership, and regulated by the state through a planning mechanism. This inheritance varied from country to country: in Poland, for instance, agricultural land had remained in largely private ownership; in Central Europe and the Baltic, where communist rule had been less extended, there was a larger nonstate sector, particularly in services, and a stronger entrepreneurial tradition. But in all of the communist-ruled countries the state had played a decisive role in production and management, and in all of the post-communist countries there were similar problems of adjustment to a very different economic environment.

Post-communist governments, for instance, were all committed to "privatization"; but some moved more quickly and further than others. Generally, East Central Europe experienced the greatest degree of change, while the former Soviet republics moved more cautiously (Russia, for instance, had as many people working in state as in private enterprises in the late 1990s, and had not yet accepted the private purchase and sale of agricultural land). The economic aspects of post-communism, however, were not limited to ownership: post-communist governments also had to create the financial and legal institutions that underpin a market economy, they had to balance their budgets, and they had to adjust to the flow of commodities and currencies between their own countries and the international economy. There were also one-off problems of adjustment, such as allowing prices to find their own level (when prices were "freed" in Russia in January 1992 they increased nearly threefold in a single month).

This, in turn, raised problems of social policy. Communist party states had been welfarist: the quality of service was often indifferent, officials had their own facilities, bribery was common, and yet basic health care was free of charge at the point of delivery. Housing was predominantly state-owned, with low rentals and cheap utilities. Education was in the hands of the state at all levels and free of charge. Many of these policies were incorporated in communist constitutions, and they formed part of the "social contract" on which the stability of communist governments appeared to be based: there were few of the democratic liberties of the West, such as competitive elections or an independent press, but in a notional exchange communist party state publics could be sure of low prices for their foodstuffs, guaranteed employment, and comprehensive social security (in this sense they were "authoritarian welfare states"). Post-communist governments made fewer promises, and tried to shift housing into the private sector and health care onto an insurance basis; but they had citizens who were not accustomed to paying for such services, and who still expected government—in the last resort—to provide them.

Communist rule, for many, had been not simply authoritarian but totalitarian: and this meant not simply that there was a single party, but that there was no protection against its excesses and no *civil society that might have balanced the power of the executive. Post-communist governments, accordingly, sought to encourage the development of an effective legal system and a society that relied more on self-regulation than on state prescription. The first steps had been taken in the last communist years: the USSR, for instance, established a "committee of constitutional supervision" in 1988 which was the forerunner of a supreme court, and the law codes themselves were changed so as (for instance) to eliminate the crime of "anti-Soviet activity." The post-communist period saw the adoption of a constitution that insisted on the separation of powers and judicial independence, new civil and criminal codes were adopted, and there was a move towards trial by jury. But the rule of law remained very weak throughout the region, with rising levels of reported crime, acute shortages of funding for the police as well as for the judicial system, and organized crime that had often established alliances with local and even national-level politicians and state officials.

The post-communist constitutions were very clear in their commitment to pluralism and human rights, and several of them (including Bulgaria, Slovakia, and Russia) also made clear that they adhered to the international conventions on such matters and that, in the event of any disagreement, conventions of this kind would have precedence over domestic legislation. They were committed, at the same time, to political diversity, and (in the words of the Czech constitution) to the "emergence and free competition of political parties." But it proved very difficult to establish democratic politics from above in place of the centralized single-party rule of the recent past. Most frequently, the post-communist countries moved towards a strongly centralized and sometimes authoritarian system based on a directly elected presidency with executive powers.

The Russian constitution that was adopted in 1993, for instance, gave the president of that country powers that compared to those of the tsar: in particular, he could nominate and dismiss the prime minister and other members of the government; the parliament had to give its assent to his nomination, but if the same candidate was rejected three times the president could dissolve the parliament and call new elections. He could also rule by decree. The post-communist countries of Central Asia went even further, establishing powerful presidencies whose terms were extended by referendum. The most egregious case was in Turkmenistan where the former Communist Party first secretary was reelected unopposed as president in 1992 with 99.5 percent of the vote, taking the title "Turkmenbashi" or father of the Turkmen people; his powers were extended until 2002 in a referendum in 1994 in which the vote in favor was a reported 99.99 percent.

Party politics were weakly developed in the post-communist world, particularly in the former Soviet republics. There were certainly bodies that called themselves parties, and that nominated candidates for public office: forty-three of them contended the Russian Duma elections in 1995, and as many as 112 in the Polish elections of 1991. But typically, across the region, they were created from above by small groups around a charismatic leader, and for this reason were often known as "Zhirinovsky's party" or "Klaus's party" rather than by their proper name. They rarely held congresses or published accounts; they were less likely than their Western counterparts—or simply less able—to establish a strong organizational presence at the local level; and they had a tendency to split, or even disappear entirely.

Post-communist parties, equally, had relatively low levels of membership, no more than tens of thousands in Central Europe and no more than half a million in the case of the largest party, the Communist Party, in the Russian Federation. Indeed there was considerable suspicion of the very concept, for reasons that included the abuse of power by a single ruling party throughout the communist period. The survey evidence typically indicated not just that parties were distrusted, but that they were the most distrusted of all political institutions; and many, for this reason, avoided the word altogether in their official title. Levels of identification were low in comparative terms; and there were higher levels of negative than of positive partisanship (see Miller et al., 1998; Rose et al., 1998). At elections themselves, large numbers opted for independents rather than party-sponsored candidates: in the Ukrainian Supreme Council elections of 1994, independents took half the seats and two-thirds of the vote; and in the Russian Duma elections of 1995, more independents were elected in the single-member-district contests (which accounted for half of all the seats) than candidates nominated by the parties.

Post-communism, accordingly, helped to identify a number of the issues that were confronted by the countries that had formerly been under communist rule; and yet it was an unsatisfactory term in many respects. For a start, the process of change was uneven throughout the region, and many elements of the communist past persisted. In the Czech Republic the economy swiftly reverted to capitalism, and the former communists had little influence. But in Romania, the movement that overthrew Nicolae Ceauşescu's authoritarian regime in December 1989 was led by former party officials, and a post-communist leadership did not emerge until the election of President Constantinescu in 1996. In Serbia, the former communist leadership (now increasingly nationalist) remained in place. In Hungary, former communists won a majority of seats in the 1994 parliamentary elections and formed the new government. In Poland and in Lithuania, they won parliamentary and presidential elections. In Russia, the Communist Party won the largest number of seats in the 1995 and 1999 Duma elections, and the president and prime minister in the early post-communist years were former members of the party's central committee.

Differences among the post-communist countries, meanwhile, were being widened by their various relationships with the outside world. Most European communist party states had been held together by the *Warsaw Treaty Organization, established in 1955 and extended for twenty years in 1985, and by the Council for Mutual Economic Assistance or Comecon, established in 1949 to encourage a process of economic integration among its member nations. Both were dissolved in 1991 as communist governments lost power throughout the region. All of the former Soviet republics, except the three Baltic republics, agreed to join a *Commonwealth of Independent States that had been established in December 1991, but it remained no more than a framework for cooperation. There were closer links among four of the member states (Russia, Belarus, Kyrgyzstan, and Kazakhstan), and particularly between Russia and Belarus, which signed a treaty of integration in 1996.

Wider international movements, moreover, were introducing new divisions by the late 1990s. Hungary, Poland, and the Czech Republic were the first of the formerly communist countries to join NATO in 1999. All three, together with Estonia and Slovenia, were among the countries that figure in the first wave of the enlargement of the European Union that was due to take place in the early years of the new century. This suggested that the countries of Central Europe would increasingly become "normal" European democracies, some of them with socialist governments but none of them usefully described as "post-communist." At the same time it raised the prospect that the post-communist countries beyond the boundaries of the newly enlarged Europe would find themselves the victims of a new division of the continent, with lower living standards and systems of government that were likely to remain centralized and authoritarian for some time to come.

(See also NINETEEN EIGHTY-NINE.)

Leslie Holmes, *Post-Communism: An Introduction* (Cambridge U.K., 1997). William L. Miller, Stephen White, and Paul Heywood, *Values and Political Change in Postcommunist Europe* (London and New York, 1998). Richard Rose, William Mishler, and Christian Haerpfer, *Democracy and Its Alternatives: Understanding Post-Communist Societies* (Baltimore, 1998). Stephen White, Judy Batt, and Paul G. Lewis, eds., *Developments in Central and East European Politics 2* (London and Durham, N.C., 1998). Richard Sakua, *Postcommunism* (Buckingham, 1999).

STEPHEN WHITE

POSTINDUSTRIAL SOCIETY. The term "post-industrial society" is associated primarily with the work of two sociologists, Daniel Bell and Alain Touraine, though paradoxically, the usages by the two have almost nothing in common.

The concept of postindustrial society was first used by Bell in 1959 in lectures at the Salzburg Seminar in American Studies, and was the explicit foundation of the Commission on the Year 2000, of the American Academy of Arts and Sciences, in its several works published in 1965 (reprinted by the M.I.T. Press in 1998) and elaborated in the book by Bell, *The Coming of Post-Industrial Society,* published by Basic Books (New York) in 1973.

Touraine's use of the term was in his book *The Post-Industrial Society,* published in France in 1969 and in English by Random House, in 1971, a collection of disparate essays in which the term appears only in the introduction.

For Bell, the term was used initially to indicate the change from a manufacturing or goods-producing economy to services (though not of the fast-food variety)—human services, education and health, professional services, business services, research, and the like. But by 1965 Bell added as the major factor, what he called its axial principle, the codification of theoretical knowledge and the new applications of science to technology as the levers of economic change.

For Touraine, the postindustrial society was the programmed society, or the complete absorption of an individual into the society. It is "more useful," he wrote, "to speak of alienation than of exploitation: the former defines a social, the latter merely an economic relationship. . . . A man is alienated when his only relationship to the social and cultural directions of his society is the one the ruling class accords him compatible with the maintenance of its own dominance."

Over the years, Touraine's conception found echoes in Europe, particularly in the emergence of *new social movements such as the Greens, while Bell's analysis, popularized initially by the futurism of Herman Kahn, but then absorbed into the literature of social and technological change, became widely used in the United States.

The major effort to supersede the work of Bell and Touraine was made by Manuel Castells in his massive three-volume work, *The Information Age: Economy, Society and Culture* (1996–1998), where Castells defines the new economy as one organized around the production and distribution of information, and technology becomes the means of expanding the role of information and knowledge in increasing productivity in the society.

While praising the scope of Castells's effort, the intellectual difficulty in Castells's analytical framework, Bell has pointed out, is the conflation of information with knowledge and the confusing interchange of the terms. Information, he has argued, is the communication of data and news and results of work, while knowledge is judgment of validity and the verification of results.

Bell's fullest presentation of his ideas is contained in his monographic essay, "The Social Framework of the Information Society," in the volume *The Computer Age,* edited by Michael L. Dertouzos and Joel Moses (M.I.T. Press, 1979), and the republication of *The Coming of Post-Industrial Society,* with a new 30,000-word foreword, by Basic Books in 1999. These statements seek to identify the differences between the industrial societies (in the West between 1750 and 1950) and the postindustrial societies of the last half of the twentieth century on to the twenty-first.

The crux of the change is in the nature of innovation. Almost all the industries of the industrial society—steel, electricity, telephone, automobile, and aviation—were all created by "talented tinkers," inventors such as Darby, Bessemer, Edison, Bell, Marconi, and the Wright brothers who knew little of or were indifferent to the work of science in their time. The industries of the postindustrial age derive from theoretical work in science, particularly in physics in the quantum revolution. The work in solid-state physics of Niels Bohr and Felix Bloch led to the transistor and the semiconductor industries and the microprocessor. The paper of Albert Einstein in 1905 on light as a quanta or pulse, not just as a wave, led to the photoelectric cell (in elevator beams and cameras) as well as the laser (an acronym: light amplified by the stimulation of the emission of radiation).

To that extent, a mechanical technology, machines and motors, gives way to an intellectual technology, algorithms which are used in computer-aided design and computer-aided manufacture. Education becomes the ladder of social ascent, so much so that in the United States in 1996, of the 126 million persons in the labor force, 36.5 million persons were professional and managers, and an additional 37.6 million were technicians, sales and administrative support persons (about 60 percent of the labor force) as against 13.5 million skilled workers and 18 million operators and laborers (or 25 percent of the labor force). The remainder are in transportation, utilities and the like.

Insofar as technology becomes the lever of changes, it becomes important to understand the differentiation of technology and its trajectories. Thus, there is a distinction between transformation technologies, extension technologies, and niches. A telephone is a transformation technology; mobile and cell phones are extensions, since they break the cord; while branch exchanges (e.g. a common number for a business or university within the organization) are niches. A computer is a transformation technology; networks, linking up the stand-alones, are extensions; while applications, such as spreadsheets, are niches. National economies are distinguished by their capacities to adapt to these changes. Niches, for example, are created by engineers or entrepreneurs, backed by venture capitalists who are risk-takers. Japan has been a society that does not encourage such individual initiatives. The United States does. And this explains, in large measure, the large lead of the United States over Japan in the trajectory of telecommunication technologies.

The world economy is shaped by such trajectories. Thus, there are distinctions between initating technology, qualitatively improving technology, and making products. The United States, because of its large research base, has led in initiating technology. Japan, because of its attention to quality, has led in improvements. But when a technology is standardized, then labor costs become the major factor and those societies, particularly in Asia, such as the Republic of Korea (South Korea) or Malaysia or Thailand, begin to take over the manufacture of goods.

In these several ways, postindustrialism, or as we have come to call it, the *information society, creates a new international division of labor and a new system of world power. Areas which cannot make the transformations, such as many of the societies in Africa, begin to lag further and further behind in the world development index. Societies begin to fragment when national authority is unable to direct change. Thus the twenty-first century begins to see new forms of world order—and disorder.

(See also DEINDUSTRIALIZATION; GLOBALIZATION; INFORMATION TECHNOLOGY.)

Herman Kahn and Anthony J. Wiener, *The Year 2000* (New York, 1971). Alain Touraine, *The Post-Industrial Society* (New York, Cambridge, Mass., 1971). Daniel Bell, *The Coming of Post-Industrial Society* (New York, 1973; the 1999 edition contains an additional foreword). Michael L. Dertouzos and Joel Moses, eds., *The Computer Age: A Twenty-Year View* (Cambridge, Mass., 1979). Simon Nora and Alain Minc, *The Computerization of Society* (Cambridge, Mass., 1980). Manuel Castells, *The Information Age: Economy, Society and Culture*, 3 vols. (Oxford, 1996–1998).

DANIEL BELL

POSTMATERIALISM. Postmaterialist values give top priority to self-expression, belonging, and the nonmaterial quality of life—as opposed to materialist values, which give top priority to economic and physical security. Throughout industrial society, people's basic values and goals are gradually shifting from giving top priority to economic growth and consumption, to placing increasing emphasis on the quality of life. The incentives that once motivated the workforce are becoming less effective than they were; the policies that once gave rise to broad political support no longer work as readily as they did; even the values that once shaped sexual behavior and child rearing are giving way to new norms. In large part, this reflects a process of intergenerational value change; it tends to pass unnoticed unless it is measured by longitudinal survey research. But its impact is pervasive. It is changing social, political, and economic life. And because it is transforming entire lifestyles, including consumer patterns, fertility rates, and the priority that people give to environmental protection, human activities have become a major factor influencing changes in the geophysical environment. It is also leading to less public support for *nationalism, less emphasis on military expenditures, and a declining willingness to fight for one's country. These changes are gradual, however, and subject to substantial short-term fluctuations.

Evidence of intergenerational value change began to be gathered on a cross-national basis in 1970 (Inglehart, 1971). It was hypothesized that, as a result of the rapid economic development and the expansion of the *welfare state following World War II, the formative experience of the younger birth cohorts differed from that of older cohorts in ways that were leading them to develop fundamentally different value priorities. Throughout most of history, the threat of severe economic deprivation or even starvation had been a crucial concern for most people. But the unprecedented degree of economic security experienced by the postwar generation in most industrial societies was leading to a gradual shift from "materialist" values (emphasizing economic and physical security above all) toward "postmaterialist" priorities (emphasizing self-expression and the quality of life).

In 1970, surveys were carried out in six West European nations to test this hypothesis. The results showed striking differences between the priorities of old and young. Among the oldest group (which had experienced the insecurity and devastation of World War I, the Great Depression, and World War II), those with materialist priorities outnumbered those

with postmaterialist priorities by more than twelve to one; but, moving from the older to younger cohorts, the proportion of materialists shrank, and the proportion of postmaterialists rose. Among the youngest group—those born after World War II—there was a shift in the balance between value types, with postmaterialists becoming more numerous than materialists.

Cohort analysis of a twenty-five-year series of surveys, in which exactly the same questions were administered to representative national samples, demonstrated that given birth cohorts did *not* become more materialist as they aged from 1970 to 1994—instead, most of these cohorts were actually a little *less* materialist at the end of this period than they had been at the start.

During the period from 1970 to 1994, the group that was aged 65+ became a group aged 89+, of whom very few survivors remained to be interviewed. They were replaced by younger individuals, who are much more postmaterialist than their elders. This has produced a net shift from materialist to postmaterialist values in the populations of these societies.

In each of the six societies first surveyed in 1970 (and also in the United States, which was first surveyed in 1972), a significant decline was found in the proportion of materialists, and an increase in the proportion of postmaterialists. The size of this shift varied from country to country, partly as a function of the economic and physical conditions that prevailed in the given country during this period, but all seven countries moved in the predicted direction. Similar results emerged from the twenty-two countries included in both the 1981 and the 1990 World Values surveys: in almost every case, there was evidence of an intergenerational shift from materialist toward postmaterialist priorities. This shift was taking place not only in Western countries but (very rapidly) in East Asia and (more slowly) in Eastern and Central Europe. It has not yet become an important factor in preindustrial societies but should eventually become increasingly significant there too, as economic development takes place.

In industrialized societies, postmaterialist values are closely related to environmental attitudes and environmentalist behavior. For example, those with postmaterialist values are four or five times as likely to be active members of environmentalist groups, or to vote for *green parties, in countries where they exist. An intergenerational shift seems to be occurring toward giving higher priority to environmental protection (Inglehart, 1977).

Similarly, because the basic goals of postmaterialists differ from those that have long prevailed in their societies, they tend to support change-oriented parties—which are usually the parties of the *Left. But this fact does not guarantee the automatic success of the Left. On the contrary, the rise of postmaterialist issues such as abortion, *environmentalism, and gay and lesbian rights often tends to split existing Left parties, with the traditional working-class base sometimes being alienated by the stand advocated by growing postmaterialist elements.

Postmaterialist values turn out to be correlated with a surprisingly wide range of other values, relating to work, leisure, gender roles, and a variety of other social and political orientations. One example of the many dimensions that are correlated with materialist/postmaterialist values is sexual restrictiveness. The formative conditions that gave rise to postmaterialist values also lead to an outlook which has less need for the security and predictability of absolute sexual rules (Inglehart, 1990). The World Values Survey data suggest that sexual norms are undergoing a similar process of intergenerational change, moving toward less restrictive orientations. They show a clear and consistent tendency for the young and the postmaterialists to have less restrictive sexual norms than the old.

The rise of postmaterialism seems to be working to erode mass support for nationalism and patriotism. Publics have become accustomed to economic and physical security, and are less likely to feel threatened by neighboring peoples. But the decline of patriotism and nationalism goes beyond the postmaterialist syndrome, for it also reflects a historical change in Western publics' orientations toward *war—a change that seems linked with the experience of World War II, on one hand, and an awareness that modern technology would make a third world war vastly more destructive than even the cataclysm of 1939–1945. Finally, in Western Europe the evolution of European Union institutions has contributed to making the perspective of the nation-state seem outmoded, giving rise to a faint but growing sense of European *citizenship.

(See also GAY AND LESBIAN POLITICS; GENDER AND POLITICS; NEW SOCIAL MOVEMENTS; PEACE MOVEMENT; POSTINDUSTRIAL SOCIETY; POSTMODERNISM; REPRODUCTIVE POLITICS.)

Ronald Inglehart, "The Silent Revolution in Europe: Intergenerational Change in Post Industrial Societies," *American Political Science Review* 65, no. 4 (December 1971); 991–1017. Ronald Inglehart, *The Silent Revolution: Changing Values and Political Styles Among Western Publics* (Princeton, N.J., 1977). Ronald Inglehart, *Culture Shift in Advanced Industrial Society* (Princeton, N.J., 1990). Ronald Inglehart, *Modernization and Postmodernization: Cultural, Economic and Political Change in 43 Societies* (Princeton, N.J., 1997).

RONALD INGLEHART

POSTMODERNISM. Postmodernism is a body of thought and sensibility that emerged in the late 1960s, and that appears alive and well at the start of the 2000s. Postmodernism has spread and thrived throughout Western Europe and the United States, especially in and around universities, among architects, artists, and performers, and in advertising and the mass media. The term *postmodern* has generated, and is still generating, an immense amount of discourse. It is often simply a vehicle for talking about "the spirit of the age," so that many people who doubt that it means anything besides chronology—say, work produced after 1965 or so—are still eager to come to symposia and conferences on it. The most original work done under a postmodern label has been in architecture, mainly in North America, and in social thought, mainly in France.

Postmodern architects and their publicists claim to have rediscovered the historic forms and styles—"the styles," in Le Corbusier's dismissive terminology—that the triumphs of Le Corbusier, Mies, and Gropius were supposed to have wiped out. But they are not just reactionary eclectics; they think they can twist and recombine architectural history in fresh and original ways that would have been unthinkable before modernism wiped the slate clean. Their sensitivity to the forms of the past enables them to design buildings and environments that are complex and ironic, contradictory and multivalent. Louis Kahn, Robert Venturi, Michael Graves, Aldo Rossi, Frank Gehry, Charles Moore, James Stirling, and Ricardo Bofill are among the stars of postmodern architecture, although all are not happy with the label.

Postmodern architecture presents various conceptual and human problems. Its way of blending past and present is in fact the central idea of modernism in literature and art: the principle of montage. This is not radical innovation, but what Harold Rosenberg called "the tradition of the new." Postmodern language explodes with images of radical breakthrough, subversion, and transgression and with claims to leave both Dada and revolutionary *Marxism far behind; but beneath the noise, one can hear a familiar refrain, a blatant, shameless self-promotion worthy of the great modernist hustlers Flaubert and Mark Twain. Philip Johnson put postmodernism over the top in the late 1970s and established it as *the* corporate idiom of the Reagan decade with his AT&T Building in New York. This skyscraper features an extravagant Chippendale top, an immense, dramatically lit stone arcade at the bottom (he said "Borromini," his critics said "Mussolini"), and fifty floors of lucrative real estate in between. Within a decade the giant AT&T was gone, and the building was reincarnated as the Sony Building, as solid an investment as ever. If this was postmodern irony, much of the public was ready for plain talk.

The most interesting postmodern social thought emanates from France, where it developed out of the Parisian uprising of 1968, the breakdown of that uprising, and the years of posttraumatic stress syndrome that French intellectuals went through. Among the most original postmodern thinkers have been Michel *Foucault, Jacques Lacan, Roland Barthes, Jean-Francois Lyotard, Jacques Derrida, Julia Kristeva, and Jean Baudrillard. These intellectuals had a distinctive aura in France: they were spectacular performers who could mesmerize large audiences with theatrical flair and they received an often frenzied public adulation. Many of their most ardent followers have been U.S. academics, who have arranged a constant round of transatlantic visits for them.

The intellectuals who began to identify themselves as postmodern in the early 1970s professed regrets for their radicalism in the 1960s, although they continued to define their work by the paradigms of resistance or revolution. The original sin of 1960s radicals, they said, was to have employed the wrong metaphysics—Derrida called it "the metaphysics of presence"—which posited the essential unity of human experience. This delusion was supposedly the source of the Western idea of *human rights. Postmodernists came to disparage the whole paradigm of human rights, because it discounted the differences between people, which they considered more important. The human differences most interesting to postmoderns so far have been sex/gender and race/ethnicity. They haven't shown much interest in class, national, or religious differences. They have been violently abusive toward Marxists who stress the importance of class-based differences.

Jean-Francois Lyotard is the paradigmatic postmodernist, the writer who has used the concept in the most ambitious and audacious ways. He says, "There is no longer a horizon of universalization, of general emancipation, before the eyes of postmodern man." The postmodern epoch is defined by "the failure of the universal" and "the disappearance of the idea of progress within rationality and freedom." To be in tune with the times (though he never explains just why we should be) is to be free from "grand narratives" (or "master narratives," "metanarratives"), from stories that supposedly give our individual or collective histories meaning beyond ourselves. We ought to give up the quest for transcendent meaning, and "just live," in a playful "eternal present." Lyotard (along with his whole generation in France) portrays Nietzsche as the prophet and hero of this new morality. The other pillar of his postmodern edifice is Ludwig Wittgenstein. Lyotard offers a highly politicized version of the late Wittgenstein's "language games": language games are bound to be heterogenous and incommensurable with each other; truth and meaning can exist only in particular communities of belief and desire; no one can transcend the community into which he or she is born. Lyotard's signature is a radical skepticism, both about what people can know and about what they can do—"skepticism of metanarrative," he calls it— which passes abruptly into dogmatism and peremptory a priori decrees about what is and what is not possible. Some critics have argued that this leap from skepticism to dogmatism typifies postmodern thinking as a whole.

As French culture veered sharply to the right in the 1970s, postmodern attacks on Marxism gradually escalated into diatribes against the French Revolution and the Declaration of Rights. Before long, the Left Bank was saturated with tracts that showed how the mass murders perpetrated by Stalinism were actually simple corollaries of the Enlightenment. Parisian intellectuals who had finally learned (often at quite advanced ages) to see through Stalinism were carried along by a momentum that propelled them, in a remarkably short time, through *liberalism as well. By the time the revolution's bicentennial arrived, it was hard to find a French intellectual who would say a good word for it. French postmodernism today is marked by a ferocious contempt for the Enlightenment, for the revolution, for humanism, for the idea of human rights, for what sometimes seems to be the whole of modern life and thought. Its emotional violence, lack of intellectual balance, and learned ignorance of the traditions it condemns suggest echoes of the Action Francaise, or the pre-1933 German "politics of cultural despair." French postmoderns look longingly across the Rhine and celebrate Martin Heidegger as their intellectual hero, while German humanists like Habermas look nervously toward Paris and fear that once more the lights are going out all over Europe.

He need not worry. True, in denying human unity and human rights, postmodernism shows an affinity with the traditional post-1789 European Right (Burke, de Maistre, Müller, et al.). However, its activists come from the post-1960s Left, and their practical activity focuses almost wholly on causes and groups that today's Left has made its own: e.g., racial and sexual equality, local and global ecology, nuclear disarmament. Still, left-wing politics from the perspective of right-wing metaphysics is bound to generate trouble, though not exactly the kind of trouble Habermas fears. Postmoderns typically work in or for *new social movements: they fight oppression and injustice against women, homosexuals, people of color, et al. But if the ideas of justice, shared humanity, and human rights are groundless, why should anyone who isn't a member of these groups identify with them, accept their claims of victimization, or care about their fate?

Postmoderns have contributed brains and energy to feminist, gay, and ecological movements, and to the Greens. They have generally pushed their movements in the separatist and sectarian directions, away from broad civil rights coalitions and from human bonds that could transcend group boundaries. If there is a coherent postmodern political vision, it is probably something like what U.S. political scientists call "interest group liberalism": an open, ever-growing aggregation of voluntary associations, some immensely powerful, others virtually powerless, none showing any concern for anyone beyond itself. French postmoderns present this view of the world as a spectacular discovery and as the key to freedom and happiness in the new pluralist, "polytheistic" world. Americans, who have lived in a political culture dominated by interest-group liberalism (at least since Tocqueville's time) and who are used to seeing vital public needs unrecognized and unfulfilled, should be forgiven if they cast a cold eye.

Both friends and enemies of postmodernism felt that it "fit" the sleazy glamour and flamboyant nihilism of the Thatcher-Reagan years. But there was one big thing that it did not fit: the struggle for human rights in Eastern Europe, and then in China, in 1989. When demonstrators in Prague went up against armed Soviet troops, bearing signs that said "Truth Will Prevail," when students in Beijing died with "We Shall Overcome" on their shirts, this wasn't in the postmodern repertory. It was too serious, too universal, too much of a "grand narrative": people weren't supposed to be doing this anymore! Postmodernism blanked out in 1989, in the face of one of the great political moments in history. On the other hand, their blankness positioned them perfectly for 1990: when revolutionary people and peoples fell apart into a hundred tribes and tribalisms, postmoderns could tell the world they'd told us so, that tribal identity and corporate privilege were all there was.

It would be foolish to predict postmodernism's fate in the twenty-first century. However, its ups and downs from 1989–1990 should make it clear that it is really less a theory than a mentality: arch sophistication, emotional flatness, weariness of life (even in the very young), certainty that everything that can happen has happened (hence the self is defined by being "post-"), talent for manipulating everything without meaning anything. In periods of political impasse and constriction, the postmodern mood appears to make sense of life. But it grows blind and dumb when men and women step into the foreground, grow innovative and resourceful in fighting for freedom, and actually create something new under the sun. When people manifest unexpected depths, postmodernism shows that deep down it's shallow.

(See also MAY 1968; MODERNITY; NINETEEN EIGHTY-NINE; POSTINDUSTRIAL SOCIETY; POSTMATERIALISM.)

Robert Venturi, *Complexity and Contradiction in Architecture* (New York, 1966). Michael Foucault, *Power/Knowledge: Selected Interviews and Other Writings, 1972–1977* (New York, 1980). Jean-François Lyotard, *The Post-Modern Condition: A Report on Knowledge,* translated by Geoff Bennington and Brian Massumi (Minneapolis, 1984). Jürgen Habermas, *The Philosophical Discourse of Modernity,* translated by Frederick Lawrence (Cambridge, Mass., 1987). Marshall Berman, "Why Modernism Still Matters" *Tikkun* 4, no. 1 (January–February 1989). Linda Nicholson, ed., *Feminism/Postmodernism* (New York, 1990). Fredric Jameson, *Postmodernism, or, the Cultural Logic of Late Capitalism* (Durham, N.C., 1991).
MARSHALL BERMAN

POTSDAM CONFERENCE. The last meeting of the *World War II Grand Alliance took place from 17 July to 2 August 1945 in Potsdam, near the destroyed German capital of Berlin. The future of Germany was the major issue facing the new president of the United States, Harry *Truman, Premier Joseph *Stalin of the Soviet Union, and Prime Minister Winston *Churchill of Britain. (After the election of 28 July, Labor Party leader Clement Attlee replaced Churchill.) The successful test of the first atomic bomb on 16 July also cast its shadow over future relations among the Big Three.

The key dispute at the conference concerned German reparations. The Soviet Union demanded significant reparations from Germany, both in industrial plant and from current production, on the scale of the US$20 billion figure established for discussion at Yalta. The Western powers favored reparations only through the dismantling and removal of industrial plant. The United States and Britain opposed reparations from current production, insisting that Germany must first become self-supporting from exports. The three countries reached a compromise that merely postponed the problem. Although Germany itself was to be treated as a single economic unit, each power was entitled to collect reparations from its respective zone. The Western zones were to provide the Soviets with one-quarter of all additional equipment not necessary for the peacetime functioning of the German economy. The zonal agreement on reparations was a first step leading to the division of Germany.

A related issue was the settlement of Germany's eastern frontier. Having already annexed a large section of eastern Poland, Stalin wanted the country to receive territorial compensation from Germany. He proposed a western border for Poland at the Oder and Neisse rivers. When asked about the millions of Germans in the territory, Stalin claimed that they had fled. Although the Western powers conceded the Oder-Neisse boundary as a "provisional solution" pending the final peace conference, the Soviets and the Poles made it permanent through the forcible expulsion of the German population.

Although word of the atomic bomb strengthened Truman's confidence at Potsdam, there is little evidence that the weapon played any decisive role in conference diplomacy. Truman informed Stalin of the existence of the new weapon in only the vaguest terms, but the Soviet leader was already aware of it through his espionage network. Despite Truman's complaints, the Soviets did not change their policy in Eastern Europe. Truman was first and foremost determined to secure Soviet involvement in the war against Japan. For his part Stalin shared with Truman information about Japanese proposals for peace. Although the Big Three issued a general warning demanding that Japan surrender, there was no specific reference to the bomb. Less than two weeks after the conclusion of the conference, the United States used the atomic bomb against *Hiroshima and Nagasaki, the Soviets entered the war against Japan, and the Japanese surrendered.

(See also COLD WAR; NUCLEAR WEAPONS; YALTA CONFERENCE.)

Herbert Feis, *Between War and Peace: The Potsdam Conference* (Princeton, N.J., 1960). Martin J. Sherwin, *A World Destroyed: The Atomic Bomb and the Grand Alliance* (New York, 1975).

THOMAS ALAN SCHWARTZ

POVERTY. See DEVELOPMENT AND UNDERDEVELOPMENT; EQUALITY AND INEQUALITY; FEMINIZATION OF POVERTY; UNDERCLASS.

POWER. Talk of power pervades the discourse and the analysis of politics, both domestic and international, yet disputes over how to define and recognize it are endless. As participants in and students of politics we want to know where it lies, how extensive it is, and how it works, yet when we reflect on it, we cannot agree on what it is. This is partly because we have different and often conflicting interests in seeking such knowledge, which lead us to look in different directions. So, for instance, one's interest may be immediately practical (whom to influence or lobby or corrupt or assassinate or avoid); it may be to pin responsibility on policy makers for the consequences of their actions and inaction, as when C. Wright Mills (in *The Power Elite* [New York, 1956]) sought to call the "men of power" to account; it may be to reveal the unobvious practices of individuals or groups, within institutions and structures, that are crucial in generating outcomes we care about (such as patterns of inequality or oppression within or across states). And it is partly because conceptions of power are not independent of their object and are thus inherently political. How we think of power may serve to reproduce and reinforce power structures and relations; or alternatively it may contest and subvert them.

At its most general, *power* simply denotes the capacity of agents to bring about changes. But which agents and which changes? In political life, the agents are individuals or collectivities (such as *elites, groups, organizations, and *states) and the changes, or outcomes of their power, are those that are somehow significant. What makes outcomes significant? Several answers to this have been given. One is that they must be *intended*. But is intention sufficient? What if, like the Stoics, I want only what I can get, or like a conformist, only what others want, or, like a sycophant, only what (I think) others want me to want? Am I powerful, as opposed to you, if the outcomes I intentionally produce occur because you have threatened or induced me, or if I only produce them at enormous cost? And are the intentions actual or hypothetical? Is my power not greater if I can produce what I might but do not actually want? And is intention necessary? Can power not be exercised in routine or unconsidered ways, as when by making investment decisions I deprive unknown people of work or provide them with it?

Another answer is that the outcomes of power affect *interests*, whether those of the powerful or of those affected by their power. The former is assumed by Realist theorists of *international relations for whom state power furthers the "national interest." It is often assumed that power adversely affects the interests of those subject to it, assuming that power signifies the presence of a zero-sum game, but some thinkers deny this, citing the example of paternalism and claiming that power can be productive and transformative or empowering. One problem here is that what counts as agents' "interests" (let alone the "national interest") is highly contestable: some assert and others deny that our interests can conflict with our preferences.

A third answer, also denying that power always registers a zero-sum relationship, sees power as generating collective action or cooperation. Thus Cicero spoke of *potestas in populo* and Hannah *Arendt identified what she saw as a distinctive tradition and vocabulary which defines it as the "human ability . . . to act in concert" (*On Violence* [New York, 1970], p. 44), referring to the Athenians, the Romans, and eighteenth-century revolutionaries, especially in the U.S.

But the concept of power typically encompasses a further sense contrasting with Arendt's—of an asymmetric relationship of power as subjection, control, or dependence, in which some have power over others, an idea captured by Spinoza's distinction between *potentia* and *potestas*, which we use when speaking of someone being "subject to the other's power" and of being "in the power of another" (*Tractatus theologico-politicus*, chap. 2, para. 9). Indeed, this further idea is inseparable from the more general idea of power over outcomes to the extent that these are only attainable through securing the compliance of others in this way. Max *Weber called this further idea *Herrschaft*, or domination, suggesting a broad distinction between that resulting from a "constellation of interests," such as the market (as in the case of monopoly) and that resulting from "authority, i.e. power to command and duty to obey" (*Economy and Society* [Berkeley, Calif., 1978], p. 943), intending by the latter structured relations between superiors and subordinates in which, however, compliance can be based on a wide variety of motives, from pure habit to the rational calculation of advantage, and obtained by a variety of means.

What are these means of securing compliance? We may distinguish five such mechanisms of power: *force* (the infliction of physical restraint or destruction which, however, in treating its victims as objects, not subjects, does not secure their compliance and is thus a limit case); *coercion* (the use of explicit or implicit threats, involving a conflict of wills and the overcoming of resistance); *manipulation* (the use of art or skill to avert, bypass, or deflect conflict and resistance); *authority* (where those subject to it accept reasons to refrain from reasoning about what they are required to do or believe); and *rational persuasion* (another limit case, since here it is, supposedly, my reasons, not my power, that persuade you what to believe or do. However, thinkers such as Nietzsche and *Foucault maintain that power and reason are inextricably fused).

There are many ways of combining these various elements into conceptions of power to make sense of our world. Among these, two contrasting strategies can be singled out. One, deriving from the behaviorist and empiricist tradition of political science in the United States, focuses on observable conflict between actors whose interests are revealed by their express preferences over contested policies. Power is exercised by overcoming resistance, by winning in decision-making situations of overt conflict. Only such evidence can put claims about "ruling elites," by writers such as C. Wright Mills, or Marxist claims about class power, to empirical test, by seeing who prevails in overt political contests over key issues. A classic in this genre was Robert Dahl's study of New Haven politics, *Who Governs?* (New Haven, Conn., 1961). Using this methodology, Dahl's conclusion was that power was distributed pluralistically in New Haven. A similar focus on overt conflict between power-seeking actors (in this case states) can be seen in Realist and Neorealist writings in international relations.

An alternative strategy is to view power as lying below the surface of conflicting preferences which are, in this view, themselves seen as liable to be shaped by power. Various traditions of inquiry have exemplified this strategy: Marx-inspired discussions of *ideology and class consciousness, Freud-inspired discussions of the impact of child-rearing practices on personality formation and the cultural roots of psychopathology, studies of the constitution of subjectivity and the formation of discursive practices of individuality in particular contexts, and the "construction" of identity and agency by recent feminist theorists and historians. In such writings power is seen as the ability to influence beliefs and desires through processes that are often neither intended nor understood and may require no deliberate activity on the part of the powerful. Here power is successful to the extent to which observable conflict is eliminated or avoided.

There is much to be said for and against each of the ways of conceiving power. But we should note that, while both claim to yield empirical knowledge, neither can plausibly claim to be "objective," in the sense of neutral between perspectives. From the standpoint of the first, the second makes speculative and untestable claims about unobservable processes. From the standpoint of the second, the first fails to capture what we may call the self-concealing character of power. For if power is the more effective the more it is hidden from view, then it will, in this aspect, systematically elude any methodology that relies on the readily or directly observable.

(See also CLASS AND POLITICS; PLURALISM; REALISM.)

Dennis Wrong, *Power: Its Forms, Bases and Uses* (New York, 1980). Keith Dowding, *Power* (Minneapolis, 1996). Barry Hindess, *Discourses of Power: From Hobbes to Foucault* (Oxford, 1996).

STEVEN LUKES

PRAGUE SPRING. Until *Gorbachev's *perestroika the Prague Spring was the most important Communist Party-led reform aimed at creating a democratic and pluralist socialism. The fact that this peaceful attempt at "within-system" reform came in *Czechoslovakia had much to do with the relatively deep roots of *socialism in that society, by comparison with the rest of Eastern and *Central Europe, as well as with the absence of strong anti-Soviet *nationalism.

The movement for radical change stemmed from a combination of economic and political factors. Economic performance began seriously to falter in the early 1960s when production actually declined. This fueled pressure for a decentralizing and marketizing economic reform that was introduced in 1967 as the New Economic System. As this fell short of what the economic reformers, led by Ota Sik, thought necessary, they lent their weight to the demands of the creative intelligentsia for political change, voiced at the writers' congress in June 1967. Within the Communist Party grievances focused on Antonín Novotný who was replaced in January 1968 as first secretary by Alexander Dubček.

A moderate Slovak party official, against whom nobody, notably Moscow, had any objections, Dubček found himself heading a motley coalition united only by opposition to Novotný and including conservatives such as Vasil Bilák as well as reformers like Josef Smrkovský. The reformers successfully encouraged what would now be called glasnost to magnify calls for the removal of conservatives from power, which hastened the replacement in March of Novotný as president (his state post) by Ludvík Svoboda. Taking advantage of the relaxation of censorship and police controls, intellectuals and students demanded more rapid and far-reaching democratization than the Dubček leadership, hampered by a largely conservative party central committee, anxious allies in Moscow, East Berlin, and Warsaw, and its own notions of acceptable reform, was able to provide. The party's action program, published in April, set out a somewhat more enlightened system of Communist Party rule. More radical political reform was outlined in theses prepared by a central committee team headed by Zdenek Mylnár; these were to be submitted to the Fourteenth Party Congress, which was preempted by the Soviet invasion and held clandestinely in August. These proposals envisaged a staged transition to a more constitutional and pluralistic system in which a more democratic Communist Party might, within a decade, share power with interest organizations rather than compete on an equal basis with opposition parties.

Growing differences between the party leadership and radical, mainly non-Communist, groups centered on the distinction between the kind of gradual democratization allowing for oppositional activity the party advocated and the competitive democracy seen as vital by the radicals. Václav *Havel, for instance, called for the creation of a democratic party based on a national moral revival, something he helped bring about in 1989. In 1968 political activity was more fragmented, with the reinvigoration of the small non-Communist parties, the revival of the social democrats, and the establishment of quasi-political clubs, such as K231 (former political prisoners) and KAN (a non-party pressure group). Seeing the need by June for more forceful civic action, a group of intellectuals signed the 2,000 Words declaration, a clarion call to the grass roots to organize themselves, help oust the conservative officials still dominating party and government, and pressure the leadership for radical institutional change. The Dubček leadership found itself squeezed between the Scylla of public pressure for faster change and the Charybdis of domestic conservative resistance supplemented by warnings from East European and Soviet allies. Following a collective *Warsaw Treaty Organization (Warsaw Pact) ultimatum in June, the Czechoslovak party leaders, under pressure at meetings in Cierna nad Tisou (July) and Bratislava (August), made pledges to curtail democratization that they found difficult to fulfill. In retrospect some, like Mylnár, have argued that had tougher restraints been imposed, Soviet intervention might have been avoided.

The Soviet politburo, after much hesitation, decided that Dubček could not control the growing tide of radical reform, which was acquiring revolutionary proportions. Apart from their concerns about the Prague Spring setting up an alternative and attractive model of democratic and humane socialism, the Soviet leaders viewed with alarm the weakening of security links and military links. At a time when it was reversing reform at home, the Brezhnev leadership was averse to running even the slightest risk of Czechoslovak change spilling over into the western republics of the Soviet Union. While the 500,000 Warsaw Pact troops encountered no more than demonstrations, the invasion of 20 August 1968 failed to install a "workers'" government. The partial restoration of censorship did not extinguish reform: spurred by nationalist sentiment, workers started to give more active support to the "renewal" of political life, as the reforms were commonly termed. October saw the establishment of a federation of Czech and Slovak republics, a goal that had preoccupied Slovak attention in preceding months. As protest against the invasion, notably the self-immolation of Jan Palach, continued into 1969, Dubček was replaced in April as first secretary by Gustav Husák, a Slovak politician with a moderately reformist reputation. Early hopes that he might emulate Hungary's János Kádár and renew change after restoring order went unfulfilled as the policy of "normalization" purged 500,000 Communists and ushered in two decades of moral and economic decay that bankrupted the chances of party-led reform. It was by human rights groups such as *Charter 77, which gave birth to Civic Forum, that society was finally mobilized in November 1989 to carry through a peaceful *revolution that saw the Prague Spring as a proud symbol of free speech—Dubček became chair of the federal parliament—but an outdated political model. The most significant impact of 1968 was felt within the group of reform-minded members of the party establishment in the Soviet Union. It was from the Prague Spring that Gorbachev and his associates drew many of their ideas of democratization and from the invasion and its aftermath that they largely derived their determination not to use force in Eastern and Central Europe, a decision that made possible the *annus mirabilis* of 1989.

(See also COMMUNIST PARTY STATES; NINETEEN EIGHTY-NINE.)

Galia Golan, *The Czechoslovak Reform Movement* (Cambridge, U.K., 1971). H. Gordon Skilling, *Czechoslovakia's Interrupted Revolution* (Princeton, N.J., 1976).

ALEX PRAVDA

PREBISCH, Raúl. Economist, policymaker, and diplomat, Raúl Prebisch (1901–1986) was among the most influential Latin Americans of the century. Prebisch had a major impact on Argentina, as the first director of the nation's central bank; on the region, as executive secretary of the UN Economic Commission for Latin America (ECLA; later the *Economic Commission for Latin America and the Caribbean, or ECLAC); on the *Third World as a whole, as the first director of the UN Conference on Trade and Development (UNCTAD); and globally, as a founder of development economics. In the postwar era, Prebisch's thesis on unequal exchange between "center" and "periphery"—his term for the industrial West and the primary-exporting Third World—has achieved wide recognition, if not universal acceptance, as the hallmark of the structuralist school of economics.

Born in Tucumán, Argentina, in 1901, Prebisch studied at the University of Buenos Aires. As a young economist, he gained favor with Argentina's political establishment, and led the country's new central bank from 1935 to 1943. The perceived inadequacy of neoclassical economics during the Great Depression of the 1930s led him to *Keynesianism, and then to his own center-periphery thesis on the world economy, developed between 1944 and 1949. Prebisch's instrument for elaborating, testing, and propagating his ideas was ECLA, which he directed from 1950 to 1962.

His first and most famous thesis appeared in *The Economic Development of Latin America and Its Principal Problems* (Spanish ed., 1949). Here he sought to explain the secular deterioration of the relative prices of primary goods in the world market. Prebisch argued that long-term productivity gains were greater and diffused more readily in industrial than in primary activities. If prices of industrial goods had fallen, Prebisch held, the effects of technical progress would have spread over the entire center-periphery system, and the terms of trade for agricultural and mineral goods would have improved. They did not do so, Prebisch asserted, because during the upswing of the business cycle, the center's working class absorbs real economic gains, but wage contracts make industrial prices "sticky" during the downswing. Because workers are poorly organized in the periphery (especially in agriculture), the periphery absorbs more of the system's income contraction during recession. (Although the terms-of-trade argument remains highly controversial today, econometric evidence of the last decade has tended to confirm secular deterioration.) Finally, Prebisch pointed to the center's monopolistic pricing of industrial goods as a cause of unequal exchange.

In the *Economic Survey of Latin America: 1949*, Prebisch further elaborated his thesis. An underlying cause of the deterioration in terms of trade was the creation of a surplus labor supply, as modern technique partially transformed the largely agricultural, procapitalist, and low-productivity sector of the periphery's economy. Such labor put downward pressure on wages and therefore on agricultural prices. For Prebisch, the very definition of "underdevelopment" was the heterogeneity of productivities.

Another reason for deterioration was that, with world income rising, the periphery demanded more industrial goods while the center wanted fewer primary goods as proportions of their total incomes. (H. W. Singer independently developed a similar thesis.) For Prebisch, a related problem was the periphery's high propensity to import, partly caused by income concentration, contributing to a perennial *balance-of-payments problem.

Thus Prebisch's analysis pointed to three negative features in the periphery's economy: structural unemployment, external disequilibrium, and deteriorating terms of trade—all of which a properly implemented policy of industrialization would help eliminate. Traditional export activities could be "taxed" for industrial development through state-directed exchange and commercial policies.

The *Economic Survey* was a point of departure for a "structuralist" school of development studies that would emphasize macroeconomics, the foreign exchange constraint, the role of the state, interdisciplinary approaches, and historical (transcyclical) changes. One such study was *Towards a Dynamic Development Policy for Latin America* (1963), in which Prebisch treated hitherto-subordinated social issues. He now called for reforms in agrarian structure and income distribution and pointed to structural problems whose recognition anticipated *dependency theory: First, income concentration in Latin America was accompanying industrialization; second, manufacturing was becoming more capital-intensive, owing to elite consumption patterns, and consequently was absorbing less labor than anticipated.

Prebisch's work at ECLA ranged far beyond his theoretical contributions. He promoted Latin American economic integration and the creation of UNCTAD, of which he was ap-

pointed first director. During his years at UNCTAD (1964–1969), Prebisch traveled the globe, propagating his ideas on unequal exchange and seeking commodity price agreements between central and peripheral countries. Subsequently Prebisch returned to ECLA, where he remained an active theorist, policy advisor, and advocate for Third World interests until his death in 1986.

Prebisch's most important later book was *Peripheral Capitalism* (1981), which can be associated with the non-Marxist version of the "dependency" tradition. He now argued that the structural features of peripheral countries prevented the full development of capitalism owing to the large and growing share of income appropriated by the center-emulating privileged classes; unequal exchange with industrial countries; and "power relations" between center and periphery (and within the periphery).

(See also IMPORT-SUBSTITUTION INDUSTRIALIZATION; UNITED NATIONS CONFERENCE ON TRADE AND DEVELOPMENT.)

United Nations Economic Commission for Latin America, *The Economic Development of Latin America and Its Principal Problems* (Lake Success, N.Y., 1950). Raúl Prebisch, *Capitalismo periférico: Crisis y transformación* (Mexico City, 1981). Raúl Prebisch, "Five Stages in My Thinking on Development," in Gerald M. Meier and Dudley Seers, eds., *Pioneers in Development* (New York, 1984), 175–192.

JOSEPH L. LOVE

PRESIDENCY, U.S. Henry Jones Ford, in his classic 1898 work *The Rise and Growth of American Government*, quoted Alexander Hamilton's prediction to a friend that the time would "assuredly come when every vital question of the state will be merged in the question, 'Who shall be the next president?' " Ford cited this remark to support his argument that, in creating the presidency, the Constitutional Convention of 1787 had "revived the oldest political institution of the race, the elective kingship."

Although there is much truth in Ford's evaluation of the U.S. presidency, it also displays a certain measure of ambivalence on a fundamental issue. Is the presidency best understood as primarily a person ("Who shall be the next president?") or an office (an "elective kingship")?

Political scientists in the twentieth century have continued to grapple with Ford's conundrum but have not resolved it. The majority probably would agree that the best answer to the person-or-office question is both: person and office, president and presidency. The office has become important mostly because its constitutional design suited it well for national leadership in the changing circumstances of history. But because the U.S. Constitution invested so much responsibility in the person who is president, that person's background, personality, and leadership skills are also consequential.

Office. The Constitutional Convention created a government marked not by *separation of powers (the traditional formulation) but rather, in the political scientist Richard Neustadt's apt phrase, by "separated institutions sharing powers." Institutional separation meant, for example, that in stark contrast to political systems based on *parliamentary democracy, which draw their executive leadership from the legislature, the president was forbidden by Article I, Section 6 of the Constitution to appoint any sitting member of Congress to the cabinet or White House staff. These severely separated branches were, however, constitutionally enjoined to share in the exercise of virtually all the powers of the national government—the president is "Commander in Chief of the Army and Navy," but Congress has the power to "declare *war"; Congress is empowered to "make all laws," but the president may veto them, or more energetically, may propose "such Measures as he shall judge necessary and expedient"; the Senate may (or may choose not to) give "Advice and Consent" concerning presidential appointments to the executive branch and the judiciary; and so on.

Powers, of course, do not define power—over time the presidency has become increasingly powerful even though the formal powers of the office have remained the same. A second cluster of constitutional decisions, those concerning the number and selection of the executive, provides much of the explanation for the presidency's expanding influence. The framers of the Constitution, after much debate, created the presidency as a one-person, not a plural or committee-style, office and provided that the president would be elected by the entire nation, independent of Congress and the state governments. In doing so, they made the president the only national officer who can plausibly claim both a political mandate to speak for the people and their government and an institutional capacity to lead with what the Pennsylvania delegate James Wilson described as "energy, unity, and responsibility."

Lead, that is, when national leadership is sought, which, during the nineteenth century, it usually was not. Historically, it took a century and a quarter—from 1789 to 1913—for parchment to become practice, that is, for all of the constitutionally enumerated powers of the presidency to come to life. Treaty making and other matters of foreign affairs aside—who but the president could represent the *United States to other nations or lead it into war?—Congress seized the lion's share of the government's shared powers nearly from the beginning, dominating even the executive appointment process. When it came to legislation, members of Congress treated with scorn most early presidential efforts to recommend or influence their consideration of bills and resolutions; nor, until Andrew Jackson in the 1830s, were presidents able to exercise the veto power without provoking a politically disabling storm of wrath on Capitol Hill.

Presidential disempowerment was, if long-lived, temporary, the logical consequence of the condition of weak national government that generally prevailed during the nineteenth century. The country, then a congeries of local economies and cultures, was not seeking what the presidential office was constitutionally designed to offer, namely, energetic leadership in behalf of national initiatives. But the conditions that sustained weak government began to change around the turn of the century. The broad extension of railroads and telegraph lines made all but inevitable the development of a national economy, and with this transformation came demands that the national government take measures variously to facilitate the spread and to tame the excesses of massive corporations. Early-twentieth-century presidents Theodore Roosevelt and Woodrow Wilson roused a popular mandate for the president to make full use of the office's constitutional powers to lead Congress and the executive branch. Franklin D. *Roosevelt, during the Great Depression of the 1930s, and more recent presidents such as Lyndon B. *Johnson

and Ronald *Reagan also have played the role of chief legislator on a grand scale. The post–World War II rise of the United States to *superpower status in a then-bipolar, now-unipolar international system lifted the presidency to center stage not just in Washington but the world.

Person. Because the presidency is important, so is the person who is the president. What background characteristics do presidents typically acquire before taking office? What manners of personality? What skills of leadership?

As to background, presidents almost always have been drawn from the ranks of white, male, married Christians who already have held high governmental office. Women, African Americans, Jews, bachelors, even nationally prominent leaders from the realms of business, education, and elsewhere in the private sector have found it hard to rouse serious interest in their potential presidential candidacies. Recent historical trends indicate both an expansion (in social terms) and a contraction (in occupational terms) of the talent pool from which Americans choose their presidents. Until John F. *Kennedy's election in 1960, for example, Roman Catholics were effectively excluded from consideration; so, until Reagan was elected in 1980, were divorced men. *Public opinion surveys indicate a growing willingness among voters to select a black, female, or Jewish president. Yet the rosters of presidential candidates in recent elections have been composed almost entirely of sitting or former senators, governors, and vice presidents.

The personality, or psychological character, that a president brings to the White House is, considering the power of the office and the pressures that weigh upon its occupant, of obvious importance. Public interest in former Senator Gary Hart's sexual behavior, Senator Joseph Biden's plagiarism, Senator Robert Dole's temper, and the purported "wimpiness" of nominees George *Bush and Michael Dukakis in the 1988 presidential election illustrates the widespread concern about presidential character. So do the efforts of James David Barber and other political scientists to develop behavioral models that relate presidential personality to presidential performance. Regrettably, however, scholarly understanding of this matter has not kept pace with public concern. Personality theory is still too murky a field to explain, much less predict, presidential character.

The skills of leadership that a president requires may be more confidently described. In relations with the rest of the executive branch, the president is called upon to be a talented manager of authority, both of lieutenants on the White House staff (whose chronic sycophancy toward the president and hostility toward the president's critics perennially threaten to overwhelm the good effects of their loyalty, talent, and hard work) and of the massive departments and agencies of the bureaucracy, whose activities lie at the heart of the president's role as chief executive.

Presidential leadership of Congress requires different, more tactical political skills. Senators and representatives, no less than the president, are politically independent and self-interested. No one has described the challenge of leading them more precisely and pithily than Neustadt: to lead is to persuade, to persuade is to bargain, and to bargain is to convince individual members of Congress that their interests and the president's are (or can be made to be) the same.

Ultimately, a president's standing with Congress and the

bureaucracy rests on the bedrock of public opinion, which makes the "presentation of self" (a phrase invented by the sociologist Erving Goffman) to the American people an important cluster of leadership skills. Presentation of self involves not just speechmaking, press conferences, and other forms of rhetoric, but dramaturgy as well. During Richard *Nixon's first term, for example, he reinforced a televised speech appealing for the support of the "silent majority" of blue-collar workers and their families by dramatically donning a hard hat before a cheering crowd (and a battery of observing cameras) at a New York construction site.

Perhaps a president's most important leadership skills involve a strategic sense of the historical possibilities of the time. These possibilities are defined both by objective conditions (such as the international situation, the budget, and the health of the economy) and by the public mood. Above all, the president must have a highly developed aptitude for what Woodrow Wilson called "interpretation"—that is, the ability to understand and articulate the varying, vaguely expressed desires of the American people for change or quiescence, material reward or moral challenge, isolation from or intervention in the problems of the world, and so on.

In the end, the background, personality, and leadership skills of the president are important because of the ways in which the Constitution and changing historical circumstances have made the presidency important. Person and office, although defined and often discussed separately, are in essence one.

(See also BUREAUCRATIC POLITICS; CARTER, JIMMY; CONGRESS, U.S.; CONSTITUTION; EISENHOWER, DWIGHT D.; INTERNATIONAL SYSTEMS; PSYCHOLOGY AND POLITICS; SUPREME COURT OF THE UNITED STATES; TRUMAN, HARRY S.)

Richard E. Neustadt, *Presidential Power* (New York, 1960). James David Barber, *The Presidential Character: Predicting Performance in the White House* (Englewood Cliffs, N.J., 1972). Erwin C. Hargrove and Michael Nelson, *Presidents, Politics, and Policy* (Baltimore and New York, 1984). Michael Nelson, ed., *The Presidency and the Political System* (Washington, D.C., 1984). Sidney M. Milkis and Michael Nelson, *The American Presidency: Origins and Development, 1776–1990* (Washington, D.C., 1990).

. MICHAEL NELSON

PRISONER'S DILEMMA. See GAME THEORY.

PRIVATIZATION. Privatization is an economic tool inexorably yoked to politics. The technical aspect of privatization, transferring all or part of a public sector function to the private sector, is dependent for its success on political will. The transfer can take many forms including total asset-sale privatization and contracting out. In this process, political proficiency is as important as the economic aspects in creating successful privatization. The considerable technical issues significant in a privatization effort can also determine success or failure and range from transition costs to difficulties in estimating market value to the continuing need for regulation after transfer is complete.

After World War II, public sectors expanded in most countries. Governments were interested in creating more market-like enterprises for political, economic, and ideological reasons. International organizations such as the *World Bank were interested in joint investments with governments rather than private companies and wanted to help promote infrastructure growth in less developed countries (Farazmand, 1999). Late in the 1970s this trend began to reverse, initially in industrialized countries and later in underdeveloped nations, giving impetus to the privatization movement. The rationale for the privatization movement in industrialized countries was ideologically driven, intended to accomplish two practical public policy objectives: reducing the size of government and decreasing budget deficits. Political leaders, such as British Prime Minister Margaret *Thatcher and U.S. President Ronald Reagan, responded with programs privatizing *inter alia* public utilities in Britain (1981–1986) and Reagan's "productivity enhancements through competition" in the 1980s.

In developing nations the privatization movement was motivated by the difficulty of *Third World countries in meeting their debt repayment schedules. Heavy budget deficits, losses from poorly performing public sector services, and programs such as social welfare put considerable pressure on governments to take action to become more efficient, productive, and streamlined.

The myriad structural formats considered as privatization are distinctly different from other public sector reforms often implemented simultaneously. In terms of microeconomics, the U.S. "reinventing government" movement has proffered strong policies of improved management and more efficient government/enterprise relations and market pricing, but has not reduced public ownership or management. Macroeconomic changes such as liberalizing markets, price deregulations, opening markets to foreign competition, and demonopolization, reduce market entry and exit barriers and promote free competition and improve the possibilities for successful privatization.

The main characteristic of privatization is the cultural shift in the *state-market relationship from a relationship that was social-utility oriented to one of private profit maximization. Forms of privatization vary. Public asset transfer can include only property or other economic elements while management and control are maintained by the government, or, as is most common, ownership and control are sold or leased along with economic elements. Government contracting, a form of privatizing management or service functions, is most successful where confidence in the reliability and stability of private service providers is high and regulation enforcement is possible. As in all situations of market competition, corruption and conflict of interest can be serious problems. Other methods include selling state enterprise stock shares on the open market as in Australia which now has the highest share ownership rates in the world. Liquidation, and sale to management or employees are other options. At the start of the twenty-first century, privatization has become a pervasive global economic-political strategy with mixed results. Privatized enterprises now provide average annual proceeds of over 1.5 percent of GDP in New Zealand to approximately 0.1 percent in Japan, with other OECD countries falling in between.

Controversy reigns, even in those countries recognized as world leaders in asset-sale privatization (Britain, New Zealand, and Australia) as to the problematic nature of controlling quality of services once privatization has occurred. The boon, however, is in the large profits obtained when the asset sale occurs. In some cases these profits have been used to reduce state debt as in Victoria, Australia, which was able to pay down two-thirds of its debt, thus reducing revenue outflows to debt service and allowing redirection to infrastructure and social program enhancements.

The contested implications of privatization can best be understood by examining the controversies surrounding its goals and representations. Proponents argue that, from an ideological standpoint, free market forces provide cost savings through competition. Private management is claimed to be more efficient in goods and services production and delivery. It attracts both foreign and national private investment. The proliferation of privatization as a mechanism to spread capitalist ideology around the world has been well funded to the tune of over US$200 billion by the World Bank to Third World countries from 1990–2000. As always, the World Bank and the *International Monetary Fund have stipulated conditionality that requires borrowing countries to adopt *structural adjustment programs including privatizing "inefficiently" run public enterprises. Such measures are intended to realize economic efficiencies that could be better spent for infrastructure and social development. Politically, privatization has been used to advance conservative, free-market ideologies. Acting as leverage for tax cut programs, government budget cuts, and cuts in *welfare assistance, government was to turn selected public sector functions over to the private sector, thereby achieving the savings and profits to pay for the reform programs.

Despite the ideological and practical justifications claimed for privatization, critics point out serious drawbacks of privatization, for instance, concentration of power in the private sector and lack of transparency leading to favoritism and *corruption. Further, political corruption which has allowed public officials to inappropriately profit from privatization has had serious impacts, especially on developing economies. Even in developed countries abuse is a pervasive issue. In the U.S., 25 percent of top government contractors have been found guilty of abusing their contracts, yet they still provide services to the different branches of the armed services. Critics cite that privatization in countries with underdeveloped economies has been used to transfer wealth from the common good of the society at large to privileged ethnic, familial, or economic groups. Often no objective consideration is given to the raison d'etre which necessitated the establishment of public enterprises in the first place, and thus the economic stimulus and social good which were to be derived are never realized.

Privatization, in both developed and developing countries, is producing mixed results whose long-term implications are not yet clear. The stakeholder benefits of well-implemented privatization are cost-savings or asset sales, expanding economic enterprise, and provision of quality services at least cost. The dangers of corruption, abuse, and runaway commercialization, however, are abundant. Furthermore, as the critics of privatization point out, it continues to impact and reshape political ideologies globally as is seen in Russia, Eastern and Central Europe, and Africa. In short, in spite of the ideological divide on privatization, the evidence to date suggests that privatization has created winners and losers in developed as well as underdeveloped countries, although clearly the negative impact is more felt in underdeveloped countries than in developed ones. The literature on privati-

zation has identified governments that are selling, consultants, financial, and legal institutions, new investor-owners, directors and managers of the new enterprises as winners. The losers, according to the same source, are former staff of privatized companies, trade unions, customers who benefitted from these enterprises, and citizens/taxpayers, as public wealth and skills are transferred to the privileged nationals and their international partners.

There is a sense of urgency, at least according to critics, to reconsider the privatization strategy. Reform is being advocated to restore, once more, the public sector's capacity to provide essential and desirable services. One strategy that researchers are advocating in this regard is public-private partnership. The "how" of this strategy and whether or not it is even feasible in the vogue of global capitalism is open to future inquiry. In the meantime, the literature on privatization suggests that underdeveloped countries carefully reconsider the goals and benefits of public sector enterprises in order to assure fulfillment of government responsibility for the welfare and security of its citizens. In developed countries, on the other hand, particular attention must be given to analyzing the long-term costs, payments, and responsibilities which may remain with the government when privatization occurs. Privatization is an economic-ideological tool requiring strategic assessment of long-term outcomes and rigorous assessment of quality on behalf of the public good.

(See also INTERNATIONAL DEBT; PARASTATALS.)

Yacob Haile-Mariam and Berhanu Mengistu, "Public enterprises and the Privatisation Thesis," *Third World Quarterly*, 10(4) October. Ali Farazmand, "Privatisation or reform? Public Enterprise Management in Transition," *International Review of Administrative Sciences*, 65(4) December (Glasgow, U.K., 1999).

BERHANU MENGISTU

PROGRESSIVE MOVEMENT, U.S. Progressivism was a political movement in the United States that was not contained within any one party or organization. Its adherents were reformers who opposed the patronage-based *political machines that dominated many levels of government. Progressives also shared a vision of a political community in which civically educated citizens were not divided by enduring class, ethnic, or party conflicts, but by temporary, well-informed disagreements on public issues. Such a diffuse movement cannot be precisely dated, but progressivism had its greatest impact between the election of 1896 and U.S. entry into World War I in 1917.

Progressivism moved from local to state to national government as individual leaders sought higher office. Support for Progressive candidates such as Seth Low (New York) or Charles Merriam (Chicago) followed earlier class and ethnic divisions. More successful Progressives, such as Newton Baker (Cleveland), were able to create new coalitions that brought together machine opponents of different social classes and ethnic groups. A new conception of efficiency, which encompassed effective service provision as well as elimination of corruption, displaced the older reform ideal of "good government," which often meant government from which non-Anglo-Saxon or working-class politicians such as Boston's James Michael Curley and New York's George Washington Plunkitt had been removed. The most enduring Progressive mayors included Baker and Tom Johnson in

Cleveland, Hazen Pingree in Detroit, and Brand Whitlock in Toledo. John Purroy Mitchel (New York) and George Alexander (Los Angeles) were more briefly successful.

At the state level, Progressives organized against what they believed were exploitative economic interests; opposition to the railroads was particularly important in the Midwest and West. Robert La Follette (Wisconsin) and Hiram Johnson (California) built farm-labor alliances to become governors of their states, and then U.S. senators. Charles Evans Hughes was elected governor of New York after leading an investigation into insurance company abuses.

Progressivism created chaos in national politics, but ultimately little was changed. In 1912, former President Theodore Roosevelt organized the Progressive Party after he lost the Republican nomination to incumbent William Howard Taft. The Republican split allowed Democrat Woodrow Wilson to win the election with a minority of the popular vote. Though Roosevelt's party claimed the label, all three candidates could be considered Progressives. In 1916, Roosevelt returned to the Republican Party, frustrating the hopes of the most radical Progressives for a new politics pitting a single Progressive party against a single conservative party. Most Progressives followed Roosevelt and supported Hughes, the Republican nominee, but an estimated twenty percent, including leaders of the radical faction, supported Wilson as he won reelection. By 1920, the national Republican majority of 1896–1908 was restored. Progressivism had a more enduring impact on the House of Representatives: a 1910 revolt against Speaker Joseph G. Cannon by Republican Progressives produced decentralization as authority shifted from the Speaker of the House to committees.

World War I disrupted Progressive politics, exacerbating ethnic conflicts that Progressive coalitions had often cut across. Progressive coalitions in some cities and states survived the effects of war; in others, Progressive innovations were adopted by the party organizations they had displaced. In national politics, progressivism became more exclusively the movement of insurgent Republicans from the Midwest and West, who fought their party's dominant Eastern wing over the tariff and other issues. Robert La Follette, the leader of this faction, received seventeen percent of the popular vote as the Progressive Party candidate for president in 1924. Progressive ideas were among the many strains contributing to Franklin *Roosevelt's *New Deal, but there was no clear political continuity between the two eras of political change: most surviving Progressive leaders actually opposed Roosevelt's policies as excessively centralist.

Because Progressives disagreed over issues like business regulation, their legacy was less evident in new policies than in new ways of making and administering policies. The New York Bureau of Municipal Research provided a model for new semipublic institutions applying expertise to governmental problems. Progressives also enacted mechanisms to weaken party organizations: the direct primary (allowing voters to choose party candidates), the initiative (allowing voters to propose measures), the referendum (allowing voters to approve measures), and the recall (allowing voters to remove officials). Local antiparty measures included nonpartisan elections, at-large rather than ward-based (district) elections, and, especially in smaller cities, replacement of mayoral systems with government by commission or city manager.

Benjamin Park De Witt, *The Progressive Movement* (1915; Seattle, 1968). Melvin G. Holli, *Reform in Detroit: Hazen S. Pingree and Urban Politics* (New York, 1969). William S. Leary, Jr., and Arthur S. Link, *The Progressive Era and the Great War, 1896–1920* (Arlington Heights, Ill., 1978). Kenneth Finegold, *Experts and Politicians: Reform Challenges to Machine Politics in New York, Cleveland, and Chicago* (Princeton, N.J., 1995). James J. Connolly, *The Triumph of Urban Progressivism: Urban Political Culture in Boston, 1900–1925* (Cambridge, Mass., 1998).

KENNETH FINEGOLD

PROPAGANDA. See PSYCHOLOGY AND POLITICS.

PROPORTIONAL REPRESENTATION. Most common in continental Europe, proportional representation is a method of electing representatives in *parliamentary democracies. In the more commonly used list system, the intent is to provide for political parties the same ratio of seats in a parliamentary body that these parties received in an election. For example, if a political party received twenty percent of the vote in an election, under proportional representation this party would receive twenty percent of the seats in the legislative body. The much less widely used Hare system (named for the nineteenth-century British political reformer Thomas Hare) is a complicated mechanism wherein individual candidates can be ranked by the voters in an order of preference.

Proportional representation differs greatly from the nonproportional single-member-district, "first-past-the-post" electoral system used in Britain, the United States, and many other Commonwealth countries. Proportional representation's origins date from the late nineteenth and early twentieth centuries when the proliferation of political parties representing specific groups in continental European societies (nobility, peasants, industrialists, workers, religions) made the Anglo-American system impractical and unfair. For example, if several districts had individual candidates from five different parties and the leading party's candidate received twenty-five percent of the vote in each of them, under the Anglo-American "first-past-the-post" rule, that party would win one hundred percent of the seats with only twenty-five percent of the votes.

The Anglo-American preference for single-member-district, "first-past-the-post" electoral systems derives from the earlier introduction of *democracy, the greater role given to individual representation, and the smaller number of parties in those countries. In fact the relationship between the number of parties and the choice between proportional representation and the Anglo-American system is somewhat of a chicken-and-egg issue. With fewer parties, there is less likelihood of a perceived need for proportional representation. Yet an entrenched single-member-district, "first-past-the-post" system is biased in favor of only two parties and thus makes the effective formation of additional parties inherently more difficult.

Most countries using proportional representation today have the political parties provide a list of candidates so that voters may choose to give their vote to the party that most closely represents their ideological preference. In other words, the party as a collective entity is the primary vehicle for organizing political expression. This system encourages parties to place candidates whom they would most like to see elected near the top of the list, as the candidates are chosen for the legislature on the basis of the proportion of their party's votes that they receive. In multiparty systems, voters often have a wider range of political choices, which often correlates with higher voter participation than in Anglo-American systems. Some countries (Sweden and the Federal Republic of Germany [FRG]) provide a minimum threshold (four percent and five percent, respectively) to prevent the proliferation of a large number of tiny parties. Other countries (Italy and Israel) have minimal (one percent) thresholds, producing large numbers of political parties. There are also variations in how candidates are chosen. For example, the FRG uses a combination of single-member districts and proportional representation, but the allocation of seats in the Bundestag still depends on the proportion of the vote that the parties obtain in the votes by party list.

The primary criticisms of proportional representation by advocates of Anglo-American systems are that there is too great a proliferation of parties and that the formation of working majorities is made more difficult. As the above examples of the threshold provision suggest, however, problems associated with a large number of parties can be avoided by building safeguards into the system.

(See also ELECTIONS AND VOTING BEHAVIOR; POLITICAL PARTIES AND PARTY COMPETITION.)

Seymour Martin Lipset and Stein Rokkan, *Party Systems and Voter Alignments* (New York, 1967).

CHRISTOPHER S. ALLEN

PROSTITUTION. Financial or material compensation for sex may be differentiated as prostitution or may be integrated in relationships such as marriage or dating. A continuum of sexual-economic exchange between women and men is a culturally and historically persistent feature of social organization. This exchange is legally defined as prostitution, and then usually as the "crime of prostitution," when "women, homosexuals or transgenders explicitly solicit money, either verbally or non-verbally, from men for specific sexual services performed in public, private or commercial space." Criminal or civil codes do not specify gender or sexual identities but policing practices invariably target subordinate groups. Almost exclusively men pay for sex (with money, goods, or other reimbursement) and largely women provide sex; when homosexual or transgender men provide sexual service this does not change the gender pattern because, like women, they service men. Significantly, those who solicit money for sex are defined by their activity as "prostitutes," an illegitimate if not illegal status, while those who pay for sex are rarely distinguished from the general male population.

Since prostitution functions as an institutionalized regulator of gender prescriptions, any transgressive behavior on the part of women or women-identified persons within a given context can call forth the stigma "prostitute" or "whore" and its punitive consequences. For example, women working or simply walking in the public sphere ("public women"/"common women") and women traveling alone or among other women ("free women"), regardless of their occupation or intention, have been branded, beaten, and sometimes arrested for prostitution as have women accused of breaching gender-discriminatory marital, migration, or dress codes.

The earliest depictions of prostitutes in modern Europe are accredited to the sixteenth-century Italian writer Pietro Aretino who developed the device of satirical dialogue between whores to mock social conventions and hypocrisies. Such dialogues form the base of the pornographic tradition in Europe, dominating the genre well into the eighteenth century. By the early nineteenth century, the function of pornography had dissolved from sexy social critique to sexual arousal alone. Revealingly, portrayals of witty subversive prostitutes were replaced by images of passive sexual stimuli for men while condemnations of the medium were recast in moral, rather than political, terms.

Like pornography, prostitution has been a site of controversy and control. Beginning with ancient societies, third parties have manipulated the sexual-economic system for their own material benefit by recruiting women and by selling, transporting, or offering them as gifts to (other) men. For centuries politicians, religious reformers, social scientists, and medical authorities have been debating whether the barter in women should be legalized, outlawed, tolerated, or abolished. Within those debates the person of the prostitute serves as symbol of social disorder, immorality, and disease.

Feminist perspectives have been as divided as those of mainstream authorities. During the last decades of the nineteenth century in Britain and France, a feminist movement took force under the leadership of Josephine Butler against state regulation of prostitution, specifically against police harassment of prostitutes and other working women. By the turn of the century the movement had been overshadowed by a social purity campaign against prostitution per se and for greater rather than lesser police powers aimed repressively at punishing prostitution customers and profiteers, on the one side, and "rescuing" and "rehabilitating" prostitutes, on the other. During the 1970s, prostitutes in the United States and Britain embraced the early feminist outrage of Butler and reawakened a movement against state criminalization and police harassment of working women. Politically identifying themselves as "sex workers," prostitutes demanded social and legal recognition of prostitution as legitimate work and of sexual service providers as legitimate citizens. Those activists and their contemporary feminist allies came into immediate clash with abolitionist feminists, inheritors of the social purity campaign, who defined sexual commerce per se as violence against women, regardless of conditions ranging from female autonomy to male coercion. Since the 1980s, the ideological and strategic tension between those who recognize prostitution as work and those who define it a priori as violence against women has become a heated political fault line of international feminism. Whereas the former are fighting alongside sex workers against conditions of exploitation and violence within the sex industry, the latter are fighting for stricter state prohibition of the industry as such. From the perspective of sex workers and their allies, increased state repression invariably leads to greater social control, physical harassment, and economic deprivation for women; from the perspective of feminist and religious abolitionists, recognition of prostitution as work reinforces the commodification of female bodies and undermines public morality.

In practice, regulations of the sex industry currently fluctuate according to four state concerns: national revenue, migration policy, colonial military occupation, and public health. Specifically, intensification of controls typically coincides with: 1) increased state dependence upon the funds generated from the sex industry at home or from the prostitution earnings sent home by migrant women; 2) state reliance upon the labor of migrant women in undocumented service sectors of the economy together with increased restrictions on legal immigration; 3) provision of sex and "entertainment" to military men and, more recently on an equally large scale, to male tourists or businessmen; 4) public clamor for control of sexually transmitted disease, notably syphilis during the nineteenth century and *AIDS today, wherein prostitutes are scapegoated for spread of disease and targeted for state medical controls despite historical demonstrations of the illogic and inefficiency of such controls.

Although prostitution is legislated predominantly on the national level, the realities of contemporary sexual economics since the 1970s have become increasingly international in character. Millions of women migrate yearly within and across state borders in search of revenue to support themselves and their families, often as an escape from coercion and exploitation at home. Given their lack of autonomous travel, labor, or immigration rights, they often must rely on more or less honest third parties who arrange the transport of women and girls from rural to urban areas and from poorer to richer countries, predominantly for placement in prostitution, domestic work, or arranged marriage. On the male side of the gender imbalance, traveling and military men from industrialized countries support a booming sex tourism industry in developing countries which has come to provide two to fourteen percent of the GDP in certain regional economies.

The current expansion of labor migration and corresponding growth of the sex industry have massively augmented the profits and abuses of the sexual-economic system. Sex workers have responded to those developments, as well as to the global AIDS epidemic, with grassroots organizing and alliance-building. A political movement of sex workers began in North America and Western Europe in the 1970s; by the mid-1980s, sex workers on all continents were denouncing violations of their human rights in national and international forums. Aided by non-governmental and governmental funding for AIDS prevention work, activist prostitutes have mobilized thousands of women in regional and transregional meetings, especially in Latin America and Asia. In protest against social and state hypocrisy, these "dialogues between whores" give political voice to women now speaking on their own behalf. They are asking for solidarity from labor, migrant, and feminist organizations, and they demand an end to harassment by public authorities and full access to civil and human rights.

(See also GENDER AND POLITICS; WOMEN AND DEVELOPMENT.)

Alain Corbin, *Misery and Prostitution in the Nineteenth and Twentieth Century* (London, 1978, 1990). Judith Walkowitz, *Prostitution and Victorian Society: Women, Class, and the State* (Cambridge, U.K., 1980). Allan Brandt, *No Magic Bullet: A Social History of Venereal Disease in the United States Since 1880* (New York, 1985). Thang-Dam Truong, *Sex, Money and Morality: The Political Economy of Prostitution and Tourism in South East Asia* (London, 1990). Lynn Hunt, ed., *The Invention of Pornography* (New York, 1996). Gail Pheterson, ed., *A Vindication of the Rights of Whores*, (Seattle, 1989); *The Prostitution Prism* (Amsterdam, 1996). Marjan Wijers and Lin Lap-Chew, *Trafficking in Women, Forced Labour and Slavery-Like Practices in Marriage, Domestic Labour and Prostitution* (Utrecht, 1997). Kamala Kempadoo and Jo Doezema, eds., *Global Sex Workers: Rights, Resistance and Redefinition* (New York, 1998). Lin Lean Lim, ed., *The Economic and Social Bases of Prostitution in Southeast Asia* (Geneva, 1998).

GAIL PHETERSON

PROTECTION. Government policies that increase the price or decrease the availability of imports *protect* domestic producers. Political contention around import protection is a durable political issue in most countries. Except manipulations of the national currency, it is the government intervention in economic activity practiced the longest. Trade politics has colored relations between nations since the Middle Ages. Debates about the wisdom of *mercantilism and other protectionist practices inspired Adam Smith, David Ricardo, Friedrich List, and many other theorists of the eighteenth and nineteenth centuries who developed the foundations for modern politico-economic theory. Questions of trade policy continue to be important in current debates about the less developed countries and the global division of labor, the distribution of income and wealth, and the wisdom and feasibility of many national policies aimed at shaping economic life.

Economic theory sometimes endorses protection. When a nation is a relatively large consumer or producer, it may exploit its market power by import or export duties to shift the terms of trade in its favor (for example, a Brazilian export duty on coffee). If workers are idle, then import restrictions can raise national income, especially if foreign retaliation against exports is not prompt or severe. Strategic trade theory sometimes claims that protection can be applied to oligopolistic industries such as commercial airliners with beneficial consequences not only for the industry but for the nation as a whole. Some scholars have suggested that protection promotes social stability and, in developed countries, raises the incomes of poorly paid workers. However, economists generally argue that intervention is either undesirable or else more efficiently accomplished in other ways. For example, a wage subsidy for low-wage, import-competing industries would protect the welfare of their workers more efficiently than a tariff, and much more efficiently than quotas or so-called voluntary export restraints.

Contrary to what might be expected, protection is common in small countries that have negligible market power, and in industries that do not fall within the scope of strategic trade theory. Although world tariff levels have declined substantially in the last twenty years, the least economically efficient forms of protection (quotas and voluntary export restraints) are increasingly prevalent substitutes.

While the economic efficiency of many protective practices is dubious, their political efficacy is not. One must understand protection as a policy intended to maximize political support for the government in power. Economic conditions are important insofar as they affect political calculations. It should not be assumed that governments are attempting to maximize national income.

Most empirical work on the *political economy of trade policy deals with the inter-industry distribution of protection within a nation. It is commonly believed that declining import-competing industries that are moderately concentrated, labor-intensive, low-wage, and employ many workers are better able to achieve protection than industries that are not. Although there is some empirical support for such claims, other factors also have strong effects: current protection generally depends on previous protection, and on reductions in protection offered by other countries in multilateral tariff negotiations.

How one thinks about the politics of protection depends on the time horizon one adopts. In the short run real economic resources, unlike financial ones, cannot inexpensively redeploy to new activities. This implies that management and labor within an industry are likely to take common positions on protective measures. (Labor's interest in protection becomes more producer-oriented as it gains bargaining strength and sector-specific skills. This, in addition to increasing exposure to the consequences of international wage disparities due to declines in transport costs and protection, might account for the historic shift of labor movements in advanced capitalist states toward more protectionist positions.) In the short run the political effects of idle capacity caused by recessions can be pronounced, particularly in nations that are large and that have geographically concentrated industries. There is also some evidence that inflation reduces protectionist pressures and that a lack of protection reduces inflationary pressures. The business cycle is thus linked to trade policy so that recession engenders protection and prosperity (or inflation) leads to liberalization, while changes in policy can affect employment or inflation. Choices of monetary and fiscal policy and economic conditions thus shape a government's trade policy choices.

Over a longer period, economic factors redeploy to new sectors, and neoclassical models become more realistic. The Stolper-Samuelson theorem (1941) argues that with two factors of production, the scarce factor in each nation benefits from protection. If politics followed these lines, trade policy would invariably be a struggle between capital and labor: In capital-scarce economies, capital would favor protection, while under labor scarcity, labor would. The evidence suggests that capital-scarce nations are much more protectionist than capital-abundant ones, an asymmetry not explained by the theorem. (The relative ease of administering a bureaucracy that taxes external trade probably contributes to the heavy reliance on such taxes in poor countries, but this cannot account for their frequent resort to non-tariff barriers that often let foreigners capture the rents that these barriers create.)

A hegemony theory of protection attempts to explain global trade policy patterns over an extended period. The gist of the theory is that open trade is a collective good, that the presence of a very large, dominant nation that benefits from openness will enhance prospects for an open global system, and that in its absence the prospects for openness are meager. (A variant of this argument is that when international trade is concentrated among a small set of trading nations, the trading system will be open.)

Hegemony theory is superficially attractive, but has several weaknesses. Empirically, the relation between U.S. or U.K. supremacy and trading system openness is weak; in both cases, openness is not closely related to hegemony (or even concentration of capabilities in a handful of nations). The conceptual difficulties are also formidable. Market access is not a collective good. As the results of multilateral tariff bargaining make clear, nations reduce protection in a way that awards rela-

tively excludable benefits to those offering reciprocal cuts. The Soviet Union and other East bloc nations were excluded from the General Agreement on Tariffs and Trade (GATT) system owing partly to the U.S. desire to do so. While this exclusion was obviously influenced by national security politics, it also had fewer negative economic consequences for the United States than for some of its allies and economic competitors in Western Europe.

Hegemony theorists have not offered a compelling reason why the hegemon should prefer an open trading system. If the hegemon were to forgo levying optimal tariffs to induce others to reduce their own, then the others also must possess substantial market power, and it is not clear what distinguishes a hegemon from them except its larger size. On the other hand, if other nations do not possess market power, then their optimal tariff is already zero, and they therefore cannot match reductions in the hegemon's optimal tariff with reductions in their own. The hegemonic state would then levy the optimal tariff, and others would "grin and bear it." The simplest basis for the claim that hegemonic nations prefer open trade is to note that such nations are capital exporters and that they must establish a trading system that permits borrowers to earn enough foreign exchange through exporting to be able to service their international debts.

Efforts to explain differences in protection across nations have been quite limited. Apart from its relation to relative capital scarcity, protection is statistically associated with large land area, plentiful unskilled labor, a high ratio of government expenditures to national income, and low levels of per capita income. Such variables account statistically for about two-thirds of the cross-national variation in tariff rates, but only one-fourth to one-fifth the variation in the ratio of imports to GNP.

Other analysts explain cross-national differences in terms of different national institutions and ideologies. Work in this vein has been limited, and has primarily addressed U.S. commercial policy. These institutional and ideological explanations are often concerned with accounting for *lack* of change—in particular, the continued alleged adherence of the United States to a policy of openness. They suggest that government officials enjoy enough freedom from interest group, party, and public pressure to exercise discretion in their policy choices, but that these choices are also constrained by the institutional forms of national governments and international organizations and law, which change much more slowly than the short-run constellations of interests in civil society. These ideas are plausible, and the notion that politicians gratify their private preferences when making policy choices has some empirical support. However, the historical narratives favored by most exponents of this approach are better suited to illustrating the argument than to testing it. Such explanations must also confront the sources of changes in institutions and ideologies in order to explain policy shifts over the long run.

Tariffs are a relatively unimportant source of contention in the current international politics of protection, because so many of them have been reduced or eliminated. However, non-tariff barriers continue to be the source of friction. Because many national policies may confer competitive advantages on national producers, attempts to eliminate or internationally control non-tariff barriers often raise fundamental questions of national sovereignty. Another way in which current international trade negotiations raise larger political questions is through the increasing tendency to treat national policies toward foreign investment as a foreign trade issue. Firms that face protective barriers abroad may leap them by direct investment in the protected economy. If foreign direct investment is easy, policies to benefit national industries are problematic—who exactly is a national producer, and who is a foreign one?

Because the post–World War II international negotiations over the reduction of trade barriers have been dominated by the developed countries, trade tends to be freest in the commodities that these countries export. Internationally negotiated reductions of protection in agriculture and basic industries such as textiles and apparel—two areas where less developed countries often enjoy a comparative advantage—have been much less thoroughgoing. Collective action by less developed countries and an increased willingness of developed countries to offer reciprocal concessions to them may improve their access to developed country markets, but without the willingness of developed countries to pay the kinds of adjustment costs that less developed countries often face when they open their economies, the prospects for a wider sharing of the benefits of an open trading system are not encouraging.

(See also INTERNATIONAL POLITICAL ECONOMY; WORLD TRADE ORGANIZATION.)

Stephen P. Magee, William A. Brock, and Leslie Young, *Black Hole Tariffs and Endogenous Policy Theory: Political Economy in General Equilibrium* (Cambridge, U.K., 1989). Robert E. Baldwin, ed, *Empirical Studies of Commercial Policy* (Chicago, 1991). Michael J. Gilligan, *Empowering Exporters: Reciprocity, Delegation, and Collective Action in American Trade Policy* (Ann Arbor, Mich., 1997). BRIDGES Weekly Trade News Digest© is published by the International Centre for Trade and Sustainable Development and edited by the Institute for Agriculture and Trade Policy. It can be found at the ICTSD Web page: http://www.ictsd.org.

TIMOTHY J. McKEOWN

PSYCHOLOGY AND POLITICS. Politics deals with relations among people; therefore it is inevitably linked with psychology, which deals with human thinking and behavior. Political analysts throughout the ages and across civilizations have been interested in the reciprocal impact of personality characteristics and political environments. Although psychological insights have been applied to the study of numerous political phenomena for thousands of years, no coherent body of knowledge has emerged. Rather, diverse theories have been employed to explain why rulers and subjects think and act as they do and how their thoughts and actions shape the course of politics.

In the pre-Christian era, for example, Confucius (551–479 B.C.E.) and Aristotle (381–322 B.C.E.) taught about the connection between psychology and politics. Aristotle's *Rhetoric* provides advice about motivating various publics to support political causes. To succeed, Aristotle said, politicians must know how to stir their audiences' emotions. Niccolò Machiavelli's *Prince* (1513) is a medieval political psychology classic. Machiavelli urged rulers to study human nature so that they could control politics by manipulating their subjects. *The Prince* is filled with practical advice about the art of political manipulation.

Human Nature and Self-Government. Judgments about the best ways to govern political entities hinge on perceptions about the psychological makeup of human beings. These perceptions moved to the forefront of the political dialogue starting in the seventeenth century, when questions about citizen control of government agitated people in the Western world. Thomas Hobbes (1588–1679), a major contributor to the debate, saw human life as nasty, brutish, and short unless people were governed by stern rulers. By contrast, later political philosophers like John Locke (1632–1704), the Baron de Montesquieu (1689–1755), and Jean-Jacques Rousseau (1712–1788) believed that ordinary citizens were capable of governing themselves and needed protection from the unbridled whims of fallible rulers. The scope of citizen control of government must be decided through negotiations between rulers and subjects and affirmed by contract. These later political philosophers laid the foundations for constitutional government in the Western world, based on the belief that all human beings, including rulers, are fallible. A system of checks and balances was needed to forestall excesses and assure governance for the public good.

Karl *Marx (1818–1883) held a different view of human nature, believing that most people will support the common good except when they have been corrupted by capitalist economic systems. The overweening desire for domination of human and material resources fostered by capitalism could be eliminated through the abolition of private property rights. People would then share resources equitably and would be devoted to the collective good. Based on Marx's ideal vision of humanity, millions of people around the world embraced communist *ideology. But not all nineteenth-century visions of human nature were as optimistic as Marx's view. Psychologists like Sigmund Freud (1856–1939) pointed to irrational elements in human personality that led to irrational political behaviors, including genocide and war. Freud believed that societal norms were required to control individual irrational drives. When these norms were internalized and became the individual's superego or conscience, individuals and civilizations prospered.

The Impact of Personality on Leadership Styles. In the twentieth century, psychopolitical analysis became more scientific. Modern psychological theories and social science research techniques replaced mere assertions and speculations about the relation between human nature and politics. Using Freudian and neo-Freudian psychoanalytic concepts, Harold Lasswell wrote his pathbreaking book *Psychopathology and Politics* (Chicago, 1930). Lasswell contended that leaders try to legitimate their actions by claiming that they are performed in the public interest. In reality, the public behavior of political leaders is usually motivated by private concerns that they cannot admit to themselves or others. Psychiatric case studies of political activists persuaded Lasswell that the psychological characteristics of political leaders frequently border on the pathological.

The political consequences of the psychological makeup and motivations of major political leaders have been of particular interest to citizens subject to their control and to scholars. Psychobiographies based on Freudian and neo-Freudian notions have been written about leaders such as *Stalin, *Roosevelt, *Churchill, *Gandhi, *Mao Zedong, and *Hitler. In Hitler's case, for instance, biographers have tried to explain the psychological urges that made him willing to plunge the world into war to accomplish his political objectives. They have tried to fathom what made him capable of ordering the deliberate extermination of millions of human beings whom he deemed racially inferior and therefore worthless or dangerous. Even more puzzling, how could mild-mannered Harry Truman, president of a society that prides itself on its high regard for human lives, order a nuclear attack on wartime enemies knowing the horrendous consequences for military and civilian targets?

Answers to such questions have been sought from psychoanalytic theories, from social learning theories, and from various behavioristic approaches to psychology. Are inborn traits or human drives the explanation, so that a leader is born with an authoritarian personality or a compulsion for grandiose acts of violence? Or should one seek causes for the behavior of political leaders in societal influences that molded their personality, particularly during their formative years? Do circumstances create heroes and leaders as well as villains and mindless followers, or will these personality characteristics surface regardless of environmental contexts? Can political leaders mold the psyches of populations under their control to benefit the leaders' political purposes? What are the elements of charisma? These and many other questions about the psychological aspects of political leadership await definitive answers.

Political Socialization. Political leaders everywhere are interested in citizens' political socialization to create basic political attitudes that generate allegiance and support for political entities. They know that it is far easier to rule populations that willingly cooperate with public officials than to govern by force, contrary to the public's wishes. Depending on the prevailing political ideology, political socialization may strive to engender a high regard for *democracy or for authoritarian rule.

Socialization efforts are based on psychoanalytic concepts and learning theories. The efforts range from relying on unwritten rules about the norms of political behavior, passed on informally by parents and teachers to successive generations, to formal measures, such as prescribed civic education classes or elaborate indoctrination programs used in authoritarian societies throughout the life cycle. Political socialization guides the perceptions, attitudes, and opinions that humans form about their political world. These attitudes and opinions then shape people's actions when they vote in elections, pay taxes, serve in the armed forces, or contribute to society's economic development. Besides conveying factual information, political socialization engages people's emotions through stirring symbols, such as flags, patriotic music, or colorful public ceremonies.

When political socialization fosters attitudes favoring international cooperation and peaceful conduct in the international sphere, international agreements can be reached more easily and peace maintained. When attitudes are chauvinistic, or when other countries are routinely depicted as enemies, international conflict may ensue. This is especially true because mirror images are common. A nation that perceives its chief antagonist as a likely aggressor is apt to be perceived in exactly the same way by this antagonist. A major problem plaguing political socialization is the fact that misperceptions are common and are spread and perpetuated through socialization processes. Because major policies, including the decision to go to war, may hinge on these perceptions, the fear of misperception is great (e.g., Ralph White, *Nobody Wanted War*, Garden City, N.Y., 1970).

The success of socialization efforts is never assured and failures may lead to disaster. For example, when citizens lack achievement motivation, their society's economic development is likely to lag (David McClelland, *The Achieving Society*, Princeton, N.J., 1961). Successful socialization often hinges on psychological predispositions of the socialized subjects as well as on the political environment in which socialization takes place. For instance, the fact that humans satisfy their needs sequentially, with survival needs taking precedence, explains why starving populations care more about free food than free speech and other democratic concerns (Abraham Maslow, *Motivation and Personality*, New York, 1954).

What is the impact of different political environments on the political thinking and behavior of various publics? Comparative studies of the political attitudes and actions of people living under various types of regimes in diverse political cultures show marked variations in citizens' political attitudes and opinions (e.g., Gabriel Almond and Sidney Verba, eds., *The Civic Culture Revisited*, Boston, 1980). Citizens' attitudes and behaviors are also affected by major political upheavals such as wars, revolutions, and economic depressions. For example, the trauma created by major economic disasters leaves people everywhere fearful of losing their jobs and eager to support social policies that they may have previously shunned.

The Context for Decision Making. Political psychologists have devoted substantial attention to decision making because leaders' decisions affect the fate of their nations and the world. Decisions are shaped by the leaders' perceptions, attitudes, and opinions as well as the political context at the time of decision (Alexander George, *Presidential Decision-Making in Foreign Policy*, Boulder, Colo., 1980). Under conditions of high tension and group pressure, decision making is subject to intense psychological constraints. The psychologist Irving Janis, for example, in *Victims of Groupthink* (2d ed., Boston, 1999), described how U.S. policy makers bungled policies designed to overthrow Cuba's Communist government because group pressures supported flawed policy proposals. Understanding such psychologically debilitating conditions permits developing remedial procedures that can ease such problems.

Of course, leaders are not the only decision makers in politics. Individual citizens make voting decisions and decisions about supporting various policies and *interest groups. These decisions are important in all societies, but especially in democracies. This is why leaders spend much time and effort to gauge the nature of these political perceptions and attitudes and to measure their prevalence. They also attempt to shape and even manipulate these perceptions through well-chosen persuasion techniques.

The Causes and Cures of Political Violence. *Political violence has always been a major political concern. Civil war, revolution, terrorism, and international war are widely condemned by many societies and glorified by others as the acme of patriotic fervor. Important psychological forces are involved in political violence. For example, it is well established that people have fewer inhibitions about acting violently when they are members of a crowd rather than acting alone. Mob psychology and crowd hysteria are common. It is also common for people who oppose committing acts of violence in their private behavior to willingly perform extremely violent acts at the behest of their governments. Even organized religious bodies that fervently preach the sanctity of life to their constituents often pray for the success of their nation's military forces.

If it is true, as is often alleged, that political violence originates in the mind, then its eradication, if desired, may require the creation of more peace-inducing psychological environments. Political psychologists have devoted considerable thought and effort to this problem since the mid-1950s. Studies have focused on attitudes relevant to international relations, including *nationalism, patriotism, images of other nations, *public opinion, decision-making processes, and interactions during international conflicts.

Psychologists have developed various models of international conflict. For example, if it is viewed as a zero-sum aggressor-defender situation, one party's gain is the other's loss. To frustrate the aggressor's plans, the defender must develop sufficient military capacity to intimidate and thereby deter the aggressor. If a conflict-spiral model is postulated, where tensions escalate in spiral fashion, one can attempt to lower tensions through a series of reciprocal steps that lower tensions gradually (Charles Osgood, *An Alternative to War or Surrender*, Urbana, Ill., 1962). The process constitutes a positive-sum solution to international problems whereby all parties benefit. Other plans to forestall war, especially nuclear war, have tried to use psychological and social pressures to suppress jingoism (e.g., Edward Tolman, *Drives toward War*, New York, 1942). Bargaining and negotiating processes that can lead to peaceful conflict resolution have also attracted the attention of scholars and political practitioners. While there have been conspicuous successes, tragic failures continue to mar political life in many parts of the world.

(See also AUTHORITARIANISM; ELITES; POLITICAL CULTURE.)

Eric Singer and Valerie Hudson, eds., *Political Psychology and Foreign Policy* (Boulder, Colo., 1992). Shanto Iyengar and William J. McGuire, eds., *Explorations in Political Psychology* (Durham, N.C., and London, 1993). Richard Ned Lebow, *The Art of Bargaining* (Baltimore, 1996). Diana C. Mutz, Paul M. Sniderman, and Richard Brody, eds., *Political Persuasion and Attitude Change* (Ann Arbor, Mich., 1996). Alexander L. George and Juliette L. George, *Presidential Personality and Performance* (Boulder, Colo., 1998).

DORIS A. GRABER

PUBLIC ASSISTANCE. See ENTITLEMENTS; MEDICARE AND MEDICAID; WELFARE; WELFARE STATE.

PUBLIC CHOICE THEORY. According to the major text in the field, *public choice* "can be defined as the economic study of nonmarket decision-making, or simply the application of economics to political science" (Mueller, 1989). The subject, then, pertains to voters, politicians, bureaucrats, *interest groups, and the environment within which they interact to produce policy outcomes. That is the political science part; the economics part is a bit more difficult to specify. In brief, the economist's basic postulate is that the human actor is driven by personal self-interest (or, in the terminology of economists, utility or satisfaction). With this as the point of

departure the public choice analyst proceeds to employ the rather formidable analytical tools of modern economics in search of truths about public or collective choice. Thus, the analyst might wish to explain voter choices; the formation of coalitions; the electoral strategies of parties; the choice of fiscal and monetary policies; the pursuit of market advantages by interest groups; the growth of government; budgetary behavior of bureaucrats; and so on.

Now a well-recognized cross-disciplinary field claiming two Nobel laureates (Kenneth J. Arrow and James M. Buchanan), the study is hardly more than forty years of age, having been created, independently, by Kenneth Arrow (1951) and Duncan Black (1948) in the late 1940s and early 1950s. Both economists were fascinated by the perplexities of elections and voting under simple majority rule. Arrow demonstrated through the use of symbolic logic that, under certain clearly specified conditions or norms, collective choices could not achieve outcomes consistent with the diverse preferences held by voters. The problem was not that a majority could not be formed, but that too many majorities would eventuate, each to negate the others; thus, "cyclical majorities" resulted. This outcome, if true, was demoralizing to any committed democrat and believer in expanding government.

Countless commentators have since found or claimed to have discovered ways around Arrow's paradox, but the single best critique was actually written shortly before Arrow's monograph was published, namely the highly original work of Duncan Black. Black argued that groups using simple majority rule could achieve a stable equilibrium or outcome if the preferences of the voters were "single-peaked," that is, if the rank-ordering of their preferences displayed a certain logic such as preferring more to less or less to more and not confusing the two by making one's second choice the very opposite of the first. Thus, a voter whose first choice is to have the largest budget possible but second choice is the smallest budget instead of the median budget is deemed inconsistent and has preferences that are not single-peaked. Black's early work produced an enduring result called the median voter theorem that says the median voter preference will generally win, thus negating Arrow's paradox.

This proposition has important normative significance as well in that it can be shown that the result generates the most utility for society possible under the circumstances. In addition, Anthony Downs (1957) claimed that electoral competition among parties would also lead to policy positions closest to those preferred by median voters; thus, "Tweedledum and Tweedledee," or, in effect, no choice at all since both parties offer the same policies.

Although this branch of public choice has gone on to further explore the formal properties and most likely outcomes of elections and various constitutional rules, other less mathematical approaches have centered on other elements of politics, including bureaucracy. James M. Buchanan has explored basic constitutional problems and "rent-seeking," i.e., the rational pursuit by interest groups of economic privileges. He has been particularly concerned with facilitating mutually beneficial exchanges among citizens and a more efficient fiscal constitution that honors more citizen preferences. His work has also emphasized the redistributional quest of the interests leading in the end to the growth of government and negative-sum games in which everyone becomes worse off. Much of his work as well as that of followers in the so-called Virginia School has produced a theory of governmental or political failure very much the logical equivalent of the market failure school. Thus, Buchanan and colleagues have deromanticized politics and, indirectly, elevated appreciation for the market and other private institutions to new heights.

Although much of the substance of public choice can be stated in intricate mathematical terms, its basic findings are, like those of economics, simple. Democratic governments are claimed to engage in a number of highly important monetary and fiscal activities that are inefficient and, often, inequitable: 1) *political business cycles are alleged to produce inflationary policies that are pursued during the months before elections while less inflationary or deflationary policies follow a successful campaign; 2) policies are enacted in which total costs exceed total benefits; 3) costs are usually diluted through time and over the general taxpaying population so they will be invisible politically, while benefits will be highly visible to those who enjoy them, i.e., shares will be substantial enough to be noticed and provided during the immediate period. Our *Social Security program illustrates each of these claims.

The political process generates inefficiencies because political behavior differs dramatically from the market process. Voters, politicians, and bureaucrats must all respond to peculiar and perverse political incentives and institutions, none of which facilitates optimal policies. Voters are constrained by having single votes that can only be cast at discontinuous elections while politicians must concern themselves with mobilizing majorities based on incompatible coalition interests. Bureaucrats must please legislatures rather than consumers in markets.

Whereas the market is able to integrate its diverse interests and make everyone better off, there is no efficient "hidden hand" in politics. In fact, politics might better be described as a veiled fist because politics is ultimately based on coercion and on forming majorities consisting of temporary alliances among powerful interests. Such an image of politics is not reassuring, but it is the one set forth by public choice analysts (Mitchell and Simmons, 1994) during the past forty years and it is one that has gained increasing influence not only among academics but in politics itself.

(See also ELECTIONS AND VOTING BEHAVIOR; GAME THEORY; POLITICAL ECONOMY; RATIONAL CHOICE.)

Duncan Black, *The Theory of Committees and Elections* (Cambridge, U.K., 1948). Kenneth J. Arrow, *Social Choice and Individual Values* (New York, 1951). Anthony Downs, *An Economic Theory of Democracy* (New York, 1957). James M. Buchanan, *The Limits of Liberty* (Chicago, 1975). Dennis Mueller, *Public Choice II: A Revised Edition of Public Choice* (Cambridge, Mass., 1989). William C. Mitchell and Randy Simmons, *Beyond Politics* (New York, 1994).

WILLIAM C. MITCHELL

PUBLIC GOOD. A good characterized by two main properties, jointness of supply and nonexcludability, is a public good. If a good is characterized by jointness of supply, then the consumption of the good by one person does not affect the consumption of others in the group. If a good is characterized by nonexcludability, then it is impossible to prevent anyone in the group from consuming it. The classic example of a public good is a lighthouse: unlike a private good, the benefits of the lighthouse are joint and, once produced, are unsusceptible to exclusion.

The general idea of public goods and the problems which they pose for society have been present in political writings for several centuries. The contemporary interest in the concept originated in welfare economics in the work of Paul Samuelson ("The Pure Theory of Public Expenditure" *Review of Economics and Statistics* 36 [November 1954]: 387–389). Samuelson focused on how the properties of jointness and nonexcludability affected our ability to determine optimal levels of *consumption* of the good. For political analysis the problem of the *provision* of public goods was prominent in Mancur Olson's analysis of the logic of collective action (*The Logic of Collective Action*, Cambridge, Mass., 1965). These initial efforts to analyze the political and economic implications of public goods have led to extensive research on the subject.

To grasp the fundamental importance of the concept, one must relax the stringent criteria for what constitutes a public good. There are very few pure public goods, goods that are truly joint in supply and that are of a form which makes exclusion from consumption impossible. But a wide range of goods—known variously as "collective," "group," or "club" goods—have properties sufficiently similar to the pure case to create collective action problems. Examples in political analysis are numerous: international stability, national defense, tax revenues, environmental concerns, union activities, *interest groups, etc. For all of these goods the problem of nonexcludability is the key: the fact that members of a group cannot be excluded from enjoying the benefits of a good, either because exclusion is too costly or because it is technically infeasible, produces two fundamental problems. First, in the classic "free-rider" problem, if any member of the group pays the costs of producing the public good, then anyone else in the group can exploit the producer and consume the good for free. Second, the free availability of the good diminishes the incentive for any individual to contribute to its production, resulting in a collectively suboptimal provision of the good. Many of the strategic implications of these problems have been investigated through the use of *game theory. The basic conflict between individual and collective rationality characterized by the provision of public goods is analogous to the "Prisoners' Dilemma" problem: the choice of noncooperation dictated by individual self-interest leads to the production of a collective outcome which is suboptimal for all of the actors.

Much of the research has focused on the problem of suboptimal provision. Solutions can be divided into those which attempt to show that individual contribution is the rational self-interested action (such as Olson's by-product theory) and those which rely on external sanctions, typically by the state, to guarantee contribution.

(See also PUBLIC CHOICE THEORY.)

Duncan Snidal, "Public Goods, Property Rights and Political Organizations" *International Studies Quarterly* 23, no. 4 (December 1979): 532–566. Russell Hardin, *Collective Action* (Baltimore, 1982). Michael Taylor, *The Possibility of Cooperation* (New York, 1987).

JACK KNIGHT

PUBLIC OPINION. Students of politics agree that public opinion is an aggregate of individual opinions on issues of political relevance that can influence individual and group behavior and the actions of leaders and governments. The term began to be used frequently in political discourse in the late eighteenth century, catalyzed by the French Revolution. Its earlier origins from ancient Greece and Rome are summarized by Wilhelm Bauer in his "Public Opinion" (in Edwin R. A. Seligman, ed., *Encyclopaedia of the Social Sciences*, vol. 12, New York, 1934).

There is less agreement about specific political meanings of public opinion: whether it refers to "mass public," "informed public," or different "attentive publics"; to the opinions of *elites, organized groups, or other "opinion leaders" who ultimately influence widely held attitudes and beliefs; or to the "climate of opinion" that individuals perceive—correctly or incorrectly (the term "pluralistic ignorance" refers to the latter)—from the information that they get through personal interactions and through the mass media. The last meaning was emphasized by Walter Lippmann (United States) and Elisabeth Noelle-Neumann (Germany).

Notwithstanding this disagreement, mass opinion has been considered an important and even "rational" force: Political actors must confront it. The claim of rationality—versus charges that the mass public is ignorant and unsophisticated about politics—occurs in research in the United States, beginning with Paul Lazarsfeld and associates at Columbia University, voting studies at the University of Michigan, and, especially, the writing of V. O. Key, Jr. The rational sources of opinion include: 1) the explicit pursuit of self-interest, which research has not found to be as predominant as economic theories have expected; 2) the pursuit of genuinely collective or national interests (e.g., individuals' concern for the nation's general well-being, not simply their own); 3) the influences of culture, core values, and ideological and symbolic concerns; 4) social characteristics and identification with groups (i.e., race and ethnicity, economic status, gender, education, etc., related to political interests); 5) the influences of trusted opinion leaders, organizations, and institutions, including elites whose opinions are conveyed through the mass media, and to friends, peers, and family members who provide cues about politics; and 6) events and changes in objective conditions that affect individuals directly, independent of the interpretations offered by others.

That public opinion is rational in this sense, does not mean that the public is wise, because processes of manipulation or deception (e.g., through propaganda, in the extreme) may misdirect the public from its true interests. This rationality offers support for greater *democracy, in which electoral accountability provides incentives for government responsiveness; in contrast, the myth of "the rational public" may be exploited by governments to exert political control and maintain power. But whether public opinion influences government or whether the latter controls the former, public consensus or compliance is necessary for effective governance.

In such a context public opinion has visible influences. It provides *legitimacy or serves as a legitimizing symbol. At times of democratic elections, the influences on public opinion described above are reflected in electoral outcomes; in this way public opinion provides a mechanism for change by replacing leaders who govern and by altering the bases of support for those elected. There is evidence that public opinion not only constrains both domestic and foreign policy–making from exceeding acceptable bounds but that on many salient issues public preferences can move governments in new di-

rections; and public opinion can also influence how government institutions formulate policies and adapt their own structures to take public opinion into account.

Political leaders, political analysts, and academic researchers learn about public opinion in many ways. These include reliance on impressionistic observations; the use of elites, organized groups, or others as informants; reports in the mass media presumed to reflect or influence public opinion; and documentary and other primary sources used by social historians. The most important means for tracking national public opinion has been the sample survey, which first came into visible use in the United States in 1935 and has since grown in significance.

Two developments suggest that public opinion polling is associated with the struggle for democracy. First, since 1960, U.S. presidents in office have been as concerned about public opinion as they had once been only during election campaigns, revealing their interest in controlling if not responding to public opinion. Second, the worldwide movement from authoritarian government to democratic processes—from Latin America to Eastern and Central Europe, the former Soviet states, and parts of Asia—has increased public opinion polling, which has emerged (or reemerged) in these countries. In some instances, polling has been used to try to help democracy along; in others, government-sponsored or -controlled polls are used to thwart democratic initiatives. As ostensibly free elections occur, political candidates seek information from polls, suggesting that concern for public opinion and the use of survey research will increasingly accompany leaders into office.

There is, therefore, currently more need than ever before for comparative analysis of public opinion and public opinion processes across nations, as the number of mass surveys conducted worldwide grows. In recognition of this and in the interest of maintaining the integrity of survey research, the World Association for Public Opinion Research, formed in 1947, began publishing in 1989 the *International Journal of Public Opinion Research*.

(See also ELECTIONS AND VOTING BEHAVIOR; IDEOLOGY; INFORMATION SOCIETY; MEDIA AND POLITICS; POLITICAL PARTIES AND PARTY COMPETITION; PSYCHOLOGY AND POLITICS; RATIONAL CHOICE.)

W. Phillips Davison and Avery Leiserson, "Public Opinion," in David Sills, ed., *International Encyclopedia of the Social Sciences*, vol. 13 (New York, 1968). Donald R. Kinder and David O. Sears, "Public Opinion and Political Action," in Gardner Lindzey and Elliot Aronson, eds., *Handbook of Social Psychology*, 3d ed., vol. 2 (New York, 1985). Paul M. Sniderman, "The New Look in Public Opinion Research," in Ada W. Finifter, ed., *Political Science: The State of the Discipline II* (Washington, D.C., 1993). Robert S. Erikson and Kent L. Tedin, *American Public Opinion: Its Origins, Content, and Impact*, 5th ed. (Boston, 1995).

ROBERT Y. SHAPIRO

PUBLIC POLICY. In its most commonly understood form public policy is the output or product of government action. It is what comes out of the governing process in terms of the selected goals of public officials and the impact on society of pursuing those goals. In this view government is the center of decision making. It is fed by popular or powerful inputs and it responds with its authoritative benefits and controls. The will of the people in democratic governments, as expressed through electoral participation, lobbying, legislative inquiry, or similar means, is supposed to be transformed in the governing process. The process ends with the passage of laws or regulations, the generation of special tax expenditures, or other products of authoritative decision making that effectively govern public life. While this output model has a value, public policy is not quite that simple. More important, it is often seen as a process, rather than a product, that begins before decisions are made and reaches to the intended public consumers or beneficiaries of the policy.

In this more current perspective, public policy has a kind of circularity. It starts and ends with the social or political groups organized around distinct areas of interest or issue areas that are likely to be affected by government action. These organized groups, numbering in the thousands in most Western societies and increasing steadily all over the world, form a system of interest-group politics. Interest groups, more than individuals, are active both in the development of legislative proposals and in the implementation of decisions. Accordingly, a diverse collection of groups representing separate private interests, or *nongovernmental organizations representing issues in the general interest such as the promotion of human rights or the protection of the environment, work to define and redefine public policy through interaction with public officials at various stages of government, but especially in the legislative and executive branches. Through court briefs and expert witness contributions they are visible in the judicial branch where policy is also influenced and occasionally revised.

Ultimately, however, public policy touches all aspects of the individual's public life through development of regularized patterns of access to public benefits or patterns of authoritative control. First, it *regulates* services such as traffic management, telephone or television access, public utilities, legal resources, and countless others. Second, it *distributes* public resources such as federal, state, and local construction contracts; public housing or land sales; scholarships; and public employment. Third, but less frequently than regulatory or distributive policy, it may also redistribute public resources in an effort to increase opportunities for the disadvantaged by indirectly drawing more from the taxes of the wealthy. While some analysts doubt that redistributive policy has ever been significant, welfare policies and programs authorizing special treatment for some groups in competitive access to schooling or employment may well fit this category. Virtually every politically sensitive person seeks to encourage some form of government regulation or distribution. Although conservatives often call for "deregulation," they encourage protective regulation for business relations and traditional social institutions.

Only the best-organized groups play an active role in the first phase of policy development, *formulation*. For example, recent national health care reform proposals in the United States and other countries brought medical associations, insurance lobbies, drug producers, and others to legislative offices for lobbying purposes. The policy *adoption* phase is obviously the most restrictive since it centers on internal governmental activity. Last, the policy *implementation* phase, in which programs are administered and tailored, should also be restricted in theory. In fact, implementation actually brings private associations and the targeted beneficiaries or consum-

ers of policies into the process of implementation. They are crucial in the administration and refinement of public programs.

Unofficially, but consistently, where government has a regulatory impact on organized groups or communities, they acquire over time a capacity to influence, if not guide, the practical application policies and program administration. Private enterprises, for example, play a large role in defining commercial policies. Educators help set education policy, mortgage lenders influence housing policies, truckers influence highway regulation, and so on. Only where people are disorganized is there little or no private power in public policy making. Unemployment recipients are an example of such an absence of organization in the United States but not in other countries such as France.

Ultimately, most political organizations seek to guide public policy by transforming an array of private interests into the constituent elements of the public interest. At base, the purpose or goal of public policy is to serve the public interest.

(See also INTEREST GROUPS; POLITICAL PARTICIPATION.)

Theodore Lowi, *The End of Liberalism*, 2d ed. (New York, 1979). George J. Gordon and Michael Milakovich, *Public Administration in America*, 5th ed. (New York, 1995). James P. Lester and Joseph Stewart, *Public Policy* (Minneapolis/St. Paul, 1996). James E. Anderson, *Public Policy making*, 3d ed. (Boston, 1997).

LORENZO MORRIS

PUERTO RICO. The story of Puerto Rico over the past century has been marked by an ongoing effort to overcome over 500 years of colonialism. Conquered in 1493 by Spain and acquired by the United States in 1898 during the Spanish-American War, this Caribbean island of 3,435 square miles (8,931 sq. km.) has never been an independent state. Officially, Puerto Rico became a U.S. commonwealth in 1952, when the island was granted limited self-government. Earlier, the Foraker Act (1900) had provided for three branches of government, vested executive authority in a presidentially appointed government, and integrated Puerto Rico into the U.S. economy. The Jones Act (1917), perceived as a war measure to ensure loyalty, conferred U.S. *citizenship on island residents but denied them participation in national elections. Although the Puerto Rican Federal Relations Act (1950) authorized a locally drafted constitution, ultimate sovereignty over island affairs was retained by the U.S. Congress. Puerto Rico's lone representative to that body, a resident commissioner in the House, has voice but no vote except in committees.

Puerto Rico has become a crossroads for some of the major ideologies of this century—nationalism, socialism, and modernization—and for the principal Western cultural heritages—African, Hispanic, Antillean, and North American. Its 3.8 million Spanish-speaking inhabitants make it one of the most densely populated regions of the world. Modernization and economic development, sometimes negatively perceived as Americanization, took off during the 1940s and 1950s led by Luis Muñoz Marín (1898–1990), the island's first elected governor. A charismatic leader, he blended nationalist, socialist, and modernization ideas into a new populism centered around the Partido Popular Democrático (PPD). He co-opted independence and statehood into populist autonomism. Nationalist sentiment, variously expressed as independence, autonomy, and statehood, has been fueled by the still-unresolved colonial status. By the 1990s, the island's economic dependency, coupled with an oversized governmental bureaucracy (28.3 percent of total employment)—the result of several decades of corporatist policies and socialist populism of the autonomist PPD, involving nationalization of public utilities (telephone, electricity, and water) as well as partial sectors of the shipping, hotel, and agriculture industries—had undermined U.S efforts to portray Puerto Rico as a showcase of development. One by-product was the encouragement of outmigration; about 3 million Puerto Ricans live in the continental United States. Pedro Roselló, a young Yale-educated physician and statehood advocate, was elected governor in 1992, when he adopted a new economic model based on the privatization of state-owned industries and the dismantling of federal tax incentives seen as corporate welfare gimmicks by a cost-conscious U.S. Republican Congress. Efforts were made to increase government efficiency by transferring some parts to private management beginning with comprehensive government-funded health insurance coverage for low-income residents (1.2 million in 1998) in which the private sector provides all medical services. In 1998, despite mounting opposition from labor unions and the independence and autonomist parties, the Puerto Rico Telephone Company, valued at over US$2 billion, was privatized, and several government-owned hotels and agriculture-related industries were also sold.

Economic progress has been accompanied by wide income disparities and intractable social problems. The per capita income of $9,674 is among the highest in Latin America, but it is less than half of the lowest in the fifty states. In the 1990s over 62 percent of the population had incomes below the federal poverty level compared to 13 percent of the U.S. median and the 25.7 percent of the poorest state, Mississippi. While the island's economy is highly integrated with that of the United States (87 percent of its exports and 60 percent of imports), a staggering federal dependency, $11.2 billion in 1999, or 29 percent of Puerto Rico's $38.2 billion GNP, rendered its economic model nonexportable. Its dynamic industrial economy became heavily dependent on exemptions from federal and local taxes. In 1999 over 44 percent of the GDP came from manufacturing and more than 38 percent from service industries; agriculture accounted for less than 1 percent and tourism for approximately 6 percent of the economy; exports of $34.9 billion exceeded imports of $25.2 billion in 1999. Tax breaks for U.S. corporations benefiting from Section 936 of the Internal Revenue Code are being phased out (to be completely terminated by 2008); the IRS lost almost $70 billion in revenue from 1988 to 1997. Island residents pay 5 percent of their personal income to state and local taxes, and no federal taxes, while stateside residents pay 10 percent of their income to the federal government. Unemployment has recently decreased from 17.7 percent (1987) to 12.5 (1999), but it still doubles that of the United States. Besides poverty and unemployment, Puerto Rico faces a serious AIDS epidemic, alcoholism, drug addiction with consequent crime, mental illness, and a host of other social problems, at rates among the highest in the nation.

Political inequality and lack of sovereignty have become both a national human rights issue and an international *decolonization issue in the 1990s and in the twenty-first century. In 1972 the Decolonization Committee of the General Assem-

bly of the United Nations recognized the inalienable right of Puerto Ricans to self-determination and independence. The United States opposed subsequent efforts to discuss the Puerto Rican case at the General Assembly, and Congress took up the debate over decolonization. Legislation was unsuccessfully introduced in the 101st Congress in 1989 to authorize a referendum on the political status of the island. In 1993 a locally sponsored referendum was held in which commonwealth—as defined by the PPD but not by Congress—was favored (48 percent) over statehood (46 percent). The three options represented by the island's three principal political parties were defined as "enhanced" commonwealth status (the PPD position), statehood (the position of the Partido Nuevo Progresista [PNP]), and independence (the position of the Partido Independentista Puertorriqueño [PIP]. In 1994 a new status bill was also unsuccessfully introduced in the 104th Congress. A similar bill introduced in the 105th Congress was passed by the House but was still pending in the Senate as of June 1998. A new consensus seems to have emerged that, in the long run, statehood is more economically advantageous, for both the island and the U.S. Treasury, than commonwealth, which is a drain on the federal government. Globalization, the future expansion of *NAFTA, and the possible normalization of U.S. relations with Cuba may erode the relative advantage of Puerto Rico's commonwealth status. It is argued that only statehood will provide the permanent political stability and dispel the uncertainties and risks of the island's present colonial status.

Although in the 1996 elections, the pro statehood PNP, led by Roselló, became a majority party by capturing 51.1 percent of the electorate, nationalist sentiment has increased as a result of the U.S. Navy training exercises which take place on Vieques. This small island is inhabited by approximately 8,000 persons and is part of the Puerto Rico archipelago. President Clinton's decision to allow a limited resumption of the Navy's practices has met with wide opposition among political and religious sectors and has served to emphasize the second-class nature of Puerto Ricans's American citizenship as well as the island's political disempowerment and disenfranchisement at the federal level. The Vieques issue is a microcosm of tensions surrounding Puerto Rico–U.S. relations. Regardless of who wins the November 2000 elections, the pro-statehood PNP or the PPD, which favors neither statehood nor independence, unless Congress sponsors a status referendum, and defines the respective alternatives realistically, Puerto Rico's decolonization efforts in favor of statehood look uncertain during the first decade of the twenty-first century.

(See also Hispanic Americans.)

Henry Wells, *The Modernization of Puerto Rico: A Political Study of Changing Values and Institutions* (Cambridge, Mass., 1969). U.S. General Accounting Office, *Tax Policy Analysis of Certain Potential Effects of Extending Federal Income Taxation to Puerto Rico* (Washington, D.C., 1996). U.S. General Accounting Office, *U.S. Insular Areas Application of the U.S. Constitution* (Washington, D.C., 1997). José Trías Monge, *Puerto Rico: The Trials of the Oldest Colony in the World* (New Haven, Conn., 1997). J. Thomas Hexner and Glenn Jenkins, *Puerto Rico: The Economic and Fiscal Dimensions* (Washington, D.C., 1998).

                                                             Luis G. Rodríguez

PURCHASING POWER PARITY. Purchasing power is the amount of goods and services bought by a unit of currency.

It is therefore the reciprocal of a price index: when prices go up, purchasing power falls. Purchasing power parity is the theory that exchange rates between currencies are determined (in equilibrium or in the long run) by the amount of goods and services that a currency can buy. If £1 in Britain buys what $1.50 buys in the United States, the equilibrium exchange rate would be £1 = $1.50. The theory was propounded by the Swedish economist Gustav Cassel (1866–1944) in 1916 when a system of free exchange rates prevailed. If the prices of tradable goods are lower in one country than in another, allowing for transport costs and tariffs, people buy these cheaper goods and sell them in the dearer country. In the cheaper country the prices of goods or the value of the exchange rate will rise. But not all goods and services are tradable (e.g., government services), and transport costs, tariffs, capital movements, and government policies interfere with the long-term tendency to equality of the purchasing power of different currencies. Another version of the theory explains *changes* in the exchange rate by *changes* in the relative purchasing power of the currencies. The explanation of the exchange rate is that it depends on supply and demand, and

purchasing power is only one of many factors that determine supply and demand.

If the purchasing power parity theory were correct, converting incomes per head of different countries at the current exchange rate would yield accurate comparisons of the command over goods and services. But since the purchasing power parity theory does not hold, the real income per head of poor countries is (for example) underestimated when converted by exchange rates. The low relative prices of many nontraded services, such as those of teachers or barbers or retailers, produces for poor countries a substantially higher purchasing power. For purposes of international comparisons indices of relative national price levels that use absolute price comparisons have some advantages. Nevertheless, the theory provides a useful benchmark for policies.

(See also DEVELOPMENT AND UNDERDEVELOPMENT.)

Rudiger Dornbusch, "Purchasing Power Parity," in John Eatwell, Murray Milgate, and Peter Newman, eds., *The New Palgrave: A Dictionary of Economics*, vol. 3 (London, 1987).

PAUL STREETEN

Q

QADDAFI, Muammar. Born in 1941 into a family of the Qadhafa tribe on the southern coastline of the Gulf of Sirte in *Libya, Muammar Qaddafi received a mosque-based early education in Misurata. Then, in the late 1950s, his family moved to Sabha, the main town of the Fezzan, where Qaddafi attended secondary school. He soon became an active Arab nationalist, after contact with Ba'thist and Nasserist ideas, especially the radical nationalist propaganda of Radio Cairo.

At school, Qaddafi participated in a small group of politically active friends—a group which was eventually to form the nucleus of the Free Officers Movement. Finally, in October 1961, he was expelled from school by the authorities after organizing a demonstration against the monarchy.

Qaddafi and the majority of his circle then decided that the only way to pursue their political objectives was through the Libyan armed forces—the only institution in the country not dominated by traditional tribal influences and with a relatively modernist outlook. So in late 1961, Qaddafi became a student at the Benghazi Military Academy. Upon graduation in 1966, he joined the communications branch of the army—away from elite units such as the Cyrenaican Defense Force which were renowned for their firm support of the monarchy.

Qaddafi continued to develop the Free Officers Movement, despite senior commanders' occasional suspicion of his activities. Eventually he was sent to Britain for further training, but even at a distance, Qaddafi pursued his political work. His military career also prospered and he was promoted to the rank of captain. Finally on 1 September 1969, when King Idris was on holiday in Turkey, the Free Officers struck. Their coup succeeded largely because the authorities did not realize how well organized the military conspiracy had become. While the king took up a comfortable exile in Cairo, Qaddafi assumed the leadership of the new republican regime, becoming head of state in 1970.

Qaddafi came to power with an Arab nationalist perspective, tinged with the egalitarianism and puritanical morality of nomadic society. This political vision evolved throughout the 1970s and by the end of the decade his personal ideology had been codified and published in a three-volume work, often known as the *Green Book*. This treatise described the "Third Universal Theory" which was to supersede capitalism and communism and which was based on the principle of "direct popular democracy." Qaddafi also considered the Third Universal Theory to be a prescription for political organization throughout the Third World. Although not explicitly Islamic, the underlying moral justification of the theory was drawn from Islamic thought.

The full rigors of the political system derived from the *Green Book* were put into operation by Qaddafi in Libya during the 1970s and 1980s. Political life in modern Libya is very much Qaddafi's personal creation. Since the start of the 1990s, opportunism has become the dominant aspect of the Libyan leader's personal political style as he confronts domestic and international hostility.

The political radicalism of Libya under Qaddafi has made him personally a notorious figure, particularly in the West, although his antagonism to most established Middle Eastern governments has isolated him there as well. Qaddafi is the Middle Eastern politician most closely associated in the popular mind with international *terrorism, although up to 1986 Libya's terrorist links had been largely with extremist Palestinian organizations and, as a priority, directed against its own nationals in exile who were opposed to the Qaddafi regime. U.S. and British hostility toward the Libyan leader has been most marked since the mid-1980s, and since then he has often been inaccurately portrayed in the Western media as an irresponsible extremist and a threat to regional security and stability.

(See also ARAB NATIONALISM; ISLAM; NASSERISM.)

Frederick Muscat, *My President, My Son* (Valletta, Malta, 1974). J. Cooley, *Libyan Sandstorm* (London, 1984).

GEORGE JOFFÉ

QATAR. See GULF STATES.

QUEBEC. The 5.8 million French speakers of Quebec represent the overwhelming majority (82 percent) of Quebec's population. At the same time, they constitute the only instance of a French-speaking majority within a Canadian province. The next largest Francophone concentration, in the province of New Brunswick, numbers about 220,000 (on the basis of home language) and constitutes less than one third of the province's population. In all the other provinces, people using French as their home language represent no more than 3 percent of the population—in most cases the percentage is far less.

This concentration of French speakers in Quebec has in recent decades provided the basis for a strong Québécois *nationalism which has spawned a movement for Quebec's political disengagement from the rest of *Canada. However, this Quebec-based nationalism is only the most recent variant of a longstanding nationalist sentiment among French speakers, born of a long history of cultural threat and economic inferiority.

The Francophone population of Quebec can be traced back to the colony of New France, founded in 1608. By the time the colony was conquered by the British, in 1759, its population had grown to 70,000. Initially, the British authorities planned to force the assimilation of the colony's French-speaking, Catholic population, following the directive of the Royal Proclamation. However, both practical and strategic concerns led them to abandon this plan. In 1774 the Quebec Act restored seigneurial rights, the tithe, and the Civil Code. In 1791, the Constitutional Act established a representative assembly, as the colony's growing English-speaking population had long demanded, but divided the colony into Lower Canada (the basis of present-day Quebec) and Upper Canada (the basis of present-day Ontario).

After being merged into the United Canadas in 1840, Quebec and Ontario joined New Brunswick and Nova Scotia in 1867 to create a new confederation, the basis of present-day Canada. Despite the confederal referent, the Canadian system is in fact federal. Even this feature was largely the result of the insistence of French-Canadian delegates who feared that a unitary system would place distinctive French-Canadian institutions at the mercy of the overwhelming English-speaking majority. Defense of provincial autonomy became a constant of Quebec political life, faithfully intoned by all provincial governments. This Quebec autonomism was reinforced by the chronic underrepresentation of French speakers in federal institutions and the steady decline of the French-speaking communities in most other provinces (usually reinforced by repressive English-only laws).

With the turn of the century Quebec began the transition to an urban, industrial society. In the 1950s, there emerged a substantial new middle class of intellectuals, administrators, engineers, and other professionals, which began to challenge the Catholic Church's control of education and social services in Quebec and to call for an end to the historical predominance of English speakers in both the ownership and management of the Quebec economy. These objectives necessarily entailed a more interventionist Quebec state.

With the 1960 election of Jean Lesage's Parti Libéral, the Quebec government was rapidly expanded, assuming direct control of education and social functions and creating a network of state enterprises. These initiatives were legitimized within a new variant of French-Canadian nationalism which defined the nation in terms of Quebec alone and called for the transformation of the provincial government into a national state. This period of Liberal government (1960–1966), commonly known as the "Quiet Revolution," saw an escalation in tension between Quebec and the rest of Canada as Quebec neonationalists contended that the existing federal system could afford the Quebec government neither the powers nor the status which befit its new role as a national state.

Proposals proliferated for a new constitutional arrangement: special status for Quebec, the construction of the federal level along binational lines, Quebec sovereignty linked to a Canadian economic association. Nonetheless, the federal government under the leadership of Pierre Elliott* Trudeau (1968–1979 and 1980–1984) roundly rejected any scheme which would recognize Quebec's specificity, instead championing the constitutional entrenchment of a variety of rights: political, legal, and linguistic. The protection of the French language minorities outside Quebec, through official bilingualism, was the centerpiece in the federal strategy for countering Quebec nationalism.

As the constitutional stalemate persisted, support steadily grew in Quebec for the Parti Québécois (PQ), founded in 1968 with René Lévesque as its leader. The PQ called for Quebec to assume political sovereignty, while remaining closely linked to the rest of Canada in an economic association. Upon its election to the Quebec government in 1976 the PQ undertook a series of social and political reforms and, in particular, reinforced through Bill 101 the law on French preeminence which had been put in place by the Liberal government of Robert Bourassa (1970–1976). But in a May 1980 referendum, the PQ government was unable to secure majority support for its proposal that it be given a mandate to negotiate sovereignty-association with the rest of Canada.

With the failure of the Quebec referendum, the federal government seized the occasion to pursue Pierre Trudeau's alternative vision of repatriating the Canadian Constitution and entrenched bill of rights. In the fall of 1981 the federal government succeeded in securing the approval of all provincial governments but Quebec to revision of the Constitution along these lines. Thus, the Constitution was revised without Quebec's formal approval.

With the return to power of the Bourassa Liberals in 1985, efforts were renewed to secure Quebec's formal adhesion to the Constitution. These efforts produced a new package of changes, commonly dubbed the Meech Lake Accord, which had the approval of all ten premiers and the Canadian prime minister. However, over the next three years, changes in provincial governments coupled with the rapid rise in English-Canadian opposition to the accord resulted in failure of two provincial legislatures to approve the accord within the three-year time limit.

This failure of the accord, coupled with the evident English-Canadian opposition to any recognition of Quebec's specificity, refueled the cause of Quebec sovereignty. Thus, after returning to power in 1994 under Jacques Parizeau, the Parti Québécois staged a second referendum on Quebec sovereignty in 1995 that almost won with a "yes" vote of 49.5 percent. Subsequently, support for sovereignty has declined, but the Parti Québécois remains in power and is formally committed to holding a third referendum on Quebec sovereignty whenever conditions are favorable.

(See also FEDERALISM; REFORM; RELIGION AND POLITICS.)

Kenneth McRoberts, *Quebec: Social Change and Political Crisis*, 3d ed. (Toronto, 1993). Guy Lachapelle, Gérald Bernier, Daniel Salée, and Luc Bernier, *The Quebec Democracy* (Montreal, 1993). Alain-G. Gagnon and Alain Noël, *L'Espace québécois* (Montreal, 1995). Robert Young, *The Secession of Quebec and the Future of Canada* (Montreal, 1995). Gilles Bourque and Jules Duchastel, *L'Identité fragmentée* (Montreal, 1996).

KENNETH MCROBERTS

R

RACE AND RACISM. See overleaf.

RATIONAL CHOICE THEORY. Rational choice theories are predicated on the notion that individual actors pursue their goals efficiently. These individuals may have a great deal of information or none at all, but based on their understanding of the alternatives before them, they select the course of action that promises to deliver the greatest net benefits. The nature of these benefits varies from one rational choice theory to the next. Sometimes individuals are said to pursue money or re-election or international security, but the ends that individuals pursue need not be self-aggrandizing in nature. Although rational choice theories tend to assume selfish goals, nothing in rational choice theory precludes the theorist from stipulating tastes for altruism. The defining characteristic of rational choice theory is not what it assumes about human motivation but rather the notion that individuals pursue their aims efficiently.

Central to rational choice theory (and foreign to many other forms of political theorizing) is the concept of equilibrium. A marketplace or political institution is said to be in equilibrium if none of the individual actors have an incentive to change his or her behavior unilaterally. If, for example, the actors in question were political parties and their objective were to win elections, their political platforms would be in equilibrium if no political party could increase its chances of winning the election by altering its platform. Rational choice theory is in large part an attempt to discern the conditions under which equilibria exist in political systems and to describe the nature of such equilibria. These theoretical statements then become the basis for empirical research, which examines whether the equilibrium predictions hold.

The allure of rational choice theory is its capacity to accumulate theoretical insights within a unified deductive framework. Assumptions about individual preferences, information, institutional incentives, sequencing of decisions, and the like may vary from model to model, but the explicit, formal character of these models makes it possible to retrace the steps of the theorist and examine the significance of any particular modeling assumption. Such deductive models of politics have grown increasingly complex since their introduction into political science in the 1950s. A limitation is the sheer analytic intractability of models that strive to depict the strategic complexity of actual political settings. Inevitably, rational choice theorists are forced to simplify the world greatly in order to generate theoretical results. Whether the resulting models comport with empirical observation is therefore an important concern. Simple, abstract renderings of politics are arresting—

when they make predictions that are both nonobvious and empirically sustainable.

Two hallmarks of rational choice theory are its methodological individualism and concern with the consequences of institutional design. Sometimes, for analytic simplicity, states, parties, and other corporate entities are assumed to be unitary actors with a coherent schedule of preferences. Nevertheless, there is constant pressure among theorists to specify the underlying microfoundations, that is, the strategic behavior of individuals who comprise these corporate entities. This concern with microfoundations is especially pressing when electoral or legislative systems or the distribution of resources in society are constituted in certain ways. In the 1950s, Kenneth Arrow pointed out that even when individuals have well-ordered preferences over outcomes, procedures designed to aggregate preferences such as majority rule may give rise to collective choices that are unstable and self-contradictory. Subsequent scholars, notably William Riker, have argued that this problem is endemic to voting systems and that the inherent instability of legislative and popular decisions makes them susceptible to manipulation by clever agenda-setters. Many scholars focus their attention on the normative implications of "preference aggregation" in democratic systems, an endeavor that lies at the heart of the field known as public choice. Scholars working at this nexus of empirical and normative concerns often seek to identify voting rules, parliamentary procedures, and counterbalancing institutions that alleviate these perverse features of democracy.

Another line of scholarship that calls attention to institutional structure and microfoundations addresses the problem of collective action. Mancur Olson argued that when a large number of individuals pursue common objectives (e.g., voters seeking to elect their preferred candidate) and any single individual's actions have little consequence for the aggregate outcome (one vote is unlikely to be decisive), these individuals will tend to "free-ride." Voters will stay home rather than incur the costs of voting because they can enjoy the benefits of the electoral outcome regardless of whether they participate. Only when these collective actors are offered "selective incentives" (side-payments to participate or punishments for nonparticipation) can collective action problems be overcome.

Collective action problems represent the largest body of study among rational choice theorists. Wherever there are public goods—national security, propitious laws, an informed citizenry—there will be a tendency for individuals to foist the costs onto others while enjoying the benefits. In international affairs, collective action problems arise in the maintenance of multilateral agreements, the exploitation of natural resources,

(cont. on p. 714)

RACE AND RACISM. The study of race and racism is a rapidly growing field in the social sciences. Over the past few decades there has been a flowering of studies of race and ethnic differences and their social meaning in various historical, social, political, and economic contexts. Theoretical and political debates have raged during this time, and have sometimes led to bitter conceptual and political arguments. At the same time the analysis of race and racism has become an established field of study in a number of social science disciplines, most notably in sociology, political science, economics, anthropology, cultural studies, and geography. The literature emanating from all these disciplines has multiplied over the years, particularly in the United States, Britain and other European societies, and South Africa.

There seem to be two major reasons for this growing interest in the study of race and racism. First, and most importantly, there has been an evident preoccupation with racial issues in a variety of societies, including the United States, South Africa, and a number of societies in Western Europe. Studies have shown that racial inequalities and injustices continue to be reproduced at a number of levels, ranging from the economic, social, and political to the cultural. Second, associated with this awareness of the persistence of racial inequalities there has been a realization that racism continues to be a vital, and some would say growing, force in contemporary societies.

Whatever the explanation for the recent flowering of interest in the study of race and racism, it is clear that current debates have led to the emergence of a variety of schools of thought. There is by no means agreement about the definition of the key concepts of race and racism, nor about their relevance for social analysis, while some have questioned whether racism exists as a unified category or is composed of a variety of political and social discourses and practices. Given these theoretical differences it is useful to explore diverse explanations of racial and ethnic phenomena in the contemporary political environment and their implications for sociopolitical change.

Theoretical and Conceptual Origins. The study of race as a field of social-scientific inquiry and research can be seen as originating in the work of a number of American social theorists, including most notably Robert E. Park, Charles S. Johnson, and E. Franklin Frazier. From a different perspective the work of black writers, most notably W.E.B. *Du Bois, helped to establish the centrality of race to the analysis of U.S. society. During the period from the 1920s to the 1950s the works of this group of writers helped to establish what came to be defined as the study of race relations, particularly through their studies of segregation, immigration, and race consciousness in the United States. During the interwar period the works of these authors helped to develop a body of sociological concepts which were later to be refined into a sociology of race relations.

Early sociological theorizing on race in the United States saw race as a relevant social category only to the extent to which cultural and social meanings were attached to the physical traits of a particular social group. This in turn helped to popularize notions about the origins of racial conflicts and prejudice which concentrated on situations of cultural contact. Emphasis in sociological studies of the race problem during these decades was on the origins of race prejudice, the interplay between prejudice and conflict, the impact of assimilation on the life of *African Americans, and the processes by which racial conflicts could be mediated or overcome.

These early studies of race did not actually talk about racism as such. This is a more recent concept and its usage was linked to the rise of Nazism in Germany. As the Nazis came to power and articulated and put into practice their ideas about racial superiority, the term "racism" came to be used to refer to ideas which defined some racial or ethnic groups as superior and others as inferior. This usage of the term was first suggested by Ruth Benedict in her book *Race and Racism* (London, 1942), which defined racism as "the dogma that one ethnic group is condemned by nature to congenital inferiority and another group is destined to congenital superiority." In this context racism was seen as referring to those sets of ideas that defined ethnic and racial groups on the basis of claims about biological nature and inherent superiority or ability.

In the post-1945 period a number of developments outside of the United States encouraged interest in the study of race and racism in other societies. An important development in this context was the emergence of migrant labor as an important social group in many West European societies. Migration from the ex-colonies and southern Europe led to the creation of racial and ethnic minorities in countries such as Britain, France, the Federal Republic of Germany (FRG), and the Netherlands. Another important development was the entrenchment of the *apartheid system in South Africa, a process which aroused the interest of both social scientists and political activists, particularly in relation to the role of the political and legal systems in enforcing racial segregation and the "separate development" of different racial groups.

In Britain and other European societies, the growth in the theorization of race and racism ran parallel to these developments. This work has provided a number of important and sophisticated analyses of the politics and *ideology of racism. There were two central concerns in these early European attempts to theorize racial and ethnic relations; first, the patterns of immigration and incorporation in the labor market of black and other ethnic communities; second, the role of colonial history in determining popular conceptions of color, race, and ethnicity in European societies. Most studies of this period concentrated on the interaction between minority and majority communities in employment, housing, and other social contexts.

Although many of these studies were influenced by the

early American theories, they also included theoretical works of some significance. Michael Banton's book *Race Relations* (London, 1967) represents a good example of texts from this period. It looked at race relations from a global and historical perspective, concentrating particularly on situations of cultural contact, beliefs about the nature of race, and the social relations constructed on the basis of racial categories. By looking at the experience of changing patterns of interaction historically, Banton argued that six basic orders of race relations could be delineated: institutionalized contact, acculturation, domination, paternalism, integration, and pluralism.

Political Sociology of Racism. An important focus of research in recent years has been the role of political institutions in shaping the position of racial minorities in particular societies. As William Julius Wilson has pointed out, political and legal frameworks are an important element in contemporary situations governed by racial domination and inequality. This is a theme which has been developed over the past three decades in the works of political sociologists who have looked at a variety of race relations situations, ranging from South Africa to Britain and the United States.

This concern with relations of *power and privilege has influenced the study of race and racism in a fundamental way. A clear example of this trend is John Rex's *Race Relations in Sociological Theory* (2d ed., London, 1983), which attempts to provide a broad theoretical framework for the study of race relations. According to Rex's analytic model, the definition of social relations between persons as race relations is encouraged by the existence of certain structural conditions: e.g., frontier situations of conflict over scarce resources, the existence of unfree, indentured, or slave labor, unusually harsh class exploitation, strict legal intergroup distinctions and occupational segregation, differential access to power and prestige, cultural diversity and limited group interaction, and migrant labor as an underclass fulfilling stigmatized roles in a metropolitan setting. From this perspective the study of race relations is concerned with situations in which such structured conditions interact with actors' definitions in such a way as to produce a racially structured social reality.

Marxism, Racism, and Class Theory. The other main conceptual framework which has influenced the study of race and racism in recent years is *Marxism. Early Marxist work on racial and ethnic divisions concentrated particularly on race and class as modes of exploitation. Oliver Cox's *Caste, Class and Race* (New York, 1948) is an early example of this focus. Cox was primarily interested in the economic interests which produce racist exploitation and ideologies historically, and explained racial inequality as an outcome of the interest of the capitalist class in super-exploiting sections of the working class. Because he saw class divisions as the fundamental source of exploitation in society, the main thrust of his work was to conceptualize racial exploitation as a special form of class exploitation. This model was subsequently to exercise a

deep influence on the work of Marxist writers on race in the United States and, to a more limited extent, in European and other societies.

The majority of recent Marxist studies, however, are critical both of the work of Cox and of classical Marxism. It has been pointed out, for example, that although the works of *Marx and Engels contain a number of scattered references to the pertinence of racial and ethnic relations in certain social formations (e.g., the reference to race as an economic factor in the slavery of the United States), they contain little historical or theoretical reflection on the role of such processes in the capitalist mode of production as a whole. Perhaps even more damaging, a number of critics have argued that several statements on race by Marx and Engels reveal traces of the dominant racial stereotypes of their time and an uncritical usage of common racist imagery. Additionally, a number of critics of Marxism have argued that the reliance by Marxists on the concept of class has precluded them from analyzing racial and ethnic phenomena in their own right, short of subsuming them under wider social relations or treating them as a kind of superstructural phenomenon.

Recent studies in the United States and Britain have focused more specifically on the role of the *state as a site for the reproduction of racially structured situations. Drawing partly on recent Marxist debates on the nature of the capitalist state, a number of studies have analyzed the interplay between politics and racism in specific historical settings. Studies of the role of state institutions in maintaining racialized structures in a number of societies, particularly the United States and South Africa, have highlighted the importance of the political context of racism. This has raised important questions and problems: What is the precise role of the state in the reproduction of racially structured social relations? How far can the state be transformed into an instrument of anti-racist political actions? These and other questions are currently being explored and debated.

As mentioned earlier, the claim that racism is a source of division within the working class was central to the work of early Marxist writers such as Cox. This theme has once again become central to contemporary debates about racism and class formation. In their study of immigrant workers in the class structure of Western Europe, Stephen Castles and Godula Kosack (*Immigrant Workers and Class Structure in Western Europe*, London, 1973) deal with the way in which the state has intervened to create two distinct strata within the working class through the system of contract labor, which denies political rights to the essentially foreign lower stratum. This lower stratum is said to perform the function of a reserve army of labor.

In Britain, the work of Robert Miles represents the most fully developed Marxist analysis of racism as a social and historical phenomenon. His writings reflect a deep concern with overcoming the potentially divisive impact of racism on

711

class organization and radical political action. His analysis was first articulated in *Racism and Migrant Labour* (London, 1982), which is perhaps the most sustained attempt to include the study of racism within the mainstream of Marxist social theory. His empirical research has focused specifically on the situation in Britain and in the rest of Western Europe, and has looked at the role of political, class, and ideological relationships in shaping our understandings of racial conflict and change in these societies.

A final aspect of recent debates about the pertinence of Marxism to the analysis of race and racism is the question of whether there is an intrinsic Eurocentric bias in the core of Marxist theory. This theme has been taken up in recent years by a number of critics of Marxism and by others who profess to be sympathetic to the Marxist tradition. Perhaps the most important statement of this position is Cedric Robinson's *Black Marxism* (London, 1983), which argues forcefully that Marxism is inextricably tied to Western European philosophical traditions which cannot easily incorporate the experience of racism and ethnic divisions. This and other studies seem certain to raise questions which will play a part in Marxist discussions for some time to come.

What seems clear is that Marxist discussion of race and racism is searching for a new agenda for the analysis of the dynamics of racial categorization, and there are some encouraging signs of development and renewal. Important contributions are being made to this debate from a number of countries, and these are helping to fashion new perspectives on the role of the state in maintaining racial domination. Good examples of such research are the numerous studies of the South African state and its part in institutionalizing the apartheid system since 1948. These studies have shown that the state and legal institutions played an integral role in the establishment and maintenance of apartheid. They have also suggested that the state must be included as a key actor in the study of racism in different national and political contexts.

Politics, Power, and Racism. Concern with the state and politics has been evident in studies of the United States and Europe as well. A key concern of a number of recent U.S. studies has been the interrelationship between relations of politics, power, and racism. As Michael Omi and Howard Winant argue in *Racial Formation in the United States* (New York, 1986), one of the most salient features of racial relations in contemporary societies is the role of political and legal relations in defining the existence of racial categories and defining the social meanings of notions such as racial inequality, racism, and *ethnicity.

This theme has been taken up in recent years in studies of the situation of black and other ethnic minorities in Europe. Such studies have looked particularly at the processes by which minority communities and migrant workers are often excluded from equal access to political institutions and are denied basic social and economic *rights. It is interesting to

note in this context that in countries such as the FRG and France a key point in recent political conflicts has been the question of whether migrant workers should be given greater political rights.

The position of black minorities in Britain represents something of a special case in this regard, and a key concern of a number of recent studies of the politics of race in Britain has been to develop a conception of racialization as a process which has specific effects on politics and ideology. Aspects of this process include the impact of racist ideologies and nationalist discourses, antiracist discourses, and the influence of black political action on political institutions and forms of political mobilization.

It is within this context that the concepts of racial categorization and racialization have been used to refer to what Robert Miles in *Racism* calls "those instances where social relations between people have been structured by the signification of human biological characteristics in such a way as to define and construct differentiated social collectivities." A number of writers have attempted to use these concepts to analyze the processes by which race has been socially and politically constructed in specific historical, political, and institutional contexts.

Good examples of such studies include attempts to critically analyze the role of race relations legislation, the emergence of black minority representation in political institutions, and the development of public policies dealing with specific aspects of racial inequality in areas such as employment and housing. The premise of such studies is that the processes by which race is given particular meanings are variable across and within national boundaries and are shaped by political, legal, and socioeconomic environments. Comparative studies of immigration policies in Europe have shown, for example, that the construction of legislation to control the arrival of specific groups of migrants was often the subject of intense political and ideological controversy.

Race, Culture, and Ethnicity. The changing form of racial ideologies in advanced industrial societies is perhaps best illustrated by the recent debates about the role of racial imagery and symbols in the mass media, literature, art, and other cultural forms. A growing body of work has been produced on the use of race as a symbol in various areas of cultural expression and experience. Reacting against what they see as the lack of an account of cultural forms of racial discourse, a number of writers have sought to develop a more rounded picture of contemporary racial imagery by looking at the role of literature, the popular media, and other cultural forms in representing changing images of race and ethnicity. As David Goldberg has pointed out (*Anatomy of Racism*, Minneapolis, 1990), "the presumption of a single monolithic racism is being displaced by a mapping of the multifarious historical formulations of *racisms.*"

This has led to growing interest in how racist ideologies

developed and in the various forms such ideologies have taken at different stages of development. Although this issue had not received much scholarly attention in the past, the renewed interest in the analysis of culture and discourse has helped to overcome this neglect, and the historical, cultural, literary, and philosophical roots of ideologies of race are coming under scrutiny. Specifically, questions are being asked about the role that ideological relations can play in providing a basis for the articulation of racist discourses and practices.

The role of the press and other popular media in shaping social images about racial and ethnic minorities has been a particular focus. A number of detailed studies have examined how press coverage of racial questions can help to construct images of racial minorities as outsiders and as a threat to social cohesion (Teun van Dijk, *Racism and the Press*, London, 1991). One interesting illustration of this process was the furor over the response of Muslim communities to the publication of Salman Rushdie's *The Satanic Verses* (London, 1989). The attempt by some Muslim community leaders to use the affair as a means of political mobilization received extensive coverage in the media and led to a wide-ranging debate about the "future of race relations" in British society. Sections of the press used the events surrounding the Rushdie affair to question the possibility of a peaceful transition toward a multiracial society. Hostile media coverage of the events surrounding the political mobilizations around the Rushdie affair thus served to reinforce the view that minorities who do not share the dominant political values of British society pose a threat to social stability and cohesion. The affair also gave added impetus to debates about the multiple cultural and political identities that have been included in the broad categorization of "black and ethnic minority communities."

Another focus has been the role of race and ethnicity as symbols in a variety of cultural forms, including literature and the cinema. This had been a neglected area of research, but in recent years this has been remedied by the publication of a number of important studies of race, culture, and identity. Originating largely from the United States, such studies have looked at a number of areas, including literature, the cinema, and other popular cultural forms, such as television and radio, along with advertising. They have sought to show that within contemporary societies our understandings of race, and the articulation of racist ideologies, cannot be reduced to economic, political, or class relations. This line of argument is exemplified by Henry Louis Gates, Jr.'s *The Signifying Monkey* (New York, 1988), which attempts to outline a framework for the analysis of images of race within the context of literature in the United States.

Apart from studies of contemporary trends, there has also been a growing interest in historical research on the origins of ideas about race and in the dynamics of race, class, and gender during the colonial period. This has been reflected in important and valuable accounts of the changing usage of racial symbols during the past few centuries and in accounts of the experiences of colonialism and their impact on our understandings of race and culture. The work of Gayatri Spivak (*In Other Worlds*, London, 1987) has helped to highlight, for example, the complex processes of racial and gender identification experienced by the colonized during the colonial and postcolonial periods. Other studies have sought to show that the oppressed themselves have produced their own discourses about race and identity in the context of their own experiences of domination and exclusion.

Conclusion. In the context of the current political environment it is likely that questions about racism will remain an important component of the political agenda in many societies. It is therefore important to analyze the changing discourses and practices about race in contemporary societies rather than assume that they can be subsumed under an ahistorical and unchanging category of racism. Developments in the United States, Europe, and South Africa point to the need to see racial ideologies as unstable and as liable to transformation and change. Indeed, in the contemporary European environment the transformations in Eastern and Central Europe have introduced a new dimension to debates about race and ethnicity, and one which existing accounts of the Western European situation seem to be singularly incapable of dealing with.

The analytical models outlined above also point to the need to broaden existing research priorities to include a multidimensional view of racial discourses. Such a view will need to include perspectives about economic, social, political, cultural, and legal expressions of ideas about race and ethnicity. Indications are that recent theoretical contributions in this field have looked more seriously at the cultural dimension and have helped shed new light on contemporary racisms which have received little attention. But recent political trends worldwide point to the urgency for us to develop more adequate conceptualizations of the workings of racisms as sets of ideas and as practices if we are to be able to challenge and overcome them.

(See also CIVIL RIGHTS MOVEMENT; CLASS AND POLITICS; COLONIAL EMPIRES; DECOLONIZATION; EQUALITY AND INEQUALITY; GENDER AND POLITICS; INTERNATIONAL MIGRATION; KING, MARTIN LUTHER, JR.; MALCOLM X.)

William Julius Wilson, *Power, Racism and Privilege* (New York, 1973). Henry Louis Gates, Jr., ed., *"Race," Writing and Difference* (Chicago, 1986). John Rex and David Mason, eds., *Theories of Race and Ethnic Relations* (Cambridge, U.K., 1986). Robert Miles, *Racism* (London, 1989). Tariq Modood and Richard Berthoud, eds., *Ethnic Minorities in Britain: Diversity and Disadvantage* (London, 1997). Martin Bulmer and John Solomos, eds., *Racism* (Oxford, 1999). John Solomos and Les Back, eds., *Theories of Race and Racism* (London, 1999). William Julius Wilson, et al., ed., *America Becoming: Racial trends and Their Consequences*, Vol. 1 (National Academy Press, 2000)

JOHN SOLOMOS
LES BACK

and balance of power between large numbers of diffuse actors and small numbers of actors with concentrated political and economic power. Rational choice theory sets itself the task of identifying these underlying problems and the institutional mechanisms by which they are or could be held in check.

Given its central concern with strategic behavior, rational choice theories are often applied to settings in which states, parties, and other groups are vying for power. Under what circumstances do international disputes escalate into war? Under what circumstances do countries enter into and abide by international agreements? This literature has been influenced greatly by rational choice theories about signaling and decision making under conditions of uncertainty. Each country has private information about its own capabilities and objectives. The actions it takes in the international arena reveal something about its aims and resolve. In equilibrium, countries distill all the information they can from the murky signals given by other countries.

Sometimes miscalculations occur, and leaders embark on wars that devastate their own countries and result in their overthrow. Whether these miscalculations stem from a rational reading of the available evidence, tastes for reckless action, or wishful thinking is a question that inevitably follows unexplained behavior. A persistent methodological issue surrounds apparent disjunctures between theory and data: Is the theoretical model wanting, or is the discrepancy between the theoretical prediction and actual observation the product of a momentary disequilibrium?

(See also GAME THEORY; PUBLIC CHOICE THEORY; PUBLIC GOOD.)

Mancur Olson, *The Logic of Collective Action* (Cambridge, Mass., 1965). Dennis C. Mueller, *Public Choice II* (Cambridge, U.K., 1989). Donald P. Green and Ian Shapiro, *Pathologies of Rational Choice Theory: A Critique of Applications in Political Science* (New Haven, Conn., 1994).

DONALD GREEN

REAGAN, Ronald Wilson. Fortieth president of the United States, from 1981 to 1989, Ronald Reagan was born on 6 February 1911 in Tampico, Illinois. After graduating from Eureka College in Illinois in 1932, the future president's first job was as a radio sports announcer in Iowa in 1933. In 1937, Reagan embarked on a thirty-year career in films and television, appearing in approximately fifty films.

The Hollywood years engendered Reagan's interest in politics. He served six terms as president of the Screen Actors Guild, speaking out against *communism and working to constrain such influences in the film industry. During World War II, Reagan attained the rank of captain in the Army Air Corps. In 1952, he publicly renounced his affiliation with the Democratic Party and became a conservative Republican. As Reagan's film career waned, he moved to television, hosting *General Electric Theater* from 1954 to 1962 and traveling as a public spokesman for GE.

At the age of 55, Reagan defeated the Democratic incumbent Edmund G. ("Pat") Brown and was sworn in as California governor in 1967. He won again in 1970, with both terms marked by a sensitivity to the need for compromise on his ideologically driven policies to allow passage of legislation. His management style as governor, one of delegation and decentralization, would be mirrored in his presidency.

After two unsuccessful attempts to win the Republican presidential nomination in 1968 and 1976, Reagan secured it in 1980 and chose George *Bush as his vice-presidential running mate. Running against Democratic incumbent President Jimmy *Carter, Reagan's campaign themes emphasized the economy, governmental growth, the budget deficit, declining U.S. prestige abroad, and the threat of the Soviet Union. Winning the White House with 51 percent of the popular vote and 489 electoral college votes, Reagan strode into the Oval Office with a new Republican majority in the Senate riding on his coattails.

The first year of Reagan's presidency stands as his most significant domestically. After recovering quickly from an assassination attempt in March 1981, Reagan advanced his supply-side economic policies through Congress. Demonstrating political acumen, he gained passage of sweeping tax reductions designed to induce economic growth. Congress enacted most of the president's proposals, cutting income tax rates, substantially increasing defense spending, and drastically shrinking non-defense expenditures. The aim of these policies was to ignite economic growth and the resultant upsurge in governmental revenue would offset the deficit and allow for a balanced federal budget. The results were not exactly as envisioned. Reagan presided over the longest peacetime economic expansion in history, yet these tax cuts and defense spending transformed America into the world's biggest debtor with the budget deficit exploding.

The conservative social agenda Reagan pursued met with limited success. On New Right issues such as abortion and school prayer, Congress refused to act and Reagan declined to push. With a Republican-controlled Senate, Reagan used his judicial appointment power to help advance his social agenda at all levels of the federal judiciary by nominating the "ideologically faithful." By his 1989 departure, Reagan had appointed over 60 percent of all federal judges and four U.S. Supreme Court justices, a significant legacy.

In foreign affairs, Reagan's stern anticommunist posture evidenced by his support for anticommunist freedom fighters in various countries and accompanied by the military buildup and his Strategic Defense Initiative, evolved into one of relative conciliation in his second term. The Intermediate Nuclear Forces (INF) treaty, the Moscow summit, and the Reagan-Gorbachev relationship placed Reagan as "peacemaker"—belying his earlier characterizations of the Soviets as an "evil empire." His forging a line of communication through several summits with new Soviet leader Mikhail *Gorbachev was instrumental in the reduction of tensions between the two superpowers and these foreign policy advances were considered profound achievements by the public. Reagan's willingness to use the military was demonstrated in the U.S. peacekeeping force in Lebanon, the intervention in Grenada, and the bombing raid of Libya.

Reagan's organizational style in the White House was to delegate much authority and policy formulation to aides with, as critics charged, inadequate oversight. He came under increasing fire for these decentralized decision-making arrangements which allowed unaccountable subordinates to dictate policy.

The Reagan White House worked assiduously at cultivation and management of image so as to maximize favorable exposure and minimize criticism. Reagan's show business experience, telegenic appearance, and genial personality dovetailed with this media operation and his reputation as "the Great Communicator" became legendary. As his time in office progressed, an increasing number of verbal gaffes by Reagan moved his staff to minimize the number of presidential unscripted media events.

In 1984, Reagan won reelection with a landslide victory over Democratic challenger Walter Mondale; he garnered 525 electoral votes, a record, and 59 percent of the popular vote. Two years later, Democrats would regain control of the Senate. On the domestic agenda, the tax reforms of 1986 were the major successes in the second term.

Reagan, with his second wife, Nancy Davis Reagan, retained high personal popularity in his second term, although the last two years were controversy-plagued. In late 1986, it was revealed that several members of Reagan's National Security Council staff had engaged in illegal activities including selling arms to Iran and diverting the profits of those sales to the Nicaraguan contras who had been denied aid by Congress. The controversy resulted in a commission investigation, congressional testimony, and temporary damage to Reagan's popularity.

After his leaving office, it was disclosed in 1994 that the former president suffered from Alzheimer's disease, an often fatal brain disorder. In 1998, to honor him, National Airport in Washington, D.C., was renamed the Ronald Reagan National Airport, and the second largest federal building, after the Pentagon, was christened the Ronald Reagan Building and International Trade Center.

Reagan will be remembered for bringing a tide of *conservatism to U.S. politics. Domestically, Reagan changed the face of campaigning and governing with imagery, symbols, and video, emphasized personal warmth and charisma, and forged success in economic growth and tax cuts and tax reform. His legacy will be tempered by long-term budget deficits and national debt and the Iran-contra scandal. Many of the tenets of Reagan's 1980 campaign, including reducing the size and scope of government and balancing the federal budget, were not realized.

Reagan's relationship with Mikhail Gorbachev dominates his *foreign policy legacy and ostensibly ushered in a new era of U.S.-Soviet relations. His promise to enhance U.S. power in the international arena was successful through the military buildup under his direction and his display of force in selected regional conflicts. The allied military success in the *Gulf War of 1991 owes much to the massive military budgets of 1981–1989. Upon Reagan's departure in 1989, well over sixty percent of Americans approved of his job performance as president.

(See also COLD WAR; CONGRESS, U.S.; NICARAGUA; PRESIDENCY, U.S.; TAXES AND TAXATION; THATCHERISM; FOREIGN POLICY, U.S.)

Sidney Blumenthal and Thomas Byrne Edsall, eds., *The Reagan Legacy* (New York, 1988). Charles O. Jones, ed., *The Reagan Legacy: Promise and Performance* (Chatham, N.J., 1988). Larry Berman, ed., *Looking Back on the Reagan Presidency* (Baltimore, 1990).

LARRY BERMAN
STEPHEN R. ROUTH

REALISM. Also known as Political Realism or Realpolitik, Realism remains one of the dominant schools of thought within the field of *international relations. With a long intellectual pedigree, dating at least from *Thucydides' (ca. 460–400 b.c.e.) history of *The Peloponnesian War* and the writings of Niccolo Machiavelli (1469–1527) and Thomas Hobbes (1588–1679), Realism is distinguished from contending approaches by three assumptions regarding the nature of international politics.

First, the *international system is anarchic and based on the principle of self-help. By *anarchy, Realists do not mean that international politics are chaotic. Indeed, some proponents argue that relations between nations do exhibit regularities and are even driven by widely accepted social norms. Rather, for Realists anarchy simply means that the international system lacks any political authority higher than the *state. Unlike domestic politics, where a hierarchical pattern of authority exists to enforce private agreements and public laws, sovereign states stand in relations of formal equality. As a result, states are ultimately dependent on their own resources to protect their interests, enforce agreements, and maintain order.

Second, states are the dominant actors in world politics. Both private actors, such as multinational corporations, and intergovernmental organizations, such as the UN, exist and influence international politics. Realists assume these actors are subordinate to states. Private entities and intergovernmental organizations act within the political arena, but they do so only with the consent of national political authorities.

Third, in Hans Morgenthau's classic statement (*Politics Among Nations: The Struggle for Power and Peace*, 5th ed., rev., New York, 1978, p. 5), "statesmen think and act in terms of interest defined as power," broadly conceived to include both material and psychological, military and economic capabilities. The "national interest," in this view, is to maximize *power. Because power exists only relationally, it follows that world politics is inherently conflictual; all countries cannot increase their power or satisfy their national interests simultaneously.

Kenneth Waltz (in *Theory of International Politics*, Reading, Mass., 1979, p. 118) has recently refined this third assumption, clarifying the ambiguity between power as a means and as an end. "At a minimum," he writes, states "seek their own preservation and, at a maximum, drive for universal domination." Only after survival is assured, he continues, can they afford to seek other goals; as a result, states act, first and foremost, to maximize *security.

Realism emerged in its modern form largely in reaction to *Idealism, a more normatively driven approach which held that countries were united in an underlying harmony of interest—a view shattered by the outbreak of World War II. Rather than study the world as it might be, Realists maintained that a science of international politics must study the world as it was—an insistence that resulted in the Realists' self-acclaimed appellation.

The generation of Realists writing immediately before and after World War II, now referred to as the classical Realists, shared an essentially pessimistic view of human nature. Reinhold Niebuhr (1892–1971), Nicholas Spykman (1893–1943), Hans Morgenthau (1904–1980), and others believed that the struggle for power was inherent in human nature. Viewing humankind as unchanging, these Realists held out little hope for any transformation of international politics. Rather, they focused on the principles of *diplomacy and mechanisms—

such as the *balance of power, international morality and world *public opinion, and *international law—which regulated and restrained the inevitable clashes of interests between states.

Contemporary Realists, often called Neorealists or Structural Realists, have sought to inject greater theoretic rigor by defining concepts more clearly and deriving testable hypotheses. Neorealists have also focused on the international system, examining how different structures—defined in terms of ordering principles, the functional differentiation of the units, and distributions of capabilities—produce varying patterns of world politics which cannot be explained simply in terms of the interests and policies of individual countries. Most fundamentally, Neorealists derive the causes of international conflict not from innate human characteristics but from anarchy. Given the necessary reliance on self-help, a state must prepare to defend itself against potential threats from others. In so preparing, however, it (perhaps unwittingly) threatens others—thereby creating a vicious cycle of increasing threat and insecurity. Thus, even though all states may possess thoroughly pacific intentions, international competition and conflict may still arise.

In the approximately forty-five years since it emerged as a clearly defined school of thought, Realism has stimulated a diverse research program. In a recent review, John A. Vasquez (*The Power of Power Politics: A Critique*, New Brunswick, N.J., 1983) identifies five foci within Realism: the study of 1) *foreign policy, which has sought both to clarify the concepts of national interest and power in the context of past and present policy problems and develop models of national decision making; 2) systemic processes, especially those that regulate international conflict; 3) the causes of *war; 4) *deterrence and bargaining, with a particular emphasis on *nuclear weapons and strategy; and 5) supranationalism, including *international organizations and international regimes. Since the early 1970s, a Realist school of *international political economy has also emerged. Focusing on the interaction of power and wealth, this school has been particularly concerned with the relationship between *hegemony, or the presence of a single dominant state, and international economic openness and closure.

Critiques of Realism. No theoretical approach to international relations, especially one as central as Realism, is without its critics. Although by no means an exhaustive list, it is possible to identify five general criticisms.

First, the predictive power of Realism, and its status as a positive theory of international relations, rests on the objective determination of the national interest—whether it be defined in terms of power or security. Only if the national interest is clear and unambiguous can the theorist discern whether countries do, in fact, adopt appropriate policies. Yet, "the trouble . . . ," as Arnold Wolfers noted in " 'National Security' as an Ambiguous Symbol" (*Political Science Quarterly* 67, no. 4 [December 1952], p. 484), "is that the term 'security' covers a range of goals so wide that highly divergent policies can be interpreted as policies of security." As a consequence, the predictive and, in turn, explanatory power of Realism is weakened.

Second, many Realists, and especially Neorealists who explicitly exclude domestic policies from their theories, have treated the state as a unitary actor. Critics have charged that even if this "billiard-ball" view was appropriate for describing international relations in an earlier era, it is of declining relevance today. With the growth of private cross-border communications and organizations, and with the rise of economic *interdependence, the "hard shell" of the state has crumbled. According to Robert Keohane and Joseph Nye in *Power and Interdependence: World Politics in Transition* (2d ed., Boston, 1989), relations between some countries and in some issue areas are better characterized by "complex interdependence"—where multiple channels connect societies, no clear hierarchy exists between the "high" politics of military security and "low" politics of economic affairs, and military force is of less utility.

Third, Neorealists have recently been criticized for being "statists," that is, assuming that states are the primary actors in world politics without explaining why they emerged as the predominant form of political organization or considering how they might evolve in the future. Fourth, and closely related, Neorealists have been challenged for not developing a dynamic theory which can explain the evolution of the international system through time. Specifically, critics within the "agent-structure" debate have argued that Neorealism must incorporate how the actions of "agents," or decision makers operating within the constraints of the system, affect in turn the structure of the system. In "Reflections on *Theory of International Politics:* A Response to My Critics" (in Robert O. Keohane, ed., *Neorealism and Its Critics*, New York, 1986), Waltz recognizes both of these problems and accepts them as inevitable limitations of relevant, "problem-solving" theory.

Finally, Realism does not adequately ground the national pursuit of power or security, however defined, in the interests and incentives of individual foreign policy decision makers. Classical Realism was developed before many of the advances in modern political science, and Neorealism seeks to derive strictly systemic theories of international politics. From a public or rational choice perspective, which accepts the methodological individualism of neoclassical economics, there is no necessary reason why the interests of self-seeking politicians should coincide with the national interest. Given the difficulties of translating social preferences into public policy, a considerable gap will often exist between the interests of the people as a whole and actual policy. To the extent that such difficulties arise, the explanatory power of Realism is further weakened.

Despite these limitations, Realism remains a powerful, simple, and elegant theory of international politics. Rather than focusing on *ideology, national *regime types, stages of economic development, and other particularistic or time-bound factors, Realism builds its explanations on the most general and enduring features of international politics—the struggle for power and security by self-seeking states within an anarchic international system—and in doing so provides both a persuasive explanation for conflict within the international arena and a guide for managing such disputes.

Normative Critique. Realism is often criticized for being amoral, and perhaps even immoral, in its elevation of the national interest over other ethical principles. Realism, as defined above, is a positive theory of international politics, and as such is not motivated primarily by normative concerns.

Yet, to the extent that Realists enter the policy arena, whether as direct participants or outside experts, this criticism is not entirely inappropriate.

Realists do consider standards of conduct at the international level to be different from those governing behavior within states. In an anarchic world, national leaders must, at times, adopt or countenance actions that would be legally or morally repugnant in relations among individuals. As the environment changes, Realists maintain, definitions of morality must change too. As George F. Kennan writes in "Morality and Foreign Affairs" (*Foreign Affairs* 64, no. 2 [Winter 1985–1986], p. 206), the "primary obligation [of a government] is to the *interests* of the national society it represents, not to the moral impulses that individual elements of that society may experience."

As always, Realists emphasize the importance of studying the world as it is rather than as we wish it to be. This commitment to "realism" carries over into the evaluation of policy. As Hans Morgenthau concludes in "Another Great Debate': The National Interest of the United States" (*American Political Science Review* 46, no. 4 [December 1952], p. 988), "The contest between utopianism and realism is not tantamount to a contest between principle and expediency, morality and immorality.... The contest is rather between one type of political morality and another type of political morality, one taking as its standard universal moral principles abstractly formulated, the other weighing these principles against the moral requirements of concrete political action, their relative merits to be decided by a prudent evaluation of the political consequences to which they are likely to lead."

Edward Hallett Carr, *The Twenty Years' Crisis, 1919–1939* (New York, 1939). Stephen D. Krasner, *Defending the National Interest: Raw Materials Investments and U.S. Foreign Policy* (Princeton, N.J., 1978). Robert Gilpin, *The Political Economy of International Relations* (Princeton, N.J., 1987). Alexander Wendt, "The Agent-Structure Problem in International Relations" *International Organization* 41, no. 3 (Summer 1987): 335–370.

DAVID A. LAKE

REBELLION. See POLITICAL VIOLENCE; GUERRILLA WARFARE.

RECIPROCITY. In *international law the term *reciprocity* refers to the principle that the *rights claimed by one state accrue to other states; or more generally, that the rights of one party accrue to comparable entities. Reciprocity is implied by the concept of *sovereignty, as developed in the fifteenth and sixteenth centuries: legally independent states, claiming authority over their own territories and populations, could not deny similar rights to other states. Astute diplomats have for centuries conceded rights to other states when, through the principle of reciprocity, they could therefore obtain equivalent rights themselves, and have refrained from claiming rights when such claims would imply more valuable comparable claims by others. As secretary of state of the United States in the early 1790s, for example, Thomas Jefferson was careful to make such use of the principle of reciprocity in his negotiations with Britain and France.

Reciprocity also refers to situations of interaction resulting from the intersection of actor strategies. Specific reciprocity refers to balanced exchanges in which each party's actions are contingent on the other's, in such a way that benefits are exchanged for benefits, but are withheld in the absence of compensation. Diffuse reciprocity refers to the observance of norms prescribing that one contribute one's fair share, or behave well toward others, for the sake of obtaining benefits for a group of which one is a part, rather than for the sake of specific conditional rewards.

In bilateral situations involving a combination of mutual interest in cooperation and conflict of interest over the distribution of gains—specifically, in what is known in *game theory as Prisoners' Dilemma—strategies of specific reciprocity can promote cooperation. Such cooperation can be seen not only in experimental games but also on such issues as international trade and *arms control. Specific reciprocity is often an appropriate principle of behavior when norms of obligation are weak because it protects participants against severe exploitation.

However, even in bilateral situations, specific reciprocity can accentuate conflict. Even moderate levels of uncertainty and misleading information ("noise") can prevent reciprocal cooperation from emerging; and reciprocity can lead to "feuds" as well as to cooperation. In multilateral situations, reciprocity can cause further difficulties, because reciprocal agreements between two parties can affect the value of previous agreements, thus engendering demands for renegotiation of older bargains. For instance, the conditional most-favored-nation (MFN) clause in U.S. trade policy before 1923 exemplified specific reciprocity: a concession given to one trading partner was not offered to others automatically, but only for negotiated compensation. The clause was eventually abandoned largely because the resulting negotiations were tedious, mutually irritating, and often fruitless.

Specific reciprocity in contemporary international politics is also complicated by differences in internal regulations among countries. For instance, in the late 1980s some members of the *European Community demanded that in order for banks from nonmember countries to have access to the Single European Market, those countries must grant reciprocal access to European banks. But the United States does not have unitary arrangements for banking, which is regulated by the states. The United States could offer "national treatment," in which European banks suffer no more restrictions in Illinois or California than New York banks do, but it could not offer specific reciprocity, providing that a New York subsidiary of a German bank could operate in Illinois or California. For its part, the European Community could not implement specific reciprocity by discriminating against U.S. subsidiaries in Germany without fragmenting the regulatory framework that it had been at pains to establish.

Specific reciprocity is not, therefore, a guarantee of cooperation. Diffuse reciprocity, in which members of a community follow accepted norms of behavior toward one another, requires much less negotiation. For example, unconditional MFN treatment provides that all benefits provided to one trade partner are immediately generalized, without compensation, to all other trade partners to which unconditional MFN applies (e.g., among members of the *General Agreement on Tariffs and Trade [GATT]).

However, governments following strategies of diffuse reciprocity may be exploited by partners that seek gains at their expense or by others attempting to benefit from general observance of norms without doing so themselves. Institutional arrangements such as GATT and the European Community incorporate elements of both specific and diffuse reciprocity in order to encourage mutually beneficial exchange while limiting opportunities for exploitation.

Reciprocity will remain a central principle of world politics as long as separate units engage in exchange in a nonhierarchical system. Under favorable conditions, either specific or diffuse reciprocity can promote cooperation, but under unfavorable conditions, conflict can result. The appropriateness of various strategies of reciprocity depends both on the configuration of actors' interests and on prevailing institutional arrangements.

(See also INTERNATIONAL COOPERATION; INTERNATIONAL POLITICAL ECONOMY; REGIME.)

Martin Wight, *Systems of States* (Leicester, 1977). Robert Axelrod, *The Evolution of Cooperation* (New York, 1984). Robert O. Keohane, "Reciprocity in International Relations" *International Organization* 40 (Winter 1986): 1–27. George W. Downs and David M. Rucke, *Tacit Bargaining, Arms Races, and Arms Control* (Ann Arbor, Mich., 1990).

ROBERT O. KEOHANE

REFORM. The goal, in some form, of countless political leaders and social movements throughout history, reform has also been a central focus of reflection for political theorists ranging from Machiavelli to Marxists of the twentieth century. Successful reforms may serve not only to reorient policy but also to change the balance of social power and the contours of political debate. Failed reforms not only ruin political careers but even, in extreme cases, set the stage for violent upheavals. It is thus important, as Machiavelli acknowledged centuries ago in *The Prince*, to understand the difficult and often dangerous process that ushers in a "new order of things."

The *Oxford English Dictionary* defines reform as "the amendment, or altering for the better, of some faulty state of things, especially of a corrupt or oppressive political institution or practice; the removal of some abuse or wrong." This definition is useful, but both its empirical and normative components are controversial. The normative issue concerns whether or not reform necessarily represents "altering for the better." In the eyes of many Marxists, for example, attempts at "reform" within the capitalist system have traditionally been viewed as futile or even counterproductive, given that they may well delay the coming of the socialist *revolution that is deemed the only genuine solution to the oppressive practices of the current system. Even within the Marxist camp, however, another strong current—the revisionists or social democrats—has argued that cumulative reforms might well be the most effective way of producing a humane socialist society.

The major empirical issue is how broad or dramatic the scope of "amendment" must be to qualify as reform. Where should one draw the line between incremental change and genuine reform? Many policymakers have been known to herald even modest changes (e.g., the restructuring of an agency) as reforms precisely because they believe attaching such a label may have symbolic value, enhancing the perceived importance of their actions. Arguably the term should be reserved for more substantial instances of policy change;

classic examples would be the 1832 Reform Act that significantly expanded the suffrage in Britain or the administrative reforms resulting from the Progressive movement in the United States during the nineteenth century.

In recent years the term reform has also been used, as in the case of the Soviet Union under Mikhail *Gorbachev, to describe an even more ambitious project: a multifaceted campaign undertaken by the government to restructure key state institutions, revamp a host of public policies, shift the balance of social power, and ultimately even change fundamental social values. According to most dictionaries, a sweeping reform of this sort should more properly be termed a "reformation," but that label is seldom employed by contemporary political analysts, no doubt owing to its inevitable association with the religious Reformation of the sixteenth century. At the expense of analytical precision, such political reformation projects—whether or not they be deemed fully successful— are now frequently referred to as "revolutions" (e.g., see Peter Jenkins, *Mrs. Thatcher's Revolution*, London, 1987, and Martin Anderson, *Revolution: The Reagan Legacy*, Stanford, Calif., 1988). A less confusing term for such phenomena, and thus the one that will be used here, is simply "great reforms."

Unlike revolutions, great reforms traditionally have not been the focus of extensive comparative analyses. However, the profusion of dramatic reform experiments over the last decade—including *Deng Xiaoping's China, Gorbachev's Soviet Union, and Margaret *Thatcher's Britain, to mention only the most prominent—has recently inspired a number of social scientists to examine the origins, dynamics, and effects of great reforms in a comparative perspective. The following is but a brief summary of some of their central findings.

First, great reforms have tended to be launched in what can be broadly described as a context of crisis. Whether the crisis stems from external threats (as in Peter the Great's Russia), economic depression (as in Franklin D. *Roosevelt's United States), political malaise, or some combination of factors, it can serve to open a window of opportunity for reformers by making action seem urgent and thus increasing support for what would otherwise be seen as excessively bold or risky ventures. Important though the facilitating role of crises has been, two caveats should be noted here: not all nations in crisis experience great reform experiments, and not all major reforms are introduced in a burst during a crisis period (in twentieth-century Sweden, for example, it was primarily the extraordinary longevity of Social Democratic rule that allowed for the implementation of great reforms; see T. J. Pempel, *Uncommon Democracies*, Ithaca, N.Y., 1990).

Second, although some reform leaders may appear to be ideologues, they generally lack a coherent blueprint for social change and act in a rather pragmatic fashion. For example, Margaret Thatcher and Ronald *Reagan were reputed to be ideological in the extreme, but political prudence led them both to shy away from or limit cuts in popular social programs (the National Health Service in Britain, Social Security in the United States) that contradicted their conservative views. Thatcher became best known for her vast program of *privatization (selling state-owned industries to private shareholders), but it was barely mentioned in her 1979 manifesto and was developed gradually in an experimental manner. Deng's reforms have proceeded in a zigzag fashion, as innovations have often been curtailed to mollify opposition. Roosevelt was famous for his experimentation and improvisation during the *New Deal of the 1930s, and Gorbachev employed a similar style.

Third, reform governments generally find it extremely difficult to maintain the support of all elements of the coalition that backed them initially. Once vague promises of reform are transformed into concrete policy, and once laundry lists of programs are reduced to manageable or affordable priorities, many erstwhile supporters become disappointed or even actively opposed to the government. Thus the New Deal coalition began to collapse in 1937, Deng found himself faced with explosive demonstrations in 1989, Thatcher was rejected by her own Conservative Party in 1990, and Gorbachev was ultimately ousted by forces who had once applauded his programs of glasnost and *perestroika.

Fourth, the effects of great reform campaigns vary enormously and are hard to gauge while they are still in progress. The administrations of Lyndon *Johnson (1963–1969) and Reagan (1981–1989) in the United States enjoyed enormous success in their early years but then stalled so badly that many would question categorizing them as examples of great reform. The Socialist government of Francois *Mitterrand in France met with a similar fate from 1981 to 1986. More dramatically, Salvador *Allende's Unidad Popular government in Chile enjoyed a promising first year of reform in 1970, but by 1973 it had been ousted in a bloody coup that led to the reversal of its initiatives and the abolition of democracy. The governments of both Deng in China and Gorbachev in the Soviet Union experienced serious problems right after scholars were beginning to portray their reforms as irreversible, and it is still too early to assess their achievements accurately. The Thatcher government illustrated how tenuous the concept of "irreversible reform" really is by privatizing enterprises that had been nationalized forty years before and had seemed destined to stay in the public sector forever. As many scholars have noted, the most durable reforms are no doubt those instituted in such a manner as to create beneficiaries (e.g., strengthened trade unions or welfare recipients) willing and able to fight for their retention years after reforms are introduced.

(See also POLITICAL REALIGNMENT.)

Samuel Huntington, *Political Order in Changing Societies* (New Haven, Conn., 1968). Adam Przeworski, *Capitalism and Social Democracy* (Cambridge, U.K. 1985). Michael Oksenberg and Bruce Dickson, "The Origins, Processes and Outcomes of Great Political Reform," in Dankwart Rustow and Kenneth Erickson, eds., *Comparative Political Dynamics* (New York, 1991), pp. 235–261. John T. S. Keeler, ed., "The Politics of Reform in Comparative Perspective,"*Comparative Political Studies* special issue (January 1993).

JOHN T. S. KEELER

REFUGEES. That refugees have always been both a cause and consequence of intercommunal conflict has been once again graphically illustrated by the events which began in 1990 when Rwandan refugees attempted to repatriate from Uganda by force. This "invasion" caused the internal displacement of 1 million people and many deaths. The prolonged state of conflict and insecurity that ensued culminated in the 1994 genocide. Furthermore, with the breakdown of the Soviet Union accompanied by the emergence of states organized along "ethnic" lines and the war in Yugoslavia, Europe

has witnessed the largest involuntary migration since the Second World War.

Since 1982, the office of the UN High Commissioner for Refugees (UNHCR) has been committed to reducing numbers through repatriations, but throughout the 1990s a growing number of conflicts around the world have kept the numbers of refugees at some 16 million. The number of persons who are displaced within national borders is conservatively estimated at 20 million. Many of these lack even the minimal assistance available to refugees. They do not have a special protected status except for what is available within the framework of general international human rights law. This raises the question whether human rights can be secured through UN intervention.

The quest for communal homogeneity along religious, ethnic, and political lines, with its attendant problems of minorities and statelessness, the persistent tendency toward the centralization of state power, and the assertion of hegemonic control of territory, resources, and populations by national groups or ruling elites lie at the root of forcible expulsions. These have been greatly exacerbated over the last decades by dramatic changes in demography, ecological decay, and the growing inequalities in the world economy. The refugee policies of receiving states continue to be animated by a composite of domestic and foreign policy calculations, pressure from domestic compatriot constituencies, the labor requirements of their economies, preservation of relations with allies, embarrassment of adversaries, and, to a certain extent, humanitarianism.

In a world in which nation-states lay increasingly firm claims to sovereign territorial control, refugees often exist both at the geographic frontiers between states and at the conceptual margins of international politics and law; they are frequently at the mercy of the capricious benevolence of asylum states and vulnerable to the political calculations of regional and international powers. Most host governments in the South are unable to provide for the basic security or subsistence needs of their own populations, let alone those of refugees. Attention to the psychological and social trauma of forced migration is rare.

Throughout the twentieth century, defining the term "refugee" has itself been a serious political and conceptual problem for states and international organizations. The currently favored definition of "refugee" is to be found in the UN Convention Relating to the Status of Refugees, drafted in 1951 and now adopted by over 100 countries. The UN Convention defines refugees as persons who are outside their country of origin owing to a well-founded fear of persecution on the basis of race, religion, nationality, membership in a social group, or political opinion. Since 1951, several regional accords, notably the Organization of African Unity Refugee Convention of 1969, have defined refugees in broader terms to include persons fleeing external aggression, occupation, foreign domination, or events seriously disturbing public order. The 1984 Cartegena Declaration makes similar liberal provisions for the Latin American region.

As a concept of *international law, the term "refugee" has evolved considerably since its entry into international affairs after World War I. Until the imposition of immigration controls which began in the late nineteenth century, there was little reason to define clearly the term "refugee." Before then, open immigration was permitted and encouraged by most states. In contrast to the present, immigrants and refugees were frequently considered crucial to economic growth and a valuable cultural and intellectual resource, not a problem. The earliest international legal instruments concerning refugees date from the 1920s and assigned refugee status to specific national groups, for example to Russians fleeing the Bolshevik Revolution. Such national groups were viewed as lacking the protection of their country of origin and in need of international protection. The Evian Conference of 1938, which addressed the flight of Jews from National Socialist Germany, marked the first instance of international recognition of the refugee as victim of persecution.

The common analytic assumption of all refugee definitions throughout the twentieth century has been that a normal bond of trust, loyalty, protection, and assistance constitutes the basic political link between the citizen and the state, the violation of which engenders refugees. Much of the current debate among states regarding refugee status revolves around whether persecution is the sole phenomenon by which the social contract can be severed or whether the absence of state protection can manifest itself in diverse ways, including the state's inability to provide public order or subsistence. It is widely agreed that even the UN's current persecution-based definition encompasses especially predatory, politically motivated economic policies, such as the denial on racial, religious, or political grounds of any opportunity for employment, and that the rigid distinction between political and so-called "economic" refugees is politically motivated and on weak jurisprudential ground, particularly in light of international legal recognition of economic and social rights as fundamental human rights.

The international refugee regime has been developing throughout the twentieth century. Originally under the League of Nations and later the UN, a series of international organizations have been established to address the refugee problem. These institutions, including UNHCR, have pursued a strategy of depoliticizing the refugee issue by emphasizing its moral and humanitarian dimensions. Solutions to the refugee's predicament pursued by UNHCR include permanent integration in a country of asylum (either within the region of origin or overseas) or eventual voluntary repatriation. UNHCR has become the largest UN agency to be entirely devoted to the human rights needs of one particular group. However, the machinery for monitoring and enforcing refugee rights remains largely ineffective, mainly due to the pressure of the main donors, who influence refugee policy in line with their own political agendas.

As with so many international political issues, the politics of refugees may be influenced in a perverse way. Owing primarily to disagreements between the Soviet Union and the Western powers over how to deal with Russian, Ukrainian, and Baltic nationals who had found themselves outside their countries of origin in the aftermath of World War II and who, for the most part, were unwilling to return, the Soviet Union declined to support the UNHCR, and control of the organization fell to the West by default, which in turn led to the politicization of the refugee issue by the West to its strategic and ideological advantage. The United States went still further by enacting legislation which, until 1980, identified refugees by definition as persons fleeing communism.

Nation-states are especially reluctant to cooperate when membership issues are at stake, as is always the case when asylum and permanent resettlement are a possibility. Although some interstate cooperation has recently emerged, mainly between countries in the North, it is essentially limited to restrictive measures. In particular, the member-states of the European Union have devised a common approach to refugees and migrants. The process of eliminating border controls and allowing free movement of capital and labor in Western Europe has taken place in the proximity of great unrest and the breakdown of old state entities and the formation of new ones. This has prompted Western European states to create "fortress Europe," characterized by fingerprinting and the use of *information technology in the sharing of information, limited access to asylum through so-called "fast track" procedures, and tightening up of border controls. Detention of asylum seekers as a form of "humane deterrence" continues to be widely practiced. Asylum as a means of securing permanent integration into the host society has been further undermined by an approach that identifies repatriation as the main solution to the refugee problem. The granting of temporary protection, a status with few rights attached, to those fleeing the conflict in the former Yugoslavia, "preventive protection" in the country of origin, and the use of coercion to repatriate refugees are manifestations of this trend.

(See also FOREIGN WORKERS; GREAT LAKES REGION; HUMANITARIAN INTERVENTION; HUMAN RIGHTS; INTERNATIONAL MIGRATION; NATIONALISM; WORLD WAR II.)

J. Bennett, *Internally Displaced People: A Global Survey* (New York, 1998). UN High Commissioner for Refugees, *The State of the World's Refugees: A Humanitarian Agenda* (New York, 1997).

BARBARA E. HARRELL-BOND
GUGLIELMO VERDIRAME

REGIME. In the second half of the twentieth century, the French word *régime*—referring to a set of rules recognized in *international law for the governance of a particular subject—was first anglicized by international lawyers, then adopted by social scientists studying international institutions. Regimes are sets of implicit or explicit principles, norms, rules, and decision-making procedures applicable to specific areas of international relations. Examples of international regimes include the international monetary arrangements established at the Bretton Woods Conference of 1944, regulations governing civil air transport and telecommunications, the rules and organizations established in the 1970s to monitor and control the proliferation of *nuclear weapons, and an emerging set of international environmental regulations. International regimes therefore operate in all major issue areas of world politics: *security, economic, environmental.

The concept of international regime helps observers to describe the rapid increase, since 1945, in the number of multilateral arrangements through which *states cooperate to regulate transborder activity. Most international regimes include at least one formal *international organization, with the tasks of providing particular services, monitoring members' compliance with rules, and serving as a forum for negotiations. Yet *international relations remains a "self-help" system, organized through interstate arrangements rather than hierarchically.

International regimes are established by states to achieve

state purposes, not to make them obsolete. The international organizations involved in regimes usually have quite restricted powers, and certainly do not act as miniature governments. When the rules of international regimes are enforced, they are enforced by states, not by international organizations themselves. International regimes have problematic relationships to state power, and two questions are particularly debatable: 1) whether international regimes must rely on the support of a single dominant power; and 2) whether the rules of the regimes have significant effects apart from the influence exerted by their supporters.

International regimes thrived during the period after World War II, which was characterized both by increasing *interdependence and by the preponderance of the United States. It is therefore difficult to disentangle the relative contributions of interdependence and U.S. dominance to their success, and whether they can continue to flourish in a more multipolar world remains to be seen. Continued high levels of interdependence will provide incentives to cooperate, and cooperation in a complex, multipolar world will require regimes. On the other hand, economic and political competition among states in such a world is likely to limit the efficacy of international rules.

The rules of international regimes reflect not only the power of states but internationally accepted principles, such as that of *sovereignty. Furthermore, over time the relative power of actors may change, while rules remain relatively fixed. Thus the outcomes to be expected on the basis of power alone often differ from those observed within the framework of international regimes. To the extent that such differences persist, and states continue to comply with regime rules, international regimes matter. When their rules become too inconsistent with the distribution of state power, however, it is to be expected that the regimes will be bypassed, deprived of substantial funding, or otherwise rendered meaningless.

International regimes are created by states for their purposes, and they operate within limits set by states. Within these limits, however, they enable systematic cooperation to occur and affect the authority patterns and the distribution of benefits in world politics.

(See also HEGEMONY; INTERNATIONAL COOPERATION; INTERNATIONAL POLITICAL ECONOMY.)

Stephen D. Krasner, ed., *International Regimes* (Ithaca, N.Y., 1983). Robert O. Keohane, *After Hegemony: Cooperation and Discord in the World Political Economy* (Princeton, N.J., 1984).

ROBERT O. KEOHANE

REGIONAL DEVELOPMENT BANKS. Four international organizations can be described as "regional development banks" (RDBs): the *Inter-American Development Bank (established 1959 in Washington, D.C.); the *African Development Bank (established 1964 in Abidjan, Côte d'Ivoire); the *Asian Development Bank (established 1966 in Manila, The Philippines); and the European Bank for Reconstruction and Development (established 1991 in London, England). Modeled on the *World Bank (established in 1944 in Washington, D.C.), the fundamental aim of all these multilateral development banks is to foster long-term development that is socially equitable and environmentally sustainable.

Two of the RDBs (the Inter-American Development Bank and the Asian Development Bank) were established during the Cold War and supported by the major Western powers in part because of the ideological struggle with communism. Nonetheless, with one exception the governing charters of the RDBs, like that of the World Bank, maintain that they are "apolitical" in character. The exception (the European Bank for Reconstruction and Development) was founded at the end of the Cold War explicitly to facilitate the transition of European countries in the former Soviet bloc to market-based, democratic societies. If the RDBs and the World Bank do have an ideological bias, this is manifested in their support of economic policies that strengthen the institutions and culture of *capitalism.

In contrast to the United Nations where each member state has equal status, but like the World Bank, the voice of each member country in the RDB's governing councils is commensurate with its shareholding, which in turn corresponds roughly to its economic size and importance. And in contrast to the World Bank, which now caters to developing and "transition" countries around the globe, the RDBs were purposely designed to serve the specific needs of developing countries in their respective continents. Moreover, unlike the World Bank, in which the developed countries have a permanent majority, two of the RDBs (the Inter-American and African) were deliberately organized so as to ensure a voting majority for the developing-country members, although in both cases the majority has been whittled down through negotiations.

Despite differences rooted in their historical and geographical circumstances, the RDBs have grown to be increasingly similar to each other and to the World Bank in their operational philosophy and practices, although a widespread view is that the World Bank is more effective than the RDBs. The tendency of these multilateral development banks, along with the *International Monetary Fund, to espouse market- and globalization-friendly economic policies, particularly in countries experiencing economic crisis, has embroiled them in controversy ever since the 1980s because such policies are also often associated with increasing disparities and poverty.

The unique potential of the RDBs is that they are institutions in which the people and countries of each region have a large stake. This enables them to make a vital contribution to long-term development based on a greater awareness of the opportunities and constraints facing the region, and to generating solutions that are more appropriate to their circumstances and reflect a high degree of local ownership.

Roy Culpeper, *Titans or Behemoths?* Volume 5 of *The Multilateral Development Banks* (Boulder Colo., and Ottawa, 1997).

ROY CULPEPER

RELIGION AND POLITICS. See overleaf.

REPRODUCTIVE POLITICS. The domain of law, policy, and social action in modern societies in which groups and individuals contend over the means, and meanings, of controlling human fertility is known as reproductive politics. Because fertility intimately involves issues regarding gender division, the status of women, sexuality, health, population, and child welfare, reproductive politics necessarily encompasses all of

(cont. on p. 726)

RELIGION AND POLITICS. Religion relates to politics in a number of ways. First, it interacts with the nation-state, which is now the standard political arrangement throughout the global community. Second, many religions are powerful worldwide forces and thus affect international arrangements. Third, religious conflicts can intensify divisions within and between states. Fourth, religious values are often invoked to justify and legitimize political action and political arrangements, and this links in with ways in which it affects voting behavior and other manifestations of political behavior or political struggle. Fifth, religious institutions themselves play a role within nations. Sixth, the behavior of political leaders often owes something to their religious beliefs. All these are often intertwined.

Whereas premodern arrangements varied widely between West and East and between North and South, the nation-state as understood today is roughly homogeneous, and by considering it in relation to religion we have a good way of surveying the global scene and preparing for longer historical analysis. In describing interactions I shall adhere to a rather traditional definition of religion, which emphasizes belief in the transcendent or supernatural, to distinguish religion from secular ideologies such as Marxism, though in fact such ideologies may function like religions.

The classical modern nation-state, as developed in nineteenth-century Europe, was linguistically and culturally based. Regions such as Germany, Italy, Norway, and Poland acquired self-consciousness in part through the creation of modernized national languages and literatures. But religious affiliation could also stand as an additional marker of identity—for instance, Catholicism in Poland helped define Polish identity, although this immediately created problems for minority groups. There could also be conflict between religion and *nationalism as with Italy, because Italian unification was bound to destroy the Papal States. Further, the ideology of much nineteenth-century nationalism was *liberalism, and the conservative traditionalism of the papacy resisted this. In Italy it was only after World War II, with the coming to power of the Christian Democrats (effectively a blend of Catholicism and liberal democratic ideology), that the Church was able or willing to play a fully effective role in Italian national politics.

In some cases the marker of national identity is itself religious or ideological. For instance, despite Protestant leadership in the nineteenth century, Ireland's nationalism has been defined through Catholicism, and in contemporary Northern Ireland the split occurs along religious lines between the two main groups. Even before the breaching of the Berlin Wall, the German Democratic Republic's raison d'être disappeared with the abandonment of Marxism-Leninism as its official ideology, given that the masses were disillusioned with it.

Where religious divisions were significant, linguistic nationalism might serve to cement the nation, itself the focus of ultimate loyalty, as in nineteenth-century Germany. In the United States, things were different: Here was a nation defined through a constitution, where the separation of church and state came to be thoroughly realized despite the religiously homogeneous, primarily Protestant, character of its history up to the nineteenth century, when Catholic and Jewish migrants began to arrive in large numbers.

Japan, though mainly a Buddhist country, reshaped itself in a different fashion through the Meiji Constitution of 1889, which defined the national ethos as being summed up in *Shinto ritual (freedom of religion was, however, entrenched in the constitution, although it declared Shinto *not* to be a religion: the doctrinal dimension of Shinto, never strong, was eliminated, but the myth of the imperial family and its divine descent was underlined). Shinto was seen as an integral part of the *kokutai*, or national essence.

The breakup of the Ottoman and Habsburg empires after World War I led to further national development, giving rise in Europe to a number of new linguistically shaped nations. The most significant long-term occurrence was the beginnings of the effective realization of a Jewish state. Although the Zionist movement was secular and socialist in ethos, the definition of Jewishness could not escape the religious question: Was it not because of the observance of Judaism that the Jews had come to be a separate people?

The position of minorities throughout the new, nationally oriented Europe was unhappy: and hypernationalism was a main factor in the growth of *anti-Semitism. Premodern religious epistemology also played its part: Lutheran and Catholic anti-Jewish thinking was predicated on the assumption that revelation was plain and so the Jews, in neglecting the Christian interpretation of the Old Testament, were willfully rejecting the truth.

The spread of colonialism contributed to the development of nationalist identity among subject peoples, taking various forms relative to religion. Pan-Arab nationalism tended toward secularism. In India a modernized Hindu ideology of tolerance of different religions as so many paths to the one truth provided the content of a new sense of India as a single, however diverse, people. After independence India's constitution was consciously pluralist, though in giving concessions to Muslims and other minorities it slowly began to provoke a backlash among Hindu nationalists. A large segment of India's Muslims, moreover, parted from the Republic of India, creating Pakistan. Like other predominantly Muslim countries it has experimented with partial imposition of Islamic law (*shari'a) and consequently has caused some problems for minority groups. But religion was not strong enough to bind East and West Pakistan together: the Bengali-speaking eastern province became Bangladesh in 1971.

But when combined with nationalist sentiment, *Islam could be highly dynamic, most notably in the case of the Ayatollah Ruhollah *Khomeini's Islamic revolution in Iran in 1979. Although secular pan-Arabism has been a powerful force, attempts to unite countries on this basis have failed, whereas Islamic revival is a growing movement in various major Arab countries, from Algeria to Egypt. A soft ideology of religious unity has proved a major instrument in governing predominantly Islamic Indonesia, which because of its geographical and cultural configuration is prone to disunity.

Many formerly Buddhist countries have come under Marxist rule. Because Marxist ideology is aggressively antireligious, traditional religions have suffered greatly in these circumstances, and especially when, as in the case of Tibet, national consciousness is religious as well as linguistico-cultural in nature. But in Vietnam, Laos, Cambodia, China, and the Democratic People's Republic of Korea (North Korea), traditional religious practice was mostly suppressed until the mid-1980s. On the other hand, a strong Sinhala Buddhist nationalism became evident not very long after the independence of Sri Lanka in 1948. In 1956 Solomon W. R. D. Bandaranaike campaigned under the slogan "Sinhala only." This linguistic enthusiasm overlay a concern to restore something like the glories of the medieval Buddhist state. It led to deteriorating relations with the Tamils, an uprising among young Sinhalese radicals (the People's Liberation Front) in 1971, and eventually civil war in 1985. Sinhalese Buddhist ideology did not have a suitable theory of the place of *Hinduism (practiced by Tamils) or other minority religions (Islam and Christianity) in a Buddhist Sri Lanka.

In sub-Saharan Africa the relation of religion to the nation is even more complex because of the ethnically irrational colonial boundaries. Because so many of the political elites were trained in mission schools, there is a presumption of Christianity as the ruling ethos; but in some areas the new states must try to balance Islamic, Christian, and indigenous African practices, as in Nigeria. An interesting evolution is that of South Africa. After the union in 1910 the humiliated Afrikaners systematically began to work for power, realized in 1948, and then for the imposition of apartheid. They had constructed a language and literature (Afrikaans) and used the ethos of the Dutch Reformed Church to underpin their conception of the political order.

Some of the effects of religion on nationalism can be seen operating in the successor states of the Soviet Union since 1989. Christianity had helped to reinforce culture in the national struggles of Armenians and Georgians against contiguous Muslim groups. Revived Orthodoxy, after its taming during the high Marxist period, intensified Russian identity, and so on.

In addition to the religious factor in the composition of national identities, there is the increasingly transnational character of major and minor religious traditions and ethnic groups. This often has great political significance, because diaspora migrants can use their economic and political influence abroad to help movements at home. For instance, in the 1980s, Sikhs in Britain, Canada, and the United States strongly supported the movement for an independent Sikh state (Khalistan) in the Punjab. Tamils abroad have taken part in the struggle for autonomy in Sri Lanka. Diaspora communities may be doubly effective: first, they are likely to be more prosperous than their coreligionists at home; and second, because their identity is ambiguous, they are likely to contain people more fanatically committed to tradition as a means of overcoming the ambiguity. This is one factor, for instance, in the migration of U.S. Jews to Israel, out of a hyperactive sense of renewed commitment to the faith, and this reinforces some of the groups, such as Gush Emunim, which combine nationalism and religious commitment.

In debating the concept of civil religion, Robert N. Bellah and others draw attention to the way in which the nation itself functions as a focus and vehicle of pieties that are analogous to those of traditional religion. Patriotism has the dimensions of religion: having a mythic or narrative dimension, an ethical, an experiential, a ritual, an organizational, and a material dimension. History as taught in high school textbooks sums up much of the myth of the nation and refers to its heroes and saints (successful generals, presidents, poets, artists, and so on). The national ethos is presented through civics and in the inculcation of the values of the good citizen (for example, willingness to fight, ability to raise a family, honesty). The experiential dimension is expressed through the feelings of glory and uplift found in the celebration of the nation. The ritual dimension is expressed through the flag, the national anthem, state ceremonies, television presentations on solemn occasions, tours of national monuments, etc. The organizational dimension is woven into the development of ritual (the military, the president, the schoolteacher, and others are significant members of the social pattern of the nation). The material dimension is found in the monuments, the land itself, the artwork and architecture of the nation, and military hardware. What is lacking in terms of the comparison is a highly developed doctrinal dimension, and this is why the nation-state, to justify the great sacrifices it demands of individuals (and we may note how the language of sacrifice pervades war memorials and political rhetoric), tends to fall back on the doctrines of religion or universal ideology (such as Marxism), and sometimes both. Consequently Britain could see itself in World War II as fighting for Christian and democratic values against paganism and *totalitarianism; the Soviet Union invoked its Marxist values, and in a more minor key the support of the Orthodox Church.

The demand for religious or ideological justification for the nation-state arises simultaneously from the great sacrifices demanded and the weakness of mere nationalism as an ideology. But insofar as the doctrines designed to fill out the doctrinal dimension of nationalism tend to be universalistic, a contradiction can easily develop between them and patriotic values. Hence Margaret Thatcher's anger at Saint Paul's Cathedral for including the Lord's Prayer in Spanish in the memorial service after the Malvinas/Falklands War. Hence too the struggles of a minority of Christians against the regime in Germany during World War II. Also, a ruling elite may try to impose an unpopular worldview at odds with the values of the majority of the population (e.g., in Poland up to 1989; in the Shah's Iran, with its ideology of *modernization and quasi-Fascist celebration of ancient glory; and in the blend of Calvinism and racism in the apartheid ideology of South Africa). But the most vital strain is represented by the essential contradictions between universal worldviews and the particularities of nationalism. So, for instance, the democratic worldview built into the U.S. Constitution and suffused palely with religious values comes into conflict with U.S. foreign policy in supporting authoritarian regimes such as that of Chile under Pinochet and Iraq under Saddam Hussein during the war in the 1980s against Iran, both out of fear of the supposed alternative. Jimmy Carter tried to reconcile his own Christian and democratic values by beginning his presidency trying to align foreign policy with the protection of *human rights. The takeover of universalistic values by nation-states helps to explain the paradox of nations' fighting each other under the flag of the same God (as with Germany and France in World War I). The Nazis overcame such contradiction by adopting a racially based ideology that undergirded a kind of nationalism writ large, and so could mobilize support among suitable ethnic groups beyond the German nation. But its intellectual power was weak, although partly compensated for by the Nazi mastery of ritual.

The universalism of religions often makes religious values a rallying point in the critique of regimes and in revolutionary movements. Thus Catholic *liberation theology has a revolutionary and reconstructive role in Latin America, modernized Shi'i Islam provided a platform for the *Iranian Revolution of 1979, and the Komeito has argued for the purification of Japanese politics. The prevalence of religious revitalization movements, ranging from the Islamic Brotherhood in Syria and Egypt to new independent churches in black Africa, and from the new Christian conservatism in the United States to the neo-Hindu nationalism of the Bharatiya Janata Party in India, is politically significant, and itself follows *secularization. Such movements are sometimes protests against religious changes consequent upon the adoption of liberal values (as in liberal Protestantism, post–Vatican II Catholicism, Islamic modernism, etc.); sometimes, as in the colonial world, revivalism represents a protest against the adventitious Western trappings of modern methods; sometimes (as in India) it is also a backlash against a pluralism whereby minorities are seen as having privileges not accorded to the majority. Also, revival movements often aspire to reestablish religious or ethnic glory perceived to have existed in the past: in earlier Islamic civilization before the onset of the colonial period; in medieval Sri Lanka; in ancient India; and so on. This may sometimes cause tension between nationalism as more narrowly considered and a wider spiritual revival: this is most evident in relation to species of Arab nationalism (for example, Egyptian, Iraqi, and Algerian) and pan-Islamic values.

Traditional relationships between religion and the political order generally have not persisted into the contemporary era; some aspects of earlier arrangements, however, have survived, albeit in modernized form, as with the monarchy in Britain. Something of older arrangements was evident in the role of the emperor in prewar Japan. But, by and large, previous modes of conceiving the relation of political and religious power have disappeared. In different ways, political power used to be religiously sanctified, though in general religious institutions had some degree of independence. In Western Europe this independence was in part expressed through the papacy: by having a spiritual monarch the Catholic Church protected its transnational status. But the feudal system also allowed for Church functionaries, for instance the abbots of powerful monarchies, to adopt something of a baronial role. The usual Buddhist schema involved a symbiosis between the *sangha* and the king. The latter was responsible for the economic well-being of the order and the purification of the system through the periodic purging of monks and nuns who did not live according to the rules. On the other hand, the *sangha* guaranteed the legitimacy of the monarch. In modern times the disappearance of monarchs from many Buddhist countries means that the state functions to control the *sangha*, often ineptly because of the different basis of political power. The Buddhist system was adapted in Hindu contexts, where the king was seen as a divine being mediating between heaven and earth: his symbolic role was managed by brahmin priests, e.g., through coronation rituals. The deep entrenchment of sacred legal values interpreted by a priestly class placed some restraints on the monarchy's absolute authority. Sometimes the political and spiritual systems were fused, as in the traditional role of the Dalai Lama in Tibet. The Chinese emperor's role was for the most part conceived within the framework of Confucian values, which also served as an ideology for the unified imperial civil service. The Confucian examination system based on classical literary and sacred texts lasted over two millennia, until its abolition in 1905. Islamic monarchy was restricted by the necessity to adhere to sharīʿa or law. In the Ottoman Empire a partially pluralist system was developed called *millet*, which gave Christian and Jewish leaders control over their own subcommunities, which could adhere to their separate systems of custom and law. By contrast, from the seventeenth century onward in Europe the usual political system was one of *cuius regio eius religio*—that is, every principality or state had its official religion to which citizens were expected to adhere, although they were not prevented from migrating to another state to practice their own religion. While fragments of such prior systems have carried over, even these have undergone profound modification. Established religion, associated with the monarchy, continues for instance in the United Kingdom, but effectively the country is pluralistic; the role of the Dalai Lama has been greatly spiritualized during his exile; the imperial functions of the Japanese emperor have been greatly diminished; the Indian maharajahs have in effect been privatized.

In modern times the influence of religious organizations on political life results in part from their weight within the interplay of institutional forces, from the ways religious values may influence voting, and from the motivations and policies of individuals among the political leadership. Instances of the first kind can be found in the effects of church lobbies on issues such as abortion and divorce in Ireland and the United States; the lobby in the United States on behalf of Israel; and revivalist Hindu pressures on the state in India. In relation to the second we may mention the historic nonconformist linkage with the emergence of the Labour Party in Britain, the tendency of pious Catholics in Italy to vote Christian Democrat (before the collapse of Christian Democracy at the end of the 1980s), and Buddhist support for the Sri Lanka Freedom Party from 1956 onwards. Finally, among influential individuals whose politics were fired by religious belief we may include Mahatma *Gandhi in India; Martin Luther *King, Jr., in the U.S. *Civil Rights Movement; the Ayatollah Khomeini in the Iranian Revolution; Alcide De Gasperi in the restoration of Italian democracy after World War II; Solomon W. R. D. Bandaranaike, a convert to *Buddhism, in the revival of Sinhala Buddhist nationalism; Dag Hammarskjöld, the mystic who was UN secretary-general; Desmond Tutu, archbishop of Cape Town, prominent in the anti-apartheid struggle; President Jimmy Carter; and Lech Wałęsa. Also important, of course, is the impact of antireligious values, as seen in the lives of such as Kemal Atatürk, Mao Zedong, and Joseph Stalin.

Modern communications elevate leading religious figures to global status and give them political influence in a wider context than would have been true even fifty years earlier: for instance, the extensive travels of Pope *John Paul II give him a political role beyond that implied by the leadership of the *Roman Catholic Church; the same holds true for the Dalai Lama and Archbishop Tutu.

The globalization of institutions also affects traditional religions. The trend is toward the formation of spiritual blocs through such organizations as the World Council of Churches, the World Fellowship of Buddhists, and the Organization of the Islamic Conference. This is accompanied by a move toward a relative homogenization of faith and practice in the different religions. These moves enhance the power of traditions to influence events. Such power may reflect demographic developments: for instance, the shift of Christianity southward, with its relative decay in the North and increase in Africa and revival in Latin America, and the fact that the great majority of Muslims live in South and Southeast Asia (with Indonesia, Pakistan, Bangladesh, and India being by far the largest Muslim countries).

Until the beginning of the 1980s there was a tendency for political scientists to ignore or downplay the force of religion in politics. This was in part ideological—attributable to, for example, the influence of Marxian ideas—and in part due to a more general secular bias within the discipline as a whole. Conversely, scholars of religion tended out of a sense of idealism to neglect the political dimension of religions. Now we can perceive more realistically the range of patterns of interaction between two critical aspects of human existence.

(See also CHRISTIAN DEMOCRACY; CONFUCIANISM; JIHAD; VATICAN II.)

Ernst Cassirer, *The Myth of the State* (London, 1946). Donald E. Smith, *Religion and Political Development* (Boston, 1970). Peter Merkl and Ninian Smart, eds., *Religion and Politics in the Contemporary World* (New York, 1983). James E. Wood, ed., *Religion and the State* (Waco, Tex., 1985). Richard T. Antoun and Mary Elaine Hegland, eds., *Religious Resurgence* (Syracuse, N.Y., 1987). Richard L. Rubenstein, ed., *Spirit Matters: The Worldwide Impact of Religion on Contemporary Politics* (New York, 1987). Ninian Smart, *Religion and the Western Mind* (Albany, N.Y., 1987). Gustavo Benavides and Martin W. Daly, eds., *Religion and Political Power* (Albany, N.Y., 1989). Eric Jones and Vernon Reynolds, eds. *Survival and Religion* (New York, 1995).

NINIAN SMART

these; and in the late twentieth century, reproductive politics came to have a dynamic international resonance as well. Since the mid-1980s, international women's movements seeking gender equality and women's empowerment have brought a human rights framework to this political domain; their theorizing and advocacy have created the concept of "reproductive and sexual *rights," now embodied in several United Nations documents.

Reproductive Rights as Human Rights. Although women have for centuries acted on the view that control over their bodies, fertility, and health ought to be in their hands, the formalization of this belief in the concept of reproductive rights is a fairly recent development. The term first emerged in feminist struggles to defend access to safe, legal abortion and contraception in North America and Europe in the 1970s but soon was adopted also by women's health movements in Latin America and the Caribbean, Asia, and Africa. In 1984, just prior to the World Population Conference in Mexico City and at the prodding of groups of activists from the global South, the International Campaign on Abortion, Sterilization and Contraception, based in Amsterdam, was renamed the Women's Global Network for Reproductive Rights (WGNRR) and given a broad mandate to address all the issues related to women's reproductive health, not only those involving family planning. Feminist advocates of reproductive rights asserted "women's right to decide whether, when and how to have children—regardless of nationality, class, race, age, religion, disability, sexuality or marital status—in the social, economic and political conditions that make such decisions possible" (from *WGNRR Statement of Purpose*, 1989). They called for access to safe, effective contraception; safe, legal abortion services for all women, regardless of income; preventive measures to end the abysmally high rates of maternal mortality and morbidity still prevalent in many parts of the world, especially measures to assure access for all women to prenatal care and good-quality, comprehensive reproductive and child health services; an end to sterilization abuse and other coercive practices by medical and family planning providers; and improved education for women of all ages about birth control, reproduction, infertility, diverse forms of sexuality, the risks and side effects of medical contraceptives, and sexually transmitted infections. They affirmed as basic *human rights women's right to decide whether and when to have children, to live self-determined sexual lives, and to be free from sexual, physical, and clinical violence.

Avowedly feminist campaigns for women's reproductive rights arose as part of the wider women's rights and health movements of the 1960s, '70s, and '80s. Contrary to a widely held misconception, these movements were not only or primarily an outgrowth of what is sometimes disparagingly termed "Western *feminism." Rather, they have developed in many countries and regions of the global South, in ways that reflect specific local conditions and policies: for example, in India, to oppose government-sponsored campaigns imposing targets for sterilization and hormonal implants; in the Philippines and much of Latin America, to oppose church-influenced policies prohibiting safe, legal contraception and abortion; in Bangladesh and Pakistan, to oppose brutal attacks on women accused by religious tribunals of transgressing sexual norms; and in Egypt, Senegal, Nigeria, and elsewhere, to oppose harmful traditional practices condoned by governments and prescribed by religious authorities, such as female genital mutilation (FGM).

In many countries and cultures, including among Northern-based communities of color ("the South within the North"), the idea that women have a "right to control over their own bodies" has become a rallying cry against two mutually hostile transnational forces. On the one hand, feminist advocates have faced neo-Malthusian population control organizations, closely tied both to medical establishments and to many government and international population agencies. For such groups, "population growth" remains one, if not the major, cause of poverty, social unrest, and environmental degradation, especially in less developed countries. The remedy for this problem, in their view, is increased spending for population programs that emphasize long-acting or permanent medical technologies (e.g., surgical or chemical sterilization or hormonal implants and injections) to reduce women's fertility, especially among the poor and immigrants.

In the opposite camp from these pronatalist influences, the 1980s and '90s saw the growing strength and consolidation, at both country and international levels, of antiabortion, "pro-family" groups associated with religious fundamentalists and conservative politicians. In many countries—especially those with a strong Roman Catholic Church, evangelical Protestant, or resurgent Islamist presence (Afghanistan, Chile, Ireland, Pakistan, the Philippines, Sudan, and the United States, to name a few)—as well as in United Nations forums, these groups have staunchly opposed women's reproductive and sexual freedom on behalf of "fetal rights," womanly duty, and the traditional authority of husbands, fathers, and religious hierarchies. What unites these two otherwise antagonistic forces is that both regard women's bodies and reproductive capacities instrumentally: either as incubators and emblems of tradition, or as pollutors and population control targets.

In contrast to both (antinatalist) population control advocates and (pronatalist) religious fundamentalists, feminist advocates and women's health activists around the world have worked to develop and implement a concept of reproductive rights whose starting point is the health, well-being, and empowerment of women. Their priority is to prevent unnecessary mortality and morbidity related to reproduction and sex for women (including that which arises from male violence and clinical abuse), as well as to maximize the enabling conditions for safe and decent childrearing and for authentic choice over whether and when to have a child and whether and when to have sex. With the rising threat of HIV/*AIDS among women, especially in Africa, Asia, and communities of color in the North, the public health dimensions of such decisions provide a grim incentive for transforming policies. But a human rights approach to reproductive rights is as much about personal and bodily self-determination as it is about prevention of illness and death; indeed, public health experts agree that women's lack of self-determination over their sexuality is one of the primary causes of their increasing exposure to heterosexually transmitted HIV. It is a sobering reminder that health and human rights are mutually dependent.

The idea of having control over one's body, or bodily integrity, which provides the philosophical foundation of reproductive and sexual rights, is not merely a derivative of Western notions of individualism and private property.

Rather, it reflects women's common experience as childbearers and nurturers who must maintain control over the conditions of their reproductive activity in order to perform it well, and as the principal victims of sexual and domestic violence. It also resonates closely with religious and cosmological traditions that value women's bodies as the source of life and nourishment or that view the human body as an integral part of the self, not separate from (or subordinate to) the soul or spirit. Above all, it is an expression of the value of self-determination, or personhood, recognizing that, if I am burdened by unwanted childbearing, domestic violence and abuse, preventable illness, malnutrition, or lack of access to normal health care and family planning information and services, it will impede my capacity to act as a responsible citizen and community member—that is, to exercise my civil and political rights. Thus, bodily integrity includes both negative rights—for example, the right to be free from sexual violence, forced marriage or pregnancy, FGM, and involuntary sterilization—and affirmative rights—for example, the right to the best available reproductive and primary health care, full information and services for safe contraception and abortion, safe birthing services, and the free expression of one's sexuality regardless of sexual orientation or marital status.

Women's movement campaigns to link reproductive rights with basic human rights principles have been part of a larger effort to secure recognition for matters of personal and bodily integrity, health, and reproduction in international instruments. They have also helped to promote the principle of the indivisibility of such personal and social rights from the more established civil and political as well as economic rights. Early documents such as the founding Charter of the *World Health Organization (1946), the Universal Declaration of Human Rights (1948), and the International Covenant on Economic, Social and Cultural Rights (1967) contain language inscribing "the enjoyment of the highest attainable standard of health" and the right to "life, liberty and security of the person" as fundamental human rights. The American Convention on Human Rights (1970) and the African Charter on Human and People's Rights (1982) also refer to the inviolability of the person and mental and physical integrity; while the Convention on the Elimination of All Forms of Discrimination Against Women (Women's Convention, 1980) prohibits its signatories from discriminating against women with regard to all the established rights including access to health care, education and information, employment, freedom in marriage, and reproductive decision-making. (At this writing, the United States remains one of a minority of countries that still has not ratified the Women's Convention.)

Through a historic series of United Nations meetings in the 1990s, women's international coalitions worked to extend these basic human rights principles to specific aspects of women's reproductive and sexual freedom and to infuse a new gender awareness into the official documents of the Vienna Conference on Human Rights in 1993, the International Conference on Population and Development (ICPD) in Cairo in 1994, and the Fourth World Conference on Women in Beijing in 1995. The women's caucuses were successful despite well-organized and determined efforts by the Vatican and its government allies from several Catholic and Islamic countries to block the new language of reproductive/sexual rights and gender equality. As a result, the international human rights vocabulary now includes not only "the basic right of all couples and individuals to decide freely and responsibly the number, spacing and timing of their children" but also freedom from "gender based violence and all forms of sexual harassment and exploitation" including "systematic rape, sexual slavery, and forced pregnancy"; freedom from FGM; and the right "to have a satisfying and safe sex life."

Paragraph 96 of the Beijing Platform for Action goes even further, stating:

The human rights of women include their right to have control over and decide freely and responsibly on matters related to their sexuality, including sexual and reproductive health, free of coercion, discrimination and violence. Equal relationships between women and men in matters of sexual relations and reproduction, including full respect for the integrity of the person, require mutual respect, consent and shared responsibility for sexual behaviour and its consequences.

Finally, the 1990s movement for women's personal and bodily rights as human rights succeeded in securing the unprecedented definition of rape as a *war crime by the War Crimes Tribunal for Bosnia and the Rome Statute of the International Criminal Court (July 1998).

Limits Constraining the Human Rights Approach. Although international women's groups have achieved significant gains in the transformation of formal human rights language and instruments, a "human rights approach" to reproductive politics still faces major obstacles to effective implementation and enforcement. First, existing international human rights mechanisms have little power to enforce accountability, especially if violators are private parties rather than state governments or officials. Given the continued weakness of international organizations, enforcement still depends largely on the cooperation of national governments, many of whom are corrupt, unstable, and lacking political will where human rights and gender equality are concerned. Moreover, implementation of women's reproductive and sexual rights has to contend with the persistence of a rigid "public"-"private" distinction in international human rights law, lending de facto immunity to all but the most blatant public violations (e.g., systematic rape of political prisoners or civilians during war). Feminists organizing on behalf of women's human rights since the 1970s have tried to break down the artificial barrier between "public" and "private" spheres, pointing out that perpetrators of violations against women's reproductive and sexual rights are most often husbands or partners, other kin, or doctors. Especially for women, whose lives in many cultures are still locked within domesticity, human rights claims must penetrate the "private sphere" where everyday violations of their bodily integrity and personhood—marital rape, FGM, virginity codes, customary repudiation of birth control—occur. Public actions of the state and its agents—for example, laws prohibiting or restricting abortion, or rape of civilians by soldiers and police—reinforce such daily life intrusions and, with them, form a continuum of systemic abuse. Yet the spaces and mechanisms for bringing complaints against this system remain elusive, shielded by those in power at every level of society.

Second, due to the globalization of capitalist markets and the retrenchment of the *welfare state, the availability and quality of public health services continue to deteriorate, especially burdening low-income women. This trend has had a deleterious impact on reproductive rights and health in many countries, even "developed" countries in the North, where increasing privatization has left many poor women without access to reproductive health services. Despite the drawbacks of government bureaucracies as health care dispensers, women's experiences with private clinics that function according to the profit motive suggest that this model is far less reliable in meeting their health needs, especially if they lack resources. Where there is no system of public accountability nor any commitment to criteria of social justice and universal standards of care, reproductive health facilities tend to become supermarkets for those who can pay, or dependent on private donors and cost-cutting insurance companies. Meanwhile, developing countries, overburdened by foreign debt, trade inequities, and structural adjustments imposed by international donor agencies, have sharply reduced their budgetary allocations to health, including reproductive health. These pressures exacerbate the chain reaction of maternal and infant mortality, not only by countering social development and deepening poverty and shortages in food and health care, but also by undermining the legitimacy of claims on the state.

Third, the post–Cold War eruption in many parts of the world of right-wing movements, racism, nationalism, and ethnic hatreds not only destabilizes governments and whole societies but creates specific and devastating threats to women's reproductive and sexual health. Chronic violence, genocidal "ethnic cleansing," and military occupation in regions such as the former Yugoslavia and Central Africa have meant mass rape, abandonment, and refugee status for thousands of women and girls (those who survive), greatly increasing their vulnerability to prostitution, sexual trafficking, unwanted pregnancy, and sexually transmitted diseases. Under such conditions, the semblance of any public institutions to deal with these problems is torn apart, and reproductive or primary health services become virtually nonexistent. At the same time, remilitarization for the purpose of defending against terrorist attacks or "rogue states" in countries as diverse as the United States, India, and Egypt also diverts scarce resources from health, education, and social service budgets.

Finally, the rise of fundamentalist political movements in many countries and in all major religious groups during the last decades of the twentieth century has reinvoked a patriarchal family culture that emphasizes female subordination, son preference, patrilineal and arranged marriages, and the condemnation of abortion and contraception freely chosen by women. These ostensibly religious movements exist worldwide and reflect a backlash everywhere against the recent gains of women's movements. Particularly in Northern countries, they dovetail in a curious way with the continued medicalization of reproductive culture, including an emphasis both on medically controlled contraceptive technologies and obstetrical imaging and intervention technologies that construct the "fetus as patient." The global antiabortion movement has had a particularly deep impact, intimidating medical providers and so far preventing United Nations agencies responsible for health, population, and development from recognizing access to safe, legal abortion as a fundamental human right.

Together, these political, economic, military, and cultural conditions construct the larger context in which women's reproductive rights will continue to be extremely difficult to achieve. Any full analysis of reproductive politics must take such external constraints into account, and strategies to define and implement women's reproductive rights must aim toward a deeper level of social change than the human rights approach has yet envisioned. Individual women cannot exercise their reproductive and sexual rights without the necessary enabling conditions for their empowerment. These include both material and infrastructural supports—such as reliable transportation, child care, and jobs as well as accessible and adequate health services—and cultural and political supports—such as access to education, self-esteem, and political power. In turn, such conditions for the vast majority would require a reordering of international and national economic policies to abandon debt servicing and militarism in favor of social welfare and primary health care; and a transformation of now dominant political cultures in a direction of equality, justice, and peace. As DAWN, a leading organization of women from the global South, puts it, "women's reproductive health must be placed within a comprehensive human development framework that promotes all people's wellbeing and women's full citizenship."

(See also GENDER AND POLITICS; INTERNATIONAL LAW; POPULATION POLICY; WOMEN AND DEVELOPMENT; WAR CRIMES TRIBUNALS.)

Ruth Dixon-Mueller, *Population Policy and Women's Rights: Transforming Reproductive Choice* (New York, 1993). Sonia Corrêa/DAWN, *Population and Reproductive Rights: Feminist Perspectives from the South* (London, 1994). Sonia Corrêa and Rosalind Petchesky, "Reproductive Rights: A Feminist Perspective," in G. Sen, A. Germain, and L. C. Chen, eds., *Population Policies Reconsidered: Health, Empowerment and Rights* (Cambridge, Mass., 1994). United Nations, *Programme of Action of the International Conference on Population and Development* (New York, 1994). Betsy Hartmann, *Reproductive Rights and Wrongs* (Boston, 1995). International Planned Parenthood Federation, *IPPF Charter on Sexual and Reproductive Rights* (London, 1995). Rosalind Pollack Petchesky, "From Population Control to Reproductive Rights: Feminist Fault Lines," in *Reproductive Health Matters* (November 1995). Julie Peters and Andrea Wolper, eds., *Women's Rights, Human Rights: International Feminist Perspectives* (New York and London, 1995). United Nations, *Beijing Declaration and Platform for Action*, adopted by the Fourth World Conference on Women (New York, 1996). Rosalind P. Petchesky and Karen Judd, eds./International Reproductive Rights Research Action Group, *Negotiating Reproductive Rights: Women's Perspectives Across Countries and Cultures* (London and New York, 1998).

ROSALIND POLLACK PETCHESKY

RESOLUTION 242. United Nations Security Council Resolution 242, passed in November 1967 in the wake of the Arab-Israeli war of June of that year, has become the internationally accepted basis for peacemaking in the Middle East. Drafted by Lord Caradon, the British ambassador to the United Nations, in consultation with the parties concerned, the resolution was an attempt to bring Israeli demands for a final, formal peace agreement together with those of Egypt, Syria, and Jordan for Israel's withdrawal from the territories—the Sinai Peninsula, Gaza Strip, Golan Heights, West Bank, and East Jerusalem—which it had occupied during the June war.

The resolution did this by a balanced emphasis on "the inadmissibility of the acquisition of territory by war and the need to work for a just and lasting peace." It therefore called for "withdrawal of Israel from territories occupied in the recent conflict," as well as for "termination of all claims or states of belligerency and respect for and acknowledgment of the sovereignty, territorial integrity and political independence of every state in the area and their right to live in peace." The resolution also called for "a just settlement of the refugee problem."

The resolution was accepted by Egypt, Jordan, and Israel from the outset, but was initially rejected by Syria. Only after the war of October 1973 did Syria accept the resolution, while all the Arab states (except Libya) accepted its principles at the Fez Arab summit conference in 1982. The most consistent rejection of Resolution 242 came from the *Palestine Liberation Organization (PLO), which from its inception in 1964 refused the principle of a peaceful settlement with Israel. After 1974, however, as the PLO moved towards accepting that principle, it came to base its objections to Resolution 242 on the fact that it dealt with the Palestinians as refugees, rather than as a people with national rights. Finally, in 1988, the PLO formally accepted Resolution 242 as the basis for a Middle East settlement.

In spite of apparently universal acceptance of Resolution 242 as the basis for an Arab-Israeli settlement, major problems remain. The Israeli Likud party, which has dominated all Israeli governments between 1977 and 1999 (except for the Labor government of 1992–1996), rejects the application of this resolution to the occupied West Bank, Gaza Strip, Arab East Jerusalem, or the Golan Heights. Over the years, moreover, a school of thought has grown increasingly influential in Israel and the United States, arguing that the principle of "land for peace" embodied in Resolution 242 is no longer relevant, and that the changes since June 1967 have become irreversible. This argument for the permanence of the status quo emerging from the 1967 war was undermined by the outbreak of the Palestinian *intifada in December 1987, which showed that the status quo in the occupied territories was in fact untenable. This in turn led to the launching of the Madrid peace conference in 1991, and to the Palestinian-Israeli accords of 1993, both of which explicitly based themselves on Security Council Resolution 242.

(See also ARAB-ISRAELI CONFLICT; PALESTINE; UNITED NATIONS.)

Arthur Lall, *The UN and the Middle East Crisis, 1967,* rev. ed. (New York, 1970). William B. Quandt, *Peace Process: American Diplomacy and the Arab-Israeli Conflict since 1967* (Washington, D.C., 1993).

RASHID I. KHALIDI

REVOLUTION. See overleaf.

RIGHT. Generally used to characterize the conservative end of the political spectrum in modern polities, the Right as a concept may be defined in part by its opposition to its political counterpart, the *Left. Political parties, movements, and ideas sharing a commitment to the advancement of conservative economic, social, and political ideas may be referred to as being of the Right. Parties such as the British Conservatives, the U.S. Republicans, and many European Christian Democrats are seen as representing the arguments of the Right. These parties are to be distinguished from those of the extreme Right (such as the Front National in France) whose philosophies commit them to a level of radical change—often

predicated on a social vision associated with racism and xenophobia—that in itself disqualifies them from consideration alongside more mainstream versions.

The Right is suspicious of the idea of progress and is generally committed to the status quo. Its preference for the existing order and resistance to substantial change can be traced to the work of the conservative thinker Edmund Burke, who, for example, rejected the principles of the French Revolution in 1789. Burke, strongly committed to personal liberty, believed that striving for liberty through revolutionary methods would inevitably fail and result in the undermining of the democratic institutions necessary for individual freedom.

Advocates of the Right reject rationalism and reason as a basis for political action, believing instead in tradition and custom as guides to behavior. Accordingly, institutional arrangements which have evolved gradually over the course of history are to be modified only with extreme prudence. Conservative principles of the Right also include the veneration of religion, loyalty, and a system of social hierarchy. In contrast to liberals and those on the Left, conservatives on the Right believe that the bases of political obligation lie in historical legitimacy and loyalty to the state and not in any sort of social contract.

Although some of its proponents look askance at changes associated with capitalist development, harking back to an era of clearly defined social and economic hierarchical allegiances, most modern advocates of the Right now accept the capitalist system. All members of the Right share a belief in the importance of private property (together with a legal system) as the foundation and enabling condition for political and economic liberty. They also share an antipathy to collectivist economic or political institutions, preferring those based in individualism.

As a political movement the Right has to some extent been eclipsed by the success of the *New Right, which has been due in part to the latter's greater attention to social issues concerning the family, for example, and women's abortion rights. In this sense, the Right has suffered a similar fate to that of the Left, as *new social movements have eroded the traditional bases of support. But democratic parties advancing arguments of the Right are still prominent electorally in Western democracies, and with the collapse of collectivist polities in Eastern and Central Europe they have received a measure of vindication and have shown renewed vitality and purpose.

(See also CHRISTIAN DEMOCRACY; CONSERVATISM; LIBERALISM.)

Michael Oakeshott, *Rationalism in Politics* (London, 1962). Noel O'Sullivan, *Conservatism* (London, 1976).

DESMOND KING

RIGHTS. As a focus of moral, political, and legal theory, the concept of *rights* has assumed an ever-increasing importance in recent decades. This significance has generated debates of great sophistication about the nature and limits of rights, engaging the most impressive philosophic and theoretical energies of this period.

The idea of rights is closely associated with the existence of a claim, either to be protected in relation to activity, as in civil and political rights, or to be confirmed as entitled by law

(cont. on p. 734)

REVOLUTION. Since ancient times, governments have been changed by force. Plato and Aristotle commented on changes in the governments of Greek city-states from aristocracies and tyrannies to democracies (and back again) in the third through sixth centuries B.C.E. The Roman republic was founded in a revolution against Etruscan kings in the sixth century B.C.E. During the European Renaissance of the sixteenth century C.E., Italians introduced the word "revolutions" (in Italian, *revoluziones*) to describe the alternating victories of the popular and aristocratic factions who fought for control of Italian states, which sometimes became republics and sometimes duchies. And in the mid-seventeenth century, the philosopher Thomas Hobbes used the English word "revolution" to describe the circular transfer of power from England's King Charles I to the Puritan Parliament under Oliver Cromwell, and after Cromwell's death back to Charles's son, King Charles II. In all these cases, "revolution" meant a transfer of power and a recasting of government, from one party and kind of government to another. But nothing in this change was necessarily permanent or progressive; power could be taken again by a group that was defeated. A monarchy could be (and often was) restored.

This view of revolution as an alternation of governments was replaced in the eighteenth and nineteenth centuries by a new view of revolution, based on the Enlightenment faith in progress. In this new view, made popular in attempts to understand the French Revolution of 1789, writers argued that society was bound to progress toward more fair and productive forms of social organization, and that revolutions were necessary to destroy the institutions and individuals who maintained, and benefited from, an outmoded and unfair social order. Revolutions, therefore, were progressive and necessary. Instead of cyclical crises of governments, revolutions marked permanent, favorable transformations of entire societies.

This view of revolution was given an enormously influential presentation in 1848 by Karl *Marx and Frederick Engels in *The Communist Manifesto*. Marx and Engels argued that all of history showed a series of revolutions that were linked to economic progress. In each revolution, a backward and oppressive economic class that benefited from outmoded economic and political institutions was turned out by a new class whose power stemmed from more advanced forms of economic production. Revolutions, therefore, were as inevitable as the improvement of economic production. In this Marxist view, the French Revolution marked one revolutionary transition, in which more productive capitalist merchants and manufacturers overturned outmoded feudal landlords. A next step was bound to come, in which capitalists were themselves thrown out by workers. Free of the exploitation of capitalist masters, workers could then develop an unfettered system of production that would serve workers' needs better than any other system. The workers' revolution would thus usher in a lasting age of genuine utopia.

By the later nineteenth century (and through most of the twentieth century) the progressive utopian view of revolution, usually in its Marxist form, had become the dominant view of the meaning of "revolution." People who described themselves as revolutionaries, as well as scholars who tried to understand revolutions, addressed themselves to the problem of the permanent transformation of entire societies. The notion of revolution as a simple crisis of government, leading to a not necessarily beneficial, and possibly reversible, change in leaders and institutions was put aside.

However, actual historical experience has not always justified faith in the progressive utopian view of revolution. The American Revolution of 1776 began with a remarkable Declaration of Independence and led to a Constitution and *Bill of Rights that have inspired the struggle for freedom and citizenship for centuries. Yet while this freedom proved durable for many, Afro-Americans and Native Americans long remained subject to slavery and conquest. The French Revolution of 1789 lost its way after Napoleon's defeats in 1812 and 1815, and France—from 1815 to 1848—was again ruled by Kings (Louis XVIII, Charles X, Louis Philippe). The *Russian Revolution of 1917, the *Chinese Revolution of 1949, and the Cambodian Revolution of 1975 destroyed millions of lives in their quest, never achieved, for a utopian society. In Russia and Cambodia, the Communist and Khmer Rouge parties who led the revolutions have been forced out of power. And while China's Communist Party remains in power, it is unlikely that its revolutionary leader, *Mao Zedong, would recognize his revolutionary ideals in today's entrepreneurial China.

At the start of the twenty-first century, there are still believers in the "utopian view" of revolution—both revolutionaries and scholars who consider revolutions to be necessary transitions for political and economic progress. However, there are also skeptics and conservatives, who believe that revolutions are neither necessary nor progressive, but are costly, often tragic events, indicating only that a government has run into a crisis.

Revolutions in the Twentieth Century. What is perhaps most striking about revolutions in the twentieth century was their sheer volume and variety. From the beginning to the end of the twentieth century, in every area of the world, revolutions shaped political life.

From 1900 through the 1920s, revolutions shook Mexico, Saudi Arabia, China, Turkey, Iran, and Russia. The Mexican Revolution led to a capitalist, populist, one-party state. Saudi Arabia's revolution was made by Islamic fundamentalists. In Turkey, Iran, and China, secular modernizers overthrew traditional monarchies and installed republican constitutions. In Russia, Lenin's Communist Party created the world's first *communist party state. Clearly, from the beginning of the century, a wide range of revolutionary ideologies and outcomes is evident. This diversity would continue throughout the century.

Western Europe also felt the impact of revolution. The German revolution of 1918, following World War I, eliminated the reign of the Kaiser, and left in place a weak and divided government that paved the way for the rise of Nazism, which itself was a revolutionary movement of the extreme nationalist right.

In the 1940s and 1950s, following World War II, communist revolutions in Eastern and Central Europe (secured by Soviet tanks) set the stage for the *Cold War, while the communist revolution in China (1949) transformed Asian politics. From 1945 through the 1960s, revolutions of national liberation and *modernization altered the maps of Africa, the Middle East, and Southeast Asia. Some of these revolutions were socialist, others capitalist; all were strongly nationalist. In the 1970s and 1980s revolutions overthrew the imperial regime in Ethiopia, semi-modern personal dictatorships in Nicaragua, Portugal, and the Philippines, and created radical Islamic states in Iran, Afghanistan, and Sudan. These revolutions ranged from socialist to Islamic fundamentalist to democratic-capitalist. Finally, the end of the 1980s and early 1990s were marked by revolutions against Communist regimes in Eastern and Central Europe and the Soviet Union, creating a host of newly independent states, and by the "peaceful revolution" that led to the end of apartheid in South Africa. Even experts on revolution have sometimes been confused by the enormous range of forms and places in which revolutions have arisen.

Given this great variety, it is difficult to find simple, common factors that created this century of revolution. However, four major factors largely account for the rising revolutionary tide: (1) weak states, (2) conflicting *elites, (3) rapid population growth, and (4) erratic international intervention.

1. Weak States. Prior to the twentieth century, most large states were long-standing, well-financed, conservative organizations. They enjoyed a tradition of power, financial means appropriate to their goals, and stable relationships with supportive elites. However, in the twentieth century, international military and economic competition greatly increased the pressures on states. The rapid rate of economic growth in some countries in the twentieth century—3 or 4 percent per year in the large advanced economies, and up to 9 or 10 percent per year in rapidly developing states in Asia and Latin America—allowed successful states to leave slower-growing states trailing in the dust. Throughout this century, many states have therefore found themselves competing with more advanced economies—Russia competing with Germany, China with Japan, Iran and Afghanistan seeking to begin catching up with Europe. As a result, leaders of traditional states undertook programs of rapid investment and restructuring, straining their finances to the utmost, alienating traditional elites, and becoming dependent on international borrowing. These conditions reduced the ability of states to maintain old loyalties and to operate freely against internal and external opponents. Straining to overcome past disadvantages, these states struggled with their economies and lost political support.

In many other cases, twentieth-century states arose as recent creations or colonial impositions, with no long tradition or well-established supporters. Personalist dictators or unpopular colonial powers often found themselves isolated, opposed by entire populations, and with their armies becoming strained and unreliable.

Long-established, economically successful states do not have revolutions. Recently established or economically struggling states often do. In the twentieth century, both of the latter became far more common.

2. Conflicting Elites. In every society certain individuals are more influential than others. They may have influence by occupying formal positions of leadership or by expressing influential views through art, journalism, or speaking. Thus army officers, political leaders and high bureaucrats, cultural and religious leaders, labor and business leaders, and intellectuals form influential elites.

In stable states, elites compete for power, but accept basic "rules of the game" for the distribution of power, wealth, and status. However, sometimes new factors emerge which upset those rules. The state may fall into the hands of one leader or one faction that seeks to exclude all others. Foreigners may displace domestic elites. Or rapid social mobility may undermine traditional pathways to office and wealth, creating challenges to established elites and opportunities for new ones. In any of these situations, elites may come into sharp conflict with each other or with the state. If the state is weak, a determined elite group, or coalition of groups, may seek to overthrow the state and change the "rules of the game"—that is, the basic political and economic institutions—in a direction they believe is better. Such elite leadership is always necessary for revolutions to become more than mere popular riots, which, as a rule, are readily suppressed.

The growth of international economic and military links in the twentieth century greatly increased the opportunities for elite conflicts. International investors, foreign aid donors, or military backers might support one person or faction in a country, excluding and alienating others. The growth of industrial and export enclaves gives new resources to business, labor, and trading elites, who might then challenge the prerogatives of landlords and rural elites. "Uneven" economic development, which favors one sector of the economy over others—industry over farming, urban over rural, factory over household manufacturing—can lead to violent elite conflicts if it makes no allowance for elites in the less favored sector to retain their positions of influence.

In sum, the explosion of international trade, investment, and foreign aid and military support in the twentieth century has greatly increased the potential for conflict among elites.

3. Rapid Population Growth. The twentieth century saw exceptionally rapid population growth, particularly in the developing countries of the Third World. A rapid fall in death rates, chiefly due to progress in vaccination and sanitation, combined with a continued high birth rate and large family size, has produced a rise in world population from 1.6 billion in 1900 to more than 6 billion today.

Although population growth is usually cited for contributing to poverty and resource exhaustion, it has profound political effects as well. The growth of populations increases the difficulty of states in providing services to an expanding population, increases the competition among elite groups for positions of power and status, and undermines the position of workers and *peasants seeking jobs and adequate land. Population growth is also generally accompanied by shifts in the composition of the population: more people generally means more young people, and they are increasingly concentrated in cities. This increases the pool of people most likely to join revolts—single young people—and concentrates them where they can easily join to demonstrate or protest. Although population growth alone does not cause revolutions, population growth can intensify the pressures on weak states and conflicting elites, making it more likely that such states and elites will enter full-scale revolutionary struggles.

4. Erratic International Intervention. A stable international balance of power, with stable policies, as prevailed in Europe in the second half of the nineteenth century, can reduce the likelihood of revolutions. Governments know they can count on international support, and challengers know they cannot. But erratic international *intervention can lead to widespread revolutionary turmoil.

In the twentieth century, the erratic swings of the Cold War, and swings in U.S. policy between internationalism and isolationism, heightened the instability of governments around the world. The collapse of the Soviet Union in 1989–1991 and the end of the Cold War further intensified pressures for change, as both former Soviet clients and local ethnic and nationalist rebels that had been held in check by Cold War maneuverings found themselves on their own.

From the 1940s through the 1980s, the Soviet Union, later aided by Cuban military support, sponsored revolutionary movements around the world. Poland, Hungary, Czechoslovakia, Cuba, Vietnam, the Democratic People's Republic of Korea (North Korea), and Afghanistan, among other countries, saw revolutionary communist regimes take power with Soviet military aid; Cuba helped to put such regimes in power in Angola and Mozambique. In response, the United States supported anticommunist, but often nondemocratic and military governments, in many developing nations.

However, in the late 1970s and the 1980s, the United States reduced its support for authoritarian regimes, which allowed revolutionary movements to succeed in Iran, in Nicaragua, and the Philippines. From the 1980s onward the Soviet Union, beset by internal weakness and then disintegration, reduced its support for communist regimes, first in Afghanistan (where an Islamic revolution displaced a communist regime), then in Eastern Europe, where anticommunist regimes were overthrown by popular movements in 1989. All these policy shifts contributed to revolutions.

The four factors listed above—weak states, conflicting elites, rapid population growth, and erratic international intervention—became widespread in the twentieth century. In many states, one or more of these conditions arose without leading to revolution. But where all four factors appeared simultaneously in one society, revolution was the likely result. Such revolutionary conjunctures became increasingly common over the course of the century, producing an extraordinary number of revolutions.

Interestingly, there is no one kind of *ideology behind the century's varied revolutions. Rather, when the four conditions noted above are all present, a revolutionary ideology emerges, combining elements of *nationalism and utopianism, plus whatever indigenous widespread beliefs can be used to oppose the ideology that supports the current regime. Thus, although there are some basic similarities among communist revolutions, or among Islamic revolu-

tions, every revolution reflects its own custom-built revolutionary ideology.

The consequences of these revolutions for twentieth-century politics were momentous. First, the communist revolutions in the Soviet Union and China led to a two-way, and sometimes three-way, competition for world influence between these states and the capitalist alliance led by the United States and the European Union. With world leaders often believing that revolutions could create a permanent move of countries into the "communist" camp, much of the world's international tensions and conflicts in the latter decades of the twentieth century revolved around whether various countries in Asia, Africa, and Latin America would "fall" to communism. However, as the realization grew that revolutions may in fact be only cyclical crises whose results may be altered with time, superpower concern over the form of other nations' governments began to diminish.

Second, the twentieth century saw so many states founded on the belief in revolutionary utopianism that an enormous amount of human and material energy was expanded in trying to make revolutionary institutions "work." No doubt the greatest portion of human misery in this century came from World Wars I and II, which were rooted in traditional plans for territorial expansion by Germany in Europe and by Japan in Asia. But close behind in sheer volume of human misery caused were the attempts of revolutionary governments to remold human beings and societies—in spite of all evidence and human will to the contrary—to fit utopian ideals. In the Soviet Union, Eastern and Central Europe, China, various countries in Africa and Asia, and most recently in Cambodia, tens of millions of people were starved, murdered, imprisoned, or stripped of their livelihoods and dignity in failed efforts to create allegiance, efficiency, and harmony in revolutionary states.

Third, the large number of revolutions in the twentieth century has created regions of local instability and political competition in Africa, the Middle East, and South Asia, leading to continued international wars between regional rivals. In the Horn of Africa, on the Iran/Iraq border, in Afghanistan, and in Southeast Asia, international wars involving revolutionary states and neighbors who either feared revolutionary expansion or sought to take advantage of revolutionary turmoil has led to decades of war, migration of *refugees, and hunger. Lack of governmental stability in these regions has made them continuous sources of international tension and military operations.

If revolutions are indeed passages on the path to progress, we should expect that the end of the twentieth century should have shown progressive results. Yet the historical record is mixed at best. Several of the East European nations that recently threw off communist rule are building brighter futures. But most of the nations and regions strongly affected by revolutions in this century—Russia and the bulk of the former Soviet Union, the Balkans, China, Cuba, Vietnam, Africa, and the Middle East—have shown remarkably little progress toward democracy and economic prosperity, the twin goals of most revolutionary utopians. The nations and regions that have made greater progress in these respects—the Pacific Rim nations of Japan, Korea, Taiwan, Singapore, and Hong Kong, and certain states in Latin America (Brazil, Chile, Venezuela, Mexico, Argentina)—had much less revolutionary upheaval. This is not to say that revolutionary states have not made great progress in industrialization, literacy, and basic health care, only that their progress toward democracy and overall economic prosperity has been deeply disappointing to their leaders and their populations, and has generally lagged well behind comparable states which undertook nonrevolutionary paths to economic development and political reform. This outcome has led to a thorough reevaluation of the causes and outcomes of revolution by scholars.

The Scholarly Analysis of Revolutions. Scholarship on revolutions has itself turned in cycles. In the first half of the twentieth century, most scholars believed that revolutions were essentially state crises and were skeptical as to whether they brought social progress—a view most elaborately presented in Crane Brinton's *Anatomy of Revolution* (New York, 1965), which described revolutions as being like a "fever." In the years from World War II to the late 1970s, however, scholars increasingly believed that revolutions were perhaps necessary to destroy traditional institutions and classes that impeded the development of modern social and economic organization. Communist revolutions were credited with promoting rapid industrialization in Russia and China, and it was hoped that in Cuba, and perhaps in Vietnam, Nicaragua, and Iran, revolutions would succeed in replacing repressive dictatorship by fairer, freer societies.

Yet the 1980s brought great disillusionment with revolutionary dreams. Cuba under Castro became a showplace for economic crisis and a personalist, dominating state. Nicaragua and Iran suffered devastated economies. Given the chance, Nicaragua's population voted its revolutionary government out of power, a step also taken by the peoples of Eastern Europe and the Soviet Union. Indeed, the collapse of the European communist governments has shown that the Russian Revolution of 1917 did not mark a permanent transformation of Russian society, but rather was the breakdown of a particular state (Russia's traditional tsarist regime), which was followed by the overturning of the Communist state itself a few decades later.

As to the revolutions of 1989–91 in East Central Europe and the Soviet Union, it would be equally unwise to assume that they mark a permanent transformation of their societies in a more progressive direction. Some successors to the fallen communist regimes, as in Poland, Hungary, the Czech Republic, Slovenia, and the Baltic states, have brought democracy and economic progress. Yet others, such as the Ukraine, Belarus, Romania, Slovakia, the new states of central Asia and the Caucasus, and even Russia, have found democracy more problematic, and prosperity more elusive. There is evidence for possible movement in either direction in the years ahead.

If contemporary scholarship has become more skeptical of the utopian potential of revolutions, it has also become more certain of particular aspects of revolution. First, certain causal principles are widely recognized, largely as a result of the work of those scholars who have shown that several specific structural characteristics and processes make states vulnerable to crises and revolution (Skocpol, 1979; Goldstone, 1991). These are the four elements mentioned above as becoming increasingly prevalent in the last century. Only the advanced industrial democracies of Western Europe and North America seem to have escaped these conditions. Weak states, conflicting elites, rapid population growth, and erratic international intervention are still frequently found in Asia, Africa, Latin America, East Europe, and the former Soviet Republics; thus revolutions and revolutionary movements should continue to occur into the twenty-first century.

In addition, scholars have come to agree on certain outcomes of revolutions. First, revolutions lead to the strengthening of feelings of nationalism and self-assertion in new revolutionary states. Second, revolutions tend to increase the ability of states to mobilize people and demand sacrifices for military and economic efforts. Regrettably, this combination of assertive nationalism and mass mobilization increases the likelihood of wars, which are common by-products of revolution. This is the expected result when a new government faces the strains of war and mass mobilization. However, this tendency makes it difficult for revolutions to maintain democratic governments.

There is a nobility to the dream of revolution as a means to achieve utopia in a single stroke. Yet the twentieth century was, as a century of widespread revolution, a harsh testing ground for that noble ideal. Revolutions sometimes spread the ideals of democracy and justice but more often spread the centralization of power, wars, and economic hardship; they revealed the decay and distress of one government only to erect, with great bloodshed and sacrifice, a state which made a mockery of utopian ideals. Indeed, with few exceptions the great anti-utopian, totalitarian police-states of the twentieth century were not the work of small-minded dictators but the outcome of revolutions guided by progressive utopian visions.

Surely we will continue to see harsh and authoritarian revolutions, as occurred in Congo/Zaire. Yet we can hope that the more peaceful and democratic revolutions in the Philippines in 1986, and in Eastern and Central Europe in 1989–1991, mark a new phase in the evolution of revolutions. Perhaps the twenty-first century will see more revolutions succeed in replacing dictatorships with more democratic and prosperous societies. What we can be certain of is that as long as weak governments, divided elites, population increase, and international intervention continue, revolutions and their effects will shape world politics.

(See also ALGERIAN WAR OF INDEPENDENCE; CLASS AND POLITICS; GUERRILLA WARFARE; GUEVARA, ERNESTO; IRANIAN REVOLUTION; LENINISM; NATIONAL LIBERATION MOVEMENTS; POLITICAL VIOLENCE.)

Theda Skocpol, *States and Social Revolutions* (Cambridge, U.K., 1979). Jack A. Goldstone, *Revolution and Rebellion in the Early Modern World* (Berkeley, Calif., 1991). Eric Selbin, *Modern Latin American Revolutions* (Boulder, Colo., 1993). James DeFronzo, *Revolutions and Revolutionary Movements*, 2d ed. (Boulder, Colo., 1996). Jack A. V. Goldstone, ed., *The Encyclopedia of Political Revolutions* (Washington, D.C., 1998).

JACK A. GOLDSTONE

or morality to certain benefits, as in social rights. Rights can either be embodied in law or expressed aspirationally. The abortion debate illustrates contradictory conceptions of rights, focusing in one instance on the right to life of the fetus, and in the other on the right to choice of the mother. Government can resolve this debate legally, but the encounter of opposed moral conceptions is basically without any means of reconciliation, especially by advocates of unconditional positions. Those who conceive of such a controversy in less polar terms are often open to compromise as to the character of the right at stake.

The importance of rights reflects centuries of popular struggle against autocratic government and other modes of coercive authority, and yet the historic success of rights should not be confused with the rise of political *democracy. An emphasis on rights is also intended to guard minorities against the tyranny of the majority or to insulate individuals against societal and cultural practices based upon intolerance. The gradual acceptance of the Western liberal notion that only constitutional government is fully legitimate contributes to the wider conviction that the claims of the governed are worthy of consideration. The essence of this claiming process is the struggle to overcome avoidable human suffering in its many forms. Such an endeavor has resulted in societal demands for limits on the authority of the *state and other agencies of control (whether it be church or employer).

The rise of the idea of *citizenship has reinforced the notion that the individual has certain rights that should be upheld regardless of the source of encroachment. The U.S. *Civil Rights Movement of the 1960s illustrates this belief. This affirmative role of the state in protecting rights remains controversial in several respects. To begin with, it is less firmly established, especially in non-Western countries that reject strict separations of church and state and regard cultural and religious notions of ethical behavior as of greater relevance than "rights" derived from state action or by reference to international standards. Moreover, the role of the state as the custodian of human welfare is currently under attack by enthusiasts of market economics, who contend that there is a tension between efficiency in the allocation of resources and welfare rights.

The history of rights as a political language is properly associated with movements of resistance to royalism, culminating in the English, American, and French revolutions. In each instance, the idea of rights emerged as a principal means to mediate between the authority of the state and the autonomy of the people subject to governmental control. At stake from the nineteenth century onwards was the basic "right" of peoples to give their consent, whether by elections or otherwise. The notion of rights is linked to ideas of *legitimacy and *sovereignty within the frame of constitutional government. The depth of this linkage has been recognized through endorsing an inherent "right" of *revolution in response to tyrannical or oppressive rule. This understanding of a reciprocal relationship based on the duty to respect law and the authority of the state on the one side and the duty of government to act in accordance with principles of fairness and respect on the other gives rise to the concept of a social contract between government and governed. These ideas of contract—a historical fiction, as the bargain was never actually struck in real time, but only presumed—rest on an even deeper foundation

in the Judeo-Christian tradition of a covenant between God and the Israelites acknowledging reciprocal duties.

The evolution of practices pertaining to rights exhibits the clear influence of political philosophy upon political behavior and institutions. John Locke's exposition of inalienable rights definitely influenced the founders of the American republic in the aftermath of the revolution against British colonial rule. Similarly, the writings of Voltaire, Rousseau, Diderot, and others were much in the minds of those who made the French Revolution, quite remarkably including those who constituted the mobs in Paris. The revolutionary spirit, carried to terroristic excess, was grounded on the need to establish a new governmental framework that would sweep away all at once the cruel and arbitrary excesses of the French monarchy, the Catholic church, and the inequities of feudal economic structures. This framework was anchored in the revolutionary espousal of "the rights of man" that took precedence over whatever stood in the way. In this regard, the eighteenth century ended with an acceptance of rights as the basis of constitutional limitation on the state.

The next phase of struggle centered on ways to impose limits on the market. The rise of labor and the challenge of *Marxism posed the issue in a variety of distinct settings. Marxist-Leninists avoided concern about rights by contending that justice and injustice were inevitable expressions of class rule, and that seizure of power on behalf of the masses was the only relevant political goal—justice being impossible in a capitalist society, injustice being impossible in a classless society. The collapse of the Soviet Union has discredited such views almost everywhere and correspondingly reaffirmed the liberal emphasis on the need to avoid abuses of power, wherever situated, by the enumeration and implementation of rights.

The failure of Marxism-Leninism has also had some spillover effect on socialist values more generally and the notion of welfare rights in particular. The view is now prevalent in many societies that the market must be freed from undue constraints, which means "rolling back" some welfare rights. For example, Sweden, long a pioneer in according welfare to all of its people, seemed in the 1990s to believe that its competitiveness in the world economy had been reduced by the conferral of excessive welfare rights.

In the period since World War II a new type of rights has achieved prominence, namely "*human rights." Starting in 1948 with the Universal Declaration of Human Rights, governments have come to affirm that all people are entitled to certain modes of protection as well as to provision of basic material needs. The impetus for human rights clearly reflected the ascendancy of an individual ethos associated with Western *liberalism, although international undertakings took some account of the more collectivist notions of *socialism as championed during the *Cold War period by the Soviet Union. The most comprehensive formulation of human rights is contained in two treaties that were opened for ratification in 1966—the International Covenant on Economic, Social and Cultural Rights and the International Covenant on Civil and Political Rights. Essentially, these documents set forth standards. There are no enforcement mechanisms, and many governments that adhered to such treaties did so despite their own gross violations. Others, including the United States, could never mobilize the political will to ratify such treaties, with opposition to adherence centering on supposed interferences of human rights with some understandings that a sovereign state should not be subject to external claims of authority. Despite these difficulties, the human rights movement has continued to gather momentum over the decades, finding expression in various treaties that, in elaborating more specialized rights, were in effect calling attention to categories of persons deemed especially vulnerable to abuse. An array of treaty instruments on such matters as racial discrimination, women, and children has resulted.

The effectiveness of human rights has surprised many observers. Governments were prepared to acknowledge that human rights generated *international law obligations, but many were not prepared to respect these rights in practice nor to negotiate arrangements that would impartially establish violations and provide for enforcement. Nevertheless, the existence of human rights embodied in international law standards came to matter in a variety of settings. For one thing, a vast network of transnational, nongovernmental organizations concerned with human rights emerged and used reliable information about gross violations to exert pressure on governments, many of which cared about their reputations. Further, *public opinion favored using economic leverage in relation to human rights, as has been the case with foreign economic assistance policy in the United States since the mid-1970s.

For another, broad currents of international politics coincided with the claims embodied in human rights standards. In the East-West setting, the *Helsinki Accords of 1975 were conceived at the time as important mainly because they officially recognized the post–World War II boundaries that existed in Europe. Provisions in the treaty relating to human rights accountability by countries in Europe were scornfully dismissed as exercises in Cold War propaganda. In operation, the annual inquiry into human rights failures in Eastern and Central Europe mandated by what came to be known as the Helsinki Process grew important both in strengthening the popular will of the people in these countries to resist and in undermining the belief of the leadership in their capacity to rule. These tendencies were strongly reinforced by the emergence of the *Gorbachev leadership in the Kremlin with its espousal of a commitment to human rights and democracy. In retrospect, the emancipation of Eastern and Central Europe and the Soviet Union reflects the relevance of human rights to political behavior.

The complexity of human rights as a topic of global scope is somewhat daunting. There is, to begin with, a variety of initiatives to carry human rights forward on a regional level, most notably in Europe, where an implementation structure enables individuals to mount certain claims against their own government. Further, there are many areas of protection in which existing standards remain insufficient or inappropriate, as in relation to the protection of indigenous peoples or with respect to gay and lesbian autonomy. Also, non-Western normative traditions are becoming more assertive, being both critical of claims of universality on behalf of human rights that hide alleged Western biases, and in some instances self-critical of cruelties embodied in hallowed cultural norms, as in the Hindu caste system or in Islamic views on corporal punishment or the status of women.

There is little doubt that the transnational ferment of recent years in relation to rights is likely to persist and influence the quality of political life. As we grow even more conscious of what it means to live in a global village, with cultures in constant contact through both modern communications and by way of intercultural migration, the pressure for tolerance and understanding will increase, and so will the appeals to rights in response to avoidable human suffering.

(See also CONSTITUTION; GAY AND LESBIAN POLITICS; LENINISM; REPRODUCTIVE POLITICS; ROE v. WADE; WELFARE STATE.)

Ronald Dworkin, *Taking Rights Seriously* (Cambridge, Mass., 1977). Joel Feinberg, *Rights, Justice, and the Bounds of Liberty* (Princeton, N.J., 1980). United Nations, Geneva Centre of Human Rights, *Human Rights: A Compilation of International Instruments* (New York, 1988).

RICHARD FALK

RIO TREATY. The Inter-American Treaty of Reciprocal Assistance, adopted in 1947 at a meeting in Rio de Janeiro, is known as the Rio Treaty. It is a mutual *security pact providing for the American states to respond to acts of aggression in the Western Hemisphere (given a precise geographic definition) with consultative procedures and, if agreed upon, certain types of assistance and *sanctions. The treaty placed on a permanent basis the prior temporary regional security arrangements adopted during World War II, with the scope of aggression broadened to include attack by other American states as well as non-American. Its procedures are closely coordinated with provisions in the charter of the *Organization of American States. The Rio Treaty began with twenty-one signatories, the United States and the then-twenty sovereign Latin American states. Cuba unilaterally abrogated the treaty in 1962, but Trinidad and Tobago later adhered, so that membership has remained at twenty-one states.

Except for one case, all treaty applications have entailed inter-American disputes; except for two, they have all involved the circum-Caribbean region. Eighteen situations were addressed between 1948 and 1979; sanctions were applied against the Dominican Republic in 1960 and Cuba in 1962 and 1964. The case of Panama versus the United States in 1964 over Canal Zone problems was the first involving a non-Latin American party. After 1979 security collaboration was minimal. Latin Americans were dissatisfied with what they viewed as U.S. domination of inter-American security processes. The Rio Treaty was not a significant factor in Central American conflict during the 1980s or involved at all in the settlement of the Beagle Channel dispute between Argentina and Chile (decided in 1984 with mediation by the Holy See). Treaty procedures were applied to armed conflict between Ecuador and Peru in 1981, and to the British-Argentine South Atlantic War (*Malvinas/Falklands War) in 1982, the only cases undertaken outside the Caribbean zone; the latter was the only one involving a non-American state. In the post–Cold War era, mutual security as defined in the Rio Treaty remained a low priority.

(See also U.S.–LATIN AMERICAN RELATIONS.)

General Secretariat of the Organization of American States, *Applications of the Inter-American Treaty of Reciprocal Assistance, 1948–1972,* 2 vols. (Washington, D.C., 1973). G. Pope Atkins, "The Inter-American System," chap. 8 in *Latin America in the International Political System,* 2d ed. (Boulder, Colo., 1989).

G. POPE ATKINS

RIOT. See POLITICAL VIOLENCE.

ROE v. WADE. The U.S. Supreme Court decision *Roe* v. *Wade* (1973) structures debate in the United States on both reproductive policy and the role of the judiciary in a constitutional democracy. Supporters of that decision hail the Supreme Court for protecting a woman's fundamental right to choose whether to carry a pregnancy to term. Critics of that decision condemn the justices for sanctioning the murder each year of approximately 1.5 million of what they believe to be unborn children. Anti-*Roe* critics condemn the justices for substituting their beliefs about abortion for those of elected officials. Many distinguished scholars agree for the most part on the policy the justices made. They claim only that the *Supreme Court of the United States had no more business making abortion policy than deciding whether the United States should intervene militarily in a foreign civil war.

By a 7–2 vote the justices in *Roe* decided that doctors had a qualified constitutional right to perform abortions. The source of this right was the due process clauses of the Fifth and Fourteenth Amendments to the Constitution of the United States, which declared that "no person shall . . . be deprived of life, liberty, or property, without due process of law." Justice Harry Blackmun's majority opinion held that states could not regulate abortion at all during the first trimester of a pregnancy, and could regulate abortion only to protect maternal health during the second trimester. He did conclude that states could ban abortion in the last trimester, but only if no significant danger to maternal health existed. Subsequent Supreme Court decisions have both expanded and qualified the particular details of the abortion right. Judicial majorities have permitted both the federal government and states to deny funding for abortion. In 1992, the justices ruled that states could regulate abortion in any way that did not unduly burden a woman's effort to terminate a pregnancy. Still, from 1973 to the present, the Supreme Court has ruled that government officials may not substantially interfere with any adult woman who has found a doctor willing to terminate her pregnancy.

The Supreme Court's decision dramatically increased access to safe and legal abortions in the United States. Before *Roe*, most states had not strictly enforced statutory bans on abortion, some states had liberalized abortion restrictions, and four states made abortion legal. Still, unless women lived in the right communities or had a close relationship with a physician, terminating a pregnancy meant risking an illegal and frequently unsafe abortion. Illegal abortion during the 1950s was the third most lucrative criminal activity in the country, next to drugs and gambling. Abortion became a public enterprise after *Roe*. Abortion clinics opened and did a thriving business, even in the face of much pro-life mayhem. Economies of scale enabled the price of a legal abortion to drop fivefold, making that practice available to any woman of some means who lived near a clinic. Access to abortion is still not universal. Poor, rural women often cannot locate an abortion provider. Judicial rulings protecting *reproductive rights have nevertheless enabled most women to plan their education and careers, knowing they will not be derailed by an unexpected pregnancy.

Judicial decisions finding a constitutional right to an abortion have been criticized on many grounds. Some pro-choice advocates believe the court has not gone far enough. Abortion, in their view, should never be restricted and should be fully funded by governing authorities. Feminists have criticized the justices for focusing on the rights of physicians and privacy rights, rather than on the vital role abortion plays in ensuring that women will be able to participate as equals in the public worlds of work and politics. The more strident criticisms have come from the political right, which sees *Roe* as violating both fetal rights and democratic governance.

These differences have had a significant impact on partisan politics in the United States. Over the past twenty years, the Democratic Party in the United States has become dominated by persons who favor abortion on demand. President Bill Clinton and many other leading party officials often seemed more committed to keeping abortion legal than ensuring the economic redistribution championed by New Deal Democrats. Most Republican Party activists favor overruling *Roe* and a strong pro-life stand is necessary for any Republican candidate to gain that party's presidential nomination. Abortion issues, however, tend to play greater roles in primaries than in general elections. Party activists may vote on abortion, but the general public tends to prefer economic issues when choosing between a pro-life Republican and a pro-choice Democrat.

Roe v. *Wade* also plays a major role in debates in the United States over the role of the judiciary in a constitutional democracy. Proponents of the decision maintain that the justices should and historically have protected fundamental rights not explicitly enumerated in the Constitution of the United States. The due process clauses of the Constitution, in one common view, protect fundamental liberty rights. If the right to abortion is such a fundamental liberty right, then the justices should protect abortion, even though the persons responsible for the constitutional text did not explicitly mention abortion or think abortion was a fundamental liberty right. Critics of *Roe* think these abstractions violate the rule of law and constitutionalism. The Constitution is meaningless, in their view, if interpreted as protecting whatever a judicial majority thinks is a fundamental liberty. Rather, the justices should protect only rights clearly mentioned in the text or clearly intended by the persons responsible for the Constitution.

These questions are not decided by the federal judiciary in isolation from the rest of the political system. Abortion has loomed large in recent presidential judicial appointment decisions and during the Senate confirmation process. Robert Bork was denied a Supreme Court seat partly because of his opposition to *Roe*. Moreover, how aggressively elected officials protect abortion rights plays a major role in determining the extent to which abortion is a practical option for women living in their jurisdictions.

Kristin Luker, *Abortion and the Politics of Motherhood* (Berkeley, Calif., 1984). Lawrence H. Tribe, *Abortion: The Clash of Absolutes* (New York, 1990). Mark A. Graber, *Rethinking Abortion: Equal Choice, the Constitution, and Reproductive Rights* (Princeton, N.J., 1996).

                                                            MARK A. GRABER

ROMAN CATHOLIC CHURCH. The Roman Catholic Church has been an actor in world affairs for two millennia. The "Christian fact," a religious community which quickly assumed an institutional status, posed a double challenge to the Graeco-Roman world. First, the church's claim on the conscience of believers was a profound challenge to the classical world's conception of the power of the *state; now there was a new standard of behavior against which a state's prescriptions and prohibitions would be tested. Second, as a social institution the church quickly became a contending locus of power in the Roman Empire.

The evolution of the relationship between spiritual and temporal power took several forms: the church and the Roman Empire; the church in the Respublica Christiana of the High Middle Ages; the church and the Catholic and Protestant states of the post-Reformation period. The Treaty of Westphalia (1648), which ended the religious wars in Europe, also symbolized the rise of the nation-state, the basic unit of world politics for the last three centuries. It is in the context of the "Westphalian system" that the issue of the Catholic Church and international politics emerges in its modern form. The nation-state posed a theoretical and a practical challenge for Catholicism. On the one hand, the claims of the sovereign state threatened fundamental Catholic teaching that bonds of human solidarity and responsibility to others exist in spite of state boundaries and these obligations must be honored in times of war and peace. In theory Catholic teaching on international affairs accorded the state real but relative moral value. The nation-state is recognized as a legitimate center of moral and political authority, but the activity of states is to be assessed in light of the moral order of rights and duties. On the other hand, at the practical diplomatic level, the church recognizes the role of nation-states and maintains formal diplomatic relations with over 170 states; this activity is directed by the Vatican's secretary of state, a cardinal who is the ranking official in the Roman Curia.

The modern diplomatic role of the Catholic Church begins with Pius XII, elected to the papacy shortly before World War II began. A diplomat by temperament and training, he was deeply involved in the *diplomacy of the war and even more so in the postwar period, until his death in 1958. Using an extensive teaching ministry and a wide range of diplomatic contacts, Pius XII was particularly known for two aspects of his policy: an unyielding opposition to Marxism and Soviet communism and an active role in the renewal of Christian Democratic parties in Western Europe. While these parties were lay organizations, the social teaching of Pius XII and the clear support of the Vatican for Christian Democracy were essential contributions to the growth of the party in the Federal Republic of Germany, Italy, and the Low Countries.

The brief pontificate of John XXIII (1958–1963) produced profound changes in Catholic teaching and practice, the effects of which continue to influence the church today. From the perspective of international politics two dimensions of this papacy stand out: the inauguration of the "Vatican Ostpolitik" and the convocation of the Second Vatican Council (1962–1965).

The term "*Ostpolitik" was never used by the Holy See, but it was appropriately applied by commentators to the change in policy of the Roman Catholic Church toward the communist regimes of Eastern and Central Europe in the 1970s and 1980s. Pius XII viewed these regimes as morally illegitimate and he followed a policy of refusing to deal with them diplomatically. By the early 1960s, it was judged by many in the church that the policy of isolating these governments also made it more difficult for the church to achieve key pastoral objectives. These included the appointment of trustworthy bishops, the increase in the number of seminarians allowed to prepare for the priesthood, and the establishment of religious education programs in parishes. John XXIII, relying upon the skillful diplomacy of Monsignor Agostino Casaroli (later cardinal-secretary of state), initiated a process of limited negotiations with states in Eastern Europe.

The policy was continued and expanded by Pope Paul VI (1963–1978), who had unsuccessfully advocated such negotiations in the 1950s. The purpose of engaging the communist regimes was to seek concrete practical steps which would improve the possibilities for Catholics to practice their faith. The diplomacy of both John XXIII and Paul VI not only changed the position of the church in dealing with communist governments, it also gave much greater weight in Vatican diplomacy to the countries of the *Third World. During the *Cold War and since its demise, the Holy See has striven to amplify the voice and express the needs of the nations and states torn by internal conflict and often excluded from the benefits of the global economy.

The decisive contribution of John XXIII to the church, however, was his quite unexpected decision to convoke an ecumenical council. The council had a significant effect on Catholicism's relationship to the political order. Its two principal documents in this regard were the *Declaration on Religious Freedom* (Dignitatis Humanae, 1965) and *The Pastoral Constitution of the Church in the Modern World* (Gaudium et Spes, 1965). The influence of *Vatican II can be assessed in terms of its teaching and in the way the teaching took shape in policies. The texts just named had the double effect of "depoliticizing" the church's role and "resocializing" its ministry. The document on religious freedom refashioned Catholic teaching on church-state relations. The basic principle of *Dignitatis Humanae* is that the church seeks one thing from the state, the freedom to fulfill its ministry. The position left behind the post-Reformation view that the state should acknowledge Catholicism as the religion of the state whenever possible. The concept of the Catholic state was designed to protect the status of the church in civil law, but it often had the consequence of tying the church to policies of states which were of dubious moral quality. *Dignitatis Humanae* "depoliticized" the church's role by distancing it from any specific government. The freedom the church gained from the policy of *Dignitatis Humanae* provided a more independent status from which to address issues of *human rights, social justice, and social policy within nations and among states.

The teaching of *Gaudium et Spes* "resocialized" the church's public ministry, providing new authority and impetus for Catholic social engagement from the parish to the papacy. The conciliar document provided the most expansive conception of the church's public role of any teaching document since the Reformation. Its decisive significance was not what it said about any specific social issue, but the way it defined the ministry of the church in the world. It tied the church's ministry to the defense of human dignity. In the theology of Vatican II, the church's primary identity is as a religious community with a goal and purpose which are found beyond human history. But the church should pursue its religious ministry in history by contributing to four objectives: protecting human dignity, promoting human rights, fostering the unity of the human family, and providing a sense of meaning to every area of human activity (*Gaudium et Spes*, 40–42). This conception of the church's role seeks a religiously based ministry which produces socially significant results.

The second Vatican Council's impact can be found in the deepening social engagement of the church at all levels of its life since 1965. This social involvement is evident in the "local church" in various parts of the world and in the ministry of Pope *John Paul II (1978–). Since Vatican II local churches throughout the world have played significant social roles in quite different ways. The Latin American example is the best known and most analyzed. This region of the church, overwhelmingly Catholic and facing massive social and economic issues, was the first to undertake a systematic review of its life and ministry after Vatican II. The occasion was the Medellin Conference of Bishops in 1968; the results of the meeting set a direction for the church on human rights and social justice throughout Latin America, particularly in Brazil and Chile in the 1970s and in Central America in the 1980s. Since the 1990s church leaders, theologians, and "base communities" of Catholics have pressed the issues of the poor and of economically vulnerable nations in the debate about globalization. The animating spirit for much of this activity was the Theology of Liberation, a method of understanding the church's role in society from the perspective of and with an "option" for the poor. The pervasive influence of the Theology of Liberation attracted the attention of the Holy See, which has supported some ideas and criticized others. Although he has often criticized this theological perspective, John Paul II has used some of its themes in his defense of the poor and advocacy for social justice.

The struggle of the Latin American church in the 1970s and 1980s was against poverty and authoritarian regimes; in the 1990s the local churches on the African continent faced more extreme poverty and the social chaos associated with "failed states." Often the religious communities were the only sources of social cohesion; no distinctive theology arose from Africa, but in many countries the church served as a substitute for institutions of government and a complement to international agencies.

In the quite different setting of the United States, where Catholics make up about 25 percent of the population, Catholic bishops have been highly visible actors in the policy debate of the 1980s and 1990s on issues of bioethics, welfare reform, capital punishment, and the ethics of military strategy from *nuclear weapons to *humanitarian intervention.

The engagement of the "local church" in social, political, and economic issues throughout the world is one of the most visible consequences of Vatican II. It has been subordinate to and complementary of the more traditional method through which Catholicism has addressed the international order, namely, through the papacy. John Paul II has been the most activist incumbent the papal office has known since the Middle Ages. The Pope has shaped a strategy of imposing tight internal discipline in the church, with a broad-ranging commitment to public issues of peace, human rights, and economic justice in the world. Continuing Vatican II, John Paul has stressed the need for the church to maintain its religious identity while simultaneously seeking to contribute to the solution of major social issues. Stressing the role of religious

freedom and the need for moral evaluation of all institutions and their policies, he has confronted virtually all of the major issues in world politics. The Pope's style of engagement is seldom directly political, but it almost always has substantial political consequences.

He has used three means to shape this activist pontificate. First, he is committed to a ministry of the word, written and spoken. He has produced three explicitly "social encyclicals"—*Laborem Exercens* (1981), *Sollicitudo Rei Socialis* (1987), and *Centesimus Annus* (1991)—and scores of other statements and speeches on a remarkable range of public issues. Second, the pope has used over eighty trips to some of the most conflicted areas of the world to strengthen the church's social and pastoral ministry. While his unique role in the defeat of the communist system in Poland and his subsequent contribution to the dismantling of the Soviet empire is widely recognized, the pontificate of John Paul II has had an impact far beyond the Soviet system. Two trips, to Cuba in 1998 and to the Middle East in 2000, illustrate the range, diversity, and impact of papal diplomacy. In Cuba he extended his well-developed critique of communist polity, seeking to provide social space for the church by his appeal to the right of religious freedom. But, characteristically, he joined this critique of communism with an equally firm opposition to the U.S.-led economic embargo of Cuba. The papal journey to the Middle East was not a diplomatic intervention but a spiritual pilgrimage in observance of the millennial celebration of the birth of Christ. Consistent with his style, however, John Paul II's apologies for centuries of *anti-Semitism in the church and his advocacy of a homeland for Palestinians were both pregnant with political significance and influence.

Third, John Paul II has been willing to engage his office and the Holy See in direct diplomatic intervention under specified conditions. He directed the church's role in mediating the Beagle Channel dispute between Chile and Argentina. He personally intervened with George Bush and Saddam Hussein on the eve of the *Gulf War, arguing against the use of force, something he continued to do throughout the war. He attempted Vatican mediation in Lebanon and Yugoslavia without much success. Finally, he is committed to two quite broad but different objectives as the post–Cold War order takes shape. On one hand, to raise up the needs and aspirations of African states and peoples, calling for appropriate responses from the international community. On the other, to help the church in Europe contribute to a distinctive conception of Europe in world affairs. Both of these objectives, in turn, are part of his developing strategy to provide a moral framework and evaluation of the process of *globalization.

The combination of the legacy of Vatican II, the ministry of local churches, and the pastoral leadership of an intellectually and diplomatically activist pope shape the religious and public role of Catholicism on the cusp of a new century.

(See also CHRISTIAN DEMOCRACY; LIBERATION THEOLOGY; RELIGION AND POLITICS; VATICAN CITY STATE.)

Ivan Vallier, "The Roman Catholic Church: A Transnational Actor," in Robert O. Keohane and Joseph S. Nye, Jr., eds., *Transnational Relations and World Politics* (Cambridge, Mass., 1973), pp. 129–152. Thomas M. Gannon, S.J., ed., *World Catholicism in Transition* (New York, 1988). J. Bryan Hehir, "Papal Foreign Policy," *Foreign Policy* 78 (Spring 1990): 26–48. Adrian Hastings, ed., *Modern Catholicism: Vatican II and After*

(New York, 1991). George Weigel, *Witness to Hope: The Biography of John Paul II* (New York, 1999).

J. BRYAN HEHIR

ROMANIA. The first Romanian states emerged from independent shepherd communities in the Carpathian Mountains in the eleventh century, about 800 years after the withdrawal of Roman legions from the province of Dacia. Its people spoke a Latin language and were Orthodox Christians. In the thirteenth and fourteenth centuries, after the Mongol conquest and withdrawal, two principalities coalesced, Moldavia and Wallachia. North and west of the Carpathians, in Transylvania, Romanian speakers were ruled by the Hungarians, and there were also German merchant cities. Wallachia and Moldavia became tributaries of the Ottoman Empire from the fifteenth to the nineteenth centuries, but kept their own princes. Serfdom was the rule, but in a heavily pastoral economy, serfs usually paid light labor dues, or else a tribute in kind.

Russian military occupation between 1828 and 1834 created the first modern administrations in the Principalities of Wallachia and Moldavia and opened up trade and cultural relations with Western Europe. Cereal exports began and caused an increase in peasant obligations. A nationalist movement modeled on the French example took root among educated nobles. In Transylvania, ruled by the Habsburgs since the seventeenth century, but dominated by the Hungarian nobility, an anti-Magyar Romanian *nationalism also developed, led at first by the Orthodox Church. Nationalist sentiment led to the Union of Moldavia and Wallachia in 1859, and to the creation of an independent Romanian kingdom in 1878. Transylvania, the Banat, Austrian Bukovina, and Russian Bessarabia were united to Romania after World War I, though these provinces had very large non-Romanian minority populations, including Hungarians, Germans, Jews, and Ukrainians.

Until World War I, Romania was a land of large estates dominated by its landowners. Though serfs were freed in 1864, they remained poor sharecroppers and staged a massive peasant uprising in 1907. After World War I, there was a land reform which resulted in a rural society characterized by dwarf holdings and economic stagnation. Despite some industrial growth, rural overpopulation and poverty continued.

Economic problems combined with increasingly tense relations between Romanian nationalists and the country's Jewish and Hungarian minorities fostered the growth of extreme right-wing nationalism. Jews (4 percent of the population) were a particular target because of their commercial and professional success. New university graduates who could not find good jobs during the Depression joined the fascists, so that by the late 1930s, the virulently xenophobic Iron Guard had become the most dynamic political movement in the country. In 1938 King Carol II established a royal dictatorship to try to stem the rise of the Iron Guard, but despite growing repression, he failed.

During World War II Romania, led by a military dictator, Marshal Antonescu, joined *Hitler in the invasion of the Soviet Union. The Soviets invaded Romania in 1944, and forced it to accept a communist government even though the Communist Party had had almost no domestic support. By 1948, Romanian Communists were in full control.

Until the early 1960s, Romania was subservient to the Soviets and engaged in the usual Stalinist projects of massive industrialization and rural *collectivization. But when Soviet and East European reform efforts tried to push Romania into specializing in light industry, agriculture, and resource extraction, Romania accelerated industrialization and took a nationalist, defiant path. Romania's Stalinists, led first by Gheorghe Gheorghiu-Dej and then, in 1965, by Nicolae Ceausescu, turned to ultranationalist intellectuals, who had been dormant since 1944, to legitimize their rule.

Under Ceausescu nationalism and self-reliance became more pronounced. Trading relations were opened with the West to free Romania of its dependence on the Soviet bloc. This produced a brief period of cosmetic liberal reforms, but by the early 1970s these were reversed in favor of a more autarkic, repressive line. Ceausescu was obsessed with the need to make Romania a great power, and one of his most outrageous policies was the prohibition of birth control and of abortion in order to promote population growth. This resulted in large numbers of unwanted, abandoned children, and humiliation for women who were forced to undergo periodic inspections to make sure that they were not obtaining illegal abortions.

By the early 1980s, Romania had amassed a large foreign debt because it had imported capital goods to promote industry. But these industries were inefficient and could not export enough to pay the debt. This was a common problem throughout Eastern Europe, but only Ceausescu took the draconian measure of forcing more food and fuel exports to pay back the debts while intensifying investments in these huge, unprofitable industries. The result was an unprecedented decline in the standard of living as Romanians began to run short of energy and food.

As the population, and eventually even the Communist Party, became disillusioned with Ceausescu, he turned to his family and cronies for support. In the 1980s, he increasingly relied on a grotesque cult of personality to sustain his legitimacy. He resurrected old right-wing mythologies about racial and national unity since the time of the Dacians (i.e., antedating the Roman Empire). He and his wife Elena presented themselves as omniscient, benevolent demigods. The culmination was a gigantic building project in Bucharest, the capital city, that displaced tens of thousands and threw them into suburban slums. Eventually, Ceausescu planned to do this in all of Romania's towns and villages, thus destroying the fabric of traditional society. But events caught up with his lunatic schemes.

In December 1989, with popular discontent rising, and communism collapsing everywhere in Eastern Europe, elements in the army, the Communist Party, and perhaps the security services as well decided that he had to go. There was a brief, violent uprising. Nicolae and Elena Ceausescu tried to flee, but were captured by the army and shot.

Former Party administrators took power under the guise of being democrats. The new regime headed by Ion Iliescu made some moves toward reforming the economy, and it allowed free elections and political dissent. But with a poor, restive population on one hand, and the old bureaucracy and security services still present on the other, *reforms were slow and limited. In 1996 a new president, Emil Constantinescu, was elected on the promise that now real privatization would occur. But to this day Romania remains very poor, beset by potentially serious ethnic divisions, and politically unstable.

Romanians hope to join the North Atlantic Treaty Organization and the European Union, but Europe is not so eager to have 23 million impoverished Romanians as their new dependents. Romania in the twenty-first century is more likely to repeat the sad political and economic history of Latin America in the twentieth than to become a prosperous Western European nation.

(See also ANTI-SEMITISM; COMMUNIST PARTY STATES; NINETEEN EIGHTY-NINE; STALINISM.)

Henry Roberts, *The Political Problems of an Agrarian State* (New Haven, Conn., 1951). Daniel Chirot, *Social Change in a Peripheral Society* (New York, 1976). Katherine Verdery, *National Ideology Under Socialism* (Berkeley, Calif., 1991). Irina Livezeanu, *Cultural Politics in Greater Romania* (Ithaca, N.Y., 1995). Gail Kligman, *The Politics of Duplicity* (Berkeley, Calif., 1998).

DANIEL CHIROT

ROME, TREATY OF. The treaty that created the European Economic Community (EEC), the Treaty of Rome remains the most historically significant instrument of regional integration. It was one of two treaties of Rome signed by Belgium, the Federal Republic of Germany, France, Italy, Luxembourg, and the Netherlands on 25 March 1957. The other created the European Atomic Energy Community (Euratom). Together with the 1951 Treaty of Paris, which created the European Coal and Steel Community (ECSC), these treaties form the basic constitutional documents of what is now the *European Union (EU).

It is unusual for an international treaty to be compared to a constitutional document, but the treaties of Paris and Rome created central decision-making institutions (the European Commission, the Council of Ministers, and the European Parliament) with the power to promulgate common legislation, plus a *European Court of Justice to rule on the interpretation of the community law that those institutions create. The court has insisted that community law must always override the national law of a member state wherever a conflict occurs, basing this view on the treaties. Thus the treaties limit the *sovereignty of the member states, and in this they differ from conventional international treaties and more closely resemble constitutional documents.

Unlike more conventional constitutional documents, however, the treaties also contain commitments to specific policies. The most well-known provision of the EEC treaty is for the creation of a common market with no internal tariffs, with a common external tariff, and with internal free movement of labor, capital, goods, and services. There are also commitments, however, regarding the creation of a common agricultural policy and a common transport policy, and regarding the coordination of economic and social policy.

The treaties were a recognition of the interdependence of the economies of the participating states, but they also strengthened that interdependence. More significantly, perhaps, the EEC treaty was a response to the perception that a large, regional domestic market was necessary if the community states were to be able to compete economically with the United States. There was also an ambition among at least some of those involved with the drawing up of the treaty to move toward a politically united Europe. The framework of community law that the treaty created, as interpreted by the European Court of Justice, has assisted this development from economic to political unity.

One effect of the treaties was to create a new category of law: not domestic law, but, because it has direct applicability in member states, not *international law either. Also, particularly since the ratification of the *Maastricht Treaty in 1993, the demarcation of what were previously domestic policy areas as the subject of joint policy-making blurred the division between foreign and domestic policy for the member states. In creating the European Community, then, the treaties created a new type of *international organization, one that remains the archetype for all efforts at regional integration and is a major new actor in international economic and political affairs.

Neill Nugent, *The Government and Politics of the European Community* (London, 1989).

STEPHEN GEORGE

ROOSEVELT, Franklin Delano. Thirty-second president of the *United States, Franklin Delano Roosevelt (1882–1945) is one of the most significant political figures of the twentieth century. He led the nation through the Great Depression of the 1930s, the most harrowing crisis in its history since the Civil War, and was the architect of the U.S. *welfare state and leader of the Allies in victory over *fascism in *World War II. His election to third and fourth terms as president was unprecedented (and now constitutionally prohibited), he was the first president to systematically utilize intellectuals in his administration (generically known as his "Brain Trust"), and he recast the electoral support for the Democratic Party through his *New Deal coalition. Yet during his lifetime FDR was a controversial figure in U.S. politics, beloved by many and referred to derisively by others as "that man in the White House." Today his personality and contributions are still contested by scholars.

Franklin Roosevelt was born in Hyde Park, New York, to a family of considerable inherited wealth. His parents, James and Sarah Delano Roosevelt, were descendants of Hudson Valley squires. Franklin was educated by private tutors, graduated from Groton School, and received a degree from Harvard University in 1904. A year later he married a distant cousin, Eleanor Roosevelt, who became the most politically prominent first lady in U.S. history and an important political figure on her own terms. A student with little intellectual commitment, Roosevelt entered Columbia Law School with the vague intention of becoming a corporate lawyer. Although he never graduated, he passed the New York bar examination in 1907. After a brief experience with a law firm, Roosevelt was elected to the New York State Senate in 1910 from a district that had not sent a Democrat to the state legislature since 1884. He received national attention by leading the opposition to the U.S. senatorial candidate supported by Tammany Hall, the Democratic Party machine in New York County, and for his sponsorship of labor and conservation legislation. President Woodrow Wilson selected him for the position of assistant secretary of the Navy in 1913, which he held until 1920 when he was nominated by the Democratic Party as its vice-presidential candidate.

In August 1921 Roosevelt was confronted with the most

momentous event in his personal life: he was stricken by polio. FDR would never walk or stand again without crutches and braces. In political terms, however, his medical exile proved to be an advantage. Roosevelt's defense of the *League of Nations in the 1920 presidential campaign was now a political liability, and his low national profile left other Democrats to struggle in a period of Republican hegemony. Roosevelt nominated Al Smith for governor of New York in 1924 and for president in 1928 and gained attention for his rousing speeches in support of the "happy warrior of the political battlefield." Although Smith was defeated by Herbert Hoover, Roosevelt won the governorship of New York by the small margin of 25,564 votes. He proved to be an able administrator who responded quickly to problems created by the depression, which deepened dramatically during his second term. For this precursor to the *New Deal Roosevelt recruited many figures who would later run bureaucracies in his presidential administrations, including Harry Hopkins, Adolf Berle, Jr., and Frances Perkins.

In 1932 the Democratic Party selected Franklin Roosevelt as its presidential nominee on the fourth ballot over his former mentor Al Smith. Roosevelt ran an aggressive campaign, promising to provide "a new deal for the American people" and calling for the formation of a "concert of interests" to fight the depression as Thomas Jefferson had done in 1800 to fight elite domination of the new federal government. While Hoover explained that the depression was an international phenomenon, Roosevelt insisted that the depression represented the failure of U.S. economic *elites. According to FDR, the president had presided over an era of profligate capitalism and people in the United States were being forced to bear the burden of this "obeisance to Mammon."

Elected by a landslide of 472 electoral votes to Hoover's 42, Roosevelt faced a demoralized nation with an economy on the verge of collapse when he took office in March 1933. In his inaugural address, the new president spoke of the "nameless, unreasonable, unjustified terror" that gripped the nation and assured the American people that "the only thing we have to fear is fear itself." Roosevelt spoke darkly of the possibility of employing dictatorial powers to meet this emergency that was as serious as invasion by a "foreign foe," and Congress delegated significant powers to the executive branch, especially in the first one hundred days of his presidency; but in the end the Roosevelt administration remained within the constitutional boundaries of the political system.

The depression proved to be a formidable challenge. Roosevelt employed a variety of measures, both cautious and bold in conception or implementation, to restore economic confidence and provide relief. Sometimes the president was pushed by Congress and by his own administrators to initiate programs, as in the case of labor and social security legislation. Frances Perkins, secretary of labor, contended that she had great difficulty in convincing the president to examine the ideological significance of unionization. Sometimes, however, the president would move in directions that surprised and angered his own advisors, such as his famous "left turn" in 1936 in which he attacked "economic royalists" who would "regiment people, their labor and their property." He contended that these same kind of elites had behaved similarly toward the populist President Andrew Jackson in the 1830s.

As "it seemed sometimes that all were against him—all but the people of the United States," so too did he "welcome the hatred" of those who would "gang up against the people's liberties." It was from this democratic antielitism that FDR built ideological support for the welfare state. He once contended that the "spirit of the frontier husking bee is found today in carefully constructed statutes."

Roosevelt's power was seriously reduced after his landslide reelection over Alfred Landon, governor of Kansas and Republican Party candidate, by both congressional and public opposition to his "court packing" proposal in 1937 and his failure to "purge" conservative Democrats running in state primaries in 1938. In regard to the latter, Roosevelt abandoned his role of honest broker among party factions by campaigning for liberals in an attempt to reform the U.S. party system into clearly defined opposing ideologies. Although this reform effort did not succeed, to the considerable anger of both Republicans like Hoover and Democrats like Smith, Roosevelt did manage to redefine *liberalism as the belief that under modern conditions the national government can actively solve problems, notably in the realm of economic and social welfare policy.

The rise of fascism, however, provided the president with a new political arena as he began to focus on international issues. In the early 1930s Roosevelt's interests were almost entirely domestic ones, although he did promote the Good Neighbor policy for Latin America. He was an internationalist early in his career but did not actively oppose the Neutrality Act of 1935, which required an arms embargo when states of belligerency occurred, despite objections from his secretary of state, Cordell Hull. His Chautauqua address of 1936, in which he warned of pursuing "fool's gold" in seeking to trade with belligerents and described "men coughing out their gassed lungs," is one of the strongest antiwar speeches ever delivered by a U.S. president.

In October 1937, however, the president spoke of the "breakdown of all international law and order" and suggested the possibility that collective action might be necessary to "quarantine" aggressors. In his controversial decision to seek reelection to a third term, FDR warned that the world crisis involved an ethical choice of "moral decency versus the firing squad" and compared the crisis he faced to the one faced by Abraham Lincoln in 1860. He hired Robert Sherwood, the author of a Broadway play about Lincoln, as speech writer and encouraged the press to follow up his analogy that as Lincoln faced a nation half slave and half free, the president faced a world so divided. His Republican opponent Wendell Willkie rejected these comparisons to Lincoln and compared Roosevelt's ambitions to those of European dictators. Put on the defensive by Willkie's charge that his reelection would mean that the United States would be at *war in six months, Roosevelt pledged that "your boys are not going to be sent into any foreign wars."

After his reelection, however, in a series of measured steps the president prepared the people for war. Japanese forces bombed U.S. military installations at Pearl Harbor in December 1941. To defend nations fighting the Nazis in Europe, Roosevelt had extracted commitments from a reluctant Congress and an isolationist public in the six months before Pearl Harbor. He told the people in a fireside chat that the lend-lease arrangement with Britain was necessary to prevent its fall to the Nazis. FDR admitted that the United States risked war as it prepared to become the "arsenal for democracy." Roosevelt declared in 1941 that he was now "Dr. Win the War" instead of "Dr. New Deal," and that August, with British leader Winston *Churchill, he defined Allied war aims in the Atlantic Charter in terms roughly equivalent to his conception of freedom developed in the New Deal.

In his prosecution of the war, Roosevelt tended to follow the same honest-broker strategy that he had undertaken in his rebuilding of the Democratic Party. He extended lend-lease aid to the Soviet Union when it was invaded by Germany and added the Soviets to an Allied coalition with the British, gave assurances to the Soviets that the Allies would open a second front against Germany in 1942, and generally refused to deal with divisive questions during the war such as territorial disputes or questions of colonial independence. FDR envisioned a postwar world built on cooperation between the great powers. This would be the animating idea behind the creation of the UN.

During the war Roosevelt's opponents found it almost impossible to challenge his domination of the political agenda, despite some regrettable policies and dangerous threats. In 1942 by executive order he incarcerated U.S. citizens of Japanese descent and told Congress that should they fail to pass economic stabilization legislation he would act himself. Although reelected to a fourth term in 1944, Roosevelt was seriously ill, and he died on 12 April 1945, shortly after attending a meeting with Allied leaders at Yalta. Although there was initial congressional support for these accords, the almost immediate advent of the *Cold War led to a reevaluation of the utility and wisdom of FDR's policy of cooperation and compromise with the Soviet Union.

FDR's legacy is still a controversial one owing in part to the fact that the two major initiatives of his administrations, the welfare state and international intervention, remain contested policies in the United States. Moreover, Roosevelt's own personal capabilities continue to be scrutinized. Many scholars and even political allies, including in varying degrees Walter Lippmann, Rexford Tugwell, and Frances Perkins, insist that a careful examination of Franklin Roosevelt's policies suggests that his political *ideology never rose much beyond that of the "country squire" from Hyde Park with some progressive sensibilities. Roosevelt himself was generally reluctant to state his views in any systematic way, insisting as he did on one occasion that he was simply "a Christian and a Democrat." Others, such as James MacGregor Burns, grant that he was a masterful politician with the characteristics of the lion and the fox that Machiavelli contended were the essential features of a leader, but maintain that he lacked any real political vision. There is certainly a sense that even in the context of political compromise there was an especially ad hoc and gimcrack quality to many New Deal programs. Still others, including Arthur Schlesinger, Jr., contend that his pragmatism itself constituted a democratic theory and that he had built a "middle way" of governance between fascism and communism. Whatever assessment is offered of Roosevelt's leadership, he clearly was a superb reader of U.S. *political culture who managed to apply all the great symbols in the American experience (both of past presidents like Jefferson, Jackson, and Lincoln and of dearly held values such as social justice and fairness) to the art of political crisis management.

(See also CONGRESS, U.S.; ISOLATIONISM; PRESIDENCY, U.S.; UNITED NATIONS; YALTA CONFERENCE.)

James MacGregor Burns, *Roosevelt: The Lion and the Fox* (New York, 1956). Rexford G. Tugwell, *The Democratic Roosevelt* (Baltimore, 1957). Philip Abbott, *The Exemplary Presidency: Franklin D. Roosevelt and the American Political Tradition* (Amherst, Mass., 1990). Frank Freidel, *Franklin D. Roosevelt: A Rendezvous with Destiny* (Boston, 1990).

PHILIP ABBOTT

RULES OF WAR. See WAR, RULES OF.

RURAL DEVELOPMENT. The term "rural development" implies a process of increasing productivity and improving standards of living in rural areas. It is a term used most frequently with reference to developing countries. In most such countries, rural areas exhibit not only very low levels of productivity but also persistent evidence of dire poverty. In the decades after World War II, many governments introduced public policies to relieve constraints on agricultural growth and to improve conditions of life in rural areas: *Nongovernmental organizations (NGOs) also experimented with a variety of means to stimulate more dynamic and equitable rural economies. Despite such interventions, rural underdevelopment proved difficult to overcome whether in socialist or capitalist economies of the *Third World. Among ongoing problems were urban bias in national development strategies, increasing population pressure on land and water resources, environmental pollution, growing incidence of landlessness and underemployment, and low investment in human resource development.

Before World War II, rural areas were often characterized by an emphasis on commercial production for export, great inequalities in the distribution of productive assets, and large portions of the population producing only for subsistence. Colonial governments, through marketing boards and taxes, captured significant benefits from export trade. Colonial economies, however, were strongly conditioned to monocrop production and were buffeted by strong boom and bust cycles. In most countries, lack of infrastructure, low life expectancy, and high rates of infant mortality, ill health, malnutrition, and illiteracy also combined to discourage rural economic growth.

After independence, many governments and development specialists anticipated that the *modernization of rural areas would follow from urban and industrial growth in the process of economic development. Modernization was expected to draw excess labor out of the agricultural sector and increase demand for food and industrial inputs that would then be reflected in greater agricultural production and potential for rural growth. The modernization of the rural sector would reflect the experience of the United States and other industrializing countries a century earlier. Many governments in the 1940s, 1950s, and 1960s sought to stimulate rural transformation through policies to encourage technological innovation in agriculture, particularly in areas of high productive potential. This emphasis was spurred through investment in physical infrastructure and efforts to encourage the adoption of new seed varieties and more extensive use of chemical fertilizers and irrigation, basic components of the *green revolution.

By the 1960s, critics of the urban and industrial bias of this "trickle-down" model pointed to evidence that only a small sector of the rural population was benefiting from government-assisted efforts to increase productivity through agricultural research, extension, credit, and infrastructure. Moreover, they pointed to increasing evidence that urban and industrial development was not absorbing excess rural labor. Concern over the apparent failure of modernization to stimulate a process of rural development, along with increased sensitivity to the potential for rural political protest, led to new emphases in government policies and the efforts of NGOs. In many countries, the problems of peasant producers and rural communities were given more focused attention. During the late 1950s and 1960s, even while governments continued to invest in ongoing agricultural modernization efforts, they also introduced community development and agrarian reform programs to encourage greater equity and more dynamic rural growth.

Community development efforts sought to unleash the productive potential of rural villages and communities through identification of felt needs, local organization, and self-help efforts, in the expectation that such activities would overcome the fatalism, powerlessness, and traditionalism thought to characterize the lives of the rural poor. A critical component of this approach was the village-level worker, who was to be a catalyst in unlocking local potential for development.

At the same time, several strands in development thinking encouraged a redistributive approach to stimulate agricultural productivity and rural development, especially in Latin America and parts of Asia. Many development specialists increasingly viewed inequity in the distribution of productive assets as the cause of the failure of technological modernization to reach poor rural villages. The rapidly growing economies of Taiwan and Japan supported the argument that greater equity in land distribution was needed before the productive potential of rural areas could be unleashed. A radical critique of modernization policies emphasized the feudal and semifeudal relations of production that encouraged landlords to eschew productivity in favor of security, status, and power and that forced *peasants into exploitative relationships, stifling their initiative. More conservative supporters of redistributive policies anticipated increased rural political stability if peasants became small market-oriented producers. In a number of countries, agrarian reform legislation was passed and agrarian reform institutes established to address difficult issues of land tenure, to redistribute land, and to build infrastructure for agrarian reform beneficiaries.

In most countries, however, agrarian reform affected only a small portion of the rural population. In practice, governments proved unwilling or unable to expropriate large landholdings, many of which had been modernized and were providing an important source of foreign exchange to the country. The capacity of both traditional and more capitalist landowners to resist the redistributive efforts of even committed governments was considerable. In addition to the political constraints of a redistributive path toward rural development, the difficulties of financing and administering access to green revolution technology, extension, and markets

were among the factors that helped dampen optimism about the potential of agrarian reform to respond effectively to rural underdevelopment. Agrarian reforms that emerged from revolutionary upheavals also faced severe organizational, administrative, and financial constraints that limited their economic and political success. Theoretical arguments for the importance of agrarian reform remained generally intact, while practical experience increased awareness of its political, administrative, and financial demands. Increasingly, government-sponsored agrarian reform initiatives were targeted only for areas where rural unrest or insurgency threatened.

The early 1970s brought new efforts to address persistent evidence of rural underdevelopment. Keynoted by *World Bank President Robert McNamara in a 1973 speech in Nairobi, "the poorest forty percent," most of whom lived in rural areas, took on new importance. Significant shortfalls in food grain production and high international commodity prices in the early 1970s focused attention on a "world food crisis" and increased interest in the provision of national food security. The decade demonstrated greater concern for peasants and villagers and new regard for their contributions to agricultural production, particularly of basic food grains. There was much increased attention to the role of women in the rural development process as well as new emphasis on the importance of nutrition, health, and education to improved standards of living. Basic human needs and integrated rural development approaches sought to counterbalance the inequities and inefficiencies introduced by ongoing modernization efforts. The *basic needs approach indicated the importance of social development if rural poverty were to be addressed, and governments sought to generate programs, often funded by international loans, to deliver increased education, health, and sanitation services to rural dwellers. Integrated rural development programs focused on the provision of social, productive, and infrastructural services in packages designed to be appropriate to the diverse needs and conditions of specific rural regions. This approach, which at times acknowledged the need for land redistribution, placed greater emphasis on the potential for technological innovation to increase peasant productive potential even on very small holdings.

Basic needs and integrated rural development approaches were widely adopted in developing countries in the 1970s, often bringing new vigor to many ministries of planning, agriculture, public works, and social services as well as to diverse agencies for research, extension, credit, and marketing. Heavy foreign borrowing often accompanied these efforts, encouraged by the programmatic concerns of many international agencies and the wide availability of easy credit during the decade. Disillusion with these new approaches to rural underdevelopment began to emerge within a few years of their adoption, however. Governments experienced great difficulty in meeting the heavy demands they made on administrative capacities for coordination and timely delivery of effective services. Moreover, evidence accumulated of the frequent appropriation of program and project benefits by better-off sectors of the rural population, leaving the poorest untouched or relatively worse off. In the wake of an international debt crisis in 1982, many governments retreated rapidly from rural investment commitments under the dual impact of foreign exchange shortages and the need to impose strict austerity on public sector budgets.

Rural development initiatives in the 1980s were dominated by concerns about the macroeconomic context of agricultural sector development and the impact of prices on incentives for production. Prior initiatives, particularly those at the sectoral level such as modernization and integrated rural development, were heavily criticized for having been pursued in macroeconomic contexts that were highly unfavorable to agriculture in general and for having introduced a variety of unsustainable subsidies that distorted national economic interactions. Throughout the decade, the potential for rural development was associated with efforts to alter rural-urban terms of trade and to introduce competitive market prices for agricultural inputs (particularly fertilizer and credit) and outputs. Considerable efforts were undertaken, often as the result of conditions set by international financial institutions, to weaken or dismantle agricultural marketing boards and to remove subsidies that had been introduced in the 1960s or 1970s to stimulate technological innovation and greater productivity. In Africa, where communal landholding systems were increasingly imperiled by poverty and population pressures, new emphasis was placed on tenure reforms thought to be essential to the stimulation of dynamic smallholder production.

Just as the rural development initiatives of the 1970s were criticized for being less concerned with price incentives and macroeconomic terms of trade than they should have been, so the emphasis on macroeconomic and pricing policies of the 1980s engendered criticism for their failure to encourage investment in social and physical infrastructure, research and extension, and poverty alleviation. Increasing concerns were voiced about natural resource degradation caused by inappropriate government policies, chemical inputs, and the interrelated impact of poverty and population pressure. Similarly, greater attention was focused on the problem of rural employment.

In the meantime, however, urban migration and population growth substantially increased the number of people living in urban and periurban areas. In many countries, particularly in Latin America and increasingly in Asia, while the probability of being poor remained greater in rural areas, the preponderance of poor people was increasingly found in cities. In terms of national development policies and political dynamics, this population shift encouraged greater attention to urban development and poverty alleviation. Although demographic change also stimulated renewed efforts to increase agricultural productivity, it tended to decrease the resources available for rural poverty alleviation, social and physical infrastructure, and employment generation.

Four or more decades of efforts to address problems of rural areas were characterized by changing analyses of the constraints on rural economic development. These were reflected in altered approaches to stimulating productivity and raising standards of living by governments and NGOs. In most cases, rural inhabitants were not the principal initiators of these interventions. International agencies and ministries of planning or finance often took the lead in defining the problems and designing the solutions. To the extent that rural interests were represented in national policy making, they were often those of larger, commercially oriented farmers and of village elites who continued to benefit from unequal resource distribution and preferential access to public goods and services. With sporadic exceptions, the majority of most rural populations continued to be not only poor but also powerless in national politics. Rural development continued to be an elusive goal in many countries, the achievement of which implied major changes in international economic exchanges, domestic political relationships, macroeconomic and agricultural sector policies, and access to productive and social assets among the rural poor.

(See also COLLECTIVIZATION; DEVELOPMENT AND UNDERDEVELOPMENT; FOOD POLITICS; LAND REFORM; WOMEN AND DEVELOPMENT.)

Robert Bates, *Markets and States in Tropical Africa* (Berkeley, Calif., 1981). Merilee S. Grindle, *State and Countryside: Development Policy and Agrarian Politics in Latin America* (Baltimore, 1986). Jean Dreze and Amartya Sen, *Hunger and Public Action* (Oxford, 1990). Thomas P. Tomich, Peter Kilby, and Bruce Johnston, *Transforming Agrarian Economies: Opportunities Seized, Opportunities Missed* (Ithaca, N.Y., 1995).

MERILEE S. GRINDLE

RUSSIA. In December 1991 the first independent Russian state since 1922 came into being in a storm of optimism. Soviet *communism was declared defunct, and Russia was to turn back onto the road of Western civilization through the establishment of a new democratic and capitalist order. At least that is how Russian president Boris *Yeltsin portrayed events at the time.

The result by October 1993 was a complete breakdown of the Russian state and open warfare on the streets of Moscow, symbolized perhaps best by the burnt-out hull of the Russian White House, where the Russian parliament used to meet. It was destroyed by repeated tank bombardments when Boris Yeltsin ordered government troops to storm the building, leaving 146 dead and up to a thousand wounded. The October 1993 tragedy was above all a conflict between institutions: in 1991 a presidential system of government had been layered on top of a functioning parliamentary system, so that each side claimed ultimate authority to issue laws. Economic policy was at the center of this institutional tug-of-war: whether to transform Russia's economy as quickly as possible through "shock therapy" (freeing prices, engaging in rapid privatization, and holding enterprises to hard budget constraints) or whether to pursue a more gradual, restrained approach to the market.

Russian government had to be invented anew at the end of 1993. Elections were held in December for a new legislature at the same time as a plebiscite was conducted on a new constitution whose rules governed those elections. The new constitution contained a number of controversial provisions that weighted the political process significantly in favor of the presidency. The turnout in the elections was relatively low (54.8 percent of eligible voters). According to the official results, the new constitution was approved by 58.4 percent of those participating, though there is some evidence that the results were rigged.

The first Russian republic was born with the heavy scars of Soviet communism. The second Russian republic that emerged out of its ashes continued to bear those scars. The new Russian system of government was patterned on the semi-presidential system of France, where the president is directly elected and enjoys significant powers, but the government through which the president rules requires the consent of the legislature. In the Russian case, however, the presidency towers over the political process, and the degree to which the legislature exercises control over the government is questionable. Indeed, the Russian government has at times been characterized as "super-presidential."

The December 1993 constitution created a bicameral legislature known as the Federal Assembly. Its upper house, the Federation Council, consists of 176 members (two from each of the eighty-nine federal subunits of Russia, excluding Chechnia). The Federation Council elected in 1993 was formed from competitive elections within federal subunits, though the constitution does not specify whether the body should be elected or appointed. A bill providing for the election of the Federation Council was approved by both houses of the legislature in June 1995, but was vetoed by Yeltsin on the grounds that it was unconstitutional. Yeltsin instead successfully insisted on an upper house formed by regional governors and heads of the legislatures, who, though locally elected, are dependent on federal subsidies and are only part-time federal legislators. The lower house, the State Duma, is composed of 450 deputies elected for four-year terms, though again the Russian constitution does not specify how elections are to take place. In 1993 a mixed electoral system was chosen in which half of the seats were determined by proportional representation (with a minimum five-percent threshold) and half by single-member-district plurality elections. This system was used as well in the 1995 legislative elections, though Yeltsin consistently pushed to reduce proportional representation, since it favored his opponents. Majorities of both houses are necessary to pass laws. But bills are usually drafted by committees of the Duma and then, once passed on the floor, make their way to the Federation Council, which has fourteen days to consider the legislation. If no action is taken, the law is regarded as passed, but if the Federation Council rejects the bill, it can be overridden by two-thirds of the Duma. All laws require the approval of the Duma, including the annual federal budget.

According to the constitution, the Russian president, who is directly elected for a four-year term and serves a maximum of two terms, is the head of state and guarantor of the constitution. Though the Duma must provide its consent to the president's choice of prime minister, the prime minister and the government are subordinate to the president, not the legislature. Individual ministers are not subject to confirmation, recall, or sanction by the legislature, and the president has the right to dissolve the legislature if the legislature rejects the president's candidate for prime minister three times. The president can entirely ignore the legislature's vote of no-confidence in the prime minister the first time it is given, and if a second no-confidence vote is made within three months, the president can choose to dissolve the legislature rather than dismiss the prime minister. The president also has the right to issue binding decrees (*ukazy*) in the absence of legislation and can veto laws passed by the legislature. These institutional arrangements effectively place the executive branch beyond the reach of the legislature.

Russia suffers from an excess of weak political parties, many of which have formed on the basis of personalistic groupings of politicians. Numerous splits have plagued both right and left of the political spectrum, while political parties remain loosely tied with social groups. Surveys conducted in 1994 indicated that 78 percent of Russians did not identify with any political party, compared with 13 percent of Americans and eight percent of British. In the 1993 elections thirteen parties were on the ballot, as well as 1,586 candidates in 224 districts, most of these running as independents. Eight parties passed the five-percent hurdle in the proportional representation part of the vote, though the combined effect of proportional representation and district races increased the number of effective parties in the legislature. Vladimir Zhirinovsky's Liberal-Democratic Party (an extremist nationalist movement) won the largest number of votes (22.9 percent), while the liberal Russia's Choice, which openly supported Yeltsin, received only 15.5 percent, performing only slightly better than the Communists (12.4 percent). The 1995 legislative elections witnessed an explosion of personalistic parties and independent candidacies, with forty-three parties on the ballot and 2,751 candidates vying for district seats. With 64.4 percent of the electorate participating, only four parties cleared the five-percent barrier: the Communists (with 22.3 percent of the vote), the Liberal-Democratic Party (11.1 percent), Our Home Is Russia (the "party of power" associated with then Prime Minister Viktor Chernomyrdin, with 10.1 percent), and Yabloko (a liberal party, with 6.9 percent). The Russian Duma has been dominated by communist and nationalist parties. Nevertheless, the presence of large numbers of independents and representatives of smaller parties elected in the districts has weakened party coherence within the legislature, as has the president's steadfast refusal to affiliate with any political party. In spite of his seemingly low popularity on the eve of reelection, Yeltsin ran against nine other opponents for president in June 1996, defeating his Communist rival Gennadii Zyuganov in a runoff election by a 53.8 percent majority (with a turnout of 68.9 percent).

Another feature of Russia's semi-democracy has been the weakness of law enforcement and legal institutions. Post-Soviet Russia has undergone major legal reform, including a significant effort to imbue courts with independent powers. But courts often continue to be dependent on local authorities, and corruption and law evasion remain widespread. In 1996, for instance, only 16 percent of Russia's taxpayers paid their taxes on time and in full, and a third of Russia's corporations failed to pay taxes. In Russia in 1996 only 59 percent of the expected amount of tax revenue was collected. It was estimated in 1998 that $12–15 billion flow out of Russia illegally every year, much of this to offshore banks to avoid taxation and regulation. As much as half of the Russian economy operates in the "shadow sector"—i.e., illegally and unregistered. The rise of organized criminal groups (according to official reports, penetrating up to half of all businesses) has accompanied the larger breakdown of political institutions that has gripped Russian society since independence.

Since the early 1990s the Russian economy has been in a state of collapse. Indeed, from 1992 to 1995 it contracted by 42 percent. The freeing of prices in early 1992 associated with "shock therapy" led to annual inflation rates of 2,500 percent in 1992, 847 percent in 1993, and 250 percent in 1994. Beginning in 1995–96 a concerted effort was made to bring inflation under control, and by 1997 inflation had dropped to 11 percent annually. In that year the Russian economy may have registered a slight positive growth rate—between 0.2 and 0.4 percent. (A major corruption scandal within the State Committee for Statistics raised questions about these figures.) By 1998 the collapse of East Asian economies and declining world oil prices (energy accounts for 45 percent of Russia's export earnings) brought about the collapse of the Russian stock market, causing Russia to seek additional loans from the International Monetary Fund to prop up its economy. Official unemployment remained below 10 percent, but there was considerable hidden unemployment. As much as a quarter of the workforce was not receiving its wages on time, and unpaid wages remained the leading cause of labor unrest in Russia.

Shock therapy created a distinctive brand of *capitalism in Russia. By 1997, 82 percent of Russian enterprises had been placed into private hands—an enormous social revolution in patterns of property ownership. A massive voucher privatization program turned more than 60 million people into shareholders of Russian businesses. However, one of the major results of the way in which *privatization was conducted was a high level of inside ownership within large enterprises. Nonmanagerial employees on average owned 39 percent of shares in Russian companies by 1995, with another 16 percent being owned by management and 13 percent by the state. In the United States 50 percent of all corporate shares are owned by households. In Russia, the corresponding figure was six percent. In many cases managers opposed the sale of stock to outsiders and instead encouraged their workers to buy enterprise stock. In turn, inside ownership reinforced managerial control over enterprises, and, according to some, is a significant obstacle to restructuring Russian firms.

The combination of patterns of economic and political organization under state socialism and modes of privatization during the transition to capitalism brought about an enormous concentration of wealth and power in Russia. The top twenty firms in the Russian economy, for instance, account for 56 percent of Russia's industrial production and employ 3.4 million out of Russia's 17 million industrial workers. While 21 percent of the population lives below the official poverty line, a small group of individuals—the so-called "new Russians"—has become fantastically rich off of privatization, with access to government being the key to how this occurred. Privatization has also led to geographically uneven patterns of development. Moscow, for instance, represents 7 percent of Russia's total population, but as of 1997 accounted for 20 percent of all privatized enterprises and 70 percent of all foreign investment.

Of Russia's 147 million inhabitants, 81 percent are ethnic Russians. The remainder consists predominantly of members of thirty-six groups with populations of 100,000 or more. The largest of these, the 5.5 million Volga Tatars, voted in a referendum in 1992 to recognize Tatarstan as a "sovereign state" and a "subject of international law." In 1994 the government of Tatarstan signed an "international" agreement with Moscow that ambiguously recognized Tatarstan as part of the Russian Federation while giving Tatarstan far-reaching "sovereignty," including the right to sign its own international treaties. A number of other ethnically-based territories have reached similar bilateral agreements with the Russian government. Russia inherited an ethnofederal structure from the for-

mer Soviet Union, and it has been moving in the direction of greater asymmetry among federal units over time. This in turn has been resented by the Russian majority. The crisis of governability that engulfed Russia in 1993 severely exacerbated relations between the center and localities and, in some opinions, nearly led to the collapse of the federation. Russia continues to suffer from considerable conflict between Moscow and its regions, one of whose manifestations is the failure of regions to send locally collected tax revenues to Moscow, exacerbating further Russia's debt problems.

Russia's most serious ethnic challenge has come from its 900,000-strong Chechen minority. In November 1991 Dzhakhar Dudaev, a former general in the former Soviet air force, imposed a personalistic dictatorship in Chechnia and refused to recognize Moscow's authority, turning Chechnia into a de facto independent state. In fall 1994 Yeltsin decided to reassert Russian control by organizing a revolt against the Dudaev government. When that revolt failed, Yeltsin ordered large-scale military action in December 1994. Instead of a quick victory, Dudaev's forces kept the Russian army pinned down in Groznyi for a month. Chechen forces eventually retreated to the mountains and fought a successful *guerrilla war. Dudaev was killed in a bombing raid in April 1996, but soon after, in June 1996, Chechen fighters retook Groznyi, moving surreptitiously into the city and driving out Russian troops. More than 80,000 people died in the war before a cease-fire and treaty were negotiated in August 1996. The agreement postponed the issue of the status of Chechnia until the year 2000, provided for a withdrawal of Russian troops, and created conditions for local elections (which guerrilla leaders overwhelmingly won). Moreover, the war demonstrated the incompetence of the Russian army (once the seemingly invincible force of a superpower) and became a larger metaphor for the breakdown of the Russian state.

Russia is no longer a global superpower, though it still possesses 21,000 nuclear warheads and the capability of launching nuclear strikes anywhere on the planet. But in the postcommunist period Russia has redefined itself as a regional power, identifying its particular zone of interest as the so-called "near-abroad"—i.e., the republics of the former *Soviet Union. Russia's assertion of its interests as a "Great Power" in the region, its stated goals of "reintegrating" the former Soviet republics, and its strident opposition to *North Atlantic Treaty Organization (NATO) expansion in East Europe are viewed by some as signs of Russia's intent to recreate the Soviet empire. Russia has also been concerned with the fate of the 26 million Russians living beyond Russia's borders in the "near-abroad." Restrictive citizenship laws in Latvia and Estonia, conflicts involving the Russian-speaking communities of the Pridniestr region, Crimea, and northern Kazakstan, and a large in-migration of Russians from Central Asia and the Caucasus have attracted the attention of Russian politicians across the political spectrum.

Russia has changed at an extraordinary pace since independence. These changes were inextricably connected with the dominance of Boris Yeltsin over Russian politics. Yeltsin invented the Russian presidency and defined Russia's partial democracy and frontier brand of capitalism. As the new millennium dawns and Yeltsin's rule gives way to others, the vector assumed by Russian politics could well alter. Widespread dissatisfaction with the current state of affairs epitomizes the public mood. Analysts disagree over the extent to which capitalism and democracy have sunk roots in Russia, the prospects for establishing a coherent state and a vibrant economy, and the possibilities of collapse into more virulent forms of dictatorship. Yet, as Russia's erratic path over the twentieth century so vividly demonstrates, in Russia the seemingly impossible has a habit of occurring with astounding frequency.

(See also DEMOCRATIC TRANSITIONS; POST-COMMUNISM; SOCIALISM AND SOCIAL DEMOCRACY.)

Stephen Handelman, *Comrade Criminal: Russia's New Mafiya* (New Haven, Conn., 1995). Tim McDaniel, *The Agony of the Russian Idea* (Princeton, N.J., 1996). Richard Sakwa, *Russian Politics and Society,* 2d ed. (New York, 1996). Joseph R. Blasi, Maya Kroumova, and Douglas Kruse, *Kremlin Capitalism: Privatizing the Russian Economy* (Ithaca, N.Y., 1997). Mary McAuley, *Russia's Politics of Uncertainty* (Cambridge U.K., 1997). David Remnick, *Resurrection: The Struggle for a New Russia* (New York, 1997). Stephen White, Richard Rose, and Ian McAllister, *How Russia Votes* (Chatham, N.J., 1997).

MARK R. BEISSINGER

RUSSIAN REVOLUTION. The revolution that took place in Russia in 1917 was actually a series of overlapping revolutions occurring in rapid succession. First, early in 1917, the Liberal or Political Revolution of the middle classes and part of the intelligentsia attempted to create a constitutional order. A provisional government, self-selected by leading members of the old tsarist parliament, the Duma, tried to govern the country and guide the revolution along a moderate track while keeping Russia in the war against Germany. Social polarization and growing discontent with the war and the policies of the provisional government attracted many workers and soldiers to the radical Bolshevik party, led by Vladimir *Lenin. The Workers' Revolution of October 1917 led to the establishment of Soviet power and a government under Lenin. Among its first acts, the new government encouraged the growing peasant movement to seize the lands and eliminate the economic and social power of the old aristocracy. The Peasant Revolution of 1918 culminated in massive land seizures, the expropriation of the nobility, and the equalization of landholding. Finally, the multiple revolts of the non-Russian peoples of the empire—the Revolutions of the Nationalities—resulted in the establishment of new nation-states that left the Bolsheviks isolated in central *Russia.

The roots of the revolution lay in deep structural tensions in the tsarist autocratic system that resisted participation of much of society in the making of state policy. By the early twentieth century many liberal and radical intellectuals, workers, and townspeople desired political *reform (or revolution) to create a more representative and responsive polity. At the same time powerful landed nobles, on whom the tsar depended most immediately for social support and high state personnel, became increasingly resistant to political reform or changes in the patterns of landholding. Peasant dissatisfaction with their small plots exploded in the revolution of 1905–1907, and workers, living under a harsh regime of all-powerful bosses and no legal expression of their grievances, responded to the radical messages of socialist revolutionaries. By the eve of World War I society was polarizing. At one extreme were the tsar and his few supporters; at the other, much of society ready for radical change. But at the same time, the most radical workers grew alienated from both liberal and moderate socialist politicians.

The final blow to the fragile structure of the empire came in the bloody test of strength from 1914–1918 with Imperial Germany when Russia's technological and productive backwardness proved inadequate to stand up to its enemies, carry on the war, and supply its cities with fuel and food. Late in February 1917, illegal meetings of women workers were held in several textile mills in Petrograd (St. Petersburg, now Leningrad). The women decided to go on strike and marched to other factories shouting "bread." By noon twenty-one factories and 50,000 workers had joined the strike. Bread shortages inflamed those in bread lines, and they joined the strikers. By the second day, 24 February, one half the industrial workers of Petrograd (200,000) were on strike. Cossacks refused to shoot down the workers. In the Duma the liberals now called for a government responsible to parliament. Once soldiers joined the workers' rebellion, tsarist power collapsed in a few days.

Liberals in the Duma were fearful of the spontaneous rebelliousness of the masses (*stikhiia*). Pavel Milyukov, leader of the liberal Constitutional Democratic Party (Kadets, *Partiia Narodnoi Svobody*), later admitted: "We did not want this revolution ... And we had desperately struggled so that this would not happen." They formed their own government, while the workers created a Soviet ("Council") of Workers' Deputies. Instead of a single center of power in Russia, the February days ended with two rival centers—one holding formal power and representing the middle and upper classes, as well as liberal public opinion; the other holding real, physical power, commanding the soldiers and workers. The new political institutions of the "dual power" (*dvoevlastie*) reproduced the social polarization of prewar tsarist society.

The first clash between the two centers of power occurred in April over disagreements about the continuation of the war. The Provisional Government wanted to carry war to a victorious end and acquire the imperial fruits of war (e.g., control over the Straits) promised by the Allies to the Tsar. But the Soviet demanded a "democratic peace" with no annexations or indemnities. When demonstrators surged into the streets to protest Foreign Minister Milyukov's note on war aims, the government fell. A coalition government was formed with a number of Soviet representatives from moderate socialist parties. The Bolsheviks remained outside the government and championed the notion of Soviet power, a government made up only of representatives of the lower classes.

Through May and June workers became more discontent with rising prices and falling real wages. The initial cooperation of the factory owners dissipated, and workers blamed the owners for their worsening situation. Soldiers were tired of the war and turned against the government when it attempted to launch an offensive in the late spring. In early July radical workers and soldiers attempted a coup in Petrograd, but the Soviet, led by the Mensheviks and Socialist Revolutionaries, managed to put it down. Bolsheviks were arrested, and Lenin went into hiding. But this short-lived dip in Bolshevik support ended with the attempt by General Lavr Kornilov to seize power and reestablish discipline in the army. By early September Bolsheviks held majorities in both the Moscow and Petrograd Soviets, and Lenin urged his followers to seize power. On 25 October 1917 (7 November), the Bolsheviks overthrew the Provisional Government, now led by Aleksandr Kerensky, and proclaimed a Soviet government.

State *capitalism (1917–1918) briefly replaced legal private capitalism, only to give way to a system of nationalized economy later called "War Communism" (1918–1921). Within the new Soviet republic ordinary people, particularly workers, eventually became part of a new ruling class of bureaucrats, party officials, and military officers. Out of the chaos of the radical *democracy that had begun to flourish in 1917, the Bolsheviks created a new and authoritarian state, which they considered to be "the dictatorship of the proletariat."

The Russian Revolution has been the classic example for Marxists of a successful workers' revolution. Indeed, a spontaneous workers' movement, aided at key moments by the soldiers of the Petrograd garrison, was the key agent in the February Revolution. The October Revolution was much more of a planned, military operation, initiated by the Bolshevik leadership, though widely supported in Petrograd by workers and soldiers. The broad alliance of social forces—workers, soldiers, some local middle-class elements in the towns, and a part of the peasantry—that had come together to support Soviet power in the fall of 1917 soon disintegrated as Russia withdrew from the war, soldiers left for home, and industrial erosion took its toll on an already-weakened working class. For many analysts, especially those who were more sympathetic to the aspirations of the Bolsheviks, the subsequent drift from a more democratic form of Soviet rule to the one-party dictatorship of 1918 and the civil war years was rooted in the traumatic circumstances of international isolation, the collapse of the old economy, and the consequent loss of a broad social base for Bolshevism. For others, particularly Western liberal and conservative writers, dictatorship was inherent in the Leninist theory of party organization, the vanguardism of the cadre party, and Bolshevik suspicion of Western parliamentary forms.

Unlike later twentieth-century revolutions—in China, Vietnam, Cuba, and elsewhere in the Third World—Russia's revolutions were primarily urban, made by a minority of the population. Lenin argued that for Soviet power to endure the party and workers had to rely on some support from the peasantry and an international revolution to aid backward Russia grow into socialism. When neither a revolution in the developed West nor uprisings in the colonial world came to Russia's aid, the party fell back upon those elements that supported it most completely and curtailed the range of free expression and political action. Key to Soviet survival after 1917 was the organization of a militant party and effective army that could wage war against socialism's enemies.

Yet for much of the twentieth century the legacy of Bolshevism went beyond the development of the powerful revolutionary weapon of the Leninist party. For Third-World Marxists the Bolsheviks were, not only the founders of the "first socialist state" and the "party of a new type," but model revolutionaries committed to the anti-imperialist struggles of the colonial peoples. *Leninism provided a view of history that saw socialism of the Soviet type, complete with party dictatorship and a nationalized economy, as a higher stage of development beyond capitalism, the market, and a democratic, representative political order of the Western type. Only in the late 1980s would the authoritarian legacy of the Russian Rev-

olution and civil war be radically revised by the heirs of the Bolsheviks themselves, but the democratic reform led by Mikhail *Gorbachev rapidly undermined the monopoly of power that the Communists had forged in the civil war and tore asunder the ideological and political links that had held the *Soviet Union together.

(See also CHINESE REVOLUTION; COMMUNIST PARTY STATES; MARXISM; POST-COMMUNISM.)

William G. Rosenberg, *Liberals in the Russian Revolution: The Constitutional Democratic Party, 1917–1921* (Princeton, N.J., 1974). Alexander Rabinowitch, *The Bolsheviks Come to Power: The Revolution of 1917 in Petrograd* (New York, 1976). Allan K. Wildman, *The End of the Russian Imperial Army*, 2 vols. (Princeton, N.J., 1980, 1987). Ronald Suny and Arthur Adams, eds., *The Russian Revolution and Bolshevik Victory: Visions and Revisions* (Lexington, Mass., 1990). Orlando Figes, *A People's Tragedy: A History of the Russian Revolution* (New York, 1996).

RONALD GRIGOR SUNY

RWANDA. Rwanda's state organization long predates European rule. In precolonial Rwanda the king ruled through a complex hierarchy of officials; pervasive patron-client relations provided mechanisms of control over land, cattle, and people. Three principal social categories—Hutu (about 84 percent of current population), Tutsi (14 percent), and Twa (less than 1 percent)—were distinguished by status and wealth but shared a common language and many other cultural features.

Rwanda was ruled by Germany before World War I, and thereafter under Belgium, first as a League of Nations mandate and later as a UN Trust Territory. While the monarchy was retained Belgian policies expanded the power and prerogatives of Tutsi chiefs, imposing taxes and labor exactions which fell heavily on rural producers, especially on Hutu. Although not all Tutsi were rich and powerful, virtually all those who attained great wealth and power during the colonial period were Tutsi.

Resentment of these class and ethnic inequalities fueled popular protests during the 1950s. In the revolution of 1959–1961, rural Hutu repudiated the authority of Tutsi chiefs and forced tens of thousands of Tutsi to flee to Uganda, Tanzania, Burundi, and Congo. In 1961 a referendum abolished the monarchy, and on 1 July 1962 Belgium ceded power to a Hutu-dominated republic headed by President Grégoire Kayibanda. Following incursions by armed Tutsi refugees seeking to overthrow the fragile new regime, in 1964 Kayibanda's government executed Tutsi members of the government and allowed the massacre of ten to twenty thousand unarmed Tutsi citizens. Such ethnic scapegoating as a response to an external threat was to reappear again in the 1990s.

Although revered among many Hutu for his dedication to the rural masses, Kayibanda is faulted by his critics for introducing single-party rule, concentrating power in the hands of individuals from his home region (central Rwanda), and failing to curtail ethnic conflicts. Aggravated by the massacre of thousands of Hutu in Burundi under a Tutsi-dominated government, ethnic and regional tensions led to a *coup d'état on 5 July 1973; Major General Juvénal Habyarimana, a Hutu from the north, assumed power.

Beyond internal politics, Rwanda faced severe structural constraints. Population density is among the highest in Africa (more than 7 million people in a country of 26,000 sq.

miles [26,000 sq. km.]), and 90 percent of the population depends on agriculture for their livelihood. With foreign assistance, the Second Republic sought to improve the transport network, promote reforestation, expand export production of coffee and tea, and establish small-scale manufacturing. Habyarimana's government also reorganized primary school education, encouraged the construction of rural health clinics, and permitted the proliferation of local associations working for development.

Some of these programs provided benefits to rural dwellers, but their main effect was often to extend the reach of the state, provide jobs to educated elites, and expand the resources of politically powerful people. Toward the end of the 1980s a series of crises undermined Rwanda's development efforts. A crash in the world price of coffee diminished government revenues and disrupted the local economy. *Famine caused several hundred deaths. The press exposed corruption and land accumulation by government officials. Consequently, in July 1990 Habyarimana announced political changes to prepare for multiparty elections.

In October 1990, however, Rwandan exiles based in Uganda attacked northern Rwanda. The Rwandan Patriotic Front (RPF) sought democratization of Rwanda's authoritarian government and the right of return for Rwandan refugees. Fearing the return of Tutsi hegemony, during the next three years Habyarimana's government initiated small-scale pogroms against Tutsi civilians. Meanwhile, hundreds of thousands of Rwandans in the north fled their homes as the RPF occupied territory there. A *structural adjustment program, including a sharp currency devaluation in November 1990, caused hunger and deprivation among both rural and urban poor.

From 1991 new political parties emerged to challenge Habyarimana's single party, the Mouvement Révolutionnaire national pour le développement (MRND); while major opposition parties called for transethnic collaboration to end the war and promote democracy, fair multiparty competition and open debate were sidetracked by military mobilization, tight security, and deepening ethnic polarization. Nonetheless in August 1993 the Arusha Accords provided for a negotiated end to the war. A UN peacekeeping force was to oversee installation of transitional institutions that would incorporate the internal opposition and the RPF, and merge the two armies. But Habyarimana delayed implementation of the accords, while extremists trained and armed militias, preparing for further violence. Splits within the internal opposition intensified after the assassination in October 1993 of Melchior Ndadaye, Burundi's first Hutu president, by elements in Burundi's Tutsi-dominated army.

Thus Rwanda was already a tinderbox when Habyarimana's plane was shot down on 6 April 1994, killing all on board. Using his death as a pretext, extremist elements in the government and the army launched a campaign of exterminating Tutsi and moderate Hutu seen as opponents of Habyarimana. The *genocide lasted one hundred days, leaving more than half a million people dead (mostly Tutsi), thousands of displaced persons, and almost 2 million refugees (mostly Hutu) in neighboring countries. Having won the war and stopped the genocide, the RPF installed a new government in July 1994.

During the two years after 1994, some 800,000 "old caseload" Rwandan refugees returned to Rwanda. These former exiles, most of them Tutsi, became an important support base for the new government, which has tried to respond to their needs for land, housing, and jobs. With substantial help from the international community the post-genocide government moved to staff government offices, repair damaged infrastructure, reopen schools, and restore a justice system to try those accused of participation in the genocide. Many Rwandan associations, especially women's groups, have organized programs to assist survivors of the genocide, promote reconstruction, and diminish violence.

The post-genocide government has made significant progress in rebuilding a shattered state and society, often in the face of recurring threats to security. Yet significant problems remain. Power is held largely by newcomers who returned to Rwanda from Uganda after the genocide, and recurrent patterns of exclusion against Hutu and against Tutsi survivors of the genocide create resentment. Many of the hundreds of thousands of Hutu refugees who were forcibly repatriated from Tanzania and the Congo (former Zaire) in 1996–1997 still lack proper housing, and the government has imposed a forced villagization policy that is unpopular with many rural Hutu. Rwanda's prisons are overflowing with more than 120,000 people still awaiting trial. And the Rwandan Patriotic Army has been accused of killing thousands of Hutu in the weeks following the RPF victory in 1994; in April 1995 while closing internally displaced persons' camps in southern Rwanda; and during the war in the Democratic Republic of *Congo (1996–1997) to overthrow Mobutu. RPA troops occupying eastern Congo since 1998 have been accused of systematic abuses against Congolese civilians.

In the years ahead Rwanda's people will continue to face daunting challenges: how to overcome the poisonous legacy of the genocide, and how to achieve democracy and improved governance in conditions where there is too little land for too many people, where inequality continues to grow rapidly, and where external economic and political environments can so sharply intensify internal difficulties.

(See also RWANDAN GENOCIDE.)

René Lemarchand, *Rwanda and Burundi* (London, 1970). Catharine Newbury, *The Cohesion of Oppression: Clientship and Ethnicity in Rwanda, 1860–1960* (New York, 1988.) Gérard Prunier, *The Rwanda Crisis: History of a Genocide*, 2d ed. (New York, 1997). Peter Uvin, *Aiding Violence: The Development Enterprise in Rwanda* (West Hartford, Conn., 1998). Alison Des Forges, *Leave None to Tell the Story: Genocide in Rwanda* (New York and Paris, 1999).

CATHARINE NEWBURY

RWANDAN GENOCIDE. The Rwandan *genocide, launched by a small group of Hutu political and military leaders on 6 April 1994, slaughtered more than half a million Tutsi, a people who comprised about 10 percent of the Rwandan population, as well as thousands of Hutu who opposed the elite in power. This *genocide resembled others in its dehumanization of the targeted people, its wartime context, and its slaughter of others besides the primary group. It differed in its rapidity—it lasted some one hundred days—and in the extent to which ordinary people, mobilized by a small elite, participated in the killing.

The genocide was sparked by the assassination of President Juvenal Habyarimana, whose airplane was shot down as he returned from a meeting about the Arusha Accords, largely inoperative since their signature in August 1993. The Accords supposedly ended a three-year-long war with the Rwandan Patriotic Front (RPF), but both sides were preparing to resume combat and did so after Habyarimana's death.

The RPF was made up mostly of Tutsi who had fled abroad after a Hutu-led revolution in 1959 ended generations of Tutsi rule. From the start of the war, Habyarimana sought to use ethnic loyalty to restore his popularity, slipping at the end of an increasingly repressive twenty-year rule. He accused Tutsi residents in *Rwanda of being "accomplices" of the RPF and arrested thousands of them. From October 1990 through 1993 officials directed a series of massacres of Tutsi, each time killing several hundred and establishing patterns for the 1994 genocide.

Habyarimana was obliged to end the official monopoly of his own party in 1991, and faced challenges from two predominantly Hutu parties which formed a bi-ethnic coalition with the RPF. Habyarimana and his supporters labeled these Hutu opponents also "accomplices" of the "enemy." Intraparty rivalry among Hutu became violent as each developed militia to disrupt meetings and to harass and even kill opponents.

At the end of 1993, an important part of the bi-ethnic opposition split off and rejoined Habyarimana under the banner of "Hutu Power." Thus fortified, Habyarimana prepared for killing Tutsi and Hutu political opponents under the guise of "self-defense." Newspapers had for years published anti-Tutsi propaganda; they were now joined by the lively and popular Radio Télévision Libre des Mille Collines (RTLM), nominally private but officially backed, which delivered increasingly virulent incitations to hate and fear Tutsi and those Hutu who were opposed to Habyarimana. Militia loyal to Habyarimana, particularly the Interahamwe of his own party and another group known as the Impuzamugambi, recruited many young men, especially among the poor and unemployed, and had them trained by army officers. Authorities distributed weapons to militia and other pro-Habyarimana community leaders.

Of the foreign nations most important in Rwanda, Belgium and the United States had ineffectually protested early massacres while France had staunchly supported Habyarimana. All three, as well as other nations represented in Rwanda, viewed preparations for mass slaughter with concern but failed to intervene. The commander of the United Nations Assistance Mission in Rwanda (UNAMIR), a peacekeeping force of 2,800 troops sent to help implement the Arusha Accords, repeatedly called for reinforcements and a stronger mandate, but the UN Security Council, under U.S. leadership, refused. The United States, haunted by the UN failure in Somalia the year before, rejected any policy that might entail great risk for the peacekeepers or increased costs for itself.

Within hours of Habyarimana's death, his supporters ordered Presidential Guards and other elite troops to slaughter Tutsi and Hutu rivals, beginning with the prime minister, Agathe Uwilingiyimana. They also killed ten Belgian peacekeepers, thus provoking a Belgian decision to withdraw its troops, leaving the peacekeeping force seriously weakened.

UN headquarters ordered the peacekeepers to defend themselves, but not Rwandans, and then withdrew most of the force. Belgian, French, and Italian troops arrived to evacuate foreigners and left quickly, reinforcing the impression that the international community would do nothing to halt the carnage.

With no prospect of outside interference, the nucleus of leaders rapidly attracted support from a larger number of military officers. Thus strengthened, they installed an interim government ready to do their bidding on April 9 and enlisted both administrators who controlled the highly developed administrative system and leaders of opposition parties. They used these military, administrative, and political leaders and their networks to mobilize the population for tracking and killing Tutsi. Radio RTLM and the national radio filled the air daily with propaganda encouraging the slaughter.

Tens of thousands of Tutsi were killed in large-scale massacres in churches, schools, and hospitals where they had sought refuge, sometimes at official direction. The military led these attacks with firearms, grenades, and even mortars. The militia, redirected from fighting party rivals to eliminating Tutsi, seconded the military and were followed by ordinary citizens who killed with machetes and similar implements.

An estimated 20,000 persons were slain in five days, testimony to the efficacy of the joint military-administrative-political direction. But in an important exception to compliance elsewhere, local administrators in central and southern Rwanda, where most Tutsi were found, resisted the genocide for nearly two weeks. After April 18, national officials removed the resisters and killed several of them. Other opponents then retreated into silence or actively led the killing. Officials punished ordinary citizens who opposed the genocide, even killing some, and rewarded participants with food, drink, drugs, money, and the property of the victims. Within three months, between 800,000 and a million people were slaughtered.

No international actor contested the legitimacy of the genocidal government: Rwanda continued to sit as a nonpermanent member of the UN *Security Council and the French president received its leaders. The UN finally approved a strengthened peacekeeping force, but it arrived after the RPF had already defeated the government and driven it from Rwanda, along with some two million refugees. In its conquest, the RPF slaughtered tens of thousands of civilians.

Leaders of many nations, as well as the UN, subsequently acknowledged their responsibility in failing to halt the genocide. The UN Security Council established the International Criminal Tribunal for Rwanda, which is currently prosecuting those accused of genocide and crimes against humanity in Rwanda during 1994.

(See also ETHNICITY; HUMANITARIAN INTERVENTION; UNITED NATIONS.)

Gerard Prunier, *The Rwanda Crisis: History of a Genocide* (New York, 1995). Howard Adelman and Astri Suhrke, eds., *The Path of a Genocide* (New Brunswick, N.J., 1999). Alison Des Forges, *Leave None to Tell the Story: Genocide in Rwanda* (New York, 1999).

ALISON DES FORGES

S

SADAT, Anwar. Born to a modest peasant family, Anwar Sadat (1918–1981) rose through the army to play a prominent part in Egyptian political life, first as a key figure in the anti-British military conspiracies of the 1940s and later as an influential government official in the 1950s and 1960s. However, Sadat did not reveal his potential for political leadership until his imposing predecessor, Gamal Abdel *Nasser, passed from the scene on 28 September 1970 and Sadat assumed the presidency in a smooth constitutional transfer of power.

Sadat soon made his own distinctive bid for leadership, breaking with Abdel Nasser's radical nationalist policies. Only six months after assuming power, he imprisoned many of his opponents on the Left, claiming that they had been plotting against him. He soon released from *Egypt's jails thousands of Islamic fundamentalists, using them as a counter to the remaining power of the Nasserist Left.

Sadat then launched an economic and political liberalization called the *infitah or "Open Door"—a policy that tried to tie Egypt's economy to the West and to give the regime a democratic face. Realizing that a full accommodation with the West remained blocked by the state of *war with Israel, Sadat expelled Egypt's Soviet advisers in 1972. Then, in October 1973, he launched a war against Israel in order to prepare the way for a peaceful settlement. Egypt's initial battlefield successes gave Sadat the prestige of "victory" in the war and enabled him to make a dramatic bid for *peace with Israel, including a personal trip to Jerusalem in November 1977. Though excoriated by many in the Arab world, Sadat continued to seek peace with Israel, eventually signing the Camp David Accords and sharing the 1978 Nobel Peace Prize with Israeli Prime Minister Menachem Begin. Continued negotiations led to a formal peace treaty in March 1979.

Many Egyptians, especially the upper classes, welcomed Sadat's economic liberalization, his relaxation of Nasserist *authoritarianism, and his achievement of peace with Israel. However, by the late 1970s limited democratization proved no substitute for real economic progress and domestic discontent mounted. When the government cut back state subsidies in 1977, riots swept several Egyptian cities, reflecting popular anger at the new rich and their foreign-influenced lifestyle, while so many Egyptians had barely enough to eat. Such policies drew critical attention to Sadat's own family: his brother had made millions on shady business deals and his wife Jihan often hosted lavish international social events.

Sadat's peace agreement with Israel had increasingly become a liability. His critics accused him of betraying the Palestinians and of gaining little substance in return. Throughout the Arab world he was an outcast. Abroad, his prestige as a Nobel laureate obscured these difficulties. The illusion was shattered on 6 October 1981 when members of an Islamic fundamentalist cell in the army assassinated the president while he was reviewing a military parade. Sadat's supporters in the West, expecting the kind of outpouring of grief that met Abdel Nasser's death, found instead that Cairo was unmoved.

Husni Mubarak, Sadat's successor, has adhered to the main lines of his predecessor's policies. The historic peace with Israel and ties to the West have held. Yet Sadat's achievements will remain problematic until a broader *Middle East peace has been achieved and Egypt's economy and political life fulfill the initial promises of Sadat's liberal reforms.

(See also ARAB-ISRAELI CONFLICT; ARAB NATIONALISM; ASSASSINATION; ISLAM; NASSERISM; NATIONALISM; REFORM.)

John Waterbury, *The Egypt of Nasser and Sadat: The Political Economy of Two Regimes* (Princeton, N.J., 1983). Raymond William Baker, *Sadat and After: Struggles for Egypt's Political Soul* (Cambridge, Mass., 1990).

RAYMOND WILLIAM BAKER

SAINT KITTS AND NEVIS. See ENGLISH-SPEAKING CARIBBEAN.

SAINT LUCIA. See ENGLISH-SPEAKING CARIBBEAN.

SAINT VINCENT AND THE GRENADINES. See ENGLISH-SPEAKING CARIBBEAN.

SALT. See STRATEGIC ARMS LIMITATION TREATIES.

SAMOA. See PACIFIC ISLANDS.

SAN MARINO. See SMALL STATES AND TERRITORIES.

SANCTIONS in relations between states are penalties threatened or imposed on a target as a consequence of its anticipated or actual failure to observe international standards or obligations. They are intended to influence the target's foreign or domestic policy and may be applied unilaterally by individual governments or multilaterally by governments acting in informal concert or within the framework of *international organizations. Sanctions may also be initiated by state, provincial, or municipal authorities and promoted by *nongovernmental organizations and other citizen-based groups. The target is usually a government, but may also be an entity seeking governmental status. A wide range of possible measures can be applied. Economic sanctions include import and export embargoes and prohibiting aid, investment, and transportation links. Target assets can be frozen and transfers of funds blocked. Political sanctions reduce diplomatic links and deny representation and membership in international organizations. Cultural sanctions limit scientific, educational, and sports contacts.

Economic deprivation used to further the interests of sender states, usually as an accompaniment to war, has a long history. *Thucydides describes a trade boycott of Megara by Athens during the Peloponnesian War in the fifth century B.C., France organized a grain boycott against Britain during the Napoleonic Wars, and in the twentieth century naval blockades were instituted by belligerents in both world wars. During the Cold War, Western countries maintained an embargo on exports of strategic goods to the Soviet Union. However, the concept of multilateral economic sanctions as a means of ensuring "collective security" was introduced by the League of Nations in 1920, and in spite of the failure of League sanctions against Italy in the 1930s, this idea was carried forward in the United Nations (UN) Charter in 1945. Chapter VII authorizes the *Security Council to order all members to impose sanctions to meet a "threat to the peace, breach of the peace or act of aggression." Sanctions resolutions require an affirmative vote of nine members of the Council, with no veto from a permanent member (Britain, China, France, Russia, the United States).

East-West rivalry brought deadlock in the Security Council for nearly four decades and comprehensive mandatory sanctions were imposed only on Southern Rhodesia (now Zimbabwe). A mandatory arms embargo was also imposed on South Arrica. In both cases the objective was the end of white minority rule. Outside the UN, extensive sanctions against South Africa were instigated by individual governments and by the Organization of African Unity (OAU), the Commonwealth, and many other groups. The thaw in East-West relations following the end of the Cold War enabled the Security Council to act quickly in August 1990 to condemn Iraq's invasion and purported annexation of Kuwait and impose a sweeping range of restrictions. Sanctions remained in force after the liberation of Kuwait with the main object of controlling Iraq's deadly weapons capability. There followed a series of Security Council orders for comprehensive measures against Yugoslavia and Haiti and selective measures on eight other countries, seven in Africa. Security Council action in all cases except the initial response to Iraq's aggression was prompted by "threats to the peace" arising from internal situations: the overthrow of elected governments (Haiti and Sierra Leone), civil conflict (Somalia, Yugoslavia, Liberia, Angola where the UNITA movement was the target, and Rwanda), and alleged responsibility for harboring terrorists (Libya, Sudan, and the Taliban movement in Afghanistan). Repressive regimes, support for international *terrorism, and nuclear proliferation have also prompted governments, particularly in the United States, to impose sanctions unilaterally or through bodies other than the UN.

The effectiveness of economic or other sanctions is open to question. To deprive a target of markets, suppliers, and other important links with the senders requires efficient national enforcement procedures which are often lacking. Nor does deprivation necessarily bring political compliance. In judging success, one relevant issue is what would work better: force means loss of life while incentives, or doing nothing, may be unacceptable. It is also difficult to separate the effects of sanc-

tions from concurrent events. Opinions differ on the role sanctions played in ending *apartheid in South Africa, and in other cases compliance followed the threat or use of force.

Multilateral measures enjoy greater legitimacy, facilitate more efficient implementation, and reduce sanctions evasion by limiting the target's access to alternative markets and suppliers. But target response is a key factor and the government under pressure will weigh the costs of sanctions against the benefits of pursuing the offending policy. Sanctions may prove counterproductive by strengthening domestic support for the target government, allowing it to blame all ills on external pressure, and by encouraging the growth of highly profitable sanctions-busting activities which erode the basis of *civil society.

Success must also be related to goals. In their major study of twentieth-century economic sanctions, Gary Hufbauer, Jeffrey Schott, and Kimberly Elliott (*Economic Sanctions Reconsidered*, 2d ed., Washington, D.C., 1990) found that in 115 cases, mainly initiated by the United States, sanctions helped to achieve senders' goals approximately one third of the time. Compliance requires a change in the target's policy; more achievable objectives are deterrence, punishment, conflict-limitation, and stigmatization. Sanctions can also serve to uphold international norms, important in respect of apartheid in South Africa and other cases involving *human rights. But senders' motives can be complex. Goals can have more to do with domestic considerations than the target's behavior, and, as Lisa Martin showed, pressure to apply sanctions often comes from allies and fellow-members of international organizations (*Coercive Cooperation: Explaining Multilateral Economic Sanctions*, Princeton, N.J., 1997).

In the 1990s old concerns about effectiveness and the domestic cost of sanctions for senders were heightened by the burden imposed on states bordering on Iraq and Yugoslavia and supplemented by new concerns about adverse effects on the civilian populations of targets. Reports of hardship in Haiti and Iraq led to calls for humanitarian exemptions for food, medicine, and other civilian goods. In 1995 the permanent members of the Security Council agreed that humanitarian issues must be addressed when sanctions are imposed and an elaborate "oil for food" scheme allowed Iraq to export oil and use the proceeds, under UN supervision, to import essential goods.

The injustice and futility of harming civilians who are powerless to affect policy in undemocratic societies leads senders to prefer selective sanctions. Arms embargoes, for instance, limit a target's war-making capability. There is also a new emphasis on targeted measures which impact directly on government personnel and elites. Financial sanctions—blocking assets and transfers of funds belonging to individuals and groups—are seen as the most promising but a study sponsored by the Swiss government on the technical aspects of financial sanctions revealed the many difficulties involved (Department of Federal Economic Affairs, *Targeting UN Financial Sanctions*, Bern, 1998, 1999). Other targeted measures include denial of participation in international meetings and travel bans. The UN has begun to experiment with targeted measures against UNITA and the Taliban but their efficacy is not yet confirmed. Nor is enforcement more assured than in the case of traditional trade sanctions.

(See also DIPLOMACY; FORCE, USE OF; FOREIGN POLICY.)

David A. Baldwin, *Economic Statecraft* (Princeton, N.J., 1985). Margaret P. Doxey, *International Sanctions in Contemporary Perspective*, 2d ed. (New York, 1996). David Cortright and George A. Lopez, *The Sanctions Decade: Assessing UN Strategies in the 1990s* (Boulder, Colo., 2000).

                                        MARGARET P. DOXEY

SÃO TOMÉ AND PRÍNCIPE. See SMALL STATES AND TERRITORIES.

SAUDI ARABIA. The Kingdom of Saudi Arabia is the third state formed by the Sa'ud family. The first—born in the mid-eighteenth century—expanded to include most of the Arabian Peninsula and even some parts of modern Iraq and Jordan. It was defeated and eradicated by an Egyptian expedition in 1818. A second state reappeared a few decades later, when a Saudi prince succeeded in reestablishing his family's rule in central Arabia, but this state was defeated by a local rival, backed by Ottoman power, in 1881.

The present Saudi state dates from 1902, when Prince 'Abd al-'Aziz ibn 'Abd al-Rahman Al Sa'ud (known as Ibn Saud) recaptured Riyadh. He spent thirty years expanding and consolidating the territories that form the modern state. These territories were officially united and proclaimed as the Kingdom of Saudi Arabia on 21 September 1932. 'Abd al-'Aziz signed an oil concession agreement with Standard Oil of California (Chevron) the following year.

This new state had been welded together by a powerful form of Islamic fundamentalism, called Wahhabism, which called for a return to the letter of the Quran. This simple, literal interpretation of Islam rallied both tribal and settled people to the Saudi banner, sweeping 'Abd al-'Aziz from one victory to another. The most zealous of his troops wanted to continue the conquests into British-controlled Iraq and Jordan, but 'Abd al-'Aziz was unwilling to risk a confrontation with London. He defeated these rebellious units in a bloody desert battle in 1929.

Saudi Arabia remains a kingdom with a monarch as its active chief of state. 'Abd al-'Aziz was succeeded upon his death in 1953 by his eldest surviving son, Saud, who was replaced by his brother Faisal in 1964. Since then two more of 'Abd al-'Aziz's sons have reigned: Khalid (1975–1982) and Fahd (1982–present). Fahd, elderly and ill, will be succeeded by one of the surviving sons of the founding king. There is no established mechanism for kingship to pass to the next Saudi generation, the grandsons of 'Abd al-'Aziz.

The king's authority, while substantial, is not unlimited. In 1992 King Fahd issued a "basic law," a constitution-like document detailing the rights of citizens and the powers of government. In 1993 he appointed the first "consultative council" in the kingdom's history, with advisory powers. A more effective limit on arbitrary power is the need for the king to build consensus among leading members of the Saud family and prominent figures in society before making major decisions. But the monarch remains the focal point of the Saudi political system.

The Saudi regime bans political parties and trade unions, and carefully supervises other elements of civil society (chambers of commerce and industry, the media, the religious establishment). From time to time, though, opposition has surfaced. The Saud family itself was split in the late 1950s and early 1960s, as Saud and Faisal competed for power and a more liberal group of princes publicly announced their opposition to the regime. The regime clamped down on public manifestations of dissent among workers (notably in the Eastern Province oil fields in the 1950s), in the armed forces (in the 1960s), and in religious circles (during and after the Gulf War of 1990–91) when they arose.

This large country, covering more than 775,000 square miles (2 million sq. km.), has a small native-born population (approximately 16 million by official Saudi estimates), though it is growing at a very high rate (approximately 3 percent per year over the last decade). To staff its oil-based economy, the kingdom has recruited a large number (approximately 6 million) of foreign workers, in the early years of the oil boom mostly from the Arab world and now increasingly from South Asia. Nearly all of the country's wage labor is performed by these foreigners, whose lives are tightly controlled. The government has not hesitated to deport those who are controversial politically. During the *Gulf War of 1990–91, up to one million Yemenis were effectively deported because of policy differences between Riyadh and Sanaa.

Ever since the first oil began to flow in 1938, Saudi Arabia has been a state built on oil revenues. When rising Saudi production met soaring prices in the period after 1974, government revenues increased astronomically. These revenues have been used for many purposes: building a countrywide modern infrastructure and an extensive welfare state, buying huge amounts of sophisticated weaponry, supporting the fabulous lifestyle of the ruling family, creating new industries around the kingdom's oil and gas resources, supplying large amounts of foreign aid in various parts of the world, and investing abroad, mainly in Europe and the United States. These uses have set off social changes in the kingdom, such as growing urbanization and widespread education, which have substantially altered Saudi society and given rise to pressures for more change.

During the 1970s and 1980s, Saudi Arabia gave away several billions of dollars every year in grants, loans, and other kinds of foreign aid, mainly to Islamic recipients. It supported governments and political groups in Muslim countries, Muslim minority groups in Europe and Asia, a wide network of mosques and Muslim educational and charitable institutions around the world, and Islamic international organizations. The Saudi government also continues to spend large amounts of money to make the Haj (pilgrimage to Mecca) a successful event each year. All these efforts seek to promote the Saudi government's own particular interpretation of *Islam, against other political interpretations like those of revolutionary Islamic Iran and against more liberal social interpretations fostered by other Muslim governments. Particularly during the 1980s, Saudi Arabia also coordinated its foreign aid programs with the United States, funding political movements in Afghanistan, Nicaragua, Mozambique, and elsewhere that the U.S. government could not afford to support or preferred to keep at arm's length.

In 1981, Saudi Arabia became the de facto leader of the Gulf Cooperation Council (GCC), a group of six Gulf States. Despite very high spending for sophisticated arms imported from the West, the GCC remained militarily weak. It was unable to defend one of its members, Kuwait, against the Iraqi invasion of 2 August 1990. That crisis made it clear that Saudi Arabia could not defend itself without the support of the

United States. In fact, the United States has been the patron of the Saudi state since the 1940s, when U.S. wartime aid helped keep the royal family's budget in balance. The House of Sa'ud, suspicious of the British, gave American oil companies the right to produce oil in the kingdom—a source of very large profits and real geostrategic leverage for the United States ever since. Even when the Saudis took control of their domestic oil industry in the 1970s, they remained close to both the American oil companies and the U.S. government.

To protect the Saudi state and monarchy, the United States has consistently provided military and security assistance. During the 1970s and 1980s the United States built a network of major military bases in the kingdom designed to accommodate foreign forces in a crisis, and it organized a powerful U.S.-based Gulf intervention force which was deployed to the region in 1990.

Saudi Arabia accounts for approximately 25 percent of the world's proven oil reserves, and is the largest producer and exporter of oil in the world. The country plays a key role in the global oil market, especially within the *Organization of Petroleum Exporting Countries (OPEC). During the Arab-Israeli War of 1973, King Faisal employed the "oil weapon," refusing for a short time to export oil to countries supporting Israel, including the United States. Since then, Saudi Arabia has shown moderation on oil pricing issues and has been reluctant to use such political boycotts. However, when oil prices fall precipitously, as they did in the late 1990s, the Saudis have taken the lead among OPEC members and other producers to try to restrict production to push prices back up.

As oil prices declined in real terms during the 1980s and 1990s, and the Saudi government spent billions of its reserve dollars on the two Gulf Wars—first to support Iraq against Iran and then to fund the international coalition's war against Iraq—the Saudi government found it more difficult to sustain the spending policies of earlier decades. Foreign aid and defense spending were reduced during the late 1990s. The Saudi bureaucracy is no longer able to absorb young Saudis entering the work force, and unemployment has become a problem in the kingdom. The generous welfare state and physical infrastructure built in the 1970s has been strained by population growth and lower revenues. As the century turned, Saudi policy makers were embarking on a new economic direction, aimed at reducing the role of the state in the economy and encouraging the private sector. This new direction includes cuts in subsidies on consumer goods, privatization of state-owned assets, and the encouragement of foreign investment. The political ramifications of these changes, both in terms of lessened government control over economy and society and in terms of the new burdens it places on Saudi citizens, will determine the future of the Saudi state.

(See also Arab-Israeli Conflict; Iran-Iraq War.)

David E. Long, *The Kingdom of Saudi Arabia* (Gainesville, Fla., 1997). Mamoun Fandy, *Saudi Arabia and the Politics of Dissent* (New York, 1999).

Ghassan Salame

SCANDINAVIA. The five Nordic countries of *Denmark, *Finland, *Iceland, *Norway, and *Sweden together constitute Scandinavia. The Nordic-Teutonic people inhabited the Nordic areas from ancient times, sharing a single language. The Viking age (800–1000 c.e.) was marked by a number of connected petty kingdoms, and during this period Iceland, the Faroe Islands, and Greenland were settled. Another group, distinct both ethnically and linguistically, settled the Finnish area (100 c.e.); later, Swedes settled there as well. In 1389, the Swedish-Finnish area fell under the rule of the queen of Denmark. This arrangement, called the Kalmar Union, broke up in 1523 and was followed by numerous Nordic wars. The two main adversaries—Denmark and Norway opposing Sweden and Finland—sided with different great powers during the Napoleonic Wars (1807–1814). In the postwar settlement, Denmark lost Norway to Sweden, which had lost Finland to Russia in 1809. Full independence was attained by Norway in 1905, Finland in 1917, and Iceland in 1918. The Faroe Islands and Greenland were granted home rule by Denmark in 1947 and 1979 respectively.

Language is a unifying factor, as Danish, Norwegian, and Swedish are mutually intelligible languages. Finland has been integrated into the Nordic world in the twentieth century, despite the language barrier. (Swedish is still an important second language there.) Religion is also a source of commonality: Christianity was adopted during the Viking age, and Lutheran Protestantism replaced Catholicism around 1530. There is also a common legal tradition: medieval Scandinavian law was a separate branch of Germanic law. *Things* (meetings of all freemen) established laws, which were recorded from the eleventh to the thirteenth centuries, then supplemented and codified in the early modern period.

Modern Nordic development has been characterized by a peaceful transition to liberal *democracy. The aristocracy was too weak to block the consolidation of peasant property rights in the preindustrial period. An independent *peasantry on small family farms formed autonomous farmers' parties. The industrial working class, with some rural support, formed social democratic parties. Their achievement was universal franchise and parliamentary democracy. In the 1930s labor movements won the support of the poorest farmers. The Nordic party systems all display a nonsocialist side, split between agrarian, liberal, conservative, and Christian populist parties. The *Left is more homogenous, dominated by social democratic parties with close connections to centralized trade union organizations. The Finnish case varies from the Scandinavian model in important ways. First, it experienced a bloody civil war in 1917–1918. In addition, its Left was split equally along communist and social democratic lines, and the trade union movement was splintered as well. Recent developments, however, bring it closer to the general Nordic pattern. Iceland's Left is also divided.

Nordic cooperation in the modern age began during the mid-nineteenth century. A monetary union existed between Denmark, Norway, and Sweden from 1873 to 1914. During World War I, bilateral trade between the three countries expanded significantly. But Finnish preoccupation with the Soviet Union, its eastern neighbor, ties to German industry in the case of Sweden, and a Norwegian orientation toward its western trade partner, Britain, blocked further integration. In the interwar period, much collaboration took place within the League of Nations. With the threat from Nazi Germany in the late 1930s, a Nordic defense union was discussed, but World War II precluded its realization. In 1948 the idea was resurrected. The Danish, Norwegian, and Icelandic governments, however, wanted support from Western great powers and opted for *North Atlantic Treaty Organization (NATO) membership instead. Sweden maintained neutrality. Finland concluded a Treaty of Friendship, Cooperation, and Mutual Assistance according to which it was to be defended by the Soviet Union if invaded by foreign troops.

Nordic collaboration has also been complicated by the effects of unequal economic development. Negotiations toward a Nordic common market began in 1948, but the process of European integration delayed the proposal until May 1959, and at that juncture the *European Free Trade Association (EFTA) was seen as a more interesting alternative. Extensive Nordic economic cooperation developed within EFTA. A more ambitious plan, Nordek, was launched in the late 1960s, inspired by the increase of intra-Nordic trade during that decade, but suddenly new prospects for extension of the European Community (EC) emerged. Finland backed out, owing to its links to the Soviet Union. Sweden believed EC membership to be incompatible with neutrality. Norway decided to withdraw its membership application following a referendum in 1972. Only Denmark joined the EC in 1972. Finland, Iceland, Norway, and Sweden later concluded trade treaties with the EC.

Nordic cooperation may, however, point to some achievements. The Nordic Council, a yearly gathering of delegations of legislators and government ministers, was founded in 1952. (Later, a separate council of ministers was set up.) Subcommittees meet more often. Finland joined in 1955. The Nordic Council is an advisory body, not mandated to deal with foreign policy, although there is some coordination of policies in the UN, in the *Council of Europe, and regarding *North-South relations. The Nordic Council adopted the Nordic Convention on Cooperation (the Helsinki convention) in 1962 (extended in 1970), an international treaty that codified the results and aims of Nordic cooperation.

The EU *European Union single market offensive of the late 1980s and the end of the Cold War (1989) led the Nordic non-EU-members to reconsider their relationship to the EU. By 1994 they had all entered into the European Economic Area (EEA) agreement with the EU. This implied full integration of their economies into the EU's single market. But already by 1995, Sweden and Finland entered the EU as full members, leaving Norway and Iceland (together with Liechtenstein) as the only participants in the EEA. With three out of five states and most of Scandinavia's population inside the EU, the Nordic Council has been restructured. Cooperation has been narrowed down to specified issue areas, and coordination of the member countries' different connections to the EU, the EEA, and broader European organizations is now a core activity.

(See also CLASS AND POLITICS; SOCIALISM AND SOCIAL DEMOCRACY.)

Erik Allardt et al., eds., *Nordic Democracy* (Copenhagen, 1981). Franz Wendt, *Cooperation in the Nordic Countries—Achievements and Obstacles* (Stockholm, 1981).

LARS MJØSET

SCHRÖDER, Gerhard. Gerhard Schröder, the chancellor of *Germany elected in 1998, is the first German political leader truly of the postwar generation. Unlike his predecessor Helmut *Kohl, who was a teenager during World War II,

Schröder was born at the war's cusp, in 1944, in the small Lower Saxony town of Rosenburg. He was however profoundly affected by the war in one sense; his father—a German soldier—was killed on the eastern front in Romania. As a young man, Gerhard Schröder had to work while he completed his education, serving a stint in a hardware store before completing the first phase of his university studies.

In his twenties, he became active in Social Democratic Party (SPD) politics, belonging to the *Jungsozialisten* (Young Socialists) or *Jusos* as they are known colloquially. Schröder embraced Marxism—as did most *Jusos* at the time—although this fact is not surprising given the Marxist roots of virtually all Social Democratic, Socialist, and Labor parties. Schröder then received his law degree from Göttingen University in 1976, and by then he had become an influential young politician in the SPD. He became a member of the *Bundestag* in 1980 and in 1990 was elected *Minister-Präsident* (governor) of Lower Saxony. Even in his early years in public life, Schröder had high ambitions. One evening in Bonn in the 1980s, Schröder—who had taken perhaps an extra glass of wine or two—was walking past the gate to the chancellor's office then occupied by Helmut Kohl, put his hands on the gate, and exclaimed: "I want to be in there!" Schröder's personal life is not without controversy, as he has been married and divorced three times, and his present wife is number four. During the 1998 campaign, the youth wing of Helmut Kohl's Christian Democratic Union used a gag slogan urging voters to reject Schröder and the SPD, stating "three women can't be wrong."

During his election campaign, Germany's new chancellor was compared with British Labour Party's Tony *Blair and even with U.S. President Bill *Clinton. Observers stressed one apparent thread that tied the three politically young (all are in their forties or fifties) political leaders together. As heads of "left" parties on their countries' respective political spectra, they seemed to share an affinity for moving away from their parties' previous more firmly left tendencies toward more centrist positions. In fact, the SPD slogan for the 1998 campaign was *"die neue Mitte"* (the New Middle), suggesting just such a moderate tendency on Schröder's and the SPD's part. Further contributing to this perception was the apparent awarding of the powerful Economics Ministry to free-market-oriented computer magnate Jost Stollman during Red-Green coalition negotiations.

Yet a funny thing happened on Schröder's way toward the center: it's called German politics. Unlike Bill Clinton who can often operate without regard to his own Democratic Party's concerns, or unlike Tony Blair who controls and shapes policy of his majority Labour Party, Gerhard Schröder is much more institutionally constrained. One constraint is that the SPD is in coalition with another party, the Greens, and does not have a majority by itself. A second constraint is the institutional structure of the SPD with its various factions and constituencies.

The Greens' position as a minority—but absolutely essential—member of the coalition government meant that some of the Clinton-like or Blair-like overtures toward the center were challenged by Greens' concerns. The Greens' leader—and new Foreign Minister—Joschka Fischer drove hard bargains in insuring that many of the Greens' environmental positions would be part of the coalition agreement.

Likewise, the SPD itself acted as a brake on some of

Schröder's more centrist-leaning tendencies. One form this brake took was in the person of Oskar Lafontaine, the chairman of the SPD and new finance minister. If Schröder is interested in more "supply side" measures as reinvigorating the economy with technological innovation and increased flexibility, Lafontaine relies on a more "demand-side" approach such as increasing the number of jobs, decreasing inequality, and targeting tax cuts and social benefits toward the working class and the powerful trade unions, the SPD's largest constituency. In fact, Lafontaine drove such a hard bargain that he persuaded Schröder to give more authority to the Finance Ministry—especially concerning EU affairs—while the Economics Ministry would see its responsibilities reduced. Stollman—the computer magnate—balked at this power shift and stepped down from consideration as a candidate for economics minister.

Lastly, however, there is one other force that may have delayed Schröder's move to the center. His father died in the war and he was brought up by his widowed mother. In that sense, he shares a surface similarity with Bill Clinton. Unlike the American president, however, who has gone on to embrace other values, Schröder retains a powerful commitment to maintaining a strong welfare state and a social benefits package that will sustain widows like his mother in their old age.

CHRISTOPHER S. ALLEN

SECESSIONIST MOVEMENTS. Secession entails the breaking of connections between a regional unit and the *state to which it is joined. Secessionist movements resist what are perceived as illegitimate rules laid down by the existing state of which they are a part. Frequently (but not always) ethnically inspired, the seceding entity rejects potential reforms within the state as insufficient and struggles instead for separate, sovereign statehood (the externalist solution). Secession, therefore, represents a radical effort on the part of a regional actor to achieve full self-determination, transforming the political structure of the existing state in the process. Not surprisingly, the uncompromising and far-reaching nature of secessionist demands often brings on a sharp response from state authorities determined to maintain the territorial integrity of the state against all challengers. Because the demands and counterdemands of secessionist and state elites are presented in nonnegotiable terms, it often proves difficult to accommodate them and intense conflict frequently results.

Despite the enormous resources at the disposal of ruling authorities, secessionist movements have been skillful in using a variety of means to oppose the extension of state power to their area. Tactics include nonpayment of taxes, unwillingness to enlist for military service, boycotts, work stoppages, emigration, sabotage, and armed violence. Ungovernability (that is, the breakdown of reciprocities and political exchange relations between state and societal elites) is frequently viewed by secessionist leaders as a precondition for radical change.

The number of successful secessions increased in recent years with the breakdown of the Soviet Union and Yugoslavia, spawning a host of new states in both multinational "empires." Whereas the *Baltic states proclaimed independence and opened negotiations with the Soviet Union regarding fu-

ture relations and the Czech Republic and Slovakia agreed to a "velvet divorce," other secessionist movements in Kurdistan, Kashmir, southern Sudan, and Kosovo have continued to wage *guerrilla warfare to achieve their goals of independence. In some of the most dramatic conflicts of our times, regional fears of central domination have led to battles between standing armies, resulting in the crushing of secessionist forces in eastern Nigeria (Biafra), a bitterly contested confrontation in Chechnya, separate de facto autonomous areas in Bosnia-Herzegovina, and victory by secessionist forces in Bangladesh. In Eritrea, a thirty-year struggle by the Eritrean People's Liberation Front to regain self-determination also led to a successful outcome, although in 1998 heavy fighting began between Eritrean and Ethiopian troops that continues to the present time to determine the border between their countries. Although most states have sufficient political, economic, and military resources at their disposal to fend off these challenges to their authority, these successes indicate that their control over their peoples and territory can no longer be taken for granted.

Certainly, the international community has played and will continue to play a critical role in sustaining or undermining the stability of states under secessionist attack. Although external governments generally refuse to extend recognition to secessionist regimes or movements, in some cases (Slovenia, Croatia, Biafra) recognition by foreign states assured a wider audience for their claims to legitimacy. External aid to secessionist movements (Belgian support for Katanga; Indian backing of the Tamils in Sri Lanka) has served to prolong encounters. External mediators and peacekeepers have intervened to facilitate a peaceful solution to state-secessionist conflicts in Cyprus and Sri Lanka. The UN, determined to bring an end to the fighting in Croatia and Bosnia-Herzegovina, put pressure on authorities in Belgrade by placing sanctions on trade and by authorizing the use of force to protect shipments of humanitarian aid. Finally, in the case of East Pakistan (now Bangladesh), the role of a supportive Indian army proved critical in thwarting efforts by the West Pakistan–led army to regain control over this noncontiguous region.

If the forces of local *nationalism have generally lacked the capacity to wrest independence from a reluctant political center, there are indications that such movements may fare better in the future. The frailness of state institutions and infrastructures, the disappointing economic performance of many countries, and the unwillingness of the industrialized countries to enforce stable relations or provide adequate economic support to desperately poor late industrializing countries all point to the prospect of a new fluidity in interstate relations. Moreover, as successful secessions create new minorities, an additional number of secession-prone movements can be anticipated. Nationalism appears to be broadening in scope at the very point in history when states seem unable to meet the minimal expectations of their publics.

(See also ERITREAN WAR OF INDEPENDENCE; ETHNICITY; FORCE, USE OF; NATIONAL LIBERATION MOVEMENTS.)

Lee C. Buchheit, *Secession: The Legitimacy of Self-Determination* (New Haven, Conn., 1978). Donald L. Horowitz, *Ethnic Groups in Conflict* (Berkeley, Calif., 1985). David A. Lake and Donald Rothchild, eds., *The International Spread of Ethnic Conflict: Fear, Diffusion, and Escalation* (Princeton, N.J., 1998).

DONALD ROTHCHILD

SECULARIZATION. The origin of the term "secularization" goes back to the Middle Ages. First used to indicate the process of alienation of Church property to the state, it soon came to be applied to the loss of temporal power by the Church. Later its meaning was extended to include the process by which priests abandoned or were forced to leave their clerical role and become laymen. Overall, then, secularization involves a transition from the religious to the nonreligious—to the secular—world.

In order for such a transition to take place, it must be possible to differentiate clearly between the two spheres, to distinguish the lay and civilian from the religious and sacred. Consequently, and inevitably, secularization implies increasing reliance on worldly criteria in the process of decision making, the jettisoning of religiously based or inspired doctrines, the rationalization of attitudes and behaviors, and the Weberian imperative to apply rationality to the goals selected and to the means utilized. Accordingly, rulers will no longer follow religious doctrines but will structure their decisions according to secular criteria. Then, in its social and political behavior, the population at large will no longer feel bound to the teachings of the Church and dependent on its representatives and their religious principles. Finally, all *ideologies, and not just religious doctrines and beliefs, will be abandoned and replaced by secular, rational behavior. Because some political ideologies have a quasi-religious character, de-ideologization may therefore come to coincide with the process of secularization.

Taken for granted and considered irresistible and irreversible, the process of secularization has encountered serious obstacles. Religious principles and criteria continue to play a significant role in the life of many individuals who generally abide by them in their social and political behavior. They can still serve as justifying principles of more than passing significance. Political ideologies may have crumbled away, but they are not necessarily replaced by rational criteria and rational processes of decision making. More important, powerful religious beliefs are still used to shape and justify the behavior of rulers both domestically and on the international scene.

Twentieth-century *fundamentalism has acted as a drag on secularizing tendencies. Fundamentalist thought aims directly at the reconstruction of temporal power for religious organizations and their leaders. It denies the separation of the religious sphere from all other spheres and especially from the political, social, and cultural domains. Indeed, fundamentalism affirms the supremacy of the religious sphere over all others and the supremacy of its interpreters over all other sociopolitical actors. It claims that religious criteria must be not only the dominant criteria but the exclusive arbiter of behavior. Thus all major principles of thought and behavior must be sought, and can be found, in the books of the prophets. Any action whatsoever should be inspired by those principles and evaluated according to those criteria. Muslim fundamentalism worldwide and, to a lesser degree, Jewish and Christian fundamentalism are contemporary phenomena that underscore the fact that secularization has not been completed. The proliferation of religious sects all over the world testifies to the resurgence of fundamentalism and throws doubt on the prospect that complete secularization will ever be accomplished. Encircled and endangered minorities may always resort to some immutable, fundamental principles to take hope, to strengthen their faith, to survive in a hostile world, and to justify death for a holy cause.

The elemental contradictions of Western rationalism and the corresponding process of secularization are exposed by current challenges. The continued significance of fundamentalism calls into question a conventional modernist view of history as continuous progress, with secularization an important constituent process. A different conception of history seems to be in order, one that makes room for the reversal of processes, the resurgence of ideologies, and the basic spiritual needs of individuals. A more subtle understanding is required of different principles and criteria for different realms of individual life, thinking, and activities. An awareness is developing that religious criteria are not the only, nor even the dominant, criteria to be used. At the same time, secular, rational criteria are not the only criteria people will apply in their behavior. Secularization, although a powerful and still-unfolding process, is not all-encompassing.

(See also MODERNITY; MODERNIZATION; RELIGION AND POLITICS; WEBER, MAX.)

Harvey Cox, *The Secular City: Secularization and Urbanization in Theological Perspective* (New York, 1966). Wolfgang Schluchter, *The Rise of Western Rationalism: Max Weber's Developmental History* (Berkeley, Calif., 1981). Gilles Kepel, *Revenge of God: The Resurgence of Islam, Christianity, and Judaism in the Modern World* (University Park, Pa., 1994).

GIANFRANCO PASQUINO

SECURITY. Although a concept that is crucial to an understanding of international politics, as is the case with most fundamental concepts, "security" is ambiguous and elastic in its meaning. In the most fundamental sense, to be secure is to feel free from threats, anxiety, or danger. Security is therefore a state of mind in which an individual, whether the highest political leader of the land or the average citizen, feels safe from harm by others. Used in this way, a *state (or its leaders and citizens) believes itself secure when it fears that nothing adverse can be done to it by other states or by other foreign nonstate actors. To define security in this fashion is to see that it is a subjective state of mind, not an objective condition of being. It describes how people feel, not whether they are justified in feeling the way they do. In this sense security depends on the perceptions people have of their position in their environment, not on an objective view of that environment.

This subjectivity explains why security can encompass so many things: what makes one individual feel secure may not be sufficient to make another feel so. Individuals differ in their tolerance for uncertainty, their ability to live with anxiety, and their capacity to cope with pressure. One person's security can well be another's insecurity.

Furthermore, although individuals differ in what makes them feel secure or insecure, most experience neither perfect security nor absolute insecurity. Rather, the subjective sense of security or insecurity varies along a continuum. Security, therefore, is not a matter of either/or—either one has it or one does not; rather, it is a matter of degree, of feeling more or less secure, more or less insecure. What is true of individuals is true of states. States are not perfectly secure or completely insecure, but rather experience either condition in degrees. For both individuals and states, then, security is a condition that comes in shades of gray, not hues of black and white.

The concern that states have for their security stems from the nature of the international political environment in which states exist. International politics is characterized by the absence of an effective government above states that has the authority and the power to make laws, to enforce them, and to resolve disputes among states. International politics is anarchic because there is no world government. In such an anarchic realm, states must be concerned first and foremost with their security—the extent to which they feel unthreatened by the actions of others. With no government to look to for protection, they must rely on their own efforts. A concern for survival thus breeds a preoccupation with security.

At the minimum, the ability to enjoy a reasonable degree of security requires that a state be certain either that it can dissuade other states from attacking it or that it can successfully defend itself if attacked. A concern for security immediately gives rise to a focus on the military power the state has relative to that of others. In a condition of *anarchy, therefore, the pursuit of security requires that states be watchful about both the balance of military power that obtains among them and the intentions of other states.

The concern for relative power is best illustrated by what is probably the oldest, and many say still the best, book on international politics—*Thucydides' The Peloponnesian Wars. Thucydides saw the root cause of the Peloponnesian Wars to be the growing power of Athens relative to that of Sparta and the danger which that growing imbalance posed to the security of Sparta. If Sparta allowed Athenian power to grow too great, Sparta would be at risk because Athens could have attacked and defeated her. Even if not attacked by Athens, its growing power, if left unchecked, could intimidate Sparta because Athens could threaten to attack and destroy Sparta whenever Athens chose. If the imbalance of power grew too great, Athens could have easily defeated Sparta and could simply threaten to do so in order to bend Sparta to its will. What was thus at stake for Sparta, if Athenian power grew too great, was not simply safety from military attack but also the protection of Sparta's moral values, its way of life, and the material prosperity of its citizens. In this sense, Sparta's security was not an end in itself; rather, what was at stake were all the things that being physically secure from attack enables a state to enjoy.

The case of Athens and Sparta demonstrates that a concern for security must ultimately focus on the potential physical danger to a state that is posed by imbalances in military power. But the case also shows why a concern for security cannot be restricted simply to military power. A state fashions the military power it deploys from many elements: the economic wealth of a nation, the quality of its political leadership, the cohesiveness of the polity, the motivation of the citizenry, the nature of its military leadership, its access to food and raw materials, and so on. It was the growth in Athenian wealth and financial and naval power, together with the democratic nature of Athens, that enabled Athens to deploy an ever-more-threatening military force. Athens was a more dynamic society than Sparta, and that was reflected in the growth of its overall power. At the end of the day, security demands military power sufficient to dissuade or defeat an attack; but so many nonmilitary elements are required to gen-

erate effective military power that a concern for security can never be restricted solely to the final military end product.

Taken together, these two factors—the nonmilitary elements required to fashion an effective military instrument and the subjective nature of security—demonstrate why security has been such an ambiguous and elastic term. Not only is there a large degree of variability in what makes individuals and states feel secure; there are also many elements required to fashion an effective military instrument. Both factors explain why states historically have never restricted their security purview simply to their armies. In the name of security, great empires have been founded and relentlessly expanded, hegemonic wars have been waged, economic self-sufficiency has been sought after, crushing armaments races have been entered into, innumerable interventions into the affairs of other states have been undertaken, alliances have been formed and broken, and great religious and ideological crusades have been launched.

For example, in the nineteenth century, Britain developed a huge empire in northeast Africa in order to protect its sea route to India that ran through Egypt via the Suez Canal, all in the name of protecting the security of the British Isles and its overseas empire. In the twentieth century, Japan annexed Korea, conquered Manchuria, waged war against China, conquered Southeast Asia and the Dutch East Indies, all in the name of creating an autarkic "Greater East Asia Co-Prosperity Sphere" that would make her secure against external threats. In the post–World War II era, the Soviet Union conquered and ruled for forty-five years Eastern and Central Europe in the name of security against another attack from the West; and the United States waged two land wars in Asia—in Korea and Vietnam—in the name of security for itself and its allies against Communism. Finally, the United States and the Soviet Union developed nuclear arsenals of tens of thousands of warheads each, all in the name of making each secure against nuclear attack by the other. In the grand sweep of history, almost the entire range of state behavior has been, in one way or another, justified in the name of security.

In the contemporary world, security has come to include two additional elements. The first involves protection of the environment from irreversible degradation by combating, among other things, acid rain, desertification, forest destruction, ozone pollution, and global warming. In a world in which environmental degradation crosses national borders with abandon, environmental security has impelled states to find cooperative rather than competitive solutions. The second element has to do with the revival of the UN and the brighter prospects for collective security. The end of the *Cold War has brought an end to the paralysis of the UN and has cleared the way for the institution to develop beyond its traditional peacekeeping role to a war-deterring one. Rather than simply sending troops and inserting them between two warring parties that have agreed to cease fighting (its peacekeeping role), many hope the UN can now create a standing military force to threaten, and punish if necessary, potential aggressors in order to stop aggression in the first place (its war-deterring or aggression-punishing role). If its collective security role worked well, its peacekeeping role would diminish dramatically.

Viewed in analytical and historical perspective, security is an all-encompassing concept. It is inevitable that it be so because of both its subjective nature and the varied elements that make it up.

(See also ALLIANCE; BALANCE OF POWER; DETERRENCE; ENVIRONMENTALISM; FORCE, USE OF; INTERNATIONAL RELATIONS; UNITED NATIONS.)

Arnold Wolfers, *Discord and Collaboration* (Baltimore, Md., 1962). Robert Jervis, *Perception and Misperception in International Politics* (Princeton, N.J., 1976). Robert Gilpin, *War and Change in World Politics* (Cambridge, U.K., 1981). Barry Buzan, *People, States and Fear* (Chapel Hill, N.C., 1983).

ROBERT J. ART

SECURITY COUNCIL. The Security Council of the *United Nations has primary responsibility under the UN Charter for the maintenance of international *peace and *security. During the first forty five years of its existence, the council was largely paralyzed by the *Cold War, but since 1990 and the thawing of the global political climate, it has been very active.

The Security Council is composed of fifteen UN member states, five of which are permanent members—United States, United Kingdom, France, the Russian Federation, and China. The permanent members have the power to veto a substantive decision of the council by voting against it. The veto is cast much less often now than it was during the Cold War, but it is still very much in use as a threat which blocks council action.

The other ten members of the council are elected by the General Assembly to two-year nonrenewable terms, with five new members elected each year. The ten elected members, known in Charter language as "nonpermanent members," are selected according to a distribution formula from each of the world's major regions.

The Security Council meets formally in both private and public sessions. The meetings normally take place in the Security Council Chamber at UN headquarters in New York, and there the council votes on resolutions and conducts other official business. The Security Council will meet occasionally in private sessions, mainly to decide on its recommendation of a candidate for the position of the UN secretary-general. Since 1990 the council has conducted most of its business in private "consultations" (informal, off-the-record meetings) which are held on most weekdays during the year. Meetings are chaired by the powerful president, an office that rotates each month on an alphabetical basis among the council's membership.

In addition to recommending to the General Assembly for a final decision the name of new secretaries-general, the council also recommends to the assembly the admission of states as new members of the UN. The council elects judges to the *International Court of Justice, jointly with the General Assembly. In the key area of peace and security, it performs three main functions. It assists in the peaceful settlement of disputes. It establishes and oversees UN peacekeeping forces. And it takes enforcement measures against recalcitrant states or other parties.

Acting under Chapter VI of the Charter, the council "shall, when it deems necessary, call upon the parties" to a dispute to settle it by peaceful means such as negotiation, mediation, conciliation, arbitration, or judicial settlement (Article 33). And it may, if all the parties to a dispute request, make recommendations to the parties with a view to a peaceful settlement (Article 38). In practice, the council often asks the secretary-general or one of his or her special representatives to mediate or negotiate under guidelines the council has established. Increasingly the council members themselves have travelled to conflict areas in an effort to negotiate settlements directly or to mediate conflicts.

Though the first UN peacekeeping force was established by the General Assembly, all subsequent forces have been established by the Security Council, which exercises authority and command over them. The council delegates to the secretary-general its powers to organize and to exercise command and control over the force, but it maintains close management and oversight over the operations—too much so in the view of many Secretariat officials and military commanders. Though the Charter does not expressly give the council any powers to establish or operate peacekeeping forces, the International Court of Justice in a 1962 case found that the council has an implied power for these purposes.

Peacekeeping forces are usually deployed by the council only after cease-fires have been agreed upon, so the peacekeepers are only lightly armed—unlike an army (military enforcement force) fighting an opposing force. In the post–Cold War period, with greater consensus among its members, the council has established far more peacekeeping operations than in the past. At a peak in the mid-1990s there were over seventy thousand peacekeepers deployed worldwide. Some large and complex operations include not only soldiers but also civilian police, election monitors, de-mining and demobilization experts, and civilian administrative personnel.

The Security Council may also take enforcement measures which are more robust than peacekeeping. These enforcement powers are contained in Chapter VII of the Charter, which authorizes the council to determine when a threat to, or breach of, the peace has occurred, and authorizes it among other things to impose economic and military sanctions against a state or other parties.

The "peace" referred to in Article 39 may involve conflicts other than those between states. At the time the Charter was established, it was envisaged that conflicts within the borders of a state could also constitute a threat to or breach of the peace, and thus that the council could order the use of enforcement measures. The council has broadened its definition of these cases over time, so that gross violations of *human rights may now be seen as a threat to the peace, as was the case with the *genocide in *Rwanda.

In exercising its enforcement powers, the Security Council has imposed economic *santions against a number of states and other parties. The great majority of these sanction regimes have been imposed in the post–Cold War period. The council imposed general trade sanction against Iraq in 1990, but since then the council has preferred to imposed more "targeted" sanctions such as arms embargoes, travel restrictions, the freezing of overseas bank accounts, restrictions on diplomatic relations, and bans on key commodities like petroleum and diamonds.

Under Article 42 of the Charter, the Security Council has the power to order the use of *force to maintain or restore peace and security. However, the collective use of force as a military sanction does not operate in the way intended. It was originally envisaged that states would conclude agreements with the UN that would enable the council to require troop contributions to a UN force that would carry out military enforcement operations. Due to the Cold War this procedure was not implemented, and more recently there has not been the political will to return to the original intentions of the Charter.

Nonetheless the Security Council has delegated its Chapter VII powers to member states who volunteer their forces to carry out the enforcement action. These delegations of power include a delegation of a power of command and control over such forces, usually to those volunteering. Recently, the council has delegated its enforcement powers to the *North Atlantic Treaty Organization (NATO) in certain Balkan conflicts, to a force assembled by the *Economic Community of West African States in Liberia, and to a multinational force led by Australia in East Timor. These are sometimes referred to as "coalitions of the willing." The best-known case is the coalition led by the United States, assembled under Resolution 678, in response to Iraq's invasion of Kuwait in 1990.

The council has delegated its Chapter VII powers to members states for the attainment of various objectives, including to counter a use of force, to carry out a naval interdiction against a state, to achieve humanitarian objectives, to protect UN-declared "safe areas," and to ensure implementation of a peace agreement. So long as there is no political will to provide the UN with a standing force, such delegations in the face of urgent crises are likely to continue.

States and nonstate actors have made a wide variety of proposals concerning potential reform of the work, size, and composition of the Security Council. Concerning size and composition, the General Assembly adopted resolution 48/26 in 1993, which established an Open-Ended Working Group to "consider all aspects of the question of increase in the membership of the Security Council." The *nonpermanent* membership of the Security Council has already been enlarged once in 1965 from six to its present ten. However, any change in the membership of the Security Council requires an amendment of the Charter, which can only take place with the consent of "all the permanent members." As such, it is highly unlikely that any formal changes concerning membership of the *permanent members* or their veto powers will be adopted.

(See also BOSNIAN WAR; GULF WAR; HUMANITARIAN INTERVENTION; KOSOVO WAR; RWANDAN GENOCIDE.)

Sydney D. Bailey and Sam Daws, *The Procedure of the UN Security Council*, 3d ed. (Oxford, 1998). David M. Malone, *Decision-Making in the UN Security Council* (Oxford, 1998). Danesh Sarooshi, *The United Nations and the Development of Collective Security: The Delegation by the UN Security Council of Its Chapter VII Powers* (Oxford, 1999).

DANESH D. SAROOSHI

SECURITY DILEMMA. The term *security dilemma* appears to have been coined by John Herz ("Idealist Internationalism and the Security Dilemma" *World Politics* 2 [January 1950]: 157–180). He referred to the condition in a "self-help" anarchic society (one without government or superordinate authority) in which groups or individuals, striving to attain *security from attack, "are driven to acquire more and more power to escape the impact of the power of others." Insecurity among the others increases, and this motivates stepped-up preparations: the "vicious circle of security and power accumulation is on." *International relations is in most respects an anarchic society, and the security dilemma is often credited as the source of *arms races and the escalation of diplomatic crises into *war, even though neither of the adversary states may have aggressive intentions toward the other.

The security dilemma operates only under particular conditions of international relations. It stems primarily from leaders' perceptions of the military circumstances, specifically whether the offense has substantial advantages over the defense and whether defensive capabilities can be distinguished from offensive ones. Geographically, mountains and bodies of water (e.g., the situations of Switzerland and Britain) facilitate defense and ease the security dilemma; plains (e.g., the western region of the former Soviet Union) exacerbate it. Technologically, strong land fortifications ease the security dilemma, and highly accurate but vulnerable *nuclear weapons exacerbate it.

In 1914 most military and civilian commanders thought that the extant technology favored an offense which could mobilize and move rapidly; these expectations contributed to rapid competitive mobilizations and war even among those who in principle preferred peace. Offensive and defensive strategies thus could not easily be distinguished. Ironically, the course of the war soon showed that perceptions of the strategic circumstances were erroneous, and that trench warfare favored the defense. Perceptions of the adversary's hostile intent and of changing strategic circumstances can also aggravate the security dilemma. German leaders in 1914 perceived a certain "window of opportunity" before expansion of the French army and modernization of the Russian army were consolidated, after which their own security dilemma would be aggravated.

Neither threats nor concessions are likely to ease a security dilemma. Threats will enhance the adversary's sense of insecurity; concessions will probably enhance one's own. Changes of strategic postures and weapons procurement in favor of the defense can help, as can better means to monitor the adversary's intentions and capabilities—if the adversary likewise has largely defensive aims. *Arms control agreements that provide for the destruction of vulnerable "first-strike" weapons, the provision of demilitarized buffer zones, and inspection procedures are helpful. The dissolution of the Soviet Union and the *Warsaw Treaty Organization have considerably eased the security dilemma in Europe. So too have arms control and *disarmament agreements to reduce offensive forces, and agreements for prior notification of maneuvers and exchange of information in crisis.

(See also ANARCHY.)

Robert Jervis, "Cooperation under the Security Dilemma" *World Politics* 30 (July 1978): 167–212.

BRUCE RUSSETT

SELF-DETERMINATION. Self-determination is the right of cohesive national groups, or "peoples," to choose their own form of political organization, free of external domination. The concept encompasses a spectrum of *rights, including independent statehood, association with other groups in a federal state, and other forms of autonomy short of independence.

The idea of self-determination as an organizing principle for the claims and actions of aggrieved nations, peoples, or groups within nations first appeared in the Enlightenment. Its emergence was connected to, if not directly caused by, the appearance of the modern European nation-state (the "Westphalian State") beginning in the middle of the seventeenth century. Self-determination achieved greater prominence and wider recognition as a political-philosophical concept following World War I when Woodrow Wilson proclaimed it to be a universal guiding principle, even as his own secretary of state, Robert Lansing, lamented its proclamation. Lansing described it as a dangerous idea, being fearful that its exercise would result in political fallout and bloodshed in empires where peace and stability formerly had been imposed by central control. The tragic conflicts in the subregions of former *Yugoslavia illustrate the scenario that Lansing feared.

There is a vast literature on the subject of self-determination both as a political concept and, in recent years, as a legal right. Some of the key issues dealt with in this literature include: (1) the scope of the right to self-determination, (2) the recognition of ethnic groups, (3) the intervention of other countries, and (4) the tension between maintaining a balance between the stability and integrity of nation-states and the exercise of democratic rights and freedoms of peoples who have been historically placed under the control of others. The growth of the literature on self-determination is related to the ebb and flow of dominations of nations by other nations or a dominant class within a state. Historically such domination has tended to continue in the face of resistance, provoking revolt by oppressed groups until the conflict is resolved in the victory of the resisting nation or group.

More recently, the development of an *international law of *human rights has helped to sharpen the focus on self-determination as a legal right. While some jurists have argued that the right to self-determination could be considered *jus cogens*, it is certain that self-determination is now considered a human right under international law. (*See* International Covenant on Economic, Social, and Cultural Rights, Dec. 16, 1966, 993 U.N.T.S.3; Internation Covenant on Civil and Political Rights, loc cit. 171. Article 1 of each covenant provides: "All peoples have the right of self-determination. By virtue of that right, they freely determine their political status and freely pursue their economic, social, and cultural development.")

Attempts have also been made to extend the concept of self-determination from the purely political sphere to include economic and social issues as well. In today's democratic era, the concept of self-determination offers a great opportunity to peoples who aspire to have a full measure of autonomy to exercise their democratic rights in different political arrangements. But political autonomy—or independence—is not sufficient for the realization of the full benefits of democracy, as many developing nations found out following the era of decolonization in the 1960s and 1970s. These nations found that their political independence was gravely compromised because their economies were dependent on the markets of developed nations of Europe and North America. Indeed, economic self-determination has been used as a rallying cry by developing nations in their quest for fair trade and increased control over their economic resources.

Given that the idea of self-determination is associated with the notion of progress, a nagging question remains: to the extent that self-determination results in the breakup of large units into smaller ones and is typically accompanied by bitter warfare, exemplified by the crises in the former Soviet Union and Yugoslavia, how can such a condition be associated with progress? At a time when the world is witnessing an ugly form of nationalism which has been the driving force behind the tragedy in the Balkan region, should we not make a distinction between a form of nationalism that demands "ethnic cleansing," as happened in Bosnia-Herzegovina and Kosovo, and one which simply demands separation from a former empire, as in Chechnya and Eritrea? What criteria do we apply in making such a distinction? The requirements made in international legal instruments, such as the ones cited above, are good first principles with which to start. However, the refinement of mechanisms and institutions for putting into practice these principles awaits further action by the world community.

(See also BOSNIAN WAR; KOSOVO WAR.)

Richard Falk et al., "Are Indigenous Peoples Entitled to International and Juridical Personality?" in *Proceedings of the American Society of International Law*, 79 (Washington, D.C., 1986), 189–208. Antonio Cassese, ed., *Self-Determination of Peoples: A Legal Reappraisal* (Cambridge, U.K., 1995).

PEREKET HABLTE SELASSIE

SELF-MANAGEMENT. See INDUSTRIAL DEMOCRACY; WORKERS' CONTROL.

SENEGAL. Small in size (approximately 76,000 sq. mi.; 197,000 sq. km.) as well as in population (8 million people), Senegal is a peasant-dominated society overwhelmed by problems of poverty and illiteracy. It is notable for having been able to maintain a multiparty system—a rarity in Africa until recently.

Senegal borders on both the Sahara desert and the Atlantic Ocean. Because of the early advent of *Islam, most Senegalese are Muslims (83 percent), and Muslim religious leaders, called Marabouts, play an important role in the political process. Although the Marabouts do not make policy, and attempts to build an Islamic party have failed, the support of the Marabouts is essential to the stability and even the viability of any government.

Senegal also has had long and continuous contact with Europe by way of the Atlantic, particularly since the country was a French colony from 1850 to 1960. As early as 1879, the residents of the major cities along the coast (Dakar, Gorée, Rufisque, and Saint Louis) were granted French *citizenship and were allowed to elect their own mayors and municipal councils and a representative to the Chamber of Deputies in Paris. After World War II, voting privileges and rights of free association were extended throughout the country. Through this process, the Senegalese acquired the habit of political debate and the skills of political mobilization, organization, and management.

Civic understanding of modern politics and the existence of a turbulent intellectual and commercial bourgeoisie explain why the Senegalese avoided the *authoritarianism that appeared elsewhere in Africa. After a brief period of de facto one-party rule following independence, Senegal's domestic political history has been pluralistic: from four parties between 1974 and 1981, Senegal has over a dozen political parties competing at the local, regional, and national levels. The system cuts across ethnic and religious lines and offers choices across the ideological spectrum. Moreover, the electoral system of proportional representation encourages the representation of diverse interests.

The recent history of the country indicates that these achievements are not enough and that sustained economic progress is critical to containing growing frustrations. When Abdou Diouf came to power in 1981 following the voluntary resignation of President Léopold Sédar Senghor, he inherited an economy in disarray. A series of severe droughts, declining prices of the nation's major exports—peanuts and phosphates—poor management of an oversized public sector, a rise in oil prices, and a steady population increase all served to lower the annual income of the average Senegalese. The decline of the rural economy fueled a rural exodus, swelling the slums of Dakar, the capital, and exacerbating existing problems.

Diouf responded to these critical problems by attempting to rewrite the post-independence social contract between the government and the population. With the help of the *International Monetary Fund and the *World Bank, he launched an economic recovery program designed to reduce quite radically the role of the government in the allocation of resources. This resulted in a substantial reduction of the bureaucracy, a gradual erosion of subsidies on foodstuffs, and an increased role for the private sector.

Economic housecleaning has not been painless, especially in urban areas. Furthermore, national income has been inadequate to repay the country's burdensome debts. Servicing of the debt continues to absorb a large portion of export earnings. In addition, the gap between the government, composed mostly of technocrats, and the rest of the population has increased, severing the link that had been maintained in the past by the populist regional leaders who had held positions in both the government and the ruling party.

The erosion of domestic support for the government, however, has had little effect on the prestige of Senegal abroad and its influence in international organizations and meetings. Before the wave of democratization across Africa in the 1990s, this influence remained relatively strong because Senegal was unusual—a multiparty *democracy in Africa—and a voice of moderation in such bodies as the *Organization of Africa Unity and the UN.

At home, the violent struggle for autonomy in the Casamance region continued to challenge Senegal's image as a stable democracy, and growing economic hardships in urban areas provided opposition parties the opportunity to mobilize support against the Diouf regime and in support of *sopi* or change. After four unsuccessful attempts as a challenger in the presidential election, Abdoulaye Wade finally made it in February 2000, by defeating Diouf in a presidential election judged free and fair by impartial observers. A major determinant of this victory, and a lesson of political maturity that the Senegalese opposition offers to the rest of Africa, was that the major opposition parties united behind a single candidate against the incumbent president. The Senegalese opposition succeeded where divided oppositions had failed elsewhere, particularly in Cameroun, Kenya, and Togo.

(See also FRANCOPHONE AFRICA.)

Donal Cruise O'Brien, *Saints and Politicians: Essays on the Organizations of a Senegalese Peasant Society* (London, 1975). Sheldon Geller, *Senegal: An African Nation between Islam and the West* (Boulder, Colo., 1982). Robert Fatton, *The Making of a Liberal Democracy: Senegal's Passive Revolution 1975–1985* (Boulder, Colo., 1987). Catherine Boone, *Merchant Capital and the Roots of State Power in Senegal, 1930–1985* (Cambridge, U.K., 1992).

SAMBA KA

SEPARATION OF POWERS is the constitutional doctrine that requires the partial or complete assignment of executive, legislative, and judicial powers to separate branches of government, provides for different means of selecting their officers, prohibits them from serving simultaneously in more than one branch, and provides each branch with sufficient checks and balances to prevent usurpation of power by the others. *Sovereignty resides in the people and no branch may claim to possess a monopoly of the sovereign powers.

Although the Greek *polis* and the Roman Republic had separate institutions, these were instituted for mixed government—the representation of different classes. The doctrine of separation of powers was developed by the French philosopher Baron de Montesquieu, author of *The Spirit of the Laws* (1748), who argued that if those who made the laws also executed them, or if those who executed the laws controlled the courts, the result would be tyranny. Only states that separated powers and placed them in different hands could remain free. Earlier the three-way division of powers (executive, legislative, and federative, meaning diplomatic) had been developed by the English political theorist John Locke in his *Second Treatise of Government* (1690).

In 1788 James Madison observed that the new U.S. Constitution (which does not contain a distributing clause) embodied partial rather than complete separation of powers. He argued in *Federalist* 51 that if Congress were to exercise all legislative powers, the other departments of government would be drawn into its "vortex." To prevent this Madison and others divided the legislative power (bicameralism) and instituted the partial separation scheme, so that the powers of the executive and judiciary would overlap with that of Congress. Thus, for example, the president recommends laws for congressional consideration; the Senate advises and consents to treaties and appointments; the president possesses a pardon power; the House impeaches and the Senate tries the case. Courts will generally uphold a law against a contrary executive order or an executive agreement concluded with another government. The Supreme Court has struck down laws that provide Congress with appointment powers to federal regulatory agencies, and removal powers over officers of the *United States, and it has ruled unconstitutional delegation of budgetary powers involving sequesters to a congressional agency. It has also ruled that the "legislative veto" of presidential or administration actions is unconstitutional unless the congressional veto resolution is passed by both chambers and submitted to the president for his approval or constitutional veto. The judiciary will not take jurisdiction over cases if Congress provides that judicial decisions are subject to revision by the legislature or reviewable by executive officials who would carry it out.

True separation of powers exists only when each institution has the constitutional power and informal authority to retain its independence from the others. In totalitarian systems there are three branches of government, but they are all under control of a single party and its ruling council. Similarly, some military regimes in developing nations place the branches of government under a military council.

In democratic political systems the major issue is not tyranny but effective and accountable governance. Separation of powers can lead to long periods of gridlock and buck-passing, punctuated by occasional periods of effective presidential leadership. In national emergencies the executive may rely on unilateral assertions of power, such as the use of an expanded conception of constitutional prerogative in the United States used by Jackson, Lincoln, and Franklin Roosevelt, the use of presidential ukase in Russia by Yeltsin, or the institution of martial rule and emergency powers.

(See also CONGRESS, U.S.; PRESIDENCY, U.S.; SUPREME COURT OF THE UNITED STATES.)

W. B. Gwyn, *The Meaning of the Separation of Powers* (New Orleans, 1965).

RICHARD M. PIOUS

SERBIA AND MONTENEGRO are two ancient South Slavic principalities that were internationally recognized as independent at the Congress of Berlin (1878) and later united within the two Yugoslav states (1918–1991); they are currently the remaining units of rump *Yugoslavia—the Federal Republic of Yugoslavia (SRJ). Serbia reached its zenith under the Nemanjić dynasty that reigned over a sovereign Serbian principality from the end of the twelfth century, then a kingdom (1217–1346), and finally an empire (1346–1371). After the Nemanjićes, the state disintegrated into a bevy of princely states, some of them vassals of the expanding Ottoman Turks, who subjoined Serbia in 1389, but permitted the vassal Serbian Despotate until its complete incorporation within the Ottoman Empire in 1459.

Montenegro (Black Mountain) is a fifteenth-century Venetian name for a fragment of the medieval Slavic principality of Dioclia (Duklja), which in the tenth century constituted the hinterland from the eastern shores of the Bay of Kotor to the estuary of the Drin River. In 1043, Byzantium recognized the sovereignty of this principality, under the new name of Zeta. From 1183 to 1186 Zeta was conquered by Nemanjić Serbia and remained within the Serbian state until its crumbling in the fourteenth century. Various princely rulers held on against—or colluded with—the Ottomans until 1496, when Montenegro became a part of the Ottoman Empire. From the seventeenth century on, the Montenegrin tribes increasingly wrested self-rule from the Turks and, from the beginning of the eighteenth century, became virtually independent under the Petrović dynasty. Likewise, Serbia regained its autonomy in the early nineteeth-century uprisings, led alternately by the Karadjordjević and Obrenović families, which became princely in the course of insurgency.

After the First World War, during which both countries were occupied by the Central Powers, Serbia subjoined Montenegro within Yugoslavia, which Serbia effectively dominated, and dethroned the Petrović dynasty—a fate shared by no other royal family on the Allied side. During the interwar period both lands were divided in attitudes toward the Belgrade regimes, which were opposed as retrograde and domineering by the political left and the nationalist opposition. The Communist movement became very strong in Montene-

gro, which was an important Partisan base in the Second World War. After 1941, most of Serbia was occupied by the Germans, who established a puppet Serbian administration. Montenegro was occupied by the Italians, who had no time to create a dependent authority, Montenegro having quickly become a cauldron of civil war between the Serb-nationalist Chetniks and Communist Partisans. In the course of the war, the Communists triumphed over the Chetniks and thereby prevented the revival of the old monarchist, Serb-dominated system. The Serbian dynasty was dethroned, Serbia and Montenegro having become two federal republics in the six-unit socialist federation. The modern borders of the two republics were fixed in 1945, Serbia having two autonomous units—Vojvodina and Kosovo, the latter predominantly Albanian—within its federal territory.

The Communists promoted separate Montenegrin identity, which was considered an anti-Serb measure by the Serbian nationalist forces. The question of Montenegrin identity had significant political consequences and became an issue in the growing Serbian alienation with *Tito's federalist system during the 1980s. Slobodan Milošević's movement of the 1980s, which was fired by resentment over Kosovar Albanian autonomy, had a signiftcant following among the pro-Serbian Montenegrins, who overthrew the anti-Milošević Communist leadership in 1989, precisely when Kosovo, too, lost its autonomy. From 1989 to 1997, as Milošević strengthened his hold over Serbia, presiding over a phony transition in which Milošević's Communist supporters transformed themselves into nationalist Socialists, Montenegro marched with Milošević. As a result, Montenegro, too, was involved in Milošević's war efforts against *Croatia and Bosnia.

Since 1997, when the autonomist premier Milo Djukanović won the presidential election in Montenegro, the Montenegrin leadership has been steadily at odds with Milošević. It did not support Milošević's brinkmanship over Kosovo in the spring of 1999 and thereby escaped the brunt of *North Atlantic Treaty Organization (NATO) air attacks, which were initiated after failed negotiations over the Kosovo issue. Milošević's brutal ethnic cleansing of Kosovo's Albanian population strengthened efforts against his regime. With the NATO-led UN mission in Kosovo, which followed the Serbian withdrawal in June 1999, Milošević was steadily under attack from a variety of oppositional forces, which found an ally in Djukanović's Montenegro. In July 2000 Milošević initiated constitutional changes that effectively eliminated equality and parity between Serbia and Montenegro in the constitutional system of rump Yugoslavia. Because these changes were rejected by Montenegro, which also refused to participate in the federal elections of September 2000, a resolution between the two federal partners could well depend on force.

The population of Serbia, according to the preliminary census results in 1991, amounted to 9,791,475, of which Serbs constituted 65.65 percent, Albanians 17.23 percent, Hungarians 3.53 percent, Yugoslavs 3.25 percent, and (Bosniak) Muslims 2.42 percent. According to the same census, the population of Montenegro was 615,267, of which Montenegrins were 61.84 percent, (Bosniak) Muslims 14.62 percent, Serbs 9.29 percent, and Albanians 4.2 percent. Most religious Serbs and Montenegrins belong to the Serbian Orthodox Church, but during the 1990s an autocephalous—and canonically unrecognized—Montenegrin Orthodox Church has been making headway among pro-independence Montenegrins. Industrial installations of Serbia were seriously damaged in the NATO campaign of 1999. Both Serbia and Montenegro are still predominantly rural, the north of Serbia proper and Vojvodina being the centers of cereal production.

(See also BOSNIA AND HERZEGOVINA; BOSNIAN WAR; KOSOVO WAR; MACEDONIA; SLOVENIA.)

Laura Silber and Allan Little, *The Death of Yugoslavia* (London, 1995). Tim Judah, *The Serbs: History, Myth and the Destruction of Yugoslavia* (New Haven, Conn., and London, 1997).

IVO BANAC

SEYCHELLES. See INDIAN OCEAN REGION.

SHARĪ'A. The generic term for Islamic law, sharī'a is to be distinguished from *fiqh*, jurisprudence, and from *qānūn*, which refers to law as statute and as legal rules in actual operation in the contemporary *Middle East. Strictly speaking, the sharī'a derives from two written sources: the Quran, the Book revealed to the Prophet Muhammad in the sixth century C.E., and the *sunna*, which is the compilation of the words and deeds of the Prophet. In actual fact, the sharī'a was formed in later centuries through arduous and systematic scholarship, developed by jurists of competing schools. Although formally based on the Quran and the *sunna*, the sharī'a generated a logic of its own as jurists had to articulate a system with internal coherence, responsive to social interests, needs, and customs.

As late as the 1970s, scholars of the contemporary sharī'a described it as being an ever more restricted domain of the law, confined essentially to matrimonial and inheritance jurisprudence. But with the advent of the Islamic revolution in Iran in 1979, traditional Islamic jurists (known as the *Āyāt Allāhs*) took over the Iranian state and sought to establish the rule of Islamic law in all walks of life. At the same time, the leaders of neighboring Pakistan tried to introduce strict sharī'a rules, while political *Islam all over the Muslim world called for the comprehensive and strict implementation of Islamic law.

In this context, the sharī'a became significant on two levels. First, because of a tradition which was rich with more than ten centuries of sophisticated writings, the sharī'a came to be associated politically with the quintessence of Islam, and the projected Islamic state was defined as a state ruled by the sharī'a. The sharī'a therefore served as the rallying point of Islamic forces across the Muslim world, even in the more conservative states like Saudi Arabia and Jordan.

Second, although the content of this Islamization was vague, significant efforts were exerted to expand the application of the sharī'a from the restricted areas of family law to wider legal subjects. Chief among these were constitutional and economic law. In the first case, the Iranian constitution became the model for governmental institutions. In economic law, the two most urgent areas for the adaptation of the sharī'a were the regulation of the production and distribution of goods in the light of a reconstruction of legal precedents, and the conception and establishment of an Islamic banking system in which interest would be banned. Various efforts in these fields have met with only mixed results, but the sway of the sharī'a has nonetheless been significantly extended.

(See also RELIGION AND POLITICS.)

Noel Coulson, *A History of Islamic Law* (Edinburgh, 1964). Joseph Schacht, *Introduction to Islamic Law* (Oxford, 1964). Norman Anderson, *Law Reform in the Muslim World* (London, 1976). Chibli Mallat, ed., *Islamic Law and Finance* (London, 1988). Chibli Mallat and Jane Connors, eds., *Islamic Family Law* (London 1990). Chibli Mallat, *The Renaissance of Islamic Law* (Cambridge, U.K., in press).

CHIBLI MALLAT

SIERRA LEONE. Contemporary Sierra Leone is a product of its history as a haven from conflicts in Africa and from slavery in the Americas; the legacies of colonialism; the economic imperatives of a mining and agricultural economy; its patrimonial internal politics since independence in 1961; and now a war that has dragged on since 1991.

The political fabric of Sierra Leone is woven from many traditions, including the legacies of indigenous political systems, some based on personal rule of powerful warriors, others that involved significant public participation in choosing leaders. There remains a remarkable degree of consensus about democratic norms among the people of Sierra Leone. It has its origins in many precolonial societies in Sierra Leone, as well as in the small settlement of returned Africans who came in 1787 to set up a self-governing "Land of Freedom." During British colonial rule a Legislative Council was appointed (1862), elections held in Freetown and surrounding villages from 1895, and the limited franchise in the colony (1924) was extended to the interior in 1957.

Competitive elections began in 1951 and a pattern of largely free and open election was established by independence in 1961 under the first prime minister, Milton Margai. Elections in 1967 saw the victory of the opposition All People's Congress (APC) over the governing Sierra Leone People's Party (SLPP) in one of the few elections in Africa by that time to see an opposition party win. That victory was brief owing to a coup which ushered in a year of military rule after which Siaka Stevens and the APC were returned to power. In 1985 Joseph Momoh was elected president in a one-party election.

The invasion of the Revolutionary United Front (RUF) and the National Patriotic Front of Liberia (NPLF) on 23 March 1991 added the problems of war to a faltering economy fed by political weakness, corruption, elite conflict, and ethnicity. By late 1991 about one-third of the country was under their control. On 29 April 1992, a coup overthrew the government of President Joseph Momoh and brought to power the National Provisional Ruling Council (NPRC). That was followed by another coup in January 1996 by soldiers promising peace and a return to civilian rule. In February and March 1996 multiparty elections were held, although much of the nation was inaccessible because of the fighting. Nearly 50 percent of the 1.6 million registered voters participated. Thirteen parties took part in the elections with five gaining seats in parliament. On 29 March 1996, the leader of the SLPP, Ahmed Tejan Kabbah, was sworn in as president.

On 25 May 1997, President Kabbah was overthrown by elements of the Sierra Leone army led by some members of the former NPRC regime working with forces of the ROF. They established the Armed Forces Revolutionary Council (AFRC).

Their claim to power was tenuous; they were not recognized by most of the international community. Following skirmishes between the AFRC's forces and Economic Community of West African States Monitoring Group (ECOMOG) troops, an offensive against the AFRC began in February 1998. After a nine-day battle the Nigerian-led forces took control of Freetown, ousting the AFRC. The government of President Ahmad Tejan Kabbah was reestablished on 10 March 1998. In late 1998 parts of Freetown were captured and destroyed by rebel forces. Although pushed out of the capital, they remain in control of much of the rest of the country. The Nigerian ECOMOG troop levels were increased to 16,000 to facilitate the war against the AFRC and RUF.

By mid-1999 the UN and relief agencies estimated there were 500,000 *refugees in the Freetown area and at least 350,000 refugees outside the country. The total number of refugees since the invasion in 1991 is over one million. Between 30,000 and 50,000 people have been killed.

About 70 percent of the 4.5 million population, living in Sierra Leone's 71,740 square miles (185,806 sq. km.), are normally in agriculture, producing one-third of the GDP. Both the agricultural and mining economy were virtually destroyed by 1999. Sierra Leone had been the second largest producer of rutile, which provided 57 percent of the country's mineral exports in 1993; by 1995 rutile production ceased. In 1994, diamond exports fell from two million carats in 1970 to 400,000. By 1998 the legal diamond trade stopped. Real GDP fell 10 percent in 1995 and has continued to fall. Total public debt increased tenfold by 1987 to more than 50 percent of GNP. By 1995 it was $1 billion or 108 percent of GDP.

Despite its early lead in education, including Fourah Bay College (1827), literacy is now less than 15 percent and the once-outstanding education system has nearly collapsed. In 1998 about 55 percent of children of school age were out of school because of the war. Sierra Leone has the highest rate of death in childbirth of those reported, with 1,800 deaths per 100,000 versus eight for the United States.

Since the war began Sierra Leone has been largely ignored by major world powers in spite of high levels of violence, atrocities, and the forced recruitment of children as soldiers, bearers, and sex slaves. External links remain strongest with the states in the *Economic Community of West African States (especially Nigeria, Guinea, and Ghana) and with Great Britain, China, Germany, Saudi Arabia, Canada, France, and the United States.

Among the most vocal critics of government policies are professionals, students, and the press. Ethnicity is becoming an increasingly important factor in politics. Although religion has occasionally been used as an election issue, it has not been a source of major conflict.

In January 1999 RUF forces again entered Freetown, gaining control of its Eastern and Central sectors, maiming and killing civilians, and looting and burning parts of the city. By mid-January ECOMOG forces had retaken the city. In May 1999 President Kabbah signed a cease-fire brokered by Jesse Jackson and the United States. On 7 July, 1999 President Kabbah and Foday Sankoh, head of the UF, signed a peace agreement brokered by the UN and the Organization of African Unity (OAU), under heavy U.S. pressure but strong opposition in Freetown. It provided four cabinet posts for the

RUF and made Sankoh a vice president and head of the commissioin to oversee diamond sales. The RUF was to disarm, as were government irregular troops. Nonetheless, fighting continued and Sankoh was slow to return to Freetown. In October a government of national unity was finally announced. A UN peacekeeping force of about 6,000 troops from India, Jordan, Ghana, and Nigeria arrived to monitor the agreement. In May 2000 about 500 UN peacekeepers were captured by the RUF. Sankoh fled his home in Freetown ahead of an angry mob and was captured several days later on 17 May in Freetown and jailed by the Sierra Leone government. British troops arrived to stabilize the situation, although the majority were to be withdrawn in June 2000. Most of the UN hostages were freed by the end of May but the situation remained chaotic.

The prospects for political stability in the short run are also limited by the legacies of war and the atrocities against the civilian population, committed in particular by the RUF. But RUF was not alone in attacks against civilians; atrocities were also committed by the AFRC, the Sierra Leone military, the Kamajor, local militias, thugs, and even ECOMOG. The country continues to be plagued by the struggle for power among elites who mouth the terminology of democracy but seem unable to agree to follow its rules themselves. This is ironic in a context in which survey research shows that the strength of mass democratic values is comparable to those in the United States. With the exception of Britian, Sierra Leone was abandoned and ignored by the West, which bears a great deal of responsibility for the deaths and carnage that have devastated the country. Given the history of the war and the lack of elite consensus, it will take the collective efforts of the world's major leaders to bring peace and security to Sierra Leone.

John R. Cartwright, *Politics in Sierra Leone, 1947–67* (Toronto, 1970). Fred M. Hayward and Jimmy D. Kandeh, "Perspectives on Twenty-five Years of Elections in Sierra Leone," in Fred M. Hayward, ed., *Elections in Independent Africa* (Boulder, Colo., 1987), pp. 25–59. Fred M. Hayward, "Sierra Leone: State Consolidation, Fragmentation and Decay," in Donal Cruise O'Brien, John Dunn, and Richard Rathbone, eds., *Contemporary West African States* (Cambridge, U.K:, 1989), pp. 165–180. Jimmy D. Kandeh, "Procedural Consensus, Governmental Performance and Democratic Prospects in Sierra Leone" *Journal of African Policy Studies* 1, no. 3 (1995): 245–261. Paul Richards, *Fighting for the Rain Forest: War, Youth, and Resources in Sierra Leone* (Oxford, 1996). Fred M. Hayward and Jimmy D. Kandeh, "Sierra Leone: Violence and Decay, April 1992 to March 1994" *Africa Contemporary Record* 24 (2000): B161–B185.

FRED M. HAYWARD

SINGAPORE. Singapore is a city-state, with a resident population of 3.9 million (1999) on a diamond-shaped island of 239 square miles (619 sq. km.). In addition to the main island there are 63 offshore islands, with a land area of 10.7 sq. mi. Per capita income in 1999 was approximately U.S. $21,800, which makes Singapore the ninth richest country in the world. Singaporeans' average life expectancy surpasses seventy-seven years, about the same as that of Austria or Scotland. Family planning has been very successful, and the fertility rate is 1.70. Singapore has depended on as many as 400,000 foreign workers to meet its labor needs.

Singapore's racial breakdown is: Chinese, 77.3 percent; Malay, 14.1 percent; Indian, 7.3 percent; other, 1.3 percent. Some 86 percent of Singaporeans live in government-built multi-racial housing estates. Each estate has a racial balance proportional to the national figures.

A dominant-party-state ruled by the People's Action Party (PAP) since the island achieved internal self-government in 1959, Singapore was part of Malaysia between 1963 and 1965 and became an independent country on 9 August 1965. Lee Kuan Yew served as prime minister from 1959 to 1990. He has retained a cabinet post as senior minister since second-generation PAP leaders came to power. Goh Chok Tong has been prime minister since 1990.

Singapore is a republic with a unicameral parliament. The president, originally a ceremonial head of state, was chosen by parliament for a four-year term. The first popular election for the president occurred in August 1993; the new term of office is six years. Parliament has eighty-one seats and voting is compulsory. Between 1968 and 1981 the PAP held all parliamentary seats. The PAP won seventy-seven of eighty-one seats and 61.0 percent of the popular vote in the August 1991 elections, the first elections under Prime Minister Goh Chok Tong. In the January 1997 elections the size of the parliament increased to eighty-three seats, the PAP increased its popular vote to 65 percent, and the opposition was halved to two elected members of parliament.

Final political authority resides with the elected prime minister and the cabinet. Up to three opposition candidates can be invited to become nonconstituent members of parliament (MPs) if fewer than three opposition candidates are elected. A 1990 law provides for up to six nominated MPs, distinguished persons who are supposed to be non-partisan. The single-member constituency format was modified shortly before the 1988 elections with the creation of Group Representation Constituencies (GRCs). The GRCs collapsed a majority of single-member constituencies into combined districts with at least one minority candidate on each electoral team. Voters vote for a team, not individual candidates, in GRCs. In the 1997 elections, there were fifteen GRCs (ranging from four to six members per team) and nine single seats.

The Judicial Committee (Repeal) Bill of February 1994 abolished all appeals to the Privy Council in London and established the Court of Appeal in Singapore as the final court. Judicial authority rests with the Supreme Court, the High Court, the Court of Appeal, and twenty-three subordinate courts, including a Family Court and a Juvenile Court. Judges are appointed by the president. Jury trial was abolished in 1970. Persons suspected of endangering security of the country can be detained without trial under the Internal Security Act (ISA) for renewable two-year terms. ISA detentions are non-existent today.

Singapore's meritocratic society has a highly trained, efficient, and well-paid civil service. The integrity of the civil service and politicians is ensured by the Corrupt Practices Investigation Bureau.

Singapore's political leadership gives importance to nurturing *political culture that stresses national identity, yet allows for some communal diversity. Emphasis also is on an orderly society that still allows for pluralism, such as through regular elections, the Feedback Unit, and town councils. The government emphasizes social stability and the family as the bedrock of economic development and a good society. The 1994 caning of American Michael Fay (four strokes only) brought much attention to Singapore, though corporal punishment is not uncommon in many countries. Caning is mandated for thirty offenses, including violent crimes and other crimes such as vandalism. Regulations announced in 1998 require caning and prison for hardcore drug addicts. Females and males over fifty and under sixteen and those physically unfit are exempted. Caning, more than the death penalty, is a major deterrent to violent crimes and deliberate socially disruptive behavior.

Singapore's goal is a widely accepted national culture that has a high regard for legitimate authority, educational achievement, stable families, social harmony, discipline, and stability. These objectives maximize economic development and allow individuals to make the optimum use of their lives and talents. Four core values widely discussed by government officials since 1989 are: 1) community over self; 2) the family as the basic building block of society; 3) solving major issues through consensus instead of contention; and 4) attention to religious and racial tolerance. Singaporeans have adopted much from the West, but the government wishes to exclude what it sees as negative aspects often accompanying Western culture, including illicit drugs, illegitimate births, violent crime, and blatant disregard for the environment such as littering. A 1998 survey of regular Feedback Unit respondents revealed 80 percent believed the government ran the country well and had the welfare of citizens at heart; only about one-third thought the government took criticism well or was open enough.

Since the early 1960s, Singapore has followed an unswerving commitment to *export-led growth. The first economic objectives after independence were to create political stability, attract investor confidence, and recruit *multinational corporations (MNCs). In 1960, nearly 90 percent of the manufacturing output was for domestic consumption, whereas today two-thirds of the output is exported.

The Second Industrial Revolution (SIR) was introduced in 1979. SIR was intended to encourage plant upgrading, automation, and relocation of labor-intensive industries. The government has subsequently pushed programs to make Singapore more attractive for MNC investment, particularly in terms of regional headquarters and as a servicing center. During the 1980s over half the workers in manufacturing were employed in foreign-owned firms, and more than 80 percent of direct exports came from these firms. Today, 70 percent of the GDP comes from the service sector, with just over 27 percent from the manufacturing sector.

The PAP government has basically succeeded in meeting Singaporeans' material needs. In 1998, its Current Account Surplus was US$18.1 billion, and during the past decade real GDP increased at nearly 9 percent annually, though 1999 growth, as a result of the economic meltdown in Asia, was 5.4 percent. Singapore remains heavily dependent on external economic forces to maintain its prosperity and growth. The faltering Asian economies in 1997–98 led the government to look for more markets outside Asia, specifically the European Union and North America.

Singapore's military strategy is geared toward deterrence. Defense spending is 5.5 percent of GDP. The 55,000-member Singapore Armed Forces (SAF) is a highly mobile, technologically sophisticated force with the most capable air force in the Association of Southeast Asian Nations (ASEAN). Mandatory two-year military service beginning at age eighteen or official exemption is required for employment. The SAF is externally oriented, and has a minimal internal security role.

The pillars of Singapore's foreign policy include trade with any state for mutual benefit, close cooperation with fellow ASEAN neighbors, and a nonaligned foreign policy. It has offered expanded facilities to the U.S. military. The foreign minister has applauded the stabilizing impact of the United States in Asia and has urged a continued U.S. presence.

(See also CONFUCIANISM; NEWLY INDUSTRIALIZING ECONOMIES.)

Thomas J. Bellows, *The People's Action Party of Singapore: Emergence of a Dominant Party System* (New Haven, Conn., 1970). Stella R. Quah, *Family in Singapore: Sociological Perspectives*, 2d. ed. (Singapore, 1998).
THOMAS J. BELLOWS

SINO-AMERICAN RELATIONS. With the establishment of the People's Republic of China (PRC) in 1949, China's new leaders opted for a close political-military alliance with the Soviet Union. This was soon followed in 1950 by Chinese decisions to endorse and support North Korean leader Kim Il Sung's war to unite all the Korean peninsula under Communist rule. These Chinese moves ended an earlier U.S. policy of disengaging from the Chinese civil war while courting the PRC in hopes of minimizing Soviet influence in Asia. The United States then intervened to keep Taiwan from PRC control. Over the next six decades U.S. links with Taiwan grew dense, creating a bond that was impossible to cut yet difficult to sustain in the face of PRC pressure.

During the 1950s U.S. policy sought to split the Sino-Soviet alliance. The deterioration of that alliance in the late 1950s failed to lead to an improvement in Sino-American relations, however, because of the preoccupation of both sides with the *Vietnam War combined with the revolutionary cast of Chinese domestic and international policy. Growing Soviet power finally brought China and the United States together in 1971. Over the next eighteen years Beijing and Washington worked to build a relationship transcending common fear of the Soviet Union. Economic, cultural, and political links thickened greatly with China's post-1978 policies of market-oriented reform and opening to the outside world. In the United States many people developed warm feelings about a China which seemed to be becoming "just like us."

The use of overwhelming military force by the Chinese government to crush the *Tiananmen Square pro-democracy movement in June 1989 had a deep impact on U.S. public opinion about China. Because a large international press corps had assembled in Beijing to cover Mikhail Gorbachev's watershed visit to China (the first such visit by a Soviet leader since 1959), images of the stark repression in Beijing were broadcast by television into American homes. As a result U.S. *public opinion on China took a pendulum swing as basic as those of 1937 when it swung toward China and against Japan in the Sino-Japanese war then under way, of 1950 when it dropped the sympathetic view of China as a wartime ally against Japan and turned against "Red China," and of 1972 when it was captivated by the urbanity of Chinese Premier Zhou Enlai and the apparent pro-Americanism of *Party Chairman Mao Zedong. A perennial characteristic of U.S. ties

with China has been a peculiarly emotional nature largely absent in U.S. relations with other global powers. After the sea change in U.S. opinion in June 1989 a major problem of U.S. administrations was how to maintain cordial relations with a Chinese regime deeply unpopular with the American public.

The peaceful relinquishment of power by *communist party states in Eastern and Central Europe and the Soviet Union further highlighted the antidemocratic nature of the Chinese Communist Eastern and Central regime. The dramatic disappearance of the Soviet threat removed the strategic basis of the Sino-American détente. It also removed the rationale for applying a more lenient standard to the Chinese regime than that previously applied to other *communist governments. As Chinese markets grew and opened rapidly in the 1990s, U.S. business wanted to avoid being shut out. U.S. leaders also understood the heavy political and possibly military costs that might ensue if Sino-American relations deteriorated too much. Yet efforts to cooperate with China came under attack by many in the United States as appeasement of an evil regime.

On the Chinese side, the collapse of the European communist regimes and of the near-revolution in China itself in 1989, plus American triumphalism at the Western victory in the *Cold War, led a portion of the leadership of the *Chinese Communist Party (CCP) to adopt a siege mentality. *Deng Xiaoping, in perhaps the last great battle of his eventful life, took the lead in rejecting that mentality. Deng insisted that China remain fully engaged in the global market economy despite the political risks that it entailed for the Chinese regime, and seek to avoid confrontation with the United States. The way to save CCP rule in China, Deng argued, was by continuing the economic growth that resulted from marketization and opening, not by building walls to keep out foreigners. The Party, Deng argued, could and should contain the challenges posed by marketization and opening.

By the mid-1990s the mainstream of the Chinese foreign policy elite had concluded that China's successful emergence as a great power required avoiding a collision with the United States, at least while China was still in an inferior position. Nevertheless, most of China's leaders remain deeply apprehensive of U.S. objectives and policies. They look forward to the day when America's position in the world is much reduced and China's relative position much stronger—a condition they refer to as multipolarity. They resent U.S. efforts to lead world affairs in the post–Cold War era, and reject U.S. efforts to uphold "universal standards" critical of China's human rights record. At the same time, they understand that the loss of American markets, capital, and technology could well cause China to fail to achieve its long-sought rise to the front rank of global wealth and power. They also realize that the somewhat nebulous but vitally important U.S. goodwill keeps places like Hong Kong and Taiwan stable, which is essential to China's economic modernization.

A small but politically influential minority of leaders based in the People's Liberation Army feel that China could successfully conduct a war with the United States over Taiwan at a sooner rather than a later date. These people point to fundamental asymmetries in the national purpose and will of China and the United States, concluding that China could outfight and out-suffer the United States in a conflict over

Taiwan. By striking swiftly and boldly, then enduring whatever punishment the United States could dish out, while imposing casualties and other costs on the United States, China could exhaust American will. The Americans would soon tire of the effort and agree to terms acceptable to China. China's development might be set back by a few years, but Taiwan would finally be incorporated into the PRC.

An additional element of volatility is provided by popular nationalism and anti-Americanism in China. As belief in Marxism-Leninism waned in China during the 1990s, nationalism gradually emerged to replace it. During the failed effort to win the 2000 Olympic Games for Beijing—a bid which the U.S. Congress formally opposed—China's government stumbled upon the legitimizing effects of representing national pride against an apparently insulting United States. As China achieved spectacular economic growth in the 1990s, many Chinese longed for international recognition. Confronted instead with continual U.S. criticism of China, many patriotic Chinese became resentful and sought ways to repay U.S. disrespect in kind. The explosion of vitriolic anti-U.S. demonstrations following the accidental U.S. bombing of the PRC embassy in Belgrade, Yugoslavia, in 1999 was an example of both elite manipulation and popular anti-Americanism.

On both sides of the Sino-American relationship, governments struggle to prevent domestic passions and conflicting interests over Taiwan from generating deeper conflict. As with earlier dyads of rival powers, the primary incentive for cooperation is negative—an awareness of the immense costs that might ensue if the rivalry is not cautiously and skillfully managed.

(See also CONTAINMENT; U.S. FOREIGN POLICY.)

JOHN W. GARVER

SLOVAKIA. Slovakia is a new Central European state, the product of the collapse of communism in 1989 and failure of the constitutional bargain that had brought the territory of Slovakia out of a thousand years of Hungarian rule and into *Czechoslovakia in 1918. The joining of predominantly Catholic Slovakia to the more secular, more populous, and more economically developed Czech lands never found a consensual institutional form, with many Slovaks chafing under the constraints of what came to be called "Prago-centrism." Although the enduring tensions between Czechs and Slovaks never reached the threshold of violence, conflict erupted in each period of twentieth-century state crisis. The defection of Slovak leaders to form their own short-lived wartime state under Hitler was symptomatic of that unresolved controversy, engendering a semi-sovereignty that bolstered institutional and elite development while tarnishing the idea of statehood itself. Under communism, the restored postwar Czechoslovakia was no more successful in resolving national tensions than the interwar state had been, despite an attempted federal solution sparked by the Prague Spring reforms of 1968. Ultimately, Czech and Slovak leaders following the collapse of communism once more found it impossible to agree on a democratized formulation of state institutions, creating a negotiating deadlock that led to the dissolution of the state, accepted by both republics' legislatures in the course of 1992.

Although many predicted the routinization of Slovak politics after independence liquidated chronic tensions with Prague, the politics of the 1990s were instead marked by nearly constant confrontation between three-time Prime Minister Vladimir Meciar and his opposition over his government's restrictions on media, cronyism in the *privatization process, harassment of the opposition, and intolerance of the sizable Hungarian minority, whose linguistic and educational rights were curtailed. The party system, although incorporating recognizable European partisan families such as social democracy, Christian democracy, and ethnic minority parties, remained polarized between these "standard" parties and Meciar's Movement for a Democratic Slovakia and its junior partners.

These battles left their constitutional mark; following years of strife between a president selected by parliament and the Meciar government, culminating in legislative deadlock over the legislative selection of a new president, Slovakia's parliamentary system was modified in 1998 to provide for direct presidential elections. Domestic tensions also drew sustained criticism from the West by the mid-1990s, hobbling Slovak aspirations to join the European Union and NATO after an initial period in which the country appeared headed for early membership. Economic eligibility was not a major stumbling block: communist policy had narrowed the developmental gap between the Czech and Slovak economies, and the Slovak post-communist economy continued to perform better than the East European norm despite what domestic and foreign observers criticized as its lack of transparency. Not until Meciar's democratically deficient government lost its majority in the 1998 elections, however, did Slovakia finally make progress toward European integration under a more responsive but unwieldy coalition government.

(See also CZECH REPUBLIC; NINETEEN EIGHTY-NINE; POST-COMMUNISM.)

CAROL SKALNIK LEFF

SLOVENIA. The Republic of Slovenia has been an independent country since 25 June 1991. The official language is Slovenian and, in the areas where there are Hungarian or Italian minorities, Hungarian and Italian respectively. Slovenia has a population of 1,986,989 of which 87.8 percent are ethnic Slovenians. No other single ethnicity accounts for more than 3 percent of the population. Slovenia borders Italy, Austria, Hungary, and *Croatia. Although it covers only 20,256 square meters, its landscape includes Alpine, Pannonian, and Mediterranean elements, which has allowed Slovenia to develop a tourist industry.

A distinct Slovenian national identity arose during the Protestant Reformation when the first books were published in Slovenian. Slovenians launched their first national program, *Zedinje Slovenije* (United Slovenia), in the March 1848 revolution. The first Slovenian state was established in 1918 but lasted only one month before it joined with the Kingdom of Serbs, Croats, and Slovenes. On 6 April 1941, Slovenia was occupied, divided into three zones (Italian, German, and Hungarian), and threatened with *genocide. The struggle for national liberation was organized by the Liberation Front under the leadership of the Communist Party of Slovenia, which was simultaneously conducting a socialist revolution. A number of Slovenians under the leadership of the Roman Catholic Church founded a special military unit, the Home Guard, which collaborated with the Nazis. Thus, the Second World War in Slovenia was also a civil war.

An extended period of Yugoslav socialism followed the Second World War. First, Slovenia had the status of federal republic in *Yugoslavia; then, in 1974, with the emergence of the self-management system, it became a confederation. After the death of *Tito in 1980, Yugoslavia began to disintegrate as a result of the movement for Serbian hegemony which strove to transform the Yugoslav federation of republics into a centralized Greater Serbia. Influenced by emerging national movements and demands for political pluralism, Slovenia held its first party elections in 1990. In 1991, its proclamation of independence was met by the aggression of the Yugoslav National Army, against which Slovenia prevailed during the Ten-Day War. In December 1991, Slovenia adopted its first constitution.

Slovenia is a parliamentary democracy with a combined electoral system. The Parliament is bicameral, comprised of the State Senate and the State Council. The Senate has ninety seats, two of which are reserved for representatives of the two national minorities. The ninety-seat State Council is made up of eighteen representatives of functional interests (interest groups) and twenty-two representatives of local interests. The largest parties in the Parliament are the Liberal Democrats, the Slovenian People's Party, the Social Democrats, the Christian Democrats, and the United List of Social Democrats. With class distinctions only beginning to emerge, religion shapes the single axis of party competition measured by proximity to the Roman Catholic Church.

Since 1992, Janez Drnovšek has served as Prime Minister; the largely ceremonial presidency has been held since 1990 by Milan Kučan, former leader of a Communist reform movement.

Slovenia became a full member of the United Nations in 1992. A year later it was accepted into the Council of Europe. It is a candidate for both the European Union and NATO. The Slovenian Army cooperates with NATO in the framework of the Partnership for Peace (EAPC). Slovenia's international influence is limited for the most part to the Balkans where it played an important role during the war in *Bosnia and Herzegovina and during the war in Kosovo.

(See also BOSNIAN WAR; MACEDONIA; KOSOVO WAR; SERBIA AND MONTENEGRO.)

Igor Luksic, "Political Culture in Slovenia," in Fritz Plasser and Andreas Pribersky, eds., *Political Culture in East Central Europe* (Aldershot, Mass., 1996), pp. 91–104. Danica Fink-Hafner and John R. Robbins, eds., *Making a New Nation* (Aldershot, Mass., 1997).

IGOR LUKSIC

SMALL STATES AND TERRITORIES. The world's political map, dominated by large states, includes many lesser-known small states and territories (SSTs). Using the World Bank benchmark of 1.5 million population, there are fifty-six small states, as well as more than a hundred small territories under the sovereign control of others. A substantial majority of these small political units are islands or island federations, like Fiji in the Pacific or Barbados in the Caribbean. But others are located on the continental mainlands, sometimes as coastal enclaves, like Monaco or *Brunei, and sometimes as landlocked (often mountainous) territories, like Swaziland or Liechtenstein.

A large number of the SSTs have emerged only recently from colonialism (or are still under foreign sovereign authority). East *Timor, for example, gained independence from Indonesian occupation only in mid-1999, while Martinique remains uneasily under French rule. On the other hand, a few SSTs have enjoyed a separate political identity for centuries. San Marino claims eleven centuries of independence, while the royal house of Grimaldi in Monaco counts 700 years of its princely rule.

The government of SSTs takes several forms. Some are fully sovereign states (though because of their small size they are likely to be under the influence of larger states, especially former colonial powers). Some are semi-sovereign—they govern their internal affairs, but important responsibilities like defense and *foreign policy are left in the hands of larger states. Some are self-governing territories that can enjoy substantial autonomy, but are under the authority of a larger sovereign power. And some are colonial or non-self-governing territories, where the larger sovereign state has full local powers. SSTs can have very quirky political arrangements. *Andorra has two co-princes, one of whom is a Spanish bishop while the other is the president of France. While some SSTs cherish their ties to a mother country, other colonial SSTs are seeking independence.

Economically, SSTs have been handicapped by very small domestic markets and many suffer from relatively underdeveloped economies. Some export agricultural products like bananas or sugar and others specialize in fishing. Historically, smuggling and piracy were economic mainstays for many SSTs. In the past forty years, thanks to international air travel, tourism has brought prosperity to some fortunate places. Oil deposits have brought riches to a few others.

In the 1990s, developments in computers and advanced telecommunications laid the basis for a new way of life for a number of SSTs based on financial services. Increasingly, these tiny territories have become "offshore" banking centers—havens for tax avoidance and money laundering. By offering a special legal environment with bank privacy guarantees, simplified corporate registry, and no taxes, some SSTs have attracted billions of dollars in offshore funds. A task force headed by the Bank for International Settlements issued a list of offshore "noncooperative" states in 2000, of which nine out of thirteen were SSTs. Millions of dollars have flowed into local SST economies as a result of offshore banking, though this prosperity has been very unequally distributed. The lion's share often goes to expatriate bankers, lawyers, and financiers.

Europe has twelve SSTs, five of which are islands or island groups. Monaco, a small urban enclave on the northern Mediterranean coast, is one of the most prosperous and best known of all small states. With just 32,000 permanent residents (8,000 of whom are citizens) and 500 acres of territory, it is famous for its high-stakes casino and elegant hotels. In recent years, though, Monaco's prosperity has increasingly relied on its role as an offshore financial haven. While Monaco is a sovereign state, its independence is somewhat limited, since its big neighbor, France, manages its foreign relations, postal services, and defense, while the French franc has served as its official currency.

In addition to Monaco, the smaller European territories of this type are: the Principality of Liechtenstein (pop. 31,000), the semi-independent statelets of Andorra (pop. 64,000) and San Marino (pop. 24,000), and four British territories—the Isle of Man (pop. 70,000), the Channel Islands (pop. 150,000), the Faeroe Islands (pop. 45,000), and Gibraltar (pop. 29,000)—as well as *Vatican City State. With just 700 residents and 109 acres, the Vatican may be the only state in the world with a diplomatic corps larger than its resident population. Europe also has three large SSTs—the islands of *Cyprus (pop. 737,000) and Malta (pop. 375,000) and the city-state of *Luxembourg (pop. 378,000).

The smaller nine all fall within the geographical boundaries of the *European Union and under the control or tutelage of EU states, but none is actually under EU jurisdiction. By escaping EU laws and regulations, they function more readily as offshore tax shelters and money-laundering havens. In every case but Vatican City, these European SSTs have enjoyed an explosion in the number of bank branches, bank deposits, legal offices, and registered corporations. The little Channel Island of Jersey (pop. 90,000) reported bank deposits of no less than £60 billion in 1996.

The Caribbean area has a number of SSTs, the majority islands. According to our adjusted World Bank figures there are fourteen states and fifteen territories in this class in the Caribbean region, ranging in size from Montserrat (pop. 6,400) to *Trinidad and Tobago (pop. 1,300,000). Belize (pop. 236,000), Suriname (pop. 431,000), French Guiana (pop. 168,000), and Guyana (pop. 705,000) are all located on the mainland. Some of the better-known islands include Aruba (pop. 80,000), Barbados (pop. 257,000), the Bahamas (pop. 284,000), Martinique (pop. 412,00), and Grenada (pop. 94,500). The Netherlands Antilles (pop. 208,000) are home of George Soros's famous Quantum hedge-fund, while Bermuda (pop. 63,000) has recently become an important center for the global insurance industry.

The tiny British self-governing territory of Cayman Islands (pop. 23,000) has risen to special prominence (some would say, notoriety) in recent decades. Until the 1970s, these three small coral islands south of Cuba were an impoverished backwater, subsisting on third-rate tourism, fishing, and smuggling. By the mid 1990s, the Caymans had metamorphosed into the world's fifth largest banking center as measured by deposits (after the United States, Japan, Britain, and France). By that time, no less than 560 banks were registered in the territory, including forty-six of the world's fifty largest (though only seventy banks actually maintained a physical presence on the islands). Many major accounting and law firms had also located branches in the Caymans. The Caymans succeeded, according to one source, because they offered "tax efficient asset protection." There are virtually no taxes, no exchange controls, and no threats to the "confidentiality" of depositors.

The Pacific Ocean region has two dozen island SSTs, ranging in size from Fiji (pop. 773,000) to tiny Tokelau, an atoll with just 1,700 residents. Some of the territories embrace hundreds of islands scattered over more than a thousand miles of ocean. The Indian Ocean is site of four large island groups, including the Maldives (pop. 245,000) and the Seychelles (pop. 79,000), as well as a number of other territories including the French island of Reunion (pop. 718,000). Among the smallest Pacific SSTs, Nauru (pop. 10,000) and Niue (2,100) have specialized in offshore finance, a field where newcomers

can have an advantage. As international pressure forces older offshore centers in Europe and the Caribbean to introduce limited regulation, states in the Pacific region have been able to offer the most radically deregulated offshore financial havens.

Africa, too, has a number of SSTs—twelve states according to the World Bank count, including the islands of Cape Verde (pop. 416,000) and São Tomé and Príncipe (pop. 142,000), coastal Djibouti (pop. 636,000), and continental Swaziland (pop. 969,000), as well as a number of territorial remnants of colonialism, like Ceuta (pop. 69,000) and Melilla (pop. 60,000), Spanish territories on Morocco's Mediterranean coast. Asia, by contrast, has relatively few SSTs, many of which are quite prosperous. The island of Bahrain (pop. 629,000), peninsular Qatar (pop. 724,000), and coastal Brunei (pop. 323,000) are all petroleum-rich monarchies.

The majority of SSTs differ from the few success stories based on top-level tourism, oil, or offshore financial havens. Many suffer from serious economic problems, including remoteness from major markets and dependence on one or two primary products for export earnings. Reduced overseas development assistance has hurt many SSTs, which relied on grants from colonial or ex-colonial states to maintain their modest living standards.

The new free trade rules embodied in the *World Trade Organization (WTO) have harmed many SSTs. One of the first big disputes submitted to WTO arbitration concerned a European Union (EU) tariff advantage for imports of bananas from Caribbean islands. The EU lost the case in 1999 and the Caribbean exporters lost their market, with devastating results for island economies. SSTs worldwide are very critical of the WTO and its efforts to further liberalize the world trading system.

Island SSTs face especially serious environmental issues such as pollution and shortages of freshwater. Runoff, sewage, and waste disposal problems have negatively affected beaches, fishing, and coral barrier reefs. Island and coastal SSTs are especially exposed to catastrophic events such as hurricanes, typhoons, and volcanic eruptions and they have been working on early-warning, preventive measures and special insurance schemes to deal with these calamities. Most threatening of all, global warming is likely to lead to the rising of sea levels which could increase storm exposure, result in territory loss, or even cause some SSTs to sink entirely beneath the waves. SST authorities have been among the most vocal proponents of intergovernmental action to address global warming.

Because of their small size, SSTs have very limited resources for governmental activity and public services. As a result, they have increasingly sought strength in numbers through cooperation with other SSTs. They seek regional cooperation for joint services in education, tourism promotion, and other fields, while they seek *international cooperation to promote common goals and development strategies in international forums.

The Caribbean region has travelled farthest along the road of cooperation. A short-lived West Indies Federation fell apart in 1962 but today joint efforts are quite advanced, due to Caricom, the Caribbean Community and Common Market (founded 1973), a grouping of fifteen mostly English-language states. Caricom states have developed a number of institutions, including the University of the West Indies, a common news agency, a common meteorological association, a common court of justice, and a free-trade zone.

The Caribbean has been a leader of international cooperation with other small states, particularly within the small island movement, which has produced AOSIS (founded 1991), the worldwide, forty-member Alliance of Small Island States. The South Pacific Forum, though originally founded in 1971 to promote regional dialogue, now has been strengthened to include its own university, tourism council, geoscience commission, and environmental program. An Indian Ocean Commission (created 1984), funded by the European Union, has followed a similar path. In addition to joint efforts in higher education, tourism, the environment, fishing, and economic integration, it has programs to study fruit flies and an initiative against dumping or accidental loss of petroleum by ships in the surrounding seas.

In the 1990s, the big intergovernmental organizations began to respond. In 1990, UNESCO set up a special directorate for relations with small member states and for special small state policy concerns. In 1994, the United Nations held a world conference on the *Sustainable Development of Small Island Developing States in Barbados, an event that focused international attention on SST problems and potential. Subsequently, a number of other conferences have taken place, including a five-year followup to the Barbados gathering in 1999 and a global conference on the Development Agenda for Small States, held in London in February 2000 under the auspices of the World Bank and the Commonwealth Secretariat. Both institutions issued an important joint paper shortly afterwards and international institutions are now implementing aid and development strategies that target SST issues.

As communication and transportation costs decline, SSTs will increasingly be able to join the mainstream of the global economic and political system. With a combined population some 5 percent of the global total and important natural resources, they will seek to take their rightful place among the world's larger nations. If they can avoid the worst effects of climate change and unsustainable development, their peoples will have new opportunities to realize a more ambitious future.

(See also COLONIAL EMPIRES; DEVELOPMENT AND UNDERDEVELOPMENT; ENGLISH-SPEAKING CARIBBEAN; ENVIRONMENTALISM; FINANCE, INTERNATIONAL; GAMBIA; GULF STATES; INDIAN OCEAN REGION; SUSTAINABLE DEVELOPMENT.)

Institute for Latin American Integration, *The Latin American and Caribbean Integration Process in 1992/93* (Buenos Aires, 1994). United Nations General Assembly, *Report of the Global Conference on the Sustainable Development of Small Island Developing States* (New York, 1994). Frank Rampersad, *The New World Trade Order: Uruguay Round Agreements and Implications for the CARICOM States* (Kingston, 1997). World Bank and the Commonwealth Secretariat, *Small States: Meeting Challenges in the Global Economy* (Washington, 2000).

JAMES A. PAUL

SOCIAL CAPITAL. The concept of social capital recently entered the study of politics through sociology, especially the sociology of education. However, the phenomena that the concept refers to—norms and networks of reciprocity, trust, and cooperation that provide opportunity for individual advancement, ethnic entrepreneurship, economic development,

civic participation, and other private and social goods—have long been central to political inquiry. Whereas physical capital describes tangible investment in infrastructure, such as factories and equipment, and human capital refers to intangible investment in individuals, such as education and skill training, social capital often describes investments in the collective capacity to achieve common goals.

This definition—the collective capacity to achieve common ends—is substantially different from the concept's original formulation. Pierre Bourdieu (1986) introduced the concept to the social sciences. For Bourdieu, social capital describes the social networks that an individual may access for personal gain, and which can be converted to and from economic, cultural, and symbolic capital. James Coleman (1998) defining social capital as social arrangements that facilitate individual goal attainment, established the concept within the field of education. For Bourdieu, and Coleman, social capital involves access to social structures that can facilitate individual pursuits. Many studies of social capital focus on varieties of reciprocal social relations that are consistent with a *rational choice approach to understanding social interactions. Revolving credit schemes and other informal credit markets, for example, where personal relations, based on locality or *ethnicity, often provide sanctions and incentives for cooperative behavior, are a common focus of studies of social capital.

Robert Putnam (1993, 2000) brought the concept to political science, and defined it in a markedly different way. He defines social capital as traditions of civic engagement that promote the success of political institutions. The attempt to expand the concept of social capital beyond the instrumental incentives of individuals to the cultural values of collectivities has been plagued by methodological flaws that are familiar to critics of *political culture approaches to the study of politics. Many suspect that stretching the concept in this way may endanger its heuristic value.

The suggestion behind the market metaphor is that the collective capacity of groups to achieve common ends may be reinvested and accumulated through responsible use or squandered and diminished through irresponsible use. To build social capital is difficult; to destroy it is easy. Social capital is also often theorized to promote more effective use of physical and human capital.

Maintenance of social capital can come with high cost to the freedom of individuals. Further, while social capital may involve pursuit of a common end, it is not always used for the common good. Social capital can be deployed for oppressive as well as for progressive ends. Loyalty to authority, shared values, and networks of reciprocity and trust have been tremendously useful to genocidal regimes and racist societies.

(See also CIVIL SOCIETY.)

Pierre Bourdieu, "The Forms of Capital," in *Handbook of Theory and Research for Sociology of Education* (New York: 1986), 241–258. James Coleman, "Social Capital in the Creation of Human Capital," *American Journal of Sociology* (1998), S95-120. Alejandro Portes, "Social Capital," *Annual Review of Sociology* (1998), 1–24. Robert Putnam, *Making Democracy Work: Civic Traditions in Modern Italy* (Princeton: 1993). Robert Putnam, *Bowling Alone: The Collapse and Revival of American Community* (New York, 2000).

CHRISTOPHER CANDLAND

SOCIAL INSURANCE. See WELFARE STATE.

SOCIAL MARKET ECONOMY. The social market economy (*soziale Marktwirtschaft* in German) is the term used to describe the set of economic policies in the post–World War II Federal Republic of *Germany (FRG). It drew its intellectual origins from the Economics Department of the University of Freiburg during the 1920s and 1930s as well as from Christian social and economic teachings characteristic of the European Catholic church. The most well-known Freiburg School theorists and practitioners of the social market economy were Wilhelm Ropke, Walter Eucken, Egon Tuchtfeldt, Ludwig Erhard, and Alfred Muller-Armack. The social market economy is often considered the linchpin in the rapid economic growth of the FRG during the 1950s and early 1960s, the period also known as the *Wirtschaftswunder* (Economic Miracle). These social market principles have also continued to shape German economic policy during the 1970s, 1980s, and 1990s.

The social market economy is sometimes referred to as simply a combination of free market economy with a considerable layer of social benefits. In reality, this set of economic policies is more complex; just situating it on a continuum between laissez-faire and state-centered policies does not do justice to the concept. In fact, its authors wanted a set of economic policies that sidestepped the shortcomings of Nazism, communism, laissez-faire, and the post–World War II set of Keynesian policies. Specifically, the primary principle behind the social market economy is one of a market system, but one in which the market is organized by a comprehensive framework that defines the boundaries of competition. Moreover, these framing policies produce a stable set of market policies that are implemented by coordination among public and private sector actors and improve—not impede—economic competitiveness. The social market economy does not lie "halfway between state and market," but represents a qualitatively different approach.

The "social" component of the social market economy also differs from those of other countries. Although the FRG has always been generous with benefits, they serve more than just distributive income transfer purposes. For example, two of the most important provisions, government savings subsidies to individuals and a comprehensive vocational education system, have direct and positive benefits for the competitiveness of the German economy.

The best way to convey the vision of the social market economy may be through the words of one of its founders, Wilhelm Ropke:

[Our program] consists of measures and institutions which impart to competition the framework, rules, and machinery of impartial supervision which a competitive system needs as much as any game or match if it is not to degenerate into a vulgar brawl. A genuine, equitable, and smoothly functioning competitive system can not in fact survive without a judicious moral and legal framework and without regular supervision of the conditions under which competition can take place pursuant to real efficiency principles. This presupposes mature economic discernment on the part of all responsible bodies and individuals and a strong impartial state. ("The Guiding Principles of the Liberal Programme," in Horst Friedrich Wunche, ed., *Standard Texts on the Social Market Economy*, p. 188.)

(See also KEYNESIANISM; POLITICAL ECONOMY; WELFARE STATE.)

Horst Friedrich Wunche, ed., *Standard Texts on the Social Market Economy* (Stuttgart and New York, 1982).

CHRISTOPHER S. ALLEN

SOCIAL MOBILITY. Societies in the modern world are divided into social classes that rank people according to *power, privileges, and prestige. Whereas the number and kinds of the social classes in a society change little over time, the membership in those social classes does change. Social mobility is the movement of some people from one social class to another. Mobility can be upward or downward along society's rank ordering. Some socially mobile people move up from underprivileged classes to privileged ones; others move down from more to less privileged classes. People whose social class position remains the same over time are immobile.

The rates of upward and downward mobility reflect both opportunity and inequality in society. Opportunity fosters mobility by creating more professional and managerial positions that can be filled by upward mobility. Equality fosters mobility by allowing the higher and lower classes to compete equally for whatever positions opportunity has created. Societies with few opportunities and much inequality have low rates of both upward and downward mobility. The privileged and the poor are locked into their social class positions throughout their lives, and children grow up to inherit the privilege or poverty of their parents.

Americans used to think of the United States as a country with more opportunity and equality than others. In the 1980s and 1990s, that sanguine view has been tempered. Many Americans now speak of diminished expectations. Survey data show that less than half of parents and would-be parents expect their children to be upwardly mobile.

Diminished expectations are consistent with recent experience. Mobility patterns in the United States have changed substantially since the 1960s. Opportunity increased and inequality decreased rapidly between 1962 and 1973. Since the stagflation of 1975–82, however, opportunity has ceased to be a major source of upward mobility. Meanwhile, inequality has continued to abate, contributing to mobility throughout that period. One important measure of inequality—the strength of the statistical association between a person's social class while growing up and his or her social class as an adult—decreased 50 percent between 1962 and 1985. This is a dramatic and unprecedented change over roughly twenty years that reflects the expansion of higher education between 1955 and 1975. Since 1985, the inequality component of social mobility has not changed while the creation of opportunity slowed.

*African-Americans had a very distinctive pattern of blocked social mobility up until 1962. African-American families that succeeded in accumulating some advantages during one generation could not pass them on to succeeding generations the way white families could. This pattern exacerbated the effects of discrimination and poverty. Since the mid-1960s, mobility patterns among African-American families have become more like those of white families, increasing the social distance between the African-American middle class and *underclass and at the same time reducing the social distance between African-American and white middle classes.

Gender is not a major factor in social mobility. Despite vast (but shrinking) differences between men's and women's labor force participation and their unequal representation in many occupations, the social distance between two women of different social classes and another is the same as the social distance between two men of those same classes.

Comparisons among European nations show that social policy affects social mobility. Some policies advance opportunity; others foster equality. Indirectly they create mobility. Case studies of public policy in Sweden and Hungary show two dramatically different approaches to opportunity and equality that have affected mobility. In Sweden, social democratic programs to promote equality have been largely successful. They have resulted in a lower association between social class background and adult social class in Sweden than anywhere else that has been studied closely. In Hungary, a politically motivated policy of advancing the children of the working class (favored by the Communist leadership) dramatically reduced the association between class background and adult social class between 1956 and 1973. The U.S. case shows the consequences of far more diffuse state-level policies. Despite a near absence of federal policies designed to promote social mobility, support for public higher education in most large states contributed to the 50 percent reduction in inequality of mobility chances between 1962 and 1985.

(See also CLASS AND POLITICS; EQUALITY AND INEQUALITY; GENDER AND POLITICS; SOCIALISM AND SOCIAL DEMOCRACY; WELFARE STATE.)

Robert Erikson and John H. Goldthorpe, *The Constant Flux: A Study of Class Mobility in Industrial Societies* (Oxford, 1992). Michael Hout, "The Politics of Mobility," in *Generating Social Stratification*, Alan C. Kerckhoff, ed. (Boulder, Colo., 1996), 293–316.

MICHAEL HOUT

SOCIAL MOVEMENTS. See CIVIL RIGHTS MOVEMENT; LABOR MOVEMENT; NEW SOCIAL MOVEMENTS.

SOCIAL POLICY; SOCIAL WELFARE. See WELFARE; WELFARE STATE.

SOCIAL SECURITY. Former Senator Bill Bradley once observed that Social Security is the best expression of community in America. He might have added that it is also the nation's most popular social policy and most effective vehicle for protecting individuals and their families against financial risks associated with retirement, disability, and survivorship.

Spawned in the midst of the nation's Great Depression, the Social Security Act of 1935 seeks to provide basic protection to Americans against what Franklin D. *Roosevelt called "the vicissitudes of life." Social Security—the Old-Age, Survivor's and Disability Insurance program (OASDI)—is built on the social insurance principles that the right to a benefit is based on the prior payroll tax contribution of employees and their employers. Where welfare programs (a.k.a. public assistance) seek to relieve immediate distress, the Social Security Act's social insurance programs—Social Security, Unemployment Insurance, and later Medicare—are oriented toward preventing poverty. Built on the principle of universal coverage, social insurance provides a social means of pooling risks. In exchange for making modest contributions over their work lives, the social insurance approach provides citizens with a floor of protection against identifiable and predictable risks.

From 1939 through the mid-1970s Social Security expanded incrementally, with survivors' protections added in 1939, coverage expanded and benefits liberalized in 1950, disability protections in 1956, benefits substantially increased from 1965 through 1972, and automatic cost-of-living protections added in 1972. Then, almost abruptly, the focus shifted to program financing. Unanticipated economic changes created short-term financing problems in the mid-1970s and again in the early 1980s. Demographic changes—including increasing longevity, declining birth rates, and the anticipated aging of 76 million baby boomers born from 1946 through 1964—fueled long-term financing problems. Legislation passed in 1977 and again in 1983 responded to these problems, though plainly there is once again need for reform.

Today, Social Security covers 149 million workers and their families, paying monthly benefits to 44 million persons including 3 million children under eighteen, mostly survivors or dependents of disabled workers. It is the main source of disability and survivors' protections for America's families. For a twenty-seven-year-old couple with two children under age four and with earnings equal to average wages, Social Security is the equivalent of a life insurance policy in excess of $300,000; a disability policy in excess of $200,000. It provides Americans with the equivalent of $12.1 trillion dollars in life insurance protection, more than the entire value ($10.8 trillion) of all the private life insurance protection in force. It is the only pension protection available to six out of ten working persons in the private sector (Ball, 1998).

The program has transformed old age in America. For the middle class, it provides the foundation of a secure retirement, ideally to be built upon by other pension coverage, private savings, sound investments, accumulated equity in their homes, and, for some, work in their later years. But even for those who are relatively well off, the roughly 4.9 million elderly households with incomes between $20,001 and $33,777 in 1996, Social Security provides nearly half of the total income going to their homes. For the bottom 60 percent of the elderly income distribution—those 14.7 million households with incomes under $20,000 in 1996—Social Security provided over 70 percent of all household income. Absent Social Security, the poverty rate among the old would increase to roughly 50 percent. Very importantly, the security of beneficiaries is protected by annual cost-of-living protection (the "COLA") which assures that benefits, once received, maintain their purchasing power into advanced old age. Indeed, the program's adequacy features—the desire to provide widespread protection and do a bit more for those who have worked many years but at low wages—have driven its success. This is not to suggest that the economic security of the old cannot be improved. In spite of the great advances in the economic status of the old, many, especially single women living to advanced old age, remain at great economic risk.

Social Security's yearly projections are revised to reflect anticipated demographic and economic change. The nation is again challenged to address an anticipated shortfall in its financing, but this time without an impending short-term crisis. Yearly revenues are substantially larger than expenditures for many years to come (a $124 billion surplus in 1999 alone). But continued improvements in longevity and expected long-run declines in the rate of growth of the economy contribute to a projected long-run shortfall. The best estimates suggest that Social Security has sufficient funds to meet all obligations until 2034. After that, its revenue stream is sufficient to pay

72 percent of its obligations over the remaining forty years in its seventy-five-year estimating period. In theory, the problem could be addressed by immediately raising the Social Security payroll tax on employers and employees from 6.2 to 7.2 percent or by reducing all future benefits by 15 percent. Of course, few would seriously suggest doing either.

Approaches to reform often reflect deep divisions in the philosophy of the extent to which the individual versus the national community should bear the risks of preparing for retirement, disability, or survivorship. The traditional view of Social Security emphasizes providing widespread protection as its fundamental purpose. From this perspective, stabilizing financing and assuring benefits that are adequate and can be counted upon regardless of inflation, business cycles, and market fluctuations are central reform objectives. Strong commitment exists here for maintaining the moderate redistribution that seeks to provide a minimally adequate floor of protection for those who have worked for many years at relatively low wages. In contrast, strong belief in the primacy of individual responsibility and freedom of choice as the preeminent organizing values of society underlies the views of those seeking to privatize Social Security. The emphasis, here, is on maximizing rates of return for individuals and reducing the role of government in a market economy. While safeguards may be built in for the most disadvantaged, such proposals provide substantially greater reward to those with higher earnings.

More realistically, many incremental changes can effectively address the financing problem without radically altering the program's basic commitments and structure. For example, President Bill Clinton proposed using Social Security surpluses to buy down the publicly-held federal debt and then turning over these obligations to Social Security, a change that would enable the program to meet all obligations through 2045. The president and others have proposed diversifying Social Security trust fund investments, allowing for a small portion of the trust fund assets to be invested by an independent board in a broad selection of private equities. This could substantially address the program's financing while also improving the rate of return on trust fund investments. Other proposals include raising the ceiling on wages subject to the payroll tax, increasing the age of eligibility for full retirement benefits, extending coverage to state and local government employees not currently included in the program, small increases in payroll taxation (e.g., by 0.25 percent in 2040), technical adjustment in the COLA, and other small benefit reductions. Plainly, there will be no pain-free solutions, but the public acceptance of reform to this popular program can be enhanced if the burdens of change are distributed equitably.

(See also NEW DEAL; WELFARE STATE.)

Eric R. Kingson and Edward D. Berkowitz, *Social Security and Medicare: A Policy Primer* (Westport, Conn., 1993). C. Eugene Steuerle and Jon M. Bakija, *Retooling Social Security for the Twenty-first Century* (Washington, D.C., 1994). Eric. R. Kingson and James H. Schulz, eds., *Social Security in the Twenty-first Century* (New York, 1997). Henry J. Aaron and Robert D. Reischauer, *Countdown to Reform: The Great Social Security Debate* (New York, 1998). Robert M. Ball, *Straight Talk About Social Security: An Analysis of the Issues in the Current Debate* (New York, 1998).
ERIC R. KINGSON

SOCIALISM AND SOCIAL DEMOCRACY. See overleaf.

SOLIDARITY. With its coordination of a mass workers' movement in *Poland against a putative workers' state and its crucial role in facilitating the collapse of communist systems in Eastern Europe, Solidarity is rightly regarded as one of the most important and innovative social movements of the twentieth century. It began as a trade union movement in August 1980, when Polish workers (particularly in large industries like shipbuilding and steel) staged massive strikes protesting price increases and demanding the right to form trade unions independent of state and Communist Party control. When general strikes in Gdańsk and Szczecin threatened to engulf the entire country, the government, already weakened by a severe economic crisis, capitulated and signed the Gdańsk Accord on 31 August, legalizing independent union activity. On 17 September, activists nationwide voted to create the "independent self-governing trade union 'Solidarity,' " led by Lech *Watłésa of Gdańsk.

Solidarity survived as a legal trade union and social movement until December 1981, when state authorities declared martial law and outlawed Solidarity. Nevertheless the organization retained a powerful hold on the popular imagination, and, in 1989, as the government faced new economic difficulties and new social protests, the authorities negotiated a power-sharing deal with the former union leaders. Elections intended to sanction the deal, however, showed so little support for the Communist Party that Solidarity representatives themselves formed a government in September 1989, a development that helped trigger the collapse of *Communist Party states throughout Eastern and *Central Europe over the next few months.

Solidarity has been interpreted variously as a militant trade union, a *new social movement, a democratic political opposition, and a Catholic fundamentalist movement for national revival—and in some sense it was all of these things, for so many people with so many different views joined Solidarity. "State vs. society" is how both Solidarity *and* the government spoke of the conflict in 1980–1981, and although such language is a sociologist's nightmare, it revealed the unusual set of social cleavages produced by communist government. By nationalizing all industry and controlling social life, the ruling party made employees out of virtually the entire population. And nearly 10 million of these employees joined the union, including skilled workers, manual laborers, teachers, doctors, lawyers, engineers, even farmers. Whereas in market societies citizens can strive to improve their own conditions at the expense of others (as in the capital-labor relationship), in communist society all claims are directed only against the state. And so these disparate social groups all entered Solidarity, which promised to vigorously defend their interests before a common employer.

But while workers dominated the union numerically, they did not always do so politically. For since Poland was also a political monopoly, all political oppositions entered Solidarity too, as the only legal institution, besides the Catholic Church, with a right to present an alternative vision of a just social order. The interconnectedness of politics and economics in communist society thus had two important consequences: it made Solidarity much larger than it would have been in a market society (indeed, in the new conditions of the early 1990s, Solidarity had about one-fourth the members of 1981);

(cont. on p. 781)

SOCIALISM AND SOCIAL DEMOCRACY. Socialists of all stripes criticize *capitalism—a combination of private ownership of productive resources with their decentralized allocation by markets—claiming that this system cannot simultaneously achieve rationality in allocating scarce resources to alternative uses and justice in distributing material welfare. Yet the specific diagnoses and the proposed remedies have been sufficiently distinct to have generated at least three alternative socialist projects: communitarian, Marxist, and social democratic. Communitarian socialism emerged in the 1830s and withered as a serious alternative when socialist *ideology became fused with Marxist theory and the working-class movement around 1890. The Second International split in the aftermath of World War I over the issue of *democracy, but Marxist socialism continued uncontested in the economic realm until the middle 1930s, when the Swedish Social Democrats first formulated their strategy. Between World War II and 1989, command socialism and social democracy offered alternative and highly antagonistic projects. With the fall of command socialism in Central and Eastern Europe, the demise of the social democratic model in Scandinavia, and the dissolution of the Soviet Union, socialists can only ask, "What is left?"

Since this question organizes my essay, the approach I adopt is not historical. Indeed, to set the framework of analysis, I begin in the first section by recouching socialist critiques of capitalism in a deliberately anachronistic language of contemporary economic theory. In the second section I briefly review the blueprints, and the weaknesses, of command socialism, social democracy, and market socialism. The concluding part gropes for an answer.

Socialist Critiques of Capitalism. Let me first restate the fundamental views of *Marx and Engels and their followers concerning capitalism. The main conclusion of their analysis, which became the guiding theory of the Second International (1889–1914), was that capitalism was at the same time irrational and unjust. It was irrational because it necessarily inhibited the development of productive resources and regularly caused a waste of already-produced assets. And it was unjust because it distributed material welfare as a function of initial wealth rather than contributions or needs.

Viewed in retrospect, socialist critiques of capitalism frequently appear quaint, often incoherent, and at times bizarre. They bear the imprint of the nineteenth century: the very notion that any decentralized social system can function in an orderly way still baffles the imagination of many socialist critics of capitalism. And they are frightfully ignorant: they dispose of arguments for capitalism with a wave of a hand. Yet paradoxically, as all variants of the really-existing socialisms have plunged into disrepute, some central arguments for the irrationality of capitalism are regaining their theoretical force.

To formulate socialist critiques in a modern way, we need to reconstruct the capitalist blueprint. The model is simple: individuals know that they need, they have endowments, they exchange and engage in production whenever they want. Moreover, in equilibrium all markets clear. Hence, the prices at which individuals exchange reflect their preferences and relative scarcities; these prices inform individuals about all the opportunities they forsake. As a result, resources are allocated in such a way that all gains from trade are exhausted, no one can be better off without someone else being worse off, and the resulting distribution of welfare would not be altered under a unanimity rule.

Reasonable socialist critiques of this model all converge on the assertion that capitalism generates "waste." Yet they evoke several alternative reasons: 1) the "anarchy" of capitalist production, 2) the "contradiction" between individual and collective rationality, and 3) the "contradiction" between forces of production and relations of production. Moreover, the waste involved in each of these explanations is different: anarchy causes waste of existing endowments and even of commodities already produced, while the waste caused by the two remaining contradictions is of opportunities. My view is that the first of these criticisms is valid but we do not know whether it is remediable under any economic system, that the second critique fails to draw some important distinctions and is misdirected once these are made, and that the third one is valid and fundamental.

The anarchy critique concerns 1) the efficiency of the competitive equilibrium and 2) the feasibility of costless adjustment to a state where the expectations under which individual agents make their decisions are simultaneously fulfilled. Both are complicated issues.

First, in the light of recent developments of neoclassical theory, markets cannot be expected to generate efficient allocation of resources. Even under perfect competition, labor and capital are underutilized and final goods markets do not clear in equilibrium because employers, lenders, and consumers must pay rents to assure that, respectively, employees, borrowers, and sellers will deliver goods and services of contracted quality. Capitalism is thus inefficient even in a competitive equilibrium.

Second, even if the competitive equilibrium were efficient, as the capitalist blueprint maintained, a costless adjustment to this equilibrium may be unfeasible either because decentralized economies are never in equilibrium or because the adjustment is gradual. Marx himself seems to have wobbled about the first point, and he firmly adhered to the second. On the first point, he asserted that capitalist markets do sometimes clear but only by accident. And he developed an elaborate theory of crises of overproduction and underconsumption that became the mainstay of the economic theory of his followers. In these crises, capital and labor lie idle and the final goods markets do not clear. The waste is of the already-available factors of production and commodities.

Hence, the anarchy critique seems vindicated by recent developments of economic theory. Yet whether this critique establishes the irrationality of capitalism depends on whether the anarchy characteristic of the capitalist markets can be remedied by some alternative economic organization. And since I doubt it can be, I do not see this critique as crucial.

The claim that under capitalism individually rational actions lead to collective suboptimality confuses two situations, and is false about the first one and misdirected concerning the second. Marx thought that competition forces individual firms to invest in such a way that the general rate of profit falls. This particular argument has been shown to be false. In general, if consumption is rival and if there are no externalities, no increasing returns to scale, and no myopia, then there is no conflict between individual and collective rationality. Only if any of these assumptions are violated does individual rationality diverge from the collective one.

In real economies, these assumptions are violated: about this much no one disagrees. But all this implies is that any reasonable blueprint of capitalism must have some ways of coping with situations under which individual and social rates of return diverge—and all such blueprints do treat this situation. One way is to introduce corrective fiscal intervention, another is to reassign property rights. Hence, even under capitalism, markets may do only what they do well, and the state may have to step in where markets fail. This observation gives comfort to many socialists who gleefully observe that capitalism cannot exist without state intervention. But in fact it dulls the critique: capitalism is not any less, or more, capable than socialism of handling all the situations in which social rates of return diverge from private ones.

Having cleared the underbrush, we arrived at the claim that capitalism leads to a systematic underutilization of the productive potential. My version of this argument asserts that capitalism is irrational because it cannot access some technically feasible distributions of welfare even if these are normatively and politically desirable. We may have technological and organizational means to feed everyone on earth, we may want to feed everyone, and yet we may be still unable to do it under capitalism. Here is the argument.

Imagine an economy in which there are two agents, capitalists and workers. If the output does not depend on rates of return to the endowments controlled by these agents, then under a given state of technology all distributions of welfare that sum up to this level of output are accessible. But under capitalism output does depend on the rates of return to endowments. If capitalists receive the entire return from capital and workers the entire return from labor, then resources will be efficiently allocated and the distribution of income will reflect marginal productivity of the two factors. But if either capitalists or workers receive less than the entire return, that is, if the distribution of income diverges from the competitive market, they will withdraw capital or labor and resources will be underutilized.

Under capitalism, endowments—capital and labor power—are privately owned, and the agents who decide whether and how to utilize them are self-interested. Private property implies that owners have the right to withdraw their endowments from productive uses if they do not expect to receive an adequate rate of return. Hence, when the final distribution of welfare diverges from the allocation that would be generated by competitive markets, resources will be underutilized, and capitalism will lead to an inefficient, that is, collectively irrational allocation.

Suppose that, instead of wasting already-produced food, we distributed it to the poor. Then the price of food would fall, farmers would be getting a lower rate of return, and they would produce less. Moreover, some people who produce food for themselves would find it more profitable to do something else and get free food. Or suppose that we paid farmers to produce, supported farm prices out of taxes, and distributed food to the poor. Then the rate of return would fall throughout the economy, and the output of other commodities would decline. In fact, we do some of both, out of compassion or other motivations. But under capitalism we do it at the cost of reducing output below its potential level.

Hence, capitalism is irrational in the sense that under this system we cannot use the full productive potential without rewarding those who control the productive endowments. Technically feasible distributions of welfare are inaccessible under the capitalist system. If a society decides that the allocation of resources or the distribution of income should obey criteria other than maximization of profit, resources will be underutilized or underdeveloped.

"Command" Socialism. According to Marx, Engels, and their followers within the Second International, the irrationality and injustice of capitalism are intrinsic to the combination of private ownership and market allocation. Capitalism cannot be reformed. In turn, these deleterious effects of capitalism, as well as many others, ranging from war through prejudice to prostitution, would be automatically eliminated by abolishing private property. Hence, when *Marxism, socialism, and the *labor movement became briefly fused in Europe between 1891 and 1914, the economic program of socialist parties consisted of one demand: to nationalize the means of production, so that all resources at society's disposal could be rationally administered to satisfy human needs.

At the same time, it is important to remember that until 1919 Marxists did not develop any blueprints for implementing this system. Only in the aftermath of World War I, as the triumph of the *Russian Revolution and the massive insurgency of workers in several European countries confronted the socialist movement with the real possibility of realizing its ideas, did several detailed proposals for administering socialist economies develop.

The central claim of the "command" model was that the dynamic potential could be fully developed only if resources were centrally allocated to satisfy human needs. This model was based on several explicit assumptions: as co-owners of the means of production, "socialist men" would truthfully reveal their needs and their productive potential and would exert effort independently of reward while planners would behave as perfect agents of the society, simply solving problems of optimal allocation.

To analyze what went wrong, we must first restate the socialist blueprint. Households have needs. Firms have the capacity to produce objects that satisfy needs. The planner learns about the needs of households and the production capacities of firms and calculates how to allocate resources among firms and how to distribute the output among households in order to satisfy needs to the extent possible given the resources. The result is rational administration of things to satisfy needs.

The critiques of this model of socialism fall into three categories: 1) Even if the planner had truthful information, the sheer complexity of the problem would make it impossible to handle. 2) If individuals are self-interested, without a market mechanism the planner cannot learn about the true needs of households and the true capacities of firms. 3) There are no incentives and no monitoring mechanisms that would force the planner to promote general welfare.

Even if the planner's problem can be resolved in principle, the task facing planners is enormous. Soviet economists envisaged a few years ago that under the reformed price system, between 1,500 and 2,000 prices of basic products would be fixed by Gosplan (the State Planning Commission), another 20,000 to 30,000 prices would be administered by specialized agencies, and the remaining prices would be determined by contracts between suppliers and users. It is difficult to imagine how so many prices could be "gotten right," even with the use of computers.

Even if the planner is able to solve the calculation problem, the case for the feasibility of socialism hinges on the assumption that once economic agents—households, firms, and planners—become coproprietors of productive wealth, they act spontaneously in ways that support collective welfare. Specifically, households truthfully reveal to the planner their needs and firms their productive capacities, while planners act as perfect agents of the public.

None of these assumptions has worked under really-existing socialism. This may not be a decisive argument, for it is easy to claim that the nondemocratic nature of economic decision making in the socialist countries subverted the very notion of social ownership. But it is obvious that this notion ignores "free rider" problems (i.e., individuals trying to avoid paying their share of the cost of providing public goods). If individuals continue to be self-interested even when they co-own the productive wealth, households overreport their needs. True, the planner need not rely on revealed preferences to decide what to produce and how to distribute. In a poor country, the urgency of some needs is apparent to any observer. The planner can rely on some theory of needs to decide that minimal calorie consumption should be assured to everyone first, followed by shelter, medical attention, education, etc. This was the original intuition behind physical *planning. These methods will not work, however, once needs become more differentiated. And if the planner relies on revealed preferences, households have an incentive to misrepresent their needs.

Likewise, firms have powerful incentives to hide some of their productive capacities, and individuals may shirk in production. At least thus far, arguments for the feasibility of socialism must rest on the assumption that socialization of the means of production causes individuals to adopt socialist preferences, and this assumption is unrealistic. Since collective ownership does create free rider problems, the hope that it would alter preferences is tenuous. Hence, command socialism is unfeasible.

When planners are misinformed and self-interested and the immediate producers shirk, the output may be inferior to capitalism at any distribution of welfare. Under socialism, we may be unable to feed everyone because we cannot produce enough.

Social Democracy. The fundamental premise of social democracy is that *nationalization of the means of production is not necessary to overcome either the irrationality or the injustice of capitalism. Governments that want to eradicate poverty while minimizing losses of efficiency are not helpless in capitalist economies. They can counteract economic fluctuations, they can steer investment, they can facilitate labor mobility, and they can deliver welfare services and maintain incomes. The degree of irrationality of capitalism is not given: governments elected with a mandate to assure the material security of all citizens do have instruments with which to pursue their mission. They can implement "functional socialism," even if ownership of productive resources remains private.

Since this understanding emerged only gradually, as a reflection on successful practice rather than implementation of prior blueprints, it may be useful to trace its origins. Ever since the 1890s, socialists had thought their irreversible electoral progress would culminate one day in a parliamentary majority that would allow them to take office and legislate their societies into socialism. They were completely unprepared for what ensued. In several countries, parties bearing social democratic, labor, or socialist labels were invited to form governments by default, without winning the majority that would have been necessary to pursue the program of nationalization, because the bourgeois parties were too divided to maintain their traditional coalitions. Indeed, the first elected socialist government in the world was formed by the Swedish Social Democrats in 1920 just as they suffered their first-ever electoral reversal.

Once in office, socialists found themselves in the embarrassing situation of not being able to pursue the only program they had—nationalization—and not having any other program that would distinguish them from their bourgeois opponents. They could and did pursue ad hoc measures designed to improve conditions for their electoral continuency: the development of public housing; the institution of unemployment relief; and the introduction of minimum wages, income and inheritance taxes, and old-age pensions. But such measures did not differ from the tradition of conservative reforms associated with Bismarck, Disraeli, or Giolitti. Socialists behaved like all other parties: with some distributional bias toward their own constituency but full of respect for the golden principles of the balanced budget, deflation, the *gold standard, etc. They formed commissions to study the feasibility of nationalization and stopped there.

By the 1930s, the problem was that resources lay fallow: engines stood idle while people were out of work. At no time was the irrationality of capitalism more blatant. As families starved, food—already-produced food—was destroyed. Coffee was burned, pigs were buried, machines rusted. And according to the economic orthodoxy of the time, this state of affairs was simply natural; the only recourse was to cut the costs of production, which meant wages. Some relief measures to assist the unemployed were obviously urgent, but such measures were not considered advisable from the economic point of view. In Britain, the Labour government actually proposed to reduce unemployment compensation: this was the condition for being bailed out by the thirties' version of the *International Monetary Fund (IMF), where the "M" stood for the Morgan Bank. But in Sweden the Social Democratic Party, having won the elections of 1932, broke the shell of orthodox monetary policy. As unemployment climbed sharply with the onset of the Great Depression, the party stumbled upon an idea that was truly new: instead of assisting the unemployed, the Swedish Social Democrats employed them.

As this new policy appeared to have generated a spectacular success, it became theoretized. Socialist parties had acquired a reason to be in office under capitalism. There was something to be done: the economy was not moving according to natural laws, the economic crises could be attenuated, the waste of resources and the material deprivation could be alleviated if the government pursued anticyclical policies. Full employment became a realistic goal that could be pursued at all times. Moreover, since the economy would be stimulated by distributing incomes to people who consume most of it, the distributional bias of the Left found a rationalization in a technical economic theory.

It was Keynes who could reconcile private ownership of the means of production with democratic management of the economy. Whether or not the Swedish Social Democrats were following Keynes's recipes when they launched their policies, this has become the credo of social democracy. The practical question that social democrats have tried to solve ever since is how simultaneously to regulate investment and income. An appropriate government policy, combining a particular tax system with a social policy, would generate a level of welfare equal to the one attainable had workers jointly owned the capital stock.

The closest this general posture came to an explicit blueprint was the so-called Rehn-Meidner Plan, which was developed in Sweden between 1951 and 1958. In this model, the unions were to keep their private wages at the competitive level, given by the increase of productivity and the rate of inflation in export-receiving countries, and to reduce wage differentials, in part to put pressure on less efficient firms. In turn, the role of the government was to maintain full employment, devalue the currency whenever wage drift pushed wages above the competitive level, facilitate labor mobility by an active labor market policy, and supply social services on a universalistic basis. The tax system, which combined a high rate of taxation on consumption and selective incentives for investment, was the main policy instrument.

There is no question that this model has been successful in practice. Statistical analyses of developed capitalist countries show repeatedly that lower income inequality, more extensive welfare services, a more favorable trade-off between employment and inflation, a more favorable trade-off between wages and investment, and a more favorable trade-off between growth and social policies are to be found in those countries that combine strong unions with social democratic control over the government. To put it simply, the only countries in the world where almost no one is poor after taxes and transfers are the countries that have pursued social democratic policies.

Yet there are several indications that the social democratic model is no longer viable. At the institutional level, it is apparent that the two cornerstones of the social democratic strategy—centralized bargaining and continued tenure in office of social democratic parties—have crumbled. Formal centralized bargaining disintegrated in Sweden and is maintained only by the insistence of governments in Norway, while electoral support for social democratic parties declined drastically, forcing them out of office. At the economic level, it is apparent that the performance of the social democratic countries deteriorated in relative terms during the 1980s.

While it is not easy to separate cause and effect, several deficiencies endogenous to the social democratic model are cited to explain this demise: 1) A high degree of regulation and discretionary interventions by governments distorted the price system and weakened incentives to save and to work. In particular, governments tended to maintain full employment by unproductive employment in the public sector. 2) Universalistic welfare programs led to excess of demand over supply and thus to the rationing of access by administrative rules. 3) High marginal tax rates led to capital flight. 4) Wage drift, which was unresponsive to economic conditions, undermined the centralized bargains.

Exogenous factors may also elucidate the demise of social democracy: 1) The changing composition of class structure, especially the numerical decline of manual labor, undermined both the traditional electoral base of socialist parties and their ability to recruit voters among other sectors of society. 2) Increasing international competition undermined the initial rationale for centralized bargaining and forced governments to align their tax policy with those of competitors.

Yet, while explanations of the collapse abound, thus far the retreat from traditional social democratic policies has been limited. It is most visible in the abandonment of the full employment policy, the adoption of the "flat" tax model, and in fiscal and monetary policy. Thus far at least, it has not extended to welfare or labor market policy.

Market Socialism. The combination of full employment, a reasonable level of investment, and material security is possible only when encompassing centralized unions cooperate with socialist governments that enjoy long tenure in office. When these political conditions are absent, the efforts of particular groups of workers to raise wages result in unemployment and inequality, while governments have no incentives to assure material security for everyone.

The case for "market socialism"—a system in which workers own their firms but resources are allocated by markets—is a political, not an economic one. That is, we still do not know if 1) forms of property have consequences for firm performance and 2) the observed distribution of forms of property, in particular the paucity of employee-owned cooperatives, is due to their performance. In spite of the popularity of the idea of market socialism, we still do not have a theory of the firm that would justify this preference.

Therefore, the putative advantages of market socialism rest on distributional considerations, which have in the past provided and in many countries continue to furnish an important impulse toward socialism of some sort. One way to see the distributional cost of capitalism to wage earners, suggested long ago by Paul Samuelson, is to look at the proportion of net income consumed by owners of capital. The net output in any capitalist economy can be partitioned into consumption of wage earners, investment, and consumption of capitalists. The last part is forever lost to wage earners; it is the cost they pay for the private ownership of productive wealth. This cost varies enormously among capitalist countries. In 1985, for every dollar of value added in manufacturing, the consumption of capitalists ranged from about ten cents in Austria and Norway to well under forty cents in Britain and the United States to about sixty cents in Brazil and seventy cents in Argentina. Hence, in purely distributional terms, Austrian and Norwegian wage earners have little to gain from nationalization or socialization. Since nationalization has some inevitable costs, they are best off relying on their market power and electoral influence. British and U.S. workers have more to gain by squeezing profits or owning productive wealth directly: they end up striking more. In turn, the distributional effect of nationalization in Argentina and Brazil would be enormous. If income differentials between the top and the bottom quintile would be limited at the factor of five in socialist Brazil, the income of the poorest twenty percent would increase tenfold. Hence, in Argentina and Brazil nationalization is attractive to wage earners for purely distributional reasons.

Yet the paradox is that those working-class movements that may have the political muscle to bring about some form of socialism by legislation have no incentives to do so, while those movements that have much to gain by transferring productive wealth into the public realm have no power to do it. Hence socialism as the program of public ownership of productive wealth is the political project only of those movements that cannot bring it about.

In the end, market socialism does appear attractive on distributional grounds. Even if we cannot exactly anticipate its effects on employment, investment, and labor productivity, a combination of cooperatives with markets would be superior to capitalism in equalizing income distribution. If we think of market socialism as a system in which there is a labor-cum-capital market, that is, if being a shareholder in a co-op constitutes simultaneously a right and the obligation to work in it and these rights-obligations can be traded, then in equilibrium the rate of return to total endowments will be uniform throughout the economy. The distribution of income associated with this equilibrium will be more egalitarian than under capitalism since employees receive the entire net income of the firm.

However, the claim that market socialism would be a system of *industrial democracy, in the sense that the process of production would be democratic, seems unfounded. If worker-owned firms compete and if one way of organizing production maximizes profits, then they will be forced to choose this organization. In turn, if more than one organization of production maximizes profits, then capitalists would be indifferent between them, and if workers prefer one, capitalists would adopt it. Hence, workers' co-ops would have nothing to change.

Moreover, since under market socialism the utilization of resources would depend on rates of return, this system would suffer from the social inaccessibility of technically feasible allocations of welfare, the same irrationality that characterizes capitalism. Hence, market socialism would be still at odds with democracy. The principle that everyone has equal economic rights is not sufficient for democracy either in production or in the economy as a whole.

What Is Left? The capitalist economy, in which owners of wealth and of the capacity to work make decentralized decisions about allocation of their endowments, regularly generates a number of effects that are experienced as profound deprivations by large segments of society. The combination of market with private ownership limits the collective sovereignty, does not assure the material security of anyone who does not own wealth, and generates drastic inequalities, including the inequality of opportunity. This has been the traditional socialist critique of capitalism. The perennial question of various strands of socialism has been what, if anything, can be done about it. And, as this review shows, none of the answers survived intact the test of time.

What is then left? By posing the question in this manner, I want to inquire whether any socialist ideals continue to 1) conform to the traditional normative commitments of socialism, 2) remain economically feasible, and 3) appeal to movements or parties that would be capable of realizing them.

Imposing these three constraints on the potential answers evokes a sense of a paradox. If a Martian were asked to pick the most efficient and humane economic systems on earth, it would certainly not choose the countries with unfettered markets. The United States is a stagnant economy in which real wages have been constant for more than a decade and the real income of the bottom 40 percent of the population has declined. It is an inhumane society in which 11.5 percent of the population, some 32 million people, including twenty percent of all children, live in absolute poverty. It is a political system with the lowest voting rates among democracies and the highest per capita prison population in the world. Yet the message about the virtues of market economy it emanates finds receptive echoes all around the world. This is even more perplexing when we observe that the worldwide turn toward a reliance on markets and away from state intervention during the 1980s has been accompanied by an equally widespread economic stagnation and increasing inequalities among and within nations.

Moreover, faith in the virtues of unfettered markets is being increasingly undermined by recent developments in the very neoclassical economic theory that used to provide theoretical foundations for the belief that markets allocate resources efficiently. As long as belief in the efficiency of market allocation was sustainable, justifications of socialism were limited either to those cases where the private and the social rates of return diverged or to claims that market allocation, while efficient, leads to other normative undesirable outcomes. Today, the observation that a complete set of markets is unfeasible and information is inevitably imperfect places political institutions at the very core of any debate about economic systems. Yet again, despite these theoretical developments, market ideology is enjoying today an unprecedented and almost uncontested hegemony.

Given the current flux of economic theory and the puzzling divergence between economic realities and economic ideologies, this is not the moment to speculate about the future of socialism. Critiques of an exclusive reliance on markets cannot be used as a vindication of the traditional socialist models analyzed above. With all their faults, markets are the only mechanism we know today for eliciting private information and for providing private incentives. Command socialism is dead. Moreover, while social democracy was an unquestionable historical success, the conditions that made it feasible have been undermined by its own dynamic or by changes in the world economy. Hence, no return to the models of the past is feasible. Let me thus limit this conclusion to normative considerations that render continuing relevance to socialism.

The fundamental motivation of socialism is the ideal of collective sovereignty. People, that is, individuals acting on the bases of their current preferences, are collectively sovereign if the alternatives open to them as a collectivity are constrained only by conditions independent of their collective capacities and by individual rights. Specifically, people are sovereign only if there exist some procedures through which they can alter the existing institutions, including the state and property, and they can allocate available resources to all feasible uses.

But why juxtapose individuals and society: is not the choice by the "society" the same as the choice by the competing individuals? The warrant for claiming that capitalism is irrational stems from the fact that individuals are simultaneously market agents and citizens. The allocation of resources they prefer as citizens does not in general coincide with that at which they arrive via the market. Capitalism is a system in which scarce resources are owned privately. Yet under capitalism property is institutionally distinct from authority. As a result, there are two mechanisms by which resources can be allocated to uses and distributed among households: the market and the *state. The market is a mechanism in which individuals cast votes for allocations with the resources they own, and these resources are always distributed unequally; the state is a system which allocates resources it does not own, and where the rights to decide are distributed differently from the market. Hence the two mechanisms lead to the same outcome only by a fluke.

Democracy in the political realm exacerbates this divergence by equalizing the right to influence the allocation of resources. Indeed, distributions of consumption used by the market and those collectively preferred by citizens must differ since democracy offers those who are poor, oppressed, or otherwise miserable as a consequence of the initial distribution of endowments an opportunity to find redress via the state.

Hence, if "the people" are sovereign, they may prefer an allocation and distribution of resources that differs from the market outcome. It is this preference that cannot be reached when endowments are allocated in a decentralized way.

Even when individuals express as citizens their collective preference for a particular allocation and when all the material conditions are present to implement this preference, the democratically chosen allocation is unreachable under capitalism. Society, by which I always mean all individuals through a democratic process, can decide collectively that needs different from those maximized by the market should be the goal of development. It is this insistence that the allocation of resources and the distribution of incomes should fall under collective control that renders continuing relevance to socialism.

Nonetheless, the notion of "the" socialism, socialism as the end of history, is untenable. The democratic process in which all individuals are equally empowered in the collective decision making is necessarily open-ended, and its verdicts are continually reversible. It cannot be based on any assumptions about human nature, and it cannot be expected to lead to predetermined outcomes. The outcome of political conflicts— and conflict is what all politics is about—may be to direct societal resources to maximize free time, maximize employment, seek beauty, or maximize consumption. Moreover, continuing disagreements about the manners in which any of these goals can be implemented, including the organization of states and markets, are inevitable and desirable.

Given that we live in an age of doubt not only about decentralized but also collective mechanisms of decision making, neither the design of markets nor of democratic institutions is obvious. Yet at the level of practical politics, this quest for collective sovereignty has two immediate consequences, both concerning the status of citizenship. One is the traditional emphasis on equality of access to the democratic process, access that entails real empowerment of individuals to participate in public affairs in an enlightened manner. This is both a call for political institutions that open a space for deliberation and for educational institutions that do not limit the knowledge of pubic affairs to those who enjoy a privileged position in the economic structure. The second is the insistence that full membership in a political community entails social *citizenship: security and opportunity for all. These two practical principles continue to distinguish socialism.

(See also COMMAND ECONOMY; COMMUNIST PARTY STATES; EQUALITY AND INEQUALITY; KEYNESIANISM; NINETEEN EIGHTY-NINE; TAXES AND TAXATION; WELFARE STATE.)

Karl Marx, *Capital*, 3 vols. (New York, 1967). Maurice Dobb, *Welfare Economics and the Economics of Socialism* (Cambridge, U.K., 1969). G. A. Cohen, *Karl Marx's Theory of History: A Defense* (Princeton, N.J., 1978). Alec Nove, *The Economics of Feasible Socialism* (London, 1983). Michael Burawoy, *The Politics of Production: Factory Regimes under Capitalism and Socialism* (London, 1985). Adam Przeworski, *Capitalism and Social Democracy* (Cambridge, U.K., 1985). Brian Barry, *Democracy, Power and Justice: Essays in Political Theory* (Oxford, 1989). Jon Elster and Karl Ove Moene, eds., *Alternatives to Capitalism* (Cambridge, U.K., 1989). Pranab Bardhan and John Roemer, *Market Socialism: A Case for Rejuvenation*, East-South System Transformations Working Paper #9 (Chicago, 1991). Peter Murell, "Can Neoclassical Economics Underpin the Reform of Centrally Planned Economies?" *Journal of Economic Perspectives* 5 (1991): 59–76.

ADAM PRZEWORSKI

and it made it impossible for Solidarity to be a trade union alone, for when the employer is the state, every economic strike is necessarily a political strike as well.

In its first months, Solidarity *tried* to be a simple trade union, seeking basic gains for its members, such as wage increases and reduced working time, and leaving "politics" to the state. Yet it quickly became clear that Solidarity's very existence threw the entire system into crisis. A planned economy cannot function when an independent union asserts workers' interests irrespective of plan provisions, and a single-party government cannot effectively govern when the majority of citizens speak freely and publicly against it. Solidarity therefore had no choice but to become a political opposition movement. Although many tendencies competed for influence, the dominant line at the national level was a rather moderate one. At the same time that it supported a fully democratic system, the national leadership did not fail to recognize geopolitical realities (possible Soviet intervention). Thus it proposed only a neocorporatist power-sharing arrangement whereby Solidarity would uphold the party's right to hold state power in return for governmental guarantees of Solidarity's right to determine key areas of social policy.

Solidarity also exhibited a profound moral dimension, which played itself out in two different ways. For some, particularly radical intellectuals, Solidarity was above all a new social movement whose primary aim was neither to defend workers' interests nor to win state power, but to build a vibrant civil society with an active citizenry and a flourishing public sphere. The early days of Solidarity most closely approximated this vision, as embodied in the union's original motto, *podmiotowość*, meaning *citizenship, autonomy, self-determination, and dignity, all rolled into one.

For others, however, Solidarity's moral mission meant making Poland a true Catholic country. This nationalist-fundamentalist tendency became increasingly strong, particularly in poorer industrial areas, in the second half of 1981, when political and economic reform appeared stalled. Scorning "compromises with Communists" and "phony geopolitical constraints," this tendency in Solidarity, harking back to the prewar era, demanded free elections to oust the Communists and favored a clericalization of public life.

The government imposed martial law in December 1981 ("to protect the country from anarchy"), and Solidarity was driven underground. But with political stalemate continuing to paralyze the country, the party declared a general amnesty in 1986 and cautiously renewed ties with Solidarity. The party now favored market reform but lacked the *legitimacy needed to implement it. Solidarity, meanwhile, now also favored the introduction of radical market reform, and it alone did have legitimacy. The basis of the neocorporatist deal began to reappear. After a series of wildcat strikes in 1988 threatened to overtake both the government *and* Solidarity, the two sides convened roundtable talks in early 1989 and struck the deal that led to parliamentary elections, a Solidarity government, and proof to other Eastern Europeans that the Soviets would no longer intervene to keep Communist parties in power.

In the end, Solidarity led a *sui generis* *revolution: nonviolent, evolutionary, but leading to a fundamental change in government and economic policy. Although "socialism" was rejected in favor of "capitalism," many collectivist values persisted, as can be seen in Solidarity's desires that capitalism be beneficial to all and that the state still intervene to make life better. Solidarity therefore leaves a very rich and diverse legacy, having proved that state socialism could be radically transformed without violent revolution.

The fall of communism has meant a profound identity crisis for Solidarity. The union initially supported the neoliberal policies of the new government, but when workers protested against declining living standards, it began criticizing these same policies. For Solidarity, however, the problem was not capitalism but that Poland had adopted the wrong kind of capitalism. In 1996 it organized a coalition of over two dozen self-identified "right-wing" parties behind a peculiar program of "moral" capitalism, entailing free enterprise, workers' benefits, and strong Church involvement in politics. It also called for strong punishment of secret collaborators with the communist regime. The coalition won parliamentary elections in 1997, but the emerging government did not drastically alter policies, and the coalition began to fragment.

(See also CORPORATISM; NINETEEN EIGHTY-NINE; ONE-PARTY SYSTEM; RELIGION AND POLITICS; ROMAN CATHOLIC CHURCH.)

Timothy Garton Ash, *The Polish Revolution* (New York, 1983). David Ost, *Solidarity and the Politics of Anti-Politics* (Philadelphia, 1990). Lawrence Goodwyn, *Breaking the Barrier: The Rise of Solidarność in Poland* (New York, 1991). Jan Kubik, *The Power of Symbols Against the Symbols of Power* (University Park, Pa., 1994).

DAVID OST

SOLOMON ISLANDS. See PACIFIC ISLANDS.

SOLZHENITSYN, Aleksandr. Born in Kislovodsk in the southern Caucasus region of *Russia on 11 December 1918, Aleksandr Solzhenitsyn was educated in mathematics and literature, and during his years in college he also became a Marxist and joined the Communist Party. After the German invasion in 1941, Solzhenitsyn entered the Red Army, where he became a battery commander and a captain in the artillery. But he was arrested near the end of the war and charged with "anti-Soviet agitation and propaganda" and "the founding of a hostile organization." The principal evidence against him was a series of letters he had written from the front in which he alluded critically to *Stalin and proposed establishing a political party to oppose the Communists. He received an eight-year term in the Soviet gulag—an experience that inspired all his subsequent creative work.

After Stalin's death in 1953, Solzhenitsyn was soon released and permitted to live in Ryazan, where he taught physics in a high school and devoted himself to writing. His first published work, *One Day in the Life of Ivan Denisovich*, landed like a bombshell in Soviet society. Nikita Khrushchev read the novella and gave his personal approval for it to appear in November 1962. The story captured the world's attention, as did Solzhenitsyn's subsequent novels, most notably *Cancer Ward* and *The First Circle*, which, like *Ivan Denisovich*, are autobiographical treatments of his years as a prisoner under Stalin.

In the 1960s, Solzhenitsyn was closely identified with exposing the full truth of Stalin's extensive labor camp system and with attempts to challenge the Kremlin's harsh censorship of literature. As a result of this defiance, Solzhenitsyn was expelled from the Union of Soviet Writers in 1969. A year later, he was awarded the Nobel Prize for literature.

By that time, a small but vigorous *human rights movement was emerging inside the Soviet Union. One of its leading figures was the physicist Andrei Sakharov, with whom Solzhenitsyn was often linked in the eyes of the West. But in 1973 Solzhenitsyn published "Letter to the Soviet Leaders." This long essay, together with subsequent public statements, made clear that Solzhenitsyn, unlike Sakharov and many other dissidents, had no use for *parliamentary democracy or political parties. Solzhenitsyn's ideas resembled the views of the nineteenth-century Russian Slavophiles, who opposed serfdom and other harsh dimensions of tsarist autocracy but also mistrusted Western forms of government.

In February 1974, Aleksandr Solzhenitsyn was arrested and charged with treason for his book *The Gulag Archipelago*, a mammoth account of Stalin's labor camp system. He was immediately expelled from the *Soviet Union and deprived of his *citizenship. With his family, Solzhenitsyn soon moved from Europe to Vermont, where he lived a secluded existence, concentrating on a cycle of novels about World War I and the Bolshevik revolution.

Under Mikhail *Gorbachev, all of Solzhenitsyn's works were published in the Soviet Union and his citizenship was restored. His unique status in Soviet society was confirmed on 18 September 1990, when two Soviet newspapers, with a combined circulation of more than 22 million readers, published his long essay *Rebuilding Russia: Toward Some Formulations* (New York, 1991). With characteristic eloquence and anger, Solzhenitsyn denounced the Soviet regime for bringing catastrophe onto the country. And he repeated his mistrust of a Western parliamentary system. Solzhenitsyn's ideas were debated in the Soviet media for several weeks. Although Mikhail Gorbachev publicly acknowledged Solzhenitsyn "to be a great man," he concluded that Solzhenitsyn was "immersed in the past."

Solzhenitsyn's exile came to an end on 27 May 1994 when he arrived in the Far Eastern city of Vladivostok. From there, he traveled by train to Moscow for eight weeks, making regular stops in order to meet ordinary people and renew contact with his homeland. Solzhenitsyn may also have been exploring a political role for himself in post-Soviet Russia. But he has not found a broad audience for his views. He hosted his own talk show on national television before it was abruptly canceled and continues to publish essays expressing bitter disappointment over the collapse of Russia's economy, corrupt government institutions, organized crime, and the maleficent influence of the West. Most Russians share this gloomy assessment, but Solzhenitsyn has offered no concrete solution to Russia's woes.

(See also PERESTROIKA; SOVIET DISSENT.)

Michael Scammell, *Solzhenitsyn* (New York, 1984). D. M. Thomas, *Alexander Solzhenitsyn: A Century in His Life* (New York, 1998).
JOSHUA RUBENSTEIN

SOMALIA. Situated at the extreme corner of northeastern Africa, contemporary Somalia is a direct product of European colonialism during the second half of the nineteenth century. Prior to this, and over many centuries, the highly homogeneous pastoral Somalis had roamed, with their livestock, the

breadth of the *Horn of Africa. This autonomy was undermined with the inception of British rule over northern Somalia (as the Somaliland Protectorate) in 1886 and Italian claims over southern Somalia in 1905. The French established their own colony (French Somaliland) in 1888; Ethiopia was ceded the Ogaden in 1897; and, later, a fifth portion of Somali territory became part of the British colony of Kenya as the Northern Frontier District.

The trauma of partition ignited Somali indignation. However, before a common counterattack could be marshaled, the Somali people, notwithstanding their one language, one religion (*Islam), and one ethnic base, had to overcome two factors: the disparate nature of a pastoral way of life and the absence of any measure of collective consciousness.

A source of inspiration for the Somali response to colonialism was sought primarily in Islam. Basing his cause on the concept of *jihad (disciplined and millenarian struggle against "infidels"), a fiery and poetically gifted Sayyid Muhammad Abdille Hassan led twenty years of fierce resistance to colonial rule, particularly by the British and Ethiopians, but lost.

With the conclusion of World War II, a new spirit of Somali nationalism came to the fore. The vectors for this revival were anticolonial organizations such as the Somali Youth League (SYL) and the Somali National League (SNL), established in 1945 and 1947 respectively. The collaborative agitation of these two organizations and other smaller ones culminated in independence for British Somaliland on 26 June 1960. Five days later, on 1 July, the new state voluntarily joined Italian Somaliland to become the new nation of the Somali Republic. In one of the first acts of union, representatives of the two regions elected Aden Abdille Osman, a key figure in Italian Somaliland politics, as the new president.

The Somali Republic began its new political life as a multiparty parliamentary state. Abdulrashid Ali Sharmarke, a leading member of the SYL, was sworn in as the first prime minister. But this initiation of democratic institutions was soon undercut by the weight of a weak civil society, tension between northerners and southerners over the new dispensation, a border war with Ethiopia in 1964, and the overall frailty of the Somali economy. This created an intense situation of interelite competition for strategic positions in the postcolonial state. This process came to a halt in 1969 with the military coup d'état led by Major General Mohamed Siyad Barre.

The new military government, named the Supreme Revolutionary Council (SRC), dismissed the Parliament, banned political parties, canceled the 1960 constitution, and promised, among other things, a rejuvenation of democracy in the near future. The SRC renamed the country the Somali Democratic Republic, with socialism as its official *ideology. Despite some notable accomplishments (e.g., the development of an official orthography for the Somali language), after six years of unilateral rule the SRC came under pressure from its main patron, the Soviet Union, to enlarge its political base. In July 1976, the Somali Revolutionary Socialist Party was created with Barre as secretary general. Whatever the form of government, however, Somalia faced increasing economic pressures.

The most fundamental and immediate element of Somali material life is the harshness of its ecological base. The climate is arid to semiarid, with annual precipitation of less than 17 inches (430 millimeters) a year. Less than 13 percent of the land (about 19.75 million acres, or about 8 million hectares) is suitable for agriculture and farming. This Sahelian environment is deteriorating fast, with severe droughts expected about every eight years.

Somalia's economy is a hybrid. Much like the postcolonial state itself, this is a consequence of a continuing clash between an ancient and indigenous kin-based production and trade system, and the commodity-ordered world economy. Pastoralism is consistent with reciprocal social systems in which production, despite its austere nature, is essentially organized for collective consumption. The commodity-ordered economy is driven by a very different logic of exchange and private control and use of resources. The articulation of these two systems has created an asymmetric relationship in which the indigenous economy has underwritten the modern sector, including the state. Approximately 60 percent of Somalia's population earn their living by raising livestock, which in turn contributes over 80 percent of the country's exports. The agricultural sector, the second largest, suffers from neglect.

In short, a worsening ecological foundation, inadequate investment in productive sectors, a rising birth rate, unwise and bloated state expenditures, an inauspicious international order, and a rising debt burden created harrowing circumstances for most citizens during the 1970s and 1980s. Average living standards continued to decline while Somalia's dependency deepened to the extent that virtually all development funds and nearly half of the government's annual budget came from external donors. All of these limiting conditions were exacerbated by two other factors with long-term consequences: war with Ethiopia and the conditions for more loans set by the *International Monetary Fund (IMF). The war, which took place in 1977–1978, cost thousands of lives, left behind many displaced people, and skewed the political economy toward militarism. One outcome of the war was the change in patron from the Soviet Union to the United States.

Since 1988, the most critical issue in contemporary Somali political economy is the intensifying combat over the state. A new threshold of confrontation was reached in the summer of that year when insurgents of the Somali National Movement (SNM) attacked Hargeysa, the northern regional capital, and other settlements. More than 30,000 people are reported to have died and nearly 400,000 civilians sought refuge across the border in Ethiopia. These clashes soon spread to southern Somalia. By January 1991, Mogadishu exploded in conflict. After fierce fighting for three weeks, Siyad Barre and his regime collapsed.

SNM forces moved into northern Somalia, forming an independent state, the Somaliland Republic, which has failed to win international recognition. In the south, internecine wars over control of the state and the replacement of Barre tore the country apart, with fighting between different warlords endangering the lives of millions of people, who were often deprived of food and other necessities. It was in this context that U.S. President George *Bush dispatched U.S. troops to Somalia in December 1992 as part of an international humanitarian intervention known as Operation Restore Hope.

In May 1993, the United Nations took over peacekeeping duties under the UN Somali operation known as UNOSOM

II. Unfortunately, the U.S.-led mission transformed its mandate from humanitarianism to an obsession with getting rid of the strongest of the Somali warlords, General Aidid. The military confrontation between the UN force and the Aidid militia between June and October 1993 ended in a bloody street fight during which eighteen American soldiers were killed. For U.S. policymakers, this was too high a price to pay for peace and stability in Somalia. The subsequent withdrawal of U.S. troops led to the withdrawal of contingents from other developed countries and a humiliation for the *United Nations. With the final withdrawal of UNOSOM II in March 1995, the chances of restoring Somali national unity under a single state authority became dim. Factional strife between clans and subclans continued. Except for de facto state rule in the breakaway northern region, Somalia entered the twenty-first century as a stateless society divided among competing and often brutal warlords, representing elites using their respective clans as a basis for acquiring state power. Meanwhile, the country continued to descend deeper into fragmentation, general pauperism, and mutual predacity.

M. Lewis, *A Pastoral Democracy: A Study of Pastoralism and Politics Among the Northern Somali of the Horn* (Oxford, 1961). Saadia Touval, *Somali Nationalism: International Politics and the Drive for Unity in the Horn of Africa* (Cambridge, 1963). Abdi Samatar, *The State and Rural Transformation in Northern Somalia, 1884–1986* (Madison, Wis., 1989). John Drysdale, *Whatever Happened to Somalia? A Tale of Tragic Blunders* (London, 1994).

AHMED I. SAMATAR

SOUTH AFRICA. In 1910 South Africa was constituted as a White Dominion in the British Empire. The South African state reflected the interests of a relatively independent, stratified white society, based on the exploitation of a black population denied any political rights. The maintenance of the "white race" as a dominant was the first principle of what was called the Native Policy. There were other aims as well, such as mediation and adjustment of differences between English and Afrikaners, between white workers and their employers, and between mining and farming interests. These contradictions were pursued in the context of the major goal, which was "making South Africa a white man's country," like other white settler colonies.

The population of South Africa is made up of the indigenous inhabitants who speak two major Bantu languages, Nguni and Sotho, and European settlers, consisting mainly of Dutch and English. There are other languages, Tswana, Venda, and Ndebela. Then there are descendants of Africans and Whites, the so-called Coloureds, and descendants of Indian indentured servants. Christianity is the dominant religion, with Hinduism, Islam, Judaism, and traditional African practices also observed.

The contemporary economic, political, and social structures have their roots in the nineteenth century when the British, by an act of conquest, assumed patrimony of South Africa. In the 1860s they had brought Indian indentured labourers to work in the sugarcane plantations of Natal. Prior to that, the Dutch East India Company had brought slaves from Malay.

Diamonds were found in 1867–8, in an area occupied by Griquas, Koranmas, and some Afrikaners. Robert Southey, the colonial secretary, declared the diamonds were "the rock on which the success of South Africa will be built." And, indeed, they were. Many of the features which would define South Africa's capitalist development first occurred in the mines: the deployment, for the first time, of large-scale imperial capital; the introduction of modern industrial technologies; the employment of migrant labourers on short term contracts, and their segregation in compounds, with their movement strictly controlled by complex pass laws. These developments all contributed to massive surplus extractions from subsistence producers confined to the reserves. And Cecil John Rhodes would make his fortune there. In 1884–6 gold was discovered in the Transvaal. In 1904 Chinese indentured laborers were imported to work in the gold mines. The agitation for and against Chinese labor aroused and hardened race prejudices, facilitated the emergence of the Afrikaner Volk Party, and laid the groundwork for the cooperation between Afrikaner *nationalism and the white labor movement. The enmity between Afrikaner *nationalism and British *imperialism led to the formation of the Nationalist Party in 1914 led by J. B. M. Hertzog, who had fought against the British in the South African War of 1899–1902. That struggle reached its apogee with the attainment of the Republic in 1961.

In South Africa, the indigenous people's resistance to conquest and its aftermath has been long and continuous. The organizational forms which emerged to express and head the resistance have their roots in the specific historical circumstances and in the incorporation of the various groups in the settler political economy. Broadly speaking, the struggle against foreign domination can be divided into three phases: the wars of resistance, the struggle against political exclusion from 1910 to 1960, and the resumption of the armed resistance that followed the banning of liberation movement in 1960. This conflict culminated in 1994, when after negotiations, a new democratic constitution was adopted and elections were held in which the African National Congress emerged triumphant.

The opening of the diamond mines in 1867 and the gold mines in the 1880s, and the defeat of African chiefdoms and kingdoms in the last quarter of the nineteenth century and the incorporation of their people as cheap labor in the economy of settlers, opened a new terrain of both national and working-class struggles. Both struggles bore the marks of their birth. Early in the twentieth century there emerged ethnically oriented organizations, the South African Indian Congress, the Coloured Peoples Organization, and in 1912 the Native National Congress (later to be renamed the African National Congress). The ANC's main goal in 1912 was to forge a national consciousness, among hitherto divided nationalities. In the meantime the incorporation of the Africans into the developing capitalist economy had stimulated the emergence of trade union consciousness. This trade union consciousness led to the formation, in 1919, of the Industrial and Commercial Workers Union. In 1921 the Communist Party of South Africa was formed.

The Congress Alliance (CA) was made up of these organizations. The CA became an omnibus movement, encompassing supporters from a variety of national groups and classes. In the 1960s, following the banning of the ANC, the various national formations gradually merged. The national struggle merged with the class struggle, even as a rigid racial hierarchy was being imposed by the apartheid laws. This would be critical for the struggles in the 1980s, which led to the election victory of the Congress Alliance in 1994.

The Sharpeville massacre of March 1960 was a turning point. It marked the end of nonviolent methods of struggle, and a turn to armed struggle. In 1963, leaders of the now underground Congress Movement were arrested, and after a long trial, Nelson *Mandela, Walter Sisulu, Govan Mbeki, and others were sentenced to life imprisonment. After Sharpeville, Oliver Thambo had been sent outside the country to mobilize the international community and to establish guerrilla training camps for the ANC partisans. For the next two decades the struggle against apartheid became three-pronged. It involved, first, internal mobilization through infiltration of trained guerrillas and, second, mobilization of the international community though the offices of the United Nations, the Organization of African Unity, the churches, and anti-apartheid formations in the United States and Western Europe. The third leg was the armed struggle waged from the Frontline States of Tanzania, Zambia, and, following the collapse of Portuguese colonialism, Mozambique and Angola. In 1980 Zimbabwe won its independence and joined the phalanx of states from which the armed struggle could be waged.

The crisis of *apartheid worsened from 1970 on due to a number of developments, including the collapse of Portuguese colonialism in Angola and Mozambique, the Soweto uprising in 1976, the escalating conflict in Namibia, the growing isolation of South Africa as a result of UN actions, the boycott movement in major European countries and the United States, and not least by the escalating armed struggle waged by Umkhonto Wesizwe (the armed wing of the ANC). In 1972, in Durban, the black working class began to flex its muscle in a series of crippling strikes. In the late 1970s the apartheid regime appointed a series of commissions (Schlebush, Riekert, Wiehan) whose conclusions paved the way for the abortive reform strategy of the early 1980s.

The reform strategy was a multipronged offensive. It included the appointment of a Presidential Council, whose task was constitutional reform, giving dictatorial powers to the executive presidency in case of a stalemate. Preferential treatment in jobs was granted to those Africans who had ten-year residence in cities, and in the Bantu homelands Africans were granted "citizenship" rights. It was to oppose the attempt to divorce Coloureds and Asians from Africans that the United Democratic Front (UDF) was formed. The popular upsurge that swept the country from 1984 to 1986 marked a watershed in the long history of struggle. The state of emergency imposed in 1985 and eventually suspended in 1990 (except in Natal) marked the terminal phase of apartheid.

The release of political prisoners such as Walter Sisulu and Govan Mbeki in 1989 paved the way for the release of Nelson Mandela, the unbanning of the liberation movement, and the beginning of tortured negotiations that led to the drafting of a new constitution and the holding of elections in 1994 that led to the unqualified victory of the ANC alliance. The second elections in 1999 marked the maturing of South Africa's democracy. Today South Africa, instead of being a polecat in the nations of the world, has become a respected member, and Mr. Mandela, its first president, has become an international statesman.

(See also Colonial Empires; Guerrilla Warfare.)

Brian Bunting, *The Rise of the South African Reich* (London, 1960). H. J. Simons and R. Simons, *Race and Class in South Africa, 1850–1950* (London, 1969). John Cell, *The Highest Stage of White Supremacy: The Origins of Segregation in South Africa and the American South* (New York, 1982). T. R. H. Davenport, *South Africa: A Modern History*, 3rd ed. (Cambridge, U.K., 1987). Bernard Magubane, *The Political Economy of Race and Class in South Africa*, 2d ed. (New York, 1990). Frank Welsh, *A History of South Africa* (New York, 1998).

BERNARD MAGUBANE

SOUTH ASIAN ASSOCIATION FOR REGIONAL COOP-ERATION. In December 1985 the South Asian Association for Regional Cooperation (SAARC) was formed by Bangladesh, Bhutan, India, Maldives, Nepal, Pakistan, and Sri Lanka to address issues of peace and development and promote regional cooperation in South Asia. Despite the establishment of a permanent Secretariat in Kathmandu, Nepal, and several regional institutions to coordinate SAARC programs and activities, the organization has achieved only limited success due to lack of commitment of India and Pakistan. SAARC's most significant initiative has been the launching of the South Asian Preferential Trading Arrangement (SAPTA) in 1995 and an agreement among SAARC leaders to create the SAARC Free Trade Area (SAFTA) by 2001.

SAARC's usefulness lies in the regularly held annual summits which provide critical opportunities for South Asian leaders to engage in informal discussion and address bilateral disputes. This informal diplomacy led to the Indo–Sri Lankan accord on the Tamil problem in 1987 and helped diffuse Indo-Pakistani border tensions in 1986, 1992, and 1997. The question remains as to whether SAARC can grow and expand its role given the current level of tension between India and Pakistan. It is important to note that unlike the Association of Southeast Asian Nations (ASEAN) and the European Union, external actors and developments played a minor role in the formation of SAARC. SAARC's future growth, like its origin, will undoubtedly be driven by the domestic political and economic dynamics of South Asia, particularly India and Pakistan. So far, the Indian and Pakistani leaders have shown scant willingness to ease tensions. Additionally, lack of strong domestic support for SAARC precludes any urgency for bold regional cooperation policy initiatives by South Asian leaders.

(See also INDIAN OCEAN REGION.)

Kishore C. Dash, "The Political Economy of Regional Cooperation in South Asia" *Pacific Affairs* 69, no. 2 (Summer 1996): 185–209. Kishore C. Dash, "Domestic Support, Weak Governments, and Regional Cooperation: A Case Study of South Asia" *Contemporary South Asia* 6, no. 1 (1997): 57–77.

KISHORE C. DASH

SOUTH KOREA. See KOREA, REPUBLIC OF.

SOUTH PACIFIC. See PACIFIC ISLANDS.

SOUTH-SOUTH COOPERATION. South-South cooperation seeks to strengthen economic relations among the newly industrialized and developing economies of Africa, Asia, Latin America, and Oceania. The objective is to reinforce and expand the mutual benefits that can be derived from deepening, more expansive interdependence among the countries of "the South." Prompting the quest for greater cooperation has been

the belief that the historically fashioned global, trade, investment, production, and financial regimes remain fundamentally biased in favor of the economic and strategic interests of the core capitalist states of North America, Western Europe, and East Asia. More immediately, South-South cooperation is propelled by slow overall growth in South-North trade, the expansion of the *European Union, and the consolidation of the *North American Free Trade Agreement (NAFTA) which, along with a general increase in protectionist measures, promise even greater obstacles to manufactured and agricultural exports from the South, growing attacks within the framework of the *World Trade Organization on trade preferences for the South, and the conviction that the concerns of smaller, weaker economies are being largely ignored in this era of global economic liberalization. South-South cooperation is seen as a way to stimulate economic growth, increase the commonly low levels of trade among Southern economies, reduce the dependency on Northern markets and capital, and, in general, place the countries of the South in the position to take greater control of their economic fortunes. Actual and potential benefits of such cooperation include coordinated and strengthened bargaining with potential investors, with suppliers, and within international economic policy-making bodies. Another key benefit is the overcoming of the political barriers to greater economic integration and rationalization, thereby enlarging the economic space for nascent and expanding South-based industries. The means for realizing South-South cooperation include preferential trade agreements, freer movement of goods, services, and people, direct investment, development assistance, joint research and development, the transfer of appropriate technology, food security and agricultural development agreements, regional transportation and communications networks, and joint negotiating positions.

The origins of South-South cooperation lie in the coming together of the newly independent African and Asian countries and the developing countries of Latin America in the 1950s and early 1960s to argue for basic reforms in the organization of world trade and finance and to fashion a political stance independent of the Cold War polarization. Notable among the early regional and interregional conferences that laid the intellectual and political foundations for South-South cooperation were the Afro-Asian Conference (Bandung, Indonesia, 1955), the First Summit of Non-Aligned Countries (Belgrade, 1961), and the Conference on Problems of Developing Countries (Cairo, 1962). New international institutions emerged. For example, between 1955 and 1964 the *Non-aligned Movement, the *Organization of Petroleum Exporting Countries, the Group of 77, and the *United Nations Conference on Trade and Development were established as organs for defining and promoting political cooperation and economic development strategies for the countries of the South. The landmark Declaration and Programme of Action on the Establishment of a New International Economic Order, adopted at the UN Sixth Special Session in 1974, provided the impetus for strengthened commitment to South-South cooperation as an integral part of the effort to fundamentally restructure global economic relations.

Inspired by the history and success of the European Union, economic integration among neighboring states is the most prominent feature of South-South cooperation. Subregional and regional free trade and preferential trade associations, common markets, and lake and river basin development associations continue to proliferate. New cooperative arrangements are being developed and once dormant associations are being revitalized. Among current South-South regional economic associations are the *Economic Community of West African States (ECOWAS), the *Southern African Development Community (SADC), the Common Market for Eastern and Southern Africa (COMESA), the Maghreb Arab Union (MAU), the *Association of Southeast Asian Nations (ASEAN), the South Asian Association for Regional Cooperation (SAARC), the South Asian Preferential Trading Agreement (SAPTA), the Gulf Cooperation Council (GCC), the Latin American Integration Association (LAIA), the Andean Common Market, the Southern Cone Common Market (MERCUSOR), the Central American Common Market (CACM), and the Caribbean Community (CARICOM).

Commitments to technical and economic cooperation among the countries of the South remain strong. For example, the United Nations Development Programme, and the South Centre, an intergovernmental organization established in 1994, are strong advocates of South-South cooperation as a core mechanism for defending the economic interests and promoting development in the current period of global economic liberalization. It is clear, however, that despite voiced commitments and formal agreements, the gains of cooperation remain elusive. Notwithstanding the growth in economic and technical relations among the countries of the South, such cooperation has not had a marked impact on the overall character of the international economic order. The South remains overwhelmingly dependent on the industrialized economies of the North for export markets, foreign investment, concessionary finance, and technology. Increasing economic differentiation and rivalry among the countries of the South, lukewarm popular support for regional integration schemes, often-intense political conflicts, and renewed efforts by competing Northern economies to integrate regions of the developing world into their economic spheres undermine the pursuit of substantive South-South cooperation. There is also a clear sentiment among the states of the South that dependent integration with the North is to be preferred to the danger of increased marginalization in the evolving, dynamic, global economic order. Nevertheless, South-South cooperation remains a salient issue in the pursuit of *sustainable development, and could emerge as a more prominent feature in the competitive struggles over the structure of the global political economy in the twenty-first century.

(See also DEVELOPMENT AND UNDERDEVELOPMENT; NORTH-SOUTH RELATIONS; PROTECTION.)

Denis Benn, "South-South Cooperation: A Strategic Dimension of International Development Cooperation," *Cooperation South* (Winter 1996). Jaime De Melo and Arvind Panagariya, eds., *New Dimensions in Regional Integration* (New York, 1996).

HASHIM T. GIBRILL

SOUTH YEMEN. See YEMEN.

SOUTHERN AFRICA includes Angola, Botswana, Lesotho, Malawi, Mozambique, Namibia, South Africa, Swaziland, Zambia, and Zimbabwe. It spans 2.3 million square miles 6 million sq. km., which covers 20 percent of the African continent. The official European language of Angola and Mozambique is Portuguese, while English is the official European language of the other countries. There are numerous official indigenous languages spoken throughout the region.

The region has a population of 110 million, representing 15 percent of the continent. The largest populated country is South Africa with 43.5 million people. Mozambique is the second, with 18 million, followed by Zimbabwe with 11.2 million. Swaziland has the smallest population with 950,000.

The emergence of modern Southern Africa has its roots in the struggle against European domination. Malawi and Zambia gained their independence from British colonial rule in 1964, Botswana and Lesotho in 1966, and Swaziland in 1968. Following a war of liberation, Angola and Mozambique won their independence from Portuguese colonial rule in 1975. Protracted wars of liberation were fought against the white minority–ruled regimes of Zimbabwe, Namibia, and South Africa. Zimbabwe became independent in 1980, Namibia in 1990, and there was a transition to black majority rule in South Africa in 1994.

The transition in South Africa brought an end to a particularly difficult era in the history of Southern Africa that began in 1975 with the independence of Angola and Mozambique. Fearful that the "white hinterland" of Southern Africa was collapsing, the *apartheid regime of South Africa used both war and diplomacy as a strategy to ensure its survival as the white regional hegemon. The war of regional destabilization against its neighbors during the decade of the 1980s was especially horrific. It began shortly after Angola, Botswana, Lesotho, Malawi, Mozambique, Swaziland, Tanzania, Zambia, and Zimbabwe established the Southern African Development Coordination Conference (SADCC), with the major objective of decreasing regional economic dependence on the apartheid regime and fostering regional *development. South Africa responded to SADCC's creation with the military invasion of capitals, the sabotage of regional infrastructures, killings and abductions, and support of dissident groups. Damage from destabilization cost the member states US$60.5 billion between 1980 and 1988. There were at least a million deaths, and millions were displaced. As a result of regional destabilization, SADCC was not able to realize its goals and objectives. Its greatest achievement during this period was in uniting the region and the world against the apartheid regime. Namibia became a member of the organization in 1990.

With the transition in South Africa, SADCC had to redefine its objectives to include a post-apartheid South Africa. In 1992, SADCC was reborn as the *Southern African Development Community (SADC). Its major objective is to enhance regional economic integration. The ultimate goal of the organization is the creation of a single regional market. South Africa joined SADC in 1994, Mauritius in 1995, and the Democratic Republic of the Congo and Seychelles in 1997.

South Africa remains the regional economic hegemon, which is most evident by the fact that its GNP is five times that of the other nine members of the region combined. As the most industrialized country in the region, South Africa is a major exporter of precious and semiprecious metals, base metals, and mineral products. Zimbabwe, the second most industrialized country, is a major exporter of tobacco, gold, and other minerals. Angola is the only country that exports petroleum, while Botswana's major export is diamonds. Other regional exports include sugar, copper, wool, shellfish, fish, tea, beef, and textiles.

South Africa's continued regional economic dominance is a controversial issue. While on the one hand the significant increase of South African technology and capital into the region since 1994 is welcomed, on the other, countries are fearful that their economies will be swallowed up by their economically powerful neighbor. Several countries have accused South Africa of being an unfair trading partner since there is a huge disparity in the amount of goods South Africa exports to its regional neighbors as opposed to what it imports from them.

South Africa, along with Botswana, Lesotho, Namibia, and Swaziland (the BLNS states), make up the Southern African Customs Union (SACU) that was created in 1910. All of these countries, with the exception of Botswana, are also members of the Common Monetary Area (CMA), which means that their currencies are linked to the South African rand. In addition, six countries are members of the Common Market for Eastern and Southern Africa (COMESA). This overlapping of membership in various regional economic organizations, including SADC, not only makes it difficult to implement a coherent regional development and integration strategy, but raises questions about the political commitment these nations have toward regional integration.

Notwithstanding the fact that several of the countries have adopted International Monetary Fund/World Bank *structural adjustment programs, the masses in the region continue to live in poverty. *Globalization is having a significant impact on the economic structures of these countries. As exporters of primary products, all the countries have been affected by declining terms of trade. The fear exists that, perhaps with the exception of South Africa, they will become more marginalized within the world economy as a result of their inability to compete under the new international trade regime following the completion of the Uruguay Round and the establishment of the *World Trade Organization.

All the countries of the region are members of the *Lomé Convention/Cotonou Agreement, although South Africa joined under a limited accession provision, which means that it does not have access to European Union (EU) aid and trade preferences. The other countries have preferential access to the EU market for the export of sugar, beef, fish, horticultural products, furniture, textiles, and clothing. These preferences, however, may be eroded as a result of the provisions of the new international trade regime.

The effort to unite the region politically dates back to the creation of the Frontline States (FLS) in 1975. The FLS, through their diplomacy and influence, helped facilitate an end to the remaining vestiges of white-settler colonial rule. The founding members of the FLS were Angola, Botswana, Mozambique, Tanzania, and Zambia. Zimbabwe became a member in 1980 and Namibia in 1990. In 1996, the SADC Organ on Politics, Defence, and Security was established to replace the FLS. The ultimate objective of the Organ is to enhance the political integration of the SADC member states.

Eight of the ten countries are republics, while Lesotho and Swaziland are kingdoms. Whereas the king of Lesotho is a constitutional monarch who has only ceremonial powers, the Swazi king has absolute power. In fact, all the regional countries, with the exception of Swaziland, have in principle adopted multiparty democratic systems of government, although in practice this is not necessarily the case. Angola, Malawi, Mozambique, Namibia, South Africa, and Zambia all made transitions to democratic rule during the early part of the 1990s.

At independence Angola and Mozambique established Marxist-Leninist regimes. During the early 1990s, however, both abandoned Marxism-Leninism. In Angola, both political stability and democracy remain illusive, while Mozambique has a fledgling democracy. Although when Zimbabwe gained its independence the government in theory adopted Marxist-Leninism, in practice this was never the case. Marxist-Leninism, however, was officially abandoned in 1990. As a one-party authoritarian state, the Zimbabwe government has been repeatedly accused of human rights violations.

The model democracies in the region are considered to be Botswana, Namibia, and South Africa. Botswana has the oldest democracy. Since the same political party has been in power since independence, the country, however, has become a one-party dominant state. Both Namibia and South Africa have the potential of becoming one-party dominant states, unless viable opposition parties develop to challenge the ruling parties.

The implementation of democracy in both Malawi and Zambia has been problematic. Since multiparty elections were held in Malawi in 1994, the government has found it extremely difficult to transcend problems, such as corruption and patronage, it inherited from thirty years of dictatorial rule by Hastings Kamuzu Banda. Zambia continues to be governed along the lines of a *one-party system. All opposition parties have been silenced and the government has been cited for *human rights violations.

With the exception of Angola, Lesotho is the most politically unstable country in the region. Such instability stems from serious rivalries between and among political parties, and as a result of the military being involved in the country's politics since 1970. On several occasions, regional countries have intervened to help resolve conflicts, or to put down mutinies by the army and/or the police.

In the tiny Kingdom of Swaziland, the king rules by decree. Elections for members of parliament are on a nonparty basis. The king appoints the cabinet, and although the current king, Mswati III, has promised political reforms, to date this has not occurred.

South Africa has the largest military force in the region with 137,000 active troops. Angola has the second largest with 82,000 active troops, followed by Zimbabwe with 45,000 and Zambia with 22,000.

The region is actively involved with the *Organization of African Unity (OAU). Zimbabwe was the venue in June 1997 of the first OAU Summit to be held in Southern Africa. President Robert Mugabe of Zimbabwe served as chair of the OAU during 1997–98. The former president of Zambia, Kenneth Kaunda, served as chair in 1987–88.

(See also DECOLONIZATION; DEMOCRATIC TRANSITIONS; DEVELOPMENT AND UNDERDEVELOPMENT.)

Christian P. Potholm and Richard Dale, eds., *Southern Africa in Perspective* (New York, 1972). Africa Institute of South Africa, *Africa at a Glance: Facts and Figures* (Pretoria, South Africa, annual). Colin Legum, ed., *Africa Contemporary Record* (New York, annual).

MARGARET C. LEE

SOUTHERN AFRICAN DEVELOPMENT COMMUNITY. In April 1980, the nine independent nations in Southern Africa (Angola, Botswana, Lesotho, Malawi, Mozambique, Swaziland, Tanzania, Zambia, and Zimbabwe) established the Southern African Development Coordination Conference (SADCC) with the major objective of decreasing regional economic dependence on South Africa and fostering regional development. Other objectives included the reduction of economic dependence in general; the forging of links to create a genuine and equitable regional integration; the mobilization of resources to promote the implementation of national, interstate, and regional policies; and concerted action to secure international cooperation within the framework of the strategy outlined for economic liberation. On independence in 1990, Namibia became the tenth member of the organization.

The strategy adopted by SADCC was functional cooperation, which is a project-by-project, or sector, approach to regional cooperation and development. It was designed to enhance the economies of member states through the development of major regional sectors: transport and communications; food, agricultural, and natural resources; industry and trade; energy; human resources; mining; and tourism. Each member state was responsible for the coordination of at least one sector or subsector.

Between 1980 and 1989, SADCC mainly served as a unifying force in the region against *apartheid *South Africa. Its greatest impact, therefore, was political, largely owing to South Africa's policy of regional destabilization, which included the military invasion of capitals, support for dissident groups, killings and abductions, and the sabotage of regional networks, including transport and communications, and energy. By 1989, the SADCC countries found themselves more dependent on the apartheid regime, especially in the area of transportation.

The negotiations for a new dispensation in South Africa that began in 1990 effectively brought an end to South Africa's policy of regional destabilization. For the first time, SADCC member states contemplated the idea that a post-apartheid South Africa could become a member of the organization. With that in mind, they determined that having as a major objective decreased dependence on the apartheid regime was no longer viable. This forced a reassessment of the goals and objectives of SADCC.

In 1992, SADCC experienced a rebirth as the Southern African Development Community (SADC). The current objectives of SADC include: deeper economic cooperation and integration, on the basis of balance, equity, and mutual benefit; common economic, political, and social values; enhanced enterprise and competitiveness; *democracy and good governance, respect for the rule of law, and the guarantee of human rights; popular participation; the alleviation of poverty; and strengthened regional solidarity, *peace, and *security.

In order to achieve these objectives, the organization proposed to adopt a new strategy—development integration—that combines market integration with development. The ultimate objective of the organization is to create a single regional market. This is achieved, according to market integration theory, through different degrees of integration: free trade areas, customs unions, common markets, economic unions, and total economic integration. In addition, the organization retained its strategy of functional cooperation. The sectors and subsectors for coordination have been expanded. They include: energy; livestock production; animal disease control; agricultural research; environment and land management; water; inland fisheries, forestry, and wildlife; tourism; culture and information; transport and communications; marine, fisheries, and resources; finance and investment; human resources development; industry and trade; mining; labor and employment; and food, agriculture, and natural resources.

South Africa became a member of SADC in 1994, Mauritius in 1995, and the Democratic Republic of the Congo and Seychelles in 1997. The headquarters of the fourteen-member organization is in Gaborone, Botswana.

In 1996, the SADC Organ on Politics, Defence and Security was created in response to the need to move toward the political integration of the region. The Organ was designed to replace the role the Frontline States (FLS) had played in the region. The FLS was established in 1975 for the major purpose of ending all vestiges of white-settler colonial rule.

As one of the wealthiest regions in the world, Southern Africa is poised for enhanced regional development, cooperation, and integration during the twenty-first century. There appears to be serious constraints, however, to implementing a strategy of market integration. The primary conditions for such integration—comparative advantage and economies of scale—do not currently exist in the region. Also, South Africa, as the regional giant, would likely be the main beneficiary of market integration. An unequitable distribution of the benefits from market integration would be untenable.

Market integration is also hindered by the fact that all SADC member states are members of other regional schemes designed to enhance regional integration. South Africa, Botswana, Lesotho, Namibia, and Swaziland, for example, are members of the Southern African Customs Union (SACU). Four of these countries are also members of the Common Monetary Area (CMA). In addition, all the SADC member states, with the exception of South Africa, Botswana, Lesotho, and Mozambique, are members of the Common Market for Eastern and Southern Africa (COMESA), which is seen as a rival to SADC. Of the fourteen members of the Cross Border Initiative (CBI), seven are SADC countries. The CBI is an extraregional strategy developed by the World Bank, the International Monetary Fund, the *African Development Bank, and the European Union that is designed to create a free trade zone among its members.

Instead of pursuing a strategy of market integration, which is unrealistic because of the constraints identified above, the SADC member states should perhaps focus on enhanced regional development and cooperation. What is most important is for the member states to have access to each other's markets with a view to enhancing economic, political, and social development.

SADC has an advantage in that internationally it is recognized as having the greatest potential for enhancing regional economic and political integration. It is also considered an important actor in the plan by the *Organization of African

Unity (OAU) to create an African Economic Community by 2025. However, a major weakness of SADC is its continued dependence on its international partners for 86 percent of revenue for project development. Regional self-reliance must become a reality in order to prevent the region from being controlled by extraregional actors.

SADC's future is promising. South Africa's membership has enhanced the capacity of the organization tremendously, although many of the member states have expressed concerns about South Africa's growing regional economic hegemony. In order for the goals and objectives of the organization to be realized, all member states, including South Africa, must make a greater political commitment to regional development, cooperation, and integration.

(See also DEVELOPMENT AND UNDERDEVELOPMENT; SOUTHERN AFRICA.)

Margaret C. Lee, *SADCC: The Political Economy of Development in Southern Africa* (Nashville, 1989). Jens Harlov, *Regional Cooperation and Integration within Industry and Trade in Southern Africa: General Approaches, SADCC and the World Bank* (Aldershot, U.K., 1997).

MARGARET C. LEE

SOVEREIGNTY. A concept central to modern political thought, sovereignty's importance is bound up with specifying the essential character of the territorial *state. Sovereignty, a complex and somewhat contested conception, combines a description of attributes with various emotive concerns for or against limitations on the internal and external discretion of the state. According to most influential lines of interpretation, sovereign states remain the primary political actors in international society, although in a condition of relative decline as compared to international institutions, transnational corporate and financial actors, and transnational citizens' associations. To varying extents, these nonstate actors are controlled by sovereign states, and cannot be properly regarded as completely independent actors. For instance, only sovereign states are eligible to become full members of the UN and most other important international organizations.

In origins and evolution, sovereignty is definitely a Western concept, and was not shared by other regions until this century. (Certain non-Western parallels do exist, however.) In contemporary discussion, the concept of sovereignty is accepted as an indispensable term in both academic and diplomatic discussions of political life throughout the world. Its importance is confirmed in Marxist, realist, and liberal political discourse, but the range of usage varies widely, reflecting differences in *ideology and political priorities.

The very centrality of sovereignty ensures its contested character. In each setting, meanings are attributed to sovereignty that accord with the interpreter's project. There is little neutral ground when it comes to sovereignty.

It is possible, of course, to throw one's weight behind a particular definition or to obscure the difficulty of providing a definition that is at once clear and authoritative. Surely, some definitions are more influential than others, and to some extent, there exists a mainstream tradition with a distinguished roster of adherents. This lineage can be traced to the classical works of Machiavelli, Bodin, Hobbes, Locke, Rousseau, and Bentham, and was carried forward by such thinkers as Max *Weber, Hans Morgenthau, Bertrand de Jouvenal, F. H. Hinsley, and Hedley Bull. Despite this corpus of distinguished scholarship, sovereignty has a history of conceptual migration. Early usage, perhaps most prominently in Jean Bodin's great work, *Six Books of a Commonwealth* (1576), was almost exclusively devoted to state/society relations, the internal dimensions of sovereignty. The doctrine of sovereignty provided a way of locating the center of authority in relation to domestic conflict, and, in the end, was a means to uphold the claims of the state as against rival feudal and ecclesiastical claimants. The state became "sovereign" because it generally succeeded in upholding this final power of decision, or as later put so influentially by Weber, because the state enjoyed a monopoly over the legitimate use of *force. Sovereignty in early modern Europe was a secularizing terminology that reflected the decline of universalist religious authority and actively encouraged belief in the territorial supremacy of the state.

Hobbes extended these aspects of sovereignty in *Leviathan* (1651), interpreting sovereignty as a status, conferring upon the state an absolute prerogative to impose its will via law on civil society, an authority derived from a hypothetical social contract that overcame the ravages of life in a state of nature. The people in any society were, in effect, protected by the sovereign against their own aggressive natures, but in exchange relinquished much of their freedom to obtain the order and serenity of a well-administered civil society.

This Hobbesian view of sovereignty was challenged by John Locke, among others. Locke feared much of what Hobbes favored. If human nature was as flawed as Hobbes believed, then it would be a disastrous error to concentrate authority in the state or in any single place. Locke, although more positive about human nature, was concerned with establishing a government as clear about the limits of its authority as about its extent. It is from Locke, and Montesquieu as well, that we owe ideas about the *separation of the powers of government, notions of checks and balances, and, most of all, the idea that citizens enjoy certain inalienable *rights which, if not upheld, lead finally to a right of *revolution that inheres in the citizenry. For Locke the locus of sovereignty was suspended somewhere between the state and society, a constitutionalist nexus that has become associated with the inner nature of legitimate government at the level of the sovereign state. So conceived, sovereignty is compatible with citizen rights and the accountability of government and officialdom, including the head of state.

Indeed, some formulations of sovereignty, tracing their lineage to Rousseau, especially those imbued with democratic ideology, go much further. They locate sovereignty in civil society or in the people, giving rise to the terminology of popular sovereignty and an associated enthusiasm for the will of "the people." This line of thinking underlay the radicalism of the French Revolution. At least rhetorically, Abraham Lincoln endorsed such a view of sovereignty when he spoke of government "of the people, by the people, for the people."

Whether or not the state is sovereign, or how to construe sovereignty in relation to civil society, is no longer an important focus of debate except when it comes to *foreign policy. Domestic controversy about governance has shifted its ground: the key concerns now revolve around the way the state is constituted, especially relations between the center and other administrative units, and the modes by which governing authority is constrained and held to account. In this regard, the idea of sovereignty as such has been generally displaced in political discourse by an emphasis on rights and duties, by arguments about the nature of *democracy, and by discussions of how to maintain political and economic independence in relation to outside forces. One partial exception to this generalization has to do with state building in the non-Western world as a preoccupation in the immediate postcolonial period. Especially in Africa and the Middle East, the idea of making the state truly "sovereign" and upholding "sovereign rights" retains relevance as a central project of both governmental and oppositional forces.

Sovereignty as a basic idea and ideal in *international relations persists. Implicit in discussions since Machiavelli and Hobbes is the conviction that the state is the ultimate arbiter of its own fate in relation to the outside world. The clash of sovereign wills in international life gives rise to ceaseless conflict, as scarcity in relation to relative power and prestige, as well as with respect to resources and markets, leads to fierce competition among states, giving international relations its zero-sum history and reputation, and accounting for the prominence of *war.

Because there is no state beyond the state—no superstate—there is no human agency capable of establishing a shared morality or an effective legal order. Each state is "sovereign" in international society, a law unto itself. By and large, such formulations of sovereignty in international relations have been associated with realist thinking, which tends to regard law, morality, and conscience as irrelevant, or of marginal relevance, to the external conduct of states.

Despite the continuing prevalence of *realism as the approach of choice among diplomats and academic specialists, conceptual and policy tensions exist and are mounting. For several centuries the states system has needed to endow agreements among its sovereign members with reliability. Sovereignty, if carried too far as a guide to behavior, undermined the reliability of mutually beneficial interaction among distinct states, whether the subject matter was diplomacy, tourism, or commerce. *International law arose to regulate such relations among states, and has expanded steadily over time in response to the growing complexity of international life. But an effective international law is not easily reconcilable with conceptions of sovereignty that underlie realist thought about international relations. Realist thinking erodes the authority of treaties as binding obligations of states and casts doubt upon the rules protecting foreign diplomats and citizens.

The recent emphasis on the international protection of *human rights is a particular challenge to sovereignty, implying that a state is not territorially supreme even with respect to the manner in which a government treats persons resident within its boundaries. Such challenges to the conventional understanding of sovereignty arise from both normative and functional pressures. The experience of Nazi persecution of the Jews and the disclosures about the *Holocaust after World War II generated a political consensus that the internal relations of state and society were no longer a matter exclusively within domestic jurisdiction, but had become a subject of legitimate international concern under certain specified conditions of abuse. This consensus has been reinforced by the rise of influential grass-roots and transnational nongovernmental organizations dedicated to the promotion and protection of human rights.

On a functional level, interdependence and globalization have made it impractical to view the world as consisting of territorial units each exerting supreme authority within its borders but not elsewhere. Technological capacity gives many states the possibility of operating beyond boundaries, including *space. Ocean activity has long been a feature of international relations. Protecting the global commons against environmental decay is widely acknowledged as taking precedence over a purely territorial conception of authority, as is the complementary need to protect the health and well-being of territorial communities against damage from extraterritorial toxic releases.

A second type of conceptual tension is also of recent origin. Sovereignty and sovereign rights are emphasized as a means to protect the weak against the strong, yet the notion of sovereignty as placing the actor beyond accountability has been relied upon by the strong to impose their will on the weak. The UN Charter illustrates the tension in theory and practice. In Article 2(1) the principle of "sovereign equality" is endorsed, and Article 2(7) affirms that even the UN is bound to respect the "domestic jurisdiction" of states; thus territorial supremacy is privileged over the enforcement of international obligations. Yet the charter, especially as combined with UN practice, undertakes to save succeeding generations from the scourge of war, to promote human rights, and to uphold the principle of *self-determination.

Recent trends in international relations are contradictory and confusing. All states, including the most powerful, give lip service to ideas of sovereign equality, nonintervention, and respect for international law. Yet the experience of international relations includes the theme of the strong exerting their will upon the weak, of repeated interventions, aggressive wars, and of indirect penetration of sovereign territory by way of capital, *diplomacy, propaganda, and culture. Even if a few states can still defend their territory against an invading army, not even the most powerful can protect its people and cities against a devastating surprise attack by guided missiles, and none can control the flow of images and ideas that shape human tastes and values. The globalized "presence" of Madonna, McDonald's, and Mickey Mouse make a mockery of sovereignty as exclusive territorial control. A few governments do their best to insulate their populations from such influences, but their efforts are growing less effective and run counter to democratizing demands that are growing more difficult to resist.

There have been many attempts in the history of political and legal thought to reconcile these conceptual and operational tensions between sovereignty as an idea and law as a source of constraint on the behavior of governments. Even Bodin, the seminal modern theorist of sovereignty, conditioned his theory of sovereignty on an acceptance of the embedded applicability of natural law to the affairs of state. Jurists and others have written about notions of "autolimitation" as inherent in sovereignty, or that sovereign authority can be flexibly redirected to satisfy state interests. Yet in the end such attempts at reconciliation seem more ingenious than convincing. Doubt persists, and properly. The fundamental claim of sovereignty is its emphasis on unrestricted governmental authority within territorial boundaries. If such authority exists, then wider obligations of the state are problematic. If such authority is denied, then sovereignty itself seems abridged or qualified. Indeed, if the state no longer is entitled to exercise such authority or fails to do so in practice, then it becomes misleading to retain sovereignty as a descriptive term.

Undoubtedly, sovereignty will continue to be used in the public discourse of international relations for the foreseeable future. It provides diplomats with a hallowed concept by which to carry on political debate, and it represents in a variety of situations the ongoing struggles of a given people for self-determination and independence. Nevertheless, its continued use in academic work seems more questionable, except possibly in the setting of describing "contending notions of sovereignty." Interdependence and the interpenetration of domestic and international politics, the mobility and globalization of capital and information, and the rising influence of transnational social movements and organizations are among the factors that make it anachronistic to analyze politics as if territorial supremacy continued to be a generalized condition or a useful fiction. In particular, sovereignty, with its stress on the inside/outside distinction as between domestic and international society, seems more misleading than illuminating under current conditions. If the role of political ideas in academic pursuits is to clarify tendencies and patterns, then the viability of sovereignty as concept and project seems increasingly dubious. When the polemical function of a concept outweighs its empirical referent, it may be time to consider scuttling the concept itself or at least severely circumscribing its use.

(See also ENVIRONMENTALISM; INFORMATION SOCIETY; INTERNATIONAL SYSTEMS; INTERVENTION; LEGITIMACY; NATIONALISM; UNITED NATIONS.)

Harold J. Laski, *Studies in the Problem of Sovereignty* (New Haven, Conn., 1917). Bertrand de Jouvenal, *Sovereignty: An Inquiry into the Political Good* (Chicago, 1957). Hedley Bull, *The Anarchical Society: A Study of Order in World Politics* (New York, 1977). Hans Morgenthau, *Politics Among Nations: The Struggle for Power and Peace*, 6th ed., edited and revised by Kenneth W. Thompson (New York, 1985). F. H. Hinsley, *Sovereignty*, 2d ed. (Cambridge, U.K., 1986). David Held, *Political Theory and the Modern State* (Stanford, Calif., 1989).

RICHARD FALK

SOVIET DISSENT. For nearly two decades, beginning in the mid-1960s, Soviet *human rights activists demanded a dialogue with their own government over the country's growing social, economic, and political problems. Dissent involved a broad range of nonconformist opinion. Nationalists in several republics pressed Soviet officials for cultural autonomy for their peoples. Religious activists wanted freedom to practice their faiths. Many Jews petitioned for the right to emigrate. Human rights activists in Moscow and Leningrad defended all these movements as well as insisting that the regime relax censorship, end the abuse of psychiatry for political purposes, and dismantle harsh labor camps for political prisoners. The Kremlin responded with arrests, harassment, and, in many cases, forcible banishment from the *Soviet Union. By the mid-1980s, the regime succeeded in crushing virtually all organized, public manifestations of dissent.

The death of Anatoly Marchenko on 8 December 1986 marked the end of this era. After a prolonged hunger strike and inadequate medical care, Marchenko, one of the most well-known human rights activists of the Brezhnev period, died in Chistopol Prison. By that time, Mikhail *Gorbachev had been in power for almost two years. Marchenko's death reminded the world that Gorbachev had inherited not only Brezhnev's failing economy, but his prisoners as well. If Gorbachev wanted to establish credibility as a reformer, he had to release them. Gorbachev turned the tragedy to his advantage. Within ten days after Marchenko's death, Gorbachev called Andrei Sakharov in Gorky, where he was forcibly confined, and invited him to return to Moscow a free man. In one dramatic gesture, Gorbachev broke with the policies of the Brezhnev era and unleashed a new program of glasnost. Sakharov's release was the first of many hundreds. In February 1987, the regime announced its readiness to release all prisoners of conscience.

Gorbachev affirmed his determination to turn the Soviet Union into a country of laws, to dismantle the power of the Communist Party, and even to remake the economy through a program of market incentives. He helped dig the country out from under *Stalinism before being pushed aside himself. Most accounts of Gorbachev's years in power focus on his dramatic struggles within the upper reaches of the Communist Party. But history must take into account how the Soviet human rights movement helped to shape Gorbachev's priorities. It was the dissidents who first introduced words like *gulag*, *glasnost*, and *samizdat* into the world's vocabulary. And it was their courage and sacrifice that set the moral agenda for Gorbachev's *reforms and the terms of his acceptance in the West.

Gorbachev allowed many former prisoners and activists to move from positions of dissent to what might be called the "loyal opposition." Andrei Sakharov was elected to the Congress of People's Deputies where, until his death in December 1989, he defended the same democratic principles that guided his years as a leading figure among the Moscow dissidents. When the Estonian nationalist Mart Niklus was released from a labor camp in 1987, his train was greeted by a crowd of thousands of people, who carried him—he was wearing his prison uniform—from the train station to his home in Tartu. Niklus soon became a prominent voice in the Estonian struggle for independence.

Other former dissidents were elected to republican legislatures. Sergei Kovalyov, who had earlier served a twelve-year term for "anti-Soviet agitation and propaganda," sat in the legislature of the Russian republic. Under Boris *Yeltsin, he became *Russia's first human rights commissioner and advocated democratic reforms in the face of official indifference. Kovalyov also became the most widely recognized opponent of Russia's two wars in Chechnya.

The life of Larisa Bogoraz exemplifies the changes that have taken place in Soviet society. The widow of Anatoly Marchenko, Bogoraz began her career as a dissident when her first husband, Yuli Daniel, was brought to trial in February 1966 for publishing his short stories in the West. Bogoraz herself was arrested in Red Square in August 1968 for demonstrating against the Warsaw Pact invasion of Czechoslovakia and sentenced to four years of internal exile. Today she participates in the organization Memorial, which has supporters throughout the country and advocates proper documentation of the *Stalin period and a suitable monument to his victims.

Other veteran activists continue to monitor politically charged trials and press for the rights of unpopular ethnic minorities. But in a society facing severe economic insecurity and unstable political institutions, the principled example of former dissidents will not be enough to insure Russia's transformation into a modern, liberal democracy.

(See also PERESTROIKA.)

Joshua Rubenstein, *Soviet Dissidents, Their Struggle for Human Rights* (Boston, 1985). Ludmilla Alexeyeva, *Soviet Dissent, Contemporary Movements for National, Religious, and Human Rights,* trans. John Glad and Carol Pearce (Middletown, Conn., 1987).

JOSHUA RUBENSTEIN

SOVIET REPUBLICS. See COMMONWEALTH OF INDEPENDENT STATES.

SOVIET UNION. From World War II until the late 1980s, the Soviet Union, alongside the United States, was a superpower, projecting a distinctive political system based on and justified by the ideology of *Marxism-*Leninism (*communism), introduced into Russia by the Bolshevik-led "Great October Socialist Revolution" of 1917. From the mid-1980s, under the dynamic leadership of Mikhail *Gorbachev, the system experienced induced change, provoking contradictions and conflicts that at times bordered on chaos and anarchy. The search for new political and economic institutions and practices led at the end of 1991 to the dissolution of the Soviet system and its replacement by a series of new states.

In its seven-decade existence, the Soviet Union possessed a distinctive political system, purportedly dedicated to the creation of a classless, stateless society. While the whole enterprise was justified in Marxist terminology, the main feature was the elimination of spontaneity, accomplished by forced methods. Copied and imposed in various parts of the world, including some remote from Russia, "Soviet communism" was a model for emulation, giving the land of its origin a powerful world role in the twentieth century.

Two principal factors influenced the formation and functioning of the Soviet polity: first, the inheritance of the Russian Empire, with its enormous landmass—some 8.65 million sq. mi. (22.4 million sq. km., one-sixth of the earth's land surface)—and the problems and opportunities it presented: its large and growing population—reaching 290 million during 1990; its multiplicity of national and ethnic groups (over 100 officially recognized), with their various traditions, languages, and cultures; and its peculiar historical experiences, including the failure to absorb the invigorating experiences of the Renaissance and the Reformation that inspired the values that inform modern Europe; second, the ideology of revolutionary communism, which created a powerful tradition in its own right.

Moreover, the Russian heritage was ambiguous about the nation's place in the world, and specifically its relationship with Europe (or more broadly the West), while the Marxist-Leninist tradition embraced both humanistic, liberating goals and cruel methods, including some unique to Russia's experience. These ambiguities and tensions emerged in the political struggle over the heritage of *Lenin and *Stalin, whose influence in the first two decades of Soviet power shaped the system and reshaped the society using novel forms of rule backed by the ancient one of cruel repression.

Origins of the System. The Soviet system appeared to represent a new type of polity. It has been identified as a form of *totalitarianism, but other terms have focused on the *ideology or the *one-party system, characterizing it as an ideocracy or partocracy. The system was established in the late 1920s and the 1930s by Joseph Stalin (1879–1953) on the basis of a legacy of ideology, political precepts, and practices bequeathed by Vladimir Lenin (1870–1924).

Its most obvious characteristic was the Communist Party's political monopoly, all other parties being prohibited within months of the revolution. From March 1921, when the Bolsheviks' tenth congress banned organized factions within the party, that principle together with "democratic centralism" (discussion of a topic should cease once a decision has been taken and orders from the center are binding) led to ideological orthodoxy. Marxism-Leninism was susceptible of only one "scientific" (and therefore "correct") interpretation, presented by the wielder of supreme political power. This authoritative figure then used the prerogative of ideological innovation to brand political opponents as "un-Marxist" or "enemies of the people" and remove them from office. From the mid-1960s, that tradition stifled dissenting opinion by condemning as "dissidents" those who thought differently. Only from the mid-1980s, under Mikhail Gorbachev, did a fresh approach permit discussion of alternative perspectives and the creation of new channels of political expression.

The Goal of "Communism." The ideology thus justified the *revolution and the system which it created; it also posited certain goals. Given Russia's undeveloped condition, economic modernization was stressed in the phrase "building a communist society." Following Stalin's policy of "socialism in one country," the Soviet Union set about industrializing the economy, partly to defend "socialism" but also because "communism" envisaged an industrial society. In 1931, Stalin warned that the country was 50 or 100 years behind the advanced countries: the lag must be overcome in ten years or it would perish. The foremost purpose of the political system therefore became economic growth, with emphasis on heavy industry. Successive leaders sustained this. In the early 1960s, Nikita Khrushchev (1894–1971) boasted that the country had embarked on the rapid building of communism: within twenty years the United States would be overtaken on many economic indicators. Such promises were quickly abandoned by his successors, Leonid Brezhnev and Aleksei Kosygin, as attempted economic reforms failed and stagnation set in. Under Gorbachev, from 1985, the aim of "acceleration of social and economic development" was replaced by that of placing the economy on a market footing—an extremely controversial goal, given the values of Marxism-Leninism, requiring the questionable existence of a pool of managerial skills and entrepreneurial values in society and the willingness of the bureaucracy to surrender its commanding position. The attainment of "communism" was postponed indefinitely.

Political Structures. In pursuit of the goal, political institutions based on control were established. Under Stalin, the leader, surrounded by a cult, was dominant; the Communist Party was used to discipline key sectors of society and to move reliable supporters into managerial and administrative positions through a system known as *nomenklatura*; the country was governed through its powerful ministerial empires, coordinated by Gosplan (the State Planning Committee); the representative institutions—Soviets of Workers' Deputies—were decorative and ceremonial; other institutions, including trade unions and the Komsomol (Young Communist League), functioned as "transmission belts" for the center's policies; and the repressive agencies, notoriously the "secret" or political police, closely scrutinized the whole society. For many, this system was authentic "socialism," referred to in the 1970s as "developed," "mature," or "real" socialism.

Under Stalin's successors, the party moved to the center of the political stage; its numbers expanded rapidly, embracing the best educated and trained citizens. By the mid-1980s, it had some 19 million members, of whom 31.8 percent possessed higher education and a mere 45.0 percent were workers. As its own propaganda boasted, the working class party had become the party of the whole people. A major political force, a significant employer, owner of substantial property including a dozen or more publishing houses, a large bureaucracy, and an institution from which millions of members and their families gained status: such was the Communist Party of the Soviet Union (CPSU) in the 1980s. Article 6 of the 1977 Constitution declared it "the leading and guiding force of Soviet society and the nucleus of its political system, of all state institutions and public organizations." It was described as a coordinator, a catalyst, a vanguard, but whatever the metaphor, the significance remained: the CPSU was a monopolistic ruling party and dominated the Soviet state, which converted party policy into law and then implemented the law under close party supervision, with party members placed in all sensitive positions throughout society.

That constellation of institutional forces ensured discipline and directed the nation's efforts along channels deemed appropriate for economic development. The industrial sector was entirely state-owned and thus politically controlled; agriculture was controlled through collective and state farms. The planning process established politically motivated production goals, which were made law and implemented under, at times, extreme pressure from the control agencies, including purges, show trials, and labor camps.

Politics consisted in *mobilization*: an attempt to change behavior patterns in compressed time as society underwent massive transformation. Before "socialism in one country," the country had a rural, agrarian, peasant-dominated social and economic structure, its people characterized by a premodern lifestyle, poverty, cultural inertia, a lack of formal schooling and of participatory political experience, mitigated by strong cultural traditions and a native wiliness; within a generation it acquired an urban, industrial, and educated population, bullied into shape but galvanized to withstand the Nazi onslaught in World War II.

The positive attainments of that era laid the groundwork for a much more complex, educated, and sophisticated society that, a generation after Stalin's death, made demands on the system beyond its capacity. The methods used, however, affected the system's ability to modify its responses to societal developments and the capacity of society to sustain reform. That legacy, defined as genuine "socialism" and embracing both an institutional configuration and a set of attitudes and values (a particular political culture), served to inhibit the whole country.

The Culture of Soviet Politics. For Lenin politics was about victory and defeat, in the final analysis about *kto kogo?* (Who shall defeat whom?); compromise with the "class enemy" (political opponents) could be only a tactic. Stalin applied this principle severely, arguing that the "class struggle" would intensify as "communism" approached, and the "class enemy" must be identified and rooted out mercilessly. He promoted administrators whose lack of sentimentality matched their sycophancy and devotion to the cause: these set the ethos of the system, inventing rules as they went along, petty dictators in their territory, subject to the whims of their own superiors. Their goal was to achieve fulfillment of central directives using whatever means necessary and to report success to the center.

The population's political role was to turn out regularly and vote for party-selected candidates, including loyal and diligent workers for whom this was a reward. The mass media were strictly censored, contacts with the outside world heavily restricted. Autonomous associations were replaced by regime-sponsored, party-led "public organizations" whose purpose was to control the expression of opinion. The secret police penetrated all groups, including even the family and the churches. Public opinion was irrelevant; political debate took place behind closed doors; representative institutions simply could not function, and the population failed to acquire political experience relevant to democratization. Yet many regarded the traditional ethos as quite authentic for a "socialist" system.

Stalinism and Late Soviet Politics. Many values, practices, and customs of the system came under sustained attack by freethinking intellectuals and by establishment figures in the Academy of Sciences and universities from the mid-1960s, most tellingly on the grounds that they now hampered further economic, scientific, and political advance (see, notably, Andrei Sakharov, *Progress, Coexistence and Intellectual Freedom*, London, 1968). The dogmatic application of the ideology; democratic centralism used to control the lower administration; the ban on factions in the Communist Party (when no alternative channels for political expression existed); the practice of party-controlled appointments to positions of responsibility and authority; *censorship of all printed materials and restrictions on imported publications—these were identified as unnecessary obstacles in modern Soviet society. Nevertheless, so strong was the traditional hostility to spontaneity in favor of planning, organization, and discipline that it took a further generation before new leaders acted. Meanwhile, the development and global projection of the country's military might continued apace; so did a program of spectacular space research.

Many administrators, party members, and conceivably ordinary citizens retained allegiance to the ideals symbolized by these practices and principles. The critique of certain aspects of *capitalism remained powerful in a society with strong collectivist traditions. Moreover, past policies had worked: society *had* been transformed in a generation; countless millions *had* benefited from the new opportunities for education and for geographic and social mobility; the nation's health and welfare *had* improved within living memory. Politically it did not matter that such opportunities have accompanied *modernization in other societies. Some concluded that, if organized and told what to do, the Soviet people could move mountains—literally, if necessary. What was required, therefore, was a return to discipline.

Another interpretation acknowledged past attainments and even justified the harshness by reference to "backwardness" and the absence of an appropriate culture. However, the society, and the problems facing it, were quite different from what existed sixty years earlier. Rapid modernization had been replaced by the task of managing a complex society. The demands on the resources of government and society were greater than ever before, and standard Western theory about interests and their political articulation was common in Soviet writings well before Leonid Brezhnev used such language in the late 1970s.

Furthermore, by 1989 over 35 million Soviet citizens had higher or specialized secondary education, and along with expanding information this presented new possibilities for participatory politics. Since Stalin's death, increased contacts with foreign countries at many levels had ended the isolation and with it the profound ignorance of the outside world. As living standards rose, the availability of the transistor radio, television, and other communications technology gave access to Western information sources, including the highly influential broadcasts of Voice of America, the British Broadcasting Corporation, and Radio Liberty. Private channels, notably émigrés in the United States, Israel, and Western Europe, further educated Soviet citizens about their own relative condition and affirmed other effective ways of organizing society. Finally, the bulk of the population (all under the age of forty-five) had by then lived their adulthood in a society that, while limiting freedom, was far less brutally repressive than that of their parents. Unlike the Brezhnev generation, they were not prepared to look back complacently at past victories: in comparison with their contemporaries elsewhere, living standards were slipping, and they wanted to catch up.

When Gorbachev allowed such concerns to be voiced, the Soviet people used political means to press their case, as new representative institutions and accompanying electoral reform gave opportunities to express dissatisfaction with the Communist Party's stewardship. Party and state officials were voted out of office, even when running unopposed. Nationalist movements, dedicated to withdrawal from the Soviet Union, won resounding victories, particularly in Lithuania and Georgia, but also in other areas; democrats also won control of soviets (councils) in key cities, including Moscow. Such councils, acting with the authority of a popular mandate, set about redefining not only their policies but their relationship with the center, provoking constitutional crises. The lessons were obvious: despite the lack of experience of competitive elections, and attempts by the apparatus to control the proceedings, the voters could use the ballot to express their political will.

Under glasnost the mass media undermined the credibility of the party and state *apparatchiki* by exposing incompetence, privilege, and corruption; old aspirations of self-determination, among certain nationalities, resurfaced as hostility to the center's mismanagement rose, exacerbated by the central authorities' heavy-handed repression of nationalist demonstrations. The program of rolling reforms led to fundamental questions about the nature of the system, its gov-

ernability, and its integrity: its very survival was thrown in doubt. By the end of 1991 the Soviet Union disintegrated under internal and external political and economic pressures.

Now seen in the broader sweep of Russian history, the painful and exhilarating experiences of the Soviet period were a time of formation. Soviet rule created the economic and social basis for modernity, gave citizens new skills and values that could not be contained within the structures that promoted them, and made possible a variety of democratic politics which is still struggling to emerge.

(See also COMMONWEALTH OF INDEPENDENT STATES; PERESTROIKA; POST-COMMUNISM; RUSSIAN REVOLUTION; SOCIALISM AND SOCIAL DEMOCRACY.)

Stephen F. Cohen, *Rethinking the Soviet Experience* (Oxford and New York, 1985). Moshe Lewin, *The Gorbachev Phenomenon* (Berkeley, Calif., 1988). Geoffrey Hosking, *The Awakening of the Soviet Union* (London and Cambridge, Mass., 1990). Mary McAuley, *Soviet Politics, 1917–1991* (London, 1992). Robert Service, *A History of Twentieth-Century Russia* (London, 1997).

RONALD J. HILL

SOWETO REBELLION. See SOUTH AFRICA.

SPACE. Since the Soviet Union launched the first artificial Earth-orbiting satellite, Sputnik 1, on 4 October 1957, eight additional countries (the United States, France, Australia, China, Japan, the United Kingdom, India, and Israel) and the European Space Agency have launched at least one satellite. Twelve humans have walked on the surface of the moon, several people have stayed in space for a year or more at a time, automated spacecraft have landed on Venus and Mars, and close-up images of five of the remaining six planets and of Halley's comet have been obtained. Earth observation satellites have obtained data essential for national *security purposes as well as for environmental management, resource location, and weather forecasting. Communications via satellite have become both a multibillion-dollar business and a vital link between military forces and their command structures. Satellites are providing precise position location on a global basis, a capability with myriad applications.

Five international treaties have come into force to provide a framework for the conduct of activities in space; the most fundamental and influential of these is the Outer Space Treaty of 1967, which set forth the basic principles that outer space was the province of all mankind, that the moon and other celestial bodies were not subject to claims of national sovereignty, and that weapons of mass destruction should not be stationed in space. A number of international and regional organizations have been formed to operate space systems, particularly communication satellites.

Underpinning the extension of humanity's sphere of activities to outer space (a sphere without clear legal definition) have been a variety of motivations. The particular mix of factors leading a nation to be active in space has varied across countries and over time, but until recently the political-military foundations of space policy have been paramount. In recent years, commercial motivations have become an increasingly strong influence on space activities.

The United States and the former Soviet Union carried out comprehensive civilian and national security space programs and are the only two countries to have developed the capability of launching humans into space. Both have orbited not only their own citizens but individuals from several other countries. With the end of the Cold War and the collapse of the Soviet Union, Russia has continued a space program, but on a more modest scale. Current U.S. space spending is an order of magnitude or more greater than the space spending of Russia, Europe, Japan, or China, the next tier of spacefaring countries. The last three of these countries have identified autonomy as a long-range space goal, i.e., the ability to carry out any space activity they choose using means under their own control. Whether any or all make the commitment of human and financial resources to achieve and maintain such autonomous capability in the twenty-first century remains to be seen. Until they do, they will remain second-level space powers except in those cases where they target their investments into particular areas of specialization.

Neither the Soviet Union nor the United States deployed complete weapons systems in space. However, space systems have become an essential part of planning for and fighting a modern *war, because they are used for early warning of attack, target identification and location, damage assessment, strategic and tactical communications, position location, and weather forecasting. Space systems are also used for optical and electronic *intelligence. Some U.S. military planners see space as a major theater for future warfighting, and are concerned about controlling access to, and activities in, orbit.

Other countries use, or plan to use, space for military purposes. For example, Britain has launched military communication satellites and China and France use observation satellites for national security objectives. The very possession of a launch vehicle capable of putting a sizable payload into orbit is an indication of the capability to launch a warhead (nuclear or nonnuclear) over significant distances in time of war.

Observation satellites also play a critical role in verifying arms control agreements; the 1972 Strategic Arms Limitation Treaty forebade the signatories from interfering with "national technical means," i.e., photointelligence satellites used to verify compliance. There have been frequent proposals for a regional or international satellite agency to monitor military activities around the world and to add confidence to various *arms control agreements.

Scientists around the world have taken advantage of the opportunity to put their instruments into space; space science has become a major arena for international technical cooperation. Objects of scientific investigation include the origins, evolution, and current condition of the moon, other planets, comets, asteroids, the universe, and life; the physical character of space itself; and the Earth's surface and atmosphere. Some suggest that a comprehensive scientific study of the Earth from space can provide the information and insights required for understanding and effective management of global environmental changes.

Certainly the single most visible space achievement to date was Project Apollo, carried out by the United States between 1961 and 1972. President John F. Kennedy, in response to Soviet successes in launching the first satellite and the first human, in May 1961 set a manned lunar landing as a high-priority U.S. goal. The Soviet Union also attempted a lunar landing program in the 1960s, but several failures convinced it to withdraw from the moon race. Having won that race, the United States launched six more lunar landing missions,

five successfully, but then chose not to continue human exploration beyond Earth orbit. Both the United States and the Soviet Union in the 1970s and 1980s confined their crewed space flights to the immediate vicinity of humanity's home planet. The experience to date of putting humans into space has not provided convincing evidence of tangible benefits from human involvement. The United States is leading a sixteen-nation effort to develop an international space station, an orbiting laboratory aimed at providing such evidence.

There is no doubt that the utilization of space for various Earth-bound purposes—communication of voice, video, and data for a variety of purposes, Earth observation, and potentially new applications such as space manufacturing, navigation services, generating electrical power from solar energy, among others—will continue. Various entrepreneurs and larger firms continue to develop profit-making enterprises based on launching payloads into orbit and using them for established and new applications. The very high costs of both access to space and space operations mean that space utilization must produce high benefits or unique advantages leading to economic return. Only if access and operating costs are lowered dramatically are activities in space other than gathering and transmitting information likely to become economically much more significant. Military utilization of space will continue, and could expand, as the focus shifts from bipolar to multipolar conflicts.

The political competition that fueled humanity's first steps on another celestial body has largely dissipated, and three decades of experience with human operations in Earth orbit have so far demonstrated few advantages beyond the symbolic and motivational of putting people into space, particularly given the high additional costs of life support for human crews. Yet the idea of human travel to other planets and of eventual establishment of permanent outposts on the moon, Mars, and perhaps beyond remains potent. Whether space activities to date are the precursor to humanity becoming a multiplanet species in the twenty-first century remains to be determined.

T. A. Heppenheimer, *Countdown: A History of Space Flight* (New York, 1997). Walter J. McDougall, *. . . the Heavens and the Earth: A Political History of the Space Age* (Baltimore, 1997). Dwayne Day, John Logsden, and Brian Latell, eds., *Eye in the Sky: The Story of the Corona Spy Satellites* (Washington, D.C., 1998).

JOHN M. LOGSDON

SPAIN. The current political regime of Spain (population 39 million) is a consolidated *democracy. The relative stability of the *constitutional monarchy, established in the aftermath of nearly four decades of right-wing authoritarian rule under Francisco *Franco (who died in November 1975), stands in contrast with the preceding century of Spanish history, throughout which Spain was incapable of maintaining a stable democracy. This political change has been accompanied by substantial socioeconomic *modernization (beginning in the 1960s), a profound decentralization of the state (beginning in 1980), and a considerable alteration in Spain's foreign relations, leading it to join both the *North Atlantic Treaty Organization (NATO) and the European Union (in the 1980s). In the end, a country sometimes regarded as on the political, social, and economic "semi-periphery" of Europe has assumed most of the features that characterize the other affluent, democratic societies of Western Europe. Only the continuing terrorist violence of the Basque-nationalist ETA (Euskadi ta Akatasuna—Basque Homeland and Liberty) remains an exceptional feature of politics in Spain.

Spain's lack of a tradition of democratic stability stemmed in part from its delayed economic *development. In the mid-1870s, when the quasi-democratic Restoration Monarchy was established, 70 percent of the labor force was active in the primary sector. Given levels of illiteracy that were high even by late-nineteenth-century standards, the rural peasantry was easily manipulated by local notables, making possible the rigging of elections and the carefully orchestrated *turno pacífico*, in which the Conservative and Liberal parties alternated in power. This system could not be regarded as democratic. It ended with a military coup in 1923. The Second Republic (1931–36) was fully democratic, but it was extremely unstable and was destroyed by the civil war of 1936–39. It was followed by nearly four decades of authoritarian rule, towards the end of which Spain began to develop economically at a rapid rate. As recently as 1950, 49 percent of the labor force was active in the primary sector. By 1997, this had fallen to 7 percent—close to the average among OECD countries. This socioeconomic transformation has not only developed the kind of social capital among Spanish citizens that many have argued is a prerequisite for stable democracy, but it has also ameliorated class divisions that had helped to polarize Spanish society in the past.

Earlier prospects for democratic stability were also undermined by two other deep social cleavages. One pitted the Castilian Spanish center against regional minorities with different languages and political cultures. The multinational nature of Spanish society derived from the very process by which the Spanish state was created—the 700-year *Reconquista* (ending in 1492), which progressively expelled Islamic Moors from the Iberian Peninsula. Even though by the sixteenth century a large and internationally powerful Spanish state had come into existence, the heterogeneity of Spain's population (resulting from the fact that the *Reconquista* had been undertaken by peoples with different languages and cultures) greatly complicated the nation-building process and gave rise to civil wars in 1640, 1700–1715, 1833–40, 1846–48, 1872–75, and 1936–39. In addition to linguistic diversity (Catalans, Valencianos, and inhabitants of the Balearic Islands speak languages with origins in the Languedoc region of France, Gallegos speak a variant of Portuguese, and Basques speak a non-Indo-European language), this instability resulted from sharply conflicting political cultures, pitting centralizing Castilian governments against Basques and Catalans who defended a tradition of regional autonomy.

Another deep-rooted cleavage involved conflicting preferences over the proper role of the *Roman Catholic Church in Spanish society and politics. Catholicism's status as an established religion and its conservative if not reactionary stands on social and political issues in the late nineteenth and early twentieth centuries fueled numerous outbreaks of anticlerical violence. Franco's victory in the 1936–39 civil war reversed the anticlericalism of the Second Republic and led to the reestablishment of the state religion. Thus, this highly contentious issue occupied a prominent place on the agenda of the post-Franco transition, along with the pent-up demands from

Basques and Catalans for a restoration of their self-government rights.

Despite the polarizing potential of these issues, the Spanish transition to democracy must be regarded as enormously successful. Unfolding largely through negotiations among representatives of the key parties, a constitutional order was established under which these and other traditionally divisive issues (such as that of monarch vs. republic) were satisfactorily resolved. All significant nationwide political parties, ranging from the Communists and their allies within the coalition Izquierda Unida to the Partido Popular (formerly Alianza Popular, founded by conservatives and former supporters of the Franco regime), have consistently behaved as responsible democratic parties. Only the anti-system stance maintained by the small revolutionary Basque nationalist party, Herri Batasuna, and the semiloyal stance initially adopted by the two more centrist Basque nationalist parties, Partido Nacionalista Vasco and Eusko Alkartasuna, represent departures from this overall pattern of firm support for the new regime and its institutions. Success in this democratic transition can largely be attributed to the responsible, stabilizing leadership of Spain's political elites, in particular: the first post-Franco democratic prime minister, Adolfo Suárez (a product of Franco's National Movement, but who, along with King Juan Carlos, engineered the dismantling of the old regime); the Communist leader, Santiago Carrillo, who led his party from clandestine opposition to Eurocommunist moderation; Felipe González, leader of the Partido Socialista Obrero Español (PSOE), who transformed that party into one of the most moderate social democratic parties in Europe; and Manuel Fraga, a prominent former Franquist minister who led his party, Alianza Popular, and the overwhelming majority of former supporters of the Franco regime to fully support the new regime.

In sharp contrast with the extreme cabinet instability of the Second Republic, governments under the current regime have been outstandingly stable. The length of time between partisan changes of government between 1977 and 1996 averaged 114 months—second only to Australia—despite the fact that only two of seven governments have held a majority of seats in parliament. In contrast with the radical policy shifts which helped to polarize and destabilize the Second Republic, there has been alternation in power (from the center-right Unión de Centro Democrático [UCD] governments of Adolfo Suárez and Leopoldo Calvo Sotelo [1977–1982], to the center-left PSOE government of Felipe González [1982–1996], and to the center-right Partido Popular government of José María Aznar [elected in 1996; reelected in 2000]) with only moderate, incremental changes in public policy.

This is not to say that there have not been important changes under this regime. Since the mid-1970s, a substantial *secularization of Spanish society has taken place. This, coupled with the general avoidance of religious issues by party elites of both left and right, has defused the once explosive religious cleavage. Basque and Catalan demands for a restoration of their self-government rights have led to a profound restructuring of the once highly centralized Franquist state and creation of the *Estado de las Autonomías*—an uneven devolution of policy-making and implementation authority to seventeen regional governments. This has satisfied the autonomist aspirations of all but a minority of Basques (who continue to support the pro-independence Herri Batasuna and ETA), although the flexible nature of the *Estado de las Autonomías*, in combination with the considerable "blackmail potential" of the Basque and Catalan nationalist parties (whose support is often necessary in order to form governments in Madrid), have meant that the allocation of powers between central and regional governments has remained an open political issue. Also reversing the excesses of the Franco regime, policies of both UCD and PSOE governments have transformed the smallest and most underfunded central government in the industrialized world (which, until the late 1970s, was incapable of providing free, compulsory elementary education to Spain's children) into one whose provision of government services is in line with other modern countries.

Finally, a major reorientation of Spain's international self-image and foreign policy has taken place. Traditionally seeing itself as a bridge to both Latin America and the Arab world, Spain shifted decisively toward European integration in the 1980s. Previously nonaligned, Spain joined NATO in 1981. The extent of its reorientation is illustrated by the altered stance of the Socialist Party: initially opposed to NATO membership (making a demand for withdrawal a campaign issue in 1982), the PSOE government which came to power in that year not only engineered a positive vote in the 1986 referendum reaffirming NATO membership, but ultimately succeeded in having one of its own, the PSOE's former foreign minister Javier Solana, selected as NATO's secretary general. Spain also became a member of the European Union in 1986, and has sided with those countries favoring greater European integration. In an effort to join the "inner circle" of EU members participating in monetary union, it adopted restrictive monetary and fiscal policies that ultimately enabled Spain to meet the criteria for entry into the *Economic and Monetary Union (EMU).

(See also AUTHORITARIANISM; DEMOCRATIC TRANSITIONS; PERIPHERAL NATIONALISM; RELIGION AND POLITICS; SPANISH CIVIL WAR.)

Richard Gunther, Goldie Shabad, and Giacomo Sani, *Spain After Franco: The Making of a Competitive Party System* (Berkeley, Calif, 1986). Stanley G. Payne, *The Franco Regime, 1936–1975* (Madison, Wis., 1987). Salvador Giner, ed., *España: Sociedad y política* (Madrid, 1990). Richard Gunther, José Ramón Montero, and Joan Botella, *Politics in Modern Spain* (forthcoming).

RICHARD GUNTHER

SPANISH CIVIL WAR. On 17 July 1936, Spanish armed forces in Morocco rose up against the legitimate government of the republic, accusing it of promoting both the "disintegration of the fatherland" and the cause of Bolshevik revolution. The uprising, proving to be only partially successful, ushered in a three-year civil war. Forces loyal to the republic, supported by working-class militias, retained control over the republic's key industrial zones of Madrid, Catalonia, Levante, and the Basque Provinces; nationalist rebels, meanwhile, consolidated their position in the agricultural, food-producing areas of the peninsula, causing chronic food shortages throughout the war in republican *Spain.

The working-class revolution that the rebel generals warned against was in fact unleashed by their own rebellion. As a result of what can be termed a spontaneous *revolution, improvised worker committees and militias surged through-

out much of the republican territory, assuming the administrative functions of the government and the military role of the army that had just been dissolved by the republican government. In the social and economic sphere, hundreds of farms and factories were collectivized. The European left-wing romantics who came to Spain to fight for the "last great cause" believed they were witnessing the rise of a new working-class civilization.

The vital dilemma of republican Spain was this: was it possible to win the war through this spontaneous revolutionary momentum, or was it imperative to create a centralized military machine as demanded by the communists? The latter believed that the social revolution should be postponed until after the military victory. The communist thesis predominated because the Soviet Union was the main supplier of arms to the republic and the Partido Comunista de España exercised sole control over these weapons. Also, their defense of private property and of a "bourgeois" order as the best way to win the war turned the communists into a barrier against social revolution and, consequently, into the champions of the middle classes. The need to create a central government and an efficient army became the principal issue in the struggle for political power in republican Spain. In the fall of 1936, the anarcho-syndicalist Confederación Nacional del Trabajo joined Francisco Largo Caballero's government, but in May 1937 the coalition was dissolved owing to the communist attempt to break up the militias and curb the social revolution. Largo Caballero's affinity with the revolutionary unions and his opposition to the communist strategy of gaining full control over republican Spain in the service of the Soviet Union's foreign policy led to his downfall.

The new government, headed by the socialist Juan Negrín, was a coalition between communists and socialists bent on destroying the power of the unions. Negrín followed the communist logic: the militias were inefficient; a disciplined army was necessary to win the war, or at least to resist until a change in international conditions would motivate France and Britain to assist the republic. Only the Soviet Union could guarantee the resources needed to implement this strategy.

Indalecio Prieto, the defeatist defense minister of the republic, maintained that "the side that has the healthier rear guard will win the war. Ours is festering in plain sight." Political unity and the morale of society in nationalist Spain were of course vital for victory. In the end, however, the winning side was the one that had the better-trained and better-supplied army, under the undisputed leadership of a prestigious general.

Even though the origins of the Spanish Civil War were strictly internal, its development clearly depended on the attitudes of the major foreign powers. France and Britain followed a nonintervention policy more as a way to prevent a large-scale European war than as a mechanism to save the Spanish republic. On the other hand, Germany and Italy did not hesitate to break the nonintervention agreements; *Mussolini supplied considerable military help to *Franco. In exchange for economic concessions, the Germans sent the Condor Legion, a force of 100 combat aircraft, to Spain. Mussolini was more generous than his German colleague and sent sizable infantry forces, tanks, and artillery.

Aid by the Soviet Union to the Spanish republic was more a foreign policy instrument aimed at restoring a European system of collective security against Germany than an effort to uphold the cause of democracy or social revolution in Spain. Also, the Communist International recruited and organized the International Brigades. The Brigades mobilized an army of antifascist workers, progressive authors, communist activists, and middle-class intellectuals; the war in Spain gave them a cause. Many came with the hope of turning Spain into a graveyard of European *fascism.

Indeed, living as we are in a post-ideological age, we can gauge the real historical meaning of the Civil War only if we see it for what it was: one of the most emotive and impassioned ideological struggles of the twentieth century. The Spanish Civil War had a significant effect on the Western conscience; its impact on the intellectuals was considerable. Very few of them, like T. S. Eliot, refused to take sides. A small minority of conservative and Catholic intellectuals defended "Franco's Crusade." The majority supported the republic as the cause of freedom and democracy. The war in the trenches was indeed accompanied by a war of pens.

The International Brigades played a decisive role in the defense of Madrid in November 1936, and also in two later campaigns (Jarama in February 1937 and Guadalajara in March of the same year). Franco's failure to bring the war to a quick end by a sweeping assault on the capital forced him to shift his efforts to the north. In the fall of 1937, the Basque Provinces succumbed to the nationalists in a campaign that had its most tragic moment in the bombardment of Guernica by the German air force. The republic attempted its own offensives in Brunete, Aragon, and Teruel but was always unable to exploit its initial gains. Franco, on the other hand, knew how to turn his counteroffensive in Teruel (early in 1938) into the beginning of his thrust toward the eastern coast and Valencia with the purpose of splitting republican Spain. In an effort to save Valencia, the republic launched its last great offensive of the war when its forces crossed the Ebro River on 24 July 1938. But as in earlier cases, the republican army failed to take advantage of the initial success of its offensive.

The last phase of the war took place in Catalonia. Weary and worn, the republican army was unable to withstand the nationalist offensive that would end with the taking of Barcelona on 25 January 1939. The military options left to the republic were practically nil, and as a result the insistence by Negrin and his communist allies on continuing the war effort was futile. On 28 March, the nationalist army entered the capital. The civil war between the two Spains, in which hundreds of thousands of Spaniards lost their lives, ended with Madrid's surrender.

Viewed from the perspective of today's new and vigorous Spanish democracy, the lesson of the Civil War is that a liberal democracy can hardly survive if it is not sustained by an advanced social structure and a broad bourgeois center. Spanish democracy in the 1930s degenerated into civil war because of its incapacity to reconcile the extremes of a highly polarized society, a society the philosopher Ortega y Gasset had defined as "Invertebrate Spain."

Raymond Carr, *The Spanish Tragedy: The Civil War in Perspective* (London, 1977). Hugh Thomas, *The Spanish Civil War*, 3d ed. (New York, 1977).

SHLOMO BEN-AMI

SRI LANKA. The island-nation of Sri Lanka, with a population of around 18 million, lies 29 miles (46 km.) off the southeastern coast of *India. The British unified the island in 1815 and governed it as the colony of Ceylon until independence in 1948. The country's name was changed to Sri Lanka in 1972.

A parliamentary system, which had been in place since independence, was replaced in 1978, when a new constitution put power in the hands of an executive president in addition to the Parliament. The executive president is elected directly by universal adult suffrage, and the Parliament is chosen by a system of proportional representation. Since the 1980s violence and intimidation have increasingly affected election campaigns and voter turnout, but the actual vote counts are generally thought to be reasonably accurate. The judiciary has some independence, but has been subjected to many political pressures and has by and large been unwilling to act as a counterweight to the executive branch. The state has since colonial times been highly centralized, with all power resting in the capital city, Colombo, but a constitutional amendment passed in 1987 gives significant political powers to provincial councils. The extent of any further decentralization of power remains a divisive political issue.

All governments since independence have been led by one of two main political parties, the United National Party (UNP) or the Sri Lanka Freedom Party (SLFP). Policy differences between the two major parties have often been minimal, but the UNP has generally followed a more pro-Western and pro-business line than the SLFP. At each of the six elections held between 1956 and 1977 the incumbent government was defeated, but after 1977 the UNP held political power for seventeen years. Chandrika Kumaratunga, the leader of the SLFP and the People's Alliance coalition, was elected president in 1994. Her victory was widely attributed to a widespread belief that the UNP had become corrupt, and to the hope that a change in government might lead to a decline in political violence. By the end of the decade, however, Kumaratunga's government was widely perceived as no more effective than its UNP predecessors.

Governments after 1977 reversed the earlier policy of tight state regulation of the economy and pursued a program of economic liberalization, which was supported generously by the international aid community. Exports were diversified away from tea, rubber, and coconuts; the massive Mahaweli irrigation project went ahead; and rice production increased. On the other hand, welfare programs were cut back, and the very poor experienced a decline in their standard of living. The People's Alliance made few changes in economic policy, and continued the privatization program begun by the UNP.

Ethnic divisions have played an important role in politics since independence, but began to threaten the integrity of the polity only after 1972, when the first republican constitution entrenched the position of the Sinhalese majority and took little account of minority interests, especially those of the Sri Lanka Tamils, who are concentrated in the northeast of the island and in urban areas. Civil war broke out after anti-Tamil riots in the majority-Sinhalese areas in 1983. Sri Lanka Tamil groups claimed a Tamil homeland (Eelam) in the northeast, and most of the fighting has been confined to this region. At first the separatists received support from India, but in 1987 the Sri Lankan and Indian governments concluded an agreement to end the violence. Under this pact the government made some concessions to Tamil demands, including the devolution of power to the provinces. An Indian peacekeeping force was stationed in the northeast, but the most powerful (and ruthless) Sri Lanka Tamil group, the Liberation Tigers of Tamil Eelam (LTTE), believed that the agreement did not go far enough. Fighting soon broke out between the LTTE and the Indians and continued until the Indian withdrawal in March 1990. After a brief period of peace, the war between the government and the LTTE resumed. There was another cease-fire when the People's Alliance replaced the UNP in 1994, but peace negotiations broke down in 1995, after which the state attempted to defeat the LTTE militarily. Although the government gained considerable territory, the LTTE remained a formidable force. At the end of the decade the prospects for peace in the near term appeared poor. Between 1983 and 1999 perhaps 60,000 people, mostly civilians living in the northeast, lost their lives in this conflict, and many more were uprooted from their homes.

In addition to the Sri Lanka Tamils, there are two other Tamil-speaking ethnic minorities, the Indian Tamils (descendants of immigrants who came to work on the plantations in the British period) and the Muslims (Moors). The Indian Tamils have generally managed to stay out of the ethnic conflict, but the Muslims have been drawn in because many of them live in the proposed Tamil homeland and dispute the LTTE's claim to represent all Tamil-speaking groups.

There are also class and generational tensions. The LTTE wages its campaign not only against Sinhalese dominance but against other Sri Lanka Tamil political groups, including those dominated by the English-speaking elite. Moreover, beginning in 1987 a Sinhalese group, the Janatha Vimukthi Peramuna (JVP), waged a violent campaign against the state. The JVP resented the Indian presence on the island and believed that the government had made too many concessions to the Tamils. It received support from young Sinhalese in rural and semiurban areas who felt excluded from the political process. The security forces succeeded in repressing the JVP in 1989, and the threat to the government receded. However, the social and economic forces that bred support for the JVP remain, and further challenges to the state from outside the democratic system are possible. Nonetheless, despite all the political violence and human rights abuses of recent years, politics continues to be characterized by a popular belief in the legitimacy of the electoral process.

(See also BUDDHISM; ETHNICITY; HINDUISM; SOUTH ASIAN ASSOCIATION FOR REGIONAL COOPERATION.)

K. M. de Silva, ed., *Sri Lanka: Problems of Governance* (Delhi, 1993). Michael Roberts, ed., *Sri Lanka: Collective Identities Revisited*, vol. 2 (Colombo, 1998).

JOHN D. ROGERS

STALIN, Joseph. General secretary of the Communist Party of the Soviet Union from 1922 to 1953 and effective dictator of the country after 1929, Joseph Stalin was born Iosif Vissarionovich Dzhugashvili on 9 December 1879 (21 December, Western style) to a working-class family in the town of Gori in what is now the Republic of Georgia. Expelled from the Orthodox seminary where he was considered willful and rebellious, he joined the nascent Russian Social-Democratic

Workers' Party, siding with its radical, Bolshevik wing led by V. I. Lenin after the split of 1903. His conspiratorial activity in Transcaucasia (including bank robberies to finance the party) brought him to Lenin's attention, and in 1912 he was coopted to be a member of the Central Committee of the Bolshevik Party and an editor of the party newspaper *Pravda*.

Arrested in 1913, Stalin was released from detention in Siberia after the fall of Tsar Nicholas II in February (March, Western style) 1917, and resumed his place in the Bolshevik leadership. Following the Bolshevik seizure of power in October (November) 1917 he was made Commissar of Nationalities in the new Soviet government. During the Civil War of 1918–1920 he served as an army political commissar and as Commissar of the Workers' and Peasants' Inspection. He was chosen a member of the Politburo of the Communist Party when it was set up in 1919.

In 1922, at Lenin's suggestion, Stalin was elevated to the new post of general secretary of the party. In his "Testament" of January 1923, shortly before his death, Lenin adjudged Stalin "too rude," but failed to remove him.

In the period 1923–1927 Stalin collaborated with the cautious faction of Communists led by Nikolai Bukharin who supported the semicapitalist New Economic Policy (NEP, 1921–1928), to fight Lev *Trotsky and the "Left Opposition" with their more proworker line. Meanwhile he built a personal power base in the professional bureaucracy or "apparatus" of the party. After expelling the Left Opposition from the party in 1927, he ousted Bukharin and the "Right Opposition" from the leadership and launched the radical programs that linked his name with the basic principles of the Soviet system for the next half century.

The "Stalin Revolution" included forcible *collectivization of the peasants; rapid expansion of heavy industry pursuant to the Five-Year Plans; and a vast increase in the labor camp system. Stalin repudiated social and artistic experimentation in favor of the propaganda of "socialist realism," embraced Russian nationalism, and abandoned the Marxian doctrines of egalitarianism and the "withering away of the state." He persecuted all religions until *World War II, when he granted limited toleration to the Russian Orthodox Church in order to gain its patriotic support.

Sensing opposition within the Communist Party leadership, Stalin used the December 1934 assassination of his heir-apparent Sergei Kirov (probably not arranged by Stalin himself, as once thought) as the excuse to launch the Great Purge of 1936–1938. This included the "Moscow Trials" that condemned his rivals of the 1920s, and the secret execution or imprisonment of one to two million members of the Soviet bureaucracy, intelligentsia, and military leadership.

Stalin toned down the Communist doctrine of world proletarian revolution, beginning with his theory of "socialism in one country" (1924), while he tightened Soviet control over the parties of the Communist International and used them as agents of influence and espionage in the service of *Soviet foreign policy.

In the mid-1930s Stalin sought alliances with the Western democracies in the name of "collective security," and ordered foreign Communist parties to support democratic governments through the "Popular Front." Then, to buy time, he concluded the German-Soviet Nonaggression Pact of August 1939 that set the stage for World War II. In 1939–1940, under cover of the pact, Stalin advanced the Soviet Union's western borders and annexed the Baltic Republics of Lithuania, Latvia, and Estonia.

Thanks to Stalin's efforts to placate Adolf *Hitler and his refusal to heed intelligence warnings, Soviet forces were taken by surprise when Germany invaded in June 1941, and suffered crushing initial defeats. Stalin at first panicked, but then assumed personal control over military operations. At war's end the Red Army had pushed back all the way to Berlin, occupying the entire band of East-Central and Southeastern European countries that had collaborated with the Nazis or had been occupied by them. Despite his promise at the *Yalta Conference of January–February 1945 to respect democratic principles in this region, Stalin proceeded to install the local Communists in power, along with the Soviet model of government and economy, thereby helping to bring on the *Cold War between the *Soviet Union and the Western powers. Communists as well as non-Communists who resisted Soviet hegemony were purged, with the exception of *Tito's Yugoslavia, which was expelled in 1948 from the Communist Information Bureau (Cominform) linking the new Communist governments.

Stalin took the victory of 1945 as vindication of his command economy, and intensified his dictatorial control instead of relaxing it as his subjects had hoped. He continued to conduct purges, particularly against ethnic minorities, foreign influences, and Jewish cultural figures. Possible further purges were cut short by his death of a stroke on 5 March 1953.

Stalin's model of government and economy was copied in China, North Korea, North Vietnam, and Cuba. The term "Neo-Stalinism" is generally applied to the antireform government of Leonid Brezhnev that followed the overthrow of Nikita Khrushchev in 1964, and to other Communist governments that followed the lead of the Brezhnev regime.

Stalin's place in history has been subject to widely differing interpretations. The official Communist line while he was still living was that he had continued the proletarian revolution and the building of *socialism begun by Lenin, crushed the "enemies of the people," and inspired every area of Soviet life and thought with his genius. This view was repudiated in part by Khrushchev in his de-Stalinization campaign of 1956–1961 emphasizing the terror of the purges, and further by Mikhail *Gorbachev during the period of "*perestroika" from 1985 to 1991, rejecting *Stalinism as a "command-administrative system" that had merely created "barracks socialism."

Since the collapse of the Soviet Union in 1991, most opinion in the formerly Communist countries has again identified Stalinism and Communism, though in a totally negative sense. A small minority of dogmatic Russian Communists continues to extol Stalin's role, particularly as a war leader.

Western evaluations of Stalin disagree as to whether he merely implemented the tyranny inherent in the Bolshevik Revolution and one-party dictatorship (the more conservative view) or whether he betrayed the Communist revolution by creating a bureaucratic dictatorship over the workers (the view of the non-Communist Left, notably of Trotskyists). Both of these schools of thought equate *Stalinism with the totalitarian system of rule, while "revisionist" scholars play down the "totalitarian model" and seek the explanation for Stalinism in Russia's social backwardness.

A composite view of Stalin is that he built on Lenin's heritage in some respects and contradicted it in others, synthesizing the most severe features of both the revolution and the tsarist regime in a postrevolutionary dictatorship that combined revolutionary rhetoric and a militarized economy with old nationalist ambitions.

By most accounts, Stalin was a man of extraordinary evil. Adept at behind-the-scenes intrigue, he was implacably vindictive toward anyone who had ever disagreed with him or outshone him, save Lenin. Foreign leaders and diplomats who dealt with Stalin found him personally charming as well as shrewd, though he enjoyed humiliating his own loyal entourage. In retrospect, his paranoid tendencies are clear, but this is an occupational disease of dictators.

Stalin's attitude toward the *ideology of *Marxism-*Leninism is still not widely understood. Most authorities assume either a doctrinaire belief that goaded him on, or a cynically propagandistic manipulation of doctrine. More likely Stalin combined an intense need for legitimation and personal acclaim with the ability to adopt any policy he chose, label it Marxism-Leninism, and destroy anyone who called this reasoning into question. He always cloaked his actions in Marxist-Leninist garb while tailoring the meaning of ideology to suit his policy decisions; the party's monopoly of public discourse made it seem to friend and foe alike that the ideology was still being followed undeviatingly.

(See also COMMUNIST PARTY STATES; RUSSIAN REVOLUTION; TOTALITARIANISM.)

Isaac Deutscher, *Stalin: A Political Biography* (New York and London, 1949). Robert C. Tucker, *Stalin as Revolutionary, 1879–1929* (New York, 1973). Roy A. Medvedev, *Let History Judge: The Origins and Consequences of Stalinism* (rev. ed., New York, 1989). Robert C. Tucker, *Stalin in Power* (New York, 1990). Robert Conquest, *Stalin: Breaker of Nations* (New York, 1991). Dmitri Volkogonov, *Stalin: Triumph and Tragedy* (New York, 1991). Robert V. Daniels, ed., *The Stalin Revolution: Foundations of the Totalitarian Era* (4th ed., Boston, 1997).

ROBERT V. DANIELS

STALINISM. Joseph *Stalin became undisputed leader of the *Soviet Union in 1929 and remained so until his death in 1953. Stalinism is the name given to the system that developed during those tumultuous years and to the attitudes that sustained and defended it. Stalinism may well be the most important historical phenomenon of the twentieth century. While the lurid evil of Nazism came and went, Stalinism created a social system whose essential elements endured for over fifty years. Stalinism was crucial to both the Allied victory in *World War II and the ensuing *Cold War, and American culture during the Cold War era cannot be understood without looking at the "red menace" that was part of its self-definition. Stalinism provided a blueprint for many other countries, all of which—including the fifteen successor states of the Soviet Union—are still struggling with its legacy. Stalinism is also crucial to ideological debates about the nature of socialism and *Marxism. Was Stalinism the logical consequence of Marxist doctrine, as both Stalin and his most vociferous critics maintain? And if socialism is *not* to blame for the disasters of the Stalin era, then what went wrong and why?

The major elements of Stalinism's own self-image were:

1. Unity. The Bolsheviks were obsessed with unity, and they had good reason to be: only their own unity and the

disunity of their many powerful opponents gave them hope for survival. Stalin emerged victorious from the leadership competition after *Lenin's death not only because of "machine politics" but because the party felt that he would guarantee this unity at whatever cost. The will to unity had an exclusive and punitive side that expressed itself as "vigilance" in unmasking "enemies of the people."

2. "There are no fortresses Bolsheviks cannot storm." This slogan typified the sense of urgency of the early 1930s, when Stalin made clear that he would go to any lengths to build up the country's strength in the shortest period of time. The ensuing violent attempts at social engineering engendered mass confusion that brought the country to the brink of ruin.

3. Construction of Socialism. Out of the chaos of breakneck industrialization and forced *collectivization arose a system of highly centralized control that reduced market forces to a minimum. During the *perestroika period, the system built up in the 1930s was labeled the administrative-command system, amid passionate debates about whether the country had ever really achieved genuine socialism.

4. Patriotism. Stalin increasingly stressed the importance of the Russian national tradition. This feature became even more prominent during the war against *Hitler. Patriotism was part of a larger dimension of Stalinism to which Nicholas Timasheff gave the name "the great retreat"—the progressive abandonment of revolutionary values in favor of traditional values such as *nationalism, family, and hierarchy.

Besides these features, outside observers tended to stress the following:

1. Gulag Prison-Camp System. "Gulag"—an acronym for Glavnoe Upravlenie Ispravitel'no-Trudovykh Lagerei ("Main Administration of Corrective Labor Camps")—is a term made world-famous by the writings of Aleksandr *Solzhenitsyn. During the Stalin years, millions of people from all levels of Soviet society were arrested on false charges and subjected to treatment that reached extremes of inhumanity.

2. Cult of the Leader. The term "cult of personality" was used in the Soviet Union after Stalin's death as a euphemism for various sins of the Stalinist period, from the replacement of collective leadership by one-man rule to the many "violations of socialist legality." But what struck foreign observers at the time was the quasi-religious cult of Stalin, which reached dizzying heights in the postwar period.

3. Cultural Repression. The Stalinist authorities maintained strict control over intellectual life of all kinds; one famous episode in particular symbolizes Stalinism's aggressive intellectual provincialism: the career of Trofim Lysenko, the charlatan who managed to convince the leadership that rejection of Mendelian genetics would lead to miraculous spurts of agricultural productivity.

4. One crucial aspect of Stalinism is almost forgotten: the "grand alliance." During World War II, the Western democracies willingly accepted Stalin as an ally. The viciousness of the war on the eastern front was incomparably greater than the war in the west: Western Europe and the United States survived with their material and moral values more or less intact partly because the Soviet Union took the brunt of the casualties and devastation. A convenient historical amnesia has removed from popular consciousness the fact that the Western powers were once Stalin's grateful allies.

Stalinism covered a period of intense change, during which the Soviet Union went from defeated pariah state to world superpower. Many of the foregoing features of Stalinism are more appropriate to some periods than others. This point can be illustrated by two novels that have done more than any amount of scholarly analysis to fix the Western image of Stalinism. Arthur Koestler's Darkness at Noon was an attempt to solve the mystery of why former party leaders confessed to imaginary crimes during the show trials of the late 1930s. George Orwell's 1984 was inspired by postwar Soviet society, with its mind-numbing barrage of xenophobic and mendacious propaganda combined with the gray poverty of a country devastated by the war.

After the war, the Stalinist system was exported more or less intact to the communist countries of Europe and Asia. *Mao Zedong's radical policies in China were sometimes seen as an alternative to Stalinism. The implied contrast, however, was to postwar Soviet society, which seemed bogged down in terminal stodginess; observers forgot about the Soviet Union's own "great leap forward" of the 1930s.

The process of de-Stalinization in the Soviet Union started immediately upon Stalin's death, beginning with the release of political prisoners and with denunciations of other flagrant crimes of the Stalin period. During the Khrushchev years (1953–1964) the scope of the critique steadily widened, until it threatened to subvert some of the fundamental features of the Soviet system. Under Brezhnev, this process of critical thinking was pushed underground. (To call the result "neo-Stalinism" is misleading: Lysenko, for example, was discredited only after Khrushchev was replaced by Brezhnev.) Under Gorbachev, the critique was renewed and widened to include the entire "administrative-command" system, including the Communist Party's political monopoly. De-Stalinization's positive program had always been "back to Lenin!"; it has been transcended to the extent that Leninist values themselves were ultimately rejected by Russian society.

A phenomenon as complex and dramatic as Stalinism has naturally given rise to many interpretive debates. Much discussion has centered on whether any valid alternatives to Stalinism existed within *Leninism. Two of Stalin's defeated opponents—Lev *Trotsky and Nikolai Bukharin—have become symbols of this possibility. The main themes of the Trotsky alternative were internal democratization for the working class leading to overthrow of the repressive bureaucracy, combined with world revolution leading to a benign international environment. Bukharin stressed the gradual and voluntary socialist transformation of agriculture.

The most serious attempt to place Stalinism in a larger comparative framework has been the concept of *totalitarianism. This concept grew out of two basic perceptions: first, that there was an essential similarity between Nazism and Stalinism, and, second, that these systems differed vastly from ordinary authoritarian dictatorships. The unprecedented monopolization of all social activity by the central leadership meant the elimination of independent alternatives in every area from politics to literature. In each sphere the leadership not only silenced opposition but demanded enthusiastic and sincere acceptance. Opponents of the totalitarianism concept argue that it encourages a view of Soviet society as merely the passive victim of the party elite. They also point to the great convenience of the term for Cold War propaganda battles.

The collapse of communism in Eastern Europe and the Soviet Union conclusively demonstrates that Stalinism was a historical dead end, and our heightened awareness of this may lead us to underestimate the seriousness of the dilemmas that gave rise to it. Any full account of Stalinism would have to give due weight not only to Bolshevik policies but also to the heritage of the Russian past, the utopian dreams of Marxist socialism, the murderous international pressures of the twentieth century, and the contradictions of forced-pace economic and cultural modernization.

(See also COMMAND ECONOMY; COMMUNIST PARTY STATES; MARXISM; POST-COMMUNISM; RUSSIAN REVOLUTION; SOCIALISM AND SOCIAL DEMOCRACY.)

Leon Trotsky, *The Revolution Betrayed: What Is the Soviet Union and Where Is It Going?* (1937; rep. New York, 1972). Nicholas S. Timasheff, *The Great Retreat: The Growth and Decline of Communism in Russia* (New York, 1946). Roy A. Medvedev, *Let History Judge: The Origins and Consequences of Stalinism*, revised and expanded edition (New York, 1989).
LARS T. LIH

STATE. There is a great deal of agreement among social scientists about how the state should be defined. A composite definition would include three elements. First, a state is a set of institutions which possess the means of violence and coercion. The state staffs such institutions with its own personnel; the continuity of such personnel over time distinguishes the state from the more transient government or administration as used in the context of U.S. politics. Second, these institutions in principle control a geographically bounded territory, usually referred to as a society. Crucially, the state looks inward to its own society and outward to larger societies in which it must make its way; its behavior in one area often can only be explained by its activities in the other. Third, the state monopolizes rule-making within its territory. This tends toward the creation of a common *political culture shared by all citizens. Differently put, the historical record witnesses an increasing pressure for the merging of nation and state. Sometimes national sentiment is created by the state, but sometimes the national principle can call into existence new states or divide the old.

It must be stressed that statehood is often an aspiration rather than an actual achievement. On the one hand, most historic states have had great difficulty in controlling their civil societies, and in particular in establishing their own monopoly of the means of violence. On the other hand, the *security of the state is compromised to an extent by broader forces which it cannot control. One such force—ably theorized by writers such as Raymond Aron, Kenneth Waltz, and Robert Gilpin—is that of the system of states, present for a thousand years in European history and now characteristic of what is genuinely a world polity. A second force, *capitalism, clearly has laws of motion all its own. Much interesting and important work is now being done in modern social science on the interrelations of capital and state, both domestically and internationally. If we are to understand the behavior of states, however, as much attention must be paid to a third variable, that of political regime, which has complex relations both to capital and to the state system.

Contesting the State. The nature of the state has been the subject of intellectual and political debate, especially in the twentieth century. The most obvious opposing views are

those of Anglo-Saxon *liberalism, *Marxism, and a looser school best dubbed Germanic *realism.

While there are many versions of liberalism, most are suspicious of the activities of the state. All that is virtuous is seen as residing in society; state forces are seen as obstacles ideally to be avoided. The most active role for the state envisaged by some liberals is that of a night watchman, protecting a framework within which market forces can then operate according to their own logic. This is the philosophy of laissez-faire; its explanations are society-based rather than state-centered because no independent reality is accorded to the polity. More sophisticated liberals emphasize the need for restrictions on state intrusion into society, but are much more aware of the visceral qualities of political *power. They seek to protect the individual against fear and arbitrariness—a position which means that the market is endorsed more for its capacity to create *pluralism and wealth than as something to be affirmed in and of itself. A similar distinction between naïveté and sophistication can be seen at work in liberal attitudes to *geopolitics. The laissez-faire "Manchester School" insisted that *peace would be assured by the growing *interdependence of the world economy; trade rather than territorial conquest was held to be the route to progress and prosperity. Less naïve liberals, following the lead of Immanuel Kant, have suggested that the era of peace will depend not just on trade but on other states recognizing the principles of *nationalism and of *democracy.

Quite clearly, Marxism displays characteristics of the naiver versions of liberalism. This can be seen most generally in the fact that Marxism offers society-based accounts of politics, and more particularly in its doctrines of eventual universal peace and of the "withering away of the state." The originality of Marxism lies in its belief that society is structured by the presence of social classes whose characters depend upon the particular mode of production in which they are embedded. This stress on class society means that Marxist hopes for both peace and the end of the state are on a different time scale than those of the naiver sort of liberal: these dreams cannot be realized until property relations are abandoned. The transition to socialism will be difficult, Marxists maintain, precisely because the modern state looks after the interests of capitalists: domestically state power is used to break working class bids for power while internationally the fact that different states seek markets for their national capitalists leads to *war.

A third perspective, Germanic realism, sees the state as an actor in its own right, able to represent the general interest in an "asocial" world of state competition. Externally, the state is seen as the guarantor of survival. Social thought in general was massively influenced by the long peace between 1815 and 1914 in which the brute social transformation of industrialization seemed all-important. But Germans achieved statehood in part because of war, and hence in the work of thinkers such as Max *Weber and Otto Hintze the impact of geopolitical transformation upon social life acquired particular prominence.

Since the 1970s, renewed interest in the state has been at the forefront of the social sciences. The exact reasons why this should be so are complex, although they certainly include modern Marxists' attempt to move beyond the instrumentalism generally characteristic of Marx's own theory to understandings, most of which proved to be unsatisfactory, of "the relatively autonomous powers" of the state. Whatever the intellectual history of the matter, there is no doubt about the outcome: the state is back.

Recent Theoretical Developments. Contemporary political analysis concerning the state will be better understood by first considering some pertinent empirical material. First, it is now generally recognized that the history of economic development beloved by both Marxists and liberals was rudely interrupted by geopolitical conflict between 1914 and 1945, and that this period profoundly changed social life. The different organization of social class in the German Democratic Republic and Federal Republic of Germany (East and West Germany) for a full half century, to cite but a single example, was the result of geopolitical settlement rather than of any logic of class formation itself. Similarly, *revolutions tend to occur in regimes which have been debilitated by excessive participation or actual defeat in war. State breakdowns give revolutionary *elites their chance.

Second, social scientists increasingly realize that the form of social movements often results from the characteristics of the state with which they interact. Working classes tend to be militant when a state excludes them from participation in civil society, i.e., workers take on the state when they are prevented from organizing industrially and confronting their immediate capitalist opponents. Thus a liberal state with full *citizenship sees no working-class revolutionary movement, whereas authoritarian and autocratic regimes see the emergence of Marxist-inspired workers: this principle helps explain the difference in working class behavior in the United States and czarist Russia at the end of the nineteenth century. The same principle—that political exclusion breeds militancy—helps explain the incidence of revolution within the *Third World since 1945. Central American societies share a mode of production, but only a few witness revolutions. The possibility of participation in a Costa Rica diffuses social conflict; its absence in Nicaragua under Somoza led to the creation of a revolutionary elite with popular support.

Contemporary analysts of the state also point to two dimensions of state power. Traditional theory concerned itself with the extent of the state's arbitrary powers, that is, the polar opposition between despotic and constitutional regimes. However, studies of agrarian states show that claims to universal power were more pretension than reality because the state had relatively few servants to penetrate and organize social life. Hence, a second dimension of state power, infrastructural power, concerns actual state capacities. Differently put, states are not free-floating. State strength is often the result of a state's ability to cooperate with groupings in civil society, and such cooperation is often ensured by some limitation on a state's despotic powers. Thus in the eighteenth century, the absolutist French state may have been autonomous in the sense of being "free from" parliamentary constraint, but it was nonetheless weaker—as the test of warfare showed—than its constitutional rival, Britain. In Britain, agreement between the upper classes and state actors allowed for higher levels of taxation and greater general efficiency, so the British state was "free to" do much more. This paradox applies equally well to the modern world: the war mobilization of Britain in *World War II exceeded that of Germany, and recent scholars of the Japanese state have stressed that

its great strength results from a "politics of reciprocal consent."

Modern social science is at its best when tracing the ways in which state power influences and is influenced by other sources of social power. An appreciation of the state complements previous understandings of socioeconomic forces, but it need not improperly seek to establish a monolithic state-centric view. We can appreciate some of the advances that have been made by scholars by turning first to historical and then to contemporary realities.

Origins of the State. Two processes have been responsible for the rise of states. Irrigation agriculture is the first. Whereas pastoralists or slash-and-burn agriculturalists can literally run away from an incipient state, the fixed investments of irrigation systems necessitate stability and thereby allow taxation, the lifeblood of the state. Second, the first states were based on temples, and recent scholarship has suggested that service of a demanding god may account for acceptance of the state.

Pristine state formation took place on only a few occasions, typically in geographically diverse places. But even early state power was so great that secondary state formation became an evolutionary necessity. Societies which did not have the protection of a state fell before those so endowed. Once the state was invented, it could not be forgotten.

As important a breakthrough in social evolution as the emergence of pristine states was the rise to world *hegemony of northwestern Europe, due to a dynamic broadly capitalist in spirit. Why this should have happened has long haunted social scientists, not least because much of the European pattern came to dominate the world. Recent research has made it possible for us to understand the role of the state and of the state system in the initial emergence of capitalism.

The European continent saw the emergence of states whose structures were conducive to the emergence of capitalism. Limits to arbitrariness meant that the state could not finally control capitalist actors, and the greater state revenue that resulted from cooperation with upper classes working through parliaments allowed for the provision of regularized justice and, in time, a revenue base.

This European development is largely explicable as the result of forces external to any single state. European states were long-lasting, and in consequence engaged in endless competition with each other. The pressure of interstate rivalry led to an increase in bureaucracy (the central development of the modern state), and in time to the creation of genuine nation-states. Under these circumstances, it was in the interest of rulers to limit predatory behavior toward capitalists whose flight would only result in an increase in the tax revenue of geopolitical rivals.

European development was exceptional in that it allowed for the emergence of capitalism and of a pluralistic society at one and the same time. This, of course, involved a long process, with extensive citizenship *rights only coming in the nineteenth and twentieth centuries. To mention this fact is to point to a darker side to the picture. The development of the modern state did not always encourage the growth of political rights. Imperial Germany sought to develop its economy and to keep its old regime in power; the people were to be integrated essentially through social rather than political citizenship, given that the state could not be controlled by parliamentary means. *Authoritarianism in tandem with a mobilized populace proved a dangerous brew. So too was the presence in multiethnic states such as Austro-Hungary of those who, convinced they could not advance through access to the imperial state, chose to play the national card so as to form their own. All in all, the dynamic which had proved so beneficial to the rise of Europe proved disastrous in 1914.

*World War I opened an era of geopolitical conflict, during the course of which it was by no means always apparent that this liberal legacy would survive. But in World War II force of arms destroyed *fascism, although it vastly enhanced—at least for nearly half a century—state socialism as well.

Liberal and Authoritarian States in the Modern World. The core of capitalist society was extended and consolidated in the settlement occasioned by the end of World War II. Japan and West Germany had liberalism imposed upon them, and they have thereafter preferred to advance via trade rather than conquest. More generally, the postwar world has seen the removal, in part at the behest of the United States, of extreme *Left and extreme *Right within the nations at the heart of capitalist society: liberalism seems triumphant. Does this mean that this core now operates on Anglo-Saxon principles—such that a concern with the state is losing much relevance? That question has gained in salience over time, for both intellectual and institutional reasons. Intellectually, a radical Right has sought to undo those elements of statist organization offering comprehensive social protections that had been retained, largely in Europe, against American wishes. Institutionally, the creation of a genuine international division of labor in combination with the freeing of financial markets from governmental regulation has suggested to many that capitalism, rather than states, now runs the world.

However, the ability of a national society to succeed within capitalism depends upon its state's ability to coordinate both workers and capitalists and to provide the necessary infrastructure such that citizens have the capacity to respond flexibly to international economic change. The practices of states in this regard are quite varied. Late industrial society does seem to benefit from high standards of education at every societal level, and increasing attention to this point is being given by economic leaders. Involvement of workers can be guaranteed in different ways, by the microcorporatism of German and Japanese firms or the macrocorporatism familiar from the Swedish model. States do not have a good record of managing firms themselves, not least because nationalized industries become powerful actors that are often able to prevent flexible responses. There is, however, every reason to believe that states can help business in myriad ways, for example by providing information about international market conditions, as is done particularly skillfully in Japan and the Republic of Korea (South Korea).

Thus, despite changes in the organization of capitalism, the evidence overwhelmingly goes against the assertion that states do not matter. They do, and any loss of their salience in certain areas of policy has been compensated for by their increased intervention in others. Organization internally and nationally enables a modern citizenry to swim in the larger sea of capitalist society; differently put, organization is needed internally because the principles of Adam Smith work externally. Competitive advantage is still created by nations.

Meanwhile, the overwhelming reality for most states in the world remains that of underdevelopment. The attempt to modernize quickly has placed liberalism at a discount. Both state socialist regimes and authoritarian regimes inside capitalism have sought to achieve development by means of centralizing power. The fate of such nations in contemporary circumstances is one of the questions of the age.

The most striking fact about state-planned industrialization is that it proves to be ineffective, even counterproductive, once the earliest stages of economic growth have been achieved. This is the fundamental fact behind attempts to liberalize authoritarian regimes. Such liberalization attempts are driven by pressures from above and from below, the exact mix between the two varying according to national circumstance: rulers wish to gain *legitimacy (and modern weaponry) through economic growth while newly educated middle-class elements, functionally ever more important in late industrial society, consistently join reformist parties. It is becoming possible to distinguish between different types of liberalization. The fact that a double transition to democracy and to capitalism has to be made in post-communist societies makes for very profound difficulties, with the distinct possibility that popular pressure might make it impossible for state leaders to implement necessary economic reforms. In this world, however, chances of success are highly variable. If biology is not, *pace* Freud, destiny, history often is: on this basis, Czechoslovakia (democratic and industrial in the interwar years) might have been expected to fare better than Romania and Poland, but for the ethnic-nationalist tensions spurring dissolution of the union.

In contrast, the transition from authoritarian regimes within capitalist society is, in principle, easier. But here too variable outcomes, again often dictated by historical legacies, can be expected. An East Asian state such as South Korea has benefited from fundamental *land reform pushed through at the time of the *Korean War, a tradition of literacy and of a state, created by Imperial Japan, concerned with infrastructural affairs; furthermore, as a result of its geopolitical vulnerability it has gained a good deal—from loans to trading privileges—from the United States. Whereas one can hope for successful liberalization there, great fears attend the "openings" in countries such as Brazil and Argentina. Racked by debt, possessed of ruling classes with reference points abroad (to which they often export capital), and bereft of a state tradition concerned with infrastructural services, it seems possible that the oscillation between democracy and *military rule will continue, at least in the near future.

In fact, the majority of states within the less developed world do not look as if they are liberalizing at all. India is exceptional in retaining democracy in such circumstances. More typical are state apparatuses which are overly developed, that is, possessed of sophisticated weapons used internally against their own people—or, as in Africa, against ethnic elements other than those comprising the ruling elite.

System of States and the Question of Hegemony. The theorists of the interstate system have in recent years added a striking coda to traditional theory. Once capitalist society becomes industrial, a leading state is needed to provide key services for capitalism as a whole—particularly a common currency and an insistence on free trade. Both Britain and the

United States are held to have provided such services; the fact of disputed hegemony after 1870 is held to be the underlying reason for international trade rivalry and full-scale geopolitical conflict thereafter.

This theory is not much of a guide to history: Britain had an economic lead but always faced genuine geopolitical rivals, but German expansionism is best explained in terms different from those suggested by the theory. The United States, on the other hand, was a genuine hegemon in 1945 in terms of both economic and military might; and it makes sense to see the theory in question, dubbed "hegemonic stability theory," as the *ideology of the postwar U.S. state elite.

U.S. hegemony has been exercised in two ways. In the period whose end was symbolized by the dollar "going off gold" in 1971, U.S. hegemony was benign. The interdependence of the world economy increased both because the United States insisted on free trade and because it provided the defense for all of capitalist society. But the glories of this period—at least for the core of capitalist society—have been replaced by much more predatory behavior on the part of the United States. The leading state has refused to satisfy its budgetary obligations to the United Nations while attempting to turn the organization to its political will, and in the last fifteen years it has absorbed most of the world's excess capital—behavior that bodes ill for both developing and liberalizing countries. Equally importantly, the United States used its mammoth influence in the aftermath of the 1997 Asian economic crisis more to serve its own economic interests than to improve the prospects of those in peril. All this has created great resentment among the allies of the United States.

At present, however, it does not seem that resentment will lead to a new age of geopolitical confrontation. *Nuclear weapons make recourse to war less rational for state actors, while trade is quite widely recognized as the best avenue to success. Furthermore, given the widespread realization that economic growth depends upon participating in an ever-larger and ever-faster international market, withdrawal from that market via protectionism (and, in consequence, trade wars) is relatively unlikely. In short, the world *political economy looks set to "muddle through."

The optimism of these last remarks amounts to saying that we can hope that there will be no World War III. But this optimism must be tempered. If major war is less likely, regional wars of ferocious intensity look ever more likely, particularly after the *Gulf War and the *Kosovo War. Large parts of the Third World possess formidable armed forces, and some will possess nuclear weapons soon; and many such countries have not benefited from economic growth. This is a dangerous mix. It suggests that war will continue to affect the historical record.

Future of the State. A current claim in scientific and political discourse is that the state is likely to lose its importance in the future. Two forces seem to have occasioned this speculation. On the one hand, the state seems to be losing its powers, in a process of "hollowing out" due to the greater *globalization of various international forces. The interdependence of the world economy, and in particular the growing share of world production taken by transnational corporations, is seen as withering the state's economic functions. In political terms, moreover, the emergence of supra-national authorities, from the *International Monetary Fund and the *World Trade Organization through, ever more dramatically, the *European Union, is seen as curtailing the state's authority in significant ways.

There is some truth to these assertions, but they need to be qualified. Full-scale state *sovereignty was never available in the European dynamic which was thereafter largely extended to the rest of the world: states always had to contend with the forces of capitalism and of interstate rivalry. The principal thrust of this essay is that the state has in myriad ways not lost its salience. Third World countries most certainly are states, and if their power is often greater in despotic than in infrastructural terms, it certainly shows no sign of diminishing. Equally, success within capitalist society seems to depend on national organization by the state. It may be that states, whether liberal or post-communist, are now less attracted to actual central *planning of industries; but a loss of state direction in that quarter is often more than made up for by an increasing emphasis on state provision of other services, from education to seed money for infant industries. Finally, capitalist society is not, so to speak, pure: its institutions are not genuinely supranational since they were created and are still controlled by the United States. Most important of all, the behavior of the United States—still half preferring to change the rules of the *international system which it dominates rather than to adopt a genuine trading strategy of its own—remains that of a great state. The world may be more complex than before, but we cannot understand it without an appreciation of the workings of the state.

(See also BUREAUCRATIC POLITICS; CLASS AND POLITICS; CORPORATISM; DEMOCRATIC TRANSITIONS; DEVELOPMENT AND UNDERDEVELOPMENT; INTERNATIONAL DEBT; INTERNATIONAL POLITICAL ECONOMY; MODERNIZATION; MULTINATIONAL CORPORATIONS; PLURALISM; POST-COMMUNISM; PROTECTION; REFORM; SOCIALISM AND SOCIAL DEMOCRACY; TAXES AND TAXATION.)

Kenneth Waltz, *Man, the State and War* (New York, 1959). Charles Tilly, ed., *The Formation of National States in Western Europe* (Princeton, N.J., 1975). Gianfranco Poggi, *The Development of the Modern State* (London, 1978). Theda Skocpol, *States and Social Revolutions* (Cambridge, U.K., 1979). Mancur Olson, *The Rise and Decline of Nations* (New Haven, Conn., 1982). Peter Katzenstein, *Small States in World Markets* (Ithaca, N.Y., 1985). Michael Mann, *States, War and Capitalism* (Oxford, 1988). John A. Hall and G. John Ikenberry, *The State* (Milton Keynes, U.K., 1989).

JOHN A. HALL

STRATEGIC ARMS LIMITATION TREATIES. See ARMS CONTROL; NUCLEAR WEAPONS.

STRATEGY. The term *strategy* refers to the means that policymakers choose to attain desired ends. Strategy is, in effect, a course of action, a plan for achieving specified goals. Although the term can be used to describe a plan for applying means to attain ends in any realm of political life, it is most frequently used in military affairs, a usage that became common during the eighteenth century.

When used in the realm of warfare, strategy refers to the art of using force to bring about desired outcomes on the battlefield. It refers to the broad questions of how, when, and where to bring *force to bear against an adversary. While the goal of a given strategy may be the destruction of the enemy's war-making potential, countries that engage in *war often pursue objectives that fall far short of destroying the enemy's military capability. The goal of a successful military strategy is to attain, in the most efficient and least costly fashion, a country's military objectives, whatever those objectives may consist of.

There are three broad types of military strategy. Offensive strategies involve taking the battle to the adversary, often to the end of destroying the enemy's fighting capability or compelling the enemy to retreat or surrender. Defensive strategies involve blocking the adversary's attack and denying the enemy its objectives. Deterrent strategies attempt to raise the cost to the adversary of continuing the battle, seeking to convince the enemy to abandon its aggressive intentions. Whereas offensive and defensive strategies focus on wearing down the enemy's military capability, deterrent strategies focus on wearing down the enemy's will. In any given campaign, military commanders may well use a mix of these strategies to attain their objectives most effectively.

Military planners formulate strategy at differing levels of generality. The term *grand strategy* refers to overarching plans that seek to balance a country's resources with its global military commitments. Formulating grand strategy involves determining the set of military objectives that devolve from a country's national interests and the threats that exist to those interests, identifying geographic and functional missions, and allocating available military resources to those missions.

During the nineteenth century, for example, British grand strategy involved maintaining a *balance of power on the European continent largely through shifting its political alignments with other European countries, while relying on the unrivaled Royal Navy to protect imperial lines of communication. During the *Cold War, U.S. grand strategy was based on the notion of *containment: preventing the Soviet Union from gaining control over the main industrial centers of Eurasia while restricting the spread of Soviet influence in the *Third World.

Grand strategy is distinct from theater strategy, which refers to planning for military operations in a specific geographic area. Theater strategy specifies how many and what types of forces are needed in a given region and how those forces would be used in battle. For example, the infamous Schlieffen plan—the strategy used by Germany at the outset of *World War I—called for German forces to hold defensive positions on the eastern front against Russia while mounting a decisive attack against France on the western front. During the Cold War, the *North Atlantic Treaty Organization's strategy for defending Western Europe against a Soviet attack called for forward defense with conventional weapons in Germany and escalation to the use of *nuclear weapons should conventional forces fail to halt the Soviet advance.

Strategy is distinct from tactics, which focus more narrowly on the actual placement and movement of troops on the battlefield. Whereas strategy seeks to identify how best to attain military objectives through the course of a campaign, tactical considerations focus on day-to-day prosecution of the battle: how to take advantage of the terrain, whether to attempt to penetrate the enemy's defensive line or to attack from the flanks, whether to retreat when under fire or to hold one's position, etc.

Military planners and scholars of military affairs have long searched for fundamental rules to govern the formulation of strategy. Inquiry has focused on a broad range of questions, including the following: What level of numerical superiority is necessary to ensure military victory? Is it preferable to be on the offensive, or does the defender enjoy tactical advantages that offset the attacker's ability to choose the time and place of battle? How important is the element of surprise?

Although some generalizations about strategy have emerged from inquiry into these questions, understanding the nature of warfare remains an intractable problem. The obstacles to a better understanding of war and a more scientific approach to formulating strategy stem in part from the unique nature of each battle. The quality and morale of opposing forces, the terrain, the climate, the technological sophistication of weaponry—these factors vary widely from case to case. Furthermore, the "fog of war"—the confusion and uncertainty that often pervade the battlefield—makes it very difficult, if not impossible, to transform the art of strategy into a science.

The term *strategic weapons* is commonly used to refer to intercontinental missiles armed with nuclear warheads. *Strategic studies* refers to scholarly inquiry into military affairs, broadly defined. In the context of *game theory, an analytic technique used to model bargaining between parties, strategy refers to the pattern of play that a given side pursues in order to attain its preferred outcome. If following a "tit-for-tat" strategy, for example, a player simply responds in kind to its opponent's move in each round of play.

(See also ALLIANCE; CLAUSEWITZ, CARL VON; DETERRENCE; FOREIGN POLICY.)

Edward Mead Earle et al., eds., *Makers of Modern Strategy* (Princeton, N.J., 1971).

CHARLES KUPCHAN

STRUCTURAL ADJUSTMENT PROGRAMS. Since the early 1980s the term "structural adjustment" has been used to label the set of orthodox economic policies imposed upon national governments by the *World Bank and *International Monetary Fund (IMF) as a condition for receiving loans. Structural adjustment programs (SAPs) emphasize a reduced role for government and expanded reliance upon free markets. They are usually undertaken in response to a syndrome of severe macroeconomic imbalances centered around *balance of payments deficits, collapsing currency values, and growth stagnation.

It is difficult to be precise about the content of SAPs because the term is often used to incorporate the related policy package known as "stabilization," which refers to short-term arrangements that stave off immediate crisis. Stabilization requires external aid, usually from the IMF, to temporarily meet external obligations and balance payments. To quickly bring a country's demand for foreign goods and services in line with its ability to pay for them, the currency is devalued and tight fiscal and monetary policies force contraction of the domestic economy. Structural adjustment proper, which involves longer-term policy changes designed to enable the economy to resume growth after the massive trauma of initial stabilization, falls formally within the purview of the World Bank. It emphasizes market liberalization (especially in international trade), *privatization of state-owned enterprises, deregulation, and a continuation of fiscal austerity, monetary tightness, and realistic exchange rates. In practice, the distinction between stabilization and structural adjustment is blurred because the two international financial institutions (IFIs) usually cooperate in designing and funding programs and the conservative economic orthodoxy that underlies both packages has been dubbed "the Washington consensus."

The controversies surrounding SAPs derive from both their roots in neoclassical economic theory and the role of the IFIs in imposing them as loan conditions. Structural adjustment loans (SALs) were first dispensed by the World Bank in 1980 in response to the payments crises induced in many developing countries by OPEC oil price increases. By 1982, they were also being used to encourage internal restructuring to cope with global recession, high interest rates, and sagging commodity prices. The World Bank's shift from funding development projects to inducing policy reform was justified by the dictum that sound projects were not possible in an unsound policy environment, especially the *import-substitution industrialization (ISI) widely practiced in developing countries. When private sources of capital dried up in the face of the Latin American debt crisis (first manifested in August 1982 in Mexico), SALs emerged as the only available source of financing, giving the World Bank enormous leverage to engineer the wholesale revolution in economic policy that swept through developing countries over the next two decades. The IMF formally undertook SALs beginning in 1986 with the establishment of the Structural Adjustment Facility, succeeded by the Enhanced Structural Adjustment Facility in 1987. In November 1999, it was renamed the Poverty Reduction and Growth Facility (PRGF), with somewhat greater attention to poverty issues and considerably more coordination with the World Bank, but no appreciable change in policy. Loans remain conditional upon acceptable progress in achieving policy reforms. As of April 2000, the PRGF had outstanding loans to thirty-one countries totaling $4.5 billion, but had disbursed about $12 billion to fifty-six countries since 1986. In fiscal year 1999, the World Bank disbursed more than $10 billion in structural adjustment loans and another $5 billion in related sector adjustment loans. The importance of SALs is considerably greater than these dollar amounts might suggest, however, because other financial institutions, national aid programs, and private actors use IMF judgments concerning the soundness of national policies as a dominant factor in allocating grants, loans, and investment. By 1990, two thirds of the states in Africa had received policy-based loans from the World Bank and thirty-one had received adjustment loans from the IMF. Meanwhile, every nation in Latin America had undertaken an adjustment of a similar style. Critics decry the power of institutions controlled by rich countries to erode the national autonomy of poor ones by dictating economic policies.

Moreover, SAPs have become the crucible of theoretical and policy clashes that have deeper political and philosophical roots. Critiques of structural adjustment have much in common with the anti-globalization arguments that have achieved center stage in public debates more recently. At issue is the universal applicability of neoclassical theoretical models that critics contend have been used to impose policies that are unnecessarily contractionary and that benefit business interests (especially *multinational corporations) at the expense of workers and the poor.

Proponents of SAPs blame governments for irresponsible spending and borrowing, failure to adjust domestic policies to external realities, and, consequently, investment shortages that reflect lack of business confidence. The goal of structural adjustment is a more externally oriented, export-led economy that both contributes to and benefits from the integrated global economy. SAPs aim to achieve a sustainable balance of payments by reducing distortions that impede efficiency, fuel excessive demand for foreign goods and services, and constrain market forces that would spur growth and incoming investment. Trade barriers and overvalued exchange rates encourage imports and discourage exports. Capital controls, overregulation, and state ownership of key industries diminish investment. Excessive state spending generates growth-sapping inflation and debt.

Critics of structural adjustment grant that these neoclassically founded diagnoses are frequently (though not always) correct, but note that they do not address the causes of economic crises that lie outside the country itself, such as weak demand and trade barriers elsewhere in the world economy and deterioration in the terms of trade. Rooted as they are in neoclassical theory rather than empirical research, all SAPs tend to look pretty much alike, even though the circumstances of nations are very different.

Furthermore, critics contend, austerity programs unnecessarily threaten the poor and weaken the state politically, since cuts in government spending usually attack social services and public investment first. Because tight fiscal and monetary policies reverse growth long before they slow the economy enough to ease inflationary pressures, stabilization and structural adjustment are said to violate the mandate of the IMF (contained in Article I of its charter) to correct maladjustments "without resorting to measures destructive of national or international prosperity." Liberalization in trade and investment benefits foreign interests but endangers small domestic producers that cannot compete and diminishes the bargaining power of labor against newly deregulated and geographically mobile capital. Privatization and other foreign investment also incur long-term liabilities. Whatever growth may result from structural adjustment exacts a high price in inequality, foreign dependence, and social instability.

(See also DEVELOPMENT AND UNDERDEVELOPMENT; EQUALITY AND INEQUALITY; EXPORT-LED GROWTH; GLOBALIZATION; INTERATIONAL DEBT; NORTH-SOUTH RELATIONS.)

G. A. Cornia, R. Jolly, and F. Stewart, eds., *Adjustment with a Human Face* (Oxford, 1987). Daniel M. Schydlowsky, ed., *Structural Adjustment: Retrospect and Prospect* (Westport, Conn., 1995).

BRUCE E. MOON

SUDAN. Sudan is geographically the largest country in Africa with a total area of 1 million square miles (2.5 million sq. km.) and a population of about 30 million people. Nine countries and the Red Sea surround the country. The

Red Sea is to the northeast; Eritrea and Ethiopia to the east; Kenya, Uganda, and the Democratic Republic of the Congo to the south; Central African Republic and Chad to the west; Libya to the northwest; and Egypt to the north. A journey backward through history would show that the modern Sudanese nation-state is a product of multivariate systems of governance and civilizations. Prominent among these systems were the pre-Christian-era Kush kingdom, the Nubian Christian kingdom that ruled Sudan for more than 700 years, the Turko-Egyptian (1821–1885), the Mahdia (1885–1898), and the Anglo-Egyptian condominium (1898–1956) from which the country gained its independence on 1 January 1956.

The country has, since independence, witnessed a political cycle of multiparty democracy alternating with military/authoritarian systems of governance. The military has had a lion's share in the political management of the modern Sudanese nation-state. There have been, for instance, three periods of military rule for a total of thirty-four years out of forty-four years of independence. The first period of military rule was during the period 1958–1964. It was overthrown through a popular uprising (intifahda) in October 1964 and followed by a period of multiparty democracy (1965–1969). The second period lasted from 1969 to April 1985, when military rule was once more overthrown through a popular uprising. The third military regime, currently in charge, came to power in June 1989.

The Sudan Communist Party and the National Islamic Front (NIF) supported the second and third military regimes, respectively. The ideological orientation of the two regimes led them to create a one-party system of governance. Legislative bodies were established. However, only members of Sudan Socialist Union (SSU), a party created by the second military regime, were allowed to contest elections, though all Sudanese were eligible to vote. Similarly, only members of the National Congress of the present military regime of General Omar Hassan Al-Beshir (head of state) and Dr. Hassan Abdalla Al-Turabi (secretary-general of the party and spiritual leader) are allowed to run for seats in the National Assembly. As of April 2000, all the political parties have been allowed to resume their political activities, though it remained unclear as to when elections for the National Assembly would be conducted.

The political cycle of civilian and military regimes of the postindependent Sudan has been dominated by a sustained struggle between traditional forces and the elite, though both belong to the same ethnic/racial group. Traditional forces have dominated political parties and multiparty democracy, while the elite and other modern forces have constituted military regimes and parties with ideological orientation, such as Communism and Islamic *fundamentalism. Both elite and traditional forces have, however, effectively utilized a narrowly based political authority to reinforce Arab hegemony in the Sudan. This is in spite of 500 ethnic groups, which speak more than a hundred languages and profess three religions—African traditional religion, Christianity, and *Islam.

The outcome of a narrow-based political authority is unequal development between the various regions of the country. Macroeconomic policy and development strategies have tended to favor central and northern Sudan, while neglecting the other regions, especially in the south and west. Most of the major development projects, such as the Gezira scheme, have been concentrated in the central region. Social services (schools and health facilities) and physical infrastructure also accompanied this concentration. Moreover, the introduction of *sharia'a, or Islamic laws, in September 1983 was seen by many political forces in southern Sudan as a way of denying them revenue from the oil that was discovered there in the late 1970s.

Islamic laws continue to be the foundation of economic policy and social development even after the second popular uprising of April 1985. This was due to the inability of the third multiparty democratic government (1986–1989) of Al-Sadig Al-Mahdi to abrogate the sharia'a in accordance with his election manifesto. And when a national consensus was emerging on the necessity to freeze the Islamic laws of 1983, at least as a temporary measure, until a constitutional conference determines the most appropriate constitution for a multiethnic Sudanese nation-state, the NIF staged a successful military coup on 30 June 1989. The NIF has transformed Sudan into a full Islamic state, which is governed by a coalition of military-civilian Islamists of the National Congress Party.

The quest for an Islamic system of governance by all the Sudanese governments that have come and gone, compounded by unequal development, has caused postindependence to be at war with itself twice now. The Sudanese internal conflicts have been between the predominantly Arab and Muslim north and African and mainly Christian south. The south, which constitutes about one third of the area of the country with a population of more than 10 million people, is rich in natural resources, such as fossil oil, timber, water, wildlife, and minerals. These resources, with the exception of oil, have not been utilized for the social well-being of ordinary Sudanese because of the civil wars. The first civil war lasted seventeen years (1955–1972), while the second has now reached its seventeenth year (1983–2000).

The second civil war is distinguished from the first in two ways. It is more devastating; it is estimated that about 2 million southern Sudanese have died as a result of the current conflict (compared with in the first). And it extends beyond the south, to southern Blue Nile, southern Kordofan, and eastern Sudan. This second feature of the Sudanese conflict, which has important political implications for both the unity of the country and governance power structure, was brought about by the Sudan People's Liberation Movement (SPLM) and its military wing the Sudan People's Liberation Army (SPLA), which are both headed by Dr. John Garang de Mabior, a southern Sudanese.

The SPLM/A calls for the establishment of a New Sudan in which all the Sudanese participate in its political, social, and economic affairs, irrespective of ethnicity, race, region, religion, or gender. In this regard, the SPLA has among its rank and file Sudanese from other regions of the country, especially southern Blue Nile and southern Kordofan. In addition, the SPLM/A has formed an alliance with other political parties and groups from northern Sudan. This is the National Democratic Alliance (NDA), which was formed in 1990 with the main objective of overthrowing the current regime. The NDA comprises the SPLM, Democratic Unionist Party (DUP), Umma Party, Union of Sudan African Parties (USAP), the Beja Congress, Sudan Communist Party, Sudan Federal Party, Sudan Alliance Forces (SAF), Sudanese Trade Unions, and the Legitimate Command of Sudanese Armed Forces.

The NDA is a potential force that would bring about fundamental political changes in the structure and orientation of the Sudanese nation-state. This would in turn restore democratic governance and sustained peace to Sudan and its neighbors. It would also restore international confidence and respect, since Sudan is considered an exporter of Islamic fundamentalism and international *terrorism.

Francis M. Deng, *War of Visions: Conflicts of Identities in the Sudan* (Washington, D.C., 1994). Elwathig Kamer, ed., *John Garang: The Vision of The New Sudan: Questions of Unity and Identity* (Cairo, 1998).

LUAL A. DENG

SUEZ CRISIS. The Suez crisis of 1956 began with President Gamal Abdel *Nasser's speech of 26 July 1956 announcing the *nationalization of the Suez Canal. This itself was a response to the U.S. decision, supported by the British, to withdraw the offer of financial assistance for *Egypt's proposed Aswan High Dam. Nationalization was bitterly resented by the British and French governments, which saw it as an act of self-aggrandizement on President Nasser's part and a threat to their vital interests. Both prepared their forces to invade Egypt while going through the motions of trying to negotiate the international management of the canal.

The crisis culminated in the coordinated military attack by Britain, France, and Israel beginning on 29 October 1956. British and French forces occupied Port Said but were forced to withdraw under intense U.S. economic pressure. A UN Emergency Force was hastily established to replace the invading armies. The canal was then cleared of the obstacles sunk by the Egyptians and reopened to traffic in April 1957. Meanwhile, Israel was forced to withdraw its forces from the Sinai Peninsula in March 1957, also under U.S. pressure.

The response of Sir Anthony Eden's British government to the crisis was dictated by its determination to use force to overthrow Nasser. But it was also anxious to do this in a way which would offend neither the United States nor the many Britons who were bitterly opposed to an attack on Egypt. Eden's mismanagement of the crisis led to his resignation as prime minister in January 1957 and his replacement by Harold Macmillan. Both Macmillan and President Dwight *Eisenhower were quick to restore the Anglo-American partnership. The Conservative Party under Macmillan then went on to win the general election of 1959 in which the Suez issue played little role. For Macmillan and his colleagues the main lessons of the crisis concerned the extent of British dependence on the United States and the lack of support from major *Commonwealth countries like India. Many were now persuaded that Britain's future lay not with its empire but with Europe.

Unlike the British, the French were almost unanimous in their belief that force should be used against Egypt, which was widely seen as the main supporter of the Algerian rebellion begun in 1955. However, the government of Guy Mollet realized that it had to act in concert with the British, and it was for this reason that, in October 1956, it suggested the idea of cooperation with Israel, to which it was already supplying arms. Many in France, including senior officers, were unhappy at being forced to stop military action before it had either secured the whole of the canal or led to the overthrow of Nasser. In this way, failure at Suez was one of the major factors exacerbating the political divisions which encouraged the collapse of the Fourth Republic in 1958, the return of President Charles de *Gaulle, and the decision to grant Algeria its independence. A second result was the belief that it was unwise to allow France to remain dependent on Britain and the United States, something which did much to stimulate the development of France's independent deterrent (the *force de frappe*) and its entry into the European Economic Community as a founding member in 1957.

U.S. policy toward the Suez crisis was guided by President Eisenhower's desire to secure a peaceful settlement without alienating his British and French allies. Once the invasion had begun, Eisenhower's aim was the immediate withdrawal of the Anglo-French force under UN auspices, followed by the reconstruction of the Western alliance. To this end, during a major run on the British pound, he held up U.S. financial assistance until military evacuation was complete. He was similarly adamant about Israeli withdrawal. Soviet and Arab reaction to the crisis then persuaded him that swift action was necessary to prevent the communists and their allies from filling the vacuum left by the retreating British and French. The result was the so-called *Eisenhower Doctrine, which stated that the United States was willing to use armed force in the Middle East in the event of communist aggression. As a result, Washington lost much of the credit that it had obtained in the Arab world for its strong stand against the invasion.

The one Great Power which was not directly involved with the crisis was the Soviet Union. This was partly because it was engaged in putting down the revolt that had broken out in Hungary just before the invasion, partly because the Soviets could derive great benefit from the affair by simply identifying themselves with a Third World country subject to imperialist aggression. Moscow's only major political intervention was on 5 November 1956 when it proposed joint action with the United States against Britain and France, accompanied by an unspecified military threat if a cease-fire was not immediately accepted. The Soviet Union was also quick to provide economic and military aid to Egypt, followed by an offer to finance Egypt's new development program and then, in October 1958, to assist in the funding and the construction of the Aswan Dam. In this way the Soviets were able to use the crisis to establish themselves as a major rival to the United States in the region and the primary source of assistance to important Middle Eastern states like Egypt, Syria, and Iraq.

In the Middle East itself, the person who benefited most from the crisis was President Nasser. Not only had he kept the canal in Egyptian hands but he also became the focus for widespread Arab support. His immediate response was to try to increase inter-Arab cooperation as well as to extend his influence into countries like Jordan, Saudi Arabia, and Iraq, which he identified as allies of the West. But the most immediate result was his acceptance of Syrian requests for political union, which culminated in the creation of the United Arab Republic (UAR) in February 1958. On the domestic front, the nationalization of British, French, and Jewish property which accompanied the invasion provided the spur to a large extension of state enterprise and, ultimately, to the move to a centrally planned economy in 1961.

Israel also derived benefit from the crisis. It obtained the right of free passage through the Gulf of Aqaba, denied by

Egypt since 1948, and so commercial access to the countries of Africa and Asia. There was also a considerable decline in the number of armed incursions from the Gaza Strip and elsewhere until the mid-1960s. More problematic was the partial security guarantee which the Israeli government obtained from the United States at the time of its military withdrawal from the Sinai Peninsula. This was not honored during the Arab-Israeli crisis which preceded the June War of 1967.

As far as the *Middle East was concerned, the Suez crisis of 1956 accelerated the decline of British and French influence and paved the way for the Soviet and U.S. domination which lasted until the decline of the Soviet position in the early 1970s. It provided an important but temporary victory for President Nasser and his type of secular *Arab nationalism and transformed the dispute between Israelis and Palestinians into one between Israel and the surrounding Arab states.

(See also ALGERIAN WAR OF INDEPENDENCE; ARAB-ISRAELI CONFLICT; NASSERISM.)

Donald Neff, *Warriors at Suez: Eisenhower Takes America into the Middle East* (New York, 1981). Muhammad H. Haykal, *Cutting the Lion's Tail: Suez Through Egyptian Eyes* (London, 1986). Wm. Roger Louis and Roger Owen, eds., *Suez 1956: The Crisis and Its Consequences* (Oxford, 1989). Keith Kyle, *The Suez Crisis: Thirty Years After* (London, 1991). Selwin Ilan Troen and Moshe Shemesh, eds., *The Suez-Sinai Crisis, 1956: Retrospective and Reappraisal* (London, 1990).

ROGER OWEN

SUPREME COURT OF THE UNITED STATES. The U.S. Constitution of 1787 sketched a bare outline of the federal judicial power. Article III established only one federal court—the Supreme Court—leaving Congress, in the Judiciary Act of 1789, to create the lower federal courts, to fix the number of justices on the high court, and to set its appellate jurisdiction. The Constitution provided that the president would appoint the justices with the advice and consent of the Senate, leaving their specific qualifications (should they be lawyers? should they have previous judicial experience? should they be native-born citizens?) undefined. This open-ended process invited the president to consider political and not just professional qualifications. The delegates to the Philadelphia Convention also clothed the justices with substantial independence by granting them tenure during good behavior and provided for their removal from office only after impeachment by the House of Representatives for "high crimes and misdemeanors" and conviction by the Senate.

In response to complaints by states' rights advocates that the proposed Constitution granted too much autonomy to the Court, Alexander Hamilton formulated his classic nationalist defense of judicial independence. Hamilton proclaimed in *Federalist* 78 (1787) that "the judiciary . . . will always be the least dangerous to the political rights of the Constitution" (Clinton Rossiter, ed., *The Federalist Papers*, p. 465). Because the Court commanded only the authority of its legal judgment instead of the power of the purse and the sword, the justices would be able to consult "nothing . . . but the Constitution and its law" (p. 471). Accordingly, he asserted that an independent federal judiciary, generally, and the Supreme Court, specifically, offered the best protection for the rights of citizens under the new Constitution. Hamilton's arguments remain compelling, even though today the justices exercise

far greater influence over political issues and public life than Hamilton anticipated.

The growth of the Supreme Court's power is attributable at least as much to the exigencies of U.S. *political culture as to any effort on the part of the justices to broaden their authority. As Alexis de Tocqueville observed in the 1830s, law in the United States is an extension of political discourse, so much so that "scarcely any political question arises in the United States that is not resolved, sooner or later, into a judicial question" (*Democracy in America*, vol. 1, ed. Phillips Bradley [1945], p. 290). The justices, however, have also played a decisive role in expanding their influence over public affairs, often doing so by disavowing that they either wanted or should have such influence. For example, in addressing a directive from Congress to seat federal judges as pension claims commissioners, Chief Justice John Jay stated in *Hayburn's Case* (1793) that Congress could assign judges only to judicial and not administrative duties. In the same year, Jay refused President George Washington's request for an advisory interpretation of the 1778 Franco-American treaty. By limiting the Court to actual rather than hypothetical disputes, the justices sought to assure themselves that when they spoke they did so in ways that would have direct rather than imagined consequences.

Chief Justice John Marshall (1803–1835) built upon this early foundation by establishing the authority of the Court to interpret conclusively the meaning of the Constitution. He did so by establishing the institution of *judicial review, doing so for federal legislation in *Marbury* v. *Madison* (1803), in which the Court declared a portion of the Judiciary Act of 1789 unconstitutional, and for state legislation in cases such as *McCulloch* v. *Maryland* (1819), which voided a Maryland law imposing a tax on the Second Bank of the United States. The cost of this heightened judicial authority over constitutional interpretation was inevitably the judiciary's greater involvement in the political system.

Throughout the remainder of the nineteenth century, Marshall's successors expanded the scope of judicial review and the prestige of the Court at the same time that they refused to adjudicate so-called political questions. In *Luther* v. *Borden* (1849), Chief Justice Roger B. Taney held that the question of which of two competing governments in Rhode Island was legitimate was entirely "political in nature." Therefore, Taney concluded, the political branches of the federal government, not the courts, could best determine whether Rhode Island or any other state had met the mandate of the Guarantee Clause of Article IV that each state have a republican form of government. The judiciary, Taney observed, had no role to play; its business was legal, not political.

As in the nineteenth century, the Court also deferred in the twentieth century to the legislative and executive branches in matters involving war and foreign affairs. In *Koremastu* v. *United States* (1944), for example, the justices invoked national security to approve the relocation of Japanese-American citizens based solely on their ancestry. The Court's actions echoed decisions during World War I that affirmed the power of the national government to proscribe political dissent to a degree unthinkable in peacetime (e.g., *Schenck* v. *United States* [1918]). In a dispute arising out of President Jimmy Carter's termination of a treaty with Taiwan, the justices in *Goldwater*

v. *Carter* (1979) refused to determine whether Congress's approval of the termination was required by the Constitution. The Court did reluctantly enter into the foreign policy arena in *Dames & Moore* v. *Regan* (1981), upholding an executive order, issued after Iran's release of American hostages, that effectively prevented the petitioner's recovery of assets from the government of Iran. Stressing the narrowness of its decision, the Court precluded further action on its decision as precedent.

The justices themselves have recognized that regulating the standards granting litigants access to the Court can influence its power. The Court has found a textual limit to its power of review in the "cases and controversies" clause of Article III. Accordingly, suits must be justiciable before the Court will decide them, and the party bringing the suit must have standing to do so. The Court will not accept friendly or collusive controversies, moot causes, and disputes lacking in ripeness. For instance, in *Muskrat* v. *United States* (1912), the justices dismissed a suit paid for the defendant, the U.S. government, because the action was a friendly controversy meant to gain an advisory opinion on the constitutionality of federal legislation. Similarly, a cause was found moot in *Atherton Mills* v. *Johnson* (1922) where the plaintiff, who initiated the suit to challenge the regulation of minor laborers, was no longer governed by the law's age limits when the case came before the Court. The action in *United Public Works* v. *Mitchell* (1947) was also beyond the Court's "judgment" because the law banning political campaigning by federal employees was challenged by plaintiffs who had not been charged with violating the statute in question. According to Justice Robert H. Jackson, a "hypothetical threat" to the plaintiffs' constitutional rights was insufficient to confer jurisdiction, and the suit was dismissed because it had not "ripened" into an actual legal contest.

Despite these examples, the justices have often honored the concept of judicial restraint more in word than deed. Perhaps the classic example was Chief Justice Taney's decision in *Dred Scott* v. *Sandford* (1857). Taney attempted to settle the politically explosive issue of slavery in the territories by declaring that persons of African descent were not citizens of the United States and that they had no rights that white men were bound to respect. Taney's position stirred outrage among free-state Republicans on the eve of the Civil War. In *Pollock* v. *Farmers Loan and Trust Company* (1895), a bare majority of the Court declared the federal income tax unconstitutional, a position that was not reversed until the ratification of the Sixteenth Amendment in 1913.

The Court, moreover, is hardly a self-regulating institution; instead, its agenda is shaped by the character of the litigation that comes before it, which is in turn the product of shifting social demands. Until 1937, for example, the justices invoked the doctrines of liberty to contract and substantive due process of law to limit governmental intervention in the economy. The Great Depression shattered the myth of laissez-faire constitutionalism and free-market economics that supported these doctrines, but even so the Court refused to extend constitutional support to Franklin D. *Roosevelt's *New Deal economic programs, initially striking down several pieces of Roosevelt's legislative program. Eventually, however, they reversed field, deciding in *West Coast Hotel* v. *Parrish* (1937) and

Jones & Laughlin Steel Corporation v. *National Labor Relations Board* (1937) that state legislatures and Congress had broad power over the economy. Having changed course, however, the Court did not go out of business; instead, civil-liberties and civil-rights activists, represented by the American Civil Liberties Union, the National Association for the Advancement of Colored People, and the National Organization of Women, demanded an increased portion of the Court's time.

Under the leadership of Chief Justice Earl Warren (1953–1969), for example, the Court became a judicial engine of social reform. Beginning with *Brown* v. *Board of Education* (1954), the justices made a permanent imprint on race relations in the United States by ordering an end to separate-but-equal public schools. Opponents of the Court retaliated by claiming that Warren and his colleagues were unelected, and therefore unaccountable, judges who sought to substitute their personal preferences for that of legislative majorities. Billboards around the country proclaimed "Impeach Earl Warren."

The dramatic expansion of judicial "judgment" for the sake of racial equality was followed by the Court's equally bold venture into the once-taboo field of "political questions." In the interest of electoral fairness, the Court in *Baker* v. *Carr* (1962) refashioned the political questions doctrine to permit judicial review of state apportionment plans. The Warren Court also departed from the historical practice of permitting the president and Congress to operate according to their own rules. In *Powell* v. *McCormack* (1969), the justices responded to an attempt, under House of Representatives rules, to exclude a duly elected member, Adam Clayton Powell, from sitting in the House. The Court held that, regardless of the House's internal procedures, the Constitution gave Congress the power only to remove a member, not to exclude.

First President Richard *Nixon and then President Ronald *Reagan won election by, among other things, campaigning against the Supreme Court. Nixon and then Reagan promised, as did the latter's Republican successor, George *Bush, to reverse the highly controversial social agenda of the Warren years and to appoint justices who would strictly interpret the meaning of the Constitution. The results were mixed at best. President Nixon's selection of Chief Justice Warren Burger and Associate Justice Harry Blackmun actually produced a Court that in some areas, such as abortion rights in *Roe* v. *Wade* (1972), was more activist than the Warren Court. President Reagan was somewhat more successful, in large measure due to his selection of Chief Justice William H. Rehnquist, who worked systematically to lead his colleagues toward an agenda designed to repudiate the Warren Court's positions on *human rights, as well as the Burger Court's decision in *Roe* v. *Wade*. As has often been the case, however, presidential expectations that new justices would reformulate constitutional law have proven unfounded. President Dwight *Eisenhower, for example, complained that his two biggest political mistakes were the appointments of two fellow Republicans, Chief Justice Warren and Associate Justice William Brennan, to the high court. Moreover, several appointees during the Reagan and Bush years, notably Sandra Day O'Connor, William Kennedy, and David Souter, have taken moderate positions in several critical cases and thereby frustrated the larger political goals of the presidents that selected them. The result has been a Court with a conservative yet mixed record on civil liberties and civil rights matters. The current justices have permitted some additional public assistance, for example, to religious schools, but they continue to resist officially sponsored devotional exercises in public schools. The current Court has refused to extend the right of privacy to homosexual privacy and physician-assisted suicide (*Washington* v. *Glucksberg* [1997]), yet the justices have also required that discrimination based on sexual preference (*Romer* v. *Evans* [1996]) be intensively scrutinized and accepted that terminally ill patients cannot be refused assisted suicide under all circumstances.

Nonetheless, the constitutional ground has shifted during the years of the Rehnquist Court. The Court now provides stronger protection to the rights of property holders against the political actions of the states (*Phillips* v. *Washington Legal Foundation* [1998]). Even more dramatic, the justices have resurrected the Eleventh Amendment and expanded the immunity of the states from lawsuits brought by private citizens (*Seminole Tribe* v. *Florida* [1996]). And a majority of the justices generally have taken the position that federalism is best understood and explained constitutionally from the perspective of the states rather than of the national government (*United States* v. *Lopez* [1995]). This position has also given the states somewhat greater leeway in treating suspects and defendants in criminal cases. Most dramatic, perhaps, the modern Court has made clear its impatience with the slow pace of executions in capital cases by limiting severely the use of habeas corpus petitions by death-row inmates (*McCleskey* v. *Zant* [1991]).

The impact of these recent developments has been most striking in the Court's image as a national symbol, not just a legal body with often sharpened political interests. Through most of its history, the Court has been more often than not a reluctant exponent of the doctrine of equal justice under law. The Warren Court years, in that regard, were something of an anomaly, in which criminal defendants, the politically unorthodox, the crusaders in support of full political expression, and racial minorities found an ally in the Constitution and a majority of the justices. Today that is not nearly so true.

By design and circumstances, the purportedly apolitical Supreme Court has emerged over the past two centuries as more than a court but less than a full-blown political institution. What its history has repeatedly shown, as both Hamilton and Tocqueville understood, is that the Court, paradoxically, has had to be of the world of politics without being in that world. Perhaps the most important measure of the Court's historic success is that, even today, it continues to cultivate its institutional strength by meeting this difficult challenge.

(See also CIVIL RIGHTS MOVEMENT; CONGRESS, U.S.; PRESIDENCY, U.S.; UNITED STATES.)

Robert G. McCloskey, *The American Supreme Court* (Chicago, 1960). Alexander Bickel, *The Least Dangerous Branch: The Supreme Court at the Bar of Politics* (Indianapolis, 1962). Kermit L. Hall, ed., *The Oxford Companion to the Supreme Court of the United States* (New York, 1992). Tinsley E. Yarbrough, *The Rehnquist Court and the Constitution* (New York, 2000).

KERMIT L. HALL

SURINAME. Once a member, together with the Netherlands Antilles, of the Tripartite Kingdom of the Netherlands, Suriname achieved its independence on 25 November 1975. For five years this small country on the north coast of South America (population approximately 450,000) was governed as a parliamentary democracy by a largely black ("Creole") government counterbalanced by a largely East Indian ("Hindustani") opposition. The existence of a number of other fairly sizeable ethnic groups (Indonesians, Bush Negroes, Amerindians, Chinese, Syrians, and Dutch) meant that neither of the two largest groups could control the government without a consociational (multiethnic) alliance of some kind. Nevertheless, the Creole-Hindustani rivalry paralyzed the system and precipitated a military coup on 25 February 1980.

Enthusiasm at the possibility of transcending ethnic politics turned to dismay as misgovernment, corruption, and human rights violations occurred. A guerrilla war of Bush Negroes (descendants of escaped slaves) broke out in the summer of 1986. This, together with financial pressure from the *Netherlands and demonstrations in the capital, Paramaribo, led the military leader, Desi Bouterse, to restore democracy in 1987. In that year, an alliance of Creole, Hindustani, and Indonesian parties handily defeated a promilitary party.

Governmental paralysis in the face of military insubordination culminated in a coup in 1990. New elections, won by the same consociational bloc, led to Bouterse's removal as military commander. But Dutch pressures for structural adjustments stymied the new government. Ironically, after the 1995 elections the promilitary party (now headed by Bouterse) managed to lure several members of the multiethnic bloc to defect.

The new government, led by Jules Wijdenbosch, aroused Dutch hostility because of its corruption and defiant refusal to prosecute drug and human rights violations. Despite some improvement in economic performance, cracks in the coalition cost this government its parliamentary majority. New elections in May 2000 were won by the consociational bloc, led by Ronald Venetiaan.

(See also CONSOCIATIONAL DEMOCRACY; GUERRILLA WARFARE.)

H. E. Chin and H. Buddingh', *Surinam: Politics, Economics, and Society* (London, 1987). E. M. Dew. *The Trouble in Suriname, 1975–1993* (Westport, Conn., 1994).

EDWARD M. DEW

SUSTAINABLE DEVELOPMENT. See overleaf.

SWAZILAND. See SOUTHERN AFRICA; SMALL STATES AND TERRITORIES.

SWEDEN. A small, affluent nation located in *Scandinavia in Northern Europe, Sweden is commonly considered the archetype of the modern *welfare state. Though Sweden's relative standing has slipped in recent years, its 8.8 million inhabitants still enjoy one of the highest standards of living in the world. From a comparative perspective, Sweden stands out as the advanced capitalist country with the most egalitarian distribution of income, before as well as after taxes and government transfers are taken into account. With unions organizing more than 85 percent of all wage earners, Sweden also represents the most thoroughly unionized of the advanced capitalist countries. Historically tied to the powerful
(cont. on p. 819)

SUSTAINABLE DEVELOPMENT. The concept of sustainable development reconciles two apparently contradictory goals—environmental conservation and economic development—and brings them into a single policy framework. It addresses the deepening global environmental crisis and the increasing social and economic imbalances that divide the world. As Klaus Töpfer, Executive Director of the United Nations Environment Programme (UNEP), has put it: "The world's population has now passed six billion, and the majority of these people live in poverty. Meanwhile, the share of the planet's resources being used by the affluent minority is also growing. These two issues—the poverty of the majority and the excessive consumption of the minority—are driving forces of environmental degradation." The sustainable development approach suggests a solution to this double crisis.

A Brief History. Throughout history many societies have worried that they may be living and consuming in the present at the expense of the future. On the walls of a monastery in Alsace, for example, researchers discovered the oldest written records of sustainable forest management, dating back to the year 1144.

In recent years, the burgeoning environmental movement spurred thinking on sustainability—for the first time on a global basis. In 1972, the Club of Rome warned of "The Limits of Growth" in its famous report, while in the same year the *United Nations held its first Conference on the Human Environment in Stockholm. In 1973, UNEP Executive Director Maurice Strong coined the term "eco-development" to describe a development strategy that safeguards the ecosystem while meeting social and economic objectives like more food, schools, and housing.

The International Union for the Conservation of Nature introduced "sustainable development" in 1980 in its World Conservation Strategy, a plan for the global environment from a biological point of view. Nevertheless, the report failed to analyze the underlying political and economic structures causing environmental degradation—*multinational corporations organizing the logging of old-growth forests, for example, or automobile companies lobbying for more roads and lower pollution standards.

In 1987, the World Commission on Environment and Development published its Brundtland Report, a milestone in sustainable development theory that combined the notion of growth and development with the idea of an ecological, non-destructive economy. But the report's definition of sustainable development remained vague and diffuse, allowing for many interpretations and eventually giving rise to a dangerous misconception that sustainable development is the same thing as sustainable or sustained growth.

In 1992, at the UN Conference on Environment and Development in Rio (also known as "The Earth Summit"), governments agreed on sustainable development as the leading political concept. They passed Agenda 21, an elaborate action plan to achieve sustainable development worldwide. Although a consensus definition of sustainable development was still lacking, the conference gained tremendous publicity

and it had great influence on policy thinking. To monitor the implementation of Agenda 21 and the related Rio Declaration, the UN created the Commission on Sustainable Development in 1993. Sustainable development had by then very broad political acceptance. Environmentalists thought they had won the day. But powerful polluting industries (autos, oil, chemicals) along with growth-oriented governments led by the United States blocked progress in the followup international negotiations and blunted the concept, so it could not serve as a viable policy tool. The business lobby made matters worse by pressing for deregulated markets and opposing new taxes and policy regulations designed to improve the environment. Agenda 21 remained largely a dead letter.

While conservative apologists insist that things are getting better (or will soon improve), the real world situation has deteriorated dramatically. According to UNEP, at the turn of the millennium over 80 percent of the world's forests had been destroyed or degraded and 25 percent of the approximately 4,630 mammal species in the world stood at risk of total extinction. Further, if present consumption patterns continue, two-thirds of the global population will live in conditions of severe water shortage by the year 2025. Global warming, severe weather events, drastic declines in fish stocks, pollution of drinking water, new diseases—these and many more signs of crisis have evoked urgent protests from scientists, environmental groups, and increasing numbers of the public. But with a few exceptions like the 1987 Montreal Protocol on the ozone layer or the Cartagena protocol on biosafety adopted in early 2000, little has been achieved on an intergovernmental basis to implement an effective sustainable development strategy.

Different Concepts. Sustainable development is neither a new development theory, nor is it a clearly defined political concept. Rather, it is a normative idea summed up by a well-known sentence of the Brundtland Report: "Sustainable development is development that meets the needs of the present without compromising the ability of future generations to meet their own needs." This definition combines an intergenerational, future-oriented aspect with a dimension oriented to the needs of the present. The consensus-oriented character of the approach was the main reason for its success in the discourse of the 1990s.

At the time of the Rio Conference, sustainable development was the rallying cry of a movement and a (relatively) clear plan of action. But today its vagueness has the quality of many political slogans—it can mean different things to different people. Generally on hearing it, no one is challenged to rethink positions or to alter preconceptions. Sustainable development is typically an empty phrase that can be understood by environmentalists, economists, business managers, and politicians according to their own separate interests. Nevertheless, the debate can be understood in terms of four main positions that offer substantially different levels of sustainability.

Pseudo-Sustainability. The weakest form of sustainability, strongly backed by the majority of the business lobby and reflected in the work of many economists and libertarian policy think-tanks, can be called "pseudo-sustainability." It assumes that the market will come up with solutions to resource depletion, pollution, or other disruption of the ecosystem. According to this view, even the reduction of biodiversity through the disappearance of species is not necessarily a problem, since market forces and especially progress in technology can be counted on for fresh solutions to compensate for the loss of natural resources. Near-extinct species can be preserved in zoos, for example, or their genetic makeup stored in gene banks for the use and appreciation of coming generations. Increasingly scarce (and polluting) fossil fuels can be replaced by new energy forms based on hydrogen, generated by solar energy, or other common substances, while food shortages will be solved by new genetically-altered seeds, new fertilizers, advanced types of irrigation, and other agricultural technologies. According to this view, any change in the natural systems of the planet can be "sustainable" as long as equivalent research and investments serve present and future generations. Sustained economic growth and minimum interference in the market are regarded as necessary preconditions for this path. Proponents see almost no limit to the use of human-made substitutes for non-renewable natural resources.

This reductionist view subordinates nature completely to a cost-benefit calculation. It stakes the future of life on the planet on a dubious theory and places humanity in the hands of financiers and corporate executives whose only goal is profit and whose time-horizon is short, especially on an ecological timescale. Evidence of the results of this approach is already visible, in the form of our present crisis. The social dimension of sustainable development also disappears almost completely in this model, as social justice depends on the invisible hand of the market, again with real world results such as mass poverty that are clear for all to see.

Sometimes called "cornucopian technocentrism," this idea of plenteous sustainability assumes an overflowing cornucopia of technology. But it is simply naïve optimism. Even modest advances in protecting the environment—air and water pollution controls, for example—have usually depended on government regulation to correct the excesses of the market. This approach also grossly underestimates the interdependence and chain reactions produced by constant human interference with the ecosystem. Today, as unprecedented natural disasters, widespread pollution, and rapid species extinction constantly remind us, the unchecked effects of capitalism on the environment leads to a wide-ranging and nonreversible deterioration of our natural heritage.

Weak Sustainability. The "enlightened" wing of the business community and its allies in government, universities, and the right wing of the environmental movement advocate what we can call "weak sustainability." They take the environmental challenge more seriously than the more conservative group and are more open to a limited role for regulation. They admit that human-engineered substitutes for natural resources are subject to certain limits. And they distinguish between essential components of the natural environment, for which no substitutes can be found (e.g., the ozone layer) and nonessential components (e.g., fossil fuels) for which substitutes are possible if they produce more benefit (and more profit) for present and future generations. These views, however, appear to be largely driven by public relations thinking and by the opportunity to gain public approval by "greenwash," presenting normal investments as environmentally friendly measures.

The concept admits the absolute limits of the ecosystem's carrying capacity but nevertheless insists on the primacy of economic growth. Sustainable development, these advocates believe, will be achieved by an "efficiency revolution," resulting in a much more cost-effective production process and management of resources. They don't think that fundamental economic changes are necessary.

This approach, sometimes called "ecological modernization" or "eco-efficiency," is prominently supported by the World Business Council on Sustainable Development and reflected in the "Factor Four" concept of Ernst-Ulrich von Weizsäcker. "Factor Four" argues that both sustainability and development can be met through "doubling wealth and halving resource use" by means of innovations like more energy-efficient motors, new kinds of buildings and lighting fixtures, reusing waste, and so on. Proponents argue that business is already aware of cost-savings and is pursuing this path to market-driven solutions. Periodic announcements by business leaders appear to confirm this view. The CEO of oil giant British Petroleum told the press not long ago that his company will reduce its energy use in refineries and throughout the production stream, saving millions of dollars in the process. Other firms have been following suit. Nevertheless, natural resource consumption continues to climb rapidly and even very modest intergovernmental targets to address global warming have not been met. The eco-efficiency argument depends on a dishonest focus on microcase success stories while studiously ignoring the larger picture.

Quantitative growth overwhelms efficiency gains and continues the overconsumption of resources. For example, the automobile industry now produces more fuel-efficient, low-pollution vehicles than it did in 1950. But in the same time, the world's automobile fleet has grown tenfold, from 53 million vehicles to about 530 million. Net pollution and resource use has thus risen substantially. No "factor four" improvement is visible here, though the stock market shares of auto firms more than quadrupled in that period.

The concept of eco-efficiency entails an optimistic belief in technological progress which underestimates the complexity of real ecological interdependence. Finally, it largely neglects the social dimension of sustainability and reflects a narrow perception of the ecological and human future of the planet. Few serious environmental scientists accept the theses of this position.

Strong Sustainability. Many environmentalists and scientists adopt a position we can call "strong sustainability." It begins with the view that the existing stock of natural resources must be maintained for future generations. Tradeoffs are only legitimate within this resource stock, for example, by substituting renewable energy sources (like wind or solar-generated electricity) for fossil fuels (like electricity from coal or oil-fired generating stations).

In this view, economic growth in the industrialized countries has to be reduced to zero to increase the opportunities for (sustainable) development in the countries of the global South, a step that can only be taken with forceful multilateral action. So the concept of strong sustainability focuses on distributive effects not only within and between generations but also between countries. It emphasizes the social dimension more than any other sustainability concept and pleads for structural changes in the patterns of production and strengthened opportunities of *political participation.

As a response to the shortcomings of the eco-efficiency concept, this approach introduces the term "sufficiency." Sufficiency is a very old concept that can be found in the Bible and other texts. It has attracted increasing attention because more material possessions and other aspects of wealth do not increase people's life satisfaction, as many opinion polls have shown. To the contrary, consumer society causes many forms of human dissatisfaction. In order to increase satisfaction and reduce resource use to a level that prevents the long term destruction of the global ecosystem, technology-based productivity improvements are not enough. Instead, proponents of strong sustainability argue that we must develop a new concept of wealth and well-being that goes beyond the present materialism and consumerism of the industrialized countries.

Ultra Sustainability. Some environmentalists subscribe to a view we can call "ultra sustainability." This idea is extremely ecocentric, stressing the primacy of resource conservation and insisting on the intrinsic values of all natural objects within the ecosphere. Consequently, proponents believe that natural resources must remain unused and nothing can be substituted for them. This position, which emerged from Western naturalist philosophy during the 1970s and 1980s, has evolved into a theory called "Deep Ecology." Its advocates have developed a radical critique of Western culture, including its anthropocentrism, belief in science and technology, and economic orientation. This school of thought views "weaker" concepts of sustainable development as unviable solutions to the accelerating human destruction of the environment. The theory proposes self-regulatory powers of the ecosystem as a possible solution to natural destruction (the Gaia hypothesis).

Many critics, including committed environmentalists, see this approach as extremely simplistic and antirational. It also does not promote equality or sufficiently take into account the economic and social situation of the poor countries and their need for a development process that results in higher material standards of life. Thus it ignores the need to eliminate social inequality—one of the major barriers to a sustainable future. Ultra sustainability, therefore, fails to provide an adequate framework for sustainable development.

Conclusion. The very different and contradictory concepts of sustainable development reflect the limits of the sustainability approach as a whole. Its broad success in the public debate comes at the expense of conceptual clarity. But still, the different theories can be judged by their multidisciplinary scope and explanatory value. The eco-efficiency approach clearly does not measure up, with its misplaced and single-minded trust in market forces. In view of the urgent environmental crisis—depletion of the ozone layer, increased global warming, further desertification, an accelerated loss of biodiversity—the business-driven approach is completely inadequate. Scientific evidence demonstrates very clearly that the operations of businesses, even when presented in a "greenwashed" fashion, lead towards a further deterioration of the global environment and human living conditions. The Chairman of Ford Motors admitted this inconsistency in a publication issued at the company's 2000 annual meeting, where he said that his best-selling product, sports utility vehicles, were dangerous and bad for the environment. He later affirmed that since billions of dollars of Ford profits depended on these products, the company would continue to advertise and produce them.

Clearly, governments or intergovernmental institutions must set effective social and environmental standards that can foster real sustainability in spite of the unsustainable tendencies of the private economy. Citizens, acting through political institutions, must promote distributive justice within and between societies and ensure the appropriate protection of nature and resources. Strong democratic institutions on the national and international level are essential to coordinate sustainable development policies and international governance.

"Strong sustainability" reflects the best potential for the concept of sustainable development. Environmental sustainability and social justice are its joint goals while economic development is seen as only a means. The concept emphasizes that sustainable development cannot be achieved by assigning primacy to the economy and it rejects a belief in progress towards this goal mainly through technological innovation.

Humanity needs increased resource productivity for sustainable development. Still more, we need fundamental structural changes in the patterns of consumption (to emphasize sufficiency) and production (to produce without harm to the environment). And we need democratic governance of political processes, both on the national and international level. Beyond all this, to achieve sustainable development, we need to reach new understanding of the quality of life and the value of the environment as a treasure for ourselves and our successors.

(See also DEVELOPMENT AND UNDERDEVELOPMENT; ENVIRONMENTALISM; FOOD POLITICS; POPULATION POLICY.)

JENS MARTENS, KLAUS SCHILDER

SUSTAINABLE DEVELOPMENT. As we embark on a new century, there are few certainties about what kind of world we will inhabit in twenty-five years, though there is no shortage of speculation. One element that seems inevitable, however, is that the earth's population will continue to expand, and that economic growth will be crucial to cope with this phenomenon. But this growth must be more sustainable than in the past—and there is increasing consensus among industry, governments, and civil societies worldwide that this is the way forward.

Sustainable development means development that meets the needs of the present without compromising the ability of future generations to meet their own needs. The concept is built on three fundamental and inseparable pillars: economic growth, environmental improvement, and social responsibility. It is a continually evolving process whereby society gradually moves to a position where these three elements interact in a self-reinforcing manner. Yet sustainable development is not a clear and easily defined objective, and varies from country to country. Depending upon local conditions, the emphasis among development, job creation, improvement in social conditions, and the environment can differ.

Over the past twenty years, the attitude of industry toward ecological preservation has evolved markedly from a defensive to a proactive stand, leading corporations to become major solution providers toward sustainability. In the 1970s and 1980s, as environmental pressure groups in industrialized countries gained influence at the policy-making level, business was obliged to pay attention to green issues and correct blatantly polluting practices. In the 1990s, firms moved beyond compliance with regulations to avoid penalties into producing eco-efficient goods, that is, "doing more with less." They discovered that using new processes which minimize environmental impact could actually boost profitability and open up new commercial opportunities. Corporate practice on sustainability has further advanced to what can be called a holistic approach that integrates socially responsible entrepreneurship into overall operating strategy.

Developing Country Conundrum. The developing world faces the most daunting challenges in pursuing sustainable economic growth. Poverty is a strong driver for environmental degradation and the developing countries need economic growth to eradicate poverty. But this growth must be different from what the newly industrialized countries experienced in their early industrialization. Population pressures, including growth of 100 million and more every year, risk adding to existing environmental degradation.

Most of the new manufacturing capacity that will be added up to the middle of this century will be in what is today developing countries. This affords us an excellent opportunity to make economic growth in these countries more sustainable. But for that to happen, they need help from the industrialized countries.

One means to achieving this lies in innovation and new technology, which have a key role to play in fostering sustainable development everywhere. Currently, all but a handful of developing nations face formidable barriers in exploiting innovation and technology, which, to flourish, require efficient information networks, a large pool of skilled human resources, and substantial investment. Wholesale technology transfer to poor country governments in an effort to help them to "leapfrog" environmentally damaging manufacturing processes is probably not the answer. In any case, the high expectations raised by this approach have not been met. In addition to providing technological hardware to resource-poor governments, there must be an emphasis on developing the software side—technical skills and knowledge—and adapting the entire package to suit local needs and budgets. Business-to-business cooperation is the best conduit for developing such a skill-based pool and, in general, for innovating in the marketplace.

Industry, while seeking out new markets, has a responsibility to make sure that the benefits of technology-driven globalization reach the world's poorest. And corporations can help to nurture a culture of sustainable development in developing countries by creating job opportunities, providing training and capacity building for employees and suppliers, and disseminating best practices in environmental and resource management.

Wherever they operate, progressive companies know that they ignore sustainable development at their peril. It is in the corporate world's interest to have people everywhere share in economic activity in a way that is kind to the environment. For if the benefits of globalization are perceived to be one-sided, business risks a backlash from stakeholders—employees, customers, community groups, and investors—with damaging consequences, as the ministerial meeting of the *World Trade Organization in Seattle demonstrated.

The Principle of Eco-Efficiency. Industry's application of eco-efficiency is a rejoinder to critics who charge that business is not in the business of sustainable development. The term was coined in 1991 by the Geneva-based World Business Council for Sustainable Development (WBCSD) to describe business practices that highlight the positive connections between economic and ecological efficiency. It is a concept that combines economic improvements with more efficient use of resources. In short, eco-efficiency seeks to add more value with less impact on the environment. It requires business to reduce material and energy inputs, cut back on toxic waste, enhance recyclability, maximize use of renewables, extend product durability, and increase the service intensity of goods.

Eco-efficiency is not only relevant to leading edge, rich-country multinationals. It is a universal concept that can be applied across all industry sectors and to all companies, be they family-run affairs, medium-sized entities, or corporations, and to all countries. The single most important requirement for companies to reap the full benefits of eco-efficiency is senior management commitment. If dedication and a vision of how to achieve sustainable development are lacking, the likelihood of success is limited. Today, the reach and influence of eco-efficiency have spread beyond business into the policy-making sphere of governments whose role is to provide the multilayered foundation needed to achieve sustainability. A case in point is that both the Organization for Economic Cooperation and Development and the European Union are using eco-efficiency as a policy concept.

Business Shifts. The Rio Earth Summit of 1992 helped to propagate an eco-efficient mind-set among corporations, and proved to be a strong catalyst for change in how they treat environmental issues. Firms, at least in the developed world, are increasingly viewing sustainable development as integral to business development, while also regarding environmental matters as companywide responsibilities as opposed to areas to be handled only by experts. They are linking sustainability with savings and opportunities, rather than with costs and liabilities. Another noticeable change is the shift from end-of-pipe approaches geared to fixing existing problems to the use of cleaner, more efficient production processes. Some companies and sectors are also pursuing by-product synergy, which entails using the by-products and wastes from one industry as raw materials and resources for another—thus creating zero waste. There is also a move to manufacture products with new and enhanced functionality and services.

On a more general level, there has been a shift from corporate confidentiality to openness, transparency, and discussions with a broad range of stakeholders. That shift is due to the revolution in communications and computer technology, giving the public instant access to information and placing multinationals under greater scrutiny on the world stage than ever before. Finally, there is evidence that those firms which take their environmental and social growth responsibilities seriously are harvesting financial rewards in the shape of better stock prices.

Eco-Efficiency in Practice. Here are a few examples.

Climate Change. While climate change is a global problem requiring global solutions, the majority of actions for reducing greenhouse gas emissions, believed to provoke climate shifts, clearly lie with industry—and industry is responding. Companies such as BP Amoco, DuPont, and Shell are investing heavily in renewable energy sources, which may not only mitigate the risks of climate change but offer greater growth prospects than the carbon fuel industry. DuPont, for example, intends to source 10 percent of its global energy use from 2010 on from renewable resources. Major energy firms have also set targets for reducing their global greenhouse gas emissions, and to hold energy use flat. In the transportation area, under the umbrella of the WBCSD, oil and auto firms including Shell, Ford, General Motors, and Toyota are behind an initiative to create a vision for future sustainable mobility.

Forestry. In South America, plantations are being established on lands abandoned because farming has failed. These "new model" plantations preserve a minimum of 20 percent of the remaining natural forests in perpetuity to maintain wildlife habitat, protect water quality, and prevent soil erosion and flooding. The remaining abandoned areas are converted to highly productive tree farms, which produce four to ten times more than the most productive forests in the Northern Hemisphere. This is no altruistic act. Most of those involved in forestry understand that to prosper, they need to manage their resource base in a sustainable fashion. Deliberately destroying the productivity of the forests which provide their raw materials is corporate suicide.

Mining. In recent years, the mining industry has made efforts to reduce the impact of its operations on the local environment, which can lead to improved relations with local communities. In addition, modern technology makes it possible to extract underground natural resources without actually setting foot in sensitive eco-regions. WMC Limited conducted flora and fauna surveys when the company carried out exploratory drilling for gold in an ecologically sensitive region in Victoria, Australia, and it intentionally excluded areas where biologically important plants were found from the exploration program. Recently, some of the world's biggest mining companies, together with the WBCSD, are spearheading the Global Mining Initiative, the aim of which is to define how the mining and minerals industry can contribute to sustainable development.

Water. Business is protecting and preventing the pollution of fresh water—a scarce resource in many areas—partly to ensure its own clean supply for manufacturing purposes and also as part of its payback to communities targeted as markets. In 1985, Nestlé South Africa helped set up Eco-Link, an association which supports many projects, one of which works to find ways to harvest limited water resources together with improving water and waste management to help combat problems attributable to waterborne diseases. The solutions include the building of water tanks and capping access to natural underground springs.

Influence of Financial Markets. One major reason why business is supporting sustainable development is because it is proving to make economic sense and to be good for the bottom line. While companies cannot be managed simply according to philanthropic principles, it is clearly in the interest of the "good performers" to be able to obtain proper recognition from the financial markets for their results. The markets hold the scorecard both when it comes to evaluating companies on the stock exchange and when pricing risks which influence interest rates and insurance premiums. The influence of financial markets in spurring sustainable development was emphasized in September 1999 when the Dow Jones Sustainability Group Index was launched. The index is based on the performance of 200 companies selected from a broad range of sectors including heavy industry, with a total market capitalization of US$4.4 trillion. Dow Jones identified this group as being leaders on sustainability. A notional back calculation of the index between 1994 and mid-1999 has shown that it would have outperformed the Dow Jones Global Index, achieving an annualized return of 17 percent compared with the Global Index's 13 percent.

Shared Responsibility. Companies are only one element in the sustainable development equation. The other two crucial players are governments and *civil society. Governments have the responsibility of creating framework conditions that allow business to be innovative and implement new management practices and new technologies. These conditions include macroeconomic stability, open markets, clear intellectual property rights, regulatory enforcement, political stability, and minimal bureaucratic red tape. Availability of natural resources, a skilled work force, and good infrastructure are also important. Governments everywhere have to be involved in dealing with complex environmental issues, be they climate change, fresh water, or biodiversity, which business, let alone individual firms, cannot tackle singlehandedly. They also need to stop subsidizing uses of resources such as water and energy which contribute to environmental problems. Such subsidies do not reflect resource scarcity and lead to a vicious spiral of waste and environmental damage, while also thwarting private initiatives that could offer solutions.

Meanwhile, consumers and *nongovernmental organizations are exerting pressure on governments to protect the environment—and they are increasingly vocal and powerful. The environment has become one of the factors influencing consumer purchasing decisions. Thus the successful journey toward sustainable development hinges on equitable partnerships between the public and private sectors and civil society.

Given their different stages on that journey, the industrialized and developing worlds inevitably have different priorities. Feedback from developing countries themselves highlights poverty alleviation, corruption, and education as being among the top priority issues that must be dealt with in order to achieve progress toward sustainability. While resource-intensive consumption patterns are an issue for industrialized countries, poor nations are struggling to meet their basic needs and combat poverty. Business needs to absorb these differences in crafting principles to fit local conditions.

Toward Responsible Entrepreneurship. As well as possessing environmentally sound credentials, forward-thinking companies realize they also need to address their social license to operate. That is why corporate social responsibility (CSR), the social pillar of sustainable development, has leapt to a prominent place on the global corporate policy agenda. Each company has its own definition of CSR, although some of the most common priorities are human rights, employee education, community involvement, and supplier relations.

Companies are reporting that a coherent CSR strategy has clear business benefits: a better alignment of corporate goals with those of society, an enhanced reputation, and reduction of risk and its associated costs.

The business case argument has another dimension. Globalization, free trade, and foreign direct investment all have their detractors who complain that social and environmental standards are being compromised in the pursuit of these goals, and that investment decisions are often insensitive to local needs and circumstances. A social policy provides business with an opportunity to demonstrate that this need not be the case, and to show its "human" face.

With companies more than ever aware that good corporate citizenship is necessary for business, the momentum in industry for working toward sustainable development is growing. Business has already made much progress, but much more needs to be delivered by all concerned parties. At the next Earth Summit in 2002, industry, governments, and civil society must convincingly and collectively show that efforts to raise environmental and social good conduct over the past decade have bred success. Whether in the next decade economic development becomes synonymous with sustainable development will depend on the breadth of these efforts.

(See also DEVELOPMENT AND UNDERDEVELOPMENT; ENVIRONMENTALISM; GLOBALIZATION; NORTH-SOUTH RELATIONS.)

BJÖRN STIGSON

confederation of blue-collar unions (*Landsorganissationen* or LO), the Social Democratic Party has dominated Swedish politics since the 1930s. From 1932 to 1976, Sweden had but three prime ministers, all Social Democrats (Per Albin Hansson, Tage Erlander, and Olof Palme). By contrast, the period since the mid-1970s has been characterized by a great deal of political volatility.

Narrow electoral defeats for the Social Democrats in 1976 and 1979 resulted in a period of coalition government by non-socialist parties, but the Social Democrats returned to power in 1982 and strong economic performance provided the basis for their continued electoral success through the 1980s. With the economy heading towards a deep recession, the Social Democrats suffered a historic setback in the election of 1991, polling 37.6 percent of the popular vote. However, nonsocialist coalition government again proved short lived: in 1994, the Social Democrats recovered their previous losses and returned to power. In the election of 1998, the Social Democrats did even worse than they had done in 1991 (36.6 percent of the popular vote), but their losses translated into gains for other Left parties, enabling the leader of the Social Democratic Party, Göran Persson, to remain as prime minister.

Political Institutions and Party Politics. Sweden became a hereditary monarchy and a national state with a unitary structure in the sixteenth century. While there exists a long tradition of municipal self-government within a national legislative framework, regional authorities have never been an important part of the Swedish system of government. At the central level, the ministries are small and have very few administrative responsibilities. The task of implementing government policy rests with state agencies (*ämbetsverk*) run by civil servants, and the ability of elected politicians to influence their activities is strictly limited. The autonomy and professionalism of the civil service constitutes an important feature of the consensual cast of Swedish politics.

Originally an assembly of estates, the *Riksdag* became a bicameral parliament in 1866, but the principle of parliamentary government did not become institutionalized until 1917, shortly before the introduction of universal suffrage in 1921. The constitution of 1809 survived the transition to *parliamentary democracy and it was not until 1974 that the *Riksdag* adopted a new constitution, formally reducing the role of the monarch to that of a figurehead. As part of the rewriting of the constitution, a unicameral Parliament, currently comprising 349 seats, was introduced in 1970. Based on *proportional representation, the electoral system has recently been reformed so as to enable voters to choose among individual candidates nominated by the parties. Also, the regular term of each Parliament has been extended from three to four years.

To be represented in Parliament, a party must gain 4 percent of the national vote or 12 percent of the vote in any one of twenty-eight electoral districts. From 1921 to 1988, there were five parliamentary parties, commonly conceived as forming two separate blocs: on the one hand, the "socialist bloc" of the Social Democrats and the Left Party (formerly known as the Communist Party); and, on the other hand, the "bourgeois bloc" of the Center Party (formerly known as the Farmers Party), the Liberals, and the Moderates (formerly known as the Conservatives). The two blocs have always been divided among themselves, however, and compromises across the socialist-bourgeois divide have been common. Although the Social Democrats have dominated Swedish party politics since the 1930s, they have held a parliamentary majority of their own on only two occasions (1940–44 and 1968–70).

Two new parliamentary parties have emerged since the late 1980s: the Christian Democrats and the Greens. Clearly identifying themselves as part of the bourgeois bloc, the Christian Democrats made major gains in the 1998 election, primarily at the expense of their centrist rivals (the Center Party and the Liberals). Rejecting any bloc affiliation in the 1980s, the Greens have increasingly come to see themselves and to be seen by voters as part of the Left. This evolution was confirmed by their decision to enter into an implicit government coalition with the Social Democrats and the Left Party following the 1998 election (in which the socialist parties alone fell one vote short of a parliamentary majority).

From an all-time high of 91.8 percent in 1976, voter turnout declined throughout the 1980s and dropped precipitously in 1998, when only 78.6 percent of eligible voters actually voted. Along with the emergence of new parties and the resurgence of electoral support for the Left Party, which polled an unprecedented 12.8 percent of the vote in 1998, the decline of voter turnout signifies persistent voter dissatisfaction with the major parties and their apparent inability to restore economic prosperity while preserving the basic principles of the so-called Swedish Model.

The Swedish Model in Transition. Sweden's postwar prosperity ultimately depended on the competitiveness of Swedish industry in world markets. Manufactured goods account for the lion's share of Swedish exports, and the manufacturing sector is in turn dominated by a small number of large companies. Alongside concentrated private ownership, the "mixed economy" that Sweden developed during the postwar period consisted of three basic components: first, government policies to promote full employment; secondly, a comprehensive welfare state based on the principle of social citizenship and providing benefits in the form of services as well as transfer payments; and, thirdly, centralized wage bargaining in pursuit of wage solidarity as well as wage restraint. Since the early 1980s, all three features of the Swedish Model have come under pressure and have been modified.

The rise of separate white-collar unions and the growing importance of the public sector as an employer have made the coordination of wage bargaining more difficult. In response to these developments and the perceived need to develop more flexible forms of remuneration, private employers successfully imposed more decentralized bargaining arrangements in the late 1980s and early 1990s and thus added to the pressure on governments to adopt a less accommodating macroeconomic stance. With unemployment rising from less than 2 percent in 1990 to about 10 percent in 1996, the goal of price stability clearly took precedence over the goal of full employment by the early 1990s. This reorientation of macroeconomic policy has been cemented by legislation which renders the Central Bank more autonomous from the government. Having embraced industry-level wage bargaining and central bank autonomy, Sweden might be said to have moved towards the German Model.

Meanwhile, bourgeois and Social Democratic governments alike have cut back welfare entitlements and employment in the public sector while cutting back marginal tax rates for high-income earners. As part of reforms designed to make the public sector more efficient and responsive, some efforts have been made to promote private alternatives to the public provision of health and other social services, and the pension reform agreed upon by the major parties in 1995 provides for private pension funds within the framework of the public pension system. Though less generous than it used to be, the welfare state still remains essentially intact and continues to enjoy broad-based popular support.

Sweden in Europe. The Swedish Model was essentially a national bargain between labor and business, premised on the ability of the national government to regulate the Swedish economy. The parameters of class compromise have changed as the Swedish economy has become integrated into a European-wide economy amd large Swedish firms have become multinational in their operations. (In relation to its domestic employment, employment abroad by the Swedish manufacturing industry increased from 12 percent in 1960 to 37 percent in 1987.)

Because of its neutrality policy, dating back to the early nineteenth century, Sweden became a member of the European Free Trade Association (EFTA) rather than the European Community (EC) in the late 1950s. Nonetheless, its trade with EC member states continued to increase: by 1985, half of Swedish exports were sold within the EC. The Single Market program adopted by the EC (renamed the *European Union or EU with the ratification of the *Moastvicht Treaty in 1993) and the subsequent collapse of the erstwhile Soviet bloc led Sweden to apply for EC membership in 1991. Following a popular referendum in November 1994 which approved membership by a margin of 52.3 percent to 46.8 percent, Sweden formally joined the EU on 1 January 1995.

Sweden's relationship to the EU remains a source of domestic political controversy. Following the referendum of 1994, public opinion turned against the EU and, largely for this reason, the government has chosen to remain outside the single-currency arrangement known as the Economic and Monetary Union (EMU). The current government reserves the option of joining the EMU at a later date, but the Left Party and the Greens are strongly opposed to EMU membership and, in the aftermath of the 1998 election, the continuation of Social Democratic government depends on the support of these parties. The 1998 election thus reinforced Sweden's position as one of the more reluctant members of the EU.

In Swedish politics, EU membership has come to be associated with welfare-state retrenchment and the employment crisis of the 1990s. However, the retreat from the social and economic policy objectives traditionally associated with the Swedish Model began prior to Sweden's entry into the EU. At present, EU membership does not require Sweden to lower its standards on environmental protection or the rights of workers, women, and immigrants. In terms of the ability of the government to pursue its own macroeconomic priorities, the constraints of economic *interdependence—in particular, the integration of financial markets—are more important than the constraints of EU membership. Over the next few years, Sweden will either recover from the current employment crisis or Swedes will come to accept mass unemployment as a more or less permanent condition. Either way, Sweden should move towards a more constructive engagement in the process of European integration.

(See also CLASS AND POLITICS; LABOR MOVEMENT; SOCIALISM AND SOCIAL DEMOCRACY; TAXES AND TAXATION.)

Gösta Esping-Andersen, *Politics Against Markets: The Social Democratic Road to Power* (Princeton, N.J., 1985). Hugh Heclo and Hendrik Madsen, *Policy and Politics in Sweden: Principled Pragmatism* (Philadelphia, 1987). Jonas Pontusson, *The Limits of Social Democracy: Investment Politics in Sweden* (Ithaca, N.Y., 1992). Christine Ingebritsen, *The Nordic States and the European Union* (Ithaca, N.Y., 1998).

JONAS PONTUSSON

SWITZERLAND. Landlocked Switzerland, in the Alpine region of Western Europe, has an area of 15,940 square miles (41,273 sq. km.) and a population of between 6 and 7 million. Most of the inhabitants speak a German dialect, but French and Italian are also recognized as official languages, and Romansh, spoken by a tiny minority, is a fourth national tongue. The population is about evenly divided between Protestants and Roman Catholics, a division that caused a number of bloody conflicts until the middle of the nineteenth century.

The origin of Switzerland can be traced to 1291, when three small forest communities, Uri, Schwyz, and Unterwalden, concluded a defensive alliance in order to preserve their local independence and individual customs. Five more cantons joined them during the following century, and an additional five by 1513. The Peace of Westphalia of 1648 officially recognized Swiss independence from the Holy Roman Empire and acknowledged frontiers that have not changed much since that time. The Napoleonic period led to some border rearrangements and brought the number of Swiss cantons to twenty-two, of which three, at various times, split into half-cantons. In 1979 the largely French-speaking Catholic part of the old canton of Bern (mainly German-speaking and Protestant) broke away, forming a separate twenty-third canton, Jura.

All the cantons originally had their own ways of governing and strongly desired to retain their traditions. As the alliance gradually grew into a federation, the many cantonal and communal differences led to frequent disputes and armed conflicts. The constitution of 1848 eventually provided a viable modern government. It was revised in 1874 and is still, with amendments, the blueprint of the present-day Swiss political structure. It emphasizes democracy, decentralization, and the sovereignty of individual cantons, which give much autonomy to individual communities. All powers not specifically granted to the federal authorities in the federal constitution are reserved to the cantons. These include schools, police, and affairs of church. The people also have a direct say in the running of their political affairs, and in some areas there still exist town meetings with legislative powers, as in Appenzell Inner-Rhodes where, in April 1990, local suffrage for women was overwhelmingly defeated by a show of (male) hands. Local, cantonal, and federal questions are frequently determined by referendum, as were such national issues as joining the UN (rejected in 1985), joining the *International Monetary Fund and the *World Bank (approved in 1992), limiting the number of *foreign workers (rejected in 1988), and allowing women to vote in federal elections (rejected in 1959 but approved in 1971).

Emphasizing the concept of *federalism and following the example of the United States, the Swiss national parliament, the *Bundesversammlung,* is bicameral. In the 200-seat *Nationalrat* every canton and half-canton is represented according to its population, with each guaranteed at least one member. Elections are held every four years under a rather complicated list system on the principle of *proportional representation. In the forty-six-member *Ständerat* every canton has two seats and every half-canton one. Methods of election and length of term are left to the discretion of each canton. Both chambers usually meet four times a year for about three to four weeks; their members are part-time legislators and receive merely a per diem compensation for their services.

The executive branch, the *Bundesrat,* or federal council, is chosen by the *Bundesversammlung* for a four-year period. Each of the seven councillors is responsible for one of these departments: finance and customs; foreign affairs (called the political department); interior; justice and police; military; public economy; and transportation and energy. Incumbents are usually automatically reelected as often as they wish, and there is no way for them to be voted out of office during their term, although some have resigned under pressure. The president of Switzerland is named by the *Bundesversammlung* from among the councillors on an annual rotating basis and holds this office in addition to any other portfolio. He may not be immediately reelected. No canton may have more than one member on the executive, and there are various additional rules to ensure that some of the larger cantons are always represented and that the non-German-speaking cantons are not neglected.

Lists of candidates for parliamentary elections are developed in each canton by the individual parties. Although as many as fifteen or twenty different lists may be presented at any given election, most of them have no chance of success. However, communists have in the past acquired a few seats, as have right-wingers who cashed in on such emotional issues as the alleged overabundance of foreign workers. In recent years the Greens have also managed to enter the legislature. But the overwhelming majority of the *Bundesversammlung* is usually made up of a combination of members of the Freisinnig-Demokratische Partei, the Christlichdemokratische Volkspartei, the Sozialdemokratische Partei, and the somewhat smaller Schweizerische Volkspartei. Since 1959, the *Bundesrat* has been composed of representatives of these four parties in what amounts to a permanent coalition, thus assuring a high degree of stability.

Early in their history the Swiss were frequently involved in wars. Following some victories, such as Morgarten in 1315 against Austria, they seemed likely to play a major military role in European affairs; but after decisive defeats two hundred years later, the concept of Swiss nonintervention and neutrality prevailed, even though Swiss mercenaries continued to participate in many foreign battles. Aided by a terrain that is largely mountainous and a highly trained army in which nearly all able-bodied males serve most of their adult lives, neutrality has become a major pillar of Swiss foreign policy. Switzerland joined the League of Nations, whose headquarters were in Geneva, but regards membership in the UN as incompatible with its neutrality. However, it has joined various UN agencies, is part of the European Free Trade As-

sociation (EFTA) and the Council of Europe, and has participated in the Organization for Security and Cooperation in Europe. Joining a lengthening queue, in May 1992 the government announced its intention to apply for membership in the *European Union. Important international organizations are still based on Swiss soil, and various international conferences, including summit meetings, are held there from time to time.

Utilizing Swiss neutrality before and during World War II, many of Hitler's victims had deposited money with Swiss banks. Switzerland now is accepting some responsibility for returning the money to survivors and heirs. Also, the German government has established accounts to compensate for gold and other property taken from victims, many of whom are making claims although others will never be identified.

George Arthur Codding, Jr., *The Federal Government of Switzerland* (Boston, 1961). Christopher Hughes, *Switzerland* (New York, 1975). Walter S. G. Kohn, *Governments and Politics of the German-speaking Countries* (Chicago, 1980). James Murray Luck, *A History of Switzerland* (Palo Alto, Calif., 1985). Rolf Kieser and Kurt R. Spillman, eds., *The New Switzerland: Problems and Policies* (Palo Alto, Calif., 1996).

WALTER S. G. KOHN

SYRIA has a geopolitical importance out of all proportion to its relatively small population, area, resource base, and economic wealth because of its formidable military power, assertive foreign policy, and location at the heart of the *Middle East, bordering Israel, Lebanon, Turkey, Iraq, and Jordan. As a result, it plays a central role in most of the Middle East's key disputes and has been one of Israel's foremost adversaries.

Syria has one of the world's richest and longest recorded histories, but the modern state was created only in 1920, when the Western powers carved it out of the Ottoman Empire, and it remained under French colonial rule until independence in 1946. The state originated through no felt need among those who lived in it, and its arbitrary boundaries bore no relationship to underlying cultural patterns or historical relationships within the region. From its inception, Syria lacked legitimacy among its inhabitants, who aspired to be part of a larger pan-Arab state. Between 1958 and 1961, Syria erased itself from the map altogether, merging with Egypt to form the United Arab Republic. Although pan-Arabism still plays an important role as a legitimating ideology for Syrian regimes, it has lost some of its power, and a coherent Syrian state, with a powerful political center and distinctive identity, has gradually emerged.

The nominally pan-Arab, socialist Ba'th (Resurrection) Party has ruled Syria without interruption since 1963, although a coup d'état in 1966 brought a leftist faction led by Salah Jadid to power, and another one in 1970, led by Hafiz al-Asad, resulted in a swing back to the center. This continuity, which contrasts sharply with the chronic instability between the late 1940s and early 1960s, has come at a high cost to civil liberties. The Ba'thist regime is, at root, an authoritarian military dictatorship in which the president stands supreme and in which members of the minority 'Alawi sect dominate key positions within the elite. The president, after a pro forma nomination by Parliament, is popularly elected to a seven-year term (Bashar al-Asad received more than 99 percent of all votes in the June 2000 election following the death of his father, Hafiz). In theory the Ba'th shares power with six kindred small parties in the National Progressive Front (NPF), but the non-Ba'thist parties are clearly subordinate members: they lack autonomy, genuine constituencies, and the right to recruit followers in the armed forces and the universities, which are exclusively reserved for the Ba'th. Beneath the presidency, the main formal political institutions are government cabinets, within which all key cabinet portfolios are awarded to Ba'this, and the People's Assembly, which is elected by popular vote. Despite their high visibility, neither commands much actual power. In the November 1998 People's Assembly elections the NPF won two thirds of all seats (its share is predetermined) and independents the rest, but the elections were neither free nor open: the Ba'th controls who gets on the ballot and, through its control of the media, who gets heard. The Ba'th has approximately 600,000–700,000 members and a formal presence in virtually every village, as well as in all large institutions, workplaces, and organizations. The party is organized hierarchically: the Regional Command is the top authority as well as the center of power within Syria. Despite its ubiquity, the Ba'th party shows evidence of enervation and decay. Discipline has declined as the party has attracted careerists and fallen victim to the corruption that infests all of public life in Syria.

Real power in Syria rests with the armed forces and internal security and intelligence agencies, which are largely commanded by officers from the 'Alawi sect. Most of the Ba'this who seized power in 1963 were officers from villages and small provincial towns, and many came from the peripheral 'Alawi and Druze communities. They replaced a traditional elite composed mainly of Damascus- and Aleppo-based large landowners and merchants, most of whom were from the majority Sunni community. Initially the putschists were inspired by class differences, not sectarian ones. However, since 1963 the regime's greatest vulnerability has been the perception that it is essentially an 'Alawi one, although Sunnis are represented within the regime at all levels. In this heterogeneous country, in which Sunni Muslims account for almost 75 percent of the population of 16 million (1999) and Arabs for 85 percent, sectarian and ethnic differences remain the source of some of the sharpest political cleavages.

After seizing power, the Ba'th, in accordance with its socialist ideology, implemented land reform and nationalized all major industrial, commercial, and financial institutions. The regime also embarked on an ambitious program of industrialization and infrastructural development, which transformed and integrated Syria's economy. The Ba'th's social development policies were equally far-reaching: an enormous expansion of education and health care opened up new opportunities and improved living conditions for many Syrians, especially in the countryside. In the 1970s, Asad liberalized the economy, which grew rapidly because of an influx of petrodollars and foreign aid. When these sources of revenue declined in the late 1970s, growth dropped sharply. In addition, rampant corruption, a bloated bureaucracy, an inefficient public sector, foreign exchange shortages, and a military machine that regularly consumed over half of the ordinary budget combined to produce severe economic problems. However, in the early 1990s GOP growth averaged 7–8 percent annually because of growing oil exports, good harvests,

and a surge in foreign aid following the Gulf War. Despite persistent demands for economic liberalization, the regime has been slow to initiate structural economic reform, maintaining that Syria already has an active private sector alongside the large mixed and public ones. Since the mid-1990s, annual GOP growth has declined to 4–6 percent.

Periodically, the regime has faced open opposition, particularly by the Muslim Brotherhood. Shortly after Syria's intervention in Lebanon in 1976, a wave of bombings and assassinations rattled the regime, whose harsh response fueled even more discontent. In 1980, the army was called into Aleppo and other leading cities to quash strikes and demonstrations that threatened to blossom into an insurrection. Two years later the regime virtually destroyed the city of Hama and killed as many as 20,000 people while suppressing a Muslim fundamentalist uprising. Since then, the opposition has been in disarray and the regime has felt more secure, but *human rights violations continue on a large scale. Prospects for political liberalization are bleak because the regime fears it would be repudiated in genuinely free elections. The ascent of thirty-four-year-old Bashar al-Asad to the presidency following the death of his father in 2000 raised widespread hopes that he would initiate reforms and bring a new generation to power. However, the ability of the inexperienced Bashar to maintain power is uncertain, despite the apparently smooth succession.

Under Hafiz al-Asad, Syria emerged as a major power in the Middle East. Syria's foreign policy has largely evolved in the context of its sense of territorial impairment, its self-conception as the birthplace of *Arab nationalism, and its conflict with Israel, with which it has fought wars in 1967, 1973, and 1982. Pan-Arabism and anti-Zionism have traditionally been the twin guiding principles of its policies in the region, as well as the justification for most of its actions. One of the overriding goals of the regime's foreign policy has been to regain the Golan Heights, which Israel occupied in 1967, and restore Palestinian rights. To that end, Syria participated in the post–Gulf War 1991 Madrid conference that marked the beginning of a new drive for peace in the region and subsequently began direct, off-on bilateral negotiations with Israel. Their talks were unsuccessful and ended in February 1996.

Despite Syria's rhetoric about Arab unity, its relations with other Arab countries have been stormy. Its alliance with Egypt in the 1973 war quickly collapsed after Egypt pursued a separate peace agreement with Israel. Relations were not restored until 1989. At least since the mid-1970s, Syria has been a bitter enemy of Iraq, where a rival wing of the Ba'th Party holds power, although a united rapprochement occurred in 1996. Syria's support for Iran in its war with Iraq between 1980 and 1988 was denounced throughout the Arab world, and its deployment of forces in Saudi Arabia following the Iraqi invasion of Kuwait in 1990 was also controversial within the region. From the mid-1970s, Syria tried repeatedly to bring Lebanon, Jordan, and the Palestinians into its orbit to increase its leverage. It was most successful in Lebanon where it intervened militarily in 1976 to bring an end to civil war. It has maintained a military presence and exerted a strong political influence in Lebanon ever since.

Syria's close relations with the Soviet Union were based on

its need for military and diplomatic support in its conflict with Israel. Asad exploited Cold War tensions to his advantage and used Soviet backing to build Syria into the powerful state that it is. The relationship between the two countries changed profoundly after Mikhail Gorbachev came to power. The Soviet Union indicated that it would not support the Asad regime's quest for military parity with Israel, undermining its central strategic doctrine. By the close of the 1980s, Syria's doubts about the reliability of the Soviet Union as an ally and recognition that only the United States could persuade Israel to withdraw from the Golan Heights prompted it to seek better relations with the United States, a pattern that intensified during the *Gulf War and continued in the postwar discussions about the Middle East.

(See also ARAB-ISRAELI CONFLICT; DECOLONIZATION; IRAN-IRAQ WAR; MILITARY RULE.)

Nikolaos van Dam, *The Struggle for Power in Syria* (London, 1981). John Devlin, *Syria* (Boulder, Colo., 1983). Moshe Ma'oz, *Asad: The Sphinx of Damascus* (New York, 1988). Patrick Seale, *Asad: The Struggle for the Middle East* (Berkeley, Calif., 1988). Raymond A. Hinnebusch, *Authoritarian Power and State Formation in Ba'thist Syria* (Boulder, Colo., 1990). Volker Perthes, *The Political Economy of Syria under Asad* (New York, 1995).

ALASDAIR DRYSDALE

T

TAIWAN. A large island that is located on the Tropic of Cancer, Taiwan is approximately 100 miles east of the South China coast. It is approximately 250 miles long and 100 miles across at its widest point. The population of 22 million in the late 1990s creates one of the highest population densities in the world, which is especially great since sparsely settled mountains occupy two-thirds of the island. On the one hand, Taiwan has long been credited with an "economic miracle" that transformed it from an impoverished agricultural economy to a prosperous industrial society during the postwar era; and its successful (and bloodless) democratic transition in the early 1990s represented another major achievement. On the other hand, its unsettled international status dating from the Chinese Civil War in the late 1940s threatens its very existence as most nations and international organizations, at least officially, now recognize the People's Republic of *China (PRC) as exercising *sovereignty over Taiwan.

Historically, Taiwan has been part of China; and almost all of the current residents are ethnically Han Chinese (about two percent are aborigines). Yet, the linkages between Taiwan and China have been somewhat tenuous for extended periods. Major Chinese settlement began in the late sixteenth century; and except for a brief period of Dutch colonization in the early seventeenth century, Taiwan was part of China for the next 400 years, albeit as a generally ignored "wild west" frontier until the late nineteenth century when China began a major modernization effort on the island to ward off imperialist predators. However, following Japan's victory in the Sino-Japanese War, Taiwan was ceded to Japan as a colony. With Japan's defeat in World War II, Taiwan reverted back to Chiang Kai-shek's Republic of China (ROC) in 1945. Following the communist victory in the Chinese Civil War, Chiang and his Nationalist or Kuomintang (KMT) Party retreated to Taiwan and a few other islands in 1949.

Both the Chinese Communist regime in Beijing and the KMT regime in Taipei claimed to be the sole legitimate government of all China. By the 1970s, though, the PRC had clearly won the battle for diplomatic recognition when it replaced the ROC in the *United Nations and gained diplomatic recognition from even the United States, Taiwan's principal *Cold War ally and patron. During the 1980s and early 1990s, relations between Taiwan and the PRC actually thawed (even though they made no move to recognize each other). In the late 1980s, Taiwan permitted its residents to visit the Chinese Mainland and its businesses to trade with and invest in the PRC. In light of the resulting explosion of cross-Strait contacts, Beijing was reassured that Taiwan was moving toward becoming part of China, and so at first looked tolerantly upon Taiwan's "pragmatic diplomacy" of upgrading its unofficial

relations and diplomatic status. Ultimately, however, both the ROC and PRC saw Taiwan's "diplomatic limbo" as threatening their basic goals (Beijing feared Taiwan's growing "independence" and Taipei feared that the PRC would be able to force its integration into the current Chinese regime). Thus, several harsh disputes broke out in the mid- and late 1990s which even reached the point of military threats and which were perhaps contained by the continuing U.S. policy of strong opposition to both a declaration of independence by Taiwan and the use of force to settle the issue by China.

Taiwan's political institutions were inherited from the 1946 Constitution of the Republic of China which created the five branches of government proposed by the KMT's founder Sun Yat-sen who supplemented the three parts of government emphasized in Western theory (the Executive, Legislative, and Judicial Yuans) with two additional branches reflecting traditional Chinese political practices (the Control Yuan which served an ombudsman function of checking on governmental abuses and the Examination Yuan for the civil service system). In addition to these five branches, the central figure in the regime is the powerful president who appoints the premier or leader of the Executive Yuan; and there is a separate National Assembly which has authority over constitutional matters and, until 1996, elected the president. Despite the democratic nature of the ROC Constitution, KMT rule in postwar Taiwan was quite authoritarian for a number of reasons. Martial law declared during the civil war was continued and, among other things, prohibited the formation of new parties (opposition figures could run as independents); because of the regime's claim to rule all of China, the vast majority of the seats in the Legislative Yuan and National Assembly were held by those elected from Mainland constituencies in the late 1940s, ensuring huge KMT majorities; and the top positions in both the government and the KMT were dominated by "Mainlanders" (i.e., the fifteen percent of the population who had come to Taiwan in the late 1940s), creating significant resentment among the "Islander" majority. Still, competitive local elections were permitted; and the KMT integrated preexisting local political factions into its lower and middle levels.

In contrast to the very limited political change during the first several decades of KMT rule, the economy proved to be extremely dynamic as Taiwan took advantage of the growing *globalization in the world economy to develop rapidly. Its annual growth rate during the second half of the twentieth century averaged 8.5 percent, one of the highest in the world. By the end of the century, it had a GNP per capita of $13,000 (almost equivalent to the poorer countries in southern Europe) and ranked fifteenth in the world in total trade and third in foreign reserves. After a brief period of *import-substitution industrialization during the 1950s (which included a radical land reform to boost agricultural production), Taiwan adopted an *export-led growth strategy in the 1960s. Taiwan's small businesses (which were almost exclusively run by Islanders) proved to be extremely entrepreneurial and competitive in the low-cost light industry niche of the world economy. *Multinational corporations (MNCs) were recruited for (and limited to) a few key sectors, particularly electronics, where local business did not have the requisite expertise. Unlike the situation in many developing countries, though, local entrepreneurs were able to move into these industries fairly quickly later on. A move into heavy industry (e.g., steel and petrochemicals) began in the 1970s, spearheaded by state corporations. By the late 1980s, Taiwan's corporations, both by themselves and in partnership with MNCs, began moving into high-tech industries; and by the mid-1990s, for example, Taiwan had become a significant player in the world semiconductor and personal computer industries. Taiwan's economic success, though, meant that it was pricing itself out of the low-wage sector of the global economy; so that by the late 1980s many of the traditional industries were moving increasingly over the 1990s "offshore," to the PRC.

Rapid economic growth brought increasing prosperity. Not only did GNP per capita rise, but by the late 1970s Taiwan had one of the least unequal income distributions in the world as the result of the land reform and rising wages that occurred once full employment was achieved in the late 1960s. This transition to a middle-class society also helped set in motion growing liberalization in the political realm as two distinct groups implicitly challenged the authoritarian system. First, the middle-class population in general became more restive over authoritarian restrictions. Second, the primary beneficiaries of the "economic miracle" were Islander business people whose new wealth created a potentially important political resource. Beginning in the 1970s and picking up speed in the 1980s, therefore, political liberalization seemed something of an ongoing (though not inevitable) social force.

In the political realm itself, *democracy was pushed both "from above" by reformers within the KMT (led by Chiang's son Chiang Ching-kuo and, after his death in 1988, by his handpicked successor Lee Teng-hui, an Islander technocrat) and "from below" by an increasingly open and aggressive opposition. Ultimately, Taiwan moved through a fairly rapid and completely bloodless democratic transition marked by the abolition of martial law (1987), the forced retirement of the "senior legislators" (1991), and the direct election of the president (1996). Unlike many ruling authoritarian parties, the KMT survived democratization quite well and remained the majority party in an increasingly competitive two-party system until the 2000 presidential elections. Such normal political cleavages as class and gender have been quite marginal in Taiwan's politics, even in the democratic era. Instead, the most important cleavage, at least until quite recently, has been the ethnic one between Mainlanders and Islanders with the KMT appealing to almost all of the former and the opposition Democratic Progressive Party appealing to the more nationalistic of the latter with its advocacy of Taiwan independence. By the late 1990s, though, even this division was moderating. The KMT had become a primarily Islander party under Lee Teng-hui; the DPP moderated its position on national identity after being punished at the polls; and the extreme positions on national identity and relations with the PRC came to be represented by minor parties.

Taiwan's move toward full democracy seemingly culminated in the March 2000 presidential elections, when DPP candidate Chen Shui-bian won a close three-way battle with the official KMT nominee and a KMT defector who ran as an independent. Domestically, the transition to Chen's presidency went quite smoothly, confirming the consolidation of Taiwan's democracy. Chen selected a multi-party cabinet of primarily technocrats and scientists. The premier was the former KMT Defense Minister; and there actually were more KMT than DPP cabinet members, although Chen specifically refused to conclude a formal coalition with the Kuomintang. Internationally, the DPP's and Chen's previous support of Taiwan independence set the stage for a crisis in cross-Strait relations. Yet, Chen took an extremely conciliatory position (significantly more so than the policy toward the PRC of outgoing President Lee Teng-hui) which seemed quite popular in Washington and, at least in the short-run, sufficient to mollify Beijing.

Steve Chan and Cal Clark, *Flexibility, Foresight, and Fortuna in Taiwan's Development* (London, 1992). John F. Copper, *Taiwan: Nation-State or Province?* (Boulder, Colo., 1996). Robert M. Marsh, *The Great Transformation: Social Change in Taipei, Taiwan since the 1960s* (Armonk, N.Y., 1996). Linda Chao and Ramon H. Myers, *The First Chinese Democracy: Political Life in the Republic of China* (Baltimore, 1998).

CAL CLARK

TAJIKISTAN. See CENTRAL ASIA.

TANZANIA. Led at independence by a philosopher-president who translated Shakespeare into Swahili and walked the countryside to mobilize peasant support, Tanzania has negotiated the transition from single-party rule to multiparty competition and from socialist aspirations to capitalist pragmatism. Its early development achievements and optimistic commitment to self-reliance, however, were succeeded by recurring economic crises, deteriorating public services, and intensified aid dependence.

A stepchild of the colonial era, Tanganyika was colonized by Germany and then ruled by Britain as a League of Nations Mandate and subsequently a United Nations Trusteeship Territory. European rule ended far less violently than it had begun. Led by Julius *Nyerere, negotiators, not guerrillas, assumed power. Independent on 9 December 1961, Tanganyika united with Zanzibar in 1964 to create the United Republic of Tanzania.

Liberal Development Strategy. Optmistic projections and World Bank advice—at independence, Tanganyika had little developed infrastructure, even less industry, and few educated citizens—spawned a liberal development strategy: relatively open economy; emphasis on export production, successful farmers, and pilot projects; increasing but still limited state role; and maintenance of friendly relations with the major powers. Events soon deflated the optimism. Popular opposition to Britain's transfer of authority to a minority Arab government in Zanzibar in December 1963 provided fertile ground for a brief but bloody coup on the islands. Shortly thereafter an army mutiny on the mainland led a vulnerable government to summon foreign troops. Before the gunsmoke had fully cleared, Nyerere and the new Zanzibar leader, Abeid Karume, negotiated the union of the two states.

Sharply declining world prices for sisal exports delayed or aborted several projects. Diplomatic ruptures with England and West Germany and conflict with the United States reduced external support and encouraged expanded relationships with socialist Europe and China. University students' dramatic 1966 protest against conscription into the National Service led Nyerere to reduce his own and other leaders' salaries, expel the students involved, and rethink the role and organization of education.

Ujamaa. Social services expanded rapidly. Although one of the world's poorest countries, Tanzania achieved nearly universal primary education and provided clean water to more of its citizens than most other African countries. Infant and maternal mortality declined, life expectancy increased, and adult illiteracy was substantially reduced.

Yet, the liberal development strategy had failed. The 1967 Arusha Declaration and related papers analyzed the failure, focusing on external dependence. Self-reliance and *ujamaa*— Tanzanian socialism loosely based on historical patterns of mutual support—became the guiding principles for a radical development strategy. The open economy was increasingly closed: in its place came *nationalizations, import restrictions, foreign exchange controls, and constraints on foreign investment. Other measures severely restricted individual accumulation and consumption, gave preferential treatment to cooperatives and socialist villages, assigned priority to basic industries, and accelerated indigenization. Foreign policy became more sharply critical of international capitalism and more Africa-oriented.

Party supremacy was institutionalized. Government and party elections held regularly from independence to 1990 employed an innovative form of single-party competition, seeking to reconcile control and participation. Having incorporated potential alternative power bases—unions, women, youth—and guaranteeing military representation, in practice the party ruled but did not govern. In 1977 the Tanganyika African National Union (TANU) merged with its Zanzibar counterpart, the Afro-Shirazi Party, becoming the Chama cha Mapinduzi (CCM) [Revolutionary Party].

With no dominant regional/ethnic group and a widely understood national language, Swahili, Tanzania's heterogeneous population has only infrequently experienced conflicts organized around racial, religious, and ethnic identities. A major source of continuity and *legitimacy, Tanzanian elections facilitated the presidential transition in 1985 from Nyerere to Ali Hassan Mwinyi, a Zanzibari whose broad support reflected the national integrative ethos.

Regional and International Leadership. Tanzania's internationalist leadership attempted to preserve the East African cooperation developed under British rule, threatened by Kenya's advantaged position and subsequently Idi Amin Dada's dictatorial rule in Uganda. Nyerere unsuccessfully sought *Organization of African Unity (OAU) support against invading Ugandan troops in 1978. Ultimately, Tanzanian soldiers expelled the Ugandans, drove the retreating army across Uganda, exiled Amin, and remained in Uganda until mid-1981 to support the transition to civilian rule.

Tanzania provided significant support to African nationalist and liberation movements, both independently and through regional and continental organizations, and made major investments—an oil pipeline, a railway, and improved roads—to reduce landlocked Zambia's dependence on the southern African infrastructure. A founding member of the Front Line States, Tanzania also provided settlements and training, communications, and education facilities for southern African liberation groups.

Transitions. Drought, sharply increased oil prices, the collapse of East African economic cooperation, and war in the 1970s jarred the radical development strategy. Starved of foreign exchange, industries operated below capacity. Depressed commodity prices and efforts to protect urban consumers stimulated extralegal trade. Successive emergency economic recovery plans in the early 1980s neither brought rapid improvements nor satisfied the policy reform demands (including devaluation, decontrol, and privatization) of the International Monetary Fund and external development assistance agencies. Nyerere's retirement from government in 1985 facilitated renewed external support, including reconciliation with the IMF, World Bank, and other aid agencies. With a massive inflow of capital, by the end of the decade inflation had slowed and the growth in production resumed. Tanzania's structural adjustment was widely termed successful. Yet, the gap between the most and least affluent, progressively reduced over a quarter century, expanded dramatically, conspicuous consumption became fashionable, and social services were increasingly jeopardized. At the same time, reduced restrictions on foreign investment, trade, and exchange facilitated rapid economic growth in Zanzibar, accompanied by political pressure to dissolve the union.

As structural adjustment replaced the radical development strategy, competitive party politics replaced single-party rule. Although a national commission found continuing support for the single-party system, the leadership managed the transition to multiparty competition and relaxed constraints on alternative media. With some confusion and bureaucratic heavy-handedness but with little violence or disruption, party flags, manifestos, and logos proliferated. Ultimately, the CCM's Benjamin Mkapa, a former journalist and foreign minister, became president in 1995, handily defeating his major opponents, a CCM dissident with significant popular support and a university professor and former presidential adviser who led a largely Zanzibar-based ticket only narrowly beaten on the islands. Electoral competition had jolted and rejuvenated the CCM, at least for a while. More electoral coalitions than integrated political formations with coherent agendas, the unsuccessful opposition parties experienced post-election factional conflicts and resignations.

A relentless activist for regional cooperation and a global advocate for Africa, former president Nyerere chaired the South Commission, an organization to promote *South-South cooperation, and sought to mediate among contending groups in Africa's Great Lakes area until his death in October 1999. As the century ended, an emerging indigenous capitalist class asserted its autonomy, flashed its wealth, and at the same time remained heavily dependent on state regulation and support and on the continuing inflow of foreign capital. Increased debt compounded the aid dependence, entrenched foreign influence, and weakened the foundation for *sustainable development.

(See also ONE-PARTY SYSTEM; SOUTHERN AFRICA; STRUCTURAL ADJUSTMENT PROGRAM.)

Joel Samoff, "Single-Party Competitive Elections in Tanzania," in Fred Hayward, ed., *Elections in Independent Africa* (Boulder, Colo., 1987), 149–186. Horace Campbell and Howard Stein, eds., *The IMF and Tanzania: The Dynamics of Liberalization* (Boulder, Colo., 1992). Mwesiga Baregu, "The Rise and Fall of the One-Party State in Tanzania," in Jennifer A. Widner, ed., *Economic Change and Political Liberalization in Sub-Saharan Africa* (Baltimore, 1994), 158–181.

JOEL SAMOFF

TARIFF. See PROTECTION; TAXES AND TAXATION.

TAXES AND TAXATION. All governments need money. Modern governments need lots of money. How to get this money and whom to take it from are some of the most difficult issues faced by governments anywhere. All states are faced with a basic dilemma: citizens, or constituents, want government services, but they resist paying for them.

Foundations of Tax Policy. There are essentially two ways to think of the role of the state with respect to taxes and taxation. The first, most eloquently represented by Anthony Downs in his seminal essay "Why Government Is Too Small in a Democracy" (*World Politics*, 1959), sees the state as trapped between the competing desires of its constituents for more spending on the one hand and lower taxes on the other. The logic here is that citizens do not generally appreciate the *public goods provided by government (roads, airports, environmental regulation, health and safety codes, etc.) as being positive goods. Public goods and services paid for by government spending are generally "assumed" and sometimes resented. So, for example, few citizens back out of their driveway each day and think to themselves: "Gee, I'm sure glad the government built this road in front of my house so that I can drive to work." Indeed if they think about the road on the way to work, they are likely to be angry that it has too many potholes, or that it is not wide enough, or that there are too few (or too many) stoplights between their home and their job.

Taxes, in contrast, are felt directly. With each paycheck and virtually every purchase from a store constituents are reminded of the costs of how much government "takes away" from them individually. Thus there is an inequality in citizens' perceptions between the costs of taxation and the benefits of public spending. This problem is exacerbated by the common public perception that when governments do spend, they obtain things that are a "waste of money." For example, a particular individual may feel that government gives too much money to military contractors and thus logically resents her taxes going for this expense. Even if the same individual may be willing to pay for more child immunization programs, she resents the fact that government "wastes" her tax dollars. Another individual may equally resent tax money being spent on "welfare cheats." Even if he thinks that we should spend more on B-1 bombers, he is likely to think that too much of "his money" goes to welfare spending and is therefore wasted.

From this Downsian perspective, we see that all governments are faced with a rather fundamental set of dilemmas. It is, after all, the responsibility of government to provide services to a variety of constituencies. So doing, however, almost certainly invokes the wrath of the very constituents that the government seeks to serve. For scholars working in this tradition, tax policy is the result of a set of institutionally structured compromises between state actors, interest groups, and voters.

The other main perspective on taxes and taxation assumes that state actors operate from a quite different orientation and motivation. James Buchanan is certainly the most well known student of taxation from the "public choice" school, which sees the state as the "Leviathan." The Leviathan (composed of the individual actors who occupy positions within the state) needs revenues to pursue its own self-interests. At least in Buchanan's more extreme "rationalist" perspective, the government is essentially seen as the enemy of the citizens and taxes are an important point of conflict between citizens and the state These authors are often active in promoting constitutional limitations on the taxing powers of the state. Other less extreme *rational choice scholars are less clear about the degree of malicious intent of state actors, but still see the state as the Leviathan whose interest is to extract resources from the economy to further its own ends. Tax policy from this perspective, then, is viewed as a set of more or less Machiavellian machinations whereby state actors must obfuscate their intentions and hoodwink citizens.

How Do Taxes Differ Across Countries? The single most important variable for understanding tax policy variation is the level of economic development. Rich and developed countries tend to collect far more revenue (as a percent of GDP) than do poor and underdeveloped countries. Moreover, while there still is a high degree of variation among taxes in advanced nations, it can still be said that they follow somewhat similar patterns. For example, all OECD nations collect at least 30 percent of GDP in taxes and rely on just four basic sources of revenue (individual and corporate income, general consumption, and social security taxes) for at least 80 percent of that revenue. Excises, tariffs, export duties, and taxes on particular goods have become relatively insignificant sources of state revenues in these advanced nations. Poorer countries, because they have less well developed systems of tax administration, and/or because they have fewer people with less money to tax, tend to rely more heavily on duties, tariffs, and taxes on specific goods.

The average tax burden in the OECD was 38 percent of GDP. The average tax burden in the developing world is less than 20 percent of GDP. In the poorest countries in particular, income taxes are extraordinarily difficult to collect. Not only do the very poor have little or no monetary income, the wealthy are often able to avoid income taxes thanks to corruption and graft. The other main source of revenue in developed countries, social security taxes, while perhaps less subject to corruption, is also of limited use in countries where 40 to 80 percent of the population work in agriculture—often at a subsistence level.

Thus governments in the developing world are left with fewer choices regarding whom to tax and how to collect it. Their specific tax structures, then, are often a product of the particular natural resource base from which they begin. For example, countries richly endowed with resources are sometimes able to tax the profits of the *multinational corporations which extract and/or export these resources. In these countries, profits taxes contribute a large share of total revenue.

Whereas profits taxes make up an average of only 7 percent of revenue in the developed world, they contribute an average of 16.5 percent of revenue in the developing world. In twelve countries profits taxes contribute over 25 percent of total taxes and in six countries they make up over one-half of all tax revenue.

The main sources of revenue in the developing world are taxes on specific goods and services and taxes on foreign trade. Taxes on specific goods or services (such as tobacco, petroleum, or salt) can be relatively easy to monitor and collect, which is especially important in countries with an inefficient or corrupt administrative apparatus. These taxes contribute an average of 25 percent of total revenue in the non-OECD world. Taxes on foreign trade (both import duties and export taxes) are also relatively easily monitored and collected. They have also been quite popular instruments of economic management (and sometimes corruption) since they can be selectively applied and thus made to favor certain domestic industries over international producers. The recent trend towards more open markets has reduced the attractiveness of some of these taxes in many countries. But given the difficulties in raising revenues from alternative sources in much of the developing world, they continue to be very important sources of revenue, contributing between 25 and 35 percent of total revenue.

Although governments in advanced countries have substantially larger economies from which to draw revenues, it does not follow that extracting revenues is easy. As implied above, democratization generates far greater demands on governments for public services *at the same time* that it increases citizens' ability to oppose tax increases. This dilemma has shaped tax policy in all rich democracies. For example, early in the century as capitalist countries became more democratic, there tended to be a common push for more progressive taxes that would impose heavy burdens on the wealthy and on corporate profits. As the twentieth century matured and more and more voters began to earn higher incomes, high rates of taxation on earned income increasingly tended to lose favor. In recent years, "hidden taxes," such as the value-added tax and taxes which are meant to finance very specific, but universally available insurance systems (e.g., Social Security), have also grown more attractive to tax policy makers.

Tax Reform. The most significant development in tax policy in recent years has been that policy makers of almost all political persuasions have grown dissatisfied with steeply progressive tax systems. Increasingly, tax policy makers have come to believe that progressive taxes do not redistribute income effectively because they are inherently easy to avoid. The virtually universal experience in the late twentieth century was that at the same time that progressive tax rates were introduced, tax incentives and tax expenditures (sometimes called "tax loopholes") were also introduced. The result was to reduce the redistributive impact of these taxes and the misallocation of national economic resources. Interestingly, a growing body of evidence suggests that large state direct expenditures can be more redistributive than steeply progressive taxes and tax policy.

The issue of "tax competition" has also grown in importance throughout the world—particularly in areas of advancing economic integration such as within the European Union.

Many argue today that growing economic competition and the lowering of the transaction costs of transnational production and distribution create a new tax policy environment which is forcing democratic governments to rethink traditional tax policy assumptions. In decades past, tax policy was largely a domestic affair. While it has long been argued that high taxes hurt economic growth, there has never been substantial evidence supporting this proposition. Increasingly, however, tax policy makers believe that they must design domestic tax policy in response to tax policy changes that are sweeping the globe. Beginning with the massive tax rate cuts during the *Thatcher and *Reagan years in Britain and the United States, virtually every single country in the world has begun to substantially cut marginal tax rates on high income earners and on corporate profits. Whereas tax rates of 80 to more than 90 percent on very high income earners and/or investment income were quite common in the 1970s, today most countries' top income tax rates are no higher than 40 percent. The distributive consequences of this new competitive tax policy environment are today very much in question.

(See also DEVELOPMENT AND UNDERDEVELOPMENT; POLITICAL ECONOMY.)

Richard Musgrave and Peggy Musgrave, *Public Finance in Theory and Practice,* 3d ed. (New York, 1980). Michael Boskin and Charles McLure, *World Tax Reform: Case Studies of Developed and Developing Countries* (San Francisco, 1990). Vito Tanzi, *Taxation in an Integrating World* (Washington, D.C., 1995). Sven Steinmo, ed., *Tax Policy* (London, 1998).

SVEN STEINMO

TERRORISM. The concept of "terrorism" has been a category of political discourse since the late eighteenth century but has been especially prominent since the 1970s. Its central meaning is the use of terror for the furthering of political ends, and it was originally used to denote the use of terror by the French revolutionary government against its opponents. This is also the sense in which it was used, and on occasion justified, by the Bolsheviks after 1917. This usage of the term, to cover terror by governments, has now become less common, though by no means irrelevant, and in most contemporary usage the term covers acts of terror by those opposed to governments. The range of activities which the term covers has been wide, but four main forms of action tend to be included: *assassinations, bombings, seizures of individuals as hostages, and the hijacking of planes. In the 1970s the term "international terrorism" began to be used to cover acts of violence committed by political groups outside the country in which they were primarily active. The other term that emerged at the same time, "state terrorism," referred to encouragement, or alleged encouragement, by states of such acts of violence.

Taking terrorism in its second, anti-state, sense, there can be said to be three main phases of its history. There is first a prehistory of terrorism, in the sense of acts which would today be called terrorist. The main form this took were acts of assassination for political and politico-religious ends: the tyrannicides of Greece and Rome, the Zealots of Palestine, the Hashashin of medieval Islam. Many of these cases were often regarded as morally legitimate. The second phase of terrorism was the use of violence by political groups in the nineteenth century, especially by anarchists and some nationalists. The assassinations of Tsar Alexander II in 1881 and of Archduke

Franz Ferdinand in 1914 were perhaps the most famous cases, but there was widespread endorsement of bombing by anarchists in Europe and the United States, as "propaganda of the deed," and a number of nationalist groups, notably the Irish and the Armenians, practiced assassination, bombing, and various forms of violent seizure and destruction of property.

A third and more complex phase of terrorism dates from the end of World War II. In a range of nationalist conflicts in the *Third World—Israel, Kenya, Cyprus, South Yemen, Algeria—officials and citizens of the colonial state were attacked as part of what in the end were successful campaigns for national independence. In other cases nationalist movements that did not succeed also used it—for example, in Palestine, the Basque region of Spain, and South Molucca. At the same time, political groups seeking various forms of revolutionary political and social change within their own countries also resorted to acts of terror: this was widespread with the urban guerrillas of Latin America—in Argentina, Brazil, Uruguay—and on a more spasmodic basis in some of the developed democracies—the Red Army Faction in the Federal Republic of Germany, the Red Brigades in Italy, the Weathermen in the United States. Most of these revolutionary groups claimed affiliation with the political *Left: but in the 1970s and 1980s there were also major campaigns of terror by right-wing groups, notably in France and Italy. The 1980s also saw the rise of religiously inspired terrorism in a number of Muslim countries.

Terrorism in this specific sense generated widespread concern in the societies affected, and, as a result of the spread of translational terrorism in the world as a whole. The publicity given to certain dramatic events, such as hijackings, and the administrative and financial costs of searching and monitoring international travel from the late 1960s onward underlined this. During the late 1970s the U.S. Congress and government made concern with terrorism a major part of its *foreign policy and compiled a list of those countries that were deemed to be supporting it. Special units were set up to cover antiterrorism, that is, measures to prevent terrorist acts, and counterterrorism, that is, measures to respond to and, where deemed appropriate, retaliate against terrorism. In August 1998, for example, the United States attacked sites in Afghanistan and Sudan that were alleged to be associated with Islamist terrorists which had bombed two U.S. embassies in Africa.

Distinct as these phenomena appeared to be, there were, however, a number of ways in which the public and international concern of the 1970s and 1980s obscured the issues involved. First, the scale of the phenomenon was distorted by a disproportionate focus on international terrorism. The far more important and costly phenomenon was not international terrorism but terrorism within communal situations, largely in Third World countries. This involved situations where people of different ethnic or religious character, who had often lived side by side for centuries, came to be locked in situations of violence and retribution, often involving massacres, mass kidnappings, forcible displacements, and so forth. Cases of this were in the conflicts between Christian and Muslim in Lebanon, between Tamil and Sinhalese in Sri Lanka, between Hindu and Sikh in Punjab, between Jews and Arabs in Israel and Palestine. Despite its Third World focus,

however, there were a number of cases in Europe—in Cyprus, Northern Ireland, and, with the breakdown of Communist authority during the late 1980s, in the Soviet Union and former Yugoslavia as well. The most pervasive and, in the long term, dangerous aspect of terrorism was this spread of communal terrorism as a product of social and economic tensions in ethnically mixed societies.

A second area of confusion concerned what were and were not acts of terrorism. Here those who opposed states and were victims of state violence were quick to revive the original, 1790s definition of the term and to argue that most of the acts of terror for political ends committed in the contemporary world were carried out by states: the victims of Nazism and *Stalinism, and of many repressive regimes in the post-1945 period, were testimony enough of that. Part of the critique of U.S. anti-terrorism policies was that it went together with connivance by Washington with death squads and other terrorist groups in Latin America. Those who analyzed forms of oppression and coercion outside the framework of state power also argued that terror played a part in establishing and maintaining these forms of domination: the use, actual and threatened, of violence by men against women was an evident case.

There was also considerable room for debate on the way in which the term "terrorist" was used to define, as distinct from merely qualify, specific political groups. Many of those involved in nationalist campaigns questioned the use of the term "terrorist" to disqualify not just specific acts but the overall *legitimacy and goals of their movements. Some revolutionary groups in developed countries appeared to have no other strategy than that of planting bombs and killing individuals, but this was not the case in the nationalist contexts where the goals, national independence, was distinct from the tactics used, of which terror was one but by no means the only one. That the Zionists, Algerians, and Palestinians used, among other tactics, terror as an instrument in independence struggles did not necessarily mean that their broader goals were illegitimate. For some critics of violence, on the other hand, all or most uses of force, even those with legitimate political ends, involved some element of terror and were, consequently, illegitimate.

Two further issues raised in discussions of terrorism were those of cause and efficacy. The search for a cause of terrorism ranged from social and economic conditions to theories based on psychology, "the terrorist personality," and religion. Given the variety of forms taken by terrorist phenomena and the diversity of conditions in which it originated, this was a fruitless exercise. The one characteristic common to terrorist acts against states was a belief, usually mistaken, that individual acts of violence could in some way accelerate change and achieve goals that other, more conventional forms of political action could not. The association with individual religions, most recently Islam, does not survive historical comparison. Assessments of the efficacy of terrorism have tended to show that, beyond publicity, it usually achieved very little, unless the goals were very specific—the release of particular prisoners, the appropriation of some money. Indeed the main result of terroristic acts was not to inflect governments in the direction the terrorists wanted but rather to harden them in the opposite direction—as Russia after 1881 and Argentina after 1975, to name but two cases, demonstrated.

(See also ANARCHY; DECOLONIZATION; GUERRILLA WARFARE; INTERNATIONAL LAW; NATIONAL LIBERATION MOVEMENTS; POLITICAL VIOLENCE; REVOLUTION.)

Richard Rubenstein, *Alchemists of Revolution: Terrorism in the Modern World* (London and New York, 1987). Walter Laqueur, *Terrorism*, 2d ed. (New York and London, 1988). Adrian Guelke, *The Age of Terrorism and the International Political System* (London, 1995). Conor Gearty, ed., *Terrorism* (Aldershot, U.K., 1996).

FRED HALLIDAY

THAILAND. Located in mainland Southeast Asia, Thailand is bordered by Burma on the west and north, by Laos and Cambodia on the east, and by Malaysia on the south. Its northern borders are only 100 miles (160 km.) from China, while Vietnam is less than 100 miles to the east. About the size of Texas and with a population approaching 65 million, Thailand can be divided into four geographic regions: the central plain with its rich alluvial soil and relatively high standard of living; the northeast where poverty and arid conditions prevail; the north with its mountains and varied ethnic hill groups; and the southern peninsula, characterized by a Malay-speaking minority.

Thailand's capital city, Bangkok, with a population of approximately 10 million, is located in the central plain near the Gulf of Siam. Bangkok, dominating every aspect of Thai society, is the kingdom's unchallenged center of political, economic, cultural, educational, and social activity.

Although about 60 percent of the Thai labor force is in the agricultural sphere of the economy, the number in rice farming is decreasing as Thai farmers have diversified into crops such as vegetables, fruits, maize, tapioca, coffee, flowers, sugar, rubber, and livestock. As *modernization has arrived, Thai farmers have become more sophisticated economic actors, moving from subsistence to surplus agriculture. Although farming areas have not developed economically as rapidly as urban areas in the past twenty years, the standard of living in the countryside has improved. Manufacturing now is responsible for a larger share of the GDP than is agriculture. The average yearly per capita income in Thailand is US$2,800.

For most Thais, the family is the most important unit of identity, although the movement toward a more urban population has undermined the traditional closeness of extended families. Rural Thais also identify with their village, a community of about 100 to 300 households, characterized by an agricultural economy, a Buddhist temple, and patron-client bonds that act as the integrative web of society.

The key element in the structure of Thai society is that of superior-subordinate relationships. These relationships are reciprocal and personal with the superior (patron) having power over the subordinate (client). Patron-client bonds stem from personal relationships such as kinship groupings, official ties within the bureaucracy, school ties, or common village origins, and are based largely on personal loyalty.

The superior is expected to be compassionate and kind and to manifest these qualities by protecting, aiding, complimenting, and giving generously to those whose status is inferior. In return, the subordinate, or client, is expected to act deferentially and to cause his patron the least amount of trouble.

At every level, from the village to the central government in Bangkok, patron-client groups perform the functions of disseminating information, allocating resources, and organizing people. These groupings form a link in a network of personal relations that extends throughout Thai society and that traditionally has formed the heart of Thai politics. Although both personalism and patron-client relationships remain important, in the past several decades Thai politics has evolved in the direction of decreased personalism and more formalized participation in the political structures.

Since 1932, when a group of civilians and military officers overthrew the absolute monarchy, the Thai military has played the dominant role in Thai politics. Of the fifty-three cabinets during the period 1932 to 1998, twenty-four were classified as military governments, ten as military-dominated, and nineteen as civilian. Civilian governments, which were the most unstable, were often replaced by military regimes following army coups d'état. Because communist insurgency has ended and because there is no viable external threat to Thai security, the major rationale for military intervention into governmental affairs has been undermined. Nevertheless, the February 1991 coup was an example of continuing military dominance. Following the overthrow of Prime Minister Chatichai's administration in 1991, the military realized that the days of direct military rule were over; hence, the generals appointed civilian Anand Panyarachun as prime minister. In May 1992 the Thai citizenry demonstrated against the military leaders, and with the support of the king forced them to retreat and to accept the return of full civilian rule.

The king deposed the generals and called for elections. As the appointed prime minister, Anand Panyarachun oversaw the first election and then stepped down. From 1992 to 1998 the prime ministers were Anand Panyarachun (1992, appointed), Chuan Leekpai (1992–1995, elected as leader of the Democratic Party), Banharn Silapa-archa (1995–1996, elected as leader of the Chart Thai Party), Chawalit Yongchaiyut (1996–1997, elected as leader of the New Aspiration Party), and Chuan Leekpai (1997–present, reelected).

For most of the contemporary era, Thailand has been a bureaucratic polity with the military holding the key positions. Although the highest-level leaders may change, often by extraconstitutional means such as military coups, the sustained role of the bureaucracy has ensured a high degree of policy continuity. The formerly exclusive role of the bureaucracy has been widened in recent years by the new role of technocrats who are highly trained and educated officials concerned more about the public good than the traditional values of hierarchy, patronage, and security. Moreover, institutions such as Parliament, political parties, and interest groups are playing a more effective role in determining public policy.

The Parliament is no longer just a rubber stamp of the prime minister. In 1997 a new reform constitution was passed overwhelmingly by the combined upper and lower houses of Parliament. The new constitution was designed to reduce corruption (politicians must declare assets before taking office), enhance human rights, decentralize the polity, make the higher legislative body, the Senate, more accountable, provide the judiciary with more authority, and strengthen political parties. The new constitution calls for senators to be directly elected. Ministers must give up their seats in Parliament before taking charge of their portfolios, a provision designed to separate the executive from the legislative branch. One hundred of the 500 members of Parliament are elected by a national vote from a national proportional list of party-nominated candidates. The other 400 candidates are elected in single-member constituencies. This provision was included to reduce the prevalence of vote buying and to strengthen the major parties.

Theoretically above politics, the Thai monarch is the national symbol, the supreme patron who reigns over all, and the leader of the Buddhist religion. The prestige and veneration of the monarchy have grown since the 1950 coronation of King Phumiphol Adunyadej, who recently became the kingdom's longest-reigning monarch as well as the present world's longest-serving king. In the 1980s, the king became more involved in Thai politics. His strong stance against coups d'état, for example, has helped to stabilize politics in Thailand. Traditionally, the Chinese-Thai minority (about 10 percent of the population) has dominated the Thai economy while the Thai majority has prevailed in politics. However, a fundamental change has occurred in Thai politics with the Chinese-Thai becoming more involved. The new Parliament includes an unprecedented number of Chinese-Thai business executives.

From the early 1960s to 1997, Thailand sustained a 7 percent growth rate, a rate equaled by few other developing nations. More remarkably, the kingdom's average annual economic growth in the late 1980s was 10 percent, among the highest of any country. Coincident with these high growth rates was the increase in the export sector, which in the late 1980s grew about 24 percent each year. Foreign investment grew at a similarly rapid rate, with Japan, Taiwan, the United States, Hong Kong, and the Republic of Korea the leading investors.

The factors responsible for the kingdom's economic successes included a commitment to free-market, export-driven policies, carried out by highly trained, and generally conservative, technocrats. These new officials were not as steeped in personalistic, clientelist politics as their predecessors. The vital involvement of Thailand's Chinese minority and the fact that Thai leaders have adhered to a consistent set of economic policies also have helped explain the vibrancy of the economy.

In July 1997 Thailand's remarkable economic growth ended abruptly when the Thai currency (the baht) lost 50 percent of its value, the stock market lost 70 percent of its worth, and bankruptcies proliferated. The causes of the debacle included *corruption, weak infrastructure, weak economic leadership, and imprudent borrowing of foreign currency. Borrowed money was spent primarily on real estate and industries that offered meager returns. Thai labor and exports became more expensive and less competitive. Speculators bet on the devaluation of the baht, selling the currency at a profit, and forcing the central bank to try to defend the currency. Foreign currency reserves fell drastically. Finally, the International Monetary Fund sponsored a $17 billion rescue package.

The greatest obstacles to ending the economic crisis are the poor state of infrastructural facilities and the depletion of natural resources, especially forests. Thai universities graduate only a third of the students needed in engineering and related "hard" sciences and technology. One further difficulty stems, ironically, from the nation's former economic success. Foreign investment and trade have made the Thai economy vulner-able to the vagaries of the world economy. The crisis affected Thailand first, but then spread to Malaysia, Indonesia, and the Philippines.

Thailand has evolved into a semidemocracy with new institutions available for more effective political participation. There is open participation, a free press, and free elections. Nevertheless, Thai society is still dominated by a small proportion of the society that controls the military, economic, and political spheres. The prospects for continued *parliamentary democracy depend on the capacity of the government to meet the needs of the people, to rekindle the formerly high level of economic development, to restrain the military, and to provide for a smooth monarchical succession. Prospects are also contingent on the ability of the state to strengthen institutions such as the Parliament and political parties and to decrease the role of patronage and corruption.

(See also ASSOCIATION OF SOUTHEAST ASIAN NATIONS; BUDDHISM; DEMOCRATIC TRANSITIONS; DEVELOPMENT AND UNDERDEVELOPMENT; MILITARY RULE; PATRON-CLIENT POLITICS; SOUTHEAST ASIA TREATY ORGANIZATION.)

Clark D. Neher and Wiwat Mungkandi, eds., *Thailand–U.S. Relations in the New International Era,* Institute of East Asian Studies Research Papers (Berkeley, Calif., 1990). Anek Laothamatas, *From Bureaucratic Polity to Liberal Corporatism: Business Associations and the New Political Economy of Thailand* (Boulder, Colo., 1991). Elliot Kulick and Dick Wilson, *Thailand's Turn: Profile of a New Dragon* (New York, 1992). Kevin Hewison, ed., *Political Change in Thailand: Democracy and Participation* (London, 1997). Pasuk Phongpaichit and C. Baker, *Thailand: Economy and Politics* (Kuala Lumpur, 1995). Ryan Bishop and Lillian S. Robinson, *Night Market: Sexual Cultures and the Thai Economic Miracle* (London, 1998).

CLARK D. NEHER

THATCHER, Margaret. The first woman prime minister in a major West European state, Margaret Thatcher is remarkable also for being the first British prime minister to win three successive general elections since Lord Liverpool in the early nineteenth century, as well as for being the longest continuously serving prime minister in twentieth-century *Britain, holding the post from May 1979 to November 1990. She has lent her name to an "ism"—*Thatcherism. This refers both to her political style—which is abrasive and direct—and her policies—tax cutting and encouraging the free market. In Britain she has also made a mark for her proclaimed break with the postwar consensus policies which she thought had produced the relative economic decline of the country.

She was born in 1925, the daughter of a shopkeeper in Grantham. She read chemistry at Oxford and later qualified as a barrister, specializing in taxation. She entered Parliament for Finchley, North London, in 1959, a seat which she held until her retirement from the House of Commons in 1992. It is interesting that she chose such male-dominated careers; at the time the Conservatives had only a handful of women members of Parliament (MPs). The Conservative Party was also dominated in these years by people from upper-class backgrounds. In this company Margaret Thatcher, although she married a well-off divorcé, Denis Thatcher, was something of an upstart. Even in 1990 she could still speak dismissively of "toffs" in the party. She also publicly referred to middle-class "guilt," which she thought held back earlier

Conservative governments from taking necessary but unpopular actions to combat inflation, social indiscipline, and abuses of trade union power. She dismissed these as "wet" Conservatives.

In the new Conservative administration of 1970 Thatcher was appointed secretary of state for education, the only female member of the cabinet. In that post she gained extra resources for her department and oversaw an expansion of the service. But she was never close to the prime minister, Edward Heath, or closely involved in major decisions. The Heath government was controversial for its adoption in 1972 of a statutory prices and incomes policy to combat inflation—in spite of an election pledge not to do so. When the Conservatives lost two general elections in 1974 Heath's position as leader came under pressure. Thatcher was the only heavyweight figure to challenge him in a leadership election in February 1975. It was a shock when she defeated him and went on to win the leadership on a second ballot among Conservative MPs. As leader of the opposition she increasingly espoused free market economic policies, in contrast to those both of the previous Conservative government and the then Labour government.

As prime minister in 1979 she broke new ground in economic policy. Income tax cuts, tough monetary targets, a reduced growth of planned public spending, and the abandonment of Keynesian fine tuning signaled a new approach. These policies were maintained despite a subsequent sharp rise in unemployment and fall in production. Measures to privatize publicly owned undertakings and weaken trade unions were also introduced. Yet soaring inflation and sharply rising unemployment made the government and the prime minister deeply unpopular. The reputation of both was helped by the recapture in June 1982 of the Malvinas/Falkland Islands from Argentina and the recovery of the economy. In the June 1983 general election, Thatcher gained a landslide election victory.

In the new Parliament the government continued with the reforms of trade unions, *privatization, and tax cuts. Industrial action by trade unions was defeated, notably a yearlong strike by miners. Inflation and unemployment turned down, thus preparing the ground for another handsome election victory in 1987.

In foreign affairs Margaret Thatcher was so assertive of British interests that she was sometimes dismissed as a "little Englander." In contrast to Edward Heath she was more of an Atlanticist than a European. Her relations with most European Community (EC) leaders were marred by acrimonious disputes over Britain's budgetary contribution and her resistance to measures to speed integration. The special relationship with the United States was largely a function of her close rapport with President Ronald *Reagan. In 1986 she courted unpopularity by allowing U.S. planes to take off from Britain to mount bombing raids in Libya.

She reduced the size and challenged the culture of the civil service and sharply reduced the role of local government, but she did little else to reform political institutions. Opinion surveys showed that she was not a much-liked figure but was much respected as a strong, decisive leader. As party leader she reasserted a long-dormant neoliberal strand in the Conservative Party and stood for a unique blend of liberal economics—a greater role for markets, income tax cuts, and less government intervention in the economy—and authoritarianism—regarding law and order and freedom of information.

As a peacetime prime minister she was distinctive. The most dominant personal premierships in this century were the wartime tenures of Lloyd George and Winston Churchill. As party leader and prime minister, Thatcher was more of a mobilizer than a conciliator, determined to take radical measures to turn the country around. For a Conservative she was oddly impatient with the state of things. She was so closely involved in pushing so many radical policies on privatization, income tax cuts, education reforms, industrial relations changes, local government finance, and resistance to British membership in the EC Exchange Rate Mechanism that it can be argued she made a difference to policy outcomes.

Thatcher appointed her supporters to key economic posts and intervened energetically in the work of departments. In this she was helped by a strengthened policy unit and above all by her own stamina, inquisitiveness, and self-confidence in the correctness of her opinions on so many issues. What she achieved at the center of British government she did largely by herself rather than through institutions. Remarkably, in a political system with a collective executive (the cabinet) she was less an advocate for the team than a figure apart, forcefully presenting her own views.

There was much irony in that her cabinets contained few true Thatcherites. Some of her close allies, notably Nigel Lawson, chancellor of the exchequer, Norman Tebbit, party chair, and Nicholas Ridley, secretary of state for trade and industry, all left in stormy circumstances. In November 1990 Sir Geoffrey Howe suddenly resigned. Sir Geoffrey was the only other member, apart from Margaret Thatcher herself, to have survived from the first government in 1979. In his resignation speech he condemned Thatcher's leadership style and forcefully repudiated her approach to Britain's relationship with the EC. The speech was seen as a challenge to Thatcher's leadership, a challenge that was accepted by her old foe Michael Heseltine. Although she won the first ballot for the party leadership her majority was not sufficient to avoid the need for a second ballot. Concerned cabinet colleagues warned that she would lose the leadership and appealed to her to stand down. This she did, and in the ensuing leadership ballot John Major was elected party leader and became prime minister.

Two questions remain for historians. First, why did the Conservative Party achieve such dominance throughout the 1980s and the first years of the 1990s? In part it was a consequence of the first-past-the-post electoral system which translated a forty-two percent share of the popular vote into some sixty percent of the seats in the House of Commons in 1983 and 1987. In part it was also due to the decline of the Labour Party and the trade unions, and in part to the division of the non-Conservative vote between the Alliance and Labour parties. Second, if Thatcher undoubtedly helped to dismantle so many of the institutions and policies of the postwar consensus, how successful was she in laying the outlines of a new settlement?

(See also CONSERVATISM; LIBERALISM; MALVINAS/FALKLANDS WAR; MONETARISM; NEW RIGHT; TAXES AND TAXATION.)

Anthony King, "Margaret Thatcher: The Style of a Prime Minister," in Anthony King, ed., *The British Prime Minister,* 2d ed. (London, 1985). Dennis Kavanagh, *Thatcherism and British Politics* (Oxford, 1989). Dennis Kavanagh, "Making Sense of Thatcherism," in Dennis Kavanagh, ed., *Politics and Personalities* (London, 1990). Hugo Young, *One of Us* (London, 1990). Margaret Thatcher, *Downing Street Years* (London, 1993).

DENNIS KAVANAGH

THATCHERISM. The phenomenon known as "Thatcherism" flourished in *Britain from the mid-1970s to the early 1990s. The term was coined when Margaret *Thatcher was elected Conservative Party leader in 1975 and became popular after she became prime minister in 1979. First used by Marxist-inspired critics, the term entered fully into everyday language by the early 1980s. Among its many meanings are: Thatcher's "conviction politics" approach to campaigning and political leadership; her right-wing "authoritarian populism" and commitment to a "free economy and strong state"; a distinctive set of neoliberal economic policies; and the more general economic and political strategies pursued by Thatcher and her close advisers in government. Many commentators have questioned whether "Thatcherism" has any real analytic value in any or all of these respects, and some regard Thatcher's policies and politics as just part of a more general shift in the 1970s and 1980s towards neoliberalism, neoconservatism, and the New Right. If so, as a distinctive British variant of this general shift, Thatcherism won as much attention as it did for four main reasons. Thatcher was the first (and, as yet, only) woman to become prime minister in Britain, had a domineering personality, won three successive election victories (helped in 1983 and 1987 by a divided opposition), and exploited more fully than most the powers given to all prime ministers under Britain's "elected dictatorship."

A distinctive Thatcherite economic strategy took some years to evolve. The initial policies comprised *monetarism, attacks on trade union privileges, and faith in market forces. Gradually a more radical economic program emerged aimed at rolling back the social democratic postwar settlement based on full employment and the *welfare state and at providing secure foundations for an enterprise society and popular capitalism. The strategy's main features were: liberalization; economic deregulation; *privatization of state-owned industries; market proxies in the residual public sector; promoting the internationalization of the economy; and lower direct taxation. From 1986–87 onwards these measures were supplemented by a more radical program of restructuring a wide range of institutions in civil society: education, the health service, the professions, the mass media, culture industries, and religion. The high point of Thatcherism seems to have been the tax-cutting budget in favor of the rich in 1987. Thereafter economic and political trends moved against the government. It also faced growing discontent over such issues as National Health Service reform, road and rail transport, privatization of water and electricity, the issue of European integration, and, most damagingly, the Thatcher-inspired "poll tax" introduced to replace the local property tax. The years 1989–90 proved to be the beginning of the end for Thatcherism, and Thatcher resigned as party leader and prime minister in November 1990, being replaced by John Major after a bruising leadership battle.

The social basis of Thatcherism was initially rooted in Thatcher's ability to voice latent petit bourgeois discontent with the postwar settlement as well as more general disillusion with the Labour government, the unions, and an increasingly visible economic decline. Thatcherism also enjoyed massive press support almost to the last. Once in office, the Conservatives used government resources to consolidate popular support—notably among skilled manual workers in the private sector and among small business people and the self-employed. Support was stronger in the prosperous south of England than in Scotland, Wales, and the declining north. Although Thatcherism's success was often explained in terms of its hegemonization of political discourse, public opinion did not seem to have shifted in an identifiably Thatcherite direction.

Thatcherism's overall impact is becoming clearer. It won major international recognition during the 1980s and inspired many other neoliberal movements in several continents. In Britain itself, the Thatcher and Major governments made some largely irreversible structural changes in the economy: they privatized most of the state-owned enterprises and forced the contracting out of public services; abolished exchange controls and deregulated finance; diverted resources from public investment into private consumption; shifted the tax burden from direct to indirect taxes and from rich to poor; disorganized the trade union movement; and severely weakened local government. Although they did boost the City of London as an international financial center, there is little evidence that their governments reversed Britain's comparative long-run economic decline. Thatcherism also maintained Britain's relative isolation from the European Union. The most important political legacy of Thatcherism is the transformation of the Labour Party into New Labour with its commitment to market forces, enterprise, and a "welfare into work reform" of the welfare state.

(See also CONSERVATISM; KEYNESIANISM; RIGHT.)

BOB JESSOP

THIRD WORLD. At the start of twenty-first century, the concept "Third World" refers to a dynamic and multifaceted phenomenon. The revolutions of 1989, the disintegration of socialist regimes, the end of the *Cold War, and globalization all have profound implications for the group of countries said to constitute the Third World. To assess the contemporary significance of this concept for *international relations, the place to begin is with its origin and alternative definitions.

Coined by French authors, the term contains an allusion to the Third Estate of prerevolutionary France—that is, to social groups other than the most privileged groups of the day, the clergy and the nobility (the First and Second Estates, respectively). Analogously, then, *Third World* refers to the marginalized strata of the international system.

Another interpretation equates the Third World with poverty in general. For the *World Bank, the Third World comprises low-income countries. These may be subdivided according to GNP per capita. But this definition is replete with empirical contradictions. Some Middle Eastern countries have a higher average per capita income than does the United States, and there is a greater incidence of poverty in some U.S. inner cities than in many parts of the Third World. Furthermore, emphasis on statistical indicators such as per capita income often deflects attention from qualitative social conditions. From a slightly different perspective, the term "Third World" means oppressed nations, suggesting the existence of states that are exploited and of others that are exploiters.

In common usage, the Third World comprises all countries not included in the First World and the Second World. The Western capitalist countries plus Japan, Australia, and New Zealand, and often Israel and South Africa as well, are widely regarded as constituting the First World. The Second World—a construction of the Cold War era—consisted of the socialist countries of Eastern and Central Europe, what was called the Soviet bloc. The Third World encompasses the nations of Africa, Asia, and Latin America, most of them former colonies which to varying degrees could be characterized as underdeveloped.

The ambiguities associated with the term "Third World" are manifold. One complication is the role of oppressed peoples outside the three continents. Are African Americans part of the Third World? Native Americans? Australian aborigines? In addition, ethnocentrism may be detected in assigning first place to the countries that rank ahead of the others according to an economic and technological yardstick. The Third World would be first if the criteria were the chronology of the human species (which begins with Africa) or total population.

Yet another source of discomfort comes from the abandonment of the notion that world politics is characterized by a struggle between two rival systems—the thinking that had dominated the four decades of the Cold War. If worlds one and two no longer exist, does it make sense to delimit a "Third World"?

To be sure, some observers reject the term "Third World" altogether. An influential commission headed by Willy Brandt, former chancellor of the Federal Republic of Germany, preferred a dichotomy, as indicated by the title of its report: *North-South: A Program for Survival* (Cambridge, Mass., 1980). This distinction is between two hemispheres, a more economically advanced "north" and a less developed "south." However, there are well-to-do nations south of the equator (Australia, New Zealand, and, more problematically, South Africa) as well as several poor countries in the "north": India, with fifteen percent of the world's population, the rest of South Asia, some of Southeast Asia, the Caribbean, Central America, and the northern region of South America. Another viewpoint is that the world should be analyzed in more unitary terms. World systems theorists such as Immanuel Wallerstein reason that there is a single world economy and that it is capitalist. The analysis that follows from this presupposition identifies three tiers of the world economy: core, periphery, and semiperiphery. The danger, however, in employing such broad strokes lies in omitting the fine detail, which is precisely what in substance must be discerned.

Clearly, the division of the world into zones is a reality. But the components are changing. Most important is the disintegration of the Second ("socialist") World. Moreover, the global political economy is increasingly differentiated, with important distinctions between the first generation of countries to have penetrated Japanese and Western markets (the "Four Tigers"—Taiwan, the Republic of Korea [South Korea], Singapore, and Hong Kong), possible competition from a second generation of *newly industrializing economies, and, on the other end of the spectrum, sub-Saharan Africa, which is the most marginalized region in the mosaic of globalization.

In sum, the Third World is a geographical and political category referring broadly to the three continents of Asia, Africa, and Latin America, not a precise analytical concept. The main drawbacks to Third Worldist thinking are sentimentality, the tendency to romanticize struggles waged by "the wretched of the earth," and the impression that only the advanced countries are the oppressors without due emphasis on locally dominant forces and transnational coalitions. Despite its pitfalls, the term "Third World" is a convenient shorthand to depict the group of countries struggling to escape from underdevelopment. Although a new order has emerged after the Cold War in which vocabulary of the past is sometimes regarded as both quaint and inappropriate, "Third World" is still widely used. As a metaphor, it describes the disadvantaged position of peoples, most of whom are of color amid large concentrations of poverty in postcolonial societies, within the ambit of a rapidly changing global political economy.

(See also DEVELOPMENT AND UNDERDEVELOPMENT; INTERNATIONAL SYSTEMS; MODERNIZATION; NORTH-SOUTH RELATIONS; RURAL DEVELOPMENT; WOMEN AND DEVELOPMENT.)

Allen H. Merriam, "Semantic Implications of the Term 'Third World.'" *International Studies Notes* 6, no. 3 (Fall 1979): 12–15. James H. Mittelman and Mustapha Kamal Pasha, *Out from Underdevelopment Revisited: Changing Global Structures and the Remaking of the Third World* (London and New York, 1997). James H. Mittelman, *The Globalization Syndrome: Transformation and Resistance* (Princeton, N.J., 2000).

JAMES H. MITTELMAN

THUCYDIDES. Considered the greatest of the classical Greek historians because of his authorship of an unfinished, untitled history of the Peloponnesian War, Thucydides evidently was trained in the dialectical modes of argument of the Sophists and influenced by the diagnostic practice of early Greek medicine. Sensitive to many themes in the Greek culture of his time, he wrote his book to be, in the rendering of his first English-language translator, Thomas Hobbes, "an everlasting possession."

His immortality as a historian derives from an exemplary commitment to descriptive accuracy, analytical depth in probing the conditions and possibilities of the human condition, and the dramatic power of his account. The book can be read as a tragic account of the rise and fall of imperial Athens, as a painfully accurate account of the dismemberment of the unifying alliances and the civilized standards of conduct of the Greek city-states in general and Athens in particular, and as a scientific history of the Peloponnesian War (431–404 B.C.E.) between Athens and Sparta, each supported by a changing coalition of allies, colonies, and even former enemies.

Ironically, his failings as a general facilitated his detailed investigation of the actions and rationales of both sides during the *war. The son of Olorus, Thucydides was an Athenian who had Thracian roots, including an interest in gold mines there. From textual evidence, Thucydides is estimated to have been born around 460 B.C.E. Having been elected one of Athens's ten *strategoi* in 424 with responsibility for the Thracian region, Thucydides had unfortunately lost the important city of Amphipolis that winter to the Spartan general Brasidas's surprising winter campaign and his effective anti-imperialist appeals. Returning to Athens, Thucydides was tried and convicted for his loss, and exiled from Athens. He appears to have returned some twenty years later, at the end of the war, and to have died shortly thereafter.

Thucydides shares with Sun Tzu and Kautilya the role of cofounders of a global discipline of international politics. In each case these writers emphasized the "realistic" importance of power politics, within a theoretical and cultural framework that acknowledged as well the importance of cultural ideals such as justice, moderation, and appropriateness. Modern Western writers have identified him with the Realist tradition of international theorizing and prudent diplomacy, citing Machiavelli, Hobbes, *Clausewitz, and Morgenthau as important successors. Except for revolutionary, anti-imperialist, or communitarian regimes, this school of international political practice has had tremendous influence—if not always great public acclaim—among the leading statesmen and stateswomen of the modern era. As Hobbes tried to justify his absolutist antidemocratic politics with references to the horrible civil strife in Corcyra, so Thucydides' insights and interpretive visions have been fitted with Neorealist, Marxist, communitarian, and even postmodernist perspectives.

(See also Balance of Power; International Relations; Postmodernism; Realism.)

Donald Kagan, *The Outbreak of the Peloponnesian War* (Ithaca, N.Y., 1969). Donald Kagan, *The Archidamian War* (Ithaca, N.Y., 1974). Donald Kagan, *The Peace of Nicias and the Sicilian Expedition* (Ithaca, N.Y., 1981). W. Robert Connor, *Thucydides* (Princeton, N.J., 1984). Donald Kagan, *The Fall of the Athenian Empire* (Ithaca, N.Y., 1987).

HAYWARD R. ALKER, JR.

TIANANMEN SQUARE. The spontaneous demonstrations that filled Beijing's Tiananmen Square, the symbolic capital of China's communist *revolution, in the spring of 1989 were unprecedented in the history of the People's Republic of *China. They revealed a high level of disillusionment with the reform program initiated in the late 1970s and exposed deep divisions within *Chinese Communist Party (CCP) leadership about future development.

The specific cause of the demonstrations was the death of the reformist ex-CCP General Secretary Hu Yaobang. But frustrations among key sectors of the urban population meant that the student actions quickly found widespread support. The stop-and-go urban economic reform program launched in late 1984 failed to turn around the urban economy and was extremely destabilizing. The industrial working class saw its privileged position coming under threat from market-based reforms; intellectuals and students were frustrated by insufficient political reform; and all were affected by inflation.

The students were the social group that first took to the streets and remained the driving force. They were alienated from the mainstream of the party-dominated society and were not concerned so directly with the financial and social problems that beset the rest of Beijing's urban population.

On 26 April, the Beijing Students Autonomous Federation was formally founded, the first such organization in the history of the People's Republic. This represented a fundamental challenge to traditional party dominance of social organizations, a challenge that was increased by the founding of the Beijing Workers Autonomous Federation in mid-May.

The stress on combating official corruption gave the movement the feel of a moral crusade, and this was important for creating broader public support. This moral image was heightened by the launching of the hunger strike on 13 May. However, the original leaders found it increasingly difficult to coordinate actions. The fragmented organizational structure made decision making cumbersome and hampered the students' capacity to act flexibly and decisively.

The party's reaction was no more coherent. The movement exposed deep divisions within the party about the reform program. The resultant inner-party struggle between conservative leaders and reformers gathered around CCP General Secretary Zhao Ziyang had to be resolved before the students could be dealt with. Zhao was marginalized and martial law was invoked on 20 May. The conservative group saw the establishment of autonomous organizations as a fundamental challenge to party rule and were unwilling to accept any political agenda that was not set by the party itself. This refusal to recognize the organizations shut out the possibility for genuine dialogue, making conflict inevitable. The decision to call in the army to crush the demonstrations on 4 June highlighted how out of touch the conservative leaders were with the process of change that the economic reforms had unleashed. Estimates of the number killed in the crackdown range from a few hundred to over 1,000.

Tiananmen remains an important symbol for all involved and provides a source of continued friction in foreign relations, especially with the United States. The current Chinese leadership defends the crackdown as necessary and as providing the stability for subsequent economic growth. However, now they rarely denounce the movement as a "counterrevolutionary uprising," the milder term "disturbance" being preferred. With rapid economic development and memories fading, the leadership hopes to close discussions without undergoing a painful day of reckoning and retribution. Zhao Ziyang, though still out of power, has subsequently referred to the violent suppression as a "serious mistake" for which the Party should apologize. Some feel that a reversal of judgment on Tiananmen could provide a new leadership with the moral authority to carry out faster economic and especially political reform. Future leaders will have to deal with these different interpretations.

(See also Deng Xiaoping; Sino-American Relations.)

Tony Saich, ed., *The Chinese People's Movement: Perspectives on Spring 1989* (Armonk, N.Y., 1990). Suzanne Ogden, Kathleen Hartford, Lawrence R. Sullivan, and David Zweig, eds., *China's Search for Democracy: The Student and Mass Movement of 1989* (Armonk, N.Y., 1991).

TONY SAICH

TIBET. From rival tribes, the Tibetans were united in the sixth century; they were led by strong tribal leaders until the thirteenth century, when Mongol khans created a theocracy under their Buddhist spiritual advisors. These Dalai Lamas held absolute power, although at times Tibet was ruled by monk regents or by agents (*amban*) sent by the Chinese government. From 1913 to 1950 Tibet was de facto independent. In 1950 Tibet was incorporated into the People's Republic of *China (PRC), and since 1 September 1965 has been known as the Tibet Autonomous Region (TAR).

The Chinese constitution stipulates that in areas where minority people make up a majority of the population, local governments will be run by the ethnic minorities and have relatively broad powers in comparison with similar regions where the ethnic Chinese predominate. The TAR represents only about one-third of the total area of ethnic Tibetan inhabitation in China and corresponds to the area of political control traditionally maintained by the Dalai Lamas. About half of China's 4 million Tibetans live in the TAR; the other half lives in twelve autonomous prefectures and counties with a Tibetan majority in the Chinese provinces of Gansu, Qinghai, Sichuan, and Yunnan.

From 1950 until an abortive revolt in 1959, the fourteenth, and current, Dalai Lama continued ruling in conjunction with Chinese officials. After the revolt, the Dalai Lama and approximately 50,000–60,000 Tibetans fled into exile in India and the surrounding region. An ad hoc government replaced the Dalai Lama until the establishment of the TAR in 1965.

The TAR government, always led by a Tibetan, is in charge of enforcing laws, making local policies, administering local finance and economic development. It also has responsibility in areas such as education, tourism, and public health. In August 1979, a Tibet Regional People's Congress, also led by Tibetans, and similar parliamentary groups at the county and municipal levels were established. There is a local court system and police force. All major decisions must be approved by the authorities in Beijing.

Real power in the TAR lies in the hands of the local *Chinese Communist Party (CCP) organization, which has never had a Tibetan leader. There are CCP branches at every level of government. In addition, Chinese military forces have considerable sway in the region owing to Tibet's strategic position, a plateau averaging 16,000 feet (4,880 meters) above sea level looking down onto the frontier with India (with whom China fought a brief war in 1962). There are also border police units and a sizable local militia. Because of recent disturbances, the central government has introduced armed police forces as well.

Chinese policies of the 1960s attempted to destroy religion and imposed arbitrary rules on the Tibetans. The Dalai Lama was portrayed by Beijing as a traitor in exile. Tibetans are devout Buddhists who universally look upon the Dalai Lama as their spiritual leader, and Chinese policies have found few followers while creating deep divisions between the two peoples. A recent influx of Chinese into the TAR has exacerbated the cleavages as the immigrants have received privileges beyond those available to the Tibetans.

These divisions are further aggravated by an effective worldwide campaign conducted by the Dalai Lama in India and his supporters in the West to achieve Tibetan independence. China believes Tibet was never independent, and the issue is historically murky. Initially aided by the Central Intelligence Agency, the Tibetan exile movement has gained a momentum of its own, and in 1990 the Dalai Lama won the Nobel Peace Prize. The exile community has been able to operate clandestinely inside Tibet as well. In 1987 violence erupted in Tibet, resulting in many Tibetan casualties and the declaration of martial law in the capital, Lhasa, in 1989, only to be lifted more than a year later. In the 1990s several bombs were detonated in Lhasa.

Tibet was a feudal state until 1959 and desperately poor. Beginning in 1951 the Chinese built roads, hospitals, schools, factories, tourist facilities, airports, and the like. However, these additions for the most part have had little effect on the local Tibetan population, and it appears that the Chinese have benefited more than the Tibetans. Tibet remains a poor, traditional, agricultural economy with little prospect for growth without a railway, which to date has remained a technological impossibility over the permafrost and 16,000-foot (4,900-meter) mountain passes.

In recent years the Dalai Lama and the Chinese government have held informal talks on various levels to negotiate the cleric's return to Tibet in order to ease ethnic strains. Many Tibetan exiles oppose the Dalai Lama's return until Tibet has achieved independence. The Dalai Lama believes that under certain conditions he can return and work with the Chinese government as he did in the 1950s and serve as a force for political stability and economic development.

Currently the hostility that Tibetans feel toward the Chinese is palpable, exacerbated by the continuing flow of Chinese into the TAR, and this tension makes any prospect of economic and political progress unlikely. Chinese officials have admitted that political autonomy has been a sham yet do little to change the situation. Military force is still deemed the best way to maintain order and stability.

(See also BUDDHISM; ETHNICITY; RELIGION AND POLITICS.)

A. Tom Grunfeld, *The Making of Modern Tibet* (London and New York, 1996). Melvyn C. Goldstein, *The Snow Lion and the Dragon: China, Tibet, and the Dalai Lama* (Berkeley, Calif., 1997).

A. TOM GRUNFELD

TIMOR. An island in the Indonesian archipelago, Timor is inhabited by people of mixed Austronesian-Melanesian ancestry. European involvement dates from the sixteenth century, and diplomatic negotiations between 1839 and 1914 partitioned the island into West (Dutch) Timor and East (Portuguese) Timor, including the enclave of Oecussi Ambeno on the northwest coast. After Japanese occupation during World War II, West Timor became part of independent *Indonesia, with the east remaining a Portuguese overseas territory. After the 1974 armed forces coup in Portugal, the small mestizo elite split over the options of independence or continued association with Portugal. In a brief civil war in August 1975, the left-wing pro-independence Frente Revolucionaria do Timor Leste Independente (Fretilin) defeated the conservative associationist forces. Fearing Fretilin's left-wing connections, Indonesia invaded the territory in September. Fretilin declared independence on 28 November, but was forced from the capital, Dili, after an Indonesian airborne attack in December 1975. The UN General Assembly called on Indonesia to withdraw and the Security Council condemned the invasion, but many observers believe that the invasion initially had the tacit approval of the United States and Australia. Indonesia formally annexed the territory on 15 July 1976.

*Guerrilla warfare under a succession of Fretilin leaders continued in the mountains. The disruption of agriculture by the war and the resettlement of villagers by Indonesian authorities as a *counterinsurgency measure led to *famine in which perhaps 100,000 people (of an original population of 650,000) died. International attention was drawn to continuing unrest in the territory when Indonesian troops killed more than 100 demonstrators at a funeral in Dili on 12 November

1991. In 1996, Jose Ramos Horta and the Timorese Catholic bishop Felipe Ximenes Belo were awarded the Nobel Peace Prize for their efforts to seek a peaceful end to the conflict.

The East Timor issue was a diplomatic liability to Indonesia under President Suharto, and in January 1999 Suharto's successor, B. J. Habibie, unexpectedly invited the East Timorese to choose between independence and far-reaching autonomy within Indonesia. On 5 May, Indonesia and Portugal agreed that the United Nations would conduct a "popular consultation" over the future of the territory, and in a referendum on 30 August 1999, held by the United Nations Mission in East Timor (UNAMET), 78.5 percent of voters supported independence. During the following weeks, local pro-Indonesian militias, backed by the Indonesian military, launched a campaign of destruction and intimidation which killed thousands of people, destroyed much of the territory's infrastructure, and drove about 250,000 *refugees into West (Indonesian) Timor. In September 1999, the UN Security Council authorized a multinational military force (INTERFET) under Australian command, to enter East Timor to restore peace and security. In mid-October 1999, Indonesia surrendered its claims to the territory and on 25 October the Security Council established the United Nations Transitional Administration in East Timor (UNTAET) to oversee a transition to independence.

Peter Carey and G. Carter Bentley, eds., *East Timor at the Crossroads: The Forging of a Nation* (Honolulu, 1995). John G. Taylor, *East Timor: The Price of Freedom* (New York, 1999).

ROBERT CRIBB

TITO. Josip Broz, known as Tito (1892–1980), was president of *Yugoslavia (1953–1980), general secretary (later president) of the Communist Party (League of Communists) of Yugoslavia (1939–1980), and marshal of Yugoslavia. He was born in the village of Kumrovec, northwest of Zagreb, Croatia, to a peasant family. Having completed his apprenticeship as a locksmith, he worked in Zagreb, where he joined the Social Democratic Party of Croatia-Slavonia in 1910, and later in Austria and Germany. During World War I he served as a sergeant in the Austro-Hungarian army on Serbian and Russian fronts. Wounded and captured by the Russians in 1915, he was a prisoner of war until 1917, when he joined the Red Guard unit in Omsk, Siberia. He returned to the newly founded Yugoslavia in 1920 as a convinced communist. Having joined the Communist Party of Yugoslavia (KPJ), he worked as a trade union organizer and in 1928, as a result of his work against party factions, became the political secretary of the Zagreb party organization.

After the assassination of Stjepan Radić, the leader of the Croatian national movement, in 1928, Tito stirred up demonstrations against the Belgrade government. In line with the growing Communist militancy of the time, he apparently planned terrorist actions (bombs were discovered in his apartment). His defiant defense at the trial increased his standing in the KPJ. After serving a prison term, he was released in 1934 and was co-opted into the KPJ's exiled Politburo in December 1934, when he assumed the pseudonym Tito. After 1937, when *Stalin decimated the exiled leadership of the KPJ, Tito increasingly emerged as the Comintern's choice for general secretary. His appointment was formalized in 1939 and

received internal confirmation at the Fifth Land Conference of the KPJ, held in Zagreb, in October 1940. Tito was already noted as a leftist who put little stock in Popular Front arrangements with non-Communists. Moreover, he was a strong federalist, seeing the solution of the nationality question in Yugoslavia in a Soviet-style federation. This led him to complain against Soviet pleas for cooperation with anti-Communist and Great Serbian Chetniks during the war and prompted him to emphasize the revolutionary seizure of power. This was at variance with Soviet policy of wartime alliance with the Western Allies and their local adherents.

In line with his insurrectionary strategy, Tito organized the Yugoslav Partisan army during the Axis occupation and dismemberment of Yugoslavia. As a result of his military successes and the expansion of the territory held by the Partisans, the Western Allies recognized Tito in 1943 as the leader of Yugoslav resistance, obliging the exiled government of King Peter II to come to terms with him. Communist power was established throughout Yugoslavia by May 1945, usually with a level of ruthlessness that was unique in Eastern Europe. In essence, unlike the countries of Eastern Europe which were occupied by the Soviet Army, Yugoslavia underwent a domestic revolution that established a regional and very militant Communist center.

In the immediate postwar period, under Tito's leadership, Yugoslavia became the most communized country of Eastern Europe. In the early years of the *Cold War Tito's militancy in the *Balkans (Albania, Greece) irritated the Soviet leadership, which was afraid that Tito might provoke a premature war with the West. Tito's independent views and base ultimately provoked the Soviet leadership to plot his overthrow. This failed, but in June 1948, after the promulgation of the Cominform resolution, Yugoslavia was expelled from the Communist family and briefly floundered in total isolation, exposed to internal challenges by pro-Soviet Communists.

After 1949, Western countries came to the aid of Tito, having determined that his "national communism" was a toxin that ought to be encouraged within the increasingly monolithic Soviet camp. For his part, Tito moderated his policies and by 1950 started introducing workers' councils into enterprises. These were meant to be the institutional basis for a return to authentic Marxist "self-management" by the producers in all areas of decision making. In fact, this was a pragmatic attempt to find an ideological alternative to Soviet socialism without embracing Western *pluralism and a market economy. Though he was himself least of all an ideologist, Tito occupied this diminishing middle ground between the Soviets and the West. Self-management, nonalignment in foreign policy, and self-reliance in defense policy were the three pillars of his system. From 1962 he increasingly favored Yugoslavia's decentralization, the high point of this effort being the semiconfederalist constitution of 1974, which was, however, predicated on the lasting rule of the Communist Party.

Having reconciled himself with the Soviet leadership in 1955, Tito continued to clash with Moscow, notably after the Hungarian uprising in 1956 and the invasion of Czechoslovakia in 1968. His relations with the West were on the whole good, with occasional cooling, as in the early 1960s. Most of his energies in foreign policy were devoted to the Third World countries. Tito's last years were a period of deepening malaise, noted for growing conflicts between the constituent nationalities, and recourse to repression. His style of charismatic personal dictatorship was increasingly anachronistic and his ideological solutions an obstacle to needed reform. Despite these failings, his reputation is experiencing a popular revival in the post-Yugoslav countries.

(See also COMMUNISM; COMMUNIST PARTY STATES; INDUSTRIAL DEMOCRACY; NONALIGNED MOVEMENT; WORKERS' CONTROL.)

Phyllis Auty, *Tito: A Biography* (New York, 1970). Duncan Wilson, *Tito's Yugoslavia* (Cambridge, U.K., 1979).

IVO BANAC

TOGO. A small West African state of 34,794 square miles (55,995 sq. km.) and roughly 4 million people located between Ghana and Benin, Togo stretches inland 320 miles (515 km.) from a 32-mile (52-kilometer) coastline along which its capital, Lomé, is located. Contested by several European powers, Germany established a protectorate in 1884 and laid much of the country's infrastructure, including railroads. In 1914 Togo fell to Anglo-French forces in the first Allied victory of World War I. Divided into two League of Nations mandates (later UN trusteeships), British Togoland opted in a 1956 plebiscite (with dissent, intermittently irredentist, among the Ewe) to merge with Ghana. French Togoland became independent on 27 April 1960 under Sylvanus Olympio, from the more economically developed coastal region.

In 1963, Olympio, who had erected a harsh single-party system and espoused fiscal orthodoxy, rejected demands by northern troops just demobilized from France's colonial armies for integration into the new Togolese army. Olympio was murdered in an armed confrontation by Sergeant Etienne (later Gnassingbe) Eyadema, and power passed to a northern party that accepted the insurgents' demands. The army in due course tripled in size, while its hand-picked head of state, Nicholas Grunitzky, was incapable of either consolidating his rule or legitimizing himself among coastal groups. In 1967 Captain Eyadema seized power and set up an initially benign but increasingly brutal dictatorship.

Until 1965, Togo had the lowest economic growth rate of all twelve former French African colonies, exporting primarily cocoa and coffee. Eyadema's reign coincided with the initiation of the export of phosphate, of which Togo is today the world's fifth-largest producer. Swollen state revenues (especially after nationalization of the industry) alleviated Togo's fiscal problems, consolidated Eyadema's rule, and permitted sustained development of the north without neglect of the south. However, patronage (used as a societal glue) led to massive *corruption; state enterprises turned chronic deficits owing to inefficiency and embezzlement; and efforts to project an image of Eyadema's popularity gave birth to a personality cult. As commodity prices fell in the 1980s, revenues contracted, the debt-servicing burden brought the economy under intense pressure, and conspiracies arose, including some involving Olympio's sons.

Throughout his very long tenure in power, Eyadema transformed what was a military dictatorship into a one-party state system under his personal rule throughout the 1970s and the 1980s. In 1991, a sovereign national conference was held, resulting in the return to multiparty politics and the election of Joseph Kokou Koffigoh as interim prime minister. Eyadema eventually succeeded in subverting the democratic proj-

ect of the national conference by rigging the next two presidential elections in his favor, in 1993 and 1998, respectively. In the process, his regime was accused of serious human rights violations, including summary executions and disappearances. Part of his success in staying in power was due to the political immaturity of the democratic opposition, whose endless divisions prevented it from uniting in a common front against the wily dictator. Fortunately for Togo, internal and external pressures have succeeded in making Eyadema promise that he will not stand for reelection when his current mandate expires in 2003.

(See also FRANCOPHONE AFRICA; MILITARY RULE.)

Robert Cornevin, *Histoire du Togo* (Paris, 1959). Samuel Decalo, *Historical Dictionary of Togo*, 2d ed. (Metuchen, N.J., 1987). Samuel Decalo, *Coups and Army Rule in Africa: Motivations and Constraints* (New Haven, Conn., 1990).

SAMUEL DECALO

TONGA. See PACIFIC ISLANDS.

TORTURE. From the Latin *torquere* (to twist), torture is best defined as a deliberate, sanctioned procedure by which official authority inflicts pain. Year after year, *Amnesty International Annual Reports reveal that torture is practiced in 100 UN member states (over half of the world's governments)—from peaceful democracies to the most repressive military regimes. The severest torture is practiced in forty-five states to obtain information, provoke confessions, induce detainees to implicate third parties, and, above all, to humiliate and destroy the victim's personhood.

Although torture occurred in the Ottoman Empire and Imperial Japan, its institutionalization is especially European: it flourished in the Greek city-republics, the Roman Empire, and the Renaissance. Under Greek civil procedure in the fifth and fourth centuries B.C.E., free citizens were not tortured, but a coerced kind of evidence was extracted by force from noncitizens—slaves and foreigners—if they had been accused of a crime. The first major Western legal provisions for torture appeared during the Roman Empire: Title 48 of the *Digest* and Title 9 of the *Code*. With these came a vastly expanded definition of treason that included injuring or diminishing the majesty of the emperor (*crimen laesae maiestatis*) and granted the imperial order extraordinary legal powers when the imperial safety was (or was imagined to be) in danger. As a result, disgraced free citizens, originally protected from torture, were increasingly vulnerable to interrogation and punishment, as Edward Peters' *Torture* (New York, 1985) describes.

Torture declined in Europe between the ninth and twelfth centuries, only to become an integral part of criminal procedures of the Latin church and of most European states between 1250 and 1800, with confession elevated to "the queen of proofs" and crimes of heresy aligned with crimes of treason. During this period torture became an integral part of criminal jurisprudence in much of Europe.

In 1754, all torture was abolished in Prussia, with Saxony, Denmark, and Poland following suit. On the heels of the 1789 French Declaration of the Rights of Man (forbidding torture "forever") and the U.S. Bill of Rights (forbidding "cruel and unusual punishment"), the practice disappeared as a legally authorized procedure in the nineteenth century. John Langbein (*Torture and the Law of Proof*, Chicago, 1977) argues that this attitudinal shift was due to the rise of prisons and work-houses, which offered alternatives to death as a punishment for serious crimes and thus diminished the need for full proof—the underpinning of torture.

Torture was revived in World War I, when state secrets became more closely guarded by state security police, such as the Deuxième Bureau in France and Scotland Yard in Britain, and by military intelligence, which became increasingly unanswerable to civilian jurisprudence. The fear of conspiracy engendered paranoia toward the enemy; accused spies and prisoners of war were tortured for information in the recesses of a new labyrinth of prisons. Secret political police used torture on suspected enemies of the state, party, and people in Mussolini's Italy after 1929, in the Stalinist Soviet Union of the 1930s, and in Nazi Germany, where torture was practiced on communists and socialists, religious and cultural prisoners, and above all on Jews, and was transformed into a medical specialty (Robert Jay Lifton, *The Nazi Doctors*, New York, 1986) and a routine part of extrajudicial procedure. During World War II, the practice of torture spread among the Allied and Axis armed forces in Europe and Asia, although the Germans and Japanese used it more often, not only because their ideologies justified it more easily but also because they had initially conquered more foreign territory and had to contend with strong movements of resistance. Some of the most terrifying incidents of torture were perpetrated against the French Resistance in German-occupied France, and were carried out under the direction of Klaus Barbie, the "Butcher of Lyon" (who would help train Bolivian security forces in the 1950s and 1960s). After World War II, the international community hoped to abolish torture. In 1948, the UN adopted the Universal Declaration of Human Rights, with Article 5 stating, "No one shall be subjected to torture or to cruel, inhuman, or degrading treatment or punishment." The 1949 Geneva Convention forbids combatants, prisoners, or civilians to be tortured; Article 3 of the 1950 European Convention on Human Rights prohibits torture and inhuman, degrading punishment.

Nonetheless, European forces fighting national resistance and liberation movements in Africa and Asia increasingly practiced torture. Refinements in the technology and psychology of torture occurred in French Indochina and Algeria, where in the 1950s the French army and police modernized the science of torment, particularly the use of electricity on and in the body. In apartheid-era South Africa (where torture was used routinely by the Dutch on blacks and whites in the 1600s but abolished with the British conquest in 1795), emergency powers and security legislation enacted to mask the routine torture of black political detainees by the police led to the destruction of the rule of law, as Anthony Mathews (*Freedom, State Security and the Rule of Law*, Cape Town, 1986) documents. In Latin America (where the Spanish Crown instituted the Inquisition in 1571), torture was part of legal proceedings until independence in the 1810s and 1820s. Its reinstitution occurred in the 1960s beginning with the military coup in Brazil in 1964. Torture became a routine part of state policy in Argentina between 1976 and 1983.

The United States became interested in torture as a result of an increased interest in national security doctrine and counterinsurgency. The U.S. Agency for International Development and the Office of Public Safety became the cover under which the *Central Intelligence Agency (CIA) developed experts in torture in the 1960s and 1970s. At the Latin American Defense College, School of the Americas, International Police Academy, and U.S. Border Patrol Academy, courses in interrogation, anatomy, and basic electricity were offered. Jaime Wright et al. (*Nunca Mais*, New York, 1986) describe incidents of U.S. advisors and U.S.-trained Latin American officers using prisoners as guinea pigs in torture classes in Brazil. In the 1980s, U.S. military and CIA officials paid Salvadoran army death squads to torture and kill citizens they identified as politically dangerous. Moreover, U.S. arms firms and the U.S. government, among other countries such as Britain, are deeply involved in the sale or transfer of torture equipment.

Similar to the expansive justifications for torture, ranging from *crimen laesae maiestatis* in the Roman Empire to heresy and treason by the Vatican and most European states between 1250 and 1800, today the doctrine of national security views all dissent as subversive and terrorist and focuses on the danger of the enemy within. Therefore, despite efforts by Amnesty International, the UN, and other international bodies to eliminate the practice, torture has not died out. Far from being the eccentric practice of deranged and psychotic military commanders or governments, torture remains routine in many states, and its legacy continues to affect civil society. Medieval and early modern torture was applied by the judiciary and restricted in its application, purpose, and technology. Today, unfortunately, it has become an official procedure of the state, unrestricted in application, purpose, or technology.

(See also HUMAN RIGHTS; INTERNATIONAL LAW; WAR CRIMES.)

Michel Foucault, *Discipline and Punishment* (New York, 1979). Nigel Rodney, *Treatment of Prisoners and International Law* (New York, 1990). Amnesty International, *A Glimpse of Hell: Reports on Torture Worldwide* (New York, 1996). Marguerite Feitlowitz, *A Lexicon of Terror: Argentina and the Legacies of Torture* (New York, 1998).

JENNIFER SCHIRMER

TOTALITARIANISM. The concept of "totalitarianism" provided a typology of what appeared to be a new kind of state that emerged in Europe in the aftermath of World War I. These new states—the Soviet Union, Fascist Italy, and National Socialist Germany were the three most obvious examples—were politically and economically highly centralized, rabidly antiliberal, highly controlling and invasive in their attitude toward their own citizens, and in practice, if not always in theory, militaristic.

The term was apparently coined by an Italian liberal named Giovanni Amendola, in May 1923. Amendola's usage contrasted the "majoritarian" Italian election law of the time with *Mussolini's "totalitarian reform," designed to achieve a super majority for the largest vote-getter in parliamentary elections, even if that party had only a modest plurality. But within a few years the term had taken on a much broader meaning in Italian politics, contrasting liberal *pluralism with the Fascist Party, which sought a total monopoly on intellectual, ethical, and religious, as well as political, power.

The term thus originated among the Italian opponents of *Fascism, who never ceased to use the term negatively, from a liberal or socialist point of view. But after the spring of 1925, the term was often employed by Fascist intellectuals like Giovanni Gentile and by Mussolini himself to characterize their "revolution." As Fascism moved away from its street-fighting origins, however, the term lost some of its initial connotations of coercion and violence and suggested ever more wholly the intent of the state to absorb every sphere of human life into itself.

It was not long before the term spread to Germany, where, as in Italy, the destruction of decadent liberalism was the issue as National Socialism was coming to power. *Hitler himself used the term "totalitarianism" only on rare occasions, as it suggested to him an Italian comparison, which he came to dislike. But right-wing intellectuals like Carl Schmitt used the term to indicate a more modern and stringent version of the antiliberal states of the premodern period, with their single-minded mission to preserve their populations from the inevitable enemies among the warring states of the European system. But in the course of the 1930s, the National Socialists entirely ceased to use the term, claiming that it failed to comprehend the dynamism of National Socialism and its racism.

The term spread to the English-speaking world in the 1930s, largely through emigration of refugee intellectuals from Italy (Gaetano Salvemini) and Germany (the philosophers of the "Frankfurt School," Paul Tillich, Franz Neumann). From about the middle of the decade on, however, it began to be applied also to the Soviet Union. At first it was largely conservatives (or at least people not of the Left) who saw parallels between the *Soviet Union and the single party, the leader cult, and the *ideology that prevailed in Italy and Germany. By the outbreak of World War II, however, men and women on the anti-Stalinist Left had begun to employ the term, led by *Trotsky and his followers and also by Menshevik émigrés, many of whom later wrote for the *New Leader* in New York.

With the onset of the *Cold War, the term became a central term in the anti-Soviet rhetoric of "Cold War liberals" such as Arthur Schlesinger, Jr., and Reinhold Niebuhr. It soon spread to the Truman administration, where it was used to promote the *Marshall Plan and the North Atlantic Treaty Organization (NATO), to resist the spread of Communism across Europe. With Germany and Italy defeated, "totalitarianism" now became virtually synonymous, particularly in the United States, with the Soviet system. But since the typology was based on a Soviet-Nazi comparison (with the Italian comparison now judged more problematical), it suggested not merely the extremity of the Soviet system, but also that it was typologically similar to that of Germany between 1933 and 1945, a comparison with considerable potential for political mobilization.

Use of the term prior to the late 1940s had been relatively journalistic, with the comparisons between the totalitarian powers rather unsystematic and various. Beginning with the publication of Hannah Arendt's *The Origins of Totalitarianism* (1951) and Carl Friedrich and Zbigniew Brzezinski's *Totalitarian Dictatorship and Autocracy* (1956), however, the term achieved intellectual ascendancy among political scientists, philosophers and even contemporary historians studying the statist regimes of the twentieth century.

As the Cold War and those who waged it came under increasing criticism in the 1960s, however, the idea of the Soviet Union (and now China and the East European "people's democracies") as totalitarian states became increasingly contested. Particularly after the death of Stalin and the onset of reform under Khrushchev, "totalitarianism" seemed to some scholars too rigid and static a category, and also too self-referential. Studies of both Nazi Germany and the Soviet Union, in Europe and the United States, developed strong revisionist wings, and for a time only a few scholars, most on the political right, availed themselves of the term.

With the collapse of the Soviet Union and its client states and the marketization of the Chinese economy, there seem to be no real totalitarian states left in the world as the twenty-first century opens. And yet the term remains, generally used in a rather diffuse way, but provoking only a fraction of its former controversy. This durability may be because ordinary people in large numbers sense that there really was something "different" about Communist and Fascist states, and that difference needs a handy and expressive term, such as "totalitarian." But the worldwide reaction against the strong states of the twentieth century has surely increased the plausibility of the idea that an all-powerful state, motivated by ideas of the utopian transformation of individuals according to an ideology, was a disease of the dreadful twentieth century and now, it may be, a thing of the past.

(See also AUTHORITARIANISM; MILITARISM.)

Abbott Gleason, *Totalitarianism: The Inner History of the Cold War* (New York, 1995). Michael Halberstam, *Totalitarianism and the Modern Conception of Politics* (New Haven, Conn., 1999).

ABBOTT GLEASON

TRADE. See WORLD TRADE ORGANIZATION.

TRANSNATIONAL CORPORATIONS. See MULTINATIONAL CORPORATIONS.

TRANSNATIONAL RELATIONS. See INTERNATIONAL SYSTEMS.

TREATY. A treaty is a written international agreement concluded between states or other subjects of *international law that is intended to create rights and obligations, or to establish relationships governed by the rules of international law. The term "treaty" is often used generically for any international instrument of a contractual character governed by the rules of international law, although several other terms are also used in international practice, among them convention, agreement, protocol, compact, charter, accord, act, general act, statute, pact, and covenant. Treaties can be bilateral instruments, which are intended to promote or regulate matters of particular interest only to two states. Treaties may also be multilateral, having more than two parties, and often create new principles or rules of international law.

Treaties are made through a process. First comes international negotiation, in which a draft text is produced by duly authorized agents. Second is adoption, which involves acceptance of the final text by the negotiators, and is authenticated by the act of signature. In the third stage, the process of ratification occurs, in which each state subjects the treaty text to its constitutional procedures for formal approval of the text. Finally, there is entry into force, in which the binding force of the treaty is initiated on its parties. Treaties effectively operate as international contracts. Accordingly, the fundamental principle in the law of treaties is *pacta sunt servanda*, which means pacts made in good faith shall be observed. This concept underlies the entire system of international legal relations among states, since the duty of honoring international obligations entails a basic condition for the existence of a legal order.

Treaties establish and maintain international institutions, global *regimes, and regional organizations, as well as regulate interstate affairs. The United Nations system is interconnected by international agreements. The UN Charter is a treaty, as are the instruments creating all specialized UN functional agencies. Nearly all regional organizations and alliances derive from treaty-based sources. Witness the European Union, Organization of American States, Organization of African Unity, and the North Atlantic Treaty Organization. The rise of *interdependence and *globalization as modern forces has fostered thousands of international agreements to facilitate economic, social, cultural, and technical relations between states. Numerous "law-making treaties" establish rules for universal application and many serve as core agreements for legal regimes that provide rules, regulations, and expectations for state conduct in transnational activities. Twenty multilateral agreements anchor the regime for international *human rights. Most states are party to the four 1949 Geneva Conventions on the laws of war. Scores of treaties regulate national activities through special regimes for use of the oceans, atmosphere, outer space, and Antarctica, as well as for protection and conservation of the global environment. International commerce is regulated by the General Agreement on Tariffs and Trade (with its World Trade Organization) and is affected by numerous multilateral treaty-based institutions, including the International Monetary Fund, the World Bank, the Organisation of Petroleum Exporting Countries, the Association of Southeast Asian Nations, and the North American Free Trade Agreement.

Treaties provide the legal sinews for international relations. While 45,000 treaties are now registered with the UN Secretariat, thousands of other agreements are also in force. The 1969 Vienna Convention on the Law of Treaties furnishes an authoritative statement on the modern law of treaties.

Jan Klabbers, *The Concept of Treaty in International Law* (The Hague, 1996). Douglas M. Johnson, *Consent and Commitment in the World Community: The Classification and Analysis of International Instruments* (Irvington-on-Hudson, N.Y., 1997). Monroe Leigh, *National Treaty Law and Practice* (Washington, D.C., 1999).

CHRISTOPHER C. JOYNER

TREATY OF ROME. See ROME, TREATY OF.

TREATY OF VERSAILLES. See WORLD WAR I.

TRIBALISM. The use of the concept of *tribalism* would seem to imply acceptance of a term which requires scientific re-evaluation. To avoid any possible misunderstanding, it is extremely important to draw a distinction between tribalism as a concept and as a putative social phenomenon. Some controversy centers on the latter, depending on the ideological and professional background of the onlooker. For historical reasons, Westerners generally take for granted the existence

of "tribalism" in Africa. In contrast, African intellectuals generally believe that this usage reflects the usual European or colonially derived stereotypes about Africa. This represents both an ideological and an epistemological disjuncture between the two points of view. It is therefore not without significance that since the 1970s African social scientists have dispensed with the concept of tribalism and have displayed great hostility to its continued use by Westerners. This is partly a subjective reaction against the Eurocentric ideological supposition that, sociologically speaking, everything African is tribal. It is also a result of an increasing awareness of the complexity and range of social formations in both precolonial and postcolonial Africa. The incongruity between this and anthropological tribal stereotypes has become a source of exasperation among African intellectuals.

Yet there are historical predispositions which account for the reflexes of apparent African detractors as well as for the demand by African intellectuals for the decolonization of African history and social science. Therefore, we do well by starting from the beginning, because all social thought is befogged by prevailing historical circumstances.

Historical Origins of the Concept of the Tribe. The tribe as a concept dates back to Greek and Roman antiquity, ending in Europe with what Karl *Marx referred to as "Germanic tribes." According to this classical view, tribes were supposed to represent a particular stage of human development characterized by the existence of self-contained, autonomous groups based on kinship or principles of consanguinity and practicing subsistence economy.

Although this concept is questionable even for ancient societies in that "self-contained" societies are a historical rarity, it is most important to grasp that according to classical notions tribes were a particular stage of political and economic organization wherein there was neither subjugation to an external authority nor reliance on external exchange. However, there was recognition of internal authorities such as chiefs and elders.

This is what European evolutionists brought with them to Africa. Their intellectual predispositions were confirmed by the reports of the early European explorers. Images of African rulers, adorned with all sorts of symbols of rank, holding court with tribal elders, with plumed warriors, prancing about in their fur anklets as symbols of power, came to typify social organization in the "Dark Continent." Colonial anthropologists succeeded in bestowing respectability upon this stereotype. In *African Political Systems* (Evans-Pritchard and Fortes, eds., 1947), an otherwise sympathetic, albeit paternalistic collection of essays, a wide range of African political formations is reduced to one denominator. But inconsistencies in terminology betray an awareness among the authors of certain differences. For instance, the presiding "tribal" authorities are variously referred to as "king," "paramount chief," and "chief," and the units they govern as "kingdom" and "chiefdom," respectively. What is not questioned, despite the implicit awareness of differences in scale and quality, is the basic assumption that they all represent tribal formations.

This is what African intellectuals and politicians have come to object to not only as a distortion of African history but also as an expression of European arrogance, if not racism. In doing so, some have gone so far as to deny the existence at all in Africa of things called tribes. Subjective responses aside, it would be premature to reject all existing concepts without first testing them rigorously. A careful analysis of African social formations would indicate that tribal formations *did* exist in Africa but that they were not characteristic of *all* regions of the continent. For instance, the kingdoms of West Africa, riverine Sudan, Ethiopia, the interlacustrine region of East Africa, and the Congo Basin had long passed the tribal stage. Far from being self-contained, their economies were mercantile or predatory. Likewise, far from being based on kinship, their polities were distinguished by well-established formal bureaucracies which depended on revenues and exploitation of servile or slave labor.

In other parts of Africa such as East, Central, and Southern Africa, with a few exceptions here and there, it can be said that tribal formations in the classical sense were the norm. But once again, all this refers only to different types of centralized political formations. Yet there existed noncentralized social formations as well, ranging from the hunters and food gatherers of Southern Africa and the Congo forest to the "Nilotic" herders of East Africa and southern Sudan. It was in recognition of the latter that David Tait and John Middleton edited the volume *Tribes Without Rulers* in 1953. The title of the book itself is a contradiction in terms because the concept of tribe refers to a particular level of political centralization, as we have seen. Under the impact of colonial ideology the most the anthropologists were able to do was to distinguish between different types of "tribes" in Africa. Indeed, it could be surmised that the obsession with tribalism in Africa among Westerners derives from the colonial ideological fixation with tribes in Africa.

Tribalism: A Basic Misconception. If the application of the concept of tribe in Africa had been flawed from the beginning, then the concept of tribalism could not but perpetuate the original fallacies. Second, having emerged, the concept is incapable of distinguishing between nationalities, regionalism, *ethnicity, and *class conflicts, especially in the urban or modern context. If we proceed from the assumption that colonial impositions undermined tribal organization in Africa by incorporating all and sundry into a broader political entity, the colonial state, then "tribalism" cannot be interpreted as a harking back to a nonexistent past. Its reference point must be something post-tribal and postcolonial. This means that it has nothing to do with tribes but rather with modern African political and economic exigencies, whose drama is largely played out in the urban areas.

This interpretation would favor the concept of ethnicity at the expense of tribalism. The former, unlike the latter, has no organic connotations but rather diffuse cultural and linguistic connotations which are subject to more than one form of expression. Unlike intertribal relations, ethnic representations are not total. They are partial, intermittent, and nontranscendental, i.e., they are subject to class manipulation, they are evoked opportunistically, and they are not aimed at overthrowing the whole system. They are a conscious maneuvering for relative advantage within the established order. If they become transcendent, as has happened in some African countries, then we must think of the problem of nationalities within given African states, the best example of which so far is Ethiopia. There might be other, less clear-cut cases such as Nigeria during the Biafran War, Uganda during the Buganda

rebellion, or Chad in its period of civil war. But these would seem to be still within the realm of ethnic conflict and a by-product of the concept of a unitary nation-state which Africans inherited from the Europeans.

It may be concluded that the concept of tribalism is erroneous in its general foundations and consequently obscures a number of issues in Africa which could be understood otherwise. The concept militates against cross-cultural comparisons regarding certain social phenomena which obtained in but are not peculiar to Africa, e.g., ethnic and class conflicts or manipulation of these in the interests of certain identifiable strata within African society at large. The persistence of ethnic identities is almost universal, as current history shows in both Western and Eastern Europe, the New World in general, and, of course, most of sub-Saharan Africa.

Therefore, the problem is not to decry a spurious category called "tribalism" but to confront the problem of *cultural pluralism* within modern nation-states which, deriving from the European historical antecedent, are supposed to be unitary. What is called "tribalism" in Africa is often an attempt by disadvantaged sociocultural groups to gain more social space within the given political and economic setup. In the circumstances democratic *pluralism is at issue rather than a dictatorial insistence on misconceived unitarism. Ethnolinguistic groups have existed throughout history but have not forestalled the emergence of different cross-cultural political and social formations over the last two thousand years. Why should they be a problem in the modern era, which is supposed to be more enlightened, more rational, and certainly more affluent than previous ages? Africa is part of the modern world, even if not by its own choice. It has to be treated as such, irrespective of any colonial prejudices or Western ideological or racist suppositions. "Tribalism" is one of those, and should be dispensed with in scientific discourse regarding Africa so as to facilitate cross-cultural comparisons or the development of more universalistic concepts for dealing with contradictions among the different peoples of the world.

(See also COLONIAL EMPIRES; RACE AND RACISM; SECESSIONIST MOVEMENTS.)

N. Paden, ed., *Values, Identities, and National Integration: Empirical Research in Africa* (Evanston, Ill., 1980). C. Coquery-Vidrovitch, "A Propos des Racines Historiques du Pouvoir: Chefferie et Tribalisme," *Pouvoir* 25 (1983): 51–56. C. Young, "Ethnicity and the Colonial and Postcolonial State in Africa," in P. Brass, ed., *Ethnic Groups and the State* (London, 1985), 57–93. A. D. Smith, *Ethnic Origin of Nations* (Oxford, 1986).

A. B. M. MAFEJE

TRINIDAD AND TOBAGO. The Republic of Trinidad and Tobago comprises two main islands located off the coast of Venezuela. It is the second largest of the *English-speaking Caribbean states (after Jamaica), with an area of 1,980 square miles (5,128 sq. km.) and a population of 1.3 million (1995). The population is divided almost evenly between the African descendants of slaves and the Indian descendants of indentured laborers, with smaller groups of European, Chinese, Syrian, and mixed races. Trinidad was a Spanish colony from 1498 until its capture by the British in 1797. Tobago was disputed by the Dutch, French, and English until it was ceded to Britain in 1814. The two islands were administratively joined in 1888; British Crown Colony government lasted until independence in 1962.

Self-government was granted in 1956, and the first mass party, the People's National Movement (PNM), was formed by Dr. Eric Williams. The PNM had its base of support in the African population whereas its opposition, the Democratic Labor Party (DLP), held sway in the Indian community. A combination of charismatic leadership, party organization, patronage, and racial distrust kept the PNM in power until 1986 when charges of corruption and mismanagement and general discontent fed by a declining economy led to its defeat at the polls. A new party, the National Alliance for Reconstruction (NAR), a merger of various opposition groups, was swept into power on a platform of economic and social reform. The NAR alliance was short-lived, and the Indian segment formed the United National Congress (UNC). The NAR came into power at a time when structural adjustment measures were seen as necessary to reorient the economy; however, the resulting social dislocation coupled with the political disunity culminated in the violent seizure of the parliament (while in session) by Black Muslim activists in 1990. After the dust had settled, a revitalized PNM returned to power in 1991. In 1995, snap elections were called to give the PNM a stronger mandate but, again largely because of social disaffection, the elections instead brought the UNC to power, in coalition with the NAR. Of great significance was the fact that this victory brought to power the first Indian-led government in Trinidad and Tobago. Although the UNC tried to some degree to appeal to all segments of the population, ethnic disunity, patronage politics, allegations of *corruption, and anti-media policies produced a level of dissatisfaction with this government as the country headed toward new elections in late 2000 or early 2001.

Trinidad and Tobago has invested heavily in industry, including methanol, iron and steel, and petrochemicals. On the other hand, agriculture, especially sugar production, has declined as a result of insufficient incentives and low international prices. Tourism has contributed less to the overall GDP of the country than in other Caribbean islands.

During the oil boom of the 1970s, Trinidad and Tobago increased its wealth considerably and was able to disburse US$250 million in loans and technical assistance to its less fortunate Caribbean neighbors. However, the country's economy declined in the 1980s and, after years of economic nationalism, Trinidad and Tobago began a process of liberalizing the economy by divesting state enterprises, encouraging foreign investment, and removing barriers to free trade, with variable results. Per capita GDP was US$4,101 in 1995.

Trinidad and Tobago plays an important role in the region. Social ties and geographical proximity have engendered a close relationship with the Eastern Caribbean islands, a relationship that soured temporarily when the country refused to participate in the 1983 invasion of Grenada. Trinidad and Tobago is a key member of the Caribbean Community and Common Market (Caricom) where it ranks with Jamaica, Guyana, and Barbados as More Developed Countries (MDCs). The country played a major role in the formation of the Association of Caribbean States (ACS) and hosts its secretariat. Trinidad and Tobago was the first English-speaking country to join the Organization of American States (OAS) in

1967. It is also active in the United Nations, the Commonwealth, and the Nonaligned Movement.

Selwyn Ryan, *The Disillusioned Electorate: The Politics of Succession in Trinidad and Tobago* (Port-of-Spain, Trinidad, 1989). Selwyn Ryan, *The Muslimeen Grab for Power: Race, Religion and Revolution in Trinidad and Tobago* (Port-of-Spain, Trinidad, 1991).

JACQUELINE ANNE BRAVEBOY-WAGNER

TROTSKY, Lev. Born Lev Davidovich Bronstein, Trotsky (1879–1940) was a distinguished theorist of *Marxism, a gifted author and historian, and a spellbinding revolutionary orator. Critical of centralized party organization, he resisted joining the Bolsheviks until 1917. In that year he was elected president of the Petrograd Soviet and coordinated the Bolshevik seizure of power. During the civil war he organized and commanded the Red Army. After the death of V. I. *Lenin in 1924, he led the left opposition in the struggle against Stalinist reaction. Deported from the *Soviet Union in 1929, Trotsky escaped Joseph *Stalin's purge trials of the 1930s but was assassinated in Mexico in 1940 by the Soviet secret police.

Trotsky interpreted the *Russian Revolution from an international perspective. In 1906 his theory of "permanent revolution" analyzed Russian history in terms of contradictions between backwardness and modernity (Leon Trotsky, *Permanent Revolution* and *Results and Prospects*, London, 1962). The capitalist class was relatively weak because the tsarist state depended on imported capital. At the same time, the proletariat was stronger than numbers suggested, being concentrated in large factories that facilitated political strikes. Trotsky concluded that Russian workers must overthrow the autocracy and make the *revolution permanent in two respects: a workers' government would pass immediately from political to socialist reforms; by repudiating tsarism's foreign debts, it would also precipitate a revolutionary crisis in Europe.

Trotsky expected socialism to create a "United States of Europe" with a planned international division of labor. When European revolutions failed to come to Russia's assistance, he turned to centralized *planning and military discipline in the factories in the hope of sustaining socialist prospects within the "capitalist encirclement" (Leon Trotsky, *Terrorism and Communism*, Ann Arbor, Mich., 1961). "War Communism" provoked widespread opposition to Trotsky and the Soviet government, leading to the New Economic Policy (NEP) in the spring of 1921. Trotsky accepted the return to market relations but continued to believe that state industry must be supported through planning.

Trotsky's critics thought planning would disrupt the market and prevent recovery. By the mid-1920s, N. I. Bukharin led the right wing of the Communist Party of the Soviet Union in arguing that agriculture must have priority over industry and must generate voluntary savings for new investments. Trotsky replied that agricultural growth depended on material incentives and manufactured consumer goods. He believed a solution to the "goods famine" lay in Soviet Russia's reintegration into the world economy: as in the tsarist period, the Soviet economy would require foreign investments and imports of machinery and goods.

By planning economic relations with the capitalist countries, Trotsky hoped to forestall a crisis of the NEP and to orient industrialization strategy on foreign trade (Richard B. Day, *Leon Trotsky and the Politics of Economic Isolation*, Cambridge, U.K., 1973). With accelerated industrial growth, he believed the working class would become a political force capable of resisting Stalinist bureaucracy. Instead, struggle between the left and right wings of the party exhausted both to the benefit of the Stalinist "center." Bukharin charged that Trotsky's theory of "permanent revolution" denied Soviet Russia's capacity for independence; Trotsky responded that Bukharin was a proponent of capitalist agriculture and an enemy of socialist industry. Stalin swept both rivals aside when he adopted Bukharin's slogan of "socialism in one country" and interpreted it to mean industrial self-sufficiency.

Stalin's ascendancy meant the end of the NEP by 1929. For material incentives Stalin substituted forced labor; for voluntary savings he substituted the fiscal apparatus of forced collectivization. In exile during the 1930s, Trotsky thought the Stalinist system was inherently unstable: it was a contradictory combination of nominally socialist property with primitive forces of production. Seeing that arbitrary plans reproduced a black market, Trotsky became one of the first Marxists to consider market *socialism. He thought the revolution's degeneration under Stalin proved that socialism required both a planned market and democratic politics.

The unifying theme of Trotsky's thought, from 1906 until his death in 1940, was the need to replace *capitalism and nation-states with socialism and international planning. His theory of *imperialism anticipated European unification and contradictions associated today with *globalization of production and markets. His view of planning exemplified a parallel contradiction within Marxism itself: *Marx thought the socialist state would "wither away" when politics was replaced by planning, yet Stalin transformed planning into rule by a bureaucracy in the service of a despot.

Trotsky concluded that socialism required the involvement of independent trade unions and several political parties in the planning process. Identifying planning with public participation, he denied that Stalinism could be reformed from above. A socialist future presupposed a second revolution to overthrow the Stalinist bureaucracy. Collapse of Mikhail *Gorbachev's *perestroika in 1991 may be said to confirm Trotsky's prediction that the most probable alternative to a second revolution was capitalist restoration.

(See also LENINISM; POST-COMMUNISM; STALINISM.)

Isaac Deutscher, *The Prophet Armed* (New York, 1965). Isaac Deutscher, *The Prophet Unarmed* (New York, 1965). Isaac Deutscher, *The Prophet Outcast* (New York, 1965). Dmitri Volkogonov, *Trotsky, the Eternal Revolutionary* (New York, 1996).

RICHARD B. DAY

TRUDEAU, Pierre. Born in Montreal on 18 October 1919, Pierre Elliott Trudeau was prime minister of *Canada from 1968 until 1979, when the Liberal Party which he led was defeated, and from 1980 until 1984, when he retired from office. His tenure was longer than any, save those of prime ministers Sir John A. MacDonald and Mackenzie King. Like them, he profoundly shaped the direction of Canadian politics.

Raised and educated in *Quebec, Trudeau was part of the important postwar generation of progressives drawn from the trade union movement, intellectual circles, and left Catholicism that determined to turn traditional elites out of power and create a modern Quebec. He played a central intellectual role in the 1950s as one of the founders of *Cité Libre*, a reliable source of critical commentary on Quebec society, and as the editor of a politically influential book about the landmark strike at Asbestos in 1949. Nevertheless, in his writings on democratic theory and Quebec society Trudeau exhibited a deep fear of all *nationalisms and a mistrust of his compatriots' commitment to what he considered fundamental democratic values. Therefore, when the nationalist movement emerged with force in the new Quebec of the mid-1960s, Trudeau—with Gérard Pelletier, a journalist, and Jean Marchand, a unionist (a group termed the Three Wise Men)—moved into politics at the national level in order to present an alternative to that movement.

Combining his stance on nationalism with a profound commitment to a liberal society, Trudeau set out to translate his vision into legislative and constitutional reality. As minister of justice and then prime minister he engineered a liberalization of the criminal code (1969), which legalized abortion and contraception, decriminalized homosexual acts between consenting adults, and relaxed the grounds for divorce. Even more important, the Official Languages Act (1969) announced the federal government's commitment to bilingualism throughout the country. Finally, the 1982 Constitution Act entrenched not only language rights but also a Charter of Rights and Freedoms in fundamental law. Having worked to defeat the 1980 referendum on sovereignty-association for Quebec in the name of "renewed *federalism" and having pushed through constitutional reform, Trudeau retired to private law practice in Montreal in 1984.

Trudeau's policies were never uncontested, of course. Significant opposition existed among provincial politicians in Quebec, who found him too federalist and individualist, and among popular opinion in the western provinces, which tagged him too pro-French. Regional tensions, especially, increased mightily throughout his years in office.

In the realm of economic policy Trudeau demonstrated little consistency. He objected to economic programs developed for nationalist reasons (to reduce the influence of the United States in Canada), but his governments also sometimes tried to develop more active industrial strategy and policy for trade diversification. Such half-measures had little success, however, and he left office in 1984 after pressure from the United States, most of the provincial governments, much of *public opinion, and a major recession forced the dramatic repudiation of a series of interventionary economic programs. The government of his successor, John Turner, presided over the first stages of the move to a Free Trade Agreement with the United States in the context of neoliberal economic thinking.

By the 1980s Pierre Trudeau had become the longest-serving leader in the West and, as such, he tried to encourage a better *North-South dialogue and an easing of East-West tensions. After leaving office he undertook a personal peace initiative to countries in both the Eastern and Western blocs, arguing for reduction of nuclear weapons and an end to the *Cold War. For these efforts, he was awarded the Albert Einstein Peace Prize. He died in September 2000.

(See also NAFTA.)

Pierre Elliott Trudeau, *Federalism and the French-Canadians* (Toronto, 1968). Pierre Elliott Trudeau, ed., *The Asbestos Strike* (Toronto, 1974).

JANE JENSEN

TRUMAN DOCTRINE. The Truman Doctrine, as set forth by President Harry S. *Truman in 1947, committed the U.S. government to a global policy aimed at stopping the spread of *communism. The seeds of the doctrine were planted on 21 February 1947, when Britain informed U.S. officials that it no longer could aid conservative forces in Greece who were fighting the National Liberation Front (which contained communist leaders) nor Turkey, which the Soviets were pressuring for treaty concessions. Realizing that the British Empire was collapsing, Truman and Undersecretary of State Dean *Acheson (who wrote the doctrine message) also realized the president himself had been weakened by economic problems and a Republican landslide victory in the 1946 congressional elections. They further believed that communist political victories could occur in war-devastated Western Europe unless vast U.S. aid was quickly extended. Truman therefore decided to ask Congress to give him $400 million for Greece and Turkey and to frame an open-ended policy that stressed how communism had to be stopped globally by "the free peoples of the world." The Republicans, pledged to cut taxes and expenditures, would then have to choose publicly whether to appropriate large amounts in Congress to fight communism wherever Truman saw the threat existing.

Internal opposition appeared. Secretary of State George Marshall and his top advisers on Soviet affairs criticized the strong anticommunist rhetoric and also noted that Yugoslav communists, not Soviet, supplied the Greek Front. Truman overruled Marshall. Acheson convinced congressional leaders privately by arguing that if communists won in Greece they would extend their power throughout the Middle East and Europe. Acheson thus anticipated the later *domino theory. Congressional critics who feared that a new global commitment could lead to huge expenditures, if not war, and to a vast expansion of presidential powers were a small minority.

Truman announced his doctrine before a congressional joint session on 12 March 1947. Congress accepted his argument by appropriating the $400 million and did so again in 1948 when it passed the $12 billion *Marshall Plan to rebuild Western Europe. Greece finally quieted in 1949 only when the Yugoslavs, for internal reasons, quit aiding the Front; nevertheless, the doctrine was seen as triumphant in its first test. Later presidents tried to revive it to conjure up domestic support for their beleaguered policies. Lyndon *Johnson, 1964 to 1967, in *Vietnam; Jimmy *Carter, 1980, in the Persian Gulf; and Ronald *Reagan, 1983, in Central America were among those presidents. Truman had used a regional crisis to increase presidential power, create a powerful anticommunist consensus in U.S. politics, and make global commitments that transformed *American foreign policy.

(See also CONTAINMENT.)

Lawrence C. Wittner, *American Intervention in Greece, 1943–1949* (New York, 1982).

WALTER LAFEBER

TRUMAN, Harry S. The thirty-third president of the United States, Harry S. Truman has become a national hero. Although he might not agree with the present evaluation, he certainly disagreed with the very critical portrayal that reigned during his presidency.

Truman, like some of his predecessors, rose to high office from humble circumstances. Descended from English and southern stock, he spent his early years near the intersection of the South, the Middle West, and the Far West—in Lamar, Missouri, his birthplace on 8 May 1884, and in Grandview and Independence, Missouri. The first child of John and Martha Truman, Harry attended the Independence public schools. Unable to afford college, he worked for several years in Kansas City and then farmed from 1906 to 1917 on the Grandview place established by his maternal grandfather, Solomon Young. Service at the front in France in 1918 affected his outlook on himself and the world and was followed by an unsuccessful business venture in downtown Kansas City.

Before the business episode, Harry had married Bess Wallace in 1919 and settled into his mother-in-law's house in Independence, and in 1924, Bess gave birth to the couple's only child, Margaret. By then he had embarked upon his political career. Raised a Southern Democrat, he had joined Kansas City's Pendergast organization before the war, and with the backing of the *political machine he was elected to the county court (an administrative agency) in 1922, defeated in 1924, and elected presiding judge in 1926. Serving two four-year terms as Jackson County's top administrator, he distinguished himself as a road builder.

Truman moved up to the U.S. Senate in 1935. Backed by the machine, he supported *Roosevelt's *New Deal and promoted regulation of the transportation system. Coming close to defeat in 1940 following the collapse of Pendergast's power, he gained fame in his second term as chair of a World War II Special Committee to Investigate the National Defense Program, and his new prestige and his ability to get along with a wide range of Democrats, along with the hostility of some leaders and factions to Vice President Henry A. Wallace, led to Truman's selection for the vice presidency in 1944.

With Roosevelt's death on 12 April 1945, Truman ascended to the presidency. As president, he saw himself basically as decision maker in chief, the person to whom his aides brought major matters for final resolution. Although capable of vacillation, he functioned in ways that pleased many of his subordinates, especially two of his secretaries of state, George C. Marshall and Dean *Acheson.

International relations dominated Truman's presidency. World War II still raged when he became president, and the major decisions about defeating Germany and establishing the UN had already been made, but he carried those tasks to completion and then made a major decision of his own concerning Japan. He decided that atomic bombs should be used to end the Pacific War (and also to influence the Soviet Union, now behaving in troubling ways in Eastern Europe).

The *Cold War soon commanded Truman's attention, and he was ultimately responsible for decisions on U.S. contributions to it. Those decisions included the dismissal of Henry Wallace as secretary of commerce in 1946, aid to Greece and Turkey, and the promise of similar assistance to other countries faced with similar pressures (the so-called *Truman Doctrine). The decisions of 1947–1948 to help economically depressed Western Europe (the *Marshall Plan) and to airlift supplies to blockaded Berlin also came to his desk, and he played a similar role in recognizing the new state of Israel in

1948 and in restraining U.S. participation in the Chinese Civil War.

By 1949, the United States was enjoying more success in Western Europe than in China, and in the next four years, with Truman functioning as decision maker, Washington enlarged and militarized its policy of *containment. In this process, Truman approved of U.S. membership in the *North Atlantic Treaty Organization and authorized the development of a hydrogen bomb. For a time, he withheld endorsement of a plan for a vast expansion of U.S. military spending (NSC 68) but then gave the go-ahead for U.S. military intervention in the war in Korea, which began in 1950. He now endorsed a major military buildup and decided, in 1951, that U.S. troops should be dispatched to Europe to strengthen a developing NATO force. He gave his stamp of approval to U.S. financial assistance to France in its battle against revolution in Indochina as well as to a U.S. alliance with Japan. And he made the decisions against General Douglas MacArthur, refusing MacArthur's proposed widening of the *Korean War and removing him from command.

Although significant chiefly in international affairs, Truman's presidency also affected domestic developments. His economic decisions helped the nation avoid a postwar depression. A series of decisions to establish a Civil Rights Committee, begin Justice Department cooperation with the National Association for the Advancement of Colored People, deliver a special presidential message on civil rights, and issue two executive orders on the treatment of minorities in the civil service and the military all assisted black Americans in their escalating efforts to change race relations in the United States. Although Congress did not pass civil rights legislation, the Supreme Court handed down decisions that favored black claims, and the military and civilian bureaucracies altered their racial practices. Congress accepted only a few items on Truman's reform agenda, labeled the Fair Deal, but his efforts prepared the way for legislative victories in the 1960s.

Truman also played roles of some importance in the Red Scare. He fanned the flames with his loyalty program, established in 1947, his Justice Department's prosecution of communist leaders in the United States, and his rhetorical attacks upon both Republicans and Henry Wallace in the 1948 election. Yet when it reached new heights in his last years in office, he tried to contain the scare by vetoing legislative manifestations of it and criticizing Senator Joseph R. McCarthy, the most prominent proponent of the charge that communists inside the United States seriously threatened the nation.

Proud to be president and regarding presidential leadership as essential, Truman had an impact on his office. He enlarged and strengthened it, increasing the number of presidential advisers, employing the veto power more often than all but two other presidents, sending troops to Korea and to Europe on his own authority, and putting down MacArthur's challenge to the presidency.

Nevertheless, Truman was not popular. He did enjoy an unexpected victory in the presidential election of 1948, but even then he obtained less than 50 percent of the popular vote. By late 1951, only 23 percent of the people approved of his performance as president, and the next year he failed to maintain Democratic control of the national government. When he left office, only 31 percent of the people approved of his handling of the job.

In the eyes of many in the United States, Truman seemed too small, but, as his farewell address in January 1953 suggests, he regarded himself as unusually successful. Emphasizing his decisions in foreign affairs, he proposed that he had prevented a repetition of the mistakes made from 1919 to 1941 that he held responsible for World War II. Henry Wallace had portrayed him as a major contributor to the coming of the Cold War; revisionist historians later repeated the charge; but Truman regarded the Cold War as the best of the available alternatives. The leading competitor was World War III, and a combination of Wallace-like weakness and MacArthur-like rashness, rather than the decisions he made, would, he maintained, have produced that war. Still further, he predicted that continuation of his containment policy would produce an American victory in the cold war.

Truman did not live long enough to see himself become a national hero. Returning to Independence in 1953, he was an active ex-president for a decade until his health, which, except for stress, had been robust, began to decline. He died in a Kansas City hospital on 26 December 1972, and his rise to hero's rank began soon thereafter.

(See also AFRICAN AMERICANS; HIROSHIMA; McCARTHYISM; NUCLEAR WEAPONS; PRESIDENCY, U.S.; UNITED NATIONS; U.S. FOREIGN POLICY.)

Richard S. Kirkendall, ed., *The Harry S. Truman Encyclopedia* (Boston, 1989). Alonzo L. Hamby, *Man of the People: A Life of Harry S. Truman* (New York, 1995).

RICHARD S. KIRKENDALL

TRUTH AND RECONCILIATION COMMISSION. The Truth and Reconciliation Commission (TRC) of *South Africa has its origin in four tumultuous years of negotiations for a new dispensation in the country. As a result of a negotiated settlement, the first multiracial elections were held in South Africa in April 1994, and the first black, Nelson *Mandela, was sworn in as president in May.

The negotiated settlement followed over 300 years of resistance to white-minority domination, which included the system of apartheid that was officially introduced when the National Party (NP) came to power in 1948. *Apartheid, which was identified as a "crime against humanity" by the United Nations, was the most brutal and inhumane racist system that existed at the end of the twentieth century. As a result of apartheid, South Africa became virtually a military state, resulting in thousands of nonwhite people being killed, maimed, imprisoned, abducted, and tortured; millions dispossessed of their land; and the majority left without political and economic power.

The decision to create what eventually became the TRC was a major compromise. Since apartheid was considered a crime against humanity, there were those who felt that a Nuremberg-type tribunal should be created to prosecute apartheid-era perpetrators. Others argued, however, that the apartheid-era security forces would make it impossible for a peaceful transition to occur if such a tribunal was established. Consequently, a compromise was reached during negotiations that called for the establishment of a commission to investigate *human rights violations committed during the apartheid era that would have the power to grant amnesty.

The TRC is one of nineteen truth commissions that have

been established to date around the world. Such commissions have become important for countries in transition, such as Chile and El Salvador, that are attempting to heal from autocratic and military regimes that were particularly brutal. It is felt that only by acknowledging the past can such countries move forward in a spirit of national unity and reconciliation.

In July 1995, the TRC was established with the Promotion of National Unity and Reconciliation Act. The commission was to be in existence for approximately two years. President Mandela appointed seventeen commissioners to the TRC, with Archbishop Desmond Tutu serving as chairperson, and Dr. Alex Boraine serving as vice chairperson. Three committees were established: Committee on Human Rights Violations; Committee on Amnesty; and Committee on Reparation and Rehabilitation.

The Committee on Human Rights investigated gross human rights violations committed within a political context between 1 March 1960 and 10 May 1994. Victims of such violations were people who were killed, tortured, abducted, or severely ill-treated; and family members or dependents of people who were killed or who disappeared. Between 15 April 1996 and 31 July 1998, the committee heard testimonies of over 20,000 victims, as well as governmental and nongovernmental entities that had supported the apartheid regime.

The Committee on Amnesty, the most important committee, was assigned the task of determining whether perpetrators of gross human rights violations should be granted amnesty. Amnesty could only be granted if the violation was committed within a political context and perpetrators told the truth. Amnesty applications were received from members of the antiapartheid liberation movement and apartheid-era political parties, security officials, and individuals who committed crimes on behalf of the state. Although the committee received over 7,000 applications, only a small percentage of applicants were granted amnesty.

The Committee on Reparation and Rehabilitation was given the tasks of assisting the victims of gross violations of human rights abuses to restore their dignity, compensating them for damages, and attempting to prevent such abuses from being repeated.

Some critics of the TRC argue that apartheid-era perpetrators have literally gotten away with murder. While some supporters of the TRC acknowledge that justice was sacrificed for truth, they contend that this was done in the spirit of national unity, reconciliation, reconstruction, and peace. Ironically, some of the strongest critics of the TRC were involved in its creation. Once established, however, they claimed that it served as a "witch-hunt" against the forces of apartheid.

Although there will never be a consensus regarding the significance of the TRC, the acknowledgment by the perpetrators of abuses during the apartheid era is an important step in creating national reconciliation. Such reconciliation, however, is likely to be difficult if the majority of whites, on whose behalf most of the perpetrators committed the abuses, are not willing to acknowledge and make amends for their tacit approval of the apartheid regime.

The TRC is unique in both its creation and operation. With respect to the former, unlike all other commissions, the TRC's establishment was democratic in that it followed months of debate on its purpose and structure within and outside of parliament. In terms of its operation, the TRC was the first truth commission given the authority to subpoena witnesses. This ability to subpoena gave the TRC the power to offer amnesty in exchange for the truth. Those who refused this offer stood in jeopardy of being prosecuted in a court of law. As a consequence of the uniqueness of the TRC, South Africans know much more about the past than would have otherwise been possible. They can now begin to build a consensus on the history of the past.

Beth S. Lyons, "Between Nuremberg and Amnesia: The Truth and Reconciliation Commission of South Africa," *Monthly Review* 49 (September 1997): 5–22. Lyn S. Graybill, "Pursuit of Truth and Reconciliation in South Africa," *Africa Today* 45, no. 1 (1998): 103–133. Sarah Nuttall and Carla Coetzee, eds., *Negotiating the Past: The Making of Memory in South Africa* (Cape Town, 1998). TRC, *Truth and Reconciliation Commission Report of South Africa* (New York, 1999).

MARGARET C. LEE

TUNISIA. Tunisia is a small North African nation, with a population of about 9 million, bordering strategic narrows between the western and eastern Mediterranean. Tunis, the capital city, has a long history as a major trading center, linking Africa with the Mediterranean basin and beyond. Tunisia today is a constitutional republic dominated by a ruling political party and a strong presidential system. Increasing ties to Europe have brought a modicum of economic prosperity, but a diverse civil society faces strong official pressures for conformity. An Islamic movement has challenged the regime in recent years, though the country remains relatively secular and the culture is open to many intellectual and political currents.

In 1881 France seized the area and ruled it as a protectorate, laying the foundations of the modern state and economy, but at heavy cost to the local population. An anticolonial movement developed in the interwar period. After World War II, it gathered force under the leadership of lawyer Habib Bourguiba, supported by a growing mass party and a militant trade union movement.

France finally withdrew in 1955–1956 and, soon after, a National Constituent Assembly proclaimed Tunisia a republic, with Bourguiba as first president. A new constitution, adopted in 1959, created a strong presidency and a weak parliament. The new leader and his associates asserted a virtual monopoly for their Neo-Destour Party, barring others from running in elections and claiming to represent the unity of the new nation.

Bourguiba, who was very influenced by French ideas, became known for his modernizing social *reforms—some of the most far-reaching in any Arab or Islamic country. He nationalized religious landholdings, and dismantled religious institutions, in the name of economic development. He also sought to improve the status of women with legal and social reforms.

Tunisia, unlike its neighbors Libya and Algeria, possessed no oil fields. With Western aid, the Bourguiba government developed the country's large deposits of phosphate, an important fertilizer, and it promoted tourism and light industry. But most of the population lived on small farms and agriculture lagged badly. Tunisia had one great economic advantage: it had a very small army and so was not burdened with high military costs. A very high proportion of state revenues were spent on social services, including education. For at least twenty-five years after independence, military influence in politics remained slight.

During the first years after independence, as French settlers left and French capital pulled out of the country, the economy floundered. Many politicians and intellectuals called for more state intervention in the economy. In 1964 the Neo-Destour changed its name to the Parti Socialiste Destourien (PSD), and the regime undertook socialist economic reforms, bringing more than half the economy under state control by the end of the decade. The most ambitious reform program, led by Economy Minister Ahmad Ben Salah, sought to bring all private farms into state-sponsored agricultural cooperatives. In 1970, amid fierce criticism from the farmers, the president abruptly dismissed his minister, accusing him of treason. A new government team dismantled many of the reforms and returned the cooperatives to private ownership.

Increasingly isolated and intolerant of criticism, Bourguiba banned all opposition political activities in 1973. Though his health was failing (he had suffered a stroke in 1967), he refused to prepare the way for a successor.

The turn away from socialism did not lead to democratization. In 1973, when unions went on strike to protest falling real wages, the government outlawed strikes and imposed fines and prison sentences. The president, often referred to in the muzzled press as the "Supreme Combatant," purged the ranks of the party. In 1975, an amendment to the constitution made him "president for life." Three years later, when the trade union confederation called a general strike to protest government repression, Bourguiba ordered out the army. Military and security forces savagely attacked the strikers, killing dozens and arresting hundreds more, including all major leaders of the union.

Though politics were troubled, the Tunisian economy grew rapidly in the 1970s. Oil was discovered in sufficient quantity to meet domestic needs and begin exports, producing nearly half of all export earnings by the end of the decade. Tunisia also attracted investments from European *multinational corporations. But continuing agricultural problems led to heavy migration out of the countryside. For the first time, urban dwellers comprised more than half of the total population. In spite of new jobs, many created by the burgeoning tourist industry, urban unemployment remained high and thousands of workers emigrated to Europe.

In international relations, Tunisia continued its close ties with the West. It also assumed a more prominent role in the Arab world during the 1980s as Tunis became headquarters of the *Arab League from 1979 to 1991 and headquarters of the *Palestine Liberation Organization from 1982 to 1994. In February 1989, Tunisia joined in forming a regional North African trade and development body, the Union du Maghreb Arabe (UMA), but increasingly liberal trade arrangements with the European Union provided a far more important opening for Tunisia's exports and economic relations.

In 1981 the government experimented with limited democratization, allowing a few officially sanctioned parties to run for office for the first time since independence. But social peace proved elusive and the economy faltered. When the *International Monetary Fund (IMF) imposed austerity measures, forcing the government to raise the price of bread and semolina in late 1983, protest riots swept the country. The government restored order only after massive intervention by the army. Though the protests were largely spontaneous, the Islamic Tendency Movement (MTI), headed by Cheikh Rached el-Ghannouchi, came to the fore as the greatest challenge to the regime.

The shaken government blamed the riots on foreign conspirators and accused the MTI of being a puppet of Iran. Bourguiba disbanded the trade unions, closed down critical newspapers, and jailed many thousands of dissidents, especially Islamists. General Zine El Abidine Ben Ali, minister of the interior and former director of military security, organized the crackdown. A major trial of Islamist leaders, some of whom received the death sentence, threatened to ignite further protests. The ailing Bourguiba insisted he would "eradicate the fundamentalist poison."

In October 1987, the president named Ben Ali as prime minister. Just one month later, the premier deposed the eighty-four-year-old Bourguiba in a bloodless coup. A politically appointed panel of doctors declared the founder of the Republic incapacitated and unable to rule, giving a semblance of legitimacy to Ben Ali's succession. Though Bourguiba departed, the Bourguibist political system remained largely intact. One difference stood out: Ben Ali brought many army and security officers into top political positions.

Ben Ali promised reforms and set in motion a modest liberalization, declaring a general amnesty for political prisoners and inviting political exiles home. He pushed through constitutional reforms limiting the presidency to three successive five-year terms, with no candidate allowed over age seventy. The new government gave Islam a more prominent role in public life, such as broadcasting the call to prayer over state television. Ben Ali also undertook a new round of *privatization of state-owned enterprises, and he eliminated price controls and devalued the currency in line with demands of the IMF and other international creditors.

In 1988 the ruling party changed its name again, to become the Democratic Constitutional Rally (RCD). In spite of the new name, the Bourguibist party remained autocratic and authoritarian, holding tightly to the power it had monopolized since 1957. In the 1989, 1994, and 1999 presidential elections, Ben Ali was declared the winner with an overwhelming vote (in 1999 with more than 94 percent of the ballots). Elections to the Chamber of Deputies and municipal councils had similar monolithic results—for instance, in 1999 the RCD won 92 percent of the parliamentary seats and in 2000 94 percent of the municipal council seats.

Economically, the regime met with success. Though oil revenues declined, tourism boomed, as over 4 million foreign visitors flocked to popular Tunisian resorts. An agreement of association with the European Union, signed in 1995, moves Tunisia toward full free-trade with the EU in 2008, bringing significant additional investments in export-oriented industries. From 1988 to 1998, Tunisia's economy more than doubled and the country's foreign debt steadily declined.

Many, though, were left out of Tunisia's economic progress—urban unemployed, poor farmers, and small business owners suddenly driven to bankruptcy by the pressure of the world market. These and others rallied to the political opposition, especially the Islamists and their main movement, the Renaissance Party (EL Nahda), successor to the MTI. A vigorous *human rights movement also challenged the excesses of the ruling party. In April 1993, two hundred intellectuals and other well-known figures published a statement denouncing restrictions on fundamental freedoms. Others circulated a demand for a general amnesty for all political prisoners. The government responded by numerous imprisonments and house arrests. Not only Islamists but also trade unionists, lawyers, journalists, human rights advocates, and many others fell victim to the police and the security services. The international human rights movement has expressed sharp criticism of the continuing violations.

As Tunisia draws nearer to Europe, its prosperity and political future are clouded by the ruling-party system built on the repressive institutions and personality cult of the early postcolonial era.

(See also COLONIAL EMPIRES; DECOLONIZATION; ISLAM; FUNDAMENTALISM; MODERNIZATION; ONE-PARTY SYSTEM.)

Harold D. Nelson, *Tunisia: A Country Study* (Washington, D.C., 1979). Lisa Anderson, *The State and Social Transformation in Tunisia and Libya* (Princeton, N.J., 1987). Susan E. Waltz, *Human Rights and Reform: Changing the Face of North African Politics* (Berkeley, Calif., 1995). John P. Entelis, ed., *Islam, Democracy and the State in North Africa* (Bloomington, Ind., 1997). Emad Eldin Shahin, *Political Ascent: Contemporary Islamic Movements in North Africa* (Boulder, Colo., 1997). Emma C. Murphy, *Economic and Political Change in Tunisia: From Bourguiba to Ben Ali* (New York, 1999).

MONCEF M. KHADDAR

TURKEY. One of the successor states that emerged out of the ruins of the Ottoman Empire after World War I, the new state of Turkey was created after a protracted nationalist struggle (1919–1922) against an invading Greek army supported by the Western powers, as well as a civil war that pitted the nationalists against the forces of the Sultan. Turkey is strategically located on the crossroads between Europe and Asia. Its control over the vital straits which join the Black Sea to the Aegean and the Mediterranean give the country a permanent and vital strategic significance. Its population (62.5 million according to the 1997 census) and size (301,380 sq. mi.; 780,575 sq. km.) make Turkey one of the largest powers in the region.

After the Treaty of Lausanne (July 1923) had confirmed their victory, the nationalists began to resolve the question of the new regime. In the struggle that followed, the radicals, led by Kemal *Atatürk, defeated the conservatives and established a republic on 29 October 1923. The Republican People's Party (RPP), founded by Atatürk and his followers in 1923, became the major instrument in the battle against conservatism. The 1924 constitution vested virtually all power in the unicameral legislature; owing to an indirect system of elections, this body was dominated by the country's elites. In 1924 the Assembly abolished the caliphate, setting off a program of secular reforms which made Turkey the first Muslim country to disestablish *Islam.

By their secularizing reforms during the twenties the Kemalists sought to create a rational society associated by the Kemalists with Western capitalism. When private business interests failed to take the initiative, the Kemalists decided that the state would carry out reform from the top. This was especially true after the world economic crisis of 1930 when—under the new ideology of *Kemalism—the state began to intervene actively in the economy in order to create an industrial infrastructure.

The policy of statism was continued until the end of World War II, when a powerful group of merchants, industrialists, landlords, and intellectuals emerged from within the RPP to challenge the hegemony of the single-party state. President Ismet İnönü and most of the Turkish elite agreed that the time had arrived for competitive multiparty politics. In 1946 the dissidents formed the Democrat Party, which went on to defeat the ruling RPP in the general election of 1950.

The Democrats ruled from 1950 to 1960. Instead of democratizing the system, however, they continued to use institutions inherited from the single-party period. However, aided by the Korean War boom, they transformed the economy, opening it to private enterprise. *Marshall Plan funds financed highway construction and provided tractors, undermining traditional agriculture and setting off a major migration of peasants to the towns and cities. Commerce also flourished as goods were imported at very favorable rates of exchange, allowing merchants to make fortunes and accumulate capital for investment.

These policies touched off inflation that especially harmed salaried civil servants and soldiers; they lost ground not only financially but also in terms of status. The young officers became dissatisfied with the performance of their politicians. Ultimately, however, it was the Democrats' impatience with the opposition and their repressive and autocratic policies which led to the first military intervention of 27 May 1960.

The soldiers had intervened in order to break the deadlock between the parties, but their allies in the universities persuaded them to oversee the restructuring of the entire political system. Before elections were held in October 1961, Turkey had been given a new, liberal Constitution which guaranteed virtually all civil rights, an election law which permitted direct elections and proportional representation (thereby breaking the grip of the old elites), and a political parties law which allowed the founding of a socialist party. Under these conditions the country began an ideological debate beyond the narrow confines of Kemalism. In 1961, trade unionists founded the Workers' Party of Turkey (WPT), and within two years the Assembly passed laws which gave the unions the right to engage in collective bargaining and to strike.

The junta had shut down the Democrat Party and arrested and tried its leaders, three of whom were executed for violating the constitution. Neo-Democrat parties, the most important of which was the Justice Party (JP), emerged to take its place. The 1960s began with coalition governments, but the JP, under Süleyman Demirel's leadership, won the elections in 1965 and 1969, and Turkey was back to the two-party system.

Perhaps the most important political development of this period was the integration of the armed forces into the political system as the guardian of the status quo. The armed forces set up a mutual fund which soon became a huge business-industrial conglomerate, the officer corps got new privileges, and a new military intelligence network came into being—all of which made a coup from below virtually impossible. Any future military intervention would be to defend stability, not promote change.

Under the watchful eye of the newly created State Planning Organization, the economy averaged a growth rate of almost seven percent between 1963 and 1973. Turkey began to industrialize, which had important political and social repercussions. On the one hand, it led to the rise of a militant working class, represented by the WPT, and a radical union movement known by the acronym DISK. On the other hand, small businesses and industries went bankrupt as a few large holding companies established their sway over the economy. As a result, the Right was fragmented; groups broke away from the JP to form parties to represent their narrow interests. The late 1960s witnessed the rise of several small parties including the neofascist Nationalist Action Party (NAP) and the Islamist National Order Party, later renamed the National Salvation Party (NSP). The center-right JP government was trapped between the criticism of an increasingly anti-American Left (after the *Cyprus crisis of 1964) and a Right which demanded *protection for small enterprise. The ensuing political instability—marked by strikes, the massive workers' demonstration of 15/16 June 1970, and acts of urban *terrorism by the student Left—led to another military intervention on 12 March 1970.

Turkey lived under martial law until the elections of October 1973. During that period, the generals attempted to restore political stability by ruthlessly crushing the Left and bolstering the Center-Right with constitutional amendments. The Workers' Party was shut down; its supporters coalesced around the RPP, now social democratic and led by the charismatic Bülent Ecevit. In the elections of 1973 the RPP emerged as the strongest party, but with insufficient seats to form a government on its own. It therefore formed a coalition with the Islamist NSP.

Intervention in Cyprus (July 1974) enhanced Ecevit's popularity, and he calculated that he would win a large majority in an early election. He resigned, but found that the opposition would not permit early polling. His coalition was replaced by a coalition of the Right in which the neofascists were partners. As the two major parties could never win sufficient seats to form governments on their own, they were forced to depend on the small parties of the Right. Chronic political and economic instability throughout the 1970s, including increasing terrorism, prepared the way for the third military intervention on 12 September 1980.

The 1970s also witnessed the triumph of social democracy, which established itself in the cities and among the unions. The Right came to see this as the main threat to the established order. The generals who seized power in 1980 decided to restructure the politics, economy, and society of Turkey so as to put an end to any such threat in the future. They abolished the 1961 constitution and replaced it by a quasi-presidential charter which eliminated virtually all rights guarantees. All parties were dissolved and ex-politicians disqualified from politics from five to ten years. The universities lost their autonomy and professional associations were not permitted to engage in political activity—the medical association could not even lobby against the death penalty. The generals' aim was to depoliticize the entire society by restricting politics to a tiny minority. Meanwhile, supported by the *International Monetary Fund and the *World Bank, Turgut Özal was charged with managing the economy. He implemented a free-market policy designed to bring down inflation by curbing demand at home and encouraging exports.

When political activity was partially restored in 1983, the generals found that depoliticization had not worked. Their party failed to win even a managed election in November; the voters elected Özal's Motherland Party because it promised the swiftest return to democracy. That trend continued throughout the eighties, but the Constitution and the new laws prevented a more rapid transition to democratic politics. By 1989 the Social Democratic Populist Party (SHP, one of the successors to the RPP) had again become the first party in the country, although not in the Assembly. Meanwhile, Özal saw that his party was likely to lose the general election. He therefore had himself elected president, but this only increased political disaffection in the country. When an early general election was held in October 1991, Demirel's True Path Party won the most votes but did not win enough seats to rule on its own. Demirel formed a coalition government with SHP, now the third party, and the Motherland Party, led by Mesut Yilmaz, went into opposition.

Political instability became even more acute following President Özal's death in April and Demirel's election as the new president in May 1993. The two center-right parties these men had led became even more fragmented without their strong personalities. Tansu Ciller succeeded as TPP's leader and became the first woman prime minister in Turkey, and formed a weak and indecisive coalition with the SHP. The Islamists took advantage of a divided and allegedly corrupt government and presented themselves as the honest party. The voters responded by supporting the Welfare Party first in the municipal elections of March 1994 and then in the indecisive general election of December 1995.

Turkey continued to be ruled by coalitions. Despite their hostility to each other, Yilmaz and Ciller agreed to form a secular, center-right coalition in March 1996—a coalition which lasted only three months. Against all expectations, Ciller now agreed to govern alongside Welfare's Necmettin Erbakan, whom she had attacked in the harshest terms. However, this coalition, which gave the Islamists power at the center, alarmed the secularists, led by the generals. Under constant pressure from the military-led National Security council, Erbakan resigned in June 1997. Yilmaz again formed another coalition, this time a caretaker government which would take the country to a general election without a strong Welfare Party and with Tansu Ciller removed from the political scene. The Constitutional Court closed down the Welfare Party in January 1998, and charges of widespread corruption were filed against Ciller and her husband. The hope was that such measures would bring about unity on the center-right, sufficient for it to win the general election slated for April 1999 and restore a semblance of political stability.

Kemal Karpat, *Turkey's Politics: Transition to a Multi-Party System* (Princeton, N.J. 1959). Niyazi Berkes, *The Development of Secularism in Turkey* (Montreal, 1964). Bernard Lewis, *The Emergence of Modern Turkey*, 2nd. ed. (Oxford, 1968). Feroz Ahmad, *The Turkish Experiment in Democracy, 1950–1975* (London, 1977). N. C. Schick and E. A. Tonak, eds., *Turkey in Transition* (New York, 1987). Feroz Ahmad, *The Making of Modern Turkey* (London, 1993).

FEROZ AHMAD

TURKMENISTAN. See CENTRAL ASIA.

TUVALU (ELLICE ISLANDS). See PACIFIC ISLANDS.

U

U.S. FOREIGN POLICY. Because the *United States is one of the most powerful nations in the world, analyses of its *foreign policy have tended to be wrapped in controversy. Thus Americans may see their foreign policy very differently from the foreigners affected by such policy, and academic analysts may see it differently from ordinary citizens. At the risk of oversimplification and missing some of the more complicated disputes, I will outline three major contending interpretations of U.S. foreign policy.

Most Americans consciously (or subliminally) endorse a *liberal* or "bourgeois-liberal" view of their own foreign policy; in such a view, the institutions of political democracy in domestic affairs lead to peaceful *international relations, and the United States is thus seen as an unusually moral actor in world affairs, fighting only when it is first attacked by someone else (as at Pearl Harbor in 1941), offering economic and political assistance to others (as in the *Marshall Plan after *World War II), a nation generally motivated by altruistic and generous motives, a "model for the world." The *Monroe Doctrine, enunciated in 1823, and U.S. participation in two world wars and in the *Cold War, are thus seen as the United States protecting the freedom and self-determination of other nations, because Americans identify with the well-being and happiness of human beings in general.

In opposition to this view, some American critics of U.S. foreign policy are joined by others around the world in adopting a Marxist or *radical* view. In this view, the economic structures of *capitalism are interpreted as causing the United States (as the preeminent capitalist country in the world) to be an unusually expansionist country, a nation engaging in more than its share of gunboat diplomacy and armed invasions, provoking international tensions and arms races. This view has captured a wide audience among the academics of Western Europe and of the *Third World, and it is intuitively endorsed by many others throughout the world. It has also, of course, been the official interpretation of U.S. foreign policy taught in *Communist Party states. The phrase "dollar diplomacy" thus has unpleasant connotations for many Latin Americans, for it is retrospectively seen as having brought the U.S. Marines into Nicaragua or Haiti in the 1920s to protect U.S. investments, and as producing many other forms of intervention.

A third view holds that the United States is neither an unusually moral country nor an unusually expansionist country, but simply an ordinary country, pursuing self-interest and power as every other major power has done. This is a power-politics or *realist* interpretation that would attach relatively little importance to either political democracy or capitalist economics as explanations for the conduct of foreign policy, but would rather see the anarchic character of world politics as dictating the basic behavior of *any* international actor: all such actors are driven to behave in the same fashion. Such an interpretation became fashionable after World War II among those U.S. academics analyzing international relations. The writings of Hans Morgenthau played a major role in introducing students in the United States to the realist school of analysis. This is also more or less the interpretation of U.S. foreign policy that would have been found persuasive by European diplomats and political elites through much of the nineteenth century, as they regarded the American declarations of a "different" approach to the world as largely hypocritical and saw the Monroe Doctrine as nothing more than the assertion of a sphere of influence. Most European political elites (perhaps rationalizing their own positions) thus sympathized with Spain in the 1898 Spanish-American War, for they saw the United States as embarking on an *imperialism no different from European imperialisms.

It is significant to note that these interpretations emphasize very different factors in the prediction or explanation of U.S. foreign policy behavior. The realist focus will emphasize military power and will often broaden this (sometimes at the risk of tautology) to include all components of national power, especially international economic power. Whatever a nation seeks, it will have to have power to obtain it, so the analysis goes; and the primary object of choice and analysis will thus be whether a nation can maintain its power and influence. In the increasingly interdependent world emerging since the 1960s, economic leverage may count for more, and military capacity for less, but the significance of coercive military power will never disappear. The 1947 Marshall Plan, and the delivery of *foreign aid in general, are interpreted as tools of power, rather than as generous and humane gestures in their own right.

The history of U.S. isolation and nonentanglement in the years before the Spanish-American War and the entry in 1917 into *World War I are thus seen, in this realist power-politics interpretation, as simply an application of the rules of *balance of power. As long as Europe was divided against itself, and as long as the Atlantic Ocean offered the United States the protection of a very wide moat (much more secure than the moat offered Britain by the English Channel), it made sense for the United States to forego heavy investments in armies and fleets. Any other country blessed with the same natural reassurance against invasion would have done the same. But the United States' "Manifest Destiny" conquest of Mexican territory in 1845 and general expansion to the Pacific is similarly seen as what any other state would do, exploiting the central position on a continent to expand to its edges, just as tsarist Russia expanded across Siberia.

Such Morgenthau-type realists see the United States as no different from Britain or other countries, but have lamented the self-assessments by which Americans, Woodrow Wilson being a most important example, have foolishly and idealistically convinced themselves that they were somehow above power politics, i.e., that U.S. foreign policy was in some way more high-minded and generous and unselfish than the foreign policy of the more traditional powers. At times, the realists almost seem to be insisting that it is impossible for any country to have a different foreign policy, and to be angry with anyone for trying to do so, as if it were somehow unnatural for a country to be interested in goals other than power. For the realists, *idealism is seen as a dangerous self-delusion, causing interventions where the beneficiary allies (as in Vietnam or El Salvador) are actually not so noble, causing the United States to be naive sometimes about "open covenants, openly arrived at," and then to be cruelly disappointed when the results, as in the Treaty of Versailles, do not match its high standards. The U.S. attempt to return self-consciously to isolation between 1919 and 1939 is interpreted by such realists as a misguided reaction to the discovery that Britain and France had imperialistically negotiated secret treaties during World War I, i.e., that the Allies were not much more moral than imperial Germany had been in its conduct of foreign policy.

The power-politics believer in the significance of international *anarchy thus sees all nations trapped in a "prisoner's dilemma," in which none can trust the other states to be restrained, and in which each thus has to reach for power for itself, as a reassurance against what other states would do with untrammeled power. As noted, the most modern of such realist analysts recognize that power can have many dimensions beyond the military, but they still would interpret economic factors mostly in terms of the influence it gives state A over state B.

A quite different emphasis on economic considerations emerges in the radical or Marxist interpretation. This view rejects the centrality of state-centered power rivalries and instead sees the economic workings of capitalism as the root cause, rather than a secondary dimension of international competition. Capitalist states are burdened by great inequalities of wealth, by periods of dangerously high unemployment, and by endemic crises of profitability caused by overproduction of commodities relative to their marketability (or underconsumption). Political elites are concerned that economic crises will spill over into the political realm. Countries like the United States therefore become desperate to find markets abroad. A prime objective becomes to force the underdeveloped countries of the world to open themselves up to U.S. investment and to the importation of surplus manufactures. Thus, expansionist foreign policy flows from underlying economic causes.

This view considers it "no accident" that the United States began a more active foreign policy, for the first time building a large navy, after 1890, because until then the open frontier and an expanding economy had amounted to a "safety valve" for periodic cycles of unemployment or underconsumption. The further capitalist industrialization proceeded in the United States, by this interpretation, the more the United States felt driven to expand abroad, doing a great deal of harm by this expansion.

This radical-Marxist interpretation thus attaches great significance to the domestic political-economic structures of the United States, but at the same time often neglects the empirical details of political behavior. It is enough to know that U.S. policy is determined by the linkages between state and class interests. Little attention therefore is assigned to elections and political or cultural trends. The triumph of "internationalist" Republicans like Vandenberg and *Eisenhower over the "isolationists" like Taft at the end of the 1940s is regarded as almost foreordained by economic drives, and explanations for interventionist policy from the *Vietnam War to the *Gulf War are sought in economic motivations.

Finally, the interpretation the majority of Americans would find the most plausible views foreign policy as a projection basically of the advantages of their domestic regime. The details of whether democratic processes have been properly executed, and how they have functioned, thus become central in the liberal view, and the *process* of foreign policy making has to be analyzed alongside the *substance* of that policy.

A typical attitude of U.S. policy makers has been that the citizens of other countries would be happier if they were free to adopt the same system of self-government and political democracy as in the United States, and that such democratic countries would then have no real difficulty in getting along internationally. Woodrow Wilson's proposals for Europe in 1918 illustrate this faith, as did Franklin *Roosevelt's vision of the world to follow World War II. And it is indeed difficult to find an example of any war between two countries as democratically governed as the United States.

This model of free compact and self-government has not just seemed appropriate for other nations in their domestic affairs but has also been applied as a model for relations among all nations. It is not surprising that the *League of Nations was the brainchild of U.S. President Woodrow Wilson. Just as Americans have confidence in the voluntary contracts of domestic law, as long as this is part of government by the consent of the governed, so they had great confidence in *international law and in international organizations such as the League of Nations and the UN.

The crucial variables for the liberal interpretation (as for the realist power-politics interpretation) are thus *political* and not economic. Although still the dominant view of foreign policy within the United States, the tenets of American liberalism have been strained in recent decades. One of the shocks of the Vietnam War (which all around the globe worked to increase the appeal of the Marxist interpretation and very much shook American liberal self-confidence) was that many analysts began in the 1960s to question whether democracy could so easily be exported to the poorer countries of the Third World. Perhaps one had to be economically rich to benefit from freedom of the press. Or perhaps one had to be conditioned by specific cultural traditions to make free elections work well. Perhaps the dominant self-analysis of U.S. foreign policy simply reflected a peculiar cultural tradition dating back to New England town meetings, and to the free-and-equal style of the frontier.

The end of the Cold War could be seen as a great victory for U.S. foreign policy, but most Americans have not shown any follow-up enthusiasm for establishing a hegemony over the world; they have rather been very cautious about deploying U.S. forces abroad to handle the "complex emergencies" that proliferated about the time of the demise of Communist ideology. This suggests again that Americans are not driven by an appetite for power; more probably they are stunned at the magnitude of their success, at the number of countries that are now formal democracies, at the frequency of overseas elections that need to be monitored for fairness, etc.

Professional political scientists sometimes scoff at the idealism and optimism of this liberal interpretation of U.S. foreign policy. In fact, the most realist of analysts may share with typical citizens a great awareness of power. Americans have spent two centuries distrusting and checking the uses of political power in domestic life, worrying that governments might shoot, imprison, and coerce individuals. The power-politics outlook merely shifts the concern about the abuse of power to foreign governments, and to what they might do if their armies were more powerful than ours. Whereas the Marxist would regard issues of economic interrelationship as much more significant than these arrangements of political and military power, the average liberal American thus shares with the power-oriented political scientist a fascination with the political arrangements by which citizens are governed and coerced. More than any other, a perspective that emphasizes issues of power in their institutional contexts pulls the fields of U.S. government, *comparative politics, and international relations (and, for that matter, even political philosophy) closer together, a perspective that treats foreign policy making as a more complicated variant of the policy process.

The processes of international economic integration are now challenging the separate sovereign prerogatives of countries all around the globe. The Communist dictatorship in Beijing finds it must liberalize somewhat politically if it wishes to produce the rising prosperity of continuing trade. But a political democracy like the United States also discovers that decisions must now be made in concert with other governments and international entities such as the *World Trade Organization, and perhaps that the demands of voters are increasingly driven by economic considerations, as a presidential campaign can key on the slogan of "It's the economy, stupid."

Some analysts after the Cold War would thus stress how economic power has taken precedence over military and other traditional forms of power. But others would stress that the pursuit of economic "plenty" may indeed have replaced any pursuit of "power" for democracies, and perhaps even for a nondemocracy like Communist China.

Yet the constraints of economic integration are still not likely to produce the "wars for markets" that Marxist analysis once predicted. Rather than resisting U.S. investment, places like China and Vietnam are now trying to attract it.

(See also GAME THEORY; ISOLATIONISM; JAPAN-U.S. RELATIONS; REALISM; UNITED NATIONS; U.S.-AFRICA RELATIONS; U.S.–LATIN AMERICAN RELATIONS.)

Frank Klingberg, "The Historical Alternation of Moods in American Foreign Policy" World Politics 4, no. 2 (January 1952): 239–273. Louis Hartz, The Liberal Tradition in America (New York, 1955). Hans Morgenthau, Politics Among Nations (New York, 1967). Gabriel Kolko, The Roots of American Foreign Policy (Boston, 1969). Thomas Cascothers, In the Name of Democracy: U.S. Policy Toward Latin America in the Reagan Years. (Berkeley, Calif., 1991). Lea Brilmayer, American Hegemony: Political Morality in a One-Superpower World (New Haven, Conn. 1994). Michael E. Brown, ed., The International Dimensions of Internal Conflicts (Cambridge, Mass., 1996).

GEORGE H. QUESTER

U.S.–AFRICA RELATIONS. The independence of African countries from European colonialism and their attempt to establish stable political regimes and developing economies provided the major post–World War II context for their international relations. The vast continent of Africa, a geopolitically important landmass connected to Europe and the Middle East, contains a critical supply of the raw materials considered important for military and industrial purposes by most economically advanced nations. To the extent that European countries were often preoccupied with their own postwar reconstruction, the United States pursued its own interests in Africa, incorporating it into the collective security framework of Western opposition to Soviet interests.

The objectives pursued by the United States involved the preservation of its access to strategic resources and geographical position. For example, U.S. policy was designed to maintain friendly relations with North African states in order to have access to military facilities that would buttress the southern flank of its NATO commitments in the Mediterranean. This position would also provide stability for American allies in the Middle East and security for oil exports from certain Arab countries. Thus, when the United States was expelled from Libya after its revolution in 1969, U.S. policy for a considerable period was directed toward securing military base rights in Somalia, Kenya, and the Indian Ocean in order to contain Soviet and Arab military pressure on U.S. allies in the Middle East region.

Likewise, the basis for American involvement in the Congo crisis of 1960–1964 was its dependence on the Congo for critical strategic minerals such as cobalt and uranium, used in its growing nuclear weapons program. The legacy of early U.S. relations with the Congo initiated a long period of support for the regime of President Mobutu Sese Seko. However, a more negative attitude developed toward the corrupt and dictatorial Mobutu regime in its latter stages, which placed the United States in a more secure position to support the collapse of that government and the emergence of Laurent Kabila, the victor in the civil war of 1997.

More important, the American posture in West Africa had long been anchored by its relations with Nigeria, the most populous African nation and a leading exporter of oil to the United States in the 1990s. Yet, the U.S. desire for democratization in Nigeria was thwarted by political instability, as General Sani Abacha came to power in a 1993 coup against the previous regime of General Ibrahim Babangida. Abacha promptly stopped the transition to civilian rule by annulling the presidential election and imprisoning the apparent civilian victor, Chief Moshood Abiola. The sudden deaths of General Abacha and the popular Abiola in June and July of 1998, respectively, caused serious civil strife, and in response, Abacha's successor, General Abdusalam Abubakar, revived the program of transition to civilian rule. Yet, the United States, jaundiced by a series of repressive actions by the Abacha regime, wielded its influence modestly because of its position as an importer of Nigerian oil as well as Nigeria's vital influence in the politics of West Africa. Nigeria's military intervention in Liberia and Sierra Leone in 1997 and 1998, as well as its crucial support for the MPLA regime in Angola in 1976, illustrates its regional importance.

U.S. policy has focused predominantly on South Africa because of the extent of American business investments and trade (especially strategic minerals such as diamonds, manganese, chromium and platinum-group metals), involvement in its $115 billion GDP, and American interest in protecting the oil routes around the Cape of Good Hope and the adjacent eastern and western coasts. Thus, the foreign policy of the United States has been designed to manage the emergence of independent states in Southern Africa without threatening its own basic interests. The challenges by Africans to Western colonial powers such as Portugal (in Angola and Mozambique) and white settlers in Zimbabwe, South Africa, and South-West Africa fomented guerrilla conflicts which found the United States and the Soviet Union supporting opposite sides. With the independence of Zimbabwe in 1980, black majority rule in South-West Africa (Namibia) in 1990 and in South Africa in 1994, and the near-resolution of the civil war in the former Portuguese territories, the region entered a new phase in the mid-1990s. U.S. policy toward South Africa changed with the adoption of the Anti-Apartheid Act in 1986, the product of the opposition of the American people to the "constructive engagement" policy of the Reagan administration. Since the emergence of Nelson *Mandela from prison and the election of the African National Congress to govern the country, the United States has strongly supported Mandela's leadership. The "national interest" that shapes foreign policy is often governed by a combination of such factors as the intensity of public opinion and the influence of decision-making institutions and professionals. In this respect, two factors are most important, one of which is the environment of policy. Some of the initial changes in the nature of American foreign policy toward Africa have been affected by the absence of Soviet competition, which has freed the United States to pursue an agenda of global economic relations involving Africa as well. Thus, for example, President Bill Clinton traveled to Africa in April 1998 in an effort to initiate a new chapter in U.S.-African relations based on trade and investment rather than solely upon economic development assistance. This direction of policy, which has bipartisan support in the Congress but has stirred up some measure of dissent among those fearful of the impact upon the American and African working classes, will most likely become the focus of American policy in Africa for some time to come.

The other important factor in shaping the "national interest" is the increasingly active engagement of representatives of the 30 million U.S. citizens of African descent and their growing role in foreign policy formulation. Their interests in Africa have evolved naturally, together with the efforts of black political leaders and foreign policy professionals in such projects as the provision of drought relief to the Sahel region of the Africa in the early 1970s, the repeal of the Byrd amendment in 1977 that allowed the United States to trade with the outlaw Rhodesian regime in contravention to UN economic sanctions, the passage of the 1986 Anti-Apartheid Act, and the African Growth and Opportunity bill introduced in Congress in 1997. In the future, as the economic importance of Africa to the United States increases, all Americans may perhaps view Africa as a more critical *foreign policy priority.

(See also COLONIAL EMPIRES; CONTAINMENT; U.S. FOREIGN POLICY.)

Vernon McKay, *Africa in World Politics* (New York, 1963). Frederick S. Arkhurst, ed., *U.S. Policy Toward Africa* (New York, 1975). Gerald J. Bender, James S. Coleman, and Richard L. Sklar, eds., *African Crisis Areas and U.S. Foreign Policy* (Berkeley, Calif., 1985). Peter J. Schraeder, *United States Foreign Policy Toward Africa: Incrementalism, Crisis and Change* (New York, 1994).

RONALD WALTERS

U.S.–CENTRAL AMERICAN RELATIONS. The history of foreign relations between the United States and Central America has been dominated by recurring cycles of intervention and neglect. These cycles, characterized by moments of intense U.S. presence in Central America, followed by relatively prolonged phases of lack of U.S. commitment to the region, have inhibited the development of a balanced relationship based on shared medium- and long-term objectives.

During the *Cold War, Central America experienced one of the greatest periods of U.S. interventionism. Towards the end of the 1980s, however, this interventionism was gradually neutralized by the coming to an end of a bipolar world. In fact, the end of the *Reagan era and the advent of the *Bush administration allowed for the strengthening of the peace and democratization process stimulated by the Esquipulas II Agreement (1987) which facilitated the negotiations that ended the civil wars in Nicaragua (1988–1990), El Salvador (1989–1992), and eventually Guatemala (1994–996). It also marked the beginning of a gradual "abandonment" of the region, which stopped being a U.S. strategic priority, particularly given increased turbulence in the Middle East and Central Europe.

The arrival of the *Clinton administration in 1993 raised some hopes in Central America for a new era of teamwork, based on a shared vision of much needed development for the peoples of the region. After all, they had felt the worst of the Cold War, therefore they deserved to have the best of a peace dividend. In 1994, when the White House assumed major responsibility for the organization of the summit of the Americas, the U.S. government undertook its first initiative of importance directed towards Central America. At the summit, held in Miami in December 1994, the Declaration Central America-USA (CONCA-USA) was signed. It was intended to initiate a new era of cooperation and dialogue between the United States and Belize, Costa Rica, Dominican Republic, El Salvador, Guatemala, Honduras, Nicaragua, and Panama.

The CONCA-USA Declaration laid the foundation for the development between 1997 and 1999 of the most intense relations between a U.S. president and his Central American counterparts. The heads of state of the area met as a group with Clinton on at least three occasions, as well as bilaterally during the Second Summit of the Americas in Santiago de Chile in 1998. More significantly Clinton visited Central America, first as part of a Latin American tour in 1997 and in 1999 in order to survey the devastation of Hurricane Mitch.

From CONCA-USA to the "Negative Agenda." The CONCA-USA Declaration highlighted environmental problems as critical issues in U.S.–Central American relations. It opened the door for the development of a proactive regional environmental strategy based on a shared vision for the future. It made possible, for example, the signing of the first hemispheric agreement on "joint implementation" between the U.S. Environmental Protection Agency (EPA) and the Central American environmental ministries. It also paved the way for the beginning of an unprecedented effort to work together in the mitigation of climatic change, which put Central America at the forefront of the agreements reached during the Kyoto Conference in 1998. These important achievements, however, did not pave the way for solutions in two areas of fundamental importance to the Central American governments: free trade and Central American emigration to the United States.

Central America wanted "trade, not aid." The region understood that in a global economy it would stand to benefit from access to the U.S. market, and took every opportunity to mention its willingness to begin free trade negotiations. Failure to achieve "*NAFTA parity", in part because of the opposition of the U.S. Congress to it, disappointed the region. In other words, all of Central America's proposals on this subject, including one to sign its own free trade agreement with the United States, were rejected. And it wasn't until well into 1999 that a diluted Caribbean Basin Initiative (CBI) enhancement was achieved. This did not resolve the region's main concern, that is, the lack of competitiveness of its products in the U.S. market with respect to Mexico and, more importantly, its lack of opportunity to compete with Mexico in attracting much needed foreign investment.

The distance between the region and the United States has grown due to the frequency with which the Central American agenda ended up being linked to U.S. domestic problems. This was especially evident when U.S. companies or citizens appealed to their congressional representatives for backing of their commercial or legal grievances against what they considered to be abuses on the part of the Central American governments. The intervention of the congress, people, lobbying groups, and "interested parties" in the actions of the Department of State and the White House ended up generating tremendous tension and new impositions in such sensitive areas as textile manufacturing and banana and tuna exports. These issues, and others, constituted a "negative agenda" which always managed to take precedence over more substantial matters.

Current Changes of Direction: Hurricane Mitch. In October of 1998 Hurricane Mitch devastated Honduras and Nicaragua, and ravaged El Salvador and Guatemala. Material damage amounted to almost one billion dollars and the total death count exceeded 10,000. The disaster destroyed 70 percent of the transportation infrastructure of Honduras and 60 percent of Nicaragua's. This was, without a doubt, one of the worst natural and social catastrophes in Central America in the last twenty-five years.

The response of the United States to the tragedy was immediate and characterized by a combination of material generosity and political symbolism. In November of 1998, scarcely two weeks after the hurricane, President Clinton supported a trip to Honduras by former President George Bush to assess the damages caused by Mitch. By December 1998, when Central American leaders met with President Clinton in Washington, the administration had already resolved to contribute $300 million dollars in emergency aid to the region,

which would include $150 million from the Department of Defense, $87 million from USAID, and $63 million from the Department of Agriculture. At this time Clinton also announced the decision to grant a waiver through January 31, 1999 to keep Honduran, Nicaraguan, and Salvadoran nationals, who were in the U.S. illegally, from being deported to their native countries. This waiver was eventually extended until March of 2000, at which time it was revoked. Finally, during his trip to Central America in March of 1999, Clinton declared his intention to request an extraordinary aid package for Central America from Congress. At that time, it was said to have amounted to about $700 million dollars, which, once it materialized, would make the United States and the European Union the two main donors in the area. Even though the administration's policy initiatives eventually weakened, their initial formulation and implementation marked a positive development with respect to U.S. interest in the region.

In other areas the Clinton administration also acted positively. Towards the end of January 1999, the president created a "task force" spearheaded by the Department of State and USAID to coordinate all U.S. activity in the region. The person responsible for carrying this out, Ambassador Wendy Sherman, summarized the U.S. objectives in the following way:

1. Support democratic stability in the entire region.
2. Revitalize the national economies of the affected countries.
3. Prevent massive emigration of Central Americans to the United States.
4. Reverse the environmental degradation in the region.

Perhaps the most striking aspect was the fact that unlike previous instances in the history of bilateral relations, this time the United States actually did come to appreciate Central America's circumstances with an understanding that transcended a mere humanitarian effort. First of all, it recognized the need to respond to regional vulnerabilities in a comprehensive and long-term way. Secondly, it proposed transferring the largest amount of development aid and resources possible using local and community organizations including municipalities and city governments. Finally it managed to clearly link the events in Central America with their potential domestic impact on the United States.

From the "political message" viewpoint, the management of the humanitarian crisis caused by Mitch constituted a powerful indicator of Washington's preferential commitment to its Central American neighbors. This commitment paved the way for, among other things, the U.S. rebuilding of its relations with the Central American armed forces, to whom they accorded a pivotal role in mitigating the disaster. A clear example of this was the way in which the United States succeeded in establishing a new bond of cooperation with the Nicaraguan army, from which it had been estranged since the fall of the Somoza regime in 1979.

It is interesting to note, however, that this positive atmosphere was quickly complicated at the end of the 1990s by a series of difficulties that clearly reflected Central America's historic limitations as an object of *U.S. foreign policy. For one thing, some of the funds promised by the Clinton administration did not necessarily come from new budget sources. Rather they represented resources that had already been appropriated for other purposes and now, because of Hurricane Mitch, would have their final destination changed by special executive action, in order to expedite their immediate disbursement without the usual delays. However, in the case of new resources such as the $700 million announced by President Clinton in Nicaragua, the administration had to appeal to Congress, where the proposal was quickly caught in a bitter partisan dispute between the Republicans and Democrats. It was only after a long and bloody political battle that the administration was able to obtain the funds for Central America and it was a much smaller amount than had originally been announced.

As Hurricane Mitch stopped being a news item in the media, the president's ability to impose his political will lessened, until it almost disappeared completely. For example, the most important means of helping Central America in the long term, that is increased access of their products to the United States market through some preferential mechanism, was overwhelmingly rejected by the Department of Commerce and the U.S. Trade Representative. This caused considerable distress among the Central American presidents, who didn't hesitate to express their disappointment openly.

Something similar happened with the relaxation of U.S. migration policies announced in December of 1998. By the beginning of February 1999, the Immigration and Naturalization Service began a new wave of deportations, which were suspended only because of President Clinton's imminent visit to Central America in the month of March. This new challenge to the President, who recognized the legal impossibility of opposing the decision made by his subordinates in the Department of Justice, caused an onslaught of protests from the presidents of El Salvador, Honduras, Guatemala, and Nicaragua. All of them attributed the principal responsibility for Central American northward migrations to the United States' actions during the Cold War years.

In addition, Central America's management of the tragedy occasioned by Hurricane Mitch was, at best, insufficient and, at worst, irresponsible. Basically, at least as far as the United States was concerned, the Central American governments were too slow and weak in backing the White House against Congress. It is also true that this situation was further aggravated by a lack of regional unity in the search for reconstruction resources, and by the absence of lobbying mechanisms capable of successfully swaying U.S. policy. These facts, however, serve only to emphasize Central America's historic difficulties in obtaining true preferential and priority treatment within the international agenda of the United States even during the most critical moments of its development.

Revitalized Hegemony: Central America as a New Security Realm. The United States' hegemonic project, abandoned in the 1990s, became revitalized at the beginning of the twenty-first century and revolves around—once again—the subject of security. This time, however, the enemy, instead of being outside the hemisphere, lives and grows in the United States' own backyard since *drug activity has replaced *communism as the new enemy.

In the current logic of U.S. security, Central America has a key role to play in obstructing the flow of drugs and undocumented people transported to the north. As the antidrug battle widened, and within the framework of the withdrawal of U.S. military bases from Panama, it became vital for the United States to deploy a renewed regional security initiative. Based on cooperation between the DEA and the police and the armed forces of Central America since the beginning of the 1990s, this initiative acquired special significance once the U.S. security border moved from the Gulf of Mexico in the north to the Gulf of Urabá and the Darién Gap in the South.

The U.S. decision to assign Central America an important strategic role in the battle against drugs is noteworthy in at least four ways. First, from a political perspective, it has redefined, reoriented, and reprioritized the cooperation agenda, which has shifted from the predominantly environmental issues of the CONCA-USA Declaration towards military or political issues where joint training, equipping, and patrolling predominate. Second, from a bureaucratic and policy formulation perspective, although the Department of State continues to be responsible for U.S. foreign relations in the area, there is today an increasing influence on the part of the DEA, the Department of Defense, and the intelligence agencies in these decision making processes. Third, from a geopolitical perspective, the focus of U.S. attention has broadened, making Central America, together with the Caribbean and Colombia, one operative unit towards which the United States seeks to act with increasingly integrated policies. Finally, from a diplomatic perspective, the United States has succeeded in reconstructing a hegemonic project with the Central American governments, which have heartily endorsed Washington's proposals. Such unanimity has not been seen since the Cold War years.

These conditions imply some risks. The greatest of them is that the "negative agenda" might give way to a one topic agenda, where security issues take on an importance disproportionate with other issues vital to guaranteeing the survival of the still very vulnerable Central American democracies, which require strong economic and social development. Washington authorities categorically deny that such a risk exists. In fact, they have repeatedly insisted on an alternative interpretation that conceives of the battle against drug activity as the very foundation of democratic consolidation in the area. They also point to the continued support afforded to Central America in areas such as the environment or the strengthening of public institutions that have little to do with security issues.

Regardless of the differing arguments, it is indisputable that U.S. drug policy has acquired an importance out of proportion with other U.S. initiatives in the region. This tendency increased with the decision of the Clinton administration to grant Colombia up to $1.6 billion dollars for the battle against drug activity and the insurgent forces supposedly linked to it. Furthermore, in 1999 the United States ratified a treaty with Costa Rica to allow U.S. representatives to accompany Costa Rican government vessels on patrol. Similar agreements with El Salvador, Panama, and Honduras are planned.

Toward a Constructive Agenda: The Near Future. One of the lessons Central America has learned in the last decades is that the only thing worse than not receiving attention from Washington is receiving negative attention. The "negative agenda" that has predominated during the second half of the 1990s has prevented the development of more balanced relations. It is foreseeable that the issues of this agenda, which cannot easily be ignored by the parties, could be addressed more effectively and fully in a more cooperative and open atmosphere. Therefore it is urgent that both the U.S. and Central America clarify their areas of convergence and divergence and define a methodology for addressing them in the medium and long term. This task should not ignore the great asymmetries that separate them, but it should also recognize the extraordinary possibilities presented by the fact that Central America is for the first time a democratic region, and there is no impending threat from another continent. As long as the United States considers Central America as nothing more than a source of environmental, human, and security problems, and is not capable of accepting it as a trustworthy partner for successfully facing common challenges together, the possibility of overcoming the "negative agenda" will continue to be slim. Therefore while establishing a joint atmosphere of cooperation requires recognizing mutual complaints, it is equally important that this recognition not obscure the will to address them in a constructive and cooperative spirit.

The signing of the CONCA-USA Declaration in 1994 was a step in the right direction. It would be even more helpful if the U.S. and Central America were able, in this same spirit, to formalize their relations to reach an understanding like the one that already exists between Mexico, Canada, and the United States. The NAFTA countries have agreed to conduct their relations within a framework of periodic consultations at the different decision making levels. These consultations facilitate discussion of complex and sensitive subjects before they lead to unnecessary confrontations. Although the consultations are not always enough to avoid conflict, establishing dialogue in any case enhances communication between the parties and deepens mutual credibility and trust. In other words, formalizing relations would also help end the intense cycles of intervention and neglect that have affected U.S.–Central American relations so profoundly.

Kenichi Ohmae in his book *El fin del Estado Nacion* foresees the end of the nation-state, to be replaced by what he calls the region-state. According to Ohmae the dynamic of the world economy is making the state based on the Westphalian model obsolete by preventing it from playing its traditional role as arbitrator of national entities. According to his analysis, bureaucratic fragmentation and regionalism are also exacerbating the deterioration of the nation-state. The growth of the metropoli whose economic power is out of proportion with that of the states that contain them, is causing "supercities" to become alternative growth points. Consequently, a new balance of power is arising that is not determined by geographical, ethnic, or cultural limits, but by the ability of these megacities to supply their outlying regions with the benefits that historically were provided by the state.

Although it is still too early to proclaim the advent of a new Middle Age, Ohmae's predictions could shape a very interesting context for reinventing relations between the United States and Central America in the first decades of the twenty-first century. In fact, Central American migration patterns towards certain U.S. cities have turned these cities, for all intents and purposes, into veritable regional enclaves in North America. Some U.S. cities are also financial and commercial magnets that could end up reconstructing the political content of the Caribbean Basin.

Even though this could take many years to materialize, it is possible to speculate that, sooner rather than later, the United States and Central America will have to face the profound changes that will occur in the nature of the nation-state. After suffering the blows of growing economic competition and new political and technological dilemmas, these countries must choose to become true partners linked by a complex regional agenda and a long-term strategy, recognizing that this association will always be asymmetrical.

Realists in the United States and Central America will argue that it is inconceivable that relations between the superpower and its immediate area of influence could change in the next few decades. From their perspective, the United States will continue to be tangled up in the administration of Central America's fragile democracies and underdeveloped economies. Furthermore, they will assume, probably to some degree correctly, that without any credible threats to question its hegemony, the United States will be able to neutralize any divisive or subversive tendencies that could eventually appear in Central America. This will remain true provided that none of these potential tensions would be sufficiently serious to endanger U.S. interests in the area.

It is clear that on the U.S. world strategic map, it will be difficult for Central America, in the twenty-first century, to be a priority area for the superpower. Central America will not even obtain the prominence within the hemisphere that other larger Latin American countries could achieve, especially those in the Southern Cone.

Nonetheless, as the events of the 1980s and 1990s proved, an unstable and violent Central America can cause significant domestic repercussions in the United States, especially if these problems generate new and massive migratory flows towards North America, or instigate tremendous economic chaos in the region. The same could be said of other phenomena that, like drug trafficking, could worsen in a context of serious political chaos in Central America.

The question, then, is not whether vital U.S. national security interests will be in any way threatened by future events in Central America. With the exception of some apocalyptic tragedy, hardly any foreseeable event could have such a far-reaching impact. Rather, the real crux of the matter is what would be the most effective and efficient way for the United States and Central America to shoulder and resolve the realities of their geopolitical proximity in a creative and positive way. We believe that these challenges would be better met within a framework of political, economic, and environmental cooperation, which is only possible in the context of functional democracies and sustainable human development.

(See also DEMOCRATIC TRANSITIONS; ENVIRONMENTALISM; GEOPOLITICS.)

Kenichi Ohmae, *The End of the Nation State* (New York, 1995). Rachel Sieder, *Central America: Fragile Transition* (London, 1996). Richard E. Feinberg, *Summitry of the Americas: A Progress Report* (Washington, D.C., 1997). Tom Farer, *Transnational Crime in the Americas* (New York, 2000). William McCallister, *Drug Diplomacy in the 20th Century* (New York, 2000).

JOSÉ MARÍA FIGUERES OLSEN
LUIS GUILLERMO SOLÍS

U.S.–LATIN AMERICAN RELATIONS. The history of U.S.–Latin American relations generally confirms *Thucydides' observation that large countries will do what they will and small countries will accept what they must, and so the analysis of inter-American relations must begin with the identification of U.S. interests in the region. These interests were first identified early in the nineteenth century, when England threatened to seize Spanish Florida and use it as a base to attack the *United States. As an act of national defense, Congress responded in 1811 by adopting the No-Transfer Resolution, the first substantial statement of U.S. policy toward Latin America. What began as an effort to keep the British out of Florida soon expanded when, in the early 1820s, the Holy Alliance authorized France to assist Spain in recovering her American colonies. This led to the *Monroe Doctrine, the cognitive bedrock of U.S. policy toward Latin America. Since that time the fundamental interest of the United States in its relations with Latin America has been to exclude extrahemispheric rivals from the region. Within this geopolitical paradigm of strategic denial, other interests—many motivated by the drive for economic advantage—have been subordinate but often complementary.

Because strategic denial directed the attention of U.S. officials to the analysis of the intentions and behavior of extrahemispheric rivals, Washington's policy toward Latin America rarely focused upon Latin Americans per se, but upon what extrahemispheric rivals might do in Latin America that would affect the *security of the United States. This view made good sense early in the nineteenth century, when Latin America was not much more than a large hunk of territory: sparsely populated by a few million humans divided into several mutually incomprehensible castes with, the notoriously unstable nations of the region lacking all but the most rudimentary forms of political organization.

Over the years since the early nineteenth century, however, Latin American states have slowly emerged as independent actors on the world stage. The principal U.S. response was to create an inter-American system to enlist the support of Latin Americans in preserving the paradigm of strategic denial. Although the initial steps were taken in the final quarter of the nineteenth century, the experience of *World War II was especially important in convincing U.S. policy makers of the need for the cooperation of Latin Americans to exclude extrahemispheric rivals. It led to the first formal U.S. peacetime mutual security alliance, the 1947 Inter-American Treaty of Reciprocal Assistance, which firmly attached Latin America to the U.S. pole. In return for their nominal allegiance, Latin Americans extracted from the United States 1) a formal pledge of nonintervention, and 2) consent to the creation of institutions to regulate the inter-American system. Foremost among these institutions was the *Organization of American States (OAS), created in 1948 by the Act of Bogotá to replace the amorphous Pan American Union.

Although the United States continued to intervene regularly in Latin America, and although the OAS and its ancillary organizations are weak, the result of these two concessions has been to strengthen Latin America when conflicts arise with the United States. They have redefined how members should act, and made deviations from expected behavior increasingly costly. One cost has been to galvanize Latin American resistance to deviations in U.S. policy, as the Contadora and Esquipulas peace processes during the 1980s suggest.

Formed at a summit meeting held on the Panamanian island of Contadora in early 1983, the Contadora Group (Colombia, Mexico, Panama, and Venezuela) pointedly excluded the United States; indeed, many of the twenty-one Contadora principles ran directly counter to U.S. policy in Central America. Although Contadora was designed in large measure to structure the process of diplomatic bargaining between the U.S. and Sandinista Nicaragua, it had the effect of restricting Washington's freedom of maneuver in Central America. Similarly, the "Procedure for the Establishment of a Firm and Lasting Peace in Central America" (known as the Esquipulas II accords after the Guatemalan town where the five Central American chiefs of state met in mid-1987 to plan a process of political reconciliation) also pointedly excluded the United States and restricted Washington's freedom by designating a date after which it became illegal for any state to assist insurgent movements such as the Nicaraguan contras.

Latin America's growing autonomy can also be seen in the content of the post–Cold War inter-American policy agenda, which consists of issues such as *drug trafficking, *international debt, illegal migration, *democratic transitions, *human rights, poverty, economic development, and trade. Given the continuing revolutions in communications and transportation, the 450 million people in the region will be in ever more intimate contact with U.S. citizens. Latin America is no longer an inert piece of territory.

In addition to emerging Latin American autonomy, a second structural change has also been occurring: a long-term process of democratization in U.S. public policy making. The rapidity of change since World War II has been especially striking. It was not easy to identify this process during the 1940s and 1950s, however, and it was only in the 1960s that sufficient space existed in public opinion for disaffected citizens to criticize Washington's tendency to interpret instability in the *Third World as an example of communist adventurism. Opposition to the *Vietnam War became the principal manifestation of this disaffection, but the erosion of support for *containment was also evident elsewhere.

The partisan debate that reached a fever pitch in the 1980s over the content of U.S. policy toward Central America was part of this process of democratization. It was produced by the slow incorporation of new groups of U.S. citizens into the policy-making process. Only a few decades ago, a small handful of officials in Washington were the only relevant participants. Today, even a minor policy issue is likely to involve a bewildering array of official participants, and major policy issues involve the public at all levels of government.

Because there are more participants, there is more diversity of opinion. This diversity may not seem immediately evident, for the policy-relevant ideological spectrum remains fairly narrow in Washington. But when *foreign policy goes beyond those issues that are amenable to a quick fix, as it did in Central America in the 1980s, or when it affects the core interests of powerful organized groups such as labor unions, as did the trade liberalization debates of the 1990s, then the diversity becomes increasingly obvious. The longer time frame permits the mobilization of a panoply of non-governmental organizations seeking to influence the policy process. Notable among them have been groups from the liberal foreign policy community—the citizens who emerged in the 1960s, 70s, and 80s to anchor the left end of the U.S. political spectrum, creating institutions (like *Amnesty International, Americas Watch, the Washington Office on Latin America, and dozens of church groups) to structure their dissent. While these liberals have been unable to carry the day on such issues as the 1989 invasion of Panama or the provision of expanded military aid to Colombia in 2000, their insistence on human rights and non-intervention has played a significant role in shaping U.S. policy toward the region.

Quite apart from the growing autonomy of Latin America and the democratization of the U.S. policy-making process, changes in *international relations also challenge the utility of strategic denial. One of these is the nature of warfare, whose history can be written as a continuous adjustment between technological change, on the one hand, and the significance of geographic proximity, on the other. Our most distant ancestors needed to be within an arm's distance of an adversary in order to inflict physical damage, but soon wooden clubs permitted rivals to strike one another from a slight distance. Not long thereafter the availability of rocks led to the discovery that one could launch a weapon rather than swing it, and with that the die was cast: all military history since then is little more than a discussion of the changing tactics and strategies surrounding the introduction of ever more sophisticated projectiles.

One consequence of the increased sophistication of offensive weapons has been the increased sophistication of defensive strategies. In the 1820s, the United States was vulnerable to attack from Latin America, and at this historical moment strategic denial earned its status as a paradigm by providing policy makers with a framework to address a problem they considered acute. Over two centuries, however, the changing nature of warfare has slowly but inexorably rendered less compelling the significance of geographic proximity and, hence, the rationale behind strategic denial.

A second change in international relations lies in the shifting standards of "success" in international relations. For most of human history, the tribe or nation that could bring the largest amount of physical power to bear on a battlefield could carry the day. For nearly half a century after the end of World War II, the Soviet Union and the United States were content to define "success" in terms of this strategy, with the focus upon the use of limited force to subdue a militarily primitive Third World nation allied with a rival superpower. In the United States during the 1980s, this strategy was called the Reagan Doctrine. With the fall of the Berlin Wall and the collapse of the Soviet Union, however, military issues have taken a back seat to economic ones, and the utility of military force to confront new threats—such as drug trafficking, immigration, and transnational crime—has increasingly been called into question.

In sum, several changes in the structure of inter-American relations combined to render strategic denial an anachronistic paradigm for U.S. policy toward Latin America at the end of the twentieth century. The 1990s was therefore a transitional decade, as officials in Washington strove to develop a new paradigm to orient U.S.–Latin American relations in the twenty-first century.

Once freed of the imperative to contain external threats in the Western hemisphere, the Clinton administration redefined the key strategic objectives of U.S. policy in terms of promoting democracy and expanding free trade. Two trends influenced this choice of priorities. First was the reestablishment of constitutional order throughout Latin America, as democratically elected governments replaced authoritarian military rulers, particularly in the Southern Cone, and negotiated settlements ended the wars that had ravaged Central America. Second, and related to the collapse of socialist models of economic organization, was the rapid globalization of the world economy, organized around free markets, advanced technology, and trade. As the world's dominant economic superpower the United States, along with a host of international financial institutions, avidly promoted market reform, privatization, and trade liberalization as the keys to solving the region's chronic problems of slow growth, hyperinflation, and debt.

The heightened faith in free trade as the key to economic prosperity found its most concrete manifestation in the conclusion of the North American Free Trade Agreement (*NAFTA) linking the economies of the United States, Mexico, and Canada. The drive to extend a free trade agreement throughout the Americas met stiff resistance within the United States, however, from protectionist forces worried about the loss of U.S. jobs, as well as liberal activists concerned about the lack of environmental and workers' protections abroad. The legitimacy of free market reforms was also called into question throughout the hemisphere, as privatization widened income disparities in a region already known for having the worst income distribution in the world. The linkage between economics and politics became ever more clear as popular frustration with the privations of economic adjustment appeared to threaten the very future of democratic governance, particularly in the Andean region.

Just as the end of the twentieth century had witnessed electoral transitions to democracy in all of Latin America except Cuba, the beginning of the twenty-first was characterized by an unprecedented effort to make the institutions of democracy function. Governments, as well as *non-governmental organizations, channeled resources and expertise to reform electoral and judicial systems and assist *civil society in making democratic participation meaningful for broader segments of the population.

Whether such an effort will prove successful remains open to question. Persistent asymmetries of power between the United States and its Latin American allies, as well as a residue of suspicion in the region of past U.S. violations of sovereignty, meant that U.S. leadership even in an effort to defend democracy was still widely questioned. The frequent declarations of mutual interest—in combating drug trafficking and *corruption, rationalizing immigration policies, and maintaining open trade regimes, for example—often masked deep divisions over the means to achieve such goals, as well as the relative priorities attached to them. In such a situation, a more appropriate framework for U.S.–Latin American relations would be that which guide U.S. relations with the industrialized countries of Europe—a policy of patient *diplomacy based upon mutual respect but frequently conflicting interests. For such a framework to become the dominant one, however, established patterns of U.S. behavior, founded on centuries of strategic denial and underlying cultural prejudice, would have to change.

(See also BAY OF PIGS INVASION; CUBAN MISSILE CRISIS; DEVELOPMENT AND UNDERDEVELOPMENT; INTERVENTION; INTER-

NATIONAL MIGRATION; LATIN AMERICAN AND CARIBBEAN REGIONAL ORGANIZATIONS; REALISM; U.S.–CENTRAL AMERICAN RELATIONS; U.S. FOREIGN POLICY.)

Samuel Flagg Bemis, *The Latin-American Policy of the United States: An Historical Interpretation* (New York, 1943). James W. Gantenbein, ed., *The Evolution of Our Latin-American Policy: A Documentary, Record* (New York, 1950). G. Pope Atkins, *Latin American in the International Political System*, 2d ed. (Boulder, Colo., 1989). Arnson, Cynthia J., *Crossroads: Congress, the President, and Central America, 1976–1993* (University Park, Penn., 1993). Schoultz, Lars, *Beneath the United States: A History of U.S. Policy Toward Latin America* (Cambridge, Mass., 1998).

LARS SCHOULTZ
CYNTHIA ARNSON

UGANDA. The configuration of historical forces that have molded Ugandan politics may be attributed to the geography of the country and to governmental policies pursued since the turn of the twentieth century. These have given Uganda its particular brand of politics, which in turn have been shaped by the pattern of uneven socioeconomic development across the country; the manipulation of ethnic consciousness; religious loyalties and ideologies; and reliance on the military as the mainstay of power. The course of political events in Uganda has borne a direct relationship to the existence or absence of a viable national* ideology or ethos and the degree of internal* legitimacy of the authorities. Yet although socioeconomic conditions have in large measure influenced the patterns of politics in the country, their tempo has been affected by the factor of leadership or personality, and this in turn has been conditioned by the international climate.

The nation-state of Uganda came into existence as a result of territorial surgery performed by European colonial powers in Eastern and Central Africa during the heyday of the new European* imperialism between 1890 and 1914. The delimitation of Ugandan territory by European colonial powers brought together an African population composed of about fifteen different ethnic groups with various socioeconomic and political characteristics. These ethnic groups can be categorized into four main language clusters: Bantu, Nilo-Sudanic, Lwo, and Atesot. In Uganda's contemporary history, both ethnic and linguistic factors have played a significant role in politics.

The relevance of *ethnicity and language to Ugandan politics is derived from economic and political policies pursued by successive administrations in the country since the beginning of the twentieth century. Preferential treatment of Buganda and Busoga by the British colonial administration allowed for the first formal political organizations on the national scene to emerge in that region of the country. After World War II, Africans began political agitation, first to demand their rights in the political process and then to challenge the pyramidal racial power structure in the country, creating a stir for a quasi-national approach to politics. In Buganda, the Bataka Party was formed in 1946 and the Uganda African Farmers' Union was inaugurated the following year; for the remainder of the 1940s these two organizations became the organs through which the African population articulated its grievances. After an insurrection by Africans in 1949, the British colonial government granted Africans in Buganda the right to elect their representatives to the Colonial National Legislative Council, on which hitherto only Europeans and Asians had sat. The action proved to be a watershed in Ugandan history and heralded populist politics against the colonial authorities in Buganda; in the decade of the 1950s, it spread to other parts of the country.

Postwar politics in Buganda—and later the rest of Uganda—grew out of an increasing awareness of the principles and practices of *democracy and African consciousness of race and class. The first mass political party, the Uganda National Congress (UNC), was founded in March 1952 during the liberal era of Governor Cohen and was a lineal descendant of the Bataka Party and the Uganda African Farmers Union. Although the UNC was initially a Buganda-based political party, its leadership identified itself with the broad aspirations of Africans across the country and it made concerted efforts to draw in representatives from the various parts of Uganda. As it expanded, its leadership became dominated by Protestants. This caused apprehension among Roman Catholics, and in 1956 they recast nationwide the Democratic Party (DP), which had been launched in Buganda in 1954 by Catholic Action to represent their interests. The formation of the DP to represent the interests of Roman Catholics reawakened the religious dimension in Uganda politics. The binding force of Catholicism was to enable the DP to win followers throughout the country.

Although the UNC was arguably the most broad-based nationalist party in the country, it was, after the formation of the DP, torn by internal division and personal bickering; this introduced the element of personality in Uganda politics. As a result of the internal disharmony within the UNC, a number of splinter parties emerged, one of which was the Uganda Peoples Union (UPU). In March 1960, the UPU and A. Milton Obote's faction of the UNC amalgamated to form the Uganda Peoples Congress (UPC), which adopted a a Pan-Africanist posture while at the same time exhibiting antipathy toward Buganda. In fact the two groups were bound together by common fear of postcolonial domination of the rest of the country by Buganda. The emergence of the UPC as an expression of anti-Kiganda nationalism has since then colored the perception of the UPC in Buganda and has injected the theme of center versus periphery into Ugandan politics, which has endured to the present time.

The general elections of March 1961, in which about 80 percent of the electorate in seventy-six rural and urban constituencies exercised their right of franchise, saw the participation of only 3 percent in the twenty-one rural constituencies of Buganda. The results of the election, favoring the Democratic Party (DP) over the UPC by forty-three seats to thirty-five, pointed to the emergence of an ideological alliance in the country along ethnoregional and religious lines. After the DP victory, the colonial government asked the leader of the DP, Benedicto Kiwanuka, to form the government and become the first African chief minister in the Legislative Council during the transitional period of self-government, while the leader of the UPC, A. Milton Obote, was recognized as leader of the opposition. The results also demonstrated that there were now only two dominant political parties in the country, and in the future they would be the locus of Ugandan politics. But because only a minuscule proportion of the population in Buganda participated in the elections, there was the distinct possibility that the Buganda Lukiiko could constitute a third force in Ugandan politics. That possibility became a reality when late in 1961 a political party representing the interests of the Buganda Lukiiko and opposed to the Catholic-based DP, the Kabaka Yekka (KY—"the King Alone"), was formed for the principal purpose of allying itself with the non-Kiganda but predominantly Protestant party, the UPC.

In the pre-independence election of April 1962, the UPC won 52.4 percent of the total vote and forty-three seats in the National Assembly, while the DP won 45.5 percent and twenty-four seats. The remaining twenty-four seats were claimed, in accordance with a provision in the constitution, by the Buganda Lukiiko for its political party, the KY, which then entered into an alliance with the UPC. Thus when Britain granted political independence to Uganda on 9 October 1962, it was the UPC-KY alliance which formed the first postcolonial government of the country. By the terms of the UPC-KY coalition, the leader of the UPC, Obote, became prime minister and thus the executive head of the government, while the *kabaka* became a non-executive president or the titular head of state.

The UPC and the KY were ill-matched partners, since on virtually every policy issue the two parties were opposed; but they were held together by their common resentment of the Catholic-dominated DP. The UPC-KY alliance poignantly demonstrated how religion can be manipulated to shift the balance of power in Ugandan politics. Within a year, strains in the UPC-KY relationship quickly developed, and the "unholy" alliance broke down irretrievably over a territorial dispute in 1964. The termination of the UPC-KY alliance after 1964 led to a bloody military confrontation between the *kabaka*'s forces and those of Obote in 1966 and the resultant demise of the Kiganda monarchy.

The end of the UPC-KY tactical political alliance both betrayed the inadequacy of religion as a cohesive factor in Ugandan politics and brought into greater prominence the divisions between center and periphery in the country. Equally significant, the absence of UPC strongholds in Buganda, where Kampala, the seat of government, is situated, compelled it to rely on the military as a mainstay of power. The use of the military by Obote to settle political differences between the UPC and the KY emboldened the army to intervene directly in politics. This was, among other things, a precondition of the *coup d'état of 25 January 1971, led by General Idi Amin Dada. The Amin regime was overthrown by a combined force of Ugandan rebels and Tanzanian troops, marking the first time that an African government has intervened to end tyranny in a neighboring state. Since the Obote coup of 1966, the equation of power has rested on the determination of the military. In July 1985, the military under General Tito Okello overthrew the second government of the UPC, and was in turn ousted on 25 January 1986 by another military organization, the National Resistance (NRA), led by Yoweri Kaguta Museveni.

The usurpation of power by Yoweri Museveni's NRA ushered in a new era of *militarism in Ugandan politics. At the same time, President Museveni has shown himself to be a man of political cunning, shrewdness, and clear military ability. Significantly, although in 1986 Museveni defeated the military junta of Tito Okello Lutwa, he still has neither won peace nor created the climate for political *pluralism in the country. In 1998, after having helped Laurent Kabila rise to power in Kinshasa, Uganda joined *Rwanda in a war of ag-gression in the Congo, presumably to stop incursions by Uganda rebels based outside the country, but in reality to plunder the Congo's natural wealth.

Although any leader must be held responsible both for his or her government's policies and for their impact, many of the actions of Ugandan leaders and politicians have been molded by the historical circumstances of the country. In brief, until the end of the twentieth century Ugandan history has been largely characterized by uneven socioeconomic development in different areas of the country, competition and conflicts along ethnic and regional lines, loyalties and divisions derived from religion, and political reliance on the military. In all likelihood this situation will continue, until democracy replaces Museveni's "no party" state.

(See also COLONIAL EMPIRES; CONGO, DEMOCRATIC REPUBLIC OF; GREAT LAKES REGION; MILITARY RULE; PAN-AFRICANISM.)

F. B. Wellbourn, *Religion and Politics in Uganda* (Nairobi, 1965). G. S. K. Ibingira, *The Forging of an African Nation: The Political and Constitutional Evolution of Uganda from Colonial Rule to Independence, 1894–1962* (New York, 1973). Nelson Kasfir, *The Shrinking Political Arena: Participation and Ethnicity in African Politics, with a Case Study of Uganda* (London, 1976). Mahmood Mamdani, *Politics and Class Formation in Uganda* (New York, 1976). Amii Omara-Otunnu, *Politics and the Military in Uganda, 1895–1985* (London, 1987). K. Rupesinghe, *Conflict Resolution in Uganda* (Oslo, 1989).

AMII OMARA-OTUNNU

UKRAINE. Ukraine became an independent state after its Supreme Rada (or Soviet, i.e., legislature) adopted a declaration of independence on 24 August 1991 which was subsequently ratified in a nationwide referendum on 1 December. Secession from the USSR was by no means unilateral, for *Russia played a crucial role in the course of events that culminated in the rise of an independent Ukraine, and the breakup of the Soviet Union as a whole, in peaceful fashion. The declaration of "sovereignty" by the parliament of the Russian Federation in June 1990 enabled its Ukrainian counterpart to do likewise in July 1990, and Boris *Yeltsin's official visit to Kiev in November 1990, during which the Russian leader recognized Ukraine as Russia's equal, was another major factor. The Soviet Union was formally dissolved on 8 December 1991 when the presidents of Ukraine and Russia, and the chairman of the Belarus parliament, abrogated the treaty of union that had been signed by their respective republics, and the Transcaucasus Federation, in December 1922. At the same time the three leaders announced the formation of the *Commonwealth of Independent States.

Like the other former *communist party states, Ukraine faced the challenge of transition to a new political system, a market economy, and a civil society. Its situation was further complicated, however by problems arising out of its particular historical experience and social and political circumstances that were not wholly part of its communist legacy.

In its first days independent Ukraine faced a potential challenge to its territorial integrity in its highly industrialized and Russian-speaking east. There an independent labor movement had emerged in the late 1980s, as it had elsewhere in the USSR; in the end, however, it did not fight for the preservation of a common Soviet state or for the region's transfer to Russia, but accepted a Ukrainian state drawn according to the borders of the former Ukrainian Soviet republic. The accident at the Chernobyl nuclear station (1986), the long-term impact of which was only gradually appreciated by the public, helped to stimulate a pro-independence mood above ethnic, linguistic, and religious divisions.

Crimea appeared to pose an even greater threat to Ukraine's territorial integrity. In the Russian-Ukrainian treaty of 1997, the Russian Federation formally recognized not only Ukrainian independence but also Ukraine's territorial integrity within its Soviet borders, that is, including Crimea and Donbas, where a majority of population was either Russian by ethnicity or spoke Russian rather than Ukrainian. Despite this formal recognition there were—and remain—many in Russia, including influential members of the political and cultural elites, who continue to uphold the traditional Russian nationalist view denying that Ukrainians are really a nation distinct from the Russians.

Ukraine in 1991 was a very different entity from that which in 1922 had joined Russia and others to form the Soviet Union. In 1991 it included areas that before 1939–1945 had belonged to Poland, Czechoslovakia, and Romania, and had been under the Austrian-Hungarian monarchy until 1919. They differed from those parts of Ukraine that had already been Soviet before 1939, and had earlier belonged to the Russian Empire.

It was especially in the western parts of Ukraine, and particularly in formerly Austrian and Polish Galicia—that is, the *oblasti* (provinces) of Lviv, Ternopil, and Ivano-Frankivs'k—that the Ukrainian national movement won mass popular support in the 1980s, during Gorbachev's *perestroika. There, an overwhelming majority had already voted for independence in the March 1991 referendum in which, all told, a majority of Ukrainian voters had favored the preservation of a reformed Soviet Union. When elements of the Communist establishment in Kiev took up the cause of independence, the anti-Communist national movement, members of which had first been elected to the Supreme Rada in 1990, did not challenge the new order: they accepted the victory of the ex-Communist Leonid Kravchuk as Ukraine's first president (1991), correctly viewing him and his comrades as the only force capable of upholding both Ukraine's independence and its territorial integrity. This "historic compromise" prevented the outbreak of a civil war that would have inevitably become a conflict between the western and eastern regions of the republic. The first constitution of independent Ukraine (adopted in 1996) was the concluding step in this process, just as the treaty with Russia in the following year laid the foundation for a stable relationship with Ukraine's most important neighbor and, after the Ukrainians, its largest ethnic group.

The results of the presidential and parliamentary elections in the years since independence clearly suggest that a process of gradual political integration, or the formation of a political or civic nation, has been under way in Ukraine. In November 1999, Leonid Kuchma won reelection as president with over fifty percent of votes in the far eastern Donetsk and over ninety percent in Lviv; in all previous Ukrainian elections, whether parliamentary or presidential, those doing well in the east suffered a crushing defeat in the west and winners in the west were sure losers in the east.

Ukraine's record in avoiding political conflicts and upheavals in the post-Communist transition compares favorably with most other formerly Soviet states. However, its record in such areas as economic reform, law enforcement, crime prevention, and the broad areas of health care or education is poor. The responsibility for these failures and Ukraine's avoidance of ethnic and social violence have common roots: the old nomenklatura which retained power as born-again Ukrainians, and most specifically the successive heads of the state, Kravchuk and Kuchma, the governments they appointed, and the parliament. Unlike Poland and Hungary, Ukraine did not have an elite capable of replacing the old cadres and at the same time capable of establishing its authority over the new state's entire territory. In a deeper sense, the present condition of Ukraine is a reflection of its underdeveloped civil society, the weakness of its political parties, and the underdevelopment and poverty of its news media and educational institutions. There is also the matter of the demographic and psychological exhaustion of its population: it has not properly recovered from the losses it suffered in the famines of 1932–1933 and 1946–1947 and in World War II, and these have been compounded by the environmental and health consequences of the Chernobyl catastrophe. Ukraine's death rates exceed those of births, and the emigration of the young further distorts the balance between age groups. Ukraine's proper recovery will take longer than one or two presidential or parliamentary terms: it is a task for a generation.

(See also CHERNOBYL NUCLEAR ACCIDENT; POST-COMMUNISM.)

Alexander Motyl and Bohdan Krawchenko, "Ukraine: From Empire to Nationhood," in Ian Bremmer and Ray Taras, eds., *New States, New Politics: Building the Post-Soviet Nations* (1997), pp. 235–275. Taras Kuzio, ed., *Contemporary Ukraine: Dynamics of Post-Soviet Transformation* (Armonk, N.Y., 1998). Roman Szporluk, *Russia, Ukraine, and The Breakup of the Soviet Union* (Stanford, Ca., 2000).

ROMAN SZPORLUK

UNCTAD. See UNITED NATIONS CONFERENCE ON TRADE AND DEVELOPMENT.

UNDERCLASS. The term *underclass* has been used to refer to the persistently poor, whose economic resources and behavioral patterns differentiate them from their fellow citizens. Although the term has primarily been used in the United States to refer to the poor in black and Hispanic urban ghettos, it has also been applied in European nations, where economic restructuring and immigration combined to produce concentrations of poverty during the 1980s.

The Swedish social scientist Gunnar Myrdal first drew attention to the term in 1962, when he warned that economic progress threatened to leave behind a sector of the population who were either unemployed or unemployable. Such people, he feared, would become increasingly marginal to the mainstream of modern society. By the late 1970s, high rates of unemployment, teen pregnancy, and increases in urban crime helped to popularize arguments about the emergence of an underclass within U.S. ghettos. The violence that accompanied the spread of drugs in the 1980s gave further credence to the notion of an American underclass.

The popular use of the term *underclass* sparked efforts to define this group more precisely. Most definitions identify four characteristics of underclass neighborhoods: high rates of school dropouts, female-headed households, welfare dependency, and irregular attachment to the labor market. Depending on how these indicators are defined, estimates of the size of the underclass in the United States have varied widely.

There is also little agreement about the causes of the existence of an underclass in the United States. Debate has centered around two contending explanations. The first argues that cultural and behavioral factors account for the existence of the underclass. In this view, the deviant behavior of the poor—including an unwillingness to work, stay in school, and postpone childbearing until marriage—creates an underclass. The second explanation highlights the role of social and economic structural forces in creating an underclass. The most prominent exponent of this perspective, William Julius Wilson, has argued that the shift from a manufacturing to a service-based economy created severe economic dislocations in the 1970s that disproportionately affected poor and minority urban communities. Combined with the gains of the *Civil Rights Movement, which allowed middle-class *African Americans to move out of inner-city ghettos, these economic forces stripped minority inner-city areas of the resources needed to sustain communities.

Despite disagreement about the causes of the existence of the underclass, the term has most often been used in public debate to signal behavioral, not economic, factors. This development has led some analysts to abandon the term altogether.

During the 1980s, rising poverty and concentrations of ethnic minorities in European cities raised concern about the growth of an underclass in some European nations. Arguments have been made most strongly in Britain, where economic decline and sharp cuts in social programs have created a new group of very poor citizens. In other nations, concentrations of poor ethnic minorities have been compared to the U.S. underclass. However, the distinctive history of race and the comparatively small *welfare state in the United States suggests that the sharp social isolation and persistent poverty characteristic of the U.S. underclass is less likely to develop in European nations.

(See also INTERNATIONAL MIGRATION.)

Christopher Jencks and Paul E. Peterson, eds., *The Urban Underclass* (Washington, D.C., 1991).

MARGARET WEIR

UNDERDEVELOPMENT. See DEVELOPMENT AND UNDERDEVELOPMENT.

UNION OF SOVIET SOCIALIST REPUBLICS. See SOVIET UNION.

UNIONS, LABOR. See LABOR MOVEMENT.

UNITED ARAB EMIRATES. See GULF STATES.

UNITED KINGDOM. See BRITAIN.

UNITED NATIONS. (See also page 859.) The United Nations (UN), born on 24 October 1945, has been the most important *international organization of the period since World War II, and the center of a wide-ranging network of international bodies. The UN emerged from the anti-Axis coalition of

World War II. On 1 January 1942, in the Washington Declaration, twenty-six Allied countries, which came to be called the United Nations, pledged to employ their full resources against Germany, Italy, and Japan. Thus World War II not only showed the need for an effective international organization to replace the unsuccessful *League of Nations (1919–1946) but also highlighted the possibilities of *international cooperation as a basis for resisting threats to the *peace. In its early years, the new body was often known as the United Nations Organization (UNO), in order to distinguish it from the wartime alliance out of which it had grown.

Charter and Structure. The formal basis for the UN's activities is the UN Charter. The product of careful consideration and intensive diplomacy on the part of the leading Allied powers in World War II (especially the United States, the United Kingdom, and the Soviet Union), the charter was finally adopted by the representatives of fifty states meeting at San Francisco on 26 June 1945, formally entering into force on 24 October of the same year. The charter reflected the view that an *international system, if it is to be stable, has to take account of the demands not just of international *security narrowly conceived but also of justice and *human rights. The 111 articles of the UN Charter established not only the purposes and principles of the organization but also its structures, tasks, finances, and procedures.

Membership was confined to states (as distinct from nongovernmental or international entities). Thus, although the charter begins with the ringing words "We the peoples of the United Nations," the UN has always had the character of being an association of governments of sovereign states. In accord with article 7 of the charter, there are six "principal organs" of the UN: the General Assembly, the *Security Council, the Economic and Social Council, the Trusteeship Council, the *International Court of Justice, and the Secretariat.

The General Assembly, established under chapter IV of the charter, is the plenary body, controlling much of the UN's work. Meeting in regular session for the last quarter of every year, it approves the budget, adopts priorities, call international conferences, oversees the work of numerous subsidiary bodies, and adopts resolutions on a wide range of issues.

The Security Council, established under chapter V of the charter, has "primary responsibility for the maintenance of international peace and security." It was originally specified as having eleven members: the "big five" permanent members (China, France, the United Kingdom, the United States, and the Soviet Union) plus six others to be elected for two-year terms by the General Assembly. In 1965, following the growth in UN membership, the council was enlarged to fifteen members, ten of whom are elected, its decisions requiring an affirmative vote of nine members. In 1992 Russia succeeded to the USSR's permanent seat. Each of the "big five" has a power of veto. It meets frequently throughout the year, and is empowered to take decisions binding on all UN members. Under the charter's crucial chapter VII (articles 39–51) it has extensive powers to take "action with respect to threats to the peace, breaches of the peace, and acts of aggression."

The Economic and Social Council (ECOSOC), established under chapter X of the charter, supervises the work of numerous commissions, committees, and expert bodies in the economic and social fields, including the Commission on Human Rights, and seeks to coordinate the activities of UN specialized agencies in these areas. Originally consisting of eighteen members elected for three-year terms by the General Assembly, it was progressively enlarged, in 1965 and 1973, to its present size of fifty-four.

The Trusteeship Council, set up under chapter XIII of the charter, superintended the transition to self-government of trust territories. In 1994, with the final ending of the Trust Territory of the Pacific Islands, it was able to suspend its operation. Because most cases of *decolonization did not involve trust territories, the UN was involved, if at all, through different bodies, such as the Special Committee on Decolonization, set up by the General Assembly in 1961.

The International Court of Justice (ICJ) in The Hague was constituted by the Statute of the ICJ, adopted at San Francisco on 26 June 1945 at the same time as the UN Charter. All UN member states are also parties to the statute. The ICJ, recognized by chapter XIV of the charter as "the principal judicial organ of the United Nations," actually came into existence in 1946, as successor to the Permanent Court of International Justice (1922–1946). It consists of fifteen judges, elected by the General Assembly and the Security Council for nine-year terms. It considers cases brought to it by states, and it also gives advisory opinions on legal questions put to it by the UN General Assembly, the Security Council, and other UN bodies. By June 2000 it had dealt with seventy contentious cases between states, and also delivered twenty-four advisory opinions.

The Secretariat, established by chapter XV of the charter, was intended to consist of "international officials responsible only to the Organization." Having grown to over 12,000 in the mid-1980s, by 1998 it comprised some 9,000 people at UN headquarters in New York and at other offices, the largest of which is Geneva. It is headed by the secretary-general. The holders of this post have been Trygve Lie (Norway, 1946–1953), Dag Hammarskjöld (Sweden, 1953–1961), U Thant (Burma, 1961–1971), Kurt Waldheim (Austria, 1972–1981), Javier Pérez Cuéllar (Peru, 1982–1991), Boutros Boutros-Ghali (Egypt, 1992–1996), and Kofi *Annan (Ghana, 1997–).

The "UN system" comprises not only the six principal organs of the UN outlined above but also the numerous subsidiary bodies and specialized agencies that operate under the UN's auspices. There are sixteen specialized agencies, each with its own constitution, membership, and budget. Apart from the main financial agencies (the *International Monetary Fund (IMF) and the *World Bank), the "big four" are the *International Labor Organization (ILO) in Geneva, the Food and Agriculture Organization (FAO) in Rome, the UN Educational, Scientific and Cultural Organization (UNESCO) in Paris, and the *World Health Organization (WHO) in Geneva. Other intergovernmental organizations associated with the UN include the International Atomic Energy Agency (IAEA) and the *World Trade Organization (WTO).

The number of member states of the UN, fifty-one at the beginning, increased dramatically in its first four decades, due mainly to the effects of successive waves of decolonization, and also the disintegration of some states. In 1999 membership reached 188. No member state has ever been expelled from the UN; nor has any left. However, in 1965–1966 Indonesia temporarily withdrew, from 1949 to 1971 China was represented only by the Nationalist government in Taiwan,

and since 1992 certain rights of Yugoslavia have been suspended.

Role and Influence. The actual role and influence of the UN have differed significantly from what was foreseen in 1945. In particular, peacekeeping and observer forces, not mentioned in the charter, have been an important aspect of UN action in numerous conflicts and crises; various issues not addressed in the charter, such as environmental management, have become more central to the work of the organization; and the secretary-general's functions have grown, especially the use of the position's "good offices" to mediate between members.

For much of the UN's first forty-five years of existence, East-West hostility prevented the Security Council from taking action on certain major issues: by the end of 1989, the Soviet Union had vetoed 114 resolutions, the United States 67, the United Kingdom 30, France 18, and China 3. The majority (103) of the Soviet vetoes were in the years before 1966; all the U.S. vetoes occurred after that, reflecting a growing U.S. perception of the organization as being dominated by hostile groupings of Third World and communist states. In the post–Cold War years 1990–99, only nine vetoes were cast: United States 5, Russia 2, and China 2.

In 1950 the UN did support decisive action, over Korea. At that time the Soviet Union had unwisely absented itself from the Security Council (in protest against China's being represented by the Nationalist delegate), so it could not use the veto. On 25 June 1950, the Security Council condemned the armed attack by the Democratic People's Republic of Korea (North Korea) on the Republic of Korea (South Korea). Two days later, Security Council Resolution (SC Res.) 83 recommended that UN members "furnish such assistance to the Republic of Korea as may be necessary to repel the armed attack." Then on 7 July 1950 SC Res. 84 approved a unified command in Korea under the United States, authorizing it to use the UN flag. When the Soviet Union resumed its place in the Security Council, the Western powers secured the passage of the "Uniting for Peace" resolution through the General Assembly, which enabled the General Assembly to act in cases where the Security Council was hamstrung by the veto.

The "Uniting for Peace" procedure was used again in 1956—against two of its original sponsors, Britain and France, after they had vetoed any Security Council action over their attack on Egypt. The General Assembly called for an immediate cease-fire and the withdrawal of forces from the Suez Canal. Britain, followed by France, acquiesced, partly owing to U.S. pressure. Another General Assembly resolution at that time called for a withdrawal of Soviet forces from Hungary: this was ignored.

The Middle East crisis of 1956 gave rise to a major innovation in UN practice: peacekeeping, or the use of multinational forces under UN command to help control and resolve conflict between hostile states or between hostile communities within a state. Since 1948 there had been a small UN Truce Supervision Organization (UNTSO) in the Middle East. This was complemented in November 1956 by the dispatch of a UN Emergency Force (UNEF-I) to the Suez Canal area, Sinai, and Gaza, by agreement with the Egyptian government. Some 6,000 soldiers drawn from many countries helped keep a precarious peace between Israel and Egypt; their withdrawal at Egypt's request in 1967 was part of the process that led to the outbreak of the June 1967 war.

In the years since 1956, peacekeeping forces have become one of the UN's most common means of assisting cease-fire and peace efforts. In 1958–1978 they were deployed mainly in the post-colonial world, including in Lebanon, Congo, West Irian, Yemen, Cyprus, Sinai, and the Golan Heights. With the gradual ending of the Cold War, and the increased possibilities of cooperation in the UN Security Council, there was an expansion of peacekeeping: in 1988 to 1999, forty new operations were established—three times as many as in the whole of the UN's previous history. Some of the new operations involved innovative efforts not merely to freeze conflicts, but also to resolve them—for example (as in Namibia and Cambodia), through assisting elections and the reconstruction of civil society. The most severe difficulties arose when peacekeepers were deployed to countries with fragile or nonexistent cease-fires. In the former Yugoslavia, the UN Protection Force (UNPROFOR, 1992–1995), the largest UN peacekeeping operation ever, became a symbol of failure: despite an important role in the delivery of humanitarian aid in the midst of the war in Bosnia-Herzegovina, it was effective neither in maintaining cease-fires nor in protecting the inhabitants of the six UN-proclaimed "safe areas." In this and other cases (including Somalia, Rwanda, and Haiti) the presence of peacekeepers alone was unable to achieve the desired results, and had to be followed by UN-authorized enforcement operations under the control of a single country or alliance. There was also a tendency for UN peacekeeping forces to be given greater authority to use force than before, but this was not always matched by appropriate resources and force structures.

One method of pressure provided for in the UN Charter (article 41) is mandatory economic *sanctions. The Security Council has applied sanctions of various kinds—whether general (covering virtually all trade and financial transactions) or more limited (taking the form, for example, of arms and/or air traffic embargoes)—in many cases, including: Rhodesia (1966–1979); South Africa (1977–1994); Iraq (1990–); former Yugoslavia (1991–1996); Serbia and Montenegro (1992–1996 and 1998–); Somalia (1992–); Libya (1992–1999); (Liberia 1992–); Khmer Rouge–held areas of Cambodia (1992–); Haiti (1993–1994); UNITA rebel movement in Angola (1993–); Rwanda (1994–); Sudan (1996–); Sierra Leone (1997–); Taliban authorities in Afghanistan (1999–); and Ethiopia and Eritrea (2000–).

In the many conflicts and crises of the post-1945 era the UN's record has been mixed. In some, especially those involving Security Council members on both sides, the UN could achieve little. This was true of the wars in Vietnam between 1946 and 1975, of the 1979 Sino-Vietnamese war, and of the long armed confrontation in Europe between the *North Atlantic Treaty Organization and the *Warsaw Treaty Organization (Warsaw Pact) states. On the other hand, in many cases the UN did enunciate important principles, as for example in SC Res. 242 of 22 November 1967, on the Arab-Israel problem; and SC Res. 502 of 3 April 1982, on the Argentine invasion of the Malvinas/Falkland Islands. Through mediation and good offices the UN contributed to the 1988

cease-fire ending the *Iran-Iraq war, and to the 1989 Soviet withdrawal from Afghanistan.

With the changes in the Soviet Union in the late 1980s, the collapse of communist rule in central and eastern Europe in 1989, and the ending of the Cold War, new possibilities of cooperation within a UN framework began to emerge. After Iraq's invasion of Kuwait on 2 August 1990, the Security Council not only imposed on Iraq extensive economic sanctions, but also authorized the use of "all necessary means" if Iraq did not quit Kuwait. In subsequent military action in January and February 1991, a coalition of countries led by the United States forced Iraq to withdraw. The Security Council then imposed tough peace terms on Iraq, including measures of nuclear and chemical disarmament. The implementation of these terms, requiring detailed verification on a long-term basis, posed many problems. The Iraq-Kuwait episode was exceptional in many ways, especially because it originated in an unusually blatant act of aggression. Yet it reinforced hopes that the UN might become much more active and interventionist in the post–Cold War era. This proved to be the case, with the UN in the 1990s becoming deeply involved in addressing civil wars, in most cases with limited results. The Security Council broke new ground by establishing criminal tribunals for the former Yugoslavia (1993) and Rwanda (1994). However, on many key issues, including Kosovo in March 1999, the Security Council was not able to agree on the military means to be used to achieve its declared goals. Even if the high hopes of the UN becoming the main center for managing international security were disappointed, it did assist in a wide range of practical tasks, from removing mines to election monitoring.

Apart from action in particular crises, the UN—through General Assembly resolutions, conferences, specialized agencies, and subsidiary bodies—has been involved in a wide range of other activities. It has assisted the development of various international agreements on human rights, and established monitoring machinery; it has played a key part in the development of *international law and legal institutions; it has become increasingly associated with the causes of *arms control and *disarmament, and has been instrumental in securing and reviewing the operation of some multilateral agreements in this field, including the 1968 Treaty on the Non-Proliferation of Nuclear Weapons; and it has provided an important venue for discussion of trade, aid, economic development, the environment, and the role of women.

The UN has been criticized from several different directions. In its early years it was seen by the Soviet Union as an instrument of Western hegemony. Later, the General Assembly, often dismissed as a talking shop, came to be viewed in the United States as hostile and as promoting conflict rather than resolving it—at least on certain issues. The growth of UN bureaucracy in the 1970s led to strong attacks on waste and inefficiency. As a protest against particular activities and practices, both the Soviet Union and the United States have at times been among the many states withholding assessed contributions to the UN budget. By 1998, the United States owed the United Nations over $1.6 billion in unpaid assessments. The total of almost $3.0 billion owed by all debtor

(cont. on p. 874)

UNITED NATIONS. The United Nations has a vital role in world affairs. For more than fifty years the UN has helped manage relations between states and regulate a broad range of human activity. It has worked to protect the security of people and promote peace and sustainable development. During the past five decades, the organization has been confronted with countless international crises and numerous challenges to its authority and relevance. Over the next half century, new and increasingly insidious threats to human security will test the UN's principles and resources.

Despite a less than perfect record over its first half century, the UN has served an irreplaceable function. How many more lives would have been lost to conflict, disease, and starvation if there was no United Nations? And can we say that we would have avoided a third world war without it?

The challenges ahead should motivate us to make the institution a stronger and truer reflection of its founding values and principles, and to better equip the organization with the tools necessary to deal effectively with existing and emerging threats to international *peace and *security.

*Globalization will not make this task any easier. An effective multilateral system must be put in place to deal with globalization's rapid change, as well as its negative consequences. Gross violations of *human rights, environmental degradation, *terrorism, transnational organized crime, infectious disease, and the *drug trade are all issues that require strong, effective, and multilateral solutions. No longer can the nation-state, not even the most powerful, go it alone. *International cooperation is essential to deal with these threats. A robust United Nations should occupy a central position in that system, for it has great potential to address the complex problems of today's world. Translating that potential into reality, however, means that the deficiencies of the UN system must be remedied.

The United Nations must have as its first order of business protecting the *rights and security of people. The UN must, as Secretary-General *Annan has said, "put people at the center of everything we do." Doing so is not a luxury; it is elemental to the organization's mandate. The realities of the modern era demand such a focus and the UN Charter permits it.

The UN *Security Council has at times failed to respond to serious crises, resulting in the lessening of its own authority and a reduced respect for the United Nations as a whole. These failures have been due in large part to the narrow definition the Security Council has afforded the concept of security. Without adopting a more encompassing definition of security that places individual rights on par with those of states, the Council will be unable to deal effectively with many modern threats to international peace and security. Canada has attempted to broaden that definition to encompass threats to human security. Placing the protection of civilians squarely on the Council's agenda was a major step in that direction.

The Secretary-General's Report on the Protection of Civilians in Armed Conflict, issued in 1999, was inspired by the tragic reality that civilians are no longer innocent casualties of war but often the deliberate targets of belligerents, who terrorize the defenseless rather than attempt peace. This landmark report is a useful primer for the direction the UN needs to go and the actions Member States must be willing to undertake in the decades to come.

The forty recommendations contained in the report outline the key measures that the Security Council, the United Nations more broadly, and the international community should take to increase both the legal and the physical protection of civilians. The report implicitly recognizes that while legal protections form the basis of people's security, they mean nothing without the potent ability to back them up. By making sure the capacity to provide for people's physical protection exists, the UN's Member States will make for a stronger, more adaptable, more effectual United Nations. More important still, they will help save lives.

One of the most important recommendations in the report is aimed at increasing the capacity of the UN to protect individuals' physical security. Giving the organization the ability to deploy rapidly by increasing the numbers of civilian police and administrators, as well as creating rapidly deployable military and police units along with a mobile mission headquarters, will improve response time to humanitarian and other crises where people's lives are in jeopardy.

Four other recommendations would help prevent imminent conflicts from erupting. Imposing arms embargoes on parties to conflict is one way of reducing the ability of combatants to wage war. Deploying preventive peacekeeping operations would keep opposing factions apart while attempts at finding a political solution are underway. Greater use of targeted *sanctions would help deter leaders of warring factions from pursuing ill-gotten gains through violence. And deploying international observers to monitor the security of internally displaced persons or refugees would help to prevent the terrorizing or recruitment of civilians by combatants in camps.

The final three major recommendations are designed to

help alleviate the suffering of individuals once conflict has broken out. The Security Council must insure that civilians have unimpeded access to humanitarian assistance and it should provide for the security and protection of humanitarian workers. It should also ensure that peacekeeping and peace enforcement operations have the right and ability to close down hate media, which can ferment antagonisms and heighten fears. And when all else fails and widespread and systematic abuses are ongoing, the Council should take robust enforcement action to end the suffering of defenseless civilians.

Intervening militarily in times of humanitarian necessity requires a major commitment of physical resources and political will. In order to muster such dedication, a serious discussion of the importance, implications, and form of intervention to end human suffering must take place. Secretary-General Annan called for such a dialogue in his groundbreaking speech opening the 54th General Assembly. Unfortunately, the international community's response has been muted. Despite the recriminations and apologies for inaction during the first years of the *Bosnian war and the entire *Rwandan genocide, the appetite of many states for taking or sponsoring action remains weak. Without a commitment by states to developing acceptable and consistent criteria, enforcement action to protect civilians will remain piecemeal, uneven, and unrefined, and may in the end pose a threat to human security as intervention is used by some states as a tool to advance a self-interested political agenda.

Even if the will is present, and a systematic approach to enforcement action has been established, effective action will depend on a strong early warning function. Too often, simmering tensions go undetected, so that devastating crises erupt, seemingly from out of nowhere. Governments must provide the UN with adequate financial and personnel resources to make sure that an effective early warning capacity exists. For its part, the UN must improve its coordination with civil society and *non-governmental organizations (NGOs), which often serve an invaluable early detection role on the ground.

While working with these new international actors, the UN should maintain its leadership role. A well-functioning and well-equipped UN should be the standard bearer—working with governments, *civil society, and NGOs to pursue a comprehensive people-centered agenda. These new international actors obviously cannot substitute for an effective UN when it comes to enforcing international peace and security.

The reticence of the Council to authorize the deployment of major operations in recent years and the increased reliance on coalitions of the willing and on regional organizations to provide peacekeeping forces is a disturbing trend. Increased dependence on regional or subregional groups for both peacekeeping and other security roles has produced uneven results and continues to represent a retreat of the UN from its mandate. Linked to this trend is the reliance on trust funds (voluntary contributions) to pay for UN peacekeeping operations. This represents a disturbing and unwelcome departure from the established practice of burden-sharing among the full membership.

Far more fundamental to the future relevance of the Organization are the threats people face on a daily basis. At the beginning of the third millennium the world's people continue to be confronted with many of the same challenges they did at the beginning of the last. Poverty, freedom from violence, access to clean water and a sure supply of food, adequate shelter, disease, a good job, and an education remain the preoccupations of the vast majority of people. These ever-present concerns are, however, compounded by new realities such as environmental degradation, rampant population growth, the scourge of small arms and light weapons, intrastate conflict, unequal access to trade, overwhelming debt burdens, and perhaps the issue that has the greatest potential to entrench inequality in the new century, the digital divide. These are the challenges that a vital and robust United Nations system must meet if it is to fulfill its promise in the new century.

Enhancing the capacity of the United Nations does not only mean adapting to new issues and technologies, it also means finding a new way of structuring the Organization to increase its effectiveness and make it more accountable.

One of the major obstacles to the United Nations asserting its proper leadership role in responding to threats to international peace and security is the disunity among Security Council members, especially the "Permanent Five" (P-5). Political and policy differences, among the P-5, combined with the use or, more frequently, the threat of use of the veto create serious barriers to action. Limiting the use of the veto to issues concerning threats to and breaches of the peace, as well as acts of aggression (Article VII of the UN Charter), would enhance the long-term effectiveness of the Council and would better respect the original intentions of the drafters of the Charter.

Central to any discussion of United Nations reform is the

question of an expanded Security Council membership. Increasing the Council's numbers has proven to be difficult and controversial. Despite this, the exercise remains a valid and important one. The addition of six to ten elected, nonpermanent seats to the Council would make it more representative, and help reinforce its credibility and authority. The addition of any permanent, nonelected members to the Council would be a step backward, and mean that the Council, at a time when democratic accountability is in ascendance, would become far less so.

One positive development on this front in recent years has been the greater openness and transparency of the Security Council. There is now an increasing trend toward holding open meetings, which allows interested nonmembers of the Council to attend formal deliberations, and opens informal consultations to non-Council members in cases where their input could have a positive effect on conflict prevention and resolution.

While the Security Council is often the focus of discussions on the effectiveness of the UN, the General Assembly, UN programmers and funds, and specialized agencies merit comment as well. The General Assembly is often maligned for being plodding and for its political theatrics. Its large membership, its chronically congested agenda, some of its working methods, and different priorities among delegations conspire to make the forum unwieldy at times and painstakingly slow in reaching consensus.

In spite of the General Assembly's shortcomings, it has a vital role to play in the United Nations system because of its universal membership and the fact that its mandate allows it to consider any matter within the broad scope of the UN Charter. The General Assembly is a forum which, if used right, can build consensus on important issues and sustain momentum in support of multilateral initiatives. As examples, General Assembly resolutions have provided important political support to human security initiatives such as the Landmines Convention and the International Criminal Court.

The United Nations funds and programs remain the Organization's most visible elements. The Children's Fund (UNICEF), the High Commissioner for Refugees (UNHCR), and the Development Programme (UNDP) are all widely known and respected institutions. The world-wide network of these organs must be preserved and in certain cases strengthened, given the valuable role each plays in the protection of people's dignity, safety, and person in situations of extreme insecurity.

The UN's Specialized Agencies also have an important function. The impact of new technologies and globalization has revitalised the work of many of these agencies given the transnational and cross-disciplinary nature of the global forces. The agencies must, however, remain independent of political influence. As technical bodies which have the mandate to create global health, safety, and regulatory systems, they must remain the domain of experts, not diplomats. Introducing sensitive political elements could detract from their ability to carry out purely technical work.

A more responsive United Nations should also be more representative. The United Nations should, therefore, continue to strengthen its ties with civil society and NGOs, giving them the opportunity to make their valuable contributions to the Organization. These groups are able to push agendas which have been impossible to advance within the UN for various political reasons. The Landmines Treaty and the International Criminal Court were both initiatives pursued outside of the UN by a unique and powerful coalition of likeminded governments, individual departments of the UN Secretariat, civil society, and the NGO community. The Ottawa Convention on landmines and the Statute of Rome of the ICC were legitimized by these non-traditional alliances and then able to be brought into the UN system.

A role for parliamentarians within the United Nations would also prove useful. Engaging with representatives of government and not just government officials would help promote support for the United Nations among those who appropriate funds and decide on policy, not just those who enact it. None of the modern threats to human security can be dealt with effectively without including these nontraditional actors at the United Nations.

The most important factor in the future success of the UN system remains the political will of the membership to work together to advance the common good of humanity. Intrinsically linked to this factor is the willingness of member states to provide the resources necessary for the UN to fulfil its role, including the timely payment of assessed contributions. Supporters of a strong and effective United Nations will have to be energetic advocates if the organization is to fulfil its promise as a vital and effective institution in the new century.

(See also ENVIRONMENTALISM; HUMANITARIAN INTERVENTION.)

LLOYD AXWORTHY

UNITED NATIONS. The United Nations is a deeply flawed institution that has, nonetheless, served foreign policy interests from time to time. Expectations at the organization's creation in 1945 were exaggerated, and expectations about its rebirth in the early 1990s were similarly overblown. What to do with the organization's accumulated baggage, what its future role should be, and how the United States should relate to it are all subjects of intense debate, unlikely to be resolved in the near future. There may in fact simply be no "solutions" to the UN's current problems. It may be that the inherent internal contradictions in the UN Charter make it impossible for the UN to function any more effectively than it now does, and, at the same time, that the prevailing international political environment makes it equally impossible to "fix" its structure to make it more effective. Thus, the most likely future role for the UN will be an approximate continuation of its muddled, incoherent, and marginally important present status.

Some UN supporters long for it to have a much larger role, one that truly constrains the international exercise of the sovereign powers of nation-states, and which selectively intervenes in the internal affairs of governments to achieve objectives they deem desirable. These advocates proclaim the impending demise of sovereignty (or at least the radical diminution of its importance in world affairs), and yearn for the United Nations to become Tennyson's "Parliament of man." What some really want, of course, is to muzzle the United States, a "*hyperpuissance*," a world hegemon, a dangerous adherent to its own national values and institutions rather than a willing participant in the flowering of "global governance." Hence, in a very real and urgent sense, the current international debate over the role and effectiveness of the United Nations is a surrogate for a larger and even more important debate about the structure of the world's politics and *"international law" over the next several centuries. This, in turn, for many Americans, raises questions and apprehensions about the democratic legitimacy of such developments.

Opinion within the United States on this subject is hardly one-dimensional. Indeed, many observers outside of the United States are mystified at the intensity of the domestic American debate, puzzled why it apparently occurs in only one major power. There are two reasons. First, the United States is differentiated from other nations by its generic distrust for governmental structures of all kinds, from the local to the international, and by its commitment to its own constitutional system of *separation of powers, unique in the contemporary world. Accordingly, any international institution that purports to assert governmental power, even indirectly, and certainly one that embodies no indicia of democratic accountability, is automatically (and properly) viewed as suspect. Second, America's frequently mentioned status as a superpower makes it acutely aware of any potential infringement on its unilateral ability to decide its own foreign policy. Neither of these broad considerations is likely to change substantially in the foreseeable future. In fact, it is precisely because of America's unique position in the world that the results of its debate matter, whether others understand it, participate in it, or even approve of it.

The very history of the United Nations itself, moreover, demonstrates why American skepticism is well grounded. Until the successful resolution of the *Cold War, the UN, and the *Security Council in particular, was gridlocked, and unable to perform any significant international function in a sustained fashion. More to the point, in the twentieth century's third world war, the struggle between Communism and the forces of freedom, the United Nations was at best essentially irrelevant, and at worst a harmful forum for the Communists and other anti-Western forces to attack American values and interests. This history cannot now be conveniently ignored by the UN's champions, much though they wish to, arguing that the end of the Cold War has liberated the organization as if it were 1945 all over again. It is this history that precisely and unambiguously demonstrates that the UN is a forum for the conflict of national interest, not a place of worship for what some believe are humanity's "higher ideals."

In fact, it is shocking to many of the UN's most ardent admirers that national interest analysis is even mentioned in connection with the organization. These are likely to be people deeply offended by both halves of the first sentence of this essay. They expect, tacitly at least, that in the hallowed chambers of the Security Council and the General Assembly, parochial national interests will be laid aside, and the member states will search selflessly for the common good. Stated somewhat less piously, these advocates expect that the member states, great and small, should temper their pursuit of national interests, and that conduct which may be commonplace outside of the United Nations context should not be acceptable within it. Hence, as a corollary, the greater the range of subject matters—military, political, economic, and social—that can be drawn into the UN's purview, the greater the circumscription of "narrow" national interests that can be obtained.

This is, of course, why the calling of "higher morality," especially in the context of the United Nations, is so troubling. Calculations of competing and often adverse national interests are at least grounded both in empirically verifiable realities and in the cold-blooded risk-return tradeoff. Mistakes, often tragic and costly, can and frequently have been made in this calculus over the years, but it does have the benefit of making opposing parties' actions somewhat more comprehensible and predictable. This is the lesson of national strength and mutual nuclear deterrence during the Cold War, an unpleasant but ultimately effective form of contest that eventually led to the collapse of Communism and the Soviet bloc without nuclear warfare. By contrast, morality and high-mindedness are uniquely personal and idiosyncratic, frequently perceived as arbitrary or even hypocritical by others, and often dangerously confusing. These are all observations that apply with great force to the UN, and they demonstrate why, in all likelihood, the UN's role will be minimal well into the foreseeable future.

In fact, this observation should lead logically to the question: what exactly is the United Nations? In practical terms, it is simply an agglomeration of member states, served (at least in theory) by a staff that has no power or autonomy— and no independent democratic or other political legitimacy— to act except as directed by the member governments. Thus understood, there really is no "United Nations"; there is no "there" there, only the shifting reflections of the several views of the members. The UN has no more legitimacy or permanence than those members, and especially the largest, most important members, choose to give it. In particular, the secretary-general is, according to Article 97 of the Charter, simply "the chief administrative officer of the Organization," and he has no independent political mandate or authority. Needless to say, the subordinate Secretariat staff has no independent legitimacy either.

In years past, efforts to claim legitimacy, especially for the often irrelevant and frequently mischievous resolutions of the General Assembly, have rested on the slogan of "one nation, one vote." Loosely derived from the concept of "sovereign equality," this slogan has functioned as an analogy to the legitimate democratic principle of "one person, one vote." But the analogy fails badly for several reasons, not the least of which is its palpable divorce from international reality, and the real relations of power and influence that govern outside of United Nations meetings. UN voting under the "one nation, one vote" system puts the United States at an enormous disadvantage. It did so during the Cold War when the Communist bloc and the *Nonaligned Movement routinely outvoted the United States on issue after issue. Even after Communism's demise (and the consequent irrelevance of "nonalignment"), these voting patterns continued. Thus, for most attentive Americans, and for those international observ-

ers not already part of the UN's priestly class, the General Assembly and similar governing bodies throughout the UN system have been backwaters for virtually all of the organization's existence.

International reality has been at least partially reflected in the Security Council, through Charter mechanisms such as the five permanent members and their veto power. Precisely for this reason, both the identities of the permanent members and their vetoes have been under constant attack from the outset. Even today, suggestions for changing the composition of the permanent membership, the overall size of the council, and eliminating or substantially modifying the veto abound, filling endless hours of conferences and the pages of journals devoted to international topics. The result so far has been another version of UN gridlock, as the various proposals for reform cancel one another out, and the status quo on the Council persists. This ongoing, internal UN political story is, of course, further proof that most nations in addition to the United States still wearyingly pursue their own national interests, rather than accepting the admonitions of UN worshipers to cast aside such worldly accoutrements.

The unwillingness or inability to face the blunt reality that the UN can never be more than what the member states want it to be has led in recent years to a fascination with the role of *non-governmental organizations. The NGOs (which in many countries are in fact often financed, directly or indirectly, from government sources) form an ephemeral universe known as *"civil society," which increasingly asserts its equivalence to member governments at least as a source of "moral" authority, as it creeps toward assuming a decision-making role as well. Although the NGOs proclaim that they are "broadening" participation in the United Nations, they represent collectively nothing more than a gathering of *interest groups, lobbying and pressuring for their own agendas. While such activity is both undeniably legitimate and desirable in national contexts, its penetration into the UN system has had profoundly undemocratic consequences, by giving some, but not all, interest groups a "second bite" at international decision-making. By participating first in their national debates, and then participating again in UN and other multilateral fora (where they represent no one but themselves) as actors with influence already exceeding that of many small governments, the NGOs are affecting substantive outcomes, as they themselves openly boast. To the unfortunate extent that their involvement in decision-making continues, they represent an unwelcome recreation of the concept of "corporatist" representation found in pre–World War II Italy, rather than a truly democratic innovation.

In practical terms, this analysis of the United Nations reveals several important lessons for the future of the organization. While written from an American perspective, these precepts apply at least by analogy to the likely conduct of the other permanent members of the Security Council, and to some of the other major UN member-states (such as Japan and India) that do not currently have that status. The fundamental U.S. interests within the UN system can be described in three ways: (1) preserving America's ability to make critical policy decisions within the democratically accountable structures of the Constitution; (2) preserving and enhancing its political, military, and economic national interests, especially the integrity of our constitutional system; and (3) maintaining an appropriate American leadership role, while safeguarding against unfair financial and other burdens. These principles to lead to the following priorities for the United States:

1. The United Nations is a potentially useful tool of U.S. foreign policy, but not the preferred (or only) tool. The UN can sometimes play a helpful role in advancing American interests, as in the *Gulf War. Although it does not follow that the Security Council should always, or even frequently, be invoked, this conclusion is now under frontal assault. In May 1999, during the Kosovo conflict, Secretary-General Kofi *Annan insisted that "unless the Security Council is restored to its pre-eminent position as the sole source of legitimacy on the use of force, we are on a dangerous path to anarchy." In his annual report a few months later, he said that military actions undertaken without council authorization constitute threats to the "very core of the international security system." Both of these statements are flatly incorrect, unsupported either by the language and history of the UN Charter, or by fifty-five years of the Charter's operation. There will almost certainly be other conflicts where the United States will decide to act without first obtaining "approval" by the council. Accordingly, the stage is now set to decide whether the secretary-general prevails, or whether the United States maintains the capability for independent—and, where necessary, unilateral—military action.

2. Only the United States can lead the United Nations effectively. As described above, the UN neither has, nor should it have, the capability for independent action. It follows that when we entrust it with responsibility for an important undertaking, the United States must understand that it alone can lead the effort to a successful conclusion. The most important example of this point is undoubtedly the fate of the UN Special Commission ("UNSCOM") to eliminate Iraq's weapons of mass destruction. When the United States provided clear leadership, UNSCOM achieved significant progress. While far from perfect, UNSCOM stood nearly unequaled as an ex-

ample of international arms control. When, however, the Clinton administration ceded de facto leadership of UNSCOM to the secretary-general, its effectiveness collapsed. Thus, if the United States is not prepared to provide sustained leadership for those ventures given to the UN, it simply cannot count on them being implemented effectively.

3. UN governance structures must change to reflect the real burdens of membership. Most UN agencies allocate their financial requirements through member "assessments," or percentages of their budgets that members are "required" to remit. The United States' share (derived under a complex and antiquated formula) is typically 25 percent (over 30 percent for peacekeeping), the largest of any member. The predictable temptation to increase agency budgets has, therefore, over the years, proven irresistible, so that UN financial decision-making is now broken almost beyond repair. The solution is either to change the "one nation, one vote" approach on financial matters, or to replace assessments with voluntary contributions. Voluntary contributions are currently used in several UN programs, and have the distinct advantage of allowing members to pay only for what they want. If UN financing does not change, dissatisfaction will persist, ultimately calling into question the utility of Sisyphean efforts at UN "reform."

4. The United Nations or other international organizations should not assume "governmental" authority. There have been considerable efforts recently to create new multilateral structures to constrain nation-states, such as the Kyoto Protocol on climate change and the Statute of Rome, creating an International Criminal Court. Several of these agreements required signatories to make changes of constitutional dimensions, and many have done so willingly. The United States has quite properly not participated in this exercise because the trend toward integration has lessened democratic accountability and weakened national constitutional protections. Where elitist politics prevail, even in democracies, this pattern may be acceptable, but it is not acceptable to Americans.

These suggestions will undoubtedly be distasteful to many, but they in fact represent a broad consensus within the American body politic, as widely and consistently reflected in Congress. Before proposing utopian plans for the additional expansion of UN functions into ever-broader areas of international and domestic policy, however, it will be an unyielding prerequisite that these American concerns be addressed. Otherwise, the best friends of the United Nations may find themselves even more dramatically reducing the already low levels of American popular and congressional support for the organization.

JOHN R. BOLTON

countries to the UN forced the organization to limit its activities.

Despite its weaknesses and perennial financial crises, the UN has become the first genuinely global international organization, bringing almost all sovereign states together under one set of principles—those of the UN Charter. States find membership of the UN and its many associated bodies indispensable and value the functional cooperation it facilitates. It is probably wrong to see the UN as a nascent world government, but it remains central to the survival and advancement of the idea that states exist as part of a universal international society.

(See also ARAB-ISRAELI CONFLICT; ECONOMIC COMMISSION FOR AFRICA; ECONOMIC COMMISSION FOR LATIN AMERICA AND THE CARIBBEAN; FORCE, USE OF; GULF WAR; KOREAN WAR; MALVINAS/FALKLANDS WAR; RESOLUTION 242; RWANDA; SANCTIONS; SOMALIA; SUEZ CRISIS; UNITED NATIONS CONFERENCE ON TRADE AND DEVELOPMENT; WORLD TRADE ORGANIZATION.)

United Nations, *Yearbook of the United Nations* (New York, annually). Inis Claude, *Swords into Ploughshares: The Problems and Progress of International Organization,* 4th ed. (New York, 1971). Paul Taylor and A. J. R. Groom, eds., *International Institutions at Work* (London, 1988). Adam Roberts and Benedict Kingsbury, eds., *United Nations, Divided World: The UN's Roles in International Relations,* 2d ed. (Oxford, 1993). United Nations, *The Blue Helmets: A Review of UN Peacekeeping,* 3rd ed. (UN, New York, 1996). Sydney Bailey and Sam Daws, *The Procedure of the United Nations Security Council,* 3rd ed. (Oxford, 1998).

ADAM ROBERTS

UNITED NATIONS CONFERENCE ON TRADE AND DEVELOPMENT. In 1964 the United Nations Conference on Trade and Development (UNCTAD) was established by the General Assembly as one of its permanent organs. The developing countries at the time were not happy either with certain developments in the world economy or with the norms, principles, and practices of postwar economic institutions (the *International Monetary Fund, the *World Bank, and the *General Agreement on Tariffs and Trade). They felt, in particular, that the latter institutions reflected essentially Western, liberal perspectives that were not wholly appropriate for developing countries and that the international economy itself was biased against their interests and needs. There was thus strong support among intellectual and political leaders of developing countries for the creation of an international economic institution that would articulate and promote their views and facilitate and accelerate their economic development. Despite opposition from Western nations, which disagreed with the need to create a new institution and with the ideas being propounded, the *Third World prevailed and UNCTAD became the institutional embodiment of a specific Third World perspective on international economic relations. UNCTAD was established as an organ of the UN General Assembly rather than as a specialized agency, largely to ensure that it would receive adequate budgetary support.

Raúl *Prebisch, the Argentine economist who subsequently became the first secretary-general of UNCTAD, developed many of the ideas that lay behind UNCTAD's creation. Prebisch argued that Third World raw material exports were facing a continuing decline in their terms of trade, that the Third World had to adopt a strategy of *import-substitution indus-

trialization in order to develop, and that relations between the developed "center" and the developing "periphery" were inherently exploitative. These ideas were sharply challenged by many economists but, to practitioners and intellectuals in the Third World, they seemed intuitively correct. In any case, Prebisch's ideas, which were also the basis of *dependency theory in many of its variations, were transformed into UNCTAD's leitmotifs: suspicions about the fairness of the Bretton Woods system, pessimism about the prospects for raw materials exports and thus an emphasis on the need to stabilize and raise prices by interventions in the markets, demand for preferential access to Western markets for Third World manufactures, and free or freer access to Western technology. These ideas were of course anathema to conservative developed-country governments strongly committed to the market—as long as they benefited from open markets—and these ideas guaranteed that UNCTAD would become an institution of confrontation, the developed countries' least favorable multilateral setting.

UNCTAD, by international standards, is not a very large organization in terms of either budget or staff (less than 400 professionals). It is, however, one of the most universal organizations as it has more than 180 member states. The conference usually meets every four years to set policy guidelines and to attempt to resolve major disputes on the issues. Between conferences, the Trade and Development Board has been responsible for providing direction and guidance. The Board, which usually meets annually, initially operated through standing committees that corresponded to divisions within the staff bureaucracy: committees dealing with manufactures, commodities, transfer of technology, development finance, economic and technical cooperation among developing countries, and the like. The committees provided direction to the staff and reviewed reports and papers prepared by the staff, but what the committees requested was also heavily influenced by what the staff itself wanted to do. Informal channels of communication between the staff and representatives of key Third World governments were and are powerful and pervasive. Recent reforms have altered the committee structure but have not greatly changed the work program of the organization.

Measured against the desire of the developing countries to restructure the international economic order, UNCTAD has not been a success. It did succeed in its early years in gaining support for the General System of Preferences, but the benefits were relatively limited and largely concentrated in a small group of newly industrializing countries. Indeed, many economists have argued that the emphasis on a combination of preferential access to Western markets and relatively closed Third World markets was itself mistaken, as it hindered or delayed efforts to make the manufactured exports of the developing countries internationally competitive. On other issues, such as commodities, transfer of technology, and shipping, UNCTAD did some useful work in its early years, largely in forming a common Third World position, but achieved limited practical results.

UNCTAD's influence surged in the 1970s as it became the major institutional setting for the Third World's effort to establish the New International Economic Order. With the *Organization of Petroleum Exporting Countries seemingly dominant and perhaps willing to use some of its power to achieve gains for other developing countries, and with the developed countries in disarray, the odds on a successful challenge to the existing order by a coalition of weak countries seemed to be as short as they were likely to get. Thus the Group of 77 in UNCTAD demanded major changes in a number of key areas. The developed countries successfully resisted these demands, partly from ideology, partly from conflicts of interest, and partly because of technical weaknesses in some of the demands.

UNCTAD's role diminished in the 1980s and after. UNCTAD's interventionist principles were increasingly out of fashion among conservative Western countries, new problems in debt and the trading regime were dealt with largely by the old Bretton Woods institutions, and sharply declining economic performance in much of the Third World tended to deflect attention from multilateral to bilateral or regional relations. UNCTAD still performs some useful functions as the "voice" of the Third World, as a source of some useful research, and as a provider of technical assistance for the least developed countries and for cooperation among developing countries. But as UNCTAD itself gradually adopted a market orientation (despite some internal resistance) and as it sought to reform itself (with limited success) in response to growing criticism from both North and South, it lost its distinct role and has had great difficulty in defining a new role—at least one that is not already being done elsewhere.

(See also INTERNATIONAL DEBT; INTERNATIONAL POLITICAL ECONOMY; NEWLY INDUSTRIALIZING ECONOMIES; NORTH-SOUTH RELATIONS; SUSTAINABLE DEVELOPMENT; UNITED NATIONS.)

Branislav Gosovic, *UNCTAD: Conflict and Compromise* (Leiden, 1972). Robert L. Rothstein, *Global Bargaining: UNCTAD and the Quest for a New International Economic Order* (Princeton, N.J., 1979).

ROBERT L. ROTHSTEIN

UNITED STATES. From their early history, the United States and its politics have been described, in the words of Alexis de Tocqueville, as "exceptional," qualitatively different from other nations. The distinction still holds. The American polity is the only one dominated by two loosely structured coalition parties, weaker as national organizations than those elsewhere. It is the only democratic system without an electorally viable socialist, social democratic, or labor party. The correlation between social class (high to low, middle-class and working-class) and party voting present in all electoral democracies is weaker than in other industrial nations. The United States is the oldest continuing *democracy (the Democratic Party has existed longer than any party in the world), and the most populist, in that over 500,000 offices are filled in elections. Nevertheless a smaller percentage of the eligible electorate vote than in other democracies, roughly 50 percent in presidential elections, 35 percent in non-presidential-year congressional contests, and even less in many local ones. The American polity is also differentiated from others in having state-conducted primary elections, in which voters who select to register in a political party choose nominees for the general elections.

Institutional Principles of American Government. The American Constitution, the oldest in the world, established a divided form of government, the presidency and two houses of Congress, which differs from those of Europe and the Commonwealth and reflects a deliberate decision by the country's founders to create a weak and internally conflicted political system. The leaders of the Revolution, with their opposition to a powerful monarchical regime, strongly distrusted the state. The first constitution, the Articles of Confederation, provided for a Congress to pass laws, but *not* for an executive.

The second and continuing one, which went into effect in 1789, divided the government into many units, each selected differently for varying periods of office. The president was to be elected every four years by an electoral college, basically local *elites. Senators, two from each state, were to be chosen by the state legislators for six-year terms, with one-third of the seats open every two years, and the popularly elected House of Representatives was to be filled every two years, with the number from each state roughly proportionate to its share of the national population. The president may veto legislation passed by Congress, but the veto can be overridden by two-thirds of each house. Changes to the Constitution require a two-thirds vote in both houses of Congress and ratification by three-quarters of the states. The Constitution provides for Supreme Court justices who are appointed by the president for life, but their nomination, like those of other federal justices, cabinet members, and high ranking officeholders, must be ratified by the Senate. The terms of office are still the same today, but the system of selecting the electoral college has been changed so that the contest for president is practically by popular vote, as is the election of senators.

Almost all other democratic nations, those in Latin America apart, have a much more unified government, with a prime minister and cabinet who must have the support of the majority of the elected members of parliament. Given that the executive must be backed by the parliamentarians who place it in office, prime ministers are much more powerful, particularly in the domestic field, than presidents.

The American system laid down in the late eighteenth century is basically intact. As noted, it has been amended to provide for direct popular election of senators, but each state still has two, regardless of differences in population size. The procedures for nominating presidential and other candidates have also become more populist. Potential nominees must run in party primaries (elections among registered party members) held some time before the general election. These first emerged in some western states around the turn of the century. They became prevalent for almost all posts after World War II. Nominees were previously chosen by party conventions, often controlled by "machines" or cabals of professional politicians. These developments were paralleled by the emergence in state and local governments of initiatives and referenda, which require the electorate's direct involvement in the passage of legislation and state constitutional amendments. These *reforms reflect a commitment to *populism, to the belief that the public, rather than professional politicians, should control as much of the policy-formation processes as possible.

Political Structure and Political Culture. Comparing causes and consequences of the divided authority presidential system with that of the more common parliamentary unified government points up the way in which values and institutions interact to produce distinct *political cultures. The

American system has intensified the commitment to individualism and concern for the protection of *rights through legal action. The *Bill of Rights, unique until recently, is designed to protect the citizenry against governmental abuse of *power. It has engendered an emphasis on personal rights and thus fosters litigiousness. As a result, Americans have a greater propensity than other peoples to go to court not only against government but against each other. The emphasis on constitutionally protected rights has led to a steady enlargement of basic freedoms in the areas of speech, assembly, and private behavior and to a variety of legal defense organizations to sustain such efforts, the most prominent of which has been the American Civil Liberties Union. The rights of blacks and other minorities, of women, even of animals and plants, have grown extensively since World War II through legal action as well as mass protest. American litigiousness may be seen in the greater frequency of appeals against convictions, as well as more malpractice, environmental, and occupational safety suits than occur elsewhere. The country has more lawyers per capita than other nations.

The disdain for authority, for conforming to the rules laid down by the state, has been related by some to other unique American traits, such as the highest crime rate, as well as the lowest level of voting participation, in the developed world. Basically the American tradition does not encourage obedience to the state and the law. This point may be illustrated by reference to efforts by the U.S. and Canadian governments to change the systems of measurements and weights, that is, to "go metric" and drop the ancient and less logical system of miles and inches, pounds and ounces. Over two decades ago, each country told its citizens that in ten years only metric measurements would be used, although both systems could be used until a given date. The Canadians, whose Tory-monarchical history and structures have made for much greater respect for and reliance on the state and who have lower per capita crime, deviance, and litigiousness rates than Americans, deferred to the decision of their leaders and now follow the metric system. Americans largely ignored the new policy, and the government abandoned the effort to change. Distances still refer to yards or miles, weights are in pounds and ounces, and temperature readings are in Fahrenheit.

The cross-national variation in voting rates may be explained in part by the different reactions of Americans and Canadians to fulfilling the obligations or duties of good *citizenship. Many voters everywhere take the time to cast a ballot for the same reason they obey a sign not to walk on the grass, wait at a red light even if no car is approaching, or do not break the law in other ways when there is little or no chance that they will be caught in a violation. Many potential voters, knowing that they will rarely, if ever, determine the outcome of an election, recognize that to devote time to cast a ballot is not rational behavior. Voting is simply encouraged as an expression of good citizenship. Americans, being less conformist, less law-abiding, than Canadians or Europeans, may be expected to vote less.

The greater emphasis on populism also appears to contribute to low turnout. In the United States, unlike Canada or other parliamentary countries, voters are asked to cast a ballot for many offices and referenda. In most states they are called on to vote twice every year in primary and general elections, sometimes more frequently if local and state balloting occurs

at different times. In almost every other country, national elections are held only every four or five years. At these and in municipal or provincial elections, the ballot contains candidates for only one office, member of parliament, or legislator.

Conformism and populism do not exhaust the factors related to low voter turnout in America. Although Americans express greater interest in politics than those polled in other democracies, it is more difficult to vote in the United States than in Canada or Europe. Americans must register to vote some time before the election, a requirement which does not exist in other countries. Adult citizens elsewhere are usually placed on a voting roll. But, although the requirement to register reduces turnout, it is not the predominant cause of low voter turnout. Some midwestern states, like North Dakota and Minnesota, have practically eliminated voter registration and, while the proportion voting there is higher than in other states, it is still lower than in most of Europe and Canada.

Religion and American Political Culture. Individualism and resistance to authority in America are also fostered by the predominant religious institutions, the Protestant sects. The United States is the *only* country in Christendom the majority of whose inhabitants adhere to *sects,* voluntary, non-state-related institutions, mainly Methodist and Baptist, but also hundreds of others. The sects are predominantly congregational; each local unit adheres voluntarily to its national denomination, which has little or no control over it. Youths are asked to make a denominational choice on reaching the age of decision, i.e., they are not members automatically by family affiliation. Ministers do not have power over their parishioners. Elsewhere *churches,* Anglican, Catholic, Lutheran, and Orthodox, dominate. They are hierarchical in structure, and membership is a birthright; parishioners are expected to follow the lead of their priests and bishops. Outside of the United States, churches have been state supported; their clergy are paid by the state, their hierarchy is formally appointed or confirmed by the government, and their schools are subsidized by taxes.

The United States was the first country in which religious groups became voluntary associations. American ministers and laity recognized that they had to foster voluntary commitments both to maintain support for the church and to foster community needs. Tocqueville concluded that voluntarism is a large part of the answer to the greater popular strength of organized religion, a phenomenon still documented by cross-national opinion polls, indicating Americans are the most God-believing, churchgoing, and fundamentalist people in the West.

These emphases in American Protestant sectarianism have both reinforced and been strengthened by social and political individualism. The sectarian is expected to follow a moral code, as determined by his or her own sense of rectitude, through a personal relationship to God, one not mediated by bishops or dictated by the state. The sectarians in Britain, who are in a minority, have been known as "dissenters" and "nonconformists," dissenting from, rather than conforming to, the doctrines of the Church of England, the established state religion.

The strength of sectarian values and their implications for the political process may be seen in reactions to the supreme test of citizenship and adherence to the national will, war.

State churches have not only legitimated government (e.g., the divine right of kings), they have invariably approved of the wars their nations have engaged in, calling on the populace to serve and obey. And the citizens have done so. Americans, however, have been different. In every war in which the United States has participated, with the exception of World War II, when the country was attacked by Japan, there has been a major antiwar movement. During the war of 1812, the New England states threatened to secede because of their opposition to the conflict. Thousands of American soldiers, including some West Point graduates, deserted during the Mexican War and joined the opposing army because they believed the Mexicans were right and the United States wrong. In the Civil War, both sides witnessed major opposition to their causes from behind the lines. There were hundreds of thousands of conscientious objectors and a large vote for antiwar Socialist Party candidates during World War I. Polls revealed massive opposition to the *Korean War. The strength of the antiwar protest movement to the *Vietnam War, which helped to end it, is well known. In his comparative historical study of opposition to American wars, Sol Tax reported that, as of 1968, the anti–Vietnam War movement only stood *fourth* on the list of significance of such efforts.

Many of the antiwar movements have had direct links to Protestant sectarianism. Conscientious objection to military service has its roots there, and the phenomenon has been much more prevalent in America than elsewhere. Still it may be recognized that a great deal of antiwar activity in the United States does not have direct Protestant sectarian origin. Jews, Catholics, and secularists, particularly political leftists, have played major, sometimes predominant, roles in such movements. But it may be argued that sectarianism has affected non-Protestants who, like foreign immigrants, have been socialized and assimilated to the prevalent ethos. Studies of American Catholicism by foreign Catholic scholars have noted the extent to which their American coreligionists, including church functionaries, have taken over the cultural patterns and individualist moralistic emphases of Protestant sectarianism. A French Dominican, R. L. Bruckberger, observes that to European Catholics, American Catholics resemble Baptists and Methodists more than they do their Continental coreligionists. Similar points have been made about Jews. American socialists during World War I and New Left antiwar activists in the Vietnam War followed scenarios laid down by Protestant sectarians.

Protestant-inspired moralism has affected not only opposition to wars. It has determined the American style in foreign relations generally, including the ways the country goes to war. Patriotism, including support for wars, is as moralistic as resistance to participation. To endorse a war, Americans must see a conflict as on God's side against Satan, for morality against evil. When Ronald *Reagan defined the struggle against *communism as an effort to destroy the "evil empire," he was as American as apple pie. The United States only goes to war against evil empires, not, in its self-perception, to defend material interests. And in such conflicts, no compromise is possible. Hence it demands "unconditional surrender" from the enemy, not negotiated peace. When it cannot destroy the satanic opponent, it tries to refuse to do business with it. Thus the United States did not recognize the Soviet Union for a decade and a half after its creation. It refused to recognize the communist People's Republic of China for over two decades. It still does not deal with Castro's Cuba.

The passion of American opposition to communism, prior to the collapse of the Soviet Union in 1991, was interpreted by some as reflecting the fact that the country is capitalist and conservative. But equally capitalist and conservative nations and leaders like *Churchill in Britain, de *Gaulle in France, and *Franco in Spain had little difficulty in coming to terms with, and trading with, communist states that the United States would not recognize. Francisco Franco, right-wing dictator, who won a bloody struggle identified by him as against atheistic communism, recognized Castro shortly after he took power in Cuba. As church, rather than sectarian, Christians, Churchill, de Gaulle, and Franco believed human beings and institutions are inherently corrupt, are never perfect. Countries with such views go to war to protect state interests, not to create the good society or eliminate evil.

The Two-Party System. The political institutions and basic values of the United States account for another aspect of American exceptionalism mentioned earlier: its two-party system, the absence of effective and electorally viable third parties. As various political scientists, notably E. E. Schattschneider, have emphasized, the American presidential system seriously discourages more than two parties. Given that only one party and person can win the presidency, voters recognize that realistically they must choose between the two strongest candidates running for office. Support for weaker third or fourth nominees or parties is a wasted choice. Hence voters who are not enthusiastic about the two major candidates still wind up supporting one of them as "the lesser evil." It is much easier for minor or new parties to gain votes in parliamentary systems, where voters elect individual members in constituencies. They do not take part in national or statewide elections for the head of government, as in the United States. The former permit smaller parties to concentrate their energies in districts in which they can win. The latter requires significant national support to be visible.

The pressure to back a potential winner produced the two-party coalitional system. Highly diverse groups have come together under the rubric of the Democratic and Republican parties. For historical reasons related to issues around the Civil War, the white South, which sought to hold down blacks, was Democratic until the post–World War II era. Blacks supported the Republicans, the party which ended slavery, until the Great Depression of the 1930s. Economic conditions led them to shift to the Democrats, who furthered state economic assistance to the poor, particularly the unemployed and sharecropping farmers. The Democrats historically have been the party of the "have-nots," which included those of recent immigrant background, Catholics, Jews, as well as organized labor. The Republicans, and before them the Whig and Federalist parties, have been the party of the "haves," the economically privileged, and those of higher-status, white Anglo-Saxon Protestant, background. Yet, prior to the Great Depression, the Republican Party included near-socialist agrarian radicals in the Midwest as well as most impoverished blacks.

What makes such heterogenous coalition parties possible has been the absence of party discipline, of the obligation of candidates and officials to follow a party line and support party leaders. This diversity is facilitated by the *separation of powers, the fact that unlike a prime minister, who must resign from office and usually call a new election if he or she loses a vote in parliament, a president stays in office no matter how many proposals are defeated in Congress. Parliamentary parties, like the British or Canadian Conservatives or the Scandinavian Social Democrats, must maintain discipline if the system is to work. Members of parliaments are expected, almost required, to vote with their party. They may have to vote for policies favored by their party leaders even when these are very unpopular in the districts they represent. An American congressperson, however, is only concerned with winning the district.

The American separation of powers allows and encourages members of Congress to vote with their constituents against their president or dominant party view. Allen Gotlieb, Canadian ambassador to the United States during the 1980s, has noted that American legislators, including congressional leaders, will vote against and help to kill bills to carry out major international agreements in response to pressure from small groups of local constituents, such as those in the scallop fishing industry or logging concerns. As former House Speaker Thomas P. (Tip) O'Neill once put it, in Congress "all politics is local."

The inability of party organizations to nominate and control legislators running and elected under their label has increased greatly since liberal reforms designed to weaken party "machines" took effect. The unanticipated results, however, were to increase the number and strengthen the influence of lobbyists and to make elected officials much more dependent on financial contributions produced by *interest groups, as the costs of campaigning have mounted in the television age.

Presidents normally have a great deal of difficulty with Congress, even when their party controls a majority of both houses, as Franklin *Roosevelt did after he won reelection by a landslide in 1936. In recent years the American electorate has divided control of the government between the two parties; the Republicans win the presidency, the Democrats dominate Congress or vice versa. By so doing the voters seemingly reinforce the Founders' desire to have the different branches of government check and balance each other. Under such conditions, the presidency is a much weaker office than the prime ministership whose party has a parliamentary majority. An American president controls foreign policy and can order troops overseas, but cannot get drafted budgets or much proposed legislation passed by Congress.

The heterogeneity of the major American parties has been enhanced by a primary system that allows representatives of antagonistic factions within the respective parties to run against each other in partywide elections. Thus in 1972, George Wallace, the former right-wing segregationist governor of Alabama, contested the Democratic Party presidential primaries. His successful rival in that year was George McGovern, a leftist populist, who was subsequently defeated by Richard *Nixon in the general election. Nixon had secured the Republican nomination by defeating a liberal, Governor Nelson Rockefeller. Jesse Jackson, a militant black and a leftist on economic issues, ran in the Democratic presidential primaries in 1984 and 1988, as did a number of moderate and liberal whites. George *Bush, running as a moderate Repub-

lican, lost to Ronald Reagan, perceived as a right-winger, in the primaries in 1980.

During periods of national crisis, left-wing near-socialist groups won control of major party nominations on state levels. Thus the Non-Partisan League formed by socialists captured the Republican Party primaries and then elected state officials and senators in North Dakota from 1916 until World War II. A similar group took control of Oklahoma, running in the Democratic primary, in the early twenties. During the Great Depression of the 1930s, organized factions in which socialists or communists played a major role controlled the Democratic Party in California, Oregon, and Washington. While overt factions have not contested primaries since World War II, candidates representing different orientations continue to compete. During the eighties and nineties, self-defined conservative caucuses and organizations have operated within the Republican Party inside and outside of Congress. The moderate and more liberal Republicans are less well organized, but they exist. Among Democrats, the moderate and more conservative forces are organized in the Democratic Leadership Council. The more numerous liberals among party activists are divided among the Americans for Democratic Action, the Coalition for Democratic Values, and Jesse Jackson's Rainbow Coalition. Interests and ideological groups function in both parties, e.g., civil rights supporters, feminists, farm blocs, labor unions, environmentalists (greens), pro- and anti-choice advocates, etc.

Why No Socialism in America? Political structures explain the absence of significant third or minor parties in America, but they do not account for the absence of social democratic and leftist class-conscious groups as political forces. A number of factors have been suggested by students of the subject, such as the strength of the classically liberal (anti-state) tradition in America and a more egalitarian social class structure, i.e., one based in status rather than economic or power terms, than exists elsewhere.

The most general approach, associated with English author and Fabian H. G. Wells and the American political scientist Louis Hartz, emphasizes the extent to which the distrust of a strong state that was the core of the revolutionary ideology continues to influence the way Americans look at politics. *Socialism, which assumes the need for a powerful state-controlled economy, is antithetical to this outlook. The radicalism which stems from the Jeffersonian view that the less government the better is close to *anarchism. Therefore, it should not be surprising that the major American *labor movement, the American Federation of Labor (AFL), was syndicalist and anti-statist rather than socialist, favoring independent workers' action. Its founding president, Samuel Gompers, who held the office for four decades, described himself as a near anarchist. The most important American radical labor movement, the Industrial Workers of the World (IWW), was anarcho-syndicalist.

Conversely, the monarchical tradition in Europe and Canada fostered Tory statism. Tory *conservatism meant belief in the *monarchy, the alliance between church and state, *mercantilism, i.e., state intervention in the economy, and noblesse oblige. The emergence of the *welfare state in Europe is associated with two conservative figures, Disraeli in Britain and Bismarck in Germany. Classical liberalism, anti-statism, laissez-faire, which has dominated American political thinking, has been a minority movement in Europe. The socialist emphasis on using the state for economic and social reforms was legitimated there by statist conservatism. Americans today are less supportive of welfare state policies than the citizens of any other nation, and, not surprisingly, their government provides less.

The failure of socialist parties and the weakness of economic class as a base for partisan cleavage have also been linked to the special character of the American status system. Unlike most European countries, with a feudal aristocratic tradition of hierarchy, where deference has been given and expected, American society, as Tocqueville noted in the nineteenth century, has been more egalitarian in terms of respect. He emphasized that equality in America also means meritocracy, a stress on equality of opportunity among individuals regardless of social origins. The United States, of course, has always been highly inegalitarian in economic and power terms, but much less so in status, social ranking, terms. In contrast to Japanese and most European languages, there are no words which must be used in America to reflect the relative status of the speakers. Lower-strata Europeans did not have to be propagandized or educated to think politically in class terms, they were socialized by their postfeudal, more status-conscious societies to react that way. In the United States the value-generating and value-sustaining institutions have negated class consciousness among whites. As political scientist Walter Dean Burnham sums up the political consequences: "No feudalism, no socialism."

While class-based movements have been weak in the United States, and the correlation between class position and party voting has been lower than in almost all other industrialized societies, the salient social bases of partisan cleavage in America, as elsewhere, have been stratification variables. As noted, the Democrats for much of their history have drawn disproportionate support from the have-not strata in occupational, ethnic, and religious terms. The Republicans represented the more socioeconomically dominant elements. However, these linkages were rarely presented in class terms until the Great Depression, when Franklin Roosevelt and the *New Deal wing of the Democratic Party appealed openly to the labor unions, the workers, the poor, the unemployed, and the less affluent rural population against the rich and economically powerful.

The association between class and party was greatly strengthened in that era. The labor organizations strongly backed the Democrats, and trade unions flourished with the help of the Roosevelt administration. Those business elements, a minority, which had previously been Democratic because of ethnic, religious, or sectional economic ties, shifted to the Republicans. The New Deal introduced, in historian Richard Hofstadter's words, "a social democratic tinge" into American politics. America now had its own welfare state, though one which never reached the proportions in other industrialized polities during this century.

Werner Sombart noted almost a century ago in his *Why No Socialism in the United States?* that the country's greater wealth undermines the socialist appeal and reduces the emphasis on class. This continued to be the case during the prolonged prosperity after World War II. America became even more affluent. It is still the richest industrialized nation in terms of per capita income, close to $20,000 per year. Although a significant population, disproportionately black and Hispanic, lives in poverty, consumption goods are more evenly spread among the remainder, particularly the white population, than is true elsewhere. The postwar increase in wealth, which continued through the 1960s, negated the stress on class divisions brought about by the Great Depression. Trade-union membership declined steadily from thirty-five percent of the employed labor force in 1955 to sixteen percent in 1991, one of the lowest such proportions in any industrialized economy. Republicans, the party identified with anti-statist laissez-faire ideologies, were able to win the presidency in five of the six presidential elections between 1968 and 1992.

Political Parties and Divided Government. From 1968 to 1992, the Democrats captured at least one, usually both, of the houses of Congress. With Bill *Clinton's election as president in 1992 and reelection in 1996, the Democrats controlled the White House but the Republicans seized control of Congress after the 1994 midterm elections. It is puzzling why a majority of the American electorate selects different parties for the presidency and Congress. Part of the answer seems to be that presidential contests involve issues of national style morality, and grant special importance to consensus or concerns about crime, family, and the economy. Alternatively, congressional campaigns are conducted in local districts where the concerns of particular (rather than broad, national) constituencies hold sway. But this is inference, not knowledge.

There is now renewed distrust of government and approval in principle of divided government by a solid majority of those polled. When survey researchers inquire whether it is better to have the presidency and both houses of Congress in the hands of one party or divided, sixty to seventy percent of the respondents reply "different parties."

This does not mean that many voters consciously opt for a president of one party and a congressperson of the other in order to check them. Rather, as in the constituency by-elections and provincial elections held elsewhere, those who vote for the governing party nationally frequently choose the opposition in special or local elections, which cannot remove the government from power. These lesser contests are used to express discontent with some policies of those who control the national administration, even though voters do not wish to remove their leaders. In the United States, the electorate behaves similarly. In off-year contests (those in which a president is not elected), the president's party almost invariably loses congressional seats. The nonpresidential party also wins by-elections and in recent presidential election years has gotten many more votes for its congressional than presidential candidates. In Canada, the party which wins federal office tends to lose in provincial contests, held soon after the national elections. Divided government, federal and provincial, does not weaken the power of the national administration in parliamentary systems such as Canada, the Federal Republic of Germany, or Spain. But in America, it produces a divided and sometimes ineffectual federal government, because Congress shares governing power with the president.

The Third Century of American Politics. As the United States moves into its third century under the same Constitution, it seemingly has the same divided form of government and, compared with the Euro-Canadian polities, value emphases. It is still classically liberal (libertarian), distrustful of government, and populist. The electorate still has more power to choose its leaders than in other democracies, which depend on unified governments to fulfill economic and welfare functions and which have fewer offices and policies directly open to electoral choice.

Yet America has obviously changed greatly since 1789. From a nation of thirteen states and 4 million people hugging the Atlantic seaboard, it has grown to a continent-spanning federation of fifty states and 270 million people. Close to 30 million live in California, a state nonexistent in 1789. It began as an overwhelmingly agrarian society with more than ninety percent of its workforce on the land, many as impoverished subsistence farmers. As it begins the twenty-first century, only two percent are farmers; the great majority live in sprawling metropolitan regions. From an underdeveloped rural economy which relied heavily on Britain for its manufactured goods, it became in the latter decades of the nineteenth century the most prosperous industrial power on earth. In real consumer income terms it still holds this position, although the emergence of other industrial countries and the reexpansion of Europe have reduced its proportion of the world's production from two-fifths immediately after World War II to a quarter. The character of its labor force has changed, first with the decline of agriculture and the expansion of industry, and more recently with the falloff in unskilled manual jobs and growth of high-tech and scientific activities accompanied by an increase in white-collar and service jobs and in positions requiring college education.

On the international scene, the United States moved from being a small, militarily weak country far from the major power centers and proud of its isolation to the strongest nation on earth, the focus of military and economic alliances and agreements. Domestically, the Civil War resolved the issue of states' rights versus federal power and resulted in a shift from the original loosely integrated federation to a highly centralized one. During and after the Great Depression and World War II, the country became an increasingly nationalized polity with funds and power concentrated in the center. Under Ronald Reagan, the Republicans tried to reverse the trend, but succeeded only in stopping its growth. The country's military and international responsibilities remain a major factor in maintaining the enhanced role of the national government.

Although the American government, as noted, remains the least involved in welfare activities and government ownership and influence on the economy of any developed country, it has moved greatly since the 1930s in the direction of providing assistance to the less privileged through programs like *Social Security, unemployment insurance, bank deposit insurance, medical aid, aid to single mothers, and college student loans. The federal and state governments are deeply involved in legislation to protect the environment, provide occupational safety, and remove economic discrimination against blacks, ethnic minorities, women, and older people.

Despite these developments, which make governing the United States infinitely more complex than in the late eighteenth and nineteenth centuries, the *form* of government has not changed. The presidency remains a much weaker office than the prime ministry and cabinet in the rest of the democratic world. Congress is much more powerful than any parliament, but, as planned by the Founders, it is a divided body. The Supreme Court, with its powers to negate legislation as unconstitutional and to limit laws, regulations, and administrative decrees with reference to the Bill of Rights and other portions of the Constitution, is the most powerful court in the world. It can and does legislate major public matters such as the suffrage, racial and gender equality, abortion, and the death penalty. And the constitutional and individualistic elements in American culture which foster litigiousness contribute to further inhibition of the powers of government.

The question is increasingly raised by political observers whether these constraints on the government will permit the United States to deal with the problems posed by a global economy; challenges from Japan and the newly industrialized countries of East Asia, European integration, the collapse of communist regimes in Eastern Europe, and the attempted industrialization of the impoverished nations of South Asia and Africa. To these may be added the domestic difficulties involved in handling the urban-based problems of housing, pollution, transportation, education, and minorities and immigrant placement. But it is not clear that a more united parliamentary system would work better under conditions of geographic and cultural heterogeneity. Canada, which has a parliamentary system and a Tory emphasis on government responsibility for welfare, also has severe governance problems. Its provinces are demanding and obtaining much more power than American states and, as noted, their electorates in recent decades have almost invariably chosen governments that are in opposition to the party in federal control.

The United States is a difficult place to govern. It is divided along sectional, economic, ethnic, racial, and religious lines. Mass immigration, approximately 800,000 annually or an increase of about four percent to the population each decade, continues. Racial polarization has not eased. The country's international responsibilities have not declined. Yet its people continue to exhibit more distrust of centralized government than do any other, and, as noted, prefer divided and conflicted government. Viewed cross-nationally, Americans are the most Whiggish, most classically liberal population among the democratic nations. They continue to stand with Thomas Jefferson in believing the less government the better. It is not surprising, therefore, that the country retains the internally divisive system established in the late eighteenth century.

(See also AFRICAN AMERICANS; AMERICAN FEDERATION OF LABOR AND CONGRESS OF INDUSTRIAL ORGANIZATIONS; CARTER, JIMMY; CIVIL RIGHTS MOVEMENT; CLASS AND POLITICS; CONGRESS, U.S.; EISENHOWER, DWIGHT D.; ELECTIONS AND VOTING BEHAVIOR; ETHNICITY; FEDERALISM; GLOBALIZATION; GREAT SOCIETY; HISPANIC AMERICANS; INTERNATIONAL MIGRATION; JOHNSON, LYNDON BAINES; KENNEDY, JOHN FITZGERALD; LIBERALISM; NATIVE AMERICANS; NEW DEAL COALITION; POLITICAL MACHINE; POLITICAL PARTIES AND PARTY COMPETITION; PRESIDENCY, U.S.; RELIGION AND POLITICS; SUPREME COURT OF THE UNITED STATES; TRUMAN, HARRY S.; U.S. FOREIGN POLICY.)

E. E. Schattschneider, *Party Government* (New York, 1942). Seymour Martin Lipset, *The First New Nation* (New York, 1963, 1979). Sol Tax, "War and the Draft," in Martin Fried, Marvin Harris, and Robert Murphy, eds., *War* (Garden City, N.Y., 1968). Raymond Wolfinger, *Who Votes?* (New Haven, Conn., 1980). Samuel Huntington, *American Poli-*

tics (Cambridge, Mass., 1981). Nelson Polsby, *Consequences of Party Reform* (New York, 1983). Byron Shafer, *Quiet Revolution: The Struggle for the Democratic Party and the Shaping of Post-Reform Politics* (New York, 1983). James Q. Wilson, *Bureaucracy* (New York, 1989). Seymour Martin Lipset, *Continental Divide: The Values and Institutions of the United States and Canada* (New York, 1990).

SEYMOUR MARTIN LIPSET

URBANIZATION. The development of modern societies is inextricably linked to the process of urbanization throughout the world. Any understanding of the politics of the world must therefore take stock of this agglomerative process and its effects.

Urbanization commenced with the Neolithic revolution in food production, some ten thousand years ago or so. The mastery over food production freed a number of persons from direct subsistence activities and created a basis for a more complex division of labor, the concentration of population in one place, and the emergence of new forms of social inequality. In this manner, the city states of classical antiquity came to develop and prosper, first in the area that is roughly coterminous with the contemporary *Middle East, and then the rest of the world.

The ancient city-states and feudal societies which followed them were incapable of maintaining the continuity in socioeconomic development, despite their impressive cultural accomplishments. This was due to a number of reasons, including their low level of technological development, territorial rivalries and conflicts, and the extreme methods of exploitation and political control. The development of *capitalism in Europe ushered in a new era in human history. The initial phase of *mercantilism facilitated capital accumulation through trade, imperialist conquests, forced labor, and plundering. This phase soon gave way to the era of competitive capitalism in the nineteenth century, in which industrial cities flourished as centers of capitalist production.

The laissez-faire philosophy of competitive capitalism translated into untold misery for the laboring classes in industrial cities. Low wages, unemployment, poverty, homelessness, and crime became part of the urban landscape. This situation was compounded by the limited scope of government intervention. It was in this context that workers, progressive and left intellectuals, and women coalesced into social movements that began to agitate for social justice. Fearful of this groundswell of opposition, the ruling classes and their political surrogates were forced to grant concessions, which eventually became institutionalized as *welfare state measures. The latter were extended to people of color, women, the aged, and other segments of the disenfranchised citizenry as a result of the popular struggles of the 1960s.

The structural crisis of capitalism that reached its peak around the 1973 "oil crisis" signaled the end of post–World War II "Cold War" liberalism, whose impulses were shaped by an unprecedented three decades of prosperity. After that a mood of retrenchment and the devolution of government set in, and has continued to shape the terms of political discourse to the present day.

While capitalist economic integration tends to transmit throughout the system any shocks occasioned by periodic crises, it is local areas that bear the brunt of the adverse consequences. In the more centralized state systems such as Britain and France, social groups that are adversely affected by economic restructuring have historically had greater political leverage in influencing national policies that can mitigate local conditions. In highly decentralized and fragmented political systems such as that of the United States, local areas are left largely to their own resources. In the case of the latter, cities are locked in a feverish competition to attract private development using subsidies that they can ill afford, given their shrinking revenue bases. Often these subsidies are financed with resources that have been withdrawn from social programs. To justify these measures, the ideological demonization of the poor assumes the rhetoric of discouraging "underclass dependencies" through punitive welfare reform policies.

In European countries, urban areas are also experiencing growing inequalities that are partly due to the process of capital restructuring and tertiarization, and partly due to the influx of new immigrant groups who have swollen the ranks of the urban poor. Thus, while in the United States the struggles for social and economic justice in the larger urban areas have constituted an essentially "racialized discourse," it would seem that a number of European metropolitan areas are increasingly confronted with a similar political trend.

In the major as well as the regional urban centers of the *Third World countries, the economic and social structural distortions are borne out by the extreme disparities in wealth between the "haves" and the "have-nots." This in turn has prompted the development of the so-called "informal sector," which complements the formal one by lowering the costs of reproduction of the urban labor force through the provision of low-cost goods and services. Given the high rate of *Third World urbanization, the informal sector also absorbs a large number of in-migrants as low-wage workers and petty commodity producers. Historically, this sector has therefore served to mitigate the conditions of inequality and poverty and has thus engendered some semblance of political stability.

However, the era of *structural adjustment programs has ushered in another cycle of instability in the major Third World cities. The structural adjustment programs imposed by the *World Bank in the 1980s mandated the reduction of the size and the costs of the public sector and the raising of the prices paid to farmers. In the urban areas, these measures wreaked havoc on the infrastructure and education, and raised the prices of staples for the middle-income groups and the poor. In response, major demonstrations and riots broke out, necessitating increasingly repressive measures. At the same time, the World Bank and the *International Monetary Fund prescribed "democratization" measures that encouraged the popular classes to mobilize against repressive regimes that had been installed at the height of the Cold War. This has resulted in very contradictory tendencies since it is these same elements who have borne the brunt of the structural adjustment policies. Today, throughout Latin America, Africa, and Asia, the major cities are on the brink of cataclysm.

Urbanization is an integral part of the process of socioeconomic development that has shaped the cultures and institutions of all societies, both historical as well as contemporary. Urban problems furnish insights into the connection between national and international politics, on the one hand,

and the spatial articulation of economic, political, and ideological relations, on the other.

(See also DEVELOPMENT AND UNDERDEVELOPMENT; MODERNIZATION; SOCIAL MOBILITY.)

Lewis Mumford *The City in History* (New York, 1961). John Mollenkopf and Manuel Castells, eds., *Dual City: Restructuring New York* (New York, 1991). Edward G. Goetz and Susan E. Clarke, eds., *The New Localism: Comparative Urban Politics in a Global Era* (Newbury Park, Calif., 1993). Charles M. Becker, Andrew M. Hamer, and Andrew R. Morrison, eds., *Beyond Urban Bias in Africa: Urbanization in an Era of Structural Adjustment* (Portsmouth, N.H., 1994). David Judge, Gerry Stoker, and Harold Wolman, eds., *Theories of Urban Politics* (Thousand Oaks, Calif., 1995).

RONALD S. EDARI

URUGUAY. The smallest country in South America with a land area approximately the size of North Dakota, Uruguay became a sovereign nation in 1828 thanks to the mediation of the British who for commercial reasons fostered the creation of a buffer state between Argentina and Brazil. The country is virtually a city-state with its capital and major port city, Montevideo, home to almost one-half the population as well as the vast majority of industrial, cultural, and educational activity. Uruguay is blessed with fertile grasslands that cover almost 90 percent of the land, and agriculture and livestock raising have always played an important role in the economy. A heterogeneous population of mostly Spanish and Italian heritage developed one of Latin America's most urban and urbane stable democracies. With a GDP of US$6,200 in 1997, a life expectancy of 72.4 years, and a literacy ratio of 96 percent, the expectation of continued democratic stability after a lapse into military dictatorship from 1973 to 1985 is a realistic expectation.

For much of the nineteenth century Uruguay resembled its neighbors with instability and civil war the norm. This was exacerbated by the continued interference of Brazil and Argentina in the country's internal affairs, frequently abetted by rival Uruguayan factions. By the 1830s, two political parties, the urban-based Colorados and the rural and more conservative Blancos, began a decades-long struggle for power, punctuated by civil wars, which would not end until the first decade of the twentieth century.

The defeat of the Blancos in the 1903–4 Civil War heralded the ascendancy of Uruguay's most important political figure, José Batlle y Ordoñez, who would serve as president from 1903 until 1907 and again from 1911 until 1915, and remain the dominant political figure in the country until his death in 1929. Batlle's state-building and nationalist vision included extensive welfare and pension programs, the separation of church and state with liberalized divorce, and an experiment with a collegial executive system in which a president shared power with a nine-member National Council and Administration which dominated domestic affairs. Economic innovations included the creation of public corporations to handle mortgage lending, insurance, and public utilities. The Great Depression with its accompanying economic crisis led to a civilian coup in the early 1930s, which returned the country to a unipersonal presidency. The economic recovery and stability of the late 1940s and early 1950s led to the fruition of Batlle's vision with the adoption of a nine-member National Council of Government (the so-called *Colegiado Integral*) in 1952. This collegial executive system would last until 1966 when economic decline and social unrest led to the readoption of a unipersonal presidency.

Uruguayan democracy soured when Vice President Jorge Pacheco Areco assumed the presidency in 1967. Pacheco cracked down on the union and student movements, using the growing threat of an urban guerrilla movement—the Tupamaros—as his justification. The 1972 elections took place in the midst of continuing economic stagnation and growing left-wing militancy. Pacheco's handpicked successor, Juan Maria Bordaberry, won the presidency. Bordaberry, a political newcomer, unleashed the military against the Left in April of 1972, decimating the Tupamaros within a few months. First challenging the president over ministerial appointments, the military took direct power in June of 1973 but chose to keep Bordaberry on as a figurehead.

The de facto military government closed Parliament, intervened in the National University, censored the press, arrested thousands, and engaged in systematic torture of political prisoners whose number by 1976 gave Uruguay the highest percentage of political prisoners per capita in the world. The military held power until 1985, when their mismanagement of the economy and failure to win a plebiscite on a new authoritarian constitution sealed their fate.

Although willing to extricate themselves from power, the military were fearful that exiled Blanco senator Wilson Ferreira Aldunate, an outspoken critic of the regime, would win the presidency. By relegalizing the Left and imprisoning Wilson, the armed forces all but assured a Colorado victory. President Julio Maria Sanguinetti, a middle-of-the-road politician, quickly restored civil liberties and reestablished Uruguay's international legitimacy. The issue of past human rights violations during the dictatorship was set aside by the passage of a law that effectively ended all legal proceedings concerning such abuses.

The divisiveness over the human rights issue and an economic slowdown during the last two years of the Sanguinetti administration led to a Blanco victory in the 1989 elections. Senator Luis Alberto Lacalle became the first member of his party to be elected president in the twentieth century. The Lacalle administration pushed a program of economic reform and supported the creation of MERCOSUR, the common market consisting of Brazil, Argentina, Uruguay, and Paraguay. Although economic growth did accelerate under Lacalle, his antilabor and strong free market rhetoric did not go down well with a fiercely middle class welfare-oriented population in an economy with 20 percent of the active labor force employed by the state.

The voters had their say in a referendum on the *privatization of the telephone company, which was defeated by a vote of 72 to 28 percent. This defeat coupled with growing charges of *corruption in the Lacalle administration led to a strong comeback by the Colorados in the 1994 elections. Julio Maria Sanguinetti was elected president for a second time.

The 1994 presidential elections turned Uruguay into a true three-party system with the Left increasing its vote to some 30 percent. Less than three percentage points separated the Colorados, Blancos, and Frente Amplio (as the leftist coalition is known). The Left solidified its hold on Montevideo by winning the mayoralty for the second consecutive time with over 40 percent of the vote in the departmental capital.

Under a second Sanguinetti administration, Uruguay enjoyed significant economic growth thanks mostly to the healthy economies of its MERCOSUR partners. The issue of the fate of individuals who disappeared under the military dictatorship did not go away, with no clear resolution offered. The Left continued to gain strength, especially among the young.

In 1996 a crucial constitutional referendum reformed Uruguay's byzantine electoral system which had historically allowed the traditional parties to each run several presidential candidates, with the most voted candidate of the party that received the most overall votes gaining the presidency, in effect a simultaneous primary and election, known in Uruguay as the "double simultaneous vote." Under the new system, party primaries and conventions will determine the sole presidential candidate for each party in the election. If no candidate receives 50 percent plus one vote on the first ballot, a runoff between the first- and second-place finishers is re-

quired. Thus, the elections in late 1999 can be won by any of Uruguay's three major parties.

Thus the elections in 1999 could have been won by any of Uruguay's three major parties. After spirited primaries the voters could choose between ex-President Lacalle of the Blanco Party, Tabaré Vázquez of the Encuentro Progresista-Frente Amplio, and Jorge Batlle of the Colorado Party. The first round was won by Tabaré Vázquez with 40 percent of the vote, Batlle finished second with 31.5 percent, and Lacalle a distant third with some 21 percent. In the required run-off (ballotage), Jorge Batlle, son of one president and grand-nephew of another, defeated Vazquez by 52 to 45 percent. Most importantly, a vibrant democracy continues to thrive.

(See also DEMOCRATIC TRANSITIONS; MILITARY RULE.)

Martin Weinstein, *Uruguay: Democracy at the Crossroads* (Boulder, Colo., 1988). Charles Guy Gillespie, *Negotiating Democracy: Politicians and Generals in Uruguay* (New York, 1991).

MARTIN WEINSTEIN

UZBEKISTAN. See CENTRAL ASIA.

V

VANUATU. See PACIFIC ISLANDS.

VARGAS, Getúlio. *Brazil's foremost political leader in this century, Getúlio Vargas governed for over two decades and left a strong legacy. He wrought basic changes in Brazil's politics, economy, and society, while his own style of leadership evolved from traditional to populist. Born in 1883 in Rio Grande do Sul, Vargas was raised in a prominent family. Disillusioned as an army cadet, he enrolled in law school. Upon graduation in 1907, he was appointed district attorney in Porto Alegre by party chiefs, and soon he won election to the state legislature.

Vargas took his first federal post in 1923, when he entered Congress, and a year later he was named chief of the state delegation because of his loyalty and skills of conciliation. After several years in national politics, Vargas was chosen to be governor of Rio Grande do Sul in 1928. His administration was remarkable for its bipartisan character and experiments with economic *planning.

In 1930 Vargas decided to run for president on a ticket supported by Rio Grande and Minas Gerais. When their candidate lost to the government candidate, younger politicians in the two states mounted an armed revolt. A reluctant revolutionist, Vargas nonetheless assumed leadership of the successful revolt and was sworn in as provisional president in November 1930.

During his first administration (1930–1937) Vargas was severely challenged by the depression, praetorian forces, a civil war in São Paulo, and former allies in Rio Grande. He remained in power by forming a new national alliance based on the army, loyal governors, and labor. During most of his first term, Vargas attempted to rule democratically, holding elections in 1933 and 1934, promulgating a liberal constitution in 1934, and working with Congress. Still, *democracy appeared chaotic in the mid-1930s and Vargas conspired to increase his own powers.

After convincing the army high command that he needed greater authority to preserve the nation, Vargas executed a coup in November 1937. He disbanded Congress, deposed a few state governors, and gave the country a new regime, named the Estado Novo after Salazar's in Portugal. He burned state flags to symbolize federal dominance and promulgated a *constitution pieced together from fascist models. In fact, Vargas did not use the Constitution but governed autocratically. His lawyers reworked labor legislation into a code, and social security expanded to cover most urban workers. Big business received favored treatment, as the government sought to spur the economy by all possible means.

These measures alienated liberals but won Vargas the support of industrialists and workers alike.

After the outbreak of World War II, Vargas initially flirted with the Axis but eventually entered the war on the side of the Allies in 1942 and sent an army division to Italy in 1944. His aim was to reap economic benefits for Brazil in terms of trade, foreign investment, and lend-lease assistance. Meanwhile, politicians at home criticized the dictatorship and called for elections. Vargas agreed in early 1945 and soon founded two parties. But before the campaign could get under way, the army high command deposed Vargas and held elections without him.

From his self-imposed exile at the family ranch, Vargas easily won election to the Senate. He soon tired of defending his administration in a hostile Congress, however, and decided to run for president. After an arduous campaign—the first modern one in Brazil's history—Vargas won a landslide victory, largely on his reputation as "father of the poor" and defender of Brazil's patrimony. When inaugurated in 1951, Vargas pledged his administration to an ambitious program of economic growth and independence from foreign capital. He stressed government planning, higher income for labor, and ownership of basic industries. He created Petrobras, a government petroleum monopoly, and several development agencies. Vargas soon ran into balance-of-payments problems, however, and found himself stymied by political opponents. The country had grown too complex for his traditional administrative style. Threatened with a military coup in August 1954, he committed suicide rather than suffer another disgrace. The working and lower middle classes believed him a martyr and revered his memory.

The Vargas era brought major changes to the country. Brazil industrialized rapidly with official encouragement, a stance called "developmental nationalism." The workforce moved to cities and became unionized. São Paulo, Rio, and Belo Horizonte formed an urban-industrial heartland. Governmental authority centralized in Rio, and the army gained a monopoly on the use of violence. Women and eighteen-year-olds gained the vote in 1932, and by the 1950s mass electoral politics had replaced the previous limited democracy. Although national parties mediated elections and managed congressional alliances, presidential elections became contests between populists—charismatic leaders pledged to help the masses and reform society. Vargas initiated most of these changes, and as late as the 1980s younger politicians still invoked his name. Vargas's long career embodies Brazil's transition from a backward rural society to a modern industrial one.

(See also POPULISM.)

John W. F. Dulles, *Vargas of Brazil: A Political Biography* (Austin, Tex., 1967). Paulo Brandi, *Vargas: da vida para a história* (Rio de Janeiro, 1983).
MICHAEL L. CONNIFF

VATICAN CITY STATE. The *Roman Catholic Church is a peculiar type of society in that its international juridical standing rests on its spiritual sovereignty. There are three distinct yet interdependent realities: the Vatican City State, the Holy See, and the Universal Church.

Until 1870, the temporal domain of the Church included the Papal States, which ceased to exist from 1870 to 1929. The Lateran Treaty, signed between *Italy and the Holy See on 11 February 1929, created the Vatican City State and "recognizes the *sovereignty of the Holy See" (Art. 2) over this atypical state. The function of this quasi-symbolic, tiny temporal sovereignty is to ensure that the Catholic Church has the minimum autonomy necessary in order to freely exercise its spiritual mission. To this end, the Italian government "guarantees" its territorial integrity. As such, the Vatican City State is a member of nine intergovernmental organizations and of many *non-governmental organizations. Nevertheless, this minuscule state is only a recent development in the history of the papacy: it is not because he is the representative of a state of forty-four hectares (109 acres) that the Sovereign Pontiff is welcomed abroad and maintains diplomatic relations, but rather because he is at the head of the Holy See, which owes its sovereignty in the international order to its spiritual mission. This state is not a nation, for one does not belong to it by *jus sanguinis* or *jus soli*, but by *jus officii*. The Holy See enjoys a status *sui generis* in *international law.

According to Canon 361 of the new Code of Canon Law promulgated in 1983 by *John Paul II, the Holy See designates "not only the Roman Pontiff, but also . . . the office of the Secretary of State . . . and the other institutions of the Roman Curia." These are the official organs of the Vatican City State.

Following changes instituted in 1988, the office of the Secretary of State, which is directed by a cardinal chosen at the Pope's discretion, was divided into two sections. The first, called the Section of General Affairs, is responsible for relations with international organizations as well as with the personnel of the pontifical administration. The other section is in charge of "relations with states," thus replacing the Council for Public Affairs of the Church. The number of countries with which the Holy See has formal diplomatic relations has risen from 100 to 164 during the last fifteen years. In addition, the Vatican is represented by fifteen delegations and twenty-four offices which work with international organizations.

Since 1929, numerous conventions attached to the Lateran Treaty have been signed. In addition, Article 7 of the Constitution of 27 December 1947 of the Italian Republic recognizes the validity of the accords agreed to by the Kingdom of Italy. Over the years, this agreement has passed from the status of a treaty giving the Vatican "guarantees" that could always be taken back by the Italian state to a bilateral accord regulated by international law.

More recently, a revision of the Lateran Accords was drafted and was signed on 18 February 1984. This agreement abrogates the first article of the treaty, which made Catholicism "the only religion of the (Italian) state." This formulation is in accord with what one finds in the accords passed during the same period with Spain, Colombia, and Ecuador. The Catholic religion asks to be recognized as a social reality of the highest importance not only because of the weight of history but also owing to its current vitality. Nevertheless, it no longer seeks to be treated as a monopolistic religion; henceforth, in a pluralist society the Catholic religion acknowledges respect on a juridical level for those who profess another religion or who manifest different ideological convictions.

For John Paul II, the Church must reinstate morality in the face of the threats of nihilism and of certain deviations of modern thinking. His first goal, to which he made a judicious contribution, was the downfall of Soviet communism.

During the post-communist years, the strategy of the Holy See has been to foster a dense, efficient network of diplomatic relations between Central and Eastern European countries, and thus facilitate legislation for freedom or religion in all former communist countries, including those of the former Soviet Union.

Under John Paul II, the Holy See has been directly involved, through its diplomatic channels, in all major political conflicts throughout the world, ranging from East-West disputes to conflicts between *Third World countries.

The papacy has hardened Church discipline. Between 1992 and 1995 the Congregation for the Doctrine of the Faith reinterpreted conciliatory ecclesiology in a more authoritarian direction, including papal authority over local churches.

(See also RELIGION AND POLITICS; POST-COMMUNISM; SECULARIZATION.)

Higinus Cardinale, *The Holy See and the International Order* (Gerrands Cross, U.K., 1976). Pierre Blet, *Histoire de la Représentation Diplomatique du Saint-Siège, des origines à l'aube du XIXe siècle*, Collectanea Archivi Vaticani 9 (Città del Vaticano, 1982). Roland Minnerath, *L'Eglise et les Etats concordataires (1846–1981). La souveraineté spirituelle* (Paris, 1983). *Code de droit canonique* (1984). Paul Poupard, *Le Vatican* (1994). Giancarlo Zizolà, *Les Papes du XXe siècle* (1996).
HENRI MADELIN

VATICAN II. Delivered on 11 October 1962 after four years of intensive preparation, Pope John XXIII's opening speech at the Vatican II ecumenical council caused a sensation. In it, he asked that the members of the council avoid multiplying condemnations and take into account the ecumenical perspective that should enlighten the council.

At its opening, over 2,400 participants were present. One hundred fifty guests from other Christian churches were also invited as silent observers; John XXIII imposed their presence despite hesitations on the part of a majority of the Curate. Among those present were a number of experts (such as theologians and liturgists) who were not permitted to intervene in the general debate but who participated in various committees, and more specifically in those which would yield the texts of Vatican II.

The first topic to be discussed was the liturgy—one of the rare issues treated from the beginning with a view to renewal, even though most of its dispositions confirmed familiar traditions: the importance given to the Word of God, active participation of the laity, use of modern languages, the celebration of the Eucharist, communion with bread and wine. Notwithstanding the numerous criticisms given by a small minority, the project was approved by 97 percent of the members of the council.

John XXIII's death at the end of the first session, on 3 June

1963, touched many people, transcending the Roman Catholic Church, and prompted speculation as to whether his successor would continue the council's work. On 21 June 1963 Giovanni Battista Montini was elected Pope Paul VI by the conclave. In full accordance with the spirit in which John XXIII had led the council, his only wish was to accelerate the council's activities and make them more efficient. One of his first decisions was to invite as "auditors" men and women representative of the laity's role in the church.

The council continued with three other sessions between September 1963 and December 1965. The works of Vatican II are remarkable not only in number—sixteen texts were adopted (four constitutions, nine decrees, and three declarations)—but also in that they reflect a profound renewal of spirit in the church, based on a revitalization of hope, an optimistic vision of the world in which God is incarnated. This is first evident in the texts concerning the internal structure of the Church—seen as the people of God before being a hierarchical organization—with a rehabilitation of the role of the laity in which each and everyone holds a specific role as member of this people. The council affirmed the Church as a communion of particular churches and allowed for a renewal of the exercise of collegiality at all levels while opening new perspectives for ecumenical research. It may be noted that today's practice is not up to the expectations of Vatican II. With the pastoral constitution *Gaudium et Spes*, the Church abandoned radical condemnation of the world and elected instead to have a presence in the debates of today's world, calling for a true alliance between the Church and all humanity.

Vatican II certainly startled many members of the church in allowing individuals to behave, in the last resort, according to personal conscience, and further, with the Declaration of Religious Liberty. This led the way to new understandings between Christians, non-Christians, and atheists, and opened the Church to more democratic mores.

The Council Fathers divided into two camps. Most, themselves quite a diverse group, were concerned, in accordance with the wishes of John XXIII, with the exigencies of the world, with the call for Christians to bear witness to their unity, with the necessity to anchor the life of the Church in the Holy Scriptures and their living tradition. The prime concern of a minority was to safeguard the faith, which, in their view, would be altered by formal change. These divisions seem to continue to mark today's Church, at least as two viewpoints that have to come to an accord when choices are to be made.

The Council's wish for independence vis-à-vis the Roman Curia, which had been in charge of its preparation and organization, was affirmed by the first working assembly. This independent spirit, displayed continually, caused sharp tensions at times. Nearly all the texts, which serve as the foundation for the Church today, were sent back to the commissions for revision when they failed to reflect the wish for openness, for dialogue, for renovation as expressed by the Pope and the Council Fathers. Their revision involved the Fathers in personal reexamination, and thereby in a deeper commitment to the spirit of the council.

Gustave Martelet, *Les Islée Maitresses de Vatican II* (Paris, 1985). Peter Hebble Thwaite, *Jean XXIII, le Pape du Concile* (Paris, 1988). Joseph Thomas, *Le Concile Vatican II* (Paris, 1989).

HENRI MADELIN

VENEZUELA. During the nineteenth century, Venezuela was a poor and politically undeveloped state. A series of regionally based strongmen, or *caudillos,* backed by private armies, controlled the central government in Caracas, but never without sporadic challenges from other *caudillos.* Most of the population lived in poverty, ignorance, and fear, although a small elite class amassed some wealth from import businesses or the export of coffee, cocoa, or hides, and negotiated an uneasy coexistence with each government.

Fundamental transformations of Venezuelan politics and economy began during the dictatorship of Juan Vicente Gómez (1908–1935), who finally defeated all other *caudillos* and created an effective national military force. Oil production also began during his rule and expanded so rapidly that Venezuela became the world's largest oil exporter and second-largest producer by 1928. The resulting inflow of wealth strengthened state capacities and contributed to the growth of a small middle class that began to demand greater participation in politics. These demands were met with brutal repression until the relatively liberal dictatorship of General Medina Angarita (1941–1945), who permitted the rapid organization of mass political parties, trade unions, and peasant leagues. The largest of the new parties, Acción Democráitica (AD), joined with junior military officers to overthrow Medina and oversee the country's first popular elections. This democratic regime failed, however, because the Catholic Church and conservative interests felt threatened by the anticlerical policies, social *reforms, and electoral dominance of the AD government, and encouraged the military to overthrow it in 1948.

As a result, Venezuela experienced ten more years of dictatorship, this time under Marcos Pérez Jiménez. This government coincided initially with continued oil-fueled economic expansion, which accelerated industrialization, urban migration, and infrastructural development. But when the economy slumped and the dictator was discredited by charges of corruption and electoral fraud in 1957, he was replaced by a military-civilian junta.

Since 1958, all Venezuelan presidents have been chosen in fair, direct elections with universal adult suffrage. The first government of this democratic regime faced frequent coup attempts but survived them all. The regime was also threatened by an armed insurgency movement beginning in 1961, but the guerrillas were mostly defeated by 1965 and returned to electoral politics in 1967. *Democracy was fully consolidated by 1969, when the ruling Acción Democrática party recognized its electoral defeat and handed over the presidency to Rafael Caldera of the Partido Social Cristiano (COPEI). These two parties alternated in the presidency for the next three terms.

The success of the transition to democracy owes much to the leadership of Rómulo Betancourt and Rafael Caldera, the founders of AD and COPEI, respectively. In order to prevent a repeat of the polarization that doomed democracy during the 1945–1948 period, the two leaders persuaded their parties to support the Pact of Punto Fijo, which calmed partisan rivalries, removed contentious issues from the political agenda, produced broad support for a common program of reforms, and committed the first presidential candidates to a national unity coalition regardless of the election results.

The stability of Venezuelan democracy from 1968 to 1988 also owed much to the nature of the two main parties. While the Social Democratic AD and Christian Democratic COPEI initially reflected the cleavage between a hegemonic reformist, anticlerical government and its conservative opposition, both parties moved towards the center by 1958, becoming overlapping center-left and center-right parties. There was greater ideological distance between these two parties and the smaller parties, particularly the Movimiento al Socialismo (MAS), a pluralistic splinter from the Communist Party. However, as AD and COPEI shared around 80 percent of the legislative vote and 90 percent of the presidential vote from 1973 to 1988, the cleavage between them was the dominant one. These two parties were also remarkably similar in the support they drew from all regions, classes, ages, and occupational groups. Their ideological proximity helped preserve the spirit of interparty consultation and consensus established in the Pact of Punto Fijo. AD and COPEI were also aggressive in enforcing party discipline in Congress and in controlling other organizations for partisan purposes. Thorough party penetration helped party leaders achieve their aim of moderating conflict in the interests of stability, but it also bred frustration with the nation's stifled organizational life.

Although Venezuela's socioeconomic inequalities are pronounced, its per capita GDP was by far the highest in Latin America for several decades thanks to the oil industry, which provides 90 percent of its export earnings and 50 to 75 percent of its central government revenues. The public sector grew strongly during the years of high oil prices (1974–1976, 1979–1981) in order to create jobs for party supporters, subsidize producers and consumers, expand social benefits, and finance ambitious industrialization and infrastructure projects. The government, however, failed to take adequate precautions to prevent indebtedness or wrenching adjustment during years of falling oil prices (1977–1978, 1981–1987). In the late 1970s the economy began a long period of decline. Growing numbers of Venezuelans blamed the two leading parties for worsening living standards and *corruption. These two parties lost most of their support in the elections of 1993–2000. The political vacuum was filled by Hugo Chávez Frías, who led an unsuccessful coup attempt in 1992 and was elected president in 1998 and 2000. A constituent assembly in 1999 strengthened the president's powers and enabled him to install supporters in all other national government bodies.

Venezuela has remained at peace with its neighbors, although it has lingering border disputes with Guyana and Colombia and there is considerable resentment of the many illegal Colombian and West Indian immigrants. It has become an influential leader in Central American and the Caribbean Basin by investing there, offering mediation, granting economic assistance, subsidizing oil shipments, and providing air links to remote islands. Relations with the United States have been friendly, as the United States has long viewed Venezuela as the model of a democratic, reformist alternative to Cuba.

(See also DEMOCRATIC TRANSITIONS; ORGANIZATION OF PETROLEUM EXPORTING COUNTRIES: U.S.–LATIN AMERICAN RELATIONS.)

David Eugene Blank, *Venezuela: Politics in a Petroleum Republic* (New York, 1984). John D. Martz and David J. Myers, eds., *Venezuela: The Democratic Experience*, 2d. ed. (New York, 1986).

MICHAEL COPPEDGE

VERSAILLES, TREATY OF. See WORLD WAR I.

VETO. Broadly speaking, the veto ("I forbid" in Latin) connotes any institutionalized ability to reject offers during political bargaining. From this perspective, the U.S. Senate has a veto over treaties negotiated by the executive, and constitutional courts have a veto over legislation. However, the term usually refers to an executive or presidential veto over legislation.

The significance of the executive veto varies dramatically across constitutional designs. In parliamentary systems, the executive is an agent of a legislative party or coalition of parties, so the veto has no role. In semipresidential systems, like that of France, an elected president with limited powers serves concurrently with a prime minister selected by the legislature. In such systems, the presidential veto, if one exists at all, usually can be overridden (reversed) by a simple legislative majority. Thus, the veto may simply delay legislation. But in systems based on the *separation of powers (so-called presidential systems), the executive veto is often a key element of the constitutional design. These systems usually require super-majority votes in both chambers of the legislature to override a presidential veto. The veto is often the executive's principal legislative power. (In some countries, though not the United States, the president may also issue decrees and introduce legislation.) A study encompassing forty-three governments in presidential and semipresidential systems in thirty-five countries found that 76 percent possessed executive vetoes with super-majority provisions (Shugart and Carey 1992).

The presidential veto in separation of powers systems may influence legislators in a variety of ways (Cameron 2000). The legislature's anticipation of a veto alters the content of bills, while vetoes and veto threats further shape important legislation. However, the veto is a potent tool only when the executive's policy preferences differ from those of the legislature, for example, during divided party government in the United States.

Matthew Shugart and John Carey, *Presidents and Assemblies* (Cambridge, U.K. 1992). Charles Cameron, *Veto Bargaining* (Cambridge, U.K. 2000).

CHARLES M. CAMERON

VIETNAM. The Socialist Republic of Vietnam (SRV), with a population over 78 million in 2000, is the world's twelfth and Southeast Asia's second most populous state. The SRV, along with China, Cuba, the Democratic People's Republic of Korea (North Korea), and Laos, are the last five remaining *communist party states. The SRV was formed following military reunification on 30 April 1975 and national elections held in July 1976 that formally united North and South.

Vietnam is situated on the rugged eastern part of the Indochinese peninsula. Laos and Cambodia lie to the west, China to the north. Vietnam's population is concentrated in two rice-growing areas, the Red River delta in the north and the Mekong River delta in the south. These are joined by the Central Mountain range, which has been likened to a peasant's bamboo carrying pole from which the two rice baskets—the river deltas—are suspended.

Vietnam is an agrarian society with over three-quarters of

the population living in rural areas engaged in agricultural pursuits. An estimated 85 percent of the population are ethnic Vietnamese. Vietnam's minority population consists of Chinese, Khmers, and a variety of highland ethnic groups. The Vietnamese people adhere to a syncretic religious tradition that is a mixture of Mahayana Buddhism, Taoism, and *Confucianism. There is a substantial Catholic minority and a small Islamic community. Most of the highlanders are animists. Vietnam has also developed its own unique religious traditions, that of Hoa Hao and Cao Dai, which are strong in the Mekong Delta and the area northwest of Saigon.

The emergence of a communist regime in Vietnam has been the end product of a prolonged process of socioeconomic transformation and modernization precipitated by the corrosive impact of French colonialism on traditional Vietnamese society. In 1930 *Ho Chi Minh founded the Vietnam Communist Party (VCP), a modern political organization dedicated to revolutionary ends. In August 1945 Ho seized power and proclaimed the formation of the Democratic Republic of Vietnam (DRV). France opposed this move and a bitter eight-year war ensued.

In 1954, Vietnam was partitioned. A pro-American regime (the Republic of Vietnam) remained in control in South Vietnam, while the Vietnam Communist Party took charge of the Democratic Republic of Vietnam in the north. The VCP quickly established a "people's democracy." This was a monoorganizational state in which the party penetrated and controlled all organizations including the bureaucracy and the military. Society at large was grouped into mass organizations for peasants, workers, women, youth, and special interest groups (for artists, journalists, intellectuals, and various religions). Together these formed the constituents of the Vietnam Fatherland Front, an umbrella organization controlled by the VCP.

After assuming state power in the north, the VCP moved to organize production along orthodox socialist lines. In 1955–56 North Vietnam conducted a Chinese-style *land reform program that went badly off course. In addition to many innocent victims whose land was confiscated, an estimated 15,000 persons were executed. In 1956–57, the regime admitted its mistakes, dismissed the officials concerned, and launched a "rectification of errors" campaign. The VCP then resumed its march toward socialism. In the 1960s, peasant farmers were organized into agricultural production cooperatives in which the major means of production were collectivized. At the same time all heavy and light industry was nationalized and placed under central state control. Handicraft production was likewise organized collectively.

The constitutional structure of the DRV initially drew its authority from the 1945 independence constitution. This was replaced by a more orthodox communist party state constitution in 1960. This document enshrined the leading role of the party and Marxist-Leninist ideology. The highest legislative body, the National Assembly, was in fact a rubber stamp controlled and directed by the VCP. All facets of the economy were placed under rigid central control under a State Planning Commission.

In the late 1950s North Vietnam became the beneficiary of large-scale Chinese and Soviet aid. Priority was now placed on developing an industrial base. This was reflected in Vietnam's first Three-Year Plan (1958–60). In September 1960, the VCP's Third National Congress decided to step up support for the Communist-led "war of national liberation" in the south. The United States responded by introducing ground troops and in 1965 initiated a sustained air war over North Vietnam which destroyed much of its industry and infrastructure.

The *Vietnam War soon became an "escalating stalemate" as North Vietnam increased its armed infiltration into the south and the United States introduced ever-increasing numbers of ground forces. Communist offensives in 1968 and 1972 failed to alter the balance on the battlefield. A peace agreement reached in 1973 led to the withdrawal of United States troops but failed to stop the fighting among the Vietnamese. In 1975 Communist forces overwhelmed South Vietnam and captured Saigon on 30 April.

Communist leaders moved quickly to integrate the south into existing northern political structures. Vietnam's endeavor to build socialism in the post–Vietnam War years was short-lived. Southern peasants resisted collectivization. Natural disasters in 1977 and 1978, coupled with gross economic mismanagement, produced an economic crisis of mammoth proportions. Large numbers of ethnic Chinese and Southern Vietnamese began to flee the country by boat or by land into southern China. At the same time, relations with neighboring Cambodia and its ally, China, deteriorated.

In late 1978 Vietnam invaded and occupied Cambodia. In early 1979 China retaliated by attacking and laying waste to Vietnam's northern frontier region. Vietnam was also subject to an aid and trade embargo by neighboring states and Western countries formerly sympathetic to South Vietnam. As a result, Vietnam became totally dependent on the Soviet Union and Eastern Europe. Just prior to its invasion of Cambodia, Vietnam and the Soviet Union signed a twenty-five-year Treaty of Friendship and Cooperation. After China's attack on Vietnam, the Soviet Union greatly increased its military aid to Vietnam and established a naval base at the former U.S. facility at Cam Ranh Bay. The regular Vietnamese army was modernized and grew in size to the fifth largest in the world, numbering over 1.2 million.

The combined effects of the Sino-Vietnamese War, coupled with distortions in the Vietnamese economy caused by dependency on Soviet subsidies and misguided economic priorities, further deepened Vietnam's socioeconomic crisis. This provoked spontaneous pressures from below to do away with the rigidities of socialist planning. Cries for reform were soon heard within the VCP itself. In the late 1970s some members of the VCP pushed for a reform package based on market mechanisms and price incentives. These efforts faced stiff opposition from party conservatives and it was only in 1986, at the VCP's Sixth National Congress, that Vietnam formally endorsed "renovation" as national policy.

Vietnam's efforts to reform the economy have resulted in restructuring of the central planning apparatus, greater decentralization, and increased emphasis on the market mechanism, the private sector, and individual initiative. After the withdrawal of Vietnamese military forces from Cambodia in September 1989, Vietnam implemented a major demobilization of its armed forces. Vietnam's reformist path, which has been defined as "developing a market economy with a socialist orientation under the direction of the state," was endorsed by the Seventh and Eighth National Party Congresses, held in 1991 and 1996, respectively. Both of these meetings also endorsed a policy of industrializing and modernizing Vietnam so it could catch up with neighbors in the early decades of the twenty-first century.

Following the signing of a comprehensive Cambodian peace agreement in October 1991, Vietnam ceased to be a pariah state. After the Soviet Union collapsed, Vietnam successfully reorientated its economy to East Asia. As a result aid and foreign investment poured in while trade grew. Vietnam also took determined steps to diversify its foreign relations under the slogan of "making friends with all countries." Relations with China were normalized in November 1991. In July 1995 Vietnam also normalized its relations with the United States and became the seventh member of the Association of Southeast Asian Nations (ASEAN).

In April 1997 the United States appointed Pete Peterson, a former Vietnam-era prisoner of war, its first ambassador to postwar Vietnam. Within three years more than 400 American companies were engaged in business. Their investments totaled US$1.3 billion in 1999, making the United States the sixth largest investor in Vietnam. In 1999, after three years of negotiations, the United States and Vietnam came very close to agreeing on the terms of a historic bilateral trade agreement. On the eve of the scheduled signing ceremony Vietnam reneged due to internal dissent by party conservatives who feared losing control over the economy. Nonetheless, a high point in bilateral relations was reached in March 2000 when William Cohen became the first U.S. secretary of defense to visit Hanoi since the end of the Vietnam War.

Vietnam's program of renovation has been accompanied by a carefully controlled process of political liberalization. In 1992 the SRV adopted a new constitution which for the first time made the VCP accountable under state law. The central government apparatus was revamped. Collective leadership was replaced by a cabinet system headed by a prime minister. Individual ministers are now held responsible for their actions. Vietnam's National Assembly has been given increased scope to shape legislation and on occasion has demonstrated its independence. Vietnam's electoral process has been opened up to permit independent nonparty candidates to stand for election. Nonetheless, the VCP leadership continues to declare its opposition to pluralism and multiparty democracy. Political dissidents are dealt with harshly.

In late 1996, Vietnam's economic growth rate began to decline for the first time since the adoption of renovation. In 1997 Vietnam experienced a marked fall in both foreign investment and trade. Late in the year violent peasant protests broke out in the northern province of Thai Binh, a bastion of the communist revolution. The VCP responded by jettisoning its aging leadership troika—Party Secretary General Do Muoi, President Le Duc Anh, and Prime Minister Vo Van Kiet. Le Kha Phieu, a career political officer in the military, became the new party chief. Under his direction Vietnam responded to the Asian financial crisis by battening down the hatches in an attempt to ride out the economic storm.

During 1998–99 five plenary meetings of the VCP Central Committee were held. All reaffirmed that economic reforms would not be permitted to undermine political stability. The seventh and eight plenums, held in August and November 1999, began preparations for the Ninth National Party Congress scheduled for the first quarter of 2001. As a consequence, economic reform efforts are likely to remain stalled as Vietnamese leaders turn inward to map socioeconomic policy for the five years following the Ninth Congress.

(See also DECOLONIZATION; NATIONAL LIBERATION MOVEMENTS.)

Gareth Porter, *Vietnam: The Politics of Bureaucratic Socialism* (Ithaca, N.Y., 1993). Adam Fforde and Stefan de Vylder, *From Plan to Market: The Economic Transition in Vietnam* (Boulder, Colo., 1996). Gabriel Kolko, *Vietnam: Anatomy of a Peace* (New York, 1997). Carlyle A. Thayer and Ramses Amer, *Vietnamese Foreign Policy in Transition* (New York, 1999).

CARLYLE A. THAYER

VIETNAM WAR. Fashioned from stark slabs of black granite, the Vietnam Veterans Memorial in Washington, D.C., perfectly represents America's collective memory of its longest *war and first defeat. The memorial, like the memory, is both somber and ambiguous.

On the polished face of the memorial appear the names of some 58,000 U.S. military personnel who died in Indochina. This was the greatest cost of the war to the *United States. There were others as well: the bitterness of over 3 million *Vietnam veterans who returned to more scorn than gratitude from their fellow citizens; the inflation that followed years of deficit financing to help cover more than $150 billion in war expenses; bruising divisions within American society about responsibility for the nation's defeat and the devastation of the peoples and lands of Indochina; and a public cynicism about government, reinforced by the *Watergate scandal, that was to mark U.S. politics for many years.

American involvement in the conflicts of Indochina was driven by a doctrinal commitment to the *containment of *communism. The goal was absolute, but it was pursued through incremental, compromise measures. From Harry *Truman to Richard *Nixon, no president could find a formula for victory at a cost in lives and resources he thought the public would endure or U.S. interests would justify. Yet throughout the war, even after it became broadly unpopular, *public opinion always opposed withdrawal if it would lead to defeat. Thus, from 1950 until 1975, as the military and political tide ran first against the French and then against a series of non-Communist governments in Vietnam, Cambodia, and Laos, American actions were sufficient only to postpone defeat.

American ambivalence about the French colonial war in Vietnam turned to active support after the triumph of communism in China in 1949. As Washington intervened in Korea in June 1950, President Truman ordered the first significant military aid to the French forces in Indochina. By 1954, the United States was covering some eighty percent of their costs.

As the French neared defeat at Dien Bien Phu in April 1954, French and American military leaders recommended a massive U.S. air strike to relieve the besieged garrison. After consulting with congressional leaders, President Dwight D. *Eisenhower refused unless Paris accelerated the independence of its Indochinese colonies and the British agreed to join in the operation. Neither condition was fulfilled.

While acquiescing in the French defeat and agreeing not to disturb the Geneva Accords (July 1954) that divided Vietnam pending elections two years later, the Eisenhower administration soon moved to buttress the anti-Communist government of Ngo Dinh Diem in the south. It formed the Southeast Asia Treaty Organization (SEATO); sent American military advisers and massive quantities of military and economic aid to the Republic of Vietnam (South Vietnam); and backed Diem's stand against holding the scheduled 1956 elections.

Like his predecessor, President John F. *Kennedy avoided sending U.S. combat troops to Vietnam. But the unpopular Diem government faltered in its war against a burgeoning insurgency and Washington greatly increased its assistance and the number of American military advisers. As U.S. advisers began to accompany government battalions into combat and took casualties, Vietnam emerged as a public issue in the United States.

By the late summer of 1963, the strategic hamlets program (modeled on a successful British *counterinsurgency program in Malaya) was failing, military operations were mixed in their results, and Diem was under increasing pressure from Buddhist groups. Kennedy encouraged a *coup d'état by South Vietnamese military leaders. Diem was assassinated during the coup (1 November 1963). His removal produced an extended period of political instability in Saigon, lasting until the presidency of Nguyen Van Thieu (1967–1975).

President Lyndon B. *Johnson cautiously increased the number of U.S. advisers in 1964 and, in August, responded to an attack by North Vietnamese patrol boats on an American destroyer in the Tonkin Gulf with the first U.S. bombing raid against the Democratic Republic of Vietnam (North Vietnam). (The raid followed claims of a second PT boat attack that were never substantiated.) Johnson used the incident to gain from Congress a nearly unanimous resolution authorizing him "to take all necessary measures" to defend U.S. forces and prevent further aggression in the region.

After his landslide reelection in 1964, Johnson moved more vigorously to head off a developing military defeat of Saigon's forces by the National Liberation Front, which was receiving increasing assistance from the North Vietnamese. In December, American bombing of infiltration routes in Laos (Operation Barrel Roll) was initiated. In February 1965, Johnson ordered a bombing campaign against North Vietnam (Rolling Thunder). This campaign was escalated incrementally over the coming years, in an effort to break Hanoi's will as well as to interdict the flow of supplies and soldiers to the south. The bases for U.S. airplanes were vulnerable to attack, and Johnson soon ordered two marine battalions to guard duty. By late spring 1965, Saigon's forces in central Vietnam were near collapse. Washington sent more American troops and by summer they were in combat.

During 1966 and 1967, American forces were gradually increased to some 500,000, matched by increasing numbers of North Vietnamese forces infiltrating the south. Each, with its southern allies, waged a brutal main force war of attrition designed more to inflict casualties than to gain and hold territory. Meanwhile, a guerrilla war in the villages was opposed by a massive, American-supported pacification program that relied on local militia and economic aid efforts. As a result of both wars, well over one million Vietnamese were forced to leave their ancestral homes for the crowded, economically pressed cities. Throughout this period, both Hanoi and Wash-

ington proclaimed their willingness to negotiate an end to the conflict, but each insisted on its own terms.

As casualties mounted, U.S. public opinion began to turn against the war. On 31 January 1968 (the Vietnamese lunar New Year, called Tet), the National Liberation Front and the North Vietnamese army launched attacks throughout the south, including a dramatic assault on the American embassy in Saigon. While the offensive fell short militarily, it shocked an American public already skeptical of Johnson's claims of progress. Attacked by the *Left for intervention and by the *Right for a failure to prevail, in late March Johnson announced that he would not seek reelection. He ordered new efforts at a negotiated solution and put a cap on the U.S. force level at under 550,000.

Promising to end the war on honorable terms, Richard Nixon won the presidency of a nation bitterly divided over the war. For the next four years, Nixon pursued a complex strategy. To convince the American public that the end was in sight, he pursued a policy of "Vietnamization" that attempted to strengthen Saigon's military forces while gradually withdrawing American troops.

To convince Hanoi to settle the war on acceptable terms, he ordered a series of military measures: increased bombing in Vietnam; the secret bombing of North Vietnamese sanctuaries in Cambodia; the April 1970 invasion of Cambodia by American and South Vietnamese troops to disrupt these sanctuaries (leading to widespread antiwar demonstrations in the United States and the fatal shooting of four student protesters at Kent State University); a disastrous invasion of Laos (to interdict North Vietnamese supply routes) in early 1971 by South Vietnamese troops; and heavy bombing as well as the mining of Hanoi's harbor, Haiphong, after a new North Vietnamese offensive in April 1972. And to help achieve a settlement, Nixon sought the assistance of Moscow and Beijing, Hanoi's patrons.

The key to ending the war were secret talks in Paris with North Vietnamese representatives. In the summer of 1969 Nixon's national security adviser, Henry *Kissinger, threatened them with punishing, new American military measures if there were no diplomatic breakthrough by 1 November. It did not move Hanoi and Washington failed to follow through on its threat. But the talks continued intermittently for the next three years, producing a compromise agreement between the two exhausted sides in October 1972. Hanoi abandoned its insistence that President Thieu be removed from power and agreed to return U.S. prisoners of war. Washington dropped its long-standing insistence that Hanoi withdraw its forces from South Vietnam when American troops left.

President Thieu balked at these terms. But after Nixon's reelection in November, a renewed bombing attack on North Vietnam in late December, and a new aid package for the South Vietnamese, the American president insisted that Thieu acquiesce in a renegotiated settlement on essentially the same terms. An ill-defined cease-fire was declared in January 1973 and the remaining American forces were withdrawn.

Both the cease-fire and talks among the Vietnamese on the political future of South Vietnam collapsed, however. In early 1975, hindered by its own poor morale and dwindling American aid, the South Vietnamese army crumbled in the face of a new North Vietnamese offensive. On 30 April 1975, Saigon fell to the Communist forces. The remaining Americans fled before them, without having arranged for the escape of most of the hundreds of thousands of South Vietnamese who had worked with them. Soon thereafter, Phnom Penh, the capital of Cambodia, was taken by the genocidal Khmer Rouge.

For a few years after the war, "Let Us Forget" better described the collective attitude of Americans than "Lest We Forget." But by the 1980s, a series of films and television programs addressed the Vietnam experience. Some found only horror in the war; others found glory in the actions of American soldiers.

Similarly, during the war and after, analysts and political leaders found very different explanations and lessons in the experience. Some found an explanation in their view of a United States bound by its drive for economic advantage in the *Third World and the power of a *military-industrial complex in Washington. Others believed there had been a simple failure of will by American presidents.

Supporters of the presidents who had engaged America in the conflict argued that the war came through an inadvertent stumbling into the Vietnam quagmire. The bureaucracy either misled its leaders or failed to warn them. But critics of this view pointed to the information available within the government, from the start, about the difficulties of engagement.

Supporters of Congress blamed an "imperial presidency" for the disaster. But critics of Congress, arguing that it must share in the blame, pointed to the passage of the Tonkin Gulf Resolution and the failure of Congress to use the power of the purse to influence presidents' behavior.

The two most influential lessons of the war helped shape the general policies of the first two postwar presidencies. For President Jimmy *Carter and many of his advisers, Vietnam was primarily a conceptual error, the result of a rigid American commitment to the containment of communism everywhere, without due regard to local realities and specific U.S. interests. Vietnam tragically illustrated the limits of American power in a changing world. To President Ronald *Reagan and many of his advisers, the United States had been right to intervene in Vietnam. The failure was not conceptual but political: a liberal press and Congress had helped create a national loss of will that made the pursuit of victory impossible. The limits to American power were primarily self-imposed.

A crucial difference between them was thus the question of whether the war was winnable. Many conservatives, pointing to the incremental nature of U.S. military involvement,

Johnson's limits on the bombing campaign, and the failure of Congress to allow generous quantities of aid to the anti-Communist governments in Vietnam and Cambodia in the months before their defeats, argued that the war could and should have been won. Liberal analysts pointed to Pentagon studies showing the limited effects of the bombing on a society with few industrial targets; to the ability of the North Vietnamese to match every American troop increase; to the dependency of the South Vietnamese government on American aid, demonstrating its lack of popular support in a war that would be decided as much by political as by military strength; and to the evident determination of Hanoi and the National Liberation Front to prevail and reunite their nation on their terms. For much of the public, the lesson was simple but ambiguous: "Win quickly or stay out," with some emphasizing the former and some the latter.

After UN forces had routed the Iraqi army in Kuwait in early 1991, President George *Bush immediately proclaimed that the specter of Vietnam had been buried forever in the desert sands of the Arabian Peninsula. To some, however, his impassioned reference to an earlier war showed how strongly it still weighed. Like the memorial on the Mall in Washington, D.C., and despite the establishment of diplomatic relations between the two nations in the mid-1990s, Vietnam continued to occupy a haunting place in the American memory, and likely will do so in the new millennium.

(See also BUREAUCRATIC POLITICS; COLONIAL EMPIRES; DECOLONIZATION; GUERRILLA WARFARE; GULF WAR; KOREAN WAR; NATIONAL LIBERATION MOVEMENTS; U.S. FOREIGN POLICY.)

George C. Herring, ed., *The Pentagon Papers* (New York, 1971; abridged ed, New York, 1993). Leslie H. Gelb with Richard K. Betts, *The Irony of Vietnam: The System Worked* (Washington, D.C., 1979). George C. Herring, *America's Longest War: The United States and Vietnam, 1950–1975*, 2nd ed. New York, 1986). Stanley Karnow, *Vietnam: A History*, Rev. ed. (New York, 1991). William J. Duiker, *Sacred War: Nationalism and Revolution in a Divided Vietnam* (New York, 1995).

ANTHONY LAKE

VIOLENCE, POLITICAL. See ASSASSINATION; POLITICAL VIOLENCE; TERRORISM; TORTURE.

VOLUNTARY EXPORT RESTRAINT. See PROTECTION.

VOTING BEHAVIOR. See ELECTIONS AND VOTING BEHAVIOR.

W

WAŁĘSA, Lech. Born 29 September 1943 in the village of Popowo near Lipno in northwest Poland, Lech Wałęsa will forever be associated with the Gdańsk shipyard and the birth of *Solidarity. Now the shipyard is in bankruptcy and he himself on the margins of Polish politics: in 1998 Solidarity is led by Marian Krzaklewski and heads a coalition government under the premiership of Jerzy Buzek. For his part Wałęsa has formed a small political party, the Christian Democracy of the Third Polish Republic, waiting the moment when the parties and groups gathered around Solidarity in government fall out and his services are once again required.

Although his own standing among at home has fallen considerably, he is assured a place in Polish history both as a Noble Peace Prize recipient and as the electrician who, after ten years of union militancy, in 1980 confronted the communist leadership and contributed to the eventual collapse of the Soviet system. Interned in 1981 under martial law, he reemerged to be the astute aboveground leader of the Solidarity opposition, in the process forging an alliance with the *Roman Catholic Church and benefiting from the personal encouragement of meetings with Pope *John Paul II in 1985 and 1987. He led Solidarity to the roundtable talks that culminated in partially free elections which contributed to the installation in September 1989 of the first noncommunist premier, Tadeusz Mazowiecki.

Later as president he exploited the different tendencies contained within the Solidarity movement, in particular between liberal secular and nationalist-clerical sentiments. Wałęsa manipulated the question of the future of the Solidarity Citizens' Committees, the grassroots power base for any noncommunist movement, and brought about the fragmentation of the Citizens' Parliamentary Caucus (OKP), the party in power.

In 1991, Wałęsa dissolved the parliament of Jan Krzysztof Bielecki and the first fully free parliamentary elections produced a parliament which included representatives of parliament of twenty-four parties. It seems in retrospect that Wałęsa was too quick to follow up the vote of no confidence in the minority government of Hannah Suchocka by again dissolving parliament in May 1993. The elections proved to be a disaster for the right and for the Church which had openly supported it, and instead ushered in a postcommunist government for the next four years.

A constitutional framework that permitted "cohabitation" preserved some power for Wałęsa to confront the postcommunist governments of Waldemar Pawiak and Jozef Oleksy as the ex-communist SLD and their PSL allies sought to take over the reins of economic as well as political power. However Wałęsa's overly aggressive election campaign of November 1995, in which he was outmaneuvered by the polished ex-communist Alexander Kwáśniewski, saw him narrowly lose office. Wałęsa's departure, accompanied by the accusations of spying against premier Oleksy, was a characteristic end to a career stronger on personal courage than on public persona.

By then Wałęsa was burdened with his own private scandals involving a million-dollar honorarium, the public behavior of members of his family, as well as continuing rumors centered around secret-police files and talk of collaboration. Wałęsa has made it clear that he will not seek the presidency again, a promise he is likely to keep since the powers accorded that office under the Constitution passed in May 1997 are too limiting. A think tank named after him as well as the honorary degrees he has collected, his continuing speaking career around the world, and a personal column in a top news weekly are a paradoxical epilogue for a man who never had much time for the intellectuals or "eggheads" who surrounded him.

(See also DEMOCRATIC TRANSITION; NINETEEN-EIGHTY-NINE; POLAND; POST COMMUNISM.)

GEORGE KOLANKIEWICZ

WAR. See overleaf.

WAR CRIMES. Grave offenses against the laws of warfare entailing criminal responsibility of individuals are known as war crimes. It is frequently asserted that every single violation of the laws of warfare amounts automatically to a war crime, but in actuality individual criminal responsibility is more restricted in scope. A war crime is typically committed by members of armed forces, but it can also be perpetrated by civilians.

There is no comprehensive and binding definition of the term *war crimes*. The basic, albeit incomplete, definition appears in Article 6 of the 1945 Charter of the International Military Tribunal (annexed to the London Agreement for the Prosecution and Punishment of the Major War Criminals of the European Axis), which also sets forth two independent categories of "crimes against peace" and "crimes against humanity." Under this provision, war crimes include—but are not limited to—"murder, ill-treatment or deportation to slave labour or for any other purpose of civilian population of or in occupied territory, murder or ill-treatment of prisoners of war or persons on the seas, killing of hostages, plunder of public or private property, wanton destruction of cities, towns or villages, or devastation not justified by military necessity."

The International Military Tribunal at Nuremberg emphasized that other acts not mentioned in Article 6—such as the

(cont. on p. 897)

WAR. War is broadly defined by Malinowski as an "armed conflict between two independent political units, by means of organized military force, in the pursuit of a tribal or national policy" (1968, p. 28). The more restricted definition used here conceptualizes war as events that produce substantial militarized arms conflict between organized military forces of independent nations. This excludes massive *domestic* conflicts such as the American Civil War (1861–1865), the Boxer Rebellion in China (1900), and the *Russian Revolution (1917–1921), guerrilla activities such as the Cuban Revolution (1959), and terrorist campaigns such as those attributed to Osama Ben Laden (1998–2000).

The focus of scholarly interest about war has been on global conflicts that escalate and produce severe consequences with high casualties. Global wars directly involve major powers on both sides, devastate world resources and populations, and threaten the very foundations of the international order. The best-known and most carefully studied cases of this very rare phenomenon are *World War I (1913–1918) and *World War II (1939–1945). Limited wars involve major powers on one side only and while consequences can be devastating for the smaller power, these conflicts are "limited" for the major power. Recall that in the *Vietnam War (1960–1975) the United States lost approximately 60,000 soldiers, but the Vietnamese counted their losses in the millions. *Peace, on the other hand, is simply the lack of militarized contests among nations. Nations are at peace even in crisis, provided that disputes are resolved by accommodation, or by forcing one side to yield to the demands of another *without* resorting to arms.

When *alliances are present, limited wars can diffuse and escalate into major wars. The German intervention in Czechoslovakia (1938) led to appeasement, but a comparable action in Poland (1939) led to World War II. The Iraqi intervention in Kuwait (1990) led to the limited *Gulf War waged by the U.S.-led alliance (1990–1991). The *Cold War between the United States and the Soviet Union (1946–1989) never escalated despite its duration. The task of theory is to anticipate conflicts before they begin and forecast their potential escalation.

A classic account of the reasons for waging war is provided by the Realist tradition in *international relations. Realists propose that the distribution of power among nations is directly related to the onset of global war. Balance of power theory, as the name implies, posits that nations face anarchy in world politics and stability is preserved as long as an equal distribution of power is maintained. A preponderant power will use its power advantage to wage war because it expects to win at a relatively low cost. Nations facing equivalent powers will not wage war because they deem the costs too high. Thus, this bold thesis proposes that asymmetric power distributions, as Waltz argues, will lead to war "because there is nothing to prevent them" (1959, p. 232).

In such an anarchic global environment all nations wish to increase their relative power to guarantee their future *security. The function of alliances is to preserve the balance of power among contending coalitions and provide the weaker nations with some measure of protection against larger foes. When alliances are balanced, opponents cannot single out and attack smaller nations, because the costs of waging war against the alliance backing the small nation are prohibitive. *Balance of power advocates concede that limited conflicts cannot be prevented *within* an alliance (e.g., the USSR intervention in Hungary, 1956). However, advocates argue that balance of power prevents global wars among equal coalitions. An important implication is that all nations are only temporary enemies and friends, and dismemberment of major powers must be avoided to preserve the fundamental flexibility needed to maintain the existing international order.

Despite its wide acceptance and influence among policy makers, formal and empirical tests of balance of power propositions produce negative and contradictory results. Balance of power logically holds only under the dubious assumptions that leaders are unwilling to take risks and that they know with certainty the outcome of a war *before* it is waged. Furthermore, empirical studies overwhelmingly show that a balance of power is *required* to wage a global war or a serious war in the periphery. Thus, instead of setting the conditions for stability, a balance of power establishes the preconditions for war.

The debate about the virtues or limitations of balance of power could be relegated to the classroom were it not for the specter of nuclear war. The seminal work of Brodie (1946) brought the threat of nuclear conflict into clear focus—classical deterrence assumes a competitive, anarchic environment where nations seek to maximize power to assure security. Mutual Assured Destruction (MAD), which evolved from balance of power theory, argues that nations are restrained when a nuclear balance is achieved because opponents can retaliate against aggression with an overwhelming nuclear strike. In such circumstances, the relative gains of a challenge pale in comparison to the potential destruction associated with a nuclear exchange. Nuclear terror ensures peace not because nations are satisfied with the international order—none are in an anarchic world—but because the costs of nuclear war are prohibitive. In a perverse sense, the obsolescence of global war is due to the increased effectiveness of the means of mass destruction. MAD is not easy to challenge because no nuclear war has been waged among nuclear powers. The logical implication of MAD is that nuclear parity *secures* peace. The controversial implication is that *nuclear proliferation also secures peace under parity*. Thus, as new members of the international community acquire a nuclear veto over their opponents, the chances of nuclear war, and specifically a global war, decline dramatically. In sum, MAD contends that the nuclear balance is directly responsible for the long peace during the Cold War (1948–1989).

The prescriptions of *deterrence that guided U.S. policy in the twentieth century no longer fit actions taken by policy makers. First of all, following the collapse of the Soviet Union, few, if any, still hold that nuclear parity has preserved the long peace since the United States is now preponderant. Instead, since 1989 the prospects of global war have diminished. Moreover, nuclear tests by India and Pakistan in 1998 were universally seen as a dangerous development that could escalate the festering conflict over Kashmir. Nuclear proliferation is not universally seen as a cure for war. Thus, instead of waging war against the former Soviet Union, as balance of power implies, the United States has led efforts to restructure and stabilize the Russian economy.

A search for successful alternatives to balance of power that can distinguish a priori dangerous from stable conditions continues. One major alternative is the power transition theory first advanced by Organski (Organski and Kugler, 1980). Unlike the balance of power perspective where world politics is dominated by anarchy and shifting coalitions, the power transition perspective proposes that the world is organized into a coherent hierarchical system. The environment of world politics consists of a large set of nations who are satisfied with the rules of the game, while a sizable minority—unhappy with their status and position in the international order—are dissatisfied nations. As some among these dissatisfied nations achieve a parity of power with the dominant nation, they become the potential challengers for world supremacy. Power transition supporters welcome an asymmetry of power dominated by a satisfied nation. In the post–Cold War era, the United States and its satisfied allies fit this role and ensure peace. Power transition relies on the structural dynamics of the international system; war is anticipated when a dissatisfied challenger overtakes the leader of the satisfied coalition and demands major adjustments in the status quo. Once they achieve a balance of power rather than preponderance, risk-prone leaders of dissatisfied nations are willing to endure high costs to change international structures when they anticipate the probability of victory is equal to or slightly larger than 50 percent. Rigorous testing indicates that the implications of power transition are consistent with observed political events. Specifically, this perspective accounts accurately for structural changes over the last two centuries. Power transition accounts equally well for the long peace in the nineteenth century, the World War periods, the Cold War period, and the post-Soviet era.

When the contest between the United States and the USSR ceased as the Soviet Union collapsed, the problems raised by nuclear proliferation elevated in importance. Unlike Mutual Assured Destruction, power transition implies that deterrence is *unstable* and *proliferation* is dangerous. As developing nations reach nuclear parity in global or regional environments, some are expected to use their nuclear capabilities to resolve extended disputes. Large nuclear arsenals do not ensure peace. The decision by India to join the nuclear club means that all the great powers that will compete for dominance in the twenty-first century are nuclear powers. In this century, some observers believe Asia will challenge for global dominance as China overtakes the United States in power first, followed by India's overtaking of China. The implication of these transitions is that the preconditions for global war will be present at least twice during this century. Nuclear weapons are likely to be used if these challengers do not become (as the EU did) satisfied members of the international community. It follows from power transition theory that attempts to prevent nuclear proliferation are of paramount importance.

In the Middle East, power transition suggests that fears of a regional nuclear war are well founded. Power transition suggests that as long as Israel is the dominant nation in the Middle East, stability should prevail. However, if dissatisfied nations like Iran or Iraq were to acquire nuclear capabilities equivalent to those of Israel—without reaching a settlement—the potential for conflict among these nations would increase, not decrease. Practitioners seem to share this insight.

Following World War II the United States, as the dominant power, had the opportunity to manage the stability of the international system through strategies that successfully ensured peace. The Marshall Plan was instituted not only to help the recovery of Europe and Japan, but also to allow democratic institutions to prosper in the land of erstwhile enemies. Faced with the Asian challenge in the twenty-first century, the United States can once more try to incorporate old opponents into the status quo. After World War II, the United States forged a new status quo by encouraging the reduction of territorial flashpoints, the adoption of market economies, and the expansion of democracy. Similar strategies can be implemented once more. First, the United States can encourage the expansion of the European Union and NATO to encompass Russia. Second, it can support Asian regional integration and economic reorganization. Third, it can encourage China to join the World Trade Organization and eventually NATO. The fundamental implication of power transition theory is that the incorporation of dissatisfied challengers into the satisfied majority can prevent global war. Since the two Asian nations, China and India, that may challenge in this century remain outside the fold of the satisfied majority, global war can best be prevented—perhaps permanently—by altering their current perceptions of the status quo. Regional conflicts, however, are likely to continue.

The structural implications of the international system cover only a small portion of research on the implementation of strategies designed to avoid war. Indeed, the *democratic peace*—the realization that democracies do not fight democracies—has become an axiom of politics. This peace is limited, however, since empirical research has shown that democracies wage war, albeit *not* against other democracies, with the same frequency as nondemocracies. In fact, democracies are involved in more severe wars than autocratic regimes, and scholars have accumulated evidence that autocracies do not wage war against other autocracies. The explanation for this peaceful behavior between democracies is attributed to the inability of leaders to amass *public opinion in favor of war, against similar regimes. The severity of conflict with nondemocracies is attributed to self-interest—democratic leaders realize that victory is essential to preserve their political futures. If democracy is a key to peace, then the democratic transitions we are currently witnessing augur well for stability in world politics. Recent work, however, challenges these conclusions, suggesting instead that consistent liberal preferences, free press, freedom of speech, and the support of human rights, rather than democracy per se, may be the key to peace.

Major studies have been made to advance scientific analysis of decisions as they relate to war initiation and escalation. Bueno de Mesquita (1981, 1997), with his pioneering work,

has developed the foundations of a predictive model of conflict. His decision analysis model can identify those crises that escalate to war, and allow policy makers to detect and implement strategies that can avoid war. The purpose of this work is to anticipate the optimal policies that leaders can employ to avert conflict. Using the position of each stakeholder in a conflict, their resources, and the importance each stakeholder attaches to the issue in dispute, these decision tools can be used to anticipate the positions that each stakeholder will adopt, and identify available options to diffuse or minimize the costs of conflict. With such techniques, it is now possible to anticipate the initiation of conflict, evaluate its intensity, and identify strategies that can alter the outcome. In sum, it is possible to anticipate the severity of the war and the cost of achieving peace. For the first time, decision makers have a tool that allows them to design effective policies to achieve their goals peacefully. Accurate assessments of the dynamics of conflicts such as the *Gulf War, *Kosovo War, and most recently the war in Chechnya, argue well for the utility of this approach.

What can be said from this short exploration of the vast scholarly literature on war? The leading paradigm used to explore war is still balance of power. Increasingly, however, theory combined with evidence is moving the field further and further from unsupported generalizations. Empirical work has flourished as data banks for the study of war have grown, resulting in the demise of many long-held beliefs about war. As we move into the future, improvements in theorizing driven by the interaction among empirical reality, formal deduction, and inductive insights will undoubtedly expand our knowledge of war. Our generation nevertheless can take credit for being the first to face the scientific challenge of empirically exploring propositions initiated by previous generations of students of war and peace. There is hope that policy makers will take advantage of such knowledge to manage war and avert or reduce its horrendous consequences.

(See also FORCE, USE OF; NUCLEAR WEAPONS; REALISM.)

Bernard Brodie, *The Absolute Weapon* (New York, 1946). Kenneth N. Waltz, *Man, the State, and War: A Theoretical Analysis* (New York, 1959). Bronislaw Malinowski, "An Anthropological Analysis of War," in Leon Bramson and George W. Goethals, eds., *War: Studies from Psychology, Sociology, Anthropology*, rev. ed. (New York, 1968). A. F. K. Organski and Jacek Kugler, *The War Ledger* (Chicago, 1980). Bruce Bueno de Mesquita, *The War Trap* (New Haven, Conn., 1981). Bruce Bueno de Mesquita, "A Decision Making Model: Its Structure and Form," *International Interactions* 23, no. 3–4 (1997): 235–266.

JACEK KUGLER

employment of poisoned weapons or the improper use of flags of truce—have historically been treated as war crimes. In fact, a number of war criminals tried after *World War II were convicted of offenses not covered by the London charter (e.g., breach of surrender terms).

The four Geneva Conventions of 1949 for the Protection of War Victims (Articles 50, 51, 130, and 147) list "grave breaches" involving specified acts committed against persons or property protected in each convention, chiefly, the wounded and sick, prisoners of *war, and civilians. Other grave breaches are enumerated in Article 85 of the 1977 Protocol Additional to the Geneva Conventions Relating to the Protection of Victims of International Armed Conflicts (Protocol I). Paragraph 5 of the latter clause proclaims that grave breaches of both the conventions and the protocol "shall be regarded as war crimes."

The 1993 Statute of the International Tribunal for the former Yugoslavia shuns the phrase "war crimes." Instead, it includes provisions covering "violations of the laws or customs of war" and "grave breaches of the Geneva Conventions of 1949" (as well as "crimes against humanity" and "genocide," but not "crimes against peace").

War crimes are punished severely. The International Military Tribunal at Nuremberg and Tokyo imposed the death sentence on a number of major criminals, as did a host of national courts. However, the current trend, as evidenced in the Yugoslav Statute, is to avoid capital punishment and to limit the penalty to imprisonment.

The punishment of war criminals requires that verdict and sentence be pronounced after a fair trial by a duly formed and impartial judicial panel. Currently, immense efforts are made to create a permanent international criminal court vested with jurisdiction over war criminals. As long as such a court is not operative, international penal proceedings can only be carried out by *ad hoc* tribunals like those that rendered judgment at Nuremberg and Tokyo or the one dealing with Yugoslav offenders.

The indictment of some war criminals on a supra-national level does not preclude the prosecution of others before national courts. Naturally, in the absence of an international tribunal endowed with jurisdiction, the only option available is that of national trials.

When states prosecute war crimes committed by members of their own armed forces, trials are generally conducted pursuant to the pertinent domestic military law. But should other states wish to institute penal proceedings, they can only do so by virtue of *international law. Under customary international law, war crimes are subject to universal jurisdiction so that all states are entitled to bring offenders to trial.

Since the *Nuremberg Trials, it has been acknowledged that war criminals cannot relieve themselves of criminal responsibility by citing official position or superior orders. Even obedience to explicit national legislation provides no protection against international law. Additionally, war crimes are not subject to the application of ordinary rules of statutes of limitations. Hence, there is no time limit on prosecution, which can commence after many decades.

War crime trials date back at least to the fifteenth century, but the issue of war crimes came to the fore mainly as a result of the countless Nazi and Japanese atrocities perpetrated in the course of World War II. Apart from the two major trials

conducted by the international military tribunals, thousands of lesser war criminals were prosecuted before national courts in more than a dozen countries.

Notwithstanding the overall success of the post–World War II trials, there was a prevailing reluctance to proceed with war crimes trials subsequent to the multiple regional wars of the Cold War era. The zeitgeist changed in the 1990s. The establishment of the Yugoslav Tribunal, and the renewal of interest in the creation of a permanent international criminal court, reflect the growing public desire to ensure that war criminals do not escape trial and punishment.

(See also GENOCIDE; WAR, RULES OF.)

Yoram Dinstein, *et al., War Crimes in International Law* (The Hague, 1996).

YORAM DINSTEIN

WAR CRIMES TRIBUNALS. War crimes trials by national tribunals date back at least to the fifteenth century (the Breisach trial of Peter of Hagenbach, in the Holy Roman Empire, in 1474). A celebrated trial was that of Captain Henry Wirz—the commandant of the Confederate prisoners of war camp at Andersonville, Georgia—by a special military commission in Washington, D.C., in 1865. In Article 228 of the 1919 Peace Treaty of Versailles, the German government recognized the right of the Allied and associated powers to prosecute war criminals before military tribunals. Parallel provisions also appeared in the other Peace Treaties of Paris, 1919–1920. But the object intended was aborted in practice.

The idea of establishing an international tribunal for prosecuting a crime connected with war originated in Article 227 of the Versailles Treaty, in which the Allied and associated powers arraigned the German Kaiser Wilhelm II "for a supreme offence against international morality and the sanctity of treaties." However, this provision remained a dead letter, inasmuch as the kaiser had found asylum in a neutral country (The Netherlands) which refused to surrender him for trial.

The first international tribunal to have actually prosecuted and punished war criminals (as well as the perpetrators of crimes against peace and crimes against humanity) was the international military tribunal at Nuremberg in 1945–1946. This trial of the major German war criminals of World War II was followed by parallel proceedings against the principal Japanese offenders, held in Tokyo in 1946–1948, before the International Military Tribunal for the Far East.

Both post–World War II international military tribunals operated ad hoc and were dissolved upon the conclusion of their work. Notwithstanding the manifest success of at least the Nuremberg trial, there was no desire to set up new international war crimes tribunals subsequent to the multiple regional wars of the Cold War era. The zeitgeist changed in the 1990s. In 1993, the United Nations Security Council established an International Tribunal for the Prosecution of Persons Responsible for Serious Violations of International Humanitarian Law Committed in the Territory of Former Yugoslavia since 1991 (with jurisdiction over violations of the laws or customs of war, grave breaches of the Geneva Conventions of 1949, crimes against humanity, and *genocide). In 1994, the Security Council established another international criminal tribunal, this time for Rwanda (with jurisdiction over genocide, crimes against humanity, and violations of Article 3 common to the Geneva Conventions and of Additional Protocol II). The two tribunals are functioning, respectively, at The Hague and Arusha (Tanzania), and have already rendered a number of important judgments. It must be emphasized that the scope of their mandates, like that of the Nuremberg and Tokyo tribunals in the 1940s, is strictly ad hoc.

In 1998, the Statute of an International Criminal Court was adopted by a United Nations Diplomatic Conference in Rome. The Court is envisaged as a permanent institution, with jurisdiction over war crimes, crimes against humanity, genocide, and in theory the crime of aggression which has been left undefined. The Rome Statute is not yet in force, and several of its key provisions—relating both to the exercise of jurisdiction and to the definition of crimes—are controversial. It is nevertheless clear that, if only in broad outlines, the new concept of a permanent international criminal court is almost universally supported. The establishment of such a court reflects growing public desire to ensure that war criminals do not escape justice.

(See also INTERNATIONAL LAW; NUREMBERG TRIALS.)

G. K. McDonald and O. Swaak-Goldman, *Substantive and Procedural Aspects of International Criminal Law: The Experience of International and National Courts*, 3 vols. (The Hague, 2000).

YORAM DINSTEIN

WAR ON POVERTY. See GREAT SOCIETY.

WAR POWERS RESOLUTION. The War Powers Resolution attempted to ensure a congressional role in the decision to commit American military forces to hostilities. The resolution was enacted over President Richard *Nixon's veto in November 1973. As a joint resolution, the measure has the force and effect of law. It was the product of an increasing congressional sentiment, spurred largely by *Watergate and the *Vietnam War, that the executive branch had come too frequently to disregard legislative prerogatives in general and the congressional war power in particular. Final enactment came after the Senate's adoption of the National Commitments Resolution in 1969 and the passage of differing versions of war powers legislation (left unreconciled) during intervening years. At the time of its enactment the resolution was seen by many as a significant reclamation of the congressional war power.

The law contains six major provisions. First, it sets forth Congress's opinion of the breadth of the president's power to use armed force without prior congressional approval. This, it provides, may be done in the event of a national emergency created by an attack on the United States, its territories or possessions, or its armed forces. The provision is nonbinding (unlike a similar, obligatory provision in the Senate version of the resolution that was dropped by the conference committee). Second, the resolution requires that the president consult with Congress before the U.S. armed forces are "introduced into hostilities or into situations where imminent involvement in hostilities is clearly indicated by the circumstances." Third, it requires that in such circumstances the president transmit a written report to Congress within forty-eight hours. Fourth, the resolution requires the president to withdraw the armed forces from hostilities within sixty days after a report is transmitted or required to be transmitted (ninety days in the event of unavoidable military necessity

incidental to the withdrawal), subject to three exceptions: a declaration of *war, specific statutory authorization, or statutory extension of the time period. Fifth, the resolution requires the president to withdraw the armed forces from hostilities when Congress so directs through the adoption of a concurrent resolution (which is not presented to the president for his signature or veto). Finally, the resolution precludes any inference of authority to introduce the armed forces into hostilities from any treaty or statute not containing specific authorization.

Presidents generally have complied with the reporting requirement of the War Powers Resolution. Consultation, however, has been more uneven. President Ronald *Reagan arguably declined to comply with the sixty-day time period during the 1988 escort operation to protect Kuwaiti shipping in the Persian Gulf. President Bill *Clinton arguably breached the time period in prosecuting hostilities against Yugoslavia for seventy-seven days in 1999. The courts have dismissed as nonjusticiable various legal challenges alleging presidential noncompliance. For all practical purposes, the resolution has thus proved judicially unenforceable.

Politically, the resolution has not worked as many had expected, in part because key provisions are vague. The term "hostilities," for example, is undefined, leaving room for good faith disagreement over whether or when hostilities have occurred. Also, presidents have transmitted reports under other provisions of the resolution, creating doubt whether the sixty-day time period was triggered. A number of remedial amendments have been proposed, but none has been adopted. Finally, a 1983 Supreme Court case casts serious doubt on the validity of the provision requiring withdrawal of the armed forces from hostilities upon the adoption of a concurrent resolution.

(See also CONGRESS, U.S.; KOSOVO WAR; PRESIDENCY, U.S.; SEPARATION OF POWERS; SUPREME COURT OF THE UNITED STATES.)

Michael J. Glennon, *Constitutional Diplomacy* (Princeton, N.J., 1990).

MICHAEL J. GLENNON

WARFARE, RULES OF. The rules of warfare are established by *international law with a view to regulating the conduct of belligerents in the course of international armed conflicts. These rules (known in the aggregate as *jus in bello*) must be distinguished from the law governing the commencement of hostilities (*jus ad bellum*). Contemporary international law prohibits the use of *force in *international relations. Nevertheless, once *war breaks out (in violation of the *jus ad bellum*), the same rules of warfare (*jus in bello*) apply to all belligerents. There must be no discrimination in the implementation of the rules of warfare between the armed forces or the civilians of the aggressor state(s) and those of the victim(s) of aggression. Aggressor(s) and victim(s) alike are equally bound by the obligations ensuing from the rules of warfare and equally entitled to benefit from the corresponding rights.

The rules of warfare are premised on the dual notion that the adverse effects of war should be alleviated as much as possible (given military necessities) and that the freedom of the parties to resort to methods and means of warfare is not unlimited. Some rules—e.g., the protection of heralds arranging truce—have their roots in ancient practice. Most, however, are a product of modern humanitarian concepts: they were devised in the last two centuries and have no antecedents in the past.

Certain rules of warfare have evolved as customary law and remain uncodified, but much of the law is currently incorporated in numerous international conventions, preeminently the two sets of The Hague Conventions, dating from 1907, and the Geneva Conventions, concluded in 1949. The latter, four in number and supplemented by a partly controversial Additional Protocol of 1977, are usually referred to as the Red Cross Conventions and labeled as "international humanitarian law." In reality, there is scarcely any justification for a substantive differentiation between the law of Geneva and the law of The Hague. The two sets of conventions are complementary, and many important provisions are actually interchangeable. All rules of warfare reflect a balance between humanitarian considerations, on the one hand, and the requirements of military necessity, on the other.

The rules of warfare draw a fundamental distinction between combatants and civilians. Civilians enjoy a qualified protection against dangers arising from military operations. Although they face the perils of warfare in many unavoidable ways (for instance, when they work in a munitions factory, which, as explained below, is a legitimate target for strategic bombing), they must not be the object of either a deliberate or even an indiscriminate attack. Special and detailed protection is offered to civilians living in territories occupied by the enemy in the course of the war.

Combatants, provided that they comply with the rules of warfare and satisfy prerequisite conditions, are entitled to the status of prisoners of war. This status is of paramount significance when combatants fall into the enemy's hands, either by choice (laying down their arms) or by force of circumstances (being wounded, sick, or shipwrecked). Prisoners of war are guaranteed their lives, health, and dignity, although they lose their liberty. During captivity, the detaining power must treat them humanely pursuant to numerous directives spelled out in the Third Geneva Convention of 1949. As a rule, prisoners of war are to be released and repatriated only after the cessation of active hostilities.

A number of weapons have been expressly forbidden for any use in warfare on the grounds that they are deemed to be excessively injurious to the immediate victims or have potentially harmful effects for others. There are various conventions prohibiting chemical, biological, and bacteriological weapons; poisons; weapons modifying or causing damage to the environment; specified types of floating mines in maritime warfare; "dumdum" (i.e., expanding) bullets; explosive or inflammable projectiles under a prescribed weight (except in air warfare); and weapons causing injury by fragments not detectable by X rays. The employment of several other weapons (primarily land mines, booby traps, and incendiary devices) is also restricted where civilians are concerned.

Recourse to some weapons is controversial. This is particularly true of nuclear devices. The rationale for proscribing them is obvious: they are not only excessively injurious to the immediate victims but have long-standing harmful effects to others as well. However, as yet, there is no comprehensive interdiction of *nuclear weapons that is legally binding. A series of conventions in force, wherein nuclear weapons are excluded from use in specific areas (for instance, Latin Amer-

ica), can be construed as implying that otherwise the employment of such weapons is permissible.

There are multiple rules concerning lawful and unlawful methods of warfare. Belligerents are allowed to resort to espionage, although, if caught in the act, the spy will not be accorded prisoner-of-war status. Siege on land, maritime blockade, and the seizure of contraband at sea are permissible. Conversely, the use of privateers at sea has been abolished. There are also injunctions against forms of deception considered perfidious (chiefly, feigning an intent to surrender; feigning noncombatant status; improper use of enemy or neutral uniforms; and abuse of emblems like the Red Cross). But there is no sweeping ban on deception in warfare. For example, there is no impediment to ambushes, camouflage, or false codes (other than distress signals). Occasionally, there are striking dissimilarities between the rules governing land and maritime warfare. Thus, whereas it is legitimate to fly a false (enemy or neutral) flag at any time prior to opening fire at sea, the equivalent tactics on land would be regarded as perfidious.

The general protection accorded to civilians has engendered a distinction between military targets (which can be attacked at discretion) and civilian objects (which are exempt from attack). This is a crucial issue in the context of strategic bombing. It is generally agreed that military targets encompass not merely military forces and installations (including depots, vehicles, aircraft, and warships) but also factories engaged in the manufacture of military supplies or central lines of communication. The presence of civilians does not shield industrial plants, airports, harbors, railroad stations, or major highways. Moreover, if a number of military objectives that are not clearly separated and distinct are located in a city or any other site inhabited by civilians, they can be looked upon as a single "target area" for the purpose of bombing. This is the juridical underpinning of the saturation bombings of the Ruhr basin in Germany during *World War II. By contrast, air raids purely designed to terrorize the civilian population or break its morale are manifestly illicit. Hence the enduring controversy relating to the legality of the overall strategic bombing policy carried out by the Allies in the course of World War II. The only possible justification was that of reprisals in response to previous violations of the law by the Axis air forces.

At all events, the following objects must not be attacked, as long as they are not used by the enemy for military purposes: hospitals, medical installations, ambulances, hospital ships, and medical aircraft; places of religious worship; cultural property, such as museums and historical monuments; undefended places (although it is debatable whether this term has much meaning in the context of strategic bombing); unarmed merchant ships not traveling in an escorted convoy (but exemption from attack does not preclude the seizure of enemy merchant ships and cargoes as prize); crops and drinking water indispensable to the survival of the civilian population; dams, nuclear electrical generating stations, and other installations containing dangerous forces; and civil defense organizations. It is also forbidden to harm the wounded and sick; medical or religious personnel; envoys bearing flags of truce; and, of late, even journalists. Pillage and the wanton destruction of enemy private property are prohibited.

In the nature of things, the evolution of the rules of warfare cannot always keep pace with technological advances in weapon systems. Unless a new convention is concluded to cope with state-of-the-art devices, they are subject to the application of traditional legal concepts (although these may be perceived by some as outdated). Interestingly enough, even when new conventions emerge—e.g., the instruments adopted in the 1930s to deal with submarine warfare—they often leave the classical legal standards essentially intact.

After every major war, all preexisting rules of warfare must be reassessed in the light of the actual practice of states. For example, the use of "exclusion zones" in maritime warfare in the 1980s, both in the *Malvinas/Falklands War and in the *Iran-Iraq War, has left several open questions. It is not always easy to determine whether persistent breaches of the rules of warfare reflect the emergence of new legal norms or should be stigmatized as violations of international law (and, in grave cases, *war crimes).

(See also GENOCIDE; NUREMBERG TRIALS.)

D. Bindschedler-Robert et al., "The Regulation of Armed Conflicts," in M. Cherif Bassiouni and Ved P. Nanda, eds., *International Criminal Law*, vol. 1 (Springfield, Ill., 1973), pp. 293–452. Richard B. Baxter, "The Duties of Combatants and the Conduct of Hostilities (Law of The Hague)," in *International Dimensions of Humanitarian Law* (Dordrecht, 1988), pp. 93–133.

YORAM DINSTEIN

WARLORDISM. The term "warlord" entered English as a translation of *Kriegsherr*, a term applied to the German emperor in the 1880s (presumably to connote a link to the medieval empires). Early in the twentieth century, "warlord" was used as a translation of the Chinese term *du-jun*. So-called warlords ruled various parts of *China from about 1912 until 1928, when Chiang Kai-shek reunified the country, absorbing various warlords into his army. These dual origins are reflected in somewhat contradictory definitions of warlord (Funk and Wagnalls):

1. A leader or high-ranking officer in a militaristic nation.
2. The warlike ruler or leader of a local region or group of bandits, especially in the Orient.

Subsequent use of the term generally reflects the second definition, according to which warlords rule autonomous regions.

The term "warlord" reappears in journalistic and scholarly coverage of Africa, and to a lesser extent Asia, in the 1980s and 1990s. Leaders in Somalia, Chad, Liberia, Sierra Leone, Zululand (South Africa), Afghanistan, and the southern Philippines, *inter alios*, are described as warlords.

Chiang Kai-shek identified five essential characteristics of warlord behavior: lack of a political principle, occupation of an area, an insatiable need for money and property, love of his own skin, and dependence on imperialist support (Charlton and May, 1989). Most politicians would appear to love their own skin, but the Chiang formulation does suggest the importance of economic factors and of external backing. Not all the Chinese warlords seem to have had significant foreign backing and the Chadian experience suggests that foreign backing can be a liability under some circumstances.

Recent usage does suggest that "lack of a political principle" is a defining characteristic. Leaders who might otherwise qualify as "warlords"—the supposed Marxist Laurent Kabila, the anti-Marxist Jonas Savimbi—were exempted if another label was available.

A fruitful approach is suggested by William Reno (1998). Contrary to the common explanation which traces warlord politics primarily to the collapse of state authority and capacity, Reno places economic factors at the center of his model and identifies warlord-like aspects in the politics of Nigeria under Abacha and Congo/Zaire under Mobutu, states which did not collapse and where full-fledged warlordism did not appear, as it did in Sierra Leone and Liberia. He argues that Liberian warlordism emerged as the result of a social coalition of enterprising strongmen, small-scale foreign commercial operators, and a small segment of the country's youth. Previous Liberian rulers influenced and changed elite social arrangements in ways that later, as external conditions changed, gave strongmen the political and financial autonomy to seek their own fortunes at the expense of a central authority. These variables help to explain why some governments continue to be structured on the principles of sovereignty and territoriality (even if they incorporate features of warlord politics), whereas in Liberia strongmen encountered less difficulty in building their authority through more purely private means.

By 1999–2000 the role of warlords in linking resources, especially diamonds, to international markets had become clear. The United Nations interposed peacekeepers between armed groups in Congo who controlled mineral resources, but attempted to deal with the insurgency of Savimbi in Angola by cutting off the conversion of diamonds into weapons. It was clear, also, that warlordism in Sierra Leone, Congo, Angola, and elsewhere could not thrive without the connivance of foreign governments.

(See also MERCENARIES; MILITARISM; TERRORISM.)

Roger Charlton and Roy May, "Warlords and Militarism in Chad," *Review of African Political Economy* 45–46 (Winter, 1989): 12–25. William Reno, *Warlord Politics and African States* (Boulder, 1998).

THOMAS TURNER

WARSAW TREATY ORGANIZATION. The Warsaw Treaty Organization (WTO), also often referred to as the Warsaw Pact, was created pursuant to a treaty signed on 14 May 1955 by the Soviet Union, Albania, Bulgaria, Hungary, the German Democratic Republic (GDR), Poland, Romania, and Czechoslovakia. The treaty followed by only nine days the accession of the Federal Republic of Germany (FRG) to the *North Atlantic Treaty Organization (NATO). The treaty established an organization comprising a joint command of the armed forces of the member states and a political consultative committee; other military and political bodies were added later. While nominally all members were equal, the Soviet Union held a dominant and controlling position in the WTO until the end of 1989.

The WTO was originally established for a period of twenty years, to be automatically extended for ten years for all members who did not denounce its continuance. Albania ceased to participate in the WTO in 1961 and withdrew in 1968. In April 1985 the WTO was extended again for twenty plus ten years by all the other members. However, as a consequence of the revolutionary transformation of its members, the GDR withdrew on the eve of its own absorption into the FRG in August 1990, the military organizational elements of the alliance were abolished as of 31 March 1991, and on 1 July 1991 the WTO was dissolved by consensus of its members.

The WTO was designed both to be a political counter to NATO and to justify continuing Soviet military presence on the territory of various WTO members. The WTO coordinated the armed forces of its members (Romania only nominally after 1963), and joint military exercises were held from 1961 through 1989.

In 1956, Soviet military intervention prevented Hungary from leaving the WTO. In 1968, military forces of the Soviet Union and several other members, although not the WTO itself, intervened in Czechoslovakia to ensure communist orthodoxy, implementing what in the West came to be called the "Brezhnev Doctrine" (after Soviet leader Leonid Brezhnev). With a new leadership in the Soviet Union under Mikhail *Gorbachev willing to permit freedom of choice to the nations of Eastern and *Central Europe, both the internal political systems of the member states and their external relations changed suddenly and drastically beginning in November 1989. For a time, with Soviet *hegemony ended and Soviet forces beginning their withdrawal, several of its members saw an interim role for a "new" WTO based on equality to serve their interests pending creation of pan-European *security arrangements. The Soviet Union encouraged such a transformation of the WTO from a military-political alliance under its control to a political consultative one. This prospect, however, proved ephemeral. The speed of *German reunification and the initiation of steps to establish a new European security order in 1990, coupled with the burdens of the pact's past role as an instrument of Soviet domination, doomed the WTO to a demise by 1991.

The WTO reflected the changing relationship of the Communist-ruled states of Eastern Europe with the Soviet Union in its origins, throughout its existence, and in its dissolution. The WTO was born of the *Cold War and died with it.

(See also NINETEEN EIGHTY-NINE; SOVIET UNION.)

Robin Alison Remington, *The Warsaw Pact: Case Studies in Communist Conflict Resolution* (Cambridge, Mass., 1971). David Holloway and Jane M. O. Sharp, eds., *The Warsaw Pact: Alliance in Transition?* (Ithaca, N.Y., 1984). General of the Army P. G. Lushev, ed., *Varshavskii dogovor: istoriia i sovremennost'* [The Warsaw Treaty: History and the Present Day] (Moscow, 1990).

RAYMOND L. GARTHOFF

WATERGATE. The most serious political scandal in modern U.S. history has come to be known as Watergate. In June 1972, burglars hired by the Committee to Re-elect the President to engage in political espionage were arrested at Democratic National Committee headquarters, located in the Watergate Hotel in Washington, D.C. The ensuing judicial proceedings, congressional investigations, and press coverage culminated in the resignation of President Richard M. *Nixon on 9 August 1974. Nixon had been forced to surrender tape recordings of conversations that he had had with several of his top aides, which revealed that he had conspired with them to obstruct justice by attempting to thwart the investigation of the burglary. The pardoning of Nixon by his successor, Gerald R. Ford, precluded criminal proceedings against him. Over

thirty Nixon administration officials, campaign staff, and contributors, however, were indicted, convicted, and imprisoned for their roles in the scandal.

Watergate encompassed wrongdoing on a wide scale, including the misuse of campaign donations and the unlawful and unethical use of the Federal Bureau of Investigation, the Internal Revenue Service, and the *Central Intelligence Agency by Nixon and his aides against their political "enemies." From 1969 to 1971 the Nixon administration authorized, without court approval, the wiretapping of government officials and journalists to uncover the sources of leaked news about the bombing of Cambodia and other "national security" matters. The "Huston plan," approved by Nixon in 1971, contemplated burglaries and the opening of mail to detect security leaks. Also in 1971, Nixon created the Special Investigations Unit (the "plumbers") to carry out such operations as breaking into the office of Daniel Ellsberg's psychiatrist. Ellsberg had given copies of the secret "Pentagon papers," documenting U.S. involvement in Indochina, to newspapers. Nixon's objective was to find derogatory information about Ellsberg before Ellsberg's espionage trial.

Scholars continue to debate the significance and long-term consequences of Watergate for the functioning of the U.S. political system. Most view it less as an aberrant event attributable to the character flaws of Nixon and his associates than as symptomatic of more deeply rooted problems of U.S. political development. One prominent view is that Watergate was the culmination of a decades-long trend toward an "imperial *presidency." With the growth of the federal government's domestic and international responsibilities, increased power, discretion, and prestige were (misguidedly) lodged in the presidency. This occurred through presidential initiative and *Congress's delegation of its powers or abdication of its responsibilities. The results included a greatly enlarged White House staff; an increase in secrecy, deception, and evasion of congressional controls in the conduct of military and covert operations abroad; the use of executive agencies to monitor and discourage political opponents and interfere in the electoral process; and the impoundment of funds appropriated by Congress. In short, along with the *Vietnam War, Watergate signaled for many the extent to which growing presidential power had endangered civil liberties and the constitutional balance between legislative and executive authority.

Watergate affected U.S. politics in a variety of ways. First, along with the war in Vietnam, it gave fresh impetus to the public's growing mistrust of government. Although the decline in trust began before Watergate and Vietnam, the largest single increase in mistrust occurred between 1972 and 1974, the period in which Watergate was a salient event. Second, Watergate, again like Vietnam, changed the relationship between the mass media and government, particularly the executive branch. The post-Watergate period has seen the demise of "objective journalism" as a professional standard, and in its place the rise of a more interpretive, skeptical, and aggressive style of reporting. For many journalists, Watergate signaled the need for a more adversarial relationship toward those in power; it also showed that such a relationship could reap professional rewards.

Third, Watergate led to changes in the internal workings of Congress. Coming on the heels of Nixon's resignation, the

1974 elections resulted in significant Democratic gains in Congress. The "Watergate babies" brought to Washington that year spearheaded a variety of reforms intended to decentralize authority by decreasing the power, in particular, of committee chairs chosen by seniority. The young cohort pushed Congress further in the direction of a legislature dominated by more individualistic, activist, issue-oriented, national politicians.

Finally, and perhaps most importantly, Watergate spurred Congress to reassert its authority vis-à-vis the president. Congress legislated a host of reforms intended to prevent a repeat of the criminal and unethical activities undertaken during the Nixon years, and to redress the perceived erosion of congressional powers that many believed had helped give rise to the aggrandizement of presidential power. Congress passed campaign finance reforms in 1974 that set a limit on how much a person or a person's family could spend on his or her candidacy, set a limit of $1,000 on the amount individuals could contribute to a candidate in any given election, outlawed cash contributions in excess of $100, and prohibited foreign contributions. All but the first provision have been upheld by the *Supreme Court. To put an end to usurpations of presidential power in foreign affairs, Congress passed the *War Powers Resolution in 1973. Its intent was to guarantee that the president could not commit troops without consulting Congress, and that if such a commitment extended beyond sixty days, Congress would be required to give its explicit approval. In domestic policy, Congress passed the Budget and Impoundment Control Act of 1974. The purposes of this legislation were to bring appropriations decisions closer to revenue decisions by centralizing the budgetary process in Congress and to give Congress the expertise (through the creation of budget committees and the Congressional Budget Office) that would allow it to operate independently of the president and his Office of Management and Budget.

The optimistic view of Watergate is that it represents a blessing in disguise. It ought to deter future presidents from breaking the law, and arrests the compulsion toward enlarging the powers and prestige of the presidency at the expense of the other branches. The ways in which the scandal was uncovered and resolved serve as a vindication of the U.S. system of institutional checks and balances and of such principles as "no one is above the law." A more pessimistic view is that, while future presidents may be deterred from acting criminally and unethically (or at least take greater care not to get caught), the presidency remains a problematic institution. Watergate did nothing to change the plebiscitary nature of the presidency, in which the public's unrealistic expectations (fueled in part by presidents themselves) create tremendous pressures on presidents to deliver. Yet presidents' capacity to control events is limited, despite the considerable, disproportionate resources and power at their disposal. As expectations inevitably outstrip their capacity, they will continue to disappoint themselves and the public, and be tempted to abuse their powers.

(See also SEPARATION OF POWERS; UNITED STATES.)

Carl Bernstein and Bob Woodward, *All the President's Men* (New York, 1974). Richard Ben-Veniste, *Stonewall: The Real Story of the Watergate Prosecution* (New York, 1977).

GARY MUCCIARONI

WEBER, Max. Although Max Weber (1864–1920) is regarded as one of the founders of twentieth-century sociology, Weber's university appointments were all in political economy (at Freiburg in 1894, Heidelberg in 1896, and Munich in 1919), and it was the mutual interaction between economic systems and law, culture, and politics that formed the subject of his major academic studies. His works stood out for their methodological sophistication, breadth of historical scholarship, and increasingly abstract conceptualization, culminating in his enormous theoretical compendium *Economy and Society* (1921). Although his reputation in his own time owed something to his controversial interventions in the political issues of Wilhelmine Germany, Weber came to articulate an ideal of value-free social science that has been highly influential on subsequent scholarship.

Weber's importance for political science and political sociology lies in his early recognition of key developments emerging in the social structure and politics of capitalist societies at the beginning of the twentieth century, and in the theoretical categories he provided for their analysis. In the field of social stratification, his threefold distinction between "class, status, and party" has provided a powerful instrument for analyzing the complexities of social structure. Weber himself used it to explain the position of an emergent middle *class of white-collar, technical, and administrative personnel between capital and labor, whose share of the economic product depended on skill and educational status rather than on the ownership of property or the power of collective organization. In opposition to Marxists, he contended that the terms of systematic class conflict in mature *capitalism could be set and regulated at the political level, and therefore was dependent for its containment on the character of the political system. At the same time he acknowledged the importance of status groups, especially those of *ethnicity and nation, in providing a basis of political allegiance and mobilization cutting across class lines.

Weber's most notable contribution, however, lay in identifying the importance of bureaucracy to modern politics. His definition of bureaucracy, not as a type of political *system* but as a continuous, professionalized, and rule-governed form of administration, showed it to be increasingly prevalent—thanks to its being uniquely equipped to handle increasingly varied and complex organizational tasks—in all spheres of modern life. On the basis of this analysis he demonstrated that the socialist ideal of a society without domination was utopian, and predicted that the replacement of the capitalist entrepreneur by the state administrator would create a monolithic power structure as oppressive as that of ancient Egypt and as economically stagnant as that of late imperial Rome. In Weber's view, the key concern about bureaucracy was not that it be replaced but that it be checked, on the one hand, within a framework of mutually limiting power structures and, on the other, by ensuring that bureaucratic organizations were themselves subordinate to the control of individual leaders selected on the basis of nonbureaucratic principles and acting under such principles.

Weber's theoretical analysis of the dangers as well as the indispensability of bureaucracy was put to practical effect in his criticisms of the Wilhelmine constitution during World War I. He was one of the most outspoken advocates of democratization, in the interests of coherent military policy and decisive national leadership alike. After the war this critique was developed into a theory of democratic politics as "competitive leadership democracy." Weber was among the first to recognize that the advent of universal suffrage had undermined the independence of the individual member of parliament in favor of the party machine, and had ensured the subordination of both to the party leader capable of winning a mass following in the struggle of an electoral campaign. In arguing that the chief function of parliaments lay in ensuring the public scrutiny of government and in providing a training ground for political leadership, he anticipated the relative decline that would take place in their importance during the course of the twentieth century.

Weber can best be characterized as a political liberal whose achievement was to provide a reformulation of *liberalism in sociological terms that were appropriate to a new age of capitalist combines, bureaucratic organization, mass politics, and working-class advance. Although he deplored the demise of the era of classical individualism, his perspective was forward- rather than backward-looking, and it was to the individual leader at the head of organizations that Weber turned to embody the creativity and dynamism that were always associated in his mind with the individual rather than the collectivity. This opposition provides the most convincing rationale for his famous antithesis between bureaucracy and charisma.

(See also BUREAUCRATIC POLITICS; MARXISM; MODERNITY.)

Max Weber, *Economy and Society*, ed. Guenther Roth and Claus Wittich (New York, 1968). Wolfgang Mommsen, *The Age of Bureaucracy* (Oxford, 1974). David Beetham, *Max Weber and the Theory of Modern Politics*, 2d ed. (Cambridge, U.K., 1985). Wolfgang Mommsen, *Max Weber and German Politics, 1890–1920* (Chicago, 1985).

DAVID BEETHAM

WELFARE. The term welfare generally refers to a variety of government programs directed to the poor and economically needy. In order to qualify for such programs, households must fall below certain income and asset levels. In addition, many of these programs are directed to particularly vulnerable population groups such as the disabled, female-headed families with children, or the elderly.

Welfare programs can be divided into those providing cash and those that provide in-kind assistance. Major cash programs in the United States include the Temporary Assistance to Needy Families program or TANF (designed for families with children under age 18), Supplemental Security Income or SSI (targeted to the aged, blind, and disabled), and General Assistance (a state-run program for those not qualifying for other forms of support). In-kind programs include Medicaid (a health insurance program for the poor), Food Stamps (providing coupons or a debit card for the purchase of food), the Free or Reduced-Price School Lunch Program, and Housing Assistance programs (providing subsidized housing). These programs are funded and administered on both a federal and a state level.

In general, the level of resources that households receive from these programs is quite modest. Their intent is not to lift the families out of poverty, but rather to provide short-term assistance to tide individuals through periods of economic vulnerability caused by events such as the loss of a job, family dissolution, or illness.

A long-standing debate in Western industrialized countries (particularly in the United States and Britain) has been the extent to which welfare programs discourage work and marriage, while at the same time encouraging out-of-wedlock births, resulting in an increased dependency upon government assistance. Recent longitudinal research has shown that while many U.S. households will at some point rely upon a welfare program, most recipients will use such assistance for relatively short periods of time, and that the effects upon marriage and family formation are minor.

Nevertheless, the fear of these negative behavioral effects was a major impetus behind the welfare reform changes that were signed into law by President Bill *Clinton in 1996 (known as the Personal Responsibility and Work Opportunity Act). The bill resulted in the Aid to Families with Dependent Children (AFDC) program being replaced by the nonentitlement TANF program, stricter work requirements for those receiving aid, a five-year lifetime limit on the use of TANF, and considerable program flexibility given to states through the use of block grants.

Since 1994, the welfare rolls in the United States have been falling, partially as a result of the above changes in the welfare system, but also as a consequence of the robust economic performance from the mid 1990s onward. However, the overall rate of poverty has declined very little during this period.

Several Western industrialized countries including Britain, the Netherlands, Australia, and New Zealand have recently modified their welfare programs in order to attempt to increase recipients' incentives to find work and leave public assistance. In addition, a number of countries are considering reducing their programmatic benefits (albeit not to U.S. levels), citing the high costs of maintaining a generous welfare state in light of increasing global economic competition.

(See also ENTITLEMENTS; MEDICARE AND MEDICAID; SOCIAL SECURITY; WELFARE STATE.)

Mark Robert Rank, *Living on the Edge: The Realities of Welfare in America* (New York, 1994). Lutz Leisering and Stephan Leibfried, *Time and Poverty in Western Welfare States: United Germany in Perspective* (Cambridge, U.K., 1999). James T. Patterson, *America's Struggle Against Poverty in the Twentieth Century* (Cambridge, Mass., 2000).

MARK R. RANK

WELFARE STATE. For more than a century welfare states have developed both in Western Europe and in North America as only the most recent stage in the long-term process of *state formation in the West. Although widely different in their legal character, ideological legitimation, institutional structure, level and scopes of benefits, and overall share in the national income, all contemporary welfare states display significant similarities in their development and functioning.

In Western capitalist *democracies, national, collective, and compulsory arrangements have emerged in order to cope with the adversities and deficiencies that affect individual citizens in industrial society. Social security constitutes the hard core of the welfare state—a system of insurance under the direct or indirect control of the national government, intended to cover the risks to wage earners and their dependents of income loss when it is impossible for them to work because of disease, disability, lack of employment opportunity, old age, or death. Levies and benefits are job-related, and accordingly the system rests on the assumption that the vast majority of the healthy, adult, male population is regularly employed from adolescence to old age. Dependents are assumed to share in the wages and, if necessary, in the benefits paid to breadwinners or their survivors.

Social security represents a functional equivalent of the providential aspects of private saving. Payroll taxes are deducted from wages and serve to finance the benefits to those who cannot work: a compulsory accumulation of transfer capital. The obligation is imposed especially on wage earners. The self-employed are usually left out of social security, and salaries are often exempt from levies beyond a certain limit. As a result, social security taxes tend to be fiscally regressive, increasing income inequality, while benefits may have a progressive effect. The most important redistributive result, however, is an overall income transfer from the young to the old.

Modern welfare states complement their social security systems with some form of social assistance (or "welfare" in the strict sense as it used in the United States). These benefits are financed from general tax funds and reserved for those who are in no position to claim social security benefits on the basis of their past working career. The main beneficiaries are single parents and aged persons (both groups largely women) and those who have been disabled before reaching working age.

In many countries family allowances are paid, increasing with the number of children, to correct a wage system based on individual achievement so as to ensure that the needs of wage earners' dependents are met. Finally, a variegated array of "human" or "welfare services" provides manifold forms of assistance, such as social work, community work, legal counseling, psychotherapy, rehabilitation, and so on.

Closely connected to the web of welfare state benefits and services are the sectors of health care and education. In most countries wage earners are insured for the costs of medical treatment, hospitalization, and medication, with varying degrees of legal compulsion and of government intervention in the delivery of care. Only in the United States has insurance against medical expense remained mostly private, although the government fully funds Medicare (1956) for the elderly and Medicaid (1965) for the poor; also there is no national insurance scheme for income loss resulting from disease, although such plans may function at the state level. In Britain, at the other extreme, nearly all medical personnel and facilities were brought under direct government control through the National Health Service (1946).

Elementary education is compulsory up to early adolescence in all welfare states, and everywhere it is closely regulated and in large part subsidized by government. The development of basic skills and vocational training in principle enables all adult citizens to earn a living, reducing dependence on welfare provisions to specific conditions of hardship.

Many welfare states have carried out, at the national or the municipal level, large public housing programs aimed at providing adequate dwellings at low rents. In the periphery of the welfare state, a multitude of government-initiated benefits, subsidies, and prevention, training, or treatment schemes provide for specific needs of separate population categories.

There is no single common denominator to define the area of the welfare state. Even within one country, a panoply of legal, ideological, and institutional characteristics intermingle to produce a conglomerate of arrangements. Private associations, church agencies, and governmental services compete and collaborate at every level, constituting a transitional zone between the private and the public realm: this coalescence is itself typical of modern welfare states.

The complexity and variety of contemporary welfare arrangements present social scientists with a challenge to establish some order and seek a systematic theoretical approach. Welfare state institutions may be analyzed from the perspective of the functions they perform. As philanthropic aid and insurance benefits were increasingly tied to a past of regular employment, they tended to reinforce the pressure on able workers to accept steady wage labor. As a consequence, social policy has been instrumental in "transforming non-wage-workers into wage-workers" (Claus Offe, *Contradictions of the Welfare State*, London, 1984) and thus has contributed to a process of "active proletarianization" by compelling already-dispossessed workers to sell their labor for a wage. Unemployment benefits and social assistance served the function of "regulating the poor" by maintaining a reserve labor force during slack periods and forcing it into employment as demand for labor picked up again (Frances Fox Piven and Richard A. Cloward, *Regulating the Poor: The Functions of Public Welfare*, London, 1972).

If these views stress the functions of the welfare state in creating and maintaining the supply of wage labor, other approaches emphasize the contribution of welfare state institutions to the maintenance of public order and the formation of modern citizens by simultaneously eradicating extreme poverty and the rebellious nonconformism of the "dangerous classes." Madhouses, workhouses, and jails all served to "punish and discipline" (Michel Foucault, *Discipline and Punish: The Birth of the Prison*, London, 1977); schoolteachers, visitors to the poor, housing supervisors, and social workers became the infantry in the campaign for "social control" (Stanley Cohen and Andrew T. Scull, eds., *Social Control and the State*, Oxford, 1983) or even a veritable "family police" (Jacques Donzelot, *The Policing of the Families*, New York, 1979).

Not only regular employment but also decent conduct; abstinence from promiscuous sex, gaudy pleasures, alcohol, and illicit drugs; and parental discipline and children's school attendance became conditions for entitlement to welfare benefits. It was expected that workers who contributed to national insurance throughout their working lives and came to rely on its benefits in times of need would strengthen their initially tenuous bonds to the national state—a foremost consideration in Bismarck's Germany and a function served most explicitly by the veterans' schemes developed in the United States after the Civil War (Theda Skocpol and John Ikenberry, "The Political Formation of the American Welfare State in Historical and Comparative Perspective," *Comparative Social Research* 6 [1983]: 87–148) and in France after World War I.

The manifold institutions of the emerging welfare state did indeed serve these functions more or less effectively, and from the early nineteenth century on large employers or concerned members of the urban middle class had in fact been motivated in growing numbers by such considerations. Moreover, overcrowding, filth, and epidemics in the sprawling inner cities strongly heightened their concern with urban industrial poverty. The twofold objectives of labor supply and public order and the corresponding motivations among the entrepreneurial and urban elites are necessary elements in the explanation of the emergence of welfare states, but by themselves they are not sufficient. Even when major social actors agreed on the objectives to be realized and on the means to bring them about, they were still divided by conflicts about the distribution of burdens and still had to overcome the paralyzing dilemmas of collective action that, time and again, have stood in the way of concerted action on the part of established elites.

In some important respects, the history of the welfare state is a continuation of the development of care for the poor in medieval and early modern Europe. During the Middle Ages, in an era of weak local and regional government and in the absence of effective central authority, the vagrant poor presented a major threat to the security of landholding *peasants. They could easily destroy harvests, set fire to barns, or cast equally terrifying magic spells (a power attributed especially to elderly women who were helpless in all other respects). Those poor who could walk, and thus roam about from one village to another, could also fight and work, which made them both fearsome and potentially useful. The vagrant poor therefore represented both a threat and an opportunity to the established ranks of society. But the established villagers could not on their own ward off the danger or exploit the potential of the poor in their midst. Generous peasants might find their farms overcrowded by beggars, whereas more miserly neighbors would profit from the relative quiet and safety thus brought about at no cost to themselves.

Under these conditions, itinerant or village priests operated as charitable entrepreneurs: by exhorting the villagers to charity and threatening ostracism and damnation, they succeeded in increasing the peasants' confidence that their neighbors would be equally generous. Ritualized and ostentatious giving provided a setting for mutual control of charitable effort. The mutual suspicion that peers might abstain from charitable effort was initially overcome by manipulating these reciprocal expectations, and once collective action got underway, it was gradually superseded by mutual confidence and the informal sanctions that operate within an emerging collectivity.

In this sense, the virtue of charity rests on expectations of the virtuousness of others. A more or less precarious charitable equilibrium might thus come into existence, provided no major external disturbances, such as harvest failure, plague, invasion, or war, interfered to undo it again. Village charity accordingly came about as the result of a process in which collective action produced both a collectivity, the parish community, and a collective good, pacification of the poor in the parish area.

In this perspective, the dilemmas of collective action belong to a phase of transition: the actors concerned are interdependent and already aware of their interdependence, but there is as yet no agency for effective coordination of their efforts. The collectivizing process may be set in motion through manipulation of expectations, by illusory expectations, or through outside intervention, and once it is underway, collective action may bring about a collectivity that can more effectively coordinate the members' efforts at creating collective goods.

A next round of the collectivizing process with respect to the care of the poor occurred at a higher level of integration in early modern Europe, when towns found themselves confronted with bands of vagrant beggars roaming the countryside and threatening their supplies. Again, municipalities hesitated to provide food and shelter lest they be overrun by the needy, and every town hoped it could profit from the efforts of its neighbors. The town walls served as much to keep out the poor, who plundered the harvests, as to defend against enemy armies. This time the dilemmas of collective action were overcome by an illusion: the workhouse, which was expected to take in the sturdy (that is, the able and dangerous) poor and make them work for their own keep without cost to the town. Although these high hopes soon proved illusory and the workhouses ended up operating at a loss, rarely succeeding in keeping the worst offenders behind their walls, the expectations prompted many municipalities in the sixteenth and seventeenth centuries to found workhouses. As workhouses spread, especially in the large cities, they absorbed a considerable number of vagrants. Although still relatively weak, central governments could persuade local authorities to continue operating their workhouses by judiciously distributing grants (e.g., the seventeenth century French *don royal*). Central governments also intervened by establishing general rules for the allocation of the poor (to their locality of birth or of residence) and, by enforcing these rules, increased the confidence of local authorities that neighboring towns would accept their shares of the burden, thus encouraging them to do likewise (e.g., the Elizabethan poor laws in England, 1601). As the central government intervened, local authorities competed in demanding its support, in the process both intensifying central intervention and promoting the expansion of the central state apparatus. By the end of the eighteenth century, European national states were deeply, albeit indirectly, involved in the care of the poor, which continued to be implemented by local authorities.

The spread of popular education in the nineteenth century represented another major advance in central state intervention in the lives of the poor and laboring classes. At its core, the elementary curriculum consists of a code for national communication, permitting any two strangers in the realm to effectively manage their encounter. A major impetus for the development of mass elementary education came from the conflict between, on the one hand, metropolitan elites, oriented toward the national state and the national market, who sought direct access to potential consumers, workers, taxpayers, recruits, and voters in the country at large, and, on the other hand, elites with a regional base who attempted to maintain their monopolistic mediation functions for their local clientele. Bureaucratic innovations such as the inspectorate, teacher certification, school subsidies, and enforcement of attendance constituted so many ramifications of the administrative apparatus into the remotest parts of the territory and into aspects of life hitherto considered outside the pale of public life. Mass education did increase the mental aptitudes and the social opportunities of the poor, but it also helped to form a state apparatus that would be equal to the intricacies of managing millions of people in contemporary social welfare systems. The experience of mass mobilization and large-scale warfare also prepared the bureaucracy for subsequent massive social interventions.

Throughout the nineteenth century the position of industrial workers was considered an anomaly, a transitory phenomenon. The established citizenry reasoned that if only laborers would learn to save, they would be able to provide against adversity and perhaps even establish themselves as independent entrepreneurs. Moral improvement and a "civilizing campaign" would teach them foresight and self-discipline. Within the radical wing of the workers' movement, on the other hand, the situation of the proletariat was equally regarded as transient—soon to be superseded by a socialist or syndicalist order in which either the state or workers' councils would run the factories and distribute the proceeds among those who had worked for them.

Only when industrial wage employment came to be considered a permanent and pervasive phenomenon of modern society did the notion of some kind of collective insurance against income loss take hold definitively. During the second half of the nineteenth century, workers' mutual funds spread rapidly, a transitory phenomenon between small, voluntary, private saving (albeit in groups and under mutual pressure) and large-scale, compulsory, collective provision. But mutual funds tended to exclude the neediest and to suffer from an accumulation of risks owing to their homogeneous membership, which was exposed to the same epidemics, laid off en masse, and reached pensionable age in the same period.

As industrialization proceeded and wage workers increased in number, attempts at solving the "social question" became the subject of intense contestation at every turn. First, there was the matter of distribution of the financial burdens that any kind of workers' insurance would entail. Second, the small bourgeoisie resisted all inroads by big business, big government, and big unions, and certainly the compulsory accumulation of transfer capital in lieu of private savings (Henri Hatzfeld, *Du Paupérisme à la Sécurité Sociale; Essai sur les Origines de la Sécurité Socialé en France, 1850-1940*, Paris, 1971). And, finally, the workers' movement was deeply divided on the issue of social insurance and government intervention—the American Federation of Labor (AFL) and the European radical socialist unions vehemently opposed the idea, whereas other unions supported it on condition that the state or the employers pay the costs.

Any lasting and adequate solution would have to match the scale of the problem: it would have to redistribute income from younger generations of workers to the retired, encompass an entire industrial sector so as not to unduly favor competitors, and maintain solvency into the distant future. Unions adamantly resisted company insurance because it tied the workers to the firm and might become insolvent with the company's demise. Management equally vehemently opposed union insurance as it would strengthen the union's grip on the workers and allow it to have a say in shop floor discipline. Both workers and employers wanted the other side to pay for the scheme. If the scheme was to be redistributive, older workers might find it even harder to get a job, for it was feared that they would soon qualify for retirement benefits from the common fund.

Employers faced the familiar dilemma of collective action: a cooperative course would weaken their position vis-à-vis their competitors, whereas an uncooperative stance would leave the overall situation at least as bad as before. External compulsion might solve the dilemma for them by forcing each and everyone to collaborate and by relieving fears that, by staying out of the insurance plan, some would improve their competitive position at others' expense.

Under these conditions an activist reformist regime might initiate legislation for social insurance, seeking the support of either progressive large entrepreneurs or moderate unions, or both. Bismarck did the former in Germany in the early 1880s, Lloyd George the latter shortly before World War I in Britain, and Franklin Delano *Roosevelt followed the third course in the early 1930s in the United States (Wolfgang J. Mommsen and W. Mock, eds., *The Emergence of the Welfare State in Britain and Germany, 1850-1950*, London, 1981; Maurice Bruce, *The Coming of the Welfare State*, London, 1961, 1968 [on the United Kingdom]; Martha Derthick, *Policymaking for Social Security*, Washington D.C., 1979 [on the United States]; Margaret Weir, Shola Orloff, and Theda Skocpol, eds., *The Politics of Social Policy in the United States*, Princeton, N.J., 1988).

The aftermath of World War II saw an extension and intensification of social security schemes throughout Western Europe, inspired by the Beveridge plan in Britain and similar schemes promising soldiers and workers a better future after the war. The appeal of the victorious Soviet Union and of communist parties throughout Europe helped to persuade centrist and conservative parties in the West that the time had come for adequate workers' insurance, if only to erase the memories of the misery that the Great Depression had caused for millions of unemployed workers, radicalized by their experience.

As a result of mobilization for total warfare, the state apparatus had increased enormously in capacity. During wartime large unions and big business had learned to cooperate with government, and afterwards this "wartime triangle" remained in place. After 1945, democratic society everywhere seemed to imply a welfare state.

In the early 1950s, once the devastations of war had been repaired, economic growth was used to finance expansion of welfare provisions. A second period of rapid growth occurred in the late 1960s and early 1970s. Throughout the postwar period "welfare state politics could lie in repose while the engine of economic growth did its work." (Hugh Heclo, "Toward a New Welfare State?" in Peter Flora and Arnold J. Heidenheimer, eds., *The Development of Welfare States in Europe and America*, New Brunswick, N.J., and London, 1981, pp. 383–406.) The clientele of welfare provisions expanded accordingly. Even voters who opposed in principle public spending and high taxation tended to oppose cuts in benefits that profited them personally much more strenuously than they supported retrenchments in general and in the abstract. In this manner, strongly motivated minorities combined to defend their interests successfully every time they were threatened by a necessarily less determined and cohesive opposition.

The second consequence of this expansion was the emergence of a stratum of professional experts and administrators who depended on collective arrangements for employment and advancement. These "new middle classes" constituted a formidable array of interest groups promoting the expansion of welfare arrangements.

A third consequence was a broad transformation of mentality among citizens of contemporary welfare states: 1) An increase in valuation of what experts and the welfare state have to offer—health, knowledge, and protection from income loss. People increasingly defined events in their daily lives in terms of the basic concepts of the professions that they expected to provide these values: a process of "proto-professionalization." 2) Increasing orientation toward the future, by deferring immediate gratification through greater self-constraint or through the acceptance of compulsion, for example, in schooling and social insurance. 3) Increasing awareness of the generalization of interdependency in modern society, a transition from a perception of events mainly in terms of religion or morality to a consciousness of the "lengthening chains of dependency"—an awareness of the ways in which the adversities and deficiencies that afflict one group affect others indirectly.

In this transition from charitable feeling to social consciousness, a sense of responsibility for the plight of others is combined with the conviction that it is not the duty of the individual to ameliorate the condition of the stranger in need. The state has become the abstract, universal, and anonymous caretaker of all members of society. Yet this "social consciousness" is not at all gratuitous. It implies silent consent to a considerable tax burden and to a significant redistribution of income between generations, between sexes, and between the active and nonactive populations. In short, social consciousness relates to charity as transfer capital to alms and as industrial production to craftsmanship.

By the mid-1970s, the powerful forces for expansion of the welfare state were checked—mainly by the budgetary deficits they helped to cause. In the following years left-wing governments such as that of François *Mitterrand in France found themselves incapable of continuing expansionist policies. Meanwhile, rightist regimes, such as Margaret *Thatcher's in Britain and Ronald *Reagan's in the United States, mostly failed in cutting back health, education, or social security expenditures. In multiparty systems, coalition politics even reinforced spending patterns: where bourgeois and social democratic parties alternated in government, as in the Netherlands, Scandinavia, and Italy, social expenditure nevertheless continued to increase (Harold L. Wilensky, "Leftism, Catholicism, and Democratic Corporatism: The Role of Parties in Recent Welfare State Development," in Flora and Heidenheimer, eds., op.cit., pp. 345–382). After a period of exponential expansion from the mid-1940s to the mid-1970s, the welfare state has not broken down, but its growth has been slowed or halted.

The main problem in the further development of welfare arrangements is the gradual erosion of the dominant pattern of a full-time, lifelong working career. Persistent unemployment, the feminization of the work force, the flexibilization of labor contracts, and part-time or casual work combine to undo the close relation between past earnings and subsequent entitlements that was at the core of the social security system. Increasingly elaborate regulations tend either to provoke evasion or to prompt inspection, thus undermining both civil confidence and civil liberties. The aging of the population, combined with pressures emanating from the global economy "which mercilessly punishes profligate governments and uncompetitive economies" (Gøsta Esping-Andersen, "After the Golden Age? Welfare State Dilemmas in a Global Economy," in Gøsta Esping-Andersen, ed., Welfare States in Transition: National Adaptations in Global Economies, London, 1998) pose additional challenges for the welfare state. Universal schemes, modeled after national pension plans that require no means test and cannot easily be defrauded, such as the minimum income or negative income tax, appear to be promising but costly new avenues.

State-controlled arrangements for social security and health care exist in many developing countries as well. But these schemes tend to be restricted to those in regular wage employment, especially the military, the civil service, professionals, and workers in indispensable industries, such as mines or railroads. Domestic workers, the self-employed, and agricultural workers are generally excluded from membership. As a consequence, the overall redistributive effect is regressive—contributions and services are paid in large part by the general taxpayer or the consumer, and benefits accrue to a small, highly-paid, urban minority (Stewart MacPherson and James Midgley, Comparative Social Policy and the Third World, New York, 1987).

The Western welfare state stands at the end of a collectivizing process that in the course of many centuries has expanded in scale from the rural village to entire nations. But the process has not gone beyond that level, and the arrangements remain national in scope. Even in the European Union, where the social policies of member states are gradually integrated and "harmonized," the constituent states so far retain full control of social insurance, health, and welfare. Transnational social policy measures, implying an enforced accumulation of transfer capital and its redistribution from rich to poor nations, so far remain utopian.

(See also CITIZENSHIP; FEMINIZATION OF POVERTY; LABOR MOVEMENT; POLITICAL ECONOMY; SOCIALISM AND SOCIAL DEMOCRACY; TAXES AND TAXATION.)

Richard M. Titmuss, Essays on "The Welfare State" (London, 1958). Harold L. Wilensky and Charles N. Lebaux, Industrial Society and Social Welfare (New York, 1958). T. H. Marshall, Social Policy in the Twentieth Century (London, 1965). Catharina Lis and Hugo Soly, Poverty and Capitalism in Pre-industrial Europe (Brighton, U.K., 1979). Michael B. Katz, In the Shadow of the Poorhouse; A Social History of Welfare in America (New York, 1986). Peter Flora, ed., Growth to Limits: The Western European Welfare States Since World War II, 5 vols. (Berlin and New York, 1987). Abram de Swaan, In Care of the State; Health Care, Education and Welfare in Europe and the USA in the Modern Era (New York and Cambridge, 1988). Gøsta Esping-Anderson, The Three Worlds of Welfare Capitalism (Cambridge, U.K., 1990).

ABRAM DE SWAAN

WEST GERMANY. See GERMANY, FEDERAL REPUBLIC OF.

WESTERN SAHARA. is a former Spanish colony (1884–1976) claimed by *Morocco. The native Arab-Berber-speaking population has reached nearly 300,000. This desert land contains considerable mineral deposits, mainly phosphates; its Atlantic coast boasts extremely rich fishing waters.

Spain never held a referendum on *self-determination; instead, Morocco and *Mauritania (until 1979) occupied the territory. The Frente Popular para la Liberación de Saguia el-Hamra y Rio de Oro (POLISARIO), the Sahrawi liberation movement, proclaimed on 27 February 1976 the creation of a state, the Sahrawi Arab Democratic Republic, which became a member of the Organization of African Unity (OAU) in 1984.

Moroccans claim Western Sahara even though neither the International Court of Justice (1975) nor any country recognizes Moroccan sovereignty over the territory. Morocco has positioned more than 100,000 troops inside electronically protected earthen walls and encouraged settlements of Moroccans; nearly 200,000 settlers live in the main Sahrawi cities. Morocco's occupation of Western Sahara has poisoned relations with Algeria, which has sheltered thousands of Sahrawi refugees and has provided military, diplomatic, and logistical support to POLISARIO. The conflict remains one of the main obstacles to regional integration.

In August 1988, the UN arranged for a peace plan that included the holding of a referendum on self-determination. Except for a promising meeting between King Hassan and POLISARIO leaders in January 1989, Morocco refused until summer 1997 to hold further direct talks with Sahrawis despite UN and OAU calls for such negotiations. The United States, which has traditionally supported Morocco, has also encouraged a negotiated settlement. The U.S. Congress seeks a resolution of the conflict, partly because of the wastefulness of the UN Mission for the Referendum in Western Sahara (MINURSO).

From 1992 to 1997, the situation remained stalemated. Morocco refused to withdraw its military and administrative forces to allow a referendum without constraints. King Hassan refused to hold a genuinely free referendum because of the uncertainty of the result but also because of Algeria's unstable domestic situation since 1992; outside powers failed to press the king to end the conflict. Morocco reneged on the conditions of the peace plan by adding tens of thousands of individuals to the list of voters initially agreed upon and created hurdles for the UN in its attempt to organize a "free and fair" referendum. Other causes of the impasse were the failure of Morocco and POLISARIO to agree on the criteria for eligibility of voters and the partiality of UN Secretary-General Boutros Boutros-Ghali in favor of the Moroccan position. By 1996, the resumption of war appeared imminent. However, Secretary-General Kofi Annan's appointment in March 1997 of James Baker as Special UN Representative for Western Sahara offered new hope for a peaceful settlement. The stature and credibility of Baker made it difficult for Morocco to refuse direct negotiations. Thus, Morocco and POLISARIO held several rounds of negotiations in London, Lisbon, and Houston. The final round in Houston in September 1997 produced an agreement on many salient issues, including the criteria for identification, the confinement of troops during the vote, and the role of the UN during the third-week transition period. It also produced a Code of Conduct to guarantee a transparent electoral process. The long-awaited referendum was set for 7 December 1998, but as has become customary, it never took place due mostly to Moroccan demands for MINURSO to include additional voters. Although the identification process was completed, Morocco introduced new demands. The UN set July 2000 as another date for the referendum. King Hassan II died in July 1999. His more liberal son, King Mohammed VI, has taken as hard a stance on Western Sahara as his father did. Though he removed Driss Basri, the all-powerful minister of the interior, who carried out the repression in the occupied territory, Mohammed VI offered Sahrawis only some vague regional autonomy under Moroccan sovereignty, an offer that Hassan had contemplated in the 1980s. Undoubtedly, short of an unlikely foreign intervention, Moroccans will never allow the holding of a referendum they are uncertain to win.

In March 2000, Annan announced that the referendum could not take place before 2002 at the earliest. In April, James Baker visited the Maghreb region to investigate the feasibility of implementing the Houston Accords and how to overcome specific problems obstructing the execution of the peace plan. Baker was pessimistic mainly because of the obstacles created by Morocco and its delaying tactics made possible by UN passivity and the hesitancy of France and the United States, fearful of destabilizing the fragile transition in Morocco. Many have shown exasperation with the constant postponement of the referendum; meanwhile, the Sahrawis contemplate resuming hostilities to break the decade-long deadlock. Obstacles on the ground have become evident since the Houston Accords. Unless Baker remains in charge, it is unlikely that the Moroccans will allow the holding of a genuinely fair referendum. As Baker stated, "It is a lot easier to agree to do certain things sometimes than it is to do them, so the proof of the pudding will be in the eating."

(See also MILITARY RULE.)

Yahia Zoubir and Daniel Volmam, eds., *International Dimensions of the Western Sahara Conflict* (Westport, Conn., 1993). Yahia H. Zoubir and Anthony G. Pazzanita, "The United Nations' Failure to Resolve the Western Sahara Conflict," *Middle East Journal* 49, no. 4 (Autumn 1995): 614–28. Martine de Froberville, *Sahara occidental: La confiance perdue* (Paris, 1996). Yahia H. Zoubir, "The Western Sahara Conflict: A Case Study in Failure of Prenegotiation and Prolongation of Conflict," *California Western International Law Journal* 26, no. 2 (Spring 1996): 173–213. Yahia H. Zoubir and Daniel Volman, "The United States and Conflict in the Maghreb," *Journal of North African Studies* 2, no. 3 (Winter 1997/98): 10–24. Yahia H. Zoubir, "Geopolitics of the Western Sahara Conflict," in Yahia H. Zoubir, ed., *North Africa in Transition: State, Society, and Economic Transformation in the 1990s* (Gainesville, Fla., 1999), pp. 195–211.

YAHIA H. ZOUBIR

WESTERN SAMOA. See PACIFIC ISLANDS.

WOMEN AND DEVELOPMENT. The focus on women within the field of development was one outcome of the *United Nations Decade for Women (1975–1986). But the origins of the Decade itself lie in the political and theoretical concerns of feminists about equality, human rights and welfare, and considerations about economic efficiency. Thus, the Decade, with its themes of equality (women's rights), development (alleviation of poverty), and *peace (elimination of all forms of violence), can be viewed as the manifestation of feminist politics within the framework of the concern of the international community with the issue of development.

The assumption underlying the launching of the First Development Decade (1961–1970) was that the process of capital accumulation and ensuing increases in the GNP would lead to the alleviation of poverty and to sustained economic growth. However, the failure of the benefits of economic growth to "trickle down" to the poor, and the increase and strengthening of the membership of *Third World governments in the UN, led to the more politically oriented International Development Strategy for the Second Decade (1971–1980). The first reference to "the full integration of women in the total development" appeared in this Strategy. It is perhaps also significant that the proclamation of 1975 as International Women's Year (IWY) by the UN occurred in the context of North-South dialogue on issues of equity in international relations and amid calls for a New International Economic Order (NIEO), a context that was to change dramatically in 1980 with the emergence of conservative governments in the industrialized countries of the North.

The UN Decade for Women provided the framework and resources for a variety of activities in the areas of research and advocacy, organizational and legislative change, and development policy and practice, much of this within the framework of the initial emphasis on increasing the participation/integration of "Women in Development" (WID). Attempts have been made to classify these approaches. Caroline Moser has identified the following: the "welfare" approach of the 1950s to 1970s; "equity" (the original WID approach, linked to the goal of equality) and "anti-poverty" (linked to the goal of development) from the mid-1970s to the mid-1980s; "efficiency" and "empowerment" in the latter half of the 1980s. Moser has also operationalized and introduced to development planning the concepts of practical and strategic gender needs (adapting from Maxine Molineux's conceptualization of practical and strategic gender interests).

However, these approaches often overlap, while the distinctions mask more fundamental differences in theoretical and political approaches over the years. The literature traces a shift from the original (WID) to Women and Development (WAD or WAND) and Gender and Development (GAD). Although they are not mutually exclusive, they reflect significant differences. In brief, WID focuses on women's programs; WAD attempts to explore the relationship between women's position and condition and development; while GAD considers the link between women and development in the context of the relationships between men and women embedded in the social relations of gender.

The WID approach is based on the liberal theory of development (and feminism) within which the Decade for Women was launched. Its main tenets are that men and women are equally endowed, have the same capacity to attain success in life, and that what they need to attain equality is "equal opportunity." It emphasizes individual effort and choice, ignoring the structural obstacles placed on women by their positions and responsibilities in society. It also tends to overlook the sociocultural and political conditions under which "development" takes place. By focusing on women's practical needs, it tended to sidestep the more challenging issues of strategic gender interests, although these were always implicit in the work of feminist-oriented researchers and practitioners.

Recognition that women, as a specific social group, required special attention was supported by the seminal work of the Swedish economist Ester Boserup, in her book *Women's Role in Economic Development* (New York, 1970), which drew attention to the importance of women's work in agriculture in many Third World countries and to the "invisibility" of much of this work to economic planners and policy makers. Women's "invisibility" in the processes of production led to their marginalization, and to the notion that they were "outside" of development, hence the emphasis on "integrating" women in development. The WID approach has led to a number of tangible benefits for women. Drawing on "welfare," "poverty," and "equity" approaches, it opened up new fields of research and teaching, documenting discrimination against women and the conditions of their lives in different countries,

cultures, and classes; it introduced new institutional arrangements, strategies, and methodologies for documenting women's work and improving women's condition; in many countries it led to changes in legislation to remove discriminatory practices; and it raised the level of awareness of the situation of women worldwide and served to mobilize women to take action on their own behalf.

The WAD/WAND approach, spearheaded and explored chiefly by Third World feminist practitioners, researchers, and advocates, attempts to extend the WID approach by questioning the mainstream concept of development itself and introducing a broader framework which acknowledges the structural and political barriers to women's participation in development. Women's exclusion from the benefits of economic development are not seen as solely created by a lack of equal opportunity, but by political systems (colonial and neocolonial), along with a structure of gender relations which, far from "excluding" women, actually benefit from the exploitation of women's time, labor, and sexuality. It emphasizes women's strategic gender interests and their empowerment, through their organizations, to promote and protect gains made within the framework of WID.

The introduction of the concept of "gender" into the discourse emerged from feminist scholars seeking, in the words of Naila Kabeer, "to steer a path somewhere between the liberal individualism of WID scholarship and the structural determinism of certain Marxist accounts, so that analysis could move beyond demonstrating the adverse/marginalizing impact of development/capitalism on women to a deeper understanding of the ways in which unequal relations between women and men may have contributed to the extent and forms of exclusion that women faced in the development process."

By the end of the UN Decade for Women, the insights, knowledge, and analyses generated by the research and action stimulated by this initiative had led to major challenges to the traditional discourse on development itself, and increasingly to the call for a new paradigm based on the reality and perspectives of women. At the cutting edge of this debate is the network of Third World feminists—women involved in research and analysis, policy making, and action—promoting Development Alternatives with Women for a New Era (DAWN), launched at the NGO Forum of the Third World Conference of Women held in Nairobi in 1985. DAWN's major contribution was to locate the situation of women within the context of colonial and neocolonial relations (*dependency) between countries and to link an understanding of women's situation to the macroeconomic framework of their governments. They introduced the concept of empowerment, asserting that only a strong women's movement with a feminist consciousness and commitment to change can promote the achievement of a more equitable and humane world.

In a wider sense it was the achievement of many of the short-term goals of the Decade that revealed their limitation: for despite changing laws, the establishment of policies and programs, special mechanisms, and projects for ensuring the increased participation of women in development activities, the situation of women continued to deteriorate in terms of a widening gap between rich and poor within and between countries, and in terms of the incidence of violence against women.

It is now increasingly recognized that the ideas and concepts guiding the policies and programs for the Decade emerged within a system that did not question the existing development model. The research and analyses carried out throughout the Decade showed that industrialization and *modernization often had an adverse effect on women's lives, jeopardizing traditional *rights and livelihoods, "domesticating" them, limiting their role and status yet giving them additional burdens as modernization and commercialization replaced family-support systems and the mutual exchange of goods and services.

Feminist scholarship also exposed the existence of gender-based hierarchies, even at the level of the poorest household, determining women's access to critical resources and services. Moreover, it was recognized that far from being outside development, the exploitation of women's time, labor, and sexuality was central to the process of capital accumulation, and that women had in fact incurred a disproportionate cost of the evolution of the world capitalist system. Their marginalization, feminists argued, was not necessarily the product of ill-conceived development planning but a logical consequence of an economic system based on the exploitation of the most vulnerable by the most powerful. Increasingly it was acknowledged that development was not a purely technical issue but one that was deeply political and ideological. These considerations were palpable when activists on issues concerning women and gender roles encountered an institutionalized male bias that dismissed research findings and, at times, rendered rational argument impossible.

The global economic crisis of the 1980s and the policies of structural adjustment adopted by most Third World countries to deal with the accumulation of international debt demonstrate, as nothing else has done, the gender and class biases inherent in a model that is focused on economic growth while ignoring social, cultural, and political factors. Macroeconomic policies which privilege economic production over social reproduction by cutting social services jeopardize women in three ways: first, by reducing employment, because it is women who predominate in the social sector; second, by reducing their access to services that are essential if they are to manage their dual roles in production and reproduction; and third, by increasing the demand on their time, as they are expected to fill the gaps created by the cuts:

Similarly, on the production side of the equation, the *export-led growth models focus in many instances on the creation of export-processing zones dependent on large supplies of cheap and compliant female labor, an ideal reserve labor force. The emphasis on export-oriented agriculture, meanwhile, jeopardized the production of food, the chief area of women's involvement in the field of agriculture and the chief source of nutrition for their families.

But the negative impact of these policies on women also highlighted how policies that hurt women spill over to the whole society. The centrality of women's role in reproduction, and the link between social reproduction and production, mean that policies which harm women undermine the economy and society in fundamental ways.

In reflecting on the field of women and development over the past twenty-five years, it is apparent that the most significant shifts have come from the strengthening of feminist politics within its leadership. In the women's movement this has led to a shift from a narrow concern for "women's" issues to a wide range of global concerns, from environment to human rights, from population to debt, structural adjustment, and trade, while at the institutional level it has widened the areas in which a focus on women is required if programs are to achieve stated objectives in regard to equity and participation.

This shift can be traced through the growth of the movement in numbers and level of sophistication and participation in the global conferences of the 1990s, culminating in the Fourth World Conference on Women held in Beijing in September 1995. Since the First World Conference on Women (Mexico City 1975) and subsequent conferences held in Copenhagen (1980) and Nairobi (1985), the agenda relating to women's stake in development had widened and deepened to elaborate programs in the areas of rural development, health, violence, and education, to name a few. However, women's organizing within the global conferences of the 1990s—Environment (Rio de Janeiro 1992), Human Rights (Vienna 1993), Population (Cario 1994), Human Settlements (Istanbul 1994), Social Development (Copenhagen 1995), and Food (Rome 1995)—marked a new point of departure for the agenda of the women's movement. Drawing on the analytical tools developed by feminist researcher-activists throughout the decade of the 1980s, conference participants succeeded in changing the terms of the debates in many of these areas, thus broadening the scope of the concept of development.

This activist approach to issues of women and development is, however, increasingly countered by the co-optation of feminist language, concepts, and agendas and by various bureaucratic devices. "Gender mainstreaming" is one such approach. Since the ending of the UN Decade for Women (1985), and given the reduced resources available for women's development programs and projects, there has been a trend toward mainstreaming of women's projects by various official agencies. Ostensibly, mainstreaming is a strategy for linking women's projects into the processes of development planning and delivery systems so that women gain access to mainstream development resources. Applied with commitment to gender equity, mainstreaming can be a powerful tool. Without this commitment, it can lead to the removal of the focus on women altogether.

Another example is in the use of gender analysis. While it can be used to highlight differences in gender roles and responsibilities, in the inequality of access to and control of resources afforded to men and women, and in the complexity of women's multiple roles and the implications for development planning, gender is being increasingly used to give more attention to men's needs. More recently the introduction of gender management systems (GMS) in the name of good governance and efficiency emphasizes a more bureaucratic approach and a denial of the political roots of the WID initiative and the feminist politics which has advanced this agenda. Indeed, although the use of gender was proposed by feminists as a way of drawing attention to the structural imbalances of responsibilities and power between men and women, the way in which it is being applied is a cause of increasing concern among feminists not only because of the fear that women will again become "invisible" but because they see this as a manifestation of the attempts to depoliticize women as a constituency in development.

These concerns must be seen within the context of the rise of fundamentalism to counter feminist politics within the women's movement. Some view this as an indication of a backlash against a movement which has perhaps become too effective in its challenge to the status quo.

(See also DEVELOPMENT AND UNDERDEVELOPMENT; EQUALITY AND INEQUALITY; FEMINIST THEORY; GENDER AND POLITICS; INTERNATIONAL DEBT; NORTH-SOUTH RELATIONS; PATRIARCHY; REPRODUCTIVE POLITICS; STRUCTURAL ADJUSTMENT PROGRAM.)

Gita Sen and Caren Grown, *Development, Crises and Alternative Visions: Third World Women's Perspectives* (New York, 1987). Caroline Moser, "Gender Planning in the Third World: Meeting Practical and Strategic Gender Needs," *World Development* 17, no. 11 (November 1989): 1799–1825. Irene Tinker, ed., *Persistent Inequalities; Women and World Development* (Oxford, 1990). Diane Elson, ed., *Male Bias in the Development Process: An Overview* (Manchester, U.K., 1991). Sonia Corrêa with Rebecca Reichmann, *Population and Reproductive Rights: Feminist Perspectives from the South* (London, 1994). Naila Kabeer, *Reversed Realities: Gender Hierarchies in Development Thought* (London, 1994).

PEGGY ANTROBUS

WORKERS' CONTROL. As David Montgomery has most cogently argued in *Workers' Control in America* (New York, 1979), workers' control over production has manifested itself from the beginnings of industrial capitalism in the chronic battles and everyday struggles of workers to control their own pace and style of work, to determine their own work group relations, and to resist the imposed routines of the clock and disciplines of the boss. In the nineteenth and early twentieth centuries, actual conflicts over control, as well as oppositional organizations and ideologies, such as anarcho-syndicalism, were most often rooted in craft cultures of skilled male workers. While challenging capitalist control, craft vision and practices were often quite traditional and exclusivist vis-à-vis less skilled and women workers.

With the political crises of World War I, however, as well as its acceleration of mass production and scientific management techniques threatening to further erode craft autonomy and shop floor discretion, skilled workers led mass movements for workers' control that included the less skilled more fully in a democratic challenge to capitalist authority in the workplace and often in the political sphere as well. In Britain, the shop stewards movement was inspired by revolutionary syndicalism, as well as the guild *socialism of G. D. H. Cole, and helped articulate a vision of socialism based on democratic workers' control of industry, in contrast to statist control emerging in the Soviet Union. In Italy, Antonio *Gramsci and other Marxists around the journal *L'Ordine Nuovo* helped radicalize the unions' internal commissions and develop a movement for revolutionary workers' control through factory committees. Much like the Dutch council communist thinker Anton Pannekoek, Gramsci argued that the unions' function of bargaining for better conditions for the sale of labor power under capitalism prevented them from effectively representing workers' interest in democratic control of production and the abolition of labor as a commodity. In this view, unions invariably enforce bureaucratic discipline among workers, and only independent factory committees can lead the struggle to democratize the workplace.

In Germany and Russia, mass movements for workers' control in the factories and mines developed in the course of political revolutions at the end of the war, and these were often supported by workers' councils and soviets that took over local political power. The Bolsheviks' theoretical and practical ambivalence to workers' control was profound, however, as I have argued in *Workers' Control and Socialist Democracy: The Soviet Experience* (London, 1982), and along with the conditions generated by years of a devastating war followed by civil war (1918–1921), this ambivalence doomed workers' control in the new regime.

But as much as the early Soviet experience continues to define for many either the myth of democratic possibilities of revolutionary workers' control or the lessons of political betrayal, it is the experiences in other major European countries that defined limits relevant for the rest of the century. Even under the tremendous strains of war-induced political crises and rapid organizational growth, unions proved resilient and often able to accommodate modified demands for workers' control, and autonomist factory council movements proved incapable of generating effective leadership and organization to preempt or displace them. Neither the craft nor resistance to Taylorism could be realistically sustained (contra Michael Piore and Charles Sabel, *The Second Industrial Divide*, New York, 1984), and industrial unionism was able to provide forms of representation and material benefits that enhanced the rights and conditions of the less skilled while compensating the more skilled. In cases such as Germany, the state was able to institutionalize workers councils (1920) with modest powers and thus helped to undercut more radical demands for workers' control. In the post–World War II period, patterns of institutionalization through unions and the state became even more pronounced and were repeated even in some less developed societies. Challenges to these patterns emerged once again during militant shop floor struggles in the late 1960s and early 1970s, and the heritage of Gramsci, Cole, and others of the earlier period was revived and widely debated. Although these shop floor protests had an important impact on union organization, the revolutionary ideologies and vocabularies of workers' control were yet again displaced, this time by a much richer array of managerial, union, and state initiatives around worker participation and *industrial democracy. And more than in previous periods, these initiatives have aimed to reorganize the work process itself, utilizing the capacities of new information technologies to do so.

(See also ANARCHISM; INFORMATION SOCIETY; LABOR MOVEMENT.)

Carmen Sirianni, "Workers' Control in Europe: A Comparative Sociological Analysis," in James Cronin and Carmen Sirianni, eds., *Work, Community, and Power* (Philadelphia, 1984), pp. 254–310.

CARMEN SIRIANNI

WORLD BANK. The World Bank, an enduring legacy of the post–World War II global economic order, is the foremost international development institution. As the single largest source of long-term lending for development, it is a principal intermediary between the advanced industrial countries and the less developed countries. As the center of development orthodoxy, it is the primary actor in the propagation and dissemination of ideas about development. The financial and intellectual resources at its command, coupled with the steady growth of its role in coping with economic adversity, have given it an increasingly influential and intrusive position in shaping policy choices of many countries. Perhaps its greatest impact in the *international political economy is one of system maintenance: It is a strategic mechanism for keeping developing countries engaged in the existing structures of finance, investment, technology, production, and exchange.

Formally the International Bank for Reconstruction and Development (IBRD), the World Bank was a product of the Bretton Woods conference of 1944. However, since the dominant concern of the architects of Bretton Woods was the postwar global monetary regime and the role of the *International Monetary Fund (IMF) in that regime, the Bank was a sideshow in the epic negotiations at that conference. While the IMF was the object of many compromises between the United States and its European allies, the Bank was in almost every respect an exclusively U.S. creation, an institution that reflected the triumph of American preferences and embodied an American vision of world order. Practically the entire spadework for the organization had already been done within the sanctums of the U.S. Treasury Department. Given the fundamental asymmetry in this relationship to the United States, other countries could only bargain for greater benefits and fewer burdens. Ultimately, it was the United States that determined the range of issues that would be subject to bargaining. On such issues as the lending capacity and the governing structure of the Bank, the only relevant debate was the debate within the United States.

American *hegemony in the organization was established in the selection of its headquarters. John Maynard Keynes, Britain's senior foreign economic policy statesman and the most influential European delegate at Bretton Woods, initially insisted that both the Bank and the Fund be located outside the United States. When that proposal encountered U.S. opposition, he fought to have them placed in New York in the hope that they could be kept at a safe distance from what he called "the politics of Congress and the nationalistic whispering galleries of the Embassies and Legations of Washington." The outcome was a foregone conclusion. The headquarters of the Bank is to this day only two blocks from the White House, a location that not only ensures that few aspects of its operations escape political scrutiny, but also gives the United States an inestimable source of influence over the agency.

The paramount conception held by the creators of the World Bank was that of an organization that would perform compensatory and catalytic functions. The ultimate rationale for such a multilateral instrumentality was the pervasive conviction that governments could not rely exclusively upon private channels to provide international financing in adequate volumes and on reasonable terms. Hence, the Bank was designed to reduce the element of risk in foreign lending at a time when international capital markets were still reeling from the disastrous experiences of the interwar decades. Its own financing activities were expected to establish an international standard for sound loans and to improve the quality of information about international investment opportunities. Thereby, it was hoped, private lenders and investors could gain sufficient confidence to venture overseas again. As late as the 1960s, the IBRD innocently described itself as a safe bridge over which private capital could move into the international field.

However, the enormity of the tasks it faced upon its inception, coupled with the operational strictures that were codified in its Articles of Agreement, left the IBRD with a limited mandate in its early years. Although the developing countries succeeded in securing at Bretton Woods the injunction that development would command an equal priority as reconstruction, the primary mission initially assigned to the Bank was to rebuild the war-ravaged economies of Europe. While the IBRD's reconstruction assistance was limited, and was quickly eclipsed by the *Marshall Plan, lending to the industrial countries accounted for more than one half of its financing even ten years after it began operations and was not phased out until 1968. When the Bank began to shift its focus to the developing countries, it adopted an extremely cautious stance on who could be considered a creditworthy borrower and on what might qualify as a sound loan. In effect, its preoccupation with securing the confidence of investors dictated adherence to conservative conventions of banking on its part and an insistence on exacting standards of economic rectitude on the part of its clients.

Lending Facilities and Organizational Structure. From the very start, the sources of financing of the IBRD have confronted it with an exceptional amalgam of constraints and opportunities that, in turn, have intimately affected many aspects of its operations. The IBRD's equity consists of capital subscriptions from its shareholders—the member countries, currently 181 in number—who literally own the Bank. The rules require that only 10 percent of a subscription be paid in, a proportion that has been reduced even further in recent years due to increases in the IBRD's capital stock. The remainder is "callable capital," subject to call to meet losses in an emergency. The Bank has never had to exercise this contingency; were it to do so, the burden would be borne by its more affluent members. However, the most important source of the IBRD's loanable funds comes from the sale of securities to private investors and central banks. The Bank has devised a panoply of borrowing and investment instruments—increasingly diversified by country, currency, maturity, and source—and has become one of the most active and sophisticated players in the international capital markets. Between 1970 and 2000, there was a rapid growth in its outstanding borrowings, from about $2 billion to $120 billion, in tandem with the huge expansion of its lending to developing countries. With conservative lending policies and prudent financial management, the Bank's bonds have consistently enjoyed a Triple-A rating, while its annual income in recent years has exceeded $1.5 billion, the bulk of it reinvested. These modalities of financing give the IBRD a substantial degree of operational latitude and administrative discretion. At the same time they make the Bank, perhaps more than any other *international organization, dependent on its standing in the financial markets. It is the judgement of bondholders, as much as the predilections of its managers, or the bidding of the United States, that defines the outer limits of what is permissible.

IBRD loans have generally been repayable over twelve to twenty years, with a grace period of five years. Both the principal and the interest on each loan are fully guaranteed by the government of the borrowing country. The rates are typically more favorable than those available from commercial banks, thanks to the IBRD's ability to borrow on extremely attractive terms. Nevertheless, IBRD loans are concentrated on higher income developing and "transition" countries, borrowers commonly regarded as more creditworthy. Towards the end of the 1990s, just ten countries accounted for more than 75 percent of its new loans each year.

Two organizational affiliates have been established to circumvent some of the limitations inherent in IBRD lending: the International Development Association (IDA) and the International Finance Corporation (IFC). IDA was set up in 1960 in response to pressures from developing countries for a soft-loan agency under the control of the United Nations. It provides credits with maturities of up to forty years with ten-year grace periods and no interest (but a service charge of less than one percent). This concessional assistance is directed toward the poorest countries, most of which cannot attract commercial financing. But for IDA, the World Bank would have had a much smaller role in most of South Asia and sub-Saharan Africa. Although its charter proclaims it to be a separate and distinct entity from the IBRD, IDA in reality is no more than a special window of the Bank. What sets it apart institutionally from the IBRD is its financial structure: IDA derives most of its lending resources through periodic donations, referred to as "replenishments," from wealthy countries. To date, IDA has had twelve such triennial replenishments, which, given the antipathy toward multilateral assistance in some countries, especially the United States, have become increasingly politicized and torturous exercises.

The IFC, founded in 1956, is dedicated to the spread of private enterprise across the world and assists developing countries in attracting venture capital, both foreign and domestic, for that purpose. Like the IBRD, the IFC obtains its resources through paid-in subscriptions and capital markets borrowings. However, unlike the Bank, the IFC makes not only loans but also equity investments. Its loans, moreover, are not backed by government guarantees. While for many years the scope and scale of IFC operations remained modest, they took off in the 1990s in line with the Bank's greater emphasis on private sector development. The IFC's larger impact is intended to be catalytic, its presence often providing a comfort to private financiers. It uses its own funds to mobilize project financing from other investors and lenders through syndications, underwritings, cofinancings, and other instruments. It also has launched financial products such as equity funds; supported infrastructure *privatizations and corporate restructurings; and provided extensive technical assistance for the development of capital markets in so-called "emerging market" economies, including the ex-communist countries of Central and Eastern Europe.

The concern with private capital led to the formation in 1988 of yet a third affiliate of the IBRD (and a fourth component of what is commonly designated as "the World Bank Group"), the Multilateral Investment Guarantee Agency (MIGA). MIGA's mandate is to stimulate the flow of foreign direct investment to developing countries by providing guarantees against political risk such as armed conflict and civil unrest, nationalization and expropriation, restrictions on currency transfer, and breaches of contract by host governments.

MIGA also operates jointly with the IFC a foreign investment advisory service to assist member states with policy and institutional issues affecting foreign investment, including strategies to attract foreign investors. As was the case with the IBRD, the avowed thrust of MIGA's activities is compensatory: to fill gaps in the market for investment insurance not occupied by other institutions and to enhance the level of coverage through such modalities as reinsurance of projects with national or private agencies.

Formally, all powers of the World Bank are vested in a board of governors, consisting of one governor from each member country. As that body meets only once a year, most of its authority is delegated to a twenty-four-member board of executive directors who meet in permanent session at the headquarters of the Bank. Nominally employees of the Bank, even drawing their salaries from the Bank, these directors are appointed by and accountable to their governments and, hence, are direct channels for the exercise of national influence in the organization. They exercise oversight of financial and operational programs and are responsible for approving all lending proposals, bond issues, the annual budget, and major policy initiatives. The stratification of power among states in the Bank is readily apparent in the composition of the executive board. While the five largest shareholders appoint their own directors, in effect occupying permanent seats on the board, the other members combine into more or less compatible caucuses to produce enough voting power to elect the remaining nineteen directors. This procedure ensures that the majority of member states are not directly represented in the highest decision-making organ of the Bank. The voice of smaller members is further diluted by the requirement that a director acting on behalf of more than one member cast all the of votes of the group as a unit.

As in the IMF, voting is weighted: the voting strength of each member of the IBRD, as well as in its affiliates, is closely related to financial contributions. The United States, which initially commanded a plurality of 35 per cent, has seen its voting power in the IBRD shrink by more than one-half. This decline is mirrored in IDA and is largely the result of an increasingly strident and successful insistence that other states undertake a greater amount of burden-sharing. However, these changes obscure more fundamental continuities. The United States still commands the power of veto, having engineered a lifting from 80 to 85 percent in the majority required to amend the Articles of Agreement. In addition, the dominant coalition of advanced industrial countries remains intact. In the IBRD, both the shares and the votes of the Big Five—the United States, Japan, Germany, France and the United Kingdom—are close to 40 percent. For the countries of the North as whole, these proportions approach 60 percent. In IDA, the hierarchy is even more pronounced and is reinforced by the official designation of the principal suppliers to the agency's coffers as "Part I countries."

The United States, moreover, continues to enjoy the preponderant influence among national actors in determining what issues do and do not dominate the organization's agenda. Although the United States has not always prevailed in preventing the Bank from denying loans to individual countries (e.g., numerous countries singled out as human rights violators) or for particular projects (e.g., agricultural projects considered to pose a threat of injury to American producers), no programmatic initiatives are undertaken by the Bank in violation of the preferences of the United States, nor are any likely to be pursued in the absence of the support of the United States. The United States does not face hegemonic contenders who espouse a fundamental alternative for the Bank. Nor does it confront serious challenges to the traditional prerogatives it has enjoyed in the organization, although such challenges could be forthcoming in the future, especially from the *European Union or Japan. It is still taken for granted that the president of the World Bank will be an American national designated by the White House. Even though they have seldom turned out to be subservient instruments of the U.S. government, such has been the practice in the selection of each of the nine presidents the Bank has had to date from the first Eugene Meyer (1946–1947), to the current president, James D. Wolfensohn (1995–).

Despite, and in part because of, the preeminence of the North, much of what the World Bank does is not simply the product of demands dictated by any state or of the bargains struck by a coalition of like-minded states. The distribution of voting rights sparks intermittent altercations among shareholders, but those votes are seldom exercised. Typically, decisions by the executive board have been consensual. Only rarely is there opposition against a lending proposal that is presented by the president to the board; even rarer is a proposal that is turned down by the directors. The ascendancy of the "management," as the secretariat of the organization is called, was established in the early years after Meyer resigned in a showdown with the executive directors over the issue of who would run the Bank. The operational decisions that determine the day-to-day activities of the Bank have since remained in the hands of the management, led by its president whose resources today include a staff of more than 4,000 development professionals. The economic and technical expertise of this staff helps to ensure considerable administrative autonomy, as does the complex repertory of decision rules the organization has crafted over the years to govern its most tangible product, development projects and programs.

Development Strategies: From Trickle-Down To Environmental Sustainability. World Bank lending for development has gone through four major phases. While there are important continuities, each phase has been marked by different sets of policy goals and policy tools. In the early years of development financing (1950–1965), the Bank concentrated on "hard hat," large-scale and capital-intensive projects in economic infrastructure—power plants, highways, railways, ports, dams, and telecommunication facilities. The bulk of its loans were spent on the foreign exchange costs of such projects, whose financial and economic benefits could be measured with relative certainty. The Bank became a steadfast champion of the view that investment in "physical overhead" sectors was the prerequisite for successful development. It tended to regard a shortage of capital as a primary obstacle to development and to define its own mission in terms of alleviating that shortage. Otherwise, it insisted that the private sector was the true engine of growth and development. The proper role of the *state in development was regarded as compensatory: to provide the institutional framework that would allow private enterprise, domestic and foreign, to function effectively. In addition, the Bank pressed developing

countries at every turn to rely on market incentives and market constraints. Reductions of various forms of price distortions, along with cost recovery through realistic user fees, were standard conditions of its loans. The emphasis on laissez-faire notwithstanding, the Bank's activities for the very outset had a barely veiled Keynesian thrust. Much of its lending underwrote a more activist role for the state in developing economies. As early as the 1950s, the Bank even gave its blessing to development *planning, maintaining the visible hand was needed to guide investment decisions in order to ensure a sounder allocation of resources.

Over the 1960s, the World Bank broadened the scope of its lending to include projects in agriculture and industry, sectors hitherto designed as "directly productive" and reserved for the private sector. In line with a growing awareness of the shortages of human skills in much of the developing world, the bank also ventured into financiing education projects. However, the major shift in its development strategy came in the 1970s under the leadership of Robert S. McNamara (1960–1981) when the agency formally espoused a new hierarchy of objectives centered on the reduction of poverty and inequality and expressed in new doctrines such as "redistribution with growth" and *"basic needs." McNamara personally took up the cause of alleviating the plight of the "bottom 40 percent," the 1 billion people thought to be living in conditions of absolute poverty.

The Bank embarked on massive lending for *rural development, a sector that at one point became the largest in IBRD and IDA allocations, displacing even transportation. The Bank also began funding projects in other areas that previously had been neglected, especially *population policy, health, nutrition, water, sanitation, small-scale enterprises, and sites and services for squatters in urban slums. The so-called "new style" rural and urban projects were explicitly aimed at benefiting masses of the rural and urban poor. Yet, despite the rhetoric, the Bank never really banked on the poor of the world. The intended and the actual beneficiaries of its poverty-oriented projects seldom reach below an upper crust of the poor, who, in contrast to the rural landless and the urban unemployed, were thought to be in a better position to pay back their loans. The new style projects were still oriented primarily toward increasing production. Hence, the original purposes of Bank financing were not replaced or recast. Rather, new objectives and new components were tagged onto the old. Moreover, these projects, despite their novelty and complexity, were not subjected to a different set of evaluative criteria. Instead, the Bank applied its traditional panoply of criteria for project evaluation. The thrust of the new style projects remained reformist through and through. In the final analysis, therefore, the newly found concern about poverty did not amount to a wholesale departure for the Bank, although it was instrumental in overturning many of the conventional assumptions once held by the organization about the process of development. It also put the Bank at the forefront of global efforts to combat poverty in developing countries. The McNamara years are still remembered as the golden era of the World Bank.

In the third phase, ushered in by the 1980s, the programmatic innovations of the 1970s were demoted in favor of a yet more ambitious undertaking: rescuing developing countries from economic perversity. The World Bank began to gear its lending to a broad array of policy reforms that fall under the rubric of "structural adjustment." These reforms have included exposing protected economies to international competition and steering them toward outward-oriented policies; reducing distortionary government interventions in virtually all areas of economic activity; privatizing state-owned enterprises and, short of that, curbing their hold on the state budget and their access to domestic credit; and creating a decent "enabling environment" for economic activity through sound legal and regulatory institutions. In pursuit of this agenda, the Bank crafted a new lending vehicle, structural adjustment loans. These loans, unlike its project finance, were not tied to specific investments; instead, they provided borrowers with quick disbursing, freely usable foreign exchange. In return for such *balance of payments support, the Bank wrested a commitment to sweeping programs of reform with conditions that went greatly beyond the stipulations typically associated with project financing. Later in the decade, the Bank deployed another instrument of policy-based lending, "sector adjustment loans." As they concentrate on policy and institutional reforms in a particular sector—such as finance trade, agriculture, or energy—these loans are somewhat narrower in scope than structural adjustment loans, but they share many of the same objectives. By the end of the decade, adjustment lending surpassed 25 percent of the organization's lending commitments.

Policy-based lending gave the World Bank a seat at the highest echelons of economic decision making in developing countries. Henceforth, it would no longer consort merely with ministers of agriculture or industry; it became an interlocutor to finance ministers and central bankers as well. Unsurprisingly, the greater profile embroiled the Bank in some of the same controversies that had plagued the IMF all along. These controversies intensified when the Bank tightened conditionality and expanded it to include not only economic liberalization but also elements of political liberalization (under the guise of such sobriquets as "governance").

Adjustment lending also increasingly pitted the Bank in conflicts with the IMF as the division of labor charted between the two agencies at Bretton Woods began to erode. The Bank and the Fund have traditionally had complementary functions and close relations. Their headquarters are on the opposite sides of the same street and they are even linked by an underground tunnel. Membership in the IMF has always been a prerequisite for membership in the Bank. The notion that the IMF would assume responsibility for short-term, macroeconomic issues while the Bank would preoccupy itself with long-term microeconomic concerns might have been credible at one time. It all but ceased to be so when the IMF began to pay more attention to "supply side" factors (e.g., the enhancement of productive capacities in specific sectors and a more efficient utilization of public revenues) that were the traditional preserve of the Bank, while the Bank infused into its lending programs a host of macroeconomic policy reforms hitherto confined largely to the wish lists contained in its country economic reports and otherwise commonly regarded as falling within the competence of the IMF. As they have been drawn into greater collaboration with each other, the Bank and the Fund also have found themselves at odds over such policies as the amount of exchange rate devaluations or the size of public spending cuts to be negotiated with borrowing countries. In part, the conflicts are expressions of turf wars, including the jockeying for a leadership mandate in lingering debt and financial crises. But they also suggest more fundamental differences in objectives and orientations among the two agencies.

In the fourth phase, which began in the early 1990s, the World Bank has elevated poverty and the environment as its overriding preoccupations. The administration of Wolfensohn, the most dynamic leader the Bank has had since McNamara, also has undertaken a major effort to enhance the effectiveness and efficiency of the organization's operations and, in the process, to restructure its relations with the many constituencies that affect and are affected by them. In proclaiming anew its commitment to reducing poverty as its primary mission, the Bank was at pains to emphasize that the fight against global poverty was stalled, while in many countries the incidence of poverty and inequality had worsened. It eschewed the "bean counts," and associated qualification exercises, that had made the "new style" projects of the McNamara era the object of considerable skepticism both inside and outside the Bank. But to poverty reduction, and to many other of its activities in the field, the Bank brought a set of objectives as demanding as any it had pursued in earlier decades. It insisted that poverty strategies must be country-driven as conditionality could not substitute for government "ownership." It called for broadening participation to include "stakeholders" such as *non-governmental organizations and other groups in *civil society. It argued for a comprehensive exploration of the determinants of poverty and of its multiple dimensions, including gender disparities, insecurity, powerlessness, and social exclusion. It stressed the need for empowering the poor through improved governance and greater accountability. And all along, it gave pride of place to rapid economic growth and market-oriented liberalization as prerequisites for alleviating poverty. In terms of its own lending, the Bank became heavily involved in building safety nets to mitigate some of the deprivations visited on the poor by structural adjustment and financial contagions. By the end of the 1990s, it could claim that lending for human development—education, health, nutrition, family planning, and social protection—accounted for the largest share of its financing activities. The implications for poverty were less than obvious, however. As in the 1970s, the thrust of its lending was oriented much less toward attacking poverty directly than toward promoting growth and efficiency.

For the first time in its history, in the 1990s the World Bank also defined environmental sustainability as part of its central mission, occasionally grouping it with poverty reduction into the superordinate objective of "environmentally sustainable poverty alleviation." The Bank was a latecomer to environmentalism. Indeed, for many years environmental concerns were treated as an irritant by most officials in charge of lending operations. The Bank's initial posture on the environment was defensive: to minimize the ecological disruptions, and the attendant political embarrassments, arising from a growing number of projects it had funded. Soon, however, it began to cast its role beyond that of damage control. It embarked on a substantial volume of financing targeted specifically toward the environment. By the end of the 1990s its portfolio of environmental projects—covering a widening spectrum activities, including pollution abatement, watershed protection, soil reclamation, and habitat protection—had surpassed $15 billion. Already, by the middle of the decade, the Bank had officially sworn itself to "mainstreaming the environment" and it began to subject more and more of its entire lending portfolio to environmental assessments. In its policies, as in its research, it dedicated itself to systematically exploring the complex linkages among issues of growth, poverty, and the environment Henceforth, development and the environment were to be treated as elements of an integral whole. It espoused the imperative of addressing environmentally *sustainable development at the sectoral and macroeconomic levels and it confronted its borrowers with the same challenge by selectively incorporating environmental questions into its "policy dialogue" with them.

The Determinants of Policy Change. An analogy often used by World Bank staffers to describe their own organization is that of a supertanker that needs several nautical miles before it is able to modify its course. The history of the Bank provides ample testimony to its propensity for torpidity. Except for joining the chorus of those who contended the *Third World faced a liquidity rather than a solvency problem, the Bank sat out the first phase of the debt crisis of the 1980s. When the Bank later moved closer to center stage, the nature of its role was defined mainly by the U.S. Treasury Department. From the strenuous defense of creditors' claims to the cautious provision of guarantees on repayment of restructured debt, its words and actions did nothing to dispel suspicions that it was a handmaiden of private bankers. Yet the supertanker does change course, often in ways that are mystifying to those of its own crew and those of other vessels. World Bank watchers usually point to hegemonic pressures to account for changes in the organization's behavior. Some changes are indeed responses to the demands of its sovereign paymasters, the United States in particular. The tightening of conditionality in the 1980s and the attention to private sector development in the 1990s are cases in point. However, two other factors have had a critical bearing on changes in strategy: policy learning and institutional rationality.

Among the bases of the first factor is the role of specialized knowledge as a definer of action in the World Bank. For more than a quarter of a century, the supreme claimants to authoritative knowledge relevant to the making and unmaking of policy in the Bank have been development professionals, especially economists, rather than bankers, lawyers, engineers, or politicians. Economists have occupied many of the senior decision making positions in the organization. Over the last two decades, the position of Chief Economist has been held by some of the leading lights in the profession, including Hollis Chenery, Anne Krueger, Stanley Fischer, Lawrence Summers, and Joseph Stiglitz. The evaluation of the unfolding experiences of development, especially the lessons to be derived from the Bank's own projects and programs, is a permanent preoccupation, and one that is institutionalized in organizational routines, although the ramifications for policy are often tenuous. While the Bank has never been polarized by ideological or doctrinal schisms, issues such as the tradeoffs between growth and equity, or the institutional prerequisites for the proper functioning of markets, are still highly contested. Policy choices have been shaped closely by professional agreements and disagreements about cause-effect and ends-means relationships in the realm of development. Few, if any,

major changes in the development strategies of the Bank have endured in the absence of a substantial consensus on these concerns.

Institutional rationality, on the other hand, suggests that support for or resistance to alternative policies are ultimately determined by estimations of the consequences for the survival and growth of the organization as an institution. The World Bank, like any complex bureaucracy, pursues certain strategic choices intended to reduce its vulnerability and further its autonomy. Over the years it has attempted to protect those commitments that it has come to regard as intrinsic to its identity. Considerations of preserving and enhancing the niches it occupies in international development policy are seldom absent in ordering priorities; more often, they are decisive. Hence, behind many of its choices is a decisional calculus geared toward its own institutional interests, interests that are not always identical with those of its shareholders. Two minimum conditions have caused the Bank to be more successful than most other international organizations in acquiring a degree of authority independent of that originally conferred on it by its creators. First, it has been allowed to exercise operational latitude as long as hegemonic preferences are not violated. Secondly, at certain junctures its executive leadership has been able to exploit crisis and uncertainty to redefine organizational competences.

The weight of policy learning and institutional rationality is illustrated in some of the shifts in development strategy over the last three decades. The adoption of the agenda of poverty in the 1970s was one of the consequences of the extensive reevaluation of international development policy at the turn of that decade. It reflected misgivings both in and out of the Bank about the consequences of the growth models of earlier years. In particular, there was a widely shared conviction that trickle-down approaches of the past had reinforced the syndrome of deprivation, marginalization, and inequality in many parts of the Third World. For many, the pathway of growth the Bank had pursued had not only bypassed the majority of the poor, it may even have left them more desperate. In addition, the programmatic innovations of the 1970s were instrumental in securing the huge expansion in lending that the McNamara regime had set as one of its objectives. That expansion would have been difficult to justify had the Bank not ventured beyond its original toolkit of infrastructure investments and beyond the traditional beneficiaries of its lending programs. By then, concentrating lending in agriculture on cattle ranchers in Argentina or on coffee growers in Kenya had become less than politically acceptable. Hence, the emphasis on making the "small farmer" (*peasants did not enter the Bank's lexicon) the beneficiary of financial credits, extension services, irrigation systems, and training programs.

However, the fragility of the intellectual consensus about the 1970s approach to poverty alleviation eventually because a source of its undoing. Project planners soon discovered they had a paucity of knowledge about the new areas of lending. As the hierarchy of objectives became more abstract, and as the emphasis gradually shifted away from purely physical-biological and technical-economic inputs, planners found it much more difficult to isolate measurable effects. They expressed growing doubts about what was manipulable. There was an admission in some quarters that rural and urban poverty projects demanded a different set of skills from what was to be found in the Bank, that these projects required insights located in disciplines other than those that had traditionally informed development policy. But there was little agreement on whether or how such steps could be pressed into designing a better product. Yet another factor contributed to the disengagement from poverty-oriented projects that took place in the 1980s. Some of those projects turned out to be organizationally disruptive. Many of them ran into trouble owing to the excessive complexity and ambitiousness with which they were designed as well as the difficulties in overcoming the political, economic, technological, and administrative obstacles encountered in the process of implementation.

The same combination of factors is evident in the shift in the focus of the World Bank toward structural adjustment in the 1980s. The triumph of neoclassical orthodoxy in the organization was to no small extent the product of a profound rethinking of development concerns that amounted to nothing less than a sea change. There were widespread expressions of the view that the public sector in many developing countries had produced disastrous economic policies. There was extensive questioning of the assistance the Bank had given to solidifying the role of the state in developing economies in earlier decades, especially after it had shed its inhibitions about lending to state-owned enterprises. There also was a pervasive suspicion that the development project, which the Bank had treated as its main policy tool, may be less consequential than it had presumed—that the overall framework of economic policies was more decisive in determining development outcomes, including the long-term successes or failures of projects themselves. Although many disputes remained about such matters as the sequencing and pacing of reforms, the appropriate roles of the state and the market, and the ways of mitigating political and social costs, a remarkable (albeit less than universal) consensus emerged on the central tenets of reformist packages. Few policy makers would challenge the need to adhere to monetary and fiscal prudence, to move away from inward-looking paths of development, to place a greater reliance on market forces, or to allow more leeway for the private sector.

While such a process of reevaluation provided the intellectual underpinning for adjustment lending, considerations of institutional maintenance were also at work. The felt need to avoid a lapse into irrelevance became acute in the World Bank with the intensification of the economic travails of the 1980s: The debt crisis not only led to the retreat of commercial creditors from the developing countries, but it also wreaked havoc with the Bank's own operational portfolio. The flow of Bank resources, as measured by the ratio of disbursements to repayments, shrank and then turned negative. Hence the balance of payments financing afforded by adjustment lending was designed to compensate for the ponderous rhythms of the project cycle and to accelerate the pace of lending, thereby preserving the "money-moving" function that the organization regards as vital to its mission. The new financing modality became a strategic response to a situational constraint.

Institutional rationality was also decisive behind the recasting of the Bank's environmental strategy in the 1990s. In this saga, knowledge and learning were conspicuous by their absence. As early as the mid-1970s, some Bank officials acknowledged that they could no longer treat ecological destruction as just another inevitable but necessary externality.

In subsequent years, others expressed the need to address ecological concerns explicitly in project design. Yet until the late 1980s these sentiments had only an episodic impact on lending choices. What triggered the internal policy reforms was external pressure from a cohesive and articulate coalition of environmental groups, often acting in concert with congressional critics of the World Bank, that produced a catalogue of environmental disasters caused by projects financed by the agency. The Polonoroeste project in the Brazilian Amazon, the transmigration scheme in Indonesia, the Singrauli power plant project in India—these and a host of other projects across the developing world were paraded in an effort to demonstrate that the World Bank was bankrolling ecological destruction, the plundering of tropical rainforests, the despoiling of wildlife habitats, and the involuntary uprooting of indigenous people. The negative publicity led to demands for accountability and oversight. The findings of an independent commission supported the complaints of the environmentalists and led to the cancellation of financing for one project, Narmada Sardar Sarovar dam and power in India, in 1993. That same year the executive directors, acting under threats from the U.S. Congress of cuts in funding for IDA, took the unusual step of approving the creation of an outside appeals mechanism, the Inspection Panel, to receive and investigate public complaints about Bank projects. Two years later, in the first claim filed with the panel, it backed charges that the proposed funding of the Arun III dam and highway project in the Himalayas of Nepal violated the Bank's own environmental guidelines, a finding that led to the withdrawal of the Bank from the project.

The coalition succeeded in making the World Bank the foremost battleground over the environment. But the external pressures also served as a catalyst for changes few had anticipated. First, they provided ammunition for the growing ranks of environmentalists within the Bank itself. Second, they led to sweeping organizational and operational changes. Among these were the establishment of a full-scale environment department, which later was placed under the wings of a "vice-presidency for environmentally and socially sustainable development"; the creation of environment subunits in each of the regional offices, the mainstay of lending operations, with growing mandates for screening financing proposals; and the adoption of a miscellany of directives and guidelines for environmental assessments and safeguards. Thirdly, and in the long run most importantly, the Bank found that the issue of the environment presented not only a threat but also an opportunity.

It is of no small irony that the Bank has become a steward in the evolving global regime for environmental governance. It is one of the principal implementing agencies of the Global Environment Facility (GEF) and the Multilateral Fund for the Montreal Protocol (MFMP), two international mechanisms for planetary problems associated with atmospheric pollution. For the Bank, these instruments represent not only additional resources for project financing but also further avenues for expanding its authority and legitimacy. By the end of the 1990s, the Bank was able to boast that it had to become the largest source of international financing for biodiversity projects. It had the largest renewable energy portfolio of any institution in the world. It also had one of the largest environmental research centers to be found anywhere. At global forums on the environment, it had ceased to be an onlooker. As the 1992 Rio Summit, formally the United Nations Conference on Environment and Development (UNCED), revealed, the Bank henceforth would be one of the leading players, helping to both define the terms of the debate and the course of action. As an indication of its growing responsibilities, in 2000 the Bank even insinuated itself as a trustee in the nascent regime for emissions trading by launching a prototype carbon fund offering private companies in industrial countries credits against future carbon dioxide emissions limits in return for investments in "climate friendly" projects in developing countries. If such roles in the global arena are any indication, despite the original intentions and inclinations, the greening of the World Bank will continue, although neither the pace nor the direction is likely to assuage its many critics.

Retrospect and Prospect. The record of the last five decades suggests that the World Bank has been quite adept at reorienting its policies in order to expand its domain. Indeed, it is probably one of the few multilateral organizations in the field of development whose authority has grown consistently. As it entered the new millennium, the Bank faced more claimants and more demands than ever before in its history. Yet it also was mindful of its limitations and contradictions. The Bank has all but abandoned the notion that it had at its disposal an armory of theoretical insights and practical tools that could be deployed to lift any and all countries out of poverty and stagnation. Such a notion was pervasice during the 1950s and the early 1960s. It resurfaced, in less exuberant form, during the free market spree of the 1980s and early 1990s. But the certitude with which the Bank once enunciated its version of the truth is much less evident. In recent years, it has expressed growing doubts about the virtues of integration and comprehensiveness in program design. It has become much more skeptical about the "blueprint" approaches that have been a hallmark of its style and it has underscored the need for adaptive learning and consensus building. It has recognized the weight of "civil society" and *"social capital." It even has engaged in a deliberate search for knowledge about the political dimensions of development. While such musings at times are little more than rhetorical devices, they also reflect diminished confidence in its traditional approaches and expanded awareness of the complexities of causation in development.

In many respects, development has proved to be a receding target for the World Bank. In the 1970s, the organization failed, at times spectacularly, in its attempt to create multisectoral and multicomponent projects combining the objectives of increasing growth and productivity with reducing poverty and inequality. In the 1980s, it had little more success in achieving the economic and social objectives it sought in adjustment lending. In the 1990s, the Bank largely failed to halt the deterioration in the quality of its projects. If sustainability, the likelihood that a project will deliver the intended results over its lifetime, is the yardstick for judging development effectiveness, the Bank is not winning the battle. By its own admission, well over one-half of its projects fail the test. Among the many reasons behind the poor performance, one factor, embedded in the organizational culture, seems paramount: the pressure to lend and to accommodate borrowers. Budgetary and career incentives have continued to reward larger volumes of lending and hence projects of larger size.

The Wolfensohn leadership, more than any of its predecessors, committed itself to replacing the "culture of approval" by a "culture of effectiveness," to emphasizing results on the ground as the ultimate test for judging organizational success. However, notwithstanding successive overhauls in management systems and operational procedures, the attempt to reinvent the Bank has been less than successful. One consequence of the hiatus between changes in policy and changes in practice is that more than a decade after the Bank resolved to avoid the public relations fiascoes over the issue of the environment, if found itself revisiting the familiar controversies. In the summer of 2000, the Bank was forced to back away from a poverty reduction project in the Qinghai province of China, by then its largest borrower, after the Inspection Panel echoed many of the complaints lodged by* human rights and environmental organizations by reporting that the project's planned resettlement of nearly 60,000 Chinese farmers into lands traditionally occupied by ethnic Tibetans violated Bank policies.

For the foreseeable future, the World Bank is likely to continue to be the linchpin of international collaboration in the area of development. It will continue to be the leading channel and coordinator of multilateral assistance to developing countries. All such roles presume that the stake that the most powerful and prosperous members have in the organization stays intact. To the extent it does and to the extent that the weaker and poorer do not have credible alternatives in the world economy, the World Bank is likely to become further engaged in contributing to the governance structures for international *public goods, in areas that are difficult to predict but of which its involvement in global environmental issues may be a harbinger. Among international organizations, it remains the principal protagonist in the process of economic reform in developing countries. And it remains the leading voice in the debate about development: Its pronouncements, though seldom commonly heeded, always command attention throughout the developing world.

(See also Development and Underdevelopment; Finance, International; Food Politics; International Debt; Modernization; North-South relations; Structural Adjustment Program.)

Edward S. Mason and Robert E. Asher, *The World Bank Since Bretton Woods* (Washington, D.C. 1973). Robert L. Ayres, *Banking on the Poor: The World Bank and World Poverty* (Cambridge, Mass., 1983). Paul Mosley, Jane Harrigan, and John Toye, *Aid and Power: The World Bank and Policy-Based Lending*, vols. 1 and 2 (New York, 1991). Bruce Rich, *Mortgaging the Earth: The World Bank, Environmental Impoverishment, and the Crisis of Development* (Boston, 1994). Catherine Caufield, *Masters of Illusion: The World Bank and the Poverty of Nations* (New York, 1997). Devesh Kapur, John P. Lewis, and Richard Webb, *The World Bank: Its First Half Century*, vol. 1, *History* (Washington, D.C., 1997). Devesh Kapur, John P. Lewis, and Richard Webb, eds., *The World Bank: Its First Half Century*, vol. 2, *Perspectives* (Washington, D.C., 1997). World Bank, *World Development Report* (Washington, D.C., annual).

Don Babai

WORLD COURT. See International Court of Justice.

WORLD HEALTH ORGANIZATION. The World Health Organization (WHO) came into existence in 1948, taking over the functions of the Office International d'Hygiène Publique (established 1907) and the Health Organization of the League of Nations (established 1919). WHO's aim is the attainment by all peoples of the highest possible level of health, to be achieved through technical collaboration with its members in the areas of disease eradication, nutrition, environmental hygiene, and health service administration. To this end, WHO maintains epidemiological and statistical services, promotes scientific cooperation, proposes international conventions, conducts research, and develops international standards for food, biological, and pharmaceutical products. A publications program ensures the wide dissemination of statistical data and policy recommendations. Membership in the organization, which is open to all, has grown from the original 61 signatories to the Constitution in 1948 to 191 members in 1998.

Like other specialized agencies of the UN, WHO raises its budget from annual assessments of members. The projected 2000–2001 budget is $842 million, but income from other sources such as the trust funds for *AIDS, tropical disease research, and onchocerciasis (river blindness) control more than doubles that sum, bringing the 2000–2001 total to $1.8 billion.

WHO consists of three constituent bodies: the large, comprehensive World Health Assembly, which meets annually to decide policy and approve the program and budget; the smaller, representative Executive Board, which meets semiannually to prepare the assembly's agenda; and the Secretariat, which is the staff. Unlike other UN specialized agencies, WHO is a decentralized organization. It maintains headquarters in Geneva, Switzerland, but vital work of the organization is performed in six regional offices, which formulate regional policies and monitor regional activities—in Brazzaville, for the African region; in Washington, D.C., for the Americas; in Alexandria, Egypt, for the Eastern Mediterranean region; in Copenhagen, for Europe; in New Delhi, for Southeast Asia; and in Manila, for the Western Pacific region.

In the mid-1970s, under the leadership of Halfdan Mahler, a social democrat from Denmark, WHO stepped into the political limelight espousing the cause of the world's sick and poor. It successfully eradicated smallpox, the first disease ever to be eliminated through human effort. It gave *Third World nations useful instruments enabling them to negotiate with multinational corporations and, for those with the political will to do so, a handle on planning their services. It challenged the infant formula industry, for example, by producing a code that restricts sales practices in the Third World, and it took on the pharmaceutical industry by publishing a list of 200 essential drugs to substitute for the average 3,500 to 5,000 marketed to underdeveloped countries.

In 1978, the organization issued a challenge: "Health for All by the Year 2000." To reach this goal, WHO proposed a primary health care service model—a package of preventive and curative services to be delivered by auxiliary personnel. This strategy seemed revolutionary coming from an organization that, until 1975, subscribed to the medical doctrine that the proper response to human health needs in developing countries was the transfer of Western biomedical technology. Primary health care thus represented progress over most of WHO's previous programs, which relied on the delivery of curative services by physicians and nurses in urban hospitals. But the strategy failed to address the real health problems of the Third World poor and led only to the "medicalization" of underdevelopment. Underscoring WHO's failure to alleviate the root causes of ill health, recurrent epidemics of cholera in Latin America and Africa killed tens of thousands of poor people living without the most elementary services in polluted, overcrowded shantytowns. Basic concerns with the provision of latrines, safe water supplies, and adequate nutrition yielded to demands for fiscal reform of service delivery.

By the end of the 1980s, state provision of primary health care was abandoned in favor of a multiplicity of microprojects run by *non-governmental organizations, which donors control more easily than direct aid to allegedly corrupt governments. This privatization of health service delivery represents a major shift in the health care paradigm, with market values replacing the vision of humanitarian aid and the state welfare model. Setting the new global health policy agenda was the *World Bank, which promoted privatization and rapidly became the largest aid agency in the health sector. WHO's influence and power declined under Hiroshi Nakajima of Japan, director-general from 1988 to 1998.

Like other specialized agencies and the UN itself, WHO tends to mirror and transmit through its programs the balance of world power and the dominance of North over South. Smallpox eradication was carried out at the request of the United States, which largely funded and staffed the program; not all Third World countries felt it was their highest priority or that it would improve overall health as measured by death rates, which failed to decline. Similarly, the Global Programme on AIDS (now UNAIDS, a joint project of the World Bank, UN Development Programme, and WHO) corresponds to U.S. interests. The United States accounts for one third of the world's cases of AIDS, and the U.S. government promotes research on heterosexual transmission of human immunodeficiency virus (HIV) rather than on care of people with AIDS under conditions of poor and scarce health resources; it also cooperates in vaccine trials with Third World governments that lack the health infrastructure needed to vaccinate their populations against HIV. WHO observed the UN Security Council embargo on Iraq during the 1991 Gulf War and played no role in the provision of essential medical supplies or care to the civilian population, which it left to nongovernmental organizations, led by the International League of Red Cross and Red Crescent Societies.

If privatization continues under Gro Harlem Brundtland of Norway, the first woman to be director-general (elected in 1998), it seems unlikely that WHO will make a lasting change in the social inequalities between North and South, including inequalities in health care and chances of survival.

Fiona Godless, "The World Health Organization," *BMJ* 1994, 309: 1424–1428; 1491–1495; 1566–1570; 1636–1639; 1995, 310:110–112; 178–182; 389–393; 583–586. Meredeth Turshen, *Privatizing Health Services in Africa* (New Brunswick, N.J., 1998).

MEREDETH TURSHEN

WORLD SYSTEM. See INTERNATIONAL SYSTEMS.

WORLD TRADE ORGANIZATION. The World Trade Organization is the principal organization responsible for the rules of global trade and the cornerstone of the global *regime for the exchange of goods and services between states. It was formally founded in 1995 as the successor to the General Agreement on Tariffs and Trade, which for four decades was the central forum for striking deals and settling disputes on trade, and which continues to serve as the main rule book for the conduct of commerce among members of the Organization. The overall purpose of both GATT and the WTO has remained constant: to boost the growth in world trade by reducing barriers in a nondiscriminatory and transparent fashion. Momentous as such a task might be, it is not one that has sufficed to endow either of them with universal endearment. While GATT and WTO have contributed to the huge growth in world trade over the last fifty years, and while they have insinuated a substantial measure of accountability and predictability in a realm once regarded as the prerogative of individual *sovereignty, their own legitimacy and credibility have been subjected to intense and searing questioning. The procedures of the WTO are cumbersome and ineffectual. The pace of its deliberations is often glacial. And much of its agenda is arcane and soporific. Yet, from bananas to beef, from Canadian asbestos to Cuban rum, from sweat shops to sea turtles—the issues before the WTO increasingly stir passionate responses among governments and publics alike. As demonstrated by the violent protests in the streets of Seattle that attended the collapse of WTO's ministerial meeting in December 1999, the WTO has become one of the foremost battlegrounds in the backlash against *globalization. It also has become one of the main foci in the crisis of governance affecting international institutions.

The conversion of GATT into the WTO represents a resurrection of an important element in the original blueprint for the global economy after World War II. The General Agreement, initially envisaged as an interim treaty and signed by twenty-odd countries in 1947, was not intended to stand alone. Rather, it was designed to be part of a comprehensive International Trade Organization (ITO) which, in turn, would have formed the third leg of the Bretton Woods tripod—along with the *International Monetary Fund (IMF) and the International Bank for Reconstruction and Development (IBRD) or *World Bank. The ITO would have had a broad mandate covering not only trade barriers but also economic development, commodity agreements, employment policy, foreign investment, and restrictive business practices. It also would have had strong enforcement powers to ensure compliance with its rules. The charter of the ITO drew the ire of the U.S. Congress and was not even submitted to it for ratification. The ITO, therefore, never came into existence. GATT emerged by default as the overseer of the rules for world trade. But it was given no teeth to perform such a role. Its scope, moreover, was limited largely to one among the gamut of issues that fall under the rubric of trade: commercial barriers on industrial products. As purists are wont to note, GATT was not even an *international organization in the strict sense of the term. *De facto*, it did become such an entity but its "provisional" status remained throughout its tenure. Only with the creation of the WTO did the trade regime acquire a fully-fledged and permanent multilateral organization and one with an explicit mandate that reaches beyond industrial barriers.

Freer and Fairer Trade. As was the case with the other institutions that underpinned the postwar international economic order, GATT reflected the preponderance and preferences of the United States. It also embodied a conviction about the imperative of avoiding a relapse into the beggarthy-neighbor policies that led to the disintegration of the world economy in the 1930s. At the heart of GATT is a code of prescriptions and proscriptions for the behavior of states in trade. The dominant thrust of the code is liberal, albeit not of the classical nineteenth century version of *liberalism. Hence, measures to liberalize and increase the flow of goods were not tethered entirely to ideals of aggregate growth and aggregate efficiency. There was a common recognition that those measures also would have to respect goals of domestic employment and price stability and, more generally, the greater responsibilities assumed by governments in protecting their economies against external disturbances. The occasional recitations of the idiom of laissez-faire orthodoxy notwithstanding, GATT was to dedicate itself not so much to free trade, but to freer and fairer trade.

The cornerstone of GATT, and of the trade regime at large, is the principle of nondiscrimination, embodied in the rule of unconditional "most-favored-nation" (MFN) treatment for all its signatories. Accordingly, any concession granted by one member to another member has to be extended automatically to all others, the so-called "contracting parties" of GATT. The rule, in effect, is intended to ensure that a country's products can enter foreign markets according to terms no less favorable than those enjoyed by any other country. Hence, any reduction or increase in trading barriers has to be generalized to all members of the regime. At the same time, according to the principles of GATT, liberalization of trade must be based on reciprocity: market opening measures negotiated between any two parties require concessions by both sides. In the jargon of GATT, liberalization is to be mutually advantageous and substantially equivalent. While the economic justification behind reciprocity is dubious, the norm has an eminently political calculus: to deflect the domestic opposition that inevitably crystallizes against unilateral and unrequited reductions in trade barriers. The General Agreement also urges its members to make the instruments of protection transparent. In general, non-tariff barriers, such as quantitative restrictions, are to be prohibited. Hence, states are to confine themselves to tariffs, which operate by price rather than by volume, are more predictable, less arbitrary, and easier to negotiate downward.

From the outset, GATT was strewn with escape clauses. The MFN rule can be suspended for customs unions and free trade areas. Thus the European Common Market, the forerunner to the *European Union (EU), was left free to engage in reductions in trade barriers among its members that would not have to be multilateralized across GATT. Exemptions from MFN were also tolerated for preferential arrangements existing before the formation of GATT, e.g. British and French imperial relations. Quantitative restrictions could be used to cope with *balance of payments difficulties. They also could be invoked for reasons of national *security. Subject to certain strictures, temporary safeguards in the form of higher tariffs or import quotas could be imposed in order to protect domestic industries threatened with a surge of imports attributable to previous concessions. Also codified in the rules, at the insistence of the United States, were allowances for a panoply of liberal practices in agriculture, including export subsides and import controls. These loopholes and exceptions grew over the years. Some of them were expected to provide an incentive to move toward greater openness; many were intended to temper the costs of international adjustments on national economies and societies and, as such, allow for an important element of flexibility in the treatment of defectors; all bore the imprint of politically influential domestic interests pushing for *protection.

Nominally in charge of this code was an entity with marginal powers. In fact, GATT was run as a club by and for the world's largest trading nations: the U.S., Western Europe, and Japan. All of these powers were determined to keep GATT on a short leash. Therefore, as an institution GATT remained no more than the sum of its parts. However, it did provide a setting for two important activities. The first is dispute settlement. GATT become a forum for the resolution of complaints about violations of its trade rules. However, its machinery for the purpose was widely regarded as ineffective: The consensual decision-making requirement that prevailed across GATT allowed disputants to block the findings of expert panels convened to handle the complaints; rulings, which could authorize retaliation by the injured party, were not considered binding; and the means of securing compliance were nonexistent. The second activity is one in which GATT has had a greater measure of success: conference diplomacy. The highlight of this diplomacy was successive rounds of multilateral trade negotiations (MTNs). The six rounds of MTNS held between the late 1940s and 1960s, culminating in the Kennedy Round of 1962–1967, paved the way for a remarkable decline in tariff barriers and an equally remarkable increase in world trade and prosperity.

Like the institution as a whole, the bargains struck through GATT in this period rested on the ability and willingness of the United States to underwrite the costs of creating a more open trade order. GATT was of limited utility in addressing the concerns of the *Third World: for most developing countries, the norms and rules of GATT, and the preoccupation of MTNs with tariff barriers on industrial products, were not relevant to their immediate priorities. Once the charter for the ITO was shelved, many of them chose to stay clear of GATT, while even those that did join for the most part remained outside the MFN process. On the other hand, GATT was instrumental in absorbing the Europeans and the Japanese into the emerging economic order. U.S. toleration of asymmetric benefits—specifically, willingness to forego an insistence on reciprocal concessions by Western Europe and Japan and, more generally, to accommodate a measure of cheating by its trading partners—helped to lower the resistance against liberalization under GATT. At the same time, despite resistance from a variety of economic and political constituencies, there was little in the GATT process that posed a serious threat to material interests at home. The United States was the driving force behind all the multilateral negotiations. To a large extent, it remains so today even though the enthusiasm for such an enterprise has waned. But for the United States, for the rest of the world—and for GATT and the WTO—the issues at stake in the project of liberalization, and more generally in the international management of trade relations, have become markedly different.

The Road to Punta del Este. In the 1970s and 1980s, the GATT-based regime was shaken at its foundations by protectionism. Protectionism did not emerge full blown in these decades. Even in prior years, the industrial countries shielded a variety of domestic producers from the pressures of foreign competition. Moreover, there never has been a wholesale and inexorable retreat from liberalization in the postwar period. By and large, protectionism has remained a selective affair and has not precluded further measures toward openness. Nevertheless, there is no mistaking the overall trend of the 1970s and 1980s: mercantilist practices proliferated, reaching levels that dwarfed those in preceding decades, with the consequence that an increasing proportion of world trade fell outside the rules of GATT. "Voluntary export restraints" (VERs) and "orderly marketing arrangements" (OMAs)—market-restricting agreements that are quotas in all but name and that are outright evasions of the MFN requirement—became pervasive in numerous industries, including steel, automobiles, textiles, footwear, semiconductors, electronic products, and machine tools. By some counts, the proportion of world trade consisting of such forms of "managed trade" may have reached as much as one-half. Most of these restrictions were imposed by the United States and Western Europe and were directed against Japan and the developing countries, especially the *newly industrializing economies (NIEs) of East Asia. A variety of other non-tariff barriers (NTBs), ranging from government procurement practices and customs procedures to health standards and environmental protection requirements, were added to the arsenal of trade policy and were often deployed for few purposes other than shutting out or slowing down foreign competition. Yet, other practices eroded the principle of nondiscrimination in GATT. Antidumping actions and countervailing duty measures became favorite weapons against individual suppliers. Some Western European countries even pressed for institutionalizing the principle of "selectivity" in the application of industrial safeguards, which would give a legal imprimatur to the practice of singling out particular competitors for punitive treatment, chiping away further at the MFN rule.

In short, the behavior of many states in world trade in the 1970s and 1980s violated both the letter and the spirit of GATT. At the same time, GATT was helpless and virtually irrelevant in defusing conflicts that erupted among its leading members. Many of these conflicts centered on areas that had not been brought under the scope of GATT. At one end of the spectrum were industrial policies aimed at developing and maintaining a comparative advantage in high technology. At the other end were the high levels of production supports and export subsidies in agriculture that helped to spark a full-scale trade war across the Atlantic. The causes behind the new protectionism and the attendant erosion of GATT rules are both numerous and complex. They include the harsh economic environment of the 1970s and 1980s, particularly the dislocations brought about by the oil price shocks, by bouts of recession and inflation, by unemployment in beleaguered industries, and by massive trade and payment imbalances. They also include the rapid changes in international competitiveness manifested in the rise of Japan and the newly industrializing economies (NIEs) and the loss of a good part of the traditional manufacturing base of Western countries to these newcomers. Also playing a part was the shift toward a more aggressive trade policy in the United States as a response to perceptions of the country's decline in the international economy in general and the loss of dominance in world trade in particular. To all these factors must be added one that lies at the doorstep of GATT itself. Unwittingly, GATT became the victim of its own success. Its one indisputable achievement has been to negotiate tariffs virtually out of existence: the average tariff in industrial countries was brought down from a level of more than 40 percent in 1947 to less than 5 percent by 1990. But once tariffs were no longer a usable instrument of trade policy, governments came under intense pressure to deploy other means in order to circumvent GATT rules. In a more general sense, the rise in protectionism has been an antidote to the realization of one of the hallowed objectives of GATT: the rapid growth in world trade. This growth has meant a sharp increase in *interdependence, which has increased sensitivity to external disturbances, accentuated the pressures on domestic industries, and complicated the management of the trade regime.

The seventh and eighth sets of MTNs under GATT, respectively the Tokyo and Uruguay rounds, were undertaken in an effort to restore a measure of coherence and stability to the regime. The Tokyo Round (1973–79) was the first systematic effort to tackle the proliferation of non-tariff barriers (NTBs). The negotiations produced codes of conduct on NTBs in a variety of areas, including export subsidies, countervailing duties, government procurement, customs valuation, product standards, and import licensing. In each case, the objective was to increase the degree of transparency and to limit the element of arbitrariness in government interventions. The extension of the scope of GATT to include the management of NTBs represented an important advance. However, the effort to devise a code that would limit the widespread evasions of GATT's safeguards provisions and thereby bring under multilateral surveillance the rash of VERs and OMAs, foundered over the issue of selectivity. This failure to agree on the rules that would reaffirm the principle of nondiscrimination underscored a further weakening of the regime. On the whole, the Tokyo Round was an exercise in damage limitation. The negotiations brought about further reductions in tariffs on manufactures. However, the primary object of the Tokyo Round was less one of continuing liberalization than of containing the drift toward protectionism. The attempt to nail down more liberal rules for trade in such areas as agricultural products made little headway.

The Uruguay Round, which opened in Punta del Este in 1986, had an agenda that in complexity and ambitiousness has been matched by few other episodes in international conference diplomacy, including the Bretton Woods Conference and the Third United Nations Conference on the *Law of the Sea. The mother of all MTNs, the Uruguay Round was charged with nothing less than tackling anew the unfinished business of past negotiations, including the increasingly contentious issues of safeguards and subsidies, while simultaneously bringing under the coverage of global rules new ones, such as trade in services and intellectual property, that had not been addressed before. The sweeping and disparate agenda reflected the widening scope of issues that had intruded into trade policy. But it also appeared to present a recipe for failure as it confronted the negotiators with daunting problems of bridging divergent positions to arrive at an agreement. The talks were divided into fifteen negotiating committees. Over the course of the negotiations, GATT's membership expanded by twenty-five countries, all demand-

ing a seat at the bargaining table. The negotiations broke down on more than one occasion. It took four years to launch the round and it also took four years longer than originally planned to bring it to a close. That a breakthrough, one that will define many aspects of global trade policy for decades to come, could have been achieved in spite of these difficulties is instructive. Behind the achievement was a growing sentiment, expressed recurringly in the *Group of 7 summit, that the rules-based trade regime faced the process of collapse. American leadership was critical to both the process and the outcome. The United States was the main force in convening the round, in constructing its broad agenda, and in maintaining the momentum of the negotiations. The Reagan administration, confronted with a swelling trade deficit, had sought the talks in an effort to deflect protectionist pressures at home and to pry open markets abroad. Its diplomats insisted on the linkage of all the issues in the package that it took to be critical, with the consequence that a partial agreement was precluded and failure to agree on one item meant derailment of the whole package. In addition, a new set of actors had developed a stake in the success of the negotiations: the developing countries. While most of them had been marginal or absent in previous MTNs, in the Uruguay Round they emerged as serious players. Moreover, their stances went beyond the dogmatic insistence on "special and differential" treatment. That principle, enshrined in GATT in 1965 as a part of a concession to its poorer members, exempted them from obligations such as reciprocity, but it also diminished their bargaining power in GATT by reducing their role to that of supplicants. The developing countries now concentrated their demands on increasing or maintaining their access to the markets of the advanced industrial countries.

The Road from Marrakesh. The Uruguay Round agreements, signed in Marrakesh, Morocco, in 1994, represents the high water mark of global trade negotiations in the twentieth century. On the whole, the agreements have served to revitalize the regime by both strengthening and extending its rules and procedures. They halted the sense of crisis and drift, thereby restoring a measure of confidence, if only short-lived, in the structures and processes of multilateral negotiations over trade issues. They also have brought about important institutional changes, including the conversion of GATT into the WTO and an overhaul of the multilateral machinery for dispute settlement. None of these changes has banished conflict from the edifice of world trade. As the road to Seattle has made clear, every one of them has helped to generate new sources of conflict.

The Uruguay Round succeeded in imposing multilateral disciplines in several areas that have been notoriously resistant to liberalization, notably agriculture and textiles. As in many other areas, the liberalization agreements are limited and tentative—for many they are instances of too little, too slow, or too late—but some of the agreements also provide a framework of commitments and a roadmap for actions that may serve as yardsticks for measuring progress and as baselines for future negotiations. In agriculture, the agreements called for major reductions in export subsidies, limitations on internal supports, and the replacement of quotas by tariffs, which, though as restrictive as non-tariff barriers, are more transparent. Developing countries wrested an agreement to eliminate the Multi-Fiber Arrangement, which for decades has controlled their sales of textiles and clothing to the industrial countries through bilateral quotas and has provided an egregious example of managed trade and one of the more embarrassing contraventions of the MFN rule. It is a limited victory: the phaseout has been stretched to 2005, after which the sector is to be brought under the normal rules of GATT; in the interim, countries are free to impose safeguards to check import surges. There has been substantial tariff-cutting, as extensive as any achieved in previous rounds, bringing the levels in more areas to zero. The rules on subsidies and countervailing (or anti-subsidy) measures have been tightened. There are now also firmer rules that limit when and how industrial safeguards can be invoked. In addition, the use of "grey area" devices such as VERs and OMAs is now prohibited. However, little has been done to reduce the scope for anti-dumping actions, which have become the weapon of choice for many countries in recent years.

Where the Uruguay Round broke new ground is in broadening the purview of the regime to cover trade in services, intellectual property, and investment. The result in each case is but a first draft that will serve as a point of departure for bargaining in the years and decades ahead. Nevertheless, the WTO now has two additional sets of rules that one day may occupy a status equal to that of the traditional rule book it is charged with administering, namely GATT. The General Agreement on Trade in Services (GATS) lays down principles and procedures for liberalizing what has become the fastest growing area of world trade. Exports of commercial services today approach $1.5 trillion, more than one-fourth of the total for merchandise exports, and encompass many sectors, ranging from banking and insurance to telecommunications and broadcasting. GATS lays down the principle of nondiscrimination, as reflected not only in the MFN rule but also in the application of the "national treatment" rule requiring equal treatment for foreign and domestic suppliers. It also requires governments to make regulations in service sectors transparent and objective. However, these rules allow for plenty of exemptions and loopholes. In addition, many sectors are not included in GATS, while the questions of what sectors should be added, how the commitment to market access ought to be secured, and to what extent the removal of restrictions on services should also allow for the free movement of the providers of those services across borders, are the subjects of intense controversies before the WTO. Some of the issues are being tackled in sector-specific negotiations, but resolution of many of the larger ones awaits another MTN.

Equally contentious are many of the issues in the Agreement on trade-related intellectual property rights (TRIPs). The most comprehensive framework for intellectual property rights, the TRIPs agreement seeks to enforce common rules, backed by the prospect of collectively authorized *sanctions, for the protection of patents, licenses, trademarks, and copyrights around the world. Some of the questions the agreement addresses are seemingly trivial, e.g. whether France can legally discriminate against exporters of foreign scallops bearing the designation *noix de Coquille Saint-Jacques*, an appellation that, according to French regulations, is reserved exclusively for the French variety. But many other questions are momentous, e.g. whether India should be forced to recognize foreign drug patents, exposing its pharmaceutical industry to competition from *multinational corporations. Many developing countries have expressed grave worries about the latter question and related ones such as the ability of foreign agricultural companies to patent and control the supply of special varieties of seed for commodities they consider vital for national food and nutrition goals. Consequently, the poorer countries have insisted on a lengthier transition period before they can be expected to comply with the new regulations for enforcing intellectual property rights. Some of the same concerns are held about the more limited and partial agreement on trade-related investment measures (TRIMs). As the collapse in 1998 of the negotiations on a Multilateral Agreement on Investment (MAI) under the auspices of the OECD suggests, any attempt to create a global regime that imposes common standards for national policies affecting foreign investment is likely to encounter considerable opposition, as would an attempt to move the MAI to the WTO itself.

The institutional legacy of the Uruguay Round is an organization that, in comparison to GATT, rests on a firmer footing. The authority of the WTO has been enhanced by endowing it not only with a wider mandate in world trade but also a more robust conflict resolution structure. The WTO also has assumed responsibilities for conducting regular reviews of the trade policies of its member countries. While these reviews are not formal exercises in surveillance, their value lies in the potential for making the behavior of states more transparent; for some states, they also may offer an additional impetus for policy reform. Membership, while not yet universal, is more inclusive: by the middle of 2000, the WTO had 136 members, accounting for more than 90 percent of world trade in goods and services. However, these members have not ceded much more autonomy to the WTO than they did to GATT. To date, proposals to make the organization less member-driven, and to boost the power of the director-general, have met with resistance For a global agency that is often portrayed as a monster with many tentacles, the resources at the command of the WTO secretariat are miniscule by comparison with those of the IMF or the World Bank. The WTO's total staff in 2000 was just above 500, while its budget was about $75 million, less than one-twentieth of the World Bank budget. Nor does the WTO have powers of enforcement. Unlike the Bretton Woods twins, it cannot offer material inducements and it cannot impose punitive sanctions. Enforcement, therefore, remains solely within the hands of its members.

Compared to the arrangements that existed in GATT, there are several striking novelties in the WTO's dispute settlement mechanism. Decisions cannot be vetoed by disputants. Hence, a country that is losing a case can no longer prevent a ruling from being adopted. Unless they are settled "out of court," cases continue to be heard by expert panels, consisting of three (sometimes five) individuals, that function much like tribunals. But whereas in the days of GATT decisions required unanimity, a stipulation that resulted in frequent failures to resolve conflicts, cases are now decided by majority vote. Either side can appeal the legal basis of a panel's rulings. The length of time allowed for settling cases has been shortened; there are now deadlines, albeit they are flexible. Unsurprisingly, no aspect of these new arrangements—from the method of the selection of panelists to the pace of the proceedings—escapes criticism. Yet in at least one crucial respect, the new system has proven to be a resounding success. The procedural reforms have led countries to avail themselves of the machinery more than ever before, so much so that there is now a chorus of complaints about the excessive judicialization of the WTO. By the end of 1999, marking the first five years of the existence of the WTO, 185 cases had been brought to its dispute settlement body. GATT, by contrast, handled only 300 disputes between 1947 and 1994. The United States has been the foremost litigant, accounting for one out of three cases filed. But developing countries also become active complainants. The rate of compliance has been respectable. Perhaps more consequential for the WTO in the long run, however, have been two developments: first, the violations of its decisions in several politically explosive cases, such as in the squabble between the United States and the European Union over hormone-treated beef; and, second, the widespread questioning of the legitimacy of the institution at large.

The Road to and From Seattle. The world trade regime on the eve of the millennium was severely tested by the intensification of protectionist pressures and by widening international conflicts over old and new issues. The WTO itself came under siege as a multiplicity of actors, including many groups from *civil society, confronted it with protests about its governance and behavior and with demands for fundamental reform. The numerous "food fights," along with the mounting squabbles over such issues as production and export subsidies, were testimony to the willingness of the major trading powers to engage in a pattern of provocation and brinkmanship. The resort to anti-dumping suits assumed epidemic proportions; the practitioners, moreover, no longer were confined to the advanced industrial countries, as they were now emulated by larger "emerging market" ones. Even voluntary export restraints, illegal under the new rules, began to resurface.

For some of the most vital areas of world trade, few, if any, governments among the developed countries showed much appetite for neutralizing powerful protectionist lobbies and building the domestic political coalitions to push ahead the project of multilateral liberalization. In agriculture, there was little consensus about the next steps, let alone about a grand bargain, for dismantling protections. On competition policy, which includes the amalgam of business practices that often restrict the ability of foreign companies to operate in a national market, the task of writing and enforcing global rules had yet to begin. The 1999 WTO ministerial meeting in Seattle, designed to prepare the groundwork for the next round of multilateral trade negotiations, the "Millennium Round," revealed a hardening of positions. The United States and the EU were not prepared to make compromises on such major issues such as agricultural barriers and anti-dumping legislation. And neither was willing to offer side payments that might narrow the wide gaps between the rich and poor countries not only over traditional questions such as the pace of removal of barriers to textile exports, but also over newer and much more vexatious ones such as the inclusion of environmental and labor standards in the trade rules of the WTO. It was the failure to agree on the minimal outlines of an agenda for a ninth round—and not the outside protests—that led to the collapse of the meeting.

However, the debacle in Seattle, including the events in the street, signified larger concerns about the functioning of the trade regime that are likely to leave lasting effects, many of them difficult to predict, on the WTO. First, it has thrown doubts about whether marathon bargaining that stretches across the better part of a decade and encompasses an expanding welter of issues is the best vehicle for reaching decisions on reforming the rules of global trade. Defenders of a process as messy and cumbersome as that of GATT/WTO MTNs have tended to regard it as part of the cost of conducting business in an increasingly interdependent world. Trade diplomats have taken it as axiomatic that comprehensive package-dealing is both imperative and inevitable: Unless countries can strike agreements across sectors, they will not agree to make concessions within sectors. And, according to this logic, thanks to the trade-offs that issue-linkage allows, the overall gains from liberalization will be greater. The MFA-TRIPs bargain at the Uruguay Round, linking the phaseout of restrictions on textiles to new rules on intellectual property, illustrates what can be achieved in talks involving a large, seemingly unmanageable, bundle of issues. However, most states today are not keen on a broad agenda for trade talks. At Seattle, some countries did want to expand the agenda; many more countries wanted to narrow it. The majority, consisting of developing countries, felt they had yet to absorb the results of the Uruguay Round and hence they did not want another round at all. While they have yet to agree on meaningful alternatives, few governments are eager about MTNs. The Uruguay Round demonstrated that these exercises have become considerably more difficult to organize and sustain. The Millennium Round promises to be even more difficult. The ambivalence on the part of state actors has not been offset by support from corporate interests. Given the mismatch between the cycles of the market place and those of multilateral diplomacy—few of the negotiators at the Uruguay Round had so much an inkling as to what "electronic commerce," covered in an annex to GATS, might entail—the private sector places little faith in the ability of such talks to yield quick results.

Secondly, the Seattle ministerial made clear that developing countries are bent on making their voices heard in these negotiations. The outcome might have been different had they been willing to follow the script written by the United States. But the meeting showed a determination to press their demands for market access and to resist efforts on the part of the developed countries to single-handedly dictate the agenda. Today, the developing countries are more informed and more prepared about the issues at stake than in previous international encounters over trade policy. They are better organized and better represented, and they also have a clearer sense of negotiating strategies. Of course, they are far from a homogenous group and they hardly have the makings of a single negotiating bloc. The disparity of interests and circumstances within their ranks helps to explain the divergences in their negotiating positions. The Uruguay Round did not fracture along North-South lines—some coalitions cut across traditional divisions—and the Millennium Round, if such a round is held, is not likely to do so either. On many aspects of services trade, the stances of Singapore and the Republic of Korea have usually been closer to those of the developed countries than to those of India or Brazil. The "Cairns Group" of states pushing for free trade in agriculture includes not only affluent exporters such as Australia and Canada but also less affluent ones such as Brazil, Colombia, Malaysia, and

Thailand. Nevertheless, the majority of developing countries, especially the smaller and poorer ones, do share the sentiment that the trade regime as a whole is biased against them and that they are excluded from much of the decision making structures of the WTO. The so-called "Green Room" process, which serves to limit participation in all important deliberations to a small number of countries and which was imported wholesale into Seattle, is especially resented. At the same time, the stake of the developing countries in the world trading system has never been greater. Collectively, they now account for 27.5 percent of world merchandise exports and close to 25 percent of commercial services exports. Over the last two decades, they have sensed that they have the most to lose from closure of the trade system. Many of them today sing from the same hymn books on globalization and liberalization. Many have instituted far-reaching market reforms, shedding layers of statist protections that had isolated from the trading system, in favor of more outward-oriented policies. These reforms have owed much to revisions in economic convictions and to the exhaustion of economic alternatives, but for some nations, they have been part of the price of admission into GATT and the WTO. And yet many developing countries also feel that there is a hiatus between what they deliver and what they receive in the trade regime. Here, the experience of the Uruguay Round casts a long shadow. They are convinced that they got the short end of the stick at that round, giving too many concessions in areas such as intellectual property and investment protection that they did not even understand properly and saddling themselves with obligations that they cannot fulfill, all in return for concessions in areas such as agriculture and textiles that were paltry and that have yet to be met. Hence, they are resolute in not placing themselves in a position of having to acquiesce to another agreement hammered out by the rich countries.

The developing countries are also adamant about avoiding the linkage of trade policy to "other" issues, especially the environment and labor. These two issues involve different concerns and they pose different dilemmas for the WTO. But what they have in common, in the view of most developing countries, is the potential for being deployed by the industrial countries as prongs for protectionism. The trade-environment linkage, which looms as one of the dominant priorities on the agenda of the WTO in the decades ahead, is more substantive than tactical. The issues of trade and the environment are inextricably and inexorably connected, in ways that are not fully understood within or outside the WTO. That there is an intimate nexus between trade liberalization and trade protectionism, on the one hand, and between environmental protection and environmental degradation, on the other hand, was brought home to GATT in 1991 when a dispute panel ruled against the United States after Mexico complained about the use of U.S. law to ban imports of tuna caught in nets that entangle dolphins. The particulars of the case, and of subsequent cases that have ruled against the application of U.S. legislation aimed at protecting sea turtles and reducing atmospheric pollution, are complex, as are the legal arguments used in each. But the cases have been distorted to the point that they have become the stuff of mythology, one consequence of which is that they have earned the WTO epithets of "the agent of globalization" and "the enemy of the environment." The WTO, in fact, is just waking up to the environment issue. All the essential questions concerning its roles and its approach in this area—e.g., its place in the expanding network of global environmental regimes, the conditions under which international trade rules are to preempt or be preempted by environmental ones, the extent to which trade measures might be explicitly designed to serve environmental objectives—remain to be resolved. The controversies defy quick and easy solutions and the WTO recognizes that they present potential flashpoints between North and South. But they also may contain the ingredients of a North-South compromise. Developing countries, in the meanwhile, remain fearful of the prospect that the trade-environmental linkage will be exploited by the rich states to legitimize barriers against their exports. The same fear is expressed, in more acute form, about the trade-labor linkage, which is rightfully seen as a barely masked pretext for protectionist pressures. Here, the linkage is more tactical than substantive. The rationale behind connecting the two issues in the context of the WTO appears all the more tenuous since the *International Labor Organization is widely recognized as the appropriate venue for addressing labor issues. In addition, U.S. proposals to nudge the WTO to examine issues such as child labor, workers' rights, and minimum wages may be no more than a political concession to a domestic constituency. Nevertheless, for developing countries the proposal evokes the nightmare scenario of the WTO enforcing labor standards under the threat of trade sanctions. It was the airing of such a proposal that precipitated a walkout by developing countries and the collapse of the Seattle ministerial.

Thirdly, and perhaps most importantly, the events in Seattle point to one of the emerging fault lines in global economic governance. The demands of the voices in the street—consisting of a motley horde of environmentalists, trade unionists, consumer activists, *human rights advocates, and self-styled anarchists—were frequently inchoate and incoherent (as was the much publicized alliance, dubbed as "Turtles and Teamsters," between the first two groups). But these demands included a call for accountability and transparency, two qualities not commonly associated with the operating modalities of the WTO. And, when they were not concentrating on chanting slogans about shutting down the organization, the demands also contained a call for "participation" and "inclusion." Thus, with a lag of five to ten years after the World Bank and the IMF found themselves in confrontation with environmental and human rights NGOs, the WTO had its first introduction to "civil society." Given that some of these demands will be echoed by state actors, the WTO will find it difficult to avoid such conundra as how far and how fast it can adapt itself to the altered political realities, whether it can undertake internal reforms while preserving its mission, whether its leadership is adequate for creatively coping with the conflicting pressures on the agency, and whether it can accommodate private actors such as NGOs in its dispute settlement process.

In the long run, the ultimate significance of the final event of the century for the WTO may be the interring of two of the premises on which GATT and many other international organizations were founded in the postwar years. The first, all but taken for granted until recently, is that *international cooperation in the management of economic policy is the preserve of state actors. For the foreseeable future, trade policy will continue to be primarily the domain of officialdom, both governmental and intergovernmental. But it will no longer be exclusively so. The second premise, associated in part with the functionalist approach to international organization, is that an issue such as trade can and should be defined in narrow, limited, technical, and specific terms. In effect, trade must be confined to trade. Such was part of the vision on which GATT was founded. The increasingly contested terrain of the WTO, and the multiplicity of actors asserting claims to redefining its agenda, all but guarantees that many more linkages are yet to be drawn between "trade" and "non-trade" issues.

Prospects. In the lore of the WTO there is a metaphor invoked by officials in the agency's headquarters in Geneva whenever the enterprise of multilateral liberalization appears to be faltering: the bicycle must keep moving; otherwise it will tip over. To some who surveyed the world trade system at the end of the 1990s, the bicycle was close to tipping. Indeed, pronouncements about the demise of the WTO became commonplace. The persistence of protectionist practices, the eruption of trade wars among the leading economies, the flouting of the rulings of dispute settlement tribunals, the fiasco of Seattle—these developments seemed to point to a vehicle more wobbly than ever.

In several important respects, however, the bicycle metaphor may be misleading, for it rests on two unwarranted assumptions: first, that liberalization and protectionism are mutually exclusive; and second, that it is the momentum of trade talks that checks the slide toward protectionism. The experience of the years since World War II, in fact, suggests that protectionism in some areas has proceeded in tandem with liberalization in other areas. Such was the case throughout the 1990s, and such is likely to be the case in the near future. If there is one maxim to be derived from the record of multilateral trade negotiations, it is that no breakthrough is final and no breakdown is fatal. Moreover, the bulwarks against protectionism are not confined to MTNs, which remain an affair among bureaucrats. The internationalization of production—spurred by corporate strategies that are spinning a complex web of transnational alliances, mergers, and cooperative agreements—has been in part a response to protectionist pressures and also a brake on the acceleration of those pressures. Protectionism no doubt has reduced the volume of world trade, but that volume has continued to grow at robust levels, typically twice as high as those of output, and it now approaches $7 trillion a year. The writ of the WTO runs wider than GATT's. WTO members are no longer free to pick and choose the disciplines to which they might be willing to commit themselves; instead, they are now formally obligated to adhere to all the rules of the regime. And there is a long queue of countries waiting for admission to the WTO. The impending admission of the country at the head of that queue, China, is hardly indicative of a tottering structure.

Yet, if the bicycle has not fallen, for the WTO two nagging questions remain: Who is the rider? And is there a destination? That neither question can be answered with certainty is testimony to the travails of the WTO in recent years. The identity of the rider is uncertain inasmuch as it is not clear whether any of the leading powers in the global economy is inclined to lead the way in furthering the drive toward market openness and in strengthening the institutional structures

of world trade. For the United States, which traditionally exercised that leadership function, these have long since ceased to be consuming priorities. The destination is uncertain because liberalization, the objective presumed in the bicycle metaphor—and by the WTO—itself entails different projects. The original norms and rules of world trade assumed a realm of buyers and sellers interacting at arm's length across national borders on the basis of comparative advantage and disadvantage. In this image, trade policy consisted of formal barriers imposed by the importing country at the border and the task of trade negotiations and trade agreements was to reduce or eliminate those barriers. In fact, an increasing proportion of world trade now takes the form of intrafirm trade in components and services produced in many different countries, often importing and exporting the same product. In this case the essence of trade policy is not import restrictions but a variety of policies and practices that affect the capacity to acquire strategic advantage in advanced technology or to secure access to foreign markets for specific firms, and that determine the terms of entry of foreign competitors in one's domestic markets. Hence, the relevant barriers are behind, not at, the border. But, as the WTO, like GATT, has discovered, it is less than clear what ought to be targets of liberalization since many of these barriers are embedded in institutions that define the relationships between state, society, economy, and culture.

The institutional alternatives to the WTO-centered regime raise further questions about this destination. As the recent record suggests, regional trade initiatives are becoming increasingly attractive: more regional trade pacts were launched in the 1990s than in the preceding four decades. Policy makers have only begun to attend to the question of the consistency of the rules of regional trade arrangements such as Mercosur or APEC with those of the multilateral trade regime. They also have yet to determine whether liberalization in regional contexts is a complement to or a substitute for that under the auspices of the WTO. The fears once expressed about a balkanization of the world trading system, a prospect that would render the WTO obsolete, are probably overstated. However, if the multilateral trade negotiating process remains stalled, the appetite for striking bargains among smaller groups of states in settings less politically charged than that of the WTO is bound to increase. Most of the world's trading nations are likely to continue to maintain a strong stake in the WTO because it represents the one and only rules-based trade regime with universal applicability. But it is not inevitable that the WTO will provide the exclusive moorings of the regime for world trade. A more likely scenario is a multilayered regime with multilateral rules coexisting and even contending with regional and bilateral rules.

(See also DEVELOPMENT AND UNDERDEVELOPMENT; ENVIRONMENTALISM; FOOD POLITICS; INTERNATIONAL POLITICAL ECONOMY; LABOR MOVEMENT; MERCANTILISM; NORTH-SOUTH RELATIONS.)

Robert E. Hudec, *The GATT Legal System and World Trade Diplomacy* (New York, 1975). Gilbert R. Winham, *International Trade and the Tokyo Round* (Princeton, N.J., 1986). Bernard M. Hoekman and Michel M. Kostecki, *The Political Economy of the World Trading System: From GATT to WTO* (Oxford, 1996). Robert Z. Lawrence, Dani Rodrik, and John Whalley, *Emerging Agenda for Global Trade: High Stakes for Developing Countries* (Washington, D.C. 1996). Jagdish Bhagwati and Mathias

Hirsch, eds., *The Uruguay Round and Beyond* (Ann Arbor, Mich., 1998). Anne O. Krueger, ed., *The WTO as an International Organization* (Chicago, 1998). World Trade Organization, *Trading into the Future*, 2nd ed. (Geneva, 1999).

Don Babai

WORLD WAR I. The fateful march toward the beginning of World War I started on 28 June 1914 in Sarajevo, Bosnia, with the assassination of Archduke Franz Ferdinand, heir to the throne of Austria-Hungary, and his wife. This terrorist act, planned in Belgrade with the knowledge of some Serbian officials, convinced Habsburg decision makers in Vienna that only a military defeat of the Serbs would curb South Slav appeals threatening the multinational state. Determined to take action, the Habsburg leadership in early July quickly gained German assurances of military support in case of a major *war. Berlin hoped this act of loyalty to its longtime ally (since 1879) would deter Russian intervention. The Austrian ultimatum, delivered on 23 July 1914 in Belgrade, was deliberately framed to be rejected. On 25 July Austria-Hungary broke diplomatic relations with Serbia; three days later Vienna declared war. The Habsburgs believed they had launched the Third Balkan War.

Russia's actions, meanwhile, were guaranteeing the war would not be localized. From the start Saint Petersburg resolved to protect its Serbian client and its own *Balkan ambitions. Russia's assertiveness during the July crisis—not surprisingly—collided with Vienna's desire for revenge and the German commitment to support its ally. On 30 July Russia ordered general mobilization, the first Great Power to do so. This decision sparked German countermeasures. The step also thwarted Britain's belated efforts for mediation. Berlin then ordered mobilization and shortly thereafter began its offensive against France. Germany's deliberate violation of Belgian neutrality convinced the British cabinet to support France against Germany. By 5 August 1914 World War I had begun, even though the major fighting was still days away.

Europe's system of *alliances (the Triple Alliance of Germany, Austria-Hungary, and Italy) and ententes (the Triple Entente of Russia, France, and Britain) had managed for a decade to avoid a direct confrontation involving all of the partners. Now after two years of constant Balkan tension, the Sarajevo murders brought all but Italy into a continental war. Rampant *militarism, press agitation, fanatical *nationalism, untested military and naval forces, and boredom combined to end a century of European stability and *peace.

The shooting had scarcely begun when the war became a genuine world war. On 23 August Japan declared war on Germany, fulfilling its alliance commitment to Britain and seizing some German holdings in the Far East. Before long, a tortuous campaign began among German and British colonial troops in Africa. Closer to Europe, the Ottoman government first proclaimed its neutrality in August, then in October joined the Central Powers (Germany and Austria-Hungary).

The Search for Allies. Both sides now started a desperate search for additional allies. The most fateful interventions would be those of Italy and the United States. From August 1914 to May 1915 Rome negotiated with both sides over possible entry. Italy's goal was unambiguous: it wanted Habsburg lands in which Italians lived transferred to Italy. To offset the claim of Italian irredentism Vienna and Berlin had little to offer but Habsburg territory. Yet Vienna's offers were never enough. Finally, on 23 May 1915, Italy entered the war against its former allies. Ultimately the Italian dead would outnumber the Italians living in the areas transferred after the war. Bulgaria and Romania remained aloof from the initial fighting. Each was courted assiduously. Eventually, in late 1915 Bulgaria entered the war to defend itself against an Anglo-French-Greek effort in Macedonia. Then in the summer of 1916 Bucharest joined the Triple Entente, only to find itself quickly routed by Austro-German forces. Neither intervention altered the course of the war.

U.S. intervention in April 1917 would be far more important. Through the war's first three years, Washington opted for neutrality while profiting handsomely from the sale of war goods to the Triple Entente powers. But in early 1915 Berlin's decisions about submarine warfare threatened to entangle the United States. The sinking of the *Lusitania* in May 1915 with the loss of 128 American lives jeopardized German-American relations, though subsequent German pledges eased the tension. Then in January 1917 Berlin resumed unrestricted submarine attacks. The Germans also launched a maladroit effort to entice Mexico into the war, exposed by the Zimmermann telegraph affair. President Woodrow Wilson believed he had no option but war. On 6 April 1917 Congress declared war on the Central Powers. The European *international system found itself fundamentally changed; henceforth, U.S. participation (or failure to do so) would be decisive. By November 1918 and the armistice, the American presence had become paramount in every phase of war and peace.

The Fighting, 1914–1917. As the diplomats added coalition partners, the military and naval leadership fought stubbornly and wastefully on land and sea. The German offensive in the west stalled in September 1914 at the Battle of the Marne. Within weeks trenches extended from Switzerland to the North Sea and cut off a substantial part of northern France and virtually all of Belgium. Horrendous efforts failed to break through the defensive positions in late 1914, then again in 1915. Each attack was seen as bringing a victory; none did. Then in 1916 came two costly efforts: Verdun and the Somme. The German high command resolved to take Verdun; the Anglo-French forces wanted to crash beyond the Somme River. Neither attack succeeded save in death and destruction; 2 million men on both sides were casualties in the Verdun-Somme battles. By late 1916 the fighting on the western front had altered almost nothing militarily, while prompting increasing domestic morale problems.

The war at sea was unspectacular. Allied blockade policies isolated Germany. Sporadic naval clashes in the North Sea brought no advantage. The admirals kept hoping for a major clash of capital ships instead of submarine warfare. But the long-awaited showdown of dreadnoughts in the Battle of Jutland on 31 May–1 June 1916 was inconclusive. Confusion, miscalculation, and hesitation produced a draw. Britain's naval blockade continued, while the Germans edged closer to an all-out submarine policy.

On the eastern front and in the Balkans the war was more dramatic. In 1914 Vienna had quickly lost territory to the Russians, only to regain some of it by 1915 with German assistance. Germany's great victory over the Russians at Tannenberg in September 1914 stemmed the Slavic tide. The Serbs retreated in 1914, then advanced, and then finally in mid-1915 were decisively routed. Bulgaria and Romania fought, lost, fought again, and the fighting along the Macedonian front altered little.

The most spectacular peripheral campaign, in failure and imagination, came with the British effort to open a second front against the Ottoman Empire in early 1915. Seizure of the Straits at Constantinople might, it was hoped, offset the stalemate in the west. From the start the Gallipoli campaign saw British and British imperial troops suffer from indecisive leadership and confusion of execution. Eventually in 1916 London abandoned the effort, just as the battles of Verdun and the Somme began.

As the stalemate in the west continued, new weapons systems emerged. None succeeded in bringing a decisive advantage. Heavy artillery pounded the trenches; airplanes fought and delivered some bombs; poison gas was tried with terrible physical and psychological damage; the truck became the tank. Still the trenches proved supreme. In the west in 1917 the armies remained deadlocked, the British and French awaiting the American troops. The Germans focused their attention eastward where events in Russia steadily dissolved the tsarist government. Everywhere discontent, malaise, and domestic hardship were commonplace. The war now consumed everything it touched.

War Aims, 1914–1917. From August 1914 to the spring of 1917 policymakers in each capital struggled to define their minimum war aims. As the casualties mounted, so also did the war aims. This vicious interaction meant that only total victory could make the increasingly fearful human cost worthwhile. In September 1914 Germany's expected victory led to schemes—east and west—that ensured Germanic hegemony on the Continent. Nor would those aims be entirely abandoned even late in 1918 with the German collapse. For France survival came first, then the expulsion of German troops from France and the return of Alsace-Lorraine, lost in 1871 to Berlin. For London, German colonies, a new *balance of power on the Continent, and protection from Russia emerged as goals. Vienna's perspective veered erratically from banishment of the Serbian menace in 1914 to mere survival by 1917–1918.

In 1914 Russia's aims had also been expansive: Constantinople, a Balkan sphere of influence, and predominance in eastern Europe. The war's continuing reverses eventually put the tsar's government on the defensive. In March 1917 the cumulative effect of court intrigue, the presence of the strange mystic Rasputin, food shortages, and mounting domestic discontent finally erupted. Within days the Romanov dynasty was gone. Ill-advised Allied and Russian attempts to prolong Russia's war effort merely condemned the country to mounting chaos. Guided by *Lenin's organizing genius and utter lack of scruples, the Bolsheviks in November 1917 seized control of the remaining organs of Russian authority. The Treaty of Brest-Litovsk on 3 March 1918 took Russia from the world war into the travail of civil war. The treaty extended German (and Austrian) power in the east almost beyond their earlier ambitions; the Ukraine, Russian Poland, the Baltic states, and Finland moved into the German orbit. Equally important, Russia had been ousted from the balance of power, at least for the moment.

In the Balkans French, British, and Greek forces continued to occupy German and Habsburg divisions. In the sands of Arabia, British efforts to dismantle Ottoman power began to succeed. On the Italian front Italians and Austrians continued to slaughter each other, with more Habsburg gains than losses but no decisive defeat of the former Italian ally.

On the western front, in early 1918, the German military, now thoroughly in command of the German government, opted for a final offensive to crush Anglo-French forces before America's full potential would be felt. The new German effort started on 21 March 1918; it nearly succeeded, only to falter once more at the Marne. Thereafter the military tide turned quickly. The arrival of U.S. forces made the difference. By September German forces were retreating. Later that month the German military asked the civilians to negotiate a respite. The German diplomats tried, only to be outmaneuvered by Woodrow Wilson, who insisted on an armistice and a new German government. With their armies retreating and the populace near open rebellion, Berlin and Vienna concluded an armistice on 11 November 1918. The Habsburg and Hohenzollern dynasties abdicated, following the Romanovs. Six months later, on 28 June 1919, a civilian German government guided by a socialist president, Friedrich Ebert, not the kaiser or his generals, signed the Treaty of Versailles. Five years after the first two deaths on the streets of Sarajevo, at least 13 million had fallen in the Great War—and possibly there were that many unknown deaths as well. The old order in Europe was forever destroyed.

Peace Treaties and the War's Consequences. The treaties of Paris ending the war ratified the collapse of the Habsburg monarchy, while spelling out the details of Germany's defeat. The latter were more important. Germany's military and naval power was drastically curtailed; Allied soldiers could occupy the left bank of the Rhine for up to fifteen years; Alsace and Lorraine were returned to France; German colonies were divided among the victors; East Prussia was separated from Germany proper by the new Poland. The German government was obliged, moreover, to pay reparations for the physical and human suffering of the war, reparations that soon became a major political and economic stumbling block to Europe's recovery and stability. Further intensifying German resentment, Article 231 of the Treaty of Versailles assigned "war guilt" to Berlin and its allies for causing the war. That historical judgment, juxtaposed with the German military's allegations that the civilians and not they had lost the war, would frame the German agenda for the 1920s.

The war also destroyed the prevailing pattern of European *diplomacy. The monarchical governments of eastern Europe disappeared, as did the Ottoman regime. Successor governments displayed few of the aristocratic traits of the old regimes. Of these the new Soviet Union was the most radical. Elsewhere in eastern and central Europe small democratic states emerged, their nationalist ambitions amply fulfilled: Poland, Czechoslovakia, Yugoslavia. The residual survivors—Austria, Hungary, Romania, Bulgaria—were also more democratic and nationalistic. Yet in none of the governments, as the interwar years revealed, were democratic roots strong. Instead authoritarian regimes would soon come to power in most.

Germany, though defeated, remained basically intact as a country. France recovered its lost provinces but was stunted for a generation by wartime population losses. Britain obtained German colonies and full command of the European seas. Yet London also faced staggering debt problems. The Italians had fought on the winning side but felt and behaved like losers. The most significant alteration came, of course, from the effect of the American presence: in the fighting, in the peacemaking, and in its future relationship to Europe, whether intimate or not. Washington had become the supreme power.

The war effort also prompted calls for the creation of a *League of Nations, a formalized collective *security system to preserve the victory against Germany and to address the evils of the old diplomacy. The balance of power would be enshrined in a new, open diplomatic system in which the great powers would seek to protect the weaker. This new structural approach dramatically affirmed the new volatility of international politics without, however, changing much actual state behavior.

If the League appeared to alter the practice of diplomacy, the economic transformation wrought by the war did so in fact. The United States had replaced Europe's traditional economic dominance. War debts, reparations issues, social and human costs, and a dispirited workforce were outcomes that made every European government, victor or defeated, dependent on the United States. New York replaced London as the center of the world economy. Henceforth, the House of Morgan and the U.S. Treasury were key players—whether openly or in secret—in the new international system.

Even in the imperial arena things had changed. To be sure, the Anglo-French victors kept and expanded their colonial holdings at German and Ottoman expense. But Woodrow Wilson's talk of self-determination and the creation of the mandate system for colonial administration put finite limits on imperial holdings. The troops furnished by Britain's colonial governments, moreover, ensured the end of the empire and the creation of the *Commonwealth. In East Asia, meanwhile, the Japanese, with their new colonial possessions, were awakened to imperial ambitions. From that development much mischief would come.

If nationalism was a principal cause of the war, the four-year struggle merely intensified its importance and worsened its debilitating effects. The collapse of the multinational Habsburg monarchy foreshadowed intensive national rivalries in eastern Europe. What had previously been contained under one sovereign monarch now existed in many. And the sheer bellicosity of the peace meant that German, French, and British nationalism was also strengthened, while that of the Italians became easily susceptible to Benito *Mussolini's bombast. While Lenin talked of the supranational idea, *communism appeared to many a more dangerous form of Russian nationalism and far more threatening to the economic order.

On the domestic side, the war's impact was as significant as on the international, perhaps more so. Death removed a generation of actual and potential leaders. State power grew at an extraordinary rate; the centralization of economic life continued. The character of the workforce changed, with more women present and with more demands for shared power. Socialism and unions were more appealing in an era of malaise, whether in the victor or the defeated states. *Democracy had won, but democratic values had received scant encouragement. Political stability was not only more difficult

to achieve, it was far more difficult to maintain. The European governments of the 1920s were like revolving doors, forever changing and with little sense of persistent direction.

Perhaps most importantly, World War I and the peace treaties transformed the agenda of international politics. For Germany the abrogation of the Treaty of Versailles now became its abiding passion; for France and the new governments in the east, the containment of Germany became their principal agenda. Britain sought to preserve its empire while slipping back into its pre-1904 balance of power stance vis-à-vis the Continent. The United States, now the effective arbiter, reverted to political but not economic isolation; this contradictory stance left a dangerous vacuum which *Hitler would carefully exploit. Everywhere the fear of Bolshevism and the Soviet Union acted as a backdrop against which diplomacy was conducted. The League of Nations represented a new approach to international politics. But with Germany, the Soviet Union, and the United States outside the League, at least initially, collective security remained bilateral and intermittent. World War I had merely set the stage for *World War II. (See also COLONIAL EMPIRES.)

Luigi Albertini, *The Origins of the War of 1914,* translated and edited by Isabella Massey, 3 vols. (London, 1952–1957). Marc Ferro, *The Great War, 1914–1918* (London, 1973). Fritz Fischer, *War of Illusions: German Policies from 1911 to 1914,* translated by Marian Jackson (New York, 1975). James Joll, *The Origins of the First World War* (London, 1984). David Stevenson, *The First World War and International Politics* (Oxford, 1988). Samuel R. Williamson, Jr., *Austria-Hungary and the Origins of the First World War* (London and New York, 1991).

SAMUEL R. WILLIAMSON, JR.

WORLD WAR II. The term *World War II* is conventionally applied to the series of overlapping military and political conflicts which began on 1 September 1939, when the armies of Nazi Germany invaded Poland, and ended on 2 September 1945, when representatives of Germany's main ally, Japan, signed an instrument of surrender. During this six-year period fighting took place on six continents and on every ocean, and 40–50 million people, most of them civilians, lost their lives. World War II was not *an* event. It was, more accurately, a nexus, a giant knot in which the strands of several preexisting conflicts and crises became entangled. Though each of these conflicts and crises had a history of its own before 1939 and many continued their course after 1945, the process of entanglement and disentanglement was a transformative one. In international politics and in the domestic politics of most of the participating *states, the *war was a moment of transition, in which existing relationships were reshaped and existing trends accelerated or reversed.

The "Last European War." Although the case has been made against the Eurocentrism of dating a world war by Germany's aggressions in Europe rather than by Japan's prior aggressions in Manchuria (1931) and China (1937), most historians still treat Germany's attack on Poland and the British and French governments' formal declarations of war on Germany as the starting point of the conflict. In those terms, it began as an exclusively European war. The analogy with the events of 1914–1918, implicit in the very term *World War II,* is misleading, because the second war was far more global than the first, but it does convey at least a partial truth: the issues at stake in the original crisis of September 1939 were recognizably akin to those at stake in *World War I. In the most immediate sense, war came as a result of the German regime's drive to create a territorial empire in continental Europe and the Western powers' refusal to allow the *balance of power to be altered in that way.

In a broader perspective, however, *Hitler's actions and British and French reactions must be seen within the context of a fundamental *destabilization of the European system of interstate relations which occurred in the late nineteenth-early twentieth century and created the conditions for both world wars. The sources of this destabilization were, among others, the decay of long-established multinational empires in Central and Eastern Europe, the rise of a unified German state, and the wide dissemination of nationalist, imperialist, and social-Darwinist *ideologies. Historians have debated long and hard as to whether the settlement that followed World War I could ever have succeeded in remedying this destabilization, but the undeniable fact is that it did not succeed, and in 1933 a man who was committed to overturning the settlement came to the head of the German state.

However one explains Adolf Hitler's foreign policy—and it has been variously interpreted as the systematic application of an ideological blueprint, the ad hoc improvisations of a skilled opportunist, or the inexorable working out of the regime's own inner logic—the objective consequences of the policy were clear. By absorbing Austria and Czechoslovakia (1938–1939) and by invading and occupying Poland (September 1939), Denmark and Norway (April 1940), and the Netherlands, Belgium, and France (May-June 1940), while signing a nonaggression pact with the Soviet Union (August 1939) and keeping the United States out of the war, Hitler accomplished much of what the German imperial government had sought but had never been able to achieve in the first war.

Operation Barbarossa and the Holocaust. At what point this traditional European conflict was transformed into something quite different is open to interpretation. Some would argue that the nature of Hitler's regime and ideology made it different from the start. Others would point to Hitler's decision to postpone invasion of the British Isles and transfer resources for an invasion of the Soviet Union (Operation Barbarossa) as a turning point. Certainly the launching of Operation Barbarossa in June 1941 dramatically expanded the scale of the conflict. It also introduced into it a more pronounced ideological and racialist dimension: the aim of the invasion was not just to expand German territory but to clear so-called inferior races from this territory and destroy the Bolshevik regime, which Hitler had long identified with Jewry. That said, Operation Barbarossa could also be fitted within the framework of traditional geopolitical and strategic calculations. On the one hand, Hitler was fulfilling a long-standing aspiration of German *nationalism (which he himself had expressed in his autobiography *Mein Kampf*) by extending the German empire into the open spaces of the Ukraine, White Russia, and the *Baltic republics; on the other hand, he was taking a strategic gamble to knock the Soviet Union out of the war before the United States was drawn in on Britain's side.

It is much more difficult to fit within any traditional framework the decision that accompanied Barbarossa to proceed with a more systematic persecution of European Jews. Historians of the *Holocaust have not reached a total consensus as to when and how the Nazis' "final solution of the Jewish problem" was agreed upon, but most would accept that during the second half of 1941, with the blocking of further Jewish emigration from German-controlled Europe and with the drawing up of plans for death camps, the Nazi leadership moved decisively toward the actual elimination of all Jews. The creation of the German territorial empire had created the conditions for a distinct war within a war, which the historian Lucy Dawidowicz has aptly termed "the war against the Jews." This genocidal campaign, unprecedented in the totality of its objectives and the methodical bureaucracy of its procedures, was inexplicable in purely military terms and, indeed, toward the end of the war diverted scarce resources away from the campaign against the Red Army.

Pearl Harbor, the Asian Crisis, and Global War. In its initial stages Operation Barbarossa was a stunning success in rational-military as well as irrational-genocidal terms. However, by November 1941, the German advance had slowed and on 5 December it came to a halt on the outskirts of Moscow. Two days later, Japan launched a surprise attack on the U.S. Pacific Fleet at Pearl Harbor, and within a few days the United States found itself at war not only with Japan but also, as a result of Hitler's precipitate declaration of war, with Germany. By the end of 1941 the metamorphosis of European war into global war was complete.

Even though the European crisis had certainly influenced events in Asia and the Pacific, this new strand in the conflict had distinct origins of its own. The underlying conjuncture had emerged in the late nineteenth century: a huge but vulnerable Chinese empire being challenged by an emerging Japan, while other powers (European colonial powers, Russia, and the United States) attempted both to exploit Chinese weakness and forestall Japanese expansionism. After World War I, the region's stability had been restored with mechanisms comparable to those employed in Europe, i.e., multilateral, international agreements that were intended to provide for peaceful and gradual change within the framework of the status quo. But, as in Europe, this status quo proved unacceptable to a significant segment of the elite and the general public within the leading revisionist state, in this case Japan. From 1931 onwards Japan attempted to establish a territorial and economic empire at the expense of China. This expansionism increasingly alienated Japan from the Western powers and from the Soviet Union and encouraged the Japanese to cooperate with the anti-status quo powers in Europe.

By September 1939, with Japan's two-year war in China continuing and its international isolation deepening, some form of further conflict in the region was highly likely, irrespective of events in Europe. However, there was nothing predetermined about the form that war would take in December 1941. Japan's civilian and military leadership was torn between a northern strategy, which gave priority to conflict with the Soviet Union, and a southern strategy, which favored expansion into European colonial territories, especially resource-rich ones like the Dutch East Indies and British Malaya. It was only in July 1941, when Japanese troops entered the southern half of French Indochina and the United States responded by organizing a Western embargo on trade with Japan, that the configuration of the future conflict became apparent. The Japanese military and civilian leadership saw two alternatives: they could either submit to economic pressure, withdraw from China, and give up their vision of a Greater East Asia Co-Prosperity Sphere; or they could follow Berlin's promptings and prepare for war against the United States and Britain. By early September 1941 they had opted definitively for the latter course.

In December 1941, then, the two sides in the global war were fixed, and, in the opinion of most historians and many contemporaries, so was the outcome. The superiority in human and material resources enjoyed by the anti-Axis alliance of the United States, the Soviet Union, and the British Commonwealth and Empire was simply too great for the Axis powers to win the war. On the other hand, both the Germans and the Japanese (who within months of Pearl Harbor had taken control of Malaya and Singapore, the Dutch East Indies, the Philippines, and Burma) were well entrenched in their positions. To dislodge them, even with all the advantages that the anti-Axis alliance had at their disposal, was bound to take a considerable time, especially once the Allies had committed themselves to accepting nothing short of unconditional surrender. That created the conditions for long and bloody campaigns over the next three and a half years—in Russia, North Africa, Italy and the Balkans, France and Poland, the Pacific islands and the Philippines, Burma and China.

Domestic Conflict: Resistance and Collaboration. The protracted nature of the struggle to defeat the German and Japanese empires had implications beyond the international and military realms. While societies under Axis occupation were essentially spectators to the global conflict, individuals within these societies were engaged in their own struggles. Their war took place not on conventional battlefields but in the political and paramilitary skirmishing that pitted occupying authorities and those who collaborated with them against those who, in one form or another, resisted.

It appears that the majority of collaborators were motivated by impulses other than slavish admiration for the invaders or their ideology. In Europe they were often products of homegrown authoritarian traditions, with personal and political agendas that carried over from the prewar period. In Asia, the strongest common denominator among those who welcomed and tried to work with the Japanese was anti-Western nationalism. Resisters, who were generally motivated in the first instance by opposition to occupation and united in their efforts to sabotage it, nonetheless came to the struggle with agendas and motives that similarly predated the war. In both theaters resistance was often politicized by splits between communists and noncommunists or by attempts to develop reformist or revolutionary ideologies for the postwar future. In Asia, even more than in Europe, resistance entailed not just opposition to the current occupation but rejection of the prewar status quo. These triangular conflicts, involving occupiers, collaborators, and resisters, would obviously not have occurred without the larger war between the Axis and the anti-Axis powers. But the forms that such conflicts took primarily reflected local conditions, and their reverberations lasted long after the foreign occupations had come to an end. In this sense, these domestic conflicts must be recognized as distinct from the international conflict that spawned them.

Impact of the War. States fight wars in order to resolve what they perceive as problems. From the perspective of the victors in World War II, this conflict solved the basic problem of the 1930s. By 1945 German and Japanese power had been utterly destroyed and the threat that these two nations posed to the international order eliminated for the foreseeable future. In virtually every other respect, however, the war seemed as much a starting point as an end point. It transformed military and political realities, but resolved remarkably little. Perhaps the two most graphic symbols of this in 1945 were the mushroom clouds hanging over *Hiroshima and Nagasaki and the political clouds hanging over Poland, for whose independence, ironically, the West had gone to war in 1939.

The transitional character of the war was nowhere more apparent than at the level of the *international system. In three respects, World War II hastened a transition which had been under way for many decades. First, it facilitated the accumulation of political, economic, and military might in what became known as *superpower states. There was nothing unexpected about the fact that this occurred where it did: the emergence of American and Russian superpowers had been predicted on numerous occasions over the course of the preceding century. But the war's global scale and protracted denouement after 1941 forced the pace of change by placing a premium on those nations (first and foremost, the United States) with the industrial, military, and demographic resources to fight such a war successfully. By the end of 1943, for example, the United States was producing almost as many arms as all the other belligerents combined and was the only power in the world capable of waging conventional war in both Europe and Asia while simultaneously investing heavily in the development of an atomic bomb.

The second element in the transition was a further decline in the status of the old system's dominant powers (something which had been going on well before 1939 but had been partially masked by the self-imposed isolation of the United States and the Soviet Union). The remarkable triumphs of the Axis in 1939–1942 had the unanticipated consequence of hastening the eclipse of all "middle" powers—not just Germany, Italy, and Japan, which were subsequently crushed under the weight of the opposing coalition, and not just France and the other states humiliated by the Axis in the early stages of the war, but even Britain. For the British, victory came at the cost of colossal economic dislocation and sacrifice, not to mention the political cost involved in surrendering remnants of global leadership to stronger allies and making concessions to colonial populations. Like their former foes, Britain and France were left with no alternative but to integrate themselves into a new system structured around the superpower rivalry—the same system into which the formerly independent powers of Central and Eastern Europe were integrated more forcefully.

Third, the war accelerated the emergence of newly independent states, especially in Asia and Africa, where the collapse of the European *colonial empires entered a critical stage. The easy successes that Japan and Germany achieved in 1939-1942 burst the bubble of European prestige outside Europe. In Asia, Japanese occupation encouraged the development of nationalist and regional consciousness and gave firsthand experience in self-rule. The economic disruptions that the war produced not only weakened the strategic capacities of the European states but in many regions (particularly in Africa) fostered rapid economic development, which had significant political and social ramifications after the war. And, of course, the change in the global balance of power elevated two states which, from their different ideological perspectives, were both fundamentally opposed to colonialism.

In most of these respects, the transforming effect of World War II is more obvious in retrospect than it was at the time. The inevitability of Europe's decline or of *decolonization was far from universally recognized in 1945. Furthermore, it could legitimately be argued that the postwar system owed at least as much to the events of the immediate postwar era as to the events of 1939–1945. The problem of German power, for example, was not so much solved by 1945 as transcended after 1945, with the emergence of a greater and more threatening "problem," that of superpower rivalry. One might make a similar argument about the long *peace that the new international system produced among developed nations (though not between developed and less developed countries) after 1945. The superpower confrontation and the unprecedented destructive power of *nuclear weapons were probably more significant deterrents to renewed conflict than the memories of World War II, however painful they might be.

Whereas the war's impact on the international system was more profound than at first recognized, its impact on state behavior has been less profound than people in 1945 might have expected (or hoped). The war prompted a renewed internationalism in many quarters, but the *international organizations that were created at the end of the war (above all the UN, founded at San Francisco in June 1945) did not fulfill these high hopes, essentially because states refused to surrender their *sovereignty to such organizations. Similarly disappointed were the hopes of those who assumed that the development of an atomic bomb, which had so revolutionized the character of warfare, would also revolutionize diplomatic realities, for example by forcing an end to the anarchic relationship between sovereign states. In fact, the actual changes proved much more modest: states possessing the bomb have tended to manage their relations with one another in a more cautious and prudential manner, but the primacy of the state has not been fundamentally altered by nuclear weapons.

The impact of the war on the domestic politics of the various states involved is the largest and most difficult question of all. The war inevitably reshaped political agendas, altered political preferences, and changed the balance of political forces. The extent of its influence and the degree to which it reinforced or reversed prewar trends are issues that historians have to assess country by country and study by study. What one can say is that in every society that experienced the war firsthand it left an enduring mark on the collective memory. In some countries, like Britain and the Soviet Union, the collective memory could be a socially cohesive one. In others, particularly those which experienced the schisms of resistance and collaboration, the memory was often bitter and divisive.

(See also CHURCHILL, WINSTON; FORCE, USE OF; GENOCIDE; HIROHITO; MILITARISM; MUSSOLINI, BENITO; NUREMBERG TRIALS; ROOSEVELT, FRANKLIN DELANO; STALIN, JOSEPH; UNITED NATIONS; WAR CRIMES.)

Gordon Wright, *The Ordeal of Total War, 1939–1945* (New York, 1968). Christopher Thorne, *The Issue of War: States, Societies, and the Far Eastern Conflict of 1941–1945* (New York, 1985). Akira Iriye, *The Origins of the Second World War in Asia and the Pacific* (London, 1987). John Keegan, *The Second World War* (New York, 1989). R. A. C. Parker, *Struggle for Survival: The History of the Second World War* (Oxford, 1990).

ANDREW SHENNAN

Y

YALTA CONFERENCE. The Black Sea resort of Yalta was the setting for the last summit conference of the original "Big Three" alliance leaders during *World War II. Winston *Churchill, Franklin *Roosevelt, and Joseph *Stalin met from 4 February to 11 February 1945 to resolve their differences over the shape of the postwar order. Soon after the conference ended, Yalta became a controversial symbol in international politics and in the domestic politics of the United States.

Battlefield conditions influenced the relative strength of the participants. The Red Army occupied much of Eastern Europe and Poland; the Americans and British had not yet crossed the Rhine. To minimize U.S. casualties in attacking Japan, the U.S. military—not knowing that the still-untested atomic bomb would make unnecessary an invasion of Japan—wanted Soviet help in dislodging the large Japanese armies in Manchuria, northern China, and Korea. Fearing that allied discord might encourage isolationism, Roosevelt placed great emphasis on good relations with Stalin, preferring to leave critical issues unsettled rather than invite public disunity. He appreciated Soviet concessions on the United Nations: Stalin agreed that permanent members of the Security Council could not block the consideration of issues although they could veto UN actions. The Soviets also received additional seats in the General Assembly for their Ukraine and Belorussian Republics.

Summit participants postponed major decisions about the future of Germany. They decided to award a zone of occupation to France, and agreed that the Soviet Union was entitled to half of all reparations, with US$20 billion as a "basis for discussion." The future of Poland received the most attention. Churchill protested Soviet repression in Poland and insisted that Stalin allow noncommunist Poles to participate in the government. Roosevelt, referring to his millions of Polish-American constituents, also urged Stalin to make some gesture, though he was unwilling to press the issue. Stalin vigorously defended Soviet policy in Poland, making reference to the Soviet Union's *security and the Western powers' dominance in Italy. His only concession was to agree to include an unspecified number of other "democratic leaders from Poland itself and from Poles abroad" in the procommunist Lublin government. Along with the "Declaration of Liberated Europe," which "guaranteed" democratic governments and free elections in Eastern Europe, these concessions brought about little change in Soviet policy, because there was no attempt to define the particular procedures or principles underlying these concepts.

The Far Eastern agreements were equally controversial. The United States obtained Stalin's commitment to enter the war two or three months after Germany's surrender. In return the Soviets received the southern half of Sakhalin, which Japan had taken from imperial Russia in 1905, and the Kuril Islands, which had never been Russian possessions. In return for a vague commitment to negotiate with the Nationalist Chinese government, the Soviets also received leaseholds on Port Arthur and Dairen, control of the main Manchurian railways, and recognition of a Soviet-controlled regime in Outer Mongolia.

Despite the hopes raised by Yalta, disillusionment developed rapidly when it became clear that the Soviet Union would impose communist rule over Eastern Europe. After the communist victory in China, Senator Joseph McCarthy charged that Roosevelt's concessions at Yalta betrayed the nationalists. French President Charles de *Gaulle later claimed Yalta was proof of American designs to divide and weaken Europe. Only with the *Gorbachev revolution in *Soviet foreign policy did Yalta gain the chance to retreat into history.

(See also COLD WAR; MCCARTHYISM; POTSDAM CONFERENCE; U.S. FOREIGN POLICY)

Athan Theoharis, *The Yalta Myths: An Issue in U.S. Politics, 1945–1955* (Columbia, Mo., 1970). Robert Dallek, *Franklin D. Roosevelt and American Foreign Policy, 1932–1945* (New York, 1979). Russell D. Buhite, *Decisions at Yalta: An Appraisal of Summit Diplomacy* (Wilmington, Del., 1986).

THOMAS ALAN SCHWARTZ

YELTSIN, Boris. In 1991, Boris Yeltsin became the first elected national leader in Russian history. Shortly thereafter he became a driving force behind the final dissolution of the *Soviet Union and then the first president of the post-Soviet Russian Federation. His remarkable career saw him achieve prominence in three radically different political environments: the pre-*perestroika Soviet Union, the revolutionary years of Mikhail *Gorbachev's perestroika, and the opening years of the post-Soviet era.

Yeltsin was born in 1931 in the Urals region of Russia. After an apolitical childhood and youth, he joined the Communist Party in 1961 as a necessary step in a career as industrial manager. He soon became involved in full-time party work and in 1976 became a provincial party secretary in the important industrial region of Sverdlovsk (now Ekaterinburg). It was unusual for someone of Yeltsin's background and relatively short party tenure to be appointed to a high party post of this kind. Yeltsin is sometimes called a "typical apparatchik," but the hallmarks of Yeltsin's political style—risk and confrontation—are not those associated with a Soviet-era party official.

Yeltsin was an early beneficiary of Gorbachev's reform program: he was promoted in 1985 to the position of party chief in Moscow and was also made a candidate member of the ruling Politburo that same year. His career took a dramatic turn in the fall of 1987 when he tendered his resignation from the Politburo because of his unhappiness with the course of reform. His resignation was a clear violation of the rules of the Soviet political game and Yeltsin was promptly subjected to an old-style ritual denunciation. Gorbachev offered him a government post but warned him that he would not be allowed back into politics.

Meanwhile, Gorbachev was busy creating a situation in which he could no longer unilaterally determine who would be allowed to play a leadership role. In 1989, Yeltsin ran for a seat in the newly created legislature of the Soviet Union. Despite, or rather because of, the opposition of the party apparatus, Yeltsin won in an overwhelming landslide. The new-found power of electoral legitimacy—coupled with the Communist Party's renunciation of its monopoly status—allowed Yeltsin to later become the first prominent political leader to leave the party (June 1990). In that same year Yeltsin made another unexpected and risky move: he left the legislature of the Soviet Union as a whole and joined the parliament of Russia. At this time, the level of the Russian republic was still a mostly meaningless middle layer in the bureaucracy. In 1991, Yeltsin won a solid majority in a direct election for the presidency of the Russian Republic.

Yeltsin's new base in *Russia transformed the political situation: the leader of the most important constituent of the Soviet Union was a determined rival of the leader of the Union as a whole. Events accelerated as Gorbachev and Yeltsin conducted negotiations for a new Union Treaty that would give much more autonomy to the republics. These negotiations were interrupted in August 1991 by the coup launched by disgruntled party and security elites. With Gorbachev quarantined in the south of Russia, Yeltsin led the resistance to the doomed coup. His dramatic defiance, symbolized by his speech atop a tank, made him a worldwide hero.

In December 1991 Yeltsin met in top secret at Belovezhsky in Belarus with the leaders of Belarus and Ukraine; the three leaders signed a treaty which set up a *Commonwealth of Independent States that replaced the old Soviet Union. The proposed commonwealth never became effective; the real meaning of the Belovezhsky Treaty was the collapse of the Soviet Union into fifteen independent states. Instead of a powerless figurehead, the Russian president was now head of state of one of the world's great powers.

The next period in Yeltsin's career (1991–1993) can be called the shock period: economic shock therapy and the political shock of armed struggle between president and legislature. Economic shock therapy—sudden freeing of previously regulated prices and forced-pace *"privatization"—was put into place by a team of young economists led by Yegor Gaidar. The "Gaidar team" had no political base beyond Yeltsin. The conflict between Yeltsin and his former allies in the Russian legislature was fueled by the resulting social upheaval. In the fall of 1993, Yeltsin stepped outside the existing constitution by dissolving the legislature in preparation for a new constitution. The legislature refused to go quietly and Yeltsin ended up by shelling the Parliament building with close to a hundred lives lost. Yeltsin argued that his actions were forced on him by an intolerable situation of polarized conflict.

The crisis of October 1993 cleared the way for the intro-

duction of a new constitution that was tailor-made for Yeltsin and his desire for wide presidential authority. Yeltsin now played a less dramatic role in a more stable situation. His most important decision during this period was the military onslaught against Chechnya in December 1994. Although a peace agreement was signed after almost two years of fighting, another invasion of Chechnya began in late 1997 at the very end of Yeltsin's tenure, this time with much greater public support. It is painful to read in Yeltsin's memoirs (written before Chechnya) his thoughts at Belovezhsky in which he blames Gorbachev for "armed interventions" in Georgia and Lithuania—incidents which appear microscopic compared to Chechnya (*The Struggle for Russia*, pp. 114–115).

Owing to Chechnya and the hardships imposed by his reform strategy, Yeltsin's popularity rating was in the single digits by early 1996, only months before the first post-Soviet presidential election. Although many observers wrote him off at this point, Yeltsin managed to achieve a resounding electoral victory. His only serious opponent was Gennadii Zyuganov, the candidate of the Russian Communist Party: faced with a choice between the old and the new, most voters chose the new, warts and all.

Russia's financial crash in August 1998 marked the beginning of the final phase of Yeltsin's political career. During this period Yeltsin was clearly on the defensive on policy questions. The major issue still to be decided was how, when, and even if Yeltsin would step down from the presidency. Although elections were scheduled for mid-2000, politicians in the Duma tried to remove Yeltsin by impeachment in May 1999. Despite a large majority, the vote fell short of the required two-thirds majority. There was also speculation that Yeltsin intended to engineer an emergency in order to postpone or cancel the elections. Yeltsin managed to surprise everyone once more by suddenly resigning the presidency on New Year's Day 2000. By this time, he had found a reliable successor in Vladimir Putin, who became acting president after Yeltsin's resignation prior to winning presidential elections several months later. Putin's very first act as acting president was to shield Yeltsin and his advisors from any criminal prosecution. Thus Yeltsin managed to place an unknown quantity in the presidential office: one more problematic heritage of the Yeltsin years.

Yeltsin's election victory was also due to the help of a handful of Russian businessmen with control over vast empires of banks, media, and other enterprises. The new prominence of these oligarchs underscored Yeltsin's failure to create any durable party structure to support reform. The election also took a toll on Yeltsin's health. Yeltsin had always relied on projecting physical strength, but he was experiencing serious heart trouble even before the votes were counted. He successfully underwent heart surgery in late 1996.

Yeltsin has written two books of memoirs, one published prior to the breakup of the Soviet Union (*Against the Grain*) and the other soon after the crisis of October 1993 (*The Struggle for Russia*). The memoirs reveal an intensely political and combative personality. In the first volume, Yeltsin's platform for Russia seemed built on negative and even simplistic planks, such as promises to remove the privileges of the party elite and contempt for Gorbachev's "half-measures." A broader vision is apparent in the second volume, although Yeltsin's discussion is hardly more concrete (for example,

Yeltsin presents no rationale for economic shock therapy). One word used constantly in the second volume may provide a clue to the core of the outlook Yeltsin had evolved by the end of 1993: *normal'nyi*, a word that indicates what things *should* be but all too rarely are. Yeltsin's sense of what is *normal'nyi* seems to come from a somewhat idealized view of Western societies, compounded by an angry rejection of the absurdities imposed by the Soviet system. Russia's burden, as Yeltsin tells it, is that "once again, we've got to catch up, strain every muscle, and make super efforts merely to become like everyone else" (*The Struggle for Russia*, p. 175).

Yeltsin has never made any secret about his desire to be on top. His critics argue that Yeltsin has never stood for anything else and that major decisions such as the destruction of the Union in late 1991 and the shelling of the legislature in 1993 were made mainly for reasons of personal rivalry. Yeltsin's desire for personal preeminence has led him to ignore the task of building a durable coalition for reform. By the end of his second term as president, he was relying heavily on family members such as his daughter Tatiana Diachenko. Without any coherent vision beyond rejection of the past, he allowed "democratic market reform" to become synonymous with parasitic corruption and a new "us vs. them" division between rulers and ruled.

His supporters maintained that Yeltsin's combative tendency to identify himself with the cause of Russia was close enough to the truth to serve the country well. He pushed wide the door opened by Gorbachev to ensure rapid democratization, he fought back communist counterrevolution in 1991, and he was willing to weather the political fallout of tough economic reform. Every revolution has costs, setbacks, and ironies, but Yeltsin consistently kept to the track of creating a workable market economy. His legacy will be gratitude for his stewardship of Russia through a painful but necessary period of destruction of the old and creation of the new.

The outcome of this clash of opinion will be heavily influenced by the quality of the omelets created by all the broken eggs of the Yeltsin era. Yeltsin's second term was scheduled to end in 2000; the Russian constitution in force in 1998 forbade a third term. While in office, Yeltsin was supported by Western governments and institutions because he seemed to guarantee stability, but the importance of a single individual with no obvious successor showed that this guarantee was a fragile one.

Boris Yeltsin, *Against the Grain* (New York, 1990). John Morrison, *Boris Yeltsin: From Bolshevik to Democrat* (New York, 1991). Boris Yeltsin, *The Struggle for Russia* (New York, 1994). Dmitry Mikheyev, *Russia Transformed* (Indianapolis, 1996).

LARS T. LIH

YEMEN. The Republic of Yemen was created in May 1990 as a result of the merger of two previously separate entities, the Yemen Arab Republic, or North Yemen, and the People's Democratic Republic of Yemen, or South Yemen. This union, initiated peacefully by agreement between the governments, but followed by civil war in 1994, brought together two rather disparate states, whose over 16 million inhabitants (1997) represented more than half the total population of the Arabian Peninsula.

The North. The mountains of Yemen have been the site of settled agricultural civilizations for thousands of years and of a succession of states claiming control of much of southern Arabia. Occupied by the Turks in 1870, who defined the area of the modern state, North Yemen emerged as a separate independent entity when the Turks withdrew in 1918. Society was divided between the tribal forces in the north of the country, loyal to the Zeidi branch of Shi'i Islam, and the Shafei population in the central and southern regions, loyal to a branch of Sunni Islam. Up to 1962 power lay in the hands of the Zeidis, whose leaders, the Hamid al-Din Imams, insulated North Yemen from the outside world and maintained an autocratic grip on the country.

In 1962 the Imamate was replaced by the Yemen Arab Republic in a nationalist coup, but resistance from the tribes, aided by Saudi Arabia and Britain, led to a civil war. Egyptian forces fought, until 1967, on the side of the republic. In 1970 a compromise peace was reached, but there was intermittent resistance from left-wing guerrillas until 1982 and from tribes opposed to the growing strength of central government. In 1978 power was assumed by Ali Abdullah Salih, a Zeidi artillery officer, who proceeded to strengthen the power of the army and the state. Although elections for a General People's Congress were allowed, parties were banned and power rested with the armed forces. In addition to left-wing and tribal resistance, there was also from the early 1980s onward widespread Islamist opposition.

In 1988 the population stood at 8.5 million. The Yemeni economy relied heavily on external funding, in particular from the remittances of hundreds of thousands of workers in the oil-producing states and from foreign aid. There has been some industrial and agricultural development, and in 1984 oil was discovered in commercial quantities by the Hunt Corporation. Estimated per capita income in 1988 was US$640.

After the end of the civil war in 1970, Yemen pursued a neutral policy in regional and international affairs. It cultivated relations with Saudi Arabia, on whom it was economically dependent and with whom there was a disputed frontier, but remained on good terms with Arab radicals. It continued to receive arms from the Soviet Union but gradually improved relations with the United States.

The South. The state of South Yemen was created as a result of the occupation by Britain of the port of Aden in 1839 and subsequently of the adjacent hinterland. Until the 1950s British attention focused almost entirely on Aden, for strategic reasons, but an attempt was then made to weld the various political entities encompassed by British rule into a Federation of South Arabia. This was finally achieved in 1962 but came under increasing pressure from radical nationalists, aided by the newly created republic in North Yemen and by Egypt. When Britain withdrew in November 1967 power was assumed by the National Liberation Front, who created a radical, one-party state.

The National Front proceeded over the ensuing two decades to try, with Soviet support and guidance, to apply socialist transformation to South Yemen. In 1970 the country was renamed the People's Democratic Republic of Yemen (PDRY). The Front itself was gradually changed to become in 1978 the Yemeni Socialist Party and the economy was subjected to centralized *planning. Education, culture, and the press were brought under state control. Reforms were introduced to spread health and education services and to improve the position of women. Islam was given a "progressive" and "anti-imperialist" interpretation. This process was, however, fraught with problems: South Yemen had a very meager economic base, and the leadership was repeatedly rent by factional differences. In the most serious of these, in January 1986, several thousand officials and party members lost their lives after two weeks of fighting.

The economy of South Yemen was precarious, with the port of Aden having lost its previous prosperity and only one percent of the land area cultivable. In 1988 the population stood at 2.4 million and per capita income at US$430. Domestic productions included fish and cotton, but the state relied on workers' remittances and foreign aid to a considerable degree. However, after 1988, oil in commercial quantities was discovered.

In foreign policy, the PDRY built close relations with the Soviet Union and relied on the Soviet bloc for much military and economic support. Aden was in the first post-independence period committed to support for radical forces in the Arabian Peninsula, including left-wing guerrillas in Oman and in North Yemen. Relations with the West were poor and those with Washington were broken in 1969, only to be restored in 1990. In the late 1970s and 1980s, however, Aden gradually improved its relations with the West and with the rest of the Arab world.

Yemeni Unity. Both Yemeni leaderships had remained committed to union of the two Yemeni states: despite their fighting wars in 1972 and again in 1979, the two Yemens pursued this policy and in May 1990 agreed on full union of the two states, into a new Republic of Yemen, to be achieved after a thirty-month transition period. By 1997 population stood at 16 million, and per capita income at US$270.

For the North unity represented an opportunity, now that it had oil reserves, to enhance its power, while for the Southern leadership it was a means to offset growing economic problems and the collapse of the Soviet bloc. Development of the country was, however, soon disrupted by the impact on Yemen of the Iraqi occupation of Kuwait, in August 1990, and the *Gulf War that followed: Yemen inclined toward Iraq and, as a result, many Yemenis in Saudi Arabia were expelled and all aid from oil producers was cut. This crisis, within the new republic and in relations with other states, was to lead to worsening relations between the Northern and Southern components of the regime. In late April 1994 the Northern authorities launched a military assault against the South leading in July to the effective unification of all Yemen under Northern control. In the aftermath of the war, social and economic problems increased and political divisions were perpetuated: in the elections of 1997 the supporters of the Socialist Party refused to vote, while the General People's Congress broke with its tribal and Islamist allies in the Reform Party. Growing corruption and rival violence from tribal and Islamist elements further threatened the stability of the country.

(See also GUERRILLA WARFARE; ONE-PARTY SYSTEM.)

Gregory Gause III, *Saudi-Yemeni Relations: Domestic Structures and Foreign Influence* (New York and Oxford, 1990). Fred Halliday, *Revolution and Foreign Policy: The Case of South Yemen, 1967–1987* (Cambridge, U.K., and New York, 1990). Manfred Werner, *The Yemen Arab Republic: Development and Change in an Ancient Land* (Boulder, Colo., 1991), E. G. H. Joffé, M. J. Hachemi, and E. W. Watkins, *Yemen Today: Crisis and Solutions* (London, 1997).

FRED HALLIDAY

YUGOSLAVIA. Established in 1918 as the national home for all the South Slavs except Bulgarians, Yugoslavia represented the union of the previously independent kingdoms of *Serbia and Montenegro and most of the South Slavic lands of Austria-Hungary (Slovenian Carniola, with portions of Styria and Carinthia; Croatia-Slavonia, Dalmatia, and *Bosnia and Herzegovina; and portions of the former counties of Baranja, Bačka, and the Banat, collectively known as the Vojvodina). After World War II, state territory expanded to include Istria, Rijeka, Zadar, and the Adriatic islands that Italy had earlier received in three unequal agreements with Yugoslavia (1920–1925).

The population in 1921 was 12,017,323, of which Serbs (including Montenegrins) constituted 38.8 percent, Croats 23.8 percent, Slovenes 8.5 percent, Bosnian Muslims 6.1 percent, Macedonians 4.9 percent, Germans 4.3 percent, Hungarians 3.9 percent, and Albanians 3.7 percent. By 1981 the population had risen to 22,427,585, but the proportions of constituent nationalities (with exceptions) remained similar: Serbs 36.3 percent (Montenegrins, counted separately, 2.6 percent), Croats 19.8 percent, Slovenes 7.8 percent, Bosnian Muslims 8.9 percent, Macedonians 6.0 percent, Hungarians 1.9 percent, and Albanians 7.7 percent, Germans having been expelled as a group after the war.

The principal religious communities in 1921 were Eastern Orthodox (Serbs, Montenegrins, Macedonians, Vlachs) 46.6 percent; Roman and Greek Catholics (Croats, Slovenes, Germans, Hungarians) 41.2 percent; Sunni Muslims (Bosnian Muslims, Albanians, Turks) 11.1 percent; Protestants (Hungarians, Germans, Slovaks) 1.8 percent; and Jews 0.5 percent. The religious affiliation of the population became much more difficult to gauge under the postwar Communist regime. The country was unevenly developed, the industrial base before the war being largely in the northwest (Slovenia, northern *Croatia), but with significant potential in grain production (northern Croatia, Vojvodina), mining (Bosnia, Serbia), and maritime transportation (southern Croatia).

Internal divisions of the Yugoslav state would have been difficult to overcome under the best of circumstances. Matters were complicated by a permanent clash of national ideologies that governed the aspirations and behavior of the principal national groups. For the Serbs, notably the governing Radical Party of Nikola Pašić, Yugoslavia was not a new state but the final product of Serbia's wars (1912–1918) for the unification of all Serbs within a single state. It was therefore only natural that Serbia's state institutions (monarchy, army, administrative apparatus) should be extended to the "newly liberated territories" of former Austria-Hungary, enabling Serbia to dominate in the political affairs of the Yugoslav state just as it did in military affairs; moreover, that this new state should be administered from a single center, without recourse to any federal arrangements. *Federalism would be permitted only after a redrawing of internal frontiers, meaning that the Serbs would then incorporate, by a combination of demographic and historical arguments, practically all areas of Yugoslavia, with the exception of *Slovenia and northwestern Croatia, within their federal unit. This was clearly not to the advantage of Croats and the unrecognized Slavic groups that the Serbs treated as assimilable (Bosnian Muslims, Macedonians, Montenegrins). The Serbian view was reinforced by the Yugoslavist unitarists, who viewed centralism as an instrument that could aid the construction of an integral Yugoslav supranation. Jointly, Serbian centralists and Yugoslavist unitarists prevailed, and brought about the centralistic Vidovdan Constitution of 1921, which was passed by a bare majority over the boycott and opposition of most Croat, Slovene, and left-wing parties.

As the most important non-Serb group with a history of limited statehood within the Habsburg Monarchy, the Croats became the leaders in the struggle against the Serbian state project. Unlike the Serbs, who were divided among several major parties, the Croats were led by the agrarian-based Croat Peasant Party (HSS) during the interwar period. The party boycotted the Constituent Assembly and opposed the installation of Serbia's Karadjordjević dynasty for the whole country, opting rather for a loose confederal arrangement in which all the historical units (Serbia, Croatia, Slovenia, Bosnia and Herzegovina, Montenegro, *Macedonia, Vojvodina) would be self-governed. The party was repressed and outlawed, but in 1925 the Pašić government exacted the recognition of the dynasty and the Constitution from imprisoned Radić, leading to the HSS's accession to the cabinet under a semblance of power holding. The arrangement did not last long. By 1927, no outstanding issues having been solved, Radić withdrew from the cabinet and pursued a new oppositional course, this time in alliance with the Serbs of Croatia. After his assassination in 1928 by a Radical deputy on the floor of the Parliament, the Vidovdan system seemed on the verge of collapse. In response, on 6 January 1929, King Alexander suspended the Constitution, the Parliament, and political parties and proclaimed his personal rule.

King Alexander's dictatorship, vestiges of which remained even after the king's assassination by Croat and Macedonian nationalists in 1934, was predicated on the ideology of Yugoslavist unitarism but effectively favored Serbian predominance. The rough handling of the opposition accomplished little. Since the successive quasi-dictatorial governments of prime ministers Bogoljub Jevtić and Milan Stojadinović (1934–1939) failed to reach an agreement with the Croats and other disaffected nationalities, Regent Paul increasingly took personal charge of the negotiations. These were all the more pressing owing to the rise of German and Italian influence in Central and southeastern Europe. In August 1939 Prince Paul accepted the agreement (*Sporazum*) between his prime minister Drag Dragiša Cvetković and Vladko Maček, Radić's successor at the helm of the HSS. The agreement created an autonomous Croatian banate (a military district under the jurisdiction of a ban, or governor) whose territory encompassed most of Croatia-Slavonia, Dalmatia, and portions of Bosnia and Herzegovina. Maček became vice-president in the Cvetković cabinet and the HSS took over the regional and local administration in the banate. The agreement was opposed by various nationalist currents among the Serbs and Croats, the former having targeted the regency of Prince Paul as a culprit in the arrangement. After the Cvetković-Maček government acceded to the Axis in March 1941, the government was overthrown in a military putsch, the regency dissolved, and King Peter II proclaimed of legal age. In response,

the Axis countries invaded Yugoslavia in April 1941, quickly overwhelmed its defenses, obliged the government and the king to flee abroad, and proceeded to dismember the country.

The Axis partners and their satellites (Germany, Italy, Hungary, and Bulgaria) either partitioned the territory of Yugoslavia among themselves or established their special occupation zones (Serbia, Banat, Montenegro). The unannexed portions of Croatia (with Bosnia and Herzegovina) formally became a new Axis ally—the Independent State of Croatia. This was, in fact, an Italo-German condominium, garrisoned by Germany and Italy, and ruled through the Ustašas (Insurgents), a minuscule Croat Fascist organization, which excelled in anti-Serb violence. (On the whole, Yugoslavia lost 1,014,000 people in the course of the war, or 5.9 percent of its population, not all because of internecine violence. The Serbs lost 487,000, or 6.9 percent; Croats 207,000, or 5.4 percent; Bosnian Muslims 86,000, or 6.8 percent; and Jews 60,000, or 77.9 percent, of their conationals.) For their part, the predominantly Serb guerrillas, or Chetniks, were themselves increasingly collaborating with the occupiers and, though ostensibly the army of the London-based Yugoslav government-in-exile, pursued a program of anti-Croat and anti-Muslim violence. Hence the inability of the London Yugoslavs to project a broader-based Yugoslav—rather than Serb—image, and the unwillingness of the non-Serbs to acknowledge this government as their own. The principal beneficiary of these troubles was the Communist Party of Yugoslavia (KPJ) under the leadership of Josip Broz (*Tito). The party's strengths were united and militant leadership; appeal to the disaffected peasantry, youth, and women; and, most importantly, a vision of an egalitarian future based on the equitable solution of the nationality question.

The Communists stressed the equality and individuality of the South Slavic nations (instead of nondescript nationalities or ethnicities) in the opposition to Serbian supremacy and Yugoslavist unitarism, thereby overthrowing the two pillars of the interwar order. They proposed to build a Soviet-style federal state based on minor modifications of historical borders. As their military successes increased and their political authority received Allied support, they extended their power at the expense of the exiled king, whose support was significant only in Serbia. After the conquest of Serbia by the Soviet army and Yugoslav Communists in October 1944, Tito encountered no significant obstacles on the road to power. The new constitution of 1945 dethroned the king and established a federal *communist party state. Though the Communists initially allowed for little self-rule, the existence of the six republics (Serbia, Croatia, Slovenia, Macedonia, Montenegro, and Bosnia and Herzegovina) and two additional autonomous provinces within Serbia (Vojvodina and Kosovo) created the framework for the affirmation of genuine statehood after the passing of administrative centralism. Still, strong central controls could not be removed at once. After the Soviet leadership expelled Yugoslavia from the Cominform (1948), thereby punishing Tito for an independent and excessively revolutionary policy while simultaneously initiating the wave of thoroughgoing Sovietization of Eastern Europe, Yugoslav Communists responded with innovative ideological measures, such as the introduction of workers' councils and self-management in enterprises, which were predicated on a modicum of decentralization. In addition, after Stalin's death,

Yugoslavia restored some of its systemic ties with the Soviet bloc while simultaneously pursuing a nonaligned foreign policy, which brought it into growing interaction with *Third World countries.

In 1962, when the dispute between the reformers (Edvard Kardelj) and dogmatists (Aleksandar Ranković) threatened the unity of the Yugoslav Communist leadership, Tito sided with the reformers and thereby initiated a new wave of decentralization. In 1966 he toppled Ranković, the leading Serbian Communist and centralist, and permitted the transfer of significant powers to the republics and autonomous provinces. Despite reversals in this policy (the purge of the Croat nationalist Communists in 1971), Tito institutionalized his decentralizing course in the Constitution of 1974, which raised Vojvodina and Kosovo to the level of virtual republics while simultaneously introducing a system of absolute parity and proportionality in the relations among the republics and in their participation in the federal organs. The Constitution had two major structural weaknesses: 1) it was predicated on the permanent rule and unity of the Communist Party, and 2) it could be changed only by absolute consensus.

Tito's perpetuum mobile kept rotating during the stagnant 1970s. After Tito's death in 1980, Serbian Communists started a campaign against Tito's Constitution. They found their pretext in Kosovo, where they exaggerated the supposed "counterrevolutionary activities" of the province's Albanian majority in order to abolish the autonomous status of Kosovo. Slobodan Milošević, leader of the Serbian Communist Party since 1987, put together a coalition of Serbian forces, representing the Orthodox Church, intelligentsia, and apparatus of the party state, with the aim of hammering through the constitutional changes. With pressure and mass mobilization he succeeded in changing the leaderships of Kosovo, Vojvodina, and Montenegro. With four votes in Yugoslavia's federal presidency in his pocket, and with the Yugoslav People's Army (JNA) on his side, he was able to neutralize the influence of the four remaining republics—Slovenia, Croatia, Bosnia and Herzegovina, and Macedonia.

The Communists of these four republics repeatedly demonstrated their weakness in failing to resist Milošević's demolition of the Yugoslav federal system. As a result of their timidity, as well as communism's collapse throughout Eastern Europe in 1989–1990, the federal Communist Party split in January 1990. Successor parties failed to retain power in Slovenia and Croatia (March–April 1990) as well as in Bosnia and Herzegovina and Macedonia (November–December 1990). In Serbia and Montenegro, however, renationalized Communists won elections (December 1990). The new leaders, notably Franjo Tudjman of Croatia, then tried to negotiate a confederal arrangement for Yugoslavia. Milošević rejected these proposals on the grounds that the sovereignty of the republics as confederal or independent states was possible only if their borders were changed to accommodate the Serb minorities that were unwilling to live outside a unitary Yugoslav or Serbian state. In order to underscore this point, Mil-

ošević stirred up Serb insurgency in Croatia, whose government played into his hands by failing to find common ground with its Serb minority (531,502, or 11.6 percent, of Croatia's population in 1981). Although the Serbs constituted a greater presence in neighboring Bosnia and Herzegovina (1,320,644 Serbs represented 32 percent of the republic's population in 1981), where they participated in the coalition government, here as in Croatia the Serb minorities were increasingly armed by the JNA.

In the spring of 1991, after negotiations between the presidents of the six republics collapsed, Serbia initiated a constitutional crisis by refusing to seat the Croat representative as chair of the federal presidency. Slovenia had already held a plebiscite on independence in December 1990, and Croatia followed suit in May 1991. In both cases overwhelming majorities opted for separation from Yugoslavia. With all the federal agencies paralyzed, Croatia and Slovenia proclaimed their independence in June 1991. The JNA staged a limited assault on Slovenia and was repulsed. In September 1991 it initiated a full-scale war against Croatia. By this time the JNA was deserted by non-Serb officers and was being supplied more and more by Serb irregulars. The growing disarray of the JNA accounts for the savagery of its assault throughout the inner rim of Croatia (Vukovar, Karlovac, Zadar, and Dubrovnik) as this predominantly Serb force carved out a third of Croatia's territory, causing vast destruction, loss of life, and emigration.

The war in Croatia prompted growing international mediation. Unprepared for a local crisis of this magnitude, practically all international agencies and individual governments failed to restrain the conflict. A UN mission, headed by former U.S. Secretary of State Cyrus Vance, won an agreement on the establishment of United Nations Protected Areas in the predominantly or significantly Serb-inhabited areas of Croatia, but its larger success is in doubt. The recognition of Slovenia, Croatia, and Bosnia and Herzegovina, initially by the European Community countries and then by the United States and most major powers (January–April 1992), did not prevent a Serbian assault on Bosnia and Herzegovina (beginning in April–May 1992) with consequences even graver than those during the war in Croatia. With the recognition of Macedonia virtually assured, the Milošević government in Belgrade initiated the constitution of a rump Yugoslav state consisting of Serbia and Montenegro.

(See also BOSNIAN WAR; KOSOVO WAR.)

Stevan K. Pavlowitch, *Yugoslavia* (New York, 1971). Jozo Tomasevich, *War and Revolution in Yugoslavia: The Chetniks* (Stanford, Calif., 1975). Dennison Rusinow, *The Yugoslav Experiment, 1948–1974* (Berkeley, Calif., 1977). Ivo Banac, *The National Question in Yugoslavia: Origins, History, Politics* (Ithaca, N.Y., 1984). Ivo Banac, *With Stalin against Tito: Cominformist Splits in Yugoslav Communism* (Ithaca, N.Y., 1988). Sabrina Ramet, *Nationalism and Federalism in Yugoslavia* (Bloomington, Ind., 1992). John R. Lampe, *Yugoslavia as History: Twice There Was a Country* (Cambridge, U.K., 1996).

IVO BANAC

Z

ZAMBIA. Located in the center of the African continent, landlocked Zambia is best known for its copper mines, its vast dry plateau, and the dramatic Victoria Falls. Four cultural/linguistic groups have dominated its history: the Bemba, the Tonga, the Ngoni, and the Lozi. In 1989, the British South Africa Company annexed the territory, which became known as Northern Rhodesia. After some initial skirmishes, the company managed to entrench its rule, often through the authority of amenable local rulers. Company officials concentrated on collecting taxes, which drove adult males into migrant labor, and established Northern Rhodesia as a labor pool for its more affluent southern neighbors. On taking over in 1924, the British colonial office initiated few changes; however, the territory's fortunes improved when its copper ores became commercially exploitable. By the mid-1930s, Northern Rhodesia was one of the world's leading copper producers. A dual economy developed, characterized by rural decline and increasing dependence on urban wage labor.

African nationalist activities initially relied on the leadership and support of African workers (particularly the mineworkers) as well as the emerging urban middle class. However, trade union and nationalist goals clashed in the late 1950s, and trade unionists for the most part withdrew from the nationalist leadership. The educated African elite came to dominate both the United National Independence Party (UNIP) and the older but less popular African National Congress (ANC) of Zambia—not to be confused with the African National Congress of South Africa.

In 1964 Northern Rhodesia obtained independence as Zambia, with Kenneth Kaunda, the head of the UNIP, as its head of state and chief executive. The UNIP dominated parliament, holding sixty-five of seventy-five seats, and ANC members rarely criticized the government. However, competition over political power exacerbated political divisions, opposition parties flourished, and political conflicts were fomented by economic difficulties.

Historically Zambia's economic ties had been with the south, and Kaunda's decision to cut those ties in an effort to help end white rule in *Southern Africa had serious economic repercussions. Between 1963 and 1968, high copper prices enabled the government to pursue this policy at little cost to its citizens. However, the subsequent slump in copper prices, combined with widespread economic mismanagement, reduced the new nation's capacity to deliver promised improvements. Political discontent increased as the economy weakened.

In an effort to contain these problems, the government nationalized the copper mines in 1969 and began to move against the political opposition. In 1973, the Second Republic was inaugurated as a one-party state. Henceforth, elections were to be contested within the UNIP. The populace accepted the change without comment, but participation in elections dropped precipitously. This apathy may have been due partly to the absence of rival parties, but it may also have reflected widespread discontent with UNIP rule, particularly in the Copperbelt. From the mid-1970s, declining commodity prices, especially for copper, declining agricultural production, and blatant mismanagement combined to bring about an economic crisis that the country has not been able to overcome. Despite the adoption of IMF *structural adjustment programes, the economy continued to falter, with education, health, and welfare for the citizenry declining precipitously. Discontent continued to grow during the 1980s, and became increasingly centered around demands for a multiparty democracy.

Although Kaunda remained in control until 1991, the forces against him grew in strength. Intellectuals, businesspersons, students, trade unionists (particularly the still powerful and articulate mineworkers' union), and some dissident members of the armed forces became increasingly disillusioned with Kaunda's rule. The mass of the people lost faith in the UNIP government as well. This discontent led to the formation of the Movement for Multiparty Democracy (MMD) and to pressure for elections. In October 1991, UNIP was decisively defeated at the polls, the Second Republic ended, and a new government led by Frederick Chiluba of the MMD was installed.

The defeat of Kaunda after twenty-seven years of personal rule was a momentous event in Zambia, but it did not change the lives of ordinary citizens for the better. There was no "democracy dividend" for Zambians, as the MMD was unable to implement its campaign promises of greater prosperity and a more open government. The economic crisis remained as intractable as before the elections, and little assistance was forthcoming from the international community to ease the country's external debt. Like UNIP, the new ruling party was accused of authoritarianism and rampant corruption. Desertions from its ranks and mounting discontent tempted former president Kaunda to make a political comeback in 1992. Fearful of losing the 1996 elections, the Chiluba regime unleashed a reign of terror and declared Kaunda a foreigner, since his parents had come from Malawi. As a result, UNIP boycotted the elections, and Chiluba was reelected with 82 percent of the vote cast. It is hoped that with both Chiluba and Kaunda absent from the presidential ballot in 2001, Zambians would be able to choose a ruler who will help the country chart a new course for the future and restore the confidence needed for economic recovery and genuine democracy.

(See also COLONIAL EMPIRES; NATIONALISM; SOUTHERN AF-RICAN DEVELOPMENT COMMUNITY.)

Andrew Roberts, *A History Of Zambia* (London, 1976). Cherry Gertzel, Carolyn Baylies, and Morris Szeftel, *The Dynamics of the One-Party State in Zambia* (Manchester, U.K., 1984). Owen Sichone and Bornwell C. Chikulo, eds., *Democracy in Zambia: Challenges to the Third Republic* (Harare, 1996).

JANE L. PARPART

ZIMBABWE. The Republic of Zimbabwe is located in the region of *Southern Africa. As a landlocked country, it borders Mozambique to the east, South Africa to the south, Botswana to the west, and Zambia to the north. The total area of the country is 150,873 square miles (390,759 sq. km.). Zimbabwe's population is around 11.2 million, and the capital city is Harare. There are two main ethnic groups, the Shona, who represent 75 percent of the population, and the Ndebele, who represent 19 percent. The official language is English, and there are four indigenous languages—Shona, Ndebele, Venda, and Tonga. The two dominant religions are traditional and Christianity.

The modern nation-state of Zimbabwe has its origin in ninety years of resistance against white-minority domination. The war of liberation against the illegal regime began in the 1960s, and in 1979, a negotiated settlement was reached that resulted in the people of Zimbabwe gaining their independence on 18 April 1980. Although the negotiated settlement, known as the Lancaster House Agreement, put in place a multiparty democracy, it was designed to protect the interests of the white minority. For example, even though they represented less than two percent of the population, the whites were granted 20 out of 100 seats in parliament for at least seven years. In addition, private property was protected, which meant that the whites were able to retain control over the best land in the country, even if it was idle. Although the war of liberation had been fought over the land question, land could only be acquired by the government on a willing-seller, willing-buyer basis. For many blacks, this seemed particularly unfair since, they argued, whites had stolen the land from them. At independence, the black majority inherited a legacy of white privilege and white economic hegemony.

The independence election of 1980 gave the Zimbabwe African National Union–Patriotic Front (ZANU-PF), under the leadership of Robert Mugabe, a sweeping mandate to rule the country. ZANU's major rival, the Patriotic Front–Zimbabwe African People's Union (PF-ZAPU), under the leadership of Joshua Nkomo, came in second place. The ongoing political rivalry between ZANU-PF and PF-ZAPU was finally resolved on 1987 December 22, when the two parties signed a Unity Accord and merged as ZANU-PF.

Although theoretically Zimbabwe has, since independence, been a multiparty, constitutional democracy, in practice this has not been the case. Instead, the country, under the leadership of Mugabe and ZANU-PF, is a de facto one-party authoritarian state, where patronage and corruption have become entrenched and institutionalized. With each national election, ZANU-PF and Mugabe have managed to increase their political dominance, and until 1999, the opposition was silenced.

Although the Lancaster House Constitution has a Bill of Rights, the government is accused by human rights organi-zations and opposition parties of abrogating the human rights of Zimbabweans. The Constitution has been amended at least sixteen times. In 1987, the provision granting whites twenty seats in parliament was removed, and in 1991, the government was authorized to acquire white land for resettlement. For years, many in the country lobbied for a constitutional conference that would allow Zimbabweans to write their own constitution. Bowing to pressure, in 1999, the government established a Constitutional Commission to draft a new constitution. The Draft Constitution was rejected by the majority of Zimbabweans during a referendum held in February 2000. This rejection followed accusations that the Draft Constitution did not reflect the views of most Zimbabweans and would further entrench the power of the president. The proposed changes would have also allowed the government to acquire land for redistribution without compensation.

Following the defeat of the proposal, the government passed the 16th amendment to the Lancaster House Constitution, giving itself authority to acquire land without compensation. In a strong show of support, following the defeat of the referendum, war veterans, backed by the government, began to invade mainly white-owned farms. This action sparked political instability throughout the country and added to the country's economic decline.

The most difficult challenge facing the government is resolving the country's economic crisis. At independence, in an attempt to rectify some of the injustices that had been perpetuated on the majority population during white-minority rule, the government implemented programs providing services to the majority population, such as free education and health care, that had heretofore been denied. A limited program of land redistribution was also implemented. By the end of the 1980s, the economic growth the country had experienced during the first few years of independence had slowed tremendously, and the country had experienced a catastrophic drought. These factors, coupled with a relatively closed economy and massive corruption, resulted in huge budget deficits.

In 1990, the government dropped Marxism-Leninism as official ideology, and signed an IMF/World Bank Structural Adjustment Agreement. With the economic liberalization imposed by the Bretton Woods institutions, the government was forced to end many of the social programs that had been put in place during the first decade of independence. Much of the socioeconomic progress that had been made was quickly reversed. It was during this period that the ruling party began to abandon its commitment to the continued social and economic improvement of the masses.

Civil society resistance to the government increased as a result of government involvement, since August 1998, in the war over power and resources in the Democratic Republic of Congo. During protests and riots from early 1998, the military was called in to quell the disturbances, resulting in numerous casualties and arrests. These and other draconian policies have resulted in Zimbabwe resembling a police state.

The political instability that followed the referendum vote in February 2000 resulted in even more deaths and increased brutality by the police and ZANU-backed war veterans. A great deal of the violence was directed at supporters of the Movement for Democratic Change (MDC) under the leadership of Morgan Tsvangirai. The MDC has posed the greatest challenge to date to ZANU-PF rule.

The road to real democracy in Zimbabwe will be long and arduous. Since no successor has been identified for the post-Mugabe era, there will likely be a divisive struggle for power among numerous contenders. While ZANU-PF will likely remain the ruling party for sometime to come, divisions within the party could result in breakaway factions. One faction would likely be those opposed to the party's authoritarian and corrupt practices. Another faction would likely be those who never approved of the ZANU-PF and PF-ZAPU merger. Such an outcome could be very serious in that ethnic rivalries between the Shona and the Ndebele, with their respective support of ZANU-PF and PF-ZAPU, could be revived. The breakaway factions could conceivably unite and form a strong opposition party.

Zimbabwe, notwithstanding its internal problems, plays a major role in the regional politics of Southern Africa. This is mainly done through its membership in the *Southern African Development Community (SADC) and the Common Market for Eastern and Southern Africa (COMESA). The country is also a member of the Organization of African Unity (OAU) and the Nonaligned Movement.

(See also COLONIAL EMPIRES; DECOLONIZATION; LAND REFORM; STRUCTURAL ADJUSTMENT PROGRAM.)

Canaan S. Banana, ed., *Turmoil and Tenacity: Zimbabwe 1890–1990* (Harare, Zimbabwe, 1989). Jeffrey Herbst, *State Politics in Zimbabwe* (Harare, Zimbabwe, 1990). Carolyn Jenkins, "The Politics of Economic Policy-Making in Zimbabwe," *Journal of Modern African Studies* 35, no. 4 (1997): 575–602. Special Issue on Zimbabwe, *Africa Insight* (Pretoria) 30, no. 1 (May 2000).

MARGARET C. LEE

ZIONISM. Although premodern Judaism idealized the "Land of *Israel" and Jewish messianism promised restoration of the ancient homeland, over the centuries the trickle of Jews who actually immigrated to *Palestine had no notion of a state-building project. Modern Jewish *nationalism, in the form of Zionism (from the Hebrew *Tziyon*, a synonym for Jerusalem), emerged only in the last third of the nineteenth century, mainly among the Jewish masses of eastern Europe, for whom it was one of several responses to socioeconomic crisis and virulent *anti-Semitism (manifested in officially sponsored pogroms in tsarist Russia in 1871 and 1881), which together blocked most avenues of individual or collective integration or advancement. In this period millions of Jews sought to escape their plight by emigrating not to Palestine but to western Europe and the Americas, and above all to the United States. While most of those who did not emigrate westward clung to traditional ways, sought assimilation, or turned to socialism, which promised the eradication of anti-Semitism, the example of other European peoples' turn toward nationalism and a midcentury Hebrew-language cultural revival paved the way for the emergence of a small "Love of Zion" movement, promoting emigration to Palestine and Jewish national-cultural revival there. This first wave of Jewish immigration to Palestine, from 1881 to 1903, led to the establishment of a number of Jewish agricultural settlements in Palestine, which survived thanks largely to the financial support of western European Jewish philanthropists.

As an organized and explicitly political nationalist move-ment, however, Zionism emerged only after 1896, when Theodor Herzl (1860–1904), a Viennese journalist, published his influential pamphlet *The Jewish State* and a year later convened the first Zionist Congress at Basel, Switzerland. The anti-Semitism which the Dreyfus affair brought to the surface even in "enlightened" France helped convince Herzl, an assimilated Jew from an affluent family, that the only solution to the "Jewish problem" was mass emigration to some territory in which the Jews could establish their own sovereign state. Herzl transformed a diffuse proto-Zionism into a modern international mass political movement, the Zionist Organization (ZO), whose main focus during his lifetime was to secure from the Ottoman Empire, which then ruled Palestine, or from one or more of the European powers, a "charter" granting Jews the right to settle in and develop Palestine. Over time the ZO developed a comprehensive network of institutions, including elected decision-making bodies, a financial apparatus, and an agency to acquire land in Palestine for Jewish settlement (the Jewish National Fund).

The main premises on which Zionism as an *ideology rests include the definition of all Jews everywhere as constituting a single nation; the inevitability of anti-Semitism wherever Jews and non-Jews live together, and its ineradicability by means of education or social reform; the irredeemable abnormality of Jewish life in "exile," a result of Jewish rootlessness and powerlessness; and the necessity of achieving the territorial concentration of all or most of the world's Jews in Palestine, where Jewish national rebirth and *sovereignty are to be realized.

Zionism was influenced by, and has many similarities with, other contemporary European nationalisms. However, because Jews did not constitute a compact majority in any specific territory in Europe wherein they could seek sovereignty, Zionism could be realized only through large-scale Jewish immigration to, and settlement in, an extra-European territory, an undertaking which the contemporaneous "new *imperialism" made both conceivable and feasible. Zionism was thus not simply a national but also a colonial-settler project, and its attitude toward Palestine's indigenous Arab population, on the verge of its own national "awakening," was profoundly influenced by contemporary European colonial discourse. The famous early Zionist slogan, "A land without a people for a people without a land," reflected a conception of Palestine as empty, because not inhabited or developed by Europeans. Later, when the existence of Palestine's Arab population and its opposition to the Zionist project became unmistakably obvious, most Zionists denied the authenticity of Palestinian *Arab nationalism while asserting a superior Jewish claim to Palestine based on historical precedence, divine promise, urgent need, and/or invested labor.

Given Ottoman, and later Palestinian and other Arab, opposition to the Zionist goal of creating a Jewish state in Palestine, the Zionist movement required a powerful European patron to provide protection and support. Only in November 1917, when Britain issued the *Balfour Declaration, did such a patron finally come forward. British support for and protection of the Zionist project lasted until 1939, when British efforts to conciliate the Arabs led to a breakdown in the alliance. By that time, however, the yishuv (the Jewish community in Palestine) was, in demographic, economic, political, and military terms, almost strong enough to stand on its own, thanks in part to increased Jewish immigration during the 1930s stimulated by the spread of European anti-Semitism (particularly the Nazi assumption of power in Germany) and channeled to Palestine when the Western democracies shut their doors.

By 1942 the Zionist movement was openly proclaiming that its goal was a Jewish state in all of Palestine, but it was only after World War II that an all-out political, diplomatic, and military campaign was launched to achieve statehood, in uniquely favorable circumstances: shocked by the Nazi extermination of some six million European Jews, the world community was sympathetic as never before to Zionism as a response to anti-Semitism; both the United States and the Soviet Union came to endorse Jewish statehood; the *United Nations, to which Britain referred the Palestine problem in February 1947, still had few Third World members who might have been more receptive to the Arab case; Jewish communities worldwide (in which Zionism now won widespread support) were effectively mobilized; and within the yishuv itself the groundwork for statehood had been laid. In November 1947 the UN General Assembly voted to recommend the partition of Palestine into independent Arab and Jewish states, touching off intercommunal warfare. In May 1948 the State of Israel was proclaimed, and when the ensuing Arab-Israeli War of 1948–49 came to an end the new Jewish state was in control of seventy-seven percent of Palestine.

Zionism has never been a monolithic movement: from its very inception it has comprised distinct and often conflicting tendencies. Herzl's "political" Zionism and its successor, the bourgeois and secular "General Zionist" tendency, were soon challenged by "labor Zionism" (or "socialist Zionism"), which stressed not big-power diplomacy but immigration and settlement work leading to the creation in Palestine of a social-democratic Jewish society; among this tendency's outstanding figures was David *Ben-Gurion (1886–1973). Though most orthodox rabbis initially denounced Zionism as false messianism and state-worshiping idolatry, a religious Zionist movement also emerged, in uneasy partnership with the ZO's secular majority. In the 1920s a right wing emerged within the Zionist movement, led by Vladimir Jabotinsky (1880–1940). Jabotinsky's "Revisionist" Zionism rejected the gradualism of the ZO's leadership, its reluctance in certain periods to openly demand a sovereign Jewish state, and its talk of compromise with the Palestinian Arabs. Initially influenced by contemporary European *fascism, the Revisionists demanded the immediate establishment, by force if necessary, of a sovereign Jewish state in all of Palestine and Transjordan.

The General Zionists played the leading role in the ZO from its inception into the early 1930s, when labor Zionism emerged as the strongest tendency. For the following four decades, with the General and religious Zionist parties as junior partners, labor Zionism dominated the ZO, the yishuv, and later Israel. The labor-Zionist movement, which stressed the gradual development of a self-sufficient yishuv, rhetorical moderation toward the Palestinians without substantive concessions, and the cultivation of international support, played a crucial role in laying the economic, social, cultural, and political foundations of the future State of Israel.

By the 1970s, however, political, social, and cultural developments within Israel (including Israel's 1967 conquest and occupation of the West Bank and Gaza, and the Right's ability to capitalize electorally on the resentment felt by many Jews originally from Arab countries about neglect and discrimination at the hands of the labor-Zionist establishment) converged to undermine labor Zionism's dominance, and in 1977 Jabotinsky's disciple Menachem Begin (1913–1992) formed Israel's first government not dominated by labor Zionists. Though the Labor Party retained considerable support, mainly among middle-class Jewish Israelis of European origin, over the following two decades the direction and tone of Israeli politics were set largely by the Zionist Right, with ultranationalist and clericalist forces gaining ground.

Although after 1948 some Israeli leaders (including Ben-Gurion) argued that there was no further need for a Zionist movement, the World Zionist Organization (as it is now called) has continued to function, promoting and raising money for Jewish immigration to Israel, carrying on Jewish educational and cultural work in the Diaspora, and lobbying on behalf of Israel. Within Israel various attitudes toward Zionism coexist, ranging from a strong commitment to the continuation of Israel's task of "ingathering the exiles" to indifference among many younger Israelis, in whose slang the word "Zionism" is a synonym for bombast. In the 1980s Israeli scholars began to challenge many long-cherished myths of Zionist and Israeli history, and later a few Israeli intellectuals even began to call themselves "post-Zionist," arguing that Zionism was no longer relevant to the kind of society and polity Israel had become. Nonetheless, Israel remains in theory and practice a Zionist state, in that Israel officially defines itself not as a state of its citizens, Jews and Arabs, but as the state of all Jews everywhere, who under Israeli law have the automatic right to immigrate to Israel, acquire citizenship, and enjoy privileges denied to Israel's non-Jewish citizens. This self-definition and the practices which flow from it, along with Israeli military rule over Palestinians in the West Bank and Gaza, were cited as justification for the controversial 1975 UN General Assembly resolution classifying Zionism as a form of racism (repealed in 1991).

Although since 1948, and especially since 1967, identification with Israel has come to be the main content of secular Jewish identity for many Jews in the Western democracies, particularly the United States which has the world's largest Jewish community, that identification is unencumbered by any sense of personal obligation to move to Israel. In fact, very few Jews from these countries have chosen to live in Israel; for most, Zionism has continued to be, as the old joke goes, a matter of "an American Jew donating money to a French Jew to fund a Russian Jew's immigration to Israel." Indeed, generally speaking, large numbers of Jews have gone to Palestine (and later to Israel) only when confronted with inequality of rights and opportunities, discrimination, or persecution in their own countries, and only when other options have been closed; even Soviet Jews emigrating in the 1970s and 1990s, if given a choice, usually expressed a preference for the United States or other Western countries. Before 1948 the Jewish communities in the Arab countries had been largely ignored by, and were generally unreceptive to, Zionism, a thoroughly European Jewish movement in leadership, orientation, and ethos; their massive immigration to Israel between 1948 and the early 1960s was the result not of Zionist conviction but of the Palestine conflict, which made their situation in their countries of origin untenable.

In one obvious sense, Zionism can be judged a tremendous success: the utopian dream of a Viennese journalist was realized some five decades later in the creation of a new nation-state which has repeatedly demonstrated its durability. Some qualification of that judgment may be in order, however. Although Zionism promised to establish a safe haven for Jews, its failure, despite repeated military triumphs, to induce the Palestinians to abandon their own drive for statehood, or to compel most Arab states to accept peace on Israel's terms, has meant that the yishuv, and then Israel, have always been embattled. Ironically, of all the world's Jewish communities, it is today in Israel that Jews face the gravest threat of physical annihilation. The apparently ineradicable persistence of the Palestinians also suggests that, even if Israel's present military superiority endures, the Zionist achievement after 1948 of a Jewish majority in Palestine is impermanent: barring mass expulsions, Arabs will probably once again be a majority in Palestine within a few decades, while the Palestinian minority within Israel's 1967 borders grows increasingly unwilling to accept the burdens of second-class citizenship imposed by the state's Zionist self-definition.

Nor have other goals of Zionism as originally envisioned—Jewish independence, unity, territorial concentration, and cultural revival—been fully realized. In conflict with much of the population over which it rules and much of the region in which it is situated, Israel's strength, if not its very survival, still depends heavily on the military, economic, and political support of a distant superpower, the United States. However, the end of the *Cold War and post–Gulf War realignments in the Middle East may put that "special relationship" into question by depriving Israel of its former role as a key U.S. ally against Soviet-backed regimes and radical-nationalist forces in the region. Israeli Jewish society is riven by conflicts along ethnic, class, ideological, and religious/secular lines as well as by bitter divisions over the issue of withdrawal from the territories occupied in 1967. The fault lines within Israel and Zionism surfaced dramatically in November 1995 when a right-wing Jewish extremist assassinated Prime Minister Yitzhak Rabin, whom the Right had accused of betraying the Jewish people by negotiating agreements with the Palestinians that provided for limited Palestinian self-rule in parts of the West Bank and Gaza. Despite widespread revulsion at Rabin's murder the Right won the subsequent elections, leading to the breakdown of movement toward Israeli-Palestinian peace envisioned in these agreements.

The majority of the world's Jews still lives outside Israel, though the wave of Jewish immigration from the Soviet Union and its successor states which began in the late 1980s has increased the proportion in Israel. Israel-Diaspora relations are often troubled, and despite the danger of assimilation many observers believe that the Diaspora fosters greater cultural vitality than Israel, where clericalist and chauvinist forces exert a growing influence. As a result, despite having overcome enormous obstacles and successfully created a strong state that has endured for half a century and enjoys widespread loyalty among Jews, the long-term prospects of the Zionist project remain uncertain.

(See also ARAB-ISRAELI CONFLICT; COLONIAL EMPIRES; GULF WAR; HOLOCAUST; INTERNATIONAL MIGRATION.)

Arthur Hertzberg, ed., *The Zionist Idea* (New York, 1959). David Vital, *The Origins of Zionism* (Oxford, 1975). David Vital, *Zionism: The Formative Years* (Oxford, 1982). David Vital, *Zionism: The Crucial Phase* (Oxford, 1987). Gershon Shafir, *Land, Labor and the Origins of the Israeli-Palestinian Conflict, 1882–1914* (Cambridge, U.K., 1989).

ZACHARY LOCKMAN

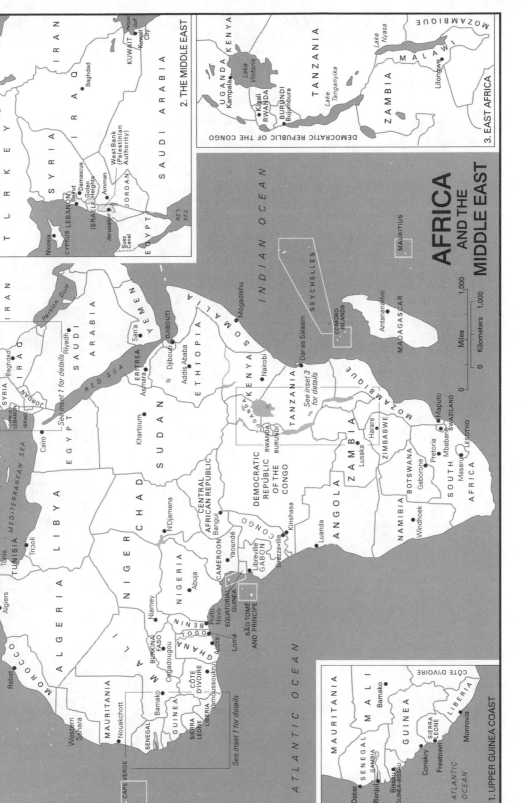

AFRICA
AND THE
MIDDLE EAST

2. THE MIDDLE EAST

3. EAST AFRICA

1. UPPER GUINEA COAST

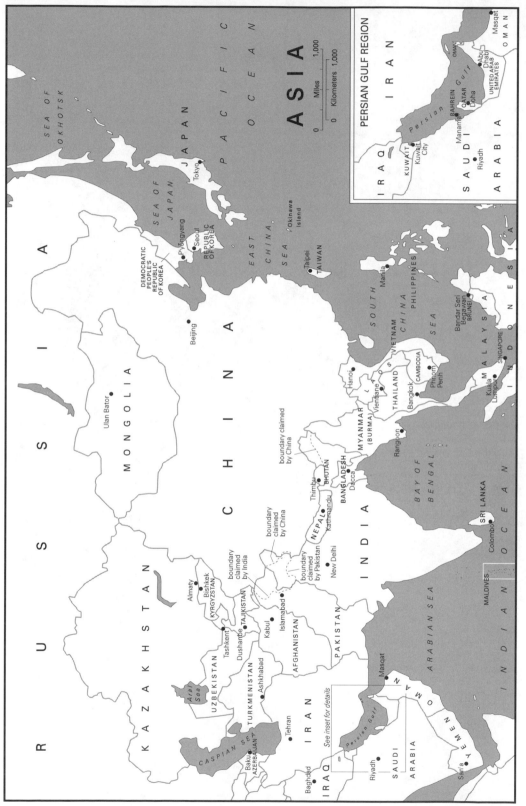

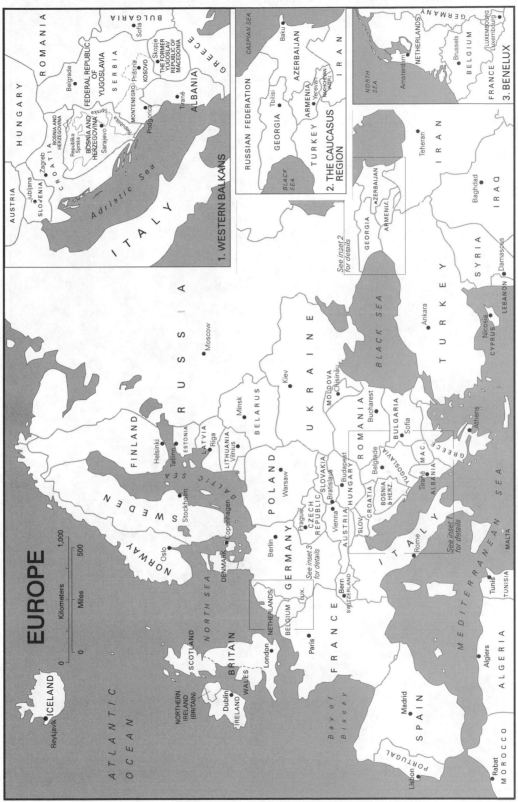

EUROPE

1. WESTERN BALKANS

2. THE CAUCASUS REGION

3. BENELUX

GREENLAND

UNITED STATES OF AMERICA

PACIFIC
OCEAN

C A N A D A

Ottawa

Washington, DC

UNITED STATES OF AMERICA

ATLANTIC
OCEAN

Gulf of Mexico

BAHAMAS

Nassau

Havana

See inset 2 for details

MEXICO

CUBA

HAITI

DOMINICAN
REPUBLIC

JAMAICA

Kingston

**NORTH AND CENTRAL
AMERICA**

Mexico City

BELIZE

GUATEMALA

HONDURAS

CARIBBEAN SEA

Caracas

| 0 | Miles | 1,000 |

| 0 | Kilometers | 1,000 |

EL
SALVADOR

NICARAGUA

VENEZUELA

COSTA RICA

PANAMA

COLOMBIA

See inset 1 for details

1. CENTRAL AMERICA

MEXICO

BELIZE
Belmopan

CARIBBEAN
SEA

GUATEMALA
Guatemala
City

HONDURAS
Tegucigalpa

San Salvador
EL
SALVADOR

NICARAGUA
Managua

PACIFIC
OCEAN

COSTA RICA
San José

Panama
Canal

PANAMA
Panama
City

2. N.W. CARIBBEAN REGION

HAITI
Port-
au-Prince

DOMINICAN
REPUBLIC
Santo
Domingo

Puerto
Rico

ANGUILLA

ANTIGUA
AND BARBUDA

Basseterre
SAINT CHRISTOPHER
(KITTS) –NEVIS
Saint Johns

Roseau
DOMINICA

CARIBBEAN SEA

Castries
SAINT LUCIA
Kingstown
SAINT VINCENT AND
THE GRENADINES

BARBADOS

Bridgetown

GRENADA
Saint George's

Caracas

Port of Spain

TRINIDAD
AND
TOBAGO

VENEZUELA

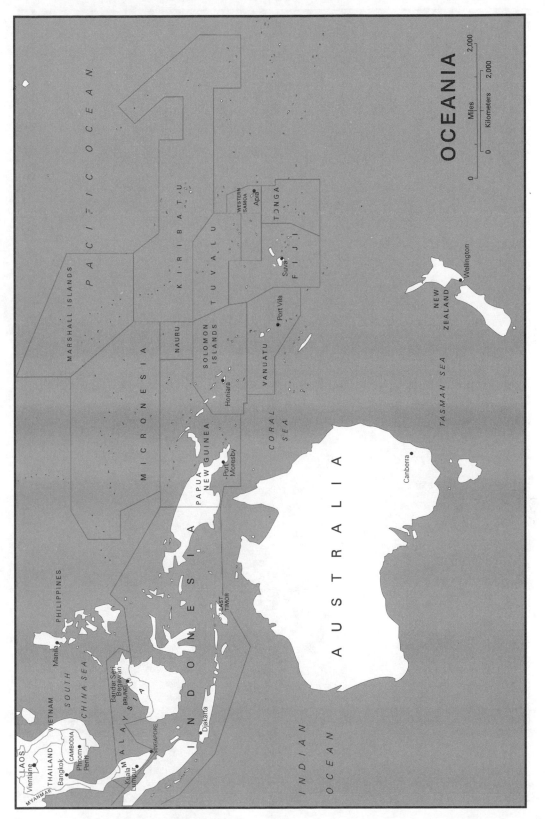

OCEANIA

SOUTH AMERICA

INDEX